W9-BEM-267

SECOND EDITION

O*NET

Dictionary of Occupational Titles

Based on information obtained from the U.S. Department of Labor, the U.S. Census Bureau, and other reliable sources

Developed under the direction of J. Michael Farr and LaVerne L. Ludden, Ed.D., with database work by Laurence Shatkin, Ph.D.

DISCARD

JIST
Works

O*NET Dictionary of Occupational Titles, Second Edition

© 2002 by JIST Publishing, Inc.

Published by JIST Works, an imprint of JIST Publishing, Inc.
8902 Otis Avenue
Indianapolis, IN 46216-1033

Phone: 1-800-648-JIST   Fax: 1-800-JIST-FAX
E-mail: editorial@jist.com   Web site: www.jist.com

About Career Materials Published by JIST

For the best information on occupations, many people—including experienced career professionals—rely on JIST. JIST has published information about careers and job search since the 1970s. JIST offers occupational references plus hundreds of other books, videos, assessment devices, and software.

Quantity discounts are available for this reference and other JIST books. Please call the JIST sales staff at 1-800-648-JIST weekdays for details.

Visit www.jist.com to find out about JIST products, get free book chapters, and link to other career-related sites. You can also learn more about JIST authors and JIST training available to professionals.

A free catalog is available to professionals at schools, institutions, and other programs. It presents hundreds of helpful publications on career, job search, self-help, and business topics from JIST and other publishers. Please call 1-800-648-JIST or visit www.jist.com to request the JIST catalog.

Editors: Susan Pines, Veda Dickerson, Lori Cates
Interior Designer: Aleata Howard
Interior Layout: Carolyn J. Newland
Cover Designer: Honeymoon Image & Design, Inc.
Proofreader: Paula Lowell

Printed in the United States of America
06 05 04 03 02 01   9 8 7 6 5 4 3 2 1

Library of Congress Cataloging-in-Publication Data

O*NET dictionary of occupational titles.—2nd ed.
    p.cm.
    "Based on information obtained from the U.S. Department of Labor, the U.S. Census Bureau, and other reliable sources."
    "Developed under the direction of J. Michael Farr and LaVerne L. Ludden, Ed.D., with database work by Laurence Shatkin, Ph.D."
    ISBN 1-56370-845-0—ISBN 1-56370-846-9
        1. Occupations—United States—Dictionaries. 2. Occupations—United States—Classification. I. Farr, J. Michael. II. Ludden, LaVerne, 1949- III. Shatkin, Laurence. IV. United States. Dept. of Labor. V. JIST Works, Inc.

HB2595 .016 2001
331.7'003—dc21   2001038356

We have been careful to provide accurate information in this book, but it is possible that errors and omissions have been introduced. Please consider this in making any career plans or other important decisions. Trust your own judgment above all else and in all things.

ISBN 1-56370-845-0 Softcover
ISBN 1-56370-846-9 Hardcover

This Book Is Easier to Use Than It Looks

Please don't be intimidated by the formal look of this book. We have worked hard to make it an easy-to-use and valuable resource for a variety of nontechnical purposes.

We believe this reference will be of great help to job seekers, students, businesses, educators, career counselors, and many others. It provides, in a practical format, a major new standard for organizing and describing occupations. It describes over 1,000 jobs and includes data on earnings, education and training required, growth, skills required, and much more.

This Book Uses the Latest Information Sources

The information database used to create this book was developed by the U.S. Department of Labor (DOL) and replaces an older information system. This new source of occupational information, called the O*NET (for the Occupational Information Network), represents a major change from the past. Many governmental, business, educational, and other organizations rely on the standardized occupational classification system developed by the DOL. The O*NET system is the standard now used in collecting data on wages, job growth, and related facts.

The O*NET is clearly an important new information source. But the amount of information in the electronic database—and the way it is presented—has limited use for many people. As a result, the DOL releases the O*NET database to developers, so they can adapt the data into print and software formats that reach a wide audience.

This book was the first to provide the O*NET material in printed form, and we hope it serves as a beneficial tool. This edition is the first to use the O*NET's new Standard Occupational Classification (SOC) structure (explained in the introduction) and other features available in the most recent O*NET database update. The changes in the latest version of the O*NET make the original O*NET system, used in the first edition of this book, obsolete.

This book is the result of cooperation between a private organization and governmental agencies. In this case, we think your taxes are being spent wisely.

Important Notice on the Limitations of Use of This Book

Occupational information in this book reflects jobs as they have been found to occur, but they may not coincide in every respect with jobs as performed in particular establishments or at certain localities. Readers demanding specific job information should supplement it with local data.

Note that the U.S. Department of Labor and JIST Publishing have no responsibility for establishing wage levels or settling jurisdictional matters for occupations. In preparing vocational definitions, no data were collected concerning these and related matters. Therefore, the occupational information in this book cannot be regarded as determining standards for any aspect of the employer-employee relationship. Data contained in this publication should not be considered a judicial or legislative standard for wages, hours, or other contractual or bargaining elements.

Credits

Although several people have their names on the cover, this book represents many years of work by hundreds of dedicated individuals. The O*NET database that serves as this book's basis was created by researchers and developers under the direction of the U.S. Department of Labor. They, in turn, were assisted by thousands of employers who provided details on the nature of work in thousands of job samplings used in the database's development.

While the O*NET database was first released several years ago, it is based on the substantial work done on an earlier database used to develop the *Dictionary of Occupational Titles* (DOT). That DOT database was first used in the 1939 DOT edition and has been continuously updated since. The DOT formed the basis for much of the occupational information used by employers, job seekers, career counselors, educational and training institutions, researchers, policy makers, and others.

Because of their large numbers, most who worked on the occupational material used in this book are not credited. Even so, we appreciate their efforts and present this book in their honor and in the honor of the good people at the U.S. Department of Labor who made the O*NET database and earlier sources of career information possible. Thanks.

Table of Contents

Quick Summary of Major Sections

Introduction. A brief overview of the O*NET system and this book. Includes a sample O*NET job description and reviews its many elements, such as job duties, education required, earnings, skills, abilities, personality type, working conditions, and more. Offers tips to help students, job seekers, career changers, employers, career counselors and others use this reference. *The introduction starts on page 1.*

O*NET Occupational Descriptions. The book's main section, providing information-packed descriptions for over 1,000 jobs in the O*NET database. Descriptions are arranged by their O*NET number and within logical groupings of related jobs. The major job groups and their corresponding code numbers are listed below. *The job descriptions start on page 23.*

Appendix: Exploring Careers Based on Interests. Very useful for uncovering career and learning options based on interests. *The appendix starts on page 665.*

Index of O*NET Job Titles. All job titles in the O*NET database (and, therefore, in this book) appear here in alphabetic order. *The index starts on page 681.*

List of O*NET Occupations in Related Job Groupings

We include this list to help you quickly locate the job descriptions that interest you. It uses the current O*NET structure that groups similar jobs together. All jobs in the current O*NET database are shown in this list within the groupings. The O*NET uses a numbering system to organize its groupings and subgroupings, and these numbers appear in the list. Finally, the O*NET assigns a unique number code to each job title, and these codes are shown also. The job descriptions are arranged in the book in the same sequence you see here. The list provides the page number where you can find each job description.

Business and Financial Operations Occupations 13-0000 51

Computer and Mathematical Occupations 15-0000 74

Architecture and Engineering Occupations 17-0000 84

Life, Physical, and Social Science Occupations 19-0000 112

Community and Social Services Occupations 21-0000 146

Legal Occupations 23-0000 155

Education, Training, and Library Occupations 25-0000 162

Contents_____

Arts, Design, Entertainment, Sports, and Media Occupations 27-0000 193

Office and Administrative Support Occupations 43-0000 335

Farming, Fishing, and Forestry Occupations 45-0000 378

Construction and Extraction Occupations 47-0000 393

Installation, Maintenance, and Repair Occupations 49-0000 436

Contents_____

Introduction

We know that many people skip the introduction and dive directly into the book. Our objective was to make this introduction easy to read and nontechnical. We admit that some information here is, well, dull. But we tried to format it so you can quickly browse the headings and disregard or read material as desired. For example, this introduction presents a sample job description with its elements pointed out and explained, which is very helpful in understanding the book's main section.

Also, please note that although there may be technical differences between the terms *occupation* and *job,* we use them interchangeably in this book.

What Is the O*NET?

The O*NET is not a book—it is a computerized database of information on occupations. Developed by the U.S. Department of Labor, O*NET is short for "The Occupational Information Network," the database's formal name.

In its current form (the one we used in this book), the O*NET database provides information on about 1,000 occupations. In the years to come, occupations will be added and deleted, and the information on all occupations will be updated regularly. For example, this second edition includes many changes made to the O*NET database since the first edition was released in 1998.

The Department of Labor has stated that its role is to create and maintain the O*NET database, and it has no plans to release it in print. The *O*NET Dictionary of Occupational Titles* was the first book to provide the O*NET in a useful printed form. This new edition is the first and only book to present the newest O*NET updates, including the new Standard Occupational Classification (SOC) system now used for organizing the O*NET jobs.

The O*NET Replaces an Older Occupational Information System

The O*NET was designed to replace an earlier occupational information system, also developed by the Department of Labor. This older system was used as the basis for a book titled the *Dictionary of Occupational Titles*, published for the final time in 1991.

The old DOT gave details on 12,741 occupational titles. While this is far more than the approximately 1,000 jobs in the O*NET database, many old DOT jobs were highly specialized or employed few people, and their descriptions were not included in the O*NET. The result is a list of O*NET occupations that is smaller and far more useful for many purposes.

The new O*NET and the old DOT systems have similarities because the new O*NET is built on the solid foundation provided by the older DOT system. If you are familiar with the *Dictionary of Occupational Titles*, you will probably feel quite comfortable with the O*NET descriptions in this book. Because this book bridges the new O*NET and the DOT, we refer to both systems in the title—*O*NET Dictionary of Occupational Titles*.

The O*NET Has Too Much Information to Be Useful for Many Purposes

Remember that the O*NET is not a book—it is a database with many details about each occupation. The O*NET database includes a narrative description of each job, plus details on almost 450 data element descriptors. If you were to print the complete O*NET information for one occupation, you would have a very long, boring, and confusing description.

Consider this: If you were asked to describe your best friend, you would most likely omit many details. For example, you probably would not mention your friend's blood type, cholesterol level, mom's name, if he or she were good at reading maps, and what he or she had for breakfast, lunch, and dinner. Instead, you would select details that you felt best described this person. More specific details could be very important to someone at some time, but not in many situations.

In a similar way, if you looked at all the information available for each occupation in the O*NET database, you would quickly understand why printing it in book form would not make sense. For example, following is the summary information on just one of the almost 450 O*NET data elements available for one occupation.

Rate control is very important for a job such as Aircraft Pilot, but it means little to most office workers, for example. So including rate control information on each occupation would not be helpful—and giving details on the almost 450 data elements for every job would create many pages of little interest to most people.

In addition, a book with all this information would be thousands of pages long and require many volumes. Who would buy or read it? For this reason, we used a variety of techniques to reduce the information provided for each occupation—and increase the usefulness of each description for most readers.

Element:	Rate Control		
Description:	The ability to time the adjustments of a movement or equipment control in anticipation of changes in the speed and/or direction of a continuously moving object or scene.		
Content Model Key:	I.A.2.b.4		
	I. Worker Characteristics		
	A. Abilities		
	2. Psychomotor Abilities		
	b. Control Movement Abilities		
	4. Rate Control		

Variable	Variable Description		File Name	Field Values	Scale, Ques Codes
A28LV00M	Rate Control-Level		Means_AB	1-7,0(NR)	LV,A

Left Label	Value	Right Value
Requires precisely timed control adjustments to random changes of a high-speed object moving in several directions.	7.00	
	6.50	Operating aircraft controls used to land a jet on an aircraft carrier in rough weather.
	4.80	Shooting a duck in flight.
	3.60	Keeping up with a car you are following when the speed of that car changes.
	2.40	Riding a bicycle alongside a jogger.
Requires timed control adjustments to a slow-moving, almost predictable object moving in a single direction.	1.00	

A28IM00M	Rate Control-Importance		Means_AB	1-5	IM,A

If You Want More Details About the O*NET Occupations

You may want more detailed information about occupations than we can provide in this book. For example, you may want to know the rate control measures for an occupation. If so, we suggest that you access the O*NET database. It is available on the Internet at http://online.onetcenter.org.

The O*NET database on the Internet can be difficult to use and understand, since it includes an enormous amount of detailed information on each job. Software from other sources, including JIST Publishing, will include the O*NET information in electronic form. In some cases, this software will make it much easier to find and use the details in the O*NET you really want. Please contact JIST if you are interested in software that includes the O*NET data; the company's information appears on page ii.

A Sample O*NET Description —and What It Includes

It would take more than 10 pages to print all the data on one job in the O*NET database. And much of that data would be in coded form that is not easy to understand without study. That's simply too much information for most people and would result in a book of more than 10,000 pages. So our challenge was to create a description of each O*NET occupation that would be useful to most people and that would be practical in book form.

We stayed up late many nights considering how to do this. The result is the carefully thought-out job descriptions you find in this book. Because a picture is worth a thousand words, we provide a sample O*NET job description next. To help you understand all that it includes, we point out its many elements and then explain each one.

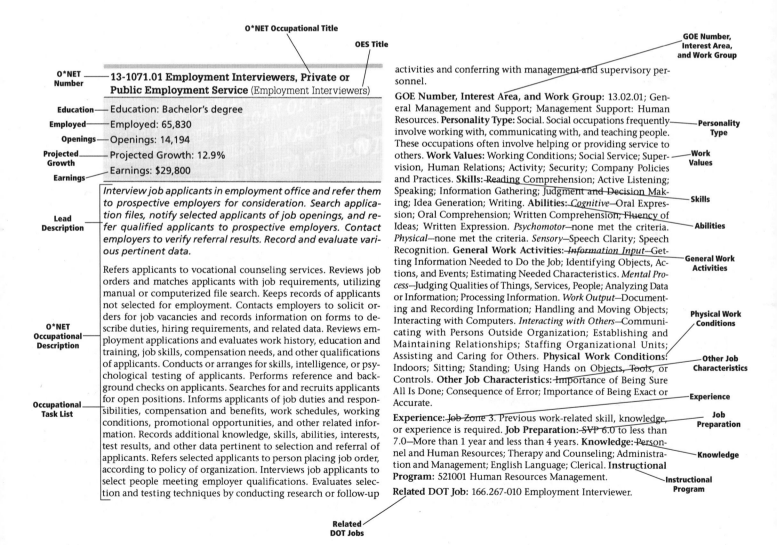

O*NET Occupational Title

OES Title

GOE Number, Interest Area, and Work Group

O*NET Number — 13-1071.01 Employment Interviewers, Private or Public Employment Service (Employment Interviewers)

Education — Education: Bachelor's degree

Employed — Employed: 65,830

Openings — Openings: 14,194

Projected Growth — Projected Growth: 12.9%

Earnings — Earnings: $29,800

Lead Description — *Interview job applicants in employment office and refer them to prospective employers for consideration. Search application files, notify selected applicants of job openings, and refer qualified applicants to prospective employers. Contact employers to verify referral results. Record and evaluate various pertinent data.*

O*NET Occupational Description — Refers applicants to vocational counseling services. Reviews job orders and matches applicants with job requirements, utilizing manual or computerized file search. Keeps records of applicants not selected for employment. Contacts employers to solicit orders for job vacancies and records information on forms to describe duties, hiring requirements, and related data. Reviews employment applications and evaluates work history, education and training, job skills, compensation needs, and other qualifications of applicants. Conducts or arranges for skills, intelligence, or psychological testing of applicants. Performs reference and background checks on applicants. Searches for and recruits applicants for open positions. Informs applicants of job duties and responsibilities, compensation and benefits, work schedules, working conditions, promotional opportunities, and other related information. Records additional knowledge, skills, abilities, interests, test results, and other data pertinent to selection and referral of applicants. Refers selected applicants to person placing job order, according to policy of organization. Interviews job applicants to select people meeting employer qualifications. Evaluates selection and testing techniques by conducting research or follow-up

Occupational Task List

activities and conferring with management and supervisory personnel.

GOE Number, Interest Area, and Work Group: 13.02.01; General Management and Support; Management Support: Human Resources. **Personality Type:** Social. Social occupations frequently involve working with, communicating with, and teaching people. These occupations often involve helping or providing service to others. **Work Values:** Working Conditions; Social Service; Supervision, Human Relations; Activity; Security; Company Policies and Practices. **Skills:** Reading Comprehension; Active Listening; Speaking; Information Gathering; Judgment and Decision Making; Idea Generation; Writing. **Abilities:** *Cognitive*—Oral Expression; Oral Comprehension; Written Comprehension; Fluency of Ideas; Written Expression. *Psychomotor*—none met the criteria. *Physical*—none met the criteria. *Sensory*—Speech Clarity; Speech Recognition. **General Work Activities:** *Information Input*—Getting Information Needed to Do the Job; Identifying Objects, Actions, and Events; Estimating Needed Characteristics. *Mental Process*—Judging Qualities of Things, Services, People; Analyzing Data or Information; Processing Information. *Work Output*—Documenting and Recording Information; Handling and Moving Objects; Interacting with Computers. *Interacting with Others*—Communicating with Persons Outside Organization; Establishing and Maintaining Relationships; Staffing Organizational Units; Assisting and Caring for Others. **Physical Work Conditions:** Indoors; Sitting; Standing; Using Hands on Objects, Tools, or Controls. **Other Job Characteristics:** Importance of Being Sure All Is Done; Consequence of Error; Importance of Being Exact or Accurate.

Experience: Job Zone 3. Previous work-related skill, knowledge, or experience is required. **Job Preparation:** SVP 6.0 to less than 7.0—More than 1 year and less than 4 years. **Knowledge:** Personnel and Human Resources; Therapy and Counseling; Administration and Management; English Language; Clerical. **Instructional Program:** 521001 Human Resources Management.

Related DOT Job: 166.267-010 Employment Interviewer.

Personality Type

Work Values

Skills

Abilities

General Work Activities

Physical Work Conditions

Other Job Characteristics

Experience

Job Preparation

Knowledge

Instructional Program

Related DOT Jobs

Details on Each Information Element in the Job Descriptions

While short, each description is packed with useful information that will be quite helpful for most readers. Most content is easy enough to understand, although some details will interest only those who require it. Other elements require some explanation. Following are details on each information element included in the job descriptions. Some of this information may be more detail than you need, so skim the content to find what you want to know.

We tried to keep our explanation nontechnical. Unfortunately, some of the O*NET is technical, and some readers have inquiring minds that want to know such details. For this reason, we felt compelled to add more information than some of you might want. Too much, too little—it's a balancing act we hope gives most of you what you need.

O*NET Number

Each O*NET occupation is assigned a unique number. These are not random numbers, because they are based on the Standard Occupational Classification (SOC) system established by the federal government. The SOC is a new structure for organizing jobs based on the work performed, and it is being adopted by all federal agencies that collect and distribute data. Since the O*NET numbering system puts job titles into groupings of related jobs, it's pretty logical to use. You can see how this system works by looking at the list of O*NET occupations in the table of contents. Occupations in this book are presented in numerical order, using their assigned O*NET number. Although some numbers appear to be missing, these absent numbers allow for future expansion of the numbering system.

Quick tip on how to use this information: The O*NET number allows you to quickly cross-reference other O*NET information sources, including the government's Web site that provides more details on the O*NET jobs.

O*NET Occupational Title

This title, which appears in bold, is assigned to the job by the Department of Labor. We include the newest O*NET titles, which are based on those used in the SOC system.

OES Title

In parenthesis is the job title used in the Occupational Employment Survey (OES) system that most closely relates to the O*NET job title. The government currently employs several systems to track information on occupations. The OES is used by U.S. Bureau of Labor Statistics (BLS) to collect wage and employment data. The O*NET system is used for most information in this book, but we used the OES system as the information source for the education requirements, employment data, projected growth, and earnings for each occupation. Therefore, you see the same education level, employment data and projections, and earnings data for jobs that share OES titles, even though their O*NET titles differ.

Quick tip on how to use this information: This alternate title may help you learn other names for this job. But the title is here more to let technical users know where we obtained key data, such as earnings.

Education

This line lists the education or training typically required for entry into a job. Please note, however, that some (or many) who work in the job may have higher or lower levels of education than indicated. Certification or licensing may be required for some jobs, but accurate information on such requirements is not available yet from the O*NET database. You need to determine such requirements from other sources, such as the *Occupational Outlook Handbook*.

The Department of Labor uses 11 levels of education or training to classify the education, training, and experience needs of a job. One of these levels is assigned to each job in this book.

The 11 Education and Training Levels

Short-term O-T-J (on-the-job) training. It is possible to work in these occupations and achieve an average level of performance within a few days or weeks through on-the-job training.

Moderate-term O-T-J (on-the-job) training. Occupations that require this type of training can be performed adequately after a 1- to 12-month period of combined on-the-job and informal training. Typically, untrained workers observe experienced workers perform tasks and are gradually moved into progressively more difficult assignments.

Long-term O-T-J (on-the-job) training. This training requires more than 12 months of on-the-job training or combined work experience and formal classroom instruction. This includes occupations that use formal apprenticeships for training workers that may take up to 4 years. It also includes intensive occupation-specific, employer-sponsored training like police academies. Furthermore, it includes occupations that require natural talent that must be developed over many years.

Work experience in a related occupation. This type of job requires experience in a related occupation. For example, police detectives are selected based on their experience as police patrol officers.

Postsecondary vocational training. This requirement can vary from training that involves a few months but is usually less than 1 year. In a few instances, there may be as many as 4 years of training.

Associate degree. This degree usually requires 2 years of full-time academic work beyond high school.

Bachelor's degree. This degree requires approximately 4 to 5 years of full-time academic work beyond high school.

Work experience, plus degree. Jobs in this category are often management-related and require some experience in a related nonmanagerial position.

Master's degree. Completion of a master's degree usually requires 1 to 2 years of full-time study beyond the bachelor's degree.

Doctoral degree. This degree normally requires 2 or more years of full-time academic work beyond the bachelor's degree.

First professional degree. This type of degree normally requires a minimum of 2 years of education beyond the bachelor's degree and frequently requires 3 years.

Quick tip on how to use this information: We put this information at the top of the description to give you a quick idea of the job's education or training requirements.

Employed

The number of people employed in the occupation can be used to estimate job availability. This information, released in 1998, comes from BLS and is the most current available.

Quick tip on how to use this information: Occupations employing a large number of people often have more openings than those employing smaller numbers. This is one useful measure of job opportunity.

Openings

The number of openings available each year for the job appears next. It is based on the new jobs created, plus openings due to resignations, terminations, retirement, and death. This data, released in 1998, comes from BLS and is the most current available.

Quick tip on how to use this information: Occupations with many annual openings often offer opportunity and may be easier to obtain.

Projected Growth

This part of the description lists the percent of projected new jobs for a 10-year period ending in 2008. The figure comes from BLS and is the most up-to-date available.

Quick tip on how to use this information: Jobs with high projected growth frequently provide many opportunities. Low and negative growth numbers may reflect stagnant or declining areas.

Earnings

This figure represents the median earnings for all people in the job. The median means that half the people earn more and half earn less. This annual amount, released in 1998, comes from BLS and is the most current available.

Quick tips on how to use this information: Earnings figures can be misleading for several reasons. For example, new or recent entrants to the occupation often earn substantially less because they usually have much less experience than the average person working in the job. Pay rates also often vary considerably in different regions of the country. In addition, smaller employers often pay less. So consider the earnings information as a guideline that may not apply to your situation. You can often obtain local earnings information from your state employment service or other sources; ask your librarian for help. You also can ask people employed in an occupation what workers in your geographic area earn at differing experience levels.

O*NET Occupational Description

This section gives you a brief but useable description for each job. The first part is the lead description, which is printed in italics. This text is sometimes followed by statements (also in italics) such as "Include wholesale or retail trade merchandising managers" or "Exclude procurement managers" that provide related titles that may be described in other O*NET occupations. This section is then followed, in regular type, by an occupational task list that describes occupational tasks specific to the job.

Quick tips on how to use this information: The brief lead information gives you a quick way to understand the job. If it interests you, the more detailed task statement gives you a good review of the work that someone in the job does.

GOE Number, Interest Area, and Work Group

The Guide for Occupational Exploration is a system for organizing jobs based on interests. Developed by the U.S.

Department of Labor, the GOE was designed as an intuitive way to help counselors, students, job seekers, career changers, and others identify occupations for further exploration. Since the GOE system is widely used for exploring career and learning options, we provide GOE information in the descriptions so you can cross-reference other systems that use it.

The GOE organizes all jobs into 14 major interest groupings and then into more specific subgroups (called *work groups*) of related jobs. Note that we use the latest GOE interest group and work group names and numbers throughout this book. This new GOE information comes from a major revision of the GOE system released in a book titled *Guide for Occupational Exploration,* Third Edition (JIST Works, 2001). The many changes and improvements make the old GOE system obsolete.

We include the six-digit GOE number for each job. The first two numbers represent the major interest area where the job is assigned. The third and fourth digits indicate the GOE work group where the job is found. The last two digits are used to provide a unique number for each job.

Here is a list of the GOE's 14 major interest areas.

The 14 GOE Interest Areas

01 Arts, Entertainment, and Media

02 Science, Math, and Engineering

03 Plants and Animals

04 Law, Law Enforcement, and Public Safety

05 Mechanics, Installers, and Repairers

06 Construction, Mining, and Drilling

07 Transportation

08 Industrial Production

09 Business Detail

10 Sales and Marketing

11 Recreation, Travel, and Other Personal Services

12 Education and Social Service

13 General Management and Support

14 Medical and Health Services

Quick tips on how to use this information: The GOE information is a very helpful way to find jobs that you might otherwise overlook. GOE codes in the job descriptions allow you to cross-reference any career information system using the new GOE structure. The appendix provides a more thorough description of the GOE system and includes a complete listing of its work groups and

other details—very useful for exploring career options. If you take an interest assessment that gives you a GOE code or group, the appendix allows you to cross-reference it to related O*NET jobs.

Personality Type

This information is useful for those who use a career interest inventory titled the *Self-Directed Search* or related career information systems based on these personality types. The SDS author developed a popular theory that suggests a person's interests can be classified into 1 of 6 personality types. Each personality type relates to jobs that fit the descriptions listed next.

The 6 Personality Types

Artistic. These occupations frequently involve working with forms, designs, and patterns. They often require self-expression, and the work can be done without following a clear set of rules.

Conventional. These occupations frequently involve following set procedures and routines. These occupations can include working with data and details more than with ideas. Usually there is a clear line of authority to follow.

Enterprising. These occupations frequently involve starting up and carrying out projects. These occupations can involve leading people and making many decisions. They sometimes require risk taking and often deal with business.

Investigative. These occupations frequently involve working with ideas and require an extensive amount of thinking. These occupations can involve searching for facts and figuring out problems mentally.

Realistic. These occupations frequently involve work activities that include practical, hands-on problems and solutions. They often deal with plants, animals, and real-world materials like wood, tools, and machinery. Many of the occupations require working outside and do not involve a lot of paperwork or working closely with others.

Social. These occupations frequently involve working with, communicating with, and teaching people. These occupations often involve helping or providing service to others.

Quick tips on how to use this information: The SDS and other career interest inventories, like the *Strong Campbell Interest Inventory* and the *Armed Services Vocational Battery*, use the SDS personality types. If you have used one of these popular tests, you might recall your personality type and can use it to identify jobs that match it. You can also use the personality type information even if you haven't taken one of the assessments. Simply read the personality type definitions and determine the one that most closely describes jobs that interest you. Then compare jobs you have held or are considering to see if they are close matches.

The Personality Types Easily Cross-Reference to GOE Interest Areas

Most career information systems use groupings of related jobs that can be easily cross-referenced. For example, here we include a table that cross-references the 14 GOE interest areas to the 6 SDS personality types. This "crosswalk" allows you to identify potential jobs based on interests and personality types. We hope you find this information interesting and useful, whatever your situation.

GOE Interest Area	Personality Type
01 Arts, Entertainment, and Media	Artistic
02 Science, Math, and Engineering	Investigative
03 Plants and Animals	Realistic
04 Law, Law Enforcement, and Public Safety	Realistic, Social
05 Mechanics, Installers, and Repairers	Realistic
06 Construction, Mining, and Drilling	Realistic
07 Transportation	Realistic
08 Industrial Production	Realistic
09 Business Detail	Conventional
10 Sales and Marketing	Enterprising
11 Recreation, Travel, and Other Personal Services	Social, Conventional
12 Education and Social Service	Social
13 General Management and Support	Enterprising, Social
14 Medical and Health Services	Investigative, Social

Work Values

The O*NET database includes information on 21 work values for each job. The work values information helps you identify jobs that match your personal values, such as wanting security or independence in the work you do. For most jobs, relatively few work values receive high ratings, so giving numeric data for all 21 values is not useful. Instead, we selected the work values with the highest ratings for each job. In most cases, we include the top 5 work values but list up to 8 if the numeric ratings are tied or very close.

The 21 work values are arranged into 6 major groupings.

The 21 Work Values

Achievement. **Occupations that satisfy these work values are results-oriented and allow employees to use their strongest abilities, giving them a feeling of accomplishment.**

Ability Utilization. Workers on this job make use of their individual abilities.

Achievement. Workers on this job get a feeling of accomplishment.

Altruism. **Occupations that satisfy these work values allow employees to provide service to others and work with coworkers in a friendly, noncompetitive environment.**

Coworkers. Workers on this job have coworkers who are easy to get along with.

Moral Values. Workers on this job are never pressured to do things that go against their sense of right and wrong.

Social Service. Workers on this job have work where they do things for other people.

Autonomy. **Occupations that satisfy this work value allow employees to work on their own and make decisions.**

Autonomy. Workers on this job plan their work with little supervision.

Creativity. Workers on this job try out their own ideas.

Responsibility. Workers on this job make decisions on their own.

Comfort. **Occupations that satisfy these work values offer job security and good working conditions.**

Activity. Workers on this job are busy all the time.

Compensation. Workers on this job are paid well in comparison with other workers.

Independence. Workers on this job do their work alone.

Security. Workers on this job have steady employment.

Variety. Workers on this job have something different to do every day.

Working Conditions. Workers on this job have good working conditions.

Safety. **Occupations that satisfy these work values offer supportive management that stands behind employees and provides a predictable and stable work environment.**

Company Policies and Practices. Workers on this job are treated fairly by the company.

Supervision, Human Relations. Workers on this job have supervisors who back up their workers with management.

Supervision, Technical. Workers on this job have supervisors who train their workers well.

(continues)

Identification of Key Causes. Identifying the things that must be changed to achieve a goal.

Identifying Downstream Consequences. Determining the long-term outcomes of a change in operations.

Implementation Planning. Developing approaches for implementing an idea.

Information Gathering. Knowing how to find information and identifying essential information.

Information Organization. Finding ways to structure or classify multiple pieces of information.

Installation. Installing equipment, machines, wiring, or programs to meet specifications.

Instructing. Teaching others how to do something.

Judgment and Decision Making. Weighing the relative costs and benefits of a potential action.

Management of Financial Resources. Determining how money will be spent to get the work done, and accounting for these expenditures.

Management of Material Resources. Obtaining and seeing to the appropriate use of equipment, facilities, and materials needed to do certain work.

Management of Personnel Resources. Motivating, developing, and directing people as they work, identifying the best people for the job.

Negotiation. Bringing others together and trying to reconcile differences.

Operation and Control. Controlling operations of equipment or systems.

Operation Monitoring. Watching gauges, dials, or other indicators to make sure a machine is working properly.

Operations Analysis. Analyzing needs and product requirements to create a design.

Persuasion. Persuading others to approach things differently.

Problem Identification. Identifying the nature of problems.

Product Inspection. Inspecting and evaluating the quality of products.

Programming. Writing computer programs for various purposes.

Repairing. Repairing machines or systems using the needed tools.

Service Orientation. Actively looking for ways to help people.

Social Perceptiveness. Being aware of others' reactions and understanding why they react the way they do.

Solution Appraisal. Observing and evaluating the outcomes of a problem solution to identify lessons learned or redirect efforts.

Synthesis and Reorganization. Reorganizing information to get a better approach to problems or tasks.

Systems Evaluation. Looking at many indicators of system performance, taking into account their accuracy.

Systems Perception. Determining when important changes have occurred in a system or are likely to occur.

Technology Design. Generating or adapting equipment and technology to serve user needs.

Testing. Conducting tests to determine whether equipment, software, or procedures are operating as expected.

Time Management. Managing one's time and the time of others.

Troubleshooting. Determining what is causing an operating error and deciding what to do about it.

Visioning. Developing an image of how a system should work under ideal conditions.

Quick tips on how to use this information: A big part of successful career decision-making depends on your knowing what skills you enjoy and are good at. So look over the list of skills and write down those that you would most like to use in your next job. These are the ones to include in your career planning as much as possible. If you are looking for a job, the skills in the job descriptions are those you should emphasize in the interview, since they are the ones likely to be valued by employers.

Abilities

This section contains "enduring attributes" that influence the job performance of workers. These attributes don't change over long periods of time. Abilities affect how quickly a person can learn new skills and the level of skill that can be achieved. Sometimes people refer to this as aptitude or even talent. Usually an ability increases your interest in learning and practicing a skill. For example, you may find that math is easy for you. So when you are taught a concept like calculating the mean and standard deviation (to help control product quality, for example) you are able to quickly learn how to use this in your job.

The O*NET database provides measures on 52 abilities for each job. (I trust that you are now beginning to understand our wisdom in including only the more important measures in each job description.) The abilities are organized into four subgroups: Cognitive (with 21 abilities), Psychomotor (10 abilities), Physical (9 abilities), and Sensory (12 abilities).

We used the O*NET's level-of-ability rating to select the top abilities in each subgroup. We set a requirement that an ability must have a measure higher than the average of that ability for all jobs. For example, the highest ranked physical abilities for Employment Interviewers include trunk strength, gross body coordination, and extent flexibility—but the numeric ratings for these abilities are only 17, 6, and 6 on a scale of 0 to 100. Obviously, these are not important abilities for an Employment Interviewer, and that is why we set the average as a minimum. When no ability has a rating higher than the average for all jobs, we write "none met the criteria."

Here are the 52 abilities that are included in the job descriptions, along with brief explanations for each.

The 52 Abilities

Cognitive Abilities. **These are mental processes that influence the acquisition and application of knowledge in problem solving.**

Category Flexibility. The ability to produce many rules so that each rule tells how to group or combine a set of things in a different way.

Deductive Reasoning. The ability to apply general rules to specific problems to come up with logical answers. It involves deciding if an answer makes sense or provides a logical explanation for why a series of seemingly unrelated events occur together.

Flexibility of Closure. The ability to identify or detect a known pattern (a figure, object, word, or sound) that is hidden in other distracting material.

Fluency of Ideas. The ability to come up with a number of ideas about a given topic. It concerns the number of ideas produced and not the quality, correctness, or creativity of the ideas.

Inductive Reasoning. The ability to combine separate pieces of information, or specific answers to problems, to form general rules or conclusions. It includes coming up with a logical explanation for why a series of seemingly unrelated events occur together.

Information Ordering. The ability to correctly follow a given rule or set of rules in order to arrange things or actions in a certain order. The things or actions can include numbers, letters, words, pictures, procedures, sentences, and mathematical or logical operations.

Mathematical Reasoning. The ability to understand and organize a problem and then to select a mathematical method or formula to solve the problem.

Memorization. The ability to remember information such as words, numbers, pictures, and procedures.

Number Facility. The ability to add, subtract, multiply, or divide quickly and correctly.

Oral Comprehension. The ability to listen to and understand information and ideas presented through spoken words and sentences.

Oral Expression. The ability to communicate information and ideas in speaking so others will understand.

Originality. The ability to come up with unusual or clever ideas about a given topic or situation, or to develop creative ways to solve a problem.

Perceptual Speed. The ability to quickly and accurately compare letters, numbers, objects, pictures, or patterns. The things to be compared may be presented at the same time or one after the other. This ability also includes comparing a presented object with a remembered object.

Problem Sensitivity. The ability to tell when something is wrong or is likely to go wrong. It does not involve solving the problem, only recognizing there is a problem.

Selective Attention. The ability to concentrate and not be distracted while performing a task over a period of time.

Spatial Orientation. The ability to know one's location in relation to the environment, or to know where other objects are in relation to one's self.

Speed of Closure. The ability to quickly make sense of information that seems to be without meaning or organization. It involves quickly combining and organizing different pieces of information into a meaningful pattern.

Time Sharing. The ability to efficiently shift back and forth between two or more activities or sources of information (such as speech, sounds, touch, or other sources).

Visualization. The ability to imagine how something will look after it is moved around or when its parts are moved or rearranged.

Written Comprehension. The ability to read and understand information and ideas presented in writing.

Written Expression. The ability to communicate information and ideas in writing so others will understand.

Psychomotor Abilities. **These abilities influence the capacity to manipulate and control objects primarily using fine motor skills.**

Arm-Hand Steadiness. The ability to keep the hand and arm steady while making an arm movement or while holding the arm and hand in one position.

Control Precision. The ability to quickly and repeatedly make precise adjustments in moving the controls of a machine or vehicle to exact positions.

Finger Dexterity. The ability to make precisely coordinated movements of the fingers of one or both hands to grasp, manipulate, or assemble very small objects.

Manual Dexterity. The ability to quickly make coordinated movements of one hand, a hand together with its arm, or two hands to grasp, manipulate, or assemble objects.

Multilimb Coordination. The ability to coordinate movements of two or more limbs together (for example, two arms, two legs, or one leg and one arm) while sitting, standing, or lying

© JIST Works

down. It does not involve performing the activities while the body is in motion.

Rate Control. The ability to time the adjustments of a movement or equipment control in anticipation of changes in the speed and/or direction of a continuously moving object or scene.

Reaction Time. The ability to quickly respond (with the hand, finger, or foot) to one signal (sound, light, picture, and so on) when it appears.

Response Orientation. The ability to choose quickly and correctly between two or more movements in response to two or more signals (lights, sounds, pictures, and so on). It includes the speed with which the correct response is started with the hand, foot, or other body parts.

Speed of Limb Movement. The ability to quickly move the arms or legs.

Wrist-Finger Speed. The ability to make fast, simple, repeated movements of the fingers, hands, and wrists.

***Physical Strength Abilities.* These abilities influence strength, endurance, flexibility, balance, and coordination.**

Dynamic Flexibility. The ability to quickly and repeatedly bend, stretch, twist, or reach out with the body, arms, and/or legs.

Dynamic Strength. The ability to exert muscle force repeatedly or continuously over time. This involves muscular endurance and resistance to muscle fatigue.

Explosive Strength. The ability to use short bursts of muscle force to propel oneself (as in jumping or sprinting) or to throw an object.

Extent Flexibility. The ability to bend, stretch, twist, or reach out with the body, arms, and/or legs.

Gross Body Coordination. The ability to coordinate the movement of the arms, legs, and torso together in activities where the whole body is in motion.

Gross Body Equilibrium. The ability to keep or regain one's body balance or stay upright when in an unstable position.

Stamina. The ability to exert one's self physically over long periods of time without getting winded or out of breath.

Static Strength. The ability to exert maximum muscle force to lift, push, pull, or carry objects.

Trunk Strength. The ability to use one's abdominal and lower back muscles to support part of the body repeatedly or continuously over time without giving out or fatiguing.

***Sensory Abilities.* These abilities influence visual, auditory, and speech perception.**

Auditory Attention. The ability to focus on a single source of auditory (hearing) information in the presence of other distracting sounds.

Depth Perception. The ability to judge which of several objects is closer or farther away from the observer, or to judge the distance between an object and the observer.

Far Vision. The ability to see details at a distance.

Glare Sensitivity. The ability to see objects in the presence of glare or bright lighting.

Hearing Sensitivity. The ability to detect or tell the difference between sounds that vary over broad ranges of pitch and loudness.

Near Vision. The ability to see details of objects at a close range (within a few feet of the observer).

Night Vision. The ability to see under low light conditions.

Peripheral Vision. The ability to see objects or movement of objects to one's side when the eyes are focused forward.

Sound Localization. The ability to tell the direction from which a sound originated.

Speech Clarity. The ability to speak clearly so that it is understandable to a listener.

Speech Recognition. The ability to identify and understand the speech of another person.

Visual Color Discrimination. The ability to match or detect differences between colors, including shades of color and brightness.

Quick tips on how to use this information: Many of the abilities are similar to the skills. This overlap should not concern you because skills and abilities are alike in some important ways. As with skills, you can select abilities that are important to you and look for career options that include them.

Abilities and Disabilities

We encourage you to use the data on abilities with care. The O*NET information does not take into account how a person with a disability might perform a job. Many jobs can be redesigned to accommodate disabilities. For this reason, the O*NET data should not be used to exclude people from jobs.

This is but one example how even carefully collected data can lead to inaccurate conclusions. Data has its limitations, and you need to use common sense in interpreting the contents of this book and other references.

General Work Activities

This section lists the general types of activities involved in performing the job described. As with the skills section, some jobs list very complex activities as well as more basic ones. There are four subgroups within general work activities: Information Input (5 activities), Mental Process (10 activities), Work Output (10 activities), and Interacting with Others (17 activities). The work activities measures provide one of the O*NET's best ways to get a flavor of the occupation. After careful consideration, we concluded that what matters most is not whether a work activity is rated above average, but rather which are the 3 or so most important activities. So, for each subgroup, we sorted all the activities for each occupation in order of importance, and then chose the top 3. In a few cases where activities tied for third place, we included as many as 5.

Here are brief descriptions for the 42 general work activities in the O*NET database.

The 42 General Work Activities

Information Input

Estimating Needed Characteristics. Estimating the characteristics of materials, products, events, or information: Estimating sizes, distances, and quantities or determining time, costs, resources, or materials needed to perform a work activity.

Getting Information Needed to Do the Job. Observing, receiving, and otherwise obtaining information from all relevant sources.

Identifying Objects, Actions, and Events. Identifying information received by making estimates or categorizations, recognizing differences or similarities, or sensing.

Inspecting Equipment, Structures, and Materials. Inspecting or diagnosing equipment, structures, or materials to identify the causes of errors or other problems or defects.

Monitoring Processes, Materials, and Surroundings. Monitoring and reviewing information from materials, events, or the environment, often to detect problems or to find out when things are finished.

Mental Process

Analyzing Data or Information. Identifying underlying principles, reasons, or facts by breaking down information or data into separate parts.

Developing Objectives and Strategies. Establishing long-range objectives and specifying the strategies and actions to achieve these objectives.

Evaluating Information Against Standards. Evaluating information against a set of standards and verifying that it is correct.

Judging Qualities of Things, Services, Other People's Work. Making judgments about or assessing the value, importance, or quality of things or people's work.

Making Decisions and Solving Problems. Combining, evaluating, and reasoning with information and data to make decisions and solve problems. These processes involve making decisions about the relative importance of information and choosing the best solution.

Organizing, Planning, and Prioritizing. Developing plans to accomplish work, and prioritizing and organizing one's work.

Processing Information. Compiling, coding, categorizing, calculating, tabulating, auditing, verifying, or processing information or data.

Scheduling Work and Activities. Scheduling events, programs, and activities, as well as the work of others.

Thinking Creatively. Originating, inventing, designing, or creating new applications, ideas, relationships, systems, or products, including artistic contributions.

Updating and Using Job-Relevant Knowledge. Keeping up-to-date technically and knowing the functions of one's job and related jobs.

Work Output

Controlling Machines and Processes. Using either control mechanisms or direct physical activity to operate machines or processes (not including computers or vehicles).

Documenting and Recording Information. Entering, transcribing, recording, storing, or maintaining information in either written form or by electronic/magnetic recording.

Drafting and Specifying Technical Devices. Providing documentation, detailed instructions, drawings, or specifications to inform others about how devices, parts, equipment, or structures are to be fabricated, constructed, assembled, modified, maintained, or used.

Handling and Moving Objects. Using one's hands and arms in handling, installing, forming, positioning, and moving materials, or in manipulating things. Includes the use of keyboards.

Implementing Ideas and Programs. Conducting or carrying out work procedures and activities in accord with one's ideas or information provided through directions/instructions for purposes of installing, modifying, preparing, delivering, constructing, integrating, finishing, or completing programs, systems, structures, or products.

Interacting with Computers. Controlling computer functions by using programs, setting up functions, writing software, or otherwise communicating with computer systems.

Operating Vehicles or Equipment. Running, maneuvering, navigating, or driving vehicles or mechanized equipment, such as forklifts, passenger vehicles, aircraft, or watercraft.

Performing General Physical Activities. Performing physical activities that require moving one's whole body, such as in climbing, lifting, balancing, walking, and stooping, where the activities often also require considerable use of the arms and legs, such as in the physical handling of materials.

Repairing and Maintaining Electrical Equipment. Fixing, servicing, adjusting, regulating, calibrating, fine-tuning, or testing machines, devices, and equipment that operate primarily on the basis of electrical or electronic (not mechanical) principles.

Repairing and Maintaining Mechanical Equipment. Fixing, servicing, aligning, setting up, adjusting, and testing machines, devices, moving parts, and equipment that operate primarily on the basis of mechanical (not electronic) principles.

Interacting with Others

Assisting and Caring for Others. Providing assistance or personal care to others.

Coaching and Developing Others. Identifying developmental needs of others and coaching or otherwise helping others to improve their knowledge or skills.

Communicating with Other Workers. Providing information to supervisors, fellow workers, and subordinates. This information can be exchanged face-to-face, in writing, or via telephone/electronic transfer.

Communicating with Persons Outside Organization. Communicating with persons outside the organization and representing the organization to customers, the public, government, and other external sources. Information can be exchanged face-to-face, in writing, or via telephone/electronic transfer.

Coordinating Work and Activities of Others. Coordinating members of a work group to accomplish tasks.

Developing and Building Teams. Encouraging and building mutual trust, respect, and cooperation among team members.

Establishing and Maintaining Relationships. Developing constructive and cooperative working relationships with others.

Guiding, Directing, and Motivating Subordinates. Providing guidance and direction to subordinates, including setting performance standards and monitoring subordinates.

Influencing Others or Selling. Convincing others to buy merchandise/goods or otherwise changing their minds or actions.

Interpreting Meaning of Information to Others. Translating or explaining what information means and how it can be understood or used to support responses or feedback to others.

Monitoring and Controlling Resources. Monitoring and controlling resources and overseeing the spending of money.

Performing Administrative Activities. Approving requests, handling paperwork, and performing day-to-day administrative tasks.

Performing for or Working with the Public. Performing for people or dealing directly with the public, including serving persons in restaurants and stores and receiving clients or guests.

Providing Consultation and Advice to Others. Providing consultation and expert advice to management or other groups on technical, systems-related, or process-related topics.

Resolving Conflict and Negotiating with Others. Handling complaints, arbitrating disputes, resolving grievances, or otherwise negotiating with others.

Staffing Organizational Units. Recruiting, interviewing, selecting, hiring, and promoting persons for the organization.

Teaching Others. Identifying educational needs, developing formal training programs or classes, and teaching or instructing others.

Quick tip on how to use this information: This information gives you a good idea of the types of activities that require higher-than-average skills for the job. So, for example, if a job requires higher-than-average skills in "staffing organizational units, " you need to decide if you have or want to develop these skills to perform well on this job.

Physical Work Conditions

The O*NET provides 26 measures on a variety of work environments and working conditions, including work setting, environmental conditions, job hazards, body positioning, and work attire. We found that many physical work conditions received a low rating in the O*NET even though it was obvious these conditions are important. That is why we selected the 3 work conditions with the highest ratings. If there were ties for the third position, we included as many as 5 conditions. Brief descriptions for each measure follow. Here are all the physical work conditions in the O*NET database, as well as brief descriptions of each.

The 26 Physical Work Conditions

Bending or Twisting the Body. Amount of bending or twisting.

Climbing Ladders, Scaffolds, Poles, etc. Covers all climbing to elevated locations.

Common Protective or Safety Attire. Examples are safety shoes, glasses, gloves, hearing protection, hard hat, and personal flotation device.

Contaminants. Contaminants present like pollutants, gases, dust, odors, and so on.

Cramped Work Space or Awkward Positions. Cramped work space that requires getting into awkward positions.

Diseases or Infections. Potential diseases/infections (for example, patient care, some laboratory work, and sanitation control).

Distracting Sounds and Noise Levels. Sounds and noise levels that are distracting and uncomfortable.

(continues)

(continued)

Extremely Bright or Inadequate Lighting. Extremely bright or inadequate lighting conditions.

Hazardous Conditions. For example, high-voltage electricity, combustibles, explosives, chemicals; does not include hazardous equipment or situations.

Hazardous Equipment. For example, saws and machinery/mechanical parts. Includes exposure to vehicular traffic but not driving a vehicle.

Hazardous Situations. Situations involving likely cuts, bites, stings, or minor burns.

High Places. For example, heights above 8 feet on ladders, poles, scaffolding, and catwalks.

Indoors. Amount job requires working indoors.

Keeping or Regaining Balance. Amount of keeping or regaining balance.

Kneeling, Crouching, or Crawling. Amount of kneeling, stooping, crouching, or crawling.

Making Repetitive Motions. Need to make repetitive motions.

Outdoors. Amount job requires working outdoors.

Radiation. Potential exposure to radiation.

Sitting. Amount of sitting required.

Special Uniform. Examples are that of a commercial pilot, nurse, police officer, or military personnel.

Specialized Protective or Safety Attire. Examples are breathing apparatus, safety harness, full protection suit, and radiation protection.

Standing. Amount of standing required.

Using Hands on Objects, Tools, or Controls. Using hands to handle, control, or feel objects, tools, or controls.

Very Hot. Very hot (above 90°F) or very cold (under 32°F) temperatures.

Walking or Running. Amount of walking or running.

Whole Body Vibration. For example, operating a jackhammer or earthmoving equipment.

Quick tips on how to use this information: For people with physical limitations or reactions to chemicals, for example, the importance of these measures is obvious. You can use this information to avoid jobs that are likely to cause you problems or provide tasks you cannot handle. All of us have limitations of some kind, and all of us have preferences for our working conditions. All jobs require some compromise, and the information here helps you clearly understand what a job may require of you.

Other Job Characteristics

This section of the job description provides other information you may find helpful. There are 8 job characteristics presented below. We included the 3 with the highest numerical measures in each job description and up to 5 if there was a tie for third place. Here are brief definitions for these characteristics.

The 8 Other Job Characteristics

Consequence of Error. The degree to which a mistake would cause a serious problem that was not readily correctable.

Frustrating Circumstances. The extent to which frustrating circumstances—roadblocks—to work are beyond the worker's control or hinder the accomplishment of this job.

Degree of Automation. The level of automation of this job.

Importance of Being Exact or Accurate. The importance of being very exact or highly accurate in performing this job.

Importance of Being Sure All Is Done. The importance of being sure that all the details of this job are performed and everything is done completely.

Importance of Being Aware of New Events. The importance of being constantly aware of either frequently changing events (for example, security guard watching for shoplifters) or infrequent events (for example, radar operator watching for tornadoes) to perform this job.

Importance of Repeating Same Tasks. The importance of repeating the same physical activities (for example, key entry) or mental activities (for example, checking entries in a ledger) over and over—without stopping.

Pace Determined by Speed of Equipment. The degree to which the pace is determined by the speed of equipment or machinery. (This does not refer to keeping busy at all times on this job.)

Quick tip on how to use this information: As you see, several of these items overlap with other data collected in the O*NET database. Still, we think you will find this information useful in helping you consider one job over another.

Experience

This section of the job description presents information the O*NET refers to as "job zones." The information presented in the O*NET job zones is a bit technical and hard to interpret, so we extracted one easily understood element from the job zones that gives the level of experience needed for each job. The O*NET assigns 1 of 5 levels of experience for each job, and we included this information in our job descriptions. Please note that sometimes discrepancies occur between the education data listed at a job description's beginning and the job zone data because the information comes from different agencies within the Department of Labor.

Here are the 5 levels the O*NET provides to help define the experience needed for entry into various jobs.

The 5 Levels of Experience

Job Zone 1. Little or no preparation needed. No previous work-related skill, knowledge, or experience is needed for these occupations. For example, a person can become a general office clerk even if the person has never worked in an office before.

Job Zone 2. Some preparation needed. Some previous work-related skill, knowledge, or experience may be helpful in these occupations but usually is not needed. For example, a drywall installer might benefit from experience installing drywall, but an inexperienced person could still learn to be an installer with little difficulty.

Job Zone 3. Medium preparation needed. Previous work-related skill, knowledge, or experience is required for these occupations. For example, an electrician must have completed 3 or 4 years of apprenticeship or several years of vocational training and often must have passed a licensing exam to perform the job.

Job Zone 4. Considerable preparation needed. A minimum of 2 to 4 years of work-related skill, knowledge, or experience is needed for these occupations. For example, an accountant must complete 4 years of college and work for several years in accounting to be considered qualified.

Job Zone 5. Extensive preparation needed. Extensive skill, knowledge, and experience are needed for these occupations. Many require more than 5 years of experience. For example, surgeons must complete 4 years of college and an additional 5 to 7 years of specialized medical training to be able to do the job.

Quick tip on how to use this information: This helps you understand the amount of training or education needed to qualify for entry into a job.

Job Preparation

The Department of Labor uses a system called the Standard Vocational Preparation (SVP) to assign 1 of 5 levels of training or education to a job. This SVP system has been used by the department for many years in standard reference systems such as the *Dictionary of Occupational Titles,* and SVP information has been included in the O*NET database. Please note that sometimes discrepancies occur between the education data listed at a job description's beginning and the job preparation data because the information comes from different agencies within the Department of Labor.

The 5 Standard Vocational Preparation (SVP) Codes

SVP below 4.0—Less than six months.

SVP 4.00 to 5.99—Six months to less than 2 years.

SVP 6.0 to less than 7.0—More than 1 year and less than 4 years.

SVP 7.0 to less than 8.0—2 years to less than 10 years.

SVP 8.0 and above—4 years to more than 10 years.

Quick tip on how to use this information: This measure is very similar to the one used for experience and can be used in a similar way to consider jobs that interest you.

Knowledge

Our job descriptions include information from the O*NET on the knowledge required to successfully perform in the occupation described. The knowledge may have been obtained from formal or informal sources, including high school or college courses or majors, training programs, self-employment, military, paid or volunteer work experience, and other life experiences. There are 33 O*NET knowledge descriptors. We selected the 5 with the highest importance ratings for each job and included as many as 8 if there was a tie.

Here are brief descriptions of the 33 knowledge items used in the O*NET and included in our job descriptions. They are arranged within the useful clusters shown here.

The 33 Knowledge Descriptors

Arts and Humanities

English Language. Knowledge of the structure and content of the English language, including the meaning and spelling of words, rules of composition, and grammar.

Fine Arts. Knowledge of theory and techniques required to produce, compose, and perform works of music, dance, visual arts, drama, and sculpture.

Foreign Language. Knowledge of the structure and content of a foreign (non-English) language, including the meaning and spelling of words, rules of composition and grammar, and pronunciation.

History and Archeology. Knowledge of past historical events and their causes, indicators, and impact on particular civilizations and cultures.

Philosophy and Theology. Knowledge of different philosophical systems and religions, including their basic principles, values, ethics, ways of thinking, customs, and practices, and their impact on human culture.

(continues)

(continued)

Business and Management

Administration and Management. Knowledge of principles and processes involved in business and organizational planning, coordination, and execution. This includes strategic planning, resource allocation, manpower modeling, leadership techniques, and production methods.

Clerical. Knowledge of administrative and clerical procedures and systems such as word-processing systems, filing and records management systems, stenography and transcription, forms design principles, and other office procedures and terminology.

Customer and Personal Service. Knowledge of principles and processes for providing customer and personal services, including needs assessment techniques, quality service standards, alternative delivery systems, and customer satisfaction evaluation techniques.

Economics and Accounting. Knowledge of economic and accounting principles and practices, the financial markets, banking, and the analysis and reporting of financial data.

Personnel and Human Resources. Knowledge of policies and practices involved in personnel/human resource functions. This includes recruitment, selection, training, and promotion regulations and procedures; compensation and benefits packages; labor relations and negotiation strategies; and personnel information systems.

Sales and Marketing. Knowledge of principles and methods involved in showing, promoting, and selling products or services. This includes marketing strategies and tactics, product demonstration and sales techniques, and sales control systems.

Communications

Communications and Media. Knowledge of media production, communication, and dissemination techniques and methods, including alternative ways to inform and entertain via written, oral, and visual media.

Telecommunications. Knowledge of transmission, broadcasting, switching, control, and operation of telecommunications systems.

Education and Training

Education and Training. Knowledge of instructional methods and training techniques, including curriculum design principles, learning theory, group and individual teaching techniques, design of individual development plans, and test design principles.

Law and Public Safety

Law, Government, and Jurisprudence. Knowledge of laws, legal codes, court procedures, precedents, government regulations, executive orders, agency rules, and the democratic political process.

Public Safety and Security. Knowledge of weaponry, public safety, and security operations, rules, regulations, precautions, prevention, and the protection of people, data, and property.

Manufacturing and Production

Building and Construction. Knowledge of materials, methods, and the appropriate tools to construct objects, structures, and buildings.

Computers and Electronics. Knowledge of electric circuit boards, processors, chips, and computer hardware and software, including applications and programming.

Design. Knowledge of design techniques, principles, tools, and instruments involved in the production and use of precision technical plans, blueprints, drawings, and models.

Engineering and Technology. Knowledge of equipment, tools, mechanical devices, and their uses to produce motion, light, power, technology, and other applications.

Food Production. Knowledge of techniques and equipment for planting, growing, and harvesting of food for consumption, including crop rotation methods, animal husbandry, and food storage/handling techniques.

Mechanical. Knowledge of machines and tools, including their designs, uses, benefits, repair, and maintenance.

Production and Processing. Knowledge of inputs, outputs, raw materials, waste, quality control, costs, and techniques for maximizing the manufacture and distribution of goods.

Mathematics and Science

Biology. Knowledge of plant and animal living tissue, cells, organisms, and entities, including their functions, interdependencies, and interactions with each other and the environment.

Chemistry. Knowledge of the composition, structure, and properties of substances and of the chemical processes and transformations that they undergo. This includes uses of chemicals and their interactions, danger signs, production techniques, and disposal methods.

Geography. Knowledge of various methods for describing the location and distribution of land, sea, and air masses, including their physical locations, relationships, and characteristics.

Mathematics. Knowledge of numbers, their operations, and interrelationships, including arithmetic, algebra, geometry, calculus, statistics, and their applications.

Medicine and Dentistry. Knowledge of the information and techniques needed to diagnose and treat injuries, diseases, and deformities. This includes symptoms, treatment alternatives, drug properties and interactions, and preventive health-care measures.

Physics. Knowledge and prediction of physical principles, laws, and applications, including air, water, material dynamics, light, atomic principles, heat, electric theory, earth formations, and meteorological and related natural phenomena.

Psychology. Knowledge of human behavior and performance, mental processes, psychological research methods, and the assessment and treatment of behavioral and affective disorders.

Sociology and Anthropology. Knowledge of group behavior and dynamics, societal trends and influences, cultures, their history, migrations, ethnicity, and origins.

Therapy and Counseling. Knowledge of information and techniques needed to rehabilitate physical and mental ailments and to provide career guidance, including alternative treatments, rehabilitation equipment and its proper use, and methods to evaluate treatment effects.

Transportation

Transportation. Knowledge of principles and methods for moving people or goods by air, rail, sea, or road, including their relative costs, advantages, and limitations.

Quick tips on how to use this information: If you are considering additional education or training, this section gives you some idea of the courses or programs that would be helpful for each job. It also helps you to identify if you have some or all knowledge needed for a new job and what you need to improve on through additional training.

Instructional Program

The Classification of Instructional Programs (CIP) is a system of naming and categorizing training and educational programs and courses. Developed by the U.S. Department of Education, the CIP is widely used in occupational, education, and training reference systems. We listed the CIP program or course names related to each occupation.

Quick tip on how to use this information: The CIP information helps you identify the names of training or educational programs that prepare you for a job. The U.S. Department of Education has a reference guide describing all of the CIP programs. Titled the *Classification of Instructional Programs*, it should be available through state libraries and directly from the Department of Education at www.ed.gov.

Related DOT Jobs

At the end of each description is one or more job titles related to the O*NET job title. We obtained these by cross-referencing the O*NET title to another occupational classification system titled the *Dictionary of Occupational Titles*. The DOT is an older occupational reference system developed by the Department of Labor that has been replaced by the O*NET. We also included the DOT number assigned to each job title to allow you to cross-reference career information systems using the DOT system.

Quick tips on how to use this information: Even if you never use the DOT, the alternative titles help you identify the wide range of specialized jobs that are available. The DOT has over 12,000 job titles, and most of them are now merged into the more general job titles used in the O*NET. This makes the O*NET much easier to use when identifying jobs that interest you, and the DOT job titles can give you ideas on more specialized jobs that may interest you even more. If you wish, you can then learn more about the more specialized DOT jobs by reading their descriptions in the *Dictionary of Occupational Titles*. One of these specialized jobs may be just what you want to do with your career.

An Explanation of Some Curious Things in the Job Descriptions

As you read the job descriptions in this book, you may notice some odd things. For example, some job descriptions do not include information found in most other descriptions. And other details here and there may not seem right to you. We explain some of these points here, although you may notice others.

The basic reason for what appears to be errors is that the job descriptions are based on data we assemble from and cross-reference to several enormous databases of information. These databases are not perfect. They may have missing data, do not provide precise cross-references to other systems, and have other limitations. We did our best to create a useful resource but had to base it on the limitations of our information sources. So here are explanations of a few things you may notice as you read the job descriptions.

Information in the Descriptions May Overlap

As you read the job descriptions that follow this introduction, you may note that information in one section of a description is similar to information in another. This is not an error on our part, since the O*NET data sometimes overlaps. For example, the general work activities statements are often similar to the occupational task list section. The skills statements may be similar to content provided elsewhere in the description.

The reason lies in how the information was developed. The occupational task lists were written specifically for each job, based on information collected from employer surveys and other sources. Work values, knowledge, abilities, skills, general work activities, and physical work conditions were created quite differently. For these, a list of characteristics was developed that applies to many or all jobs. Each occupation was given a numerical rating for each characteristic, with higher numbers referring to higher levels of competence. Since there are so many measures, listing them all for each job would be impractical and, we think, confusing. Instead, we developed a method for listing the more important characteristics for each job—the ones that are most important to have or develop.

"None Met the Criteria"

The criteria we used to select data for inclusion in the job descriptions differs from one part to another. These criteria were explained earlier in this introduction.

When you see the statement, "none met the criteria" in the abilities or other parts of a job description, this doesn't mean abilities are not important in these jobs. Rather, the job had no measure high enough to meet our criteria for inclusion. We adjusted our criteria to avoid this situation from occurring too often, but you see this statement in some descriptions.

Information That Seems Incorrect

You may notice that some information in a job descriptions seems contradictory, inaccurate, or incorrect. This is simply a reflection of the data that was available from the database. So, as you review the descriptions, keep in mind that data has its limitations.

For example, you may notice that several jobs in a row share the same education, openings, growth, and salary data. Although the O*NET system is used for most information in this book, we use the OES system explained earlier as the source for the education requirements, employment projections, and earnings. Therefore, you see the same education, employment information, and salary data for jobs that share OES titles (listed in parentheses), even though their O*NET titles differ.

"No Data Available"

When you see this statement in a job description, it means just what it says. This tends to happen for recent O*NET job entries, where the data has not yet been collected or processed for one or more of that job's measures.

"Partial List"

You see this statement at the end of some job descriptions in the Related DOT Jobs section. We did this only when there is a very long list of similar or related DOT jobs. When this is so, we listed the first 20 DOT job titles. Since this section's purpose is to introduce you to the many specialized jobs related to each O*NET title, we think that listing 20 specialized job titles gives you a good idea of the many related occupations. For some O*NET job titles, there are hundreds of related DOT titles. Many of these jobs are similar to each other, like "Manager, Bakery" and "Manager, Cemetery," and going on and on with similar job titles isn't helpful.

Some Job Descriptions Are Shorter Than Others

Some job descriptions are substantially shorter others. When this occurs, you see the statement, "The Department of Labor has not collected some data for this job, so it has fewer details than the other descriptions."

One reason for the shorter descriptions is that some jobs have been recently added to the O*NET database, and these do not yet have data available for them.

Another reason is that sometimes one job title encapsulates other detailed jobs as part of the numbering structure, and the one job title has a briefer description. To get full information, you need to review the detailed jobs' descriptions. For example, Accountants and Auditors is listed as one job (with a shorter description), but it is then followed by longer, separate descriptions for Accountants and then Auditors.

O*NET Job Title Is Followed by the Same or Similar Title in Parentheses

We know this looks odd when it occurs, but the second title is the OES title, and this is sometimes the same as the O*NET title. We considered moving the OES title down in the description where it would not be as noticeable. We may do that in a future revision, but decided to put it where it is since the OES title is the source of some key data on earnings and other points.

Tips for Using This Book

The O*NET is now the major and most authoritative source of occupational information for employers, job seekers, students, career changers, and many others. Most occupational information sources will rely on or cross-reference to the O*NET as the standard for detailed, reliable data on jobs.

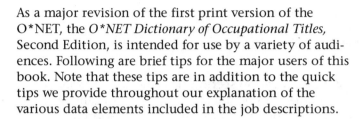

As a major revision of the first print version of the O*NET, the *O*NET Dictionary of Occupational Titles, Second Edition,* is intended for use by a variety of audiences. Following are brief tips for the major users of this book. Note that these tips are in addition to the quick tips we provide throughout our explanation of the various data elements included in the job descriptions.

Tips for Employers and Human Resource Development Professionals

The O*NET descriptions in this book provide a variety of valuable information for use in business. Some of these uses include the following.

- **Write job descriptions.** Each O*NET description has been carefully constructed to accurately reflect the tasks, skills, abilities, and other attributes required. These details provide an excellent source of objective information to use in writing job descriptions. As an example, look back at the sample description for Employment Interviewers presented earlier in the introduction. You find the key skills needed in the position, the responsibility level required, the education and training required, and the knowledge needed to succeed in the job—most of the content for a solid job description. Of course, you will need to customize the information for your organization, but the O*NET descriptions provide an excellent starting point.

- **Structure employment interviews and hiring decisions.** You can use the O*NET descriptions to identify key skills and experiences to look for when screening applicants during interviews. This can be done informally, or a formal list of required competencies could be developed and then used by interviewers to more objectively rate each applicant. Of course, employer-specific requirements should be added as needed to the basic requirements for job performance provided by the O*NET descriptions.

- **Set pay levels.** We have noted the limitations for using pay information, and those same cautions apply when used by employers setting pay levels. The salary information does, however, provide some guidance on the pay rate for an experienced worker. Entry-level workers are often be paid less (sometimes much less), and local conditions often determine the going rate to attract the employee skills needed. There are no hard guidelines, so use your judgment.

- **Identify training requirements.** You can use the descriptions to identify training needed for current or prospective employees to gain proficiency in various jobs. You may also identify skills or other weaknesses in a potential employee that can be corrected through brief training and, therefore, increase the applicant pool for certain positions. The O*NET information is also helpful for existing employees seeking upward mobility to a more challenging or different job with the same employer. It can help them identify skills, training, knowledge, and other factors that they need to develop for success.

Tips for People Exploring Career Alternatives

Virtually all workers in North America work in one of the occupations described in this book. While the descriptions are quite brief, they provide substantial information that can be used as a preliminary source for identifying one or more career options to explore more thoroughly.

If you are using this book to explore career options, the best way to begin is by identifying clusters of jobs that interest you most. We suggest you do this by looking at the list of jobs in the table of contents. The occupations there are arranged into groups of similar jobs, with the groups presented in bold type. Once you locate a group of jobs that seems interesting to you, identify specific job titles within the same or similar groups for further exploration. In this way, you will often identify jobs that you may otherwise not consider. Read the O*NET descriptions for those jobs that most interest you and, for those you want to know even more about, use one of the resources that follow:

- **Read the *Occupational Outlook Handbook.*** Each O*NET description includes a reference to one or more job titles found in a separate book titled the *Occupational Outlook Handbook.* We like the OOH and recommend it highly. Its descriptions are longer and provide details that are useful to anyone considering the occupation. The OOH is available in most libraries and through many bookstores. The OOH descriptions are also provided in a book titled *America's Top 300 Jobs* (JIST Works). One of these books should be available in most libraries and bookstores.

- **Read the *Dictionary of Occupational Titles* and the *Guide for Occupational Exploration.*** The DOT and GOE are widely used reference books with organizational systems cross-referenced by many other books, interest inventories, and other materials. The O*NET descriptions in this book include related DOT and GOE numbers and job titles or interest groups, allowing you to cross-reference these important systems. The DOT was published by the U.S. Department of Labor and provides brief descriptions for over 12,000 job titles. The last edition of the DOT was released in 1991. Since the O*NET database replaces the older DOT database of occupational information, there are no plans to update the DOT in the future. Even so, it will remain a rich source of information on many specific job titles that are simply not described elsewhere. The *Guide for Occupational Exploration,* Third Edition (JIST Works), organizes jobs into groupings based on interests and provides useful information on these groupings and the jobs within the groups.

● **Get additional information from the library or the Internet.** Ask a librarian to direct you to books, periodicals, and other sources of information on an occupation that interests you. Professional journals are often available for a wide variety of occupations and industries. You can also often obtain substantial information from professional associations and sources on the Internet. JIST's Web site provides links to other career-related sites. Visit the company at www.jist.com.

● **Talk to people who work in the jobs that interest you.** The best source of information is often overlooked—the people who work in jobs that interest you. They are often willing to answer your questions and to give you sources of additional information.

Tips for Those Considering Education or Training Options

People with more training or education tend to earn more than those with less. While most training and education benefits you in some way, too many people do not spend enough time investigating such an important decision. Before you spend substantial time and money on courses or training programs, spend some time investigating what you hope to gain.

Each O*NET description provides several sources of education and training information. The education section of each job description is the most obvious one, but additional information is found in the knowledge and instructional programs sections. Following are some details on how each of these sections can be used to better understand the training or education needed for a given job.

● **The education section.** This includes information on the training or education level typically required for entry into the listed occupation.

● **The knowledge section.** This section gives you some idea of the courses or programs that would be helpful for each job.

● **The instructional program section.** Each occupational description includes a CIP code and title. This refers to the Classification of Instructional Programs, a widely used system for organizing training and education programs. The CIP code and title tell you the type of training or educational programs typically available for preparing for that occupation. Program names used in various schools and training programs may differ from those listed in the CIP, but the CIP information gives you some idea of the programs available.

While the O*NET descriptions provide some information on the level of training, education, and experience required for various occupations, you obviously need more detail. As with occupational data, a wide variety of training and education information is available. Bookstores and libraries have many books on the topic; much is available on the Internet; and local schools and training programs provide orientation and admission information. All these resources should be used before making an important decision on education or training.

Tips for Job Seekers

The O*NET job descriptions in this book can help you in two important ways:

● **Identify new job targets.** Many job seekers miss employment opportunities by overlooking jobs they can do but with which they are not familiar. For this reason, you should carefully review all the O*NET job titles, with particular emphasis on those in clusters you are already considering. A listing of O*NET jobs within clusters appears in the table of contents. Review it if you are looking for a job. As you identify possible new job targets, look up their O*NET descriptions to determine if you might qualify. If so, you should consider pursuing these jobs. In the interview, point out the qualities that you have and state that you can quickly learn any needed skills.

- **Prepare for interviews.** The O*NET descriptions offer very useful information in preparing for interviews. For example, once you have set up an interview for a position, carefully review the O*NET description for that job. Doing so helps you identify skills and experience you should emphasize. We also encourage you to carefully review the O*NET descriptions of jobs you have held in the past. Doing so identifies skills and other characteristics that you can present in your interview for a new position.

Even past jobs that seem unrelated to your current interests often provide skills and experience that you can use to convince an employer that you can handle the position you seek. Careful interview preparation can make the difference between getting a job offer or not. We have often found that better-prepared job seekers get jobs over those with superior credentials. The difference is in how well they present themselves in interviews. Those who read and understand the skills they have to do the job they seek—and communicate this to an employer—have a distinct advantage.

Tips for Teachers and Educators

O*NET descriptions provide excellent information on the skill and knowledge needed to succeed in a given job. If you are responsible for developing or teaching a course or curriculum for a school or training program, the descriptions provide exact points that need to be learned. An outcome-oriented program could be developed to teach specific, measurable knowledge or competencies. Remember that the O*NET database provides specific measures for many elements included in this book, and these measures can be obtained by accessing the database itself.

Tips for Those Researching Technical and Legal Issues—"Caveat Datum"

You have probably heard of "caveat emptor," which is Latin for "let the buyer beware." We think "caveat datum," which loosely translated means "beware of the data," is particularly appropriate as our advice regarding the O*NET data as the basis for settling legal and other important issues.

The O*NET database—and the O*NET descriptions in this book—provide substantial technical information on jobs and their many characteristics and requirements. The U.S. government provides this information, and great care has been taken to make it both accurate and reliable. Even so,

the information does have limitations. For example, the O*NET job title Sales Managers has enormous differences in requirements from one employer to another in such points as responsibility, stress, travel requirements, computer literacy requirements, product knowledge, and physical lifting of samples. These differences can simply not be included in one description database, and many job-to-job differences exist. That is why the U.S. Department of Labor has never approved or encouraged the use of its occupational information to support formal litigation or as the final, authoritative basis for legal and other formal matters.

In a similar way, we urge you to understand that the validity of the underlying information has limitations. For example, an occupation that lists a bachelor's degree as a typical training requirement for entry often has some or even many people successfully working in the job with less education—or much more.

One information source can simply not cover all variations of a given job. Too many differences exist in the requirements for the same job title among different employers. That is why we recommend that you use your own judgment in understanding the information. While it has been carefully collected and reviewed, it has limitations and should not be used as the final authoritative source for legal or technical issues.

The Appendix—Useful for Career Exploration Based on Interests!

We know that hardly anyone pays attention to an appendix, but this book's appendix is an exception. The reason is that it can be used by you to explore career options based on your interests. You can use it as a type of assessment inventory, and it's free. We provide additional details on how to use the information in the appendix itself, but here is a brief review.

The appendix presents some very useful information based on the *Guide for Occupational Exploration*, Third Edition, revised by JIST Works in 2001. The GOE is a career reference originally developed by the U.S. Department of Labor to help people explore career options.

The appendix begins with a brief description of 14 interest areas used in the GOE. Just pick one or more of these areas that sound most appealing to you. Next comes a very helpful list of GOE groupings of related jobs. This arrangement allows you to quickly find the types of jobs that appeal to you. Each job grouping then lists job titles from two standard reference sources, the OOH and, of course, the O*NET.

Since all the job titles are from standard reference sources, you can easily get additional information on any job title you find—and descriptions of the O*NET jobs are in this very book.

Your Suggestions Are Welcome

While it was impractical to include details on all data elements for each occupation found in the O*NET database, the O*NET descriptions in this book include substantial details in a useful format. In addition to the narrative description, we include higher-than-average requirements for many data elements for each occupation—plus the crosswalk information for the GOE, CIP, and DOT (all explained earlier). While some compromises were involved in constructing helpful descriptions, we think the information is valuable for many uses. We hope you agree.

Because we intend to revise this book as updated O*NET data becomes available, please let us know what you would like us to include in future editions. Please send your comments and suggestions to Editor, *O*NET Dictionary of Occupational Titles,* JIST Works, 8902 Otis Ave., Indianapolis, IN 46216-1033. You can also send an e-mail to ONET@jist.com. Thanks!

O*NET Occupational Descriptions

This is the book's main section, and it provides information-packed descriptions for the 1,000-plus jobs in the O*NET database. Descriptions are arranged by their O*NET number and in logical groupings of related jobs.

See the introduction for more details on how this section is organized. In addition, a sample job description points out the important features of each entry. The introduction also offers helpful information on how to use and interpret the descriptions.

If you are looking for a list of the job descriptions included here, see the table of contents. Also, all job titles appear alphabetically in the index.

11-0000
Management Occupations

11-1000 Top Executives

11-1011.00 Chief Executives (General Managers and Top Executives)

Education: Work experience, plus degree
Employed: 3,362,395
Openings: 421,006
Projected Growth: 16.4%
Earnings: $55,890

Determine and formulate policies and provide the overall direction of companies or private and public sector organizations within the guidelines set up by a board of directors or similar governing body. Plan, direct, or coordinate operational activities at the highest level of management with the help of subordinate executives and staff managers.

GOE Number, Interest Area, and Work Group: 13.01.01; General Management and Support; General Management Work and Management of Support Functions. **Instructional Programs:** 440401 Public Administration; 500704 Arts Management; 520201 Business Administration and Management, General; 520701 Enterprise Management and Operation, General; 521101 International Business. **Note:** The Department of Labor has not collected some data for this job, so it has fewer details than the other descriptions.

11-1011.01 Government Service Executives (General Managers and Top Executives)

Education: Work experience, plus degree
Employed: 3,362,395
Openings: 421,006
Projected Growth: 16.4%
Earnings: $55,890

Determine and formulate policies and provide overall direction of federal, state, local, or international government activities. Plan, direct, and coordinate operational activities at the highest level of management with the help of subordinate managers.

Plans, promotes, organizes, and coordinates public community service program and maintains cooperative working relationships among public and agency participants. Directs organization charged with administering and monitoring regulated activities to interpret and clarify laws and ensure compliance with laws. Prepares budget and directs and monitors expenditures of department funds. Directs and conducts studies and research, and prepares reports and other publications relating to operational trends and program objectives and accomplishments. Negotiates contracts and agreements with federal and state agencies and other organizations and prepares budget for funding and implementation of programs. Implements corrective action plan to solve problems. Establishes and maintains comprehensive and current record keeping system of activities and operational procedures in business office. Delivers speeches, writes articles, and presents information for organization at meetings or conventions to promote services, exchange ideas, and accomplish objectives. Participates in activities to promote business and expand services, and provides technical assistance in conducting of conferences, seminars, and workshops. Testifies in court, before control or review board, or at legislature. Develops, plans, organizes, and administers policies and procedures for organization to ensure administrative and operational objectives are met. Reviews and analyzes legislation, laws, and public policy and recommends changes to promote and support interests of general population, as well as special groups. Directs and coordinates activities of workers in public organization to ensure continuing operations, maximize returns on investments, and increase productivity. Develops, directs, and coordinates testing, hiring, training, and evaluation of staff personnel. Consults with staff and others in government, business, and private organizations to discuss issues, coordinate activities, and resolve problems.

GOE Number, Interest Area, and Work Group: 13.01.01; General Management and Support; General Management Work and Management of Support Functions. **Personality Type:** Enterprising. Enterprising occupations frequently involve starting up and carrying out projects. These occupations can involve leading people and making many decisions. They sometimes require risk taking and often deal with business. **Work Values:** Authority; Working Conditions; Responsibility; Activity; Autonomy; Ability Utilization. **Skills:** Coordination; Judgment and Decision Making; Problem Identification; Identification of Key Causes; Identifying Downstream Consequences; Critical Thinking; Monitoring; Solution Appraisal. **Abilities:** *Cognitive*—Oral Expression; Oral Comprehension; Written Comprehension; Written Expression; Inductive Reasoning. *Psychomotor*—none met the criteria. *Physical*—Trunk Strength. *Sensory*—Speech Clarity; Near Vision; Speech Recognition. **General Work Activities:** *Information Input*—Getting Information Needed to Do the Job; Identifying Objects, Actions, and Events; Estimating Needed Characteristics. *Mental Process*—Analyzing Data or Information; Processing Information; Making Decisions and Solving Problems. *Work Output*—Implementing Ideas and Programs; Documenting and Recording Information; Interacting with Computers. *Interacting with Others*—Communicating with Other Workers; Coordinating Work and Activities of Others; Guiding, Directing and Motivating Subordinates; Communicating with Persons Outside Organization; Performing Administrative Activities. **Physical Work Conditions:** Indoors; Sitting; Standing. **Other Job Characteristics:** Consequence of Error; Frustrating Circumstances; Importance of Being Exact or Accurate; Importance of Being Sure All Is Done.

Experience: Job Zone 4. A minimum of two to four years of work-related skill, knowledge, or experience is needed. **Job Preparation:** SVP 7.0 to less than 8.0—2 years to less than 10 years. **Knowledge:** Administration and Management; Law, Government and Jurisprudence; English Language; Education and Training; Economics and Accounting; Personnel and Human Resources. **Instructional Programs:** 440401 Public Administration; 500704 Arts Management; 520201 Business Administration and Management, General; 520701 Enterprise Management and Operation, General; 521101 International Business.

Related DOT Jobs: 050.117-010 Director, Employment Research and Planning; 079.167-010 Community-Services-and-Health-Education Officer; 137.137-010 Director, Translation; 168.167-090 Manager, Regulated Program; 169.117-010 Executive Secretary, State Board of Nursing; 185.167-062 Supervisor, Liquor Stores and Agencies; 186.117-022 Deputy Insurance Commissioner; 187.117-018 Director, Institution; 187.117-054 Superintendent, Recreation; 188.117-014 Business-Enterprise Officer; 188.117-018 Chief, Fishery Division; 188.117-022 Civil Preparedness Officer; 188.117-026 Commissioner, Conservation of Resources; 188.117-030 Commissioner, Public Works; 188.117-034 Director, Aeronautics Commission; 188.117-038 Director, Agricultural Services; 188.117-042 Director, Arts-and-Humanities Council; 188.117-046 Director, Compliance; 188.117-050 Director, Consumer Affairs; 188.117-054 Director, Correctional Agency (partial list; see the introduction for sources of the complete list).

11-1011.02 Private Sector Executives (General Managers and Top Executives)

Education: Work experience, plus degree

Employed: 3,362,395

Openings: 421,006

Projected Growth: 16.4%

Earnings: $55,890

Determine and formulate policies and business strategies and provide overall direction of private sector organizations. Plan, direct, and coordinate operational activities at the highest level of management with the help of subordinate managers.

Screens, selects, hires, transfers, and discharges employees. Confers with board members, organization officials, and staff members to establish policies and formulate plans. Directs activities of organization to plan procedures, establish responsibilities, and coordinate functions among departments and sites. Reviews financial statements and sales and activity reports to ensure that organization's objectives are achieved. Assigns or delegates responsibilities to subordinates. Directs and coordinates activities of business involved with buying and selling investment products and financial services. Presides over or serves on board of directors, management committees, or other governing boards. Negotiates or approves contracts with suppliers and distributors, and with maintenance, janitorial, and security providers. Promotes objectives of institution or business before associations, the public, government agencies, or community groups. Analyzes operations to evaluate performance of company and staff and to determine areas of cost reduction and program improvement. Directs inservice training of staff. Establishes internal control procedures. Prepares reports and budgets. Directs non-merchandising departments of business, such as advertising, purchasing, credit, and accounting. Directs and coordinates activities of business or department concerned with production, pricing, sales, and/or distribution of products. Directs and coordinates organization's financial and budget activities to fund operations, maximize investments, and increase efficiency. Directs, plans, and implements policies and objectives of organization or business in accordance with charter and board of directors. Administers program for selection of sites, construction of buildings, and provision of equipment and supplies.

GOE Number, Interest Area, and Work Group: 13.01.01; General Management and Support; General Management Work and Management of Support Functions. **Personality Type:** Enterprising. Enterprising occupations frequently involve starting up and carrying out projects. These occupations can involve leading people and making many decisions. They sometimes require risk taking and often deal with business. **Work Values:** Authority; Autonomy; Working Conditions; Responsibility; Activity; Social Status; Compensation. **Skills:** Judgment and Decision Making; Coordination; Systems Perception; Identification of Key Causes; Identifying Downstream Consequences; Solution Appraisal; Systems Evaluation. **Abilities:** *Cognitive*—Oral Comprehension; Oral Expression; Written Comprehension; Written Expression; Number Facility; Problem Sensitivity. *Psychomotor*—none met the criteria. *Physical*—Trunk Strength. *Sensory*—Speech Clarity; Near Vision; Speech Recognition. **General Work Activities:** *Information Input*—Getting Information Needed to Do the Job; Identifying Objects, Actions, and Events; Monitoring Processes, Materials, and Surroundings. *Mental Process*—Developing Objectives and Strategies; Making Decisions and Solving Problems; Organizing, Planning, and Prioritizing. *Work Output*—Implementing Ideas and Programs; Interacting with Computers; Documenting and Recording Information. *Interacting with Others*—Monitoring and Controlling Resources; Communicating with Other Workers; Performing Administrative Activities; Providing Consultation and Advice to Others; Influencing Others or Selling; Developing and Building Teams. **Physical Work Conditions:** Indoors; Sitting; Walking or Running; Standing. **Other Job Characteristics:** Consequence of Error; Importance of Being Sure All Is Done; Frustrating Circumstances.

Experience: Job Zone 5. Extensive skill, knowledge, and experience are needed. Very advanced communication and organizational skills are required. **Job Preparation:** SVP 8.0 and above—4 years to more than 10 years. **Knowledge:** Administration and Management; Economics and Accounting; English Language; Sales and Marketing; Production and Processing; Mathematics. **Instructional Programs:** 440401 Public Administration; 500704 Arts Management; 520201 Business Administration and Management, General; 520701 Enterprise Management and Operation, General; 521101 International Business.

Related DOT Jobs: 090.117-034 President, Educational Institution; 099.117-022 Superintendent, Schools; 137.137-010 Director, Translation; 185.117-010 Manager, Department Store; 186.117-034 Manager, Brokerage Office; 186.117-054 President, Financial Institution; 187.167-074 Manager, Cemetery; 189.117-022 Manager, Industrial Organization; 189.117-026 President; 189.117-034 Vice President; 189.117-038 User Representative, International Accounting; 189.117-046 Manager, Bakery; 189.167-022 Manager, Department; 189.167-030 Program Manager.

11-1021.00 General and Operations Managers
(General Managers and Top Executives)

Education: Work experience, plus degree

Employed: 3,362,395

Openings: 421,006

Projected Growth: 16.4%

Earnings: $55,890

Plan, direct, or coordinate the operations of companies or public and private sector organizations. Duties and responsibilities include formulating policies, managing daily operations, and planning the use of materials and human resources, but are too diverse and general in nature to be classified in any one functional area of management or administration, such as personnel, purchasing, or administrative services. Includes owners and managers who head small business establishments whose duties are primarily managerial.

GOE Number, Interest Area, and Work Group: 13.01.01; General Management and Support; General Management Work and Management of Support Functions. **Instructional Programs:** 440401 Public Administration; 500704 Arts Management; 520201 Business Administration and Management, General; 520701 Enterprise Management and Operation, General; 521101 International Business. **Note:** The Department of Labor has not collected some data for this job, so it has fewer details than the other descriptions.

11-1031.00 Legislators (All Other Professional, Paraprofessional, and Technical Workers)

Education: No data available.
Employed: 818,200
Openings: No data available.
Projected Growth: No data available.
Earnings: $36,790

Develop laws and statutes at the federal, state, or local level.

GOE Number, Interest Area, and Work Group: 13.01.01; General Management and Support; General Management Work and Management of Support Functions. **Instructional Programs:** 451001 Political Science, General; 451002 American Government and Politics. **Note:** The Department of Labor has not collected some data for this job, so it has fewer details than the other descriptions.

11-2000 Advertising, Marketing, Promotions, Public Relations, and Sales Managers

11-2011.00 Advertising and Promotions Managers
(Advertising, Marketing, Promotions, Public Relations, and Sales Managers)

Education: Work experience, plus degree
Employed: 485,214
Openings: 89,237
Projected Growth: 23%
Earnings: $57,300

Plan and direct advertising policies and programs or produce collateral materials, such as posters, contests, coupons, or giveaways, to create extra interest in the purchase of a product or service for a department, an entire organization, or on an account basis.

Inspects premises of assigned stores for adequate security and compliance with safety codes and ordinances. Directs conversion of products from USA to foreign standards. Represents company at trade association meetings to promote products. Confers with clients to provide marketing or technical advice. Directs activities of workers engaged in developing and producing advertisements. Contacts organizations to explain services and facilities offered or to secure props, audio visual materials, and sound effects. Inspects layouts and advertising copy and edits scripts, audio and video tapes, and other promotional material for adherence to specifications. Reads trade journals and professional literature to stay informed on trends, innovations, and changes that affect media planning. Confers with department heads and/or staff to discuss topics such as contracts, selection of advertising media, or product to be advertised. Directs product research and development. Consults publications to learn about conventions and social functions and organizes prospect files for promotional purposes. Supervises and trains service representatives. Monitors and analyzes sales promotion results to determine cost effectiveness of promotion campaign. Formulates plans to extend business with established accounts and transacts business as agent for advertising accounts. Plans and prepares advertising and promotional material. Plans and executes advertising policies of organization. Coordinates activities of departments, such as sales, graphic arts, media, finance, and research. Adjusts broadcasting schedules due to program cancellation.

GOE Number, Interest Area, and Work Group: 10.01.01; Sales and Marketing; Managerial Work in Sales and Marketing. **Personality Type:** Artistic. Artistic occupations frequently involve working with forms, designs, and patterns. These occupations often require self-expression, and the work can be done without following a clear set of rules. **Work Values:** Working Conditions; Creativity; Authority; Ability Utilization; Achievement. **Skills:** Coordination; Solution Appraisal; Identification of Key Causes; Information Gathering; Problem Identification; Reading Comprehension. **Abilities:** *Cognitive*—Oral Expression; Written Expression; Originality; Fluency of Ideas; Oral Comprehension; Written Comprehension. *Psychomotor*—Response Orientation. *Physical*—Trunk Strength. *Sensory*—Speech Clarity; Near Vision; Speech Recognition. **General Work Activities:** *Information Input*—Getting Information Needed to Do the Job; Identifying Objects, Actions, and Events; Monitoring Processes, Materials, and Surroundings; Estimating Needed Characteristics. *Mental Process*—Making Decisions and Solving Problems; Organizing, Planning, and Prioritizing; Developing Objectives and Strategies. *Work Output*—Implementing Ideas and Programs; Documenting and Recording Information; Interacting with Computers. *Interacting with Others*—Influencing Others or Selling; Communicating with Other Workers; Communicating with Persons Outside Organization. **Physical Work Conditions:** Indoors; Sitting; Standing. **Other Job Characteristics:** Consequence of Error; Importance of Being Sure All Is Done; Frustrating Circumstances.

Experience: Job Zone 4. A minimum of two to four years of work-related skill, knowledge, or experience is needed. **Job Preparation:** SVP 7.0 to less than 8.0—2 years to less than 10 years. **Knowledge:** Sales and Marketing; Administration and Management; Communications and Media; Customer and Personal Service; English Language. **Instructional Programs:** 080101 Apparel and Accessories Marketing Operations, General; 080102 Fashion Merchandising; 080204 Business Services Marketing Operations; 080902 Hotel/Motel Services Marketing Operations; 081208 Vehicle Marketing Operations; 090201 Advertising; 090501 Public Relations and Organizational Communications; 500704 Arts Management; 520201 Business Administration and Management, General; 521401 Business Marketing and Marketing Management; 521402 Marketing Research; 521403 International Business Marketing; 521499 Marketing Management and Research, Other.

Related DOT Jobs: 159.167-022 Executive Producer, Promos; 163.117-018 Manager, Promotion; 164.117-010 Manager, Advertising; 164.117-014 Manager, Advertising Agency; 164.117-018 Media Director; 164.167-010 Account Executive.

11-2021.00 Marketing Managers (Advertising, Marketing, Promotions, Public Relations, and Sales Managers)

Education: Work experience, plus degree	
Employed: 485,214	
Openings: 89,237	
Projected Growth: 23%	
Earnings: $57,300	

Determine the demand for products and services offered by a firm and its competitors and identify potential customers. Develop pricing strategies with the goal of maximizing the firm's profits or share of the market while ensuring the firm's customers are satisfied. Oversee product development or monitor trends that indicate the need for new products and services.

Prepares report of marketing activities. Analyzes business developments and consults trade journals to monitor market trends and determine market opportunities for products. Coordinates promotional activities and shows to market products and services. Consults with buying personnel to gain advice regarding the types of products or services that are expected to be in demand. Advises business and other groups on local, national, and international factors affecting the buying and selling of products and services. Compiles list describing product or service offerings and sets prices or fees. Confers with legal staff to resolve problems, such as copyright infringement and royalty sharing with outside producers and distributors. Conducts economic and commercial surveys to identify potential markets for products and services. Coordinates and publicizes marketing activities to promote products and services. Develops marketing strategy, based on knowledge of establishment policy, nature or market, and cost and markup factors. Selects products and accessories to be displayed at trade or special production shows.

GOE Number, Interest Area, and Work Group: 10.01.01; Sales and Marketing; Managerial Work in Sales and Marketing. **Personality Type:** Enterprising. Enterprising occupations frequently involve starting up and carrying out projects. These occupations can involve leading people and making many decisions. They

sometimes require risk taking and often deal with business. **Work Values:** Working Conditions; Creativity; Ability Utilization; Autonomy; Achievement. **Skills:** Visioning; Systems Perception; Identifying Downstream Consequences; Coordination; Information Gathering; Judgment and Decision Making. **Abilities:** *Cognitive—*Oral Comprehension; Originality; Oral Expression; Fluency of Ideas; Written Comprehension. *Psychomotor—*Response Orientation. *Physical—*Trunk Strength. *Sensory—*Speech Clarity; Near Vision; Speech Recognition. **General Work Activities:** *Information Input—*Getting Information Needed to Do the Job; Identifying Objects, Actions, and Events; Estimating Needed Characteristics. *Mental Process—*Making Decisions and Solving Problems; Developing Objectives and Strategies; Analyzing Data or Information. *Work Output—*Implementing Ideas and Programs; Documenting and Recording Information; Interacting with Computers. *Interacting with Others—*Communicating with Other Workers; Providing Consultation and Advice to Others; Communicating with Persons Outside Organization. **Physical Work Conditions:** Indoors; Sitting; Standing. **Other Job Characteristics:** Consequence of Error; Frustrating Circumstances; Importance of Being Sure All Is Done.

Experience: Job Zone 4. A minimum of two to four years of work-related skill, knowledge, or experience is needed. **Job Preparation:** SVP 7.0 to less than 8.0—2 years to less than 10 years. **Knowledge:** Sales and Marketing; Administration and Management; Mathematics; Communications and Media; English Language. **Instructional Programs:** 080101 Apparel and Accessories Marketing Operations, General; 080102 Fashion Merchandising; 080204 Business Services Marketing Operations; 080902 Hotel/Motel Services Marketing Operations; 081208 Vehicle Marketing Operations; 090201 Advertising; 090501 Public Relations and Organizational Communications; 500704 Arts Management; 520201 Business Administration and Management, General; 521401 Business Marketing and Marketing Management; 521402 Marketing Research; 521403 International Business Marketing; 521499 Marketing Management and Research, Other.

Related DOT Jobs: 162.117-034 Media Buyer; 163.117-022 Director, Media Marketing; 164.117-022 Media Planner; 185.157-010 Fashion Coordinator; 185.157-014 Supervisor of Sales; 187.167-170 Manager, World Trade and Maritime Division.

11-2022.00 Sales Managers (Advertising, Marketing, Promotions, Public Relations, and Sales Managers)

Education: Work experience, plus degree	
Employed: 485,214	
Openings: 89,237	
Projected Growth: 23%	
Earnings: $57,300	

Direct the actual distribution or movement of a product or service to the customer. Coordinate sales distribution by establishing sales territories, quotas, and goals and establish training programs for sales representatives. Analyze sales statistics gathered by staff to determine sales potential and inventory requirements and monitor the preferences of customers.

Direct conversion of products from USA to foreign standards. Analyzes marketing potential of new and existing store locations, sales statistics, and expenditures to formulate policy. Directs, coordinates, and reviews activities in sales and service accounting and record keeping, and receiving and shipping operations. Plans and directs staffing, training, and performance evaluations to develop and control sales and service programs. Reviews operational records and reports to project sales and determine profitability. Directs foreign sales and service outlets of organization. Directs clerical staff to maintain export correspondence, bid requests, and credit collections and current information on tariffs, licenses, and restrictions. Resolves customer complaints regarding sales and service. Inspects premises of assigned stores for adequate security exits and compliance with safety codes and ordinances. Represents company at trade association meetings to promote products. Confers with potential customers regarding equipment needs and advises customers on types of equipment to purchase. Visits franchised dealers to stimulate interest in establishment or expansion of leasing programs. Directs and coordinates activities involving sales of manufactured goods, service outlets, technical services, operating retail chain, and advertising services for publication. Confers or consults with department heads to plan advertising services, secure information on appliances and equipment, and customer required specifications. Directs product research and development. Advises dealers and distributors on policies and operating procedures to ensure functional effectiveness of business.

GOE Number, Interest Area, and Work Group: 10.01.01; Sales and Marketing; Managerial Work in Sales and Marketing. **Personality Type:** Enterprising. Enterprising occupations frequently involve starting up and carrying out projects. These occupations can involve leading people and making many decisions. They sometimes require risk taking and often deal with business. **Work Values:** Compensation; Authority; Activity; Working Conditions; Autonomy. **Skills:** Speaking; Coordination; Monitoring; Active Listening; Time Management; Information Gathering; Identification of Key Causes; Problem Identification; Solution Appraisal. **Abilities:** *Cognitive*—Oral Expression; Oral Comprehension; Written Comprehension; Mathematical Reasoning; Deductive Reasoning; Number Facility. *Psychomotor*—none met the criteria. *Physical*—Trunk Strength. *Sensory*—Speech Clarity; Speech Recognition; Near Vision. **General Work Activities:** *Information Input*—Getting Information Needed to Do the Job; Identifying Objects, Actions, and Events; Monitoring Processes, Materials, and Surroundings. *Mental Process*—Analyzing Data or Information; Making Decisions and Solving Problems; Updating and Using Job-Relevant Knowledge; Organizing, Planning, and Prioritizing. *Work Output*—Implementing Ideas and Programs; Documenting and Recording Information; Interacting with Computers. *Interacting with Others*—Influencing Others or Selling; Communicating with Persons Outside Organization; Staffing Organizational Units; Communicating with Other Workers; Establishing and Maintaining Relationships. **Physical Work Conditions:** Indoors; Sitting; Walking or Running; Standing. **Other Job Characteristics:** Consequence of Error; Importance of Being Sure All Is Done; Frustrating Circumstances; Importance of Being Exact or Accurate.

Experience: Job Zone 4. A minimum of two to four years of work-related skill, knowledge, or experience is needed. **Job Preparation:** SVP 7.0 to less than 8.0—2 years to less than 10 years. **Knowledge:** Administration and Management; Sales and Marketing; Customer and Personal Service; English Language; Mathematics. **Instructional Programs:** 080101 Apparel and Accessories Marketing Operations, General; 080102 Fashion Merchandising; 080204 Business Services Marketing Operations; 080902 Hotel/Motel Services Marketing Operations; 081208 Vehicle Marketing Operations; 090201 Advertising; 090501 Public Relations and Organizational Communications; 500704 Arts Management; 520201 Business Administration and Management, General; 521401 Business Marketing and Marketing Management; 521402 Marketing Research; 521403 International Business Marketing; 521499 Marketing Management and Research, Other.

Related DOT Jobs: 163.117-014 Manager, Export; 163.167-010 Manager, Advertising; 163.167-018 Manager, Sales; 163.167-022 Manager, Utility Sales and Service; 163.267-010 Field Representative; 185.117-014 Area Supervisor, Retail Chain Store; 185.167-042 Manager, Professional Equipment Sales-and-Service; 187.167-162 Manager, Vehicle Leasing and Rental; 189.117-018 Manager, Customer Technical Services.

11-2031.00 Public Relations Managers (Advertising, Marketing, Promotions, Public Relations, and Sales Managers)

Education: Work experience, plus degree	
Employed: 485,214	
Openings: 89,237	
Projected Growth: 23%	
Earnings: $57,300	

Plan and direct public relations programs designed to create and maintain a favorable public image for employer or client; or if engaged in fundraising, plan and direct activities to solicit and maintain funds for special projects and nonprofit organizations.

GOE Number, Interest Area, and Work Group: 13.01.01; General Management and Support; General Management Work and Management of Support Functions. **Instructional Programs:** 080101 Apparel and Accessories Marketing Operations, General; 080102 Fashion Merchandising; 080204 Business Services Marketing Operations; 080902 Hotel/Motel Services Marketing Operations; 081208 Vehicle Marketing Operations; 090201 Advertising; 090501 Public Relations and Organizational Communications; 500704 Arts Management; 520201 Business Administration and Management, General; 521401 Business Marketing and Marketing Management; 521402 Marketing Research; 521403 International Business Marketing; 521499 Marketing Management and Research, Other. **Note:** The Department of Labor has not collected some data for this job, so it has fewer details than the other descriptions.

11-3000 Operations Specialties Managers

11-3011.00 Administrative Services Managers
(Administrative Services Managers)

Education: Work experience, plus degree

Employed: 364,259

Openings: 46,558

Projected Growth: 18.1%

Earnings: $44,370

Plan, direct, or coordinate supportive services of an organization, such as recordkeeping, mail distribution, telephone operator/receptionist, and other office support services. May oversee facilities planning and maintenance and custodial operations.

Prepares and reviews operational reports and schedules to ensure accuracy and efficiency. Recommends cost-saving methods, such as supply changes and disposal of records to improve efficiency of department. Conducts classes to teach procedures to staff. Formulates budgetary reports. Analyzes internal processes and plans or implements procedural and policy changes to improve operations. Coordinates activities of clerical and administrative personnel in establishment or organization. Hires and terminates clerical and administrative personnel.

GOE Number, Interest Area, and Work Group: 09.01.01; Business Detail; Managerial Work in Business Detail. **Personality Type:** Enterprising. Enterprising occupations frequently involve starting up and carrying out projects. These occupations can involve leading people and making many decisions. They sometimes require risk taking and often deal with business. **Work Values:** Authority; Working Conditions; Company Policies and Practices; Responsibility; Security; Autonomy. **Skills:** Reading Comprehension; Coordination; Writing; Speaking; Information Gathering; Monitoring; Idea Evaluation; Judgment and Decision Making; Management of Personnel Resources; Learning Strategies. **Abilities:** *Cognitive*—Oral Expression; Oral Comprehension; Written Comprehension; Written Expression; Information Ordering. *Psychomotor*—Wrist-Finger Speed; Response Orientation. *Physical*—Trunk Strength. *Sensory*—Speech Clarity; Near Vision; Speech Recognition. **General Work Activities:** *Information Input*—Getting Information Needed to Do the Job; Monitoring Processes, Materials, and Surroundings; Identifying Objects, Actions, and Events. *Mental Process*—Analyzing Data or Information; Processing Information; Making Decisions and Solving Problems; Organizing, Planning, and Prioritizing. *Work Output*—Documenting and Recording Information; Implementing Ideas and Programs; Interacting with Computers. *Interacting with Others*—Communicating with Other Workers; Staffing Organizational Units; Coordinating Work and Activities of Others; Performing Administrative Activities; Providing Consultation and Advice to Others. **Physical Work Conditions:** Indoors; Sitting; Standing. **Other Job Characteristics:** Consequence of Error; Degree of Automation; Importance of Being Sure All Is Done.

Experience: Job Zone 4. A minimum of two to four years of work-related skill, knowledge, or experience is needed. **Job Preparation:** SVP 7.0 to less than 8.0—2 years to less than 10 years. **Knowledge:** Administration and Management; Personnel and Human Resources; Economics and Accounting; English Language; Clerical. **Instructional Programs:** 440401 Public Administration; 520201 Business Administration and Management, General; 520202 Purchasing, Procurement and Contracts Management; 520203 Logistics and Materials Management.

Related DOT Jobs: 169.167-034 Manager, Office; 187.117-062 Radiology Administrator; 188.117-130 Court Administrator; 189.167-014 Director, Service.

11-3021.00 Computer and Information Systems Managers (Engineering, Natural Science, and Computer and Information Systems Managers)

Education: Work experience, plus degree

Employed: 326,229

Openings: 54,120

Projected Growth: 43.5%

Earnings: $75,320

Plan, direct, or coordinate activities in such fields as electronic data processing, information systems, systems analysis, and computer programming.

Analyzes workflow and assigns or schedules work to meet priorities and goals. Prepares and reviews operational reports or project progress reports. Consults with users, management, vendors, and technicians to determine computing needs and system requirements. Approves, prepares, monitors, and adjusts operational budget. Meets with department heads, managers, supervisors, vendors, and others to solicit cooperation and resolve problems. Develops performance standards and evaluates work in light of established standards. Participates in staffing decisions. Directs training of subordinates. Develops and interprets organizational goals, policies, and procedures, and reviews project plans. Evaluates data processing project proposals and assesses project feasibility. Directs daily operations of department and coordinates project activities with other departments.

GOE Number, Interest Area, and Work Group: 02.01.01; Science, Math, and Engineering; Managerial Work in Science, Math, and Engineering. **Personality Type:** Enterprising. Enterprising occupations frequently involve starting up and carrying out projects. These occupations can involve leading people and making many decisions. They sometimes require risk taking and often deal with business. **Work Values:** Working Conditions; Authority; Security; Ability Utilization; Responsibility. **Skills:** Problem Identification; Solution Appraisal; Coordination; Management of Material Resources; Management of Personnel Resources; Reading Comprehension; Information Gathering. **Abilities:** *Cognitive*—Oral Expression; Oral Comprehension; Written Comprehension; Written Expression; Mathematical Reasoning; Number Facility. *Psychomotor*—Wrist-Finger Speed; Finger Dexterity; Response Orientation. *Physical*—Trunk Strength. *Sensory*—Speech Clarity; Near Vision; Speech Recognition. **General Work Activities:** *Information Input*—Getting Information Needed to Do the Job; Estimating Needed Characteristics; Monitoring Processes, Materials, and Surroundings. *Mental Process*—Making Decisions and Solving Problems; Updating and Using Job-Relevant Knowledge; Scheduling Work and Activities. *Work Output*—Implementing Ideas and Programs; Interacting with Computers; Documenting and Recording Information. *Interacting with Others*—Guiding, Directing and Motivating Subordinates; Establishing and Maintaining Relationships; Coordinating Work and Activities of Others. **Physical Work Conditions:** Indoors; Sitting; Standing. **Other Job Characteristics:** Consequence of Error; Importance of Being Sure All Is Done; Importance of Being Exact or Accurate.

Experience: Job Zone 5. Extensive skill, knowledge, and experience are needed. Very advanced communication and organizational skills are required. **Job Preparation:** SVP 8.0 and above—4 years to more than 10 years. **Knowledge:** Administration and Management; Computers and Electronics; Mathematics; English Language; Economics and Accounting. **Instructional Program:** 143001 Engineering/Industrial Management.

Related DOT Jobs: 169.167-030 Manager, Data Processing; 169.167-082 Manager, Computer Operations.

11-3031.00 Financial Managers (Financial Managers)

Education: Work experience, plus degree

Employed: 693,291

Openings: 78,071

Projected Growth: 14%

Earnings: $55,070

Plan, direct, and coordinate accounting, investing, banking, insurance, securities, and other financial activities of a branch, office, or department of an establishment.

GOE Number, Interest Area, and Work Group: 13.01.01; General Management and Support; General Management Work and Management of Support Functions. **Instructional Programs:** 520801 Finance, General; 520806 International Finance; 520807 Investments and Securities; 520808 Public Finance; 520899 Financial Management and Services, Other. **Note:** The Department of Labor has not collected some data for this job, so it has fewer details than the other descriptions.

11-3031.01 Treasurers, Controllers, and Chief Financial Officers (Financial Managers)

Education: Work experience, plus degree

Employed: 693,291

Openings: 78,071

Projected Growth: 14%

Earnings: $55,070

Plan, direct, and coordinate the financial activities of an organization at the highest level of management. Includes financial reserve officers.

Interprets current policies and practices and plans and implements new operating procedures to improve efficiency and reduce costs. Ensures that institution reserves meet legal requirements. Arranges audits of company accounts. Evaluates need for procurement of funds and investment of surplus. Delegates authority for receipt, disbursement, banking, protection and custody of funds, securities, and financial instruments. Prepares reports or directs preparation of reports summarizing organization's current and forecasted financial position, business activity, and reports required by regulatory agencies. Coordinates and directs financial planning, budgeting, procurement, and investment activities of organization. Advises management on economic objectives and policies, investments, and loans for short- and long-range financial plans. Analyzes past, present, and expected operations.

GOE Number, Interest Area, and Work Group: 13.01.01; General Management and Support; General Management Work and Management of Support Functions. **Personality Type:** Enterprising. Enterprising occupations frequently involve starting up and carrying out projects. These occupations can involve leading people and making many decisions. They sometimes require risk taking and often deal with business. **Work Values:** Working Conditions; Authority; Activity; Ability Utilization; Company Policies and Practices. **Skills:** Management of Financial Resources; Problem Identification; Information Gathering; Judgment and Decision Making; Systems Perception. **Abilities:** *Cognitive*—Written Comprehension; Mathematical Reasoning; Deductive Reasoning; Oral Comprehension; Oral Expression; Written Expression. *Psychomotor*—none met the criteria. *Physical*—Trunk Strength. *Sensory*—Near Vision; Speech Clarity; Speech Recognition. **General Work Activities:** *Information Input*—Getting Information Needed to Do the Job; Estimating Needed Characteristics; Identifying Objects, Actions, and Events. *Mental Process*—Analyzing Data or Information; Making Decisions and Solving Problems; Developing Objectives and Strategies; Organizing, Planning, and Prioritizing. *Work Output*—Documenting and Recording Information; Implementing Ideas and Programs; Interacting with Computers. *Interacting with Others*—Communicating with Other Workers; Providing Consultation and Advice to Others; Monitoring and Controlling Resources; Interpreting Meaning of Information to Others; Coordinating Work and Activities of Others. **Physical Work Conditions:** Indoors; Sitting; Standing. **Other Job Characteristics:** Consequence of Error; Importance of Being Exact or Accurate; Importance of Being Sure All Is Done.

Experience: Job Zone 5. Extensive skill, knowledge, and experience are needed. Very advanced communication and organizational skills are required. **Job Preparation:** SVP 8.0 and above—4 years to more than 10 years. **Knowledge:** Economics and Accounting; Administration and Management; Mathematics; Law, Government and Jurisprudence; English Language. **Instructional Programs:** 520801 Finance, General; 520806 International Finance; 520807 Investments and Securities; 520808 Public Finance; 520899 Financial Management and Services, Other.

Related DOT Jobs: 160.167-058 Controller; 161.117-018 Treasurer; 186.117-070 Treasurer, Financial Institution; 186.117-078 Vice President, Financial Institution; 186.167-054 Reserve Officer.

11-3031.02 Financial Managers, Branch or Department (Financial Managers)

Education: Work experience, plus degree

Employed: 693,291

Openings: 78,071

Projected Growth: 14%

Earnings: $55,070

Direct and coordinate financial activities of workers in a branch, office, or department of an establishment, such as branch bank, brokerage firm, risk and insurance department, or credit department.

Directs insurance negotiations, selects insurance brokers and carriers, and places insurance. Submits delinquent accounts to attorney or outside agency for collection. Examines, evaluates, and processes loan applications. Establishes credit limitations on customer account. Reviews reports of securities transactions and price lists to analyze market conditions. Monitors order flow and transactions that brokerage firm executes on floor of exchange. Evaluates data pertaining to costs to plan budget. Evaluates effectiveness of current collection policies and procedures. Establishes procedures for custody and control of assets, records, loan collateral, and securities to ensure safekeeping. Prepares operational and risk reports for management analysis. Selects appropriate technique to minimize loss, such as avoidance and loss prevention and reduction. Analyzes and classifies risks as to frequency and financial impact of risk on company. Prepares financial and regulatory reports required by law, regulations, and board of directors. Directs and coordinates activities to implement institution policies, procedures, and practices concerning granting or extending lines of credit and loans. Manages branch or office of financial institution. Plans, directs, and coordinates risk and insurance programs of establishment to control risks and losses. Directs and coordinates activities of workers engaged in conducting credit investigations and collecting delinquent accounts of customers. Directs floor operations of brokerage firm engaged in buying and selling securities at exchange. Reviews collection reports to ascertain status of collections and balances outstanding.

GOE Number, Interest Area, and Work Group: 13.01.01; General Management and Support; General Management Work and Management of Support Functions. **Personality Type:** Enterprising. Enterprising occupations frequently involve starting up and carrying out projects. These occupations can involve leading people and making many decisions. They sometimes require risk taking and often deal with business. **Work Values:** Authority; Working Conditions; Company Policies and Practices; Activity; Ability Utilization. **Skills:** Problem Identification; Solution Appraisal; Management of Financial Resources; Writing; Monitoring. **Abilities:** *Cognitive*—Written Expression; Oral Comprehension; Written Comprehension; Mathematical Reasoning; Oral Expression. *Psychomotor*—Wrist-Finger Speed; Response Orientation. *Physical*—Trunk Strength. *Sensory*—Near Vision; Speech Clarity; Speech Recognition. **General Work Activities:** *Information Input*—Getting Information Needed to Do the Job; Identifying Objects, Actions, and Events; Estimating Needed Characteristics. *Mental Process*—Analyzing Data or Information; Judging Qualities

of Things, Services, People; Processing Information; Making Decisions and Solving Problems; Organizing, Planning, and Prioritizing. *Work Output*—Documenting and Recording Information; Interacting with Computers; Implementing Ideas and Programs. *Interacting with Others*—Performing Administrative Activities; Communicating with Other Workers; Coordinating Work and Activities of Others; Monitoring and Controlling Resources; Providing Consultation and Advice to Others; Guiding, Directing and Motivating Subordinates. **Physical Work Conditions:** Indoors; Sitting; Standing. **Other Job Characteristics:** Consequence of Error; Importance of Being Exact or Accurate; Degree of Automation.

Experience: Job Zone 4. A minimum of two to four years of work-related skill, knowledge, or experience is needed. **Job Preparation:** SVP 7.0 to less than 8.0—2 years to less than 10 years. **Knowledge:** Economics and Accounting; Administration and Management; Mathematics; English Language; Law, Government and Jurisprudence. **Instructional Programs:** 520801 Finance, General; 520806 International Finance; 520807 Investments and Securities; 520808 Public Finance; 520899 Financial Management and Services, Other.

Related DOT Jobs: 169.167-086 Manager, Credit and Collection; 186.117-066 Risk and Insurance Manager; 186.117-074 Trust Officer; 186.117-082 Foreign-Exchange Dealer; 186.117-086 Manager, Exchange Floor; 186.137-014 Operations Officer; 186.167-070 Assistant Branch Manager, Financial Institution; 186.167-082 Factor; 186.167-086 Manager, Financial Institution.

11-3040.00 Human Resources Managers (Human Resources Managers)

Education: Work experience, plus degree

Employed: 229,594

Openings: 32,929

Projected Growth: 19.4%

Earnings: $49,010

Plan, direct, and coordinate human resource management activities of an organization to maximize the strategic use of human resources and maintain functions such as employee compensation, recruitment, personnel policies, and regulatory compliance.

Prepares budget for personnel operations. Plans and conducts new employee orientation to foster positive attitude toward organizational objectives. Writes directives advising department managers of organization policy in personnel matters such as equal employment opportunity, sexual harassment, and discrimination. Studies legislation, arbitration decisions, and collective bargaining contracts to assess industry trends. Maintains records and compiles statistical reports concerning personnel-related data such as hires, transfers, performance appraisals, and absenteeism rates. Analyzes statistical data and reports to identify and determine causes of personnel problems and develop recommendations for improvement of organization's personnel policies and practices. Represents organization at personnel-related hearings and investigations. Contracts with vendors to provide employee services, such as canteen, transportation, or relocation service. Conducts exit interviews to identify reasons for employee termination and writes separation notices. Investigates industrial accidents and prepares reports for insurance carrier. Plans, directs, supervises, and coordinates work activities of subordinates and staff relating to employment, compensation, labor relations, and employee relations. Meets with shop stewards and supervisors to resolve grievances. Directs preparation and distribution of written and verbal information to inform employees of benefits, compensation, and personnel policies. Evaluates and modifies benefits policies to establish competitive programs and to ensure compliance with legal requirements. Analyzes compensation policies, government regulations, and prevailing wage rates to develop competitive compensation plan. Develops methods to improve employment policies, processes, and practices and recommends changes to management. Prepares personnel forecast to project employment needs. Negotiates bargaining agreements and resolves labor disputes.

GOE Number, Interest Area, and Work Group: 13.01.01; General Management and Support; General Management Work and Management of Support Functions. **Personality Type:** Enterprising. Enterprising occupations frequently involve starting up and carrying out projects. These occupations can involve leading people and making many decisions. They sometimes require risk taking and often deal with business. **Work Values:** Working Conditions; Ability Utilization; Authority; Autonomy; Activity; Responsibility; Security. **Skills:** Management of Personnel Resources; Identification of Key Causes; Problem Identification; Identifying Downstream Consequences; Systems Perception; Visioning; Solution Appraisal; Information Gathering. **Abilities:** *Cognitive*— Written Comprehension; Written Expression; Oral Expression; Oral Comprehension; Deductive Reasoning. *Psychomotor*—Reaction Time; Response Orientation. *Physical*—Gross Body Coordination; Gross Body Equilibrium. *Sensory*—Near Vision; Speech Clarity; Far Vision. **General Work Activities:** *Information Input*— Getting Information Needed to Do the Job; Identifying Objects, Actions, and Events; Estimating Needed Characteristics. *Mental Process*—Judging Qualities of Things, Services, People; Developing Objectives and Strategies; Evaluating Information Against Standards; Analyzing Data or Information; Making Decisions and Solving Problems. *Work Output*—Implementing Ideas and Programs; Documenting and Recording Information; Interacting with Computers. *Interacting with Others*—Communicating with Other Workers; Performing Administrative Activities; Staffing Organizational Units; Resolving Conflict and Negotiating with Others. **Physical Work Conditions:** Indoors; Sitting; Standing. **Other Job Characteristics:** Consequence of Error; Importance of Being Sure All Is Done; Importance of Being Exact or Accurate.

Experience: Job Zone 4. A minimum of two to four years of work-related skill, knowledge, or experience is needed. **Job Preparation:** SVP 7.0 to less than 8.0—2 years to less than 10 years. **Knowledge:** Personnel and Human Resources; Administration and Management; Mathematics; English Language; Education and Training. **Instructional Programs:** 440401 Public Administration; 521001 Human Resources Management; 521002 Labor/Personnel Relations and Studies.

Related DOT Jobs: 166.117-010 Director, Industrial Relations; 166.117-018 Manager, Personnel; 166.167-030 Manager, Employment; 188.117-086 Director, Merit System.

11-3041.00 Compensation and Benefits Managers
(Human Resources Managers)

Education: Work experience, plus degree
Employed: 229,594
Openings: 32,929
Projected Growth: 19.4%
Earnings: $49,010

Plan, direct, or coordinate compensation and benefits activities and staff of an organization.

Writes directives advising department managers of organization policy in personnel matters such as equal employment opportunity, sexual harassment, and discrimination. Contracts with vendors to provide employee services, such as canteen, transportation, or relocation service. Develops methods to improve employment policies, processes, and practices and recommends changes to management. Prepares personnel forecast to project employment needs. Prepares and delivers presentations and reports to corporate officers or other management regarding human resource management policies and practices and recommendations for change. Meets with shop stewards and supervisors to resolve grievances. Plans and conducts new employee orientation to foster positive attitude toward organizational objectives. Analyzes statistical data and reports to identify and determine causes of personnel problems and develop recommendations for improvement of organization's personnel policies and practices. Represents organization at personnel-related hearings and investigations. Analyzes compensation policies, government regulations, and prevailing wage rates to develop competitive compensation plan. Evaluates and modifies benefits policies to establish competitive programs and to ensure compliance with legal requirements. Formulates policies and procedures for recruitment, testing, placement, classification, orientation, benefits, and labor and industrial relations. Studies legislation, arbitration decisions, and collective bargaining contracts to assess industry trends. Directs preparation and distribution of written and verbal information to inform employees of benefits, compensation, and personnel policies. Investigates industrial accidents and prepares reports for insurance carrier. Prepares budget for personnel operations. Negotiates bargaining agreements and resolves labor disputes. Conducts exit interviews to identify reasons for employee termination and writes separation notices.

GOE Number, Interest Area, and Work Group: 13.01.01; General Management and Support; General Management Work and Management of Support Functions. **Personality Type:** Enterprising. Enterprising occupations frequently involve starting up and carrying out projects. These occupations can involve leading people and making many decisions. They sometimes require risk taking and often deal with business. **Work Values:** Working Conditions; Ability Utilization; Autonomy; Authority; Responsibility; Activity; Security. **Skills:** Management of Personnel Resources; Identification of Key Causes; Problem Identification; Solution Appraisal; Information Gathering; Identifying Downstream Consequences; Systems Perception; Visioning. **Abilities:** *Cognitive*— Written Comprehension; Oral Expression; Oral Comprehension; Written Expression; Deductive Reasoning. *Psychomotor*—Response

Orientation; Reaction Time. *Physical*—Gross Body Coordination; Gross Body Equilibrium. *Sensory*—Near Vision; Far Vision; Speech Clarity. **General Work Activities:** *Information Input*—Getting Information Needed to Do the Job; Identifying Objects, Actions, and Events; Estimating Needed Characteristics. *Mental Process*—Developing Objectives and Strategies; Judging Qualities of Things, Services, People; Evaluating Information Against Standards; Analyzing Data or Information; Making Decisions and Solving Problems. *Work Output*—Implementing Ideas and Programs; Documenting and Recording Information; Interacting with Computers. *Interacting with Others*—Communicating with Other Workers; Performing Administrative Activities; Resolving Conflict and Negotiating with Others; Staffing Organizational Units. **Physical Work Conditions:** Indoors; Sitting; Standing. **Other Job Characteristics:** Consequence of Error; Importance of Being Sure All Is Done; Importance of Being Exact or Accurate.

Experience: Job Zone 4. A minimum of two to four years of work-related skill, knowledge, or experience is needed. **Job Preparation:** SVP 7.0 to less than 8.0—2 years to less than 10 years. **Knowledge:** Personnel and Human Resources; Administration and Management; Mathematics; English Language; Education and Training. **Instructional Programs:** 440401 Public Administration; 521001 Human Resources Management; 521002 Labor/Personnel Relations and Studies.

Related DOT Jobs: 166.167-018 Manager, Benefits; 166.167-022 Manager, Compensation.

11-3042.00 Training and Development Managers
(Human Resources Managers)

Education: Work experience, plus degree

Employed: 229,594

Openings: 32,929

Projected Growth: 19.4%

Earnings: $49,010

Plan, direct, or coordinate the training and development activities and staff of an organization.

Develops and organizes training manuals, multimedia visual aids, and other educational materials. Confers with management and supervisory personnel to identify training needs based on projected production processes, changes, and other factors. Interprets and clarifies regulatory policies governing apprenticeship training programs, and provides information and assistance to trainees and labor and management representatives. Trains instructors and supervisors in effective training techniques. Prepares training budget for department or organization. Reviews and evaluates training and apprenticeship programs for compliance with government standards. Coordinates established courses with technical and professional courses provided by community schools and designates training procedures. Analyzes training needs to develop new training programs or modify and improve existing programs. Evaluates effectiveness of training programs and instructor performance. Formulates training policies and schedules, utilizing knowledge of identified training needs. Plans and develops training procedures utilizing knowledge of relative effectiveness of individual training, classroom training, demon-strations, on-the-job training, meetings, conferences, and workshops. Develops testing and evaluation procedures.

GOE Number, Interest Area, and Work Group: 13.01.01; General Management and Support; General Management Work and Management of Support Functions. **Personality Type:** Enterprising. Enterprising occupations frequently involve starting up and carrying out projects. These occupations can involve leading people and making many decisions. They sometimes require risk taking and often deal with business. **Work Values:** Authority; Working Conditions; Coworkers; Achievement; Company Policies and Practices; Supervision, Human Relations; Social Service. **Skills:** Critical Thinking; Reading Comprehension; Visioning; Speaking; Idea Evaluation; Learning Strategies; Implementation Planning; Management of Personnel Resources; Information Gathering; Instructing. **Abilities:** *Cognitive*—Deductive Reasoning; Oral Expression; Oral Comprehension; Inductive Reasoning; Written Expression; Written Comprehension. *Psychomotor*—Response Orientation; Rate Control. *Physical*—none met the criteria. *Sensory*—Near Vision; Far Vision; Speech Clarity. **General Work Activities:** *Information Input*—Getting Information Needed to Do the Job; Identifying Objects, Actions, and Events; Monitoring Processes, Materials, and Surroundings; Estimating Needed Characteristics. *Mental Process*—Judging Qualities of Things, Services, People; Developing Objectives and Strategies; Making Decisions and Solving Problems; Evaluating Information Against Standards; Organizing, Planning, and Prioritizing. *Work Output*—Implementing Ideas and Programs; Documenting and Recording Information; Handling and Moving Objects; Interacting with Computers. *Interacting with Others*—Teaching Others; Coaching and Developing Others; Providing Consultation and Advice to Others; Communicating with Other Workers. **Physical Work Conditions:** Indoors; Sitting; Standing. **Other Job Characteristics:** Consequence of Error; Importance of Being Sure All Is Done; Importance of Being Exact or Accurate.

Experience: Job Zone 4. A minimum of two to four years of work-related skill, knowledge, or experience is needed. **Job Preparation:** SVP 7.0 to less than 8.0—2 years to less than 10 years. **Knowledge:** Education and Training; Administration and Management; Personnel and Human Resources; English Language; Law, Government and Jurisprudence; Psychology. **Instructional Programs:** 440401 Public Administration; 521001 Human Resources Management; 521002 Labor/Personnel Relations and Studies.

Related DOT Jobs: 166.167-026 Manager, Education and Training; 188.117-010 Apprenticeship Consultant; 375.167-054 Police Academy Program Coordinator.

11-3051.00 Industrial Production Managers (Industrial Production Managers)

Education: Bachelor's degree

Employed: 208,345

Openings: 20,865

Projected Growth: –0.9%

Earnings: $56,320

Plan, direct, or coordinate the work activities and resources necessary for manufacturing products in accordance with cost, quality, and quantity specifications.

Negotiates materials prices with suppliers. Initiates and coordinates inventory and cost control programs. Reviews operations and confers with technical or administrative staff to resolve production or processing problems. Analyzes production, quality control, maintenance, and other operational reports to detect production problems. Reviews plans and confers with research and support staff to develop new products and processes or the quality of existing products. Examines samples of raw products or directs testing during processing to ensure finished products conform to prescribed quality standards. Hires, trains, evaluates, and discharges staff. Resolves personnel grievances. Develops budgets and approves expenditures for supplies, materials, and human resources. Coordinates and recommends procedures for facility and equipment maintenance or modification. Directs and coordinates production, processing, distribution, and marketing activities of industrial organization. Reviews processing schedules and production orders to determine staffing requirements, work procedures, and duty assignments. Prepares and maintains production reports and personnel records.

GOE Number, Interest Area, and Work Group: 08.01.01; Industrial Production; Managerial Work in Industrial Production. **Personality Type:** Enterprising. Enterprising occupations frequently involve starting up and carrying out projects. These occupations can involve leading people and making many decisions. They sometimes require risk taking and often deal with business. **Work Values:** Authority; Autonomy; Activity; Responsibility; Company Policies and Practices. **Skills:** Product Inspection; Coordination; Judgment and Decision Making; Management of Personnel Resources; Identification of Key Causes. **Abilities:** *Cognitive*—Oral Expression; Oral Comprehension; Written Comprehension; Written Expression; Inductive Reasoning. *Psychomotor*—Control Precision; Response Orientation; Reaction Time. *Physical*—Trunk Strength; Gross Body Equilibrium. *Sensory*—Near Vision; Speech Clarity; Visual Color Discrimination. **General Work Activities:** *Information Input*—Getting Information Needed to Do the Job; Monitoring Processes, Materials, and Surroundings; Estimating Needed Characteristics. *Mental Process*—Making Decisions and Solving Problems; Analyzing Data or Information; Judging Qualities of Things, Services, People. *Work Output*—Implementing Ideas and Programs; Documenting and Recording Information; Interacting with Computers. *Interacting with Others*—Coordinating Work and Activities of Others; Communicating with Other Workers; Resolving Conflict and Negotiating with Others. **Physical Work Conditions:** Indoors; Sitting; Walking or Running; Standing. **Other Job Characteristics:** Consequence of Error; Importance of Being Sure All Is Done; Importance of Being Exact or Accurate.

Experience: Job Zone 4. A minimum of two to four years of work-related skill, knowledge, or experience is needed. **Job Preparation:** SVP 7.0 to less than 8.0—2 years to less than 10 years. **Knowledge:** Production and Processing; Administration and Management; Personnel and Human Resources; English Language; Food Production. **Instructional Programs:** 520201 Business Administration and Management, General; 520205 Operations Management and Supervision.

Related DOT Jobs: 180.167-054 Superintendent; 182.167-022 Superintendent, Concrete-Mixing Plant; 183.117-010 Manager, Branch; 183.117-014 Production Superintendent; 183.161-014 Wine Maker; 183.167-010 Brewing Director; 183.167-014 General Superintendent, Milling; 183.167-018 General Supervisor; 183.167-022 General Supervisor; 183.167-026 Manager, Food Processing Plant; 183.167-034 Superintendent, Car Construction; 187.167-090 Manager, Dental Laboratory; 188.167-094 Superintendent, Industries, Correctional Facility.

11-3061.00 Purchasing Managers (Purchasing Managers)

Education: Work experience, plus degree
Employed: 175,977
Openings: 24,516
Projected Growth: 7.1%
Earnings: $41,830

Plan, direct, or coordinate the activities of buyers, purchasing officers, and related workers involved in purchasing materials, products, and services.

Determines merchandise costs and formulates and coordinates merchandising policies and activities to ensure profit. Prepares report regarding market conditions and merchandise costs. Analyzes market and delivery systems to determine present and future material availability. Represents company in formulating policies and negotiating contracts with suppliers. Conducts inventory and directs buyers in purchase of products, materials, and supplies. Develops and implements office, operations, and systems instructions, policies, and procedures. Directs and coordinates activities of personnel engaged in buying, selling, and distributing materials, equipment, machinery, and supplies. Prepares, reviews, and processes requisitions and purchase orders for supplies and equipment.

GOE Number, Interest Area, and Work Group: 13.01.01; General Management and Support; General Management Work and Management of Support Functions. **Personality Type:** Enterprising. Enterprising occupations frequently involve starting up and carrying out projects. These occupations can involve leading people and making many decisions. They sometimes require risk taking and often deal with business. **Work Values:** Working Conditions; Activity; Company Policies and Practices; Authority; Coworkers; Autonomy; Responsibility. **Skills:** Information Gathering; Judgment and Decision Making; Writing; Coordination; Management of Material Resources; Management of Personnel Resources. **Abilities:** *Cognitive*—Oral Expression; Mathematical Reasoning; Deductive Reasoning; Written Comprehension; Written Expression; Number Facility. *Psychomotor*—none met the criteria. *Physical*—none met the criteria. *Sensory*—Speech Clarity; Speech Recognition. **General Work Activities:** *Information Input*—Getting Information Needed to Do the Job; Monitoring Processes, Materials, and Surroundings; Estimating Needed Characteristics; Identifying Objects, Actions, and Events. *Mental Process*—Making Decisions and Solving Problems; Analyzing Data or Information; Scheduling Work and Activities; Processing Information; Organizing, Planning, and Prioritizing. *Work Output*—

Implementing Ideas and Programs; Documenting and Recording Information; Interacting with Computers. *Interacting with Others* —Monitoring and Controlling Resources; Communicating with Other Workers; Communicating with Persons Outside Organization. **Physical Work Conditions:** Indoors; Sitting; Walking or Running; Standing. **Other Job Characteristics:** Consequence of Error; Importance of Being Exact or Accurate; Importance of Being Sure All Is Done.

Experience: Job Zone 4. A minimum of two to four years of work-related skill, knowledge, or experience is needed. **Job Preparation:** SVP 7.0 to less than 8.0—2 years to less than 10 years. **Knowledge:** Administration and Management; Economics and Accounting; Mathematics; Sales and Marketing; Production and Processing; English Language. **Instructional Programs:** 080705 General Retailing Operations; 520201 Business Administration and Management, General; 520202 Purchasing, Procurement and Contracts Management.

Related DOT Jobs: 162.167-014 Buyer, Tobacco, Head; 162.167-022 Manager, Procurement Services; 184.117-078 Superintendent, Commissary; 185.167-034 Manager, Merchandise.

11-3071.00 Transportation, Storage, and Distribution Managers (Communication, Transportation, and Utilities Operations Managers)

Education: Work experience, plus degree

Employed: 195,951

Openings: 25,388

Projected Growth: 19.3%

Earnings: $52,810

Plan, direct, or coordinate transportation, storage, or distribution activities in accordance with governmental policies and regulations.

GOE Number, Interest Area, and Work Group: 13.01.01; General Management and Support; General Management Work and Management of Support Functions. **Instructional Programs:** 440401 Public Administration; 449999 Public Administration and Services, Other; 490104 Aviation Management; 520201 Business Administration and Management, General; 520203 Logistics and Materials Management. **Note:** The Department of Labor has not collected some data for this job, so it has fewer details than the other descriptions.

11-3071.01 Transportation Managers (Communication, Transportation, and Utilities Operations Managers)

Education: Work experience, plus degree

Employed: 195,951

Openings: 25,388

Projected Growth: 19.3%

Earnings: $52,810

Plan, direct, and coordinate the transportation operations within an organization or the activities of organizations that provide transportation services.

Enforces compliance of operations personnel with administrative policies, procedures, safety rules, and government regulations. Analyzes expenditures and other financial reports to develop plans, policies, and budgets for increasing profits and improving services. Oversees activities relating to dispatching, routing, and tracking transportation vehicles, such as aircraft and railroad cars. Prepares management recommendations, such as need for increasing fares, tariffs, or expansion or changes to existing schedules. Oversees procurement process, including research and testing of equipment, vendor contacts, and approval of requisitions. Conducts investigations in cooperation with government agencies to determine causes of transportation accidents and to improve safety procedures. Confers and cooperates with management and other in formulating and implementing administrative, operational and customer relations, policies and procedures. Reviews transportation schedules, worker assignments and routes to ensure compliance with standards for personnel selection, safety, and union contract terms. Oversees process of investigation and response to customer or shipper complaints relating to operations department. Oversees workers assigning tariff classifications, and preparing billing according to mode of transportation and destination of shipment. Inspects or oversees repairs and maintenance to equipment, vehicles, and facilities to enforce standards for safety, efficiency, cleanliness, and appearance. Negotiates and authorizes contracts with equipment and materials suppliers. Participates in union contract negotiations and settlement of grievances. Directs and coordinates, through subordinates, activities of operations department to obtain use of equipment, facilities, and human resources. Acts as organization representative before commissions or regulatory bodies during hearings, such as to increase rates and change routes and schedules.

GOE Number, Interest Area, and Work Group: 07.01.01; Transportation; Managerial Work in Transportation. **Personality Type:** Enterprising. Enterprising occupations frequently involve starting up and carrying out projects. These occupations can involve leading people and making many decisions. They sometimes require risk taking and often deal with business. **Work Values:** Autonomy; Authority; Ability Utilization; Activity; Security. **Skills:** Reading Comprehension; Coordination; Management of Personnel Resources; Management of Material Resources; Judgment and Decision Making. **Abilities:** *Cognitive*—Oral Expression; Problem Sensitivity; Oral Comprehension; Written Comprehension; Mathematical Reasoning. *Psychomotor*—none met the criteria. *Physical*— none met the criteria. *Sensory*—Speech Clarity; Speech Recognition; Glare Sensitivity. **General Work Activities:** *Information Input*—Getting Information Needed to Do the Job; Monitoring Processes, Materials, and Surroundings; Estimating Needed Characteristics; Inspecting Equipment, Structures, Materials. *Mental Process*—Evaluating Information Against Standards; Making Decisions and Solving Problems; Analyzing Data or Information. *Work Output*—Implementing Ideas and Programs; Interacting with Computers; Documenting and Recording Information; Handling and Moving Objects. *Interacting with Others*—Communicating with Other Workers; Guiding, Directing and Motivating Subordinates; Monitoring and Controlling Resources. **Physical Work Conditions:** Indoors; Sitting; Standing. **Other Job Characteristics:** Consequence of Error; Importance of Being Sure All Is Done; Frustrating Circumstances.

Experience: Job Zone 4. A minimum of two to four years of work-related skill, knowledge, or experience is needed. **Job Preparation:** SVP 7.0 to less than 8.0—2 years to less than 10 years. **Knowledge:** Transportation; Administration and Management; Mathematics; Economics and Accounting; Personnel and Human Resources. **Instructional Programs:** 440401 Public Administration; 449999 Public Administration and Services, Other; 490104 Aviation Management; 520201 Business Administration and Management, General; 520203 Logistics and Materials Management.

Related DOT Jobs: 180.167-062 Manager, Aerial Planting and Cultivation; 184.117-014 Director, Transportation; 184.117-018 District Supervisor; 184.117-026 Manager, Airport; 184.117-034 Manager, Automotive Services; 184.117-038 Manager, Flight Operations; 184.117-042 Manager, Harbor Department; 184.117-050 Manager, Operations; 184.117-054 Manager, Regional; 184.117-058 Manager, Schedule Planning; 184.117-066 Manager, Traffic; 184.117-086 Manager, Car Inspection and Repair; 184.117-090 Regional Superintendent, Railroad Car Inspection and Repair; 184.167-010 Boat Dispatcher; 184.167-042 General Agent, Operations; 184.167-054 Manager, Bus Transportation; 184.167-058 Manager, Cargo-and-Ramp-Services; 184.167-066 Manager, Flight Control; 184.167-070 Manager, Flight-Reservations; 184.167-082 Manager, Station (partial list; see the introduction for sources of the complete list).

11-3071.02 Storage and Distribution Managers
(Communication, Transportation, and Utilities Operations Managers)

Education: Work experience, plus degree
Employed: 195,951
Openings: 25,388
Projected Growth: 19.3%
Earnings: $52,810

Plan, direct, and coordinate the storage and distribution operations within an organization or the activities of organizations that are engaged in storing and distributing materials and products.

Develops and implements plans for facility modification or expansion, such as equipment purchase or changes in space allocation or structural design. Confers with department heads to coordinate warehouse activities, such as production, sales, records control, and purchasing. Negotiates contracts, settlements, and freight-handling agreements to resolve problems between foreign and domestic shippers. Inspects physical condition of warehouse and equipment and prepares work orders for testing, maintenance, or repair. Supervises the activities of worker engaged in receiving, storing, testing, and shipping products or materials. Reviews invoices, work orders, consumption reports, and demand forecasts to estimate peak delivery periods and issue work assignments. Interviews, selects, and trains warehouse and supervisory personnel. Schedules air or surface pickup, delivery, or distribution of products or materials. Prepares or directs preparation of correspondence, reports, and operations, maintenance,

and safety manuals. Establishes standard and emergency operating procedures for receiving, handling, storing, shipping, or salvaging products or materials. Interacts with customers or shippers to solicit new business, answer questions about services offered or required, and investigate complaints. Examines products or materials to estimate quantities or weight and type of container required for storage or transport. Plans, develops, and implements warehouse safety and security programs and activities. Examines invoices and shipping manifests for conformity to tariff and customs regulations and contacts customs officials to effect release of shipments.

GOE Number, Interest Area, and Work Group: 13.01.01; General Management and Support; General Management Work and Management of Support Functions. **Personality Type:** Enterprising. Enterprising occupations frequently involve starting up and carrying out projects. These occupations can involve leading people and making many decisions. They sometimes require risk taking and often deal with business. **Work Values:** Authority; Autonomy; Responsibility; Security; Company Policies and Practices. **Skills:** Problem Identification; Management of Personnel Resources; Negotiation; Systems Perception; Product Inspection; Implementation Planning; Coordination; Writing. **Abilities:** *Cognitive*—Oral Comprehension; Written Comprehension; Oral Expression; Written Expression; Problem Sensitivity. *Psychomotor*—none met the criteria. *Physical*—none met the criteria. *Sensory*—Speech Clarity; Speech Recognition. **General Work Activities:** *Information Input*—Estimating Needed Characteristics; Inspecting Equipment, Structures, Materials; Getting Information Needed to Do the Job. *Mental Process*—Scheduling Work and Activities; Making Decisions and Solving Problems; Organizing, Planning, and Prioritizing. *Work Output*—Implementing Ideas and Programs; Performing General Physical Activities; Handling and Moving Objects. *Interacting with Others*—Communicating with Other Workers; Coordinating Work and Activities of Others; Guiding, Directing and Motivating Subordinates. **Physical Work Conditions:** Indoors; Sitting; Standing. **Other Job Characteristics:** Consequence of Error; Frustrating Circumstances; Importance of Being Sure All Is Done.

Experience: Job Zone 4. A minimum of two to four years of work-related skill, knowledge, or experience is needed. **Job Preparation:** SVP 7.0 to less than 8.0—2 years to less than 10 years. **Knowledge:** Administration and Management; Transportation; Personnel and Human Resources; Mathematics; Production and Processing. **Instructional Programs:** 440401 Public Administration; 449999 Public Administration and Services, Other; 490104 Aviation Management; 520201 Business Administration and Management, General; 520203 Logistics and Materials Management.

Related DOT Jobs: 181.117-010 Manager, Bulk Plant; 184.117-022 Import-Export Agent; 184.167-038 Dispatcher, Chief I; 184.167-114 Manager, Warehouse; 184.167-118 Operations Manager; 184.167-146 Superintendent, Compressor Stations; 184.167-190 Superintendent, Measurement; 189.167-038 Superintendent, Ammunition Storage.

11-9000 Other Management Occupations

11-9011.00 Farm, Ranch, and Other Agricultural Managers (First-Line Supervisors and Managers/Supervisors—Agricultural, Forestry, Fishing, and Related Workers)

Education: No data available.

Employed: 51,350

Openings: No data available.

Projected Growth: No data available.

Earnings: $27,410

On a paid basis, manage farms, ranches, aquacultural operations, greenhouses, nurseries, timber tracts, cotton gins, packing houses, or other agricultural establishments for employers. Carry out production, financial, and marketing decisions relating to the managed operations following guidelines from the owner. May contract tenant farmers or producers to carry out the day-to-day activities of the managed operation. May supervise planting, cultivating, harvesting, and marketing activities. May prepare cost, production, and other records. May perform physical work and operate machinery.

GOE Number, Interest Area, and Work Group: 13.01.01; General Management and Support; General Management Work and Management of Support Functions. **Instructional Programs:** 010104 Farm and Ranch Management; 010199 Agricultural Business and Management, Other; 010301 Agricultural Production Workers and Managers, General; 010302 Agricultural Animal Husbandry and Production Management; 010304 Crop Production Operations and Management; 010399 Agricultural Production Workers and Managers, Other; 019999 Agricultural Business and Production, Other; 020201 Animal Sciences, General; 020202 Agricultural Animal Breeding and Genetics; 020204 Agricultural Animal Nutrition; 020206 Dairy Science; 020209 Poultry Science; 020401 Plant Sciences, General; 020402 Agronomy and Crop Science; 020409 Range Science and Management. **Note:** The Department of Labor has not collected some data for this job, so it has fewer details than the other descriptions.

11-9011.01 Nursery and Greenhouse Managers (Nursery and Greenhouse Managers)

Education: Work experience in a related occupation

Employed: 5,154

Openings: 583

Projected Growth: 15.1%

Earnings: $25,360

Plan, organize, direct, control, and coordinate activities of workers engaged in propagating, cultivating, and harvesting horticultural specialties, such as trees, shrubs, flowers, mushrooms, and other plants.

Coordinates clerical, record keeping, inventory, requisition, and marketing activities. Considers such factors as whether plants need hothouse/greenhouse or natural weather growing conditions. Selects and purchases seed, plant nutrients, and disease control chemicals. Grows horticultural plants under controlled conditions hydroponically. Tours work areas to observe work being done, to inspect crops, and to evaluate plant and soil conditions. Negotiates contracts for lease of lands or trucks or for purchase of trees. Confers with horticultural personnel in planning facility renovations or additions. Manages nursery to grow horticultural plants for sale to trade or retail customers, for display or exhibition, or for research. Hires workers and directs supervisors and workers planting seeds, controlling plant growth and disease, potting, or cutting plants for marketing. Determines type and quantity of horticultural plants to be grown, such as trees, shrubs, flowers, ornamental plants, or vegetables, based on budget, projected sales volume, or executive directive.

GOE Number, Interest Area, and Work Group: 03.01.02; Plants and Animals; Managerial Work: Nursery, Groundskeeping, and Logging. **Personality Type:** Enterprising. Enterprising occupations frequently involve starting up and carrying out projects. These occupations can involve leading people and making many decisions. They sometimes require risk taking and often deal with business. **Work Values:** Authority; Autonomy; Moral Values; Ability Utilization; Creativity; Responsibility. **Skills:** Management of Personnel Resources; Coordination; Implementation Planning; Active Listening; Reading Comprehension; Speaking. **Abilities:** *Cognitive*—Oral Expression; Written Comprehension; Oral Comprehension; Written Expression; Number Facility; Deductive Reasoning. *Psychomotor*—none met the criteria. *Physical*—Trunk Strength; Gross Body Coordination; Gross Body Equilibrium. *Sensory*—Speech Clarity; Speech Recognition; Visual Color Discrimination. **General Work Activities:** *Information Input*—Getting Information Needed to Do the Job; Monitoring Processes, Materials, and Surroundings; Identifying Objects, Actions, and Events. *Mental Process*—Making Decisions and Solving Problems; Judging Qualities of Things, Services, People; Organizing, Planning, and Prioritizing. *Work Output*—Performing General Physical Activities; Handling and Moving Objects; Implementing Ideas and Programs. *Interacting with Others*—Guiding, Directing and Motivating Subordinates; Communicating with Other Workers; Communicating with Persons Outside Organization; Coordinating Work and Activities of Others. **Physical Work Conditions:** Indoors; Standing; Kneeling, Crouching, or Crawling; Outdoors. **Other Job Characteristics:** Importance of Being Sure All Is Done; Consequence of Error; Frustrating Circumstances; Importance of Being Aware of New Events.

Experience: Job Zone 4. A minimum of two to four years of work-related skill, knowledge, or experience is needed. **Job Preparation:** SVP 7.0 to less than 8.0—2 years to less than 10 years. **Knowledge:** Administration and Management; Biology; Personnel and Human Resources; Chemistry; English Language. **Instructional Programs:** 010101 Agricultural Business and Management, General; 010102 Agricultural Business/Agribusiness Operations; 010601 Horticulture Services Operations and Management, General; 010603 Ornamental Horticulture Operations and Management; 010604 Greenhouse Operations and Management; 010606 Nursery Operations and Management; 020403 Horticulture Science.

Related DOT Jobs: 180.117-010 Manager, Christmas-Tree Farm; 180.161-014 Superintendent, Horticulture; 180.167-042 Manager, Nursery.

11-9011.02 Agricultural Crop Farm Managers (First-Line Supervisors and Managers/Supervisors—Agricultural, Forestry, Fishing, and Related Workers)

Education: No data available.
Employed: 51,350
Openings: No data available.
Projected Growth: No data available.
Earnings: $27,410

Direct and coordinate, through subordinate supervisory personnel, activities of workers engaged in agricultural crop production for corporations, cooperatives, or other owners.

Inspects equipment to ensure proper functioning. Negotiates with bank officials to obtain credit from bank. Evaluates financial statements and makes budget proposals. Confers with purchasers and arranges for sale of crops. Records information, such as production, farm management practices, and parent stock, and prepares financial and operational reports. Determines procedural changes in drying, grading, storage, and shipment for greater efficiency and accuracy. Analyzes soil to determine type and quantity of fertilizer required for maximum production. Plans and directs development and production of hybrid plant varieties with high yield or disease and insect resistant characteristics. Purchases machinery, equipment, and supplies, such as tractors, seed, fertilizer, and chemicals. Hires, discharges, transfers, and promotes workers, enforces safety regulations, and interprets policies. Coordinates growing activities with those of engineering, equipment maintenance, packing houses, and other related departments. Analyzes market conditions to determine acreage allocations. Directs and coordinates worker activities, such as planting, irrigation, chemical application, harvesting, grading, payroll, and record keeping. Contracts with farmers or independent owners for raising of crops or for management of crop production. Inspects orchards and fields to determine maturity dates of crops or to estimate potential crop damage from weather.

GOE Number, Interest Area, and Work Group: 03.01.01; Plants and Animals; Managerial Work: Farming and Fishing. **Personality Type:** Enterprising. Enterprising occupations frequently involve starting up and carrying out projects. These occupations can involve leading people and making many decisions. They sometimes require risk taking and often deal with business. **Work Values:** Autonomy; Authority; Responsibility; Creativity; Ability Utilization; Activity. **Skills:** Coordination; Speaking; Management of Personnel Resources; Negotiation; Writing; Management of Financial Resources. **Abilities:** *Cognitive*—Oral Expression; Deductive Reasoning; Oral Comprehension; Written Comprehension; Written Expression. *Psychomotor*—none met the criteria. *Physical*—Trunk Strength. *Sensory*—Near Vision; Speech Clarity; Far Vision. **General Work Activities:** *Information Input*—Getting Information Needed to Do the Job; Identifying Objects, Actions, and Events; Estimating Needed Characteristics; Monitoring Processes, Materials, and Surroundings; Inspecting Equipment, Structures,

Materials. *Mental Process*—Judging Qualities of Things, Services, People; Organizing, Planning, and Prioritizing; Developing Objectives and Strategies; Analyzing Data or Information; Making Decisions and Solving Problems. *Work Output*—Documenting and Recording Information; Implementing Ideas and Programs; Performing General Physical Activities. *Interacting with Others*—Coordinating Work and Activities of Others; Communicating with Other Workers; Communicating with Persons Outside Organization. **Physical Work Conditions:** Standing; Indoors; Outdoors. **Other Job Characteristics:** Consequence of Error; Importance of Being Sure All Is Done; Importance of Being Exact or Accurate.

Experience: Job Zone 4. A minimum of two to four years of work-related skill, knowledge, or experience is needed. **Job Preparation:** SVP 7.0 to less than 8.0—2 years to less than 10 years. **Knowledge:** Food Production; Administration and Management; Personnel and Human Resources; Economics and Accounting; Production and Processing. **Instructional Programs:** 010104 Farm and Ranch Management; 010199 Agricultural Business and Management, Other; 010301 Agricultural Production Workers and Managers, General; 010302 Agricultural Animal Husbandry and Production Management; 010304 Crop Production Operations and Management; 010399 Agricultural Production Workers and Managers, Other; 019999 Agricultural Business and Production, Other; 020201 Animal Sciences, General; 020202 Agricultural Animal Breeding and Genetics; 020204 Agricultural Animal Nutrition; 020206 Dairy Science; 020209 Poultry Science; 020401 Plant Sciences, General; 020402 Agronomy and Crop Science; 020409 Range Science and Management.

Related DOT Jobs: 180.161-010 Manager, Production, Seed Corn; 180.167-018 General Manager, Farm; 180.167-058 Superintendent, Production; 180.167-066 Manager, Orchard.

11-9011.03 Fish Hatchery Managers (First-Line Supervisors and Managers/Supervisors—Agricultural, Forestry, Fishing, and Related Workers)

Education: No data available.
Employed: 51,350
Openings: No data available.
Projected Growth: No data available.
Earnings: $27,410

Direct and coordinate, through subordinate supervisory personnel, activities of workers engaged in fish hatchery production for corporations, cooperatives, or other owners.

Accounts for and dispenses funds. Confers with biologists and other fishery personnel to obtain data concerning fish habits, food, and environmental requirements. Collects information regarding techniques for collecting, fertilizing, incubating spawn, and treatment of spawn and fry. Oversees movement of mature fish to lakes, ponds, streams or commercial tanks. Prepares budget reports. Approves employment and discharge of employees, signs payrolls, and performs personnel duties. Prepares reports required by state and federal laws. Determines, administers, and executes policies relating to administration, standards of hatchery operations, and facility maintenance. Oversees trapping and spawning of fish, egg incubation, and fry rearing, applying knowledge of management and fish culturing techniques.

GOE Number, Interest Area, and Work Group: 03.01.01; Plants and Animals; Managerial Work: Farming and Fishing. **Personality Type:** Enterprising. Enterprising occupations frequently involve starting up and carrying out projects. These occupations can involve leading people and making many decisions. They sometimes require risk taking and often deal with business. **Work Values:** Autonomy; Responsibility; Authority; Creativity; Achievement; Variety; Compensation. **Skills:** Reading Comprehension; Management of Financial Resources; Writing; Critical Thinking. **Abilities:** *Cognitive*—Oral Expression; Oral Comprehension; Written Comprehension; Information Ordering; Written Expression. *Psychomotor*—Reaction Time; Response Orientation; Speed of Limb Movement. *Physical*—Gross Body Coordination; Gross Body Equilibrium. *Sensory*—Near Vision; Far Vision; Speech Clarity. **General Work Activities:** *Information Input*—Getting Information Needed to Do the Job; Monitoring Processes, Materials, and Surroundings; Identifying Objects, Actions, and Events. *Mental Process*—Making Decisions and Solving Problems; Evaluating Information Against Standards; Organizing, Planning, and Prioritizing; Judging Qualities of Things, Services, People; Scheduling Work and Activities. *Work Output*—Documenting and Recording Information; Implementing Ideas and Programs; Controlling Machines and Processes. *Interacting with Others*—Coordinating Work and Activities of Others; Guiding, Directing and Motivating Subordinates; Monitoring and Controlling Resources. **Physical Work Conditions:** Sitting; Standing; Outdoors. **Other Job Characteristics:** Consequence of Error; Importance of Being Sure All Is Done; Importance of Being Exact or Accurate.

Experience: Job Zone 4. A minimum of two to four years of work-related skill, knowledge, or experience is needed. **Job Preparation:** SVP 7.0 to less than 8.0—2 years to less than 10 years. **Knowledge:** Food Production; Administration and Management; Economics and Accounting; Personnel and Human Resources; Biology. **Instructional Programs:** 010104 Farm and Ranch Management; 010199 Agricultural Business and Management, Other; 010301 Agricultural Production Workers and Managers, General; 010302 Agricultural Animal Husbandry and Production Management; 010304 Crop Production Operations and Management; 010399 Agricultural Production Workers and Managers, Other; 019999 Agricultural Business and Production, Other; 020201 Animal Sciences, General; 020202 Agricultural Animal Breeding and Genetics; 020204 Agricultural Animal Nutrition; 020206 Dairy Science; 020209 Poultry Science; 020401 Plant Sciences, General; 020402 Agronomy and Crop Science; 020409 Range Science and Management.

Related DOT Job: 180.167-030 Manager, Fish Hatchery.

11-9012.00 Farmers and Ranchers (First-Line Supervisors and Managers/Supervisors —Agricultural, Forestry, Fishing, and Related Workers)

Education: No data available.

Employed: 51,350

Openings: No data available.

Projected Growth: No data available.

Earnings: $27,410

On an ownership or rental basis, operate farms, ranches, greenhouses, nurseries, timber tracts, or other agricultural production establishments that produce crops, horticultural specialties, livestock, poultry, finfish, shellfish, or animal specialties. May plant, cultivate, harvest, perform post-harvest activities, and market crops and livestock. May hire, train, and supervise farm workers or supervise a farm labor contractor. May prepare cost, production, and other records. May maintain and operate machinery and perform physical work.

Selects and purchases supplies and equipment, such as seed, tree stock, fertilizers, farm machinery, implements, livestock, and feed. Lubricates, adjusts, and makes minor repairs on farm equipment, using oilcan, grease gun, and hand tools. Grows out of season crops in greenhouse or early crops in cold-frame bed, or buds and grafts plant stock. Destroys diseased or superfluous crops, such as queen bee cells, bee colonies, parasites, and vermin. Installs irrigation systems and irrigates fields. Demonstrates and explains farm work techniques and safety regulations to workers. Maintains employee and financial records. Grades and packages crop for marketing. Hires and directs workers engaged in planting, cultivating, irrigating, harvesting, and marketing crops and raising livestock. Arranges with buyers for sale and shipment of crops. Breeds and raises stock, such as animals, poultry, honeybees, or earthworms. Determines kind and quantity of crops or livestock to be raised, according to market conditions, weather, and farm size. Harvests crops and collects specialty products, such as royal jelly from queen bee cells and honey from honeycombs. Inspects growing environment to maintain optimum growing or breeding conditions. Assembles, positions, and secures structures, such as trellises or beehives, using hand tools. Sets up and operates farm machinery to till soil, plant, prune, fertilize, apply herbicides and pesticides, and haul harvested crops. Plans harvesting considering ripeness and maturity of crop and weather conditions.

GOE Number, Interest Area, and Work Group: 03.01.01; Plants and Animals; Managerial Work: Farming and Fishing. **Personality Type:** Realistic. Realistic occupations frequently involve work activities that include practical, hands-on problems and solutions. These occupations often deal with plants, animals, and real-world materials like wood, tools, and machinery. Many of the occupations require working outside and do not involve a lot of paperwork or working closely with others. **Work Values:** Autonomy; Responsibility; Creativity; Achievement; Moral Values; Authority. **Skills:** Equipment Selection; Coordination; Operation and Control; Management of Financial Resources; Product Inspection. **Abilities:** *Cognitive*—Information Ordering; Deductive Reasoning; Oral Expression; Number Facility; Problem Sensitivity. *Psychomotor*—Control Precision; Manual Dexterity; Wrist-Finger Speed; Multilimb Coordination. *Physical*—Static Strength; Trunk Strength; Dynamic Strength; Stamina. *Sensory*—Near Vision; Speech Clarity; Far Vision. **General Work Activities:** *Information Input*—Monitoring Processes, Materials, and Surroundings; Identifying Objects, Actions, and Events; Getting Information Needed to Do the Job. *Mental Process*—Making Decisions and Solving Problems; Organizing, Planning, and Prioritizing; Scheduling Work and Activities; Updating and Using Job-Relevant Knowledge; Analyzing Data or Information. *Work Output*—Operating Vehicles or Equipment; Performing General Physical Activities; Repairing and Maintaining Mechanical Equipment. *Interacting with Others*–Monitoring and Controlling Resources; Coordinating Work and Activities of Others; Teaching Others. **Physical Work Conditions:** Using Hands on Objects, Tools, or Controls; Outdoors; Standing. **Other Job Characteristics:** Consequence of Error; Importance of Being Sure All Is Done; Frustrating Circumstances.

Experience: Job Zone 3. Previous work-related skill, knowledge, or experience is required. **Job Preparation:** SVP 6.0 to less than 7.0–More than 1 year and less than 4 years. **Knowledge:** Food Production; Personnel and Human Resources; Production and Processing; Biology; Sales and Marketing. **Instructional Programs:** 010104 Farm and Ranch Management; 010199 Agricultural Business and Management, Other; 010301 Agricultural Production Workers and Managers, General; 010302 Agricultural Animal Husbandry and Production Management; 010304 Crop Production Operations and Management; 010399 Agricultural Production Workers and Managers, Other; 019999 Agricultural Business and Production, Other; 020201 Animal Sciences, General; 020202 Agricultural Animal Breeding and Genetics; 020204 Agricultural Animal Nutrition; 020206 Dairy Science; 020209 Poultry Science; 020401 Plant Sciences, General; 020402 Agronomy and Crop Science; 020409 Range Science and Management.

Related DOT Jobs: 401.161-010 Farmer, Cash Grain; 402.161-010 Farmer, Vegetable; 403.161-010 Farmer, Tree-Fruit-and-Nut Crops; 403.161-014 Farmer, Fruit Crops, Bush and Vine; 404.161-010 Farmer, Field Crop; 407.161-010 Farmer, Diversified Crops; 413.161-010 Beekeeper; 413.161-018 Worm Grower; 421.161-010 Farmer, General.

11-9021.00 Construction Managers (Construction Managers)

Education: Bachelor's degree
Employed: 270,041
Openings: 32,841
Projected Growth: 14%
Earnings: $47,610

Plan, direct, coordinate, or budget, usually through subordinate supervisory personnel, activities concerned with the construction and maintenance of structures, facilities, and systems. Participate in the conceptual development of a construction project and oversee its organization, scheduling, and implementation.

Studies job specifications to plan and approve construction of project. Confers with supervisory personnel to discuss such matters as work procedures, complaints, and construction problems. Inspects and reviews construction work, repair projects, and reports to ensure work conforms to specifications. Requisitions supplies and materials to complete construction project. Interprets and explains plans and contract terms to administrative staff, workers, and clients. Directs and supervises workers on construction site to ensure project meets specifications. Formulates reports concerning such areas as work progress, costs, and scheduling. Dispatches workers to construction sites to work on specified project. Investigates reports of damage at construction sites to ensure proper procedures are being carried out. Plans, organizes, and directs activities concerned with construction and maintenance of structures, facilities, and systems. Contracts workers to perform construction work in accordance with specifications.

GOE Number, Interest Area, and Work Group: 06.01.01; Construction, Mining, and Drilling; Managerial Work in Construction, Mining, and Drilling. **Personality Type:** Enterprising. Enterprising occupations frequently involve starting up and carrying out projects. These occupations can involve leading people and making many decisions. They sometimes require risk taking and often deal with business. **Work Values:** Authority; Autonomy; Responsibility; Compensation; Ability Utilization; Variety. **Skills:** Coordination; Management of Personnel Resources; Time Management; Mathematics; Product Inspection. **Abilities:** *Cognitive*–Oral Comprehension; Oral Expression; Written Comprehension; Written Expression; Problem Sensitivity. *Psychomotor*–none met the criteria. *Physical*–none met the criteria. *Sensory*–Near Vision; Speech Recognition; Speech Clarity. **General Work Activities:** *Information Input*–Monitoring Processes, Materials, and Surroundings; Getting Information Needed to Do the Job; Inspecting Equipment, Structures, Materials. *Mental Process*–Making Decisions and Solving Problems; Organizing, Planning, and Prioritizing; Developing Objectives and Strategies. *Work Output*–Implementing Ideas and Programs; Performing General Physical Activities; Documenting and Recording Information. *Interacting with Others*–Coordinating Work and Activities of Others; Guiding, Directing and Motivating Subordinates; Developing and Building Teams. **Physical Work Conditions:** Sitting; Outdoors; Distracting Sounds and Noise Levels; Indoors; Standing. **Other Job Characteristics:** Consequence of Error; Importance of Being Sure All Is Done; Importance of Being Exact or Accurate.

Experience: Job Zone 4. A minimum of two to four years of work-related skill, knowledge, or experience is needed. **Job Preparation:** SVP 7.0 to less than 8.0–2 years to less than 10 years. **Knowledge:** Administration and Management; Building and Construction; Personnel and Human Resources; Mechanical; Public Safety and Security. **Instructional Programs:** 151001 Construction/Building Technology/Technician.

Related DOT Jobs: 182.167-010 Contractor; 182.167-018 Railroad-Construction Director; 182.167-026 Superintendent, Construction; 182.167-030 Superintendent, Maintenance of Way; 182.167-034 Supervisor, Bridges and Buildings.

11-9031.00 Education Administrators, Preschool and Child Care Center/Program (Education Administrators)

Education: Work experience, plus degree
Employed: 447,158
Openings: 60,229
Projected Growth: 13%
Earnings: $60,400

Plan, direct, or coordinate the academic and nonacademic activities of preschool and child care centers or programs.

Counsels and provides guidance to students regarding personal, academic, or behavioral problems. Determines allocations of funds for staff, supplies, materials, and equipment and authorizes purchases. Reviews and approves new programs or recommends modifications to existing programs. Plans, directs, and monitors instructional methods and content for educational, vocational, or student activity programs. Evaluates programs to determine effectiveness, efficiency, and utilization and to ensure activities comply with federal, state, and local regulations. Collects and analyzes survey data, regulatory information, and demographic and employment trends to forecast enrollment patterns and curriculum changes. Contacts and addresses commercial, community, or political groups to promote educational programs and services or lobby for legislative changes. Writes articles, manuals, and other publications and assists in the distribution of promotional literature. Confers with parents and staff to discuss educational activities, policies, and student behavioral or learning problems. Coordinates outreach activities with businesses, communities, and other institutions or organizations to identify educational needs, and establish and coordinate programs. Reviews and interprets government codes and develops programs to ensure facility safety, security, and maintenance. Determines scope of educational program offerings and prepares drafts of course schedules and descriptions to estimate staffing and facility requirements. Prepares and submits budget requests or grant proposals to solicit program funding. Directs and coordinates activities of teachers or administrators at daycare centers, schools, public agencies, and institutions. Organizes and directs committees of specialists, volunteers, and staff to provide technical and advisory assistance for programs. Recruits, hires, trains, and evaluates primary and supplemental staff and recommends personnel actions for programs and services.

GOE Number, Interest Area, and Work Group: 12.01.01; Education and Social Service; Managerial Work in Education and Social Service. **Personality Type:** Social. Social occupations frequently involve working with, communicating with, and teaching people. These occupations often involve helping or providing service to others. **Work Values:** Ability Utilization; Activity; Achievement; Security; Social Status; Working Conditions; Company Policies and Practices; Authority. **Skills:** Writing; Coordination; Learning Strategies; Reading Comprehension; Management of Personnel Resources. **Abilities:** *Cognitive*—Written Expression; Oral Expression; Written Comprehension; Oral Comprehension; Fluency of Ideas. *Psychomotor*—none met the criteria. *Physical*—none met the criteria. *Sensory*—Speech Clarity; Near Vision; Speech Recognition. **General Work Activities:** *Information Input*—Getting Information Needed to Do the Job; Identifying Objects, Actions, and Events; Monitoring Processes, Materials, and Surroundings. *Mental Process*—Developing Objectives and Strategies; Organizing, Planning, and Prioritizing; Making Decisions and Solving Problems; Analyzing Data or Information. *Work Output*—Implementing Ideas and Programs; Documenting and Recording Information; Interacting with Computers. *Interacting with Others*—Communicating with Persons Outside Organization; Communicating with Other Workers; Providing Consultation and Advice to Others. **Physical Work Conditions:** Indoors; Sitting; Standing. **Other Job Characteristics:** Consequence of Error; Frustrating Circumstances; Importance of Being Sure All Is Done.

Experience: Job Zone 4. A minimum of two to four years of work-related skill, knowledge, or experience is needed. **Job Preparation:** SVP 7.0 to less than 8.0—2 years to less than 10 years. **Knowledge:** Education and Training; Administration and Management; English Language; Personnel and Human Resources; Sales and Marketing. **Instructional Programs:** 130101 Education, General; 130401 Education Administration and Supervision, General; 130402 Administration of Special Education; 130403 Adult and Continuing Education Administration; 130404 Educational Supervision; 130405 Elementary, Middle and Secondary Education Administration; 130406 Higher Education Administration; 130407 Community and Junior College Administration; 130499 Education Administration and Supervision, Other.

Related DOT Jobs: 092.167-010 Director, Day Care Center; 094.167-014 Director, Special Education; 097.167-010 Director, Vocational Training; 099.117-010 Director, Educational Program; 099.117-018 Principal.

11-9032.00 Education Administrators, Elementary and Secondary School (Education Administrators)

Education: Work experience, plus degree

Employed: 447,158

Openings: 60,229

Projected Growth: 13%

Earnings: $60,400

Plan, direct, or coordinate the academic, clerical, or auxiliary activities of public or private elementary or secondary level schools.

Plans, directs, and monitors instructional methods and content for educational, vocational, or student activity programs. Directs and coordinates activities of teachers or administrators at daycare centers, schools, public agencies, and institutions. Coordinates outreach activities with businesses, communities, and other institutions or organizations to identify educational needs, and establish and coordinate programs. Collects and analyzes survey data, regulatory information, and demographic and employment trends to forecast enrollment patterns and curriculum changes. Determines scope of educational program offerings and prepares drafts of course schedules and descriptions to estimate staffing and facility requirements. Prepares and submits budget requests or grant proposals to solicit program funding. Evaluates programs to determine effectiveness, efficiency, and utilization and to ensure activities comply with federal, state, and local regulations. Counsels and provides guidance to students regarding personal, academic, or behavioral problems. Reviews and interprets government codes and develops programs to ensure facility safety, security, and maintenance. Reviews and approves new programs or recommends modifications to existing programs. Determines allocations of funds for staff, supplies, materials, and equipment and authorizes purchases. Organizes and directs committees of specialists, volunteers, and staff to provide technical and advisory assistance for programs. Plans and coordinates consumer research and educational services to assist organizations in product development and marketing. Recruits, hires, trains, and evaluates primary and supplemental staff and recommends personnel actions for programs and services. Contacts and addresses commercial, community, or political groups to promote educational programs and services or lobby for legislative changes. Writes articles, manuals, and other publications and assists in the distribution of promotional literature.

GOE Number, Interest Area, and Work Group: 12.01.01; Education and Social Service; Managerial Work in Education and Social Service. **Personality Type:** Social. Social occupations frequently involve working with, communicating with, and teaching people. These occupations often involve helping or providing service to others. **Work Values:** Ability Utilization; Activity; Achievement; Social Status; Working Conditions; Security; Authority; Company Policies and Practices. **Skills:** Writing; Coordination; Learning Strategies; Reading Comprehension; Management of Personnel Resources. **Abilities:** *Cognitive*—Oral Expression; Written Expression; Written Comprehension; Oral Comprehension; Fluency of Ideas. *Psychomotor*—none met the criteria. *Physical*—none met the criteria. *Sensory*—Speech Clarity; Near Vision; Speech Recognition. **General Work Activities:** *Information Input*—Getting Information Needed to Do the Job; Identifying Objects, Actions, and Events; Monitoring Processes, Materials, and Surroundings. *Mental Process*—Developing Objectives and Strategies; Organizing, Planning, and Prioritizing; Analyzing Data or Information; Making Decisions and Solving Problems. *Work Output*—Implementing Ideas and Programs; Documenting and Recording Information; Interacting with Computers. *Interacting with Others*—Communicating with Persons Outside Organization; Communicating with Other Workers; Providing Consultation and Advice to Others. **Physical Work Conditions:** Indoors; Sitting; Standing. **Other Job Characteristics:** Consequence of Error; Frustrating Circumstances; Importance of Being Sure All Is Done.

Experience: Job Zone 4. A minimum of two to four years of work-related skill, knowledge, or experience is needed. **Job Preparation:** SVP 7.0 to less than 8.0—2 years to less than 10 years. **Knowledge:** Education and Training; Administration and Management; English Language; Personnel and Human Resources; Sales and Marketing. **Instructional Programs:** 130101 Education, General; 130401 Education Administration and Supervision, General; 130402 Administration of Special Education; 130403 Adult and Continuing Education Administration; 130404 Educational Supervision; 130405 Elementary, Middle and Secondary Education Administration; 130406 Higher Education Administration; 130407 Community and Junior College Administration; 130499 Education Administration and Supervision, Other.

Related DOT Jobs: 091.107-010 Assistant Principal; 094.117-010 Director, Commission for the Blind; 094.167-014 Director, Special Education; 097.167-010 Director, Vocational Training; 099.117-010 Director, Educational Program; 099.117-018 Principal.

11-9033.00 Education Administrators, Postsecondary
(Education Administrators)

Education: Work experience, plus degree

Employed: 447,158

Openings: 60,229

Projected Growth: 13%

Earnings: $60,400

Plan, direct, or coordinate research, instructional, student administration and services, and other educational activities at postsecondary institutions, including universities, colleges, and junior and community colleges.

Confers with other academic staff to explain admission requirements and transfer credit policies, and compares course equivalencies to university/college curriculum. Represents college/university as liaison officer with accrediting agencies and to exchange information between academic institutions and in community. Evaluates personnel and physical plant operations, student programs, and statistical and research data to implement procedures or modifications to administrative policies. Advises staff and students on problems relating to policies, program administration, and financial and personal matters, and recommends solutions. Estimates and allocates department funding based on financial success of previous courses and other pertinent factors. Consults with staff, students, alumni, and subject experts to determine needs/feasibility, and to formulate admission policies and educational programs. Completes and submits operating budget for approval, controls expenditures, and maintains financial reports and records. Meets with academic and administrative personnel to disseminate information, identify problems, monitor progress reports, and ensure adherence to goals/objectives. Negotiates with foundation and industry representatives to secure loans for university and identify costs and materials for building construction. Directs work activities of personnel engaged in administration of academic institutions, departments, and alumni organizations. Establishes operational policies and procedures and develops academic objectives. Recruits, employs, trains, and terminates department personnel. Reviews student misconduct reports requiring disciplinary action and counsels students to ensure conformance to university policies. Coordinates alumni functions and encourages alumni endorsement of recruiting and fund raising activities. Plans and promotes athletic policies, sports events, ticket sales, and student participation in social, cultural, and recreational activities.

GOE Number, Interest Area, and Work Group: 12.01.01; Education and Social Service; Managerial Work in Education and Social Service. **Personality Type:** Enterprising. Enterprising occupations frequently involve starting up and carrying out projects. These occupations can involve leading people and making many decisions. They sometimes require risk taking and often deal with business. **Work Values:** Working Conditions; Social Status; Ability Utilization; Authority; Activity. **Skills:** Identification of Key Causes; Management of Financial Resources; Coordination; Monitoring; Systems Evaluation; Judgment and Decision Making; Reading Comprehension. **Abilities:** *Cognitive*—Written Expression; Oral Comprehension; Written Comprehension; Oral Expression; Deductive Reasoning. *Psychomotor*—none met the criteria. *Physical*—Trunk Strength. *Sensory*—Speech Clarity; Near Vision; Speech Recognition. **General Work Activities:** *Information Input*—Getting Information Needed to Do the Job; Estimating Needed Characteristics; Identifying Objects, Actions, and Events. *Mental Process*—Making Decisions and Solving Problems; Analyzing Data or Information; Developing Objectives and Strategies; Processing Information. *Work Output*—Documenting and Recording Information; Implementing Ideas and Programs; Interacting with Computers. *Interacting with Others*—Performing Administrative Activities; Communicating with Persons Outside Organization; Establishing and Maintaining Relationships. **Physical Work Conditions:** Sitting; Indoors; Standing; Walking or Running. **Other Job Characteristics:** Consequence of Error; Importance of Being Sure All Is Done; Importance of Being Exact or Accurate.

Experience: Job Zone 5. Extensive skill, knowledge, and experience are needed. Very advanced communication and organizational skills are required. **Job Preparation:** SVP 8.0 and above—4 years to more than 10 years. **Knowledge:** Administration and Management; Education and Training; Economics and Accounting; English Language; Personnel and Human Resources. **Instructional Programs:** 130101 Education, General; 130401 Education Administration and Supervision, General; 130402 Administration of Special Education; 130403 Adult and Continuing Education Administration; 130404 Educational Supervision; 130405 Elementary, Middle and Secondary Education Administration; 130406 Higher Education Administration; 130407 Community and Junior College Administration; 130499 Education Administration and Supervision, Other.

Related DOT Jobs: 090.117-010 Academic Dean; 090.117-014 Alumni Secretary; 090.117-018 Dean of Students; 090.117-022 Director, Athletic; 090.117-026 Director, Extension Work; 090.117-030 Financial-Aid Officer; 090.167-010 Department Head, College or University; 090.167-014 Director of Admissions; 090.167-018 Director of Institutional Research; 090.167-022 Director of Student Affairs; 090.167-026 Director, Summer Sessions; 090.167-030 Registrar, College or University; 186.117-010 Business Manager, College or University.

11-9041.00 Engineering Managers (Engineering, Natural Science, and Computer and Information Systems Managers)

Education: Work experience, plus degree
Employed: 326,229
Openings: 54,120
Projected Growth: 43.5%
Earnings: $75,320

Plan, direct, or coordinate activities in such fields as architecture and engineering, or manage research and development in these fields.

Plans, directs, and coordinates survey work with activities of other staff, certifies survey work, and writes land legal descriptions. Confers with and prepares reports for officials and speaks to public to solicit support. Administers highway planning, construction, and maintenance, and reviews and recommends or approves contracts and cost estimates. Analyzes technology, resource needs, and market demand, and confers with management, production, and marketing staff to plan and assess feasibility of project. Plans and directs oil field development, gas and oil production, and geothermal drilling. Directs, reviews, and approves product design and changes, and directs testing. Plans and directs installation, maintenance, testing, and repair of facilities and equipment. Evaluates contract proposals, directs negotiation of research contracts, and prepares bids and contracts. Establishes procedures, and directs testing, operation, maintenance, and repair of trans-

mitter equipment. Plans, coordinates, and directs engineering project, organizes and assigns staff, and directs integration of technical activities with products. Directs engineering of water control, treatment, and distribution projects.

GOE Number, Interest Area, and Work Group: 02.01.01; Science, Math, and Engineering; Managerial Work in Science, Math, and Engineering. **Personality Type:** Enterprising. Enterprising occupations frequently involve starting up and carrying out projects. These occupations can involve leading people and making many decisions. They sometimes require risk taking and often deal with business. **Work Values:** Autonomy; Compensation; Authority; Working Conditions; Company Policies and Practices; Ability Utilization. **Skills:** Coordination; Operations Analysis; Visioning; Information Gathering; Testing; Science. **Abilities:** *Cognitive*—Oral Comprehension; Written Comprehension; Oral Expression; Written Expression; Deductive Reasoning. *Psychomotor*—Response Orientation. *Physical*—Trunk Strength; Gross Body Equilibrium. *Sensory*—Speech Clarity; Near Vision; Speech Recognition. **General Work Activities:** *Information Input*—Getting Information Needed to Do the Job; Identifying Objects, Actions, and Events; Estimating Needed Characteristics; Monitoring Processes, Materials, and Surroundings. *Mental Process*—Organizing, Planning, and Prioritizing; Analyzing Data or Information; Making Decisions and Solving Problems. *Work Output*—Implementing Ideas and Programs; Interacting with Computers; Drafting and Specifying Technical Devices. *Interacting with Others*—Guiding, Directing and Motivating Subordinates; Coordinating Work and Activities of Others; Providing Consultation and Advice to Others. **Physical Work Conditions:** Indoors; Sitting; Outdoors; Standing; Walking or Running. **Other Job Characteristics:** Consequence of Error; Importance of Being Exact or Accurate; Importance of Being Sure All Is Done; Frustrating Circumstances.

Experience: Job Zone 5. Extensive skill, knowledge, and experience are needed. Very advanced communication and organizational skills are required. **Job Preparation:** SVP 8.0 and above—4 years to more than 10 years. **Knowledge:** Engineering and Technology; Administration and Management; Design; Physics; Mathematics. **Instructional Program:** 143001 Engineering/Industrial Management.

Related DOT Jobs: 003.167-034 Engineer-in-Charge, Transmitter; 003.167-070 Engineering Manager, Electronics; 005.167-010 Chief Engineer, Waterworks; 005.167-022 Highway-Administrative Engineer; 007.167-014 Plant Engineer; 010.161-014 Chief Petroleum Engineer; 010.167-018 Superintendent, Oil-Well Services; 018.167-022 Manager, Land Surveying; 019.167-014 Project Engineer; 162.117-030 Research-Contracts Supervisor.

11-9051.00 Food Service Managers (Food Service and Lodging Managers)

Education: Work experience in a related occupation
Employed: 594,642
Openings: 138,826
Projected Growth: 16.3%
Earnings: $26,700

Plan, direct, or coordinate activities of an organization or department that serves food and beverages.

Monitors budget, payroll records, and reviews financial transactions to ensure expenditures are authorized and budgeted. Coordinates assignments of cooking personnel to ensure economical use of food and timely preparation. Investigates and resolves complaints regarding food quality, service, or accommodations. Reviews menus and analyzes recipes to determine labor and overhead costs, and assigns prices to menu items. Establishes and enforces nutrition standards for dining establishment based on accepted industry standards. Keeps records required by government agencies regarding sanitation and regarding food subsidies where indicated. Tests cooked food by tasting and smelling to ensure palatability and flavor conformity. Monitors food preparation and methods, size of portions, and garnishing and presentation of food to ensure food is prepared and presented in accepted manner. Estimates food, liquor, wine, and other beverage consumption to anticipate amount to be purchased or requisitioned. Organizes and directs worker training programs, resolves personnel problems, hires new staff, and evaluates employee performance in dining and lodging facilities. Plans menus and food utilization based on anticipated number of guests, nutritional value, palatability, popularity, and costs. Monitors compliance with health and fire regulations regarding food preparation and serving and building maintenance in lodging and dining facility. Creates specialty dishes and develops recipes to be used in dining facility.

GOE Number, Interest Area, and Work Group: 11.01.01; Recreation, Travel, and Other Personal Services; Managerial Work in Recreation, Travel, and Other Personal Services. **Personality Type:** Enterprising. Enterprising occupations frequently involve starting up and carrying out projects. These occupations can involve leading people and making many decisions. They sometimes require risk taking and often deal with business. **Work Values:** Authority; Security; Autonomy; Responsibility; Creativity. **Skills:** Coordination; Management of Personnel Resources; Problem Identification; Time Management; Speaking; Monitoring. **Abilities:** *Cognitive*—Oral Expression; Oral Comprehension; Written Comprehension; Deductive Reasoning; Number Facility; Mathematical Reasoning. *Psychomotor*—Wrist-Finger Speed; Arm-Hand Steadiness; Reaction Time. *Physical*—Trunk Strength; Gross Body Equilibrium; Stamina. *Sensory*—Near Vision; Speech Clarity; Visual Color Discrimination. **General Work Activities:** *Information Input*—Identifying Objects, Actions, and Events; Monitoring Processes, Materials, and Surroundings; Getting Information Needed to Do the Job; Estimating Needed Characteristics. *Mental Process*—Updating and Using Job-Relevant Knowledge; Scheduling Work and Activities; Evaluating Information Against Standards. *Work Output*—Documenting and Recording Information; Handling and Moving Objects; Performing General Physical Activities. *Interacting with Others*—Monitoring and Controlling Resources; Communicating with Other Workers; Guiding, Directing and Motivating Subordinates. **Physical Work Conditions:** Indoors; Standing; Walking or Running; Sitting. **Other Job Characteristics:** Importance of Being Sure All Is Done; Consequence of Error; Frustrating Circumstances.

Experience: Job Zone 4. A minimum of two to four years of work-related skill, knowledge, or experience is needed. **Job Preparation:** SVP 7.0 to less than 8.0—2 years to less than 10 years. **Knowledge:** Administration and Management; Customer and Personal Service; Economics and Accounting; Mathematics; Education

and Training; Public Safety and Security; Law, Government and Jurisprudence; Personnel and Human Resources. **Instructional Programs:** 080901 Hospitality and Recreation Marketing Operations, General; 080906 Food Sales Operations; 120504 Food and Beverage/Restaurant Operations Manager; 190505 Food Systems Administration; 200401 Institutional Food Workers and Administrators, General; 200405 Food Caterer; 200409 Institutional Food Services Administrator; 520702 Franchise Operation; 520901 Hospitality/Administration Management; 520902 Hotel/Motel and Restaurant Management.

Related DOT Jobs: 185.137-010 Manager, Fast Food Services; 187.161-010 Executive Chef; 187.167-026 Director, Food Services; 187.167-050 Manager, Agricultural-Labor Camp; 187.167-066 Manager, Camp; 187.167-106 Manager, Food Service; 187.167-126 Manager, Liquor Establishment; 187.167-206 Dietary Manager; 187.167-210 Director, Food and Beverage; 319.137-014 Manager, Flight Kitchen; 319.137-018 Manager, Industrial Cafeteria; 320.137-010 Manager, Boarding House.

11-9061.00 Funeral Directors (Funeral Directors and Morticians)

Education: Associate degree
Employed: 27,527
Openings: 3,972
Projected Growth: 16.1%
Earnings: $35,040

Perform various tasks to arrange and direct funeral services, such as coordinating transportation of body to mortuary for embalming, interviewing family or other authorized person to arrange details, selecting pallbearers, procuring official for religious rites, and providing transportation for mourners.

Arranges and directs funeral services. Directs preparations and shipment of body for out-of-state burial. Plans placement of casket in parlor or chapel and adjusts lights, fixtures, and floral displays. Interviews family or other authorized person to arrange details, such as selection of casket and location and time of burial. Closes casket and leads funeral cortege to church or burial site. Directs placement and removal of casket from hearse.

GOE Number, Interest Area, and Work Group: 13.01.01; General Management and Support; General Management Work and Management of Support Functions. **Personality Type:** Enterprising. Enterprising occupations frequently involve starting up and carrying out projects. These occupations can involve leading people and making many decisions. They sometimes require risk taking and often deal with business. **Work Values:** Autonomy; Security; Social Service; Compensation; Achievement; Authority. **Skills:** Social Perceptiveness; Coordination; Active Listening; Speaking; Service Orientation; Reading Comprehension. **Abilities:** *Cognitive*—Oral Expression; Oral Comprehension; Problem Sensitivity; Written Comprehension; Written Expression. *Psychomotor*—none met the criteria. *Physical*—none met the criteria. **General Work Activities:** *Information Input*—Getting Information Needed to Do the Job; Estimating Needed Characteristics; Monitoring Processes, Materials, and Surroundings. *Mental Process*—Making Decisions and Solving Problems; Organizing,

Planning, and Prioritizing; Scheduling Work and Activities. *Work Output*—Implementing Ideas and Programs; Documenting and Recording Information; Handling and Moving Objects; Performing General Physical Activities. *Interacting with Others*—Communicating with Persons Outside Organization; Coordinating Work and Activities of Others; Performing Administrative Activities; Communicating with Other Workers. **Physical Work Conditions:** Indoors; Sitting; Standing. **Other Job Characteristics:** Importance of Being Sure All Is Done; Consequence of Error; Importance of Being Exact or Accurate.

Experience: Job Zone 4. A minimum of two to four years of work-related skill, knowledge, or experience is needed. **Job Preparation:** SVP 7.0 to less than 8.0—2 years to less than 10 years. **Knowledge:** Administration and Management; Customer and Personal Service; Transportation; Sales and Marketing; English Language; Psychology. **Instructional Program:** 120301 Funeral Services and Mortuary Science.

Related DOT Job: 187.167-030 Director, Funeral.

11-9071.00 Gaming Managers (All Other Managers and Administrators)

Education: No data available.

Employed: 946,190

Openings: No data available.

Projected Growth: No data available.

Earnings: $49,220

Plan, organize, direct, control, or coordinate gaming operations in a casino. Formulate gaming policies for their area of responsibility.

Directs workers compiling summary sheets for each race or event to show amount wagered and amount to be paid to winners. Observes and supervises operation to ensure that employees render prompt and courteous service to patrons. Resolves customer complaints regarding service. Establishes policies on types of gambling offered, odds, extension of credit, and serving food and beverages. Interviews and hires workers. Explains and interprets house rules, such as game rules and betting limits, to patrons. Records, issues receipts for, and pays off bets. Trains new workers and evaluates their performance. Review operational expenses, budget estimates, betting accounts, and collection reports for accuracy. Prepares work schedules, assigns work stations, and keeps attendance records.

GOE Number, Interest Area, and Work Group: 11.01.01; Recreation, Travel, and Other Personal Services; Managerial Work in Recreation, Travel, and Other Personal Services. **Personality Type:** Enterprising. Enterprising occupations frequently involve starting up and carrying out projects. These occupations can involve leading people and making many decisions. They sometimes require risk taking and often deal with business. **Work Values:** Responsibility; Authority; Working Conditions; Security; Autonomy. **Skills:** Management of Personnel Resources; Management of Financial Resources; Critical Thinking; Speaking. **Abilities:** *Cognitive*—Oral Expression; Number Facility; Mathematical Reasoning; Time Sharing; Deductive Reasoning; Information Ordering. *Psychomotor*—none met the criteria. *Physical*—none met the

criteria. *Sensory*—Near Vision; Far Vision; Night Vision; Sound Localization; Peripheral Vision. **General Work Activities:** *Information Input*—Getting Information Needed to Do the Job; Monitoring Processes, Materials, and Surroundings; Identifying Objects, Actions, and Events. *Mental Process*—Making Decisions and Solving Problems; Scheduling Work and Activities; Developing Objectives and Strategies. *Work Output*—Documenting and Recording Information; Implementing Ideas and Programs; Controlling Machines and Processes; Handling and Moving Objects. *Interacting with Others*—Performing Administrative Activities; Coordinating Work and Activities of Others; Communicating with Other Workers. **Physical Work Conditions:** Indoors; Sitting; Standing. **Other Job Characteristics:** Consequence of Error; Importance of Being Exact or Accurate; Importance of Being Sure All Is Done.

Experience: Job Zone 3. Previous work-related skill, knowledge, or experience is required. **Job Preparation:** SVP 6.0 to less than 7.0—More than 1 year and less than 4 years. **Knowledge:** Administration and Management; Economics and Accounting; Personnel and Human Resources; Customer and Personal Service; Mathematics. **Instructional Programs:** 080301 Entrepreneurship; 310301 Parks, Recreation and Leisure Facilities Management; 440201 Community Organization, Resources and Services; 440401 Public Administration; 500704 Arts Management; 520101 Business, General; 520201 Business Administration and Management, General; 520203 Logistics and Materials Management; 520206 Non-Profit and Public Management; 520299 Business Administration and Management, Other; 520701 Enterprise Management and Operation, General; 520702 Franchise Operation; 520799 Enterprise Management and Operation, Other; 520903 Travel-Tourism Management; 520999 Hospitality Services Management, Other.

Related DOT Jobs: 187.167-014 Bookmaker; 187.167-070 Manager, Casino; 187.167-134 Manager, Mutuel Department; 343.137-010 Manager, Cardroom.

11-9081.00 Lodging Managers (Food Service and Lodging Managers)

Education: Work experience in a related occupation

Employed: 594,642

Openings: 138,826

Projected Growth: 16.3%

Earnings: $26,700

Plan, direct, or coordinate activities of an organization or department that provides lodging and other accommodations.

Answers inquiries pertaining to hotel policies and services and resolves occupants' complaints. Arranges telephone answering service, delivers mail and packages, and answers questions regarding locations for eating and entertainment. Receives and processes advance registration payments, sends out letters of confirmation, and returns checks when registration cannot be accepted. Shows, rents, or assigns accommodations. Collects payment and records data pertaining to funds and expenditures. Confers and cooperates with other department heads to ensure coordination of hotel activities. Greets and registers guests. Observes and monitors performance to ensure efficient operations and adherence to facility's policies and procedures. Inspects guest rooms, public areas, and grounds for cleanliness and appearance. Assigns duties to workers and schedules shifts. Interviews and hires applicants. Manages and maintains temporary or permanent lodging facilities. Coordinates front-office activities of hotel or motel and resolves problems. Purchases supplies and arranges for outside services, such as deliveries, laundry, maintenance and repair, and trash collection.

GOE Number, Interest Area, and Work Group: 11.01.01; Recreation, Travel, and Other Personal Services; Managerial Work in Recreation, Travel, and Other Personal Services. **Personality Type:** Enterprising. Enterprising occupations frequently involve starting up and carrying out projects. These occupations can involve leading people and making many decisions. They sometimes require risk taking and often deal with business. **Work Values:** Autonomy; Authority; Responsibility; Working Conditions; Security. **Skills:** Coordination; Service Orientation; Time Management; Management of Material Resources; Management of Personnel Resources; Speaking; Problem Identification. **Abilities:** *Cognitive*—Oral Expression; Number Facility; Oral Comprehension; Written Comprehension; Problem Sensitivity; Information Ordering. *Psychomotor*—Wrist-Finger Speed; Arm-Hand Steadiness; Response Orientation. *Physical*—Static Strength; Extent Flexibility; Trunk Strength. *Sensory*—Near Vision; Speech Recognition; Speech Clarity. **General Work Activities:** *Information Input*—Getting Information Needed to Do the Job; Inspecting Equipment, Structures, Materials; Monitoring Processes, Materials, and Surroundings. *Mental Process*—Scheduling Work and Activities; Organizing, Planning, and Prioritizing; Processing Information; Making Decisions and Solving Problems. *Work Output*—Documenting and Recording Information; Interacting with Computers; Performing General Physical Activities. *Interacting with Others*—Monitoring and Controlling Resources; Establishing and Maintaining Relationships; Performing for or Working with the Public. **Physical Work Conditions:** Indoors; Standing; Sitting; Walking or Running. **Other Job Characteristics:** Importance of Being Sure All Is Done; Consequence of Error; Importance of Being Exact or Accurate; Frustrating Circumstances.

Experience: Job Zone 3. Previous work-related skill, knowledge, or experience is required. **Job Preparation:** SVP 6.0 to less than 7.0—More than 1 year and less than 4 years. **Knowledge:** Administration and Management; Customer and Personal Service; Personnel and Human Resources; Public Safety and Security; English Language; Clerical; Economics and Accounting. **Instructional Programs:** 080901 Hospitality and Recreation Marketing Operations, General; 080906 Food Sales Operations; 120504 Food and Beverage/Restaurant Operations Manager; 190505 Food Systems Administration; 200401 Institutional Food Workers and Administrators, General; 200405 Food Caterer; 200409 Institutional Food Services Administrator; 520702 Franchise Operation; 520901 Hospitality/Administration Management; 520902 Hotel/Motel and Restaurant Management.

Related DOT Jobs: 187.117-038 Manager, Hotel or Motel; 187.137-018 Manager, Front Office; 320.137-014 Manager, Lodging Facilities.

11-9111.00 Medical and Health Services Managers
(Medical and Health Services Managers)

Education: Work experience, plus degree
Employed: 222,441
Openings: 31,238
Projected Growth: 33.3%
Earnings: $48,870

Plan, direct, or coordinate medicine and health services in hospitals, clinics, managed care organizations, public health agencies, or similar organizations.

Develops instructional materials and conducts in-service and community-based educational programs. Develops organizational policies and procedures and establishes evaluative or operational criteria for facility or medical unit. Develops and maintains computerized records management system to store or process personnel, activity, or personnel data. Consults with medical, business, and community groups to discuss service problems, coordinate activities and plans, and promote health programs. Directs and coordinates activities of medical, nursing, technical, clerical, service, and maintenance personnel of health care facility or mobile unit. Inspects facilities for emergency readiness and compliance of access, safety, and sanitation regulations and recommends building or equipment modifications. Reviews and analyzes facility activities and data to aid planning and cash and risk management and to improve service utilization. Prepares activity reports to inform management of the status and implementation plans of programs, services, and quality initiatives. Implements and administers programs and services for health care or medical facility. Develops or expands medical programs or health services for research, rehabilitation, and community health promotion. Administers fiscal operations, such as planning budgets, authorizing expenditures and coordinating financial reporting. Establishes work schedules and assignments for staff, according to workload, space and equipment availability. Recruits, hires, and evaluates the performance of medical staff and auxiliary personnel.

GOE Number, Interest Area, and Work Group: 14.01.01; Medical and Health Services; Managerial Work in Medical and Health Services. **Personality Type:** Enterprising. Enterprising occupations frequently involve starting up and carrying out projects. These occupations can involve leading people and making many decisions. They sometimes require risk taking and often deal with business. **Work Values:** Security; Working Conditions; Authority; Responsibility; Autonomy. **Skills:** Systems Perception; Systems Evaluation; Management of Financial Resources; Identification of Key Causes; Reading Comprehension; Implementation Planning; Coordination. **Abilities:** *Cognitive*—Oral Expression; Oral Comprehension; Written Comprehension; Written Expression; Mathematical Reasoning; Problem Sensitivity. *Psychomotor*—none met the criteria. *Physical*—none met the criteria. *Sensory*—Speech Clarity; Speech Recognition; Far Vision. **General Work Activities:** *Information Input*—Getting Information Needed to Do the Job; Identifying Objects, Actions, and Events; Inspecting Equipment, Structures, Materials. *Mental Process*—Making

Decisions and Solving Problems; Analyzing Data or Information; Scheduling Work and Activities; Processing Information. *Work Output*—Interacting with Computers; Implementing Ideas and Programs; Documenting and Recording Information. *Interacting with Others*—Communicating with Other Workers; Guiding, Directing and Motivating Subordinates; Communicating with Persons Outside Organization; Performing Administrative Activities; Staffing Organizational Units. **Physical Work Conditions:** Indoors; Sitting; Standing. **Other Job Characteristics:** Consequence of Error; Importance of Being Sure All Is Done; Importance of Being Exact or Accurate; Importance of Being Aware of New Events.

Experience: Job Zone 4. A minimum of two to four years of work-related skill, knowledge, or experience is needed. **Job Preparation:** SVP 7.0 to less than 8.0—2 years to less than 10 years. **Knowledge:** Administration and Management; Personnel and Human Resources; Education and Training; Economics and Accounting; Mathematics. **Instructional Programs:** 510701 Health System/Health Services Administration; 510702 Hospital/Health Facilities Administration; 510704 Health Unit Manager/Ward Supervisor; 510706 Medical Records Administration; 510799 Health and Medical Administrative Services, Other; 511602 Nursing Administration (Post-R.N.); 512201 Public Health, General; 520201 Business Administration and Management, General.

Related DOT Jobs: 076.117-010 Coordinator of Rehabilitation Services; 079.117-010 Emergency Medical Services Coordinator; 079.167-014 Medical-Record Administrator; 169.167-090 Quality Assurance Coordinator; 187.117-010 Administrator, Health Care Facility; 187.117-058 Director, Outpatient Services.

11-9121.00 Natural Sciences Managers (Engineering, Natural Science, and Computer and Information Systems Managers)

Education: Work experience, plus degree

Employed: 326,229

Openings: 54,120

Projected Growth: 43.5%

Earnings: $75,320

Plan, direct, or coordinate activities in such fields as life sciences, physical sciences, mathematics, statistics, and manage research and development in these fields.

Coordinates successive phases of problem analysis, solution proposals, and testing. Provides technical assistance to agencies conducting environmental studies. Advises and assists in obtaining patents or other legal requirements. Confers with scientists, engineers, regulators, and others to plan and review projects, and to provide technical assistance. Prepares and administers budget, approves and reviews expenditures, and prepares financial reports. Plans and directs research, development, and production activities of chemical plant. Schedules, directs, and assigns duties to engineers, technicians, researchers, and other staff. Reviews project activities and prepares and reviews research, testing, and operational reports.

GOE Number, Interest Area, and Work Group: 02.01.01; Science, Math, and Engineering; Managerial Work in Science, Math, and Engineering. **Personality Type:** Investigative. Investigative

occupations frequently involve working with ideas and require an extensive amount of thinking. These occupations can involve searching for facts and figuring out problems mentally. **Work Values:** Working Conditions; Autonomy; Responsibility; Ability Utilization; Authority. **Skills:** Coordination; Reading Comprehension; Solution Appraisal; Management of Material Resources; Problem Identification; Science. **Abilities:** *Cognitive*—Oral Comprehension; Written Comprehension; Oral Expression; Written Expression; Number Facility; Fluency of Ideas. *Psychomotor*—none met the criteria. *Physical*—none met the criteria. *Sensory*—Speech Clarity; Near Vision; Speech Recognition. **General Work Activities:** *Information Input*—Getting Information Needed to Do the Job; Estimating Needed Characteristics; Monitoring Processes, Materials, and Surroundings. *Mental Process*—Analyzing Data or Information; Making Decisions and Solving Problems; Developing Objectives and Strategies; Updating and Using Job-Relevant Knowledge. *Work Output*—Documenting and Recording Information; Implementing Ideas and Programs; Interacting with Computers. *Interacting with Others*—Communicating with Other Workers; Providing Consultation and Advice to Others; Developing and Building Teams. **Physical Work Conditions:** Indoors; Sitting; Standing. **Other Job Characteristics:** Consequence of Error; Importance of Being Sure All Is Done; Importance of Being Exact or Accurate.

Experience: Job Zone 5. Extensive skill, knowledge, and experience are needed. Very advanced communication and organizational skills are required. **Job Preparation:** SVP 8.0 and above—4 years to more than 10 years. **Knowledge:** Administration and Management; Mathematics; English Language; Chemistry; Economics and Accounting. **Instructional Program:** 143001 Engineering/Industrial Management.

Related DOT Jobs: 008.167-010 Technical Director, Chemical Plant; 022.161-010 Chemical Laboratory Chief; 029.167-014 Project Manager, Environmental Research.

11-9131.00 Postmasters and Mail Superintendents (Postmasters and Mail Superintendents)

Education: Work experience in a related occupation

Employed: 26,362

Openings: 3,256

Projected Growth: 3%

Earnings: $44,730

Direct and coordinate operational, administrative, management, and supportive services of a U.S. post office or coordinate activities of workers engaged in postal and related work in assigned post office.

Selects, trains, and evaluates performance of employees and prepares work schedules. Organizes and supervises directly, or through subordinates, such activities as processing incoming and outgoing mail to ensure efficient service to patrons. Resolves customer complaints and informs public of postal laws and regulations. Selects, trains, and terminates postmasters and managers of associate postal units. Negotiates labor disputes. Confers with suppliers to obtain bids for proposed purchases, requisitions supplies, and disburses funds as specified by law. Prepares and submits detailed and summary reports of post office activities to designated supervisors. Directs and coordinates operational, management, and supportive services of associate post offices within district area known as sectional center. Directs and coordinates operations of several sectional centers within district.

GOE Number, Interest Area, and Work Group: 13.01.01; General Management and Support; General Management Work and Management of Support Functions. **Personality Type:** Enterprising. Enterprising occupations frequently involve starting up and carrying out projects. These occupations can involve leading people and making many decisions. They sometimes require risk taking and often deal with business. **Work Values:** Security; Authority; Company Policies and Practices; Working Conditions; Moral Values; Activity; Compensation. **Skills:** Systems Evaluation; Negotiation; Solution Appraisal; Coordination; Monitoring; Management of Personnel Resources; Management of Financial Resources; Problem Identification. **Abilities:** *Cognitive*—Oral Expression; Written Expression; Oral Comprehension; Written Comprehension; Problem Sensitivity. *Psychomotor*—none met the criteria. *Physical*—none met the criteria. *Sensory*—Speech Clarity; Speech Recognition. **General Work Activities:** *Information Input*—Getting Information Needed to Do the Job; Monitoring Processes, Materials, and Surroundings; Estimating Needed Characteristics; Identifying Objects, Actions, and Events. *Mental Process*—Making Decisions and Solving Problems; Scheduling Work and Activities; Judging Qualities of Things, Services, Other People's Work; Organizing, Planning, and Prioritizing. *Work Output*—Implementing Ideas and Programs; Documenting and Recording Information; Drafting and Specifying Technical Devices; Controlling Machines and Processes; Handling and Moving Objects; Performing General Physical Activities. *Interacting with Others*—Communicating with Other Workers; Coordinating Work and Activities of Others; Guiding, Directing and Motivating Subordinates. **Physical Work Conditions:** Indoors; Special Uniform; Sitting. **Other Job Characteristics:** Consequence of Error; Importance of Being Exact or Accurate; Importance of Being Sure All Is Done.

Experience: Job Zone 4. A minimum of two to four years of work-related skill, knowledge, or experience is needed. **Job Preparation:** SVP 7.0 to less than 8.0—2 years to less than 10 years. **Knowledge:** Administration and Management; Personnel and Human Resources; Transportation; Law, Government and Jurisprudence; English Language; Education and Training. **Instructional Programs:** 440401 Public Administration; 520201 Business Administration and Management, General.

Related DOT Jobs: 188.167-066 Postmaster; 188.167-086 Sectional Center Manager, Postal Service.

11-9141.00 Property, Real Estate, and Community Association Managers (Property, Real Estate, and Community Association Managers)

Education: Bachelor's degree
Employed: 315,461
Openings: 47,581
Projected Growth: 13.7%
Earnings: $29,860

Plan, direct, or coordinate selling, buying, leasing, or governance activities of commercial, industrial, or residential real estate properties.

Purchases building and maintenance supplies, equipment, or furniture. Develops and administers annual operating budget. Meets with prospective leasers to show property, explain terms of occupancy, and provide information about local area. Prepares reports summarizing financial and operational status of property or facility. Maintains contact with insurance carrier, fire and police departments, and other agencies to ensure protection and compliance with codes and regulations. Confers with legal authority to ensure transactions and terminations of contracts and agreements are in accordance with court orders, laws, and regulations. Assembles and analyzes construction and vendor service contract bids. Negotiates for sale, lease, or development of property, and completes or reviews appropriate documents and forms. Manages and oversees operations, maintenance, and administrative functions for commercial, industrial, or residential properties. Directs and coordinates the activities of staff and contract personnel and evaluates performance. Recruits, hires, and trains managerial, clerical, and maintenance staff, or contracts with vendors for security, maintenance, extermination, or groundskeeping personnel. Investigates complaints, disturbances, and violations and resolves problems following management rules and regulations. Plans, schedules, and coordinates general maintenance, major repairs, and remodeling or construction projects for commercial or residential property. Meets with clients to negotiate management and service contracts, determine priorities, and discuss financial and operational status of property. Directs collection of monthly assessments, rental fees and deposits, and payment of insurance premiums, mortgage, taxes, and incurred operating expenses. Inspects facilities and equipment and inventories building contents to document damage and determine repair needs.

GOE Number, Interest Area, and Work Group: 13.01.01; General Management and Support; General Management Work and Management of Support Functions. **Personality Type:** Enterprising. Enterprising occupations frequently involve starting up and carrying out projects. These occupations can involve leading people and making many decisions. They sometimes require risk taking and often deal with business. **Work Values:** Autonomy; Activity; Responsibility; Authority; Working Conditions. **Skills:** Management of Financial Resources; Coordination; Judgment and Decision Making; Management of Personnel Resources; Writing; Active Listening; Reading Comprehension. **Abilities:** *Cognitive*—Oral Comprehension; Number Facility; Written Comprehension; Oral Expression; Mathematical Reasoning. *Psychomotor*—none met the criteria. *Physical*—none met the criteria. *Sensory*—Speech Recognition; Speech Clarity; Auditory Attention. **General Work Activities:** *Information Input*—Getting Information Needed to Do the Job; Identifying Objects, Actions, and Events; Inspecting Equipment, Structures, Materials. *Mental Process*—Evaluating Information Against Standards; Scheduling Work and Activities; Making Decisions and Solving Problems; Organizing, Planning, and Prioritizing. *Work Output*—Documenting and Recording Information; Implementing Ideas and Programs; Performing General Physical Activities. *Interacting with Others*—Communicating with Other Workers; Communicating with Persons Outside Or-

  **49**

ganization; Coordinating Work and Activities of Others; Monitoring and Controlling Resources; Performing Administrative Activities. **Physical Work Conditions:** Indoors; Sitting; Walking or Running. **Other Job Characteristics:** Consequence of Error; Importance of Being Sure All Is Done; Frustrating Circumstances.

Experience: Job Zone 4. A minimum of two to four years of work-related skill, knowledge, or experience is needed. **Job Preparation:** SVP 7.0 to less than 8.0—2 years to less than 10 years. **Knowledge:** Administration and Management; English Language; Law, Government and Jurisprudence; Personnel and Human Resources; Mathematics. **Instructional Program:** 521501 Real Estate.

Related DOT Jobs: 186.117-062 Rental Manager, Public Events Facilities; 186.167-018 Manager, Apartment House; 186.167-030 Manager, Housing Project; 186.167-042 Manager, Market; 186.167-046 Manager, Property; 186.167-062 Condominium Manager; 186.167-066 Manager, Real-Estate Firm; 187.167-190 Superintendent, Building.

11-9151.00 Social and Community Service Managers
(All Other Managers and Administrators)

Education: No data available.

Employed: 946,190

Openings: No data available.

Projected Growth: No data available.

Earnings: $49,220

Plan, organize, or coordinate the activities of a social service program or community outreach organization. Oversee the program or organization's budget and policies regarding participant involvement, program requirements, and benefits. Work may involve directing social workers, counselors, or probation officers.

Plans, directs, and prepares fund-raising activities and public relations materials. Determines organizational policies, defines scope of services offered, and administration of procedures. Establishes and maintains relationships with other agencies and organizations in community to meet and not duplicate community needs and services. Participates in program activities to serve clients of agency. Researches and analyzes member or community needs as basis for community development. Assigns duties to staff or volunteers. Speaks to community groups to explain and interpret agency purpose, programs, and policies. Advises volunteers and volunteer leaders to ensure quality of programs and effective use of resources. Instructs and trains agency staff or volunteers in skills required to provide services. Interviews, recruits, or hires volunteers and staff. Observes workers to evaluate performance and ensure work meets established standards. Confers and consults with individuals, groups, and committees to determine needs, and plan, implement, and extend organization's programs and services. Coordinates volunteer service programs, such as Red Cross, hospital volunteers, or vocational training for disabled individuals. Prepares, distributes, and maintains records and reports, such as budgets, personnel records, or training manuals.

GOE Number, Interest Area, and Work Group: 12.01.01; Education and Social Service; Managerial Work in Education and Social Service. **Personality Type:** Social. Social occupations frequently involve working with, communicating with, and teaching people. These occupations often involve helping or providing service to others. **Work Values:** Social Service; Security; Autonomy; Activity; Company Policies and Practices; Authority; Achievement. **Skills:** Speaking; Coordination; Idea Generation; Visioning; Problem Identification; Reading Comprehension. **Abilities:** *Cognitive*—Oral Comprehension; Written Comprehension; Oral Expression; Written Expression; Problem Sensitivity. *Psychomotor*—Response Orientation. *Physical*—Gross Body Equilibrium. *Sensory*—Near Vision; Speech Clarity; Far Vision; Speech Recognition. **General Work Activities:** *Information Input*—Getting Information Needed to Do the Job; Identifying Objects, Actions, and Events; Estimating Needed Characteristics. *Mental Process*—Judging Qualities of Things, Services, Other People's Work; Developing Objectives and Strategies; Making Decisions and Solving Problems; Analyzing Data or Information. *Work Output*—Implementing Ideas and Programs; Documenting and Recording Information; Performing General Physical Activities. *Interacting with Others*—Communicating with Persons Outside Organization; Communicating with Other Workers; Monitoring and Controlling Resources; Guiding, Directing and Motivating Subordinates. **Physical Work Conditions:** Indoors; Sitting; Standing. **Other Job Characteristics:** Consequence of Error; Frustrating Circumstances; Importance of Being Sure All Is Done.

Experience: Job Zone 4. A minimum of two to four years of work-related skill, knowledge, or experience is needed. **Job Preparation:** SVP 7.0 to less than 8.0—2 years to less than 10 years. **Knowledge:** Administration and Management; Customer and Personal Service; Education and Training; Personnel and Human Resources; English Language. **Instructional Programs:** 080301 Entrepreneurship; 310301 Parks, Recreation and Leisure Facilities Management; 440201 Community Organization, Resources and Services; 440401 Public Administration; 500704 Arts Management; 520101 Business, General; 520201 Business Administration and Management, General; 520203 Logistics and Materials Management; 520206 Non-Profit and Public Management; 520299 Business Administration and Management, Other; 520701 Enterprise Management and Operation, General; 520702 Franchise Operation; 520799 Enterprise Management and Operation, Other; 520903 Travel-Tourism Management; 520999 Hospitality Services Management, Other.

Related DOT Jobs: 187.117-022 District Adviser; 187.117-026 Executive Director, Sheltered Workshop; 187.117-046 Program Director, Group Work; 187.117-066 Executive Director, Red Cross; 187.167-022 Coordinator, Volunteer Services; 187.167-038 Director, Volunteer Services; 187.167-214 Director, Service; 187.167-234 Director, Community Organization; 195.117-010 Administrator, Social Welfare; 195.167-022 Director, Field; 195.167-038 Rehabilitation Center Manager.

13-0000
Business and Financial Operations Occupations

13-1000 Business Operations Specialists

13-1011.00 Agents and Business Managers of Artists, Performers, and Athletes (Advertising, Marketing, Promotions, Public Relations, and Sales Managers)

Education: Work experience, plus degree
Employed: 485,214
Openings: 89,237
Projected Growth: 23%
Earnings: $57,300

Represent and promote artists, performers, and athletes to prospective employers. Handle contract negotiation and other business matters for clients.

Prepares periodic accounting statements for clients concerning financial affairs. Advises clients on financial and legal matters, such as investments and taxes. Schedules promotional or performance engagements for clients. Manages business affairs for clients, such as obtaining travel and lodging accommodations, selling tickets, marketing and advertising, and paying expenses. Collects fees, commission, or other payment, according to contract terms. Hires trainer or coach to advise client on performance matters, such as training techniques or presentation of act. Obtains information and inspects facilities, equipment, and accommodations of potential performance venue. Negotiates with management, promoters, union officials, and other persons, to obtain contracts for clients, such as entertainers, artists, and athletes. Conducts auditions or interviews new clients.

GOE Number, Interest Area, and Work Group: 01.01.01; Arts, Entertainment, and Media; Managerial Work in Arts, Entertainment, and Media. **Personality Type:** Enterprising. Enterprising occupations frequently involve starting up and carrying out projects. These occupations can involve leading people and making many decisions. They sometimes require risk taking and often deal with business. **Work Values:** Autonomy; Working Conditions; Social Service; Compensation; Achievement. **Skills:** Negotiation; Speaking; Reading Comprehension; Time Management; Active Listening; Coordination; Critical Thinking; Information Gathering. **Abilities:** *Cognitive*—Oral Expression; Oral Comprehension; Written Comprehension; Number Facility; Mathematical Reasoning; Written Expression. *Psychomotor*—none met the criteria. *Physical*—none met the criteria. *Sensory*—Speech Clarity; Speech Recognition; Auditory Attention. **General Work Activities:** *Information Input*—Getting Information Needed to Do the Job; Identifying Objects, Actions, and Events; Estimating Needed Characteristics. *Mental Process*—Organizing, Planning, and Prioritizing; Scheduling Work and Activities; Making Decisions and Solving Problems. *Work Output*—Documenting and Recording Information; Implementing Ideas and Programs; Performing General Physical Activities; Interacting with Computers. *Interacting with Others*—Resolving Conflict and Negotiating with Others; Communicating with Persons Outside Organization; Establishing and Maintaining Relationships. **Physical Work Conditions:** Indoors; Sitting; Standing. **Other Job Characteristics:** Frustrating Circumstances; Consequence of Error; Importance of Being Sure All Is Done.

Experience: Job Zone 3. Previous work-related skill, knowledge, or experience is required. **Job Preparation:** SVP 6.0 to less than 7.0—More than 1 year and less than 4 years. **Knowledge:** Administration and Management; Economics and Accounting; Sales and Marketing; Personnel and Human Resources; Mathematics. **Instructional Programs:** 080101 Apparel and Accessories Marketing Operations, General; 080102 Fashion Merchandising; 080204 Business Services Marketing Operations; 080902 Hotel/Motel Services Marketing Operations; 081208 Vehicle Marketing Operations; 090201 Advertising; 090501 Public Relations and Organizational Communications; 500704 Arts Management; 520201 Business Administration and Management, General; 521401 Business Marketing and Marketing Management; 521402 Marketing Research; 521403 International Business Marketing; 521499 Marketing Management and Research, Other.

Related DOT Jobs: 153.117-014 Manager, Athlete; 191.117-010 Artist's Manager; 191.117-014 Booking Manager; 191.117-018 Business Manager; 191.117-022 Circus Agent; 191.117-026 Jockey Agent; 191.117-034 Literary Agent; 191.117-038 Manager, Touring Production; 191.167-010 Advance Agent.

13-1021.00 Purchasing Agents and Buyers, Farm Products (Purchasing Agents)

Education: Bachelor's degree
Employed: 224,149
Openings: 42,342
Projected Growth: 10.8%
Earnings: $38,040

Purchase farm products either for further processing or for resale.

Coordinates and directs activities or workers engaged in cutting, transporting, storing, or milling products and in maintaining records. Reviews orders and determines product types and quantities required to meet demand. Arranges sales, loans, or financing for supplies, such as equipment, seed, feed, fertilizer, and chemicals. Plans and arranges for transportation for crops, milk, or other products to dairy or processing facility. Advises farm groups and growers on land preparation and livestock care to maximize quantity and quality of production. Estimates production possibilities by surveying property and studying factors such as history of crop rotation, soil fertility, and irrigation facilities. Maintains records of business transactions. Inspects and tests crops or other farm products to determine quality and to detect evidence of disease or insect damage. Negotiates contracts with farmers for production or purchase of agricultural products such as milk, grains, and Christmas trees. Writes articles for publication.

GOE Number, Interest Area, and Work Group: 13.02.02; General Management and Support; Management Support: Purchasing. **Personality Type:** Enterprising. Enterprising occupations frequently involve starting up and carrying out projects. These occupations can involve leading people and making many decisions. They sometimes require risk taking and often deal with business. **Work Values:** Coworkers; Responsibility; Autonomy; Company Policies and Practices; Achievement; Ability Utilization. **Skills:** Writing; Information Gathering; Speaking; Mathematics; Reading Comprehension. **Abilities:** *Cognitive*—Oral Expression; Oral Comprehension; Written Expression; Number Facility; Written Comprehension. *Psychomotor*—none met the criteria. *Physical*—Gross Body Equilibrium; Stamina. *Sensory*—Near Vision; Speech Clarity; Speech Recognition. **General Work Activities:** *Information Input*—Identifying Objects, Actions, and Events; Inspecting Equipment, Structures, Materials; Getting Information Needed to Do the Job. *Mental Process*—Judging Qualities of Things, Services, People; Analyzing Data or Information; Making Decisions and Solving Problems. *Work Output*—Documenting and Recording Information; Implementing Ideas and Programs; Interacting with Computers. *Interacting with Others*—Monitoring and Controlling Resources; Establishing and Maintaining Relationships; Communicating with Persons Outside Organization. **Physical Work Conditions:** Indoors; Sitting; Standing; Using Hands on Objects, Tools, or Controls; Walking or Running. **Other Job Characteristics:** Consequence of Error; Importance of Being Exact or Accurate; Importance of Being Sure All Is Done; Frustrating Circumstances.

Experience: Job Zone 4. A minimum of two to four years of work-related skill, knowledge, or experience is needed. **Job Preparation:** SVP 7.0 to less than 8.0—2 years to less than 10 years. **Knowledge:** English Language; Mathematics; Production and Processing; Food Production; Communications and Media; Economics and Accounting. **Instructional Programs:** 080704 General Buying Operations; 520202 Purchasing, Procurement and Contracts Management.

Related DOT Jobs: 162.117-010 Christmas-Tree Contractor; 162.117-022 Field Contractor; 162.117-026 Field-Contact Technician; 162.167-010 Buyer, Grain; 162.167-018 Clean-Rice Broker.

13-1022.00 Wholesale and Retail Buyers, Except Farm Products (Purchasing Agents)

Education: Bachelor's degree
Employed: 224,149
Openings: 42,342
Projected Growth: 10.8%
Earnings: $38,040

Buy merchandise or commodities, other than farm products, for resale to consumers at the wholesale or retail level, including both durable and nondurable goods. Analyze past buying trends, sales records, price, and quality of merchandise to determine value and yield. Select, order, and authorize payment for merchandise according to contractual agreements. Conduct meetings with sales personnel and introduce new products.

Provides clerks with information, such as price, mark-ups or mark-downs, manufacturer number, season code, and style number to print on price tags. Examines, selects, orders, and purchases merchandise from suppliers or other merchants. Confers with sales and purchasing personnel to obtain information about customer needs and preferences. Analyzes sales records and trends to determine current or expected demand and minimum inventory required. Sets or recommends mark-up rates, mark-down rates, and selling prices for merchandise. Trains purchasing or sales personnel. Consults with store or merchandise managers about budget and goods to be purchased. Approves advertising materials. Conducts staff meetings with sales personnel to introduce new merchandise. Authorizes payment of invoices or return of merchandise. Inspects, grades, or approves merchandise or products to determine value or yield. Arranges for transportation of purchases.

GOE Number, Interest Area, and Work Group: 13.02.02; General Management and Support; Management Support: Purchasing. **Personality Type:** Enterprising. Enterprising occupations frequently involve starting up and carrying out projects. These occupations can involve leading people and making many decisions. They sometimes require risk taking and often deal with business. **Work Values:** Working Conditions; Company Policies and Practices; Activity; Responsibility; Moral Values. **Skills:** Speaking; Management of Material Resources; Information Gathering; Product Inspection; Reading Comprehension; Active Listening. **Abilities:** *Cognitive*—Oral Expression; Oral Comprehension; Written Comprehension; Deductive Reasoning; Number Facility. *Psychomotor*—none met the criteria. *Physical*—Extent Flexibility; Trunk Strength. *Sensory*—Near Vision; Speech Recognition; Visual Color Discrimination. **General Work Activities:** *Information Input*—Identifying Objects, Actions, and Events; Getting Information Needed to Do the Job; Estimating Needed Characteristics. *Mental Process*—Analyzing Data or Information; Updating and Using Job-Relevant Knowledge; Judging Qualities of Things, Services, People; Developing Objectives and Strategies; Organizing, Planning, and Prioritizing. *Work Output*—Documenting and Recording Information; Implementing Ideas and Programs; Handling and Moving Objects. *Interacting with Others*—Communicating with Other Workers; Monitoring and Controlling Resources; Teaching Others. **Physical Work Conditions:** Indoors; Sitting; Standing. **Other Job Characteristics:** Consequence of Error; Frustrating Circumstances; Importance of Being Exact or Accurate; Importance of Being Sure All Is Done.

Experience: Job Zone 3. Previous work-related skill, knowledge, or experience is required. **Job Preparation:** SVP 6.0 to less than 7.0—More than 1 year and less than 4 years. **Knowledge:** Sales and Marketing; Mathematics; Administration and Management; Customer and Personal Service; English Language; Economics and Accounting; Transportation. **Instructional Programs:** 080704 General Buying Operations; 520202 Purchasing, Procurement and Contracts Management.

Related DOT Jobs: 162.157-018 Buyer; 162.157-022 Buyer, Assistant.

13-1023.00 Purchasing Agents, Except Wholesale, Retail, and Farm Products (Purchasing Agents)

Education: Bachelor's degree
Employed: 224,149
Openings: 42,342
Projected Growth: 10.8%
Earnings: $38,040

Purchase machinery, equipment, tools, parts, supplies, or services necessary for the operation of an establishment. Purchase raw or semifinished materials for manufacturing.

Arbitrates claims and resolves complaints generated during performance of contract. Prepares purchase orders or bid proposals and reviews requisitions for goods and services. Evaluates and monitors contract performance to determine need for changes and to ensure compliance with contractual obligations. Maintains and reviews computerized or manual records of items purchased, costs, delivery, product performance, and inventories. Confers with personnel, users, and vendors to discuss defective or unacceptable goods or services and determines corrective action. Directs and coordinates workers' activities involving bid proposals and procurement of goods and services. Analyzes price proposals, financial reports, and other data and information to determine reasonable prices. Locates and arranges for purchase of goods and services necessary for efficient operation of organization. Negotiates or renegotiates, and administers contracts with suppliers, vendors, and other representatives. Formulates policies and procedures for bid proposals and procurement of goods and services.

GOE Number, Interest Area, and Work Group: 13.02.02; General Management and Support; Management Support: Purchasing. **Personality Type:** Enterprising. Enterprising occupations frequently involve starting up and carrying out projects. These occupations can involve leading people and making many decisions. They sometimes require risk taking and often deal with business. **Work Values:** Activity; Ability Utilization; Achievement; Autonomy; Compensation; Working Conditions. **Skills:** Judgment and Decision Making; Reading Comprehension; Management of Financial Resources; Negotiation; Problem Identification; Writing; Mathematics; Active Listening. **Abilities:** *Cognitive*—Oral Expression; Oral Comprehension; Written Comprehension; Written Expression; Mathematical Reasoning. *Psychomotor*—none met the criteria. *Physical*—none met the criteria. *Sensory*—Speech Recognition. **General Work Activities:** *Information Input*—Getting Information Needed to Do the Job; Monitoring Processes, Materials, and Surroundings; Identifying Objects, Actions, and Events. *Mental Process*—Judging Qualities of Things, Services, People; Making Decisions and Solving Problems; Analyzing Data or Information. *Work Output*—Documenting and Recording Information; Implementing Ideas and Programs; Interacting with Computers. *Interacting with Others*—Resolving Conflict and Negotiating with Others; Communicating with Other Workers; Communicating with Persons Outside Organization. **Physical Work Conditions:** Indoors; Sitting; Using Hands on Objects, Tools, or Controls. **Other Job Characteristics:** Consequence of Error; Importance of Being Exact or Accurate; Importance of Being Sure All Is Done.

Experience: Job Zone 4. A minimum of two to four years of work-related skill, knowledge, or experience is needed. **Job Preparation:** SVP 7.0 to less than 8.0—2 years to less than 10 years. **Knowledge:** Administration and Management; Mathematics; Economics and Accounting; English Language; Computers and Electronics; Clerical. **Instructional Programs:** 080704 General Buying Operations; 520202 Purchasing, Procurement and Contracts Management.

Related DOT Jobs: 162.117-018 Contract Specialist; 162.157-030 Outside Property Agent; 162.157-038 Purchasing Agent; 163.117-010 Manager, Contracts.

13-1031.00 Claims Adjusters, Examiners, and Investigators (Insurance Adjusters, Examiners, and Investigators)

Education: Long-term O-T-J training	
Employed: 180,112	
Openings: 16,055	
Projected Growth: 20.4%	
Earnings: $38,290	

Review settled claims to determine that payments and settlements have been made in accordance with company practices and procedures, ensuring that proper methods have been followed. Report overpayments, underpayments, and other irregularities. Confer with legal counsel on claims requiring litigation.

GOE Number, Interest Area, and Work Group: 13.02.04; General Management and Support; Management Support: Investigation and Analysis. **Instructional Programs:** 081001 Insurance Marketing Operations; 520805 Insurance and Risk Management. **Note:** The Department of Labor has not collected some data for this job, so it has fewer details than the other descriptions.

13-1031.01 Claims Examiners, Property and Casualty Insurance (Property and Casualty Insurance Claims Examiners)

Education: Bachelor's degree	
Employed: 48,746	
Openings: 3,838	
Projected Growth: 12.5%	
Earnings: $40,110	

Review settled insurance claims to determine that payments and settlements have been made in accordance with company practices and procedures. Report overpayments, underpayments, and other irregularities. Confer with legal counsel on claims requiring litigation.

Analyzes data used in settling claim to determine its validity in payment of claims. Reports overpayments, underpayments, and other irregularities. Confers with legal counsel on claims requiring litigation.

GOE Number, Interest Area, and Work Group: 13.02.04; General Management and Support; Management Support: Investigation and Analysis. **Personality Type:** Conventional. Conventional occupations frequently involve following set procedures and routines. These occupations can include working with data and details more than with ideas. Usually there is a clear line of authority to follow. **Work Values:** Company Policies and Practices; Supervision, Human Relations; Working Conditions; Advancement; Security. **Skills:** Reading Comprehension; Information Gathering; Problem Identification; Mathematics; Writing. **Abilities:** *Cognitive*—Written Comprehension; Mathematical Reasoning; Problem Sensitivity; Number Facility; Written Expression; Oral Comprehension. *Psychomotor*—none met the criteria. *Physical*—

none met the criteria. *Sensory*—Speech Clarity. **General Work Activities:** *Information Input*—Getting Information Needed to Do the Job; Identifying Objects, Actions, and Events; Monitoring Processes, Materials, and Surroundings. *Mental Process*—Evaluating Information Against Standards; Analyzing Data or Information; Judging Qualities of Things, Services, Other People's Work. *Work Output*—Documenting and Recording Information; Interacting with Computers; Implementing Ideas and Programs. *Interacting with Others*—Communicating with Other Workers; Communicating with Persons Outside Organization; Performing Administrative Activities; Interpreting Meaning of Information to Others. **Physical Work Conditions:** Indoors; Sitting; Walking or Running. **Other Job Characteristics:** Importance of Being Sure All Is Done; Consequence of Error; Importance of Being Exact or Accurate.

Experience: Job Zone 4. A minimum of two to four years of work-related skill, knowledge, or experience is needed. **Job Preparation:** SVP 7.0 to less than 8.0—2 years to less than 10 years. **Knowledge:** Mathematics; Law, Government and Jurisprudence; English Language; Computers and Electronics; Administration and Management; Economics and Accounting; Communications and Media. **Instructional Program:** 520805 Insurance and Risk Management.

Related DOT Job: 168.267-014 Claim Examiner.

13-1031.02 Insurance Adjusters, Examiners, and Investigators (Insurance Adjusters, Examiners, and Investigators)

Education: Long-term O-T-J training
Employed: 180,112
Openings: 16,055
Projected Growth: 20.4%
Earnings: $38,290

Investigate, analyze, and determine the extent of insurance company's liability concerning personal, casualty, or property loss or damages. Attempt to effect settlement with claimants. Correspond with or interview medical specialists, agents, witnesses, or claimants to compile information. Calculate benefit payments and approve payment of claims within a certain monetary limit.

Examines claims form and other records to determine insurance coverage. Negotiates claim settlements and recommends litigation when settlement cannot be negotiated. Interviews or corresponds with claimant and witnesses, consults police and hospital records, and inspects property damage to determine extent of liability. Analyzes information gathered by investigation and reports findings and recommendations. Interviews or corresponds with agents and claimants to correct errors or omissions and to investigate questionable entries. Obtains credit information from banks and other credit services. Prepares report of findings of investigation. Communicates with former associates to verify employment record and to obtain background information regarding persons or businesses applying for credit. Collects evidence to support contested claims in court. Investigates and

assesses damage to property. Examines titles to property to determine validity and acts as company agent in transactions with property owners. Refers questionable claims to investigator or claims adjuster for investigation or settlement.

GOE Number, Interest Area, and Work Group: 13.02.04; General Management and Support; Management Support: Investigation and Analysis. **Personality Type:** Enterprising. Enterprising occupations frequently involve starting up and carrying out projects. These occupations can involve leading people and making many decisions. They sometimes require risk taking and often deal with business. **Work Values:** Company Policies and Practices; Advancement; Ability Utilization; Supervision, Human Relations; Responsibility; Achievement; Activity. **Skills:** Active Listening; Information Gathering; Reading Comprehension; Writing; Critical Thinking. **Abilities:** *Cognitive*—Written Comprehension; Written Expression; Oral Expression; Oral Comprehension; Inductive Reasoning. *Psychomotor*—none met the criteria. *Physical*—none met the criteria. *Sensory*—Near Vision; Speech Clarity; Far Vision; Speech Recognition. **General Work Activities:** *Information Input*—Getting Information Needed to Do the Job; Identifying Objects, Actions, and Events; Monitoring Processes, Materials, and Surroundings. *Mental Process*—Analyzing Data or Information; Evaluating Information Against Standards; Judging Qualities of Things, Services, Other People's Work. *Work Output*—Documenting and Recording Information; Interacting with Computers; Implementing Ideas and Programs; Handling and Moving Objects. *Interacting with Others*—Communicating with Persons Outside Organization; Communicating with Other Workers; Interpreting Meaning of Information to Others. **Physical Work Conditions:** Indoors; Sitting; Standing. **Other Job Characteristics:** Frustrating Circumstances; Importance of Being Sure All Is Done; Importance of Being Exact or Accurate; Consequence of Error.

Experience: Job Zone 3. Previous work-related skill, knowledge, or experience is required. **Job Preparation:** SVP 6.0 to less than 7.0—More than 1 year and less than 4 years. **Knowledge:** Law, Government and Jurisprudence; Mathematics; Economics and Accounting; Public Safety and Security; English Language. **Instructional Programs:** 081001 Insurance Marketing Operations; 520805 Insurance and Risk Management.

Related DOT Jobs: 191.167-014 Claim Agent; 241.217-010 Claim Adjuster; 241.267-018 Claim Examiner.

13-1032.00 Insurance Appraisers, Auto Damage (Auto Insurance Appraisers)

Education: Long-term O-T-J training
Employed: 10,452
Openings: 871
Projected Growth: 16%
Earnings: $40,000

Appraise automobile or other vehicle damage to determine cost of repair for insurance claim settlement. Seek agreement with automotive repair shop on cost of repair. Prepare insurance forms to indicate repair cost or cost estimates and recommendations.

Evaluates practicality of repair as opposed to payment of market value of vehicle before accident. Examines damaged vehicle to determine extent of structural, body, mechanical, electrical, or interior damage. Reviews repair-cost estimates with automobile-repair shop to secure agreement on cost of repairs. Arranges to have damage appraised by another appraiser to resolve disagreement with shop on repair cost. Prepares insurance forms to indicate repair-cost estimates and recommendations. Estimates parts and labor to repair damage, using standard automotive labor and parts-cost manuals and knowledge of automotive repair. Determines salvage value on total-loss vehicle.

GOE Number, Interest Area, and Work Group: 13.02.04; General Management and Support; Management Support: Investigation and Analysis. **Personality Type:** Conventional. Conventional occupations frequently involve following set procedures and routines. These occupations can include working with data and details more than with ideas. Usually there is a clear line of authority to follow. **Work Values:** Company Policies and Practices; Supervision, Human Relations; Advancement; Responsibility; Security. **Skills:** Mathematics; Reading Comprehension; Problem Identification; Judgment and Decision Making; Speaking; Writing; Active Listening. **Abilities:** *Cognitive*–Number Facility; Mathematical Reasoning; Written Comprehension; Written Expression; Oral Comprehension. *Psychomotor*–none met the criteria. *Physical*–Gross Body Coordination. *Sensory*–Speech Recognition. **General Work Activities:** *Information Input*–Getting Information Needed to Do the Job; Inspecting Equipment, Structures, Materials; Identifying Objects, Actions, and Events. *Mental Process*–Processing Information; Evaluating Information Against Standards; Making Decisions and Solving Problems; Judging Qualities of Things, Services, Other People's Work. *Work Output*–Documenting and Recording Information; Handling and Moving Objects; Performing General Physical Activities. *Interacting with Others*–Performing Administrative Activities; Communicating with Persons Outside Organization; Communicating with Other Workers; Establishing and Maintaining Relationships; Interpreting Meaning of Information to Others. **Physical Work Conditions:** Sitting; Indoors; Standing. **Other Job Characteristics:** Importance of Being Exact or Accurate; Importance of Being Sure All Is Done; Consequence of Error.

Experience: Job Zone 4. A minimum of two to four years of work-related skill, knowledge, or experience is needed. **Job Preparation:** SVP 7.0 to less than 8.0—2 years to less than 10 years. **Knowledge:** Mathematics; Clerical; Mechanical; Economics and Accounting; English Language; Administration and Management. **Instructional Program:** 081001 Insurance Marketing Operations.

Related DOT Job: 241.267-014 Appraiser, Automobile Damage.

13-1041.00 Compliance Officers, Except Agriculture, Construction, Health and Safety, and Transportation
(Inspectors and Compliance Officers)

Education: Work experience in a related occupation
Employed: 176,175
Openings: 19,910
Projected Growth: 10.5%
Earnings: $36,820

Examine, evaluate, and investigate eligibility for or conformity with laws and regulations governing contract compliance of licenses and permits. Perform other compliance and enforcement inspection activities not classified elsewhere.

GOE Number, Interest Area, and Work Group: 04.04.02; Law, Law Enforcement, and Public Safety; Public Safety: Regulations Enforcement. **Instructional Programs:** 030203 Natural Resources Law Enforcement and Protective Services; 150701 Occupational Safety and Health Technology/Technician; 521601 Taxation. **Note:** The Department of Labor has not collected some data for this job, so it has fewer details than the other descriptions.

13-1041.01 Environmental Compliance Inspectors
(Inspectors and Compliance Officers)

Education: Work experience in a related occupation
Employed: 176,175
Openings: 19,910
Projected Growth: 10.5%
Earnings: $36,820

Inspect and investigate sources of pollution to protect the public and environment. Ensure conformance with federal, state, and local regulations and ordinances.

Examines permits, licenses, applications, and records to ensure compliance with licensing requirements. Advises individuals and groups concerning pollution control regulations, inspection and investigation findings, and encourages voluntary action to correct problems or issues citations for violations. Studies laws and statutes to determine nature of code violation and type of action to be taken. Evaluates label information for accuracy and conformance to regulatory requirements. Reviews and evaluates applications for registration of products containing dangerous materials or pollution control discharge permits. Assists in development of spill prevention programs and hazardous waste rules and regulations, and recommends corrective action in event of hazardous spill. Interviews individuals to determine nature of suspected violations and to obtain evidence of violation. Investigates complaints and suspected violations concerning illegal dumping, pollution, pesticides, product quality, or labeling laws. Inspects establishments to ensure that handling, storage, and disposal of fertilizers, pesticides, and other hazardous chemicals conform with regulations. Conducts field tests and collects samples for laboratory analysis. Inspects solid waste disposal and treatment facilities, wastewater treatment facilities, or other water courses or sites for conformance with regulations. Conducts research on hazardous waste management projects to determine magnitude of disposal problem, treatment, and disposal alternatives and costs. Prepares, organizes, and maintains records to document activities, recommend action, provide reference materials, and prepare technical and evidentiary reports.

GOE Number, Interest Area, and Work Group: 04.04.02; Law, Law Enforcement, and Public Safety; Public Safety: Regulations Enforcement. **Personality Type:** Investigative. Investigative occupations frequently involve working with ideas and require an extensive amount of thinking. These occupations can involve searching for facts and figuring out problems mentally. **Work**

Values: Supervision, Human Relations; Achievement; Security; Company Policies and Practices; Activity; Autonomy. **Skills:** Reading Comprehension; Information Gathering; Problem Identification; Speaking; Critical Thinking. **Abilities:** *Cognitive*—Written Comprehension; Oral Expression; Problem Sensitivity; Written Expression; Oral Comprehension; Inductive Reasoning. *Psychomotor*—Multilimb Coordination. *Physical*—Gross Body Coordination; Gross Body Equilibrium. *Sensory*—Near Vision; Speech Clarity; Visual Color Discrimination; Speech Recognition. **General Work Activities:** *Information Input*—Getting Information Needed to Do the Job; Identifying Objects, Actions, and Events; Inspecting Equipment, Structures, Materials. *Mental Process*—Evaluating Information Against Standards; Analyzing Data or Information; Judging Qualities of Things, Services, People; Processing Information; Updating and Using Job-Relevant Knowledge. *Work Output*—Documenting and Recording Information; Implementing Ideas and Programs; Handling and Moving Objects. *Interacting with Others*—Communicating with Persons Outside Organization; Interpreting Meaning of Information to Others; Providing Consultation and Advice to Others; Communicating with Other Workers. **Physical Work Conditions:** Indoors; Contaminants; Using Hands on Objects, Tools, or Controls; Standing. **Other Job Characteristics:** Consequence of Error; Importance of Being Exact or Accurate; Importance of Being Sure All Is Done.

Experience: Job Zone 3. Previous work-related skill, knowledge, or experience is required. **Job Preparation:** SVP 6.0 to less than 7.0—More than 1 year and less than 4 years. **Knowledge:** Chemistry; Public Safety and Security; Law, Government and Jurisprudence; Mathematics; Production and Processing; English Language. **Instructional Programs:** 030203 Natural Resources Law Enforcement and Protective Services; 150701 Occupational Safety and Health Technology/Technician; 521601 Taxation.

Related DOT Jobs: 168.267-054 Inspector, Industrial Waste; 168.267-082 Agricultural-Chemicals Inspector; 168.267-086 Hazardous-Waste Management Specialist; 168.267-090 Inspector, Water-Pollution Control; 168.267-098 Pesticide-Control Inspector; 168.267-106 Registration Specialist, Agricultural Chemicals; 168.267-110 Sanitation Inspector.

13-1041.02 Licensing Examiners and Inspectors
(Inspectors and Compliance Officers)

Education: Work experience in a related occupation
Employed: 176,175
Openings: 19,910
Projected Growth: 10.5%
Earnings: $36,820

Examine, evaluate, and investigate eligibility for, conformity with, or liability under licenses or permits.

Provides information and answers questions of individuals or groups concerning licensing, permit, or passport regulations. Scores tests and rates ability of applicant through observation of equipment operation and control. Visits establishments to determine that valid licenses and permits are displayed and that licensing standards are being upheld. Issues licenses to individuals meeting standards. Confers with officials, technical, or professional specialists and interviews individuals to obtain informa-

tion or clarify facts. Prepares reports of activities, evaluations, recommendations, and decisions. Warns violators of infractions or penalties. Determines eligibility or liability and approves or disallows application or license. Administers oral, written, road, or flight test to determine applicant's eligibility for licensing. Evaluates applications, records, and documents to determine relevant eligibility information or liability incurred. Prepares correspondence to inform concerned parties of decisions made and appeal rights.

GOE Number, Interest Area, and Work Group: 04.04.02; Law, Law Enforcement, and Public Safety; Public Safety: Regulations Enforcement. **Personality Type:** Conventional. Conventional occupations frequently involve following set procedures and routines. These occupations can include working with data and details more than with ideas. Usually there is a clear line of authority to follow. **Work Values:** Company Policies and Practices; Security; Supervision, Human Relations; Responsibility; Autonomy. **Skills:** Reading Comprehension; Speaking; Active Listening; Information Gathering; Monitoring; Writing. **Abilities:** *Cognitive*—Oral Expression; Written Comprehension; Written Expression; Oral Comprehension; Problem Sensitivity; Memorization. *Psychomotor*—none met the criteria. *Physical*—Gross Body Coordination. *Sensory*—Near Vision; Speech Clarity; Speech Recognition. **General Work Activities:** *Information Input*—Getting Information Needed to Do the Job; Identifying Objects, Actions, and Events; Monitoring Processes, Materials, and Surroundings. *Mental Process*—Judging Qualities of Things, Services, People; Evaluating Information Against Standards; Making Decisions and Solving Problems. *Work Output*—Documenting and Recording Information; Implementing Ideas and Programs; Handling and Moving Objects. *Interacting with Others*—Communicating with Persons Outside Organization; Interpreting Meaning of Information to Others; Providing Consultation and Advice to Others; Performing for or Working with the Public. **Physical Work Conditions:** Indoors; Sitting; Using Hands on Objects, Tools, or Controls. **Other Job Characteristics:** Consequence of Error; Importance of Being Sure All Is Done; Importance of Being Exact or Accurate.

Experience: Job Zone 3. Previous work-related skill, knowledge, or experience is required. **Job Preparation:** SVP 6.0 to less than 7.0—More than 1 year and less than 4 years. **Knowledge:** English Language; Law, Government and Jurisprudence; Clerical; Mathematics; Communications and Media. **Instructional Programs:** 030203 Natural Resources Law Enforcement and Protective Services; 150701 Occupational Safety and Health Technology/Technician; 521601 Taxation.

Related DOT Jobs: 168.167-074 Reviewing Officer, Driver's License; 168.267-034 Driver's License Examiner; 168.267-066 License Inspector; 169.267-014 Examiner; 169.267-030 Passport-Application Examiner; 196.163-010 Flight-Operations Inspector.

13-1041.03 Equal Opportunity Representatives and Officers (Inspectors and Compliance Officers)

Education: Work experience in a related occupation
Employed: 176,175
Openings: 19,910
Projected Growth: 10.5%
Earnings: $36,820

Monitor and evaluate compliance with equal opportunity laws, guidelines, and policies. Ensure that employment practices and contracting arrangements give equal opportunity without regard to race, religion, color, national origin, sex, age, or disability.

Studies equal opportunity complaints to clarify issues. Reviews contracts to determine company actions required to meet governmental equal opportunity provisions. Develops guidelines for nondiscriminatory employment practices for use by employers. Acts as representative between minority placement agencies and employers. Conducts surveys and evaluates findings to determine existence of systematic discrimination. Interprets civil rights laws and equal opportunity governmental regulations for individuals and employers. Consults with community representatives to develop technical assistance agreements in accordance with governmental regulations. Confers with management or other personnel to resolve or settle equal opportunity issues and disputes. Investigates employment practices and alleged violations of law to document and correct discriminatory factors. Prepares report of findings and recommendations for corrective action.

GOE Number, Interest Area, and Work Group: 04.04.02; Law, Law Enforcement, and Public Safety; Public Safety: Regulations Enforcement. **Personality Type:** Social. Social occupations frequently involve working with, communicating with, and teaching people. These occupations often involve helping or providing service to others. **Work Values:** Working Conditions; Company Policies and Practices; Responsibility; Achievement; Supervision, Human Relations. **Skills:** Information Gathering; Reading Comprehension; Writing; Speaking; Active Listening. **Abilities:** *Cognitive*—Written Comprehension; Oral Comprehension; Oral Expression; Written Expression; Problem Sensitivity. *Psychomotor*—none met the criteria. *Physical*—Gross Body Equilibrium. *Sensory*—Speech Clarity; Near Vision; Speech Recognition. **General Work Activities:** *Information Input*—Getting Information Needed to Do the Job; Monitoring Processes, Materials, and Surroundings; Identifying Objects, Actions, and Events. *Mental Process*—Evaluating Information Against Standards; Processing Information; Analyzing Data or Information. *Work Output*—Documenting and Recording Information; Implementing Ideas and Programs; Interacting with Computers. *Interacting with Others*—Communicating with Persons Outside Organization; Interpreting Meaning of Information to Others; Providing Consultation and Advice to Others; Communicating with Other Workers. **Physical Work Conditions:** Indoors; Sitting; Standing. **Other Job Characteristics:** Frustrating Circumstances; Importance of Being Sure All Is Done; Importance of Being Exact or Accurate; Consequence of Error.

Experience: Job Zone 4. A minimum of two to four years of work-related skill, knowledge, or experience is needed. **Job Preparation:** SVP 7.0 to less than 8.0—2 years to less than 10 years. **Knowledge:** Personnel and Human Resources; Law, Government and Jurisprudence; English Language; Mathematics; Communications and Media. **Instructional Programs:** 030203 Natural Resources Law Enforcement and Protective Services; 150701 Occupational Safety and Health Technology/Technician; 521601 Taxation.

Related DOT Jobs: 168.167-014 Equal-Opportunity Representative; 168.267-114 Equal Opportunity Officer.

13-1041.04 Government Property Inspectors and Investigators (Inspectors and Compliance Officers)

Education: Work experience in a related occupation
Employed: 176,175
Openings: 19,910
Projected Growth: 10.5%
Earnings: $36,820

Investigate or inspect government property to ensure compliance with contract agreements and government regulations.

Locates and interviews plaintiffs, witnesses, or representatives of business or government to gather facts relevant to inspection or alleged violation. Testifies in court or at administrative proceedings concerning findings of investigation. Submits samples of product to government laboratory for testing as indicated by departmental procedures. Prepares correspondence, reports of inspections or investigations, and recommendations for administrative or legal authorities. Inspects manufactured or processed products to ensure compliance with contract specifications and legal requirements. Examines records, reports, and documents to establish facts and detect discrepancies. Inspects government-owned equipment and materials in hands of private contractors to prevent waste, damage, theft, and other irregularities. Investigates regulated activities to detect violation of law relating to such activities as revenue collection, employment practices, or fraudulent benefit claims. Investigates character of applicant for special license or permit and misuses of license or permit.

GOE Number, Interest Area, and Work Group: 04.04.02; Law, Law Enforcement, and Public Safety; Public Safety: Regulations Enforcement. **Personality Type:** Enterprising. Enterprising occupations frequently involve starting up and carrying out projects. These occupations can involve leading people and making many decisions. They sometimes require risk taking and often deal with business. **Work Values:** Security; Company Policies and Practices; Supervision, Human Relations; Advancement; Variety; Social Status. **Skills:** Speaking; Reading Comprehension; Writing; Judgment and Decision Making; Critical Thinking; Information Gathering; Problem Identification. **Abilities:** *Cognitive*—Problem Sensitivity; Written Expression; Oral Expression; Written Comprehension; Oral Comprehension; Deductive Reasoning. *Psychomotor*—Wrist-Finger Speed; Multilimb Coordination. *Physical*—Trunk Strength; Gross Body Coordination; Dynamic Strength. *Sensory*—Near Vision; Speech Clarity; Speech Recognition. **General Work Activities:** *Information Input*—Getting Information Needed to Do the Job; Identifying Objects, Actions, and Events; Inspecting Equipment, Structures, Materials. *Mental Process*—Evaluating Information Against Standards; Judging Qualities of Things, Services, People; Updating and Using Job-Relevant Knowledge; Analyzing Data or Information. *Work Output*—Documenting and Recording Information; Implementing Ideas and Programs; Handling and Moving Objects. *Interacting with Others*—Communicating with Persons Outside Organization; Interpreting Meaning of Information to Others; Communicating with Other Workers. **Physical Work Conditions:** Indoors; Standing; Sitting; Using Hands on Objects, Tools, or Controls. **Other Job Characteristics:** Consequence of Error; Importance of Being Sure All Is Done; Importance of Being Exact or Accurate.

Experience: Job Zone 3. Previous work-related skill, knowledge, or experience is required. **Job Preparation:** SVP 6.0 to less than 7.0—More than 1 year and less than 4 years. **Knowledge:** Law, Government and Jurisprudence; English Language; Mathematics; Public Safety and Security; Personnel and Human Resources. **Instructional Programs:** 030203 Natural Resources Law Enforcement and Protective Services; 150701 Occupational Safety and Health Technology/Technician; 521601 Taxation.

Related DOT Jobs: 168.267-050 Inspector, Government Property; 168.267-062 Investigator; 168.287-014 Inspector, Quality Assurance.

13-1041.05 Pressure Vessel Inspectors (Inspectors and Compliance Officers)

Education: Work experience in a related occupation
Employed: 176,175
Openings: 19,910
Projected Growth: 10.5%
Earnings: $36,820

Inspect pressure vessel equipment for conformance with safety laws and standards regulating their design, fabrication, installation, repair, and operation.

Witnesses acceptance and installation tests. Calculates allowable limits of pressure, strength, and stresses. Keeps records and prepares reports of inspections and investigations for administrative or legal authorities. Confers with engineers, manufacturers, contractors, owners, and operators concerning problems in construction, operation, and repair. Investigates accidents to determine causes and to develop methods of preventing recurrences. Examines permits and inspection records to determine that inspection schedule and remedial actions conform to procedures and regulations. Inspects drawings, designs, and specifications for piping, boilers and other vessels. Performs standard tests to verify condition of equipment and calibration of meters and gauges, using test equipment and hand tools. Inspects gas mains to determine that rate of flow, pressure, location, construction, or installation conform to standards. Evaluates factors, such as materials used, safety devices, regulators, construction quality, riveting, welding, pitting, corrosion, cracking, and safety valve operation. Recommends or orders actions to correct violations of legal requirements or to eliminate unsafe conditions.

GOE Number, Interest Area, and Work Group: 02.08.02; Science, Math, and Engineering; Engineering Technology: Industrial and Safety. **Personality Type:** Realistic. Realistic occupations frequently involve work activities that include practical, hands-on problems and solutions. These occupations often deal with plants, animals, and real-world materials like wood, tools, and machinery. Many of the occupations require working outside and do not involve a lot of paperwork or working closely with others. **Work Values:** Independence; Autonomy; Supervision, Human Relations; Responsibility; Security. **Skills:** Mathematics; Product Inspection; Writing; Testing; Identification of Key Causes; Active Listening. **Abilities:** *Cognitive*—Problem Sensitivity; Oral Expres-

sion; Written Expression; Written Comprehension; Oral Comprehension. *Psychomotor*—none met the criteria. *Physical*—none met the criteria. **General Work Activities:** *Information Input*—Inspecting Equipment, Structures, Materials; Getting Information Needed to Do the Job; Monitoring Processes, Materials, and Surroundings. *Mental Process*—Evaluating Information Against Standards; Processing Information; Judging Qualities of Things, Services, People; Making Decisions and Solving Problems. *Work Output*—Documenting and Recording Information; Controlling Machines and Processes; Performing General Physical Activities; Handling and Moving Objects. *Interacting with Others*—Communicating with Other Workers; Communicating with Persons Outside Organization; Performing Administrative Activities; Providing Consultation and Advice to Others; Interpreting Meaning of Information to Others. **Physical Work Conditions:** Indoors; Standing; Common Protective or Safety Attire; Using Hands on Objects, Tools, or Controls. **Other Job Characteristics:** Consequence of Error; Importance of Being Exact or Accurate; Importance of Being Sure All Is Done.

Experience: Job Zone 4. A minimum of two to four years of work-related skill, knowledge, or experience is needed. **Job Preparation:** SVP 7.0 to less than 8.0—2 years to less than 10 years. **Knowledge:** Public Safety and Security; Physics; Mathematics; Mechanical; Engineering and Technology. **Instructional Programs:** 030203 Natural Resources Law Enforcement and Protective Services; 150701 Occupational Safety and Health Technology/Technician; 521601 Taxation.

Related DOT Jobs: 168.167-026 Inspector, Boiler; 168.264-018 Gas Inspector.

13-1041.06 Coroners (Inspectors and Compliance Officers)

Education: Work experience in a related occupation
Employed: 176,175
Openings: 19,910
Projected Growth: 10.5%
Earnings: $36,820

Direct activities such as autopsies, pathological and toxicological analyses, and inquests, relating to the investigation of deaths occurring within a legal jurisdiction, to determine cause of death or to fix responsibility for accidental, violent, or unexplained deaths.

Confers with officials of public health and law enforcement agencies to coordinate interdepartmental activities. Provides information concerning death circumstance to relatives of deceased. Testifies at inquests, hearings, and court trials. Directs activities of workers involved in preparing documents for permanent records. Directs investigations into circumstances of deaths to fix responsibility for accidental, violent, or unexplained death. Directs activities of physicians and technologists conducting autopsies and pathological and toxicological analyses to determine cause of death. Coordinates activities for disposition of unclaimed corpse and personal effects of deceased.

GOE Number, Interest Area, and Work Group: 14.01.01; Medical and Health Services; Managerial Work in Medical and Health

Services. **Personality Type:** Investigative. Investigative occupations frequently involve working with ideas and require an extensive amount of thinking. These occupations can involve searching for facts and figuring out problems mentally. **Work Values:** Autonomy; Security; Responsibility; Ability Utilization; Authority. **Skills:** Information Gathering; Science; Reading Comprehension; Speaking; Writing; Critical Thinking; Problem Identification. **Abilities:** *Cognitive*—Inductive Reasoning; Oral Expression; Problem Sensitivity; Oral Comprehension; Written Expression. *Psychomotor*—Manual Dexterity; Arm-Hand Steadiness; Finger Dexterity; Wrist-Finger Speed. *Physical*—Gross Body Coordination. *Sensory*—Near Vision; Speech Clarity; Visual Color Discrimination. **General Work Activities:** *Information Input*—Getting Information Needed to Do the Job; Identifying Objects, Actions, and Events; Monitoring Processes, Materials, and Surroundings. *Mental Process*—Analyzing Data or Information; Making Decisions and Solving Problems; Updating and Using Job-Relevant Knowledge. *Work Output*—Implementing Ideas and Programs; Handling and Moving Objects; Documenting and Recording Information. *Interacting with Others*—Communicating with Other Workers; Coordinating Work and Activities of Others; Communicating with Persons Outside Organization. **Physical Work Conditions:** Common Protective or Safety Attire; Using Hands on Objects, Tools, or Controls; Standing; Indoors. **Other Job Characteristics:** Consequence of Error; Importance of Being Sure All Is Done; Frustrating Circumstances.

Experience: Job Zone 4. A minimum of two to four years of work-related skill, knowledge, or experience is needed. **Job Preparation:** SVP 7.0 to less than 8.0—2 years to less than 10 years. **Knowledge:** Biology; Medicine and Dentistry; Administration and Management; English Language; Law, Government and Jurisprudence. **Instructional Programs:** 030203 Natural Resources Law Enforcement and Protective Services; 150701 Occupational Safety and Health Technology/Technician; 521601 Taxation.

Related DOT Job: 168.161-010 Coroner.

13-1051.00 Cost Estimators (Cost Estimators)

Education: Bachelor's degree
Employed: 151,687
Openings: 27,649
Projected Growth: 13%
Earnings: $40,590

Prepare cost estimates for product manufacturing, construction projects, or services, to aid management in bidding on or determining price of product or service. Specialize according to particular service performed or type of product manufactured.

Prepares estimates for selecting vendors or subcontractors, and determining cost effectiveness. Conducts special studies to develop and establish standard hour and related cost data or to effect cost reduction. Consults with clients, vendors, or other individuals to discuss and formulate estimates and resolve issues. Computes cost factors used for preparing estimates for management and determining cost effectiveness. Reviews data to determine material and labor requirements, and prepares itemized list. Analyzes blueprints, specifications, proposals, and other documentation, to prepare time, cost, and labor estimates. Prepares estimates used for management purposes, such as planning, organizing, and scheduling work. Prepares time, cost, and labor estimates for products, projects, or services, applying specialized methodologies, techniques, or processes.

GOE Number, Interest Area, and Work Group: 13.02.04; General Management and Support; Management Support: Investigation and Analysis. **Personality Type:** Conventional. Conventional occupations frequently involve following set procedures and routines. These occupations can include working with data and details more than with ideas. Usually there is a clear line of authority to follow. **Work Values:** Working Conditions; Independence; Responsibility; Autonomy; Supervision, Human Relations; Security; Company Policies and Practices; Ability Utilization. **Skills:** Information Gathering; Mathematics; Reading Comprehension; Writing; Identifying Downstream Consequences; Active Learning. **Abilities:** *Cognitive*—Mathematical Reasoning; Number Facility; Written Comprehension; Oral Expression; Oral Comprehension. *Psychomotor*—none met the criteria. *Physical*—none met the criteria. *Sensory*—Speech Clarity; Speech Recognition. **General Work Activities:** *Information Input*—Estimating Needed Characteristics; Getting Information Needed to Do the Job; Identifying Objects, Actions, and Events. *Mental Process*—Processing Information; Analyzing Data or Information; Making Decisions and Solving Problems. *Work Output*—Documenting and Recording Information; Implementing Ideas and Programs; Handling and Moving Objects. *Interacting with Others*—Providing Consultation and Advice to Others; Communicating with Other Workers; Communicating with Persons Outside Organization. **Physical Work Conditions:** Indoors; Sitting; Using Hands on Objects, Tools, or Controls. **Other Job Characteristics:** Consequence of Error; Importance of Being Exact or Accurate; Importance of Being Sure All Is Done.

Experience: Job Zone 4. A minimum of two to four years of work-related skill, knowledge, or experience is needed. **Job Preparation:** SVP 7.0 to less than 8.0—2 years to less than 10 years. **Knowledge:** Mathematics; Production and Processing; Economics and Accounting; Administration and Management; Building and Construction. **Instructional Program:** 520202 Purchasing, Procurement and Contracts Management.

Related DOT Job: 169.267-038 Estimator.

13-1061.00 Emergency Management Specialists (All Other Managers and Administrators)

Education: No data available.
Employed: 946,190
Openings: No data available.
Projected Growth: No data available.
Earnings: $49,220

Coordinate disaster response or crisis management activities. Provide disaster preparedness training. Prepare emergency plans and procedures for natural (for example, hurricanes, floods, or earthquakes), wartime, or technological (for example, nuclear power plant emergencies or hazardous materials spills) disasters or hostage situations.

GOE Number, Interest Area, and Work Group: 04.01.01; Law, Law Enforcement, and Public Safety; Managerial Work in Law, Law Enforcement, and Public Safety. **Instructional Programs:** 080301 Entrepreneurship; 310301 Parks, Recreation and Leisure Facilities Management; 440201 Community Organization, Resources and Services; 440401 Public Administration; 500704 Arts Management; 520101 Business, General; 520201 Business Administration and Management, General; 520203 Logistics and Materials Management; 520206 Non-Profit and Public Management; 520299 Business Administration and Management, Other; 520701 Enterprise Management and Operation, General; 520702 Franchise Operation; 520799 Enterprise Management and Operation, Other; 520903 Travel-Tourism Management; 520999 Hospitality Services Management, Other. **Note:** The Department of Labor has not collected some data for this job, so it has fewer details than the other descriptions.

13-1071.00 Employment, Recruitment, and Placement Specialists (Human Resources, Training, and Labor Relations Specialists)

Education: Bachelor's degree
Employed: 367,370
Openings: 82,760
Projected Growth: 17.9%
Earnings: $37,710

Recruit and place workers.

GOE Number, Interest Area, and Work Group: 13.02.01; General Management and Support; Management Support: Human Resources. **Instructional Programs:** 521001 Human Resources Management; 521002 Labor/Personnel Relations and Studies; 521003 Organizational Behavior Studies; 521099 Human Resources Management, Other. **Note:** The Department of Labor has not collected some data for this job, so it has fewer details than the other descriptions.

13-1071.01 Employment Interviewers, Private or Public Employment Service (Employment Interviewers)

Education: Bachelor's degree
Employed: 65,830
Openings: 14,194
Projected Growth: 12.9%
Earnings: $29,800

Interview job applicants in employment office and refer them to prospective employers for consideration. Search application files, notify selected applicants of job openings, and refer qualified applicants to prospective employers. Contact employers to verify referral results. Record and evaluate various pertinent data.

Refers applicants to vocational counseling services. Reviews job orders and matches applicants with job requirements, utilizing manual or computerized file search. Keeps records of applicants not selected for employment. Contacts employers to solicit orders for job vacancies and records information on forms to describe duties, hiring requirements, and related data. Reviews employment applications and evaluates work history, education and training, job skills, compensation needs, and other qualifications of applicants. Conducts or arranges for skills, intelligence, or psychological testing of applicants. Performs reference and background checks on applicants. Searches for and recruits applicants for open positions. Informs applicants of job duties and responsibilities, compensation and benefits, work schedules, working conditions, promotional opportunities, and other related information. Records additional knowledge, skills, abilities, interests, test results, and other data pertinent to selection and referral of applicants. Refers selected applicants to person placing job order, according to policy of organization. Interviews job applicants to select people meeting employer qualifications. Evaluates selection and testing techniques by conducting research or follow-up activities and conferring with management and supervisory personnel.

GOE Number, Interest Area, and Work Group: 13.02.01; General Management and Support; Management Support: Human Resources. **Personality Type:** Social. Social occupations frequently involve working with, communicating with, and teaching people. These occupations often involve helping or providing service to others. **Work Values:** Working Conditions; Social Service; Supervision, Human Relations; Activity; Security; Company Policies and Practices. **Skills:** Reading Comprehension; Active Listening; Speaking; Information Gathering; Judgment and Decision Making; Idea Generation; Writing. **Abilities:** *Cognitive*—Oral Expression; Oral Comprehension; Written Comprehension; Fluency of Ideas; Written Expression. *Psychomotor*—none met the criteria. *Physical*—none met the criteria. *Sensory*—Speech Clarity; Speech Recognition. **General Work Activities:** *Information Input*—Getting Information Needed to Do the Job; Identifying Objects, Actions, and Events; Estimating Needed Characteristics. *Mental Process*—Judging Qualities of Things, Services, People; Analyzing Data or Information; Processing Information. *Work Output*—Documenting and Recording Information; Handling and Moving Objects; Interacting with Computers. *Interacting with Others*—Communicating with Persons Outside Organization; Establishing and Maintaining Relationships; Staffing Organizational Units; Assisting and Caring for Others. **Physical Work Conditions:** Indoors; Sitting; Standing; Using Hands on Objects, Tools, or Controls. **Other Job Characteristics:** Importance of Being Sure All Is Done; Consequence of Error; Importance of Being Exact or Accurate.

Experience: Job Zone 3. Previous work-related skill, knowledge, or experience is required. **Job Preparation:** SVP 6.0 to less than 7.0—More than 1 year and less than 4 years. **Knowledge:** Personnel and Human Resources; Therapy and Counseling; Administration and Management; English Language; Clerical. **Instructional Program:** 521001 Human Resources Management.

Related DOT Job: 166.267-010 Employment Interviewer.

13-1071.02 Personnel Recruiters (Human Resources, Training, and Labor Relations Specialists)

Education: Bachelor's degree
Employed: 367,370
Openings: 82,760
Projected Growth: 17.9%
Earnings: $37,710

Seek out, interview, and screen applicants to fill existing and future job openings and to promote career opportunities within an organization.

Assists and advises establishment management in organizing, preparing, and implementing recruiting and retention programs. Reviews and evaluates applicant qualifications or eligibility for specified licensing, according to established guidelines and designated licensing codes. Contacts college representatives to arrange for and schedule on-campus interviews with students. Conducts reference and background checks on applicants. Provides potential applicants with information regarding facilities, operations, benefits, and job or career opportunities in organization. Arranges for interviews and travel and lodging for selected applicants at company expense. Evaluates recruitment and selection criteria to ensure conformance to professional, statistical, and testing standards, and recommends revision as needed. Speaks to civic, social, and other groups to provide information concerning job possibilities and career opportunities. Prepares and maintains employment records and authorizes paperwork assigning applicant to positions. Corrects and scores portions of examinations used to screen and select applicants. Projects yearly recruitment expenditures for budgetary consideration and control. Notifies applicants by mail or telephone to inform them of employment possibilities, consideration, and selection. Interviews applicants to obtain work history, training, education, job skills, and other background information. Hires or refers applicant to other hiring personnel in organization.

GOE Number, Interest Area, and Work Group: 13.02.01; General Management and Support; Management Support: Human Resources. **Personality Type:** Enterprising. Enterprising occupations frequently involve starting up and carrying out projects. These occupations can involve leading people and making many decisions. They sometimes require risk taking and often deal with business. **Work Values:** Working Conditions; Company Policies and Practices; Supervision, Human Relations; Activity; Achievement. **Skills:** Active Listening; Reading Comprehension; Writing; Speaking; Visioning. **Abilities:** *Cognitive*—Oral Comprehension; Oral Expression; Written Comprehension; Written Expression; Mathematical Reasoning. *Psychomotor*—none met the criteria. *Physical*—none met the criteria. *Sensory*—Speech Clarity; Near Vision; Speech Recognition. **General Work Activities:** *Information Input*—Getting Information Needed to Do the Job; Identifying Objects, Actions, and Events; Estimating Needed Characteristics. *Mental Process*—Judging Qualities of Things, Services, People; Organizing, Planning, and Prioritizing; Making Decisions and Solving Problems; Analyzing Data or Information. *Work Output*—Documenting and Recording Information; Implementing Ideas and Programs; Interacting with Computers. *Interacting with Oth-*

ers—Staffing Organizational Units; Communicating with Persons Outside Organization; Communicating with Other Workers. **Physical Work Conditions:** Indoors; Sitting; Walking or Running; Standing. **Other Job Characteristics:** Consequence of Error; Frustrating Circumstances; Importance of Being Exact or Accurate; Importance of Being Sure All Is Done.

Experience: Job Zone 3. Previous work-related skill, knowledge, or experience is required. **Job Preparation:** SVP 6.0 to less than 7.0—More than 1 year and less than 4 years. **Knowledge:** Personnel and Human Resources; Psychology; Sales and Marketing; English Language; Mathematics; Administration and Management. **Instructional Programs:** 521001 Human Resources Management; 521002 Labor/Personnel Relations and Studies; 521003 Organizational Behavior Studies; 521099 Human Resources Management, Other.

Related DOT Jobs: 099.167-010 Certification and Selection Specialist; 166.267-026 Recruiter; 166.267-038 Personnel Recruiter; 205.367-050 Supervisor, Contingents.

13-1072.00 Compensation, Benefits, and Job Analysis Specialists (Human Resources, Training, and Labor Relations Specialists)

Education: Bachelor's degree
Employed: 367,370
Openings: 82,760
Projected Growth: 17.9%
Earnings: $37,710

Conduct compensation and benefits programs and job analysis for employer. Specialize in specific areas such as position classification or pension programs.

Researches job and worker requirements, structural and functional relationships among jobs and occupations, and occupational trends. Plans and develops curricula and materials for training programs and conducts training. Observes and interviews employees to collect job, organizational, and occupational information. Prepares reports such as job descriptions, organization, and flow charts, and career path reports, to summarize job analysis information. Analyzes organizational, occupational, and industrial data to facilitate organizational functions and provide technical information to business, industry, and government. Evaluates and improves methods and techniques for selecting, promoting, evaluating, and training workers. Consults with business, industry, government, and union officials to arrange for, plan, and design occupational studies and surveys. Prepares research results for publication in form of journals, books, manuals, and film. Determines need for and develops job analysis instruments and materials.

GOE Number, Interest Area, and Work Group: 13.02.01; General Management and Support; Management Support: Human Resources. **Personality Type:** Investigative. Investigative occupations frequently involve working with ideas and require an extensive amount of thinking. These occupations can involve searching for facts and figuring out problems mentally. **Work Values:** Working Conditions; Responsibility; Ability Utilization; Achievement; Autonomy; Coworkers. **Skills:** Writing; Information Gathering; Reading Comprehension; Identification of Key Causes; Systems Evaluation; Speaking. **Abilities:** *Cognitive*—Oral Comprehension; Written Expression; Oral Expression; Deductive Reasoning; Written Comprehension. *Psychomotor*—none met the criteria. *Physical*—none met the criteria. *Sensory*—Near Vision; Speech Clarity; Far Vision. **General Work Activities:** *Information Input*—Getting Information Needed to Do the Job; Identifying Objects, Actions, and Events; Monitoring Processes, Materials, and Surroundings. *Mental Process*—Analyzing Data or Information; Judging Qualities of Things, Services, People; Making Decisions and Solving Problems; Updating and Using Job-Relevant Knowledge. *Work Output*—Documenting and Recording Information; Implementing Ideas and Programs; Interacting with Computers. *Interacting with Others*—Communicating with Persons Outside Organization; Providing Consultation and Advice to Others; Communicating with Other Workers. **Physical Work Conditions:** Indoors; Sitting; Standing. **Other Job Characteristics:** Importance of Being Exact or Accurate; Importance of Being Sure All Is Done; Frustrating Circumstances.

Experience: Job Zone 3. Previous work-related skill, knowledge, or experience is required. **Job Preparation:** SVP 6.0 to less than 7.0—More than 1 year and less than 4 years. **Knowledge:** Mathematics; Psychology; English Language; Personnel and Human Resources; Computers and Electronics. **Instructional Programs:** 521001 Human Resources Management; 521002 Labor/Personnel Relations and Studies; 521003 Organizational Behavior Studies; 521099 Human Resources Management, Other.

Related DOT Jobs: 166.067-010 Occupational Analyst; 166.267-018 Job Analyst.

13-1073.00 Training and Development Specialists
(Human Resources, Training, and Labor Relations Specialists)

Education: Bachelor's degree
Employed: 367,370
Openings: 82,760
Projected Growth: 17.9%
Earnings: $37,710

Conduct training and development programs for employees.

Assigns instructors to conduct training and assists them in obtaining required training materials. Evaluates training materials, such as outlines, text, and handouts, prepared by instructors. Confers with managers, instructors, or customer representatives of industrial or commercial establishment to determine training needs. Organizes and develops training procedure manuals and guides. Attends meetings and seminars to obtain information useful to train staff and to inform management of training programs and goals. Maintains records and writes reports to monitor and evaluate training activities and program effectiveness. Monitors training costs to ensure budget is not exceeded, and prepares budget report to justify expenditures. Refers trainees with social problems to appropriate service agency. Screens, hires, and assigns workers to positions based on qualifications. Schedules classes based on availability of classrooms, equipment, and instructors. Develops and conducts orientation and training for

employees or customers of industrial or commercial establishment. Coordinates recruitment and placement of participants in skill training. Supervises instructors, monitors and evaluates instructor performance, and refers instructors to classes for skill development.

GOE Number, Interest Area, and Work Group: 13.02.01; General Management and Support; Management Support: Human Resources. **Personality Type:** Social. Social occupations frequently involve working with, communicating with, and teaching people. These occupations often involve helping or providing service to others. **Work Values:** Working Conditions; Coworkers; Authority; Responsibility; Achievement; Company Policies and Practices. **Skills:** Problem Identification; Learning Strategies; Writing; Speaking; Management of Financial Resources; Monitoring; Active Listening; Information Gathering; Solution Appraisal. **Abilities:** *Cognitive*—Oral Expression; Oral Comprehension; Written Expression; Written Comprehension; Originality. *Psychomotor*—Wrist-Finger Speed. *Physical*—none met the criteria. *Sensory*—Speech Clarity; Near Vision; Night Vision. **General Work Activities:** *Information Input*—Getting Information Needed to Do the Job; Monitoring Processes, Materials, and Surroundings; Identifying Objects, Actions, and Events. *Mental Process*—Judging Qualities of Things, Services, People; Organizing, Planning, and Prioritizing; Scheduling Work and Activities. *Work Output*—Documenting and Recording Information; Implementing Ideas and Programs; Handling and Moving Objects. *Interacting with Others*—Staffing Organizational Units; Coaching and Developing Others; Communicating with Other Workers. **Physical Work Conditions:** Indoors; Sitting; Standing. **Other Job Characteristics:** Frustrating Circumstances; Importance of Being Sure All Is Done; Consequence of Error.

Experience: Job Zone 4. A minimum of two to four years of work-related skill, knowledge, or experience is needed. **Job Preparation:** SVP 7.0 to less than 8.0—2 years to less than 10 years. **Knowledge:** Education and Training; Personnel and Human Resources; Psychology; English Language; Administration and Management; Sales and Marketing; Clerical; Economics and Accounting. **Instructional Programs:** 521001 Human Resources Management; 521002 Labor/Personnel Relations and Studies; 521003 Organizational Behavior Studies; 521099 Human Resources Management, Other.

Related DOT Jobs: 079.127-010 Inservice Coordinator, Auxiliary Personnel; 166.167-038 Port Purser; 166.167-054 Technical Training Coordinator; 169.167-062 Coordinator, Skill-Training Program; 239.137-010 Commercial-Instructor Supervisor.

13-1081.00 Logisticians (Management Analysts)

Education: Work experience, plus degree
Employed: 344,494
Openings: 23,831
Projected Growth: 28.4%
Earnings: $49,470

Analyze and coordinate the logistical functions of a firm or organization. Assume responsibility for the entire life cycle of a product, including acquisition, distribution, internal allocation, delivery, and final disposal of resources.

GOE Number, Interest Area, and Work Group: 13.02.04; General Management and Support; Management Support: Investigation and Analysis. **Instructional Program:** 520201 Business Administration and Management, General. **Note:** The Department of Labor has not collected some data for this job, so it has fewer details than the other descriptions.

13-1111.00 Management Analysts (Management Analysts)

Education: Work experience, plus degree

Employed: 344,494

Openings: 23,831

Projected Growth: 28.4%

Earnings: $49,470

Conduct organizational studies and evaluations, design systems and procedures, conduct work simplifications and measurement studies, and prepare operations and procedures manuals to assist management in operating more efficiently and effectively. Includes program analysts and management consultants.

Recommends purchase of storage equipment, and designs area layout to locate equipment in space available. Interviews personnel and conducts on-site observation to ascertain unit functions, work performed, and methods, equipment, and personnel used. Designs, evaluates, recommends, and approves changes of forms and reports. Plans study of work problems and procedures, such as organizational change, communications, information flow, integrated production methods, inventory control, or cost analysis. Confers with personnel concerned to ensure successful functioning of newly implemented systems or procedures. Analyzes data gathered and develops solutions or alternative methods of proceeding. Reviews forms and reports, and confers with management and users about format, distribution, and purpose, and to identify problems and improvements. Gathers and organizes information on problems or procedures. Prepares manuals and trains workers in use of new forms, reports, procedures or equipment, according to organizational policy. Develops and implements records management program for filing, protection, and retrieval of records, and assures compliance with program. Documents findings of study and prepares recommendations for implementation of new systems, procedures, or organizational changes.

GOE Number, Interest Area, and Work Group: 13.02.04; General Management and Support; Management Support: Investigation and Analysis. **Personality Type:** Enterprising. Enterprising occupations frequently involve starting up and carrying out projects. These occupations can involve leading people and making many decisions. They sometimes require risk taking and often deal with business. **Work Values:** Working Conditions; Achievement; Creativity; Compensation; Ability Utilization; Autonomy. **Skills:** Identification of Key Causes; Systems Evaluation; Problem Identification; Information Gathering; Information Organization. **Abilities:** *Cognitive*—Oral Expression; Written Expression; Problem Sensitivity; Oral Comprehension; Written Comprehension. *Psychomotor*—Wrist-Finger Speed. *Physical*—none met the criteria. *Sensory*—Near Vision; Speech Clarity; Speech

Recognition. **General Work Activities:** *Information Input*—Getting Information Needed to Do the Job; Monitoring Processes, Materials, and Surroundings; Identifying Objects, Actions, and Events. *Mental Process*—Analyzing Data or Information; Making Decisions and Solving Problems; Organizing, Planning, and Prioritizing. *Work Output*—Implementing Ideas and Programs; Documenting and Recording Information; Interacting with Computers. *Interacting with Others*—Providing Consultation and Advice to Others; Communicating with Other Workers; Establishing and Maintaining Relationships. **Physical Work Conditions:** Indoors; Sitting; Standing. **Other Job Characteristics:** Consequence of Error; Importance of Being Sure All Is Done; Frustrating Circumstances.

Experience: Job Zone 4. A minimum of two to four years of work-related skill, knowledge, or experience is needed. **Job Preparation:** SVP 7.0 to less than 8.0—2 years to less than 10 years. **Knowledge:** Administration and Management; English Language; Education and Training; Mathematics; Personnel and Human Resources. **Instructional Program:** 520201 Business Administration and Management, General.

Related DOT Jobs: 161.117-014 Director, Records Management; 161.167-010 Management Analyst; 161.167-014 Manager, Forms Analysis; 161.167-018 Manager, Records Analysis; 161.167-022 Manager, Reports Analysis; 161.267-010 Clerical-Methods Analyst; 161.267-018 Forms Analyst; 161.267-022 Records-Management Analyst; 161.267-026 Reports Analyst.

13-1121.00 Meeting and Convention Planners (All Other Management Support Workers)

Education: No data available.

Employed: 792,150

Openings: No data available.

Projected Growth: No data available.

Earnings: $37,060

Coordinate activities of staff and convention personnel to make arrangements for group meetings and conventions.

Reads trade publications, attends seminars, and consults with other meeting professionals to keep abreast of meeting management standards and trends. Plans and develops programs, budgets, and services, such as lodging, catering, and entertainment, according to customer requirements. Maintains records of events. Reviews bills for accuracy and approves payment. Consults with customer to determine objectives and requirements for events, such as meetings, conferences, and conventions. Obtains permits from fire and health departments to erect displays and exhibits and serve food at events. Inspects rooms and displays for conformance to customer requirements, and conducts post-meeting evaluations to improve future events. Evaluates and selects providers of services, such as meeting facilities, speakers, and transportation, according to customer requirements. Directs and coordinates activities of staff and convention personnel to make arrangements, prepare facilities, and provide services for events. Negotiates contracts with such providers as hotels, convention centers, and speakers. Speaks with attendees and resolves complaints to maintain goodwill.

GOE Number, Interest Area, and Work Group: 11.01.01; Recreation, Travel, and Other Personal Services; Managerial Work in Recreation, Travel, and Other Personal Services. **Personality Type:** Enterprising. Enterprising occupations frequently involve starting up and carrying out projects. These occupations can involve leading people and making many decisions. They sometimes require risk taking and often deal with business. **Work Values:** Working Conditions; Responsibility; Autonomy; Achievement; Variety; Authority; Recognition; Creativity. **Skills:** Coordination; Management of Personnel Resources; Implementation Planning; Speaking; Service Orientation. **Abilities:** *Cognitive*—Oral Expression; Oral Comprehension; Written Comprehension; Problem Sensitivity; Written Expression; Information Ordering. *Psychomotor*—none met the criteria. *Physical*—none met the criteria. *Sensory*—Speech Clarity; Speech Recognition; Auditory Attention. **General Work Activities:** *Information Input*—Getting Information Needed to Do the Job; Identifying Objects, Actions, and Events; Estimating Needed Characteristics. *Mental Process*—Organizing, Planning, and Prioritizing; Scheduling Work and Activities; Making Decisions and Solving Problems. *Work Output*—Implementing Ideas and Programs; Documenting and Recording Information; Drafting and Specifying Technical Devices. *Interacting with Others*—Coordinating Work and Activities of Others; Communicating with Other Workers; Establishing and Maintaining Relationships; Communicating with Persons Outside Organization. **Physical Work Conditions:** Sitting; Indoors; Standing. **Other Job Characteristics:** Importance of Being Sure All Is Done; Frustrating Circumstances; Consequence of Error.

Experience: Job Zone 4. A minimum of two to four years of work-related skill, knowledge, or experience is needed. **Job Preparation:** SVP 7.0 to less than 8.0—2 years to less than 10 years. **Knowledge:** Administration and Management; Customer and Personal Service; English Language; Communications and Media; Sales and Marketing. **Instructional Programs:** 440501 Public Policy Analysis; 520401 Administrative Assistant/Secretarial Science, General; 520402 Executive Assistant/Secretary.

Related DOT Jobs: 169.117-022 Meeting Planner; 187.167-078 Manager, Convention.

13-2000 Financial Specialists

13-2011.00 Accountants and Auditors (Accountants and Auditors)

Education: Bachelor's degree
Employed: 1,079,726
Openings: 129,566
Projected Growth: 11.3%
Earnings: $37,860

Examine, analyze, and interpret accounting records for the purpose of giving advice or preparing statements. Install or advise on systems of recording costs or other financial and budgetary data.

GOE Number, Interest Area, and Work Group: 13.02.03; General Management and Support; Management Support: Account-

ing and Auditing. **Instructional Programs:** 520301 Accounting; 521601 Taxation. **Note:** The Department of Labor has not collected some data for this job, so it has fewer details than the other descriptions.

13-2011.01 Accountants (Accountants and Auditors)

Education: Bachelor's degree
Employed: 1,079,726
Openings: 129,566
Projected Growth: 11.3%
Earnings: $37,860

Analyze financial information and prepare financial reports to determine or maintain record of assets, liabilities, profit and loss, or tax liability. Perform other financial activities within an organization.

Analyzes records of financial transactions to determine accuracy and completeness of entries, using computer. Reports finances of establishment to management, and advises management about resource utilization, tax strategies, and assumptions underlying budget forecasts. Develops, maintains, and analyzes budgets, and prepares periodic reports comparing budgeted costs to actual costs. Develops, implements, modifies, and documents budgeting, cost, general, property, and tax accounting systems. Establishes table of accounts, and assigns entries to proper accounts. Audits contracts, and prepares reports to substantiate transactions prior to settlement. Prepares forms and manuals for workers performing accounting and bookkeeping tasks. Adapts accounting and record keeping functions to current technology of computerized accounting systems. Directs activities of workers performing accounting and bookkeeping tasks. Computes taxes owed, ensures compliance with tax payment, reporting, and other tax requirements, and represents establishment before taxing authority. Surveys establishment operations to ascertain accounting needs. Predicts revenues and expenditures, and submits reports to management. Analyzes operations, trends, costs, revenues, financial commitments, and obligations incurred, to project future revenues and expenses, using computer. Prepares balance sheet, profit and loss statement, amortization and depreciation schedules, and other financial reports, using calculator or computer. Appraises, evaluates, and inventories real property and equipment, and records description, value, location, and other information.

GOE Number, Interest Area, and Work Group: 13.02.03; General Management and Support; Management Support: Accounting and Auditing. **Personality Type:** Conventional. Conventional occupations frequently involve following set procedures and routines. These occupations can include working with data and details more than with ideas. Usually there is a clear line of authority to follow. **Work Values:** Working Conditions; Compensation; Security; Activity; Social Status; Ability Utilization. **Skills:** Information Gathering; Management of Financial Resources; Solution Appraisal; Problem Identification; Identifying Downstream Consequences; Judgment and Decision Making; Mathematics; Systems Evaluation. **Abilities:** *Cognitive*—Number Facility; Written Comprehension; Written Expression; Mathematical Reasoning; Information Ordering. *Psychomotor*—Finger Dexterity. *Physical*—none met the criteria. *Sensory*—Near Vision; Speech Clarity; Far Vision. **General Work Activities:** *Information Input*—Getting Information Needed to Do the Job; Identifying Objects, Actions, and Events; Estimating Needed Characteristics. *Mental Process*—Analyzing Data or Information; Processing Information; Evaluating Information Against Standards. *Work Output*—Interacting with Computers; Documenting and Recording Information; Implementing Ideas and Programs. *Interacting with Others*—Communicating with Other Workers; Providing Consultation and Advice to Others; Monitoring and Controlling Resources. **Physical Work Conditions:** Indoors; Sitting; Using Hands on Objects, Tools, or Controls. **Other Job Characteristics:** Importance of Being Exact or Accurate; Consequence of Error; Importance of Being Sure All Is Done.

Experience: Job Zone 4. A minimum of two to four years of work-related skill, knowledge, or experience is needed. **Job Preparation:** SVP 7.0 to less than 8.0—2 years to less than 10 years. **Knowledge:** Mathematics; Economics and Accounting; Administration and Management; English Language; Clerical. **Instructional Programs:** 520301 Accounting; 521601 Taxation.

Related DOT Jobs: 160.162-010 Accountant, Tax; 160.162-018 Accountant; 160.162-022 Accountant, Budget; 160.162-026 Accountant, Cost; 160.167-022 Accountant, Property; 160.167-026 Accountant, Systems; 160.167-042 Bursar.

13-2011.02 Auditors (Accountants and Auditors)

Education: Bachelor's degree

Employed: 1,079,726

Openings: 129,566

Projected Growth: 11.3%

Earnings: $37,860

Examine and analyze accounting records to determine financial status of establishment and to prepare financial reports concerning operating procedures.

Inspects account books and system for efficiency, effectiveness, and use of accepted accounting procedures to record transactions. Confers with company officials about financial and regulatory matters. Audits records to determine unemployment insurance premiums, liabilities, and compliance with tax laws. Reviews taxpayer accounts, and conducts audits on-site, by correspondence, or by summoning taxpayer to office. Evaluates taxpayer finances to determine tax liability, using knowledge of interest and discount, annuities, valuation of stocks and bonds, and amortization valuation of depletable assets. Analyzes annual reports, financial statements, and other records, using accepted accounting and statistical procedures, to determine financial condition. Verifies journal and ledger entries by examining inventory. Inspects cash on hand, notes receivable and payable, negotiable securities, and canceled checks. Examines records and interviews workers to ensure recording of transactions and compliance with laws and regulations. Supervises auditing of establishments, and determines scope of investigation required. Examines records, tax returns, and related documents pertaining to settlement of decedent's estate regulations. Examines payroll and personnel

records to determine worker's compensation coverage. Analyzes data for deficient controls, duplicated effort, extravagance, fraud, or non-compliance with laws, regulations, and management policies. Reports to management about asset utilization and audit results, and recommends changes in operations and financial activities. Reviews data about material assets, net worth, liabilities, capital stock, surplus, income, and expenditures. Directs activities of personnel engaged in filing, recording, compiling and transmitting financial records.

GOE Number, Interest Area, and Work Group: 13.02.03; General Management and Support; Management Support: Accounting and Auditing. **Personality Type:** Conventional. Conventional occupations frequently involve following set procedures and routines. These occupations can include working with data and details more than with ideas. Usually there is a clear line of authority to follow. **Work Values:** Working Conditions; Compensation; Company Policies and Practices; Security; Ability Utilization. **Skills:** Systems Evaluation; Information Gathering; Problem Identification; Identification of Key Causes; Critical Thinking. **Abilities:** *Cognitive*—Number Facility; Written Comprehension; Problem Sensitivity; Mathematical Reasoning; Written Expression; Oral Expression. *Psychomotor*—Finger Dexterity; Control Precision; Multilimb Coordination. *Physical*—none met the criteria. *Sensory*—Near Vision; Speech Clarity; Speech Recognition. **General Work Activities:** *Information Input*—Getting Information Needed to Do the Job; Identifying Objects, Actions, and Events; Monitoring Processes, Materials, and Surroundings. *Mental Process*—Processing Information; Analyzing Data or Information; Evaluating Information Against Standards; Updating and Using Job-Relevant Knowledge. *Work Output*—Documenting and Recording Information; Interacting with Computers; Implementing Ideas and Programs. *Interacting with Others*—Providing Consultation and Advice to Others; Interpreting Meaning of Information to Others; Communicating with Other Workers; Monitoring and Controlling Resources. **Physical Work Conditions:** Indoors; Sitting; Using Hands on Objects, Tools, or Controls. **Other Job Characteristics:** Consequence of Error; Importance of Being Exact or Accurate; Importance of Being Sure All Is Done.

Experience: Job Zone 4. A minimum of two to four years of work-related skill, knowledge, or experience is needed. **Job Preparation:** SVP 7.0 to less than 8.0—2 years to less than 10 years. **Knowledge:** Economics and Accounting; Mathematics; Administration and Management; Law, Government and Jurisprudence; English Language. **Instructional Programs:** 520301 Accounting; 521601 Taxation.

Related DOT Jobs: 160.167-030 Auditor, County or City; 160.167-034 Auditor, Internal; 160.167-038 Auditor, Tax; 160.167-054 Auditor; 160.267-014 Director, Utility Accounts.

13-2021.00 Appraisers and Assessors of Real Estate
(Real Estate Appraisers)

Education: Bachelor's degree

Employed: 47,896

Openings: 6,383

Projected Growth: 11.2%

Earnings: $40,290

Appraise real property to determine its fair value. Assess taxes in accordance with prescribed schedules.

GOE Number, Interest Area, and Work Group: 13.02.04; General Management and Support; Management Support: Investigation and Analysis. **Instructional Program:** 521501 Real Estate. **Note:** The Department of Labor has not collected some data for this job, so it has fewer details than the other descriptions.

13-2021.01 Assessors (Assessors)

Education: Bachelor's degree

Employed: 22,397

Openings: 1,807

Projected Growth: 11.8%

Earnings: $29,830

Appraise real and personal property to determine its fair value. Assess taxes in accordance with prescribed schedules.

Inspects property, considering factors such as market value, location, and building or replacement costs, to determine appraisal value. Assesses and computes taxes according to prescribed tax tables and schedules. Appraises real and personal property, such as aircraft, marine craft, buildings, and land to determine fair value. Interprets property laws, formulates operational policies, and directs assessment office activities. Writes and submits appraisal and tax reports for public record.

GOE Number, Interest Area, and Work Group: 13.02.04; General Management and Support; Management Support: Investigation and Analysis. **Personality Type:** Conventional. Conventional occupations frequently involve following set procedures and routines. These occupations can include working with data and details more than with ideas. Usually there is a clear line of authority to follow. **Work Values:** Independence; Responsibility; Security; Autonomy; Compensation. **Skills:** Reading Comprehension; Information Gathering; Judgment and Decision Making; Writing; Product Inspection. **Abilities:** *Cognitive*—Number Facility; Written Expression; Mathematical Reasoning; Written Comprehension; Inductive Reasoning. *Psychomotor*—none met the criteria. *Physical*—Gross Body Equilibrium. *Sensory*—Speech Clarity; Far Vision. **General Work Activities:** *Information Input*—Estimating Needed Characteristics; Getting Information Needed to Do the Job; Identifying Objects, Actions, and Events. *Mental Process*—Processing Information; Judging Qualities of Things, Services, People; Analyzing Data or Information; Evaluating Information Against Standards. *Work Output*—Documenting and Recording Information; Performing General Physical Activities; Implementing Ideas and Programs. *Interacting with Others*—Interpreting Meaning of Information to Others; Communicating with Other Workers; Communicating with Persons Outside Organization; Providing Consultation and Advice to Others. **Physical Work Conditions:** Outdoors; Standing; Indoors; Walking or Running; Sitting. **Other Job Characteristics:** Importance of Being Exact or Accurate; Importance of Being Sure All Is Done; Consequence of Error.

Experience: Job Zone 4. A minimum of two to four years of work-related skill, knowledge, or experience is needed. **Job Preparation:** SVP 7.0 to less than 8.0—2 years to less than 10 years.

Knowledge: Mathematics; Economics and Accounting; Law, Government and Jurisprudence; English Language; Building and Construction. **Instructional Program:** 521501 Real Estate.

Related DOT Job: 188.167-010 Appraiser.

13-2021.02 Appraisers, Real Estate (Real Estate Appraisers)

Education: Bachelor's degree

Employed: 47,896

Openings: 6,383

Projected Growth: 11.2%

Earnings: $40,290

Appraise real property to determine its value for purchase, sales, investment, mortgage, or loan purposes.

Considers such factors as depreciation, value comparison of similar property, and income potential, when computing final estimation of property value. Photographs interiors and exteriors of property to assist in estimating property value, to substantiate finding, and to complete appraisal report. Inspects property for construction, condition, and functional design and takes property measurements. Interviews persons familiar with property and immediate surroundings, such as contractors, home owners, and other realtors to obtain pertinent information. Searches public records for transactions, such as sales, leases, and assessments. Prepares written report, utilizing data collected, and submits report to corroborate value established. Considers location and trends or impending changes that could influence future value of property.

GOE Number, Interest Area, and Work Group: 13.02.04; General Management and Support; Management Support: Investigation and Analysis. **Personality Type:** Enterprising. Enterprising occupations frequently involve starting up and carrying out projects. These occupations can involve leading people and making many decisions. They sometimes require risk taking and often deal with business. **Work Values:** Responsibility; Autonomy; Independence; Ability Utilization; Working Conditions. **Skills:** Information Gathering; Writing; Reading Comprehension; Mathematics; Active Listening; Speaking. **Abilities:** *Cognitive*—Oral Comprehension; Oral Expression; Written Expression; Deductive Reasoning; Written Comprehension. *Psychomotor*—Wrist-Finger Speed. *Physical*—none met the criteria. *Sensory*—Speech Clarity; Far Vision; Speech Recognition. **General Work Activities:** *Information Input*—Getting Information Needed to Do the Job; Identifying Objects, Actions, and Events; Inspecting Equipment, Structures, Materials. *Mental Process*—Judging Qualities of Things, Services, People; Updating and Using Job-Relevant Knowledge; Making Decisions and Solving Problems. *Work Output*—Documenting and Recording Information; Implementing Ideas and Programs; Performing General Physical Activities; Interacting with Computers. *Interacting with Others*—Communicating with Other Workers; Communicating with Persons Outside Organization; Establishing and Maintaining Relationships; Performing Administrative Activities; Providing Consultation and Advice to Others. **Physical Work Conditions:** Sitting; Standing; Outdoors; Indoors; Walking or Running. **Other Job Characteristics:** Importance of

Being Exact or Accurate; Importance of Being Sure All Is Done; Consequence of Error.

Experience: Job Zone 4. A minimum of two to four years of work-related skill, knowledge, or experience is needed. **Job Preparation:** SVP 7.0 to less than 8.0—2 years to less than 10 years. **Knowledge:** Building and Construction; Mathematics; Economics and Accounting; English Language; Clerical. **Instructional Program:** 521501 Real Estate.

Related DOT Job: 191.267-010 Appraiser, Real Estate.

13-2031.00 Budget Analysts (Budget Analysts)

Education: Bachelor's degree
Employed: 59,173
Openings: 9,617
Projected Growth: 13.7%
Earnings: $44,950

Examine budget estimates for completeness, accuracy, and conformance with procedures and regulations. Analyze budgeting and accounting reports for the purpose of maintaining expenditure controls.

Recommends approval or disapproval of requests for funds. Analyzes costs in relation to services performed during previous fiscal years to prepare comparative analyses of operating programs. Advises staff on cost analysis and fiscal allocations. Directs preparation of regular and special budget reports to interpret budget directives and to establish policies for carrying out directives. Directs compilation of data based on statistical studies and analyses of past and current years to prepare budgets. Testifies regarding proposed budgets before examining and fund-granting authorities to clarify reports and gain support for estimated budget needs. Correlates appropriations for specific programs with appropriations for divisional programs and includes items for emergency funds. Reviews operating budgets periodically to analyze trends affecting budget needs. Analyzes accounting records to determine financial resources required to implement program and submits recommendations for budget allocations. Consults with unit heads to ensure adjustments are made in accordance with program changes to facilitate long-term planning.

GOE Number, Interest Area, and Work Group: 13.02.04; General Management and Support; Management Support: Investigation and Analysis. **Personality Type:** Conventional. Conventional occupations frequently involve following set procedures and routines. These occupations can include working with data and details more than with ideas. Usually there is a clear line of authority to follow. **Work Values:** Working Conditions; Supervision, Human Relations; Advancement; Activity; Ability Utilization; Company Policies and Practices. **Skills:** Problem Identification; Management of Financial Resources; Judgment and Decision Making; Information Gathering; Identifying Downstream Consequences; Solution Appraisal; Systems Perception; Mathematics. **Abilities:** *Cognitive*—Number Facility; Mathematical Reasoning; Written Comprehension; Oral Comprehension; Written Expression; Oral Expression. *Psychomotor*—none met the criteria. *Physical*—none met the criteria. *Sensory*—Near Vision; Speech Clarity; Speech Recognition. **General Work Activities:** *Information In-*

put—Getting Information Needed to Do the Job; Identifying Objects, Actions, and Events; Estimating Needed Characteristics. *Mental Process*—Analyzing Data or Information; Making Decisions and Solving Problems; Processing Information. *Work Output*—Implementing Ideas and Programs; Documenting and Recording Information; Interacting with Computers. *Interacting with Others*—Monitoring and Controlling Resources; Communicating with Other Workers; Providing Consultation and Advice to Others. **Physical Work Conditions:** Indoors; Sitting; Using Hands on Objects, Tools, or Controls. **Other Job Characteristics:** Consequence of Error; Importance of Being Exact or Accurate; Importance of Being Sure All Is Done.

Experience: Job Zone 4. A minimum of two to four years of work-related skill, knowledge, or experience is needed. **Job Preparation:** SVP 7.0 to less than 8.0—2 years to less than 10 years. **Knowledge:** Mathematics; Economics and Accounting; Administration and Management; Computers and Electronics; English Language. **Instructional Programs:** 520301 Accounting; 520801 Finance, General; 520808 Public Finance.

Related DOT Jobs: 161.117-010 Budget Officer; 161.267-030 Budget Analyst.

13-2041.00 Credit Analysts (Credit Analysts)

Education: Bachelor's degree
Employed: 41,971
Openings: 7,260
Projected Growth: 19.9%
Earnings: $35,590

Analyze current credit data and financial statements of individuals or firms to determine the degree of risk involved in extending credit or lending money. Prepare reports with this credit information for use in decision-making.

Compares liquidity, profitability, and credit history with similar establishments of same industry and geographic location. Analyzes financial data, such as income growth, quality of management, and market share to determine profitability of loan. Evaluates customer records and recommends payment plan based on earnings, savings data, payment history, and purchase activity. Completes loan application, including credit analysis and summary of loan request, and submits to loan committee for approval. Confers with credit association and other business representatives to exchange credit information. Consults with customers to resolve complaints and verify financial and credit transactions and adjust accounts as needed. Analyzes credit data and financial statements to determine degree of risk involved in extending credit or lending money. Reviews individual or commercial customer files to identify and select delinquent accounts for collection. Generates financial ratios, using computer program, to evaluate customer's financial status.

GOE Number, Interest Area, and Work Group: 13.02.04; General Management and Support; Management Support: Investigation and Analysis. **Personality Type:** Conventional. Conventional occupations frequently involve following set procedures and routines. These occupations can include working with data and details more than with ideas. Usually there is a clear line of authority to follow. **Work Values:** Working Conditions; Supervision, Human Relations; Company Policies and Practices; Advancement; Activity. **Skills:** Reading Comprehension; Problem Identification; Information Gathering; Critical Thinking; Active Listening. **Abilities:** *Cognitive*—Mathematical Reasoning; Written Comprehension; Number Facility; Problem Sensitivity; Oral Expression; Deductive Reasoning. *Psychomotor*—none met the criteria. *Physical*—none met the criteria. *Sensory*—Near Vision; Speech Recognition; Speech Clarity. **General Work Activities:** *Information Input*—Getting Information Needed to Do the Job; Identifying Objects, Actions, and Events; Monitoring Processes, Materials, and Surroundings. *Mental Process*—Analyzing Data or Information; Processing Information; Evaluating Information Against Standards. *Work Output*—Interacting with Computers; Documenting and Recording Information; Implementing Ideas and Programs. *Interacting with Others*—Communicating with Persons Outside Organization; Communicating with Other Workers; Performing Administrative Activities; Establishing and Maintaining Relationships. **Physical Work Conditions:** Indoors; Sitting; Using Hands on Objects, Tools, or Controls. **Other Job Characteristics:** Consequence of Error; Frustrating Circumstances; Importance of Being Exact or Accurate; Importance of Being Sure All Is Done.

Experience: Job Zone 4. A minimum of two to four years of work-related skill, knowledge, or experience is needed. **Job Preparation:** SVP 7.0 to less than 8.0—2 years to less than 10 years. **Knowledge:** Economics and Accounting; Mathematics; Computers and Electronics; English Language; Law, Government and Jurisprudence; Customer and Personal Service; Geography. **Instructional Program:** 520801 Finance, General.

Related DOT Jobs: 160.267-022 Credit Analyst; 186.267-022 Loan Review Analyst; 241.267-022 Credit Analyst.

13-2051.00 Financial Analysts (Statisticians)

Education:	Master's degree
Employed:	16,529
Openings:	1,635
Projected Growth:	2.3%
Earnings:	$48,540

Conduct quantitative analyses of information affecting investment programs of public or private institutions.

Draws charts and graphs to illustrate reports, using computer. Interprets data concerning price, yield, stability, and future trends in investment risks and economic influences pertinent to investments. Calls brokers and purchases investments for company, according to company policy. Recommends investment timing and buy-and-sell orders to company or to staff of investment establishment. Analyzes financial information to forecast business, industry, and economic conditions, for use in making investment decisions. Gathers information such as industry, regulatory, and economic information, company financial statements, financial periodicals, and newspapers.

GOE Number, Interest Area, and Work Group: 13.02.04; General Management and Support; Management Support: Investigation and Analysis. **Personality Type:** Investigative. Investigative occupations frequently involve working with ideas and require

an extensive amount of thinking. These occupations can involve searching for facts and figuring out problems mentally. **Work Values:** Autonomy; Compensation; Ability Utilization; Working Conditions; Company Policies and Practices. **Skills:** Judgment and Decision Making; Information Gathering; Reading Comprehension; Critical Thinking; Active Learning; Identifying Downstream Consequences. **Abilities:** *Cognitive*—Number Facility; Written Comprehension; Mathematical Reasoning; Deductive Reasoning; Written Expression. *Psychomotor*—none met the criteria. *Physical*—Trunk Strength. *Sensory*—Near Vision; Speech Clarity; Speech Recognition. **General Work Activities:** *Information Input*—Getting Information Needed to Do the Job; Identifying Objects, Actions, and Events; Monitoring Processes, Materials, and Surroundings. *Mental Process*—Analyzing Data or Information; Updating and Using Job-Relevant Knowledge; Making Decisions and Solving Problems; Judging Qualities of Things, Services, Other People's Work. *Work Output*—Interacting with Computers; Documenting and Recording Information; Implementing Ideas and Programs. *Interacting with Others*—Providing Consultation and Advice to Others; Interpreting Meaning of Information to Others; Communicating with Other Workers; Communicating with Persons Outside Organization. **Physical Work Conditions:** Indoors; Sitting; Using Hands on Objects, Tools, or Controls; Standing. **Other Job Characteristics:** Consequence of Error; Importance of Being Exact or Accurate; Degree of Automation.

Experience: Job Zone 5. Extensive skill, knowledge, and experience are needed. Very advanced communication and organizational skills are required. **Job Preparation:** SVP 8.0 and above—4 years to more than 10 years. **Knowledge:** Economics and Accounting; Mathematics; Computers and Electronics; English Language; Law, Government and Jurisprudence. **Instructional Programs:** 260615 Biostatistics; 270101 Mathematics; 270301 Applied Mathematics, General; 270501 Mathematical Statistics; 521302 Business Statistics.

Related DOT Job: 160.267-026 Investment Analyst.

13-2052.00 Personal Financial Advisors (All Other Financial Specialists)

Education:	No data available.
Employed:	264,640
Openings:	No data available.
Projected Growth:	No data available.
Earnings:	$39,490

Advise clients on financial plans, utilizing knowledge of tax and investment strategies, securities, insurance, pension plans, and real estate. Assess clients' assets, liabilities, cash flow, insurance coverage, tax status, and financial objectives, to establish investment strategies.

Counsels client on financial problems, such as excessive spending and borrowing of funds. Establishes payment priorities to plan payoff method and estimate time for debt liquidation. Calculates amount of debt and funds available. Determines amount of aid to be granted, considering such factors as funds available, extent of demand, and needs of students. Contacts creditors to arrange for payment adjustments so that payments are feasible for client and agreeable to creditors. Interviews students to obtain information and compares data on students' applications with eligibility requirements to determine eligibility for assistance program. Opens account for client and disburses funds from account to creditors as agent for client. Prepares required records and reports. Authorizes release of funds to students. Interviews client with debt problems to determine available monthly income after living expenses to meet credit obligations. Assists in selection of candidates for specific financial awards or aid. Explains to individuals and groups financial assistance available to college and university students, such as loans, grants, and scholarships.

GOE Number, Interest Area, and Work Group: 12.03.01; Education and Social Service; Educational Services: Counseling and Evaluation. **Personality Type:** Social. Social occupations frequently involve working with, communicating with, and teaching people. These occupations often involve helping or providing service to others. **Work Values:** Working Conditions; Social Service; Achievement; Security; Company Policies and Practices; Coworkers; Autonomy; Responsibility. **Skills:** Speaking; Active Listening; Reading Comprehension; Problem Identification; Mathematics; Critical Thinking; Judgment and Decision Making; Service Orientation; Information Gathering. **Abilities:** *Cognitive*—Number Facility; Problem Sensitivity; Oral Comprehension; Oral Expression; Mathematical Reasoning. *Psychomotor*—none met the criteria. *Physical*—none met the criteria. *Sensory*—Speech Clarity; Speech Recognition. **General Work Activities:** *Information Input*—Getting Information Needed to Do the Job; Identifying Objects, Actions, and Events; Estimating Needed Characteristics. *Mental Process*—Processing Information; Analyzing Data or Information; Developing Objectives and Strategies; Evaluating Information Against Standards; Making Decisions and Solving Problems. *Work Output*—Documenting and Recording Information; Implementing Ideas and Programs; Interacting with Computers. *Interacting with Others*—Communicating with Persons Outside Organization; Providing Consultation and Advice to Others; Interpreting Meaning of Information to Others; Establishing and Maintaining Relationships; Assisting and Caring for Others. **Physical Work Conditions:** Indoors; Sitting; Standing. **Other Job Characteristics:** Consequence of Error; Importance of Being Exact or Accurate; Importance of Being Sure All Is Done.

Experience: Job Zone 3. Previous work-related skill, knowledge, or experience is required. **Job Preparation:** SVP 6.0 to less than 7.0—More than 1 year and less than 4 years. **Knowledge:** Economics and Accounting; Mathematics; Administration and Management; Customer and Personal Service; English Language. **Instructional Programs:** 520801 Finance, General; 520804 Financial Planning; 520806 International Finance.

Related DOT Jobs: 160.207-010 Credit Counselor; 169.267-018 Financial-Aid Counselor.

13-2053.00 Insurance Underwriters (Insurance Underwriters)

Education:	Bachelor's degree
Employed:	96,949
Openings:	3,771
Projected Growth:	2.7%
Earnings:	$38,710

Review individual applications for insurance, to evaluate degree of risk involved and determine acceptance of applications.

Declines excessive risks. Evaluates possibility of losses due to catastrophe or excessive insurance. Decreases value of policy when risk is substandard and specifies applicable endorsements or applies rating to ensure safe profitable distribution of risks, using reference materials. Authorizes reinsurance of policy when risk is high. Writes to field representatives, medical personnel, and others to obtain further information, quote rates, or explain company underwriting policies. Examines documents to determine degree of risk from such factors as applicant financial standing and value and condition of property. Reviews company records to determine amount of insurance in force on single risk or group of closely related risks.

GOE Number, Interest Area, and Work Group: 13.02.04; General Management and Support; Management Support: Investigation and Analysis. **Personality Type:** Conventional. Conventional occupations frequently involve following set procedures and routines. These occupations can include working with data and details more than with ideas. Usually there is a clear line of authority to follow. **Work Values:** Company Policies and Practices; Supervision, Human Relations; Responsibility; Working Conditions; Security; Advancement. **Skills:** Judgment and Decision Making; Information Gathering; Mathematics; Reading Comprehension; Critical Thinking. **Abilities:** *Cognitive*—Written Comprehension; Problem Sensitivity; Written Expression; Oral Expression; Oral Comprehension. *Psychomotor*—none met the criteria. *Physical*—none met the criteria. *Sensory*—Near Vision. **General Work Activities:** *Information Input*—Getting Information Needed to Do the Job; Identifying Objects, Actions, and Events; Estimating Needed Characteristics. *Mental Process*—Judging Qualities of Things, Services, People; Making Decisions and Solving Problems; Evaluating Information Against Standards; Processing Information. *Work Output*—Documenting and Recording Information; Implementing Ideas and Programs; Interacting with Computers. *Interacting with Others*—Communicating with Other Workers; Communicating with Persons Outside Organization; Performing Administrative Activities. **Physical Work Conditions:** Indoors; Sitting; Standing; Making Repetitive Motions; Using Hands on Objects, Tools, or Controls. **Other Job Characteristics:** Consequence of Error; Importance of Being Sure All Is Done; Importance of Being Exact or Accurate.

Experience: Job Zone 4. A minimum of two to four years of work-related skill, knowledge, or experience is needed. **Job Preparation:** SVP 7.0 to less than 8.0—2 years to less than 10 years. **Knowledge:** Mathematics; English Language; Economics and Accounting; Clerical; Administration and Management. **Instructional Programs:** 520801 Finance, General; 520805 Insurance and Risk Management.

Related DOT Job: 169.267-046 Underwriter.

13-2061.00 Financial Examiners (Inspectors and Compliance Officers)

Education: Work experience in a related occupation
Employed: 176,175
Openings: 19,910
Projected Growth: 10.5%
Earnings: $36,820

Enforce or ensure compliance with laws and regulations governing financial and securities institutions and governing financial and real estate transactions. Examine, verify correctness of, or establish authenticity of records.

Recommends action to ensure compliance with laws and regulations or to protect solvency of institution. Investigates activities of institutions to enforce laws and regulations and to ensure legality of transactions and operations or financial solvency. Determines if application action is in public interest and in accordance with regulations, and recommends acceptance or rejection of application. Establishes guidelines for and directs implementation of procedures and policies to comply with new and revised regulations. Reviews applications for merger, acquisition, establishment of new institution, acceptance in Federal Reserve System, or registration of securities sales. Reviews, analyzes, and interprets new, proposed, or revised laws, regulations, policies, and procedures. Directs workers engaged in designing, writing, and publishing guidelines, manuals, bulletins, and reports. Conducts or arranges for educational classes and training programs. Confers with officials of real estate, securities, or financial institution industries to exchange views and discuss issues or pending cases. Schedules audits and examines records and reports to determine regulatory compliance.

GOE Number, Interest Area, and Work Group: 04.04.02; Law, Law Enforcement, and Public Safety; Public Safety: Regulations Enforcement. **Personality Type:** Enterprising. Enterprising occupations frequently involve starting up and carrying out projects. These occupations can involve leading people and making many decisions. They sometimes require risk taking and often deal with business. **Work Values:** Working Conditions; Activity; Security; Compensation; Advancement; Autonomy; Social Status; Responsibility. **Skills:** Reading Comprehension; Problem Identification; Writing; Judgment and Decision Making; Information Gathering. **Abilities:** *Cognitive*—Written Comprehension; Oral Expression; Problem Sensitivity; Number Facility; Deductive Reasoning; Oral Comprehension. *Psychomotor*—none met the criteria. *Physical*—Trunk Strength. *Sensory*—Near Vision; Speech Clarity; Speech Recognition. **General Work Activities:** *Information Input*—Getting Information Needed to Do the Job; Identifying Objects, Actions, and Events; Monitoring Processes, Materials, and Surroundings. *Mental Process*—Evaluating Information Against Standards; Judging Qualities of Things, Services, People; Making Decisions and Solving Problems. *Work Output*—Implementing Ideas and Programs; Documenting and Recording Information; Interacting with Computers. *Interacting with Others*—Communicating with Persons Outside Organization; Communicating with Other Workers; Providing Consultation and Advice to Others;

Interpreting Meaning of Information to Others. **Physical Work Conditions:** Indoors; Sitting; Using Hands on Objects, Tools, or Controls. **Other Job Characteristics:** Consequence of Error; Importance of Being Sure All Is Done; Importance of Being Exact or Accurate.

Experience: Job Zone 4. A minimum of two to four years of work-related skill, knowledge, or experience is needed. **Job Preparation:** SVP 7.0 to less than 8.0—2 years to less than 10 years. **Knowledge:** Economics and Accounting; Mathematics; English Language; Education and Training; Law, Government and Jurisprudence. **Instructional Programs:** 030203 Natural Resources Law Enforcement and Protective Services; 150701 Occupational Safety and Health Technology/Technician; 521601 Taxation.

Related DOT Jobs: 160.167-046 Chief Bank Examiner; 186.117-090 Compliance Officer; 188.167-038 Director, Securities and Real Estate.

13-2071.00 Loan Counselors (Loan Counselors and Officers)

Education: Bachelor's degree
Employed: 227,410
Openings: 39,836
Projected Growth: 21.2%
Earnings: $35,340

Provide guidance to prospective loan applicants who have problems qualifying for traditional loans, including determining the best type of loan and explaining loan requirements or restrictions.

Confers with underwriters to aid in resolving mortgage application problems. Interviews applicant and requests specified information for loan application. Computes payment schedule. Ensures loan agreements are complete and accurate according to policy. Approves loan within specified limits. Refers loan to loan committee for approval. Arranges for maintenance and liquidation of delinquent property. Negotiates payment arrangements with customers for delinquent loan balance. Supervises loan personnel. Submits application to credit analyst for verification and recommendation. Petitions court to transfer title and deeds of collateral to bank. Analyzes applicant's financial status, credit, and property evaluation to determine feasibility of granting loan. Contacts applicant or creditors to resolve questions regarding application information. Analyzes potential loan markets to develop prospects for loans.

GOE Number, Interest Area, and Work Group: 13.02.04; General Management and Support; Management Support: Investigation and Analysis. **Personality Type:** Enterprising. Enterprising occupations frequently involve starting up and carrying out projects. These occupations can involve leading people and making many decisions. They sometimes require risk taking and often deal with business. **Work Values:** Working Conditions; Advancement; Coworkers; Responsibility; Company Policies and Practices. **Skills:** Reading Comprehension; Information Gathering; Speaking; Active Listening; Problem Identification; Mathematics; Writing; Judgment and Decision Making; Critical Thinking.

Abilities: *Cognitive*—Written Comprehension; Number Facility; Oral Comprehension; Oral Expression; Written Expression. *Psychomotor*—Wrist-Finger Speed; Response Orientation. *Physical*—none met the criteria. *Sensory*—Near Vision; Speech Clarity; Speech Recognition. **General Work Activities:** *Information Input*—Getting Information Needed to Do the Job; Identifying Objects, Actions, and Events; Monitoring Processes, Materials, and Surroundings. *Mental Process*—Evaluating Information Against Standards; Analyzing Data or Information; Processing Information. *Work Output*—Documenting and Recording Information; Interacting with Computers; Implementing Ideas and Programs. *Interacting with Others*—Performing Administrative Activities; Communicating with Other Workers; Communicating with Persons Outside Organization; Establishing and Maintaining Relationships. **Physical Work Conditions:** Indoors; Sitting; Walking or Running; Standing. **Other Job Characteristics:** Consequence of Error; Importance of Being Exact or Accurate; Importance of Being Sure All Is Done.

Experience: Job Zone 4. A minimum of two to four years of work-related skill, knowledge, or experience is needed. **Job Preparation:** SVP 7.0 to less than 8.0—2 years to less than 10 years. **Knowledge:** Economics and Accounting; Mathematics; English Language; Clerical; Law, Government and Jurisprudence; Customer and Personal Service. **Instructional Programs:** 080401 Financial Services Marketing Operations; 520801 Finance, General.

Related DOT Jobs: No data available.

13-2072.00 Loan Officers (Loan Counselors and Officers)

Education: Bachelor's degree
Employed: 227,410
Openings: 39,836
Projected Growth: 21.2%
Earnings: $35,340

Evaluate, authorize, or recommend approval of commercial, real estate, or credit loans. Advise borrowers on financial status and methods of payments. Includes mortgage loan officers and agents, collection analysts, loan servicing officers, and loan underwriters.

Computes payment schedule. Refers loan to loan committee for approval. Interviews applicant and requests specified information for loan application. Contacts applicant or creditors to resolve questions regarding application information. Petitions court to transfer title and deeds of collateral to bank. Negotiates payment arrangements with customers for delinquent loan balance. Analyzes potential loan markets to develop prospects for loans. Arranges for maintenance and liquidation of delinquent property. Confers with underwriters to aid in resolving mortgage application problems. Submits application to credit analyst for verification and recommendation. Ensures loan agreements are complete and accurate according to policy. Analyzes applicant's financial status, credit, and property evaluation to determine feasibility of granting loan. Supervises loan personnel. Approves loan within specified limits.

GOE Number, Interest Area, and Work Group: 13.02.04; General Management and Support; Management Support: Investigation and Analysis. **Personality Type:** Enterprising. Enterprising occupations frequently involve starting up and carrying out projects. These occupations can involve leading people and making many decisions. They sometimes require risk taking and often deal with business. **Work Values:** Working Conditions; Advancement; Coworkers; Company Policies and Practices; Responsibility. **Skills:** Reading Comprehension; Speaking; Information Gathering; Active Listening; Judgment and Decision Making; Problem Identification; Writing; Mathematics. **Abilities:** *Cognitive*—Written Comprehension; Number Facility; Oral Comprehension; Oral Expression; Written Expression. *Psychomotor*—Wrist-Finger Speed; Response Orientation. *Physical*—none met the criteria. *Sensory*—Near Vision; Speech Clarity; Speech Recognition. **General Work Activities:** *Information Input*—Getting Information Needed to Do the Job; Identifying Objects, Actions, and Events; Monitoring Processes, Materials, and Surroundings. *Mental Process*—Evaluating Information Against Standards; Analyzing Data or Information; Processing Information. *Work Output*—Documenting and Recording Information; Interacting with Computers; Implementing Ideas and Programs. *Interacting with Others*—Performing Administrative Activities; Communicating with Other Workers; Communicating with Persons Outside Organization; Establishing and Maintaining Relationships. **Physical Work Conditions:** Indoors; Sitting; Walking or Running; Standing. **Other Job Characteristics:** Importance of Being Sure All Is Done; Importance of Being Exact or Accurate; Consequence of Error.

Experience: Job Zone 4. A minimum of two to four years of work-related skill, knowledge, or experience is needed. **Job Preparation:** SVP 7.0 to less than 8.0—2 years to less than 10 years. **Knowledge:** Economics and Accounting; Mathematics; English Language; Clerical; Customer and Personal Service; Law, Government and Jurisprudence. **Instructional Programs:** 080401 Financial Services Marketing Operations; 520801 Finance, General.

Related DOT Jobs: 186.167-078 Commercial Loan Collection Officer; 186.267-018 Loan Officer; 186.267-026 Underwriter, Mortgage Loan.

13-2081.00 Tax Examiners, Collectors, and Revenue Agents (Tax Examiners, Collectors, and Revenue Agents)

Education: Bachelor's degree
Employed: 62,246
Openings: 5,057
Projected Growth: 5.4%
Earnings: $39,540

Determine tax liability of or collect taxes from individuals or business firms according to prescribed laws and regulations.

Serves as member of regional appeals board to reexamine unresolved issues in terms of relevant laws and regulations. Investigates legal instruments, other documents, financial transactions, operation methods, and industry practices to assess inclusiveness of accounting records and tax returns. Analyzes accounting books and records to determine appropriateness of accounting methods employed and compliance with statutory provisions. Secures taxpayer's agreement to discharge tax assessment or submits contested determination to other administrative or judicial conferees for appeals hearings. Selects appropriate remedy, such as partial-payment agreement, offer of compromise, or seizure and sale of property. Examines selected tax returns to determine nature and extent of audits to be performed. Conducts independent field audits and investigations of federal income tax returns to verify or amend tax liabilities. Directs service of legal documents, such as subpoenas, warrants, notices of assessment and garnishments. Participates in informal appeals hearings on contested cases from other agents. Recommends criminal prosecutions and civil penalties. Examines and analyzes tax assets and liabilities to determine resolution of delinquent tax problems. Confers with taxpayer or representative to explain issues involved and applicability of pertinent tax laws and regulations.

GOE Number, Interest Area, and Work Group: 13.02.03; General Management and Support; Management Support: Accounting and Auditing. **Personality Type:** Conventional. Conventional occupations frequently involve following set procedures and routines. These occupations can include working with data and details more than with ideas. Usually there is a clear line of authority to follow. **Work Values:** Working Conditions; Security; Company Policies and Practices; Supervision, Human Relations; Responsibility; Autonomy. **Skills:** Problem Identification; Reading Comprehension; Information Gathering; Mathematics; Judgment and Decision Making; Critical Thinking. **Abilities:** *Cognitive*—Number Facility; Written Comprehension; Mathematical Reasoning; Oral Expression; Oral Comprehension. *Psychomotor*—none met the criteria. *Physical*—none met the criteria. *Sensory*—Near Vision; Speech Recognition; Speech Clarity. **General Work Activities:** *Information Input*—Getting Information Needed to Do the Job; Identifying Objects, Actions, and Events; Estimating Needed Characteristics. *Mental Process*—Analyzing Data or Information; Evaluating Information Against Standards; Making Decisions and Solving Problems. *Work Output*—Implementing Ideas and Programs; Documenting and Recording Information; Interacting with Computers. *Interacting with Others*—Communicating with Persons Outside Organization; Interpreting Meaning of Information to Others; Communicating with Other Workers; Providing Consultation and Advice to Others. **Physical Work Conditions:** Indoors; Sitting; Standing; Using Hands on Objects, Tools, or Controls. **Other Job Characteristics:** Consequence of Error; Importance of Being Exact or Accurate; Importance of Being Sure All Is Done.

Experience: Job Zone 4. A minimum of two to four years of work-related skill, knowledge, or experience is needed. **Job Preparation:** SVP 7.0 to less than 8.0—2 years to less than 10 years. **Knowledge:** Economics and Accounting; Mathematics; Law, Government and Jurisprudence; English Language; Administration and Management. **Instructional Program:** 520301 Accounting.

Related DOT Jobs: 160.167-050 Revenue Agent; 188.167-074 Revenue Officer.

13-2082.00 Tax Preparers (Tax Preparers)

Education: Moderate-term O-T-J training
Employed: 79,378
Openings: 13,654
Projected Growth: 19.3%
Earnings: $27,960

Prepare tax returns for individuals or small businesses, without having the background or responsibilities of an accredited or certified public accountant.

Verifies totals on forms prepared by others to detect errors in arithmetic or procedure, as needed. Computes taxes owed, using adding machine or personal computer, and completes entries on forms, following tax form instructions and tax tables. Calculates form preparation fee according to complexity of return and amount of time required to prepare forms. Reviews financial records, such as income statements and documentation of expenditures to determine forms needed to prepare return. Interviews client to obtain additional information on taxable income and deductible expenses and allowances. Consults tax law handbook or bulletins to determine procedure for preparation of atypical returns.

GOE Number, Interest Area, and Work Group: 09.03.01; Business Detail; Bookkeeping, Auditing, and Accounting. **Personality Type:** Conventional. Conventional occupations frequently involve following set procedures and routines. These occupations can include working with data and details more than with ideas. Usually there is a clear line of authority to follow. **Work Values:** Working Conditions; Independence; Company Policies and Practices; Supervision, Human Relations; Activity. **Skills:** Reading Comprehension; Mathematics; Active Listening; Speaking; Information Gathering. **Abilities:** *Cognitive*—Number Facility; Mathematical Reasoning; Oral Comprehension; Deductive Reasoning; Written Comprehension; Oral Expression. *Psychomotor*—none met the criteria. *Physical*—none met the criteria. *Sensory*—Near Vision; Speech Clarity; Speech Recognition. **General Work Activities:** *Information Input*—Getting Information Needed to Do the Job; Identifying Objects, Actions, and Events; Estimating Needed Characteristics. *Mental Process*—Processing Information; Updating and Using Job-Relevant Knowledge; Evaluating Information Against Standards. *Work Output*—Documenting and Recording Information; Handling and Moving Objects; Implementing Ideas and Programs. *Interacting with Others*—Performing Administrative Activities; Communicating with Persons Outside Organization; Performing for or Working with the Public. **Physical Work Conditions:** Sitting; Indoors; Making Repetitive Motions. **Other Job Characteristics:** Importance of Being Exact or Accurate; Importance of Being Sure All Is Done; Consequence of Error.

Experience: Job Zone 2. Some previous work-related skill, knowledge, or experience may be helpful, but usually is not needed. **Job Preparation:** SVP 4.00 to 5.99—6 months to less than 2 years. **Knowledge:** Mathematics; Economics and Accounting; Law, Government and Jurisprudence; Clerical; Computers and Electronics; English Language. **Instructional Programs:** 520302 Accounting Technician; 521601 Taxation.

Related DOT Job: 219.362-070 Tax Preparer.

15-0000

Computer and Mathematical Occupations

15-1000 Computer Specialists

15-1011.00 Computer and Information Scientists, Research (Computer Scientists)

Education: Bachelor's degree
Employed: 97,493
Openings: 27,942
Projected Growth: 117.5%
Earnings: $46,670

Conduct research into fundamental computer and information science as theorists, designers, or inventors. Solve or develop solutions to problems in the field of computer hardware and software.

GOE Number, Interest Area, and Work Group: 02.06.01; Science, Math, and Engineering; Mathematics and Computers: Data Processing. **Instructional Programs:** 110101 Computer and Information Sciences, General; 110201 Computer Programming; 110301 Data Processing Technology/Technician; 110401 Information Sciences and Systems; 110501 Computer Systems Analysis; 110701 Computer Science; 119999 Computer and Information Sciences, Other; 521202 Business Computer Programming/Programmer; 521203 Business Systems Analysis and Design; 521204 Business Systems Networking and Telecommunications; 521299 Business Information and Data Processing Services, Other. **Note:** The Department of Labor has not collected some data for this job, so it has fewer details than the other descriptions.

15-1021.00 Computer Programmers (Computer Programmers)

Education: Bachelor's degree
Employed: 647,783
Openings: 74,773
Projected Growth: 29.5%
Earnings: No data available.

Convert project specifications and convert statements of problems and procedures into detailed, logical flow charts for coding into computer language. Develop and write computer programs to store, locate, and retrieve specific documents, data, and information. Program Web sites.

Collaborates with computer manufacturers and other users to develop new programming methods. Converts detailed logical flow chart to language processible by computer. Develops programs from workflow charts or diagrams, considering computer storage capacity, speed, and intended use of output data. Consults with managerial and engineering and technical personnel to clarify program intent, identify problems, and suggest changes. Prepares records and reports. Assists computer operators or system analysts to resolve problems in running computer program. Assigns, coordinates, and reviews work and activities of programming personnel. Trains subordinates in programming and program coding. Compiles and writes documentation of program

development and subsequent revisions. Revises or directs revision of existing programs to increase operating efficiency or adapt to new requirements. Prepares or receives detailed workflow chart and diagram to illustrate sequence of steps to describe input, output, and logical operation. Resolves symbolic formulations, prepares flow charts and block diagrams, and encodes resultant equations for processing. Analyzes, reviews, and rewrites programs, using workflow chart and diagram, applying knowledge of computer capabilities, subject matter, and symbolic logic. Writes instructions to guide operating personnel during production runs.

GOE Number, Interest Area, and Work Group: 02.06.01; Science, Math, and Engineering; Mathematics and Computers: Data Processing. **Personality Type:** Investigative. Investigative occupations frequently involve working with ideas and require an extensive amount of thinking. These occupations can involve searching for facts and figuring out problems mentally. **Work Values:** Creativity; Ability Utilization; Security; Autonomy; Achievement; Company Policies and Practices; Compensation. **Skills:** Programming; Problem Identification; Information Organization; Troubleshooting; Reading Comprehension. **Abilities:** *Cognitive*—Oral Expression; Oral Comprehension; Written Comprehension; Written Expression; Deductive Reasoning; Mathematical Reasoning. *Psychomotor*—Wrist-Finger Speed; Finger Dexterity. *Physical*—Trunk Strength. *Sensory*—Near Vision; Speech Clarity; Visual Color Discrimination. **General Work Activities:** *Information Input*—Getting Information Needed to Do the Job; Identifying Objects, Actions, and Events; Monitoring Processes, Materials, and Surroundings. *Mental Process*—Analyzing Data or Information; Thinking Creatively; Updating and Using Job-Relevant Knowledge; Processing Information. *Work Output*—Interacting with Computers; Implementing Ideas and Programs; Documenting and Recording Information. *Interacting with Others*—Providing Consultation and Advice to Others; Communicating with Other Workers; Teaching Others; Guiding, Directing and Motivating Subordinates. **Physical Work Conditions:** Indoors; Sitting; Standing; Making Repetitive Motions. **Other Job Characteristics:** Degree of Automation; Importance of Being Sure All Is Done; Consequence of Error.

Experience: Job Zone 4. A minimum of two to four years of work-related skill, knowledge, or experience is needed. **Job Preparation:** SVP 7.0 to less than 8.0—2 years to less than 10 years. **Knowledge:** Computers and Electronics; Mathematics; English Language; Education and Training; Clerical. **Instructional Programs:** 110201 Computer Programming; 110201 Computer Programming; 521201 Management Information Systems and Business Data Processing, General; 521201 Management Information Systems and Business Data Processing, General; 521202 Business Computer Programming/Programmer.

Related DOT Jobs: 030.162-010 Computer Programmer; 030.162-018 Programmer, Engineering and Scientific; 030.167-010 Chief, Computer Programmer.

15-1031.00 Computer Software Engineers, Applications (Computer Engineers)

Education: Bachelor's degree
Employed: 299,308
Openings: 81,337
Projected Growth: 107.9%
Earnings: $61,910

Develop, create, and modify general computer applications software or specialized utility programs. Analyze user needs and develop software solutions. Design software or customize software for client use with the aim of optimizing operational efficiency. Analyze and design databases within an application area, working individually or coordinating database development as part of a team.

Analyzes information to determine, recommend, and plan layout for type of computers and peripheral equipment modifications to existing systems. Monitors functioning of equipment to ensure system operates in conformance with specifications. Enters data into computer terminal to store, retrieve, and manipulate data for analysis of system capabilities and requirements. Recommends purchase of equipment to control dust, temperature, and humidity in area of system installation. Specifies power supply requirements and configuration. Trains users to use new or modified equipment. Coordinates installation of software system. Develops and directs software system testing procedures, programming, and documentation. Consults with engineering staff to evaluate interface between hardware and software and operational and performance requirements of overall system. Evaluates factors such as reporting formats required, cost constraints, and need for security restrictions to determine hardware configuration. Formulates and designs software system, using scientific analysis and mathematical models to predict and measure outcome and consequences of design. Analyzes software requirements to determine feasibility of design within time and cost constraints. Consults with customer concerning maintenance of software system. Confers with data processing and project managers to obtain information on limitations and capabilities for data processing projects.

GOE Number, Interest Area, and Work Group: 02.07.01; Science, Math, and Engineering; Engineering: Research and Systems Design. **Personality Type:** Investigative. Investigative occupations frequently involve working with ideas and require an extensive amount of thinking. These occupations can involve searching for facts and figuring out problems mentally. **Work Values:** Ability Utilization; Working Conditions; Creativity; Responsibility; Social Status; Achievement; Autonomy; Activity. **Skills:** Troubleshooting; Programming; Active Learning; Testing; Mathematics. **Abilities:** *Cognitive*—Written Comprehension; Oral Comprehension; Inductive Reasoning; Oral Expression; Written Expression; Mathematical Reasoning. *Psychomotor*—Wrist-Finger Speed; Response Orientation. *Physical*—Gross Body Coordination. *Sensory*—Near Vision; Speech Clarity; Speech Recognition. **General Work Activities:** *Information Input*—Getting Information Needed to Do the Job; Identifying Objects, Actions, and Events; Monitoring Processes, Materials, and Surroundings; Estimating Needed Characteristics. *Mental Process*—Updating and Using Job-Relevant Knowledge; Thinking Creatively; Analyzing Data or Information. *Work Output*—Interacting with Computers; Drafting and Specifying Technical Devices; Implementing Ideas and Programs; Documenting and Recording Information. *Interacting with Others*—Providing Consultation and Advice to Others; Communicating with Other Workers; Communicating with Persons Outside Organization. **Physical Work Conditions:** Indoors; Sitting; Using Hands on Objects, Tools, or Controls. **Other Job Characteristics:** Degree of Automation; Importance of Being Exact or Accurate; Importance of Being Sure All Is Done.

Experience: Job Zone 4. A minimum of two to four years of work-related skill, knowledge, or experience is needed. **Job Preparation:** SVP 7.0 to less than 8.0—2 years to less than 10 years. **Knowledge:** Computers and Electronics; Engineering and Technology; Mathematics; English Language; Administration and Management; Design; Education and Training. **Instructional Programs:** 110401 Information Sciences and Systems; 140901 Computer Engineering.

Related DOT Job: 030.062-010 Software Engineer.

15-1032.00 Computer Software Engineers, Systems Software (Computer Engineers)

Education: Bachelor's degree

Employed: 299,308

Openings: 81,337

Projected Growth: 107.9%

Earnings: $61,910

Research, design, develop, and test operating, systems-level software, compilers, and network distribution software for medical, industrial, military, communications, aerospace, business, scientific, and general computing applications. Set operational specifications; formulate and analyze software requirements. Apply principles and techniques of computer science, engineering, and mathematical analysis.

Specifies power supply requirements and configuration. Confers with data processing and project managers to obtain information on limitations and capabilities for data processing projects. Formulates and designs software system, using scientific analysis and mathematical models to predict and measure outcome and consequences of design. Develops and directs software system testing procedures, programming, and documentation. Coordinates installation of software system. Monitors functioning of equipment to ensure system operates in conformance with specifications. Consults with customer concerning maintenance of software system. Recommends purchase of equipment to control dust, temperature, and humidity in area of system installation. Trains users to use new or modified equipment. Consults with engineering staff to evaluate interface between hardware and software and operational and performance requirements of overall system. Evaluates factors such as reporting formats required, cost constraints, and need for security restrictions to determine hardware configuration. Analyzes software requirements to determine feasibility of design within time and cost constraints. Enters data into computer terminal to store, retrieve, and manipulate data for analysis of system capabilities and requirements. Analyzes information to determine, recommend, and plan layout for type of computers and peripheral equipment modifications to existing systems.

GOE Number, Interest Area, and Work Group: 02.07.01; Science, Math, and Engineering; Engineering: Research and Systems Design. **Personality Type:** Investigative. Investigative occupations frequently involve working with ideas and require an extensive amount of thinking. These occupations can involve searching for facts and figuring out problems mentally. **Work Values:** Ability Utilization; Working Conditions; Creativity; Responsibility;

Achievement; Autonomy; Activity; Social Status. **Skills:** Programming; Troubleshooting; Active Learning; Testing; Mathematics. **Abilities:** *Cognitive*—Written Comprehension; Oral Comprehension; Inductive Reasoning; Mathematical Reasoning; Oral Expression; Written Expression. *Psychomotor*—Wrist-Finger Speed; Response Orientation. *Physical*—Gross Body Coordination. *Sensory*—Near Vision; Speech Clarity; Speech Recognition. **General Work Activities:** *Information Input*—Identifying Objects, Actions, and Events; Getting Information Needed to Do the Job; Monitoring Processes, Materials, and Surroundings; Estimating Needed Characteristics. *Mental Process*—Updating and Using Job-Relevant Knowledge; Thinking Creatively; Analyzing Data or Information. *Work Output*—Interacting with Computers; Drafting and Specifying Technical Devices; Implementing Ideas and Programs; Documenting and Recording Information. *Interacting with Others*—Providing Consultation and Advice to Others; Communicating with Persons Outside Organization; Communicating with Other Workers. **Physical Work Conditions:** Indoors; Sitting; Using Hands on Objects, Tools, or Controls. **Other Job Characteristics:** Degree of Automation; Importance of Being Exact or Accurate; Importance of Being Sure All Is Done.

Experience: Job Zone 4. A minimum of two to four years of work-related skill, knowledge, or experience is needed. **Job Preparation:** SVP 7.0 to less than 8.0—2 years to less than 10 years. **Knowledge:** Computers and Electronics; Mathematics; Engineering and Technology; English Language; Administration and Management; Education and Training; Design. **Instructional Programs:** 110401 Information Sciences and Systems; 140901 Computer Engineering.

Related DOT Job: 030.062-010 Software Engineer.

15-1041.00 Computer Support Specialists (Computer Support Specialists)

Education: Associate degree

Employed: 429,316

Openings: 113,041

Projected Growth: 102.3%

Earnings: $37,120

Provide technical assistance to computer-system users. Answer questions or resolve computer problems for clients in person, via telephone, or from remote location. Provide assistance concerning the use of computer hardware and software, including printing, installation, word processing, electronic mail, and operating systems.

Develops training materials and procedures, and conducts training programs. Confers with staff, users, and management to determine requirements for new systems or modifications. Refers major hardware or software problems or defective products to vendors or technicians for service. Maintains record of daily data communication transactions, problems and remedial action taken, and installation activities. Conducts office automation feasibility studies, including workflow analysis, space design, and cost comparison analysis. Reads trade magazines and technical manuals, and attends conferences and seminars to maintain knowledge of hardware and software. Inspects equipment and reads order sheets to prepare for delivery to users. Tests and monitors software, hardware, and peripheral equipment to evaluate use, effectiveness, and adequacy of product for user. Prepares evaluations of software and hardware, and submits recommendations to management for review. Enters commands and observes system functioning to verify correct operations and detect errors. Installs and performs minor repairs to hardware, software, and peripheral equipment, following design or installation specifications. Reads technical manuals, confers with users, and conducts computer diagnostics to determine nature of problems and provide technical assistance. Supervises and coordinates workers engaged in problem solving, monitoring, and installing data communication equipment and software.

GOE Number, Interest Area, and Work Group: 02.06.01; Science, Math, and Engineering; Mathematics and Computers: Data Processing. **Personality Type:** Investigative. Investigative occupations frequently involve working with ideas and require an extensive amount of thinking. These occupations can involve searching for facts and figuring out problems mentally. **Work Values:** Autonomy; Working Conditions; Security; Company Policies and Practices; Achievement; Compensation; Advancement; Variety. **Skills:** Testing; Reading Comprehension; Information Organization; Troubleshooting; Programming; Active Learning. **Abilities:** *Cognitive*—Oral Comprehension; Written Comprehension; Oral Expression; Problem Sensitivity; Mathematical Reasoning; Written Expression. *Psychomotor*—Finger Dexterity; Arm-Hand Steadiness; Manual Dexterity; Wrist-Finger Speed. *Physical*—Extent Flexibility; Gross Body Coordination. *Sensory*—Near Vision; Speech Clarity; Visual Color Discrimination. **General Work Activities:** *Information Input*—Getting Information Needed to Do the Job; Identifying Objects, Actions, and Events; Inspecting Equipment, Structures, Materials. *Mental Process*—Updating and Using Job-Relevant Knowledge; Making Decisions and Solving Problems; Analyzing Data or Information; Judging Qualities of Things, Services, Other People's Work. *Work Output*—Interacting with Computers; Repairing and Maintaining Electrical Equipment; Handling and Moving Objects. *Interacting with Others*—Communicating with Other Workers; Providing Consultation and Advice to Others; Interpreting Meaning of Information to Others; Teaching Others. **Physical Work Conditions:** Indoors; Using Hands on Objects, Tools, or Controls; Sitting. **Other Job Characteristics:** Degree of Automation; Importance of Being Exact or Accurate; Consequence of Error.

Experience: Job Zone 4. A minimum of two to four years of work-related skill, knowledge, or experience is needed. **Job Preparation:** SVP 7.0 to less than 8.0—2 years to less than 10 years. **Knowledge:** Computers and Electronics; Education and Training; English Language; Telecommunications; Mathematics; Engineering and Technology. **Instructional Programs:** 110401 Information Sciences and Systems; 521201 Management Information Systems and Business Data Processing, General; 521204 Business Systems Networking and Telecommunications.

Related DOT Jobs: 031.132-010 Supervisor, Network Control Operators; 031.262-014 Network Control Operator; 032.132-010 User Support Analyst Supervisor; 032.262-010 User Support Analyst; 033.162-018 Technical Support Specialist; 039.264-010 Microcomputer Support Specialist.

15-1051.00 Computer Systems Analysts (Systems Analysts)

Education: Bachelor's degree
Employed: 616,915
Openings: 154,157
Projected Growth: 93.6%
Earnings: $52,180

Analyze science, engineering, business, and all other data-processing problems for application to electronic data-processing systems. Analyze user requirements, procedures, and problems to automate or improve existing systems and to review computer system capabilities, workflow, and scheduling limitations. Analyze or recommend commercially available software. Supervise computer programmers.

Trains staff and users to use computer system and its programs. Consults with staff and users to identify operating procedure problems. Devises flow charts and diagrams to illustrate steps and to describe logical operational steps of program. Writes and revises program and system design procedures, test procedures, and quality standards. Reviews and analyzes computer printouts and performance indications to locate code problems. Analyzes and tests computer programs or system to identify errors and ensure conformance to standard. Assists staff and users to solve computer related problems, such as malfunctions and program problems. Coordinates installation of computer programs and operating systems, and tests, maintains, and monitors computer system. Reads manuals, periodicals, and technical reports to learn how to develop programs to meet staff and user requirements. Writes documentation to describe and develop installation and operating procedures of programs. Formulates and reviews plans outlining steps required to develop programs to meet staff and user requirements. Modifies program to correct errors by correcting computer codes.

GOE Number, Interest Area, and Work Group: 02.06.01; Science, Math, and Engineering; Mathematics and Computers: Data Processing. **Personality Type:** Investigative. Investigative occupations frequently involve working with ideas and require an extensive amount of thinking. These occupations can involve searching for facts and figuring out problems mentally. **Work Values:** Company Policies and Practices; Ability Utilization; Security; Autonomy; Responsibility; Creativity; Compensation. **Skills:** Troubleshooting; Testing; Programming; Reading Comprehension; Writing; Problem Identification. **Abilities:** *Cognitive*—Written Comprehension; Written Expression; Mathematical Reasoning; Oral Comprehension; Deductive Reasoning. *Psychomotor*—Wrist-Finger Speed; Response Orientation; Reaction Time; Arm-Hand Steadiness. *Physical*—Trunk Strength. *Sensory*—Near Vision; Speech Clarity; Visual Color Discrimination. **General Work Activities:** *Information Input*—Getting Information Needed to Do the Job; Identifying Objects, Actions, and Events; Monitoring Processes, Materials, and Surroundings. *Mental Process*—Updating and Using Job-Relevant Knowledge; Thinking Creatively; Analyzing Data or Information. *Work Output*—Interacting with Computers; Implementing Ideas and Programs; Documenting and Recording Information. *Interacting with Others*—Communicating with Other Workers; Providing Consultation and Advice to Others; Communicating with Persons Outside Organization; Teaching Others. **Physical Work Conditions:** Indoors; Sitting; Using Hands on Objects, Tools, or Controls. **Other Job Characteristics:** Degree of Automation; Importance of Being Sure All Is Done; Consequence of Error.

Experience: Job Zone 3. Previous work-related skill, knowledge, or experience is required. **Job Preparation:** SVP 6.0 to less than 7.0—More than 1 year and less than 4 years. **Knowledge:** Computers and Electronics; English Language; Education and Training; Mathematics; Customer and Personal Service. **Instructional Programs:** 110101 Computer and Information Sciences, General; 110201 Computer Programming; 110501 Computer Systems Analysis; 521201 Management Information Systems and Business Data Processing, General; 521202 Business Computer Programming/Programmer; 521203 Business Systems Analysis and Design.

Related DOT Jobs: 030.162-014 Programmer-Analyst; 030.162-022 Systems Programmer; 030.167-014 Systems Analyst; 033.262-010 Quality Assurance Analyst.

15-1061.00 Database Administrators (Database Administrators)

Education: Bachelor's degree
Employed: 87,421
Openings: 19,027
Projected Growth: 77.2%
Earnings: $47,980

Coordinate changes to computer databases. Test and implement the database, applying knowledge of database-management systems. Plan, coordinate, and implement security measures to safeguard computer databases.

Trains users and answers questions. Develops data model describing data elements and how they are used, following procedures using pen, template or computer software. Reviews workflow charts developed by programmer analyst to understand tasks computer will perform, such as updating records. Reviews procedures in data base management system manuals for making changes to data base. Confers with coworkers to determine scope and limitations of project. Revises company definition of data as defined in data dictionary. Specifies user and user access levels for each segment of data base. Directs programmers and analysts to make changes to data base management system. Writes logical and physical data base descriptions including location, space, access method, and security. Establishes and calculates optimum values for data base parameters, using manuals and calculator. Selects and enters codes to monitor data base performance and to create production data base. Tests, corrects errors, and modifies changes to programs or to data base. Codes data base descriptions and specifies identifiers of data base to management system or directs others in coding descriptions. Reviews project request describing data base user needs, estimating time and cost required to accomplish project.

GOE Number, Interest Area, and Work Group: 02.06.01; Science, Math, and Engineering; Mathematics and Computers: Data Processing. **Personality Type:** Investigative. Investigative occupations frequently involve working with ideas and require an extensive amount of thinking. These occupations can involve searching for facts and figuring out problems mentally. **Work Values:** Security; Company Policies and Practices; Compensation; Responsibility; Ability Utilization; Working Conditions. **Skills:** Programming; Mathematics; Information Organization; Critical Thinking; Reading Comprehension; Operations Analysis. **Abilities:** *Cognitive*—Written Comprehension; Oral Expression; Mathematical Reasoning; Deductive Reasoning; Information Ordering. *Psychomotor*—Wrist-Finger Speed; Manual Dexterity; Finger Dexterity. *Physical*—Trunk Strength. *Sensory*—Near Vision; Auditory Attention; Glare Sensitivity; Sound Localization. **General Work Activities:** *Information Input*—Getting Information Needed to Do the Job; Monitoring Processes, Materials, and Surroundings; Identifying Objects, Actions, and Events. *Mental Process*—Analyzing Data or Information; Updating and Using Job-Relevant Knowledge; Processing Information; Making Decisions and Solving Problems. *Work Output*—Interacting with Computers; Implementing Ideas and Programs; Documenting and Recording Information. *Interacting with Others*—Communicating with Other Workers; Providing Consultation and Advice to Others; Interpreting Meaning of Information to Others. **Physical Work Conditions:** Indoors; Sitting; Using Hands on Objects, Tools, or Controls. **Other Job Characteristics:** Importance of Being Sure All Is Done; Consequence of Error; Frustrating Circumstances; Degree of Automation.

Experience: Job Zone 4. A minimum of two to four years of work-related skill, knowledge, or experience is needed. **Job Preparation:** SVP 7.0 to less than 8.0—2 years to less than 10 years. **Knowledge:** Computers and Electronics; Administration and Management; English Language; Mathematics; Education and Training. **Instructional Programs:** 110101 Computer and Information Sciences, General; 110401 Information Sciences and Systems; 521201 Management Information Systems and Business Data Processing, General.

Related DOT Jobs: 039.162-010 Data Base Administrator; 039.162-014 Data Base Design Analyst; 109.067-010 Information Scientist.

15-1071.00 Network and Computer Systems Administrators (All Other Management Support Workers)

Education: No data available.

Employed: 792,150

Openings: No data available.

Projected Growth: No data available.

Earnings: $37,060

Install, configure, and support an organization's local area network (LAN), wide area network (WAN), and Internet system, or a segment of a network system. Maintain network hardware and software. Monitor network to ensure network availability to all system users. Perform necessary maintenance to support network availability. Supervise other network-support and client-server specialists. Plan, coordinate, and implement network security measures.

GOE Number, Interest Area, and Work Group: 02.06.01; Science, Math, and Engineering; Mathematics and Computers: Data

Processing. **Instructional Programs:** 440501 Public Policy Analysis; 520401 Administrative Assistant/Secretarial Science, General; 520402 Executive Assistant/Secretary. **Note:** The Department of Labor has not collected some data for this job, so it has fewer details than the other descriptions.

15-1071.01 Computer Security Specialists (All Other Management Support Workers)

Education: No data available.

Employed: 792,150

Openings: No data available.

Projected Growth: No data available.

Earnings: $37,060

Plan, coordinate, and implement security measures for information systems, to regulate access to computer data files and to prevent unauthorized modification, destruction, or disclosure of information.

Tests data processing system to ensure functioning of data processing activities and security measures. Coordinates implementation of computer system plan with establishment personnel and outside vendors. Modifies computer security files to incorporate new software, correct errors, or change individual access status. Monitors use of data files and regulates access to safeguard information in computer files. Confers with personnel to discuss issues such as computer data access needs, security violations, and programming changes. Develops plans to safeguard computer files against accidental or unauthorized modification, destruction, or disclosure and to meet emergency data processing needs. Writes reports to document computer security and emergency measures policies, procedures, and test results.

GOE Number, Interest Area, and Work Group: 02.06.01; Science, Math, and Engineering; Mathematics and Computers: Data Processing. **Personality Type:** Investigative. Investigative occupations frequently involve working with ideas and require an extensive amount of thinking. These occupations can involve searching for facts and figuring out problems mentally. **Work Values:** Working Conditions; Compensation; Responsibility; Ability Utilization; Autonomy. **Skills:** Programming; Writing; Operations Analysis; Idea Generation; Mathematics; Implementation Planning; Technology Design. **Abilities:** *Cognitive*—Deductive Reasoning; Oral Comprehension; Written Comprehension; Oral Expression; Information Ordering; Written Expression. *Psychomotor*—none met the criteria. *Physical*—none met the criteria. *Sensory*—Near Vision; Speech Clarity; Far Vision. **General Work Activities:** *Information Input*—Monitoring Processes, Materials, and Surroundings; Getting Information Needed to Do the Job; Identifying Objects, Actions, and Events; Inspecting Equipment, Structures, Materials. *Mental Process*—Making Decisions and Solving Problems; Updating and Using Job-Relevant Knowledge; Analyzing Data or Information; Developing Objectives and Strategies. *Work Output*—Interacting with Computers; Documenting and Recording Information; Implementing Ideas and Programs. *Interacting with Others*—Providing Consultation and Advice to Others; Communicating with Other Workers; Monitoring and Controlling Resources; Coordinating Work and Activities of Others. **Physical Work Conditions:** Indoors; Sitting; Using Hands on Objects,

Tools, or Controls; Standing. **Other Job Characteristics:** Consequence of Error; Importance of Being Sure All Is Done; Importance of Being Exact or Accurate.

Experience: Job Zone 4. A minimum of two to four years of work-related skill, knowledge, or experience is needed. **Job Preparation:** SVP 7.0 to less than 8.0—2 years to less than 10 years. **Knowledge:** Computers and Electronics; Public Safety and Security; English Language; Administration and Management; Mathematics. **Instructional Programs:** 440501 Public Policy Analysis; 520401 Administrative Assistant/Secretarial Science, General; 520402 Executive Assistant/Secretary.

Related DOT Jobs: 033.162-010 Computer Security Coordinator; 033.162-014 Data Recovery Planner; 033.362-010 Computer Security Specialist.

15-1081.00 Network Systems and Data Communications Analysts (Computer Scientists)

Education: Bachelor's degree

Employed: 97,493

Openings: 27,942

Projected Growth: 117.5%

Earnings: $46,670

Analyze, design, test, and evaluate network systems such as local area networks (LAN), wide area networks (WAN), Internet, intranet, and other data communications systems. Perform network modeling, analysis, and planning. Research and recommend network and data communications hardware and software. Supervise computer programmers. Includes telecommunications specialists who deal with the interfacing of computer and communications equipment.

Identifies areas of operation which need upgraded equipment, such as modems, fiber optic cables, and telephone wires. Assists users to identify and solve data communication problems. Trains users in use of equipment. Visits vendors to learn about available products or services. Conducts survey to determine user needs. Develops and writes procedures for installation, use, and solving problems of communications hardware and software. Tests and evaluates hardware and software to determine efficiency, reliability, and compatibility with existing system. Reads technical manuals and brochures to determine equipment which meets establishment requirements. Analyzes test data and recommends hardware or software for purchase. Monitors system performance.

GOE Number, Interest Area, and Work Group: 02.06.01; Science, Math, and Engineering; Mathematics and Computers: Data Processing. **Personality Type:** Investigative. Investigative occupations frequently involve working with ideas and require an extensive amount of thinking. These occupations can involve searching for facts and figuring out problems mentally. **Work Values:** Compensation; Ability Utilization; Company Policies and Practices; Autonomy; Working Conditions; Security. **Skills:** Testing; Reading Comprehension; Troubleshooting; Management of Material Resources; Writing. **Abilities:** *Cognitive*—Written Comprehension; Oral Expression; Oral Comprehension; Written Expression; Information Ordering. *Psychomotor*—Wrist-Finger Speed;

Finger Dexterity; Control Precision. *Physical*—none met the criteria. *Sensory*—Near Vision; Speech Clarity; Speech Recognition. **General Work Activities:** *Information Input*—Getting Information Needed to Do the Job; Monitoring Processes, Materials, and Surroundings; Identifying Objects, Actions, and Events. *Mental Process*—Updating and Using Job-Relevant Knowledge; Analyzing Data or Information; Making Decisions and Solving Problems; Judging Qualities of Things, Services, Other People's Work. *Work Output*—Interacting with Computers; Drafting and Specifying Technical Devices; Implementing Ideas and Programs. *Interacting with Others*—Providing Consultation and Advice to Others; Interpreting Meaning of Information to Others; Communicating with Other Workers. **Physical Work Conditions:** Indoors; Sitting; Using Hands on Objects, Tools, or Controls. **Other Job Characteristics:** Consequence of Error; Degree of Automation; Frustrating Circumstances.

Experience: Job Zone 4. A minimum of two to four years of work-related skill, knowledge, or experience is needed. **Job Preparation:** SVP 7.0 to less than 8.0—2 years to less than 10 years. **Knowledge:** Computers and Electronics; Telecommunications; Mathematics; Education and Training; Public Safety and Security. **Instructional Programs:** 110101 Computer and Information Sciences, General; 110201 Computer Programming; 110301 Data Processing Technology/Technician; 110401 Information Sciences and Systems; 110501 Computer Systems Analysis; 110701 Computer Science; 119999 Computer and Information Sciences, Other; 521202 Business Computer Programming/Programmer; 521203 Business Systems Analysis and Design; 521204 Business Systems Networking and Telecommunications; 521299 Business Information and Data Processing Services, Other.

Related DOT Job: 031.262-010 Data Communications Analyst.

15-2000 Mathematical Science Occupations

15-2011.00 Actuaries (Actuaries)

Education: Bachelor's degree

Employed: 16,160

Openings: 1,712

Projected Growth: 7.1%

Earnings: $65,560

Analyze statistical data such as mortality, accident, sickness, disability, and retirement rates; construct probability tables to forecast risk and liability for payment of future benefits. Ascertain premium rates required and cash reserves necessary to ensure payment of future benefits.

Determines mortality, accident, sickness, disability, and retirement rates. Constructs probability tables regarding fire, natural disasters, and unemployment, based on analysis of statistical data and other pertinent information. Designs or reviews insurance and pension plans and calculates premiums. Ascertains premium rates required and cash reserves and liabilities necessary to ensure payment of future benefits. Determines equitable basis for distributing surplus earnings under participating insurance and annuity contracts in mutual companies.

GOE Number, Interest Area, and Work Group: 02.06.02; Science, Math, and Engineering; Mathematics and Computers: Data Analysis. **Personality Type:** Conventional. Conventional occupations frequently involve following set procedures and routines. These occupations can include working with data and details more than with ideas. Usually there is a clear line of authority to follow. **Work Values:** Working Conditions; Autonomy; Company Policies and Practices; Security; Ability Utilization; Supervision, Human Relations; Independence. **Skills:** Information Gathering; Mathematics; Information Organization; Reading Comprehension; Critical Thinking. **Abilities:** *Cognitive*—Number Facility; Mathematical Reasoning; Deductive Reasoning; Written Comprehension; Inductive Reasoning. *Psychomotor*—Wrist-Finger Speed; Finger Dexterity; Manual Dexterity. *Physical*—none met the criteria. *Sensory*—Near Vision; Glare Sensitivity. **General Work Activities:** *Information Input*—Getting Information Needed to Do the Job; Identifying Objects, Actions, and Events; Estimating Needed Characteristics. *Mental Process*—Analyzing Data or Information; Processing Information; Evaluating Information Against Standards. *Work Output*—Implementing Ideas and Programs; Documenting and Recording Information; Interacting with Computers. *Interacting with Others*—Monitoring and Controlling Resources; Providing Consultation and Advice to Others; Performing Administrative Activities; Interpreting Meaning of Information to Others. **Physical Work Conditions:** Sitting; Indoors; Using Hands on Objects, Tools, or Controls. **Other Job Characteristics:** Importance of Being Exact or Accurate; Importance of Being Sure All Is Done; Consequence of Error.

Experience: Job Zone 5. Extensive skill, knowledge, and experience are needed. Very advanced communication and organizational skills are required. **Job Preparation:** SVP 8.0 and above—4 years to more than 10 years. **Knowledge:** Mathematics; Economics and Accounting; Clerical; Computers and Electronics; English Language. **Instructional Program:** 520802 Actuarial Science.

Related DOT Job: 020.167-010 Actuary.

15-2021.00 Mathematicians (Mathematicians)

Education: Master's degree

Employed: 14,036

Openings: 1,304

Projected Growth: –5.5%

Earnings: No data available.

Conduct research in fundamental mathematics or in the application of mathematical techniques to science, management, and other fields. Solve or direct solutions to problems in various fields by mathematical methods.

Conducts research in fundamental mathematics and in application of mathematical techniques to science, management and other fields. Utilizes knowledge of such subjects or fields as physics, engineering, astronomy, biology, economics, business and industrial management, or cryptography. Acts as advisor or consultant to research personnel concerning mathematical methods and applications. Applies mathematics or mathematical methods of numerical analysis, and operates or directs operation of desk calculators and mechanical and other functional areas. Operates or directs operation of desk calculators and mechanical and electronic computation machines, analyzers, and plotters in solving problem support of mathematical, scientific or industrial research. Performs computations and applies methods of numerical analysis. Conceives or directs ideas for application of mathematics to wide variety of fields, including science, engineering, military planning, electronic data processing, and management. Studies and tests hypotheses and alternative theories. Conducts research in such branches of mathematics as algebra, geometry, number theory, logic and topology.

GOE Number, Interest Area, and Work Group: 02.06.02; Science, Math, and Engineering; Mathematics and Computers: Data Analysis. **Personality Type:** Investigative. Investigative occupations frequently involve working with ideas and require an extensive amount of thinking. These occupations can involve searching for facts and figuring out problems mentally. **Work Values:** Autonomy; Ability Utilization; Independence; Working Conditions; Responsibility. **Skills:** Mathematics; Active Learning; Learning Strategies; Information Gathering; Idea Generation; Solution Appraisal. **Abilities:** *Cognitive*—Mathematical Reasoning; Number Facility; Deductive Reasoning; Inductive Reasoning; Oral Comprehension; Written Comprehension. *Psychomotor*—none met the criteria. *Physical*—none met the criteria. *Sensory*—Speech Clarity. **General Work Activities:** *Information Input*—Getting Information Needed to Do the Job; Identifying Objects, Actions, and Events; Estimating Needed Characteristics. *Mental Process*—Processing Information; Analyzing Data or Information; Thinking Creatively. *Work Output*—Interacting with Computers; Documenting and Recording Information; Handling and Moving Objects. *Interacting with Others*—Interpreting Meaning of Information to Others; Communicating with Other Workers; Providing Consultation and Advice to Others. **Physical Work Conditions:** Indoors; Sitting; Standing; Using Hands on Objects, Tools, or Controls. **Other Job Characteristics:** Consequence of Error; Importance of Being Exact or Accurate; Importance of Being Sure All Is Done.

Experience: Job Zone 5. Extensive skill, knowledge, and experience are needed. Very advanced communication and organizational skills are required. **Job Preparation:** SVP 8.0 and above—4 years to more than 10 years. **Knowledge:** Mathematics; Computers and Electronics; Administration and Management; Physics; Engineering and Technology; English Language. **Instructional Programs:** 270101 Mathematics; 270301 Applied Mathematics, General; 400801 Physics, General; 400810 Theoretical and Mathematical Physics.

Related DOT Job: 020.067-014 Mathematician.

15-2031.00 Operations Research Analysts (Operations Research Analysts)

Education: Master's degree

Employed: 76,320

Openings: 5,355

Projected Growth: 8.7%

Earnings: $49,070

Formulate and apply mathematical modeling and other optimizing methods, using a computer to develop and interpret information that assists management with decision making, policy formulation, or other managerial functions. Develop related software, services, or products. Collect and analyze data, and develop decision-support software. Develop and supply optimal time, cost, or logistics networks for program evaluation, review, or implementation.

Designs, conducts, and evaluates experimental operational models where insufficient data exists to formulate model. Develops and applies time and cost networks to plan and control large projects. Defines data requirements and gathers and validates information, applying judgment and statistical tests. Studies information and selects plan from competitive proposals that afford maximum probability of profit or effectiveness relating to cost or risk. Evaluates implementation and effectiveness of research. Performs validation and testing of model to ensure adequacy, or determines need for reformulation. Specifies manipulative or computational methods to be applied to model. Prepares model of problem in form of one or several equations that relates constants and variables, restrictions, alternatives, conflicting objectives and their numerical parameters. Analyzes problem in terms of management information and conceptualizes and defines problem. Prepares for management reports defining problem, evaluation, and possible solution.

GOE Number, Interest Area, and Work Group: 02.06.02; Science, Math, and Engineering; Mathematics and Computers: Data Analysis. **Personality Type:** Investigative. Investigative occupations frequently involve working with ideas and require an extensive amount of thinking. These occupations can involve searching for facts and figuring out problems mentally. **Work Values:** Autonomy; Ability Utilization; Creativity; Responsibility; Working Conditions; Company Policies and Practices. **Skills:** Systems Evaluation; Mathematics; Problem Identification; Identification of Key Causes; Visioning; Solution Appraisal; Monitoring; Critical Thinking; Judgment and Decision Making. **Abilities:** *Cognitive*—Mathematical Reasoning; Written Comprehension; Oral Comprehension; Written Expression; Deductive Reasoning. *Psychomotor*—none met the criteria. *Physical*—none met the criteria. **General Work Activities:** *Information Input*—Getting Information Needed to Do the Job; Identifying Objects, Actions, and Events; Estimating Needed Characteristics; Monitoring Processes, Materials, and Surroundings. *Mental Process*—Making Decisions and Solving Problems; Analyzing Data or Information; Updating and Using Job-Relevant Knowledge; Processing Information. *Work Output*—Interacting with Computers; Implementing Ideas and Programs; Documenting and Recording Information. *Interacting with Others*—Providing Consultation and Advice to Others; Communicating with Other Workers; Communicating with Persons Outside Organization. **Physical Work Conditions:** Indoors; Sitting; Using Hands on Objects, Tools, or Controls. **Other Job Characteristics:** Consequence of Error; Importance of Being Sure All Is Done; Importance of Being Exact or Accurate.

Experience: Job Zone 4. A minimum of two to four years of work-related skill, knowledge, or experience is needed. **Job Preparation:** SVP 7.0 to less than 8.0—2 years to less than 10 years. **Knowledge:** Mathematics; Administration and Management; Computers and Electronics; Economics and Accounting; English Language. **Instructional Programs:** 270301 Applied Mathematics, General; 270302 Operations Research; 521301 Management Science; 521399 Business Quantitative Methods and Management Science, Other.

Related DOT Job: 020.067-018 Operations-Research Analyst.

15-2041.00 Statisticians (Statisticians)

Education:	Master's degree
Employed:	16,529
Openings:	1,635
Projected Growth:	2.3%
Earnings:	$48,540

Engage in the development of mathematical theory. Apply statistical theory and methods to collect, organize, interpret, and summarize numerical data that provide usable information. Specialize in fields such as biostatistics, agricultural statistics, business statistics, economic statistics, or other fields.

Analyzes and interprets statistics to identify significant differences in relationships among sources of information. Examines theories, such as those of probability and inference, to discover mathematical bases for new or improved methods of obtaining and evaluating numerical data. Investigates, evaluates, and reports on applicability, efficiency, and accuracy of statistical methods used to obtain and evaluate data. Evaluates reliability of source information, adjusts and weighs raw data, and organizes results into form compatible with analysis by computers or other methods. Develops statistical methodology. Applies statistical methodology to provide information for scientific research and statistical analysis. Develops and tests experimental designs, sampling techniques, and analytical methods, and prepares recommendations concerning their use. Conducts surveys utilizing sampling techniques or complete enumeration bases. Plans methods to collect information and develops questionnaire techniques according to survey design. Presents numerical information by computer readouts, graphs, charts, tables, written reports or other methods. Describes sources of information and limitations on reliability and usability.

GOE Number, Interest Area, and Work Group: 02.06.02; Science, Math, and Engineering; Mathematics and Computers: Data Analysis. **Personality Type:** Investigative. Investigative occupations frequently involve working with ideas and require an extensive amount of thinking. These occupations can involve searching for facts and figuring out problems mentally. **Work Values:** Autonomy; Ability Utilization; Independence; Working Conditions; Responsibility. **Skills:** Mathematics; Information Gathering; Critical Thinking; Active Learning; Solution Appraisal; Idea Evaluation; Idea Generation; Information Organization. **Abilities:** *Cognitive*—Number Facility; Mathematical Reasoning; Deductive Reasoning; Written Expression; Inductive Reasoning. *Psychomotor*—Finger Dexterity; Wrist-Finger Speed; Control Precision. *Physical*—none met the criteria. *Sensory*—Near Vision; Speech Clarity; Glare Sensitivity. **General Work Activities:** *Information Input*—Getting Information Needed to Do the Job; Identifying Objects, Actions, and Events; Estimating Needed Characteristics. *Mental Process*—Analyzing Data or Information; Processing Information; Evaluating Information Against Standards. *Work Output*—Interacting with Computers; Documenting and Recording Information; Implementing Ideas and Programs. *Interacting with Others*—Interpreting Meaning of Information to Others; Communicating with Other Workers; Providing Consultation and Advice to Others. **Physical Work Conditions:** Indoors; Sitting; Using Hands on Objects, Tools, or Controls. **Other Job Characteristics:** Importance of Being Exact or Accurate; Importance of Being Sure All Is Done; Degree of Automation; Consequence of Error.

Experience: Job Zone 4. A minimum of two to four years of work-related skill, knowledge, or experience is needed. **Job Preparation:** SVP 7.0 to less than 8.0—2 years to less than 10 years. **Knowledge:** Mathematics; Computers and Electronics; English Language; Clerical; Economics and Accounting; Administration and Management. **Instructional Programs:** 260615 Biostatistics; 270101 Mathematics; 270301 Applied Mathematics, General; 270501 Mathematical Statistics; 521302 Business Statistics.

Related DOT Jobs: 020.067-022 Statistician, Mathematical; 020.167-026 Statistician, Applied.

15-3011.00 Mathematical Technicians (Mathematical Technicians)

Education: No data available.

Employed: 2,530

Openings: No data available.

Projected Growth: No data available.

Earnings: $30,460

Apply standardized mathematical formulas, principles, and methodology to technological problems in engineering and physical sciences, in relation to specific industrial and research objectives, processes, equipment, and products.

Analyzes raw data from computer or recorded on photographic film or other media. Translates data into numerical values, equations, flow charts, graphs or other media. Modifies standard formulas to conform to data processing method selected. Confers with professional scientific, and engineering personnel to plan project. Selects most economical and reliable combination of manual, mechanical, or data processing methods and equipment consistent with data reduction requirements. Selects most fea-

sible combination and sequence of computational methods to reduce raw data to meaningful and manageable terms. Calculates data for analysis, using computer or calculator. Analyzes processed data to detect errors.

GOE Number, Interest Area, and Work Group: 02.06.02; Science, Math, and Engineering; Mathematics and Computers: Data Analysis. **Personality Type:** Investigative. Investigative occupations frequently involve working with ideas and require an extensive amount of thinking. These occupations can involve searching for facts and figuring out problems mentally. **Work Values:** Ability Utilization; Working Conditions; Moral Values; Supervision, Human Relations; Advancement; Security. **Skills:** Mathematics; Critical Thinking; Active Learning; Active Listening; Reading Comprehension; Synthesis/Reorganization. **Abilities:** *Cognitive*—Number Facility; Mathematical Reasoning; Deductive Reasoning; Oral Expression; Oral Comprehension. *Psychomotor*—Wrist-Finger Speed. *Physical*—none met the criteria. *Sensory*—Near Vision; Speech Clarity; Glare Sensitivity. **General Work Activities:** *Information Input*—Getting Information Needed to Do the Job; Identifying Objects, Actions, and Events; Estimating Needed Characteristics. *Mental Process*—Processing Information; Analyzing Data or Information; Updating and Using Job-Relevant Knowledge; Making Decisions and Solving Problems. *Work Output*—Interacting with Computers; Implementing Ideas and Programs; Documenting and Recording Information. *Interacting with Others*—Communicating with Other Workers; Interpreting Meaning of Information to Others; Providing Consultation and Advice to Others. **Physical Work Conditions:** Indoors; Sitting; Using Hands on Objects, Tools, or Controls. **Other Job Characteristics:** Importance of Being Exact or Accurate; Importance of Being Sure All Is Done; Degree of Automation.

Experience: Job Zone 4. A minimum of two to four years of work-related skill, knowledge, or experience is needed. **Job Preparation:** SVP 7.0 to less than 8.0—2 years to less than 10 years. **Knowledge:** Mathematics; Computers and Electronics; English Language; Engineering and Technology; Clerical. **Instructional Program:** 270301 Applied Mathematics, General.

Related DOT Job: 020.162-010 Mathematical Technician.

17-0000
Architecture and Engineering Occupations

17-1000 Architects, Surveyors, and Cartographers

17-1011.00 Architects, Except Landscape and Naval
(Architects)

Education: Bachelor's degree
Employed: 99,162
Openings: 7,762
Projected Growth: 18.9%
Earnings: $47,710

Plan and design structures such as private residences, office buildings, theaters, factories, and other structural property.

Conducts periodic on-site observation of work during construction to monitor compliance with plans. Represents client in obtaining bids and awarding construction contracts. Prepares contract documents for building contractors. Administers construction contracts. Prepares operating and maintenance manuals, studies, and reports. Consults with client to determine functional and spatial requirements of structure. Integrates engineering element into unified design. Plans layout of project. Prepares information regarding design, structure specifications, materials, color, equipment, estimated costs, and construction time. Prepares scale drawings. Directs activities of workers engaged in preparing drawings and specification documents.

GOE Number, Interest Area, and Work Group: 02.07.03; Science, Math, and Engineering; Engineering: Design. **Personality Type:** Artistic. Artistic occupations frequently involve working with forms, designs, and patterns. These occupations often require self-expression, and the work can be done without following a clear set of rules. **Work Values:** Ability Utilization; Creativity; Achievement; Recognition; Social Status. **Skills:** Coordination; Reading Comprehension; Mathematics; Active Listening; Writing. **Abilities:** *Cognitive*–Visualization; Written Expression; Deductive Reasoning; Fluency of Ideas; Number Facility; Oral Expression. *Psychomotor*–Wrist-Finger Speed; Arm-Hand Steadiness; Response Orientation. *Physical*–Trunk Strength; Gross Body Equilibrium; Stamina. *Sensory*–Near Vision; Far Vision; Visual Color Discrimination. **General Work Activities:** *Information Input*–Estimating Needed Characteristics; Getting Information Needed to Do the Job; Identifying Objects, Actions, and Events. *Mental Process*–Thinking Creatively; Evaluating Information Against Standards; Processing Information. *Work Output*–Drafting and Specifying Technical Devices; Implementing Ideas and Programs; Documenting and Recording Information. *Interacting with Others*–Communicating with Persons Outside Organization; Providing Consultation and Advice to Others; Establishing and Maintaining Relationships. **Physical Work Conditions:** Indoors; Sitting; Using Hands on Objects, Tools, or Controls. **Other Job Characteristics:** Consequence of Error; Importance of Being Exact or Accurate; Importance of Being Sure All Is Done.

Experience: Job Zone 4. A minimum of two to four years of work-related skill, knowledge, or experience is needed. **Job Preparation:** SVP 7.0 to less than 8.0–2 years to less than 10 years.

Knowledge: Design; Building and Construction; Administration and Management; Mathematics; English Language. **Instructional Programs:** 040201 Architecture; 040401 Architectural Environmental Design; 049999 Architecture and Related Programs, Other. **Related DOT Jobs:** 001.061-010 Architect; 001.167-010 School-Plant Consultant.

17-1012.00 Landscape Architects (Landscape Architects)

Education: Bachelor's degree
Employed: 22,060
Openings: 1,605
Projected Growth: 14.5%
Earnings: $37,930

Plan and design land areas for such projects as parks, other recreational facilities, airports, highways, hospitals, schools, land subdivisions, commercial sites, industrial sites, and residential sites.

Prepares site plans, specifications, and cost estimates for land development, coordinating arrangement of existing and proposed land features and structures. Compiles and analyzes data on conditions, such as location, drainage, and location of structures for environmental reports and landscaping plans. Inspects landscape work to ensure compliance with specifications, approve quality of materials and work, and advise client and construction personnel. Confers with clients, engineering personnel, and architects on overall program.

GOE Number, Interest Area, and Work Group: 02.07.03; Science, Math, and Engineering; Engineering: Design. **Personality Type:** Artistic. Artistic occupations frequently involve working with forms, designs, and patterns. These occupations often require self-expression, and the work can be done without following a clear set of rules. **Work Values:** Ability Utilization; Creativity; Social Status; Achievement; Moral Values; Autonomy; Recognition. **Skills:** Idea Generation; Judgment and Decision Making; Solution Appraisal; Critical Thinking; Information Gathering; Visioning; Active Listening; Idea Evaluation; Active Learning. **Abilities:** *Cognitive*–Visualization; Oral Comprehension; Originality; Oral Expression; Written Expression. *Psychomotor*–none met the criteria. *Physical*–Dynamic Flexibility; Stamina; Gross Body Equilibrium. *Sensory*–Far Vision; Visual Color Discrimination; Speech Clarity. **General Work Activities:** *Information Input*–Getting Information Needed to Do the Job; Identifying Objects, Actions, and Events; Estimating Needed Characteristics. *Mental Process*–Thinking Creatively; Making Decisions and Solving Problems; Analyzing Data or Information. *Work Output*–Drafting and Specifying Technical Devices; Implementing Ideas and Programs; Documenting and Recording Information. *Interacting with Others*–Providing Consultation and Advice to Others; Communicating with Persons Outside Organization; Communicating with Other Workers. **Physical Work Conditions:** Sitting; Indoors; Using Hands on Objects, Tools, or Controls. **Other Job Characteristics:** Consequence of Error; Frustrating Circumstances; Importance of Being Exact or Accurate; Importance of Being Sure All Is Done.

Experience: Job Zone 5. Extensive skill, knowledge, and experience are needed. Very advanced communication and organizational skills are required. **Job Preparation:** SVP 8.0 and above—4 years to more than 10 years. **Knowledge:** Design; Mathematics; Engineering and Technology; Administration and Management; Biology. **Instructional Programs:** 040401 Architectural Environmental Design; 040601 Landscape Architecture.

Related DOT Job: 001.061-018 Landscape Architect.

17-1021.00 Cartographers and Photogrammetrists
(Surveyors, Cartographers, and Photogrammetrists)

Education: Bachelor's degree
Employed: 41,333
Openings: 7,467
Projected Growth: 1.4%
Earnings: $37,640

Collect, analyze, and interpret geographic information provided by geodetic surveys, aerial photographs, and satellite data. Research, study, and prepare maps and other spatial data in digital or graphic form, for legal, social, political, educational, and design purposes. Work with Geographic Information Systems (GIS). Design and evaluate algorithms, data structures, and user interfaces for GIS and mapping systems.

Studies legal records to establish boundaries of local, national and international properties. Revises existing maps and charts and corrects maps in various stages of compilation. Determines guidelines for source material to be used, such as maps, automated mapping products, photographic survey data, and place names. Travels over photographed area to observe, identify, record and verify all features shown and not shown in photograph. Develops design concept of map product. Identifies, scales, and orients geodetic points, elevations, and other planimetric or topographic features, applying standard math formulas. Determines and defines production specifications, such as projection, scale, size, and colors of map product. Prepares mosaic prints, contour maps, profile sheets, and related cartographic material applying mastery of photogrammetric techniques and principles. Analyzes survey data, source maps and photos, computer or automated mapping products, and other records to determine location and name of features.

GOE Number, Interest Area, and Work Group: 02.08.03; Science, Math, and Engineering; Engineering Technology: Design. **Personality Type:** Conventional. Conventional occupations frequently involve following set procedures and routines. These occupations can include working with data and details more than with ideas. Usually there is a clear line of authority to follow. **Work Values:** Autonomy; Moral Values; Ability Utilization; Responsibility; Achievement; Working Conditions. **Skills:** Information Gathering; Information Organization; Reading Comprehension; Mathematics; Writing; Synthesis/Reorganization. **Abilities:** *Cognitive*—Mathematical Reasoning; Written Comprehension; Number Facility; Flexibility of Closure; Spatial Orientation. *Psychomotor*—Arm-Hand Steadiness; Wrist-Finger Speed; Finger Dexterity. *Physical*—Stamina; Gross Body Coordination;

Gross Body Equilibrium. *Sensory*—Near Vision; Far Vision; Visual Color Discrimination. **General Work Activities:** *Information Input*—Getting Information Needed to Do the Job; Identifying Objects, Actions, and Events; Estimating Needed Characteristics. *Mental Process*—Analyzing Data or Information; Processing Information; Updating and Using Job-Relevant Knowledge. *Work Output*—Documenting and Recording Information; Drafting and Specifying Technical Devices; Implementing Ideas and Programs. *Interacting with Others*—Interpreting Meaning of Information to Others; Communicating with Persons Outside Organization; Communicating with Other Workers; Performing Administrative Activities. **Physical Work Conditions:** Indoors; Sitting; Outdoors. **Other Job Characteristics:** Importance of Being Exact or Accurate; Importance of Being Sure All Is Done; Consequence of Error.

Experience: Job Zone 4. A minimum of two to four years of work-related skill, knowledge, or experience is needed. **Job Preparation:** SVP 7.0 to less than 8.0—2 years to less than 10 years. **Knowledge:** Geography; Mathematics; Design; Law, Government and Jurisprudence; Computers and Electronics. **Instructional Programs:** 151102 Surveying; 450702 Cartography.

Related DOT Jobs: 018.131-010 Supervisor, Cartography; 018.261-010 Drafter, Cartographic; 018.261-026 Photogrammetrist; 018.262-010 Field-Map Editor.

17-1022.00 Surveyors (Surveyors, Cartographers, and Photogrammetrists)

Education: Bachelor's degree
Employed: 41,333
Openings: 7,467
Projected Growth: 1.4%
Earnings: $37,640

Make exact measurements and determine property boundaries. Provide data relevant to the shape, contour, gravitation, location, elevation, or dimension of land or land features on or near the earth's surface, for engineering, mapmaking, mining, land evaluation, construction, and other purposes.

Coordinates findings with work of engineering and architectural personnel, clients, and others concerned with project. Prepares charts and tables and makes precise determinations of elevations and records other characteristics of terrain. Computes geodetic measurements and interprets survey data to determine position, shape, and elevations of geomorphic and topographic features. Conducts research in surveying and mapping methods using knowledge of techniques of photogrammetric map compilation, electronic data processing, and flight and control planning. Locates and marks sites selected for geophysical prospecting activities, such as locating petroleum or mineral products. Estimates cost of survey. Studies weight, shape, size, and mass of earth, and variations in earth's gravitational field, using astronomic observations and complex computation. Takes instrument readings of sun or stars and calculates longitude and latitude to determine specific area location. Establishes fixed points for use in making maps, using geodetic and engineering instruments. Determines appropriate and economical methods and procedures for establishing survey control. Drafts or directs others to draft maps of survey data. Prepares survey proposal or directs one or more phases of survey proposal preparation. Analyzes survey objectives and specifications, utilizing knowledge of survey uses. Surveys water bodies to determine navigable channels and to secure data for construction of breakwaters, piers, and other marine structures. Determines photographic equipment to be used, altitude from which to photograph terrain, and directs aerial surveys of specified geographical area. Plans ground surveys designed to establish base lines, elevations, and other geodetic measurements. Keeps accurate notes, records, and sketches to describe and certify work performed. Computes data necessary for driving and connecting underground passages, underground storage, and volume of underground deposits.

GOE Number, Interest Area, and Work Group: 02.08.01; Science, Math, and Engineering; Engineering Technology: Surveying. **Personality Type:** Investigative. Investigative occupations frequently involve working with ideas and require an extensive amount of thinking. These occupations can involve searching for facts and figuring out problems mentally. **Work Values:** Moral Values; Achievement; Autonomy; Ability Utilization; Responsibility; Security. **Skills:** Mathematics; Information Gathering; Science; Reading Comprehension; Active Learning. **Abilities:** *Cognitive*—Written Expression; Mathematical Reasoning; Number Facility; Written Comprehension; Oral Expression. *Psychomotor*—Arm-Hand Steadiness; Control Precision; Multilimb Coordination. *Physical*—Stamina; Gross Body Coordination; Gross Body Equilibrium. *Sensory*—Far Vision; Near Vision; Speech Clarity. **General Work Activities:** *Information Input*—Getting Information Needed to Do the Job; Estimating Needed Characteristics; Identifying Objects, Actions, and Events. *Mental Process*—Analyzing Data or Information; Processing Information; Making Decisions and Solving Problems. *Work Output*—Documenting and Recording Information; Drafting and Specifying Technical Devices; Handling and Moving Objects. *Interacting with Others*—Communicating with Other Workers; Communicating with Persons Outside Organization; Interpreting Meaning of Information to Others. **Physical Work Conditions:** Indoors; Standing; Outdoors; Using Hands on Objects, Tools, or Controls. **Other Job Characteristics:** Importance of Being Exact or Accurate; Importance of Being Sure All Is Done; Consequence of Error.

Experience: Job Zone 4. A minimum of two to four years of work-related skill, knowledge, or experience is needed. **Job Preparation:** SVP 7.0 to less than 8.0—2 years to less than 10 years. **Knowledge:** Mathematics; Geography; Physics; Design; Administration and Management. **Instructional Programs:** 151102 Surveying; 450702 Cartography.

Related DOT Jobs: 018.161-010 Surveyor, Mine; 018.167-018 Land Surveyor; 018.167-026 Photogrammetric Engineer; 018.167-038 Surveyor, Geodetic; 018.167-042 Surveyor, Geophysical Prospecting; 018.167-046 Surveyor, Marine; 024.061-014 Geodesist; 184.167-026 Director, Photogrammetry Flight Operations.

17-2000 Engineers

17-2011.00 Aerospace Engineers (Aerospace Engineers)

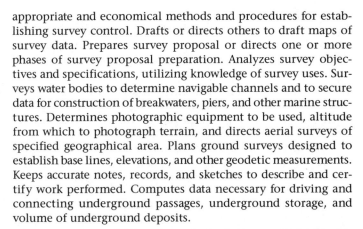

Education: Bachelor's degree
Employed: 53,035
Openings: 1,606
Projected Growth: 8.8%
Earnings: $66,950

Perform a variety of engineering work in designing, constructing, and testing aircraft, missiles, and spacecraft. Conduct basic and applied research to evaluate adaptability of materials and equipment to aircraft design and manufacture. Recommend improvements in testing equipment and techniques.

Maintains records of performance reports for future reference. Formulates mathematical models or other methods of computer analysis to develop, evaluate, or modify design according to customer engineering requirements. Evaluates product data and design from inspections and reports for conformance to engineering principles, customer requirements, and quality standards. Writes technical reports and other documentation, such as handbooks and bulletins, for use by engineering staff, management, and customers. Evaluates and approves selection of vendors by study of past performance and new advertisements. Directs research and development programs to improve production methods, parts, and equipment technology and reduce costs. Directs and coordinates activities of engineering or technical personnel designing, fabricating, modifying, or testing of aircraft or aerospace products. Develops design criteria for aeronautical or aerospace products or systems, including testing methods, production costs, quality standards, and completion dates. Plans and conducts experimental, environmental, operational and stress tests on models and prototypes of aircraft and aerospace systems and equipment. Formulates conceptual design of aeronautical or aerospace products or systems to meet customer requirements. Analyzes project requests and proposals and engineering data to determine feasibility, producibility, cost, and production time of aerospace or aeronautical product. Reviews performance reports and documentation from customers and field engineers, and inspects malfunctioning or damaged products to determine problem. Plans and coordinates activities concerned with investigating and resolving customers reports of technical problems with aircraft or aerospace vehicles.

GOE Number, Interest Area, and Work Group: 02.07.04; Science, Math, and Engineering; Engineering: General Engineering. **Personality Type:** Investigative. Investigative occupations frequently involve working with ideas and require an extensive amount of thinking. These occupations can involve searching for facts and figuring out problems mentally. **Work Values:** Ability Utilization; Creativity; Social Status; Responsibility; Autonomy. **Skills:** Mathematics; Science; Technology Design; Active Learning; Writing. **Abilities:** *Cognitive*—Written Comprehension; Oral Comprehension; Oral Expression; Written Expression; Number Facility; Mathematical Reasoning. *Psychomotor*—Control Precision.

Physical—none met the criteria. *Sensory*—Speech Clarity; Speech Recognition; Visual Color Discrimination; Depth Perception. **General Work Activities:** *Information Input*—Getting Information Needed to Do the Job; Identifying Objects, Actions, and Events; Monitoring Processes, Materials, and Surroundings. *Mental Process*—Thinking Creatively; Updating and Using Job-Relevant Knowledge; Evaluating Information Against Standards; Processing Information. *Work Output*—Drafting and Specifying Technical Devices; Documenting and Recording Information; Implementing Ideas and Programs; Interacting with Computers. *Interacting with Others*—Providing Consultation and Advice to Others; Interpreting Meaning of Information to Others; Communicating with Other Workers. **Physical Work Conditions:** Sitting; Indoors; Standing. **Other Job Characteristics:** Consequence of Error; Importance of Being Exact or Accurate; Importance of Being Sure All Is Done.

Experience: Job Zone 5. Extensive skill, knowledge, and experience are needed. Very advanced communication and organizational skills are required. **Job Preparation:** SVP 8.0 and above—4 years to more than 10 years. **Knowledge:** Engineering and Technology; Physics; Mathematics; Administration and Management; English Language. **Instructional Program:** 140201 Aerospace, Aeronautical and Astronautical Engineering.

Related DOT Jobs: 002.061-010 Aerodynamicist; 002.061-014 Aeronautical Engineer; 002.061-018 Aeronautical Test Engineer; 002.061-022 Aeronautical-Design Engineer; 002.061-026 Aeronautical-Research Engineer; 002.061-030 Stress Analyst; 002.167-010 Value Engineer; 002.167-014 Field-Service Engineer; 002.167-018 Aeronautical Project Engineer.

17-2021.00 Agricultural Engineers (Agricultural Engineers)

Education: No data available.

Employed: 3,190

Openings: No data available.

Projected Growth: No data available.

Earnings: $52,510

Apply knowledge of engineering technology and biological science to agricultural problems concerned with power and machinery, electrification, structures, soil and water conservation, and processing of agricultural products.

Conducts tests on agricultural machinery and equipment. Plans and directs construction of rural electric-power distribution systems, and irrigation, drainage, and flood control systems for soil and water conservation. Develops criteria for design, manufacture, or construction of equipment, structures, and facilities. Designs and supervises installation of equipment and instruments used to evaluate and process farm products, and to automate agricultural operations. Designs and supervises erection of crop storage, animal shelter, and residential structures and heating, lighting, cooling, plumbing, and waste disposal systems. Designs agricultural machinery and equipment. Designs sensing, measuring, and recording devices and instrumentation used to study plant or animal life. Studies such problems as effect of temperature, humidity, and light on plants and animals and effectiveness of different insecticides. Designs and directs manufacture of equipment for land tillage and fertilization, plant and animal disease and insect control, and for harvesting or moving commodities. Conducts research to develop agricultural machinery and equipment.

GOE Number, Interest Area, and Work Group: 02.07.01; Science, Math, and Engineering; Engineering: Research and Systems Design. **Personality Type:** Investigative. Investigative occupations frequently involve working with ideas and require an extensive amount of thinking. These occupations can involve searching for facts and figuring out problems mentally. **Work Values:** Ability Utilization; Creativity; Responsibility; Autonomy; Social Status; Achievement. **Skills:** Mathematics; Idea Generation; Science; Active Learning; Operations Analysis. **Abilities:** *Cognitive*—Deductive Reasoning; Visualization; Information Ordering; Oral Expression; Originality. *Psychomotor*—Finger Dexterity; Control Precision; Multilimb Coordination. *Physical*—Dynamic Flexibility; Gross Body Coordination. *Sensory*—Near Vision; Speech Clarity; Far Vision. **General Work Activities:** *Information Input*—Identifying Objects, Actions, and Events; Getting Information Needed to Do the Job; Monitoring Processes, Materials, and Surroundings. *Mental Process*—Thinking Creatively; Analyzing Data or Information; Updating and Using Job-Relevant Knowledge; Evaluating Information Against Standards. *Work Output*—Drafting and Specifying Technical Devices; Implementing Ideas and Programs; Handling and Moving Objects; Documenting and Recording Information. *Interacting with Others*—Providing Consultation and Advice to Others; Coordinating Work and Activities of Others; Communicating with Other Workers. **Physical Work Conditions:** Indoors; Sitting; Outdoors; Using Hands on Objects, Tools, or Controls. **Other Job Characteristics:** Consequence of Error; Importance of Being Exact or Accurate; Importance of Being Sure All Is Done.

Experience: Job Zone 5. Extensive skill, knowledge, and experience are needed. Very advanced communication and organizational skills are required. **Job Preparation:** SVP 8.0 and above—4 years to more than 10 years. **Knowledge:** Engineering and Technology; Design; Biology; Mathematics; Mechanical. **Instructional Program:** 140301 Agricultural Engineering.

Related DOT Jobs: 013.061-010 Agricultural Engineer; 013.061-014 Agricultural-Research Engineer; 013.061-018 Design-Engineer, Agricultural Equipment; 013.061-022 Test Engineer, Agricultural Equipment.

17-2031.00 Biomedical Engineers (All Other Professional, Paraprofessional, and Technical Workers)

Education: No data available.

Employed: 818,200

Openings: No data available.

Projected Growth: No data available.

Earnings: $36,790

Apply knowledge of engineering, biology, and biomechanical principles to the design, development, and evaluation of biological and health systems and products, such as artificial organs, prostheses, instrumentation, medical information systems, and health management and care-delivery systems.

GOE Number, Interest Area, and Work Group: 02.07.04; Science, Math, and Engineering; Engineering: General Engineering. **Instructional Program:** 140501 Bioengineering and Biomedical Engineering. **Note:** The Department of Labor has not collected some data for this job, so it has fewer details than the other descriptions.

17-2041.00 Chemical Engineers (Chemical Engineers)

Education: Bachelor's degree

Employed: 48,363

Openings: 3,892

Projected Growth: 9.5%

Earnings: $64,760

Design chemical-plant equipment. Devise processes for manufacturing chemicals and products such as gasoline, synthetic rubber, plastics, detergents, cement, paper, and pulp, by applying principles and technology of chemistry, physics, and engineering.

Develops safety procedures to be employed by workers operating equipment or working in close proximity to on-going chemical reactions. Prepares estimate of production costs and production progress reports for management. Determines most effective arrangement of operations, such as mixing, crushing, heat transfer, distillation, and drying. Designs measurement and control systems for chemical plants based on data collected in laboratory experiments and in pilot plant operations. Designs and plans layout of equipment. Develops processes to separate components of liquids or gases or generate electrical currents, using controlled chemical processes. Directs activities of workers who operate or who are engaged in constructing and improving absorption, evaporation, or electromagnetic equipment. Performs laboratory studies of steps in manufacture of new product and tests proposed process in small scale operation (pilot plant). Performs tests throughout stages of production to determine degree of control over variables, including temperature, density, specific gravity, and pressure. Conducts research to develop new and improved chemical manufacturing processes.

GOE Number, Interest Area, and Work Group: 02.07.01; Science, Math, and Engineering; Engineering: Research and Systems Design. **Personality Type:** Investigative. Investigative occupations frequently involve working with ideas and require an extensive amount of thinking. These occupations can involve searching for facts and figuring out problems mentally. **Work Values:** Ability Utilization; Creativity; Responsibility; Social Status; Autonomy. **Skills:** Science; Reading Comprehension; Operations Analysis; Active Learning; Testing. **Abilities:** *Cognitive*—Deductive Reasoning; Written Comprehension; Mathematical Reasoning; Written Expression; Originality; Inductive Reasoning. *Psychomotor*—Control Precision; Reaction Time; Response Orientation. *Physical*—Extent Flexibility; Gross Body Equilibrium. *Sensory*—Near Vision; Visual Color Discrimination; Speech Clarity. **General Work Activities:** *Information Input*—Monitoring Processes, Materials, and Surroundings; Identifying Objects, Actions, and Events; Getting Information Needed to Do the Job. *Mental Process*—Analyzing Data or Information; Making Decisions and Solving Problems; Updating and Using Job-Relevant Knowledge; Organizing, Planning, and Prioritizing. *Work Output*—Drafting and Specifying Technical Devices; Implementing Ideas and Programs; Documenting and Recording Information. *Interacting with Others*—Communicating with Other Workers; Providing Consultation and Advice to Others; Interpreting Meaning of Information to Others; Establishing and Maintaining Relationships; Coordinating Work and Activities of Others. **Physical Work Conditions:** Indoors; Common Protective or Safety Attire; Using Hands on Objects, Tools, or Controls. **Other Job Characteristics:** Consequence of Error; Importance of Being Exact or Accurate; Degree of Automation.

Experience: Job Zone 5. Extensive skill, knowledge, and experience are needed. Very advanced communication and organizational skills are required. **Job Preparation:** SVP 8.0 and above—4 years to more than 10 years. **Knowledge:** Chemistry; Engineering and Technology; Physics; Mathematics; Design. **Instructional Program:** 140701 Chemical Engineering.

Related DOT Jobs: 008.061-010 Absorption-and-Adsorption Engineer; 008.061-014 Chemical Design Engineer, Processes; 008.061-018 Chemical Engineer; 008.061-022 Chemical Research Engineer; 008.061-026 Chemical-Test Engineer.

17-2051.00 Civil Engineers (Civil Engineers)

Education: Bachelor's degree

Employed: 195,028

Openings: 20,603

Projected Growth: 20.9%

Earnings: $53,450

Perform engineering duties in planning, designing, and overseeing construction and maintenance of building structures and facilities such as roads, railroads, airports, bridges, harbors, channels, dams, irrigation projects, pipelines, power plants, water and sewage systems, and waste disposal units. Includes architectural, structural, traffic, ocean, and geotechnical engineers.

Inspects project sites to monitor progress and ensure conformance to design specifications and safety or sanitation standards. Computes load and grade requirements, water flow rates, and material stress factors to determine design specifications. Directs or participates in surveying to lay out installations and establish reference points, grades, and elevations to guide construction. Directs construction, operations, and maintenance activities at project site. Plans and designs transportation or hydraulic systems and structures, following construction and government standards, using design software and drawing tools. Conducts studies of traffic patterns or environmental conditions to identify engineering problems and assess the potential impact of projects. Tests soils and materials to determine the adequacy and strength of foundations, concrete, asphalt, or steel. Provides technical advice regarding design, construction, or program modifications and structural repairs to industrial and managerial personnel. Prepares or presents public reports, such as bid proposals, deeds, environmental impact statements, and property and right-of-way descriptions. Analyzes survey reports, maps, drawings, blueprints, aerial photography, and other topographical or geologic data to plan projects. Estimates quantities and cost of materials, equipment, or labor to determine project feasibility.

GOE Number, Interest Area, and Work Group: 02.07.04; Science, Math, and Engineering; Engineering: General Engineering. **Personality Type:** Realistic. Realistic occupations frequently involve work activities that include practical, hands-on problems and solutions. These occupations often deal with plants, animals, and real-world materials like wood, tools, and machinery. Many of the occupations require working outside and do not involve a lot of paperwork or working closely with others. **Work Values:** Ability Utilization; Autonomy; Achievement; Social Status; Creativity. **Skills:** Mathematics; Operations Analysis; Implementation Planning; Reading Comprehension; Problem Identification; Solution Appraisal; Information Gathering; Speaking; Writing; Critical Thinking. **Abilities:** *Cognitive*—Deductive Reasoning; Inductive Reasoning; Written Comprehension; Oral Expression; Oral Comprehension; Mathematical Reasoning. *Psychomotor*—Multilimb Coordination; Response Orientation. *Physical*—Trunk Strength. *Sensory*—Near Vision; Speech Clarity; Far Vision. **General Work Activities:** *Information Input*—Getting Information Needed to Do the Job; Inspecting Equipment, Structures, Materials; Estimating Needed Characteristics. *Mental Process*—Analyzing Data or Information; Making Decisions and Solving Problems; Processing Information. *Work Output*—Drafting and Specifying Technical Devices; Implementing Ideas and Programs; Interacting with Computers; Documenting and Recording Information. *Interacting with Others*—Communicating with Other Workers; Providing Consultation and Advice to Others; Coordinating Work and Activities of Others. **Physical Work Conditions:** Indoors; Sitting; Outdoors; Standing. **Other Job Characteristics:** Consequence of Error; Importance of Being Sure All Is Done; Importance of Being Exact or Accurate.

Experience: Job Zone 4. A minimum of two to four years of work-related skill, knowledge, or experience is needed. **Job Preparation:** SVP 7.0 to less than 8.0—2 years to less than 10 years. **Knowledge:** Engineering and Technology; Design; Administration and Management; Physics; Building and Construction. **Instructional Programs:** 140401 Architectural Engineering; 140801 Civil Engineering, General; 140802 Geotechnical Engineering; 140803 Structural Engineering; 140804 Transportation and Highway Engineering; 140805 Water Resources Engineering; 140899 Civil Engineering, Other.

Related DOT Jobs: 005.061-010 Airport Engineer; 005.061-014 Civil Engineer; 005.061-018 Hydraulic Engineer; 005.061-022 Irrigation Engineer; 005.061-026 Railroad Engineer; 005.061-030 Sanitary Engineer; 005.061-034 Structural Engineer; 005.061-038 Transportation Engineer; 005.167-014 Drainage-Design Coordinator; 005.167-018 Forest Engineer; 005.167-026 Production Engineer, Track; 019.167-018 Resource-Recovery Engineer.

17-2061.00 Computer Hardware Engineers (Electrical and Electronics Engineers)

Education: Bachelor's degree
Employed: 356,954
Openings: 29,636
Projected Growth: 25.9%
Earnings: $62,260

Research, design, develop, and test computer or computer-related equipment for commercial, industrial, military, or scientific use. Supervise the manufacturing and installation of computer or computer-related equipment and components.

Formulates and designs software system, using scientific analysis and mathematical models to predict and measure outcome and consequences of design. Enters data into computer terminal to store, retrieve, and manipulate data for analysis of system capabilities and requirements. Consults with engineering staff to evaluate interface between hardware and software and operational and performance requirements of overall system. Analyzes information to determine, recommend, and plan layout for type of computers and peripheral equipment modifications to existing systems. Confers with data processing and project managers to obtain information on limitations and capabilities for data processing projects. Coordinates installation of software system. Consults with customer concerning maintenance of software system. Trains users to use new or modified equipment. Recommends purchase of equipment to control dust, temperature, and humidity in area of system installation. Specifies power supply requirements and configuration. Develops and directs software system testing procedures, programming, and documentation. Evaluates factors such as reporting formats required, cost constraints, and need for security restrictions to determine hardware configuration. Analyzes software requirements to determine feasibility of design within time and cost constraints. Monitors functioning of equipment to ensure system operates in conformance with specifications.

GOE Number, Interest Area, and Work Group: 02.07.01; Science, Math, and Engineering; Engineering: Research and Systems Design. **Personality Type:** Investigative. Investigative occupations frequently involve working with ideas and require an extensive amount of thinking. These occupations can involve searching for facts and figuring out problems mentally. **Work Values:** Ability Utilization; Working Conditions; Creativity; Responsibility; Achievement; Social Status; Activity; Autonomy. **Skills:** Programming; Troubleshooting; Active Learning; Testing; Mathematics. **Abilities:** *Cognitive*—Written Comprehension; Oral Comprehension; Inductive Reasoning; Oral Expression; Written Expression; Mathematical Reasoning. *Psychomotor*—Wrist-Finger Speed; Response Orientation. *Physical*—Gross Body Coordination. *Sensory*—Near Vision; Speech Clarity; Speech Recognition. **General Work Activities:** *Information Input*—Getting Information Needed to Do the Job; Identifying Objects, Actions, and Events; Monitoring Processes, Materials, and Surroundings; Estimating Needed Characteristics. *Mental Process*—Updating and Using Job-Relevant Knowledge; Thinking Creatively; Analyzing Data or Information. *Work Output*—Interacting with Computers; Drafting and Specifying Technical Devices; Documenting and Recording Information; Implementing Ideas and Programs. *Interacting with Others*—Providing Consultation and Advice to Others; Communicating with Other Workers; Communicating with Persons Outside Organization. **Physical Work Conditions:** Indoors; Sitting; Using Hands on Objects, Tools, or Controls. **Other Job Characteristics:** Degree of Automation; Importance of Being Exact or Accurate; Importance of Being Sure All Is Done.

Experience: Job Zone 4. A minimum of two to four years of work-related skill, knowledge, or experience is needed. **Job Prepara-**

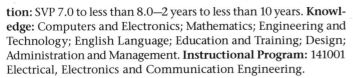

tion: SVP 7.0 to less than 8.0—2 years to less than 10 years. **Knowledge:** Computers and Electronics; Mathematics; Engineering and Technology; English Language; Education and Training; Design; Administration and Management. **Instructional Program:** 141001 Electrical, Electronics and Communication Engineering.

Related DOT Jobs: No data available.

17-2071.00 Electrical Engineers (Electrical and Electronics Engineers)

Education: Bachelor's degree
Employed: 356,954
Openings: 29,636
Projected Growth: 25.9%
Earnings: $62,260

Design, develop, test, or supervise the manufacturing and installation of electrical equipment, components, or systems, for commercial, industrial, military, or scientific use.

Designs electrical instruments, equipment, facilities, components, products, and systems for commercial, industrial, and domestic purposes. Compiles data and writes reports regarding existing and potential engineering studies and projects. Develops applications of controls, instruments, and systems for new commercial, domestic, and industrial uses. Plans and implements research methodology and procedures to apply principles of electrical theory to engineering projects. Plans layout of electric power generating plants and distribution lines and stations. Performs detailed calculations to compute and establish manufacturing, construction, and installation standards and specifications. Estimates labor, material, and construction costs, and prepares specifications for purchase of materials and equipment. Collects data relating to commercial and residential development, population, and power system interconnection to determine operating efficiency of electrical systems. Operates computer-assisted engineering and design software and equipment to perform engineering tasks. Investigates customer or public complaints, determines nature and extent of problem, and recommends remedial measures. Inspects completed installations and observes operations for conformance to design and equipment specifications, and operational and safety standards. Evaluates and analyzes data regarding electric power systems and stations, and recommends changes to improve operating efficiency. Confers with engineers, customers, and others to discuss existing or potential engineering projects and products. Conducts field surveys and studies maps, graphs, diagrams, and other data to identify and correct power system problems. Prepares and studies technical drawings, specifications of electrical systems, and topographical maps to ensure installation and operations conform to standards and customer requirements.

GOE Number, Interest Area, and Work Group: 02.07.04; Science, Math, and Engineering; Engineering: General Engineering. **Personality Type:** Investigative. Investigative occupations frequently involve working with ideas and require an extensive amount of thinking. These occupations can involve searching for facts and figuring out problems mentally. **Work Values:** Ability Utilization; Responsibility; Creativity; Autonomy; Social Sta-

tus. **Skills:** Mathematics; Critical Thinking; Reading Comprehension; Active Learning; Writing. **Abilities:** *Cognitive*—Number Facility; Written Comprehension; Oral Expression; Deductive Reasoning; Mathematical Reasoning; Oral Comprehension. *Psychomotor*—Finger Dexterity; Manual Dexterity; Wrist-Finger Speed. *Physical*—Trunk Strength; Gross Body Coordination; Stamina. *Sensory*—Near Vision; Speech Clarity; Visual Color Discrimination. **General Work Activities:** *Information Input*—Getting Information Needed to Do the Job; Identifying Objects, Actions, and Events; Inspecting Equipment, Structures, Materials. *Mental Process*—Analyzing Data or Information; Making Decisions and Solving Problems; Updating and Using Job-Relevant Knowledge. *Work Output*—Drafting and Specifying Technical Devices; Implementing Ideas and Programs; Interacting with Computers. *Interacting with Others*—Communicating with Persons Outside Organization; Coordinating Work and Activities of Others; Providing Consultation and Advice to Others; Communicating with Other Workers. **Physical Work Conditions:** Indoors; Sitting; Using Hands on Objects, Tools, or Controls. **Other Job Characteristics:** Consequence of Error; Importance of Being Sure All Is Done; Importance of Being Exact or Accurate.

Experience: Job Zone 5. Extensive skill, knowledge, and experience are needed. Very advanced communication and organizational skills are required. **Job Preparation:** SVP 8.0 and above—4 years to more than 10 years. **Knowledge:** Engineering and Technology; Computers and Electronics; Mathematics; Design; Building and Construction; Production and Processing. **Instructional Program:** 141001 Electrical, Electronics and Communication Engineering.

Related DOT Jobs: 003.061-010 Electrical Engineer; 003.061-014 Electrical Test Engineer; 003.061-018 Electrical-Design Engineer; 003.061-022 Electrical-Prospecting Engineer; 003.061-026 Electrical-Research Engineer; 003.061-046 Illuminating Engineer; 003.167-014 Distribution-Field Engineer; 003.167-018 Electrical Engineer, Power System; 003.167-022 Electrolysis-and-Corrosion-Control Engineer; 003.167-026 Engineer of System Development; 003.167-038 Induction-Coordination Power Engineer; 003.167-046 Power-Distribution Engineer; 003.167-050 Power-Transmission Engineer; 003.167-054 Protection Engineer.

17-2072.00 Electronics Engineers, Except Computer (Electrical and Electronics Engineers)

Education: Bachelor's degree
Employed: 356,954
Openings: 29,636
Projected Growth: 25.9%
Earnings: $62,260

Research, design, develop, and test electronic components and systems for commercial, industrial, military, or scientific use, applying knowledge of electronic theory and materials properties. Design electronic circuits and components for use in fields such as telecommunications, aerospace guidance and propulsion control, acoustics, or instruments and controls.

Reviews or prepares budget and cost estimates for equipment, construction, and installation projects, and controls expenditures.

Prepares, reviews, and maintains maintenance schedules and operational reports and charts. Provides technical assistance to field and laboratory staff regarding equipment standards and problems, and applications of transmitting and receiving methods. Inspects electronic equipment, instruments, products, and systems to ensure conformance to specifications, safety standards, and applicable codes and regulations. Analyzes system requirements, capacity, cost, and customer needs to determine feasibility of project and develop system plan. Plans and develops applications and modifications for electronic properties used in components, products, and systems, to improve technical performance. Confers with engineers, customers, and others to discuss existing and potential engineering projects or products. Directs and coordinates activities concerned with manufacture, construction, installation, maintenance, operation, and modification of electronic equipment, products, and systems. Develops operational, maintenance, and testing procedures for electronic products, components, equipment, and systems. Determines material and equipment needs and orders supplies. Designs electronic components, products and systems for commercial, industrial, medical, military, and scientific applications. Investigates causes of personal injury resulting from contact with high voltage communications equipment. Plans and implements research, methodology, and procedures to apply principles of electronic theory to engineering projects. Evaluates operational systems and recommends repair or design modifications based on factors, such as environment, service, cost, and system capabilities. Conducts studies to gather information regarding current services, equipment capacities, traffic data, and acquisition and installation costs.

GOE Number, Interest Area, and Work Group: 02.07.04; Science, Math, and Engineering; Engineering: General Engineering. **Personality Type:** Investigative. Investigative occupations frequently involve working with ideas and require an extensive amount of thinking. These occupations can involve searching for facts and figuring out problems mentally. **Work Values:** Ability Utilization; Responsibility; Creativity; Autonomy; Working Conditions. **Skills:** Mathematics; Reading Comprehension; Writing; Science; Judgment and Decision Making. **Abilities:** *Cognitive*—Written Comprehension; Oral Expression; Mathematical Reasoning; Oral Comprehension; Number Facility; Deductive Reasoning. *Psychomotor*—Wrist-Finger Speed; Finger Dexterity; Manual Dexterity. *Physical*—Gross Body Coordination; Dynamic Flexibility. *Sensory*—Near Vision; Speech Clarity; Visual Color Discrimination; Speech Recognition; Far Vision. **General Work Activities:** *Information Input*—Getting Information Needed to Do the Job; Inspecting Equipment, Structures, Materials; Monitoring Processes, Materials, and Surroundings; Identifying Objects, Actions, and Events. *Mental Process*—Analyzing Data or Information; Making Decisions and Solving Problems; Thinking Creatively; Updating and Using Job-Relevant Knowledge. *Work Output*—Drafting and Specifying Technical Devices; Implementing Ideas and Programs; Interacting with Computers; Repairing and Maintaining Electrical Equipment. *Interacting with Others*—Communicating with Other Workers; Coordinating Work and Activities of Others; Communicating with Persons Outside Organization. **Physical Work Conditions:** Indoors; Using Hands on Objects, Tools, or Controls; Sitting. **Other Job Characteristics:** Consequence of Error; Importance of Being Sure All Is Done; Importance of Being Exact or Accurate.

Experience: Job Zone 5. Extensive skill, knowledge, and experience are needed. Very advanced communication and organizational skills are required. **Job Preparation:** SVP 8.0 and above—4 years to more than 10 years. **Knowledge:** Engineering and Technology; Design; Mathematics; Computers and Electronics; Production and Processing; Telecommunications. **Instructional Program:** 141001 Electrical, Electronics and Communication Engineering.

Related DOT Jobs: 003.061-030 Electronics Engineer; 003.061-034 Electronics-Design Engineer; 003.061-038 Electronics-Research Engineer; 003.061-042 Electronics-Test Engineer; 003.061-050 Planning Engineer, Central Office Facilities; 003.167-010 Cable Engineer, Outside Plant; 003.167-030 Engineer-in-Charge, Studio Operations; 003.167-042 Outside-Plant Engineer; 003.167-058 Supervisor, Microwave; 003.167-066 Transmission-and-Protection Engineer; 003.187-010 Central-Office Equipment Engineer; 003.187-014 Commercial Engineer; 003.187-018 Customer-Equipment Engineer; 031.167-018 Telecommunications Specialist.

17-2081.00 Environmental Engineers (Civil Engineers)

Education: Bachelor's degree
Employed: 195,028
Openings: 20,603
Projected Growth: 20.9%
Earnings: $53,450

Design, plan, or perform engineering duties in the prevention, control, and remediation of environmental health hazards utilizing various engineering disciplines. Use waste treatment, site remediation, or pollution control technology.

GOE Number, Interest Area, and Work Group: 02.07.04; Science, Math, and Engineering; Engineering: General Engineering. **Instructional Programs:** 140401 Architectural Engineering; 140801 Civil Engineering, General; 140802 Geotechnical Engineering; 140803 Structural Engineering; 140804 Transportation and Highway Engineering; 140805 Water Resources Engineering; 140899 Civil Engineering, Other. **Note:** The Department of Labor has not collected some data for this job, so it has fewer details than the other descriptions.

17-2111.00 Health and Safety Engineers, Except Mining Safety Engineers and Inspectors (Safety Engineers, Except Mining)

Education: No data available.
Employed: 21,940
Openings: No data available.
Projected Growth: No data available.
Earnings: $50,990

Promote worksite or product safety by applying knowledge of industrial processes, mechanics, chemistry, psychology, and industrial health and safety laws.

GOE Number, Interest Area, and Work Group: 02.07.04; Science, Math, and Engineering; Engineering: General Engineering. **Instructional Program:** 140101 Engineering, General. **Note:** The Department of Labor has not collected some data for this job, so it has fewer details than the other descriptions.

17-2111.01 Industrial Safety and Health Engineers
(Safety Engineers, Except Mining)

Education: No data available.

Employed: 21,940

Openings: No data available.

Projected Growth: No data available.

Earnings: $50,990

Plan, implement, and coordinate safety programs requiring application of engineering principles and technology, to prevent or correct unsafe environmental working conditions.

Designs and builds safety devices for machinery or safety clothing. Inspects facilities, machinery, and safety equipment to identify and correct potential hazards, and ensure compliance with safety regulations. Conducts or directs testing of air quality, noise, temperature, or radiation to verify compliance with health and safety regulations. Investigates causes of industrial accidents or injuries to develop solutions to minimize or prevent recurrence. Checks floors of plant to ensure they are strong enough to support heavy machinery. Compiles, analyzes, and interprets statistical data related to exposure factors concerning occupational illnesses and accidents. Examines plans and specifications for new machinery or equipment to determine if all safety requirements have been included. Conducts plant or area surveys to determine safety levels for exposure to materials and conditions. Installs or directs installation of safety devices on machinery. Provides technical guidance to organizations regarding how to handle health-related problems, such as water and air pollution. Conducts or coordinates training of workers concerning safety laws and regulations, use of safety equipment, devices, and clothing, and first aid. Devises and implements safety or industrial health program to prevent, correct, or control unsafe environmental conditions. Prepares reports of findings from investigation of accidents, inspection of facilities, or testing of environment. Maintains liaison with outside organizations, such as fire departments, mutual aid societies, and rescue teams.

GOE Number, Interest Area, and Work Group: 02.07.02; Science, Math, and Engineering; Engineering: Industrial and Safety. **Personality Type:** Investigative. Investigative occupations frequently involve working with ideas and require an extensive amount of thinking. These occupations can involve searching for facts and figuring out problems mentally. **Work Values:** Responsibility; Ability Utilization; Autonomy; Social Status; Creativity. **Skills:** Mathematics; Problem Identification; Operations Analysis; Instructing; Identification of Key Causes; Monitoring; Technology Design; Idea Evaluation; Critical Thinking; Reading Comprehension. **Abilities:** *Cognitive*—Written Comprehension; Oral Comprehension; Inductive Reasoning; Deductive Reasoning; Mathematical Reasoning; Written Expression. *Psychomotor*—Control Precision; Multilimb Coordination. *Physical*—Extent Flexibility; Trunk Strength; Gross Body Coordination. *Sensory*—Near Vision; Speech Clarity; Speech Recognition. **General Work Activities:** *Information Input*—Getting Information Needed to Do the Job; Inspecting Equipment, Structures, Materials; Identifying Objects, Actions, and Events. *Mental Process*—Processing Information; Making Decisions and Solving Problems; Evaluating Information Against Standards. *Work Output*—Implementing Ideas and Programs; Drafting and Specifying Technical Devices; Interacting with Computers; Handling and Moving Objects. *Interacting with Others*—Providing Consultation and Advice to Others; Interpreting Meaning of Information to Others; Communicating with Other Workers; Communicating with Persons Outside Organization. **Physical Work Conditions:** Indoors; Sitting; Standing. **Other Job Characteristics:** Consequence of Error; Importance of Being Exact or Accurate; Importance of Being Sure All Is Done.

Experience: Job Zone 4. A minimum of two to four years of work-related skill, knowledge, or experience is needed. **Job Preparation:** SVP 7.0 to less than 8.0—2 years to less than 10 years. **Knowledge:** Engineering and Technology; Public Safety and Security; Design; Physics; Administration and Management. **Instructional Program:** 140101 Engineering, General.

Related DOT Jobs: 012.061-014 Safety Engineer; 012.167-034 Industrial-Health Engineer; 012.167-058 Safety Manager.

17-2111.02 Fire-Prevention and Protection Engineers
(Safety Engineers, Except Mining)

Education: No data available.

Employed: 21,940

Openings: No data available.

Projected Growth: No data available.

Earnings: $50,990

Research causes of fires. Determine fire-protection methods. Design or recommend materials or equipment such as structural components or fire-detection equipment, to assist organizations in safeguarding life and property against fire, explosion, and related hazards.

Designs fire detection equipment, alarm systems, fire extinguishing devices and systems, or structural components protection. Conducts research on fire retardants and fire safety of materials and devices to determine cause and methods of fire prevention. Organizes and trains personnel to carry out fire protection programs. Evaluates fire departments and laws and regulations affecting fire prevention or fire safety. Recommends and advises on use of fire detection equipment, extinguishing devices, or methods to alleviate conditions conducive to fire. Studies buildings to evaluate fire prevention factors, resistance of construction, contents, water supply and delivery, and exits. Determines fire causes and methods of fire prevention. Advises and plans for prevention of destruction by fire, wind, water, or other causes of damage.

GOE Number, Interest Area, and Work Group: 02.07.02; Science, Math, and Engineering; Engineering: Industrial and Safety. **Personality Type:** Investigative. Investigative occupations frequently involve working with ideas and require an extensive amount of thinking. These occupations can involve searching for facts and figuring out problems mentally. **Work Values:** Responsibility; Autonomy; Achievement; Ability Utilization; Social Status. **Skills:** Technology Design; Instructing; Reading Comprehension; Active Learning; Information Gathering; Speaking; Operations Analysis. **Abilities:** *Cognitive*—Oral Expression; Deductive Reasoning; Inductive Reasoning; Problem Sensitivity; Written Expression; Written Comprehension. *Psychomotor*—none met the criteria. *Physical*—none met the criteria. *Sensory*—Speech Clarity; Depth Perception; Night Vision. **General Work Activities:** *Information Input*—Getting Information Needed to Do the Job; Identifying Objects, Actions, and Events; Monitoring Processes, Materials, and Surroundings. *Mental Process*—Making Decisions and Solving Problems; Analyzing Data or Information; Updating and Using Job-Relevant Knowledge; Processing Information. *Work Output*—Drafting and Specifying Technical Devices; Implementing Ideas and Programs; Documenting and Recording Information. *Interacting with Others*—Communicating with Persons Outside Organization; Providing Consultation and Advice to Others; Interpreting Meaning of Information to Others. **Physical Work Conditions:** Indoors; Sitting; Standing. **Other Job Characteristics:** Consequence of Error; Importance of Being Exact or Accurate; Importance of Being Sure All Is Done.

Experience: Job Zone 4. A minimum of two to four years of work-related skill, knowledge, or experience is needed. **Job Preparation:** SVP 7.0 to less than 8.0—2 years to less than 10 years. **Knowledge:** Public Safety and Security; Education and Training; Chemistry; Engineering and Technology; Law, Government and Jurisprudence. **Instructional Program:** 140101 Engineering, General.

Related DOT Jobs: 012.167-022 Fire-Prevention Research Engineer; 012.167-026 Fire-Protection Engineer.

17-2111.03 Product Safety Engineers (Safety Engineers, Except Mining)

Education: No data available.
Employed: 21,940
Openings: No data available.
Projected Growth: No data available.
Earnings: $50,990

Develop and conduct tests to evaluate product safety levels; recommend measures to reduce or eliminate hazards.

Prepares reports of findings from investigation of accidents. Advises and recommends procedures for detection, prevention, and elimination of physical, chemical, or other product hazards. Evaluates potential health hazards or damage which could occur from misuse of product and engineers solutions to improve safety. Participates in preparation of product usage and precautionary label instructions. Conducts research to evaluate safety levels for products. Investigates causes of accidents, injuries, or illnesses from product usage to develop solutions to minimize or prevent recurrence.

GOE Number, Interest Area, and Work Group: 02.07.02; Science, Math, and Engineering; Engineering: Industrial and Safety. **Personality Type:** Investigative. Investigative occupations frequently involve working with ideas and require an extensive

amount of thinking. These occupations can involve searching for facts and figuring out problems mentally. **Work Values:** Achievement; Ability Utilization; Autonomy; Creativity; Responsibility. **Skills:** Information Gathering; Testing; Solution Appraisal; Mathematics; Problem Identification; Active Learning; Writing. **Abilities:** *Cognitive*—Written Expression; Problem Sensitivity; Deductive Reasoning; Oral Expression; Inductive Reasoning; Oral Comprehension. *Psychomotor*—none met the criteria. *Physical*—none met the criteria. *Sensory*—Speech Clarity; Speech Recognition; Sound Localization; Visual Color Discrimination. **General Work Activities:** *Information Input*—Identifying Objects, Actions, and Events; Getting Information Needed to Do the Job; Inspecting Equipment, Structures, Materials. *Mental Process*—Processing Information; Evaluating Information Against Standards; Analyzing Data or Information. *Work Output*—Documenting and Recording Information; Implementing Ideas and Programs; Interacting with Computers. *Interacting with Others*—Providing Consultation and Advice to Others; Interpreting Meaning of Information to Others; Communicating with Other Workers. **Physical Work Conditions:** Indoors; Sitting; Using Hands on Objects, Tools, or Controls. **Other Job Characteristics:** Consequence of Error; Importance of Being Exact or Accurate; Importance of Being Sure All Is Done.

Experience: Job Zone 5. Extensive skill, knowledge, and experience are needed. Very advanced communication and organizational skills are required. **Job Preparation:** SVP 8.0 and above—4 years to more than 10 years. **Knowledge:** Public Safety and Security; Chemistry; Engineering and Technology; Physics; English Language. **Instructional Program:** 140101 Engineering, General.

Related DOT Job: 012.061-010 Product-Safety Engineer.

17-2112.00 Industrial Engineers (Industrial Engineers)

Education: Bachelor's degree
Employed: 126,303
Openings: 13,125
Projected Growth: 12.8%
Earnings: $52,610

Design, develop, test, and evaluate integrated systems for managing industrial production processes including human work factors, quality control, inventory control, logistics and material flow, cost analysis, and production coordination.

Evaluates precision and accuracy of production and testing equipment and engineering drawings to formulate corrective action plan. Drafts and designs layout of equipment, materials, and workspace to illustrate maximum efficiency, using drafting tools and computer. Reviews production schedules, engineering specifications, orders, and related information to obtain knowledge of manufacturing methods, procedures, and activities. Formulates sampling procedures and designs and develops forms and instructions for recording, evaluating, and reporting quality and reliability data. Coordinates quality control objectives and activities to resolve production problems, maximize product reliability, and minimize cost. Completes production reports, purchase orders, and material, tool, and equipment lists. Regulates and alters workflow schedules according to established manufacturing sequences and lead times to expedite production operations. Records or oversees recording of information to ensure currency of engineering drawings and documentation of production problems. Implements methods and procedures for disposition of discrepant material and defective or damaged parts, and assesses cost and responsibility. Plans and establishes sequence of operations to fabricate and assemble parts or products and to promote efficient utilization of resources. Confers with vendors, staff, and management personnel regarding purchases, procedures, product specifications, manufacturing capabilities, and project status. Develops manufacturing methods, labor utilization standards, and cost analysis systems to promote efficient staff and facility utilization. Studies operations sequence, material flow, functional statements, organization charts, and project information to determine worker functions and responsibilities. Applies statistical methods and performs mathematical calculations to determine manufacturing processes, staff requirements, and production standards.

GOE Number, Interest Area, and Work Group: 02.07.02; Science, Math, and Engineering; Engineering: Industrial and Safety. **Personality Type:** Enterprising. Enterprising occupations frequently involve starting up and carrying out projects. These occupations can involve leading people and making many decisions. They sometimes require risk taking and often deal with business. **Work Values:** Ability Utilization; Creativity; Autonomy; Responsibility; Authority; Social Status; Activity. **Skills:** Mathematics; Reading Comprehension; Management of Material Resources; Systems Evaluation; Information Gathering. **Abilities:** *Cognitive*—Written Comprehension; Written Expression; Oral Comprehension; Oral Expression; Deductive Reasoning; Fluency of Ideas. *Psychomotor*—none met the criteria. *Physical*—none met the criteria. *Sensory*—Speech Recognition; Speech Clarity; Depth Perception. **General Work Activities:** *Information Input*—Getting Information Needed to Do the Job; Identifying Objects, Actions, and Events; Monitoring Processes, Materials, and Surroundings. *Mental Process*—Processing Information; Analyzing Data or Information; Making Decisions and Solving Problems. *Work Output*—Documenting and Recording Information; Implementing Ideas and Programs; Interacting with Computers. *Interacting with Others*—Communicating with Other Workers; Providing Consultation and Advice to Others; Coordinating Work and Activities of Others. **Physical Work Conditions:** Indoors; Sitting; Using Hands on Objects, Tools, or Controls. **Other Job Characteristics:** Consequence of Error; Importance of Being Sure All Is Done; Importance of Being Aware of New Events.

Experience: Job Zone 4. A minimum of two to four years of work-related skill, knowledge, or experience is needed. **Job Preparation:** SVP 7.0 to less than 8.0—2 years to less than 10 years. **Knowledge:** Mathematics; Engineering and Technology; Production and Processing; Administration and Management; Design. **Instructional Programs:** 141701 Industrial/Manufacturing Engineering; 143001 Engineering/Industrial Management.

Related DOT Jobs: 011.161-010 Supervisor, Metallurgical-and-Quality-Control-Testing; 012.061-018 Standards Engineer; 012.067-010 Metrologist; 012.167-010 Configuration Management Analyst; 012.167-014 Manager, Quality Control; 012.167-018 Factory Lay-Out Engineer; 012.167-030 Industrial Engineer; 012.167-038 Liaison Engineer; 012.167-042 Manufacturing Engineer; 012.167-046 Production Engineer; 012.167-050 Production Planner; 012.167-054 Quality Control Engineer; 012.167-062 Supervisor, Vendor Quality; 012.167-070 Time-Study Engineer; 012.167-074 Tool Planner; 012.167-078 Documentation Engineer; 012.167-082 Material Scheduler; 012.187-014 Shoe-Lay-Out Planner; 019.167-010 Logistics Engineer; 822.261-014 Equipment Inspector.

17-2121.00 Marine Engineers and Naval Architects
(Marine Engineers)

Education: No data available.

Employed: 3,890

Openings: No data available.

Projected Growth: No data available.

Earnings: $48,050

Design, develop, and evaluate the operation of marine vessels, ship machinery, and related equipment, such as power supply and propulsion systems.

GOE Number, Interest Area, and Work Group: 02.07.03; Science, Math, and Engineering; Engineering: Design. **Instructional Program:** 142201 Naval Architecture and Marine Engineering. **Note:** The Department of Labor has not collected some data for this job, so it has fewer details than the other descriptions.

17-2121.01 Marine Engineers (Marine Engineers)

Education: No data available.

Employed: 3,890

Openings: No data available.

Projected Growth: No data available.

Earnings: $48,050

Design, develop, and take responsibility for the installation of ship machinery and related equipment, including propulsion machines and power-supply systems.

Maintains and coordinates repair of marine machinery and equipment for installation on vessels. Prepares technical reports for use by engineering, management, or sales personnel. Prepares or directs preparation of product or system layout and detailed drawings and schematics. Conducts analytical, environmental, operational, or performance studies to develop design for products, such as marine engines, equipment, and structures. Confers with research personnel to clarify or resolve problems and develop or modify design. Inspects marine equipment and machinery to draw up work requests and job specifications. Reviews work requests and compares them with previous work completed on ship to ensure costs are economically sound. Coordinates activities with those of regulatory bodies to ensure repairs and alterations are at minimum cost, consistent with safety. Procures materials needed to repair marine equipment and machinery. Conducts environmental, operational, or performance tests on marine machinery and equipment. Designs and oversees testing, installation, and repair of marine apparatus and equipment. Determines conditions under which tests are to be conducted and sequences and phases of test operations. Evaluates operation of marine equipment during acceptance testing and shakedown cruises. Investigates and observes tests on machinery and equipment for compliance with standards. Analyzes data to determine feasibility of product proposal. Maintains contact and formulates reports for contractors and clients to ensure completion of work at minimum cost.

GOE Number, Interest Area, and Work Group: 02.07.01; Science, Math, and Engineering; Engineering: Research and Systems Design. **Personality Type:** Realistic. Realistic occupations frequently involve work activities that include practical, hands-on problems and solutions. These occupations often deal with plants, animals, and real-world materials like wood, tools, and machinery. Many of the occupations require working outside and do not involve a lot of paperwork or working closely with others. **Work Values:** Ability Utilization; Autonomy; Creativity; Responsibility; Social Status. **Skills:** Mathematics; Reading Comprehension; Writing; Testing; Science. **Abilities:** *Cognitive*—Oral Expression; Written Expression; Visualization; Written Comprehension; Problem Sensitivity; Inductive Reasoning. *Psychomotor*—Control Precision; Finger Dexterity; Manual Dexterity. *Physical*—Gross Body Equilibrium; Gross Body Coordination. *Sensory*—Near Vision; Speech Clarity; Far Vision. **General Work Activities:** *Information Input*—Inspecting Equipment, Structures, Materials; Getting Information Needed to Do the Job; Identifying Objects, Actions, and Events. *Mental Process*—Evaluating Information Against Standards; Updating and Using Job-Relevant Knowledge; Making Decisions and Solving Problems. *Work Output*—Implementing Ideas and Programs; Drafting and Specifying Technical Devices; Repairing and Maintaining Mechanical Equipment. *Interacting with Others*—Communicating with Other Workers; Providing Consultation and Advice to Others; Coordinating Work and Activities of Others. **Physical Work Conditions:** Using Hands on Objects, Tools, or Controls; Sitting; Indoors. **Other Job Characteristics:** Consequence of Error; Importance of Being Sure All Is Done; Importance of Being Exact or Accurate.

Experience: Job Zone 5. Extensive skill, knowledge, and experience are needed. Very advanced communication and organizational skills are required. **Job Preparation:** SVP 8.0 and above—4 years to more than 10 years. **Knowledge:** Engineering and Technology; Mechanical; Mathematics; Physics; Design; Administration and Management. **Instructional Program:** 142201 Naval Architecture and Marine Engineering.

Related DOT Jobs: 014.061-010 Design Engineer, Marine Equipment; 014.061-014 Marine Engineer; 014.061-018 Research Engineer, Marine Equipment; 014.061-022 Test Engineer, Marine Equipment; 014.167-010 Marine Surveyor; 014.167-014 Port Engineer.

17-2121.02 Marine Architects (Architects)

Education: Bachelor's degree

Employed: 99,162

Openings: 7,762

Projected Growth: 18.9%

Earnings: $47,710

Design and oversee construction and repair of marine craft and floating structures such as ships, barges, tugs, dredges, submarines, torpedoes, floats, and buoys. Confer with marine engineers.

Designs complete hull and superstructure according to specifications and test data, in conformity with standards of safety, efficiency, and economy. Confers with marine engineering personnel to establish arrangement of boiler room equipment and propulsion machinery, heating and ventilating systems, refrigeration equipment, piping, and other functional equipment. Studies design proposals and specifications to establish basic characteristics of craft, such as size, weight, speed, propulsion, displacement, and draft. Designs layout of craft interior, including cargo space, passenger compartments, ladder wells, and elevators. Oversees construction and testing of prototype in model basin and develops sectional and waterline curves of hull to establish center of gravity, ideal hull form, and buoyancy and stability data. Evaluates performance of craft during dock and sea trials to determine design changes and conformance with national and international standards.

GOE Number, Interest Area, and Work Group: 02.07.03; Science, Math, and Engineering; Engineering: Design. **Personality Type:** Realistic. Realistic occupations frequently involve work activities that include practical, hands-on problems and solutions. These occupations often deal with plants, animals, and real-world materials like wood, tools, and machinery. Many of the occupations require working outside and do not involve a lot of paperwork or working closely with others. **Work Values:** Ability Utilization; Creativity; Achievement; Social Status; Autonomy. **Skills:** Mathematics; Testing; Active Learning; Monitoring; Solution Appraisal; Reading Comprehension; Critical Thinking; Idea Evaluation. **Abilities:** *Cognitive*—Visualization; Deductive Reasoning; Written Comprehension; Originality; Information Ordering; Oral Comprehension. *Psychomotor*—Finger Dexterity; Manual Dexterity; Multilimb Coordination. *Physical*—Gross Body Equilibrium; Gross Body Coordination; Dynamic Flexibility. *Sensory*—Far Vision; Near Vision; Speech Clarity. **General Work Activities:** *Information Input*—Getting Information Needed to Do the Job; Inspecting Equipment, Structures, Materials; Identifying Objects, Actions, and Events. *Mental Process*—Making Decisions and Solving Problems; Thinking Creatively; Updating and Using Job-Relevant Knowledge; Analyzing Data or Information. *Work Output*—Drafting and Specifying Technical Devices; Implementing Ideas and Programs; Handling and Moving Objects. *Interacting with Others*—Communicating with Other Workers; Coordinating Work and Activities of Others; Interpreting Meaning of Information to Others; Establishing and Maintaining Relationships. **Physical Work Conditions:** Indoors; Sitting; Using Hands on Objects, Tools, or Controls. **Other Job Characteristics:** Consequence of Error; Importance of Being Exact or Accurate; Importance of Being Sure All Is Done.

Experience: Job Zone 5. Extensive skill, knowledge, and experience are needed. Very advanced communication and organizational skills are required. **Job Preparation:** SVP 8.0 and above—4 years to more than 10 years. **Knowledge:** Design; Engineering and Technology; Mathematics; Physics; Building and Construction. **Instructional Programs:** 040201 Architecture; 040401

Architectural Environmental Design; 049999 Architecture and Related Programs, Other.
Related DOT Job: 001.061-014 Architect, Marine.

17-2131.00 Materials Engineers (Materials Engineers)

Education: Bachelor's degree
Employed: 19,654
Openings: 1,567
Projected Growth: 9%
Earnings: $57,970

Evaluate materials and develop machinery and processes to manufacture materials for use in products that must meet specialized design and performance specifications. Develop new uses for known materials. Includes engineers working with composite materials or specializing in one type of material such as graphite, metal and metal alloys, ceramics and glass, plastics and polymers, and naturally occurring materials.

Evaluates technical and economic factors relating to process or product design objectives. Confers with producers of material during investigation and evaluation of material for product applications. Reviews product failure data and interprets laboratory test results to determine material or process causes. Plans and implements laboratory operations to develop material and fabrication procedures that maintain cost and performance standards. Reviews new product plans and makes recommendations for material selection based on design objectives and cost.

GOE Number, Interest Area, and Work Group: 02.07.02; Science, Math, and Engineering; Engineering: Industrial and Safety. **Personality Type:** Investigative. Investigative occupations frequently involve working with ideas and require an extensive amount of thinking. These occupations can involve searching for facts and figuring out problems mentally. **Work Values:** Ability Utilization; Creativity; Autonomy; Responsibility; Moral Values. **Skills:** Mathematics; Science; Solution Appraisal; Operations Analysis; Judgment and Decision Making. **Abilities:** *Cognitive*—Written Comprehension; Deductive Reasoning; Inductive Reasoning; Problem Sensitivity; Oral Expression; Written Expression. *Psychomotor*—Control Precision; Rate Control. *Physical*—none met the criteria. *Sensory*—Speech Clarity. **General Work Activities:** *Information Input*—Getting Information Needed to Do the Job; Identifying Objects, Actions, and Events; Estimating Needed Characteristics. *Mental Process*—Making Decisions and Solving Problems; Processing Information; Analyzing Data or Information. *Work Output*—Implementing Ideas and Programs; Drafting and Specifying Technical Devices; Documenting and Recording Information. *Interacting with Others*—Providing Consultation and Advice to Others; Communicating with Other Workers; Interpreting Meaning of Information to Others. **Physical Work Conditions:** Indoors; Sitting; Using Hands on Objects, Tools, or Controls. **Other Job Characteristics:** Consequence of Error; Importance of Being Exact or Accurate; Importance of Being Sure All Is Done.

Experience: Job Zone 5. Extensive skill, knowledge, and experience are needed. Very advanced communication and organizational skills are required. **Job Preparation:** SVP 8.0 and above—4 years to more than 10 years. **Knowledge:** Engineering and Technology; Mathematics; Design; English Language; Production and Processing. **Instructional Programs:** 140601 Ceramic Sciences and Engineering; 141801 Material Engineering; 142001 Metallurgical Engineering; 143101 Materials Science; 400701 Metallurgy. **Related DOT Job:** 019.061-014 Materials Engineer.

17-2141.00 Mechanical Engineers (Mechanical Engineers)

Education: Bachelor's degree
Employed: 219,654
Openings: 9,388
Projected Growth: 16.4%
Earnings: $53,290

Perform engineering duties in planning and designing tools, engines, machines, and other mechanically functioning equipment. Oversee installation, operation, maintenance, and repair of such equipment as centralized heat, gas, water, and steam systems.

Tests ability of machines to perform tasks. Develops models of alternate processing methods to test feasibility or new applications of system components, and recommends implementation of procedures. Confers with establishment personnel and engineers to implement operating procedures and resolve system malfunctions, and to provide technical information. Plans and directs engineering personnel in fabrication of test control apparatus and equipment, and develops procedures for testing products. Researches and analyzes data, such as customer design proposal, specifications, and manuals to determine feasibility of design or application. Determines parts supply, maintenance tasks, safety procedures, and service schedule required to maintain machines and equipment in prescribed condition. Designs products and systems to meet process requirements, applying knowledge of engineering principles. Selects or designs tools to meet specifications, using manuals, drafting tools, computer, and specialized software programs. Studies industrial processes to determine where and how application of equipment can be made. Conducts experiments to test and analyze existing designs and equipment to obtain data on performance of product, and prepares reports. Alters or modifies design to obtain specified functional and operational performance. Investigates equipment failures and difficulties, diagnoses faulty operation, and makes recommendations to maintenance crew. Inspects, evaluates, and arranges field installations and recommends design modifications to eliminate machine or system malfunctions. Coordinates building, fabrication, and installation of product design and operation, maintenance, and repair activities to utilize machines and equipment. Specifies system components or directs modification of products to ensure conformance with engineering design and performance specifications. Oversees installation to ensure machines and equipment are installed and functioning according to specifications.

GOE Number, Interest Area, and Work Group: 02.07.04; Science, Math, and Engineering; Engineering: General Engineering. **Personality Type:** Realistic. Realistic occupations frequently involve work activities that include practical, hands-on problems and solutions. These occupations often deal with plants, animals, and real-world materials like wood, tools, and machinery. Many of the occupations require working outside and do not involve a lot of paperwork or working closely with others. **Work Values:** Autonomy; Ability Utilization; Responsibility; Creativity; Social Status; Achievement. **Skills:** Mathematics; Active Learning; Reading Comprehension; Problem Identification; Science; Technology Design. **Abilities:** *Cognitive*—Mathematical Reasoning; Deductive Reasoning; Written Comprehension; Number Facility; Visualization. *Psychomotor*—Arm-Hand Steadiness; Finger Dexterity; Manual Dexterity. *Physical*—Extent Flexibility; Trunk Strength; Gross Body Equilibrium. *Sensory*—Near Vision; Visual Color Discrimination; Speech Clarity. **General Work Activities:** *Information Input*—Getting Information Needed to Do the Job; Inspecting Equipment, Structures, Materials; Identifying Objects, Actions, and Events. *Mental Process*—Analyzing Data or Information; Thinking Creatively; Processing Information; Making Decisions and Solving Problems; Updating and Using Job-Relevant Knowledge. *Work Output*—Drafting and Specifying Technical Devices; Interacting with Computers; Implementing Ideas and Programs. *Interacting with Others*—Providing Consultation and Advice to Others; Communicating with Other Workers; Interpreting Meaning of Information to Others. **Physical Work Conditions:** Indoors; Sitting; Hazardous Equipment; Using Hands on Objects, Tools, or Controls. **Other Job Characteristics:** Consequence of Error; Importance of Being Exact or Accurate; Degree of Automation.

Experience: Job Zone 4. A minimum of two to four years of work-related skill, knowledge, or experience is needed. **Job Preparation:** SVP 7.0 to less than 8.0—2 years to less than 10 years. **Knowledge:** Engineering and Technology; Design; Mathematics; Computers and Electronics; Physics. **Instructional Program:** 141901 Mechanical Engineering.

Related DOT Jobs: 007.061-010 Automotive Engineer; 007.061-014 Mechanical Engineer; 007.061-018 Mechanical-Design Engineer, Facilities; 007.061-022 Mechanical-Design Engineer, Products; 007.061-026 Tool Designer; 007.061-030 Tool-Designer Apprentice; 007.061-034 Utilization Engineer; 007.061-038 Applications Engineer, Manufacturing; 007.061-042 Stress Analyst; 007.161-022 Mechanical Research Engineer; 007.161-034 Test Engineer, Mechanical Equipment; 007.161-038 Solar-Energy-Systems Designer.

17-2151.00 Mining and Geological Engineers, Including Mining Safety Engineers (Mining Engineers)

Education: Bachelor's degree
Employed: 4,444
Openings: 282
Projected Growth: –12.6%
Earnings: $56,090

Determine the location and plan the extraction of coal, metallic ores, nonmetallic minerals, and building materials such as stone and gravel. Conduct preliminary surveys of deposits or undeveloped mines and plan their development. Examine deposits or mines to determine whether they can be worked at a profit. Make geological and topographical surveys. Evolve methods of mining best suited to character, type, and size of deposits. Supervise mining operations.

Trains mine personnel in safe working practices and first aid. Evaluates data to develop new mining products, equipment, or processes. Designs, implements, and monitors facility projects, such as water, communication, ventilation, drainage, power supply, and conveyor systems. Conducts or collaborates in geological exploration and reviews maps and drilling logs to determine location, size, accessibility, and value of mineral deposits, or optimal oil and gas reservoir locations. Determines methods to extract minerals, considering factors, such as safety, optimal costs, and deposit characteristics. Provides technical consultation during drilling operations. Tests air to detect toxic gases and recommends alterations or installation of ventilation shafts, partitions, or equipment, to remedy problem. Designs and maintains protective and rescue equipment and safety devices. Inspects mining areas for unsafe structures, equipment, and working conditions. Devises methods to solve environmental problems and reclaim mine sites. Plans, conducts, or directs others in performing mining experiments to test or prove research findings. Plans and coordinates mining processes and labor utilization. Lays out and directs mine construction operations. Prepares technical reports for use by mining, engineering, and management personnel. Monitors production rate of gas, oil, or minerals from wells or mines.

GOE Number, Interest Area, and Work Group: 02.07.02; Science, Math, and Engineering; Engineering: Industrial and Safety. **Personality Type:** Investigative. Investigative occupations frequently involve working with ideas and require an extensive amount of thinking. These occupations can involve searching for facts and figuring out problems mentally. **Work Values:** Responsibility; Autonomy; Ability Utilization; Social Status; Authority; Achievement. **Skills:** Operations Analysis; Active Learning; Judgment and Decision Making; Equipment Selection; Mathematics. **Abilities:** *Cognitive*—Oral Expression; Deductive Reasoning; Oral Comprehension; Visualization; Problem Sensitivity; Originality. *Psychomotor*—Finger Dexterity; Manual Dexterity; Control Precision. *Physical*—Explosive Strength; Gross Body Equilibrium. *Sensory*—Near Vision; Speech Clarity; Far Vision. **General Work Activities:** *Information Input*—Getting Information Needed to Do the Job; Inspecting Equipment, Structures, Materials; Identifying Objects, Actions, and Events. *Mental Process*—Making Decisions and Solving Problems; Updating and Using Job-Relevant Knowledge; Analyzing Data or Information. *Work Output*—Drafting and Specifying Technical Devices; Implementing Ideas and Programs; Documenting and Recording Information. *Interacting with Others*—Communicating with Other Workers; Coordinating Work and Activities of Others; Guiding, Directing and Motivating Subordinates. **Physical Work Conditions:** Indoors; Sitting; Common Protective or Safety Attire. **Other Job Characteristics:** Consequence of Error; Importance of Being Sure All Is Done; Importance of Being Exact or Accurate.

Experience: Job Zone 4. A minimum of two to four years of work-related skill, knowledge, or experience is needed. **Job Preparation:** SVP 7.0 to less than 8.0—2 years to less than 10 years. **Knowledge:** Engineering and Technology; Mathematics; Physics; Administration and Management; Design. **Instructional Program:** 142101 Mining and Mineral Engineering.

Related DOT Jobs: 010.061-010 Design Engineer, Mining-and-Oil-Field Equipment; 010.061-014 Mining Engineer; 010.061-022

Research Engineer, Mining-and-Oil-Well Equipment; 010.061-026 Safety Engineer, Mines; 010.061-030 Test Engineer, Mining-and-Oil-Field Equipment.

17-2161.00 Nuclear Engineers (Nuclear Engineers)

Education: Bachelor's degree

Employed: 11,694

Openings: 882

Projected Growth: 5.8%

Earnings: $71,310

Conduct research on nuclear engineering problems. Apply principles and theory of nuclear science to problems concerned with release, control, and utilization of nuclear energy and nuclear waste disposal.

Directs operating and maintenance activities of operational nuclear facility. Writes operational instructions relative to nuclear plant operation and nuclear fuel and waste handling and disposal. Maintains reports to summarize work and document plant operations. Designs and develops nuclear machinery and equipment, such as reactor cores, radiation shielding, and associated instrumentation and control mechanisms. Inspects nuclear fuels, waste, equipment, test-reactor vessel and related systems, and control instrumentation to identify potential problems or hazards. Evaluates research findings to develop new concepts of thermonuclear analysis and new uses of radioactive models. Conducts tests to research nuclear fuel behavior and nuclear machinery and equipment performance. Analyzes available data and consults with other scientists to determine parameters of experimentation and suitability of analytical models. Plans and designs nuclear research to discover facts, or to test, prove, or modify known nuclear theories. Performs experiments to determine acceptable methods of nuclear material usage, nuclear fuel reclamation, and waste disposal. Determines potential hazard and accident conditions which may exist in fuel handling and storage and recommends preventive measures. Formulates equations that describe phenomena occurring during fission of nuclear fuels and develops analytical models for research. Examines accidents and obtains data to formulate preventive measures. Synthesizes analyses of tests results and prepares technical reports of findings and recommendations. Monitors nuclear operations to identify potential or inherent design, construction, or operational problems to ensure safe operations. Designs and oversees construction and operation of nuclear fuels reprocessing systems and reclamation systems. Formulates and initiates corrective actions and orders plant shut down in emergency situations.

GOE Number, Interest Area, and Work Group: 02.07.01; Science, Math, and Engineering; Engineering: Research and Systems Design. **Personality Type:** Investigative. Investigative occupations frequently involve working with ideas and require an extensive amount of thinking. These occupations can involve searching for facts and figuring out problems mentally. **Work Values:** Ability Utilization; Creativity; Responsibility; Social Status; Activity; Autonomy; Security. **Skills:** Science; Information Gathering; Mathematics; Product Inspection; Active Learning; Judgment and Decision Making; Operations Analysis. **Abilities:** *Cognitive*—Mathematical Reasoning; Problem Sensitivity; Deductive Reasoning; Written Expression; Oral Expression; Written Comprehension. *Psychomotor*—Control Precision; Response Orientation; Reaction Time. *Physical*—none met the criteria. *Sensory*—Speech Clarity; Near Vision; Auditory Attention; Speech Recognition. **General Work Activities:** *Information Input*—Getting Information Needed to Do the Job; Monitoring Processes, Materials, and Surroundings; Inspecting Equipment, Structures, Materials. *Mental Process*—Analyzing Data or Information; Making Decisions and Solving Problems; Evaluating Information Against Standards; Processing Information. *Work Output*—Implementing Ideas and Programs; Drafting and Specifying Technical Devices; Documenting and Recording Information. *Interacting with Others*—Communicating with Other Workers; Providing Consultation and Advice to Others; Interpreting Meaning of Information to Others. **Physical Work Conditions:** Indoors; Sitting; Hazardous Conditions. **Other Job Characteristics:** Consequence of Error; Importance of Being Exact or Accurate; Importance of Being Sure All Is Done.

Experience: Job Zone 5. Extensive skill, knowledge, and experience are needed. Very advanced communication and organizational skills are required. **Job Preparation:** SVP 8.0 and above—4 years to more than 10 years. **Knowledge:** Engineering and Technology; Physics; Mathematics; Design; Administration and Management; English Language. **Instructional Program:** 142301 Nuclear Engineering.

Related DOT Jobs: 005.061-042 Waste-Management Engineer, Radioactive Materials; 015.061-010 Design Engineer, Nuclear Equipment; 015.061-014 Nuclear Engineer; 015.061-018 Research Engineer, Nuclear Equipment; 015.061-022 Test Engineer, Nuclear Equipment; 015.061-026 Nuclear-Fuels Reclamation Engineer; 015.061-030 Nuclear-Fuels Research Engineer; 015.067-010 Nuclear-Criticality Safety Engineer; 015.137-010 Radiation-Protection Engineer; 015.167-010 Nuclear-Plant Technical Advisor; 015.167-014 Nuclear-Test-Reactor Program Coordinator.

17-2171.00 Petroleum Engineers (Petroleum Engineers)

Education: Bachelor's degree

Employed: 12,061

Openings: 802

Projected Growth: –3.6%

Earnings: $74,260

Devise methods to improve oil and gas well production. Determine the need for new or modified tool designs. Oversee drilling. Offer technical advice to achieve economical and satisfactory progress.

Conducts engineering research experiments to improve or modify mining and oil machinery and operations. Inspects oil and gas wells to determine that installations are completed. Monitors production rates, and plans rework processes to improve production. Assists engineering and other personnel to solve operating problems. Interprets drilling and testing information for personnel. Tests machinery and equipment to ensure conformance to performance specifications and to ensure safety. Writes technical reports for engineering and management personnel. Assigns work to staff to obtain maximum utilization of personnel. Coordinates activities of workers engaged in research, planning, and development. Evaluates findings to develop, design, or test equipment or processes. Confers with scientific, engineering, and technical personnel to resolve design, research, and testing problems. Develops plans for oil and gas field drilling, and for product recovery and treatment. Designs or modifies mining and oil field machinery and tools, applying engineering principles. Analyzes data to recommend placement of wells and supplementary processes to enhance production.

GOE Number, Interest Area, and Work Group: 02.07.04; Science, Math, and Engineering; Engineering: General Engineering. **Personality Type:** Realistic. Realistic occupations frequently involve work activities that include practical, hands-on problems and solutions. These occupations often deal with plants, animals, and real-world materials like wood, tools, and machinery. Many of the occupations require working outside and do not involve a lot of paperwork or working closely with others. **Work Values:** Ability Utilization; Autonomy; Social Status; Creativity; Responsibility. **Skills:** Mathematics; Writing; Information Gathering; Problem Identification; Product Inspection; Critical Thinking; Science; Operations Analysis; Judgment and Decision Making; Reading Comprehension. **Abilities:** *Cognitive*—Written Comprehension; Oral Expression; Inductive Reasoning; Oral Comprehension; Written Expression; Problem Sensitivity. *Psychomotor*—Manual Dexterity; Wrist-Finger Speed; Control Precision; Finger Dexterity. *Physical*—Gross Body Equilibrium; Dynamic Strength; Trunk Strength. *Sensory*—Near Vision; Speech Clarity; Auditory Attention; Hearing Sensitivity. **General Work Activities:** *Information Input*—Getting Information Needed to Do the Job; Monitoring Processes, Materials, and Surroundings; Identifying Objects, Actions, and Events. *Mental Process*—Analyzing Data or Information; Making Decisions and Solving Problems; Updating and Using Job-Relevant Knowledge; Processing Information. *Work Output*—Implementing Ideas and Programs; Drafting and Specifying Technical Devices; Documenting and Recording Information. *Interacting with Others*—Communicating with Other Workers; Providing Consultation and Advice to Others; Coordinating Work and Activities of Others. **Physical Work Conditions:** Using Hands on Objects, Tools, or Controls; Sitting; Indoors. **Other Job Characteristics:** Consequence of Error; Importance of Being Sure All Is Done; Importance of Being Exact or Accurate.

Experience: Job Zone 5. Extensive skill, knowledge, and experience are needed. Very advanced communication and organizational skills are required. **Job Preparation:** SVP 8.0 and above—4 years to more than 10 years. **Knowledge:** Engineering and Technology; Physics; English Language; Mathematics; Administration and Management. **Instructional Program:** 142501 Petroleum Engineering.

Related DOT Jobs: 010.061-010 Design Engineer, Mining-and-Oil-Field Equipment; 010.061-018 Petroleum Engineer; 010.061-022 Research Engineer, Mining-and-Oil-Well Equipment; 010.061-030 Test Engineer, Mining-and-Oil-Field Equipment; 010.161-010 Chief Engineer, Research; 010.167-010 Chief Engineer; 010.167-014 District Supervisor, Mud-Analysis Well Logging.

17-3000 Drafters, Engineering, and Mapping Technicians

17-3011.00 Architectural and Civil Drafters (Drafters)

Education: No data available.

Employed: 263,770

Openings: No data available.

Projected Growth: No data available.

Earnings: $32,170

Prepare detailed drawings of architectural and structural features of buildings. Prepare drawings and topographical relief maps used in civil engineering projects such as highways, bridges, and public works. Use knowledge of building materials, engineering practices, and mathematics to complete drawings.

GOE Number, Interest Area, and Work Group: 02.08.03; Science, Math, and Engineering; Engineering Technology: Design. **Instructional Programs:** 480101 Drafting, General; 480102 Architectural Drafting; 480103 Civil/Structural Drafting; 480104 Electrical/Electronics Drafting; 480105 Mechanical Drafting; 480199 Drafting, Other. **Note:** The Department of Labor has not collected some data for this job, so it has fewer details than the other descriptions.

17-3011.01 Architectural Drafters (Drafters)

Education: No data available.

Employed: 263,770

Openings: No data available.

Projected Growth: No data available.

Earnings: $32,170

Prepare detailed drawings of architectural designs and plans for buildings and structures, according to specifications provided by architect.

Calculates heat loss and gain of buildings and structures to determine required equipment specifications, following standard procedures. Prepares colored drawings of landscape and interior designs for presentation to client. Lays out and plans interior room arrangements for commercial buildings, and draws charts, forms, and records, using computer assisted equipment. Develops diagrams for construction, fabrication, and installation of equipment, structures, components, and systems, using field documents and specifications. Traces copies of plans and drawings, using transparent paper or cloth, ink, pencil, and standard drafting instruments for reproduction purposes. Drafts and corrects topographical maps to represent geological stratigraphy, mineral deposits, and pipeline systems, using survey data and aerial photographs. Lays out schematics and wiring diagrams used to erect, install, and repair establishment cable and electrical systems, using computer equipment. Draws rough and detailed scale plans, to scale, for foundations, buildings, and structures, according to specifications. Builds landscape models, using data provided by landscape architect.

GOE Number, Interest Area, and Work Group: 02.08.03; Science, Math, and Engineering; Engineering Technology: Design. **Personality Type:** Realistic. Realistic occupations frequently involve work activities that include practical, hands-on problems and solutions. These occupations often deal with plants, animals, and real-world materials like wood, tools, and machinery. Many of the occupations require working outside and do not involve a lot of paperwork or working closely with others. **Work Values:** Working Conditions; Moral Values; Ability Utilization; Independence; Compensation. **Skills:** Mathematics; Visioning; Programming; Reading Comprehension; Information Gathering; Active Learning; Operations Analysis. **Abilities:** *Cognitive*—Visualization; Written Comprehension; Written Expression; Deductive Reasoning; Number Facility; Mathematical Reasoning. *Psychomotor*—Arm-Hand Steadiness; Manual Dexterity; Finger Dexterity. *Physical*—Trunk Strength; Dynamic Strength. *Sensory*—Near Vision; Visual Color Discrimination; Far Vision. **General Work Activities:** *Information Input*—Getting Information Needed to Do the Job; Identifying Objects, Actions, and Events; Estimating Needed Characteristics. *Mental Process*—Processing Information; Thinking Creatively; Analyzing Data or Information. *Work Output*—Drafting and Specifying Technical Devices; Interacting with Computers; Handling and Moving Objects. *Interacting with Others*—Interpreting Meaning of Information to Others; Communicating with Other Workers; Providing Consultation and Advice to Others. **Physical Work Conditions:** Indoors; Using Hands on Objects, Tools, or Controls; Sitting. **Other Job Characteristics:** Importance of Being Exact or Accurate; Importance of Being Sure All Is Done; Consequence of Error.

Experience: Job Zone 4. A minimum of two to four years of work-related skill, knowledge, or experience is needed. **Job Preparation:** SVP 7.0 to less than 8.0—2 years to less than 10 years. **Knowledge:** Design; Mathematics; Engineering and Technology; Computers and Electronics; Physics. **Instructional Programs:** 480101 Drafting, General; 480102 Architectural Drafting; 480103 Civil/Structural Drafting; 480104 Electrical/Electronics Drafting; 480105 Mechanical Drafting; 480199 Drafting, Other.

Related DOT Jobs: 001.261-010 Drafter, Architectural; 001.261-014 Drafter, Landscape; 005.281-014 Drafter, Structural; 014.281-010 Drafter, Marine; 017.261-026 Drafter, Commercial; 017.261-034 Drafter, Heating and Ventilating; 017.261-038 Drafter, Plumbing; 017.281-018 Drafter, Assistant; 017.281-030 Drafter, Oil and Gas.

17-3011.02 Civil Drafters (Drafters)

Education: No data available.
Employed: 263,770
Openings: No data available.
Projected Growth: No data available.
Earnings: $32,170

Prepare drawings and topographical and relief maps used in civil engineering projects such as highways, bridges, pipelines, flood control projects, and water and sewage control systems.

Correlates, interprets, and modifies data obtained from topographical surveys, well logs, and geophysical prospecting reports. Draws maps, diagrams, and profiles, using cross-sections and surveys, to represent elevations, topographical contours, subsurface formations and structures. Plots boreholes for oil and gas wells from photographic subsurface survey recordings and other data, using computer assisted drafting equipment. Drafts plans and detailed drawings for structures, installations, and construction projects, such as highways, sewage disposal systems, and dikes. Computes and represents characteristics and dimensions of borehole, such as depth, degree, and direction of inclination. Accompanies field survey crew to locate grading markers or to collect data required to revise construction drawings. Calculates excavation tonnage and prepares graphs and fill-hauling diagrams used in earth-moving operations. Reviews rough sketches, drawings, specifications, and other engineering data received from civil engineer. Identifies symbols located on topographical surveys to denote geological and geophysical formations or oil field installations. Finishes and duplicates drawings, according to required mediums and specifications for reproduction, using blueprinting, photographing, or other duplicating methods.

GOE Number, Interest Area, and Work Group: 02.08.03; Science, Math, and Engineering; Engineering Technology: Design. **Personality Type:** Realistic. Realistic occupations frequently involve work activities that include practical, hands-on problems and solutions. These occupations often deal with plants, animals, and real-world materials like wood, tools, and machinery. Many of the occupations require working outside and do not involve a lot of paperwork or working closely with others. **Work Values:** Moral Values; Ability Utilization; Working Conditions; Activity; Achievement. **Skills:** Mathematics; Reading Comprehension; Information Gathering; Active Learning; Visioning; Operations Analysis; Information Organization. **Abilities:** *Cognitive*—Inductive Reasoning; Number Facility; Mathematical Reasoning; Information Ordering; Written Comprehension. *Psychomotor*—Wrist-Finger Speed; Arm-Hand Steadiness; Finger Dexterity. *Physical*—Trunk Strength. *Sensory*—Near Vision; Speech Clarity; Visual Color Discrimination; Speech Recognition; Far Vision. **General Work Activities:** *Information Input*—Getting Information Needed to Do the Job; Identifying Objects, Actions, and Events; Estimating Needed Characteristics. *Mental Process*—Processing Information; Updating and Using Job-Relevant Knowledge; Analyzing Data or Information. *Work Output*—Drafting and Specifying Technical Devices; Interacting with Computers; Handling and Moving Objects. *Interacting with Others*—Communicating with Other Workers; Interpreting Meaning of Information to Others; Providing Consultation and Advice to Others. **Physical Work Conditions:** Indoors; Sitting; Using Hands on Objects, Tools, or Controls. **Other Job Characteristics:** Consequence of Error; Importance of Being Exact or Accurate; Importance of Being Sure All Is Done.

Experience: Job Zone 3. Previous work-related skill, knowledge, or experience is required. **Job Preparation:** SVP 6.0 to less than 7.0—More than 1 year and less than 4 years. **Knowledge:** Design; Mathematics; Engineering and Technology; Computers and Electronics; Physics. **Instructional Programs:** 480101 Drafting, General; 480102 Architectural Drafting; 480103 Civil/Structural Drafting; 480104 Electrical/Electronics Drafting; 480105 Mechanical Drafting; 480199 Drafting, Other.

Related DOT Jobs: 005.281-010 Drafter, Civil; 010.281-010 Drafter, Directional Survey; 010.281-014 Drafter, Geological; 010.281-018 Drafter, Geophysical.

17-3012.00 Electrical and Electronics Drafters
(Drafters)

Education: No data available.

Employed: 263,770

Openings: No data available.

Projected Growth: No data available.

Earnings: $32,170

Prepare wiring diagrams, circuit-board assembly diagrams, and layout drawings used for manufacture, installation, and repair of electrical equipment in factories, power plants, and buildings.

GOE Number, Interest Area, and Work Group: 02.08.03; Science, Math, and Engineering; Engineering Technology: Design. **Instructional Programs:** 480101 Drafting, General; 480102 Architectural Drafting; 480103 Civil/Structural Drafting; 480104 Electrical/Electronics Drafting; 480105 Mechanical Drafting; 480199 Drafting, Other. **Note:** The Department of Labor has not collected some data for this job, so it has fewer details than the other descriptions.

17-3012.01 Electronic Drafters (Drafters)

Education: No data available.

Employed: 263,770

Openings: No data available.

Projected Growth: No data available.

Earnings: $32,170

Draw wiring diagrams, circuit-board assembly diagrams, schematics, and layout drawings used for manufacture, installation, and repair of electronic equipment.

Examines electronic schematics and analyzes logic diagrams and design documents to plan layout of printed circuit board components and circuitry. Compiles data, computes quantities, and prepares cost estimates to determine equipment needs, and requisitions materials as required. Creates master layout of design components and circuitry and printed circuit boards, according to specifications, and utilizing computer-assisted equipment. Consults with engineers to discuss and interpret design concepts, and determine requirements of detailed working drawings. Plots electrical test points on layout sheet, using pencil, and draws schematics to wire test fixture heads to frame. Copies drawings of printed circuit board fabrication, using print machine or blueprinting procedure. Selects drill size to drill test head, according to test design and specifications, and submits guide layout to designated department. Generates computer tapes of final layout design to produce layered photo masks and photo plotting design onto film. Examines and verifies master layout for electrical and mechanical accuracy. Keys and programs specified commands and engineering specifications into computer system to change functions and test final layout. Reviews work orders and procedural manuals and confers with vendors and design staff to resolve problems and modify design. Locates files relating to specified design projection data base library, loads program into computer, and records completed job data. Supervises and coordinates work activities of workers engaged in drafting, designing layouts, assembling, and testing printed circuit boards. Reviews blueprints to determine customer requirements and consults with assembler regarding schematics, wiring procedures, and conductor paths. Drafts detail and assembly drawings and designs of electromechanical equipment and related data processing systems.

GOE Number, Interest Area, and Work Group: 02.08.03; Science, Math, and Engineering; Engineering Technology: Design. **Personality Type:** Realistic. Realistic occupations frequently involve work activities that include practical, hands-on problems and solutions. These occupations often deal with plants, animals, and real-world materials like wood, tools, and machinery. Many of the occupations require working outside and do not involve a lot of paperwork or working closely with others. **Work Values:** Working Conditions; Ability Utilization; Moral Values; Compensation; Company Policies and Practices; Activity. **Skills:** Mathematics; Operations Analysis; Reading Comprehension; Technology Design; Problem Identification; Testing; Programming; Information Organization. **Abilities:** *Cognitive*—Information Ordering; Visualization; Oral Expression; Written Comprehension; Oral Comprehension; Number Facility. *Psychomotor*—Arm-Hand Steadiness; Wrist-Finger Speed; Manual Dexterity. *Physical*—Trunk Strength. *Sensory*—Near Vision; Visual Color Discrimination; Speech Clarity. **General Work Activities:** *Information Input*—Getting Information Needed to Do the Job; Inspecting Equipment, Structures, Materials; Identifying Objects, Actions, and Events. *Mental Process*—Processing Information; Analyzing Data or Information; Evaluating Information Against Standards. *Work Output*—Drafting and Specifying Technical Devices; Interacting with Computers; Implementing Ideas and Programs. *Interacting with Others*—Communicating with Other Workers; Coordinating Work and Activities of Others; Guiding, Directing and Motivating Subordinates. **Physical Work Conditions:** Indoors; Using Hands on Objects, Tools, or Controls; Sitting. **Other Job Characteristics:** Importance of Being Exact or Accurate; Consequence of Error; Importance of Being Sure All Is Done.

Experience: Job Zone 3. Previous work-related skill, knowledge, or experience is required. **Job Preparation:** SVP 6.0 to less than 7.0—More than 1 year and less than 4 years. **Knowledge:** Design; Computers and Electronics; Mathematics; Engineering and Technology; English Language; Administration and Management. **Instructional Programs:** 480101 Drafting, General; 480102 Architectural Drafting; 480103 Civil/Structural Drafting; 480104 Electrical/Electronics Drafting; 480105 Mechanical Drafting; 480199 Drafting, Other.

Related DOT Jobs: 003.131-010 Supervisor, Drafting and Printed Circuit Design; 003.261-018 Integrated Circuit Layout Designer; 003.261-022 Printed Circuit Designer; 003.281-014 Drafter, Electronic; 003.362-010 Design Technician, Computer-Aided; 017.261-014 Design Drafter, Electromechanisms; 726.364-014 Test Fixture Designer.

17-3012.02 Electrical Drafters (Estimators and Drafters, Utilities)

Education: No data available.

Employed: 5,270

Openings: No data available.

Projected Growth: No data available.

Earnings: $46,010

Develop specifications and instructions for installation of voltage transformers, overhead or underground cables, and related electrical equipment used to conduct electrical energy from transmission lines or high-voltage distribution lines to consumers.

Estimates labor and material costs for installation of electrical equipment and distribution systems. Visits site of proposed installation and draws rough sketch of location. Drafts sketches to scale. Takes measurements, such as distances to be spanned by wire and cable, which affect installation and arrangement of equipment. Drafts working drawing, wiring diagrams, wiring connections or cross section of underground cables, as required for instructions to installation crew. Studies work order request to determine type of service, such as lighting or power, demanded by installation. Reviews completed construction drawings and cost estimates for accuracy and conformity to standards and regulations. Draws master sketch showing relation of proposed installation to existing facilities. Confers with engineering staff and other personnel to resolve problems.

GOE Number, Interest Area, and Work Group: 02.08.03; Science, Math, and Engineering; Engineering Technology: Design. **Personality Type:** Conventional. Conventional occupations frequently involve following set procedures and routines. These occupations can include working with data and details more than with ideas. Usually there is a clear line of authority to follow. **Work Values:** Ability Utilization; Moral Values; Autonomy; Company Policies and Practices; Achievement. **Skills:** Operations Analysis; Judgment and Decision Making; Information Organization; Mathematics; Synthesis/Reorganization; Equipment Selection; Management of Personnel Resources; Reading Comprehension; Idea Generation. **Abilities:** *Cognitive*—Number Facility; Deductive Reasoning; Visualization; Oral Expression; Spatial Orientation; Mathematical Reasoning. *Psychomotor*—Finger Dexterity. *Physical*—Trunk Strength; Stamina; Dynamic Flexibility. *Sensory*—Near Vision; Far Vision; Depth Perception; Night Vision. **General Work Activities:** *Information Input*—Getting Information Needed to Do the Job; Estimating Needed Characteristics; Inspecting Equipment, Structures, Materials. *Mental Process*—Evaluating Information Against Standards; Making Decisions and Solving Problems; Analyzing Data or Information. *Work Output*—Drafting and Specifying Technical Devices; Documenting and Recording Information; Implementing Ideas and Programs. *Interacting with Others*—Communicating with Other Workers; Providing Consultation and Advice to Others; Interpreting Meaning of Information to Others; Guiding, Directing and Motivating Subordinates. **Physical Work Conditions:** Sitting; Indoors; Hazardous Conditions. **Other Job Characteristics:** Importance of Being Sure All Is Done; Consequence of Error; Importance of Being Exact or Accurate.

Experience: Job Zone 4. A minimum of two to four years of work-related skill, knowledge, or experience is needed. **Job Preparation:** SVP 7.0 to less than 8.0—2 years to less than 10 years. **Knowledge:** Design; Engineering and Technology; Administration and Management; Mathematics; Building and Construction. **Instructional Programs:** 480103 Civil/Structural Drafting; 480104 Electrical/Electronics Drafting.

Related DOT Jobs: 003.281-010 Drafter, Electrical; 019.161-010 Supervisor, Estimator and Drafter; 019.261-014 Estimator and Drafter.

17-3013.00 Mechanical Drafters (Drafters)

Education: No data available.

Employed: 263,770

Openings: No data available.

Projected Growth: No data available.

Earnings: $32,170

Prepare detailed working diagrams of machinery and mechanical devices including dimensions, fastening methods, and other engineering information.

Computes mathematical formulas to develop and design detailed specifications for components or machinery, using computer-assisted equipment. Lays out and draws schematic, orthographic, or angle views to depict functional relationships of components, assemblies, systems, and machines. Lays out, draws, and reproduces illustrations for reference manuals and technical publications to describe operation and maintenance of mechanical systems. Modifies and revises designs to correct operating deficiencies or to reduce production problems. Observes set-up and gauges during programmed machine or equipment trial run to verify conformance of signals and systems to specifications. Measures machine set-up and parts during production to ensure compliance with design specifications, using precision measuring instruments. Compiles and analyzes test data to determine effect of machine design on various factors, such as temperature and pressure. Coordinates and works in conjunction with other workers to design, layout, or detail components and systems. Directs work activities of detailer and confers with staff and supervisors to resolve design or other problems. Positions instructions and comments onto drawings and illustrates and describes installation and maintenance details. Reviews and analyzes specifications, sketches, engineering drawings, ideas, and related design data to determine factors affecting component designs. Shades or colors drawings to clarify and emphasize details and dimensions and eliminate background, using ink, crayon, airbrush, and overlays. Draws freehand sketches of designs and traces finished drawings onto designated paper for reproduction of blueprints. Develops detailed design drawings and specifications for mechanical equipment, dies/tools, and controls, according to engineering sketches and design proposals. Confers with customer representatives to review schematics and answer questions pertaining to installation of systems.

GOE Number, Interest Area, and Work Group: 02.08.03; Science, Math, and Engineering; Engineering Technology: Design. **Personality Type:** Realistic. Realistic occupations frequently involve work activities that include practical, hands-on problems and solutions. These occupations often deal with plants, animals, and real-world materials like wood, tools, and machinery. Many of the occupations require working outside and do not involve a lot of paperwork or working closely with others. **Work Values:** Moral Values; Working Conditions; Ability Utilization; Activity; Achievement; Company Policies and Practices. **Skills:** Mathematics; Operations Analysis; Information Gathering; Product Inspection; Solution Appraisal; Information Organization; Critical Thinking. **Abilities:** *Cognitive*—Visualization; Written Comprehension; Oral Comprehension; Deductive Reasoning; Written Expression; Number Facility. *Psychomotor*—Arm-Hand Steadiness; Manual Dexterity; Finger Dexterity. *Physical*—Trunk Strength; Gross Body Coordination. *Sensory*—Near Vision; Visual Color Discrimination; Speech Clarity. **General Work Activities:** *Information Input*—Getting Information Needed to Do the Job; Identifying Objects, Actions, and Events; Inspecting Equipment, Structures, Materials. *Mental Process*—Evaluating Information Against Standards; Analyzing Data or Information; Updating and Using Job-Relevant Knowledge. *Work Output*—Drafting and Specifying Technical Devices; Handling and Moving Objects; Interacting with Computers; Implementing Ideas and Programs. *Interacting with Others*—Communicating with Other Workers; Communicating with Persons Outside Organization; Interpreting Meaning of Information to Others. **Physical Work Conditions:** Sitting; Indoors; Using Hands on Objects, Tools, or Controls. **Other Job Characteristics:** Importance of Being Sure All Is Done; Importance of Being Exact or Accurate; Consequence of Error.

Experience: Job Zone 4. A minimum of two to four years of work-related skill, knowledge, or experience is needed. **Job Preparation:** SVP 7.0 to less than 8.0—2 years to less than 10 years. **Knowledge:** Design; Engineering and Technology; Mathematics; Computers and Electronics; English Language. **Instructional Programs:** 480101 Drafting, General; 480102 Architectural Drafting; 480103 Civil/Structural Drafting; 480104 Electrical/Electronics Drafting; 480105 Mechanical Drafting; 480199 Drafting, Other.

Related DOT Jobs: 002.261-010 Drafter, Aeronautical; 003.261-014 Controls Designer; 007.161-010 Die Designer; 007.161-014 Die-Designer Apprentice; 007.161-018 Engineering Assistant, Mechanical Equipment; 007.261-014 Drafter, Castings; 007.261-018 Drafter, Patent; 007.261-022 Drafter, Tool Design; 007.281-010 Drafter, Mechanical; 017.261-018 Detailer; 017.261-022 Detailer, Furniture; 017.261-030 Drafter, Detail; 017.261-042 Drafter, Automotive Design; 017.281-010 Auto-Design Detailer; 017.281-014 Drafter Apprentice; 017.281-026 Drafter, Automotive Design Layout; 017.281-034 Technical Illustrator.

17-3021.00 Aerospace Engineering and Operations Technicians (All Other Engineering and Related Technicians and Technologists)

Education: No data available.
Employed: 253,980
Openings: No data available.
Projected Growth: No data available.
Earnings: $37,420

Operate, install, calibrate, and maintain integrated computer or communications systems consoles, simulators, and other data-acquisition, test, and measurement instruments and equipment to launch, track, position, and evaluate air and space vehicles. Record and interpret test data.

Constructs and maintains test facilities for aircraft parts and systems, according to specifications, using hand tools, power tools, and test instruments. Inspects, diagnoses, maintains, and operates test setup and equipment to detect malfunctions, and adjusts, repairs, or replaces faulty components. Sets up, operates, maintains, and monitors computer systems and devices for data acquisition and analysis to detect malfunctions. Discusses test data requirements and results with other personnel, determines data required, and calculates and modifies test parameters or equipment. Fabricates and installs parts and systems to be tested in test equipment, using hand tools, power tools, and test instruments. Records and interprets test data on parts, assemblies, and mechanisms, and confers with engineering personnel regarding test procedures and results. Tests aircraft systems under simulated operational conditions, using test instrumentation and equipment, to determine design or fabrication parameters. Determines data required, plans data acquisition operations, and sets up required data acquisition, test, and measurement equipment. Inputs commands and data into computer systems to modify programs for specific test requirements or for equipment maintenance and calibration.

GOE Number, Interest Area, and Work Group: 02.08.04; Science, Math, and Engineering; Engineering Technology: General. **Personality Type:** Investigative. Investigative occupations frequently involve working with ideas and require an extensive amount of thinking. These occupations can involve searching for facts and figuring out problems mentally. **Work Values:** Activity; Moral Values; Achievement; Working Conditions; Compensation; Ability Utilization; Security. **Skills:** Science; Mathematics; Equipment Maintenance; Testing; Operation Monitoring; Operation and Control; Product Inspection; Installation. **Abilities:** *Cognitive*—Deductive Reasoning; Information Ordering; Written Comprehension; Visualization; Inductive Reasoning. *Psychomotor*—Wrist-Finger Speed; Arm-Hand Steadiness; Finger Dexterity; Control Precision. *Physical*—Trunk Strength; Extent Flexibility; Stamina. *Sensory*—Near Vision; Speech Clarity; Far Vision. **General Work Activities:** *Information Input*—Getting Information Needed to Do the Job; Inspecting Equipment, Structures, Materials; Identifying Objects, Actions, and Events. *Mental Process*—Processing Information; Analyzing Data or Information; Making Decisions and Solving Problems. *Work Output*—Interacting with Computers; Documenting and Recording Information; Controlling Machines and Processes; Implementing Ideas and Programs; Drafting and Specifying Technical Devices. *Interacting with Others*—Interpreting Meaning of Information to Others; Communicating with Other Workers; Providing Consultation and Advice to Others. **Physical Work Conditions:** Indoors; Using Hands on Objects, Tools, or Controls; Sitting. **Other Job Characteristics:** Consequence of Error; Importance of Being Sure All Is Done; Importance of Being Exact or Accurate.

Experience: Job Zone 4. A minimum of two to four years of work-related skill, knowledge, or experience is needed. **Job Preparation:** SVP 7.0 to less than 8.0—2 years to less than 10 years.

Knowledge: Engineering and Technology; Computers and Electronics; Mathematics; Physics; Mechanical. **Instructional Programs:** 100104 Radio and Television Broadcasting Technology/Technician; 100199 Communications Technol./Technicians, Other; 150101 Architectural Engineering Technology/Technician; 150304 Laser and Optical Technology/Technician; 150503 Energy Management and Systems Technology/Technician; 150505 Solar Technology/Technician; 150506 Water Quality and Wastewater Treatment Technology/Technician; 150507 Environmental and Pollution Control Technology/Technician; 150599 Environmental Control Technol./Technicians, Other; 150607 Plastics Technology/Technician; 150611 Metallurgical Technology/Technician; 150699 Industrial Production Technol./Technicians, Other; 150801 Aeronautical and Aerospace Engineering Technology/Technician; 150899 Mechanical Engineering-Related Technol./Technicians, Other; 150901 Mining Technology/Technician.

Related DOT Jobs: 002.261-014 Research Mechanic; 002.262-010 Flight-Test Data Acquisition Technician; 710.361-014 Test Equipment Mechanic; 869.261-026 Wind Tunnel Mechanic.

17-3022.00 Civil Engineering Technicians (Civil Engineering Technicians and Technologists)

Education: No data available.

Employed: 72,480

Openings: No data available.

Projected Growth: No data available.

Earnings: $34,420

Apply theory and principles of civil engineering in planning, designing, and overseeing construction and maintenance of structures and facilities under the direction of engineering staff or physical scientists.

Evaluates facility to determine suitability for occupancy and square footage availability. Analyzes proposed site factors and designs maps, graphs, tracings, and diagrams to illustrate findings. Plans and conducts field surveys to locate new sites and analyze details of project sites. Calculates dimensions, square footage, profile and component specifications, and material quantities, using calculator or computer. Reports maintenance problems occurring at project site to supervisor and negotiates changes to resolve system conflicts. Conducts materials test and analysis, using tools and equipment, and applying engineering knowledge. Confers with supervisor to determine project details, such as plan preparation, acceptance testing, and evaluation of field conditions. Responds to public suggestions and complaints. Develops plans and estimates costs for installation of systems, utilization of facilities, or construction of structures. Reads and reviews project blueprints and structural specifications to determine dimensions of structure or system and material requirements. Drafts detailed dimensional drawings and designs layouts for projects and to ensure conformance to specifications. Inspects project site and evaluates contractor work to detect design malfunctions and ensure conformance to design specifications and applicable codes. Prepares reports and documents project activities and data.

GOE Number, Interest Area, and Work Group: 02.08.04; Science, Math, and Engineering; Engineering Technology: General.

Personality Type: Realistic. Realistic occupations frequently involve work activities that include practical, hands-on problems and solutions. These occupations often deal with plants, animals, and real-world materials like wood, tools, and machinery. Many of the occupations require working outside and do not involve a lot of paperwork or working closely with others. **Work Values:** Moral Values; Activity; Working Conditions; Ability Utilization; Supervision, Human Relations. **Skills:** Operations Analysis; Mathematics; Reading Comprehension; Idea Evaluation; Information Organization. **Abilities:** *Cognitive*—Problem Sensitivity; Number Facility; Mathematical Reasoning; Written Comprehension; Written Expression; Oral Comprehension. *Psychomotor*—Control Precision; Multilimb Coordination; Rate Control. *Physical*—Gross Body Equilibrium. *Sensory*—Speech Clarity; Near Vision; Depth Perception. **General Work Activities:** *Information Input*—Getting Information Needed to Do the Job; Identifying Objects, Actions, and Events; Monitoring Processes, Materials, and Surroundings. *Mental Process*—Making Decisions and Solving Problems; Evaluating Information Against Standards; Organizing, Planning, and Prioritizing; Processing Information; Analyzing Data or Information. *Work Output*—Drafting and Specifying Technical Devices; Implementing Ideas and Programs; Documenting and Recording Information. *Interacting with Others*—Communicating with Other Workers; Interpreting Meaning of Information to Others; Communicating with Persons Outside Organization; Establishing and Maintaining Relationships. **Physical Work Conditions:** Indoors; Sitting; Standing; Outdoors. **Other Job Characteristics:** Importance of Being Sure All Is Done; Importance of Being Exact or Accurate; Consequence of Error.

Experience: Job Zone 4. A minimum of two to four years of work-related skill, knowledge, or experience is needed. **Job Preparation:** SVP 7.0 to less than 8.0—2 years to less than 10 years. **Knowledge:** Engineering and Technology; Design; Mathematics; Building and Construction; English Language. **Instructional Programs:** 150101 Architectural Engineering Technology/Technician; 150201 Civil Engineering/Civil Technology/Technician; 151001 Construction/Building Technology/Technician.

Related DOT Jobs: 005.261-014 Civil Engineering Technician; 019.261-018 Facility Planner; 019.261-026 Fire-Protection Engineering Technician; 199.261-014 Parking Analyst.

17-3023.00 Electrical and Electronic Engineering Technicians (Electrical and Electronic Technicians)

Education: Associate degree

Employed: 334,810

Openings: 42,572

Projected Growth: 16.8%

Earnings: $35,970

Apply electrical and electronic theory and related knowledge to design, build, repair, calibrate, and modify electrical components, circuitry, controls, and machinery for subsequent evaluation and use by engineering staff in making engineering design decisions. Work under the direction of engineering staff.

GOE Number, Interest Area, and Work Group: 02.08.04; Science, Math, and Engineering; Engineering Technology: General. Instructional Programs: 150301 Computer Engineering Technology/Technician; 150303 Electrical, Electronic and Communications Engin. Technology/Technician; 150399 Electrical and Electronic Engin.-Related Technol./Technician; 150403 Electromechanical Technology/Technician; 150404 Instrumentation Technology/Technician; 150405 Robotics Technology/Technician; 150801 Aeronautical and Aerospace Engineering Technology/ Technician. Note: The Department of Labor has not collected some data for this job, so it has fewer details than the other descriptions.

17-3023.01 Electronics Engineering Technicians
(Electrical and Electronic Technicians)

Education: Associate degree

Employed: 334,810

Openings: 42,572

Projected Growth: 16.8%

Earnings: $35,970

Lay out, build, test, troubleshoot, repair, and modify developmental and production electronic components, parts, equipment, and systems, such as computer equipment, missile-control instrumentation, electron tubes, test equipment, and machine tool numerical controls. Apply principles and theories of electronics, electrical circuitry, engineering mathematics, electronic and electrical testing, and physics. Work under direction of engineering staff.

Assembles circuitry or electronic components, according to engineering instructions, technical manuals, and knowledge of electronics using hand tools and power tools. Adjusts and replaces defective or improperly functioning circuitry and electronics components, using hand tools and soldering iron. Assists engineers in development of testing techniques, laboratory equipment, and circuitry or installation specifications, by writing reports and recording data. Designs basic circuitry and sketches for design documentation, as directed by engineers, using drafting instruments and computer aided design equipment. Fabricates parts, such as coils, terminal boards, and chassis, using bench lathes, drills, or other machine tools. Reads blueprints, wiring diagrams, schematic drawings, and engineering instructions for assembling electronics units, applying knowledge of electronic theory and components. Tests electronics unit, using standard test equipment, to evaluate performance and determine needs for adjustments.

GOE Number, Interest Area, and Work Group: 02.08.04; Science, Math, and Engineering; Engineering Technology: General. Personality Type: Realistic. Realistic occupations frequently involve work activities that include practical, hands-on problems and solutions. These occupations often deal with plants, animals, and real-world materials like wood, tools, and machinery. Many of the occupations require working outside and do not involve a lot of paperwork or working closely with others. Work Values: Moral Values; Working Conditions; Ability Utilization; Activity;

Achievement. Skills: Problem Identification; Testing; Mathematics; Active Learning; Operations Analysis; Information Gathering. Abilities: *Cognitive*—Written Comprehension; Visualization; Deductive Reasoning; Problem Sensitivity; Written Expression; Oral Comprehension. *Psychomotor*—Arm-Hand Steadiness; Control Precision; Finger Dexterity. *Physical*—none met the criteria. *Sensory*—Speech Clarity; Sound Localization. General Work Activities: *Information Input*—Getting Information Needed to Do the Job; Inspecting Equipment, Structures, Materials; Identifying Objects, Actions, and Events. *Mental Process*—Updating and Using Job-Relevant Knowledge; Evaluating Information Against Standards; Making Decisions and Solving Problems; Analyzing Data or Information. *Work Output*—Repairing and Maintaining Electrical Equipment; Drafting and Specifying Technical Devices; Documenting and Recording Information; Handling and Moving Objects. *Interacting with Others*—Communicating with Other Workers; Communicating with Persons Outside Organization; Performing Administrative Activities. Physical Work Conditions: Indoors; Using Hands on Objects, Tools, or Controls; Standing. Other Job Characteristics: Degree of Automation; Importance of Being Exact or Accurate; Consequence of Error.

Experience: Job Zone 4. A minimum of two to four years of work-related skill, knowledge, or experience is needed. Job Preparation: SVP 7.0 to less than 8.0—2 years to less than 10 years. Knowledge: Computers and Electronics; Engineering and Technology; Design; Mathematics; English Language. Instructional Programs: 150301 Computer Engineering Technology/Technician; 150303 Electrical, Electronic and Communications Engin. Technology/Technician; 150399 Electrical and Electronic Engin.-Related Technol./Technician; 150403 Electromechanical Technology/Technician; 150404 Instrumentation Technology/Technician; 150405 Robotics Technology/Technician; 150801 Aeronautical and Aerospace Engineering Technology/Technician.

Related DOT Jobs: 003.161-014 Electronics Technician; 003.161-018 Technician, Semiconductor Development; 725.381-010 Tube Rebuilder; 726.261-010 Electronics Assembler, Developmental.

17-3023.02 Calibration and Instrumentation Technicians (Electrical and Electronic Technicians)

Education: Associate degree

Employed: 334,810

Openings: 42,572

Projected Growth: 16.8%

Earnings: $35,970

Develop, test, calibrate, operate, and repair electrical, mechanical, electromechanical, electrohydraulic, or electronic measuring and recording instruments, apparatus, and equipment.

Sets up test equipment and conducts tests on performance and reliability of mechanical, structural, or electromechanical equipment. Performs preventative and corrective maintenance of test apparatus and peripheral equipment. Confers with engineers, supervisor, and other technical workers to assist with equipment installation, maintenance, and repair techniques. Sketches plans for developing jigs, fixtures, instruments, and related nonstandard apparatus. Selects sensing, telemetering, and recording instrumentation and circuitry. Modifies performance and operation of component parts and circuitry to specifications, using test equipment and precision instruments. Plans sequence of testing and calibration program for instruments and equipment according to blueprints, schematics, technical manuals, and other specifications. Analyzes and converts test data, using mathematical formulas, and reports results and proposed modifications. Disassembles and reassembles instruments and equipment, using hand tools, and inspects instruments and equipment for defects.

GOE Number, Interest Area, and Work Group: 02.08.04; Science, Math, and Engineering; Engineering Technology: General. **Personality Type:** Realistic. Realistic occupations frequently involve work activities that include practical, hands-on problems and solutions. These occupations often deal with plants, animals, and real-world materials like wood, tools, and machinery. Many of the occupations require working outside and do not involve a lot of paperwork or working closely with others. **Work Values:** Moral Values; Supervision, Human Relations; Activity; Working Conditions; Company Policies and Practices; Security. **Skills:** Technology Design; Equipment Selection; Product Inspection; Equipment Maintenance; Testing; Information Gathering. **Abilities:** *Cognitive*—Mathematical Reasoning; Written Comprehension; Information Ordering; Problem Sensitivity; Deductive Reasoning. *Psychomotor*—Control Precision; Finger Dexterity; Wrist-Finger Speed. *Physical*—none met the criteria. *Sensory*—Visual Color Discrimination. **General Work Activities:** *Information Input*—Getting Information Needed to Do the Job; Monitoring Processes, Materials, and Surroundings; Inspecting Equipment, Structures, Materials. *Mental Process*—Analyzing Data or Information; Updating and Using Job-Relevant Knowledge; Processing Information. *Work Output*—Repairing and Maintaining Mechanical Equipment; Controlling Machines and Processes; Handling and Moving Objects; Repairing and Maintaining Electrical Equipment. *Interacting with Others*—Communicating with Other Workers; Assisting and Caring for Others; Establishing and Maintaining Relationships. **Physical Work Conditions:** Indoors; Sitting; Standing. **Other Job Characteristics:** Importance of Being Exact or Accurate; Consequence of Error; Importance of Being Sure All Is Done.

Experience: Job Zone 4. A minimum of two to four years of work-related skill, knowledge, or experience is needed. **Job Preparation:** SVP 7.0 to less than 8.0—2 years to less than 10 years. **Knowledge:** Design; Mathematics; Mechanical; Engineering and Technology; Computers and Electronics. **Instructional Programs:** 150301 Computer Engineering Technology/Technician; 150303 Electrical, Electronic and Communications Engin. Technology/Technician; 150399 Electrical and Electronic Engin.-Related Technol./Technician; 150403 Electromechanical Technology/Technician; 150404 Instrumentation Technology/Technician; 150405 Robotics Technology/Technician; 150801 Aeronautical and Aerospace Engineering Technology/Technician.

Related DOT Jobs: 003.261-010 Instrumentation Technician; 019.281-010 Calibration Laboratory Technician; 828.261-018 Senior Technician, Controls.

17-3023.03 Electrical Engineering Technicians
(Electrical and Electronic Technicians)

Education: Associate degree
Employed: 334,810
Openings: 42,572
Projected Growth: 16.8%
Earnings: $35,970

Apply electrical theory and related knowledge to test and modify developmental or operational electrical machinery and electrical control equipment and circuitry, in industrial or commercial plants and laboratories. Work under direction of engineering staff.

Assembles electrical and electronic systems and prototypes according to engineering data and knowledge of electrical principles, using hand tools and measuring instruments. Analyzes and interprets test information. Collaborates with electrical engineer and other personnel to solve developmental problems. Draws diagrams and writes engineering specifications to clarify design details and functional criteria of experimental electronics units. Modifies electrical prototypes, parts, assemblies, and systems to correct functional deviations. Plans method and sequence of operations for testing and developing experimental electronic and electrical equipment. Sets up and operates test equipment to evaluate performance of developmental parts, assemblies, or systems under simulated operating conditions. Maintains and repairs testing equipment.

GOE Number, Interest Area, and Work Group: 02.08.04; Science, Math, and Engineering; Engineering Technology: General. **Personality Type:** Realistic. Realistic occupations frequently involve work activities that include practical, hands-on problems and solutions. These occupations often deal with plants, animals, and real-world materials like wood, tools, and machinery. Many of the occupations require working outside and do not involve a lot of paperwork or working closely with others. **Work Values:** Moral Values; Working Conditions; Activity; Ability Utilization; Achievement. **Skills:** Technology Design; Active Learning; Troubleshooting; Operations Analysis; Problem Identification. **Abilities:** *Cognitive*—Written Comprehension; Oral Comprehension; Information Ordering; Deductive Reasoning; Written Expression. *Psychomotor*—Manual Dexterity; Control Precision; Wrist-Finger Speed. *Physical*—none met the criteria. *Sensory*—Visual Color Discrimination; Speech Recognition. **General Work Activities:** *Information Input*—Inspecting Equipment, Structures, Materials; Getting Information Needed to Do the Job; Monitoring Processes, Materials, and Surroundings. *Mental Process*—Analyzing Data or Information; Updating and Using Job-Relevant Knowledge; Processing Information. *Work Output*—Repairing and Maintaining Electrical Equipment; Drafting and Specifying Technical Devices; Handling and Moving Objects. *Interacting with Others*—Communicating with Other Workers; Providing Consultation and Advice to Others; Establishing and Maintaining Relationships. **Physical Work Conditions:** Indoors; Sitting; Using Hands on Objects, Tools, or Controls. **Other Job Characteristics:** Consequence of Error; Importance of Being Sure All Is Done; Importance of Being Exact or Accurate.

Experience: Job Zone 4. A minimum of two to four years of work-related skill, knowledge, or experience is needed. **Job Preparation:** SVP 7.0 to less than 8.0—2 years to less than 10 years. **Knowledge:** Engineering and Technology; Mathematics; Design; Computers and Electronics; Physics. **Instructional Programs:** 150301 Computer Engineering Technology/Technician; 150303 Electrical, Electronic and Communications Engin. Technology/Technician; 150399 Electrical and Electronic Engin.-Related Technol./Technician; 150403 Electromechanical Technology/Technician; 150404 Instrumentation Technology/Technician; 150405 Robotics Technology/Technician; 150801 Aeronautical and Aerospace Engineering Technology/Technician.

Related DOT Jobs: 003.161-010 Electrical Technician; 726.261-014 Electrician, Research.

17-3024.00 Electro-Mechanical Technicians
(Electromechanical Equipment Assemblers, Precision)

Education: Work experience in a related occupation

Employed: 49,541

Openings: 9,529

Projected Growth: 5.7%

Earnings: $23,250

Operate, test, and maintain unmanned, automated, servo-mechanical, or electromechanical equipment. Operate unmanned submarines, aircraft, or other equipment at worksites such as oil rigs, deep ocean exploration, or hazardous waste removal. Assist engineers in testing and designing robotics equipment.

Installs electrical and electronic parts and hardware in housing or assembly, using soldering equipment and hand tools. Verifies dimensions and clearances of parts to ensure conformance to specifications, using precision measuring instruments. Inspects parts for surface defects. Repairs, reworks, and calibrates assemblies to meet operational specifications and tolerances. Reads blueprints, schematics, diagrams, and technical orders to determine method and sequence of assembly. Aligns, fits, and assembles component parts, using hand tools, power tools, fixtures, templates, and microscope. Operates metalworking machines to fabricate housings, jigs, fittings, and fixtures. Analyzes and records test results and prepares written documentation. Tests performance of electromechanical assembly, using test instruments such as oscilloscope, electronic voltmeter, and bridge.

GOE Number, Interest Area, and Work Group: 02.08.04; Science, Math, and Engineering; Engineering Technology: General. **Personality Type:** Realistic. Realistic occupations frequently involve work activities that include practical, hands-on problems and solutions. These occupations often deal with plants, animals, and real-world materials like wood, tools, and machinery. Many of the occupations require working outside and do not involve a lot of paperwork or working closely with others. **Work Values:** Moral Values; Independence; Company Policies and Practices; Supervision, Human Relations; Activity. **Skills:** Troubleshooting; Repairing; Product Inspection; Testing; Equipment Maintenance. **Abilities:** *Cognitive*—Information Ordering; Visualization; Problem Sensitivity; Written Comprehension; Written Expression.

Psychomotor—Finger Dexterity; Manual Dexterity; Arm-Hand Steadiness. *Physical*—Extent Flexibility; Trunk Strength; Static Strength. *Sensory*—Near Vision; Visual Color Discrimination; Depth Perception. **General Work Activities:** *Information Input*—Getting Information Needed to Do the Job; Inspecting Equipment, Structures, Materials; Monitoring Processes, Materials, and Surroundings. *Mental Process*—Evaluating Information Against Standards; Analyzing Data or Information; Updating and Using Job-Relevant Knowledge; Making Decisions and Solving Problems; Judging Qualities of Things, Services, Other People's Work. *Work Output*—Handling and Moving Objects; Repairing and Maintaining Electrical Equipment; Controlling Machines and Processes. *Interacting with Others*—Communicating with Other Workers; Performing Administrative Activities; Interpreting Meaning of Information to Others. **Physical Work Conditions:** Indoors; Using Hands on Objects, Tools, or Controls; Hazardous Equipment. **Other Job Characteristics:** Importance of Being Sure All Is Done; Importance of Being Exact or Accurate; Degree of Automation.

Experience: Job Zone 4. A minimum of two to four years of work-related skill, knowledge, or experience is needed. **Job Preparation:** SVP 7.0 to less than 8.0—2 years to less than 10 years. **Knowledge:** Mechanical; Engineering and Technology; Production and Processing; Computers and Electronics; Design. **Instructional Programs:** 150403 Electromechanical Technology/Technician; 150405 Robotics Technology/Technician; 150499 Electromechanical Instrumentation and Maintenance Technol./Technicians, Other.

Related DOT Jobs: 710.281-018 Electromechanical Technician; 828.381-018 Assembler, Electromechanical.

17-3025.00 Environmental Engineering Technicians
(All Other Engineering and Related Technicians and Technologists)

Education: No data available.

Employed: 253,980

Openings: No data available.

Projected Growth: No data available.

Earnings: $37,420

Apply theory and principles of environmental engineering to modify, test, and operate equipment and devices used in the prevention, control, and remediation of environmental pollution, including waste treatment and site remediation. Assist in the development of environmental pollution remediation devices under direction of engineer.

GOE Number, Interest Area, and Work Group: 02.08.04; Science, Math, and Engineering; Engineering Technology: General. **Instructional Programs:** 100104 Radio and Television Broadcasting Technology/Technician; 100199 Communications Technol./Technicians, Other; 150101 Architectural Engineering Technology/Technician; 150304 Laser and Optical Technology/Technician; 150503 Energy Management and Systems Technology/Technician; 150505 Solar Technology/Technician; 150506 Water Quality and Wastewater Treatment Technology/Technician; 150507 Environmental and Pollution Control Technology/Technician; 150599 Environmental Control Technol./Technicians,

Other; 150607 Plastics Technology/Technician; 150611 Metallurgical Technology/Technician; 150699 Industrial Production Technol./Technicians, Other; 150801 Aeronautical and Aerospace Engineering Technology/Technician; 150899 Mechanical Engineering-Related Technol./Technicians, Other; 150901 Mining Technology/Technician. **Note:** The Department of Labor has not collected some data for this job, so it has fewer details than the other descriptions.

17-3026.00 Industrial Engineering Technicians
(Industrial Engineering Technicians and Technologists)

Education: No data available.

Employed: 31,260

Openings: No data available.

Projected Growth: No data available.

Earnings: $38,320

Apply engineering theory and principles to problems of industrial layout or manufacturing production. Study and record time, motion, method, and speed involved in performance of production, maintenance, clerical, and other worker operations for such purposes as establishing standard production rates or improving efficiency. Work under the direction of engineering staff.

Selects products for tests at specified stages in production process, and tests products for performance characteristics and adherence to specifications. Records test data, applying statistical quality control procedures. Recommends modifications to existing quality or production standards to achieve optimum quality within limits of equipment capability. Interprets engineering drawings, schematic diagrams, or formulas and confers with management or engineering staff to determine quality and reliability standards. Compiles and evaluates statistical data to determine and maintain quality and reliability of products. Aids in planning work assignments in accordance with worker performance, machine capacity, production schedules, and anticipated delays. Prepares charts, graphs, and diagrams to illustrate workflow, routing, floor layouts, material handling, and machine utilization. Reads worker logs, product processing sheets, and specification sheets, to verify that records adhere to quality assurance specifications. Studies time, motion, methods, and speed involved in maintenance, production, and other operations to establish standard production rate and improve efficiency. Prepares graphs or charts of data or enters data into computer for analysis. Observes workers operating equipment or performing tasks to determine time involved and fatigue rate, using timing devices. Recommends revision to methods of operation, material handling, equipment layout, or other changes to increase production or improve standards. Observes worker using equipment to verify that equipment is being operated and maintained according to quality assurance standards. Evaluates data and writes reports to validate or indicate deviations from existing standards.

GOE Number, Interest Area, and Work Group: 02.08.02; Science, Math, and Engineering; Engineering Technology: Industrial and Safety. **Personality Type:** Investigative. Investigative occupations frequently involve working with ideas and require

an extensive amount of thinking. These occupations can involve searching for facts and figuring out problems mentally. **Work Values:** Moral Values; Supervision, Human Relations; Activity; Achievement; Ability Utilization; Company Policies and Practices. **Skills:** Mathematics; Reading Comprehension; Product Inspection; Systems Evaluation; Testing; Monitoring; Critical Thinking; Identification of Key Causes; Writing; Idea Evaluation. **Abilities:** *Cognitive*—Number Facility; Information Ordering; Mathematical Reasoning; Written Expression; Problem Sensitivity. *Psychomotor*—Finger Dexterity; Manual Dexterity. *Physical*—Gross Body Coordination; Dynamic Flexibility; Gross Body Equilibrium. *Sensory*—Near Vision; Far Vision; Speech Clarity. **General Work Activities:** *Information Input*—Getting Information Needed to Do the Job; Monitoring Processes, Materials, and Surroundings; Identifying Objects, Actions, and Events. *Mental Process*—Evaluating Information Against Standards; Processing Information; Judging Qualities of Things, Services, Other People's Work. *Work Output*—Documenting and Recording Information; Implementing Ideas and Programs; Interacting with Computers. *Interacting with Others*—Communicating with Other Workers; Interpreting Meaning of Information to Others; Providing Consultation and Advice to Others. **Physical Work Conditions:** Indoors; Sitting; Distracting Sounds and Noise Levels; Using Hands on Objects, Tools, or Controls; Standing. **Other Job Characteristics:** Importance of Being Exact or Accurate; Consequence of Error; Degree of Automation; Importance of Being Sure All Is Done.

Experience: Job Zone 3. Previous work-related skill, knowledge, or experience is required. **Job Preparation:** SVP 6.0 to less than 7.0—More than 1 year and less than 4 years. **Knowledge:** Engineering and Technology; Production and Processing; Mathematics; Design; English Language. **Instructional Programs:** 150603 Industrial/Manufacturing Technology/Technician; 150702 Quality Control Technology/Technician.

Related DOT Jobs: 012.261-014 Quality Control Technician; 012.267-010 Industrial Engineering Technician; 168.367-022 Personnel Quality Assurance Auditor.

17-3027.00 Mechanical Engineering Technicians
(Mechanical Engineering Technicians and Technologists)

Education: No data available.

Employed: 87,450

Openings: No data available.

Projected Growth: No data available.

Earnings: $39,170

Apply theory and principles of mechanical engineering to modify, develop, and test machinery and equipment, under direction of engineering staff or physical scientists.

Confers with technicians and submits reports of test results to engineering department and recommends design or material changes. Sets up prototype and test apparatus and operates test controlling equipment to observe and record prototype test results. Reviews project instructions and specifications to identify, modify and plan requirements fabrication, assembly and testing. Discusses changes in design, method of manufacture and assembly, and drafting techniques and procedures with staff and coordinates corrections. Calculates required capacities for equipment of proposed system to obtain specified performance and submits data to engineering personnel for approval. Drafts detail drawing or sketch for drafting room completion or to request parts fabrication by machine, sheet or wood shops. Records test procedures and results, numerical and graphical data, and recommendations for changes in product or test methods. Sets up and conducts tests of complete units and components under operational conditions to investigate proposals for improving equipment performance. Reviews project instructions and blueprints to ascertain test specifications, procedures, objectives, and tests nature of technical problems, such as redesign. Operates drill press, grinders, engine lathe, or other machines to modify parts tested or to fabricate experimental parts for testing. Reads dials and meters to determine amperage, voltage, electrical out and input at specific operating temperature to analyze parts performance. Prepares parts sketches and writes work orders and purchase requests to be furnished by outside contractors. Inspects lines and figures for clarity and returns erroneous drawings to designer for correction. Estimates cost factors, including labor and material for purchased and fabricated parts and costs for assembly, testing, and installing. Analyzes tests results in relation to design or rated specifications and test objectives and modifies or adjusts equipment to meet specifications.

GOE Number, Interest Area, and Work Group: 02.08.04; Science, Math, and Engineering; Engineering Technology: General. **Personality Type:** Realistic. Realistic occupations frequently involve work activities that include practical, hands-on problems and solutions. These occupations often deal with plants, animals, and real-world materials like wood, tools, and machinery. Many of the occupations require working outside and do not involve a lot of paperwork or working closely with others. **Work Values:** Moral Values; Achievement; Activity; Supervision, Human Relations; Advancement; Security; Company Policies and Practices. **Skills:** Mathematics; Technology Design; Operation and Control; Testing; Reading Comprehension; Idea Evaluation. **Abilities:** *Cognitive*—Written Comprehension; Written Expression; Oral Expression; Oral Comprehension; Mathematical Reasoning; Number Facility. *Psychomotor*—Wrist-Finger Speed; Control Precision; Manual Dexterity. *Physical*—Explosive Strength; Gross Body Coordination; Dynamic Flexibility; Dynamic Strength. *Sensory*—Speech Clarity; Speech Recognition; Visual Color Discrimination; Far Vision; Auditory Attention. **General Work Activities:** *Information Input*—Inspecting Equipment, Structures, Materials; Getting Information Needed to Do the Job; Monitoring Processes, Materials, and Surroundings. *Mental Process*—Updating and Using Job-Relevant Knowledge; Processing Information; Analyzing Data or Information. *Work Output*—Controlling Machines and Processes; Drafting and Specifying Technical Devices; Handling and Moving Objects. *Interacting with Others*—Communicating with Other Workers; Interpreting Meaning of Information to Others; Monitoring and Controlling Resources. **Physical Work Conditions:** Indoors; Using Hands on Objects, Tools, or Controls; Sitting; Hazardous Equipment. **Other Job Characteristics:** Importance of Being Exact or Accurate; Importance of Being Sure All Is Done; Consequence of Error.

Experience: Job Zone 4. A minimum of two to four years of work-related skill, knowledge, or experience is needed. **Job**

Preparation: SVP 7.0 to less than 8.0—2 years to less than 10 years. **Knowledge:** Engineering and Technology; Mechanical; Design; Mathematics; Physics. **Instructional Programs:** 150403 Electromechanical Technology/Technician; 150501 Heating, Air Conditioning and Refrigeration Technology/Technician; 150803 Automotive Engineering Technology/Technician; 150805 Mechanical Engineering/Mechanical Technology/Technician.

Related DOT Jobs: 007.161-026 Mechanical-Engineering Technician; 007.161-030 Optomechanical Technician; 007.167-010 Die-Drawing Checker; 007.181-010 Heat-Transfer Technician; 007.267-010 Drawings Checker, Engineering; 007.267-014 Tool Design Checker; 017.261-010 Auto-Design Checker.

17-3031.00 Surveying and Mapping Technicians
(Surveying and Mapping Technicians)

Education: Moderate-term O-T-J training	
Employed: 68,674	
Openings: 15,057	
Projected Growth: 21.8%	
Earnings: $25,940	

Perform surveying and mapping duties, usually under the direction of a surveyor, cartographer, or photogrammetrist to obtain data used for construction, mapmaking, boundary location, mining, or other purposes. Calculate mapmaking information and create maps from source data such as surveying notes, aerial photography, satellite data, or other maps, to show topographical features, political boundaries, and other features. Verify accuracy and completeness of topographical maps.

GOE Number, Interest Area, and Work Group: 02.08.01; Science, Math, and Engineering; Engineering Technology: Surveying. **Instructional Programs:** 151102 Surveying; 450702 Cartography. **Note:** The Department of Labor has not collected some data for this job, so it has fewer details than the other descriptions.

17-3031.01 Surveying Technicians (Surveying and Mapping Technicians)

Education: Moderate-term O-T-J training	
Employed: 68,674	
Openings: 15,057	
Projected Growth: 21.8%	
Earnings: $25,940	

Adjust and operate surveying instruments such as theodolite and electronic distance-measuring equipment. Compile notes, make sketches, and enter data into computers.

Directs work of subordinate members of party, performing surveying duties not requiring licensure. Compiles notes, sketches, and records of survey data obtained and work performed. Obtains land survey data, such as angles, elevations, points, and contours, using electronic distance measuring equipment and other surveying instruments.

GOE Number, Interest Area, and Work Group: 02.08.01; Science, Math, and Engineering; Engineering Technology: Surveying. **Personality Type:** Realistic. Realistic occupations frequently involve work activities that include practical, hands-on problems and solutions. These occupations often deal with plants, animals, and real-world materials like wood, tools, and machinery. Many of the occupations require working outside and do not involve a lot of paperwork or working closely with others. **Work Values:** Moral Values; Company Policies and Practices; Security; Authority; Supervision, Human Relations. **Skills:** Mathematics; Information Organization; Reading Comprehension; Information Gathering; Writing. **Abilities:** *Cognitive*—Written Expression; Oral Expression; Spatial Orientation; Information Ordering; Number Facility. *Psychomotor*—none met the criteria. *Physical*—none met the criteria. *Sensory*—Far Vision; Depth Perception. **General Work Activities:** *Information Input*—Getting Information Needed to Do the Job; Identifying Objects, Actions, and Events; Monitoring Processes, Materials, and Surroundings. *Mental Process*—Processing Information; Analyzing Data or Information; Updating and Using Job-Relevant Knowledge. *Work Output*—Documenting and Recording Information; Controlling Machines and Processes; Performing General Physical Activities. *Interacting with Others*—Communicating with Other Workers; Guiding, Directing and Motivating Subordinates; Coordinating Work and Activities of Others. **Physical Work Conditions:** Outdoors; Standing; Using Hands on Objects, Tools, or Controls. **Other Job Characteristics:** Importance of Being Exact or Accurate; Importance of Being Sure All Is Done; Consequence of Error.

Experience: Job Zone 4. A minimum of two to four years of work-related skill, knowledge, or experience is needed. **Job Preparation:** SVP 7.0 to less than 8.0—2 years to less than 10 years. **Knowledge:** Engineering and Technology; Mathematics; Design; Computers and Electronics; Geography. **Instructional Programs:** 151102 Surveying; 450702 Cartography.

Related DOT Jobs: 018.167-010 Chief of Party; 018.167-034 Surveyor Assistant, Instruments.

17-3031.02 Mapping Technicians (Surveying and Mapping Technicians)

Education: Moderate-term O-T-J training
Employed: 68,674
Openings: 15,057
Projected Growth: 21.8%
Earnings: $25,940

Calculate mapmaking information from field notes; draw and verify accuracy of topographical maps.

Analyzes aerial photographs to detect and interpret significant military, industrial, resource, or topographical data. Lays out and matches aerial photographs in sequence taken, looking for missing areas. Marks errors and makes corrections, such as numbering grid lines or lettering names of rivers or towns. Trims, aligns, and joins prints to form photographic mosaic, maintaining scaled distances between reference points. Calculates latitude, longitude, angles, areas, and other information for mapmaking from survey field notes, using reference tables and computer. Supervises and coordinates activities of workers engaged in drafting maps or in production of blueprints, photostats, and photographs. Verifies identification of topographical features and accuracy of contour lines by comparison with aerial photographs, old maps, and other reference materials. Forms three-dimensional image of aerial photographs taken from different locations, using mathematical and aides and plotting instruments. Computes and measures scaled distances between reference points to establish exact relative position of adjoining prints. Traces contours and topographical details to produce map. Stores, retrieves, and compares map information, using computers and data banks.

GOE Number, Interest Area, and Work Group: 02.08.01; Science, Math, and Engineering; Engineering Technology: Surveying. **Personality Type:** Conventional. Conventional occupations frequently involve following set procedures and routines. These occupations can include working with data and details more than with ideas. Usually there is a clear line of authority to follow. **Work Values:** Moral Values; Activity; Achievement; Autonomy; Working Conditions; Ability Utilization; Authority; Security. **Skills:** Mathematics; Information Organization; Synthesis/Reorganization; Information Gathering; Monitoring; Active Learning. **Abilities:** *Cognitive*—Written Comprehension; Inductive Reasoning; Mathematical Reasoning; Number Facility; Written Expression; Information Ordering. *Psychomotor*—Wrist-Finger Speed; Arm-Hand Steadiness; Finger Dexterity. *Physical*—none met the criteria. *Sensory*—Near Vision; Visual Color Discrimination; Far Vision. **General Work Activities:** *Information Input*—Identifying Objects, Actions, and Events; Getting Information Needed to Do the Job; Inspecting Equipment, Structures, Materials. *Mental Process*—Processing Information; Analyzing Data or Information; Updating and Using Job-Relevant Knowledge. *Work Output*—Interacting with Computers; Drafting and Specifying Technical Devices; Implementing Ideas and Programs; Documenting and Recording Information. *Interacting with Others*—Guiding, Directing and Motivating Subordinates; Communicating with Other Workers; Coordinating Work and Activities of Others. **Physical Work Conditions:** Indoors; Using Hands on Objects, Tools, or Controls; Sitting. **Other Job Characteristics:** Importance of Being Exact or Accurate; Importance of Being Sure All Is Done; Consequence of Error.

Experience: Job Zone 3. Previous work-related skill, knowledge, or experience is required. **Job Preparation:** SVP 6.0 to less than 7.0—More than 1 year and less than 4 years. **Knowledge:** Geography; Mathematics; Design; Computers and Electronics; Engineering and Technology. **Instructional Programs:** 151102 Surveying; 450702 Cartography.

Related DOT Jobs: 018.167-014 Geodetic Computator; 018.167-030 Supervisor, Mapping; 018.261-018 Editor, Map; 018.261-022 Mosaicist; 018.281-010 Stereo-Plotter Operator; 029.167-010 Aerial-Photograph Interpreter.

19-0000
Life, Physical, and Social Science Occupations

19-1000 Life Scientists

19-1011.00 Animal Scientists (Agricultural and Food Scientists)

Education: Bachelor's degree
Employed: 21,468
Openings: 1,639
Projected Growth: 10.9%
Earnings: $42,340

Conduct research in the genetics, nutrition, reproduction, growth, and development of domestic farm animals.

Develops improved practices in feeding, housing, sanitation, and parasite and disease control of animals and poultry. Researches and controls selection and breeding practices to increase efficiency of production and improve quality of animals. Determines generic composition of animal population, and heritability of traits, utilizing principles of genetics. Develops improved practices in incubation, brooding, and artificial insemination. Studies effects of management practices, processing methods, feed, and environmental conditions on quality and quantity of animal products, such as eggs and milk. Studies nutritional requirements of animals and nutritive value of feed materials for animals and poultry. Crossbreeds animals with existing strains, or crosses strains to obtain new combinations of desirable characteristics.

GOE Number, Interest Area, and Work Group: 02.03.01; Science, Math, and Engineering; Life Sciences: Animal Specialization. **Personality Type:** Investigative. Investigative occupations frequently involve working with ideas and require an extensive amount of thinking. These occupations can involve searching for facts and figuring out problems mentally. **Work Values:** Autonomy; Independence; Responsibility; Ability Utilization; Creativity; Achievement. **Skills:** Information Gathering; Science; Reading Comprehension; Active Learning; Critical Thinking. **Abilities:** *Cognitive*—Written Comprehension; Inductive Reasoning; Deductive Reasoning; Mathematical Reasoning; Oral Comprehension; Written Expression. *Psychomotor*—none met the criteria. *Physical*—none met the criteria. *Sensory*—Near Vision; Speech Clarity; Speech Recognition. **General Work Activities:** *Information Input*—Getting Information Needed to Do the Job; Identifying Objects, Actions, and Events; Monitoring Processes, Materials, and Surroundings. *Mental Process*—Making Decisions and Solving Problems; Processing Information; Analyzing Data or Information. *Work Output*—Implementing Ideas and Programs; Controlling Machines and Processes; Handling and Moving Objects. *Interacting with Others*—Interpreting Meaning of Information to Others; Communicating with Persons Outside Organization; Communicating with Other Workers. **Physical Work Conditions:** Indoors; Sitting; Hazardous Situations; Standing. **Other Job Characteristics:** Consequence of Error; Importance of Being Exact or Accurate; Importance of Being Sure All Is Done.

Experience: Job Zone 5. Extensive skill, knowledge, and experience are needed. Very advanced communication and organizational skills are required. **Job Preparation:** SVP 8.0 and above—4 years to more than 10 years. **Knowledge:** Biology; Food Production; Mathematics; English Language; Chemistry. **Instructional Programs:** 020101 Agriculture/Agricultural Sciences, General; 020102 Agricultural Extension; 020201 Animal Sciences, General; 020202 Agricultural Animal Breeding and Genetics; 020203 Agricultural Animal Health; 020204 Agricultural Animal Nutrition; 020205 Agricultural Animal Physiology; 020206 Dairy Science; 020209 Poultry Science; 020299 Animal Sciences, Other; 020301 Food Sciences and Technology; 020401 Plant Sciences, General; 020402 Agronomy and Crop Science; 020403 Horticulture Science; 020405 Plant Breeding and Genetics.

Related DOT Jobs: 040.061-014 Animal Scientist; 040.061-018 Dairy Scientist; 040.061-042 Poultry Scientist; 041.061-014 Animal Breeder.

19-1012.00 Food Scientists and Technologists (Agricultural and Food Scientists)

Education: Bachelor's degree
Employed: 21,468
Openings: 1,639
Projected Growth: 10.9%
Earnings: $42,340

Use chemistry, microbiology, engineering, and other sciences to study the principles underlying the processing and deterioration of foods. Analyze food content to determine levels of vitamins, fat, sugar, and protein. Discover new food sources. Research ways to make processed foods safe, palatable, and healthful. Apply knowledge of food science to determine best ways to process, package, preserve, store, and distribute food.

Confers with process engineers, flavor experts, and packaging and marketing specialists to resolve problems in product development. Develops new and improved methods and systems for food processing, production, quality control, packaging, and distribution. Conducts research on new products and development of foods, applying scientific and engineering principles. Tests new products in test kitchen. Develops food standards, safety and sanitary regulations, and waste management and water supply specifications. Studies methods to improve physical, chemical, and microbiological composition of foods. Studies methods to improve quality of foods, such as flavor, color, texture, nutritional value, and convenience.

GOE Number, Interest Area, and Work Group: 02.03.04; Science, Math, and Engineering; Life Sciences: Food Research. **Personality Type:** Investigative. Investigative occupations frequently involve working with ideas and require an extensive amount of thinking. These occupations can involve searching for facts and figuring out problems mentally. **Work Values:** Autonomy; Security; Responsibility; Ability Utilization; Creativity. **Skills:** Science; Active Learning; Reading Comprehension; Idea Generation; Idea Evaluation; Solution Appraisal. **Abilities:** *Cognitive*—Written Comprehension; Oral Comprehension; Number Facility; Oral Expression; Written Expression; Deductive Reasoning. *Psychomotor*—none met the criteria. *Physical*—none met the criteria. *Sensory*—Speech Clarity. **General Work Activities:** *Information Input*—Identifying Objects, Actions, and Events; Getting Information Needed to Do the Job; Monitoring Processes, Materials, and Surroundings. *Mental Process*—Analyzing Data or Information; Judging Qualities of Things, Services, Other People's Work; Making Decisions and Solving Problems. *Work Output*—Implementing Ideas and Programs; Handling and Moving Objects; Documenting and Recording Information. *Interacting with Others*—Providing Consultation and Advice to Others; Communicating with Other Workers; Interpreting Meaning of Information to Others. **Physical Work Conditions:** Indoors; Sitting; Using Hands on Objects, Tools, or Controls. **Other Job Characteristics:** Consequence of Error; Importance of Being Exact or Accurate; Importance of Being Sure All Is Done.

Experience: Job Zone 4. A minimum of two to four years of work-related skill, knowledge, or experience is needed. **Job Preparation:** SVP 7.0 to less than 8.0—2 years to less than 10 years. **Knowledge:** Production and Processing; Food Production; Biology; Chemistry; English Language. **Instructional Programs:** 020101 Agriculture/Agricultural Sciences, General; 020102 Agricultural Extension; 020201 Animal Sciences, General; 020202 Agricultural Animal Breeding and Genetics; 020203 Agricultural Animal Health; 020204 Agricultural Animal Nutrition; 020205 Agricultural Animal Physiology; 020206 Dairy Science; 020209 Poultry Science; 020299 Animal Sciences, Other; 020301 Food Sciences and Technology; 020401 Plant Sciences, General; 020402 Agronomy and Crop Science; 020403 Horticulture Science; 020405 Plant Breeding and Genetics.

Related DOT Job: 041.081-010 Food Technologist.

19-1013.00 Soil and Plant Scientists (Agricultural and Food Scientists)

Education: Bachelor's degree

Employed: 21,468

Openings: 1,639

Projected Growth: 10.9%

Earnings: $42,340

Conduct research in breeding, physiology, production, yield, and management of crops and agricultural plants. Conduct research on the growth of crops and plants in soils and on the control of pests. Study the chemical, physical, biological, and mineralogical composition of soils as they relate to plant or crop growth. Classify and map soils. Investigate effects of alternative practices on soil and crop productivity.

GOE Number, Interest Area, and Work Group: 02.03.02; Science, Math, and Engineering; Life Sciences: Plant Specialization. **Instructional Programs:** 020101 Agriculture/Agricultural Sciences, General; 020102 Agricultural Extension; 020201 Animal Sciences, General; 020202 Agricultural Animal Breeding and Genetics; 020203 Agricultural Animal Health; 020204 Agricultural Animal Nutrition; 020205 Agricultural Animal Physiology; 020206 Dairy Science; 020209 Poultry Science; 020299 Animal Sciences, Other; 020301 Food Sciences and Technology; 020401 Plant Sciences, General; 020402 Agronomy and Crop Science; 020403 Horticulture Science; 020405 Plant Breeding and Genetics. **Note:** The Department of Labor has not collected some data for this job, so it has fewer details than the other descriptions.

19-1013.01 Plant Scientists (Agricultural and Food Scientists)

Education: Bachelor's degree

Employed: 21,468

Openings: 1,639

Projected Growth: 10.9%

Earnings: $42,340

Conduct research in breeding, production, and yield of plants or crops. Conduct research on the control of pests.

Studies crop production to discover effects of various climatic and soil conditions on crops. Studies insect distribution and habitat and recommends methods to prevent importation and spread of injurious species. Experiments to develop new or improved varieties of products having specific features, such as higher yield, resistance to disease, size, or maturity. Aids in control and elimination of agricultural, structural and forest pests by developing new and improved pesticides. Conducts experiments regarding causes of bee diseases and factors affecting yields of nectar pollen on various plants visited by bees. Develops methods for control of noxious weeds, crop diseases, and insect pests. Identifies and classifies species of insects and allied forms, such as mites and spiders. Conducts research to determine best methods of planting, spraying, cultivating, and harvesting horticultural products. Improves bee strains, utilizing selective breeding by artificial insemination. Conducts experiments and investigations to determine methods of storing, processing, and transporting horticultural products.

GOE Number, Interest Area, and Work Group: 02.03.02; Science, Math, and Engineering; Life Sciences: Plant Specialization. **Personality Type:** Investigative. Investigative occupations frequently involve working with ideas and require an extensive amount of thinking. These occupations can involve searching for facts and figuring out problems mentally. **Work Values:** Autonomy; Independence; Responsibility; Ability Utilization; Creativity. **Skills:** Information Gathering; Science; Writing; Critical Thinking; Reading Comprehension. **Abilities:** *Cognitive*—Written Comprehension; Deductive Reasoning; Oral Comprehension; Inductive Reasoning; Information Ordering. *Psychomotor*—none met the criteria. *Physical*—none met the criteria. *Sensory*—Speech Clarity; Visual Color Discrimination; Far Vision; Speech Recognition. **General Work Activities:** *Information Input*—Identifying Objects, Actions, and Events; Getting Information Needed to Do the Job; Monitoring Processes, Materials, and Surroundings. *Mental Process*—Processing Information; Analyzing Data or Information; Making Decisions and Solving Problems; Updating and Using Job-Relevant Knowledge. *Work Output*—Implementing Ideas and Programs; Documenting and Recording Information; Handling and Moving Objects. *Interacting with Others*—Interpreting Meaning of Information to Others; Providing Consultation and Advice to Others; Communicating with Persons Outside Organization. **Physical Work Conditions:** Sitting; Indoors; Outdoors. **Other Job Characteristics:** Consequence of Error; Importance of Being Exact or Accurate; Importance of Being Sure All Is Done.

Experience: Job Zone 5. Extensive skill, knowledge, and experience are needed. Very advanced communication and organizational skills are required. **Job Preparation:** SVP 8.0 and above—4 years to more than 10 years. **Knowledge:** Food Production; Biology; English Language; Chemistry; Education and Training; Communications and Media. **Instructional Programs:** 020101 Agriculture/Agricultural Sciences, General; 020102 Agricultural Extension; 020201 Animal Sciences, General; 020202 Agricultural Animal Breeding and Genetics; 020203 Agricultural Animal Health; 020204 Agricultural Animal Nutrition; 020205 Agricultural Animal Physiology; 020206 Dairy Science; 020209 Poultry Science; 020299 Animal Sciences, Other; 020301 Food Sciences and Technology; 020401 Plant Sciences, General; 020402 Agronomy and Crop Science; 020403 Horticulture Science; 020405 Plant Breeding and Genetics.

Related DOT Jobs: 040.061-010 Agronomist; 040.061-038 Horticulturist; 041.061-018 Apiculturist; 041.061-046 Entomologist; 041.061-082 Plant Breeder.

19-1013.02 Soil Scientists (Agricultural and Food Scientists)

Education: Bachelor's degree
Employed: 21,468
Openings: 1,639
Projected Growth: 10.9%
Earnings: $42,340

Research or study soil characteristics; map soil types; investigate responses of soils to known management practices. Determine use capabilities of soils and effects of alternative practices on soil productivity.

Provides advice on rural or urban land use. Investigates responses of specific soil types to soil management practices, such as fertilization, crop rotation, and industrial waste control. Performs chemical analysis on microorganism content of soil to determine microbial reactions and chemical mineralogical relationship to plant growth. Studies soil characteristics and classifies soils according to standard types. Conducts experiments on farms or experimental stations to determine best soil types for different plants.

GOE Number, Interest Area, and Work Group: 02.03.02; Science, Math, and Engineering; Life Sciences: Plant Specialization. **Personality Type:** Investigative. Investigative occupations frequently involve working with ideas and require an extensive amount of thinking. These occupations can involve searching for facts and figuring out problems mentally. **Work Values:** Autonomy; Independence; Creativity; Moral Values; Ability Utilization. **Skills:** Reading Comprehension; Science; Writing; Critical Thinking; Active Learning. **Abilities:** *Cognitive*—Deductive Reasoning; Inductive Reasoning; Written Comprehension; Category Flexibility; Mathematical Reasoning. *Psychomotor*—none met the criteria. *Physical*—none met the criteria. *Sensory*—Speech Clarity; Speech Recognition. **General Work Activities:** *Information Input*—Identifying Objects, Actions, and Events; Getting Information Needed to Do the Job; Monitoring Processes, Materials, and Surroundings. *Mental Process*—Analyzing Data or Information;

Making Decisions and Solving Problems; Processing Information. *Work Output*—Implementing Ideas and Programs; Handling and Moving Objects; Controlling Machines and Processes; Documenting and Recording Information. *Interacting with Others*—Providing Consultation and Advice to Others; Interpreting Meaning of Information to Others; Communicating with Persons Outside Organization. **Physical Work Conditions:** Indoors; Sitting; Outdoors; Using Hands on Objects, Tools, or Controls. **Other Job Characteristics:** Importance of Being Exact or Accurate; Importance of Being Sure All Is Done; Consequence of Error.

Experience: Job Zone 5. Extensive skill, knowledge, and experience are needed. Very advanced communication and organizational skills are required. **Job Preparation:** SVP 8.0 and above—4 years to more than 10 years. **Knowledge:** Chemistry; Biology; Food Production; Mathematics; English Language. **Instructional Programs:** 020101 Agriculture/Agricultural Sciences, General; 020102 Agricultural Extension; 020201 Animal Sciences, General; 020202 Agricultural Animal Breeding and Genetics; 020203 Agricultural Animal Health; 020204 Agricultural Animal Nutrition; 020205 Agricultural Animal Physiology; 020206 Dairy Science; 020209 Poultry Science; 020299 Animal Sciences, Other; 020301 Food Sciences and Technology; 020401 Plant Sciences, General; 020402 Agronomy and Crop Science; 020403 Horticulture Science; 020405 Plant Breeding and Genetics.

Related DOT Job: 040.061-058 Soil Scientist.

19-1020.01 Biologists (Biological Scientists)

Education: Doctoral degree
Employed: 80,950
Openings: 10,417
Projected Growth: 35%
Earnings: $46,140

Research or study basic principles of plant and animal life, such as origin, relationship, development, anatomy, and functions.

Develops methods and apparatus for securing representative plant, animal, aquatic, or soil samples. Prepares environmental impact reports for industry, government, or publication. Identifies, classifies, and studies structure, behavior, ecology, physiology, nutrition, culture, and distribution of plant and animal species. Studies reactions of plants, animals, and marine species to parasites. Studies aquatic plants and animals and environmental conditions affecting them, such as radioactivity or pollution. Investigates and develops pest management and control measures. Communicates test results to state and federal representatives and general public. Plans and administers biological research programs for government, research firms, medical industries, or manufacturing firms. Researches environmental effects of present and potential uses of land and water areas and determines methods of improving environment or crop yields. Studies basic principles of plant and animal life, such as origin, relationship, development, anatomy, and functions. Develops methods of extracting drugs from aquatic plants and animals. Measures salinity, acidity, light, oxygen content, and other physical conditions of water to determine their relationship to aquatic life. Studies and manages wild animal populations. Cultivates, breeds, and grows aquatic life, such as lobsters, clams, or fish farming. Collects and analyzes biological data about relationship among and between organisms and their environment.

GOE Number, Interest Area, and Work Group: 02.03.03; Science, Math, and Engineering; Life Sciences: Plant and Animal Specialization. **Personality Type:** Investigative. Investigative occupations frequently involve working with ideas and require an extensive amount of thinking. These occupations can involve searching for facts and figuring out problems mentally. **Work Values:** Autonomy; Ability Utilization; Achievement; Creativity; Independence. **Skills:** Science; Reading Comprehension; Writing; Mathematics; Critical Thinking; Active Learning; Information Organization. **Abilities:** *Cognitive*—Deductive Reasoning; Inductive Reasoning; Information Ordering; Written Expression; Written Comprehension. *Psychomotor*—Response Orientation. *Physical*—Extent Flexibility; Trunk Strength; Stamina. *Sensory*—Near Vision; Speech Clarity; Far Vision. **General Work Activities:** *Information Input*—Identifying Objects, Actions, and Events; Getting Information Needed to Do the Job; Monitoring Processes, Materials, and Surroundings. *Mental Process*—Analyzing Data or Information; Processing Information; Updating and Using Job-Relevant Knowledge. *Work Output*—Documenting and Recording Information; Controlling Machines and Processes; Implementing Ideas and Programs. *Interacting with Others*—Providing Consultation and Advice to Others; Communicating with Persons Outside Organization; Communicating with Other Workers. **Physical Work Conditions:** Indoors; Using Hands on Objects, Tools, or Controls; Common Protective or Safety Attire. **Other Job Characteristics:** Consequence of Error; Importance of Being Sure All Is Done; Importance of Being Exact or Accurate.

Experience: Job Zone 5. Extensive skill, knowledge, and experience are needed. Very advanced communication and organizational skills are required. **Job Preparation:** SVP 8.0 and above—4 years to more than 10 years. **Knowledge:** Biology; Mathematics; Chemistry; English Language; Physics. **Instructional Programs:** 020401 Plant Sciences, General; 020406 Agricultural Plant Pathology; 020407 Agricultural Plant Physiology; 260101 Biology, General; 260202 Biochemistry; 260203 Biophysics; 260301 Botany, General; 260305 Plant Pathology; 260307 Plant Physiology; 260399 Botany, Other; 260401 Cell Biology; 260402 Molecular Biology; 260499 Cell and Molecular Biology, Other; 260501 Microbiology/Bacteriology; 260601 Anatomy.

Related DOT Jobs: 041.061-022 Aquatic Biologist; 041.061-030 Biologist; 041.061-066 Nematologist.

19-1021.00 Biochemists and Biophysicists (Biological Scientists)

Education: Doctoral degree
Employed: 80,950
Openings: 10,417
Projected Growth: 35%
Earnings: $46,140

Study the chemical composition and physical principles of living cells and organisms, their electrical and mechanical energy, and related phenomena. Conduct research to further understanding of the complex chemical combinations and reactions involved in metabolism, reproduction, growth, and heredity. Determine the effects of foods, drugs, serums, hormones, and other substances on the tissues and vital processes of living organisms.

GOE Number, Interest Area, and Work Group: 02.03.03; Science, Math, and Engineering; Life Sciences: Plant and Animal Specialization. **Instructional Programs:** 020401 Plant Sciences, General; 020406 Agricultural Plant Pathology; 020407 Agricultural Plant Physiology; 260101 Biology, General; 260202 Biochemistry; 260203 Biophysics; 260301 Botany, General; 260305 Plant Pathology; 260307 Plant Physiology; 260399 Botany, Other; 260401 Cell Biology; 260402 Molecular Biology; 260499 Cell and Molecular Biology, Other; 260501 Microbiology/Bacteriology; 260601 Anatomy. **Note:** The Department of Labor has not collected some data for this job, so it has fewer details than the other descriptions.

19-1021.01 Biochemists (Biological Scientists)

Education: Doctoral degree
Employed: 80,950
Openings: 10,417
Projected Growth: 35%
Earnings: $46,140

Research or study chemical composition and processes of living organisms that affect vital processes such as growth and aging. Determine the effects of chemical actions on organisms, such as the action of foods, drugs, or other substances on body functions and tissues.

Analyzes foods to determine nutritional value and effects of cooking, canning, and processing on this value. Researches methods of transferring characteristics, such as resistance to disease, from one organism to another. Examines chemical aspects of formation of antibodies, and researches chemistry of cells and blood corpuscles. Develops methods to process, store, and use food, drugs, and chemical compounds. Develops and executes tests to detect disease, genetic disorders, or other abnormalities. Isolates, analyzes, and identifies hormones, vitamins, allergens, minerals, and enzymes, and determines their effects on body functions. Researches and determines chemical action of substances, such as drugs, serums, hormones, and food on tissues and vital processes. Cleans, purifies, refines, and otherwise prepares pharmaceutical compounds for commercial distribution. Develops and tests new drugs and medications used for commercial distribution. Prepares reports and recommendations based upon research outcomes. Studies chemistry of living processes, such as cell development, breathing and digestion, and living energy changes, such as growth, aging, and death. Designs and builds laboratory equipment needed for special research projects.

GOE Number, Interest Area, and Work Group: 02.03.03; Science, Math, and Engineering; Life Sciences: Plant and Animal Specialization. **Personality Type:** Investigative. Investigative occupations frequently involve working with ideas and require an extensive amount of thinking. These occupations can involve searching for facts and figuring out problems mentally. **Work Values:** Ability Utilization; Autonomy; Creativity; Responsibility; Independence; Security. **Skills:** Science; Reading Comprehension; Writing; Critical Thinking; Active Learning; Information Gathering. **Abilities:** *Cognitive*—Inductive Reasoning; Written Comprehension; Deductive Reasoning; Written Expression; Information Ordering. *Psychomotor*—Finger Dexterity; Arm-Hand Steadiness. *Physical*—Trunk Strength. *Sensory*—Near Vision; Visual Color Discrimination; Depth Perception. **General Work Activities:** *Information Input*—Getting Information Needed to Do the Job; Identifying Objects, Actions, and Events; Monitoring Processes, Materials, and Surroundings. *Mental Process*—Processing Information; Analyzing Data or Information; Updating and Using Job-Relevant Knowledge. *Work Output*—Documenting and Recording Information; Implementing Ideas and Programs; Controlling Machines and Processes. *Interacting with Others*—Interpreting Meaning of Information to Others; Providing Consultation and Advice to Others; Communicating with Other Workers. **Physical Work Conditions:** Indoors; Using Hands on Objects, Tools, or Controls; Sitting. **Other Job Characteristics:** Consequence of Error; Importance of Being Exact or Accurate; Importance of Being Sure All Is Done.

Experience: Job Zone 5. Extensive skill, knowledge, and experience are needed. Very advanced communication and organizational skills are required. **Job Preparation:** SVP 8.0 and above—4 years to more than 10 years. **Knowledge:** Chemistry; Biology; Mathematics; English Language; Building and Construction. **Instructional Programs:** 020401 Plant Sciences, General; 020406 Agricultural Plant Pathology; 020407 Agricultural Plant Physiology; 260101 Biology, General; 260202 Biochemistry; 260203 Biophysics; 260301 Botany, General; 260305 Plant Pathology; 260307 Plant Physiology; 260399 Botany, Other; 260401 Cell Biology; 260402 Molecular Biology; 260499 Cell and Molecular Biology, Other; 260501 Microbiology/Bacteriology; 260601 Anatomy.

Related DOT Job: 041.061-026 Biochemist.

19-1021.02 Biophysicists (Biological Scientists)

Education: Doctoral degree
Employed: 80,950
Openings: 10,417
Projected Growth: 35%
Earnings: $46,140

Research or study physical principles of living cells and organisms, their electrical and mechanical energy, and related phenomena.

Investigates dynamics of seeing and hearing. Studies physical principles of living cells and organisms and their electrical and mechanical energy. Researches transformation of substances in cells, using atomic isotopes. Researches manner in which characteristics of plants and animals are carried through successive generations. Studies spatial configuration of submicroscopic molecules, such as proteins, using X-ray and electron microscope. Studies absorption of light by chlorophyll in photosynthesis or by pigments of eye involved in vision. Analyzes functions of electronic

and human brains, such as learning, thinking, and memory. Investigates transmission of electrical impulses along nerves and muscles. Investigates damage to cells and tissues caused by X rays and nuclear particles. Researches cancer treatment, using radiation and nuclear particles.

GOE Number, Interest Area, and Work Group: 02.03.03; Science, Math, and Engineering; Life Sciences: Plant and Animal Specialization. **Personality Type:** Investigative. Investigative occupations frequently involve working with ideas and require an extensive amount of thinking. These occupations can involve searching for facts and figuring out problems mentally. **Work Values:** Autonomy; Ability Utilization; Responsibility; Independence; Security. **Skills:** Science; Reading Comprehension; Writing; Information Gathering; Idea Generation; Active Learning; Mathematics. **Abilities:** *Cognitive*—Written Comprehension; Deductive Reasoning; Inductive Reasoning; Information Ordering; Memorization. *Psychomotor*—Arm-Hand Steadiness; Finger Dexterity; Control Precision. *Physical*—Trunk Strength. *Sensory*—Near Vision; Visual Color Discrimination; Depth Perception. **General Work Activities:** *Information Input*—Monitoring Processes, Materials, and Surroundings; Getting Information Needed to Do the Job; Identifying Objects, Actions, and Events. *Mental Process*—Analyzing Data or Information; Processing Information; Making Decisions and Solving Problems. *Work Output*—Documenting and Recording Information; Implementing Ideas and Programs; Controlling Machines and Processes. *Interacting with Others*—Interpreting Meaning of Information to Others; Monitoring and Controlling Resources; Providing Consultation and Advice to Others. **Physical Work Conditions:** Indoors; Using Hands on Objects, Tools, or Controls; Common Protective or Safety Attire. **Other Job Characteristics:** Importance of Being Sure All Is Done; Importance of Being Exact or Accurate; Consequence of Error.

Experience: Job Zone 5. Extensive skill, knowledge, and experience are needed. Very advanced communication and organizational skills are required. **Job Preparation:** SVP 8.0 and above—4 years to more than 10 years. **Knowledge:** Biology; Physics; Mathematics; Chemistry; English Language. **Instructional Programs:** 020401 Plant Sciences, General; 020406 Agricultural Plant Pathology; 020407 Agricultural Plant Physiology; 260101 Biology, General; 260202 Biochemistry; 260203 Biophysics; 260301 Botany, General; 260305 Plant Pathology; 260307 Plant Physiology; 260399 Botany, Other; 260401 Cell Biology; 260402 Molecular Biology; 260499 Cell and Molecular Biology, Other; 260501 Microbiology/Bacteriology; 260601 Anatomy.

Related DOT Job: 041.061-034 Biophysicist.

19-1022.00 Microbiologists (Biological Scientists)

Education: Doctoral degree
Employed: 80,950
Openings: 10,417
Projected Growth: 35%
Earnings: $46,140

Investigate the growth, structure, development, and other characteristics of microscopic organisms such as bacteria, algae, or fungi. Includes medical microbiologists who study the relationship between organisms and disease or the effects of antibiotics on microorganisms.

Prepares technical reports and recommendations based upon research outcomes. Studies growth structure and development of viruses and rickettsiae. Observes action of microorganisms upon living tissues of plants, higher animals, and other microorganisms, and on dead organic matter. Examines physiological, morphological, and cultural characteristics, using microscope, to identify microorganisms. Researches use of bacteria and microorganisms to develop vitamins, antibiotics, amino acids, grain alcohol, sugars, and polymers. Conducts chemical analyses of substances, such as acids, alcohols, and enzymes. Studies growth, structure, development, and general characteristics of bacteria and other microorganisms. Isolates and makes cultures of bacteria or other microorganisms in prescribed media, controlling moisture, aeration, temperature, and nutrition.

GOE Number, Interest Area, and Work Group: 02.03.03; Science, Math, and Engineering; Life Sciences: Plant and Animal Specialization. **Personality Type:** Investigative. Investigative occupations frequently involve working with ideas and require an extensive amount of thinking. These occupations can involve searching for facts and figuring out problems mentally. **Work Values:** Autonomy; Ability Utilization; Independence; Working Conditions; Responsibility; Creativity. **Skills:** Science; Writing; Reading Comprehension; Problem Identification; Information Gathering; Active Learning. **Abilities:** *Cognitive*—Deductive Reasoning; Inductive Reasoning; Written Comprehension; Written Expression; Information Ordering. *Psychomotor*—Arm-Hand Steadiness; Manual Dexterity; Finger Dexterity; Control Precision. *Physical*—Extent Flexibility; Gross Body Coordination. *Sensory*—Near Vision; Speech Clarity; Visual Color Discrimination. **General Work Activities:** *Information Input*—Getting Information Needed to Do the Job; Identifying Objects, Actions, and Events; Monitoring Processes, Materials, and Surroundings. *Mental Process*—Analyzing Data or Information; Processing Information; Organizing, Planning, and Prioritizing. *Work Output*—Controlling Machines and Processes; Documenting and Recording Information; Implementing Ideas and Programs. *Interacting with Others*—Interpreting Meaning of Information to Others; Providing Consultation and Advice to Others; Communicating with Other Workers; Communicating with Persons Outside Organization. **Physical Work Conditions:** Indoors; Diseases or Infections; Using Hands on Objects, Tools, or Controls; Common Protective or Safety Attire. **Other Job Characteristics:** Consequence of Error; Importance of Being Exact or Accurate; Importance of Being Sure All Is Done.

Experience: Job Zone 5. Extensive skill, knowledge, and experience are needed. Very advanced communication and organizational skills are required. **Job Preparation:** SVP 8.0 and above—4 years to more than 10 years. **Knowledge:** Biology; Mathematics; Chemistry; Administration and Management; English Language. **Instructional Programs:** 020401 Plant Sciences, General; 020406 Agricultural Plant Pathology; 020407 Agricultural Plant Physiology; 260101 Biology, General; 260202 Biochemistry; 260203 Biophysics; 260301 Botany, General; 260305 Plant Pathology; 260307 Plant Physiology; 260399 Botany, Other; 260401 Cell Biology; 260402 Molecular Biology; 260499 Cell and Molecular Biology, Other; 260501 Microbiology/Bacteriology; 260601 Anatomy. **Related DOT Job:** 041.061-058 Microbiologist.

19-1023.00 Zoologists and Wildlife Biologists
(Biological Scientists)

Education: Doctoral degree
Employed: 80,950
Openings: 10,417
Projected Growth: 35%
Earnings: $46,140

Study the origins, behavior, diseases, genetics, and life processes of animals and wildlife. Specialize in wildlife research and management, including collecting and analyzing biological data to determine the environmental effects of present and potential use of land and water areas.

Prepares collections of preserved specimens or microscopic slides for species identification and study of species development or animal disease. Studies animals in their natural habitats, and assesses effects of environment on animals. Analyzes characteristics of animals to identify and classify animals. Conducts experimental studies, using chemicals and various types of scientific equipment. Studies origin, interrelationships, classification, life histories and diseases, development, genetics, and distribution of animals. Collects and dissects animal specimens and examines specimens under microscope. Raises specimens for study and observation or for use in experiments.

GOE Number, Interest Area, and Work Group: 02.03.01; Science, Math, and Engineering; Life Sciences: Animal Specialization. **Personality Type:** Investigative. Investigative occupations frequently involve working with ideas and require an extensive amount of thinking. These occupations can involve searching for facts and figuring out problems mentally. **Work Values:** Autonomy; Achievement; Ability Utilization; Responsibility; Creativity. **Skills:** Reading Comprehension; Science; Information Gathering; Problem Identification; Active Learning; Idea Generation; Information Organization; Writing. **Abilities:** *Cognitive*—Deductive Reasoning; Category Flexibility; Inductive Reasoning; Written Comprehension; Problem Sensitivity; Information Ordering. *Psychomotor*—Arm-Hand Steadiness; Reaction Time; Finger Dexterity; Manual Dexterity. *Physical*—Static Strength; Gross Body Coordination; Dynamic Strength; Stamina. *Sensory*—Near Vision; Auditory Attention; Far Vision. **General Work Activities:** *Information Input*—Identifying Objects, Actions, and Events; Getting Information Needed to Do the Job; Monitoring Processes, Materials, and Surroundings. *Mental Process*—Analyzing Data or Information; Processing Information; Updating and Using Job-Relevant Knowledge; Organizing, Planning, and Prioritizing. *Work Output*—Documenting and Recording Information; Controlling Machines and Processes; Handling and Moving Objects. *Interacting with Others*—Interpreting Meaning of Information to Others; Monitoring and Controlling Resources; Communicating with Other Workers; Performing Administrative Activities. **Physical Work Conditions:** Using Hands on Objects, Tools, or Controls; Indoors; Outdoors; Hazardous Situations; Common Protective or Safety Attire. **Other Job Characteristics:** Importance of Being Sure All Is Done; Importance of Being Exact or Accurate; Consequence of Error.

Experience: Job Zone 5. Extensive skill, knowledge, and experience are needed. Very advanced communication and organizational skills are required. **Job Preparation:** SVP 8.0 and above—4 years to more than 10 years. **Knowledge:** Biology; Mathematics; Chemistry; English Language; Clerical. **Instructional Programs:** 020401 Plant Sciences, General; 020406 Agricultural Plant Pathology; 020407 Agricultural Plant Physiology; 260101 Biology, General; 260202 Biochemistry; 260203 Biophysics; 260301 Botany, General; 260305 Plant Pathology; 260307 Plant Physiology; 260399 Botany, Other; 260401 Cell Biology; 260402 Molecular Biology; 260499 Cell and Molecular Biology, Other; 260501 Microbiology/Bacteriology; 260601 Anatomy.

Related DOT Job: 041.061-090 Zoologist.

19-1031.00 Conservation Scientists (Conservation Scientists and Foresters)

Education: Bachelor's degree
Employed: 38,949
Openings: 3,328
Projected Growth: 17.9%
Earnings: $42,750

Manage, improve, and protect natural resources to maximize their use without damaging the environment. Conduct soil surveys and develop plans to eliminate soil erosion or to protect rangelands from fire and rodent damage. Instruct farmers, agricultural production managers, or ranchers in the best use of crop rotation, contour plowing, or terracing to conserve soil and water; in the number and kind of livestock and forage plants best suited to particular ranges; and in range and farm improvements such as fences and water reservoirs.

GOE Number, Interest Area, and Work Group: 02.03.03; Science, Math, and Engineering; Life Sciences: Plant and Animal Specialization. **Instructional Programs:** 020409 Range Science and Management; 020501 Soil Sciences; 030101 Natural Resources Conservation, General; 030201 Natural Resources Management and Policy; 030203 Natural Resources Law Enforcement and Protective Services; 030299 Natural Resources Management and Protective Services, Other; 030501 Forestry, General; 030502 Forestry Sciences; 030506 Forest Management; 030509 Wood Science and Pulp/Paper Technology; 030599 Forestry and Related Sciences, Other; 039999 Conservation and Renewable Natural Resources, Other. **Note:** The Department of Labor has not collected some data for this job, so it has fewer details than the other descriptions.

19-1031.01 Soil Conservationists (Conservation Scientists and Foresters)

Education: Bachelor's degree
Employed: 38,949
Openings: 3,328
Projected Growth: 17.9%
Earnings: $42,750

Plan and develop coordinated practices for soil erosion control, soil and water conservation, and sound land use.

Surveys property to mark locations and measurements, using surveying instruments. Conducts surveys and investigations of various land uses, such as rural or urban, agriculture, construction, forestry or mining. Computes design specification for implementation of conservation practices, using survey and field information technical guides, engineering manuals, and calculator. Develops or participates in environmental studies. Computes cost estimates of different conservation practices based on needs of land users, maintenance requirements, and life expectancy of practices. Revisits land users to view implemented land use practices and plans. Monitors projects during and after construction to ensure projects conform to design specifications. Analyzes results of investigations to determine measures needed to maintain or restore proper soil management. Develops plans for conservation, such as conservation cropping systems, woodlands management, pasture planning and engineering systems. Plans soil management practices, such as crop rotation, reforestation, permanent vegetation, contour plowing, or terracing, to maintain soil and conserve water. Discusses conservation plans, problems, and alternative solutions with land users, applying knowledge of agronomy, soil science, forestry, or agricultural sciences.

GOE Number, Interest Area, and Work Group: 02.03.02; Science, Math, and Engineering; Life Sciences: Plant Specialization. **Personality Type:** Investigative. Investigative occupations frequently involve working with ideas and require an extensive amount of thinking. These occupations can involve searching for facts and figuring out problems mentally. **Work Values:** Autonomy; Ability Utilization; Responsibility; Creativity; Independence; Achievement. **Skills:** Implementation Planning; Identifying Downstream Consequences; Monitoring; Judgment and Decision Making; Mathematics; Solution Appraisal; Reading Comprehension. **Abilities:** *Cognitive*—Deductive Reasoning; Oral Expression; Oral Comprehension; Inductive Reasoning; Problem Sensitivity. *Psychomotor*—Multilimb Coordination; Finger Dexterity. *Physical*—Gross Body Equilibrium. *Sensory*—Far Vision; Near Vision; Speech Clarity. **General Work Activities:** *Information Input*—Getting Information Needed to Do the Job; Identifying Objects, Actions, and Events; Monitoring Processes, Materials, and Surroundings. *Mental Process*—Making Decisions and Solving Problems; Analyzing Data or Information; Processing Information. *Work Output*—Implementing Ideas and Programs; Documenting and Recording Information; Performing General Physical Activities; Drafting and Specifying Technical Devices. *Interacting with Others*—Providing Consultation and Advice to Others; Communicating with Persons Outside Organization; Interpreting Meaning of Information to Others. **Physical Work Conditions:** Outdoors; Using Hands on Objects, Tools, or Controls; Sitting; Indoors; Standing. **Other Job Characteristics:** Consequence of Error; Frustrating Circumstances; Importance of Being Sure All Is Done.

Experience: Job Zone 4. A minimum of two to four years of work-related skill, knowledge, or experience is needed. **Job Preparation:** SVP 7.0 to less than 8.0—2 years to less than 10 years. **Knowledge:** Biology; Mathematics; Engineering and Technology; Food Production; English Language. **Instructional Programs:** 020409 Range Science and Management; 020501 Soil Sciences; 030101 Natural Resources Conservation, General; 030201

Natural Resources Management and Policy; 030203 Natural Resources Law Enforcement and Protective Services; 030299 Natural Resources Management and Protective Services, Other; 030501 Forestry, General; 030502 Forestry Sciences; 030506 Forest Management; 030509 Wood Science and Pulp/Paper Technology; 030599 Forestry and Related Sciences, Other; 039999 Conservation and Renewable Natural Resources, Other.

Related DOT Jobs: 040.061-054 Soil Conservationist; 040.261-010 Soil-Conservation Technician.

19-1031.02 Range Managers (Conservation Scientists and Foresters)

Education: Bachelor's degree

Employed: 38,949

Openings: 3,328

Projected Growth: 17.9%

Earnings: $42,750

Research or study rangeland management practices to provide sustained production of forage, livestock, and wildlife.

Studies rangelands to determine number and kind of livestock that can be most profitably grazed. Develops methods for protecting range from fire and rodent damage. Studies forage plants and their growth requirements to determine varieties best suited to particular range. Develops improved practices for range reseeding. Studies rangelands to determine best grazing seasons. Plans and directs construction of range improvements, such as fences, corrals, water reservoirs and soil-erosion control structures. Plans and directs maintenance of range improvements. Develops methods for controlling poisonous plants in rangelands.

GOE Number, Interest Area, and Work Group: 02.03.02; Science, Math, and Engineering; Life Sciences: Plant Specialization. **Personality Type:** Investigative. Investigative occupations frequently involve working with ideas and require an extensive amount of thinking. These occupations can involve searching for facts and figuring out problems mentally. **Work Values:** Autonomy; Independence; Ability Utilization; Creativity; Responsibility. **Skills:** Judgment and Decision Making; Identification of Key Causes; Idea Evaluation; Problem Identification; Solution Appraisal; Implementation Planning. **Abilities:** *Cognitive*—Oral Expression; Inductive Reasoning; Problem Sensitivity; Deductive Reasoning; Spatial Orientation; Visualization. *Psychomotor*—none met the criteria. *Physical*—Stamina. *Sensory*—Far Vision; Speech Clarity; Peripheral Vision. **General Work Activities:** *Information Input*—Getting Information Needed to Do the Job; Estimating Needed Characteristics; Monitoring Processes, Materials, and Surroundings. *Mental Process*—Making Decisions and Solving Problems; Analyzing Data or Information; Developing Objectives and Strategies. *Work Output*—Implementing Ideas and Programs; Drafting and Specifying Technical Devices; Documenting and Recording Information; Performing General Physical Activities. *Interacting with Others*—Communicating with Other Workers; Providing Consultation and Advice to Others; Interpreting Meaning of Information to Others; Coordinating Work and Activities of Others. **Physical Work Conditions:** Outdoors; Walking or Running; Standing. **Other Job Characteristics:** Consequence of Error; Frus-

trating Circumstances; Importance of Being Exact or Accurate; Importance of Being Sure All Is Done.

Experience: Job Zone 5. Extensive skill, knowledge, and experience are needed. Very advanced communication and organizational skills are required. **Job Preparation:** SVP 8.0 and above—4 years to more than 10 years. **Knowledge:** Administration and Management; Biology; Food Production; Mathematics; Geography; Building and Construction. **Instructional Programs:** 020409 Range Science and Management; 020501 Soil Sciences; 030101 Natural Resources Conservation, General; 030201 Natural Resources Management and Policy; 030203 Natural Resources Law Enforcement and Protective Services; 030299 Natural Resources Management and Protective Services, Other; 030501 Forestry, General; 030502 Forestry Sciences; 030506 Forest Management; 030509 Wood Science and Pulp/Paper Technology; 030599 Forestry and Related Sciences, Other; 039999 Conservation and Renewable Natural Resources, Other.

Related DOT Job: 040.061-046 Range Manager.

19-1031.03 Park Naturalists (Conservation Scientists and Foresters)

Education: Bachelor's degree

Employed: 38,949

Openings: 3,328

Projected Growth: 17.9%

Earnings: $42,750

Plan, develop, and conduct programs to inform public of historical, natural, and scientific features of national, state, or local park.

Takes photographs and motion pictures to illustrate lectures and publications and to develop displays. Interviews specialists in desired fields to obtain and develop data for park information programs. Confers with park staff to determine subjects to be presented to public. Prepares and presents illustrated lectures of park features. Surveys park to determine distribution and abundance of fauna and flora. Conducts field trips to point out scientific, historic, and natural features of park. Performs emergency duties to protect human life, government property, and natural features of park. Plans and organizes activities of seasonal staff members. Surveys park to determine forest conditions. Constructs historical, scientific, and nature visitor-center displays. Maintains official park photographic and information files. Plans and develops audiovisual devices for public programs.

GOE Number, Interest Area, and Work Group: 12.01.01; Education and Social Service; Managerial Work in Education and Social Service. **Personality Type:** Social. Social occupations frequently involve working with, communicating with, and teaching people. These occupations often involve helping or providing service to others. **Work Values:** Autonomy; Moral Values; Responsibility; Achievement; Ability Utilization; Creativity. **Skills:** Writing; Speaking; Service Orientation; Implementation Planning; Reading Comprehension; Active Listening; Information Gathering. **Abilities:** *Cognitive*—Oral Comprehension; Oral Expression; Written Expression; Written Comprehension; Memorization; Visualization. *Psychomotor*—Rate Control. *Physical*—Stamina;

Dynamic Strength; Static Strength. *Sensory*—Speech Clarity; Far Vision; Hearing Sensitivity; Auditory Attention. **General Work Activities:** *Information Input*—Getting Information Needed to Do the Job; Identifying Objects, Actions, and Events; Monitoring Processes, Materials, and Surroundings. *Mental Process*—Processing Information; Analyzing Data or Information; Organizing, Planning, and Prioritizing. *Work Output*—Performing General Physical Activities; Implementing Ideas and Programs; Documenting and Recording Information. *Interacting with Others*—Performing for or Working with the Public; Communicating with Persons Outside Organization; Teaching Others. **Physical Work Conditions:** Outdoors; Walking or Running; Standing. **Other Job Characteristics:** Importance of Being Sure All Is Done; Importance of Being Exact or Accurate; Frustrating Circumstances.

Experience: Job Zone 4. A minimum of two to four years of work-related skill, knowledge, or experience is needed. **Job Preparation:** SVP 7.0 to less than 8.0—2 years to less than 10 years. **Knowledge:** Biology; Education and Training; English Language; History and Archeology; Communications and Media; Administration and Management; Geography. **Instructional Programs:** 020409 Range Science and Management; 020501 Soil Sciences; 030101 Natural Resources Conservation, General; 030201 Natural Resources Management and Policy; 030203 Natural Resources Law Enforcement and Protective Services; 030299 Natural Resources Management and Protective Services, Other; 030501 Forestry, General; 030502 Forestry Sciences; 030506 Forest Management; 030509 Wood Science and Pulp/Paper Technology; 030599 Forestry and Related Sciences, Other; 039999 Conservation and Renewable Natural Resources, Other.

Related DOT Job: 049.127-010 Park Naturalist.

19-1032.00 Foresters (Conservation Scientists and Foresters)

Education: Bachelor's degree
Employed: 38,949
Openings: 3,328
Projected Growth: 17.9%
Earnings: $42,750

Manage forested lands for economic, recreational, and conservation purposes. Inventory the type, amount, and location of standing timber. Appraise the timber's worth, negotiate the purchase, and draw up contracts for procurement. Determine how to conserve wildlife habitats, creek beds, water quality, and soil stability, and how best to comply with environmental regulations. Devise plans for planting and growing new trees; monitor trees for healthy growth; determine the best time for harvesting. Develop forest-management plans for public and privately owned forested lands.

Conducts public educational programs on forest care and conservation. Plans and directs construction and maintenance of recreation facilities, fire towers, trails, roads, and fire breaks. Participates in environmental studies and prepares environmental reports. Maps forest areas and estimates standing timber and future growth. Analyzes forest conditions to determine reason for prevalence of different variety of trees. Plans cutting programs to assure continuous production or to assist timber companies to achieve production goals. Suggests methods of processing wood for various uses. Studies classification, life history, light and soil requirements and resistance to disease and insects of different tree species. Researches forest propagation and culture affecting tree growth rates, yield, and duration and seed production, growth viability, and germination of different species. Determines methods of cutting and removing timber with minimum waste and environmental damage. Plans and directs forestation and reforestation projects. Assists in planning and implementing projects for control of floods, soil erosion, tree diseases, infestation, and forest fire. Investigates adaptability of different tree species to new environmental conditions, such as soil type, climate and altitude. Supervises activities of other forestry workers. Manages tree nurseries and thins forest to encourage natural growth of sprouts or seedlings of desired varieties. Develops techniques for measuring and identifying trees. Advises landowners on forestry management techniques. Directs suppression of forest fires and fights forest fires.

GOE Number, Interest Area, and Work Group: 02.03.02; Science, Math, and Engineering; Life Sciences: Plant Specialization. **Personality Type:** Realistic. Realistic occupations frequently involve work activities that include practical, hands-on problems and solutions. These occupations often deal with plants, animals, and real-world materials like wood, tools, and machinery. Many of the occupations require working outside and do not involve a lot of paperwork or working closely with others. **Work Values:** Autonomy; Responsibility; Ability Utilization; Achievement; Creativity. **Skills:** Solution Appraisal; Identifying Downstream Consequences; Identification of Key Causes; Systems Perception; Information Gathering; Judgment and Decision Making; Implementation Planning. **Abilities:** *Cognitive*—Oral Expression; Deductive Reasoning; Spatial Orientation; Written Expression; Visualization; Written Comprehension. *Psychomotor*—Control Precision; Speed of Limb Movement; Multilimb Coordination. *Physical*—Trunk Strength; Static Strength; Stamina. *Sensory*—Far Vision; Night Vision; Near Vision; Speech Clarity. **General Work Activities:** *Information Input*—Getting Information Needed to Do the Job; Identifying Objects, Actions, and Events; Monitoring Processes, Materials, and Surroundings. *Mental Process*—Analyzing Data or Information; Developing Objectives and Strategies; Updating and Using Job-Relevant Knowledge; Making Decisions and Solving Problems. *Work Output*—Performing General Physical Activities; Drafting and Specifying Technical Devices; Implementing Ideas and Programs; Documenting and Recording Information. *Interacting with Others*—Providing Consultation and Advice to Others; Communicating with Other Workers; Communicating with Persons Outside Organization. **Physical Work Conditions:** Outdoors; Standing; Special Uniform. **Other Job Characteristics:** Consequence of Error; Importance of Being Sure All Is Done; Importance of Being Aware of New Events.

Experience: Job Zone 4. A minimum of two to four years of work-related skill, knowledge, or experience is needed. **Job Preparation:** SVP 7.0 to less than 8.0—2 years to less than 10 years. **Knowledge:** Biology; Administration and Management; English Language; Chemistry; Mathematics; Education and Training. **Instructional Programs:** 020409 Range Science and Management; 020501 Soil Sciences; 030101 Natural Resources Conservation, General; 030201 Natural Resources Management and Policy;

030203 Natural Resources Law Enforcement and Protective Services; 030299 Natural Resources Management and Protective Services, Other; 030501 Forestry, General; 030502 Forestry Sciences; 030506 Forest Management; 030509 Wood Science and Pulp/Paper Technology; 030599 Forestry and Related Sciences, Other; 039999 Conservation and Renewable Natural Resources, Other.

Related DOT Jobs: 040.061-030 Forest Ecologist; 040.061-050 Silviculturist; 040.167-010 Forester.

19-1041.00 Epidemiologists (Medical Scientists)

Education: Doctoral degree

Employed: 31,139

Openings: 3,214

Projected Growth: 24.6%

Earnings: $50,410

Investigate and describe the determinants and distribution of disease, disability, and other health outcomes. Develop the means for prevention and control.

Analyzes data, applying statistical techniques and scientific knowledge; prepares reports; and presents findings. Supervises activities of clerical and statistical or laboratory personnel. Examines organs, tissues, cell structures, or microorganisms by systematic observation or using microscope. Prepares and analyzes samples for toxicity, bacteria, or microorganisms or to study cell structure and properties. Studies effects of drugs, gases, pesticides, parasites, or microorganisms, or health and physiological processes of animals and humans. Standardizes drug dosages, methods of immunization, and procedures for manufacture of drugs and medicinal compounds. Conducts research to develop methodologies, instrumentation, or identification, diagnosing, and treatment procedures for medical application. Confers with health department, industry personnel, physicians, and others to develop health safety standards and programs to improve public health. Plans methodological design of research study and arranges for data collection. Investigates cause, progress, life cycle, or mode of transmission of diseases or parasites. Plans and directs studies to investigate human or animal disease, preventive methods, and treatments for disease. Consults with and advises physicians, educators, researchers, and others regarding medical applications of sciences such as physics, biology, and chemistry. Teaches principles of medicine and medical laboratory procedures to physicians, residents, students, and technicians.

GOE Number, Interest Area, and Work Group: 02.03.01; Science, Math, and Engineering; Life Sciences: Animal Specialization. **Personality Type:** Investigative. Investigative occupations frequently involve working with ideas and require an extensive amount of thinking. These occupations can involve searching for facts and figuring out problems mentally. **Work Values:** Achievement; Social Status; Ability Utilization; Security; Responsibility; Autonomy; Compensation. **Skills:** Active Learning; Instructing; Reading Comprehension; Writing; Science; Information Gathering. **Abilities:** *Cognitive*—Oral Expression; Inductive Reasoning; Oral Comprehension; Written Expression; Problem Sensitivity. *Psychomotor*—Arm-Hand Steadiness; Finger Dexterity; Control Precision. *Physical*—none met the criteria. *Sensory*—Speech

Clarity; Near Vision; Auditory Attention; Far Vision; Visual Color Discrimination. **General Work Activities:** *Information Input*—Identifying Objects, Actions, and Events; Getting Information Needed to Do the Job; Monitoring Processes, Materials, and Surroundings. *Mental Process*—Analyzing Data or Information; Making Decisions and Solving Problems; Updating and Using Job-Relevant Knowledge; Processing Information. *Work Output*—Implementing Ideas and Programs; Documenting and Recording Information; Handling and Moving Objects. *Interacting with Others*—Communicating with Other Workers; Interpreting Meaning of Information to Others; Communicating with Persons Outside Organization; Teaching Others. **Physical Work Conditions:** Indoors; Using Hands on Objects, Tools, or Controls; Sitting; Diseases or Infections. **Other Job Characteristics:** Consequence of Error; Importance of Being Exact or Accurate; Importance of Being Sure All Is Done.

Experience: Job Zone 4. A minimum of two to four years of work-related skill, knowledge, or experience is needed. **Job Preparation:** SVP 7.0 to less than 8.0—2 years to less than 10 years. **Knowledge:** Mathematics; Biology; Chemistry; Computers and Electronics; English Language; Medicine and Dentistry. **Instructional Programs:** 260705 Pharmacology, Human and Animal; 511301 Medical Anatomy; 511302 Medical Biochemistry; 511303 Medical Biomathematics and Biometrics; 511304 Medical Physics/Biophysics; 511305 Medical Cell Biology; 511306 Medical Genetics; 511307 Medical Immunology; 511308 Medical Microbiology; 511309 Medical Molecular Biology; 511310 Medical Neurobiology; 511311 Medical Nutrition; 511312 Medical Pathology; 511313 Medical Physiology; 511314 Medical Toxicology.

Related DOT Jobs: 041.061-054 Histopathologist; 041.167-010 Environmental Epidemiologist.

19-1042.00 Medical Scientists, Except Epidemiologists (Medical Scientists)

Education: Doctoral degree

Employed: 31,139

Openings: 3,214

Projected Growth: 24.6%

Earnings: $50,410

Conduct research dealing with human diseases and the improvement of human health. Engage in clinical investigation or other research, production, technical writing, or related activities.

Analyzes data, applying statistical techniques and scientific knowledge, prepares reports, and presents findings. Studies effects of drugs, gases, pesticides, parasites, or microorganisms, or health and physiological processes of animals and humans. Investigates cause, progress, life cycle, or mode of transmission of diseases or parasites. Plans methodological design of research study and arranges for data collection. Confers with health department, industry personnel, physicians, and others to develop health safety standards and programs to improve public health. Standardizes drug dosages, methods of immunization, and procedures for manufacture of drugs and medicinal compounds. Supervises activities of clerical and statistical or laboratory personnel. Consults with and advises physicians, educators, researchers, and others regarding medical applications of sciences, such as physics, biology, and chemistry. Prepares and analyzes samples for toxicity, bacteria, or microorganisms or to study cell structure and properties. Examines organs, tissues, cell structures, or microorganisms by systematic observation or using microscope. Plans and directs studies to investigate human or animal disease, preventive methods, and treatments for disease. Conducts research to develop methodologies, instrumentation, or identification, diagnosing, and treatment procedures for medical application. Teaches principles of medicine and medical and laboratory procedures to physicians, residents, students, and technicians.

GOE Number, Interest Area, and Work Group: 02.03.01; Science, Math, and Engineering; Life Sciences: Animal Specialization. **Personality Type:** Investigative. Investigative occupations frequently involve working with ideas and require an extensive amount of thinking. These occupations can involve searching for facts and figuring out problems mentally. **Work Values:** Social Status; Achievement; Security; Ability Utilization; Autonomy; Responsibility; Compensation. **Skills:** Instructing; Active Learning; Reading Comprehension; Writing; Information Gathering; Science. **Abilities:** *Cognitive*—Oral Expression; Inductive Reasoning; Oral Comprehension; Written Expression; Problem Sensitivity. *Psychomotor*—Arm-Hand Steadiness; Finger Dexterity; Control Precision. *Physical*—none met the criteria. *Sensory*—Speech Clarity; Near Vision; Visual Color Discrimination; Far Vision; Auditory Attention. **General Work Activities:** *Information Input*—Identifying Objects, Actions, and Events; Getting Information Needed to Do the Job; Monitoring Processes, Materials, and Surroundings. *Mental Process*—Analyzing Data or Information; Updating and Using Job-Relevant Knowledge; Processing Information; Making Decisions and Solving Problems. *Work Output*—Implementing Ideas and Programs; Documenting and Recording Information; Handling and Moving Objects. *Interacting with Others*—Interpreting Meaning of Information to Others; Communicating with Other Workers; Teaching Others; Communicating with Persons Outside Organization. **Physical Work Conditions:** Indoors; Sitting; Diseases or Infections; Using Hands on Objects, Tools, or Controls. **Other Job Characteristics:** Consequence of Error; Importance of Being Exact or Accurate; Importance of Being Sure All Is Done.

Experience: Job Zone 4. A minimum of two to four years of work-related skill, knowledge, or experience is needed. **Job Preparation:** SVP 7.0 to less than 8.0—2 years to less than 10 years. **Knowledge:** Mathematics; Chemistry; Biology; English Language; Medicine and Dentistry; Computers and Electronics. **Instructional Programs:** 260705 Pharmacology, Human and Animal; 511301 Medical Anatomy; 511302 Medical Biochemistry; 511303 Medical Biomathematics and Biometrics; 511304 Medical Physics/Biophysics; 511305 Medical Cell Biology; 511306 Medical Genetics; 511307 Medical Immunology; 511308 Medical Microbiology; 511309 Medical Molecular Biology; 511310 Medical Neurobiology; 511311 Medical Nutrition; 511312 Medical Pathology; 511313 Medical Physiology; 511314 Medical Toxicology.

Related DOT Jobs: 041.061-010 Anatomist; 041.061-070 Parasitologist; 041.061-074 Pharmacologist; 041.067-010 Medical Coordinator, Pesticide Use; 079.021-014 Medical Physicist.

19-2000 Physical Scientists

19-2011.00 Astronomers (Physicists and Astronomers)

Education: Doctoral degree
Employed: 17,932
Openings: 1,164
Projected Growth: 2.2%
Earnings: $73,240

Observe, research, and interpret celestial and astronomical phenomena to increase basic knowledge. Apply such information to practical problems.

Calculates orbits and determines sizes, shapes, brightness, and motions of different celestial bodies. Determines exact time by celestial observations and conducts research into relationships between time and space. Analyzes wave lengths of radiation from celestial bodies, as observed in all ranges of spectrum. Develops mathematical tables giving positions of sun, moon, planets, and stars at given times for use by air and sea navigators. Studies history, structure, extent, and evolution of stars, stellar systems, and universe. Studies celestial phenomena from ground or above atmosphere, using various optical devices, such as telescopes situated on ground or attached to satellites. Computes positions of sun, moon, planets, stars, nebulae, and galaxies. Designs optical, mechanical, and electronic instruments for astronomical research.

GOE Number, Interest Area, and Work Group: 02.02.01; Science, Math, and Engineering; Physical Sciences. **Personality Type:** Investigative. Investigative occupations frequently involve working with ideas and require an extensive amount of thinking. These occupations can involve searching for facts and figuring out problems mentally. **Work Values:** Autonomy; Independence; Moral Values; Ability Utilization; Responsibility; Creativity. **Skills:** Science; Mathematics; Information Gathering; Critical Thinking; Active Learning. **Abilities:** *Cognitive*—Mathematical Reasoning; Written Comprehension; Inductive Reasoning; Deductive Reasoning; Number Facility. *Psychomotor*—Control Precision. *Physical*—none met the criteria. *Sensory*—Depth Perception; Night Vision; Far Vision. **General Work Activities:** *Information Input*—Identifying Objects, Actions, and Events; Getting Information Needed to Do the Job; Monitoring Processes, Materials, and Surroundings. *Mental Process*—Analyzing Data or Information; Processing Information; Making Decisions and Solving Problems. *Work Output*—Implementing Ideas and Programs; Controlling Machines and Processes; Drafting and Specifying Technical Devices; Documenting and Recording Information. *Interacting with Others*—Interpreting Meaning of Information to Others; Communicating with Other Workers; Providing Consultation and Advice to Others. **Physical Work Conditions:** Sitting; Outdoors; Indoors. **Other Job Characteristics:** Importance of Being Exact or Accurate; Importance of Being Aware of New Events; Consequence of Error.

Experience: Job Zone 5. Extensive skill, knowledge, and experience are needed. Very advanced communication and organizational skills are required. **Job Preparation:** SVP 8.0 and above—4 years to more than 10 years. **Knowledge:** Physics; Mathematics;

Computers and Electronics; Design; English Language; Engineering and Technology. **Instructional Programs:** 400201 Astronomy; 400301 Astrophysics; 400801 Physics, General; 400802 Chemical and Atomic/Molecular Physics; 400804 Elementary Particle Physics; 400805 Plasma and High-Temperature Physics; 400806 Nuclear Physics; 400807 Optics; 400808 Solid State and Low-Temperature Physics; 400809 Acoustics; 400810 Theoretical and Mathematical Physics; 400899 Physics, Other.

Related DOT Job: 021.067-010 Astronomer.

19-2012.00 Physicists (Physicists and Astronomers)

Education: Doctoral degree

Employed: 17,932

Openings: 1,164

Projected Growth: 2.2%

Earnings: $73,240

Conduct research into the phases of physical phenomena. Develop theories and laws on the basis of observation and experiments. Devise methods to apply laws and theories to industry and other fields.

Consults other scientists regarding innovations to ensure equipment or plant design conforms to health physics standards for protection of personnel. Assists with development of manufacturing, assembly, and fabrication processes of lasers, masers, infrared, and other light-emitting and light-sensitive devices. Assists in developing standards of permissible concentrations of radioisotopes in liquids and gases. Incorporates methods for maintenance and repair of components and designs, and develops test instrumentation and test procedures. Advises authorities in procedures to be followed in radiation incidents or hazards, and assists in civil defense planning. Directs testing and monitoring of contamination of radioactive equipment and recording of personnel and plant area radiation exposure data. Designs electronic circuitry and optical components with scientific characteristics to fit within specified mechanical limits and perform according to specifications. Conducts application analysis to determine commercial, industrial, scientific, medical, military, or other uses for electro-optical devices. Analyzes results of experiments designed to detect and measure previously unobserved physical phenomena. Describes and expresses observations and conclusions in mathematical terms. Observes structure and properties of matter and transformation and propagation of energy, using masers, lasers, telescopes and other equipment. Conducts instrumental analyses to determine physical properties of materials. Conducts research pertaining to potential environmental impact of proposed atomic energy related industrial development to determine qualifications for licensing.

GOE Number, Interest Area, and Work Group: 02.02.01; Science, Math, and Engineering; Physical Sciences. **Personality Type:** Investigative. Investigative occupations frequently involve working with ideas and require an extensive amount of thinking. These occupations can involve searching for facts and figuring out problems mentally. **Work Values:** Ability Utilization; Autonomy; Creativity; Achievement; Recognition; Working Conditions. **Skills:** Mathematics; Science; Writing; Reading Comprehension; Active Learning. **Abilities:** *Cognitive*—Written Comprehension; Written

Expression; Oral Comprehension; Inductive Reasoning; Oral Expression; Mathematical Reasoning. *Psychomotor*—none met the criteria. *Physical*—none met the criteria. *Sensory*—Speech Clarity; Speech Recognition; Hearing Sensitivity. **General Work Activities:** *Information Input*—Getting Information Needed to Do the Job; Identifying Objects, Actions, and Events; Monitoring Processes, Materials, and Surroundings. *Mental Process*—Analyzing Data or Information; Processing Information; Making Decisions and Solving Problems. *Work Output*—Drafting and Specifying Technologynical Devices; Implementing Ideas and Programs; Documenting and Recording Information. *Interacting with Others*—Interpreting Meaning of Information to Others; Communicating with Other Workers; Providing Consultation and Advice to Others. **Physical Work Conditions:** Indoors; Sitting; Using Hands on Objects, Tools, or Controls. **Other Job Characteristics:** Consequence of Error; Importance of Being Exact or Accurate; Importance of Being Sure All Is Done.

Experience: Job Zone 5. Extensive skill, knowledge, and experience are needed. Very advanced communication and organizational skills are required. **Job Preparation:** SVP 8.0 and above—4 years to more than 10 years. **Knowledge:** Physics; Mathematics; English Language; Education and Training; Engineering and Technology. **Instructional Programs:** 400201 Astronomy; 400301 Astrophysics; 400801 Physics, General; 400802 Chemical and Atomic/Molecular Physics; 400804 Elementary Particle Physics; 400805 Plasma and High-Temperature Physics; 400806 Nuclear Physics; 400807 Optics; 400808 Solid State and Low-Temperature Physics; 400809 Acoustics; 400810 Theoretical and Mathematical Physics; 400899 Physics, Other.

Related DOT Jobs: 015.021-010 Health Physicist; 023.061-010 Electro-Optical Engineer; 023.061-014 Physicist; 023.067-010 Physicist, Theoretical.

19-2021.00 Atmospheric and Space Scientists (Atmospheric Scientists)

Education: Bachelor's degree

Employed: 8,419

Openings: 683

Projected Growth: 14.6%

Earnings: $54,430

Investigate atmospheric phenomena and interpret meteorological data gathered by surface and air stations, satellites, and radar; prepare reports and forecasts for public and other uses.

Prepares special forecasts and briefings for air and sea transportation, agriculture, fire prevention, air-pollution control, and school groups. Studies and interprets synoptic reports, maps, photographs, and prognostic charts to predict long and short range weather conditions. Operates computer graphic equipment to produce weather reports and maps for analysis, distribution, or use in televised weather broadcast. Directs forecasting services at weather station, or at radio or television broadcasting facility. Issues hurricane and other severe weather warnings. Conducts basic or applied research in meteorology. Analyzes and interprets meteorological data gathered by surface and upper air stations, satellites, and radar to prepare reports and forecasts. Broadcasts weather forecast over television or radio.

GOE Number, Interest Area, and Work Group: 02.02.01; Science, Math, and Engineering; Physical Sciences. **Personality Type:** Investigative. Investigative occupations frequently involve working with ideas and require an extensive amount of thinking. These occupations can involve searching for facts and figuring out problems mentally. **Work Values:** Moral Values; Security; Autonomy; Ability Utilization; Responsibility. **Skills:** Science; Information Gathering; Information Organization; Active Learning; Critical Thinking; Reading Comprehension. **Abilities:** *Cognitive*—Oral Expression; Written Comprehension; Speed of Closure; Inductive Reasoning; Oral Comprehension. *Psychomotor*—Finger Dexterity. *Physical*—none met the criteria. *Sensory*—Speech Clarity; Far Vision; Visual Color Discrimination. **General Work Activities:** *Information Input*—Getting Information Needed to Do the Job; Monitoring Processes, Materials, and Surroundings; Identifying Objects, Actions, and Events. *Mental Process*—Analyzing Data or Information; Updating and Using Job-Relevant Knowledge; Processing Information. *Work Output*—Interacting with Computers; Handling and Moving Objects; Documenting and Recording Information. *Interacting with Others*—Interpreting Meaning of Information to Others; Communicating with Other Workers; Communicating with Persons Outside Organization; Performing for or Working with the Public. **Physical Work Conditions:** Indoors; Sitting; Using Hands on Objects, Tools, or Controls. **Other Job Characteristics:** Importance of Being Aware of New Events; Degree of Automation; Importance of Being Sure All Is Done; Importance of Being Exact or Accurate.

Experience: Job Zone 4. A minimum of two to four years of work-related skill, knowledge, or experience is needed. **Job Preparation:** SVP 7.0 to less than 8.0—2 years to less than 10 years. **Knowledge:** Communications and Media; Physics; Geography; Mathematics; Computers and Electronics; English Language. **Instructional Program:** 400401 Atmospheric Sciences and Meteorology.

Related DOT Job: 025.062-010 Meteorologist.

19-2031.00 Chemists (Chemists)

Education: Bachelor's degree
Employed: 96,372
Openings: 8,137
Projected Growth: 13.9%
Earnings: $46,220

Conduct qualitative and quantitative chemical analyses or chemical experiments in laboratories for quality or process control or to develop new products or knowledge.

Writes technical papers and reports and prepares standards and specifications for processes, facilities, products, and tests. Confers with scientists and engineers to conduct analyses of research projects, interpret test results, or develop nonstandard tests. Induces changes in composition of substances by introducing heat, light, energy, and chemical catalysts for quantitative and qualitative analysis. Compiles and analyzes test information to determine process or equipment operating efficiency and to diagnose malfunctions. Analyzes organic and inorganic compounds to determine chemical and physical properties, composition, structure,

relationships, and reactions, utilizing chromatography, spectroscopy, and spectrophotometry techniques. Studies effects of various methods of processing, preserving, and packaging on composition and properties of foods. Develops, improves, and customizes products, equipment, formulas, processes, and analytical methods. Prepares test solutions, compounds, and reagents for laboratory personnel to conduct test. Directs, coordinates, and advises personnel in test procedures for analyzing components and physical properties of materials.

GOE Number, Interest Area, and Work Group: 02.02.01; Science, Math, and Engineering; Physical Sciences. **Personality Type:** Investigative. Investigative occupations frequently involve working with ideas and require an extensive amount of thinking. These occupations can involve searching for facts and figuring out problems mentally. **Work Values:** Ability Utilization; Creativity; Autonomy; Responsibility; Security; Achievement. **Skills:** Science; Reading Comprehension; Writing; Information Gathering; Active Learning. **Abilities:** *Cognitive*—Deductive Reasoning; Mathematical Reasoning; Written Comprehension; Oral Expression; Written Expression. *Psychomotor*—Arm-Hand Steadiness; Finger Dexterity; Response Orientation. *Physical*—none met the criteria. *Sensory*—Near Vision; Speech Clarity; Visual Color Discrimination. **General Work Activities:** *Information Input*—Monitoring Processes, Materials, and Surroundings; Getting Information Needed to Do the Job; Identifying Objects, Actions, and Events. *Mental Process*—Analyzing Data or Information; Processing Information; Updating and Using Job-Relevant Knowledge. *Work Output*—Documenting and Recording Information; Controlling Machines and Processes; Implementing Ideas and Programs. *Interacting with Others*—Communicating with Other Workers; Interpreting Meaning of Information to Others; Coordinating Work and Activities of Others. **Physical Work Conditions:** Indoors; Hazardous Conditions; Contaminants. **Other Job Characteristics:** Consequence of Error; Importance of Being Exact or Accurate; Importance of Being Sure All Is Done.

Experience: Job Zone 4. A minimum of two to four years of work-related skill, knowledge, or experience is needed. **Job Preparation:** SVP 7.0 to less than 8.0—2 years to less than 10 years. **Knowledge:** Chemistry; Mathematics; English Language; Computers and Electronics; Physics; Administration and Management; Engineering and Technology. **Instructional Programs:** 400501 Chemistry, General; 400502 Analytical Chemistry; 400503 Inorganic Chemistry; 400504 Organic Chemistry; 400505 Medicinal/Pharmaceutical Chemistry; 400506 Physical and Theoretical Chemistry; 400507 Polymer Chemistry; 400599 Chemistry, Other.

Related DOT Jobs: 022.061-010 Chemist; 022.061-014 Chemist, Food; 022.137-010 Laboratory Supervisor.

19-2032.00 Materials Scientists (All Other Physical Scientists)

Education: No data available.
Employed: 68,060
Openings: No data available.
Projected Growth: No data available.
Earnings: $48,990

Research and study the structures and chemical properties of various natural and manmade materials, including metals, alloys, rubber, ceramics, semiconductors, polymers, and glass. Determine ways to strengthen or combine materials or develop new materials with new or specific properties, for use in a variety of products and applications.

Studies structures and properties of materials such as metals, alloys, polymers, and ceramics to obtain research data. Plans laboratory experiments to confirm feasibility of processes and techniques to produce materials having special characteristics. Reports materials-study findings for other scientists and requesters. Guides technical staff engaged in developing materials for specific use in projected product or device.

GOE Number, Interest Area, and Work Group: 02.02.01; Science, Math, and Engineering; Physical Sciences. **Personality Type:** Investigative. Investigative occupations frequently involve working with ideas and require an extensive amount of thinking. These occupations can involve searching for facts and figuring out problems mentally. **Work Values:** Autonomy; Ability Utilization; Creativity; Working Conditions; Responsibility. **Skills:** Science; Active Learning; Writing; Reading Comprehension; Mathematics. **Abilities:** *Cognitive*—Written Expression; Written Comprehension; Mathematical Reasoning; Originality; Oral Expression; Deductive Reasoning. *Psychomotor*—none met the criteria. *Physical*—none met the criteria. *Sensory*—Near Vision; Visual Color Discrimination. **General Work Activities:** *Information Input*—Getting Information Needed to Do the Job; Identifying Objects, Actions, and Events; Monitoring Processes, Materials, and Surroundings. *Mental Process*—Processing Information; Analyzing Data or Information; Updating and Using Job-Relevant Knowledge. *Work Output*—Documenting and Recording Information; Controlling Machines and Processes; Implementing Ideas and Programs. *Interacting with Others*—Guiding, Directing and Motivating Subordinates; Communicating with Other Workers; Interpreting Meaning of Information to Others. **Physical Work Conditions:** Indoors; Sitting; Using Hands on Objects, Tools, or Controls. **Other Job Characteristics:** Importance of Being Exact or Accurate; Importance of Being Sure All Is Done; Frustrating Circumstances.

Experience: Job Zone 4. A minimum of two to four years of work-related skill, knowledge, or experience is needed. **Job Preparation:** SVP 7.0 to less than 8.0—2 years to less than 10 years. **Knowledge:** Engineering and Technology; Mathematics; Chemistry; English Language; Physics. **Instructional Program:** 030102 Environmental Science/Studies.

Related DOT Job: 029.081-014 Materials Scientist.

19-2041.00 Environmental Scientists and Specialists, Including Health (All Other Physical Scientists)

Education: No data available.

Employed: 68,060

Openings: No data available.

Projected Growth: No data available.

Earnings: $48,990

Conduct research or perform investigation for the purpose of identifying, abating, or eliminating sources of pollutants or hazards that affect either the environment or the health of the population. Apply knowledge of various scientific disciplines to collect, synthesize, study, report, and take action based on data derived from measurements or observations of air, food, soil, water, and other sources.

Collects, identifies and analyzes data to assess sources of pollution, determine their effects, and establish standards. Prepares graphs or charts from data samples and advises enforcement personnel on proper standards and regulations. Plans and develops research models using knowledge of mathematical and statistical concepts. Determines data collection methods to be employed in research projects and surveys.

GOE Number, Interest Area, and Work Group: 02.03.03; Science, Math, and Engineering; Life Sciences: Plant and Animal Specialization. **Personality Type:** Investigative. Investigative occupations frequently involve working with ideas and require an extensive amount of thinking. These occupations can involve searching for facts and figuring out problems mentally. **Work Values:** Autonomy; Ability Utilization; Achievement; Creativity; Responsibility; Independence. **Skills:** Idea Generation; Information Gathering; Active Learning; Mathematics; Science; Reading Comprehension. **Abilities:** *Cognitive*—Mathematical Reasoning; Written Expression; Written Comprehension; Problem Sensitivity; Inductive Reasoning. *Psychomotor*—none met the criteria. *Physical*—none met the criteria. **General Work Activities:** *Information Input*—Getting Information Needed to Do the Job; Identifying Objects, Actions, and Events; Monitoring Processes, Materials, and Surroundings. *Mental Process*—Analyzing Data or Information; Processing Information; Making Decisions and Solving Problems. *Work Output*—Interacting with Computers; Documenting and Recording Information; Implementing Ideas and Programs. *Interacting with Others*—Interpreting Meaning of Information to Others; Communicating with Other Workers; Communicating with Persons Outside Organization; Providing Consultation and Advice to Others. **Physical Work Conditions:** Indoors; Outdoors; Contaminants. **Other Job Characteristics:** Importance of Being Sure All Is Done; Consequence of Error; Importance of Being Exact or Accurate.

Experience: Job Zone 5. Extensive skill, knowledge, and experience are needed. Very advanced communication and organizational skills are required. **Job Preparation:** SVP 8.0 and above—4 years to more than 10 years. **Knowledge:** Mathematics; Biology; Chemistry; English Language; Physics. **Instructional Program:** 030102 Environmental Science/Studies.

Related DOT Jobs: 019.081-018 Pollution-Control Engineer; 029.081-010 Environmental Analyst.

19-2042.00 Geoscientists, Except Hydrologists and Geographers (Geologists, Geophysicists, and Oceanographers)

Education: Bachelor's degree

Employed: 43,880

Openings: 3,613

Projected Growth: 15.5%

Earnings: $53,890

Study the composition, structure, and other physical aspects of the earth. Use knowledge of geology, physics, and mathematics in exploring for oil, gas, minerals, or underground water, or in disposing of waste, reclaiming land, or solving other environmental problems. Study the earth's internal composition, atmospheres, and oceans, and its magnetic, electrical, and gravitational forces.

GOE Number, Interest Area, and Work Group: 02.02.01; Science, Math, and Engineering; Physical Sciences. **Instructional Programs:** 400601 Geology; 400602 Geochemistry; 400603 Geophysics and Seismology; 400604 Paleontology; 400699 Geological and Related Sciences, Other; 400702 Oceanography; 400703 Earth and Planetary Sciences. **Note:** The Department of Labor has not collected some data for this job, so it has fewer details than the other descriptions.

19-2042.01 Geologists (Geologists, Geophysicists, and Oceanographers)

Education: Bachelor's degree
Employed: 43,880
Openings: 3,613
Projected Growth: 15.5%
Earnings: $53,890

Study composition, structure, and history of the earth's crust. Examine rocks, minerals, and fossil remains to identify and determine the sequence of processes affecting the development of the earth.

Studies, examines, measures, and classifies composition, structure, and history of earth's crust, including rocks, minerals, fossils, soil, and ocean floor. Recommends and prepares reports on foundation design, acquisition, retention, or release of property leases, or areas of further research. Identifies and determines sequence of processes affecting development of earth. Prepares geological reports, maps, charts, and diagrams. Inspects proposed construction site and sets up test equipment and drilling machinery. Measures characteristics of earth, using seismograph, gravimeter, torsion balance, magnetometer, pendulum devices, and electrical resistivity apparatus. Analyzes engineering problems at construction projects, such as dams, tunnels, and large buildings, applying geological knowledge. Tests industrial diamonds and abrasives, soil, or rocks to determine geological characteristics, using optical, X-ray, heat, acid, and precision instruments. Interprets research data, and recommends further study or action. Locates and estimates probable gas and oil deposits, using aerial photographs, charts, and research and survey results. Develops instruments for geological work, such as diamond tool and dies, jeweled bearings, and grinding laps and wheels.

GOE Number, Interest Area, and Work Group: 02.02.01; Science, Math, and Engineering; Physical Sciences. **Personality Type:** Investigative. Investigative occupations frequently involve working with ideas and require an extensive amount of thinking. These occupations can involve searching for facts and figuring out problems mentally. **Work Values:** Moral Values; Ability Utilization; Responsibility; Autonomy; Achievement. **Skills:** Technology Design; Mathematics; Information Gathering; Writing; Active Learning; Reading Comprehension. **Abilities:** *Cognitive*—Written Expression; Written Comprehension; Inductive Reasoning; Number Facility; Mathematical Reasoning; Deductive Reasoning. *Psychomotor*—Control Precision; Arm-Hand Steadiness; Finger Dexterity. *Physical*—none met the criteria. *Sensory*—Near Vision; Visual Color Discrimination; Depth Perception. **General Work Activities:** *Information Input*—Getting Information Needed to Do the Job; Identifying Objects, Actions, and Events; Monitoring Processes, Materials, and Surroundings. *Mental Process*—Processing Information; Analyzing Data or Information; Making Decisions and Solving Problems. *Work Output*—Implementing Ideas and Programs; Handling and Moving Objects; Controlling Machines and Processes. *Interacting with Others*—Interpreting Meaning of Information to Others; Communicating with Other Workers; Providing Consultation and Advice to Others. **Physical Work Conditions:** Sitting; Outdoors; Indoors. **Other Job Characteristics:** Importance of Being Exact or Accurate; Consequence of Error; Importance of Being Sure All Is Done.

Experience: Job Zone 5. Extensive skill, knowledge, and experience are needed. Very advanced communication and organizational skills are required. **Job Preparation:** SVP 8.0 and above—4 years to more than 10 years. **Knowledge:** Physics; Mathematics; Chemistry; Engineering and Technology; English Language. **Instructional Programs:** 400601 Geology; 400602 Geochemistry; 400603 Geophysics and Seismology; 400604 Paleontology; 400699 Geological and Related Sciences, Other; 400702 Oceanography; 400703 Earth and Planetary Sciences.

Related DOT Jobs: 024.061-010 Crystallographer; 024.061-018 Geologist; 024.061-022 Geologist, Petroleum; 024.061-026 Geophysical Prospector; 024.061-038 Mineralogist; 024.061-042 Paleontologist; 024.061-046 Petrologist; 024.061-054 Stratigrapher; 024.161-010 Engineer, Soils; 024.284-010 Prospector.

19-2043.00 Hydrologists (Geologists, Geophysicists, and Oceanographers)

Education: Bachelor's degree
Employed: 43,880
Openings: 3,613
Projected Growth: 15.5%
Earnings: $53,890

Research the distribution, circulation, and physical properties of underground and surface waters. Study the form and intensity of precipitation, its rate of infiltration into the soil, its movement through the earth, and its return to the ocean and atmosphere.

Prepares and issues maps and reports indicating areas of seismic risk to existing or proposed construction or development. Studies, maps, and charts distribution, disposition, and development of waters of land areas, including form and intensity of precipitation. Studies, measures, and interprets seismic, gravitational, electrical, thermal, and magnetic forces and data affecting the earth. Evaluates data in reference to project planning, such as flood and drought control, water power and supply, drainage, irrigation, and inland navigation. Studies waters of land areas to determine modes of return to ocean and atmosphere. Investigates origin and activity of glaciers, volcanoes, and earthquakes. Studies and analyzes physical aspects of earth, including atmosphere and hydrosphere, and interior structure. Compiles and evaluates data to prepare navigational charts and maps, predict atmospheric conditions, and prepare environmental reports.

GOE Number, Interest Area, and Work Group: 02.02.01; Science, Math, and Engineering; Physical Sciences. **Personality Type:** Investigative. Investigative occupations frequently involve working with ideas and require an extensive amount of thinking. These occupations can involve searching for facts and figuring out problems mentally. **Work Values:** Autonomy; Ability Utilization; Moral Values; Responsibility; Independence. **Skills:** Mathematics; Science; Writing; Information Gathering; Critical Thinking; Active Learning. **Abilities:** *Cognitive*—Written Comprehension; Deductive Reasoning; Mathematical Reasoning; Number Facility; Inductive Reasoning; Oral Comprehension. *Psychomotor*—none met the criteria. *Physical*—none met the criteria. *Sensory*—Depth Perception. **General Work Activities:** *Information Input*—Getting Information Needed to Do the Job; Identifying Objects, Actions, and Events; Monitoring Processes, Materials, and Surroundings. *Mental Process*—Processing Information; Analyzing Data or Information; Making Decisions and Solving Problems. *Work Output*—Documenting and Recording Information; Implementing Ideas and Programs; Interacting with Computers. *Interacting with Others*—Interpreting Meaning of Information to Others; Providing Consultation and Advice to Others; Communicating with Other Workers. **Physical Work Conditions:** Sitting; Indoors; Outdoors. **Other Job Characteristics:** Importance of Being Exact or Accurate; Consequence of Error; Importance of Being Sure All Is Done.

Experience: Job Zone 5. Extensive skill, knowledge, and experience are needed. Very advanced communication and organizational skills are required. **Job Preparation:** SVP 8.0 and above—4 years to more than 10 years. **Knowledge:** Physics; Mathematics; Geography; Chemistry; English Language. **Instructional Programs:** 400601 Geology; 400602 Geochemistry; 400603 Geophysics and Seismology; 400604 Paleontology; 400699 Geological and Related Sciences, Other; 400702 Oceanography; 400703 Earth and Planetary Sciences.

Related DOT Jobs: 024.061-030 Geophysicist; 024.061-034 Hydrologist; 024.061-050 Seismologist; 024.167-010 Geophysical-Laboratory Chief.

19-3000 Social Scientists and Related Workers

19-3011.00 Economists (Economists and Marketing Research Analysts)

Education: Bachelor's degree
Employed: 70,032
Openings: 11,550
Projected Growth: 18.4%
Earnings: $48,330

Conduct research, prepare reports, or formulate plans to help solve economic problems arising from production and distribution of goods and services. Collect and process economic and statistical data, using econometric and sampling techniques.

Studies economic and statistical data in area of specialization, such as finance, labor, or agriculture. Provides advice and consultation to business and public and private agencies. Reviews and analyzes data to prepare reports, to forecast future marketing trends, and to stay abreast of economic changes. Organizes research data into report format, including graphic illustrations of research findings. Compiles data relating to research area, such as employment, productivity, and wages and hours. Supervises research projects and students' study projects. Testifies at regulatory or legislative hearings to present recommendations. Teaches theories, principles, and methods of economics. Assigns work to staff. Devises methods and procedures for collecting and processing data, using various econometric and sampling techniques. Formulates recommendations, policies, or plans to interpret markets or solve economic problems. Develops economic guidelines and standards and preparing points of view used in forecasting trends and formulating economic policy.

GOE Number, Interest Area, and Work Group: 02.04.02; Science, Math, and Engineering; Social Sciences: Economics, Public Policy, and History. **Personality Type:** Investigative. Investigative occupations frequently involve working with ideas and require an extensive amount of thinking. These occupations can involve searching for facts and figuring out problems mentally. **Work Values:** Autonomy; Ability Utilization; Working Conditions; Achievement; Security; Responsibility. **Skills:** Systems Evaluation; Problem Identification; Information Gathering; Systems Perception; Solution Appraisal; Visioning. **Abilities:** *Cognitive*—Mathematical Reasoning; Written Comprehension; Written Expression; Number Facility; Oral Expression. *Psychomotor*—none met the criteria. *Physical*—none met the criteria. *Sensory*—Speech Clarity; Near Vision; Speech Recognition. **General Work Activities:** *Information Input*—Getting Information Needed to Do the Job; Identifying Objects, Actions, and Events; Monitoring Processes, Materials, and Surroundings. *Mental Process*—Updating and Using Job-Relevant Knowledge; Processing Information; Analyzing Data or Information. *Work Output*—Documenting and Recording Information; Implementing Ideas and Programs; Interacting with Computers. *Interacting with Others*—Communicating with Other Workers; Providing Consultation and Advice to Others; Teaching Others; Interpreting Meaning of Information to Others; Communicating with Persons Outside Organization. **Physical Work Conditions:** Indoors; Sitting; Standing. **Other Job Characteristics:** Consequence of Error; Importance of Being Exact or Accurate; Importance of Being Aware of New Events.

Experience: Job Zone 5. Extensive skill, knowledge, and experience are needed. Very advanced communication and organizational skills are required. **Job Preparation:** SVP 8.0 and above—4 years to more than 10 years. **Knowledge:** Mathematics; Economics and Accounting; English Language; Education and Training; Production and Processing; Computers and Electronics; Administration and Management. **Instructional Programs:** 010103 Agricultural Economics; 450601 Economics, General; 450602

Applied and Resource Economics; 450603 Econometrics and Quantitative Economics; 450604 Development Economics and International Development; 450605 International Economics; 450699 Economics, Other; 520601 Business/Managerial Economics.

Related DOT Job: 050.067-010 Economist.

19-3021.00 Market Research Analysts (Economists and Marketing Research Analysts)

Education: Bachelor's degree

Employed: 70,032

Openings: 11,550

Projected Growth: 18.4%

Earnings: $48,330

Research market conditions in local, regional, or national areas to determine potential sales of a product or service. Gather information on competitors, prices, and sales, and on methods of marketing and distribution. Use survey results to create a marketing campaign based on regional preferences and buying habits.

Prepares reports and graphic illustrations of findings. Attends staff conferences to submit findings and proposals to management for consideration. Translates complex numerical data into non-technical, written text. Gathers data on competitors and analyzes prices, sales, and method of marketing and distribution. Establishes research methodology. Designs format for data gathering, such as surveys, opinion polls, or questionnaires. Examines and analyzes statistical data to forecast future marketing trends and to identify potential markets. Checks consumer reaction to new or improved products or services. Collects data on customer preferences and buying habits.

GOE Number, Interest Area, and Work Group: 13.02.04; General Management and Support; Management Support: Investigation and Analysis. **Personality Type:** Investigative. Investigative occupations frequently involve working with ideas and require an extensive amount of thinking. These occupations can involve searching for facts and figuring out problems mentally. **Work Values:** Autonomy; Working Conditions; Ability Utilization; Company Policies and Practices; Recognition. **Skills:** Writing; Information Gathering; Mathematics; Identifying Downstream Consequences; Reading Comprehension; Information Organization. **Abilities:** *Cognitive*–Mathematical Reasoning; Number Facility; Written Expression; Written Comprehension; Oral Expression. *Psychomotor*–none met the criteria. *Physical*–none met the criteria. *Sensory*–Near Vision; Speech Clarity; Auditory Attention. **General Work Activities:** *Information Input*–Getting Information Needed to Do the Job; Identifying Objects, Actions, and Events; Estimating Needed Characteristics; Monitoring Processes, Materials, and Surroundings. *Mental Process*–Analyzing Data or Information; Processing Information; Making Decisions and Solving Problems. *Work Output*–Documenting and Recording Information; Interacting with Computers; Implementing Ideas and Programs. *Interacting with Others*–Interpreting Meaning of Information to Others; Communicating with Other Workers; Communicating with Persons Outside Organization. **Physical Work Conditions:** Indoors; Sitting; Using Hands on Objects, Tools, or

Controls. **Other Job Characteristics:** Consequence of Error; Importance of Being Exact or Accurate; Frustrating Circumstances.

Experience: Job Zone 4. A minimum of two to four years of work-related skill, knowledge, or experience is needed. **Job Preparation:** SVP 7.0 to less than 8.0—2 years to less than 10 years. **Knowledge:** Mathematics; Sales and Marketing; English Language; Computers and Electronics; Economics and Accounting; Geography. **Instructional Programs:** 010103 Agricultural Economics; 450601 Economics, General; 450602 Applied and Resource Economics; 450603 Econometrics and Quantitative Economics; 450604 Development Economics and International Development; 450605 International Economics; 450699 Economics, Other; 520601 Business/Managerial Economics.

Related DOT Jobs: 050.067-014 Market-Research Analyst I; 169.267-034 Research Analyst.

19-3022.00 Survey Researchers (Economists and Marketing Research Analysts)

Education: Bachelor's degree

Employed: 70,032

Openings: 11,550

Projected Growth: 18.4%

Earnings: $48,330

Design or conduct surveys. Supervise interviewers who conduct the survey in person or over the telephone. Present survey results to client.

GOE Number, Interest Area, and Work Group: 02.04.02; Science, Math, and Engineering; Social Sciences: Economics, Public Policy, and History. **Instructional Programs:** 010103 Agricultural Economics; 450601 Economics, General; 450602 Applied and Resource Economics; 450603 Econometrics and Quantitative Economics; 450604 Development Economics and International Development; 450605 International Economics; 450699 Economics, Other; 520601 Business/Managerial Economics. **Note:** The Department of Labor has not collected some data for this job, so it has fewer details than the other descriptions.

19-3031.00 Clinical, Counseling, and School Psychologists (Psychologists)

Education: Master's degree

Employed: 165,827

Openings: 21,473

Projected Growth: 11.4%

Earnings: $48,050

Diagnose and treat mental disorders and learning disabilities. Diagnose and treat cognitive, behavioral, and emotional problems. Use individual, child, family, and group therapies. Design and implement behavior-modification programs.

GOE Number, Interest Area, and Work Group: 12.02.02; Education and Social Service; Social Services: Counseling and Social Work. **Instructional Programs:** 420101 Psychology, General; 420201 Clinical Psychology; 420301 Cognitive Psychology and

Psycholinguistics; 420401 Community Psychology; 420601 Counseling Psychology; 420701 Developmental and Child Psychology; 420801 Experimental Psychology; 420901 Industrial and Organizational Psychology; 421101 Physiological Psychology/Psychobiology; 421601 Social Psychology; 421701 School Psychology; 429999 Psychology, Other; 512705 Psychoanalysis. **Note:** The Department of Labor has not collected some data for this job, so it has fewer details than the other descriptions.

19-3031.01 Educational Psychologists (Psychologists)

Education: Master's degree

Employed: 165,827

Openings: 21,473

Projected Growth: 11.4%

Earnings: $48,050

Investigate processes of learning and teaching. Develop psychological principles and techniques applicable to educational problems.

Evaluates needs, limitations, and potentials of child, through observation, review of school records, and consultation with parents and school personnel. Collaborates with education specialists in developing curriculum content and methods of organizing and conducting classroom work. Recommends placement of students in classes and treatment programs based on individual needs. Counsels pupils individually and in groups, to assist pupils to achieve personal, social, and emotional adjustment. Advises school board, superintendent, administrative committees, and parent-teacher groups regarding provision of psychological services within educational system or school. Analyzes characteristics and adjustment needs of students having various mental abilities and recommends educational program to promote maximum adjustment. Administers standardized tests to evaluate intelligence, achievement, and personality and to diagnose disabilities and difficulties among students. Advises teachers and other school personnel on methods to enhance school and classroom atmosphere to maximize student learning and motivation. Investigates traits, attitudes, and feelings of teachers to predict conditions that affect teacher's mental health and success with students. Formulates achievement, diagnostic, and predictive tests to aid teachers in planning methods and content of instruction. Plans remedial classes and testing programs designed to meet needs of special students. Interprets and explains test results, in terms of norms, reliability, and validity, to teachers, counselors, students, and other entitled parties. Conducts research to aid introduction of programs in schools to meet current psychological, educational, and sociological needs of children. Conducts experiments to study educational problems, such as motivation, adjustment, teacher training, and individual differences in mental abilities.

GOE Number, Interest Area, and Work Group: 12.03.01; Education and Social Service; Educational Services: Counseling and Evaluation. **Personality Type:** Investigative. Investigative occupations frequently involve working with ideas and require an extensive amount of thinking. These occupations can involve searching for facts and figuring out problems mentally. **Work Values:** Autonomy; Ability Utilization; Achievement; Creativity;

Social Service. **Skills:** Social Perceptiveness; Problem Identification; Identification of Key Causes; Information Gathering; Learning Strategies; Reading Comprehension; Writing. **Abilities:** *Cognitive*—Oral Expression; Inductive Reasoning; Problem Sensitivity; Written Comprehension; Written Expression. *Psychomotor*—Reaction Time; Response Orientation. *Physical*—none met the criteria. *Sensory*—Near Vision; Speech Clarity; Auditory Attention. **General Work Activities:** *Information Input*—Getting Information Needed to Do the Job; Identifying Objects, Actions, and Events; Monitoring Processes, Materials, and Surroundings. *Mental Process*—Judging Qualities of Things, Services, Other People's Work; Analyzing Data or Information; Making Decisions and Solving Problems. *Work Output*—Implementing Ideas and Programs; Documenting and Recording Information; Interacting with Computers. *Interacting with Others*—Communicating with Other Workers; Interpreting Meaning of Information to Others; Providing Consultation and Advice to Others; Communicating with Persons Outside Organization. **Physical Work Conditions:** Indoors; Sitting; Using Hands on Objects, Tools, or Controls. **Other Job Characteristics:** Consequence of Error; Importance of Being Sure All Is Done; Frustrating Circumstances; Importance of Being Exact or Accurate.

Experience: Job Zone 4. A minimum of two to four years of work-related skill, knowledge, or experience is needed. **Job Preparation:** SVP 7.0 to less than 8.0—2 years to less than 10 years. **Knowledge:** Psychology; Education and Training; English Language; Therapy and Counseling; Mathematics. **Instructional Programs:** 420101 Psychology, General; 420201 Clinical Psychology; 420301 Cognitive Psychology and Psycholinguistics; 420401 Community Psychology; 420601 Counseling Psychology; 420701 Developmental and Child Psychology; 420801 Experimental Psychology; 420901 Industrial and Organizational Psychology; 421101 Physiological Psychology/Psychobiology; 421601 Social Psychology; 421701 School Psychology; 429999 Psychology, Other; 512705 Psychoanalysis.

Related DOT Jobs: 045.067-010 Psychologist, Educational; 045.067-018 Psychometrist; 045.107-034 Psychologist, School.

19-3031.02 Clinical Psychologists (Psychologists)

Education: Master's degree

Employed: 165,827

Openings: 21,473

Projected Growth: 11.4%

Earnings: $48,050

Diagnose or evaluate mental and emotional disorders of individuals through observation, interview, and psychological tests. Formulate and administer programs of treatment.

Assists clients to gain insight, define goals, and plan action to achieve effective personal, social, educational, and vocational development and adjustment. Responds to client reactions, evaluates effectiveness of counseling or treatment, and modifies plan as needed. Interviews individuals, couples, or families, and reviews records to obtain information on medical, psychological, emotional, relationship, or other problems. Selects, administers, scores, and interprets psychological tests to obtain information on individual's intelligence, achievement, interest, and personality. Utilizes treatment methods, such as psychotherapy, hypnosis, behavior modification, stress reduction therapy, psychodrama, and play therapy. Plans and develops accredited psychological service programs in psychiatric center or hospital, in collaboration with psychiatrists and other professional staff. Consults reference material such as textbooks, manuals, and journals, to identify symptoms, make diagnoses, and develop approach to treatment. Provides occupational, educational, and other information to enable individual to formulate realistic educational and vocational plans. Plans, supervises, and conducts psychological research in fields such as personality development, and diagnosis, treatment, and prevention of mental disorders. Directs, coordinates, and evaluates activities of psychological staff and student interns engaged in patient evaluation and treatment in psychiatric facility. Provides psychological services and advice to private firms and community agencies on individual cases or mental health programs. Develops, directs, and participates in staff training programs. Develops treatment plan, including type, frequency, intensity, and duration of therapy, in collaboration with psychiatrist and other specialists. Observes individual at play, in group interactions, or other situations to detect indications of mental deficiency, abnormal behavior, or maladjustment.

GOE Number, Interest Area, and Work Group: 12.02.02; Education and Social Service; Social Services: Counseling and Social Work. **Personality Type:** Investigative. Investigative occupations frequently involve working with ideas and require an extensive amount of thinking. These occupations can involve searching for facts and figuring out problems mentally. **Work Values:** Social Service; Autonomy; Responsibility; Ability Utilization; Creativity. **Skills:** Social Perceptiveness; Active Listening; Problem Identification; Reading Comprehension; Speaking; Information Gathering; Identification of Key Causes. **Abilities:** *Cognitive*—Oral Comprehension; Written Comprehension; Oral Expression; Problem Sensitivity; Inductive Reasoning. *Psychomotor*—none met the criteria. *Physical*—none met the criteria. *Sensory*—Near Vision; Speech Clarity; Speech Recognition. **General Work Activities:** *Information Input*—Identifying Objects, Actions, and Events; Getting Information Needed to Do the Job; Monitoring Processes, Materials, and Surroundings. *Mental Process*—Making Decisions and Solving Problems; Analyzing Data or Information; Updating and Using Job-Relevant Knowledge. *Work Output*—Implementing Ideas and Programs; Documenting and Recording Information; Interacting with Computers. *Interacting with Others*—Communicating with Persons Outside Organization; Teaching Others; Establishing and Maintaining Relationships. **Physical Work Conditions:** Indoors; Sitting; Standing. **Other Job Characteristics:** Consequence of Error; Importance of Being Sure All Is Done; Frustrating Circumstances.

Experience: Job Zone 4. A minimum of two to four years of work-related skill, knowledge, or experience is needed. **Job Preparation:** SVP 7.0 to less than 8.0—2 years to less than 10 years. **Knowledge:** Psychology; Therapy and Counseling; English Language; Administration and Management; Customer and Personal Service. **Instructional Programs:** 420101 Psychology, General; 420201 Clinical Psychology; 420301 Cognitive Psychology and Psycholinguistics; 420401 Community Psychology; 420601 Counseling Psychology; 420701 Developmental and Child Psychology;

420801 Experimental Psychology; 420901 Industrial and Organizational Psychology; 421101 Physiological Psychology/Psychobiology; 421601 Social Psychology; 421701 School Psychology; 429999 Psychology, Other; 512705 Psychoanalysis.
Related DOT Jobs: 045.107-022 Clinical Psychologist; 045.107-046 Psychologist, Chief; 045.107-050 Clinical Therapist.

19-3031.03 Counseling Psychologists (Psychologists)

Education: Master's degree
Employed: 165,827
Openings: 21,473
Projected Growth: 11.4%
Earnings: $48,050

Assess and evaluate individuals' problems through the use of case history, interview, and observation. Provide individual or group counseling services to assist individuals in achieving more effective personal, social, educational, and vocational development and adjustment.

Analyzes data such as interview notes, test results, and reference manuals and texts to identify symptoms and diagnose the nature of client's problems. Evaluates results of counseling methods to determine the reliability and validity of treatments. Conducts research to develop or improve diagnostic or therapeutic counseling techniques. Consults with other professionals to discuss therapy or treatment, counseling resources or techniques, and to share occupational information. Develops therapeutic and treatment plans based on individual interests, abilities, or needs of clients. Advises clients on the potential benefits of counseling or makes referrals to specialists or other institutions for non-counseling problems. Counsels clients to assist them in understanding personal or interactive problems, defining goals, and developing realistic action plans. Selects, administers, or interprets psychological tests to assess intelligence, aptitude, ability, or interests. Collects information about individuals or clients, using interviews, case histories, observational techniques, and other assessment methods.

GOE Number, Interest Area, and Work Group: 12.02.02; Education and Social Service; Social Services: Counseling and Social Work. **Personality Type:** Social. Social occupations frequently involve working with, communicating with, and teaching people. These occupations often involve helping or providing service to others. **Work Values:** Social Service; Autonomy; Achievement; Ability Utilization; Creativity; Working Conditions. **Skills:** Social Perceptiveness; Active Listening; Reading Comprehension; Critical Thinking; Active Learning; Problem Identification; Information Gathering; Learning Strategies. **Abilities:** *Cognitive*—Problem Sensitivity; Oral Comprehension; Oral Expression; Inductive Reasoning; Written Expression; Written Comprehension. *Psychomotor*—none met the criteria. *Physical*—none met the criteria. *Sensory*—Speech Clarity; Speech Recognition. **General Work Activities:** *Information Input*—Getting Information Needed to Do the Job; Identifying Objects, Actions, and Events; Monitoring Processes, Materials, and Surroundings. *Mental Process*—Making Decisions and Solving Problems; Analyzing Data or Information; Processing Information. *Work Output*—Documenting and Recording Information; Interacting with Computers; Handling and Moving Objects. *Interacting with Others*—Assisting and Caring for Others; Establishing and Maintaining Relationships; Communicating with Persons Outside Organization. **Physical Work Conditions:** Indoors; Sitting; Standing. **Other Job Characteristics:** Consequence of Error; Frustrating Circumstances; Importance of Being Sure All Is Done.

Experience: Job Zone 5. Extensive skill, knowledge, and experience are needed. Very advanced communication and organizational skills are required. **Job Preparation:** SVP 8.0 and above—4 years to more than 10 years. **Knowledge:** Psychology; Therapy and Counseling; Mathematics; Communications and Media; English Language. **Instructional Programs:** 420101 Psychology, General; 420201 Clinical Psychology; 420301 Cognitive Psychology and Psycholinguistics; 420401 Community Psychology; 420601 Counseling Psychology; 420701 Developmental and Child Psychology; 420801 Experimental Psychology; 420901 Industrial and Organizational Psychology; 421101 Physiological Psychology/Psychobiology; 421601 Social Psychology; 421701 School Psychology; 429999 Psychology, Other; 512705 Psychoanalysis.

Related DOT Jobs: 045.107-026 Psychologist, Counseling; 045.107-054 Counselor, Marriage and Family.

19-3032.00 Industrial-Organizational Psychologists
(Psychologists)

Education: Master's degree

Employed: 165,827

Openings: 21,473

Projected Growth: 11.4%

Earnings: $48,050

Apply principles of psychology to personnel, administration, management, sales, and marketing problems. Participate in policy planning. Participate in employee screening, training, and development, and in organizational development and analysis. Work with management to reorganize the work setting to improve worker productivity.

Conducts research studies of physical work environments, organizational structure, communication systems, group interaction, morale, and motivation to assess organizational functioning. Analyzes job requirements to establish criteria for classification, selection, training, and other related personnel functions. Plans, develops, and organizes training programs, applying principles of learning and individual differences. Analyzes data, using statistical methods and applications, to evaluate and measure the effectiveness of program implementation or training. Studies consumer reaction to new products and package designs, using surveys and tests, and measures the effectiveness of advertising media. Advises management in strategic changes to personnel, managerial, and marketing policies and practices to improve organizational effectiveness and efficiency. Develops interview Technologyniques, rating scales, and psychological tests to assess skills, abilities, and interests as aids in selection, placement and promotion. Observes and interviews workers to identify the physical, mental, and educational requirements of job.

GOE Number, Interest Area, and Work Group: 02.04.01; Science, Math, and Engineering; Social Sciences: Psychology, Sociology, and Anthropology. **Personality Type:** Investigative. Investigative occupations frequently involve working with ideas and require an extensive amount of thinking. These occupations can involve searching for facts and figuring out problems mentally. **Work Values:** Autonomy; Working Conditions; Creativity; Compensation; Achievement; Ability Utilization. **Skills:** Identification of Key Causes; Systems Evaluation; Reading Comprehension; Information Gathering; Problem Identification. **Abilities:** *Cognitive*—Oral Comprehension; Written Comprehension; Oral Expression; Written Expression; Originality; Mathematical Reasoning. *Psychomotor*—none met the criteria. *Physical*—none met the criteria. *Sensory*—Speech Clarity; Speech Recognition. **General Work Activities:** *Information Input*—Getting Information Needed to Do the Job; Identifying Objects, Actions, and Events; Monitoring Processes, Materials, and Surroundings; Estimating Needed Characteristics. *Mental Process*—Processing Information; Analyzing Data or Information; Making Decisions and Solving Problems. *Work Output*—Documenting and Recording Information; Implementing Ideas and Programs; Interacting with Computers. *Interacting with Others*—Providing Consultation and Advice to Others; Communicating with Other Workers; Teaching Others. **Physical Work Conditions:** Indoors; Sitting; Standing. **Other Job Characteristics:** Consequence of Error; Importance of Being Sure All Is Done; Importance of Being Exact or Accurate; Frustrating Circumstances.

Experience: Job Zone 5. Extensive skill, knowledge, and experience are needed. Very advanced communication and organizational skills are required. **Job Preparation:** SVP 8.0 and above—4 years to more than 10 years. **Knowledge:** Psychology; Personnel and Human Resources; Education and Training; Mathematics; Administration and Management. **Instructional Programs:** 420101 Psychology, General; 420201 Clinical Psychology; 420301 Cognitive Psychology and Psycholinguistics; 420401 Community Psychology; 420601 Counseling Psychology; 420701 Developmental and Child Psychology; 420801 Experimental Psychology; 420901 Industrial and Organizational Psychology; 421101 Physiological Psychology/Psychobiology; 421601 Social Psychology; 421701 School Psychology; 429999 Psychology, Other; 512705 Psychoanalysis.

Related DOT Jobs: 045.061-014 Psychologist, Engineering; 045.107-030 Psychologist, Industrial-Organizational.

19-3041.00 Sociologists (Social Scientists)

Education: Master's degree

Employed: 50,108

Openings: 6,928

Projected Growth: 12.7%

Earnings: No data available.

Study human society and social behavior by examining the groups and social institutions that people form, as well as various social, religious, political, and business organizations. Study the behavior and interaction of groups, trace their origin and growth, and analyze the influence of group activities on individual members.

Develops approaches to solution of group's problems, based on findings and incorporating sociological research and study in related disciplines. Analyzes and evaluates data. Consults with lawmakers, administrators, and other officials who deal with problems of social change. Interprets methods employed and findings to individuals within agency and community. Prepares publications and reports on subjects, such as social factors which affect health, demographic characteristics, and social and racial discrimination in society. Monitors group interaction and role affiliations to evaluate progress and to determine need for additional change. Collaborates with research workers in other disciplines. Directs work of statistical clerks, statisticians, and others. Develops intervention procedures, utilizing Technologyniques such as interviews, consultations, role playing, and participant observation of group interaction, to facilitate solution. Collects information and makes judgments through observation, interview, and review of documents. Observes group interaction and interviews group members to identify problems and collect data related to factors, such as group organization and authority relationships. Constructs and tests methods of data collection. Plans and directs research on crime and prevention, group relations in industrial organization, urban communities, and physical environment and Technologynology. Collects and analyzes scientific data concerning social phenomena, such as community, associations, social institutions, ethnic minorities, and social change. Develops research designs on basis of existing knowledge and evolving theory.

GOE Number, Interest Area, and Work Group: 02.04.01; Science, Math, and Engineering; Social Sciences: Psychology, Sociology, and Anthropology. **Personality Type:** Investigative. Investigative occupations frequently involve working with ideas and require an extensive amount of thinking. These occupations can involve searching for facts and figuring out problems mentally. **Work Values:** Autonomy; Responsibility; Creativity; Working Conditions; Ability Utilization. **Skills:** Writing; Information Gathering; Reading Comprehension; Mathematics; Critical Thinking; Active Learning; Problem Identification. **Abilities:** *Cognitive*—Written Expression; Oral Comprehension; Written Comprehension; Oral Expression; Deductive Reasoning. *Psychomotor*—none met the criteria. *Physical*—none met the criteria. *Sensory*—Speech Clarity; Speech Recognition; Auditory Attention. **General Work Activities:** *Information Input*—Getting Information Needed to Do the Job; Identifying Objects, Actions, and Events; Monitoring Processes, Materials, and Surroundings. *Mental Process*—Analyzing Data or Information; Processing Information; Making Decisions and Solving Problems. *Work Output*—Implementing Ideas and Programs; Documenting and Recording Information; Interacting with Computers. *Interacting with Others*—Providing Consultation and Advice to Others; Interpreting Meaning of Information to Others; Communicating with Other Workers. **Physical Work Conditions:** Indoors; Sitting; Standing. **Other Job Characteristics:** Consequence of Error; Importance of Being Exact or Accurate; Importance of Being Sure All Is Done; Frustrating Circumstances; Importance of Being Aware of New Events.

Experience: Job Zone 3. Previous work-related skill, knowledge, or experience is required. **Job Preparation:** SVP 6.0 to less than 7.0—More than 1 year and less than 4 years. **Knowledge:** Sociol-

ogy and Anthropology; English Language; Education and Training; Administration and Management; Psychology; Mathematics. **Instructional Programs:** 450501 Demography/Population Studies; 451001 Political Science, General; 451101 Sociology.
Related DOT Jobs: 054.067-010 Research Worker, Social Welfare; 054.067-014 Sociologist; 054.107-010 Clinical Sociologist.

19-3051.00 Urban and Regional Planners (Urban and Regional Planners)

Education: Master's degree
Employed: 34,702
Openings: 5,057
Projected Growth: 17.4%
Earnings: $42,860

Develop comprehensive plans and programs for use of land and physical facilities of local jurisdictions, such as towns, cities, counties, and metropolitan areas.

Advises planning officials on feasibility, cost effectiveness, regulatory conformance, and alternative recommendations for project. Prepares or requisitions graphic and narrative report on land use data. Recommends governmental measures affecting land use, public utilities, community facilities, housing, and transportation. Conducts field investigations, economic or public-opinion surveys, demographic studies, or other research to gather required information. Maintains collection of socioeconomic, environmental, and regulatory data related to land use for governmental and private sectors. Discusses purpose of land-use projects, such as transportation, conservation, residential, commercial, industrial, and community use, with planning officials. Evaluates information to determine feasibility of proposals or to identify factors requiring amendment. Compiles, organizes, and analyzes data on economic, social, and physical factors affecting land use, using statistical methods. Develops alternative plans with recommendations for program or project. Reviews and evaluates environmental impact reports applying to specific private and public planning projects and programs. Determines regulatory limitations on project.

GOE Number, Interest Area, and Work Group: 02.04.02; Science, Math, and Engineering; Social Sciences: Economics, Public Policy, and History. **Personality Type:** Investigative. Investigative occupations frequently involve working with ideas and require an extensive amount of thinking. These occupations can involve searching for facts and figuring out problems mentally. **Work Values:** Autonomy; Ability Utilization; Achievement; Creativity; Security; Social Status; Working Conditions. **Skills:** Idea Evaluation; Information Gathering; Implementation Planning; Solution Appraisal; Judgment and Decision Making; Idea Generation. **Abilities:** *Cognitive*—Inductive Reasoning; Deductive Reasoning; Written Comprehension; Oral Expression; Written Expression; Oral Comprehension. *Psychomotor*—none met the criteria. *Physical*—Gross Body Coordination; Dynamic Flexibility; Gross Body Equilibrium. *Sensory*—Near Vision; Speech Clarity; Far Vision. **General Work Activities:** *Information Input*—Getting Information Needed to Do the Job; Identifying Objects, Actions, and Events; Estimating Needed Characteristics. *Mental Process*—

Processing Information; Analyzing Data or Information; Organizing, Planning, and Prioritizing. *Work Output*—Documenting and Recording Information; Implementing Ideas and Programs; Interacting with Computers. *Interacting with Others*—Providing Consultation and Advice to Others; Communicating with Persons Outside Organization; Communicating with Other Workers. **Physical Work Conditions:** Sitting; Indoors; Using Hands on Objects, Tools, or Controls. **Other Job Characteristics:** Frustrating Circumstances; Importance of Being Sure All Is Done; Importance of Being Exact or Accurate.

Experience: Job Zone 4. A minimum of two to four years of work-related skill, knowledge, or experience is needed. **Job Preparation:** SVP 7.0 to less than 8.0—2 years to less than 10 years. **Knowledge:** Sociology and Anthropology; Mathematics; English Language; Law, Government and Jurisprudence; Administration and Management; Economics and Accounting; Building and Construction. **Instructional Programs:** 040301 City/Urban, Community and Regional Planning; 040701 Architectural Urban Design and Planning.

Related DOT Jobs: 188.167-110 Planner, Program Services; 199.167-014 Urban Planner.

19-3091.00 Anthropologists and Archeologists (Social Scientists)

Education: Master's degree
Employed: 50,108
Openings: 6,928
Projected Growth: 12.7%
Earnings: No data available.

Study the origin, development, and behavior of humans. Study the way of life, language, or physical characteristics of existing people in various parts of the world. Engage in systematic recovery and examination of remaining material evidence, such as tools or pottery, from past human cultures, in order to determine the history, customs, and living habits of earlier civilizations.

GOE Number, Interest Area, and Work Group: 02.04.01; Science, Math, and Engineering; Social Sciences: Psychology, Sociology, and Anthropology. **Instructional Programs:** 450201 Anthropology; 450301 Archeology; 450501 Demography/Population Studies; 450901 International Relations and Affairs; 451101 Sociology. **Note:** The Department of Labor has not collected some data for this job, so it has fewer details than the other descriptions.

19-3091.01 Anthropologists (Social Scientists)

Education: Master's degree
Employed: 50,108
Openings: 6,928
Projected Growth: 12.7%
Earnings: No data available.

Research or study the origins and physical, social, and cultural development and behavior of humans. Research or study the cultures and organizations humans have created.

Studies relationships between language and culture and socialinguistic studies, relationship between individual personality and culture, or complex industrialized societies. Studies museum collections of skeletal remains and human fossils to determine their meaning in terms of long-range human evolution. Studies physical and physiological adaptations to differing environments and hereditary characteristics of living populations. Studies cultures, particularly preindustrial and non-Western societies, including religion, economics, mythology and traditions, and intellectual and artistic life. Applies anthropological concepts to current problems. Formulates general laws of cultural development, general rules of social and cultural behavior, or general value orientations. Observes and measures bodily variations and physical attributes of existing human types. Studies growth patterns, sexual differences, and aging phenomena of human groups, current and past. Gathers, analyzes, and reports data on human physique, social customs, and artifacts, such as weapons, tools, pottery, and clothing. Applies anthropological data and techniques to solution of problems in human relations.

GOE Number, Interest Area, and Work Group: 02.04.01; Science, Math, and Engineering; Social Sciences: Psychology, Sociology, and Anthropology. **Personality Type:** Investigative. Investigative occupations frequently involve working with ideas and require an extensive amount of thinking. These occupations can involve searching for facts and figuring out problems mentally. **Work Values:** Autonomy; Ability Utilization; Creativity; Responsibility; Achievement. **Skills:** Writing; Information Gathering; Information Organization; Synthesis/Reorganization; Active Learning. **Abilities:** *Cognitive*—Oral Comprehension; Written Expression; Inductive Reasoning; Written Comprehension; Fluency of Ideas. *Psychomotor*—none met the criteria. *Physical*—none met the criteria. *Sensory*—Speech Clarity; Near Vision; Speech Recognition. **General Work Activities:** *Information Input*—Getting Information Needed to Do the Job; Identifying Objects, Actions, and Events; Estimating Needed Characteristics. *Mental Process*—Analyzing Data or Information; Processing Information; Judging Qualities of Things, Services, Other People's Work. *Work Output*—Implementing Ideas and Programs; Documenting and Recording Information; Handling and Moving Objects. *Interacting with Others*—Interpreting Meaning of Information to Others; Communicating with Other Workers; Providing Consultation and Advice to Others. **Physical Work Conditions:** Indoors; Sitting; Using Hands on Objects, Tools, or Controls; Outdoors. **Other Job Characteristics:** Importance of Being Exact or Accurate; Importance of Being Sure All Is Done; Importance of Being Aware of New Events.

Experience: Job Zone 4. A minimum of two to four years of work-related skill, knowledge, or experience is needed. **Job Preparation:** SVP 7.0 to less than 8.0—2 years to less than 10 years. **Knowledge:** Sociology and Anthropology; History and Archeology; English Language; Geography; Biology. **Instructional Programs:** 450201 Anthropology; 450301 Archeology; 450501 Demography/Population Studies; 450901 International Relations and Affairs; 451101 Sociology.

Related DOT Jobs: 055.067-010 Anthropologist; 055.067-014 Anthropologist, Physical; 055.067-022 Ethnologist.

19-3091.02 Archeologists (Social Scientists)

Education: Master's degree

Employed: 50,108

Openings: 6,928

Projected Growth: 12.7%

Earnings: No data available.

Conduct research to reconstruct the record of past human life and culture from human remains, artifacts, architectural features, and structures recovered through excavation, underwater recovery, or other means of discovery.

Studies artifacts, architectural features, and types of structures recovered by excavation in order to determine age and cultural identity. Classifies and interprets artifacts, architectural features, and types of structures recovered by excavation, to determine age and cultural identity. Establishes chronological sequence of development of each culture from simpler to more advanced levels.

GOE Number, Interest Area, and Work Group: 02.04.01; Science, Math, and Engineering; Social Sciences: Psychology, Sociology, and Anthropology. **Personality Type:** Investigative. Investigative occupations frequently involve working with ideas and require an extensive amount of thinking. These occupations can involve searching for facts and figuring out problems mentally. **Work Values:** Autonomy; Achievement; Responsibility; Creativity; Ability Utilization. **Skills:** Information Organization; Synthesis/Reorganization; Reading Comprehension; Information Gathering; Active Learning; Writing. **Abilities:** *Cognitive*—Inductive Reasoning; Category Flexibility; Information Ordering; Deductive Reasoning; Written Comprehension. *Psychomotor*—none met the criteria. *Physical*—Extent Flexibility; Gross Body Coordination; Gross Body Equilibrium. *Sensory*—Visual Color Discrimination; Depth Perception; Peripheral Vision. **General Work Activities:** *Information Input*—Identifying Objects, Actions, and Events; Getting Information Needed to Do the Job; Estimating Needed Characteristics. *Mental Process*—Processing Information; Analyzing Data or Information; Judging Qualities of Things, Services, Other People's Work. *Work Output*—Documenting and Recording Information; Handling and Moving Objects; Performing General Physical Activities. *Interacting with Others*—Interpreting Meaning of Information to Others; Communicating with Persons Outside Organization; Communicating with Other Workers. **Physical Work Conditions:** Outdoors; Using Hands on Objects, Tools, or Controls; Indoors. **Other Job Characteristics:** Importance of Being Exact or Accurate; Consequence of Error; Importance of Being Sure All Is Done; Importance of Being Aware of New Events.

Experience: Job Zone 4. A minimum of two to four years of work-related skill, knowledge, or experience is needed. **Job Preparation:** SVP 7.0 to less than 8.0—2 years to less than 10 years. **Knowledge:** History and Archeology; Sociology and Anthropology; Geography; English Language; Clerical; Philosophy and Theology. **Instructional Programs:** 450201 Anthropology; 450301 Archeology.

Related DOT Job: 055.067-018 Archeologist.

19-3092.00 Geographers (All Other Physical Scientists)

Education: No data available.

Employed: 68,060

Openings: No data available.

Projected Growth: No data available.

Earnings: $48,990

Study nature and the use of areas of the earth's surface; relate and interpret interactions of physical and cultural phenomena. Conduct research on physical aspects of a region, including land forms, climates, soils, plants, and animals. Conduct research on the spatial implications of human activities within a given area, including social characteristics, economic activities, and political organization. Research interdependence between regions on scales ranging from local to global.

Collects data on physical characteristics of specified area, such as geological formation, climate, and vegetation, using surveying or meteorological equipment. Constructs and interprets maps, graphs, and diagrams. Studies population characteristics within area, such as ethnic distribution and economic activity. Uses surveying equipment to assess geology, physics, and biology within given area. Advises governments and organizations on ethnic and natural boundaries between nation or administrative areas. Prepares environmental impact reports based on results of study.

GOE Number, Interest Area, and Work Group: 02.02.01; Science, Math, and Engineering; Physical Sciences. **Personality Type:** Investigative. Investigative occupations frequently involve working with ideas and require an extensive amount of thinking. These occupations can involve searching for facts and figuring out problems mentally. **Work Values:** Autonomy; Ability Utilization; Moral Values; Responsibility; Independence; Achievement. **Skills:** Writing; Information Gathering; Reading Comprehension; Information Organization; Critical Thinking; Mathematics. **Abilities:** *Cognitive*—Oral Expression; Written Expression; Written Comprehension; Oral Comprehension; Problem Sensitivity; Deductive Reasoning. *Psychomotor*—Arm-Hand Steadiness; Rate Control. *Physical*—none met the criteria. *Sensory*—Far Vision; Visual Color Discrimination; Night Vision. **General Work Activities:** *Information Input*—Getting Information Needed to Do the Job; Estimating Needed Characteristics; Identifying Objects, Actions, and Events. *Mental Process*—Processing Information; Analyzing Data or Information; Updating and Using Job-Relevant Knowledge; Evaluating Information Against Standards. *Work Output*—Documenting and Recording Information; Handling and Moving Objects; Controlling Machines and Processes. *Interacting with Others*—Communicating with Other Workers; Communicating with Persons Outside Organization; Interpreting Meaning of Information to Others. **Physical Work Conditions:** Outdoors; Sitting; Indoors. **Other Job Characteristics:** Importance of Being Exact or Accurate; Importance of Being Sure All Is Done; Consequence of Error; Frustrating Circumstances.

Experience: Job Zone 4. A minimum of two to four years of work-related skill, knowledge, or experience is needed. **Job Preparation:** SVP 7.0 to less than 8.0—2 years to less than 10 years.

Knowledge: Geography; Sociology and Anthropology; Biology; Physics; Mathematics. **Instructional Program:** 030102 Environmental Science/Studies.

Related DOT Jobs: 029.067-010 Geographer; 029.067-014 Geographer, Physical.

19-3093.00 Historians (Social Scientists)

Education: Master's degree
Employed: 50,108
Openings: 6,928
Projected Growth: 12.7%
Earnings: No data available.

Research, analyze, record, and interpret the past, as recorded in sources such as government and institution records, newspapers and other periodicals, photographs, interviews, films, and unpublished manuscripts such as personal diaries and letters.

Advises or consults with individuals, institutions, and commercial organizations on technological evolution or customs peculiar to certain historical period. Organizes and evaluates data on basis of authenticity and relative significance. Consults experts or witnesses of historical events. Translates or requests translation of reference materials. Speaks before various groups, organizations, and clubs to promote societal aims and activities. Edits society publications. Reviews publications and exhibits prepared by others prior to public release in order to ensure historical accuracy of presentations. Consults with or advises other individuals on historical authenticity of various materials. Reviews and collects data, such as books, pamphlets, periodicals, and rare newspapers, to provide source material for research. Traces historical development in fields, such as economics, sociology, or philosophy. Assembles historical data by consulting sources, such as archives, court records, diaries, news files, and miscellaneous published and unpublished materials. Conducts historical research on subjects of import to society and presents finding and theories in textbooks, journals, and other publications. Coordinates activities of workers engaged in cataloging and filing materials.

GOE Number, Interest Area, and Work Group: 02.04.02; Science, Math, and Engineering; Social Sciences: Economics, Public Policy, and History. **Personality Type:** Investigative. Investigative occupations frequently involve working with ideas and require an extensive amount of thinking. These occupations can involve searching for facts and figuring out problems mentally. **Work Values:** Autonomy; Working Conditions; Achievement; Ability Utilization; Responsibility. **Skills:** Information Gathering; Writing; Reading Comprehension; Information Organization; Speaking. **Abilities:** *Cognitive*—Written Comprehension; Written Expression; Oral Expression; Oral Comprehension; Memorization. *Psychomotor*—none met the criteria. *Physical*—none met the criteria. *Sensory*—Speech Clarity; Near Vision; Speech Recognition. **General Work Activities:** *Information Input*—Getting Information Needed to Do the Job; Identifying Objects, Actions, and Events; Estimating Needed Characteristics. *Mental Process*—Analyzing Data or Information; Processing Information; Judging Qualities of Things, Services, Other People's Work. *Work Out-*

put—Documenting and Recording Information; Implementing Ideas and Programs; Interacting with Computers. *Interacting with Others*—Interpreting Meaning of Information to Others; Communicating with Persons Outside Organization; Providing Consultation and Advice to Others; Communicating with Other Workers. **Physical Work Conditions:** Indoors; Sitting; Standing. **Other Job Characteristics:** Importance of Being Exact or Accurate; Consequence of Error; Importance of Being Sure All Is Done.

Experience: Job Zone 4. A minimum of two to four years of work-related skill, knowledge, or experience is needed. **Job Preparation:** SVP 7.0 to less than 8.0—2 years to less than 10 years. **Knowledge:** History and Archeology; English Language; Administration and Management; Sociology and Anthropology; Communications and Media. **Instructional Programs:** 500701 Art, General; 500704 Arts Management; 520201 Business Administration and Management, General.

Related DOT Jobs: 052.067-014 Director, State-Historical Society; 052.067-022 Historian; 052.067-026 Historian, Dramatic Arts; 052.167-010 Director, Research.

19-3094.00 Political Scientists (Social Scientists)

Education: Master's degree
Employed: 50,108
Openings: 6,928
Projected Growth: 12.7%
Earnings: No data available.

Study the origin, development, and operation of political systems. Research a wide range of subjects such as relations between the United States and foreign countries, the beliefs and institutions of foreign nations, or the politics of small towns or a major metropolis. Study topics such as public opinion, political decision making, and ideology. Analyze the structure and operation of governments and various political entities. Conduct public-opinion surveys, analyze election results, or analyze public documents.

Consults with government officials, civic bodies, research agencies, and political parties. Prepares reports detailing findings and conclusions. Recommends programs and policies to institutions and organizations. Organizes and conducts public opinion surveys and interprets results. Conducts research into political philosophy and theories of political systems, such as governmental institutions, public laws, and international law. Analyzes and interprets results of studies; prepares reports detailing findings, recommendations, or conclusions.

GOE Number, Interest Area, and Work Group: 02.04.02; Science, Math, and Engineering; Social Sciences: Economics, Public Policy, and History. **Personality Type:** Investigative. Investigative occupations frequently involve working with ideas and require an extensive amount of thinking. These occupations can involve searching for facts and figuring out problems mentally. **Work Values:** Autonomy; Working Conditions; Responsibility; Ability Utilization; Creativity. **Skills:** Writing; Identifying Downstream Consequences; Reading Comprehension; Information Gathering; Mathematics. **Abilities:** *Cognitive*—Written Comprehension; Oral Comprehension; Oral Expression; Written Expression; Deductive Reasoning; Inductive Reasoning. *Psychomotor*—none met the criteria. *Physical*—none met the criteria. *Sensory*—Speech Clarity; Speech Recognition; Auditory Attention. **General Work Activities:** *Information Input*—Getting Information Needed to Do the Job; Identifying Objects, Actions, and Events; Monitoring Processes, Materials, and Surroundings; Estimating Needed Characteristics. *Mental Process*—Analyzing Data or Information; Processing Information; Making Decisions and Solving Problems. *Work Output*—Implementing Ideas and Programs; Interacting with Computers; Documenting and Recording Information. *Interacting with Others*—Providing Consultation and Advice to Others; Communicating with Persons Outside Organization; Communicating with Other Workers. **Physical Work Conditions:** Indoors; Sitting; Standing. **Other Job Characteristics:** Importance of Being Aware of New Events; Importance of Being Exact or Accurate; Consequence of Error; Importance of Being Sure All Is Done.

Experience: Job Zone 5. Extensive skill, knowledge, and experience are needed. Very advanced communication and organizational skills are required. **Job Preparation:** SVP 8.0 and above—4 years to more than 10 years. **Knowledge:** Law, Government and Jurisprudence; English Language; Communications and Media; Philosophy and Theology; Mathematics. **Instructional Programs:** 450901 International Relations and Affairs; 451001 Political Science, General; 451002 American Government and Politics; 451099 Political Science and Government, Other.

Related DOT Job: 051.067-010 Political Scientist.

19-4000 Life, Physical, and Social Science Technicians

19-4011.00 Agricultural and Food Science Technicians (Biological, Agricultural, and Food Technicians and Technologists, Except Health)

Education: No data available.

Employed: 40,480

Openings: No data available.

Projected Growth: No data available.

Earnings: $27,430

Work with agricultural scientists in food, fiber, and animal research, production, and processing. Assist with animal breeding and nutrition. Work under supervision. Conduct tests and experiments to improve yield and quality of crops or to increase the resistance of plants and animals to disease or insects. Includes technicians who assist food scientists or food technologists in the research, development, production technology, quality control, packaging, processing, and use of foods.

GOE Number, Interest Area, and Work Group: 02.03.04; Science, Math, and Engineering; Life Sciences: Food Research. **Instructional Programs:** 010302 Agricultural Animal Husbandry and Production Management; 010304 Crop Production Operations and Management; 020201 Animal Sciences, General; 020202 Agricultural Animal Breeding and Genetics; 020204 Agricultural Animal Nutrition; 020206 Dairy Science; 020301 Food Sciences

and Technology; 020401 Plant Sciences, General; 020402 Agronomy and Crop Science; 410101 Biological Technology/Technician. **Note:** The Department of Labor has not collected some data for this job, so it has fewer details than the other descriptions.

19-4011.01 Agricultural Technicians (Biological, Agricultural, and Food Technicians and Technologists, Except Health)

Education: No data available.

Employed: 40,480

Openings: No data available.

Projected Growth: No data available.

Earnings: $27,430

Set up and maintain laboratory. Collect and record data to assist scientist in biology or related agricultural science experiments.

Records production and test data for evaluation by personnel. Examines animals and specimens to determine presence of disease or other problems. Waters and feeds rations to livestock and laboratory animals. Measures or weighs ingredients used in testing or as animal feed. Pricks animals, and collects blood samples for testing, using hand-held devices. Plants seeds in specified area, and counts plants that grow, to determine germination rate of seeds. Cleans and maintains laboratory and field equipment and work areas. Sets up laboratory and field equipment to assist research workers. Adjusts testing equipment and prepares culture media, following standard procedures.

GOE Number, Interest Area, and Work Group: 02.03.04; Science, Math, and Engineering; Life Sciences: Food Research. **Personality Type:** Realistic. Realistic occupations frequently involve work activities that include practical, hands-on problems and solutions. These occupations often deal with plants, animals, and real-world materials like wood, tools, and machinery. Many of the occupations require working outside and do not involve a lot of paperwork or working closely with others. **Work Values:** Moral Values; Company Policies and Practices; Supervision, Technical; Activity; Supervision, Human Relations; Security. **Skills:** Mathematics; Reading Comprehension; Science; Problem Identification; Active Listening; Information Gathering; Information Organization. **Abilities:** *Cognitive*—Oral Comprehension; Written Expression; Problem Sensitivity; Category Flexibility; Information Ordering; Deductive Reasoning. *Psychomotor*—Manual Dexterity; Finger Dexterity; Control Precision; Arm-Hand Steadiness. *Physical*—Static Strength; Extent Flexibility; Dynamic Strength. *Sensory*—Sound Localization. **General Work Activities:** *Information Input*—Identifying Objects, Actions, and Events; Getting Information Needed to Do the Job; Monitoring Processes, Materials, and Surroundings; Inspecting Equipment, Structures, Materials. *Mental Process*—Evaluating Information Against Standards; Processing Information; Analyzing Data or Information. *Work Output*—Documenting and Recording Information; Handling and Moving Objects; Repairing and Maintaining Mechanical Equipment; Performing General Physical Activities; Controlling Machines and Processes. *Interacting with Others*—Communicating with Other Workers; Performing Administrative Activities; Assisting and

Caring for Others. **Physical Work Conditions:** Indoors; Using Hands on Objects, Tools, or Controls; Standing; Diseases or Infections. **Other Job Characteristics:** Importance of Being Exact or Accurate; Importance of Being Sure All Is Done; Consequence of Error.

Experience: Job Zone 2. Some previous work-related skill, knowledge, or experience may be helpful, but usually is not needed. **Job Preparation:** SVP 4.00 to 5.99—6 months to less than 2 years. **Knowledge:** Biology; Mathematics; Food Production; Clerical; Medicine and Dentistry. **Instructional Programs:** 010302 Agricultural Animal Husbandry and Production Management; 010304 Crop Production Operations and Management; 020201 Animal Sciences, General; 020202 Agricultural Animal Breeding and Genetics; 020204 Agricultural Animal Nutrition; 020206 Dairy Science; 020301 Food Sciences and Technology; 020401 Plant Sciences, General; 020402 Agronomy and Crop Science; 410101 Biological Technology/Technician.

Related DOT Jobs: 040.361-014 Seed Analyst; 049.364-010 Feed-Research Aide; 049.364-018 Biological Aide; 411.364-010 Blood Tester, Fowl; 559.384-010 Laboratory Assistant, Culture Media.

19-4011.02 Food Science Technicians (Biological, Agricultural, and Food Technicians and Technologists, Except Health)

Education: No data available.

Employed: 40,480

Openings: No data available.

Projected Growth: No data available.

Earnings: $27,430

Perform standardized qualitative and quantitative tests to determine physical or chemical properties of food or beverage products.

Prepares slides and incubates slides with cell cultures. Examines chemical and biological samples to identify cell structure, bacteria, or extraneous material, using microscope. Records and compiles test results, and prepares graphs, charts, and reports. Cleans and sterilizes laboratory equipment. Analyzes test results to classify product, or compares results with standard tables. Mixes, blends, or cultivates ingredients to make reagents or to manufacture food or beverage products. Computes moisture or salt content, percentage of ingredients, formulas, or other product factors, using mathematical and chemical procedures. Tastes or smells food or beverages to ensure flavor meets specifications or to select samples with specific characteristics. Conducts standardized tests on food, beverages, additives, and preservatives to ensure compliance to standards for factors such as color, texture, nutrients, and coloring. Orders supplies to maintain inventory in laboratory or in storage facility of food or beverage processing plant. Measures, tests, and weighs bottles, cans, and other containers to ensure hardness, strength, and dimensions meet specifications.

GOE Number, Interest Area, and Work Group: 02.03.04; Science, Math, and Engineering; Life Sciences: Food Research. **Personality Type:** Realistic. Realistic occupations frequently involve worl activities that include practical, hands-on problems and solutions. These occupations often deal with plants, animals, and real-world materials like wood, tools, and machinery. Many of the occupations require working outside and do not involve a lot of paperwork or working closely with others. **Work Values:** Moral Values; Security; Working Conditions; Supervision, Human Relations; Activity. **Skills:** Mathematics; Reading Comprehension; Product Inspection; Information Gathering; Science; Active Learning; Writing. **Abilities:** *Cognitive*—Number Facility; Information Ordering; Written Expression; Deductive Reasoning; Mathematical Reasoning; Written Comprehension. *Psychomotor*—Manual Dexterity; Control Precision; Arm-Hand Steadiness. *Physical*—Extent Flexibility; Gross Body Coordination. *Sensory*—Near Vision; Visual Color Discrimination; Depth Perception. **General Work Activities:** *Information Input*—Identifying Objects, Actions, and Events; Getting Information Needed to Do the Job; Monitoring Processes, Materials, and Surroundings. *Mental Process*—Judging Qualities of Things, Services, Other People's Work; Processing Information; Analyzing Data or Information. *Work Output*—Handling and Moving Objects; Controlling Machines and Processes; Documenting and Recording Information. *Interacting with Others*—Interpreting Meaning of Information to Others; Monitoring and Controlling Resources; Performing Administrative Activities. **Physical Work Conditions:** Indoors; Using Hands on Objects, Tools, or Controls; Sitting. **Other Job Characteristics:** Importance of Being Exact or Accurate; Importance of Being Sure All Is Done; Consequence of Error.

Experience: Job Zone 2. Some previous work-related skill, knowledge, or experience may be helpful, but usually is not needed. **Job Preparation:** SVP 4.00 to 5.99—6 months to less than 2 years. **Knowledge:** Chemistry; Biology; Mathematics; English Language; Food Production. **Instructional Programs:** 010302 Agricultural Animal Husbandry and Production Management; 010304 Crop Production Operations and Management; 020201 Animal Sciences, General; 020202 Agricultural Animal Breeding and Genetics; 020204 Agricultural Animal Nutrition; 020206 Dairy Science; 020301 Food Sciences and Technology; 020401 Plant Sciences, General; 020402 Agronomy and Crop Science; 410101 Biological Technology/Technician.

Related DOT Jobs: 022.261-014 Malt-Specifications-Control Assistant; 022.381-010 Yeast-Culture Developer; 029.361-010 Bottle-House Quality-Control Technician; 029.361-014 Food Tester; 199.251-010 Tester, Food Products; 526.381-018 Baker, Test.

19-4021.00 Biological Technicians (Biological, Agricultural, and Food Technicians and Technologists, Except Health)

Education: No data available.

Employed: 40,480

Openings: No data available.

Projected Growth: No data available.

Earnings: $27,430

Assist biological and medical scientists in laboratories. Set up, operate, and maintain laboratory instruments and equipment. Monitor experiments, make observations, and calculate and record results. Analyze organic substances such as blood, food, and drugs.

Pricks animals, and collects blood samples for testing, using hand-held devices. Cleans and maintains laboratory and field equipment and work areas. Examines animals and specimens to determine presence of disease or other problems. Waters and feeds rations to livestock and laboratory animals. Adjusts testing equipment and prepares culture media, following standard procedures. Records production and test data for evaluation by personnel. Plants seeds in specified area, and counts plants that grow, to determine germination rate of seeds. Sets up laboratory and field equipment to assist research workers. Measures or weighs ingredients used in testing or as animal feed.

GOE Number, Interest Area, and Work Group: 02.05.02; Science, Math, and Engineering; Laboratory Technology: Life Sciences. **Personality Type:** Realistic. Realistic occupations frequently involve work activities that include practical, hands-on problems and solutions. These occupations often deal with plants, animals, and real-world materials like wood, tools, and machinery. Many of the occupations require working outside and do not involve a lot of paperwork or working closely with others. **Work Values:** Moral Values; Supervision, Technical; Company Policies and Practices; Activity; Security; Supervision, Human Relations. **Skills:** Reading Comprehension; Mathematics; Science; Problem Identification; Active Listening; Information Gathering; Information Organization. **Abilities:** *Cognitive*—Oral Compre-hension; Written Expression; Category Flexibility; Problem Sensitivity; Information Ordering; Deductive Reasoning. *Psychomotor*—Manual Dexterity; Finger Dexterity; Control Precision; Arm-Hand Steadiness. *Physical*—Static Strength; Extent Flexibility; Dynamic Strength. *Sensory*—Sound Localization. **General Work Activities:** *Information Input*—Identifying Objects, Actions, and Events; Getting Information Needed to Do the Job; Monitoring Processes, Materials, and Surroundings; Inspecting Equipment, Structures, Materials. *Mental Process*—Evaluating Information Against Standards; Processing Information; Analyzing Data or Information. *Work Output*—Documenting and Recording Information; Handling and Moving Objects; Repairing and Maintaining Mechanical Equipment; Performing General Physical Activities; Controlling Machines and Processes. *Interacting with Others*—Communicating with Other Workers; Performing Administrative Activities; Assisting and Caring for Others. **Physical Work Conditions:** Indoors; Using Hands on Objects, Tools, or Controls; Diseases or Infections; Standing. **Other Job Characteristics:** Importance of Being Sure All Is Done; Importance of Being Exact or Accurate; Consequence of Error.

Experience: Job Zone 2. Some previous work-related skill, knowledge, or experience may be helpful, but usually is not needed. **Job Preparation:** SVP 4.00 to 5.99–6 months to less than 2 years. **Knowledge:** Biology; Mathematics; Food Production; Clerical; Medicine and Dentistry. **Instructional Programs:** 010302 Agricultural Animal Husbandry and Production Management; 010304 Crop Production Operations and Management; 020201 Animal Sciences, General; 020202 Agricultural Animal Breeding and Genetics; 020204 Agricultural Animal Nutrition; 020206 Dairy Science; 020301 Food Sciences and Technology; 020401 Plant Sciences, General; 020402 Agronomy and Crop Science; 410101 Biological Technology/Technician.

Related DOT Jobs: 040.361-014 Seed Analyst; 049.364-010 Feed-Research Aide; 049.364-018 Biological Aide; 411.364-010 Blood Tester, Fowl; 559.384-010 Laboratory Assistant, Culture Media.

19-4031.00 Chemical Technicians (Chemical Technicians and Technologists, Except Health)

Education: No data available.

Employed: 76,210

Openings: No data available.

Projected Growth: No data available.

Earnings: $31,450

Conduct chemical and physical laboratory tests to assist scientists in making qualitative and quantitative analyses of solid, liquid, and gaseous materials for purposes such as research and development of new products or processes, quality control, maintenance of environmental standards, and other work involving experimental, theoretical, or practical application of chemistry and related sciences.

Directs other workers in compounding and distilling chemicals. Cleans and sterilizes laboratory equipment. Reviews process paperwork for products to ensure compliance to standards and specifications. Sets up and calibrates laboratory equipment and instruments used for testing, process control, product development, and research. Prepares chemical solutions for products and processes, following standardized formulas or creates experimental formulas. Tests and analyzes chemical and physical properties of liquids, solids, gases, radioactive and biological materials, and products such as perfumes. Documents results of tests and analyses, and writes technical reports or prepares graphs and charts.

GOE Number, Interest Area, and Work Group: 02.05.01; Science, Math, and Engineering; Laboratory Technology: Physical Sciences. **Personality Type:** Realistic. Realistic occupations frequently involve work activities that include practical, hands-on problems and solutions. These occupations often deal with plants, animals, and real-world materials like wood, tools, and machinery. Many of the occupations require working outside and do not involve a lot of paperwork or working closely with others. **Work Values:** Moral Values; Activity; Security; Supervision, Human Relations; Ability Utilization; Working Conditions. **Skills:** Science; Reading Comprehension; Critical Thinking; Mathematics; Writing; Active Listening. **Abilities:** *Cognitive*—Information Ordering; Written Comprehension; Written Expression; Number Facility; Deductive Reasoning; Mathematical Reasoning. *Psychomotor*—Control Precision; Arm-Hand Steadiness; Manual Dexterity. *Physical*—Trunk Strength; Gross Body Coordination; Explosive Strength. *Sensory*—Near Vision; Visual Color Discrimination; Depth Perception. **General Work Activities:** *Information Input*—Monitoring Processes, Materials, and Surroundings; Getting Information Needed to Do the Job; Inspecting Equipment, Structures, Materials; Identifying Objects, Actions, and Events. *Mental Process*—Analyzing Data or Information; Updating and Using Job-Relevant Knowledge; Evaluating Information Against Standards; Processing Information. *Work Output*—Controlling Machines and Processes; Handling and Moving Objects; Implementing Ideas and Programs. *Interacting with Others*—Communicating with Other Workers; Assisting and Caring for Others; Coordinating Work and Activities of Others; Establishing and Maintaining Relationships. **Physical Work Conditions:** Indoors; Using Hands on Objects, Tools, or Controls; Contaminants;

Sitting; Hazardous Conditions. **Other Job Characteristics:** Importance of Being Exact or Accurate; Importance of Being Sure All Is Done; Consequence of Error.

Experience: Job Zone 3. Previous work-related skill, knowledge, or experience is required. **Job Preparation:** SVP 6.0 to less than 7.0—More than 1 year and less than 4 years. **Knowledge:** Chemistry; Mathematics; English Language; Physics; Engineering and Technology. **Instructional Programs:** 020301 Food Sciences and Technology; 150701 Occupational Safety and Health Technology/Technician; 410301 Chemical Technology/Technician; 510802 Medical Laboratory Assistant.

Related DOT Jobs: 019.261-030 Laboratory Technician; 022.161-018 Perfumer; 022.261-010 Chemical Laboratory Technician; 029.261-010 Laboratory Tester.

19-4041.00 Geological and Petroleum Technicians
(Petroleum Technicians and Technologists)

Education: No data available.

Employed: 8,020

Openings: No data available.

Projected Growth: No data available.

Earnings: $40,120

Assist scientists in the use of electrical, sonic, or nuclear measuring instruments in both laboratory and production activities, to obtain data indicating potential sources of metallic ore, gas, or petroleum. Analyze mud and drill cuttings. Chart pressure, temperature, and other characteristics of wells or bore holes. Investigate and collect information leading to the possible discovery of new oil fields.

GOE Number, Interest Area, and Work Group: 02.05.01; Science, Math, and Engineering; Laboratory Technology: Physical Sciences. **Instructional Programs:** 150903 Petroleum Technology/Technician; 410399 Physical Science Technology/Technicians, Other. **Note:** The Department of Labor has not collected some data for this job, so it has fewer details than the other descriptions.

19-4041.01 Geological Data Technicians (Petroleum Technicians and Technologists)

Education: No data available.

Employed: 8,020

Openings: No data available.

Projected Growth: No data available.

Earnings: $40,120

Measure, record, and evaluate geological data, using sonic, electronic, electrical, seismic, or gravity-measuring instruments, to prospect for oil or gas. Collect and evaluate core samples and cuttings.

Assembles, maintains, and distributes information for library or record system. Interviews individuals and researches public databases to obtain information. Plans and directs activities of workers who operate equipment to collect data, or operates equipment.

Develops and prints photographic recordings of information, using equipment. Diagnoses and repairs malfunctioning instruments and equipment, using manufacturers' manuals and hand tools. Develops and designs packing materials and handling procedures for shipping of objects. Sets up or directs set-up of instruments used to collect geological data. Collects samples and cuttings, using equipment and hand tools. Reads and studies reports to compile information and data for geological and geophysical prospecting. Evaluates and interprets core samples and cuttings, and other geological data used in prospecting for oil or gas. Records readings to obtain data used in prospecting for oil or gas. Measures geological characteristics used in prospecting for oil or gas, using measuring instruments. Prepares and attaches packing instructions to shipping container. Operates and adjusts equipment and apparatus to obtain geological data.

GOE Number, Interest Area, and Work Group: 02.05.01; Science, Math, and Engineering; Laboratory Technology: Physical Sciences. **Personality Type:** Realistic. Realistic occupations frequently involve work activities that include practical, hands-on problems and solutions. These occupations often deal with plants, animals, and real-world materials like wood, tools, and machinery. Many of the occupations require working outside and do not involve a lot of paperwork or working closely with others. **Work Values:** Moral Values; Company Policies and Practices; Activity; Ability Utilization; Security; Compensation. **Skills:** Reading Comprehension; Information Gathering; Information Organization; Speaking; Mathematics. **Abilities:** *Cognitive*—Written Comprehension; Information Ordering; Inductive Reasoning; Written Expression; Oral Expression. *Psychomotor*—Control Precision; Wrist-Finger Speed; Arm-Hand Steadiness; Finger Dexterity; Manual Dexterity. *Physical*—Extent Flexibility; Static Strength; Gross Body Coordination. *Sensory*—Near Vision; Speech Clarity; Visual Color Discrimination; Far Vision. **General Work Activities:** *Information Input*—Getting Information Needed to Do the Job; Identifying Objects, Actions, and Events; Estimating Needed Characteristics. *Mental Process*—Analyzing Data or Information; Processing Information; Organizing, Planning, and Prioritizing. *Work Output*—Handling and Moving Objects; Documenting and Recording Information; Controlling Machines and Processes. *Interacting with Others*—Communicating with Other Workers; Coordinating Work and Activities of Others; Communicating with Persons Outside Organization; Interpreting Meaning of Information to Others. **Physical Work Conditions:** Outdoors; Using Hands on Objects, Tools, or Controls; Standing. **Other Job Characteristics:** Consequence of Error; Importance of Being Exact or Accurate; Frustrating Circumstances.

Experience: Job Zone 3. Previous work-related skill, knowledge, or experience is required. **Job Preparation:** SVP 6.0 to less than 7.0—More than 1 year and less than 4 years. **Knowledge:** Physics; Mathematics; Engineering and Technology; Mechanical; Administration and Management; English Language; Production and Processing. **Instructional Programs:** 150903 Petroleum Technology/Technician; 410399 Physical Science Technology/Technicians, Other.

Related DOT Jobs: 010.161-018 Observer, Seismic Prospecting; 010.261-014 Observer, Electrical Prospecting; 010.261-018 Observer, Gravity Prospecting; 010.261-022 Surveyor, Oil-Well Directional; 010.267-010 Scout; 024.267-010 Geological Aide; 194.382-010 Section-Plotter Operator; 930.167-010 Technical Operator.

19-4041.02 Geological Sample Test Technicians
(Petroleum Technicians and Technologists)

Education: No data available.

Employed: 8,020

Openings: No data available.

Projected Growth: No data available.

Earnings: $40,120

Test and analyze geological samples, crude oil, or petroleum products, to detect presence of petroleum, gas, or mineral deposits indicating potential for exploration and production or to determine physical and chemical properties to ensure that products meet quality standards.

Assembles and disassembles testing, measuring, and mechanical equipment and devices. Inspects engines for wear and defective parts, using equipment and measuring devices. Supervises and coordinates activities of workers, including initiating and recommending personnel actions. Adjusts and repairs testing, electrical, and mechanical equipment and devices. Collects solid and fluid samples from oil- or gas-bearing formations for analysis. Analyzes samples to determine presence, quantity, and quality of products, such as oil or gases. Tests samples for content and characteristics, using laboratory apparatus and testing equipment. Records testing and operational data for review and further analysis.

GOE Number, Interest Area, and Work Group: 02.05.01; Science, Math, and Engineering; Laboratory Technology: Physical Sciences. **Personality Type:** Realistic. Realistic occupations frequently involve work activities that include practical, hands-on problems and solutions. These occupations often deal with plants, animals, and real-world materials like wood, tools, and machinery. Many of the occupations require working outside and do not involve a lot of paperwork or working closely with others. **Work Values:** Moral Values; Company Policies and Practices; Compensation; Advancement; Security; Supervision, Human Relations. **Skills:** Science; Information Gathering; Coordination; Testing; Mathematics. **Abilities:** *Cognitive*—Information Ordering; Oral Expression; Deductive Reasoning; Problem Sensitivity; Written Expression. *Psychomotor*—Wrist-Finger Speed; Manual Dexterity; Arm-Hand Steadiness; Finger Dexterity. *Physical*—Extent Flexibility; Stamina; Dynamic Strength; Gross Body Coordination. *Sensory*—Near Vision; Visual Color Discrimination; Speech Clarity. **General Work Activities:** *Information Input*—Getting Information Needed to Do the Job; Identifying Objects, Actions, and Events; Estimating Needed Characteristics; Monitoring Processes, Materials, and Surroundings; Inspecting Equipment, Structures, Materials. *Mental Process*—Analyzing Data or Information; Processing Information; Updating and Using Job-Relevant Knowledge. *Work Output*—Documenting and Recording Information; Controlling Machines and Processes; Repairing and Maintaining Mechanical Equipment. *Interacting with Others*— Communicating with Other Workers; Interpreting Meaning of Information to Others; Coordinating Work and Activities of Others. **Physical Work Conditions:** Using Hands on Objects, Tools, or Controls; Outdoors; Indoors. **Other Job Characteristics:** Consequence of Error; Importance of Being Exact or Accurate; Importance of Being Sure All Is Done.

Experience: Job Zone 3. Previous work-related skill, knowledge, or experience is required. **Job Preparation:** SVP 6.0 to less than 7.0—More than 1 year and less than 4 years. **Knowledge:** Mechanical; Physics; Engineering and Technology; Mathematics; Personnel and Human Resources. **Instructional Programs:** 150903 Petroleum Technology/Technician; 410399 Physical Science Technology/Technicians, Other.

Related DOT Jobs: 010.131-010 Well-Logging Captain, Mud Analysis; 010.261-010 Field Engineer, Specialist; 010.261-026 Test-Engine Evaluator; 010.281-022 Well-Logging Operator, Mud Analysis; 024.381-010 Laboratory Assistant; 029.261-018 Test-Engine Operator; 029.261-022 Tester.

19-4051.00 Nuclear Technicians (Nuclear Technicians and Technologists)

Education: No data available.

Employed: 3,550

Openings: No data available.

Projected Growth: No data available.

Earnings: $45,970

Assist scientists in both laboratory and production. Perform technical tasks involving nuclear physics, primarily in operation, maintenance, production, and quality-control support activities.

GOE Number, Interest Area, and Work Group: 02.05.01; Science, Math, and Engineering; Laboratory Technology: Physical Sciences. **Instructional Programs:** 410204 Industrial Radiologic Technology/Technician; 410205 Nuclear/Nuclear Power Technology/Technician; 410299 Nuclear and Industrial Radiologic Technology/Technicians, Other. **Note:** The Department of Labor has not collected some data for this job, so it has fewer details than the other descriptions.

19-4051.01 Nuclear Equipment Operation Technicians (Nuclear Technicians and Technologists)

Education: No data available.

Employed: 3,550

Openings: No data available.

Projected Growth: No data available.

Earnings: $45,970

Operate equipment used for the release, control, and utilization of nuclear energy, to assist scientists in laboratory and production activities.

Writes summary of activities or records experiment data in log for further analysis by engineers, scientists, or customers, or for future reference. Controls laboratory compounding equipment enclosed in protective hot cell to prepare radioisotopes and other radioactive materials. Transfers experimental materials to and from specified containers and to tube, chamber or tunnel, using slave manipulators or extension tools. Sets up and operates machines to saw fuel elements to size or to cut and polish test pieces, following blueprints and other specifications. Withdraws radioactive sample for analysis, fills container with prescribed quantity of material for shipment, or removes spent fuel elements. Adjusts controls of equipment to control particle beam, chain reaction, or radiation, according to specifications. Communicates with maintenance personnel to ensure readiness of support systems and to warn of radiation hazards. Sets control panel switches and activates equipment, such as nuclear reactor, particle accelerator, or gamma radiation equipment, according to specifications. Modifies, devises, and maintains equipment used in operations. Installs instrumentation leads in reactor core to measure operating temperature and pressure according to mockups, blueprints, and diagrams. Positions fuel elements in reactor or environmental chamber, according to specified configuration, using slave manipulators or extension tools. Reviews experiment schedule to determine specifications, such as subatomic particle parameters, radiation time, dosage, and gamma intensity. Monitors instruments, gauges, and recording devices in control room during operation of equipment, under direction of nuclear experimenter. Calculates equipment operating factors, such as radiation time, dosage, temperature, and pressure, using standard formulas and conversion tables.

GOE Number, Interest Area, and Work Group: 02.05.01; Science, Math, and Engineering; Laboratory Technology: Physical Sciences. **Personality Type:** Realistic. Realistic occupations frequently involve work activities that include practical, hands-on problems and solutions. These occupations often deal with plants, animals, and real-world materials like wood, tools, and machinery. Many of the occupations require working outside and do not involve a lot of paperwork or working closely with others. **Work Values:** Compensation; Company Policies and Practices; Supervision, Human Relations; Ability Utilization; Activity; Independence; Moral Values; Security. **Skills:** Mathematics; Science; Operation and Control; Reading Comprehension; Installation. **Abilities:** *Cognitive*—Problem Sensitivity; Information Ordering; Perceptual Speed; Written Comprehension; Number Facility. *Psychomotor*—Control Precision; Arm-Hand Steadiness; Manual Dexterity; Reaction Time. *Physical*—Static Strength; Extent Flexibility; Trunk Strength. *Sensory*—Near Vision; Far Vision; Visual Color Discrimination. **General Work Activities:** *Information Input*—Getting Information Needed to Do the Job; Monitoring Processes, Materials, and Surroundings; Inspecting Equipment, Structures, Materials. *Mental Process*—Updating and Using Job-Relevant Knowledge; Processing Information; Evaluating Information Against Standards; Making Decisions and Solving Problems. *Work Output*—Controlling Machines and Processes; Handling and Moving Objects; Implementing Ideas and Programs. *Interacting with Others*—Communicating with Other Workers; Performing Administrative Activities; Coordinating Work and Activities of Others. **Physical Work Conditions:** Indoors; Using Hands on Objects, Tools, or Controls; Common Protective or Safety Attire; Radiation. **Other Job Characteristics:** Consequence of Error; Importance of Being Exact or Accurate; Importance of Being Sure All Is Done.

Experience: Job Zone 3. Previous work-related skill, knowledge, or experience is required. **Job Preparation:** SVP 6.0 to less than 7.0—More than 1 year and less than 4 years. **Knowledge:** Engineering and Technology; Physics; Public Safety and Security; Mathematics; Chemistry. **Instructional Programs:** 410204 Indus-

trial Radiologic Technology/Technician; 410205 Nuclear/Nuclear Power Technology/Technician; 410299 Nuclear and Industrial Radiologic Technology/Technicians, Other.

Related DOT Jobs: 015.362-010 Accelerator Operator; 015.362-014 Gamma-Facilities Operator; 015.362-018 Hot-Cell Technician; 015.362-022 Radioisotope-Production Operator; 015.362-026 Reactor Operator, Test-and-Research.

19-4051.02 Nuclear Monitoring Technicians (Nuclear Technicians and Technologists)

Education: No data available.

Employed: 3,550

Openings: No data available.

Projected Growth: No data available.

Earnings: $45,970

Collect and test samples to monitor results of nuclear experiments and contamination of humans, facilities, and environment.

Weighs and mixes decontamination chemical solutions in tank and immerses objects in solution for specified time, using hoist. Instructs personnel in radiation safety procedures and demonstrates use of protective clothing and equipment. Confers with scientist directing project to determine significant events to watch for during test. Prepares reports on contamination tests, material and equipment decontaminated, and methods used in decontamination process. Decontaminates objects by cleaning with soap or solvents or by abrading, using wire brush, buffing wheel or sandblasting machine. Observes projected photographs to locate particle tracks and events and compiles lists of events from particle detectors. Enters data into computer to record characteristics of nuclear events and locating coordinates of particles. Informs supervisors to take action when individual exposures or area radiation levels approach maximum permissible limits. Monitors personnel for length and intensity of exposure to radiation for health and safety purposes. Calibrates and maintains chemical instrumentation sensing elements and sampling system equipment, using calibrations instruments and hand tools. Scans photographic emulsions exposed to direct radiation to compute track properties from standard formulas, using microscope with scales and protractors. Calculates safe radiation exposure time for personnel, using plant contamination readings and prescribed safe levels of radiation. Assists in setting-up equipment that automatically detects area radiation deviations and tests detection equipment to ensure accuracy. Collects samples of air, water, gases and solids to determine radioactivity levels of contamination. Measures intensity and identifies type of radiation in work areas, equipment, and materials, using radiation detectors and other instruments. Places radioactive waste, such as sweepings and broken sample bottles, into containers for disposal.

GOE Number, Interest Area, and Work Group: 04.04.02; Law, Law Enforcement, and Public Safety; Public Safety: Regulations Enforcement. **Personality Type:** Realistic. Realistic occupations frequently involve work activities that include practical, hands-on problems and solutions. These occupations often deal with plants, animals, and real-world materials like wood, tools, and machinery. Many of the occupations require working outside and do not involve a lot of paperwork or working closely with others. **Work Values:** Compensation; Company Policies and Practices; Security; Supervision, Human Relations; Activity; Ability Utilization; Supervision, Technical; Social Status. **Skills:** Science; Information Gathering; Mathematics; Problem Identification; Speaking; Reading Comprehension. **Abilities:** *Cognitive*—Problem Sensitivity; Oral Expression; Inductive Reasoning; Number Facility; Written Comprehension. *Psychomotor*—Control Precision; Manual Dexterity; Finger Dexterity. *Physical*—Extent Flexibility; Static Strength; Dynamic Strength; Stamina; Dynamic Flexibility. *Sensory*—Near Vision; Speech Clarity; Far Vision. **General Work Activities:** *Information Input*—Getting Information Needed to Do the Job; Monitoring Processes, Materials, and Surroundings; Identifying Objects, Actions, and Events. *Mental Process*—Evaluating Information Against Standards; Processing Information; Judging Qualities of Things, Services, Other People's Work; Analyzing Data or Information. *Work Output*—Handling and Moving Objects; Controlling Machines and Processes; Implementing Ideas and Programs. *Interacting with Others*—Communicating with Other Workers; Providing Consultation and Advice to Others; Teaching Others. **Physical Work Conditions:** Indoors; Specialized Protective or Safety Attire; Contaminants; Using Hands on Objects, Tools, or Controls. **Other Job Characteristics:** Consequence of Error; Importance of Being Sure All Is Done; Importance of Being Exact or Accurate.

Experience: Job Zone 3. Previous work-related skill, knowledge, or experience is required. **Job Preparation:** SVP 6.0 to less than 7.0—More than 1 year and less than 4 years. **Knowledge:** Physics; Mathematics; Public Safety and Security; Chemistry; Education and Training. **Instructional Programs:** 410204 Industrial Radiologic Technology/Technician; 410205 Nuclear/Nuclear Power Technology/Technician; 410299 Nuclear and Industrial Radiologic Technology/Technicians, Other.

Related DOT Jobs: 015.261-010 Chemical-Radiation Technician; 015.384-010 Scanner; 199.167-010 Radiation Monitor; 199.384-010 Decontaminator.

19-4061.00 Social Science Research Assistants (All Other Professional, Paraprofessional, and Technical Workers)

Education: No data available.

Employed: 818,200

Openings: No data available.

Projected Growth: No data available.

Earnings: $36,790

Assist social scientists in laboratory, survey, and other social research. Perform publication activities, laboratory analysis, quality control, or data management. Work under the direct supervision of a social scientist, assisting in those activities that are more routine.

GOE Number, Interest Area, and Work Group: 02.04.02; Science, Math, and Engineering; Social Sciences: Economics, Public Policy, and History. **Instructional Programs:** 451001 Political Science, General; 451002 American Government and Politics;

451101 Sociology; 459999 Social Sciences and History, Other. **Note:** The Department of Labor has not collected some data for this job, so it has fewer details than the other descriptions.

19-4061.01 City Planning Aides (All Other Professional, Paraprofessional, and Technical Workers)

Education: No data available.

Employed: 818,200

Openings: No data available.

Projected Growth: No data available.

Earnings: $36,790

Compile data from various sources such as maps, reports, and field and file investigations, for use by city planner in making planning studies.

Summarizes information from maps, reports, investigations, and books. Conducts interviews and surveys and observes conditions which affect land usage. Prepares and updates files and records. Answers public inquiries. Prepares reports, using statistics, charts, and graphs, to illustrate planning studies in areas, such as population, land use, or zoning.

GOE Number, Interest Area, and Work Group: 02.04.02; Science, Math, and Engineering; Social Sciences: Economics, Public Policy, and History. **Personality Type:** Conventional. Conventional occupations frequently involve following set procedures and routines. These occupations can include working with data and details more than with ideas. Usually there is a clear line of authority to follow. **Work Values:** Working Conditions; Company Policies and Practices; Supervision, Human Relations; Advancement; Security. **Skills:** Writing; Mathematics; Information Gathering; Reading Comprehension; Active Listening. **Abilities:** *Cognitive*—Written Comprehension; Written Expression; Oral Comprehension; Oral Expression; Information Ordering; Mathematical Reasoning. *Psychomotor*—none met the criteria. *Physical*—none met the criteria. *Sensory*—Near Vision; Speech Clarity; Speech Recognition. **General Work Activities:** *Information Input*—Getting Information Needed to Do the Job; Estimating Needed Characteristics; Identifying Objects, Actions, and Events. *Mental Process*—Analyzing Data or Information; Processing Information; Evaluating Information Against Standards. *Work Output*—Documenting and Recording Information; Handling and Moving Objects; Interacting with Computers. *Interacting with Others*—Communicating with Other Workers; Communicating with Persons Outside Organization; Performing Administrative Activities. **Physical Work Conditions:** Indoors; Sitting; Standing. **Other Job Characteristics:** Importance of Being Exact or Accurate; Consequence of Error; Importance of Being Sure All Is Done.

Experience: Job Zone 3. Previous work-related skill, knowledge, or experience is required. **Job Preparation:** SVP 6.0 to less than 7.0—More than 1 year and less than 4 years. **Knowledge:** Geography; Mathematics; Clerical; English Language; Administration and Management. **Instructional Program:** 150201 Civil Engineering/ Civil Technology/Technician.

Related DOT Job: 199.364-010 City Planning Aide.

19-4091.00 Environmental Science and Protection Technicians, Including Health (Chemical Technicians and Technologists, Except Health)

Education: No data available.

Employed: 76,210

Openings: No data available.

Projected Growth: No data available.

Earnings: $31,450

Perform laboratory and field tests to monitor the environment and to investigate sources of pollution, including those that affect health. Under direction of an environmental scientist or specialist, collect samples of gases, soil, water, and other materials for testing; take corrective actions as assigned.

Calibrates microscopes and test instruments. Calculates amount of pollutant in samples or computes air pollution or gas flow in industrial processes, using chemical and mathematical formulas. Conducts standardized tests to ensure materials and supplies used throughout power supply system meet processing and safety specifications. Weighs, analyzes, and measures collected sample particles, such as lead, coal dust, or rock, to determine concentration of pollutants. Sets up equipment or station to monitor and collect pollutants from sites, such as smoke stacks, manufacturing plants, or mechanical equipment. Records test data and prepares reports, summaries, and charts, that interpret test results and recommend changes. Develops procedures and directs activities of workers in laboratory. Collects samples of gases, soils, water, industrial wastewater, and asbestos products to conduct tests on pollutant levels. Determines amounts and kinds of chemicals to use in destroying harmful organisms and removing impurities from purification systems. Discusses test results and analyses with customers. Examines and analyzes material for presence and concentration of contaminants such as asbestos in environment, using variety of microscopes. Performs chemical and physical laboratory and field tests on collected samples to assess compliance with pollution standards, using test instruments. Prepares samples or photomicrographs for testing and analysis.

GOE Number, Interest Area, and Work Group: 02.05.02; Science, Math, and Engineering; Laboratory Technology: Life Sciences. **Personality Type:** Investigative. Investigative occupations frequently involve working with ideas and require an extensive amount of thinking. These occupations can involve searching for facts and figuring out problems mentally. **Work Values:** Security; Independence; Company Policies and Practices; Activity; Responsibility; Supervision, Human Relations. **Skills:** Science; Mathematics; Information Gathering; Reading Comprehension; Writing. **Abilities:** *Cognitive*—Information Ordering; Number Facility; Written Comprehension; Mathematical Reasoning; Deductive Reasoning; Written Expression. *Psychomotor*—Control Precision; Finger Dexterity; Arm-Hand Steadiness; Manual Dexterity. *Physical*—Trunk Strength; Static Strength; Explosive Strength. *Sensory*—Near Vision; Far Vision; Speech Clarity. **General Work Activities:** *Information Input*—Getting Information Needed to Do the Job; Monitoring Processes, Materials, and Surroundings; Identifying Objects, Actions, and Events. *Mental Process*—Analyzing Data or Information; Processing Information; Making Decisions and Solving Problems; Evaluating Information Against Standards; Judging Qualities of Things, Services, Other People's Work. *Work Output*—Documenting and Recording Information; Implementing Ideas and Programs; Handling and Moving Objects; Controlling Machines and Processes. *Interacting with Others*—Providing Consultation and Advice to Others; Communicating with Other Workers; Communicating with Persons Outside Organization; Interpreting Meaning of Information to Others. **Physical Work Conditions:** Using Hands on Objects, Tools, or Controls; Contaminants; Indoors. **Other Job Characteristics:** Consequence of Error; Importance of Being Exact or Accurate; Importance of Being Sure All Is Done.

Experience: Job Zone 3. Previous work-related skill, knowledge, or experience is required. **Job Preparation:** SVP 6.0 to less than 7.0—More than 1 year and less than 4 years. **Knowledge:** Chemistry; Mathematics; Public Safety and Security; English Language; Computers and Electronics. **Instructional Programs:** 020301 Food Sciences and Technology; 150701 Occupational Safety and Health Technology/Technician; 410301 Chemical Technology/Technician; 510802 Medical Laboratory Assistant.

Related DOT Jobs: 012.261-010 Air Analyst; 012.281-010 Smoke Tester; 022.261-018 Chemist, Instrumentation; 022.261-022 Chemist, Wastewater-Treatment Plant; 022.281-014 Chemist, Water Purification; 029.261-014 Pollution-Control Technician; 029.261-030 Microscopist, Asbestos; 029.361-018 Laboratory Assistant.

19-4092.00 Forensic Science Technicians (All Other Physical and Life Science Technicians and Technologists)

Education: No data available.

Employed: 99,710

Openings: No data available.

Projected Growth: No data available.

Earnings: $31,250

Collect, identify, classify, and analyze physical evidence related to criminal investigations. Perform tests on weapons or on substances such as fiber, hair, and tissue, to determine significance to investigation. Testify as expert witnesses on evidence or crime laboratory techniques. Serve as specialists in area of expertise, such as ballistics, fingerprinting, handwriting, or biochemistry.

Prepares reports or presentations of findings, investigative methods, or laboratory techniques. Collects and preserves criminal evidence used to solve cases. Confers with ballistics, fingerprinting, handwriting, documents, electronics, medical, chemical, or metallurgical experts concerning evidence and its interpretation. Reconstructs crime scene to determine relationships among pieces of evidence. Testifies as expert witness on evidence or laboratory techniques in trials or hearings. Examines, tests, and analyzes tissue samples, chemical substances, physical materials, and ballistics evidence, using recording, measuring, and testing equipment. Interprets laboratory findings and test results to identify and classify substances, materials, and other evidence collected at crime scene.

GOE Number, Interest Area, and Work Group: 04.03.02; Law, Law Enforcement, and Public Safety; Law Enforcement: Technology. **Personality Type:** Investigative. Investigative occupations frequently involve working with ideas and require an extensive amount of thinking. These occupations can involve searching for facts and figuring out problems mentally. **Work Values:** Autonomy; Achievement; Ability Utilization; Security; Recognition; Variety. **Skills:** Science; Reading Comprehension; Information Gathering; Problem Identification; Mathematics; Information Organization; Speaking; Writing; Critical Thinking. **Abilities:** *Cognitive*—Inductive Reasoning; Information Ordering; Oral Expression; Category Flexibility; Written Expression; Flexibility of Closure. *Psychomotor*—Arm-Hand Steadiness; Manual Dexterity; Wrist-Finger Speed. *Physical*—Trunk Strength; Gross Body Coordination; Dynamic Strength. *Sensory*—Near Vision; Speech Clarity; Visual Color Discrimination. **General Work Activities:** *Information Input*—Getting Information Needed to Do the Job; Identifying Objects, Actions, and Events; Estimating Needed Characteristics; Monitoring Processes, Materials, and Surroundings; Inspecting Equipment, Structures, Materials. *Mental Process*—Analyzing Data or Information; Judging Qualities of Things, Services, Other People's Work; Making Decisions and Solving Problems. *Work Output*—Documenting and Recording Information; Handling and Moving Objects; Controlling Machines and Processes. *Interacting with Others*—Communicating with Other Workers; Communicating with Persons Outside Organization; Interpreting Meaning of Information to Others. **Physical Work Conditions:** Indoors; Using Hands on Objects, Tools, or Controls; Sitting; Outdoors; Standing. **Other Job Characteristics:** Importance of Being Exact or Accurate; Consequence of Error; Frustrating Circumstances; Importance of Being Sure All Is Done.

Experience: Job Zone 4. A minimum of two to four years of work-related skill, knowledge, or experience is needed. **Job Preparation:** SVP 7.0 to less than 8.0—2 years to less than 10 years. **Knowledge:** Public Safety and Security; Chemistry; English Language; Law, Government and Jurisprudence; Computers and Electronics. **Instructional Programs:** 020301 Food Sciences and Technology; 030102 Environmental Science/Studies; 150701 Occupational Safety and Health Technology/Technician; 410399 Physical Science Technology/Technicians, Other; 419999 Science Technology/Technicians, Other; 430106 Forensic Technology/Technician.

Related DOT Jobs: 029.261-026 Criminalist; 199.267-010 Ballistics Expert, Forensic.

19-4093.00 Forest and Conservation Technicians
(Forest and Conservation Workers)

Education: Short-term O-T-J training
Employed: 32,667
Openings: 5,265
Projected Growth: 0.7%
Earnings: $23,140

Compile data pertaining to size, content, condition, and other characteristics of forest tracts. Work under direction of foresters. Train and lead forest workers in forest propagation and in fire prevention and suppression. Assist conservation scientists in managing, improving, and protecting rangelands and wildlife habitats. Help provide technical assistance regarding the conservation of soil, water, and related natural resources.

GOE Number, Interest Area, and Work Group: 03.03.02; Plants and Animals; Hands-on Work: Forestry and Logging. **Instructional Programs:** 030101 Natural Resources Conservation, General; 030201 Natural Resources Management and Policy; 030203 Natural Resources Law Enforcement and Protective Services; 030299 Natural Resources Management and Protective Services, Other; 030401 Forest Harvesting and Production Technology/Technician; 030501 Forestry, General; 030502 Forestry Sciences; 030506 Forest Management; 030509 Wood Science and Pulp/Paper Technology; 030599 Forestry and Related Sciences, Other; 039999 Conservation and Renewable Natural Resources, Other. **Note:** The Department of Labor has not collected some data for this job, so it has fewer details than the other descriptions.

21-0000
Community and Social Services Occupations

21-1000 Counselors, Social Workers, and Other Community and Social Service Specialists

21-1011.00 Substance Abuse and Behavioral Disorder Counselors (Social Workers, Medical and Psychiatric)

Education: No data available.

Employed: 218,170

Openings: No data available.

Projected Growth: No data available.

Earnings: $31,620

Counsel and advise individuals with alcohol, tobacco, drug, or other problems such as gambling and eating disorders. Counsel individuals, families, or groups. Engage in prevention programs.

Interviews clients, reviews records, and confers with other professionals to evaluate mental or physical condition of client or patient. Plans and conducts programs to prevent substance abuse or improve health and counseling services in community. Intervenes as advocate for client or patient to resolve emergency problems in crisis situation. Counsels clients and patients, individually and in group sessions, to assist in overcoming dependencies, adjusting to life, and making changes. Counsels family members to assist in understanding, dealing with, and supporting client or patient. Formulates or coordinates program plan for treatment, care, and rehabilitation of client or patient, based on social work experience and knowledge. Monitors, evaluates, and records client progress according to measurable goals described in treatment and care plan. Modifies treatment plan to comply with changes in client's status. Supervises and directs other workers providing services to client or patient. Refers patient, client, or family to community resources to assist in recovery from mental or physical illness.

GOE Number, Interest Area, and Work Group: 12.02.02; Education and Social Service; Social Services: Counseling and Social Work. Personality Type: Social. Social occupations frequently involve working with, communicating with, and teaching people. These occupations often involve helping or providing service to others. Work Values: Social Service; Activity; Achievement; Autonomy; Responsibility; Security; Ability Utilization. Skills: Social Perceptiveness; Critical Thinking; Service Orientation; Management of Financial Resources; Problem Identification; Active Listening; Reading Comprehension. Abilities: *Cognitive*—Oral Comprehension; Oral Expression; Problem Sensitivity; Written Comprehension; Fluency of Ideas. *Psychomotor*—none met the criteria. *Physical*—none met the criteria. *Sensory*—Speech Clarity; Near Vision; Speech Recognition. General Work Activities: *Information Input*—Getting Information Needed to Do the Job; Identifying Objects, Actions, and Events; Monitoring Processes, Materials, and Surroundings. *Mental Process*—Making Decisions and Solving Problems; Evaluating Information Against Standards; Processing Information; Analyzing Data or Information. *Work*

Output—Documenting and Recording Information; Implementing Ideas and Programs; Handling and Moving Objects; Interacting with Computers. *Interacting with Others*—Communicating with Persons Outside Organization; Establishing and Maintaining Relationships; Assisting and Caring for Others. Physical Work Conditions: Sitting; Indoors; Standing. Other Job Characteristics: Consequence of Error; Importance of Being Sure All Is Done; Frustrating Circumstances.

Experience: Job Zone 4. A minimum of two to four years of work-related skill, knowledge, or experience is needed. Job Preparation: SVP 7.0 to less than 8.0—2 years to less than 10 years. Knowledge: Therapy and Counseling; Psychology; Customer and Personal Service; Education and Training; English Language. Instructional Programs: 440701 Social Work; 511503 Clinical and Medical Social Work.

Related DOT Job: 045.107-058 Substance Abuse Counselor.

21-1012.00 Educational, Vocational, and School Counselors (Counselors)

Education: Master's degree

Employed: 182,260

Openings: 21,279

Projected Growth: 25%

Earnings: $38,650

Counsel individuals and provide group educational and vocational guidance services.

Establishes and maintains relationships with employers and personnel from supportive service agencies to develop opportunities for counselees. Compiles and studies occupational, educational, and economic information to assist counselees in making and carrying out vocational and educational objectives. Interprets program regulations or benefit requirements and assists counselees in obtaining needed supportive services. Collects and evaluates information about counselees' abilities, interests, and personality characteristics, using records, tests, and interviews. Advises counselees to assist them in understanding and overcoming personal and social problems. Teaches vocational and educational guidance classes. Addresses community groups and faculty members to explain counseling services. Refers qualified counselees to employer or employment service for placement. Advises counselees to assist them in developing their educational and vocational objectives. Conducts follow-up interviews with counselees and maintains case records. Plans and conducts orientation programs and group conferences to promote adjustment of individuals to new life experiences.

GOE Number, Interest Area, and Work Group: 12.03.01; Education and Social Service; Educational Services: Counseling and Evaluation. Personality Type: Social. Social occupations frequently involve working with, communicating with, and teaching people. These occupations often involve helping or providing service to others. Work Values: Social Service; Achievement; Working Conditions; Autonomy; Responsibility; Authority. Skills: Active Listening; Social Perceptiveness; Reading Comprehension; Service Orientation; Speaking; Problem Identification. Abilities: *Cognitive*—Oral Expression; Oral Comprehension; Written Expression; Written Comprehension; Problem Sensitivity. *Psychomotor—* none met the criteria. *Physical—*none met the criteria. *Sensory—* Speech Clarity; Speech Recognition. **General Work Activities:** *Information Input—*Getting Information Needed to Do the Job; Identifying Objects, Actions, and Events; Monitoring Processes, Materials, and Surroundings. *Mental Process—*Making Decisions and Solving Problems; Analyzing Data or Information; Judging Qualities of Things, Services, People. *Work Output—*Documenting and Recording Information; Implementing Ideas and Programs; Interacting with Computers. *Interacting with Others—* Assisting and Caring for Others; Establishing and Maintaining Relationships; Interpreting Meaning of Information to Others; Providing Consultation and Advice to Others; Communicating with Persons Outside Organization; Performing for or Working with the Public. **Physical Work Conditions:** Indoors; Sitting; Standing. **Other Job Characteristics:** Importance of Being Sure All Is Done; Importance of Being Exact or Accurate; Consequence of Error.

Experience: Job Zone 4. A minimum of two to four years of work-related skill, knowledge, or experience is needed. **Job Preparation:** SVP 7.0 to less than 8.0—2 years to less than 10 years. **Knowledge:** Therapy and Counseling; Education and Training; Psychology; English Language; Personnel and Human Resources. **Instructional Programs:** 131101 Counselor Education Counseling and Guidance Services; 131102 College/Postsecondary Student Counseling and Personnel Services; 421701 School Psychology; 512310 Vocational Rehabilitation Counseling.

Related DOT Jobs: 045.107-010 Counselor; 045.107-014 Counselor, Nurses' Association; 045.107-018 Director of Counseling; 045.107-038 Residence Counselor; 045.107-042 Vocational Rehabilitation Counselor; 045.117-010 Director of Guidance in Public Schools; 090.107-010 Foreign-Student Adviser; 094.224-022 Employment Training Specialist; 169.267-026 Supervisor, Special Services; 187.167-198 Veterans Contact Representative.

21-1013.00 Marriage and Family Therapists
(Counselors)

Education: Master's degree
Employed: 182,260
Openings: 21,279
Projected Growth: 25%
Earnings: $38,650

Diagnose and treat mental and emotional disorders, whether cognitive, affective, or behavioral, within the context of marriage and family systems. Apply psychotherapeutic and family-systems theories and techniques in the delivery of professional services to individuals, couples, and families, for the purpose of treating diagnosed nervous and mental disorders.

GOE Number, Interest Area, and Work Group: 12.02.02; Education and Social Service; Social Services: Counseling and Social Work. **Instructional Programs:** 131101 Counselor Education Counseling and Guidance Services; 131102 College/Postsecondary Student Counseling and Personnel Services; 421701 School Psychology; 512310 Vocational Rehabilitation Counseling. **Note:** The

Department of Labor has not collected some data for this job, so it has fewer details than the other descriptions.

21-1014.00 Mental Health Counselors (Social Workers, Medical and Psychiatric)

Education: No data available.
Employed: 218,170
Openings: No data available.
Projected Growth: No data available.
Earnings: $31,620

Counsel with emphasis on prevention. Work with individuals and groups to promote optimum mental health. Help individuals deal with addictions and substance abuse; family, parenting, and marital problems; suicide; stress-management; problems with self-esteem; and issues associated with aging and with mental and emotional health.

Monitors, evaluates, and records client progress according to measurable goals described in treatment and care plan. Counsels clients and patients, individually and in group sessions, to assist in overcoming dependencies, adjusting to life, and making changes. Refers patient, client, or family to community resources to assist in recovery from mental or physical illness. Formulates or coordinates program plan for treatment, care, and rehabilitation of client or patient, based on social work experience and knowledge. Plans and conducts programs to prevent substance abuse or improve health and counseling services in community. Supervises and directs other workers providing services to client or patient. Intervenes as advocate for client or patient to resolve emergency problems in crisis situation. Modifies treatment plan to comply with changes in client's status. Interviews clients, reviews records, and confers with other professionals to evaluate mental or physical condition of client or patient. Counsels family members to assist in understanding, dealing with, and supporting client or patient.

GOE Number, Interest Area, and Work Group: 12.02.02; Education and Social Service; Social Services: Counseling and Social Work. **Personality Type:** Social. Social occupations frequently involve working with, communicating with, and teaching people. These occupations often involve helping or providing service to others. **Work Values:** Social Service; Achievement; Activity; Autonomy; Ability Utilization; Security; Responsibility. **Skills:** Social Perceptiveness; Reading Comprehension; Critical Thinking; Service Orientation; Problem Identification; Management of Financial Resources; Active Listening. **Abilities:** *Cognitive—*Oral Comprehension; Oral Expression; Problem Sensitivity; Written Comprehension; Fluency of Ideas. *Psychomotor—*none met the criteria. *Physical—*none met the criteria. *Sensory—*Speech Clarity; Near Vision; Speech Recognition. **General Work Activities:** *Information Input—*Getting Information Needed to Do the Job; Identifying Objects, Actions, and Events; Monitoring Processes, Materials, and Surroundings. *Mental Process—*Making Decisions and Solving Problems; Analyzing Data or Information; Evaluating Information Against Standards; Processing Information. *Work Output—*Documenting and Recording Information; Implementing Ideas and Programs; Handling and Moving Objects; Interacting with Computers. *Interacting with Others*—Communicating with Persons Outside Organization; Establishing and Maintaining Relationships; Assisting and Caring for Others. **Physical Work Conditions:** Sitting; Indoors; Standing. **Other Job Characteristics:** Consequence of Error; Importance of Being Sure All Is Done; Frustrating Circumstances.

Experience: Job Zone 4. A minimum of two to four years of work-related skill, knowledge, or experience is needed. **Job Preparation:** SVP 7.0 to less than 8.0—2 years to less than 10 years. **Knowledge:** Therapy and Counseling; Psychology; Customer and Personal Service; Education and Training; English Language. **Instructional Programs:** 440701 Social Work; 511503 Clinical and Medical Social Work.

Related DOT Job: 195.107-050 Bereavement Counselor.

21-1015.00 Rehabilitation Counselors (Social Workers, Medical and Psychiatric)

Education: No data available.
Employed: 218,170
Openings: No data available.
Projected Growth: No data available.
Earnings: $31,620

Counsel individuals to maximize the independence and employability of persons coping with personal, social, and vocational difficulties that result from birth defects, illness, disease, accidents, or the stress of daily life. Coordinate activities for residents of care and treatment facilities. Assess client needs. Design and implement rehabilitation programs that may include personal and vocational counseling, training, and job placement.

GOE Number, Interest Area, and Work Group: 12.02.02; Education and Social Service; Social Services: Counseling and Social Work. **Instructional Programs:** 440701 Social Work; 511503 Clinical and Medical Social Work. **Note:** The Department of Labor has not collected some data for this job, so it has fewer details than the other descriptions.

21-1021.00 Child, Family, and School Social Workers (Social Workers)

Education: No data available.
Employed: 365,600
Openings: No data available.
Projected Growth: No data available.
Earnings: $29,960

Provide social services and assistance to improve the social and psychological functioning of children and their families, to maximize the family well-being, and to maximize the academic functioning of children. Assist single parents, arrange adoptions, and find foster homes for abandoned or abused children. In schools, address problems such as teenage pregnancy, misbehavior, and truancy. Advise teachers on how to deal with problem children.

Refers client to community resources for needed assistance. Develops program content, organizes, and leads activities planned to enhance social development of individual members and accomplishment of group goals. Counsels parents with child rearing problems and children and youth with difficulties in social adjustments. Leads group counseling sessions to provide support in such areas as grief, stress, or chemical dependency. Counsels students whose behavior, school progress, or mental or physical impairment indicates need for assistance. Interviews individuals to assess social and emotional capabilities, physical and mental impairments, and financial needs. Arranges for medical, psychiatric, and other tests that may disclose cause of difficulties and indicate remedial measures. Consults with parents, teachers, and other school personnel to determine causes of problems and effect solutions. Serves as liaison between student, home, school, family service agencies, child guidance clinics, courts, protective services, doctors, and clergy members. Investigates home conditions to determine suitability of foster or adoptive home, or to protect children from harmful environment. Determines client's eligibility for financial assistance. Reviews service plan and performs follow-up to determine quantity and quality of service provided to client. Places children in foster or adoptive homes, institutions, or medical treatment centers. Evaluates personal characteristics of foster home or adoption applicants. Maintains case history records and prepares reports. Assists travelers, including runaways, migrants, transients, refugees, repatriated Americans, and problem families. Arranges for day care, homemaker service, prenatal care, and child planning programs for clients in need of such services. Counsels individuals or family members regarding behavior modifications, rehabilitation, social adjustments, financial assistance, vocational training, child care, or medical care.

GOE Number, Interest Area, and Work Group: 12.02.02; Education and Social Service; Social Services: Counseling and Social Work. **Personality Type:** Social. Social occupations frequently involve working with, communicating with, and teaching people. These occupations often involve helping or providing service to others. **Work Values:** Social Service; Activity; Autonomy; Achievement; Security. **Skills:** Social Perceptiveness; Service Orientation; Problem Identification; Active Listening; Speaking; Solution Appraisal; Information Gathering; Reading Comprehension. **Abilities:** *Cognitive*—Oral Expression; Oral Comprehension; Problem Sensitivity; Written Expression; Written Comprehension. *Psychomotor*—none met the criteria. *Physical*—none met the criteria. *Sensory*—Speech Clarity; Speech Recognition. **General Work Activities:** *Information Input*—Getting Information Needed to Do the Job; Monitoring Processes, Materials, and Surroundings; Identifying Objects, Actions, and Events. *Mental Process*—Judging Qualities of Things, Services, Other People's Work; Making Decisions and Solving Problems; Analyzing Data or Information. *Work Output*—Implementing Ideas and Programs; Documenting and Recording Information; Interacting with Computers. *Interacting with Others*—Establishing and Maintaining Relationships; Assisting and Caring for Others; Communicating with Persons Outside Organization. **Physical Work Conditions:** Indoors; Sitting; Standing. **Other Job Characteristics:** Frustrating Circumstances; Consequence of Error; Importance of Being Sure All Is Done.

Experience: Job Zone 4. A minimum of two to four years of work-related skill, knowledge, or experience is needed. **Job Preparation:** SVP 7.0 to less than 8.0—2 years to less than 10 years. **Knowledge:** Therapy and Counseling; Psychology; English Language; Sociology and Anthropology; Administration and Management. **Instructional Programs:** 440201 Community Organization, Resources and Services; 440701 Social Work.

Related DOT Jobs: 195.107-010 Caseworker; 195.107-014 Caseworker, Child Welfare; 195.107-018 Caseworker, Family; 195.107-022 Social Group Worker; 195.107-026 Social Worker, Delinquency Prevention; 195.107-038 Social Worker, School; 195.137-010 Casework Supervisor.

21-1022.00 Medical and Public Health Social Workers
(Social Workers)

Education: No data available.

Employed: 365,600

Openings: No data available.

Projected Growth: No data available.

Earnings: $29,960

Provide persons, families, or vulnerable populations with the psychosocial support needed to cope with chronic, acute, or terminal illnesses such as Alzheimer's, cancer, or AIDS. Advise family caregivers, provide patient education and counseling, and make necessary referrals for other social services.

Modifies treatment plan to comply with changes in client's status. Intervenes as advocate for client or patient to resolve emergency problems in crisis situation. Refers patient, client, or family to community resources to assist in recovery from mental or physical illness. Plans and conducts programs to prevent substance abuse or improve health and counseling services in community. Interviews clients, reviews records, and confers with other professionals to evaluate mental or physical condition of client or patient. Monitors, evaluates, and records client progress according to measurable goals described in treatment and care plan. Formulates or coordinates program plan for treatment, care, and rehabilitation of client or patient, based on social work experience and knowledge. Counsels clients and patients, individually and in group sessions, to assist in overcoming dependencies, adjusting to life, and making changes. Supervises and directs other workers providing services to client or patient. Counsels family members to assist in understanding, dealing with, and supporting client or patient.

GOE Number, Interest Area, and Work Group: 12.02.02; Education and Social Service; Social Services: Counseling and Social Work. **Personality Type:** Social. Social occupations frequently involve working with, communicating with, and teaching people. These occupations often involve helping or providing service to others. **Work Values:** Social Service; Activity; Achievement; Autonomy; Ability Utilization; Responsibility; Security. **Skills:** Social Perceptiveness; Critical Thinking; Service Orientation; Management of Financial Resources; Problem Identification; Active Listening; Reading Comprehension. **Abilities:** *Cognitive*—Oral Comprehension; Problem Sensitivity; Oral Expression; Written Comprehension; Fluency of Ideas. *Psychomotor*—none met the

criteria. *Physical*—none met the criteria. *Sensory*—Speech Clarity; Near Vision; Speech Recognition. **General Work Activities:** *Information Input*—Getting Information Needed to Do the Job; Identifying Objects, Actions, and Events; Monitoring Processes, Materials, and Surroundings. *Mental Process*—Making Decisions and Solving Problems; Analyzing Data or Information; Evaluating Information Against Standards; Processing Information. *Work Output*—Documenting and Recording Information; Implementing Ideas and Programs; Interacting with Computers; Handling and Moving Objects. *Interacting with Others*—Communicating with Persons Outside Organization; Establishing and Maintaining Relationships; Assisting and Caring for Others. **Physical Work Conditions:** Sitting; Indoors; Standing. **Other Job Characteristics:** Consequence of Error; Frustrating Circumstances; Importance of Being Sure All Is Done.

Experience: Job Zone 4. A minimum of two to four years of work-related skill, knowledge, or experience is needed. **Job Preparation:** SVP 7.0 to less than 8.0—2 years to less than 10 years. **Knowledge:** Therapy and Counseling; Psychology; Customer and Personal Service; Education and Training; English Language. **Instructional Programs:** 440201 Community Organization, Resources and Services; 440701 Social Work.

Related DOT Job: 195.107-030 Social Worker, Medical.

21-1023.00 Mental Health and Substance Abuse Social Workers (Social Workers)

Education: No data available.

Employed: 365,600

Openings: No data available.

Projected Growth: No data available.

Earnings: $29,960

Assess and treat individuals with mental, emotional, or substance-abuse problems, including abuse of alcohol, tobacco, and/or other drugs. Provide individual and group therapy, crisis intervention, case management, client advocacy, abuse prevention, and education.

Supervises and directs other workers providing services to client or patient. Plans and conducts programs to prevent substance abuse or improve health and counseling services in community. Modifies treatment plan to comply with changes in client's status. Refers patient, client, or family to community resources to assist in recovery from mental or physical illness. Interviews clients, reviews records, and confers with other professionals to evaluate mental or physical condition of client or patient. Counsels family members to assist in understanding, dealing with, and supporting client or patient. Counsels clients and patients, individually and in group sessions, to assist in overcoming dependencies, adjusting to life, and making changes. Formulates or coordinates program plan for treatment, care, and rehabilitation of client or patient, based on social work experience and knowledge. Intervenes as advocate for client or patient to resolve emergency problems in crisis situation. Monitors, evaluates, and records client progress according to measurable goals described in treatment and care plan.

GOE Number, Interest Area, and Work Group: 12.02.02; Education and Social Service; Social Services: Counseling and Social Work. **Personality Type:** Social. Social occupations frequently involve working with, communicating with, and teaching people. These occupations often involve helping or providing service to others. **Work Values:** Social Service; Activity; Achievement; Autonomy; Ability Utilization; Security; Responsibility. **Skills:** Social Perceptiveness; Problem Identification; Critical Thinking; Active Listening; Service Orientation; Management of Financial Resources; Reading Comprehension. **Abilities:** *Cognitive*—Oral Comprehension; Problem Sensitivity; Oral Expression; Written Comprehension; Fluency of Ideas. *Psychomotor*—none met the criteria. *Physical*—none met the criteria. *Sensory*—Speech Clarity; Near Vision; Speech Recognition. **General Work Activities:** *Information Input*—Getting Information Needed to Do the Job; Identifying Objects, Actions, and Events; Monitoring Processes, Materials, and Surroundings. *Mental Process*—Making Decisions and Solving Problems; Analyzing Data or Information; Processing Information; Evaluating Information Against Standards. *Work Output*—Documenting and Recording Information; Implementing Ideas and Programs; Interacting with Computers; Handling and Moving Objects. *Interacting with Others*—Communicating with Persons Outside Organization; Establishing and Maintaining Relationships; Assisting and Caring for Others. **Physical Work Conditions:** Sitting; Indoors; Standing. **Other Job Characteristics:** Consequence of Error; Frustrating Circumstances; Importance of Being Sure All Is Done.

Experience: Job Zone 4. A minimum of two to four years of work-related skill, knowledge, or experience is needed. **Job Preparation:** SVP 7.0 to less than 8.0—2 years to less than 10 years. **Knowledge:** Therapy and Counseling; Customer and Personal Service; Psychology; Education and Training; English Language. **Instructional Programs:** 440201 Community Organization, Resources and Services; 440701 Social Work.

Related DOT Jobs: 195.107-034 Social Worker, Psychiatric; 195.167-050 Case Manager.

21-1091.00 Health Educators (Social Workers, Medical and Psychiatric)

Education: No data available.

Employed: 218,170

Openings: No data available.

Projected Growth: No data available.

Earnings: $31,620

Promote, maintain, and improve individual and community health by assisting individuals and communities to adopt healthy behaviors. Collect and analyze data to identify community needs; plan, implement, monitor, and evaluate programs to encourage healthy lifestyles, policies, and environments. Serve as a resource for professionals, other individuals, or the community. Administer fiscal resources for health education programs.

Promotes health discussions in schools, industry, and community agencies. Conducts community surveys to ascertain health needs, develop desirable health goals, and determine availability of professional health services. Prepares and disseminates educational and informational materials. Collaborates with health specialists and civic groups to ascertain community health needs, to determine availability of services, and to develop goals. Plans and provides educational opportunities for health personnel. Develops and maintains cooperation between public, civic, professional, and voluntary agencies.

GOE Number, Interest Area, and Work Group: 14.08.01; Medical and Health Services; Health Protection and Promotion. **Personality Type:** Social. Social occupations frequently involve working with, communicating with, and teaching people. These occupations often involve helping or providing service to others. **Work Values:** Achievement; Social Service; Working Conditions; Responsibility; Ability Utilization; Autonomy; Social Status. **Skills:** Speaking; Coordination; Writing; Information Gathering; Active Listening. **Abilities:** *Cognitive*—Oral Expression; Written Comprehension; Written Expression; Oral Comprehension; Inductive Reasoning. *Psychomotor*—none met the criteria. *Physical*—none met the criteria. *Sensory*—Speech Clarity; Speech Recognition; Night Vision. **General Work Activities:** *Information Input*—Getting Information Needed to Do the Job; Identifying Objects, Actions, and Events; Estimating Needed Characteristics. *Mental Process*—Making Decisions and Solving Problems; Updating and Using Job-Relevant Knowledge; Processing Information. *Work Output*—Implementing Ideas and Programs; Documenting and Recording Information; Interacting with Computers. *Interacting with Others*—Communicating with Persons Outside Organization; Establishing and Maintaining Relationships; Teaching Others. **Physical Work Conditions:** Indoors; Sitting; Standing. **Other Job Characteristics:** Consequence of Error; Importance of Being Exact or Accurate; Importance of Being Sure All Is Done; Frustrating Circumstances.

Experience: Job Zone 5. Extensive skill, knowledge, and experience are needed. Very advanced communication and organizational skills are required. **Job Preparation:** SVP 8.0 and above—4 years to more than 10 years. **Knowledge:** Education and Training; English Language; Communications and Media; Customer and Personal Service; Medicine and Dentistry; Therapy and Counseling. **Instructional Programs:** 440701 Social Work; 511503 Clinical and Medical Social Work.

Related DOT Job: 079.117-014 Public Health Educator.

21-1092.00 Probation Officers and Correctional Treatment Specialists (Social Workers, Except Medical and Psychiatric)

Education: No data available.

Employed: 365,600

Openings: No data available.

Projected Growth: No data available.

Earnings: $29,960

Provide social services to assist in rehabilitating law offenders who are in custody, on probation, or on parole. Recommend a rehabilitation and treatment plan for the offender, including conditional release and education and employment stipulations.

Develops and prepares informational packets of social agencies and assistance organizations and programs, for inmate or offender. Counsels offender and refers offender to social resources of community for assistance. Consults with attorneys, judges, and institution personnel to evaluate inmate's social progress. Informs offender or inmate of requirements of conditional release, such as office visits, restitution payments, or educational and employment stipulations. Confers with inmate's or offender's family to identify needs and problems, and to ensure that family and business are attended to. Makes recommendations concerning conditional release or institutionalization of offender or inmate. Assists offender or inmate with matters concerning detainers, sentences in other jurisdictions, writs, and applications for social assistance. Conducts prehearing or presentencing investigations and testifies in court. Determines nature and extent of inmate's or offender's criminal record and current and prospective social problems. Reviews and evaluates legal and social history and progress of offender or inmate. Conducts follow-up interview with offender or inmate to ascertain progress made. Provides guidance to inmates or offenders, such as development of vocational and educational plans and available social services. Formulates rehabilitation plan for each assigned offender or inmate. Prepares and maintains case folder for each assigned inmate or offender. Interviews offender or inmate to determine social progress, individual problems, needs, interests, and attitude.

GOE Number, Interest Area, and Work Group: 12.02.02; Education and Social Service; Social Services: Counseling and Social Work. **Personality Type:** Social. Social occupations frequently involve working with, communicating with, and teaching people. These occupations often involve helping or providing service to others. **Work Values:** Social Service; Security; Activity; Supervision, Human Relations; Company Policies and Practices. **Skills:** Active Listening; Speaking; Service Orientation; Identification of Key Causes; Judgment and Decision Making; Idea Evaluation; Problem Identification; Reading Comprehension. **Abilities:** *Cognitive—* Oral Expression; Oral Comprehension; Problem Sensitivity; Written Comprehension; Written Expression. *Psychomotor—*none met the criteria. *Physical—*none met the criteria. *Sensory—*Speech Clarity; Speech Recognition; Glare Sensitivity. **General Work Activities:** *Information Input—*Getting Information Needed to Do the Job; Identifying Objects, Actions, and Events; Monitoring Processes, Materials, and Surroundings. *Mental Process—*Making Decisions and Solving Problems; Judging Qualities of Things, Services, Other People's Work; Developing Objectives and Strategies. *Work Output—*Documenting and Recording Information; Implementing Ideas and Programs; Interacting with Computers. *Interacting with Others—*Communicating with Persons Outside Organization; Assisting and Caring for Others; Establishing and Maintaining Relationships. **Physical Work Conditions:** Indoors; Sitting; Walking or Running. **Other Job Characteristics:** Consequence of Error; Importance of Being Exact or Accurate; Importance of Being Sure All Is Done.

Experience: Job Zone 3. Previous work-related skill, knowledge, or experience is required. **Job Preparation:** SVP 6.0 to less than 7.0—More than 1 year and less than 4 years. **Knowledge:** Therapy and Counseling; Psychology; Law, Government and Jurisprudence; English Language; Public Safety and Security. **Instructional Programs:** 440201 Community Organization, Resources and Services; 440701 Social Work.

Related DOT Jobs: 166.267-022 Prisoner-Classification Interviewer; 195.107-042 Correctional-Treatment Specialist; 195.107-046 Probation-and-Parole Officer; 195.367-026 Preparole-Counseling Aide.

21-1093.00 Social and Human Service Assistants
(Human Service Workers and Assistants)

Education: Moderate-term O-T-J training

Employed: 268,444

Openings: 91,824

Projected Growth: 52.7%

Earnings: $21,360

Assist professionals from a wide variety of fields, such as psychology, rehabilitation, or social work, to provide client services and support for families. Assist clients in identifying and obtaining available benefits and social and community services. Assist social workers with developing, organizing, and conducting programs to prevent and resolve problems involving substance abuse, human relationships, rehabilitation, or adult daycare.

Assists in planning of food budget, utilizing charts and sample budgets. Demonstrates use and care of equipment for tenant use. Explains rules established by owner or management, such as sanitation and maintenance requirements, and parking regulations. Transports and accompanies clients to shopping area and to appointments, using automobile. Oversees day-to-day group activities of residents in institution. Consults with supervisor concerning programs for individual families. Cares for children in client's home during client's appointments. Assists clients with preparation of forms, such as tax or rent forms. Informs tenants of facilities, such as laundries and playgrounds. Observes and discusses meal preparation and suggests alternate methods of food preparation. Keeps records and prepares reports for owner or management concerning visits with clients. Meets with youth groups to acquaint them with consequences of delinquent acts. Observes clients' food selections and recommends alternate economical and nutritional food choices. Monitors free, supplementary meal program to ensure that the facility is clean and that eligibility guidelines are met for persons receiving meals. Assists in locating housing for displaced individuals. Provides information on and refers individuals to public or private agencies and community services for assistance. Advises clients regarding food stamps, child care, food, money management, sanitation, and housekeeping. Visits individuals in homes or attends group meetings to provide information on agency services, requirements and procedures. Submits to and reviews reports and problems with superior. Interviews individuals and family members to compile information on social, educational, criminal, institutional, or drug history.

GOE Number, Interest Area, and Work Group: 12.02.02; Education and Social Service; Social Services: Counseling and Social Work. **Personality Type:** Social. Social occupations frequently involve working with, communicating with, and teaching people. These occupations often involve helping or providing service to others. **Work Values:** Social Service; Supervision, Human Relations; Company Policies and Practices; Working Conditions; Variety; Activity. **Skills:** Social Perceptiveness; Service Orientation; Speaking; Active Listening; Reading Comprehension. **Abilities:** *Cognitive*—Oral Expression; Oral Comprehension; Written Expression; Written Comprehension; Problem Sensitivity. *Psychomotor*—none met the criteria. *Physical*—none met the criteria. *Sensory*—Speech Recognition. **General Work Activities:** *Information Input*—Getting Information Needed to Do the Job; Identifying Objects, Actions, and Events; Monitoring Processes, Materials, and Surroundings. *Mental Process*—Making Decisions and Solving Problems; Analyzing Data or Information; Organizing, Planning, and Prioritizing. *Work Output*—Documenting and Recording Information; Implementing Ideas and Programs; Performing General Physical Activities. *Interacting with Others*—Assisting and Caring for Others; Communicating with Persons Outside Organization; Providing Consultation and Advice to Others. **Physical Work Conditions:** Indoors; Sitting; Standing. **Other Job Characteristics:** Frustrating Circumstances; Consequence of Error; Importance of Being Sure All Is Done.

Experience: Job Zone 2. Some previous work-related skill, knowledge, or experience may be helpful, but usually is not needed. **Job Preparation:** SVP 4.00 to 5.99—6 months to less than 2 years. **Knowledge:** Customer and Personal Service; Therapy and Counseling; Education and Training; Psychology; Clerical. **Instructional Programs:** 510301 Community Health Liaison; 511501 Alcohol/Drug Abuse Counseling; 511599 Mental Health Services, Other.

Related DOT Jobs: 195.367-010 Case Aide; 195.367-014 Management Aide; 195.367-022 Food-Management Aide; 195.367-034 Social-Services Aide.

21-2000 Religious Workers

21-2011.00 Clergy (Clergy)

Education: First professional degree

Employed: 149,179

Openings: 14,197

Projected Growth: 13.4%

Earnings: $28,850

Conduct religious worship services. Perform various spiritual functions associated with the beliefs and practices of a religious faith or denomination. Provide spiritual and moral guidance and assistance to members.

Interprets doctrine of religion. Counsels those in spiritual need. Visits the sick and shut-ins, and helps the poor. Engages in interfaith, community, civic, educational, and recreational activities sponsored by or related to interest of denomination. Writes articles for publication. Prepares and delivers sermons and other talks. Administers religious rites or ordinances. Leads congregation in worship services. Conducts wedding and funeral services. Instructs people who seek conversion to faith.

GOE Number, Interest Area, and Work Group: 12.02.01; Education and Social Service; Social Services: Religious. **Personality Type:** Social. Social occupations frequently involve working with, communicating with, and teaching people. These occupations often involve helping or providing service to others. **Work Val-**ues: Social Status; Autonomy; Achievement; Social Service; Security. **Skills:** Social Perceptiveness; Speaking; Service Orientation; Active Listening; Writing; Reading Comprehension. **Abilities:** *Cognitive*—Oral Expression; Written Expression; Written Comprehension; Problem Sensitivity; Oral Comprehension. *Psychomotor*—none met the criteria. *Physical*—none met the criteria. *Sensory*—Speech Clarity; Speech Recognition. **General Work Activities:** *Information Input*—Getting Information Needed to Do the Job; Identifying Objects, Actions, and Events; Monitoring Processes, Materials, and Surroundings. *Mental Process*—Organizing, Planning, and Prioritizing; Judging Qualities of Things, Services, Other People's Work; Making Decisions and Solving Problems. *Work Output*—Implementing Ideas and Programs; Handling and Moving Objects; Documenting and Recording Information. *Interacting with Others*—Establishing and Maintaining Relationships; Assisting and Caring for Others; Interpreting Meaning of Information to Others. **Physical Work Conditions:** Indoors; Standing; Special Uniform. **Other Job Characteristics:** Consequence of Error; Importance of Being Sure All Is Done; Frustrating Circumstances.

Experience: Job Zone 5. Extensive skill, knowledge, and experience are needed. Very advanced communication and organizational skills are required. **Job Preparation:** SVP 8.0 and above—4 years to more than 10 years. **Knowledge:** Philosophy and Theology; Education and Training; Psychology; English Language; Therapy and Counseling. **Instructional Programs:** 390601 Theology/Theological Studies; 390602 Divinity/Ministry (B.D., M.Div.); 390604 Pre-Theological/Pre-Ministerial Studies; 390701 Pastoral Counseling and Specialized Ministries; 399999 Theological Studies and Religious Vocations, Other.

Related DOT Job: 120.107-010 Clergy Member.

21-2021.00 Directors, Religious Activities and Education (Directors of Religious Activities and Education)

Education: Bachelor's degree

Employed: 111,599

Openings: 13,292

Projected Growth: 25.1%

Earnings: $24,970

Direct and coordinate activities of a denominational group to meet the religious needs of students. Plan, direct, or coordinate church-school programs to promote religious education among church membership. Provide counseling and guidance relative to marital, health, financial, and religious problems.

Interprets policies of university to community religious workers. Plans congregational activities and projects to encourage participation in religious education programs. Counsels individuals regarding marital, health, financial, and religious problems. Assists and advises groups in promoting interfaith understanding. Plans and conducts conferences dealing with interpretation of religious ideas and convictions. Solicits support, participation, and interest in religious education programs from congregation members, organizations, officials, and clergy. Analyzes member participation and changes in congregation emphasis to determine needs for religious education. Develops, organizes, and directs study courses and religious education programs within congregation. Analyzes revenue and program cost data to determine budget priorities. Orders and distributes school supplies. Supervises instructional staff in religious education program. Promotes student participation in extracurricular congregational activities. Coordinates activities with religious advisers, councils, and university officials to meet religious needs of students. Interprets religious education to public through speaking, leading discussions, and writing articles for local and national publications.

GOE Number, Interest Area, and Work Group: 12.02.01; Education and Social Service; Social Services: Religious. **Personality Type:** Social. Social occupations frequently involve working with, communicating with, and teaching people. These occupations often involve helping or providing service to others. **Work Values:** Social Service; Social Status; Achievement; Working Conditions; Autonomy. **Skills:** Social Perceptiveness; Active Listening; Service Orientation; Writing; Reading Comprehension; Speaking. **Abilities:** *Cognitive*—Oral Expression; Oral Comprehension; Written Expression; Problem Sensitivity; Written Comprehension. *Psychomotor*—none met the criteria. *Physical*—none met the criteria. *Sensory*—Speech Clarity; Speech Recognition. **General Work Activities:** *Information Input*—Getting Information Needed to Do the Job; Identifying Objects, Actions, and Events; Estimating Needed Characteristics; Monitoring Processes, Materials, and Surroundings. *Mental Process*—Organizing, Planning, and Prioritizing; Scheduling Work and Activities; Analyzing Data or Information. *Work Output*—Implementing Ideas and Programs; Documenting and Recording Information; Interacting with Computers; Performing General Physical Activities. *Interacting with Others*—Communicating with Other Workers; Communicating with Persons Outside Organization; Teaching Others; Establishing and Maintaining Relationships; Assisting and Caring for Others; Providing Consultation and Advice to Others. **Physical Work Conditions:** Indoors; Sitting; Standing. **Other Job Characteristics:** Consequence of Error; Frustrating Circumstances; Importance of Being Exact or Accurate; Importance of Being Sure All Is Done.

Experience: Job Zone 5. Extensive skill, knowledge, and experience are needed. Very advanced communication and organizational skills are required. **Job Preparation:** SVP 8.0 and above—4 years to more than 10 years. **Knowledge:** Administration and Management; Therapy and Counseling; Psychology; Education and Training; Sociology and Anthropology; Philosophy and Theology; English Language. **Instructional Programs:** 390201 Bible/Biblical Studies; 390301 Missions/Missionary Studies and Misology; 390401 Religious Education.

Related DOT Jobs: 129.107-018 Director of Religious Activities; 129.107-022 Director, Religious Education.

23-0000
Legal Occupations

23-1000 Lawyers, Judges, and Related Workers

23-1011.00 Lawyers (Lawyers)

Education: First professional degree
Employed: 680,955
Openings: 38,182
Projected Growth: 17.2%
Earnings: $78,170

Represent clients in criminal and civil litigation and other legal proceedings. Draw up legal documents. Advise clients on or manage legal transactions. Specialize in a single area or practice broadly in many areas of law.

Prepares opinions on legal issues. Prepares and drafts legal documents, such as wills, deeds, patent applications, mortgages, leases, and contracts. Prepares and files legal briefs. Interprets laws, rulings, and regulations for individuals and business. Presents evidence to defend client in civil or criminal litigation. Acts as agent, trustee, guardian, or executor for business or individuals. Confers with colleagues with specialty in area of legal issue to establish and verify basis for legal proceeding. Searches for and examines public and other legal records to write opinions or establish ownership. Presents evidence to prosecute defendant in civil or criminal litigation. Advises clients concerning business transactions, claim liability, advisability of prosecuting or defending law suits, or legal rights and obligations. Probates wills and represents and advises executors and administrators of estates. Gathers evidence to formulate defense or to initiate legal actions. Interviews clients and witnesses to ascertain facts of case. Examines legal data to determine advisability of defending or prosecuting lawsuit. Studies constitution, statutes, decisions, regulations, and ordinances of quasi-judicial bodies. Evaluates findings and develops strategy and arguments in preparation for presentation of case. Represents client in court or before government agency. Conducts case, examining and cross-examining witnesses; summarizes case to judge or jury.

GOE Number, Interest Area, and Work Group: 04.02.01; Law, Law Enforcement, and Public Safety; Law: Legal Practice and Justice Administration. **Personality Type:** Enterprising. Enterprising occupations frequently involve starting up and carrying out projects. These occupations can involve leading people and making many decisions. They sometimes require risk taking and often deal with business. **Work Values:** Autonomy; Ability Utilization; Compensation; Responsibility; Achievement. **Skills:** Persuasion; Reading Comprehension; Synthesis/Reorganization; Speaking; Critical Thinking. **Abilities:** *Cognitive*—Oral Comprehension; Written Comprehension; Oral Expression; Written Expression; Deductive Reasoning. *Psychomotor*—none met the criteria. *Physical*—none met the criteria. *Sensory*—Speech Clarity; Speech Recognition; Auditory Attention. **General Work Activities:** *Information Input*—Getting Information Needed to Do the Job; Identifying Objects, Actions, and Events; Estimating Needed Characteristics. *Mental Process*—Updating and Using Job-Relevant Knowledge; Evaluating Information Against Standards; Making Decisions and Solving Problems. *Work Output*—Implementing Ideas and Programs; Documenting and Recording Information; Interacting with Computers. *Interacting with Others*—Interpreting Meaning of Information to Others; Communicating with Persons Outside Organization; Providing Consultation and Advice to Others; Influencing Others or Selling; Communicating with Other Workers. **Physical Work Conditions:** Indoors; Sitting; Standing. **Other Job Characteristics:** Consequence of Error; Importance of Being Exact or Accurate; Importance of Being Sure All Is Done.

Experience: Job Zone 5. Extensive skill, knowledge, and experience are needed. Very advanced communication and organizational skills are required. **Job Preparation:** SVP 8.0 and above—4 years to more than 10 years. **Knowledge:** Law, Government and Jurisprudence; English Language; Administration and Management; Education and Training; Clerical. **Instructional Programs:** 220101 Law (LL.B., J.D.); 220104 Juridical Science/Legal Specialization (LL.M.,M.C.L.,J.S.D./S; 220199 Law and Legal Studies, Other.

Related DOT Jobs: 110.107-010 Lawyer; 110.107-014 Lawyer, Criminal; 110.117-010 District Attorney; 110.117-014 Insurance Attorney; 110.117-018 Lawyer, Admiralty; 110.117-022 Lawyer, Corporation; 110.117-026 Lawyer, Patent; 110.117-030 Lawyer, Probate; 110.117-034 Lawyer, Real Estate; 110.117-038 Tax Attorney; 110.117-042 Title Attorney.

23-1021.00 Administrative Law Judges, Adjudicators, and Hearing Officers (Adjudicators, Hearings Officers, and Judicial Reviewers)

Education: No data available.
Employed: 57,990
Openings: No data available.
Projected Growth: No data available.
Earnings: $33,870

Conduct hearings to decide or recommend decisions on claims concerning government programs or other government-related matters. Prepare decisions. Determine penalties or the existence and amount of liability. Recommend the acceptance or rejection of claims or compromise settlements.

Researches laws, regulations, policies and precedent decisions to prepare for hearings. Notifies claimant of denied claim and appeal rights. Determines existence and amount of liability, according to law, administrative and judicial precedents and evidence. Counsels parties and recommends acceptance or rejection of compromise settlement offers. Prepares written opinions and decisions. Reviews and evaluates data on documents, such as claim applications, birth or death certificates, and physician or employer records. Authorizes payment of valid claims. Questions witnesses to obtain information. Conducts studies of appeals procedures in field agencies to ensure adherence to legal requirements and to facilitate determination of cases. Interviews or corresponds with claimants or agents to elicit information. Analyzes evidence and applicable law, regulations, policy, and precedent decisions to determine conclusions. Rules on exceptions, motions, and admissibility of evidence. Participates in court proceedings. Arranges and conducts hearings to obtain information and evidence relative to disposition of claim. Obtains additional information to clarify evidence. Issues subpoenas and administers oaths to prepare for formal hearing.

GOE Number, Interest Area, and Work Group: 04.02.01; Law, Law Enforcement, and Public Safety; Law: Legal Practice and Justice Administration. **Personality Type:** Enterprising. Enterprising occupations frequently involve starting up and carrying out projects. These occupations can involve leading people and making many decisions. They sometimes require risk taking and often deal with business. **Work Values:** Autonomy; Working Conditions; Security; Responsibility; Ability Utilization. **Skills:** Active Listening; Judgment and Decision Making; Critical Thinking; Reading Comprehension; Information Gathering. **Abilities:** *Cognitive*—Oral Comprehension; Written Comprehension; Oral Expression; Written Expression; Memorization; Inductive Reasoning. *Psychomotor*—none met the criteria. *Physical*—none met the criteria. *Sensory*—Speech Clarity; Speech Recognition; Auditory Attention. **General Work Activities:** *Information Input*—Getting Information Needed to Do the Job; Identifying Objects, Actions, and Events; Monitoring Processes, Materials, and Surroundings. *Mental Process*—Making Decisions and Solving Problems; Evaluating Information Against Standards; Processing Information; Analyzing Data or Information. *Work Output*—Documenting and Recording Information; Implementing Ideas and Programs; Interacting with Computers. *Interacting with Others*—Interpreting Meaning of Information to Others; Communicating with Other Workers; Communicating with Persons Outside Organization. **Physical Work Conditions:** Indoors; Sitting; Standing. **Other Job Characteristics:** Importance of Being Sure All Is Done; Importance of Being Exact or Accurate; Consequence of Error; Frustrating Circumstances.

Experience: Job Zone 5. Extensive skill, knowledge, and experience are needed. Very advanced communication and organizational skills are required. **Job Preparation:** SVP 8.0 and above—4 years to more than 10 years. **Knowledge:** Law, Government and Jurisprudence; English Language; Administration and Management; Psychology; Education and Training; Computers and Electronics; Mathematics. **Instructional Programs:** 220101 Law (LL.B., J.D.); 220199 Law and Legal Studies, Other.

Related DOT Jobs: 119.107-010 Hearing Officer; 119.117-010 Appeals Reviewer, Veteran; 119.167-010 Adjudicator; 119.267-014 Appeals Referee; 169.267-010 Claims Adjudicator.

23-1022.00 Arbitrators, Mediators, and Conciliators
(Adjudicators, Hearings Officers, and Judicial Reviewers)

Education: No data available.

Employed: 57,990

Openings: No data available.

Projected Growth: No data available.

Earnings: $33,870

Facilitate negotiation and conflict resolution through dialogue. Resolve conflicts outside the court system by mutual consent of parties involved.

Counsels parties and recommends acceptance or rejection of compromise settlement offers. Participates in court proceedings. Conducts studies of appeals procedures in field agencies to ensure adherence to legal requirements and to facilitate determination of cases. Analyzes evidence and applicable law, regulations, policy and precedent decisions to determine conclusions. Rules on exceptions, motions and admissibility of evidence. Notifies claimant of denied claim and appeal rights. Determines existence and amount of liability, according to law, administrative and judicial precedents and evidence. Authorizes payment of valid claims. Issues subpoenas and administers oaths to prepare for formal hearing. Researches laws, regulations, policies and precedent decisions to prepare for hearings. Reviews and evaluates data on documents, such as claim applications, birth or death certificates, and physician or employer records. Interviews or corresponds with claimants or agents to elicit information. Prepares written opinions and decisions. Arranges and conducts hearings to obtain information and evidence relative to disposition of claim. Obtains additional information to clarify evidence. Questions witnesses to obtain information.

GOE Number, Interest Area, and Work Group: 04.02.01; Law, Law Enforcement, and Public Safety; Law: Legal Practice and Justice Administration. **Personality Type:** Enterprising. Enterprising occupations frequently involve starting up and carrying out projects. These occupations can involve leading people and making many decisions. They sometimes require risk taking and often deal with business. **Work Values:** Autonomy; Working Conditions; Security; Responsibility; Ability Utilization. **Skills:** Active Listening; Critical Thinking; Judgment and Decision Making; Reading Comprehension; Information Gathering. **Abilities:** *Cognitive*—Written Comprehension; Oral Expression; Oral Comprehension; Written Expression; Inductive Reasoning; Memorization. *Psychomotor*—none met the criteria. *Physical*—none met the criteria. *Sensory*—Speech Clarity; Speech Recognition; Auditory Attention. **General Work Activities:** *Information Input*—Getting Information Needed to Do the Job; Identifying Objects, Actions, and Events; Monitoring Processes, Materials, and Surroundings. *Mental Process*—Making Decisions and Solving Problems; Evaluating Information Against Standards; Processing Information; Analyzing Data or Information. *Work Output*—Documenting and Recording Information; Interacting with Computers; Implementing Ideas and Programs. *Interacting with Others*—Interpreting Meaning of Information to Others; Communicating with Other Workers; Communicating with Persons Outside Organization. **Physical Work Conditions:** Indoors; Sitting; Standing. **Other Job Characteristics:** Importance of Being Sure All Is Done; Importance of Being Exact or Accurate; Consequence of Error; Frustrating Circumstances.

Experience: Job Zone 5. Extensive skill, knowledge, and experience are needed. Very advanced communication and organizational skills are required. **Job Preparation:** SVP 8.0 and above—4 years to more than 10 years. **Knowledge:** Law, Government and Jurisprudence; Administration and Management; English Language; Psychology; Education and Training; Computers and Electronics; Mathematics. **Instructional Programs:** 220101 Law (LL.B., J.D.); 220199 Law and Legal Studies, Other.

Related DOT Jobs: No data available.

23-1023.00 Judges, Magistrate Judges, and Magistrates (Judges and Magistrates)

Education: No data available.

Employed: 24,850

Openings: No data available.

Projected Growth: No data available.

Earnings: $66,900

Arbitrate, advise, adjudicate, or administer justice in a court of law. Sentence defendant in criminal cases according to government statutes. Determine liability of defendant in civil cases. Issue marriage licenses and perform wedding ceremonies.

Sentences defendant in criminal cases, on conviction by jury, according to statutes of state or federal government. Establishes rules of procedure on questions for which standard procedures have not been established by law or by superior court. Awards judicial relief to litigants in civil cases in relation to findings by jury or by court. Settles disputes between opposing attorneys. Performs wedding ceremonies. Rules on admissibility of evidence and methods of conducting testimony. Conducts preliminary hearings in felony cases to determine reasonable and probable cause to hold defendant for further proceedings or trial. Instructs jury on applicable law and directs jury to deduce facts from evidence presented. Listens to presentation of case or allegations of plaintiff. Examines evidence in criminal cases to determine if evidence will support charges.

GOE Number, Interest Area, and Work Group: 04.02.01; Law, Law Enforcement, and Public Safety; Law: Legal Practice and Justice Administration. **Personality Type:** Enterprising. Enterprising occupations frequently involve starting up and carrying out projects. These occupations can involve leading people and making many decisions. They sometimes require risk taking and often deal with business. **Work Values:** Responsibility; Autonomy; Social Status; Security; Working Conditions. **Skills:** Judgment and Decision Making; Reading Comprehension; Active Listening; Critical Thinking; Active Learning. **Abilities:** *Cognitive*—Written Comprehension; Inductive Reasoning; Oral Expression; Oral Comprehension; Deductive Reasoning. *Psychomotor*—none met the criteria. *Physical*—none met the criteria. *Sensory*—Speech Clarity; Near Vision; Speech Recognition. **General Work Activities:** *Information Input*—Getting Information Needed to Do the Job; Identifying Objects, Actions, and Events; Monitoring Processes, Materials, and Surroundings. *Mental Process*—Evaluating Information Against Standards; Analyzing Data or Information; Judging Qualities of Things, Services, Other People's Work. *Work Output*—Implementing Ideas and Programs; Documenting and Recording Information; Performing General Physical Activities. *Interacting with Others*—Resolving Conflict and Negotiating with Others; Interpreting Meaning of Information to Others; Performing for or Working with the Public. **Physical Work Conditions:** Indoors; Special Uniform; Sitting. **Other Job Characteristics:** Consequence of Error; Frustrating Circumstances; Importance of Being Sure All Is Done.

Experience: Job Zone 5. Extensive skill, knowledge, and experience are needed. Very advanced communication and organizational skills are required. **Job Preparation:** SVP 8.0 and above—4 years to more than 10 years. **Knowledge:** Law, Government and Jurisprudence; English Language; Public Safety and Security; Administration and Management; Sociology and Anthropology. **Instructional Programs:** 220101 Law (LL.B., J.D.); 220199 Law and Legal Studies, Other.

Related DOT Jobs: 111.107-010 Judge; 111.107-014 Magistrate.

23-2000 Legal Support Workers

23-2011.00 Paralegals and Legal Assistants (Paralegals and Legal Assistants)

Education: Associate degree

Employed: 136,045

Openings: 33,971

Projected Growth: 62%

Earnings: $32,760

Assist lawyers by researching legal precedent, investigating facts, or preparing legal documents. Conduct research to support a legal proceeding, to formulate a defense, or to initiate legal action.

Presents arguments and evidence to support appeal at appeal hearing. Prepares affidavits or other documents, maintains document file, and files pleadings with court clerk. Answers questions regarding legal issues pertaining to civil service hearings. Directs and coordinates law office activity, including delivery of subpoenas. Prepares legal documents, including briefs, pleadings, appeals, wills, contracts, and real estate closing statements. Keeps and monitors legal volumes to ensure that law library is up-to-date. Calls upon witnesses to testify at hearing. Investigates facts and law of cases to determine causes of action and to prepare cases. Appraises and inventories real and personal property for estate planning. Gathers and analyzes research data, such as statutes, decisions, and legal articles, codes, and documents. Arbitrates disputes between parties and assists in real estate closing process.

GOE Number, Interest Area, and Work Group: 04.02.02; Law, Law Enforcement, and Public Safety; Law: Legal Support. **Personality Type:** Enterprising. Enterprising occupations frequently involve starting up and carrying out projects. These occupations can involve leading people and making many decisions. They sometimes require risk taking and often deal with business. **Work Values:** Working Conditions; Activity; Company Policies and Practices; Ability Utilization; Security; Autonomy. **Skills:** Reading Comprehension; Critical Thinking; Information Gathering; Speaking; Synthesis/Reorganization; Writing. **Abilities:** *Cognitive*—Written Comprehension; Oral Comprehension; Written Expression; Oral Expression; Deductive Reasoning. *Psychomotor*—Wrist-Finger Speed. *Physical*—none met the criteria. *Sensory*—Near Vision; Speech Clarity. **General Work Activities:** *Information Input*—Getting Information Needed to Do the Job; Identifying Objects, Actions, and Events; Estimating Needed Characteristics; Monitoring Processes, Materials, and Surroundings. *Mental Process—*Analyzing Data or Information; Evaluating Information Against Standards; Making Decisions and Solving Problems. *Work Output—*Documenting and Recording Information; Implementing Ideas and Programs; Handling and Moving Objects. *Interacting with Others—*Communicating with Other Workers; Communicating with Persons Outside Organization; Establishing and Maintaining Relationships. **Physical Work Conditions:** Indoors; Sitting; Standing. **Other Job Characteristics:** Consequence of Error; Importance of Being Sure All Is Done; Importance of Being Exact or Accurate.

Experience: Job Zone 4. A minimum of two to four years of work-related skill, knowledge, or experience is needed. **Job Preparation:** SVP 7.0 to less than 8.0—2 years to less than 10 years. **Knowledge:** Law, Government and Jurisprudence; Clerical; English Language; Computers and Electronics; Administration and Management. **Instructional Program:** 220103 Paralegal/Legal Assistant.

Related DOT Jobs: 119.167-014 Patent Agent; 119.267-022 Legal Investigator; 119.267-026 Paralegal.

23-2091.00 Court Reporters (Court Reporters, Medical Transcriptionists, and Stenographers)

Education: Postsecondary vocational training

Employed: 109,953

Openings: 15,612

Projected Growth: 9.7%

Earnings: $25,430

Use verbatim methods and equipment to capture, store, retrieve, and transcribe pretrial and trial proceedings or other information. Includes stenocaptioners who operate computerized stenographic captioning equipment to provide captions of live or prerecorded broadcasts for hearing-impaired viewers.

GOE Number, Interest Area, and Work Group: 09.07.02; Business Detail; Records Processing: Preparation and Maintenance. **Instructional Programs:** 510708 Medical Transcription; 520405 Court Reporter. **Note:** The Department of Labor has not collected some data for this job, so it has fewer details than the other descriptions.

23-2092.00 Law Clerks (Law Clerks)

Education: No data available.

Employed: 43,770

Openings: No data available.

Projected Growth: No data available.

Earnings: $27,430

Assist lawyers or judges by researching or preparing legal documents. Meet with clients or assist lawyers and judges in court.

Appraises and inventories real and personal property for estate planning. Delivers or directs delivery of subpoenas to witness and parties to action. Prepares real estate closing statement and assists in closing process. Stores, catalogs, and maintains currency of legal volumes. Prepares affidavits of documents and maintains document file. Searches patent files to ascertain originality of parent application. Investigates facts and law of case to determine causes of action and to prepare case accordingly. Files pleadings with court clerk. Researches and analyzes law sources to prepare legal documents for review, approval, and use by attorney. Communicates and arbitrates disputes between opposing parties.

GOE Number, Interest Area, and Work Group: 04.02.02; Law, Law Enforcement, and Public Safety; Law: Legal Support. **Personality Type:** Enterprising. Enterprising occupations frequently involve starting up and carrying out projects. These occupations can involve leading people and making many decisions. They sometimes require risk taking and often deal with business. **Work Values:** Working Conditions; Activity; Company Policies and Practices; Security; Achievement; Supervision, Human Relations; Advancement; Ability Utilization. **Skills:** Critical Thinking; Reading Comprehension; Writing; Information Gathering; Active Listening; Active Learning; Information Organization. **Abilities:** *Cognitive—*Written Comprehension; Oral Expression; Written Expression; Oral Comprehension; Number Facility. *Psychomotor—*none met the criteria. *Physical—*none met the criteria. *Sensory—*Near Vision; Speech Clarity; Speech Recognition. **General Work Activities:** *Information Input—*Getting Information Needed to Do the Job; Identifying Objects, Actions, and Events; Monitoring Processes, Materials, and Surroundings; Estimating Needed Characteristics. *Mental Process—*Analyzing Data or Information; Evaluating Information Against Standards; Making Decisions and Solving Problems. *Work Output—*Documenting and Recording Information; Implementing Ideas and Programs; Interacting with Computers. *Interacting with Others—*Communicating with Other Workers; Communicating with Persons Outside Organization; Performing Administrative Activities. **Physical Work Conditions:** Indoors; Sitting; Using Hands on Objects, Tools, or Controls; Walking or Running; Standing. **Other Job Characteristics:** Importance of Being Sure All Is Done; Consequence of Error; Importance of Being Exact or Accurate.

Experience: Job Zone 4. A minimum of two to four years of work-related skill, knowledge, or experience is needed. **Job Preparation:** SVP 7.0 to less than 8.0—2 years to less than 10 years. **Knowledge:** Law, Government and Jurisprudence; English Language; Clerical; Communications and Media; Mathematics; Computers and Electronics. **Instructional Program:** 220101 Law (LL.B., J.D.).

Related DOT Job: 119.267-026 Paralegal.

23-2093.00 Title Examiners, Abstractors, and Searchers (Title Examiners and Abstractors)

Education: No data available.

Employed: 16,820

Openings: No data available.

Projected Growth: No data available.

Earnings: $29,100

Search real estate records, examine titles, or summarize pertinent legal or insurance details for a variety of purposes. Compile lists of mortgages, contracts, and other instruments pertaining to titles by searching public and private records for law firms, real estate agencies, or title insurance companies.

GOE Number, Interest Area, and Work Group: 04.02.02; Law, Law Enforcement, and Public Safety; Law: Legal Support. **Instructional Program:** 220103 Paralegal/Legal Assistant. **Note:** The Department of Labor has not collected some data for this job, so it has fewer details than the other descriptions.

23-2093.01 Title Searchers (Title Searchers)

Education: No data available.

Employed: 11,000

Openings: No data available.

Projected Growth: No data available.

Earnings: $23,930

Compile list (chain) of mortgages, deeds, contracts, judgments, and other instruments pertaining to title by searching public and private records of real estate or title insurance company.

Prepares title commitment and final policy of title insurance based on information compiled from title search. Reads search request to ascertain type of title evidence required and to obtain description of property and names of involved parties. Compiles information and documents required for title binder. Confers with realtors, lending institution personnel, buyers, sellers, contractors, surveyors, and courthouse personnel to obtain additional information. Retrieves and examines closing files for accuracy, to ensure that information included is recorded and executed according to regulations. Prepares closing statement, utilizing knowledge and expertise in real estate procedures. Examines title to determine if there are restrictions limiting use of property, lists restrictions, and indicates action needed for clear title. Uses computerized system to retrieve additional documentation needed to complete real estate transaction. Requisitions maps or drawings delineating property from company title plant, county surveyor, or assessor's office. Searches lot books, geographic and general indices, and assessor's rolls to compile lists of transactions pertaining to property. Compares legal description of property with legal description contained in records and indices, to verify such factors as deed ownership.

GOE Number, Interest Area, and Work Group: 04.02.02; Law, Law Enforcement, and Public Safety; Law: Legal Support. **Personality Type:** Conventional. Conventional occupations frequently involve following set procedures and routines. These occupations can include working with data and details more than with ideas. Usually there is a clear line of authority to follow. **Work Values:** Independence; Company Policies and Practices; Working Conditions; Moral Values; Supervision, Human Relations; Security. **Skills:** Information Gathering; Reading Comprehension; Writing; Speaking; Information Organization. **Abilities:** *Cognitive*—Written Comprehension; Written Expression; Oral Comprehension; Oral Expression; Perceptual Speed; Speed of Closure. *Psychomotor*—Wrist-Finger Speed. *Physical*—none met the criteria. *Sensory*—Near Vision. **General Work Activities:** *Information Input*—Getting Information Needed to Do the Job; Identifying Objects, Actions, and Events; Estimating Needed Characteristics. *Mental Process*—Evaluating Information Against Standards; Processing Information; Analyzing Data or Information. *Work Output*—Documenting and Recording Information; Interacting with Computers; Handling and Moving Objects. *Interacting with Others*—Communicating with Persons Outside Organization; Establishing and Maintaining Relationships; Interpreting Meaning of Information to Others. **Physical Work Conditions:** Indoors; Sitting; Using Hands on Objects, Tools, or Controls. **Other Job Characteristics:** Importance of Being Exact or Accurate; Importance of Being Sure All Is Done; Degree of Automation.

Experience: Job Zone 2. Some previous work-related skill, knowledge, or experience may be helpful, but usually is not needed. **Job Preparation:** SVP 4.00 to 5.99—6 months to less than 2 years. **Knowledge:** Law, Government and Jurisprudence; Clerical; English Language; Computers and Electronics; Geography. **Instructional Program:** 220103 Paralegal/Legal Assistant.

Related DOT Job: 209.367-046 Title Searcher.

23-2093.02 Title Examiners and Abstractors (Title Examiners and Abstractors)

Education: No data available.

Employed: 16,820

Openings: No data available.

Projected Growth: No data available.

Earnings: $29,100

Title Examiners search public records and examine titles to determine legal condition of property title. Copy or prepare summaries (abstracts) of recorded documents that affect condition of title to property, such as mortgages, trust deeds, and contracts. Prepare and issue policy that guarantees legality of title. Abstractors summarize pertinent legal or insurance details or sections of statutes or case law from reference books, for purpose of examination, proof, or ready reference. Search out titles, to determine whether title deed is correct.

Confers with interested parties to resolve problems and impart information. Analyzes encumbrances to title, statutes and case law, and prepares report outlining encumbrances and actions required to clear title. Examines mortgages, liens, judgments, easements, plat books, maps, contracts, and agreements to verify legal description, ownership, restrictions, or conformity to requirements. Prepares correspondence and other records. Prepares and issues title insurance policy. Searches records to determine if delinquent taxes are due. Copies or summarizes recorded documents, such as mortgages, trust deeds, and contracts, affecting title to property. Directs activities of workers searching records and examining titles to real property.

GOE Number, Interest Area, and Work Group: 04.02.02; Law, Law Enforcement, and Public Safety; Law: Legal Support. **Personality Type:** Conventional. Conventional occupations frequently involve following set procedures and routines. These occupations can include working with data and details more than with ideas. Usually there is a clear line of authority to follow. **Work Values:** Company Policies and Practices; Independence; Security; Working Conditions; Supervision, Human Relations; Autonomy. **Skills:** Reading Comprehension; Information Gathering; Information Organization; Writing; Critical Thinking. **Abilities:** *Cognitive*—Written Comprehension; Written Expression; Oral Expression; Deductive Reasoning; Number Facility. *Psychomotor*—none met the criteria. *Physical*—none met the criteria. *Sensory*—Near Vision; Speech Clarity; Speech Recognition. **General Work Activities:** *Information Input*—Getting Information Needed to Do the Job; Identifying Objects, Actions, and Events; Estimating Needed Characteristics. *Mental Process*—Analyzing Data or Information; Processing Information; Evaluating Information Against Standards. *Work Output*—Documenting and Recording Information; Implementing Ideas and Programs; Handling and Moving Objects. *Interacting with Others*—Interpreting Meaning of Information to Others; Resolving Conflict and Negotiating with Others; Communicating with Persons Outside Organization. **Physical Work Conditions:** Indoors; Sitting; Using Hands on Objects, Tools, or Controls. **Other Job Characteristics:** Importance of Being Exact or Accurate; Consequence of Error; Importance of Being Sure All Is Done.

Experience: Job Zone 3. Previous work-related skill, knowledge, or experience is required. **Job Preparation:** SVP 6.0 to less than 7.0—More than 1 year and less than 4 years. **Knowledge:** Law, Government and Jurisprudence; English Language; Clerical; Mathematics; Computers and Electronics; Administration and Management. **Instructional Program:** 220103 Paralegal/Legal Assistant.

Related DOT Jobs: 119.167-018 Title Supervisor; 119.267-010 Abstractor; 119.287-010 Title Examiner; 162.267-010 Title Clerk.

25-0000
Education, Training, and Library Occupations

25-1000 Postsecondary Teachers

25-1011.00 Business Teachers, Postsecondary (College and University Faculty)

Education: Doctoral degree

Employed: 865,356

Openings: 139,101

Projected Growth: 22.6%

Earnings: No data available.

Teach courses in business administration and management, such as accounting, finance, human resources, labor relations, marketing, and operations research.

GOE Number, Interest Area, and Work Group: 12.03.02; Education and Social Service; Educational Services: Postsecondary and Adult Teaching and Instructing. **Instructional Programs:** 520101 Business, General; 520201 Business Administration and Management, General; 520301 Accounting. **Note:** The Department of Labor has not collected some data for this job, so it has fewer details than the other descriptions.

25-1021.00 Computer Science Teachers, Postsecondary (College and University Faculty)

Education: Doctoral degree

Employed: 865,356

Openings: 139,101

Projected Growth: 22.6%

Earnings: No data available.

Teach courses in computer science. Specialize in a field of computer science, such as the design and function of computers or operations and research analysis.

Conducts research in particular field of knowledge and publishes findings in professional journals. Prepares and delivers lectures to students. Compiles bibliographies of specialized materials for outside reading assignments. Stimulates class discussions. Compiles, administers, and grades examinations, or assigns this work to others. Serves on faculty committee providing professional consulting services to government and industry. Advises students on academic and vocational curricula. Directs research of other teachers or graduate students working for advanced academic degrees. Acts as adviser to student organizations.

GOE Number, Interest Area, and Work Group: 12.03.02; Education and Social Service; Educational Services: Postsecondary and Adult Teaching and Instructing. **Personality Type:** Investigative. Investigative occupations frequently involve working with ideas and require an extensive amount of thinking. These occupations can involve searching for facts and figuring out problems mentally. **Work Values:** Achievement; Ability Utilization; Authority; Working Conditions; Autonomy. **Skills:** Instructing;

Reading Comprehension; Writing; Information Gathering; Active Learning. **Abilities:** *Cognitive*—Written Comprehension; Oral Expression; Written Expression; Oral Comprehension; Information Ordering; Deductive Reasoning. *Psychomotor*—Finger Dexterity; Wrist-Finger Speed; Multilimb Coordination; Response Orientation. *Physical*—Gross Body Coordination; Gross Body Equilibrium. *Sensory*—Speech Clarity; Far Vision; Near Vision. **General Work Activities:** *Information Input*—Getting Information Needed to Do the Job; Identifying Objects, Actions, and Events; Monitoring Processes, Materials, and Surroundings. *Mental Process*—Updating and Using Job-Relevant Knowledge; Evaluating Information Against Standards; Processing Information; Analyzing Data or Information; Making Decisions and Solving Problems. *Work Output*—Interacting with Computers; Handling and Moving Objects; Documenting and Recording Information. *Interacting with Others*—Teaching Others; Communicating with Persons Outside Organization; Interpreting Meaning of Information to Others. **Physical Work Conditions:** Indoors; Sitting; Using Hands on Objects, Tools, or Controls. **Other Job Characteristics:** Frustrating Circumstances; Degree of Automation; Importance of Being Exact or Accurate; Importance of Being Sure All Is Done.

Experience: Job Zone 5. Extensive skill, knowledge, and experience are needed. Very advanced communication and organizational skills are required. **Job Preparation:** SVP 8.0 and above—4 years to more than 10 years. **Knowledge:** Computers and Electronics; Education and Training; Mathematics; English Language; Administration and Management. **Instructional Programs:** 110101 Computer and Information Sciences, General; 110201 Computer Programming; 110401 Information Sciences and Systems; 110501 Computer Systems Analysis; 110701 Computer Science.

Related DOT Job: 090.227-010 Faculty Member, College or University.

25-1022.00 Mathematical Science Teachers, Postsecondary (College and University Faculty)

Education: Doctoral degree

Employed: 865,356

Openings: 139,101

Projected Growth: 22.6%

Earnings: No data available.

Teach courses pertaining to mathematical concepts, statistics, and actuarial science. Teach courses pertaining to the application of original and standardized mathematical techniques in solving specific problems and situations.

Serves on faculty committee providing professional consulting services to government and industry. Compiles, administers, and grades examinations, or assigns this work to others. Stimulates class discussions. Acts as adviser to student organizations. Advises students on academic and vocational curricula. Compiles bibliographies of specialized materials for outside reading assignments. Prepares and delivers lectures to students. Directs research of other teachers or graduate students working for advanced academic degrees. Conducts research in particular field of knowledge and publishes findings in professional journals.

GOE Number, Interest Area, and Work Group: 12.03.02; Education and Social Service; Educational Services: Postsecondary and Adult Teaching and Instructing. **Personality Type:** Investigative. Investigative occupations frequently involve working with ideas and require an extensive amount of thinking. These occupations can involve searching for facts and figuring out problems mentally. **Work Values:** Achievement; Ability Utilization; Authority; Working Conditions; Autonomy. **Skills:** Mathematics; Reading Comprehension; Learning Strategies; Instructing; Active Learning; Writing. **Abilities:** *Cognitive*—Written Comprehension; Mathematical Reasoning; Oral Expression; Written Expression; Number Facility; Oral Comprehension. *Psychomotor*—none met the criteria. *Physical*—none met the criteria. *Sensory*—Speech Clarity. **General Work Activities:** *Information Input*—Getting Information Needed to Do the Job; Monitoring Processes, Materials, and Surroundings; Estimating Needed Characteristics; Identifying Objects, Actions, and Events. *Mental Process*—Updating and Using Job-Relevant Knowledge; Judging Qualities of Things, Services, Other People's Work; Organizing, Planning, and Prioritizing. *Work Output*—Implementing Ideas and Programs; Documenting and Recording Information; Interacting with Computers. *Interacting with Others*—Teaching Others; Interpreting Meaning of Information to Others; Communicating with Other Workers. **Physical Work Conditions:** Indoors; Standing; Sitting. **Other Job Characteristics:** Importance of Being Sure All Is Done; Importance of Being Exact or Accurate; Consequence of Error.

Experience: Job Zone 5. Extensive skill, knowledge, and experience are needed. Very advanced communication and organizational skills are required. **Job Preparation:** SVP 8.0 and above—4 years to more than 10 years. **Knowledge:** Education and Training; Mathematics; English Language; Computers and Electronics; Administration and Management; Clerical. **Instructional Program:** 300801 Mathematics and Computer Science.

Related DOT Job: 090.227-010 Faculty Member, College or University.

25-1031.00 Architecture Teachers, Postsecondary
(College and University Faculty)

Education: Doctoral degree
Employed: 865,356
Openings: 139,101
Projected Growth: 22.6%
Earnings: No data available.

Teach courses in architecture and architectural design, such as architectural environmental design, interior architecture/design, and landscape architecture.

GOE Number, Interest Area, and Work Group: 12.03.02; Education and Social Service; Educational Services: Postsecondary and Adult Teaching and Instructing. **Instructional Program:** 040201 Architecture. **Note:** The Department of Labor has not collected some data for this job, so it has fewer details than the other descriptions.

25-1032.00 Engineering Teachers, Postsecondary
(College and University Faculty)

Education: Doctoral degree
Employed: 865,356
Openings: 139,101
Projected Growth: 22.6%
Earnings: No data available.

Teach courses pertaining to the application of physical laws and principles of engineering to the development of machines, materials, instruments, processes, and services. Includes teachers of subjects such as chemical, civil, electrical, industrial, mechanical, mineral, and petroleum engineering. Includes both teachers primarily engaged in teaching and those who do a combination of teaching and research.

Directs research of other teachers or graduate students working for advanced academic degrees. Compiles bibliographies of specialized materials for outside reading assignments. Stimulates class discussions. Compiles, administers, and grades examinations, or assigns this work to others. Acts as adviser to student organizations. Conducts research in particular field of knowledge and publishes findings in professional journals. Advises students on academic and vocational curricula. Prepares and delivers lectures to students. Serves on faculty committee providing professional consulting services to government and industry.

GOE Number, Interest Area, and Work Group: 12.03.02; Education and Social Service; Educational Services: Postsecondary and Adult Teaching and Instructing. **Personality Type:** Investigative. Investigative occupations frequently involve working with ideas and require an extensive amount of thinking. These occupations can involve searching for facts and figuring out problems mentally. **Work Values:** Ability Utilization; Achievement; Authority; Working Conditions; Responsibility; Autonomy. **Skills:** Mathematics; Reading Comprehension; Active Learning; Science; Critical Thinking. **Abilities:** *Cognitive*—Oral Comprehension; Written Comprehension; Oral Expression; Written Expression; Mathematical Reasoning. *Psychomotor*—none met the criteria. *Physical*—none met the criteria. *Sensory*—Speech Clarity; Far Vision; Speech Recognition. **General Work Activities:** *Information Input*—Getting Information Needed to Do the Job; Estimating Needed Characteristics; Identifying Objects, Actions, and Events. *Mental Process*—Updating and Using Job-Relevant Knowledge; Processing Information; Judging Qualities of Things, Services, Other People's Work; Analyzing Data or Information. *Work Output*—Documenting and Recording Information; Implementing Ideas and Programs; Interacting with Computers. *Interacting with Others*—Teaching Others; Interpreting Meaning of Information to Others; Communicating with Other Workers. **Physical Work Conditions:** Indoors; Sitting; Standing. **Other Job Characteristics:** Importance of Being Exact or Accurate; Importance of Being Sure All Is Done; Consequence of Error.

Experience: Job Zone 5. Extensive skill, knowledge, and experience are needed. Very advanced communication and organizational skills are required. **Job Preparation:** SVP 8.0 and above—4 years to more than 10 years. **Knowledge:** Engineering and Technology; Education and Training; Mathematics; Physics; Design; English Language. **Instructional Programs:** 140101 Engineering, General; 140201 Aerospace, Aeronautical and Astronautical Engineering; 140301 Agricultural Engineering; 140401 Architectural Engineering; 140501 Bioengineering and Biomedical Engineering; 140701 Chemical Engineering; 140801 Civil Engineering, General; 140802 Geotechnical Engineering; 140803 Structural Engineering; 140804 Transportation and Highway Engineering; 140805 Water Resources Engineering; 140901 Computer Engineering; 141001 Electrical, Electronics and Communication Engineering; 141101 Engineering Mechanics; 141201 Engineering Physics.

Related DOT Job: 090.227-010 Faculty Member, College or University.

25-1041.00 Agricultural Sciences Teachers, Postsecondary (College and University Faculty)

Education: Doctoral degree
Employed: 865,356
Openings: 139,101
Projected Growth: 22.6%
Earnings: No data available.

Teach courses in the agricultural sciences. Includes teachers of agronomy, dairy sciences, fisheries management, horticultural sciences, poultry sciences, range management, and agricultural soil conservation.

Advises students on academic and vocational curricula. Stimulates class discussions. Directs research of other teachers or graduate students working for advanced academic degrees. Compiles bibliographies of specialized materials for outside reading assignments. Acts as adviser to student organizations. Compiles, administers, and grades examinations, or assigns this work to others. Prepares and delivers lectures to students. Serves on faculty committee providing professional consulting services to government and industry. Conducts research in particular field of knowledge and publishes findings in professional journals.

GOE Number, Interest Area, and Work Group: 12.03.02; Education and Social Service; Educational Services: Postsecondary and Adult Teaching and Instructing. **Personality Type:** Investigative. Investigative occupations frequently involve working with ideas and require an extensive amount of thinking. These occupations can involve searching for facts and figuring out problems mentally. **Work Values:** Achievement; Ability Utilization; Authority; Responsibility; Social Service; Social Status; Autonomy; Working Conditions. **Skills:** Reading Comprehension; Instructing; Learning Strategies; Writing; Active Learning; Science; Critical Thinking. **Abilities:** *Cognitive*—Oral Expression; Written Expression; Written Comprehension; Oral Comprehension; Deductive Reasoning; Fluency of Ideas. *Psychomotor*—none met the criteria. *Physical*—none met the criteria. *Sensory*—Speech Clarity; Speech Recognition. **General Work Activities:** *Information Input*—Getting Information Needed to Do the Job; Identifying Objects, Actions, and Events; Estimating Needed Characteristics. *Mental Process*— Judging Qualities of Things, Services, Other People's Work; Processing Information; Updating and Using Job-Relevant Knowledge; Organizing, Planning, and Prioritizing; Ana-

lyzing Data or Information. *Work Output*—Implementing Ideas and Programs; Documenting and Recording Information; Handling and Moving Objects. *Interacting with Others*—Teaching Others; Coaching and Developing Others; Communicating with Other Workers. **Physical Work Conditions:** Indoors; Sitting; Standing. **Other Job Characteristics:** Importance of Being Sure All Is Done; Consequence of Error; Importance of Being Exact or Accurate.

Experience: Job Zone 5. Extensive skill, knowledge, and experience are needed. Very advanced communication and organizational skills are required. **Job Preparation:** SVP 8.0 and above—4 years to more than 10 years. **Knowledge:** Education and Training; Biology; Psychology; Chemistry; English Language. **Instructional Programs:** 020101 Agriculture/Agricultural Sciences, General; 020201 Animal Sciences, General; 020202 Agricultural Animal Breeding and Genetics; 020203 Agricultural Animal Health; 020204 Agricultural Animal Nutrition; 020206 Dairy Science; 020209 Poultry Science; 020301 Food Sciences and Tech.; 020401 Plant Sciences, General; 020402 Agronomy and Crop Science; 020403 Horticulture Science; 020405 Plant Breeding and Genetics; 020406 Agricultural Plant Pathology; 020407 Agricultural Plant Physiology; 020408 Plant Protection (Pest Management).

Related DOT Job: 090.227-010 Faculty Member, College or University.

25-1042.00 Biological Science Teachers, Postsecondary (College and University Faculty)

Education: Doctoral degree
Employed: 865,356
Openings: 139,101
Projected Growth: 22.6%
Earnings: No data available.

Teach courses in biological sciences.

Acts as adviser to student organizations. Compiles bibliographies of specialized materials for outside reading assignments. Stimulates class discussions. Advises students on academic and vocational curricula. Serves on faculty committee providing professional consulting services to government and industry. Directs research of other teachers or graduate students working for advanced academic degrees. Compiles, administers, and grades examinations, or assigns this work to others. Prepares and delivers lectures to students. Conducts research in particular field of knowledge and publishes findings in professional journals.

GOE Number, Interest Area, and Work Group: 12.03.02; Education and Social Service; Educational Services: Postsecondary and Adult Teaching and Instructing. **Personality Type:** Investigative. Investigative occupations frequently involve working with ideas and require an extensive amount of thinking. These occupations can involve searching for facts and figuring out problems mentally. **Work Values:** Achievement; Ability Utilization; Authority; Autonomy; Creativity; Social Status; Responsibility; Working Conditions. **Skills:** Reading Comprehension; Instructing; Learning Strategies; Active Learning; Science; Critical Thinking; Writing. **Abilities:** *Cognitive*—Oral Expression; Written Expression; Written Comprehension; Oral Comprehension; Fluency of Ideas; Deductive Reasoning. *Psychomotor*—none met the criteria. *Physical*—none met the criteria. *Sensory*—Speech Clarity; Speech Recognition. **General Work Activities:** *Information Input*—Getting Information Needed to Do the Job; Estimating Needed Characteristics; Identifying Objects, Actions, and Events. *Mental Process*—Judging Qualities of Things, Services, Other People's Work; Processing Information; Updating and Using Job-Relevant Knowledge; Organizing, Planning, and Prioritizing; Analyzing Data or Information. *Work Output*—Implementing Ideas and Programs; Documenting and Recording Information; Handling and Moving Objects. *Interacting with Others*—Teaching Others; Coaching and Developing Others; Communicating with Other Workers. **Physical Work Conditions:** Indoors; Sitting; Standing. **Other Job Characteristics:** Importance of Being Sure All Is Done; Consequence of Error; Importance of Being Exact or Accurate.

Experience: Job Zone 5. Extensive skill, knowledge, and experience are needed. Very advanced communication and organizational skills are required. **Job Preparation:** SVP 8.0 and above—4 years to more than 10 years. **Knowledge:** Education and Training; Biology; Psychology; Chemistry; English Language. **Instructional Programs:** 260101 Biology, General; 260202 Biochemistry; 260203 Biophysics; 260301 Botany, General; 260305 Plant Pathology; 260401 Cell Biology; 260402 Molecular Biology; 260501 Microbiology/Bacteriology; 260601 Anatomy; 260603 Ecology; 260607 Marine/Aquatic Biology; 260608 Neuroscience; 260609 Nutritional Sciences; 260610 Parasitology; 260611 Radiation Biology/Radiobiology.

Related DOT Job: 090.227-010 Faculty Member, College or University.

25-1043.00 Forestry and Conservation Science Teachers, Postsecondary (College and University Faculty)

Education: Doctoral degree
Employed: 865,356
Openings: 139,101
Projected Growth: 22.6%
Earnings: No data available.

Teach courses in environmental and conservation science.

Compiles, administers, and grades examinations, or assigns this work to others. Serves on faculty committee providing professional consulting services to government and industry. Compiles bibliographies of specialized materials for outside reading assignments. Stimulates class discussions. Prepares and delivers lectures to students. Conducts research in particular field of knowledge and publishes findings in professional journals. Advises students on academic and vocational curricula. Directs research of other teachers or graduate students working for advanced academic degrees. Acts as adviser to student organizations.

GOE Number, Interest Area, and Work Group: 12.03.02; Education and Social Service; Educational Services: Postsecondary and Adult Teaching and Instructing. **Personality Type:** Investigative. Investigative occupations frequently involve working with ideas and require an extensive amount of thinking. These occupations can involve searching for facts and figuring out problems mentally. **Work Values:** Achievement; Ability Utilization; Authority; Social Status; Autonomy; Creativity; Responsibility; Working Conditions. **Skills:** Reading Comprehension; Instructing; Learning Strategies; Critical Thinking; Active Learning; Science; Writing. **Abilities:** *Cognitive*—Oral Expression; Written Expression; Written Comprehension; Oral Comprehension; Deductive Reasoning; Fluency of Ideas. *Psychomotor*—none met the criteria. *Physical*—none met the criteria. *Sensory*—Speech Clarity; Speech Recognition. **General Work Activities:** *Information Input*—Getting Information Needed to Do the Job; Identifying Objects, Actions, and Events; Estimating Needed Characteristics. *Mental Process*—Judging Qualities of Things, Services, Other People's Work; Processing Information; Analyzing Data or Information; Organizing, Planning, and Prioritizing; Updating and Using Job-Relevant Knowledge. *Work Output*—Implementing Ideas and Programs; Documenting and Recording Information; Handling and Moving Objects. *Interacting with Others*—Teaching Others; Coaching and Developing Others; Communicating with Other Workers. **Physical Work Conditions:** Indoors; Sitting; Standing. **Other Job Characteristics:** Importance of Being Sure All Is Done; Consequence of Error; Importance of Being Exact or Accurate.

Experience: Job Zone 5. Extensive skill, knowledge, and experience are needed. Very advanced communication and organizational skills are required. **Job Preparation:** SVP 8.0 and above—4 years to more than 10 years. **Knowledge:** Education and Training; Biology; Psychology; Chemistry; English Language. **Instructional Programs:** 030501 Forestry, General; 030502 Forestry Sciences; 030506 Forest Management; 030601 Wildlife and Wildlands Management.

Related DOT Job: 090.227-010 Faculty Member, College or University.

25-1051.00 Atmospheric, Earth, Marine, and Space Sciences Teachers, Postsecondary (College and University Faculty)

Education: Doctoral degree
Employed: 865,356
Openings: 139,101
Projected Growth: 22.6%
Earnings: No data available.

Teach courses in the physical sciences, except chemistry and physics.

GOE Number, Interest Area, and Work Group: 12.03.02; Education and Social Service; Educational Services: Postsecondary and Adult Teaching and Instructing. **Instructional Programs:** 400401 Atmospheric Sciences and Meteorology; 400601 Geology; 400602 Geochemistry; 400603 Geophysics and Seismology; 400604 Paleontology; 400699 Geological and Related Sciences, Other; 400703 Earth and Planetary Sciences. **Note:** The Department of Labor has not collected some data for this job, so it has fewer details than the other descriptions.

25-1052.00 Chemistry Teachers, Postsecondary
(College and University Faculty)

Education: Doctoral degree
Employed: 865,356
Openings: 139,101
Projected Growth: 22.6%
Earnings: No data available.

Teach courses pertaining to the chemical and physical properties and compositional changes of substances. Provide instruction in the methods of qualitative and quantitative chemical analysis. Includes both teachers primarily engaged in teaching and those who do a combination of teaching and research.

Advises students on academic and vocational curricula. Compiles, administers, and grades examinations, or assigns this work to others. Stimulates class discussions. Compiles bibliographies of specialized materials for outside reading assignments. Serves on faculty committee providing professional consulting services to government and industry. Conducts research in particular field of knowledge and publishes findings in professional journals. Directs research of other teachers or graduate students working for advanced academic degrees. Prepares and delivers lectures to students. Acts as adviser to student organizations.

GOE Number, Interest Area, and Work Group: 12.03.02; Education and Social Service; Educational Services: Postsecondary and Adult Teaching and Instructing. **Personality Type:** Investigative. Investigative occupations frequently involve working with ideas and require an extensive amount of thinking. These occupations can involve searching for facts and figuring out problems mentally. **Work Values:** Achievement; Ability Utilization; Autonomy; Authority; Working Conditions; Creativity; Social Status; Responsibility. **Skills:** Writing; Reading Comprehension; Instructing; Learning Strategies; Active Learning. **Abilities:** *Cognitive*—Oral Expression; Written Comprehension; Oral Comprehension; Written Expression; Information Ordering. *Psychomotor*—Finger Dexterity; Arm-Hand Steadiness; Manual Dexterity. *Physical*—none met the criteria. *Sensory*—Speech Clarity; Far Vision; Near Vision. **General Work Activities:** *Information Input*—Getting Information Needed to Do the Job; Identifying Objects, Actions, and Events; Monitoring Processes, Materials, and Surroundings. *Mental Process*—Analyzing Data or Information; Updating and Using Job-Relevant Knowledge; Processing Information. *Work Output*—Documenting and Recording Information; Handling and Moving Objects; Interacting with Computers; Implementing Ideas and Programs. *Interacting with Others*—Teaching Others; Interpreting Meaning of Information to Others; Communicating with Persons Outside Organization. **Physical Work Conditions:** Indoors; Sitting; Standing. **Other Job Characteristics:** Frustrating Circumstances; Importance of Being Exact or Accurate; Importance of Being Sure All Is Done; Consequence of Error.

Experience: Job Zone 5. Extensive skill, knowledge, and experience are needed. Very advanced communication and organizational skills are required. **Job Preparation:** SVP 8.0 and above—4 years to more than 10 years. **Knowledge:** Chemistry; Mathematics; Education and Training; English Language; Administration

and Management. **Instructional Programs:** 400501 Chemistry, General; 400502 Analytical Chemistry; 400503 Inorganic Chemistry; 400504 Organic Chemistry; 400505 Medicinal/Pharmaceutical Chemistry; 400507 Polymer Chemistry.

Related DOT Job: 090.227-010 Faculty Member, College or University.

25-1053.00 Environmental Science Teachers, Postsecondary (College and University Faculty)

Education: Doctoral degree
Employed: 865,356
Openings: 139,101
Projected Growth: 22.6%
Earnings: No data available.

Teach courses in environmental science.

GOE Number, Interest Area, and Work Group: 12.03.02; Education and Social Service; Educational Services: Postsecondary and Adult Teaching and Instructing. **Instructional Program:** 030102 Environmental Science/Studies. **Note:** The Department of Labor has not collected some data for this job, so it has fewer details than the other descriptions.

25-1054.00 Physics Teachers, Postsecondary (College and University Faculty)

Education: Doctoral degree
Employed: 865,356
Openings: 139,101
Projected Growth: 22.6%
Earnings: No data available.

Teach courses pertaining to the laws of matter and energy. Includes both teachers primarily engaged in teaching and those who do a combination of teaching and research.

Acts as adviser to student organizations. Serves on faculty committee providing professional consulting services to government and industry. Compiles, administers, and grades examinations, or assigns this work to others. Stimulates class discussions. Directs research of other teachers or graduate students working for advanced academic degrees. Prepares and delivers lectures to students. Conducts research in particular field of knowledge and publishes findings in professional journals. Advises students on academic and vocational curricula. Compiles bibliographies of specialized materials for outside reading assignments.

GOE Number, Interest Area, and Work Group: 12.03.02; Education and Social Service; Educational Services: Postsecondary and Adult Teaching and Instructing. **Personality Type:** Investigative. Investigative occupations frequently involve working with ideas and require an extensive amount of thinking. These occupations can involve searching for facts and figuring out problems mentally. **Work Values:** Achievement; Ability Utilization; Authority; Autonomy; Working Conditions; Creativity; Social Status; Responsibility. **Skills:** Reading Comprehension; Writing; Instructing; Science; Learning Strategies. **Abilities:** *Cognitive*—Oral

Expression; Written Comprehension; Oral Comprehension; Number Facility; Deductive Reasoning. *Psychomotor*–Reaction Time; Response Orientation; Rate Control. *Physical*–none met the criteria. *Sensory*–Speech Clarity; Near Vision; Far Vision. **General Work Activities:** *Information Input*–Getting Information Needed to Do the Job; Identifying Objects, Actions, and Events; Estimating Needed Characteristics; Monitoring Processes, Materials, and Surroundings. *Mental Process*–Analyzing Data or Information; Processing Information; Updating and Using Job-Relevant Knowledge. *Work Output*–Documenting and Recording Information; Implementing Ideas and Programs; Interacting with Computers; Handling and Moving Objects. *Interacting with Others*–Teaching Others; Interpreting Meaning of Information to Others; Communicating with Persons Outside Organization. **Physical Work Conditions:** Indoors; Sitting; Using Hands on Objects, Tools, or Controls. **Other Job Characteristics:** Frustrating Circumstances; Importance of Being Sure All Is Done; Importance of Being Exact or Accurate; Degree of Automation; Consequence of Error.

Experience: Job Zone 5. Extensive skill, knowledge, and experience are needed. Very advanced communication and organizational skills are required. **Job Preparation:** SVP 8.0 and above—4 years to more than 10 years. **Knowledge:** Physics; Education and Training; Mathematics; English Language; Administration and Management. **Instructional Programs:** 400101 Physical Sciences, General; 400101 Physical Sciences, General; 400101 Physical Sciences, General; 400201 Astronomy; 400301 Astrophysics.

Related DOT Job: 090.227-010 Faculty Member, College or University.

25-1061.00 Anthropology and Archeology Teachers, Postsecondary (College and University Faculty)

Education: Doctoral degree

Employed: 865,356

Openings: 139,101

Projected Growth: 22.6%

Earnings: No data available.

Teach courses in anthropology or archeology.

Acts as adviser to student organizations. Compiles, administers, and grades examinations, or assigns this work to others. Compiles bibliographies of specialized materials for outside reading assignments. Stimulates class discussions. Conducts research in particular field of knowledge and publishes findings in professional journals. Serves on faculty committee providing professional consulting services to government and industry. Directs research of other teachers or graduate students working for advanced academic degrees. Prepares and delivers lectures to students. Advises students on academic and vocational curricula.

GOE Number, Interest Area, and Work Group: 12.03.02; Education and Social Service; Educational Services: Postsecondary and Adult Teaching and Instructing. **Personality Type:** Social. Social occupations frequently involve working with, communicating with, and teaching people. These occupations often involve helping or providing service to others. **Work Values:** Achievement; Authority; Ability Utilization; Responsibility; Autonomy. **Skills:** Reading Comprehension; Instructing; Speaking;

Active Learning; Active Listening; Writing; Learning Strategies. **Abilities:** *Cognitive*–Oral Expression; Written Comprehension; Written Expression; Oral Comprehension; Deductive Reasoning. *Psychomotor*–none met the criteria. *Physical*–none met the criteria. *Sensory*–Speech Clarity; Speech Recognition; Far Vision. **General Work Activities:** *Information Input*–Getting Information Needed to Do the Job; Identifying Objects, Actions, and Events; Estimating Needed Characteristics. *Mental Process*–Judging Qualities of Things, Services, Other People's Work; Organizing, Planning, and Prioritizing; Processing Information; Developing Objectives and Strategies; Updating and Using Job-Relevant Knowledge. *Work Output*–Implementing Ideas and Programs; Documenting and Recording Information; Interacting with Computers. *Interacting with Others*–Teaching Others; Communicating with Other Workers; Coaching and Developing Others. **Physical Work Conditions:** Indoors; Sitting; Standing. **Other Job Characteristics:** Importance of Being Sure All Is Done; Consequence of Error; Importance of Being Exact or Accurate.

Experience: Job Zone 5. Extensive skill, knowledge, and experience are needed. Very advanced communication and organizational skills are required. **Job Preparation:** SVP 8.0 and above—4 years to more than 10 years. **Knowledge:** Education and Training; Sociology and Anthropology; English Language; Psychology; History and Archeology. **Instructional Programs:** 450201 Anthropology; 450301 Archeology.

Related DOT Job: 090.227-010 Faculty Member, College or University.

25-1062.00 Area, Ethnic, and Cultural Studies Teachers, Postsecondary (College and University Faculty)

Education: Doctoral degree

Employed: 865,356

Openings: 139,101

Projected Growth: 22.6%

Earnings: No data available.

Teach courses pertaining to the culture and development of an area (for example, Latin America), an ethnic group, or any other group (for example, urban affairs or women's studies).

Serves on faculty committee providing professional consulting services to government and industry. Stimulates class discussions. Advises students on academic and vocational curricula. Compiles bibliographies of specialized materials for outside reading assignments. Acts as adviser to student organizations. Conducts research in particular field of knowledge and publishes findings in professional journals. Prepares and delivers lectures to students. Compiles, administers, and grades examinations, or assigns this work to others. Directs research of other teachers or graduate students working for advanced academic degrees.

GOE Number, Interest Area, and Work Group: 12.03.02; Education and Social Service; Educational Services: Postsecondary and Adult Teaching and Instructing. **Personality Type:** Social. Social occupations frequently involve working with, communicating with, and teaching people. These occupations often involve helping or providing service to others. **Work Values:**

Achievement; Ability Utilization; Authority; Responsibility; Autonomy. **Skills:** Reading Comprehension; Instructing; Speaking; Active Learning; Active Listening; Writing; Learning Strategies. **Abilities:** *Cognitive*—Oral Expression; Written Comprehension; Written Expression; Oral Comprehension; Deductive Reasoning. *Psychomotor*—none met the criteria. *Physical*—none met the criteria. *Sensory*—Speech Clarity; Speech Recognition; Far Vision. **General Work Activities:** *Information Input*—Getting Information Needed to Do the Job; Estimating Needed Characteristics; Identifying Objects, Actions, and Events. *Mental Process*—Judging Qualities of Things, Services, Other People's Work; Organizing, Planning, and Prioritizing; Updating and Using Job-Relevant Knowledge; Developing Objectives and Strategies; Processing Information. *Work Output*—Implementing Ideas and Programs; Documenting and Recording Information; Interacting with Computers. *Interacting with Others*—Teaching Others; Communicating with Other Workers; Coaching and Developing Others. **Physical Work Conditions:** Indoors; Sitting; Standing. **Other Job Characteristics:** Importance of Being Sure All Is Done; Consequence of Error; Importance of Being Exact or Accurate.

Experience: Job Zone 5. Extensive skill, knowledge, and experience are needed. Very advanced communication and organizational skills are required. **Job Preparation:** SVP 8.0 and above—4 years to more than 10 years. **Knowledge:** Education and Training; Sociology and Anthropology; History and Archeology; English Language; Psychology. **Instructional Programs:** 050101 African Studies; 050102 American Studies/Civilization; 050103 Asian Studies; 050104 East Asian Studies; 050105 Eastern European Area Studies; 050107 Latin American Studies; 050108 Middle Eastern Studies; 050109 Pacific Area Studies; 050110 Russian and Slavic Area Studies; 050111 Scandinavian Area Studies; 050112 South Asian Studies; 050113 Southeast Asian Studies; 050114 Western European Studies; 050115 Canadian Studies; 050201 Afro-American (Black) Studies.

Related DOT Job: 090.227-010 Faculty Member, College or University.

25-1063.00 Economics Teachers, Postsecondary
(College and University Faculty)

Education: Doctoral degree
Employed: 865,356
Openings: 139,101
Projected Growth: 22.6%
Earnings: No data available.

Teach courses in economics.

Conducts research in particular field of knowledge and publishes findings in professional journals. Stimulates class discussions. Advises students on academic and vocational curricula. Directs research of other teachers or graduate students working for advanced academic degrees. Compiles, administers, and grades examinations, or assigns this work to others. Acts as adviser to student organizations. Serves on faculty committee providing professional consulting services to government and industry. Prepares and delivers lectures to students. Compiles bibliographies of specialized materials for outside reading assignments.

GOE Number, Interest Area, and Work Group: 12.03.02; Education and Social Service; Educational Services: Postsecondary and Adult Teaching and Instructing. **Personality Type:** Social. Social occupations frequently involve working with, communicating with, and teaching people. These occupations often involve helping or providing service to others. **Work Values:** Achievement; Ability Utilization; Authority; Autonomy; Responsibility. **Skills:** Reading Comprehension; Instructing; Speaking; Active Learning; Learning Strategies; Active Listening; Writing. **Abilities:** *Cognitive*—Oral Expression; Written Comprehension; Written Expression; Oral Comprehension; Deductive Reasoning. *Psychomotor*—none met the criteria. *Physical*—none met the criteria. *Sensory*—Speech Clarity; Speech Recognition; Far Vision. **General Work Activities:** *Information Input*—Getting Information Needed to Do the Job; Estimating Needed Characteristics; Identifying Objects, Actions, and Events. *Mental Process*—Judging Qualities of Things, Services, Other People's Work; Organizing, Planning, and Prioritizing; Processing Information; Developing Objectives and Strategies; Updating and Using Job-Relevant Knowledge. *Work Output*—Implementing Ideas and Programs; Documenting and Recording Information; Interacting with Computers. *Interacting with Others*—Teaching Others; Communicating with Other Workers; Coaching and Developing Others. **Physical Work Conditions:** Indoors; Sitting; Standing. **Other Job Characteristics:** Importance of Being Sure All Is Done; Consequence of Error; Importance of Being Exact or Accurate.

Experience: Job Zone 5. Extensive skill, knowledge, and experience are needed. Very advanced communication and organizational skills are required. **Job Preparation:** SVP 8.0 and above—4 years to more than 10 years. **Knowledge:** Education and Training; Sociology and Anthropology; Psychology; History and Archeology; English Language. **Instructional Programs:** 450601 Economics, General; 450602 Applied and Resource Economics; 450603 Econometrics and Quantitative Economics; 450604 Development Economics and International Development; 450605 International Economics.

Related DOT Job: 090.227-010 Faculty Member, College or University.

25-1064.00 Geography Teachers, Postsecondary
(College and University Faculty)

Education: Doctoral degree
Employed: 865,356
Openings: 139,101
Projected Growth: 22.6%
Earnings: No data available.

Teach courses in geography.

GOE Number, Interest Area, and Work Group: 12.03.02; Education and Social Service; Educational Services: Postsecondary and Adult Teaching and Instructing. **Instructional Programs:** 450701 Geography; 450702 Cartography. **Note:** The Department of Labor has not collected some data for this job, so it has fewer details than the other descriptions.

25-1065.00 Political Science Teachers, Postsecondary
(College and University Faculty)

Education: Doctoral degree

Employed: 865,356

Openings: 139,101

Projected Growth: 22.6%

Earnings: No data available.

Teach courses in political science, international affairs, and international relations.

Acts as adviser to student organizations. Compiles bibliographies of specialized materials for outside reading assignments. Stimulates class discussions. Prepares and delivers lectures to students. Compiles, administers, and grades examinations, or assigns this work to others. Directs research of other teachers or graduate students working for advanced academic degrees. Serves on faculty committee providing professional consulting services to government and industry. Conducts research in particular field of knowledge and publishes findings in professional journals. Advises students on academic and vocational curricula.

GOE Number, Interest Area, and Work Group: 12.03.02; Education and Social Service; Educational Services: Postsecondary and Adult Teaching and Instructing. **Personality Type:** Social. Social occupations frequently involve working with, communicating with, and teaching people. These occupations often involve helping or providing service to others. **Work Values:** Achievement; Ability Utilization; Authority; Responsibility; Autonomy. **Skills:** Reading Comprehension; Instructing; Active Learning; Speaking; Learning Strategies; Writing; Active Listening. **Abilities:** *Cognitive*—Oral Expression; Written Comprehension; Written Expression; Oral Comprehension; Deductive Reasoning. *Psychomotor*—none met the criteria. *Physical*—none met the criteria. *Sensory*—Speech Clarity; Speech Recognition; Far Vision. **General Work Activities:** *Information Input*—Getting Information Needed to Do the Job; Estimating Needed Characteristics; Identifying Objects, Actions, and Events. *Mental Process*—Judging Qualities of Things, Services, Other People's Work; Organizing, Planning, and Prioritizing; Updating and Using Job-Relevant Knowledge; Processing Information; Developing Objectives and Strategies. *Work Output*—Implementing Ideas and Programs; Documenting and Recording Information; Interacting with Computers. *Interacting with Others*—Teaching Others; Communicating with Other Workers; Coaching and Developing Others. **Physical Work Conditions:** Indoors; Sitting; Standing. **Other Job Characteristics:** Importance of Being Sure All Is Done; Consequence of Error; Importance of Being Exact or Accurate.

Experience: Job Zone 5. Extensive skill, knowledge, and experience are needed. Very advanced communication and organizational skills are required. **Job Preparation:** SVP 8.0 and above—4 years to more than 10 years. **Knowledge:** Education and Training; Sociology and Anthropology; Psychology; English Language; History and Archeology. **Instructional Programs:** 450901 International Relations and Affairs; 451001 Political Science, General; 451002 American Government and Politics.

Related DOT Job: 090.227-010 Faculty Member, College or University.

25-1066.00 Psychology Teachers, Postsecondary
(College and University Faculty)

Education: Doctoral degree

Employed: 865,356

Openings: 139,101

Projected Growth: 22.6%

Earnings: No data available.

Teach courses in psychology, such as child, clinical, and developmental psychology. Teach courses in psychological counseling.

Conducts research in particular field of knowledge and publishes findings in professional journals. Compiles, administers, and grades examinations, or assigns this work to others. Stimulates class discussions. Directs research of other teachers or graduate students working for advanced academic degrees. Acts as adviser to student organizations. Advises students on academic and vocational curricula. Compiles bibliographies of specialized materials for outside reading assignments. Prepares and delivers lectures to students. Serves on faculty committee providing professional consulting services to government and industry.

GOE Number, Interest Area, and Work Group: 12.03.02; Education and Social Service; Educational Services: Postsecondary and Adult Teaching and Instructing. **Personality Type:** Social. Social occupations frequently involve working with, communicating with, and teaching people. These occupations often involve helping or providing service to others. **Work Values:** Achievement; Ability Utilization; Authority; Autonomy; Responsibility. **Skills:** Reading Comprehension; Instructing; Active Learning; Speaking; Learning Strategies; Writing; Active Listening. **Abilities:** *Cognitive*—Oral Expression; Written Comprehension; Written Expression; Oral Comprehension; Deductive Reasoning. *Psychomotor*—none met the criteria. *Physical*—none met the criteria. *Sensory*—Speech Clarity; Speech Recognition; Far Vision. **General Work Activities:** *Information Input*—Getting Information Needed to Do the Job; Estimating Needed Characteristics; Identifying Objects, Actions, and Events. *Mental Process*—Judging Qualities of Things, Services, Other People's Work; Organizing, Planning, and Prioritizing; Processing Information; Developing Objectives and Strategies; Updating and Using Job-Relevant Knowledge. *Work Output*—Implementing Ideas and Programs; Documenting and Recording Information; Interacting with Computers. *Interacting with Others*—Teaching Others; Communicating with Other Workers; Coaching and Developing Others. **Physical Work Conditions:** Indoors; Sitting; Standing. **Other Job Characteristics:** Importance of Being Sure All Is Done; Consequence of Error; Importance of Being Exact or Accurate.

Experience: Job Zone 5. Extensive skill, knowledge, and experience are needed. Very advanced communication and organizational skills are required. **Job Preparation:** SVP 8.0 and above—4 years to more than 10 years. **Knowledge:** Education and Training; Sociology and Anthropology; Psychology; History and Archeology; English Language. **Instructional Programs:** 420101 Psychology, General; 420201 Clinical Psychology; 420301 Cognitive Psychology and Psycholinguistics; 420401 Community Psychology; 420601 Counseling Psychology; 420801 Experimental Psychology; 420901 Industrial and Organizational Psychology; 421101 Physiological Psychology/Psychobiology; 421601 Social Psychology; 421701 School Psychology.

Related DOT Job: 090.227-010 Faculty Member, College or University.

25-1067.00 Sociology Teachers, Postsecondary
(College and University Faculty)

Education: Doctoral degree
Employed: 865,356
Openings: 139,101
Projected Growth: 22.6%
Earnings: No data available.

Teach courses in sociology.

Conducts research in particular field of knowledge and publishes findings in professional journals. Acts as adviser to student organizations. Compiles, administers, and grades examinations, or assigns this work to others. Stimulates class discussions. Serves on faculty committee providing professional consulting services to government and industry. Prepares and delivers lectures to students. Directs research of other teachers or graduate students working for advanced academic degrees. Compiles bibliographies of specialized materials for outside reading assignments. Advises students on academic and vocational curricula.

GOE Number, Interest Area, and Work Group: 12.03.02; Education and Social Service; Educational Services: Postsecondary and Adult Teaching and Instructing. **Personality Type:** Social. Social occupations frequently involve working with, communicating with, and teaching people. These occupations often involve helping or providing service to others. **Work Values:** Achievement; Authority; Ability Utilization; Responsibility; Autonomy. **Skills:** Reading Comprehension; Instructing; Speaking; Active Learning; Learning Strategies; Active Listening; Writing. **Abilities:** *Cognitive*—Oral Expression; Written Comprehension; Written Expression; Oral Comprehension; Deductive Reasoning. *Psychomotor*—none met the criteria. *Physical*—none met the criteria. *Sensory*—Speech Clarity; Speech Recognition; Far Vision. **General Work Activities:** *Information Input*—Getting Information Needed to Do the Job; Identifying Objects, Actions, and Events; Estimating Needed Characteristics. *Mental Process*—Judging Qualities of Things, Services, Other People's Work; Organizing, Planning, and Prioritizing; Processing Information; Developing Objectives and Strategies; Updating and Using Job-Relevant Knowledge. *Work Output*—Implementing Ideas and Programs; Documenting and Recording Information; Interacting with Computers. *Interacting with Others*—Teaching Others; Communicating with Other Workers; Coaching and Developing Others. **Physical Work Conditions:** Indoors; Sitting; Standing. **Other Job Characteristics:** Importance of Being Sure All Is Done; Consequence of Error; Importance of Being Exact or Accurate.

Experience: Job Zone 5. Extensive skill, knowledge, and experience are needed. Very advanced communication and organizational skills are required. **Job Preparation:** SVP 8.0 and above—4 years to more than 10 years. **Knowledge:** Education and Training; Sociology and Anthropology; English Language; History and

Archeology; Psychology. **Instructional Programs:** 451101 Sociology; 451201 Urban Affairs/Studies.

Related DOT Job: 090.227-010 Faculty Member, College or University.

25-1071.00 Health Specialties Teachers, Postsecondary (College and University Faculty)

Education: Doctoral degree
Employed: 865,356
Openings: 139,101
Projected Growth: 22.6%
Earnings: No data available.

Teach courses in health specialties such as veterinary medicine, dentistry, pharmacy, therapy, laboratory technology, and public health.

Directs research of other teachers or graduate students working for advanced academic degrees. Stimulates class discussions. Compiles bibliographies of specialized materials for outside reading assignments. Compiles, administers, and grades examinations, or assigns this work to others. Serves on faculty committee providing professional consulting services to government and industry. Conducts research in particular field of knowledge and publishes findings in professional journals. Advises students on academic and vocational curricula. Prepares and delivers lectures to students. Acts as adviser to student organizations.

GOE Number, Interest Area, and Work Group: 12.03.02; Education and Social Service; Educational Services: Postsecondary and Adult Teaching and Instructing. **Personality Type:** Investigative. Investigative occupations frequently involve working with ideas and require an extensive amount of thinking. These occupations can involve searching for facts and figuring out problems mentally. **Work Values:** Achievement; Authority; Ability Utilization; Responsibility; Autonomy. **Skills:** Reading Comprehension; Writing; Science; Instructing; Information Gathering. **Abilities:** *Cognitive*—Oral Expression; Written Expression; Written Comprehension; Oral Comprehension; Deductive Reasoning; Fluency of Ideas. *Psychomotor*—none met the criteria. *Physical*—none met the criteria. *Sensory*—Speech Clarity; Speech Recognition; Auditory Attention. **General Work Activities:** *Information Input*—Getting Information Needed to Do the Job; Identifying Objects, Actions, and Events; Monitoring Processes, Materials, and Surroundings. *Mental Process*—Updating and Using Job-Relevant Knowledge; Organizing, Planning, and Prioritizing; Judging Qualities of Things, Services, Other People's Work. *Work Output*—Implementing Ideas and Programs; Documenting and Recording Information; Handling and Moving Objects; Interacting with Computers. *Interacting with Others*—Teaching Others; Communicating with Other Workers; Coaching and Developing Others. **Physical Work Conditions:** Indoors; Standing; Sitting. **Other Job Characteristics:** Importance of Being Exact or Accurate; Importance of Being Sure All Is Done; Frustrating Circumstances.

Experience: Job Zone 5. Extensive skill, knowledge, and experience are needed. Very advanced communication and organizational skills are required. **Job Preparation:** SVP 8.0 and above—4 years to more than 10 years. **Knowledge:** Education and Training;

Biology; Medicine and Dentistry; English Language; Therapy and Counseling. **Instructional Programs:** 510101 Chiropractic (D.C., D.C.M.); 511301 Medical Anatomy; 511302 Medical Biochemistry; 511303 Medical Biomathematics and Biometrics; 511304 Medical Physics/Biophysics; 511304 Medical Physics/Biophysics; 511305 Medical Cell Biology; 511306 Medical Genetics; 511307 Medical Immunology; 511308 Medical Microbiology; 511309 Medical Molecular Biology; 511310 Medical Neurobiology; 511311 Medical Nutrition; 511312 Medical Pathology; 511313 Medical Physiology; 511314 Medical Toxicology; 511399 Basic Medical Sciences, Other; 512202 Environmental Health; 512203 Epidemiology.

Related DOT Job: 090.227-010 Faculty Member, College or University.

25-1072.00 Nursing Instructors and Teachers, Postsecondary (College and University Faculty)

Education: Doctoral degree

Employed: 865,356

Openings: 139,101

Projected Growth: 22.6%

Earnings: No data available.

Demonstrate and teach patient care in classroom and clinical units to nursing students. Includes both teachers primarily engaged in teaching and those who do a combination of teaching and research.

Instructs and lectures nursing students in principles and application of physical, biological, and psychological subjects related to nursing. Prepares and administers examinations to nursing students. Issues assignments to students. Conducts and supervises laboratory work. Cooperates with medical and nursing personnel in evaluating and improving teaching and nursing practices. Conducts classes for patients in health practices and procedures. Directs seminars and panels. Participates in planning curriculum, teaching schedule, and course outline with medical and nursing personnel. Supervises student nurses and demonstrates patient care in clinical units of hospital. Evaluates student progress and maintains records of student classroom and clinical experience.

GOE Number, Interest Area, and Work Group: 12.03.02; Education and Social Service; Educational Services: Postsecondary and Adult Teaching and Instructing. **Personality Type:** Social. Social occupations frequently involve working with, communicating with, and teaching people. These occupations often involve helping or providing service to others. **Work Values:** Achievement; Authority; Ability Utilization; Autonomy; Social Status; Social Service; Working Conditions; Coworkers. **Skills:** Learning Strategies; Instructing; Reading Comprehension; Science; Speaking. **Abilities:** *Cognitive*—Oral Expression; Written Expression; Written Comprehension; Inductive Reasoning; Oral Comprehension. *Psychomotor*—Arm-Hand Steadiness; Manual Dexterity; Reaction Time. *Physical*—Static Strength; Extent Flexibility; Trunk Strength. *Sensory*—Speech Clarity; Near Vision; Visual Color Discrimination. **General Work Activities:** *Information Input*—Getting Information Needed to Do the Job; Monitoring Processes, Materials, and Surroundings; Identifying Objects, Actions, and Events. *Mental Process*—Updating and Using Job-Rel-

evant Knowledge; Judging Qualities of Things, Services, Other People's Work; Evaluating Information Against Standards. *Work Output*—Documenting and Recording Information; Handling and Moving Objects; Performing General Physical Activities. *Interacting with Others*—Teaching Others; Interpreting Meaning of Information to Others; Coaching and Developing Others. **Physical Work Conditions:** Indoors; Special Uniform; Diseases or Infections; Standing. **Other Job Characteristics:** Consequence of Error; Importance of Being Exact or Accurate; Importance of Being Sure All Is Done.

Experience: Job Zone 5. Extensive skill, knowledge, and experience are needed. Very advanced communication and organizational skills are required. **Job Preparation:** SVP 8.0 and above—4 years to more than 10 years. **Knowledge:** Education and Training; Medicine and Dentistry; Biology; English Language; Psychology. **Instructional Programs:** 511601 Nursing (R.N. Training); 511603 Nursing, Adult Health (Post-R.N.); 511604 Nursing Anesthetist (Post-R.N.); 511605 Nursing, Family Practice (Post-R.N.); 511606 Nursing, Maternal/Child Health (Post-R.N.); 511608 Nursing Science (Post-R.N.); 511609 Nursing, Pediatric (Post-R.N.); 511610 Nursing, Psychiatric/Mental Health (Post-R.N.); 511611 Nursing, Public Health (Post-R.N.); 511612 Nursing, Surgical (Post-R.N.).

Related DOT Job: 075.124-018 Nurse, Instructor.

25-1081.00 Education Teachers, Postsecondary (College and University Faculty)

Education: Doctoral degree

Employed: 865,356

Openings: 139,101

Projected Growth: 22.6%

Earnings: No data available.

Teach courses pertaining to education, such as counseling, curriculum, guidance, instruction, teacher education, and teaching English as a second language.

GOE Number, Interest Area, and Work Group: 12.03.02; Education and Social Service; Educational Services: Postsecondary and Adult Teaching and Instructing. **Instructional Programs:** 130101 Education, General; 130301 Curriculum and Instruction; 130401 Education Administration and Supervision, General. **Note:** The Department of Labor has not collected some data for this job, so it has fewer details than the other descriptions.

25-1082.00 Library Science Teachers, Postsecondary (College and University Faculty)

Education: Doctoral degree

Employed: 865,356

Openings: 139,101

Projected Growth: 22.6%

Earnings: No data available.

Teach courses in library science.

GOE Number, Interest Area, and Work Group: 12.03.02; Education and Social Service; Educational Services: Postsecondary and Adult Teaching and Instructing. **Instructional Program:** 250101 Library Science/Librarianship. **Note:** The Department of Labor has not collected some data for this job, so it has fewer details than the other descriptions.

25-1111.00 Criminal Justice and Law Enforcement Teachers, Postsecondary (College and University Faculty)

Education: Doctoral degree
Employed: 865,356
Openings: 139,101
Projected Growth: 22.6%
Earnings: No data available.

Teach courses in criminal justice, corrections, and law enforcement administration.

GOE Number, Interest Area, and Work Group: 12.03.02; Education and Social Service; Educational Services: Postsecondary and Adult Teaching and Instructing. **Instructional Programs:** 430102 Corrections/Correctional Administration; 430103 Criminal Justice/Law Enforcement Administration; 430104 Criminal Justice Studies. **Note:** The Department of Labor has not collected some data for this job, so it has fewer details than the other descriptions.

25-1112.00 Law Teachers, Postsecondary (College and University Faculty)

Education: Doctoral degree
Employed: 865,356
Openings: 139,101
Projected Growth: 22.6%
Earnings: No data available.

Teach courses in law.

GOE Number, Interest Area, and Work Group: 12.03.02; Education and Social Service; Educational Services: Postsecondary and Adult Teaching and Instructing. **Instructional Programs:** 220101 Law (LL.B., J.D.); 220104 Juridical Science/Legal Specialization (LL.M.,M.C.L.,J.S.D./S.J.D.). **Note:** The Department of Labor has not collected some data for this job, so it has fewer details than the other descriptions.

25-1113.00 Social Work Teachers, Postsecondary (College and University Faculty)

Education: Doctoral degree
Employed: 865,356
Openings: 139,101
Projected Growth: 22.6%
Earnings: No data available.

Teach courses in social work.

GOE Number, Interest Area, and Work Group: 12.03.02; Education and Social Service; Educational Services: Postsecondary

and Adult Teaching and Instructing. **Instructional Program:** 440701 Social Work. **Note:** The Department of Labor has not collected some data for this job, so it has fewer details than the other descriptions.

25-1121.00 Art, Drama, and Music Teachers, Postsecondary (College and University Faculty)

Education: Doctoral degree
Employed: 865,356
Openings: 139,101
Projected Growth: 22.6%
Earnings: No data available.

Teach courses in drama, music, and the arts, including fine and applied art, such as painting and sculpture, or design and crafts.

Acts as adviser to student organizations. Compiles, administers, and grades examinations, or assigns this work to others. Compiles bibliographies of specialized materials for outside reading assignments. Serves on faculty committee providing professional consulting services to government and industry. Advises students on academic and vocational curricula. Directs research of other teachers or graduate students working for advanced academic degrees. Conducts research in particular field of knowledge and publishes findings in professional journals. Prepares and delivers lectures to students. Stimulates class discussions.

GOE Number, Interest Area, and Work Group: 12.03.02; Education and Social Service; Educational Services: Postsecondary and Adult Teaching and Instructing. **Personality Type:** Artistic. Artistic occupations frequently involve working with forms, designs, and patterns. These occupations often require self-expression, and the work can be done without following a clear set of rules. **Work Values:** Achievement; Ability Utilization; Authority; Autonomy; Working Conditions. **Skills:** Instructing; Reading Comprehension; Writing; Speaking; Learning Strategies. **Abilities:** *Cognitive*—Oral Expression; Written Comprehension; Written Expression; Oral Comprehension; Fluency of Ideas. *Psychomotor*—Wrist-Finger Speed. *Physical*—Stamina. *Sensory*—Visual Color Discrimination; Speech Clarity; Near Vision. **General Work Activities:** *Information Input*—Getting Information Needed to Do the Job; Identifying Objects, Actions, and Events; Monitoring Processes, Materials, and Surroundings. *Mental Process*—Thinking Creatively; Organizing, Planning, and Prioritizing; Scheduling Work and Activities. *Work Output*—Implementing Ideas and Programs; Documenting and Recording Information; Handling and Moving Objects. *Interacting with Others*—Teaching Others; Communicating with Other Workers; Coaching and Developing Others. **Physical Work Conditions:** Indoors; Sitting; Using Hands on Objects, Tools, or Controls. **Other Job Characteristics:** Importance of Being Sure All Is Done; Importance of Being Exact or Accurate; Consequence of Error; Frustrating Circumstances.

Experience: Job Zone 5. Extensive skill, knowledge, and experience are needed. Very advanced communication and organizational skills are required. **Job Preparation:** SVP 8.0 and above—4 years to more than 10 years. **Knowledge:** Education and Training; Fine Arts; English Language; Communications and Media;

Administration and Management. **Instructional Programs:** 500501 Drama/Theater Arts, General; 500502 Technical Theater/Theater Design and Stagecraft; 500503 Acting and Directing; 500504 Playwriting and Screenwriting; 500505 Drama/Theater Literature, History and Criticism; 500602 Film-Video Making/Cinematography and Production; 500605 Photography; 500701 Art, General; 500701 Art, General; 500702 Fine/Studio Arts; 500703 Art History, Criticism and Conservation; 500704 Arts Management; 500704 Arts Management; 500705 Drawing; 500706 Intermedia.

Related DOT Job: 090.227-010 Faculty Member, College or University.

25-1122.00 Communications Teachers, Postsecondary (College and University Faculty)

Education: Doctoral degree

Employed: 865,356

Openings: 139,101

Projected Growth: 22.6%

Earnings: No data available.

Teach courses in communications, such as organizational communications, public relations, radio/television broadcasting, and journalism.

GOE Number, Interest Area, and Work Group: 12.03.02; Education and Social Service; Educational Services: Postsecondary and Adult Teaching and Instructing. **Instructional Programs:** 090101 Communications, General; 090201 Advertising; 090401 Journalism; 090402 Broadcast Journalism; 090403 Mass Communications; 090499 Journalism and Mass Communication, Other; 090501 Public Relations and Organizational Communications; 090701 Radio and Television Broadcasting; 099999 Communications, Other. **Note:** The Department of Labor has not collected some data for this job, so it has fewer details than the other descriptions.

25-1123.00 English Language and Literature Teachers, Postsecondary (College and University Faculty)

Education: Doctoral degree

Employed: 865,356

Openings: 139,101

Projected Growth: 22.6%

Earnings: No data available.

Teach courses in English language and literature, including linguistics and comparative literature.

Directs research of other teachers or graduate students working for advanced academic degrees. Compiles, administers, and grades examinations, or assigns this work to others. Compiles bibliographies of specialized materials for outside reading assignments. Stimulates class discussions. Acts as adviser to student organizations. Serves on faculty committee providing professional consulting services to government and industry. Conducts research in particular field of knowledge and publishes findings in professional journals. Prepares and delivers lectures to students. Advises students on academic and vocational curricula.

GOE Number, Interest Area, and Work Group: 12.03.02; Education and Social Service; Educational Services: Postsecondary and Adult Teaching and Instructing. **Personality Type:** Artistic. Artistic occupations frequently involve working with forms, designs, and patterns. These occupations often require self-expression, and the work can be done without following a clear set of rules. **Work Values:** Achievement; Ability Utilization; Authority; Autonomy; Social Service; Responsibility; Working Conditions. **Skills:** Reading Comprehension; Speaking; Instructing; Learning Strategies; Writing. **Abilities:** *Cognitive*—Oral Expression; Oral Comprehension; Written Comprehension; Written Expression; Fluency of Ideas. *Psychomotor*—none met the criteria. *Physical*—none met the criteria. *Sensory*—Speech Clarity; Speech Recognition; Sound Localization. **General Work Activities:** *Information Input*—Getting Information Needed to Do the Job; Identifying Objects, Actions, and Events; Estimating Needed Characteristics. *Mental Process*—Judging Qualities of Things, Services, Other People's Work; Processing Information; Organizing, Planning, and Prioritizing. *Work Output*—Implementing Ideas and Programs; Documenting and Recording Information; Interacting with Computers. *Interacting with Others*—Teaching Others; Communicating with Other Workers; Establishing and Maintaining Relationships; Interpreting Meaning of Information to Others. **Physical Work Conditions:** Indoors; Sitting; Standing. **Other Job Characteristics:** Importance of Being Sure All Is Done; Importance of Being Exact or Accurate; Consequence of Error.

Experience: Job Zone 5. Extensive skill, knowledge, and experience are needed. Very advanced communication and organizational skills are required. **Job Preparation:** SVP 8.0 and above—4 years to more than 10 years. **Knowledge:** English Language; Education and Training; Foreign Language; Communications and Media; Clerical; Computers and Electronics. **Instructional Programs:** 230101 English Language and Literature, General; 230301 Comparative Literature; 230401 English Composition; 230501 English Creative Writing; 230701 American Literature (United States).

Related DOT Job: 090.227-010 Faculty Member, College or University.

25-1124.00 Foreign Language and Literature Teachers, Postsecondary (College and University Faculty)

Education: Doctoral degree

Employed: 865,356

Openings: 139,101

Projected Growth: 22.6%

Earnings: No data available.

Teach courses in foreign (that is, other than English) languages and literature.

Acts as adviser to student organizations. Compiles bibliographies of specialized materials for outside reading assignments. Stimulates class discussions. Compiles, administers, and grades examinations, or assigns this work to others. Advises students on academic and vocational curricula. Conducts research in particular field of knowledge and publishes findings in professional journals. Directs research of other teachers or graduate students working for advanced academic degrees. Prepares and delivers lectures to students. Serves on faculty committee providing professional consulting services to government and industry.

GOE Number, Interest Area, and Work Group: 12.03.02; Education and Social Service; Educational Services: Postsecondary and Adult Teaching and Instructing. **Personality Type:** Artistic. Artistic occupations frequently involve working with forms, designs, and patterns. These occupations often require self-expression, and the work can be done without following a clear set of rules. **Work Values:** Achievement; Ability Utilization; Authority; Autonomy; Working Conditions; Responsibility; Social Service. **Skills:** Reading Comprehension; Speaking; Instructing; Learning Strategies; Writing. **Abilities:** *Cognitive*—Oral Expression; Oral Comprehension; Written Comprehension; Written Expression; Fluency of Ideas. *Psychomotor*—none met the criteria. *Physical*—none met the criteria. *Sensory*—Speech Clarity; Speech Recognition; Sound Localization. **General Work Activities:** *Information Input*—Getting Information Needed to Do the Job; Identifying Objects, Actions, and Events; Estimating Needed Characteristics. *Mental Process*—Judging Qualities of Things, Services, Other People's Work; Processing Information; Organizing, Planning, and Prioritizing. *Work Output*—Implementing Ideas and Programs; Documenting and Recording Information; Interacting with Computers. *Interacting with Others*—Teaching Others; Communicating with Other Workers; Establishing and Maintaining Relationships; Interpreting Meaning of Information to Others. **Physical Work Conditions:** Indoors; Sitting; Standing. **Other Job Characteristics:** Importance of Being Sure All Is Done; Importance of Being Exact or Accurate; Consequence of Error.

Experience: Job Zone 5. Extensive skill, knowledge, and experience are needed. Very advanced communication and organizational skills are required. **Job Preparation:** SVP 8.0 and above—4 years to more than 10 years. **Knowledge:** Education and Training; English Language; Foreign Language; Communications and Media; Computers and Electronics; Clerical. **Instructional Programs:** 160103 Foreign Language Interpretation and Translation; 160301 Chinese Language and Literature; 160302 Japanese Language and Literature; 160399 East and Southeast Asian Languages and Literatures, Other; 160402 Russian Language and Literature; 160499 East European Languages and Literatures, Other; 160501 German Language and Literature; 160502 Scandinavian Languages and Literatures; 160599 Germanic Languages and Literatures, Other; 160601 Greek Language and Literature (Modern); 160703 South Asian Languages and Literatures; 160901 French Language and Literature; 160902 Italian Language and Literature; 160904 Portuguese Language and Literature; 160905 Spanish Language and Literature.

Related DOT Job: 090.227-010 Faculty Member, College or University.

25-1125.00 History Teachers, Postsecondary (College and University Faculty)

Education: Doctoral degree
Employed: 865,356
Openings: 139,101
Projected Growth: 22.6%
Earnings: No data available.

Teach courses in human history and historiography.

Conducts research in particular field of knowledge and publishes findings in professional journals. Compiles bibliographies of specialized materials for outside reading assignments. Serves on faculty committee providing professional consulting services to government and industry. Directs research of other teachers or graduate students working for advanced academic degrees. Stimulates class discussions. Advises students on academic and vocational curricula. Compiles, administers, and grades examinations, or assigns this work to others. Prepares and delivers lectures to students. Acts as adviser to student organizations.

GOE Number, Interest Area, and Work Group: 12.03.02; Education and Social Service; Educational Services: Postsecondary and Adult Teaching and Instructing. **Personality Type:** Social. Social occupations frequently involve working with, communicating with, and teaching people. These occupations often involve helping or providing service to others. **Work Values:** Achievement; Authority; Ability Utilization; Autonomy; Responsibility. **Skills:** Reading Comprehension; Instructing; Speaking; Active Learning; Learning Strategies; Writing; Active Listening. **Abilities:** *Cognitive*—Oral Expression; Written Comprehension; Written Expression; Oral Comprehension; Deductive Reasoning. *Psychomotor*—none met the criteria. *Physical*—none met the criteria. *Sensory*—Speech Clarity; Speech Recognition; Far Vision. **General Work Activities:** *Information Input*—Getting Information Needed to Do the Job; Estimating Needed Characteristics; Identifying Objects, Actions, and Events. *Mental Process*—Judging Qualities of Things, Services, Other People's Work; Organizing, Planning, and Prioritizing; Developing Objectives and Strategies; Updating and Using Job-Relevant Knowledge; Processing Information. *Work Output*—Implementing Ideas and Programs; Documenting and Recording Information; Interacting with Computers. *Interacting with Others*—Teaching Others; Communicating with Other Workers; Coaching and Developing Others. **Physical Work Conditions:** Indoors; Sitting; Standing. **Other Job Characteristics:** Importance of Being Sure All Is Done; Consequence of Error; Importance of Being Exact or Accurate.

Experience: Job Zone 5. Extensive skill, knowledge, and experience are needed. Very advanced communication and organizational skills are required. **Job Preparation:** SVP 8.0 and above—4 years to more than 10 years. **Knowledge:** Education and Training; Sociology and Anthropology; History and Archeology; English Language; Psychology. **Instructional Programs:** 450801 History, General; 450802 American (United States) History; 450803 European History; 450804 History and Philosophy of Science and Tech.; 450805 Public/Applied History and Archival Administration.

Related DOT Job: 090.227-010 Faculty Member, College or University.

25-1126.00 Philosophy and Religion Teachers, Postsecondary (College and University Faculty)

Education: Doctoral degree
Employed: 865,356
Openings: 139,101
Projected Growth: 22.6%
Earnings: No data available.

Teach courses in philosophy, religion, and theology.

GOE Number, Interest Area, and Work Group: 12.03.02; Education and Social Service; Educational Services: Postsecondary and Adult Teaching and Instructing. **Instructional Programs:** 380101 Philosophy; 380201 Religion/Religious Studies; 389999 Philosophy and Religion; 390101 Biblical and Other Theological Languages and Literatures; 390201 Bible/Biblical Studies; 390401 Religious Education; 390501 Religious/Sacred Music; 390601 Theology/Theological Studies; 390602 Divinity/Ministry (B.D., M.Div.); 390604 Pre-Theological/Pre-Ministerial Studies; 390605. **Note:** The Department of Labor has not collected some data for this job, so it has fewer details than the other descriptions.

25-1191.00 Graduate Teaching Assistants (College and University Faculty)

Education: Doctoral degree
Employed: 865,356
Openings: 139,101
Projected Growth: 22.6%
Earnings: No data available.

Assist department chairperson, faculty members, or other professional staff members in college or university by performing teaching or teaching-related duties such as teaching lower-level courses, developing teaching materials, preparing and giving examinations, and grading examinations or papers. Must be enrolled in a graduate-school program.

Assists faculty member or staff with laboratory or field research. Grades examinations and papers. Prepares and gives examinations. Assists library staff in maintaining library collection. Teaches lower-level courses. Develops teaching materials such as syllabi and visual aids. Assists faculty member or staff with student conferences.

GOE Number, Interest Area, and Work Group: 12.03.02; Education and Social Service; Educational Services: Postsecondary and Adult Teaching and Instructing. **Personality Type:** Social. Social occupations frequently involve working with, communicating with, and teaching people. These occupations often involve helping or providing service to others. **Work Values:** Coworkers; Working Conditions; Achievement; Social Service; Authority; Ability Utilization. **Skills:** Reading Comprehension; Instructing; Speaking; Writing; Learning Strategies. **Abilities:** *Cognitive*—Oral Expression; Written Comprehension; Oral Com-

prehension; Written Expression; Fluency of Ideas. *Psychomotor*—none met the criteria. *Physical*—none met the criteria. *Sensory*—Speech Clarity; Speech Recognition. **General Work Activities:** *Information Input*—Getting Information Needed to Do the Job; Identifying Objects, Actions, and Events; Estimating Needed Characteristics. *Mental Process*—Judging Qualities of Things, Services, Other People's Work; Processing Information; Analyzing Data or Information. *Work Output*—Documenting and Recording Information; Implementing Ideas and Programs; Handling and Moving Objects; Interacting with Computers. *Interacting with Others*—Teaching Others; Communicating with Other Workers; Establishing and Maintaining Relationships. **Physical Work Conditions:** Indoors; Standing; Sitting. **Other Job Characteristics:** Importance of Being Sure All Is Done; Importance of Being Exact or Accurate; Consequence of Error.

Experience: Job Zone 5. Extensive skill, knowledge, and experience are needed. Very advanced communication and organizational skills are required. **Job Preparation:** SVP 8.0 and above—4 years to more than 10 years. **Knowledge:** Education and Training; English Language; Mathematics; Clerical; Computers and Electronics. **Instructional Program:** 130101 Education, General.

Related DOT Job: 090.227-014 Graduate Assistant.

25-1192.00 Home Economics Teachers, Postsecondary (College and University Faculty)

Education: Doctoral degree
Employed: 865,356
Openings: 139,101
Projected Growth: 22.6%
Earnings: No data available.

Teach courses in child care, family relations, finance, nutrition, and related subjects pertaining to home management.

GOE Number, Interest Area, and Work Group: 12.03.02; Education and Social Service; Educational Services: Postsecondary and Adult Teaching and Instructing. **Instructional Programs:** 190101 Home Economics, General; 190201 Business Home Economics; 190202 Home Economics Communications; 190301 Family and Community Studies; 190401 Family Resource Management Studies; 190402 Consumer Economics and Science; 190499 Family/Consumer Resource Management, Other; 190501 Foods and Nutrition Studies, General; 190502 Foods and Nutrition Science; 190503 Dietetics/Human Nutritional Services; 190505 Food Systems Administration; 190599 Foods and Nutrition Studies, Other; 190601 Housing Studies, General; 190603 Interior Environments; 190699 Housing Studies, Other; 190701 Individual and Family Development Studies, General; 190703 Family and Marriage Counseling; 190704 Family Life and Relations Studies; 190705 Gerontological Services; 190706 Child Growth, Care and Development Studies; 190799 Individual and Family Development Studies, Other; 190901 Clothing/Apparel and Textile Studies; 199999 Home Economics, Other. **Note:** The Department of Labor has not collected some data for this job, so it has fewer details than the other descriptions.

25-1193.00 Recreation and Fitness Studies Teachers, Postsecondary (College and University Faculty)

Education: Doctoral degree
Employed: 865,356
Openings: 139,101
Projected Growth: 22.6%
Earnings: No data available.

Teach courses pertaining to recreation, leisure, and fitness studies, including exercise physiology and facilities management.

GOE Number, Interest Area, and Work Group: 12.03.02; Education and Social Service; Educational Services: Postsecondary and Adult Teaching and Instructing. **Instructional Programs:** 310501 Health and Physical Education, General; 310504 Sport and Fitness Administration/Management; 310101 Parks, Recreation and Leisure Studies; 310505 Exercise Sciences/Physiology and Movement Studies; 310506 Socio-Psychological Sports Studies; 310599 Health and Physical Education/Fitness, Other. **Note:** The Department of Labor has not collected some data for this job, so it has fewer details than the other descriptions.

25-1194.00 Vocational Education Teachers, Postsecondary (Vocational Education Teachers and Instructors)

Education: Work experience in a related occupation
Employed: 419,625
Openings: 106,468
Projected Growth: 11%
Earnings: $34,430

Teach or instruct vocational or occupational subjects at the postsecondary level (but at less than the baccalaureate level) to students who have graduated or left high school. Includes correspondence-school instructors; industrial, commercial, and government training instructors; and adult education teachers and instructors who prepare persons to operate industrial machinery and equipment and transportation and communications equipment. Teaching may take place in public or private schools whose primary business is education or in a school associated with an organization whose primary business is other than education.

Arranges for lectures by subject matter experts in designated fields. Reviews enrollment applications and corresponds with applicants. Presents lectures and conducts discussions to increase students' knowledge and competence, using visual aids such as graphs, charts, videotapes, and slides. Plans course content and method of instruction. Determines training needs of students or workers. Corrects, grades, and comments on lesson assignments. Prepares reports and maintains records such as student grades, attendance, training activities, production records, and supply or equipment inventories. Participates in meetings, seminars, and training sessions and integrates relevant information into training program. Conducts on-the-job training, classes, or training sessions to teach and demonstrate principles, techniques, procedures, or methods of designated subjects. Solves operational problems and provides technical assistance with equipment and process techniques. Develops teaching aids such as instructional software, multimedia visual aids, computer tutorials, or study materials for instruction in vocational or occupational subjects. Selects and assembles books, materials, supplies, and equipment for training, courses, or projects. Administers oral, written, or performance tests to measure progress and to evaluate effectiveness of training. Prepares outline of instructional program and training schedule and establishes course goals. Observes and evaluates students' work to determine progress, provide feedback, and make suggestions for improvement. Recommends advancement, transfer, or termination of student or trainee based on mastery of subject.

GOE Number, Interest Area, and Work Group: 12.03.02; Education and Social Service; Educational Services: Postsecondary and Adult Teaching and Instructing. **Personality Type:** Social. Social occupations frequently involve working with, communicating with, and teaching people. These occupations often involve helping or providing service to others. **Work Values:** Authority; Achievement; Social Service; Working Conditions; Creativity; Responsibility. **Skills:** Speaking; Writing; Reading Comprehension; Instructing; Active Listening. **Abilities:** *Cognitive*—Oral Expression; Oral Comprehension; Written Comprehension; Written Expression; Problem Sensitivity; Number Facility. *Psychomotor*—none met the criteria. *Physical*—none met the criteria. *Sensory*—Speech Clarity; Near Vision; Auditory Attention. **General Work Activities:** *Information Input*—Getting Information Needed to Do the Job; Monitoring Processes, Materials, and Surroundings; Identifying Objects, Actions, and Events. *Mental Process*—Updating and Using Job-Relevant Knowledge; Scheduling Work and Activities; Developing Objectives and Strategies; Thinking Creatively; Judging Qualities of Things, Services, Other People's Work; Organizing, Planning, and Prioritizing. *Work Output*—Implementing Ideas and Programs; Documenting and Recording Information; Controlling Machines and Processes; Interacting with Computers. *Interacting with Others*—Teaching Others; Interpreting Meaning of Information to Others; Communicating with Persons Outside Organization; Establishing and Maintaining Relationships; Assisting and Caring for Others. **Physical Work Conditions:** Indoors; Standing; Walking or Running; Sitting. **Other Job Characteristics:** Importance of Being Sure All Is Done; Importance of Being Exact or Accurate; Consequence of Error.

Experience: Job Zone 4. A minimum of two to four years of work-related skill, knowledge, or experience is needed. **Job Preparation:** SVP 7.0 to less than 8.0—2 years to less than 10 years. **Knowledge:** Education and Training; English Language; Mathematics; Administration and Management; Clerical. **Instructional Programs:** 130101 Education, General; 131201 Adult and Continuing Teacher Education; 131205 Secondary Teacher Education; 131301 Agricultural Teacher Education (Vocational); 131303 Business Teacher Education (Vocational); 131308 Home Economics Teacher Education (Vocational); 131310 Marketing Operations Teacher Ed./Mkt. & Distribution Teacher; 131319 Technical Teacher Education (Vocational); 131320 Trade and Industrial Teacher Education (Vocational); 131327 Health Occupations Teacher Education (Vocational).

Related DOT Jobs: 075.127-010 Instructor, Psychiatric Aide; 090.222-010 Instructor, Business Education; 097.221-010 Instructor, Vocational Training; 099.227-014 Instructor, Correspondence School; 099.227-018 Instructor, Ground Services; 166.221-010 Instructor, Technical Training; 166.227-010 Training Representative; 235.222-010 Private-Branch-Exchange Service Adviser; 239.227-010 Customer-Service-Representative Instructor; 375.227-010 Police-Academy Instructor; 378.227-010 Marksmanship Instructor; 522.264-010 Training Technician; 621.221-010 Field-Service Representative; 683.222-010 Instructor, Weaving; 689.324-010 Instructor; 715.221-010 Instructor, Watch Assembly; 740.221-010 Instructor, Decorating; 788.222-010 Instructor; 789.222-010 Instructor, Apparel Manufacture; 919.223-010 Instructor, Bus, Trolley, and Taxi (partial list; see the introduction for sources of the complete list).

25-2000 Primary, Secondary, and Special Education School Teachers

25-2011.00 Preschool Teachers, Except Special Education (Preschool Teachers)

Education: Bachelor's degree

Employed: 345,575

Openings: 41,894

Projected Growth: 26.5%

Earnings: $17,310

Instruct children (normally up to 5 years of age) in activities designed to promote social, physical, and intellectual growth needed for primary school, in a preschool, day-care center, or other child development facility. Obtain required state certification.

Plans instructional activities for teacher aide. Structures play activities to instill concepts of respect and concern for others. Administers tests to determine each child's level of development according to design of test. Attends staff meetings. Confers with parents to explain preschool program and to discuss ways they can develop their child's interest. Monitors individual and/or group activities to prevent accidents and promote social skills. Demonstrates activity. Instructs children in activities designed to promote social, physical, and intellectual growth in facility, such as preschool or day care center. Plans individual and group activities for children, such as learning to listen to instructions, playing with others, and using play equipment. Reads books to entire class or to small groups.

GOE Number, Interest Area, and Work Group: 12.03.03; Education and Social Service; Educational Services: Pre-school, Elementary, and Secondary Teaching and Instructing. **Personality Type:** Social. Social occupations frequently involve working with, communicating with, and teaching people. These occupations often involve helping or providing service to others. **Work Values:** Authority; Social Service; Achievement; Responsibility; Creativity. **Skills:** Learning Strategies; Monitoring; Social Perceptiveness; Active Listening; Information Organization; Read-

ing Comprehension; Speaking. **Abilities:** *Cognitive*—Oral Expression; Oral Comprehension; Problem Sensitivity; Time Sharing; Written Comprehension. *Psychomotor*—Reaction Time; Response Orientation. *Physical*—Static Strength; Trunk Strength; Extent Flexibility. *Sensory*—Near Vision; Far Vision; Speech Clarity. **General Work Activities:** *Information Input*—Getting Information Needed to Do the Job; Monitoring Processes, Materials, and Surroundings; Identifying Objects, Actions, and Events. *Mental Process*—Thinking Creatively; Organizing, Planning, and Prioritizing; Scheduling Work and Activities. *Work Output*—Performing General Physical Activities; Documenting and Recording Information; Implementing Ideas and Programs; Handling and Moving Objects. *Interacting with Others*—Teaching Others; Assisting and Caring for Others; Establishing and Maintaining Relationships. **Physical Work Conditions:** Indoors; Standing; Sitting. **Other Job Characteristics:** Importance of Being Sure All Is Done; Importance of Being Exact or Accurate; Consequence of Error.

Experience: Job Zone 4. A minimum of two to four years of work-related skill, knowledge, or experience is needed. **Job Preparation:** SVP 7.0 to less than 8.0—2 years to less than 10 years. **Knowledge:** Education and Training; Customer and Personal Service; English Language; Psychology; Fine Arts. **Instructional Programs:** 130101 Education, General; 130201 Bilingual/Bicultural Education; 200201 Child Care and Guidance Workers and Managers, General.

Related DOT Job: 092.227-018 Teacher, Preschool.

25-2012.00 Kindergarten Teachers, Except Special Education (Kindergarten Teachers)

Education: Bachelor's degree

Employed: 183,560

Openings: 18,836

Projected Growth: 13.4%

Earnings: $33,590

Teach elemental natural and social science, personal hygiene, music, art, and literature to children from ages 4 to 6 years. Promote physical, mental, and social development. Obtain required state certification.

Instructs children in practices of personal cleanliness and self care. Supervises student activities, such as field visits, to stimulate student interest and broaden understanding of physical and social environment. Organizes and conducts games and group projects to develop cooperative behavior and to assist children in forming satisfying relationships. Alternates periods of strenuous activity with periods of rest or light activity to avoid over stimulation and fatigue. Observes children to detect signs of ill health or emotional disturbance and to evaluate progress. Encourages students in activities such as singing, dancing, and rhythmic activities, to promote self-expression and appreciation of esthetic experience. Teaches elemental science, personal hygiene, and humanities to children to promote physical, mental, and social development. Discusses student problems and progress with parents.

GOE Number, Interest Area, and Work Group: 12.03.03; Education and Social Service; Educational Services: Pre-school, Elementary, and Secondary Teaching and Instructing. **Personality**

Type: Social. Social occupations frequently involve working with, communicating with, and teaching people. These occupations often involve helping or providing service to others. **Work Values:** Authority; Social Service; Achievement; Creativity; Responsibility. **Skills:** Learning Strategies; Monitoring; Active Listening; Reading Comprehension; Speaking; Social Perceptiveness. **Abilities:** *Cognitive*—Oral Expression; Problem Sensitivity; Oral Comprehension; Written Comprehension; Written Expression; Fluency of Ideas. *Psychomotor*—Arm-Hand Steadiness; Finger Dexterity; Reaction Time. *Physical*—Trunk Strength; Extent Flexibility; Static Strength. *Sensory*—Far Vision; Near Vision; Speech Clarity. **General Work Activities:** *Information Input*—Getting Information Needed to Do the Job; Monitoring Processes, Materials, and Surroundings; Identifying Objects, Actions, and Events. *Mental Process*—Thinking Creatively; Organizing, Planning, and Prioritizing; Developing Objectives and Strategies; Updating and Using Job-Relevant Knowledge. *Work Output*—Documenting and Recording Information; Performing General Physical Activities; Implementing Ideas and Programs. *Interacting with Others*—Teaching Others; Assisting and Caring for Others; Establishing and Maintaining Relationships. **Physical Work Conditions:** Indoors; Standing; Sitting. **Other Job Characteristics:** Consequence of Error; Importance of Being Aware of New Events; Frustrating Circumstances.

Experience: Job Zone 4. A minimum of two to four years of work-related skill, knowledge, or experience is needed. **Job Preparation:** SVP 7.0 to less than 8.0—2 years to less than 10 years. **Knowledge:** Education and Training; Customer and Personal Service; English Language; Psychology; Fine Arts. **Instructional Programs:** 130101 Education, General; 130201 Bilingual/Bicultural Education.

Related DOT Job: 092.227-014 Teacher, Kindergarten.

25-2021.00 Elementary School Teachers, Except Special Education (Elementary School Teachers)

Education: Bachelor's degree
Employed: 1,754,475
Openings: 204,210
Projected Growth: 11.7%
Earnings: $36,110

Teach elementary-level pupils, in public or private schools, basic academic, social, and other formative skills.

Attends staff meetings, serves on committees, and attends workshops or in-service training activities. Prepares, administers, and corrects tests, and records results. Teaches subjects such as math, science, or social studies. Keeps attendance and grade records and prepares reports as required by school. Counsels pupils when adjustment and academic problems arise. Supervises outdoor and indoor play activities. Teaches combined-grade classes. Prepares bulletin boards. Teaches rules of conduct and maintains discipline and suitable learning environment in classroom and on playground. Evaluates student performance and discusses pupil academic and behavioral attitudes and achievements with parents. Assigns lessons, corrects papers, and hears oral presentations. Lectures, demonstrates, and uses audiovisual aids and computers to present academic, social, and motor skill subject matter to class. Prepares course objectives and outline for course of study, following curriculum guidelines or requirements of state and school. Coordinates class field trips.

GOE Number, Interest Area, and Work Group: 12.03.03; Education and Social Service; Educational Services: Pre-school, Elementary, and Secondary Teaching and Instructing. **Personality Type:** Social. Social occupations frequently involve working with, communicating with, and teaching people. These occupations often involve helping or providing service to others. **Work Values:** Authority; Social Service; Achievement; Responsibility; Creativity. **Skills:** Learning Strategies; Instructing; Social Perceptiveness; Reading Comprehension; Speaking. **Abilities:** *Cognitive*—Oral Expression; Written Comprehension; Written Expression; Oral Comprehension; Number Facility. *Psychomotor*—Arm-Hand Steadiness; Reaction Time; Response Orientation. *Physical*—Static Strength; Trunk Strength; Gross Body Coordination. *Sensory*—Speech Clarity; Far Vision; Near Vision. **General Work Activities:** *Information Input*—Getting Information Needed to Do the Job; Identifying Objects, Actions, and Events; Monitoring Processes, Materials, and Surroundings. *Mental Process*—Thinking Creatively; Developing Objectives and Strategies; Updating and Using Job-Relevant Knowledge. *Work Output*—Documenting and Recording Information; Implementing Ideas and Programs; Interacting with Computers. *Interacting with Others*—Teaching Others; Establishing and Maintaining Relationships; Interpreting Meaning of Information to Others; Assisting and Caring for Others. **Physical Work Conditions:** Indoors; Sitting; Standing. **Other Job Characteristics:** Importance of Being Sure All Is Done; Importance of Being Exact or Accurate; Frustrating Circumstances.

Experience: Job Zone 4. A minimum of two to four years of work-related skill, knowledge, or experience is needed. **Job Preparation:** SVP 7.0 to less than 8.0—2 years to less than 10 years. **Knowledge:** Education and Training; English Language; Mathematics; Psychology; History and Archeology; Customer and Personal Service. **Instructional Programs:** 130101 Education, General; 130201 Bilingual/Bicultural Education; 131202 Elementary Teacher Education; 131302 Art Teacher Education; 131305 English Teacher Education; 131306 Foreign Languages Teacher Education; 131311 Mathematics Teacher Education; 131312 Music Teacher Education; 131315 Reading Teacher Education; 131324 Drama and Dance Teacher Education; 131325 French Language Teacher Education; 131326 German Language Teacher Education; 131330 Spanish Language Teacher Education; 131331 Speech Teacher Education; 131399 Teacher Education, Specific Academic and Vocational Programs.

Related DOT Job: 092.227-010 Teacher, Elementary School.

25-2022.00 Middle School Teachers, Except Special and Vocational Education (Secondary School Teachers)

Education: Bachelor's degree
Employed: 1,426,213
Openings: 133,585
Projected Growth: 22.6%
Earnings: $37,890

Teach students, in public or private schools, in one or more subjects, at the middle, intermediate, or junior high level, which falls between elementary and senior high school as defined by applicable state laws and regulations.

Uses audiovisual aids and other materials to supplement presentations. Instructs students, using various teaching methods, such as lecture and demonstration. Assigns lessons and corrects homework. Prepares course outlines and objectives according to curriculum guidelines or state and local requirements. Develops and administers tests. Evaluates, records, and reports student progress. Performs advisory duties such as sponsoring student organizations or clubs, helping students select courses, and counseling students with problems. Selects, stores, orders, issues, and inventories classroom equipment, materials, and supplies. Keeps attendance records. Participates in faculty and professional meetings, educational conferences, and teacher training workshops. Confers with students, parents, and school counselors to resolve behavioral and academic problems. Maintains discipline in classroom.

GOE Number, Interest Area, and Work Group: 12.03.03; Education and Social Service; Educational Services: Pre-school, Elementary, and Secondary Teaching and Instructing. **Personality Type:** Social. Social occupations frequently involve working with, communicating with, and teaching people. These occupations often involve helping or providing service to others. **Work Values:** Social Service; Authority; Achievement; Responsibility; Ability Utilization; Creativity. **Skills:** Learning Strategies; Speaking; Reading Comprehension; Instructing; Mathematics. **Abilities:** *Cognitive*—Oral Expression; Written Expression; Oral Comprehension; Written Comprehension; Number Facility. *Psychomotor*—none met the criteria. *Physical*—none met the criteria. *Sensory*—Speech Clarity; Speech Recognition; Auditory Attention. **General Work Activities:** *Information Input*—Getting Information Needed to Do the Job; Identifying Objects, Actions, and Events; Monitoring Processes, Materials, and Surroundings. *Mental Process*—Updating and Using Job-Relevant Knowledge; Processing Information; Making Decisions and Solving Problems; Thinking Creatively. *Work Output*—Documenting and Recording Information; Implementing Ideas and Programs; Handling and Moving Objects. *Interacting with Others*—Teaching Others; Communicating with Persons Outside Organization; Interpreting Meaning of Information to Others. **Physical Work Conditions:** Indoors; Standing; Sitting. **Other Job Characteristics:** Importance of Being Exact or Accurate; Importance of Being Sure All Is Done; Consequence of Error; Frustrating Circumstances.

Experience: Job Zone 4. A minimum of two to four years of work-related skill, knowledge, or experience is needed. **Job Preparation:** SVP 7.0 to less than 8.0—2 years to less than 10 years. **Knowledge:** Education and Training; English Language; Mathematics; Therapy and Counseling; Psychology; Clerical. **Instructional Programs:** 130101 Education, General; 131203 Junior High/Intermediate/Middle School Teacher Education; 131205 Secondary Teacher Education; 131301 Agricultural Teacher Education (Vocational); 131302 Art Teacher Education; 131303 Business Teacher Education (Vocational); 131304 Driver and Safety Teacher Education; 131305 English Teacher Education; 131306 Foreign Languages Teacher Education; 131307 Health Teacher Education; 131308 Home Economics Teacher Education (Vocational); 131309 Technology Teacher Education/Industrial Arts Teacher Education;

131310 Marketing Operations Teacher Ed./Mkt. & Distribution Teacher; 131311 Mathematics Teacher Education; 131312 Music Teacher Education.

Related DOT Jobs: 091.227-010 Teacher, Secondary School; 099.224-010 Instructor, Physical Education.

25-2023.00 Vocational Education Teachers, Middle School (Vocational Education Teachers and Instructors)

Education: Work experience in a related occupation
Employed: 419,625
Openings: 106,468
Projected Growth: 11%
Earnings: $34,430

Teach or instruct vocational or occupational subjects at the middle school level.

Prepares course outlines and objectives according to curriculum guidelines or state and local requirements. Assigns lessons and corrects homework. Develops and administers tests. Confers with students, parents, and school counselors to resolve behavioral and academic problems. Maintains discipline in classroom. Instructs students, using various teaching methods, such as lecture and demonstration. Uses audiovisual aids and other materials to supplement presentations. Participates in faculty and professional meetings, educational conferences, and teacher training workshops. Selects, stores, orders, issues, and inventories classroom equipment, materials, and supplies. Keeps attendance records. Performs advisory duties such as sponsoring student organizations or clubs, helping students select courses, and counseling students with problems. Evaluates, records, and reports student progress.

GOE Number, Interest Area, and Work Group: 12.03.03; Education and Social Service; Educational Services: Pre-school, Elementary, and Secondary Teaching and Instructing. **Personality Type:** Social. Social occupations frequently involve working with, communicating with, and teaching people. These occupations often involve helping or providing service to others. **Work Values:** Authority; Social Service; Achievement; Responsibility; Creativity; Ability Utilization. **Skills:** Learning Strategies; Speaking; Reading Comprehension; Instructing; Mathematics. **Abilities:** *Cognitive*—Oral Expression; Written Expression; Oral Comprehension; Written Comprehension; Number Facility. *Psychomotor*—none met the criteria. *Physical*—none met the criteria. *Sensory*—Speech Clarity; Speech Recognition; Auditory Attention. **General Work Activities:** *Information Input*—Getting Information Needed to Do the Job; Identifying Objects, Actions, and Events; Monitoring Processes, Materials, and Surroundings. *Mental Process*—Updating and Using Job-Relevant Knowledge; Processing Information; Making Decisions and Solving Problems; Thinking Creatively. *Work Output*—Documenting and Recording Information; Implementing Ideas and Programs; Handling and Moving Objects. *Interacting with Others*—Teaching Others; Communicating with Persons Outside Organization; Interpreting Meaning of Information to Others. **Physical Work Conditions:** Indoors; Standing; Sitting. **Other Job Characteristics:** Importance of Being Exact or Accurate; Importance of Being Sure All Is Done; Consequence of Error; Frustrating Circumstances.

Experience: Job Zone 4. A minimum of two to four years of work-related skill, knowledge, or experience is needed. **Job Preparation:** SVP 7.0 to less than 8.0—2 years to less than 10 years. **Knowledge:** Education and Training; English Language; Mathematics; Therapy and Counseling; Psychology; Clerical. **Instructional Programs:** 130101 Education, General; 131201 Adult and Continuing Teacher Education; 131205 Secondary Teacher Education; 131301 Agricultural Teacher Education (Vocational); 131303 Business Teacher Education (Vocational); 131308 Home Economics Teacher Education (Vocational); 131310 Marketing Operations Teacher Ed./Mkt. & Distribution Teacher; 131319 Technical Teacher Education (Vocational); 131320 Trade and Industrial Teacher Education (Vocational); 131327 Health Occupations Teacher Education (Vocational).

Related DOT Job: 091.221-010 Teacher, Industrial Arts.

25-2031.00 Secondary School Teachers, Except Special and Vocational Education (Secondary School Teachers)

Education: Bachelor's degree

Employed: 1,426,213

Openings: 133,585

Projected Growth: 22.6%

Earnings: $37,890

Instruct secondary-level students, in public or private schools, in one or more subjects such as English, mathematics, or social studies. Specialize in a designated subject such as typing, commerce, or English.

Prepares course outlines and objectives according to curriculum guidelines or state and local requirements. Develops and administers tests. Confers with students, parents, and school counselors to resolve behavioral and academic problems. Maintains discipline in classroom. Assigns lessons and corrects homework. Uses audiovisual aids and other materials to supplement presentations. Selects, stores, orders, issues, and inventories classroom equipment, materials, and supplies. Keeps attendance records. Performs advisory duties, such as sponsoring student organizations or clubs, helping students select courses, and counseling students with problems. Instructs students, using various teaching methods, such as lecture and demonstration. Evaluates, records, and reports student progress. Participates in faculty and professional meetings, educational conferences, and teacher training workshops.

GOE Number, Interest Area, and Work Group: 12.03.03; Education and Social Service; Educational Services: Pre-school, Elementary, and Secondary Teaching and Instructing. **Personality Type:** Social. Social occupations frequently involve working with, communicating with, and teaching people. These occupations often involve helping or providing service to others. **Work Values:** Authority; Social Service; Achievement; Responsibility; Creativity; Ability Utilization. **Skills:** Learning Strategies; Speaking; Reading Comprehension; Instructing; Mathematics. **Abilities:** *Cognitive*—Oral Expression; Oral Comprehension; Written Comprehension; Written Expression; Number Facility. *Psychomotor*—none met the criteria. *Physical*—none met the criteria.

Sensory—Speech Clarity; Speech Recognition; Auditory Attention. **General Work Activities:** *Information Input*—Getting Information Needed to Do the Job; Identifying Objects, Actions, and Events; Monitoring Processes, Materials, and Surroundings. *Mental Process*—Updating and Using Job-Relevant Knowledge; Processing Information; Making Decisions and Solving Problems; Thinking Creatively. *Work Output*—Documenting and Recording Information; Implementing Ideas and Programs; Handling and Moving Objects. *Interacting with Others*—Teaching Others; Communicating with Persons Outside Organization; Interpreting Meaning of Information to Others. **Physical Work Conditions:** Indoors; Standing; Sitting. **Other Job Characteristics:** Importance of Being Exact or Accurate; Importance of Being Sure All Is Done; Frustrating Circumstances; Consequence of Error.

Experience: Job Zone 4. A minimum of two to four years of work-related skill, knowledge, or experience is needed. **Job Preparation:** SVP 7.0 to less than 8.0—2 years to less than 10 years. **Knowledge:** Education and Training; English Language; Mathematics; Therapy and Counseling; Psychology; Clerical. **Instructional Programs:** 130101 Education, General; 131203 Junior High/Intermediate/Middle School Teacher Education; 131205 Secondary Teacher Education; 131301 Agricultural Teacher Education (Vocational); 131302 Art Teacher Education; 131303 Business Teacher Education (Vocational); 131304 Driver and Safety Teacher Education; 131305 English Teacher Education; 131306 Foreign Languages Teacher Education; 131307 Health Teacher Education; 131308 Home Economics Teacher Education (Vocational); 131309 Technology Teacher Education/Industrial Arts Teacher Education; 131310 Marketing Operations Teacher Ed./Mkt. & Distribution Teacher; 131311 Mathematics Teacher Education; 131312 Music Teacher Education.

Related DOT Jobs: 091.227-010 Teacher, Secondary School; 099.224-010 Instructor, Physical Education; 099.227-022 Instructor, Military Science.

25-2032.00 Vocational Education Teachers, Secondary School (Vocational Education Teachers and Instructors)

Education: Work experience in a related occupation

Employed: 419,625

Openings: 106,468

Projected Growth: 11%

Earnings: $34,430

Teach or instruct vocational or occupational subjects at the secondary school level.

Keeps attendance records. Prepares course outlines and objectives according to curriculum guidelines or state and local requirements. Assigns lessons and corrects homework. Uses audiovisual aids and other materials to supplement presentations. Participates in faculty and professional meetings, educational conferences, and teacher training workshops. Develops and administers tests. Performs advisory duties, such as sponsoring student organizations or clubs, helping students select courses, and counseling students with problems. Selects, stores, orders, issues, and inventories classroom equipment, materials, and supplies.

Maintains discipline in classroom. Evaluates, records, and reports student progress. Instructs students, using various teaching methods, such as lecture and demonstration. Confers with students, parents, and school counselors to resolve behavioral and academic problems.

GOE Number, Interest Area, and Work Group: 12.03.03; Education and Social Service; Educational Services: Pre-school, Elementary, and Secondary Teaching and Instructing. **Personality Type:** Social. Social occupations frequently involve working with, communicating with, and teaching people. These occupations often involve helping or providing service to others. **Work Values:** Social Service; Authority; Achievement; Responsibility; Ability Utilization; Creativity. **Skills:** Learning Strategies; Speaking; Reading Comprehension; Instructing; Mathematics. **Abilities:** *Cognitive*—Oral Expression; Oral Comprehension; Written Comprehension; Written Expression; Number Facility. *Psychomotor*—none met the criteria. *Physical*—none met the criteria. *Sensory*—Speech Clarity; Speech Recognition; Auditory Attention. **General Work Activities:** *Information Input*—Getting Information Needed to Do the Job; Identifying Objects, Actions, and Events; Monitoring Processes, Materials, and Surroundings. *Mental Process*—Updating and Using Job-Relevant Knowledge; Processing Information; Making Decisions and Solving Problems; Thinking Creatively. *Work Output*—Documenting and Recording Information; Implementing Ideas and Programs; Handling and Moving Objects. *Interacting with Others*—Teaching Others; Communicating with Persons Outside Organization; Interpreting Meaning of Information to Others. **Physical Work Conditions:** Indoors; Standing; Sitting. **Other Job Characteristics:** Importance of Being Exact or Accurate; Importance of Being Sure All Is Done; Frustrating Circumstances; Consequence of Error.

Experience: Job Zone 4. A minimum of two to four years of work-related skill, knowledge, or experience is needed. **Job Preparation:** SVP 7.0 to less than 8.0—2 years to less than 10 years. **Knowledge:** Education and Training; English Language; Mathematics; Therapy and Counseling; Psychology; Clerical. **Instructional Programs:** 130101 Education, General; 131201 Adult and Continuing Teacher Education; 131205 Secondary Teacher Education; 131301 Agricultural Teacher Education (Vocational); 131303 Business Teacher Education (Vocational); 131308 Home Economics Teacher Education (Vocational); 131310 Marketing Operations Teacher Ed./Mkt. & Distribution Teacher; 131319 Technical Teacher Education (Vocational); 131320 Trade and Industrial Teacher Education (Vocational); 131327 Health Occupations Teacher Education (Vocational).

Related DOT Job: 091.221-010 Teacher, Industrial Arts.

25-2041.00 Special Education Teachers, Preschool, Kindergarten, and Elementary School (Special Education Teachers)

Education: Bachelor's degree

Employed: 406,036

Openings: 36,540

Projected Growth: 33.8%

Earnings: $37,850

Teach elementary school and preschool subjects to educationally and physically handicapped students. Includes teachers who specialize and work with audibly and visually handicapped students and those who teach basic academic and life-processes skills to the mentally impaired.

Confers with other staff members to plan programs designed to promote educational, physical, and social development of students. Instructs students in daily living skills required for independent maintenance and economic self-sufficiency, such as hygiene, safety, and food preparation. Plans curriculum and other instructional materials to meet students' needs, considering such factors as physical, emotional, and educational abilities. Instructs students in academic subjects, utilizing various teaching techniques, such as phonetics, multisensory learning, and repetition, to reinforce learning. Instructs students, using special educational strategies and techniques to improve sensory-motor and perceptual-motor development, memory, language, and cognition. Confers with parents, administrators, testing specialists, social workers, and others to develop individual educational plan for student. Works with students to increase motivation. Provides consistent reinforcement to learning, and continuous feedback to students. Observes, evaluates, and prepares reports on progress of students. Meets with parents to provide support, guidance in using community resources, and skills in dealing with students' learning impairments. Selects and teaches reading material and math problems related to everyday life of individual student. Teaches socially acceptable behavior, employing techniques such as behavior modification and positive reinforcement. Administers and interprets results of ability and achievement tests.

GOE Number, Interest Area, and Work Group: 12.03.03; Education and Social Service; Educational Services: Pre-school, Elementary, and Secondary Teaching and Instructing. **Personality Type:** Social. Social occupations frequently involve working with, communicating with, and teaching people. These occupations often involve helping or providing service to others. **Work Values:** Social Service; Achievement; Authority; Responsibility; Ability Utilization. **Skills:** Learning Strategies; Social Perceptiveness; Instructing; Monitoring; Speaking; Active Listening. **Abilities:** *Cognitive*—Oral Expression; Written Comprehension; Problem Sensitivity; Oral Comprehension; Written Expression. *Psychomotor*—none met the criteria. *Physical*—none met the criteria. *Sensory*—Speech Clarity; Speech Recognition; Auditory Attention. **General Work Activities:** *Information Input*—Getting Information Needed to Do the Job; Identifying Objects, Actions, and Events; Monitoring Processes, Materials, and Surroundings. *Mental Process*—Making Decisions and Solving Problems; Thinking Creatively; Analyzing Data or Information; Updating and Using Job-Relevant Knowledge. *Work Output*—Implementing Ideas and Programs; Documenting and Recording Information; Handling and Moving Objects. *Interacting with Others*—Teaching Others; Interpreting Meaning of Information to Others; Establishing and Maintaining Relationships. **Physical Work Conditions:** Indoors; Sitting; Standing. **Other Job Characteristics:** Frustrating Circumstances; Importance of Being Exact or Accurate; Importance of Being Sure All Is Done; Consequence of Error; Importance of Being Aware of New Events.

Experience: Job Zone 4. A minimum of two to four years of work-related skill, knowledge, or experience is needed. **Job Prepara-**

tion: SVP 7.0 to less than 8.0—2 years to less than 10 years. **Knowledge:** Education and Training; Psychology; Therapy and Counseling; English Language; Customer and Personal Service. **Instructional Programs:** 130101 Education, General; 131001 Special Education, General; 131003 Education of the Deaf and Hearing Impaired; 131005 Education of the Emotionally Handicapped; 131006 Education of the Mentally Handicapped; 131007 Education of the Multiple Handicapped; 131008 Education of the Physically Handicapped; 131009 Education of the Blind and Visually Handicapped; 131011 Education of the Specific Learning Disabled; 131012 Education of the Speech Impaired; 131013 Education of the Autistic; 131099 Special Education, Other.

Related DOT Jobs: 094.224-010 Teacher, Hearing Impaired; 094.224-014 Teacher, Physically Impaired; 094.224-018 Teacher, Visually Impaired; 094.227-010 Teacher, Emotionally Impaired; 094.227-022 Teacher, Mentally Impaired; 094.227-030 Teacher, Learning Disabled; 099.227-042 Teacher, Resource.

25-2042.00 Special Education Teachers, Middle School (Special Education Teachers)

Education: Bachelor's degree
Employed: 406,036
Openings: 36,540
Projected Growth: 33.8%
Earnings: $37,850

Teach middle school subjects to educationally and physically handicapped students. Includes teachers who specialize and work with audibly and visually handicapped students and those who teach basic academic and life-processes skills to the mentally impaired.

Works with students to increase motivation. Observes, evaluates, and prepares reports on progress of students. Instructs students, using special educational strategies and techniques to improve sensory-motor and perceptual-motor development, memory, language, and cognition. Instructs students in daily living skills required for independent maintenance and economic self-sufficiency, such as hygiene, safety, and food preparation. Confers with parents, administrators, testing specialists, social workers, and others to develop individual educational plan for student. Meets with parents to provide support, guidance in using community resources, and skills in dealing with students' learning impairments. Confers with other staff members to plan programs designed to promote educational, physical, and social development of students. Teaches socially acceptable behavior, employing techniques such as behavior modification and positive reinforcement. Administers and interprets results of ability and achievement tests. Selects and teaches reading material and math problems related to everyday life of individual student. Plans curriculum and other instructional materials to meet student's needs, considering such factors as physical, emotional, and educational abilities. Instructs students in academic subjects, utilizing various teaching techniques such as phonetics, multisensory learning, and repetition, to reinforce learning. Provides consistent reinforcement to learning and continuous feedback to students.

GOE Number, Interest Area, and Work Group: 12.03.03; Education and Social Service; Educational Services: Pre-school, Elementary, and Secondary Teaching and Instructing. **Personality Type:** Social. Social occupations frequently involve working with, communicating with, and teaching people. These occupations often involve helping or providing service to others. **Work Values:** Social Service; Achievement; Authority; Ability Utilization; Responsibility. **Skills:** Learning Strategies; Social Perceptiveness; Instructing; Speaking; Active Listening; Monitoring. **Abilities:** *Cognitive*—Oral Expression; Written Comprehension; Problem Sensitivity; Oral Comprehension; Written Expression. *Psychomotor*—none met the criteria. *Physical*—none met the criteria. *Sensory*—Speech Clarity; Speech Recognition; Auditory Attention. **General Work Activities:** *Information Input*—Getting Information Needed to Do the Job; Monitoring Processes, Materials, and Surroundings; Identifying Objects, Actions, and Events. *Mental Process*—Making Decisions and Solving Problems; Thinking Creatively; Updating and Using Job-Relevant Knowledge; Analyzing Data or Information. *Work Output*—Implementing Ideas and Programs; Documenting and Recording Information; Handling and Moving Objects. *Interacting with Others*—Teaching Others; Establishing and Maintaining Relationships; Interpreting Meaning of Information to Others. **Physical Work Conditions:** Indoors; Sitting; Standing. **Other Job Characteristics:** Frustrating Circumstances; Importance of Being Exact or Accurate; Importance of Being Aware of New Events; Consequence of Error; Importance of Being Sure All Is Done.

Experience: Job Zone 4. A minimum of two to four years of work-related skill, knowledge, or experience is needed. **Job Preparation:** SVP 7.0 to less than 8.0—2 years to less than 10 years. **Knowledge:** Education and Training; Therapy and Counseling; Psychology; English Language; Customer and Personal Service. **Instructional Programs:** 130101 Education, General; 131001 Special Education, General; 131003 Education of the Deaf and Hearing Impaired; 131005 Education of the Emotionally Handicapped; 131006 Education of the Mentally Handicapped; 131007 Education of the Multiple Handicapped; 131008 Education of the Physically Handicapped; 131009 Education of the Blind and Visually Handicapped; 131011 Education of the Specific Learning Disabled; 131012 Education of the Speech Impaired; 131013 Education of the Autistic; 131099 Special Education, Other.

Related DOT Jobs: 094.224-010 Teacher, Hearing Impaired; 094.224-014 Teacher, Physically Impaired; 094.227-010 Teacher, Emotionally Impaired; 094.227-022 Teacher, Mentally Impaired; 094.227-026 Teacher, Vocational Training; 094.227-030 Teacher, Learning Disabled; 099.227-042 Teacher, Resource.

25-2043.00 Special Education Teachers, Secondary School (Special Education Teachers)

Education: Bachelor's degree
Employed: 406,036
Openings: 36,540
Projected Growth: 33.8%
Earnings: $37,850

Teach secondary school subjects to educationally and physically handicapped students. Includes teachers who specialize and work with audibly and visually handicapped students and those who teach basic academic and life-processes skills to the mentally impaired.

Provides consistent reinforcement to learning, and continuous feedback to student. Plans curriculum and other instructional materials to meet student's needs, considering such factors as physical, emotional, and educational abilities. Instructs students in daily living skills required for independent maintenance and economic self-sufficiency, such as hygiene, safety, and food preparation. Instructs students in academic subjects, utilizing various teaching techniques such as phonetics, multisensory learning, and repetition, to reinforce learning. Instructs students, using special educational strategies and techniques to improve sensory-motor and perceptual-motor development, memory, language, and cognition. Confers with parents, administrators, testing specialists, social workers, and others to develop individual educational plan for student. Works with students to increase motivation. Observes, evaluates, and prepares reports on progress of students. Meets with parents to provide support, guidance in using community resources, and skills in dealing with student's learning impairment. Selects and teaches reading material and math problems related to everyday life of individual student. Administers and interprets results of ability and achievement tests. Teaches socially acceptable behavior, employing techniques such as behavior modification and positive reinforcement. Confers with other staff members to plan programs designed to promote educational, physical, and social development of students.

GOE Number, Interest Area, and Work Group: 12.03.03; Education and Social Service; Educational Services: Pre-school, Elementary, and Secondary Teaching and Instructing. **Personality Type:** Social. Social occupations frequently involve working with, communicating with, and teaching people. These occupations often involve helping or providing service to others. **Work Values:** Achievement; Social Service; Authority; Responsibility; Ability Utilization. **Skills:** Learning Strategies; Social Perceptiveness; Instructing; Monitoring; Speaking; Active Listening. **Abilities:** *Cognitive*—Oral Expression; Written Comprehension; Oral Comprehension; Written Expression; Problem Sensitivity. *Psychomotor*—none met the criteria. *Physical*—none met the criteria. *Sensory*—Speech Clarity; Speech Recognition; Auditory Attention. **General Work Activities:** *Information Input*—Getting Information Needed to Do the Job; Monitoring Processes, Materials, and Surroundings; Identifying Objects, Actions, and Events. *Mental Process*—Making Decisions and Solving Problems; Thinking Creatively; Analyzing Data or Information; Updating and Using Job-Relevant Knowledge. *Work Output*—Implementing Ideas and Programs; Documenting and Recording Information; Handling and Moving Objects. *Interacting with Others*—Teaching Others; Interpreting Meaning of Information to Others; Establishing and Maintaining Relationships. **Physical Work Conditions:** Indoors; Sitting; Standing. **Other Job Characteristics:** Frustrating Circumstances; Importance of Being Exact or Accurate; Consequence of Error; Importance of Being Sure All Is Done; Importance of Being Aware of New Events.

Experience: Job Zone 4. A minimum of two to four years of work-related skill, knowledge, or experience is needed. **Job Prepara-**tion: SVP 7.0 to less than 8.0—2 years to less than 10 years. **Knowledge:** Education and Training; Therapy and Counseling; Psychology; English Language; Customer and Personal Service. **Instructional Programs:** 130101 Education, General; 131001 Special Education, General; 131003 Education of the Deaf and Hearing Impaired; 131005 Education of the Emotionally Handicapped; 131006 Education of the Mentally Handicapped; 131007 Education of the Multiple Handicapped; 131008 Education of the Physically Handicapped; 131009 Education of the Blind and Visually Handicapped; 131011 Education of the Specific Learning Disabled; 131012 Education of the Speech Impaired; 131013 Education of the Autistic; 131099 Special Education, Other.

Related DOT Jobs: 094.107-010 Work-Study Coordinator, Special Education; 094.224-010 Teacher, Hearing Impaired; 094.224-014 Teacher, Physically Impaired; 094.224-018 Teacher, Visually Impaired; 094.227-010 Teacher, Emotionally Impaired; 094.227-022 Teacher, Mentally Impaired; 094.227-030 Teacher, Learning Disabled; 099.227-042 Teacher, Resource.

25-3000 Other Teachers and Instructors

25-3011.00 Adult Literacy, Remedial Education, and GED Teachers and Instructors (Adult Education Instructors)

Education: Work experience in a related occupation
Employed: 168,046
Openings: 46,224
Projected Growth: 20.9%
Earnings: $24,790

Teach or instruct out-of-school youth and adults in remedial education classes, preparatory classes for the General Educational Development test, literacy, or English as a second language. Teaching may or may not take place in a traditional educational institution.

Selects and assembles books, materials, and supplies for courses or projects. Adapts course of study and training methods to meet students' needs and abilities. Administers oral, written, and performance tests and issues grades in accordance with performance. Prepares outline of instructional program, lesson plans, and establishes course goals. Observes and evaluates students' work to determine progress and makes suggestions for improvement. Directs and supervises student project activities, performances, tournaments, exhibits, contests, or plays. Observes students to determine and evaluate qualifications, limitations, abilities, interests, aptitudes, temperament, and individual characteristics. Confers with leaders of government and other groups to coordinate training or to assist students to fulfill required criteria. Maintains records such as student grades, attendance, and supply inventory. Writes instructional articles on designated subjects. Conducts classes, workshops, and demonstrations to teach principles, techniques, procedures, or methods of designated subject. Orders, stores, and inventories books, materials, and supplies. Evaluates success of instruction, based on number and enthusiasm of participants; recommends retaining or eliminating course in future. Plans and conducts field trips to enrich instructional programs. Presents lectures and conducts discussions to increase students' knowledge and competence. Plans course content and method of instruction.

GOE Number, Interest Area, and Work Group: 12.03.02; Education and Social Service; Educational Services: Postsecondary and Adult Teaching and Instructing. **Personality Type:** Social. Social occupations frequently involve working with, communicating with, and teaching people. These occupations often involve helping or providing service to others. **Work Values:** Authority; Achievement; Social Service; Working Conditions; Creativity; Responsibility; Ability Utilization. **Skills:** Writing; Speaking; Instructing; Reading Comprehension; Active Listening. **Abilities:** *Cognitive*—Oral Expression; Oral Comprehension; Written Comprehension; Written Expression; Time Sharing; Fluency of Ideas. *Psychomotor*—none met the criteria. *Physical*—Gross Body Equilibrium. *Sensory*—Speech Clarity; Speech Recognition; Auditory Attention. **General Work Activities:** *Information Input*—Getting Information Needed to Do the Job; Monitoring Processes, Materials, and Surroundings; Identifying Objects, Actions, and Events. *Mental Process*—Making Decisions and Solving Problems; Scheduling Work and Activities; Updating and Using Job-Relevant Knowledge; Thinking Creatively. *Work Output*—Implementing Ideas and Programs; Documenting and Recording Information; Performing General Physical Activities; Handling and Moving Objects; Interacting with Computers. *Interacting with Others*—Teaching Others; Establishing and Maintaining Relationships; Communicating with Persons Outside Organization; Coaching and Developing Others. **Physical Work Conditions:** Indoors; Sitting; Standing. **Other Job Characteristics:** Importance of Being Exact or Accurate; Importance of Being Sure All Is Done; Frustrating Circumstances.

Experience: Job Zone 4. A minimum of two to four years of work-related skill, knowledge, or experience is needed. **Job Preparation:** SVP 7.0 to less than 8.0—2 years to less than 10 years. **Knowledge:** Education and Training; English Language; Administration and Management; Mathematics; Economics and Accounting; Computers and Electronics; Sociology and Anthropology; Psychology. **Instructional Programs:** 130101 Education, General; 131201 Adult and Continuing Teacher Education; 131304 Driver and Safety Teacher Education; 131401 Teaching English as a Second Language/Foreign Language.

Related DOT Job: 099.227-030 Teacher, Adult Education.

25-3021.00 Self-Enrichment Education Teachers
(Adult Education Instructors)

Education: Work experience in a related occupation

Employed: 168,046

Openings: 46,224

Projected Growth: 20.9%

Earnings: $24,790

Teach or instruct courses other than those that normally lead to an occupational objective or degree, such as courses in self-improvement and in nonvocational and nonacademic subjects. Teaching may or may not take place in a traditional educational institution.

Evaluates success of instruction, based on number and enthusiasm of participants; recommends retaining or eliminating course in future. Plans course content and method of instruction. Administers oral, written, and performance tests and issues grades in accordance with performance. Observes students to determine and evaluate qualifications, limitations, abilities, interests, aptitudes, temperament, and individual characteristics. Confers with leaders of government and other groups to coordinate training or to assist students to fulfill required criteria. Presents lectures and conducts discussions to increase students' knowledge and competence. Orders, stores, and inventories books, materials, and supplies. Maintains records such as student grades, attendance, and supply inventory. Plans and conducts field trips to enrich instructional programs. Directs and supervises student project activities, performances, tournaments, exhibits, contests, or plays. Selects and assembles books, materials, and supplies for courses or projects. Conducts classes, workshops, and demonstrations to teach principles, techniques, procedures, or methods of designated subject. Writes instructional articles on designated subjects. Prepares outline of instructional program, lesson plans, and establishes course goals.

GOE Number, Interest Area, and Work Group: 12.03.02; Education and Social Service; Educational Services: Postsecondary and Adult Teaching and Instructing. **Personality Type:** Social. Social occupations frequently involve working with, communicating with, and teaching people. These occupations often involve helping or providing service to others. **Work Values:** Authority; Achievement; Social Service; Ability Utilization; Creativity; Working Conditions; Responsibility. **Skills:** Speaking; Writing; Reading Comprehension; Instructing; Active Listening. **Abilities:** *Cognitive*—Oral Expression; Oral Comprehension; Written Expression; Written Comprehension; Fluency of Ideas; Time Sharing. *Psychomotor*—none met the criteria. *Physical*—Gross Body Equilibrium. *Sensory*—Speech Clarity; Auditory Attention; Speech Recognition. **General Work Activities:** *Information Input*—Getting Information Needed to Do the Job; Monitoring Processes, Materials, and Surroundings; Identifying Objects, Actions, and Events. *Mental Process*—Updating and Using Job-Relevant Knowledge; Scheduling Work and Activities; Making Decisions and Solving Problems; Thinking Creatively. *Work Output*—Documenting and Recording Information; Implementing Ideas and Programs; Performing General Physical Activities; Handling and Moving Objects; Interacting with Computers. *Interacting with Others*—Teaching Others; Establishing and Maintaining Relationships; Communicating with Persons Outside Organization; Coaching and Developing Others. **Physical Work Conditions:** Indoors; Standing; Sitting. **Other Job Characteristics:** Importance of Being Exact or Accurate; Importance of Being Sure All Is Done; Frustrating Circumstances.

Experience: Job Zone 4. A minimum of two to four years of work-related skill, knowledge, or experience is needed. **Job Preparation:** SVP 7.0 to less than 8.0—2 years to less than 10 years. **Knowledge:** Education and Training; English Language; Administration and Management; Mathematics; Computers and Electronics; Sociology and Anthropology; Psychology; Economics and Accounting. **Instructional Programs:** 130101 Education, General; 131201 Adult and Continuing Teacher Education; 131304 Driver and Safety Teacher Education; 131401 Teaching English as a Second Language/Foreign Language.

Related DOT Jobs: 097.227-010 Instructor, Flying II; 099.223-010 Instructor, Driving; 099.224-014 Teacher, Adventure Education; 099.227-026 Instructor, Modeling; 099.227-030 Teacher, Adult Education; 099.227-038 Teacher; 149.021-010 Teacher, Art; 150.027-014 Teacher, Drama; 151.027-014 Instructor, Dancing; 152.021-010 Teacher, Music; 159.227-010 Instructor, Bridge; 169.127-010 Civil Preparedness Training Officer.

25-4000 Librarians, Curators, and Archivists

25-4011.00 Archivists (Archivists, Curators, Museum Technicians, and Conservators)

Education: Master's degree
Employed: 23,202
Openings: 4,118
Projected Growth: 12.6%
Earnings: $31,750

Appraise, edit, and direct the safekeeping of permanent records and historically valuable documents. Participate in research activities based on archival materials.

Establishes policy guidelines concerning public access and use of materials. Selects and edits documents for publication and display, according to knowledge of subject, literary expression, and techniques for presentation and display. Directs filing and cross indexing of selected documents in alphabetical and chronological order. Directs acquisition and physical arrangement of new materials. Analyzes documents by ascertaining date of writing, author, or original recipient of letter to appraise value to posterity. Requests or recommends pertinent materials available in libraries, private collections, or other archives. Prepares document descriptions and reference aids for use of archives, such as accession lists, bibliographies, abstracts, and microfilmed documents. Directs activities of workers engaged in cataloging and safekeeping of valuable materials and disposition of worthless materials. Advises government agencies, scholars, journalists, and others conducting research by supplying available materials and information.

GOE Number, Interest Area, and Work Group: 12.03.04; Education and Social Service; Educational Services: Library and Museum. **Personality Type:** Investigative. Investigative occupations frequently involve working with ideas and require an extensive amount of thinking. These occupations can involve searching for facts and figuring out problems mentally. **Work Values:** Working Conditions; Moral Values; Ability Utilization; Autonomy; Authority; Achievement; Company Policies and Practices. **Skills:** Information Gathering; Writing; Information Organization; Reading Comprehension; Judgment and Decision Making; Management of Personnel Resources; Active Listening; Speaking. **Abilities:** *Cognitive*—Written Comprehension; Written Expression; Oral Expression; Information Ordering; Oral Comprehension. *Psychomotor*—none met the criteria. *Physical*—none met the criteria. *Sensory*—Near Vision; Speech Clarity. **General Work Activities:** *Information Input*—Getting Information Needed to Do the Job; Identifying Objects, Actions, and Events; Estimating Needed

Characteristics. *Mental Process*—Judging Qualities of Things, Services, Other People's Work; Processing Information; Analyzing Data or Information. *Work Output*—Documenting and Recording Information; Implementing Ideas and Programs; Handling and Moving Objects. *Interacting with Others*—Providing Consultation and Advice to Others; Communicating with Other Workers; Interpreting Meaning of Information to Others. **Physical Work Conditions:** Indoors; Sitting; Standing. **Other Job Characteristics:** Importance of Being Exact or Accurate; Importance of Being Sure All Is Done; Consequence of Error.

Experience: Job Zone 5. Extensive skill, knowledge, and experience are needed. Very advanced communication and organizational skills are required. **Job Preparation:** SVP 8.0 and above—4 years to more than 10 years. **Knowledge:** History and Archeology; English Language; Administration and Management; Clerical; Communications and Media. **Instructional Programs:** 301401 Museology/Museum Studies; 450805 Public/Applied History and Archival Administration; 500703 Art History, Criticism and Conservation.

Related DOT Job: 101.167-010 Archivist.

25-4012.00 Curators (Archivists, Curators, Museum Technicians, and Conservators)

Education: Master's degree
Employed: 23,202
Openings: 4,118
Projected Growth: 12.6%
Earnings: $31,750

Administer affairs of museum. Conduct research programs. Direct instructional, research, and public-service activities of institution.

Inspects premises for evidence of deterioration and need for repair. Develops and maintains institution's registration, cataloging, and basic record-keeping systems. Negotiates and authorizes purchase, sale, exchange, or loan of collections. Directs and coordinates activities of curatorial, personnel, fiscal, technical, research, and clerical staff. Writes and reviews grant proposals, journal articles, institutional reports, and publicity materials. Conducts or organizes tours, workshops, and instructional sessions to acquaint individuals with use of institution's facilities and materials. Arranges insurance coverage for objects on loan or special exhibits and recommends changes in coverage for entire collection. Schedules special events at facility and organizes details such as refreshment, entertainment, and decorations. Plans and organizes acquisition, storage, and exhibition of collections and related educational materials. Studies, examines, and tests acquisitions to authenticate their origin, composition, history, and current value. Confers with institution's board of directors to formulate and interpret policies, determine budget requirements, and plan overall operations. Plans and conducts special research projects. Attends meetings, conventions, and civic events to promote use of institution's services, seek financing, and maintain community alliances. Reserves facilities for group tours and social events and collects admission fees.

GOE Number, Interest Area, and Work Group: 12.03.04; Education and Social Service; Educational Services: Library and Museum. **Personality Type:** Artistic. Artistic occupations frequently involve working with forms, designs, and patterns. These occupations often require self-expression, and the work can be done without following a clear set of rules. **Work Values:** Working Conditions; Authority; Creativity; Responsibility; Moral Values; Activity; Achievement; Ability Utilization. **Skills:** Writing; Coordination; Judgment and Decision Making; Reading Comprehension; Implementation Planning; Management of Financial Resources; Problem Identification; Speaking; Identification of Key Causes; Management of Personnel Resources. **Abilities:** *Cognitive*—Written Expression; Oral Expression; Oral Comprehension; Written Comprehension; Information Ordering; Category Flexibility. *Psychomotor*—none met the criteria. *Physical*—none met the criteria. *Sensory*—Speech Clarity; Far Vision; Auditory Attention. **General Work Activities:** *Information Input*—Getting Information Needed to Do the Job; Identifying Objects, Actions, and Events; Inspecting Equipment, Structures, Materials. *Mental Process*—Judging Qualities of Things, Services, Other People's Work; Organizing, Planning, and Prioritizing; Making Decisions and Solving Problems. *Work Output*—Implementing Ideas and Programs; Documenting and Recording Information; Performing General Physical Activities; Handling and Moving Objects. *Interacting with Others*—Monitoring and Controlling Resources; Communicating with Persons Outside Organization; Establishing and Maintaining Relationships. **Physical Work Conditions:** Indoors; Standing; Sitting. **Other Job Characteristics:** Consequence of Error; Importance of Being Sure All Is Done; Importance of Being Exact or Accurate.

Experience: Job Zone 4. A minimum of two to four years of work-related skill, knowledge, or experience is needed. **Job Preparation:** SVP 7.0 to less than 8.0—2 years to less than 10 years. **Knowledge:** History and Archeology; Administration and Management; English Language; Fine Arts; Economics and Accounting; Communications and Media; Sociology and Anthropology; Mathematics. **Instructional Programs:** 301401 Museology/Museum Studies; 450805 Public/Applied History and Archival Administration; 500703 Art History, Criticism and Conservation.

Related DOT Jobs: 099.167-030 Educational Resource Coordinator; 102.017-010 Curator; 102.117-010 Supervisor, Historic Sites; 102.117-014 Director, Museum-or-Zoo; 102.167-014 Historic-Site Administrator; 102.167-018 Registrar, Museum.

25-4013.00 Museum Technicians and Conservators
(Archivists, Curators, Museum Technicians, and Conservators)

Education: Master's degree
Employed: 23,202
Openings: 4,118
Projected Growth: 12.6%
Earnings: $31,750

Prepare specimens such as fossils, skeletal parts, lace, and textiles, for museum collection and exhibits. Restore documents or install, arrange, and exhibit materials.

Prepares reports of activities; documents methods of preservation and repair. Recommends preservation measures, such as control of temperature, humidity, and exposure to light, to curatorial and building maintenance staff. Cleans objects such as paper, textiles, wood, metal, glass, rock, pottery, and furniture, using cleansers, solvents, soap solutions, and polishes. Studies descriptive information on object or conducts standard chemical and physical tests to determine age, composition, and original appearance. Repairs or reassembles broken objects, using glue, solder, hand tools, power tools, and small machines. Constructs skeletal mounts of fossils, replicas of archaeological artifacts, or duplicate specimens, using variety of materials and hand tools. Evaluates need for repair and determines safest and most effective method of treating surface of object. Repairs and restores surfaces of artifacts to regain original appearance and to prevent deterioration, according to accepted procedures. Designs and fabricates missing or broken parts. Preserves or directs preservation of objects, using plaster, resin, sealants, hardeners, and shellac. Installs, arranges, assembles, and prepares artifacts for exhibition. Cuts and welds metal sections in reconstruction or renovation of exterior structural sections and accessories of exhibits. Plans and conducts research to develop and improve methods of restoring and preserving specimens. Builds, repairs, and installs wooden steps, scaffolds, and walkways to gain access to or permit improved view of exhibited equipment. Estimates cost of restoration work. Directs curatorial and technical staff in handling, mounting, care, and storage of art objects. Notifies superior when restoration of artifact requires outside experts.

GOE Number, Interest Area, and Work Group: 12.03.04; Education and Social Service; Educational Services: Library and Museum. **Personality Type:** Artistic. Artistic occupations frequently involve working with forms, designs, and patterns. These occupations often require self-expression, and the work can be done without following a clear set of rules. **Work Values:** Moral Values; Working Conditions; Ability Utilization; Achievement; Coworkers. **Skills:** Reading Comprehension; Writing; Information Gathering; Repairing; Product Inspection. **Abilities:** *Cognitive*—Visualization; Written Expression; Oral Expression; Deductive Reasoning; Information Ordering; Oral Comprehension. *Psychomotor*—Wrist-Finger Speed; Manual Dexterity; Arm-Hand Steadiness. *Physical*—Explosive Strength; Dynamic Strength; Dynamic Flexibility. *Sensory*—Visual Color Discrimination; Near Vision; Speech Clarity. **General Work Activities:** *Information Input*—Getting Information Needed to Do the Job; Identifying Objects, Actions, and Events; Inspecting Equipment, Structures, Materials; Estimating Needed Characteristics. *Mental Process*—Making Decisions and Solving Problems; Judging Qualities of Things, Services, Other People's Work; Analyzing Data or Information. *Work Output*—Handling and Moving Objects; Implementing Ideas and Programs; Documenting and Recording Information; Drafting and Specifying Technical Devices. *Interacting with Others*—Communicating with Other Workers; Coordinating Work and Activities of Others; Interpreting Meaning of Information to Others; Performing Administrative Activities; Providing Consultation and Advice to Others. **Physical Work Conditions:** Indoors; Using Hands on Objects, Tools, or Controls; Sitting; Standing. **Other Job Characteristics:** Importance of Being Sure All Is Done; Consequence of Error; Importance of Being Exact or Accurate.

Experience: Job Zone 3. Previous work-related skill, knowledge, or experience is required. **Job Preparation:** SVP 6.0 to less than 7.0—More than 1 year and less than 4 years. **Knowledge:** History and Archeology; Building and Construction; Design; Chemistry; Mechanical; Mathematics. **Instructional Programs:** 301401 Museology/Museum Studies; 450805 Public/Applied History and Archival Administration; 500703 Art History, Criticism and Conservation.

Related DOT Jobs: 055.381-010 Conservator, Artifacts; 102.167-010 Art Conservator; 102.261-010 Conservation Technician; 102.361-010 Restorer, Lace and Textiles; 102.361-014 Restorer, Ceramic; 102.367-010 Fine Arts Packer; 102.381-010 Museum Technician; 109.281-010 Armorer Technician; 109.361-010 Restorer, Paper-and-Prints; 779.381-018 Repairer, Art Objects; 899.384-010 Transportation-Equipment-Maintenance Worker; 979.361-010 Document Restorer.

25-4021.00 Librarians (Librarians)

Education: Master's degree
Employed: 152,094
Openings: 24,798
Projected Growth: 4.8%
Earnings: $38,470

Administer libraries and perform related library services. Work in a variety of settings, including public libraries, schools, colleges and universities, museums, corporations, government agencies, law firms, nonprofit organizations, and healthcare providers. Select, acquire, catalogue, classify, circulate, and maintain library materials. Furnish reference, bibliographical, and readers' advisory services. Perform in-depth, strategic research; synthesize, analyze, edit, and filter information. Set up or work with databases and information systems to catalogue and access information.

Reviews, compiles, and publishes listing of library materials, including bibliographies and book reviews, to notify users. Manages library program for children and other special groups. Directs and trains library staff in duties, including receiving, shelving, researching, cataloging, and equipment use. Keys information into computer to store or search for selected material or data bases. Compiles lists of overdue materials and notifies borrowers. Confers with teachers, parents, and community organizations to develop, plan, and conduct programs in reading, viewing, and communication skills. Researches, retrieves, and disseminates information from books, periodicals, reference materials or commercial data bases in response to requests. Explains use of library facilities, resources, equipment, and services, and provides information governing library use and policies. Manages library resources stored in files, on film, or in computer data bases for research information. Codes, classifies, and catalogs books, publications, films, audiovisual aids, and other library materials. Reviews and evaluates resource material to select and order books, periodicals, audiovisual aids, and other materials for acquisition. Assists patrons in selecting books and informational material and in research problems. Organizes collections of books, publications, documents, audiovisual aids, and other reference materials for convenient access. Assembles and arranges display materials.

GOE Number, Interest Area, and Work Group: 12.03.04; Education and Social Service; Educational Services: Library and Mu-

seum. **Personality Type:** Artistic. Artistic occupations frequently involve working with forms, designs, and patterns. These occupations often require self-expression, and the work can be done without following a clear set of rules. **Work Values:** Working Conditions; Moral Values; Autonomy; Authority; Responsibility; Security; Coworkers. **Skills:** Reading Comprehension; Information Gathering; Information Organization; Active Listening; Speaking. **Abilities:** *Cognitive*—Category Flexibility; Written Comprehension; Information Ordering; Oral Expression; Written Expression. *Psychomotor*—Wrist-Finger Speed; Manual Dexterity; Response Orientation. *Physical*—Extent Flexibility; Static Strength; Trunk Strength. *Sensory*—Near Vision; Speech Clarity; Speech Recognition. **General Work Activities:** *Information Input*—Getting Information Needed to Do the Job; Estimating Needed Characteristics; Identifying Objects, Actions, and Events. *Mental Process*—Processing Information; Updating and Using Job-Relevant Knowledge; Judging Qualities of Things, Services, Other People's Work; Thinking Creatively. *Work Output*—Handling and Moving Objects; Documenting and Recording Information; Interacting with Computers. *Interacting with Others*—Communicating with Persons Outside Organization; Performing for or Working with the Public; Providing Consultation and Advice to Others; Establishing and Maintaining Relationships. **Physical Work Conditions:** Indoors; Sitting; Standing. **Other Job Characteristics:** Importance of Being Sure All Is Done; Degree of Automation; Importance of Being Exact or Accurate.

Experience: Job Zone 4. A minimum of two to four years of work-related skill, knowledge, or experience is needed. **Job Preparation:** SVP 7.0 to less than 8.0—2 years to less than 10 years. **Knowledge:** English Language; Customer and Personal Service; Education and Training; Clerical; Administration and Management. **Instructional Programs:** 250101 Library Science/Librarianship; 259999 Library Science, Other.

Related DOT Jobs: 100.117-010 Library Director; 100.127-010 Chief Librarian, Branch or Department; 100.127-014 Librarian; 100.167-010 Audiovisual Librarian; 100.167-014 Bookmobile Librarian; 100.167-018 Children's Librarian; 100.167-022 Institution Librarian; 100.167-026 Librarian, Special Library; 100.167-030 Media Specialist, School Library; 100.167-034 Young-Adult Librarian; 100.167-038 News Librarian; 100.267-010 Acquisitions Librarian; 100.267-014 Librarian, Special Collections; 100.367-022 Music Librarian; 100.367-026 Music Librarian, International Broadcast.

25-4031.00 Library Technicians (Library Technicians)

Education: Short-term O-T-J training
Employed: 72,254
Openings: 9,478
Projected Growth: 18.2%
Earnings: $21,730

Assist librarians by helping readers in the use of library catalogs, databases, and indexes to locate books and other materials and by answering questions that require only brief consultation of standard reference. Compile records; sort and shelve books; remove or repair damaged books; register patrons; check materials in and out of the circulation process.

Replace materials in shelving area (stacks) or files. Includes bookmobile drivers who operate bookmobiles or light trucks that pull trailers to specific locations on a predetermined schedule and assist with providing services in mobile libraries.

Composes explanatory summaries of contents of books or other reference materials. Processes print and nonprint library materials, and classifies and catalogs materials. Reviews subject matter of materials to be classified and selects classification numbers and headings according to classification system. Issues identification card to borrowers and checks materials in and out. Directs activities of library clerks and aides. Assists patrons in operating equipment, obtaining library materials and services, and explains use of reference tools. Prepares order slips for materials, follows up on orders, and compiles lists of materials acquired or withdrawn. Designs posters and special displays to promote use of library facilities or specific reading program at library. Files catalog cards according to system used. Verifies bibliographical data, including author, title, publisher, publication date, and edition on computer terminal. Compiles and maintains records relating to circulation, materials, and equipment.

GOE Number, Interest Area, and Work Group: 12.03.04; Education and Social Service; Educational Services: Library and Museum. **Personality Type:** Conventional. Conventional occupations frequently involve following set procedures and routines. These occupations can include working with data and details more than with ideas. Usually there is a clear line of authority to follow. **Work Values:** Working Conditions; Moral Values; Social Service; Coworkers; Company Policies and Practices. **Skills:** Information Organization; Reading Comprehension; Information Gathering; Active Listening; Writing. **Abilities:** *Cognitive*—Oral Expression; Information Ordering; Category Flexibility; Written Expression; Written Comprehension. *Psychomotor*—Finger Dexterity. *Physical*—Extent Flexibility; Dynamic Flexibility. *Sensory*—Near Vision; Speech Clarity; Far Vision. **General Work Activities:** *Information Input*—Getting Information Needed to Do the Job; Identifying Objects, Actions, and Events; Monitoring Processes, Materials, and Surroundings. *Mental Process*—Processing Information; Analyzing Data or Information; Organizing, Planning, and Prioritizing. *Work Output*—Documenting and Recording Information; Handling and Moving Objects; Interacting with Computers. *Interacting with Others*—Communicating with Persons Outside Organization; Communicating with Other Workers; Performing for or Working with the Public. **Physical Work Conditions:** Indoors; Sitting; Using Hands on Objects, Tools, or Controls. **Other Job Characteristics:** Importance of Being Exact or Accurate; Importance of Being Sure All Is Done; Consequence of Error.

Experience: Job Zone 2. Some previous work-related skill, knowledge, or experience may be helpful, but usually is not needed. **Job Preparation:** SVP 4.00 to 5.99—6 months to less than 2 years. **Knowledge:** Clerical; Customer and Personal Service; English Language; Computers and Electronics; Mathematics; Communications and Media. **Instructional Program:** 250301 Library Assistant.

Related DOT Jobs: 100.367-010 Bibliographer; 100.367-014 Classifier; 100.367-018 Library Technical Assistant; 100.387-010 Catalog Librarian.

25-9000 Other Education, Training, and Library Occupations

25-9011.00 Audio-Visual Collections Specialists
(Library Technicians)

Education: Short-term O-T-J training
Employed: 72,254
Openings: 9,478
Projected Growth: 18.2%
Earnings: $21,730

Prepare, plan, and operate audio-visual teaching aids for use in education. Record, catalogue, and file audio-visual materials.

Constructs and positions properties, sets, lighting equipment, and other equipment. Develops production ideas based on assignment or generates own ideas based on objectives and interest. Executes, or directs assistants to execute, rough and finished graphics and graphic designs. Directs and coordinates activities of assistants and other personnel during production. Locates and secures settings, properties, effects, and other production necessities. Conducts training sessions on selection, use, and design of audiovisual materials, and operation of presentation equipment. Determines format, approach, content, level, and medium to meet objectives most effectively within budgetary constraints, utilizing research, knowledge, and training. Sets up, adjusts, and operates equipment such as cameras, sound mixers, and recorders during production. Plans and develops preproduction ideas into outlines, scripts, continuity, story boards, and graphics, or directs assistants to develop ideas. Performs narration or presents announcements. Develops manuals, texts, workbooks, or related materials for use in conjunction with production materials.

GOE Number, Interest Area, and Work Group: 12.03.04; Education and Social Service; Educational Services: Library and Museum. **Personality Type:** Conventional. Conventional occupations frequently involve following set procedures and routines. These occupations can include working with data and details more than with ideas. Usually there is a clear line of authority to follow. **Work Values:** Working Conditions; Moral Values; Ability Utilization; Authority; Coworkers. **Skills:** Information Organization; Writing; Synthesis/Reorganization; Learning Strategies; Solution Appraisal; Implementation Planning; Idea Evaluation; Speaking; Reading Comprehension. **Abilities:** *Cognitive*—Oral Expression; Visualization; Originality; Written Expression; Information Ordering. *Psychomotor*—Control Precision; Wrist-Finger Speed; Reaction Time. *Physical*—Extent Flexibility; Static Strength; Explosive Strength. *Sensory*—Speech Clarity; Hearing Sensitivity; Speech Recognition; Glare Sensitivity. **General Work Activities:** *Information Input*—Monitoring Processes, Materials, and Surroundings; Getting Information Needed to Do the Job; Identifying Objects, Actions, and Events. *Mental Process*—Thinking Creatively; Organizing, Planning, and Prioritizing; Updating and Using Job-Relevant Knowledge. *Work Output*—Implementing Ideas and

Programs; Drafting and Specifying Technical Devices; Handling and Moving Objects; Controlling Machines and Processes. *Interacting with Others*—Establishing and Maintaining Relationships; Teaching Others; Communicating with Other Workers. **Physical Work Conditions:** Indoors; Using Hands on Objects, Tools, or Controls; Standing; Sitting. **Other Job Characteristics:** Degree of Automation; Importance of Being Exact or Accurate; Consequence of Error.

Experience: Job Zone 4. A minimum of two to four years of work-related skill, knowledge, or experience is needed. **Job Preparation:** SVP 7.0 to less than 8.0—2 years to less than 10 years. **Knowledge:** Communications and Media; Education and Training; Telecommunications; English Language; Computers and Electronics. **Instructional Program:** 250301 Library Assistant.

Related DOT Job: 149.061-010 Audiovisual Production Specialist.

25-9021.00 Farm and Home Management Advisors
(Farm and Home Management Advisors)

Education: Bachelor's degree

Employed: 9,977

Openings: 2,270

Projected Growth: –2.2%

Earnings: $37,200

Advise, instruct, and assist individuals and families engaged in agriculture, agriculture-related processes, or home-economics activities. Demonstrate procedures and apply research findings to solve problems; instruct and train in product development, sales, and the utilization of machinery and equipment to promote general welfare. Includes county agricultural agents, feed and farm management advisers, home economists, and extension service advisors.

Delivers lectures to organizations or talks over radio and television to disseminate information and promote objectives of program. Collects and evaluates data to ascertain needs and develop programs beneficial to community. Prepares leaflets, pamphlets, and visual aids for educational and informational purposes. Plans, develops, organizes, and evaluates training programs in subjects, such as home management, horticulture, and consumer information. Advises individuals and families on home management practices such as budget planning, meal preparation, energy conservation, clothing, and home furnishings. Conducts classes to educate others in subjects such as nutrition, home management, home furnishing, child care, and farming techniques. Advises farmers in matters such as feeding and health maintenance of livestock, cultivation, growing and harvesting practices, and budgeting. Organizes, advises, and participates in community activities and organizations such as county and state fair events and 4-H Clubs.

GOE Number, Interest Area, and Work Group: 12.03.02; Education and Social Service; Educational Services: Postsecondary and Adult Teaching and Instructing. **Personality Type:** Social. Social occupations frequently involve working with, communicating with, and teaching people. These occupations often involve helping or providing service to others. **Work Values:** Autonomy; Achievement; Social Service; Responsibility; Ability Utilization; Creativity. **Skills:** Reading Comprehension; Writing; Persuasion; Idea Evaluation; Solution Appraisal; Problem Identification; Active Learning; Learning Strategies; Instructing; Information Gathering. **Abilities:** *Cognitive*—Oral Expression; Oral Comprehension; Written Expression; Mathematical Reasoning; Problem Sensitivity. *Psychomotor*—Multilimb Coordination. *Physical*—Stamina; Gross Body Equilibrium. *Sensory*—Speech Clarity; Near Vision; Far Vision; Speech Recognition. **General Work Activities:** *Information Input*—Getting Information Needed to Do the Job; Identifying Objects, Actions, and Events; Estimating Needed Characteristics. *Mental Process*—Making Decisions and Solving Problems; Organizing, Planning, and Prioritizing; Analyzing Data or Information. *Work Output*—Implementing Ideas and Programs; Documenting and Recording Information; Interacting with Computers; Handling and Moving Objects. *Interacting with Others*—Communicating with Persons Outside Organization; Providing Consultation and Advice to Others; Teaching Others. **Physical Work Conditions:** Indoors; Standing; Sitting. **Other Job Characteristics:** Importance of Being Sure All Is Done; Consequence of Error; Frustrating Circumstances.

Experience: Job Zone 4. A minimum of two to four years of work-related skill, knowledge, or experience is needed. **Job Preparation:** SVP 7.0 to less than 8.0—2 years to less than 10 years. **Knowledge:** Food Production; Administration and Management; Education and Training; Economics and Accounting; Mathematics. **Instructional Programs:** 010101 Agricultural Business and Management, General; 010102 Agricultural Business/Agribusiness Operations; 010104 Farm and Ranch Management; 010302 Agricultural Animal Husbandry and Production Management; 010304 Crop Production Operations and Management; 020102 Agricultural Extension; 020204 Agricultural Animal Nutrition; 190101 Home Economics, General; 190201 Business Home Economics; 190202 Home Economics Communications; 190301 Family and Community Studies; 190401 Family Resource Management Studies; 190402 Consumer Economics and Science; 190499 Family/Consumer Resource Management, Other; 190601 Housing Studies, General.

Related DOT Jobs: 096.121-010 County Home-Demonstration Agent; 096.121-014 Home Economist; 096.127-010 County-Agricultural Agent; 096.127-014 Extension Service Specialist; 096.127-018 Feed and Farm Management Adviser; 096.127-022 Four-H Club Agent.

25-9031.00 Instructional Coordinators (Instructional Coordinators)

Education: No data available.

Employed: 87,730

Openings: No data available.

Projected Growth: No data available.

Earnings: $38,870

Develop instructional material, coordinate educational content, and incorporate current technology in specialized fields that provide guidelines to educators and instructors for developing curricula and conducting courses.

Prepares or assists in preparation of grant proposals, budgets, and program policies and goals. Confers with school officials, teachers, and administrative staff to plan and develop curricula and establish guidelines for educational programs. Prepares or approves manuals, guidelines, and reports on state educational policies and practices for distribution to school districts. Plans, conducts, and evaluates training programs and conferences for teachers to study new classroom procedures, instructional materials, and teaching aids. Advises school officials on implementation of state and federal programs and procedures. Conducts or participates in workshops, committees, and conferences designed to promote intellectual, social, and physical welfare of students. Coordinates activities of workers engaged in cataloging, distributing, and maintaining educational materials and equipment in curriculum library and laboratory. Interprets and enforces provisions of state education codes and rules and regulations of State Board of Education. Reviews student files and confers with educators, parents, and other concerned parties to decide student placement and provision of services. Inspects and authorizes repair of instructional equipment such as musical instruments. Advises teaching and administrative staff in assessment, curriculum development, management of student behavior, and use of materials and equipment. Observes, evaluates, and recommends changes in work of teaching staff to strengthen teaching skills in classroom. Confers with educational committees and advisory groups to gather information on instructional methods and materials related to specific academic subjects. Orders or authorizes purchase of instructional materials, supplies, equipment, and visual aids designed to meet educational needs of students. Researches, evaluates, and prepares recommendations on curricula, instructional methods, and materials for school system.

GOE Number, Interest Area, and Work Group: 12.01.01; Education and Social Service; Managerial Work in Education and Social Service. **Personality Type:** Social. Social occupations frequently involve working with, communicating with, and teaching people. These occupations often involve helping or providing service to others. **Work Values:** Autonomy; Achievement; Responsibility; Authority; Creativity; Working Conditions. **Skills:** Learning Strategies; Speaking; Instructing; Reading Comprehension; Writing. **Abilities:** *Cognitive*—Oral Expression; Written Comprehension; Written Expression; Oral Comprehension; Deductive Reasoning. *Psychomotor*—none met the criteria. *Physical*—none met the criteria. *Sensory*—Speech Clarity; Speech Recognition. **General Work Activities:** *Information Input*—Getting Information Needed to Do the Job; Monitoring Processes, Materials, and Surroundings; Identifying Objects, Actions, and Events. *Mental Process*—Analyzing Data or Information; Making Decisions and Solving Problems; Judging Qualities of Things, Services, Other People's Work; Processing Information; Organizing, Planning, and Prioritizing. *Work Output*—Implementing Ideas and Programs; Interacting with Computers; Documenting and Recording Information. *Interacting with Others*—Communicating with Persons Outside Organization; Providing Consultation and Advice to Others; Communicating with Other Workers; Teaching Others. **Physical Work Conditions:** Indoors; Sitting; Standing. **Other Job Characteristics:** Consequence of Error; Importance of Being Exact or Accurate; Importance of Being Sure All Is Done.

Experience: Job Zone 5. Extensive skill, knowledge, and experience are needed. Very advanced communication and organizational skills are required. **Job Preparation:** SVP 8.0 and above—4 years to more than 10 years. **Knowledge:** Education and Training; English Language; Administration and Management; Psychology; Personnel and Human Resources. **Instructional Programs:** 130101 Education, General; 130301 Curriculum and Instruction; 130501 Educational/Instructional Media Design.

Related DOT Jobs: 094.167-010 Supervisor, Special Education; 099.117-026 Supervisor, Education; 099.167-014 Consultant, Education; 099.167-018 Director, Instructional Material; 099.167-022 Educational Specialist; 099.167-026 Music Supervisor.

25-9041.00 Teacher Assistants (Teacher Assistants)

Education: Short-term O-T-J training
Employed: 1,191,790
Openings: 343,831
Projected Growth: 31.5%
Earnings: No data available.

Perform duties that are instructional in nature or that deliver direct services to students and/or parents. Serve in a position for which a teacher or another professional has ultimate responsibility for the design and implementation of educational programs and services.

Presents subject matter to students, using lecture, discussion, or supervised role playing methods. Discusses assigned teaching area with classroom teacher to coordinate instructional efforts. Confers with parents on progress of students. Prepares, administers, and grades examinations. Helps students, individually or in groups, with lesson assignments, to present or reinforce learning concepts. Prepares lesson outline and plan in assigned area and submits outline to teacher for review. Plans, prepares, and develops various teaching aids, such as bibliographies, charts, and graphs.

GOE Number, Interest Area, and Work Group: 12.03.03; Education and Social Service; Educational Services: Pre-school, Elementary, and Secondary Teaching and Instructing. **Personality Type:** Social. Social occupations frequently involve working with, communicating with, and teaching people. These occupations often involve helping or providing service to others. **Work Values:** Social Service; Achievement; Working Conditions; Coworkers; Moral Values; Supervision, Human Relations. **Skills:** Learning Strategies; Speaking; Active Listening; Reading Comprehension; Instructing. **Abilities:** *Cognitive*—Oral Expression; Written Expression; Oral Comprehension; Written Comprehension; Fluency of Ideas; Problem Sensitivity. *Psychomotor*—none met the criteria. *Physical*—none met the criteria. *Sensory*—Speech Clarity; Auditory Attention; Speech Recognition. **General Work Activities:** *Information Input*—Getting Information Needed to Do the Job; Identifying Objects, Actions, and Events; Monitoring Processes, Materials, and Surroundings. *Mental Process*—Scheduling Work and Activities; Thinking Creatively; Evaluating Information Against Standards; Updating and Using Job-Relevant Knowledge. *Work Output*—Implementing Ideas and Programs; Documenting and Recording Information; Handling and Moving Objects. *Interact-*

ing with Others—Teaching Others; Communicating with Persons Outside Organization; Establishing and Maintaining Relationships. **Physical Work Conditions:** Indoors; Sitting; Standing. **Other Job Characteristics:** Frustrating Circumstances; Importance of Being Sure All Is Done; Importance of Being Exact or Accurate.

Experience: Job Zone 3. Previous work-related skill, knowledge, or experience is required. **Job Preparation:** SVP 6.0 to less than 7.0—More than 1 year and less than 4 years. **Knowledge:** Education and Training; English Language; Mathematics; Clerical; Psychology; Customer and Personal Service. **Instructional Programs:** 130101 Education, General; 130201 Bilingual/Bicultural Education; 131501 Teacher Assistant/Aide.

Related DOT Job: 099.327-010 Teacher Aide I.

27-0000

Arts, Design, Entertainment, Sports, and Media Occupations

27-1000 Art and Design Workers

27-1011.00 Art Directors (Designers)

Education: Bachelor's degree

Employed: 335,260

Openings: 57,787

Projected Growth: 27.1%

Earnings: $29,190

Formulate design concepts and presentation approaches. Direct workers engaged in art work, layout design, and copy writing, for visual communications media such as magazines, books, newspapers, and packaging.

Draws custom illustrations for project. Confers with creative, art, copy writing, or production department heads to discuss client requirements, outline presentation concepts, and coordinate creative activities. Presents final layouts to client for approval. Prepares detailed storyboard showing sequence and timing of story development for television production. Marks up, pastes, and completes layouts to prepare for printing. Writes typography instructions, such as margin widths and type sizes, and submits for typesetting or printing. Reviews illustrative material and confers with client concerning objectives, budget, background information, and presentation approaches, styles, and techniques. Reviews and approves art and copy materials developed by staff, and proofs of printed copy. Assigns and directs staff members to develop design concepts into art layouts or prepare layouts for printing. Formulates basic layout design or presentation approach, and conceives material details, such as style and size of type, photographs, graphics, and arrangement.

GOE Number, Interest Area, and Work Group: 01.01.01; Arts, Entertainment, and Media; Managerial Work in Arts, Entertainment, and Media. **Personality Type:** Artistic. Artistic occupations frequently involve working with forms, designs, and patterns. These occupations often require self-expression, and the work can be done without following a clear set of rules. **Work Values:** Ability Utilization; Creativity; Achievement; Autonomy; Responsibility. **Skills:** Visioning; Coordination; Operations Analysis; Speaking; Active Learning. **Abilities:** *Cognitive*—Originality; Oral Expression; Visualization; Fluency of Ideas; Oral Comprehension; Written Expression. *Psychomotor*—Wrist-Finger Speed; Arm-Hand Steadiness; Finger Dexterity. *Physical*—none met the criteria. *Sensory*—Near Vision; Visual Color Discrimination; Speech Clarity. **General Work Activities:** *Information Input*—Getting Information Needed to Do the Job; Estimating Needed Characteristics; Identifying Objects, Actions, and Events. *Mental Process*—Thinking Creatively; Organizing, Planning, and Prioritizing; Making Decisions and Solving Problems. *Work Output*—Handling and Moving Objects; Drafting and Specifying Technical Devices; Implementing Ideas and Programs. *Interacting with Others*—Communicating with Other Workers; Communicating with Persons Outside Organization; Coordinating Work and Activities of Others. **Physical Work Conditions:** Indoors; Sitting; Using Hands on Objects, Tools, or Controls. **Other Job Characteristics:** Importance of Being Exact or Accurate; Importance of Being Sure All Is Done; Consequence of Error.

Experience: Job Zone 4. A minimum of two to four years of work-related skill, knowledge, or experience is needed. **Job Preparation:** SVP 7.0 to less than 8.0—2 years to less than 10 years. **Knowledge:** Design; Fine Arts; Administration and Management; Telecommunications; Communications and Media; English Language; Sales and Marketing. **Instructional Programs:** 080503 Floristry Marketing Operations; 200301 Clothing, Apparel and Textile Workers and Managers, General; 500401 Design and Visual Communications; 500404 Industrial Design; 500407 Fashion Design and Illustration; 500499 Design and Applied Arts, Other; 500502 Technical Theater/Theater Design and Stagecraft.

Related DOT Jobs: 141.031-010 Art Director; 141.067-010 Creative Director; 141.137-010 Production Manager, Advertising.

27-1012.00 Craft Artists (Artists and Commercial Artists)

Education: Work experience, plus degree

Employed: 308,496

Openings: 58,769

Projected Growth: 25.7%

Earnings: $31,690

Create or reproduce handmade objects for sale and exhibition, using a variety of techniques such as welding, weaving, pottery, and needlecraft.

GOE Number, Interest Area, and Work Group: 01.06.01; Arts, Entertainment, and Media; Craft Arts. **Instructional Programs:** 500201 Crafts, Folk Art and Artisanry; 500402 Graphic Design, Commercial Art and Illustration; 500502 Technical Theater/Theater Design and Stagecraft; 500701 Art, General; 500702 Fine/Studio Arts; 500705 Drawing; 500706 Intermedia; 500708 Painting; 500709 Sculpture; 500710 Printmaking; 500711 Ceramics Arts and Ceramics; 500712 Fiber, Textile and Weaving Arts; 500713 Metal and Jewelry Arts; 500799 Fine Arts and Art Studies, Other; 512703 Medical Illustrating. **Note:** The Department of Labor has not collected some data for this job, so it has fewer details than the other descriptions.

27-1013.00 Fine Artists, Including Painters, Sculptors, and Illustrators (Artists and Commercial Artists)

Education: Work experience, plus degree

Employed: 308,496

Openings: 58,769

Projected Growth: 25.7%

Earnings: $31,690

Create original artwork using any of a wide variety of mediums and techniques, such as painting and sculpture.

GOE Number, Interest Area, and Work Group: 01.04.01; Arts, Entertainment, and Media; Visual Arts: Studio Art. **Instructional Programs:** 500201 Crafts, Folk Art and Artisanry; 500402 Graphic Design, Commercial Art and Illustration; 500502 Technical Theater/Theater Design and Stagecraft; 500701 Art, General; 500702

Fine/Studio Arts; 500705 Drawing; 500706 Intermedia; 500708 Painting; 500709 Sculpture; 500710 Printmaking; 500711 Ceramics Arts and Ceramics; 500712 Fiber, Textile and Weaving Arts; 500713 Metal and Jewelry Arts; 500799 Fine Arts and Art Studies, Other; 512703 Medical Illustrating. **Note:** The Department of Labor has not collected some data for this job, so it has fewer details than the other descriptions.

27-1013.01 Painters and Illustrators (Artists and Commercial Artists)

Education: Work experience, plus degree
Employed: 308,496
Openings: 58,769
Projected Growth: 25.7%
Earnings: $31,690

Paint or draw subject material to produce original artwork or illustrations, using watercolors, oils, acrylics, tempera, or other paint mediums.

Assembles, leads, and solders finished glass to fabricate stained glass article. Brushes or sprays protective or decorative finish on completed background panels, informational legends, exhibit accessories, or finished painting. Integrates and develops visual elements such as line, space, mass, color, and perspective to produce desired effect. Studies style, techniques, colors, textures, and materials used by artist to maintain consistency in reconstruction or retouching procedures. Removes painting from frame or paint layer from canvas to restore artwork, following specified technique and equipment. Examines surfaces of paintings and proofs of artwork, using magnifying device, to determine method of restoration or needed corrections. Installs finished stained glass in window or door frame. Performs tests to determine factors, such as age, structure, pigment stability, and probable reaction to various cleaning agents and solvents. Confers with professional personnel or client to discuss objectives of artwork, develop illustration ideas, and theme to be portrayed. Etches, carves, paints, or draws artwork on material such as stone, glass, canvas, wood, and linoleum. Develops drawings, paintings, diagrams, and models of medical or biological subjects for use in publications, exhibits, consultations, research, and teaching. Renders drawings, illustrations, and sketches of buildings, manufactured products, or models, working from sketches, blueprints, memory, or reference materials. Paints scenic backgrounds, murals, and portraiture for motion picture and television production sets, glass artworks, and exhibits. Applies select solvents and cleaning agents to clean surface of painting and remove accretions, discolorations, and deteriorated varnish.

GOE Number, Interest Area, and Work Group: 01.04.01; Arts, Entertainment, and Media; Visual Arts: Studio Art. **Personality Type:** Artistic. Artistic occupations frequently involve working with forms, designs, and patterns. These occupations often require self-expression, and the work can be done without following a clear set of rules. **Work Values:** Ability Utilization; Creativity; Autonomy; Achievement; Independence. **Skills:** Idea Generation; Active Listening; Operations Analysis; Idea Evaluation; Product Inspection; Visioning. **Abilities:** *Cognitive*—Originality; Visualiza-

tion; Fluency of Ideas; Deductive Reasoning; Oral Comprehension. *Psychomotor*—Arm-Hand Steadiness; Finger Dexterity; Wrist-Finger Speed; Manual Dexterity. *Physical*—Extent Flexibility; Trunk Strength; Gross Body Coordination. *Sensory*—Visual Color Discrimination; Depth Perception. **General Work Activities:** *Information Input*—Getting Information Needed to Do the Job; Identifying Objects, Actions, and Events; Estimating Needed Characteristics. *Mental Process*—Thinking Creatively; Making Decisions and Solving Problems; Judging Qualities of Things, Services, Other People's Work. *Work Output*—Handling and Moving Objects; Implementing Ideas and Programs; Controlling Machines and Processes. *Interacting with Others*—Communicating with Persons Outside Organization; Providing Consultation and Advice to Others; Establishing and Maintaining Relationships; Communicating with Other Workers. **Physical Work Conditions:** Indoors; Using Hands on Objects, Tools, or Controls; Sitting. **Other Job Characteristics:** Consequence of Error; Importance of Being Sure All Is Done; Frustrating Circumstances.

Experience: Job Zone 4. A minimum of two to four years of work-related skill, knowledge, or experience is needed. **Job Preparation:** SVP 7.0 to less than 8.0—2 years to less than 10 years. **Knowledge:** Fine Arts; Design; Chemistry; Customer and Personal Service; History and Archeology; Communications and Media. **Instructional Programs:** 500201 Crafts, Folk Art and Artisanry; 500402 Graphic Design, Commercial Art and Illustration; 500502 Technical Theater/Theater Design and Stagecraft; 500701 Art, General; 500702 Fine/Studio Arts; 500705 Drawing; 500706 Intermedia; 500708 Painting; 500709 Sculpture; 500710 Printmaking; 500711 Ceramics Arts and Ceramics; 500712 Fiber, Textile and Weaving Arts; 500713 Metal and Jewelry Arts; 500799 Fine Arts and Art Studies, Other; 512703 Medical Illustrating.

Related DOT Jobs: 102.261-014 Paintings Restorer; 141.061-014 Fashion Artist; 141.061-022 Illustrator; 141.061-026 Illustrator, Medical and Scientific; 141.061-030 Illustrator, Set; 144.061-010 Painter; 144.061-014 Printmaker; 149.261-010 Exhibit Artist; 970.281-014 Delineator.

27-1013.02 Sketch Artists (Artists and Commercial Artists)

Education: Work experience, plus degree
Employed: 308,496
Openings: 58,769
Projected Growth: 25.7%
Earnings: $31,690

Sketch likenesses of subjects according to observation or descriptions to assist law enforcement agencies in identifying suspects, to depict courtroom scenes, or to entertain patrons, using mediums such as pencil, charcoal, and pastels.

Operates photocopy or similar machine to reproduce composite image. Interviews crime victims and witnesses to obtain descriptive information concerning physical build, sex, nationality, and facial features of unidentified suspect. Prepares series of simple line drawings conforming to description of suspect and presents drawings to informant for selection of sketch. Alters copy of composite image until witness or victim is satisfied that composite is best possible representation of suspect. Assembles and arranges outlines of features to form composite image, according to information provided by witness or victim. Poses subject to accentuate most pleasing features or profile. Measures distances and develops sketches of crime scene from photograph and measurements. Classifies and codes components of image, using established system, to help identify suspect. Draws sketch, profile, or likeness of posed subject or photograph, using pencil, charcoal, pastels, or other medium. Searches police photograph records, using classification and coding system to determine if existing photograph of suspects is available.

GOE Number, Interest Area, and Work Group: 01.04.01; Arts, Entertainment, and Media; Visual Arts: Studio Art. **Personality Type:** Artistic. Artistic occupations frequently involve working with forms, designs, and patterns. These occupations often require self-expression, and the work can be done without following a clear set of rules. **Work Values:** Ability Utilization; Achievement; Creativity; Autonomy; Moral Values. **Skills:** Active Listening; Information Organization; Speaking; Synthesis/Reorganization; Information Gathering. **Abilities:** *Cognitive*—Visualization; Oral Comprehension; Inductive Reasoning; Flexibility of Closure; Oral Expression; Fluency of Ideas. *Psychomotor*—Arm-Hand Steadiness; Finger Dexterity; Manual Dexterity. *Physical*—none met the criteria. *Sensory*—Auditory Attention; Hearing Sensitivity; Depth Perception. **General Work Activities:** *Information Input*—Getting Information Needed to Do the Job; Identifying Objects, Actions, and Events; Estimating Needed Characteristics. *Mental Process*—Thinking Creatively; Analyzing Data or Information; Making Decisions and Solving Problems. *Work Output*—Handling and Moving Objects; Implementing Ideas and Programs; Controlling Machines and Processes. *Interacting with Others*—Communicating with Persons Outside Organization; Interpreting Meaning of Information to Others; Performing for or Working with the Public; Communicating with Other Workers; Establishing and Maintaining Relationships. **Physical Work Conditions:** Indoors; Sitting; Using Hands on Objects, Tools, or Controls. **Other Job Characteristics:** Importance of Being Exact or Accurate; Consequence of Error; Importance of Being Sure All Is Done.

Experience: Job Zone 3. Previous work-related skill, knowledge, or experience is required. **Job Preparation:** SVP 6.0 to less than 7.0—More than 1 year and less than 4 years. **Knowledge:** Fine Arts; Design; English Language; Clerical; Communications and Media; Customer and Personal Service; Public Safety and Security. **Instructional Programs:** 500201 Crafts, Folk Art and Artisanry; 500402 Graphic Design, Commercial Art and Illustration; 500502 Technical Theater/Theater Design and Stagecraft; 500701 Art, General; 500702 Fine/Studio Arts; 500705 Drawing; 500706 Intermedia; 500708 Painting; 500709 Sculpture; 500710 Printmaking; 500711 Ceramics Arts and Ceramics; 500712 Fiber, Textile and Weaving Arts; 500713 Metal and Jewelry Arts; 500799 Fine Arts and Art Studies, Other; 512703 Medical Illustrating.

Related DOT Jobs: 141.061-034 Police Artist; 149.041-010 Quick Sketch Artist; 149.051-010 Silhouette Artist; 970.361-018 Artist, Suspect.

27-1013.03 Cartoonists (Artists and Commercial Artists)

Education: Work experience, plus degree
Employed: 308,496
Openings: 58,769
Projected Growth: 25.7%
Earnings: $31,690

Create original artwork using any of a wide variety of mediums and techniques, such as painting and sculpture.

Renders sequential drawings of characters or other subject material which when photographed and projected at specific speed becomes animated. Creates and prepares sketches and model drawings of characters, providing details from memory, live models, manufactured products, or reference material. Develops personal ideas for cartoons, comic strips, or animations, or reads written material to develop ideas. Develops color patterns and moods and paints background layouts to dramatize action for animated cartoon scenes. Labels each section with designated colors when colors are used. Sketches and submits cartoon or animation for approval. Discusses ideas for cartoons, comic strips, or animations with editor or publisher's representative. Makes changes and corrections to cartoon, comic strip, or animation as necessary.

GOE Number, Interest Area, and Work Group: 01.04.01; Arts, Entertainment, and Media; Visual Arts: Studio Art. **Personality Type:** Artistic. Artistic occupations frequently involve working with forms, designs, and patterns. These occupations often require self-expression, and the work can be done without following a clear set of rules. **Work Values:** Creativity; Ability Utilization; Autonomy; Achievement; Independence; Working Conditions. **Skills:** Idea Generation; Idea Evaluation; Active Listening; Reading Comprehension; Product Inspection; Writing. **Abilities:** *Cognitive*—Originality; Fluency of Ideas; Visualization; Oral Comprehension; Written Comprehension. *Psychomotor*—Arm-Hand Steadiness; Finger Dexterity. *Physical*—none met the criteria. *Sensory*—Visual Color Discrimination; Near Vision; Speech Clarity. **General Work Activities:** *Information Input*—Getting Information Needed to Do the Job; Identifying Objects, Actions, and Events; Estimating Needed Characteristics. *Mental Process*—Thinking Creatively; Making Decisions and Solving Problems; Analyzing Data or Information; Judging Qualities of Things, Services, Other People's Work. *Work Output*—Handling and Moving Objects; Implementing Ideas and Programs; Drafting and Specifying Technical Devices. *Interacting with Others*—Communicating with Other Workers; Communicating with Persons Outside Organization; Establishing and Maintaining Relationships. **Physical Work Conditions:** Sitting; Indoors; Using Hands on Objects, Tools, or Controls. **Other Job Characteristics:** Frustrating Circumstances; Importance of Being Sure All Is Done; Importance of Being Aware of New Events; Consequence of Error.

Experience: Job Zone 4. A minimum of two to four years of work-related skill, knowledge, or experience is needed. **Job Preparation:** SVP 7.0 to less than 8.0—2 years to less than 10 years. **Knowledge:** Fine Arts; Communications and Media; Design; English Language; Telecommunications; Computers and Electronics; Sales and Marketing. **Instructional Programs:** 500201 Crafts, Folk Art and Artisanry; 500402 Graphic Design, Commercial Art and Illustration; 500502 Technical Theater/Theater Design and Stagecraft; 500701 Art, General; 500702 Fine/Studio Arts; 500705 Drawing; 500706 Intermedia; 500708 Painting; 500709 Sculpture; 500710 Printmaking; 500711 Ceramics Arts and Ceramics; 500712 Fiber, Textile and Weaving Arts; 500713 Metal and Jewelry Arts; 500799 Fine Arts and Art Studies, Other; 512703 Medical Illustrating.

Related DOT Jobs: 141.061-010 Cartoonist; 141.081-010 Cartoonist, Motion Pictures.

27-1013.04 Sculptors (Artists and Commercial Artists)

Education: Work experience, plus degree
Employed: 308,496
Openings: 58,769
Projected Growth: 25.7%
Earnings: $31,690

Design and construct three-dimensional art works, using materials such as stone, wood, plaster, and metal, and employing various manual and tool techniques.

Carves objects from stone, concrete, plaster, wood, or other material, using abrasives and tools such as chisels, gouges, and mall. Constructs artistic forms from metal or stone, using metalworking, welding, or masonry tools and equipment. Cuts, bends, laminates, arranges, and fastens individual or mixed raw and manufactured materials and products to form works of art. Models substances, such as clay or wax, using fingers and small hand tools to form objects.

GOE Number, Interest Area, and Work Group: 01.04.01; Arts, Entertainment, and Media; Visual Arts: Studio Art. **Personality Type:** Artistic. Artistic occupations frequently involve working with forms, designs, and patterns. These occupations often require self-expression, and the work can be done without following a clear set of rules. **Work Values:** Creativity; Independence; Ability Utilization; Autonomy; Achievement. **Skills:** Idea Generation; Idea Evaluation; Monitoring; Implementation Planning; Equipment Selection. **Abilities:** *Cognitive*—Originality; Visualization; Fluency of Ideas; Information Ordering; Flexibility of Closure. *Psychomotor*—Manual Dexterity; Finger Dexterity; Arm-Hand Steadiness. *Physical*—Extent Flexibility; Static Strength; Trunk Strength. *Sensory*—Depth Perception. **General Work Activities:** *Information Input*—Getting Information Needed to Do the Job; Estimating Needed Characteristics; Monitoring Processes, Materials, and Surroundings. *Mental Process*—Thinking Creatively; Judging Qualities of Things, Services, Other People's Work; Making Decisions and Solving Problems. *Work Output*—Handling and Moving Objects; Implementing Ideas and Programs; Performing General Physical Activities. *Interacting with Others*—Influencing Others or Selling; Monitoring and Controlling Resources; Performing for or Working with the Public. **Physical Work Conditions:** Using Hands on Objects, Tools, or Controls; Indoors; Standing. **Other Job Characteristics:** Consequence of Error; Frustrating Circumstances; Importance of Being Sure All Is Done.

Experience: Job Zone 5. Extensive skill, knowledge, and experience are needed. Very advanced communication and organizational skills are required. **Job Preparation:** SVP 8.0 and above—4

years to more than 10 years. **Knowledge:** Fine Arts; Design; Engineering and Technology; Building and Construction; English Language. **Instructional Programs:** 500201 Crafts, Folk Art and Artisanry; 500402 Graphic Design, Commercial Art and Illustration; 500502 Technical Theater/Theater Design and Stagecraft; 500701 Art, General; 500702 Fine/Studio Arts; 500705 Drawing; 500706 Intermedia; 500708 Painting; 500709 Sculpture; 500710 Printmaking; 500711 Ceramics Arts and Ceramics; 500712 Fiber, Textile and Weaving Arts; 500713 Metal and Jewelry Arts; 500799 Fine Arts and Art Studies, Other; 512703 Medical Illustrating.

Related DOT Job: 144.061-018 Sculptor.

27-1014.00 Multi-Media Artists and Animators
(Artists and Commercial Artists)

Education: Work experience, plus degree
Employed: 308,496
Openings: 58,769
Projected Growth: 25.7%
Earnings: $31,690

Create special effects, animation, or other visual images, using film, video, computers, or other electronic tools and media, for use in products or creations such as computer games, movies, music videos, and commercials.

GOE Number, Interest Area, and Work Group: 01.04.02; Arts, Entertainment, and Media; Visual Arts: Design. **Instructional Programs:** 500201 Crafts, Folk Art and Artisanry; 500402 Graphic Design, Commercial Art and Illustration; 500502 Technical Theater/Theater Design and Stagecraft; 500701 Art, General; 500702 Fine/Studio Arts; 500705 Drawing; 500706 Intermedia; 500708 Painting; 500709 Sculpture; 500710 Printmaking; 500711 Ceramics Arts and Ceramics; 500712 Fiber, Textile and Weaving Arts; 500713 Metal and Jewelry Arts; 500799 Fine Arts and Art Studies, Other; 512703 Medical Illustrating. **Note:** The Department of Labor has not collected some data for this job, so it has fewer details than the other descriptions.

27-1021.00 Commercial and Industrial Designers
(Designers)

Education: Bachelor's degree
Employed: 335,260
Openings: 57,787
Projected Growth: 27.1%
Earnings: $29,190

Develop and design manufactured products such as cars, home appliances, and children's toys. Combine artistic talent with research on product use, marketing, and materials, to create the most functional and appealing product design.

Designs packaging and containers for products such as foods, beverages, toiletries, or medicines. Evaluates design ideas for feasibility based on factors such as appearance, function, serviceability, budget, production costs/methods, and market characteristics. Presents design to customer or design committee for approval and discusses need for modification. Fabricates model or sample in paper, wood, glass, fabric, plastic, or metal, using hand and power tools. Prepares itemized production requirements to produce item. Reads publications, attends showings, and studies traditional, period, and contemporary design styles and motifs to obtain perspective and design concepts. Directs and coordinates preparation of detailed drawings from sketches or fabrication of models or samples. Creates and designs graphic material for use as ornamentation, illustration, or advertising on manufactured materials and packaging. Integrates findings and concepts; sketches design ideas. Prepares detailed drawings, illustrations, artwork, or blueprints, using drawing instruments or paints and brushes. Confers with engineering, marketing, production, or sales department, or customer to establish design concepts for manufactured products. Modifies design to conform with customer specifications, production limitations, or changes in design trends.

GOE Number, Interest Area, and Work Group: 01.04.02; Arts, Entertainment, and Media; Visual Arts: Design. **Personality Type:** Artistic. Artistic occupations frequently involve working with forms, designs, and patterns. These occupations often require self-expression, and the work can be done without following a clear set of rules. **Work Values:** Achievement; Ability Utilization; Creativity; Working Conditions; Autonomy. **Skills:** Reading Comprehension; Active Learning; Critical Thinking; Equipment Selection; Information Organization. **Abilities:** *Cognitive*—Written Comprehension; Originality; Oral Comprehension; Oral Expression; Fluency of Ideas; Visualization. *Psychomotor*—Arm-Hand Steadiness; Finger Dexterity; Wrist-Finger Speed. *Physical*—Gross Body Coordination; Gross Body Equilibrium. *Sensory*—Near Vision; Visual Color Discrimination; Speech Clarity; Speech Recognition. **General Work Activities:** *Information Input*—Getting Information Needed to Do the Job; Identifying Objects, Actions, and Events; Estimating Needed Characteristics. *Mental Process*—Thinking Creatively; Updating and Using Job-Relevant Knowledge; Organizing, Planning, and Prioritizing. *Work Output*—Drafting and Specifying Technical Devices; Implementing Ideas and Programs; Handling and Moving Objects. *Interacting with Others*—Communicating with Persons Outside Organization; Communicating with Other Workers; Establishing and Maintaining Relationships. **Physical Work Conditions:** Indoors; Using Hands on Objects, Tools, or Controls; Sitting. **Other Job Characteristics:** Consequence of Error; Importance of Being Exact or Accurate; Importance of Being Sure All Is Done.

Experience: Job Zone 4. A minimum of two to four years of work-related skill, knowledge, or experience is needed. **Job Preparation:** SVP 7.0 to less than 8.0—2 years to less than 10 years. **Knowledge:** Design; Sales and Marketing; Fine Arts; Production and Processing; Mechanical. **Instructional Programs:** 080503 Floristry Marketing Operations; 200301 Clothing, Apparel and Textile Workers and Managers, General; 500401 Design and Visual Communications; 500404 Industrial Design; 500407 Fashion Design and Illustration; 500499 Design and Applied Arts, Other; 500502 Technical Theater/Theater Design and Stagecraft.

Related DOT Jobs: 141.061-038 Commercial Designer; 142.061-010 Bank-Note Designer; 142.061-014 Cloth Designer; 142.061-022 Furniture Designer; 142.061-026 Industrial Designer; 142.061-030 Memorial Designer; 142.061-034 Ornamental-Metalwork Designer; 142.061-038 Safety-Clothing-and-Equipment

Developer; 142.061-054 Stained Glass Artist; 142.081-018 Package Designer.

27-1022.00 Fashion Designers (Designers)

Education: Bachelor's degree
Employed: 335,260
Openings: 57,787
Projected Growth: 27.1%
Earnings: $29,190

Design clothing and accessories. Create original garments; design garments that follow well-established fashion trends. Develop the line of color and kinds of materials.

Arranges for showing of sample garments at sales meetings or fashion shows. Integrates findings of analysis and discussion, and personal tastes and knowledge of design, to originate design ideas. Sketches rough and detailed drawings of apparel or accessories, and writes specifications such as color scheme, construction, or material type. Examines sample garment on and off model, and modifies design to achieve desired effect. Confers with sales and management executives, or clients regarding design ideas. Sews together sections to form mockup or sample of garment or article, using sewing equipment. Designs custom garments for clients. Draws pattern for article designed, cuts pattern, and cuts material according to pattern, using measuring and drawing instruments, and scissors. Attends fashion shows and reviews garment magazines and manuals to analyze fashion trends, predictions, and consumer preferences. Directs and coordinates workers who draw and cut patterns, and construct sample or finished garment.

GOE Number, Interest Area, and Work Group: 01.04.02; Arts, Entertainment, and Media; Visual Arts: Design. **Personality Type:** Artistic. Artistic occupations frequently involve working with forms, designs, and patterns. These occupations often require self-expression, and the work can be done without following a clear set of rules. **Work Values:** Creativity; Ability Utilization; Achievement; Responsibility; Autonomy. **Skills:** Idea Generation; Identifying Downstream Consequences; Coordination; Judgment and Decision Making; Identification of Key Causes; Active Learning; Product Inspection; Operations Analysis; Persuasion; Information Gathering. **Abilities:** *Cognitive*—Fluency of Ideas; Originality; Visualization; Oral Comprehension; Written Comprehension; Oral Expression. *Psychomotor*—Finger Dexterity; Arm-Hand Steadiness; Manual Dexterity. *Physical*—Gross Body Equilibrium. *Sensory*—Visual Color Discrimination; Near Vision; Speech Clarity. **General Work Activities:** *Information Input*—Getting Information Needed to Do the Job; Identifying Objects, Actions, and Events; Estimating Needed Characteristics. *Mental Process*—Thinking Creatively; Judging Qualities of Things, Services, Other People's Work; Updating and Using Job-Relevant Knowledge. *Work Output*—Implementing Ideas and Programs; Drafting and Specifying Technical Devices; Handling and Moving Objects. *Interacting with Others*—Communicating with Other Workers; Communicating with Persons Outside Organization; Coordinating Work and Activities of Others. **Physical Work Conditions:** Indoors; Using Hands on Objects, Tools, or Controls; Sitting. **Other Job Characteristics:**

Consequence of Error; Importance of Being Sure All Is Done; Importance of Being Exact or Accurate.

Experience: Job Zone 3. Previous work-related skill, knowledge, or experience is required. **Job Preparation:** SVP 6.0 to less than 7.0—More than 1 year and less than 4 years. **Knowledge:** Design; Fine Arts; Sales and Marketing; Sociology and Anthropology; Psychology; Customer and Personal Service. **Instructional Programs:** 080503 Floristry Marketing Operations; 200301 Clothing, Apparel and Textile Workers and Managers, General; 500401 Design and Visual Communications; 500404 Industrial Design; 500407 Fashion Design and Illustration; 500499 Design and Applied Arts, Other; 500502 Technical Theater/Theater Design and Stagecraft.

Related DOT Jobs: 142.061-018 Fashion Designer; 142.081-014 Fur Designer; 142.281-010 Copyist.

27-1023.00 Floral Designers (Designers)

Education: Bachelor's degree

Employed: 335,260

Openings: 57,787

Projected Growth: 27.1%

Earnings: $29,190

Design, cut, and arrange live, dried, or artificial flowers and foliage.

Decorates buildings, halls, churches, or other facilities where events are planned. Confers with client regarding price and type of arrangement desired. Selects flora and foliage for arrangement. Estimates costs and prices arrangements. Conducts classes, demonstrations, or trains other workers. Packs and wraps completed arrangements. Plans arrangement according to client's requirements, utilizing knowledge of design and properties of materials, or selects appropriate standard design pattern. Trims material and arranges bouquets, wreaths, terrariums, and other items using trimmers, shapers, wire, pin, floral tape, foam, and other materials.

GOE Number, Interest Area, and Work Group: 01.04.02; Arts, Entertainment, and Media; Visual Arts: Design. **Personality Type:** Artistic. Artistic occupations frequently involve working with forms, designs, and patterns. These occupations often require self-expression, and the work can be done without following a clear set of rules. **Work Values:** Creativity; Moral Values; Achievement; Ability Utilization; Autonomy. **Skills:** Service Orientation; Learning Strategies; Identification of Key Causes; Problem Identification; Writing. **Abilities:** *Cognitive*—Originality; Oral Comprehension; Visualization; Oral Expression; Fluency of Ideas. *Psychomotor*—Arm-Hand Steadiness; Finger Dexterity; Multilimb Coordination. *Physical*—Extent Flexibility; Gross Body Coordination; Gross Body Equilibrium. *Sensory*—Visual Color Discrimination; Speech Clarity; Speech Recognition. **General Work Activities:** *Information Input*—Estimating Needed Characteristics; Getting Information Needed to Do the Job; Identifying Objects, Actions, and Events. *Mental Process*—Thinking Creatively; Organizing, Planning, and Prioritizing; Judging Qualities of Things, Services, Other People's Work. *Work Output*—Handling and Moving Objects; Implementing Ideas and Programs; Performing General Physical Activities. *Interacting with Others*—Communicating

with Persons Outside Organization; Performing for or Working with the Public; Providing Consultation and Advice to Others. **Physical Work Conditions:** Using Hands on Objects, Tools, or Controls; Indoors; Standing. **Other Job Characteristics:** Importance of Being Sure All Is Done; Consequence of Error; Frustrating Circumstances.

Experience: Job Zone 2. Some previous work-related skill, knowledge, or experience may be helpful, but usually is not needed. **Job Preparation:** SVP 4.00 to 5.99—6 months to less than 2 years. **Knowledge:** Fine Arts; Customer and Personal Service; Design; Biology; Education and Training. **Instructional Programs:** 080503 Floristry Marketing Operations; 200301 Clothing, Apparel and Textile Workers and Managers, General; 500401 Design and Visual Communications; 500404 Industrial Design; 500407 Fashion Design and Illustration; 500499 Design and Applied Arts, Other; 500502 Technical Theater/Theater Design and Stagecraft.

Related DOT Jobs: 142.081-010 Floral Designer; 899.364-014 Artificial-Foliage Arranger.

27-1024.00 Graphic Designers (Artists and Commercial Artists)

Education: Work experience, plus degree

Employed: 308,496

Openings: 58,769

Projected Growth: 25.7%

Earnings: $31,690

Design or create graphics to meet a client's specific commercial or promotional needs, such as packaging, displays, or logos. Use various mediums to achieve artistic or decorative effects.

Prepares series of drawings to illustrate sequence and timing of story development for television production. Reviews final layout and suggests improvements as needed. Arranges layout based upon available space, knowledge of layout principles, and esthetic design concepts. Determines size and arrangement of illustrative material and copy, and selects style and size of type. Keys information into computer equipment to create layouts for client or supervisor. Marks up, pastes, and assembles final layouts to prepare layouts for printer. Draws and prints charts, graphs, illustrations, and other artwork, using computer. Confers with client regarding layout design. Draws sample of finished layout and presents sample to art director for approval. Photographs layouts, using camera, to make layout prints for supervisor or client. Prepares notes and instructions for workers who assemble and prepare final layouts for printing. Develops negatives and prints, using negative and print developing equipment and tools and work aids to produce layout photographs. Prepares illustrations or rough sketches of material according to instructions of client or supervisor. Produces still and animated graphic formats for on-air and taped portions of television news broadcasts, using electronic video equipment. Studies illustrations and photographs to plan presentation of material, product, or service.

GOE Number, Interest Area, and Work Group: 01.04.02; Arts, Entertainment, and Media; Visual Arts: Design. **Personality Type:** Artistic. Artistic occupations frequently involve working with forms, designs, and patterns. These occupations often require self-expression, and the work can be done without following a clear set of rules. **Work Values:** Ability Utilization; Achievement; Creativity; Working Conditions; Autonomy; Recognition. **Skills:** Idea Generation; Reading Comprehension; Information Organization; Active Listening; Equipment Selection; Speaking. **Abilities:** *Cognitive*—Originality; Fluency of Ideas; Visualization; Oral Expression; Oral Comprehension. *Psychomotor*—Control Precision; Finger Dexterity. *Physical*—Trunk Strength. *Sensory*—Visual Color Discrimination; Speech Recognition; Speech Clarity. **General Work Activities:** *Information Input*—Getting Information Needed to Do the Job; Identifying Objects, Actions, and Events; Estimating Needed Characteristics. *Mental Process*—Thinking Creatively; Judging Qualities of Things, Services, Other People's Work; Evaluating Information Against Standards; Processing Information; Making Decisions and Solving Problems. *Work Output*—Drafting and Specifying Technical Devices; Interacting with Computers; Handling and Moving Objects. *Interacting with Others*—Communicating with Persons Outside Organization; Communicating with Other Workers; Interpreting Meaning of Information to Others. **Physical Work Conditions:** Indoors; Sitting; Using Hands on Objects, Tools, or Controls. **Other Job Characteristics:** Consequence of Error; Frustrating Circumstances; Importance of Being Exact or Accurate; Importance of Being Sure All Is Done.

Experience: Job Zone 4. A minimum of two to four years of work-related skill, knowledge, or experience is needed. **Job Preparation:** SVP 7.0 to less than 8.0—2 years to less than 10 years. **Knowledge:** Fine Arts; Communications and Media; Design; Computers and Electronics; English Language. **Instructional Programs:** 500201 Crafts, Folk Art and Artisanry; 500402 Graphic Design, Commercial Art and Illustration; 500502 Technical Theater/Theater Design and Stagecraft; 500701 Art, General; 500702 Fine/Studio Arts; 500705 Drawing; 500706 Intermedia; 500708 Painting; 500709 Sculpture; 500710 Printmaking; 500711 Ceramics Arts and Ceramics; 500712 Fiber, Textile and Weaving Arts; 500713 Metal and Jewelry Arts; 500799 Fine Arts and Art Studies, Other; 512703 Medical Illustrating.

Related DOT Job: 141.061-018 Graphic Designer.

27-1025.00 Interior Designers (Interior Designers)

Education: Bachelor's degree
Employed: 53,291
Openings: 9,201
Projected Growth: 27.2%
Earnings: $31,760

Plan, design, and furnish interiors of residential, commercial, or industrial buildings. Formulate design which is practical, aesthetic, and conducive to intended purposes, such as raising productivity, selling merchandise, or improving lifestyle. Specialize in a particular field, style, or phase of interior design.

Advises client on interior design factors such as space planning, layout and utilization of furnishings and equipment, and color coordination. Selects or designs and purchases furnishings, art works, and accessories. Plans and designs interior environments for boats, planes, buses, trains, and other enclosed spaces. Subcontracts fabrication, installation, and arrangement of carpeting, fixtures, accessories, draperies, paint and wall coverings, art work, furniture, and related items. Estimates material requirements and costs, and presents design to client for approval. Confers with client to determine factors affecting planning interior environments, such as budget, architectural preferences, and purpose and function. Formulates environmental plan to be practical, esthetic, and conducive to intended purposes such as raising productivity or selling merchandise. Renders design ideas in form of paste ups or drawings.

GOE Number, Interest Area, and Work Group: 01.04.02; Arts, Entertainment, and Media; Visual Arts: Design. **Personality Type:** Artistic. Artistic occupations frequently involve working with forms, designs, and patterns. These occupations often require self-expression, and the work can be done without following a clear set of rules. **Work Values:** Creativity; Ability Utilization; Achievement; Autonomy; Recognition. **Skills:** Coordination; Active Listening; Operations Analysis; Speaking; Identification of Key Causes; Idea Generation; Management of Financial Resources; Mathematics. **Abilities:** *Cognitive*—Visualization; Originality; Fluency of Ideas; Oral Expression; Oral Comprehension. *Psychomotor*—none met the criteria. *Physical*—none met the criteria. *Sensory*—Visual Color Discrimination; Speech Recognition; Depth Perception. **General Work Activities:** *Information Input*—Getting Information Needed to Do the Job; Estimating Needed Characteristics; Identifying Objects, Actions, and Events. *Mental Process*—Thinking Creatively; Making Decisions and Solving Problems; Updating and Using Job-Relevant Knowledge; Judging Qualities of Things, Services, Other People's Work. *Work Output*—Drafting and Specifying Technical Devices; Implementing Ideas and Programs; Documenting and Recording Information; Handling and Moving Objects. *Interacting with Others*—Establishing and Maintaining Relationships; Providing Consultation and Advice to Others; Monitoring and Controlling Resources; Communicating with Persons Outside Organization. **Physical Work Conditions:** Indoors; Sitting; Using Hands on Objects, Tools, or Controls. **Other Job Characteristics:** Consequence of Error; Importance of Being Exact or Accurate; Importance of Being Sure All Is Done.

Experience: Job Zone 4. A minimum of two to four years of work-related skill, knowledge, or experience is needed. **Job Preparation:** SVP 7.0 to less than 8.0—2 years to less than 10 years. **Knowledge:** Design; Administration and Management; Mathematics; Sales and Marketing; Fine Arts. **Instructional Programs:** 040501 Interior Architecture; 190603 Interior Environments; 200501 Home Furnishings and Equipment Installers and Consultants, General; 200599 Home Furnishings and Equipment Installers and Consultants, Other; 500408 Interior Design.

Related DOT Jobs: 141.051-010 Color Expert; 142.051-014 Interior Designer.

27-1026.00 Merchandise Displayers and Window Trimmers (Merchandise Displayers and Window Dressers)

Education: Moderate-term O-T-J training
Employed: 34,056
Openings: 5,067
Projected Growth: 12.7%
Earnings: $18,180

Plan and erect commercial displays such as those in windows and interiors of retail stores and at trade exhibitions.

Constructs or assembles prefabricated display properties from fabric, glass, paper, and plastic, using hand tools and woodworking power tools, according to specifications. Dresses mannequins for use in displays. Installs booths, exhibits, displays, carpets, and drapes, as guided by floor plan of building and specifications. Develops layout and selects theme, lighting, colors, and props to be used. Installs decorations such as flags, banners, festive lights, and bunting, on or in building, street, exhibit hall, or booth. Places price and descriptive signs on backdrop, fixtures, merchandise, or floor. Arranges properties, furniture, merchandise, backdrop, and other accessories, as shown in prepared sketch. Consults with advertising and sales staff to determine type of merchandise to be featured and time and place for each display. Originates ideas for merchandise display or window decoration. Prepares sketches or floor plans of proposed displays. Cuts out designs on cardboard, hard board, and plywood, according to motif of event.

GOE Number, Interest Area, and Work Group: 01.04.02; Arts, Entertainment, and Media; Visual Arts: Design. **Personality Type:** Artistic. Artistic occupations frequently involve working with forms, designs, and patterns. These occupations often require self-expression, and the work can be done without following a clear set of rules. **Work Values:** Ability Utilization; Creativity; Moral Values; Achievement; Working Conditions. **Skills:** Idea Evaluation; Idea Generation; Installation; Product Inspection; Equipment Selection. **Abilities:** *Cognitive*—Visualization; Originality; Fluency of Ideas; Information Ordering; Category Flexibility. *Psychomotor*—Manual Dexterity; Multilimb Coordination; Speed of Limb Movement. *Physical*—Extent Flexibility; Static Strength; Explosive Strength; Trunk Strength. *Sensory*—Visual Color Discrimination; Depth Perception; Far Vision. **General Work Activities:** *Information Input*—Getting Information Needed to Do the Job; Estimating Needed Characteristics; Identifying Objects, Actions, and Events. *Mental Process*—Thinking Creatively; Judging Qualities of Things, Services, Other People's Work; Organizing, Planning, and Prioritizing. *Work Output*—Implementing Ideas and Programs; Handling and Moving Objects; Performing General Physical Activities. *Interacting with Others*—Influencing Others or Selling; Communicating with Other Workers; Communicating with Persons Outside Organization. **Physical Work Conditions:** Using Hands on Objects, Tools, or Controls; Indoors; Standing. **Other Job Characteristics:** Importance of Being Sure All Is Done; Importance of Being Exact or Accurate; Frustrating Circumstances.

Experience: Job Zone 3. Previous work-related skill, knowledge, or experience is required. **Job Preparation:** SVP 6.0 to less than 7.0—More than 1 year and less than 4 years. **Knowledge:** Sales and Marketing; Fine Arts; Design; Mechanical; Communications and Media. **Instructional Programs:** 200501 Home Furnishings and Equipment Installers and Consultants, General; 500401 Design and Visual Communications.

Related DOT Jobs: 142.031-014 Manager, Display; 298.081-010 Displayer, Merchandise; 298.381-010 Decorator.

27-1027.00 Set and Exhibit Designers (Designers)

Education: Bachelor's degree
Employed: 335,260
Openings: 57,787
Projected Growth: 27.1%
Earnings: $29,190

Design special exhibits and movie, television, and theater sets. Study scripts, confer with directors, and conduct research to determine appropriate architectural styles.

GOE Number, Interest Area, and Work Group: 01.04.02; Arts, Entertainment, and Media; Visual Arts: Design. **Instructional Programs:** 080503 Floristry Marketing Operations; 200301 Clothing, Apparel and Textile Workers and Managers, General; 500401 Design and Visual Communications; 500404 Industrial Design; 500407 Fashion Design and Illustration; 500499 Design and Applied Arts, Other; 500502 Technical Theater/Theater Design and Stagecraft. **Note:** The Department of Labor has not collected some data for this job, so it has fewer details than the other descriptions.

27-1027.01 Set Designers (Designers)

Education: Bachelor's degree
Employed: 335,260
Openings: 57,787
Projected Growth: 27.1%
Earnings: $29,190

Design sets for theatrical, motion picture, and television productions.

Presents drawings for approval and makes changes and corrections as directed. Designs and builds scale models of set design or miniature sets used in filming backgrounds or special effects. Prepares rough draft and scale working drawings of sets, including floor plans, scenery, and properties to be constructed. Selects furniture, draperies, pictures, lamps, and rugs for decorative quality and appearance. Confers with heads of production and direction to establish budget, schedules, and discuss design ideas. Examines dressed set to ensure props and scenery do not interfere with movements of cast or view of camera. Directs and coordinates set construction, erection, or decoration activities to ensure conformance to design, budget, and schedule requirements. Reads script to determine location, set, or decoration requirements. Estimates costs of design materials and construction, or rental of location or props. Researches and consults experts to determine architectural and furnishing styles to depict given periods or locations. Integrates requirements including script, research, budget, and available locations to develop design. Assigns staff to complete design ideas and prepare sketches, illustrations, and detailed drawings of sets, or graphics and animation.

GOE Number, Interest Area, and Work Group: 01.04.02; Arts, Entertainment, and Media; Visual Arts: Design. **Personality Type:** Artistic. Artistic occupations frequently involve working with forms, designs, and patterns. These occupations often require self-expression, and the work can be done without following a clear set of rules. **Work Values:** Ability Utilization; Creativity; Achievement; Autonomy; Moral Values. **Skills:** Information Gathering; Reading Comprehension; Management of Material Resources; Coordination; Implementation Planning; Visioning; Identification of Key Causes; Active Listening. **Abilities:** *Cognitive*—Visualization; Written Comprehension; Oral Expression; Originality; Oral Comprehension. *Psychomotor*—Arm-Hand Steadiness; Finger Dexterity; Manual Dexterity; Wrist-Finger Speed. *Physical*—Extent Flexibility; Gross Body Equilibrium; Static Strength. *Sensory*—Visual Color Discrimination; Near Vision; Auditory Attention; Far Vision. **General Work Activities:** *Information Input*—Estimating Needed Characteristics; Getting Information Needed to Do the Job; Identifying Objects, Actions, and Events. *Mental Process*—Thinking Creatively; Organizing, Planning, and Prioritizing; Making Decisions and Solving Problems. *Work Output*—Drafting and Specifying Technical Devices; Implementing Ideas and Programs; Handling and Moving Objects. *Interacting with Others*—Coordinating Work and Activities of Others; Communicating with Other Workers; Communicating with Persons Outside Organization. **Physical Work Conditions:** Indoors; Standing; Using Hands on Objects, Tools, or Controls. **Other Job Characteristics:** Consequence of Error; Frustrating Circumstances; Importance of Being Sure All Is Done.

Experience: Job Zone 5. Extensive skill, knowledge, and experience are needed. Very advanced communication and organizational skills are required. **Job Preparation:** SVP 8.0 and above—4 years to more than 10 years. **Knowledge:** Design; Fine Arts; Building and Construction; Psychology; Sociology and Anthropology; English Language. **Instructional Programs:** 080503 Floristry Marketing Operations; 200301 Clothing, Apparel and Textile Workers and Managers, General; 500401 Design and Visual Communications; 500404 Industrial Design; 500407 Fashion Design and Illustration; 500499 Design and Applied Arts, Other; 500502 Technical Theater/Theater Design and Stagecraft.

Related DOT Jobs: 142.061-042 Set Decorator; 142.061-046 Set Designer; 142.061-050 Set Designer; 142.061-062 Art Director; 149.031-010 Supervisor, Scenic Arts.

27-1027.02 Exhibit Designers (Designers)

Education: Bachelor's degree

Employed: 335,260

Openings: 57,787

Projected Growth: 27.1%

Earnings: $29,190

Plan, design, and oversee construction and installation of permanent and temporary exhibits and displays.

Oversees preparation of artwork, construction of exhibit components, and placement of collection to ensure intended interpretation of concepts and conformance to specifications. Designs display to decorate streets, fairgrounds, building or other places for celebrations, using paper, cloth, plastic, or other materials. Submits plans for approval, and adapts plan to serve intended purpose or to conform to budget or fabrication restrictions. Prepares preliminary drawings of proposed exhibit, including detailed construction, layout, material specifications, or special effects diagrams. Confers with client or staff regarding theme, interpretative or informational purpose, planned location, budget, materials, or promotion. Designs, draws, paints, or sketches backgrounds and fixtures for use in windows or interior displays. Inspects installed exhibit for conformance to specifications and satisfactory operation of special effects components. Arranges for acquisition of specimens or graphics, or building of exhibit structures by outside contractors to complete exhibit.

GOE Number, Interest Area, and Work Group: 01.04.02; Arts, Entertainment, and Media; Visual Arts: Design. **Personality Type:** Artistic. Artistic occupations frequently involve working with forms, designs, and patterns. These occupations often require self-expression, and the work can be done without following a clear set of rules. **Work Values:** Creativity; Achievement; Ability Utilization; Autonomy; Moral Values. **Skills:** Information Organization; Idea Evaluation; Identification of Key Causes; Writing; Coordination. **Abilities:** *Cognitive*—Originality; Visualization; Oral Expression; Fluency of Ideas; Oral Comprehension. *Psychomotor*—Arm-Hand Steadiness; Wrist-Finger Speed; Manual Dexterity; Control Precision. *Physical*—Extent Flexibility; Gross Body Coordination; Stamina. *Sensory*—Visual Color Discrimination; Near Vision; Far Vision. **General Work Activities:** *Information Input*—Getting Information Needed to Do the Job; Monitoring Processes, Materials, and Surroundings; Estimating Needed Characteristics. *Mental Process*—Thinking Creatively; Organizing, Planning, and Prioritizing; Evaluating Information Against Standards. *Work Output*—Drafting and Specifying Technical Devices; Implementing Ideas and Programs; Handling and Moving Objects. *Interacting with Others*—Coordinating Work and Activities of Others; Communicating with Persons Outside Organization; Monitoring and Controlling Resources. **Physical Work Conditions:** Indoors; Standing; Using Hands on Objects, Tools, or Controls; Walking or Running. **Other Job Characteristics:** Consequence of Error; Frustrating Circumstances; Importance of Being Sure All Is Done.

Experience: Job Zone 4. A minimum of two to four years of work-related skill, knowledge, or experience is needed. **Job Preparation:** SVP 7.0 to less than 8.0—2 years to less than 10 years. **Knowledge:** Design; Fine Arts; Building and Construction; Psychology; Mathematics; Mechanical; English Language. **Instructional Programs:** 080503 Floristry Marketing Operations; 200301 Clothing, Apparel and Textile Workers and Managers, General; 500401 Design and Visual Communications; 500404 Industrial Design; 500407 Fashion Design and Illustration; 500499 Design and Applied Arts, Other; 500502 Technical Theater/Theater Design and Stagecraft.

Related DOT Jobs: 142.051-010 Display Designer; 142.061-058 Exhibit Designer.

27-2000 Entertainers and Performers, Sports and Related Workers

27-2011.00 Actors (Actors, Directors, and Producers)

Education: Long-term O-T-J training
Employed: 160,024
Openings: 31,279
Projected Growth: 23.8%
Earnings: $27,370

Play parts in stage, television, radio, video, or motion picture productions, for entertainment, information, or instruction. Interpret serious or comic role, through speech, gesture, and body movement, to entertain or inform audience. Dance and sing.

Portrays and interprets role, using speech, gestures, and body movements, to entertain radio, film, television, or live audience. Reads and rehearses role from script to learn lines, stunts, and cues as directed. Tells jokes, performs comic dances and songs, impersonates mannerisms and voice of others, contorts face and uses other devices to amuse audience. Performs original and stock tricks of illusion to entertain and mystify audience, occasionally including audience members as participants. Dresses in comical clown costume and makeup and performs comedy routines to entertain audience. Prepares for and performs action stunts for motion picture, television, or stage production. Reads from script or book to narrate action, inform, or entertain audience, utilizing few or no stage props. Sings or dances during dramatic or comedy performance. Manipulates string, wire, rod, or fingers to animate puppet or dummy in synchronization to talking, singing, or recorded program. Signals start and introduces performers to stimulate excitement and to coordinate smooth transition of acts during circus performance. Constructs puppets and ventriloquist dummies, and sews accessory clothing, using hand tools and machines. Writes original or adapted material for drama, comedy, puppet show, narration, or other performance. Performs humorous and serious interpretations of emotions, actions, and situations, using only body movements, facial expressions, and gestures.

GOE Number, Interest Area, and Work Group: 01.05.01; Arts, Entertainment, and Media; Performing Arts, Drama: Directing, Performing, Narrating, and Announcing. **Personality Type:** Artistic. Artistic occupations frequently involve working with forms, designs, and patterns. These occupations often require self-expression, and the work can be done without following a clear set of rules. **Work Values:** Ability Utilization; Achievement; Recognition; Creativity; Variety. **Skills:** Speaking; Monitoring; Reading Comprehension; Coordination; Social Perceptiveness; Active Learning. **Abilities:** *Cognitive*—Oral Expression; Memorization; Originality; Written Comprehension; Fluency of Ideas. *Psychomotor*—Reaction Time; Wrist-Finger Speed; Speed of Limb Movement. *Physical*—Gross Body Coordination; Explosive Strength; Dynamic Flexibility. *Sensory*—Near Vision; Speech Clarity; Far Vision. **General Work Activities:** *Information Input*—Getting Information Needed to Do the Job; Monitoring Processes, Materials, and Surroundings; Identifying Objects, Actions, and Events. *Mental Process*—Thinking Creatively; Judging Qualities of Things, Services, Other People's Work; Making Decisions and Solving Problems. *Work Output*—Performing General Physical Activities; Implementing Ideas and Programs; Handling and Moving Objects. *Interacting with Others*—Performing for or Working with the Public; Communicating with Other Workers; Communicating with Persons Outside Organization. **Physical Work Conditions:** Indoors; Special Uniform; Standing. **Other Job Characteristics:** Importance of Being Exact or Accurate; Importance of Being Sure All Is Done; Consequence of Error.

Experience: Job Zone 3. Previous work-related skill, knowledge, or experience is required. **Job Preparation:** SVP 6.0 to less than 7.0—More than 1 year and less than 4 years. **Knowledge:** Fine Arts; English Language; Communications and Media; Psychology; Building and Construction. **Instructional Programs:** 090701 Radio and Television Broadcasting; 500501 Drama/Theater Arts, General; 500503 Acting and Directing; 500504 Playwriting and Screenwriting; 500505 Drama/Theater Literature, History and Criticism; 500599 Dramatic/Theater Arts and Stagecraft, Other; 500601 Film/Cinema Studies; 500602 Film-Video Making/Cinematography and Production.

Related DOT Jobs: 150.047-010 Actor; 150.147-010 Narrator; 159.041-010 Magician; 159.041-014 Puppeteer; 159.044-010 Ventriloquist; 159.047-010 Clown; 159.047-014 Comedian; 159.047-018 Impersonator; 159.047-022 Mime; 159.341-014 Stunt Performer; 159.367-010 Ring Conductor.

27-2012.00 Producers and Directors (Actors, Directors, and Producers)

Education: Long-term O-T-J training
Employed: 160,024
Openings: 31,279
Projected Growth: 23.8%
Earnings: $27,370

Produce or direct stage, television, radio, video, or motion picture productions for entertainment, information, or instruction. Assume responsibility for creative decisions affecting interpretation of script, choice of guests, set design, sound, special effects, and choreography.

GOE Number, Interest Area, and Work Group: 01.01.01; Arts, Entertainment, and Media; Managerial Work in Arts, Entertainment, and Media. **Instructional Programs:** 090701 Radio and Television Broadcasting; 500501 Drama/Theater Arts, General; 500503 Acting and Directing; 500504 Playwriting and Screenwriting; 500505 Drama/Theater Literature, History and Criticism; 500599 Dramatic/Theater Arts and Stagecraft, Other; 500601 Film/Cinema Studies; 500602 Film-Video Making/Cinematography and Production. **Note:** The Department of Labor has not collected some data for this job, so it has fewer details than the other descriptions.

27-2012.01 Producers (Actors, Directors, and Producers)

Education: Long-term O-T-J training

Employed: 160,024

Openings: 31,279

Projected Growth: 23.8%

Earnings: $27,370

Plan and coordinate various aspects of radio, television, stage, or motion picture production. Select script; coordinate writing, directing, and editing; and arrange financing.

Reviews film, recordings, or rehearsals to ensure conformance to production and broadcast standards. Conducts meetings with staff to discuss production progress and to ensure production objectives are attained. Directs activities of one or more departments of motion picture studio and prepares rehearsal call sheets and reports of activities and operating costs. Selects and hires cast and staff members and arbitrates personnel disputes. Produces shows for special occasions, such as holiday or testimonial. Obtains and distributes costumes, props, music, and studio equipment to complete production. Reads manuscript and selects play for stage performance. Represents network or company in negotiations with independent producers. Distributes rehearsal call sheets and copies of script, arranges for rehearsal quarters, and contacts cast members to verify readiness for rehearsal. Times scene and calculates program timing. Establishes management policies, production schedules, and operating budgets for production. Coordinates various aspects of production, such as audio and camera work, music, timing, writing, and staging. Composes and edits script, or outlines story for screenwriter to write script. Selects scenes from taped program to be used for promotional purposes.

GOE Number, Interest Area, and Work Group: 01.01.01; Arts, Entertainment, and Media; Managerial Work in Arts, Entertainment, and Media. **Personality Type:** Artistic. Artistic occupations frequently involve working with forms, designs, and patterns. These occupations often require self-expression, and the work can be done without following a clear set of rules. **Work Values:** Autonomy; Achievement; Responsibility; Creativity; Authority; Ability Utilization. **Skills:** Coordination; Reading Comprehension; Speaking; Management of Personnel Resources; Writing. **Abilities:** *Cognitive*—Oral Expression; Written Comprehension; Written Expression; Originality; Problem Sensitivity; Oral Comprehension. *Psychomotor*—none met the criteria. *Physical*—none met the criteria. *Sensory*—Near Vision; Speech Clarity; Speech Recognition. **General Work Activities:** *Information Input*—Getting Information Needed to Do the Job; Monitoring Processes, Materials, and Surroundings; Identifying Objects, Actions, and Events. *Mental Process*—Making Decisions and Solving Problems; Scheduling Work and Activities; Organizing, Planning, and Prioritizing; Thinking Creatively. *Work Output*—Implementing Ideas and Programs; Drafting and Specifying Technical Devices; Handling and Moving Objects; Documenting and Recording Information. *Interacting with Others*—Coordinating Work and Activities of Others; Communicating with Other Workers; Staffing Organizational Units; Resolving Conflict and Negotiating with Others. **Physical Work Conditions:** Indoors; Sitting; Standing. **Other Job**

Characteristics: Consequence of Error; Frustrating Circumstances; Importance of Being Exact or Accurate; Importance of Being Sure All Is Done.

Experience: Job Zone 4. A minimum of two to four years of work-related skill, knowledge, or experience is needed. **Job Preparation:** SVP 7.0 to less than 8.0—2 years to less than 10 years. **Knowledge:** Communications and Media; Administration and Management; Personnel and Human Resources; English Language; Fine Arts. **Instructional Programs:** 090701 Radio and Television Broadcasting; 500501 Drama/Theater Arts, General; 500503 Acting and Directing; 500504 Playwriting and Screenwriting; 500505 Drama/Theater Literature, History and Criticism; 500599 Dramatic/Theater Arts and Stagecraft, Other; 500601 Film/Cinema Studies; 500602 Film-Video Making/Cinematography and Production.

Related DOT Jobs: 159.117-010 Producer; 187.167-174 Producer; 187.167-178 Producer; 187.167-182 Producer, Assistant; 962.167-014 Program Assistant.

27-2012.02 Directors—Stage, Motion Pictures, Television, and Radio (Actors, Directors, and Producers)

Education: Long-term O-T-J training

Employed: 160,024

Openings: 31,279

Projected Growth: 23.8%

Earnings: $27,370

Interpret script, conduct rehearsals, and direct activities of cast and technical crew for stage, motion pictures, television, or radio programs.

Writes and compiles letters, memos, notes, scripts, and other program material, using computer. Directs live broadcasts, films and recordings, or nonbroadcast programming for public entertainment or education. Directs cast, crew, and technicians during production or recording and filming in studio or on location. Establishes pace of program and sequences of scenes according to time requirements and cast and set accessibility. Approves equipment and elements required for production, such as scenery, lights, props, costumes, choreography, and music. Auditions and selects cast and technical staff. Reads and rehearses cast to develop performance based on script interpretations. Reviews educational material to gather information for scripts. Compiles cue words and phrases and cues announcers, cast members, and technicians during performances. Interprets stage-set diagrams to determine stage layout and supervises placement of equipment and scenery. Coaches performers in acting techniques to develop and improve performance and image. Confers with technical directors, managers, and writers to discuss details of production, such as photography, script, music, sets, and costumes. Cuts and edits film or tape to integrate component parts of film into desired sequence.

GOE Number, Interest Area, and Work Group: 01.05.01; Arts, Entertainment, and Media; Performing Arts, Drama: Directing, Performing, Narrating, and Announcing. **Personality Type:** Artistic. Artistic occupations frequently involve working with forms, designs, and patterns. These occupations often require self-expression, and the work can be done without following a clear set of rules. **Work Values:** Authority; Achievement; Responsibility; Creativity; Autonomy; Recognition; Ability Utilization. **Skills:** Coordination; Reading Comprehension; Instructing; Idea Generation; Idea Evaluation; Speaking. **Abilities:** *Cognitive*—Oral Expression; Oral Comprehension; Written Comprehension; Time Sharing; Visualization. *Psychomotor*—Reaction Time; Response Orientation; Rate Control. *Physical*—Gross Body Coordination; Gross Body Equilibrium; Dynamic Flexibility. *Sensory*—Speech Clarity; Near Vision; Far Vision. **General Work Activities:** *Information Input*—Identifying Objects, Actions, and Events; Getting Information Needed to Do the Job; Monitoring Processes, Materials, and Surroundings. *Mental Process*—Thinking Creatively; Scheduling Work and Activities; Making Decisions and Solving Problems; Judging Qualities of Things, Services, Other People's Work. *Work Output*—Implementing Ideas and Programs; Drafting and Specifying Technical Devices; Interacting with Computers. *Interacting with Others*—Communicating with Other Workers; Coordinating Work and Activities of Others; Staffing Organizational Units. **Physical Work Conditions:** Indoors; Outdoors; Sitting; Standing; Using Hands on Objects, Tools, or Controls. **Other Job Characteristics:** Consequence of Error; Importance of Being Sure All Is Done; Frustrating Circumstances; Importance of Being Exact or Accurate.

Experience: Job Zone 4. A minimum of two to four years of work-related skill, knowledge, or experience is needed. **Job Preparation:** SVP 7.0 to less than 8.0—2 years to less than 10 years. **Knowledge:** Fine Arts; Administration and Management; Communications and Media; English Language; Computers and Electronics; Clerical. **Instructional Programs:** 090701 Radio and Television Broadcasting; 500501 Drama/Theater Arts, General; 500503 Acting and Directing; 500504 Playwriting and Screenwriting; 500505 Drama/Theater Literature, History and Criticism; 500599 Dramatic/Theater Arts and Stagecraft, Other; 500601 Film/Cinema Studies; 500602 Film-Video Making/Cinematography and Production.

Related DOT Jobs: 139.167-010 Program Coordinator; 150.027-010 Dramatic Coach; 150.067-010 Director, Stage; 159.067-010 Director, Motion Picture; 159.067-014 Director, Television; 159.167-014 Director, Radio; 159.167-018 Manager, Stage.

27-2012.03 Program Directors (Actors, Directors, and Producers)

Education: Long-term O-T-J training

Employed: 160,024

Openings: 31,279

Projected Growth: 23.8%

Earnings: $27,370

Direct and coordinate activities of personnel engaged in preparation of radio or television station program schedules and programs such as sports or news.

Coordinates activities between departments, such as news and programming. Plans and schedules programming and event coverage based on length of broadcast and available station or network time. Reviews, corrects, and advises member stations concerning programs and schedules. Directs and coordinates activities of personnel engaged in broadcast news, sports, or programming. Directs setup of remote facilities and installs or cancels programs at remote stations. Confers with directors and production staff to discuss issues such as production and casting problems, budget, policy, and news coverage. Originates feature ideas and researches program topics for implementation. Examines expenditures to ensure programming and broadcasting activities are within budget. Writes news copy, notes, letters, and memos, using computer. Monitors and reviews news and programming copy and film, using audio or video equipment. Establishes work schedules and hires, assigns, and evaluates staff. Evaluates length, content, and suitability of programs for broadcast.

GOE Number, Interest Area, and Work Group: 01.01.01; Arts, Entertainment, and Media; Managerial Work in Arts, Entertainment, and Media. **Personality Type:** Enterprising. Enterprising occupations frequently involve starting up and carrying out projects. These occupations can involve leading people and making many decisions. They sometimes require risk taking and often deal with business. **Work Values:** Authority; Autonomy; Responsibility; Variety; Creativity; Achievement. **Skills:** Coordination; Writing; Management of Personnel Resources; Reading Comprehension; Implementation Planning. **Abilities:** *Cognitive*—Oral Expression; Written Expression; Oral Comprehension; Written Comprehension; Deductive Reasoning. *Psychomotor*—Wrist-Finger Speed; Response Orientation. *Physical*—Trunk Strength. *Sensory*—Near Vision; Speech Clarity; Far Vision. **General Work Activities:** *Information Input*—Identifying Objects, Actions, and Events; Monitoring Processes, Materials, and Surroundings; Getting Information Needed to Do the Job. *Mental Process*—Scheduling Work and Activities; Organizing, Planning, and Prioritizing; Judging Qualities of Things, Services, Other People's Work; Making Decisions and Solving Problems. *Work Output*—Implementing Ideas and Programs; Documenting and Recording Information; Controlling Machines and Processes; Interacting with Computers. *Interacting with Others*—Monitoring and Controlling Resources; Guiding, Directing and Motivating Subordinates; Coordinating Work and Activities of Others. **Physical Work Conditions:** Indoors; Sitting; Standing. **Other Job Characteristics:** Importance of Being Sure All Is Done; Importance of Being Exact or Accurate; Consequence of Error.

Experience: Job Zone 5. Extensive skill, knowledge, and experience are needed. Very advanced communication and organizational skills are required. **Job Preparation:** SVP 8.0 and above—4 years to more than 10 years. **Knowledge:** Communications and Media; Administration and Management; Personnel and Human Resources; English Language; Economics and Accounting. **Instructional Programs:** 090701 Radio and Television Broadcasting; 500501 Drama/Theater Arts, General; 500503 Acting and Directing; 500504 Playwriting and Screenwriting; 500505 Drama/Theater Literature, History and Criticism; 500599 Dramatic/Theater Arts and Stagecraft, Other; 500601 Film/Cinema Studies; 500602 Film-Video Making/Cinematography and Production.

Related DOT Jobs: 184.117-010 Director, Public Service; 184.167-014 Director, News; 184.167-022 Director, Operations, Broadcast; 184.167-030 Director, Program; 184.167-034 Director, Sports.

27-2012.04 Talent Directors (Actors, Directors, and Producers)

Education: Long-term O-T-J training
Employed: 160,024
Openings: 31,279
Projected Growth: 23.8%
Earnings: $27,370

Audition and interview performers to select most appropriate talent for parts in stage, television, radio, or motion picture productions.

Directs recording sessions for musical artists. Arranges for screen tests or auditions for new performers. Selects performer or submits list of suitable performers to producer or director for final selection. Promotes record sales by personal appearances and contacts with broadcasting personalities. Maintains talent file, including information about personalities, such as specialties, past performances, and availability. Auditions and interviews performers to identify most suitable talent for broadcasting, stage, or musical production. Negotiates contract agreements with performers.

GOE Number, Interest Area, and Work Group: 01.05.02; Arts, Entertainment, and Media; Performing Arts, Music: Directing, Composing and Arranging, and Performing. **Personality Type:** Artistic. Artistic occupations frequently involve working with forms, designs, and patterns. These occupations often require self-expression, and the work can be done without following a clear set of rules. **Work Values:** Responsibility; Autonomy; Working Conditions; Ability Utilization; Variety; Authority. **Skills:** Speaking; Negotiation; Active Listening; Social Perceptiveness; Reading Comprehension. **Abilities:** *Cognitive*—Oral Expression; Memorization; Deductive Reasoning; Oral Comprehension; Time Sharing; Selective Attention. *Psychomotor*—none met the criteria. *Physical*—none met the criteria. *Sensory*—Near Vision; Hearing Sensitivity; Speech Clarity. **General Work Activities:** *Information Input*—Getting Information Needed to Do the Job; Identifying Objects, Actions, and Events; Monitoring Processes, Materials, and Surroundings. *Mental Process*—Judging Qualities of Things, Services, Other People's Work; Making Decisions and Solving Problems; Thinking Creatively. *Work Output*—Documenting and Recording Information; Implementing Ideas and Programs; Controlling Machines and Processes. *Interacting with Others*—Communicating with Persons Outside Organization; Resolving Conflict and Negotiating with Others; Establishing and Maintaining Relationships. **Physical Work Conditions:** Indoors; Sitting; Standing. **Other Job Characteristics:** Importance of Being Exact or Accurate; Importance of Being Sure All Is Done; Consequence of Error.

Experience: Job Zone 3. Previous work-related skill, knowledge, or experience is required. **Job Preparation:** SVP 6.0 to less than 7.0—More than 1 year and less than 4 years. **Knowledge:** Fine Arts; Sales and Marketing; Personnel and Human Resources; Communications and Media; Administration and Management. **Instructional Programs:** 090701 Radio and Television Broadcasting; 500501 Drama/Theater Arts, General; 500503 Acting and Directing; 500504 Playwriting and Screenwriting; 500505 Drama/Theater Literature, History and Criticism; 500599 Dramatic/Theater Arts and Stagecraft, Other; 500601 Film/Cinema Studies; 500602 Film-Video Making/Cinematography and Production.

Related DOT Jobs: 159.167-010 Artist and Repertoire Manager; 159.267-010 Director, Casting; 166.167-010 Contestant Coordinator.

27-2012.05 Technical Directors/Managers (Actors, Directors, and Producers)

Education: Long-term O-T-J training
Employed: 160,024
Openings: 31,279
Projected Growth: 23.8%
Earnings: $27,370

Coordinate activities of technical departments such as taping, editing, engineering, and maintenance to produce radio or television programs.

Trains workers in use of equipment such as switcher, camera, monitor, microphones, and lights. Coordinates activities of radio or television studio and control-room personnel to ensure technical quality of programs. Supervises and assigns duties to workers engaged in technical control and production of radio and television programs. Observes picture through monitor and directs camera and video staff concerning shading and composition. Monitors broadcast to ensure that programs conform with station or network policies and regulations. Operates equipment to produce programs or broadcast live programs from remote locations. Directs personnel in auditioning talent and programs. Coordinates elements of program, such as audio, camera, special effects, timing, and script, to ensure production objectives are met. Schedules use of studio and editing facilities for producers and engineering and maintenance staff.

GOE Number, Interest Area, and Work Group: 01.01.01; Arts, Entertainment, and Media; Managerial Work in Arts, Entertainment, and Media. **Personality Type:** Realistic. Realistic occupations frequently involve work activities that include practical, hands-on problems and solutions. These occupations often deal with plants, animals, and real-world materials like wood, tools, and machinery. Many of the occupations require working outside and do not involve a lot of paperwork or working closely with others. **Work Values:** Autonomy; Authority; Ability Utilization; Responsibility; Achievement. **Skills:** Coordination; Speaking; Management of Personnel Resources; Operation and Control; Equipment Selection. **Abilities:** *Cognitive*—Oral Expression; Oral Comprehension; Selective Attention; Time Sharing; Deductive Reasoning; Information Ordering. *Psychomotor*—Reaction Time; Control Precision; Response Orientation. *Physical*—Gross Body Coordination; Dynamic Flexibility; Gross Body Equilibrium. *Sensory*—Near Vision; Far Vision; Visual Color Discrimination; Speech Clarity. **General Work Activities:** *Information Input*—Monitoring Processes, Materials, and Surroundings; Identifying Objects, Actions, and Events; Getting Information Needed to Do the Job. *Mental Process*—Scheduling Work and Activities; Judging Qualities of Things, Services, Other People's Work; Making Decisions and Solving Problems. *Work Output*—Controlling Machines and Processes; Implementing Ideas and Programs; Handling and Moving Objects. *Interacting with Others*—Coordinating Work and Activities of Others; Guiding, Directing and Motivating Subordinates; Communicating with Other Workers. **Physical Work Conditions:** Indoors; Sitting; Using Hands on Objects, Tools, or Controls. **Other Job Characteristics:** Consequence of Error; Importance of Being Sure All Is Done; Importance of Being Exact or Accurate.

Experience: Job Zone 4. A minimum of two to four years of work-related skill, knowledge, or experience is needed. **Job Preparation:** SVP 7.0 to less than 8.0—2 years to less than 10 years. **Knowledge:** Administration and Management; Communications and Media; Telecommunications; Education and Training; English Language. **Instructional Programs:** 090701 Radio and Television Broadcasting; 500501 Drama/Theater Arts, General; 500503 Acting and Directing; 500504 Playwriting and Screenwriting; 500505 Drama/Theater Literature, History and Criticism; 500599 Dramatic/Theater Arts and Stagecraft, Other; 500601 Film/Cinema Studies; 500602 Film-Video Making/Cinematography and Production.

Related DOT Jobs: 184.162-010 Manager, Production; 962.162-010 Director, Technical.

27-2021.00 Athletes and Sports Competitors (Athletes, Coaches, and Umpires)

Education: Long-term O-T-J training

Employed: 51,922

Openings: 19,465

Projected Growth: 27.9%

Earnings: $22,210

Compete in athletic events.

Participates in athletic events and competitive sports, according to established rules and regulations. Plays professional sport and is identified according to sport played, such as football, basketball, baseball, hockey, or boxing. Represents team or professional sports club, speaking to groups involved in activities such as sports clinics and fund raisers. Exercises and practices under direction of athletic trainer or professional coach to prepare and train for competitive events.

GOE Number, Interest Area, and Work Group: 01.10.01; Arts, Entertainment, and Media; Sports: Coaching, Instructing, Officiating, and Performing. **Personality Type:** Enterprising. Enterprising occupations frequently involve starting up and carrying out projects. These occupations can involve leading people and making many decisions. They sometimes require risk taking and often deal with business. **Work Values:** Ability Utilization; Recognition; Compensation; Social Status; Achievement. **Skills:** Monitoring; Coordination; Active Learning; Speaking; Learning Strategies; Social Perceptiveness; Active Listening. **Abilities:** *Cognitive*—Oral Comprehension; Spatial Orientation; Time Sharing; Memorization; Selective Attention. *Psychomotor*—Speed of Limb Movement; Reaction Time; Multilimb Coordination. *Physical*—Stamina; Trunk Strength; Dynamic Strength. *Sensory*—Depth Perception; Auditory Attention; Glare Sensitivity; Far Vision. **General Work Activities:** *Information Input*—Getting Information Needed to Do the Job; Identifying Objects, Actions, and Events; Monitoring Processes, Materials, and Surroundings. *Men-*

tal Process—Updating and Using Job-Relevant Knowledge; Making Decisions and Solving Problems; Organizing, Planning, and Prioritizing; Processing Information; Analyzing Data or Information. *Work Output*—Performing General Physical Activities; Handling and Moving Objects; Implementing Ideas and Programs. *Interacting with Others*—Communicating with Other Workers; Establishing and Maintaining Relationships; Performing for or Working with the Public; Communicating with Persons Outside Organization. **Physical Work Conditions:** Special Uniform; Walking or Running; Standing. **Other Job Characteristics:** Importance of Being Aware of New Events; Frustrating Circumstances; Consequence of Error.

Experience: Job Zone 3. Previous work-related skill, knowledge, or experience is required. **Job Preparation:** SVP 6.0 to less than 7.0—More than 1 year and less than 4 years. **Knowledge:** Biology; Physics; Communications and Media; Psychology; English Language; Education and Training. **Instructional Programs:** 120204 Umpires and Other Sports Officials; 131314 Physical Education Teaching and Coaching; 310501 Health and Physical Education, General; 310503 Athletic Training and Sports Medicine.

Related DOT Job: 153.341-010 Professional Athlete.

27-2022.00 Coaches and Scouts (Athletes, Coaches, and Umpires)

Education: Long-term O-T-J training

Employed: 51,922

Openings: 19,465

Projected Growth: 27.9%

Earnings: $22,210

Instruct or coach groups or individuals in the fundamentals of sports. Demonstrate techniques and methods of participation. Evaluate athletes' strengths and weaknesses to identify possible recruits, to improve the athletes' techniques, and to prepare athletes for competition.

Prepares scouting reports detailing information such as selection or rejection of athletes and locations identified for future recruitment. Observes athletes to determine areas of deficiency and need for individual or team improvement. Instructs athletes, individually or in groups, demonstrating sport techniques and game strategies. Evaluates athletes' skills and discusses or recommends acquisition, trade, or position assignment of players. Evaluates team and opposition capabilities to develop and plan game strategy. Analyzes athletes' performance and reviews game statistics or records to determine fitness and potential for professional sports. Plans and directs physical conditioning program for athletes to achieve maximum athletic performance. Negotiates with professional athletes or representatives to obtain services and arrange contracts.

GOE Number, Interest Area, and Work Group: 01.10.01; Arts, Entertainment, and Media; Sports: Coaching, Instructing, Officiating, and Performing. **Personality Type:** Enterprising. Enterprising occupations frequently involve starting up and carrying out projects. These occupations can involve leading people and making many decisions. They sometimes require risk taking and often deal with business. **Work Values:** Responsibility; Autonomy;

Achievement; Recognition; Authority. **Skills:** Instructing; Negotiation; Information Gathering; Management of Personnel Resources; Writing; Identification of Key Causes. **Abilities:** *Cognitive*—Oral Expression; Problem Sensitivity; Visualization; Deductive Reasoning; Written Expression; Written Comprehension. *Psychomotor*—Speed of Limb Movement; Manual Dexterity; Reaction Time. *Physical*—Explosive Strength; Gross Body Coordination; Extent Flexibility. *Sensory*—Depth Perception; Far Vision; Speech Clarity; Near Vision. **General Work Activities:** *Information Input*—Getting Information Needed to Do the Job; Identifying Objects, Actions, and Events; Monitoring Processes, Materials, and Surroundings. *Mental Process*—Making Decisions and Solving Problems; Judging Qualities of Things, Services, Other People's Work; Developing Objectives and Strategies; Analyzing Data or Information. *Work Output*—Documenting and Recording Information; Implementing Ideas and Programs; Handling and Moving Objects. *Interacting with Others*—Coaching and Developing Others; Communicating with Other Workers; Developing and Building Teams. **Physical Work Conditions:** Outdoors; Standing; Walking or Running. **Other Job Characteristics:** Consequence of Error; Importance of Being Aware of New Events; Frustrating Circumstances.

Experience: Job Zone 5. Extensive skill, knowledge, and experience are needed. Very advanced communication and organizational skills are required. **Job Preparation:** SVP 8.0 and above—4 years to more than 10 years. **Knowledge:** Education and Training; Sales and Marketing; Psychology; English Language; Administration and Management. **Instructional Programs:** 120204 Umpires and Other Sports Officials; 131314 Physical Education Teaching and Coaching; 310501 Health and Physical Education, General; 310503 Athletic Training and Sports Medicine.

Related DOT Jobs: 153.117-010 Head Coach; 153.117-018 Scout, Professional Sports; 153.227-010 Coach, Professional Athletes.

27-2023.00 Umpires, Referees, and Other Sports Officials (Athletes, Coaches, and Umpires)

Education: Long-term O-T-J training

Employed: 51,922

Openings: 19,465

Projected Growth: 27.9%

Earnings: $22,210

Officiate at competitive athletic or sporting events. Detect infractions of rules and decide penalties according to established regulations.

Confers with other sporting officials and facility managers to provide information, coordinate activities, and discuss problems. Resolves claims of rule infractions, or complaints lodged by participants, and assesses penalties based on established regulations. Signals participants or other officials to facilitate identification of infractions or otherwise regulate play or competition. Directs participants to assigned areas such as starting blocks or penalty areas. Makes qualifying determinations regarding participants, such as qualifying order or handicap. Inspects sporting equipment or examines participants to ensure compliance to regulations and safety of participants and spectators. Prepares reports to regulating organization concerning sporting activities, com-

plaints, and actions taken or needed, such as fines or other disciplinary actions. Records and maintains information regarding participants and sporting activities. Observes actions of participants at athletic and sporting events to regulate competition and detect infractions of rules. Clocks events according to established standards for play, or to measure performance of participants.

GOE Number, Interest Area, and Work Group: 01.10.01; Arts, Entertainment, and Media; Sports: Coaching, Instructing, Officiating, and Performing. **Personality Type:** Enterprising. Enterprising occupations frequently involve starting up and carrying out projects. These occupations can involve leading people and making many decisions. They sometimes require risk taking and often deal with business. **Work Values:** Responsibility; Authority; Achievement; Ability Utilization; Autonomy. **Skills:** Coordination; Active Listening; Speaking; Reading Comprehension; Writing. **Abilities:** *Cognitive*—Oral Expression; Selective Attention; Oral Comprehension; Time Sharing; Problem Sensitivity. *Psychomotor*—Reaction Time; Response Orientation; Speed of Limb Movement. *Physical*—Gross Body Coordination; Stamina; Extent Flexibility; Trunk Strength. *Sensory*—Far Vision; Speech Clarity; Near Vision; Auditory Attention; Glare Sensitivity. **General Work Activities:** *Information Input*—Getting Information Needed to Do the Job; Monitoring Processes, Materials, and Surroundings; Identifying Objects, Actions, and Events. *Mental Process*—Making Decisions and Solving Problems; Evaluating Information Against Standards; Analyzing Data or Information. *Work Output*—Documenting and Recording Information; Performing General Physical Activities; Implementing Ideas and Programs. *Interacting with Others*—Communicating with Other Workers; Communicating with Persons Outside Organization; Resolving Conflict and Negotiating with Others. **Physical Work Conditions:** Special Uniform; Standing; Walking or Running. **Other Job Characteristics:** Importance of Being Aware of New Events; Importance of Being Exact or Accurate; Importance of Being Sure All Is Done.

Experience: Job Zone 3. Previous work-related skill, knowledge, or experience is required. **Job Preparation:** SVP 6.0 to less than 7.0—More than 1 year and less than 4 years. **Knowledge:** Mathematics; English Language; Clerical; Administration and Management; Public Safety and Security. **Instructional Programs:** 120204 Umpires and Other Sports Officials; 131314 Physical Education Teaching and Coaching; 310501 Health and Physical Education, General; 310503 Athletic Training and Sports Medicine.

Related DOT Jobs: 153.117-022 Steward, Racetrack; 153.167-010 Paddock Judge; 153.167-014 Pit Steward; 153.167-018 Racing Secretary and Handicapper; 153.267-010 Horse-Race Starter; 153.267-014 Patrol Judge; 153.267-018 Umpire; 153.287-010 Hoof and Shoe Inspector; 153.367-010 Clocker; 153.367-014 Horse-Race Timer; 153.387-010 Identifier, Horse; 153.387-014 Scorer; 153.467-010 Clerk-of-Scales; 153.667-010 Starter; 219.267-010 Handicapper, Harness Racing; 349.367-010 Kennel Manager, Dog Track; 349.367-014 Receiving-Barn Custodian; 349.665-010 Scoreboard Operator.

27-2031.00 Dancers (Dancers and Choreographers)

Education: Postsecondary vocational training

Employed: 28,651

Openings: 5,099

Projected Growth: 13.6%

Earnings: $21,420

Perform dances. Sing or act.

Auditions for parts in production. Works with choreographer to refine or modify dance steps. Harmonizes body movements to rhythm of musical accompaniment. Studies and practices dance moves required in role. Performs classical, modern, or acrobatic dances in productions. Coordinates dancing with that of partner or dance ensemble. Rehearses solo or with partners or troupe members. Devises and choreographs dance for self or others.

GOE Number, Interest Area, and Work Group: 01.05.03; Arts, Entertainment, and Media; Performing Arts, Dance: Performing and Choreography. **Personality Type:** Artistic. Artistic occupations frequently involve working with forms, designs, and patterns. These occupations often require self-expression, and the work can be done without following a clear set of rules. **Work Values:** Moral Values; Ability Utilization; Achievement; Recognition; Creativity. **Skills:** Active Learning; Active Listening. **Abilities:** *Cognitive*—Spatial Orientation; Memorization; Originality; Fluency of Ideas; Oral Expression; Information Ordering. *Psychomotor*—Speed of Limb Movement; Multilimb Coordination; Arm-Hand Steadiness. *Physical*—Gross Body Coordination; Dynamic Strength; Stamina. *Sensory*—Peripheral Vision; Auditory Attention; Depth Perception. **General Work Activities:** *Information Input*—Getting Information Needed to Do the Job; Identifying Objects, Actions, and Events; Monitoring Processes, Materials, and Surroundings. *Mental Process*—Thinking Creatively; Updating and Using Job-Relevant Knowledge; Organizing, Planning, and Prioritizing. *Work Output*—Performing General Physical Activities; Implementing Ideas and Programs; Handling and Moving Objects; Drafting and Specifying Technical Devices. *Interacting with Others*—Performing for or Working with the Public; Coordinating Work and Activities of Others; Communicating with Other Workers. **Physical Work Conditions:** Indoors; Standing; Walking or Running. **Other Job Characteristics:** Importance of Being Exact or Accurate; Importance of Being Sure All Is Done; Importance of Repeating Same Tasks.

Experience: Job Zone 4. A minimum of two to four years of work-related skill, knowledge, or experience is needed. **Job Preparation:** SVP 7.0 to less than 8.0—2 years to less than 10 years. **Knowledge:** Fine Arts; Communications and Media; Mathematics; Design; Therapy and Counseling; English Language. **Instructional Program:** 500301 Dance.

Related DOT Job: 151.047-010 Dancer.

27-2032.00 Choreographers (Dancers and Choreographers)

Education: Postsecondary vocational training
Employed: 28,651
Openings: 5,099
Projected Growth: 13.6%
Earnings: $21,420

Create and teach dance. Direct and stage presentations.

Creates original dance routines for ballets, musicals, or other forms of entertainment. Determines dance movements designed to suggest story, interpret emotion, or enliven show. Studies story line and music to envision and devise dance movements. Directs and

stages dance presentations for various forms of entertainment. Auditions performers for one or more dance parts. Instructs cast in dance movements at rehearsals to achieve desired effect.

GOE Number, Interest Area, and Work Group: 01.05.03; Arts, Entertainment, and Media; Performing Arts, Dance: Performing and Choreography. **Personality Type:** Artistic. Artistic occupations frequently involve working with forms, designs, and patterns. These occupations often require self-expression, and the work can be done without following a clear set of rules. **Work Values:** Creativity; Responsibility; Authority; Ability Utilization; Autonomy; Moral Values. **Skills:** Instructing; Idea Generation; Coordination; Reading Comprehension; Monitoring. **Abilities:** *Cognitive*—Originality; Oral Expression; Fluency of Ideas; Spatial Orientation; Visualization. *Psychomotor*—Multilimb Coordination; Speed of Limb Movement; Arm-Hand Steadiness. *Physical*—Gross Body Coordination; Dynamic Strength; Dynamic Flexibility. *Sensory*—Peripheral Vision; Depth Perception; Speech Clarity. **General Work Activities:** *Information Input*—Getting Information Needed to Do the Job; Identifying Objects, Actions, and Events; Monitoring Processes, Materials, and Surroundings. *Mental Process*—Thinking Creatively; Judging Qualities of Things, Services, Other People's Work; Making Decisions and Solving Problems. *Work Output*—Implementing Ideas and Programs; Performing General Physical Activities; Documenting and Recording Information. *Interacting with Others*—Coordinating Work and Activities of Others; Teaching Others; Coaching and Developing Others; Interpreting Meaning of Information to Others; Establishing and Maintaining Relationships; Communicating with Other Workers. **Physical Work Conditions:** Indoors; Standing; Walking or Running; Bending or Twisting the Body. **Other Job Characteristics:** Frustrating Circumstances; Consequence of Error; Importance of Being Sure All Is Done.

Experience: Job Zone 5. Extensive skill, knowledge, and experience are needed. Very advanced communication and organizational skills are required. **Job Preparation:** SVP 8.0 and above—4 years to more than 10 years. **Knowledge:** Fine Arts; Education and Training; Personnel and Human Resources; Communications and Media; English Language. **Instructional Program:** 500301 Dance.

Related DOT Job: 151.027-010 Choreographer.

27-2041.00 Music Directors and Composers (Musicians)

Education: Long-term O-T-J training
Employed: 273,327
Openings: 44,774
Projected Growth: 14.8%
Earnings: No data available.

Conduct, direct, plan, and lead instrumental or vocal performances by musical groups such as orchestras, choirs, and glee clubs. Includes arrangers, composers, choral directors, and orchestrators.

GOE Number, Interest Area, and Work Group: 01.05.02; Arts, Entertainment, and Media; Performing Arts, Music: Directing, Composing and Arranging, and Performing. **Instructional Programs:** 500901 Music, General; 500902 Music History and

Literature; 500903 Music—General Performance; 500904 Music Theory and Composition; 500905 Musicology and Ethnomusicology; 500906 Music Conducting; 500907 Music—Piano and Organ Performance; 500908 Music—Voice and Choral/Opera Performance; 500909 Music Business Management and Merchandising; 500999 Music, Other. **Note:** The Department of Labor has not collected some data for this job, so it has fewer details than the other descriptions.

27-2041.01 Music Directors (Musicians)

Education: Long-term O-T-J training

Employed: 273,327

Openings: 44,774

Projected Growth: 14.8%

Earnings: No data available.

Direct and conduct instrumental or vocal performances by musical groups such as orchestras or choirs.

Transcribes musical compositions and melodic lines to adapt them to or create particular style for group. Engages services of composer to write score. Auditions and selects vocal and instrumental groups for musical presentations. Positions members within group to obtain balance among instrumental sections. Directs group at rehearsals and live or recorded performances to achieve desired effects such as tonal and harmonic balance dynamics, rhythm, and tempo. Selects vocal, instrumental, and recorded music suitable to type of performance requirements to accommodate ability of group. Issues assignments and reviews work of staff in such areas as scoring, arranging, and copying music, lyric and vocal coaching.

GOE Number, Interest Area, and Work Group: 01.05.02; Arts, Entertainment, and Media; Performing Arts, Music: Directing, Composing and Arranging, and Performing. **Personality Type:** Artistic. Artistic occupations frequently involve working with forms, designs, and patterns. These occupations often require self-expression, and the work can be done without following a clear set of rules. **Work Values:** Ability Utilization; Autonomy; Achievement; Responsibility; Creativity. **Skills:** Coordination; Management of Personnel Resources; Time Management; Monitoring; Instructing. **Abilities:** *Cognitive*—Oral Expression; Oral Comprehension; Written Comprehension; Originality; Memorization; Written Expression. *Psychomotor*—none met the criteria. *Physical*—Dynamic Flexibility. *Sensory*—Hearing Sensitivity; Sound Localization; Auditory Attention. **General Work Activities:** *Information Input*—Getting Information Needed to Do the Job; Identifying Objects, Actions, and Events; Monitoring Processes, Materials, and Surroundings. *Mental Process*—Thinking Creatively; Judging Qualities of Things, Services, Other People's Work; Scheduling Work and Activities. *Work Output*—Implementing Ideas and Programs; Performing General Physical Activities; Documenting and Recording Information; Handling and Moving Objects. *Interacting with Others*—Coordinating Work and Activities of Others; Communicating with Other Workers; Coaching and Developing Others. **Physical Work Conditions:** Indoors; Standing; Sitting. **Other Job Characteristics:** Importance of Being Exact or Accurate; Importance of Being Sure All Is Done; Importance of Repeating Same Tasks.

Experience: Job Zone 5. Extensive skill, knowledge, and experience are needed. Very advanced communication and organizational skills are required. **Job Preparation:** SVP 8.0 and above—4 years to more than 10 years. **Knowledge:** Fine Arts; Personnel and Human Resources; Administration and Management; English Language; Communications and Media; Foreign Language; Education and Training; Transportation. **Instructional Programs:** 390501 Religious/Sacred Music; 500901 Music, General; 500903 Music—General Performance; 500906 Music Conducting; 500908 Music—Voice and Choral/Opera Performance.

Related DOT Jobs: 152.047-010 Choral Director; 152.047-014 Conductor, Orchestra; 152.047-018 Director, Music.

27-2041.02 Music Arrangers and Orchestrators (Musicians)

Education: Long-term O-T-J training

Employed: 273,327

Openings: 44,774

Projected Growth: 14.8%

Earnings: No data available.

Write and transcribe musical scores.

Copies parts from score for individual performers. Determines voice, instrument, harmonic structure, rhythm, tempo, and tone balance to achieve desired effect. Adapts musical composition for orchestra, band, choral group, or individual to style for which it was not originally written. Composes musical scores for orchestra, band, choral group, or individual instrumentalist or vocalist, using knowledge of music theory and instrumental and vocal capabilities. Transposes music from one voice or instrument to another to accommodate particular musician in musical group. Transcribes musical parts from score written by arranger or orchestrator for each instrument or voice, using knowledge of music composition.

GOE Number, Interest Area, and Work Group: 01.05.02; Arts, Entertainment, and Media; Performing Arts, Music: Directing, Composing and Arranging, and Performing. **Personality Type:** Artistic. Artistic occupations frequently involve working with forms, designs, and patterns. These occupations often require self-expression, and the work can be done without following a clear set of rules. **Work Values:** Ability Utilization; Autonomy; Achievement; Creativity; Independence; Moral Values; Responsibility. **Skills:** Coordination; Idea Generation; Writing; Idea Evaluation; Synthesis/Reorganization. **Abilities:** *Cognitive*—Originality; Written Expression; Fluency of Ideas; Written Comprehension; Oral Expression. *Psychomotor*—none met the criteria. *Physical*—none met the criteria. *Sensory*—Hearing Sensitivity; Sound Localization; Auditory Attention. **General Work Activities:** *Information Input*—Getting Information Needed to Do the Job; Identifying Objects, Actions, and Events; Monitoring Processes, Materials, and Surroundings. *Mental Process*—Thinking Creatively; Processing Information; Judging Qualities of Things, Services, Other People's Work. *Work Output*—Implementing Ideas and Programs; Documenting and Recording Information; Handling and Moving Objects. *Interacting with Others*—Interpreting Meaning of Information to Others; Communicating with Persons Outside Organization;

Communicating with Other Workers. **Physical Work Conditions:** Indoors; Sitting; Using Hands on Objects, Tools, or Controls; Standing. **Other Job Characteristics:** Importance of Being Exact or Accurate; Importance of Being Sure All Is Done; Consequence of Error.

Experience: Job Zone 4. A minimum of two to four years of work-related skill, knowledge, or experience is needed. **Job Preparation:** SVP 7.0 to less than 8.0—2 years to less than 10 years. **Knowledge:** Fine Arts; English Language; Mathematics; Communications and Media; Clerical. **Instructional Programs:** 500901 Music, General; 500904 Music Theory and Composition.

Related DOT Jobs: 152.067-010 Arranger; 152.067-022 Orchestrator; 152.267-010 Copyist.

27-2041.03 Composers (Musicians)

Education: Long-term O-T-J training

Employed: 273,327

Openings: 44,774

Projected Growth: 14.8%

Earnings: No data available.

Compose music for orchestra, choral group, or band.

Creates original musical form or writes within circumscribed musical form such as sonata, symphony, or opera. Transcribes or records musical ideas into notes on scored music paper. Develops pattern of harmony, applying knowledge of music theory. Creates musical and tonal structure, applying elements of music theory, such as instrumental and vocal capabilities. Determines basic pattern of melody, applying knowledge of music theory. Synthesizes ideas for melody of musical scores for choral group, or band.

GOE Number, Interest Area, and Work Group: 01.05.02; Arts, Entertainment, and Media; Performing Arts, Music: Directing, Composing and Arranging, and Performing. **Personality Type:** Artistic. Artistic occupations frequently involve working with forms, designs, and patterns. These occupations often require self-expression, and the work can be done without following a clear set of rules. **Work Values:** Creativity; Ability Utilization; Autonomy; Independence; Moral Values. **Skills:** Idea Generation; Idea Evaluation; Information Organization; Implementation Planning; Synthesis/Reorganization. **Abilities:** *Cognitive*—Originality; Fluency of Ideas; Written Expression; Written Comprehension; Oral Comprehension; Flexibility of Closure. *Psychomotor*—none met the criteria. *Physical*—none met the criteria. *Sensory*—Hearing Sensitivity; Auditory Attention; Sound Localization. **General Work Activities:** *Information Input*—Getting Information Needed to Do the Job; Identifying Objects, Actions, and Events; Estimating Needed Characteristics. *Mental Process*—Thinking Creatively; Making Decisions and Solving Problems; Updating and Using Job-Relevant Knowledge; Judging Qualities of Things, Services, Other People's Work; Evaluating Information Against Standards. *Work Output*—Implementing Ideas and Programs; Documenting and Recording Information; Handling and Moving Objects. *Interacting with Others*—Interpreting Meaning of Information to Others; Communicating with Persons Outside Organization; Establishing and Maintaining Relationships; Communicating with Other

Workers; Performing for or Working with the Public. **Physical Work Conditions:** Indoors; Sitting; Outdoors; Standing. **Other Job Characteristics:** Importance of Being Sure All Is Done; Importance of Being Exact or Accurate; Consequence of Error; Frustrating Circumstances; Degree of Automation.

Experience: Job Zone 5. Extensive skill, knowledge, and experience are needed. Very advanced communication and organizational skills are required. **Job Preparation:** SVP 8.0 and above—4 years to more than 10 years. **Knowledge:** Fine Arts; Mathematics; English Language; Clerical; Communications and Media. **Instructional Programs:** 500901 Music, General; 500904 Music Theory and Composition.

Related DOT Job: 152.067-014 Composer.

27-2042.00 Musicians and Singers (Musicians)

Education: Long-term O-T-J training

Employed: 273,327

Openings: 44,774

Projected Growth: 14.8%

Earnings: No data available.

Play one or more musical instruments or entertain by singing songs in recital, in accompaniment, or as a member of an orchestra, band, or other musical group. Entertain on stage, radio, TV, film, or video, or record in studios.

GOE Number, Interest Area, and Work Group: 01.05.02; Arts, Entertainment, and Media; Performing Arts, Music: Directing, Composing and Arranging, and Performing. **Instructional Programs:** 500901 Music, General; 500903 Music—General Performance; 500904 Music Theory and Composition; 500905 Musicology and Ethnomusicology; 500906 Music Conducting; 500907 Music—Piano and Organ Performance; 500908 Music—Voice and Choral/Opera Performance. **Note:** The Department of Labor has not collected some data for this job, so it has fewer details than the other descriptions.

27-2042.01 Singers (Musicians)

Education: Long-term O-T-J training

Employed: 273,327

Openings: 44,774

Projected Growth: 14.8%

Earnings: No data available.

Sing songs on stage, radio, or television, or in motion pictures.

Sings before audience or recipient of message as soloist or in group, as member of vocal ensemble. Interprets or modifies music, applying knowledge of harmony, melody, rhythm, and voice production, to individualize presentation and maintain audience interest. Memorizes musical selections and routines, or sings following printed text, musical notation, or customer instructions. Sings a cappella or with musical accompaniment. Practices songs and routines to maintain and improve vocal skills. Observes choral leader or prompter for cues or directions in vocal presentation.

GOE Number, Interest Area, and Work Group: 01.05.02; Arts, Entertainment, and Media; Performing Arts, Music: Directing, Composing and Arranging, and Performing. **Personality Type:** Artistic. Artistic occupations frequently involve working with forms, designs, and patterns. These occupations often require self-expression, and the work can be done without following a clear set of rules. **Work Values:** Ability Utilization; Achievement; Moral Values; Recognition; Autonomy; Creativity. **Skills:** Active Listening; Coordination; Speaking; Reading Comprehension; Active Learning. **Abilities:** *Cognitive*—Memorization; Written Comprehension; Oral Comprehension; Oral Expression; Originality. *Psychomotor*—none met the criteria. *Physical*—none met the criteria. *Sensory*—Hearing Sensitivity; Speech Clarity; Auditory Attention. **General Work Activities:** *Information Input*—Getting Information Needed to Do the Job; Identifying Objects, Actions, and Events; Monitoring Processes, Materials, and Surroundings. *Mental Process*—Thinking Creatively; Organizing, Planning, and Prioritizing; Making Decisions and Solving Problems. *Work Output*—Implementing Ideas and Programs; Performing General Physical Activities; Handling and Moving Objects. *Interacting with Others*—Performing for or Working with the Public; Communicating with Persons Outside Organization; Communicating with Other Workers. **Physical Work Conditions:** Indoors; Standing; Sitting. **Other Job Characteristics:** Importance of Being Exact or Accurate; Importance of Being Aware of New Events; Importance of Repeating Same Tasks.

Experience: Job Zone 2. Some previous work-related skill, knowledge, or experience may be helpful, but usually is not needed. **Job Preparation:** SVP 4.00 to 5.99—6 months to less than 2 years. **Knowledge:** Fine Arts; English Language; Communications and Media; Customer and Personal Service; Education and Training; Foreign Language; Physics; Mathematics. **Instructional Programs:** 500901 Music, General; 500903 Music—General Performance; 500908 Music—Voice and Choral/Opera Performance.

Related DOT Jobs: 152.047-022 Singer; 230.647-010 Singing Messenger.

27-2042.02 Musicians, Instrumental (Musicians)

Education: Long-term O-T-J training

Employed: 273,327

Openings: 44,774

Projected Growth: 14.8%

Earnings: No data available.

Play one or more musical instruments in recital, in accompaniment, or as members of an orchestra, band, or other musical group.

Plays from memory or by following score. Practices performance on musical instrument to maintain and improve skills. Transposes music to play in alternate key or to fit individual style or purposes. Studies and rehearses music to learn and interpret score. Improvises music during performance. Memorizes musical scores. Directs band/orchestra. Teaches music for specific instruments. Plays musical instrument as soloist or as member of musical group such as orchestra or band, to entertain audience. Composes new musical scores.

GOE Number, Interest Area, and Work Group: 01.05.02; Arts, Entertainment, and Media; Performing Arts, Music: Directing, Composing and Arranging, and Performing. **Personality Type:** Artistic. Artistic occupations frequently involve working with forms, designs, and patterns. These occupations often require self-expression, and the work can be done without following a clear set of rules. **Work Values:** Ability Utilization; Achievement; Moral Values; Recognition; Creativity. **Skills:** Coordination; Visioning; Instructing; Active Learning; Learning Strategies; Monitoring. **Abilities:** *Cognitive*—Memorization; Speed of Closure; Originality; Time Sharing; Selective Attention; Oral Expression. *Psychomotor*—Wrist-Finger Speed; Finger Dexterity; Multilimb Coordination. *Physical*—Trunk Strength; Extent Flexibility; Static Strength. *Sensory*—Hearing Sensitivity; Auditory Attention; Sound Localization. **General Work Activities:** *Information Input*—Getting Information Needed to Do the Job; Identifying Objects, Actions, and Events; Monitoring Processes, Materials, and Surroundings. *Mental Process*—Thinking Creatively; Organizing, Planning, and Prioritizing; Judging Qualities of Things, Services, Other People's Work; Evaluating Information Against Standards; Scheduling Work and Activities. *Work Output*—Handling and Moving Objects; Implementing Ideas and Programs; Performing General Physical Activities. *Interacting with Others*—Performing for or Working with the Public; Developing and Building Teams; Teaching Others. **Physical Work Conditions:** Indoors; Using Hands on Objects, Tools, or Controls; Sitting. **Other Job Characteristics:** Importance of Being Exact or Accurate; Importance of Being Sure All Is Done; Frustrating Circumstances.

Experience: Job Zone 5. Extensive skill, knowledge, and experience are needed. Very advanced communication and organizational skills are required. **Job Preparation:** SVP 8.0 and above—4 years to more than 10 years. **Knowledge:** Fine Arts; Education and Training; Mathematics; English Language; Psychology. **Instructional Programs:** 390501 Religious/Sacred Music; 500901 Music, General; 500903 Music—General Performance; 500907 Music—Piano and Organ Performance.

Related DOT Job: 152.041-010 Musician, Instrumental.

27-3000 Media and Communication Workers

27-3011.00 Radio and Television Announcers (Announcers, Radio and Television)

Education: No data available.

Employed: 49,130

Openings: No data available.

Projected Growth: No data available.

Earnings: $17,950

Talk on radio or television. Interview guests, act as master of ceremonies, read news flashes, identify station by giving call letters, or announce song title and artist.

Cues worker to transmit program from network central station or other pick-up points according to schedule. Reads news flashes to inform audience of important events. Comments on music and other matters such as weather, time, or traffic conditions. Discusses various topics over telephone with viewers or listeners. Selects recordings to be played based on program specialty, knowledge of audience taste, or listening-audience requests. Describes or demonstrates products that viewers may purchase by telephoning show or by mail or that they may purchase in stores. Rewrites news bulletin from wire service teletype to fit specific time slot. Keeps daily program log to provide information on all elements aired during broadcast, such as musical selections and station promotions. Operates control console. Hosts civic, charitable, or promotional events that are broadcast over television or radio. Announces musical selections, station breaks, commercials, or public-service information, and accepts listening-audience requests. Memorizes script, reads, interviews, or ad-libs to identify station, introduce and close shows. Describes public event such as parade or convention. Moderates panel or discussion show to entertain audience. Asks questions of contestants, or manages play or game, to enable contestants to win prizes. Interviews show guests about their lives, their work, or topics of current interest. Discusses and prepares program content with producer and assistants.

GOE Number, Interest Area, and Work Group: 01.05.01; Arts, Entertainment, and Media; Performing Arts, Drama: Directing, Performing, Narrating, and Announcing. **Personality Type:** Artistic. Artistic occupations frequently involve working with forms, designs, and patterns. These occupations often require self-expression, and the work can be done without following a clear set of rules. **Work Values:** Working Conditions; Recognition; Ability Utilization; Supervision, Human Relations; Creativity; Achievement. **Skills:** Speaking; Active Listening; Writing; Reading Comprehension; Information Gathering. **Abilities:** *Cognitive*—Oral Expression; Oral Comprehension; Memorization; Written Comprehension; Fluency of Ideas. *Psychomotor*—none met the criteria. *Physical*—none met the criteria. *Sensory*—Speech Clarity; Speech Recognition; Auditory Attention. **General Work Activities:** *Information Input*—Getting Information Needed to Do the Job; Identifying Objects, Actions, and Events; Estimating Needed Characteristics; Monitoring Processes, Materials, and Surroundings. *Mental Process*—Thinking Creatively; Organizing, Planning, and Prioritizing; Scheduling Work and Activities. *Work Output*—Controlling Machines and Processes; Implementing Ideas and Programs; Handling and Moving Objects; Documenting and Recording Information. *Interacting with Others*—Communicating with Persons Outside Organization; Performing for or Working with the Public; Communicating with Other Workers. **Physical Work Conditions:** Indoors; Sitting; Using Hands on Objects, Tools, or Controls. **Other Job Characteristics:** Importance of Being Exact or Accurate; Importance of Being Sure All Is Done; Consequence of Error.

Experience: Job Zone 2. Some previous work-related skill, knowledge, or experience may be helpful, but usually is not needed. **Job Preparation:** SVP 4.00 to 5.99—6 months to less than 2 years. **Knowledge:** Communications and Media; Telecommunications; English Language; Computers and Electronics; Sales and Marketing. **Instructional Programs:** 090402 Broadcast Journalism; 090701 Radio and Television Broadcasting.

Related DOT Jobs: 159.147-010 Announcer; 159.147-014 Disc Jockey; 159.147-018 Show Host/Hostess.

27-3012.00 Public Address System and Other Announcers (Actors, Directors, and Producers)

Education: Long-term O-T-J training
Employed: 160,024
Openings: 31,279
Projected Growth: 23.8%
Earnings: $27,370

Make announcements over loud speaker, at sporting or other public events. Act as master of ceremonies or disc jockey at weddings, parties, clubs, or other gathering places.

Announces program and substitutions or other changes to patrons. Observes event to provide running commentary of activities, such as play-by-play description or explanation of official decisions. Speaks extemporaneously to audience on items of interest, such as background and history of event or past record of participants. Informs patrons of coming events or emergency calls. Reads prepared script to describe acts or tricks during performance. Provide information about event to cue operation of scoreboard or control board. Furnishes information concerning play to scoreboard operator.

GOE Number, Interest Area, and Work Group: 01.05.01; Arts, Entertainment, and Media; Performing Arts, Drama: Directing, Performing, Narrating, and Announcing. **Personality Type:** Social. Social occupations frequently involve working with, communicating with, and teaching people. These occupations often involve helping or providing service to others. **Work Values:** Recognition; Working Conditions; Achievement; Moral Values; Responsibility. **Skills:** Reading Comprehension; Speaking; Social Perceptiveness; Monitoring; Information Organization; Coordination; Active Listening. **Abilities:** *Cognitive*—Oral Expression; Written Comprehension; Selective Attention; Speed of Closure; Time Sharing; Fluency of Ideas. *Psychomotor*—Reaction Time; Response Orientation. *Physical*—none met the criteria. *Sensory*—Speech Clarity; Far Vision; Near Vision. **General Work Activities:** *Information Input*—Getting Information Needed to Do the Job; Monitoring Processes, Materials, and Surroundings; Identifying Objects, Actions, and Events. *Mental Process*—Updating and Using Job-Relevant Knowledge; Thinking Creatively; Judging Qualities of Things, Services, Other People's Work. *Work Output*—Documenting and Recording Information; Implementing Ideas and Programs; Handling and Moving Objects. *Interacting with Others*—Performing for or Working with the Public; Communicating with Persons Outside Organization; Interpreting Meaning of Information to Others. **Physical Work Conditions:** Sitting; Indoors; Outdoors. **Other Job Characteristics:** Importance of Being Aware of New Events; Frustrating Circumstances; Degree of Automation; Importance of Being Exact or Accurate.

Experience: Job Zone 3. Previous work-related skill, knowledge, or experience is required. **Job Preparation:** SVP 6.0 to less than 7.0—More than 1 year and less than 4 years. **Knowledge:** Communications and Media; English Language; Computers and Electronics; Mathematics; Telecommunications. **Instructional Programs:** 090701 Radio and Television Broadcasting; 500501 Drama/Theater Arts, General; 500503 Acting and Directing;

500504 Playwriting and Screenwriting; 500505 Drama/Theater Literature, History and Criticism; 500599 Dramatic/Theater Arts and Stagecraft, Other; 500601 Film/Cinema Studies; 500602 Film-Video Making/Cinematography and Production.

Related DOT Job: 159.347-010 Announcer.

27-3021.00 Broadcast News Analysts (Broadcast News Analysts)

Education: No data available.

Employed: 6,130

Openings: No data available.

Projected Growth: No data available.

Earnings: $31,580

Analyze, interpret, and broadcast news received from various sources.

Examines news items of local, national, and international significance to determine selection, or is assigned items for broadcast by editorial staff. Records commentary or presents commentary or news live when working in broadcast medium. Edits material for available time or space. Gathers information and develops subject perspective through research, interview, observation, and experience. Analyzes and interprets information to formulate and outline story ideas. Selects material most pertinent to presentation and organizes material into acceptable media form and format. Writes commentary, column, or script, using computer.

GOE Number, Interest Area, and Work Group: 01.03.01; Arts, Entertainment, and Media; News, Broadcasting, and Public Relations. **Personality Type:** Artistic. Artistic occupations frequently involve working with forms, designs, and patterns. These occupations often require self-expression, and the work can be done without following a clear set of rules. **Work Values:** Achievement; Working Conditions; Ability Utilization; Recognition; Creativity. **Skills:** Writing; Speaking; Information Gathering; Reading Comprehension; Active Listening. **Abilities:** *Cognitive*—Oral Expression; Written Expression; Oral Comprehension; Written Comprehension; Inductive Reasoning. *Psychomotor*—none met the criteria. *Physical*—none met the criteria. *Sensory*—Speech Clarity; Speech Recognition; Auditory Attention. **General Work Activities:** *Information Input*—Getting Information Needed to Do the Job; Identifying Objects, Actions, and Events; Monitoring Processes, Materials, and Surroundings. *Mental Process*—Judging Qualities of Things, Services, Other People's Work; Analyzing Data or Information; Processing Information. *Work Output*—Documenting and Recording Information; Implementing Ideas and Programs; Interacting with Computers. *Interacting with Others*—Performing for or Working with the Public; Interpreting Meaning of Information to Others; Communicating with Persons Outside Organization. **Physical Work Conditions:** Indoors; Sitting; Standing. **Other Job Characteristics:** Importance of Being Exact or Accurate; Importance of Being Sure All Is Done; Importance of Being Aware of New Events.

Experience: Job Zone 4. A minimum of two to four years of work-related skill, knowledge, or experience is needed. **Job Preparation:** SVP 7.0 to less than 8.0—2 years to less than 10 years. **Knowledge:** Communications and Media; English Language;

Computers and Electronics; Telecommunications; Geography; Clerical. **Instructional Programs:** 090401 Journalism; 090402 Broadcast Journalism; 090701 Radio and Television Broadcasting; 230501 English Creative Writing.

Related DOT Jobs: 131.067-010 Columnist/Commentator; 131.262-010 Newscaster.

27-3022.00 Reporters and Correspondents (Reporters and Correspondents)

Education: No data available.

Employed: 52,380

Openings: No data available.

Projected Growth: No data available.

Earnings: $26,040

Collect and analyze facts about newsworthy events by interview, investigation, or observation. Report and write stories for newspaper, news magazine, radio, or television.

Writes news stories for publication or broadcast from written or recorded notes provided by reporting staff, following prescribed editorial style and format standards. Transmits information to writing staff to write story. Takes photographs or shoots video to illustrate stories. Receives assignment or evaluates news leads and news tips to develop story idea. Conducts taped or filmed interviews or narratives. Reviews and evaluates notes to isolate pertinent facts and details. Organizes material and determines slant or emphasis. Gathers and verifies factual information regarding story, through interview, observation, and research. Edits or assists in editing videos for broadcast.

GOE Number, Interest Area, and Work Group: 01.03.01; Arts, Entertainment, and Media; News, Broadcasting, and Public Relations. **Personality Type:** Artistic. Artistic occupations frequently involve working with forms, designs, and patterns. These occupations often require self-expression, and the work can be done without following a clear set of rules. **Work Values:** Ability Utilization; Achievement; Recognition; Creativity; Security; Variety; Company Policies and Practices; Advancement. **Skills:** Writing; Information Gathering; Reading Comprehension; Active Listening; Synthesis/Reorganization. **Abilities:** *Cognitive*—Oral Expression; Written Expression; Oral Comprehension; Written Comprehension; Fluency of Ideas. *Psychomotor*—none met the criteria. *Physical*—Stamina. *Sensory*—Near Vision; Speech Clarity; Speech Recognition. **General Work Activities:** *Information Input*—Getting Information Needed to Do the Job; Identifying Objects, Actions, and Events; Monitoring Processes, Materials, and Surroundings. *Mental Process*—Judging Qualities of Things, Services, Other People's Work; Analyzing Data or Information; Organizing, Planning, and Prioritizing. *Work Output*—Documenting and Recording Information; Implementing Ideas and Programs; Handling and Moving Objects. *Interacting with Others*—Communicating with Persons Outside Organization; Performing for or Working with the Public; Communicating with Other Workers; Establishing and Maintaining Relationships. **Physical Work Conditions:** Standing; Outdoors; Indoors. **Other Job Characteristics:** Importance of Being Exact or Accurate; Importance of Being Sure All Is Done; Consequence of Error; Frustrating Circumstances.

Experience: Job Zone 4. A minimum of two to four years of work-related skill, knowledge, or experience is needed. **Job Preparation:** SVP 7.0 to less than 8.0—2 years to less than 10 years. **Knowledge:** English Language; Communications and Media; Computers and Electronics; Telecommunications; Clerical; Sociology and Anthropology. **Instructional Programs:** 090401 Journalism; 090402 Broadcast Journalism; 090403 Mass Communications; 090499 Journalism and Mass Communication, Other.

Related DOT Jobs: 131.262-014 Newswriter; 131.262-018 Reporter.

27-3031.00 Public Relations Specialists (Public Relations Specialists)

Education: Bachelor's degree

Employed: 122,329

Openings: 25,334

Projected Growth: 24.6%

Earnings: $34,550

Engage in promoting or creating goodwill for individuals, groups, or organizations, by writing or selecting favorable publicity material and releasing it through various communications media. Prepare and arrange displays. Make speeches.

Consults with advertising agencies or staff to arrange promotional campaigns in all types of media for products, organizations, or individuals. Confers with production and support personnel to coordinate production of advertisements and promotions. Studies needs, objectives, and policies of organization or individual seeking to influence public opinion or promote specific products. Conducts market and public-opinion research to introduce or test specific products or measure public opinion. Counsels clients in effective ways of communicating with public. Purchases advertising space and time as required to promote client's product or agenda. Arranges for and conducts public-contact programs designed to meet client's objectives. Plans and directs development and communication of informational programs designed to keep public informed of client's products, accomplishments, or agenda. Prepares or edits organizational publications such as newsletters to employees or public or stockholders' reports to favorably present client's viewpoint. Promotes sales and/or creates goodwill for client's products, services, or persona by coordinating exhibits, lectures, contests, or public appearances. Prepares and distributes fact sheets, news releases, photographs, scripts, motion pictures, or tape recordings to media representatives and others. Represents client during community projects and at public, social, and business gatherings.

GOE Number, Interest Area, and Work Group: 01.03.01; Arts, Entertainment, and Media; News, Broadcasting, and Public Relations. **Personality Type:** Enterprising. Enterprising occupations frequently involve starting up and carrying out projects. These occupations can involve leading people and making many decisions. They sometimes require risk taking and often deal with business. **Work Values:** Creativity; Ability Utilization; Achievement; Recognition; Compensation; Working Conditions; Responsibility. **Skills:** Speaking; Writing; Information Gathering; Visioning; Persuasion; Reading Comprehension; Idea Evaluation.

Abilities: *Cognitive*—Oral Expression; Written Expression; Oral Comprehension; Fluency of Ideas; Written Comprehension; Originality. *Psychomotor*—none met the criteria. *Physical*—none met the criteria. *Sensory*—Speech Clarity; Near Vision; Speech Recognition. **General Work Activities:** *Information Input*—Getting Information Needed to Do the Job; Identifying Objects, Actions, and Events; Estimating Needed Characteristics. *Mental Process*—Making Decisions and Solving Problems; Judging Qualities of Things, Services, Other People's Work; Organizing, Planning, and Prioritizing. *Work Output*—Implementing Ideas and Programs; Handling and Moving Objects; Documenting and Recording Information; Interacting with Computers. *Interacting with Others*—Communicating with Persons Outside Organization; Establishing and Maintaining Relationships; Influencing Others or Selling; Communicating with Other Workers. **Physical Work Conditions:** Indoors; Sitting; Outdoors; Standing. **Other Job Characteristics:** Consequence of Error; Frustrating Circumstances; Importance of Being Sure All Is Done.

Experience: Job Zone 4. A minimum of two to four years of work-related skill, knowledge, or experience is needed. **Job Preparation:** SVP 7.0 to less than 8.0—2 years to less than 10 years. **Knowledge:** Sales and Marketing; Communications and Media; Telecommunications; Mathematics; Psychology. **Instructional Programs:** 080204 Business Services Marketing Operations; 090501 Public Relations and Organizational Communications.

Related DOT Jobs: 165.017-010 Lobbyist; 165.167-010 Sales-Service Promoter; 165.167-014 Public-Relations Representative.

27-3041.00 Editors (Writers and Editors)

Education: Bachelor's degree

Employed: 340,805

Openings: 52,971

Projected Growth: 24.4%

Earnings: No data available.

Perform variety of editorial duties such as layout, indexing, and revision of written materials, in preparation for final publication.

Reads copy or proof to detect and correct errors in spelling, punctuation, and syntax; indicates corrections, using standard proofreading and typesetting symbols. Determines placement of stories based on relative significance, available space, and knowledge of layout principles. Selects and crops photographs and illustrative materials to conform to space and subject matter requirements. Verifies facts, dates, and statistics, using standard reference sources. Selects local, state, national, and international news items received by wire from press associations. Compiles index cross-references and related items such as glossaries, bibliographies, and footnotes. Reviews and approves proofs submitted by composing room. Confers with management and editorial staff members regarding placement of developing news stories. Writes and rewrites headlines, captions, columns, articles, and stories to conform to publication's style, editorial policy, and publishing requirements. Reads and evaluates manuscripts or other materials submitted for publication and confers with authors regarding changes or publication. Plans and prepares page layouts to position and space articles and photographs or illustrations. Arranges topical or alphabetical list of index items, according to page or chapter, indicating location of item in text. Reads material to determine items to be included in index of book or other publication.

GOE Number, Interest Area, and Work Group: 01.02.01; Arts, Entertainment, and Media; Writing and Editing. **Personality Type:** Artistic. Artistic occupations frequently involve working with forms, designs, and patterns. These occupations often require self-expression, and the work can be done without following a clear set of rules. **Work Values:** Creativity; Achievement; Ability Utilization; Autonomy; Responsibility. **Skills:** Writing; Reading Comprehension; Critical Thinking; Coordination; Product Inspection; Information Organization; Active Learning. **Abilities:** *Cognitive*—Written Comprehension; Written Expression; Problem Sensitivity; Information Ordering; Deductive Reasoning; Oral Expression. *Psychomotor*—none met the criteria. *Physical*—none met the criteria. *Sensory*—Near Vision; Speech Clarity. **General Work Activities:** *Information Input*—Getting Information Needed to Do the Job; Identifying Objects, Actions, and Events; Monitoring Processes, Materials, and Surroundings. *Mental Process*—Judging Qualities of Things, Services, Other People's Work; Making Decisions and Solving Problems; Evaluating Information Against Standards. *Work Output*—Implementing Ideas and Programs; Drafting and Specifying Technical Devices; Interacting with Computers; Handling and Moving Objects. *Interacting with Others*—Communicating with Other Workers; Providing Consultation and Advice to Others; Performing Administrative Activities. **Physical Work Conditions:** Indoors; Sitting; Using Hands on Objects, Tools, or Controls. **Other Job Characteristics:** Importance of Being Sure All Is Done; Importance of Being Exact or Accurate; Consequence of Error.

Experience: Job Zone 4. A minimum of two to four years of work-related skill, knowledge, or experience is needed. **Job Preparation:** SVP 7.0 to less than 8.0—2 years to less than 10 years. **Knowledge:** English Language; Communications and Media; Clerical; Computers and Electronics; Administration and Management. **Instructional Program:** 230501 English Creative Writing.

Related DOT Jobs: 132.067-022 Editor, Greeting Card; 132.067-026 Editor, News; 132.267-010 Editor, Telegraph; 132.267-014 Editorial Assistant; 132.367-010 Editor, Index.

27-3042.00 Technical Writers (Writers and Editors)

Education: Bachelor's degree

Employed: 340,805

Openings: 52,971

Projected Growth: 24.4%

Earnings: No data available.

Write technical materials such as equipment manuals, appendices, or operating and maintenance instructions. Assist in layout work.

Maintains records and files of work and revisions. Studies drawings, specifications, mock ups, and product samples to integrate and delineate technology, operating procedure, and production sequence and detail. Interviews production and engineering personnel and reads journals and other material to become familiar with product technologies and production methods. Assists in laying out material for publication. Reviews published materials and recommends revisions or changes in scope, format, content, and methods of reproduction and binding. Reviews manufacturer and trade catalogs, drawings, and other data relative to operation, maintenance, and service of equipment. Analyzes developments in specific field to determine need for revisions in previously published materials and development of new material. Draws sketches to illustrate specified materials or assembly sequence. Arranges for typing, duplication, and distribution of material. Selects photographs, drawings, sketches, diagrams, and charts to illustrate material. Observes production, developmental, and experimental activities to determine operating procedure and detail. Edits, standardizes, or makes changes to material prepared by other writers or establishment personnel. Organizes material and completes writing assignment according to set standards regarding order, clarity, conciseness, style, and terminology. Confers with customer representatives, vendors, plant executives, or publisher to establish technical specifications and to determine subject material to be developed for publication.

GOE Number, Interest Area, and Work Group: 01.02.01; Arts, Entertainment, and Media; Writing and Editing. **Personality Type:** Artistic. Artistic occupations frequently involve working with forms, designs, and patterns. These occupations often require self-expression, and the work can be done without following a clear set of rules. **Work Values:** Ability Utilization; Achievement; Responsibility; Creativity; Working Conditions. **Skills:** Writing; Reading Comprehension; Synthesis/Reorganization; Information Gathering; Active Learning; Active Listening. **Abilities:** *Cognitive*—Written Expression; Written Comprehension; Information Ordering; Originality; Speed of Closure; Oral Comprehension. *Psychomotor*—none met the criteria. *Physical*—none met the criteria. *Sensory*—Near Vision; Speech Clarity; Visual Color Discrimination; Speech Recognition. **General Work Activities:** *Information Input*—Getting Information Needed to Do the Job; Monitoring Processes, Materials, and Surroundings; Identifying Objects, Actions, and Events. *Mental Process*—Processing Information; Updating and Using Job-Relevant Knowledge; Thinking Creatively. *Work Output*—Documenting and Recording Information; Drafting and Specifying Technical Devices; Handling and Moving Objects. *Interacting with Others*—Interpreting Meaning of Information to Others; Communicating with Other Workers; Communicating with Persons Outside Organization. **Physical Work Conditions:** Indoors; Sitting; Using Hands on Objects, Tools, or Controls. **Other Job Characteristics:** Importance of Being Exact or Accurate; Frustrating Circumstances; Importance of Being Sure All Is Done.

Experience: Job Zone 5. Extensive skill, knowledge, and experience are needed. Very advanced communication and organizational skills are required. **Job Preparation:** SVP 8.0 and above—4 years to more than 10 years. **Knowledge:** English Language; Communications and Media; Computers and Electronics; Education and Training; Design. **Instructional Program:** 150101 Architectural Engineering Technology/Technician.

Related DOT Jobs: 019.267-010 Specification Writer; 131.267-026 Writer, Technical Publications; 132.017-018 Editor, Technical and Scientific Publications.

27-3043.00 Writers and Authors (Writers and Editors)

Education: Bachelor's degree
Employed: 340,805
Openings: 52,971
Projected Growth: 24.4%
Earnings: No data available.

Originate and prepare written material such as scripts, stories, advertisements, and other material.

GOE Number, Interest Area, and Work Group: 01.02.01; Arts, Entertainment, and Media; Writing and Editing. **Instructional Programs:** 230101 English Language and Literature, General; 230301 Comparative Literature; 230401 English Composition; 230501 English Creative Writing; 230701 American Literature (United States); 230801 English Literature (British and Commonwealth); 231001 Speech and Rhetorical Studies; 231101 English Technical and Business Writing; 239999 English Language and Literature/Letters, Other. **Note:** The Department of Labor has not collected some data for this job, so it has fewer details than the other descriptions.

27-3043.01 Poets and Lyricists (Writers and Editors)

Education: Bachelor's degree
Employed: 340,805
Openings: 52,971
Projected Growth: 24.4%
Earnings: No data available.

Write poetry or song lyrics for publication or performance.

Chooses subject matter and suitable form to express personal feeling and experience or ideas or to narrate story or event. Writes narrative, dramatic, lyric, or other types of poetry for publication. Writes words to fit musical compositions, including lyrics for operas, musical plays, and choral works. Adapts text to accommodate musical requirements of composer and singer.

GOE Number, Interest Area, and Work Group: 01.02.01; Arts, Entertainment, and Media; Writing and Editing. **Personality Type:** Artistic. Artistic occupations frequently involve working with forms, designs, and patterns. These occupations often require self-expression, and the work can be done without following a clear set of rules. **Work Values:** Creativity; Independence; Ability Utilization; Autonomy; Achievement. **Skills:** Writing; Reading Comprehension; Idea Generation; Learning Strategies; Idea Evaluation; Monitoring. **Abilities:** *Cognitive*—Originality; Written Expression; Fluency of Ideas; Oral Expression; Written Comprehension; Oral Comprehension. *Psychomotor*—none met the criteria. *Physical*—none met the criteria. *Sensory*—Hearing Sensitivity; Auditory Attention. **General Work Activities:** *Information Input*—Identifying Objects, Actions, and Events; Getting Information Needed to Do the Job; Monitoring Processes, Materials, and Surroundings. *Mental Process*—Thinking Creatively; Judging Qualities of Things, Services, Other People's Work; Making Decisions and Solving Problems. *Work Output*—Implementing Ideas and Programs; Documenting and Recording Information; Interacting with Comput-

ers. *Interacting with Others*—Communicating with Persons Outside Organization; Interpreting Meaning of Information to Others; Establishing and Maintaining Relationships. **Physical Work Conditions:** Indoors; Sitting; Using Hands on Objects, Tools, or Controls. **Other Job Characteristics:** Importance of Being Sure All Is Done; Consequence of Error; Frustrating Circumstances; Degree of Automation.

Experience: Job Zone 4. A minimum of two to four years of work-related skill, knowledge, or experience is needed. **Job Preparation:** SVP 7.0 to less than 8.0—2 years to less than 10 years. **Knowledge:** Fine Arts; English Language; Communications and Media; Psychology; Sociology and Anthropology; Customer and Personal Service. **Instructional Program:** 230501 English Creative Writing.

Related DOT Jobs: 131.067-030 Librettist; 131.067-034 Lyricist; 131.067-042 Poet.

27-3043.02 Creative Writers (Writers and Editors)

Education: Bachelor's degree
Employed: 340,805
Openings: 52,971
Projected Growth: 24.4%
Earnings: No data available.

Create original written works such as plays or prose, for publication or performance.

Writes fiction or nonfiction prose work, such as short story, novel, biography, article, descriptive or critical analysis, or essay. Develops factors such as theme, plot, characterization, psychological analysis, historical environment, action, and dialogue, to create material. Reviews, submits for approval, and revises written material to meet personal standards and satisfy needs of client, publisher, director, or producer. Confers with client, publisher, or producer to discuss development changes or revisions. Collaborates with other writers on specific projects. Conducts research to obtain factual information and authentic detail, utilizing sources such as newspaper accounts, diaries, and interviews. Selects subject or theme for writing project based on personal interest and writing specialty, or assignment from publisher, client, producer, or director. Organizes material for project, plans arrangement or outline, and writes synopsis. Writes play or script for moving pictures or television, based on original ideas or adapted from fictional, historical, or narrative sources. Writes humorous material for publication or performance, such as comedy routines, gags, comedy shows, or scripts for entertainers.

GOE Number, Interest Area, and Work Group: 01.02.01; Arts, Entertainment, and Media; Writing and Editing. **Personality Type:** Artistic. Artistic occupations frequently involve working with forms, designs, and patterns. These occupations often require self-expression, and the work can be done without following a clear set of rules. **Work Values:** Creativity; Ability Utilization; Achievement; Autonomy; Independence; Working Conditions; Recognition. **Skills:** Writing; Reading Comprehension; Idea Generation; Idea Evaluation; Critical Thinking; Coordination. **Abilities:** *Cognitive*—Written Expression; Originality; Written Comprehension; Fluency of Ideas; Oral Comprehension; Information Ordering.

Psychomotor—none met the criteria. *Physical*—none met the criteria. *Sensory*—Near Vision. **General Work Activities:** *Information Input*—Getting Information Needed to Do the Job; Identifying Objects, Actions, and Events; Estimating Needed Characteristics. *Mental Process*—Thinking Creatively; Judging Qualities of Things, Services, Other People's Work; Evaluating Information Against Standards. *Work Output*—Implementing Ideas and Programs; Interacting with Computers; Documenting and Recording Information. *Interacting with Others*—Communicating with Other Workers; Communicating with Persons Outside Organization; Providing Consultation and Advice to Others. **Physical Work Conditions:** Indoors; Sitting; Using Hands on Objects, Tools, or Controls. **Other Job Characteristics:** Importance of Being Sure All Is Done; Frustrating Circumstances; Consequence of Error.

Experience: Job Zone 4. A minimum of two to four years of work-related skill, knowledge, or experience is needed. **Job Preparation:** SVP 7.0 to less than 8.0—2 years to less than 10 years. **Knowledge:** English Language; Communications and Media; Computers and Electronics; Fine Arts; Psychology; Clerical. **Instructional Program:** 231101 English Technical and Business Writing.

Related DOT Jobs: 052.067-010 Biographer; 131.067-026 Humorist; 131.067-038 Playwright; 131.067-046 Writer, Prose, Fiction and Nonfiction; 131.067-050 Screen Writer; 131.087-010 Continuity Writer; 139.087-010 Crossword-Puzzle Maker.

27-3043.03 Caption Writers (Writers and Editors)

Education: Bachelor's degree

Employed: 340,805

Openings: 52,971

Projected Growth: 24.4%

Earnings: No data available.

Write caption phrases of dialogue for hearing-impaired and foreign-language–speaking viewers of movie or television productions.

Operates computerized captioning system for movies or television productions for hearing-impaired and foreign language speaking viewers. Edits translations for correctness of grammar, punctuation, and clarity of expression. Enters commands to synchronize captions with dialogue and place on the screen. Oversees encoding of captions to master tape of television production. Translates foreign language dialogue into English language captions or English dialogue into foreign language captions. Discusses captions with directors or producers of movie and television productions. Writes captions to describe music and background noises. Watches production and reviews captions simultaneously to determine which caption phrases require editing.

GOE Number, Interest Area, and Work Group: 01.03.01; Arts, Entertainment, and Media; News, Broadcasting, and Public Relations. **Personality Type:** Artistic. Artistic occupations frequently involve working with forms, designs, and patterns. These occupations often require self-expression, and the work can be done without following a clear set of rules. **Work Values:** Working Conditions; Ability Utilization; Achievement; Moral Values; Independence; Autonomy. **Skills:** Writing; Reading Comprehension;

Active Listening; Monitoring; Operation and Control; Speaking; Critical Thinking. **Abilities:** *Cognitive*—Written Expression; Written Comprehension; Oral Comprehension; Oral Expression; Speed of Closure; Perceptual Speed. *Psychomotor*—Wrist-Finger Speed. *Physical*—none met the criteria. *Sensory*—Near Vision; Speech Clarity; Speech Recognition. **General Work Activities:** *Information Input*—Monitoring Processes, Materials, and Surroundings; Identifying Objects, Actions, and Events; Getting Information Needed to Do the Job. *Mental Process*—Evaluating Information Against Standards; Thinking Creatively; Judging Qualities of Things, Services, Other People's Work. *Work Output*—Interacting with Computers; Controlling Machines and Processes; Implementing Ideas and Programs. *Interacting with Others*—Interpreting Meaning of Information to Others; Communicating with Other Workers; Communicating with Persons Outside Organization. **Physical Work Conditions:** Indoors; Sitting; Making Repetitive Motions; Using Hands on Objects, Tools, or Controls. **Other Job Characteristics:** Importance of Being Exact or Accurate; Importance of Being Sure All Is Done; Consequence of Error.

Experience: Job Zone 3. Previous work-related skill, knowledge, or experience is required. **Job Preparation:** SVP 6.0 to less than 7.0—More than 1 year and less than 4 years. **Knowledge:** English Language; Foreign Language; Communications and Media; Computers and Electronics; Clerical. **Instructional Programs:** 160101 Foreign Languages and Literatures, General; 160103 Foreign Language Interpretation and Translation.

Related DOT Job: 203.362-026 Caption Writer.

27-3043.04 Copy Writers (Writers and Editors)

Education: Bachelor's degree

Employed: 340,805

Openings: 52,971

Projected Growth: 24.4%

Earnings: No data available.

Write advertising copy for use by publication or broadcast media to promote sale of goods and services.

Obtains additional background and current development information through research and interview. Consults with sales media and marketing representatives to obtain information on product or service and discuss style and length of advertising copy. Prepares advertising copy, using computer. Writes articles, bulletins, sales letters, speeches, and other related informative and promotional material. Reviews advertising trends, consumer surveys, and other data regarding marketing of goods and services to formulate approach. Writes advertising copy for use by publication or broadcast media and revises copy according to supervisor's instructions.

GOE Number, Interest Area, and Work Group: 01.02.01; Arts, Entertainment, and Media; Writing and Editing. **Personality Type:** Artistic. Artistic occupations frequently involve working with forms, designs, and patterns. These occupations often require self-expression, and the work can be done without following a clear set of rules. **Work Values:** Creativity; Ability Utilization; Responsibility; Achievement; Working Conditions. **Skills:** Writing; Reading Comprehension; Idea Generation; Active Learning; Critical

Thinking. **Abilities:** *Cognitive*—Written Expression; Written Comprehension; Oral Comprehension; Originality; Oral Expression; Fluency of Ideas. *Psychomotor*—Wrist-Finger Speed. *Physical*—Trunk Strength. *Sensory*—Near Vision; Speech Clarity; Sound Localization. **General Work Activities:** *Information Input*—Getting Information Needed to Do the Job; Identifying Objects, Actions, and Events; Monitoring Processes, Materials, and Surroundings. *Mental Process*—Judging Qualities of Things, Services, Other People's Work; Evaluating Information Against Standards; Analyzing Data or Information. *Work Output*—Interacting with Computers; Handling and Moving Objects; Implementing Ideas and Programs. *Interacting with Others*—Communicating with Other Workers; Providing Consultation and Advice to Others; Influencing Others or Selling. **Physical Work Conditions:** Indoors; Sitting; Using Hands on Objects, Tools, or Controls. **Other Job Characteristics:** Importance of Being Sure All Is Done; Importance of Being Exact or Accurate; Consequence of Error.

Experience: Job Zone 4. A minimum of two to four years of work-related skill, knowledge, or experience is needed. **Job Preparation:** SVP 7.0 to less than 8.0—2 years to less than 10 years. **Knowledge:** Sales and Marketing; English Language; Computers and Electronics; Communications and Media; Clerical. **Instructional Program:** 090201 Advertising.

Related DOT Job: 131.067-014 Copy Writer.

27-3091.00 Interpreters and Translators (All Other Professional, Paraprofessional, and Technical Workers)

Education: No data available.

Employed: 818,200

Openings: No data available.

Projected Growth: No data available.

Earnings: $36,790

Translate or interpret written, oral, or sign-language text into another language for others.

Translates responses from second language to first. Reads written material such as legal documents, scientific works, or news reports; rewrites material into specified language, according to established rules of grammar. Receives information on subject to be discussed prior to interpreting session. Listens to statements of speaker to ascertain meaning and to remember what is said, using electronic audio system. Translates approximate or exact message of speaker into specified language, orally or by using hand signs for hearing impaired.

GOE Number, Interest Area, and Work Group: 01.03.01; Arts, Entertainment, and Media; News, Broadcasting, and Public Relations. **Personality Type:** Artistic. Artistic occupations frequently involve working with forms, designs, and patterns. These occupations often require self-expression, and the work can be done without following a clear set of rules. **Work Values:** Ability Utilization; Achievement; Social Service; Working Conditions; Autonomy. **Skills:** Active Listening; Writing; Reading Comprehension; Speaking; Service Orientation. **Abilities:** *Cognitive*—Oral Comprehension; Oral Expression; Written Comprehension; Written Expression; Memorization; Selective Attention. *Psychomotor*—none met the criteria. *Physical*—none met the crite-

ria. *Sensory*—Speech Recognition; Speech Clarity; Auditory Attention. **General Work Activities:** *Information Input*—Getting Information Needed to Do the Job; Identifying Objects, Actions, and Events; Monitoring Processes, Materials, and Surroundings. *Mental Process*—Processing Information; Updating and Using Job-Relevant Knowledge; Thinking Creatively. *Work Output*—Documenting and Recording Information; Handling and Moving Objects; Interacting with Computers. *Interacting with Others*—Interpreting Meaning of Information to Others; Communicating with Persons Outside Organization; Establishing and Maintaining Relationships. **Physical Work Conditions:** Indoors; Sitting; Standing. **Other Job Characteristics:** Importance of Being Exact or Accurate; Importance of Being Sure All Is Done; Consequence of Error.

Experience: Job Zone 3. Previous work-related skill, knowledge, or experience is required. **Job Preparation:** SVP 6.0 to less than 7.0—More than 1 year and less than 4 years. **Knowledge:** Foreign Language; English Language; Communications and Media; Sociology and Anthropology; Customer and Personal Service. **Instructional Programs:** 160101 Foreign Languages and Literatures, General; 160103 Foreign Language Interpretation and Translation.

Related DOT Jobs: 137.267-010 Interpreter; 137.267-014 Interpreter, Deaf; 137.267-018 Translator.

27-4000 Media and Communication Equipment Workers

27-4011.00 Audio and Video Equipment Technicians (Audio-Visual Specialists)

Education: No data available.

Employed: 14,010

Openings: No data available.

Projected Growth: No data available.

Earnings: $32,970

Set up, or set up and operate, audio and video equipment including microphones, sound speakers, video screens, projectors, video monitors, recording equipment, connecting wires and cables, sound and mixing boards, and related electronic equipment for concerts, sports events, meetings and conventions, presentations, and news conferences. Set up and operate associated spotlights and other custom lighting systems.

Develops production ideas based on assignment or generates own ideas based on objectives and interest. Sets up, adjusts, and operates equipment such as cameras, sound mixers, and recorders during production. Plans and develops preproduction ideas into outlines, scripts, continuity, story boards, and graphics, or directs assistants to develop ideas. Executes or directs assistants to execute rough and finished graphics and graphic designs. Performs narration or presents announcements. Conducts training sessions on selection, use, and design of audiovisual materials and on operation of presentation equipment. Develops manuals, texts, workbooks, or related materials for use in conjunction with production materials. Constructs and positions properties, sets, lighting equipment, and other equipment. Locates and secures settings, properties, effects, and other production necessities. Determines format, approach, content, level, and medium to meet objectives most effectively within budgetary constraints, utilizing research, knowledge, and training. Directs and coordinates activities of assistants and other personnel during production.

GOE Number, Interest Area, and Work Group: 01.08.01; Arts, Entertainment, and Media; Media Technology. **Personality Type:** Conventional. Conventional occupations frequently involve following set procedures and routines. These occupations can include working with data and details more than with ideas. Usually there is a clear line of authority to follow. **Work Values:** Working Conditions; Moral Values; Ability Utilization; Authority; Coworkers. **Skills:** Writing; Synthesis/Reorganization; Information Organization; Learning Strategies; Implementation Planning; Solution Appraisal; Idea Evaluation; Speaking; Reading Comprehension. **Abilities:** *Cognitive*—Oral Expression; Visualization; Originality; Written Expression; Information Ordering. *Psychomotor*—Control Precision; Wrist-Finger Speed; Reaction Time. *Physical*—Extent Flexibility; Static Strength; Explosive Strength. *Sensory*—Speech Clarity; Hearing Sensitivity; Speech Recognition; Glare Sensitivity. **General Work Activities:** *Information Input*—Monitoring Processes, Materials, and Surroundings; Getting Information Needed to Do the Job; Identifying Objects, Actions, and Events. *Mental Process*—Thinking Creatively; Updating and Using Job-Relevant Knowledge; Organizing, Planning, and Prioritizing. *Work Output*—Implementing Ideas and Programs; Drafting and Specifying Technical Devices; Controlling Machines and Processes; Handling and Moving Objects. *Interacting with Others*—Establishing and Maintaining Relationships; Teaching Others; Communicating with Other Workers. **Physical Work Conditions:** Indoors; Using Hands on Objects, Tools, or Controls; Sitting; Standing. **Other Job Characteristics:** Degree of Automation; Importance of Being Exact or Accurate; Consequence of Error.

Experience: Job Zone 4. A minimum of two to four years of work-related skill, knowledge, or experience is needed. **Job Preparation:** SVP 7.0 to less than 8.0—2 years to less than 10 years. **Knowledge:** Communications and Media; Education and Training; Telecommunications; Computers and Electronics; English Language. **Instructional Programs:** 100101 Educational/Instructional Media Technology/Technician; 130501 Educational/Instructional Media Design.

Related DOT Jobs: No data available.

27-4012.00 Broadcast Technicians (Broadcast and Sound Technicians)

Education: Postsecondary vocational training
Employed: 36,607
Openings: 3,042
Projected Growth: 6%
Earnings: $25,260

Set up, operate, and maintain the electronic equipment used to transmit radio and television programs. Control audio equipment to regulate volume level and quality of sound during radio and television broadcasts. Operate radio transmitter to broadcast radio and television programs.

Reads television programming log to ascertain program to be recorded or aired. Previews scheduled program to ensure that signal is functioning and program is ready for transmission. Maintains log, as required by station management and Federal Communications Commission. Edits manuals, schedules programs, and prepares reports outlining past and future programs, including content. Instructs trainees how to use television production equipment, to film events, and to copy/edit graphics or sound onto videotape. Produces educational and training films and videotapes, including selection of equipment and preparation of script. Observes monitors and converses with station personnel to set audio and video levels and to verify station is on-air. Selects source, such as satellite or studio, from which program will be recorded. Performs preventive and minor equipment maintenance, using hand tools. Monitors transmission of news event to station and adjusts equipment as needed to maintain quality broadcast. Aligns antennae with receiving dish to obtain clearest signal for transmission of news event to station. Lays electrical cord and audio and video cables between vehicle, microphone, camera, and reporter or person to be interviewed. Drives news van to location of news events. Sets up, operates, and maintains radio and television production equipment to broadcast programs or events.

GOE Number, Interest Area, and Work Group: 01.08.01; Arts, Entertainment, and Media; Media Technology. **Personality Type:** Realistic. Realistic occupations frequently involve work activities that include practical, hands-on problems and solutions. These occupations often deal with plants, animals, and real-world materials like wood, tools, and machinery. Many of the occupations require working outside and do not involve a lot of paperwork or working closely with others. **Work Values:** Company Policies and Practices; Moral Values; Working Conditions; Supervision, Human Relations; Ability Utilization; Achievement; Security. **Skills:** Reading Comprehension; Instructing; Writing; Learning Strategies; Monitoring; Information Organization. **Abilities:** *Cognitive*—Written Expression; Written Comprehension; Information Ordering; Oral Comprehension; Oral Expression. *Psychomotor*—Control Precision; Response Orientation; Reaction Time. *Physical*—Static Strength; Extent Flexibility; Trunk Strength; Gross Body Coordination. *Sensory*—Near Vision; Speech Recognition; Hearing Sensitivity. **General Work Activities:** *Information Input*—Monitoring Processes, Materials, and Surroundings; Inspecting Equipment, Structures, Materials; Identifying Objects, Actions, and Events. *Mental Process*—Judging Qualities of Things, Services, Other People's Work; Making Decisions and Solving Problems; Evaluating Information Against Standards; Organizing, Planning, and Prioritizing. *Work Output*—Operating Vehicles or Equipment; Handling and Moving Objects; Documenting and Recording Information. *Interacting with Others*—Communicating with Other Workers; Teaching Others; Communicating with Persons Outside Organization. **Physical Work Conditions:** Using Hands on Objects, Tools, or Controls; Standing; Indoors. **Other Job Characteristics:** Consequence of Error; Importance of Being Sure All Is Done; Importance of Being Exact or Accurate; Degree of Automation.

Experience: Job Zone 4. A minimum of two to four years of work-related skill, knowledge, or experience is needed. **Job Preparation:** SVP 7.0 to less than 8.0—2 years to less than 10 years.

Knowledge: Telecommunications; Communications and Media; Computers and Electronics; Mechanical; Transportation. **Instructional Programs:** 100104 Radio and Television Broadcasting Technology/Technician; 100199 Communications Technology/Technicians, Other.

Related DOT Jobs: 193.167-014 Field Supervisor, Broadcast; 193.262-018 Field Engineer; 194.062-010 Television Technician; 194.122-010 Access Coordinator, Cable Television; 194.262-010 Audio Operator; 194.262-022 Master Control Operator; 194.282-010 Video Operator; 194.362-018 Telecine Operator; 194.362-022 Technician, News Gathering; 194.381-010 Technical Testing Engineer; 194.382-018 Videotape Operator.

27-4013.00 Radio Operators (Electrical and Electronic Technicians)

Education: Associate degree
Employed: 334,810
Openings: 42,572
Projected Growth: 16.8%
Earnings: $35,970

Receive and transmit communications using radiotelegraph or radiotelephone equipment in accordance with government regulations. Repair equipment.

Communicates with receiving operator to give and receive instruction for transmission. Monitors emergency frequency for distress calls and dispatches emergency equipment. Coordinates radio searches for overdue or lost airplanes. Maintains station log of messages transmitted and received for activities such as flight testing and fire locations. Establishes and maintains standards of operation by periodic inspections of equipment and routine tests. Reviews company and Federal Aviation Authority regulations regarding radio communications and reports violations. Examines and operates new equipment prior to installation in airport radio stations. Determines and obtains bearings of source from which signal originated, using direction-finding procedures and equipment. Repairs transmitting equipment, using electronic testing equipment, hand tools, and power tools, to maintain communication system in operative condition. Turns controls or throws switches to activate power, adjust voice volume and modulation, and set transmitter on specified frequency. Communicates by radio with test pilot, engineering personnel, and others during flight testing to relay information. Operates sound-recording equipment to record signals and preserve broadcast for analysis by intelligence personnel.

GOE Number, Interest Area, and Work Group: 01.08.01; Arts, Entertainment, and Media; Media Technology. **Personality Type:** Realistic. Realistic occupations frequently involve work activities that include practical, hands-on problems and solutions. These occupations often deal with plants, animals, and real-world materials like wood, tools, and machinery. Many of the occupations require working outside and do not involve a lot of paperwork or working closely with others. **Work Values:** Moral Values; Company Policies and Practices; Achievement; Supervision, Human Relations; Security. **Skills:** Active Listening; Speaking; Reading Comprehension; Operation Monitoring; Coordination. **Abilities:** *Cognitive*—Oral Comprehension; Oral Expression; Written Comprehension; Flexibility of Closure; Problem Sensitivity. *Psychomotor*—Reaction Time; Control Precision; Response Orientation. *Physical*—none met the criteria. *Sensory*—Auditory Attention; Speech Clarity; Speech Recognition. **General Work Activities:** *Information Input*—Monitoring Processes, Materials, and Surroundings; Getting Information Needed to Do the Job; Identifying Objects, Actions, and Events. *Mental Process*—Processing Information; Analyzing Data or Information; Making Decisions and Solving Problems. *Work Output*—Documenting and Recording Information; Repairing and Maintaining Electrical Equipment; Handling and Moving Objects. *Interacting with Others*—Communicating with Other Workers; Interpreting Meaning of Information to Others; Performing Administrative Activities; Establishing and Maintaining Relationships. **Physical Work Conditions:** Indoors; Sitting; Using Hands on Objects, Tools, or Controls. **Other Job Characteristics:** Consequence of Error; Importance of Being Exact or Accurate; Importance of Being Sure All Is Done.

Experience: Job Zone 3. Previous work-related skill, knowledge, or experience is required. **Job Preparation:** SVP 6.0 to less than 7.0—More than 1 year and less than 4 years. **Knowledge:** Telecommunications; Computers and Electronics; Communications and Media; English Language; Law, Government and Jurisprudence; Mathematics. **Instructional Programs:** 150301 Computer Engineering Technology/Technician; 150303 Electrical, Electronic and Communications Engin. Technology/Technician; 150399 Electrical and Electronic Engin.-Related Technology/Technician; 150403 Electromechanical Technology/Technician; 150404 Instrumentation Technology/Technician; 150405 Robotics Technology/Technician; 150801 Aeronautical and Aerospace Engineering Technology/Technician.

Related DOT Jobs: 193.162-022 Airline-Radio Operator, Chief; 193.262-010 Airline-Radio Operator; 193.262-014 Dispatcher; 193.262-022 Radio Officer; 193.262-026 Radio Station Operator; 193.262-030 Radiotelegraph Operator; 193.262-034 Radiotelephone Operator; 193.362-010 Photoradio Operator; 193.362-014 Radio-Intelligence Operator; 193.382-010 Electronic Intelligence Operations Specialist.

27-4014.00 Sound Engineering Technicians (All Other Engineering and Related Technicians and Technologists)

Education: No data available.
Employed: 253,980
Openings: No data available.
Projected Growth: No data available.
Earnings: $37,420

Operate machines and equipment to record, synchronize, mix, or reproduce music, voices, or sound effects in sporting arenas, theater productions, recording studios, or movie and video productions.

Synchronizes and equalizes prerecorded dialog, music, and sound effects with visual action of motion picture or television production, using control console. Keeps log of recordings. Sets up, adjusts, and tests recording equipment to prepare for recording session. Maintains recording equipment. Records speech, music, and other sounds on recording media, using recording equipment. Reproduces and duplicates sound recordings from original recording media, using sound editing and duplication equipment. Mixes and edits voices, music, and taped sound effects, during stage performances, using sound mixing board. Regulates volume level and quality of sound during motion picture, phonograph, television, or radio production recording sessions, using control console.

GOE Number, Interest Area, and Work Group: 01.08.01; Arts, Entertainment, and Media; Media Technology. **Personality Type:** Realistic. Realistic occupations frequently involve work activities that include practical, hands-on problems and solutions. These occupations often deal with plants, animals, and real-world materials like wood, tools, and machinery. Many of the occupations require working outside and do not involve a lot of paperwork or working closely with others. **Work Values:** Moral Values; Working Conditions; Company Policies and Practices; Ability Utilization; Security; Activity. **Skills:** Operation and Control; Operation Monitoring; Equipment Selection; Equipment Maintenance; Active Listening. **Abilities:** *Cognitive*—Oral Comprehension; Time Sharing; Information Ordering; Selective Attention; Written Comprehension. *Psychomotor*—Reaction Time; Control Precision; Response Orientation. *Physical*—Gross Body Coordination; Dynamic Flexibility; Gross Body Equilibrium. *Sensory*—Hearing Sensitivity; Auditory Attention; Sound Localization. **General Work Activities:** *Information Input*—Monitoring Processes, Materials, and Surroundings; Identifying Objects, Actions, and Events; Getting Information Needed to Do the Job; Inspecting Equipment, Structures, Materials. *Mental Process*—Judging Qualities of Things, Services, Other People's Work; Thinking Creatively; Analyzing Data or Information. *Work Output*—Controlling Machines and Processes; Handling and Moving Objects; Documenting and Recording Information; Implementing Ideas and Programs. *Interacting with Others*—Communicating with Other Workers; Coordinating Work and Activities of Others; Guiding, Directing and Motivating Subordinates. **Physical Work Conditions:** Indoors; Using Hands on Objects, Tools, or Controls; Sitting. **Other Job Characteristics:** Importance of Being Sure All Is Done; Consequence of Error; Degree of Automation; Importance of Being Exact or Accurate.

Experience: Job Zone 3. Previous work-related skill, knowledge, or experience is required. **Job Preparation:** SVP 6.0 to less than 7.0—More than 1 year and less than 4 years. **Knowledge:** Engineering and Technology; Computers and Electronics; Telecommunications; Communications and Media; Administration and Management. **Instructional Programs:** 100104 Radio and Television Broadcasting Technology/Technician; 100199 Communications Technology/Technicians, Other; 150101 Architectural Engineering Technology/Technician; 150304 Laser and Optical Technology/Technician; 150503 Energy Management and Systems Technology/Technician; 150505 Solar Technology/Technician; 150506 Water Quality and Wastewater Treatment Technology/Technician; 150507 Environmental and Pollution Control Technology/Technician; 150599 Environmental Control Technology/Technicians, Other; 150607 Plastics Technology/Technician; 150611 Metallurgical Technology/Technician; 150699 Industrial Production Technology/Technicians, Other; 150801 Aeronautical and Aerospace Engineering Technology/Technician; 150899 Mechanical Engineering-Related Technology/Technicians, Other; 150901 Mining Technology/Technician.

Related DOT Jobs: 194.262-014 Sound Controller; 194.262-018 Sound Mixer; 194.362-010 Recording Engineer; 194.362-014 Rerecording Mixer; 194.382-014 Tape Transferrer; 962.167-010 Manager, Sound Effects; 962.382-010 Recordist.

27-4021.00 Photographers (Photographers)

Education: Postsecondary vocational training
Employed: 149,378
Openings: 19,839
Projected Growth: 7.7%
Earnings: $20,940

Photograph persons, subjects, merchandise, or other commercial products. Develop negatives and produce finished prints.

GOE Number, Interest Area, and Work Group: 01.08.01; Arts, Entertainment, and Media; Media Technology. **Instructional Programs:** 500406 Commercial Photography; 500605 Photography; 500699 Film/Video and Photographic Arts, Other. **Note:** The Department of Labor has not collected some data for this job, so it has fewer details than the other descriptions.

27-4021.01 Professional Photographers (Photographers)

Education: Postsecondary vocational training
Employed: 149,378
Openings: 19,839
Projected Growth: 7.7%
Earnings: $20,940

Photograph subjects or newsworthy events using still cameras, color or black-and-white film, and various photographic accessories.

Frames subject matter and background in lens to capture desired image. Arranges subject material in desired position. Directs activities of workers assisting in setting up photographic equipment. Selects and assembles equipment and required background properties, according to subject, materials, and conditions. Focuses camera and adjusts settings based on lighting, subject material, distance, and film speed. Estimates or measures light level, distance, and number of exposures needed, using measuring devices and formulas.

GOE Number, Interest Area, and Work Group: 01.08.01; Arts, Entertainment, and Media; Media Technology. **Personality Type:** Artistic. Artistic occupations frequently involve working with forms, designs, and patterns. These occupations often require self-expression, and the work can be done without following a clear set of rules. **Work Values:** Creativity; Ability Utilization; Achievement; Autonomy; Responsibility. **Skills:** Equipment Selection; Visioning; Monitoring; Product Inspection; Mathematics; Information Organization; Operation and Control; Coordination; Identification of Key Causes; Idea Generation. **Abilities:** *Cognitive*—Visualization; Fluency of Ideas; Information Ordering; Originality; Oral Expression; Oral Comprehension. *Psychomotor*—Arm-Hand Steadiness; Rate Control; Reaction Time. *Physical*—Extent Flexibility; Trunk Strength; Static Strength; Gross Body

Coordination. *Sensory*—Near Vision; Far Vision; Depth Perception. **General Work Activities:** *Information Input*—Identifying Objects, Actions, and Events; Getting Information Needed to Do the Job; Monitoring Processes, Materials, and Surroundings. *Mental Process*—Thinking Creatively; Judging Qualities of Things, Services, Other People's Work; Making Decisions and Solving Problems. *Work Output*—Handling and Moving Objects; Controlling Machines and Processes; Performing General Physical Activities. *Interacting with Others*—Communicating with Persons Outside Organization; Coordinating Work and Activities of Others; Establishing and Maintaining Relationships. **Physical Work Conditions:** Using Hands on Objects, Tools, or Controls; Standing; Indoors. **Other Job Characteristics:** Importance of Being Sure All Is Done; Importance of Being Exact or Accurate; Consequence of Error; Frustrating Circumstances.

Experience: Job Zone 3. Previous work-related skill, knowledge, or experience is required. **Job Preparation:** SVP 6.0 to less than 7.0—More than 1 year and less than 4 years. **Knowledge:** Fine Arts; Chemistry; Geography; Communications and Media; Mathematics; English Language. **Instructional Programs:** 500406 Commercial Photography; 500605 Photography; 500699 Film/Video and Photographic Arts, Other.

Related DOT Jobs: 143.062-014 Photographer, Aerial; 143.062-018 Photographer, Apprentice; 143.062-030 Photographer, Still; 143.062-034 Photojournalist; 143.382-014 Photographer, Finish.

27-4021.02 Photographers, Scientific (Photographers)

Education: Postsecondary vocational training

Employed: 149,378

Openings: 19,839

Projected Growth: 7.7%

Earnings: $20,940

Photograph variety of subject material to illustrate or record scientific or medical data or phenomena, utilizing knowledge of scientific procedures and photographic technology and techniques.

Photographs variety of subject material to illustrate or record scientific or medical data or phenomena related to an area of interest. Sights and focuses camera to take picture of subject material to illustrate or record scientific or medical data or phenomena. Observes and arranges subject material to desired position. Engages in research to develop new photographic procedure, materials, and scientific data. Sets up, mounts, or installs photographic equipment and cameras. Plans methods and procedures for photographing subject material and set-up of required equipment. Removes exposed film and develops film, using chemicals, touch up tools, and equipment.

GOE Number, Interest Area, and Work Group: 02.05.02; Science, Math, and Engineering; Laboratory Technology: Life Sciences. **Personality Type:** Artistic. Artistic occupations frequently involve working with forms, designs, and patterns. These occupations often require self-expression, and the work can be done without following a clear set of rules. **Work Values:** Ability Utilization; Achievement; Autonomy; Creativity; Independence. **Skills:** Reading Comprehension; Equipment Selection; Information Gathering; Science; Active Learning. **Abilities:** *Cognitive*—Information Ordering; Visualization; Fluency of Ideas; Deductive Reasoning; Originality. *Psychomotor*—Arm-Hand Steadiness; Reaction Time; Control Precision. *Physical*—Trunk Strength; Static Strength; Gross Body Coordination. *Sensory*—Visual Color Discrimination; Near Vision; Far Vision. **General Work Activities:** *Information Input*—Identifying Objects, Actions, and Events; Monitoring Processes, Materials, and Surroundings; Getting Information Needed to Do the Job. *Mental Process*—Thinking Creatively; Organizing, Planning, and Prioritizing; Judging Qualities of Things, Services, Other People's Work. *Work Output*—Handling and Moving Objects; Implementing Ideas and Programs; Controlling Machines and Processes. *Interacting with Others*—Communicating with Other Workers; Communicating with Persons Outside Organization; Monitoring and Controlling Resources; Providing Consultation and Advice to Others. **Physical Work Conditions:** Using Hands on Objects, Tools, or Controls; Indoors; Standing. **Other Job Characteristics:** Importance of Being Sure All Is Done; Importance of Being Exact or Accurate; Degree of Automation.

Experience: Job Zone 3. Previous work-related skill, knowledge, or experience is required. **Job Preparation:** SVP 6.0 to less than 7.0—More than 1 year and less than 4 years. **Knowledge:** Chemistry; Fine Arts; Physics; Biology; Medicine and Dentistry; Communications and Media. **Instructional Programs:** 500406 Commercial Photography; 500605 Photography; 500699 Film/Video and Photographic Arts, Other.

Related DOT Jobs: 029.280-010 Photo-Optics Technician; 143.062-026 Photographer, Scientific; 143.362-010 Biological Photographer; 143.362-014 Ophthalmic Photographer.

27-4031.00 Camera Operators, Television, Video, and Motion Picture (Camera Operators, Television, Motion Picture, Video)

Education: Moderate-term O-T-J training

Employed: 11,349

Openings: 1,893

Projected Growth: 29%

Earnings: $21,520

Operate television, video, or motion picture camera to photograph images or scenes for various purposes such as TV broadcasts, advertising, video production, or motion pictures.

Instructs camera operators regarding camera setup, angles, distances, movement, and other variables and cues for starting and stopping filming. Adjusts position and controls of camera, printer, and related equipment to produce desired effects, using precision measuring instruments. Views film to resolve problems of exposure control, subject and camera movement, changes in subject distance, and related variables. Sets up cameras, optical printers and related equipment to produce photographs and special effects. Analyzes specifications to determine work procedures, sequence of operations, and machine setup. Reads charts and computes ratios to determine variables such as lighting, shutter angles, filter factors, and camera distance. Exposes frames of film in sequential order and regulates exposures and aperture to obtain special effects. Confers with director and electrician regarding interpretation of scene, desired effects, filming and lighting requirements. Reads work order to determine specifications and location of subject material. Selects cameras, accessories, equipment, and film stock to use during filming, using knowledge of filming techniques, requirements, and computations. Observes set or location to ascertain potential problems and to determine filming and lighting requirements.

GOE Number, Interest Area, and Work Group: 01.08.01; Arts, Entertainment, and Media; Media Technology. **Personality Type:** Artistic. Artistic occupations frequently involve working with forms, designs, and patterns. These occupations often require self-expression, and the work can be done without following a clear set of rules. **Work Values:** Ability Utilization; Achievement; Recognition; Working Conditions; Variety; Moral Values. **Skills:** Technology Design; Operation and Control; Product Inspection; Reading Comprehension; Mathematics; Equipment Selection; Problem Identification. **Abilities:** *Cognitive*—Visualization; Oral Comprehension; Written Comprehension; Oral Expression; Spatial Orientation; Problem Sensitivity. *Psychomotor*—Arm-Hand Steadiness; Control Precision; Rate Control. *Physical*—Static Strength; Dynamic Strength; Gross Body Coordination. *Sensory*—Far Vision; Visual Color Discrimination; Speech Clarity. **General Work Activities:** *Information Input*—Getting Information Needed to Do the Job; Monitoring Processes, Materials, and Surroundings; Estimating Needed Characteristics; Identifying Objects, Actions, and Events. *Mental Process*—Updating and Using Job-Relevant Knowledge; Making Decisions and Solving Problems; Judging Qualities of Things, Services, Other People's Work; Thinking Creatively. *Work Output*—Controlling Machines and Processes; Handling and Moving Objects; Drafting and Specifying Technical Devices; Implementing Ideas and Programs. *Interacting with Others*—Communicating with Other Workers; Guiding, Directing and Motivating Subordinates; Coordinating Work and Activities of Others; Establishing and Maintaining Relationships. **Physical Work Conditions:** Indoors; Using Hands on Objects, Tools, or Controls; Standing. **Other Job Characteristics:** Importance of Being Aware of New Events; Frustrating Circumstances; Importance of Being Sure All Is Done.

Experience: Job Zone 4. A minimum of two to four years of work-related skill, knowledge, or experience is needed. **Job Preparation:** SVP 7.0 to less than 8.0—2 years to less than 10 years. **Knowledge:** Fine Arts; Telecommunications; Physics; Mathematics; Communications and Media. **Instructional Programs:** 100103 Photographic Technology/Technician; 100199 Communications Technol./Technicians, Other; 500406 Commercial Photography; 500602 Film-Video Making/Cinematography and Production.

Related DOT Jobs: 143.062-010 Director of Photography; 143.062-022 Camera Operator; 143.260-010 Optical-Effects-Camera Operator; 143.382-010 Camera Operator, Animation; 976.382-010 Camera Operator, Title.

27-4032.00 Film and Video Editors (Film Editors)

Education: No data available.

Employed: 10,240

Openings: No data available.

Projected Growth: No data available.

Earnings: $38,770

Edit motion picture soundtracks, film, and video.

Reviews assembled film or edited video tape on screen or monitor; makes corrections. Edits film and video tape to insert music, dialogue, and sound effects and to correct errors, using editing equipment. Studies script and confers with producers and directors concerning layout or editing to increase dramatic or entertainment value of production. Supervises and coordinates activities of workers engaged in editing and assembling filmed scenes photographed by others. Evaluates and selects scenes in terms of dramatic and entertainment value and story continuity. Trims film segments to specified lengths and reassembles segments in sequence that presents story with maximum effect.

GOE Number, Interest Area, and Work Group: 01.08.01; Arts, Entertainment, and Media; Media Technology. **Personality Type:** Artistic. Artistic occupations frequently involve working with forms, designs, and patterns. These occupations often require self-expression, and the work can be done without following a clear set of rules. **Work Values:** Autonomy; Social Status; Responsibility; Recognition; Achievement; Creativity. **Skills:** Critical Thinking; Synthesis/Reorganization; Information Organization; Monitoring; Coordination; Active Listening; Reading Comprehension; Active Learning. **Abilities:** *Cognitive*—Visualization; Information Ordering; Problem Sensitivity; Oral Comprehension; Perceptual Speed; Oral Expression. *Psychomotor*—Control Precision; Arm-Hand Steadiness; Reaction Time. *Physical*—Gross Body Coordination; Dynamic Flexibility; Stamina; Gross Body Equilibrium. *Sensory*—Night Vision; Hearing Sensitivity; Near Vision. **General Work Activities:** *Information Input*—Getting Information Needed to Do the Job; Identifying Objects, Actions, and Events; Monitoring Processes, Materials, and Surroundings. *Mental Process*—Thinking Creatively; Judging Qualities of Things, Services, Other People's Work; Making Decisions and Solving Problems. *Work Output*—Controlling Machines and Processes; Implementing Ideas and Programs; Handling and Moving Objects. *Interacting with Others*—Communicating with Other Workers; Coordinating Work and Activities of Others; Interpreting Meaning of Information to Others; Providing Consultation and Advice to Others; Guiding, Directing and Motivating Subordinates. **Physical Work Conditions:** Indoors; Using Hands on Objects, Tools, or Controls; Sitting. **Other Job Characteristics:** Degree of Automation; Importance of Being Exact or Accurate; Consequence of Error; Importance of Being Sure All Is Done.

Experience: Job Zone 4. A minimum of two to four years of work-related skill, knowledge, or experience is needed. **Job Preparation:** SVP 7.0 to less than 8.0—2 years to less than 10 years. **Knowledge:** Communications and Media; Fine Arts; Computers and Electronics; English Language; Telecommunications. **Instructional Programs:** 100104 Radio and Television Broadcasting Technology/Technician; 100199 Communications Technol./Technicians, Other; 500602 Film-Video Making/Cinematography and Production.

Related DOT Jobs: 962.132-010 Supervising Film-or-Videotape Editor; 962.262-010 Film or Videotape Editor; 962.361-010 Optical-Effects Layout Person; 962.382-014 Sound Cutter.

29-0000
Healthcare Practitioners and Technical Occupations

29-1000 Health Diagnosing and Treating Practitioners

29-1011.00 Chiropractors (Chiropractors)

Education: First professional degree

Employed: 46,256

Openings: 2,516

Projected Growth: 22.8%

Earnings: $63,930

Adjust spinal column and other articulations of the human body to correct abnormalities believed to be caused by interference with the nervous system. Examine patient to determine nature and extent of disorder. Manipulate spine or other involved areas. Utilize supplementary measures such as exercise, rest, water, light, heat, and nutritional therapy.

Performs diagnostic procedures, including physical, neurologic, and orthopedic examinations, and laboratory tests, using instruments and equipment such as X-ray machine and electrocardiograph. Utilizes supplementary measures, such as exercise, rest, water, light, heat, and nutritional therapy. Manipulates spinal column and other extremities to adjust, align, or correct abnormalities caused by neurologic and kinetic articular dysfunction. Examines patient to determine nature and extent of disorder.

GOE Number, Interest Area, and Work Group: 14.04.01; Medical and Health Services; Health Specialties. **Personality Type:** Investigative. Investigative occupations frequently involve working with ideas and require an extensive amount of thinking. These occupations can involve searching for facts and figuring out problems mentally. **Work Values:** Responsibility; Social Service; Autonomy; Ability Utilization; Achievement. **Skills:** Reading Comprehension; Problem Identification; Solution Appraisal; Active Learning; Judgment and Decision Making; Information Gathering; Active Listening. **Abilities:** *Cognitive*—Problem Sensitivity; Inductive Reasoning; Deductive Reasoning; Oral Expression; Oral Comprehension. *Psychomotor*—Manual Dexterity; Finger Dexterity; Wrist-Finger Speed. *Physical*—Static Strength; Extent Flexibility; Dynamic Strength. *Sensory*—Near Vision; Speech Clarity; Visual Color Discrimination. **General Work Activities:** *Information Input*—Identifying Objects, Actions, and Events; Getting Information Needed to Do the Job; Monitoring Processes, Materials, and Surroundings. *Mental Process*—Making Decisions and Solving Problems; Analyzing Data or Information; Updating and Using Job-Relevant Knowledge. *Work Output*—Handling and Moving Objects; Performing General Physical Activities; Implementing Ideas and Programs. *Interacting with Others*—Assisting and Caring for Others; Establishing and Maintaining Relationships; Performing for or Working with the Public; Communicating with Persons Outside Organization; Interpreting Meaning of Information to Others. **Physical Work Conditions:** Indoors; Using Hands on Objects, Tools, or Controls; Standing; Special Uniform. **Other Job Characteristics:** Consequence of Error; Importance of Being Exact or Accurate; Importance of Being Sure All Is Done.

Experience: Job Zone 5. Extensive skill, knowledge, and experience are needed. Very advanced communication and organizational skills are required. **Job Preparation:** SVP 8.0 and above—4 years to more than 10 years. **Knowledge:** Medicine and Dentistry; Biology; English Language; Customer and Personal Service; Therapy and Counseling. **Instructional Program:** 510101 Chiropractic (D.C., D.C.M.).

Related DOT Job: 079.101-010 Chiropractor.

29-1021.00 Dentists, General (Dentists)

Education: First professional degree

Employed: 160,139

Openings: 2,301

Projected Growth: 3.1%

Earnings: $110,160

Diagnose and treat diseases, injuries, and malformations of teeth, gums, and related oral structures. Treat diseases of nerves, pulp, and other dental tissues affecting vitality of teeth.

Removes pathologic tissue or diseased tissue using surgical instruments. Formulates plan of treatment for patient's teeth and mouth tissue. Restores natural color of teeth by bleaching, cleaning, and polishing. Analyzes and evaluates dental needs to determine changes and trends in patterns of dental disease. Counsels and advises patients about growth and development of dental problems and preventive oral healthcare services. Fabricates prosthodontic appliances, such as space maintainers, bridges, dentures, and obturating appliances. Fits and adjusts prosthodontic appliances in patient's mouth. Plans, organizes, and maintains dental health programs. Eliminates irritating margins of fillings and corrects occlusions, using dental instruments. Examines teeth, gums, and related tissues to determine condition, using dental instruments, X rays, and other diagnostic equipment. Fills pulp chamber and canal with endodontic materials. Treats exposure of pulp by pulp capping, removal of pulp from pulp chamber, or root canal, using dental instruments. Applies fluoride and sealants to teeth. Fills, extracts, and replaces teeth, using rotary and hand instruments, dental appliances, medications, and surgical implements. Produces and evaluates dental health educational materials. Treats infected root canal and related tissues.

GOE Number, Interest Area, and Work Group: 14.03.01; Medical and Health Services; Dentistry. **Personality Type:** Investigative. Investigative occupations frequently involve working with ideas and require an extensive amount of thinking. These occupations can involve searching for facts and figuring out problems mentally. **Work Values:** Responsibility; Social Service; Achievement; Ability Utilization; Social Status. **Skills:** Reading Comprehension; Problem Identification; Critical Thinking; Active Learning; Science. **Abilities:** *Cognitive*—Oral Comprehension; Problem Sensitivity; Oral Expression; Information Ordering; Written Expression. *Psychomotor*—Control Precision; Arm-Hand Steadiness; Finger Dexterity. *Physical*—none met the criteria. *Sensory*—Near Vision; Visual Color Discrimination. **General Work Activities:** *Information Input*—Getting Information Needed to Do the Job; Identifying Objects, Actions, and Events; Monitoring Processes, Materials, and Surroundings. *Mental Process*—Making Decisions and Solving Problems; Judging Qualities of Things,

Services, Other People's Work; Updating and Using Job-Relevant Knowledge. *Work Output*—Handling and Moving Objects; Implementing Ideas and Programs; Documenting and Recording Information. *Interacting with Others*—Assisting and Caring for Others; Communicating with Persons Outside Organization; Establishing and Maintaining Relationships. **Physical Work Conditions:** Indoors; Special Uniform; Common Protective or Safety Attire; Using Hands on Objects, Tools, or Controls. **Other Job Characteristics:** Importance of Being Exact or Accurate; Consequence of Error; Importance of Being Sure All Is Done.

Experience: Job Zone 5. Extensive skill, knowledge, and experience are needed. Very advanced communication and organizational skills are required. **Job Preparation:** SVP 8.0 and above—4 years to more than 10 years. **Knowledge:** Medicine and Dentistry; Biology; English Language; Chemistry; Administration and Management. **Instructional Programs:** 510401 Dentistry (D.D.S., D.M.D.); 510501 Dental Clinical Sciences/Graduate Dentistry (M.S., Ph.D.); 512801 Dental/Oral Surgery Specialty; 512802 Dental Public Health Specialty; 512803 Endodontics Specialty; 512804 Oral Pathology Specialty; 512805 Orthodontics Specialty; 512806 Pedodontics Specialty; 512807 Periodontics Specialty; 512808 Prosthodontics Specialty; 512899 Dental Residency Programs, Other.

Related DOT Jobs: 072.101-010 Dentist; 072.101-014 Endodontist; 072.101-026 Pediatric Dentist; 072.101-030 Periodontist; 072.101-038 Public-Health Dentist.

29-1022.00 Oral and Maxillofacial Surgeons (Dentists)

Education: First professional degree
Employed: 160,139
Openings: 2,301
Projected Growth: 3.1%
Earnings: $110,160

Perform surgery on mouth, jaws, and related head and neck structure to execute difficult and multiple extractions of teeth, to remove tumors and other abnormal growths, to correct abnormal jaw relations by mandibular or maxillary revision, to prepare mouth for insertion of dental prosthesis, or to treat fractured jaws.

Removes tumors and other abnormal growths, using surgical instruments. Treats fractures of jaws. Administers general and local anesthetics. Performs preprosthetic surgery to prepare mouth for insertion of dental prosthesis. Executes difficult and multiple extraction of teeth. Corrects abnormal jaw relations by mandibular or maxillary revision.

GOE Number, Interest Area, and Work Group: 14.03.01; Medical and Health Services; Dentistry. **Personality Type:** Investigative. Investigative occupations frequently involve working with ideas and require an extensive amount of thinking. These occupations can involve searching for facts and figuring out problems mentally. **Work Values:** Social Service; Responsibility; Achievement; Social Status; Ability Utilization. **Skills:** Reading Comprehension; Critical Thinking; Judgment and Decision Making; Problem Identification; Science. **Abilities:** *Cognitive*—Problem Sensitivity; Visualization; Oral Expression; Oral Com-

prehension; Deductive Reasoning. *Psychomotor*—Arm-Hand Steadiness; Finger Dexterity; Manual Dexterity; Control Precision. *Physical*—none met the criteria. *Sensory*—Near Vision; Visual Color Discrimination. **General Work Activities:** *Information Input*—Monitoring Processes, Materials, and Surroundings; Getting Information Needed to Do the Job; Identifying Objects, Actions, and Events. *Mental Process*—Making Decisions and Solving Problems; Judging Qualities of Things, Services, Other People's Work; Updating and Using Job-Relevant Knowledge. *Work Output*—Handling and Moving Objects; Implementing Ideas and Programs; Controlling Machines and Processes; Documenting and Recording Information. *Interacting with Others*—Assisting and Caring for Others; Communicating with Other Workers; Communicating with Persons Outside Organization; Establishing and Maintaining Relationships. **Physical Work Conditions:** Indoors; Special Uniform; Using Hands on Objects, Tools, or Controls. **Other Job Characteristics:** Consequence of Error; Importance of Being Exact or Accurate; Importance of Being Sure All Is Done.

Experience: Job Zone 5. Extensive skill, knowledge, and experience are needed. Very advanced communication and organizational skills are required. **Job Preparation:** SVP 8.0 and above—4 years to more than 10 years. **Knowledge:** Medicine and Dentistry; Biology; Chemistry; English Language; Psychology. **Instructional Programs:** 510401 Dentistry (D.D.S., D.M.D.); 510501 Dental Clinical Sciences/Graduate Dentistry (M.S., Ph.D.); 512801 Dental/Oral Surgery Specialty; 512802 Dental Public Health Specialty; 512803 Endodontics Specialty; 512804 Oral Pathology Specialty; 512805 Orthodontics Specialty; 512806 Pedodontics Specialty; 512807 Periodontics Specialty; 512808 Prosthodontics Specialty; 512899 Dental Residency Programs, Other.

Related DOT Job: 072.101-018 Oral and Maxillofacial Surgeon.

29-1023.00 Orthodontists (Dentists)

Education: First professional degree
Employed: 160,139
Openings: 2,301
Projected Growth: 3.1%
Earnings: $110,160

Examine, diagnose, and treat dental malocclusions and oral cavity anomalies. Design and fabricate appliances to realign teeth and jaws, for producing and maintaining normal function and for improving appearance.

Diagnoses teeth and jaw or other dental-facial abnormalities. Plans treatment, using cephalometric, height, and weight records, dental X rays and front and lateral dental photographs. Examines patient's mouth to determine position of teeth, and jaw development. Fits dental appliances in patients mouth to alter position and relationship of teeth and jaws and to realign teeth. Designs and fabricates appliances, such as space maintainers, retainers, and labial and lingual arch wires. Adjusts dental appliances periodically to produce and maintain normal function.

GOE Number, Interest Area, and Work Group: 14.03.01; Medical and Health Services; Dentistry. **Personality Type:** Investigative. Investigative occupations frequently involve working with ideas and require an extensive amount of thinking. These occupations can involve searching for facts and figuring out problems mentally. **Work Values:** Responsibility; Social Service; Social Status; Achievement; Ability Utilization. **Skills:** Reading Comprehension; Active Learning; Problem Identification; Science; Critical Thinking. **Abilities:** *Cognitive*—Problem Sensitivity; Oral Comprehension; Oral Expression; Visualization; Deductive Reasoning. *Psychomotor*—Arm-Hand Steadiness; Control Precision; Manual Dexterity. *Physical*—none met the criteria. **General Work Activities:** *Information Input*—Getting Information Needed to Do the Job; Identifying Objects, Actions, and Events; Monitoring Processes, Materials, and Surroundings. *Mental Process*—Making Decisions and Solving Problems; Updating and Using Job-Relevant Knowledge; Developing Objectives and Strategies. *Work Output*—Handling and Moving Objects; Implementing Ideas and Programs; Documenting and Recording Information. *Interacting with Others*—Assisting and Caring for Others; Communicating with Persons Outside Organization; Communicating with Other Workers. **Physical Work Conditions:** Indoors; Special Uniform; Using Hands on Objects, Tools, or Controls; Standing. **Other Job Characteristics:** Consequence of Error; Importance of Being Exact or Accurate; Importance of Being Sure All Is Done.

Experience: Job Zone 5. Extensive skill, knowledge, and experience are needed. Very advanced communication and organizational skills are required. **Job Preparation:** SVP 8.0 and above—4 years to more than 10 years. **Knowledge:** Medicine and Dentistry; Biology; Administration and Management; Design; Customer and Personal Service; Chemistry; Therapy and Counseling. **Instructional Programs:** 510401 Dentistry (D.D.S., D.M.D.); 510501 Dental Clinical Sciences/Graduate Dentistry (M.S., Ph.D.); 512801 Dental/Oral Surgery Specialty; 512802 Dental Public Health Specialty; 512803 Endodontics Specialty; 512804 Oral Pathology Specialty; 512805 Orthodontics Specialty; 512806 Pedodontics Specialty; 512807 Periodontics Specialty; 512808 Prosthodontics Specialty; 512899 Dental Residency Programs, Other.

Related DOT Job: 072.101-022 Orthodontist.

29-1024.00 Prosthodontists (Dentists)

Education: First professional degree

Employed: 160,139

Openings: 2,301

Projected Growth: 3.1%

Earnings: $110,160

Construct oral prostheses to replace missing teeth and other oral structures, for correcting natural and acquired deformation of mouth and jaws, for restoring and maintaining oral function such as chewing and speaking, and for improving appearance.

Adjusts prostheses to fit patient. Records physiologic position of jaws to determine shape and size of dental prostheses, using face bows, dental articulators, and recording devices. Corrects natural and acquired deformation of mouth and jaws through use of prosthetic appliances. Designs and fabricates dental prostheses. Replaces missing teeth and associated oral structures with artificial teeth to improve chewing, speech, and appearance.

GOE Number, Interest Area, and Work Group: 14.03.01; Medical and Health Services; Dentistry. **Personality Type:** Investigative. Investigative occupations frequently involve working with ideas and require an extensive amount of thinking. These occupations can involve searching for facts and figuring out problems mentally. **Work Values:** Responsibility; Social Service; Achievement; Ability Utilization; Autonomy. **Skills:** Reading Comprehension; Problem Identification; Critical Thinking; Science; Judgment and Decision Making; Solution Appraisal. **Abilities:** *Cognitive*—Visualization; Information Ordering; Written Expression; Problem Sensitivity; Oral Expression; Deductive Reasoning. *Psychomotor*—Control Precision; Arm-Hand Steadiness; Finger Dexterity. *Physical*—none met the criteria. *Sensory*—Near Vision; Visual Color Discrimination. **General Work Activities:** *Information Input*—Getting Information Needed to Do the Job; Identifying Objects, Actions, and Events; Estimating Needed Characteristics. *Mental Process*—Making Decisions and Solving Problems; Updating and Using Job-Relevant Knowledge; Analyzing Data or Information; Judging Qualities of Things, Services, Other People's Work. *Work Output*—Handling and Moving Objects; Implementing Ideas and Programs; Documenting and Recording Information. *Interacting with Others*—Assisting and Caring for Others; Communicating with Persons Outside Organization; Establishing and Maintaining Relationships. **Physical Work Conditions:** Indoors; Special Uniform; Using Hands on Objects, Tools, or Controls. **Other Job Characteristics:** Importance of Being Exact or Accurate; Consequence of Error; Importance of Being Sure All Is Done.

Experience: Job Zone 5. Extensive skill, knowledge, and experience are needed. Very advanced communication and organizational skills are required. **Job Preparation:** SVP 8.0 and above—4 years to more than 10 years. **Knowledge:** Medicine and Dentistry; Biology; Chemistry; English Language; Design. **Instructional Programs:** 510401 Dentistry (D.D.S., D.M.D.); 510501 Dental Clinical Sciences/Graduate Dentistry (M.S., Ph.D.); 512801 Dental/Oral Surgery Specialty; 512802 Dental Public Health Specialty; 512803 Endodontics Specialty; 512804 Oral Pathology Specialty; 512805 Orthodontics Specialty; 512806 Pedodontics Specialty; 512807 Periodontics Specialty; 512808 Prosthodontics Specialty; 512899 Dental Residency Programs, Other.

Related DOT Job: 072.101-034 Prosthodontist.

29-1031.00 Dietitians and Nutritionists (Dietitians and Nutritionists)

Education: Bachelor's degree

Employed: 53,972

Openings: 8,153

Projected Growth: 19.1%

Earnings: $35,040

Plan and conduct food service or nutritional programs to assist in the promotion of health and the control of disease. Supervise activities of a department providing quantity food services. Counsel individuals. Conduct nutritional research.

Plans and prepares grant proposals to request program funding. Monitors food service operations and ensures conformance to nutritional and quality standards. Instructs patients and their families in nutritional principles, dietary plans, and food selection and preparation. Consults with physicians and healthcare personnel to determine nutritional needs and diet restrictions of patient or client. Plans, organizes, and conducts training programs in dietetics, nutrition, and institutional management and administration for medical students and hospital personnel. Inspects meals served for conformance to prescribed diets and standards of palatability and appearance. Writes research reports and other publications to document and communicate research findings. Confers with design, building, and equipment personnel to plan for construction and remodeling of food service units. Evaluates nutritional care plans and provides follow-up on continuity of care. Plans, conducts, and evaluates dietary, nutritional, and epidemiological research, and analyzes findings for practical applications. Supervises activities of workers engaged in planning, preparing, and serving meals. Develops and implements dietary-care plans based on assessments of nutritional needs, diet restrictions, and other current health plans. Develops curriculum and prepares manuals, visual aids, course outlines, and other materials used in teaching.

GOE Number, Interest Area, and Work Group: 14.08.01; Medical and Health Services; Health Protection and Promotion. **Personality Type:** Investigative. Investigative occupations frequently involve working with ideas and require an extensive amount of thinking. These occupations can involve searching for facts and figuring out problems mentally. **Work Values:** Social Service; Ability Utilization; Achievement; Authority; Working Conditions; Security. **Skills:** Writing; Reading Comprehension; Management of Financial Resources; Critical Thinking; Active Learning; Information Gathering. **Abilities:** *Cognitive*—Oral Expression; Written Expression; Written Comprehension; Inductive Reasoning; Information Ordering; Oral Comprehension. *Psychomotor*—Wrist-Finger Speed. *Physical*—Gross Body Equilibrium. *Sensory*—Speech Clarity; Near Vision; Auditory Attention; Far Vision. **General Work Activities:** *Information Input*—Getting Information Needed to Do the Job; Identifying Objects, Actions, and Events; Monitoring Processes, Materials, and Surroundings. *Mental Process*—Making Decisions and Solving Problems; Analyzing Data or Information; Updating and Using Job-Relevant Knowledge. *Work Output*—Documenting and Recording Information; Implementing Ideas and Programs; Interacting with Computers. *Interacting with Others*—Communicating with Persons Outside Organization; Communicating with Other Workers; Interpreting Meaning of Information to Others; Teaching Others. **Physical Work Conditions:** Indoors; Standing; Sitting. **Other Job Characteristics:** Importance of Being Exact or Accurate; Importance of Being Sure All Is Done; Consequence of Error.

Experience: Job Zone 4. A minimum of two to four years of work-related skill, knowledge, or experience is needed. **Job Preparation:** SVP 7.0 to less than 8.0—2 years to less than 10 years. **Knowledge:** English Language; Biology; Education and Training; Administration and Management; Food Production. **Instructional Programs:** 190501 Foods and Nutrition Studies, General; 190502 Foods and Nutrition Science; 190503 Dietetics/Human Nutritional Services; 190505 Food Systems Administration; 190599 Foods and Nutrition Studies, Other; 512702 Medical Dietician.

Related DOT Jobs: 077.061-010 Dietitian, Research; 077.117-010 Dietitian, Chief; 077.127-010 Community Dietitian; 077.127-014 Dietitian, Clinical; 077.127-018 Dietitian, Consultant; 077.127-022 Dietitian, Teaching.

29-1041.00 Optometrists (Optometrists)

Education: First professional degree
Employed: 37,889
Openings: 1,532
Projected Growth: 10.6%
Earnings: $68,480

Diagnose, manage, and treat conditions and diseases of the human eye and visual system. Examine eyes and visual system; diagnose problems or impairments; prescribe corrective lenses; provide treatment. Prescribe therapeutic drugs to treat specific eye conditions.

Prescribes medications to treat eye diseases if state laws permit. Consults with and refers patients to ophthalmologist or other healthcare practitioner if additional medical treatment is determined necessary. Prescribes eyeglasses, contact lenses, and other vision aids or therapeutic procedures to correct or conserve vision. Examines eyes to determine visual acuity and perception and to diagnose diseases and other abnormalities, such as glaucoma and color blindness.

GOE Number, Interest Area, and Work Group: 14.04.01; Medical and Health Services; Health Specialties. **Personality Type:** Investigative. Investigative occupations frequently involve working with ideas and require an extensive amount of thinking. These occupations can involve searching for facts and figuring out problems mentally. **Work Values:** Social Service; Ability Utilization; Responsibility; Achievement; Autonomy. **Skills:** Reading Comprehension; Active Listening; Instructing; Science; Writing; Mathematics. **Abilities:** *Cognitive*—Oral Expression; Written Comprehension; Problem Sensitivity; Oral Comprehension; Written Expression. *Psychomotor*—Control Precision; Finger Dexterity. *Physical*—Trunk Strength; Gross Body Coordination. *Sensory*—Near Vision; Speech Clarity; Visual Color Discrimination. **General Work Activities:** *Information Input*—Getting Information Needed to Do the Job; Identifying Objects, Actions, and Events; Monitoring Processes, Materials, and Surroundings. *Mental Process*—Updating and Using Job-Relevant Knowledge; Making Decisions and Solving Problems; Analyzing Data or Information. *Work Output*—Handling and Moving Objects; Documenting and Recording Information; Implementing Ideas and Programs. *Interacting with Others*—Assisting and Caring for Others; Interpreting Meaning of Information to Others; Providing Consultation and Advice to Others. **Physical Work Conditions:** Indoors; Sitting; Using Hands on Objects, Tools, or Controls; Standing. **Other Job Characteristics:** Importance of Being Exact or Accurate; Consequence of Error; Importance of Being Sure All Is Done.

Experience: Job Zone 4. A minimum of two to four years of work-related skill, knowledge, or experience is needed. **Job Preparation:** SVP 7.0 to less than 8.0—2 years to less than 10 years. **Knowledge:** Medicine and Dentistry; Biology; English Language; Customer and Personal Service; Mathematics; Chemistry. **Instructional Program:** 511701 Optometry (O.D.).

Related DOT Job: 079.101-018 Optometrist.

29-1051.00 Pharmacists (Pharmacists)

Education: First professional degree
Employed: 185,324
Openings: 6,382
Projected Growth: 7.3%
Earnings: $66,220

Compound and dispense medications, following prescriptions issued by physicians, dentists, or other authorized medical practitioners.

Maintains established procedures concerning quality assurance, security of controlled substances, and disposal of hazardous waste. Assays prepared radiopharmaceutical, using instruments and equipment to verify rate of drug disintegration and ensure patient receives required dose. Maintains records, such as pharmacy files, charge system, inventory, and control records for radioactive nuclei. Oversees preparation and dispensation of experimental drugs. Verifies that specified radioactive substance and reagent will give desired results in examination or treatment procedures. Consults medical staff to advise on drug applications and characteristics and to review and evaluate quality and effectiveness of radiopharmaceuticals. Calculates volume of radioactive pharmaceutical required to provide patient desired level of radioactivity at prescribed time. Answers questions and provides information to pharmacy customers on drug interactions, side effects, dosage, and storage of pharmaceuticals. Compounds radioactive substances and reagents to prepare radiopharmaceutical, following radiopharmacy laboratory procedures. Plans and implements procedures in pharmacy, such as mixing, packaging, and labeling pharmaceuticals according to policies and legal requirements. Reviews prescription to assure accuracy and determine ingredients needed and suitability of radiopharmaceutical prescriptions. Compounds medications, using standard formulas and processes, such as weighing, measuring, and mixing ingredients. Analyzes records to indicate prescribing trends and excessive usage.

GOE Number, Interest Area, and Work Group: 14.02.01; Medical and Health Services; Medicine and Surgery. **Personality Type:** Investigative. Investigative occupations frequently involve working with ideas and require an extensive amount of thinking. These occupations can involve searching for facts and figuring out problems mentally. **Work Values:** Ability Utilization; Security; Social Status; Achievement; Working Conditions. **Skills:** Reading Comprehension; Writing; Mathematics; Science; Active Learning; Instructing. **Abilities:** *Cognitive*—Written Comprehension; Information Ordering; Oral Comprehension; Oral Expression; Mathematical Reasoning; Written Expression. *Psychomotor*—Control Precision. *Physical*—none met the criteria. *Sensory*—Speech Recognition. **General Work Activities:** *Information Input*—Getting Information Needed to Do the Job; Identifying Objects, Actions, and Events; Estimating Needed Characteristics. *Mental Process*—Updating and Using Job-Relevant Knowledge; Evaluating Information Against Standards; Processing Information. *Work Output*—Implementing Ideas and Programs; Handling and Moving Objects; Documenting and Recording Information. *Interacting with Others*—Communicating with Other Workers; Communicating with Persons Outside Organization; Interpreting Meaning of Information to Others. **Physical Work Conditions:** Indoors; Special Uniform; Using Hands on Objects, Tools, or Controls. **Other Job Characteristics:** Consequence of Error; Importance of Being Exact or Accurate; Importance of Being Sure All Is Done.

Experience: Job Zone 4. A minimum of two to four years of work-related skill, knowledge, or experience is needed. **Job Preparation:** SVP 7.0 to less than 8.0—2 years to less than 10 years. **Knowledge:** Chemistry; Medicine and Dentistry; Biology; Administration and Management; English Language; Computers and Electronics. **Instructional Programs:** 512001 Pharmacy (B. Pharm., Pharm.D.); 512002 Pharmacy Administration and Pharmaceutics; 512003 Medical Pharmacology and Pharmaceutical Sciences; 512099 Pharmacy, Other.

Related DOT Jobs: 074.161-010 Pharmacist; 074.161-014 Radiopharmacist; 074.167-010 Director, Pharmacy Services.

29-1061.00 Anesthesiologists (Physicians)

Education: First professional degree
Employed: 576,870
Openings: 32,563
Projected Growth: 21.2%
Earnings: No data available.

Administer anesthetics during surgery or other medical procedures.

Examines patient to determine risk during surgical, obstetrical, and other medical procedures. Positions patient on operating table to maximize patient comfort and surgical accessibility. Confers with medical professional to determine type and method of anesthetic or sedation to render patient insensible to pain. Monitors patient before, during, and after anesthesia and counteracts adverse reactions or complications. Administers anesthetic or sedation during medical procedures, using local, intravenous, spinal, or caudal methods. Informs students and staff of types and methods of anesthesia administration, signs of complications, and emergency methods to counteract reactions. Records type and amount of anesthesia and patient condition throughout procedure.

GOE Number, Interest Area, and Work Group: 14.02.01; Medical and Health Services; Medicine and Surgery. **Personality Type:** Investigative. Investigative occupations frequently involve working with ideas and require an extensive amount of thinking. These occupations can involve searching for facts and figuring out problems mentally. **Work Values:** Social Service; Ability Utilization; Achievement; Compensation; Social Status. **Skills:** Reading Comprehension; Problem Identification; Judgment and Decision Making; Critical Thinking; Speaking; Active Learning; Information Gathering; Monitoring; Coordination; Solution Appraisal. **Abilities:** *Cognitive*—Problem Sensitivity; Oral Comprehension; Information Ordering; Deductive Reasoning; Written Comprehension; Written Expression. *Psychomotor*—Control Precision; Arm-Hand Steadiness; Reaction Time. *Physical*—none met the criteria. *Sensory*—Speech Clarity. **General Work Activities:** *Information Input*—Monitoring Processes, Materials, and Surroundings; Getting Information Needed to Do the Job; Identifying Objects, Actions, and Events. *Mental Process*—Updating and Using Job-Relevant Knowledge; Making Decisions and Solving Problems; Analyzing Data or Information. *Work Output*—Controlling Machines and Processes; Documenting and Recording Information; Implementing Ideas and Programs. *Interacting with Others*—Assisting and Caring for Others; Interpreting Meaning of Information to Others; Communicating with Other Workers. **Physical Work Conditions:** Indoors; Special Uniform; Common Protective or Safety Attire. **Other Job Characteristics:** Consequence of Error; Importance of Being Sure All Is Done; Importance of Being Exact or Accurate.

Experience: Job Zone 5. Extensive skill, knowledge, and experience are needed. Very advanced communication and organizational skills are required. **Job Preparation:** SVP 8.0 and above—4 years to more than 10 years. **Knowledge:** Medicine and Dentistry; Biology; Chemistry; Mathematics; English Language. **Instructional Programs:** 511201 Medicine (M.D.); 511307 Medical Immunology; 511901 Osteopathic Medicine (D.O.); 512705 Psychoanalysis; 512901 Aerospace Medicine Residency; 512902 Allergies and Immunology Residency; 512903 Anesthesiology Residency; 512904 Blood Banking Residency; 512905 Cardiology Residency; 512906 Chemical Pathology Residency; 512907 Child/Pediatric Neurology Residency; 512908 Child Psychiatry Residency; 512909 Colon and Rectal Surgery Residency; 512910 Critical Care Anesthesiology Residency; 512911 Critical Care Medicine Residency.

Related DOT Job: 070.101-010 Anesthesiologist.

29-1062.00 Family and General Practitioners
(Physicians)

Education: First professional degree

Employed: 576,870

Openings: 32,563

Projected Growth: 21.2%

Earnings: No data available.

Diagnose, treat, and help prevent diseases and injuries that commonly occur in the general population.

Plans, implements, or administers health programs or standards in hospital, business, or community for information, prevention, or treatment of injury or illness. Prescribes or administers treatment, therapy, medication, vaccination, and other specialized medical care to treat or prevent illness, disease, or injury. Collects, records, and maintains patient information, such as medical history, reports, and examination results. Operates on patients to remove, repair, or improve functioning of diseased or injured body parts and systems and delivers babies. Analyzes records, reports, test results, or examination information to diagnose medical condition of patient. Directs and coordinates activities of nurses, students, assistants, specialists, therapists, and other medical staff. Prepares reports for government or management of birth, death, and disease statistics, workforce evaluations, or medical status of individuals. Conducts research to study anatomy and develop or test medications, treatments, or procedures to prevent, or control disease or injury. Refers patient to medical specialist or other practitioner when necessary. Advises patients and community concerning diet, activity, hygiene, and disease prevention. Examines or conducts tests on patient to provide information on medical condition. Explains procedures and discusses test results on prescribed treatments with patients.

GOE Number, Interest Area, and Work Group: 14.02.01; Medical and Health Services; Medicine and Surgery. **Personality Type:** Investigative. Investigative occupations frequently involve working with ideas and require an extensive amount of thinking. These occupations can involve searching for facts and figuring out problems mentally. **Work Values:** Social Service; Ability Utilization; Achievement; Social Status; Responsibility. **Skills:** Reading Comprehension; Problem Identification; Science; Active Learning; Judgment and Decision Making; Identification of Key Causes. **Abilities:** *Cognitive*—Inductive Reasoning; Oral Expression; Problem Sensitivity; Written Comprehension; Information Ordering; Oral Comprehension. *Psychomotor*—Manual Dexterity; Arm-Hand Steadiness; Finger Dexterity. *Physical*—Static Strength; Dynamic Strength; Stamina. *Sensory*—Speech Clarity; Near Vision; Visual Color Discrimination. **General Work Activities:** *Information Input*—Monitoring Processes, Materials, and Surroundings; Getting Information Needed to Do the Job; Identifying Objects, Actions, and Events. *Mental Process*—Analyzing Data or Information; Making Decisions and Solving Problems; Updating and Using Job-Relevant Knowledge. *Work Output*—Documenting and Recording Information; Implementing Ideas and Programs; Handling and Moving Objects. *Interacting with Others*—Assisting and Caring for Others; Communicating with Persons Outside Organization; Communicating with Other Workers; Performing for or Working with the Public. **Physical Work Conditions:** Indoors; Special Uniform; Diseases or Infections. **Other Job Characteristics:** Consequence of Error; Importance of Being Exact or Accurate; Importance of Being Sure All Is Done.

Experience: Job Zone 5. Extensive skill, knowledge, and experience are needed. Very advanced communication and organizational skills are required. **Job Preparation:** SVP 8.0 and above—4 years to more than 10 years. **Knowledge:** Medicine and Dentistry; Biology; English Language; Therapy and Counseling; Administration and Management. **Instructional Programs:** 511201 Medicine (M.D.); 511307 Medical Immunology; 511901 Osteopathic Medicine (D.O.); 512705 Psychoanalysis; 512901 Aerospace Medicine Residency; 512902 Allergies and Immunology Residency; 512903 Anesthesiology Residency; 512904 Blood Banking Residency; 512905 Cardiology Residency; 512906 Chemical Pathology Residency; 512907 Child/Pediatric Neurology Residency; 512908 Child Psychiatry Residency; 512909 Colon and Rectal Surgery Residency; 512910 Critical Care Anesthesiology Residency; 512911 Critical Care Medicine Residency.

Related DOT Jobs: 070.101-022 General Practitioner; 070.101-026 Family Practitioner; 070.101-046 Public Health Physician; 070.101-078 Physician, Occupational; 070.101-082 Police Surgeon.

29-1063.00 Internists, General (Physicians)

Education: First professional degree

Employed: 576,870

Openings: 32,563

Projected Growth: 21.2%

Earnings: No data available.

Diagnose and provide nonsurgical treatment of diseases and injuries of internal organ systems. Provide care mainly for adults who have a wide range of problems associated with the internal organs.

Prescribes or administers treatment, therapy, medication, vaccination, and other specialized medical care to treat or prevent illness, disease, or injury. Directs and coordinates activities of nurses, students, assistants, specialists, therapists, and other medical staff. Analyzes records, reports, test results, or examination information to diagnose medical condition of patient. Explains procedures and discusses test results on prescribed treatments with patients. Monitors patients' condition and progress and re-evaluates treatments as necessary. Collects, records, and maintains patient information, such as medical history, reports, and examination results. Advises patients and community concerning diet, activity, hygiene, and disease prevention. Conducts research to study anatomy and develop or test medications, treatments, or procedures to prevent, or control disease or injury. Prepares reports for government or management of birth, death, and disease statistics, workforce evaluations, or medical status of individuals. Plans, implements, or administers health programs or standards in hospital, business, or community for information, prevention, or treatment of injury or illness. Operates on patients to remove, repair, or improve functioning of diseased or injured body parts and systems and delivers babies. Examines or conducts tests on patient to provide information on medical condition. Refers patient to medical specialist or other practitioner when necessary.

GOE Number, Interest Area, and Work Group: 14.02.01; Medical and Health Services; Medicine and Surgery. **Personality Type:** Investigative. Investigative occupations frequently involve working with ideas and require an extensive amount of thinking. These occupations can involve searching for facts and figuring out problems mentally. **Work Values:** Achievement; Ability Utilization; Social Status; Social Service; Responsibility. **Skills:** Reading Comprehension; Science; Problem Identification; Active Learning; Judgment and Decision Making; Identification of Key Causes. **Abilities:** *Cognitive*—Inductive Reasoning; Problem Sensitivity; Oral Expression; Written Comprehension; Information Ordering; Oral Comprehension. *Psychomotor*—Manual Dexterity; Arm-Hand Steadiness; Finger Dexterity. *Physical*—Static Strength; Dynamic Strength; Stamina. *Sensory*—Speech Clarity; Near Vision; Visual Color Discrimination. **General Work Activities:** *Information Input*—Monitoring Processes, Materials, and Surroundings; Getting Information Needed to Do the Job; Identifying Objects, Actions, and Events. *Mental Process*—Analyzing Data or Information; Making Decisions and Solving Problems; Updating and Using Job-Relevant Knowledge. *Work Output*—Implementing Ideas and Programs; Documenting and Recording Information; Handling and Moving Objects. *Interacting with Others*—Assisting and Caring for Others; Communicating with Persons Outside Organization; Performing for or Working with the Public; Communicating with Other Workers. **Physical Work Conditions:** Indoors; Special Uniform; Diseases or Infections. **Other Job Characteristics:** Consequence of Error; Importance of Being Exact or Accurate; Importance of Being Sure All Is Done.

Experience: Job Zone 5. Extensive skill, knowledge, and experience are needed. Very advanced communication and organiza-tional skills are required. **Job Preparation:** SVP 8.0 and above—4 years to more than 10 years. **Knowledge:** Medicine and Dentistry; Biology; English Language; Therapy and Counseling; Administration and Management. **Instructional Programs:** 511201 Medicine (M.D.); 511307 Medical Immunology; 511901 Osteopathic Medicine (D.O.); 512705 Psychoanalysis; 512901 Aerospace Medicine Residency; 512902 Allergies and Immunology Residency; 512903 Anesthesiology Residency; 512904 Blood Banking Residency; 512905 Cardiology Residency; 512906 Chemical Pathology Residency; 512907 Child/Pediatric Neurology Residency; 512908 Child Psychiatry Residency; 512909 Colon and Rectal Surgery Residency; 512910 Critical Care Anesthesiology Residency; 512911 Critical Care Medicine Residency.

Related DOT Job: 070.101-042 Internist.

29-1064.00 Obstetricians and Gynecologists
(Physicians)

Education: First professional degree

Employed: 576,870

Openings: 32,563

Projected Growth: 21.2%

Earnings: No data available.

Diagnose, treat, and help prevent diseases of women, especially those affecting the reproductive system and the process of childbirth.

Plans, implements, or administers health programs or standards in hospital, business, or community for information, prevention, or treatment of injury or illness. Operates on patients to remove, repair, or improve functioning of diseased or injured body parts and systems and delivers babies. Prescribes or administers treatment, therapy, medication, vaccination, and other specialized medical care to treat or prevent illness, disease, or injury. Analyzes records, reports, test results, or examination information to diagnose medical condition of patient. Directs and coordinates activities of nurses, students, assistants, specialists, therapists, and other medical staff. Collects, records, and maintains patient information, such as medical history, reports, and examination results. Explains procedures and discusses test results on prescribed treatments with patients. Advises patients and community concerning diet, activity, hygiene, and disease prevention. Refers patient to medical specialist or other practitioner when necessary. Examines or conducts tests on patient to provide information on medical condition. Monitors patients' condition and progress and re-evaluates treatments as necessary. Prepares reports for government or management of birth, death, and disease statistics, workforce evaluations, or medical status of individuals. Conducts research to study anatomy and develop or test medications, treatments, or procedures to prevent, or control disease or injury.

GOE Number, Interest Area, and Work Group: 14.02.01; Medical and Health Services; Medicine and Surgery. **Personality Type:** Investigative. Investigative occupations frequently involve working with ideas and require an extensive amount of thinking. These occupations can involve searching for facts and figuring out problems mentally. **Work Values:** Achievement; Ability Utilization; Social Status; Social Service; Responsibility. **Skills:** Reading Comprehension; Science; Problem Identification; Active Learning; Identification of Key Causes; Judgment and Decision Making. **Abilities:** *Cognitive*–Inductive Reasoning; Oral Expression; Problem Sensitivity; Written Comprehension; Oral Comprehension; Information Ordering. *Psychomotor*–Manual Dexterity; Arm-Hand Steadiness; Finger Dexterity. *Physical*–Static Strength; Dynamic Strength; Stamina. *Sensory*–Speech Clarity; Near Vision; Visual Color Discrimination. **General Work Activities:** *Information Input*–Monitoring Processes, Materials, and Surroundings; Identifying Objects, Actions, and Events; Getting Information Needed to Do the Job. *Mental Process*–Analyzing Data or Information; Making Decisions and Solving Problems; Updating and Using Job-Relevant Knowledge. *Work Output*–Documenting and Recording Information; Implementing Ideas and Programs; Handling and Moving Objects. *Interacting with Others*–Assisting and Caring for Others; Communicating with Persons Outside Organization; Performing for or Working with the Public; Communicating with Other Workers. **Physical Work Conditions:** Indoors; Special Uniform; Diseases or Infections. **Other Job Characteristics:** Consequence of Error; Importance of Being Exact or Accurate; Importance of Being Sure All Is Done.

Experience: Job Zone 5. Extensive skill, knowledge, and experience are needed. Very advanced communication and organizational skills are required. **Job Preparation:** SVP 8.0 and above—4 years to more than 10 years. **Knowledge:** Medicine and Dentistry; Biology; English Language; Therapy and Counseling; Administration and Management. **Instructional Programs:** 511201 Medicine (M.D.); 511307 Medical Immunology; 511901 Osteopathic Medicine (D.O.); 512705 Psychoanalysis; 512901 Aerospace Medicine Residency; 512902 Allergies and Immunology Residency; 512903 Anesthesiology Residency; 512904 Blood Banking Residency; 512905 Cardiology Residency; 512906 Chemical Pathology Residency; 512907 Child/Pediatric Neurology Residency; 512908 Child Psychiatry Residency; 512909 Colon and Rectal Surgery Residency; 512910 Critical Care Anesthesiology Residency; 512911 Critical Care Medicine Residency.

Related DOT Jobs: 070.101-034 Gynecologist; 070.101-054 Obstetrician.

29-1065.00 Pediatricians, General (Physicians)

Education: First professional degree

Employed: 576,870

Openings: 32,563

Projected Growth: 21.2%

Earnings: No data available.

Diagnose, treat, and help prevent children's diseases and injuries.

Plans, implements, or administers health programs or standards in hospital, business, or community for information, prevention, or treatment of injury or illness. Monitors patients' condition and progress and re-evaluates treatments as necessary. Analyzes records, reports, test results, or examination information to diagnose medical condition of patient. Refers patient to medical specialist or other practitioner when necessary. Prepares reports for government or management of birth, death, and disease statistics, workforce evaluations, or medical status of individuals. Conducts

research to study anatomy and develop or test medications, treatments, or procedures to prevent, or control disease or injury. Advises patients and community concerning diet, activity, hygiene, and disease prevention. Examines or conducts tests on patient to provide information on medical condition. Collects, records, and maintains patient information, such as medical history, reports, and examination results. Explains procedures and discusses test results on prescribed treatments with patients. Prescribes or administers treatment, therapy, medication, vaccination, and other specialized medical care to treat or prevent illness, disease, or injury. Directs and coordinates activities of nurses, students, assistants, specialists, therapists, and other medical staff. Operates on patients to remove, repair, or improve functioning of diseased or injured body parts and systems and delivers babies.

GOE Number, Interest Area, and Work Group: 14.02.01; Medical and Health Services; Medicine and Surgery. **Personality Type:** Investigative. Investigative occupations frequently involve working with ideas and require an extensive amount of thinking. These occupations can involve searching for facts and figuring out problems mentally. **Work Values:** Social Service; Ability Utilization; Achievement; Social Status; Responsibility. **Skills:** Reading Comprehension; Science; Problem Identification; Active Learning; Judgment and Decision Making; Identification of Key Causes. **Abilities:** *Cognitive*–Inductive Reasoning; Problem Sensitivity; Oral Expression; Written Comprehension; Information Ordering; Oral Comprehension. *Psychomotor*–Manual Dexterity; Arm-Hand Steadiness; Finger Dexterity. *Physical*–Static Strength; Dynamic Strength; Stamina. *Sensory*–Speech Clarity; Near Vision; Visual Color Discrimination. **General Work Activities:** *Information Input*–Monitoring Processes, Materials, and Surroundings; Identifying Objects, Actions, and Events; Getting Information Needed to Do the Job. *Mental Process*–Analyzing Data or Information; Making Decisions and Solving Problems; Updating and Using Job-Relevant Knowledge. *Work Output*–Implementing Ideas and Programs; Documenting and Recording Information; Handling and Moving Objects. *Interacting with Others*–Assisting and Caring for Others; Communicating with Persons Outside Organization; Performing for or Working with the Public; Communicating with Other Workers. **Physical Work Conditions:** Indoors; Special Uniform; Diseases or Infections. **Other Job Characteristics:** Consequence of Error; Importance of Being Exact or Accurate; Importance of Being Sure All Is Done.

Experience: Job Zone 5. Extensive skill, knowledge, and experience are needed. Very advanced communication and organizational skills are required. **Job Preparation:** SVP 8.0 and above—4 years to more than 10 years. **Knowledge:** Medicine and Dentistry; Biology; English Language; Therapy and Counseling; Administration and Management. **Instructional Programs:** 511201 Medicine (M.D.); 511307 Medical Immunology; 511901 Osteopathic Medicine (D.O.); 512705 Psychoanalysis; 512901 Aerospace Medicine Residency; 512902 Allergies and Immunology Residency; 512903 Anesthesiology Residency; 512904 Blood Banking Residency; 512905 Cardiology Residency; 512906 Chemical Pathology Residency; 512907 Child/Pediatric Neurology Residency; 512908 Child Psychiatry Residency; 512909 Colon and Rectal Surgery Residency; 512910 Critical Care Anesthesiology Residency; 512911 Critical Care Medicine Residency.

Related DOT Job: 070.101-066 Pediatrician.

29-1066.00 Psychiatrists (Physicians)

Education: First professional degree

Employed: 576,870

Openings: 32,563

Projected Growth: 21.2%

Earnings: No data available.

Diagnose, treat, and help prevent disorders of the mind.

Prescribes, directs, and administers psychotherapeutic treatments or medications to treat mental, emotional, or behavioral disorders. Examines or conducts laboratory or diagnostic tests on patient to provide information on general physical condition and mental disorder. Reviews and evaluates treatment procedures and outcomes of other psychiatrists and medical professionals. Prepares case reports and summaries for government agencies. Teaches, conducts research, and publishes findings to increase understanding of mental, emotional, behavioral states and disorders. Gathers and maintains patient information and records, including social and medical history obtained from patient, relatives, and other professionals. Analyzes and evaluates patient data and test or examination findings to diagnose nature and extent of mental disorder. Advises and informs guardians, relatives, and significant others of patient's condition and treatment.

GOE Number, Interest Area, and Work Group: 14.02.01; Medical and Health Services; Medicine and Surgery. **Personality Type:** Investigative. Investigative occupations frequently involve working with ideas and require an extensive amount of thinking. These occupations can involve searching for facts and figuring out problems mentally. **Work Values:** Social Service; Responsibility; Achievement; Ability Utilization; Autonomy. **Skills:** Social Perceptiveness; Reading Comprehension; Problem Identification; Writing; Judgment and Decision Making; Identification of Key Causes. **Abilities:** *Cognitive*—Oral Comprehension; Written Comprehension; Oral Expression; Written Expression; Problem Sensitivity. *Psychomotor*—none met the criteria. *Physical*—none met the criteria. *Sensory*—Speech Clarity; Near Vision; Speech Recognition. **General Work Activities:** *Information Input*—Getting Information Needed to Do the Job; Identifying Objects, Actions, and Events; Monitoring Processes, Materials, and Surroundings. *Mental Process*—Analyzing Data or Information; Making Decisions and Solving Problems; Updating and Using Job-Relevant Knowledge; Processing Information. *Work Output*—Documenting and Recording Information; Implementing Ideas and Programs; Performing General Physical Activities. *Interacting with Others*—Establishing and Maintaining Relationships; Assisting and Caring for Others; Communicating with Persons Outside Organization; Providing Consultation and Advice to Others. **Physical Work Conditions:** Indoors; Sitting; Standing. **Other Job Characteristics:** Consequence of Error; Importance of Being Sure All Is Done; Importance of Being Exact or Accurate.

Experience: Job Zone 5. Extensive skill, knowledge, and experience are needed. Very advanced communication and organizational skills are required. **Job Preparation:** SVP 8.0 and above—4 years to more than 10 years. **Knowledge:** Therapy and Counseling; Psychology; Medicine and Dentistry; English Language; Education and Training. **Instructional Programs:** 511201 Medicine (M.D.); 511307 Medical Immunology; 511901 Osteopathic Medicine (D.O.); 512705 Psychoanalysis; 512901 Aerospace Medicine Residency; 512902 Allergies and Immunology Residency; 512903 Anesthesiology Residency; 512904 Blood Banking Residency; 512905 Cardiology Residency; 512906 Chemical Pathology Residency; 512907 Child/Pediatric Neurology Residency; 512908 Child Psychiatry Residency; 512909 Colon and Rectal Surgery Residency; 512910 Critical Care Anesthesiology Residency; 512911 Critical Care Medicine Residency.

Related DOT Job: 070.107-014 Psychiatrist.

29-1067.00 Surgeons (Physicians)

Education: First professional degree

Employed: 576,870

Openings: 32,563

Projected Growth: 21.2%

Earnings: No data available.

Treat diseases, injuries, and deformities by using invasive methods such as manual manipulation or by using instruments and appliances.

Examines instruments, equipment, and operating room to ensure sterility. Examines patient to provide information on medical condition and patient's surgical risk. Refers patient to medical specialist or other practitioners when necessary. Operates on patient to correct deformities, repair injuries, prevent diseases, or improve or restore patient's functions. Conducts research to develop and test surgical techniques to improve operating procedures and outcomes. Analyzes patient's medical history, medication allergies, physical condition, and examination results to verify operation's necessity and to determine best procedure. Directs and coordinates activities of nurses, assistants, specialists, and other medical staff.

GOE Number, Interest Area, and Work Group: 14.02.01; Medical and Health Services; Medicine and Surgery. **Personality Type:** Investigative. Investigative occupations frequently involve working with ideas and require an extensive amount of thinking. These occupations can involve searching for facts and figuring out problems mentally. **Work Values:** Achievement; Ability Utilization; Social Status; Social Service; Recognition; Responsibility. **Skills:** Reading Comprehension; Science; Judgment and Decision Making; Problem Identification; Coordination; Writing; Critical Thinking. **Abilities:** *Cognitive*—Written Comprehension; Problem Sensitivity; Oral Expression; Deductive Reasoning; Inductive Reasoning; Information Ordering. *Psychomotor*—Manual Dexterity; Arm-Hand Steadiness; Finger Dexterity. *Physical*—Dynamic Strength; Trunk Strength; Extent Flexibility. *Sensory*—Near Vision; Depth Perception; Speech Clarity. **General Work Activities:** *Information Input*—Getting Information Needed to Do the Job; Identifying Objects, Actions, and Events; Inspecting Equipment, Structures, Materials. *Mental Process*—Analyzing Data or Information; Making Decisions and Solving Problems; Evaluating Information Against Standards; Updating and Using Job-Relevant Knowledge. *Work Output*—Handling and Moving Objects; Performing General Physical Activities; Implementing Ideas and Programs. *Interacting with Others*—Assisting and Caring for Others; Coordinating Work and Activities of Others; Communicating with Other Workers. **Physical Work Conditions:** Indoors; Special Uniform; Using Hands on Objects, Tools, or Controls. **Other Job Characteristics:** Consequence of Error; Importance of Being Exact or Accurate; Importance of Being Sure All Is Done.

Experience: Job Zone 5. Extensive skill, knowledge, and experience are needed. Very advanced communication and organizational skills are required. **Job Preparation:** SVP 8.0 and above—4 years to more than 10 years. **Knowledge:** Medicine and Dentistry; Biology; Chemistry; Administration and Management; Psychology. **Instructional Programs:** 511201 Medicine (M.D.); 511307 Medical Immunology; 511901 Osteopathic Medicine (D.O.); 512705 Psychoanalysis; 512901 Aerospace Medicine Residency; 512902 Allergies and Immunology Residency; 512903 Anesthesiology Residency; 512904 Blood Banking Residency; 512905 Cardiology Residency; 512906 Chemical Pathology Residency; 512907 Child/Pediatric Neurology Residency; 512908 Child Psychiatry Residency; 512909 Colon and Rectal Surgery Residency; 512910 Critical Care Anesthesiology Residency; 512911 Critical Care Medicine Residency.

Related DOT Job: 070.101-094 Surgeon.

29-1071.00 Physician Assistants (Physician Assistants)

Education: Bachelor's degree
Employed: 66,263
Openings: 6,142
Projected Growth: 48%
Earnings: $47,090

Provide healthcare services typically performed by a physician, under the supervision of a physician. Conduct complete physicals, provide treatment, and counsel patients. Prescribe medication, in some cases. Graduate from an accredited educational program for physician assistants.

Performs therapeutic procedures, such as injections, immunizations, suturing and wound care, and managing infection. Develops and implements patient management plans, records progress notes, and assists in provision of continuity of care. Interprets diagnostic test results for deviations from normal. Counsels patients regarding prescribed therapeutic regimens, normal growth and development, family planning, emotional problems of daily living, and health maintenance. Compiles patient medical data, including health history and results of physical examination. Examines patient. Administers or orders diagnostic tests, such as X-ray, electrocardiogram, and laboratory tests.

GOE Number, Interest Area, and Work Group: 14.02.01; Medical and Health Services; Medicine and Surgery. **Personality Type:** Investigative. Investigative occupations frequently involve working with ideas and require an extensive amount of thinking. These occupations can involve searching for facts and figuring out problems mentally. **Work Values:** Social Service; Achievement; Activity; Ability Utilization; Coworkers. **Skills:** Reading Comprehension; Problem Identification; Information Gathering; Active Listening; Active Learning. **Abilities:** *Cognitive*—Problem Sensitivity; Oral Comprehension; Oral Expression; Information Ordering; Written Expression. *Psychomotor*—Arm-Hand Steadiness;

Manual Dexterity; Finger Dexterity; Control Precision. *Physical*—none met the criteria. *Sensory*—Near Vision; Speech Clarity; Speech Recognition. **General Work Activities:** *Information Input*—Getting Information Needed to Do the Job; Identifying Objects, Actions, and Events; Monitoring Processes, Materials, and Surroundings. *Mental Process*—Making Decisions and Solving Problems; Updating and Using Job-Relevant Knowledge; Judging Qualities of Things, Services, Other People's Work; Processing Information. *Work Output*—Handling and Moving Objects; Documenting and Recording Information; Implementing Ideas and Programs; Controlling Machines and Processes. *Interacting with Others*—Assisting and Caring for Others; Communicating with Other Workers; Establishing and Maintaining Relationships. **Physical Work Conditions:** Indoors; Special Uniform; Standing. **Other Job Characteristics:** Consequence of Error; Importance of Being Exact or Accurate; Importance of Being Sure All Is Done.

Experience: Job Zone 4. A minimum of two to four years of work-related skill, knowledge, or experience is needed. **Job Preparation:** SVP 7.0 to less than 8.0—2 years to less than 10 years. **Knowledge:** Medicine and Dentistry; Biology; Chemistry; Therapy and Counseling; Psychology. **Instructional Program:** 510807 Physician Assistant.

Related DOT Jobs: 079.364-018 Physician Assistant; 079.367-018 Medical-Service Technician.

29-1081.00 Podiatrists (Podiatrists)

Education: First professional degree
Employed: 13,904
Openings: 562
Projected Growth: 10.5%
Earnings: $79,530

Diagnose and treat diseases and deformities of the human foot.

Treats bone, muscle, and joint disorders. Prescribes drugs. Refers patients to physician when symptoms indicative of systemic disorders, such as arthritis or diabetes, are observed in feet and legs. Performs surgery. Treats deformities by mechanical and electrical methods, such as whirlpool or paraffin baths and short wave and low voltage currents. Advises patients concerning continued treatment of disorders and foot care to prevent recurrence of disorders. Prescribes corrective footwear. Treats conditions, such as corns, calluses, ingrown nails, tumors, shortened tendons, bunions, cysts, and abscesses by surgical methods. Corrects deformities by means of plaster casts and strapping. Diagnoses ailments, such as tumors, ulcers, fractures, skin or nail diseases, and deformities, utilizing urinalysis, blood tests, and X rays. Makes and fits prosthetic appliances.

GOE Number, Interest Area, and Work Group: 14.04.01; Medical and Health Services; Health Specialties. **Personality Type:** Social. Social occupations frequently involve working with, communicating with, and teaching people. These occupations often involve helping or providing service to others. **Work Values:** Responsibility; Autonomy; Social Service; Achievement; Ability Utilization. **Skills:** Reading Comprehension; Active Learning; Judgment and Decision Making; Solution Appraisal; Active

Listening. **Abilities:** *Cognitive*—Deductive Reasoning; Oral Expression; Problem Sensitivity; Inductive Reasoning; Oral Comprehension. *Psychomotor*—Manual Dexterity; Control Precision; Finger Dexterity. *Physical*—Static Strength; Extent Flexibility; Dynamic Strength. *Sensory*—Near Vision; Depth Perception; Speech Clarity. **General Work Activities:** *Information Input*—Getting Information Needed to Do the Job; Identifying Objects, Actions, and Events; Monitoring Processes, Materials, and Surroundings. *Mental Process*—Analyzing Data or Information; Making Decisions and Solving Problems; Updating and Using Job-Relevant Knowledge. *Work Output*—Handling and Moving Objects; Implementing Ideas and Programs; Performing General Physical Activities. *Interacting with Others*—Assisting and Caring for Others; Communicating with Persons Outside Organization; Interpreting Meaning of Information to Others; Performing for or Working with the Public. **Physical Work Conditions:** Indoors; Diseases or Infections; Common Protective or Safety Attire; Special Uniform; Using Hands on Objects, Tools, or Controls. **Other Job Characteristics:** Consequence of Error; Importance of Being Sure All Is Done; Importance of Being Exact or Accurate.

Experience: Job Zone 4. A minimum of two to four years of work-related skill, knowledge, or experience is needed. **Job Preparation:** SVP 7.0 to less than 8.0—2 years to less than 10 years. **Knowledge:** Medicine and Dentistry; Biology; Chemistry; Therapy and Counseling; English Language. **Instructional Program:** 512101 Podiatry (D.P.M., D.P., Pod.D.).

Related DOT Job: 079.101-022 Podiatrist.

29-1111.00 Registered Nurses (Registered Nurses)

Education: Associate degree

Employed: 2,078,810

Openings: 195,231

Projected Growth: 21.7%

Earnings: $40,690

Assess patient health problems and needs, develop and implement nursing-care plans, and maintain medical records. Administer nursing care to ill, injured, convalescent, or disabled patients. Advise patients on health maintenance and disease prevention; provide case management. Obtain required licensing or registration. Includes advance practice nurses such as nurse practitioners, clinical nurse specialists, certified nurse midwives, and certified registered nurse anesthetists. Acquire specialized, formal, post-basic nursing education. Function in highly autonomous and specialized roles.

Refers students or patients to community agencies furnishing assistance and cooperates with agencies. Informs physician of patient's condition during anesthesia. Prescribes or recommends drugs or other forms of treatment, such as physical therapy, inhalation therapy, or related therapeutic procedures. Conducts specified laboratory tests. Maintains stock of supplies. Directs and coordinates infection control program in hospital. Contracts independently to render nursing care, usually to one patient, in hospital or private home. Provides prenatal and postnatal care to obstetrical patients under supervision of obstetrician. Discusses cases with physician or obstetrician. Advises and consults with

specified personnel concerning necessary precautions to be taken to prevent possible contamination or infection. Instructs on topics, such as health education, disease prevention, child birth, and home nursing and develops health improvement programs. Delivers infants and performs postpartum examinations and treatment. Orders, interprets, and evaluates diagnostic tests to identify and assess patient's condition. Prepares rooms, sterile instruments, equipment and supplies, and hands items to surgeon. Prepares patients for and assists with examinations. Records patient's medical information and vital signs. Administers stipulated emergency measures, and contacts obstetrician when deviations from standard are encountered during pregnancy or delivery. Observes patient's skin color, dilation of pupils, and computerized equipment to monitor vital signs. Provides health care, first aid, and immunization in facilities such as schools, hospitals, and industries. Administers local, inhalation, intravenous, and other anesthetics.

GOE Number, Interest Area, and Work Group: 14.02.01; Medical and Health Services; Medicine and Surgery. **Personality Type:** Social. Social occupations frequently involve working with, communicating with, and teaching people. These occupations often involve helping or providing service to others. **Work Values:** Social Service; Coworkers; Activity; Ability Utilization; Achievement. **Skills:** Reading Comprehension; Active Listening; Speaking; Service Orientation; Instructing. **Abilities:** *Cognitive*—Oral Expression; Oral Comprehension; Problem Sensitivity; Written Comprehension; Written Expression. *Psychomotor*—Reaction Time; Arm-Hand Steadiness; Manual Dexterity. *Physical*—Static Strength; Extent Flexibility; Trunk Strength. *Sensory*—Near Vision; Speech Clarity; Speech Recognition; Visual Color Discrimination. **General Work Activities:** *Information Input*—Monitoring Processes, Materials, and Surroundings; Getting Information Needed to Do the Job; Identifying Objects, Actions, and Events. *Mental Process*—Updating and Using Job-Relevant Knowledge; Making Decisions and Solving Problems; Evaluating Information Against Standards. *Work Output*—Documenting and Recording Information; Performing General Physical Activities; Handling and Moving Objects. *Interacting with Others*—Communicating with Other Workers; Assisting and Caring for Others; Establishing and Maintaining Relationships. **Physical Work Conditions:** Special Uniform; Indoors; Standing. **Other Job Characteristics:** Consequence of Error; Importance of Being Exact or Accurate; Importance of Being Sure All Is Done.

Experience: Job Zone 4. A minimum of two to four years of work-related skill, knowledge, or experience is needed. **Job Preparation:** SVP 7.0 to less than 8.0—2 years to less than 10 years. **Knowledge:** Medicine and Dentistry; Biology; Customer and Personal Service; Chemistry; Therapy and Counseling. **Instructional Programs:** 511601 Nursing (R.N. Training); 511603 Nursing, Adult Health (Post-R.N.); 511604 Nursing Anesthetist (Post-R.N.); 511605 Nursing, Family Practice (Post-R.N.); 511606 Nursing, Maternal/Child Health (Post-R.N.); 511607 Nursing Midwifery (Post-R.N.); 511608 Nursing Science (Post-R.N.); 511609 Nursing, Pediatric (Post-R.N.); 511610 Nursing, Psychiatric/Mental Health (Post-R.N.); 511611 Nursing, Public Health (Post-R.N.); 511612 Nursing, Surgical (Post-R.N.); 511699 Nursing, Other.

Related DOT Jobs: 075.124-010 Nurse, School; 075.124-014 Nurse, Community Health; 075.127-014 Nurse, Consultant; 075.127-026

Nurse Supervisor, Community-Health Nursing; 075.127-030 Nurse Supervisor, Evening-or-Night; 075.127-034 Nurse, Infection Control; 075.137-010 Nurse Supervisor, Occupational Health Nursing; 075.137-014 Nurse, Head; 075.167-010 Nurse, Supervisor; 075.264-010 Nurse Practitioner; 075.264-014 Nurse-Midwife; 075.364-010 Nurse, General Duty; 075.371-010 Nurse Anesthetist; 075.374-014 Nurse, Office; 075.374-018 Nurse, Private Duty; 075.374-022 Nurse, Staff, Occupational Health Nursing.

29-1121.00 Audiologists (Speech-Language Pathologists and Audiologists)

Education: Master's degree
Employed: 105,024
Openings: 9,862
Projected Growth: 38.5%
Earnings: $43,080

Assess and treat persons with hearing and related disorders. Fit hearing aids and provide auditory training. Perform research related to hearing problems.

Evaluates hearing and speech/language test results and medical or background information to determine hearing or speech impairment and treatment. Counsels and instructs clients in techniques to improve speech or hearing impairment, including sign language or lipreading. Conducts or directs research and reports findings on speech or hearing topics to develop procedures, technology, or treatments. Records and maintains reports of speech or hearing research or treatments. Participates in conferences or training to update or share knowledge of new hearing or speech disorder treatment methods or technology. Refers clients to additional medical or educational services if needed. Advises educators or other medical staff on speech or hearing topics. Administers hearing or speech/language evaluations, tests, or examinations to patients to collect information on type and degree of impairment. Plans and conducts prevention and treatment programs for clients' hearing or speech problems.

GOE Number, Interest Area, and Work Group: 14.06.01; Medical and Health Services; Medical Therapy. **Personality Type:** Social. Social occupations frequently involve working with, communicating with, and teaching people. These occupations often involve helping or providing service to others. **Work Values:** Social Service; Achievement; Ability Utilization; Coworkers; Authority; Creativity. **Skills:** Reading Comprehension; Writing; Instructing; Speaking; Problem Identification; Information Organization; Information Gathering; Learning Strategies; Active Learning; Critical Thinking. **Abilities:** *Cognitive*—Oral Expression; Oral Comprehension; Written Comprehension; Written Expression; Deductive Reasoning. *Psychomotor*—none met the criteria. *Physical*—none met the criteria. *Sensory*—Speech Clarity; Speech Recognition; Auditory Attention. **General Work Activities:** *Information Input*—Getting Information Needed to Do the Job; Identifying Objects, Actions, and Events; Monitoring Processes, Materials, and Surroundings. *Mental Process*—Making Decisions and Solving Problems; Updating and Using Job-Relevant Knowledge; Processing Information. *Work Output*—Documenting and Recording Information; Implementing Ideas and Programs; Handling and Moving Objects. *Interacting with Others*—Assisting and

Caring for Others; Interpreting Meaning of Information to Others; Establishing and Maintaining Relationships; Communicating with Persons Outside Organization; Providing Consultation and Advice to Others. **Physical Work Conditions:** Indoors; Sitting; Using Hands on Objects, Tools, or Controls. **Other Job Characteristics:** Importance of Being Exact or Accurate; Importance of Being Sure All Is Done; Consequence of Error; Importance of Being Aware of New Events.

Experience: Job Zone 4. A minimum of two to four years of work-related skill, knowledge, or experience is needed. **Job Preparation:** SVP 7.0 to less than 8.0—2 years to less than 10 years. **Knowledge:** Therapy and Counseling; English Language; Medicine and Dentistry; Education and Training; Personnel and Human Resources; Administration and Management. **Instructional Programs:** 510201 Communication Disorders, General; 510202 Audiology/Hearing Sciences; 510203 Speech-Language Pathology; 510204 Speech-Language Pathology and Audiology; 510299 Communication Disorders Sciences and Services, Other.

Related DOT Jobs: 076.101-010 Audiologist; 076.101-014 Director, Speech-and-Hearing Clinic.

29-1122.00 Occupational Therapists (Occupational Therapists)

Education: Bachelor's degree
Employed: 73,123
Openings: 6,484
Projected Growth: 34.2%
Earnings: $48,230

Assess, plan, organize, and participate in rehabilitative programs that help restore general independence and vocational, homemaking, and daily living skills to disabled persons.

Consults with rehabilitation team to select activity programs and coordinate occupational therapy with other therapeutic activities. Teaches individuals skills and techniques required for participation in activities and evaluates individual's progress. Requisitions supplies and equipment. Designs and constructs special equipment, such as splints and braces. Completes and maintains necessary records. Lays out materials for individual's use and cleans and repairs tools after therapy sessions. Recommends changes in individual's work or living environment, consistent with needs and capabilities. Selects activities which will help individual learn work skills within limits of individual's mental and physical capabilities. Plans programs and social activities to help patients learn work skills and adjust to handicaps. Plans, organizes, and conducts occupational therapy program in hospital, institutional, or community setting. Trains nurses and other medical staff in therapy techniques and objectives.

GOE Number, Interest Area, and Work Group: 14.06.01; Medical and Health Services; Medical Therapy. **Personality Type:** Social. Social occupations frequently involve working with, communicating with, and teaching people. These occupations often involve helping or providing service to others. **Work Values:** Social Service; Achievement; Ability Utilization; Coworkers; Social Status. **Skills:** Instructing; Implementation Planning; Active Listening; Social Perceptiveness; Speaking. **Abilities:** *Cogni-*

tive—Oral Expression; Oral Comprehension; Written Comprehension; Deductive Reasoning; Written Expression; Problem Sensitivity. *Psychomotor*—Multilimb Coordination. *Physical*—Static Strength; Extent Flexibility; Trunk Strength. *Sensory*—Speech Recognition. **General Work Activities:** *Information Input*—Getting Information Needed to Do the Job; Identifying Objects, Actions, and Events; Monitoring Processes, Materials, and Surroundings. *Mental Process*—Analyzing Data or Information; Updating and Using Job-Relevant Knowledge; Processing Information; Making Decisions and Solving Problems. *Work Output*—Performing General Physical Activities; Documenting and Recording Information; Handling and Moving Objects. *Interacting with Others*—Assisting and Caring for Others; Providing Consultation and Advice to Others; Teaching Others. **Physical Work Conditions:** Indoors; Sitting; Special Uniform. **Other Job Characteristics:** Frustrating Circumstances; Consequence of Error; Importance of Being Sure All Is Done; Importance of Being Aware of New Events.

Experience: Job Zone 4. A minimum of two to four years of work-related skill, knowledge, or experience is needed. **Job Preparation:** SVP 7.0 to less than 8.0—2 years to less than 10 years. **Knowledge:** Therapy and Counseling; Education and Training; Administration and Management; Psychology; Medicine and Dentistry; Customer and Personal Service; Clerical; English Language. **Instructional Program:** 512306 Occupational Therapy.

Related DOT Jobs: 076.121-010 Occupational Therapist; 076.167-010 Industrial Therapist.

29-1123.00 Physical Therapists (Physical Therapists)

Education: Master's degree

Employed: 119,999

Openings: 10,602

Projected Growth: 34%

Earnings: $56,600

Assess, plan, organize, and participate in rehabilitative programs that improve mobility, relieve pain, increase strength, and decrease or prevent deformity of patients suffering from disease or injury.

Evaluates, fits, and adjusts prosthetic and orthotic devices and recommends modification to orthotist. Evaluates effects of treatment at various stages and adjusts treatments to achieve maximum benefit. Tests and measures patient's strength, motor development, sensory perception, functional capacity, and respiratory and circulatory efficiency and records data. Instructs patient and family in treatment procedures to be continued at home. Plans and prepares written treatment program based on evaluation of patient data. Administers treatment involving application of physical agents, using equipment, moist packs, ultraviolet and infrared lamps, and ultrasound machines. Records treatment, response, and progress in patient's chart or enters information into computer. Administers traction to relieve pain, using traction equipment. Instructs, motivates, and assists patient to perform various physical activities and use supportive devices, such as crutches, canes, and prostheses. Administers massage, applying knowledge of massage techniques and body physiology. Administers manual exercises to improve and maintain function. Reviews physician's referral and patient's condition and medical records to determine physical therapy treatment required. Confers with medical practitioners to obtain additional information, suggest revisions in treatment, and integrate physical therapy into patient's care.

GOE Number, Interest Area, and Work Group: 14.06.01; Medical and Health Services; Medical Therapy. **Personality Type:** Social. Social occupations frequently involve working with, communicating with, and teaching people. These occupations often involve helping or providing service to others. **Work Values:** Social Service; Achievement; Ability Utilization; Coworkers; Social Status. **Skills:** Reading Comprehension; Writing; Judgment and Decision Making; Problem Identification; Active Listening. **Abilities:** *Cognitive*—Oral Expression; Problem Sensitivity; Written Expression; Oral Comprehension; Deductive Reasoning. *Psychomotor*—Manual Dexterity; Wrist-Finger Speed; Multilimb Coordination; Reaction Time. *Physical*—Static Strength; Trunk Strength; Explosive Strength; Dynamic Strength. *Sensory*—Speech Clarity; Speech Recognition. **General Work Activities:** *Information Input*—Getting Information Needed to Do the Job; Identifying Objects, Actions, and Events; Monitoring Processes, Materials, and Surroundings. *Mental Process*—Making Decisions and Solving Problems; Judging Qualities of Things, Services, Other People's Work; Updating and Using Job-Relevant Knowledge. *Work Output*—Handling and Moving Objects; Implementing Ideas and Programs; Performing General Physical Activities. *Interacting with Others*—Assisting and Caring for Others; Establishing and Maintaining Relationships; Coaching and Developing Others; Communicating with Persons Outside Organization. **Physical Work Conditions:** Indoors; Special Uniform; Standing. **Other Job Characteristics:** Consequence of Error; Importance of Being Sure All Is Done; Importance of Being Exact or Accurate.

Experience: Job Zone 4. A minimum of two to four years of work-related skill, knowledge, or experience is needed. **Job Preparation:** SVP 7.0 to less than 8.0—2 years to less than 10 years. **Knowledge:** Therapy and Counseling; Medicine and Dentistry; English Language; Psychology; Administration and Management. **Instructional Program:** 512308 Physical Therapy.

Related DOT Job: 076.121-014 Physical Therapist.

29-1124.00 Radiation Therapists (Radiation Therapists)

Education: Associate degree

Employed: 12,366

Openings: 829

Projected Growth: 16.7%

Earnings: $39,640

Provide radiation therapy to patients as prescribed by a radiologist according to established practices and standards. Review prescription and diagnosis. Act as liaison between physician and supportive care personnel. Prepare equipment such as immobilization, treatment, and protection devices. Maintain records, reports, and files. Assist in dosimetry procedures and tumor localization.

Maintains records, reports, and files as required. Observes and reassures patient during treatment and reports unusual reactions to physician. Acts as liaison with physicist and supportive care personnel. Prepares equipment, such as immobilization, treatment, and protection devices, and positions patient according to prescription. Enters data into computer and sets controls to operate and adjust equipment and regulate dosage. Follows principles of radiation protection for patient, self, and others. Reviews prescription, diagnosis, patient chart, and identification. Photographs treated area of patient and processes film.

GOE Number, Interest Area, and Work Group: 14.06.01; Medical and Health Services; Medical Therapy. **Personality Type:** Social. Social occupations frequently involve working with, communicating with, and teaching people. These occupations often involve helping or providing service to others. **Work Values:** Moral Values; Coworkers; Social Service; Security; Ability Utilization. **Skills:** Reading Comprehension; Science; Operation and Control; Critical Thinking; Coordination; Writing; Active Listening. **Abilities:** *Cognitive*—Written Comprehension; Problem Sensitivity; Deductive Reasoning; Oral Comprehension; Information Ordering. *Psychomotor*—Control Precision; Response Orientation; Wrist-Finger Speed. *Physical*—Extent Flexibility; Static Strength; Trunk Strength. *Sensory*—Near Vision; Speech Clarity; Far Vision. **General Work Activities:** *Information Input*—Monitoring Processes, Materials, and Surroundings; Getting Information Needed to Do the Job; Identifying Objects, Actions, and Events. *Mental Process*—Evaluating Information Against Standards; Making Decisions and Solving Problems; Processing Information. *Work Output*—Interacting with Computers; Documenting and Recording Information; Controlling Machines and Processes. *Interacting with Others*—Assisting and Caring for Others; Communicating with Other Workers; Communicating with Persons Outside Organization. **Physical Work Conditions:** Indoors; Common Protective or Safety Attire; Radiation; Special Uniform. **Other Job Characteristics:** Consequence of Error; Importance of Being Sure All Is Done; Importance of Being Exact or Accurate.

Experience: Job Zone 4. A minimum of two to four years of work-related skill, knowledge, or experience is needed. **Job Preparation:** SVP 7.0 to less than 8.0—2 years to less than 10 years. **Knowledge:** Medicine and Dentistry; Computers and Electronics; Therapy and Counseling; English Language; Clerical. **Instructional Program:** 510905 Nuclear Medical Technology/Technician.

Related DOT Job: 078.361-034 Radiation Therapist.

29-1125.00 Recreational Therapists (Recreational Therapists)

Education: Bachelor's degree
Employed: 38,737
Openings: 2,439
Projected Growth: 13.4%
Earnings: $27,760

Plan, direct, or coordinate medically approved recreation programs such as sports, trips, dramatics, social activities, and arts and crafts for patients in hospitals, nursing homes, or other institutions. Assess patient's condition and recommend appropriate recreational activity.

Confers with members of treatment team to determine patient's needs, capabilities, and interests, and to determine objectives of therapy. Conducts therapy sessions to improve patient's mental and physical well-being. Modifies content of patient's treatment program based on observation and evaluation of progress. Prepares and submits reports and charts to treatment team to reflect patient's reactions and evidence of progress or regression. Instructs patient in activities and techniques, such as sports, dance, gardening, music, or art, designed to meet his or her specific physical or psychological needs. Observes and confers with patient to assess patient's needs, capabilities, and interests and to devise treatment plan. Develops treatment plan to meet needs of patient, based on needs assessment and objectives of therapy. Plans, organizes, and participates in treatment programs and activities to facilitate the physical, mental, or emotional rehabilitation or health of patient. Evaluates patient's reactions to treatment experiences to assess progress or regression and effectiveness of treatment plan. Counsels and encourages patient to develop leisure activities.

GOE Number, Interest Area, and Work Group: 14.06.01; Medical and Health Services; Medical Therapy. **Personality Type:** Social. Social occupations frequently involve working with, communicating with, and teaching people. These occupations often involve helping or providing service to others. **Work Values:** Social Service; Achievement; Coworkers; Ability Utilization; Creativity. **Skills:** Monitoring; Service Orientation; Instructing; Social Perceptiveness; Learning Strategies; Solution Appraisal; Critical Thinking; Active Listening. **Abilities:** *Cognitive*—Oral Comprehension; Oral Expression; Written Expression; Inductive Reasoning; Problem Sensitivity. *Psychomotor*—Reaction Time; Response Orientation; Multilimb Coordination; Speed of Limb Movement. *Physical*—Gross Body Coordination; Explosive Strength; Stamina. *Sensory*—Speech Clarity; Near Vision; Visual Color Discrimination; Speech Recognition. **General Work Activities:** *Information Input*—Getting Information Needed to Do the Job; Monitoring Processes, Materials, and Surroundings; Identifying Objects, Actions, and Events. *Mental Process*—Scheduling Work and Activities; Organizing, Planning, and Prioritizing; Judging Qualities of Things, Services, Other People's Work; Making Decisions and Solving Problems. *Work Output*—Performing General Physical Activities; Documenting and Recording Information; Implementing Ideas and Programs. *Interacting with Others*—Assisting and Caring for Others; Establishing and Maintaining Relationships; Teaching Others. **Physical Work Conditions:** Indoors; Diseases or Infections; Standing. **Other Job Characteristics:** Frustrating Circumstances; Consequence of Error; Importance of Being Aware of New Events.

Experience: Job Zone 4. A minimum of two to four years of work-related skill, knowledge, or experience is needed. **Job Preparation:** SVP 7.0 to less than 8.0—2 years to less than 10 years. **Knowledge:** Therapy and Counseling; Psychology; Medicine and Dentistry; Education and Training; English Language. **Instructional Programs:** 310502 Adapted Physical Education/Therapeutic Recreation; 512309 Recreational Therapy.

Related DOT Jobs: 076.124-014 Recreational Therapist; 076.124-018 Horticultural Therapist; 076.127-010 Art Therapist; 076.127-014 Music Therapist; 076.127-018 Dance Therapist.

29-1126.00 Respiratory Therapists (Respiratory Therapists)

Education: Associate degree
Employed: 86,449
Openings: 8,553
Projected Growth: 42.6%
Earnings: $34,830

Assess, treat, and care for patients with breathing disorders. Assume primary responsibility for all respiratory care modalities, including the supervision of respiratory therapy technicians. Initiate and conduct therapeutic procedures; maintain patient records; and select, assemble, check, and operate equipment.

Determines requirements for treatment, such as type and duration of therapy, and medication and dosages. Monitors patient's physiological responses to therapy, such as vital signs, arterial blood gases, and blood chemistry changes. Determines most suitable method of administering inhalants, precautions to be observed, and potential modifications needed, compatible with physician's orders. Performs bronchopulmonary drainage and assists patient in performing breathing exercises. Consults with physician in event of adverse reactions. Maintains patient's chart that contains pertinent identification and therapy information. Orders repairs when necessary. Inspects and tests respiratory therapy equipment to ensure equipment is functioning safely and efficiently. Performs pulmonary function and adjusts equipment to obtain optimum results to therapy. Reads prescription, measures arterial blood gases, and reviews patient information to assess patient condition. Operates equipment to administer medicinal gases and aerosol drugs to patients following specified parameters of treatment. Sets up and operates devices, such as mechanical ventilators, therapeutic gas administration apparatus, environmental control systems, and aerosol generators. Demonstrates respiratory care procedures to trainees and other healthcare personnel.

GOE Number, Interest Area, and Work Group: 14.06.01; Medical and Health Services; Medical Therapy. **Personality Type:** Investigative. Investigative occupations frequently involve working with ideas and require an extensive amount of thinking. These occupations can involve searching for facts and figuring out problems mentally. **Work Values:** Social Service; Achievement; Coworkers; Ability Utilization; Activity; Security. **Skills:** Reading Comprehension; Problem Identification; Service Orientation; Monitoring; Active Listening. **Abilities:** *Cognitive*—Oral Comprehension; Written Comprehension; Problem Sensitivity; Oral Expression; Deductive Reasoning; Written Expression. *Psychomotor*—Control Precision; Reaction Time. *Physical*—none met the criteria. **General Work Activities:** *Information Input*—Monitoring Processes, Materials, and Surroundings; Getting Information Needed to Do the Job; Identifying Objects, Actions, and Events. *Mental Process*—Judging Qualities of Things, Services, Other People's Work; Evaluating Information Against Standards; Making Decisions and Solving Problems; Updating and Using Job-Relevant Knowledge. *Work Output*—Documenting and Recording Information; Handling and Moving Objects; Controlling Machines and Processes. *Interacting with Others*—Assisting and Caring for Others; Communicating with Other Workers; Establishing and

Maintaining Relationships. **Physical Work Conditions:** Indoors; Special Uniform; Using Hands on Objects, Tools, or Controls. **Other Job Characteristics:** Consequence of Error; Importance of Being Exact or Accurate; Importance of Being Sure All Is Done.

Experience: Job Zone 3. Previous work-related skill, knowledge, or experience is required. **Job Preparation:** SVP 6.0 to less than 7.0—More than 1 year and less than 4 years. **Knowledge:** Medicine and Dentistry; Biology; Therapy and Counseling; Chemistry; Psychology. **Instructional Program:** 510908 Respiratory Therapy Technician.

Related DOT Job: 076.361-014 Respiratory Therapist.

29-1127.00 Speech-Language Pathologists (Speech-Language Pathologists and Audiologists)

Education: Master's degree
Employed: 105,024
Openings: 9,862
Projected Growth: 38.5%
Earnings: $43,080

Assess and treat persons with speech, language, voice, and fluency disorders. Select alternative communication systems and teach their use. Perform research related to speech and language problems.

Advises educators or other medical staff on speech or hearing topics. Evaluates hearing and speech/language test results and medical or background information to determine hearing or speech impairment and treatment. Counsels and instructs clients in techniques to improve speech or hearing impairment, including sign language or lipreading. Conducts or directs research and reports findings on speech or hearing topics to develop procedures, technology, or treatments. Records and maintains reports of speech or hearing research or treatments. Administers hearing or speech/language evaluations, tests, or examinations to patients to collect information on type and degree of impairment. Participates in conferences or training to update or share knowledge of new hearing or speech disorder treatment methods or technology. Refers clients to additional medical or educational services if needed.

GOE Number, Interest Area, and Work Group: 14.06.01; Medical and Health Services; Medical Therapy. **Personality Type:** Social. Social occupations frequently involve working with, communicating with, and teaching people. These occupations often involve helping or providing service to others. **Work Values:** Social Service; Achievement; Ability Utilization; Coworkers; Authority; Creativity. **Skills:** Reading Comprehension; Writing; Instructing; Speaking; Critical Thinking; Information Organization; Information Gathering; Problem Identification; Learning Strategies; Active Learning. **Abilities:** *Cognitive*—Oral Expression; Oral Comprehension; Written Comprehension; Written Expression; Deductive Reasoning. *Psychomotor*—none met the criteria. *Physical*—none met the criteria. *Sensory*—Speech Clarity; Speech Recognition; Auditory Attention. **General Work Activities:** *Information Input*—Getting Information Needed to Do the Job; Identifying Objects, Actions, and Events; Monitoring Processes, Materials, and Surroundings. *Mental Process*—Making Decisions and Solving Problems; Updating and Using Job-Relevant Knowledge; Processing Information. *Work Output*—Documenting and

Recording Information; Implementing Ideas and Programs; Handling and Moving Objects. *Interacting with Others*—Assisting and Caring for Others; Interpreting Meaning of Information to Others; Communicating with Persons Outside Organization; Establishing and Maintaining Relationships; Providing Consultation and Advice to Others. **Physical Work Conditions:** Indoors; Sitting; Using Hands on Objects, Tools, or Controls. **Other Job Characteristics:** Importance of Being Exact or Accurate; Importance of Being Sure All Is Done; Consequence of Error; Importance of Being Aware of New Events.

Experience: Job Zone 4. A minimum of two to four years of work-related skill, knowledge, or experience is needed. **Job Preparation:** SVP 7.0 to less than 8.0—2 years to less than 10 years. **Knowledge:** Therapy and Counseling; English Language; Medicine and Dentistry; Education and Training; Personnel and Human Resources; Administration and Management. **Instructional Programs:** 510201 Communication Disorders, General; 510202 Audiology/Hearing Sciences; 510203 Speech-Language Pathology; 510204 Speech-Language Pathology and Audiology; 510299 Communication Disorders Sciences and Services, Other.

Related DOT Jobs: 076.101-014 Director, Speech-and-Hearing Clinic; 076.104-010 Voice Pathologist; 076.107-010 Speech Pathologist.

29-1131.00 Veterinarians (Veterinarians)

Education: First professional degree
Employed: 57,038
Openings: 3,227
Projected Growth: 24.7%
Earnings: $50,950

Diagnose and treat diseases and dysfunctions of animals. Engage in a particular function such as research and development, consultation, administration, technical writing, the sale or production of commercial products, or the rendering of technical services to commercial firms or other organizations. Includes veterinarians who inspect livestock.

Exchanges information with zoos and aquariums concerning care, transfer, sale, or trade of animals to maintain all-species, nationwide inventory. Conducts postmortem studies and analysis results to determine cause of death. Inspects housing and advises animal owners regarding sanitary measures, feeding, and general care to promote health of animals. Trains personnel in handling and care of animals. Ensures compliance with regulations governing humane and ethical treatment of animals used in scientific research. Oversees activities concerned with feeding, care, and maintenance of animal quarters to ensure compliance with laboratory regulations. Participates in research projects, plans procedures, and selects animals for scientific research based on knowledge of species and research principles. Establishes and conducts quarantine and testing procedures to prevent spread of disease and compliance with governmental regulations. Inspects and tests horses, sheep, poultry flocks, and other animals for diseases and inoculates animals against various diseases, including rabies. Examines animal to detect and determine nature of disease or injury and treats animal surgically or medically. Participates in planning and executing nutrition and reproduction programs for animals.

GOE Number, Interest Area, and Work Group: 03.02.01; Plants and Animals; Animal Care and Training. **Personality Type:** Investigative. Investigative occupations frequently involve working with ideas and require an extensive amount of thinking. These occupations can involve searching for facts and figuring out problems mentally. **Work Values:** Ability Utilization; Achievement; Responsibility; Autonomy; Social Status; Recognition. **Skills:** Reading Comprehension; Problem Identification; Active Learning; Science; Solution Appraisal; Information Gathering. **Abilities:** *Cognitive*—Deductive Reasoning; Problem Sensitivity; Inductive Reasoning; Oral Expression; Oral Comprehension. *Psychomotor*—Manual Dexterity; Finger Dexterity; Arm-Hand Steadiness. *Physical*—Static Strength; Extent Flexibility; Explosive Strength; Dynamic Strength. *Sensory*—Near Vision; Speech Clarity; Hearing Sensitivity. **General Work Activities:** *Information Input*—Identifying Objects, Actions, and Events; Getting Information Needed to Do the Job; Monitoring Processes, Materials, and Surroundings. *Mental Process*—Making Decisions and Solving Problems; Analyzing Data or Information; Updating and Using Job-Relevant Knowledge. *Work Output*—Implementing Ideas and Programs; Performing General Physical Activities; Handling and Moving Objects. *Interacting with Others*—Assisting and Caring for Others; Interpreting Meaning of Information to Others; Teaching Others. **Physical Work Conditions:** Indoors; Hazardous Situations; Common Protective or Safety Attire. **Other Job Characteristics:** Consequence of Error; Frustrating Circumstances; Importance of Being Sure All Is Done.

Experience: Job Zone 5. Extensive skill, knowledge, and experience are needed. Very advanced communication and organizational skills are required. **Job Preparation:** SVP 8.0 and above—4 years to more than 10 years. **Knowledge:** Biology; Medicine and Dentistry; English Language; Chemistry; Education and Training; Mathematics. **Instructional Programs:** 512401 Veterinary Medicine (D.V.M.); 512501 Veterinary Clinical Sciences (M.S., Ph.D.); 513001 Veterinary Anesthesiology; 513002 Veterinary Dentistry; 513003 Veterinary Dermatology; 513004 Veterinary Emergency and Critical Care Medicine; 513005 Veterinary Internal Medicine; 513006 Laboratory Animal Medicine; 513007 Veterinary Microbiology; 513008 Veterinary Nutrition; 513009 Veterinary Ophthalmology; 513010 Veterinary Pathology; 513011 Veterinary Practice; 513012 Veterinary Preventive Medicine; 513013 Veterinary Radiology.

Related DOT Jobs: 073.061-010 Veterinarian, Laboratory Animal Care; 073.101-010 Veterinarian; 073.101-014 Veterinarian, Poultry; 073.101-018 Zoo Veterinarian.

29-2000 Health Technologists and Technicians

29-2011.00 Medical and Clinical Laboratory Technologists (Clinical Laboratory Technologists and Technicians)

Education: Bachelor's degree
Employed: 313,040
Openings: 20,441
Projected Growth: 17%
Earnings: No data available.

Perform complex medical laboratory tests for diagnosis, treatment, and prevention of disease. Train or supervise staff.

Cultivates, isolates, and assists in identifying microbial organisms, and performs various tests on these microorganisms. Cuts images of chromosomes from photograph and identifies and arranges them in numbered pairs on karyotype chart, using standard practices. Examines slides under microscope to detect deviations from norm and to report abnormalities for further study. Selects and prepares specimen and media for cell culture, using aseptic technique and knowledge of medium components and cell requirements. Examines and tests human, animal, or other materials for microbial organisms. Conducts chemical analysis of body fluids, including blood, urine, and spinal fluid, to determine presence of normal and abnormal components. Performs tests to determine blood group, type, and compatibility for transfusion purposes. Studies blood cells, number of blood cells, and morphology, using microscopic technique. Conducts research under direction of Microbiologist or Biochemist. Communicates with physicians, family members, and researchers requesting technical information regarding test results. Calibrates and maintains equipment used in quantitative and qualitative analysis, such as spectrophotometers, calorimeters, flame photometers, and computer-controlled analyzers. Enters analysis of medical tests and clinical results into computer for storage. Prepares slide of cell culture to identify chromosomes, views and photographs slide under photo- microscope, and prints picture. Analyzes samples of biological material for chemical content or reaction. Harvests cell culture at optimum time sequence based on knowledge of cell cycle differences and culture conditions. Cuts, stains, and mounts biological material on slides for microscopic study and diagnosis, following standard laboratory procedures. Sets up, cleans, and maintains laboratory equipment.

GOE Number, Interest Area, and Work Group: 14.05.01; Medical and Health Services; Medical Technology. **Personality Type:** Investigative. Investigative occupations frequently involve working with ideas and require an extensive amount of thinking. These occupations can involve searching for facts and figuring out problems mentally. **Work Values:** Ability Utilization; Activity; Security; Achievement; Moral Values; Working Conditions. **Skills:** Reading Comprehension; Science; Writing; Active Learning; Information Gathering. **Abilities:** *Cognitive*—Written Expression; Information Ordering; Oral Expression; Oral Comprehension; Written Comprehension. *Psychomotor*—Arm-Hand Steadiness; Control Precision; Finger Dexterity. *Physical*—none met the criteria. *Sensory*—Near Vision; Speech Clarity; Visual Color Discrimination. **General Work Activities:** *Information Input*—Identifying Objects, Actions, and Events; Getting Information Needed to Do the Job; Monitoring Processes, Materials, and Surroundings. *Mental Process*—Updating and Using Job-Relevant Knowledge; Evaluating Information Against Standards; Analyzing Data or Information. *Work Output*—Documenting and Recording Information; Controlling Machines and Processes; Handling and Moving Objects. *Interacting with Others*—Communicating with Other Workers; Communicating with Persons Outside Organization; Interpreting Meaning of Information to Others. **Physical Work Conditions:** Common Protective or Safety Attire; Sitting; Indoors. **Other Job Characteristics:** Importance of Being Exact or Accurate; Importance of Being Sure All Is Done; Degree of Automation.

Experience: Job Zone 4. A minimum of two to four years of work-related skill, knowledge, or experience is needed. **Job Preparation:** SVP 7.0 to less than 8.0—2 years to less than 10 years. **Knowledge:** Biology; Chemistry; English Language; Medicine and Dentistry; Education and Training. **Instructional Program:** 511005 Medical Technology.

Related DOT Jobs: 078.121-010 Medical Technologist, Teaching Supervisor; 078.161-010 Medical Technologist, Chief; 078.261-010 Biochemistry Technologist; 078.261-014 Microbiology Technologist; 078.261-026 Cytogenetic Technologist; 078.261-030 Histotechnologist; 078.261-038 Medical Technologist; 078.261-046 Immunohematologist; 078.281-010 Cytotechnologist.

29-2012.00 Medical and Clinical Laboratory Technicians (Clinical Laboratory Technologists and Technicians)

Education: Bachelor's degree
Employed: 313,040
Openings: 20,441
Projected Growth: 17%
Earnings: No data available.

Perform routine medical laboratory tests for the diagnosis, treatment, and prevention of disease. Work under the supervision of a medical technologist.

Prepares standard volumetric solutions and reagents used in testing. Performs blood counts, using microscope. Incubates bacteria for specified period and prepares vaccines and serums by standard laboratory methods. Inoculates fertilized eggs, broths, or other bacteriological media with organisms. Tests vaccines for sterility and virus inactivity. Conducts quantitative and qualitative chemical analyses of body fluids, such as blood, urine, and spinal fluid. Conducts blood tests for transfusion purposes. Draws blood from patient, observing principles of asepsis to obtain blood sample.

GOE Number, Interest Area, and Work Group: 14.05.01; Medical and Health Services; Medical Technology. **Personality Type:** Realistic. Realistic occupations frequently involve work activities that include practical, hands-on problems and solutions. These occupations often deal with plants, animals, and real-world materials like wood, tools, and machinery. Many of the occupations require working outside and do not involve a lot of paperwork or working closely with others. **Work Values:** Ability Utilization; Moral Values; Security; Activity; Achievement. **Skills:** Science; Reading Comprehension; Product Inspection; Mathematics; Equipment Selection; Testing. **Abilities:** *Cognitive*—Information Ordering; Oral Comprehension; Written Comprehension; Flexibility of Closure; Number Facility. *Psychomotor*—Arm-Hand Steadiness; Wrist-Finger Speed; Control Precision; Finger Dexterity. *Physical*—Extent Flexibility; Trunk Strength. *Sensory*—Near Vision; Visual Color Discrimination; Speech Clarity. **General Work Activities:** *Information Input*—Identifying Objects, Actions, and Events; Monitoring Processes, Materials, and Surroundings; Getting Information Needed to Do the Job. *Mental Process*—Evaluating Information Against Standards; Processing Information; Updating and Using Job-Relevant Knowledge. *Work Output*—Controlling Machines and Processes; Documenting and Recording

Information; Handling and Moving Objects. *Interacting with Others*—Communicating with Other Workers; Performing Administrative Activities; Communicating with Persons Outside Organization. **Physical Work Conditions:** Indoors; Common Protective or Safety Attire; Diseases or Infections. **Other Job Characteristics:** Importance of Being Exact or Accurate; Consequence of Error; Importance of Being Sure All Is Done.

Experience: Job Zone 2. Some previous work-related skill, knowledge, or experience may be helpful, but usually is not needed. **Job Preparation:** SVP 4.00 to 5.99—6 months to less than 2 years. **Knowledge:** Chemistry; Biology; Medicine and Dentistry; Mathematics; Public Safety and Security. **Instructional Program:** 511005 Medical Technology.

Related DOT Jobs: 078.367-014 Specimen Processor; 078.381-014 Medical-Laboratory Technician; 078.687-010 Laboratory Assistant, Blood and Plasma; 559.361-010 Laboratory Technician, Pharmaceutical.

29-2021.00 Dental Hygienists (Dental Hygienists)

Education: Associate degree

Employed: 143,342

Openings: 15,372

Projected Growth: 40.5%

Earnings: $45,890

Clean teeth and examine oral areas, head, and neck for signs of oral disease. Educate patients on oral hygiene; take and develop X rays; apply fluoride or sealants.

Makes impressions for study casts. Applies fluorides and other cavity preventing agents to arrest dental decay. Conducts dental health clinics for community groups to augment services of dentist. Charts conditions of decay and disease for diagnosis and treatment by dentist. Places, carves, and finishes amalgam restorations. Removes sutures and dressings. Exposes and develops X-ray film. Examines gums, using probes, to locate periodontal recessed gums and signs of gum disease. Feels lymph nodes under patient's chin to detect swelling or tenderness that could indicate presence of oral cancer. Places and removes rubber dams, matrices, and temporary restorations. Removes excess cement from coronal surfaces of teeth. Provides clinical services and health education to improve and maintain oral health of school children. Cleans calcareous deposits, accretions, and stains from teeth and beneath margins of gums, using dental instruments. Administers local anesthetic agents. Feels and visually examines gums for sores and signs of disease.

GOE Number, Interest Area, and Work Group: 14.03.01; Medical and Health Services; Dentistry. **Personality Type:** Social. Social occupations frequently involve working with, communicating with, and teaching people. These occupations often involve helping or providing service to others. **Work Values:** Social Service; Moral Values; Security; Coworkers; Ability Utilization; Achievement. **Skills:** Reading Comprehension; Problem Identification; Active Learning; Service Orientation; Speaking; Science; Critical Thinking. **Abilities:** *Cognitive*—Oral Expression; Information Ordering; Problem Sensitivity; Oral Comprehension; Written Expression. *Psychomotor*—Arm-Hand Steadiness; Manual Dexterity; Finger Dexterity; Control Precision. *Physical*—none met the criteria. *Sensory*—Speech Clarity; Visual Color Discrimination. **General Work Activities:** *Information Input*—Identifying Objects, Actions, and Events; Getting Information Needed to Do the Job; Monitoring Processes, Materials, and Surroundings; Inspecting Equipment, Structures, Materials. *Mental Process*—Updating and Using Job-Relevant Knowledge; Processing Information; Judging Qualities of Things, Services, Other People's Work. *Work Output*—Handling and Moving Objects; Implementing Ideas and Programs; Controlling Machines and Processes; Documenting and Recording Information. *Interacting with Others*—Assisting and Caring for Others; Communicating with Other Workers; Performing for or Working with the Public. **Physical Work Conditions:** Indoors; Special Uniform; Common Protective or Safety Attire. **Other Job Characteristics:** Consequence of Error; Importance of Being Sure All Is Done; Importance of Being Exact or Accurate.

Experience: Job Zone 3. Previous work-related skill, knowledge, or experience is required. **Job Preparation:** SVP 6.0 to less than 7.0—More than 1 year and less than 4 years. **Knowledge:** Medicine and Dentistry; Biology; Education and Training; English Language; Customer and Personal Service. **Instructional Program:** 510602 Dental Hygienist.

Related DOT Job: 078.361-010 Dental Hygienist.

29-2031.00 Cardiovascular Technologists and Technicians (Cardiovascular Technologists and Technicians)

Education: Associate degree

Employed: 20,803

Openings: 3,458

Projected Growth: 39.4%

Earnings: $35,770

Conduct tests on patients' pulmonary or cardiovascular systems, for diagnostic purposes. Conduct or assist in electrocardiograms, cardiac catheterizations, pulmonary function tests, lung capacity tests, and similar tests.

Alerts physician to abnormalities or changes in patient responses. Explains testing procedures to patient to obtain cooperation and reduce anxiety. Records test results and other data into patient s record. Reviews test results with physician. Operates monitor to measure and record functions of cardiovascular and pulmonary systems, as part of cardiac catheterization team. Adjusts equipment and controls according to physicians' orders or established protocol. Prepares and positions patients for testing. Records analyses of heart and related structures, using ultrasound equipment. Compares measurements of heart wall thickness and chamber sizes to standard norms to identify abnormalities. Observes ultrasound display screen and listens to signals to acquire data for measurement of blood flow velocities. Records variations in action of heart muscle, using electrocardiograph. Observes gauges, recorder, and video screens of data analysis system, during imaging of cardiovascular system. Conducts tests of pulmonary system, using spirometer and other respiratory testing equipment. Conducts electrocardiogram, phonocardiogram, echocardiogram, stress testing, and other cardiovascular tests, using specialized electronic test equipment, recording devices, and laboratory instruments. Injects contrast medium into blood vessels of patient.

Activates fluoroscope and camera to produce images used to guide catheter through cardiovascular system. Operates diagnostic imaging equipment to produce contrast enhanced radiographs of heart and cardiovascular system. Enters factors such as amount and quality of radiation beam, and filming sequence, into computer. Assesses cardiac physiology and calculates valve areas from blood flow velocity measurements.

GOE Number, Interest Area, and Work Group: 14.05.01; Medical and Health Services; Medical Technology. **Personality Type:** Investigative. Investigative occupations frequently involve working with ideas and require an extensive amount of thinking. These occupations can involve searching for facts and figuring out problems mentally. **Work Values:** Social Service; Moral Values; Company Policies and Practices; Compensation; Security; Ability Utilization; Achievement. **Skills:** Reading Comprehension; Operation Monitoring; Mathematics; Operation and Control; Science; Active Listening; Writing. **Abilities:** *Cognitive*—Written Comprehension; Oral Comprehension; Oral Expression; Problem Sensitivity; Information Ordering. *Psychomotor*—Control Precision; Finger Dexterity; Reaction Time. *Physical*—none met the criteria. *Sensory*—Hearing Sensitivity; Auditory Attention; Visual Color Discrimination. **General Work Activities:** *Information Input*—Monitoring Processes, Materials, and Surroundings; Identifying Objects, Actions, and Events; Getting Information Needed to Do the Job. *Mental Process*—Making Decisions and Solving Problems; Updating and Using Job-Relevant Knowledge; Processing Information. *Work Output*—Documenting and Recording Information; Handling and Moving Objects; Controlling Machines and Processes. *Interacting with Others*—Communicating with Other Workers; Assisting and Caring for Others; Interpreting Meaning of Information to Others. **Physical Work Conditions:** Indoors; Special Uniform; Standing. **Other Job Characteristics:** Consequence of Error; Importance of Being Exact or Accurate; Importance of Being Sure All Is Done.

Experience: Job Zone 3. Previous work-related skill, knowledge, or experience is required. **Job Preparation:** SVP 6.0 to less than 7.0—More than 1 year and less than 4 years. **Knowledge:** Medicine and Dentistry; Computers and Electronics; Biology; Mathematics; English Language. **Instructional Programs:** 510901 Cardiovascular Technology/Technician; 510906 Perfusion Technology/Technician.

Related DOT Jobs: 078.161-014 Cardiopulmonary Technologist, Chief; 078.262-010 Pulmonary-Function Technician; 078.264-010 Holter Scanning Technician; 078.362-030 Cardiopulmonary Technologist; 078.362-034 Perfusionist; 078.362-050 Special Procedures Technologist, Cardiac Catheterization; 078.362-062 Stress Test Technician; 078.364-014 Echocardiograph Technician; 078.365-010 Cardiac Monitor Technician.

29-2032.00 Diagnostic Medical Sonographers (All Other Health Professionals, Paraprofessionals, and Technicians)

Education: No data available.
Employed: 459,490
Openings: No data available.
Projected Growth: No data available.
Earnings: $27,260

Produce ultrasonic recordings of internal organs, for use by physicians.

GOE Number, Interest Area, and Work Group: 14.05.01; Medical and Health Services; Medical Technology. **Instructional Programs:** 510899 Health and Medical Assistants, Other; 510910 Diagnostic Medical Sonography; 510999 Health and Medical Diagnostic and Treatment Services, Other; 511804 Orthoptics; 512601 Health Aide; 519999 Health Professions and Related Sciences, Other. **Note:** The Department of Labor has not collected some data for this job, so it has fewer details than the other descriptions.

29-2033.00 Nuclear Medicine Technologists (Nuclear Medicine Technologists)

Education: Associate degree
Employed: 13,967
Openings: 833
Projected Growth: 11.6%
Earnings: $39,610

Prepare, administer, and measure radioactive isotopes in therapeutic, diagnostic, and tracer studies using a variety of radioisotope equipment. Prepare stock solutions of radioactive materials and calculate doses to be administered by radiologists. Subject patients to radiation. Execute studies of blood volume, red cell survival, and fat absorption, following standard laboratory techniques.

Calculates, measures, prepares, and records radiation dosage or radiopharmaceuticals, using computer and following physician's prescription and X rays. Positions radiation fields, radiation beams, and patient to develop most effective treatment of patient's disease, using computer. Develops treatment procedures for nuclear medicine treatment programs. Disposes of radioactive materials and stores radiopharmaceuticals, following radiation safety procedures. Measures glandular activity, blood volume, red cell survival, and radioactivity of patient, using scanners, Geiger counters, scintillometers, and other laboratory equipment. Administers radiopharmaceuticals or radiation to patient to detect or treat diseases, using radioisotope equipment, under direction of physician. Maintains and calibrates radioisotope and laboratory equipment.

GOE Number, Interest Area, and Work Group: 14.05.01; Medical and Health Services; Medical Technology. **Personality Type:** Investigative. Investigative occupations frequently involve working with ideas and require an extensive amount of thinking. These occupations can involve searching for facts and figuring out problems mentally. **Work Values:** Moral Values; Ability Utilization; Achievement; Security; Social Service; Coworkers. **Skills:** Reading Comprehension; Mathematics; Instructing; Science; Speaking; Active Listening. **Abilities:** *Cognitive*—Oral Comprehension; Written Comprehension; Problem Sensitivity; Oral Expression; Written Expression. *Psychomotor*—Control Precision; Arm-Hand Steadiness; Finger Dexterity. *Physical*—Trunk Strength; Extent Flexibility. *Sensory*—Speech Clarity; Speech Recognition. **General Work Activities:** *Information Input*—Monitoring Processes, Materials, and Surroundings; Getting Information Needed to Do the Job; Identifying Objects, Actions, and Events. *Mental Process*—

Analyzing Data or Information; Processing Information; Making Decisions and Solving Problems; Updating and Using Job-Relevant Knowledge. *Work Output*—Interacting with Computers; Handling and Moving Objects; Documenting and Recording Information. *Interacting with Others*—Communicating with Other Workers; Interpreting Meaning of Information to Others; Coordinating Work and Activities of Others. **Physical Work Conditions:** Indoors; Radiation; Specialized Protective or Safety Attire. **Other Job Characteristics:** Consequence of Error; Importance of Being Exact or Accurate; Importance of Being Sure All Is Done.

Experience: Job Zone 4. A minimum of two to four years of work-related skill, knowledge, or experience is needed. **Job Preparation:** SVP 7.0 to less than 8.0—2 years to less than 10 years. **Knowledge:** Medicine and Dentistry; Biology; Computers and Electronics; Mathematics; Chemistry. **Instructional Program:** 510905 Nuclear Medical Technology/Technician.

Related DOT Jobs: 078.131-010 Chief Technologist, Nuclear Medicine; 078.261-034 Medical Radiation Dosimetrist; 078.361-018 Nuclear Medicine Technologist.

29-2034.00 Radiologic Technologists and Technicians (Radiologic Technologists and Technicians)

Education: Associate degree

Employed: 161,662

Openings: 11,306

Projected Growth: 20.1%

Earnings: $32,880

Take X rays and CAT scans or administer nonradioactive materials into patient's blood stream for diagnostic purposes. Includes technologists who specialize in other modalities such as computed tomography and magnetic resonance. Includes workers whose primary duties are to demonstrate portions of the human body on X-ray film or fluoroscopic screen.

GOE Number, Interest Area, and Work Group: 14.05.01; Medical and Health Services; Medical Technology. **Instructional Program:** 510907 Medical Radiologic Technology/Technician. **Note:** The Department of Labor has not collected some data for this job, so it has fewer details than the other descriptions.

29-2034.01 Radiologic Technologists (Radiologic Technologists and Technicians)

Education: Associate degree

Employed: 161,662

Openings: 11,306

Projected Growth: 20.1%

Earnings: $32,880

Take X rays and CAT scans or administer nonradioactive materials into patient's blood stream for diagnostic purposes. Includes technologists who specialize in other modalities such as computed tomography, ultrasound, and magnetic resonance.

Assigns duties to radiologic staff to maintain patient flows and achieve production goals. Administers oral or injected contrast media to patients. Keys commands and data into computer to document and specify scan sequences, adjust transmitters and receivers, or photograph certain images. Monitors use of radiation safety measures to comply with government regulations and to ensure safety of patients and staff. Reviews and evaluates developed X rays, video tape, or computer generated information for technical quality. Develops departmental operating budget and coordinates purchase of supplies and equipment. Demonstrates new equipment, procedures, and techniques and provides technical assistance to staff. Positions and immobilizes patient on examining table. Operates or oversees operation of radiologic and magnetic imaging equipment to produce photographs of the body for diagnostic purposes. Positions imaging equipment and adjusts controls to set exposure time and distance, according to specification of examination. Operates fluoroscope to aid physician to view and guide wire or catheter through blood vessels to area of interest. Monitors video display of area being scanned and adjusts density or contrast to improve picture quality. Explains procedures and observes patients to ensure safety and comfort during scan.

GOE Number, Interest Area, and Work Group: 14.05.01; Medical and Health Services; Medical Technology. **Personality Type:** Realistic. Realistic occupations frequently involve work activities that include practical, hands-on problems and solutions. These occupations often deal with plants, animals, and real-world materials like wood, tools, and machinery. Many of the occupations require working outside and do not involve a lot of paperwork or working closely with others. **Work Values:** Ability Utilization; Security; Moral Values; Achievement; Coworkers; Social Service. **Skills:** Reading Comprehension; Operation and Control; Operation Monitoring; Problem Identification; Critical Thinking; Active Listening; Mathematics; Equipment Selection. **Abilities:** *Cognitive*—Oral Expression; Written Comprehension; Oral Comprehension; Problem Sensitivity; Number Facility. *Psychomotor*—Wrist-Finger Speed; Control Precision; Finger Dexterity. *Physical*—none met the criteria. *Sensory*—Near Vision; Speech Clarity; Visual Color Discrimination. **General Work Activities:** *Information Input*—Monitoring Processes, Materials, and Surroundings; Getting Information Needed to Do the Job; Identifying Objects, Actions, and Events. *Mental Process*—Judging Qualities of Things, Services, Other People's Work; Updating and Using Job-Relevant Knowledge; Making Decisions and Solving Problems; Evaluating Information Against Standards. *Work Output*—Controlling Machines and Processes; Handling and Moving Objects; Documenting and Recording Information. *Interacting with Others*—Assisting and Caring for Others; Communicating with Persons Outside Organization; Interpreting Meaning of Information to Others. **Physical Work Conditions:** Special Uniform; Indoors; Radiation. **Other Job Characteristics:** Consequence of Error; Importance of Being Exact or Accurate; Importance of Being Sure All Is Done.

Experience: Job Zone 4. A minimum of two to four years of work-related skill, knowledge, or experience is needed. **Job Preparation:** SVP 7.0 to less than 8.0—2 years to less than 10 years. **Knowledge:** Medicine and Dentistry; Computers and Electronics; Biology; Chemistry; Public Safety and Security. **Instructional Program:** 510907 Medical Radiologic Technology/Technician.

Related DOT Jobs: 078.162-010 Radiologic Technologist, Chief; 078.362-026 Radiologic Technologist; 078.362-046 Special Procedures Technologist, Angiogram; 078.362-054 Special Procedures Technologist, Ct Scan; 078.362-058 Special Procedures Technologist, Magnetic Resonance Imaging (MRI); 078.364-010 Ultrasound Technologist.

29-2034.02 Radiologic Technicians (Radiologic Technologists and Technicians)

Education: Associate degree

Employed: 161,662

Openings: 11,306

Projected Growth: 20.1%

Earnings: $32,880

Maintain and use equipment and supplies necessary to demonstrate portions of the human body on X-ray film or fluoroscopic screen for diagnostic purposes.

Positions patient on examining table and adjusts equipment to obtain optimum view of specific body area requested by physician. Moves X-ray equipment into position and adjusts controls to set exposure factors, such as time and distance. Explains procedures to patient to reduce anxieties and obtain patient cooperation. Uses beam-restrictive devices and patient-shielding skills to minimize radiation exposure to patient and staff. Operates mobile X-ray equipment in operating room, emergency room, or at patient's bedside.

GOE Number, Interest Area, and Work Group: 14.05.01; Medical and Health Services; Medical Technology. **Personality Type:** Realistic. Realistic occupations frequently involve work activities that include practical, hands-on problems and solutions. These occupations often deal with plants, animals, and real-world materials like wood, tools, and machinery. Many of the occupations require working outside and do not involve a lot of paperwork or working closely with others. **Work Values:** Moral Values; Social Service; Security; Coworkers; Company Policies and Practices. **Skills:** Reading Comprehension; Active Listening; Operation and Control; Social Perceptiveness; Speaking. **Abilities:** *Cognitive*—Oral Expression; Written Comprehension; Oral Comprehension; Information Ordering; Memorization; Visualization. *Psychomotor*—Control Precision; Multilimb Coordination. *Physical*—Static Strength; Gross Body Coordination; Extent Flexibility. **General Work Activities:** *Information Input*—Getting Information Needed to Do the Job; Monitoring Processes, Materials, and Surroundings; Estimating Needed Characteristics. *Mental Process*—Processing Information; Updating and Using Job-Relevant Knowledge; Making Decisions and Solving Problems. *Work Output*—Controlling Machines and Processes; Handling and Moving Objects; Documenting and Recording Information; Performing General Physical Activities. *Interacting with Others*—Assisting and Caring for Others; Interpreting Meaning of Information to Others; Communicating with Other Workers. **Physical Work Conditions:** Indoors; Radiation; Special Uniform. **Other Job Characteristics:** Consequence of Error; Importance of Being Exact or Accurate; Importance of Being Sure All Is Done.

Experience: Job Zone 4. A minimum of two to four years of work-related skill, knowledge, or experience is needed. **Job Prepara-**

tion: SVP 7.0 to less than 8.0—2 years to less than 10 years. **Knowledge:** Medicine and Dentistry; Biology; English Language; Computers and Electronics; Customer and Personal Service. **Instructional Program:** 510907 Medical Radiologic Technology/Technician.

Related DOT Job: 078.362-026 Radiologic Technologist.

29-2041.00 Emergency Medical Technicians and Paramedics (Emergency Medical Technicians)

Education: Postsecondary vocational training

Employed: 149,961

Openings: 23,138

Projected Growth: 31.6%

Earnings: $20,290

Assess injuries, administer emergency medical care, and extricate trapped individuals. Transport injured or sick persons to medical facilities.

Monitors patient's condition, using electrocardiograph. Assists in removal and transport of victims to treatment center. Assists treatment center personnel to obtain information relating to circumstances of emergency. Observes, records, and reports patient's condition, and reactions to drugs and treatment, to physician. Assesses nature and extent of illness or injury to establish and prioritize medical procedures. Maintains vehicles and medical and communication equipment, and replenishes first-aid equipment and supplies. Assists treatment center personnel to obtain and record victim's vital statistics, and to administer emergency treatment. Administers first-aid treatment and life support care to sick or injured persons in prehospital setting. Communicates with treatment center personnel to arrange reception of victims and to receive instructions for further treatment. Drives mobile intensive care unit to specified location, following instructions from emergency medical dispatcher.

GOE Number, Interest Area, and Work Group: 04.04.01; Law, Law Enforcement, and Public Safety; Public Safety: Emergency Responding. **Personality Type:** Social. Social occupations frequently involve working with, communicating with, and teaching people. These occupations often involve helping or providing service to others. **Work Values:** Social Service; Achievement; Coworkers; Ability Utilization; Security; Variety. **Skills:** Coordination; Service Orientation; Problem Identification; Judgment and Decision Making; Social Perceptiveness; Active Listening. **Abilities:** *Cognitive*—Problem Sensitivity; Oral Expression; Oral Comprehension; Speed of Closure; Deductive Reasoning. *Psychomotor*—Reaction Time; Manual Dexterity; Control Precision. *Physical*—Static Strength; Extent Flexibility; Explosive Strength; Trunk Strength. *Sensory*—Speech Recognition; Speech Clarity. **General Work Activities:** *Information Input*—Monitoring Processes, Materials, and Surroundings; Identifying Objects, Actions, and Events; Getting Information Needed to Do the Job. *Mental Process*—Updating and Using Job-Relevant Knowledge; Making Decisions and Solving Problems; Processing Information; Analyzing Data or Information. *Work Output*—Performing General Physical Activities; Handling and Moving Objects; Operating Vehicles or Equipment. *Interacting with Others*—Assisting and Caring for Others; Communicating with Other Workers; Performing for or Working with the Public; Establishing and Maintaining Relationships. **Physical Work Conditions:** Special Uniform; Common Protective or Safety Attire; Using Hands on Objects, Tools, or Controls; Diseases or Infections. **Other Job Characteristics:** Consequence of Error; Importance of Being Exact or Accurate; Importance of Being Sure All Is Done.

Experience: Job Zone 2. Some previous work-related skill, knowledge, or experience may be helpful, but usually is not needed. **Job Preparation:** SVP 4.00 to 5.99—6 months to less than 2 years. **Knowledge:** Medicine and Dentistry; Therapy and Counseling; Transportation; Biology; Telecommunications. **Instructional Program:** 510904 Emergency Medical Technology/Technician.

Related DOT Jobs: 079.364-026 Paramedic; 079.374-010 Emergency Medical Technician.

29-2051.00 Dietetic Technicians (Dietetic Technicians)

Education: No data available.

Employed: 23,950

Openings: No data available.

Projected Growth: No data available.

Earnings: $19,520

Assist dietitians in the provision of food service and nutritional programs. Under the supervision of dietitians, plan and produce meals based on established guidelines, teach principles of food and nutrition, or counsel individuals.

Supervises food production and service. Standardizes recipes and tests new products for use in facility. Selects, schedules, and conducts orientation and in-service education programs. Obtains and evaluates dietary histories of individuals to plan nutritional programs. Plans menus based on established guidelines. Develops job specifications, job descriptions, and work schedules. Assists in referrals for continuity of patient care. Guides individuals and families in food selection, preparation, and menu planning, based upon nutritional needs. Assists in implementing established cost control procedures.

GOE Number, Interest Area, and Work Group: 14.08.01; Medical and Health Services; Health Protection and Promotion. **Personality Type:** Social. Social occupations frequently involve working with, communicating with, and teaching people. These occupations often involve helping or providing service to others. **Work Values:** Coworkers; Social Service; Working Conditions; Moral Values; Security. **Skills:** Reading Comprehension; Writing; Learning Strategies; Active Listening; Speaking. **Abilities:** *Cognitive*—Oral Expression; Fluency of Ideas; Oral Comprehension; Written Comprehension; Information Ordering. *Psychomotor*—Multilimb Coordination. *Physical*—none met the criteria. *Sensory*—Speech Clarity; Far Vision; Auditory Attention. **General Work Activities:** *Information Input*—Getting Information Needed to Do the Job; Identifying Objects, Actions, and Events; Monitoring Processes, Materials, and Surroundings. *Mental Process*—Evaluating Information Against Standards; Analyzing Data or Information; Scheduling Work and Activities; Making Decisions and Solving Problems. *Work Output*—Implementing Ideas and Programs; Documenting and Recording Information; Performing General Physical Activities. *Interacting with Others*—Assisting and Caring for

Others; Teaching Others; Performing for or Working with the Public. **Physical Work Conditions:** Indoors; Sitting; Special Uniform; Using Hands on Objects, Tools, or Controls; Hazardous Situations; Standing. **Other Job Characteristics:** Importance of Being Sure All Is Done; Consequence of Error; Importance of Being Exact or Accurate.

Experience: Job Zone 4. A minimum of two to four years of work-related skill, knowledge, or experience is needed. **Job Preparation:** SVP 7.0 to less than 8.0—2 years to less than 10 years. **Knowledge:** Customer and Personal Service; Education and Training; Biology; English Language; Administration and Management. **Instructional Programs:** 190501 Foods and Nutrition Studies, General; 190502 Foods and Nutrition Science; 190503 Dietetics/Human Nutritional Services; 200404 Dietician Assistant.

Related DOT Job: 077.124-010 Dietetic Technician.

29-2052.00 Pharmacy Technicians (Pharmacy Technicians)

Education: Moderate-term O-T-J training

Employed: 108,690

Openings: 14,132

Projected Growth: 15.7%

Earnings: No data available.

Prepare medications under the direction of a pharmacist. Measure, mix, count out, label, and record amounts and dosages of medications.

Counts stock and enters data in computer to maintain inventory records. Receives and stores incoming supplies. Processes records of medication and equipment dispensed to hospital patient, computes charges, and enters data in computer. Prepares intravenous (IV) packs, using sterile technique, under supervision of hospital pharmacist. Assists pharmacist in preparing and dispensing medication. Mixes pharmaceutical preparations, fills bottles with prescribed tablets and capsules, and types labels for bottles. Cleans equipment and sterilizes glassware according to prescribed methods.

GOE Number, Interest Area, and Work Group: 14.02.01; Medical and Health Services; Medicine and Surgery. **Personality Type:** Conventional. Conventional occupations frequently involve following set procedures and routines. These occupations can include working with data and details more than with ideas. Usually there is a clear line of authority to follow. **Work Values:** Working Conditions; Coworkers; Moral Values; Activity; Security. **Skills:** Reading Comprehension; Active Listening; Mathematics; Science; Problem Identification. **Abilities:** *Cognitive*—Number Facility; Information Ordering; Oral Comprehension; Written Comprehension; Written Expression; Category Flexibility. *Psychomotor*—none met the criteria. *Physical*—none met the criteria. *Sensory*—Near Vision. **General Work Activities:** *Information Input*—Getting Information Needed to Do the Job; Identifying Objects, Actions, and Events; Monitoring Processes, Materials, and Surroundings. *Mental Process*—Processing Information; Evaluating Information Against Standards; Updating and Using Job-Relevant Knowledge. *Work Output*—Handling and Moving Objects; Implementing Ideas and Programs; Documenting and Recording Information. *Inter-*

acting with Others—Communicating with Other Workers; Performing Administrative Activities; Monitoring and Controlling Resources. **Physical Work Conditions:** Indoors; Standing; Sitting; Using Hands on Objects, Tools, or Controls. **Other Job Characteristics:** Consequence of Error; Importance of Being Exact or Accurate; Importance of Being Sure All Is Done.

Experience: Job Zone 2. Some previous work-related skill, knowledge, or experience may be helpful, but usually is not needed. **Job Preparation:** SVP 4.00 to 5.99—6 months to less than 2 years. **Knowledge:** Clerical; Medicine and Dentistry; Mathematics; Computers and Electronics; Chemistry. **Instructional Program:** 510805 Pharmacy Technician/Assistant.

Related DOT Jobs: 074.381-010 Pharmacist Assistant; 074.382-010 Pharmacy Technician.

29-2053.00 Psychiatric Technicians (Psychiatric Technicians)

Education: Postsecondary vocational training

Employed: 66,045

Openings: 15,167

Projected Growth: 10.9%

Earnings: $20,890

Care for mentally impaired or emotionally disturbed individuals, following physicians' instructions and hospital procedures. Monitor patients' physical and emotional well-being; report to medical staff. Participate in rehabilitation and treatment programs, help with personal hygiene, and administer oral medications and hypodermic injections.

Contacts patient's relatives by telephone to arrange family conferences. Observes patients to detect behavior patterns and reports observations to medical staff. Administers oral medications and hypodermic injections, following physician's prescriptions and hospital procedures. Completes initial admittance forms for new patients. Leads prescribed individual or group therapy sessions as part of specific therapeutic procedures. Intervenes to restrain violent or potentially violent or suicidal patients by verbal or physical means as required. Helps patients with their personal hygiene, such as bathing and keeping beds, clothing, and living areas clean. Issues medications from dispensary and maintains records in accordance with specified procedures. Takes and records measures of patient's general physical condition, such as pulse, temperature, and respiration, to provide daily information.

GOE Number, Interest Area, and Work Group: 14.07.01; Medical and Health Services; Patient Care and Assistance. **Personality Type:** Social. Social occupations frequently involve working with, communicating with, and teaching people. These occupations often involve helping or providing service to others. **Work Values:** Social Service; Coworkers; Supervision, Human Relations; Security; Company Policies and Practices. **Skills:** Social Perceptiveness; Reading Comprehension; Service Orientation; Active Listening; Speaking. **Abilities:** *Cognitive*—Problem Sensitivity; Oral Comprehension; Oral Expression; Written Comprehension; Selective Attention; Written Expression. *Psychomotor*—Reaction Time. *Physical*—Explosive Strength. *Sensory*—Speech Recognition. **General Work Activities:** *Information Input*—Getting Informa-

tion Needed to Do the Job; Identifying Objects, Actions, and Events; Monitoring Processes, Materials, and Surroundings. *Mental Process*—Judging Qualities of Things, Services, Other People's Work; Updating and Using Job-Relevant Knowledge; Making Decisions and Solving Problems. *Work Output*—Performing General Physical Activities; Documenting and Recording Information; Handling and Moving Objects. *Interacting with Others*—Assisting and Caring for Others; Communicating with Other Workers; Establishing and Maintaining Relationships. **Physical Work Conditions:** Indoors; Special Uniform; Standing. **Other Job Characteristics:** Consequence of Error; Importance of Being Exact or Accurate; Importance of Being Sure All Is Done.

Experience: Job Zone 3. Previous work-related skill, knowledge, or experience is required. **Job Preparation:** SVP 6.0 to less than 7.0—More than 1 year and less than 4 years. **Knowledge:** Psychology; Therapy and Counseling; Customer and Personal Service; Medicine and Dentistry; Clerical. **Instructional Program:** 511502 Psychiatric/Mental Health Services Technician.

Related DOT Job: 079.374-026 Psychiatric Technician.

29-2054.00 Respiratory Therapy Technicians (All Other Health Professionals, Paraprofessionals, and Technicians)

Education: No data available.

Employed: 459,490

Openings: No data available.

Projected Growth: No data available.

Earnings: $27,260

Provide specific, well-defined respiratory care procedures, under the direction of respiratory therapists and physicians.

GOE Number, Interest Area, and Work Group: 14.06.01; Medical and Health Services; Medical Therapy. **Instructional Programs:** 510899 Health and Medical Assistants, Other; 510910 Diagnostic Medical Sonography; 510999 Health and Medical Diagnostic and Treatment Services, Other; 511804 Orthoptics; 512601 Health Aide; 519999 Health Professions and Related Sciences, Other. **Note:** The Department of Labor has not collected some data for this job, so it has fewer details than the other descriptions.

29-2055.00 Surgical Technologists (Surgical Technologists)

Education: Postsecondary vocational training

Employed: 54,038

Openings: 9,182

Projected Growth: 41.8%

Earnings: $25,780

Assist in operations, under the supervision of surgeons, registered nurses, or other surgical personnel. Help set up operating room. Prepare and transport patients for surgery. Adjust lights and equipment. Pass instruments and other supplies to surgeons and surgeons' assistants. Hold retractors and cut sutures. Help count sponges, needles, supplies, and instruments.

Maintains supply of fluids, such as plasma, saline, blood, and glucose for use during operation. Washes and sterilizes equipment, using germicides and sterilizers. Hands instruments and supplies to surgeon, holds retractors and cuts sutures, and performs other tasks as directed by surgeon during operation. Counts sponges, needles, and instruments before and after operation. Cleans operating room. Aids team to don gowns and gloves. Assists team members to place and position patient on table. Places equipment and supplies in operating room and arranges instruments, according to instruction. Puts dressings on patient following surgery. Scrubs arms and hands and dons gown and gloves.

GOE Number, Interest Area, and Work Group: 14.02.01; Medical and Health Services; Medicine and Surgery. **Personality Type:** Realistic. Realistic occupations frequently involve work activities that include practical, hands-on problems and solutions. These occupations often deal with plants, animals, and real-world materials like wood, tools, and machinery. Many of the occupations require working outside and do not involve a lot of paperwork or working closely with others. **Work Values:** Moral Values; Security; Social Service; Supervision, Human Relations; Company Policies and Practices. **Skills:** Reading Comprehension; Active Listening; Coordination; Critical Thinking; Active Learning. **Abilities:** *Cognitive*—Oral Comprehension; Information Ordering; Number Facility; Oral Expression; Written Comprehension. *Psychomotor*—Arm-Hand Steadiness; Finger Dexterity; Reaction Time. *Physical*—none met the criteria. **General Work Activities:** *Information Input*—Getting Information Needed to Do the Job; Estimating Needed Characteristics; Monitoring Processes, Materials, and Surroundings. *Mental Process*—Processing Information; Evaluating Information Against Standards; Updating and Using Job-Relevant Knowledge. *Work Output*—Handling and Moving Objects; Implementing Ideas and Programs; Performing General Physical Activities. *Interacting with Others*—Assisting and Caring for Others; Communicating with Other Workers; Monitoring and Controlling Resources. **Physical Work Conditions:** Indoors; Special Uniform; Standing. **Other Job Characteristics:** Consequence of Error; Importance of Being Sure All Is Done; Importance of Being Exact or Accurate.

Experience: Job Zone 3. Previous work-related skill, knowledge, or experience is required. **Job Preparation:** SVP 6.0 to less than 7.0—More than 1 year and less than 4 years. **Knowledge:** Medicine and Dentistry; Biology; English Language; Mathematics; Chemistry. **Instructional Program:** 510909 Surgical/Operating Room Technician.

Related DOT Job: 079.374-022 Surgical Technician.

29-2056.00 Veterinary Technologists and Technicians (Veterinary Technologists and Technicians)

Education: Associate degree
Employed: 32,035
Openings: 2,822
Projected Growth: 16.2%
Earnings: $19,870

Perform medical tests in a laboratory environment for use in the treatment and diagnosis of diseases in animals. Prepare vaccines and serums for prevention of diseases. Prepare tissue samples and take blood samples. Execute laboratory tests such as urinalysis and blood counts. Clean and sterilize instruments and materials; maintain equipment and machines.

GOE Number, Interest Area, and Work Group: 03.02.01; Plants and Animals; Animal Care and Training. **Instructional Program:** 510808 Veterinarian Assistant/Animal Health Technician. **Note:** The Department of Labor has not collected some data for this job, so it has fewer details than the other descriptions.

29-2061.00 Licensed Practical and Licensed Vocational Nurses (Licensed Practical Nurses)

Education: Postsecondary vocational training
Employed: 691,953
Openings: 43,314
Projected Growth: 19.7%
Earnings: $26,940

Care for ill, injured, convalescent, or disabled persons in hospitals, nursing homes, clinics, private homes, group homes, and similar institutions. Work under the supervision of a registered nurse. Obtain required licensing.

Assembles and uses such equipment as catheters, tracheotomy tubes, and oxygen suppliers. Provides medical treatment and personal care to patients in private home settings. Takes and records patients' vital signs. Inventories and requisitions supplies. Collects samples, such as urine, blood, and sputum, from patients for testing and performs routine laboratory tests on samples. Sterilizes equipment and supplies, using germicides, sterilizer, or autoclave. Records food and fluid intake and output. Assists in delivery, care, and feeding of infants. Cleans rooms, makes beds, and answers patients' calls. Washes and dresses bodies of deceased persons. Administers specified medication, orally or by subcutaneous or intramuscular injection, and notes time and amount on patients' charts. Applies compresses, ice bags, and hot water bottles. Observes patients and reports adverse reactions to medication or treatment to medical personnel in charge. Dresses wounds, gives enemas, douches, alcohol rubs, and massages. Prepares or examines food trays for prescribed diet and feeds patients. Bathes, dresses, and assists patients in walking and turning.

GOE Number, Interest Area, and Work Group: 14.07.01; Medical and Health Services; Patient Care and Assistance. **Personality Type:** Social. Social occupations frequently involve working with, communicating with, and teaching people. These occupations often involve helping or providing service to others. **Work Values:** Social Service; Coworkers; Achievement; Activity; Ability Utilization. **Skills:** Service Orientation; Reading Comprehension; Social Perceptiveness; Problem Identification; Critical Thinking; Active Listening. **Abilities:** *Cognitive*—Oral Expression; Oral Comprehension; Problem Sensitivity; Number Facility; Written Comprehension; Time Sharing. *Psychomotor*—Reaction Time; Arm-Hand Steadiness. *Physical*—Static Strength; Stamina. *Sensory*—Sound Localization. **General Work Activities:** *Information Input*—Monitoring Processes, Materials, and Surroundings; Identifying Objects, Actions, and Events; Getting Information Needed to Do the Job. *Mental Process*—Updating and Using Job-Relevant

Knowledge; Making Decisions and Solving Problems; Evaluating Information Against Standards; Judging Qualities of Things, Services, Other People's Work. *Work Output*—Performing General Physical Activities; Handling and Moving Objects; Documenting and Recording Information. *Interacting with Others*—Assisting and Caring for Others; Communicating with Other Workers; Communicating with Persons Outside Organization; Establishing and Maintaining Relationships. **Physical Work Conditions:** Indoors; Special Uniform; Standing. **Other Job Characteristics:** Consequence of Error; Importance of Being Exact or Accurate; Importance of Being Sure All Is Done.

Experience: Job Zone 3. Previous work-related skill, knowledge, or experience is required. **Job Preparation:** SVP 6.0 to less than 7.0—More than 1 year and less than 4 years. **Knowledge:** Medicine and Dentistry; Customer and Personal Service; Biology; Psychology; Chemistry; Clerical. **Instructional Program:** 511613 Practical Nurse (L.P.N. Training).

Related DOT Job: 079.374-014 Nurse, Licensed Practical.

29-2071.00 Medical Records and Health Information Technicians (Medical Records and Health Information Technicians)

Education: Associate degree

Employed: 92,366

Openings: 11,453

Projected Growth: 43.9%

Earnings: $20,590

Compile, process, and maintain medical records of hospital and clinic patients in a manner consistent with medical, administrative, ethical, legal, and regulatory requirements of the healthcare system. Process, maintain, compile, and report patient information for health requirements and standards.

Maintains variety of health record indexes and storage and retrieval systems. Compiles medical care and census data for statistical reports on diseases treated, surgery performed, and use of hospital beds. Reviews records for completeness and to abstract and code data, using standard classification systems, and to identify and compile patient data. Assists in special studies or research, as needed. Contacts discharged patients, their families, and physicians to maintain registry with follow-up information, such as quality of life and length of survival of cancer patients. Enters data, such as demographic characteristics, history and extent of disease, diagnostic procedures and treatment into computer. Compiles and maintains medical records of patients to document condition and treatment and to provide data for research studies. Prepares statistical reports, narrative reports and graphic presentations of tumor registry data for use by hospital staff, researchers, and other users.

GOE Number, Interest Area, and Work Group: 09.07.02; Business Detail; Records Processing: Preparation and Maintenance. **Personality Type:** Conventional. Conventional occupations frequently involve following set procedures and routines. These occupations can include working with data and details more than with ideas. Usually there is a clear line of authority to follow. **Work Values:** Moral Values; Working Conditions; Activity; Secu-

rity; Supervision, Human Relations. **Skills:** Information Organization; Reading Comprehension; Writing; Information Gathering; Active Listening; Speaking. **Abilities:** *Cognitive*—Written Comprehension; Written Expression; Oral Comprehension; Mathematical Reasoning; Information Ordering. *Psychomotor*—Wrist-Finger Speed. *Physical*—none met the criteria. *Sensory*—Near Vision. **General Work Activities:** *Information Input*—Getting Information Needed to Do the Job; Identifying Objects, Actions, and Events; Monitoring Processes, Materials, and Surroundings. *Mental Process*—Processing Information; Evaluating Information Against Standards; Updating and Using Job-Relevant Knowledge. *Work Output*—Documenting and Recording Information; Interacting with Computers; Handling and Moving Objects. *Interacting with Others*—Performing Administrative Activities; Communicating with Other Workers; Communicating with Persons Outside Organization. **Physical Work Conditions:** Indoors; Sitting; Special Uniform. **Other Job Characteristics:** Consequence of Error; Importance of Being Exact or Accurate; Importance of Being Sure All Is Done.

Experience: Job Zone 3. Previous work-related skill, knowledge, or experience is required. **Job Preparation:** SVP 6.0 to less than 7.0—More than 1 year and less than 4 years. **Knowledge:** Clerical; Computers and Electronics; Mathematics; English Language; Medicine and Dentistry. **Instructional Program:** 510707 Medical Records Technology/Technician.

Related DOT Jobs: 079.262-014 Medical Record Coder; 079.362-014 Medical Record Technician; 079.362-018 Tumor Registrar; 169.167-046 Public Health Registrar.

29-2081.00 Opticians, Dispensing (Dispensing Opticians)

Education: Moderate-term O-T-J training

Employed: 71,467

Openings: 5,799

Projected Growth: 13.8%

Earnings: $22,440

Design, measure, fit, and adapt lenses and frames for client, according to written optical prescription or specification. Assist client in selecting frames. Measure customer for size of eyeglasses; coordinate frames with facial and eye measurements and optical prescription. Prepare work order for optical laboratory, including instructions for grinding and mounting lenses in frames. Verify exactness of finished lens spectacles. Adjust frame and lens position to fit client. Shape or reshape frames.

Fabricates lenses to prescription specifications. Instructs clients in adapting to wearing and caring for eyeglasses. Prepares work order and instructions for grinding lenses and fabricating eyeglasses. Determines client's current lens prescription, when necessary, using lensometer or lens analyzer and client's eyeglasses. Evaluates prescription in conjunction with client's vocational and avocational visual requirements. Measures client's bridge and eye size, temple length, vertex distance, pupillary distance, and optical centers of eyes, using measuring devices. Assists client in selecting frames according to style and color, coordinating frames with facial and eye measurements and optical prescription.

Repairs damaged frames. Heats, shapes, or bends plastic or metal frames to adjust eyeglasses to fit client, using pliers and hands. Recommends specific lenses, lens coatings, and frames to suit client needs. Verifies finished lenses are ground to specification. Grinds lens edges or applies coating to lenses.

GOE Number, Interest Area, and Work Group: 14.04.01; Medical and Health Services; Health Specialties. **Personality Type:** Enterprising. Enterprising occupations frequently involve starting up and carrying out projects. These occupations can involve leading people and making many decisions. They sometimes require risk taking and often deal with business. **Work Values:** Social Service; Achievement; Security; Social Status; Responsibility. **Skills:** Problem Identification; Reading Comprehension; Critical Thinking; Product Inspection; Time Management; Mathematics; Writing. **Abilities:** *Cognitive*—Oral Expression; Oral Comprehension; Written Comprehension; Problem Sensitivity; Number Facility. *Psychomotor*—Control Precision; Arm-Hand Steadiness; Finger Dexterity. *Physical*—none met the criteria. *Sensory*—Speech Recognition. **General Work Activities:** *Information Input*—Getting Information Needed to Do the Job; Identifying Objects, Actions, and Events; Estimating Needed Characteristics. *Mental Process*—Evaluating Information Against Standards; Judging Qualities of Things, Services, Other People's Work; Analyzing Data or Information; Updating and Using Job-Relevant Knowledge. *Work Output*—Implementing Ideas and Programs; Handling and Moving Objects; Documenting and Recording Information. *Interacting with Others*—Performing for or Working with the Public; Assisting and Caring for Others; Communicating with Persons Outside Organization. **Physical Work Conditions:** Indoors; Sitting; Using Hands on Objects, Tools, or Controls. **Other Job Characteristics:** Importance of Being Exact or Accurate; Importance of Being Sure All Is Done; Consequence of Error.

Experience: Job Zone 4. A minimum of two to four years of work-related skill, knowledge, or experience is needed. **Job Preparation:** SVP 7.0 to less than 8.0—2 years to less than 10 years. **Knowledge:** Administration and Management; Customer and Personal Service; Sales and Marketing; English Language; Production and Processing. **Instructional Program:** 511801 Opticianry/Dispensing Optician.

Related DOT Jobs: 299.361-010 Optician, Dispensing; 299.361-014 Optician Apprentice, Dispensing.

29-2091.00 Orthotists and Prosthetists (All Other Health Professionals, Paraprofessionals, and Technicians)

Education: No data available.

Employed: 459,490

Openings: No data available.

Projected Growth: No data available.

Earnings: $27,260

Assist patients with disabling conditions of limbs and spine or with partial or total absence of limb by fitting and preparing orthopedic braces or prostheses.

Repairs and maintains orthopedic prosthetic devices, using hand tools. Designs orthopedic and prosthetic devices, according to physician's prescription. Examines, measures, and evaluates patients' needs in relation to disease and functional loss. Maintains patients' records. Instructs patients in use of orthopedic or prosthetic devices. Selects materials and components, and makes cast measurements, model modifications, and layouts, using measuring equipment. Assists physician in formulating specifications and prescription for orthopedic and/or prosthetic devices. Supervises laboratory activities or activities of prosthetic assistants and support staff relating to development of orthopedic or prosthetic devices. Lectures and demonstrates to colleagues and other professionals concerned with orthopedics or prosthetics. Participates in research to modify design, fit, and function of orthopedic or prosthetic devices. Fits patients for device, using static and dynamic alignments. Evaluates device on patient and makes adjustments to assure fit, function, comfort, and quality.

GOE Number, Interest Area, and Work Group: 14.05.01; Medical and Health Services; Medical Technology. **Personality Type:** Social. Social occupations frequently involve working with, communicating with, and teaching people. These occupations often involve helping or providing service to others. **Work Values:** Social Service; Achievement; Ability Utilization; Moral Values; Security; Company Policies and Practices; Working Conditions; Compensation. **Skills:** Speaking; Active Listening; Reading Comprehension; Social Perceptiveness; Product Inspection; Technology Design. **Abilities:** *Cognitive*—Oral Expression; Oral Comprehension; Written Comprehension; Visualization; Written Expression. *Psychomotor*—Control Precision; Arm-Hand Steadiness; Manual Dexterity. *Physical*—Extent Flexibility; Gross Body Coordination; Explosive Strength; Stamina. *Sensory*—Speech Clarity; Near Vision; Speech Recognition. **General Work Activities:** *Information Input*—Getting Information Needed to Do the Job; Inspecting Equipment, Structures, Materials; Monitoring Processes, Materials, and Surroundings. *Mental Process*—Updating and Using Job-Relevant Knowledge; Analyzing Data or Information; Making Decisions and Solving Problems. *Work Output*—Drafting and Specifying Technical Devices; Performing General Physical Activities; Handling and Moving Objects; Documenting and Recording Information. *Interacting with Others*—Assisting and Caring for Others; Communicating with Persons Outside Organization; Communicating with Other Workers. **Physical Work Conditions:** Indoors; Using Hands on Objects, Tools, or Controls; Standing. **Other Job Characteristics:** Importance of Being Exact or Accurate; Importance of Being Sure All Is Done; Consequence of Error.

Experience: Job Zone 3. Previous work-related skill, knowledge, or experience is required. **Job Preparation:** SVP 6.0 to less than 7.0—More than 1 year and less than 4 years. **Knowledge:** Medicine and Dentistry; Design; Therapy and Counseling; Customer and Personal Service; Education and Training; Building and Construction. **Instructional Programs:** 510899 Health and Medical Assistants, Other; 510910 Diagnostic Medical Sonography; 510999 Health and Medical Diagnostic and Treatment Services, Other; 511804 Orthoptics; 512601 Health Aide; 519999 Health Professions and Related Sciences, Other.

Related DOT Jobs: 078.261-018 Orthotist; 078.261-022 Prosthetist; 078.361-022 Orthotics Assistant; 078.361-026 Prosthetics Assistant; 078.664-010 Orthopedic Assistant.

29-9000 Other Healthcare Practitioners and Technical Occupations

29-9011.00 Occupational Health and Safety Specialists (All Other Health Professionals, Paraprofessionals, and Technicians)

Education: No data available.

Employed: 459,490

Openings: No data available.

Projected Growth: No data available.

Earnings: $27,260

Review, evaluate, and analyze work environments. Design programs and procedures to control, eliminate, and prevent disease or injury caused by chemical, physical, and biological agents or ergonomic factors. Conduct inspections and enforce adherence to laws and regulations governing the health and safety of individuals. Work in the public or private sector.

Recommends measures to ensure maximum employee protection. Participates in educational meetings to instruct employees in matters pertaining to occupational health and prevention of accidents. Conducts evaluations of exposure to ionizing and non-ionizing radiation and to noise. Prepares reports including observations, analysis of contaminants, and recommendation for control and correction of hazards. Collaborates with engineers and physicians to institute control and remedial measures for hazardous and potentially hazardous conditions of equipment. Collects samples of dust, gases, vapors, and other potentially toxic materials for analysis. Reviews physicians' reports and conducts worker studies to determine if diseases or illnesses are job related. Prepares and calibrates equipment used to collect and analyze samples. Prepares documents to be used in legal proceedings and gives testimony in court proceedings. Investigates adequacy of ventilation, exhaust equipment, lighting, and other conditions which may affect employee health, comfort, or efficiency. Uses cost-benefit analysis to justify money spent.

GOE Number, Interest Area, and Work Group: 04.04.02; Law, Law Enforcement, and Public Safety; Public Safety: Regulations Enforcement. **Personality Type:** Social. Social occupations frequently involve working with, communicating with, and teaching people. These occupations often involve helping or providing service to others. **Work Values:** Autonomy; Ability Utilization; Company Policies and Practices; Responsibility; Achievement; Working Conditions; Security; Compensation. **Skills:** Speaking; Reading Comprehension; Writing; Information Gathering; Problem Identification; Science. **Abilities:** *Cognitive*—Written Comprehension; Problem Sensitivity; Oral Expression; Oral Comprehension; Written Expression. *Psychomotor*—Manual Dexterity; Finger Dexterity; Control Precision; Wrist-Finger Speed. *Physical*—Trunk Strength; Gross Body Coordination. *Sensory*—Near Vision; Speech Clarity; Visual Color Discrimination; Speech Recognition. **General Work Activities:** *Information Input*—Getting Information Needed to Do the Job; Inspecting Equipment, Structures, Materials; Identifying Objects, Actions, and Events. *Mental Process*—Judging Qualities of Things, Services, Other People's Work; Evaluating Information Against Standards; Analyzing Data or Information. *Work Output*—Documenting and Recording Information; Implementing Ideas and Programs; Handling and Moving Objects; Drafting and Specifying Technical Devices. *Interacting with Others*—Communicating with Persons Outside Organization; Communicating with Other Workers; Providing Consultation and Advice to Others. **Physical Work Conditions:** Indoors; Contaminants; Using Hands on Objects, Tools, or Controls. **Other Job Characteristics:** Consequence of Error; Importance of Being Sure All Is Done; Importance of Being Exact or Accurate.

Experience: Job Zone 5. Extensive skill, knowledge, and experience are needed. Very advanced communication and organizational skills are required. **Job Preparation:** SVP 8.0 and above—4 years to more than 10 years. **Knowledge:** Public Safety and Security; Chemistry; Medicine and Dentistry; Education and Training; Law, Government and Jurisprudence; Physics. **Instructional Programs:** 510899 Health and Medical Assistants, Other; 510910 Diagnostic Medical Sonography; 510999 Health and Medical Diagnostic and Treatment Services, Other; 511804 Orthoptics; 512601 Health Aide; 519999 Health Professions and Related Sciences, Other.

Related DOT Job: 079.161-010 Industrial Hygienist.

29-9012.00 Occupational Health and Safety Technicians (All Other Health Professionals, Paraprofessionals, and Technicians)

Education: No data available.

Employed: 459,490

Openings: No data available.

Projected Growth: No data available.

Earnings: $27,260

Collect data on work environments for analysis by occupational health and safety specialists. Implement and conduct evaluation of programs designed to limit chemical, physical, biological, and ergonomic risks to workers.

GOE Number, Interest Area, and Work Group: 04.04.02; Law, Law Enforcement, and Public Safety; Public Safety: Regulations Enforcement. **Instructional Programs:** 510899 Health and Medical Assistants, Other; 510910 Diagnostic Medical Sonography; 510999 Health and Medical Diagnostic and Treatment Services, Other; 511804 Orthoptics; 512601 Health Aide; 519999 Health Professions and Related Sciences, Other. **Note:** The Department of Labor has not collected some data for this job, so it has fewer details than the other descriptions.

29-9091.00 Athletic Trainers (All Other Health Professionals and Paraprofessionals)

Education: Associate degree

Employed: 509,525

Openings: 79,627

Projected Growth: 35%

Earnings: No data available.

Evaluate, advise, and treat athletes in recovering from injury, avoiding injury, or maintaining peak physical fitness.

Evaluates physical condition of athletes and advises or prescribes routine and corrective exercises to strengthen muscles. Administers emergency first aid, treats minor chronic disabilities, or refers injured person to physician. Recommends special diets to improve health, increase stamina, and reduce weight of athletes. Wraps ankles, fingers, wrists or other body parts with synthetic skin, gauze, or adhesive tape to support muscles and ligaments. Massages body parts to relieve soreness, strains, and bruises.

GOE Number, Interest Area, and Work Group: 14.08.01; Medical and Health Services; Health Protection and Promotion. **Personality Type:** Social. Social occupations frequently involve working with, communicating with, and teaching people. These occupations often involve helping or providing service to others. **Work Values:** Social Service; Autonomy; Ability Utilization; Achievement; Variety; Responsibility; Working Conditions; Supervision, Human Relations. **Skills:** Active Listening; Speaking; Problem Identification; Service Orientation; Information Gathering; Reading Comprehension. **Abilities:** *Cognitive*—Problem Sensitivity; Oral Expression; Information Ordering; Inductive Reasoning; Oral Comprehension. *Psychomotor*—Wrist-Finger Speed; Manual Dexterity; Multilimb Coordination. *Physical*—Extent Flexibility; Static Strength; Stamina. *Sensory*—Speech Clarity; Auditory Attention; Speech Recognition. **General Work Activities:** *Information Input*—Getting Information Needed to Do the Job; Identifying Objects, Actions, and Events; Monitoring Processes, Materials, and Surroundings. *Mental Process*—Making Decisions and Solving Problems; Updating and Using Job-Relevant Knowledge; Judging Qualities of Things, Services, Other People's Work; Analyzing Data or Information. *Work Output*—Performing General Physical Activities; Handling and Moving Objects; Implementing Ideas and Programs. *Interacting with Others*—Assisting and Caring for Others; Establishing and Maintaining Relationships; Communicating with Other Workers. **Physical Work Conditions:** Standing; Using Hands on Objects, Tools, or Controls; Indoors. **Other Job Characteristics:** Consequence of Error; Importance of Being Sure All Is Done; Frustrating Circumstances.

Experience: Job Zone 5. Extensive skill, knowledge, and experience are needed. Very advanced communication and organizational skills are required. **Job Preparation:** SVP 8.0 and above—4 years to more than 10 years. **Knowledge:** Biology; Therapy and Counseling; Medicine and Dentistry; Customer and Personal Service; Education and Training; Psychology. **Instructional Programs:** 310501 Health and Physical Education, General; 310503 Athletic Training and Sports Medicine.

Related DOT Job: 153.224-010 Athletic Trainer.

31-0000
Healthcare Support Occupations

31-1000 Nursing, Psychiatric, and Home Health Aides

31-1011.00 Home Health Aides (Personal Care and Home Health Aides)

Education: Short-term O-T-J training

Employed: 745,671

Openings: 249,694

Projected Growth: 58.1%

Earnings: No data available.

Provide routine, personal health care, such as bathing, dressing, or grooming, to elderly, convalescent, or disabled persons, in the patients' homes or in a residential care facility.

Entertains patient, reads aloud, and plays cards and other games with patient. Performs variety of miscellaneous duties as requested, such as obtaining household supplies and running errands. Purchases, prepares, and serves food for patient and other members of family, following special prescribed diets. Changes bed linens, washes and irons patient's laundry, and cleans patient's quarters. Administers prescribed oral medication under written direction of physician or as directed by home care nurse and aide. Maintains records of services performed and of apparent condition of patient. Assists patients into and out of bed, automobiles, or wheelchair, to lavatory, and up and down stairs. Massages patient and applies preparations and treatment, such as liniment or alcohol rubs and heat-lamp stimulation.

GOE Number, Interest Area, and Work Group: 14.07.01; Medical and Health Services; Patient Care and Assistance. **Personality Type:** Social. Social occupations frequently involve working with, communicating with, and teaching people. These occupations often involve helping or providing service to others. **Work Values:** Social Service; Moral Values; Security; Independence; Achievement; Variety. **Skills:** Service Orientation; Reading Comprehension; Social Perceptiveness; Monitoring; Problem Identification; Critical Thinking; Speaking; Active Listening. **Abilities:** *Cognitive*—Oral Comprehension; Oral Expression; Problem Sensitivity; Written Comprehension; Information Ordering. *Psychomotor*—Finger Dexterity. *Physical*—Static Strength; Dynamic Strength; Trunk Strength. *Sensory*—Sound Localization. **General Work Activities:** *Information Input*—Monitoring Processes, Materials, and Surroundings; Getting Information Needed to Do the Job; Estimating Needed Characteristics; Identifying Objects, Actions, and Events. *Mental Process*—Organizing, Planning, and Prioritizing; Evaluating Information Against Standards; Making Decisions and Solving Problems. *Work Output*—Performing General Physical Activities; Handling and Moving Objects; Documenting and Recording Information. *Interacting with Others*—Assisting and Caring for Others; Establishing and Maintaining Relationships; Communicating with Persons Outside Organization. **Physical Work Conditions:** Indoors; Standing; Sitting. **Other Job Characteristics:** Consequence of Error; Importance of Being Exact or Accurate; Importance of Being Sure All Is Done.

Experience: Job Zone 1. No previous work-related skill, knowledge, or experience is needed. **Job Preparation:** SVP Below 4.0— Less than 6 months. **Knowledge:** Customer and Personal Service; Medicine and Dentistry; Psychology; Therapy and Counseling; Clerical. **Instructional Programs:** 200601 Custodial, Housekeeping and Home Services Workers and Managers; 200602 Elder Care Provider/Companion; 200606 Homemaker's Aide; 511614 Nurse Assistant/Aide; 511615 Home Health Aide.

Related DOT Job: 354.377-014 Home Attendant.

31-1012.00 Nursing Aides, Orderlies, and Attendants (Nursing Aides, Orderlies, and Attendants)

Education: Short-term O-T-J training

Employed: 1,366,632

Openings: 349,640

Projected Growth: 23.8%

Earnings: $16,620

Provide basic patient care under direction of nursing staff. Feed, bathe, dress, groom, or move patients; change linens.

Sterilizes equipment and supplies. Assists patient to walk. Turns and repositions bedfast patients, alone or with assistance, to prevent bedsores. Administers massages and alcohol rubs. Administers catheterizations, bladder irrigations, enemas, and douches. Stores, prepares, and issues dressing packs, treatment trays, and other supplies. Cleans room and changes linen. Measures and records vital signs. Measures and records food and liquid intake and output. Feeds patients unable to feed themselves. Bathes, grooms, and dresses patients. Prepares food trays. Sets up equipment, such as oxygen tents, portable X-ray machines, and overhead irrigation bottles. Administers medication as directed by physician or nurse. Transports patient to areas such as operating and X-ray rooms.

GOE Number, Interest Area, and Work Group: 14.07.01; Medical and Health Services; Patient Care and Assistance. **Personality Type:** Social. Social occupations frequently involve working with, communicating with, and teaching people. These occupations often involve helping or providing service to others. **Work Values:** Social Service; Moral Values; Co-workers; Security; Activity. **Skills:** Social Perceptiveness; Active Listening; Reading Comprehension; Service Orientation; Speaking. **Abilities:** *Cognitive*—Oral Comprehension; Oral Expression; Written Comprehension; Information Ordering; Spatial Orientation; Written Expression. *Psychomotor*—Arm-Hand Steadiness; Reaction Time; Manual Dexterity. *Physical*—Static Strength; Extent Flexibility; Trunk Strength. *Sensory*—Near Vision; Speech Recognition; Speech Clarity; Visual Color Discrimination; Night Vision. **General Work Activities:** *Information Input*—Identifying Objects, Actions, and Events; Getting Information Needed to Do the Job; Monitoring Processes, Materials, and Surroundings. *Mental Process*—Evaluating Information Against Standards; Processing Information; Updating and Using Job-Relevant Knowledge. *Work Output*—Performing General Physical Activities; Documenting and Recording Information; Handling and Moving Objects. *Interacting with Others*—Assisting and Caring for Others; Establishing and Maintaining Relationships; Communicating with Other Workers. **Physical Work Conditions:** Special Uniform; Indoors; Diseases or Infections. **Other Job Characteristics:** Consequence of Error;

Importance of Being Sure All Is Done; Importance of Being Exact or Accurate.

Experience: Job Zone 2. Some previous work-related skill, knowledge, or experience may be helpful, but usually is not needed. **Job Preparation:** SVP 4.00 to 5.99—6 months to less than 2 years. **Knowledge:** Customer and Personal Service; Medicine and Dentistry; Chemistry; Public Safety and Security; Therapy and Counseling. **Instructional Program:** 511614 Nurse Assistant/Aide.

Related DOT Jobs: 354.374-010 Nurse, Practical; 355.374-014 Certified Medication Technician; 355.674-014 Nurse Assistant; 355.674-018 Orderly.

31-1013.00 Psychiatric Aides (Psychiatric Aides)

Education: Short-term O-T-J training
Employed: 94,709
Openings: 21,129
Projected Growth: 7.7%
Earnings: $22,170

Assist mentally impaired or emotionally disturbed patients. Work under direction of nursing and medical staff.

Accompanies patients to and from wards for medical and dental treatments, shopping trips, and to religious and recreational events. Assists patients in becoming accustomed to hospital routine. Demonstrates and assists patients in bathing, dressing, and grooming. Serves meals and feeds patients needing assistance. Administers prescribed medications, measures vital signs, and performs other nursing duties, such as collecting specimens and drawing blood samples. Encourages patients to participate in social, educational, and recreational activities. Monitors patients to ensure patients remain in assigned areas and aids or restrains patients to prevent injuries. Notes and maintains records of patients' activities, such as vital signs, eating habits, and daily behavior.

GOE Number, Interest Area, and Work Group: 14.07.01; Medical and Health Services; Patient Care and Assistance. **Personality Type:** Social. Social occupations frequently involve working with, communicating with, and teaching people. These occupations often involve helping or providing service to others. **Work Values:** Social Service; Security; Co-workers; Supervision, Human Relations; Activity; Moral Values. **Skills:** Active Listening; Speaking; Social Perceptiveness; Reading Comprehension; Writing; Problem Identification. **Abilities:** *Cognitive*—Oral Expression; Oral Comprehension; Problem Sensitivity; Time Sharing; Written Comprehension; Information Ordering. *Psychomotor*—Arm-Hand Steadiness; Manual Dexterity; Multilimb Coordination; Reaction Time; Speed of Limb Movement. *Physical*—Static Strength; Trunk Strength; Gross Body Coordination. *Sensory*—Speech Clarity; Speech Recognition; Visual Color Discrimination. **General Work Activities:** *Information Input*—Monitoring Processes, Materials, and Surroundings; Identifying Objects, Actions, and Events; Getting Information Needed to Do the Job. *Mental Process*—Judging Qualities of Things, Services, Other People's Work; Organizing, Planning, and Prioritizing; Processing Information; Updating and Using Job-Relevant Knowledge. *Work Output*—Performing General Physical Activities; Handling and Moving Objects; Implementing Ideas and Programs; Documenting and Recording Information.

Interacting with Others—Assisting and Caring for Others; Establishing and Maintaining Relationships; Communicating with Persons Outside Organization. **Physical Work Conditions:** Indoors; Special Uniform; Walking or Running. **Other Job Characteristics:** Frustrating Circumstances; Consequence of Error; Importance of Being Aware of New Events.

Experience: Job Zone 2. Some previous work-related skill, knowledge, or experience may be helpful, but usually is not needed. **Job Preparation:** SVP 4.00 to 5.99—6 months to less than 2 years. **Knowledge:** Customer and Personal Service; Psychology; Therapy and Counseling; Medicine and Dentistry; Chemistry. **Instructional Program:** 511502 Psychiatric/Mental Health Services Technician.

Related DOT Jobs: 355.377-014 Psychiatric Aide; 355.377-018 Mental-Retardation Aide.

31-2000 Occupational and Physical Therapist Assistants and Aides

31-2011.00 Occupational Therapist Assistants
(Occupational Therapy Assistants and Aides)

Education: Associate degree
Employed: 18,619
Openings: 3,106
Projected Growth: 39.8%
Earnings: $28,690

Assist occupational therapists in providing occupational therapy treatments and procedures. Assist in development of treatment plans, carry out routine functions, direct activity programs, and document the progress of treatments, in accordance with state laws. Obtain required formal training.

Transports patient to and from occupational therapy work area. Maintains observed information in client records and prepares written reports. Assists educational specialist or clinical psychologist in administering situational or diagnostic tests to measure client's abilities or progress. Fabricates splints and other assistant devices. Prepares work material, assembles and maintains equipment, and orders supplies. Helps professional staff demonstrate therapy techniques, such as manual and creative arts, and games. Instructs or assists in instructing patient and family in home programs and basic living skills as well as care and use of adaptive equipment. Assists in evaluation of physically, developmentally, mentally retarded, or emotionally disabled client's daily living skills and capacities. Reports information and observations to supervisor verbally. Assists occupational therapist to plan, implement, and administer educational, vocational, and recreational activities to restore, reinforce, and enhance task performances. Designs and adapts equipment and working-living environment.

GOE Number, Interest Area, and Work Group: 14.06.01; Medical and Health Services; Medical Therapy. **Personality Type:** Social. Social occupations frequently involve working with, communicating with, and teaching people. These occupations often involve helping or providing service to others. **Work Val-**

ues: Social Service; Security; Moral Values; Achievement; Supervision, Human Relations. **Skills:** Social Perceptiveness; Reading Comprehension; Service Orientation; Speaking; Active Listening. **Abilities:** *Cognitive*–Problem Sensitivity; Oral Expression; Oral Comprehension; Written Comprehension; Memorization; Deductive Reasoning. *Psychomotor*–Multilimb Coordination; Rate Control. *Physical*–Static Strength; Extent Flexibility; Trunk Strength; Gross Body Coordination. *Sensory*–Speech Recognition; Speech Clarity; Hearing Sensitivity. **General Work Activities:** *Information Input*–Getting Information Needed to Do the Job; Identifying Objects, Actions, and Events; Monitoring Processes, Materials, and Surroundings. *Mental Process*–Analyzing Data or Information; Making Decisions and Solving Problems; Thinking Creatively; Processing Information; Judging Qualities of Things, Services, Other People's Work; Updating and Using Job-Relevant Knowledge. *Work Output*–Performing General Physical Activities; Documenting and Recording Information; Implementing Ideas and Programs. *Interacting with Others*–Assisting and Caring for Others; Communicating with Other Workers; Teaching Others. **Physical Work Conditions:** Indoors; Standing; Using Hands on Objects, Tools, or Controls; Sitting. **Other Job Characteristics:** Consequence of Error; Importance of Being Sure All Is Done; Importance of Being Aware of New Events.

Experience: Job Zone 2. Some previous work-related skill, knowledge, or experience may be helpful, but usually is not needed. **Job Preparation:** SVP 4.00 to 5.99–6 months to less than 2 years. **Knowledge:** Therapy and Counseling; Education and Training; Medicine and Dentistry; Psychology; English Language; Customer and Personal Service. **Instructional Program:** 510803 Occupational Therapy Assistant.

Related DOT Job: 076.364-010 Occupational Therapy Assistant.

31-2012.00 Occupational Therapist Aides
(Occupational Therapy Assistants and Aides)

Education: Associate degree

Employed: 18,619

Openings: 3,106

Projected Growth: 39.8%

Earnings: $28,690

Perform only delegated, selected, or routine tasks in specific situations. Prepare patient and treatment room. Work under close supervision of an occupational therapist or occupational therapy assistant.

Designs and adapts equipment and working-living environment. Assists occupational therapist to plan, implement, and administer educational, vocational, and recreational activities to restore, reinforce, and enhance task performances. Helps professional staff demonstrate therapy techniques, such as manual and creative arts, and games. Assists educational specialist or clinical psychologist in administering situational or diagnostic tests to measure client's abilities or progress. Prepares work material, assembles and maintains equipment, and orders supplies. Maintains observed information in client records and prepares written reports. Transports patient to and from occupational therapy work area. Reports information and observations to supervisor verbally. Instructs or assists in instructing patient and family in home programs and basic living skills as well as care and use of adaptive equipment. Assists in evaluation of physically, developmentally, mentally retarded, or emotionally disabled client's daily living skills and capacities. Fabricates splints and other assistant devices.

GOE Number, Interest Area, and Work Group: 14.06.01; Medical and Health Services; Medical Therapy. **Personality Type:** Social. Social occupations frequently involve working with, communicating with, and teaching people. These occupations often involve helping or providing service to others. **Work Values:** Social Service; Security; Moral Values; Achievement; Supervision, Human Relations. **Skills:** Social Perceptiveness; Reading Comprehension; Active Listening; Service Orientation; Speaking. **Abilities:** *Cognitive*–Problem Sensitivity; Oral Comprehension; Oral Expression; Written Comprehension; Deductive Reasoning; Memorization. *Psychomotor*–Multilimb Coordination; Rate Control. *Physical*–Static Strength; Extent Flexibility; Trunk Strength; Gross Body Coordination. *Sensory*–Speech Recognition; Speech Clarity; Hearing Sensitivity. **General Work Activities:** *Information Input*–Getting Information Needed to Do the Job; Identifying Objects, Actions, and Events; Monitoring Processes, Materials, and Surroundings. *Mental Process*–Analyzing Data or Information; Making Decisions and Solving Problems; Judging Qualities of Things, Services, Other People's Work; Thinking Creatively; Updating and Using Job-Relevant Knowledge; Processing Information. *Work Output*–Performing General Physical Activities; Documenting and Recording Information; Implementing Ideas and Programs. *Interacting with Others*–Assisting and Caring for Others; Communicating with Other Workers; Teaching Others. **Physical Work Conditions:** Indoors; Standing; Sitting; Using Hands on Objects, Tools, or Controls. **Other Job Characteristics:** Importance of Being Sure All Is Done; Consequence of Error; Importance of Being Aware of New Events.

Experience: Job Zone 2. Some previous work-related skill, knowledge, or experience may be helpful, but usually is not needed. **Job Preparation:** SVP 4.00 to 5.99–6 months to less than 2 years. **Knowledge:** Therapy and Counseling; Education and Training; Medicine and Dentistry; Customer and Personal Service; English Language; Psychology. **Instructional Program:** 510803 Occupational Therapy Assistant.

Related DOT Job: 355.377-010 Occupational Therapy Aide.

31-2021.00 Physical Therapist Assistants (Physical Therapy Assistants and Aides)

Education: Associate degree

Employed: 82,147

Openings: 14,195

Projected Growth: 43.7%

Earnings: $21,870

Assist physical therapists in providing physical therapy treatments and procedures. In accordance with state laws, assist in the development of treatment plans, carry out routine functions, document the progress of treatment, and modify specific treatments in accordance with patient status and within the scope of treatment plans established by a physical therapist. Obtain required formal training.

Transports patients to and from treatment area. Trains patients in use and care of orthopedic braces, prostheses, and supportive devices, such as crutches. Measures patient's range-of-joint motion, body parts, and vital signs to determine effects of treatments or for patient evaluations. Observes patients during treatments and compiles and evaluates data on patients' responses to treatments and progress, and reports to physical therapist. Secures patients into or onto therapy equipment. Confers with physical therapy staff and others to discuss and evaluate patient information for planning, modifying, and coordinating treatment. Assists patients to dress, undress, and put on and remove supportive devices, such as braces, splints, and slings. Provides routine treatments, such as hydrotherapy, hot and cold packs, and paraffin bath. Adjusts fit of supportive devices for patients, as instructed. Instructs, motivates, and assists patients to learn and improve functional activities, such as perambulation, transfer, ambulation, and daily-living activities. Administers traction to relieve neck and back pain, using intermittent and static traction equipment. Records treatment given and equipment used. Cleans work area and equipment after treatment. Performs clerical duties, such as taking inventory, ordering supplies, answering telephone, taking messages, and filling out forms. Fits patients for orthopedic braces, prostheses, and supportive devices, such as crutches. Safeguards, motivates, and assists patients practicing exercises and functional activities under direction of professional staff. Administers active and passive manual therapeutic exercises, therapeutic massage, and heat, light, sound, water, and electrical modality treatments, such as ultrasound.

GOE Number, Interest Area, and Work Group: 14.06.01; Medical and Health Services; Medical Therapy. **Personality Type:** Social. Social occupations frequently involve working with, communicating with, and teaching people. These occupations often involve helping or providing service to others. **Work Values:** Social Service; Security; Moral Values; Achievement; Supervision, Human Relations. **Skills:** Reading Comprehension; Learning Strategies; Problem Identification; Service Orientation; Instructing; Active Listening. **Abilities:** *Cognitive*—Oral Expression; Oral Comprehension; Problem Sensitivity; Written Comprehension; Written Expression. *Psychomotor*—Wrist-Finger Speed; Arm-Hand Steadiness. *Physical*—Static Strength; Stamina. *Sensory*—Speech Clarity; Speech Recognition. **General Work Activities:** *Information Input*—Monitoring Processes, Materials, and Surroundings; Identifying Objects, Actions, and Events; Getting Information Needed to Do the Job. *Mental Process*—Making Decisions and Solving Problems; Judging Qualities of Things, Services, Other People's Work; Updating and Using Job-Relevant Knowledge. *Work Output*—Performing General Physical Activities; Handling and Moving Objects; Documenting and Recording Information. *Interacting with Others*—Assisting and Caring for Others; Communicating with Other Workers; Establishing and Maintaining Relationships. **Physical Work Conditions:** Indoors; Standing; Special Uniform. **Other Job Characteristics:** Importance of Being Sure All Is Done; Consequence of Error; Importance of Being Exact or Accurate.

Experience: Job Zone 2. Some previous work-related skill, knowledge, or experience may be helpful, but usually is not needed.
Job Preparation: SVP 4.00 to 5.99—6 months to less than 2 years.
Knowledge: Therapy and Counseling; Customer and Personal

Service; Education and Training; Biology; Psychology; Clerical.
Instructional Program: 510806 Physical Therapy Assistant.
Related DOT Job: 076.224-010 Physical Therapist Assistant.

31-2022.00 Physical Therapist Aides (Physical Therapy Assistants and Aides)

Education: Associate degree
Employed: 82,147
Openings: 14,195
Projected Growth: 43.7%
Earnings: $21,870

Perform only delegated, selected, or routine tasks in specific situations. Prepare patient and treatment area. Work under close supervision of a physical therapist or physical therapy assistant.

Cleans work area and equipment after treatment. Transports patients to and from treatment area. Fits patients for orthopedic braces, prostheses, and supportive devices, such as crutches. Records treatment given and equipment used. Assists patients to dress, undress, and put on and remove supportive devices, such as braces, splints, and slings. Measures patient's range-of-joint motion, body parts, and vital signs to determine effects of treatments or for patient evaluations. Confers with physical therapy staff and others to discuss and evaluate patient information for planning, modifying, and coordinating treatment. Administers traction to relieve neck and back pain, using intermittent and static traction equipment. Secures patients into or onto therapy equipment. Provides routine treatments, such as hydrotherapy, hot and cold packs, and paraffin bath. Adjusts fit of supportive devices for patients, as instructed. Trains patients in use and care of orthopedic braces, prostheses, and supportive devices, such as crutches. Observes patients during treatment and compiles and evaluates data on patients' responses to treatments and progress, and reports to physical therapist. Instructs, motivates, and assists patients to learn and improve functional activities, such as perambulation, transfer, ambulation, and daily-living activities. Performs clerical duties, such as taking inventory, ordering supplies, answering telephone, taking messages, and filling out forms. Administers active and passive manual therapeutic exercises, therapeutic massage, and heat, light, sound, water, and electrical modality treatments, such as ultrasound. Safeguards, motivates, and assists patients practicing exercises and functional activities under direction of professional staff.

GOE Number, Interest Area, and Work Group: 14.06.01; Medical and Health Services; Medical Therapy. **Personality Type:** Social. Social occupations frequently involve working with, communicating with, and teaching people. These occupations often involve helping or providing service to others. **Work Values:** Social Service; Moral Values; Security; Achievement; Supervision, Human Relations. **Skills:** Reading Comprehension; Service Orientation; Learning Strategies; Problem Identification; Instructing; Active Listening. **Abilities:** *Cognitive*—Oral Expression; Oral Comprehension; Problem Sensitivity; Written Comprehension; Written Expression. *Psychomotor*—Wrist-Finger Speed; Arm-Hand Steadiness. *Physical*—Static Strength; Stamina. *Sensory*—Speech

Clarity; Speech Recognition. **General Work Activities:** *Information Input*—Monitoring Processes, Materials, and Surroundings; Identifying Objects, Actions, and Events; Getting Information Needed to Do the Job. *Mental Process*—Making Decisions and Solving Problems; Judging Qualities of Things, Services, Other People's Work; Updating and Using Job-Relevant Knowledge. *Work Output*—Performing General Physical Activities; Handling and Moving Objects; Documenting and Recording Information. *Interacting with Others*—Assisting and Caring for Others; Communicating with Other Workers; Establishing and Maintaining Relationships. **Physical Work Conditions:** Indoors; Special Uniform; Standing. **Other Job Characteristics:** Importance of Being Sure All Is Done; Consequence of Error; Importance of Being Exact or Accurate.

Experience: Job Zone 2. Some previous work-related skill, knowledge, or experience may be helpful, but usually is not needed. **Job Preparation:** SVP 4.00 to 5.99—6 months to less than 2 years. **Knowledge:** Therapy and Counseling; Customer and Personal Service; Education and Training; Biology; Clerical; Psychology. **Instructional Program:** 510806 Physical Therapy Assistant.

Related DOT Job: 355.354-010 Physical Therapy Aide.

31-9000 Other Healthcare Support Occupations

31-9011.00 Massage Therapists (All Other Health Professionals, Paraprofessionals, and Technicians)

Education: No data available.

Employed: 459,490

Openings: No data available.

Projected Growth: No data available.

Earnings: $27,260

Massage customers for hygienic or remedial purposes.

GOE Number, Interest Area, and Work Group: 14.06.01; Medical and Health Services; Medical Therapy. **Instructional Programs:** 510899 Health and Medical Assistants, Other; 510910 Diagnostic Medical Sonography; 510999 Health and Medical Diagnostic and Treatment Services, Other; 511804 Orthoptics; 512601 Health Aide; 519999 Health Professions and Related Sciences, Other. **Note:** The Department of Labor has not collected some data for this job, so it has fewer details than the other descriptions.

31-9091.00 Dental Assistants (Dental Assistants)

Education: Moderate-term O-T-J training

Employed: 228,877

Openings: 56,389

Projected Growth: 42.2%

Earnings: $22,640

Assist dentist, set up patient and equipment, and keep records.

Instructs patients in oral hygiene and plaque control programs. Exposes dental diagnostic X rays. Applies protective coating of fluoride to teeth. Makes preliminary impressions for study casts and occlusal registrations for mounting study casts. Cleans and polishes removable appliances. Schedules appointments, prepares bills and receives payment for dental services, completes insurance forms, and maintains records, manually or using computer. Cleans teeth, using dental instruments. Pours, trims, and polishes study casts. Provides postoperative instructions prescribed by dentist. Records treatment information in patient records. Assists dentist in management of medical and dental emergencies. Takes and records medical and dental histories and vital signs of patients. Prepares patient, sterilizes and disinfects instruments, sets up instrument trays, prepares materials, and assists dentist during dental procedures. Fabricates temporary restorations and custom impressions from preliminary impressions.

GOE Number, Interest Area, and Work Group: 14.03.01; Medical and Health Services; Dentistry. **Personality Type:** Social. Social occupations frequently involve working with, communicating with, and teaching people. These occupations often involve helping or providing service to others. **Work Values:** Social Service; Security; Moral Values; Working Conditions; Co-workers. **Skills:** Reading Comprehension; Active Listening; Speaking; Writing; Problem Identification. **Abilities:** *Cognitive*—Oral Comprehension; Information Ordering; Oral Expression; Number Facility; Written Expression. *Psychomotor*—Control Precision; Arm-Hand Steadiness; Finger Dexterity. *Physical*—none met the criteria. *Sensory*—Near Vision; Speech Recognition. **General Work Activities:** *Information Input*—Inspecting Equipment, Structures, Materials; Monitoring Processes, Materials, and Surroundings; Getting Information Needed to Do the Job. *Mental Process*—Processing Information; Scheduling Work and Activities; Updating and Using Job-Relevant Knowledge. *Work Output*—Handling and Moving Objects; Documenting and Recording Information; Implementing Ideas and Programs. *Interacting with Others*—Communicating with Other Workers; Assisting and Caring for Others; Communicating with Persons Outside Organization. **Physical Work Conditions:** Indoors; Special Uniform; Using Hands on Objects, Tools, or Controls. **Other Job Characteristics:** Importance of Being Exact or Accurate; Importance of Being Sure All Is Done; Consequence of Error.

Experience: Job Zone 3. Previous work-related skill, knowledge, or experience is required. **Job Preparation:** SVP 6.0 to less than 7.0—More than 1 year and less than 4 years. **Knowledge:** Medicine and Dentistry; Clerical; English Language; Mathematics; Customer and Personal Service. **Instructional Program:** 510601 Dental Assistant.

Related DOT Job: 079.361-018 Dental Assistant.

31-9092.00 Medical Assistants (Medical Assistants)

Education: Moderate-term O-T-J training

Employed: 252,246

Openings: 49,015

Projected Growth: 57.8%

Earnings: $20,680

Perform administrative and certain clinical duties under the direction of physician. Schedule appointments. Maintain medical records, billing, and coding for insurance purposes. Take and record patients' vital signs and medical histories. Prepare patients for examination, draw blood, and administer medications as directed by physician.

Operates X-ray, electrocardiograph (EKG), and other equipment to administer routine diagnostic tests. Gives physiotherapy treatments, such as diathermy, galvanics, and hydrotherapy. Maintains medical records. Interviews patients, measures vital signs, weight, and height, and records information. Schedules appointments. Hands instruments and materials to physician. Inventories and orders medical supplies and materials. Lifts and turns patients. Prepares treatment rooms for examination of patients. Receives payment for bills. Gives injections or treatments to patients. Performs routine laboratory tests. Contacts medical facility or department to schedule patients for tests. Computes and mails monthly statements to patients and records transactions. Cleans and sterilizes instruments. Completes insurance forms.

GOE Number, Interest Area, and Work Group: 14.02.01; Medical and Health Services; Medicine and Surgery. **Personality Type:** Social. Social occupations frequently involve working with, communicating with, and teaching people. These occupations often involve helping or providing service to others. **Work Values:** Moral Values; Social Service; Security; Co-workers; Supervision, Human Relations. **Skills:** Reading Comprehension; Active Listening; Service Orientation; Information Gathering; Speaking. **Abilities:** *Cognitive*—Oral Comprehension; Information Ordering; Written Comprehension; Oral Expression; Written Expression; Number Facility. *Psychomotor*—Arm-Hand Steadiness; Control Precision; Finger Dexterity; Reaction Time. *Physical*—Static Strength; Extent Flexibility; Trunk Strength. *Sensory*—Near Vision; Speech Recognition; Speech Clarity. **General Work Activities:** *Information Input*—Getting Information Needed to Do the Job; Monitoring Processes, Materials, and Surroundings; Identifying Objects, Actions, and Events. *Mental Process*—Evaluating Information Against Standards; Processing Information; Updating and Using Job-Relevant Knowledge; Judging Qualities of Things, Services, Other People's Work. *Work Output*—Performing General Physical Activities; Documenting and Recording Information; Controlling Machines and Processes. *Interacting with Others*—Assisting and Caring for Others; Communicating with Other Workers; Establishing and Maintaining Relationships. **Physical Work Conditions:** Indoors; Special Uniform; Common Protective or Safety Attire; Diseases or Infections. **Other Job Characteristics:** Consequence of Error; Importance of Being Sure All Is Done; Importance of Being Exact or Accurate.

Experience: Job Zone 3. Previous work-related skill, knowledge, or experience is required. **Job Preparation:** SVP 6.0 to less than 7.0—More than 1 year and less than 4 years. **Knowledge:** Medicine and Dentistry; Clerical; Biology; English Language; Therapy and Counseling. **Instructional Programs:** 510705 Medical Office Management; 510801 Medical Assistant; 510804 Ophthalmic Medical Assistant; 510899 Health and Medical Assistants, Other; 511804 Orthoptics; 511899 Ophthalmic/Optometric Services, Other.

Related DOT Jobs: 079.362-010 Medical Assistant; 079.364-010 Chiropractor Assistant; 079.374-018 Podiatric Assistant.

31-9093.00 Medical Equipment Preparers (All Other Health Service Workers)

Education: Short-term O-T-J training
Employed: 184,924
Openings: 35,998
Projected Growth: 22.3%
Earnings: $19,160

Prepare, sterilize, install, or clean laboratory or healthcare equipment. Perform routine laboratory tasks; operate or inspect equipment.

Examines equipment to detect leaks, worn or loose parts, or other indications of disrepair. Installs and sets up equipment, using hand tools. Disinfects, and sterilizes equipment, such as respirators, hospital beds, and wheelchairs, and oxygen and dialysis equipment, using cleansing and sterilizing solutions. Connects equipment to water source and flushes water through system to purge equipment of wastes. Delivers equipment to specified hospital location or to patient's private residence. Starts equipment and observes gauges and equipment operation to detect malfunctions and assure equipment is operating to prescribed standards. Maintains inventory and equipment usage records.

GOE Number, Interest Area, and Work Group: 14.05.01; Medical and Health Services; Medical Technology. **Personality Type:** Realistic. Realistic occupations frequently involve work activities that include practical, hands-on problems and solutions. These occupations often deal with plants, animals, and real-world materials like wood, tools, and machinery. Many of the occupations require working outside and do not involve a lot of paperwork or working closely with others. **Work Values:** Moral Values; Independence; Security; Supervision, Technical; Supervision, Human Relations. **Skills:** Installation; Equipment Maintenance; Troubleshooting; Equipment Selection; Operation and Control; Operation Monitoring; Technology Design. **Abilities:** *Cognitive*—Problem Sensitivity; Information Ordering; Written Expression; Deductive Reasoning; Written Comprehension. *Psychomotor*—Control Precision; Manual Dexterity; Finger Dexterity. *Physical*—Static Strength; Extent Flexibility; Dynamic Strength; Stamina. *Sensory*—Speech Clarity; Hearing Sensitivity; Glare Sensitivity. **General Work Activities:** *Information Input*—Inspecting Equipment, Structures, Materials; Getting Information Needed to Do the Job; Monitoring Processes, Materials, and Surroundings; Identifying Objects, Actions, and Events. *Mental Process*—Evaluating Information Against Standards; Updating and Using Job-Relevant Knowledge; Judging Qualities of Things, Services, Other People's Work. *Work Output*—Handling and Moving Objects; Performing General Physical Activities; Controlling Machines and Processes. *Interacting with Others*—Monitoring and Controlling Resources; Performing Administrative Activities; Communicating with Other Workers; Establishing and Maintaining Relationships; Assisting and Caring for Others; Performing for or Working with the Public. **Physical Work Conditions:** Indoors; Using Hands on Objects, Tools, or Controls; Standing; Common Protective or Safety Attire; Diseases or Infections. **Other Job Characteristics:** Consequence of Error; Importance of Being Sure All Is Done; Importance of Being Exact or Accurate.

Experience: Job Zone 2. Some previous work-related skill, knowledge, or experience may be helpful, but usually is not needed. **Job Preparation:** SVP 4.00 to 5.99—6 months to less than 2 years. **Knowledge:** Mechanical; Chemistry; Customer and Personal Service; English Language; Engineering and Technology; Computers and Electronics; Clerical. **Instructional Program:** 510802 Medical Laboratory Assistant.

Related DOT Jobs: 355.674-022 Respiratory-Therapy Aide; 359.363-010 Health-Equipment Servicer; 599.584-010 Reuse Technician.

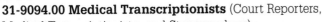

31-9094.00 Medical Transcriptionists (Court Reporters, Medical Transcriptionists, and Stenographers)

Education: Postsecondary vocational training

Employed: 109,953

Openings: 15,612

Projected Growth: 9.7%

Earnings: $25,430

Use transcribing machines with headset and foot pedal to listen to recordings by physicians and other healthcare professionals dictating a variety of medical reports, such as emergency room visits, diagnostic imaging studies, operations, chart reviews, and final summaries. Transcribe dictated reports and translate medical jargon and abbreviations into their expanded forms. Edit as necessary; return reports in either printed or electronic form to the physician or other healthcare professional for review and signature or for correction.

GOE Number, Interest Area, and Work Group: 09.07.02; Business Detail; Records Processing: Preparation and Maintenance. **Instructional Programs:** 510708 Medical Transcription; 520405 Court Reporter. **Note:** The Department of Labor has not collected some data for this job, so it has fewer details than the other descriptions.

31-9095.00 Pharmacy Aides (Pharmacy Technicians)

Education: Moderate-term O-T-J training

Employed: 108,690

Openings: 14,132

Projected Growth: 15.7%

Earnings: No data available.

Record drugs delivered to the pharmacy, store incoming merchandise, and inform the supervisor of stock needs. Operate cash register and accept prescriptions for filling.

GOE Number, Interest Area, and Work Group: 14.02.01; Medical and Health Services; Medicine and Surgery. **Instructional Program:** 510805 Pharmacy Technician/Assistant. **Note:** The Department of Labor has not collected some data for this job, so it has fewer details than the other descriptions.

31-9096.00 Veterinary Assistants and Laboratory Animal Caretakers (Veterinary Assistants)

Education: Short-term O-T-J training

Employed: 44,598

Openings: 14,770

Projected Growth: 28%

Earnings: $16,200

Feed, water, and examine pets and other nonfarm animals for signs of illness, disease, or injury in laboratories, animal hospitals, and clinics. Clean and disinfect cages and work areas; sterilize laboratory and surgical equipment. Provide routine post-operative care; administer medication orally or topically; prepare samples for laboratory examination under the supervision of veterinary or laboratory animal technologists or technicians, veterinarians, or scientists.

Assists veterinarian during surgical procedures, passing instruments and materials in accordance with oral instructions. Prepares patient, medications, equipment, and instruments for surgical procedures, using specialized knowledge. Prepares examination or treatment room, and holds or restrains animal during procedures. Assists professional personnel with research projects in commercial, public health, or research laboratories. Inspects products or carcasses to ensure compliance with health standards, when employed in food processing plant. Assists veterinarian in variety of animal health care duties, including injections, venipunctures, and wound dressings. Completes routine laboratory tests and cares for and feeds laboratory animals.

GOE Number, Interest Area, and Work Group: 03.02.01; Plants and Animals; Animal Care and Training. **Personality Type:** Realistic. Realistic occupations frequently involve work activities that include practical, hands-on problems and solutions. These occupations often deal with plants, animals, and real-world materials like wood, tools, and machinery. Many of the occupations require working outside and do not involve a lot of paperwork or working closely with others. **Work Values:** Moral Values; Security; Variety; Supervision, Technical; Achievement. **Skills:** Reading Comprehension; Active Listening; Social Perceptiveness; Speaking; Product Inspection; Science. **Abilities:** *Cognitive*—Oral Comprehension; Problem Sensitivity; Speed of Closure; Information Ordering; Selective Attention; Deductive Reasoning. *Psychomotor*—Finger Dexterity; Arm-Hand Steadiness; Manual Dexterity. *Physical*—Static Strength; Extent Flexibility; Trunk Strength. *Sensory*—Near Vision; Visual Color Discrimination; Speech Clarity. **General Work Activities:** *Information Input*—Getting Information Needed to Do the Job; Monitoring Processes, Materials, and Surroundings; Identifying Objects, Actions, and Events. *Mental Process*—Evaluating Information Against Standards; Processing Information; Analyzing Data or Information. *Work Output*—Performing General Physical Activities; Handling and Moving Objects; Documenting and Recording Information. *Interacting with Others*—Assisting and Caring for Others; Communicating with Other Workers; Establishing and Maintaining Relationships. **Physical Work Conditions:** Indoors; Common Protective or Safety Attire; Standing; Hazardous Situations; Using Hands on Objects, Tools, or Controls. **Other Job Characteristics:** Importance of Being Sure All Is Done; Consequence of Error; Frustrating Circumstances; Importance of Being Exact or Accurate.

Experience: Job Zone 3. Previous work-related skill, knowledge, or experience is required. **Job Preparation:** SVP 6.0 to less than 7.0—More than 1 year and less than 4 years. **Knowledge:** Biology; Medicine and Dentistry; Therapy and Counseling; Mathematics; English Language. **Instructional Program:** 510808 Veterinarian Assistant/Animal Health Technician.

Related DOT Job: 079.361-014 Veterinary Technician.

33-0000
Protective Service Occupations

33-1000 First-Line Supervisors/ Managers, Protective Service Workers

33-1011.00 First-Line Supervisors/Managers of Correctional Officers (All Other Protective Service Workers)

Education: Short-term O-T-J training

Employed: 166,335

Openings: 23,282

Projected Growth: 19%

Earnings: $17,470

Supervise and coordinate activities of correctional officers and jailers.

GOE Number, Interest Area, and Work Group: 04.01.01; Law, Law Enforcement, and Public Safety; Managerial Work in Law, Law Enforcement, and Public Safety. **Instructional Programs:** 430102 Corrections/Correctional Administration; 430106 Forensic Technology/Technician; 430199 Criminal Justice and Corrections, Other; 439999 Protective Services, Other. **Note:** The Department of Labor has not collected some data for this job, so it has fewer details than the other descriptions.

33-1012.00 First-Line Supervisors/Managers of Police and Detectives (Police and Detective Supervisors)

Education: Work experience in a related occupation

Employed: 110,812

Openings: 14,034

Projected Growth: 12%

Earnings: $48,700

Supervise and coordinate activities of members of police force.

Trains staff. Directs release or transfer of prisoners. Investigates charges of misconduct against staff. Directs collection, preparation, and handling of evidence and personal property of prisoners. Inspects facilities, supplies, vehicles, and equipment to ensure conformance to standards. Prepares news releases and responds to police correspondence. Cooperates with court personnel and officials from other law enforcement agencies and testifies in court. Conducts raids and orders detention of witnesses and suspects for questioning. Meets with civic, educational, and community groups to develop community programs and events; addresses groups concerning law enforcement subjects. Supervises and coordinates investigation of criminal cases. Reviews contents of written orders to ensure adherence to legal requirements. Prepares work schedules, assigns duties, and develops and revises departmental procedures. Disciplines staff for violation of department rules and regulations. Monitors and evaluates job performance of subordinates. Investigates and resolves personnel problems within organization. Prepares reports and directs preparation, handling, and maintenance of departmental records. Prepares budgets and manages expenditures of department funds. Requisitions and issues department equipment and supplies. Assists subordinates in performing job duties.

GOE Number, Interest Area, and Work Group: 04.01.01; Law, Law Enforcement, and Public Safety; Managerial Work in Law, Law Enforcement, and Public Safety. **Personality Type:** Enterprising. Enterprising occupations frequently involve starting up and carrying out projects. These occupations can involve leading people and making many decisions. They sometimes require risk taking and often deal with business. **Work Values:** Authority; Achievement; Social Status; Responsibility; Autonomy; Security. **Skills:** Judgment and Decision Making; Management of Personnel Resources; Coordination; Management of Financial Resources; Time Management; Social Perceptiveness. **Abilities:** *Cognitive*—Oral Expression; Inductive Reasoning; Written Expression; Oral Comprehension; Problem Sensitivity. *Psychomotor*—Reaction Time; Response Orientation; Speed of Limb Movement. *Physical*—Static Strength; Explosive Strength; Stamina. *Sensory*—Speech Clarity; Near Vision; Night Vision. **General Work Activities:** *Information Input*—Getting Information Needed to Do the Job; Monitoring Processes, Materials, and Surroundings; Identifying Objects, Actions, and Events. *Mental Process*—Organizing, Planning, and Prioritizing; Analyzing Data or Information; Making Decisions and Solving Problems. *Work Output*—Documenting and Recording Information; Performing General Physical Activities; Operating Vehicles or Equipment. *Interacting with Others*—Performing for or Working with the Public; Communicating with Persons Outside Organization; Resolving Conflict and Negotiating with Others. **Physical Work Conditions:** Special Uniform; Indoors; Sitting. **Other Job Characteristics:** Consequence of Error; Frustrating Circumstances; Importance of Being Sure All Is Done.

Experience: Job Zone 4. A minimum of two to four years of work-related skill, knowledge, or experience is needed. **Job Preparation:** SVP 7.0 to less than 8.0—2 years to less than 10 years. **Knowledge:** Public Safety and Security; Administration and Management; Law, Government and Jurisprudence; Personnel and Human Resources; English Language. **Instructional Programs:** 430102 Corrections/Correctional Administration; 430103 Criminal Justice/Law Enforcement Administration; 430104 Criminal Justice Studies.

Related DOT Jobs: 372.137-010 Correction Officer, Head; 372.167-018 Jailer, Chief; 375.133-010 Police Sergeant, Precinct I; 375.137-010 Commander, Identification and Records; 375.137-014 Desk Officer; 375.137-018 Police Lieutenant, Community Relations; 375.137-026 Traffic Sergeant; 375.137-030 Commander, Police Reserves; 375.137-034 Commanding Officer, Police; 375.163-010 Commanding Officer, Motorized Squad; 375.167-010 Commanding Officer, Homicide Squad; 375.167-014 Commanding Officer, Investigation Division; 375.167-022 Detective Chief; 375.167-030 Launch Commander, Harbor Police; 375.167-034 Police Captain, Precinct; 375.167-038 Police Lieutenant, Patrol; 375.167-046 Traffic Lieutenant; 375.167-050 Commander, Internal Affairs; 377.134-010 Supervisor, Identification and Communications; 377.137-010 Deputy Sheriff, Commander, Civil Division (partial list; see the introduction for sources of the complete list).

33-1021.00 First-Line Supervisors/Managers of Fire Fighting and Prevention Workers (Fire Fighting and Prevention Supervisors)

Education: Work experience in a related occupation

Employed: 59,934

Openings: 9,147

Projected Growth: 10.7%

Earnings: $44,830

Supervise and coordinate activities of workers engaged in fire fighting and fire prevention and control.

GOE Number, Interest Area, and Work Group: 04.01.01; Law, Law Enforcement, and Public Safety; Managerial Work in Law, Law Enforcement, and Public Safety. **Instructional Programs:** 430201 Fire Protection and Safety Technology/Technician; 430202 Fire Services Administration; 430203 Fire Science/Firefighting. **Note:** The Department of Labor has not collected some data for this job, so it has fewer details than the other descriptions.

33-1021.01 Municipal Fire Fighting and Prevention Supervisors (Fire Fighting and Prevention Supervisors)

Education: Work experience in a related occupation

Employed: 59,934

Openings: 9,147

Projected Growth: 10.7%

Earnings: $44,830

Supervise fire fighters who control and extinguish municipal fires, protect life and property, and conduct rescue efforts.

Writes and submits proposal for new equipment or for modification of existing equipment. Compiles report of fire call, listing location, type, probable cause, estimated damage, and disposition. Trains subordinates in use of equipment, methods of extinguishing fires, and rescue operations. Inspects fire stations, equipment, and records to ensure efficiency and enforcement of departmental regulations. Confers with civic representatives, and plans talks and demonstrations of fire safety to direct fire prevention information program. Orders and directs fire drills for occupants of buildings. Keeps equipment and personnel records. Directs building inspections to ensure compliance with fire and safety regulations. Evaluates efficiency and performance of employees, and recommends awards for service. Directs investigation of cases of suspected arson, hazards, and false alarms. Assesses nature and extent of fire, condition of building, danger to adjacent buildings, and water supply to determine crew or company requirements. Coordinates and supervises fire fighting and rescue activities, and reports events to supervisor, using two-way radio. Oversees review of new building plans to ensure compliance with laws, ordinances, and administrative rules for public fire safety. Studies and interprets fire safety codes to establish procedures for issuing permits regulating storage or use of hazardous or flammable substances.

GOE Number, Interest Area, and Work Group: 04.01.01; Law, Law Enforcement, and Public Safety; Managerial Work in Law, Law Enforcement, and Public Safety. **Personality Type:** Realistic. Realistic occupations frequently involve work activities that include practical, hands-on problems and solutions. These occupations often deal with plants, animals, and real-world materials like wood, tools, and machinery. Many of the occupations require working outside and do not involve a lot of paperwork or working closely with others. **Work Values:** Achievement; Authority; Co-workers; Social Status; Responsibility. **Skills:** Coordination; Implementation Planning; Active Listening; Problem Identification; Solution Appraisal. **Abilities:** *Cognitive*—Oral Expression; Time Sharing; Problem Sensitivity; Deductive Reasoning; Oral Comprehension. *Psychomotor*—Response Orientation; Reaction Time; Control Precision; Multilimb Coordination. *Physical*—Static Strength; Stamina; Dynamic Strength; Explosive Strength. *Sensory*—Auditory Attention; Far Vision; Near Vision. **General Work Activities:** *Information Input*—Getting Information Needed to Do the Job; Inspecting Equipment, Structures, Materials; Identifying Objects, Actions, and Events. *Mental Process*—Judging Qualities of Things, Services, Other People's Work; Making Decisions and Solving Problems; Evaluating Information Against Standards; Analyzing Data or Information. *Work Output*—Documenting and Recording Information; Performing General Physical Activities; Controlling Machines and Processes. *Interacting with Others*—Communicating with Other Workers; Coordinating Work and Activities of Others; Communicating with Persons Outside Organization; Teaching Others. **Physical Work Conditions:** Special Uniform; Outdoors; Common Protective or Safety Attire; Very Hot. **Other Job Characteristics:** Consequence of Error; Frustrating Circumstances; Importance of Being Sure All Is Done; Importance of Being Aware of New Events.

Experience: Job Zone 4. A minimum of two to four years of work-related skill, knowledge, or experience is needed. **Job Preparation:** SVP 7.0 to less than 8.0—2 years to less than 10 years. **Knowledge:** Public Safety and Security; Education and Training; Personnel and Human Resources; Mechanical; Transportation; Administration and Management. **Instructional Programs:** 430201 Fire Protection and Safety Technology/Technician; 430202 Fire Services Administration; 430203 Fire Science/Firefighting.

Related DOT Jobs: 373.134-010 Fire Captain; 373.167-010 Battalion Chief; 373.167-014 Captain, Fire-Prevention Bureau; 373.167-018 Fire Marshal.

33-1021.02 Forest Fire Fighting and Prevention Supervisors (Fire Fighting and Prevention Supervisors)

Education: Work experience in a related occupation

Employed: 59,934

Openings: 9,147

Projected Growth: 10.7%

Earnings: $44,830

Supervise fire fighters who control and suppress fires in forests or vacant public land.

Parachutes to major fire locations and directs fire containment and suppression activities. Observes fire and crews from air to determine force requirements and note changing conditions. Directs loading of fire suppression equipment into aircraft and parachuting of equipment to crews on ground. Trains workers in parachute jumping, fire suppression, aerial observation, and radio communication. Dispatches crews according to reported size, location, and condition of forest fires. Maintains radio communication with crews at fire scene to inform crew and base of changing conditions and learn of casualties.

GOE Number, Interest Area, and Work Group: 04.01.01; Law, Law Enforcement, and Public Safety; Managerial Work in Law, Law Enforcement, and Public Safety. **Personality Type:** Realistic. Realistic occupations frequently involve work activities that include practical, hands-on problems and solutions. These occupations often deal with plants, animals, and real-world materials like wood, tools, and machinery. Many of the occupations require working outside and do not involve a lot of paperwork or working closely with others. **Work Values:** Authority; Achievement; Responsibility; Social Status; Autonomy. **Skills:** Coordination; Implementation Planning; Management of Personnel Resources; Judgment and Decision Making; Systems Perception. **Abilities:** *Cognitive*—Oral Expression; Problem Sensitivity; Time Sharing; Spatial Orientation; Flexibility of Closure; Speed of Closure. *Psychomotor*—Rate Control; Speed of Limb Movement; Reaction Time. *Physical*—Static Strength; Stamina; Gross Body Coordination. *Sensory*—Far Vision; Auditory Attention; Night Vision. **General Work Activities:** *Information Input*—Getting Information Needed to Do the Job; Estimating Needed Characteristics; Identifying Objects, Actions, and Events; Monitoring Processes, Materials, and Surroundings. *Mental Process*—Making Decisions and Solving Problems; Analyzing Data or Information; Judging Qualities of Things, Services, Other People's Work; Scheduling Work and Activities; Organizing, Planning, and Prioritizing. *Work Output*—Performing General Physical Activities; Handling and Moving Objects; Operating Vehicles or Equipment. *Interacting with Others*—Coordinating Work and Activities of Others; Communicating with Other Workers; Teaching Others. **Physical Work Conditions:** Special Uniform; Common Protective or Safety Attire; Outdoors. **Other Job Characteristics:** Consequence of Error; Frustrating Circumstances; Importance of Being Sure All Is Done.

Experience: Job Zone 5. Extensive skill, knowledge, and experience are needed. Very advanced communication and organizational skills are required. **Job Preparation:** SVP 8.0 and above—4 years to more than 10 years. **Knowledge:** Public Safety and Security; Transportation; Administration and Management; Education and Training; Telecommunications. **Instructional Programs:** 430201 Fire Protection and Safety Technology/Technician; 430202 Fire Services Administration; 430203 Fire Science/Firefighting. **Related DOT Job:** 452.134-010 Smoke Jumper Supervisor.

33-2000 Fire Fighting and Prevention Workers

33-2011.00 Fire Fighters (Fire Fighters)

Education: Long-term O-T-J training
Employed: 239,320
Openings: 9,989
Projected Growth: 4.7%
Earnings: $31,150

Control and extinguish fires or respond to emergency situations where life, property, or the environment is at risk. Provide fire prevention, emergency medical service, hazardous material response, search and rescue, and disaster management.

GOE Number, Interest Area, and Work Group: 04.04.01; Law, Law Enforcement, and Public Safety; Public Safety: Emergency Responding. **Instructional Programs:** 430203 Fire Science/Firefighting; 430299 Fire Protection, Other. **Note:** The Department of Labor has not collected some data for this job, so it has fewer details than the other descriptions.

33-2011.01 Municipal Fire Fighters (Firefighters)

Education: Long-term O-T-J training
Employed: 239,320
Openings: 9,989
Projected Growth: 4.7%
Earnings: $31,150

Control and extinguish municipal fires, protect life and property, and conduct rescue efforts.

Inspects buildings for fire hazards and compliance with fire prevention ordinances. Establishes firelines to prevent unauthorized persons from entering area. Drives and operates fire fighting vehicles and equipment. Maintains fire fighting equipment and apparatus, vehicles, hydrants, and fire station. Assesses fire and situation, reports to superior, and receives instructions, using two-way radio. Participates in courses in hydraulics, pump operation, and fire fighting techniques. Responds to fire alarms and other emergency calls. Administers first aid and cardiopulmonary resuscitation to injured persons and those overcome by fire and smoke. Selects hose nozzle, depending on type of fire, and directs stream of water or chemicals onto fire. Creates openings in buildings for ventilation or entrance, using ax, chisel, crowbar, electric saw, or core cutter. Protects property from water and smoke, using waterproof salvage covers, smoke ejectors, and deodorants. Positions and climbs ladders to gain access to upper levels of buildings or to rescue individuals from burning structures. Participates in fire drills and demonstrations of fire fighting techniques. Sprays foam onto runway, extinguishes fire, and rescues aircraft crew and passengers in air-crash emergency.

GOE Number, Interest Area, and Work Group: 04.04.01; Law, Law Enforcement, and Public Safety; Public Safety: Emergency Responding. **Personality Type:** Realistic. Realistic occupations frequently involve work activities that include practical, hands-on problems and solutions. These occupations often deal with plants, animals, and real-world materials like wood, tools, and machinery. Many of the occupations require working outside and do not involve a lot of paperwork or working closely with others. **Work Values:** Achievement; Social Status; Moral Values; Co-workers; Security; Supervision, Human Relations. **Skills:** Service Orientation; Coordination; Critical Thinking; Problem Identification; Judgment and Decision Making; Idea Evaluation. **Abilities:** *Cognitive*—Oral Comprehension; Oral Expression; Information Ordering; Flexibility of Closure; Spatial Orientation; Problem Sensitivity. *Psychomotor*—Reaction Time; Response Orientation; Control Precision. *Physical*—Static Strength; Explosive Strength; Dynamic Strength. *Sensory*—Sound Localization; Auditory Attention; Far Vision. **General Work Activities:** *Information Input*—Getting Information Needed to Do the Job; Identifying Objects, Actions, and Events; Monitoring Processes, Materials, and Surroundings; Estimating Needed Characteristics. *Mental Process*—Judging Qualities of Things, Services, Other People's Work; Evaluating Information Against Standards; Updating and Using Job-Relevant Knowledge. *Work Output*—Performing General Physical Activities; Operating Vehicles or Equipment; Handling and Moving Objects. *Interacting with Others*—Communicating with Other Workers; Assisting and Caring for Others; Establishing and Maintaining Relationships. **Physical Work Conditions:** Common Protective or Safety Attire; Special Uniform; Using Hands on Objects, Tools, or Controls; Hazardous Situations; Specialized Protective or Safety Attirei. **Other Job Characteristics:** Consequence of Error; Frustrating Circumstances; Importance of Being Sure All Is Done.

Experience: Job Zone 2. Some previous work-related skill, knowledge, or experience may be helpful, but usually is not needed. **Job Preparation:** SVP 4.00 to 5.99—6 months to less than 2 years. **Knowledge:** Public Safety and Security; Medicine and Dentistry; Transportation; Therapy and Counseling; Mechanical. **Instructional Programs:** 430203 Fire Science/Firefighting; 430299 Fire Protection, Other.

Related DOT Jobs: 373.363-010 Fire Chief's Aide; 373.364-010 Fire Fighter; 373.663-010 Fire Fighter, Crash, Fire, and Rescue.

33-2011.02 Forest Fire Fighters (Firefighters)

Education: Long-term O-T-J training

Employed: 239,320

Openings: 9,989

Projected Growth: 4.7%

Earnings: $31,150

Control and suppress fires in forests or vacant public land.

Fells trees, cuts and clears brush, and digs trenches, to contain fire, using ax, chain saw, or shovel. Extinguishes flames and embers to suppress fire, using shovel, or engine or hand-driven water or chemical pumps. Ascertains best method for attacking fire, and communicates plan to airplane or base camp, using two-way radio. Patrols burned area after fire to watch for hot spots that may restart fire. Works as member of fire fighting crew. Orients self in relation to fire, using compass and map, and collects supplies and equipment dropped by parachute. Packs parachutes. Parachutes from aircraft and guides direction of fall toward clear landing area near scene of fire.

GOE Number, Interest Area, and Work Group: 04.04.01; Law, Law Enforcement, and Public Safety; Public Safety: Emergency Responding. **Personality Type:** Realistic. Realistic occupations frequently involve work activities that include practical, hands-on problems and solutions. These occupations often deal with plants, animals, and real-world materials like wood, tools, and machinery. Many of the occupations require working outside and do not involve a lot of paperwork or working closely with others. **Work Values:** Achievement; Co-workers; Moral Values; Social Status; Supervision, Human Relations; Security. **Skills:** Coordination; Service Orientation; Critical Thinking; Problem Identification;

Solution Appraisal; Monitoring; Speaking. **Abilities:** *Cognitive*—Oral Expression; Spatial Orientation; Problem Sensitivity; Speed of Closure; Oral Comprehension; Deductive Reasoning. *Psychomotor*—Response Orientation; Speed of Limb Movement; Reaction Time. *Physical*—Static Strength; Stamina; Explosive Strength; Trunk Strength. *Sensory*—Far Vision; Auditory Attention; Night Vision. **General Work Activities:** *Information Input*—Monitoring Processes, Materials, and Surroundings; Estimating Needed Characteristics; Getting Information Needed to Do the Job. *Mental Process*—Judging Qualities of Things, Services, Other People's Work; Making Decisions and Solving Problems; Updating and Using Job-Relevant Knowledge. *Work Output*—Performing General Physical Activities; Handling and Moving Objects; Controlling Machines and Processes. *Interacting with Others*—Communicating with Other Workers; Assisting and Caring for Others; Interpreting Meaning of Information to Others. **Physical Work Conditions:** Common Protective or Safety Attire; Outdoors; Standing; Special Uniform. **Other Job Characteristics:** Consequence of Error; Frustrating Circumstances; Importance of Being Sure All Is Done.

Experience: Job Zone 2. Some previous work-related skill, knowledge, or experience may be helpful, but usually is not needed. **Job Preparation:** SVP 4.00 to 5.99—6 months to less than 2 years. **Knowledge:** Public Safety and Security; Transportation; Telecommunications; Engineering and Technology; English Language; Computers and Electronics. **Instructional Programs:** 430203 Fire Science/Firefighting; 430299 Fire Protection, Other.

Related DOT Jobs: 452.364-014 Smoke Jumper; 452.687-014 Forest-Fire Fighter.

33-2021.00 Fire Inspectors and Investigators (Fire Inspectors)

Education: No data available.

Employed: 8,980

Openings: No data available.

Projected Growth: No data available.

Earnings: $41,110

Inspect buildings to detect fire hazards and enforce local ordinances and state laws. Investigate and gather facts to determine cause of fires and explosions.

GOE Number, Interest Area, and Work Group: 04.04.02; Law, Law Enforcement, and Public Safety; Public Safety: Regulations Enforcement. **Instructional Programs:** 430201 Fire Protection and Safety Technology/Technician; 430202 Fire Services Administration; 430203 Fire Science/Firefighting. **Note:** The Department of Labor has not collected some data for this job, so it has fewer details than the other descriptions.

33-2021.01 Fire Inspectors (Fire Inspectors)

Education: Work experience in a related occupation

Employed: 14,516

Openings: 900

Projected Growth: 17.2%

Earnings: No data available.

Inspect buildings and equipment to detect fire hazards and enforce state and local regulations.

Discusses violations and unsafe conditions with facility representative, makes recommendations, and instructs in fire safety practices. Collects fees for permits and licenses. Prepares reports, such as inspections performed, code violations, and recommendations for eliminating fire hazards. Issues permits and summons, and enforces fire codes. Inspects interiors and exteriors of buildings to detect hazardous conditions or violations of fire codes. Gives first aid in emergencies. Tests equipment such as gasoline storage tanks, air compressors, and fire-extinguishing and fire-protection equipment to ensure conformance to fire and safety codes.

GOE Number, Interest Area, and Work Group: 04.04.02; Law, Law Enforcement, and Public Safety; Public Safety: Regulations Enforcement. **Personality Type:** Conventional. Conventional occupations frequently involve following set procedures and routines. These occupations can include working with data and details more than with ideas. Usually there is a clear line of authority to follow. **Work Values:** Achievement; Security; Social Status; Ability Utilization; Responsibility; Moral Values; Company Policies and Practices. **Skills:** Problem Identification; Writing; Critical Thinking; Reading Comprehension; Idea Evaluation; Information Gathering. **Abilities:** *Cognitive*—Oral Expression; Problem Sensitivity; Written Expression; Inductive Reasoning; Oral Comprehension. *Psychomotor*—Reaction Time; Multilimb Coordination; Speed of Limb Movement. *Physical*—Static Strength; Stamina; Extent Flexibility. *Sensory*—Near Vision; Visual Color Discrimination; Far Vision. **General Work Activities:** *Information Input*—Inspecting Equipment, Structures, Materials; Identifying Objects, Actions, and Events; Getting Information Needed to Do the Job. *Mental Process*—Evaluating Information Against Standards; Judging Qualities of Things, Services, Other People's Work; Processing Information; Making Decisions and Solving Problems; Organizing, Planning, and Prioritizing; Updating and Using Job-Relevant Knowledge. *Work Output*—Performing General Physical Activities; Documenting and Recording Information; Drafting and Specifying Technical Devices. *Interacting with Others*—Communicating with Persons Outside Organization; Providing Consultation and Advice to Others; Interpreting Meaning of Information to Others. **Physical Work Conditions:** Special Uniform; Standing; Indoors. **Other Job Characteristics:** Consequence of Error; Importance of Being Sure All Is Done; Importance of Being Exact or Accurate.

Experience: Job Zone 2. Some previous work-related skill, knowledge, or experience may be helpful, but usually is not needed. **Job Preparation:** SVP 4.00 to 5.99—6 months to less than 2 years. **Knowledge:** Public Safety and Security; Law, Government and Jurisprudence; English Language; Building and Construction; Engineering and Technology. **Instructional Program:** 460403 Construction/Building Inspector.

Related DOT Jobs: 168.267-010 Building Inspector; 373.267-010 Fire Inspector; 373.367-010 Fire Inspector; 379.687-010 Fire-Extinguisher-Sprinkler Inspector.

33-2021.02 Fire Investigators (Fire Inspectors)

Education: Work experience in a related occupation
Employed: 14,516
Openings: 900
Projected Growth: 17.2%
Earnings: No data available.

Conduct investigations to determine causes of fires and explosions.

Tests site and materials to establish facts such as burn patterns and flash points of materials, using test equipment. Instructs children about dangers of fire. Testifies in court for cases involving fires, suspected arson, and false alarms. Prepares and maintains reports of investigation results and records of convicted arsonists and arson suspects. Analyzes evidence and other information to determine probable cause of fire or explosion. Conducts internal investigation to determine negligence and violation of laws and regulations by fire department employees. Subpoenas and interviews witnesses, property owners, and building occupants to obtain information and sworn testimony. Photographs damage and evidence relating to cause of fire or explosion, for future reference. Examines site and collects evidence to gather information relating to cause of fire, explosion, or false alarm. Swears out warrants and arrests, logs, fingerprints, and detains suspected arsonists.

GOE Number, Interest Area, and Work Group: 04.03.01; Law, Law Enforcement, and Public Safety; Law Enforcement: Investigation and Protection. **Personality Type:** Investigative. Investigative occupations frequently involve working with ideas and require an extensive amount of thinking. These occupations can involve searching for facts and figuring out problems mentally. **Work Values:** Achievement; Ability Utilization; Responsibility; Security; Social Status. **Skills:** Information Gathering; Active Listening; Critical Thinking; Writing; Problem Identification; Speaking. **Abilities:** *Cognitive*—Inductive Reasoning; Oral Expression; Problem Sensitivity; Written Expression; Flexibility of Closure; Oral Comprehension. *Psychomotor*—Arm-Hand Steadiness; Speed of Limb Movement. *Physical*—Gross Body Equilibrium; Extent Flexibility; Static Strength. *Sensory*—Speech Clarity; Far Vision; Near Vision. **General Work Activities:** *Information Input*—Getting Information Needed to Do the Job; Inspecting Equipment, Structures, Materials; Identifying Objects, Actions, and Events. *Mental Process*—Analyzing Data or Information; Making Decisions and Solving Problems; Organizing, Planning, and Prioritizing; Evaluating Information Against Standards. *Work Output*—Documenting and Recording Information; Performing General Physical Activities; Handling and Moving Objects. *Interacting with Others*—Communicating with Persons Outside Organization; Communicating with Other Workers; Interpreting Meaning of Information to Others. **Physical Work Conditions:** Special Uniform; Standing; Common Protective or Safety Attire; Indoors. **Other Job Characteristics:** Importance of Being Sure All Is Done; Consequence of Error; Importance of Being Exact or Accurate; Frustrating Circumstances.

Experience: Job Zone 4. A minimum of two to four years of work-related skill, knowledge, or experience is needed. **Job Preparation:** SVP 7.0 to less than 8.0—2 years to less than 10 years. **Knowledge:** Public Safety and Security; English Language; Law, Government and Jurisprudence; Building and Construction; Chemistry. **Instructional Program:** 430202 Fire Services Administration.

Related DOT Jobs: 373.267-014 Fire Marshal; 373.267-018 Fire-Investigation Lieutenant.

33-2022.00 Forest Fire Inspectors and Prevention Specialists (Fire Inspectors)

Education: Work experience in a related occupation
Employed: 14,516
Openings: 900
Projected Growth: 17.2%
Earnings: No data available.

Enforce fire regulations and inspect for forest fire hazards. Report forest fires and weather conditions.

Inspects camp sites to ensure camper compliance with forest use regulations. Gives directions to crew on fireline during forest fire. Observes instruments and reports meteorological data, such as temperature, relative humidity, wind direction and velocity, and types of cloud formations. Restricts public access and recreational use of forest lands during critical fire season. Directs maintenance and repair of firefighting equipment; requisitions new equipment. Maintains records and logbooks. Extinguishes smaller fires with portable extinguisher, shovel, and ax. Inspects forest tracts and logging areas for fire hazards such as accumulated wastes, mishandling of combustibles, or defective exhaust systems. Estimates size and characteristics of fire and reports findings to base camp by radio or telephone. Examines and inventories firefighting equipment, such as axes, firehoses, shovels, pumps, buckets, and fire extinguishers to determine amount and condition. Patrols and maintains surveillance, looking for forest fires, hazardous conditions, and weather phenomena. Relays messages relative to emergencies, accidents, location of crew and personnel, weather forecasts, and fire hazard conditions. Locates forest fires on area map, using azimuth sighter and known landmarks. Gives directives and instructions regarding sanitation, fire prevention, violation corrections, and related forest regulations.

GOE Number, Interest Area, and Work Group: 04.04.02; Law, Law Enforcement, and Public Safety; Public Safety: Regulations Enforcement. **Personality Type:** Realistic. Realistic occupations frequently involve work activities that include practical, hands-on problems and solutions. These occupations often deal with plants, animals, and real-world materials like wood, tools, and machinery. Many of the occupations require working outside and do not involve a lot of paperwork or working closely with others. **Work Values:** Achievement; Ability Utilization; Security; Responsibility; Social Status; Moral Values. **Skills:** Critical Thinking; Coordination; Monitoring; Information Gathering; Problem Identification; Active Learning; Judgment and Decision Making; Systems Perception. **Abilities:** *Cognitive*—Problem Sensitivity; Oral Expression; Speed of Closure; Selective Attention; Spatial Orientation; Flexibility of Closure. *Psychomotor*—Reaction Time; Multilimb Coordination; Wrist-Finger Speed; Response Orientation; Speed of Limb Movement. *Physical*—Static Strength; Trunk Strength; Stamina. *Sensory*—Far Vision; Night Vision; Glare Sensitivity. **General Work Activities:** *Information Input*—Getting Information Needed to Do the Job; Monitoring Processes, Materials, and Surroundings; Inspecting Equipment, Structures, Materials. *Mental Process*—Judging Qualities of Things, Services, Other People's Work; Making Decisions and Solving Problems; Analyzing Data or Information. *Work Output*—Performing General Physical Activities; Documenting and Recording Information; Handling and Moving Objects. *Interacting with Others*—Communicating with Persons Outside Organization; Communicating with Other Workers; Assisting and Caring for Others; Performing for or Working with the Public. **Physical Work Conditions:** Outdoors; Special Uniform; Standing; Walking or Running; Common Protective or Safety Attire; Contaminants. **Other Job Characteristics:** Consequence of Error; Frustrating Circumstances; Importance of Being Aware of New Events; Importance of Being Sure All Is Done.

Experience: Job Zone 2. Some previous work-related skill, knowledge, or experience may be helpful, but usually is not needed. **Job Preparation:** SVP 4.00 to 5.99—6 months to less than 2 years. **Knowledge:** Public Safety and Security; Geography; Education and Training; Physics; Telecommunications. **Instructional Programs:** 030203 Natural Resources Law Enforcement and Protective Services; 430202 Fire Services Administration.

Related DOT Jobs: 452.167-010 Fire Warden; 452.367-010 Fire Lookout; 452.367-014 Fire Ranger.

33-3000 Law Enforcement Workers

33-3011.00 Bailiffs (Bailiffs)

Education: No data available.
Employed: 8,870
Openings: No data available.
Projected Growth: No data available.
Earnings: $23,230

Maintain order in courts of law.

Announces entrance of judge. Stops people from entering courtroom while judge charges jury. Enforces courtroom rules of behavior and warns persons not to smoke or disturb court procedure. Guards lodging of sequestered jury. Provides jury escort to restaurant and other areas outside of courtroom to prevent jury contact with public. Maintains order in courtroom during trial and guards jury from outside contact. Checks courtroom for security and cleanliness and assures availability of sundry supplies for use of judge. Collects and retains unauthorized firearms from persons entering courtroom. Reports need for police or medical assistance to sheriff's office.

GOE Number, Interest Area, and Work Group: 04.03.01; Law, Law Enforcement, and Public Safety; Law Enforcement: Investigation and Protection. **Personality Type:** Social. Social occupations frequently involve working with, communicating with, and teaching people. These occupations often involve helping or providing service to others. **Work Values:** Security; Supervision, Human Relations; Company Policies and Practices; Moral Values; Co-workers. **Skills:** Monitoring; Social Perceptiveness; Active Listening; Problem Identification; Speaking. **Abilities:** *Cognitive*—Oral Expression; Selective Attention; Problem Sensitivity; Oral Comprehension; Time Sharing. *Psychomotor*—Reaction Time; Speed of Limb Movement; Response Orientation. *Physical*—Static Strength; Gross Body Coordination; Explosive Strength. *Sensory*—Far Vision; Speech Clarity; Peripheral Vision. **General Work Activities:** *Information Input*—Monitoring Processes, Materials, and Surroundings; Getting Information Needed to Do the Job; Inspecting Equipment, Structures, Materials; Identifying Objects, Actions, and Events. *Mental Process*—Making Decisions and Solving Problems; Judging Qualities of Things, Services, Other People's Work; Evaluating Information Against Standards. *Work Output*—Performing General Physical Activities; Handling and Moving Objects; Implementing Ideas and Programs. *Interacting with Others*—Performing for or Working with the Public; Communicating with Persons Outside Organization; Resolving Conflict and Negotiating with Others; Communicating with Other Workers. **Physical Work Conditions:** Indoors; Special Uniform; Standing. **Other Job Characteristics:** Consequence of Error; Importance of Being Aware of New Events; Importance of Being Sure All Is Done.

Experience: Job Zone 1. No previous work-related skill, knowledge, or experience is needed. **Job Preparation:** SVP Below 4.0—Less than 6 months. **Knowledge:** Public Safety and Security; Law, Government and Jurisprudence; Psychology; Customer and Personal Service; English Language; Administration and Management. **Instructional Program:** 430107 Law Enforcement/Police Science.

Related DOT Job: 377.667-010 Bailiff.

33-3012.00 Correctional Officers and Jailers
(Correctional Officers)

Education: Long-term O-T-J training
Employed: 383,408
Openings: 64,835
Projected Growth: 38.7%
Earnings: $28,540

Guard inmates in penal or rehabilitative institution in accordance with established regulations and procedures. Guard prisoners in transit between jail, courtroom, prison, or other point. Includes deputy sheriffs and police who spend the majority of their time guarding prisoners in correctional institutions.

Serves meals and distributes commissary items to prisoners. Searches prisoners, cells, and vehicles for weapons, valuables, or drugs. Uses weapons, handcuffs, and physical force to maintain discipline and order among prisoners. Takes prisoner into custody and escorts to locations within and outside of facility, such as visiting room, courtroom, or airport. Guards facility entrance to screen visitors. Records information such as prisoner identification and charges and incidences of inmate disturbance. Monitors conduct of prisoners, according to established policies, regulations, and procedures, to prevent escape or violence. Inspects locks, window bars, grills, doors, and gates at correctional facility, to prevent escape.

GOE Number, Interest Area, and Work Group: 04.03.01; Law, Law Enforcement, and Public Safety; Law Enforcement: Investigation and Protection. **Personality Type:** Realistic. Realistic occupations frequently involve work activities that include practical, hands-on problems and solutions. These occupations often deal with plants, animals, and real-world materials like wood, tools, and machinery. Many of the occupations require working outside and do not involve a lot of paperwork or working closely with others. **Work Values:** Security; Supervision, Human Relations; Company Policies and Practices; Activity; Co-workers. **Skills:** Social Perceptiveness; Speaking; Active Listening; Problem Identification; Identification of Key Causes; Coordination; Reading Comprehension. **Abilities:** *Cognitive*—Problem Sensitivity; Oral Expression; Selective Attention; Inductive Reasoning; Flexibility of Closure; Deductive Reasoning. *Psychomotor*—Reaction Time; Speed of Limb Movement; Response Orientation. *Physical*—Static Strength; Explosive Strength; Dynamic Strength. *Sensory*—Far Vision; Peripheral Vision; Near Vision; Speech Clarity. **General Work Activities:** *Information Input*—Monitoring Processes, Materials, and Surroundings; Inspecting Equipment, Structures, Materials; Getting Information Needed to Do the Job; Identifying Objects, Actions, and Events. *Mental Process*—Evaluating Information Against Standards; Updating and Using Job-Relevant Knowledge; Processing Information; Analyzing Data or Information; Making Decisions and Solving Problems. *Work Output*—Performing General Physical Activities; Handling and Moving Objects; Documenting and Recording Information. *Interacting with Others*—Assisting and Caring for Others; Communicating with Persons Outside Organization; Communicating with Other Workers. **Physical Work Conditions:** Special Uniform; Indoors; Walking or Running; Standing. **Other Job Characteristics:** Consequence of Error; Importance of Being Aware of New Events; Importance of Being Sure All Is Done.

Experience: Job Zone 2. Some previous work-related skill, knowledge, or experience may be helpful, but usually is not needed. **Job Preparation:** SVP 4.00 to 5.99—6 months to less than 2 years. **Knowledge:** Public Safety and Security; Medicine and Dentistry; Law, Government and Jurisprudence; English Language; Sociology and Anthropology; Psychology. **Instructional Programs:** 430102 Corrections/Correctional Administration; 430107 Law Enforcement/Police Science; 430199 Criminal Justice and Corrections, Other.

Related DOT Jobs: 372.367-014 Jailer; 372.567-014 Guard, Immigration; 372.667-018 Correction Officer; 372.677-010 Patrol Conductor; 375.367-010 Police Officer II.

33-3021.00 Detectives and Criminal Investigators
(Detectives and Criminal Investigators)

Education: Work experience in a related occupation
Employed: 79,167
Openings: 8,048
Projected Growth: 21%
Earnings: No data available.

Conduct investigations related to suspected violations of federal, state, or local laws, to prevent or solve crimes.

GOE Number, Interest Area, and Work Group: 04.03.01; Law, Law Enforcement, and Public Safety; Law Enforcement: Investigation and Protection. **Instructional Programs:** 430106 Forensic Technology/Technician; 430107 Law Enforcement/Police Science. **Note:** The Department of Labor has not collected some data for this job, so it has fewer details than the other descriptions.

33-3021.01 Police Detectives (Detectives and Criminal Investigators)

Education: Work experience in a related occupation

Employed: 79,167

Openings: 8,048

Projected Growth: 21%

Earnings: No data available.

Conduct investigations to prevent crimes or solve criminal cases.

Prepares assigned cases for court and charges or responses to charges, according to formalized procedures. Reviews governmental agency files to obtain identifying data pertaining to suspects or establishments suspected of violating laws. Maintains surveillance of establishments to attain identifying information on suspects. Arrests or assists in arrest of criminals or suspects. Observes and photographs narcotic purchase transaction to compile evidence and protect undercover investigators. Examines scene of crime to obtain clues and gather evidence. Schedules polygraph test for consenting parties, and records results of test interpretations for presentation with findings. Records progress of investigation, maintains informational files on suspects, and submits reports to commanding officer or magistrate to authorize warrants. Interviews complainant, witnesses, and accused persons to obtain facts or statements. Investigates establishments or persons to establish facts supporting complainant or accused, using supportive information from witnesses or tangible evidence. Testifies before court and grand jury and appears in court as witness.

GOE Number, Interest Area, and Work Group: 04.03.01; Law, Law Enforcement, and Public Safety; Law Enforcement: Investigation and Protection. **Personality Type:** Enterprising. Enterprising occupations frequently involve starting up and carrying out projects. These occupations can involve leading people and making many decisions. They sometimes require risk taking and often deal with business. **Work Values:** Security; Responsibility; Ability Utilization; Achievement; Supervision, Human Relations. **Skills:** Information Gathering; Critical Thinking; Information Organization; Synthesis/Reorganization; Active Learning; Social Perceptiveness; Speaking; Active Listening. **Abilities:** *Cognitive*—Inductive Reasoning; Oral Comprehension; Deductive Reasoning; Oral Expression; Written Expression. *Psychomotor*—Reaction Time; Wrist-Finger Speed; Control Precision. *Physical*—Gross Body Coordination; Extent Flexibility; Explosive Strength. *Sensory*—Near Vision; Sound Localization; Speech Clarity; Auditory Attention; Speech Recognition; Far Vision. **General Work Activities:** *Information Input*—Getting Information Needed to Do the Job; Identifying Objects, Actions, and Events; Monitoring Processes, Materials, and Surroundings. *Mental Process*—Analyzing Data or

Information; Making Decisions and Solving Problems; Updating and Using Job-Relevant Knowledge; Processing Information. *Work Output*—Documenting and Recording Information; Performing General Physical Activities; Handling and Moving Objects. *Interacting with Others*—Performing for or Working with the Public; Communicating with Other Workers; Communicating with Persons Outside Organization. **Physical Work Conditions:** Special Uniform; Indoors; Sitting. **Other Job Characteristics:** Frustrating Circumstances; Importance of Being Exact or Accurate; Consequence of Error.

Experience: Job Zone 4. A minimum of two to four years of work-related skill, knowledge, or experience is needed. **Job Preparation:** SVP 7.0 to less than 8.0—2 years to less than 10 years. **Knowledge:** Public Safety and Security; Law, Government and Jurisprudence; Psychology; English Language; Clerical. **Instructional Program:** 430107 Law Enforcement/Police Science.

Related DOT Jobs: 375.267-010 Detective; 375.267-014 Detective, Narcotics and Vice; 375.267-018 Investigator, Narcotics; 375.267-022 Investigator, Vice; 375.267-034 Investigator, Internal Affairs.

33-3021.02 Police Identification and Records Officers (Detectives and Criminal Investigators)

Education: Work experience in a related occupation

Employed: 79,167

Openings: 8,048

Projected Growth: 21%

Earnings: No data available.

Collect evidence at crime scene, classify and identify fingerprints, and photograph evidence for use in criminal and civil cases.

Develops film and prints, using photographic developing equipment. Submits evidence to supervisor. Photographs, records physical description, and fingerprints homicide victims and suspects for identification. Classifies and files fingerprints. Lifts prints from crime site, using special tape. Dusts selected areas of crime scene to locate and reveal latent fingerprints. Photographs crime or accident scene to obtain record of evidence.

GOE Number, Interest Area, and Work Group: 04.03.02; Law, Law Enforcement, and Public Safety; Law Enforcement: Technology. **Personality Type:** Conventional. Conventional occupations frequently involve following set procedures and routines. These occupations can include working with data and details more than with ideas. Usually there is a clear line of authority to follow. **Work Values:** Supervision, Human Relations; Security; Company Policies and Practices; Moral Values; Co-workers; Activity. **Skills:** Information Organization; Information Gathering; Active Listening; Operation and Control; Equipment Selection. **Abilities:** *Cognitive*—Category Flexibility; Information Ordering; Deductive Reasoning; Inductive Reasoning; Written Comprehension. *Psychomotor*—Control Precision; Arm-Hand Steadiness; Multilimb Coordination. *Physical*—Extent Flexibility; Trunk Strength. *Sensory*—Near Vision; Visual Color Discrimination; Night Vision. **General Work Activities:** *Information Input*—Getting Information Needed to Do the Job; Identifying Objects, Actions, and Events; Monitoring Processes, Materials, and Surroundings. *Men-*

tal Process—Processing Information; Updating and Using Job-Relevant Knowledge; Analyzing Data or Information; Making Decisions and Solving Problems. *Work Output*—Documenting and Recording Information; Controlling Machines and Processes; Handling and Moving Objects. *Interacting with Others*—Communicating with Other Workers; Interpreting Meaning of Information to Others; Communicating with Persons Outside Organization. **Physical Work Conditions:** Indoors; Standing; Special Uniform. **Other Job Characteristics:** Importance of Being Exact or Accurate; Importance of Being Sure All Is Done; Consequence of Error.

Experience: Job Zone 3. Previous work-related skill, knowledge, or experience is required. **Job Preparation:** SVP 6.0 to less than 7.0—More than 1 year and less than 4 years. **Knowledge:** Public Safety and Security; Clerical; Law, Government and Jurisprudence; English Language; Chemistry. **Instructional Program:** 430107 Law Enforcement/Police Science.

Related DOT Jobs: 375.384-010 Police Officer, Identification and Records; 375.387-010 Fingerprint Classifier.

33-3021.03 Criminal Investigators and Special Agents (Detectives and Criminal Investigators)

Education: Work experience in a related occupation
Employed: 79,167
Openings: 8,048
Projected Growth: 21%
Earnings: No data available.

Investigate alleged or suspected criminal violations of federal, state, or local laws, to determine whether evidence is sufficient to recommend prosecution.

Photographs, fingerprints, and measures height and weight of arrested suspects, noting physical characteristics, and posts data on record for filing. Compares crime scene fingerprints with those of suspect or fingerprint files to identify perpetrator, using computer. Assists in determining scope, timing, and direction of investigation. Examines records to detect links in chain of evidence or information. Searches for evidence, dusts surfaces to reveal latent fingerprints, and collects and records evidence and documents, using cameras and investigative equipment. Obtains and uses search and arrest warrants. Analyzes charge, complaint, or allegation of law violation to identify issues involved and types of evidence needed. Develops and uses informants to get leads to information. Maintains surveillance and performs undercover assignments. Reports critical information to and coordinates activities with other offices or agencies when applicable. Serves subpoenas or other official papers. Testifies before grand juries. Obtains and verifies evidence or establishes facts by interviewing, observing, and interrogating suspects and witnesses and analyzing records. Presents findings in reports.

GOE Number, Interest Area, and Work Group: 04.03.01; Law, Law Enforcement, and Public Safety; Law Enforcement: Investigation and Protection. **Personality Type:** Enterprising. Enterprising occupations frequently involve starting up and carrying out projects. These occupations can involve leading people and making many decisions. They sometimes require risk taking and of-

ten deal with business. **Work Values:** Security; Achievement; Ability Utilization; Social Status; Company Policies and Practices; Supervision, Human Relations. **Skills:** Active Listening; Information Gathering; Speaking; Synthesis/Reorganization; Social Perceptiveness; Problem Identification; Reading Comprehension; Critical Thinking; Writing. **Abilities:** *Cognitive*—Inductive Reasoning; Oral Comprehension; Oral Expression; Written Expression; Flexibility of Closure. *Psychomotor*—Multilimb Coordination; Response Orientation; Speed of Limb Movement; Rate Control. *Physical*—Explosive Strength; Gross Body Coordination; Dynamic Flexibility; Stamina. *Sensory*—Near Vision; Speech Recognition; Far Vision; Speech Clarity. **General Work Activities:** *Information Input*—Getting Information Needed to Do the Job; Identifying Objects, Actions, and Events; Monitoring Processes, Materials, and Surroundings. *Mental Process*—Analyzing Data or Information; Judging Qualities of Things, Services, Other People's Work; Organizing, Planning, and Prioritizing; Making Decisions and Solving Problems. *Work Output*—Documenting and Recording Information; Implementing Ideas and Programs; Handling and Moving Objects. *Interacting with Others*—Communicating with Other Workers; Interpreting Meaning of Information to Others; Establishing and Maintaining Relationships. **Physical Work Conditions:** Standing; Outdoors; Indoors; Walking or Running. **Other Job Characteristics:** Importance of Being Sure All Is Done; Consequence of Error; Importance of Being Aware of New Events; Frustrating Circumstances; Importance of Being Exact or Accurate.

Experience: Job Zone 4. A minimum of two to four years of work-related skill, knowledge, or experience is needed. **Job Preparation:** SVP 7.0 to less than 8.0—2 years to less than 10 years. **Knowledge:** Public Safety and Security; Law, Government and Jurisprudence; Sociology and Anthropology; English Language; Telecommunications; Psychology. **Instructional Program:** 430107 Law Enforcement/Police Science.

Related DOT Jobs: 375.167-042 Special Agent; 377.264-010 Identification Officer.

33-3021.04 Child Support, Missing Persons, and Unemployment Insurance Fraud Investigators (All Other Protective Service Workers)

Education: Short-term O-T-J training
Employed: 166,335
Openings: 23,282
Projected Growth: 19%
Earnings: $17,470

Conduct investigations to locate, arrest, and return fugitives and persons wanted for nonpayment of support payments and unemployment insurance fraud. Conduct investigations to locate missing persons.

Prepares file indicating data such as wage records of accused, witnesses, and blood test results. Completes reports to document information acquired during criminal and child support cases and actions taken. Monitors child support payments awarded by court to ensure compliance and enforcement of child support laws. Examines case file to determine that divorce decree and court-ordered judgment for payment are in order. Examines medical and dental X rays, fingerprints, and other information to identify bodies held in morgue. Testifies in court to present evidence regarding cases. Computes amount of child support payments. Obtains extradition papers to bring about return of fugitive. Contacts employers, neighbors, relatives, and law enforcement agencies to locate person sought and verify information gathered about case. Interviews client to obtain information such as relocation of absent parent, amount of child support awarded, and names of witnesses. Reviews files and criminal records to develop possible leads, such as previous addresses and aliases. Serves warrants and makes arrests to return persons sought in connection with crimes or for nonpayment of child support. Interviews and discusses case with parent charged with nonpayment of support to resolve issues in lieu of filing court proceedings. Determines types of court jurisdiction, according to facts and circumstances surrounding case; files court action. Confers with prosecuting attorney to prepare court case and with court clerk to obtain arrest warrant and schedule court date.

GOE Number, Interest Area, and Work Group: 04.03.01; Law, Law Enforcement, and Public Safety; Law Enforcement: Investigation and Protection. **Personality Type:** Enterprising. Enterprising occupations frequently involve starting up and carrying out projects. These occupations can involve leading people and making many decisions. They sometimes require risk taking and often deal with business. **Work Values:** Achievement; Security; Ability Utilization; Activity; Supervision, Human Relations. **Skills:** Active Listening; Speaking; Information Gathering; Reading Comprehension; Critical Thinking. **Abilities:** *Cognitive*—Oral Comprehension; Written Comprehension; Problem Sensitivity; Oral Expression; Written Expression. *Psychomotor*—none met the criteria. *Physical*—none met the criteria. *Sensory*—Speech Clarity; Near Vision; Speech Recognition. **General Work Activities:** *Information Input*—Getting Information Needed to Do the Job; Identifying Objects, Actions, and Events; Monitoring Processes, Materials, and Surroundings. *Mental Process*—Processing Information; Evaluating Information Against Standards; Making Decisions and Solving Problems; Organizing, Planning, and Prioritizing. *Work Output*—Documenting and Recording Information; Implementing Ideas and Programs; Performing General Physical Activities. *Interacting with Others*—Communicating with Persons Outside Organization; Establishing and Maintaining Relationships; Communicating with Other Workers. **Physical Work Conditions:** Indoors; Sitting; Walking or Running. **Other Job Characteristics:** Frustrating Circumstances; Consequence of Error; Importance of Being Exact or Accurate; Importance of Being Sure All Is Done.

Experience: Job Zone 4. A minimum of two to four years of work-related skill, knowledge, or experience is needed. **Job Preparation:** SVP 7.0 to less than 8.0—2 years to less than 10 years. **Knowledge:** Law, Government and Jurisprudence; Public Safety and Security; Economics and Accounting; English Language; Mathematics. **Instructional Programs:** 430102 Corrections/Correctional Administration; 430106 Forensic Technology/Technician; 430199 Criminal Justice and Corrections, Other; 439999 Protective Services, Other.

Related DOT Jobs: 195.267-022 Child Support Officer; 375.267-038 Police Officer III.

33-3021.05 Immigration and Customs Inspectors
(Inspectors and Compliance Officers)

Education: Work experience in a related occupation
Employed: 176,175
Openings: 19,910
Projected Growth: 10.5%
Earnings: $36,820

Investigate and inspect persons, common carriers, goods, and merchandise arriving in or departing from the United States or moving between states, to detect violations of immigration and customs laws and regulations.

Examines, classifies, weighs, measures, and appraises merchandise to enforce regulations of U.S. Customs Service and to prevent illegal importing and exporting. Examines visas and passports and interviews persons to determine eligibility for admission, residence, and travel in U.S. Determines investigative and seizure techniques to be used, and seizes contraband, undeclared merchandise, vehicles, and air or sea craft carrying smuggled merchandise. Keeps records and writes reports of activities, findings, transactions, violations, discrepancies, and decisions. Determines duty and taxes to be paid, investigates applications for duty refunds, or petitions for remission or mitigation of penalties. Collects samples of merchandise for examination, appraising, or testing; requests laboratory analyses. Issues or denies permits. Institutes civil and criminal prosecutions and assists other governmental agencies with regulation violation issues. Interprets and explains laws and regulations to others. Reviews private and public records and documents to establish, assemble, and verify facts and secure legal evidence. Inspects cargo, baggage, personal articles, and common carriers entering or leaving U.S. for compliance with revenue laws and U.S. Customs Service regulations. Testifies in administrative and judicial proceedings. Arrests, detains, paroles, or arranges for deportation of persons in violation of customs or immigration laws.

GOE Number, Interest Area, and Work Group: 04.03.01; Law, Law Enforcement, and Public Safety; Law Enforcement: Investigation and Protection. **Personality Type:** Conventional. Conventional occupations frequently involve following set procedures and routines. These occupations can include working with data and details more than with ideas. Usually there is a clear line of authority to follow. **Work Values:** Supervision, Human Relations; Security; Company Policies and Practices; Supervision, Technical; Activity. **Skills:** Problem Identification; Information Gathering; Writing; Speaking; Reading Comprehension. **Abilities:** *Cognitive*—Oral Expression; Problem Sensitivity; Written Comprehension; Written Expression; Oral Comprehension. *Psychomotor*—none met the criteria. *Physical*—Extent Flexibility; Static Strength; Stamina; Gross Body Coordination. *Sensory*—Near Vision; Speech Clarity; Far Vision. **General Work Activities:** *Information Input*—Getting Information Needed to Do the Job; Identifying Objects, Actions, and Events; Monitoring Processes, Materials, and Surroundings; Inspecting Equipment, Structures, Materials. *Mental Process*—Evaluating Information Against Standards; Judging Qualities of Things, Services, Other People's Work; Making Decisions and Solving Problems. *Work Output*—Documenting and Recording Information; Handling and Moving Objects; Implementing Ideas and Programs. *Interacting with Others—*Communicating with Persons Outside Organization; Interpreting Meaning of Information to Others; Communicating with Other Workers. **Physical Work Conditions:** Indoors; Standing; Using Hands on Objects, Tools, or Controls. **Other Job Characteristics:** Consequence of Error; Importance of Being Aware of New Events; Importance of Being Exact or Accurate; Importance of Being Sure All Is Done.

Experience: Job Zone 3. Previous work-related skill, knowledge, or experience is required. **Job Preparation:** SVP 6.0 to less than 7.0—More than 1 year and less than 4 years. **Knowledge:** Law, Government and Jurisprudence; English Language; Public Safety and Security; Communications and Media; Mathematics. **Instructional Programs:** 030203 Natural Resources Law Enforcement and Protective Services; 150701 Occupational Safety and Health Technology/Technician; 521601 Taxation.

Related DOT Jobs: 168.167-022 Immigration Inspector; 168.267-018 Customs Import Specialist; 168.267-022 Customs Inspector; 168.387-010 Opener-Verifier-Packer, Customs; 188.167-090 Special Agent, Customs.

33-3031.00 Fish and Game Wardens (Fish and Game Wardens)

Education: No data available.

Employed: 7,080

Openings: No data available.

Projected Growth: No data available.

Earnings: $35,040

Patrol assigned area to prevent violations of fish and game law. Investigate reports of damage to crops or property by wildlife. Compile biological data.

Traps beavers, dynamites beaver dams, and tranquilizes animals to implement approved control measures. Ensures method and equipment used are lawful and apprehends violators. Investigates hunting accidents and reports of fish and game law violations, issues warnings or citations, and files reports. Collects and reports information on population and condition of fish and wildlife in their habitat, availability of game food and cover, and suspected pollution. Searches area of reported property damage for animal tracks, leavings, and other evidence to identify specie of animal responsible. Serves warrants, makes arrests, and prepares and presents evidence in court actions. Seizes equipment used in fish and game law violations and arranges for disposition of fish and game illegally taken or possessed. Resurveys area and totals bag counts of hunters to determine effectiveness of control measures. Assists in promoting hunter safety training. Photographs extent of damage, documents other evidence, estimates financial loss, and recommends compensation. Addresses schools and civic groups to disseminate wildlife information and promote public relations. Patrols assigned area by car, boat, airplane, horse, or on foot to observe persons engaged in taking fish and game. Recommends revisions or changes in hunting and trapping regulations or seasons, animal relocation and release to obtain balance of wildlife and habitat.

GOE Number, Interest Area, and Work Group: 04.03.01; Law, Law Enforcement, and Public Safety; Law Enforcement: Investigation and Protection. **Personality Type:** Realistic. Realistic occupations frequently involve work activities that include practical, hands-on problems and solutions. These occupations often deal with plants, animals, and real-world materials like wood, tools, and machinery. Many of the occupations require working outside and do not involve a lot of paperwork or working closely with others. **Work Values:** Responsibility; Security; Achievement; Authority; Autonomy; Ability Utilization; Variety. **Skills:** Speaking; Identification of Key Causes; Active Listening; Reading Comprehension; Critical Thinking; Information Gathering; Problem Identification. **Abilities:** *Cognitive—*Oral Expression; Inductive Reasoning; Spatial Orientation; Problem Sensitivity; Selective Attention. *Psychomotor—*Rate Control; Control Precision; Speed of Limb Movement; Multilimb Coordination; Reaction Time. *Physical—*Static Strength; Stamina; Dynamic Strength; Trunk Strength. *Sensory—*Speech Clarity; Night Vision; Far Vision. **General Work Activities:** *Information Input—*Getting Information Needed to Do the Job; Identifying Objects, Actions, and Events; Monitoring Processes, Materials, and Surroundings. *Mental Process—*Analyzing Data or Information; Evaluating Information Against Standards; Making Decisions and Solving Problems; Organizing, Planning, and Prioritizing. *Work Output—*Performing General Physical Activities; Documenting and Recording Information; Implementing Ideas and Programs. *Interacting with Others—*Performing for or Working with the Public; Communicating with Persons Outside Organization; Resolving Conflict and Negotiating with Others. **Physical Work Conditions:** Special Uniform; Outdoors; Walking or Running; Hazardous Situations. **Other Job Characteristics:** Consequence of Error; Importance of Being Aware of New Events; Importance of Being Sure All Is Done; Frustrating Circumstances.

Experience: Job Zone 3. Previous work-related skill, knowledge, or experience is required. **Job Preparation:** SVP 6.0 to less than 7.0—More than 1 year and less than 4 years. **Knowledge:** Biology; Law, Government and Jurisprudence; Public Safety and Security; Mathematics; Administration and Management. **Instructional Programs:** 010303 Aquaculture Operations and Production Management; 030203 Natural Resources Law Enforcement and Protective Services; 030301 Fishing and Fisheries Sciences and Management; 030601 Wildlife and Wildlands Management.

Related DOT Jobs: 379.167-010 Fish and Game Warden; 379.267-010 Wildlife Control Agent.

33-3041.00 Parking Enforcement Workers (Parking Enforcement Officers)

Education: No data available.

Employed: 10,100

Openings: No data available.

Projected Growth: No data available.

Earnings: $24,850

Patrol assigned area such as public parking lot or section of city to issue tickets to overtime parking violators and illegally parked vehicles.

Writes violation tickets for illegally parked vehicles. Winds parking meter clocks. Prepares required forms and records. Chalks tires of vehicles, records time, and returns at specific intervals. Reports missing traffic signals or signs to superior at end of shift. Collects coins deposited in meters.

GOE Number, Interest Area, and Work Group: 04.03.01; Law, Law Enforcement, and Public Safety; Law Enforcement: Investigation and Protection. **Personality Type:** Conventional. Conventional occupations frequently involve following set procedures and routines. These occupations can include working with data and details more than with ideas. Usually there is a clear line of authority to follow. **Work Values:** Security; Independence; Supervision, Human Relations; Company Policies and Practices; Supervision, Technical; Activity; Moral Values. **Skills:** Writing; Reading Comprehension; Operation and Control. **Abilities:** *Cognitive*—Written Expression; Memorization; Number Facility; Written Comprehension; Information Ordering; Spatial Orientation. *Psychomotor*—Finger Dexterity. *Physical*—Gross Body Coordination; Stamina. *Sensory*—Glare Sensitivity. **General Work Activities:** *Information Input*—Getting Information Needed to Do the Job; Monitoring Processes, Materials, and Surroundings; Identifying Objects, Actions, and Events. *Mental Process*—Processing Information; Making Decisions and Solving Problems; Analyzing Data or Information. *Work Output*—Documenting and Recording Information; Performing General Physical Activities; Operating Vehicles or Equipment; Handling and Moving Objects. *Interacting with Others*—Communicating with Other Workers; Performing Administrative Activities; Performing for or Working with the Public. **Physical Work Conditions:** Special Uniform; Outdoors; Standing. **Other Job Characteristics:** Importance of Being Sure All Is Done; Importance of Being Aware of New Events; Importance of Repeating Same Tasks; Importance of Being Exact or Accurate.

Experience: Job Zone 1. No previous work-related skill, knowledge, or experience is needed. **Job Preparation:** SVP Below 4.0—Less than 6 months. **Knowledge:** Clerical; Law, Government and Jurisprudence; Geography; Mathematics; Public Safety and Security; Communications and Media. **Instructional Program:** 430107 Law Enforcement/Police Science.

Related DOT Job: 375.587-010 Parking Enforcement Officer.

33-3051.00 Police and Sheriff's Patrol Officers (Police Patrol Officers)

Education: Long-term O-T-J training

Employed: 445,632

Openings: 51,739

Projected Growth: 31.6%

Earnings: $37,710

Maintain order, enforce laws and ordinances, and protect life and property in an assigned patrol district. Patrol a specific area on foot or in a vehicle; direct traffic; issue traffic summonses; investigate accidents; apprehend and arrest suspects; serve legal processes of courts.

GOE Number, Interest Area, and Work Group: 04.03.01; Law, Law Enforcement, and Public Safety; Law Enforcement: Investigation and Protection. **Instructional Program:** 430107 Law Enforcement/Police Science. **Note:** The Department of Labor has not collected some data for this job, so it has fewer details than the other descriptions.

33-3051.01 Police Patrol Officers (Police Patrol Officers)

Education: Long-term O-T-J training

Employed: 445,632

Openings: 51,739

Projected Growth: 31.6%

Earnings: $37,710

Patrol assigned area to enforce laws and ordinances, regulate traffic, control crowds, prevent crime, and arrest violators.

Expedites processing of prisoners, and prepares and maintains records of prisoner bookings and prisoner status during booking and pretrial process. Maintains order, responds to emergencies, protects people and property, and enforces motor vehicle and criminal law. Testifies in court to present evidence or act as witness in traffic and criminal cases. Records facts and prepares reports to document activities. Renders aid to accident victims and other persons requiring first aid for physical injuries. Interviews principal and eye witnesses. Photographs crime or accident scene. Draws diagram of crime or accident scene. Relays complaint and emergency-request information to appropriate agency dispatcher. Arrests perpetrator of criminal act or submits citation or warning to violator of motor vehicle ordinance. Patrols specific area on foot, horseback, or motorized conveyance. Provides road information to assist motorists. Investigates traffic accidents and other accidents to determine causes and to determine if crime has been committed. Evaluates complaint and emergency-request information to determine response requirements. Reviews facts to determine if criminal act or statute violation is involved. Directs traffic flow and reroutes traffic in case of emergencies. Monitors traffic to ensure motorists observe traffic regulations and exhibit safe driving procedures.

GOE Number, Interest Area, and Work Group: 04.03.01; Law, Law Enforcement, and Public Safety; Law Enforcement: Investigation and Protection. **Personality Type:** Social. Social occupations frequently involve working with, communicating with, and teaching people. These occupations often involve helping or providing service to others. **Work Values:** Security; Achievement; Company Policies and Practices; Supervision, Human Relations; Variety. **Skills:** Active Listening; Problem Identification; Critical Thinking; Information Gathering; Service Orientation; Social Perceptiveness. **Abilities:** *Cognitive*—Oral Expression; Inductive Reasoning; Written Expression; Problem Sensitivity; Time Sharing; Oral Comprehension. *Psychomotor*—Reaction Time; Response Orientation; Speed of Limb Movement. *Physical*—Static Strength; Explosive Strength; Stamina. *Sensory*—Far Vision; Speech Clarity; Speech Recognition; Near Vision; Peripheral Vision. **General Work Activities:** *Information Input*—Getting Information Needed to Do the Job; Identifying Objects, Actions, and Events; Monitoring Processes, Materials, and Surroundings. *Mental Process*—Analyzing Data or Information; Evaluating Information Against Standards; Updating and Using Job-Relevant Knowledge; Making Decisions and Solving Problems. *Work Output*—Documenting and Recording Information; Operating Vehicles or Equipment; Performing

General Physical Activities. *Interacting with Others*—Performing for or Working with the Public; Assisting and Caring for Others; Resolving Conflict and Negotiating with Others. **Physical Work Conditions:** Special Uniform; Outdoors; Walking or Running. **Other Job Characteristics:** Consequence of Error; Frustrating Circumstances; Importance of Being Aware of New Events.

Experience: Job Zone 3. Previous work-related skill, knowledge, or experience is required. **Job Preparation:** SVP 6.0 to less than 7.0—More than 1 year and less than 4 years. **Knowledge:** Public Safety and Security; Law, Government and Jurisprudence; English Language; Medicine and Dentistry; Psychology. **Instructional Program:** 430107 Law Enforcement/Police Science.

Related DOT Jobs: 168.167-010 Customs Patrol Officer; 169.167-042 Park Ranger; 372.363-010 Protective Officer; 375.263-010 Accident-Prevention-Squad Police Officer; 375.263-014 Police Officer I; 375.263-018 State-Highway Police Officer; 375.264-010 Police Officer, Crime Prevention; 375.267-030 Police Inspector II; 375.267-042 Police Officer, Safety Instruction; 375.363-010 Border Guard; 375.367-014 Complaint Evaluation Officer; 375.367-018 Police Officer, Booking; 379.263-014 Public-Safety Officer.

33-3051.02 Highway Patrol Pilots (Police Patrol Officers)

Education: Long-term O-T-J training
Employed: 445,632
Openings: 51,739
Projected Growth: 31.6%
Earnings: $37,710

Pilot aircraft to patrol highway and to enforce traffic laws.

Reviews facts to determine if criminal act or statute violation involved. Renders aid to accident victims and other persons requiring first aid for physical injuries. Relays complaint and emergency request information to appropriate agency dispatcher. Prepares reports to document activities. Expedites processing of prisoners, prepares and maintains records of prisoner bookings, and maintains record of prisoner status during booking and pre-trial process. Testifies in court to present evidence or act as witness in traffic and criminal cases. Evaluates complaint and emergency request information to determine response requirements. Records facts, photographs and diagrams crime or accident scene, and interviews witnesses to gather information for possible use in legal action or safety programs. Pilots airplane to maintain order, respond to emergencies, to enforce traffic and criminal laws, and apprehend criminals. Arrests perpetrator of criminal act or submits citation or warning to violator of motor vehicle ordinance. Investigates traffic accidents and other accidents to determine causes and to determine if crimes were committed. Informs ground personnel of traffic congestion or unsafe driving conditions to ensure traffic flow and reduce incidence of accidents. Informs ground personnel where to reroute traffic in case of emergencies.

GOE Number, Interest Area, and Work Group: 04.03.01; Law, Law Enforcement, and Public Safety; Law Enforcement: Investigation and Protection. **Personality Type:** Realistic. Realistic occupations frequently involve work activities that include practical, hands-on problems and solutions. These occupations often deal with plants, animals, and real-world materials like wood, tools, and machinery. Many of the occupations require working outside and do not involve a lot of paperwork or working closely with others. **Work Values:** Achievement; Security; Company Policies and Practices; Supervision, Human Relations; Responsibility; Ability Utilization. **Skills:** Operation and Control; Social Perceptiveness; Active Listening; Reading Comprehension; Problem Identification. **Abilities:** *Cognitive*—Oral Expression; Oral Comprehension; Spatial Orientation; Written Expression; Problem Sensitivity. *Psychomotor*—Reaction Time; Response Orientation; Rate Control. *Physical*—Static Strength; Extent Flexibility; Explosive Strength. *Sensory*—Far Vision; Depth Perception; Glare Sensitivity. **General Work Activities:** *Information Input*—Getting Information Needed to Do the Job; Identifying Objects, Actions, and Events; Monitoring Processes, Materials, and Surroundings. *Mental Process*—Judging Qualities of Things, Services, Other People's Work; Updating and Using Job-Relevant Knowledge; Analyzing Data or Information. *Work Output*—Documenting and Recording Information; Operating Vehicles or Equipment; Performing General Physical Activities. *Interacting with Others*—Communicating with Persons Outside Organization; Performing for or Working with the Public; Assisting and Caring for Others; Communicating with Other Workers. **Physical Work Conditions:** Special Uniform; Using Hands on Objects, Tools, or Controls; Outdoors; Sitting. **Other Job Characteristics:** Consequence of Error; Importance of Being Sure All Is Done; Importance of Being Aware of New Events; Degree of Automation.

Experience: Job Zone 3. Previous work-related skill, knowledge, or experience is required. **Job Preparation:** SVP 6.0 to less than 7.0—More than 1 year and less than 4 years. **Knowledge:** Public Safety and Security; Transportation; Law, Government and Jurisprudence; Telecommunications; Geography. **Instructional Program:** 430107 Law Enforcement/Police Science.

Related DOT Job: 375.163-014 Pilot, Highway Patrol.

33-3051.03 Sheriffs and Deputy Sheriffs (Sheriffs and Deputy Sheriffs)

Education: Long-term O-T-J training
Employed: 91,479
Openings: 3,130
Projected Growth: 34.2%
Earnings: $28,270

Enforce law and order in rural or unincorporated districts; serve legal processes of courts. Patrol courthouse, guard court, or grand jury; escort defendants.

Maintains records and submits reports of dispositions and logs daily activities. Confiscates real or personal property by court order, and posts notices in public places. Arranges delivery of prisoner's arrest records from criminal investigation unit, at District Attorney's request. Notifies patrol units to take violators into custody, or provide needed assistance or medical aid. Takes control of accident scene to maintain traffic flow, assist accident victims, and investigate causes. Investigates illegal or suspicious activities of persons. Transports or escorts prisoners or defendants between courtroom, prison or jail, District Attorney's offices, or medical facilities. Executes arrest warrants, locating and taking persons into custody and issues citations. Serves subpoenas and summonses. Patrols and guards courthouse, grand-jury room, or assigned areas to provide security, enforce laws, maintain order, and arrest violators. Questions individuals entering secured areas to determine purpose of business and directs or reroutes individuals to destinations.

GOE Number, Interest Area, and Work Group: 04.03.01; Law, Law Enforcement, and Public Safety; Law Enforcement: Investigation and Protection. **Personality Type:** Social. Social occupations frequently involve working with, communicating with, and teaching people. These occupations often involve helping or providing service to others. **Work Values:** Security; Supervision, Human Relations; Achievement; Responsibility; Company Policies and Practices. **Skills:** Social Perceptiveness; Active Listening; Speaking; Information Gathering; Problem Identification. **Abilities:** *Cognitive*—Oral Expression; Oral Comprehension; Written Comprehension; Inductive Reasoning; Deductive Reasoning; Information Ordering. *Psychomotor*—Multilimb Coordination; Reaction Time; Response Orientation. *Physical*—Trunk Strength; Extent Flexibility; Stamina; Gross Body Coordination. *Sensory*—Near Vision; Night Vision; Far Vision. **General Work Activities:** *Information Input*—Getting Information Needed to Do the Job; Monitoring Processes, Materials, and Surroundings; Identifying Objects, Actions, and Events. *Mental Process*—Making Decisions and Solving Problems; Updating and Using Job-Relevant Knowledge; Analyzing Data or Information; Judging Qualities of Things, Services, Other People's Work; Processing Information. *Work Output*—Performing General Physical Activities; Documenting and Recording Information; Operating Vehicles or Equipment; Handling and Moving Objects. *Interacting with Others*—Performing for or Working with the Public; Communicating with Persons Outside Organization; Communicating with Other Workers. **Physical Work Conditions:** Special Uniform; Outdoors; Indoors. **Other Job Characteristics:** Consequence of Error; Frustrating Circumstances; Importance of Being Exact or Accurate; Importance of Being Sure All Is Done; Importance of Being Aware of New Events.

Experience: Job Zone 2. Some previous work-related skill, knowledge, or experience may be helpful, but usually is not needed. **Job Preparation:** SVP 4.00 to 5.99—6 months to less than 2 years. **Knowledge:** Public Safety and Security; Law, Government and Jurisprudence; Psychology; Geography; Clerical. **Instructional Program:** 430107 Law Enforcement/Police Science.

Related DOT Jobs: 377.263-010 Sheriff, Deputy; 377.363-010 Deputy Sheriff, Grand Jury; 377.667-014 Deputy Sheriff, Building Guard; 377.667-018 Deputy Sheriff, Civil Division.

33-3052.00 Transit and Railroad Police (Railroad and Transit Police and Special Agents)

Education: No data available.

Employed: 5,140

Openings: No data available.

Projected Growth: No data available.

Earnings: $40,360

Protect and police railroad and transit property, employees, or passengers.

Directs and coordinates the daily activities and training of security staff. Investigates or directs investigations of freight theft, suspicious damage or loss of passenger's valuables, and other crimes on railroad property. Guards, patrols, and polices railroad yards, cars, stations, and other facilities to protect company property and shipments and to maintain order. Examines credentials of unauthorized persons attempting to enter secured areas. Records and verifies seal numbers from boxcars containing high pilferage items such as cigarettes and liquor, to detect tampering. Apprehends or coordinates with local enforcement personnel to apprehend or remove trespassers or thieves from rail property. Seals empty boxcars by twisting nails in door hasps, using nail twister. Plans and implements special safety and preventive programs, such as fire and accident prevention. Prepares reports documenting the results and activities concerned with investigations. Directs security activities at derailments, fires, floods, and strikes involving railroad property. Interviews neighbors, associates, and former employers of job applicants to verify personal references and obtain work history data.

GOE Number, Interest Area, and Work Group: 04.03.01; Law, Law Enforcement, and Public Safety; Law Enforcement: Investigation and Protection. **Personality Type:** Enterprising. Enterprising occupations frequently involve starting up and carrying out projects. These occupations can involve leading people and making many decisions. They sometimes require risk taking and often deal with business. **Work Values:** Responsibility; Security; Achievement; Company Policies and Practices; Co-workers; Ability Utilization; Activity; Authority. **Skills:** Active Listening; Speaking; Information Gathering; Coordination; Writing; Critical Thinking; Problem Identification. **Abilities:** *Cognitive*—Inductive Reasoning; Oral Expression; Problem Sensitivity; Written Expression; Deductive Reasoning. *Psychomotor*—Speed of Limb Movement; Response Orientation; Reaction Time. *Physical*—Static Strength; Explosive Strength; Stamina. *Sensory*—Night Vision; Near Vision; Far Vision. **General Work Activities:** *Information Input*—Getting Information Needed to Do the Job; Monitoring Processes, Materials, and Surroundings; Identifying Objects, Actions, and Events. *Mental Process*—Making Decisions and Solving Problems; Evaluating Information Against Standards; Analyzing Data or Information. *Work Output*—Performing General Physical Activities; Documenting and Recording Information; Handling and Moving Objects. *Interacting with Others*—Communicating with Other Workers; Communicating with Persons Outside Organization; Coordinating Work and Activities of Others. **Physical Work Conditions:** Outdoors; Standing; Walking or Running. **Other Job Characteristics:** Consequence of Error; Importance of Being Aware of New Events; Importance of Being Sure All Is Done.

Experience: Job Zone 2. Some previous work-related skill, knowledge, or experience may be helpful, but usually is not needed. **Job Preparation:** SVP 4.00 to 5.99—6 months to less than 2 years. **Knowledge:** Public Safety and Security; Law, Government and Jurisprudence; Administration and Management; English Language; Clerical; Sociology and Anthropology; Transportation; Psychology. **Instructional Program:** 430109 Security and Loss Prevention Services.

Related DOT Jobs: 372.267-010 Special Agent; 376.167-010 Special Agent-in-Charge; 376.667-018 Patroller.

33-9000 Other Protective Service Workers

33-9011.00 Animal Control Workers (All Other Protective Service Workers)

Education: Short-term O-T-J training

Employed: 166,335

Openings: 23,282

Projected Growth: 19%

Earnings: $17,470

Handle animals, for the purpose of investigating mistreatment or for the purpose of controlling abandoned, dangerous, or unattended animals.

Writes reports of activities, and maintains files of impoundment and disposition of animals. Instructs handlers in dog health care and handler's responsibilities. Conducts tours of facility, demonstrates dog handling techniques, and explains use of dogs in police work, using trained dog. Euthanatizes rabid, unclaimed, or severely injured animals. Supplies animals with food, water, and personal care. Examines animal licenses and inspects establishments housing animals, for compliance with laws; issues warnings or summonses to violators. Removes animals from vehicle and places animal in shelter cage or other enclosure. Investigates animal bites and alleged violations, interviews witnesses, and reports violations to police or requests arrest of violators. Examines animals for injuries or malnutrition and arranges for medical treatment. Captures or removes stray, uncontrolled, or abused animals from undesirable conditions and transports to shelter. Trains police officers in dog handling and training techniques for tracking, crowd control, and narcotics and bomb detection.

GOE Number, Interest Area, and Work Group: 04.03.03; Law, Law Enforcement, and Public Safety; Law Enforcement: Security. **Personality Type:** Social. Social occupations frequently involve working with, communicating with, and teaching people. These occupations often involve helping or providing service to others. **Work Values:** Security; Moral Values; Supervision, Human Relations; Achievement; Company Policies and Practices; Supervision, Technical; Authority. **Skills:** Active Listening; Instructing; Problem Identification; Critical Thinking; Reading Comprehension; Learning Strategies. **Abilities:** *Cognitive*—Oral Expression; Written Expression; Oral Comprehension; Written Comprehension; Deductive Reasoning; Inductive Reasoning. *Psychomotor*—Reaction Time; Rate Control; Speed of Limb Movement. *Physical*—Static Strength; Explosive Strength; Stamina. *Sensory*—Far Vision; Near Vision; Speech Clarity. **General Work Activities:** *Information Input*—Getting Information Needed to Do the Job; Identifying Objects, Actions, and Events; Monitoring Processes, Materials, and Surroundings. *Mental Process*—Evaluating Information Against Standards; Judging Qualities of Things, Services, Other People's Work; Processing Information. *Work Output*—Performing General Physical Activities; Documenting and Recording Information; Handling and Moving Objects. *Interacting with Others*—Assisting and Caring for Others; Teaching Others; Communicating with Persons Outside Organization. **Physical Work Conditions:** Hazardous Situations; Standing; Indoors. **Other Job Characteristics:** Consequence of Error; Frustrating Circumstances; Importance of Being Sure All Is Done.

Experience: Job Zone 2. Some previous work-related skill, knowledge, or experience may be helpful, but usually is not needed. **Job Preparation:** SVP 4.00 to 5.99—6 months to less than 2 years. **Knowledge:** Biology; Education and Training; English Language; Customer and Personal Service; Administration and Management; Computers and Electronics; Clerical. **Instructional Programs:** 430102 Corrections/Correctional Administration; 430106 Forensic Technology/Technician; 430199 Criminal Justice and Corrections, Other; 439999 Protective Services, Other.

Related DOT Jobs: 379.137-010 Supervisor, Animal Cruelty Investigation; 379.227-010 Instructor-Trainer, Canine Service; 379.263-010 Animal Treatment Investigator; 379.673-010 Dog Catcher.

33-9021.00 Private Detectives and Investigators (Private Detectives and Investigators)

Education: Work experience in a related occupation

Employed: 60,771

Openings: 14,675

Projected Growth: 24.3%

Earnings: $21,020

Detect occurrences of unlawful acts or infractions of rules in a private establishment; seek, examine, and compile information for client.

Alerts staff and superiors of presence of suspect in establishment. Locates persons using phone or mail directories to collect money owed or to serve legal papers. Examines crime scene for clues or fingerprints and submits evidence to laboratory for analysis. Warns and ejects troublemakers from premises and apprehends and releases suspects to authorities or security personnel. Obtains and analyzes information on suspects, crimes, and disturbances to solve cases, identify criminal activity, and maintain public peace and order. Counts cash and reviews transactions, sales checks, and register tapes to verify amount of cash and shortages. Confers with establishment officials, security department, police, or postal officials to identify problems, provide information, and receive instructions. Testifies at hearings and court trials to present evidence. Enforces conformance to establishment rules and protects persons or property. Evaluates performance and honesty of employees by posing as customer or employee and comparing employee to standards. Assists victims, police, fire department, and others during emergencies. Observes employees or customers and patrols premises to detect violations and obtain evidence, using binoculars, cameras, and television. Questions persons to obtain evidence for cases of divorce, child custody, or missing persons, or individuals character or financial status. Writes reports and case summaries to document investigations or inform supervisors.

GOE Number, Interest Area, and Work Group: 04.03.03; Law, Law Enforcement, and Public Safety; Law Enforcement: Security. **Personality Type:** Enterprising. Enterprising occupations frequently involve starting up and carrying out projects. These occupations can involve leading people and making many decisions.

They sometimes require risk taking and often deal with business. **Work Values:** Ability Utilization; Achievement; Responsibility; Security; Company Policies and Practices. **Skills:** Active Listening; Problem Identification; Critical Thinking; Writing; Speaking. **Abilities:** *Cognitive*—Oral Comprehension; Inductive Reasoning; Oral Expression; Problem Sensitivity; Written Expression. *Psychomotor*—Reaction Time; Speed of Limb Movement; Response Orientation. *Physical*—Static Strength; Explosive Strength; Stamina. *Sensory*—Near Vision; Far Vision; Speech Clarity. **General Work Activities:** *Information Input*—Getting Information Needed to Do the Job; Monitoring Processes, Materials, and Surroundings; Identifying Objects, Actions, and Events. *Mental Process*—Analyzing Data or Information; Processing Information; Making Decisions and Solving Problems. *Work Output*—Documenting and Recording Information; Performing General Physical Activities; Handling and Moving Objects. *Interacting with Others*—Communicating with Other Workers; Communicating with Persons Outside Organization; Establishing and Maintaining Relationships. **Physical Work Conditions:** Standing; Indoors; Outdoors; Walking or Running. **Other Job Characteristics:** Consequence of Error; Importance of Being Aware of New Events; Importance of Being Exact or Accurate; Importance of Being Sure All Is Done.

Experience: Job Zone 2. Some previous work-related skill, knowledge, or experience may be helpful, but usually is not needed. **Job Preparation:** SVP 4.00 to 5.99—6 months to less than 2 years. **Knowledge:** Public Safety and Security; English Language; Law, Government and Jurisprudence; Telecommunications; Customer and Personal Service; Communications and Media. **Instructional Program:** 430107 Law Enforcement/Police Science.

Related DOT Jobs: 186.267-010 Bonding Agent; 241.367-026 Skip Tracer; 343.367-014 Gambling Monitor; 376.267-010 Investigator, Cash Shortage; 376.267-014 Investigator, Fraud; 376.267-018 Investigator, Private; 376.267-022 Shopping Investigator; 376.367-010 Alarm Investigator; 376.367-014 Detective I; 376.367-018 House Officer; 376.367-022 Investigator; 376.367-026 Undercover Operator; 376.667-014 Detective II.

33-9031.00 Gaming Surveillance Officers and Gaming Investigators (All Other Supervisors and Managers/Supervisors—Service Workers)

Education: No data available.

Employed: 732,280

Openings: No data available.

Projected Growth: No data available.

Earnings: $23,320

Act as oversight and security agent for management and customers. Observe casino or casino hotel operation for irregular activities such as cheating or theft by either employees or patrons. Utilize one-way mirrors from above the casino floor, from a cashier's cage, and from the desk. Use audio-video equipment to observe operation of the business. Provide verbal and written reports of all violations and suspicious behavior to supervisor.

GOE Number, Interest Area, and Work Group: 04.03.03; Law, Law Enforcement, and Public Safety; Law Enforcement: Security.

Instructional Programs: 080903 Recreation Products/Services Marketing Operations; 200401 Institutional Food Workers and Administrators, General; 200409 Institutional Food Services Administrator; 310504 Sport and Fitness Administration/Management. **Note:** The Department of Labor has not collected some data for this job, so it has fewer details than the other descriptions.

33-9032.00 Security Guards (Guards)

Education: Short-term O-T-J training

Employed: 1,026,723

Openings: 256,671

Projected Growth: 28.6%

Earnings: $16,240

Guard, patrol, or monitor premises to prevent theft, violence, or infractions of rules.

Circulates among visitors, patrons, and employees to preserve order and protect property. Inspects and adjusts security systems, equipment, and machinery to ensure operational use and to detect evidence of tampering. Answers alarms and investigates disturbances. Drives and guards armored vehicle to transport money and valuables to prevent theft and ensure safe delivery. Writes reports of daily activities and irregularities, such as equipment or property damage, theft, presence of unauthorized persons, or unusual occurrences. Monitors and adjusts controls that regulate building systems such as air conditioning, furnace, or boiler. Answers telephone calls to take messages, answer questions, and provide information during nonbusiness hours or when switchboard is closed. Operates detecting devices to screen individuals and prevent passage of prohibited articles into restricted areas. Calls police or fire departments in cases of emergency, such as fire or presence of unauthorized persons. Warns persons of rule infractions or violations, and apprehends or evicts violators from premises, using force when necessary. Patrols industrial and commercial premises to prevent and detect signs of intrusion and ensure security of doors, windows, and gates. Escorts or drives motor vehicle to transport individuals to specified locations and to provide personal protection. Monitors and authorizes entrance and departure of employees, visitors, and other persons to guard against theft and maintain security of premises.

GOE Number, Interest Area, and Work Group: 04.03.03; Law, Law Enforcement, and Public Safety; Law Enforcement: Security. **Personality Type:** Social. Social occupations frequently involve working with, communicating with, and teaching people. These occupations often involve helping or providing service to others. **Work Values:** Moral Values; Supervision, Human Relations; Company Policies and Practices; Security; Independence. **Skills:** Active Listening; Problem Identification; Critical Thinking; Speaking; Writing. **Abilities:** *Cognitive*—Oral Expression; Oral Comprehension; Time Sharing; Selective Attention; Problem Sensitivity. *Psychomotor*—Response Orientation; Reaction Time; Control Precision. *Physical*—Static Strength; Explosive Strength; Trunk Strength. *Sensory*—Sound Localization; Far Vision; Night Vision. **General Work Activities:** *Information Input*—Monitoring Processes, Materials, and Surroundings; Getting Information Needed to Do the Job; Identifying Objects, Actions, and Events. *Mental Process*—Making Decisions and Solving Problems; Judging Qualities of Things, Services, Other People's Work; Processing Information; Analyzing Data or Information; Evaluating Information Against Standards. *Work Output*—Performing General Physical Activities; Operating Vehicles or Equipment; Documenting and Recording Information. *Interacting with Others*—Performing Administrative Activities; Performing for or Working with the Public; Monitoring and Controlling Resources. **Physical Work Conditions:** Special Uniform; Indoors; Outdoors; Walking or Running; Standing. **Other Job Characteristics:** Consequence of Error; Importance of Being Aware of New Events; Importance of Being Sure All Is Done.

Experience: Job Zone 1. No previous work-related skill, knowledge, or experience is needed. **Job Preparation:** SVP Below 4.0—Less than 6 months. **Knowledge:** Public Safety and Security; Law, Government and Jurisprudence; English Language; Customer and Personal Service; Telecommunications. **Instructional Program:** 430109 Security and Loss Prevention Services.

Related DOT Jobs: 372.563-010 Armored-Car Guard and Driver; 372.567-010 Armored-Car Guard; 372.667-010 Airline Security Representative; 372.667-014 Bodyguard; 372.667-030 Gate Guard; 372.667-034 Guard, Security; 372.667-038 Merchant Patroller; 376.667-010 Bouncer; 379.667-010 Golf-Course Ranger.

33-9091.00 Crossing Guards (Crossing Guards)

Education: Short-term O-T-J training

Employed: 54,341

Openings: 9,951

Projected Growth: 4%

Earnings: $14,940

Guide or control vehicular or pedestrian traffic at such places as street and railroad crossings and construction sites.

Distributes traffic control and caution signs and markers at designated points. Records license numbers of vehicles disregarding traffic signals and reports infractions to police. Informs drivers of detour routes through construction sites. Discusses traffic routing plans, and type and location of control points with superior. Waves flags, signs, or lanterns in emergencies. Directs movement of traffic through site, using signs, flags, and hand signals. Activates warning signal lights, lowers crossing gates until train passes, and raises gate when crossing is clear. Directs actions of pedestrians and traffic at intersections. Escorts pedestrians across street.

GOE Number, Interest Area, and Work Group: 04.03.03; Law, Law Enforcement, and Public Safety; Law Enforcement: Security. **Personality Type:** Social. Social occupations frequently involve working with, communicating with, and teaching people. These occupations often involve helping or providing service to others. **Work Values:** Moral Values; Independence; Supervision, Technical; Security; Supervision, Human Relations. **Skills:** Speaking; Coordination; Active Listening; Service Orientation. **Abilities:** *Cognitive*—Time Sharing; Problem Sensitivity; Oral Expression; Selective Attention; Oral Comprehension. *Psychomotor*—Reaction Time; Multilimb Coordination; Response Orientation. *Physical*—Gross Body Coordination; Stamina; Dynamic Flexibility. *Sensory*—Far Vision; Peripheral Vision; Night Vision. **General Work Activities:** *Information Input*—Monitoring Processes, Materials, and

Surroundings; Getting Information Needed to Do the Job; Identifying Objects, Actions, and Events. *Mental Process*—Making Decisions and Solving Problems; Updating and Using Job-Relevant Knowledge; Processing Information; Analyzing Data or Information. *Work Output*—Handling and Moving Objects; Performing General Physical Activities; Controlling Machines and Processes. *Interacting with Others*—Performing for or Working with the Public; Communicating with Persons Outside Organization; Assisting and Caring for Others. **Physical Work Conditions:** Outdoors; Standing; Special Uniform. **Other Job Characteristics:** Consequence of Error; Importance of Being Aware of New Events; Importance of Being Exact or Accurate.

Experience: Job Zone 1. No previous work-related skill, knowledge, or experience is needed. **Job Preparation:** SVP Below 4.0—Less than 6 months. **Knowledge:** Public Safety and Security; Law, Government and Jurisprudence; English Language; Customer and Personal Service; Geography. **Instructional Program:** 430107 Law Enforcement/Police Science.

Related DOT Jobs: 371.567-010 Guard, School-Crossing; 371.667-010 Crossing Tender; 372.667-022 Flagger.

33-9092.00 Lifeguards, Ski Patrol, and Other Recreational Protective Service Workers
(Ski Patrol Workers and Life Guards)

Education: Short-term O-T-J training

Employed: 166,335

Openings: 23,282

Projected Growth: 19%

Earnings: $17,470

Monitor recreational areas such as pools, beaches, or ski slopes to provide assistance and protection to participants. Includes lifeguards and ski patrollers.

Examines injured persons and administers first aid or cardiopulmonary resuscitation, utilizing training and medical supplies and equipment. Instructs participants in skiing, swimming, or other recreational activity. Inspects recreational equipment such as rope tows, T-bar, J-bar, and chair lifts, for safety hazards and damage or wear. Inspects facilities for cleanliness and maintains order in recreational areas. Maintains information on emergency medical treatment and weather and beach conditions, using report forms. Rescues distressed persons, using rescue techniques and equipment. Contacts emergency medical services in case of serious injury. Observes activities in assigned area with binoculars to detect hazards, disturbances, or safety infractions. Patrols or monitors recreational areas such as trails, slopes, and swimming areas, on foot, in vehicle, or from tower. Participates in recreational demonstrations to entertain resort guests. Cautions recreational participant regarding inclement weather, unsafe areas, or illegal conduct.

GOE Number, Interest Area, and Work Group: 04.03.03; Law, Law Enforcement, and Public Safety; Law Enforcement: Security. **Personality Type:** Realistic. Realistic occupations frequently involve work activities that include practical, hands-on problems and solutions. These occupations often deal with plants, animals, and real-world materials like wood, tools, and machinery. Many of the occupations require working outside and do not involve a lot of paperwork or working closely with others. **Work Values:** Moral Values; Social Service; Achievement; Company Policies and Practices; Authority; Supervision, Human Relations; Supervision, Technical; Variety. **Skills:** Problem Identification; Service Orientation; Learning Strategies; Instructing; Critical Thinking. **Abilities:** *Cognitive*—Problem Sensitivity; Oral Expression; Information Ordering; Spatial Orientation; Oral Comprehension. *Psychomotor*—Reaction Time; Response Orientation; Multilimb Coordination; Speed of Limb Movement. *Physical*—Stamina; Explosive Strength; Gross Body Coordination. *Sensory*—Far Vision; Sound Localization; Glare Sensitivity. **General Work Activities:** *Information Input*—Monitoring Processes, Materials, and Surroundings; Inspecting Equipment, Structures, Materials; Getting Information Needed to Do the Job. *Mental Process*—Making Decisions and Solving Problems; Updating and Using Job-Relevant Knowledge; Judging Qualities of Things, Services, Other People's Work. *Work Output*—Performing General Physical Activities; Handling and Moving Objects; Documenting and Recording Information; Operating Vehicles or Equipment. *Interacting with Others*—Assisting and Caring for Others; Performing for or Working with the Public; Communicating with Persons Outside Organization. **Physical Work Conditions:** Outdoors; Special Uniform; Walking or Running. **Other Job Characteristics:** Consequence of Error; Importance of Being Aware of New Events; Importance of Being Exact or Accurate.

Experience: Job Zone 2. Some previous work-related skill, knowledge, or experience may be helpful, but usually is not needed. **Job Preparation:** SVP 4.00 to 5.99—6 months to less than 2 years. **Knowledge:** Public Safety and Security; Medicine and Dentistry; Mechanical; Customer and Personal Service; Education and Training. **Instructional Programs:** 430102 Corrections/Correctional Administration; 430106 Forensic Technology/Technician; 430199 Criminal Justice and Corrections, Other; 439999 Protective Services, Other.

Related DOT Jobs: 379.364-014 Beach Lifeguard; 379.664-010 Ski Patroller; 379.667-014 Lifeguard.

35-0000
Food Preparation and Serving Related Occupations

35-1000 Supervisors, Food Preparation and Serving Workers

35-1011.00 Chefs and Head Cooks (Food Service and Lodging Managers)

Education: Work experience in a related occupation
Employed: 594,642
Openings: 138,826
Projected Growth: 16.3%
Earnings: $26,700

Direct the preparation, seasoning, and cooking of salads, soups, fish, meats, vegetables, desserts, or other foods. Plan and price menu items, order supplies, and keep records and accounts. Participate in cooking.

Collaborates with specified personnel and plans and develops recipes and menus. Inspects supplies, equipment, and work areas to ensure conformance to established standards. Records production and operational data on specified forms. Determines production schedules and worker-time requirements to ensure timely delivery of services. Estimates amounts and costs; requisitions supplies and equipment to ensure efficient operation. Trains and otherwise instructs cooks and workers in proper food preparation procedures. Observes workers and work procedures to ensure compliance with established standards. Helps cooks and workers cook and prepare food on demand. Supervises and coordinates activities of cooks and workers engaged in food preparation. Evaluates and solves procedural problems to ensure safe and efficient operations.

GOE Number, Interest Area, and Work Group: 11.05.01; Recreation, Travel, and Other Personal Services; Food and Beverage Services: Preparing. Personality Type: Enterprising. Enterprising occupations frequently involve starting up and carrying out projects. These occupations can involve leading people and making many decisions. They sometimes require risk taking and often deal with business. Work Values: Authority; Responsibility; Moral Values; Achievement; Autonomy. Skills: Coordination; Management of Financial Resources; Management of Material Resources; Instructing; Problem Identification; Management of Personnel Resources. Abilities: *Cognitive*—Oral Expression; Problem Sensitivity; Information Ordering; Deductive Reasoning; Oral Comprehension; Number Facility. *Psychomotor*—Manual Dexterity; Finger Dexterity; Wrist-Finger Speed. *Physical*—Extent Flexibility; Static Strength; Trunk Strength. *Sensory*—Visual Color Discrimination; Speech Clarity; Speech Recognition; Far Vision. General Work Activities: *Information Input*—Monitoring Processes, Materials, and Surroundings; Identifying Objects, Actions, and Events; Getting Information Needed to Do the Job. *Mental Process*—Scheduling Work and Activities; Judging Qualities of Things, Services, Other People's Work; Evaluating Information Against Standards. *Work Output*—Handling and Moving Objects; Documenting and Recording Information; Implementing Ideas

and Programs. *Interacting with Others*—Communicating with Other Workers; Coordinating Work and Activities of Others; Guiding, Directing and Motivating Subordinates. Physical Work Conditions: Indoors; Using Hands on Objects, Tools, or Controls; Standing. Other Job Characteristics: Consequence of Error; Importance of Being Sure All Is Done; Importance of Being Exact or Accurate.

Experience: Job Zone 4. A minimum of two to four years of work-related skill, knowledge, or experience is needed. Job Preparation: SVP 7.0 to less than 8.0—2 years to less than 10 years. Knowledge: Administration and Management; Personnel and Human Resources; Mathematics; Education and Training; Economics and Accounting. Instructional Programs: 080901 Hospitality and Recreation Marketing Operations, General; 080906 Food Sales Operations; 120504 Food and Beverage/Restaurant Operations Manager; 190505 Food Systems Administration; 200401 Institutional Food Workers and Administrators, General; 200405 Food Caterer; 200409 Institutional Food Services Administrator; 520702 Franchise Operation; 520901 Hospitality/Administration Management; 520902 Hotel/Motel and Restaurant Management.

Related DOT Jobs: 313.131-010 Baker, Head; 313.131-014 Chef; 313.131-018 Cook, Head, School Cafeteria; 313.131-022 Pastry Chef; 313.131-026 Sous Chef; 315.131-010 Cook, Chief; 315.131-014 Pastry Chef; 315.137-010 Chef, Passenger Vessel; 315.137-014 Sous Chef.

35-1012.00 First-Line Supervisors/Managers of Food Preparation and Serving Workers (Food Service and Lodging Managers)

Education: Work experience in a related occupation
Employed: 594,642
Openings: 138,826
Projected Growth: 16.3%
Earnings: $26,700

Supervise workers engaged in preparing and serving food.

Supervises and coordinates activities of workers engaged in preparing and serving food and other related duties. Receives, issues, and takes inventory of supplies and equipment, and reports shortages to designated personnel. Trains workers in proper food preparation and service procedures. Recommends measures to improve work procedures and worker performance to increase quality of services and job safety. Records production and operational data on specified forms. Purchases or requisitions supplies and equipment to ensure quality and timely delivery of services. Resolves customer complaints regarding food service. Initiates personnel actions, such as hires and discharges, to ensure proper staffing. Analyzes operational problems, such as theft and wastage, and establishes controls. Schedules parties and reservations, and greets and escorts guests to seating arrangements. Specifies food portions and courses, production and time sequences, and work station and equipment arrangements. Inspects supplies, equipment, and work areas, to ensure efficient service and conformance to standards. Collaborates with specified personnel to plan menus, serving arrangements, and other related details.

Observes and evaluates workers and work procedures to ensure quality standards and service. Assigns duties, responsibilities, and work stations to employees, following work requirements.

GOE Number, Interest Area, and Work Group: 11.01.01; Recreation, Travel, and Other Personal Services; Managerial Work in Recreation, Travel, and Other Personal Services. **Personality Type:** Enterprising. Enterprising occupations frequently involve starting up and carrying out projects. These occupations can involve leading people and making many decisions. They sometimes require risk taking and often deal with business. **Work Values:** Authority; Responsibility; Co-workers; Moral Values; Autonomy; Activity. **Skills:** Management of Personnel Resources; Coordination; Speaking; Time Management; Problem Identification; Identification of Key Causes; Active Listening; Systems Perception. **Abilities:** *Cognitive*—Oral Expression; Oral Comprehension; Written Comprehension; Written Expression; Number Facility. *Psychomotor*—Response Orientation. *Physical*—Stamina; Dynamic Flexibility; Gross Body Equilibrium. *Sensory*—Speech Clarity; Near Vision; Auditory Attention. **General Work Activities:** *Information Input*—Monitoring Processes, Materials, and Surroundings; Getting Information Needed to Do the Job; Identifying Objects, Actions, and Events. *Mental Process*—Scheduling Work and Activities; Judging Qualities of Things, Services, Other People's Work; Making Decisions and Solving Problems. *Work Output*—Documenting and Recording Information; Implementing Ideas and Programs; Handling and Moving Objects. *Interacting with Others*—Coordinating Work and Activities of Others; Communicating with Other Workers; Communicating with Persons Outside Organization; Guiding, Directing and Motivating Subordinates. **Physical Work Conditions:** Indoors; Standing; Using Hands on Objects, Tools, or Controls; Walking or Running. **Other Job Characteristics:** Importance of Being Sure All Is Done; Consequence of Error; Importance of Being Exact or Accurate.

Experience: Job Zone 3. Previous work-related skill, knowledge, or experience is required. **Job Preparation:** SVP 6.0 to less than 7.0—More than 1 year and less than 4 years. **Knowledge:** Administration and Management; Customer and Personal Service; Personnel and Human Resources; English Language; Education and Training; Production and Processing; Food Production; Clerical. **Instructional Programs:** 080901 Hospitality and Recreation Marketing Operations, General; 080906 Food Sales Operations; 120504 Food and Beverage/Restaurant Operations Manager; 190505 Food Systems Administration; 200401 Institutional Food Workers and Administrators, General; 200405 Food Caterer; 200409 Institutional Food Services Administrator; 520702 Franchise Operation; 520901 Hospitality/Administration Management; 520902 Hotel/Motel and Restaurant Management.

Related DOT Jobs: 310.137-018 Steward/Stewardess; 310.137-022 Steward/Stewardess, Banquet; 310.137-026 Steward/Stewardess, Railroad Dining Car; 311.137-010 Counter Supervisor; 311.137-014 Waiter/Waitress, Banquet, Head; 311.137-018 Waiter/Waitress, Captain; 311.137-022 Waiter/Waitress, Head; 318.137-010 Kitchen Steward/Stewardess; 319.137-010 Food-Service Supervisor; 319.137-022 Supervisor, Commissary Production; 319.137-026 Supervisor, Kosher Dietary Service; 319.137-030 Kitchen Supervisor; 350.137-010 Headwaiter/Headwaitress; 350.137-014 Steward/Stewardess, Chief, Cargo Vessel.

35-2000 Cooks and Food Preparation Workers

35-2011.00 Cooks, Fast Food (Short Order and Fast Food Cooks)

Education: Short-term O-T-J training
Employed: 676,576
Openings: 226,320
Projected Growth: 18.4%
Earnings: No data available.

Prepare and cook food in a fast-food restaurant with a limited menu. Prepare a few basic items and operate large-volume, single-purpose cooking equipment.

Prepares and serves beverages such as coffee and fountain drinks. Cleans work area and food preparation equipment. Serves orders to customers at window or counter. Measures required ingredients needed for specific food item being prepared. Reads food order slip or receives verbal instructions as to food required by patron; prepares and cooks food according to instructions. Prepares specialty foods such as pizzas, fish and chips, sandwiches, and tacos, following specific methods, usually requiring short preparation time. Slices meats, cheeses, and vegetables, using knives and food slicing machines. Prepares dough, following recipe.

GOE Number, Interest Area, and Work Group: 11.05.01; Recreation, Travel, and Other Personal Services; Food and Beverage Services: Preparing. **Personality Type:** Realistic. Realistic occupations frequently involve work activities that include practical, hands-on problems and solutions. These occupations often deal with plants, animals, and real-world materials like wood, tools, and machinery. Many of the occupations require working outside and do not involve a lot of paperwork or working closely with others. **Work Values:** Moral Values; Activity; Co-workers; Security; Company Policies and Practices; Supervision, Human Relations; Supervision, Technical. **Skills:** Operation and Control. **Abilities:** *Cognitive*—Oral Comprehension; Written Comprehension; Information Ordering; Oral Expression; Time Sharing; Problem Sensitivity. *Psychomotor*—Wrist-Finger Speed. *Physical*—none met the criteria. **General Work Activities:** *Information Input*—Monitoring Processes, Materials, and Surroundings; Getting Information Needed to Do the Job; Identifying Objects, Actions, and Events. *Mental Process*—Evaluating Information Against Standards; Judging Qualities of Things, Services, Other People's Work; Processing Information; Making Decisions and Solving Problems; Organizing, Planning, and Prioritizing. *Work Output*—Handling and Moving Objects; Controlling Machines and Processes; Performing General Physical Activities. *Interacting with Others*—Performing for or Working with the Public; Communicating with Persons Outside Organization; Establishing and Maintaining Relationships; Communicating with Other Workers. **Physical Work Conditions:** Indoors; Standing; Special Uniform. **Other Job Characteristics:** Importance of Being Sure All Is Done; Importance of Being Exact or Accurate; Degree of Automation.

Experience: Job Zone 2. Some previous work-related skill, knowledge, or experience may be helpful, but usually is not needed. **Job Preparation:** SVP 4.00 to 5.99—6 months to less than 2 years. **Knowledge:** Customer and Personal Service; English Language; Mathematics; Food Production; Law, Government and Jurisprudence. **Instructional Program:** 120505 Kitchen Personnel/Cook and Assistant Training.

Related DOT Jobs: 313.361-026 Cook, Specialty; 313.374-010 Cook, Fast Food; 313.381-014 Baker, Pizza.

35-2012.00 Cooks, Institution and Cafeteria
(Institution and Cafeteria Cooks)

Education: Long-term O-T-J training
Employed: 418,355
Openings: 124,088
Projected Growth: 2.9%
Earnings: $16,090

Prepare and cook large quantities of food for institutions such as schools, hospitals, or cafeterias.

Directs activities of one or more workers who assist in preparing and serving meals. Cleans and inspects galley equipment, kitchen appliances, and work areas for cleanliness and functional operation. Prepares and cooks vegetables, salads, dressings, and desserts. Bakes breads, rolls, and other pastries. Compiles and maintains food-cost records and accounts. Washes pots, pans, dishes, utensils, and other cooking equipment. Apportions and serves food to residents, employees, or patrons. Requisitions food supplies, kitchen equipment and appliances, and other supplies; receives deliveries. Cleans, cuts, and cooks meat, fish, and poultry. Cooks foodstuffs according to menu, special dietary or nutritional restrictions, and number of persons to be served. Plans menus, taking advantage of in-season foods and local availability.

GOE Number, Interest Area, and Work Group: 11.05.01; Recreation, Travel, and Other Personal Services; Food and Beverage Services: Preparing. **Personality Type:** Realistic. Realistic occupations frequently involve work activities that include practical, hands-on problems and solutions. These occupations often deal with plants, animals, and real-world materials like wood, tools, and machinery. Many of the occupations require working outside and do not involve a lot of paperwork or working closely with others. **Work Values:** Moral Values; Activity; Security; Co-workers; Responsibility. **Skills:** Active Learning; Critical Thinking; Management of Personnel Resources; Coordination; Mathematics; Solution Appraisal. **Abilities:** *Cognitive*—Information Ordering; Oral Expression; Time Sharing; Oral Comprehension; Number Facility; Problem Sensitivity. *Psychomotor*—Wrist-Finger Speed; Manual Dexterity. *Physical*—Stamina. *Sensory*—Visual Color Discrimination. **General Work Activities:** *Information Input*—Monitoring Processes, Materials, and Surroundings; Estimating Needed Characteristics; Getting Information Needed to Do the Job. *Mental Process*—Making Decisions and Solving Problems; Judging Qualities of Things, Services, Other People's Work; Organizing, Planning, and Prioritizing; Evaluating Information Against Standards. *Work Output*—Handling and Moving Objects; Implementing Ideas and Programs;

Performing General Physical Activities. *Interacting with Others*—Monitoring and Controlling Resources; Communicating with Other Workers; Performing Administrative Activities. **Physical Work Conditions:** Indoors; Using Hands on Objects, Tools, or Controls; Standing. **Other Job Characteristics:** Importance of Being Sure All Is Done; Importance of Being Exact or Accurate; Consequence of Error.

Experience: Job Zone 2. Some previous work-related skill, knowledge, or experience may be helpful, but usually is not needed. **Job Preparation:** SVP 4.00 to 5.99—6 months to less than 2 years. **Knowledge:** Customer and Personal Service; Administration and Management; Mathematics; Food Production; Production and Processing; Personnel and Human Resources; Clerical; Economics and Accounting. **Instructional Programs:** 120505 Kitchen Personnel/Cook and Assistant Training; 120599 Culinary Arts and Related Services, Other; 200409 Institutional Food Services Administrator.

Related DOT Jobs: 313.381-030 Cook, School Cafeteria; 315.361-010 Cook; 315.371-010 Cook, Mess; 315.381-010 Cook; 315.381-022 Cook, Third; 315.381-026 Second Cook and Baker.

35-2013.00 Cooks, Private Household (Food Preparation Workers)

Education: Short-term O-T-J training
Employed: 1,256,251
Openings: 529,498
Projected Growth: 10.4%
Earnings: $13,700

Prepare meals in private homes.

GOE Number, Interest Area, and Work Group: 11.08.01; Recreation, Travel, and Other Personal Services; Other Personal Services. **Instructional Programs:** 120505 Kitchen Personnel/Cook and Assistant Training; 200401 Institutional Food Workers and Administrators, General; 200405 Food Caterer. **Note:** The Department of Labor has not collected some data for this job, so it has fewer details than the other descriptions.

35-2014.00 Cooks, Restaurant (Restaurant Cooks)

Education: Long-term O-T-J training
Employed: 783,180
Openings: 262,535
Projected Growth: 18.7%
Earnings: $16,250

Prepare, season, and cook soups, meats, vegetables, desserts, or other foodstuffs in restaurants. Order supplies; keep records and accounts; price items on menu; plan menu.

Observes and tests food to determine that it is cooked, by tasting, smelling, or piercing; turns or stirs food if necessary. Inspects food preparation and serving areas to ensure observance of safe, sanitary food-handling practices. Plans items on menu. Carves and trims meats such as beef, veal, ham, pork, and lamb, for hot or cold service or for sandwiches. Butchers and dresses animals, fowl, or shellfish; cuts and bones meat prior to cooking. Estimates food consumption and requisitions; purchases supplies or procures food from storage. Portions, arranges, and garnishes food; serves food to waiter or patron. Bakes, roasts, broils, and steams meats, fish, vegetables, and other foods. Regulates temperature of ovens, broilers, grills, and roasters. Seasons and cooks food according to recipes or personal judgment and experience. Weighs, measures, and mixes ingredients according to recipe or personal judgment, using various kitchen utensils and equipment. Bakes bread, rolls, cakes, and pastry. Washes, peels, cuts, and seeds fruits and vegetables to prepare fruits and vegetables for use.

GOE Number, Interest Area, and Work Group: 11.05.01; Recreation, Travel, and Other Personal Services; Food and Beverage Services: Preparing. **Personality Type:** Realistic. Realistic occupations frequently involve work activities that include practical, hands-on problems and solutions. These occupations often deal with plants, animals, and real-world materials like wood, tools, and machinery. Many of the occupations require working outside and do not involve a lot of paperwork or working closely with others. **Work Values:** Moral Values; Co-workers; Responsibility; Achievement; Creativity. **Skills:** Active Learning; Coordination; Speaking; Learning Strategies; Monitoring. **Abilities:** *Cognitive*—Information Ordering; Memorization; Written Comprehension; Oral Expression; Number Facility; Visualization. *Psychomotor*—Wrist-Finger Speed; Manual Dexterity; Arm-Hand Steadiness. *Physical*—Static Strength; Extent Flexibility; Trunk Strength. *Sensory*—Near Vision; Visual Color Discrimination; Peripheral Vision; Night Vision. **General Work Activities:** *Information Input*—Identifying Objects, Actions, and Events; Estimating Needed Characteristics; Monitoring Processes, Materials, and Surroundings. *Mental Process*—Thinking Creatively; Judging Qualities of Things, Services, Other People's Work; Organizing, Planning, and Prioritizing. *Work Output*—Handling and Moving Objects; Performing General Physical Activities; Controlling Machines and Processes. *Interacting with Others*—Monitoring and Controlling Resources; Coordinating Work and Activities of Others; Guiding, Directing and Motivating Subordinates. **Physical Work Conditions:** Indoors; Standing; Special Uniform. **Other Job Characteristics:** Importance of Being Sure All Is Done; Consequence of Error; Importance of Being Exact or Accurate.

Experience: Job Zone 3. Previous work-related skill, knowledge, or experience is required. **Job Preparation:** SVP 6.0 to less than 7.0—More than 1 year and less than 4 years. **Knowledge:** Customer and Personal Service; Mathematics; Public Safety and Security; Food Production; Education and Training; Production and Processing; Personnel and Human Resources. **Instructional Program:** 120503 Culinary Arts/Chef Training.

Related DOT Jobs: 313.281-010 Chef De Froid; 313.361-014 Cook; 313.361-018 Cook Apprentice; 313.361-030 Cook, Specialty, Foreign Food; 313.361-034 Garde Manger; 313.381-022 Cook, Barbecue; 313.381-034 Ice-Cream Chef; 315.361-022 Cook, Station; 315.381-014 Cook, Larder; 315.381-018 Cook, Railroad.

35-2015.00 Cooks, Short Order (Short Order and Fast Food Cooks)

Education: Short-term O-T-J training
Employed: 676,576
Openings: 226,320
Projected Growth: 18.4%
Earnings: No data available.

Prepare and cook to order a variety of foods that require only a short preparation time. Take orders from customers and serve patrons at counters or tables.

Completes order from steamtable and serves customer at table or counter. Accepts payment and makes change, or writes charge slip. Cleans food preparation equipment, work area, and counter or tables. Takes order from customer and cooks foods requiring short preparation time, according to customer requirements. Carves meats, makes sandwiches, and brews coffee.

GOE Number, Interest Area, and Work Group: 11.05.01; Recreation, Travel, and Other Personal Services; Food and Beverage Services: Preparing. **Personality Type:** Realistic. Realistic occupations frequently involve work activities that include practical, hands-on problems and solutions. These occupations often deal with plants, animals, and real-world materials like wood, tools, and machinery. Many of the occupations require working outside and do not involve a lot of paperwork or working closely with others. **Work Values:** Moral Values; Activity; Co-workers; Security; Company Policies and Practices; Supervision, Human Relations. **Skills:** Service Orientation; Operation and Control. **Abilities:** *Cognitive*—Oral Comprehension; Number Facility; Time Sharing; Information Ordering; Mathematical Reasoning; Problem Sensitivity. *Psychomotor*—Wrist-Finger Speed. *Physical*—none met the criteria. **General Work Activities:** *Information Input*—Getting Information Needed to Do the Job; Monitoring Processes, Materials, and Surroundings; Estimating Needed Characteristics. *Mental Process*—Organizing, Planning, and Prioritizing; Judging Qualities of Things, Services, Other People's Work; Processing Information. *Work Output*—Handling and Moving Objects; Controlling Machines and Processes; Implementing Ideas and Programs. *Interacting with Others*—Performing for or Working with the Public; Communicating with Persons Outside Organization; Establishing and Maintaining Relationships. **Physical Work Conditions:** Indoors; Standing; Using Hands on Objects, Tools, or Controls. **Other Job Characteristics:** Importance of Being Exact or Accurate; Importance of Being Sure All Is Done; Consequence of Error.

Experience: Job Zone 1. No previous work-related skill, knowledge, or experience is needed. **Job Preparation:** SVP Below 4.0—Less than 6 months. **Knowledge:** Customer and Personal Service; Mathematics; English Language; Food Production; Law, Government and Jurisprudence. **Instructional Program:** 120505 Kitchen Personnel/Cook and Assistant Training.

Related DOT Job: 313.374-014 Cook, Short Order.

35-2021.00 Food Preparation Workers (Food Preparation Workers)

Education: Short-term O-T-J training
Employed: 1,256,251
Openings: 529,498
Projected Growth: 10.4%
Earnings: $13,700

Perform a variety of food preparation duties other than cooking, such as preparing cold foods and shellfish, slicing meat, and brewing coffee or tea.

Cleans, cuts, slices, or disjoints meats and poultry to prepare for cooking. Requisitions, stores, and distributes food supplies, equipment, and utensils. Distributes food to waiters and waitresses to serve to customers. Butchers and cleans fowl, fish, poultry, and shellfish to prepare for cooking or serving. Cleans and maintains work areas, equipment, and utensils. Stores food in designated containers and storage areas to prevent spoilage. Prepares variety of foods according to customers' orders or instructions of superior, following approved procedures. Prepares and serves variety of beverages such as coffee, tea, and soft drinks. Cleans and portions, and cuts or peels various foods to prepare for cooking or serving. Portions and arranges food on serving dishes, trays, carts, or conveyor belts. Carries food supplies, equipment, and utensils to and from storage and work areas.

GOE Number, Interest Area, and Work Group: 11.05.01; Recreation, Travel, and Other Personal Services; Food and Beverage Services: Preparing. **Personality Type:** Realistic. Realistic occupations frequently involve work activities that include practical, hands-on problems and solutions. These occupations often deal with plants, animals, and real-world materials like wood, tools, and machinery. Many of the occupations require working outside and do not involve a lot of paperwork or working closely with others. **Work Values:** Moral Values; Activity; Co-workers; Supervision, Human Relations; Security; Supervision, Technical; Company Policies and Practices. **Skills:** Service Orientation; Active Listening; Writing. **Abilities:** *Cognitive*—Information Ordering; Oral Comprehension; Memorization; Visualization; Oral Expression. *Psychomotor*—Wrist-Finger Speed; Manual Dexterity; Arm-Hand Steadiness. *Physical*—Trunk Strength; Extent Flexibility; Static Strength. *Sensory*—Visual Color Discrimination; Speech Recognition; Hearing Sensitivity. **General Work Activities:** *Information Input*—Monitoring Processes, Materials, and Surroundings; Estimating Needed Characteristics; Getting Information Needed to Do the Job. *Mental Process*—Evaluating Information Against Standards; Judging Qualities of Things, Services, Other People's Work; Organizing, Planning, and Prioritizing. *Work Output*—Handling and Moving Objects; Performing General Physical Activities; Controlling Machines and Processes. *Interacting with Others*—Communicating with Other Workers; Establishing and Maintaining Relationships; Monitoring and Controlling Resources. **Physical Work Conditions:** Indoors; Using Hands on Objects, Tools, or Controls; Standing. **Other Job Characteristics:** Importance of Being Sure All Is Done; Consequence of Error; Importance of Being Exact or Accurate.

Experience: Job Zone 1. No previous work-related skill, knowledge, or experience is needed. **Job Preparation:** SVP Below 4.0—Less than 6 months. **Knowledge:** Customer and Personal Service; Food Production; Public Safety and Security; Mechanical; Chemistry. **Instructional Programs:** 120505 Kitchen Personnel/Cook and Assistant Training; 200401 Institutional Food Workers and Administrators, General; 200405 Food Caterer.

Related DOT Jobs: 311.674-014 Raw Shellfish Preparer; 313.684-010 Baker Helper; 313.687-010 Cook Helper, Pastry; 316.661-010 Carver; 316.684-010 Butcher, Chicken and Fish; 316.684-014 Deli Cutter-Slicer; 317.384-010 Salad Maker; 317.664-010 Sandwich Maker; 317.684-010 Coffee Maker; 317.684-014 Pantry Goods Maker; 317.687-010 Cook Helper; 319.484-010 Food Assembler, Kitchen; 319.677-010 Caterer Helper.

35-3000 Food and Beverage Serving Workers

35-3011.00 Bartenders (Bartenders)

Education: Short-term O-T-J training
Employed: 403,828
Openings: 85,583
Projected Growth: 1.9%
Earnings: $12,990

Mix and serve drinks to patrons, directly or through waitstaff.

Serves wine and draft or bottled beer. Cleans glasses, utensils, and bar equipment. Prepares appetizers such as pickles, cheese, and cold meats. Arranges bottles and glasses to make attractive display. Slices and pits fruit for garnishing drinks. Collects money for drinks served. Mixes ingredients such as liquor, soda, water, sugar, and bitters, to prepare cocktails and other drinks. Orders or requisitions liquors and supplies.

GOE Number, Interest Area, and Work Group: 11.05.02; Recreation, Travel, and Other Personal Services; Food and Beverage Services: Serving. **Personality Type:** Enterprising. Enterprising occupations frequently involve starting up and carrying out projects. These occupations can involve leading people and making many decisions. They sometimes require risk taking and often deal with business. **Work Values:** Moral Values; Social Service; Working Conditions; Supervision, Technical; Co-workers. **Skills:** Service Orientation; Mathematics; Social Perceptiveness; Active Listening; Speaking; Writing. **Abilities:** *Cognitive*—Memorization; Information Ordering; Number Facility; Oral Comprehension; Oral Expression. *Psychomotor*—Wrist-Finger Speed; Manual Dexterity; Arm-Hand Steadiness. *Physical*—Extent Flexibility; Trunk Strength; Static Strength. *Sensory*—Speech Recognition; Auditory Attention; Night Vision. **General Work Activities:** *Information Input*—Getting Information Needed to Do the Job; Monitoring Processes, Materials, and Surroundings; Identifying Objects, Actions, and Events. *Mental Process*—Updating and Using Job-Relevant Knowledge; Thinking Creatively; Evaluating Information Against Standards. *Work Output*—Handling and Moving Objects; Controlling Machines and Processes; Performing General Physical Activities. *Interacting with Others*—Establishing and Maintaining Relationships; Performing for or Working with the Public; Communicating with Persons Outside Organization; Monitoring and Controlling Resources. **Physical Work Conditions:** Standing; Indoors; Using Hands on Objects, Tools, or Controls. **Other Job Characteristics:** Importance of Being Exact or Accurate; Importance of Being Sure All Is Done; Consequence of Error; Frustrating Circumstances.

Experience: Job Zone 1. No previous work-related skill, knowledge, or experience is needed. **Job Preparation:** SVP Below 4.0—Less than 6 months. **Knowledge:** Customer and Personal Service; Sales and Marketing; Law, Government and Jurisprudence; Mathematics; English Language. **Instructional Program:** 120502 Bartender/Mixologist.

Related DOT Jobs: 312.474-010 Bartender; 312.477-010 Bar Attendant; 312.677-010 Taproom Attendant.

35-3021.00 Combined Food Preparation and Serving Workers, Including Fast Food (Food Preparation Workers)

Education: Short-term O-T-J training

Employed: 1,256,251

Openings: 529,498

Projected Growth: 10.4%

Earnings: $13,700

Perform duties that combine both food preparation and food service, with no more than 80 percent of time being spent in either job area.

Notifies kitchen personnel of shortages or of special orders. Makes and serves hot and cold beverages or desserts. Requests and records customer order and computes bill. Receives payment. Selects food items from serving or storage areas and places food and beverage items on serving tray or in takeout bag. Cooks or reheats food items such as french fries.

GOE Number, Interest Area, and Work Group: 11.05.02; Recreation, Travel, and Other Personal Services; Food and Beverage Services: Serving. **Personality Type:** Realistic. Realistic occupations frequently involve work activities that include practical, hands-on problems and solutions. These occupations often deal with plants, animals, and real-world materials like wood, tools, and machinery. Many of the occupations require working outside and do not involve a lot of paperwork or working closely with others. **Work Values:** Moral Values; Activity; Co-workers; Independence; Company Policies and Practices; Supervision, Human Relations. **Skills:** Mathematics. **Abilities:** *Cognitive*—Oral Comprehension; Number Facility; Information Ordering; Oral Expression; Written Comprehension. *Psychomotor*—Wrist-Finger Speed; Arm-Hand Steadiness; Reaction Time. *Physical*—Extent Flexibility; Static Strength; Trunk Strength. *Sensory*—Speech Recognition; Visual Color Discrimination; Hearing Sensitivity. **General Work Activities:** *Information Input*—Getting Information Needed to Do the Job; Monitoring Processes, Materials, and Surroundings; Identifying Objects, Actions, and Events. *Mental Process*—Processing Information; Evaluating Information Against Standards; Judging Qualities of Things, Services, Other People's Work. *Work Output*—Handling and Moving Objects; Performing General Physical Activities; Controlling Machines and Processes. *Interacting with Others*—Communicating with Persons Outside Organization; Performing for or Working with the Public; Establishing and Main-

taining Relationships. **Physical Work Conditions:** Indoors; Standing; Walking or Running. **Other Job Characteristics:** Importance of Being Exact or Accurate; Importance of Being Sure All Is Done; Frustrating Circumstances; Degree of Automation.

Experience: Job Zone 1. No previous work-related skill, knowledge, or experience is needed. **Job Preparation:** SVP Below 4.0—Less than 6 months. **Knowledge:** Customer and Personal Service; Mathematics; Sales and Marketing; English Language; Clerical. **Instructional Programs:** 120505 Kitchen Personnel/Cook and Assistant Training; 200401 Institutional Food Workers and Administrators, General; 200405 Food Caterer.

Related DOT Job: 311.472-010 Fast-Foods Worker.

35-3022.00 Counter Attendants, Cafeteria, Food Concession, and Coffee Shop (Food Counter and Fountain Workers)

Education: Short-term O-T-J training

Employed: 2,024,626

Openings: 944,970

Projected Growth: 12.2%

Earnings: No data available.

Serve food to diners at counter or from a steam table. Does not include counter attendants who also wait tables.

Orders items to replace stocks. Calls order to kitchen and picks up and serves order when it is ready. Prepares and serves soft drinks and ice cream dishes such as sundaes, using memorized formulas and methods of following directions. Serves salads, vegetables, meat, breads, and cocktails, ladles soups and sauces, portions desserts, and fills beverage cups and glasses. Writes items ordered on tickets, totals orders, passes orders to cook, and gives ticket stubs to customers to identify filled orders. Serves sandwiches, salads, beverages, desserts, and candies to employees in industrial establishment. Wraps menu items such as sandwiches, hot entrees, and desserts. Prepares sandwiches, salads, and other shortorder items. Adds relishes and garnishes according to instructions. Scrubs and polishes counters, steamtables, and other equipment; cleans glasses, dishes, and fountain equipment; polishes metalwork on fountain. Carves meat. Accepts payment for food, using cash register or adding machine to total check. Replenishes foods at serving stations. Serves food, beverages, or desserts to customers in variety of settings, such as take-out counter of restaurant or lunchroom. Brews coffee and tea and fills containers with requested beverages.

GOE Number, Interest Area, and Work Group: 11.05.02; Recreation, Travel, and Other Personal Services; Food and Beverage Services: Serving. **Personality Type:** Social. Social occupations frequently involve working with, communicating with, and teaching people. These occupations often involve helping or providing service to others. **Work Values:** Moral Values; Co-workers; Supervision, Technical; Social Service; Activity. **Skills:** Writing; Social Perceptiveness; Service Orientation; Problem Identification. **Abilities:** *Cognitive*—Oral Comprehension; Number Facility; Oral Expression; Written Expression; Time Sharing; Problem Sensitivity. *Psychomotor*—Wrist-Finger Speed; Speed of Limb Movement. *Physical*—Stamina. **General Work Activities:** *Information Input*—

Getting Information Needed to Do the Job; Identifying Objects, Actions, and Events; Monitoring Processes, Materials, and Surroundings. *Mental Process*—Processing Information; Updating and Using Job-Relevant Knowledge; Organizing, Planning, and Prioritizing. *Work Output*—Handling and Moving Objects; Performing General Physical Activities; Implementing Ideas and Programs. *Interacting with Others*—Performing for or Working with the Public; Communicating with Persons Outside Organization; Communicating with Other Workers. **Physical Work Conditions:** Indoors; Standing; Special Uniform. **Other Job Characteristics:** Importance of Being Exact or Accurate; Importance of Being Sure All Is Done; Consequence of Error.

Experience: Job Zone 1. No previous work-related skill, knowledge, or experience is needed. **Job Preparation:** SVP Below 4.0—Less than 6 months. **Knowledge:** Customer and Personal Service; English Language; Mathematics; Sales and Marketing; Production and Processing. **Instructional Programs:** 080901 Hospitality and Recreation Marketing Operations, General; 080906 Food Sales Operations.

Related DOT Jobs: 311.477-014 Counter Attendant, Lunchroom or Coffee Shop; 311.477-038 Waiter/Waitress, Take Out; 311.674-010 Canteen Operator; 311.677-014 Counter Attendant, Cafeteria; 319.474-010 Fountain Server.

35-3031.00 Waiters and Waitresses (Waiters and Waitresses)

Education: Short-term O-T-J training

Employed: 2,018,569

Openings: 758,122

Projected Growth: 15%

Earnings: $12,200

Take food orders and serve food and beverages to patrons in dining establishments.

Prepares salads, appetizers, and cold dishes; portions desserts; brews coffee; and performs other services as determined by establishment's size and practices. Takes order from patron for food or beverage, writing order down or memorizing it. Presents menu to patron, suggests food or beverage selections, and answers questions regarding preparation and service. Serves, or assists patrons to serve themselves, at buffet or smorgasbord table. Prepares hot, cold, and mixed drinks for patrons; chills bottles of wine. Garnishes and decorates dishes preparatory to serving. Cleans and arranges assigned station, including side stands, chairs, and table pieces such as linen, silverware, and glassware. Carves meats, bones fish and fowl, and prepares special dishes and desserts at work station or patron's table. Accepts payment and returns change, or refers patron to cashier. Removes dishes and glasses from table or counter and takes them to kitchen for cleaning. Computes cost of meal or beverage. Obtains and replenishes supplies of food, tableware, and linen. Observes patrons to respond to additional requests and to determine when meal has been completed or beverage consumed. Serves meals or beverages to patrons. Fills salt, pepper, sugar, cream, condiment, and napkin containers. Relays order to kitchen or enters order into computer.

GOE Number, Interest Area, and Work Group: 11.05.02; Recreation, Travel, and Other Personal Services; Food and Beverage Services: Serving. **Personality Type:** Social. Social occupations frequently involve working with, communicating with, and teaching people. These occupations often involve helping or providing service to others. **Work Values:** Moral Values; Co-workers; Supervision, Technical; Social Service; Activity. **Skills:** Active Listening; Service Orientation; Mathematics; Problem Identification; Writing. **Abilities:** *Cognitive*—Oral Expression; Oral Comprehension; Memorization; Written Expression; Number Facility. *Psychomotor*—Arm-Hand Steadiness; Wrist-Finger Speed; Speed of Limb Movement. *Physical*—Trunk Strength; Static Strength; Extent Flexibility. *Sensory*—Speech Recognition; Speech Clarity; Auditory Attention. **General Work Activities:** *Information Input*—Getting Information Needed to Do the Job; Monitoring Processes, Materials, and Surroundings; Identifying Objects, Actions, and Events. *Mental Process*—Processing Information; Updating and Using Job-Relevant Knowledge; Analyzing Data or Information; Evaluating Information Against Standards. *Work Output*—Performing General Physical Activities; Handling and Moving Objects; Documenting and Recording Information. *Interacting with Others*—Performing for or Working with the Public; Establishing and Maintaining Relationships; Communicating with Persons Outside Organization. **Physical Work Conditions:** Indoors; Standing; Walking or Running. **Other Job Characteristics:** Importance of Being Sure All Is Done; Frustrating Circumstances; Consequence of Error; Importance of Being Exact or Accurate.

Experience: Job Zone 1. No previous work-related skill, knowledge, or experience is needed. **Job Preparation:** SVP Below 4.0—Less than 6 months. **Knowledge:** Customer and Personal Service; Mathematics; English Language; Sales and Marketing; Psychology. **Instructional Program:** 120507 Waiter/Waitress and Dining Room Manager.

Related DOT Jobs: 311.477-018 Waiter/Waitress, Bar; 311.477-022 Waiter/Waitress, Dining Car; 311.477-026 Waiter/Waitress, Formal; 311.477-030 Waiter/Waitress, Informal; 311.674-018 Waiter/Waitress, Buffet; 350.677-010 Mess Attendant; 350.677-026 Steward/Stewardess, Wine; 350.677-030 Waiter/Waitress; 352.677-018 Waiter/Waitress, Club.

35-3041.00 Food Servers, Nonrestaurant (Food Servers, Outside)

Education: No data available.

Employed: 63,170

Openings: No data available.

Projected Growth: No data available.

Earnings: $14,300

Serve food to patrons outside of a restaurant environment, such as in hotels, hospital rooms, or cars.

Removes tray and stacks dishes for return to kitchen. Pushes carts to rooms and serves trays to patients or guests. Reads orders to determine items to place on food tray. Totals and presents check to customer and accepts payment for service. Restocks service counter with items such as ice, napkins, and straws. Washes dishes and cleans work area, tables, cabinets, and ovens. Prepares fountain drinks such as sodas, milkshakes, and malted milks. Prepares food items such as sandwiches, salads, soups, and beverages; places items such as eating utensils, napkins, and condiments on trays. Carries silverware, linen, and food on tray or uses cart. Apportions and places food servings on plates and trays according to order or instructions. Takes order and relays order to kitchen or serving counter to be filled. Examines filled tray for completeness. Prepares and delivers food trays. Records amount and types of special food items served to customers.

GOE Number, Interest Area, and Work Group: 11.05.02; Recreation, Travel, and Other Personal Services; Food and Beverage Services: Serving. **Personality Type:** Social. Social occupations frequently involve working with, communicating with, and teaching people. These occupations often involve helping or providing service to others. **Work Values:** Moral Values; Co-workers; Social Service; Supervision, Technical; Company Policies and Practices. **Skills:** Service Orientation; Reading Comprehension; Active Listening; Writing. **Abilities:** *Cognitive*—Number Facility; Oral Expression; Oral Comprehension; Information Ordering; Written Expression; Memorization. *Psychomotor*—Wrist-Finger Speed; Speed of Limb Movement. *Physical*—Static Strength; Stamina. *Sensory*—Sound Localization. **General Work Activities:** *Information Input*—Getting Information Needed to Do the Job; Identifying Objects, Actions, and Events; Monitoring Processes, Materials, and Surroundings. *Mental Process*—Evaluating Information Against Standards; Processing Information; Judging Qualities of Things, Services, Other People's Work; Organizing, Planning, and Prioritizing. *Work Output*—Handling and Moving Objects; Performing General Physical Activities; Implementing Ideas and Programs. *Interacting with Others*—Performing for or Working with the Public; Communicating with Other Workers; Communicating with Persons Outside Organization. **Physical Work Conditions:** Standing; Special Uniform; Using Hands on Objects, Tools, or Controls. **Other Job Characteristics:** Importance of Being Exact or Accurate; Importance of Being Sure All Is Done; Consequence of Error.

Experience: Job Zone 1. No previous work-related skill, knowledge, or experience is needed. **Job Preparation:** SVP Below 4.0—Less than 6 months. **Knowledge:** Customer and Personal Service; Mathematics; English Language; Sales and Marketing; Chemistry. **Instructional Program:** 120507 Waiter/Waitress and Dining Room Manager.

Related DOT Jobs: 311.477-010 Car Hop; 311.477-034 Waiter/Waitress, Room Service; 319.677-014 Food-Service Worker, Hospital.

35-9000 Other Food Preparation and Serving Related Workers

35-9011.00 Dining Room and Cafeteria Attendants and Bartender Helpers (Dining Room and Cafeteria Attendants and Bar Helpers)

Education: Short-term O-T-J training
Employed: 405,469
Openings: 181,922
Projected Growth: 4%
Earnings: $12,580

Facilitate food service. Clean tables; carry dirty dishes; replace soiled table linens; set tables; replenish supply of clean linens, silverware, glassware, and dishes; supply service bar with food; serve water, butter, and coffee to patrons.

Circulates among diners and serves coffee. Stocks refrigerating units with wines and bottled beer; replaces empty beer kegs; and slices and pits fruit used to garnish drinks. Carries food, dishes, trays, and silverware from kitchen and supply departments to serving counters. Replenishes supply of clean linens, silverware, glassware, and dishes in dining room. Keeps assigned area and equipment clean, makes coffee, fills fruit juice dispensers, and stocks vending machines with food in automat. Washes glasses, bar, and equipment; polishes bar fixtures; mops floors; removes empty bottles and trash. Mixes and prepares flavors for mixed drinks. Carries dirty dishes to kitchen and wipes tables and seats with dampened cloth. Sets tables with clean linens, sugar bowls, and condiments. Carries trays from food counters to tables for cafeteria patrons and serves ice water and butter to patrons. Cleans bar and equipment; replenishes bar supplies such as liquor, fruit, ice, and dishes. Replenishes food and equipment at steamtables and serving counters of cafeteria to facilitate service to patrons. Garnishes and positions foods on table to ensure visibility to patrons and convenience in serving.

GOE Number, Interest Area, and Work Group: 11.05.02; Recreation, Travel, and Other Personal Services; Food and Beverage Services: Serving. **Personality Type:** Realistic. Realistic occupations frequently involve work activities that include practical, hands-on problems and solutions. These occupations often deal with plants, animals, and real-world materials like wood, tools, and machinery. Many of the occupations require working outside and do not involve a lot of paperwork or working closely with others. **Work Values:** Moral Values; Co-workers; Supervision, Technical; Social Service; Company Policies and Practices; Activity; Supervision, Human Relations. **Skills:** Service Orientation. **Abilities:** *Cognitive*—Time Sharing; Oral Comprehension; Oral Expression; Problem Sensitivity; Written Comprehension; Memorization. *Psychomotor*—Wrist-Finger Speed; Speed of Limb Movement. *Physical*—Static Strength; Stamina; Gross Body Coordination. *Sensory*—Peripheral Vision. **General Work Activities:** *Information Input*—Monitoring Processes, Materials, and Surroundings; Getting Information Needed to Do the Job; Identifying Objects, Actions, and Events. *Mental Process*—Making Decisions and Solving Problems; Judging Qualities of Things, Services, Other People's Work; Organizing, Planning, and Prioritizing. *Work Output*—Handling and Moving Objects; Performing General Physical Activities; Implementing Ideas and Programs. *Interacting with Others*—Performing for or Working with the Public; Communicating with Other Workers; Communicating with Persons Outside Organization. **Physical Work Conditions:** Indoors; Standing; Walking or Running; Using Hands on Objects, Tools, or Controls. **Other Job Characteristics:** Importance of Being Sure All Is Done; Importance of Repeating Same Tasks; Importance of Being Exact or Accurate.

Experience: Job Zone 1. No previous work-related skill, knowledge, or experience is needed. **Job Preparation:** SVP Below 4.0—Less than 6 months. **Knowledge:** Customer and Personal Service; Law, Government and Jurisprudence; English Language; Chemistry; Food Production. **Instructional Programs:** 120502 Bartender/Mixologist; 120507 Waiter/Waitress and Dining Room Manager.

Related DOT Jobs: 311.677-010 Cafeteria Attendant; 311.677-018 Dining Room Attendant; 312.687-010 Bartender Helper; 319.687-010 Counter-Supply Worker.

35-9021.00 Dishwashers (Food Preparation Workers)

Education: Short-term O-T-J training

Employed: 1,256,251

Openings: 529,498

Projected Growth: 10.4%

Earnings: $13,700

Clean dishes, kitchen, food preparation equipment, or utensils.

Carries or transfers supplies and equipment between storage and work areas, using handtruck. Cleans and prepares various foods for cooking or serving. Sets up banquet tables. Loads or unloads trucks used in delivering or picking up food and supplies. Removes garbage and trash and places refuse in designated pick-up area. Prepares and packages individual place settings. Cleans and maintains work areas, equipment, and utensils. Stocks serving stations with food and utensils.

GOE Number, Interest Area, and Work Group: 11.05.01; Recreation, Travel, and Other Personal Services; Food and Beverage Services: Preparing. **Personality Type:** Realistic. Realistic occupations frequently involve work activities that include practical, hands-on problems and solutions. These occupations often deal with plants, animals, and real-world materials like wood, tools, and machinery. Many of the occupations require working outside and do not involve a lot of paperwork or working closely with others. **Work Values:** Moral Values; Co-workers; Activity; Independence; Security; Supervision, Human Relations. **Skills:** none met the criteria. **Abilities:** *Cognitive*—Information Ordering; Oral Comprehension; Spatial Orientation; Category Flexibility; Memorization. *Psychomotor*—Wrist-Finger Speed; Manual Dexterity; Multilimb Coordination. *Physical*—Trunk Strength; Extent Flexibility; Static Strength. *Sensory*—Peripheral Vision; Far Vision; Hearing Sensitivity; Depth Perception. **General Work Activities:** *Information Input*—Getting Information Needed to Do the Job; Monitoring Processes, Materials, and Surroundings; Estimating Needed Characteristics. *Mental Process*—Evaluating Information Against Standards; Judging Qualities of Things, Services, Other People's Work; Analyzing Data or Information; Organizing, Planning, and Prioritizing. *Work Output*—Handling and Moving Objects; Performing General Physical Activities; Controlling Machines and Processes. *Interacting with Others*—Communicating with Other Workers; Monitoring and Controlling Resources; Establishing and Maintaining Relationships. **Physical Work Conditions:** Indoors; Standing; Walking or Running. **Other Job Characteristics:** Importance of Being Sure All Is Done; Importance of Being Exact or Accurate; Degree of Automation.

Experience: Job Zone 1. No previous work-related skill, knowledge, or experience is needed. **Job Preparation:** SVP Below 4.0—Less than 6 months. **Knowledge:** Food Production; Customer and Personal Service; Public Safety and Security; Mechanical; Chemistry; English Language. **Instructional Programs:** 120505 Kitchen Personnel/Cook and Assistant Training; 200401 Institutional Food Workers and Administrators, General; 200405 Food Caterer.

Related DOT Jobs: 318.687-010 Kitchen Helper; 318.687-014 Scullion; 318.687-018 Silver Wrapper.

35-9031.00 Hosts and Hostesses, Restaurant, Lounge, and Coffee Shop (Restaurant Hosts and Hostesses)

Education: Short-term O-T-J training

Employed: 297,190

Openings: 110,848

Projected Growth: 18.2%

Earnings: $13,400

Welcome patrons, seat them at tables or in lounge, and help ensure quality of facilities and service.

Schedules dining reservations and arranges parties or special service for diners. Assigns work tasks and coordinates activities of dining room personnel to ensure prompt and courteous service to patrons. Adjusts complaints of patrons. Requisitions table linens and other supplies for tables and serving stations. Greets and escorts guests to tables, and provides menus. Inspects dining room serving stations for neatness and cleanliness.

GOE Number, Interest Area, and Work Group: 11.05.02; Recreation, Travel, and Other Personal Services; Food and Beverage Services: Serving. **Personality Type:** Enterprising. Enterprising occupations frequently involve starting up and carrying out projects. These occupations can involve leading people and making many decisions. They sometimes require risk taking and often deal with business. **Work Values:** Moral Values; Co-workers; Supervision, Technical; Social Service; Activity; Working Conditions. **Skills:** Time Management; Problem Identification; Management of Personnel Resources; Coordination; Learning Strategies; Speaking. **Abilities:** *Cognitive*—Oral Expression; Oral Comprehension; Number Facility; Problem Sensitivity; Written Expression; Selective Attention. *Psychomotor*—none met the criteria. *Physical*—none met the criteria. *Sensory*—Speech Clarity; Speech Recognition; Far Vision. **General Work Activities:** *Information Input*—Monitoring Processes, Materials, and Surroundings; Getting Information Needed to Do the Job; Identifying Objects, Actions, and Events. *Mental Process*—Scheduling Work and Activities; Judging Qualities of Things, Services, Other People's Work; Making Decisions and Solving Problems. *Work Output*—Performing General Physical Activities; Documenting and Recording Information; Handling and Moving Objects; Implementing Ideas and Programs. *Interacting with Others*—Communicating with Other Workers; Establishing and Maintaining Relationships; Performing for or Working with the Public. **Physical Work Conditions:** Indoors; Standing; Special Uniform. **Other Job Characteristics:** Importance of Being Exact or Accurate; Importance of Being Sure All Is Done; Consequence of Error.

Experience: Job Zone 3. Previous work-related skill, knowledge, or experience is required. **Job Preparation:** SVP 6.0 to less than 7.0—More than 1 year and less than 4 years. **Knowledge:** Customer and Personal Service; Administration and Management; Mathematics; Personnel and Human Resources; English Language. **Instructional Program:** 120507 Waiter/Waitress and Dining Room Manager.

Related DOT Job: 310.137-010 Host/Hostess, Restaurant.

37-0000
Building and Grounds Cleaning and Maintenance Occupations

37-1000 Supervisors, Building and Grounds Cleaning and Maintenance Workers

37-1011.00 First-Line Supervisors/Managers of Housekeeping and Janitorial Workers (Housekeeping Supervisors)

Education: Work experience in a related occupation

Employed: 87,412

Openings: 9,030

Projected Growth: 10.5%

Earnings: $19,590

GOE Number, Interest Area, and Work Group: 11.01.01; Recreation, Travel, and Other Personal Services; Managerial Work in Recreation, Travel, and Other Personal Services. **Instructional Programs:** 200601 Custodial, Housekeeping and Home Services Workers and Managers; 200605 Executive Housekeeper. **Note:** The Department of Labor has not collected some data for this job, so it has fewer details than the other descriptions.

37-1011.01 Housekeeping Supervisors (Institutional Cleaning Supervisors)

Education: Work experience in a related occupation

Employed: 87,412

Openings: 9,030

Projected Growth: 10.5%

Earnings: $19,590

Supervise work activities of cleaning personnel to ensure clean, orderly, and attractive rooms in hotels, hospitals, educational institutions, and similar establishments. Assign duties, inspect work, and investigate complaints regarding housekeeping service and equipment; take corrective action. Purchase housekeeping supplies and equipment, take periodic inventories, screen applicants, train new employees, and recommend dismissals.

Prepares reports concerning room occupancy, payroll, and department expenses. Investigates complaints regarding housekeeping service and equipment, and takes corrective action. Coordinates work activities among departments. Records data regarding work assignments, personnel actions, and time cards, and prepares periodic reports. Conducts orientation training and in-service training to explain policies and work procedures and to demonstrate use and maintenance of equipment. Evaluates records to forecast department personnel requirements. Attends staff meetings to discuss company policies and patrons' complaints. Makes recommendations to improve service and ensure more efficient operation. Examines building to determine need for repairs or replacement of furniture or equipment; makes recommendations to management. Selects and purchases new furnishings. Inventories stock to ensure adequate supplies. Issues supplies and equipment to workers. Establishes standards and procedures for work

of housekeeping staff. Advises manager, desk clerk, or admitting personnel of rooms ready for occupancy. Screens job applicants; hires new employees; recommends promotions, transfers, and dismissals. Obtains list of rooms to be cleaned immediately and list of prospective check-outs or discharges to prepare work assignments. Assigns workers their duties and inspects work for conformance to prescribed standards of cleanliness. Performs cleaning duties in cases of emergency or staff shortage.

GOE Number, Interest Area, and Work Group: 11.01.01; Recreation, Travel, and Other Personal Services; Managerial Work in Recreation, Travel, and Other Personal Services. **Personality Type:** Enterprising. Enterprising occupations frequently involve starting up and carrying out projects. These occupations can involve leading people and making many decisions. They sometimes require risk taking and often deal with business. **Work Values:** Authority; Moral Values; Co-workers; Activity; Working Conditions; Responsibility; Security; Autonomy. **Skills:** Problem Identification; Time Management; Management of Personnel Resources; Reading Comprehension; Speaking; Coordination. **Abilities:** *Cognitive—* Oral Expression; Oral Comprehension; Written Expression; Written Comprehension; Fluency of Ideas; Number Facility. *Psychomotor—*none met the criteria. *Physical—*none met the criteria. *Sensory—*Speech Clarity. **General Work Activities:** *Information Input—*Estimating Needed Characteristics; Identifying Objects, Actions, and Events; Getting Information Needed to Do the Job; Inspecting Equipment, Structures, Materials; Monitoring Processes, Materials, and Surroundings. *Mental Process—*Making Decisions and Solving Problems; Evaluating Information Against Standards; Judging Qualities of Things, Services, Other People's Work; Organizing, Planning, and Prioritizing. *Work Output—*Implementing Ideas and Programs; Documenting and Recording Information; Performing General Physical Activities. *Interacting with Others—*Coordinating Work and Activities of Others; Guiding, Directing and Motivating Subordinates; Communicating with Other Workers; Monitoring and Controlling Resources. **Physical Work Conditions:** Indoors; Sitting; Standing. **Other Job Characteristics:** Importance of Being Sure All Is Done; Importance of Being Exact or Accurate; Consequence of Error.

Experience: Job Zone 4. A minimum of two to four years of work-related skill, knowledge, or experience is needed. **Job Preparation:** SVP 7.0 to less than 8.0—2 years to less than 10 years. **Knowledge:** Customer and Personal Service; Personnel and Human Resources; Administration and Management; Education and Training; English Language. **Instructional Programs:** 200601 Custodial, Housekeeping and Home Services Workers and Managers; 200605 Executive Housekeeper.

Related DOT Jobs: 187.167-046 Executive Housekeeper; 321.137-010 Housekeeper.

37-1011.02 Janitorial Supervisors (Institutional Cleaning Supervisors)

Education: Work experience in a related occupation

Employed: 87,412

Openings: 9,030

Projected Growth: 10.5%

Earnings: $19,590

Supervise work activities of janitorial personnel in commercial and industrial establishments. Assign duties, inspect work, and investigate complaints regarding janitorial services; take corrective action. Purchase janitorial supplies and equipment, take periodic inventories, screen applicants, train new employees, and recommend dismissals.

Assigns janitorial work to employees, following material and work requirements. Supervises and coordinates activities of workers engaged in janitorial services. Inspects work performed to ensure conformance to specifications and established standards. Issues janitorial supplies and equipment to workers to ensure quality and timely delivery of services. Recommends personnel actions such as hires and discharges, to ensure proper staffing. Records personnel data on specified forms. Confers with staff to resolve production and personnel problems. Trains workers in janitorial methods and procedures and proper operation of equipment.

GOE Number, Interest Area, and Work Group: 11.01.01; Recreation, Travel, and Other Personal Services; Managerial Work in Recreation, Travel, and Other Personal Services. **Personality Type:** Enterprising. Enterprising occupations frequently involve starting up and carrying out projects. These occupations can involve leading people and making many decisions. They sometimes require risk taking and often deal with business. **Work Values:** Authority; Moral Values; Autonomy; Activity; Responsibility; Security. **Skills:** Coordination; Management of Personnel Resources; Time Management; Speaking; Social Perceptiveness; Writing. **Abilities:** *Cognitive*—Oral Expression; Oral Comprehension; Problem Sensitivity; Information Ordering; Time Sharing. *Psychomotor*—Manual Dexterity; Multilimb Coordination. *Physical*—Trunk Strength; Dynamic Strength. *Sensory*—Speech Clarity. **General Work Activities:** *Information Input*—Getting Information Needed to Do the Job; Inspecting Equipment, Structures, Materials; Monitoring Processes, Materials, and Surroundings. *Mental Process*—Scheduling Work and Activities; Judging Qualities of Things, Services, Other People's Work; Evaluating Information Against Standards; Making Decisions and Solving Problems; Organizing, Planning, and Prioritizing. *Work Output*—Implementing Ideas and Programs; Performing General Physical Activities; Documenting and Recording Information. *Interacting with Others*—Coordinating Work and Activities of Others; Communicating with Other Workers; Guiding, Directing and Motivating Subordinates. **Physical Work Conditions:** Standing; Indoors; Using Hands on Objects, Tools, or Controls; Walking or Running. **Other Job Characteristics:** Importance of Being Sure All Is Done; Consequence of Error; Importance of Being Exact or Accurate.

Experience: Job Zone 3. Previous work-related skill, knowledge, or experience is required. **Job Preparation:** SVP 6.0 to less than 7.0—More than 1 year and less than 4 years. **Knowledge:** Administration and Management; Personnel and Human Resources; Education and Training; Customer and Personal Service; Chemistry; English Language; Mechanical. **Instructional Programs:** 200601 Custodial, Housekeeping and Home Services Workers and Managers; 200605 Executive Housekeeper.

Related DOT Jobs: 381.137-010 Supervisor, Janitorial Services; 382.137-010 Supervisor, Maintenance; 389.137-010 Supervisor, Home Restoration Service.

37-1012.00 First-Line Supervisors/Managers of Landscaping, Lawn Service, and Groundskeeping Workers (First-Line Supervisors and Managers/Supervisors—Agricultural, Forestry, Fishing, and Related Workers)

Education: No data available.

Employed: 51,350

Openings: No data available.

Projected Growth: No data available.

Earnings: $27,410

GOE Number, Interest Area, and Work Group: 03.01.02; Plants and Animals; Managerial Work: Nursery, Groundskeeping, and Logging. **Instructional Programs:** 010104 Farm and Ranch Management; 010199 Agricultural Business and Management, Other; 010301 Agricultural Production Workers and Managers, General; 010302 Agricultural Animal Husbandry and Production Management; 010304 Crop Production Operations and Management; 010399 Agricultural Production Workers and Managers, Other; 019999 Agricultural Business and Production, Other; 020201 Animal Sciences, General; 020202 Agricultural Animal Breeding and Genetics; 020204 Agricultural Animal Nutrition; 020206 Dairy Science; 020209 Poultry Science; 020401 Plant Sciences, General; 020402 Agronomy and Crop Science; 020409 Range Science and Management. **Note:** The Department of Labor has not collected some data for this job, so it has fewer details than the other descriptions.

37-1012.01 Lawn Service Managers (Lawn Service Managers)

Education: Work experience in a related occupation

Employed: 86,354

Openings: 10,385

Projected Growth: 20%

Earnings: $25,410

Plan, direct, and coordinate activities of workers engaged in pruning trees and shrubs, cultivating lawns, and applying pesticides and other chemicals according to service contract specifications.

Schedules work for crew according to weather conditions, availability of equipment, and seasonal limitations. Spot checks completed work to improve quality of service and to ensure contract compliance. Investigates customer complaints. Prepares work activity and personnel reports. Answers customers' questions about groundskeeping care requirements. Reviews contracts to ascertain service, machine, and workforce requirements for job. Supervises workers who provide groundskeeping services on a contract basis. Suggests changes in work procedures and orders corrective work done. Prepares service cost estimates for customers.

GOE Number, Interest Area, and Work Group: 03.01.02; Plants and Animals; Managerial Work: Nursery, Groundskeeping, and Logging. **Personality Type:** Enterprising. Enterprising occupations frequently involve starting up and carrying out projects. These occupations can involve leading people and making many decisions. They sometimes require risk taking and often deal with business. **Work Values:** Authority; Autonomy; Responsibility; Moral Values; Company Policies and Practices; Ability Utilization. **Skills:** Time Management; Management of Personnel Resources; Implementation Planning; Coordination; Problem Identification. **Abilities:** *Cognitive*—Oral Comprehension; Written Comprehension; Oral Expression; Number Facility; Written Expression; Information Ordering. *Psychomotor*—none met the criteria. *Physical*—none met the criteria. *Sensory*—Speech Clarity; Glare Sensitivity. **General Work Activities:** *Information Input*—Estimating Needed Characteristics; Getting Information Needed to Do the Job; Monitoring Processes, Materials, and Surroundings. *Mental Process*—Making Decisions and Solving Problems; Organizing, Planning, and Prioritizing; Scheduling Work and Activities. *Work Output*—Implementing Ideas and Programs; Performing General Physical Activities; Handling and Moving Objects; Documenting and Recording Information. *Interacting with Others*—Guiding, Directing and Motivating Subordinates; Coordinating Work and Activities of Others; Establishing and Maintaining Relationships. **Physical Work Conditions:** Outdoors; Standing; Very Hot; Using Hands on Objects, Tools, or Controls. **Other Job Characteristics:** Importance of Being Sure All Is Done; Consequence of Error; Importance of Being Exact or Accurate.

Experience: Job Zone 4. A minimum of two to four years of work-related skill, knowledge, or experience is needed. **Job Preparation:** SVP 7.0 to less than 8.0—2 years to less than 10 years. **Knowledge:** Administration and Management; Customer and Personal Service; Personnel and Human Resources; Economics and Accounting; English Language. **Instructional Programs:** 010601 Horticulture Services Operations and Management, General; 010603 Ornamental Horticulture Operations and Management; 010607 Turf Management.

Related DOT Job: 408.131-010 Supervisor, Spray, Lawn and Tree Service.

37-1012.02 First-Line Supervisors and Manager/Supervisors—Landscaping Workers (First-Line Supervisors and Managers/Supervisors—Agricultural and Related Workers)

Education: Work experience in a related occupation

Employed: 91,546

Openings: 11,813

Projected Growth: 6.2%

Earnings: No data available.

Directly supervise and coordinate activities of landscaping workers. Manager/Supervisors are generally found in smaller establishments where they perform both supervisory and management functions such as accounting, marketing, and personnel work and may also engage in the same landscaping work as the workers they supervise.

Interviews, hires, and discharges workers. Keeps employee time records, and records daily work performed. Assists workers in performing work when completion is critical. Confers with manager to develop plans and schedules for maintenance and improve-ment of grounds. Trains workers in tasks such as transplanting and pruning trees and shrubs, finishing cement, using equipment, and caring for turf. Determines work priority and crew and equipment requirements; assigns workers tasks such as planting, fertilizing, irrigating, and mowing. Observes ongoing work to ascertain if work is being performed according to instructions and will be completed on time. Directs and assists workers engaged in maintenance and repair of equipment such as powermower and backhoe, using hand tools and power tools. Directs workers in maintenance and repair of driveways, walkways, benches, graves, and mausoleums. Mixes and prepares spray and dust solutions, and directs application of fertilizer, insecticide, and fungicide. Tours grounds such as park, botanical garden, cemetery, or golf course to inspect conditions.

GOE Number, Interest Area, and Work Group: 03.01.02; Plants and Animals; Managerial Work: Nursery, Groundskeeping, and Logging. **Personality Type:** Realistic. Realistic occupations frequently involve work activities that include practical, hands-on problems and solutions. These occupations often deal with plants, animals, and real-world materials like wood, tools, and machinery. Many of the occupations require working outside and do not involve a lot of paperwork or working closely with others. **Work Values:** Authority; Responsibility; Autonomy; Activity; Moral Values. **Skills:** Coordination; Management of Personnel Resources; Speaking; Problem Identification; Time Management; Instructing. **Abilities:** *Cognitive*—Oral Expression; Oral Comprehension; Visualization; Information Ordering; Number Facility; Written Expression. *Psychomotor*—Manual Dexterity; Wrist-Finger Speed; Multilimb Coordination; Control Precision. *Physical*—Static Strength; Trunk Strength; Extent Flexibility. *Sensory*—Speech Clarity; Near Vision; Visual Color Discrimination. **General Work Activities:** *Information Input*—Getting Information Needed to Do the Job; Monitoring Processes, Materials, and Surroundings; Inspecting Equipment, Structures, Materials. *Mental Process*—Scheduling Work and Activities; Making Decisions and Solving Problems; Organizing, Planning, and Prioritizing. *Work Output*—Performing General Physical Activities; Handling and Moving Objects; Documenting and Recording Information. *Interacting with Others*—Coordinating Work and Activities of Others; Guiding, Directing and Motivating Subordinates; Communicating with Other Workers. **Physical Work Conditions:** Outdoors; Standing; Walking or Running; Contaminants. **Other Job Characteristics:** Importance of Being Sure All Is Done; Consequence of Error; Frustrating Circumstances.

Experience: Job Zone 3. Previous work-related skill, knowledge, or experience is required. **Job Preparation:** SVP 6.0 to less than 7.0—More than 1 year and less than 4 years. **Knowledge:** Administration and Management; Personnel and Human Resources; Chemistry; Biology; Mechanical. **Instructional Programs:** 010601 Horticulture Services Operations and Management, General; 010605 Landscaping Operations and Management; 010607 Turf Management.

Related DOT Jobs: 406.134-010 Supervisor, Cemetery Workers; 406.134-014 Supervisor, Landscape; 406.137-010 Greenskeeper I; 406.137-014 Superintendent, Greens; 408.137-014 Supervisor, Tree-Trimming.

37-2000 Building Cleaning and Pest Control Workers

37-2011.00 Janitors and Cleaners, Except Maids and Housekeeping Cleaners (Janitors, Cleaners, Maids and Housekeeping Cleaners)

Education: Short-term O-T-J training
Employed: 3,183,804
Openings: 735,967
Projected Growth: 11.5%
Earnings: No data available.

Keep buildings in clean and orderly condition. Perform heavy cleaning duties such as cleaning floors, shampooing rugs, washing walls and glass, and removing rubbish. Tend furnace and boiler, perform routine maintenance activities, notify management of need for repairs, and clean snow or debris from sidewalk.

Dusts furniture, walls, machines, and equipment. Drives vehicles such as van, industrial truck, or industrial vacuum cleaner. Cleans chimneys, flues, and connecting pipes, using power and hand tools. Cleans and restores building interiors damaged by fire, smoke, or water, using commercial cleaning equipment. Services and repairs cleaning and maintenance equipment and machinery; performs minor routine painting, plumbing, electrical, and related activities. Moves items between departments, manually or using handtruck. Requisitions supplies and equipment used in cleaning and maintenance duties. Applies waxes or sealers to wood or concrete floors. Mixes water and detergents or acids in container to prepare cleaning solutions, according to specifications. Sets up, arranges, and removes decorations, tables, chairs, ladders, and scaffolding, for events such as banquets and social functions. Gathers and empties trash. Mows and trims lawns and shrubbery, using mowers and hand and power trimmers, and clears debris from grounds. Cleans or polishes walls, ceilings, windows, plant equipment and building fixtures, using steam cleaning equipment, scrapers, brooms, and a variety of hand and power tools. Removes snow from sidewalks, driveways, and parking areas, using snowplow, snowblower, and snow shovel; spreads snow-melting chemicals. Tends, cleans, adjusts and services furnaces, air conditioners, boilers, and other building heating and cooling systems. Sweeps, mops, scrubs, and vacuums floors of buildings, using cleaning solutions, tools, and equipment. Notifies management personnel concerning need for major repairs or additions to building operating systems. Sprays insecticides and fumigants to prevent insect and rodent infestation. Cleans laboratory equipment such as glassware and metal instruments, using solvents, brushes, rags, and power cleaning equipment.

GOE Number, Interest Area, and Work Group: 11.07.01; Recreation, Travel, and Other Personal Services; Cleaning and Building Services. **Personality Type:** Realistic. Realistic occupations frequently involve work activities that include practical, hands-on problems and solutions. These occupations often deal with plants, animals, and real-world materials like wood, tools, and machinery. Many of the occupations require working outside and do not involve a lot of paperwork or working closely with others. **Work Values:** Moral Values; Independence; Company Policies and Practices; Activity; Security. **Skills:** Equipment Maintenance; Repairing; Equipment Selection; Troubleshooting; Installation; Operation and Control. **Abilities:** *Cognitive*—Information Ordering; Visualization; Spatial Orientation; Problem Sensitivity; Oral Expression. *Psychomotor*—Multilimb Coordination; Manual Dexterity; Wrist-Finger Speed. *Physical*—Extent Flexibility; Static Strength; Trunk Strength. *Sensory*—Depth Perception; Hearing Sensitivity; Visual Color Discrimination. **General Work Activities:** *Information Input*—Getting Information Needed to Do the Job; Inspecting Equipment, Structures, Materials; Estimating Needed Characteristics. *Mental Process*—Judging Qualities of Things, Services, Other People's Work; Organizing, Planning, and Prioritizing; Analyzing Data or Information. *Work Output*—Performing General Physical Activities; Handling and Moving Objects; Repairing and Maintaining Mechanical Equipment. *Interacting with Others*—Monitoring and Controlling Resources; Communicating with Other Workers; Establishing and Maintaining Relationships. **Physical Work Conditions:** Indoors; Standing; Contaminants. **Other Job Characteristics:** Importance of Being Sure All Is Done; Consequence of Error; Frustrating Circumstances.

Experience: Job Zone 1. No previous work-related skill, knowledge, or experience is needed. **Job Preparation:** SVP Below 4.0—Less than 6 months. **Knowledge:** Mechanical; Chemistry; Customer and Personal Service; Building and Construction; Mathematics. **Instructional Program:** 200601 Custodial, Housekeeping and Home Services Workers and Managers.

Related DOT Jobs: 358.687-010 Change-House Attendant; 381.687-014 Cleaner, Commercial or Institutional; 381.687-018 Cleaner, Industrial; 381.687-022 Cleaner, Laboratory Equipment; 381.687-026 Cleaner, Wall; 381.687-030 Patch Worker; 381.687-034 Waxer, Floor; 382.664-010 Janitor; 389.664-010 Cleaner, Home Restoration Service; 389.667-010 Sexton; 389.683-010 Sweeper-Cleaner, Industrial; 389.687-014 Cleaner, Window; 891.684-018 Swimming-Pool Servicer; 891.687-010 Chimney Sweep; 891.687-018 Project-Crew Worker.

37-2012.00 Maids and Housekeeping Cleaners (Janitors, Cleaners, Maids and Housekeeping Cleaners)

Education: Short-term O-T-J training
Employed: 3,183,804
Openings: 735,967
Projected Growth: 11.5%
Earnings: No data available.

Perform any combination of light cleaning duties to maintain private households or commercial establishments such as hotels, restaurants, and hospitals, in a clean and orderly manner. Make beds, replenish linens, clean rooms and halls, and vacuum.

Prepares sample rooms for sales meetings. Replaces light bulbs. Washes windows, door panels, and sills. Delivers television sets, ironing boards, baby cribs, and rollaway beds to guests rooms. Cleans swimming pool with vacuum. Transports trash and waste to disposal area. Replenishes supplies such as drinking glasses, writing supplies, and bathroom items. Moves and arranges furniture, turns mattresses, hangs draperies, dusts venetian blinds, and polishes metalwork to ready hotel facilities for occupancy. Washes beds and mattresses, and remakes beds after dismissal of hospital patients. Sweeps, scrubs, waxes, and polishes floors, using brooms and mops and powered scrubbing and waxing machines. Dusts furniture and equipment. Arranges decorations, apparatus, or furniture for banquets and social functions. Cleans rugs, carpets, upholstered furniture, and draperies, using vacuum cleaner. Empties wastebaskets, and empties and cleans ashtrays. Collects soiled linens for laundering, and receives and stores linen supplies in linen closet. Washes walls, ceiling, and woodwork. Polishes metalwork such as fixtures and fittings. Cleans and removes debris from driveway and garage areas. Cleans rooms, hallways, lobbies, lounges, restrooms, corridors, elevators, stairways, locker rooms, and other work areas.

GOE Number, Interest Area, and Work Group: 11.07.01; Recreation, Travel, and Other Personal Services; Cleaning and Building Services. **Personality Type:** Realistic. Realistic occupations frequently involve work activities that include practical, hands-on problems and solutions. These occupations often deal with plants, animals, and real-world materials like wood, tools, and machinery. Many of the occupations require working outside and do not involve a lot of paperwork or working closely with others. **Work Values:** Moral Values; Independence; Activity; Co-workers; Security. **Skills:** none met the criteria. **Abilities:** *Cognitive*—Problem Sensitivity; Information Ordering; Spatial Orientation; Visualization; Oral Comprehension. *Psychomotor*—Wrist-Finger Speed; Multilimb Coordination; Speed of Limb Movement. *Physical*—Trunk Strength; Static Strength; Stamina. **General Work Activities:** *Information Input*—Inspecting Equipment, Structures, Materials; Estimating Needed Characteristics; Identifying Objects, Actions, and Events; Monitoring Processes, Materials, and Surroundings; Getting Information Needed to Do the Job. *Mental Process*—Organizing, Planning, and Prioritizing; Judging Qualities of Things, Services, Other People's Work; Evaluating Information Against Standards. *Work Output*—Handling and Moving Objects; Performing General Physical Activities; Controlling Machines and Processes. *Interacting with Others*—Communicating with Other Workers; Assisting and Caring for Others; Performing for or Working with the Public; Monitoring and Controlling Resources. **Physical Work Conditions:** Standing; Indoors; Walking or Running. **Other Job Characteristics:** Importance of Being Sure All Is Done; Consequence of Error; Importance of Being Exact or Accurate.

Experience: Job Zone 1. No previous work-related skill, knowledge, or experience is needed. **Job Preparation:** SVP Below 4.0—Less than 6 months. **Knowledge:** Customer and Personal Service; Chemistry; Public Safety and Security; Mechanical; Mathematics; Physics; Geography; Transportation. **Instructional Program:** 200601 Custodial, Housekeeping and Home Services Workers and Managers.

Related DOT Jobs: 323.687-010 Cleaner, Hospital; 323.687-014 Cleaner, Housekeeping; 323.687-018 Housecleaner.

37-2021.00 Pest Control Workers (Pest Control Workers)

Education: Moderate-term O-T-J training
Employed: 51,865
Openings: 7,983
Projected Growth: 25.4%
Earnings: $22,490

Spray or release chemical solutions or toxic gases and set traps to kill pests and vermin such as mice, termites, and roaches that infest buildings and surrounding areas.

Drives truck equipped with power spraying equipment. Studies preliminary reports and diagrams of infested area and determines treatment type required to eliminate and prevent recurrence of infestation. Inspects premises to identify infestation source and extent of damage to property, wall, and roof porosity, and access to infested locations. Measures area dimensions requiring treatment, using rule; calculates fumigant requirements; and estimates cost for service. Cleans and removes blockages from infested areas to facilitate spraying procedure and provide drainage, using broom, mop, shovel, and rake. Positions and fastens edges of tarpaulins over building, tapes vents to ensure air-tight environment, and checks for leaks. Posts warning signs; locks building doors to secure area to be fumigated. Sprays or dusts chemical solutions, powders, or gases into rooms, onto clothing, furnishings or wood, and over marshlands, ditches, catch-basins. Digs up and burns or sprays weeds with herbicides. Directs and/or assists other workers in treatment and extermination processes to eliminate and control rodents, insects, and weeds. Cuts or bores openings in building or surrounding concrete, accesses infested areas, inserts nozzle, and injects pesticide to impregnate ground. Sets mechanical traps and places poisonous paste or bait in sewers, burrows, and ditches. Cleans work site after completion of job. Records work activities performed.

GOE Number, Interest Area, and Work Group: 03.03.04; Plants and Animals; Hands-on Work: Nursery, Groundskeeping, and Pest Control. **Personality Type:** Realistic. Realistic occupations frequently involve work activities that include practical, hands-on problems and solutions. These occupations often deal with plants, animals, and real-world materials like wood, tools, and machinery. Many of the occupations require working outside and do not involve a lot of paperwork or working closely with others. **Work Values:** Independence; Moral Values; Supervision, Technical; Security; Company Policies and Practices. **Skills:** Mathematics; Problem Identification; Reading Comprehension; Operation and Control; Judgment and Decision Making. **Abilities:** *Cognitive*—Information Ordering; Problem Sensitivity; Number Facility; Oral Comprehension; Written Expression. *Psychomotor*—Multilimb Coordination. *Physical*—Extent Flexibility; Trunk Strength; Static Strength. *Sensory*—Depth Perception; Peripheral Vision. **General Work Activities:** *Information Input*—Inspecting Equipment, Structures, Materials; Getting Information Needed to Do the Job; Estimating Needed Characteristics. *Mental Process*—Making Decisions and Solving Problems; Analyzing Data or Information; Organizing, Planning, and Prioritizing. *Work Output*—Performing General Physical Activities; Handling and Moving Objects; Controlling Machines and Processes. *Interacting with Others*—Communicating with Other Workers; Communicating with Persons Outside Organization; Performing for or Working with the Public; Coordinating Work and Activities of Others; Performing Administrative Activities; Establishing and Maintaining Relationships. **Physical Work Conditions:** Indoors; Contaminants; Standing; Hazardous Conditions. **Other Job Characteristics:** Importance of Being Sure All Is Done; Consequence of Error; Importance of Being Exact or Accurate.

Experience: Job Zone 2. Some previous work-related skill, knowledge, or experience may be helpful, but usually is not needed.

Job Preparation: SVP 4.00 to 5.99—6 months to less than 2 years. **Knowledge:** Chemistry; Mechanical; Customer and Personal Service; Biology; Mathematics. **Instructional Program:** 010501 Agricultural Supplies Retailing and Wholesaling.

Related DOT Jobs: 379.687-014 Mosquito Sprayer; 383.361-010 Fumigator; 383.364-010 Exterminator, Termite; 383.684-010 Exterminator Helper; 383.687-010 Exterminator Helper, Termite; 389.684-010 Exterminator.

37-3000 Grounds Maintenance Workers

37-3011.00 Landscaping and Groundskeeping Workers (Landscaping and Groundskeeping Workers)

Education: Short-term O-T-J training

Employed: 1,129,934

Openings: 283,459

Projected Growth: 20.7%

Earnings: $17,140

Landscape or maintain grounds of property using hand or power tools or equipment. Perform a variety of tasks, including laying sod, mowing, trimming, planting, watering, fertilizing, digging, raking, installing sprinklers, and installing mortarless segmental concrete masonry wall units.

Seeds and fertilizes lawns. Waters lawns, trees, and plants, using portable sprinkler system, hose, or watering can. Applies herbicides, fungicides, fertilizers, and pesticides, using spreaders or spray equipment. Shovels snow from walks and driveways. Maintains tools and equipment. Decorates garden with stones and plants. Hauls or spreads topsoil, and spreads straw over seeded soil to hold soil in place. Trims and picks flowers and cleans flower beds. Digs holes for plants, mixes fertilizer or lime with dirt in holes, inserts plants, and fills holes with dirt. Mows lawns, using power mower. Attaches wires from planted trees to support stakes. Builds forms and mixes and pours cement to form garden borders.

GOE Number, Interest Area, and Work Group: 03.03.04; Plants and Animals; Hands-on Work: Nursery, Groundskeeping, and Pest Control. **Personality Type:** Realistic. Realistic occupations frequently involve work activities that include practical, hands-on problems and solutions. These occupations often deal with plants, animals, and real-world materials like wood, tools, and machinery. Many of the occupations require working outside and do not involve a lot of paperwork or working closely with others. **Work Values:** Moral Values; Independence; Activity; Variety; Supervision, Human Relations; Co-workers; Working Conditions; Security. **Skills:** Operation and Control; Equipment Selection; Equipment Maintenance. **Abilities:** *Cognitive*—Category Flexibility; Visualization; Information Ordering; Problem Sensitivity; Originality; Oral Comprehension. *Psychomotor*—Manual Dexterity; Multilimb Coordination; Speed of Limb Movement. *Physical*—Trunk Strength; Stamina; Static Strength. *Sensory*—Glare Sensitivity; Peripheral Vision. **General Work Activities:** *Information Input*—Getting Information Needed to Do the Job; Monitoring Processes, Materials, and Surroundings; Estimating Needed Characteristics. *Mental Process*—Judging Qualities of Things, Services, Other People's Work; Making Decisions and Solving Problems; Organizing, Planning, and Prioritizing. *Work Output*—Performing General Physical Activities; Handling and Moving Objects; Operating Vehicles or Equipment. *Interacting with Others*—Communicating with Persons Outside Organization; Communicating with Other Workers; Monitoring and Controlling Resources. **Physical Work Conditions:** Outdoors; Using Hands on Objects, Tools, or Controls; Standing; Walking or Running. **Other Job Characteristics:** Importance of Being Sure All Is Done; Consequence of Error; Importance of Being Exact or Accurate.

Experience: Job Zone 1. No previous work-related skill, knowledge, or experience is needed. **Job Preparation:** SVP Below 4.0—Less than 6 months. **Knowledge:** Chemistry; Mechanical; Building and Construction; Biology; Physics. **Instructional Programs:** 010601 Horticulture Services Operations and Management, General; 010603 Ornamental Horticulture Operations and Management; 010604 Greenhouse Operations and Management; 010606 Nursery Operations and Management.

Related DOT Jobs: 405.684-014 Horticultural Worker I; 405.687-010 Flower Picker; 405.687-018 Transplanter, Orchid; 408.364-010 Plant-Care Worker; 408.687-014 Laborer, Landscape; 408.687-018 Tree-Surgeon Helper II; 952.687-010 Hydroelectric-Plant Maintainer.

37-3012.00 Pesticide Handlers, Sprayers, and Applicators, Vegetation (Sprayers and Applicators)

Education: Moderate-term O-T-J training

Employed: 18,771

Openings: 5,167

Projected Growth: 23.6%

Earnings: $21,650

Mix or apply pesticides, herbicides, fungicides, or insecticides through sprays, dusts, vapors, soil incorporation, or chemical application on trees, shrubs, lawns, or botanical crops. Obtain required, specific training. Obtain state or federal certification.

Covers area to specified depth, applying knowledge of weather conditions, droplet size, elevation-to-distance ratio, and obstructions. Connects hoses and nozzles, selected according to terrain, distribution pattern requirements, type of infestation, and velocity. Gives driving instructions to truck driver, using hand and horn signals, to ensure complete coverage of designated area. Sprays livestock with pesticides. Plants grass with seed spreader and operates straw blower to cover seeded area with asphalt and straw mixture. Cleans and services machinery to ensure operating efficiency, using water, gasoline, lubricants, and hand tools. Fills sprayer tank with water and chemicals, according to formula. Lifts, pushes, and swings nozzle, hose, and tube to direct spray over designated area. Starts motor and engages machinery such as sprayer agitator and pump.

GOE Number, Interest Area, and Work Group: 03.03.04; Plants and Animals; Hands-on Work: Nursery, Groundskeeping, and Pest

Control. **Personality Type:** Realistic. Realistic occupations frequently involve work activities that include practical, hands-on problems and solutions. These occupations often deal with plants, animals, and real-world materials like wood, tools, and machinery. Many of the occupations require working outside and do not involve a lot of paperwork or working closely with others. **Work Values:** Moral Values; Independence; Supervision, Technical; Activity; Supervision, Human Relations; Co-workers; Company Policies and Practices. **Skills:** Operation and Control; Mathematics; Coordination; Equipment Maintenance; Equipment Selection. **Abilities:** *Cognitive*—Information Ordering; Memorization; Oral Comprehension; Deductive Reasoning; Spatial Orientation; Number Facility. *Psychomotor*—Manual Dexterity; Wrist-Finger Speed; Arm-Hand Steadiness; Finger Dexterity; Multilimb Coordination. *Physical*—Explosive Strength; Dynamic Flexibility; Static Strength. **General Work Activities:** *Information Input*—Estimating Needed Characteristics; Getting Information Needed to Do the Job; Monitoring Processes, Materials, and Surroundings; Identifying Objects, Actions, and Events. *Mental Process*—Making Decisions and Solving Problems; Evaluating Information Against Standards; Analyzing Data or Information; Judging Qualities of Things, Services, Other People's Work. *Work Output*—Performing General Physical Activities; Handling and Moving Objects; Controlling Machines and Processes. *Interacting with Others*—Communicating with Other Workers; Establishing and Maintaining Relationships; Coordinating Work and Activities of Others; Communicating with Persons Outside Organization. **Physical Work Conditions:** Outdoors; Contaminants; Standing. **Other Job Characteristics:** Importance of Being Sure All Is Done; Consequence of Error; Importance of Being Exact or Accurate; Importance of Repeating Same Tasks.

Experience: Job Zone 2. Some previous work-related skill, knowledge, or experience may be helpful, but usually is not needed. **Job Preparation:** SVP 4.00 to 5.99—6 months to less than 2 years. **Knowledge:** Chemistry; Mechanical; Engineering and Technology; Mathematics; Biology; Physics; Food Production. **Instructional Programs:** 010304 Crop Production Operations and Management; 010605 Landscaping Operations and Management; 010606 Nursery Operations and Management; 010607 Turf Management.

Related DOT Jobs: 408.662-010 Hydro-Sprayer Operator; 408.684-014 Sprayer, Hand.

37-3013.00 Tree Trimmers and Pruners (Pruners)

Education: Short-term O-T-J training

Employed: 45,058

Openings: 10,504

Projected Growth: 12.1%

Earnings: $22,070

Cut away dead or excess branches from trees or shrubs to maintain right-of-way for roads, sidewalks, or utilities or to improve appearance, health, and value of tree. Prune or treat trees or shrubs using handsaws, pruning hooks, shears, and clippers. Use truck-mounted lifts and power pruners. Fill cavities in trees to promote healing and to prevent deterioration.

Prunes, cuts down, fertilizes, and sprays trees as directed by tree surgeon. Climbs trees, using climbing hooks and belts; climbs ladders to gain access to work area. Uses truck-mounted hydraulic lifts and pruners and power pruners. Applies tar or other protective substances to cut surfaces to seal surfaces against insects. Cuts away dead and excess branches from trees, using handsaws, pruning hooks, shears, and clippers. Scrapes decayed matter from cavities in trees and fills holes with cement to promote healing and to prevent further deterioration.

GOE Number, Interest Area, and Work Group: 03.03.04; Plants and Animals; Hands-on Work: Nursery, Groundskeeping, and Pest Control. **Personality Type:** Realistic. Realistic occupations frequently involve work activities that include practical, hands-on problems and solutions. These occupations often deal with plants, animals, and real-world materials like wood, tools, and machinery. Many of the occupations require working outside and do not involve a lot of paperwork or working closely with others. **Work Values:** Moral Values; Independence; Supervision, Technical; Activity; Supervision, Human Relations; Company Policies and Practices; Security; Co-workers. **Skills:** Operation and Control; Equipment Selection. **Abilities:** *Cognitive*—Oral Comprehension; Information Ordering; Memorization; Problem Sensitivity; Deductive Reasoning; Category Flexibility. *Psychomotor*—Multilimb Coordination; Manual Dexterity; Arm-Hand Steadiness. *Physical*—Extent Flexibility; Static Strength; Explosive Strength. *Sensory*—Glare Sensitivity. **General Work Activities:** *Information Input*—Identifying Objects, Actions, and Events; Getting Information Needed to Do the Job; Monitoring Processes, Materials, and Surroundings. *Mental Process*—Judging Qualities of Things, Services, Other People's Work; Making Decisions and Solving Problems; Analyzing Data or Information; Evaluating Information Against Standards. *Work Output*—Performing General Physical Activities; Handling and Moving Objects; Controlling Machines and Processes. *Interacting with Others*—Communicating with Other Workers; Communicating with Persons Outside Organization; Establishing and Maintaining Relationships; Monitoring and Controlling Resources. **Physical Work Conditions:** Outdoors; High Places; Hazardous Situations. **Other Job Characteristics:** Importance of Being Sure All Is Done; Consequence of Error; Importance of Being Exact or Accurate.

Experience: Job Zone 2. Some previous work-related skill, knowledge, or experience may be helpful, but usually is not needed. **Job Preparation:** SVP 4.00 to 5.99—6 months to less than 2 years. **Knowledge:** Biology; Mechanical; Chemistry; Engineering and Technology; English Language. **Instructional Programs:** 010304 Crop Production Operations and Management; 010699 Horticulture Services Operations and Management, Other.

Related DOT Jobs: 408.181-010 Tree Surgeon; 408.684-018 Tree Pruner.

39-0000
Personal Care and Service Occupations

39-1000 Supervisors, Personal Care and Service Workers

39-1011.00 Gaming Supervisors (All Other Supervisors and Managers/Supervisors—Service Workers)

Education: No data available.

Employed: 732,280

Openings: No data available.

Projected Growth: No data available.

Earnings: $23,320

Supervise gaming operations and personnel in an assigned area. Circulate among tables and observe operations. Ensure that stations and games are covered for each shift. Explain and interpret operating rules of house to patrons. Plan and organize activities and create friendly atmosphere for guests in hotels/casinos. Adjust service complaints.

Resolves customer complaints regarding service. Records, issues receipts for, and pays off bets. Explains and interprets house rules, such as game rules and betting limits, to patrons. Interviews and hires workers. Prepares work schedules, assigns work stations, and keeps attendance records. Directs workers compiling summary sheets for each race or event, to show amount wagered and amount to be paid to winners. Establishes policies on types of gambling offered, odds, extension of credit, and serving food and beverages. Observes and supervises operation to ensure that employees render prompt and courteous service to patrons. Review operational expenses, budget estimates, betting accounts, and collection reports for accuracy. Trains new workers and evaluates their performance.

GOE Number, Interest Area, and Work Group: 11.01.01; Recreation, Travel, and Other Personal Services; Managerial Work in Recreation, Travel, and Other Personal Services. **Personality Type:** Enterprising. Enterprising occupations frequently involve starting up and carrying out projects. These occupations can involve leading people and making many decisions. They sometimes require risk taking and often deal with business. **Work Values:** Authority; Responsibility; Working Conditions; Security; Autonomy. **Skills:** Management of Personnel Resources; Management of Financial Resources; Critical Thinking; Speaking; Mathematics; Time Management; Monitoring; Reading Comprehension; Identification of Key Causes; Idea Generation. **Abilities:** *Cognitive*—Oral Expression; Number Facility; Mathematical Reasoning; Time Sharing; Deductive Reasoning; Information Ordering. *Psychomotor*—none met the criteria. *Physical*—none met the criteria. *Sensory*—Near Vision; Far Vision; Sound Localization; Night Vision. **General Work Activities:** *Information Input*—Getting Information Needed to Do the Job; Monitoring Processes, Materials, and Surroundings; Identifying Objects, Actions, and Events. *Mental Process*—Making Decisions and Solving Problems; Scheduling Work and Activities; Developing Objectives and Strategies. *Work Output*—Documenting and Recording Information; Implementing Ideas and Programs; Handling and Moving Objects; Controlling Machines and Processes. *Interacting with Others*—Coordinating Work and Activities of Others; Performing Administrative Activi-

ties; Communicating with Other Workers. **Physical Work Conditions:** Indoors; Sitting; Standing. **Other Job Characteristics:** Consequence of Error; Importance of Being Exact or Accurate; Importance of Being Sure All Is Done.

Experience: Job Zone 3. Previous work-related skill, knowledge, or experience is required. **Job Preparation:** SVP 6.0 to less than 7.0—More than 1 year and less than 4 years. **Knowledge:** Administration and Management; Economics and Accounting; Personnel and Human Resources; Customer and Personal Service; Mathematics. **Instructional Programs:** 080903 Recreation Products/Services Marketing Operations; 200401 Institutional Food Workers and Administrators, General; 200409 Institutional Food Services Administrator; 310504 Sport and Fitness Administration/Management.

Related DOT Job: 343.137-014 Supervisor, Cardroom.

39-1012.00 Slot Key Persons (All Other Service Workers)

Education: No data available.

Employed: 346,480

Openings: No data available.

Projected Growth: No data available.

Earnings: $15,950

Coordinate/supervise functions of slot department workers to provide service to patrons. Handle and settle complaints of players. Verify and pay off jackpots. Reset slot machines after payoffs. Make minor repairs or adjustments to slot machines. Recommend removal of slot machines for repair. Report hazards and enforce safety rules.

GOE Number, Interest Area, and Work Group: 11.02.01; Recreation, Travel, and Other Personal Services; Recreational Services. **Instructional Programs:** 080901 Hospitality and Recreation Marketing Operations, General; 080999 Hospitality and Recreation Marketing Operations, Other; 120405 Massage; 200404 Dietician Assistant. **Note:** The Department of Labor has not collected some data for this job, so it has fewer details than the other descriptions.

39-1021.00 First-Line Supervisors/Managers of Personal Service Workers (Food Service and Lodging Managers)

Education: Work experience in a related occupation

Employed: 594,642

Openings: 138,826

Projected Growth: 16.3%

Earnings: $26,700

Supervise and coordinate activities of personal service workers such as supervisors of flight attendants, hairdressers, or caddies.

Analyzes and records personnel and operational data and writes activity reports. Requisitions supplies, equipment, and designated services, to ensure quality and timely service and efficient operations. Observes and evaluates workers' appearance and performance to ensure quality service and compliance with specifications. Resolves customer complaints regarding worker performance and services rendered. Furnishes customers with information on events and activities. Inspects work areas and operating equipment to ensure conformance to established standards. Supervises and coordinates activities of workers engaged in lodging and personal services. Collaborates with personnel to plan and develop programs of events, schedules of activities, and menus. Trains workers in proper operational procedures and functions, and explains company policy. Assigns work schedules, following work requirements, to ensure quality and timely delivery of services. Informs workers about interests of specific groups.

GOE Number, Interest Area, and Work Group: 11.01.01; Recreation, Travel, and Other Personal Services; Managerial Work in Recreation, Travel, and Other Personal Services. **Personality Type:** Enterprising. Enterprising occupations frequently involve starting up and carrying out projects. These occupations can involve leading people and making many decisions. They sometimes require risk taking and often deal with business. **Work Values:** Authority; Activity; Autonomy; Working Conditions; Moral Values; Responsibility; Co-workers. **Skills:** Coordination; Service Orientation; Active Listening; Time Management; Speaking. **Abilities:** *Cognitive*—Oral Expression; Oral Comprehension; Information Ordering; Problem Sensitivity; Perceptual Speed; Time Sharing. *Psychomotor*—Response Orientation. *Physical*—Trunk Strength. *Sensory*—Near Vision; Speech Clarity; Far Vision. **General Work Activities:** *Information Input*—Getting Information Needed to Do the Job; Inspecting Equipment, Structures, Materials; Identifying Objects, Actions, and Events. *Mental Process*—Scheduling Work and Activities; Organizing, Planning, and Prioritizing; Making Decisions and Solving Problems. *Work Output*—Performing General Physical Activities; Documenting and Recording Information; Implementing Ideas and Programs; Handling and Moving Objects. *Interacting with Others*—Coordinating Work and Activities of Others; Communicating with Other Workers; Resolving Conflict and Negotiating with Others; Guiding, Directing and Motivating Subordinates; Performing for or Working with the Public. **Physical Work Conditions:** Indoors; Standing; Sitting. **Other Job Characteristics:** Importance of Being Sure All Is Done; Importance of Being Exact or Accurate; Consequence of Error.

Experience: Job Zone 3. Previous work-related skill, knowledge, or experience is required. **Job Preparation:** SVP 6.0 to less than 7.0—More than 1 year and less than 4 years. **Knowledge:** Administration and Management; Customer and Personal Service; English Language; Personnel and Human Resources; Education and Training. **Instructional Programs:** 080901 Hospitality and Recreation Marketing Operations, General; 080906 Food Sales Operations; 120504 Food and Beverage/Restaurant Operations Manager; 190505 Food Systems Administration; 200401 Institutional Food Workers and Administrators, General; 200405 Food Caterer; 200409 Institutional Food Services Administrator; 520702 Franchise Operation; 520901 Hospitality/Administration Management; 520902 Hotel/Motel and Restaurant Management.

Related DOT Jobs: 321.137-014 Inspector; 323.137-010 Supervisor, Housecleaner; 324.137-010 Baggage Porter, Head; 324.137-014 Bell Captain; 329.137-010 Superintendent, Service; 344.137-010 Usher, Head; 350.137-018 Steward/Stewardess, Chief, Passenger Ship; 350.137-022 Steward/Stewardess, Second; 350.137-026 Steward/Stewardess, Third; 352.137-010 Supervisor, Airplane-Flight Attendant; 353.137-010 Guide, Chief Airport; 358.137-010 Checkroom Chief; 388.367-010 Elevator Starter.

39-2000 Animal Care and Service Workers

39-2011.00 Animal Trainers (Animal Trainers)

Education: No data available.

Employed: 4,120

Openings: No data available.

Projected Growth: No data available.

Earnings: $21,160

Train animals for riding, harness, security, performance, obedience, or assisting persons with disabilities. Accustom animals to human voice and contact and condition animals to respond to commands. Train animals according to prescribed standards for show or competition. Train animals to carry pack loads or work as part of pack team.

Feeds, exercises, and gives general care to animal. Conducts training program to develop desired behavior. Rehearses animal according to script for motion picture or television film or stage or circus program. Observes animal's physical condition to detect illness or unhealthy condition requiring medical care. Arranges for mating of stallions and mares, and assists mares during foaling. Cues or signals animal during performance. Trains guard dog to protect property and teaches guide dog and its master to function as team. Evaluates animal to determine temperament, ability, and aptitude for training. Trains animals to protect property, compete in shows or races, obey commands, or perform tricks to entertain audience. Trains horses for riding, show, work, or racing. Trains horses as independent operator and advises owners regarding purchase of horses.

GOE Number, Interest Area, and Work Group: 03.02.01; Plants and Animals; Animal Care and Training. **Personality Type:** Social. Social occupations frequently involve working with, communicating with, and teaching people. These occupations often involve helping or providing service to others. **Work Values:** Responsibility; Autonomy; Independence; Moral Values; Creativity. **Skills:** Learning Strategies; Instructing; Solution Appraisal; Monitoring; Problem Identification; Active Learning; Speaking; Active Listening; Identification of Key Causes. **Abilities:** *Cognitive*—Oral Expression; Problem Sensitivity; Information Ordering; Selective Attention; Time Sharing; Memorization. *Psychomotor*—Speed of Limb Movement; Reaction Time; Response Orientation. *Physical*—Static Strength; Extent Flexibility; Gross Body Coordination. *Sensory*—Far Vision; Speech Clarity; Auditory Attention. **General Work Activities:** *Information Input*—Getting Information Needed to Do the Job; Identifying Objects, Actions, and Events; Monitoring Processes, Materials, and Surroundings. *Mental Process*—Judging Qualities of Things, Services, Other People's Work; Developing Objectives and Strategies; Organizing, Planning, and Prioritizing; Thinking Creatively. *Work Output*—Performing General Physical Activities; Implementing Ideas and Programs; Handling and

Moving Objects. *Interacting with Others*—Establishing and Maintaining Relationships; Performing for or Working with the Public; Assisting and Caring for Others. **Physical Work Conditions:** Standing; Hazardous Situations; Outdoors; Indoors; Kneeling, Crouching, or Crawling; Walking or Running. **Other Job Characteristics:** Frustrating Circumstances; Importance of Being Sure All Is Done; Consequence of Error.

Experience: Job Zone 3. Previous work-related skill, knowledge, or experience is required. **Job Preparation:** SVP 6.0 to less than 7.0—More than 1 year and less than 4 years. **Knowledge:** Education and Training; Biology; Customer and Personal Service; Therapy and Counseling; Medicine and Dentistry; Public Safety and Security. **Instructional Programs:** 010505 Animal Trainer; 010507 Equestrian/Equine Studies, Horse Management and Training.

Related DOT Jobs: 159.224-010 Animal Trainer; 419.224-010 Horse Trainer.

39-2021.00 Nonfarm Animal Caretakers (Animal Caretakers, Except Farm)

Education: Short-term O-T-J training
Employed: 136,754
Openings: 43,263
Projected Growth: 21.6%
Earnings: $14,820

Feed, water, groom, bathe, exercise, or otherwise care for pets and other nonfarm animals such as dogs, cats, ornamental fish or birds, zoo animals, and mice. Work in settings such as kennels, animal shelters, zoos, circuses, and aquariums. Keep records of feedings, treatments, and animals received or discharged. Clean, disinfect, and repair cages, pens, or fish tanks.

Transfers animals between enclosures for breeding, birthing, shipping, or rearranging exhibits. Mixes food, liquid formulas, medications, or food supplements according to instructions, prescriptions, and knowledge of animal species. Examines and observes animals for signs of illness, disease, or injury and provides treatment or informs veterinarian. Adjusts controls to regulate specified temperature and humidity of animal quarters, nursery, or exhibit area. Exercises animals to maintain their fitness and health, or trains animals to perform certain tasks. Washes, brushes, clips, trims, and grooms animals. Cleans and disinfects animal quarters such as pens, stables, cages, and yards. Cleans and disinfects surgical or other equipment such as saddles and bridles. Anesthetizes and inoculates animals, according to instructions. Orders, unloads, and stores feed and supplies. Saddles and shoes animals. Responds to questions from patrons and provides information about animals, such as behavior, habitat, breeding habits, or facility activities. Observes and cautions children petting and feeding animals in designated area. Installs equipment in animal care facility, such as infrared lights, feeding devices, or cribs. Feeds and waters animal according to schedules and feeding instructions. Repairs fences, cages or pens. Records information about animals, such as weight, size, physical condition, diet, medications, and food intake.

GOE Number, Interest Area, and Work Group: 03.02.01; Plants and Animals; Animal Care and Training. **Personality Type:** Real-

istic. Realistic occupations frequently involve work activities that include practical, hands-on problems and solutions. These occupations often deal with plants, animals, and real-world materials like wood, tools, and machinery. Many of the occupations require working outside and do not involve a lot of paperwork or working closely with others. **Work Values:** Moral Values; Independence; Activity; Company Policies and Practices; Supervision, Human Relations; Supervision, Technical. **Skills:** Active Listening; Speaking; Mathematics; Service Orientation; Problem Identification. **Abilities:** *Cognitive*—Oral Expression; Problem Sensitivity; Oral Comprehension; Written Expression; Information Ordering. *Psychomotor*—Control Precision; Reaction Time; Speed of Limb Movement. *Physical*—Static Strength; Dynamic Strength; Extent Flexibility. *Sensory*—Speech Clarity; Sound Localization; Hearing Sensitivity. **General Work Activities:** *Information Input*—Monitoring Processes, Materials, and Surroundings; Getting Information Needed to Do the Job; Identifying Objects, Actions, and Events. *Mental Process*—Analyzing Data or Information; Updating and Using Job-Relevant Knowledge; Organizing, Planning, and Prioritizing; Evaluating Information Against Standards; Processing Information; Making Decisions and Solving Problems. *Work Output*—Performing General Physical Activities; Handling and Moving Objects; Documenting and Recording Information. *Interacting with Others*—Communicating with Persons Outside Organization; Interpreting Meaning of Information to Others; Communicating with Other Workers; Performing for or Working with the Public. **Physical Work Conditions:** Standing; Outdoors; Indoors; Contaminants; Using Hands on Objects, Tools, or Controls. **Other Job Characteristics:** Importance of Being Sure All Is Done; Consequence of Error; Importance of Being Aware of New Events.

Experience: Job Zone 1. No previous work-related skill, knowledge, or experience is needed. **Job Preparation:** SVP Below 4.0—Less than 6 months. **Knowledge:** Biology; Medicine and Dentistry; Building and Construction; English Language; Mechanical. **Instructional Programs:** 010501 Agricultural Supplies Retailing and Wholesaling; 010507 Equestrian/Equine Studies, Horse Management and Training.

Related DOT Jobs: 410.674-010 Animal Caretaker; 410.674-022 Stable Attendant; 412.674-010 Animal Keeper; 412.674-014 Animal-Nursery Worker.

39-3000 Entertainment Attendants and Related Workers

39-3011.00 Gaming Dealers (Amusement and Recreation Attendants)

Education: Short-term O-T-J training
Employed: 337,273
Openings: 141,783
Projected Growth: 30.2%
Earnings: $12,860

Assist operators or customers in conducting games of chance.

Seats patrons at gaming tables. Prepares collection report for submission to supervisor. Sells food, beverages, and tobacco to players. Exchanges paper currency for playing chips or coin money and collects game fees or wagers. Conducts gambling table or game such as dice, roulette, cards, or keno; ensures that game rules are followed. Participates in game for gambling establishment to provide minimum complement of players at table. Verifies, computes, and pays out winnings.

GOE Number, Interest Area, and Work Group: 11.02.01; Recreation, Travel, and Other Personal Services; Recreational Services. **Personality Type:** Enterprising. Enterprising occupations frequently involve starting up and carrying out projects. These occupations can involve leading people and making many decisions. They sometimes require risk taking and often deal with business. **Work Values:** Activity; Supervision, Technical; Co-workers; Working Conditions; Compensation; Independence. **Skills:** Service Orientation; Monitoring; Social Perceptiveness; Mathematics; Reading Comprehension. **Abilities:** *Cognitive*—Number Facility; Information Ordering; Oral Expression; Time Sharing; Selective Attention. *Psychomotor*—Wrist-Finger Speed; Response Orientation; Manual Dexterity; Finger Dexterity. *Physical*—Dynamic Strength. *Sensory*—Auditory Attention; Near Vision; Speech Recognition. **General Work Activities:** *Information Input*—Identifying Objects, Actions, and Events; Getting Information Needed to Do the Job; Monitoring Processes, Materials, and Surroundings. *Mental Process*—Evaluating Information Against Standards; Judging Qualities of Things, Services, Other People's Work; Processing Information. *Work Output*—Handling and Moving Objects; Controlling Machines and Processes; Documenting and Recording Information. *Interacting with Others*—Performing for or Working with the Public; Communicating with Persons Outside Organization; Establishing and Maintaining Relationships. **Physical Work Conditions:** Indoors; Standing; Special Uniform. **Other Job Characteristics:** Importance of Being Exact or Accurate; Importance of Being Sure All Is Done; Consequence of Error.

Experience: Job Zone 2. Some previous work-related skill, knowledge, or experience may be helpful, but usually is not needed. **Job Preparation:** SVP 4.00 to 5.99—6 months to less than 2 years. **Knowledge:** Customer and Personal Service; Mathematics; Sales and Marketing; English Language; Law, Government and Jurisprudence; Education and Training. **Instructional Program:** 120203 Card Dealer.

Related DOT Job: 343.464-010 Gambling Dealer.

39-3012.00 Gaming and Sports Book Writers and Runners (Amusement and Recreation Attendants)

Education: Short-term O-T-J training

Employed: 337,273

Openings: 141,783

Projected Growth: 30.2%

Earnings: $12,860

Conduct games of chance such as dice, roulette, or cards. Perform a variety of tasks such as collecting bets or wagers, paying winnings, and explaining rules to customers.

Seats patrons at gaming tables. Exchanges paper currency for playing chips or coin money and collects game fees or wagers. Sells food, beverages, and tobacco to players. Participates in game for gambling establishment to provide minimum complement of players at table. Verifies, computes, and pays out winnings. Conducts gambling table or game such as dice, roulette, cards, or keno; ensures that game rules are followed. Prepares collection report for submission to supervisor.

GOE Number, Interest Area, and Work Group: 11.02.01; Recreation, Travel, and Other Personal Services; Recreational Services. **Personality Type:** Enterprising. Enterprising occupations frequently involve starting up and carrying out projects. These occupations can involve leading people and making many decisions. They sometimes require risk taking and often deal with business. **Work Values:** Supervision, Technical; Activity; Working Conditions; Co-workers; Independence; Compensation. **Skills:** Service Orientation; Monitoring; Reading Comprehension; Mathematics; Social Perceptiveness. **Abilities:** *Cognitive*—Number Facility; Oral Expression; Information Ordering; Time Sharing; Selective Attention. *Psychomotor*—Wrist-Finger Speed; Response Orientation; Finger Dexterity; Manual Dexterity. *Physical*—Dynamic Strength. *Sensory*—Auditory Attention; Speech Recognition; Near Vision. **General Work Activities:** *Information Input*—Identifying Objects, Actions, and Events; Getting Information Needed to Do the Job; Monitoring Processes, Materials, and Surroundings. *Mental Process*—Evaluating Information Against Standards; Judging Qualities of Things, Services, Other People's Work; Processing Information. *Work Output*—Handling and Moving Objects; Controlling Machines and Processes; Documenting and Recording Information. *Interacting with Others*—Performing for or Working with the Public; Communicating with Persons Outside Organization; Establishing and Maintaining Relationships. **Physical Work Conditions:** Indoors; Standing; Special Uniform. **Other Job Characteristics:** Importance of Being Exact or Accurate; Importance of Being Sure All Is Done; Consequence of Error.

Experience: Job Zone 2. Some previous work-related skill, knowledge, or experience may be helpful, but usually is not needed. **Job Preparation:** SVP 4.00 to 5.99—6 months to less than 2 years. **Knowledge:** Customer and Personal Service; Mathematics; Sales and Marketing; English Language; Law, Government and Jurisprudence; Education and Training. **Instructional Program:** 120203 Card Dealer.

Related DOT Jobs: 343.467-010 Cardroom Attendant I; 343.467-022 Keno Writer.

39-3021.00 Motion Picture Projectionists (Motion Picture Projectionists)

Education: Short-term O-T-J training

Employed: 9,323

Openings: 1,460

Projected Growth: –21.8%

Earnings: $15,420

Set up and operate motion picture projection and related sound reproduction equipment.

Sets up and operates motion picture projection and sound-re-producing equipment to project or produce pictures and sound effects on screen. Cleans lenses and maintains and performs minor repairs on projectors and equipment; notifies maintenance personnel to correct major malfunctions. Coordinates equipment operation with presentation of supplemental material such as music, oral commentary, or sound effects. Positions, installs, and connects auxiliary equipment such as microphones, amplifiers, and lights. Inspects and repairs faulty sections of film and re-winds film onto reels automatically or by hand. Regulates and adjusts projection light and focus, volume, tone, and timing of projection equipment. Inserts film into top magazine reel or threads film through the projector and onto automatic spool of projector. Monitors equipment operation and changes projectors without interruption to showing. Operates special-effects equipment such as stereopticon, to project pictures on screen.

GOE Number, Interest Area, and Work Group: 11.02.01; Recreation, Travel, and Other Personal Services; Recreational Services. **Personality Type:** Realistic. Realistic occupations frequently involve work activities that include practical, hands-on problems and solutions. These occupations often deal with plants, animals, and real-world materials like wood, tools, and machinery. Many of the occupations require working outside and do not involve a lot of paperwork or working closely with others. **Work Values:** Moral Values; Independence; Working Conditions; Company Policies and Practices; Supervision, Human Relations. **Skills:** Installation; Operation and Control; Operation Monitoring; Product Inspection; Repairing. **Abilities:** *Cognitive*—Problem Sensitivity; Selective Attention; Visualization; Information Ordering; Time Sharing; Deductive Reasoning. *Psychomotor*—Arm-Hand Steadiness; Control Precision; Finger Dexterity. *Physical*—none met the criteria. *Sensory*—Hearing Sensitivity; Auditory Atten-tion; Visual Color Discrimination. **General Work Activities:** *Information Input*—Monitoring Processes, Materials, and Surroundings; Getting Information Needed to Do the Job; Inspecting Equipment, Structures, Materials. *Mental Process*—Judging Qualities of Things, Services, Other People's Work; Evaluating Information Against Standards; Processing Information. *Work Output*—Controlling Machines and Processes; Handling and Moving Objects; Repairing and Maintaining Mechanical Equipment; Performing General Physical Activities. *Interacting with Others*—Communicating with Other Workers; Performing for or Working with the Public; Establishing and Maintaining Relationships. **Physical Work Conditions:** Indoors; Sitting; Using Hands on Objects, Tools, or Controls. **Other Job Characteristics:** Degree of Automation; Pace Determined by Speed of Equipment; Consequence of Error.

Experience: Job Zone 2. Some previous work-related skill, knowledge, or experience may be helpful, but usually is not needed. **Job Preparation:** SVP 4.00 to 5.99—6 months to less than 2 years. **Knowledge:** Communications and Media; Fine Arts; Computers and Electronics; Telecommunications; Engineering and Technology. **Instructional Programs:** 100101 Educational/Instructional Media Technology/Technician; 470103 Communication Systems Installer and Repairer.

Related DOT Jobs: 960.362-010 Motion-Picture Projectionist; 960.382-010 Audiovisual Technician.

39-3031.00 Ushers, Lobby Attendants, and Ticket Takers (Ushers, Lobby Attendants, and Ticket Takers)

Education: Short-term O-T-J training
Employed: 84,337
Openings: 22,505
Projected Growth: 17.6%
Earnings: $12,520

Assist patrons at entertainment events by performing duties such as collecting admission tickets and passes from patrons, assisting patrons in finding seats, searching for lost articles, and locating such facilities as rest rooms and telephones.

Monitors patrons' activities to prevent disorderly conduct and rowdiness and to detect infractions of rules. Verifies credentials of patrons desiring entrance into press box and permits only authorized persons to enter. Assists patrons to find seats, search for lost articles, and locate facilities such as rest rooms and telephones. Counts and records number of tickets collected. Serves patrons at refreshment stand during intermission. Collects admission tickets and passes from patrons at entertainment events. Assists other workers in changing advertising display. Distributes programs to patrons. Distributes door checks to patrons temporarily leaving establishment. Greets patrons desiring to attend entertainment events. Refuses admittance to patrons who do not have a ticket or pass or who are undesirable for reasons such as intoxication or improper attire. Runs errand for patrons of press box, such as obtaining refreshments and carrying news releases. Examines ticket or pass to verify authenticity, using criteria such as color and date issued.

GOE Number, Interest Area, and Work Group: 11.02.01; Recreation, Travel, and Other Personal Services; Recreational Services. **Personality Type:** Social. Social occupations frequently involve working with, communicating with, and teaching people. These occupations often involve helping or providing service to others. **Work Values:** Moral Values; Co-workers; Social Service; Working Conditions; Supervision, Technical. **Skills:** Active Listening; Service Orientation; Social Perceptiveness. **Abilities:** *Cognitive*—Oral Expression; Oral Comprehension; Spatial Orientation; Perceptual Speed; Written Comprehension. *Psychomotor*—none met the criteria. *Physical*—none met the criteria. *Sensory*—Night Vision. **General Work Activities:** *Information Input*—Getting Information Needed to Do the Job; Identifying Objects, Actions, and Events; Monitoring Processes, Materials, and Surroundings. *Mental Process*—Processing Information; Making Decisions and Solving Problems; Evaluating Information Against Standards. *Work Output*—Handling and Moving Objects; Documenting and Recording Information; Performing General Physical Activities. *Interacting with Others*—Performing for or Working with the Public; Communicating with Persons Outside Organization; Assisting and Caring for Others. **Physical Work Conditions:** Special Uniform; Indoors; Standing. **Other Job Characteristics:** Importance of Being Exact or Accurate; Importance of Being Sure All Is Done; Importance of Repeating Same Tasks.

Experience: Job Zone 1. No previous work-related skill, knowledge, or experience is needed. **Job Preparation:** SVP Below 4.0—Less than 6 months. **Knowledge:** Customer and Personal Service;

English Language; Clerical; Psychology; Sales and Marketing. **Instructional Program:** 129999 Personal and Miscellaneous Services, Other.

Related DOT Jobs: 344.667-010 Ticket Taker; 344.677-010 Press-Box Custodian; 344.677-014 Usher; 349.673-010 Drive-in Theater Attendant; 349.677-018 Children's Attendant.

39-3091.00 Amusement and Recreation Attendants
(Amusement and Recreation Attendants)

Education: Short-term O-T-J training

Employed: 337,273

Openings: 141,783

Projected Growth: 30.2%

Earnings: $12,860

Perform variety of attending duties at amusement or recreation facility. Schedule use of recreation facilities. Maintain and provide equipment to participants of sporting events or recreational pursuits. Operate amusement concessions and rides.

Launches, moors, and demonstrates use of boats, such as rowboats, canoes, and motorboats, or caddies for golfers. Monitors activities to ensure adherence to rules and safety procedures, to protect environment and maintain order; ejects unruly patrons. Attends animals, performing such tasks as harnessing, saddling, feeding, watering, and grooming, and drives horse-drawn vehicle for entertainment or advertising purposes. Records details of attendance, sales, receipts, reservations, and repair activities. Directs patrons of establishment to rides, seats, or attractions, or escorts patrons on tours of points of interest. Sells tickets and collects fees from customers, and collects or punches tickets. Provides entertainment services such as guessing patron's weight, conducting games, explaining use of arcade game machines, and photographing patrons. Rents, sells, and issues sports equipment and supplies such as bowling shoes, golf balls, swim suits, and beach chairs. Operates, drives, or explains use of mechanical riding devices or other automatic equipment in amusement parks, carnivals, or recreation areas. Sells and serves refreshments to customers. Attends amusement booth in parks, carnivals, or stadiums; awards prizes to winning players. Cleans sporting equipment, vehicles, rides, booths, facilities, and grounds. Inspects, repairs, adjusts, tests, fuels, and oils sporting and recreation equipment, game machines, and amusement rides. Provides information about facilities, entertainment options, and rules and regulations. Assists patrons in getting on and off amusement rides, boats, or ski lifts, and in mounting and riding animals. Fastens or directs patrons to fasten safety devices. Schedules use of recreation facilities such as golf courses, tennis courts, bowling alleys, and softball diamonds. Receives, retrieves, replaces, and stores sports equipment and supplies; arranges items in designated areas; and erects or removes equipment.

GOE Number, Interest Area, and Work Group: 11.02.01; Recreation, Travel, and Other Personal Services; Recreational Services. **Personality Type:** Realistic. Realistic occupations frequently involve work activities that include practical, hands-on problems and solutions. These occupations often deal with plants, animals,

and real-world materials like wood, tools, and machinery. Many of the occupations require working outside and do not involve a lot of paperwork or working closely with others. **Work Values:** Moral Values; Co-workers; Supervision, Technical; Social Service; Activity. **Skills:** Active Listening; Operation and Control; Service Orientation; Repairing; Operation Monitoring. **Abilities:** *Cognitive*—Oral Expression; Oral Comprehension; Information Ordering; Number Facility; Spatial Orientation; Time Sharing. *Psychomotor*—Reaction Time; Control Precision; Rate Control. *Physical*—Static Strength; Extent Flexibility; Trunk Strength. *Sensory*—Speech Recognition; Speech Clarity; Near Vision. **General Work Activities:** *Information Input*—Monitoring Processes, Materials, and Surroundings; Inspecting Equipment, Structures, Materials; Getting Information Needed to Do the Job. *Mental Process*—Scheduling Work and Activities; Evaluating Information Against Standards; Processing Information. *Work Output*—Controlling Machines and Processes; Performing General Physical Activities; Handling and Moving Objects. *Interacting with Others*—Communicating with Persons Outside Organization; Performing for or Working with the Public; Establishing and Maintaining Relationships. **Physical Work Conditions:** Outdoors; Standing; Walking or Running. **Other Job Characteristics:** Degree of Automation; Consequence of Error; Importance of Being Exact or Accurate; Importance of Being Sure All Is Done.

Experience: Job Zone 1. No previous work-related skill, knowledge, or experience is needed. **Job Preparation:** SVP Below 4.0—Less than 6 months. **Knowledge:** Customer and Personal Service; Sales and Marketing; Public Safety and Security; Mechanical; Mathematics. **Instructional Program:** 120203 Card Dealer.

Related DOT Jobs: 195.367-030 Recreation Aide; 340.367-010 Desk Clerk, Bowling Floor; 340.477-010 Racker; 341.367-010 Recreation-Facility Attendant; 341.464-010 Skate-Shop Attendant; 341.665-010 Ski-Tow Operator; 341.677-010 Caddie; 341.683-010 Golf-Range Attendant; 342.357-010 Weight Guesser; 342.657-010 Barker; 342.657-014 Game Attendant; 342.663-010 Ride Operator; 342.665-010 Fun-House Operator; 342.667-010 Wharf Attendant; 342.667-014 Attendant, Arcade; 342.677-010 Ride Attendant; 343.467-014 Floor Attendant; 343.577-010 Cardroom Attendant II; 349.477-010 Jinrikisha Driver; 349.664-010 Amusement Park Worker (partial list; see the introduction for sources of the complete list).

39-3092.00 Costume Attendants (Wardrobe, and Locker and Dressing Room Attendants)

Education: No data available.

Employed: 7,600

Openings: No data available.

Projected Growth: No data available.

Earnings: $15,330

Select, fit, and take care of costumes for cast members. Aid entertainers.

Purchases or rents costumes and other wardrobe accessories from vendor. Inventories stock to determine types and condition of costuming available and selects costumes based on historical analysis and studies. Repairs, alters, cleans, presses, and refits costume prior to performance; cleans and stores costume following performance. Analyzes or reviews analysis of script to determine locale of story, period, number of characters, and costumes required per character. Examines costume fit on cast member, and sketches or writes notes for alterations. Assists cast in donning costumes or assigns cast dresser to assist specific cast members with costume changes. Designs and constructs costume or sends it to tailor for construction or major repairs and alterations. Studies books, pictures, and examples of period clothing to determine styles worn during specific period in history. Arranges or directs cast dresser to arrange costumes on clothing racks in sequence of appearance.

GOE Number, Interest Area, and Work Group: 01.09.01; Arts, Entertainment, and Media; Modeling and Personal Appearance. **Personality Type:** Artistic. Artistic occupations frequently involve working with forms, designs, and patterns. These occupations often require self-expression, and the work can be done without following a clear set of rules. **Work Values:** Moral Values; Creativity; Autonomy; Responsibility; Working Conditions. **Skills:** Reading Comprehension; Idea Generation; Product Inspection; Speaking; Synthesis/Reorganization; Information Organization; Information Gathering. **Abilities:** *Cognitive*—Visualization; Originality; Information Ordering; Inductive Reasoning; Perceptual Speed. *Psychomotor*—Arm-Hand Steadiness; Wrist-Finger Speed; Finger Dexterity; Control Precision; Manual Dexterity. *Physical*—Extent Flexibility; Dynamic Flexibility; Dynamic Strength. *Sensory*—Visual Color Discrimination; Near Vision; Far Vision. **General Work Activities:** *Information Input*—Getting Information Needed to Do the Job; Inspecting Equipment, Structures, Materials; Identifying Objects, Actions, and Events. *Mental Process*—Thinking Creatively; Analyzing Data or Information; Judging Qualities of Things, Services, Other People's Work. *Work Output*—Implementing Ideas and Programs; Drafting and Specifying Technical Devices; Handling and Moving Objects. *Interacting with Others*—Monitoring and Controlling Resources; Communicating with Other Workers; Providing Consultation and Advice to Others. **Physical Work Conditions:** Indoors; Standing; Using Hands on Objects, Tools, or Controls. **Other Job Characteristics:** Consequence of Error; Importance of Being Sure All Is Done; Importance of Being Exact or Accurate.

Experience: Job Zone 4. A minimum of two to four years of work-related skill, knowledge, or experience is needed. **Job Preparation:** SVP 7.0 to less than 8.0—2 years to less than 10 years. **Knowledge:** Design; Fine Arts; English Language; Customer and Personal Service; Geography; Sociology and Anthropology; History and Archeology. **Instructional Programs:** 200301 Clothing, Apparel and Textile Workers and Managers, General; 200305 Custom Tailor.

Related DOT Jobs: 346.261-010 Costumer; 346.361-010 Wardrobe Supervisor.

39-3093.00 Locker Room, Coatroom, and Dressing Room Attendants (Wardrobe, and Locker and Dressing Room Attendants)

Education: No data available.
Employed: 7,600
Openings: No data available.
Projected Growth: No data available.
Earnings: $15,330

Provide personal items to patrons or customers in locker rooms, dressing rooms, or coatrooms.

Stores personal possessions for patrons, issues a claim check for articles stored, and returns articles on receipt of check. Cleans and polishes footwear, using brush, sponge, cleaning fluid, polish, wax, liquid, or sole dressing, and dauber. Assists customer in tub or steam room, bathes or massages them, using water, brush, mitt, sponge, and towel, to clean skin. Conducts body conditioning therapy such as steam or electric shock, using physical or visual stimuli. Packs equipment and uniforms and attends to needs of individual athletes in clubhouse. Interviews, evaluates, and advises client to develop personal improvement plan such as weight loss, using scales, measures, and recommended guidelines. Schedules appointments for client sessions, registers guests, and assigns accommodations. Inspects building and grounds, and reports or removes unauthorized or undesirable persons. Issues keys, athletic equipment, or supplies such as soap, towels, and weight-loss aids. Assists persons in establishments such as apartments, hotels, or hospitals, by opening doors, carrying bags, and performing related services. Transports customers and baggage, using motor vehicle. Records and reviews client's activities to assure program is followed. Sells service-related products and collects fees for services, rent, products, or supplies. Secures boat to dock, using mooring lines, connects utility lines to boat, and pumps water from boat for patrons. Arranges, supervises, and provides valet services such as pressing clothes, shining shoes, sending and receiving mail, and parking cars. Explains nature and cost of services and facilities available, demonstrates use of equipment, and answers customer inquiries. Performs general cleaning and maintenance of facilities and equipment, using mop, broom, lawn mower, and other cleaning aids.

GOE Number, Interest Area, and Work Group: 11.07.01; Recreation, Travel, and Other Personal Services; Cleaning and Building Services. **Personality Type:** Social. Social occupations frequently involve working with, communicating with, and teaching people. These occupations often involve helping or providing service to others. **Work Values:** Social Service; Moral Values; Working Conditions; Security; Independence. **Skills:** Service Orientation; Speaking; Active Listening; Social Perceptiveness; Coordination. **Abilities:** *Cognitive*—Oral Expression; Oral Comprehension; Memorization; Information Ordering; Number Facility; Time Sharing. *Psychomotor*—Reaction Time; Multilimb Coordination; Response Orientation. *Physical*—Extent Flexibility; Trunk Strength; Gross Body Coordination. *Sensory*—Speech Clarity; Speech Recognition; Auditory Attention. **General Work Activities:** *Information Input*—Identifying Objects, Actions, and Events; Getting Information Needed to Do the Job; Monitoring Processes, Materials, and Surroundings. *Mental Process*—Scheduling Work and Activities; Judging Qualities of Things, Services, Other People's Work; Making Decisions and Solving Problems; Organizing, Planning, and Prioritizing; Updating and Using Job-Relevant Knowledge; Processing Information. *Work Output*—Handling and Moving Objects; Performing General Physical Activities; Documenting and Recording Information. *Interacting with Others*—Communicating with Persons Outside Organization; Assisting and Caring for Others; Performing for or Working with the Public. **Physical Work Conditions:** Indoors; Standing; Walking or Running. **Other Job Characteristics:** Importance of Being Sure

All Is Done; Importance of Repeating Same Tasks; Importance of Being Aware of New Events; Frustrating Circumstances; Importance of Being Exact or Accurate.

Experience: Job Zone 1. No previous work-related skill, knowledge, or experience is needed. **Job Preparation:** SVP Below 4.0—Less than 6 months. **Knowledge:** Customer and Personal Service; Sales and Marketing; Mechanical; Mathematics; English Language; Transportation; Psychology; Clerical. **Instructional Program:** 129999 Personal and Miscellaneous Services, Other.

Related DOT Jobs: 324.577-010 Room-Service Clerk; 324.677-014 Doorkeeper; 329.467-010 Attendant, Lodging Facilities; 329.677-010 Porter, Marina; 334.374-010 Masseur/Masseuse; 334.677-010 Rubber; 358.677-010 Checkroom Attendant; 358.677-014 Locker-Room Attendant; 359.367-014 Weight-Reduction Specialist; 359.567-010 Reducing-Salon Attendant; 359.567-014 Tanning Salon Attendant; 366.677-010 Shoe Shiner.

39-4000 Funeral Service Workers

39-4011.00 Embalmers (Funeral Directors and Morticians)

Education: Associate degree

Employed: 27,527

Openings: 3,972

Projected Growth: 16.1%

Earnings: $35,040

Prepare bodies for interment, in conformity with legal requirements.

Washes and dries body, using germicidal soap and towels or hot air drier. Incises stomach and abdominal walls and probes internal organs, using trocar, to withdraw blood and waste matter from organs. Attaches trocar to pump-tube, starts pump, and repeats probing to force embalming fluid into organs. Makes incision in arm or thigh and drains blood from circulatory system and replaces blood with embalming fluid, using pump. Presses diaphragm to evacuate air from lungs. Joins lips, using needle and thread or wire. Maintains records such as itemized list of clothing or valuables delivered with body and names of persons embalmed. Dresses and places body in casket. Reshapes or reconstructs disfigured or maimed bodies, using materials such as clay, cotton, plaster of paris, and wax. Packs body orifices with cotton saturated with embalming fluid to prevent escape of gases or waste matter. Applies cosmetics to impart lifelike appearance. Closes incisions, using needle and suture. Inserts convex celluloid or cotton between eyeball and eyelid to prevent slipping and sinking of eyelid.

GOE Number, Interest Area, and Work Group: 11.08.01; Recreation, Travel, and Other Personal Services; Other Personal Services. **Personality Type:** Realistic. Realistic occupations frequently involve work activities that include practical, hands-on problems and solutions. These occupations often deal with plants, animals, and real-world materials like wood, tools, and machinery. Many of the occupations require working outside and do not involve a lot of paperwork or working closely with others. **Work Values:**

Independence; Security; Moral Values; Autonomy; Social Service; Supervision, Human Relations. **Skills:** Monitoring; Identification of Key Causes; Reading Comprehension; Social Perceptiveness; Judgment and Decision Making; Equipment Selection. **Abilities:** *Cognitive*—Written Expression; Visualization; Deductive Reasoning; Information Ordering; Written Comprehension; Oral Expression. *Psychomotor*—Finger Dexterity; Arm-Hand Steadiness; Manual Dexterity. *Physical*—Static Strength; Extent Flexibility; Dynamic Flexibility; Dynamic Strength. *Sensory*—Visual Color Discrimination; Auditory Attention; Hearing Sensitivity; Depth Perception. **General Work Activities:** *Information Input*—Getting Information Needed to Do the Job; Estimating Needed Characteristics; Identifying Objects, Actions, and Events; Monitoring Processes, Materials, and Surroundings. *Mental Process*—Judging Qualities of Things, Services, Other People's Work; Organizing, Planning, and Prioritizing; Updating and Using Job-Relevant Knowledge. *Work Output*—Handling and Moving Objects; Performing General Physical Activities; Documenting and Recording Information. *Interacting with Others*—Assisting and Caring for Others; Communicating with Persons Outside Organization; Performing Administrative Activities; Establishing and Maintaining Relationships. **Physical Work Conditions:** Indoors; Using Hands on Objects, Tools, or Controls; Contaminants. **Other Job Characteristics:** Importance of Being Sure All Is Done; Consequence of Error; Importance of Being Exact or Accurate.

Experience: Job Zone 4. A minimum of two to four years of work-related skill, knowledge, or experience is needed. **Job Preparation:** SVP 7.0 to less than 8.0—2 years to less than 10 years. **Knowledge:** Biology; Chemistry; Customer and Personal Service; Law, Government and Jurisprudence; Public Safety and Security. **Instructional Program:** 120301 Funeral Services and Mortuary Science.

Related DOT Jobs: 338.371-010 Embalmer Apprentice; 338.371-014 Embalmer.

39-4021.00 Funeral Attendants (Funeral Attendants)

Education: No data available.

Employed: 22,520

Openings: No data available.

Projected Growth: No data available.

Earnings: $15,260

Perform variety of tasks during funeral, such as placing casket in parlor or chapel prior to service, arranging floral offerings or lights around casket, directing or escorting mourners, closing casket, and issuing and storing funeral equipment.

Carries flowers to hearse or limousine for transportation to place of interment. Directs or escorts mourners to parlor or chapel in which wake or funeral is being held. Assists in closing casket. Arranges floral offerings or lights around casket. Assists mourners in and out of limousines. Issues and stores funeral equipment. Places casket in parlor or chapel prior to wake or funeral. Assists in carrying casket.

GOE Number, Interest Area, and Work Group: 11.08.01; Recreation, Travel, and Other Personal Services; Other Personal Services. **Personality Type:** Social. Social occupations frequently involve working with, communicating with, and teaching people. These occupations often involve helping or providing service to others. **Work Values:** Moral Values; Security; Social Service; Company Policies and Practices; Autonomy; Supervision, Human Relations; Compensation; Independence. **Skills:** Social Perceptiveness; Service Orientation; Active Listening; Coordination; Speaking. **Abilities:** *Cognitive*—Oral Expression; Oral Comprehension; Spatial Orientation; Visualization; Category Flexibility; Information Ordering. *Psychomotor*—Speed of Limb Movement; Rate Control. *Physical*—Static Strength; Extent Flexibility; Trunk Strength. *Sensory*—Speech Clarity; Depth Perception; Glare Sensitivity; Peripheral Vision; Night Vision. **General Work Activities:** *Information Input*—Getting Information Needed to Do the Job; Monitoring Processes, Materials, and Surroundings; Identifying Objects, Actions, and Events. *Mental Process*—Thinking Creatively; Making Decisions and Solving Problems; Judging Qualities of Things, Services, Other People's Work. *Work Output*—Performing General Physical Activities; Handling and Moving Objects; Implementing Ideas and Programs. *Interacting with Others*—Communicating with Persons Outside Organization; Assisting and Caring for Others; Performing for or Working with the Public. **Physical Work Conditions:** Indoors; Standing; Walking or Running. **Other Job Characteristics:** Importance of Being Sure All Is Done; Consequence of Error; Importance of Being Exact or Accurate.

Experience: Job Zone 1. No previous work-related skill, knowledge, or experience is needed. **Job Preparation:** SVP Below 4.0—Less than 6 months. **Knowledge:** Customer and Personal Service; Psychology; English Language; Sociology and Anthropology; Transportation. **Instructional Program:** 129999 Personal and Miscellaneous Services, Other.

Related DOT Jobs: 359.677-014 Funeral Attendant; 359.687-010 Pallbearer.

39-5000 Personal Appearance Workers

39-5011.00 Barbers (Barbers)

Education: Postsecondary vocational training

Employed: 54,288

Openings: 1,946

Projected Growth: –7.3%

Earnings: $18,460

Cut, trim, shampoo, and style patron's hair. Trim beards or give shaves.

Sells lotions, tonics, or other cosmetic supplies. Cleans work area and work tools. Questions patron regarding services and style of haircut desired. Performs other tonsorial services such as applying hairdressings or lotions, dyeing, shampooing, singeing, or styling hair, and massaging face, neck, or scalp. Records service on ticket or receives payment. Cuts, shapes, trims, and tapers hair, using clippers, comb, blow-out gun, and scissors. Orders supplies. Drapes and pins protective cloth around customer's shoulders. Applies lather and shaves beard or shapes hair contour (outline) on temple and neck, using razor.

GOE Number, Interest Area, and Work Group: 11.04.01; Recreation, Travel, and Other Personal Services; Barber and Beauty Services. **Personality Type:** Realistic. Realistic occupations frequently involve work activities that include practical, hands-on problems and solutions. These occupations often deal with plants, animals, and real-world materials like wood, tools, and machinery. Many of the occupations require working outside and do not involve a lot of paperwork or working closely with others. **Work Values:** Social Service; Moral Values; Autonomy; Achievement; Independence; Security. **Skills:** Active Listening; Service Orientation; Social Perceptiveness; Product Inspection; Identification of Key Causes; Problem Identification. **Abilities:** *Cognitive*—Oral Comprehension; Visualization; Oral Expression; Selective Attention; Information Ordering. *Psychomotor*—Arm-Hand Steadiness; Finger Dexterity; Manual Dexterity. *Physical*—Extent Flexibility; Trunk Strength; Gross Body Coordination. *Sensory*—Speech Recognition; Visual Color Discrimination. **General Work Activities:** *Information Input*—Getting Information Needed to Do the Job; Estimating Needed Characteristics; Monitoring Processes, Materials, and Surroundings; Identifying Objects, Actions, and Events. *Mental Process*—Thinking Creatively; Scheduling Work and Activities; Organizing, Planning, and Prioritizing; Updating and Using Job-Relevant Knowledge. *Work Output*—Handling and Moving Objects; Performing General Physical Activities; Controlling Machines and Processes. *Interacting with Others*—Performing for or Working with the Public; Communicating with Persons Outside Organization; Establishing and Maintaining Relationships. **Physical Work Conditions:** Indoors; Standing; Using Hands on Objects, Tools, or Controls. **Other Job Characteristics:** Importance of Being Sure All Is Done; Importance of Repeating Same Tasks; Consequence of Error.

Experience: Job Zone 3. Previous work-related skill, knowledge, or experience is required. **Job Preparation:** SVP 6.0 to less than 7.0—More than 1 year and less than 4 years. **Knowledge:** Customer and Personal Service; Sales and Marketing; Economics and Accounting; English Language; Mathematics; Clerical; Biology. **Instructional Program:** 120402 Barber/Hairstylist.

Related DOT Jobs: 330.371-010 Barber; 330.371-014 Barber Apprentice.

39-5012.00 Hairdressers, Hairstylists, and Cosmetologists (Hairdressers, Hairstylists, and Cosmetologists)

Education: Postsecondary vocational training

Employed: 605,165

Openings: 73,177

Projected Growth: 10.2%

Earnings: $15,150

Shampoo, cut, color, and style patron's hair. Massage and treat scalp. Apply makeup, dress wigs, perform hair removal, and provide nail and skin care services.

Cleans, shapes, and polishes fingernails and toenails, using files and nail polish. Applies water and setting or waving solutions to hair; winds hair on curlers or rollers. Bleaches, dyes, or tints hair, using applicator or brush. Shampoos, rinses, and dries hair and scalp or hair pieces with water, liquid soap, or other solutions. Combs, brushes, and sprays hair or wigs to set style. Administers therapeutic medication and advises patron to seek medical treatment for chronic or contagious scalp conditions. Shapes and colors eyebrows or eyelashes and removes facial hair, using depilatory cream and tweezers. Updates and maintains customer information records such as beauty services provided. Analyzes patron's hair and other physical features or reads makeup instructions to determine and recommend beauty treatment. Massages and treats scalp for hygienic and remedial purposes, using hands, fingers, or vibrating equipment. Attaches wig or hairpiece to model head and dresses wigs and hairpieces according to instructions, samples, sketches, or photographs. Cuts, trims and shapes hair or hair pieces, using clippers, scissors, trimmers, and razors. Recommends and applies cosmetics, lotions, and creams to patron to soften and lubricate skin and to enhance and restore natural appearance.

GOE Number, Interest Area, and Work Group: 11.04.01; Recreation, Travel, and Other Personal Services; Barber and Beauty Services. **Personality Type:** Enterprising. Enterprising occupations frequently involve starting up and carrying out projects. These occupations can involve leading people and making many decisions. They sometimes require risk taking and often deal with business. **Work Values:** Social Service; Moral Values; Achievement; Autonomy; Recognition; Creativity; Independence. **Skills:** Service Orientation; Problem Identification; Judgment and Decision Making; Active Listening; Social Perceptiveness; Equipment Selection; Time Management. **Abilities:** *Cognitive*—Oral Expression; Visualization; Oral Comprehension; Originality; Fluency of Ideas. *Psychomotor*—Arm-Hand Steadiness; Manual Dexterity; Finger Dexterity. *Physical*—Extent Flexibility; Trunk Strength; Dynamic Strength. *Sensory*—Visual Color Discrimination; Far Vision; Speech Recognition. **General Work Activities:** *Information Input*—Getting Information Needed to Do the Job; Monitoring Processes, Materials, and Surroundings; Estimating Needed Characteristics. *Mental Process*—Thinking Creatively; Updating and Using Job-Relevant Knowledge; Organizing, Planning, and Prioritizing. *Work Output*—Handling and Moving Objects; Implementing Ideas and Programs; Performing General Physical Activities. *Interacting with Others*—Communicating with Persons Outside Organization; Performing for or Working with the Public; Establishing and Maintaining Relationships. **Physical Work Conditions:** Indoors; Standing; Using Hands on Objects, Tools, or Controls. **Other Job Characteristics:** Frustrating Circumstances; Consequence of Error; Importance of Being Sure All Is Done.

Experience: Job Zone 3. Previous work-related skill, knowledge, or experience is required. **Job Preparation:** SVP 6.0 to less than 7.0—More than 1 year and less than 4 years. **Knowledge:** Customer and Personal Service; Clerical; Sales and Marketing; English Language; Medicine and Dentistry; Psychology; Mathematics. **Instructional Programs:** 120401 Cosmetic Services, General; 120402 Barber/Hairstylist; 120403 Cosmetologist; 120404 Electrolysis Technician; 120406 Make-Up Artist.

Related DOT Jobs: 332.271-010 Cosmetologist; 332.271-014 Cosmetologist Apprentice; 332.271-018 Hair Stylist; 332.361-010 Wig Dresser; 339.361-010 Mortuary Beautician.

39-5091.00 Makeup Artists, Theatrical and Performance (Hairdressers, Hairstylists, and Cosmetologists)

Education: Postsecondary vocational training
Employed: 605,165
Openings: 73,177
Projected Growth: 10.2%
Earnings: $15,150

Apply makeup to performers to reflect period, setting, and situation of their roles.

Applies makeup to performers to alter their appearance to accord with their roles. Examines sketches, photographs, and plaster models to obtain desired character image depiction. Studies production information such as character, period settings, and situations to determine makeup requirements. Attaches prostheses to performer and applies makeup to change physical features and depict desired character. Confers with stage or motion picture officials and performers to determine dress or makeup alterations. Selects desired makeup shades from stock or mixes oil, grease, and coloring to achieve special color effects. Designs rubber or plastic prostheses and requisitions materials such as wigs, beards, and special cosmetics. Creates character drawings or models, based upon independent research to augment period production files.

GOE Number, Interest Area, and Work Group: 01.09.01; Arts, Entertainment, and Media; Modeling and Personal Appearance. **Personality Type:** Artistic. Artistic occupations frequently involve working with forms, designs, and patterns. These occupations often require self-expression, and the work can be done without following a clear set of rules. **Work Values:** Moral Values; Social Service; Creativity; Achievement; Ability Utilization. **Skills:** Coordination; Reading Comprehension; Active Listening; Information Gathering; Equipment Selection; Solution Appraisal; Idea Generation. **Abilities:** *Cognitive*—Originality; Visualization; Information Ordering; Deductive Reasoning; Fluency of Ideas; Written Comprehension. *Psychomotor*—Arm-Hand Steadiness; Finger Dexterity; Manual Dexterity. *Physical*—Trunk Strength; Dynamic Strength; Dynamic Flexibility; Gross Body Coordination. *Sensory*—Visual Color Discrimination; Near Vision; Speech Recognition; Far Vision. **General Work Activities:** *Information Input*—Getting Information Needed to Do the Job; Estimating Needed Characteristics; Identifying Objects, Actions, and Events. *Mental Process*—Thinking Creatively; Making Decisions and Solving Problems; Judging Qualities of Things, Services, Other People's Work. *Work Output*—Handling and Moving Objects; Implementing Ideas and Programs; Drafting and Specifying Technical Devices. *Interacting with Others*—Assisting and Caring for Others; Communicating with Other Workers; Communicating with Persons Outside Organization. **Physical Work Conditions:** Using Hands on Objects, Tools, or Controls; Indoors; Standing; Sitting. **Other Job Characteristics:** Importance of Being Exact or Accurate; Frustrating Circumstances; Importance of Being Sure All Is Done.

Experience: Job Zone 2. Some previous work-related skill, knowledge, or experience may be helpful, but usually is not needed. **Job Preparation:** SVP 4.00 to 5.99—6 months to less than 2 years. **Knowledge:** Fine Arts; Customer and Personal Service; Design; Sociology and Anthropology; English Language; Communications and Media. **Instructional Programs:** 120401 Cosmetic Services, General; 120402 Barber/Hairstylist; 120403 Cosmetologist; 120404 Electrolysis Technician; 120406 Make-Up Artist.

Related DOT Jobs: 333.071-010 Make-Up Artist; 333.271-010 Body-Make-Up Artist.

39-5092.00 Manicurists and Pedicurists (Manicurists)

Education: Postsecondary vocational training

Employed: 48,851

Openings: 7,081

Projected Growth: 26%

Earnings: $13,480

Clean and shape customers' fingernails and toenails. Polish or decorate nails.

Whitens underside of nails with white paste or pencil. Cleans customers' nails in soapy water, using swabs, files, and orange sticks. Forms artificial fingernails on customer's fingers. Polishes nails, using powdered polish and buffer. Removes paper forms and shapes and smoothes edges of nails, using rotary abrasive wheel. Softens nail cuticles with water and oil, pushes back cuticles, using cuticle knife, and trims cuticles, using scissors or nippers. Attaches paper forms to tips of customer's fingers to support and shape artificial nails. Roughens surfaces of fingernails, using abrasive wheel. Applies clear or colored liquid polish onto nails with brush. Shapes and smoothes ends of nails, using scissors, files, and emery boards. Removes previously applied nail polish, using liquid remover and swabs. Brushes coats of powder and solvent onto nails and paper forms with handbrush to maintain nail appearance and to extend nails to desired length.

GOE Number, Interest Area, and Work Group: 11.04.01; Recreation, Travel, and Other Personal Services; Barber and Beauty Services. **Personality Type:** Enterprising. Enterprising occupations frequently involve starting up and carrying out projects. These occupations can involve leading people and making many decisions. They sometimes require risk taking and often deal with business. **Work Values:** Social Service; Moral Values; Autonomy; Independence; Working Conditions. **Skills:** Service Orientation; Monitoring; Active Listening; Social Perceptiveness; Product Inspection; Time Management. **Abilities:** *Cognitive*—Oral Expression; Information Ordering; Deductive Reasoning; Selective Attention; Visualization. *Psychomotor*—Arm-Hand Steadiness; Finger Dexterity. *Physical*—none met the criteria. *Sensory*—Visual Color Discrimination; Hearing Sensitivity; Glare Sensitivity. **General Work Activities:** *Information Input*—Getting Information Needed to Do the Job; Identifying Objects, Actions, and Events; Monitoring Processes, Materials, and Surroundings. *Mental Process*—Scheduling Work and Activities; Judging Qualities of Things, Services, Other People's Work; Thinking Creatively. *Work Output*—Handling and Moving Objects; Performing General Physical Activities; Implementing Ideas and Programs; Controlling Machines and Processes. *Interacting with Others*—Performing for or Working with the Public; Establishing and Maintaining Relationships; Assisting and Caring for Others. **Physical Work Conditions:** Indoors; Sitting; Using Hands on Objects, Tools, or Controls. **Other Job Characteristics:** Importance of Being Sure All Is Done; Importance of Being Exact or Accurate; Consequence of Error.

Experience: Job Zone 1. No previous work-related skill, knowledge, or experience is needed. **Job Preparation:** SVP Below 4.0—Less than 6 months. **Knowledge:** Customer and Personal Service; Chemistry; Psychology; English Language; Sociology and Anthropology. **Instructional Program:** 120403 Cosmetologist.

Related DOT Jobs: 331.674-010 Manicurist; 331.674-014 Fingernail Former.

39-5093.00 Shampooers (All Other Service Workers)

Education: No data available.

Employed: 346,480

Openings: No data available.

Projected Growth: No data available.

Earnings: $15,950

Shampoo and rinse customers' hair.

GOE Number, Interest Area, and Work Group: 11.04.01; Recreation, Travel, and Other Personal Services; Barber and Beauty Services. **Instructional Programs:** 080901 Hospitality and Recreation Marketing Operations, General; 080999 Hospitality and Recreation Marketing Operations, Other; 120405 Massage; 200404 Dietician Assistant. **Note:** The Department of Labor has not collected some data for this job, so it has fewer details than the other descriptions.

39-5094.00 Skin Care Specialists (All Other Service Workers)

Education: No data available.

Employed: 346,480

Openings: No data available.

Projected Growth: No data available.

Earnings: $15,950

Provide skin care treatments to patron's face and body to enhance individual's appearance.

GOE Number, Interest Area, and Work Group: 11.04.01; Recreation, Travel, and Other Personal Services; Barber and Beauty Services. **Instructional Programs:** 080901 Hospitality and Recreation Marketing Operations, General; 080999 Hospitality and Recreation Marketing Operations, Other; 120405 Massage; 200404 Dietician Assistant. **Note:** The Department of Labor has not collected some data for this job, so it has fewer details than the other descriptions.

39-6000 Transportation, Tourism, and Lodging Attendants

39-6011.00 Baggage Porters and Bellhops (Baggage Porters and Bellhops)

Education: Short-term O-T-J training

Employed: 39,814

Openings: 10,287

Projected Growth: 13.7%

Earnings: $13,330

Handle baggage for travelers at transportation terminals or for guests at hotels or similar establishments.

Delivers, carries, or transfers luggage, trunks, and packages to/from rooms, loading areas, vehicles, or transportation terminals. Runs errands for guests. Escorts incoming hotel guests to their rooms. Sets up display tables, racks, or shelves, and arranges merchandise display for sales personnel. Pages guests in hotel lobby, dining room, or other areas; delivers messages and room service orders. Arranges for clothing of hotel guests to be cleaned, laundered, or repaired. Completes and attaches baggage claim checks and completes baggage insurance forms. Weighs and bills baggage and parcels for shipment, and arranges for freight to be shipped. Transports guests about premises and local area, or calls taxicabs. Computes and completes charge slips for services rendered; maintains records. Supplies guests or travelers with directions, travel information, and other information such as available services and points of interest. Inspects guest's room and explains features such as night lock and operation of television.

GOE Number, Interest Area, and Work Group: 11.03.01; Recreation, Travel, and Other Personal Services; Transportation and Lodging Services. **Personality Type:** Enterprising. Enterprising occupations frequently involve starting up and carrying out projects. These occupations can involve leading people and making many decisions. They sometimes require risk taking and often deal with business. **Work Values:** Social Service; Moral Values; Independence; Working Conditions; Co-workers. **Skills:** Service Orientation; Active Listening; Reading Comprehension; Writing; Social Perceptiveness. **Abilities:** *Cognitive*—Oral Expression; Oral Comprehension; Spatial Orientation; Written Expression; Number Facility; Written Comprehension. *Psychomotor*—none met the criteria. *Physical*—Static Strength; Trunk Strength; Stamina. **General Work Activities:** *Information Input*—Getting Information Needed to Do the Job; Identifying Objects, Actions, and Events; Inspecting Equipment, Structures, Materials. *Mental Process*—Processing Information; Organizing, Planning, and Prioritizing; Updating and Using Job-Relevant Knowledge. *Work Output*—Performing General Physical Activities; Handling and Moving Objects; Documenting and Recording Information. *Interacting with Others*—Assisting and Caring for Others; Performing for or Working with the Public; Communicating with Persons Outside Organization. **Physical Work Conditions:** Special Uniform; Standing; Indoors; Using Hands on Objects, Tools, or Controls. **Other Job Characteristics:** Importance of Being Sure All Is Done; Importance of Being Exact or Accurate; Consequence of Error.

Experience: Job Zone 1. No previous work-related skill, knowledge, or experience is needed. **Job Preparation:** SVP Below 4.0—Less than 6 months. **Knowledge:** Customer and Personal Service; English Language; Transportation; Geography; Mathematics. **Instructional Program:** 129999 Personal and Miscellaneous Services, Other.

Related DOT Jobs: 324.477-010 Porter, Baggage; 324.677-010 Bellhop; 357.477-010 Baggage Checker; 357.677-010 Porter.

39-6012.00 Concierges (All Other Service Workers)

Education: No data available.

Employed: 346,480

Openings: No data available.

Projected Growth: No data available.

Earnings: $15,950

Assist patrons with personal services at hotel, apartment, or office building. Take messages. Arrange or give advice on transportation, business services, or entertainment. Monitor guest requests for housekeeping and maintenance.

GOE Number, Interest Area, and Work Group: 11.03.01; Recreation, Travel, and Other Personal Services; Transportation and Lodging Services. **Instructional Programs:** 080901 Hospitality and Recreation Marketing Operations, General; 080999 Hospitality and Recreation Marketing Operations, Other; 120405 Massage; 200404 Dietician Assistant. **Note:** The Department of Labor has not collected some data for this job, so it has fewer details than the other descriptions.

39-6021.00 Tour Guides and Escorts (Guides)

Education: No data available.

Employed: 26,270

Openings: No data available.

Projected Growth: No data available.

Earnings: $15,500

Escort individuals or groups on sightseeing tours or through places of interest such as industrial establishments, public buildings, and art galleries.

Carries equipment, luggage, or sample cases for visitors and provides errand service. Distributes brochures, conveys background information, and explains establishment processes and operations at tour site. Provides directions and other pertinent information to visitors. Plans rest stops and refreshment items. Drives motor vehicle to transport visitors to establishments and tour site locations. Speaks foreign language to communicate with foreign visitors. Solicits tour patronage and collects fees and tickets from group members. Monitors facilities and notifies establishment personnel of need for maintenance. Greets and registers visitors and issues identification badges and safety devices. Monitors visitors' activities and cautions visitors not complying with establishment regulations. Escorts group on city and establishment tours, describes points of interest, and responds to questions. Assumes responsibility for safety of group. Performs clerical duties such as filing, typing, operating switchboard, and delivering and collecting mail and messages.

GOE Number, Interest Area, and Work Group: 11.02.01; Recreation, Travel, and Other Personal Services; Recreational Services. **Personality Type:** Social. Social occupations frequently involve working with, communicating with, and teaching people. These occupations often involve helping or providing service to others. **Work Values:** Social Service; Moral Values; Variety; Authority; Working Conditions. **Skills:** Service Orientation; Active Listening; Social Perceptiveness; Speaking; Reading Comprehension. **Abilities:** *Cognitive*—Oral Expression; Oral Comprehension; Number Facility; Spatial Orientation; Memorization. *Psychomotor*—Reaction Time; Response Orientation; Rate Control. *Physical*—none met the criteria. *Sensory*—Speech Clarity; Speech Recognition; Far Vision. **General Work Activities:** *Information Input*—Monitoring Processes, Materials, and Surroundings; Getting Information Needed to Do the Job; Estimating Needed Characteristics; Identifying Objects, Actions, and Events. *Mental Process*—Scheduling

Work and Activities; Making Decisions and Solving Problems; Evaluating Information Against Standards; Processing Information; Organizing, Planning, and Prioritizing. *Work Output—*Performing General Physical Activities; Operating Vehicles or Equipment; Handling and Moving Objects. *Interacting with Others—*Communicating with Persons Outside Organization; Interpreting Meaning of Information to Others; Performing for or Working with the Public. **Physical Work Conditions:** Walking or Running; Outdoors; Standing; Sitting. **Other Job Characteristics:** Importance of Being Sure All Is Done; Consequence of Error; Importance of Being Aware of New Events; Frustrating Circumstances.

Experience: Job Zone 1. No previous work-related skill, knowledge, or experience is needed. **Job Preparation:** SVP Below 4.0—Less than 6 months. **Knowledge:** Customer and Personal Service; English Language; Foreign Language; Clerical; Communications and Media. **Instructional Program:** 080903 Recreation Products/Services Marketing Operations.

Related DOT Jobs: 109.367-010 Museum Attendant; 353.363-010 Guide, Sightseeing; 353.367-010 Guide; 353.367-014 Guide, Establishment; 353.367-018 Guide, Plant; 353.367-022 Page; 353.667-010 Escort.

39-6022.00 Travel Guides (Guides)

Education: No data available.

Employed: 26,270

Openings: No data available.

Projected Growth: No data available.

Earnings: $15,500

Plan, organize, and conduct long distance cruises, tours, and expeditions for individuals and groups.

Verifies quantity and quality of equipment to ensure prerequisite needs for expeditions and tours have been met. Arranges for transportation, accommodations, activity equipment, and services of medical personnel. Obtains or assists tourists in obtaining permits and documents such as visas, passports, and health certificates and in converting currency. Administers first aid to injured group participants. Sells or rents equipment, clothing, and supplies. Pilots airplane or drives land and water vehicles to transport tourists to activity/tour site. Pitches camp and prepares meals for tour group members. Plans tour itinerary, applying knowledge of travel routes and destination sites. Instructs novices in climbing techniques, mountaineering, and wilderness survival, and demonstrates use of hunting, fishing, and climbing equipment. Selects activity tour sites and leads individuals or groups to location and describes points of interest. Explains hunting and fishing laws to group to ensure compliance.

GOE Number, Interest Area, and Work Group: 11.02.01; Recreation, Travel, and Other Personal Services; Recreational Services. **Personality Type:** Enterprising. Enterprising occupations frequently involve starting up and carrying out projects. These occupations can involve leading people and making many decisions. They sometimes require risk taking and often deal with business. **Work Values:** Social Service; Variety; Autonomy; Moral Values; Working Conditions; Creativity; Responsibility. **Skills:** Service Orientation; Implementation Planning; Coordination; Active Listening; Operation and Control; Information Gathering; Problem

Identification; Instructing; Management of Material Resources; Time Management. **Abilities:** *Cognitive—*Oral Expression; Oral Comprehension; Written Comprehension; Time Sharing; Number Facility; Memorization. *Psychomotor—*Reaction Time; Multilimb Coordination; Response Orientation; Rate Control. *Physical—*Trunk Strength; Stamina; Dynamic Strength; Gross Body Coordination. *Sensory—*Speech Clarity; Glare Sensitivity; Auditory Attention. **General Work Activities:** *Information Input—*Getting Information Needed to Do the Job; Estimating Needed Characteristics; Identifying Objects, Actions, and Events. *Mental Process—*Scheduling Work and Activities; Developing Objectives and Strategies; Making Decisions and Solving Problems; Updating and Using Job-Relevant Knowledge; Judging Qualities of Things, Services, Other People's Work. *Work Output—*Performing General Physical Activities; Operating Vehicles or Equipment; Implementing Ideas and Programs; Handling and Moving Objects. *Interacting with Others—*Performing for or Working with the Public; Communicating with Persons Outside Organization; Assisting and Caring for Others. **Physical Work Conditions:** Outdoors; Walking or Running; Standing. **Other Job Characteristics:** Consequence of Error; Frustrating Circumstances; Importance of Being Sure All Is Done.

Experience: Job Zone 2. Some previous work-related skill, knowledge, or experience may be helpful, but usually is not needed. **Job Preparation:** SVP 4.00 to 5.99—6 months to less than 2 years. **Knowledge:** Customer and Personal Service; Geography; Transportation; English Language; Communications and Media. **Instructional Program:** 080903 Recreation Products/Services Marketing Operations.

Related DOT Jobs: 353.161-010 Guide, Hunting and Fishing; 353.164-010 Guide, Alpine; 353.167-010 Guide, Travel; 353.364-010 Dude Wrangler.

39-6031.00 Flight Attendants (Flight Attendants)

Education: Long-term O-T-J training

Employed: 99,053

Openings: 5,376

Projected Growth: 30.1%

Earnings: $37,800

Provide personal services to ensure the safety and comfort of airline passengers during flight. Greet passengers, verify tickets, explain use of safety equipment, and serve food or beverages.

Prepares reports showing place of departure and destination, passenger ticket numbers, meal and beverages inventories, and lost and found articles. Walks aisle of plane to verify that passengers have complied with federal regulations prior to take off. Assists passengers to store carry-on luggage in overhead, garment, or under-seat storage. Explains use of safety equipment to passengers. Administers first aid to passengers in distress, when needed. Collects money for meals and beverages. Greets passengers, verifies tickets, records destinations, and directs passengers to assigned seats. Serves prepared meals and beverages.

GOE Number, Interest Area, and Work Group: 11.03.01; Recreation, Travel, and Other Personal Services; Transportation and Lodging Services. **Personality Type:** Enterprising. Enterprising occupations frequently involve starting up and carrying out projects. These occupations can involve leading people and making many decisions. They sometimes require risk taking and often deal with business. **Work Values:** Social Service; Supervision, Technical; Co-workers; Moral Values; Company Policies and Practices. **Skills:** Social Perceptiveness; Service Orientation; Reading Comprehension; Active Listening; Coordination. **Abilities:** *Cognitive*—Oral Expression; Oral Comprehension; Problem Sensitivity; Number Facility; Selective Attention. *Psychomotor*—Reaction Time; Response Orientation. *Physical*—Gross Body Coordination; Gross Body Equilibrium; Stamina. *Sensory*—Speech Clarity; Speech Recognition; Auditory Attention. **General Work Activities:** *Information Input*—Monitoring Processes, Materials, and Surroundings; Identifying Objects, Actions, and Events; Getting Information Needed to Do the Job. *Mental Process*—Evaluating Information Against Standards; Organizing, Planning, and Prioritizing; Judging Qualities of Things, Services, Other People's Work; Making Decisions and Solving Problems. *Work Output*—Handling and Moving Objects; Performing General Physical Activities; Documenting and Recording Information. *Interacting with Others*—Performing for or Working with the Public; Assisting and Caring for Others; Communicating with Persons Outside Organization. **Physical Work Conditions:** Special Uniform; Indoors; Standing. **Other Job Characteristics:** Importance of Being Sure All Is Done; Consequence of Error; Importance of Being Exact or Accurate.

Experience: Job Zone 2. Some previous work-related skill, knowledge, or experience may be helpful, but usually is not needed. **Job Preparation:** SVP 4.00 to 5.99—6 months to less than 2 years. **Knowledge:** Customer and Personal Service; Public Safety and Security; Medicine and Dentistry; English Language; Law, Government and Jurisprudence; Transportation. **Instructional Program:** 490106 Flight Attendant.

Related DOT Jobs: 352.367-010 Airplane-Flight Attendant; 352.367-014 Flight Attendant, Ramp.

39-6032.00 Transportation Attendants, Except Flight Attendants and Baggage Porters (Transportation Attendants, Except Flight Attendants and Baggage Porters)

Education: No data available.
Employed: 21,110
Openings: No data available.
Projected Growth: No data available.
Earnings: $17,620

Provide services to ensure the safety and comfort of passengers aboard ships, buses, or trains, or within the station or terminal. Greet passengers, explain the use of safety equipment, serve meals or beverages, or answer questions related to travel.

Issues and collects passenger boarding passes and transfers and tears or punches tickets to prevent reuse. Inspects kitchen and dining area to ensure adherence to sanitation requirements. Serves snacks, lunch, and refreshments. Provides seating arrangements, and straightens and adjusts window shades and seat cushions to accommodate requests of passengers. Demonstrates safety procedures. Distributes sports and game equipment, magazines, newspapers, pillows, blankets, and other items to passengers and guests. Greets passengers boarding mode of transportation and announces stops. Counts and verifies tickets and seat reservations, and records number of passengers boarding and leaving mode of transportation. Cleans rooms and bathroom facilities, changes linens, and replenishes supplies to washroom. Carries baggage to assigned rooms or to station platform. Mails letters or arranges for dispatch of telegrams to assist passengers. Responds to passengers' questions, requests, or complaints. Signals transportation operator to stop or proceed, opens and closes doors, and establishes order among passengers.

GOE Number, Interest Area, and Work Group: 11.03.01; Recreation, Travel, and Other Personal Services; Transportation and Lodging Services. **Personality Type:** Enterprising. Enterprising occupations frequently involve starting up and carrying out projects. These occupations can involve leading people and making many decisions. They sometimes require risk taking and often deal with business. **Work Values:** Social Service; Moral Values; Security; Co-workers; Supervision, Technical. **Skills:** Problem Identification; Service Orientation; Active Listening; Critical Thinking; Speaking. **Abilities:** *Cognitive*—Oral Expression; Problem Sensitivity; Oral Comprehension; Written Comprehension; Spatial Orientation; Number Facility. *Psychomotor*—Reaction Time. *Physical*—Static Strength; Gross Body Equilibrium; Extent Flexibility. *Sensory*—Speech Clarity; Speech Recognition; Glare Sensitivity; Night Vision. **General Work Activities:** *Information Input*—Monitoring Processes, Materials, and Surroundings; Getting Information Needed to Do the Job; Inspecting Equipment, Structures, Materials. *Mental Process*—Evaluating Information Against Standards; Processing Information; Analyzing Data or Information; Making Decisions and Solving Problems; Organizing, Planning, and Prioritizing. *Work Output*—Handling and Moving Objects; Performing General Physical Activities; Documenting and Recording Information. *Interacting with Others*—Performing for or Working with the Public; Assisting and Caring for Others; Communicating with Persons Outside Organization. **Physical Work Conditions:** Indoors; Walking or Running; Special Uniform. **Other Job Characteristics:** Consequence of Error; Importance of Being Aware of New Events; Importance of Being Sure All Is Done.

Experience: Job Zone 1. No previous work-related skill, knowledge, or experience is needed. **Job Preparation:** SVP Below 4.0—Less than 6 months. **Knowledge:** Customer and Personal Service; Transportation; Public Safety and Security; English Language; Clerical; Communications and Media; Mathematics. **Instructional Program:** 081105 Travel Services Marketing Operations.

Related DOT Jobs: 350.677-014 Passenger Attendant; 350.677-018 Steward/Stewardess, Bath; 350.677-022 Steward/Stewardess; 351.677-010 Service Attendant, Sleeping Car; 352.577-010 Bus Attendant; 352.677-010 Passenger Service Representative I; 910.367-026 Passenger Representative; 910.667-014 Conductor; 910.677-010 Passenger Service Representative II.

39-9000 Other Personal Care and Service Workers

39-9011.00 Child Care Workers (Child Care Workers)

Education: Short-term O-T-J training

Employed: 904,542

Openings: 328,786

Projected Growth: 26.1%

Earnings: $13,750

Attend to children at schools, businesses, private households, and child care institutions. Dress, feed, and bathe children; oversee play.

Wheels handicapped children to classes or other areas of facility; secures them in equipment such as chairs and slings. Organizes and participates in recreational activities such as games. Places or hoists children into baths or pools. Monitors children on life-support equipment to detect malfunctioning of equipment; calls for medical assistance when needed. Reads to children and teaches them simple painting, drawing, handwork, and songs. Assists in preparing food for children; serves meals and refreshments to children; regulates rest periods. Disciplines children and recommends or initiates other measures to control behavior, such as caring for own clothing and picking up toys and books. Cares for children in institutional settings such as group homes, nursery schools, private businesses, or schools for the handicapped. Instructs children regarding desirable health and personal habits, such as eating, resting, and toilet habits.

GOE Number, Interest Area, and Work Group: 12.03.03; Education and Social Service; Educational Services: Pre-school, Elementary, and Secondary Teaching and Instructing. **Personality Type:** Social. Social occupations frequently involve working with, communicating with, and teaching people. These occupations often involve helping or providing service to others. **Work Values:** Social Service; Activity; Security; Moral Values; Company Policies and Practices; Co-workers; Working Conditions. **Skills:** Reading Comprehension; Learning Strategies; Active Listening; Service Orientation; Social Perceptiveness; Monitoring. **Abilities:** *Cognitive*—Oral Expression; Oral Comprehension; Problem Sensitivity; Written Comprehension; Time Sharing. *Psychomotor*—none met the criteria. *Physical*—Static Strength; Trunk Strength; Stamina. *Sensory*—Speech Clarity; Sound Localization; Peripheral Vision. **General Work Activities:** *Information Input*—Monitoring Processes, Materials, and Surroundings; Identifying Objects, Actions, and Events; Getting Information Needed to Do the Job. *Mental Process*—Making Decisions and Solving Problems; Organizing, Planning, and Prioritizing; Judging Qualities of Things, Services, Other People's Work. *Work Output*—Performing General Physical Activities; Handling and Moving Objects; Implementing Ideas and Programs. *Interacting with Others*—Assisting and Caring for Others; Communicating with Other Workers; Establishing and Maintaining Relationships. **Physical Work Conditions:** Indoors; Standing; Sitting. **Other Job Characteristics:** Consequence of Error; Importance of Being Sure All Is Done; Importance of Being Exact or Accurate.

Experience: Job Zone 1. No previous work-related skill, knowledge, or experience is needed. **Job Preparation:** SVP Below 4.0—Less than 6 months. **Knowledge:** Customer and Personal Service; Psychology; Education and Training; English Language; Administration and Management. **Instructional Programs:** 200201 Child Care and Guidance Workers and Managers, General; 200202 Child Care Provider/Assistant; 200299 Child Care and Guidance Workers and Managers, Other.

Related DOT Jobs: 355.674-010 Child-Care Attendant, School; 359.677-010 Attendant, Children's Institution; 359.677-018 Nursery School Attendant; 359.677-026 Playroom Attendant.

39-9021.00 Personal and Home Care Aides (Personal Care and Home Health Aides)

Education: Short-term O-T-J training

Employed: 745,671

Openings: 249,694

Projected Growth: 58.1%

Earnings: No data available.

Assist elderly or disabled adults with daily living activities at the person's home or in a daytime nonresidential facility. Keep house at a place of residence, including making beds, doing laundry, and washing dishes; prepare meals. Provide meals and supervised activities at nonresidential care facilities. Advise families, the elderly, and the disabled on such things as nutrition, cleanliness, and household utilities.

Types correspondence and reports. Prepares and maintains records of assistance rendered. Evaluates needs of individuals served and plans for continuing services. Assists client with dressing, undressing, and toilet activities. Assists parents in establishing good study habits for children. Drives motor vehicle to transport client to specified locations. Obtains information for client, for personal and business purposes. Assigns housekeeping duties according to children's capabilities. Gives bedside care to incapacitated individuals and trains family members to provide bedside care. Assists in training children. Advises and assists family members in planning nutritious meals, purchasing and preparing foods, and utilizing commodities from surplus food programs. Explains fundamental hygiene principles.

GOE Number, Interest Area, and Work Group: 11.08.01; Recreation, Travel, and Other Personal Services; Other Personal Services. **Personality Type:** Social. Social occupations frequently involve working with, communicating with, and teaching people. These occupations often involve helping or providing service to others. **Work Values:** Social Service; Moral Values; Company Policies and Practices; Autonomy; Security; Independence. **Skills:** Service Orientation; Social Perceptiveness; Speaking; Learning Strategies; Active Listening; Problem Identification. **Abilities:** *Cognitive*—Oral Expression; Oral Comprehension; Problem Sensitivity; Written Expression; Fluency of Ideas. *Psychomotor*—Response Orientation. *Physical*—Static Strength. *Sensory*—Speech Clarity. **General Work Activities:** *Information Input*—Getting Information Needed to Do the Job; Monitoring Processes, Materials, and Surroundings; Identifying Objects, Actions, and Events. *Mental Process*—Making Decisions and Solving Problems; Developing Objectives and Strategies; Judging Qualities of Things, Services, Other People's Work; Organizing, Planning, and Prioritizing. *Work Output*—Performing General Physical Activities; Handling and Moving Objects; Implementing Ideas and Programs; Documenting and Recording Information. *Interacting with Others*—Assisting and Caring for Others; Establishing and Maintaining Relationships; Teaching Others. **Physical Work Conditions:** Indoors; Standing; Walking or Running. **Other Job Characteristics:** Importance of Being Sure All Is Done; Consequence of Error; Frustrating Circumstances.

Experience: Job Zone 2. Some previous work-related skill, knowledge, or experience may be helpful, but usually is not needed. **Job Preparation:** SVP 4.00 to 5.99—6 months to less than 2 years. **Knowledge:** Customer and Personal Service; Medicine and Dentistry; Education and Training; Administration and Management; Clerical. **Instructional Programs:** 200201 Child Care and Guidance Workers and Managers, General; 200202 Child Care Provider/Assistant; 200601 Custodial, Housekeeping and Home Services Workers and Managers; 200602 Elder Care Provider/Companion; 200606 Homemaker's Aide.

Related DOT Jobs: 309.354-010 Homemaker; 359.573-010 Blind Aide.

39-9031.00 Fitness Trainers and Aerobics Instructors
(Sports and Physical Training Instructors and Coaches)

Education: Moderate-term O-T-J training

Employed: 358,512

Openings: 104,431

Projected Growth: 28.4%

Earnings: $22,230

Instruct or coach groups or individuals in exercise activities and the fundamentals of sports. Demonstrate techniques and methods of participation. Observe participants and inform them of corrective measures necessary to improve their skills.

Advises participants in use of heat or ultraviolet treatments and hot baths. Explains and enforces safety rules and regulations. Selects, stores, orders, issues, and inventories equipment, materials, and supplies. Organizes and conducts competition and tournaments. Plans physical education program to promote development of participant physical attributes and social skills. Organizes, leads, instructs, and referees indoor and outdoor games such as volleyball, baseball, and basketball. Teaches individual and team sports to participants, utilizing knowledge of sports techniques and of physical capabilities of participants. Teaches and demonstrates use of gymnastic and training apparatus such as trampolines and weights.

GOE Number, Interest Area, and Work Group: 01.10.01; Arts, Entertainment, and Media; Sports: Coaching, Instructing, Officiating, and Performing. **Personality Type:** Social. Social occupations frequently involve working with, communicating with, and teaching people. These occupations often involve helping or providing service to others. **Work Values:** Creativity; Authority; Achievement; Responsibility; Social Service. **Skills:** Coordination; Instructing; Learning Strategies; Speaking; Monitoring; Social

Perceptiveness. **Abilities:** *Cognitive*—Oral Expression; Time Sharing; Oral Comprehension; Information Ordering; Written Comprehension. *Psychomotor*—Multilimb Coordination; Speed of Limb Movement; Response Orientation. *Physical*—Extent Flexibility; Stamina; Trunk Strength; Explosive Strength; Dynamic Strength. *Sensory*—Depth Perception; Peripheral Vision; Far Vision. **General Work Activities:** *Information Input*—Monitoring Processes, Materials, and Surroundings; Getting Information Needed to Do the Job; Identifying Objects, Actions, and Events. *Mental Process*—Judging Qualities of Things, Services, Other People's Work; Organizing, Planning, and Prioritizing; Making Decisions and Solving Problems. *Work Output*—Performing General Physical Activities; Implementing Ideas and Programs; Handling and Moving Objects. *Interacting with Others*—Establishing and Maintaining Relationships; Coaching and Developing Others; Teaching Others. **Physical Work Conditions:** Standing; Outdoors; Indoors. **Other Job Characteristics:** Consequence of Error; Importance of Being Sure All Is Done; Importance of Being Aware of New Events.

Experience: Job Zone 3. Previous work-related skill, knowledge, or experience is required. **Job Preparation:** SVP 6.0 to less than 7.0—More than 1 year and less than 4 years. **Knowledge:** Education and Training; Psychology; Customer and Personal Service; Biology; English Language. **Instructional Programs:** 130101 Education, General; 131314 Physical Education Teaching and Coaching; 310501 Health and Physical Education, General.

Related DOT Jobs: 099.224-010 Instructor, Physical Education; 153.227-014 Instructor, Physical; 153.227-018 Instructor, Sports.

39-9032.00 Recreation Workers (Recreation Workers)

Education: Bachelor's degree

Employed: 240,651

Openings: 43,829

Projected Growth: 19.2%

Earnings: $16,500

Conduct recreation activities with groups, in public, private, or volunteer agencies, or in recreation facilities. Organize and promote activities such as arts and crafts, sports, games, music, dramatics, social recreation, camping, and hobbies, taking into account the needs and interests of individual members.

Enforces rules and regulations of facility, maintains discipline, and ensures safety. Organizes, leads, and promotes interest in facility activities such as arts, crafts, sports, games, camping, and hobbies. Schedules facility activities and maintains record of programs. Greets and introduces new arrivals to other guests, acquaints arrivals with facilities, and encourages group participation. Tests and documents content of swimming pool water and schedules maintenance and use of facilities. Supervises and coordinates work activities of personnel, trains staff, and assigns duties. Schedules maintenance and use of facilities. Evaluates staff performance and records reflective information on performance evaluation forms. Completes and maintains time and attendance forms and inventory lists. Administers first aid, according to prescribed procedures, or notifies emergency medical personnel when necessary. Assists management to resolve complaints. Ascertains and interprets group interests, evaluates equipment and facilities, and adapts activities to meet participant needs. Meets and collaborates with agency personnel, community organizations, and other professional personnel to plan balanced recreational programs for participants. Explains principles, techniques, and safety procedures of facility activities to participants and demonstrates use of material and equipment. Conducts recreational activities and instructs participants to develop skills in provided activities. Arranges for activity requirements such as entertainment and setting up equipment and decorations. Meets with staff to discuss rules, regulations, and work-related problems.

GOE Number, Interest Area, and Work Group: 11.02.01; Recreation, Travel, and Other Personal Services; Recreational Services. **Personality Type:** Social. Social occupations frequently involve working with, communicating with, and teaching people. These occupations often involve helping or providing service to others. **Work Values:** Social Service; Autonomy; Co-workers; Creativity; Activity; Moral Values; Responsibility; Variety. **Skills:** Coordination; Speaking; Implementation Planning; Service Orientation; Social Perceptiveness; Time Management. **Abilities:** *Cognitive*—Oral Expression; Oral Comprehension; Fluency of Ideas; Written Expression; Written Comprehension. *Psychomotor*—Response Orientation; Multilimb Coordination; Speed of Limb Movement. *Physical*—Trunk Strength; Gross Body Coordination; Extent Flexibility. *Sensory*—Near Vision; Speech Recognition; Speech Clarity. **General Work Activities:** *Information Input*—Getting Information Needed to Do the Job; Identifying Objects, Actions, and Events; Estimating Needed Characteristics; Monitoring Processes, Materials, and Surroundings. *Mental Process*—Organizing, Planning, and Prioritizing; Thinking Creatively; Judging Qualities of Things, Services, Other People's Work; Scheduling Work and Activities. *Work Output*—Performing General Physical Activities; Implementing Ideas and Programs; Documenting and Recording Information. *Interacting with Others*—Coordinating Work and Activities of Others; Establishing and Maintaining Relationships; Communicating with Persons Outside Organization. **Physical Work Conditions:** Indoors; Standing; Outdoors. **Other Job Characteristics:** Importance of Being Sure All Is Done; Consequence of Error; Frustrating Circumstances; Importance of Being Exact or Accurate.

Experience: Job Zone 3. Previous work-related skill, knowledge, or experience is required. **Job Preparation:** SVP 6.0 to less than 7.0—More than 1 year and less than 4 years. **Knowledge:** Customer and Personal Service; Administration and Management; Education and Training; English Language; Psychology. **Instructional Programs:** 200201 Child Care and Guidance Workers and Managers, General; 200202 Child Care Provider/Assistant; 310101 Parks, Recreation and Leisure Studies; 310301 Parks, Recreation and Leisure Facilities Management; 310501 Health and Physical Education, General; 310504 Sport and Fitness Administration/Management; 310599 Health and Physical Education/Fitness, Other; 319999 Parks, Recreation, Leisure and Fitness Studies, Other.

Related DOT Jobs: 159.124-010 Counselor, Camp; 187.167-238 Recreation Supervisor; 195.167-026 Director, Recreation Center; 195.227-010 Program Aide, Group Work; 195.227-014 Recreation Leader; 352.167-010 Director, Social.

39-9041.00 Residential Advisors (Residential Counselors)

Education: Bachelor's degree
Employed: 189,875
Openings: 27,865
Projected Growth: 46.3%
Earnings: $18,840

Coordinate activities for residents of boarding schools, college fraternities or sororities, college dormitories, or similar establishments. Order supplies and determine need for maintenance, repairs, and furnishings. Maintain household records and assign rooms. Refer residents to counseling resources if needed.

Plans menus of meals for residents of establishment. Counsels residents in identifying and resolving social and other problems. Compiles records of daily activities of residents. Escorts individuals on trips outside establishment for shopping or to obtain medical or dental services. Answers telephone. Assigns room, assists in planning recreational activities, and supervises work and study programs. Hires and supervises activities of housekeeping personnel. Chaperons group-sponsored trips and social functions. Ascertains need for and secures service of physician. Orders supplies and determines need for maintenance, repairs, and furnishings. Sorts and distributes mail.

GOE Number, Interest Area, and Work Group: 12.02.02; Education and Social Service; Social Services: Counseling and Social Work. **Personality Type:** Social. Social occupations frequently involve working with, communicating with, and teaching people. These occupations often involve helping or providing service to others. **Work Values:** Social Service; Supervision, Human Relations; Working Conditions; Autonomy; Achievement. **Skills:** Social Perceptiveness; Active Listening; Problem Identification; Coordination; Speaking. **Abilities:** *Cognitive*—Oral Expression; Problem Sensitivity; Oral Comprehension; Speed of Closure; Perceptual Speed; Information Ordering. *Psychomotor*—Reaction Time; Response Orientation; Rate Control. *Physical*—none met the criteria. *Sensory*—Far Vision; Speech Clarity; Speech Recognition. **General Work Activities:** *Information Input*—Monitoring Processes, Materials, and Surroundings; Getting Information Needed to Do the Job; Identifying Objects, Actions, and Events; Inspecting Equipment, Structures, Materials. *Mental Process*—Making Decisions and Solving Problems; Scheduling Work and Activities; Judging Qualities of Things, Services, Other People's Work. *Work Output*—Documenting and Recording Information; Performing General Physical Activities; Implementing Ideas and Programs. *Interacting with Others*—Establishing and Maintaining Relationships; Assisting and Caring for Others; Providing Consultation and Advice to Others. **Physical Work Conditions:** Indoors; Sitting; Standing. **Other Job Characteristics:** Frustrating Circumstances; Importance of Being Aware of New Events; Consequence of Error.

Experience: Job Zone 3. Previous work-related skill, knowledge, or experience is required. **Job Preparation:** SVP 6.0 to less than 7.0—More than 1 year and less than 4 years. **Knowledge:** Customer and Personal Service; Psychology; Therapy and Counseling; Administration and Management; Personnel and Human Resources. **Instructional Programs:** 200201 Child Care and Guidance Workers and Managers, General; 200202 Child Care Provider/Assistant; 200203 Child Care Services Manager.

Related DOT Job: 187.167-186 Residence Supervisor.

41-0000
Sales and Related Occupations

41-1000 Supervisors, Sales Workers

41-1011.00 First-Line Supervisors/Managers of Retail Sales Workers (Marketing and Sales Worker Supervisors)

Education: Work experience in a related occupation

Employed: 2,583,772

Openings: 410,550

Projected Growth: 10.2%

Earnings: $29,570

Directly supervise sales workers in a retail establishment or department. Perform management functions such as purchasing, budgeting, accounting, and personnel work, in addition to supervisory duties.

Prepares rental or lease agreement, specifying charges and payment procedures, for use of machinery, tools, or other such items. Listens to and resolves customer complaints regarding service, product, or personnel. Keeps records pertaining to purchases, sales, and requisitions. Plans and prepares work schedules and assigns employees to specific duties. Examines merchandise to ensure that it is correctly priced, displayed or functions as advertised. Keeps records of employees' work schedules and time cards. Formulates pricing policies on merchandise according to requirements for profitability of store operations. Inventories stock and reorders when inventories drop to specified level. Prepares sales and inventory reports for management and budget departments. Assists sales staff in completing complicated and difficult sales. Hires, trains, and evaluates personnel in sales or marketing establishment. Coordinates sales promotion activities and prepares merchandise displays and advertising copy. Directs and supervises employees engaged in sales, inventory-taking, reconciling cash receipts, or performing specific service such as pumping gasoline for customers. Confers with company officials to develop methods and procedures to increase sales, expand markets, and promote business. Examines products purchased for resale or received for storage to determine condition of product or item.

GOE Number, Interest Area, and Work Group: 10.01.01; Sales and Marketing; Managerial Work in Sales and Marketing. **Personality Type:** Enterprising. Enterprising occupations frequently involve starting up and carrying out projects. These occupations can involve leading people and making many decisions. They sometimes require risk taking and often deal with business. **Work Values:** Authority; Responsibility; Working Conditions; Autonomy; Ability Utilization; Activity; Creativity. **Skills:** Active Listening; Speaking; Coordination; Problem Identification; Reading Comprehension; Mathematics; Management of Personnel Resources. **Abilities:** *Cognitive*—Oral Expression; Oral Comprehension; Written Comprehension; Written Expression; Deductive Reasoning; Originality. *Psychomotor*—none met the criteria. *Physical*—none met the criteria. *Sensory*—Speech Clarity. **General Work Activities:** *Information Input*—Getting Information Needed to Do the Job; Identifying Objects, Actions, and Events; Monitoring Processes, Materials, and Surroundings. *Mental Process*—Scheduling Work and Activities; Analyzing Data or Information; Making Decisions and Solving Problems. *Work Output*—Documenting and Recording Information; Interacting with Computers; Implementing Ideas and Programs; Handling and Moving Objects. *Interacting with Others*—Monitoring and Controlling Resources; Communicating with Other Workers; Staffing Organizational Units. **Physical Work Conditions:** Indoors; Standing; Sitting. **Other Job Characteristics:** Importance of Being Sure All Is Done; Importance of Being Aware of New Events; Consequence of Error.

Experience: Job Zone 3. Previous work-related skill, knowledge, or experience is required. **Job Preparation:** SVP 6.0 to less than 7.0—More than 1 year and less than 4 years. **Knowledge:** Administration and Management; Personnel and Human Resources; Mathematics; Sales and Marketing; Economics and Accounting. **Instructional Programs:** 080101 Apparel and Accessories Marketing Operations, General; 080204 Business Services Marketing Operations; 080299 Business and Personal Services Marketing Operations, Other; 080705 General Retailing Operations; 080706 General Selling Skills and Sales Operations; 080709 General Distribution Operations; 080799 General Retailing and Wholesaling Operations and Skills, Other; 080809 Home Products Marketing Operations; 080810 Office Products Marketing Operations; 081203 Vehicle Parts and Accessories Marketing Operations.

Related DOT Jobs: 185.167-010 Commissary Manager; 185.167-014 Manager, Automobile Service Station; 185.167-022 Manager, Food Concession; 185.167-026 Manager, Machinery-or-Equipment, Rental and Leasing; 185.167-038 Manager, Parts; 185.167-046 Manager, Retail Store; 185.167-066 Vending-Stand Supervisor; 299.137-010 Manager, Department; 299.137-026 Supervisor, Marina Sales and Service.

41-1012.00 First-Line Supervisors/Managers of Non-Retail Sales Workers (Marketing and Sales Worker Supervisors)

Education: Work experience in a related occupation

Employed: 2,583,772

Openings: 410,550

Projected Growth: 10.2%

Earnings: $29,570

Directly supervise and coordinate activities of sales workers other than retail sales workers. Perform duties such as budgeting, accounting, and personnel work, in addition to supervisory duties.

Examines products purchased for resale or received for storage to determine condition of product or item. Hires, trains, and evaluates personnel in sales or marketing establishment. Plans and prepares work schedules and assigns employees to specific duties. Coordinates sales promotion activities and prepares merchandise displays and advertising copy. Prepares sales and inventory reports for management and budget departments. Examines merchandise to ensure that it is correctly priced, displayed or functions as advertised. Prepares rental or lease agreement, specifying charges and payment procedures, for use of machinery, tools, or other such items. Formulates pricing policies on merchandise according to requirements for profitability of store operations. Keeps records pertaining to purchases, sales, and requisitions. Assists sales staff in completing complicated and difficult sales. Confers with company officials to develop methods and procedures to increase sales, expand markets, and promote business. Directs and supervises employees engaged in sales, inventory-taking, reconciling cash receipts, or performing specific service such as pumping gasoline for customers. Inventories stock and reorders when inventories drop to specified level. Listens to and resolves customer complaints regarding service, product, or personnel.

GOE Number, Interest Area, and Work Group: 10.01.01; Sales and Marketing; Managerial Work in Sales and Marketing. **Personality Type:** Enterprising. Enterprising occupations frequently involve starting up and carrying out projects. These occupations can involve leading people and making many decisions. They sometimes require risk taking and often deal with business. **Work Values:** Responsibility; Authority; Autonomy; Working Conditions; Activity; Ability Utilization; Creativity. **Skills:** Speaking; Coordination; Active Listening; Management of Personnel Resources; Mathematics; Reading Comprehension; Problem Identification. **Abilities:** *Cognitive*—Oral Expression; Oral Comprehension; Written Comprehension; Written Expression; Originality; Deductive Reasoning. *Psychomotor*—none met the criteria. *Physical*—none met the criteria. *Sensory*—Speech Clarity. **General Work Activities:** *Information Input*—Getting Information Needed to Do the Job; Identifying Objects, Actions, and Events; Monitoring Processes, Materials, and Surroundings. *Mental Process*—Scheduling Work and Activities; Analyzing Data or Information; Making Decisions and Solving Problems. *Work Output*—Documenting and Recording Information; Interacting with Computers; Handling and Moving Objects; Implementing Ideas and Programs. *Interacting with Others*—Monitoring and Controlling Resources; Staffing Organizational Units; Communicating with Other Workers. **Physical Work Conditions:** Indoors; Standing; Sitting. **Other Job Characteristics:** Importance of Being Sure All Is Done; Importance of Being Aware of New Events; Consequence of Error.

Experience: Job Zone 3. Previous work-related skill, knowledge, or experience is required. **Job Preparation:** SVP 6.0 to less than 7.0—More than 1 year and less than 4 years. **Knowledge:** Administration and Management; Personnel and Human Resources; Mathematics; Sales and Marketing; Economics and Accounting. **Instructional Programs:** 080101 Apparel and Accessories Marketing Operations, General; 080204 Business Services Marketing Operations; 080299 Business and Personal Services Marketing Operations, Other; 080705 General Retailing Operations; 080706 General Selling Skills and Sales Operations; 080709 General Distribution Operations; 080799 General Retailing and Wholesaling Operations and Skills, Other; 080809 Home Products Marketing Operations; 080810 Office Products Marketing Operations; 081203 Vehicle Parts and Accessories Marketing Operations.

Related DOT Jobs: 163.167-014 Manager, Circulation; 169.167-038 Order Department Supervisor; 180.167-010 Artificial-Breeding Distributor; 185.157-018 Wholesaler II; 185.167-030 Manager, Meat Sales and Storage; 185.167-038 Manager, Parts; 185.167-050 Manager, Textile Conversion; 185.167-054 Manager, Tobacco Warehouse; 185.167-070 Wholesaler I; 186.167-034 Manager, Insurance Office; 187.167-098 Manager, Employment Agency; 187.167-138 Manager, Sales; 230.137-010 Supervisor, Advertising-Material Distributors; 291.157-010 Subscription Crew Leader; 293.137-010 Supervisor, Blood-Donor Recruiters; 299.137-014 Sales Supervisor, Malt Liquors.

41-2000 Retail Sales Workers

41-2011.00 Cashiers (Cashiers)

Education: Short-term O-T-J training
Employed: 3,197,813
Openings: 1,290,302
Projected Growth: 17.4%
Earnings: $13,690

Receive and disburse money in establishments other than financial institutions. Use electronic scanners, cash registers, or related equipment. Process credit or debit card transactions and validate checks.

Bags, boxes, or wraps merchandise. Monitors checkout stations, issues and removes cash as needed, and assigns workers to reduce customer delay. Sells tickets and other items to customer. Sorts, counts, and wraps currency and coins. Keeps periodic balance sheet of amount and number of transactions. Computes and records totals of transactions. Operates cash register or electronic scanner. Receives sales slip, cash, check, voucher, or charge payments and issues receipts, refunds, credits, or change due to customer. Cashes checks. Resolves customer's complaints. Answers questions and provides information to customers. Learns prices, stocks shelves, marks prices, weighs items, issues trading stamps, and redeems food stamps and coupons. Compiles and maintains non-monetary reports and records.

GOE Number, Interest Area, and Work Group: 09.05.01; Business Detail; Customer Service. **Personality Type:** Conventional. Conventional occupations frequently involve following set procedures and routines. These occupations can include working with data and details more than with ideas. Usually there is a clear line of authority to follow. **Work Values:** Co-workers; Supervision, Technical; Moral Values; Security; Supervision, Human Relations. **Skills:** Active Listening; Problem Identification; Mathematics; Reading Comprehension; Service Orientation; Writing; Speaking. **Abilities:** *Cognitive*—Oral Expression; Number Facility; Oral Comprehension; Information Ordering; Memorization. *Psychomotor*—Wrist-Finger Speed; Finger Dexterity; Manual Dexterity. *Physical*—Trunk Strength; Extent Flexibility; Dynamic Flexibility. *Sensory*—Near Vision; Speech Clarity; Speech Recognition; Visual Color Discrimination. **General Work Activities:** *Information Input*—Identifying Objects, Actions, and Events; Monitoring Processes, Materials, and Surroundings; Getting Information Needed to Do the Job. *Mental Process*—Updating and Using Job-Relevant Knowledge; Processing Information; Evaluating Information Against Standards. *Work Output*—Controlling Machines and Processes; Handling and Moving Objects; Documenting and Recording Information. *Interacting with Others*—Communicating with Persons Outside Organization; Performing for or Working with the Public; Establishing and Maintaining Relationships. **Physical Work Conditions:** Indoors; Standing; Using Hands on Objects, Tools, or Controls; Sitting. **Other Job Characteristics:** Importance of Being Exact or Accurate; Degree of Automation; Importance of Being Sure All Is Done.

Experience: Job Zone 1. No previous work-related skill, knowledge, or experience is needed. **Job Preparation:** SVP Below 4.0—Less than 6 months. **Knowledge:** Customer and Personal Service; Mathematics; Clerical; English Language; Computers and Electronics. **Instructional Programs:** 080601 Food Products Retailing and Wholesaling Operations; 080705 General Retailing Operations.

Related DOT Jobs: 211.367-010 Paymaster of Purses; 211.462-010 Cashier II; 211.462-014 Cashier-Checker; 211.462-018 Cashier-Wrapper; 211.462-022 Cashier, Gambling; 211.462-026 Check Cashier; 211.462-030 Drivers-Cash Clerk; 211.462-034 Teller; 211.462-038 Toll Collector; 211.467-010 Cashier, Courtesy Booth; 211.467-014 Money Counter; 211.467-018 Parimutuel-Ticket Cashier; 211.467-022 Parimutuel-Ticket Seller; 211.467-026 Sheet Writer; 211.467-030 Ticket Seller; 211.467-034 Change Person; 211.482-010 Cashier, Tube Room; 211.482-014 Food Checker; 249.467-010 Information Clerk-Cashier; 294.567-010 Auction Clerk.

41-2012.00 Gaming Change Persons and Booth Cashiers (Cashiers)

Education: Short-term O-T-J training

Employed: 3,197,813

Openings: 1,290,302

Projected Growth: 17.4%

Earnings: $13,690

Exchange coins and tokens for patron's money. Issue payoffs and obtain customer's signature on receipt when winnings exceed the amount held in the slot machine. Operate a booth in the slot machine area. Furnish change-persons with money-bank at the start of the shift, or count and audit money in drawers.

GOE Number, Interest Area, and Work Group: 09.05.01; Business Detail; Customer Service. **Instructional Programs:** 080601 Food Products Retailing and Wholesaling Operations; 080705 General Retailing Operations. **Note:** The Department of Labor has not collected some data for this job, so it has fewer details than the other descriptions.

41-2021.00 Counter and Rental Clerks (Counter and Rental Clerks)

Education: Short-term O-T-J training

Employed: 468,686

Openings: 199,406

Projected Growth: 23.1%

Earnings: $14,510

Receive orders for repairs, rentals, and services. Describe available options, compute cost, and accept payment.

Collects deposit or payment or records credit charges. Recommends to customer items offered by rental facility that meet customer needs. Reserves items for requested time and keeps record of items rented. Inspects and adjusts rental items to meet needs of customer. Answers telephone and receives orders by phone. Explains rental fees and provides information about rented items, such as operation or description. Computes charges based on rental rate. Prepares rental forms, obtaining customer signature and other information, such as required licenses. Receives, examines, and tags articles to be altered, cleaned, stored, or repaired. Rents item or arranges for provision of service to customer. Greets customers of agency that rents items, such as apparel, tools, and conveyances or that provide services, such as rug cleaning.

GOE Number, Interest Area, and Work Group: 09.05.01; Business Detail; Customer Service. **Personality Type:** Conventional. Conventional occupations frequently involve following set procedures and routines. These occupations can include working with data and details more than with ideas. Usually there is a clear line of authority to follow. **Work Values:** Working Conditions; Co-workers; Moral Values; Supervision, Technical; Supervision, Human Relations. **Skills:** Service Orientation; Reading Comprehension; Active Listening; Mathematics; Speaking; Information Organization; Writing. **Abilities:** *Cognitive*—Oral Comprehension; Oral Expression; Number Facility; Information Ordering; Written Comprehension. *Psychomotor*—Control Precision; Response Orientation. *Physical*—Static Strength; Trunk Strength; Extent Flexibility. *Sensory*—Near Vision; Speech Clarity; Speech Recognition. **General Work Activities:** *Information Input*—Getting Information Needed to Do the Job; Inspecting Equipment, Structures, Materials; Identifying Objects, Actions, and Events. *Mental Process*—Processing Information; Scheduling Work and Activities; Updating and Using Job-Relevant Knowledge. *Work Output*—Documenting and Recording Information; Controlling Machines and Processes; Handling and Moving Objects. *Interacting with Others*—Communicating with Persons Outside Organization; Performing for or Working with the Public; Establishing and Maintaining Relationships; Influencing Others or Selling. **Physical Work Conditions:** Indoors; Standing; Sitting. **Other Job Characteristics:** Importance of Being Exact or Accurate; Importance of Being Sure All Is Done; Consequence of Error; Degree of Automation.

Experience: Job Zone 1. No previous work-related skill, knowledge, or experience is needed. **Job Preparation:** SVP Below 4.0—Less than 6 months. **Knowledge:** Customer and Personal Service; Clerical; Sales and Marketing; English Language; Mathematics. **Instructional Programs:** 080705 General Retailing Operations; 080706 General Selling Skills and Sales Operations; 081299 Vehicle and Petroleum Products Marketing Operations, Other.

Related DOT Jobs: 216.482-030 Laundry Pricing Clerk; 249.362-010 Counter Clerk; 249.366-010 Counter Clerk; 290.477-010 Coupon-Redemption Clerk; 290.477-018 Sales Clerk, Food; 295.357-010 Apparel-Rental Clerk; 295.357-014 Tool-and-Equipment-Rental Clerk; 295.357-018 Furniture-Rental Consultant; 295.367-010 Airplane-Charter Clerk; 295.367-014 Baby-Stroller and Wheelchair Rental Clerk; 295.367-026 Storage-Facility Rental Clerk; 295.467-010 Bicycle-Rental Clerk; 295.467-014 Boat-Rental Clerk; 295.467-018 Hospital-Television-Rental Clerk; 295.467-022 Trailer-Rental Clerk; 295.467-026 Automobile Rental Clerk; 299.367-018 Watch-and-Clock-Repair Clerk; 369.367-010 Fur-Storage Clerk; 369.367-014 Rug Measurer; 369.467-010 Manager, Branch Store (partial list; see the introduction for sources of the complete list).

41-2022.00 Parts Salespersons (Parts Salespersons)

Education: Moderate-term O-T-J training

Employed: 299,688

Openings: 35,323

Projected Growth: 1.2%

Earnings: $22,730

Sell spare and replacement parts and equipment in repair shop or parts store.

Examines returned part for defects, and exchanges defective part or refunds money. Takes inventory of stock. Receives and fills telephone orders for parts. Demonstrates equipment to customer and explains functioning of equipment. Discusses use and features of various parts, based on knowledge of machine or equipment. Measures parts, using precision measuring instruments to determine whether similar parts may be machined to required size. Places new merchandise on display. Marks and stores parts in stockroom according to prearranged system. Determines replacement part required, according to inspection of old part, customer request, or customer description of malfunction. Receives payment or obtains credit authorization. Fills customer orders from stock. Reads catalog, microfiche viewer, or computer display to determine replacement part stock number and price. Advises customer on substitution or modification of part when identical replacement is not available. Repairs parts or equipment. Prepares sales slip or sales contract.

GOE Number, Interest Area, and Work Group: 10.03.01; Sales and Marketing; General Sales. **Personality Type:** Enterprising. Enterprising occupations frequently involve starting up and carrying out projects. These occupations can involve leading people and making many decisions. They sometimes require risk taking and often deal with business. **Work Values:** Working Conditions; Co-workers; Supervision, Human Relations; Supervision, Technical; Independence; Advancement; Company Policies and Practices. **Skills:** Product Inspection; Active Listening; Reading Comprehension; Repairing; Service Orientation. **Abilities:** *Cognitive*—Oral Expression; Oral Comprehension; Written Comprehension; Number Facility; Information Ordering. *Psychomotor*—Finger Dexterity; Wrist-Finger Speed; Manual Dexterity. *Physical*—Extent Flexibility; Static Strength; Trunk Strength. *Sensory*—Near Vision; Speech Recognition; Visual Color Discrimination; Speech Clarity. **General Work Activities:** *Information Input*—Getting Information Needed to Do the Job; Inspecting Equipment, Structures, Materials; Estimating Needed Characteristics. *Mental Process*—Processing Information; Analyzing Data or Information; Updating and Using Job-Relevant Knowledge. *Work Output*—Documenting and Recording Information; Performing General Physical Activities; Handling and Moving Objects. *Interacting with Others*—Communicating with Persons Outside Organization; Influencing Others or Selling; Performing for or Working with the Public. **Physical Work Conditions:** Indoors; Standing; Using Hands on Objects, Tools, or Controls. **Other Job Characteristics:** Importance of Being Exact or Accurate; Importance of Being Sure All Is Done; Degree of Automation; Consequence of Error.

Experience: Job Zone 2. Some previous work-related skill, knowledge, or experience may be helpful, but usually is not needed.

Job Preparation: SVP 4.00 to 5.99—6 months to less than 2 years. **Knowledge:** Mechanical; Customer and Personal Service; English Language; Sales and Marketing; Clerical; Mathematics. **Instructional Programs:** 010501 Agricultural Supplies Retailing and Wholesaling; 080705 General Retailing Operations; 080706 General Selling Skills and Sales Operations; 081203 Vehicle Parts and Accessories Marketing Operations; 081208 Vehicle Marketing Operations.

Related DOT Job: 279.357-062 Salesperson, Parts.

41-2031.00 Retail Salespersons (Retail Salespersons)

Education: Short-term O-T-J training

Employed: 4,056,472

Openings: 1,305,317

Projected Growth: 13.9%

Earnings: $15,830

Sell merchandise such as furniture, motor vehicles, appliances, or apparel, in a retail establishment.

Wraps merchandise. Estimates cost of repair or alteration of merchandise. Estimates and quotes trade-in allowances. Maintains records related to sales. Tickets, arranges, and displays merchandise to promote sales. Estimates quantity and cost of merchandise required, such as paint or floor covering. Greets customer. Totals purchases, receives payment, makes change, or processes credit transaction. Rents merchandise to customers. Fits or assists customers in trying on merchandise. Sells or arranges for delivery, insurance, financing, or service contracts for merchandise. Requisitions new stock. Cleans shelves, counters, and tables. Prepares sales slip or sales contract. Demonstrates use or operation of merchandise. Recommends, selects, and obtains merchandise based on customer needs and desires. Describes merchandise and explains use, operation, and care of merchandise to customers. Computes sales price of merchandise. Inventories stock.

GOE Number, Interest Area, and Work Group: 10.03.01; Sales and Marketing; General Sales. **Personality Type:** Enterprising. Enterprising occupations frequently involve starting up and carrying out projects. These occupations can involve leading people and making many decisions. They sometimes require risk taking and often deal with business. **Work Values:** Co-workers; Supervision, Technical; Working Conditions; Supervision, Human Relations; Advancement. **Skills:** Active Listening; Service Orientation; Problem Identification; Speaking; Mathematics. **Abilities:** *Cognitive*—Oral Expression; Oral Comprehension; Number Facility; Information Ordering; Written Expression; Memorization. *Psychomotor*—Manual Dexterity; Finger Dexterity; Response Orientation. *Physical*—Extent Flexibility; Trunk Strength; Static Strength. *Sensory*—Near Vision; Speech Recognition; Speech Clarity. **General Work Activities:** *Information Input*—Getting Information Needed to Do the Job; Identifying Objects, Actions, and Events; Monitoring Processes, Materials, and Surroundings. *Mental Process*—Updating and Using Job-Relevant Knowledge; Processing Information; Analyzing Data or Information. *Work Output*—Documenting and Recording Information; Controlling Machines and Processes; Handling and Moving Objects. *Interacting with Others*—Influencing Others or Selling; Performing for or Working with the Public; Communicating with Persons Outside Organization. **Physical Work Conditions:** Indoors; Standing; Walking or Running. **Other Job Characteristics:** Importance of Being Sure All Is Done; Importance of Being Exact or Accurate; Consequence of Error; Degree of Automation.

Experience: Job Zone 2. Some previous work-related skill, knowledge, or experience may be helpful, but usually is not needed. **Job Preparation:** SVP 4.00 to 5.99—6 months to less than 2 years. **Knowledge:** Sales and Marketing; Customer and Personal Service; Mathematics; English Language; Clerical. **Instructional Programs:** 010501 Agricultural Supplies Retailing and Wholesaling; 080101 Apparel and Accessories Marketing Operations, General; 080102 Fashion Merchandising; 080199 Apparel and Accessories Marketing Operations, Other; 080503 Floristry Marketing Operations; 080601 Food Products Retailing and Wholesaling Operations; 080705 General Retailing Operations; 080706 General Selling Skills and Sales Operations; 080809 Home Products Marketing Operations; 080903 Recreation Products/Services Marketing Operations; 081203 Vehicle Parts and Accessories Marketing Operations; 081208 Vehicle Marketing Operations; 081301 Health Products and Services Marketing Operations; 089999 Marketing Operations/Marketing and Distribution, Other; 200306 Fashion and Fabric Consultant.

Related DOT Jobs: 260.357-026 Salesperson, Flowers; 261.351-010 Salesperson, Wigs; 261.354-010 Salesperson, Corsets; 261.357-042 Salesperson, Furs; 261.357-046 Salesperson, Infants' and Children's Wear; 261.357-050 Salesperson, Men's and Boys' Clothing; 261.357-054 Salesperson, Men's Furnishings; 261.357-058 Salesperson, Millinery; 261.357-062 Salesperson, Shoes; 261.357-066 Salesperson, Women's Apparel and Accessories; 261.357-070 Salesperson, Yard Goods; 261.357-074 Salesperson, Leather-and-Suede Apparel-and-Accessories; 262.357-018 Salesperson, Cosmetics and Toiletries; 270.352-010 Salesperson, Sewing Machines; 270.357-018 Salesperson, China and Silverware; 270.357-022 Salesperson, Curtains and Draperies; 270.357-026 Salesperson, Floor Coverings; 270.357-030 Salesperson, Furniture; 270.357-034 Salesperson, Household Appliances; 270.357-038 Salesperson, Stereo Equipment (partial list; see the introduction for sources of the complete list).

41-3000 Sales Representatives, Services

41-3011.00 Advertising Sales Agents (Sales Agents, Advertising)

Education: No data available.

Employed: 128,360

Openings: No data available.

Projected Growth: No data available.

Earnings: $31,850

Sell or solicit advertising, including graphic art, advertising space in publications, custom-made signs, or TV and radio advertising time. Obtain leases for outdoor advertising sites. Persuade retailers to use sales promotion display items.

Writes copy as part of layout. Computes job costs. Plans and sketches layouts to meet customer needs. Prepares promotional plans, sales literature, and sales contracts, using computer. Collects payments due. Obtains pertinent information concerning prospect's past and current advertising for use in sales presentation. Prepares list of prospects for classified and display space for publication from leads in other papers and from old accounts. Sells signs to be made according to customers' specifications, utilizing knowledge of lettering, color harmony, and sign making processes. Calls on advertisers and sales promotion people to obtain information concerning prospects for current advertising and sales promotion. Delivers advertising or illustration proofs to customer for approval. Informs customer of types of artwork available by providing samples. Calls on prospects and presents outlines of various programs or commercial announcements. Draws up contract covering arrangements for designing, fabricating, erecting, and maintaining sign or display. Visits advertisers to point out advantages of publication. Exhibits prepared layouts with mats and copy with headings. Advises customer in advantages of various types of programming and methods of composing layouts and designs for signs and displays. Arranges for and accompanies prospect to commercial taping sessions.

GOE Number, Interest Area, and Work Group: 10.02.02; Sales and Marketing; Sales Technology: Intangible Sales. **Personality Type:** Enterprising. Enterprising occupations frequently involve starting up and carrying out projects. These occupations can involve leading people and making many decisions. They sometimes require risk taking and often deal with business. **Work Values:** Achievement; Working Conditions; Ability Utilization; Autonomy; Variety; Creativity. **Skills:** Speaking; Persuasion; Writing; Idea Generation; Reading Comprehension. **Abilities:** *Cognitive*—Oral Comprehension; Oral Expression; Fluency of Ideas; Written Expression; Written Comprehension. *Psychomotor*—none met the criteria. *Physical*—none met the criteria. *Sensory*—Near Vision; Speech Recognition; Speech Clarity. **General Work Activities:** *Information Input*—Getting Information Needed to Do the Job; Identifying Objects, Actions, and Events; Estimating Needed Characteristics. *Mental Process*—Thinking Creatively; Organizing, Planning, and Prioritizing; Making Decisions and Solving Problems. *Work Output*—Implementing Ideas and Programs; Interacting with Computers; Documenting and Recording Information; Drafting and Specifying Technical Devices; Handling and Moving Objects. *Interacting with Others*—Influencing Others or Selling; Communicating with Persons Outside Organization; Establishing and Maintaining Relationships. **Physical Work Conditions:** Indoors; Sitting; Standing. **Other Job Characteristics:** Importance of Being Sure All Is Done; Importance of Being Exact or Accurate; Consequence of Error.

Experience: Job Zone 3. Previous work-related skill, knowledge, or experience is required. **Job Preparation:** SVP 6.0 to less than 7.0—More than 1 year and less than 4 years. **Knowledge:** Sales and Marketing; English Language; Communications and Media; Fine Arts; Mathematics. **Instructional Programs:** 080204 Business Services Marketing Operations; 090201 Advertising.

Related DOT Jobs: 254.251-010 Sales Representative, Graphic Art; 254.257-010 Sales Representative, Signs and Displays; 254.357-014 Sales Representative, Advertising; 254.357-022 Sales Representative, Signs; 259.357-018 Sales Representative, Radio and Television Time.

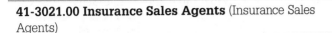

41-3021.00 Insurance Sales Agents (Insurance Sales Agents)

Education: Bachelor's degree
Employed: 387,295
Openings: 39,330
Projected Growth: 2.2%
Earnings: $34,370

Sell life, property, casualty, health, automotive, or other types of insurance. Refer clients to independent brokers, work as independent broker, or be employed by an insurance company.

Selects company that offers type of coverage requested by client to underwrite policy. Establishes client's method of payment. Calls on policyholders to deliver and explain policy, to suggest additions or changes in insurance program, or to change beneficiaries. Explains group insurance programs to promote sale of insurance plan. Explains necessary bookkeeping requirements for customer to implement and provide group insurance program. Advises clients of broker (independent agent) in selecting casualty, life, or property insurance. Contacts underwriter and submits forms to obtain binder coverage. Plans and oversees incorporation of insurance program into bookkeeping system of company. Discusses advantages and disadvantages of various policies. Installs bookkeeping systems and resolves system problems.

GOE Number, Interest Area, and Work Group: 10.02.02; Sales and Marketing; Sales Technology: Intangible Sales. **Personality Type:** Enterprising. Enterprising occupations frequently involve starting up and carrying out projects. These occupations can involve leading people and making many decisions. They sometimes require risk taking and often deal with business. **Work Values:** Working Conditions; Responsibility; Advancement; Autonomy; Ability Utilization; Company Policies and Practices. **Skills:** Speaking; Reading Comprehension; Critical Thinking; Persuasion; Active Listening; Identification of Key Causes. **Abilities:** *Cognitive*—Oral Expression; Written Comprehension; Oral Comprehension; Written Expression; Number Facility. *Psychomotor*—none met the criteria. *Physical*—none met the criteria. *Sensory*—Speech Clarity; Speech Recognition; Auditory Attention. **General Work Activities:** *Information Input*—Getting Information Needed to Do the Job; Identifying Objects, Actions, and Events; Estimating Needed Characteristics. *Mental Process*—Judging Qualities of Things, Services, Other People's Work; Evaluating Information Against Standards; Analyzing Data or Information. *Work Output*—Documenting and Recording Information; Interacting with Computers; Implementing Ideas and Programs. *Interacting with Others*—Influencing Others or Selling; Communicating with Persons Outside Organization; Performing for or Working with the Public. **Physical Work Conditions:** Indoors; Sitting; Standing. **Other Job Characteristics:** Importance of Being Sure All Is Done; Consequence of Error; Importance of Being Exact or Accurate.

Experience: Job Zone 3. Previous work-related skill, knowledge, or experience is required. **Job Preparation:** SVP 6.0 to less than 7.0—More than 1 year and less than 4 years. **Knowledge:** Sales and Marketing; Clerical; Mathematics; English Language; Administration and Management. **Instructional Programs:** 081001 Insurance Marketing Operations; 520805 Insurance and Risk Management.

Related DOT Jobs: 169.167-050 Special Agent, Group Insurance; 186.167-010 Estate Planner; 239.267-010 Placer; 250.257-010 Sales Agent, Insurance.

41-3031.00 Securities, Commodities, and Financial Services Sales Agents (Securities, Commodities, and Financial Services Sales Agents)

Education: Bachelor's degree
Employed: 303,053
Openings: 61,084
Projected Growth: 41%
Earnings: $48,090

Buy and sell securities in investment and trading firms, or call upon businesses and individuals to sell financial services. Provide financial services such as loan, tax, and securities counseling. Advise securities customers about such things as stocks, bonds, and market conditions.

GOE Number, Interest Area, and Work Group: 10.02.02; Sales and Marketing; Sales Technology: Intangible Sales. **Instructional Programs:** 080401 Financial Services Marketing Operations; 520804 Financial Planning; 520807 Investments and Securities. **Note:** The Department of Labor has not collected some data for this job, so it has fewer details than the other descriptions.

41-3031.01 Sales Agents, Securities and Commodities (Securities, Commodities, and Financial Services Sales Agents)

Education: Bachelor's degree
Employed: 303,053
Openings: 61,084
Projected Growth: 41%
Earnings: $48,090

Buy and sell securities in investment and trading firms; develop and implement financial plans for individuals, businesses, and organizations.

Identifies potential clients, using advertising campaigns, mailing lists, and personal contacts and solicits business. Contacts exchange or brokerage firm to execute order or buys and sell securities based on market quotation and competition in market. Analyzing market conditions to determine optimum time to execute securities transactions. Reviews all securities transactions to ensure accuracy of information and that trades conform to regulations of governing agencies. Prepares documents to implement plan selected by client. Completes sales order tickets and submits for processing of client requested transaction. Prepares financial reports to monitor client or corporate finances. Reads corporate reports and calculates ratios to determine best prospects for profit on stock purchase and to monitor client account. Interviews client to determine client's assets, liabilities, cash flow, insurance coverage, tax status, and financial objectives. Keeps informed about political and economic trends that influence stock prices. Records transactions accurately and keeps client informed about transactions. Develops financial plan based on analysis of client's financial status, and discusses financial options with client. Informs and advises concerned parties regarding fluctuations and securities transactions affecting plan or account.

GOE Number, Interest Area, and Work Group: 10.02.02; Sales and Marketing; Sales Technology: Intangible Sales. **Personality Type:** Enterprising. Enterprising occupations frequently involve starting up and carrying out projects. These occupations can involve leading people and making many decisions. They sometimes require risk taking and often deal with business. **Work Values:** Compensation; Recognition; Working Conditions; Responsibility; Autonomy. **Skills:** Identifying Downstream Consequences; Information Gathering; Systems Perception; Management of Financial Resources; Systems Evaluation. **Abilities:** *Cognitive*—Deductive Reasoning; Oral Comprehension; Written Comprehension; Written Expression; Oral Expression; Number Facility. *Psychomotor*—none met the criteria. *Physical*—none met the criteria. *Sensory*—Near Vision; Speech Recognition; Speech Clarity. **General Work Activities:** *Information Input*—Getting Information Needed to Do the Job; Identifying Objects, Actions, and Events; Estimating Needed Characteristics. *Mental Process*—Updating and Using Job-Relevant Knowledge; Analyzing Data or Information; Judging Qualities of Things, Services, Other People's Work; Processing Information. *Work Output*—Documenting and Recording Information; Implementing Ideas and Programs; Interacting with Computers. *Interacting with Others*—Providing Consultation and Advice to Others; Communicating with Persons Outside Organization; Monitoring and Controlling Resources. **Physical Work Conditions:** Indoors; Sitting; Using Hands on Objects, Tools, or Controls. **Other Job Characteristics:** Consequence of Error; Frustrating Circumstances; Importance of Being Exact or Accurate.

Experience: Job Zone 4. A minimum of two to four years of work-related skill, knowledge, or experience is needed. **Job Preparation:** SVP 7.0 to less than 8.0—2 years to less than 10 years. **Knowledge:** Economics and Accounting; Mathematics; Sales and Marketing; English Language; Customer and Personal Service; Clerical. **Instructional Programs:** 080401 Financial Services Marketing Operations; 520804 Financial Planning; 520807 Investments and Securities.

Related DOT Jobs: 162.157-010 Broker-and-Market Operator, Grain; 162.167-034 Floor Broker; 162.167-038 Securities Trader; 250.257-014 Financial Planner; 250.257-018 Registered Representative.

41-3031.02 Sales Agents, Financial Services (Securities, Commodities, and Financial Services Sales Agents)

Education: Bachelor's degree
Employed: 303,053
Openings: 61,084
Projected Growth: 41%
Earnings: $48,090

Sell financial services such as loan, tax, and securities counseling to customers of financial institutions and business establishments.

Prepares forms or agreement to complete sale. Sells services and equipment, such as trust, investment, and check processing services. Makes presentations on financial services to groups to attract new clients. Evaluates costs and revenue of agreements to determine continued profitability. Develops prospects from current commercial customers, referral leads, and sales and trade meetings. Contacts prospective customers to present information and explain available services. Determines customers' financial services needs and prepares proposals to sell services. Reviews business trends and advises customers regarding expected fluctuations.

GOE Number, Interest Area, and Work Group: 10.02.02; Sales and Marketing; Sales Technology: Intangible Sales. **Personality Type:** Enterprising. Enterprising occupations frequently involve starting up and carrying out projects. These occupations can involve leading people and making many decisions. They sometimes require risk taking and often deal with business. **Work Values:** Compensation; Working Conditions; Recognition; Responsibility; Autonomy. **Skills:** Systems Perception; Persuasion; Information Gathering; Active Learning; Monitoring. **Abilities:** *Cognitive*—Oral Expression; Number Facility; Deductive Reasoning; Written Comprehension; Mathematical Reasoning. *Psychomotor*—none met the criteria. *Physical*—none met the criteria. *Sensory*—Near Vision; Speech Clarity; Speech Recognition. **General Work Activities:** *Information Input*—Getting Information Needed to Do the Job; Identifying Objects, Actions, and Events; Monitoring Processes, Materials, and Surroundings. *Mental Process*—Making Decisions and Solving Problems; Updating and Using Job-Relevant Knowledge; Judging Qualities of Things, Services, Other People's Work. *Work Output*—Documenting and Recording Information; Implementing Ideas and Programs; Handling and Moving Objects. *Interacting with Others*—Communicating with Persons Outside Organization; Influencing Others or Selling; Interpreting Meaning of Information to Others. **Physical Work Conditions:** Indoors; Sitting; Standing; Using Hands on Objects, Tools, or Controls. **Other Job Characteristics:** Consequence of Error; Importance of Being Exact or Accurate; Importance of Being Sure All Is Done.

Experience: Job Zone 3. Previous work-related skill, knowledge, or experience is required. **Job Preparation:** SVP 6.0 to less than 7.0—More than 1 year and less than 4 years. **Knowledge:** Economics and Accounting; Sales and Marketing; Mathematics; English Language; Law, Government and Jurisprudence. **Instructional Programs:** 080401 Financial Services Marketing Operations; 520804 Financial Planning; 520807 Investments and Securities.

Related DOT Jobs: 250.257-022 Sales Representative, Financial Services; 250.357-026 Sales Agent, Financial-Report Service.

41-3041.00 Travel Agents (Travel Agents)

Education: Postsecondary vocational training
Employed: 137,897
Openings: 17,019
Projected Growth: 18.4%
Earnings: $23,010

Plan and sell transportation and accommodations for travel agency customers. Determine destination, modes of transportation, travel dates, costs, and accommodations required.

Converses with customer to determine destination, mode of transportation, travel dates, financial considerations, and accommodations required. Prints or requests transportation carrier tickets, using computer printer system or system link to travel carrier. Provides customer with brochures and publications containing travel information, such as local customs, points of interest, or foreign country regulations. Books transportation and hotel reservations, using computer terminal or telephone. Computes cost of travel and accommodations, using calculator, computer, carrier tariff books, and hotel rate books, or quotes package tour's costs. Plans, describes, arranges, and sells itinerary tour packages and promotional travel incentives offered by various travel carriers. Collects payment for transportation and accommodations from customer.

GOE Number, Interest Area, and Work Group: 10.03.01; Sales and Marketing; General Sales. **Personality Type:** Enterprising. Enterprising occupations frequently involve starting up and carrying out projects. These occupations can involve leading people and making many decisions. They sometimes require risk taking and often deal with business. **Work Values:** Working Conditions; Moral Values; Autonomy; Social Service; Achievement; Recognition. **Skills:** Reading Comprehension; Service Orientation; Active Listening; Problem Identification; Speaking; Critical Thinking; Coordination; Information Gathering. **Abilities:** *Cognitive*—Oral Expression; Oral Comprehension; Fluency of Ideas; Written Comprehension; Mathematical Reasoning. *Psychomotor*—none met the criteria. *Physical*—none met the criteria. *Sensory*—Speech Recognition. **General Work Activities:** *Information Input*—Getting Information Needed to Do the Job; Identifying Objects, Actions, and Events; Estimating Needed Characteristics. *Mental Process*—Processing Information; Updating and Using Job-Relevant Knowledge; Scheduling Work and Activities. *Work Output*—Interacting with Computers; Documenting and Recording Information; Handling and Moving Objects. *Interacting with Others*—Influencing Others or Selling; Performing for or Working with the Public; Communicating with Persons Outside Organization. **Physical Work Conditions:** Indoors; Sitting; Using Hands on Objects, Tools, or Controls. **Other Job Characteristics:** Importance of Being Exact or Accurate; Consequence of Error; Importance of Being Sure All Is Done.

Experience: Job Zone 2. Some previous work-related skill, knowledge, or experience may be helpful, but usually is not needed. **Job Preparation:** SVP 4.00 to 5.99—6 months to less than 2 years. **Knowledge:** Customer and Personal Service; Geography; Transportation; Computers and Electronics; Sales and Marketing. **Instructional Program:** 081105 Travel Services Marketing Operations. **Related DOT Job:** 252.152-010 Travel Agent.

41-4000 Sales Representatives, Wholesale and Manufacturing

41-4011.00 Sales Representatives, Wholesale and Manufacturing, Technical and Scientific Products
(Sales Representatives, Except Retail and Scientific and Related Products and Services)

Education: No data available.

Employed: 1,137,880

Openings: No data available.

Projected Growth: No data available.

Earnings: $36,540

Sell goods for wholesalers or manufacturers where technical or scientific knowledge is required, in such areas as biology, engineering, chemistry, and electronics, normally obtained from at least 2 years of postsecondary education.

GOE Number, Interest Area, and Work Group: 10.02.01; Sales and Marketing; Sales Technology: Technical Sales. **Instructional Programs:** 010501 Agricultural Supplies Retailing and Wholesaling; 080101 Apparel and Accessories Marketing Operations, General; 080102 Fashion Merchandising; 080199 Apparel and Accessories Marketing Operations, Other; 080299 Business and Personal Services Marketing Operations, Other; 080601 Food Products Retailing and Wholesaling Operations; 080705 General Retailing Operations; 080706 General Selling Skills and Sales Operations; 080799 General Retailing and Wholesaling Operations and Skills, Other; 080810 Office Products Marketing Operations; 089999 Marketing Operations/Marketing and Distribution, Other; 200306 Fashion and Fabric Consultant. **Note:** The Department of Labor has not collected some data for this job, so it has fewer details than the other descriptions.

41-4011.01 Sales Representatives, Agricultural
(Sales Representatives, Scientific and Related Products and Services, Except Retail)

Education: No data available.

Employed: 441,570

Openings: No data available.

Projected Growth: No data available.

Earnings: $44,690

Sell agricultural products and services such as animal feeds, farm and garden equipment, and dairy, poultry, and veterinarian supplies.

Consults with customer regarding installation, set-up, or layout of agricultural equipment and machines. Compiles lists of prospective customers for use as sales leads. Quotes prices and credit terms. Displays or shows customer agricultural related products. Prepares sales contracts for orders obtained. Demonstrates use of agricultural equipment or machines. Prepares reports of business transactions. Solicits orders from customers in person or by phone. Recommends changes in customer use of agricultural products to improve production. Informs customer of estimated delivery schedule, service contracts, warranty, or other information pertaining to purchased products.

GOE Number, Interest Area, and Work Group: 10.02.01; Sales and Marketing; Sales Technology: Technical Sales. **Personality Type:** Enterprising. Enterprising occupations frequently involve starting up and carrying out projects. These occupations can involve leading people and making many decisions. They sometimes require risk taking and often deal with business. **Work Values:** Achievement; Responsibility; Moral Values; Ability Utilization; Autonomy. **Skills:** Active Listening; Speaking; Writing; Reading Comprehension; Mathematics; Problem Identification; Persuasion. **Abilities:** *Cognitive*—Oral Expression; Oral Comprehension; Written Expression; Written Comprehension; Fluency of Ideas. *Psychomotor*—none met the criteria. *Physical*—none met the criteria. *Sensory*—Speech Recognition; Speech Clarity. **General Work Activities:** *Information Input*—Getting Information Needed to Do the Job; Estimating Needed Characteristics; Identifying Objects, Actions, and Events. *Mental Process*—Updating and Using Job-Relevant Knowledge; Organizing, Planning, and Prioritizing; Thinking Creatively. *Work Output*—Handling and Moving Objects; Documenting and Recording Information; Controlling Machines and Processes. *Interacting with Others*—Influencing Others or Selling; Communicating with Persons Outside Organization; Establishing and Maintaining Relationships; Performing for or Working with the Public. **Physical Work Conditions:** Standing; Indoors; Using Hands on Objects, Tools, or Controls. **Other Job Characteristics:** Consequence of Error; Importance of Being Sure All Is Done; Importance of Being Exact or Accurate.

Experience: Job Zone 2. Some previous work-related skill, knowledge, or experience may be helpful, but usually is not needed. **Job Preparation:** SVP 4.00 to 5.99—6 months to less than 2 years. **Knowledge:** Sales and Marketing; Mathematics; Economics and Accounting; English Language; Customer and Personal Service. **Instructional Programs:** 010501 Agricultural Supplies Retailing and Wholesaling; 080705 General Retailing Operations; 080706 General Selling Skills and Sales Operations; 080810 Office Products Marketing Operations; 081301 Health Products and Services Marketing Operations.

Related DOT Jobs: 272.357-010 Sales Representative, Animal-Feed Products; 272.357-014 Sales Representative, Farm and Garden Equipment and Supplies; 272.357-018 Sales Representative, Poultry Equipment and Supplies; 274.357-030 Sales Representative, Dairy Supplies; 276.357-018 Sales Representative, Veterinarian Supplies; 299.251-010 Sales-Service Representative, Milking Machines.

41-4011.02 Sales Representatives, Chemical and Pharmaceutical (Sales Representatives, Scientific and Related Products and Services, Except Retail)

Education: No data available.

Employed: 441,570

Openings: No data available.

Projected Growth: No data available.

Earnings: $44,690

Sell chemical or pharmaceutical products or services such as acids, industrial chemicals, agricultural chemicals, medicines, drugs, and water treatment supplies.

Promotes and sells pharmaceutical and chemical products to potential customers. Distributes drug samples to customer and takes orders for pharmaceutical supply items from customer. Explains water treatment package benefits to customer and sells chemicals to treat and resolve water process problems. Discusses characteristics and clinical studies pertaining to pharmaceutical products with physicians, dentists, hospitals, and retail/wholesale establishments. Inspects, tests, and observes chemical changes in water system equipment, utilizing test kit, reference manual, and knowledge of chemical treatment. Estimates and advises customer of service costs to correct water-treatment process problems.

GOE Number, Interest Area, and Work Group: 10.02.01; Sales and Marketing; Sales Technology: Technical Sales. **Personality Type:** Enterprising. Enterprising occupations frequently involve starting up and carrying out projects. These occupations can involve leading people and making many decisions. They sometimes require risk taking and often deal with business. **Work Values:** Compensation; Moral Values; Achievement; Ability Utilization; Autonomy; Recognition; Working Conditions; Responsibility. **Skills:** Speaking; Active Listening; Reading Comprehension; Persuasion; Science; Critical Thinking; Social Perceptiveness. **Abilities:** *Cognitive*—Oral Expression; Oral Comprehension; Written Comprehension; Information Ordering; Written Expression. *Psychomotor*—none met the criteria. *Physical*—none met the criteria. *Sensory*—Speech Clarity; Speech Recognition. **General Work Activities:** *Information Input*—Inspecting Equipment, Structures, Materials; Getting Information Needed to Do the Job; Estimating Needed Characteristics. *Mental Process*—Updating and Using Job-Relevant Knowledge; Organizing, Planning, and Prioritizing; Making Decisions and Solving Problems; Evaluating Information Against Standards; Processing Information. *Work Output*—Documenting and Recording Information; Handling and Moving Objects; Performing General Physical Activities; Controlling Machines and Processes. *Interacting with Others*—Communicating with Persons Outside Organization; Influencing Others or Selling; Establishing and Maintaining Relationships. **Physical Work Conditions:** Indoors; Sitting; Standing. **Other Job Characteristics:** Consequence of Error; Frustrating Circumstances; Importance of Being Exact or Accurate; Importance of Being Sure All Is Done.

Experience: Job Zone 3. Previous work-related skill, knowledge, or experience is required. **Job Preparation:** SVP 6.0 to less than 7.0—More than 1 year and less than 4 years. **Knowledge:** Sales and Marketing; Chemistry; Mathematics; English Language; Economics and Accounting. **Instructional Programs:** 010501 Agricultural Supplies Retailing and Wholesaling; 080705 General Retailing Operations; 080706 General Selling Skills and Sales Operations; 080810 Office Products Marketing Operations; 081301 Health Products and Services Marketing Operations.

Related DOT Jobs: 262.157-010 Pharmaceutical Detailer; 262.357-010 Sales Representative, Chemicals and Drugs; 262.357-022 Sales Representative, Water-Treatment Chemicals.

41-4011.03 Sales Representatives, Electrical/Electronic (Sales Representatives, Scientific and Related Products and Services, Except Retail)

Education: No data available.

Employed: 441,570

Openings: No data available.

Projected Growth: No data available.

Earnings: $44,690

Sell electrical, electronic, or related products or services such as communication equipment, radiographic-inspection equipment and services, ultrasonic equipment, electronics parts, computers, and EDP systems.

Recommends equipment to meet customer requirements, considering salable features, such as flexibility, cost, capacity, and economy of operation. Negotiates terms of sale and services with customer. Analyzes communication needs of customer and consults with staff engineers regarding technical problems. Sells electrical or electronic equipment, such as computers, data processing and radiographic equipment to businesses and industrial establishments. Trains establishment personnel in equipment use, utilizing knowledge of electronics and product sold.

GOE Number, Interest Area, and Work Group: 10.02.01; Sales and Marketing; Sales Technology: Technical Sales. **Personality Type:** Enterprising. Enterprising occupations frequently involve starting up and carrying out projects. These occupations can involve leading people and making many decisions. They sometimes require risk taking and often deal with business. **Work Values:** Working Conditions; Moral Values; Achievement; Ability Utilization; Autonomy; Compensation. **Skills:** Persuasion; Active Listening; Instructing; Speaking; Problem Identification. **Abilities:** *Cognitive*—Oral Expression; Oral Comprehension; Written Comprehension; Number Facility; Deductive Reasoning. *Psychomotor*—Control Precision. *Physical*—none met the criteria. *Sensory*—Speech Clarity; Speech Recognition. **General Work Activities:** *Information Input*—Getting Information Needed to Do the Job; Estimating Needed Characteristics; Identifying Objects, Actions, and Events. *Mental Process*—Analyzing Data or Information; Updating and Using Job-Relevant Knowledge; Making Decisions and Solving Problems. *Work Output*—Interacting with Computers; Handling and Moving Objects; Performing General Physical Activities. *Interacting with Others*—Influencing Others or Selling; Communicating with Persons Outside Organization; Performing for or Working with the Public. **Physical Work Conditions:** Indoors; Standing; Sitting. **Other Job Characteristics:** Consequence of Error; Frustrating Circumstances; Importance of Being Aware of New Events.

Experience: Job Zone 2. Some previous work-related skill, knowledge, or experience may be helpful, but usually is not needed. **Job Preparation:** SVP 4.00 to 5.99—6 months to less than 2 years. **Knowledge:** Sales and Marketing; Computers and Electronics; Economics and Accounting; Mathematics; Education and Training. **Instructional Programs:** 010501 Agricultural Supplies Retailing and Wholesaling; 080705 General Retailing Operations; 080706 General Selling Skills and Sales Operations; 080810 Office Products Marketing Operations; 081301 Health Products and Services Marketing Operations.

Related DOT Jobs: 271.257-010 Sales Representative, Communication Equipment; 271.352-010 Sales Representative, Radiographic-Inspection Equipment and Services; 271.352-014 Sales Representative, Ultrasonic Equipment; 271.357-010 Sales Representative, Electronics Parts; 275.257-010 Sales Representative, Computers and EDP Systems.

41-4011.04 Sales Representatives, Mechanical Equipment and Supplies (Sales Representatives, Scientific and Related Products and Services, Except Retail)

Education: No data available.

Employed: 441,570

Openings: No data available.

Projected Growth: No data available.

Earnings: $44,690

Sell mechanical equipment, machinery, materials, and supplies such as aircraft and railroad equipment and parts, construction machinery, material-handling equipment, industrial machinery, and welding equipment.

Appraises equipment and verifies customer credit rating to establish trade-in value and contract terms. Contacts current and potential customers, visits establishments to evaluate needs, and promotes sale of products and services. Submits orders for product and follows up on order to verify material list accuracy and delivery schedule meets project deadline. Reviews existing machinery/equipment placement and diagrams proposal to illustrate efficient space utilization, using standard measuring devices and templates. Attends sales and trade meetings and reads related publications to obtain current market condition information, business trends, and industry developments. Demonstrates and explains use of installed equipment and production processes. Arranges for installation and test-operation of machinery and recommends solutions to product-related problems. Computes installation or production costs, estimates savings, and prepares and submits bid specifications to customer for review and approval. Recommends and sells textile, industrial, construction, railroad, and oil field machinery, equipment, materials, and supplies, and services utilizing knowledge of machine operations. Inspects establishment premises to verify installation feasibility, and obtains building blueprints and elevator specifications to submit to engineering department for bid.

GOE Number, Interest Area, and Work Group: 10.02.01; Sales and Marketing; Sales Technology: Technical Sales. **Personality Type:** Enterprising. Enterprising occupations frequently involve starting up and carrying out projects. These occupations can involve leading people and making many decisions. They sometimes require risk taking and often deal with business. **Work Values:** Autonomy; Achievement; Company Policies and Practices; Variety; Compensation. **Skills:** Active Listening; Speaking; Reading Comprehension; Equipment Selection; Operations Analysis. **Abilities:** *Cognitive*—Number Facility; Mathematical Reasoning; Oral Expression; Oral Comprehension; Written Comprehension. *Psychomotor*—none met the criteria. *Physical*—none met the criteria. *Sensory*—Speech Clarity; Speech Recognition; Auditory Attention. **General Work Activities:** *Information Input*—Getting

Information Needed to Do the Job; Estimating Needed Characteristics; Inspecting Equipment, Structures, Materials; Identifying Objects, Actions, and Events. *Mental Process*—Updating and Using Job-Relevant Knowledge; Processing Information; Evaluating Information Against Standards. *Work Output*—Performing General Physical Activities; Controlling Machines and Processes; Handling and Moving Objects. *Interacting with Others*—Influencing Others or Selling; Communicating with Persons Outside Organization; Establishing and Maintaining Relationships. **Physical Work Conditions:** Indoors; Standing; Sitting. **Other Job Characteristics:** Frustrating Circumstances; Consequence of Error; Importance of Being Sure All Is Done.

Experience: Job Zone 2. Some previous work-related skill, knowledge, or experience may be helpful, but usually is not needed. **Job Preparation:** SVP 4.00 to 5.99—6 months to less than 2 years. **Knowledge:** Sales and Marketing; Mathematics; Economics and Accounting; Mechanical; Communications and Media. **Instructional Programs:** 010501 Agricultural Supplies Retailing and Wholesaling; 080705 General Retailing Operations; 080706 General Selling Skills and Sales Operations; 080810 Office Products Marketing Operations; 081301 Health Products and Services Marketing Operations.

Related DOT Jobs: 259.257-014 Sales Representative, Electroplating; 273.253-010 Sales Representative, Aircraft; 273.357-010 Sales Representative, Aircraft Equipment and Parts; 273.357-026 Sales Representative, Railroad Equipment and Supplies; 274.157-010 Sales Representative, Elevators, Escalators, and Dumbwaiters; 274.257-010 Sales Representative, Foundry and Machine Shop Products; 274.357-010 Sales Representative, Abrasives; 274.357-018 Sales Representative, Building Equipment and Supplies; 274.357-022 Sales Representative, Construction Machinery; 274.357-038 Sales Representative, Industrial Machinery; 274.357-046 Sales Representative, Lubricating Equipment; 274.357-050 Sales Representative, Material-Handling Equipment; 274.357-054 Sales Representative, Metals; 274.357-058 Sales Representative, Oil Field Supplies and Equipment; 274.357-070 Sales Representative, Textile Machinery; 274.357-074 Sales Representative, Welding Equipment; 274.357-078 Sales Representative, Wire Rope.

41-4011.05 Sales Representatives, Medical (Sales Representatives, Scientific and Related Products and Services, Except Retail)

Education: No data available.

Employed: 441,570

Openings: No data available.

Projected Growth: No data available.

Earnings: $44,690

Sell medical equipment, products, and services. Does not include pharmaceutical sales representatives.

Designs and fabricates custom-made medical appliances. Advises customer regarding office layout, legal and insurance regulations, cost analysis, and collection methods. Selects surgical appliances from stock and fits and sells appliance to customer. Promotes sale of medical and dental equipment, supplies, and services to doctors, dentists, hospitals, medical schools, and retail establishments. Writes specifications to order custom-made surgical appliances, using customer measurements and physician prescriptions. Studies data describing new products to accurately recommend purchase of equipment and supplies.

GOE Number, Interest Area, and Work Group: 10.02.01; Sales and Marketing; Sales Technology: Technical Sales. **Personality Type:** Enterprising. Enterprising occupations frequently involve starting up and carrying out projects. These occupations can involve leading people and making many decisions. They sometimes require risk taking and often deal with business. **Work Values:** Autonomy; Compensation; Company Policies and Practices; Achievement; Working Conditions. **Skills:** Active Listening; Reading Comprehension; Writing; Speaking; Persuasion; Equipment Selection; Operations Analysis; Problem Identification. **Abilities:** *Cognitive*—Oral Expression; Oral Comprehension; Written Expression; Written Comprehension; Mathematical Reasoning. *Psychomotor*—none met the criteria. *Physical*—none met the criteria. *Sensory*—Speech Recognition; Speech Clarity. **General Work Activities:** *Information Input*—Getting Information Needed to Do the Job; Estimating Needed Characteristics; Identifying Objects, Actions, and Events. *Mental Process*—Updating and Using Job-Relevant Knowledge; Analyzing Data or Information; Processing Information; Making Decisions and Solving Problems. *Work Output*—Handling and Moving Objects; Drafting and Specifying Technical Devices; Implementing Ideas and Programs. *Interacting with Others*—Influencing Others or Selling; Communicating with Persons Outside Organization; Establishing and Maintaining Relationships. **Physical Work Conditions:** Indoors; Standing; Sitting. **Other Job Characteristics:** Consequence of Error; Importance of Being Exact or Accurate; Importance of Being Sure All Is Done.

Experience: Job Zone 3. Previous work-related skill, knowledge, or experience is required. **Job Preparation:** SVP 6.0 to less than 7.0—More than 1 year and less than 4 years. **Knowledge:** Sales and Marketing; Mathematics; Engineering and Technology; Design; Economics and Accounting. **Instructional Programs:** 010501 Agricultural Supplies Retailing and Wholesaling; 080705 General Retailing Operations; 080706 General Selling Skills and Sales Operations; 080810 Office Products Marketing Operations; 081301 Health Products and Services Marketing Operations.

Related DOT Jobs: 276.257-010 Sales Representative, Dental and Medical Equipment and Supplies; 276.257-022 Salesperson, Surgical Appliances.

41-4011.06 Sales Representatives, Instruments (Sales Representatives, Scientific and Related Products and Services, Except Retail)

Education: No data available.

Employed: 441,570

Openings: No data available.

Projected Growth: No data available.

Earnings: $44,690

Sell precision instruments such as dynamometers and spring scales, and laboratory, navigation, and surveying instruments.

Assists customer with product selection, utilizing knowledge of engineering specifications and catalog resources. Sells weighing and other precision instruments, such as spring scales, dynamometers, and laboratory, navigational, and surveying instruments to customer. Evaluates customer needs and emphasizes product features based on technical knowledge of product capabilities and limitations.

GOE Number, Interest Area, and Work Group: 10.02.01; Sales and Marketing; Sales Technology: Technical Sales. **Personality Type:** Enterprising. Enterprising occupations frequently involve starting up and carrying out projects. These occupations can involve leading people and making many decisions. They sometimes require risk taking and often deal with business. **Work Values:** Autonomy; Working Conditions; Achievement; Compensation; Responsibility; Recognition; Company Policies and Practices; Supervision, Human Relations. **Skills:** Persuasion; Active Listening; Speaking; Reading Comprehension; Mathematics; Instructing; Service Orientation. **Abilities:** *Cognitive*—Oral Expression; Oral Comprehension; Written Comprehension; Number Facility; Deductive Reasoning. *Psychomotor*—none met the criteria. *Physical*—none met the criteria. *Sensory*—Speech Clarity; Speech Recognition. **General Work Activities:** *Information Input*—Getting Information Needed to Do the Job; Identifying Objects, Actions, and Events; Estimating Needed Characteristics. *Mental Process*—Updating and Using Job-Relevant Knowledge; Analyzing Data or Information; Processing Information. *Work Output*—Handling and Moving Objects; Controlling Machines and Processes; Performing General Physical Activities. *Interacting with Others*—Influencing Others or Selling; Communicating with Persons Outside Organization; Establishing and Maintaining Relationships; Providing Consultation and Advice to Others. **Physical Work Conditions:** Indoors; Standing; Sitting. **Other Job Characteristics:** Frustrating Circumstances; Importance of Being Exact or Accurate; Consequence of Error.

Experience: Job Zone 3. Previous work-related skill, knowledge, or experience is required. **Job Preparation:** SVP 6.0 to less than 7.0—More than 1 year and less than 4 years. **Knowledge:** Sales and Marketing; English Language; Customer and Personal Service; Computers and Electronics; Mechanical; Engineering and Technology. **Instructional Programs:** 010501 Agricultural Supplies Retailing and Wholesaling; 080705 General Retailing Operations; 080706 General Selling Skills and Sales Operations; 080810 Office Products Marketing Operations; 081301 Health Products and Services Marketing Operations.

Related DOT Jobs: 276.257-014 Sales Representative, Weighing and Force-Measurement Instruments; 276.357-014 Sales Representative, Precision Instruments.

41-4012.00 Sales Representatives, Wholesale and Manufacturing, Except Technical and Scientific Products (Sales Representatives, Except Retail and Scientific and Related Products and Services)

Education: No data available.

Employed: 1,137,880

Openings: No data available.

Projected Growth: No data available.

Earnings: $36,540

Sell goods for wholesalers or manufacturers to businesses or groups of individuals. Have substantial knowledge of items sold.

Assists and advises retail dealers in use of sales promotion techniques. Recommends products to customers, based on customer's specific needs and interests. Answers questions about products, prices, durability and credit terms. Estimates delivery dates and arranges delivery schedules. Obtains credit information on prospective customers. Oversees delivery or installation of products or equipment. Instructs customers in use of products. Investigates and resolves customer complaints. Meets with customers to demonstrate and explain features of products. Completes sales contracts or forms to record sales information. Contacts regular and prospective customers to solicit orders. Forwards orders to manufacturer. Reviews sales records and current market information to determine value or sales potential of product. Prepares lists of prospective customers. Prepares drawings, estimates, and bids to meet specific needs of customer. Writes reports on sales and products. Assembles and stocks product displays in retail stores.

GOE Number, Interest Area, and Work Group: 10.03.01; Sales and Marketing; General Sales. **Personality Type:** Enterprising. Enterprising occupations frequently involve starting up and carrying out projects. These occupations can involve leading people and making many decisions. They sometimes require risk taking and often deal with business. **Work Values:** Autonomy; Achievement; Supervision, Human Relations; Compensation; Working Conditions; Company Policies and Practices. **Skills:** Speaking; Problem Identification; Writing; Information Gathering; Active Listening. **Abilities:** *Cognitive*—Oral Expression; Oral Comprehension; Written Expression; Memorization; Written Comprehension. *Psychomotor*—Response Orientation; Multilimb Coordination; Reaction Time. *Physical*—Static Strength; Extent Flexibility; Trunk Strength. *Sensory*—Near Vision; Speech Clarity; Speech Recognition. **General Work Activities:** *Information Input*—Getting Information Needed to Do the Job; Estimating Needed Characteristics; Identifying Objects, Actions, and Events. *Mental Process*—Organizing, Planning, and Prioritizing; Developing Objectives and Strategies; Updating and Using Job-Relevant Knowledge. *Work Output*—Documenting and Recording Information; Implementing Ideas and Programs; Drafting and Specifying Technical Devices. *Interacting with Others*—Influencing Others or Selling; Communicating with Persons Outside Organization; Establishing and Maintaining Relationships. **Physical Work Conditions:** Indoors; Sitting; Standing. **Other Job Characteristics:** Frustrating Circumstances; Consequence of Error; Importance of Being Sure All Is Done.

Experience: Job Zone 2. Some previous work-related skill, knowledge, or experience may be helpful, but usually is not needed. **Job Preparation:** SVP 4.00 to 5.99—6 months to less than 2 years. **Knowledge:** Sales and Marketing; Customer and Personal Service; English Language; Communications and Media; Mathematics. **Instructional Programs:** 010501 Agricultural Supplies Retailing and Wholesaling; 080101 Apparel and Accessories Marketing Operations, General; 080102 Fashion Merchandising; 080199 Apparel and Accessories Marketing Operations, Other; 080299 Business and Personal Services Marketing Operations, Other;

080601 Food Products Retailing and Wholesaling Operations; 080705 General Retailing Operations; 080706 General Selling Skills and Sales Operations; 080799 General Retailing and Wholesaling Operations and Skills, Other; 080810 Office Products Marketing Operations; 089999 Marketing Operations/Marketing and Distribution, Other; 200306 Fashion and Fabric Consultant.

Related DOT Jobs: 162.157-026 Commission Agent, Livestock; 260.257-010 Sales Representative, Livestock; 260.357-010 Commission Agent, Agricultural Produce; 260.357-014 Sales Representative, Food Products; 260.357-018 Sales Representative, Malt Liquors; 260.357-022 Sales Representative, Tobacco Products and Smoking Supplies; 261.357-010 Sales Representative, Apparel Trimmings; 261.357-014 Sales Representative, Canvas Products; 261.357-018 Sales Representative, Footwear; 261.357-022 Sales Representative, Men's and Boys' Apparel; 261.357-026 Sales Representative, Safety Apparel and Equipment; 261.357-030 Sales Representative, Textiles; 261.357-034 Sales Representative, Uniforms; 261.357-038 Sales Representative, Women's and Girls' Apparel; 262.357-014 Sales Representative, Toilet Preparations; 269.357-010 Sales Representative, Fuels; 269.357-014 Sales Representative, Petroleum Products; 270.357-010 Sales Representative, Home Furnishings; 270.357-014 Sales Representative, Household Appliances; 271.357-014 Sales Representative, Videotape (partial list; see the introduction for sources of the complete list).

41-9000 Other Sales and Related Workers

41-9011.00 Demonstrators and Product Promoters
(Models, Demonstrators, and Product Promoters)

Education: Moderate-term O-T-J training

Employed: 91,566

Openings: 27,574

Projected Growth: 32.3%

Earnings: No data available.

Demonstrate merchandise and answer questions for the purpose of creating public interest in buying the product. Sell demonstrated merchandise.

Wears costume or sign boards and walks in public to attract attention to advertise merchandise, services, or belief. Drives truck and trailer to transport exhibit. Attends trade, traveling, promotional, educational, or amusement exhibit to answer visitors' questions and to protect exhibit against theft or damage. Answers telephone and written requests from customers for information about product use and writes articles and pamphlets on product. Prepares reports of services rendered and visits made. Collects fees or accepts donations. Lectures and shows slides to users of company product. Advises customers on homemaking problems related to products or services offered by company. Visits homes, community organizations, stores, and schools to demonstrate products or services. Instructs customers in alteration of products. Develops list of prospective clients from sources, such as newspaper items, company records, local merchants, and customers. Solicits new organization membership. Demonstrates and explains products, methods, or services to persuade customers to purchase products or utilize services available, and answers questions. Trains demonstrators to present company's products or services. Conducts guided tours of plant where product is made. Suggests product improvements to employer and product to purchase to customer. Gives product samples or token gifts to customers, and distributes handbills, brochures, or gift certificates to passers-by. Sets up and arranges display to attract attention of prospective customers. Contacts businesses and civic establishments and arranges to exhibit and sell merchandise made by disadvantaged persons.

GOE Number, Interest Area, and Work Group: 10.04.01; Sales and Marketing; Personal Soliciting. **Personality Type:** Enterprising. Enterprising occupations frequently involve starting up and carrying out projects. These occupations can involve leading people and making many decisions. They sometimes require risk taking and often deal with business. **Work Values:** Independence; Variety; Moral Values; Supervision, Technical; Activity; Company Policies and Practices. **Skills:** Speaking; Persuasion; Social Perceptiveness; Active Learning; Writing; Learning Strategies. **Abilities:** *Cognitive*—Oral Expression; Oral Comprehension; Written Expression; Memorization; Fluency of Ideas. *Psychomotor*—Control Precision; Multilimb Coordination; Response Orientation. *Physical*—Static Strength; Stamina; Gross Body Equilibrium. *Sensory*—Speech Clarity; Speech Recognition; Far Vision. **General Work Activities:** *Information Input*—Getting Information Needed to Do the Job; Identifying Objects, Actions, and Events; Estimating Needed Characteristics. *Mental Process*—Organizing, Planning, and Prioritizing; Scheduling Work and Activities; Judging Qualities of Things, Services, Other People's Work. *Work Output*—Handling and Moving Objects; Implementing Ideas and Programs; Performing General Physical Activities. *Interacting with Others*—Performing for or Working with the Public; Influencing Others or Selling; Establishing and Maintaining Relationships; Communicating with Persons Outside Organization. **Physical Work Conditions:** Indoors; Standing; Using Hands on Objects, Tools, or Controls; Outdoors; Walking or Running. **Other Job Characteristics:** Frustrating Circumstances; Importance of Being Sure All Is Done; Consequence of Error; Importance of Being Exact or Accurate; Importance of Being Aware of New Events; Importance of Repeating Same Tasks.

Experience: Job Zone 1. No previous work-related skill, knowledge, or experience is needed. **Job Preparation:** SVP Below 4.0—Less than 6 months. **Knowledge:** Sales and Marketing; Communications and Media; English Language; Education and Training; Customer and Personal Service. **Instructional Programs:** 080705 General Retailing Operations; 080706 General Selling Skills and Sales Operations.

Related DOT Jobs: 279.357-010 Sales Exhibitor; 293.357-018 Goodwill Ambassador; 297.354-010 Demonstrator; 297.354-014 Demonstrator, Knitting; 297.357-010 Demonstrator, Electric-Gas Appliances; 297.367-010 Exhibit-Display Representative; 297.451-010 Instructor, Painting; 297.454-010 Demonstrator, Sewing Techniques; 299.687-014 Sandwich-Board Carrier.

41-9012.00 Models (Models, Demonstrators, and Product Promoters)

Education: Moderate-term O-T-J training
Employed: 91,566
Openings: 27,574
Projected Growth: 32.3%
Earnings: No data available.

Model garments and other apparel to display clothing before photographers or prospective buyers at fashion shows, private showings, or retail establishments. Pose for photos to be used for advertising purposes. Pose as subject for paintings, sculptures, and other types of artistic expression.

Applies makeup to face and styles hair to enhance appearance, considering such factors as color, camera techniques, and facial features. Wears character costumes and impersonates characters portrayed to amuse children and adults. Stands, turns, and walks to demonstrate features of garment to observers at fashion shows, private showings, and retail establishments. Poses as directed or strikes suitable interpretive poses for promoting and selling merchandise or fashions during photo session. Dresses in sample or completed garments and selects own accessories. Informs prospective purchasers as to model, number, and price of garments and department where garment can be purchased. Poses as subject for paintings, sculptures, and other types of art for translation into plastic or pictorial values. Hands out samples or presents, demonstrates toys, and converses with children and adults while dressed in costume.

GOE Number, Interest Area, and Work Group: 01.09.01; Arts, Entertainment, and Media; Modeling and Personal Appearance. **Personality Type:** Artistic. Artistic occupations frequently involve working with forms, designs, and patterns. These occupations often require self-expression, and the work can be done without following a clear set of rules. **Work Values:** Recognition; Compensation; Moral Values; Social Status; Achievement; Working Conditions. **Skills:** Social Perceptiveness; Speaking; Active Listening; Coordination; Idea Evaluation. **Abilities:** *Cognitive*—Oral Comprehension; Oral Expression; Selective Attention; Visualization; Time Sharing; Memorization. *Psychomotor*—Arm-Hand Steadiness; Finger Dexterity; Speed of Limb Movement. *Physical*—Gross Body Coordination; Dynamic Flexibility; Stamina. *Sensory*—Glare Sensitivity; Visual Color Discrimination; Auditory Attention. **General Work Activities:** *Information Input*—Getting Information Needed to Do the Job; Identifying Objects, Actions, and Events; Monitoring Processes, Materials, and Surroundings. *Mental Process*—Thinking Creatively; Organizing, Planning, and Prioritizing; Updating and Using Job-Relevant Knowledge. *Work Output*—Performing General Physical Activities; Handling and Moving Objects; Implementing Ideas and Programs; Documenting and Recording Information. *Interacting with Others*—Performing for or Working with the Public; Communicating with Persons Outside Organization; Establishing and Maintaining Relationships. **Physical Work Conditions:** Standing; Indoors; Walking or Running. **Other Job Characteristics:** Frustrating Circumstances; Importance of Being Exact or Accurate; Importance of Being Sure All Is Done; Importance of Repeating Same Tasks.

Experience: Job Zone 1. No previous work-related skill, knowledge, or experience is needed. **Job Preparation:** SVP Below 4.0—Less than 6 months. **Knowledge:** Sales and Marketing; Communications and Media; Fine Arts; Customer and Personal Service; Education and Training; Sociology and Anthropology. **Instructional Programs:** 080101 Apparel and Accessories Marketing Operations, General; 080102 Fashion Merchandising; 080103 Fashion Modeling.

Related DOT Jobs: 297.667-014 Model; 299.647-010 Impersonator, Character; 961.367-010 Model, Photographers'; 961.667-010 Model, Artists'.

41-9021.00 Real Estate Brokers (Brokers, Real Estate)

Education: Work experience in a related occupation
Employed: 62,745
Openings: 8,589
Projected Growth: 13.5%
Earnings: $45,640

Operate real estate office, or work for commercial real estate firm, overseeing real estate transactions. Sell real estate, rent properties, and arrange loans.

GOE Number, Interest Area, and Work Group: 10.03.01; Sales and Marketing; General Sales. **Instructional Program:** 521501 Real Estate. **Note:** The Department of Labor has not collected some data for this job, so it has fewer details than the other descriptions.

41-9022.00 Real Estate Sales Agents (Sales Agents, Real Estate)

Education: Postsecondary vocational training
Employed: 284,627
Openings: 36,977
Projected Growth: 9%
Earnings: $28,020

Rent, buy, or sell property for clients. Perform duties such as studying property listings, interviewing prospective clients, accompanying clients to property site, discussing conditions of sale, and drawing up real estate contracts. Includes agents who represent buyer.

Searches public records to ascertain that client has clear title to property. Oversees signing of real estate documents, disburses funds, and coordinates closing activities. Answers client's questions regarding work under construction, financing, maintenance, repairs, and appraisals. Solicits and compiles listings of available rental property. Reviews plans and recommends to client construction features, and enumerates options on new home sales. Interviews prospective tenants and records information to ascertain needs and qualifications. Appraises client's unimproved property to determine loan value. Plans and organizes sales promotion programs and materials, including newspaper advertisements and real estate promotional booklets. Investigates client's financial and credit status to determine eligibility for financing. Reviews trade journals and relevant literature and attends staff and association meetings to remain knowledgeable about real estate market. Inspects condition of premises and arranges for or notifies owner of necessary maintenance. Secures construction financing with own firm or mortgage company. Contacts utility companies for service hookup to client's property. Conducts seminars and training sessions for sales agents to improve sales techniques. Locates and appraises undeveloped areas for building sites, based on evaluation of area market conditions. Prepares real estate contracts, such as closing statements, deeds, leases, and mortgages, and negotiates loans on property. Displays and explains features of property to client and discusses conditions of sale or terms of lease. Collects rental deposit.

GOE Number, Interest Area, and Work Group: 10.03.01; Sales and Marketing; General Sales. **Personality Type:** Enterprising. Enterprising occupations frequently involve starting up and carrying out projects. These occupations can involve leading people and making many decisions. They sometimes require risk taking and often deal with business. **Work Values:** Responsibility; Compensation; Autonomy; Recognition; Ability Utilization; Working Conditions. **Skills:** Active Listening; Persuasion; Speaking; Reading Comprehension; Judgment and Decision Making; Mathematics. **Abilities:** *Cognitive*—Written Comprehension; Oral Expression; Oral Comprehension; Number Facility; Problem Sensitivity; Written Expression. *Psychomotor*—none met the criteria. *Physical*—none met the criteria. *Sensory*—Near Vision; Speech Clarity; Speech Recognition. **General Work Activities:** *Information Input*—Getting Information Needed to Do the Job; Identifying Objects, Actions, and Events; Inspecting Equipment, Structures, Materials. *Mental Process*—Judging Qualities of Things, Services, Other People's Work; Evaluating Information Against Standards; Updating and Using Job-Relevant Knowledge. *Work Output*—Documenting and Recording Information; Implementing Ideas and Programs; Interacting with Computers. *Interacting with Others*—Influencing Others or Selling; Establishing and Maintaining Relationships; Performing for or Working with the Public; Communicating with Persons Outside Organization. **Physical Work Conditions:** Indoors; Sitting; Standing. **Other Job Characteristics:** Importance of Being Sure All Is Done; Importance of Being Exact or Accurate; Consequence of Error.

Experience: Job Zone 2. Some previous work-related skill, knowledge, or experience may be helpful, but usually is not needed. **Job Preparation:** SVP 4.00 to 5.99—6 months to less than 2 years. **Knowledge:** Sales and Marketing; Law, Government and Jurisprudence; Economics and Accounting; English Language; Administration and Management; Mathematics. **Instructional Program:** 521501 Real Estate.

Related DOT Jobs: 250.157-010 Superintendent, Sales; 250.357-010 Building Consultant; 250.357-014 Leasing Agent, Residence; 250.357-018 Sales Agent, Real Estate.

41-9031.00 Sales Engineers (Sales Engineers)

Education: Bachelor's degree
Employed: 79,437
Openings: 3,039
Projected Growth: 15.7%
Earnings: $54,600

Sell business goods or services, the selling of which requires a technical background equivalent to a baccalaureate degree in engineering.

Draws up or proposes changes in equipment, processes, materials, or services resulting in cost reduction or improvement in customer operations. Draws up sales or service contract for products or services. Demonstrates and explains product or service to customer representatives, such as engineers, architects, and other professionals. Calls on management representatives at commercial, industrial, and other establishments to convince prospective client to buy products or services offered. Assists sales force in sale of company products. Provides technical services to clients relating to use, operation, and maintenance of equipment. Diagnoses problems with equipment installed. Provides technical training to employees of client. Designs and drafts variations of standard products in order to meet customer needs. Arranges for trial installations of equipment. Assists in development of custom-made machinery. Reviews customer documents to develop and prepare cost estimates or projected production increases from use of proposed equipment or services.

GOE Number, Interest Area, and Work Group: 02.07.04; Science, Math, and Engineering; Engineering: General Engineering. **Personality Type:** Enterprising. Enterprising occupations frequently involve starting up and carrying out projects. These occupations can involve leading people and making many decisions. They sometimes require risk taking and often deal with business. **Work Values:** Ability Utilization; Achievement; Responsibility; Working Conditions; Moral Values; Activity. **Skills:** Speaking; Active Learning; Operations Analysis; Reading Comprehension; Technology Design; Troubleshooting; Mathematics. **Abilities:** *Cognitive*—Oral Comprehension; Oral Expression; Written Comprehension; Written Expression; Visualization. *Psychomotor*—Reaction Time; Response Orientation; Control Precision. *Physical*—Extent Flexibility; Trunk Strength; Static Strength. *Sensory*—Speech Clarity; Near Vision; Speech Recognition. **General Work Activities:** *Information Input*—Estimating Needed Characteristics; Getting Information Needed to Do the Job; Inspecting Equipment, Structures, Materials; Identifying Objects, Actions, and Events. *Mental Process*—Updating and Using Job-Relevant Knowledge; Analyzing Data or Information; Making Decisions and Solving Problems. *Work Output*—Drafting and Specifying Technical Devices; Implementing Ideas and Programs; Documenting and Recording Information. *Interacting with Others*—Communicating with Persons Outside Organization; Influencing Others or Selling; Communicating with Other Workers. **Physical Work Conditions:** Indoors; Sitting; Using Hands on Objects, Tools, or Controls. **Other Job Characteristics:** Degree of Automation; Consequence of Error; Importance of Being Sure All Is Done.

Experience: Job Zone 5. Extensive skill, knowledge, and experience are needed. Very advanced communication and organizational skills are required. **Job Preparation:** SVP 8.0 and above—4 years to more than 10 years. **Knowledge:** Sales and Marketing; Engineering and Technology; Customer and Personal Service; Design; English Language. **Instructional Programs:** 140201 Aerospace, Aeronautical and Astronautical Engineering; 140301 Agricultural Engineering; 140601 Ceramic Sciences and Engineering; 140701 Chemical Engineering; 141001 Electrical, Electronics and Communication Engineering; 141901 Mechanical Engineering;

142101 Mining and Mineral Engineering; 142201 Naval Architecture and Marine Engineering; 142301 Nuclear Engineering; 142701 Systems Engineering.

Related DOT Jobs: 002.151-010 Sales Engineer, Aeronautical Products; 003.151-010 Sales-Engineer, Electrical Products; 003.151-014 Sales-Engineer, Electronics Products and Systems; 006.151-010 Sales Engineer, Ceramic Products; 007.151-010 Sales Engineer, Mechanical Equipment; 008.151-010 Chemical-Equipment Sales Engineer; 010.151-010 Sales Engineer, Mining-and-Oil-Well Equipment and Services; 013.151-010 Sales Engineer, Agricultural Equipment; 014.151-010 Sales Engineer, Marine Equipment; 015.151-010 Sales Engineer, Nuclear Equipment.

41-9041.00 Telemarketers (Telemarketers, Door-To-Door Sales Workers, News and Street Vendors, and Other Related Workers)

Education: No data available.

Employed: 450,430

Openings: No data available.

Projected Growth: No data available.

Earnings: $17,090

Solicit orders for goods or services over the telephone.

Circulates among potential customers or travels by foot, truck, automobile, or bicycle to deliver or sell merchandise or services. Explains products or services and prices and demonstrates use of products. Writes orders for merchandise or enters order into computer. Distributes product samples or literature that details products or services. Maintains records of accounts and orders and develops prospect lists. Arranges buying party and solicits sponsorship of parties to sell merchandise. Orders or purchases supplies and stocks cart or stand. Sets up and displays sample merchandise at parties or stands. Contacts customers by phone, mail, or in person to offer or persuade them to purchase merchandise or services. Delivers merchandise, serves customer, collects money, and makes change.

GOE Number, Interest Area, and Work Group: 10.04.01; Sales and Marketing; Personal Soliciting. **Personality Type:** Enterprising. Enterprising occupations frequently involve starting up and carrying out projects. These occupations can involve leading people and making many decisions. They sometimes require risk taking and often deal with business. **Work Values:** Independence; Autonomy; Moral Values; Achievement; Compensation; Activity; Supervision, Technical; Supervision, Human Relations. **Skills:** Persuasion; Speaking; Identification of Key Causes; Service Orientation; Mathematics; Social Perceptiveness. **Abilities:** *Cognitive*—Oral Comprehension; Oral Expression; Written Expression; Number Facility; Mathematical Reasoning; Written Comprehension. *Psychomotor*—none met the criteria. *Physical*—Stamina. *Sensory*—Speech Clarity; Speech Recognition; Visual Color Discrimination; Auditory Attention. **General Work Activities:** *Information Input*—Identifying Objects, Actions, and Events; Getting Information Needed to Do the Job; Estimating Needed Characteristics; Inspecting Equipment, Structures, Materials. *Mental Process*—Updating and Using Job-Relevant Knowledge; Processing Information; Scheduling Work and Activities. *Work Output*—Docu-

menting and Recording Information; Performing General Physical Activities; Handling and Moving Objects; Operating Vehicles or Equipment. *Interacting with Others*—Communicating with Persons Outside Organization; Influencing Others or Selling; Performing for or Working with the Public. **Physical Work Conditions:** Outdoors; Walking or Running; Standing. **Other Job Characteristics:** Frustrating Circumstances; Importance of Being Sure All Is Done; Importance of Being Aware of New Events; Importance of Being Exact or Accurate.

Experience: Job Zone 1. No previous work-related skill, knowledge, or experience is needed. **Job Preparation:** SVP Below 4.0—Less than 6 months. **Knowledge:** Sales and Marketing; Customer and Personal Service; Economics and Accounting; English Language; Mathematics; Communications and Media; Telecommunications. **Instructional Programs:** 080705 General Retailing Operations; 080708 General Marketing Operations; 080809 Home Products Marketing Operations.

Related DOT Job: 299.357-014 Telephone Solicitor.

41-9091.00 Door-To-Door Sales Workers, News and Street Vendors, and Related Workers (Telemarketers, Door-To-Door Sales Workers, News and Street Vendors, and Other Related Workers)

Education: No data available.

Employed: 450,430

Openings: No data available.

Projected Growth: No data available.

Earnings: $17,090

Sell goods or services door-to-door or on the street.

Maintains records of accounts and orders and develops prospect lists. Contacts customers by phone, mail, or in person to offer or persuade them to purchase merchandise or services. Explains products or services and prices and demonstrates use of products. Writes orders for merchandise or enters order into computer. Distributes product samples or literature that details products or services. Delivers merchandise, serves customer, collects money, and makes change. Arranges buying party and solicits sponsorship of parties to sell merchandise. Circulates among potential customers or travels by foot, truck, automobile, or bicycle to deliver or sell merchandise or services. Sets up and displays sample merchandise at parties or stands. Orders or purchases supplies and stocks cart or stand.

GOE Number, Interest Area, and Work Group: 10.04.01; Sales and Marketing; Personal Soliciting. **Personality Type:** Enterprising. Enterprising occupations frequently involve starting up and carrying out projects. These occupations can involve leading people and making many decisions. They sometimes require risk taking and often deal with business. **Work Values:** Independence; Autonomy; Moral Values; Achievement; Compensation; Activity; Supervision, Human Relations; Supervision, Technical. **Skills:** Persuasion; Speaking; Identification of Key Causes; Service Orientation; Mathematics; Social Perceptiveness. **Abilities:** *Cognitive*—Oral Comprehension; Oral Expression; Written Expression; Number Facility; Written Comprehension; Mathematical Reasoning. *Psychomotor*—none met the criteria. *Physical*—Stamina. *Sensory*—Speech Clarity; Speech Recognition; Auditory Attention; Visual Color Discrimination. **General Work Activities:** *Information Input*—Identifying Objects, Actions, and Events; Getting Information Needed to Do the Job; Inspecting Equipment, Structures, Materials; Estimating Needed Characteristics. *Mental Process*—Updating and Using Job-Relevant Knowledge; Processing Information; Scheduling Work and Activities. *Work Output*—Documenting and Recording Information; Performing General Physical Activities; Operating Vehicles or Equipment; Handling and Moving Objects. *Interacting with Others*—Communicating with Persons Outside Organization; Influencing Others or Selling; Performing for or Working with the Public. **Physical Work Conditions:** Outdoors; Walking or Running; Standing. **Other Job Characteristics:** Frustrating Circumstances; Importance of Be-

ing Sure All Is Done; Importance of Being Aware of New Events; Importance of Being Exact or Accurate.

Experience: Job Zone 1. No previous work-related skill, knowledge, or experience is needed. **Job Preparation:** SVP Below 4.0—Less than 6 months. **Knowledge:** Sales and Marketing; Customer and Personal Service; English Language; Economics and Accounting; Telecommunications; Mathematics; Communications and Media. **Instructional Programs:** 080705 General Retailing Operations; 080708 General Marketing Operations; 080809 Home Products Marketing Operations.

Related DOT Jobs: 279.357-038 Salesperson-Demonstrator, Party Plan; 291.357-010 Sales Representative, Door-To-Door; 291.454-010 Lei Seller; 291.457-010 Cigarette Vendor; 291.457-014 Lounge-Car Attendant; 291.457-018 Peddler; 291.457-022 Vendor; 292.457-010 Newspaper Carrier.

43-0000
Office and Administrative Support Occupations

43-1000 Supervisors, Office and Administrative Support Workers

43-1011.00 First-Line Supervisors/Managers of Office and Administrative Support Workers (Office and Administrative Support Supervisors)

Education: Work experience in a related occupation

Employed: 1,610,814

Openings: 238,168

Projected Growth: 19.4%

Earnings: $31,090

Supervise and coordinate the activities of clerical and administrative support workers.

GOE Number, Interest Area, and Work Group: 09.01.01; Business Detail; Managerial Work in Business Detail. **Instructional Program:** 520204 Office Supervision and Management. **Note:** The Department of Labor has not collected some data for this job, so it has fewer details than the other descriptions.

43-1011.01 First-Line Supervisors, Customer Service (Office and Administrative Support Supervisors)

Education: Work experience in a related occupation

Employed: 1,610,814

Openings: 238,168

Projected Growth: 19.4%

Earnings: $31,090

Supervise and coordinate activities of workers involved in providing customer service.

Observes and evaluates workers' performance. Reviews and checks work of subordinates such as reports, records, and applications for accuracy and content, and corrects errors. Prepares, maintains, and submits reports and records, such as budgets and operational and personnel reports. Makes recommendations to management concerning staff and improvement of procedures. Plans and develops improved procedures. Requisitions or purchases supplies. Resolves complaints and answers questions of customers regarding services and procedures. Interprets and communicates work procedures and company policies to staff. Issues instructions and assigns duties to workers. Hires and discharges workers. Trains and instructs employees. Plans, prepares, and devises work schedules, according to budgets and workloads. Supervises and coordinates activities of workers engaged in customer service activities. Communicates with other departments and management to resolve problems and expedite work. Helps workers in resolving problems and completing work.

GOE Number, Interest Area, and Work Group: 09.01.01; Business Detail; Managerial Work in Business Detail. **Personality Type:** Enterprising. Enterprising occupations frequently involve starting up and carrying out projects. These occupations can involve leading people and making many decisions. They sometimes require risk taking and often deal with business. **Work Values:** Autonomy; Authority; Activity; Working Conditions; Responsibility; Achievement. **Skills:** Management of Personnel Resources; Coordination; Problem Identification; Speaking; Critical Thinking; Monitoring. **Abilities:** *Cognitive*—Oral Expression; Oral Comprehension; Written Comprehension; Written Expression; Number Facility. *Psychomotor*—Wrist-Finger Speed; Finger Dexterity; Response Orientation. *Physical*—Trunk Strength. *Sensory*—Near Vision; Speech Recognition; Speech Clarity. **General Work Activities:** *Information Input*—Getting Information Needed to Do the Job; Estimating Needed Characteristics; Identifying Objects, Actions, and Events; Monitoring Processes, Materials, and Surroundings. *Mental Process*—Scheduling Work and Activities; Making Decisions and Solving Problems; Organizing, Planning, and Prioritizing; Analyzing Data or Information. *Work Output*—Documenting and Recording Information; Implementing Ideas and Programs; Interacting with Computers; Handling and Moving Objects. *Interacting with Others*—Staffing Organizational Units; Guiding, Directing and Motivating Subordinates; Communicating with Other Workers; Establishing and Maintaining Relationships. **Physical Work Conditions:** Indoors; Sitting; Walking or Running; Standing. **Other Job Characteristics:** Frustrating Circumstances; Importance of Being Sure All Is Done; Consequence of Error.

Experience: Job Zone 3. Previous work-related skill, knowledge, or experience is required. **Job Preparation:** SVP 6.0 to less than 7.0—More than 1 year and less than 4 years. **Knowledge:** Administration and Management; Customer and Personal Service; Personnel and Human Resources; Clerical; English Language; Education and Training. **Instructional Program:** 520204 Office Supervision and Management.

Related DOT Jobs: 168.167-058 Manager, Customer Service; 205.137-014 Supervisor, Survey Workers; 205.162-010 Admitting Officer; 209.132-014 Technical Coordinator; 209.137-014 Meter Reader, Chief; 211.132-010 Teller, Head; 211.137-010 Supervisor, Cashiers; 211.137-014 Supervisor, Food Checkers and Cashiers; 211.137-022 Supervisor, Tellers; 214.137-010 Documentation Supervisor; 214.137-014 Supervisor, Statement Clerks; 214.137-022 Supervisor, Accounts Receivable; 216.137-014 Transfer Clerk, Head; 222.137-014 Linen-Room Supervisor; 222.137-026 Petroleum-Inspector Supervisor; 230.137-018 Supervisor, Mail Carriers; 235.132-010 Central-Office-Operator Supervisor; 237.137-010 Supervisor, Telephone Information; 237.137-014 Supervisor, Travel-Information Center; 238.137-010 Manager, Reservations (partial list; see the introduction for sources of the complete list).

43-1011.02 First-Line Supervisors, Administrative Support (Office and Administrative Support Supervisors)

Education: Work experience in a related occupation

Employed: 1,610,814

Openings: 238,168

Projected Growth: 19.4%

Earnings: $31,090

Supervise and coordinate activities of workers involved in providing administrative support.

Identifies and resolves discrepancies or errors. Verifies completeness and accuracy of subordinates' work, computations, and records. Requisitions supplies. Computes figures such as balances, totals, and commissions. Analyzes financial activities of establishment or department and assists in planning budget. Inspects equipment for defects and notifies maintenance personnel or outside service contractors for repairs. Compiles reports and information required by management or governmental agencies. Reviews records and reports pertaining to such activities as production, operation, payroll, customer accounts, and shipping. Oversees, coordinates, or performs activities associated with shipping, receiving, distribution, and transportation. Plans layout of stockroom, warehouse, or other storage areas, considering turnover, size, weight, and related factors pertaining to items stored. Consults with supervisor and other personnel to resolve problems such as equipment performance, output quality, and work schedules. Trains employees in work and safety procedures and company policies. Participates in work of subordinates to facilitate productivity or overcome difficult aspects of work. Examines procedures and recommends changes to save time, labor, and other costs and to improve quality control and operating efficiency. Maintains records of such matters as inventory, personnel, orders, supplies, and machine maintenance. Plans, prepares, and revises work schedules and duty assignments according to budget allotments, customer needs, problems, work loads, and statistical forecasts. Evaluates subordinates' job performance and conformance to regulations, and recommends appropriate personnel action. Supervises and coordinates activities of workers engaged in clerical or administrative support activities. Interviews, selects, and discharges employees.

GOE Number, Interest Area, and Work Group: 09.01.01; Business Detail; Managerial Work in Business Detail. **Personality Type:** Enterprising. Enterprising occupations frequently involve starting up and carrying out projects. These occupations can involve leading people and making many decisions. They sometimes require risk taking and often deal with business. **Work Values:** Authority; Autonomy; Activity; Responsibility; Working Conditions. **Skills:** Monitoring; Active Listening; Coordination; Management of Personnel Resources; Time Management; Speaking; Writing; Reading Comprehension. **Abilities:** *Cognitive*—Oral Expression; Oral Comprehension; Written Expression; Written Comprehension; Number Facility; Mathematical Reasoning. *Psychomotor*—Wrist-Finger Speed; Finger Dexterity; Manual Dexterity. *Physical*—Extent Flexibility; Static Strength; Explosive Strength. *Sensory*—Near Vision; Speech Clarity; Speech Recognition. **General Work Activities:** *Information Input*—Getting Information Needed to Do the Job; Estimating Needed Characteristics; Identifying Objects, Actions, and Events. *Mental Process*—Organizing, Planning, and Prioritizing; Evaluating Information Against Standards; Scheduling Work and Activities. *Work Output*—Documenting and Recording Information; Interacting with Computers; Implementing Ideas and Programs. *Interacting with Others*—Coordinating Work and Activities of Others; Guiding, Directing and Motivating Subordinates; Performing Administrative Activities; Coaching and Developing Others; Establishing and Maintaining Relationships. **Physical Work Conditions:** Indoors; Sitting; Standing. **Other Job Characteristics:** Frustrating Circumstances; Consequence of Error; Importance of Being Exact or Accurate; Importance of Being Sure All Is Done.

Experience: Job Zone 3. Previous work-related skill, knowledge, or experience is required. **Job Preparation:** SVP 6.0 to less than 7.0—More than 1 year and less than 4 years. **Knowledge:** Administration and Management; Clerical; English Language; Mathematics; Personnel and Human Resources; Education and Training. **Instructional Program:** 520204 Office Supervision and Management.

Related DOT Jobs: 109.137-010 Shelving Supervisor; 202.132-010 Supervisor, Steno Pool; 203.132-010 Supervisor, Telegraphic-Typewriter Operators; 203.132-014 Supervisor, Transcribing Operators; 203.137-010 Supervisor, Word Processing; 203.137-014 Typing Section Chief; 206.137-010 Supervisor, Files; 207.137-010 Chief Clerk, Print Shop; 209.132-010 Supervisor, Personnel Clerks; 209.137-010 Mailroom Supervisor; 209.137-018 Supervisor, Agency Appointments; 209.137-026 Supervisor, Marking Room; 210.132-010 Supervisor, Audit Clerks; 211.137-018 Supervisor, Money-Room; 213.132-010 Supervisor, Computer Operations; 214.137-018 Rate Supervisor; 215.137-010 Crew Scheduler, Chief; 215.137-014 Supervisor, Payroll; 215.137-018 Supervisor, Force Adjustment; 216.132-010 Supervisor, Accounting Clerks (partial list; see the introduction for sources of the complete list).

43-2000 Communications Equipment Operators

43-2011.00 Switchboard Operators, Including Answering Service (Switchboard Operators)

Education:	Short-term O-T-J training
Employed:	214,464
Openings:	47,120
Projected Growth:	–13.9%
Earnings:	$18,220

Operate telephone business systems equipment or switchboards to relay incoming, outgoing, and interoffice calls. Supply information to callers and record messages.

Date-stamps and files messages. Keeps records of calls placed and charges incurred, if any. Records messages, suggesting rewording for clarity and conciseness. Receives visitors and obtains name and nature of business. Operates communication system such as telephone, switchboard, intercom, two-way radio, or public address. Greets caller, furnishes information to caller or visitor, and relays calls. Performs clerical duties such as typing, proofreading, accepting orders, scheduling appointments, and sorting mail. Places telephone calls as instructed. Relays and routes messages.

GOE Number, Interest Area, and Work Group: 09.06.01; Business Detail; Communications. **Personality Type:** Conventional. Conventional occupations frequently involve following set procedures and routines. These occupations can include working with data and details more than with ideas. Usually there is a clear line of authority to follow. **Work Values:** Moral Values; Activity; Independence; Supervision, Human Relations; Working Conditions. **Skills:** Active Listening; Reading Comprehension; Speaking; Social Perceptiveness. **Abilities:** *Cognitive*—Oral Comprehension; Oral Expression; Selective Attention; Written Comprehension; Memorization; Written Expression. *Psychomotor*—Wrist-Finger Speed; Response Orientation; Reaction Time; Multilimb Coordination. *Physical*—none met the criteria. *Sensory*—Speech Recognition; Auditory Attention; Speech Clarity. **General Work Activities:** *Information Input*—Getting Information Needed to Do the Job; Identifying Objects, Actions, and Events; Monitoring Processes, Materials, and Surroundings. *Mental Process*—Processing Information; Evaluating Information Against Standards; Judging Qualities of Things, Services, Other People's Work. *Work Output*—Documenting and Recording Information; Handling and Moving Objects; Controlling Machines and Processes. *Interacting with Others*—Communicating with Persons Outside Organization; Performing for or Working with the Public; Performing Administrative Activities. **Physical Work Conditions:** Indoors; Sitting; Using Hands on Objects, Tools, or Controls. **Other Job Characteristics:** Importance of Being Sure All Is Done; Importance of Being Exact or Accurate; Degree of Automation.

Experience: Job Zone 1. No previous work-related skill, knowledge, or experience is needed. **Job Preparation:** SVP Below 4.0—Less than 6 months. **Knowledge:** Clerical; English Language; Telecommunications; Customer and Personal Service; Computers and Electronics. **Instructional Program:** 520406 Receptionist.

Related DOT Jobs: 235.562-014 Switchboard Operator, Police District; 235.662-014 Communication-Center Operator; 235.662-022 Telephone Operator; 235.662-026 Telephone-Answering-Service Operator; 239.362-010 Telephone Clerk, Telegraph Office.

43-2021.00 Telephone Operators (Switchboard Operators)

Education: Short-term O-T-J training

Employed: 214,464

Openings: 47,120

Projected Growth: −13.9%

Earnings: $18,220

Provide information by accessing alphabetical and geographical directories. Assist customers with special billing requests, such as charges to a third party and credits or refunds for incorrectly dialed numbers or bad connections. Handle emergency calls and assist children or people with physical disabilities in making telephone calls.

GOE Number, Interest Area, and Work Group: 09.06.01; Business Detail; Communications. **Instructional Program:** 520406 Receptionist. **Note:** The Department of Labor has not collected some data for this job, so it has fewer details than the other descriptions.

43-2021.01 Directory Assistance Operators (Directory Assistance Operators)

Education: Moderate-term O-T-J training

Employed: 23,413

Openings: 4,668

Projected Growth: −31.1%

Earnings: $30,530

Provide telephone information from central office switchboard. Refer to alphabetical or geographical reels or directories to answer questions or suggest answer sources.

Refers to alphabetical or geographical reels or directories to answer questions and provide telephone information. Types location and spelling of name on computer terminal keyboard, and scans directory or microfilm viewer to locate number. Plugs in headphones when signal light flashes on cord switchboard, or pushes switch keys on cordless switchboard to make connections. Keeps reels and directories up-to-date. Maintains record of calls received. Suggests alternate locations and spellings under which number could be listed.

GOE Number, Interest Area, and Work Group: 09.06.01; Business Detail; Communications. **Personality Type:** Conventional. Conventional occupations frequently involve following set procedures and routines. These occupations can include working with data and details more than with ideas. Usually there is a clear line of authority to follow. **Work Values:** Independence; Activity; Supervision, Technical; Moral Values; Supervision, Human Relations. **Skills:** Active Listening; Reading Comprehension; Speaking; Service Orientation; Writing. **Abilities:** *Cognitive*—Oral Expression; Oral Comprehension; Perceptual Speed; Written Comprehension; Information Ordering. *Psychomotor*—Reaction Time; Wrist-Finger Speed; Response Orientation; Finger Dexterity. *Physical*—Extent Flexibility. *Sensory*—Near Vision; Speech Clarity; Speech Recognition. **General Work Activities:** *Information Input*—Getting Information Needed to Do the Job; Identifying Objects, Actions, and Events; Monitoring Processes, Materials, and Surroundings. *Mental Process*—Processing Information; Updating and Using Job-Relevant Knowledge; Analyzing Data or Information; Evaluating Information Against Standards. *Work Output*—Handling and Moving Objects; Interacting with Computers; Controlling Machines and Processes. *Interacting with Others*—Communicating with Persons Outside Organization; Performing for or Working with the Public; Establishing and Maintaining Relationships. **Physical Work Conditions:** Indoors; Sitting; Using Hands on Objects, Tools, or Controls. **Other Job Characteristics:** Degree of Automation; Importance of Being Exact or Accurate; Importance of Being Sure All Is Done.

Experience: Job Zone 1. No previous work-related skill, knowledge, or experience is needed. **Job Preparation:** SVP Below 4.0—Less than 6 months. **Knowledge:** Customer and Personal Service; Telecommunications; English Language; Computers and Electronics; Clerical. **Instructional Programs:** 520406 Receptionist; 129999 Personal and Miscellaneous Services, Other.

Related DOT Job: 235.662-018 Directory-Assistance Operator.

43-2021.02 Central Office Operators (Central Office Operators)

Education: Moderate-term O-T-J training

Employed: 23,023

Openings: 4,983

Projected Growth: −16.6%

Earnings: $26,220

Operate telephone switchboard to establish or assist customers in establishing local or long-distance telephone connections.

Requests coin deposits for calls. Calculates and quotes charges on long-distance connections. Observes signal light on switchboard, plugs cords into trunk-jack, and dials or presses button to make connections. Consults charts to determine charges for calls from pay telephones. Gives information regarding subscribers' telephone numbers. Inserts tickets in calculagraph (time-stamping device) to record time of toll calls.

GOE Number, Interest Area, and Work Group: 09.06.01; Business Detail; Communications. **Personality Type:** Conventional. Conventional occupations frequently involve following set procedures and routines. These occupations can include working with data and details more than with ideas. Usually there is a clear line of authority to follow. **Work Values:** Moral Values; Supervision, Technical; Independence; Activity; Supervision, Human Relations. **Skills:** Active Listening; Operation and Control; Speaking; Mathematics; Service Orientation. **Abilities:** *Cognitive*—Oral Expression; Oral Comprehension; Number Facility; Selective Attention; Mathematical Reasoning. *Psychomotor*—Wrist-Finger Speed. *Physical*—none met the criteria. *Sensory*—Speech Recognition; Speech Clarity. **General Work Activities:** *Information Input*—Getting Information Needed to Do the Job; Monitoring Processes, Materials, and Surroundings; Identifying Objects, Actions, and Events. *Mental Process*—Processing Information; Making Decisions and Solving Problems; Updating and Using Job-Relevant Knowledge. *Work Output*—Handling and Moving Objects; Controlling Machines and Processes; Documenting and Recording Information. *Interacting with Others*—Communicating with Persons Outside Organization; Performing for or Working with the Public; Assisting and Caring for Others. **Physical Work Conditions:** Indoors; Sitting; Using Hands on Objects, Tools, or Controls. **Other Job Characteristics:** Importance of Being Exact or Accurate; Importance of Being Sure All Is Done; Degree of Automation; Consequence of Error.

Experience: Job Zone 1. No previous work-related skill, knowledge, or experience is needed. **Job Preparation:** SVP Below 4.0—Less than 6 months. **Knowledge:** Telecommunications; English Language; Customer and Personal Service; Mathematics; Computers and Electronics; Clerical. **Instructional Programs:** 520401 Administrative Assistant/Secretarial Science, General; 520406 Receptionist.

Related DOT Job: 235.462-010 Central-Office Operator.

43-3000 Financial Clerks

43-3011.00 Bill and Account Collectors (Bill and Account Collectors)

Education: Short-term O-T-J training
Employed: 310,774
Openings: 106,068
Projected Growth: 35.3%
Earnings: $22,540

Locate and notify customers of delinquent accounts, by mail, telephone, or personal visit, to solicit payment. Receive payment; post amount to customer's account; prepare statements to credit department if customer fails to respond; initiate repossession proceedings or service disconnection; keep records of collection and status of accounts.

Confers with customer by telephone or in person to determine reason for overdue payment and to review terms of sales, service, or credit contract. Receives payments and posts amount paid to customer account, using computer or paper records. Records information about financial status of customer and status of collection efforts. Traces delinquent customer to new address by inquiring at post office or questioning neighbors. Drives vehicle to visit customer, return merchandise to creditor, or deliver bills. Persuades customer to pay amount due on credit account, damage claim, or nonpayable check, or negotiates extension of credit. Notifies credit department, orders merchandise repossession or service disconnection, or turns over account to attorney if customer fails to respond. Mails form letters to customers to encourage payment of delinquent accounts. Sorts and files correspondence, and performs miscellaneous clerical duties.

GOE Number, Interest Area, and Work Group: 09.05.01; Business Detail; Customer Service. **Personality Type:** Conventional. Conventional occupations frequently involve following set procedures and routines. These occupations can include working with data and details more than with ideas. Usually there is a clear line of authority to follow. **Work Values:** Supervision, Human Relations; Activity; Company Policies and Practices; Security; Autonomy; Supervision, Technical; Variety; Compensation. **Skills:** Active Listening; Problem Identification; Speaking; Information Organization; Persuasion. **Abilities:** *Cognitive*—Number Facility; Oral Comprehension; Oral Expression; Problem Sensitivity; Written Comprehension. *Psychomotor*—Wrist-Finger Speed; Response Orientation; Rate Control. *Physical*—none met the criteria. *Sensory*—Speech Clarity; Speech Recognition; Auditory Attention. **General Work Activities:** *Information Input*—Getting Information Needed to Do the Job; Identifying Objects, Actions, and Events; Monitoring Processes, Materials, and Surroundings. *Mental Process*—Organizing, Planning, and Prioritizing; Developing Objectives and Strategies; Evaluating Information Against Standards; Processing Information; Scheduling Work and Activities. *Work Output*—Documenting and Recording Information; Operating Vehicles or Equipment; Interacting with Computers; Implementing Ideas and Programs. *Interacting with Others*—Communicating with Persons Outside Organization; Resolving Conflict and Negotiating with Others; Performing for or Working with the Public; Influencing Others or Selling. **Physical Work Conditions:** Indoors; Sitting; Outdoors. **Other Job Characteristics:** Frustrating Circumstances; Consequence of Error; Importance of Being Exact or Accurate; Importance of Being Sure All Is Done.

Experience: Job Zone 2. Some previous work-related skill, knowledge, or experience may be helpful, but usually is not needed. **Job Preparation:** SVP 4.00 to 5.99—6 months to less than 2 years. **Knowledge:** Clerical; Mathematics; Economics and Accounting; Computers and Electronics; English Language. **Instructional Program:** 520803 Banking and Financial Support Services.

Related DOT Jobs: 241.357-010 Collection Clerk; 241.367-010 Collector; 241.367-022 Repossessor.

43-3021.00 Billing and Posting Clerks and Machine Operators (Billing and Posting Clerks and Machine Operators)

Education: Short-term O-T-J training
Employed: 106,559
Openings: 10,750
Projected Growth: –2.6%
Earnings: $20,560

Compile, compute, and record billing, accounting, statistical, and other numerical data for billing purposes. Prepare billing invoices for services rendered or for delivery or shipment of goods.

GOE Number, Interest Area, and Work Group: 09.03.01; Business Detail; Bookkeeping, Auditing, and Accounting. **Instructional Program:** 520302 Accounting Technician. **Note:** The Department of Labor has not collected some data for this job, so it has fewer details than the other descriptions.

43-3021.01 Statement Clerks (Statement Clerks)

Education: Short-term O-T-J training
Employed: 15,647
Openings: 2,501
Projected Growth: –22.3%
Earnings: $18,630

Prepare and distribute bank statements to customers, answer inquiries, and reconcile discrepancies in records and accounts.

Encodes and cancels checks, using machine. Routes statements for mailing or over-the-counter delivery to customers. Inserts statements and canceled checks in envelopes and affixes postage, or stuffs envelopes and meters postage. Keeps canceled checks and customer signature files. Posts stop-payment notices to prevent payment of protested checks. Matches statement with batch of canceled checks by account number. Compares previously prepared bank statements with canceled checks, prepares statements for distribution to customers, and reconciles discrepancies in records and accounts. Recovers checks returned to customer in error, adjusts customer account, and answers inquiries. Takes orders for imprinted checks.

GOE Number, Interest Area, and Work Group: 09.03.01; Business Detail; Bookkeeping, Auditing, and Accounting. **Personality Type:** Conventional. Conventional occupations frequently involve following set procedures and routines. These occupations can include working with data and details more than with ideas. Usually there is a clear line of authority to follow. **Work Values:** Working Conditions; Moral Values; Activity; Supervision, Human Relations; Company Policies and Practices; Security. **Skills:** Reading Comprehension; Active Listening; Problem Identification; Information Organization; Mathematics. **Abilities:** *Cognitive*—Perceptual Speed; Number Facility; Written Comprehension; Oral Expression; Problem Sensitivity; Oral Comprehension. *Psychomotor*—Control Precision; Multilimb Coordination. *Physical*—none

met the criteria. *Sensory*—Near Vision; Hearing Sensitivity; Depth Perception. **General Work Activities:** *Information Input*—Getting Information Needed to Do the Job; Identifying Objects, Actions, and Events; Inspecting Equipment, Structures, Materials. *Mental Process*—Processing Information; Evaluating Information Against Standards; Analyzing Data or Information. *Work Output*—Documenting and Recording Information; Handling and Moving Objects; Controlling Machines and Processes. *Interacting with Others*—Communicating with Persons Outside Organization; Interpreting Meaning of Information to Others; Performing for or Working with the Public. **Physical Work Conditions:** Indoors; Sitting; Using Hands on Objects, Tools, or Controls. **Other Job Characteristics:** Importance of Being Exact or Accurate; Importance of Being Sure All Is Done; Degree of Automation.

Experience: Job Zone 2. Some previous work-related skill, knowledge, or experience may be helpful, but usually is not needed. **Job Preparation:** SVP 4.00 to 5.99—6 months to less than 2 years. **Knowledge:** Clerical; Mathematics; Economics and Accounting; Customer and Personal Service; Computers and Electronics. **Instructional Program:** 520302 Accounting Technician. **Related DOT Job:** 214.362-046 Statement Clerk.

43-3021.02 Billing, Cost, and Rate Clerks (Billing, Cost, and Rate Clerks)

Education: Short-term O-T-J training
Employed: 342,278
Openings: 63,239
Projected Growth: 14.6%
Earnings: $22,670

Compile data, compute fees and charges, and prepare invoices for billing purposes. Compute costs and calculate rates for goods, services, and shipment of goods; post data.

Compiles cost factor reports such as labor, production, storage, and equipment. Computes amounts due from such documents as purchase orders, sales tickets, and charge slips. Compiles and computes credit terms, discounts, and purchase prices for billing documents. Keeps records of invoices and support documents. Types billing documents, shipping labels, credit memorandums, and credit forms, using typewriter or computer. Verifies compiled data from vendor invoices to ensure accuracy and revises billing data when errors are found. Consults manuals which include rates, rules, regulations, and government tax and tariff information. Answers mail and telephone inquiries regarding rates, routing, and procedures. Estimates market value of product or services. Updates manuals when rates, rules, or regulations are amended. Resolves discrepancies on accounting records.

GOE Number, Interest Area, and Work Group: 09.03.01; Business Detail; Bookkeeping, Auditing, and Accounting. **Personality Type:** Conventional. Conventional occupations frequently involve following set procedures and routines. These occupations can include working with data and details more than with ideas. Usually there is a clear line of authority to follow. **Work Values:** Working Conditions; Independence; Activity; Company Policies and Practices; Security. **Skills:** Mathematics; Reading Comprehension; Active Listening; Writing; Information Gathering; Information Organization. **Abilities:** *Cognitive*—Number Facility; Mathematical Reasoning; Written Expression; Written Comprehension; Information Ordering. *Psychomotor*—Wrist-Finger Speed; Finger Dexterity; Control Precision. *Physical*—Trunk Strength. *Sensory*—Near Vision; Speech Recognition; Speech Clarity. **General Work Activities:** *Information Input*—Getting Information Needed to Do the Job; Estimating Needed Characteristics; Identifying Objects, Actions, and Events. *Mental Process*—Processing Information; Evaluating Information Against Standards; Updating and Using Job-Relevant Knowledge. *Work Output*—Documenting and Recording Information; Interacting with Computers; Handling and Moving Objects. *Interacting with Others*—Performing Administrative Activities; Communicating with Persons Outside Organization; Communicating with Other Workers. **Physical Work Conditions:** Indoors; Sitting; Making Repetitive Motions; Using Hands on Objects, Tools, or Controls. **Other Job Characteristics:** Degree of Automation; Importance of Being Exact or Accurate; Importance of Being Sure All Is Done.

Experience: Job Zone 2. Some previous work-related skill, knowledge, or experience may be helpful, but usually is not needed. **Job Preparation:** SVP 4.00 to 5.99—6 months to less than 2 years. **Knowledge:** Clerical; Economics and Accounting; Mathematics; English Language; Customer and Personal Service. **Instructional Programs:** 520302 Accounting Technician; 520408 General Office/Clerical and Typing Services.

Related DOT Jobs: 184.387-010 Wharfinger; 191.367-010 Personal Property Assessor; 214.267-010 Rate Analyst, Freight; 214.362-010 Demurrage Clerk; 214.362-014 Documentation-Billing Clerk; 214.362-022 Insurance Clerk; 214.362-026 Invoice-Control Clerk; 214.362-038 Traffic-Rate Clerk; 214.362-042 Billing Clerk; 214.382-014 Billing Typist; 214.382-018 C.O.D. Clerk; 214.382-022 Interline Clerk; 214.382-026 Revising Clerk; 214.382-030 Settlement Clerk; 214.387-010 Billing-Control Clerk; 214.387-014 Rate Reviewer; 214.387-018 Services Clerk; 214.467-010 Foreign Clerk; 214.467-014 Pricer, Message and Delivery Service; 214.482-014 Deposit-Refund Clerk (partial list; see the introduction for sources of the complete list).

43-3021.03 Billing, Posting, and Calculating Machine Operators (Billing and Posting Clerks and Machine Operators)

Education: Short-term O-T-J training
Employed: 106,559
Openings: 10,750
Projected Growth: –2.6%
Earnings: $20,560

Operate machines that automatically perform mathematical processes such as addition, subtraction, multiplication, and division, to calculate and record billing, accounting, statistical, and other numerical data. Operate special billing machines to prepare statements, bills, and invoices. Operate bookkeeping machines to copy and post data, make computations, and compile records of transactions.

Transfers data from machine, such as encoding machine, to computer. Observes operation of sorter to note document machine cannot read, and manually records amount, using keyboard. Encodes and adds amounts of transaction documents such as checks or money orders, using encoding machine. Sorts and microfilms transaction documents such as checks, using sorting machine. Compares machine totals to records for errors, and encodes correct amount or prepares correction record if error is found. Posts totals to records and prepares bill or invoice to be sent to customers, using billing machine. Bundles sorted documents to prepare those drawn on other banks for collection. Transcribes data from office records, using specified forms, billing machine, and transcribing machine. Calculates accounting and other numerical data such as amounts customers owe, sales totals, and inventory data, using calculating machine. Manually sorts and lists items for proof or collection. Cleans machines such as encoding or sorting machines and replaces ribbons, film, and tape.

GOE Number, Interest Area, and Work Group: 09.09.01; Business Detail; Clerical Machine Operation. **Personality Type:** Conventional. Conventional occupations frequently involve following set procedures and routines. These occupations can include working with data and details more than with ideas. Usually there is a clear line of authority to follow. **Work Values:** Independence; Moral Values; Activity; Supervision, Human Relations; Supervision, Technical; Company Policies and Practices; Security; Working Conditions. **Skills:** Mathematics; Operation and Control; Product Inspection; Problem Identification; Information Gathering; Reading Comprehension. **Abilities:** *Cognitive*—Number Facility; Mathematical Reasoning; Problem Sensitivity; Written Comprehension; Information Ordering. *Psychomotor*—Wrist-Finger Speed. *Physical*—none met the criteria. *Sensory*—Near Vision. **General Work Activities:** *Information Input*—Monitoring Processes, Materials, and Surroundings; Getting Information Needed to Do the Job; Identifying Objects, Actions, and Events. *Mental Process*—Processing Information; Evaluating Information Against Standards; Analyzing Data or Information. *Work Output*—Handling and Moving Objects; Documenting and Recording Information; Controlling Machines and Processes; Interacting with Computers. *Interacting with Others*—Performing Administrative Activities; Establishing and Maintaining Relationships; Interpreting Meaning of Information to Others; Communicating with Other Workers. **Physical Work Conditions:** Indoors; Sitting; Making Repetitive Motions. **Other Job Characteristics:** Importance of Being Exact or Accurate; Importance of Repeating Same Tasks; Importance of Being Sure All Is Done.

Experience: Job Zone 1. No previous work-related skill, knowledge, or experience is needed. **Job Preparation:** SVP Below 4.0—Less than 6 months. **Knowledge:** Clerical; Computers and Electronics; Mathematics; Economics and Accounting; English Language. **Instructional Program:** 520302 Accounting Technician.

Related DOT Jobs: 214.462-010 Accounts-Adjustable Clerk; 214.482-010 Billing-Machine Operator; 216.482-018 Audit-Machine Operator; 216.482-022 Calculating-Machine Operator; 217.382-010 Proof-Machine Operator.

43-3031.00 Bookkeeping, Accounting, and Auditing Clerks (Bookkeeping, Accounting, and Auditing Clerks)

Education: Moderate-term O-T-J training

Employed: 2,077,615

Openings: 325,366

Projected Growth: –3.9%

Earnings: $23,190

Compute, classify, and record numerical data to keep financial records complete. Perform any combination of routine calculating, posting, and verifying duties to obtain primary financial data for use in maintaining accounting records. Check the accuracy of figures, calculations, and postings pertaining to business transactions recorded by other workers.

Debits or credits accounts. Compiles reports and tables to show statistics related to cash receipts, expenditures, accounts payable and receivable, and profit and loss. Verifies balances and entries, calculations, and postings recorded by other workers. Processes negotiable instruments such as checks and vouchers. Complies with federal, state, and company policies, procedures, and regulations. Performs financial calculations such as amounts due, balances, discounts, equity, and principal. Records financial transactions and other account information to update and maintain accounting records. Evaluates records for accuracy of balances, postings, calculations, and other records pertaining to business or operating transactions and reconciles, or notes discrepancies.

GOE Number, Interest Area, and Work Group: 09.03.01; Business Detail; Bookkeeping, Auditing, and Accounting. **Personality Type:** Conventional. Conventional occupations frequently involve following set procedures and routines. These occupations can include working with data and details more than with ideas. Usually there is a clear line of authority to follow. **Work Values:** Working Conditions; Independence; Activity; Company Policies and Practices; Autonomy; Security. **Skills:** Reading Comprehension; Mathematics; Information Organization; Problem Identification; Active Listening. **Abilities:** *Cognitive*—Number Facility; Mathematical Reasoning; Written Comprehension; Perceptual Speed; Information Ordering. *Psychomotor*—Wrist-Finger Speed; Finger Dexterity; Control Precision. *Physical*—none met the criteria. *Sensory*—Near Vision; Speech Clarity; Speech Recognition. **General Work Activities:** *Information Input*—Getting Information Needed to Do the Job; Identifying Objects, Actions, and Events; Estimating Needed Characteristics. *Mental Process*—Processing Information; Analyzing Data or Information; Judging Qualities of Things, Services, Other People's Work. *Work Output*—Documenting and Recording Information; Interacting with Computers; Handling and Moving Objects. *Interacting with Others*—Communicating with Other Workers; Performing Administrative Activities; Interpreting Meaning of Information to Others. **Physical Work Conditions:** Indoors; Sitting; Using Hands on Objects, Tools, or Controls. **Other Job Characteristics:** Importance of Being Exact or Accurate; Consequence of Error; Importance of Being Sure All Is Done.

Experience: Job Zone 2. Some previous work-related skill, knowledge, or experience may be helpful, but usually is not needed. **Job Preparation:** SVP 4.00 to 5.99—6 months to less than 2 years.

Knowledge: Economics and Accounting; Clerical; Mathematics; English Language; Computers and Electronics. **Instructional Programs:** 520302 Accounting Technician; 520399 Accounting, Other.

Related DOT Jobs: 210.362-010 Distribution-Accounting Clerk; 210.367-010 Account-Information Clerk; 210.367-014 Foreign-Exchange-Position Clerk; 210.382-010 Audit Clerk; 210.382-014 Bookkeeper; 210.382-042 Fixed-Capital Clerk; 210.382-046 General-Ledger Bookkeeper; 210.382-054 Night Auditor; 210.382-062 Securities Clerk; 216.362-014 Collection Clerk; 216.362-022 Food-and-Beverage Controller; 216.362-034 Reserves Clerk; 216.362-038 Electronic Funds Transfer Coordinator; 216.362-042 Margin Clerk I; 216.367-014 Trust-Vault Clerk; 216.382-022 Budget Clerk; 216.482-010 Accounting Clerk; 219.367-042 Canceling and Cutting Control Clerk; 219.367-050 Letter-of-Credit Clerk.

43-3041.00 Gaming Cage Workers (All Other Service Workers)

Education: No data available.

Employed: 346,480

Openings: No data available.

Projected Growth: No data available.

Earnings: $15,950

In a gaming establishment, conduct financial transactions for patrons. Reconcile daily summaries of transactions to balance books. Accept patron's credit application and verify credit references to provide check-cashing authorization or to establish house credit accounts. Sell gambling chips, tokens, or tickets to patrons or to other workers for resale to patrons. Convert gaming chips, tokens, or tickets to currency upon patron's request. Use a cash register or computer to record transaction.

GOE Number, Interest Area, and Work Group: 09.05.01; Business Detail; Customer Service. **Instructional Programs:** 080901 Hospitality and Recreation Marketing Operations, General; 080999 Hospitality and Recreation Marketing Operations, Other; 120405 Massage; 200404 Dietician Assistant. **Note:** The Department of Labor has not collected some data for this job, so it has fewer details than the other descriptions.

43-3051.00 Payroll and Timekeeping Clerks (Payroll and Timekeeping Clerks)

Education: Short-term O-T-J training

Employed: 171,512

Openings: 15,425

Projected Growth: –6.2%

Earnings: $24,560

Compute wages and post wage data to payroll records. Keep daily records showing time of arrival and departure from work of employees. Compute earnings from time sheets and work tickets using calculator. Operate posting machine to compute and subtract payroll deductions. Enter net wages on earnings record card, check stub, and payroll sheet.

Processes and issues paychecks to employees. Records employee information such as exemptions, transfers, leave pay, and insurance coverage, to maintain and update payroll records. Verifies attendance, hours worked, and pay adjustments; posts information onto designated records. Calculates or computes wages and deductions and enters data into computer. Compiles employee time, production, and payroll data from time sheets and other records. Compares wage computations, logs, and time sheets to detect and reconcile payroll discrepancies. Reviews time sheets, work charts, timecards, and union agreements for completeness and to determine payroll factors and pay rates. Compiles and submits payroll status and other reports to designated departments.

GOE Number, Interest Area, and Work Group: 09.03.01; Business Detail; Bookkeeping, Auditing, and Accounting. **Personality Type:** Conventional. Conventional occupations frequently involve following set procedures and routines. These occupations can include working with data and details more than with ideas. Usually there is a clear line of authority to follow. **Work Values:** Working Conditions; Independence; Supervision, Human Relations; Company Policies and Practices; Security. **Skills:** Mathematics; Reading Comprehension; Writing; Problem Identification; Information Gathering; Active Listening. **Abilities:** *Cognitive*—Number Facility; Mathematical Reasoning; Written Comprehension; Information Ordering; Written Expression. *Psychomotor*—Wrist-Finger Speed; Finger Dexterity. *Physical*—Trunk Strength. **General Work Activities:** *Information Input*—Getting Information Needed to Do the Job; Identifying Objects, Actions, and Events; Monitoring Processes, Materials, and Surroundings. *Mental Process*—Processing Information; Evaluating Information Against Standards; Analyzing Data or Information. *Work Output*—Documenting and Recording Information; Interacting with Computers; Handling and Moving Objects. *Interacting with Others*—Communicating with Other Workers; Performing Administrative Activities; Monitoring and Controlling Resources. **Physical Work Conditions:** Indoors; Sitting; Making Repetitive Motions. **Other Job Characteristics:** Importance of Being Exact or Accurate; Importance of Being Sure All Is Done; Consequence of Error.

Experience: Job Zone 2. Some previous work-related skill, knowledge, or experience may be helpful, but usually is not needed. **Job Preparation:** SVP 4.00 to 5.99—6 months to less than 2 years. **Knowledge:** Clerical; Mathematics; Economics and Accounting; Personnel and Human Resources; Computers and Electronics; English Language; Administration and Management. **Instructional Program:** 520302 Accounting Technician.

Related DOT Jobs: 215.362-018 Flight-Crew-Time Clerk; 215.362-022 Timekeeper; 215.382-014 Payroll Clerk.

43-3061.00 Procurement Clerks (Procurement Clerks)

Education: Short-term O-T-J training

Employed: 58,103

Openings: 9,795

Projected Growth: –14.8%

Earnings: $22,630

Compile information and records to draw up purchase orders for procurement of materials and services.

Verifies bills from suppliers with bids and purchase orders. Reads catalogs and interviews suppliers to obtain prices and specifications. Compiles records of items purchased or transferred between departments. Compares prices, specifications, and delivery dates, and awards contract to supplier with best bid. Computes total cost of items purchased, using calculator. Types or writes purchase order and sends copy to supplier and department originating request. Determines if material is on hand in sufficient quantity. Approves bills for payment. Confers with suppliers concerning late deliveries. Verifies terminology and specifications of purchase requests. Types or writes invitation-of-bid forms; mails forms to supplier firms or distributes forms for public posting.

GOE Number, Interest Area, and Work Group: 09.07.02; Business Detail; Records Processing: Preparation and Maintenance. **Personality Type:** Conventional. Conventional occupations frequently involve following set procedures and routines. These occupations can include working with data and details more than with ideas. Usually there is a clear line of authority to follow. **Work Values:** Moral Values; Working Conditions; Activity; Company Policies and Practices; Independence. **Skills:** Speaking; Reading Comprehension; Information Organization; Information Gathering; Active Listening. **Abilities:** *Cognitive*—Written Expression; Written Comprehension; Number Facility; Oral Expression; Oral Comprehension; Perceptual Speed. *Psychomotor*—Finger Dexterity. *Physical*—none met the criteria. *Sensory*—Near Vision; Speech Clarity. **General Work Activities:** *Information Input*—Getting Information Needed to Do the Job; Identifying Objects, Actions, and Events; Estimating Needed Characteristics. *Mental Process*—Processing Information; Analyzing Data or Information; Updating and Using Job-Relevant Knowledge; Evaluating Information Against Standards. *Work Output*—Documenting and Recording Information; Implementing Ideas and Programs; Handling and Moving Objects. *Interacting with Others*—Monitoring and Controlling Resources; Communicating with Persons Outside Organization; Establishing and Maintaining Relationships. **Physical Work Conditions:** Indoors; Sitting; Using Hands on Objects, Tools, or Controls; Standing. **Other Job Characteristics:** Importance of Being Sure All Is Done; Importance of Being Exact or Accurate; Frustrating Circumstances.

Experience: Job Zone 1. No previous work-related skill, knowledge, or experience is needed. **Job Preparation:** SVP Below 4.0—Less than 6 months. **Knowledge:** Clerical; Mathematics; English Language; Economics and Accounting; Computers and Electronics. **Instructional Program:** 520408 General Office/Clerical and Typing Services.

Related DOT Jobs: 249.367-066 Procurement Clerk; 976.567-010 Film-Replacement Orderer.

43-3071.00 Tellers (Bank Tellers)

Education: Short-term O-T-J training

Employed: 559,778

Openings: 106,674

Projected Growth: –5.5%

Earnings: $17,200

Receive and pay out money. Keep records of money and negotiable instruments involved in a financial institution's various transactions.

Receives checks and cash for deposit, verifies amount, and examines checks for endorsements. Quotes unit exchange rate, following daily international rate sheet or computer display. Removes deposits from automated teller machine and night depository; counts and balances cash in them. Gives information to customer about foreign-currency regulations; computes exchange value and transaction fee for currency exchange. Explains, promotes, or sells products or services such as travelers checks, savings bonds, money orders, and cashier's checks. Composes, types, and mails correspondence relating to discrepancies, errors, and outstanding unpaid items. Balances currency, coin, and checks in cash drawer at end of shift and calculates daily transactions. Issues checks to bond owners, in settlement of transactions. Counts currency, coins, and checks received, for deposit, shipment to branch banks, or Federal Reserve Bank, by hand or using currency-counting machine. Prepares daily inventory of currency, drafts, and travelers' checks. Enters customers' transactions into computer to record transactions; issues computer-generated receipts. Cashes checks and pays out money after verification of signatures and customer balances. Examines coupons and bills presented for payment, to verify issue, payment date, and amount due.

GOE Number, Interest Area, and Work Group: 09.05.01 Business Detail, Customer Service. **Personality Type:** Conventional. Conventional occupations frequently involve following set procedures and routines. These occupations can include working with data and details more than with ideas. Usually there is a clear line of authority to follow. **Work Values:** Working Conditions; Co-workers; Supervision, Human Relations; Security; Supervision, Technical; Company Policies and Practices; Moral Values. **Skills:** Active Listening; Speaking; Mathematics; Reading Comprehension; Service Orientation. **Abilities:** *Cognitive*—Number Facility; Oral Expression; Information Ordering; Perceptual Speed; Oral Comprehension. *Psychomotor*—Wrist-Finger Speed; Response Orientation. *Physical*—Extent Flexibility; Trunk Strength. *Sensory*—Near Vision; Speech Recognition; Speech Clarity. **General Work Activities:** *Information Input*—Getting Information Needed to Do the Job; Identifying Objects, Actions, and Events; Monitoring Processes, Materials, and Surroundings. *Mental Process*—Processing Information; Evaluating Information Against Standards; Judging Qualities of Things, Services, People. *Work Output*—Documenting and Recording Information; Interacting with Computers; Handling and Moving Objects. *Interacting with Others*—Communicating with Persons Outside Organization; Monitoring and Controlling Resources; Performing for or Working with the Public. **Physical Work Conditions:** Indoors; Sitting; Using Hands on Objects, Tools, or Controls; Standing. **Other Job Characteristics:** Importance of Being Exact or Accurate; Importance of Being Sure All Is Done; Degree of Automation.

Experience: Job Zone 2. Some previous work-related skill, knowledge, or experience may be helpful, but usually is not needed. **Job Preparation:** SVP 4.00 to 5.99—Six months to less than two years. **Knowledge:** Mathematics; Economics and Accounting; Customer and Personal Service; Clerical; Computers and Electronics. **Instructional Programs:** 080401 Financial Services Marketing Operations; 520803 Banking and Financial Support Services.

Related DOT Jobs: 211.366-014 Foreign Banknote Teller-Trader; 211.382-010 Teller, Vault; 211.362.018 Teller; 219.462.010 Coupon Clerk.

43-4000 Information and Record Clerks

43-4011.00 Brokerage Clerks (Brokerage Clerks)

Education: Moderate-term O-T-J training
Employed: 76,512
Openings: 17,895
Projected Growth: 28.4%
Earnings: $27,920

Perform clerical duties involving the purchase or sale of securities. Write orders for stock purchases and sales; compute transfer taxes; verify stock transactions; accept and deliver securities; track stock price fluctuations; compute equity; distribute dividends; keep records of daily transactions and holdings.

Monitors daily stock prices and computes fluctuations to determine the need for additional collateral to secure loans. Prepares reports summarizing daily transactions and earnings for individual customer accounts. Files, types, and operates standard office machines. Corresponds with customers and confers with coworkers to answer inquiries, discuss market fluctuations, and resolve account problems. Computes total holdings, dividends, interest, transfer taxes, brokerage fees, and commissions and allocates appropriate payments to customers. Schedules and coordinates transfer and delivery of security certificates between companies, departments, and customers. Prepares forms, such as receipts, withdrawal orders, transmittal papers, and transfer confirmations, based on transaction requests from stockholders. Records and documents security transactions, such as purchases, sales, conversions, redemptions, and payments, using computers, accounting ledgers, and certificate records. Verifies ownership and transaction information and dividend distribution instructions to ensure conformance with governmental regulations, using stock records and reports.

GOE Number, Interest Area, and Work Group: 09.03.01; Business Detail; Bookkeeping, Auditing, and Accounting. **Personality Type:** Conventional. Conventional occupations frequently involve following set procedures and routines. These occupations can include working with data and details more than with ideas. Usually there is a clear line of authority to follow. **Work Values:** Working Conditions; Activity; Security; Moral Values; Company Policies and Practices; Supervision, Human Relations; Co-workers. **Skills:** Active Listening; Reading Comprehension; Mathematics; Speaking; Writing. **Abilities:** *Cognitive*—Written Expression; Number Facility; Mathematical Reasoning; Oral Expression; Written Comprehension. *Psychomotor*—Wrist-Finger Speed. *Physical*—none met the criteria. *Sensory*—Near Vision; Speech Clarity; Speech Recognition. **General Work Activities:** *Information Input*—Getting Information Needed to Do the Job; Identifying Objects, Actions, and Events; Monitoring Processes, Materials, and Surroundings. *Mental Process*—Processing Information; Updating and Using Job-Relevant Knowledge; Evaluating Information Against Standards. *Work Output*—Documenting and Recording Information; Interacting with Computers; Implementing Ideas and Programs. *Interacting with Others*—Communicating with Persons Outside Organization; Communicating with Other Workers; Establishing and Maintaining Relationships; Performing Administrative Activities; Interpreting Meaning of Information to Others. **Physical Work Conditions:** Indoors; Sitting; Standing. **Other Job Characteristics:** Consequence of Error; Frustrating Circumstances; Importance of Being Sure All Is Done; Importance of Being Aware of New Events.

Experience: Job Zone 2. Some previous work-related skill, knowledge, or experience may be helpful, but usually is not needed. **Job Preparation:** SVP 4.00 to 5.99—6 months to less than 2 years. **Knowledge:** Economics and Accounting; Clerical; Mathematics; English Language; Computers and Electronics. **Instructional Program:** 520302 Accounting Technician.

Related DOT Jobs: 216.362-046 Transfer Clerk; 216.382-046 Margin Clerk II; 216.482-034 Dividend Clerk; 219.362-018 Brokerage Clerk II; 219.362-054 Securities Clerk; 219.482-010 Brokerage Clerk I.

43-4021.00 Correspondence Clerks (Correspondence Clerks)

Education: Short-term O-T-J training

Employed: 24,877

Openings: 4,276

Projected Growth: 12.2%

Earnings: $22,270

Compose letters in reply to requests for merchandise, damage claims, credit and other information, delinquent accounts, incorrect billings, or unsatisfactory services. Gather data to formulate reply; type correspondence.

Compiles data from records to prepare periodic reports. Completes form letters in response to request or problem identified by correspondence. Compiles data pertinent to manufacture of special products for customers. Routes correspondence to other departments for reply. Maintains files and control records to show status of action in processing correspondence. Investigates discrepancies in reports and records; confers with personnel in affected departments to ensure accuracy and compliance with procedures. Reads incoming correspondence to ascertain nature of writer's concern and determine disposition of correspondence. Reviews records pertinent to resolution of problem for completeness and accuracy and attaches records to correspondence for reply by others. Processes orders for goods requested in correspondence. Types acknowledgment letter to person sending correspondence. Gathers data to formulate reply. Composes letter in response to request or problem identified by correspondence. Confers with company personnel regarding feasibility of complying with writer's request.

GOE Number, Interest Area, and Work Group: 09.07.02; Business Detail; Records Processing: Preparation and Maintenance. **Personality Type:** Conventional. Conventional occupations frequently involve following set procedures and routines. These occupations can include working with data and details more than with ideas. Usually there is a clear line of authority to follow. **Work Values:** Working Conditions; Company Policies and Practices; Activity; Moral Values; Supervision, Human Relations. **Skills:** Reading Comprehension; Writing; Problem Identification; Information Gathering; Active Listening. **Abilities:** *Cognitive*—Written Expression; Written Comprehension; Oral Comprehension; Oral Expression; Problem Sensitivity. *Psychomotor*—Wrist-Finger Speed. *Physical*—none met the criteria. *Sensory*—Near Vision. **General Work Activities:** *Information Input*—Getting Information Needed to Do the Job; Identifying Objects, Actions, and Events; Monitoring Processes, Materials, and Surroundings; Estimating Needed Characteristics. *Mental Process*—Processing Information; Evaluating Information Against Standards; Making Decisions and Solving Problems. *Work Output*—Documenting and Recording Information; Implementing Ideas and Programs; Handling and Moving Objects; Interacting with Computers. *Interacting with Others*—Performing Administrative Activities; Communicating with Persons Outside Organization; Communicating with Other Workers. **Physical Work Conditions:** Indoors; Sitting; Using Hands on Objects, Tools, or Controls. **Other Job Characteristics:** Importance of Being Sure All Is Done; Importance of Being Exact or Accurate; Consequence of Error.

Experience: Job Zone 2. Some previous work-related skill, knowledge, or experience may be helpful, but usually is not needed. **Job Preparation:** SVP 4.00 to 5.99—6 months to less than 2 years. **Knowledge:** Clerical; English Language; Economics and Accounting; Computers and Electronics; Communications and Media; Mathematics. **Instructional Program:** 520408 General Office/Clerical and Typing Services.

Related DOT Jobs: 209.362-034 Correspondence Clerk; 209.367-018 Correspondence-Review Clerk; 209.387-034 Suggestion Clerk; 221.367-062 Sales Correspondent.

43-4031.00 Court, Municipal, and License Clerks (Court Clerks)

Education: Short-term O-T-J training

Employed: 51,209

Openings: 13,394

Projected Growth: 10.8%

Earnings: $22,960

Perform clerical duties in courts of law, municipalities, and governmental licensing agencies and bureaus. Prepare docket of cases to be called; secure information for judges and court; prepare draft agendas or bylaws for town or city council; answer official correspondence; keep fiscal records and accounts; issue licenses or permits; record data; administer tests; collect fees.

GOE Number, Interest Area, and Work Group: 09.02.01; Business Detail; Administrative Detail: Administration. **Instructional Program:** 520405 Court Reporter. **Note:** The Department of Labor has not collected some data for this job, so it has fewer details than the other descriptions.

43-4031.01 Court Clerks (Court Clerks)

Education: Short-term O-T-J training

Employed: 51,209

Openings: 13,394

Projected Growth: 10.8%

Earnings: $22,960

Perform clerical duties in court of law; prepare docket of cases to be called.

Collects court fees or fines and records amounts collected. Prepares case folders; posts, files, or routes documents. Secures information for judges; contacts witnesses, attorneys, and litigants to obtain information for court. Examines legal documents submitted to court for adherence to law or court procedures. Records case disposition, court orders, and arrangement for payment of court fees. Administers oath to witnesses. Notifies district attorney's office of cases prosecuted by district attorney. Records minutes of court proceedings, using stenotype machine or shorthand; transcribes testimony, using typewriter or computer. Explains procedures or forms to parties in case. Prepares docket or calendar of cases to be called, using typewriter or computer. Instructs parties when to appear in court.

GOE Number, Interest Area, and Work Group: 09.02.01; Business Detail; Administrative Detail: Administration. **Personality Type:** Conventional. Conventional occupations frequently involve following set procedures and routines. These occupations can include working with data and details more than with ideas. Usually there is a clear line of authority to follow. **Work Values:** Activity; Security; Supervision, Human Relations; Working Conditions; Company Policies and Practices; Moral Values. **Skills:** Reading Comprehension; Active Listening; Information Organization; Writing; Speaking. **Abilities:** *Cognitive*—Written Expression; Oral Comprehension; Oral Expression; Written Comprehension; Information Ordering. *Psychomotor*—Wrist-Finger Speed; Finger Dexterity. *Physical*—none met the criteria. *Sensory*—Near Vision; Speech Recognition. **General Work Activities:** *Information Input*—Getting Information Needed to Do the Job; Monitoring Processes, Materials, and Surroundings; Identifying Objects, Actions, and Events. *Mental Process*—Evaluating Information Against Standards; Processing Information; Organizing, Planning, and Prioritizing; Judging Qualities of Things, Services, Other People's Work; Scheduling Work and Activities. *Work Output*—Documenting and Recording Information; Handling and Moving Objects; Implementing Ideas and Programs. *Interacting with Others*—Performing Administrative Activities; Communicating with Persons Outside Organization; Performing for or Working with the Public; Communicating with Other Workers. **Physical Work Conditions:** Sitting; Indoors; Using Hands on Objects, Tools, or Controls. **Other Job Characteristics:** Importance of Being Exact or Accurate; Importance of Being Sure All Is Done; Consequence of Error.

Experience: Job Zone 3. Previous work-related skill, knowledge, or experience is required. **Job Preparation:** SVP 6.0 to less than 7.0—More than 1 year and less than 4 years. **Knowledge:** Clerical; Law, Government and Jurisprudence; English Language; Computers and Electronics; Mathematics. **Instructional Program:** 520405 Court Reporter.

Related DOT Job: 243.362-010 Court Clerk.

43-4031.02 Municipal Clerks (Municipal Clerks)

Education: Short-term O-T-J training

Employed: 24,795

Openings: 6,545

Projected Growth: 11.9%

Earnings: $22,810

Draft agendas and bylaws for town or city council; record minutes of council meetings.

Prepares agendas and bylaws for town council. Prepares reports on civic needs. Records minutes of council meetings. Keeps fiscal records and accounts. Answers official correspondence.

GOE Number, Interest Area, and Work Group: 09.02.01; Business Detail; Administrative Detail: Administration. **Personality Type:** Conventional. Conventional occupations frequently involve following set procedures and routines. These occupations can include working with data and details more than with ideas. Usually there is a clear line of authority to follow. **Work Values:** Moral Values; Supervision, Human Relations; Working Conditions; Company Policies and Practices; Security. **Skills:** Writing; Reading Comprehension; Active Listening; Critical Thinking; Mathematics; Information Gathering. **Abilities:** *Cognitive*—Oral Comprehension; Written Expression; Number Facility; Written Comprehension; Information Ordering. *Psychomotor*—Wrist-Finger Speed; Reaction Time. *Physical*—none met the criteria. *Sensory*—Far Vision; Auditory Attention; Speech Recognition. **General Work Activities:** *Information Input*—Getting Information Needed to Do the Job; Monitoring Processes, Materials, and Surroundings; Identifying Objects, Actions, and Events. *Mental Process*—Processing Information; Scheduling Work and Activities; Organizing, Planning, and Prioritizing; Evaluating Information Against Standards; Analyzing Data or Information. *Work Output*—Documenting and Recording Information; Handling and Moving Objects; Interacting with Computers. *Interacting with Others*—Communicating with Persons Outside Organization; Performing Administrative Activities; Communicating with Other Workers. **Physical Work Conditions:** Indoors; Sitting; Using Hands on Objects, Tools, or Controls. **Other Job Characteristics:** Importance of Being Exact or Accurate; Importance of Being Sure All Is Done; Frustrating Circumstances.

Experience: Job Zone 2. Some previous work-related skill, knowledge, or experience may be helpful, but usually is not needed. **Job Preparation:** SVP 4.00 to 5.99—6 months to less than 2 years. **Knowledge:** Clerical; Economics and Accounting; English Language; Mathematics; Administration and Management. **Instructional Program:** 520402 Executive Assistant/Secretary.

Related DOT Job: 243.367-018 Town Clerk.

43-4031.03 License Clerks (License Clerks)

Education: Short-term O-T-J training

Employed: 24,103

Openings: 6,424

Projected Growth: 13.1%

Earnings: $22,900

Issue licenses or permits to qualified applicants. Obtain necessary information; record data.

Counts collected fees and applications. Collects prescribed fee. Submits fees and reports to government for record. Evaluates information obtained to determine applicant qualification for licensure. Questions applicant to obtain information such as name, address, and age; records data on prescribed forms. Conducts oral, visual, written, or performance test to determine applicant qualifications. Issues driver, automobile, marriage, dog, or other license.

GOE Number, Interest Area, and Work Group: 09.02.01; Business Detail; Administrative Detail: Administration. **Personality Type:** Conventional. Conventional occupations frequently involve following set procedures and routines. These occupations can include working with data and details more than with ideas. Usually there is a clear line of authority to follow. **Work Values:** Supervision, Human Relations; Activity; Moral Values; Company Policies and Practices; Security; Working Conditions. **Skills:** Speaking; Active Listening; Reading Comprehension; Information Gathering; Writing; Monitoring. **Abilities:** *Cognitive*—Oral Comprehension; Oral Expression; Written Expression; Written Comprehension; Perceptual Speed. *Psychomotor*—none met the criteria. *Physical*—none met the criteria. *Sensory*—Far Vision; Auditory Attention; Glare Sensitivity. **General Work Activities:** *Information Input*—Getting Information Needed to Do the Job; Identifying Objects, Actions, and Events; Estimating Needed Characteristics. *Mental Process*—Evaluating Information Against Standards; Processing Information; Analyzing Data or Information. *Work Output*—Documenting and Recording Information; Handling and Moving Objects; Implementing Ideas and Programs; Interacting with Computers; Performing General Physical Activities. *Interacting with Others*—Performing for or Working with the Public; Communicating with Persons Outside Organization; Establishing and Maintaining Relationships. **Physical Work Conditions:** Indoors; Sitting; Standing. **Other Job Characteristics:** Importance of Being Sure All Is Done; Importance of Being Exact or Accurate; Degree of Automation.

Experience: Job Zone 2. Some previous work-related skill, knowledge, or experience may be helpful, but usually is not needed. **Job Preparation:** SVP 4.00 to 5.99—6 months to less than 2 years. **Knowledge:** Clerical; Mathematics; Law, Government and Jurisprudence; Customer and Personal Service; English Language. **Instructional Program:** 520408 General Office/Clerical and Typing Services.

Related DOT Jobs: 205.367-034 License Clerk; 249.367-030 Dog Licenser; 379.137-014 Supervisor, Dog License Officer.

43-4041.00 Credit Authorizers, Checkers, and Clerks (Credit Authorizers)

Education: Short-term O-T-J training

Employed: 16,906

Openings: 3,693

Projected Growth: –10.7%

Earnings: $22,990

Authorize credit charges against customers' accounts. Investigate history and credit standing of individuals or business establishments applying for credit. Interview applicants to obtain personal and financial data; determine credit worthiness; process applications; notify customers of acceptance or rejection of credit.

GOE Number, Interest Area, and Work Group: 09.07.01; Business Detail; Records Processing: Verification and Proofing. **Instructional Program:** 520803 Banking and Financial Support Services. **Note:** The Department of Labor has not collected some data for this job, so it has fewer details than the other descriptions.

43-4041.01 Credit Authorizers (Credit Authorizers)

Education: Short-term O-T-J training

Employed: 16,906

Openings: 3,693

Projected Growth: –10.7%

Earnings: $22,990

Authorize credit charges against customers' accounts.

Receives charge slip or credit application by mail, or receives information from salespeople or merchants by phone. Verifies credit standing of customer from information in files; approves or disapproves credit, based on predetermined standards. Files sales slips in customer's ledger for billing purposes. Keeps record of customer's charges and payments; mails charge statement to customer. Prepares credit cards or charge account plates.

GOE Number, Interest Area, and Work Group: 09.07.01; Business Detail; Records Processing: Verification and Proofing. **Personality Type:** Conventional. Conventional occupations frequently involve following set procedures and routines. These occupations can include working with data and details more than with ideas. Usually there is a clear line of authority to follow. **Work Values:** Working Conditions; Moral Values; Security; Activity; Supervision, Human Relations. **Skills:** Active Listening; Reading Comprehension; Information Organization; Information Gathering; Writing; Speaking. **Abilities:** *Cognitive*—Number Facility; Written Comprehension; Oral Comprehension; Oral Expression; Written Expression. *Psychomotor*—Wrist-Finger Speed. *Physical*—none met the criteria. *Sensory*—Speech Clarity; Glare Sensitivity. **General Work Activities:** *Information Input*—Getting Information Needed to Do the Job; Identifying Objects, Actions, and Events; Estimating Needed Characteristics. *Mental Process*—Evaluating Information Against Standards; Processing Information; Making Decisions and Solving Problems. *Work Output*—Documenting and Recording Information; Interacting with Computers; Implementing Ideas and Programs. *Interacting with Others*—Communicating with Persons Outside Organization; Establishing and Maintaining Relationships; Interpreting Meaning of Information to Others; Performing Administrative Activities; Resolving Conflict and Negotiating with Others. **Physical Work Conditions:** Indoors; Sitting; Using Hands on Objects, Tools, or Controls. **Other Job Characteristics:** Importance of Being Exact or Accurate; Importance of Being Sure All Is Done; Degree of Automation.

Experience: Job Zone 1. No previous work-related skill, knowledge, or experience is needed. **Job Preparation:** SVP Below 4.0—Less than 6 months. **Knowledge:** Clerical; Mathematics; Economics and Accounting; Computers and Electronics; Telecommunications; English Language. **Instructional Program:** 520803 Banking and Financial Support Services.

Related DOT Job: 249.367-022 Credit Authorizer.

43-4041.02 Credit Checkers (Credit Checkers)

Education: Short-term O-T-J training
Employed: 40,955
Openings: 9,293
Projected Growth: 1.5%
Earnings: $21,550

Investigate history and credit standing of individuals or business establishments applying for credit. Telephone or write to credit departments of business and service establishments to obtain information about applicant's credit standing.

Examines city directories and public records to verify residence property ownership, bankruptcies, liens, arrest record, or unpaid taxes of applicant. Prepares reports of findings and recommendations, using typewriter or computer. Telephones subscriber to relay requested information or sends subscriber credit report. Compiles and analyzes credit information gathered by investigation. Obtains information from banks, credit bureaus, and other credit services and provides reciprocal information if requested. Interviews credit applicant by telephone or in person to obtain financial and personal data for credit report. Contacts former employers and other acquaintances to verify references, employment, health history, and social behavior.

GOE Number, Interest Area, and Work Group: 09.07.01; Business Detail; Records Processing: Verification and Proofing. **Personality Type:** Conventional. Conventional occupations frequently involve following set procedures and routines. These occupations can include working with data and details more than with ideas. Usually there is a clear line of authority to follow. **Work Values:** Working Conditions; Activity; Moral Values; Security; Supervision, Human Relations. **Skills:** Speaking; Active Listening; Writing; Information Gathering; Judgment and Decision Making; Information Organization; Reading Comprehension. **Abilities:** *Cognitive*—Oral Comprehension; Oral Expression; Written Comprehension; Problem Sensitivity; Inductive Reasoning; Written Expression. *Psychomotor*—Wrist-Finger Speed. *Physical*—

Gross Body Equilibrium. *Sensory*—Speech Clarity. **General Work Activities:** *Information Input*—Getting Information Needed to Do the Job; Identifying Objects, Actions, and Events; Monitoring Processes, Materials, and Surroundings. *Mental Process*—Processing Information; Analyzing Data or Information; Evaluating Information Against Standards. *Work Output*—Documenting and Recording Information; Interacting with Computers; Implementing Ideas and Programs. *Interacting with Others*—Communicating with Persons Outside Organization; Interpreting Meaning of Information to Others; Communicating with Other Workers; Performing Administrative Activities. **Physical Work Conditions:** Indoors; Sitting; Standing. **Other Job Characteristics:** Frustrating Circumstances; Importance of Being Sure All Is Done; Importance of Being Exact or Accurate.

Experience: Job Zone 1. No previous work-related skill, knowledge, or experience is needed. **Job Preparation:** SVP Below 4.0—Less than 6 months. **Knowledge:** Clerical; Mathematics; English Language; Telecommunications; Economics and Accounting. **Instructional Program:** 520803 Banking and Financial Support Services.

Related DOT Jobs: 209.362-018 Credit Reference Clerk; 237.367-014 Call-Out Operator; 241.267-030 Investigator.

43-4051.00 Customer Service Representatives
(Customer Service Representatives, Utilities)

Education: No data available.
Employed: 201,350
Openings: No data available.
Projected Growth: No data available.
Earnings: $28,030

Interact with customers to provide information in response to inquiries about products and services and to handle and resolve complaints.

GOE Number, Interest Area, and Work Group: 09.05.01; Business Detail; Customer Service. **Instructional Program:** 520406 Receptionist. **Note:** The Department of Labor has not collected some data for this job, so it has fewer details than the other descriptions.

43-4051.01 Adjustment Clerks (Adjustment Clerks)

Education: Short-term O-T-J training
Employed: 479,015
Openings: 141,670
Projected Growth: 34%
Earnings: $22,040

Investigate and resolve customers' inquiries concerning merchandise, service, billing, or credit rating. Examine pertinent information to determine accuracy of customers' complaints and responsibility for errors. Notify customers and appropriate personnel of findings, adjustments, and recommendations, such as exchange of merchandise, refund of money, credit to customers' accounts, or adjustment to customers' bills.

Compares merchandise with original requisition and information on invoice; prepares invoice for returned goods. Trains dealers or service personnel in construction of products, service operations, and customer service. Writes work order. Reviews claims adjustments with dealer; examines parts claimed to be defective; approves or disapproves of dealer's claim. Examines weather conditions, number of days in billing period, and reviews meter accounts for errors which might explain high utility charges. Notifies customer and designated personnel of findings and recommendations, such as exchanging merchandise, refunding money, or adjusting bill. Orders tests to detect product malfunction and determines if defect resulted from faulty construction. Prepares reports showing volume, types, and disposition of claims handled.

GOE Number, Interest Area, and Work Group: 09.05.01; Business Detail; Customer Service. **Personality Type:** Conventional. Conventional occupations frequently involve following set procedures and routines. These occupations can include working with data and details more than with ideas. Usually there is a clear line of authority to follow. **Work Values:** Working Conditions; Supervision, Human Relations; Activity; Co-workers; Moral Values; Company Policies and Practices; Security. **Skills:** Speaking; Problem Identification; Active Listening; Writing; Instructing; Reading Comprehension. **Abilities:** *Cognitive*—Oral Expression; Written Comprehension; Oral Comprehension; Written Expression; Deductive Reasoning. *Psychomotor*—Wrist-Finger Speed. *Physical*—none met the criteria. *Sensory*—Near Vision; Speech Recognition; Speech Clarity. **General Work Activities:** *Information Input*—Getting Information Needed to Do the Job; Identifying Objects, Actions, and Events; Inspecting Equipment, Structures, Materials. *Mental Process*—Making Decisions and Solving Problems; Judging Qualities of Things, Services, Other People's Work; Processing Information; Analyzing Data or Information. *Work Output*—Documenting and Recording Information; Handling and Moving Objects; Implementing Ideas and Programs. *Interacting with Others*—Performing for or Working with the Public; Resolving Conflict and Negotiating with Others; Communicating with Persons Outside Organization. **Physical Work Conditions:** Indoors; Sitting; Standing; Using Hands on Objects, Tools, or Controls. **Other Job Characteristics:** Importance of Being Sure All Is Done; Consequence of Error; Importance of Being Exact or Accurate.

Experience: Job Zone 2. Some previous work-related skill, knowledge, or experience may be helpful, but usually is not needed. **Job Preparation:** SVP 4.00 to 5.99—6 months to less than 2 years. **Knowledge:** English Language; Customer and Personal Service; Mathematics; Education and Training; Economics and Accounting. **Instructional Programs:** 081203 Vehicle Parts and Accessories Marketing Operations; 520408 General Office/Clerical and Typing Services.

Related DOT Jobs: 191.167-022 Service Representative; 209.587-042 Return-To-Factory Clerk; 221.387-014 Complaint Clerk; 241.267-034 Investigator, Utility-Bill Complaints; 241.367-014 Customer-Complaint Clerk; 241.367-034 Tire Adjuster; 241.387-010 Claims Clerk.

43-4051.02 Customer Service Representatives, Utilities (Customer Service Representatives, Utilities)

Education: No data available.
Employed: 201,350
Openings: No data available.
Projected Growth: No data available.
Earnings: $28,030

Interview applicants for water, gas, electric, or telephone service. Talk with customer by phone or in person and receive orders for installation, turn-on, discontinuance, or change in services.

Confers with customer by phone or in person to receive orders for installation, turn-on, discontinuance, or change in service. Completes contract forms; prepares change of address records; issues discontinuance orders, using computer. Determines charges for service requested; collects deposits. Solicits sale of new or additional utility services. Resolves billing or service complaints and refers grievances to designated departments for investigation.

GOE Number, Interest Area, and Work Group: 09.05.01; Business Detail; Customer Service. **Personality Type:** Conventional. Conventional occupations frequently involve following set procedures and routines. These occupations can include working with data and details more than with ideas. Usually there is a clear line of authority to follow. **Work Values:** Security; Supervision, Human Relations; Moral Values; Working Conditions; Company Policies and Practices. **Skills:** Active Listening; Speaking; Problem Identification; Service Orientation; Writing. **Abilities:** *Cognitive*—Oral Comprehension; Oral Expression; Number Facility; Mathematical Reasoning; Written Expression. *Psychomotor*—Wrist-Finger Speed. *Physical*—none met the criteria. *Sensory*—Near Vision; Speech Clarity; Speech Recognition; Auditory Attention. **General Work Activities:** *Information Input*—Getting Information Needed to Do the Job; Identifying Objects, Actions, and Events; Estimating Needed Characteristics. *Mental Process*—Processing Information; Analyzing Data or Information; Making Decisions and Solving Problems. *Work Output*—Documenting and Recording Information; Interacting with Computers; Handling and Moving Objects. *Interacting with Others*—Communicating with Persons Outside Organization; Performing for or Working with the Public; Performing Administrative Activities. **Physical Work Conditions:** Indoors; Sitting; Using Hands on Objects, Tools, or Controls. **Other Job Characteristics:** Importance of Being Sure All Is Done; Importance of Being Exact or Accurate; Importance of Repeating Same Tasks; Degree of Automation.

Experience: Job Zone 2. Some previous work-related skill, knowledge, or experience may be helpful, but usually is not needed. **Job Preparation:** SVP 4.00 to 5.99—6 months to less than 2 years. **Knowledge:** Customer and Personal Service; English Language; Sales and Marketing; Mathematics; Telecommunications. **Instructional Program:** 520406 Receptionist.

Related DOT Job: 239.362-014 Customer Service Representative.

43-4061.00 Eligibility Interviewers, Government Programs (Welfare Eligibility Workers and Interviewers)

Education: Moderate-term O-T-J training
Employed: 108,675
Openings: 1,986
Projected Growth: −7.6%
Earnings: $33,100

Determine eligibility of persons applying to receive assistance from government programs and agency resources, such as welfare, unemployment benefits, social security, and public housing.

GOE Number, Interest Area, and Work Group: 09.02.03; Business Detail; Administrative Detail: Interviewing. **Instructional Program:** 440701 Social Work. **Note:** The Department of Labor has not collected some data for this job, so it has fewer details than the other descriptions.

43-4061.01 Claims Takers, Unemployment Benefits (Claims Takers, Unemployment Benefits)

Education: No data available.
Employed: 10,500
Openings: No data available.
Projected Growth: No data available.
Earnings: $31,110

Interview unemployed workers and compile data to determine eligibility for unemployment benefits.

Interviews claimants returning at specified intervals to certify claimants for continuing benefits. Schedules unemployment insurance claimants for adjudication interview when question of eligibility arises. Assists applicants in filling out forms, using knowledge of information required or native language of applicant. Answers questions concerning registration for jobs or application for unemployment benefits. Reviews data on job application or claim forms to ensure completeness. Refers applicants to job opening or interview with other staff, in accordance with administrative guidelines or office procedure. Assists applicants completing application forms for job referrals or unemployment compensation claims.

GOE Number, Interest Area, and Work Group: 09.02.03; Business Detail; Administrative Detail: Interviewing. **Personality Type:** Conventional. Conventional occupations frequently involve following set procedures and routines. These occupations can include working with data and details more than with ideas. Usually there is a clear line of authority to follow. **Work Values:** Security; Social Service; Supervision, Human Relations; Supervision, Technical; Activity; Working Conditions. **Skills:** Speaking; Reading Comprehension; Active Listening; Information Gathering; Social Perceptiveness; Service Orientation; Writing. **Abilities:** *Cognitive*—Oral Expression; Oral Comprehension; Written Comprehension; Written Expression; Inductive Reasoning; Selective Attention. *Psychomotor*—none met the criteria. *Physical*—none met the crite-

ria. *Sensory*—Near Vision; Speech Clarity; Speech Recognition. **General Work Activities:** *Information Input*—Getting Information Needed to Do the Job; Identifying Objects, Actions, and Events; Monitoring Processes, Materials, and Surroundings. *Mental Process*—Processing Information; Evaluating Information Against Standards; Analyzing Data or Information. *Work Output*—Documenting and Recording Information; Implementing Ideas and Programs; Handling and Moving Objects; Controlling Machines and Processes. *Interacting with Others*—Performing for or Working with the Public; Communicating with Persons Outside Organization; Interpreting Meaning of Information to Others. **Physical Work Conditions:** Sitting; Indoors; Using Hands on Objects, Tools, or Controls. **Other Job Characteristics:** Importance of Being Sure All Is Done; Importance of Being Exact or Accurate; Frustrating Circumstances.

Experience: Job Zone 2. Some previous work-related skill, knowledge, or experience may be helpful, but usually is not needed. **Job Preparation:** SVP 4.00 to 5.99—6 months to less than 2 years. **Knowledge:** Personnel and Human Resources; Clerical; Customer and Personal Service; English Language; Law, Government and Jurisprudence; Therapy and Counseling. **Instructional Programs:** 440401 Public Administration; 521001 Human Resources Management.

Related DOT Job: 169.367-010 Employment-and-Claims Aide.

43-4061.02 Welfare Eligibility Workers and Interviewers (Welfare Eligibility Workers and Interviewers)

Education: Moderate-term O-T-J training
Employed: 108,675
Openings: 1,986
Projected Growth: −7.6%
Earnings: $33,100

Interview and investigate applicants and recipients to determine eligibility for use of social programs and agency resources. Record and evaluate personal and financial data obtained from individuals; initiate procedures to grant, modify, deny, or terminate eligibility for various aid programs.

Interprets and explains rules and regulations governing eligibility and grants, payment methods, and applicant's legal rights. Records and evaluates personal and financial data to determine initial or continuing eligibility. Selects and refers eligible applicants to public assistance or public housing agencies. Prepares regular and special reports, keeps records of assigned cases, and submits individual recommendations. Prepares and assists applicants in completion of routine intake and personnel forms. Explains eligibility requirements, form completion requirements, community resources for financial assistance, housing opportunities, and tenant selection methods. Reviews training approval forms and payment vouchers for completeness and accuracy. Conducts annual, interim, and special housing reviews and home visits to ensure conformance to regulations. Computes public housing rent in proportion to eligible tenant's income. Authorizes amounts of grants, money payments, food stamps, medical care, or other general assistance. Interviews and investigates applicants for public assistance to gather information pertinent to their application. Initiates procedures to grant, modify, deny, or terminate eligibility and grants for various assistance programs. Receives and records security deposits and advance rents from selected tenants.

GOE Number, Interest Area, and Work Group: 09.02.03; Business Detail; Administrative Detail: Interviewing. **Personality Type:** Social. Social occupations frequently involve working with, communicating with, and teaching people. These occupations often involve helping or providing service to others. **Work Values:** Social Service; Security; Activity; Achievement; Supervision, Human Relations. **Skills:** Service Orientation; Judgment and Decision Making; Information Gathering; Active Listening; Problem Identification; Speaking; Writing. **Abilities:** *Cognitive*—Oral Expression; Oral Comprehension; Written Comprehension; Written Expression; Number Facility. *Psychomotor*—none met the criteria. *Physical*—none met the criteria. *Sensory*—Speech Clarity; Speech Recognition. **General Work Activities:** *Information Input*—Getting Information Needed to Do the Job; Identifying Objects, Actions, and Events; Monitoring Processes, Materials, and Surroundings. *Mental Process*—Processing Information; Analyzing Data or Information; Making Decisions and Solving Problems. *Work Output*—Documenting and Recording Information; Implementing Ideas and Programs; Interacting with Computers. *Interacting with Others*—Assisting and Caring for Others; Communicating with Persons Outside Organization; Interpreting Meaning of Information to Others. **Physical Work Conditions:** Indoors; Sitting; Walking or Running; Standing. **Other Job Characteristics:** Frustrating Circumstances; Importance of Being Sure All Is Done; Importance of Being Exact or Accurate; Consequence of Error.

Experience: Job Zone 2. Some previous work-related skill, knowledge, or experience may be helpful, but usually is not needed. **Job Preparation:** SVP 4.00 to 5.99—6 months to less than 2 years. **Knowledge:** English Language; Therapy and Counseling; Clerical; Law, Government and Jurisprudence; Mathematics; Psychology; Administration and Management. **Instructional Program:** 440701 Social Work.

Related DOT Jobs: 168.267-038 Eligibility-and-Occupancy Interviewer; 169.167-018 Contact Representative; 195.267-010 Eligibility Worker; 195.267-018 Patient-Resources-and-Reimbursement Agent; 205.367-046 Rehabilitation Clerk.

43-4071.00 File Clerks (File Clerks)

Education: Short-term O-T-J training

Employed: 272,113

Openings: 117,451

Projected Growth: 9.6%

Earnings: $16,830

File correspondence, cards, invoices, receipts, and other records in alphabetical or numerical order or according to the filing system used. Locate and remove material from file when requested.

Removes or destroys outdated materials in accordance with file maintenance schedules or legal requirements. Locates and retrieves files upon request from authorized users. Inserts additional data on file records. Authorizes or documents materials movement, using logbook or computer; traces missing files. Assigns and records or stamps identification numbers or codes to index materials for filing. Inspects or examines materials or files for accuracy, legibility, or damage. Scans or reads incoming materials to determine filing order or location. Sorts or classifies information according to content, purpose, user criteria, or chronological, alphabetical, or numerical order. Photographs or makes copies of data and records, using photocopying or microfilming equipment. Places materials into storage receptacles such as file cabinets, boxes, bins, or drawers, according to classification and identification information.

GOE Number, Interest Area, and Work Group: 09.07.02; Business Detail; Records Processing: Preparation and Maintenance. **Personality Type:** Conventional. Conventional occupations frequently involve following set procedures and routines. These occupations can include working with data and details more than with ideas. Usually there is a clear line of authority to follow. **Work Values:** Moral Values; Working Conditions; Company Policies and Practices; Activity; Supervision, Human Relations. **Skills:** Information Organization; Reading Comprehension; Information Gathering; Writing; Active Listening. **Abilities:** *Cognitive*—Written Comprehension; Information Ordering; Category Flexibility; Oral Comprehension; Inductive Reasoning; Number Facility. *Psychomotor*—none met the criteria. *Physical*—none met the criteria. *Sensory*—Near Vision. **General Work Activities:** *Information Input*—Identifying Objects, Actions, and Events; Getting Information Needed to Do the Job; Inspecting Equipment, Structures, Materials. *Mental Process*—Processing Information; Judging Qualities of Things, Services, Other People's Work; Evaluating Information Against Standards. *Work Output*—Documenting and Recording Information; Handling and Moving Objects; Interacting with Computers; Implementing Ideas and Programs. *Interacting with Others*—Performing Administrative Activities; Communicating with Other Workers; Communicating with Persons Outside Organization. **Physical Work Conditions:** Indoors; Sitting; Making Repetitive Motions. **Other Job Characteristics:** Importance of Being Exact or Accurate; Importance of Being Sure All Is Done; Consequence of Error.

Experience: Job Zone 1. No previous work-related skill, knowledge, or experience is needed. **Job Preparation:** SVP Below 4.0—Less than 6 months. **Knowledge:** Clerical; Computers and Electronics; English Language; Law, Government and Jurisprudence; Mathematics. **Instructional Program:** 520408 General Office/Clerical and Typing Services.

Related DOT Jobs: 206.367-014 File Clerk II; 206.367-018 Tape Librarian; 206.387-010 Classification Clerk; 206.387-014 Fingerprint Clerk II; 206.387-022 Record Clerk; 206.387-034 File Clerk I.

43-4081.00 Hotel, Motel, and Resort Desk Clerks
(Hotel, Motel, and Resort Desk Clerks)

Education: Short-term O-T-J training

Employed: 158,662

Openings: 60,382

Projected Growth: 13.5%

Earnings: $15,160

Accommodate hotel, motel, and resort patrons by registering and assigning rooms to guests, issuing room keys, transmitting and receiving messages, keeping records of occupied rooms and guests' accounts, making and confirming reservations, and presenting statements to and collecting payments from departing guests.

Deposits guests' valuables in hotel safe or safe-deposit box. Keeps records of room availability and guests' accounts, manually or using computer. Posts charges such as room, food, liquor, or telephone, to ledger, manually or using computer. Transmits and receives messages, using telephone or telephone switchboard. Makes and confirms reservations. Computes bill, collects payment, and makes change for guests. Answers inquiries pertaining to hotel services. Date-stamps, sorts, and racks incoming mail and messages. Greets, registers, and assigns rooms to guests of hotel or motel. Issues room key and escort instructions to bellhop.

GOE Number, Interest Area, and Work Group: 11.03.01; Recreation, Travel, and Other Personal Services; Transportation and Lodging Services. **Personality Type:** Conventional. Conventional occupations frequently involve following set procedures and routines. These occupations can include working with data and details more than with ideas. Usually there is a clear line of authority to follow. **Work Values:** Working Conditions; Moral Values; Supervision, Human Relations; Social Service; Company Policies and Practices. **Skills:** Service Orientation; Active Listening; Problem Identification; Reading Comprehension; Information Organization; Coordination. **Abilities:** *Cognitive*—Oral Expression; Oral Comprehension; Number Facility; Written Comprehension; Mathematical Reasoning; Selective Attention. *Psychomotor*—none met the criteria. *Physical*—none met the criteria. *Sensory*—Speech Recognition. **General Work Activities:** *Information Input*—Getting Information Needed to Do the Job; Identifying Objects, Actions, and Events; Monitoring Processes, Materials, and Surroundings. *Mental Process*—Processing Information; Updating and Using Job-Relevant Knowledge; Making Decisions and Solving Problems. *Work Output*—Documenting and Recording Information; Interacting with Computers; Handling and Moving Objects. *Interacting with Others*—Communicating with Persons Outside Organization; Assisting and Caring for Others; Performing for or Working with the Public. **Physical Work Conditions:** Special Uniform; Standing; Indoors. **Other Job Characteristics:** Importance of Being Exact or Accurate; Importance of Being Sure All Is Done; Consequence of Error.

Experience: Job Zone 2. Some previous work-related skill, knowledge, or experience may be helpful, but usually is not needed. **Job Preparation:** SVP 4.00 to 5.99—6 months to less than 2 years. **Knowledge:** Customer and Personal Service; Clerical; English Language; Mathematics; Computers and Electronics. **Instructional Programs:** 080901 Hospitality and Recreation Marketing Operations, General; 080902 Hotel/Motel Services Marketing Operations.

Related DOT Job: 238.367-038 Hotel Clerk.

43-4111.00 Interviewers, Except Eligibility and Loan
(Interviewing Clerks)

Education: Short-term O-T-J training
Employed: 128,057
Openings: 44,483
Projected Growth: 23.3%
Earnings: $18,540

Interview persons by telephone, mail, in person, or by other means for the purpose of completing forms, applications, or questionnaires. Ask specific questions, record answers, and assist persons with completing form. Sort, classify, and file forms.

Explains reason for questioning, and other specified information. Assists person in filling out application or questionnaire. Compiles and sorts data from interview and reviews to correct errors. Contacts persons at home, place of business, or field location, by telephone, mail, or in person. Asks questions to obtain various specified information such as person's name, address, age, religion, and state of residency. Records results and data from interview or survey, using computer or specified form.

GOE Number, Interest Area, and Work Group: 09.02.03; Business Detail; Administrative Detail: Interviewing. **Personality Type:** Conventional. Conventional occupations frequently involve following set procedures and routines. These occupations can include working with data and details more than with ideas. Usually there is a clear line of authority to follow. **Work Values:** Moral Values; Independence; Working Conditions; Activity; Supervision, Human Relations. **Skills:** Speaking; Active Listening; Reading Comprehension; Information Gathering; Social Perceptiveness. **Abilities:** *Cognitive*—Oral Expression; Oral Comprehension; Written Expression; Written Comprehension; Information Ordering. *Psychomotor*—Wrist-Finger Speed. *Physical*—none met the criteria. *Sensory*—Speech Clarity; Speech Recognition. **General Work Activities:** *Information Input*—Getting Information Needed to Do the Job; Identifying Objects, Actions, and Events; Monitoring Processes, Materials, and Surroundings. *Mental Process*—Processing Information; Evaluating Information Against Standards; Organizing, Planning, and Prioritizing; Analyzing Data or Information. *Work Output*—Documenting and Recording Information; Interacting with Computers; Handling and Moving Objects. *Interacting with Others*—Communicating with Persons Outside Organization; Performing for or Working with the Public; Assisting and Caring for Others. **Physical Work Conditions:** Indoors; Sitting; Standing. **Other Job Characteristics:** Importance of Being Sure All Is Done; Importance of Being Exact or Accurate; Frustrating Circumstances.

Experience: Job Zone 1. No previous work-related skill, knowledge, or experience is needed. **Job Preparation:** SVP Below 4.0—Less than 6 months. **Knowledge:** Clerical; Computers and Electronics; English Language; Telecommunications; Personnel and Human Resources; Mathematics. **Instructional Program:** 520406 Receptionist.

Related DOT Jobs: 205.362-018 Hospital-Admitting Clerk; 205.367-014 Charge-Account Clerk; 205.367-026 Creel Clerk; 205.367-042 Registration Clerk; 205.367-054 Survey Worker; 205.367-058 Traffic Checker.

43-4121.00 Library Assistants, Clerical (Library Assistants and Bookmobile Drivers)

Education: Short-term O-T-J training

Employed: 126,691

Openings: 35,994

Projected Growth: 16.5%

Earnings: $16,980

Compile records; sort and shelve books; issue and receive library materials such as pictures, cards, slides, and microfilm. Locate library materials for loan; replace material in shelving area, stacks, or files, according to identification number and title. Register patrons to permit them to borrow books, periodicals, and other library materials.

Prepares, stores, and retrieves classification and catalog information, lecture notes, or other documents related to document stored, using computer. Drives bookmobile to specified locations following library services schedule and to garage for preventive maintenance and repairs. Sorts books, publications, and other items according to procedure and returns them to shelves, files, or other designated storage area. Maintains records of items received, stored, issued, and returned and files catalog cards according to system used. Classifies and catalogs items according to contents and purpose. Issues books to patrons and records or scans information on borrower's card. Reviews records such as microfilm and issue cards, to determine title of overdue materials and to identify borrower. Inspects returned books for damage, verifies due date, and computes and receives overdue fines. Answers routine inquiries and refers patrons who need professional assistance to librarian. Locates library materials for patrons, such as books, periodicals, tape cassettes, Braille volumes, and pictures. Delivers and retrieves items to and from departments by hand or push cart. Selects substitute titles, following criteria such as age, education, and interest, when requested materials are unavailable. Repairs books, using mending tape and paste and brush; places plastic covers on new books. Prepares address labels for books to be mailed, overdue notices, and duty schedules, using computer or typewriter. Operates and maintains audio-visual equipment and explains use of reference equipment to patrons. Places books in mailing container, affixes address label, and secures container with straps for mailing to blind library patrons. Issues borrower's identification card according to established procedures.

GOE Number, Interest Area, and Work Group: 12.03.04; Education and Social Service; Educational Services: Library and Museum. **Personality Type:** Conventional. Conventional occupations frequently involve following set procedures and routines. These occupations can include working with data and details more than with ideas. Usually there is a clear line of authority to follow. **Work Values:** Moral Values; Working Conditions; Supervision, Human Relations; Supervision, Technical; Security. **Skills:** Information Organization; Reading Comprehension; Active Listening; Service Orientation; Information Gathering. **Abilities:** *Cognitive*—Information Ordering; Category Flexibility; Oral Expression; Oral Comprehension; Written Comprehension. *Psychomotor*—Wrist-Finger Speed; Reaction Time; Response Orientation. *Physical*—

Extent Flexibility; Dynamic Flexibility; Gross Body Equilibrium. *Sensory*—Near Vision; Speech Clarity; Visual Color Discrimination. **General Work Activities:** *Information Input*—Getting Information Needed to Do the Job; Inspecting Equipment, Structures, Materials; Identifying Objects, Actions, and Events. *Mental Process*—Processing Information; Analyzing Data or Information; Evaluating Information Against Standards. *Work Output*—Handling and Moving Objects; Documenting and Recording Information; Operating Vehicles or Equipment. *Interacting with Others*—Communicating with Persons Outside Organization; Assisting and Caring for Others; Performing for or Working with the Public. **Physical Work Conditions:** Indoors; Sitting; Bending or Twisting the Body. **Other Job Characteristics:** Importance of Being Sure All Is Done; Importance of Being Exact or Accurate; Importance of Repeating Same Tasks.

Experience: Job Zone 1. No previous work-related skill, knowledge, or experience is needed. **Job Preparation:** SVP Below 4.0—Less than 6 months. **Knowledge:** Clerical; English Language; Customer and Personal Service; Computers and Electronics; Communications and Media. **Instructional Program:** 250301 Library Assistant.

Related DOT Jobs: 209.387-026 Library Clerk, Talking Books; 222.367-026 Film-or-Tape Librarian; 222.587-014 Braille-and-Talking Books Clerk; 249.363-010 Bookmobile Driver; 249.365-010 Registration Clerk; 249.367-046 Library Assistant; 249.687-014 Page.

43-4131.00 Loan Interviewers and Clerks (Loan and Credit Clerks)

Education: Short-term O-T-J training

Employed: 179,306

Openings: 46,537

Projected Growth: 11.8%

Earnings: $22,580

Interview loan applicants to elicit information; investigate applicants' backgrounds; verify references; prepare loan request papers; forward findings, reports, and documents to appraisal department. Review loan papers to ensure completeness; complete transactions between loan establishment, borrowers, and sellers, upon approval of loan.

Reviews customer accounts to determine whether payments are made on time and whether other loan terms are being followed. Presents loan and repayment schedule to customer. Schedules and conducts closing of mortgage transaction. Submits loan application with recommendation for underwriting approval. Establishes credit limit and grants extension of credit on overdue accounts. Files and maintains loan records. Orders property insurance or mortgage insurance policies to ensure protection against loss on mortgaged property. Accepts payment on accounts. Answers questions and advises customer regarding loans and transactions. Checks value of customer collateral to be held as loan security. Contacts customer by mail, telephone, or in person concerning acceptance or rejection of application. Records applications for loan and credit, loan information, and disbursement of funds, using computer. Prepares and types loan applications, closing documents, legal documents, letters, forms, government notices, and checks, using computer. Assembles and compiles documents for closing, such as title abstract, insurance form, loan form, and tax receipt. Interviews loan applicant to obtain personal and financial data and to assist in filling out application. Verifies and examines information and accuracy of loan application and closing documents. Contacts credit bureaus, employers, and other sources to check applicant credit and personal references. Calculates, reviews, and corrects errors on interest, principal, payment, and closing costs, using computer or calculator.

GOE Number, Interest Area, and Work Group: 09.02.03; Business Detail; Administrative Detail: Interviewing. **Personality Type:** Conventional. Conventional occupations frequently involve following set procedures and routines. These occupations can include working with data and details more than with ideas. Usually there is a clear line of authority to follow. **Work Values:** Working Conditions; Moral Values; Activity; Supervision, Human Relations; Company Policies and Practices. **Skills:** Active Listening; Speaking; Reading Comprehension; Mathematics; Writing. **Abilities:** *Cognitive*—Number Facility; Information Ordering; Oral Expression; Written Comprehension; Mathematical Reasoning. *Psychomotor*—Wrist-Finger Speed; Response Orientation. *Physical*—Trunk Strength. *Sensory*—Near Vision; Speech Recognition; Speech Clarity. **General Work Activities:** *Information Input*—Getting Information Needed to Do the Job; Identifying Objects, Actions, and Events; Monitoring Processes, Materials, and Surroundings. *Mental Process*—Evaluating Information Against Standards; Processing Information; Judging Qualities of Things, Services, Other People's Work; Updating and Using Job-Relevant Knowledge. *Work Output*—Documenting and Recording Information; Interacting with Computers; Handling and Moving Objects. *Interacting with Others*—Communicating with Persons Outside Organization; Performing Administrative Activities; Establishing and Maintaining Relationships. **Physical Work Conditions:** Indoors; Sitting; Using Hands on Objects, Tools, or Controls. **Other Job Characteristics:** Importance of Being Exact or Accurate; Importance of Being Sure All Is Done; Degree of Automation.

Experience: Job Zone 2. Some previous work-related skill, knowledge, or experience may be helpful, but usually is not needed. **Job Preparation:** SVP 4.00 to 5.99—6 months to less than 2 years. **Knowledge:** Economics and Accounting; Clerical; Mathematics; English Language; Law, Government and Jurisprudence. **Instructional Program:** 520803 Banking and Financial Support Services.

Related DOT Jobs: 205.367-022 Credit Clerk; 219.362-038 Mortgage-Closing Clerk; 219.367-046 Disbursement Clerk; 249.362-014 Mortgage Clerk; 249.362-018 Mortgage Loan Closer; 249.362-022 Mortgage Loan Processor.

43-4141.00 New Accounts Clerks (Banking New Accounts Clerks)

Education: Work experience in a related occupation

Employed: 111,041

Openings: 36,231

Projected Growth: 14.7%

Earnings: $21,340

Interview persons desiring to open bank accounts. Explain banking services available to prospective customers and assist them in preparing application form.

Collects and records fees and funds for deposit from customer; issues receipt, using computer. Issues initial and replacement safe-deposit key to customer, and admits customer to vault. Investigates and corrects errors upon customer request, according to customer and bank records, using calculator or computer. Executes wire transfers of funds. Obtains credit records from reporting agency. Enters account information in computer, and files forms or other documents. Answers customer questions; explains available services such as deposit accounts, bonds, and securities. Assists customer in completing application forms for loans, accounts, or safe-deposit boxes, using typewriter or computer; obtains signature. Interviews customer to obtain information needed to open account or rent safe-deposit box. Schedules repairs for locks on safe-deposit box.

GOE Number, Interest Area, and Work Group: 09.05.01; Business Detail; Customer Service. **Personality Type:** Conventional. Conventional occupations frequently involve following set procedures and routines. These occupations can include working with data and details more than with ideas. Usually there is a clear line of authority to follow. **Work Values:** Working Conditions; Supervision, Human Relations; Co-workers; Security; Moral Values. **Skills:** Active Listening; Speaking; Mathematics; Reading Comprehension; Information Gathering. **Abilities:** *Cognitive*—Oral Expression; Oral Comprehension; Written Comprehension; Number Facility; Mathematical Reasoning; Information Ordering. *Psychomotor*—Wrist-Finger Speed. *Physical*—none met the criteria. *Sensory*—Near Vision; Speech Recognition. **General Work Activities:** *Information Input*—Getting Information Needed to Do the Job; Identifying Objects, Actions, and Events; Estimating Needed Characteristics. *Mental Process*—Processing Information; Updating and Using Job-Relevant Knowledge; Evaluating Information Against Standards. *Work Output*—Documenting and Recording Information; Interacting with Computers; Handling and Moving Objects. *Interacting with Others*—Communicating with Persons Outside Organization; Performing Administrative Activities; Performing for or Working with the Public. **Physical Work Conditions:** Indoors; Sitting; Standing. **Other Job Characteristics:** Importance of Being Sure All Is Done; Importance of Being Exact or Accurate; Consequence of Error.

Experience: Job Zone 2. Some previous work-related skill, knowledge, or experience may be helpful, but usually is not needed. **Job Preparation:** SVP 4.00 to 5.99—6 months to less than 2 years. **Knowledge:** Customer and Personal Service; Clerical; Economics and Accounting; Computers and Electronics; Mathematics. **Instructional Program:** 520803 Banking and Financial Support Services.

Related DOT Jobs: 205.362-026 Customer Service Representative; 295.367-022 Safe-Deposit-Box Rental Clerk.

43-4151.00 Order Clerks (Order Clerks)

Education: Short-term O-T-J training

Employed: 361,879

Openings: 57,374

Projected Growth: 4.6%

Earnings: $21,550

Receive and process incoming orders for materials, merchandise, classified ads, or services such as repairs, installations, or rental of facilities. Inform customers of receipt, prices, shipping dates, and delays; prepare contracts and handle complaints.

Checks inventory control to determine availability of merchandise and notifies department of order that would deplete stock. Receives and handles customer complaints. Informs customer by mail or phone of information such as unit price, shipping date, anticipated delay, and additional information needed. Prepares invoices and shipping documents. Writes or types information on form to record customer's requests and specifications. Reviews orders for completeness according to reporting procedures; forwards incomplete orders for further processing. Files copies of orders received or posts order on records. Calculates and compiles statistics and prepares reports for management. Collects charge vouchers and cash for service and keeps record of transaction. Inspects outgoing work for compliance with customer's specifications. Recommends type of packing or labeling needed on order. Attempts to sell additional merchandise or service to prospective or current customers by phone or through visits. Recommends merchandise or services to customer. Computes total charge for merchandise or services and shipping charges. Routes or relays orders to specified department or unit to prepare and ship orders to designated locations. Confers with production, sales, shipping, warehouse, or common carrier personnel to expedite or trace merchandise or delayed shipments.

GOE Number, Interest Area, and Work Group: 09.05.01; Business Detail; Customer Service. **Personality Type:** Conventional. Conventional occupations frequently involve following set procedures and routines. These occupations can include working with data and details more than with ideas. Usually there is a clear line of authority to follow. **Work Values:** Moral Values; Activity; Supervision, Human Relations; Company Policies and Practices; Supervision, Technical. **Skills:** Problem Identification; Active Listening; Service Orientation; Speaking; Mathematics; Writing. **Abilities:** *Cognitive*—Oral Comprehension; Written Comprehension; Oral Expression; Number Facility; Mathematical Reasoning. *Psychomotor*—none met the criteria. *Physical*—none met the criteria. *Sensory*—Speech Clarity; Speech Recognition; Auditory Attention. **General Work Activities:** *Information Input*—Getting Information Needed to Do the Job; Identifying Objects, Actions, and Events; Monitoring Processes, Materials, and Surroundings; Estimating Needed Characteristics. *Mental Process*—Processing Information; Evaluating Information Against Standards; Updating and Using Job-Relevant Knowledge; Analyzing Data or Information. *Work Output*—Documenting and Recording Information; Interacting with Computers; Implementing Ideas and Programs. *Interacting with Others*—Communicating with Persons Outside Organization; Communicating with Other Workers; Performing for or Working with the Public. **Physical Work Conditions:** Indoors; Sitting; Using Hands on Objects, Tools, or Controls. **Other Job Characteristics:** Frustrating Circumstances; Importance of Being Sure All Is Done; Importance of Being Exact or Accurate.

Experience: Job Zone 2. Some previous work-related skill, knowledge, or experience may be helpful, but usually is not needed. **Job Preparation:** SVP 4.00 to 5.99—6 months to less than 2 years.

Knowledge: Clerical; Sales and Marketing; English Language; Telecommunications; Economics and Accounting. **Instructional Program:** 520408 General Office/Clerical and Typing Services.

Related DOT Jobs: 209.387-018 Contact Clerk; 209.567-014 Order Clerk, Food and Beverage; 245.367-026 Order-Control Clerk, Blood Bank; 249.362-026 Order Clerk; 249.367-042 Gas-Distribution-and-Emergency Clerk; 295.367-018 Film-Rental Clerk; 659.462-010 Electrotype Servicer.

43-4161.00 Human Resources Assistants, Except Payroll and Timekeeping (Human Resources Assistants, Except Payroll and Timekeeping)

Education: Short-term O-T-J training
Employed: 141,775
Openings: 21,844
Projected Growth: 2%
Earnings: $24,360

Compile and keep personnel records. Record data for each employee, such as address, weekly earnings, absences, amount of sales or production, supervisory reports on ability, and date of and reason for termination. Compile and type reports from employment records. File employment records. Search employee files and furnish information to authorized persons.

Communicates with employees or applicants to explain company personnel policies and procedures. Records employee data such as address, rate of pay, absences, and benefits, using personal computer. Compiles and types reports from employment records. Maintains and updates employee records to document personnel actions and changes in employee status. Prepares listing of vacancies and notifies eligible workers of position availability. Administers and scores employee aptitude, skills, personality, and interests tests. Explains company insurance policies and options to employees and files claim and cancellation forms. Selects applicants having specified job requirements and refers to employing official. Requests information from law enforcement officials, previous employers, and other references to determine applicant's employment acceptability. Interviews applicants to obtain and verify information. Answers questions regarding examinations, eligibility, salaries, benefits, and other pertinent information. Examines employee files to answer inquiries and provide information for personnel actions. Processes and reviews employment application to evaluate qualifications or eligibility of applicant.

GOE Number, Interest Area, and Work Group: 09.07.02; Business Detail; Records Processing: Preparation and Maintenance. **Personality Type:** Conventional. Conventional occupations frequently involve following set procedures and routines. These occupations can include working with data and details more than with ideas. Usually there is a clear line of authority to follow. **Work Values:** Working Conditions; Moral Values; Supervision, Human Relations; Company Policies and Practices; Activity. **Skills:** Reading Comprehension; Speaking; Information Organization; Active Listening; Information Gathering; Equipment Selection. **Abilities:** *Cognitive*—Oral Comprehension; Written Comprehension; Oral Expression; Written Expression; Perceptual Speed; Selective Attention. *Psychomotor*—Response Orientation. *Physical*—Gross Body Coordination; Gross Body Equilibrium. *Sensory*—Near Vision; Speech Clarity; Speech Recognition. **General Work Activities:** *Information Input*—Getting Information Needed to Do the Job; Identifying Objects, Actions, and Events; Monitoring Processes, Materials, and Surroundings. *Mental Process*—Processing Information; Evaluating Information Against Standards; Judging Qualities of Things, Services, Other People's Work. *Work Output*—Documenting and Recording Information; Interacting with Computers; Handling and Moving Objects. *Interacting with Others*—Communicating with Other Workers; Communicating with Persons Outside Organization; Staffing Organizational Units. **Physical Work Conditions:** Indoors; Sitting; Using Hands on Objects, Tools, or Controls. **Other Job Characteristics:** Importance of Being Exact or Accurate; Importance of Being Sure All Is Done; Consequence of Error.

Experience: Job Zone 2. Some previous work-related skill, knowledge, or experience may be helpful, but usually is not needed. **Job Preparation:** SVP 4.00 to 5.99—6 months to less than 2 years. **Knowledge:** Personnel and Human Resources; Clerical; English Language; Mathematics; Computers and Electronics. **Instructional Program:** 520408 General Office/Clerical and Typing Services.

Related DOT Jobs: 205.362-010 Civil-Service Clerk; 205.362-014 Employment Clerk; 205.362-022 Identification Clerk; 205.367-062 Referral Clerk, Temporary Help Agency; 205.567-010 Benefits Clerk II; 209.362-026 Personnel Clerk; 241.267-010 Agent-Contract Clerk; 249.367-090 Assignment Clerk.

43-4171.00 Receptionists and Information Clerks
(Receptionists and Information Clerks)

Education: Short-term O-T-J training
Employed: 1,293,450
Openings: 386,806
Projected Growth: 23.6%
Earnings: $18,620

Answer inquiries and obtain information for general public, customers, visitors, and other interested parties. Provide information regarding activities conducted at establishment and regarding location of departments, offices, and employees within organization.

Enrolls individuals to participate in programs; prepares lists; notifies individuals of acceptance in programs; arranges and schedules space and equipment for participants. Types memos, correspondence, travel vouchers, or other documents. Calculates and quotes rates for tours, stocks, insurance policies, and other products and services. Records, compiles, enters, and retrieves information, by hand or using computer. Provides information to public regarding tours, classes, workshops, and other programs. Files and maintains records. Greets persons entering establishment, determines nature and purpose of visit, and directs visitor to specific destination, or answers questions and provides information. Collects and distributes messages for employees of organization. Answers telephone to schedule future appointments, provide information, or forward call. Conducts tours or delivers talks describing features of public facility such as historic site or national park. Receives payment and records receipts for services. Monitors facility to ensure compliance with regulations. Performs duties such as taking care of plants and straightening magazines to maintain lobby or reception area. Registers visitors of public facility such as national park or military base; collects fees; explains regulations; assigns sites. Operates telephone switchboard to receive incoming calls. Transmits information or documents to customer, using computer, mail, or facsimile. Analyzes data to determine answer to customer or public inquiry. Hears and resolves complaints from customers and public. Provides information to public concerning available land leases, land classification, or mineral resources.

GOE Number, Interest Area, and Work Group: 09.05.01; Business Detail; Customer Service. **Personality Type:** Conventional. Conventional occupations frequently involve following set procedures and routines. These occupations can include working with data and details more than with ideas. Usually there is a clear line of authority to follow. **Work Values:** Company Policies and Practices; Activity; Moral Values; Working Conditions; Supervision, Human Relations. **Skills:** Active Listening; Reading Comprehension; Service Orientation; Speaking; Writing. **Abilities:** *Cognitive*—Oral Expression; Oral Comprehension; Written Comprehension; Written Expression; Information Ordering. *Psychomotor*—Wrist-Finger Speed; Finger Dexterity; Response Orientation. *Physical*—Trunk Strength. *Sensory*—Near Vision; Speech Recognition; Speech Clarity. **General Work Activities:** *Information Input*—Getting Information Needed to Do the Job; Identifying Objects, Actions, and Events; Monitoring Processes, Materials, and Surroundings. *Mental Process*—Scheduling Work and Activities; Processing Information; Evaluating Information Against Standards. *Work Output*—Documenting and Recording Information; Interacting with Computers; Handling and Moving Objects; Controlling Machines and Processes. *Interacting with Others*—Performing for or Working with the Public; Communicating with Persons Outside Organization; Establishing and Maintaining Relationships. **Physical Work Conditions:** Indoors; Sitting; Standing. **Other Job Characteristics:** Degree of Automation; Importance of Being Exact or Accurate; Importance of Being Sure All Is Done.

Experience: Job Zone 1. No previous work-related skill, knowledge, or experience is needed. **Job Preparation:** SVP Below 4.0—Less than 6 months. **Knowledge:** Clerical; Customer and Personal Service; English Language; Telecommunications; Mathematics. **Instructional Programs:** 081104 Tourism Promotion Operations; 510703 Health Unit Coordinator/Ward Clerk; 520406 Receptionist; 520408 General Office/Clerical and Typing Services.

Related DOT Jobs: 203.362-014 Credit Reporting Clerk; 205.367-038 Registrar; 237.267-010 Information Clerk, Automobile Club; 237.367-010 Appointment Clerk; 237.367-018 Information Clerk; 237.367-022 Information Clerk; 237.367-038 Receptionist; 237.367-042 Referral-and-Information Aide; 237.367-046 Telephone Quotation Clerk; 238.367-022 Space Scheduler; 238.367-034 Scheduler; 239.367-034 Utility Clerk; 249.262-010 Policyholder-Information Clerk; 249.367-082 Park Aide.

43-4181.00 Reservation and Transportation Ticket Agents and Travel Clerks (Reservation and Transportation Ticket Agents)

Education: No data available.
Employed: 202,930
Openings: No data available.
Projected Growth: No data available.
Earnings: $22,770

Make and confirm reservations and sell tickets to passengers for large hotel or motel chains. Check baggage; direct passengers to designated concourse, pier, or track; make reservations; deliver tickets; arrange for visas; contact individuals and groups to inform them of package tours; provide tourists with travel information such as points of interest, restaurants, rates, and emergency service.

GOE Number, Interest Area, and Work Group: 11.03.01; Recreation, Travel, and Other Personal Services; Transportation and Lodging Services. **Instructional Programs:** 081105 Travel Services Marketing Operations; 081199 Tourism and Travel Services Marketing Operations, Other. **Note:** The Department of Labor has not collected some data for this job, so it has fewer details than the other descriptions.

43-4181.01 Travel Clerks (Travel Clerks)

Education: No data available.
Employed: 18,360
Openings: No data available.
Projected Growth: No data available.
Earnings: $18,090

Provide tourists with travel information such as points of interest, restaurants, rates, and emergency service. Answer inquiries; offer suggestions; provide literature pertaining to trips, excursions, sporting events, concerts, and plays. Make reservations; deliver tickets; arrange for visas; contact individuals and groups to inform them of package tours.

Provides information concerning fares, availability of travel, and accommodations, either orally or by using guides, brochures, and maps. Confirms travel arrangements and reservations. Plans itinerary for travel and accommodations, using knowledge of routes, types of carriers, and regulations. Assists client in preparing required documents and forms for travel, such as visas. Calculates estimated travel rates and expenses, using items such as rate tables and calculators. Contacts motel, hotel, resort, and travel operators by mail or telephone to obtain advertising literature. Informs client of travel dates, times, connections, baggage limits, medical and visa requirements, and emergency information. Confers with customers by telephone, writing, or in person, to answer questions regarding services and determine travel preferences. Provides customers with travel suggestions and information such as guides, directories, brochures, and maps. Obtains reservations for air, train, or car travel and hotel or other housing accommodations. Studies maps, directories, routes, and rate tables to determine travel route and cost and availability of accommodations.

GOE Number, Interest Area, and Work Group: 09.05.01; Business Detail; Customer Service. **Personality Type:** Conventional. Conventional occupations frequently involve following set procedures and routines. These occupations can include working with data and details more than with ideas. Usually there is a clear line of authority to follow. **Work Values:** Working Conditions; Moral Values; Activity; Company Policies and Practices; Supervision, Human Relations; Social Service. **Skills:** Service Orientation; Active Listening; Speaking; Reading Comprehension; Coordination; Writing; Mathematics. **Abilities:** *Cognitive*—Oral Expression; Oral Comprehension; Written Comprehension; Written Expression; Fluency of Ideas. *Psychomotor*—Wrist-Finger Speed. *Physical*—Trunk Strength. *Sensory*—Near Vision; Speech Clarity; Auditory Attention. **General Work Activities:** *Information Input*—Getting Information Needed to Do the Job; Estimating Needed Characteristics; Identifying Objects, Actions, and Events. *Mental Process*—Scheduling Work and Activities; Processing Information; Making Decisions and Solving Problems. *Work Output*—Documenting and Recording Information; Interacting with Computers; Implementing Ideas and Programs. *Interacting with Others*—Communicating with Persons Outside Organization; Performing for or Working with the Public; Assisting and Caring for Others; Establishing and Maintaining Relationships. **Physical Work Conditions:** Sitting; Indoors; Using Hands on Objects, Tools, or Controls. **Other Job Characteristics:** Importance of Being Sure All Is Done; Importance of Being Exact or Accurate; Consequence of Error.

Experience: Job Zone 2. Some previous work-related skill, knowledge, or experience may be helpful, but usually is not needed. **Job Preparation:** SVP 4.00 to 5.99—6 months to less than 2 years. **Knowledge:** Customer and Personal Service; Geography; Mathematics; Transportation; Telecommunications. **Instructional Programs:** 081104 Tourism Promotion Operations; 081105 Travel Services Marketing Operations; 081199 Tourism and Travel Services Marketing Operations, Other.

Related DOT Jobs: 214.362-030 Rate Clerk, Passenger; 237.367-050 Tourist-Information Assistant; 238.167-010 Travel Clerk; 238.167-014 Travel Counselor, Automobile Club; 238.362-014 Reservation Clerk; 238.367-030 Travel Clerk.

43-4181.02 Reservation and Transportation Ticket Agents (Reservation and Transportation Ticket Agents)

Education: No data available.
Employed: 202,930
Openings: No data available.
Projected Growth: No data available.
Earnings: $22,770

Make and confirm reservations for passengers. Sell tickets for transportation agencies such as airlines, bus companies, railroads, and steamship lines. Check baggage and direct passengers to designated concourse, pier, or track.

Checks baggage and directs passenger to designated location for loading. Assigns specified space to customers and maintains computerized inventory of passenger space available. Assists passengers requiring special assistance to board or depart conveyance. Announces arrival and departure information, using public-address system. Informs travel agents in other locations of space reserved or available. Sells travel insurance. Determines whether space is available on travel dates requested by customer. Answers inquiries made to travel agencies or transportation firms such as airlines, bus companies, railroad companies, and steamship lines. Plans route and computes ticket cost, using schedules, rate books, and computer. Sells and assembles tickets for transmittal or mailing to customers. Reads coded data on tickets to ascertain destination; marks tickets; assigns boarding pass. Telephones customer or ticket agent to advise of changes with travel conveyance or to confirm reservation. Arranges reservations and routing for passengers at request of ticket agent. Examines passenger ticket or pass to direct passenger to specified area for loading.

GOE Number, Interest Area, and Work Group: 11.03.01; Recreation, Travel, and Other Personal Services; Transportation and Lodging Services. **Personality Type:** Conventional. Conventional occupations frequently involve following set procedures and routines. These occupations can include working with data and details more than with ideas. Usually there is a clear line of authority to follow. **Work Values:** Supervision, Human Relations; Moral Values; Company Policies and Practices; Working Conditions; Activity. **Skills:** Service Orientation; Active Listening; Reading Comprehension; Speaking; Problem Identification; Coordination. **Abilities:** *Cognitive*—Oral Expression; Oral Comprehension; Memorization; Written Comprehension; Selective Attention; Number Facility. *Psychomotor*—Wrist-Finger Speed; Arm-Hand Steadiness; Finger Dexterity. *Physical*—Static Strength; Trunk Strength. *Sensory*—Near Vision; Speech Recognition; Speech Clarity. **General Work Activities:** *Information Input*—Getting Information Needed to Do the Job; Identifying Objects, Actions, and Events; Monitoring Processes, Materials, and Surroundings. *Mental Process*—Scheduling Work and Activities; Processing Information; Making Decisions and Solving Problems. *Work Output*—Interacting with Computers; Documenting and Recording Information; Handling and Moving Objects. *Interacting with Others*—Assisting and Caring for Others; Establishing and Maintaining Relationships; Communicating with Persons Outside Organization. **Physical Work Conditions:** Indoors; Special Uniform; Standing. **Other Job Characteristics:** Consequence of Error; Degree of Automation; Importance of Being Exact or Accurate; Importance of Being Sure All Is Done.

Experience: Job Zone 2. Some previous work-related skill, knowledge, or experience may be helpful, but usually is not needed. **Job Preparation:** SVP 4.00 to 5.99—6 months to less than 2 years. **Knowledge:** Customer and Personal Service; Transportation; Geography; Clerical; English Language; Mathematics; Computers and Electronics. **Instructional Programs:** 081105 Travel Services Marketing Operations; 081199 Tourism and Travel Services Marketing Operations, Other.

Related DOT Jobs: 238.367-010 Gate Agent; 238.367-014 Reservation Clerk; 238.367-018 Reservations Agent; 238.367-026 Ticket Agent; 248.382-010 Ticketing Clerk.

43-5000 Material Recording, Scheduling, Dispatching, and Distributing Workers

43-5011.00 Cargo and Freight Agents (Transportation Agents)

Education: No data available.
Employed: 26,980
Openings: No data available.
Projected Growth: No data available.
Earnings: $23,050

Expedite and route movement of incoming and outgoing cargo and freight shipments in airline, train, and trucking terminals and on shipping docks. Take orders from customers and arrange pickup of freight and cargo for delivery to loading platform. Prepare and examine bills of lading to determine shipping charges and tariffs.

Oversees or participates in loading cargo to ensure completeness of load and even distribution of weight. Prepares manifest showing baggage, mail, freight weights, and number of passengers on airplane; teletypes data to destination. Arranges for delivery of freight and baggage to consignees. Removes ramp, and signals pilot that personnel and equipment are clear of plane. Unloads inbound freight and baggage; notifies consignees of arrival of shipments. Positions ramp for loading of airplane. Verifies passengers' tickets as they board plane. Prepares airway bill of lading on freight from consignors and routes freight on first available flight. Obtains flight number, airplane number, and names of crew members from dispatcher; records data on flight papers of airplane. Forces conditioned air into interior of plane for passenger comfort prior to departure, using mobile aircraft-air-conditioning unit.

GOE Number, Interest Area, and Work Group: 09.08.01; Business Detail; Records and Materials Processing. **Personality Type:** Conventional. Conventional occupations frequently involve following set procedures and routines. These occupations can include working with data and details more than with ideas. Usually there is a clear line of authority to follow. **Work Values:** Moral Values; Supervision, Human Relations; Company Policies and Practices; Supervision, Technical; Security. **Skills:** Coordination; Service Orientation; Operation and Control; Reading Comprehension; Monitoring; Problem Identification; Critical Thinking; Information Organization. **Abilities:** *Cognitive*—Oral Comprehension; Oral Expression; Written Expression; Problem Sensitivity; Information Ordering; Written Comprehension. *Psychomotor*—Manual Dexterity. *Physical*—Static Strength; Trunk Strength; Dynamic Strength. **General Work Activities:** *Information Input*—Getting Information Needed to Do the Job; Monitoring Processes, Materials, and Surroundings; Identifying Objects, Actions, and Events. *Mental Process*—Evaluating Information Against Standards; Processing Information; Organizing, Planning, and Prioritizing. *Work Output*—Documenting and Recording Information; Handling and Moving Objects; Performing General Physical Activities. *Interacting with Others*—Communicating with Other Workers; Performing for or Working with the Public; Communicating with Persons Outside Organization. **Physical Work Conditions:** Special Uniform; Indoors; Standing. **Other Job Characteristics:** Consequence of Error; Importance of Being Exact or Accurate; Importance of Being Sure All Is Done.

Experience: Job Zone 2. Some previous work-related skill, knowledge, or experience may be helpful, but usually is not needed. **Job Preparation:** SVP 4.00 to 5.99—6 months to less than 2 years. **Knowledge:** Transportation; Clerical; Customer and Personal Service; Mathematics; Telecommunications. **Instructional Programs:** 080709 General Distribution Operations; 520408 General Office/Clerical and Typing Services.

Related DOT Jobs: 248.367-018 Cargo Agent; 912.367-014 Transportation Agent.

43-5021.00 Couriers and Messengers (Couriers and Messengers)

Education: Short-term O-T-J training
Employed: 119,729
Openings: 35,082
Projected Growth: 8.8%
Earnings: $16,680

Pick up and carry messages, documents, packages, and other items between offices or departments within an establishment or to other business concerns. Travel by foot, bicycle, motorcycle, automobile, or public conveyance.

Monitors fluid levels and replenishes fuel to maintain delivery vehicle. Walks, rides bicycle, drives vehicle, or uses public conveyance to reach destination, to deliver message or materials in person. Receives message or materials to be delivered. Receives information on recipient, such as name, address, and telephone number. Obtains signature, receipt, or payment from recipient for articles delivered. Records information such as items received and delivered. Records recipient's replies to message. Delivers messages and items such as documents, packages, and food, between establishment departments and to other establishments and private homes. Calls by telephone to deliver verbal messages.

GOE Number, Interest Area, and Work Group: 09.08.01; Business Detail; Records and Materials Processing. **Personality Type:** Realistic. Realistic occupations frequently involve work activities that include practical, hands-on problems and solutions. These occupations often deal with plants, animals, and real-world materials like wood, tools, and machinery. Many of the occupations require working outside and do not involve a lot of paperwork or working closely with others. **Work Values:** Independence; Moral Values; Supervision, Human Relations; Company Policies and Practices; Security; Social Service. **Skills:** Service Orientation; Speaking; Writing; Reading Comprehension; Active Listening. **Abilities:** *Cognitive*—Oral Comprehension; Written Comprehension; Oral Expression; Memorization; Information Ordering; Spatial Orientation. *Psychomotor*—Response Orientation; Reaction Time; Multilimb Coordination. *Physical*—Stamina; Extent Flexibility; Gross Body Coordination. *Sensory*—Far Vision; Speech Recognition; Night Vision. **General Work Activities:** *Information Input*—Getting Information Needed to Do the Job; Identifying Objects, Actions, and Events; Monitoring Processes, Materials, and Surroundings. *Mental Process*—Evaluating Information Against Standards; Organizing, Planning, and Prioritizing; Making Decisions and Solving Problems. *Work Output*—Performing General Physical Activities; Operating Vehicles or Equipment; Documenting and Recording Information. *Interacting with Others*—Communicating with Persons Outside Organization; Communicating with Other Workers; Performing Administrative Activities; Monitoring and Controlling Resources. **Physical Work Conditions:** Outdoors; Walking or Running; Hazardous Equipment; Using Hands on Objects, Tools, or Controls; Standing; Indoors. **Other Job Characteristics:** Frustrating Circumstances; Importance of Being Sure All Is Done; Importance of Being Exact or Accurate.

Experience: Job Zone 1. No previous work-related skill, knowledge, or experience is needed. **Job Preparation:** SVP Below 4.0—Less than 6 months. **Knowledge:** Transportation; Geography; Telecommunications; Customer and Personal Service; English Language. **Instructional Program:** 129999 Personal and Miscellaneous Services, Other.

Related DOT Jobs: 215.563-010 Caller; 230.663-010 Deliverer, Outside; 239.567-010 Office Helper; 239.677-010 Messenger, Copy; 239.687-010 Route Aide; 239.687-014 Tube Operator; 299.477-010 Deliverer, Merchandise.

43-5031.00 Police, Fire, and Ambulance Dispatchers (Dispatchers, Police, Fire, and Ambulance)

Education: Moderate-term O-T-J training
Employed: 85,438
Openings: 15,874
Projected Growth: 8%
Earnings: $23,670

Receive complaints from public concerning crimes and police emergencies. Broadcast orders to police patrol units in vicinity of complaint to investigate. Operate radio, telephone, or computer equipment to receive reports of fires and medical emergencies; relay information or orders to proper officials.

Records details of calls, dispatches, and messages; maintains logs and files, using computer. Monitors alarm system to detect fires, illegal entry into establishments, or other emergencies. Coordinates emergency requests; dispatches response units to emergency, using radio or alarm system. Contacts officers to verify assignment locations. Questions caller to determine nature of problem and type and number of personnel and equipment needed. Scans status charts and computer screen to determine emergency units available for response. Questions caller, observes alarm register, and scans map, to determine if emergency is within service area. Receives incoming calls by telephone or alarm system. Determines response needed to emergency. Provides instructions to caller, utilizing knowledge of emergency medical care. Operates telecommunication equipment to relay information and messages to and from emergency site, and between law enforcement agencies. Tests and adjusts communication and alarm systems, and reports malfunctions to maintenance units.

GOE Number, Interest Area, and Work Group: 09.06.01; Business Detail; Communications. **Personality Type:** Social. Social occupations frequently involve working with, communicating with, and teaching people. These occupations often involve helping or providing service to others. **Work Values:** Security; Supervision, Human Relations; Authority; Supervision, Technical; Social Service. **Skills:** Problem Identification; Active Listening; Service Orientation; Information Gathering; Coordination; Speaking. **Abilities:** *Cognitive*—Oral Comprehension; Speed of Closure; Selective Attention; Oral Expression; Problem Sensitivity; Time Sharing. *Psychomotor*—Wrist-Finger Speed; Reaction Time; Multilimb Coordination. *Physical*—none met the criteria. *Sensory*—Speech Clarity; Speech Recognition; Near Vision. **General Work Activities:** *Information Input*—Getting Information Needed to Do the Job; Monitoring Processes, Materials, and Surroundings; Identifying Objects, Actions, and Events. *Mental Process*—Making Decisions and Solving Problems; Updating and Using Job-Relevant Knowledge; Processing Information; Analyzing Data or Information. *Work Output*—Handling and Moving Objects; Documenting and Recording Information; Interacting with Computers; Controlling Machines and Processes. *Interacting with Others*—Communicating with Other Workers; Communicating with Persons Outside Organization; Assisting and Caring for Others. **Physical Work Conditions:** Indoors; Sitting; Using Hands on Objects, Tools, or Controls. **Other Job Characteristics:** Consequence of Error; Importance of Being Sure All Is Done; Importance of Being Exact or Accurate; Frustrating Circumstances.

Experience: Job Zone 2. Some previous work-related skill, knowledge, or experience may be helpful, but usually is not needed. **Job Preparation:** SVP 4.00 to 5.99—6 months to less than 2 years. **Knowledge:** Telecommunications; Computers and Electronics; English Language; Communications and Media; Geography. **Instructional Programs:** 520401 Administrative Assistant/Secretarial Science, General; 520406 Receptionist.

Related DOT Jobs: 379.162-010 Alarm Operator; 379.362-010 Dispatcher, Radio; 379.362-014 Protective-Signal Operator; 379.362-018 Telecommunicator.

43-5032.00 Dispatchers, Except Police, Fire, and Ambulance (Dispatchers, Police, Fire, and Ambulance)

Education: Moderate-term O-T-J training
Employed: 85,438
Openings: 15,874
Projected Growth: 8%
Earnings: $23,670

Schedule and dispatch workers, work crews, equipment, or service vehicles for conveyance of materials, freight, or passengers, or for normal installation, service, or emergency repairs rendered outside the place of business. Use radio, telephone, or computer to transmit assignments; compile statistics and reports on work progress.

Maintains files and records regarding customer requests, work or services performed, charges, expenses, inventory, and other dispatch information. Relays work orders, messages, and informa-tion to or from work crews, supervisors, and field inspectors, using telephone or two-way radio. Receives or prepares work orders, according to customer request or specifications. Orders supplies and equipment, and issues them to personnel. Confers with customer or supervising personnel regarding questions, problems, and requests for service or equipment. Routes or assigns workers or equipment to appropriate location, according to customer request, specifications, or needs. Determines types or amount of equipment, vehicles, materials or personnel required, according to work order or specifications.

GOE Number, Interest Area, and Work Group: 09.06.01; Business Detail; Communications. **Personality Type:** Conventional. Conventional occupations frequently involve following set procedures and routines. These occupations can include working with data and details more than with ideas. Usually there is a clear line of authority to follow. **Work Values:** Moral Values; Security; Supervision, Technical; Supervision, Human Relations; Working Conditions; Authority; Independence; Company Policies and Practices. **Skills:** Problem Identification; Active Listening; Coordination; Equipment Selection; Time Management. **Abilities:** *Cognitive*—Oral Comprehension; Oral Expression; Written Comprehension; Information Ordering; Written Expression. *Psychomotor*—Reaction Time; Response Orientation. *Physical*—none met the criteria. *Sensory*—Speech Clarity; Speech Recognition; Auditory Attention. **General Work Activities:** *Information Input*—Getting Information Needed to Do the Job; Identifying Objects, Actions, and Events; Estimating Needed Characteristics. *Mental Process*—Making Decisions and Solving Problems; Scheduling Work and Activities; Processing Information; Analyzing Data or Information. *Work Output*—Documenting and Recording Information; Handling and Moving Objects; Controlling Machines and Processes; Interacting with Computers. *Interacting with Others*—Communicating with Other Workers; Coordinating Work and Activities of Others; Communicating with Persons Outside Organization. **Physical Work Conditions:** Indoors; Sitting; Using Hands on Objects, Tools, or Controls. **Other Job Characteristics:** Consequence of Error; Importance of Being Exact or Accurate; Importance of Being Sure All Is Done.

Experience: Job Zone 2. Some previous work-related skill, knowledge, or experience may be helpful, but usually is not needed. **Job Preparation:** SVP 4.00 to 5.99—6 months to less than 2 years. **Knowledge:** Telecommunications; Customer and Personal Service; Transportation; Clerical; English Language. **Instructional Programs:** 520401 Administrative Assistant/Secretarial Science, General; 520406 Receptionist.

Related DOT Jobs: 215.167-010 Car Clerk, Pullman; 215.367-018 Taxicab Coordinator; 221.362-014 Dispatcher, Relay; 221.367-070 Service Clerk; 221.367-082 Work-Order-Sorting Clerk; 239.167-014 Dispatcher; 239.367-014 Dispatcher, Maintenance Service; 239.367-022 Receiver-Dispatcher; 239.367-030 Dispatcher, Street Department; 248.367-026 Dispatcher, Ship Pilot; 249.167-014 Dispatcher, Motor Vehicle; 249.367-070 Routing Clerk; 910.167-014 Train Dispatcher, Assistant Chief; 910.367-018 Engine Dispatcher; 911.167-010 Dispatcher, Tugboat; 913.167-010 Bus Dispatcher, Interstate; 913.367-010 Taxicab Starter; 914.167-014 Dispatcher, Oil; 919.162-010 Dispatcher, Traffic or System; 932.167-010 Dispatcher (partial list; see the introduction for sources of the complete list).

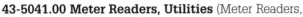

43-5041.00 Meter Readers, Utilities (Meter Readers, Utilities)

Education: Short-term O-T-J training
Employed: 50,382
Openings: 11,359
Projected Growth: 0.4%
Earnings: $25,380

Read meter and record consumption of electricity, gas, water, or steam.

Inspects meters for defects, damage, and unauthorized connections. Walks or drives truck over established route and takes readings of meter dials. Reads electric meter. Reads gas meter. Reads water meter. Collects bills in arrears. Turns service off for nonpayment of charges in vacant premises, or on for new occupants. Verifies readings to locate abnormal consumption and records reasons for fluctuations. Returns route book to business office for billing purposes. Reads steam meter. Indicates irregularities on forms for necessary action by service department.

GOE Number, Interest Area, and Work Group: 09.04.01; Business Detail; Material Control. **Personality Type:** Conventional. Conventional occupations frequently involve following set procedures and routines. These occupations can include working with data and details more than with ideas. Usually there is a clear line of authority to follow. **Work Values:** Independence; Moral Values; Supervision, Technical; Supervision, Human Relations; Company Policies and Practices; Security. **Skills:** Mathematics; Problem Identification; Reading Comprehension; Writing; Information Gathering; Operation Monitoring. **Abilities:** *Cognitive*—Written Expression; Number Facility; Written Comprehension; Problem Sensitivity; Deductive Reasoning. *Psychomotor*—Rate Control. *Physical*—Stamina. **General Work Activities:** *Information Input*—Getting Information Needed to Do the Job; Inspecting Equipment, Structures, Materials; Identifying Objects, Actions, and Events. *Mental Process*—Evaluating Information Against Standards; Processing Information; Organizing, Planning, and Prioritizing. *Work Output*—Documenting and Recording Information; Performing General Physical Activities; Operating Vehicles or Equipment. *Interacting with Others*—Performing Administrative Activities; Communicating with Persons Outside Organization; Communicating with Other Workers. **Physical Work Conditions:** Outdoors; Standing; Special Uniform. **Other Job Characteristics:** Importance of Being Exact or Accurate; Consequence of Error; Importance of Being Sure All Is Done.

Experience: Job Zone 1. No previous work-related skill, knowledge, or experience is needed. **Job Preparation:** SVP Below 4.0—Less than 6 months. **Knowledge:** Clerical; Mathematics; Geography; Mechanical; Computers and Electronics. **Instructional Programs:** No data available.

Related DOT Job: 209.567-010 Meter Reader.

43-5051.00 Postal Service Clerks (Postal Service Clerks)

Education: Short-term O-T-J training
Employed: 72,812
Openings: 4,767
Projected Growth: 6.8%
Earnings: $35,100

Perform any combination of tasks in a post office. Receive letters and parcels; sell postage and revenue stamps, postal cards, and stamped envelopes; fill out and sell money orders. Place mail in pigeon holes of mail rack or in bags, according to state, address, or other scheme; examine mail for correct postage.

Posts announcements on centrally located bulletin board to distribute government-related information to general public. Weighs and computes mailing costs of letters and parcels based on type, weight, and destination. Examines mail for correct postage. Calibrates postage meters. Receives, registers, and refers for investigation complaints regarding mail theft, delivery, lost mail, and damaged mail. Registers and insures letters and parcels. Transports mail from one work station to another within same postal office. Feeds mail into electric-electronic postage-canceling device, or hand stamps mail to cancel postage. Answers questions pertaining to mail regulations, procedures, postage rates, and mail delivery. Collects payment for postage stamps, postal cards, stamped envelopes, metered postage, and money orders. Sorts mail according to groups and destination, by hand or by operating electronic mail-sorting or scanning device. Assists public in complying with federal regulations of Postal Service and other federal agencies, such as registration of aliens.

GOE Number, Interest Area, and Work Group: 09.09.01; Business Detail; Clerical Machine Operation. **Personality Type:** Conventional. Conventional occupations frequently involve following set procedures and routines. These occupations can include working with data and details more than with ideas. Usually there is a clear line of authority to follow. **Work Values:** Security; Supervision, Human Relations; Supervision, Technical; Moral Values; Company Policies and Practices. **Skills:** Active Listening; Information Organization; Speaking; Problem Identification; Mathematics; Service Orientation; Reading Comprehension. **Abilities:** *Cognitive*—Oral Comprehension; Number Facility; Oral Expression; Perceptual Speed; Written Comprehension. *Psychomotor*—Rate Control. *Physical*—Extent Flexibility; Static Strength; Trunk Strength. *Sensory*—Near Vision; Speech Clarity; Glare Sensitivity. **General Work Activities:** *Information Input*—Getting Information Needed to Do the Job; Identifying Objects, Actions, and Events; Monitoring Processes, Materials, and Surroundings; Inspecting Equipment, Structures, Materials. *Mental Process*—Processing Information; Evaluating Information Against Standards; Updating and Using Job-Relevant Knowledge; Analyzing Data or Information. *Work Output*—Handling and Moving Objects; Controlling Machines and Processes; Performing General Physical Activities. *Interacting with Others*—Performing for or Working with the Public; Assisting and Caring for Others; Communicating with Persons Outside Organization. **Physical Work Conditions:** Indoors; Standing; Making Repetitive Motions. **Other Job Charac-**

teristics: Importance of Being Sure All Is Done; Importance of Being Exact or Accurate; Consequence of Error; Degree of Automation.

Experience: Job Zone 2. Some previous work-related skill, knowledge, or experience may be helpful, but usually is not needed. **Job Preparation:** SVP 4.00 to 5.99—6 months to less than 2 years. **Knowledge:** Clerical; Customer and Personal Service; English Language; Geography; Mathematics. **Instructional Program:** 520408 General Office/Clerical and Typing Services.

Related DOT Jobs: 209.687-014 Mail Handler; 243.367-014 Post-Office Clerk.

43-5052.00 Postal Service Mail Carriers (Postal Mail Carriers)

Education: Short-term O-T-J training

Employed: 331,981

Openings: 7,250

Projected Growth: 7.4%

Earnings: $34,840

Sort mail for delivery. Deliver mail on established route, by vehicle or on foot.

Delivers mail to residences and business establishments along route. Enters changes of address in route book and re-addresses mail to be forwarded. Picks up outgoing mail. Sells stamps and issues money orders. Completes delivery forms, collects charges, and obtains signature on receipts for delivery of specified types of mail. Inserts mail into slots of mail rack to sort mail for delivery. Drives vehicle over established route.

GOE Number, Interest Area, and Work Group: 09.08.01; Business Detail; Records and Materials Processing. **Personality Type:** Conventional. Conventional occupations frequently involve following set procedures and routines. These occupations can include working with data and details more than with ideas. Usually there is a clear line of authority to follow. **Work Values:** Independence; Security; Supervision, Human Relations; Moral Values; Company Policies and Practices. **Skills:** Reading Comprehension; Synthesis/Reorganization; Writing; Time Management; Mathematics; Active Listening; Service Orientation. **Abilities:** *Cognitive*—Written Comprehension; Perceptual Speed; Spatial Orientation; Information Ordering; Category Flexibility; Number Facility. *Psychomotor*—Response Orientation; Rate Control. *Physical*—Static Strength; Stamina. *Sensory*—Far Vision; Glare Sensitivity. **General Work Activities:** *Information Input*—Getting Information Needed to Do the Job; Identifying Objects, Actions, and Events; Estimating Needed Characteristics; Monitoring Processes, Materials, and Surroundings. *Mental Process*—Evaluating Information Against Standards; Processing Information; Organizing, Planning, and Prioritizing. *Work Output*—Performing General Physical Activities; Operating Vehicles or Equipment; Handling and Moving Objects. *Interacting with Others*—Performing for or Working with the Public; Communicating with Persons Outside Organization; Interpreting Meaning of Information to Others; Communicating with Other Workers; Assisting and Caring for Others. **Physical Work Conditions:** Special Uniform; Outdoors; Walking or Running. **Other Job Characteristics:** Importance of Being Exact or

Accurate; Importance of Being Sure All Is Done; Frustrating Circumstances.

Experience: Job Zone 1. No previous work-related skill, knowledge, or experience is needed. **Job Preparation:** SVP Below 4.0—Less than 6 months. **Knowledge:** Geography; Mathematics; Transportation; Clerical; English Language; Customer and Personal Service. **Instructional Programs:** No data available.

Related DOT Jobs: 230.363-010 Rural Mail Carrier; 230.367-010 Mail Carrier.

43-5053.00 Postal Service Mail Sorters, Processors, and Processing Machine Operators (Postal Service Clerks)

Education: Short-term O-T-J training

Employed: 72,812

Openings: 4,767

Projected Growth: 6.8%

Earnings: $35,100

Prepare incoming and outgoing mail for distribution. Examine, sort, and route mail by state, type of mail, or other scheme. Load, operate, and occasionally adjust and repair mail processing, sorting, and canceling machinery. Keep records of shipments, pouches, and sacks. Perform other duties related to mail handling within the postal service. Must complete a competitive exam.

GOE Number, Interest Area, and Work Group: 09.08.01; Business Detail; Records and Materials Processing. **Instructional Program:** 520408 General Office/Clerical and Typing Services. **Note:** The Department of Labor has not collected some data for this job, so it has fewer details than the other descriptions.

43-5061.00 Production, Planning, and Expediting Clerks (Production, Planning, and Expediting Clerks)

Education: Short-term O-T-J training

Employed: 248,148

Openings: 61,817

Projected Growth: 0.4%

Earnings: $29,270

Coordinate and expedite the flow of work and materials within or between departments of an establishment according to production schedule. Review and distribute production, work, and shipment schedules; confer with department supervisors to determine progress of work and completion dates; compile reports on progress of work, inventory levels, costs, and production problems.

Examines documents, materials, and products. Monitors work processes for completeness, accuracy, and conformance to standards and specifications. Requisitions and maintains inventory of materials and supplies to meet production demands. Arranges for delivery and distributes supplies and parts to expedite flow of materials to meet production schedules. Calculates figures such as labor and materials amounts, manufacturing costs, and wages, using pricing schedules, adding machine, or calculator. Compiles schedules and orders such as personnel assignments, production, work flow, transportation, maintenance, and repair. Completes status reports such as production progress, customer information, and materials inventory. Confers with establishment personnel, vendors, and customers to coordinate processing and shipping and to resolve complaints. Reviews documents such as production schedules, staffing tables, and specifications, to obtain information such as materials, priorities, and personnel requirements. Maintains files such as maintenance records, bills of lading, and cost reports. Monitors work progress, provides services such as furnishing permits, tickets, and union information; directs workers, to expedite work flow.

GOE Number, Interest Area, and Work Group: 09.04.01; Business Detail; Material Control. **Personality Type:** Conventional. Conventional occupations frequently involve following set procedures and routines. These occupations can include working with data and details more than with ideas. Usually there is a clear line of authority to follow. **Work Values:** Supervision, Human Relations; Activity; Moral Values; Company Policies and Practices; Supervision, Technical; Security. **Skills:** Information Organization; Reading Comprehension; Active Listening; Writing; Time Management; Implementation Planning; Monitoring; Management of Material Resources. **Abilities:** *Cognitive*—Number Facility; Information Ordering; Written Expression; Mathematical Reasoning; Oral Comprehension; Oral Expression. *Psychomotor*—Wrist-Finger Speed. *Physical*—none met the criteria. *Sensory*—Near Vision; Speech Recognition; Speech Clarity. **General Work Activities:** *Information Input*—Getting Information Needed to Do the Job; Monitoring Processes, Materials, and Surroundings; Estimating Needed Characteristics; Identifying Objects, Actions, and Events. *Mental Process*—Evaluating Information Against Standards; Processing Information; Analyzing Data or Information. *Work Output*—Documenting and Recording Information; Handling and Moving Objects; Interacting with Computers. *Interacting with Others*—Communicating with Other Workers; Communicating with Persons Outside Organization; Performing Administrative Activities. **Physical Work Conditions:** Indoors; Sitting; Using Hands on Objects, Tools, or Controls. **Other Job Characteristics:** Consequence of Error; Importance of Being Exact or Accurate; Importance of Being Sure All Is Done.

Experience: Job Zone 2. Some previous work-related skill, knowledge, or experience may be helpful, but usually is not needed. **Job Preparation:** SVP 4.00 to 5.99—6 months to less than 2 years. **Knowledge:** Clerical; Production and Processing; Mathematics; Economics and Accounting; Transportation. **Instructional Program:** 520408 General Office/Clerical and Typing Services.

Related DOT Jobs: 199.382-010 Television-Schedule Coordinator; 215.362-010 Crew Scheduler; 215.362-014 Dispatcher Clerk; 215.367-010 Assignment Clerk; 215.367-014 Personnel Scheduler; 219.362-030 Extension Clerk; 219.387-010 Assignment Clerk; 221.162-010 Production Scheduler, Paperboard Products; 221.167-010 Copy Cutter; 221.167-014 Material Coordinator; 221.167-018 Production Coordinator; 221.167-022 Retort-Load Expediter; 221.167-026 Customer Services Coordinator; 221.362-018 Estimator, Paperboard Boxes; 221.362-022 Progress Clerk; 221.362-030 Computer Processing Scheduler; 221.367-010 Alterations Work-

room Clerk; 221.367-014 Estimator, Printing; 221.367-018 Follow-Up Clerk; 221.367-026 Line-Up Worker (partial list; see the introduction for sources of the complete list).

43-5071.00 Shipping, Receiving, and Traffic Clerks
(Shipping, Receiving, and Traffic Clerks)

Education:	Short-term O-T-J training
Employed:	999,864
Openings:	242,666
Projected Growth:	3.1%
Earnings:	$22,500

Verify and keep records on incoming and outgoing shipments. Prepare items for shipment. Assemble, address, stamp, and ship merchandise or material. Receive, unpack, verify, and record incoming merchandise or material. Arrange for the transportation of products.

Confers and corresponds with establishment representatives to rectify problems such as damages, shortages, and nonconformance to specifications. Packs, seals, labels, and affixes postage to prepare materials for shipping, using work devices such as hand tools, power tools, and postage meter. Prepares documents such as work orders, bills of lading, and shipping orders to route materials. Computes amounts such as space available and shipping, storage, and demurrage charges, using calculator or price list. Requisitions and stores shipping materials and supplies to maintain inventory of stock. Contacts carrier representative to make arrangements and to issue instructions for shipping and delivery of materials. Determines shipping method for materials, using knowledge of shipping procedures, routes, and rates. Records shipment data such as weight, charges, space availability, damages, and discrepancies, for reporting, accounting, and record-keeping purposes. Examines contents and compares with records such as manifests, invoices, or orders, to verify accuracy of incoming or outgoing shipment. Delivers or routes materials to departments, using work devices such as handtruck, conveyor, or sorting bins.

GOE Number, Interest Area, and Work Group: 09.08.01; Business Detail; Records and Materials Processing. **Personality Type:** Conventional. Conventional occupations frequently involve following set procedures and routines. These occupations can include working with data and details more than with ideas. Usually there is a clear line of authority to follow. **Work Values:** Moral Values; Supervision, Human Relations; Company Policies and Practices; Activity; Independence; Security; Co-workers. **Skills:** Reading Comprehension; Critical Thinking; Information Organization; Mathematics; Service Orientation; Implementation Planning. **Abilities:** *Cognitive*—Written Comprehension; Written Expression; Oral Expression; Perceptual Speed; Mathematical Reasoning; Oral Comprehension. *Psychomotor*—Manual Dexterity; Wrist-Finger Speed; Control Precision; Arm-Hand Steadiness. *Physical*—Static Strength; Trunk Strength; Extent Flexibility. *Sensory*—Near Vision; Speech Recognition; Speech Clarity. **General Work Activities:** *Information Input*—Getting Information Needed to Do the Job; Estimating Needed Characteristics; Identifying Objects, Actions, and Events. *Mental Process*—Evaluating Information Against Standards; Making Decisions and Solving Problems; Processing Information. *Work Output*—Handling and Moving Objects; Documenting and Recording Information; Performing General Physical Activities; Controlling Machines and Processes. *Interacting with Others*—Communicating with Persons Outside Organization; Performing Administrative Activities; Communicating with Other Workers; Monitoring and Controlling Resources. **Physical Work Conditions:** Indoors; Using Hands on Objects, Tools, or Controls; Sitting; Standing. **Other Job Characteristics:** Importance of Being Exact or Accurate; Degree of Automation; Importance of Being Sure All Is Done; Consequence of Error.

Experience: Job Zone 1. No previous work-related skill, knowledge, or experience is needed. **Job Preparation:** SVP Below 4.0—Less than 6 months. **Knowledge:** Transportation; Production and Processing; Clerical; Mathematics; Computers and Electronics; English Language; Economics and Accounting. **Instructional Program:** 520408 General Office/Clerical and Typing Services.

Related DOT Jobs: 209.367-042 Reconsignment Clerk; 214.587-014 Traffic Clerk; 219.367-022 Paper-Control Clerk; 219.367-030 Shipping-Order Clerk; 221.367-022 Industrial-Order Clerk; 222.367-066 Truckload Checker; 222.387-014 Car Checker; 222.387-022 Gun-Repair Clerk; 222.387-050 Shipping and Receiving Clerk; 222.567-010 Grain Elevator Clerk; 222.567-014 Ship Runner; 222.587-018 Distributing Clerk; 222.587-034 Route-Delivery Clerk; 222.587-058 Vault Worker; 222.687-022 Routing Clerk; 222.687-030 Shipping Checker; 248.362-010 Incoming-Freight Clerk; 248.367-014 Booking Clerk; 248.367-022 Container Coordinator; 976.687-018 Photofinishing Laboratory Worker.

43-5081.00 Stock Clerks and Order Fillers (Stock Clerks and Order Fillers)

Education: No data available.

Employed: No data available.

Openings: No data available.

Projected Growth: No data available.

Earnings: No data available.

Receive, store, and issue sales-floor merchandise, materials, equipment, and other items from stockroom, warehouse, or storage yard to fill shelves, racks, tables, or customers' orders. Mark prices on merchandise and set up sales displays.

GOE Number, Interest Area, and Work Group: 09.08.01; Business Detail; Records and Materials Processing. **Instructional Programs:** No data available. **Note:** The Department of Labor has not collected some data for this job, so it has fewer details than the other descriptions.

43-5081.01 Stock Clerks, Sales Floor (Stock Clerks and Order Fillers)

Education: No data available.

Employed: No data available.

Openings: No data available.

Projected Growth: No data available.

Earnings: No data available.

Receive, store, and issue sales-floor merchandise. Stock shelves, racks, cases, bins, and tables with merchandise; arrange merchandise displays to attract customers. Periodically take physical count of stock; check and mark merchandise.

Sets up advertising signs and displays merchandise on shelves, counters, or tables to attract customers and promote sales. Transports packages to customer vehicle. Takes inventory or examines merchandise to identify items to be reordered or replenished. Requisitions merchandise from supplier based on available space, merchandise on hand, customer demand, or advertised specials. Itemizes and totals customer merchandise selection at checkout counter, using cash register; accepts cash or charge card for purchases. Cuts lumber, screening, glass, and related materials to size requested by customer. Answers questions and advises customer in selection of merchandise. Receives, opens, and unpacks cartons or crates of merchandise; checks invoice against items received. Stamps, attaches, or changes price tags on merchandise, referring to price list. Cleans display cases, shelves, and aisles. Stocks storage areas and displays with new or transferred merchandise. Packs customer purchases in bags or cartons.

GOE Number, Interest Area, and Work Group: 10.03.01; Sales and Marketing; General Sales. **Personality Type:** Realistic. Realistic occupations frequently involve work activities that include practical, hands-on problems and solutions. These occupations often deal with plants, animals, and real-world materials like wood, tools, and machinery. Many of the occupations require working outside and do not involve a lot of paperwork or working closely with others. **Work Values:** Moral Values; Independence; Activity; Company Policies and Practices; Supervision, Technical; Supervision, Human Relations. **Skills:** Mathematics; Service Orientation; Social Perceptiveness; Active Listening; Reading Comprehension. **Abilities:** *Cognitive*—Oral Comprehension; Oral Expression; Number Facility; Category Flexibility; Information Ordering. *Psychomotor*—Manual Dexterity; Speed of Limb Movement; Finger Dexterity; Arm-Hand Steadiness; Multilimb Coordination. *Physical*—Static Strength; Extent Flexibility; Trunk Strength. *Sensory*—Near Vision; Speech Clarity; Far Vision; Speech Recognition. **General Work Activities:** *Information Input*—Getting Information Needed to Do the Job; Estimating Needed Characteristics; Identifying Objects, Actions, and Events. *Mental Process*—Processing Information; Updating and Using Job-Relevant Knowledge; Evaluating Information Against Standards. *Work Output*—Handling and Moving Objects; Documenting and Recording Information; Implementing Ideas and Programs. *Interacting with Others*—Establishing and Maintaining Relationships; Performing for or Working with the Public; Communicating with Persons Outside Organization. **Physical Work Conditions:** Indoors; Standing; Walking or Running. **Other Job Characteristics:** Consequence of Error; Frustrating Circumstances; Importance of Being Exact or Accurate.

Experience: Job Zone 1. No previous work-related skill, knowledge, or experience is needed. **Job Preparation:** SVP Below 4.0—Less than 6 months. **Knowledge:** Clerical; Customer and Personal Service; Mathematics; Sales and Marketing; English Language. **Instructional Programs:** 080601 Food Products Retailing and Wholesaling Operations; 080705 General Retailing Operations.

Related DOT Jobs: 299.367-014 Stock Clerk; 299.677-014 Sales Attendant, Building Materials.

43-5081.02 Marking Clerks (Stock Clerks and Order Fillers)

Education: No data available.

Employed: No data available.

Openings: No data available.

Projected Growth: No data available.

Earnings: No data available.

Print and attach price tickets to articles of merchandise, using one or several methods such as marking price on tickets by hand or using ticket-printing machine.

Keeps records of production, returned goods, and related transactions. Indicates price, size, style, color, and inspection results on tags, tickets, and labels, using rubber stamp or writing instrument. Performs other clerical tasks during periods between auction sales. Records number and types of articles marked; packs articles in boxes. Prints information on tickets, using ticket-printing machine. Records price, buyer, and grade of product on tickets attached to products auctioned. Pins, pastes, sews, ties, or staples tickets, tags, or labels to article, using tagging mechanism. Marks selling price by hand on boxes containing merchandise or on price tickets. Compares printed price tickets with entries on purchase order to verify accuracy; notifies supervisor of discrepancies.

GOE Number, Interest Area, and Work Group: 09.08.01; Business Detail; Records and Materials Processing. **Personality Type:** Conventional. Conventional occupations frequently involve following set procedures and routines. These occupations can include working with data and details more than with ideas. Usually there is a clear line of authority to follow. **Work Values:** Moral Values; Independence; Activity; Supervision, Human Relations; Working Conditions. **Skills:** Mathematics; Product Inspection; Problem Identification; Reading Comprehension; Writing. **Abilities:** *Cognitive*—Written Expression; Information Ordering; Number Facility; Category Flexibility; Written Comprehension. *Psychomotor*—none met the criteria. *Physical*—none met the criteria. **General Work Activities:** *Information Input*—Getting Information Needed to Do the Job; Identifying Objects, Actions, and Events; Estimating Needed Characteristics. *Mental Process*—Updating and Using Job-Relevant Knowledge; Evaluating Information Against Standards; Processing Information. *Work Output*—Handling and Moving Objects; Documenting and Recording Information; Performing General Physical Activities. *Interacting with Others*—Performing Administrative Activities; Communicating with Other Workers; Interpreting Meaning of Information to Others; Communicating with Persons Outside Organization. **Physical Work Conditions:** Indoors; Using Hands on Objects, Tools, or Controls; Standing. **Other Job Characteristics:** Consequence of Error; Importance of Being Exact or Accurate; Importance of Repeating Same Tasks.

Experience: Job Zone 1. No previous work-related skill, knowledge, or experience is needed. **Job Preparation:** SVP Below 4.0—Less than 6 months. **Knowledge:** Clerical; Mathematics; Mechanical; English Language; Sales and Marketing; Production and Processing. **Instructional Programs:** No data available.

Related DOT Jobs: 209.587-034 Marker; 216.567-010 Ticket Marker; 222.387-054 Sorter-Pricer; 229.587-018 Ticketer.

43-5081.03 Stock Clerks—Stockroom, Warehouse, or Storage Yard (Stock Clerks and Order Fillers)

Education: No data available.

Employed: No data available.

Openings: No data available.

Projected Growth: No data available.

Earnings: No data available.

Receive, store, and issue materials, equipment, and other items from stockroom, warehouse, or storage yard. Keep records and compile stock reports.

Compares office inventory records with sales orders, invoices, or requisitions to verify accuracy and receipt of items. Cleans and maintains supplies, tools, equipment, instruments, and storage areas, to ensure compliance to safety regulations. Records nature, quantity, value, or location of material, supplies, or equipment received, shipped, used, or issued to workers. Compiles, reviews, and maintains data from contracts, purchase orders, requisitions, and other documents, to determine supply needs. Determines method of storage, identification, and stock location based on turnover, environmental factors, and physical capacity of facility. Verifies computations against physical count of stock, adjusts for errors, or investigates discrepancies. Receives and fills orders; sells supplies, materials, and products to customers. Adjusts, repairs, assembles, or prepares products, supplies, equipment, or other items, according to specifications or customer requirements. Assists or directs to other stockroom, warehouse, or storage yard workers. Drives truck to pick up incoming stock or deliver parts to designated locations. Confers with engineering and purchasing personnel and vendors regarding procurement and stock availability. Examines and inspects stock items for wear or defects, reports damage to supervisor, and disposes of or returns items to vendor. Purchases or prepares documents to purchase new or additional stock and recommends disposal of excess, defective, or obsolete stock. Prepares documents such as inventory balance, price lists, shortages, expenditures, and periodic reports, using computer, typewriter, or calculator. Delivers products, supplies, and equipment to designated area; determines sequence and release of back orders according to stock availability. Locates and selects material, supplies, tools, equipment, or other articles from stock, or issues stock item to workers. Receives, counts, and stores stock items and records data, manually or using computer.

GOE Number, Interest Area, and Work Group: 09.08.01; Business Detail; Records and Materials Processing. **Personality Type:** Conventional. Conventional occupations frequently involve following set procedures and routines. These occupations can include working with data and details more than with ideas. Usually there is a clear line of authority to follow. **Work Values:** Moral Values; Independence; Supervision, Human Relations; Supervision, Technical; Security; Company Policies and Practices. **Skills:** Reading Comprehension; Mathematics; Information Organization; Problem Identification; Writing; Information Gathering. **Abilities:** *Cognitive*—Information Ordering; Category Flexibility; Written Comprehension; Memorization; Written Expression. *Psychomotor*—Manual Dexterity; Wrist-Finger Speed; Multilimb

Coordination. *Physical*—Extent Flexibility; Static Strength; Trunk Strength. *Sensory*—Near Vision; Far Vision; Speech Recognition; Visual Color Discrimination. **General Work Activities:** *Information Input*—Identifying Objects, Actions, and Events; Getting Information Needed to Do the Job; Monitoring Processes, Materials, and Surroundings; Inspecting Equipment, Structures, Materials. *Mental Process*—Processing Information; Making Decisions and Solving Problems; Judging Qualities of Things, Services, Other People's Work; Evaluating Information Against Standards. *Work Output*—Handling and Moving Objects; Documenting and Recording Information; Performing General Physical Activities; Implementing Ideas and Programs. *Interacting with Others*—Monitoring and Controlling Resources; Communicating with Other Workers; Performing Administrative Activities. **Physical Work Conditions:** Indoors; Using Hands on Objects, Tools, or Controls; Walking or Running. **Other Job Characteristics:** Importance of Being Exact or Accurate; Importance of Being Sure All Is Done; Frustrating Circumstances.

Experience: Job Zone 2. Some previous work-related skill, knowledge, or experience may be helpful, but usually is not needed. **Job Preparation:** SVP 4.00 to 5.99—6 months to less than 2 years. **Knowledge:** Clerical; Mathematics; Computers and Electronics; Economics and Accounting; Production and Processing; English Language. **Instructional Program:** 080709 General Distribution Operations.

Related DOT Jobs: 219.367-018 Merchandise Distributor; 219.387-026 Space-and-Storage Clerk; 219.387-030 Stock Control Clerk; 221.587-018 Odd-Piece Checker; 221.587-022 Outsole Scheduler; 222.367-014 Cut-File Clerk; 222.367-038 Magazine Keeper; 222.367-042 Parts Clerk; 222.367-050 Prescription Clerk, Lens-and-Frames; 222.367-062 Tool-Crib Attendant; 222.387-018 Fuel-Oil Clerk; 222.387-026 Inventory Clerk; 222.387-030 Linen-Room Attendant; 222.387-034 Material Clerk; 222.387-042 Property Custodian; 222.387-058 Stock Clerk; 222.387-062 Storekeeper; 222.487-010 Checker, Bakery Products; 222.587-022 Kitchen Clerk; 222.587-054 Transformer-Stock Clerk (partial list; see the introduction for sources of the complete list).

43-5081.04 Order Fillers, Wholesale and Retail Sales
(Stock Clerks and Order Fillers)

Education: No data available.

Employed: No data available.

Openings: No data available.

Projected Growth: No data available.

Earnings: No data available.

Fill customers' mail and telephone orders from stored merchandise in accordance with specifications on sales slips or order forms. Compute prices of items; complete order receipts; keep records of outgoing orders; requisition additional materials, supplies, and equipment.

Places merchandise on conveyor leading to wrapping area. Obtains merchandise from bins or shelves. Computes price of each group of items. Reads order to ascertain catalog number, size, color, and quantity of merchandise.

GOE Number, Interest Area, and Work Group: 09.08.01; Business Detail; Records and Materials Processing. **Personality Type:** Conventional. Conventional occupations frequently involve following set procedures and routines. These occupations can include working with data and details more than with ideas. Usually there is a clear line of authority to follow. **Work Values:** Moral Values; Supervision, Human Relations; Independence; Activity; Working Conditions; Company Policies and Practices. **Skills:** Mathematics; Reading Comprehension. **Abilities:** *Cognitive*—Number Facility; Mathematical Reasoning; Written Comprehension; Oral Comprehension; Information Ordering. *Psychomotor*—none met the criteria. *Physical*—Static Strength. *Sensory*—Speech Recognition. **General Work Activities:** *Information Input*—Getting Information Needed to Do the Job; Identifying Objects, Actions, and Events; Estimating Needed Characteristics. *Mental Process*—Processing Information; Evaluating Information Against Standards; Making Decisions and Solving Problems. *Work Output*—Handling and Moving Objects; Documenting and Recording Information; Performing General Physical Activities. *Interacting with Others*—Performing Administrative Activities; Monitoring and Controlling Resources; Communicating with Persons Outside Organization. **Physical Work Conditions:** Indoors; Standing; Making Repetitive Motions. **Other Job Characteristics:** Importance of Being Exact or Accurate; Importance of Being Sure All Is Done; Degree of Automation.

Experience: Job Zone 2. Some previous work-related skill, knowledge, or experience may be helpful, but usually is not needed. **Job Preparation:** SVP 4.00 to 5.99—6 months to less than 2 years. **Knowledge:** Clerical; English Language; Mathematics; Production and Processing; Customer and Personal Service. **Instructional Programs:** No data available.

Related DOT Jobs: 222.487-014 Order Filler; 299.387-014 Stamp Analyst.

43-5111.00 Weighers, Measurers, Checkers, and Samplers, Recordkeeping (Weighers, Measurers, Checkers, and Samplers, Recordkeeping)

Education: Short-term O-T-J training

Employed: 50,591

Openings: 11,529

Projected Growth: 1.5%

Earnings: $22,300

Weigh, measure, and check materials, supplies, and equipment, for the purpose of keeping relevant records. Perform duties that are primarily clerical by nature.

Sorts products or materials into predetermined sequence or groupings for packing, shipping, or storage. Counts or estimates quantities of materials, parts, or products received or shipped. Documents quantity, quality, type, weight, and value of materials or products to maintain shipping, receiving, and production records and files. Prepares measurement tables and conversion charts, using standard formulae. Maintains perpetual inventory of samples and replenishes stock to maintain required levels. Collects and prepares product samples for laboratory analysis or testing. Fills orders for products and samples, following order tickets;

forwards or mails items. Compares product labels, tags, or tickets. Computes product totals and charges for shipments, using calculator. Weighs or measures materials or products, using volume meters, scales, rules, and calipers. Examines blueprints; prepares plans, layouts, or drawings of facility or finished products, to identify storage locations or verify parts assemblies. Operates or tends machines to clean or sanitize equipment, or manually washes equipment, using detergent, brushes, and hoses. Works with, signals, or instructs other workers to weigh, move, or check products. Communicates with customers and vendors to exchange information regarding products, materials, and services. Collects fees and issues receipts for payments. Removes products or loads not meeting quality standards from stock; notifies supervisor or appropriate department of discrepancy or shortage. Transports materials, products, or samples to processing, shipping, or storage areas, manually or by using conveyors, pumps, or handtrucks. Unloads or unpacks incoming shipments; arranges, packs, or prepares materials and products for display, distribution, outgoing shipment, or storage. Collects, prepares, or attaches measurement, weight, or identification labels or tickets to products.

GOE Number, Interest Area, and Work Group: 09.08.01; Business Detail; Records and Materials Processing. **Personality Type:** Conventional. Conventional occupations frequently involve following set procedures and routines. These occupations can include working with data and details more than with ideas. Usually there is a clear line of authority to follow. **Work Values:** Moral Values; Supervision, Human Relations; Security; Company Policies and Practices; Supervision, Technical; Independence. **Skills:** Product Inspection; Operation and Control; Equipment Selection; Mathematics; Operation Monitoring. **Abilities:** *Cognitive*—Category Flexibility; Information Ordering; Number Facility; Perceptual Speed; Problem Sensitivity; Written Comprehension. *Psychomotor*—Manual Dexterity; Control Precision; Multilimb Coordination. *Physical*—Extent Flexibility; Static Strength; Gross Body Coordination; Trunk Strength; Explosive Strength. *Sensory*—Near Vision; Hearing Sensitivity; Speech Clarity. **General Work Activities:** *Information Input*—Getting Information Needed to Do the Job; Identifying Objects, Actions, and Events; Estimating Needed Characteristics; Inspecting Equipment, Structures, Materials; Monitoring Processes, Materials, and Surroundings. *Mental Process*—Evaluating Information Against Standards; Processing Information; Judging Qualities of Things, Services, Other People's Work. *Work Output*—Documenting and Recording Information; Performing General Physical Activities; Handling and Moving Objects. *Interacting with Others*—Performing Administrative Activities; Communicating with Persons Outside Organization; Communicating with Other Workers. **Physical Work Conditions:** Using Hands on Objects, Tools, or Controls; Indoors; Standing. **Other Job Characteristics:** Importance of Being Exact or Accurate; Importance of Being Sure All Is Done; Consequence of Error.

Experience: Job Zone 1. No previous work-related skill, knowledge, or experience is needed. **Job Preparation:** SVP Below 4.0—Less than 6 months. **Knowledge:** Clerical; Mathematics; Production and Processing; Transportation; Design. **Instructional Program:** 520408 General Office/Clerical and Typing Services.

Related DOT Jobs: 206.587-010 Brand Recorder; 209.587-046 Sample Clerk, Paper; 216.462-010 Booking Prizer; 219.367-010

Checker, Dump Grounds; 221.467-010 Gin Clerk; 221.482-018 Ticket Worker; 221.487-010 Lumber Scaler; 221.587-010 Checker; 221.587-026 Recorder; 221.587-030 Tallier; 221.587-034 Tare Weigher; 221.587-046 Wheel-Press Clerk; 221.687-014 Ticket Puller; 222.367-010 Cargo Checker; 222.387-010 Aircraft-Shipping Checker; 222.387-066 Sample Clerk; 222.387-074 Shipping-and-Receiving Weigher; 222.485-010 Milk-Receiver, Tank Truck; 222.585-010 Milk Receiver; 222.587-042 Sampler, Wool (partial list; see the introduction for sources of the complete list).

43-6000 Secretaries and Administrative Assistants

43-6011.00 Executive Secretaries and Administrative Assistants (Secretaries)

Education: Moderate-term O-T-J training
Employed: 2,690,424
Openings: 358,379
Projected Growth: 0%
Earnings: $23,550

Provide high-level administrative support. Conduct research; prepare statistical reports; handle information requests; perform clerical functions such as preparing correspondence, receiving visitors, arranging conference calls, and scheduling meetings. Train and supervise lower-level clerical staff.

Coordinates and directs office services such as records and budget preparation, personnel, and housekeeping, to aid executives. Prepares records and reports such as recommendations for solutions of administrative problems and annual reports. Analyzes operating practices and procedures to create new methods or to revise existing methods. Studies management methods to improve workflow, simplify reporting procedures, or implement cost reductions. Reads and answers correspondence. Plans conferences. Files and retrieves corporation documents, records, and reports. Interprets administrative and operating policies and procedures for employees.

GOE Number, Interest Area, and Work Group: 09.02.02; Business Detail; Administrative Detail: Secretarial Work. **Personality Type:** Conventional. Conventional occupations frequently involve following set procedures and routines. These occupations can include working with data and details more than with ideas. Usually there is a clear line of authority to follow. **Work Values:** Working Conditions; Company Policies and Practices; Moral Values; Supervision, Human Relations; Security; Activity. **Skills:** Reading Comprehension; Coordination; Writing; Information Organization; Active Listening; Problem Identification. **Abilities:** *Cognitive*—Written Comprehension; Information Ordering; Oral Comprehension; Written Expression; Oral Expression. *Psychomotor*—Wrist-Finger Speed. *Physical*—Trunk Strength. *Sensory*—Near Vision; Speech Clarity; Far Vision; Speech Recognition. **General Work Activities:** *Information Input*—Getting Information Needed to Do the Job; Monitoring Processes, Materials, and Surroundings; Identifying Objects, Actions, and Events. *Mental Process*—Analyzing Data or Information; Processing Information; Making

Decisions and Solving Problems; Scheduling Work and Activities. *Work Output*—Interacting with Computers; Implementing Ideas and Programs; Documenting and Recording Information. *Interacting with Others*—Performing Administrative Activities; Communicating with Other Workers; Coordinating Work and Activities of Others; Monitoring and Controlling Resources; Interpreting Meaning of Information to Others. **Physical Work Conditions:** Indoors; Sitting; Using Hands on Objects, Tools, or Controls; Making Repetitive Motions. **Other Job Characteristics:** Importance of Being Sure All Is Done; Consequence of Error; Importance of Being Exact or Accurate.

Experience: Job Zone 4. A minimum of two to four years of work-related skill, knowledge, or experience is needed. **Job Preparation:** SVP 7.0 to less than 8.0—2 years to less than 10 years. **Knowledge:** Clerical; Administration and Management; Computers and Electronics; English Language; Mathematics; Economics and Accounting. **Instructional Program:** 520401 Administrative Assistant/Secretarial Science, General.

Related DOT Jobs: 169.167-010 Administrative Assistant; 169.167-014 Administrative Secretary.

43-6012.00 Legal Secretaries (Legal Secretaries)

Education: Postsecondary vocational training

Employed: 285,120

Openings: 44,130

Projected Growth: 13%

Earnings: $30,050

Perform secretarial duties, utilizing legal terminology, procedures, and documents. Prepare legal papers and correspondence such as summonses, complaints, motions, and subpoenas. Assist with legal research.

Attends legal meetings such as client interviews, hearings, or depositions; takes notes. Submits articles and information from searches to attorneys for review and approval for use. Reviews legal publications and performs database searches to identify laws and court decisions relevant to pending cases. Drafts and types office memos. Organizes and maintains law libraries, document files, and case files. Assists attorneys in collecting information such as employment, medical, and other records. Schedules and makes appointments. Mails, faxes, or arranges for delivery of legal correspondence to clients, witnesses, and court officials. Completes various forms such as accident reports, trial and courtroom requests, and applications, for clients. Prepares and processes legal documents and papers such as summonses, subpoenas, complaints, appeals, motions, and pretrial agreements. Receives and places telephone calls. Makes photocopies of correspondence, document, and other printed matter.

GOE Number, Interest Area, and Work Group: 09.02.02; Business Detail; Administrative Detail: Secretarial Work. **Personality Type:** Conventional. Conventional occupations frequently involve following set procedures and routines. These occupations can include working with data and details more than with ideas. Usually there is a clear line of authority to follow. **Work Values:** Working Conditions; Activity; Company Policies and Practices; Security; Moral Values. **Skills:** Reading Comprehension; Writing;

Information Organization; Active Listening; Critical Thinking. **Abilities:** *Cognitive*—Written Comprehension; Oral Comprehension; Written Expression; Oral Expression; Information Ordering. *Psychomotor*—Wrist-Finger Speed; Response Orientation. *Physical*—none met the criteria. *Sensory*—Near Vision; Speech Recognition; Speech Clarity. **General Work Activities:** *Information Input*—Getting Information Needed to Do the Job; Identifying Objects, Actions, and Events; Monitoring Processes, Materials, and Surroundings. *Mental Process*—Scheduling Work and Activities; Processing Information; Judging Qualities of Things, Services, Other People's Work; Evaluating Information Against Standards. *Work Output*—Documenting and Recording Information; Handling and Moving Objects; Interacting with Computers. *Interacting with Others*—Communicating with Other Workers; Communicating with Persons Outside Organization; Performing Administrative Activities. **Physical Work Conditions:** Sitting; Indoors; Using Hands on Objects, Tools, or Controls. **Other Job Characteristics:** Importance of Being Sure All Is Done; Importance of Being Exact or Accurate; Consequence of Error.

Experience: Job Zone 3. Previous work-related skill, knowledge, or experience is required. **Job Preparation:** SVP 6.0 to less than 7.0—More than 1 year and less than 4 years. **Knowledge:** Clerical; Law, Government and Jurisprudence; English Language; Computers and Electronics; Communications and Media; Telecommunications. **Instructional Programs:** 520401 Administrative Assistant/Secretarial Science, General; 520403 Legal Administrative Assistant/Secretary.

Related DOT Job: 201.362-010 Legal Secretary.

43-6013.00 Medical Secretaries (Medical Secretaries)

Education: Postsecondary vocational training

Employed: 219,309

Openings: 33,608

Projected Growth: 12%

Earnings: $22,390

Perform secretarial duties, utilizing specific knowledge of medical terminology and of hospital, clinic, or laboratory procedures. Schedule appointments, bill patients, and compile and record medical charts, reports, and correspondence.

Routes messages and documents such as laboratory results to appropriate staff. Transcribes recorded messages and practitioner's diagnosis and recommendations into patient's medical record. Answers telephone and directs call to appropriate staff. Prepares and transmits patients' bills. Greets visitors, ascertains purpose of visits, and directs to appropriate staff. Transmits correspondence and medical records by mail, e-mail, or fax. Takes dictation in shorthand. Schedules patient diagnostic appointments and medical consultations. Compiles and records medical charts, reports, and correspondence, using typewriter or personal computer. Maintains medical records and correspondence files.

GOE Number, Interest Area, and Work Group: 09.02.02; Business Detail; Administrative Detail: Secretarial Work. **Personality Type:** Conventional. Conventional occupations frequently involve following set procedures and routines. These occupations can include working with data and details more than with ideas. Usually there is a clear line of authority to follow. **Work Values:** Activity; Working Conditions; Moral Values; Company Policies and Practices; Security. **Skills:** Reading Comprehension; Active Listening; Writing; Speaking; Information Organization. **Abilities:** *Cognitive*—Oral Comprehension; Oral Expression; Written Comprehension; Information Ordering; Written Expression. *Psychomotor*—Wrist-Finger Speed. *Physical*—none met the criteria. *Sensory*—Speech Recognition. **General Work Activities:** *Information Input*—Getting Information Needed to Do the Job; Identifying Objects, Actions, and Events; Estimating Needed Characteristics. *Mental Process*—Processing Information; Scheduling Work and Activities; Evaluating Information Against Standards. *Work Output*—Documenting and Recording Information; Interacting with Computers; Handling and Moving Objects. *Interacting with Others*—Performing Administrative Activities; Communicating with Other Workers; Communicating with Persons Outside Organization. **Physical Work Conditions:** Indoors; Sitting; Using Hands on Objects, Tools, or Controls. **Other Job Characteristics:** Importance of Being Sure All Is Done; Importance of Being Exact or Accurate; Consequence of Error.

Experience: Job Zone 3. Previous work-related skill, knowledge, or experience is required. **Job Preparation:** SVP 6.0 to less than 7.0—More than 1 year and less than 4 years. **Knowledge:** Clerical; Computers and Electronics; English Language; Mathematics; Customer and Personal Service. **Instructional Programs:** 510705 Medical Office Management; 510708 Medical Transcription; 520401 Administrative Assistant/Secretarial Science, General; 520404 Medical Administrative Assistant/Secretary.

Related DOT Job: 201.362-014 Medical Secretary.

43-6014.00 Secretaries, Except Legal, Medical, and Executive (Secretaries)

Education: Moderate-term O-T-J training
Employed: 2,690,424
Openings: 358,379
Projected Growth: 0%
Earnings: $23,550

Perform routine clerical and administrative functions. Draft correspondence; schedule appointments; organize and maintain paper and electronic files; provide information to callers.

Locates and attaches appropriate file to incoming correspondence requiring reply. Orders and dispenses supplies. Maintains calendar and coordinates conferences and meetings. Opens incoming mail and routes mail to appropriate individuals. Greets and welcomes visitors, determines nature of business, and conducts visitors to employer or appropriate person. Compiles and maintains lists and records, using typewriter or computer. Records and types minutes of meetings, using typewriter or computer. Compiles and types statistical reports, using typewriter or computer. Mails newsletters, promotional material, and other information. Schedules appointments. Prepares and mails checks. Composes and distributes meeting notes, correspondence, and reports. Answers routine correspondence. Takes dictation in shorthand or by machine; transcribes information. Files correspondence and other records. Arranges travel schedules and reservations. Makes copies of correspondence and other printed matter. Provides customer

services such as order placement and account information. Collects and disburses funds from cash account and keeps records. Answers telephone and gives information to callers; takes messages; transfers calls to appropriate individuals.

GOE Number, Interest Area, and Work Group: 09.02.02; Business Detail; Administrative Detail: Secretarial Work. **Personality Type:** Conventional. Conventional occupations frequently involve following set procedures and routines. These occupations can include working with data and details more than with ideas. Usually there is a clear line of authority to follow. **Work Values:** Moral Values; Working Conditions; Activity; Company Policies and Practices; Supervision, Human Relations; Security. **Skills:** Reading Comprehension; Active Listening; Information Organization; Service Orientation; Writing. **Abilities:** *Cognitive*—Oral Expression; Oral Comprehension; Written Comprehension; Information Ordering; Written Expression. *Psychomotor*—Wrist-Finger Speed; Finger Dexterity; Manual Dexterity. *Physical*—Trunk Strength; Dynamic Strength; Gross Body Equilibrium. *Sensory*—Near Vision; Speech Recognition; Speech Clarity. **General Work Activities:** *Information Input*—Getting Information Needed to Do the Job; Identifying Objects, Actions, and Events; Monitoring Processes, Materials, and Surroundings. *Mental Process*—Processing Information; Evaluating Information Against Standards; Scheduling Work and Activities. *Work Output*—Interacting with Computers; Documenting and Recording Information; Handling and Moving Objects. *Interacting with Others*—Communicating with Other Workers; Communicating with Persons Outside Organization; Establishing and Maintaining Relationships. **Physical Work Conditions:** Indoors; Sitting; Using Hands on Objects, Tools, or Controls. **Other Job Characteristics:** Importance of Being Sure All Is Done; Importance of Being Exact or Accurate; Consequence of Error; Degree of Automation.

Experience: Job Zone 2. Some previous work-related skill, knowledge, or experience may be helpful, but usually is not needed. **Job Preparation:** SVP 4.00 to 5.99—6 months to less than 2 years. **Knowledge:** Clerical; English Language; Computers and Electronics; Customer and Personal Service; Telecommunications. **Instructional Program:** 520401 Administrative Assistant/Secretarial Science, General.

Related DOT Jobs: 201.162-010 Social Secretary; 201.362-018 Membership Secretary; 201.362-022 School Secretary; 201.362-026 Script Supervisor; 201.362-030 Secretary; 219.362-074 Trust Operations Assistant.

43-9000 Other Office and Administrative Support Workers

43-9011.00 Computer Operators (Computer Operators, Except Peripheral Equipment)

Education: Moderate-term O-T-J training
Employed: 223,893
Openings: 28,712
Projected Growth: –24.1%
Earnings: $25,030

Monitor and control electronic, computer, and peripheral electronic data-processing equipment to process business, scientific, engineering, and other data according to operating instructions. Enter commands at a computer terminal and set controls on computer and peripheral devices. Monitor and respond to operating and error messages.

Reads job setup instructions to determine equipment to be used and order of use. Notifies supervisor of errors or equipment stoppage. Loads peripheral equipment with selected materials for operating runs, or oversees loading of peripheral equipment by peripheral equipment operators. Observes peripheral equipment operation and error messages displayed on terminal monitor to detect faulty output or machine stoppage. Answers telephone calls to assist computer users encountering problems. Assists workers in classifying, cataloging, and maintaining tapes. Clears equipment at end of operating run and reviews schedule to determine next assignment. Records information such as computer operating time and problems which occurred, such as down time and actions taken. Diagnoses reasons for equipment malfunction and enters commands to correct error or stoppage and resume operations. Enters commands, using computer terminal, and activates controls on computer and peripheral equipment to integrate and operate equipment. Enters commands to clear computer system and start operation, using keyboard of computer terminal. Separates output, when needed, and sends data to specified users.

GOE Number, Interest Area, and Work Group: 09.09.01; Business Detail; Clerical Machine Operation. **Personality Type:** Conventional. Conventional occupations frequently involve following set procedures and routines. These occupations can include working with data and details more than with ideas. Usually there is a clear line of authority to follow. **Work Values:** Moral Values; Working Conditions; Supervision, Human Relations; Independence; Company Policies and Practices. **Skills:** Reading Comprehension; Active Listening; Problem Identification; Critical Thinking; Equipment Selection. **Abilities:** *Cognitive*—Written Comprehension; Information Ordering; Oral Comprehension; Oral Expression; Problem Sensitivity. *Psychomotor*—Wrist-Finger Speed; Finger Dexterity; Control Precision. *Physical*—Extent Flexibility; Trunk Strength; Dynamic Flexibility. *Sensory*—Near Vision; Speech Recognition; Speech Clarity. **General Work Activities:** *Information Input*—Getting Information Needed to Do the Job; Monitoring Processes, Materials, and Surroundings; Identifying Objects, Actions, and Events. *Mental Process*—Updating and Using Job-Relevant Knowledge; Evaluating Information Against Standards; Processing Information. *Work Output*—Interacting with Computers; Handling and Moving Objects; Repairing and Maintaining Electrical Equipment. *Interacting with Others*—Communicating with Other Workers; Performing Administrative Activities; Establishing and Maintaining Relationships. **Physical Work Conditions:** Indoors; Sitting; Using Hands on Objects, Tools, or Controls. **Other Job Characteristics:** Degree of Automation; Consequence of Error; Importance of Being Exact or Accurate; Importance of Being Sure All Is Done.

Experience: Job Zone 3. Previous work-related skill, knowledge, or experience is required. **Job Preparation:** SVP 6.0 to less than 7.0—More than 1 year and less than 4 years. **Knowledge:** Computers and Electronics; Clerical; English Language; Customer and

Personal Service; Telecommunications. **Instructional Programs:** 110301 Data Processing Technology/Technician; 521205 Business Computer Facilities Operator.

Related DOT Job: 213.362-010 Computer Operator.

43-9021.00 Data Entry Keyers (Data Entry Keyers, Except Composing)

Education: No data available.

Employed: 399,000

Openings: No data available.

Projected Growth: No data available.

Earnings: $19,170

Operate data-entry device such as keyboard or photo composing perforator. Verify data and prepare materials for printing.

Keeps record of completed work. Reenters data in verification format to detect errors. Selects materials needed to complete work assignment. Resolves garbled or indecipherable messages, using cryptographic procedures and equipment. Loads machine with required input or output media such as paper, cards, disk, tape, or Braille media. Deletes incorrectly entered data. Compiles, sorts, and verifies accuracy of data to be entered. Compares data entered with source documents. Enters data from source documents into computer or onto tape or disk for subsequent entry, using keyboard or scanning device. Files completed documents.

GOE Number, Interest Area, and Work Group: 09.09.01; Business Detail; Clerical Machine Operation. **Personality Type:** Conventional. Conventional occupations frequently involve following set procedures and routines. These occupations can include working with data and details more than with ideas. Usually there is a clear line of authority to follow. **Work Values:** Moral Values; Independence; Activity; Supervision, Human Relations; Working Conditions; Security; Company Policies and Practices. **Skills:** Reading Comprehension; Product Inspection; Information Organization; Operation and Control; Problem Identification. **Abilities:** *Cognitive*—Written Comprehension; Category Flexibility; Information Ordering; Problem Sensitivity; Written Expression. *Psychomotor*—Wrist-Finger Speed. *Physical*—none met the criteria. *Sensory*—Near Vision. **General Work Activities:** *Information Input*—Identifying Objects, Actions, and Events; Getting Information Needed to Do the Job; Estimating Needed Characteristics. *Mental Process*—Evaluating Information Against Standards; Processing Information; Organizing, Planning, and Prioritizing. *Work Output*—Interacting with Computers; Handling and Moving Objects; Documenting and Recording Information. *Interacting with Others*—Performing Administrative Activities; Establishing and Maintaining Relationships; Interpreting Meaning of Information to Others. **Physical Work Conditions:** Indoors; Sitting; Making Repetitive Motions. **Other Job Characteristics:** Importance of Being Exact or Accurate; Importance of Being Sure All Is Done; Importance of Repeating Same Tasks.

Experience: Job Zone 2. Some previous work-related skill, knowledge, or experience may be helpful, but usually is not needed.

Job Preparation: SVP 4.00 to 5.99—6 months to less than 2 years. **Knowledge:** Clerical; Computers and Electronics; English Language; Mathematics; Communications and Media. **Instructional Program:** 520407 Information Processing/Data Entry Technician.

Related DOT Jobs: 203.582-010 Braille Operator; 203.582-014 Braille Typist; 203.582-018 Cryptographic-Machine Operator; 203.582-038 Perforator Typist; 203.582-054 Data Entry Clerk.

43-9022.00 Word Processors and Typists (Word Processors and Typists)

Education: Moderate-term O-T-J training

Employed: 458,910

Openings: 65,143

Projected Growth: –20.4%

Earnings: $22,590

Use word processor/computer or typewriter to type letters, reports, forms, or other material from rough draft, corrected copy, or voice recording. Perform other clerical duties as assigned.

Collates pages of reports and other documents prepared. Addresses envelopes or prepares envelope labels, using typewriter or computer. Types from recorded dictation. Adjusts settings for format, page layout, line spacing, and other style requirements. Answers telephone. Files and stores completed documents. Gathers and arranges material to be typed, following instructions. Sorts and distributes mail. Transmits work electronically to other locations. Computes and verifies totals on report forms, requisitions, or bills, using adding machine or calculator. Keeps records of work performed. Uses data entry device, such as optical scanner, to input data into computer for revision or editing. Stores completed documents on computer hard drive or data storage medium such as disk. Transcribes stenotyped notes of court proceedings. Checks completed work for spelling, grammar, punctuation, and format. Types from rough draft, corrected copy, or previous version displayed on screen, using computer or typewriter. Prints and makes copy of work. Operates duplicating machine.

GOE Number, Interest Area, and Work Group: 09.09.01; Business Detail; Clerical Machine Operation. **Personality Type:** Conventional. Conventional occupations frequently involve following set procedures and routines. These occupations can include working with data and details more than with ideas. Usually there is a clear line of authority to follow. **Work Values:** Moral Values; Working Conditions; Company Policies and Practices; Activity; Supervision, Human Relations; Independence. **Skills:** Reading Comprehension; Active Listening; Information Organization; Writing; Speaking; Mathematics. **Abilities:** *Cognitive*—Oral Comprehension; Written Comprehension; Perceptual Speed; Category Flexibility; Information Ordering; Selective Attention. *Psychomotor*—Wrist-Finger Speed; Finger Dexterity; Manual Dexterity. *Physical*—Trunk Strength. *Sensory*—Near Vision; Speech Recognition; Auditory Attention; Speech Clarity. **General Work Activities:** *Information Input*—Getting Information Needed to Do the Job; Identifying Objects, Actions, and Events; Monitoring Processes, Materials, and Surroundings. *Mental Process*—Evaluating Information Against Standards; Processing Information; Judging Qualities of Things, Services, Other People's Work; Organizing, Planning, and Prioritizing. *Work Output*—Handling and Moving Objects; Interacting with Computers; Documenting and Recording Information. *Interacting with Others*—Performing Administrative Activities; Establishing and Maintaining Relationships; Communicating with Persons Outside Organization. **Physical Work Conditions:** Indoors; Sitting; Making Repetitive Motions. **Other Job Characteristics:** Degree of Automation; Importance of Being Exact or Accurate; Importance of Repeating Same Tasks; Importance of Being Sure All Is Done.

Experience: Job Zone 2. Some previous work-related skill, knowledge, or experience may be helpful, but usually is not needed. **Job Preparation:** SVP 4.00 to 5.99—6 months to less than 2 years. **Knowledge:** Clerical; English Language; Computers and Electronics; Telecommunications; Mathematics. **Instructional Program:** 520408 General Office/Clerical and Typing Services.

Related DOT Jobs: 203.362-010 Clerk-Typist; 203.382-030 Word Processing Machine Operator; 203.582-058 Transcribing-Machine Operator; 203.582-066 Typist; 203.582-078 Notereader; 209.382-010 Continuity Clerk; 209.587-010 Addresser.

43-9031.00 Desktop Publishers (Desktop Publishing Specialists)

Education: Long-term O-T-J training

Employed: 25,607

Openings: 7,546

Projected Growth: 72.6%

Earnings: $29,130

Format typescript and graphic elements, using computer software to produce publication-ready material.

Views monitors for visual representation of work in progress and for instructions and feedback throughout process. Studies layout or other instructions to determine work to be done and sequence of operations. Loads floppy disks or tapes containing information into system. Creates special effects such as vignettes, mosaics, and image combining. Saves completed work on floppy disks or magnetic tape. Enters digitized data into electronic prepress system computer memory, using scanner, camera, keyboard, or mouse. Enters data such as coordinates of images and color specifications, into system to retouch and make color corrections. Enters data such as background color, shapes, and coordinates of images. Activates options such as masking, pixel (picture element) editing, airbrushing, or image retouching. Activates options such as masking or text processing.

GOE Number, Interest Area, and Work Group: 01.07.01; Arts, Entertainment, and Media; Graphic Arts. **Personality Type:** Realistic. Realistic occupations frequently involve work activities that include practical, hands-on problems and solutions. These occupations often deal with plants, animals, and real-world materials like wood, tools, and machinery. Many of the occupations require working outside and do not involve a lot of paperwork or working closely with others. **Work Values:** Moral Values; Working Conditions; Independence; Security; Supervision, Human Relations. **Skills:** Equipment Selection; Implementation Planning; Operation and Control; Reading Comprehension; Monitoring; Operations Analysis; Information Organization. **Abilities:** *Cognitive*—Visualization; Written Comprehension; Information Ordering; Speed of Closure; Perceptual Speed. *Psychomotor*—Wrist-Finger Speed; Control Precision; Arm-Hand Steadiness; Finger Dexterity. *Physical*—none met the criteria. *Sensory*—Near Vision; Visual Color Discrimination; Night Vision; Glare Sensitivity. **General Work Activities:** *Information Input*—Getting Information Needed to Do the Job; Identifying Objects, Actions, and Events; Estimating Needed Characteristics; Monitoring Processes, Materials, and Surroundings. *Mental Process*—Thinking Creatively; Evaluating Information Against Standards; Updating and Using Job-Relevant Knowledge. *Work Output*—Interacting with Computers; Handling and Moving Objects; Implementing Ideas and Programs. *Interacting with Others*—Communicating with Other Workers; Providing Consultation and Advice to Others; Establishing and Maintaining Relationships; Monitoring and Controlling Resources. **Physical Work Conditions:** Indoors; Sitting; Using Hands on Objects, Tools, or Controls. **Other Job Characteristics:** Degree of Automation; Importance of Being Sure All Is Done; Importance of Being Exact or Accurate.

Experience: Job Zone 4. A minimum of two to four years of work-related skill, knowledge, or experience is needed. **Job Preparation:** SVP 7.0 to less than 8.0—2 years to less than 10 years. **Knowledge:** Computers and Electronics; Clerical; Communications and Media; English Language; Production and Processing; Design. **Instructional Programs:** 480211 Computer Typography and Composition Equipment Operator; 480212 Desktop Publishing Equipment Operator.

Related DOT Job: 979.282-010 Electronic Prepress System Operator.

43-9041.00 Insurance Claims and Policy Processing Clerks (Insurance Policy Processing Clerks)

Education: Moderate-term O-T-J training
Employed: 169,806
Openings: 33,119
Projected Growth: 7.9%
Earnings: $23,960

Process new insurance policies, modifications to existing policies, and claims forms. Obtain information from policyholders to verify the accuracy and completeness of information on claims forms, applications, related documents, and company records. Update existing policies and company records to reflect changes requested by policyholders and insurance company representatives.

GOE Number, Interest Area, and Work Group: 09.07.01; Business Detail; Records Processing: Verification and Proofing. **Instructional Program:** 520408 General Office/Clerical and Typing Services. **Note:** The Department of Labor has not collected some data for this job, so it has fewer details than the other descriptions.

43-9041.01 Insurance Claims Clerks (Insurance Claims Clerks)

Education: Moderate-term O-T-J training
Employed: 159,506
Openings: 12,974
Projected Growth: 14.5%
Earnings: $24,010

Obtain information from insured or designated persons for purpose of settling claim with insurance carrier.

Reviews insurance policy to determine coverage. Contacts insured or other involved persons for missing information. Posts or attaches information to claim file. Calculates amount of claim. Transmits claims for payment or for further investigation. Prepares and reviews insurance claim forms and related documents for completeness.

GOE Number, Interest Area, and Work Group: 09.07.01; Business Detail; Records Processing: Verification and Proofing. **Personality Type:** Conventional. Conventional occupations frequently involve following set procedures and routines. These occupations can include working with data and details more than with ideas. Usually there is a clear line of authority to follow. **Work Values:** Moral Values; Supervision, Human Relations; Working Conditions; Activity; Company Policies and Practices. **Skills:** Speaking; Reading Comprehension; Active Listening; Information Gathering; Mathematics; Information Organization. **Abilities:** *Cognitive*—Number Facility; Written Comprehension; Oral Comprehension; Information Ordering; Oral Expression. *Psychomotor*—Wrist-Finger Speed. *Physical*—none met the criteria. *Sensory*—Near Vision; Speech Recognition; Speech Clarity. **General Work Activities:** *Information Input*—Getting Information Needed to Do the Job; Identifying Objects, Actions, and Events; Monitoring Processes, Materials, and Surroundings. *Mental Process*—Processing Information; Evaluating Information Against Standards; Making Decisions and Solving Problems. *Work Output*—Documenting and Recording Information; Interacting with Computers; Handling and Moving Objects. *Interacting with Others*—Communicating with Persons Outside Organization; Performing Administrative Activities; Establishing and Maintaining Relationships; Interpreting Meaning of Information to Others. **Physical Work Conditions:** Indoors; Sitting; Making Repetitive Motions; Using Hands on Objects, Tools, or Controls; Standing. **Other Job Characteristics:** Importance of Being Exact or Accurate; Importance of Being Sure All Is Done; Degree of Automation.

Experience: Job Zone 2. Some previous work-related skill, knowledge, or experience may be helpful, but usually is not needed. **Job Preparation:** SVP 4.00 to 5.99—6 months to less than 2 years. **Knowledge:** Clerical; Mathematics; English Language; Telecommunications; Customer and Personal Service; Economics and Accounting. **Instructional Program:** 520408 General Office/Clerical and Typing Services.

Related DOT Jobs: 205.367-018 Claims Clerk II; 241.362-010 Claims Clerk I.

43-9041.02 Insurance Policy Processing Clerks
(Insurance Policy Processing Clerks)

Education: Moderate-term O-T-J training

Employed: 169,806

Openings: 33,119

Projected Growth: 7.9%

Earnings: $23,960

Process applications for, changes to, reinstatement of, and cancellation of insurance policies. Review insurance applications to ensure that all questions have been answered. Compile data on insurance policy changes. Change policy records to conform to insured party's specifications. Compile data on lapsed insurance policies to determine automatic reinstatement according to company policies. Cancel insurance policies as requested by agents. Verify the accuracy of insurance company records.

Notifies insurance agent and accounting department of policy cancellation. Compares information from application to criteria for policy reinstatement and approves reinstatement when criteria are met. Calculates premiums, refunds, commissions, adjustments, and new reserve requirements, using insurance rate standards. Transcribes data to worksheets and enters data into computer for use in preparing documents and adjusting accounts. Collects initial premiums, issues receipts, and compiles periodic reports for management. Receives computer printout of policy cancellations or obtains cancellation card from file. Corresponds with insured or agent to obtain information or to inform of status or changes to application of account. Checks computations of interest accrued, premiums due, and settlement surrender on loan values. Reviews and verifies data such as age, name, address, and principal sum and value of property on insurance applications and policies. Examines letters from policyholders or agents, original insurance applications, and other company documents to determine changes needed and effects of changes.

GOE Number, Interest Area, and Work Group: 09.07.01; Business Detail; Records Processing: Verification and Proofing. **Personality Type:** Conventional. Conventional occupations frequently involve following set procedures and routines. These occupations can include working with data and details more than with ideas. Usually there is a clear line of authority to follow. **Work Values:** Working Conditions; Moral Values; Supervision, Human Relations; Activity; Company Policies and Practices. **Skills:** Reading Comprehension; Mathematics; Active Listening; Writing; Speaking. **Abilities:** *Cognitive*—Written Comprehension; Mathematical Reasoning; Number Facility; Oral Expression; Oral Comprehension. *Psychomotor*—Wrist-Finger Speed. *Physical*—none met the criteria. *Sensory*—Speech Clarity. **General Work Activities:** *Information Input*—Getting Information Needed to Do the Job; Identifying Objects, Actions, and Events; Estimating Needed Characteristics; Monitoring Processes, Materials, and Surroundings. *Mental Process*—Evaluating Information Against Standards; Processing Information; Analyzing Data or Information. *Work Output*—Documenting and Recording Information; Interacting with Computers; Implementing Ideas and Programs. *Interacting with Others*—Communicating with Other Workers; Communicating

with Persons Outside Organization; Performing Administrative Activities. **Physical Work Conditions:** Indoors; Sitting; Using Hands on Objects, Tools, or Controls. **Other Job Characteristics:** Importance of Being Exact or Accurate; Importance of Being Sure All Is Done; Consequence of Error.

Experience: Job Zone 2. Some previous work-related skill, knowledge, or experience may be helpful, but usually is not needed. **Job Preparation:** SVP 4.00 to 5.99—6 months to less than 2 years. **Knowledge:** Mathematics; Clerical; Computers and Electronics; Telecommunications; Law, Government and Jurisprudence; Economics and Accounting; English Language. **Instructional Program:** 520408 General Office/Clerical and Typing Services.

Related DOT Jobs: 203.382-014 Cancellation Clerk; 209.382-014 Special-Certificate Dictator; 209.687-018 Reviewer; 219.362-042 Policy-Change Clerk; 219.362-050 Revival Clerk; 219.482-014 Insurance Checker.

43-9051.00 Mail Clerks and Mail Machine Operators, Except Postal Service (Mail Clerks, Except Mail Machine Operators and Postal Service)

Education: Short-term O-T-J training

Employed: 127,581

Openings: 26,426

Projected Growth: 9.5%

Earnings: $17,660

Prepare incoming and outgoing mail for distribution. Use hands or mail-handling machines to time stamp, open, read, sort, and route incoming mail and to address, seal, stamp, fold, stuff, and affix postage to outgoing mail or packages. Keep necessary records and complete forms.

GOE Number, Interest Area, and Work Group: 09.09.01; Business Detail; Clerical Machine Operation. **Instructional Program:** 520408 General Office/Clerical and Typing Services. **Note:** The Department of Labor has not collected some data for this job, so it has fewer details than the other descriptions.

43-9051.01 Mail Machine Operators, Preparation and Handling (Mail Machine Operators, Preparation and Handling)

Education: No data available.

Employed: 57,450

Openings: No data available.

Projected Growth: No data available.

Earnings: $17,250

Operate machines that emboss names, addresses, and other matter onto metal plates, for use in addressing machines. Operate machines that print names, addresses, and similar information onto items such as envelopes, accounting forms, and advertising literature.

Positions plates, stencils, or tapes in machine magazine. Selects type of die size. Starts machine. Removes printed material from machine, such as labeled articles, postmarked envelopes or tape, and folded sheets. Checks ink level, adds ink, and fills paste reservoir. Observes machine operation to detect evidence of malfunctions during production run. Makes adjustments to machine and inspects output for defects. Reads production order to determine type and size of items scheduled for printing and mailing. Inserts material for printing or addressing into loading rack on machine. Changes machine ribbon. Adjusts machine guides, rollers, and card insert prior to starting machine. Operates embossing machine or typewriter to make corrections, additions, and changes on address plates. Places folded sheets into envelopes preparatory to mailing.

GOE Number, Interest Area, and Work Group: 09.09.01; Business Detail; Clerical Machine Operation. **Personality Type:** Realistic. Realistic occupations frequently involve work activities that include practical, hands-on problems and solutions. These occupations often deal with plants, animals, and real-world materials like wood, tools, and machinery. Many of the occupations require working outside and do not involve a lot of paperwork or working closely with others. **Work Values:** Moral Values; Independence; Supervision, Human Relations; Supervision, Technical; Activity. **Skills:** Operation and Control; Reading Comprehension; Equipment Selection; Product Inspection; Problem Identification; Operation Monitoring. **Abilities:** *Cognitive*—Written Comprehension; Information Ordering; Perceptual Speed; Problem Sensitivity; Category Flexibility. *Psychomotor*—Manual Dexterity; Reaction Time; Rate Control. *Physical*—Dynamic Flexibility. *Sensory*—Near Vision; Peripheral Vision. **General Work Activities:** *Information Input*—Monitoring Processes, Materials, and Surroundings; Inspecting Equipment, Structures, Materials; Getting Information Needed to Do the Job. *Mental Process*—Evaluating Information Against Standards; Judging Qualities of Things, Services, Other People's Work; Processing Information. *Work Output*—Controlling Machines and Processes; Handling and Moving Objects; Performing General Physical Activities. *Interacting with Others*—Communicating with Other Workers; Performing Administrative Activities; Establishing and Maintaining Relationships. **Physical Work Conditions:** Indoors; Using Hands on Objects, Tools, or Controls; Standing. **Other Job Characteristics:** Degree of Automation; Pace Determined by Speed of Equipment; Importance of Repeating Same Tasks; Consequence of Error; Importance of Being Sure All Is Done; Importance of Being Exact or Accurate.

Experience: Job Zone 1. No previous work-related skill, knowledge, or experience is needed. **Job Preparation:** SVP Below 4.0—Less than 6 months. **Knowledge:** Production and Processing; Mechanical; Engineering and Technology; English Language; Computers and Electronics; Clerical. **Instructional Program:** 520408 General Office/Clerical and Typing Services.

Related DOT Jobs: 208.462-010 Mailing-Machine Operator; 208.582-010 Addressing-Machine Operator; 208.685-014 Folding-Machine Operator; 208.685-018 Inserting-Machine Operator; 208.685-026 Sealing-and-Canceling-Machine Operator; 208.685-034 Wing-Mailer-Machine Operator.

43-9051.02 Mail Clerks, Except Mail Machine Operators and Postal Service (Mail Clerks)

Education: Short-term O-T-J training
Employed: 127,581
Openings: 26,426
Projected Growth: 9.5%
Earnings: $17,660

Prepare incoming and outgoing mail for distribution. Time stamp, open, read, sort, and route incoming mail. Seal, stamp, and affix postage to outgoing mail or packages.

Receives request for merchandise samples or promotional literature, prepares shipping slips, and mails samples or literature. Inspects wrapping, address, and appearance of outgoing package or letter, for conformance to standards and for accuracy. Answers inquiries regarding shipping or mailing policies. Stacks bundles of bulk printed matter for shipment, and loads and unloads from trucks and conveyors. Releases packages or letters to customer upon presentation of written notice or other identification. Addresses packages or letters by hand, or using addressing machine, label, or stamp. Records and maintains records of information such as charges and destination of insured, registered or c.o.d. packages. Affixes postage to packages or letter by hand, or stamps with postage meter; dispatches mail. Seals or opens envelopes by hand or machine. Stamps date and time of receipt of incoming mail; distributes and collects mail. Sorts letters or packages into sacks or bins; places identifying tag on sack or bin, according to destination and type. Weighs packages or letters, computes charges, and accepts payment, using weight scale and rate chart. Wraps packages or bundles by hand or using tying machine.

GOE Number, Interest Area, and Work Group: 09.08.01; Business Detail; Records and Materials Processing. **Personality Type:** Conventional. Conventional occupations frequently involve following set procedures and routines. These occupations can include working with data and details more than with ideas. Usually there is a clear line of authority to follow. **Work Values:** Moral Values; Security; Supervision, Human Relations; Activity; Company Policies and Practices; Supervision, Technical. **Skills:** Information Organization; Reading Comprehension; Service Orientation; Problem Identification; Active Listening. **Abilities:** *Cognitive*—Perceptual Speed; Number Facility; Written Comprehension; Category Flexibility; Written Expression. *Psychomotor*—Wrist-Finger Speed; Manual Dexterity; Multilimb Coordination. *Physical*—Extent Flexibility; Trunk Strength; Static Strength. *Sensory*—Speech Clarity; Auditory Attention. **General Work Activities:** *Information Input*—Getting Information Needed to Do the Job; Identifying Objects, Actions, and Events; Inspecting Equipment, Structures, Materials. *Mental Process*—Processing Information; Evaluating Information Against Standards; Analyzing Data or Information. *Work Output*—Handling and Moving Objects; Performing General Physical Activities; Documenting and Recording Information. *Interacting with Others*—Communicating with Persons Outside Organization; Performing for or Working with the Public; Communicating with Other Workers. **Physical Work Conditions:** Indoors; Using Hands on Objects, Tools, or Controls; Standing; Making Repetitive Motions. **Other Job Characteristics:** Importance of Being Exact or Accurate; Importance of Repeating Same Tasks; Degree of Automation.

Experience: Job Zone 1. No previous work-related skill, knowledge, or experience is needed. **Job Preparation:** SVP Below 4.0—Less than 6 months. **Knowledge:** Geography; Clerical; Mathematics; Customer and Personal Service; English Language. **Instructional Program:** 520408 General Office/Clerical and Typing Services.

Related DOT Jobs: 209.587-018 Direct-Mail Clerk; 209.687-026 Mail Clerk; 222.367-022 Express Clerk; 222.387-038 Parcel Post

Clerk; 222.567-018 Slot-Tag Inserter; 222.587-030 Mailer; 222.587-032 Mailer Apprentice; 249.687-010 Office Copy Selector.

43-9061.00 Office Clerks, General (General Office Clerks)

Education: Short-term O-T-J training

Employed: 3,020,975

Openings: 745,378

Projected Growth: 15.3%

Earnings: $19,580

Perform duties too varied and diverse to be classified in any specific office clerical occupation, requiring limited knowledge of office management systems and procedures. Perform clerical duties assigned in accordance with the office procedures of individual establishments. Answer telephones; do bookkeeping. Type or do word processing, stenography, office-machine operation, and filing.

Orders materials, supplies, and services, and completes records and reports. Completes and mails bills, contracts, policies, invoices, or checks. Answers telephone, responds to requests, delivers messages, and runs errands. Reviews files, records, and other documents to obtain information to respond to requests. Completes work schedules and arranges appointments for staff and students. Collects, counts, and disburses money, completes banking transactions, and processes payroll. Transcribes dictation and composes and types letters and other correspondence, using typewriter or computer. Stuffs envelopes; addresses, stamps, sorts, and distributes mail, packages, and other materials. Operates office machines such as photocopier, telecopier, and personal computer. Compiles, copies, sorts, and files records of office activities, business transactions, and other activities. Computes, records, and proofreads data and other information such as records or reports. Communicates with customers, employees, and other individuals to disseminate or explain information.

GOE Number, Interest Area, and Work Group: 09.07.02; Business Detail; Records Processing: Preparation and Maintenance. **Personality Type:** Conventional. Conventional occupations frequently involve following set procedures and routines. These occupations can include working with data and details more than with ideas. Usually there is a clear line of authority to follow. **Work Values:** Moral Values; Activity; Working Conditions; Supervision, Human Relations; Co-workers; Advancement. **Skills:** Reading Comprehension; Active Listening; Information Organization; Mathematics; Writing. **Abilities:** *Cognitive*—Oral Expression; Oral Comprehension; Number Facility; Information Ordering; Written Comprehension. *Psychomotor*—Wrist-Finger Speed; Finger Dexterity; Response Orientation. *Physical*—Trunk Strength. *Sensory*—Near Vision; Speech Recognition; Speech Clarity. **General Work Activities:** *Information Input*—Getting Information Needed to Do the Job; Identifying Objects, Actions, and Events; Estimating Needed Characteristics. *Mental Process*—Processing Information; Evaluating Information Against Standards; Analyzing Data or Information. *Work Output*—Documenting and Recording Information; Interacting with Computers; Handling and Moving Objects. *Interacting with Others*—Communicating with Persons Outside Organization; Performing Administrative Activities; Communicating with Other Workers. **Physical Work Con-**ditions: Indoors; Sitting; Making Repetitive Motions. **Other Job Characteristics:** Degree of Automation; Importance of Being Exact or Accurate; Importance of Being Sure All Is Done.

Experience: Job Zone 1. No previous work-related skill, knowledge, or experience is needed. **Job Preparation:** SVP Below 4.0—Less than 6 months. **Knowledge:** Clerical; Customer and Personal Service; English Language; Mathematics; Computers and Electronics; Economics and Accounting. **Instructional Program:** 520408 General Office/Clerical and Typing Services.

Related DOT Jobs: 162.167-026 Prize Coordinator; 205.367-010 Admissions Evaluator; 205.367-030 Election Clerk; 209.362-010 Circulation Clerk; 209.362-014 Control Clerk, Auditing; 209.362-022 Identification Clerk; 209.362-030 Congressional-District Aide; 209.367-010 Agent-Licensing Clerk; 209.367-026 Fingerprint Clerk I; 209.367-034 Lost-Charge-Card Clerk; 209.367-038 News Assistant; 209.367-050 Trip Follower; 209.367-054 Yard Clerk; 209.382-022 Traffic Clerk; 209.387-022 Data-Examination Clerk; 209.562-010 Clerk, General; 209.587-014 Credit-Card Clerk; 209.587-022 History-Card Clerk; 209.587-030 Map Clerk; 209.587-050 Wrong-Address Clerk (partial list; see the introduction for sources of the complete list).

43-9071.00 Office Machine Operators, Except Computer (All Other Office Machine Operators)

Education: No data available.

Employed: 78,160

Openings: No data available.

Projected Growth: No data available.

Earnings: $22,040

Operate one or more of a variety of office machines such as photocopying, photographic, and duplicating machines.

GOE Number, Interest Area, and Work Group: 09.09.01; Business Detail; Clerical Machine Operation. **Instructional Program:** 520408 General Office/Clerical and Typing Services. **Note:** The Department of Labor has not collected some data for this job, so it has fewer details than the other descriptions.

43-9071.01 Duplicating Machine Operators (Duplicating Machine Operators)

Education: No data available.

Employed: 53,510

Openings: No data available.

Projected Growth: No data available.

Earnings: $19,530

Operate one of a variety of office machines such as photocopying, photographic, mimeograph, and duplicating machines, to make copies.

Loads machine with blank paper or film and places paper roll in holding tray or rack of machine. Places original copy in feed tray, feeds originals into feed rolls, or positions originals on table beneath camera lens. Adjusts machine to regulate ink flow, speed, paper size, focus, exposure, and camera distance from document.

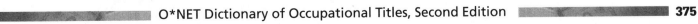

Selects type, embossed plate, or paper stock, according to size, color, thickness, and quantity specified. Cuts copies apart and writes identifying information on copies. Cleans and oils machine and printing plate. Records number of copies made. Sets controls for number of copies and presses buttons to start machine. Moves heat unit and clamping frame over screen bed to form Braille impression on page.

GOE Number, Interest Area, and Work Group: 09.09.01; Business Detail; Clerical Machine Operation. **Personality Type:** Conventional. Conventional occupations frequently involve following set procedures and routines. These occupations can include working with data and details more than with ideas. Usually there is a clear line of authority to follow. **Work Values:** Moral Values; Independence; Supervision, Human Relations; Supervision, Technical; Activity; Company Policies and Practices. **Skills:** Repairing; Operation and Control; Operation Monitoring; Equipment Maintenance. **Abilities:** *Cognitive*—Visualization; Written Comprehension; Information Ordering; Problem Sensitivity; Number Facility; Deductive Reasoning. *Psychomotor*—Control Precision; Finger Dexterity. *Physical*—none met the criteria. *Sensory*—Visual Color Discrimination; Glare Sensitivity. **General Work Activities:** *Information Input*—Getting Information Needed to Do the Job; Inspecting Equipment, Structures, Materials; Monitoring Processes, Materials, and Surroundings. *Mental Process*—Organizing, Planning, and Prioritizing; Processing Information; Judging Qualities of Things, Services, Other People's Work; Evaluating Information Against Standards. *Work Output*—Controlling Machines and Processes; Handling and Moving Objects; Repairing and Maintaining Mechanical Equipment. *Interacting with Others*—Performing Administrative Activities; Performing for or Working with the Public; Establishing and Maintaining Relationships; Assisting and Caring for Others. **Physical Work Conditions:** Indoors; Using Hands on Objects, Tools, or Controls; Standing. **Other Job Characteristics:** Degree of Automation; Pace Determined by Speed of Equipment; Importance of Being Sure All Is Done.

Experience: Job Zone 1. No previous work-related skill, knowledge, or experience is needed. **Job Preparation:** SVP Below 4.0—Less than 6 months. **Knowledge:** Computers and Electronics; Clerical; Mathematics; Mechanical; English Language; Customer and Personal Service; Production and Processing. **Instructional Program:** 520408 General Office/Clerical and Typing Services.

Related DOT Jobs: 207.682-010 Duplicating-Machine Operator I; 207.682-014 Duplicating-Machine Operator II; 207.682-018 Offset-Duplicating-Machine Operator; 207.685-010 Braille-Duplicating-Machine Operator; 207.685-014 Photocopying-Machine Operator; 207.685-018 Photographic-Machine Operator.

43-9081.00 Proofreaders and Copy Markers
(Proofreaders and Copy Markers)

Education: Short-term O-T-J training

Employed: 41,401

Openings: 8,537

Projected Growth: –17.1%

Earnings: $18,620

Read transcript or proof type setup to detect and mark for correction any grammatical, typographical, or compositional errors.

Reads proofs against copy and corrects errors in type, arrangement, grammar, punctuation, or spelling, using proofreader marks. Corrects or records omissions, errors, or inconsistencies found. Compares information or figures on one record against same data on other records or with original copy to detect errors. Calls attention to discrepancies between copy and proof. Places proof and copy side by side on reading board. Measures dimensions, spacing, and positioning of page elements (copy and illustrations) to verify conformance to specifications, using printer's ruler. Consults reference books or secures aid of reader to check references to rules of grammar and composition. Marks proof to correct errors, using standard printer's marks. Routes proofs with marked corrections to be reprinted; reads corrected copies or proofs. Reads proofsheet aloud, calling out punctuation marks and spelling unusual words and proper names.

GOE Number, Interest Area, and Work Group: 09.07.01; Business Detail; Records Processing: Verification and Proofing. **Personality Type:** Conventional. Conventional occupations frequently involve following set procedures and routines. These occupations can include working with data and details more than with ideas. Usually there is a clear line of authority to follow. **Work Values:** Moral Values; Working Conditions; Company Policies and Practices; Activity; Independence. **Skills:** Reading Comprehension; Writing; Information Organization; Product Inspection; Speaking. **Abilities:** *Cognitive*—Written Comprehension; Memorization; Perceptual Speed; Written Expression; Problem Sensitivity. *Psychomotor*—none met the criteria. *Physical*—none met the criteria. *Sensory*—Near Vision; Speech Clarity. **General Work Activities:** *Information Input*—Identifying Objects, Actions, and Events; Getting Information Needed to Do the Job; Monitoring Processes, Materials, and Surroundings; Inspecting Equipment, Structures, Materials. *Mental Process*—Evaluating Information Against Standards; Processing Information; Judging Qualities of Things, Services, Other People's Work. *Work Output*—Documenting and Recording Information; Handling and Moving Objects; Interacting with Computers; Implementing Ideas and Programs. *Interacting with Others*—Communicating with Other Workers; Providing Consultation and Advice to Others; Performing Administrative Activities. **Physical Work Conditions:** Indoors; Sitting; Using Hands on Objects, Tools, or Controls. **Other Job Characteristics:** Importance of Being Exact or Accurate; Importance of Being Sure All Is Done; Consequence of Error.

Experience: Job Zone 2. Some previous work-related skill, knowledge, or experience may be helpful, but usually is not needed. **Job Preparation:** SVP 4.00 to 5.99—6 months to less than 2 years. **Knowledge:** English Language; Mathematics; Computers and Electronics; Telecommunications; Clerical. **Instructional Programs:** 480201 Graphic and Printing Equipment Operator, General; 520501 Business Communications.

Related DOT Jobs: 209.387-030 Proofreader; 209.667-010 Copy Holder; 209.687-010 Checker II; 247.667-010 Production Proofreader.

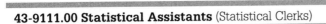

43-9111.00 Statistical Assistants (Statistical Clerks)

Education: Moderate-term O-T-J training
Employed: 72,143
Openings: 5,308
Projected Growth: –4.5%
Earnings: $23,380

Compile and compute data according to statistical formulas, for use in statistical studies. Perform actuarial computations and compile charts and graphs for use by actuaries. Includes actuarial clerks.

Prepares reports and graphs to show comparisons or survey results of statistical information obtained. Operates computer to enter and retrieve data and prepare correspondence and reports. Compiles statistics from source materials such as production, sales, and personnel records, surveys, and questionnaires. Computes statistical data according to formulas, using computer or calculator. Posts and files charts. Verifies completeness and accuracy of source data. Assembles and classifies statistics, following prescribed procedures.

GOE Number, Interest Area, and Work Group: 02.06.02; Science, Math, and Engineering; Mathematics and Computers: Data Analysis. **Personality Type:** Conventional. Conventional occupations frequently involve following set procedures and routines. These occupations can include working with data and details more than with ideas. Usually there is a clear line of authority to follow. **Work Values:** Independence; Moral Values; Working Conditions; Activity; Supervision, Human Relations; Company Policies and Practices; Security. **Skills:** Mathematics; Information Organization; Information Gathering; Writing; Reading Comprehension. **Abilities:** *Cognitive*—Number Facility; Mathematical Reasoning; Written Expression; Written Comprehension; Information Ordering. *Psychomotor*—Wrist-Finger Speed. *Physical*—none met the criteria. *Sensory*—Glare Sensitivity. **General Work Activities:** *Information Input*—Getting Information Needed to Do the Job; Identifying Objects, Actions, and Events; Estimating Needed Characteristics. *Mental Process*—Analyzing Data or Information; Processing Information; Evaluating Information Against Standards. *Work Output*—Interacting with Computers; Handling and Moving Objects; Documenting and Recording Information. *Interacting with Others*—Interpreting Meaning of Information to Others; Communicating with Other Workers; Performing Administrative Activities. **Physical Work Conditions:** Indoors; Sitting; Making Repetitive Motions. **Other Job Characteristics:** Importance of Being Exact or Accurate; Importance of Being Sure All Is Done; Importance of Repeating Same Tasks.

Experience: Job Zone 2. Some previous work-related skill, knowledge, or experience may be helpful, but usually is not needed. **Job Preparation:** SVP 4.00 to 5.99—6 months to less than 2 years. **Knowledge:** Mathematics; Computers and Electronics; Clerical; English Language; Communications and Media. **Instructional Program:** 520302 Accounting Technician.

Related DOT Jobs: 209.387-014 Compiler; 214.487-010 Chart Calculator; 216.382-062 Statistical Clerk; 216.382-066 Statistical Clerk, Advertising; 219.387-022 Planimeter Operator; 221.382-010 Chart Clerk; 221.584-010 Chart Changer.

45-0000
Farming, Fishing, and Forestry Occupations

45-1000 Supervisors, Farming, Fishing, and Forestry Workers

45-1011.00 First-Line Supervisors/Managers of Farming, Fishing, and Forestry Workers (First-Line Supervisors and Managers/Supervisors—Agricultural, Forestry, Fishing, and Related Workers)

Education: No data available.

Employed: 51,350

Openings: No data available.

Projected Growth: No data available.

Earnings: $27,410

Directly supervise and coordinate the activities of agricultural, forestry, aquacultural, and related workers.

GOE Number, Interest Area, and Work Group: 03.01.01; Plants and Animals; Managerial Work: Farming and Fishing. **Instructional Programs:** 010104 Farm and Ranch Management; 010199 Agricultural Business and Management, Other; 010301 Agricultural Production Workers and Managers, General; 010302 Agricultural Animal Husbandry and Production Management; 010304 Crop Production Operations and Management; 010399 Agricultural Production Workers and Managers, Other; 019999 Agricultural Business and Production, Other; 020201 Animal Sciences, General; 020202 Agricultural Animal Breeding and Genetics; 020204 Agricultural Animal Nutrition; 020206 Dairy Science; 020209 Poultry Science; 020401 Plant Sciences, General; 020402 Agronomy and Crop Science; 020409 Range Science and Management. **Note:** The Department of Labor has not collected some data for this job, so it has fewer details than the other descriptions.

45-1011.01 First-Line Supervisors and Manager/Supervisors—Agricultural Crop Workers (First-Line Supervisors and Managers/Supervisors—Agricultural and Related Workers)

Education: Work experience in a related occupation

Employed: 91,546

Openings: 11,813

Projected Growth: 6.2%

Earnings: No data available.

Directly supervise and coordinate activities of agricultural crop workers. Manager/Supervisors are generally found in smaller establishments where they perform both supervisory and management functions, such as accounting, marketing, and personnel work, and may also engage in the same agricultural work as the workers they supervise.

Prepares time, payroll, and production reports, such as farm conditions, amount of yield, machinery breakdowns, and labor problems. Recruits, hires, and discharges workers. Issues farm implements and machinery, ladders, or containers to workers and collects them at end of workday. Inspects crops and fields to determine maturity, yield, infestation, or work requirements, such as cultivating, spraying, weeding, or harvesting. Determines number and kind of workers needed to perform required work, and schedules activities. Trains workers in methods of field work and safety regulations, and briefs them on identifying characteristics of insects and diseases. Directs or assists in adjustment, repair, and maintenance of farm machinery and equipment. Requisitions and purchases farm supplies such as insecticides, machine parts or lubricants, and tools. Drives and operates farm machinery such as trucks, tractors, or self-propelled harvesters, to transport workers or to cultivate and harvest fields. Opens gate to permit entry of water into ditches or pipes, and signals worker to start flow of water to irrigate fields. Investigates grievances and settles disputes to maintain harmony among workers. Contracts with seasonal workers and farmers to provide employment and arranges for transportation, equipment, and living quarters. Assigns duties such as tilling soil, planting, irrigating, storing crops, and maintaining machines; assigns fields or rows to workers. Observes workers to detect inefficient and unsafe work procedures or identify problems; initiates actions to correct improper procedure or solve problem. Confers with manager to evaluate weather and soil conditions and to develop and revise plans and procedures.

GOE Number, Interest Area, and Work Group: 03.01.01; Plants and Animals; Managerial Work: Farming and Fishing. **Personality Type:** Enterprising. Enterprising occupations frequently involve starting up and carrying out projects. These occupations can involve leading people and making many decisions. They sometimes require risk taking and often deal with business. **Work Values:** Authority; Responsibility; Autonomy; Activity; Moral Values; Achievement. **Skills:** Management of Personnel Resources; Coordination; Speaking; Time Management; Problem Identification; Instructing; Equipment Selection; Product Inspection; Mathematics; Management of Material Resources. **Abilities:** *Cognitive*—Oral Expression; Oral Comprehension; Deductive Reasoning; Inductive Reasoning; Information Ordering. *Psychomotor*—Control Precision; Multilimb Coordination; Wrist-Finger Speed. *Physical*—Extent Flexibility; Static Strength; Trunk Strength. *Sensory*—Near Vision; Speech Clarity; Far Vision. **General Work Activities:** *Information Input*—Identifying Objects, Actions, and Events; Monitoring Processes, Materials, and Surroundings; Getting Information Needed to Do the Job. *Mental Process*—Making Decisions and Solving Problems; Scheduling Work and Activities; Organizing, Planning, and Prioritizing; Processing Information. *Work Output*—Performing General Physical Activities; Documenting and Recording Information; Repairing and Maintaining Mechanical Equipment; Operating Vehicles or Equipment. *Interacting with Others*—Coordinating Work and Activities of Others; Communicating with Other Workers; Guiding, Directing and Motivating Subordinates; Staffing Organizational Units. **Physical Work Conditions:** Standing; Outdoors; Using Hands on Objects, Tools, or Controls. **Other Job Characteristics:** Consequence of Error; Importance of Being Sure All Is Done; Frustrating Circumstances.

Experience: Job Zone 3. Previous work-related skill, knowledge, or experience is required. **Job Preparation:** SVP 6.0 to less than 7.0—More than 1 year and less than 4 years. **Knowledge:** Food Production; Administration and Management; Personnel and Human Resources; Mechanical; English Language; Biology. **Instructional Programs:** 010301 Agricultural Production Workers and Managers, General; 010304 Crop Production Operations and Management; 010501 Agricultural Supplies Retailing and Wholesaling.

Related DOT Jobs: 180.167-014 Field Supervisor, Seed Production; 180.167-022 Group Leader; 180.167-050 Migrant Leader; 401.137-010 Supervisor, Area; 401.137-014 Supervisor, Detasseling Crew; 402.131-010 Supervisor, Vegetable Farming; 403.131-010 Supervisor, Tree-Fruit-and-Nut Farming; 403.131-014 Supervisor, Vine-Fruit Farming; 404.131-010 Supervisor, Field-Crop Farming; 404.131-014 Supervisor, Shed Workers; 407.131-010 Supervisor, Diversified Crops; 408.137-010 Supervisor, Insect and Disease Inspection; 409.117-010 Harvest Contractor; 409.131-010 Supervisor, Picking Crew; 409.137-010 Irrigator, Head; 409.137-014 Row Boss, Hoeing; 929.137-034 Yard Supervisor, Cotton Gin.

45-1011.02 First-Line Supervisors and Manager/Supervisors—Animal Husbandry Workers (First-Line Supervisors and Managers/Supervisors—Agricultural and Related Workers)

Education: Work experience in a related occupation

Employed: 91,546

Openings: 11,813

Projected Growth: 6.2%

Earnings: No data available.

Directly supervise and coordinate activities of animal husbandry workers. Manager/Supervisors are generally found in smaller establishments where they perform both supervisory and management functions, such as accounting, marketing, and personnel work, and may also engage in the same animal husbandry work as the workers they supervise.

Inspects buildings, fences, fields or range, supplies, and equipment to determine work to be done. Studies feed, weight, health, genetic, or milk production records to determine feed formula and rations or breeding schedule. Plans and prepares work schedules. Recruits, hires, and pays workers. Prepares animal condition, production, feed consumption, and worker attendance reports. Requisitions equipment, materials, and supplies. Transports or arranges for transport of animals, equipment, food, animal feed, and other supplies to and from worksite. Treats animal illness or injury, following experience or instructions of veterinarian. Monitors eggs and adjusts incubator thermometer and gauges, to ascertain hatching progress and maintain specified conditions. Notifies veterinarian and manager of serious illnesses or injuries to animals. Trains workers in animal care, artificial insemination techniques, egg candling and sorting, and transfer of animals. Observes animals such as cattle, sheep, poultry, or game animals, for signs of illness, injury, nervousness, or unnatural behavior. Confers with manager to discuss and ascertain production requirements, condition of equipment and supplies, and work schedules. Assigns workers to tasks such as feeding and treating animals, cleaning quarters, transferring animals, and maintaining facilities. Inseminates livestock artificially to produce desired offspring and to demonstrate techniques to farmers. Oversees animal care, maintenance, breeding, or packing and transfer activities, to ensure work is done correctly and to identify and solve problems.

GOE Number, Interest Area, and Work Group: 03.01.01; Plants and Animals; Managerial Work: Farming and Fishing. **Personality Type:** Enterprising. Enterprising occupations frequently involve starting up and carrying out projects. These occupations can involve leading people and making many decisions. They sometimes require risk taking and often deal with business. **Work Values:** Authority; Responsibility; Activity; Autonomy; Achievement; Moral Values. **Skills:** Problem Identification; Coordination; Instructing; Equipment Selection; Speaking; Time Management; Management of Personnel Resources; Implementation Planning. **Abilities:** *Cognitive*—Oral Expression; Problem Sensitivity; Written Comprehension; Memorization; Oral Comprehension; Deductive Reasoning. *Psychomotor*—Manual Dexterity; Arm-Hand Steadiness; Control Precision; Finger Dexterity; Wrist-Finger Speed. *Physical*—Static Strength; Trunk Strength; Extent Flexibility. *Sensory*—Near Vision; Visual Color Discrimination; Far Vision; Auditory Attention. **General Work Activities:** *Information Input*—Getting Information Needed to Do the Job; Identifying Objects, Actions, and Events; Monitoring Processes, Materials, and Surroundings. *Mental Process*—Scheduling Work and Activities; Making Decisions and Solving Problems; Organizing, Planning, and Prioritizing. *Work Output*—Handling and Moving Objects; Documenting and Recording Information; Performing General Physical Activities. *Interacting with Others*—Communicating with Other Workers; Guiding, Directing and Motivating Subordinates; Coordinating Work and Activities of Others. **Physical Work Conditions:** Standing; Outdoors; Using Hands on Objects, Tools, or Controls. **Other Job Characteristics:** Importance of Being Sure All Is Done; Consequence of Error; Frustrating Circumstances; Importance of Being Exact or Accurate.

Experience: Job Zone 3. Previous work-related skill, knowledge, or experience is required. **Job Preparation:** SVP 6.0 to less than 7.0—More than 1 year and less than 4 years. **Knowledge:** Food Production; Administration and Management; Biology; Personnel and Human Resources; Medicine and Dentistry. **Instructional Programs:** 010301 Agricultural Production Workers and Managers, General; 010302 Agricultural Animal Husbandry and Production Management; 010507 Equestrian/Equine Studies, Horse Management and Training.

Related DOT Jobs: 410.131-010 Barn Boss; 410.131-014 Supervisor, Artificial Breeding Ranch; 410.131-018 Supervisor, Dairy Farm; 410.131-022 Supervisor, Stock Ranch; 410.134-010 Supervisor, Livestock-Yard; 410.134-014 Supervisor, Wool-Shearing; 410.134-022 Supervisor, Research Dairy Farm; 410.137-010 Camp Tender; 410.137-014 Top Screw; 411.131-010 Supervisor, Poultry Farm; 411.137-010 Supervisor, Poultry Hatchery; 412.131-010 Supervisor, Game Farm.

45-1011.03 First-Line Supervisors and Manager/Supervisors—Animal Care Workers, Except Livestock (First-Line Supervisors and Managers/Supervisors—Agricultural and Related Workers)

Education: Work experience in a related occupation

Employed: 91,546

Openings: 11,813

Projected Growth: 6.2%

Earnings: No data available.

Directly supervise and coordinate activities of animal care workers. Manager/Supervisors are generally found in smaller establishments where they perform both supervisory and management functions, such as accounting, marketing, and personnel work, and may also engage in the same animal care work as the workers they supervise.

Investigates complaints of animal neglect or cruelty and follows up on complaints appearing to justify prosecution. Monitors animal care and inspects facilities to identify problems; discusses solutions with workers. Establishes work schedule and procedures of animal care. Trains workers in animal care procedures, maintenance duties, and safety precautions. Plans budget; arranges for purchase of animals, feed, or supplies. Prepares reports concerning activity of facility, employees' time records, and animal treatment. Delivers lectures to public to stimulate interest in animals and to communicate humane philosophy to public. Observes and examines animals to detect signs of illness and determine need of services from veterinarian. Directs and assists workers in maintenance and repair of facilities. Assigns workers to tasks such as feeding and treatment of animals, and cleaning and maintenance of animal quarters. Operates euthanasia equipment to destroy animals.

GOE Number, Interest Area, and Work Group: 03.01.01; Plants and Animals; Managerial Work: Farming and Fishing. **Personality Type:** Realistic. Realistic occupations frequently involve work activities that include practical, hands-on problems and solutions. These occupations often deal with plants, animals, and real-world materials like wood, tools, and machinery. Many of the occupations require working outside and do not involve a lot of paperwork or working closely with others. **Work Values:** Authority; Autonomy; Responsibility; Activity; Security; Achievement. **Skills:** Instructing; Writing; Speaking; Coordination; Problem Identification. **Abilities:** *Cognitive*—Oral Expression; Problem Sensitivity; Written Comprehension; Written Expression; Oral Comprehension. *Psychomotor*—Manual Dexterity; Control Precision; Finger Dexterity; Wrist-Finger Speed. *Physical*—Extent Flexibility; Static Strength; Trunk Strength; Gross Body Coordination. *Sensory*—Speech Clarity; Far Vision; Auditory Attention. **General Work Activities:** *Information Input*—Getting Information Needed to Do the Job; Monitoring Processes, Materials, and Surroundings; Identifying Objects, Actions, and Events. *Mental Process*—Making Decisions and Solving Problems; Organizing, Planning, and Prioritizing; Scheduling Work and Activities. *Work Output*—Implementing Ideas and Programs; Performing General Physical Activities; Documenting and Recording Information. *Interacting with Others*—Coordinating Work and Activities of Others; Communicating with Other Workers; Communicating with Persons Outside Organization; Guiding, Directing and Motivating Subordinates. **Physical Work Conditions:** Standing; Indoors; Hazardous Situations; Outdoors; Using Hands on Objects, Tools, or Controls. **Other Job Characteristics:** Importance of Being Sure All Is Done; Importance of Being Exact or Accurate; Consequence of Error.

Experience: Job Zone 3. Previous work-related skill, knowledge, or experience is required. **Job Preparation:** SVP 6.0 to less than 7.0—More than 1 year and less than 4 years. **Knowledge:** Administration and Management; Biology; English Language; Medicine and Dentistry; Personnel and Human Resources. **Instructional**

Programs: 010101 Agricultural Business and Management, General; 010102 Agricultural Business/Agribusiness Operations; 010104 Farm and Ranch Management; 020401 Plant Sciences, General; 020409 Range Science and Management.

Related DOT Jobs: 180.167-038 Manager, Game Preserve; 187.167-218 Manager, Animal Shelter; 410.134-018 Supervisor, Kennel; 410.137-018 Supervisor, Animal Maintenance; 412.137-010 Animal Keeper, Head; 418.137-010 Supervisor, Laboratory Animal Facility; 418.137-014 Supervisor, Research Kennel.

45-1011.04 First-Line Supervisors and Manager/Supervisors—Horticultural Workers (First-Line Supervisors and Managers/Supervisors—Agricultural and Related Workers)

Education: Work experience in a related occupation
Employed: 91,546
Openings: 11,813
Projected Growth: 6.2%
Earnings: No data available.

Directly supervise and coordinate activities of horticultural workers. Manager/Supervisors are generally found in smaller establishments were they perform both supervisory and management functions, such as accounting, marketing, and personnel work, and may also engage in the same horticultural work as the workers they supervise.

Observes plants, flowers, shrubs, and trees in greenhouses, cold frames, or fields to ascertain condition. Confers with management to report conditions, to plan planting and harvesting schedules, and to discuss changes in fertilizer, herbicides, or cultivating techniques. Inspects facilities to determine maintenance needs such as malfunctioning environmental-control system, clogged sprinklers, or missing glass panes in greenhouse. Estimates work-hour requirements to plant, cultivate, or harvest; prepares work schedule. Reads inventory records, customer orders, and shipping schedules to ascertain day's activities. Reviews employees' work to ascertain quality and quantity of work performed. Drives and operates heavy machinery such as dump truck, tractor, or growth-media tiller, to transport materials and supplies. Prepares and submits written or oral reports of personnel actions, such as performance evaluations, hires, promotions, and disciplines. Assigns workers to duties such as cultivation, harvesting, maintenance, grading and packing products, or altering greenhouse environmental conditions. Trains employees in horticultural techniques such as transplanting and weeding, shearing and harvesting trees, and grading and packing flowers. Maintains records of employees' hours worked and work completed.

GOE Number, Interest Area, and Work Group: 03.01.02; Plants and Animals; Managerial Work: Nursery, Groundskeeping, and Logging. **Personality Type:** Realistic. Realistic occupations frequently involve work activities that include practical, hands-on problems and solutions. These occupations often deal with plants, animals, and real-world materials like wood, tools, and machinery. Many of the occupations require working outside and do not involve a lot of paperwork or working closely with others. **Work Values:** Authority; Autonomy; Responsibility; Activity; Moral

Values. **Skills:** Coordination; Instructing; Management of Personnel Resources; Problem Identification; Time Management; Reading Comprehension; Implementation Planning; Learning Strategies; Product Inspection; Speaking. **Abilities:** *Cognitive*—Oral Expression; Written Comprehension; Problem Sensitivity; Deductive Reasoning; Oral Comprehension. *Psychomotor*—Control Precision; Multilimb Coordination; Manual Dexterity. *Physical*—Static Strength; Trunk Strength; Gross Body Coordination; Dynamic Strength. *Sensory*—Speech Clarity; Near Vision; Visual Color Discrimination. **General Work Activities:** *Information Input*—Identifying Objects, Actions, and Events; Getting Information Needed to Do the Job; Inspecting Equipment, Structures, Materials. *Mental Process*—Making Decisions and Solving Problems; Judging Qualities of Things, Services, Other People's Work; Scheduling Work and Activities; Organizing, Planning, and Prioritizing; Analyzing Data or Information. *Work Output*—Performing General Physical Activities; Handling and Moving Objects; Documenting and Recording Information. *Interacting with Others*—Coordinating Work and Activities of Others; Guiding, Directing and Motivating Subordinates; Communicating with Other Workers. **Physical Work Conditions:** Outdoors; Standing; Using Hands on Objects, Tools, or Controls. **Other Job Characteristics:** Consequence of Error; Importance of Being Sure All Is Done; Importance of Being Exact or Accurate.

Experience: Job Zone 3. Previous work-related skill, knowledge, or experience is required. **Job Preparation:** SVP 6.0 to less than 7.0—More than 1 year and less than 4 years. **Knowledge:** Administration and Management; Biology; Food Production; Personnel and Human Resources; English Language. **Instructional Programs:** 010301 Agricultural Production Workers and Managers, General; 010304 Crop Production Operations and Management; 010601 Horticulture Services Operations and Management, General; 010603 Ornamental Horticulture Operations and Management; 010604 Greenhouse Operations and Management; 020401 Plant Sciences, General; 020403 Horticulture Science.

Related DOT Jobs: 405.131-010 Supervisor, Horticultural-Specialty Farming; 405.137-010 Supervisor, Rose-Grading; 451.137-010 Forest Nursery Supervisor; 451.137-014 Supervisor, Christmas-Tree Farm.

45-1011.05 First-Line Supervisors and Manager/Supervisors—Logging Workers (First-Line Supervisors and Managers/Supervisors—Agricultural and Related Workers)

Education: Work experience in a related occupation

Employed: 91,546

Openings: 11,813

Projected Growth: 6.2%

Earnings: No data available.

Directly supervise and coordinate activities of logging workers. Manager/Supervisors are generally found in smaller establishments where they perform both supervisory and management functions, such as accounting, marketing, and personnel work, and may also engage in the same logging work as the workers they supervise.

Changes logging operations or methods to eliminate unsafe conditions, and warns or disciplines workers disregarding safety regulations. Coordinates selection and movement of logs from storage areas, according to transportation schedules or production requirements of wood products plant. Determines methods for logging operations, size of crew, and equipment requirements. Coordinates dismantling, moving, and setting up equipment at new worksite. Confers with mill, company, and government forestry officials to determine safest and most efficient method of logging tract. Trains workers in felling and bucking trees, operating tractors and loading machines, yarding and loading techniques, and safety regulations. Plans and schedules logging operations such as felling and bucking trees, grading and sorting logs, and yarding and loading logs. Prepares production and personnel time records for management. Oversees logging operations to identify and solve problems, and ensure safety and company regulations are being followed. Assigns workers to duties such as trees to be cut, cutting sequence and specifications, and loading of trucks, railcars, or rafts.

GOE Number, Interest Area, and Work Group: 03.01.02; Plants and Animals; Managerial Work: Nursery, Groundskeeping, and Logging. **Personality Type:** Realistic. Realistic occupations frequently involve work activities that include practical, hands-on problems and solutions. These occupations often deal with plants, animals, and real-world materials like wood, tools, and machinery. Many of the occupations require working outside and do not involve a lot of paperwork or working closely with others. **Work Values:** Authority; Autonomy; Responsibility; Activity; Moral Values. **Skills:** Coordination; Problem Identification; Instructing; Management of Personnel Resources; Time Management; Implementation Planning. **Abilities:** *Cognitive*—Information Ordering; Oral Expression; Problem Sensitivity; Written Expression; Oral Comprehension. *Psychomotor*—Multilimb Coordination; Control Precision; Rate Control. *Physical*—Static Strength; Explosive Strength; Dynamic Strength; Trunk Strength; Extent Flexibility. *Sensory*—Far Vision; Auditory Attention; Near Vision. **General Work Activities:** *Information Input*—Getting Information Needed to Do the Job; Inspecting Equipment, Structures, Materials; Estimating Needed Characteristics; Identifying Objects, Actions, and Events; Monitoring Processes, Materials, and Surroundings. *Mental Process*—Making Decisions and Solving Problems; Scheduling Work and Activities; Developing Objectives and Strategies. *Work Output*—Performing General Physical Activities; Handling and Moving Objects; Documenting and Recording Information; Operating Vehicles or Equipment. *Interacting with Others*—Communicating with Other Workers; Coordinating Work and Activities of Others; Guiding, Directing and Motivating Subordinates. **Physical Work Conditions:** Outdoors; Standing; Hazardous Equipment; Common Protective or Safety Attire. **Other Job Characteristics:** Consequence of Error; Frustrating Circumstances; Importance of Being Sure All Is Done.

Experience: Job Zone 4. A minimum of two to four years of work-related skill, knowledge, or experience is needed. **Job Preparation:** SVP 7.0 to less than 8.0—2 years to less than 10 years. **Knowledge:** Administration and Management; Production and Processing; Mechanical; Personnel and Human Resources; Education and Training. **Instructional Programs:** 030405 Logging/Timber Harvesting; 030404 Forest Products Technology/Technician; 030401 Forest Harvesting and Production Technology/Technician.

Related DOT Jobs: 183.167-038 Superintendent, Logging; 454.134-010 Supervisor, Felling-Bucking; 455.134-010 Supervisor, Log Sorting; 459.133-010 Supervisor, Logging; 459.137-010 Woods Boss; 921.131-010 Hook Tender.

45-1011.06 First-Line Supervisors and Manager/Supervisors—Fishery Workers (Fishing Vessel Captains and Officers)

Education: Work experience in a related occupation

Employed: 11,370

Openings: 2,378

Projected Growth: −18.6%

Earnings: No data available.

Directly supervise and coordinate activities of fishery workers. Manager/Supervisors are generally found in smaller establishments where they perform both supervisory and management functions, such as accounting, marketing, and personnel work, and may also engage in the same fishery work as the workers they supervise.

Trains workers in spawning, rearing, cultivating, and harvesting methods, and use of equipment. Oversees worker activities such as treatment and rearing of fingerlings, maintenance of equipment, and harvesting of fish or shellfish. Plans work schedules according to availability of personnel and equipment, tidal levels, feeding schedules, or need for transfer or harvest. Observes fish and beds or ponds to detect diseases, determine quality of fish, or determine completeness of harvesting. Confers with manager to determine time and place of seed planting and of cultivating, feeding, or harvesting of fish or shellfish. Directs workers to correct deviations or problems such as disease, quality of seed distribution, or adequacy of cultivation. Assigns workers to duties such as fertilizing and incubating spawn, feeding and transferring fish, and planting, cultivating, and harvesting shellfish beds. Records number and type of fish or shellfish reared and harvested; keeps workers' time records.

GOE Number, Interest Area, and Work Group: 03.01.01; Plants and Animals; Managerial Work: Farming and Fishing. **Personality Type:** Realistic. Realistic occupations frequently involve work activities that include practical, hands-on problems and solutions. These occupations often deal with plants, animals, and real-world materials like wood, tools, and machinery. Many of the occupations require working outside and do not involve a lot of paperwork or working closely with others. **Work Values:** Authority; Responsibility; Activity; Autonomy; Achievement; Moral Values. **Skills:** Instructing; Implementation Planning; Coordination; Time Management; Management of Personnel Resources. **Abilities:** *Cognitive*—Oral Expression; Problem Sensitivity; Oral Comprehension; Information Ordering; Deductive Reasoning. *Psychomotor*—Wrist-Finger Speed; Arm-Hand Steadiness; Control Precision; Manual Dexterity. *Physical*—Trunk Strength; Static Strength; Extent Flexibility. *Sensory*—Near Vision; Far Vision; Speech Clarity; Depth Perception. **General Work Activities:** *Information Input*—Monitoring Processes, Materials, and Surroundings; Getting Information Needed to Do the Job; Identifying Objects, Actions, and Events. *Mental Process*—Scheduling Work and Activities; Making Decisions and Solving Problems; Organizing, Planning, and Prioritizing; Analyzing Data or Information. *Work Output*—Documenting and Recording Information; Implementing Ideas and Programs; Performing General Physical Activities. *Interacting with Others*—Communicating with Other Workers; Coordinating Work and Activities of Others; Teaching Others. **Physical Work Conditions:** Outdoors; Sitting; Standing; Using Hands on Objects, Tools, or Controls. **Other Job Characteristics:** Frustrating Circumstances; Consequence of Error; Importance of Being Sure All Is Done.

Experience: Job Zone 3. Previous work-related skill, knowledge, or experience is required. **Job Preparation:** SVP 6.0 to less than 7.0—More than 1 year and less than 4 years. **Knowledge:** Food Production; Biology; Administration and Management; Personnel and Human Resources; English Language. **Instructional Programs:** 010301 Agricultural Production Workers and Managers, General; 010303 Aquaculture Operations and Production Management; 030301 Fishing and Fisheries Sciences and Management.

Related DOT Jobs: 446.133-010 Supervisor, Shellfish Farming; 446.134-010 Supervisor, Fish Hatchery.

45-2000 Agricultural Workers

45-2011.00 Agricultural Inspectors (Inspectors and Compliance Officers)

Education: Work experience in a related occupation

Employed: 176,175

Openings: 19,910

Projected Growth: 10.5%

Earnings: $36,820

Inspect agricultural commodities, processing equipment, processing facilities, and fish and logging operations, to ensure compliance with regulations and laws governing health, quality, and safety.

Testifies in legal proceedings. Inspects livestock to determine effectiveness of medication and feeding programs. Inspects horticultural products or livestock to detect harmful disease, infestation, or growth rate. Collects sample of pests or suspected diseased animals or materials and routes to laboratory for identification and analysis. Writes reports of findings and recommendations and advises farmer, grower, or processor of corrective action to be taken. Inspects facilities and equipment for adequacy, sanitation, and compliance with regulations. Examines, weighs, and measures commodities such as poultry, eggs, meat, and seafood to certify wholesomeness, grade, and weight. Advises farmers and growers of development programs or new equipment and techniques to aid in quality production, applying agricultural knowledge.

GOE Number, Interest Area, and Work Group: 04.04.02; Law, Law Enforcement, and Public Safety; Public Safety: Regulations Enforcement. **Personality Type:** Realistic. Realistic occupations frequently involve work activities that include practical, hands-on problems and solutions. These occupations often deal with plants, animals, and real-world materials like wood, tools, and machinery. Many of the occupations require working outside and do not involve a lot of paperwork or working closely with others. **Work Values:** Responsibility; Security; Autonomy; Independence; Moral Values; Activity; Company Policies and Practices; Supervision, Human Relations. **Skills:** Product Inspection; Reading Comprehension; Writing; Problem Identification; Information Gathering. **Abilities:** *Cognitive*—Problem Sensitivity; Written Comprehension; Oral Expression; Written Expression; Deductive Reasoning. *Psychomotor*—Wrist-Finger Speed; Arm-Hand Steadiness; Manual Dexterity. *Physical*—Trunk Strength; Extent Flexibility; Static Strength; Gross Body Coordination. *Sensory*—Near Vision; Speech Clarity; Far Vision; Visual Color Discrimination. **General Work Activities:** *Information Input*—Getting Information Needed to Do the Job; Identifying Objects, Actions, and Events; Inspecting Equipment, Structures, Materials. *Mental Process*—Evaluating Information Against Standards; Judging Qualities of Things, Services, Other People's Work; Making Decisions and Solving Problems. *Work Output*—Documenting and Recording Information; Implementing Ideas and Programs; Handling and Moving Objects. *Interacting with Others*—Communicating with Persons Outside Organization; Providing Consultation and Advice to Others; Interpreting Meaning of Information to Others. **Physical Work Conditions:** Standing; Outdoors; Walking or Running. **Other Job Characteristics:** Consequence of Error; Importance of Being Sure All Is Done; Frustrating Circumstances; Importance of Being Exact or Accurate.

Experience: Job Zone 4. A minimum of two to four years of work-related skill, knowledge, or experience is needed. **Job Preparation:** SVP 7.0 to less than 8.0—2 years to less than 10 years. **Knowledge:** Food Production; English Language; Production and Processing; Law, Government and Jurisprudence; Biology. **Instructional Programs:** 030203 Natural Resources Law Enforcement and Protective Services; 150701 Occupational Safety and Health Technology/Technician; 521601 Taxation.

Related DOT Jobs: 168.287-010 Inspector, Agricultural Commodities; 411.267-010 Field Service Technician, Poultry.

45-2021.00 Animal Breeders (Animal Breeders)

Education: No data available.

Employed: 1,450

Openings: No data available.

Projected Growth: No data available.

Earnings: $22,440

Breed animals, including cattle, goats, horses, sheep, swine, poultry, dogs, cats, or pet birds. Select and breed animals according to their genealogy, characteristics, and offspring. Have knowledge of artificial insemination techniques and equipment use. Keep records on heats, birth intervals, or pedigree.

Clips or shears hair on animals. Selects animals to be bred, according to knowledge of animals, genealogy, traits, and offspring desired. Milks cows and goats. Builds and maintains hutches, pens, and fenced yards. Exhibits animals at shows. Kills animals, removes their pelts, and arranges for sale of pelts. Arranges for sale of animals to hospitals, research centers, pet shops, and food processing plants. Brands, tags, dehorns, tattoos, or castrates animals. Treats minor injuries and ailments and engages veterinarian to treat animals with serious illnesses or injuries. Feeds and waters animals; cleans pens, cages, yards, and hutches. Examines animals to detect symptoms of illness or injury. Records weight, diet, and other breeding data. Adjusts controls to maintain specific temperature in building.

GOE Number, Interest Area, and Work Group: 03.02.01; Plants and Animals; Animal Care and Training. **Personality Type:** Realistic. Realistic occupations frequently involve work activities that include practical, hands-on problems and solutions. These occupations often deal with plants, animals, and real-world materials like wood, tools, and machinery. Many of the occupations require working outside and do not involve a lot of paperwork or working closely with others. **Work Values:** Responsibility; Independence; Autonomy; Moral Values; Activity. **Skills:** Equipment Selection; Product Inspection; Science; Judgment and Decision Making; Information Gathering; Problem Identification; Active Listening; Reading Comprehension. **Abilities:** *Cognitive*—Deductive Reasoning; Problem Sensitivity; Oral Comprehension; Written Comprehension; Oral Expression. *Psychomotor*—Control Precision; Speed of Limb Movement. *Physical*—Static Strength; Extent Flexibility; Trunk Strength. *Sensory*—Peripheral Vision. **General Work Activities:** *Information Input*—Identifying Objects, Actions, and Events; Getting Information Needed to Do the Job; Monitoring Processes, Materials, and Surroundings. *Mental Process*—Judging Qualities of Things, Services, Other People's Work; Making Decisions and Solving Problems; Updating and Using Job-Relevant Knowledge. *Work Output*—Handling and Moving Objects; Performing General Physical Activities; Documenting and Recording Information. *Interacting with Others*—Monitoring and Controlling Resources; Communicating with Persons Outside Organization; Influencing Others or Selling. **Physical Work Conditions:** Hazardous Situations; Outdoors; Using Hands on Objects, Tools, or Controls; Standing. **Other Job Characteristics:** Consequence of Error; Importance of Being Aware of New Events; Frustrating Circumstances; Importance of Being Exact or Accurate; Importance of Being Sure All Is Done.

Experience: Job Zone 3. Previous work-related skill, knowledge, or experience is required. **Job Preparation:** SVP 6.0 to less than 7.0—More than 1 year and less than 4 years. **Knowledge:** Biology; Food Production; Sales and Marketing; Medicine and Dentistry; Administration and Management; Mechanical. **Instructional Program:** 010302 Agricultural Animal Husbandry and Production Management.

Related DOT Jobs: 410.161-010 Animal Breeder; 410.161-014 Fur Farmer; 410.161-018 Livestock Rancher; 410.161-022 Hog-Confinement-System Manager; 411.161-010 Canary Breeder; 411.161-014 Poultry Breeder; 413.161-014 Reptile Farmer.

45-2031.00 Farm Labor Contractors (First-Line Supervisors and Managers/Supervisors—Agricultural, Forestry, Fishing, and Related Workers)

Education: No data available.

Employed: 51,350

Openings: No data available.

Projected Growth: No data available.

Earnings: $27,410

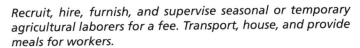

Recruit, hire, furnish, and supervise seasonal or temporary agricultural laborers for a fee. Transport, house, and provide meals for workers.

GOE Number, Interest Area, and Work Group: 03.01.01; Plants and Animals; Managerial Work: Farming and Fishing. **Instructional Programs:** 010104 Farm and Ranch Management; 010199 Agricultural Business and Management, Other; 010301 Agricultural Production Workers and Managers, General; 010302 Agricultural Animal Husbandry and Production Management; 010304 Crop Production Operations and Management; 010399 Agricultural Production Workers and Managers, Other; 019999 Agricultural Business and Production, Other; 020201 Animal Sciences, General; 020202 Agricultural Animal Breeding and Genetics; 020204 Agricultural Animal Nutrition; 020206 Dairy Science; 020209 Poultry Science; 020401 Plant Sciences, General; 020402 Agronomy and Crop Science; 020409 Range Science and Management. **Note:** The Department of Labor has not collected some data for this job, so it has fewer details than the other descriptions.

45-2041.00 Graders and Sorters, Agricultural Products (Graders and Sorters, Agricultural Products)

Education: No data available.

Employed: 70,300

Openings: No data available.

Projected Growth: No data available.

Earnings: $13,400

Grade, sort, or classify unprocessed food and other agricultural products by size, weight, color, or condition.

Examines product fibers through microscope to determine maturity and spirality of fibers. Pulls product sample apart between fingers to determine fiber quality. Records grade on tag or shipping, receiving, or sales sheet. Discards inferior or defective products and foreign matter and places acceptable products in containers for further processing. Estimates weight of product, visually and by feel. Segregates products on conveyor belt or table, according to grade, color, size, fiber quality, species, deformities, and sex. Grades and sorts products, according to factors such as color, length, width, appearance, feel, and smell. Weighs and places products in containers, according to grade; marks grade on containers.

GOE Number, Interest Area, and Work Group: 08.03.06; Industrial Production; Production Work: Hands-on Work, Assorted Materials. **Personality Type:** Realistic. Realistic occupations frequently involve work activities that include practical, hands-on problems and solutions. These occupations often deal with plants, animals, and real-world materials like wood, tools, and machinery. Many of the occupations require working outside and do not involve a lot of paperwork or working closely with others. **Work Values:** Moral Values; Independence; Supervision, Human Relations; Activity; Company Policies and Practices. **Skills:** Product Inspection. **Abilities:** *Cognitive*—Category Flexibility; Information Ordering; Perceptual Speed; Problem Sensitivity; Selective Attention; Deductive Reasoning. *Psychomotor*—Finger Dexterity; Manual Dexterity; Arm-Hand Steadiness. *Physical*—Extent Flexibility; Static

Strength; Explosive Strength; Trunk Strength. *Sensory*—Near Vision; Visual Color Discrimination; Hearing Sensitivity; Depth Perception. **General Work Activities:** *Information Input*—Identifying Objects, Actions, and Events; Inspecting Equipment, Structures, Materials; Getting Information Needed to Do the Job. *Mental Process*—Judging Qualities of Things, Services, Other People's Work; Evaluating Information Against Standards; Making Decisions and Solving Problems; Processing Information. *Work Output*—Handling and Moving Objects; Documenting and Recording Information; Controlling Machines and Processes. *Interacting with Others*—Monitoring and Controlling Resources; Performing Administrative Activities; Communicating with Other Workers. **Physical Work Conditions:** Using Hands on Objects, Tools, or Controls; Indoors; Making Repetitive Motions. **Other Job Characteristics:** Importance of Being Exact or Accurate; Importance of Repeating Same Tasks; Degree of Automation; Importance of Being Sure All Is Done.

Experience: Job Zone 1. No previous work-related skill, knowledge, or experience is needed. **Job Preparation:** SVP Below 4.0—Less than 6 months. **Knowledge:** Production and Processing; Mathematics; Food Production; Clerical; Engineering and Technology; English Language. **Instructional Programs:** 010401 Agricultural and Food Products Processing Operations and Management; 010501 Agricultural Supplies Retailing and Wholesaling.

Related DOT Jobs: 409.687-010 Inspector-Grader, Agricultural Establishment; 410.687-026 Wool-Fleece Sorter; 411.687-010 Chick Grader; 411.687-014 Chick Sexer; 429.387-010 Cotton Classer; 429.587-010 Cotton Classer Aide; 446.687-010 Clam Sorter; 522.384-010 Fish Roe Technician; 529.687-074 Egg Candler; 529.687-186 Sorter, Agricultural Produce; 589.387-014 Wool Sorter; 589.687-054 Wool-Fleece Grader.

45-2091.00 Agricultural Equipment Operators (Farm Workers)

Education: Short-term O-T-J training

Employed: 850,533

Openings: 157,331

Projected Growth: –6.6%

Earnings: No data available.

Drive and control farm equipment to till soil and to plant, cultivate, and harvest crops. Participate in crop baling or hay bucking. Operate stationary equipment to perform post-harvest tasks such as husking, shelling, threshing, and ginning.

Walks beside or rides on planting machine while inserting plants in planter mechanism at specified intervals. Drives truck to haul harvested crops, supplies, tools, or farm workers. Sprays fertilizer or pesticide solutions, using hand sprayer, to control insects, fungus and weed growth, and diseases. Positions boxes or attaches bags at discharge end of machinery to catch products, places lids on boxes, and closes sacks. Hand picks fruit such as apples, oranges, or strawberries. Oversees work crew engaged in planting, weeding, or harvesting activities. Thins, hoes, weeds, or prunes row crops, fruit trees, or vines, using hand implements. Loads hoppers, containers, or conveyor to feed machine with products, using suction gates, shovel, or pitchfork. Adjusts, repairs, lubricates, and services farm machinery; notifies supervisor or appropriate personnel when machinery malfunctions. Drives truck, or tractor with trailer attached, alongside crew loading crop or adjacent to harvesting machine. Irrigates soil, using portable pipe or ditch system; maintains ditch or pipe and pumps. Manipulates controls to set, activate, and regulate mechanisms on machinery such as self-propelled machines, conveyors, separators, cleaners, and dryers. Observes and listens to machinery operation to detect equipment malfunction; removes obstruction to avoid damage to product or machinery. Discards diseased or rotting product; guides product on conveyor to regulate flow through machine. Attaches farm implements such as plow, disc, sprayer, or harvester, to tractor, using bolts and mechanic's hand tools. Weighs crop-filled containers and records weights and other identifying information. Loads and unloads crops or containers of materials, manually or using conveyors, handtruck, forklift, or transfer auger. Mixes specified materials or chemicals and dumps solutions, powders, or seeds into planter or sprayer machinery.

GOE Number, Interest Area, and Work Group: 03.03.01; Plants and Animals; Hands-on Work: Farming. **Personality Type:** Realistic. Realistic occupations frequently involve work activities that include practical, hands-on problems and solutions. These occupations often deal with plants, animals, and real-world materials like wood, tools, and machinery. Many of the occupations require working outside and do not involve a lot of paperwork or working closely with others. **Work Values:** Moral Values; Independence; Activity; Autonomy; Variety; Responsibility; Achievement. **Skills:** Operation and Control; Repairing; Equipment Maintenance; Operation Monitoring; Time Management; Systems Perception. **Abilities:** *Cognitive*—Problem Sensitivity; Information Ordering; Oral Expression; Spatial Orientation; Number Facility; Written Expression. *Psychomotor*—Multilimb Coordination; Control Precision; Manual Dexterity. *Physical*—Static Strength; Trunk Strength; Extent Flexibility. *Sensory*—Hearing Sensitivity; Far Vision; Speech Clarity; Visual Color Discrimination; Night Vision. **General Work Activities:** *Information Input*—Monitoring Processes, Materials, and Surroundings; Inspecting Equipment, Structures, Materials; Identifying Objects, Actions, and Events. *Mental Process*—Judging Qualities of Things, Services, Other People's Work; Organizing, Planning, and Prioritizing; Evaluating Information Against Standards; Making Decisions and Solving Problems; Updating and Using Job-Relevant Knowledge. *Work Output*—Operating Vehicles or Equipment; Performing General Physical Activities; Controlling Machines and Processes. *Interacting with Others*—Communicating with Other Workers; Coordinating Work and Activities of Others; Guiding, Directing and Motivating Subordinates. **Physical Work Conditions:** Outdoors; Hazardous Equipment; Using Hands on Objects, Tools, or Controls. **Other Job Characteristics:** Consequence of Error; Degree of Automation; Frustrating Circumstances.

Experience: Job Zone 2. Some previous work-related skill, knowledge, or experience may be helpful, but usually is not needed. **Job Preparation:** SVP 4.00 to 5.99—6 months to less than 2 years. **Knowledge:** Mechanical; Food Production; Production and Processing; Chemistry; Transportation. **Instructional Programs:** 010301 Agricultural Production Workers and Managers, General; 010304 Crop Production Operations and Management.

Related DOT Jobs: 401.683-010 Farmworker, Grain I; 401.683-014 Farmworker, Rice; 402.663-010 Farmworker, Vegetable I; 403.683-010 Farmworker, Fruit I; 404.663-010 Farmworker, Field Crop I; 404.685-010 Seed-Potato Arranger; 405.683-010 Farmworker, Bulbs; 405.683-014 Growth-Media Mixer, Mushroom; 407.663-010 Farmworker, Diversified Crops I; 409.683-010 Farm-Machine Operator; 409.683-014 Field Hauler; 409.685-010 Farm-Machine Tender; 409.686-010 Farmworker, Machine; 421.683-010 Farmworker, General I; 429.685-010 Ginner; 429.685-014 Thresher, Broomcorn.

45-2092.00 Farmworkers and Laborers, Crop, Nursery, and Greenhouse (Farmworkers, Food and Fiber Crops)

Education: No data available.

Employed: 178,710

Openings: No data available.

Projected Growth: No data available.

Earnings: $12,580

Manually plant, cultivate, and harvest vegetables, fruits, nuts, horticultural specialties, and field crops. Use hand tools such as shovels, trowels, hoes, tampers, pruning hooks, shears, and knives. Till soil and apply fertilizers; transplant, weed, thin, or prune crops; apply pesticides; clean, grade, sort, pack, and load harvested products. Construct trellises; repair fences and farm buildings; participate in irrigation activities.

GOE Number, Interest Area, and Work Group: 03.03.01; Plants and Animals; Hands-on Work: Farming. **Instructional Program:** 010301 Agricultural Production Workers and Managers, General. **Note:** The Department of Labor has not collected some data for this job, so it has fewer details than the other descriptions.

45-2092.01 Nursery Workers (All Other Agricultural, Forestry, Fishing, and Related Workers)

Education: No data available.

Employed: 89,750

Openings: No data available.

Projected Growth: No data available.

Earnings: $18,150

Work in nursery facilities or at customer location. Plant, cultivate, harvest, and transplant trees, shrubs, or plants.

Moves containerized shrubs, plants, and trees, using wheelbarrow. Folds and staples corrugated forms to make boxes used for packing horticultural products. Digs, rakes, and screens soil and fills cold frames and hot beds to prepare them for planting. Plants, sprays, weeds, and waters plants, shrubs, and trees, using hand tools and gardening tools. Cuts and opens incision in rootstock, using budding knife; inserts and ties bud. Traps and destroys pests such as moles, gophers, and mice, using pesticides. Ties, bunches, wraps roots, and packs flowers, plants, shrubs, and trees to fill orders. Inspects bud tie to ensure quality. Fills growing tanks with water. Sows grass seed or plants plugs of grass and cuts, rolls, and stacks sod. Hauls and spreads topsoil, fertilizer, peat moss, and other materials to condition soil, using wheelbarrow or cart and shovel. Dips rose cuttings into vat to disinfect prior to storage.

GOE Number, Interest Area, and Work Group: 03.03.04; Plants and Animals; Hands-on Work: Nursery, Groundskeeping, and Pest Control. **Personality Type:** Realistic. Realistic occupations frequently involve work activities that include practical, hands-on problems and solutions. These occupations often deal with plants, animals, and real-world materials like wood, tools, and machinery. Many of the occupations require working outside and do not involve a lot of paperwork or working closely with others. **Work Values:** Moral Values; Supervision, Human Relations; Company Policies and Practices; Supervision, Technical; Independence. **Skills:** Equipment Selection. **Abilities:** *Cognitive*—Information Ordering; Flexibility of Closure; Problem Sensitivity; Visualization; Spatial Orientation; Perceptual Speed. *Psychomotor*—Speed of Limb Movement; Manual Dexterity; Arm-Hand Steadiness; Wrist-Finger Speed. *Physical*—Extent Flexibility; Trunk Strength; Static Strength. *Sensory*—Visual Color Discrimination; Hearing Sensitivity; Depth Perception; Far Vision. **General Work Activities:** *Information Input*—Inspecting Equipment, Structures, Materials; Estimating Needed Characteristics; Monitoring Processes, Materials, and Surroundings. *Mental Process*—Judging Qualities of Things, Services, Other People's Work; Evaluating Information Against Standards; Thinking Creatively; Organizing, Planning, and Prioritizing. *Work Output*—Performing General Physical Activities; Handling and Moving Objects; Implementing Ideas and Programs. *Interacting with Others*—Communicating with Persons Outside Organization; Performing for or Working with the Public; Monitoring and Controlling Resources. **Physical Work Conditions:** Using Hands on Objects, Tools, or Controls; Outdoors; Standing. **Other Job Characteristics:** Importance of Being Sure All Is Done; Importance of Being Exact or Accurate; Consequence of Error.

Experience: Job Zone 1. No previous work-related skill, knowledge, or experience is needed. **Job Preparation:** SVP Below 4.0—Less than 6 months. **Knowledge:** Biology; Chemistry; Production and Processing; Mechanical; Food Production. **Instructional Programs:** 010501 Agricultural Supplies Retailing and Wholesaling; 010599 Agricultural Supplies and Related Services, Other.

Related DOT Jobs: 405.684-010 Budder; 405.687-014 Horticultural Worker II.

45-2092.02 General Farmworkers (Farm Workers)

Education: Short-term O-T-J training
Employed: 850,533
Openings: 157,331
Projected Growth: –6.6%
Earnings: No data available.

Apply pesticides, herbicides, and fertilizer to crops and livestock; plant, maintain, and harvest food crops.

Repairs farm buildings, fences, and other structures. Feeds, waters, grooms, and otherwise cares for livestock and poultry. Harvests fruits and vegetables by hand. Clears and maintains irrigation ditches. Operates truck to haul livestock and products to market. Sets up and operates irrigation equipment. Loads agricultural products into trucks for transport. Cleans barns, stables, pens, and kennels. Administers simple medications to animals and fowls. Repairs and maintains farm vehicles, implements, and mechanical equipment. Operates tractors, tractor-drawn machinery, and self-propelled machinery, to plow, harrow, and fertilize soil and to plant, cultivate, spray, and harvest crops. Digs and transplants seedlings by hand. Oversees casual and seasonal help during planting and harvesting.

GOE Number, Interest Area, and Work Group: 03.03.01; Plants and Animals; Hands-on Work: Farming. **Personality Type:** Realistic. Realistic occupations frequently involve work activities that include practical, hands-on problems and solutions. These occupations often deal with plants, animals, and real-world materials like wood, tools, and machinery. Many of the occupations require working outside and do not involve a lot of paperwork or working closely with others. **Work Values:** Moral Values; Independence; Variety; Activity; Achievement. **Skills:** Repairing; Operation and Control; Equipment Maintenance; Problem Identification; Operation Monitoring. **Abilities:** *Cognitive*—Information Ordering; Oral Expression; Spatial Orientation; Problem Sensitivity; Visualization; Category Flexibility. *Psychomotor*—Control Precision; Multilimb Coordination; Response Orientation. *Physical*—Static Strength; Extent Flexibility; Trunk Strength. *Sensory*—Hearing Sensitivity; Depth Perception; Near Vision. **General Work Activities:** *Information Input*—Estimating Needed Characteristics; Identifying Objects, Actions, and Events; Monitoring Processes, Materials, and Surroundings. *Mental Process*—Organizing, Planning, and Prioritizing; Making Decisions and Solving Problems; Judging Qualities of Things, Services, Other People's Work. *Work Output*—Performing General Physical Activities; Handling and Moving Objects; Operating Vehicles or Equipment; Repairing and Maintaining Mechanical Equipment. *Interacting with Others*—Monitoring and Controlling Resources; Guiding, Directing and Motivating Subordinates; Establishing and Maintaining Relationships; Coordinating Work and Activities of Others. **Physical Work Conditions:** Outdoors; Standing; Hazardous Equipment; Using Hands on Objects, Tools, or Controls; Contaminants; Walking or Running. **Other Job Characteristics:** Consequence of Error; Frustrating Circumstances; Importance of Being Sure All Is Done.

Experience: Job Zone 1. No previous work-related skill, knowledge, or experience is needed. **Job Preparation:** SVP Below 4.0—Less than 6 months. **Knowledge:** Food Production; Mechanical; Biology; Building and Construction; Chemistry. **Instructional Programs:** 010204 Agricultural Power Machinery Operator; 010204 Agricultural Power Machinery Operator; 010301 Agricultural Production Workers and Managers, General; 010301 Agricultural Production Workers and Managers, General; 010302 Agricultural Animal Husbandry and Production Management; 010304 Crop Production Operations and Management; 010304 Crop Production Operations and Management.

Related DOT Jobs: 421.683-010 Farmworker, General I; 421.687-010 Farmworker, General II.

45-2093.00 Farmworkers, Farm and Ranch Animals
(Farm Workers)

Education: Short-term O-T-J training

Employed: 850,533

Openings: 157,331

Projected Growth: –6.6%

Earnings: No data available.

Attend to live farm, ranch, or aquacultural animals, including cattle, sheep, swine, goats, horses and other equines, poultry, finfish, shellfish, and bees. Attend to animals produced for animal products such as meat, fur, skins, feathers, eggs, milk, and honey. Feed, water, herd, graze, castrate, brand, debeak, weigh, catch, and load animals. Maintain records on animals; examine animals to detect diseases and injuries; assist in birth deliveries; and administer medications, vaccinations, or insecticides as appropriate. Clean and maintain animal housing areas.

Sprays livestock with disinfectants and insecticides. Collects, inspects, packs, or places eggs in incubator. Milks farm animals such as cows and goats, by hand or using milking machine. Marks livestock to identify ownership and grade, using brands, tags, paint, or tattoos. Herds livestock to pasture for grazing or to scales, trucks, or other enclosures. Cleans stalls, pens, and equipment, using disinfectant solutions, brushes, shovels, and water hoses. Fills feed troughs with feed. Applies or administers medications and vaccinates animals. Mixes feed, additives, and medicines in prescribed portions. Examines animals to detect disease and injuries. Waters livestock. Inspects and repairs fences, stalls, and pens. Moves equipment, poultry, or livestock manually or using truck or cart from one location to another. Grooms, clips, and trims animals. Segregates animals according to weight, age, color, and physical condition. Debeaks and trims wings of poultry. Assists with birthing of animals. Castrates or docks ears and tails of animals. Maintains growth, feeding, production, and cost records. Maintains equipment and machinery.

GOE Number, Interest Area, and Work Group: 03.03.01; Plants and Animals; Hands-on Work: Farming. **Personality Type:** Realistic. Realistic occupations frequently involve work activities that include practical, hands-on problems and solutions. These occupations often deal with plants, animals, and real-world materials like wood, tools, and machinery. Many of the occupations require working outside and do not involve a lot of paperwork or working closely with others. **Work Values:** Moral Values; Independence; Activity; Variety; Achievement. **Skills:** Repairing; Equipment Maintenance; Equipment Selection; Product Inspection; Operation and Control; Problem Identification; Writing. **Abilities:** *Cognitive*—Problem Sensitivity; Deductive Reasoning; Number Facility; Category Flexibility; Written Expression. *Psychomotor*—Multilimb Coordination; Manual Dexterity; Arm-Hand Steadiness. *Physical*—Static Strength; Trunk Strength; Dynamic Strength. *Sensory*—Depth Perception; Sound Localization; Glare Sensitivity; Night Vision. **General Work Activities:** *Information Input*—Monitoring Processes, Materials, and Surroundings; Getting Information Needed to Do the Job; Inspecting Equipment, Structures, Materials. *Mental Process*—Judging Qualities of Things, Services, Other People's Work; Evaluating Information Against Standards; Processing Information; Organizing, Planning, and Prioritizing. *Work Output*—Performing General Physical Activities; Handling and Moving Objects; Controlling Machines and Processes. *Interacting with Others*—Monitoring and Controlling Resources; Communicating with Other Workers; Performing Administrative Activities; Interpreting Meaning of Information to Others. **Physical Work Conditions:** Outdoors; Standing; Walking or Running; Hazardous Situations. **Other Job Characteristics:** Consequence of Error; Importance of Being Sure All Is Done; Frustrating Circumstances; Importance of Being Exact or Accurate.

Experience: Job Zone 1. No previous work-related skill, knowledge, or experience is needed. **Job Preparation:** SVP Below 4.0—Less than 6 months. **Knowledge:** Biology; Food Production; Mechanical; Building and Construction; Medicine and Dentistry. **Instructional Programs:** 010301 Agricultural Production Workers and Managers, General; 010302 Agricultural Animal Husbandry and Production Management.

Related DOT Jobs: 410.364-010 Lamber; 410.664-010 Farmworker, Livestock; 410.674-014 Cowpuncher; 410.674-018 Livestock-Yard Attendant; 410.684-010 Farmworker, Dairy; 410.684-014 Sheep Shearer; 410.685-010 Milker, Machine; 410.687-010 Fleece Tier; 410.687-014 Goat Herder; 410.687-022 Sheep Herder; 411.161-018 Poultry Farmer; 411.364-014 Poultry Tender; 411.584-010 Farmworker, Poultry; 411.684-010 Caponizer; 411.684-014 Poultry Vaccinator; 411.687-018 Laborer, Poultry Farm; 411.687-022 Laborer, Poultry Hatchery; 411.687-026 Poultry Debeaker; 412.684-010 Game-Farm Helper; 413.687-014 Worm-Farm Laborer (partial list; see the introduction for sources of the complete list).

45-3000 Fishing and Hunting Workers

45-3011.00 Fishers and Related Fishing Workers (All Other Agricultural, Forestry, Fishing, and Related Workers)

Education: No data available.

Employed: 89,750

Openings: No data available.

Projected Growth: No data available.

Earnings: $18,150

Use nets, fishing rods, traps, or other equipment to catch and gather fish or other aquatic animals from rivers, lakes, or oceans, for human consumption or other uses. Haul game onto ship.

Stands lookout for schools of fish and for steering and engine-room watches. Pulls and guides nets, traps, and lines onto vessel, by hand or using hoisting equipment. Attaches nets, slings, hooks, blades, and lifting devices to cables, booms, hoists, and dredges. Hits fish with club or hooks fish with gaff to assist in hauling large fish from water. Loads and unloads equipment and supplies aboard vessel, by hand or using hoisting equipment. Removes catch from fishing equipment and uses measuring equipment to ensure compliance with legal size. Connects accessories such as floats, weights, flags, lights, or markers, to nets, lines, or traps. Steers vessel in fishing area. Puts fishing equipment into water and anchors or tows equipment according to method of fishing. Sorts and cleans marine life, and returns undesirable or illegal catch to sea. Places catch in containers and stows in hold with salt and ice. Rows boats and dinghies and operates skiffs to transport fishers, divers, and sponge hookers and to tow and position fishing equipment. Records date, harvest area, and yield in logbook. Washes deck, conveyors, knives, and other equipment, using brush, detergent, and water. Lubricates, adjusts, and makes minor repairs to engines and fishing equipment. Negotiates with buyers for sale of catch. Cultivates and harvests or gathers marine life such as sponges, abalone, or oysters, from sea bottom, using diving or dredging equipment or barge. Signals other workers to move, hoist, and position loads.

GOE Number, Interest Area, and Work Group: 03.03.03; Plants and Animals; Hands-on Work: Hunting and Fishing. **Personality Type:** Realistic. Realistic occupations frequently involve work activities that include practical, hands-on problems and solutions. These occupations often deal with plants, animals, and real-world materials like wood, tools, and machinery. Many of the occupations require working outside and do not involve a lot of paperwork or working closely with others. **Work Values:** Moral Values; Activity; Co-workers; Supervision, Technical; Autonomy; Variety. **Skills:** Equipment Maintenance; Coordination; Equipment Selection; Repairing; Negotiation. **Abilities:** *Cognitive*—Flexibility of Closure; Spatial Orientation; Number Facility; Information Ordering; Perceptual Speed; Category Flexibility. *Psychomotor*—Manual Dexterity; Multilimb Coordination; Wrist-Finger Speed. *Physical*—Static Strength; Extent Flexibility; Trunk Strength; Dynamic Strength. *Sensory*—Far Vision; Near Vision; Glare Sensitivity. **General Work Activities:** *Information Input*—Monitoring Processes, Materials, and Surroundings; Identifying Objects, Actions, and Events; Getting Information Needed to Do the Job. *Mental Process*—Evaluating Information Against Standards; Judging Qualities of Things, Services, Other People's Work; Organizing, Planning, and Prioritizing; Making Decisions and Solving Problems. *Work Output*—Operating Vehicles or Equipment; Performing General Physical Activities; Handling and Moving Objects. *Interacting with Others*—Communicating with Other Workers; Influencing Others or Selling; Resolving Conflict and Negotiating with Others. **Physical Work Conditions:** Using Hands on Objects, Tools, or Controls; Outdoors; Standing. **Other Job Characteristics:** Consequence of Error; Importance of Being Sure All Is Done; Frustrating Circumstances.

Experience: Job Zone 1. No previous work-related skill, knowledge, or experience is needed. **Job Preparation:** SVP Below 4.0—Less than 6 months. **Knowledge:** Food Production; Transportation; Biology; Mechanical; Mathematics. **Instructional Programs:** 010501 Agricultural Supplies Retailing and Wholesaling; 010599 Agricultural Supplies and Related Services, Other.

Related DOT Jobs: 441.132-010 Boatswain, Otter Trawler; 441.683-010 Skiff Operator; 441.684-010 Fisher, Net; 441.684-014 Fisher, Pot; 441.684-018 Fisher, Terrapin; 441.684-022 Fisher, Weir; 442.684-010 Fisher, Line; 443.664-010 Fisher, Diving; 443.684-010 Fisher, Spear; 446.161-014 Shellfish Grower; 446.663-010 Shellfish Dredge Operator; 446.684-014 Shellfish-Bed Worker; 449.664-010 Net Repairer; 449.667-010 Deckhand, Fishing Vessel; 449.687-010 Oyster Floater.

45-3021.00 Hunters and Trappers (All Other Agricultural, Forestry, Fishing, and Related Workers)

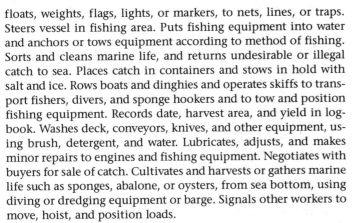

Education: No data available.
Employed: 89,750
Openings: No data available.
Projected Growth: No data available.
Earnings: $18,150

Hunt and trap wild animals for human consumption, fur, feed, bait, or other purposes.

Kills quarry for pelts or bounty, using club, poison, gun, or drowning method. Releases quarry from trap or net and transfers it to cage, or secures identification tag to quarry and releases it. Drives quarry into traps, nets, or killing area, using dogs or prods. Skins quarry, using knife, and stretches pelts on frames to be cured. Restrains quarry with arms or nets; rigs net or sling under catch to permit hoisting without bodily injury. Patrols trapline or nets to inspect settings, remove catch, and reset or relocate traps. Washes and sorts pelts according to species, color, and quality. Packs pelts in containers and loads containers onto trucks for transporting. Removes designated parts such as ears or tail, from slain quarry as evidence for killing bounty, using knife. Trains dogs for hunting. Scrapes fat, blubber, or flesh from skin side of pelt with knife or hand scraper; cures pelts with salt and boric acid. Stands watch to observe behavior of captured quarry. Traps or captures quarry alive for identification, relocation, or live sale. Selects, baits, and sets traps according to species, size, habits, and environs of bird or animal and according to reason for trapping.

GOE Number, Interest Area, and Work Group: 03.03.03; Plants and Animals; Hands-on Work: Hunting and Fishing. **Personality Type:** Realistic. Realistic occupations frequently involve work activities that include practical, hands-on problems and solutions. These occupations often deal with plants, animals, and real-world materials like wood, tools, and machinery. Many of the occupations require working outside and do not involve a lot of paperwork or working closely with others. **Work Values:** Independence; Autonomy; Moral Values; Variety; Responsibility. **Skills:** Equipment Selection; Monitoring; Instructing. **Abilities:** *Cognitive*—Spatial Orientation; Information Ordering; Flexibility of Closure; Perceptual Speed; Category Flexibility; Selective Attention. *Psychomotor*—Speed of Limb Movement; Wrist-Finger Speed; Manual Dexterity. *Physical*—Static Strength; Trunk Strength; Explosive Strength; Dynamic Strength; Extent Flexibility. *Sensory*—Near Vision; Far Vision; Depth Perception. **General Work Activities:** *Information Input*—Monitoring Processes, Materials, and Surroundings; Getting Information Needed to Do the Job; Identifying Objects, Actions, and Events. *Mental Process*—Judging Qualities of Things, Services, Other People's Work; Making Decisions and Solving Problems; Evaluating Information Against Standards. *Work Output*—Performing General Physical Activities; Implementing Ideas and Programs; Handling and Moving Objects. *Interacting with Others*—Monitoring and Controlling Resources; Teaching Others; Communicating with Other Workers; Communicating with Persons Outside Organization. **Physical Work Conditions:** Outdoors; Using Hands on Objects, Tools, or Controls; Standing; Hazardous Situations. **Other Job Characteristics:** Importance of

Being Sure All Is Done; Consequence of Error; Frustrating Circumstances.

Experience: Job Zone 2. Some previous work-related skill, knowledge, or experience may be helpful, but usually is not needed. **Job Preparation:** SVP 4.00 to 5.99—6 months to less than 2 years. **Knowledge:** Public Safety and Security; Geography; Sales and Marketing; Education and Training; Law, Government and Jurisprudence; Engineering and Technology. **Instructional Programs:** 010501 Agricultural Supplies Retailing and Wholesaling; 010599 Agricultural Supplies and Related Services, Other.

Related DOT Jobs: 461.134-010 Expedition Supervisor; 461.661-010 Predatory-Animal Hunter; 461.664-010 Underwater Hunter-Trapper; 461.684-010 Sealer; 461.684-014 Trapper, Animal; 461.684-018 Trapper, Bird.

45-4000 Forest, Conservation, and Logging Workers

45-4011.00 Forest and Conservation Workers
(Forest and Conservation Workers)

Education: Short-term O-T-J training

Employed: 32,667

Openings: 5,265

Projected Growth: 0.7%

Earnings: $23,140

Under supervision, perform manual labor necessary to develop, maintain, or protect forest, forested areas, and woodlands. Raise and transport tree seedlings; combat insects, pests, and diseases harmful to trees; build erosion and water-control structures to prevent leaching of forest soil.

Erects signs and fences, using posthole digger, shovel, or other hand tools. Selects and cuts trees according to markings or size, species, and grade. Sprays or injects trees, brush, and weeds with herbicides to combat insects, pests, and harmful diseases. Identifies and cuts diseased, weak, and other undesirable trees to protect forested areas. Prunes or shears tree tops and limbs to control growth, increase density, and improve shape. Helps forest survey crews by clearing site lines, holding measuring tools, and setting stakes. Drags cut trees from cutting area and loads trees onto truck. Gathers, bundles, sacks, and delivers forest products to buyer. Clears and piles brush, limbs, and other debris from roadside, fire trails, camping areas, and planting areas. Examines and grades trees according to standard chart; staples color-coded grade tags to limbs. Fells trees, clears brush from fire breaks, and extinguishes flames and embers to suppress fires. Sorts and separates tree seedlings, discarding substandard seedlings, according to standard chart and verbal instructions. Plants, cultivates, and harvests trees and tree seedlings to reforest land. Maintains campsites and recreational areas, replenishing firewood and other supplies and cleaning kitchens and restrooms.

GOE Number, Interest Area, and Work Group: 03.03.02; Plants and Animals; Hands-on Work: Forestry and Logging. **Personality Type:** Realistic. Realistic occupations frequently involve work activities that include practical, hands-on problems and solutions.

These occupations often deal with plants, animals, and real-world materials like wood, tools, and machinery. Many of the occupations require working outside and do not involve a lot of paperwork or working closely with others. **Work Values:** Moral Values; Achievement; Independence; Company Policies and Practices; Activity. **Skills:** Reading Comprehension; Judgment and Decision Making; Information Organization; Identification of Key Causes; Systems Perception; Coordination; Problem Identification; Equipment Selection; Visioning; Active Learning. **Abilities:** *Cognitive*—Problem Sensitivity; Spatial Orientation; Category Flexibility; Information Ordering; Flexibility of Closure. *Psychomotor*—Manual Dexterity; Multilimb Coordination; Speed of Limb Movement. *Physical*—Static Strength; Dynamic Strength; Trunk Strength. *Sensory*—Far Vision; Visual Color Discrimination. **General Work Activities:** *Information Input*—Identifying Objects, Actions, and Events; Getting Information Needed to Do the Job; Estimating Needed Characteristics. *Mental Process*—Judging Qualities of Things, Services, Other People's Work; Making Decisions and Solving Problems; Organizing, Planning, and Prioritizing. *Work Output*—Performing General Physical Activities; Handling and Moving Objects; Implementing Ideas and Programs. *Interacting with Others*—Communicating with Other Workers; Communicating with Persons Outside Organization; Monitoring and Controlling Resources. **Physical Work Conditions:** Outdoors; Standing; Hazardous Situations. **Other Job Characteristics:** Consequence of Error; Importance of Being Sure All Is Done; Importance of Being Exact or Accurate.

Experience: Job Zone 1. No previous work-related skill, knowledge, or experience is needed. **Job Preparation:** SVP Below 4.0—Less than 6 months. **Knowledge:** Biology; Mechanical; Public Safety and Security; Chemistry; Geography. **Instructional Programs:** 030101 Natural Resources Conservation, General; 030201 Natural Resources Management and Policy; 030203 Natural Resources Law Enforcement and Protective Services; 030299 Natural Resources Management and Protective Services, Other; 030401 Forest Harvesting and Production Tech./Technician; 030501 Forestry, General; 030502 Forestry Sciences; 030506 Forest Management; 030509 Wood Science and Pulp/Paper Tech.; 030599 Forestry and Related Sciences, Other; 039999 Conservation and Renewable Natural Resources, Other.

Related DOT Jobs: 451.687-010 Christmas-Tree Farm Worker; 451.687-014 Christmas-Tree Grader; 451.687-018 Seedling Puller; 451.687-022 Seedling Sorter; 452.687-010 Forest Worker; 452.687-018 Tree Planter; 453.687-010 Forest-Products Gatherer; 453.687-014 Laborer, Tree Tapping.

45-4021.00 Fallers (Fallers and Buckers)

Education: Short-term O-T-J training

Employed: 18,415

Openings: 2,475

Projected Growth: –11.5%

Earnings: $23,510

Use axes or chainsaws to fell trees, using knowledge of tree characteristics and cutting techniques to control direction of fall and minimize tree damage.

Tags unsafe trees with high visibility ribbon. Cuts limbs from felled trees, using chain saw or ax. Saws back-cuts, leaving sufficient sound wood to control direction of fall. Determines position, direction, and depth of cuts to be made; determines placement of wedges or jacks. Measures and marks felled trees for cutting into log lengths. Places supporting limbs or poles under felled tree to avoid splitting underside and to prevent log from rolling. Loads logs or wood onto trucks, by hand or using winch. Inserts jacks or drives wedge behind saw to prevent binding of saw and start tree falling. Secures cables to logs; drives tractor to drag logs to landing. Clears brush from work area and escape route; cuts sapling and other trees from direction of fall, using ax and chain saw. Splits logs, using ax, wedges, and maul; stacks wood in rick or cord lots. Stops saw engine as tree falls, pulls cutting bar from cut, and runs to safe location to avoid injury. Cuts felled trees into log lengths, using chain saw and ax. Scores cutting lines with ax, saws undercut along scored lines with chain saw, and knocks slabs from cuts with ax. Appraises tree for characteristics such as twist, rot, and heavy limb growth; gauges amount and direction of lean.

GOE Number, Interest Area, and Work Group: 03.03.02; Plants and Animals; Hands-on Work: Forestry and Logging. **Personality Type:** Realistic. Realistic occupations frequently involve work activities that include practical, hands-on problems and solutions. These occupations often deal with plants, animals, and real-world materials like wood, tools, and machinery. Many of the occupations require working outside and do not involve a lot of paperwork or working closely with others. **Work Values:** Moral Values; Activity; Company Policies and Practices; Supervision, Technical; Independence; Supervision, Human Relations. **Skills:** Coordination; Equipment Selection; Problem Identification; Product Inspection; Operation and Control; Monitoring. **Abilities:** *Cognitive*—Information Ordering; Spatial Orientation; Visualization; Deductive Reasoning; Problem Sensitivity. *Psychomotor*—Control Precision; Speed of Limb Movement; Wrist-Finger Speed; Reaction Time; Manual Dexterity; Arm-Hand Steadiness. *Physical*—Static Strength; Explosive Strength; Trunk Strength. *Sensory*—Far Vision; Depth Perception; Peripheral Vision; Auditory Attention. **General Work Activities:** *Information Input*—Estimating Needed Characteristics; Identifying Objects, Actions, and Events; Getting Information Needed to Do the Job. *Mental Process*—Judging Qualities of Things, Services, Other People's Work; Making Decisions and Solving Problems; Organizing, Planning, and Prioritizing; Analyzing Data or Information. *Work Output*—Handling and Moving Objects; Performing General Physical Activities; Controlling Machines and Processes. *Interacting with Others*—Communicating with Other Workers; Establishing and Maintaining Relationships; Assisting and Caring for Others. **Physical Work Conditions:** Outdoors; Hazardous Equipment; Standing. **Other Job Characteristics:** Consequence of Error; Importance of Being Aware of New Events; Importance of Repeating Same Tasks.

Experience: Job Zone 1. No previous work-related skill, knowledge, or experience is needed. **Job Preparation:** SVP Below 4.0—Less than 6 months. **Knowledge:** Mechanical; Public Safety and Security; Building and Construction; Physics; Engineering and Technology; Production and Processing. **Instructional Program:** 030405 Logging/Timber Harvesting.

Related DOT Jobs: 454.384-010 Faller I; 454.684-010 Bucker; 454.684-014 Faller II; 454.684-018 Logger, All-Round; 454.684-026 Tree Cutter; 454.687-010 Chain Saw Operator.

45-4022.00 Logging Equipment Operators
(Log-Handling Equipment Operators)

Education: No data available.

Employed: 19,770

Openings: No data available.

Projected Growth: No data available.

Earnings: $23,670

Drive logging tractor or wheeled vehicle equipped with one or more accessories such as bulldozer blade, frontal shear, grapple, logging arch, cable winches, hoisting rack, or crane boom. Fell trees; skid, load, unload, or stack logs; pull stumps; clear brush.

GOE Number, Interest Area, and Work Group: 03.03.02; Plants and Animals; Hands-on Work: Forestry and Logging. **Instructional Program:** 030405 Logging/Timber Harvesting. **Note:** The Department of Labor has not collected some data for this job, so it has fewer details than the other descriptions.

45-4022.01 Logging Tractor Operators (Logging Tractor Operators)

Education: No data available.

Employed: 17,350

Openings: No data available.

Projected Growth: No data available.

Earnings: $22,750

Drive tractor equipped with one or more accessories such as bulldozer blade, frontal hydraulic shear, grapple, logging arch, cable winches, hoisting rack, or crane boom. Fell trees; skid, load, unload, or stack logs; pull stumps; clear brush.

Gives or receives signals from coworkers to move logs. Saws felled trees into lengths. Drives tractor to build or repair logging and skid roads. Drives and maneuvers tractor and activates shear to cut and fell trees. Controls hydraulic tractor equipped with tree clamp and boom to lift, swing, and bunch sheared trees. Controls equipment to load, unload, or stack logs, pull stumps, and clear brush.

GOE Number, Interest Area, and Work Group: 03.03.02; Plants and Animals; Hands-on Work: Forestry and Logging. **Personality Type:** Realistic. Realistic occupations frequently involve work activities that include practical, hands-on problems and solutions. These occupations often deal with plants, animals, and real-world materials like wood, tools, and machinery. Many of the occupations require working outside and do not involve a lot of paperwork or working closely with others. **Work Values:** Moral Values; Co-workers; Company Policies and Practices; Supervision, Human Relations; Activity; Supervision, Technical. **Skills:** Operation and Control; Coordination; Operation Monitoring.

Abilities: *Cognitive*—Oral Comprehension; Deductive Reasoning; Spatial Orientation; Information Ordering; Problem Sensitivity; Selective Attention. *Psychomotor*—Control Precision; Reaction Time; Multilimb Coordination. *Physical*—Trunk Strength; Extent Flexibility; Static Strength. *Sensory*—Depth Perception; Far Vision; Peripheral Vision. **General Work Activities:** *Information Input*—Getting Information Needed to Do the Job; Monitoring Processes, Materials, and Surroundings; Identifying Objects, Actions, and Events; Inspecting Equipment, Structures, Materials. *Mental Process*—Making Decisions and Solving Problems; Judging Qualities of Things, Services, Other People's Work; Analyzing Data or Information. *Work Output*—Controlling Machines and Processes; Operating Vehicles or Equipment; Performing General Physical Activities. *Interacting with Others*—Communicating with Other Workers; Establishing and Maintaining Relationships; Coordinating Work and Activities of Others. **Physical Work Conditions:** Outdoors; Using Hands on Objects, Tools, or Controls; Sitting. **Other Job Characteristics:** Consequence of Error; Importance of Being Exact or Accurate; Importance of Being Sure All Is Done.

Experience: Job Zone 2. Some previous work-related skill, knowledge, or experience may be helpful, but usually is not needed. **Job Preparation:** SVP 4.00 to 5.99—6 months to less than 2 years. **Knowledge:** Mechanical; Engineering and Technology; English Language; Physics; Transportation; Public Safety and Security. **Instructional Program:** 030405 Logging/Timber Harvesting.

Related DOT Jobs: 454.683-010 Tree-Shear Operator; 929.663-010 Logging-Tractor Operator.

45-4023.00 Log Graders and Scalers (Log Graders and Scalers)

Education: No data available.

Employed: 4,270

Openings: No data available.

Projected Growth: No data available.

Earnings: $22,950

Grade logs or estimate the marketable content or value of logs or pulpwood, in sorting yards, millpond, log deck, or similar locations. Inspect logs for defects or measure logs to determine volume.

Measures wood to determine dimensions or quantity, using measuring device and conversion table. Paints mark on logs to identify grade and species; calls out grade. Jabs log with scale stick and inspects log to detect defects and to ascertain characteristics. Weighs log trucks before and after unloading; records weight; records identity of supplier. Estimates and calculates total volume, waste volume, and marketable volume of log, using measurements and conversion table; records results. Evaluates log's characteristics and determines grade, using established criteria. Tends conveyor chain to move logs to and from scaling station.

GOE Number, Interest Area, and Work Group: 08.02.03; Industrial Production; Production Technology: Inspection. **Personality Type:** Realistic. Realistic occupations frequently involve work activities that include practical, hands-on problems and solutions. These occupations often deal with plants, animals, and real-world materials like wood, tools, and machinery. Many of the occupations require working outside and do not involve a lot of paperwork or working closely with others. **Work Values:** Moral Values; Independence; Activity; Supervision, Human Relations; Company Policies and Practices; Responsibility. **Skills:** Product Inspection; Mathematics; Information Gathering; Judgment and Decision Making; Information Organization. **Abilities:** *Cognitive*—Number Facility; Category Flexibility; Problem Sensitivity; Mathematical Reasoning; Perceptual Speed. *Psychomotor*—Arm-Hand Steadiness; Reaction Time; Multilimb Coordination. *Physical*—Static Strength; Gross Body Coordination; Explosive Strength. *Sensory*—Visual Color Discrimination; Depth Perception; Peripheral Vision; Night Vision. **General Work Activities:** *Information Input*—Inspecting Equipment, Structures, Materials; Identifying Objects, Actions, and Events; Estimating Needed Characteristics. *Mental Process*—Judging Qualities of Things, Services, Other People's Work; Processing Information; Making Decisions and Solving Problems. *Work Output*—Documenting and Recording Information; Handling and Moving Objects; Performing General Physical Activities. *Interacting with Others*—Communicating with Other Workers; Interpreting Meaning of Information to Others; Monitoring and Controlling Resources. **Physical Work Conditions:** Outdoors; Standing; Using Hands on Objects, Tools, or Controls. **Other Job Characteristics:** Importance of Being Exact or Accurate; Importance of Being Sure All Is Done; Consequence of Error.

Experience: Job Zone 2. Some previous work-related skill, knowledge, or experience may be helpful, but usually is not needed. **Job Preparation:** SVP 4.00 to 5.99—6 months to less than 2 years. **Knowledge:** Mathematics; Biology; Clerical; Mechanical; Building and Construction. **Instructional Program:** 030404 Forest Products Technology/Technician.

Related DOT Jobs: 455.367-010 Log Grader; 455.487-010 Log Scaler.

47-0000
Construction and Extraction Occupations

47-1000 Supervisors, Construction and Extraction Workers

47-1011.00 First-Line Supervisors/Managers of Construction Trades and Extraction Workers (First-Line Supervisors and Managers/Supervisors—Production, Construction, Maintenance, and Related Workers)

Education: Work experience in a related occupation
Employed: 2,197,772
Openings: 216,115
Projected Growth: 8.9%
Earnings: No data available.

Directly supervise and coordinate activities of construction or extraction workers.

GOE Number, Interest Area, and Work Group: 06.01.01; Construction, Mining, and Drilling; Managerial Work in Construction, Mining, and Drilling. **Instructional Programs:** 460499 Construction and Building Finishers and Managers, Other; 150901 Mining Technology/Technician; 150903 Petroleum Technology/Technician. **Note:** The Department of Labor has not collected some data for this job, so it has fewer details than the other descriptions.

47-1011.01 First-Line Supervisors and Manager/Supervisors—Construction Trades Workers (Blue-Collar Worker Supervisors)

Education: Work experience in a related occupation
Employed: 2,197,772
Openings: 216,115
Projected Growth: 8.9%
Earnings: No data available.

Directly supervise and coordinate activities of construction trades workers and their helpers. Manager/Supervisors are generally found in smaller establishments where they perform both supervisory and management functions, such as accounting, marketing, and personnel work, and may also engage in the same construction trades work as the workers they supervise.

Records information such as personnel, production, and operational data, on specified forms and reports. Confers with staff and worker to ensure production and personnel problems are resolved. Directs and leads workers engaged in construction activities. Estimates material and worker requirements to complete job. Reads specifications such as blueprints and data, to determine construction requirements. Analyzes and plans installation and construction of equipment and structures. Locates, measures, and marks location and placement of structures and equipment. Trains workers in construction methods and operation of equipment. Recommends measures to improve production methods and equipment performance to increase efficiency and safety. Assists workers engaged in construction activities, using hand tools and equipment. Analyzes and resolves worker problems and recommends motivational plans. Examines and inspects work progress, equipment and construction sites to verify safety and ensure that specifications are met. Suggests and initiates personnel actions such as promotions, transfers, and hires. Supervises and coordinates activities of construction trades workers. Assigns work to employees, using material and worker requirements data.

GOE Number, Interest Area, and Work Group: 06.01.01; Construction, Mining, and Drilling; Managerial Work in Construction, Mining, and Drilling. **Personality Type:** Enterprising. Enterprising occupations frequently involve starting up and carrying out projects. These occupations can involve leading people and making many decisions. They sometimes require risk taking and often deal with business. **Work Values:** Authority; Responsibility; Autonomy; Coworkers; Activity. **Skills:** Product Inspection; Management of Personnel Resources; Coordination; Time Management; Equipment Selection; Instructing. **Abilities:** *Cognitive*—Oral Expression; Oral Comprehension; Problem Sensitivity; Information Ordering; Written Comprehension. *Psychomotor*—Manual Dexterity; Control Precision; Wrist-Finger Speed; Arm-Hand Steadiness. *Physical*—Static Strength; Extent Flexibility; Explosive Strength. *Sensory*—Near Vision; Far Vision; Auditory Attention; Visual Color Discrimination; Depth Perception. **General Work Activities:** *Information Input*—Getting Information Needed to Do the Job; Inspecting Equipment, Structures, Materials; Monitoring Processes, Materials, and Surroundings. *Mental Process*—Evaluating Information Against Standards; Making Decisions and Solving Problems; Scheduling Work and Activities. *Work Output*—Documenting and Recording Information; Performing General Physical Activities; Handling and Moving Objects. *Interacting with Others*—Communicating with Other Workers; Guiding, Directing and Motivating Subordinates; Coordinating Work and Activities of Others. **Physical Work Conditions:** Outdoors; Standing; Common Protective or Safety Attire. **Other Job Characteristics:** Importance of Being Sure All Is Done; Consequence of Error; Frustrating Circumstances; Importance of Being Exact or Accurate.

Experience: Job Zone 4. A minimum of two to four years of work-related skill, knowledge, or experience is needed. **Job Preparation:** SVP 7.0 to less than 8.0—2 years to less than 10 years. **Knowledge:** Administration and Management; Building and Construction; Personnel and Human Resources; Design; Engineering and Technology; English Language. **Instructional Program:** 460499 Construction and Building Finishers and Managers, Other.

Related DOT Jobs: 184.167-234 Supervisor of Way; 801.131-010 Supervisor, Chimney Construction; 801.134-010 Supervisor, Reinforced-Steel-Placing; 809.131-014 Supervisor, Ornamental Ironworking; 809.131-018 Supervisor, Structural-Steel Erection; 821.131-022 Steel-Post-Installer Supervisor; 824.137-010 Electrician, Chief; 825.131-010 Electrician Supervisor; 829.131-014 Electrician Supervisor; 840.131-010 Supervisor, Painting; 840.131-014 Supervisor, Painting, Shipyard; 841.137-010 Supervisor, Billposting; 842.131-010 Supervisor, Dry-Wall Application; 842.131-014 Supervisor, Lathing; 842.131-018 Supervisor, Plastering; 842.134-010 Supervisor, Taping; 843.134-010 Supervisor, Doping; 843.137-010 Supervisor, Waterproofing; 850.133-010 Supervisor, Reclamation; 850.137-014 Supervisor, Labor Gang (partial list; see the introduction for sources of the complete list).

47-1011.02 First-Line Supervisors and Manager/Supervisors—Extractive Workers (Blue-Collar Worker Supervisors)

Education: Work experience in a related occupation

Employed: 2,197,772

Openings: 216,115

Projected Growth: 8.9%

Earnings: No data available.

Directly supervise and coordinate activities of extractive workers and their helpers. Manager/Supervisors are generally found in smaller establishments where they perform both supervisory and management functions, such as accounting, marketing, and personnel work, and may also engage in the same extractive work as the workers they supervise.

Locates, measures, and marks materials and site location, using measuring and marking equipment. Analyzes and resolves worker problems and recommends motivational plans. Confers with staff and workers to ensure production personnel problems are resolved. Analyzes and plans extraction process of geological materials. Suggests and initiates personnel actions such as promotions, transfers, and hires. Records information such as personnel, production, and operational data on specified forms. Assists workers engaged in extraction activities, using hand tools and equipment. Examines and inspects equipment, site, and materials, to verify specifications are met. Supervises and coordinates activities of workers engaged in the extraction of geological materials. Trains workers in construction methods and operation of equipment. Recommends measures to improve production methods and equipment performance, to increase efficiency and safety. Assigns work to employees, using material and worker requirements data. Directs and leads workers engaged in extraction of geological materials. Orders materials, supplies, and repair of equipment and machinery.

GOE Number, Interest Area, and Work Group: 06.01.01; Construction, Mining, and Drilling; Managerial Work in Construction, Mining, and Drilling. **Personality Type:** Enterprising. Enterprising occupations frequently involve starting up and carrying out projects. These occupations can involve leading people and making many decisions. They sometimes require risk taking and often deal with business. **Work Values:** Authority; Responsibility; Autonomy; Activity; Coworkers; Variety; Achievement. **Skills:** Management of Personnel Resources; Instructing; Coordination; Solution Appraisal; Time Management; Information Gathering; Monitoring; Identifying Downstream Consequences; Judgment and Decision Making; Speaking. **Abilities:** *Cognitive*—Oral Expression; Deductive Reasoning; Problem Sensitivity; Information Ordering; Inductive Reasoning. *Psychomotor*—Manual Dexterity; Control Precision; Response Orientation. *Physical*—Trunk Strength; Stamina; Dynamic Strength. *Sensory*—Near Vision; Speech Clarity; Far Vision. **General Work Activities:** *Information Input*—Monitoring Processes, Materials, and Surroundings; Getting Information Needed to Do the Job; Identifying Objects, Actions, and Events. *Mental Process*—Organizing, Plan-

ning, and Prioritizing; Scheduling Work and Activities; Analyzing Data or Information; Making Decisions and Solving Problems; Judging Qualities of Things, Services, Other People's Work. *Work Output*—Handling and Moving Objects; Implementing Ideas and Programs; Performing General Physical Activities; Documenting and Recording Information. *Interacting with Others*—Coordinating Work and Activities of Others; Communicating with Other Workers; Guiding, Directing and Motivating Subordinates. **Physical Work Conditions:** Standing; Common Protective or Safety Attire; Outdoors. **Other Job Characteristics:** Consequence of Error; Importance of Being Sure All Is Done; Importance of Being Exact or Accurate.

Experience: Job Zone 3. Previous work-related skill, knowledge, or experience is required. **Job Preparation:** SVP 6.0 to less than 7.0—More than 1 year and less than 4 years. **Knowledge:** Administration and Management; Personnel and Human Resources; English Language; Engineering and Technology; Education and Training. **Instructional Programs:** 150901 Mining Technology/Technician; 150903 Petroleum Technology/Technician.

Related DOT Jobs: 850.137-010 Supervisor, Core Drilling; 930.130-010 Tool Pusher; 930.131-010 Field Supervisor, Oil-Well Services; 930.134-010 Quarry Supervisor, Dimension Stone; 932.132-010 Bank Boss; 939.131-010 Quarry Supervisor, Open Pit; 939.132-010 Dredge Operator Supervisor; 939.132-014 Oil-Well-Services Supervisor; 939.137-014 Pit Supervisor; 939.137-018 Section Supervisor; 939.137-022 Supervisor, Harvesting.

47-2000 Construction Trades Workers

47-2011.00 Boilermakers (Boilermakers)

Education: Long-term O-T-J training

Employed: 18,298

Openings: 2,094

Projected Growth: 1.6%

Earnings: $38,380

Construct, assemble, maintain, and repair stationary steam boilers and boiler house auxiliaries. Align structures or plate sections to assemble boiler frame tanks or vats, following blueprints. Use hand and power tools, plumb bobs, levels, wedges, dogs, or turnbuckles. Assist in testing assembled vessels. Direct cleaning of boilers and boiler furnaces. Inspect and repair boiler fittings such as safety valves, regulators, automatic-control mechanisms, water columns, and auxiliary machines.

Locates and marks reference points for columns or plates on foundation, using master straightedge, square, transit, and measuring instruments. Bolts or arc welds pressure-vessel structures and parts together, using wrenches and welding equipment. Straightens or reshapes bent pressure-vessel plates and structure parts, using hammer, jacks, and torch. Bells, beads with power hammer, or welds pressure-vessel tube ends, to ensure leakproof joints. Inspects assembled vessels for faulty accessories; pressure tests for leakage. Maintains and repairs stationary steam boilers and boiler house auxiliaries, using hand tools and power tools. Repairs insulation of pressure vessel with cement. Fabricates parts such as stacks, uptakes, and chutes, to adapt pressure vessel to premises. Attaches rigging; signals crane operator to lift pressure-vessel parts to specified position. Installs refractory brick and other heat resistant materials in firebox of pressure vessel. Studies blueprints to determine location, relationship, and dimensions of parts, to assemble pressure vessels such as boilers, tanks, and vats. Shapes seams, joints, and irregular edges of pressure-vessel sections and structural parts, to attain specified fit, using cutting torch, file, and power grinder. Repairs or replaces defective pressure-vessel parts, using torch, jacks, caulking hammers, power saw, threading die, and welding equipment. Installs manholes, handholes, valves, gauges, and feedwater connections in drums of water tube boilers, using hand tools. Positions, aligns, and secures structural parts and related assemblies of pressure vessels, using plumb bobs, levels, wedges, and turnbuckles. Cleans pressure-vessel equipment, using scrapers, wire brush, and cleaning solvent.

GOE Number, Interest Area, and Work Group: 06.02.02; Construction, Mining, and Drilling; Construction: Construction and Maintenance. **Personality Type:** Realistic. Realistic occupations frequently involve work activities that include practical, hands-on problems and solutions. These occupations often deal with plants, animals, and real-world materials like wood, tools, and machinery. Many of the occupations require working outside and do not involve a lot of paperwork or working closely with others. **Work Values:** Moral Values; Company Policies and Practices; Supervision, Human Relations; Compensation; Ability Utilization; Activity; Supervision, Technical. **Skills:** Installation; Repairing; Equipment Maintenance; Product Inspection; Troubleshooting. **Abilities:** *Cognitive*—Visualization; Selective Attention; Information Ordering; Problem Sensitivity; Deductive Reasoning. *Psychomotor*—Manual Dexterity; Finger Dexterity; Control Precision; Multilimb Coordination. *Physical*—Static Strength; Extent Flexibility; Dynamic Strength; Trunk Strength. *Sensory*—Auditory Attention; Depth Perception; Night Vision. **General Work Activities:** *Information Input*—Inspecting Equipment, Structures, Materials; Getting Information Needed to Do the Job; Monitoring Processes, Materials, and Surroundings; Identifying Objects, Actions, and Events. *Mental Process*—Evaluating Information Against Standards; Making Decisions and Solving Problems; Judging Qualities of Things, Services, Other People's Work. *Work Output*—Repairing and Maintaining Mechanical Equipment; Handling and Moving Objects; Performing General Physical Activities. *Interacting with Others*—Communicating with Other Workers; Coordinating Work and Activities of Others; Establishing and Maintaining Relationships. **Physical Work Conditions:** Using Hands on Objects, Tools, or Controls; Indoors; Standing; Hazardous Equipment. **Other Job Characteristics:** Consequence of Error; Importance of Being Sure All Is Done; Importance of Being Exact or Accurate.

Experience: Job Zone 4. A minimum of two to four years of work-related skill, knowledge, or experience is needed. **Job Preparation:** SVP 7.0 to less than 8.0—2 years to less than 10 years. **Knowledge:** Mechanical; Building and Construction; Engineering and Technology; Mathematics; Public Safety and Security. **Instructional Program:** 470303 Industrial Machinery Maintenance and Repairer.

Related DOT Jobs: 805.261-010 Boilermaker Apprentice; 805.261-014 Boilermaker I; 805.361-010 Boilerhouse Mechanic; 805.361-014 Boilermaker Fitter; 805.381-010 Boilermaker II.

47-2021.00 Brickmasons and Blockmasons
(Bricklayers, Blockmasons, and Stonemasons)

Education: Long-term O-T-J training
Employed: 156,986
Openings: 29,721
Projected Growth: 12.3%
Earnings: No data available.

Lay and bind building materials such as brick, structural tile, concrete block, cinder block, glass block, and terra-cotta block, with mortar and other substances, to construct or repair walls, partitions, arches, sewers, and other structures.

Sprays or spreads refractory material over brickwork to protect against deterioration. Mixes specified amount of sand, clay, dirt, or mortar powder with water to form refractory mixture. Calculates angles and courses and determines vertical and horizontal alignment of courses. Breaks or cuts bricks, tiles, or blocks to size, using edge of trowel, hammer, or power saw. Removes burned or damaged brick or mortar, using sledgehammer, crowbar, chipping gun, or chisel. Fastens or fuses brick or other building material to structure with wire clamps, anchor holes, torch, or cement. Examines brickwork or structure to determine need for repair. Measures distance from reference points; marks guidelines to lay out work, using plumb bobs and levels. Applies and smoothes mortar or other mixture over work surface and removes excess, using trowel and hand tools. Lays and aligns bricks, blocks, or tiles to build or repair structures or high temperature equipment such as cupola, kilns, ovens, or furnaces. Cleans working surface to remove scale, dust, soot, or chips of brick and mortar, using broom, wire brush, or scrapper.

GOE Number, Interest Area, and Work Group: 06.02.01; Construction, Mining, and Drilling; Construction: Masonry, Stone, and Brick Work. **Personality Type:** Realistic. Realistic occupations frequently involve work activities that include practical, hands-on problems and solutions. These occupations often deal with plants, animals, and real-world materials like wood, tools, and machinery. Many of the occupations require working outside and do not involve a lot of paperwork or working closely with others. **Work Values:** Moral Values; Compensation; Independence; Achievement; Ability Utilization. **Skills:** Mathematics; Equipment Selection; Repairing; Product Inspection; Monitoring. **Abilities:** *Cognitive*—Information Ordering; Visualization; Number Facility; Deductive Reasoning; Problem Sensitivity. *Psychomotor*—Manual Dexterity; Arm-Hand Steadiness; Wrist-Finger Speed. *Physical*—Extent Flexibility; Trunk Strength; Dynamic Strength. *Sensory*—Depth Perception; Peripheral Vision; Glare Sensitivity. **General Work Activities:** *Information Input*—Getting Information Needed to Do the Job; Inspecting Equipment, Structures, Materials; Monitoring Processes, Materials, and Surroundings. *Mental Process*—Judging Qualities of Things, Services, Other People's Work; Analyzing Data or Information; Processing Information. *Work Output*—Performing General Physical Activities;

Handling and Moving Objects; Controlling Machines and Processes. *Interacting with Others*—Communicating with Other Workers; Monitoring and Controlling Resources; Performing for or Working with the Public; Assisting and Caring for Others; Communicating with Persons Outside Organization; Establishing and Maintaining Relationships. **Physical Work Conditions:** Using Hands on Objects, Tools, or Controls; Standing; Outdoors. **Other Job Characteristics:** Consequence of Error; Importance of Being Sure All Is Done; Importance of Being Exact or Accurate.

Experience: Job Zone 3. Previous work-related skill, knowledge, or experience is required. **Job Preparation:** SVP 6.0 to less than 7.0—More than 1 year and less than 4 years. **Knowledge:** Building and Construction; Mechanical; Mathematics; Physics; Engineering and Technology. **Instructional Program:** 460101 Mason and Tile Setter.

Related DOT Jobs: 573.684-010 Kiln-Door Builder; 709.684-046 Hot-Top Liner; 861.381-010 Acid-Tank Liner; 861.381-014 Bricklayer; 861.381-018 Bricklayer; 861.381-022 Bricklayer Apprentice; 861.381-026 Bricklayer, Firebrick and Refractory Tile; 861.684-010 Cupola Patcher; 861.684-014 Patcher; 861.684-022 Repairer, Kiln Car; 899.364-010 Chimney Repairer.

47-2022.00 Stonemasons (Bricklayers, Blockmasons, and Stonemasons)

Education: Long-term O-T-J training
Employed: 156,986
Openings: 29,721
Projected Growth: 12.3%
Earnings: No data available.

Build stone structures such as piers, walls, and abutments. Lay walks, curbstones, or special types of masonry for vats, tanks, and floors.

Aligns and levels stone or marble, using measuring devices such as rule, square, and plumbline. Shapes, trims, faces, and cuts marble or stone, preparatory to setting, using power saws, cutting equipment, and hand tools. Sets stone or marble in place, according to layout or pattern. Mixes mortar or grout. Pours or spreads mortar or grout on marble slabs, stone, or foundation. Cleans excess mortar or grout from surface of marble, stone, or monument, using sponge, brush, water, or acid. Lines interiors of molds with treated paper and fills molds with composition-stone mixture. Drills holes in marble or ornamental stone; anchors bracket. Repairs cracked or chipped areas of ornamental stone or marble surface, using blowtorch and mastic. Removes sections of monument from truck bed and guides stone onto foundation, using skids, hoist, or truck crane. Positions mold along guidelines of wall, presses mold in place, and removes mold and paper from wall. Smoothes, polishes, and bevels surfaces, using hand tools and power tools. Finishes joints between stones, using trowel. Lays out wall pattern or foundation of monument, using straight edge, rule, or staked lines. Digs trench for foundation of monument, using pick and shovel.

GOE Number, Interest Area, and Work Group: 06.02.01; Construction, Mining, and Drilling; Construction: Masonry, Stone, and Brick Work. **Personality Type:** Realistic. Realistic occupa-

tions frequently involve work activities that include practical, hands-on problems and solutions. These occupations often deal with plants, animals, and real-world materials like wood, tools, and machinery. Many of the occupations require working outside and do not involve a lot of paperwork or working closely with others. **Work Values:** Moral Values; Compensation; Achievement; Independence; Ability Utilization. **Skills:** Equipment Selection; Operation and Control; Product Inspection; Repairing. **Abilities:** *Cognitive*—Visualization; Problem Sensitivity; Oral Comprehension; Originality; Information Ordering. *Psychomotor*—Wrist-Finger Speed; Speed of Limb Movement; Multilimb Coordination. *Physical*—Static Strength; Dynamic Strength; Extent Flexibility. *Sensory*—Depth Perception; Visual Color Discrimination; Glare Sensitivity. **General Work Activities:** *Information Input*—Getting Information Needed to Do the Job; Monitoring Processes, Materials, and Surroundings; Inspecting Equipment, Structures, Materials. *Mental Process*—Processing Information; Organizing, Planning, and Prioritizing; Judging Qualities of Things, Services, Other People's Work; Evaluating Information Against Standards. *Work Output*—Handling and Moving Objects; Performing General Physical Activities; Controlling Machines and Processes. *Interacting with Others*—Coordinating Work and Activities of Others; Communicating with Other Workers; Communicating with Persons Outside Organization; Establishing and Maintaining Relationships; Assisting and Caring for Others. **Physical Work Conditions:** Using Hands on Objects, Tools, or Controls; Outdoors; Kneeling, Crouching, or Crawling; Common Protective or Safety Attire; Making Repetitive Motions; Standing. **Other Job Characteristics:** Importance of Being Exact or Accurate; Importance of Being Sure All Is Done; Consequence of Error.

Experience: Job Zone 4. A minimum of two to four years of work-related skill, knowledge, or experience is needed. **Job Preparation:** SVP 7.0 to less than 8.0—2 years to less than 10 years. **Knowledge:** Building and Construction; Mechanical; Design; Mathematics; Public Safety and Security; Chemistry. **Instructional Program:** 460101 Mason and Tile Setter.

Related DOT Jobs: 861.361-010 Composition-Stone Applicator; 861.361-014 Monument Setter; 861.381-030 Marble Setter; 861.381-038 Stonemason; 861.381-042 Stonemason Apprentice.

47-2031.00 Carpenters (Carpenters)

Education: Long-term O-T-J training
Employed: 1,070,759
Openings: 236,108
Projected Growth: 6.9%
Earnings: No data available.

Construct, erect, install, or repair structures and fixtures made of wood, such as concrete forms, building frameworks (including partitions, joists, studding, and rafters), wood stairways, window and door frames, and hardwood floors. Install cabinets, siding, drywall, and batt or roll insulation. Includes brattice builders who build doors or brattices (ventilation walls or partitions) in underground passageways to control the proper circulation of air through the passageways and to the working places.

GOE Number, Interest Area, and Work Group: 06.02.02; Construction, Mining, and Drilling; Construction: Construction and Maintenance. **Instructional Program:** 460201 Carpenter. **Note:** The Department of Labor has not collected some data for this job, so it has fewer details than the other descriptions.

47-2031.01 Construction Carpenters (Carpenters)

Education: Long-term O-T-J training

Employed: 1,070,759

Openings: 236,108

Projected Growth: 6.9%

Earnings: No data available.

Construct, erect, install, and repair structures and fixtures of wood, plywood, and wallboard, using carpenter's hand tools and power tools.

Fills cracks and other defects in plaster or plasterboard. Sands patch, using patching plaster, trowel, and sanding tool. Finishes surfaces of woodworking or wallboard in houses and buildings, using paint, hand tools, and paneling. Measures and marks cutting lines on materials, using ruler, pencil, chalk, and marking gauge. Studies specifications in blueprints, sketches, or building plans to determine materials required and dimensions of structure to be fabricated. Inspects ceiling or floor tile, wall coverings, siding, glass, or woodwork to detect broken or damaged structures. Estimates amount and kind of lumber or other materials required, and selects and orders them. Prepares layout according to blueprint or oral instructions, using rule, framing square, and calipers. Shapes or cuts materials to specified measurements, using hand tools, machines, or power saw. Removes damaged or defective parts or sections of structure and repairs or replaces, using hand tools. Builds or repairs cabinets, doors, frameworks, floors, and other wooden fixtures used in buildings, using woodworking machines, carpenter's hand tools, and power tools. Installs structures and fixtures, such as windows, frames, floorings, and trim, or installs hardware, using carpenter's hand and power tools. Assembles and fastens materials, using hand tools and wood screws, nails, dowel pins, or glue, to make framework or props. Verifies trueness of structure, using plumb bob and level.

GOE Number, Interest Area, and Work Group: 06.02.02; Construction, Mining, and Drilling; Construction: Construction and Maintenance. **Personality Type:** Realistic. Realistic occupations frequently involve work activities that include practical, hands-on problems and solutions. These occupations often deal with plants, animals, and real-world materials like wood, tools, and machinery. Many of the occupations require working outside and do not involve a lot of paperwork or working closely with others. **Work Values:** Moral Values; Compensation; Ability Utilization; Activity; Achievement; Variety. **Skills:** Installation; Repairing; Product Inspection; Management of Material Resources; Mathematics. **Abilities:** *Cognitive*—Visualization; Information Ordering; Written Comprehension; Spatial Orientation; Problem Sensitivity. *Psychomotor*—Manual Dexterity; Arm-Hand Steadiness; Multilimb Coordination; Wrist-Finger Speed. *Physical*—Static Strength; Dynamic Strength; Extent Flexibility. *Sensory*—Depth Perception; Far Vision; Glare Sensitivity; Peripheral Vision. **General Work Activities:** *Information Input*—Getting Information Needed to Do the Job; Inspecting Equipment, Structures, Materials; Estimating Needed Characteristics. *Mental Process*—Evaluating Information Against Standards; Judging Qualities of Things, Services, Other People's Work; Making Decisions and Solving Problems; Processing Information. *Work Output*—Performing General Physical Activities; Handling and Moving Objects; Controlling Machines and Processes. *Interacting with Others*—Monitoring and Controlling Resources; Communicating with Other Workers; Establishing and Maintaining Relationships; Providing Consultation and Advice to Others. **Physical Work Conditions:** Using Hands on Objects, Tools, or Controls; Standing; Hazardous Equipment; Common Protective or Safety Attire. **Other Job Characteristics:** Importance of Being Exact or Accurate; Importance of Being Sure All Is Done; Consequence of Error.

Experience: Job Zone 4. A minimum of two to four years of work-related skill, knowledge, or experience is needed. **Job Preparation:** SVP 7.0 to less than 8.0—2 years to less than 10 years. **Knowledge:** Building and Construction; Design; Mechanical; Engineering and Technology; Mathematics. **Instructional Program:** 460201 Carpenter.

Related DOT Jobs: 860.281-010 Carpenter, Maintenance; 860.381-022 Carpenter; 860.381-026 Carpenter Apprentice; 860.381-034 Carpenter, Mold; 860.381-038 Carpenter, Railcar; 869.381-010 House Repairer; 962.281-010 Prop Maker.

47-2031.02 Rough Carpenters (Carpenters)

Education: Long-term O-T-J training

Employed: 1,070,759

Openings: 236,108

Projected Growth: 6.9%

Earnings: No data available.

Build rough wooden structures such as concrete forms, scaffolds, tunnel supports, bridge supports, sewer supports, billboard signs, and temporary frame shelters, according to sketches, blueprints, or oral instructions.

Erects forms of prefabricated forms, framework, scaffolds, hoists, roof supports, or chutes, using hand tools, plumb rule, and level. Anchors and braces forms and other structures in place, using nails, bolts, anchor rods, steel cables, planks, wedges, and timbers. Cuts or saws boards, timbers, or plywood to required size, using handsaw, power saw, or woodworking machine. Fabricates parts, using woodworking and metalworking machines. Digs or directs digging of post holes, and sets pole to support structure. Installs rough door and window frames, subflooring, fixtures, or temporary supports in structures undergoing construction or repair. Bores boltholes in timber with masonry or concrete walls, using power drill. Assembles and fastens material together to construct wood or metal framework of structure, using bolts, nails, or screws. Measures materials or distances, using square, measuring tape, or rule to lay out work. Studies blueprints and diagrams to determine dimensions of structure or form to be constructed or erected. Examines structural timbers and supports to detect decay; replaces timber, using hand tools, nuts, and bolts.

GOE Number, Interest Area, and Work Group: 06.02.02; Construction, Mining, and Drilling; Construction: Construction and Maintenance. **Personality Type:** Realistic. Realistic occupations frequently involve work activities that include practical, hands-on problems and solutions. These occupations often deal with plants, animals, and real-world materials like wood, tools, and machinery. Many of the occupations require working outside and do not involve a lot of paperwork or working closely with others. **Work Values:** Moral Values; Activity; Compensation; Ability Utilization; Variety; Achievement; Security. **Skills:** Installation; Mathematics; Product Inspection; Operation and Control; Active Listening; Equipment Selection. **Abilities:** *Cognitive*—Visualization; Information Ordering; Oral Comprehension; Number Facility; Problem Sensitivity; Written Comprehension. *Psychomotor*—Manual Dexterity; Control Precision; Wrist-Finger Speed; Speed of Limb Movement. *Physical*—Static Strength; Extent Flexibility; Trunk Strength. *Sensory*—Near Vision; Depth Perception; Far Vision. **General Work Activities:** *Information Input*—Inspecting Equipment, Structures, Materials; Getting Information Needed to Do the Job; Identifying Objects, Actions, and Events. *Mental Process*—Evaluating Information Against Standards; Organizing, Planning, and Prioritizing; Judging Qualities of Things, Services, Other People's Work; Making Decisions and Solving Problems. *Work Output*—Performing General Physical Activities; Handling and Moving Objects; Controlling Machines and Processes. *Interacting with Others*—Communicating with Other Workers; Coordinating Work and Activities of Others; Guiding, Directing and Motivating Subordinates. **Physical Work Conditions:** Using Hands on Objects, Tools, or Controls; Outdoors; Standing. **Other Job Characteristics:** Consequence of Error; Importance of Being Exact or Accurate; Importance of Being Sure All Is Done.

Experience: Job Zone 3. Previous work-related skill, knowledge, or experience is required. **Job Preparation:** SVP 6.0 to less than 7.0—More than 1 year and less than 4 years. **Knowledge:** Building and Construction; Engineering and Technology; Design; Mechanical; Mathematics. **Instructional Program:** 460201 Carpenter.

Related DOT Jobs: 860.381-030 Carpenter, Bridge; 860.381-042 Carpenter, Rough; 860.381-046 Form Builder; 869.361-018 Sign Erector-and-Repairer; 869.381-034 Timber Framer.

47-2031.03 Carpenter Assemblers and Repairers
(Carpenters)

Education: Long-term O-T-J training

Employed: 1,070,759

Openings: 236,108

Projected Growth: 6.9%

Earnings: No data available.

Perform a variety of tasks requiring a limited knowledge of carpentry, such as applying siding and weatherboard to building exteriors or assembling and erecting prefabricated buildings.

Realigns windows and screens to fit casements; oils moving parts. Aligns and fastens materials together, using hand tools and power tools, to form building or bracing. Cuts sidings and moldings, sections of weatherboard, openings in sheetrock, and lumber, using hand tools and power tools. Repairs or replaces defective locks, hinges, cranks, and pieces of wood, using glue, hand tools, and power tools. Measures cut materials to determine conformance to specifications, using tape measure. Examines wood surfaces for defects such as nicks, cracks, or blisters. Fills cracks, seams, depressions, and nail holes with filler. Moves panel or roof section to other work stations or to storage or shipping area, using electric hoist. Directs crane operator in positioning floor, wall, ceiling, and roof panel on house foundation. Applies stain, paint, or crayons to defects and filter to touch up the repaired area. Measures and marks location of studs, leaders, and receptacle openings, using tape measure, template, and marker. Trims overlapping edges of wood and weatherboard, using portable router or power saw and hand tools. Removes surface defects, using knife, scraper, wet sponge, electric iron, and sanding tools. Installs prefabricated windows and doors, insulation, wall, ceiling and floor panels or siding, using adhesives, hoists, hand tools, and power tools. Studies blueprints, specification sheets, and drawings, to determine style and type of window or wall panel required. Lays out and aligns materials on worktable or in assembly jig according to specified instructions.

GOE Number, Interest Area, and Work Group: 06.04.01; Construction, Mining, and Drilling; Hands-on Work: Construction, Extraction, and Maintenance. **Personality Type:** Realistic. Realistic occupations frequently involve work activities that include practical, hands-on problems and solutions. These occupations often deal with plants, animals, and real-world materials like wood, tools, and machinery. Many of the occupations require working outside and do not involve a lot of paperwork or working closely with others. **Work Values:** Moral Values; Activity; Security; Achievement; Supervision, Human Relations; Independence; Coworkers; Variety. **Skills:** Repairing; Product Inspection; Installation; Operation and Control; Reading Comprehension; Mathematics. **Abilities:** *Cognitive*—Visualization; Spatial Orientation; Information Ordering; Written Comprehension; Problem Sensitivity; Memorization. *Psychomotor*—Manual Dexterity; Arm-Hand Steadiness; Multilimb Coordination. *Physical*—Static Strength; Explosive Strength; Dynamic Strength; Extent Flexibility. *Sensory*—Depth Perception; Far Vision; Visual Color Discrimination. **General Work Activities:** *Information Input*—Getting Information Needed to Do the Job; Identifying Objects, Actions, and Events; Monitoring Processes, Materials, and Surroundings. *Mental Process*—Evaluating Information Against Standards; Updating and Using Job-Relevant Knowledge; Making Decisions and Solving Problems. *Work Output*—Performing General Physical Activities; Handling and Moving Objects; Controlling Machines and Processes. *Interacting with Others*—Communicating with Other Workers; Assisting and Caring for Others; Coordinating Work and Activities of Others. **Physical Work Conditions:** Using Hands on Objects, Tools, or Controls; Standing; Hazardous Equipment. **Other Job Characteristics:** Importance of Being Sure All Is Done; Importance of Being Exact or Accurate; Consequence of Error.

Experience: Job Zone 2. Some previous work-related skill, knowledge, or experience may be helpful, but usually is not needed. **Job Preparation:** SVP 4.00 to 5.99—6 months to less than 2 years. **Knowledge:** Building and Construction; Mechanical; Engineering and Technology; Design; Mathematics. **Instructional Program:** 460201 Carpenter.

Related DOT Jobs: 769.684-038 Repairer, Assembled Wood Products; 860.664-010 Carpenter I; 860.681-010 Carpenter II; 860.684-010 Builder, Beam; 860.684-014 Sider; 863.684-010 Composition-Weatherboard Applier; 863.684-014 Sider; 869.684-018 Assembler, Subassembly; 869.684-034 Lay-Out Worker; 869.684-038 Panel Installer; 869.684-042 Roof Assembler I; 869.684-062 Stull Installer; 869.684-066 Trimmer; 899.684-042 Window Repairer; 920.684-010 Crater.

47-2031.04 Ship Carpenters and Joiners (Carpenters)

Education: Long-term O-T-J training

Employed: 1,070,759

Openings: 236,108

Projected Growth: 6.9%

Earnings: No data available.

Fabricate, assemble, install, or repair wooden furnishings in ships or boats.

Cuts wood or glass to specified dimensions, using hand tools and power tools. Shapes and laminates wood to form parts of ship, using steam chambers, clamps, glue, and jigs. Repairs structural woodwork and replaces defective parts and equipment, using hand tools and power tools. Transfers dimensions or measurements of wood parts or bulkhead on plywood, using measuring instruments and marking devices. Greases gears and other moving parts of machines on ship. Shapes irregular parts and trims excess material from bulkhead and furnishings to ensure fit meets specifications. Assembles and installs hardware, gaskets, floors, furnishings, or insulation, using adhesive, hand tools, and power tools. Reads blueprints to determine dimensions of furnishings in ships or boats. Constructs floors, doors, and partitions, using woodworking machines, hand tools, and power tools.

GOE Number, Interest Area, and Work Group: 06.02.02; Construction, Mining, and Drilling; Construction: Construction and Maintenance. **Personality Type:** Realistic. Realistic occupations frequently involve work activities that include practical, hands-on problems and solutions. These occupations often deal with plants, animals, and real-world materials like wood, tools, and machinery. Many of the occupations require working outside and do not involve a lot of paperwork or working closely with others. **Work Values:** Moral Values; Activity; Independence; Compensation; Supervision, Human Relations; Ability Utilization. **Skills:** Installation; Repairing; Mathematics; Monitoring; Information Gathering; Equipment Selection. **Abilities:** *Cognitive*—Visualization; Information Ordering; Number Facility; Written Comprehension; Flexibility of Closure; Problem Sensitivity. *Psychomotor*—Manual Dexterity; Control Precision; Wrist-Finger Speed. *Physical*—Dynamic Flexibility; Extent Flexibility; Static Strength. *Sensory*—Near Vision; Depth Perception; Far Vision. **General Work Activities:** *Information Input*—Getting Information Needed to Do the Job; Monitoring Processes, Materials, and Surroundings; Identifying Objects, Actions, and Events. *Mental Process*—Making Decisions and Solving Problems; Evaluating Information Against Standards; Organizing, Planning, and Prioritizing; Analyzing Data or Information. *Work Output*—Handling and Moving Objects; Performing General Physical Activities; Controlling Machines and Processes. *Interacting with Others*—Communicating with Other Workers; Establishing and Maintaining Relationships; Performing Administrative Activities; Assisting and Caring for Others; Interpreting Meaning of Information to Others; Resolving Conflict and Negotiating with Others. **Physical Work Conditions:** Using Hands on Objects, Tools, or Controls; Standing; Hazardous Equipment; Common Protective or Safety Attire. **Other Job Characteristics:** Importance of Being Sure All Is Done; Consequence of Error; Importance of Being Exact or Accurate.

Experience: Job Zone 3. Previous work-related skill, knowledge, or experience is required. **Job Preparation:** SVP 6.0 to less than 7.0—More than 1 year and less than 4 years. **Knowledge:** Building and Construction; Design; Engineering and Technology; Mechanical; Mathematics. **Instructional Programs:** 460201 Carpenter; 490306 Marine Maintenance and Ship Repairer.

Related DOT Jobs: 806.281-058 Carpenter, Prototype; 860.281-014 Carpenter, Ship; 860.381-050 Joiner; 860.381-054 Joiner Apprentice.

47-2031.05 Boat Builders and Shipwrights (Carpenters)

Education: Long-term O-T-J training

Employed: 1,070,759

Openings: 236,108

Projected Growth: 6.9%

Earnings: No data available.

Construct and repair ships or boats, according to blueprints.

Attaches hoist to sections of hull, and directs hoist operator to align parts over blocks, according to layout of boat. Marks outline of boat on building dock, shipway, or mold loft according to blueprint specifications, using measuring instruments and crayon. Constructs and shapes wooden frames, structures, and other parts according to blueprint specifications, using hand tools, power tools, and measuring instruments. Assembles and installs hull timbers and other structures in ship, using adhesive, measuring instruments, and hand tools or power tools. Cuts out defects, using power tools and hand tools, and fits and secures replacement parts, using caulking gun, adhesive, or hand tools. Inspects boat to determine location and extent of defect. Cuts and forms parts such as keel, ribs, sidings, and support structures and blocks, using woodworking hand tools and power tools. Establishes dimensional reference points on layout and hull to make template of parts and locate machinery and equipment. Positions and secures support structures on construction area. Measures and marks dimensional lines on lumber, following template and using scriber. Smoothes and finishes ship surfaces, using power sander, broadax, adz, and paint; waxes and buffs surface to specified finish. Attaches metal parts such as fittings, plates, and bulkheads to ship, using brace and bits, augers, and wrenches. Consults with customer or supervisor and reads blueprint to determine necessary repairs.

GOE Number, Interest Area, and Work Group: 06.02.02; Construction, Mining, and Drilling; Construction: Construction and Maintenance. **Personality Type:** Realistic. Realistic occupations frequently involve work activities that include practical, hands-on problems and solutions. These occupations often deal with plants, animals, and real-world materials like wood, tools, and machinery. Many of the occupations require working outside and do not involve a lot of paperwork or working closely with others. **Work Values:** Moral Values; Achievement; Ability Utilization; Activity; Compensation. **Skills:** Equipment Selection; Mathematics; Product Inspection; Operations Analysis; Repairing; Installation. **Abilities:** *Cognitive*–Visualization; Information Ordering; Number Facility; Oral Comprehension; Written Comprehension. *Psychomotor*–Manual Dexterity; Arm-Hand Steadiness; Control Precision. *Physical*–Static Strength; Extent Flexibility; Dynamic Strength; Trunk Strength. *Sensory*–Near Vision; Speech Recognition; Depth Perception; Visual Color Discrimination. **General Work Activities:** *Information Input*–Getting Information Needed to Do the Job; Inspecting Equipment, Structures, Materials; Estimating Needed Characteristics. *Mental Process*–Judging Qualities of Things, Services, Other People's Work; Making Decisions and Solving Problems; Evaluating Information Against Standards; Organizing, Planning, and Prioritizing. *Work Output*–Handling and Moving Objects; Performing General Physical Activities; Implementing Ideas and Programs; Controlling Machines and Processes. *Interacting with Others*–Communicating with Other Workers; Communicating with Persons Outside Organization; Providing Consultation and Advice to Others. **Physical Work Conditions:** Using Hands on Objects, Tools, or Controls; Standing; Outdoors. **Other Job Characteristics:** Importance of Being Sure All Is Done; Consequence of Error; Importance of Being Exact or Accurate.

Experience: Job Zone 4. A minimum of two to four years of work-related skill, knowledge, or experience is needed. **Job Preparation:** SVP 7.0 to less than 8.0–2 years to less than 10 years. **Knowledge:** Building and Construction; Mechanical; Design; Engineering and Technology; Production and Processing. **Instructional Program:** 490306 Marine Maintenance and Ship Repairer.

Related DOT Jobs: 807.361-014 Boat Repairer; 860.361-010 Boatbuilder, Wood; 860.361-014 Boatbuilder Apprentice, Wood; 860.381-058 Shipwright; 860.381-062 Shipwright Apprentice.

47-2031.06 Brattice Builders (Carpenters)

Education: Long-term O-T-J training

Employed: 1,070,759

Openings: 236,108

Projected Growth: 6.9%

Earnings: No data available.

Build doors or brattices (ventilation walls or partitions) in underground passageways to control the proper circulation of air through the passageways and to the working places.

Installs rigid and flexible air ducts to transport air to work areas. Erects partitions to support roof in areas unsuited to timbering or bolting. Drills and blasts obstructing boulders to reopen ventilation shafts.

GOE Number, Interest Area, and Work Group: 06.02.03; Construction, Mining, and Drilling; Construction: General. **Personality Type:** Realistic. Realistic occupations frequently involve work activities that include practical, hands-on problems and solutions. These occupations often deal with plants, animals, and real-world materials like wood, tools, and machinery. Many of

the occupations require working outside and do not involve a lot of paperwork or working closely with others. **Work Values:** Moral Values; Supervision, Human Relations; Company Policies and Practices; Activity; Supervision, Technical. **Skills:** Installation; Product Inspection; Equipment Selection; Coordination; Operations Analysis; Technology Design. **Abilities:** *Cognitive*–Problem Sensitivity; Deductive Reasoning; Spatial Orientation; Oral Comprehension; Visualization; Memorization. *Psychomotor*–Control Precision; Multilimb Coordination; Arm-Hand Steadiness; Wrist-Finger Speed. *Physical*–Extent Flexibility; Static Strength; Trunk Strength. *Sensory*–Depth Perception. **General Work Activities:** *Information Input*–Getting Information Needed to Do the Job; Identifying Objects, Actions, and Events; Inspecting Equipment, Structures, Materials. *Mental Process*–Judging Qualities of Things, Services, Other People's Work; Making Decisions and Solving Problems; Analyzing Data or Information. *Work Output*–Performing General Physical Activities; Handling and Moving Objects; Controlling Machines and Processes. *Interacting with Others*–Communicating with Other Workers; Establishing and Maintaining Relationships; Developing and Building Teams; Coordinating Work and Activities of Others. **Physical Work Conditions:** Standing; Using Hands on Objects, Tools, or Controls; Common Protective or Safety Attire. **Other Job Characteristics:** Consequence of Error; Importance of Being Sure All Is Done; Importance of Being Exact or Accurate.

Experience: Job Zone 2. Some previous work-related skill, knowledge, or experience may be helpful, but usually is not needed. **Job Preparation:** SVP 4.00 to 5.99–6 months to less than 2 years. **Knowledge:** Building and Construction; Mechanical; Physics; Engineering and Technology; Design. **Instructional Program:** 460201 Carpenter.

Related DOT Job: 869.684-058 Stopping Builder.

47-2041.00 Carpet Installers (Carpet Installers)

Education: Moderate-term O-T-J training

Employed: 84,524

Openings: 11,240

Projected Growth: 3.6%

Earnings: $26,480

Lay and install carpet from rolls or blocks on floors. Install padding; trim flooring materials.

Cuts carpet padding to size and installs padding, following prescribed method. Sews sections of carpeting together by hand, when necessary. Nails tack strips around area to be carpeted or uses old strips to attach edges of new carpet. Fastens metal treads across door openings or where carpet meets flooring, to hold carpet in place. Moves furniture from area to be carpeted and removes old carpet and padding. Joins edges of carpet that meet at openings, using tape with glue and heated carpet iron. Cuts and trims carpet to fit along wall edges, openings, and projections. Measures and cuts carpeting to size according to floor sketches, using carpet knife. Installs carpet on some floors using adhesive, following prescribed method. Stretches carpet to ensure smooth surface and presses carpet in place over tack strips. Studies floor sketches to determine area to be carpeted and amount of material needed to complete job.

GOE Number, Interest Area, and Work Group: 06.02.02; Construction, Mining, and Drilling; Construction: Construction and Maintenance. **Personality Type:** Realistic. Realistic occupations frequently involve work activities that include practical, hands-on problems and solutions. These occupations often deal with plants, animals, and real-world materials like wood, tools, and machinery. Many of the occupations require working outside and do not involve a lot of paperwork or working closely with others. **Work Values:** Moral Values; Independence; Working Conditions; Supervision, Human Relations; Achievement; Coworkers; Security; Company Policies and Practices. **Skills:** Mathematics; Product Inspection; Installation; Problem Identification; Information Gathering; Information Organization; Solution Appraisal; Equipment Selection; Monitoring. **Abilities:** *Cognitive*—Number Facility; Visualization; Mathematical Reasoning; Information Ordering; Spatial Orientation; Written Comprehension. *Psychomotor*—Arm-Hand Steadiness; Multilimb Coordination; Speed of Limb Movement. *Physical*—Static Strength; Extent Flexibility; Explosive Strength; Dynamic Strength; Trunk Strength. *Sensory*—Visual Color Discrimination; Far Vision; Depth Perception. **General Work Activities:** *Information Input*—Getting Information Needed to Do the Job; Estimating Needed Characteristics; Monitoring Processes, Materials, and Surroundings. *Mental Process*—Evaluating Information Against Standards; Judging Qualities of Things, Services, Other People's Work; Processing Information; Analyzing Data or Information. *Work Output*—Handling and Moving Objects; Performing General Physical Activities; Implementing Ideas and Programs. *Interacting with Others*—Communicating with Persons Outside Organization; Monitoring and Controlling Resources; Performing for or Working with the Public. **Physical Work Conditions:** Indoors; Kneeling, Crouching, or Crawling; Using Hands on Objects, Tools, or Controls. **Other Job Characteristics:** Importance of Being Sure All Is Done; Consequence of Error; Frustrating Circumstances.

Experience: Job Zone 4. A minimum of two to four years of work-related skill, knowledge, or experience is needed. **Job Preparation:** SVP 7.0 to less than 8.0—2 years to less than 10 years. **Knowledge:** Building and Construction; Design; Mechanical; Mathematics; Physics; Transportation. **Instructional Program:** 469999 Construction Trades, Other.

Related DOT Job: 864.381-010 Carpet Layer.

47-2042.00 Floor Layers, Except Carpet, Wood, and Hard Tiles (Floor Layers, Except Carpet, Wood, and Hard Tiles)

Education: No data available.

Employed: 13,310

Openings: No data available.

Projected Growth: No data available.

Earnings: $26,900

Apply blocks, strips, or sheets of shock-absorbing, sound-deadening, or decorative coverings to floors.

Removes excess cement to clean finished surface and applies grout to seal joints of tile. Applies adhesive cement onto floor or wall material to join and adhere foundation material. Cuts covering and foundation materials, according to blueprints and sketches, and cuts pattern around floor obstructions. Heats and softens floor covering materials to patch cracks and form floor coverings around irregular surfaces, using blow torch. Measures and marks guidelines on surfaces or foundations, using chalklines and dividers. Disconnects and removes appliances, light fixtures, and worn floor and wall covering from floors, walls, and cabinets. Trims excess covering materials, tacks edges, and joins sections of covering material to form tight joint. Brushes waterproof compound onto surface and fills cracks with plaster, putty, or grout to seal pores and form smooth foundation. Lays out, positions, and applies tile and other decorative material to floors, walls, and cabinets. Rolls and presses sheet wall and floor covering into cement base to smooth and finish surface, using hand roller. Sweeps, scrapes, sands, or chips dirt and irregularities to clean base surfaces.

GOE Number, Interest Area, and Work Group: 06.02.01; Construction, Mining, and Drilling; Construction: Masonry, Stone, and Brick Work. **Personality Type:** Realistic. Realistic occupations frequently involve work activities that include practical, hands-on problems and solutions. These occupations often deal with plants, animals, and real-world materials like wood, tools, and machinery. Many of the occupations require working outside and do not involve a lot of paperwork or working closely with others. **Work Values:** Moral Values; Supervision, Human Relations; Independence; Achievement; Working Conditions. **Skills:** Installation; Mathematics; Equipment Selection; Product Inspection. **Abilities:** *Cognitive*—Visualization; Information Ordering; Number Facility; Deductive Reasoning; Problem Sensitivity. *Psychomotor*—Manual Dexterity; Control Precision; Multilimb Coordination; Finger Dexterity; Arm-Hand Steadiness. *Physical*—Extent Flexibility; Static Strength; Trunk Strength. *Sensory*—Depth Perception. **General Work Activities:** *Information Input*—Estimating Needed Characteristics; Getting Information Needed to Do the Job; Monitoring Processes, Materials, and Surroundings. *Mental Process*—Judging Qualities of Things, Services, Other People's Work; Making Decisions and Solving Problems; Evaluating Information Against Standards; Processing Information. *Work Output*—Performing General Physical Activities; Handling and Moving Objects; Implementing Ideas and Programs. *Interacting with Others*—Communicating with Other Workers; Monitoring and Controlling Resources; Teaching Others; Communicating with Persons Outside Organization; Performing Administrative Activities. **Physical Work Conditions:** Indoors; Using Hands on Objects, Tools, or Controls; Kneeling, Crouching, or Crawling. **Other Job Characteristics:** Importance of Being Sure All Is Done; Consequence of Error; Importance of Being Exact or Accurate.

Experience: Job Zone 3. Previous work-related skill, knowledge, or experience is required. **Job Preparation:** SVP 6.0 to less than 7.0—More than 1 year and less than 4 years. **Knowledge:** Building and Construction; Mechanical; Mathematics; Design; Physics. **Instructional Program:** 469999 Construction Trades, Other.

Related DOT Jobs: 622.381-026 Floor-Covering Layer; 861.381-034 Soft-Tile Setter; 864.481-010 Floor Layer; 864.481-014 Floor-Layer Apprentice.

47-2043.00 Floor Sanders and Finishers (Construction Helpers)

Education: Short-term O-T-J training
Employed: 575,959
Openings: 167,103
Projected Growth: 7.3%
Earnings: No data available.

Scrape and sand wooden floors to smooth the surfaces, using floor scraper and floor sanding machine. Apply coats of finish.

Applies filler compound to floor to seal wood. Scrapes and sands floor edges and areas inaccessible to floor sander, using scraper and disk-type sander. Guides machine over surface of floor until surface is smooth. Attaches sandpaper to roller of sanding machine.

GOE Number, Interest Area, and Work Group: 06.02.02; Construction, Mining, and Drilling; Construction: Construction and Maintenance. **Personality Type:** Realistic. Realistic occupations frequently involve work activities that include practical, hands-on problems and solutions. These occupations often deal with plants, animals, and real-world materials like wood, tools, and machinery. Many of the occupations require working outside and do not involve a lot of paperwork or working closely with others. **Work Values:** Moral Values; Independence; Supervision, Human Relations; Security; Supervision, Technical; Activity; Coworkers. **Skills:** Equipment Selection; Operation and Control; Product Inspection; Equipment Maintenance. **Abilities:** *Cognitive*—Information Ordering; Spatial Orientation; Problem Sensitivity; Deductive Reasoning; Memorization; Flexibility of Closure. *Psychomotor*—Manual Dexterity; Multilimb Coordination; Control Precision. *Physical*—Static Strength; Trunk Strength; Dynamic Strength; Stamina. *Sensory*—Far Vision; Depth Perception; Peripheral Vision. **General Work Activities:** *Information Input*—Monitoring Processes, Materials, and Surroundings; Getting Information Needed to Do the Job; Inspecting Equipment, Structures, Materials; Identifying Objects, Actions, and Events. *Mental Process*—Organizing, Planning, and Prioritizing; Judging Qualities of Things, Services, Other People's Work; Updating and Using Job-Relevant Knowledge. *Work Output*—Performing General Physical Activities; Controlling Machines and Processes; Handling and Moving Objects. *Interacting with Others*—Communicating with Other Workers; Communicating with Persons Outside Organization; Coordinating Work and Activities of Others; Performing for or Working with the Public. **Physical Work Conditions:** Using Hands on Objects, Tools, or Controls; Contaminants; Indoors. **Other Job Characteristics:** Degree of Automation; Importance of Repeating Same Tasks; Pace Determined by Speed of Equipment; Frustrating Circumstances.

Experience: Job Zone 2. Some previous work-related skill, knowledge, or experience may be helpful, but usually is not needed. **Job Preparation:** SVP 4.00 to 5.99—6 months to less than 2 years. **Knowledge:** Mechanical; Building and Construction; Engineering and Technology; Transportation; Customer and Personal Service. **Instructional Programs:** 460408 Painter and Wall Coverer; 460408 Painter and Wall Coverer; 460408 Painter and Wall Coverer; 460408 Painter and Wall Coverer; 460408 Painter and Wall

Coverer; 469999 Construction Trades, Other; 469999 Construction Trades, Other; 469999 Construction Trades, Other; 469999 Construction Trades, Other; 470201 Heating, Air Conditioning and Refrigeration Mechanic and Repairer; 470201 Heating, Air Conditioning and Refrigeration Mechanic and Repairer; 470201 Heating, Air Conditioning and Refrigeration Mechanic and Repairer; 470201 Heating, Air Conditioning and Refrigeration Mechanic and Repairer; 470201 Heating, Air Conditioning and Refrigeration Mechanic and Repairer.
Related DOT Job: 869.664-014 Construction Worker I.

47-2044.00 Tile and Marble Setters (Hard Tile Setters)

Education: Long-term O-T-J training
Employed: 28,660
Openings: 5,348
Projected Growth: 8.7%
Earnings: $33,810

Apply hard tile, marble, and wood tile to walls, floors, ceilings, and roof decks.

Tacks lath to wall and ceiling surfaces, using staple gun or hammer. Cuts tile backing to required size, using shears. Spreads mastic or other adhesive base on roof deck to form base for promenade tile, using serrated spreader. Spreads plaster or concrete over surface to form tile base and levels to specified thickness, using brush, trowel, and screed. Measures and marks surfaces to be tiled and lays out work, following blueprints. Selects tile and other items to be installed, such as bathroom accessories, walls, panels, and cabinets, according to specifications. Mixes and applies mortar or cement to edges and ends of drain tiles, to seal halves and joints. Brushes glue onto manila paper on which design has been drawn and positions tiles finished-side-down onto paper. Wipes grout between tiles and removes excess, using wet sponge. Measures and cuts metal lath to size for walls and ceilings, using tin snips. Positions and presses or taps tile with trowel handle to affix tile to plaster or adhesive base. Cuts and shapes tile, using tile cutters and biters. Installs and anchors fixtures in designated positions, using hand tools.

GOE Number, Interest Area, and Work Group: 06.02.01; Construction, Mining, and Drilling; Construction: Masonry, Stone, and Brick Work. **Personality Type:** Realistic. Realistic occupations frequently involve work activities that include practical, hands-on problems and solutions. These occupations often deal with plants, animals, and real-world materials like wood, tools, and machinery. Many of the occupations require working outside and do not involve a lot of paperwork or working closely with others. **Work Values:** Moral Values; Independence; Achievement; Company Policies and Practices; Compensation; Activity. **Skills:** Product Inspection; Mathematics; Equipment Selection; Installation; Monitoring. **Abilities:** *Cognitive*—Visualization; Information Ordering; Category Flexibility; Spatial Orientation; Mathematical Reasoning; Flexibility of Closure. *Psychomotor*—Arm-Hand Steadiness; Manual Dexterity; Control Precision; Finger Dexterity; Multilimb Coordination. *Physical*—Extent Flexibility; Static Strength; Trunk Strength. *Sensory*—Visual Color Discrimination; Depth Perception; Night Vision. **General Work Activi-**

ties: *Information Input*—Getting Information Needed to Do the Job; Estimating Needed Characteristics; Identifying Objects, Actions, and Events. *Mental Process*—Evaluating Information Against Standards; Analyzing Data or Information; Judging Qualities of Things, Services, Other People's Work. *Work Output*—Handling and Moving Objects; Performing General Physical Activities; Implementing Ideas and Programs. *Interacting with Others*—Monitoring and Controlling Resources; Communicating with Other Workers; Communicating with Persons Outside Organization; Establishing and Maintaining Relationships. **Physical Work Conditions:** Using Hands on Objects, Tools, or Controls; Standing; Hazardous Situations. **Other Job Characteristics:** Importance of Being Exact or Accurate; Importance of Being Sure All Is Done; Consequence of Error.

Experience: Job Zone 2. Some previous work-related skill, knowledge, or experience may be helpful, but usually is not needed. **Job Preparation:** SVP 4.00 to 5.99—6 months to less than 2 years. **Knowledge:** Building and Construction; Design; Mathematics; Mechanical; Physics. **Instructional Program:** 460101 Mason and Tile Setter.

Related DOT Jobs: 779.381-014 Mosaic Worker; 861.381-054 Tile Setter; 861.381-058 Tile Setter Apprentice; 861.381-062 Tile-Conduit Layer; 861.684-018 Tile Setter.

47-2051.00 Cement Masons and Concrete Finishers
(Cement Masons, Concrete Finishers, and Terrazzo Workers)

Education: Long-term O-T-J training

Employed: 139,194

Openings: 14,084

Projected Growth: 6.1%

Earnings: $25,770

Smooth and finish surfaces of poured concrete, such as floors, walks, sidewalks, roads, or curbs, using a variety of hand and power tools. Align forms for sidewalks, curbs, or gutters; patch voids; use saws to cut expansion joints.

Cuts metal division strips, and presses them into terrazzo base so that top edges form desired design or pattern. Sprinkles colored marble or stone chips, powdered steel, or coloring powder over surface to produce prescribed finish. Wets concrete surface, and rubs with stone to smooth surface and obtain specified finish. Wets surface to prepare for bonding, fills holes and cracks with grout or slurry, and smoothes, using trowel. Cleans chipped area, using wire brush, and feels and observes surface to detect rough or uneven surface. Spreads, levels, and smoothes concrete, using rake, shovel, hand or power trowel, hand or power screed, and float. Signals truck driver to position truck to facilitate pouring concrete, and moves chute to direct concrete on forms. Spreads roofing paper on surface of foundation, and spreads concrete onto roofing paper with trowel to form terrazzo base. Polishes surface, using polishing or surfacing machine. Produces rough concrete surface, using broom. Chips, scrapes, and grinds high spots, ridges, and rough projections to finish concrete, using pneumatic chisel, hand chisel, or hand tools. Pushes roller over surface to imbed chips in surface. Builds wooden molds, and clamps molds around area to be repaired, using hand tools. Cuts out damaged areas, drills holes for reinforcing rods, and positions reinforcing rods

to repair concrete, using power saw and drill. Mixes cement, sand, and water to produce concrete, grout, or slurry, using hoe, trowel, tamper, scraper, or concrete-mixing machine. Molds expansion joints and edges, using edging tools, jointers, and straightedge. Applies muriatic acid to clean surface, and rinses with water.

GOE Number, Interest Area, and Work Group: 06.02.01; Construction, Mining, and Drilling; Construction: Masonry, Stone, and Brick Work. **Personality Type:** Realistic. Realistic occupations frequently involve work activities that include practical, hands-on problems and solutions. These occupations often deal with plants, animals, and real-world materials like wood, tools, and machinery. Many of the occupations require working outside and do not involve a lot of paperwork or working closely with others. **Work Values:** Moral Values; Ability Utilization; Compensation; Company Policies and Practices; Coworkers; Achievement. **Skills:** Product Inspection; Operations Analysis; Mathematics; Identification of Key Causes; Equipment Selection. **Abilities:** *Cognitive*—Information Ordering; Written Comprehension; Oral Expression; Visualization; Problem Sensitivity; Deductive Reasoning. *Psychomotor*—Manual Dexterity; Wrist-Finger Speed; Multilimb Coordination; Arm-Hand Steadiness. *Physical*—Static Strength; Trunk Strength; Extent Flexibility. *Sensory*—Visual Color Discrimination; Far Vision; Auditory Attention. **General Work Activities:** *Information Input*—Getting Information Needed to Do the Job; Inspecting Equipment, Structures, Materials; Monitoring Processes, Materials, and Surroundings. *Mental Process*—Judging Qualities of Things, Services, Other People's Work; Evaluating Information Against Standards; Organizing, Planning, and Prioritizing. *Work Output*—Performing General Physical Activities; Handling and Moving Objects; Controlling Machines and Processes. *Interacting with Others*—Communicating with Other Workers; Coordinating Work and Activities of Others; Monitoring and Controlling Resources; Performing for or Working with the Public; Establishing and Maintaining Relationships; Communicating with Persons Outside Organization. **Physical Work Conditions:** Outdoors; Using Hands on Objects, Tools, or Controls; Standing. **Other Job Characteristics:** Consequence of Error; Frustrating Circumstances; Importance of Being Exact or Accurate; Importance of Being Sure All Is Done.

Experience: Job Zone 3. Previous work-related skill, knowledge, or experience is required. **Job Preparation:** SVP 6.0 to less than 7.0—More than 1 year and less than 4 years. **Knowledge:** Building and Construction; Mechanical; Design; Engineering and Technology; Chemistry. **Instructional Program:** 460499 Construction and Building Finishers and Managers, Other.

Related DOT Jobs: 844.364-010 Cement Mason; 844.364-014 Cement-Mason Apprentice; 844.461-010 Concrete-Stone Finisher; 844.684-010 Concrete Rubber.

47-2053.00 Terrazzo Workers and Finishers (Cement Masons, Concrete Finishers, and Terrazzo Workers)

Education: Long-term O-T-J training

Employed: 139,194

Openings: 14,084

Projected Growth: 6.1%

Earnings: $25,770

Apply a mixture of cement, sand, pigment, or marble chips to floors, stairways, and cabinet fixtures to fashion durable and decorative surfaces.

Wets concrete surface, and rubs with stone to smooth surface and obtain specified finish. Builds wooden molds, and clamps molds around area to be repaired, using hand tools. Signals truck driver to position truck to facilitate pouring concrete; moves chute to direct concrete on forms. Mixes cement, sand, and water to produce concrete, grout, or slurry, using hoe, trowel, tamper, scraper, or concrete-mixing machine. Applies muriatic acid to clean surface, and rinses with water. Molds expansion joints and edges, using edging tools, jointers, and straightedge. Sprinkles colored marble or stone chips, powdered steel, or coloring powder over surface to produce prescribed finish. Cuts out damaged areas, drills holes for reinforcing rods, and positions reinforcing rods to repair concrete, using power saw and drill. Cleans chipped area, using wire brush, and feels and observes surface to detect rough or uneven surface. Spreads, levels, and smoothes concrete, using rake, shovel, hand or power trowel, hand or power screed, and float. Produces rough concrete surface, using broom. Spreads roofing paper on surface of foundation, and spreads concrete onto roofing paper with trowel to form terrazzo base. Pushes roller over surface to imbed chips in surface. Polishes surface, using polishing or surfacing machine. Chips, scrapes, and grinds high spots, ridges, and rough projections to finish concrete, using pneumatic chisel, hand chisel, or hand tools. Wets surface to prepare for bonding, fills holes and cracks with grout or slurry, and smoothes, using trowel. Cuts metal division strips, and presses them into terrazzo base so that top edges form desired design or pattern.

GOE Number, Interest Area, and Work Group: 06.02.01; Construction, Mining, and Drilling; Construction: Masonry, Stone, and Brick Work. **Personality Type:** Realistic. Realistic occupations frequently involve work activities that include practical, hands-on problems and solutions. These occupations often deal with plants, animals, and real-world materials like wood, tools, and machinery. Many of the occupations require working outside and do not involve a lot of paperwork or working closely with others. **Work Values:** Moral Values; Company Policies and Practices; Compensation; Ability Utilization; Coworkers; Achievement. **Skills:** Product Inspection; Operations Analysis; Mathematics; Identification of Key Causes; Equipment Selection. **Abilities:** *Cognitive*—Information Ordering; Written Comprehension; Oral Expression; Visualization; Problem Sensitivity; Deductive Reasoning. *Psychomotor*—Manual Dexterity; Wrist-Finger Speed; Multilimb Coordination; Arm-Hand Steadiness. *Physical*—Static Strength; Trunk Strength; Extent Flexibility. *Sensory*—Visual Color Discrimination; Far Vision; Auditory Attention. **General Work Activities:** *Information Input*—Getting Information Needed to Do the Job; Inspecting Equipment, Structures, Materials; Monitoring Processes, Materials, and Surroundings. *Mental Process*—Judging Qualities of Things, Services, Other People's Work; Evaluating Information Against Standards; Organizing, Planning, and Prioritizing. *Work Output*—Performing General Physical Activities; Handling and Moving Objects; Controlling Machines and Processes. *Interacting with Others*—Communicating with Other Workers; Coordinating Work and Activities of Others; Communicating with Persons Outside Organization; Establishing and Maintaining Relationships; Monitoring and Controlling Resources; Performing for or Working with the Public. **Physical Work Conditions:** Outdoors; Using Hands on Objects, Tools, or Controls; Standing. **Other Job Characteristics:** Consequence of Error; Frustrating Circumstances; Importance of Being Exact or Accurate; Importance of Being Sure All Is Done.

Experience: Job Zone 3. Previous work-related skill, knowledge, or experience is required. **Job Preparation:** SVP 6.0 to less than 7.0—More than 1 year and less than 4 years. **Knowledge:** Building and Construction; Design; Mechanical; Engineering and Technology; Chemistry. **Instructional Program:** 460499 Construction and Building Finishers and Managers, Other.

Related DOT Jobs: 861.381-046 Terrazzo Worker; 861.381-050 Terrazzo-Worker Apprentice.

47-2061.00 Construction Laborers (All Other Construction Trades Workers)

Education: No data available.

Employed: 89,770

Openings: No data available.

Projected Growth: No data available.

Earnings: $24,600

Perform tasks involving physical labor at building, highway, and heavy construction projects, at tunnel and shaft excavations, and at demolition sites. Operate hand and power tools of all types: air hammers, earth tampers, cement mixers, small mechanical hoists, surveying and measuring equipment, and a variety of other equipment and instruments. Clean and prepare sites; dig trenches. Set braces to support the sides of excavations; erect scaffolding. Clean up rubble and debris; remove asbestos, lead, and other hazardous waste materials. Assist other craft workers.

Mops, brushes, or spreads paints, cleaning solutions, or other compounds over surfaces, to clean or provide protection. Smoothes and finishes freshly poured cement or concrete, using float, trowel, screed, or powered cement-finishing tool. Applies caulking compounds by hand or with caulking gun to seal crevices. Tends machine that pumps concrete, grout, cement, sand, plaster, or stucco through spray gun for application to ceilings and walls. Lubricates, cleans, and repairs machinery, equipment, and tools. Sprays materials such as water, sand, steam, vinyl, paint, or stucco through hose, to clean, coat, or seal surfaces. Razes buildings and salvages useful materials. Cleans construction site to eliminate possible hazards. Mixes concrete, using portable mixer. Mixes ingredients to create compounds used to cover or clean surfaces. Tends pumps, compressors, and generators to provide power for tools, machinery, and equipment or to heat and move materials such as asphalt. Erects and disassembles scaffolding, shoring, braces, and other temporary structures. Grinds, scrapes, sands, or polishes surfaces such as concrete, marble, terrazzo, or wood flooring, using abrasive tools or machines. Builds and positions forms for pouring concrete and dismantles forms after use, using saws, hammers, nails, or bolts. Signals equipment operators to facilitate alignment, movement, and adjustment of machinery, equipment, and materials. Digs ditches and levels earth to grade specifications, using pick and shovel. Positions, joins, aligns, and seals structural components such as concrete wall sections and pipes. Loads and unloads trucks; hauls and hoists materials. Measures, marks, and records openings and distances to lay out area to be graded or to erect building structures.

GOE Number, Interest Area, and Work Group: 06.04.01; Construction, Mining, and Drilling; Hands-on Work: Construction, Extraction, and Maintenance. **Personality Type:** Realistic. Realistic occupations frequently involve work activities that include practical, hands-on problems and solutions. These occupations often deal with plants, animals, and real-world materials like wood, tools, and machinery. Many of the occupations require working outside and do not involve a lot of paperwork or working closely with others. **Work Values:** Moral Values; Coworkers; Activity; Supervision, Technical; Supervision, Human Relations; Company Policies and Practices. **Skills:** Equipment Maintenance; Mathematics; Equipment Selection; Operation and Control; Product Inspection. **Abilities:** *Cognitive*—Information Ordering; Problem Sensitivity; Oral Comprehension; Number Facility; Oral Expression; Time Sharing. *Psychomotor*—Control Precision; Speed of Limb Movement; Arm-Hand Steadiness; Multilimb Coordination. *Physical*—Static Strength; Trunk Strength; Dynamic Strength. *Sensory*—Glare Sensitivity. **General Work Activities:** *Information Input*—Monitoring Processes, Materials, and Surroundings; Inspecting Equipment, Structures, Materials; Getting Information Needed to Do the Job. *Mental Process*—Updating and Using Job-Relevant Knowledge; Evaluating Information Against Standards; Making Decisions and Solving Problems. *Work Output*—Performing General Physical Activities; Handling and Moving Objects; Controlling Machines and Processes. *Interacting with Others*—Communicating with Other Workers; Assisting and Caring for Others; Establishing and Maintaining Relationships; Communicating with Persons Outside Organization. **Physical Work Conditions:** Outdoors; Standing; Using Hands on Objects, Tools, or Controls. **Other Job Characteristics:** Consequence of Error; Importance of Being Exact or Accurate; Importance of Being Sure All Is Done.

Experience: Job Zone 2. Some previous work-related skill, knowledge, or experience may be helpful, but usually is not needed. **Job Preparation:** SVP 4.00 to 5.99—6 months to less than 2 years. **Knowledge:** Building and Construction; Mechanical; Engineering and Technology; Mathematics; Design. **Instructional Programs:** 460501 Plumber and Pipefitter; 469999 Construction Trades, Other; 490202 Construction Equipment Operator.

Related DOT Jobs: 800.684-010 Riveter; 800.684-014 Riveter, Pneumatic; 842.665-010 Plaster-Machine Tender; 849.665-010 Pump Tender, Cement Based Materials; 850.467-010 Grade Checker; 853.665-010 Asphalt-Distributor Tender; 853.685-010 Asphalt-Heater Tender; 864.684-010 Floor and Wall Applier, Liquid; 869.487-010 Measurer; 869.664-010 Concrete-Building Assembler; 869.664-014 Construction Worker I; 869.665-010 Auxiliary-Equipment Tender; 869.667-010 Column Precaster; 869.684-082 Asbestos Removal Worker; 891.684-022 Building Cleaner; 891.685-010 Steam-Cleaning-Machine Operator; 899.684-046 Maintenance Worker, Municipal.

47-2071.00 Paving, Surfacing, and Tamping Equipment Operators (Paving, Surfacing, and Tamping Equipment Operators)

Education: Moderate-term O-T-J training
Employed: 73,980
Openings: 13,780
Projected Growth: 10.6%
Earnings: $24,510

Operate equipment used for applying concrete, asphalt, or other materials to road beds, parking lots, airport runways, and airport taxiways. Operate equipment used for tamping gravel, dirt, or other materials. Includes concrete and asphalt paving machine operators, form tampers, tamping machine operators, and stone spreader operators.

Operates machine to spread, smooth, or steel-reinforce stone, concrete, or asphalt. Operates machine to mix and spray binding, waterproofing, and curing compounds. Operates machine to clean or cut expansion joints in concrete or asphalt and to rout out cracks in pavement. Starts machine, engages clutch, pushes and moves levers, and turns wheels to control and guide machine along forms or guidelines. Drives and operates curbing machine to extrude concrete or asphalt curbing. Monitors machine operation and observes distribution of paving material to adjust machine settings or material flow. Installs dies, cutters, and extensions to screed onto machine, using hand tools. Drives machine onto truck trailer and drives truck to transport machine to and from job site. Operates machine or manually rolls surfaces to compact earth fills, foundation forms, and finished road materials, according to grade specifications. Fills tank, hopper, or machine with paving materials. Cleans, maintains, and repairs equipment, according to specifications, using mechanic's hand tools; reports malfunction to supervisor. Sets up forms and lays out guidelines for curbs, according to written specifications, using string, spray paint, and concrete-water mix. Lights burner or starts heating unit of machine and regulates temperature.

GOE Number, Interest Area, and Work Group: 06.02.03; Construction, Mining, and Drilling; Construction: General. **Personality Type:** Realistic. Realistic occupations frequently involve work activities that include practical, hands-on problems and solutions. These occupations often deal with plants, animals, and real-world materials like wood, tools, and machinery. Many of the occupations require working outside and do not involve a lot of paperwork or working closely with others. **Work Values:** Moral Values; Independence; Supervision, Technical; Supervision, Human Relations; Compensation. **Skills:** Operation and Control; Equipment Selection; Operation Monitoring; Product Inspection; Equipment Maintenance. **Abilities:** *Cognitive*—Information Ordering; Problem Sensitivity; Visualization; Spatial Orientation; Time Sharing. *Psychomotor*—Control Precision; Manual Dexterity; Reaction Time. *Physical*—Static Strength; Extent Flexibility; Trunk Strength; Explosive Strength. *Sensory*—Far Vision; Depth Perception; Peripheral Vision. **General Work Activities:** *Information Input*—Monitoring Processes, Materials, and Surroundings; Getting Information Needed to Do the Job; Inspecting Equipment, Structures, Materials. *Mental Process*—Evaluating Information

Against Standards; Updating and Using Job-Relevant Knowledge; Making Decisions and Solving Problems; Judging Qualities of Things, Services, Other People's Work; Organizing, Planning, and Prioritizing. *Work Output*—Controlling Machines and Processes; Operating Vehicles or Equipment; Handling and Moving Objects. *Interacting with Others*—Communicating with Other Workers; Coordinating Work and Activities of Others; Assisting and Caring for Others; Interpreting Meaning of Information to Others; Performing Administrative Activities. **Physical Work Conditions:** Outdoors; Using Hands on Objects, Tools, or Controls; Hazardous Equipment. **Other Job Characteristics:** Degree of Automation; Consequence of Error; Importance of Being Sure All Is Done.

Experience: Job Zone 2. Some previous work-related skill, knowledge, or experience may be helpful, but usually is not needed. **Job Preparation:** SVP 4.00 to 5.99—6 months to less than 2 years. **Knowledge:** Mechanical; Transportation; Building and Construction; Physics; Production and Processing. **Instructional Program:** 490202 Construction Equipment Operator.

Related DOT Jobs: 853.663-010 Asphalt-Paving-Machine Operator; 853.663-014 Concrete-Paving-Machine Operator; 853.663-018 Road-Oiling-Truck Driver; 853.663-022 Stone-Spreader Operator; 853.683-010 Curb-Machine Operator; 853.683-014 Heater-Planer Operator; 853.683-018 Joint-Cleaning-and-Grooving-Machine Operator; 859.683-022 Reinforcing-Steel-Machine Operator; 859.683-026 Road-Mixer Operator; 859.683-030 Road-Roller Operator; 869.683-010 Form-Tamper Operator; 869.683-018 Tamping-Machine Operator.

47-2072.00 Pile-Driver Operators (Pile-Driver Operators)

Education: No data available.

Employed: 2,280

Openings: No data available.

Projected Growth: No data available.

Earnings: $42,870

Operate pile drivers mounted on skids, barges, crawler treads, or locomotive cranes to drive pilings for retaining walls, bulkheads, and foundations of structures such as buildings, bridges, and piers.

Moves levers and turns valves to activate power hammer or to raise and lower drophammer which drives piles to required depth. Moves hand and foot levers, to control hoisting equipment to position piling leads, hoist piling into leads, and position hammer over piling.

GOE Number, Interest Area, and Work Group: 06.02.03; Construction, Mining, and Drilling; Construction: General. **Personality Type:** Realistic. Realistic occupations frequently involve work activities that include practical, hands-on problems and solutions. These occupations often deal with plants, animals, and real-world materials like wood, tools, and machinery. Many of the occupations require working outside and do not involve a lot of paperwork or working closely with others. **Work Values:** Moral Values; Independence; Supervision, Technical; Supervision, Human Relations; Activity. **Skills:** Operation and Control; Operation Monitoring. **Abilities:** *Cognitive*—Information Ordering; Spatial Orientation; Written Expression; Visualization; Selective Attention. *Psychomotor*—Multilimb Coordination; Control Preci-

sion; Speed of Limb Movement. *Physical*—Extent Flexibility; Explosive Strength; Dynamic Flexibility; Gross Body Coordination. *Sensory*—Depth Perception; Far Vision; Glare Sensitivity; Peripheral Vision. **General Work Activities:** *Information Input*—Getting Information Needed to Do the Job; Monitoring Processes, Materials, and Surroundings; Identifying Objects, Actions, and Events. *Mental Process*—Evaluating Information Against Standards; Processing Information; Analyzing Data or Information. *Work Output*—Controlling Machines and Processes; Operating Vehicles or Equipment; Handling and Moving Objects. *Interacting with Others*—Communicating with Other Workers; Developing and Building Teams; Establishing and Maintaining Relationships. **Physical Work Conditions:** Outdoors; Using Hands on Objects, Tools, or Controls; Whole Body Vibration; Sitting; Hazardous Equipment; Distracting Sounds and Noise Levels. **Other Job Characteristics:** Degree of Automation; Consequence of Error; Pace Determined by Speed of Equipment; Importance of Being Sure All Is Done; Importance of Being Exact or Accurate.

Experience: Job Zone 2. Some previous work-related skill, knowledge, or experience may be helpful, but usually is not needed. **Job Preparation:** SVP 4.00 to 5.99—6 months to less than 2 years. **Knowledge:** Building and Construction; Mechanical; Engineering and Technology; Physics; Public Safety and Security. **Instructional Program:** 490202 Construction Equipment Operator.

Related DOT Job: 859.682-018 Pile-Driver Operator.

47-2073.00 Operating Engineers and Other Construction Equipment Operators (Operating Engineers)

Education: Moderate-term O-T-J training

Employed: 125,500

Openings: 19,524

Projected Growth: 7.9%

Earnings: $35,260

Operate one or several types of power construction equipment, such as motor graders, bulldozers, scrapers, compressors, pumps, derricks, shovels, tractors, or front-end loaders, to excavate, move, and grade earth, to erect structures, or to pour concrete or other hard surface pavement. Repair and maintain equipment.

GOE Number, Interest Area, and Work Group: 06.02.03; Construction, Mining, and Drilling; Construction: General. **Instructional Program:** 490202 Construction Equipment Operator. **Note:** The Department of Labor has not collected some data for this job, so it has fewer details than the other descriptions.

47-2073.01 Grader, Bulldozer, and Scraper Operators (Grader, Bulldozer, and Scraper Operators)

Education: Moderate-term O-T-J training

Employed: 121,788

Openings: 5,729

Projected Growth: 5.7%

Earnings: $26,920

Operate machines or vehicles equipped with blades, to remove, distribute, level, or grade earth.

Aligns machine, cutterhead, or depth-gauge marker with reference stakes and guidelines on ground; positions equipment following hand signals of assistant. Connects hydraulic hoses, belts, mechanical linkage, or power takeoff shaft to tractor. Signals operator to guide movement of tractor-drawn machine. Greases, oils, and performs minor repairs on tractor, using grease gun, oilcans, and hand tools. Fastens bulldozer blade or other attachment to tractor, using hitches. Starts engine; moves throttle, switches, and levers; depresses pedals, to operate machines, equipment, and attachments. Drives equipment in successive passes over working area to achieve specified result such as grading terrain or removing, dumping, or spreading earth and rock.

GOE Number, Interest Area, and Work Group: 06.02.03; Construction, Mining, and Drilling; Construction: General. **Personality Type:** Realistic. Realistic occupations frequently involve work activities that include practical, hands-on problems and solutions. These occupations often deal with plants, animals, and real-world materials like wood, tools, and machinery. Many of the occupations require working outside and do not involve a lot of paperwork or working closely with others. **Work Values:** Moral Values; Independence; Supervision, Human Relations; Company Policies and Practices; Compensation; Achievement; Supervision, Technical. **Skills:** Operation and Control; Equipment Selection; Operation Monitoring; Repairing; Equipment Maintenance. **Abilities:** *Cognitive*—Problem Sensitivity; Spatial Orientation; Information Ordering; Visualization; Selective Attention; Time Sharing. *Psychomotor*—Control Precision; Reaction Time; Manual Dexterity. *Physical*—Static Strength; Trunk Strength; Explosive Strength; Dynamic Strength. *Sensory*—Far Vision; Depth Perception; Glare Sensitivity; Peripheral Vision. **General Work Activities:** *Information Input*—Monitoring Processes, Materials, and Surroundings; Identifying Objects, Actions, and Events; Estimating Needed Characteristics. *Mental Process*—Organizing, Planning, and Prioritizing; Updating and Using Job-Relevant Knowledge; Evaluating Information Against Standards. *Work Output*—Operating Vehicles or Equipment; Handling and Moving Objects; Performing General Physical Activities; Implementing Ideas and Programs. *Interacting with Others*—Communicating with Other Workers; Coordinating Work and Activities of Others; Assisting and Caring for Others. **Physical Work Conditions:** Outdoors; Using Hands on Objects, Tools, or Controls; Hazardous Equipment; Whole Body Vibration; Sitting. **Other Job Characteristics:** Degree of Automation; Consequence of Error; Frustrating Circumstances.

Experience: Job Zone 2. Some previous work-related skill, knowledge, or experience may be helpful, but usually is not needed. **Job Preparation:** SVP 4.00 to 5.99—6 months to less than 2 years. **Knowledge:** Mechanical; Transportation; Physics; Engineering and Technology; Production and Processing; Building and Construction. **Instructional Program:** 490202 Construction Equipment Operator.

Related DOT Jobs: 850.663-014 Elevating-Grader Operator; 850.663-022 Motor-Grader Operator; 850.683-010 Bulldozer Operator I; 850.683-014 Ditcher Operator; 850.683-022 Form-Grader Operator; 850.683-038 Scraper Operator; 850.683-046 Utility-Tractor Operator; 955.463-010 Sanitary Landfill Operator.

47-2073.02 Operating Engineers (Operating Engineers)

Education: Moderate-term O-T-J training
Employed: 125,500
Openings: 19,524
Projected Growth: 7.9%
Earnings: $35,260

Operate several types of power construction equipment, such as compressors, pumps, hoists, derricks, cranes, shovels, tractors, scrapers, or motor graders, to excavate, move, and grade earth, to erect structures, or to pour concrete or other hard surface pavement. Repair and maintain equipment.

Adjusts handwheels and depresses pedals to drive machines and control attachments such as blades, buckets, scrapers, and swing booms. Turns valves to control air and water output of compressors and pumps. Repairs and maintains equipment.

GOE Number, Interest Area, and Work Group: 06.02.03; Construction, Mining, and Drilling; Construction: General. **Personality Type:** Realistic. Realistic occupations frequently involve work activities that include practical, hands-on problems and solutions. These occupations often deal with plants, animals, and real-world materials like wood, tools, and machinery. Many of the occupations require working outside and do not involve a lot of paperwork or working closely with others. **Work Values:** Moral Values; Independence; Supervision, Technical; Company Policies and Practices; Activity; Compensation; Supervision, Human Relations. **Skills:** Operation and Control; Equipment Maintenance; Repairing; Operation Monitoring; Troubleshooting. **Abilities:** *Cognitive*—Problem Sensitivity; Visualization; Information Ordering; Deductive Reasoning; Oral Expression. *Psychomotor*—Control Precision; Multilimb Coordination; Reaction Time; Response Orientation. *Physical*—Static Strength; Trunk Strength; Explosive Strength. *Sensory*—Depth Perception. **General Work Activities:** *Information Input*—Monitoring Processes, Materials, and Surroundings; Identifying Objects, Actions, and Events; Getting Information Needed to Do the Job; Inspecting Equipment, Structures, Materials. *Mental Process*—Organizing, Planning, and Prioritizing; Judging Qualities of Things, Services, Other People's Work; Making Decisions and Solving Problems. *Work Output*—Controlling Machines and Processes; Handling and Moving Objects; Repairing and Maintaining Mechanical Equipment; Operating Vehicles or Equipment. *Interacting with Others*—Influencing Others or Selling; Communicating with Persons Outside Organization; Communicating with Other Workers. **Physical Work Conditions:** Hazardous Equipment; Using Hands on Objects, Tools, or Controls; Common Protective or Safety Attire; Outdoors. **Other Job Characteristics:** Consequence of Error; Degree of Automation; Importance of Being Sure All Is Done.

Experience: Job Zone 3. Previous work-related skill, knowledge, or experience is required. **Job Preparation:** SVP 6.0 to less than 7.0—More than 1 year and less than 4 years. **Knowledge:** Mechanical; Building and Construction; Engineering and Technology; Physics; Sales and Marketing. **Instructional Program:** 490202 Construction Equipment Operator.

Related DOT Jobs: 859.683-010 Operating Engineer; 859.683-014 Operating-Engineer Apprentice.

47-2081.00 Drywall and Ceiling Tile Installers
(Drywall Installers)

Education: No data available.

Employed: 85,910

Openings: No data available.

Projected Growth: No data available.

Earnings: $29,150

Apply plasterboard or other wallboard to ceilings or interior walls of buildings. Apply or mount acoustical tiles, or blocks, strips, or sheets of shock-absorbing materials, to ceilings and walls of buildings, to reduce or reflect sound. Apply or mount materials of a decorative quality. Includes lathers who fasten wooden, metal, or rockboard lath to walls, ceilings, or partitions of buildings, to provide support base for plaster, fireproofing, or acoustical material.

GOE Number, Interest Area, and Work Group: 06.02.02; Construction, Mining, and Drilling; Construction: Construction and Maintenance. **Instructional Program:** 469999 Construction Trades, Other. **Note:** The Department of Labor has not collected some data for this job, so it has fewer details than the other descriptions.

47-2081.01 Ceiling Tile Installers (Ceiling Tile Installers and Acoustical Carpenters)

Education: Moderate-term O-T-J training

Employed: 15,580

Openings: 3,499

Projected Growth: 8.9%

Earnings: $31,750

Apply plasterboard or other wallboard to ceilings or interior walls of buildings. Apply or mount acoustical tiles, or blocks, strips, or sheets of shock-absorbing materials, to ceilings and walls of buildings, to reduce or reflect sound. Apply or mount materials of a decorative quality. Includes lathers who fasten wooden, metal, or rockboard lath to walls, ceilings, or partitions of buildings, to provide support base for plaster, fireproofing, or acoustical material.

Hangs dry lines (stretched string) to wall molding to guide positioning of main runners. Nails channels or wood furring strips to surfaces to provide mounting for tile. Measures and marks surface to lay out work according to blueprints and drawings. Washes concrete surfaces with washing soda and zinc sulfate solution before mounting tile to increase adhesive qualities of surfaces. Cuts tiles for fixture and borders, using keyhole saw; inserts tiles into supporting framework. Scribes and cuts edges of tile to fit wall where wall molding is not specified. Applies cement to back of tile and presses tile into place, aligning with layout marks and joints of previously laid tile. Nails or screws molding to wall to support; seals joint between ceiling tile and wall. Applies acoustical tiles or shock-absorbing materials to ceilings and walls of buildings to reduce or reflect sound and to decorate rooms. Inspects furrings, mechanical mountings, and masonry surface for plumbness and level, using spirit or water level.

GOE Number, Interest Area, and Work Group: 06.02.02; Construction, Mining, and Drilling; Construction: Construction and Maintenance. **Personality Type:** Realistic. Realistic occupations frequently involve work activities that include practical, hands-on problems and solutions. These occupations often deal with plants, animals, and real-world materials like wood, tools, and machinery. Many of the occupations require working outside and do not involve a lot of paperwork or working closely with others. **Work Values:** Moral Values; Independence; Supervision, Human Relations; Company Policies and Practices; Activity; Compensation. **Skills:** Mathematics; Product Inspection; Visioning; Equipment Selection; Information Organization; Solution Appraisal. **Abilities:** *Cognitive*—Visualization; Problem Sensitivity; Perceptual Speed; Deductive Reasoning; Mathematical Reasoning; Written Comprehension. *Psychomotor*—Arm-Hand Steadiness; Multilimb Coordination; Manual Dexterity. *Physical*—Extent Flexibility; Static Strength; Gross Body Equilibrium; Dynamic Flexibility; Explosive Strength; Dynamic Strength. *Sensory*—Depth Perception; Visual Color Discrimination; Peripheral Vision; Night Vision. **General Work Activities:** *Information Input*—Inspecting Equipment, Structures, Materials; Getting Information Needed to Do the Job; Estimating Needed Characteristics. *Mental Process*—Making Decisions and Solving Problems; Processing Information; Evaluating Information Against Standards. *Work Output*—Handling and Moving Objects; Performing General Physical Activities; Implementing Ideas and Programs. *Interacting with Others*—Monitoring and Controlling Resources; Establishing and Maintaining Relationships; Communicating with Other Workers. **Physical Work Conditions:** Using Hands on Objects, Tools, or Controls; Indoors; Standing. **Other Job Characteristics:** Importance of Being Sure All Is Done; Importance of Being Exact or Accurate; Consequence of Error.

Experience: Job Zone 4. A minimum of two to four years of work-related skill, knowledge, or experience is needed. **Job Preparation:** SVP 7.0 to less than 8.0—2 years to less than 10 years. **Knowledge:** Building and Construction; Mathematics; Design; Engineering and Technology; Mechanical. **Instructional Program:** 460201 Carpenter.

Related DOT Job: 860.381-010 Acoustical Carpenter.

47-2081.02 Drywall Installers (Drywall Installers)

Education: No data available.

Employed: 85,910

Openings: No data available.

Projected Growth: No data available.

Earnings: $29,150

Apply plasterboard or other wallboard to ceilings and interior walls of buildings.

Installs blanket insulation between studs and tacks plastic moisture barrier over insulation. Reads blueprints and other specifications to determine method of installation, work procedures, and material and tool requirements. Measures and marks cutting lines on framing, drywall, and trim, using tape measure, straightedge, square, and marking devices. Cuts metal or wood framing, angle and channel iron, and trim, to size, using cutting tools. Suspends angle iron grid and channel iron from ceiling, using wire. Trims rough edges from wallboard to maintain even joints, using knife. Lays out reference lines and points, computes position of framing and furring channels; marks position, using chalkline. Removes plaster, drywall, or paneling, using crowbar and hammer. Installs horizontal and vertical metal or wooden studs for attachment of wallboard on interior walls, using hand tools. Cuts openings into board for electrical outlets, windows, vents, or fixtures, using keyhole saw or other cutting tools. Fits and fastens wallboard or sheetrock into specified position, using hand tools, portable power tools, or adhesive. Assembles and installs metal framing and decorative trim for windows, doorways, and bents.

GOE Number, Interest Area, and Work Group: 06.02.02; Construction, Mining, and Drilling; Construction: Construction and Maintenance. **Personality Type:** Realistic. Realistic occupations frequently involve work activities that include practical, hands-on problems and solutions. These occupations often deal with plants, animals, and real-world materials like wood, tools, and machinery. Many of the occupations require working outside and do not involve a lot of paperwork or working closely with others. **Work Values:** Moral Values; Supervision, Human Relations; Activity; Independence; Company Policies and Practices. **Skills:** Installation; Equipment Selection; Product Inspection; Mathematics; Reading Comprehension. **Abilities:** *Cognitive*—Written Comprehension; Information Ordering; Deductive Reasoning; Number Facility; Visualization. *Psychomotor*—Control Precision; Manual Dexterity; Multilimb Coordination; Wrist-Finger Speed. *Physical*—Extent Flexibility; Static Strength; Trunk Strength. **General Work Activities:** *Information Input*—Getting Information Needed to Do the Job; Estimating Needed Characteristics; Inspecting Equipment, Structures, Materials. *Mental Process*—Evaluating Information Against Standards; Making Decisions and Solving Problems; Analyzing Data or Information; Organizing, Planning, and Prioritizing; Judging Qualities of Things, Services, Other People's Work; Processing Information. *Work Output*—Performing General Physical Activities; Handling and Moving Objects; Controlling Machines and Processes. *Interacting with Others*—Communicating with Other Workers; Establishing and Maintaining Relationships; Communicating with Persons Outside Organization. **Physical Work Conditions:** Indoors; Using Hands on Objects, Tools, or Controls; Standing. **Other Job Characteristics:** Importance of Being Sure All Is Done; Importance of Being Exact or Accurate; Consequence of Error.

Experience: Job Zone 2. Some previous work-related skill, knowledge, or experience may be helpful, but usually is not needed. **Job Preparation:** SVP 4.00 to 5.99—6 months to less than 2 years. **Knowledge:** Building and Construction; Design; Mechanical; Engineering and Technology; Mathematics. **Instructional Program:** 469999 Construction Trades, Other.

Related DOT Jobs: 842.361-030 Dry-Wall Applicator; 842.684-014 Dry-Wall Applicator; 869.684-050 Sheetrock Applicator.

47-2082.00 Tapers (Tapers)

Education: No data available.
Employed: 34,910
Openings: No data available.
Projected Growth: No data available.
Earnings: $32,060

Seal joints between plasterboard or other wallboard to prepare wall surface for painting or papering.

Countersinks nails or screws below surface of wall prior to applying sealing compound, using hammer or screwdriver. Tapes joint, using mechanical applicator that spreads compound and embeds tape in one operation. Presses paper tape over joint to embed tape into sealing compound and seal joint. Spreads and smoothes cementing material over tape, using trowel or floating machine to blend joint with wall surface. Applies texturizing compound and primer to walls and ceiling preparatory to final finishing, using brushes, roller, or spray gun. Fills cracks and holes in walls and ceiling with sealing compound. Installs metal molding at corners in lieu of sealant and tape. Sands rough spots after cement has dried. Spreads sealing compound between boards, using trowel, broadknife, or spatula. Mixes sealing compound by hand or with portable electric mixer.

GOE Number, Interest Area, and Work Group: 06.02.03; Construction, Mining, and Drilling; Construction: General. **Personality Type:** Realistic. Realistic occupations frequently involve work activities that include practical, hands-on problems and solutions. These occupations often deal with plants, animals, and real-world materials like wood, tools, and machinery. Many of the occupations require working outside and do not involve a lot of paperwork or working closely with others. **Work Values:** Moral Values; Independence; Company Policies and Practices; Supervision, Human Relations; Activity. **Skills:** Coordination; Equipment Selection; Product Inspection. **Abilities:** *Cognitive*—Deductive Reasoning; Information Ordering; Mathematical Reasoning; Visualization; Category Flexibility; Selective Attention. *Psychomotor*—Manual Dexterity; Wrist-Finger Speed; Arm-Hand Steadiness. *Physical*—Extent Flexibility; Explosive Strength; Gross Body Equilibrium; Dynamic Flexibility. *Sensory*—Depth Perception; Night Vision; Glare Sensitivity; Peripheral Vision. **General Work Activities:** *Information Input*—Getting Information Needed to Do the Job; Inspecting Equipment, Structures, Materials; Monitoring Processes, Materials, and Surroundings. *Mental Process*—Evaluating Information Against Standards; Organizing, Planning, and Prioritizing; Analyzing Data or Information; Making Decisions and Solving Problems; Judging Qualities of Things, Services, Other People's Work. *Work Output*—Performing General Physical Activities; Handling and Moving Objects; Controlling Machines and Processes. *Interacting with Others*—Communicating with Other Workers; Establishing and Maintaining Relationships; Assisting and Caring for Others. **Physical Work Conditions:** Using Hands on Objects, Tools, or Controls; Indoors; Standing. **Other Job Characteristics:** Importance of Being Sure All Is Done; Importance of Being Exact or Accurate; Consequence of Error; Frustrating Circumstances.

Experience: Job Zone 2. Some previous work-related skill, knowledge, or experience may be helpful, but usually is not needed. **Job Preparation:** SVP 4.00 to 5.99—6 months to less than 2 years. **Knowledge:** Building and Construction; Engineering and Technology; Chemistry; English Language; Mechanical; Public Safety and Security. **Instructional Program:** 469999 Construction Trades, Other.

Related DOT Job: 842.664-010 Taper.

47-2111.00 Electricians (Electricians)

Education: Long-term O-T-J training

Employed: 656,151

Openings: 92,734

Projected Growth: 10.3%

Earnings: $35,310

Install, maintain, and repair electrical wiring, equipment, and fixtures. Ensure that work is in accordance with relevant codes. Install or service street lights, intercom systems, or electrical control systems.

Installs electrical wiring, equipment, apparatus, and fixtures, using hand tools and power tools. Climbs ladder to install, maintain, or repair electrical wiring, equipment, and fixtures. Inspects systems and electrical parts to detect hazards, defects, and need for adjustments or repair. Plans layout and installation of electrical wiring, equipment, and fixtures consistent with specifications and local codes. Maintains, repairs, or replaces wiring, equipment, and fixtures, using hand tools. Readies and assembles electrical wiring, equipment, and fixtures, using specifications and hand tools. Prepares sketches of location of wiring and equipment, or follows blueprints, to determine location of equipment and conformance to safety codes. Constructs and fabricates parts, using hand tools and specifications. Possesses electrician's license or identification card to meet governmental regulations. Directs and trains workers to install, maintain, or repair electrical wiring, equipment, and fixtures. Drives vehicle, operates flood lights, and places flares during power failure or emergency. Diagnoses malfunctioning systems, apparatus, and components, using test equipment and hand tools. Tests electrical systems and continuity of circuits in electrical wiring, equipment, and fixtures, using testing devices such as ohmmeter, voltmeter, and oscilloscope.

GOE Number, Interest Area, and Work Group: 06.02.02; Construction, Mining, and Drilling; Construction: Construction and Maintenance. **Personality Type:** Realistic. Realistic occupations frequently involve work activities that include practical, hands-on problems and solutions. These occupations often deal with plants, animals, and real-world materials like wood, tools, and machinery. Many of the occupations require working outside and do not involve a lot of paperwork or working closely with others. **Work Values:** Moral Values; Ability Utilization; Compensation; Responsibility; Activity. **Skills:** Installation; Repairing; Equipment Selection; Testing; Troubleshooting; Mathematics. **Abilities:** *Cognitive*—Problem Sensitivity; Information Ordering; Written Comprehension; Memorization; Oral Expression. *Psychomotor*—Finger Dexterity; Arm-Hand Steadiness; Manual Dexterity. *Physical*—Extent Flexibility; Trunk Strength; Static Strength. *Sensory*—Near Vision; Visual Color Discrimination; Speech Clarity. **General Work Activities:** *Information Input*—Getting Information Needed to Do the Job; Inspecting Equipment, Structures, Materials; Monitoring Processes, Materials, and Surroundings. *Mental Process*—Making Decisions and Solving Problems; Updating and Using Job-Relevant Knowledge; Judging Qualities of Things, Services, Other People's Work. *Work Output*—Handling and Moving Objects; Repairing and Maintaining Electrical Equipment; Implementing Ideas and Programs. *Interacting with Others*—Communicating with Other Workers; Teaching Others; Coordinating Work and Activities of Others. **Physical Work Conditions:** Using Hands on Objects, Tools, or Controls; Indoors; Standing; Hazardous Conditions; Common Protective or Safety Attire; Hazardous Equipment. **Other Job Characteristics:** Consequence of Error; Importance of Being Sure All Is Done; Importance of Being Exact or Accurate.

Experience: Job Zone 3. Previous work-related skill, knowledge, or experience is required. **Job Preparation:** SVP 6.0 to less than 7.0—More than 1 year and less than 4 years. **Knowledge:** Design; Engineering and Technology; Computers and Electronics; Building and Construction; Education and Training; Mechanical; Physics. **Instructional Programs:** 460302 Electrician; 460303 Lineworker; 490306 Marine Maintenance and Ship Repairer.

Related DOT Jobs: 729.381-018 Street-Light Repairer; 822.361-018 Protective-Signal Installer; 822.361-022 Protective-Signal Repairer; 824.261-010 Electrician; 824.261-014 Electrician Apprentice; 824.281-010 Airport Electrician; 824.281-018 Neon-Sign Servicer; 824.381-010 Street-Light Servicer; 824.681-010 Electrician; 825.281-014 Electrician; 825.381-030 Electrician; 825.381-034 Electrician Apprentice; 829.261-018 Electrician, Maintenance.

47-2121.00 Glaziers (Glaziers)

Education: Long-term O-T-J training

Employed: 44,266

Openings: 7,699

Projected Growth: 3.9%

Earnings: $26,410

Install glass in windows, skylights, store fronts, and display cases, or on surfaces such as building fronts, interior walls, ceilings, and tabletops.

Moves furniture to clear work site and covers floors and furnishings with drop cloths. Sets glass doors into frame and bolts metal hinges, handles, locks, and other hardware onto glass doors. Attaches mounting strips and moldings to surface and applies mastic cement, putty, or screws to secure mirrors into position. Measures, cuts, fits, and presses antiglare adhesive film to glass; sprays glass with tinting solution to prevent light glare. Covers mirrors with protective material to prevent damage. Loads and arranges mirrors on truck, following sequence of deliveries. Drives truck to installation site and unloads mirrors, equipment, and tools. Measures mirror and dimensions of area to be covered and determines plumb of walls or ceilings, using plumb line and level. Fastens glass panes into wood sash and spreads and smoothes putty around edge of pane with knife to seal joints. Attaches backing and leveling devices to wall surface, using nails and screws, and cuts mounting strips and moldings to required lengths. Installs preassembled framework for windows or doors designed to be fitted with glass panels, including stained glass windows, using hand tools. Marks outline or pattern on glass, cuts glass, and breaks off excess glass by hand or with notched tool. Assembles, fits, and attaches metal-framed glass enclosures for showers or bathtubs to framing around bath enclosure.

GOE Number, Interest Area, and Work Group: 06.02.02; Construction, Mining, and Drilling; Construction: Construction and Maintenance. **Personality Type:** Realistic. Realistic occupations frequently involve work activities that include practical, hands-on problems and solutions. These occupations often deal with plants, animals, and real-world materials like wood, tools, and machinery. Many of the occupations require working outside and do not involve a lot of paperwork or working closely with others. **Work Values:** Moral Values; Compensation; Autonomy; Company Policies and Practices; Security; Activity; Achievement. **Skills:** Mathematics; Installation; Product Inspection; Coordination; Technology Design; Equipment Selection. **Abilities:** *Cognitive*—Information Ordering; Mathematical Reasoning; Number Facility; Visualization; Deductive Reasoning; Category Flexibility. *Psychomotor*—Arm-Hand Steadiness; Finger Dexterity; Multilimb Coordination; Reaction Time; Wrist-Finger Speed. *Physical*—Static Strength; Extent Flexibility; Gross Body Coordination. *Sensory*—Far Vision; Visual Color Discrimination; Glare Sensitivity; Depth Perception; Peripheral Vision. **General Work Activities:** *Information Input*—Inspecting Equipment, Structures, Materials; Getting Information Needed to Do the Job; Monitoring Processes, Materials, and Surroundings. *Mental Process*—Evaluating Information Against Standards; Processing Information; Judging Qualities of Things, Services, Other People's Work; Making Decisions and Solving Problems. *Work Output*—Handling and Moving Objects; Performing General Physical Activities; Operating Vehicles or Equipment. *Interacting with Others*—Communicating with Persons Outside Organization; Performing for or Working with the Public; Establishing and Maintaining Relationships; Resolving Conflict and Negotiating with Others. **Physical Work Conditions:** Standing; Using Hands on Objects, Tools, or Controls; Hazardous Situations. **Other Job Characteristics:** Consequence of Error; Importance of Being Exact or Accurate; Importance of Being Sure All Is Done.

Experience: Job Zone 3. Previous work-related skill, knowledge, or experience is required. **Job Preparation:** SVP 6.0 to less than 7.0—More than 1 year and less than 4 years. **Knowledge:** Building and Construction; Engineering and Technology; Transportation; Mechanical; Design. **Instructional Program:** 469999 Construction Trades, Other.

Related DOT Jobs: 865.361-010 Mirror Installer; 865.381-010 Glazier; 865.381-014 Glazier Apprentice.

47-2131.00 Insulation Workers, Floor, Ceiling, and Wall (Insulation Workers)

Education: Moderate-term O-T-J training

Employed: 66,614

Openings: 7,014

Projected Growth: 7.5%

Earnings: $25,490

Line and cover structures with insulating materials. Work with batt, roll, or blown insulation materials.

Evenly distributes insulating materials into small spaces within floors, ceilings, or walls, using blower and hose attachments or cement mortar. Measures and cuts insulation for covering surfaces, using tape measure, handsaw, knife or scissors. Moves controls, buttons, or levers to start blower and regulate flow of materials through nozzle. Covers, seals, or finishes insulated surfaces or access holes with plastic covers, canvas ships, sealant,

tape, cement, or asphalt mastic. Fills blower hopper with insulating materials. Prepares surfaces for insulation application by brushing or spreading on adhesives, cement, or asphalt or by attaching metal pins to surfaces. Fits, wraps, or attaches insulating materials to structures of surfaces, using hand tools or wires, following blueprint specifications. Reads blueprints and selects appropriate insulation, based on the heat retaining or excluding characteristics of the material.

GOE Number, Interest Area, and Work Group: 06.02.02; Construction, Mining, and Drilling; Construction: Construction and Maintenance. **Personality Type:** Realistic. Realistic occupations frequently involve work activities that include practical, hands-on problems and solutions. These occupations often deal with plants, animals, and real-world materials like wood, tools, and machinery. Many of the occupations require working outside and do not involve a lot of paperwork or working closely with others. **Work Values:** Moral Values; Independence; Supervision, Human Relations; Supervision, Technical; Company Policies and Practices; Activity. **Skills:** Equipment Selection; Product Inspection; Mathematics; Operation and Control; Coordination. **Abilities:** *Cognitive*—Number Facility; Written Comprehension; Information Ordering; Problem Sensitivity; Oral Comprehension; Spatial Orientation. *Psychomotor*—Control Precision. *Physical*—Trunk Strength; Static Strength; Gross Body Coordination. **General Work Activities:** *Information Input*—Getting Information Needed to Do the Job; Estimating Needed Characteristics; Monitoring Processes, Materials, and Surroundings. *Mental Process*—Organizing, Planning, and Prioritizing; Updating and Using Job-Relevant Knowledge; Making Decisions and Solving Problems. *Work Output*—Handling and Moving Objects; Performing General Physical Activities; Implementing Ideas and Programs. *Interacting with Others*—Communicating with Other Workers; Monitoring and Controlling Resources; Performing for or Working with the Public; Performing Administrative Activities. **Physical Work Conditions:** Standing; Indoors; Using Hands on Objects, Tools, or Controls. **Other Job Characteristics:** Importance of Being Sure All Is Done; Consequence of Error; Importance of Being Exact or Accurate.

Experience: Job Zone 3. Previous work-related skill, knowledge, or experience is required. **Job Preparation:** SVP 6.0 to less than 7.0—More than 1 year and less than 4 years. **Knowledge:** Building and Construction; Mechanical; Mathematics; Production and Processing; Design; Physics. **Instructional Program:** 469999 Construction Trades, Other.

Related DOT Jobs: 863.364-010 Insulation-Worker Apprentice; 863.364-014 Insulation Worker; 863.381-010 Cork Insulator, Refrigeration Plant; 863.664-010 Blower Insulator; 863.685-010 Insulation-Power-Unit Tender.

47-2132.00 Insulation Workers, Mechanical (Insulation Workers)

Education: Moderate-term O-T-J training

Employed: 66,614

Openings: 7,014

Projected Growth: 7.5%

Earnings: $25,490

Apply insulating materials to pipes, ductwork, or other mechanical systems to help control and maintain temperature.

Evenly distributes insulating materials into small spaces within floors, ceilings, or walls, using blower and hose attachments or cement mortar. Moves controls, buttons, or levers to start blower and regulate flow of materials through nozzle. Fills blower hopper with insulating materials. Measures and cuts insulation for covering surfaces, using tape measure, handsaw, knife, or scissors. Covers, seals, or finishes insulated surfaces or access holes with plastic covers, canvas ships, sealant, tape, cement, or asphalt mastic. Reads blueprints and selects appropriate insulation, based on the heat retaining or excluding characteristics of the material. Fits, wraps, or attaches insulating materials to structures of surfaces, using hand tools or wires, following blueprint specifications. Prepares surfaces for insulation application, by brushing or spreading on adhesives, cement, or asphalt, or by attaching metal pins to surfaces.

GOE Number, Interest Area, and Work Group: 06.02.02; Construction, Mining, and Drilling; Construction: Construction and Maintenance. **Personality Type:** Realistic. Realistic occupations frequently involve work activities that include practical, hands-on problems and solutions. These occupations often deal with plants, animals, and real-world materials like wood, tools, and machinery. Many of the occupations require working outside and do not involve a lot of paperwork or working closely with others. **Work Values:** Moral Values; Independence; Supervision, Human Relations; Supervision, Technical; Company Policies and Practices; Activity. **Skills:** Equipment Selection; Mathematics; Product Inspection; Coordination; Operation and Control. **Abilities:** *Cognitive*—Written Comprehension; Number Facility; Information Ordering; Spatial Orientation; Problem Sensitivity; Oral Comprehension. *Psychomotor*—Control Precision. *Physical*—Trunk Strength; Static Strength; Gross Body Coordination. **General Work Activities:** *Information Input*—Getting Information Needed to Do the Job; Monitoring Processes, Materials, and Surroundings; Estimating Needed Characteristics. *Mental Process*—Organizing, Planning, and Prioritizing; Making Decisions and Solving Problems; Updating and Using Job-Relevant Knowledge. *Work Output*—Handling and Moving Objects; Performing General Physical Activities; Implementing Ideas and Programs. *Interacting with Others*—Communicating with Other Workers; Monitoring and Controlling Resources; Performing for or Working with the Public; Performing Administrative Activities. **Physical Work Conditions:** Standing; Using Hands on Objects, Tools, or Controls; Indoors. **Other Job Characteristics:** Importance of Being Sure All Is Done; Consequence of Error; Importance of Being Exact or Accurate.

Experience: Job Zone 3. Previous work-related skill, knowledge, or experience is required. **Job Preparation:** SVP 6.0 to less than 7.0—More than 1 year and less than 4 years. **Knowledge:** Building and Construction; Mechanical; Mathematics; Production and Processing; Physics; Design. **Instructional Program:** 469999 Construction Trades, Other.

Related DOT Jobs: 863.364-010 Insulation-Worker Apprentice; 863.364-014 Insulation Worker; 863.381-014 Pipe Coverer and Insulator.

47-2141.00 Painters, Construction and Maintenance
(Painters and Paperhangers)

Education: Moderate-term O-T-J training
Employed: 475,937
Openings: 86,538
Projected Growth: 8.6%
Earnings: $25,110

Paint walls, equipment, buildings, bridges, and other structural surfaces, using brushes, rollers, and spray guns. Remove old paint to prepare surface prior to painting. Mix colors or oils to obtain desired color or consistency.

Reads work order or receives instructions from supervisor or homeowner. Applies paint to simulate wood grain, marble, brick, or stonework. Bakes finish on painted and enameled articles in baking oven. Mixes and matches colors of paint, stain, or varnish. Washes and treats surfaces with oil, turpentine, mildew remover, or other preparations. Fills cracks, holes, and joints with caulk putty, plaster, or other filler, using caulking gun or putty knife. Erects scaffolding or sets up ladders to work above ground level. Covers surfaces with dropcloths or masking tape and paper to protect surface during painting. Removes fixtures, such as pictures and electric switchcovers, from walls prior to painting. Sprays or brushes hot plastics or pitch onto surfaces. Smoothes surfaces, using sandpaper, scrapers, brushes, steel wool, or sanding machine. Cuts stencils; brushes and sprays lettering and decorations on surfaces. Paints surfaces, using brushes, spray gun, or rollers. Sands surfaces between coats and polishes final coat to specified finish. Burns off old paint, using blowtorch.

GOE Number, Interest Area, and Work Group: 06.02.02; Construction, Mining, and Drilling; Construction: Construction and Maintenance. **Personality Type:** Realistic. Realistic occupations frequently involve work activities that include practical, hands-on problems and solutions. These occupations often deal with plants, animals, and real-world materials like wood, tools, and machinery. Many of the occupations require working outside and do not involve a lot of paperwork or working closely with others. **Work Values:** Moral Values; Independence; Activity; Achievement; Company Policies and Practices. **Skills:** Mathematics; Equipment Selection; Product Inspection; Coordination. **Abilities:** *Cognitive*—Written Comprehension; Visualization; Oral Comprehension; Information Ordering; Problem Sensitivity. *Psychomotor*—Wrist-Finger Speed; Arm-Hand Steadiness; Multilimb Coordination. *Physical*—Dynamic Strength; Static Strength; Stamina; Extent Flexibility. *Sensory*—Visual Color Discrimination. **General Work Activities:** *Information Input*—Getting Information Needed to Do the Job; Estimating Needed Characteristics; Monitoring Processes, Materials, and Surroundings. *Mental Process*—Organizing, Planning, and Prioritizing; Judging Qualities of Things, Services, Other People's Work; Making Decisions and Solving Problems; Thinking Creatively. *Work Output*—Performing General Physical Activities; Handling and Moving Objects; Controlling Machines and Processes. *Interacting with Others*—Communicating with Other Workers; Communicating with Persons Outside Organization; Performing for or Working with the Public. **Physical Work Conditions:** Standing; Using Hands on Objects, Tools, or Controls;

Making Repetitive Motions. **Other Job Characteristics:** Importance of Being Sure All Is Done; Importance of Being Exact or Accurate; Consequence of Error.

Experience: Job Zone 4. A minimum of two to four years of work-related skill, knowledge, or experience is needed. **Job Preparation:** SVP 7.0 to less than 8.0—2 years to less than 10 years. **Knowledge:** Building and Construction; Customer and Personal Service; Chemistry; Fine Arts; Mechanical. **Instructional Program:** 460408 Painter and Wall Coverer.

Related DOT Jobs: 840.381-010 Painter; 840.381-014 Painter Apprentice, Shipyard; 840.381-018 Painter, Shipyard; 840.681-010 Painter, Stage Settings.

47-2142.00 Paperhangers (Painters and Paperhangers)

Education: Moderate-term O-T-J training

Employed: 475,937

Openings: 86,538

Projected Growth: 8.6%

Earnings: $25,110

Cover interior walls and ceilings of rooms with decorative wallpaper or fabric. Attach advertising posters on surfaces such as walls and billboards. Remove old materials from surface to be papered.

Erects and works from scaffold. Mixes paste, using paste-powder and water; brushes paste onto surface. Measures and cuts strips from roll of wallpaper or fabric, using shears or razor. Smoothes strips or poster sections with brush or roller to remove wrinkles and bubbles and to smooth joints. Marks vertical guideline on wall to align first strip, using plumb bob and chalkline. Smoothes rough spots on walls and ceilings, using sandpaper. Removes old paper, using water, steam machine, or chemical remover and scraper. Fills holes and cracks with plaster, using trowel. Measures walls and ceiling to compute number and length of strips required to cover surface. Applies acetic acid to damp plaster to prevent lime from bleeding through paper. Trims excess material at ceiling or baseboard, using knife. Aligns and places strips or poster sections of billboard on surface to match adjacent edges. Trims rough edges from strips, using straightedge and trimming knife. Applies thinned glue to waterproof porous surfaces, using brush, roller, or pasting machine. Removes paint, varnish, and grease from surfaces, using paint remover and water-soda solution. Staples or tacks advertising posters onto fences, walls, or poles.

GOE Number, Interest Area, and Work Group: 06.02.02; Construction, Mining, and Drilling; Construction: Construction and Maintenance. **Personality Type:** Realistic. Realistic occupations frequently involve work activities that include practical, hands-on problems and solutions. These occupations often deal with plants, animals, and real-world materials like wood, tools, and machinery. Many of the occupations require working outside and do not involve a lot of paperwork or working closely with others. **Work Values:** Moral Values; Activity; Independence; Company Policies and Practices; Achievement. **Skills:** Mathematics; Equipment Selection; Product Inspection. **Abilities:** *Cognitive*—Number Facility; Information Ordering; Visualization; Problem Sensitiv-

ity; Oral Comprehension. *Psychomotor*—Arm-Hand Steadiness; Manual Dexterity; Multilimb Coordination. *Physical*—Extent Flexibility; Stamina; Static Strength. **General Work Activities:** *Information Input*—Getting Information Needed to Do the Job; Estimating Needed Characteristics; Monitoring Processes, Materials, and Surroundings. *Mental Process*—Organizing, Planning, and Prioritizing; Processing Information; Evaluating Information Against Standards. *Work Output*—Handling and Moving Objects; Performing General Physical Activities; Implementing Ideas and Programs. *Interacting with Others*—Monitoring and Controlling Resources; Communicating with Other Workers; Performing Administrative Activities. **Physical Work Conditions:** Standing; Indoors; Making Repetitive Motions; Using Hands on Objects, Tools, or Controls; Climbing Ladders, Scaffolds, Poles, etc. **Other Job Characteristics:** Importance of Being Exact or Accurate; Importance of Being Sure All Is Done; Consequence of Error.

Experience: Job Zone 2. Some previous work-related skill, knowledge, or experience may be helpful, but usually is not needed. **Job Preparation:** SVP 4.00 to 5.99—6 months to less than 2 years. **Knowledge:** Building and Construction; Design; Mathematics; Chemistry; Mechanical. **Instructional Program:** 460408 Painter and Wall Coverer.

Related DOT Jobs: 841.381-010 Paperhanger; 841.684-010 Billposter.

47-2151.00 Pipelayers (Pipelayers)

Education: No data available.

Employed: 47,650

Openings: No data available.

Projected Growth: No data available.

Earnings: $24,880

Lay pipe for storm or sanitation sewers, drains, and water mains. Grade trenches or culverts; position pipe; seal joints.

Checks slope, using carpenter's level or lasers. Lays pipes in trenches and welds, cements, glues, or otherwise connects pieces together. Lays out route of pipe, following written instructions or blueprints. Covers pipe with earth or other materials. Digs trenches to desired or required depth by hand or using trenching tool. Grades and levels base of trench, using tamping machine and hand tools. Taps and drills holes into pipe to introduce auxiliary lines or devices.

GOE Number, Interest Area, and Work Group: 06.02.03; Construction, Mining, and Drilling; Construction: General. **Personality Type:** Realistic. Realistic occupations frequently involve work activities that include practical, hands-on problems and solutions. These occupations often deal with plants, animals, and real-world materials like wood, tools, and machinery. Many of the occupations require working outside and do not involve a lot of paperwork or working closely with others. **Work Values:** Moral Values; Supervision, Technical; Company Policies and Practices; Activity; Supervision, Human Relations. **Skills:** Equipment Selection; Product Inspection; Operation and Control; Problem Identification; Coordination; Mathematics; Active Listening; Equipment Maintenance; Installation. **Abilities:** *Cognitive*—Visualization; Spatial Orientation; Information Ordering; Problem Sensitivity; Written Comprehension. *Psychomotor*—Manual

Dexterity; Multilimb Coordination; Speed of Limb Movement. *Physical*—Trunk Strength; Static Strength; Dynamic Strength. *Sensory*—Far Vision; Depth Perception; Glare Sensitivity; Visual Color Discrimination. **General Work Activities:** *Information Input*—Getting Information Needed to Do the Job; Monitoring Processes, Materials, and Surroundings; Identifying Objects, Actions, and Events. *Mental Process*—Judging Qualities of Things, Services, Other People's Work; Organizing, Planning, and Prioritizing; Making Decisions and Solving Problems; Analyzing Data or Information; Updating and Using Job-Relevant Knowledge; Evaluating Information Against Standards. *Work Output*—Performing General Physical Activities; Handling and Moving Objects; Implementing Ideas and Programs. *Interacting with Others*—Coordinating Work and Activities of Others; Communicating with Other Workers; Performing Administrative Activities; Assisting and Caring for Others. **Physical Work Conditions:** Using Hands on Objects, Tools, or Controls; Outdoors; Standing. **Other Job Characteristics:** Consequence of Error; Degree of Automation; Frustrating Circumstances.

Experience: Job Zone 2. Some previous work-related skill, knowledge, or experience may be helpful, but usually is not needed. **Job Preparation:** SVP 4.00 to 5.99—6 months to less than 2 years. **Knowledge:** Mechanical; Building and Construction; Design; Engineering and Technology; Physics. **Instructional Program:** 460501 Plumber and Pipefitter.

Related DOT Jobs: 851.383-010 Irrigation System Installer; 869.664-014 Construction Worker I.

47-2152.00 Plumbers, Pipefitters, and Steamfitters
(Plumbers, Pipefitters, and Steamfitters)

Education: Long-term O-T-J training
Employed: 426,325
Openings: 58,261
Projected Growth: 5.3%
Earnings: $34,670

Assemble, install, alter, and repair pipelines or pipe systems that carry water, steam, air, or other liquids or gases. Install heating and cooling equipment and mechanical control systems.

GOE Number, Interest Area, and Work Group: 06.02.02; Construction, Mining, and Drilling; Construction: Construction and Maintenance. **Instructional Program:** 460501 Plumber and Pipefitter. **Note:** The Department of Labor has not collected some data for this job, so it has fewer details than the other descriptions.

47-2152.01 Pipe Fitters (Plumbers, Pipefitters, and
Steamfitters)

Education: Long-term O-T-J training
Employed: 426,325
Openings: 58,261
Projected Growth: 5.3%
Earnings: $34,670

Lay out, assemble, install, and maintain pipe systems, pipe supports, and related hydraulic and pneumatic equipment, for steam, hot water, heating, cooling, lubricating, sprinkling, and industrial production and processing systems.

Modifies and maintains pipe systems and related machines and equipment components following specifications, using hand tools and power tools. Cuts, threads, and hammers pipe to specifications, using tools such as saws, cutting torches, and pipe threaders and benders. Attaches pipes to walls, structures, and fixtures such as radiators or tanks, using brackets, clamps, tools, or welding equipment. Measures and marks pipes for cutting and threading. Inspects, examines, and tests installed systems and pipe lines, using pressure gauge, hydrostatic testing, observation, or other methods. Selects pipe sizes and types and related materials such as supports, hangers, and hydraulic cylinders, according to specifications. Inspects work site to determine presence of obstruction and to ensure that holes will not cause structural weakness. Coats nonferrous piping materials by dipping in mixture of molten tin and lead, to prevent erosion or galvanic and electrolytic action. Assembles pipes, tubes, and fittings, according to specifications. Cuts and bores holes in structures such as bulkheads, decks, walls, and mains, using hand and power tools, prior to pipe installation. Turns valve to shut off steam, water, or other gases or liquids from pipe section, using valve key or wrenches. Operates motorized pump to remove water from flooded manholes, basements, or facility floors. Plans pipe system layout, installation, or repair according to specifications. Lays out full scale drawings of pipe systems, supports, and related equipment, following blueprints.

GOE Number, Interest Area, and Work Group: 06.02.02; Construction, Mining, and Drilling; Construction: Construction and Maintenance. **Personality Type:** Realistic. Realistic occupations frequently involve work activities that include practical, hands-on problems and solutions. These occupations often deal with plants, animals, and real-world materials like wood, tools, and machinery. Many of the occupations require working outside and do not involve a lot of paperwork or working closely with others. **Work Values:** Moral Values; Independence; Ability Utilization; Security; Company Policies and Practices; Activity. **Skills:** Product Inspection; Installation; Problem Identification; Equipment Selection; Operation and Control. **Abilities:** *Cognitive*—Visualization; Information Ordering; Perceptual Speed; Problem Sensitivity; Deductive Reasoning. *Psychomotor*—Arm-Hand Steadiness; Wrist-Finger Speed; Speed of Limb Movement; Finger Dexterity. *Physical*—Static Strength; Extent Flexibility; Explosive Strength; Dynamic Strength; Trunk Strength; Stamina. *Sensory*—Near Vision; Far Vision; Depth Perception. **General Work Activities:** *Information Input*—Getting Information Needed to Do the Job; Inspecting Equipment, Structures, Materials; Identifying Objects, Actions, and Events. *Mental Process*—Evaluating Information Against Standards; Organizing, Planning, and Prioritizing; Judging Qualities of Things, Services, Other People's Work; Analyzing Data or Information; Making Decisions and Solving Problems. *Work Output*—Handling and Moving Objects; Performing General Physical Activities; Controlling Machines and Processes; Repairing and Maintaining Mechanical Equipment. *Interacting with Others*—Monitoring and Controlling Resources; Communicating with Other Workers; Coordinating Work and Activities of

Others; Performing Administrative Activities; Providing Consultation and Advice to Others; Interpreting Meaning of Information to Others. **Physical Work Conditions:** Using Hands on Objects, Tools, or Controls; Common Protective or Safety Attire; Indoors. **Other Job Characteristics:** Consequence of Error; Importance of Being Exact or Accurate; Importance of Being Sure All Is Done.

Experience: Job Zone 4. A minimum of two to four years of work-related skill, knowledge, or experience is needed. **Job Preparation:** SVP 7.0 to less than 8.0—2 years to less than 10 years. **Knowledge:** Building and Construction; Mechanical; Design; Engineering and Technology; Mathematics. **Instructional Program:** 460501 Plumber and Pipefitter.

Related DOT Jobs: 862.261-010 Pipe Fitter; 862.281-010 Coppersmith; 862.281-014 Coppersmith Apprentice; 862.281-022 Pipe Fitter; 862.281-026 Pipe-Fitter Apprentice; 862.361-014 Gas-Main Fitter; 862.361-018 Pipe Fitter, Diesel Engine I; 862.361-022 Steam Service Inspector; 862.381-014 Industrial-Gas Fitter; 862.381-022 Pipe Fitter, Diesel Engine II.

47-2152.02 Plumbers (Plumbers, Pipefitters, and Steamfitters)

Education: Long-term O-T-J training

Employed: 426,325

Openings: 58,261

Projected Growth: 5.3%

Earnings: $34,670

Assemble, install, and repair pipes, fittings, and fixtures of heating, water, and drainage systems, according to specifications and plumbing codes.

Repairs and maintains plumbing by replacing defective washers, replacing or mending broken pipes, and opening clogged drains. Assembles pipe sections, tubing and fittings, using screws, bolts, solder, plastic solvent, and caulking. Cuts opening in structures to accommodate pipe and pipe fittings, using hand and power tools. Locates and marks position of pipe installations and passage holes in structures, using measuring instruments such as ruler and level. Studies building plans and inspects structure to determine required materials and equipment and sequence of pipe installations. Installs pipe assemblies, fittings, valves, and fixtures such as sinks, toilets, and tubs, using hand and power tools. Cuts, threads, and bends pipe to required angle, using pipe cutters, pipe-threading machine, and pipe-bending machine. Fills pipes or plumbing fixtures with water or air and observes pressure gauges to detect and locate leaks. Directs workers engaged in pipe cutting and preassembly and installation of plumbing systems and components.

GOE Number, Interest Area, and Work Group: 06.02.02; Construction, Mining, and Drilling; Construction: Construction and Maintenance. **Personality Type:** Realistic. Realistic occupations frequently involve work activities that include practical, hands-on problems and solutions. These occupations often deal with plants, animals, and real-world materials like wood, tools, and machinery. Many of the occupations require working outside and

do not involve a lot of paperwork or working closely with others. **Work Values:** Compensation; Moral Values; Responsibility; Authority; Achievement. **Skills:** Installation; Coordination; Repairing; Equipment Selection; Problem Identification; Operation and Control; Equipment Maintenance; Active Listening. **Abilities:** *Cognitive*—Visualization; Information Ordering; Deductive Reasoning; Problem Sensitivity; Perceptual Speed. *Psychomotor*—Arm-Hand Steadiness; Finger Dexterity; Manual Dexterity. *Physical*—Extent Flexibility; Static Strength; Trunk Strength. *Sensory*—Near Vision; Far Vision; Depth Perception. **General Work Activities:** *Information Input*—Getting Information Needed to Do the Job; Inspecting Equipment, Structures, Materials; Monitoring Processes, Materials, and Surroundings. *Mental Process*—Making Decisions and Solving Problems; Organizing, Planning, and Prioritizing; Updating and Using Job-Relevant Knowledge. *Work Output*—Handling and Moving Objects; Performing General Physical Activities; Repairing and Maintaining Mechanical Equipment. *Interacting with Others*—Communicating with Other Workers; Establishing and Maintaining Relationships; Coordinating Work and Activities of Others. **Physical Work Conditions:** Using Hands on Objects, Tools, or Controls; Standing; Indoors. **Other Job Characteristics:** Importance of Being Sure All Is Done; Consequence of Error; Importance of Being Exact or Accurate.

Experience: Job Zone 3. Previous work-related skill, knowledge, or experience is required. **Job Preparation:** SVP 6.0 to less than 7.0—More than 1 year and less than 4 years. **Knowledge:** Mechanical; Building and Construction; Engineering and Technology; Mathematics; Design. **Instructional Program:** 460501 Plumber and Pipefitter.

Related DOT Jobs: 862.381-030 Plumber; 862.381-034 Plumber Apprentice; 862.681-010 Plumber.

47-2152.03 Pipelaying Fitters (Pipelaying Fitters)

Education: No data available.

Employed: 5,690

Openings: No data available.

Projected Growth: No data available.

Earnings: $34,290

Align pipeline section in preparation of welding. Signal tractor driver for placement of pipeline sections in proper alignment. Insert steel spacer.

Inserts spacers between pipe ends. Corrects misalignment of pipe, using sledge hammer. Inspects joint to verify uniformity of spacing and alignment of pipe surfaces. Guides pipe into trench and signals hoist operator to move pipe until specified alignment with other pipes is achieved.

GOE Number, Interest Area, and Work Group: 06.02.03; Construction, Mining, and Drilling; Construction: General. **Personality Type:** Realistic. Realistic occupations frequently involve work activities that include practical, hands-on problems and solutions. These occupations often deal with plants, animals, and real-world materials like wood, tools, and machinery. Many of the occupations require working outside and do not involve a lot of paperwork or working closely with others. **Work Values:** Moral

Values; Company Policies and Practices; Independence; Activity; Security; Supervision, Human Relations; Supervision, Technical. **Skills:** Product Inspection; Equipment Selection; Equipment Maintenance; Installation. **Abilities:** *Cognitive*—Problem Sensitivity; Information Ordering; Spatial Orientation; Visualization; Perceptual Speed. *Psychomotor*—Manual Dexterity; Arm-Hand Steadiness; Speed of Limb Movement; Multilimb Coordination; Reaction Time. *Physical*—Explosive Strength; Gross Body Coordination; Trunk Strength; Static Strength. *Sensory*—Depth Perception; Far Vision; Visual Color Discrimination; Peripheral Vision. **General Work Activities:** *Information Input*—Monitoring Processes, Materials, and Surroundings; Inspecting Equipment, Structures, Materials; Identifying Objects, Actions, and Events. *Mental Process*—Updating and Using Job-Relevant Knowledge; Evaluating Information Against Standards; Judging Qualities of Things, Services, Other People's Work; Making Decisions and Solving Problems; Organizing, Planning, and Prioritizing. *Work Output*—Performing General Physical Activities; Handling and Moving Objects; Implementing Ideas and Programs. *Interacting with Others*—Communicating with Other Workers; Coordinating Work and Activities of Others; Establishing and Maintaining Relationships; Assisting and Caring for Others. **Physical Work Conditions:** Outdoors; Standing; Using Hands on Objects, Tools, or Controls. **Other Job Characteristics:** Frustrating Circumstances; Importance of Being Sure All Is Done; Importance of Being Exact or Accurate; Consequence of Error.

Experience: Job Zone 2. Some previous work-related skill, knowledge, or experience may be helpful, but usually is not needed. **Job Preparation:** SVP 4.00 to 5.99—6 months to less than 2 years. **Knowledge:** Mechanical; Building and Construction; Physics; Engineering and Technology; Production and Processing; Food Production; Communications and Media. **Instructional Program:** 460501 Plumber and Pipefitter.

Related DOT Job: 869.664-014 Construction Worker I.

47-2161.00 Plasterers and Stucco Masons (Plasterers and Stucco Masons)

Education: Long-term O-T-J training

Employed: 40,316

Openings: 7,984

Projected Growth: 17.1%

Earnings: $29,390

Apply interior or exterior plaster, cement, stucco, or similar materials. Set ornamental plaster.

Installs guidewires on exterior surface of buildings to indicate thickness of plaster or stucco. Molds and installs ornamental plaster pieces, panels, and trim. Directs workers to mix plaster to desired consistency and to erect scaffolds. Applies weatherproof, decorative covering to exterior surfaces of building. Mixes mortar to desired consistency and puts up scaffolds. Creates decorative textures in finish coat, using sand, pebbles, or stones. Applies coats of plaster or stucco to walls, ceilings, or partitions of buildings, using trowel, brush, or spray gun.

GOE Number, Interest Area, and Work Group: 06.02.02; Construction, Mining, and Drilling; Construction: Construction and

Maintenance. **Personality Type:** Realistic. Realistic occupations frequently involve work activities that include practical, hands-on problems and solutions. These occupations often deal with plants, animals, and real-world materials like wood, tools, and machinery. Many of the occupations require working outside and do not involve a lot of paperwork or working closely with others. **Work Values:** Moral Values; Company Policies and Practices; Coworkers; Compensation; Achievement. **Skills:** Coordination; Time Management; Monitoring; Equipment Selection; Problem Identification; Product Inspection; Identification of Key Causes. **Abilities:** *Cognitive*—Information Ordering; Deductive Reasoning; Oral Comprehension; Visualization; Written Comprehension; Oral Expression. *Psychomotor*—Manual Dexterity; Wrist-Finger Speed; Multilimb Coordination; Arm-Hand Steadiness. *Physical*—Extent Flexibility; Static Strength; Dynamic Strength. *Sensory*—Speech Clarity; Depth Perception; Glare Sensitivity; Visual Color Discrimination. **General Work Activities:** *Information Input*—Getting Information Needed to Do the Job; Monitoring Processes, Materials, and Surroundings; Identifying Objects, Actions, and Events. *Mental Process*—Analyzing Data or Information; Thinking Creatively; Organizing, Planning, and Prioritizing. *Work Output*—Handling and Moving Objects; Performing General Physical Activities; Implementing Ideas and Programs. *Interacting with Others*—Communicating with Other Workers; Coordinating Work and Activities of Others; Communicating with Persons Outside Organization; Establishing and Maintaining Relationships. **Physical Work Conditions:** Using Hands on Objects, Tools, or Controls; Climbing Ladders, Scaffolds, Poles, etc.; Indoors; Contaminants; Standing. **Other Job Characteristics:** Importance of Being Sure All Is Done; Importance of Being Exact or Accurate; Frustrating Circumstances.

Experience: Job Zone 4. A minimum of two to four years of work-related skill, knowledge, or experience is needed. **Job Preparation:** SVP 7.0 to less than 8.0—2 years to less than 10 years. **Knowledge:** Building and Construction; Mathematics; Design; Mechanical; Engineering and Technology; English Language; Education and Training. **Instructional Program:** 469999 Construction Trades, Other.

Related DOT Jobs: 842.361-018 Plasterer; 842.361-022 Plasterer Apprentice; 842.361-026 Plasterer, Molding; 842.381-014 Stucco Mason.

47-2171.00 Reinforcing Iron and Rebar Workers (Reinforcing Metal Workers)

Education: No data available.

Employed: 21,770

Openings: No data available.

Projected Growth: No data available.

Earnings: $32,850

Position and secure steel bars or mesh in concrete forms to reinforce concrete. Use a variety of fasteners, rod-bending machines, blowtorches, and hand tools.

Determines number, sizes, shapes, and locations of reinforcing rods from blueprints, sketches, or oral instructions. Welds reinforcing bars together, using arch-welding equipment. Reinforces concrete with wire mesh. Cuts rods to required lengths, using hacksaw, bar cutters, or acetylene torch. Selects and places rods in forms, spacing and fastening them together, using wire and pliers. Bends steel rods with hand tools and rodbending machine.

GOE Number, Interest Area, and Work Group: 06.02.03; Construction, Mining, and Drilling; Construction: General. **Personality Type:** Realistic. Realistic occupations frequently involve work activities that include practical, hands-on problems and solutions. These occupations often deal with plants, animals, and real-world materials like wood, tools, and machinery. Many of the occupations require working outside and do not involve a lot of paperwork or working closely with others. **Work Values:** Moral Values; Independence; Company Policies and Practices; Activity; Supervision, Technical; Security; Supervision, Human Relations. **Skills:** Active Listening; Reading Comprehension. **Abilities:** *Cognitive*—Visualization; Spatial Orientation; Oral Comprehension; Written Comprehension; Information Ordering; Number Facility. *Psychomotor*—Multilimb Coordination; Wrist-Finger Speed; Control Precision. *Physical*—Static Strength; Extent Flexibility; Explosive Strength. *Sensory*—Glare Sensitivity; Speech Clarity; Depth Perception; Speech Recognition. **General Work Activities:** *Information Input*—Getting Information Needed to Do the Job; Identifying Objects, Actions, and Events; Monitoring Processes, Materials, and Surroundings. *Mental Process*—Analyzing Data or Information; Organizing, Planning, and Prioritizing; Making Decisions and Solving Problems; Evaluating Information Against Standards. *Work Output*—Handling and Moving Objects; Performing General Physical Activities; Controlling Machines and Processes. *Interacting with Others*—Monitoring and Controlling Resources; Communicating with Other Workers; Establishing and Maintaining Relationships. **Physical Work Conditions:** Using Hands on Objects, Tools, or Controls; Common Protective or Safety Attire; Outdoors; Standing; Hazardous Situations. **Other Job Characteristics:** Consequence of Error; Importance of Being Sure All Is Done; Importance of Being Exact or Accurate.

Experience: Job Zone 3. Previous work-related skill, knowledge, or experience is required. **Job Preparation:** SVP 6.0 to less than 7.0—More than 1 year and less than 4 years. **Knowledge:** Building and Construction; Design; Engineering and Technology; Mathematics; Physics. **Instructional Program:** 460499 Construction and Building Finishers and Managers, Other.

Related DOT Job: 801.684-026 Reinforcing-Metal Worker.

47-2181.00 Roofers (Roofers)

Education: Moderate-term O-T-J training

Employed: 157,774

Openings: 28,797

Projected Growth: 12%

Earnings: $25,340

Cover roofs of structures with shingles, slate, asphalt, aluminum, wood, and related materials. Spray roofs, sidings, and walls with material to bind, seal, insulate, or soundproof sections of structures.

Cuts roofing paper to size and nails or staples paper to roof in overlapping strips to form base for roofing materials. Insulates, soundproofs, and seals buildings with foam, using spray gun, air compressor, and heater. Applies alternate layers of hot asphalt or tar and roofing paper until roof covering is completed as specified. Aligns roofing material with edge of roof. Cuts strips of flashing and fits them into angles formed by walls, vents, and intersecting roof surfaces. Punches holes in slate, tile, terra-cotta, or wooden shingles, using punch and hammer. Fastens composition shingles or sheets to roof with asphalt, cement, or nails. Applies gravel or pebbles over top layer, using rake or stiff-bristled broom. Cleans and maintains equipment. Mops or pours hot asphalt or tar onto roof base when applying asphalt or tar and gravel to roof. Overlaps successive layers of roofing material, determining distance of overlap, using chalkline, gauge on shingling hatchet, or lines on shingles. Removes snow, water, or debris from roofs prior to applying roofing materials.

GOE Number, Interest Area, and Work Group: 06.02.02; Construction, Mining, and Drilling; Construction: Construction and Maintenance. **Personality Type:** Realistic. Realistic occupations frequently involve work activities that include practical, hands-on problems and solutions. These occupations often deal with plants, animals, and real-world materials like wood, tools, and machinery. Many of the occupations require working outside and do not involve a lot of paperwork or working closely with others. **Work Values:** Moral Values; Activity; Compensation; Coworkers; Achievement; Independence. **Skills:** Coordination; Equipment Selection; Operation and Control; Repairing; Product Inspection; Installation. **Abilities:** *Cognitive*—Information Ordering; Deductive Reasoning; Spatial Orientation; Visualization; Memorization; Oral Comprehension. *Psychomotor*—Manual Dexterity; Wrist-Finger Speed; Multilimb Coordination. *Physical*—Extent Flexibility; Static Strength; Gross Body Equilibrium. *Sensory*—Depth Perception; Peripheral Vision; Glare Sensitivity. **General Work Activities:** *Information Input*—Getting Information Needed to Do the Job; Estimating Needed Characteristics; Identifying Objects, Actions, and Events. *Mental Process*—Making Decisions and Solving Problems; Judging Qualities of Things, Services, Other People's Work; Organizing, Planning, and Prioritizing. *Work Output*—Performing General Physical Activities; Handling and Moving Objects; Implementing Ideas and Programs. *Interacting with Others*—Communicating with Other Workers; Communicating with Persons Outside Organization; Establishing and Maintaining Relationships. **Physical Work Conditions:** Outdoors; High Places; Using Hands on Objects, Tools, or Controls. **Other Job Characteristics:** Consequence of Error; Importance of Repeating Same Tasks; Importance of Being Exact or Accurate; Importance of Being Sure All Is Done.

Experience: Job Zone 3. Previous work-related skill, knowledge, or experience is required. **Job Preparation:** SVP 6.0 to less than 7.0—More than 1 year and less than 4 years. **Knowledge:** Building and Construction; Mechanical; Engineering and Technology; Physics; Design. **Instructional Program:** 469999 Construction Trades, Other.

Related DOT Jobs: 866.381-010 Roofer; 866.381-014 Roofer Apprentice; 866.684-010 Roofer Applicator.

47-2211.00 Sheet Metal Workers (Sheet Metal Workers and Duct Installers)

Education: Moderate-term O-T-J training

Employed: 229,700

Openings: 22,680

Projected Growth: 14.1%

Earnings: No data available.

Fabricate, assemble, install, and repair sheet metal products and equipment, such as ducts, control boxes, drainpipes, and furnace casings. Set up and operate fabricating machines to cut, bend, and straighten sheet metal. Shape metal over anvils, blocks, or forms, using hammer. Operate soldering and welding equipment to join sheet metal parts. Inspect, assemble, and smooth seams and joints of burred surfaces.

Inspects assemblies and installation for conformance to specifications, using measuring instruments such as calipers, scales, dial indicators, gauges, and micrometers. Trims, files, grinds, deburrs, buffs, and smoothes surfaces, using hand tools and portable power tools. Shapes metal material over anvil, block, or other form, using hand tools. Determines sequence and methods of fabricating, assembling, and installing sheet metal products, using blueprints, sketches, or product specifications. Selects gauge and type of sheet metal or nonmetallic material, according to product specifications. Lays out and marks dimensions and reference lines on material, using scribes, dividers, squares, and rulers. Welds, solders, bolts, rivets, screws, clips, caulks, or bonds component parts to assemble products, using hand tools, power tools, and equipment. Sets up and operates fabricating machines such as shears, brakes, presses, and routers, to cut, bend, block, and form materials. Installs assemblies in supportive framework according to blueprints, using hand tools, power tools, and lifting and handling devices.

GOE Number, Interest Area, and Work Group: 06.02.02; Construction, Mining, and Drilling; Construction: Construction and Maintenance. **Personality Type:** Realistic. Realistic occupations frequently involve work activities that include practical, hands-on problems and solutions. These occupations often deal with plants, animals, and real-world materials like wood, tools, and machinery. Many of the occupations require working outside and do not involve a lot of paperwork or working closely with others. **Work Values:** Moral Values; Company Policies and Practices; Supervision, Human Relations; Independence; Activity. **Skills:** Installation; Mathematics; Equipment Selection; Product Inspection; Coordination; Operation and Control. **Abilities:** *Cognitive—* Information Ordering; Visualization; Written Comprehension; Deductive Reasoning; Number Facility; Problem Sensitivity. *Psychomotor—*Control Precision; Manual Dexterity; Arm-Hand Steadiness. *Physical—*Static Strength; Trunk Strength; Explosive Strength. **General Work Activities:** *Information Input—*Getting Information Needed to Do the Job; Identifying Objects, Actions, and Events; Inspecting Equipment, Structures, Materials. *Mental Process—*Evaluating Information Against Standards; Judging Qualities of Things, Services, Other People's Work; Organizing, Planning, and Prioritizing. *Work Output—*Handling and Moving Objects; Controlling Machines and Processes; Performing General Physical Activities. *Interacting with Others—*Monitoring and Controlling Resources; Interpreting Meaning of Information to Others; Coordinating Work and Activities of Others; Performing Administrative Activities. **Physical Work Conditions:** Indoors; Using Hands on Objects, Tools, or Controls; Hazardous Equipment. **Other Job Characteristics:** Importance of Being Exact or Accurate; Consequence of Error; Degree of Automation.

Experience: Job Zone 3. Previous work-related skill, knowledge, or experience is required. **Job Preparation:** SVP 6.0 to less than 7.0—More than 1 year and less than 4 years. **Knowledge:** Production and Processing; Mechanical; Computers and Electronics; Building and Construction; Design. **Instructional Programs:** 469999 Construction Trades, Other; 480506 Sheet Metal Worker.

Related DOT Jobs: 804.281-010 Sheet-Metal Worker; 804.281-014 Sheet-Metal-Worker Apprentice; 804.481-010 Hood Maker.

47-2221.00 Structural Iron and Steel Workers (Structural Metal Workers)

Education: No data available.

Employed: 59,060

Openings: No data available.

Projected Growth: No data available.

Earnings: $32,890

Raise, place, and unite iron or steel girders, columns, and other structural members to form completed structures or structural frameworks. Erect metal storage tanks; assemble prefabricated metal buildings.

Inserts sealing strips, wiring, insulating material, ladders, flanges, gauges, and valves, depending on type of structure being assembled. Verifies vertical and horizontal alignment of structural-steel members, using plumb bob and level. Pulls, pushes, or pries structural-steel member into approximate position while member is supported by hoisting device. Drives drift pins through rivet holes to align rivet holes in structural-steel member with corresponding holes in previously placed member. Forces structural-steel members into final position, using turnbuckles, crowbars, jacks, and hand tools. Bolts aligned structural-steel members in position until they can be permanently riveted, bolted, or welded in place. Fastens structural-steel members to cable of hoist, using chain, cable, or rope. Signals worker operating hoisting equipment to lift and place structural-steel member. Catches hot rivets tossed by Rivet Heater in bucket and inserts rivets in holes, using tongs. Cuts and welds steel members to make alterations, using oxyacetylene welding equipment. Sets up hoisting equipment for raising and placing structural-steel members. Guides structural-steel member, using tab line (rope), or rides on member, to guide it into position. Bucks (holds) rivets while Riveter, Pneumatic uses air-hammer to form heads on rivets.

GOE Number, Interest Area, and Work Group: 06.02.03; Construction, Mining, and Drilling; Construction: General. **Personality Type:** Realistic. Realistic occupations frequently involve work activities that include practical, hands-on problems and solutions. These occupations often deal with plants, animals, and real-world materials like wood, tools, and machinery. Many of the occupations require working outside and do not involve a lot of paperwork or working closely with others. **Work Values:** Moral Values; Company Policies and Practices; Activity; Coworkers; Supervision, Human Relations. **Skills:** Coordination; Installation; Product Inspection; Equipment Selection; Operation and Control. **Abilities:** *Cognitive*—Visualization; Information Ordering; Spatial Orientation; Oral Expression; Deductive Reasoning; Oral Comprehension. *Psychomotor*—Manual Dexterity; Multilimb Coordination; Reaction Time. *Physical*—Static Strength; Dynamic Strength; Gross Body Equilibrium. *Sensory*—Far Vision; Depth Perception; Peripheral Vision. **General Work Activities:** *Information Input*—Inspecting Equipment, Structures, Materials; Monitoring Processes, Materials, and Surroundings; Getting Information Needed to Do the Job; Estimating Needed Characteristics. *Mental Process*—Judging Qualities of Things, Services, Other People's Work; Updating and Using Job-Relevant Knowledge; Making Decisions and Solving Problems. *Work Output*—Performing General Physical Activities; Handling and Moving Objects; Controlling Machines and Processes. *Interacting with Others*—Communicating with Other Workers; Coordinating Work and Activities of Others; Establishing and Maintaining Relationships. **Physical Work Conditions:** Common Protective or Safety Attire; Standing; Using Hands on Objects, Tools, or Controls. **Other Job Characteristics:** Consequence of Error; Importance of Being Sure All Is Done; Importance of Being Exact or Accurate.

Experience: Job Zone 3. Previous work-related skill, knowledge, or experience is required. **Job Preparation:** SVP 6.0 to less than 7.0—More than 1 year and less than 4 years. **Knowledge:** Building and Construction; Mechanical; Public Safety and Security; Engineering and Technology; Physics; Mathematics. **Instructional Program:** 469999 Construction Trades, Other.

Related DOT Jobs: 801.361-014 Structural-Steel Worker; 801.361-018 Structural-Steel-Worker Apprentice; 801.361-022 Tank Setter; 801.381-010 Assembler, Metal Building.

47-3000 Helpers, Construction Trades

47-3011.00 Helpers—Brickmasons, Blockmasons, Stonemasons, and Tile and Marble Setters
(Construction Helpers)

Education: Short-term O-T-J training

Employed: 575,959

Openings: 167,103

Projected Growth: 7.3%

Earnings: No data available.

Help brickmasons, blockmasons, stonemasons, or tile and marble setters by performing duties of lesser skill. Use, supply, or hold materials or tools; clean work area and equipment.

Removes excess grout and residue from tile or brick joints with wet sponge or trowel. Transports materials, tools, and machines to installation site, manually or using conveyance equipment. Mixes mortar, plaster and grout, manually or using a machine, according to standard formulae. Selects materials for installation, following numbered sequence or drawings. Arranges and stores materials, machines, tools, and equipment. Cuts materials to specified size for installation, using power saw or tile cutter. Applies caulk, sealants, or other agents to installed surface. Moves or positions marble slabs and ingot covers, using crane, hoist, or dolly. Corrects surface imperfections or fills chipped, cracked, or broken bricks or tiles, using fillers, adhesives, and grouting materials. Cleans installation surfaces, equipment, tools work site, and storage areas, using water, chemical solutions, oxygen lance, or polishing machines. Applies grout between joints of bricks or tiles, using grouting trowel. Removes damaged tile, brick, or mortar, and prepares installation surfaces, using pliers, chipping hammers, chisels, drills, and metal wire anchors. Assists in the preparation, installation, repair, or rebuilding of tile, brick, or stone surfaces. Erects scaffolding or other installation structures. Modifies material moving, mixing, grouting, grinding, polishing, or cleaning procedures, according to the type of installation or materials required.

GOE Number, Interest Area, and Work Group: 06.04.01; Construction, Mining, and Drilling; Hands-on Work: Construction, Extraction, and Maintenance. **Personality Type:** Realistic. Realistic occupations frequently involve work activities that include practical, hands-on problems and solutions. These occupations often deal with plants, animals, and real-world materials like wood, tools, and machinery. Many of the occupations require working outside and do not involve a lot of paperwork or working closely with others. **Work Values:** Moral Values; Supervision, Technical; Activity; Coworkers; Advancement. **Skills:** Installation; Coordination; Equipment Selection; Operation and Control; Product Inspection. **Abilities:** *Cognitive*—Number Facility; Oral Comprehension; Information Ordering; Visualization; Problem Sensitivity. *Psychomotor*—Wrist-Finger Speed; Multilimb Coordination; Speed of Limb Movement. *Physical*—Static Strength; Dynamic Strength; Extent Flexibility. *Sensory*—Sound Localization; Glare Sensitivity; Peripheral Vision. **General Work Activities:** *Information Input*—Getting Information Needed to Do the Job; Inspecting Equipment, Structures, Materials; Monitoring Processes, Materials, and Surroundings. *Mental Process*—Evaluating Information Against Standards; Judging Qualities of Things, Services, Other People's Work; Processing Information. *Work Output*—Handling and Moving Objects; Performing General Physical Activities; Controlling Machines and Processes. *Interacting with Others*—Assisting and Caring for Others; Communicating with Other Workers; Establishing and Maintaining Relationships. **Physical Work Conditions:** Outdoors; Using Hands on Objects, Tools, or Controls; Kneeling, Crouching, or Crawling. **Other Job Characteristics:** Consequence of Error; Importance of Being Sure All Is Done; Importance of Being Exact or Accurate.

Experience: Job Zone 1. No previous work-related skill, knowledge, or experience is needed. **Job Preparation:** SVP Below 4.0—Less than 6 months. **Knowledge:** Building and Construction; Mechanical; Mathematics; Design; Engineering and Technology; English Language; Physics. **Instructional Programs:** No data available.

Related DOT Jobs: 709.687-018 Hot-Top-Liner Helper; 861.664-010 Marble Finisher; 861.664-018 Tile Finisher; 861.687-010 Bricklayer Helper, Firebrick and Refractory Tile; 861.687-014 Patcher Helper.

47-3012.00 Helpers—Carpenters (Construction Helpers)

Education: Short-term O-T-J training

Employed: 575,959

Openings: 167,103

Projected Growth: 7.3%

Earnings: No data available.

Help carpenters by performing duties of lesser skill. Use, supply, or hold materials or tools; clean work area and equipment.

Drills holes in timbers or lumber. Cuts and installs insulating or sound-absorbing material. Glues and clamps edges or joints of assembled parts. Smoothes and sands surfaces to remove ridges, tool marks, glue, or caulking. Spreads adhesives on flooring to install tile or linoleum. Fastens timbers and/or lumber with glue, screws, pegs, or nails. Cuts tile or linoleum to fit. Covers surfaces with laminated plastic covering material. Selects needed tools, equipment, and materials from storage and transports items to work site. Erects scaffolding, shoring, and braces. Hews timbers. Positions and holds timbers, lumber, and paneling in place for fastening or cutting. Holds plumb bobs, sighting rods, and other equipment to aid in establishing reference points and lines. Cuts timbers, lumber, and/or paneling to specified dimensions.

GOE Number, Interest Area, and Work Group: 06.04.01; Construction, Mining, and Drilling; Hands-on Work: Construction, Extraction, and Maintenance. **Personality Type:** Realistic. Realistic occupations frequently involve work activities that include practical, hands-on problems and solutions. These occupations often deal with plants, animals, and real-world materials like wood, tools, and machinery. Many of the occupations require working outside and do not involve a lot of paperwork or working closely with others. **Work Values:** Moral Values; Coworkers; Advancement; Activity; Supervision, Technical. **Skills:** Repairing; Mathematics; Equipment Selection. **Abilities:** *Cognitive*—Visualization; Information Ordering; Spatial Orientation; Oral Comprehension; Number Facility; Category Flexibility. *Psychomotor*—Manual Dexterity; Reaction Time; Arm-Hand Steadiness. *Physical*—Static Strength; Dynamic Strength; Trunk Strength. *Sensory*—Far Vision; Peripheral Vision; Depth Perception. **General Work Activities:** *Information Input*—Getting Information Needed to Do the Job; Monitoring Processes, Materials, and Surroundings; Inspecting Equipment, Structures, Materials. *Mental Process*—Thinking Creatively; Judging Qualities of Things, Services, Other People's Work; Evaluating Information Against Standards; Organizing, Planning, and Prioritizing. *Work Output*—Performing General Physical Activities; Handling and Moving Objects; Controlling Machines and Processes. *Interacting with Others*—Communicating with Other Workers; Establishing and Maintaining Relationships; Assisting and Caring for Others. **Physical Work Conditions:** Using Hands on Objects, Tools, or Controls; Common Protective or Safety Attire; Standing. **Other Job Characteristics:** Importance of Being Sure All Is Done; Importance of Being Exact or Accurate; Consequence of Error.

Experience: Job Zone 1. No previous work-related skill, knowledge, or experience is needed. **Job Preparation:** SVP Below 4.0—Less than 6 months. **Knowledge:** Building and Construction;

Mechanical; Public Safety and Security; Engineering and Technology; Mathematics. **Instructional Programs:** No data available.

Related DOT Jobs: 764.687-050 Cooper Helper; 860.664-014 Joiner Helper; 860.664-018 Shipwright Helper; 869.664-014 Construction Worker I; 869.687-026 Construction Worker II; 869.687-042 Timber-Framer Helper.

47-3013.00 Helpers—Electricians (Construction Helpers)

Education: Short-term O-T-J training

Employed: 575,959

Openings: 167,103

Projected Growth: 7.3%

Earnings: No data available.

Help electricians by performing duties of lesser skill. Use, supply, or hold materials or tools; clean work area and equipment.

Drills holes for wiring, using power drill, and pulls or pushes wiring through opening. Traces out short circuits in wiring, using test meter. Measures, cuts, and bends wire and conduit, using measuring instruments and hand tools. Transports tools, materials, equipment, and supplies to work site, manually or by using handtruck or driving truck. Bolts component parts together to form tower assemblies, using hand tools. Solders electrical connections, using soldering iron. Rigs scaffolds, hoists, and shoring, erects barricades, and digs trenches. Strings transmission lines or cables through ducts or conduits, underground, through equipment, or to towers. Disassembles defective electrical equipment, replaces defective or worn parts, and reassembles equipment, using hand tools. Threads conduit ends, connects couplings, and fabricates and secures conduit support brackets, using hand tools. Breaks up concrete to facilitate installation or repair of equipment, using airhammer. Trims trees and clears undergrowth along right-of-way. Raises, lowers, or positions equipment, tools, and materials for installation or use, using hoist, handline, or block and tackle. Maintains tools and equipment, washes parts, and keeps supplies and parts in order. Strips insulation from wire ends, using wire stripping pliers, and attaches wires to terminals for subsequent soldering. Examines electrical units for loose connections and broken insulation and tightens connections, using hand tools.

GOE Number, Interest Area, and Work Group: 05.03.01; Mechanics, Installers, and Repairers; Mechanical Work: Vehicles and Facilities. **Personality Type:** Realistic. Realistic occupations frequently involve work activities that include practical, hands-on problems and solutions. These occupations often deal with plants, animals, and real-world materials like wood, tools, and machinery. Many of the occupations require working outside and do not involve a lot of paperwork or working closely with others. **Work Values:** Moral Values; Supervision, Technical; Advancement; Activity; Coworkers. **Skills:** Equipment Selection; Equipment Maintenance; Mathematics; Installation; Repairing. **Abilities:** *Cognitive*—Spatial Orientation; Information Ordering; Visualization; Oral Comprehension; Memorization; Problem Sensitivity. *Psychomotor*—Manual Dexterity; Arm-Hand Steadiness; Finger Dexterity; Multilimb Coordination. *Physical*—Static Strength;

Explosive Strength; Trunk Strength. *Sensory*—Near Vision; Visual Color Discrimination; Depth Perception. **General Work Activities:** *Information Input*—Identifying Objects, Actions, and Events; Getting Information Needed to Do the Job; Monitoring Processes, Materials, and Surroundings; Inspecting Equipment, Structures, Materials. *Mental Process*—Judging Qualities of Things, Services, Other People's Work; Organizing, Planning, and Prioritizing; Updating and Using Job-Relevant Knowledge. *Work Output*—Handling and Moving Objects; Repairing and Maintaining Electrical Equipment; Performing General Physical Activities. *Interacting with Others*—Assisting and Caring for Others; Communicating with Other Workers; Establishing and Maintaining Relationships. **Physical Work Conditions:** Using Hands on Objects, Tools, or Controls; Common Protective or Safety Attire; Standing; Hazardous Conditions. **Other Job Characteristics:** Consequence of Error; Degree of Automation; Importance of Being Sure All Is Done.

Experience: Job Zone 2. Some previous work-related skill, knowledge, or experience may be helpful, but usually is not needed. **Job Preparation:** SVP 4.00 to 5.99—6 months to less than 2 years. **Knowledge:** Mechanical; Engineering and Technology; Computers and Electronics; Building and Construction; Public Safety and Security. **Instructional Programs:** No data available.

Related DOT Jobs: 821.667-010 Helper, Electrical; 821.684-014 Tower Erector Helper; 822.664-010 Protective-Signal-Installer Helper; 822.684-014 Protective-Signal-Repairer Helper; 825.684-010 Electrician Helper, Automotive; 829.684-022 Electrician Helper; 829.684-026 Electrician Helper.

47-3014.00 Helpers—Painters, Paperhangers, Plasterers, and Stucco Masons (Construction Helpers)

Education: Short-term O-T-J training
Employed: 575,959
Openings: 167,103
Projected Growth: 7.3%
Earnings: No data available.

Help painters, paperhangers, plasterers, or stucco masons by performing duties of lesser skill. Use, supply, or hold materials or tools; clean work area and equipment.

Performs any combination of support duties to assist painter, paperhanger, plasterer, or mason. Covers surfaces of articles not to be painted with masking tape prior to painting. Smoothes surfaces of articles to be painted, using sanding and buffing tools and equipment. Fills cracks or breaks in surfaces of plaster articles with putty or epoxy compounds. Removes articles such as cabinets, metal furniture, and paint containers, from stripping tanks after prescribed period of time. Pours specified amounts of chemical solutions into stripping tanks. Places articles to be stripped into stripping tanks.

GOE Number, Interest Area, and Work Group: 06.04.01; Construction, Mining, and Drilling; Hands-on Work: Construction, Extraction, and Maintenance. **Personality Type:** Realistic. Realistic occupations frequently involve work activities that include practical, hands-on problems and solutions. These occupations often deal with plants, animals, and real-world materials like wood,

tools, and machinery. Many of the occupations require working outside and do not involve a lot of paperwork or working closely with others. **Work Values:** Moral Values; Supervision, Technical; Activity; Coworkers; Advancement. **Skills:** Coordination; Equipment Selection. **Abilities:** *Cognitive*—Oral Comprehension; Information Ordering; Problem Sensitivity; Number Facility; Oral Expression. *Psychomotor*—Manual Dexterity. *Physical*—Static Strength; Dynamic Strength; Extent Flexibility. *Sensory*—Visual Color Discrimination. **General Work Activities:** *Information Input*—Getting Information Needed to Do the Job; Inspecting Equipment, Structures, Materials; Monitoring Processes, Materials, and Surroundings. *Mental Process*—Updating and Using Job-Relevant Knowledge; Evaluating Information Against Standards; Organizing, Planning, and Prioritizing. *Work Output*—Performing General Physical Activities; Handling and Moving Objects; Controlling Machines and Processes. *Interacting with Others*—Assisting and Caring for Others; Communicating with Other Workers; Establishing and Maintaining Relationships. **Physical Work Conditions:** Using Hands on Objects, Tools, or Controls; Indoors; Standing; Contaminants; Common Protective or Safety Attire. **Other Job Characteristics:** Consequence of Error; Importance of Being Sure All Is Done; Importance of Being Exact or Accurate.

Experience: Job Zone 1. No previous work-related skill, knowledge, or experience is needed. **Job Preparation:** SVP Below 4.0—Less than 6 months. **Knowledge:** Building and Construction; Mechanical; Mathematics; Chemistry; Engineering and Technology; Production and Processing. **Instructional Programs:** No data available.

Related DOT Job: 840.687-010 Painter Helper, Shipyard.

47-3015.00 Helpers—Pipelayers, Plumbers, Pipefitters, and Steamfitters (Construction Helpers)

Education: Short-term O-T-J training
Employed: 575,959
Openings: 167,103
Projected Growth: 7.3%
Earnings: No data available.

Help plumbers, pipefitters, steamfitters, or pipelayers by performing duties of lesser skill. Use, supply, or hold materials or tools; clean work area and equipment.

Disassembles and removes damaged or worn pipe. Mounts brackets and hangers on walls and ceilings to hold pipes. Cuts or drills holes in walls to accommodate passage of pipes, using pneumatic drill. Immerses pipe in chemical solution to remove dirt, oil, and scale. Assists in installing gas burner to convert furnaces from wood, coal, or oil. Requisitions tools and equipment and selects type and size of pipe. Fits or assists in fitting valves, couplings, or assemblies to tanks, pumps, or systems, using hand tools. Cleans shop, work area, and machines, using solvent and rags. Fills pipe with sand or resin to prevent distortion, and holds pipes during bending and installation.

GOE Number, Interest Area, and Work Group: 06.04.01; Construction, Mining, and Drilling; Hands-on Work: Construction, Extraction, and Maintenance. **Personality Type:** Realistic. Realistic occupations frequently involve work activities that include practical, hands-on problems and solutions. These occupations often deal with plants, animals, and real-world materials like wood, tools, and machinery. Many of the occupations require working outside and do not involve a lot of paperwork or working closely with others. **Work Values:** Moral Values; Supervision, Technical; Advancement; Activity; Supervision, Human Relations; Coworkers; Security. **Skills:** Equipment Selection; Equipment Maintenance; Installation; Repairing; Coordination. **Abilities:** *Cognitive*—Oral Comprehension; Information Ordering; Visualization; Problem Sensitivity; Spatial Orientation; Oral Expression. *Psychomotor*—Manual Dexterity; Arm-Hand Steadiness; Control Precision; Multilimb Coordination. *Physical*—Static Strength; Extent Flexibility; Trunk Strength. *Sensory*—Depth Perception; Far Vision; Visual Color Discrimination. **General Work Activities:** *Information Input*—Getting Information Needed to Do the Job; Monitoring Processes, Materials, and Surroundings; Identifying Objects, Actions, and Events; Estimating Needed Characteristics. *Mental Process*—Updating and Using Job-Relevant Knowledge; Organizing, Planning, and Prioritizing; Judging Qualities of Things, Services, Other People's Work. *Work Output*—Handling and Moving Objects; Controlling Machines and Processes; Performing General Physical Activities. *Interacting with Others*—Assisting and Caring for Others; Communicating with Other Workers; Establishing and Maintaining Relationships. **Physical Work Conditions:** Using Hands on Objects, Tools, or Controls; Indoors; Standing. **Other Job Characteristics:** Degree of Automation; Consequence of Error; Importance of Being Sure All Is Done.

Experience: Job Zone 2. Some previous work-related skill, knowledge, or experience may be helpful, but usually is not needed. **Job Preparation:** SVP 4.00 to 5.99—6 months to less than 2 years. **Knowledge:** Mechanical; Building and Construction; Engineering and Technology; Production and Processing; Chemistry; Physics. **Instructional Programs:** No data available.

Related DOT Jobs: 862.684-018 Pipe-Fitter Helper; 862.684-022 Pipe-Fitter Helper.

47-3016.00 Helpers—Roofers (Helpers, Roofers)

Education: No data available.

Employed: 29,820

Openings: No data available.

Projected Growth: No data available.

Earnings: $16,900

Help roofers by performing duties of lesser skill. Use, supply, or hold materials or tools; clean work area and equipment.

GOE Number, Interest Area, and Work Group: 06.04.01; Construction, Mining, and Drilling; Hands-on Work: Construction, Extraction, and Maintenance. **Instructional Programs:** No data available. **Note:** The Department of Labor has not collected some data for this job, so it has fewer details than the other descriptions.

47-4000 Other Construction and Related Workers

47-4011.00 Construction and Building Inspectors
(Construction and Building Inspectors)

Education: Work experience in a related occupation

Employed: 68,104

Openings: 3,515

Projected Growth: 15.7%

Earnings: $37,540

Inspect structures, using engineering skills to determine structural soundness and compliance with specifications, building codes, and other regulations. Conduct inspections that are general in nature or that are limited to a specific area such as electrical systems or plumbing.

Records and notifies owners, violators, and authorities of violations of construction specifications and building codes. Computes estimates of work completed and approves payment for contractors. Evaluates premises for cleanliness, including garbage disposal and lack of vermin infestation. Maintains daily logs, inventory, and inspection and construction records; prepares reports. Reviews complaints, obtains evidence, and testifies in court that construction does not conform to code. Issues violation notices, stop-work orders, and permits for construction and occupancy. Approves and signs plans that meet required specifications. Measures dimensions and verifies level, alignment, and elevation of structures and fixtures to ensure compliance to building plans and codes. Reviews and interprets plans, blueprints, specifications, and construction methods to ensure compliance to legal requirements. Inspects bridges, dams, highways, building, wiring, plumbing, electrical circuits, sewer, heating system, and foundation for conformance to specifications and codes. Confers with owners, violators, and authorities to explain regulations and recommend alterations in construction or specifications.

GOE Number, Interest Area, and Work Group: 02.08.02; Science, Math, and Engineering; Engineering Technology: Industrial and Safety. **Personality Type:** Conventional. Conventional occupations frequently involve following set procedures and routines. These occupations can include working with data and details more than with ideas. Usually there is a clear line of authority to follow. **Work Values:** Responsibility; Autonomy; Independence; Security; Supervision, Human Relations; Company Policies and Practices; Activity; Ability Utilization. **Skills:** Product Inspection; Speaking; Problem Identification; Active Listening; Active Learning; Critical Thinking; Writing; Reading Comprehension. **Abilities:** *Cognitive*—Problem Sensitivity; Oral Expression; Written Expression; Written Comprehension; Deductive Reasoning. *Psychomotor*—Speed of Limb Movement. *Physical*—Gross Body Equilibrium; Stamina; Extent Flexibility. *Sensory*—Near Vision; Far Vision; Visual Color Discrimination. **General Work Activities:** *Information Input*—Inspecting Equipment, Structures, Materials; Getting Information Needed to Do the Job; Identifying Objects, Actions, and Events. *Mental Process*—Evaluating Information

Against Standards; Judging Qualities of Things, Services, Other People's Work; Making Decisions and Solving Problems. *Work Output*—Documenting and Recording Information; Handling and Moving Objects; Performing General Physical Activities. *Interacting with Others*—Communicating with Persons Outside Organization; Performing Administrative Activities; Interpreting Meaning of Information to Others. **Physical Work Conditions:** Standing; Indoors; Outdoors. **Other Job Characteristics:** Consequence of Error; Importance of Being Sure All Is Done; Importance of Being Exact or Accurate.

Experience: Job Zone 3. Previous work-related skill, knowledge, or experience is required. **Job Preparation:** SVP 6.0 to less than 7.0—More than 1 year and less than 4 years. **Knowledge:** Building and Construction; Public Safety and Security; Mathematics; Design; Mechanical. **Instructional Program:** 460403 Construction/Building Inspector.

Related DOT Jobs: 168.167-030 Inspector, Building; 168.167-034 Inspector, Electrical; 168.167-046 Inspector, Heating and Refrigeration; 168.167-050 Inspector, Plumbing; 168.267-102 Plan Checker; 168.367-018 Code Inspector; 182.267-010 Construction Inspector.

47-4021.00 Elevator Installers and Repairers (Elevator Installers and Repairers)

Education: Long-term O-T-J training

Employed: 29,608

Openings: 5,088

Projected Growth: 12.2%

Earnings: $47,860

Assemble, install, repair, or maintain electric or hydraulic freight or passenger elevators, escalators, or dumbwaiters.

Operates elevator to determine power demand and tests power consumption to detect overload factors. Adjusts safety controls, counter weights, and mechanism of doors. Connects electrical wiring to control panels and electric motors. Disassembles defective unit and repairs or replaces parts such as locks, gears, cables, and electric wiring. Lubricates bearings and other parts to minimize friction. Locates malfunction in brakes, motor, switches, and signal and control systems, using test equipment. Completes service reports to verify conformance to prescribed standards. Cuts prefabricated sections of framework, rails, and other components to specified dimensions. Studies blueprints to determine layout of framework and foundations. Inspects wiring connections, control panel hookups, door installation, and alignment and clearance of car hoistway. Installs safety and control devices, cables, drives, rails, motors, and elevator cars.

GOE Number, Interest Area, and Work Group: 05.02.01; Mechanics, Installers, and Repairers; Electrical and Electronic Systems: Installation and Repair. **Personality Type:** Realistic. Realistic occupations frequently involve work activities that include practical, hands-on problems and solutions. These occupations often deal with plants, animals, and real-world materials like wood, tools, and machinery. Many of the occupations require working outside and do not involve a lot of paperwork or working closely with others. **Work Values:** Moral Values; Independence; Com-

pany Policies and Practices; Security; Compensation; Responsibility; Supervision, Technical. **Skills:** Installation; Repairing; Product Inspection; Troubleshooting; Equipment Maintenance. **Abilities:** *Cognitive*—Deductive Reasoning; Problem Sensitivity; Information Ordering; Visualization; Written Comprehension. *Psychomotor*—Manual Dexterity; Control Precision; Finger Dexterity. *Physical*—Extent Flexibility; Static Strength; Trunk Strength; Dynamic Strength. *Sensory*—Hearing Sensitivity; Night Vision; Depth Perception; Visual Color Discrimination. **General Work Activities:** *Information Input*—Inspecting Equipment, Structures, Materials; Getting Information Needed to Do the Job; Identifying Objects, Actions, and Events. *Mental Process*—Evaluating Information Against Standards; Making Decisions and Solving Problems; Updating and Using Job-Relevant Knowledge. *Work Output*—Repairing and Maintaining Mechanical Equipment; Handling and Moving Objects; Repairing and Maintaining Electrical Equipment. *Interacting with Others*—Communicating with Other Workers; Performing Administrative Activities; Communicating with Persons Outside Organization. **Physical Work Conditions:** Indoors; Using Hands on Objects, Tools, or Controls; Hazardous Equipment; Standing. **Other Job Characteristics:** Consequence of Error; Importance of Being Sure All Is Done; Importance of Being Exact or Accurate.

Experience: Job Zone 4. A minimum of two to four years of work-related skill, knowledge, or experience is needed. **Job Preparation:** SVP 7.0 to less than 8.0—2 years to less than 10 years. **Knowledge:** Mechanical; Building and Construction; Engineering and Technology; Public Safety and Security; Mathematics. **Instructional Program:** 470303 Industrial Machinery Maintenance and Repairer.

Related DOT Jobs: 825.261-014 Elevator Examiner-and-Adjuster; 825.281-030 Elevator Repairer; 825.281-034 Elevator-Repairer Apprentice; 825.361-010 Elevator Constructor.

47-4031.00 Fence Erectors (Fence Erectors)

Education: No data available.

Employed: 18,300

Openings: No data available.

Projected Growth: No data available.

Earnings: $19,820

Erect and repair metal and wooden fences and fence gates around highways, industrial establishments, residences, or farms, using hand and power tools.

Cuts metal tubing, using pipe cutter. Attaches fence rail support to post, using hammer and pliers. Inserts metal tubing through rail supports. Attaches fencing to frame. Nails top and bottom rails to fence posts, or inserts them in slots on posts. Stretches wire, wire mesh, or chain link fencing between posts. Completes top fence rail of metal fence by connecting tube sections, using metal sleeves. Welds metal parts together, using portable gas welding equipment. Blasts rock formations with dynamite to facilitate digging of postholes. Lays out fence line, using tape measure; marks positions for postholes. Erects alternate panel, basket weave, and louvered fences. Sets metal or wooden post in upright position in posthole. Mixes and pours concrete around base of post or tamps soil into posthole to embed post. Assembles gate and fastens gate in position, using hand tools. Saws required lengths of lumber to make rails for wooden fence. Digs postholes with spade, posthole digger, or power-driven auger. Aligns posts, by using line or by sighting; verifies vertical alignment of posts with plumb bob or spirit level. Nails pointed slats to rails to construct picket fence. Attaches rails or tension wire along bottoms of posts to form fencing frame.

GOE Number, Interest Area, and Work Group: 06.02.03; Construction, Mining, and Drilling; Construction: General. **Personality Type:** Realistic. Realistic occupations frequently involve work activities that include practical, hands-on problems and solutions. These occupations often deal with plants, animals, and real-world materials like wood, tools, and machinery. Many of the occupations require working outside and do not involve a lot of paperwork or working closely with others. **Work Values:** Moral Values; Activity; Supervision, Human Relations; Independence; Supervision, Technical. **Skills:** Mathematics; Equipment Selection; Repairing; Operation and Control. **Abilities:** *Cognitive*—Visualization; Spatial Orientation; Information Ordering; Selective Attention; Number Facility. *Psychomotor*—Manual Dexterity; Wrist-Finger Speed; Multilimb Coordination. *Physical*—Static Strength; Extent Flexibility; Trunk Strength. *Sensory*—Depth Perception; Glare Sensitivity; Peripheral Vision; Night Vision; Sound Localization. **General Work Activities:** *Information Input*—Getting Information Needed to Do the Job; Estimating Needed Characteristics; Identifying Objects, Actions, and Events. *Mental Process*—Making Decisions and Solving Problems; Organizing, Planning, and Prioritizing; Evaluating Information Against Standards; Analyzing Data or Information. *Work Output*—Performing General Physical Activities; Handling and Moving Objects; Implementing Ideas and Programs. *Interacting with Others*—Performing for or Working with the Public; Communicating with Persons Outside Organization; Monitoring and Controlling Resources. **Physical Work Conditions:** Outdoors; Using Hands on Objects, Tools, or Controls; Standing. **Other Job Characteristics:** Importance of Being Sure All Is Done; Importance of Being Exact or Accurate; Frustrating Circumstances; Consequence of Error.

Experience: Job Zone 2. Some previous work-related skill, knowledge, or experience may be helpful, but usually is not needed. **Job Preparation:** SVP 4.00 to 5.99—6 months to less than 2 years. **Knowledge:** Building and Construction; Mechanical; Mathematics; Design; Engineering and Technology. **Instructional Program:** 010201 Agricultural Mechanization, General.

Related DOT Job: 869.684-022 Fence Erector.

47-4041.00 Hazardous Materials Removal Workers
(Hazardous Materials Removal Workers)

Education: Moderate-term O-T-J training

Employed: 37,725

Openings: 5,470

Projected Growth: 19.3%

Earnings: $27,620

Identify, remove, pack, transport, or dispose of hazardous materials, including asbestos, lead-based paint, waste oil, fuel, transmission fluid, radioactive materials, and contaminated

soil. Operate earth-moving equipment or trucks. Obtain required specialized training and certification in hazardous materials handling; obtain required confined-entry permit.

GOE Number, Interest Area, and Work Group: 06.02.03; Construction, Mining, and Drilling; Construction: General. **Instructional Program:** 469999 Construction Trades, Other. **Note:** The Department of Labor has not collected some data for this job, so it has fewer details than the other descriptions.

47-4041.01 Irradiated-Fuel Handlers (Hazardous Materials Removal Workers)

Education: Moderate-term O-T-J training

Employed: 37,725

Openings: 5,470

Projected Growth: 19.3%

Earnings: $27,620

Package, store, and convey irradiated fuels and wastes, using hoists, mechanical arms, shovels, and industrial truck.

Drives truck to convey contaminated waste to designated sea or ground location. Loads and unloads materials into containers and onto trucks, using hoists or forklift. Mixes and pours concrete into forms to encase waste material for disposal. Records number of containers stored at disposal site, and specifies amount and type of equipment and waste disposed. Cleans contaminated equipment for reuse, using detergents and solvents, sandblasters, filter pumps, and steam cleaners. Operates machines and equipment to package, store, or transport loads of waste materials. Follows prescribed safety procedures and complies with federal laws regulating waste disposal methods.

GOE Number, Interest Area, and Work Group: 08.07.01; Industrial Production; Hands-on Work: Loading, Moving, Hoisting, and Conveying. **Personality Type:** Realistic. Realistic occupations frequently involve work activities that include practical, hands-on problems and solutions. These occupations often deal with plants, animals, and real-world materials like wood, tools, and machinery. Many of the occupations require working outside and do not involve a lot of paperwork or working closely with others. **Work Values:** Moral Values; Supervision, Technical; Independence; Supervision, Human Relations; Compensation; Security; Company Policies and Practices. **Skills:** Reading Comprehension; Operation and Control; Writing. **Abilities:** *Cognitive*—Information Ordering; Number Facility; Oral Comprehension; Written Comprehension; Written Expression. *Psychomotor*—Control Precision; Multilimb Coordination; Reaction Time. *Physical*—Static Strength; Gross Body Coordination. **General Work Activities:** *Information Input*—Monitoring Processes, Materials, and Surroundings; Identifying Objects, Actions, and Events; Getting Information Needed to Do the Job; Inspecting Equipment, Structures, Materials. *Mental Process*—Evaluating Information Against Standards; Processing Information; Making Decisions and Solving Problems. *Work Output*—Handling and Moving Objects; Performing General Physical Activities; Controlling Machines and Processes; Documenting and Recording Information. *Interacting with Others*—Performing Administrative Activities; Communicating with Other Workers; Communicating with Persons Outside Organization; Establishing and Maintaining Relationships; Assisting and Caring for Others; Providing Consultation and Advice to Others. **Physical Work Conditions:** Contaminants; Outdoors; Radiation. **Other Job Characteristics:** Consequence of Error; Importance of Being Sure All Is Done; Importance of Being Exact or Accurate.

Experience: Job Zone 2. Some previous work-related skill, knowledge, or experience may be helpful, but usually is not needed. **Job Preparation:** SVP 4.00 to 5.99—6 months to less than 2 years. **Knowledge:** Transportation; Production and Processing; Chemistry; Public Safety and Security; Law, Government and Jurisprudence. **Instructional Program:** 410205 Nuclear/Nuclear Power Technology/Technician.

Related DOT Jobs: 921.663-034 Irradiated-Fuel Handler; 955.383-010 Waste-Disposal Attendant.

47-4051.00 Highway Maintenance Workers (Highway Maintenance Workers)

Education: Short-term O-T-J training

Employed: 155,284

Openings: 20,512

Projected Growth: 11.1%

Earnings: $24,490

Maintain highways, municipal and rural roads, airport runways, and rights-of-way. Patch broken or eroded pavement. Repair guard rails, highway markers, and snow fences. Mow or clear brush from along road; plow snow from roadway.

Blends compounds to form adhesive mixture, using spoon. Drives tractor with mower attachment to cut grass. Dumps, spreads, and tamps asphalt, using pneumatic tamper to patch broken pavement. Measures and marks locations for installation of markers, using tape, string, or chalk. Erects, installs, and repairs guardrails, highway markers, button-type lane markers, and snow fences, using hand tools and power tools. Verifies alignment of markers by sight. Drives truck or tractor equipped with adjustable snow plow and blower unit. Drives truck to transport crew and equipment to work site. Sets signs and cones around work area to divert traffic.

GOE Number, Interest Area, and Work Group: 06.04.01; Construction, Mining, and Drilling; Hands-on Work: Construction, Extraction, and Maintenance. **Personality Type:** Realistic. Realistic occupations frequently involve work activities that include practical, hands-on problems and solutions. These occupations often deal with plants, animals, and real-world materials like wood, tools, and machinery. Many of the occupations require working outside and do not involve a lot of paperwork or working closely with others. **Work Values:** Moral Values; Supervision, Human Relations; Company Policies and Practices; Coworkers; Compensation; Independence; Security; Activity. **Skills:** Operation and Control; Repairing; Installation; Equipment Selection; Coordination. **Abilities:** *Cognitive*—Spatial Orientation; Selective Attention; Problem Sensitivity; Oral Comprehension; Time Sharing; Number Facility. *Psychomotor*—Reaction Time; Multilimb Coordination. Response Orientation. *Physical*—Static Strength; Trunk Strength; Dynamic Strength. *Sensory*—Far Vision; Depth Perception; Glare Sensitivity. **General Work Activities:** *Information Input*—Getting Information Needed to Do the Job; Monitoring Processes, Materials, and Surroundings; Inspecting Equipment, Structures, Materials. *Mental Process*—Evaluating Information Against Standards; Judging Qualities of Things, Services, Other People's Work; Analyzing Data or Information. *Work Output*—Performing General Physical Activities; Operating Vehicles or Equipment; Handling and Moving Objects. *Interacting with Others*—Communicating with Other Workers; Establishing and Maintaining Relationships; Assisting and Caring for Others; Coordinating Work and Activities of Others. **Physical Work Conditions:** Outdoors; Using Hands on Objects, Tools, or Controls; Standing. **Other Job Characteristics:** Consequence of Error; Importance of Being Sure All Is Done; Frustrating Circumstances.

Experience: Job Zone 1. No previous work-related skill, knowledge, or experience is needed. **Job Preparation:** SVP Below 4.0—Less than 6 months. **Knowledge:** Building and Construction; Public Safety and Security; Mechanical; Mathematics; Geography. **Instructional Program:** 010605 Landscaping Operations and Management.

Related DOT Jobs: 859.684-010 Lane-Marker Installer; 899.684-014 Highway-Maintenance Worker.

47-4061.00 Rail-Track Laying and Maintenance Equipment Operators (Rail-Track Laying and Maintenance Equipment Operators)

Education: No data available.

Employed: 15,670

Openings: No data available.

Projected Growth: No data available.

Earnings: $34,330

Lay, repair, and maintain track for standard or narrow-gauge railroad equipment used in regular railroad service or in plant yards, quarries, sand and gravel pits, and mines. Includes ballast cleaning machine operators and road bed tamping machine operators.

Strings and attaches wire-guidelines machine to rails to level or align track or rails. Pushes control to close grasping device on track or rail section to raise or move section to specified location. Observes leveling indicator arms to verify levelness and alignment of track. Lubricates machines, changes oil, and fills hydraulic reservoirs to specified levels. Drives graders, tamping machines, brooms, and ballast-cleaning-and-spreading machines to redistribute gravel and ballast between rails. Turns wheels of machine, using lever controls, to adjust guidelines for track alignments and grades, following specifications. Adjusts controls of machines that spread, shape, raise, level, and align track, according to specifications. Drives vehicle that automatically moves and lays track or rails over section of track to be constructed, repaired, or maintained. Engages mechanism that lays track or rail to specified gauge.

GOE Number, Interest Area, and Work Group: 06.02.03; Construction, Mining, and Drilling; Construction: General. **Personality Type:** Realistic. Realistic occupations frequently involve work activities that include practical, hands-on problems and solutions. These occupations often deal with plants, animals, and real-world materials like wood, tools, and machinery. Many of the occupations require working outside and do not involve a lot of paperwork or working closely with others. **Work Values:** Moral Values; Supervision, Human Relations; Company Policies and Practices; Supervision, Technical; Compensation. **Skills:** Operation and Control; Operation Monitoring; Equipment Maintenance; Monitoring; Product Inspection; Judgment and Decision Making; Equipment Selection. **Abilities:** *Cognitive*—Visualization; Information Ordering; Selective Attention; Spatial Orientation; Time Sharing; Inductive Reasoning. *Psychomotor*—Control Precision; Multilimb Coordination; Reaction Time. *Physical*—Static Strength; Explosive Strength; Gross Body Coordination. *Sensory*—Depth Perception; Peripheral Vision; Far Vision. **General Work Activities:** *Information Input*—Getting Information Needed to Do the Job; Inspecting Equipment, Structures, Materials; Monitoring Processes, Materials, and Surroundings. *Mental Process*—Evaluating Information Against Standards; Analyzing Data or Information; Processing Information; Judging Qualities of Things, Services, Other People's Work. *Work Output*—Operating Vehicles or Equipment; Controlling Machines and Processes; Handling and Moving Objects. *Interacting with Others*—Establishing and Maintaining Relationships; Communicating with Other Workers; Monitoring and Controlling Resources. **Physical Work Conditions:** Outdoors; Using Hands on Objects, Tools, or Controls; Hazardous Equipment. **Other Job Characteristics:** Consequence of Error; Degree of Automation; Importance of Being Sure All Is Done.

Experience: Job Zone 1. No previous work-related skill, knowledge, or experience is needed. **Job Preparation:** SVP Below 4.0—Less than 6 months. **Knowledge:** Building and Construction; Mechanical; Engineering and Technology; Transportation; Physics. **Instructional Programs:** 470302 Heavy Equipment Maintenance and Repairer; 490202 Construction Equipment Operator.

Related DOT Jobs: 859.683-018 Railway-Equipment Operator; 910.663-010 Track-Moving-Machine Operator; 910.683-018 Track-Surfacing-Machine Operator.

47-4071.00 Septic Tank Servicers and Sewer Pipe Cleaners (Septic Tank Servicers and Sewer Pipe Cleaners)

Education: No data available.

Employed: 10,450

Openings: No data available.

Projected Growth: No data available.

Earnings: $25,410

Clean and repair septic tanks, sewer lines, or drains. Patch walls and partitions of tank; replace damaged drain tile; repair breaks in underground piping.

Services, adjusts, and makes minor repairs to equipment, machines, and attachments. Inspects manholes to locate stoppage of sewer line and repaired sewer line joints to ensure tightness, prior to backfilling. Cleans sewage collection points and sanitary lines and repairs catch basins, manholes, culverts, and storm drains. Cleans and disinfects domestic basements and other areas flooded as result of sewer stoppages. Installs rotary knives on flexible cable, mounted on reel of machine, according to diameter of pipe to be cleaned. Withdraws cable and observes residue for evidence of mud, roots, grease, and other deposits indicating broken or clogged sewer line. Operates sewer-cleaning equipment, including power rodder, high velocity water jet, sewer flusher, bucket machine, wayne ball, and vac-all. Starts machine to feed revolving cable or rods into opening, stopping machine and changing knives to conform to pipe size. Cuts damaged section of pipe with cutters, removes broken section from ditch, and replaces pipe section, using pipe sleeve. Measures distance of excavation site, using plumbers' snake, tapeline, or length of cutting head within sewer and marks trenching area. Covers repaired pipe with dirt and packs backfilled excavation, using air and gasoline tamper. Breaks asphalt and other pavement, using airhammer, pick, and shovel. Notifies coworkers to dig out ruptured line; digs out shallow sewers, using shovel. Requisitions tools and equipment and prepares records showing actions taken. Drives pickup trucks to haul crew, materials, and equipment. Updates sewer maps and manhole charting. Communicates with supervisor and other workers, using radio telephone. Rotates cleaning rods manually with turning pin. Taps mainline sewers to install sewer saddles.

GOE Number, Interest Area, and Work Group: 06.04.01; Construction, Mining, and Drilling; Hands-on Work: Construction, Extraction, and Maintenance. **Personality Type:** Realistic. Realistic occupations frequently involve work activities that include practical, hands-on problems and solutions. These occupations often deal with plants, animals, and real-world materials like wood, tools, and machinery. Many of the occupations require working outside and do not involve a lot of paperwork or working closely with others. **Work Values:** Moral Values; Independence; Supervision, Technical; Security; Company Policies and Practices; Supervision, Human Relations. **Skills:** Operation and Control; Installation; Mathematics; Repairing; Equipment Selection. **Abilities:** *Cognitive*—Oral Comprehension; Oral Expression; Deductive Reasoning; Problem Sensitivity; Inductive Reasoning; Written Comprehension. *Psychomotor*—Wrist-Finger Speed; Manual Dexterity; Arm-Hand Steadiness; Control Precision. *Physical*—Static Strength; Extent Flexibility; Trunk Strength. *Sensory*—Depth Perception. **General Work Activities:** *Information Input*—Inspecting Equipment, Structures, Materials; Getting Information Needed to Do the Job; Estimating Needed Characteristics. *Mental Process*—Making Decisions and Solving Problems; Analyzing Data or Information; Judging Qualities of Things, Services, Other People's Work. *Work Output*—Performing General Physical Activities; Handling and Moving Objects; Controlling Machines and Processes. *Interacting with Others*—Communicating with Other Workers; Communicating with Persons Outside Organization; Establishing and Maintaining Relationships. **Physical Work Conditions:** Outdoors; Using Hands on Objects, Tools, or Controls; Standing. **Other Job Characteristics:** Consequence of Error; Importance of Being Sure All Is Done; Frustrating Circumstances.

Experience: Job Zone 2. Some previous work-related skill, knowledge, or experience may be helpful, but usually is not needed. **Job Preparation:** SVP 4.00 to 5.99—6 months to less than 2 years. **Knowledge:** Mechanical; Building and Construction; Engineering and Technology; Mathematics; Clerical; Physics; Economics and Accounting. **Instructional Program:** 460501 Plumber and Pipefitter.

Related DOT Jobs: 869.664-018 Sewer-Line Repairer; 899.664-014 Sewer-Pipe Cleaner.

47-4091.00 Segmental Pavers (Paving, Surfacing, and Tamping Equipment Operators)

Education: Moderate-term O-T-J training

Employed: 73,980

Openings: 13,780

Projected Growth: 10.6%

Earnings: $24,510

Lay out, cut, and paste segmental paving units. Includes installers of bedding and restraining materials for the paving units.

GOE Number, Interest Area, and Work Group: 06.02.03; Construction, Mining, and Drilling; Construction: General. **Instructional Program:** 490202 Construction Equipment Operator. **Note:** The Department of Labor has not collected some data for this job, so it has fewer details than the other descriptions.

47-5000 Extraction Workers

47-5011.00 Derrick Operators, Oil and Gas (Derrick Operators, Oil and Gas Extraction)

Education: No data available.

Employed: 13,110

Openings: No data available.

Projected Growth: No data available.

Earnings: $26,060

Rig derrick equipment and operate pumps to circulate mud through drill hole.

Starts pumps that circulate mud through drill pipe and borehole to cool drill bit and flush out drill cuttings. Cleans and oils pulleys, blocks, and cables. Sets and bolts crown block to posts at top of derrick. Strings cables through pulleys and blocks. Weighs clay. Repairs pumps. Clamps holding fixture on end of hoisting cable. Mixes drilling mud, using portable power mixer.

GOE Number, Interest Area, and Work Group: 06.03.01; Construction, Mining, and Drilling; Mining and Drilling. **Personality Type:** Realistic. Realistic occupations frequently involve work activities that include practical, hands-on problems and solutions. These occupations often deal with plants, animals, and real-world materials like wood, tools, and machinery. Many of the occupations require working outside and do not involve a lot of paperwork or working closely with others. **Work Values:** Moral Values; Company Policies and Practices; Supervision, Human Relations; Supervision, Technical; Compensation; Activity. **Skills:** Repairing; Operation and Control; Equipment Maintenance; Troubleshooting; Operation Monitoring; Equipment Selection. **Abilities:** *Cognitive*—Visualization; Information Ordering; Spatial Orientation; Deductive Reasoning; Selective Attention; Flexibility of Closure. *Psychomotor*—Multilimb Coordination; Speed of Limb Movement; Rate Control. *Physical*—Static Strength; Extent Flexibility; Trunk Strength. *Sensory*—Depth Perception; Peripheral Vision; Glare Sensitivity. **General Work Activities:** *Information*

Input—Monitoring Processes, Materials, and Surroundings; Inspecting Equipment, Structures, Materials; Getting Information Needed to Do the Job. *Mental Process*—Judging Qualities of Things, Services, Other People's Work; Updating and Using Job-Relevant Knowledge; Making Decisions and Solving Problems; Analyzing Data or Information. *Work Output*—Controlling Machines and Processes; Performing General Physical Activities; Handling and Moving Objects. *Interacting with Others*—Communicating with Other Workers; Influencing Others or Selling; Assisting and Caring for Others; Establishing and Maintaining Relationships; Monitoring and Controlling Resources. **Physical Work Conditions:** Outdoors; Hazardous Equipment; Using Hands on Objects, Tools, or Controls; Standing. **Other Job Characteristics:** Degree of Automation; Consequence of Error; Importance of Being Sure All Is Done; Frustrating Circumstances.

Experience: Job Zone 2. Some previous work-related skill, knowledge, or experience may be helpful, but usually is not needed. **Job Preparation:** SVP 4.00 to 5.99—6 months to less than 2 years. **Knowledge:** Mechanical; Building and Construction; Public Safety and Security; Physics; Engineering and Technology. **Instructional Program:** 490299 Vehicle and Equipment Operators, Other.

Related DOT Job: 930.382-022 Rotary Derrick Operator.

47-5012.00 Rotary Drill Operators, Oil and Gas (Rotary Drill Operators, Oil and Gas Extraction)

Education: No data available.

Employed: 9,160

Openings: No data available.

Projected Growth: No data available.

Earnings: $31,940

Set up or operate a variety of drills to remove petroleum products from the earth and to find and remove core samples for testing during oil and gas exploration.

Connects sections of drill pipe, using hand tools and powered wrenches and tongs. Selects and changes drill bits according to nature of strata, using hand tools. Pushes levers and brake pedals to control draw works which lower and raise drill pipe and casing in and out of well. Positions truck-mounted derrick at drilling area specified on field map. Counts sections of drill rod to determine depth of borehole. Withdraws core barrel from hole and extracts core from barrel. Lowers and explodes charge in borehole to start flow of oil from well. Examines operation of slush pumps to ensure circulation and consistency of mud (drilling fluid) in well. Observes pressure gauge and moves control to regulate speed of rotary table and pressure of tools at bottom of borehole. Examines drillings or core samples from bottom of well to determine nature of strata. Repairs or replaces defective parts of machinery, using hand tools. Keeps record of footage drilled, location and nature of strata penetrated, and materials used. Caps well or turns valves to regulate outflow of oil from well. Fishes for and recovers lost or broken bits, casing, and drill pipes from well, using special tools.

GOE Number, Interest Area, and Work Group: 06.03.01; Construction, Mining, and Drilling; Mining and Drilling. **Personality Type:** Realistic. Realistic occupations frequently involve work activities that include practical, hands-on problems and solutions. These occupations often deal with plants, animals, and real-world materials like wood, tools, and machinery. Many of the occupations require working outside and do not involve a lot of paperwork or working closely with others. **Work Values:** Moral Values; Company Policies and Practices; Supervision, Human Relations; Compensation; Activity; Supervision, Technical. **Skills:** Repairing; Operation and Control; Operation Monitoring; Equipment Selection; Problem Identification; Equipment Maintenance. **Abilities:** *Cognitive*–Perceptual Speed; Inductive Reasoning; Spatial Orientation; Information Ordering; Selective Attention; Deductive Reasoning. *Psychomotor*–Control Precision; Multilimb Coordination; Manual Dexterity. *Physical*–Static Strength; Extent Flexibility; Trunk Strength. *Sensory*–Depth Perception; Far Vision; Visual Color Discrimination. **General Work Activities:** *Information Input*–Monitoring Processes, Materials, and Surroundings; Inspecting Equipment, Structures, Materials; Getting Information Needed to Do the Job. *Mental Process*–Analyzing Data or Information; Making Decisions and Solving Problems; Processing Information. *Work Output*–Controlling Machines and Processes; Handling and Moving Objects; Performing General Physical Activities. *Interacting with Others*–Communicating with Other Workers; Establishing and Maintaining Relationships; Performing Administrative Activities. **Physical Work Conditions:** Outdoors; Hazardous Equipment; Using Hands on Objects, Tools, or Controls. **Other Job Characteristics:** Degree of Automation; Consequence of Error; Importance of Being Sure All Is Done.

Experience: Job Zone 3. Previous work-related skill, knowledge, or experience is required. **Job Preparation:** SVP 6.0 to less than 7.0–More than 1 year and less than 4 years. **Knowledge:** Mechanical; Engineering and Technology; Mathematics; Physics; Geography. **Instructional Program:** 490299 Vehicle and Equipment Operators, Other.

Related DOT Jobs: 930.382-018 Prospecting Driller; 930.382-026 Rotary Driller; 950.382-022 Rotary-Rig Engine Operator.

47-5013.00 Service Unit Operators, Oil, Gas, and Mining (Service Unit Operators)

Education: No data available.
Employed: 13,190
Openings: No data available.
Projected Growth: No data available.
Earnings: $22,390

Operate equipment to increase oil flow from producing wells or to remove stuck pipe, casing, tools, or other obstructions from drilling wells. Perform similar services in mining exploration operations.

Observes variations on gauges, mud pumps, and pressure indicators, and listens to equipment to detect faulty operations or unusual conditions. Moves controls to back off pipe or to sever pipe at point of obstruction. Operates equipment to remove stuck pipe, casing, tools, or other obstructions from drilling wells, using specialized subsurface tools and instruments. Starts pumps which circulate water, oil, or other fluid through well, removing sand and other materials obstructing free flow of oil. Plans fishing methods and selects tools for removing obstacles such as liners, broken casing, screens, and drill pipe from wells. Confers with other personnel to gather information regarding size of pipes and tools and borehole conditions in wells. Perforates well casing or sidewall of borehole with explosive charge. Analyzes conditions of unserviceable oil or gas wells and directs recovery of lost equipment and other obstacles from boreholes. Directs drilling crew in installation of well-bottom equipment. Directs other workers to assemble and connect pipe and hydraulic lines of flushing equipment to wellhead. Directs activities of preparing for and drilling around lodged obstacles or specified earth formations with specialized tools and whipstocks. Prepares reports of services rendered, tools used, and time required. Interprets instrument readings to ascertain depth of obstruction. Assembles and operates sound-wave generating and detecting mechanisms for determining fluid level in wells. Assembles and lowers detection instruments into wells having drill pipe, drilling tools, or other obstructions wedged in well. Operates equipment to increase oil flow from producing wells. Operates hoist to lower and raise tools. Directs lowering of specialized equipment to point of obstruction.

GOE Number, Interest Area, and Work Group: 06.03.01; Construction, Mining, and Drilling; Mining and Drilling. **Personality Type:** Realistic. Realistic occupations frequently involve work activities that include practical, hands-on problems and solutions. These occupations often deal with plants, animals, and real-world materials like wood, tools, and machinery. Many of the occupations require working outside and do not involve a lot of paperwork or working closely with others. **Work Values:** Moral Values; Supervision, Human Relations; Compensation; Supervision, Technical; Company Policies and Practices. **Skills:** Equipment Selection; Operation and Control; Operation Monitoring; Active Listening; Critical Thinking; Monitoring; Problem Identification. **Abilities:** *Cognitive*–Oral Expression; Inductive Reasoning; Time Sharing; Visualization; Information Ordering; Oral Comprehension. *Psychomotor*–Control Precision; Multilimb Coordination; Reaction Time. *Physical*–Static Strength; Extent Flexibility; Dynamic Flexibility. *Sensory*–Depth Perception; Hearing Sensitivity; Auditory Attention. **General Work Activities:** *Information Input*–Getting Information Needed to Do the Job; Inspecting Equipment, Structures, Materials; Monitoring Processes, Materials, and Surroundings. *Mental Process*–Making Decisions and Solving Problems; Analyzing Data or Information; Updating and Using Job-Relevant Knowledge. *Work Output*–Controlling Machines and Processes; Performing General Physical Activities; Handling and Moving Objects. *Interacting with Others*–Communicating with Other Workers; Coordinating Work and Activities of Others; Establishing and Maintaining Relationships; Guiding, Directing and Motivating Subordinates. **Physical Work Conditions:** Outdoors; Using Hands on Objects, Tools, or Controls; Hazardous Equipment. **Other Job Characteristics:** Frustrating Circumstances; Consequence of Error; Importance of Being Sure All Is Done.

Experience: Job Zone 4. A minimum of two to four years of work-related skill, knowledge, or experience is needed. **Job Preparation:** SVP 7.0 to less than 8.0–2 years to less than 10 years. **Knowledge:** Mechanical; Engineering and Technology; Physics; Administration and Management; English Language; Mathematics. **Instructional Program:** 490299 Vehicle and Equipment Operators, Other.

Related DOT Jobs: 930.261-010 Fishing-Tool Technician, Oil Well; 930.361-010 Service-Unit Operator, Oil Well.

47-5021.00 Earth Drillers, Except Oil and Gas
(Earth Drillers, Except Oil and Gas)

Education: No data available.

Employed: 16,510

Openings: No data available.

Projected Growth: No data available.

Earnings: $27,890

Operate a variety of drills, such as rotary, churn, and pneumatic, to tap subsurface water and salt deposits, to remove core samples during mineral exploration or soil testing, and to facilitate the use of explosives in mining or construction. Use explosives. Includes horizontal and earth-boring machine operators.

GOE Number, Interest Area, and Work Group: 06.03.01; Construction, Mining, and Drilling; Mining and Drilling. **Instructional Program:** 490202 Construction Equipment Operator. **Note:** The Department of Labor has not collected some data for this job, so it has fewer details than the other descriptions.

47-5021.01 Construction Drillers (Earth Drillers, Except Oil and Gas)

Education: No data available.

Employed: 16,510

Openings: No data available.

Projected Growth: No data available.

Earnings: $27,890

Operate machine to drill or bore through earth or rock.

Operates machine to flush earth cuttings, or blows dust from hole. Monitors drilling operation and strata being drilled to determine need to adjust drilling or insert casing into hole. Retracts auger to force discharge dirt from hole. Operates hoist to lift powerline poles into position. Signals crane operator to move equipment. Assembles and positions machine, augers, and casing pipes. Drives truck or tractor to work site. Starts, stops, and controls drilling speed of machine and insertion of casing into hole. Verifies depth and level of boring position.

GOE Number, Interest Area, and Work Group: 06.03.01; Construction, Mining, and Drilling; Mining and Drilling. **Personality Type:** Realistic. Realistic occupations frequently involve work activities that include practical, hands-on problems and solutions. These occupations often deal with plants, animals, and real-world materials like wood, tools, and machinery. Many of the occupations require working outside and do not involve a lot of paperwork or working closely with others. **Work Values:** Moral Values; Company Policies and Practices; Supervision, Technical; Independence; Activity; Coworkers; Supervision, Human Relations. **Skills:** Operation and Control; Operation Monitoring; Equipment Selection; Equipment Maintenance. **Abilities:** *Cognitive*—Information Ordering; Spatial Orientation; Oral Comprehension;

Visualization; Oral Expression. *Psychomotor*—Control Precision; Response Orientation; Reaction Time. *Physical*—Static Strength; Trunk Strength; Dynamic Strength. *Sensory*—Auditory Attention; Depth Perception; Far Vision. **General Work Activities:** *Information Input*—Monitoring Processes, Materials, and Surroundings; Identifying Objects, Actions, and Events; Getting Information Needed to Do the Job; Inspecting Equipment, Structures, Materials. *Mental Process*—Making Decisions and Solving Problems; Judging Qualities of Things, Services, Other People's Work; Updating and Using Job-Relevant Knowledge. *Work Output*—Controlling Machines and Processes; Operating Vehicles or Equipment; Performing General Physical Activities. *Interacting with Others*—Communicating with Other Workers; Coordinating Work and Activities of Others; Establishing and Maintaining Relationships. **Physical Work Conditions:** Outdoors; Hazardous Equipment; Common Protective or Safety Attire. **Other Job Characteristics:** Degree of Automation; Consequence of Error; Importance of Being Sure All Is Done.

Experience: Job Zone 2. Some previous work-related skill, knowledge, or experience may be helpful, but usually is not needed. **Job Preparation:** SVP 4.00 to 5.99—6 months to less than 2 years. **Knowledge:** Mechanical; Engineering and Technology; Transportation; Public Safety and Security; Geography. **Instructional Program:** 490202 Construction Equipment Operator.

Related DOT Jobs: 850.662-010 Horizontal-Earth-Boring-Machine Operator; 850.662-014 Rock-Drill Operator II; 850.683-034 Rock-Drill Operator I; 859.682-010 Earth-Boring-Machine Operator; 859.682-014 Foundation-Drill Operator.

47-5021.02 Well and Core Drill Operators
(Earth Drillers, Except Oil and Gas)

Education: No data available.

Employed: 16,510

Openings: No data available.

Projected Growth: No data available.

Earnings: $27,890

Operate machine to drill wells and to take samples or cores for analysis of strata.

Records drilling progress and geological data. Starts and controls drilling action and lowering of well casing into well bore. Monitors operation of drilling equipment to determine changes in strata or variations in drilling. Withdraws drill rod from hole and extracts core sample. Changes drill bits as needed. Pours water into well or pumps water or slush into well to cool drill bit and remove drillings. Retrieves lost equipment from bore holes, using retrieval tools and equipment. Fabricates well casings. Lubricates machine, splices worn or broken cables, replaces parts, and builds up and repairs drill bits. Drives or guides truck-mounted equipment into position, levels and stabilizes rig, and extends telescoping derrick. Inspects core samples to determine nature of strata, or takes samples to laboratory for analysis. Couples additional lengths of drill rod as bit advances. Assembles non-truck-mounted drilling equipment, using hand tools and power tools.

GOE Number, Interest Area, and Work Group: 06.03.01; Construction, Mining, and Drilling; Mining and Drilling. **Personal-**

ity Type: Realistic. Realistic occupations frequently involve work activities that include practical, hands-on problems and solutions. These occupations often deal with plants, animals, and real-world materials like wood, tools, and machinery. Many of the occupations require working outside and do not involve a lot of paperwork or working closely with others. **Work Values:** Moral Values; Independence; Company Policies and Practices; Supervision, Human Relations; Activity; Supervision, Technical. **Skills:** Operation Monitoring; Operation and Control; Equipment Maintenance; Repairing; Equipment Selection. **Abilities:** *Cognitive*—Information Ordering; Visualization; Spatial Orientation; Problem Sensitivity; Perceptual Speed. *Psychomotor*—Control Precision; Response Orientation; Multilimb Coordination; Reaction Time. *Physical*—Static Strength; Trunk Strength; Extent Flexibility. *Sensory*—Depth Perception; Near Vision; Visual Color Discrimination. **General Work Activities:** *Information Input*—Monitoring Processes, Materials, and Surroundings; Identifying Objects, Actions, and Events; Getting Information Needed to Do the Job. *Mental Process*—Judging Qualities of Things, Services, Other People's Work; Evaluating Information Against Standards; Making Decisions and Solving Problems. *Work Output*—Controlling Machines and Processes; Performing General Physical Activities; Handling and Moving Objects. *Interacting with Others*—Communicating with Other Workers; Monitoring and Controlling Resources; Performing Administrative Activities. **Physical Work Conditions:** Common Protective or Safety Attire; Distracting Sounds and Noise Levels; Outdoors; Standing. **Other Job Characteristics:** Consequence of Error; Degree of Automation; Importance of Being Sure All Is Done.

Experience: Job Zone 3. Previous work-related skill, knowledge, or experience is required. **Job Preparation:** SVP 6.0 to less than 7.0—More than 1 year and less than 4 years. **Knowledge:** Mechanical; Engineering and Technology; Physics; Transportation; English Language. **Instructional Program:** 490202 Construction Equipment Operator.

Related DOT Jobs: 859.362-010 Well-Drill Operator; 930.662-014 Core-Drill Operator.

47-5031.00 Explosives Workers, Ordnance Handling Experts, and Blasters (Blasters and Explosives Workers)

Education: No data available.

Employed: 4,420

Openings: No data available.

Projected Growth: No data available.

Earnings: $30,910

Place and detonate explosives to demolish structures or to loosen, remove, or displace earth, rock, or other materials. Perform specialized handling, storage, and accounting procedures. Includes seismograph shooters.

Sets up and operates radio or telephone equipment to receive blast information. Loads specified amount of explosives into blast holes, manually, or using rope or hoist. Cuts specified lengths or primacord and attaches primer to end of cord. Lays primacord between rows of charged blast holes and ties cord into main line to form blast pattern. Plants explosive charge in structures or outside, using rope and safety harness for climbing. Lights fuse, drops detonating device into well, or connects wires to firing device and activates device to set off blast. Sets up and operates pneumatic drilling equipment to drill blast holes. Marks location and depth of charge holes for drilling, and measures depth of drilled blast holes. Operates equipment such as hoist, jackhammer, or drill to bore charge holes. Assembles equipment, primer, explosives, and blasting cap; loads perforating gun with explosives. Places safety cones around blast area to alert other workers. Ties specified lengths of delaying fuses into pattern to time sequence of explosions. Drives truck to transport explosives and blasting equipment to blasting site. Moves, stores, and maintains inventories of high explosives. Repairs and services blasting and automotive equipment and electrical instruments, using hand tools. Observes control panel to verify detonation of charge or listens for sound of blast. Examines blast area to determine amount and kind of explosive needed and to ensure safety prior to detonation. Fills and tamps blasting hole. Signals workers to clear area; signals hoist operator to raise equipment and sample from blast hole after detonation.

GOE Number, Interest Area, and Work Group: 06.02.03; Construction, Mining, and Drilling; Construction: General. **Personality Type:** Realistic. Realistic occupations frequently involve work activities that include practical, hands-on problems and solutions. These occupations often deal with plants, animals, and real-world materials like wood, tools, and machinery. Many of the occupations require working outside and do not involve a lot of paperwork or working closely with others. **Work Values:** Moral Values; Supervision, Technical; Compensation; Supervision, Human Relations; Company Policies and Practices. **Skills:** Operation and Control; Operation Monitoring; Equipment Selection; Mathematics; Equipment Maintenance. **Abilities:** *Cognitive*—Information Ordering; Mathematical Reasoning; Oral Expression; Number Facility; Problem Sensitivity; Spatial Orientation. *Psychomotor*—Reaction Time; Arm-Hand Steadiness; Response Orientation. *Physical*—Extent Flexibility; Static Strength; Gross Body Coordination; Explosive Strength; Trunk Strength. *Sensory*—Far Vision; Visual Color Discrimination; Depth Perception. **General Work Activities:** *Information Input*—Monitoring Processes, Materials, and Surroundings; Estimating Needed Characteristics; Inspecting Equipment, Structures, Materials; Getting Information Needed to Do the Job. *Mental Process*—Making Decisions and Solving Problems; Evaluating Information Against Standards; Updating and Using Job-Relevant Knowledge. *Work Output*—Handling and Moving Objects; Performing General Physical Activities; Controlling Machines and Processes. *Interacting with Others*—Communicating with Other Workers; Monitoring and Controlling Resources; Performing Administrative Activities; Communicating with Persons Outside Organization. **Physical Work Conditions:** Hazardous Conditions; Outdoors; Common Protective or Safety Attire. **Other Job Characteristics:** Consequence of Error; Importance of Being Exact or Accurate; Importance of Being Sure All Is Done.

Experience: Job Zone 2. Some previous work-related skill, knowledge, or experience may be helpful, but usually is not needed. **Job Preparation:** SVP 4.00 to 5.99—6 months to less than 2 years. **Knowledge:** Public Safety and Security; Physics; Engineering and Technology; Mechanical; Chemistry; Transportation; Building and

Construction. **Instructional Program:** 490202 Construction Equipment Operator.

Related DOT Jobs: 850.381-010 Miner; 859.261-010 Blaster; 931.261-010 Blaster; 931.361-010 Sample-Taker Operator; 931.361-014 Shooter; 931.361-018 Shooter, Seismograph; 931.382-010 Perforator Operator, Oil Well; 931.664-010 Tier-and-Detonator; 931.667-010 Powder Loader.

47-5041.00 Continuous Mining Machine Operators
(Continuous Mining Machine Operators)

Education: No data available.

Employed: 5,770

Openings: No data available.

Projected Growth: No data available.

Earnings: $34,740

Operate self-propelled mining machines to rip coal, metal ores, nonmetal ores, rock, stone, or sand from the face, and to load it onto conveyors or into shuttle cars in a continuous operation.

Starts machine to gather coal and convey it to floor or shuttle car. Moves lever to raise and lower hydraulic safety bar that supports roof above machine until other workers complete their framing. Repairs, oils, and adjusts machine; changes cutting teeth, using wrench. Moves levers to sump (advance) ripper bar or boring head into face of coal seam. Drives machine into position at working face.

GOE Number, Interest Area, and Work Group: 06.03.01; Construction, Mining, and Drilling; Mining and Drilling. **Personality Type:** Realistic. Realistic occupations frequently involve work activities that include practical, hands-on problems and solutions. These occupations often deal with plants, animals, and real-world materials like wood, tools, and machinery. Many of the occupations require working outside and do not involve a lot of paperwork or working closely with others. **Work Values:** Moral Values; Supervision, Human Relations; Company Policies and Practices; Activity; Supervision, Technical. **Skills:** Operation and Control; Repairing; Equipment Maintenance; Coordination; Operation Monitoring. **Abilities:** *Cognitive*—Information Ordering; Flexibility of Closure; Visualization; Spatial Orientation; Written Expression; Mathematical Reasoning. *Psychomotor*—Multilimb Coordination; Control Precision; Reaction Time. *Physical*—Static Strength; Explosive Strength; Gross Body Coordination. *Sensory*—Depth Perception; Night Vision; Far Vision. **General Work Activities:** *Information Input*—Monitoring Processes, Materials, and Surroundings; Inspecting Equipment, Structures, Materials; Getting Information Needed to Do the Job. *Mental Process*—Analyzing Data or Information; Updating and Using Job-Relevant Knowledge; Organizing, Planning, and Prioritizing. *Work Output*—Controlling Machines and Processes; Operating Vehicles or Equipment; Repairing and Maintaining Mechanical Equipment. *Interacting with Others*—Communicating with Other Workers; Assisting and Caring for Others; Coaching and Developing Others. **Physical Work Conditions:** Outdoors; Using Hands on Objects, Tools, or Controls; Common Protective or Safety Attire. **Other Job Characteristics:** Consequence of Error; Degree of Automation; Importance of Being Exact or Accurate.

Experience: Job Zone 2. Some previous work-related skill, knowledge, or experience may be helpful, but usually is not needed. **Job Preparation:** SVP 4.00 to 5.99—6 months to less than 2 years. **Knowledge:** Mechanical; Engineering and Technology; Public Safety and Security; Production and Processing; Physics; Transportation. **Instructional Program:** 490299 Vehicle and Equipment Operators, Other.

Related DOT Job: 930.683-010 Continuous-Mining-Machine Operator.

47-5042.00 Mine Cutting and Channeling Machine Operators (Mine Cutting and Channeling Machine Operators)

Education: No data available.

Employed: 2,680

Openings: No data available.

Projected Growth: No data available.

Earnings: $32,920

Operate machinery such as longwall shears, plows, and cutting machines, to cut or channel along the face or seams of coal mines, stone quarries, or other mining surfaces to facilitate blasting, separating, or removing minerals or materials from mines or from the earth's surface.

Observes and listens to operation to detect binding or stoppage of tool or equipment malfunction. Moves controls, to start and position drill cutter or torch and to advance tool into mine or quarry face. Repositions machine and moves controls to make additional holes or cuts. Drives mobile, truck-mounted, or track-mounted drilling or cutting machine in mine, quarry, or construction site. Determines location, boundaries, and depth of holes or channels to be cut. Moves controls to start and regulate movement of conveyors, to move or load material. Guides and assists crew laying track for machine and resetting supports and blocking, using jacks, shovel, sledge, and pinch bar. Charges and sets off explosives in blasting holes. Replaces worn or broken tools and machine parts and lubricates machine. Installs casing to prevent cave-ins.

GOE Number, Interest Area, and Work Group: 06.03.01; Construction, Mining, and Drilling; Mining and Drilling. **Personality Type:** Realistic. Realistic occupations frequently involve work activities that include practical, hands-on problems and solutions. These occupations often deal with plants, animals, and real-world materials like wood, tools, and machinery. Many of the occupations require working outside and do not involve a lot of paperwork or working closely with others. **Work Values:** Moral Values; Supervision, Technical; Supervision, Human Relations; Company Policies and Practices; Activity; Coworkers. **Skills:** Operation and Control; Operation Monitoring; Repairing; Coordination; Equipment Maintenance. **Abilities:** *Cognitive*—Spatial Orientation; Oral Expression; Problem Sensitivity; Selective Attention; Flexibility of Closure; Information Ordering. *Psychomotor*—Multilimb Coordination; Control Precision; Reaction Time; Speed of Limb Movement; Arm-Hand Steadiness. *Physical*—Static Strength; Extent Flexibility; Explosive Strength. *Sensory*—Depth Perception; Hearing Sensitivity; Speech Clarity. **General Work Activities:**

Information Input—Getting Information Needed to Do the Job; Monitoring Processes, Materials, and Surroundings; Inspecting Equipment, Structures, Materials; Identifying Objects, Actions, and Events. *Mental Process*—Analyzing Data or Information; Making Decisions and Solving Problems; Updating and Using Job-Relevant Knowledge; Organizing, Planning, and Prioritizing. *Work Output*—Controlling Machines and Processes; Operating Vehicles or Equipment; Performing General Physical Activities; Repairing and Maintaining Mechanical Equipment. *Interacting with Others*—Communicating with Other Workers; Coordinating Work and Activities of Others; Establishing and Maintaining Relationships. **Physical Work Conditions:** Outdoors; Common Protective or Safety Attire; Using Hands on Objects, Tools, or Controls. **Other Job Characteristics:** Consequence of Error; Degree of Automation; Importance of Being Sure All Is Done.

Experience: Job Zone 2. Some previous work-related skill, knowledge, or experience may be helpful, but usually is not needed. **Job Preparation:** SVP 4.00 to 5.99—6 months to less than 2 years. **Knowledge:** Mechanical; Engineering and Technology; Building and Construction; Physics; Public Safety and Security. **Instructional Programs:** 490202 Construction Equipment Operator; 490299 Vehicle and Equipment Operators, Other.

Related DOT Jobs: 930.382-010 Driller, Machine; 930.383-010 Channeling-Machine Runner; 930.482-010 Drilling-Machine Operator; 930.662-010 Long-Wall Shear Operator; 930.663-010 Shale Planer Operator; 930.683-014 Cutter Operator; 930.684-010 Flame Channeler.

47-5051.00 Rock Splitters, Quarry (Rock Splitters, Quarry)

Education: No data available.

Employed: 2,530

Openings: No data available.

Projected Growth: No data available.

Earnings: $22,030

Separate blocks of rough-dimension stone from quarry mass, using jackhammer and wedges.

Inserts wedges and feathers into holes; drives wedges with sledgehammer to split stone from mass. Drills holes along outline, using jackhammer. Cuts groove along outline, using chisel. Marks desired dimensions on stone, using rule and chalkline.

GOE Number, Interest Area, and Work Group: 06.03.01; Construction, Mining, and Drilling; Mining and Drilling. **Personality Type:** Realistic. Realistic occupations frequently involve work activities that include practical, hands-on problems and solutions. These occupations often deal with plants, animals, and real-world materials like wood, tools, and machinery. Many of the occupations require working outside and do not involve a lot of paperwork or working closely with others. **Work Values:** Moral Values; Independence; Coworkers; Company Policies and Practices; Supervision, Human Relations; Activity. **Skills:** Operation and Control; Equipment Selection. **Abilities:** *Cognitive*—Visualization; Category Flexibility; Number Facility; Mathematical Reasoning; Selective Attention. *Psychomotor*—Wrist-Finger Speed; Speed of Limb Movement. *Physical*—Static Strength; Trunk Strength; Ex-

plosive Strength; Dynamic Strength. *Sensory*—Depth Perception; Auditory Attention; Glare Sensitivity. **General Work Activities:** *Information Input*—Getting Information Needed to Do the Job; Monitoring Processes, Materials, and Surroundings; Identifying Objects, Actions, and Events. *Mental Process*—Making Decisions and Solving Problems; Analyzing Data or Information; Organizing, Planning, and Prioritizing. *Work Output*—Performing General Physical Activities; Handling and Moving Objects; Controlling Machines and Processes. *Interacting with Others*—Communicating with Other Workers; Coordinating Work and Activities of Others; Assisting and Caring for Others. **Physical Work Conditions:** Outdoors; Common Protective or Safety Attire; Using Hands on Objects, Tools, or Controls. **Other Job Characteristics:** Consequence of Error; Importance of Being Exact or Accurate; Importance of Being Sure All Is Done.

Experience: Job Zone 2. Some previous work-related skill, knowledge, or experience may be helpful, but usually is not needed. **Job Preparation:** SVP 4.00 to 5.99—6 months to less than 2 years. **Knowledge:** Mechanical; Public Safety and Security; Mathematics; Physics; Engineering and Technology; Building and Construction. **Instructional Program:** 490299 Vehicle and Equipment Operators, Other.

Related DOT Job: 930.684-022 Quarry Plug-and-Feather Driller.

47-5061.00 Roof Bolters, Mining (Roof Bolters)

Education: No data available.

Employed: 3,890

Openings: No data available.

Projected Growth: No data available.

Earnings: $36,420

Operate machinery to install roof-support bolts in underground mine.

Positions self-propelled bolting machine, inserts drill bit in chuck, and starts drill. Tightens ends of anchored truss bolts, using turnbuckle. Installs truss bolts traversing entire ceiling span. Positions safety jack to support underground mine roof until bolts can be installed. Rotates chuck to turn bolt and open expansion head against rock formation. Forces bolt into hole, using hydraulic mechanism of self-propelled bolting machine. Removes drill bit from chuck and inserts bolt into chuck. Drills hole into roof, according to specifications. Tests bolt for specified tension, using torque wrench.

GOE Number, Interest Area, and Work Group: 06.03.01; Construction, Mining, and Drilling; Mining and Drilling. **Personality Type:** Realistic. Realistic occupations frequently involve work activities that include practical, hands-on problems and solutions. These occupations often deal with plants, animals, and real-world materials like wood, tools, and machinery. Many of the occupations require working outside and do not involve a lot of paperwork or working closely with others. **Work Values:** Moral Values; Supervision, Technical; Supervision, Human Relations; Company Policies and Practices; Activity. **Skills:** Product Inspection; Operation and Control; Problem Identification; Installation. **Abilities:** *Cognitive*—Deductive Reasoning; Memorization; Problem Sensitivity; Spatial Orientation; Information Ordering. *Psychomo-*

tor—Control Precision; Manual Dexterity; Arm-Hand Steadiness. *Physical*—Extent Flexibility; Trunk Strength; Static Strength. *Sensory*—Depth Perception. **General Work Activities:** *Information Input*—Getting Information Needed to Do the Job; Monitoring Processes, Materials, and Surroundings; Inspecting Equipment, Structures, Materials; Identifying Objects, Actions, and Events. *Mental Process*—Evaluating Information Against Standards; Judging Qualities of Things, Services, Other People's Work; Analyzing Data or Information. *Work Output*—Performing General Physical Activities; Handling and Moving Objects; Controlling Machines and Processes. *Interacting with Others*—Communicating with Other Workers; Coaching and Developing Others; Establishing and Maintaining Relationships. **Physical Work Conditions:** Outdoors; Using Hands on Objects, Tools, or Controls; Common Protective or Safety Attire; Standing. **Other Job Characteristics:** Consequence of Error; Importance of Being Exact or Accurate; Importance of Being Sure All Is Done.

Experience: Job Zone 2. Some previous work-related skill, knowledge, or experience may be helpful, but usually is not needed. **Job Preparation:** SVP 4.00 to 5.99—6 months to less than 2 years. **Knowledge:** Mechanical; Engineering and Technology; Building and Construction; Physics; Design; Mathematics. **Instructional Program:** 490299 Vehicle and Equipment Operators, Other.

Related DOT Job: 930.683-026 Roof Bolter.

47-5071.00 Roustabouts, Oil and Gas (Roustabouts, Oil and Gas)

Education: Short-term O-T-J training

Employed: 29,562

Openings: 1,562

Projected Growth: –21.1%

Earnings: $19,780

Assemble or repair oil-field equipment, using hand and power tools.

Unscrews or tightens pipe, casing, tubing, and pump rods, using hand and power wrenches and tongs. Connects tanks and flow lines, using wrenches. Dismantles and assembles boilers and steam engine parts, using hand tools and power tools. Digs holes, sets forms, and mixes and pours concrete into forms to make foundations for wood or steel derricks. Bolts or nails together wood or steel framework to erect derrick. Bolts together pump and engine parts.

GOE Number, Interest Area, and Work Group: 06.03.01; Construction, Mining, and Drilling; Mining and Drilling. **Personality Type:** Realistic. Realistic occupations frequently involve work activities that include practical, hands-on problems and solutions. These occupations often deal with plants, animals, and real-world materials like wood, tools, and machinery. Many of the occupations require working outside and do not involve a lot of paperwork or working closely with others. **Work Values:** Moral Values; Supervision, Human Relations; Company Policies and Practices; Supervision, Technical; Activity; Coworkers. **Skills:** Repairing; Installation; Troubleshooting; Equipment Selection; Equipment Maintenance. **Abilities:** *Cognitive*—Visualization; Information

Ordering; Mathematical Reasoning; Flexibility of Closure; Speed of Closure; Problem Sensitivity. *Psychomotor*—Manual Dexterity; Finger Dexterity; Wrist-Finger Speed. *Physical*—Static Strength; Dynamic Strength; Explosive Strength; Trunk Strength; Extent Flexibility. *Sensory*—Depth Perception; Auditory Attention; Hearing Sensitivity; Glare Sensitivity; Peripheral Vision. **General Work Activities:** *Information Input*—Getting Information Needed to Do the Job; Inspecting Equipment, Structures, Materials; Identifying Objects, Actions, and Events. *Mental Process*—Updating and Using Job-Relevant Knowledge; Making Decisions and Solving Problems; Analyzing Data or Information. *Work Output*—Performing General Physical Activities; Handling and Moving Objects; Repairing and Maintaining Mechanical Equipment. *Interacting with Others*—Communicating with Other Workers; Establishing and Maintaining Relationships; Coordinating Work and Activities of Others; Coaching and Developing Others; Assisting and Caring for Others; Monitoring and Controlling Resources. **Physical Work Conditions:** Outdoors; Using Hands on Objects, Tools, or Controls; Standing; Hazardous Equipment. **Other Job Characteristics:** Consequence of Error; Importance of Being Sure All Is Done; Importance of Being Exact or Accurate.

Experience: Job Zone 2. Some previous work-related skill, knowledge, or experience may be helpful, but usually is not needed. **Job Preparation:** SVP 4.00 to 5.99—6 months to less than 2 years. **Knowledge:** Mechanical; Engineering and Technology; Building and Construction; Physics; Public Safety and Security. **Instructional Program:** 470399 Industrial Equipment Maintenance and Repairers, Other.

Related DOT Job: 869.684-046 Roustabout.

47-5081.00 Helpers—Extraction Workers (Helpers, Extractive Workers)

Education: No data available.

Employed: 13,770

Openings: No data available.

Projected Growth: No data available.

Earnings: $20,660

Help extraction craft workers such as earth drillers, blasters, explosives workers, derrick operators, and mining-machine operators by performing duties of lesser skill. Supply equipment; clean work area.

Repairs and maintains automotive and drilling equipment, using hand tools. Observes and monitors equipment operation during extraction process. Examines and collects geological matter, using hand tools and testing devices. Loads materials into gas or well hole; loads equipment, using hand tools. Signals workers to start extraction or boring process of geological materials. Sets-up and adjusts equipment used to excavate geological materials. Drives moving equipment to transport materials and parts to excavation site. Unloads materials, devices, and machine parts, using hand tools. Assists workers to extract geological materials, using hand tools and equipment. Organizes materials and prepares site for excavation or boring, using hand tools. Dismantles extracting and boring equipment used for excavation, using hand tools.

GOE Number, Interest Area, and Work Group: 06.04.01; Construction, Mining, and Drilling; Hands-on Work: Construction, Extraction, and Maintenance. **Personality Type:** Realistic. Realistic occupations frequently involve work activities that include practical, hands-on problems and solutions. These occupations often deal with plants, animals, and real-world materials like wood, tools, and machinery. Many of the occupations require working outside and do not involve a lot of paperwork or working closely with others. **Work Values:** Moral Values; Supervision, Technical; Advancement; Supervision, Human Relations; Activity. **Skills:** Equipment Maintenance; Operation Monitoring; Repairing; Equipment Selection; Operation and Control. **Abilities:** *Cognitive*—Oral Expression; Information Ordering; Problem Sensitivity; Oral Comprehension; Time Sharing. *Psychomotor*—Manual Dexterity; Multilimb Coordination; Wrist-Finger Speed. *Physical*—Static Strength; Extent Flexibility; Explosive Strength. *Sensory*—Auditory Attention; Depth Perception; Glare Sensitivity. **General Work Activities:** *Information Input*—Monitoring Processes, Materials, and Surroundings; Getting Information Needed to Do the Job; Inspecting Equipment, Structures, Materials. *Mental Process*—Updating and Using Job-Relevant Knowledge; Judging Qualities of Things, Services, Other People's Work; Making Decisions and Solving Problems. *Work Output*—Repairing and Maintaining Mechanical Equipment; Handling and Moving Objects; Performing General Physical Activities. *Interacting with Others*—Communicating with Other Workers; Assisting and Caring for Others; Establishing and Maintaining Relationships. **Physical Work Conditions:** Outdoors; Using Hands on Objects, Tools, or Controls; Standing; Whole Body Vibration; Contaminants; Distracting Sounds and Noise Levels. **Other Job Characteristics:** Consequence of Error; Importance of Being Exact or Accurate; Importance of Being Sure All Is Done.

Experience: Job Zone 1. No previous work-related skill, knowledge, or experience is needed. **Job Preparation:** SVP Below 4.0—Less than 6 months. **Knowledge:** Mechanical; Production and Processing; Engineering and Technology; Physics; Transportation. **Instructional Programs:** No data available.

Related DOT Jobs: 859.687-010 Blaster Helper; 930.664-014 Clean-Out-Driller Helper; 930.666-010 Driller Helper; 930.666-014 Tailer; 930.667-010 Shale Planer Operator Helper; 930.684-026 Rotary-Driller Helper; 930.687-010 Bottom-Hole-Pressure-Recording-Operator Helper; 939.364-010 Observer Helper, Seismic Prospecting; 939.663-010 Observer Helper, Gravity Prospecting.

49-0000
Installation, Maintenance, and Repair Occupations

49-1000 Supervisors of Installation, Maintenance, and Repair Workers

49-1011.00 First-Line Supervisors/Managers of Mechanics, Installers, and Repairers (Blue-Collar Worker Supervisors)

Education: Work experience in a related occupation
Employed: 2,197,772
Openings: 216,115
Projected Growth: 8.9%
Earnings: No data available.

Supervise and coordinate the activities of mechanics, installers, and repairers.

Computes estimates and actual costs of factors such as materials, labor, and outside contractors; prepares budgets. Confers with personnel such as management, engineering, quality control, customers, and workers' representatives to coordinate work activities and resolve problems. Recommends or initiates personnel actions, such as employment, performance evaluations, promotions, transfers, discharges, and disciplinary measures. Directs, coordinates, and assists in performance of workers' activities, such as engine tune-up, hydroelectric turbine repair, or circuit-breaker installation. Examines object, system, or facilities, such as telephone, air conditioning, or industrial plant, and analyzes information, to determine installation, service, or repair needed. Monitors operations; inspects, tests, and measures completed work, using devices such as hand tools, gauges, and specifications, to verify conformance to standards. Completes and maintains reports such as time and production records, inventories, and test results. Trains workers in methods, procedures, and use of equipment and work aids such as blueprints, hand tools, and test equipment. Patrols work area and examines tools and equipment to detect unsafe conditions or violations of safety rules. Requisitions materials and supplies such as tools, equipment, and replacement parts, for work activities. Establishes or adjusts work methods and procedures to meet production schedules, using knowledge of capacities of machines, equipment, and personnel. Interprets specifications, blueprints, and job orders, and constructs templates and lays out reference points for workers. Assigns workers to perform activities such as servicing appliances, repairing and maintaining vehicles, and installing machinery and equipment. Recommends measures such as procedural changes, service manuals revisions, and equipment purchases, to improve work performance and minimize operating costs.

GOE Number, Interest Area, and Work Group: 05.01.01; Mechanics, Installers, and Repairers; Managerial Work in Mechanics, Installers, and Repairers. **Personality Type:** Enterprising. Enterprising occupations frequently involve starting up and carrying out projects. These occupations can involve leading people and making many decisions. They sometimes require risk taking and often deal with business. **Work Values:** Authority; Responsibility; Autonomy; Activity; Coworkers; Security. **Skills:** Management of Personnel Resources; Coordination; Reading Comprehension; Management of Material Resources; Management of Financial Resources; Time Management; Product Inspection; Monitoring; Active Listening; Writing. **Abilities:** *Cognitive*—Oral Expression; Oral Comprehension; Information Ordering; Deductive Reasoning; Written Comprehension. *Psychomotor*—Manual Dexterity; Finger Dexterity; Wrist-Finger Speed. *Physical*—Trunk Strength; Static Strength. *Sensory*—Near Vision; Speech Clarity; Hearing Sensitivity. **General Work Activities:** *Information Input*—Getting Information Needed to Do the Job; Monitoring Processes, Materials, and Surroundings; Identifying Objects, Actions, and Events. *Mental Process*—Making Decisions and Solving Problems; Evaluating Information Against Standards; Scheduling Work and Activities; Organizing, Planning, and Prioritizing. *Work Output*—Implementing Ideas and Programs; Handling and Moving Objects; Documenting and Recording Information. *Interacting with Others*—Guiding, Directing and Motivating Subordinates; Coordinating Work and Activities of Others; Communicating with Other Workers. **Physical Work Conditions:** Indoors; Standing; Common Protective or Safety Attire; Using Hands on Objects, Tools, or Controls. **Other Job Characteristics:** Consequence of Error; Importance of Being Sure All Is Done; Importance of Being Exact or Accurate.

Experience: Job Zone 4. A minimum of two to four years of work-related skill, knowledge, or experience is needed. **Job Preparation:** SVP 7.0 to less than 8.0—2 years to less than 10 years. **Knowledge:** Administration and Management; Mechanical; Personnel and Human Resources; English Language; Engineering and Technology. **Instructional Programs:** 520201 Business Administration and Management, General; 520205 Operations Management and Supervision.

Related DOT Jobs: 169.167-074 Preventive Maintenance Coordinator; 184.167-050 Maintenance Supervisor; 184.167-194 Superintendent, Meters; 185.164-010 Service Manager; 185.167-058 Service Manager; 185.167-074 Manager, Auto Specialty Services; 187.167-010 Appliance-Service Supervisor; 187.167-130 Manager, Marine Service; 187.167-142 Manager, Service Department; 189.167-046 Superintendent, Maintenance; 375.167-018 Commanding Officer, Motor Equipment; 620.131-010 Supervisor, Endless Track Vehicle; 620.131-014 Supervisor, Garage; 620.131-018 Supervisor, Motorcycle Repair Shop; 620.137-010 Tank and Amphibian Tractor Operations Chief; 621.131-010 Supercharger-Repair Supervisor; 621.131-014 Supervisor, Aircraft Maintenance; 622.131-010 Supervisor, Railroad Car Repair; 622.131-014 Supervisor, Roundhouse; 622.131-018 Supervisor, Wheel Shop (partial list; see the introduction for sources of the complete list).

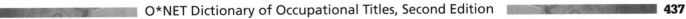

49-2000 Electrical and Electronic Equipment Mechanics, Installers, and Repairers

49-2011.00 Computer, Automated Teller, and Office Machine Repairers (Electronics Repairers, Commercial and Industrial Equipment)

Education: Postsecondary vocational training

Employed: 71,558

Openings: 9,744

Projected Growth: 12.7%

Earnings: $35,590

Repair, maintain, or install computers, word-processing systems, automated teller machines, and electronic office machines such as duplicating and fax machines.

GOE Number, Interest Area, and Work Group: 05.02.02; Mechanics, Installers, and Repairers; Electrical and Electronic Systems: Equipment Repair. **Instructional Programs:** 150402 Computer Maintenance Technology/Technician; 470101 Electrical and Electronics Equipment Installer and Repairer, General; 470102 Business Machine Repairer; 470104 Computer Installer and Repairer; 470105 Industrial Electronics Installer and Repairer; 470609 Aviation Systems and Avionics Main. Technologist/Technician. **Note:** The Department of Labor has not collected some data for this job, so it has fewer details than the other descriptions.

49-2011.01 Automatic Teller Machine Servicers
(All Other Protective Service Workers)

Education: Short-term O-T-J training

Employed: 166,335

Openings: 23,282

Projected Growth: 19%

Earnings: $17,470

Collect deposits and replenish automatic teller machines with cash and supplies.

Corrects malfunctions such as jammed cash or paper, or calls repair personnel when ATM needs repair. Records transaction information on form or log, and notifies designated personnel of discrepancies. Counts cash and items deposited by customers; compares to transactions indicated on transaction tape from ATM. Removes money canisters from ATM; replenishes machine supplies such as deposit envelopes, receipt paper, and cash. Tests machine functions. Balances machine cash account, using electronic keypad.

GOE Number, Interest Area, and Work Group: 09.09.01; Business Detail; Clerical Machine Operation. **Personality Type:** Realistic. Realistic occupations frequently involve work activities that include practical, hands-on problems and solutions. These occupations often deal with plants, animals, and real-world materials like wood, tools, and machinery. Many of the occupations require working outside and do not involve a lot of paperwork or working closely with others. **Work Values:** Independence; Moral Values; Company Policies and Practices; Security; Supervision, Human Relations. **Skills:** Mathematics; Writing; Information Gathering; Reading Comprehension; Problem Identification; Monitoring. **Abilities:** *Cognitive*—Number Facility; Information Ordering; Oral Expression; Mathematical Reasoning; Problem Sensitivity; Written Comprehension. *Psychomotor*—Manual Dexterity; Finger Dexterity; Multilimb Coordination. *Physical*—Stamina. *Sensory*—Near Vision; Visual Color Discrimination; Sound Localization. **General Work Activities:** *Information Input*—Getting Information Needed to Do the Job; Identifying Objects, Actions, and Events; Monitoring Processes, Materials, and Surroundings; Inspecting Equipment, Structures, Materials. *Mental Process*—Evaluating Information Against Standards; Processing Information; Analyzing Data or Information. *Work Output*—Documenting and Recording Information; Handling and Moving Objects; Performing General Physical Activities; Controlling Machines and Processes. *Interacting with Others*—Communicating with Other Workers; Performing Administrative Activities; Communicating with Persons Outside Organization; Establishing and Maintaining Relationships. **Physical Work Conditions:** Standing; Using Hands on Objects, Tools, or Controls; Indoors. **Other Job Characteristics:** Importance of Being Exact or Accurate; Consequence of Error; Importance of Being Sure All Is Done.

Experience: Job Zone 3. Previous work-related skill, knowledge, or experience is required. **Job Preparation:** SVP 6.0 to less than 7.0—More than 1 year and less than 4 years. **Knowledge:** Mathematics; Computers and Electronics; Clerical; Geography; Telecommunications. **Instructional Programs:** 430102 Corrections/Correctional Administration; 430106 Forensic Technology/Technician; 430199 Criminal Justice and Corrections, Other; 439999 Protective Services, Other.

Related DOT Job: 211.367-014 Automatic Teller Machine (ATM) Servicer.

49-2011.02 Data Processing Equipment Repairers
(Data Processing Equipment Repairers)

Education: Postsecondary vocational training

Employed: 79,337

Openings: 20,080

Projected Growth: 47%

Earnings: $29,340

Repair, maintain, and install computer hardware such as peripheral equipment and word-processing systems.

Replaces defective components and wiring. Tests faulty equipment and applies knowledge of functional operation of electronic units and systems to diagnose cause of malfunction. Aligns, adjusts, and calibrates equipment according to specifications. Converses with equipment operators to ascertain problems with equipment before breakdown or to ascertain cause of breakdown. Tests electronic components and circuits to locate defects, using oscilloscopes, signal generators, ammeters, and voltmeters. Adjusts mechanical parts, using hand tools and soldering iron. Maintains records of repairs, calibrations, and tests. Enters information into computer to copy program from one electronic component to another, or to draw, modify, or store schematics. Calibrates testing instruments.

GOE Number, Interest Area, and Work Group: 05.02.02; Mechanics, Installers, and Repairers; Electrical and Electronic Systems: Equipment Repair. **Personality Type:** Realistic. Realistic occupations frequently involve work activities that include practical, hands-on problems and solutions. These occupations often deal with plants, animals, and real-world materials like wood, tools, and machinery. Many of the occupations require working outside and do not involve a lot of paperwork or working closely with others. **Work Values:** Moral Values; Security; Variety; Working Conditions; Ability Utilization; Independence. **Skills:** Installation; Repairing; Troubleshooting; Problem Identification; Testing; Reading Comprehension. **Abilities:** *Cognitive*—Inductive Reasoning; Problem Sensitivity; Information Ordering; Deductive Reasoning; Oral Comprehension; Written Comprehension. *Psychomotor*—Finger Dexterity; Control Precision; Manual Dexterity. *Physical*—Extent Flexibility; Trunk Strength; Explosive Strength. *Sensory*—Near Vision; Visual Color Discrimination; Hearing Sensitivity. **General Work Activities:** *Information Input*—Inspecting Equipment, Structures, Materials; Getting Information Needed to Do the Job; Monitoring Processes, Materials, and Surroundings. *Mental Process*—Updating and Using Job-Relevant Knowledge; Evaluating Information Against Standards; Making Decisions and Solving Problems; Analyzing Data or Information; Judging Qualities of Things, Services, Other People's Work. *Work Output*—Interacting with Computers; Repairing and Maintaining Electrical Equipment; Handling and Moving Objects. *Interacting with Others*—Interpreting Meaning of Information to Others; Communicating with Other Workers; Establishing and Maintaining Relationships; Performing Administrative Activities; Providing Consultation and Advice to Others. **Physical Work Conditions:** Indoors; Using Hands on Objects, Tools, or Controls; Sitting. **Other Job Characteristics:** Degree of Automation; Importance of Being Sure All Is Done; Importance of Being Exact or Accurate; Consequence of Error.

Experience: Job Zone 4. A minimum of two to four years of work-related skill, knowledge, or experience is needed. **Job Preparation:** SVP 7.0 to less than 8.0—2 years to less than 10 years. **Knowledge:** Computers and Electronics; Mechanical; Telecommunications; Mathematics; Design. **Instructional Programs:** 150402 Computer Maintenance Technology/Technician; 470102 Business Machine Repairer; 470104 Computer Installer and Repairer.

Related DOT Jobs: 828.261-022 Electronics Mechanic; 828.261-026 Electronics-Mechanic Apprentice.

49-2011.03 Office Machine and Cash Register Servicers (Office Machine and Cash Register Servicers)

Education: Long-term O-T-J training
Employed: 58,383
Openings: 2,931
Projected Growth: 15.6%
Earnings: $27,830

Repair and service office machines such as adding, accounting, calculating, duplicating, and typewriting machines. Repair manual, electrical, and electronic office machines.

Assembles and installs machine according to specifications, using hand tools, power tools, and measuring devices. Instructs operators and servicers in operation, maintenance, and repair of machine. Reads specifications such as blueprints, charts, and schematics, to determine machine settings and adjustments. Operates machine such as typewriter, cash register, or adding machine, to test functioning of parts and mechanisms. Repairs, adjusts, or replaces electrical and mechanical components and parts, using hand tools, power tools, and soldering or welding equipment. Tests machine to locate cause of electrical problems, using testing devices such as voltmeter, ohmmeter, and circuit test equipment. Disassembles machine and examines parts such as wires, gears, and bearings for wear and defects, using hand tools, power tools, and measuring devices. Cleans and oils mechanical parts to maintain machine.

GOE Number, Interest Area, and Work Group: 05.02.02; Mechanics, Installers, and Repairers; Electrical and Electronic Systems: Equipment Repair. **Personality Type:** Realistic. Realistic occupations frequently involve work activities that include practical, hands-on problems and solutions. These occupations often deal with plants, animals, and real-world materials like wood, tools, and machinery. Many of the occupations require working outside and do not involve a lot of paperwork or working closely with others. **Work Values:** Moral Values; Independence; Supervision, Technical; Security; Supervision, Human Relations. **Skills:** Instructing; Reading Comprehension; Equipment Maintenance; Problem Identification; Repairing; Troubleshooting; Installation; Learning Strategies. **Abilities:** *Cognitive*—Written Comprehension; Deductive Reasoning; Information Ordering; Oral Expression; Visualization; Problem Sensitivity. *Psychomotor*—Finger Dexterity; Control Precision; Arm-Hand Steadiness; Manual Dexterity. *Physical*—Static Strength; Explosive Strength; Dynamic Flexibility; Gross Body Coordination. *Sensory*—Visual Color Discrimination; Near Vision; Speech Clarity. **General Work Activities:** *Information Input*—Getting Information Needed to Do the Job; Inspecting Equipment, Structures, Materials; Identifying Objects, Actions, and Events. *Mental Process*—Updating and Using Job-Relevant Knowledge; Making Decisions and Solving Problems; Analyzing Data or Information. *Work Output*—Repairing and Maintaining Electrical Equipment; Repairing and Maintaining Mechanical Equipment; Handling and Moving Objects; Controlling Machines and Processes. *Interacting with Others*—Communicating with Persons Outside Organization; Teaching Others; Communicating with Other Workers. **Physical Work Conditions:** Indoors; Using Hands on Objects, Tools, or Controls; Hazardous Equipment; Standing; Sitting. **Other Job Characteristics:** Consequence of Error; Importance of Being Sure All Is Done; Degree of Automation.

Experience: Job Zone 3. Previous work-related skill, knowledge, or experience is required. **Job Preparation:** SVP 6.0 to less than 7.0—More than 1 year and less than 4 years. **Knowledge:** Mechanical; Computers and Electronics; Engineering and Technology; Design; Education and Training. **Instructional Program:** 470102 Business Machine Repairer.

Related DOT Jobs: 633.261-010 Assembly Technician; 633.261-014 Mail-Processing-Equipment Mechanic; 633.281-010 Cash-Register Servicer; 633.281-014 Dictating-Transcribing-Machine Servicer; 633.281-018 Office-Machine Servicer; 633.281-022 Office-Machine-Servicer Apprentice; 633.281-030 Statistical-Machine Servicer; 706.381-010 Aligner, Typewriter; 706.381-030 Repairer, Typewriter.

49-2021.00 Radio Mechanics (Radio Mechanics)

Education: Postsecondary vocational training

Employed: 7,030

Openings: 811

Projected Growth: –1.4%

Earnings: $30,590

Test or repair mobile or stationary radio transmitting and receiving equipment and two-way radio communications systems used in ship-to-shore communications and found in service and emergency vehicles.

Removes and replaces defective units that are not repairable. Tests batteries with hydrometer and ammeter, and charges batteries. Tests noise level and audio quality, using audiometer. Monitors radio range station to detect flaws in transmission; adjusts controls to eliminate flaws. Adjusts receivers for maximum sensitivity and transmitters for maximum output, using frequency meter. Inserts plugs into receptacles. Bolts or screws leads to terminals to connect equipment to power source, using hand tools. Installs, tests, adjusts, modifies, and repairs intercommunication systems. Replaces defective components such as conductors, resistors, semiconductors, and integrated circuits, using soldering iron, wire cutters, and hand tools. Tests equipment for power output, frequency, and calibration, using oscilloscope, circuit analyzer, frequency meter, wattmeter, ammeter, and voltmeter. Inspects wiring and soldering; performs repairs, using soldering iron, wire cutters, pliers, and wiring diagram. Locates defects such as loose connections, broken wires, or burned-out components, using schematic diagrams, test equipment, and inspection tags. Tests emergency transmitter to ensure readiness for immediate use.

GOE Number, Interest Area, and Work Group: 05.02.02; Mechanics, Installers, and Repairers; Electrical and Electronic Systems: Equipment Repair. **Personality Type:** Realistic. Realistic occupations frequently involve work activities that include practical, hands-on problems and solutions. These occupations often deal with plants, animals, and real-world materials like wood, tools, and machinery. Many of the occupations require working outside and do not involve a lot of paperwork or working closely with others. **Work Values:** Moral Values; Independence; Security; Company Policies and Practices; Responsibility; Compensation; Activity; Supervision, Technical. **Skills:** Testing; Troubleshooting; Installation; Repairing; Problem Identification; Product Inspection; Critical Thinking; Monitoring; Equipment Maintenance. **Abilities:** *Cognitive*—Problem Sensitivity; Visualization; Flexibility of Closure; Information Ordering; Written Comprehension; Deductive Reasoning. *Psychomotor*—Finger Dexterity; Manual Dexterity; Control Precision; Arm-Hand Steadiness. *Physical*—Static Strength; Explosive Strength; Dynamic Strength. *Sensory*—Near Vision; Visual Color Discrimination; Hearing Sensitivity. **General Work Activities:** *Information Input*—Monitoring Processes, Materials, and Surroundings; Inspecting Equipment, Structures, Materials; Getting Information Needed to Do the Job. *Mental Process*—Evaluating Information Against Standards; Analyzing Data or Information; Updating and Using Job-Relevant Knowledge. *Work Output*—Repairing and Maintaining Electrical Equipment; Handling and Moving Objects; Implementing Ideas and Programs. *Interacting with Others*—Providing Consultation and Advice to Others; Communicating with Other Workers; Coaching and Developing Others; Communicating with Persons Outside Organization. **Physical Work Conditions:** Using Hands on Objects, Tools, or Controls; Indoors; Hazardous Situations; Sitting. **Other Job Characteristics:** Importance of Being Sure All Is Done; Consequence of Error; Importance of Being Exact or Accurate.

Experience: Job Zone 3. Previous work-related skill, knowledge, or experience is required. **Job Preparation:** SVP 6.0 to less than 7.0—More than 1 year and less than 4 years. **Knowledge:** Computers and Electronics; Telecommunications; Mechanical; Engineering and Technology; Physics; Mathematics; Design. **Instructional Programs:** 470101 Electrical and Electronics Equipment Installer and Repairer, General; 470103 Communication Systems Installer and Repairer.

Related DOT Jobs: 726.381-014 Electronic Equipment Repairer; 823.261-018 Radio Mechanic; 823.281-014 Electrician, Radio.

49-2022.00 Telecommunications Equipment Installers and Repairers, Except Line Installers
(Central Office and PBX Installers and Repairers)

Education: Postsecondary vocational training

Employed: 44,437

Openings: 4,617

Projected Growth: 32.3%

Earnings: $43,680

Set up, rearrange, or remove switching and dialing equipment used in central offices. Service or repair telephones and other communication equipment on customer's property. Install equipment in new locations; install wiring and telephone jacks in buildings under construction.

GOE Number, Interest Area, and Work Group: 05.02.01; Mechanics, Installers, and Repairers; Electrical and Electronic Systems: Installation and Repair. **Instructional Program:** 470103 Communication Systems Installer and Repairer. **Note:** The Department of Labor has not collected some data for this job, so it has fewer details than the other descriptions.

49-2022.01 Central Office and PBX Installers and Repairers (Central Office and PBX Installers and Repairers)

Education: Postsecondary vocational training

Employed: 44,437

Openings: 4,617

Projected Growth: 32.3%

Earnings: $43,680

Test, analyze, and repair telephone or telegraph circuits and equipment at a central office location, using test meters and hand tools. Analyze and repair defects in communications equipment on customer's premises, using circuit diagrams, polarity probes, meters, and a telephone test set. Install equipment.

Routes cables and trunklines from entry points to specified equipment, following diagrams. Installs preassembled or partially assembled switching equipment, switchboards, wiring frames, and power apparatus according to floor plans. Retests repaired equipment to ensure that malfunction has been corrected. Enters codes to correct programming of electronic switching systems. Tests and adjusts installed equipment to ensure circuit continuity and operational performance, using test instruments. Repairs or replaces defective components such as switches, relays, amplifiers, and circuit boards, using hand tools and soldering iron. Analyzes test readings, computer printouts, and trouble reports, to determine method of repair. Tests circuits and components of malfunctioning telecommunication equipment to isolate source of malfunction, using test instruments and circuit diagrams. Connects wires to equipment, using hand tools, soldering iron, or wire wrap gun. Removes and remakes connections on wire distributing frame to change circuit layout, following diagrams.

GOE Number, Interest Area, and Work Group: 05.02.01; Mechanics, Installers, and Repairers; Electrical and Electronic Systems: Installation and Repair. **Personality Type:** Realistic. Realistic occupations frequently involve work activities that include practical, hands-on problems and solutions. These occupations often deal with plants, animals, and real-world materials like wood, tools, and machinery. Many of the occupations require working outside and do not involve a lot of paperwork or working closely with others. **Work Values:** Moral Values; Company Policies and Practices; Security; Supervision, Technical; Supervision, Human Relations. **Skills:** Repairing; Installation; Problem Identification; Troubleshooting; Mathematics. **Abilities:** *Cognitive*—Problem Sensitivity; Inductive Reasoning; Written Comprehension; Information Ordering; Deductive Reasoning. *Psychomotor*—Finger Dexterity; Arm-Hand Steadiness; Control Precision; Manual Dexterity. *Physical*—Stamina. *Sensory*—Near Vision; Visual Color Discrimination; Hearing Sensitivity. **General Work Activities:** *Information Input*—Getting Information Needed to Do the Job; Inspecting Equipment, Structures, Materials; Identifying Objects, Actions, and Events. *Mental Process*—Analyzing Data or Information; Making Decisions and Solving Problems; Updating and Using Job-Relevant Knowledge. *Work Output*—Repairing and Maintaining Electrical Equipment; Handling and Moving Objects; Performing General Physical Activities. *Interacting with Others*—Coordinating Work and Activities of Others; Communicating with Other Workers; Communicating with Persons Outside Organization. **Physical Work Conditions:** Indoors; Sitting; Using Hands on Objects, Tools, or Controls. **Other Job Characteristics:** Importance of Being Exact or Accurate; Importance of Being Sure All Is Done; Consequence of Error.

Experience: Job Zone 4. A minimum of two to four years of work-related skill, knowledge, or experience is needed. **Job Preparation:** SVP 7.0 to less than 8.0—2 years to less than 10 years. **Knowledge:** Computers and Electronics; Telecommunications; Engineering and Technology; Design; Mechanical. **Instructional Program:** 470103 Communication Systems Installer and Repairer.

Related DOT Jobs: 822.281-014 Central-Office Repairer; 822.281-022 Private-Branch-Exchange Repairer; 822.361-014 Central-Office Installer; 822.381-018 Private-Branch-Exchange Installer; 822.381-022 Telegraph-Plant Maintainer.

49-2022.02 Frame Wirers, Central Office
(Frame Wirers, Central Office)

Education: No data available.

Employed: 14,500

Openings: No data available.

Projected Growth: No data available.

Earnings: $46,110

Connect wires from telephone lines and cables to distributing frames in telephone-company central office, using soldering iron and other hand tools.

Cleans switches and replaces contact points, using vacuum hose, solvents, and hand tools. Strings distributing frames with connecting wires. Assists in locating and correcting malfunction in wiring on distributing frame. Lubricates moving switch parts. Tests circuit connections, using voltmeter or ammeter. Solders connections, following diagram or oral instructions. Removes and remakes connections to change circuit layouts.

GOE Number, Interest Area, and Work Group: 05.02.01; Mechanics, Installers, and Repairers; Electrical and Electronic Systems: Installation and Repair. **Personality Type:** Realistic. Realistic occupations frequently involve work activities that include practical, hands-on problems and solutions. These occupations often deal with plants, animals, and real-world materials like wood, tools, and machinery. Many of the occupations require working outside and do not involve a lot of paperwork or working closely with others. **Work Values:** Moral Values; Supervision, Technical; Security; Supervision, Human Relations; Company Policies and Practices. **Skills:** Installation; Testing; Product Inspection; Problem Identification; Troubleshooting; Equipment Selection. **Abilities:** *Cognitive*—Oral Comprehension; Visualization; Deductive Reasoning; Information Ordering; Problem Sensitivity. *Psychomotor*—Arm-Hand Steadiness; Finger Dexterity; Multilimb Coordination. *Physical*—Extent Flexibility; Trunk Strength. **General Work Activities:** *Information Input*—Getting Information Needed to Do the Job; Monitoring Processes, Materials, and Surroundings; Identifying Objects, Actions, and Events; Inspecting Equipment, Structures, Materials. *Mental Process*—Making Decisions and Solving Problems; Judging Qualities of Things, Services, Other People's Work; Updating and Using Job-Relevant Knowledge; Analyzing Data or Information. *Work Output*—Handling and Moving Objects; Repairing and Maintaining Electrical Equipment; Implementing Ideas and Programs. *Interacting with Others*—Communicating with Other Workers; Establishing and Maintaining Relationships; Providing Consultation and Advice to Others; Assisting and Caring for Others. **Physical Work Conditions:** Indoors; Using Hands on Objects, Tools, or Controls; Standing. **Other Job Characteristics:** Importance of Being Sure All Is Done; Importance of Being Exact or Accurate; Consequence of Error.

Experience: Job Zone 2. Some previous work-related skill, knowledge, or experience may be helpful, but usually is not needed.

Job Preparation: SVP 4.00 to 5.99—6 months to less than 2 years. **Knowledge:** Telecommunications; Engineering and Technology; Mechanical; Computers and Electronics; Design. **Instructional Program:** 470103 Communication Systems Installer and Repairer.

Related DOT Job: 822.684-010 Frame Wirer.

49-2022.03 Communication Equipment Mechanics, Installers, and Repairers (Telegraph and Teletype Installers and Maintainers)

Education: No data available.

Employed: 1,030

Openings: No data available.

Projected Growth: No data available.

Earnings: $44,570

Install, maintain, test, and repair communication cables and equipment.

Measures distance from landmarks to identify exact installation site. Answers customers' inquiries or complaints. Disassembles equipment to adjust, repair, or replace parts, using hand tools. Evaluates quality of performance of installed equipment, by observance and by using test equipment. Performs routine maintenance on equipment, which includes adjustment, repair, and painting. Reviews work orders, building permits, manufacturer's instructions, and ordinances, to move, change, install, repair, or remove communication equipment. Climbs poles and ladders. Communicates with base, using telephone or two-way radio, to receive instructions or technical advise or to report unauthorized use of equipment. Cleans and maintains tools, test equipment, and motor vehicle. Repairs, replaces, or adjusts defective components. Examines and tests malfunctioning equipment to determine defects, using blueprints and electrical measuring instruments. Demonstrates equipment and instructs customer in use of equipment. Plans layout and installation of data communications equipment. Adjusts or modifies equipment in accordance with customer request or to enhance performance of equipment. Measures, cuts, splices, connects, solders, and installs wires and cables. Tests installed equipment for conformance to specifications, using test equipment. Assembles and installs communication equipment such as data-communication lines and equipment, computer systems, and antennas and towers, using hand tools. Digs holes or trenches. Determines viability of site through observation; discusses site location and construction requirements with customer.

GOE Number, Interest Area, and Work Group: 05.02.01; Mechanics, Installers, and Repairers; Electrical and Electronic Systems: Installation and Repair. **Personality Type:** Realistic. Realistic occupations frequently involve work activities that include practical, hands-on problems and solutions. These occupations often deal with plants, animals, and real-world materials like wood, tools, and machinery. Many of the occupations require working outside and do not involve a lot of paperwork or working closely with others. **Work Values:** Moral Values; Supervision, Technical; Variety; Security; Company Policies and Practices; Activity; Supervision, Human Relations. **Skills:** Repairing; Troubleshooting; Installation; Equipment Maintenance; Product Inspection; Test-

ing. **Abilities:** *Cognitive*—Problem Sensitivity; Oral Expression; Written Comprehension; Information Ordering; Oral Comprehension. *Psychomotor*—Manual Dexterity; Finger Dexterity; Wrist-Finger Speed; Response Orientation; Control Precision. *Physical*—Dynamic Strength; Static Strength; Trunk Strength. *Sensory*—Visual Color Discrimination; Depth Perception; Hearing Sensitivity. **General Work Activities:** *Information Input*—Inspecting Equipment, Structures, Materials; Getting Information Needed to Do the Job; Monitoring Processes, Materials, and Surroundings. *Mental Process*—Evaluating Information Against Standards; Updating and Using Job-Relevant Knowledge; Making Decisions and Solving Problems. *Work Output*—Repairing and Maintaining Electrical Equipment; Handling and Moving Objects; Performing General Physical Activities. *Interacting with Others*—Communicating with Other Workers; Communicating with Persons Outside Organization; Performing Administrative Activities. **Physical Work Conditions:** Using Hands on Objects, Tools, or Controls; Hazardous Conditions; Standing; Outdoors. **Other Job Characteristics:** Importance of Being Sure All Is Done; Consequence of Error; Importance of Being Exact or Accurate.

Experience: Job Zone 3. Previous work-related skill, knowledge, or experience is required. **Job Preparation:** SVP 6.0 to less than 7.0—More than 1 year and less than 4 years. **Knowledge:** Telecommunications; Mechanical; Computers and Electronics; Design; Mathematics. **Instructional Program:** 470103 Communication Systems Installer and Repairer.

Related DOT Jobs: 722.281-010 Instrument Repairer; 821.261-010 Cable Television Line Technician; 822.261-010 Electrician, Office; 822.281-030 Technician, Plant and Maintenance; 822.281-034 Technician, Submarine Cable Equipment; 823.261-022 Antenna Installer, Satellite Communications; 823.261-030 Data Communications Technician; 823.281-022 Rigger.

49-2022.04 Telecommunications Facility Examiners (All Other Communications Equipment Mechanics, Installers, and Repairers)

Education: No data available.

Employed: 41,740

Openings: No data available.

Projected Growth: No data available.

Earnings: $41,260

Examine telephone transmission facilities to determine equipment requirements for providing subscribers with new or additional telephone services.

Designates cables available for use. Climbs telephone poles or stands on truck-mounted boom to examine terminal boxes for available connections. Visits subscribers' premises to arrange for new installations such as telephone booths and telephone poles. Examines telephone transmission facilities to determine requirements for new or additional telephone services.

GOE Number, Interest Area, and Work Group: 05.02.01; Mechanics, Installers, and Repairers; Electrical and Electronic Systems: Installation and Repair. **Personality Type:** Realistic. Realistic occupations frequently involve work activities that include practical, hands-on problems and solutions. These occupations often deal with plants, animals, and real-world materials like wood, tools, and machinery. Many of the occupations require working outside and do not involve a lot of paperwork or working closely with others. **Work Values:** Moral Values; Security; Supervision, Technical; Supervision, Human Relations; Responsibility; Independence. **Skills:** Product Inspection; Equipment Selection; Technology Design; Problem Identification; Reading Comprehension; Active Listening. **Abilities:** *Cognitive*—Deductive Reasoning; Oral Comprehension; Written Comprehension; Information Ordering; Oral Expression; Spatial Orientation. *Psychomotor*—Multilimb Coordination; Arm-Hand Steadiness. *Physical*—Dynamic Strength; Extent Flexibility; Gross Body Coordination. *Sensory*—Visual Color Discrimination; Night Vision; Hearing Sensitivity; Glare Sensitivity. **General Work Activities:** *Information Input*—Inspecting Equipment, Structures, Materials; Getting Information Needed to Do the Job; Identifying Objects, Actions, and Events; Estimating Needed Characteristics. *Mental Process*—Making Decisions and Solving Problems; Evaluating Information Against Standards; Analyzing Data or Information. *Work Output*—Performing General Physical Activities; Documenting and Recording Information; Handling and Moving Objects. *Interacting with Others*—Communicating with Persons Outside Organization; Communicating with Other Workers; Performing for or Working with the Public. **Physical Work Conditions:** Climbing Ladders, Scaffolds, Poles, etc.; High Places; Outdoors. **Other Job Characteristics:** Consequence of Error; Importance of Being Sure All Is Done; Importance of Being Exact or Accurate.

Experience: Job Zone 3. Previous work-related skill, knowledge, or experience is required. **Job Preparation:** SVP 6.0 to less than 7.0—More than 1 year and less than 4 years. **Knowledge:** Telecommunications; Computers and Electronics; English Language; Engineering and Technology; Customer and Personal Service. **Instructional Program:** 470103 Communication Systems Installer and Repairer.

Related DOT Job: 959.367-014 Facility Examiner.

49-2022.05 Station Installers and Repairers, Telephone (All Other Communications Equipment Mechanics, Installers, and Repairers)

Education: No data available.

Employed: 41,740

Openings: No data available.

Projected Growth: No data available.

Earnings: $41,260

Install and repair telephone station equipment such as telephones, coin collectors, telephone booths, and switching-key equipment.

Analyzes equipment operation, using testing devices to locate and diagnose nature of malfunction and ascertain needed repairs. Disassembles components. Replaces, cleans, adjusts, and repairs parts, wires, switches, relays, circuits, or signaling units, using hand tools. Repairs cables, lays out plans for new equipment, and estimates material required. Climbs poles to install or repair outside service lines. Installs communication equipment such as intercommunication systems and related apparatus, using schematic diagrams, testing devices, and hand tools. Operates and tests equipment to ensure elimination of malfunction. Assembles telephone equipment, mounts brackets, and connects wire leads, using hand tools and following installation diagrams or work order.

GOE Number, Interest Area, and Work Group: 05.02.01; Mechanics, Installers, and Repairers; Electrical and Electronic Systems: Installation and Repair. **Personality Type:** Realistic. Realistic occupations frequently involve work activities that include practical, hands-on problems and solutions. These occupations often deal with plants, animals, and real-world materials like wood, tools, and machinery. Many of the occupations require working outside and do not involve a lot of paperwork or working closely with others. **Work Values:** Moral Values; Security; Supervision, Technical; Company Policies and Practices; Supervision, Human Relations; Independence. **Skills:** Troubleshooting; Repairing; Installation; Problem Identification; Testing. **Abilities:** *Cognitive*—Problem Sensitivity; Written Comprehension; Information Ordering; Deductive Reasoning; Visualization; Spatial Orientation. *Psychomotor*—Finger Dexterity; Arm-Hand Steadiness; Control Precision; Manual Dexterity. *Physical*—Dynamic Strength; Stamina; Gross Body Equilibrium; Gross Body Coordination; Static Strength. *Sensory*—Visual Color Discrimination; Sound Localization; Glare Sensitivity. **General Work Activities:** *Information Input*—Getting Information Needed to Do the Job; Identifying Objects, Actions, and Events; Inspecting Equipment, Structures, Materials. *Mental Process*—Making Decisions and Solving Problems; Analyzing Data or Information; Evaluating Information Against Standards; Organizing, Planning, and Prioritizing. *Work Output*—Handling and Moving Objects; Performing General Physical Activities; Repairing and Maintaining Electrical Equipment. *Interacting with Others*—Communicating with Other Workers; Coordinating Work and Activities of Others; Establishing and Maintaining Relationships; Monitoring and Controlling Resources. **Physical Work Conditions:** Using Hands on Objects, Tools, or Controls; Standing; Common Protective or Safety Attire. **Other Job Characteristics:** Importance of Being Sure All Is Done; Importance of Being Exact or Accurate; Consequence of Error.

Experience: Job Zone 4. A minimum of two to four years of work-related skill, knowledge, or experience is needed. **Job Preparation:** SVP 7.0 to less than 8.0—2 years to less than 10 years. **Knowledge:** Telecommunications; Computers and Electronics; Mechanical; Engineering and Technology; Design. **Instructional Program:** 470103 Communication Systems Installer and Repairer.

Related DOT Jobs: 822.261-022 Station Installer-and-Repairer; 822.281-018 Maintenance Mechanic, Telephone.

49-2091.00 Avionics Technicians (Commercial and Industrial Electronics Equipment Repairers)

Education: Postsecondary vocational training

Employed: 71,558

Openings: 9,744

Projected Growth: 12.7%

Earnings: $35,590

Install, inspect, test, adjust, or repair avionics equipment such as radar, radio, navigation, and missile-control systems, in aircraft or space vehicles.

Installs electrical and electronic components, assemblies, and systems in aircraft, using hand tools, power tools, and soldering iron. Tests components or assemblies, using circuit tester, oscilloscope, and voltmeter. Adjusts, repairs, or replaces malfunctioning components or assemblies, using hand tools and soldering iron. Interprets flight-test data to diagnose malfunctions and systemic performance problems. Fabricates parts and test aids as required. Sets up and operates ground support and test equipment to perform functional flight test of electrical and electronic systems. Lays out installation of assemblies and systems in aircraft, according to blueprints and wiring diagrams, using scribe, scale, and protractor. Assembles components such as switches, electrical controls, and junction boxes, using hand tools and soldering iron. Connects components to assemblies such as radio systems, instruments, magnetos, inverters, and in-flight refueling systems, using hand tools and soldering iron.

GOE Number, Interest Area, and Work Group: 05.02.01; Mechanics, Installers, and Repairers; Electrical and Electronic Systems: Installation and Repair. **Personality Type:** Realistic. Realistic occupations frequently involve work activities that include practical, hands-on problems and solutions. These occupations often deal with plants, animals, and real-world materials like wood, tools, and machinery. Many of the occupations require working outside and do not involve a lot of paperwork or working closely with others. **Work Values:** Moral Values; Supervision, Human Relations; Compensation; Company Policies and Practices; Security; Independence. **Skills:** Repairing; Troubleshooting; Testing; Operation Monitoring; Operation and Control; Installation; Equipment Maintenance; Mathematics. **Abilities:** *Cognitive*—Information Ordering; Problem Sensitivity; Written Comprehension; Visualization; Deductive Reasoning; Number Facility. *Psychomotor*—Arm-Hand Steadiness; Finger Dexterity; Manual Dexterity. *Physical*—Extent Flexibility; Static Strength; Trunk Strength. *Sensory*—Near Vision; Visual Color Discrimination; Far Vision. **General Work Activities:** *Information Input*—Monitoring Processes, Materials, and Surroundings; Getting Information Needed to Do the Job; Inspecting Equipment, Structures, Materials. *Mental Process*—Evaluating Information Against Standards; Updating and Using Job-Relevant Knowledge; Analyzing Data or Information; Judging Qualities of Things, Services, Other People's Work. *Work Output*—Handling and Moving Objects; Repairing and Maintaining Electrical Equipment; Controlling Machines and Processes. *Interacting with Others*—Communicating with Other Workers; Interpreting Meaning of Information to Others; Coordinating Work and Activities of Others. **Physical Work Conditions:** Using Hands on Objects, Tools, or Controls; Standing; Indoors; Hazardous Conditions. **Other Job Characteristics:** Consequence of Error; Importance of Being Exact or Accurate; Importance of Being Sure All Is Done.

Experience: Job Zone 4. A minimum of two to four years of work-related skill, knowledge, or experience is needed. **Job Preparation:** SVP 7.0 to less than 8.0—2 years to less than 10 years. **Knowledge:** Computers and Electronics; Engineering and Technology; Mechanical; Design; Physics. **Instructional Programs:** 150402 Computer Maintenance Technology/Technician; 470101 Electrical and Electronics Equipment Installer and Repairer, General; 470102 Business Machine Repairer; 470104 Computer Installer and Repairer; 470105 Industrial Electronics Installer and Repairer; 470609 Aviation Systems and Avionics Main. Technologist/Technician.

Related DOT Jobs: 825.261-018 Electrician, Aircraft; 825.381-010 Aircraft Mechanic, Electrical and Radio; 829.281-018 In-Flight Refueling System Repairer.

49-2092.00 Electric Motor, Power Tool, and Related Repairers (Electric Motor, Transformer, and Related Repairers)

Education: No data available.

Employed: 17,230

Openings: No data available.

Projected Growth: No data available.

Earnings: $27,730

Repair, maintain, or install electric motors, wiring, or switches.

GOE Number, Interest Area, and Work Group: 05.02.02; Mechanics, Installers, and Repairers; Electrical and Electronic Systems: Equipment Repair. **Instructional Programs:** 460302 Electrician; 470101 Electrical and Electronics Equipment Installer and Repairer, General; 470199 Electrical and Electronics Equipment Installer and Repairer, Other. **Note:** The Department of Labor has not collected some data for this job, so it has fewer details than the other descriptions.

49-2092.01 Electric Home Appliance and Power Tool Repairers (Electric Home Appliance and Power Tool Repairers)

Education: No data available.

Employed: 30,220

Openings: No data available.

Projected Growth: No data available.

Earnings: $24,160

Repair, adjust, and install all types of electric household appliances.

Measures and performs minor carpentry procedures to area where appliance is to be installed. Cleans, lubricates, and touches up minor scratches on newly installed or repaired appliance. Observes and examines appliance during operation to detect specific malfunction such as loose parts or leaking fluid. Connects appliance to power source and uses test instruments to calibrate timers and thermostats and to adjust contact points. Reassembles unit, making necessary adjustments to ensure efficient operation. Replaces worn and defective parts such as switches, bearings, transmissions, belts, gears, circuit boards, or defective wiring. Records nature of maintenance or repair in log and returns to business office for further assignments. Traces electrical circuits, following diagram, to locate shorts and grounds, using electrical-circuit testers. Instructs customer regarding operation and care of appliance and provides emergency service number. Disassembles appliance to examine specific mechanical and electrical parts to diagnose problem. Maintains stock of parts used in on-site installation, maintenance, and repair of appliance.

GOE Number, Interest Area, and Work Group: 05.02.02; Mechanics, Installers, and Repairers; Electrical and Electronic Systems: Equipment Repair. **Personality Type:** Realistic. Realistic occupations frequently involve work activities that include practical, hands-on problems and solutions. These occupations often deal with plants, animals, and real-world materials like wood, tools, and machinery. Many of the occupations require working outside and do not involve a lot of paperwork or working closely with others. **Work Values:** Moral Values; Independence; Variety; Security; Working Conditions. **Skills:** Troubleshooting; Installation; Repairing; Problem Identification; Mathematics; Operation Monitoring; Equipment Maintenance. **Abilities:** *Cognitive*—Problem Sensitivity; Information Ordering; Oral Expression; Oral Comprehension; Visualization. *Psychomotor*—Arm-Hand Steadiness; Finger Dexterity; Control Precision. *Physical*—Static Strength; Extent Flexibility; Trunk Strength. *Sensory*—Visual Color Discrimination. **General Work Activities:** *Information Input*—Inspecting Equipment, Structures, Materials; Monitoring Processes, Materials, and Surroundings; Getting Information Needed to Do the Job. *Mental Process*—Judging Qualities of Things, Services, Other People's Work; Organizing, Planning, and Prioritizing; Updating and Using Job-Relevant Knowledge. *Work Output*—Handling and Moving Objects; Repairing and Maintaining Electrical Equipment; Performing General Physical Activities. *Interacting with Others*—Communicating with Persons Outside Organization; Performing for or Working with the Public; Teaching Others. **Physical Work Conditions:** Indoors; Using Hands on Objects, Tools, or Controls; Sitting. **Other Job Characteristics:** Importance of Being Exact or Accurate; Importance of Being Sure All Is Done; Consequence of Error.

Experience: Job Zone 3. Previous work-related skill, knowledge, or experience is required. **Job Preparation:** SVP 6.0 to less than 7.0—More than 1 year and less than 4 years. **Knowledge:** Mechanical; Building and Construction; Engineering and Technology; Computers and Electronics; Education and Training; Customer and Personal Service. **Instructional Programs:** 470101 Electrical and Electronics Equipment Installer and Repairer, General; 470106 Major Appliance Installer and Repairer; 470199 Electrical and Electronics Equipment Installer and Repairer, Other; 470499 Miscellaneous Mechanics and Repairers, Other.

Related DOT Jobs: 637.261-010 Air-Conditioning Installer-Servicer, Window Unit; 723.381-010 Electrical-Appliance Repairer; 723.381-014 Vacuum Cleaner Repairer; 723.584-010 Appliance Repairer; 729.281-022 Electric-Tool Repairer; 827.261-010 Electrical-Appliance Servicer; 827.261-014 Electrical-Appliance-Servicer Apprentice.

49-2092.02 Electric Motor and Switch Assemblers and Repairers (Industrial Machinery Mechanics)

Education: Long-term O-T-J training
Employed: 535,469
Openings: 36,778
Projected Growth: 4.4%
Earnings: No data available.

Test, repair, rebuild, and assemble electric motors, generators, and equipment.

Records repairs required, parts used, and labor time. Adjusts working parts such as fan-belt tension, voltage output, contacts and springs, using hand tools. Verifies corrections, using gauges. Rewinds coils on core while core is in slots, or makes replacement coils, using coil-winding machine. Installs, secures, and aligns parts, using hand tools, welding equipment, and electrical meters. Reassembles repaired electric motors to specified requirements and ratings, using hand tools and electrical meters. Measures velocity, horsepower, r.p.m., amperage, circuitry, and voltage of unit or parts, using electrical meters and mechanical testing devices. Inspects parts for wear or damage, or reads work order or schematic drawings to determine required repairs. Cuts and forms insulation and inserts insulation into armature, rotor, or stator slots. Refaces, reams, and polishes commutators and machine parts to specified tolerances, using machine tools. Tests for overheating, using speed gauges and thermometers. Scrapes and cleans units or parts, using cleaning solvent, and lubricates moving parts. Lifts units or parts such as motors or generators, using crane or chain hoist. Repairs and rebuilds defective mechanical parts in electric motors, generators, and related equipment, using hand tools and power tools. Replaces defective parts such as coil leads, carbon brushes, and connecting wires, using soldering equipment. Rewires electrical systems; repairs or replaces electrical accessories. Disassembles defective unit, using hand tools. Cuts and removes parts such as defective coils and insulation. Tests charges and replaces batteries. Assembles electrical parts such as alternators, generators, starting devices, and switches, following schematic drawings, using hand, machine, and power tools.

GOE Number, Interest Area, and Work Group: 05.02.02; Mechanics, Installers, and Repairers; Electrical and Electronic Systems: Equipment Repair. **Personality Type:** Realistic. Realistic occupations frequently involve work activities that include practical, hands-on problems and solutions. These occupations often deal with plants, animals, and real-world materials like wood, tools, and machinery. Many of the occupations require working outside and do not involve a lot of paperwork or working closely with others. **Work Values:** Moral Values; Independence; Security; Activity; Supervision, Human Relations; Compensation; Company Policies and Practices; Supervision, Technical. **Skills:** Repairing; Installation; Product Inspection; Troubleshooting; Science; Operation and Control; Operation Monitoring. **Abilities:** *Cognitive*—Information Ordering; Written Comprehension; Visualization; Problem Sensitivity; Deductive Reasoning; Number Facility. *Psychomotor*—Finger Dexterity; Arm-Hand Steadiness; Control Precision. *Physical*—Extent Flexibility; Static Strength; Trunk Strength; Explosive Strength. *Sensory*—Near Vision; Visual Color Discrimination; Hearing Sensitivity. **General Work Activities:** *Information Input*—Inspecting Equipment, Structures, Materials; Getting Information Needed to Do the Job; Monitoring Processes, Materials, and Surroundings. *Mental Process*—Evaluating Information Against Standards; Judging Qualities of Things, Services, Other People's Work; Making Decisions and Solving Problems. *Work Output*—Handling and Moving Objects; Repairing and Maintaining Electrical Equipment; Repairing and Maintaining Mechanical Equipment; Performing General Physical Activities. *Interacting with Others*—Communicating with Other Workers; Performing Administrative Activities; Monitoring and Controlling Resources. **Physical Work Conditions:** Indoors; Using Hands on Objects, Tools, or Controls; Hazardous Equipment. **Other Job Characteristics:** Consequence of Error; Degree of Automation; Importance of Being Sure All Is Done.

Experience: Job Zone 3. Previous work-related skill, knowledge, or experience is required. **Job Preparation:** SVP 6.0 to less than 7.0—More than 1 year and less than 4 years. **Knowledge:** Mechanical; Computers and Electronics; Engineering and Technology; Design; Mathematics. **Instructional Program:** 470101 Electrical and Electronics Equipment Installer and Repairer, General.

Related DOT Jobs: 620.261-026 Electric-Golf-Cart Repairer; 721.261-010 Electric-Motor Analyst; 721.281-010 Automotive-Generator-and-Starter Repairer; 721.281-014 Electric-Motor Assembler and Tester; 721.281-018 Electric-Motor Repairer; 721.281-026 Propulsion-Motor-and-Generator Repairer; 721.381-010 Electric-Motor Fitter; 724.381-010 Adjuster, Electrical Contacts; 729.684-038 Repairer, Switchgear; 821.381-018 Wind-Generating-Electric-Power Installer.

49-2092.03 Battery Repairers (Industrial Machinery Mechanics)

Education: Long-term O-T-J training

Employed: 535,469

Openings: 36,778

Projected Growth: 4.4%

Earnings: No data available.

Inspect, repair, recharge, and replace batteries.

Installs recharged or repaired battery or cells, using hand tools. Repairs battery-charging equipment. Replaces defective parts such as cell plates, fuses, lead parts, switches, wires, anodes, cathodes, and rheostat. Adds water and acid to battery cells to obtain specified concentration. Positions and levels, or signals worker to position and level, cell, anode, or cathode, using hoist and leveling jacks. Secures cell on rocker mechanism or attaches assemblies, using bolts or cement. Inspects battery for defects such as dented cans, damaged carbon rods and terminals, and defective seals. Measures cathode blade and anode, using ruler. Measures rate of mercury flow, using stopwatch. Tests condition, fluid level, and specific gravity of electrolyte cells, using voltmeter, hydrometer, and thermometer. Seals joints with putty, mortar, and asbestos, using putty extruder and knife. Compiles operating and maintenance records. Cleans cells, cell assemblies, glassware, leads, electrical connections, and battery poles, using scraper, steam, water, emery cloth, power grinder, or acid. Disconnects electrical leads and removes battery, using hand tools and hoist. Repairs or adjusts defective parts, using hand tools or power tools. Connects battery to battery charger and adjusts rheostat to start flow of electricity into battery. Removes and disassembles cells and cathode assembly, using tension handles, prybars, and hoist; cuts wires to faulty cells. Inspects electrical connections, wiring-charging relays, charging-resistance box, and storage batteries, following wiring diagram. Fabricates and assembles electrolytic cell parts for storage batteries.

GOE Number, Interest Area, and Work Group: 05.02.02; Mechanics, Installers, and Repairers; Electrical and Electronic Systems: Equipment Repair. **Personality Type:** Realistic. Realistic occupations frequently involve work activities that include practical, hands-on problems and solutions. These occupations often deal with plants, animals, and real-world materials like wood, tools, and machinery. Many of the occupations require working outside and do not involve a lot of paperwork or working closely with others. **Work Values:** Moral Values; Security; Supervision, Technical; Activity; Independence; Supervision, Human Relations. **Skills:** Repairing; Product Inspection; Installation; Troubleshooting; Equipment Selection; Equipment Maintenance; Testing. **Abilities:** *Cognitive*—Problem Sensitivity; Written Comprehension; Information Ordering; Deductive Reasoning; Selective Attention; Written Expression. *Psychomotor*—Manual Dexterity; Reaction Time; Finger Dexterity. *Physical*—Explosive Strength; Static Strength; Dynamic Strength. *Sensory*—Visual Color Discrimination; Peripheral Vision. **General Work Activities:** *Information Input*—Inspecting Equipment, Structures, Materials; Monitoring Processes, Materials, and Surroundings; Getting Information Needed to Do the Job. *Mental Process*—Judging Qualities of Things, Services, Other People's Work; Evaluating Information Against Standards; Processing Information; Analyzing Data or Information. *Work Output*—Handling and Moving Objects; Repairing and Maintaining Electrical Equipment; Controlling Machines and Processes. *Interacting with Others*—Communicating with Other Workers; Performing Administrative Activities; Monitoring and Controlling Resources; Establishing and Maintaining Relationships. **Physical Work Conditions:** Using Hands on Objects, Tools, or Controls; Indoors; Hazardous Situations. **Other Job Characteristics:** Consequence of Error; Importance of Being Sure All Is Done; Importance of Being Exact or Accurate.

Experience: Job Zone 2. Some previous work-related skill, knowledge, or experience may be helpful, but usually is not needed. **Job Preparation:** SVP 4.00 to 5.99—6 months to less than 2 years. **Knowledge:** Computers and Electronics; Mechanical; Engineering and Technology; Chemistry; Mathematics. **Instructional Program:** 470101 Electrical and Electronics Equipment Installer and Repairer, General.

Related DOT Jobs: 727.381-014 Battery Repairer; 727.684-018 Cell Repairer; 820.381-010 Battery Maintainer, Large Emergency Storage; 825.684-018 Battery Charger; 826.384-010 Cell Repairer; 826.684-014 Cell Changer; 826.684-018 Cell Installer; 829.684-010 Battery Inspector.

49-2092.04 Transformer Repairers (Electric Motor, Transformer, and Related Repairers)

Education: No data available.

Employed: 17,230

Openings: No data available.

Projected Growth: No data available.

Earnings: $27,730

Clean and repair electrical transformers.

Drains and filters transformer oil. Winds replacement coils, using coil-winding machine. Disassembles distribution, streetlight, or instrument transformers. Fills reassembled transformer with oil until coils are submerged. Dismantles lamination assembly, preparatory to cleaning and inspection. Signals crane operator to raise heavy transformer component subassemblies. Inspects transformer for defects such as cracked weldments. Replaces worn or defective parts, using hand tools. Cleans transformer case, using scrapers and solvent. Reassembles transformer. Secures input and output wires in position.

GOE Number, Interest Area, and Work Group: 05.02.02; Mechanics, Installers, and Repairers; Electrical and Electronic Systems: Equipment Repair. **Personality Type:** Realistic. Realistic occupations frequently involve work activities that include practical, hands-on problems and solutions. These occupations often deal with plants, animals, and real-world materials like wood, tools, and machinery. Many of the occupations require working outside and do not involve a lot of paperwork or working closely with others. **Work Values:** Moral Values; Security; Supervision, Technical; Company Policies and Practices; Activity; Supervision, Human Relations. **Skills:** Repairing; Installation; Troubleshooting; Equipment Maintenance; Equipment Selection; Product Inspection. **Abilities:** *Cognitive*—Problem Sensitivity; Information Ordering; Deductive Reasoning; Oral Expression; Oral Comprehension. *Psychomotor*—Manual Dexterity; Reaction Time; Finger Dexterity. *Physical*—Dynamic Strength; Extent Flexibility; Static Strength. *Sensory*—Visual Color Discrimination; Depth Perception; Night Vision. **General Work Activities:** *Information Input*—Inspecting Equipment, Structures, Materials; Getting Information Needed to Do the Job; Identifying Objects, Actions, and Events. *Mental Process*—Judging Qualities of Things, Services, Other People's Work; Evaluating Information Against Standards; Updating and Using Job-Relevant Knowledge. *Work Output*—Handling and Moving Objects; Repairing and Maintaining Electrical Equipment; Performing General Physical Activities. *Interacting with Others*—Communicating with Other Workers; Coordinating Work and Activities of Others; Establishing and Maintaining Relationships. **Physical Work Conditions:** Outdoors; Using Hands on Objects, Tools, or Controls; Standing. **Other Job Characteristics:** Consequence of Error; Importance of Being Sure All Is Done; Importance of Being Exact or Accurate.

Experience: Job Zone 4. A minimum of two to four years of work-related skill, knowledge, or experience is needed. **Job Preparation:** SVP 7.0 to less than 8.0—2 years to less than 10 years. **Knowledge:** Mechanical; Engineering and Technology; Computers and Electronics; Telecommunications; Physics. **Instructional Programs:** 460302 Electrician; 470101 Electrical and Electronics Equipment Installer and Repairer, General; 470199 Electrical and Electronics Equipment Installer and Repairer, Other.

Related DOT Jobs: 724.381-018 Transformer Repairer; 821.361-034 Power-Transformer Repairer.

49-2092.05 Electrical Parts Reconditioners (Commercial and Industrial Electronics Equipment Repairers)

Education: Postsecondary vocational training
Employed: 71,558
Openings: 9,744
Projected Growth: 12.7%
Earnings: $35,590

Recondition and rebuild salvaged electrical parts of equipment; wind new coils on armatures of used generators and motors.

Cleans and polishes parts, using solvent and buffing wheel. Winds new coils on armatures of generators and motors. Cuts insulating material to fit slots on armature core, and places material in bottom of core slots. Replaces broken and defective parts. Disassembles salvaged equipment used in electric-power systems such as air circuit breakers and lightning arresters, using hand tools; discards nonrepairable parts. Tests armatures and motors to ensure proper operation. Bolts porcelain insulators to wood parts to assemble hot stools. Inserts and hammers ready-made coils in place. Solders, wraps, and coats wires to ensure proper insulation. Solders ends of coils to commutator segments.

GOE Number, Interest Area, and Work Group: 05.02.02; Mechanics, Installers, and Repairers; Electrical and Electronic Systems: Equipment Repair. **Personality Type:** Realistic. Realistic occupations frequently involve work activities that include practical, hands-on problems and solutions. These occupations often deal with plants, animals, and real-world materials like wood, tools, and machinery. Many of the occupations require working outside and do not involve a lot of paperwork or working closely with others. **Work Values:** Moral Values; Independence; Activity; Security; Company Policies and Practices; Supervision, Human Relations; Supervision, Technical. **Skills:** Repairing; Product Inspection; Installation; Testing; Equipment Maintenance; Equipment Selection. **Abilities:** *Cognitive*—Problem Sensitivity; Deductive Reasoning; Visualization; Information Ordering; Flexibility of Closure; Originality. *Psychomotor*—Finger Dexterity; Manual Dexterity; Wrist-Finger Speed. *Physical*—Extent Flexibility; Static Strength; Explosive Strength. *Sensory*—Visual Color Discrimination; Sound Localization. **General Work Activities:** *Information Input*—Inspecting Equipment, Structures, Materials; Identifying Objects, Actions, and Events; Getting Information Needed to Do the Job. *Mental Process*—Judging Qualities of Things, Services, Other People's Work; Making Decisions and Solving Problems; Organizing, Planning, and Prioritizing; Analyzing Data or Information. *Work Output*—Handling and Moving Objects; Performing General Physical Activities; Repairing and Maintaining Mechanical Equipment; Controlling Machines and Processes. *Interacting with Others*—Communicating with Other Workers; Establishing and Maintaining Relationships; Interpreting Meaning of Information to Others; Monitoring and Controlling Resources. **Physical Work Conditions:** Indoors; Using Hands on Objects, Tools, or Controls; Sitting. **Other Job Characteristics:** Importance of Being Exact or Accurate; Importance of Being Sure All Is Done; Consequence of Error.

Experience: Job Zone 2. Some previous work-related skill, knowledge, or experience may be helpful, but usually is not needed. **Job Preparation:** SVP 4.00 to 5.99—6 months to less than 2 years. **Knowledge:** Mechanical; Engineering and Technology; Computers and Electronics; Production and Processing; Building and Construction. **Instructional Programs:** 150402 Computer Maintenance Technology/Technician; 470101 Electrical and Electronics Equipment Installer and Repairer, General; 470102 Business Machine Repairer; 470104 Computer Installer and Repairer; 470105 Industrial Electronics Installer and Repairer; 470609 Aviation Systems and Avionics Main. Technologist/Technician.

Related DOT Jobs: 724.684-018 Armature Winder, Repair; 729.384-018 Salvage Repairer II.

49-2092.06 Hand and Portable Power Tool Repairers
(Electric Home Appliance and Power Tool Repairers)

Education: No data available.

Employed: 30,220

Openings: No data available.

Projected Growth: No data available.

Earnings: $24,160

Repair and adjust hand and power tools.

Examines and tests tools to determine defects or cause of malfunction, using hand and power tools, observation, and experience. Records nature and extent of repairs performed. Sharpens tools such as picks, shovels, screwdrivers, and scoops, using bench grinder and emery wheel. Verifies and adjusts alignment and dimensions of parts, using gauges and tracing lathe. Maintains stock of parts. Repairs or replaces tools and defective parts such as handles, vises, pliers, or metal buckets, using soldering tool, gas torch, power tools, or hand tools. Sprays, brushes, or recoats surface of polishing wheel and places it in oven to dry. Cleans polishing and buffing wheels, using steam cleaning machine, to remove abrasives and bonding materials; salvages cloth from wheel. Disassembles and reassembles tools, using hand tools, power tools, or arbor press.

GOE Number, Interest Area, and Work Group: 05.03.02; Mechanics, Installers, and Repairers; Mechanical Work: Machinery Repair. **Personality Type:** Realistic. Realistic occupations frequently involve work activities that include practical, hands-on problems and solutions. These occupations often deal with plants, animals, and real-world materials like wood, tools, and machinery. Many of the occupations require working outside and do not involve a lot of paperwork or working closely with others. **Work Values:** Moral Values; Independence; Activity; Security; Responsibility. **Skills:** Problem Identification; Repairing; Product Inspection; Equipment Selection; Operation and Control. **Abilities:** *Cognitive*—Visualization; Information Ordering; Problem Sensitivity; Memorization; Perceptual Speed; Flexibility of Closure. *Psychomotor*—Manual Dexterity; Finger Dexterity; Wrist-Finger Speed. *Physical*—Trunk Strength; Stamina; Explosive Strength. *Sensory*—Hearing Sensitivity; Depth Perception; Sound Localization. **General Work Activities:** *Information Input*—Inspecting Equipment, Structures, Materials; Getting Information Needed to Do the Job; Monitoring Processes, Materials, and Surroundings; Identifying Objects, Actions, and Events. *Mental Process*—Judging Qualities of Things, Services, Other People's Work; Updating and Using Job-Relevant Knowledge; Evaluating Information Against Standards. *Work Output*—Handling and Moving Objects; Repairing and Maintaining Mechanical Equipment; Performing General Physical Activities. *Interacting with Others*—Monitoring and Controlling Resources; Performing Administrative Activities; Communicating with Other Workers. **Physical Work Conditions:** Using Hands on Objects, Tools, or Controls; Indoors; Common Protective or Safety Attire. **Other Job Characteristics:** Importance of Being Sure All Is Done; Consequence of Error; Importance of Being Exact or Accurate.

Experience: Job Zone 2. Some previous work-related skill, knowledge, or experience may be helpful, but usually is not needed.

Job Preparation: SVP 4.00 to 5.99—6 months to less than 2 years. **Knowledge:** Mechanical; Engineering and Technology; Clerical; Mathematics; Physics. **Instructional Programs:** 470101 Electrical and Electronics Equipment Installer and Repairer, General; 470106 Major Appliance Installer and Repairer; 470199 Electrical and Electronics Equipment Installer and Repairer, Other; 470499 Miscellaneous Mechanics and Repairers, Other.

Related DOT Jobs: 519.684-026 Tool Repairer; 701.381-010 Repairer, Handtools; 701.384-010 Tool-Maintenance Worker; 701.684-010 Calibrator; 739.684-030 Buffing-and-Polishing-Wheel Repairer.

49-2093.00 Electrical and Electronics Installers and Repairers, Transportation Equipment (Commercial and Industrial Electronics Equipment Repairers)

Education: Postsecondary vocational training

Employed: 71,558

Openings: 9,744

Projected Growth: 12.7%

Earnings: $35,590

Install, adjust, or maintain mobile electronics communication equipment, including sound, sonar, security, navigation, and surveillance systems on trains, watercraft, or other mobile equipment.

Repairs or rebuilds starters, generators, distributors, or door controls, using electrician's tools. Installs electrical equipment such as air-conditioning systems, heating systems, ignition systems, generator brushes, and commutators, using hand tools. Splices wires with knife or cutting pliers; solders connections to fixtures, outlets, and equipment. Installs fixtures, outlets, terminal boards, switches, and wall boxes, using hand tools. Confers with customer to determine nature of malfunction. Estimates cost of repairs based on parts and labor charges. Visually inspects and tests electrical system or equipment, using testing devices such as oscilloscope, voltmeter, and ammeter, to determine malfunctions. Cuts openings and drills holes for fixtures, outlet boxes, and fuse holders, using electric drill and router. Adjusts, repairs, or replaces defective wiring and relays in ignition, lighting, air-conditioning, and safety control systems, using electrician's tools. Measures, cuts, and installs framework and conduit, to support and connect wiring, control panels, and junction boxes, using hand tools.

GOE Number, Interest Area, and Work Group: 05.02.01; Mechanics, Installers, and Repairers; Electrical and Electronic Systems: Installation and Repair. **Personality Type:** Realistic. Realistic occupations frequently involve work activities that include practical, hands-on problems and solutions. These occupations often deal with plants, animals, and real-world materials like wood, tools, and machinery. Many of the occupations require working outside and do not involve a lot of paperwork or working closely with others. **Work Values:** Moral Values; Security; Supervision, Human Relations; Activity; Company Policies and Practices. **Skills:** Repairing; Installation; Equipment Selection; Reading Comprehension; Problem Identification; Testing. **Abilities:** *Cognitive*—Problem Sensitivity; Information Ordering; Deductive Reasoning; Number Facility; Visualization. *Psychomotor*—Manual Dexterity;

Arm-Hand Steadiness; Finger Dexterity. *Physical*—Extent Flexibility; Trunk Strength; Static Strength. *Sensory*—Near Vision; Visual Color Discrimination; Hearing Sensitivity. **General Work Activities:** *Information Input*—Inspecting Equipment, Structures, Materials; Monitoring Processes, Materials, and Surroundings; Getting Information Needed to Do the Job. *Mental Process*—Updating and Using Job-Relevant Knowledge; Judging Qualities of Things, Services, Other People's Work; Making Decisions and Solving Problems. *Work Output*—Repairing and Maintaining Electrical Equipment; Handling and Moving Objects; Implementing Ideas and Programs. *Interacting with Others*—Communicating with Persons Outside Organization; Communicating with Other Workers; Performing for or Working with the Public. **Physical Work Conditions:** Using Hands on Objects, Tools, or Controls; Indoors; Standing; Kneeling, Crouching, or Crawling; Hazardous Equipment. **Other Job Characteristics:** Importance of Being Sure All Is Done; Consequence of Error; Importance of Being Exact or Accurate.

Experience: Job Zone 3. Previous work-related skill, knowledge, or experience is required. **Job Preparation:** SVP 6.0 to less than 7.0—More than 1 year and less than 4 years. **Knowledge:** Mechanical; Computers and Electronics; Engineering and Technology; Building and Construction; Public Safety and Security. **Instructional Programs:** 150402 Computer Maintenance Technology/Technician; 470101 Electrical and Electronics Equipment Installer and Repairer, General; 470102 Business Machine Repairer; 470104 Computer Installer and Repairer; 470105 Industrial Electronics Installer and Repairer; 470609 Aviation Systems and Avionics Main. Technologist/Technician.

Related DOT Jobs: 825.281-026 Electrician, Locomotive; 825.381-018 Controller Repairer-and-Tester; 829.684-014 Body Wirer.

49-2094.00 Electrical and Electronics Repairers, Commercial and Industrial Equipment (All Other Electrical and Electronic Equipment Mechanics, Installers, and Repairers)

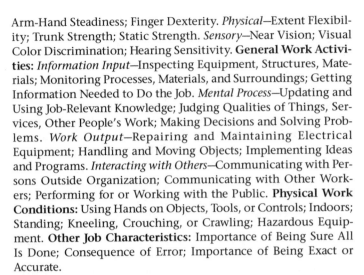

Education: No data available.

Employed: 64,500

Openings: No data available.

Projected Growth: No data available.

Earnings: $34,000

Repair, test, adjust, or install electronic equipment such as industrial controls, transmitters, and antennas.

Inspects components of equipment for defects such as loose connections and frayed wire and for accuracy of assembly and installation. Installs equipment in industrial or military establishments and in aircraft and missiles. Studies blueprints, schematics, manuals, and other specifications to determine installation procedures. Adjusts defective components, using hand tools and technical documents. Calibrates testing instruments and installed or repaired equipment to prescribed specifications. Replaces or repairs defective components, using hand tools and technical documents. Determines feasibility of using standardized equipment, and develops specifications for equipment required to perform addi-

tional functions. Operates equipment to demonstrate use of equipment and to analyze malfunctions. Maintains records of repairs, calibrations, and tests. Enters information into computer to copy program or to draw, modify, or store schematics, applying knowledge of software package used. Consults with customer, supervisor, and engineers to plan layout of equipment and to resolve problems in system operation and maintenance. Signs overhaul documents for equipment replaced or repaired. Tests faulty equipment, using test equipment and applying knowledge of functional operation of electronic unit and systems, to diagnose malfunction. Analyzes technical requirements of customer desiring to utilize electronic equipment, and performs installation and maintenance duties. Advises management regarding customer satisfaction, product performance, and suggestions for product improvements. Converses with equipment operators to ascertain whether mechanical or human error contributed to equipment breakdown.

GOE Number, Interest Area, and Work Group: 05.02.01; Mechanics, Installers, and Repairers; Electrical and Electronic Systems: Installation and Repair. **Personality Type:** Realistic. Realistic occupations frequently involve work activities that include practical, hands-on problems and solutions. These occupations often deal with plants, animals, and real-world materials like wood, tools, and machinery. Many of the occupations require working outside and do not involve a lot of paperwork or working closely with others. **Work Values:** Moral Values; Security; Supervision, Human Relations; Compensation; Company Policies and Practices; Ability Utilization; Variety. **Skills:** Equipment Maintenance; Troubleshooting; Installation; Repairing; Testing. **Abilities:** *Cognitive*—Oral Expression; Oral Comprehension; Written Comprehension; Deductive Reasoning; Visualization; Problem Sensitivity. *Psychomotor*—Finger Dexterity; Control Precision; Manual Dexterity. *Physical*—none met the criteria. *Sensory*—Near Vision; Visual Color Discrimination; Hearing Sensitivity. **General Work Activities:** *Information Input*—Inspecting Equipment, Structures, Materials; Getting Information Needed to Do the Job; Monitoring Processes, Materials, and Surroundings; Identifying Objects, Actions, and Events. *Mental Process*—Making Decisions and Solving Problems; Analyzing Data or Information; Evaluating Information Against Standards; Updating and Using Job-Relevant Knowledge. *Work Output*—Repairing and Maintaining Electrical Equipment; Handling and Moving Objects; Implementing Ideas and Programs. *Interacting with Others*—Communicating with Other Workers; Communicating with Persons Outside Organization; Teaching Others; Interpreting Meaning of Information to Others. **Physical Work Conditions:** Indoors; Using Hands on Objects, Tools, or Controls; Sitting. **Other Job Characteristics:** Consequence of Error; Importance of Being Exact or Accurate; Importance of Being Sure All Is Done.

Experience: Job Zone 3. Previous work-related skill, knowledge, or experience is required. **Job Preparation:** SVP 6.0 to less than 7.0—More than 1 year and less than 4 years. **Knowledge:** Computers and Electronics; Design; Telecommunications; Engineering and Technology; Mathematics; Physics. **Instructional Programs:** 150499 Electromechanical Instrumentation and Maintenance Technol./Technicians, Other; 470101 Electrical and Electronics Equipment Installer and Repairer, General; 470401 Instrument Calibration and Repairer.

Related DOT Jobs: 823.261-026 Avionics Technician; 828.251-010 Electronic-Sales-and-Service Technician; 828.261-014 Field Service Engineer; 828.261-022 Electronics Mechanic; 828.261-026 Electronics-Mechanic Apprentice; 828.281-022 Radioactivity-Instrument Maintenance Technician; 828.281-026 Computerized Environmental Control Installer.

49-2095.00 Electrical and Electronics Repairers, Powerhouse, Substation, and Relay (Commercial and Industrial Electronics Equipment Repairers)

Education: Postsecondary vocational training

Employed: 71,558

Openings: 9,744

Projected Growth: 12.7%

Earnings: $35,590

Inspect, test, repair, or maintain electrical equipment in generating stations, substations, and in-service relays.

Repairs or rebuilds circuit breakers, transformers, and lightning arresters by replacing worn parts. Inspects and tests equipment and circuits to identify malfunction or defect, using wiring diagrams and testing devices such as ohmmeters, voltmeters, or ammeters. Tests insulators and bushings of equipment by inducing voltage across insulation, using testing apparatus, and calculating insulation loss. Notifies personnel of need for equipment shutdown requiring changes from normal operation to maintain service. Analyzes test data to diagnose malfunctions and evaluate effect of system modifications. Prepares reports of work performed. Disconnects voltage regulators, bolts, and screws, and connects replacement regulators to high-voltage lines. Repairs, replaces, and cleans equipment such as brushes, commutators, windings, bearings, relays, switches, controls, and instruments. Paints, repairs, and maintains buildings; sets forms and pours concrete footings for installation of heavy equipment. Tests oil in circuit breakers and transformers for dielectric strength, and periodically refills.

GOE Number, Interest Area, and Work Group: 05.02.02; Mechanics, Installers, and Repairers; Electrical and Electronic Systems: Equipment Repair. **Personality Type:** Realistic. Realistic occupations frequently involve work activities that include practical, hands-on problems and solutions. These occupations often deal with plants, animals, and real-world materials like wood, tools, and machinery. Many of the occupations require working outside and do not involve a lot of paperwork or working closely with others. **Work Values:** Moral Values; Company Policies and Practices; Security; Variety; Responsibility. **Skills:** Equipment Maintenance; Testing; Troubleshooting; Problem Identification; Repairing. **Abilities:** *Cognitive*—Deductive Reasoning; Information Ordering; Problem Sensitivity; Time Sharing; Perceptual Speed. *Psychomotor*—Control Precision; Reaction Time; Manual Dexterity. *Physical*—Extent Flexibility; Static Strength; Dynamic Strength. *Sensory*—Visual Color Discrimination; Hearing Sensitivity; Auditory Attention. **General Work Activities:** *Information Input*—Inspecting Equipment, Structures, Materials; Monitoring Processes, Materials, and Surroundings; Getting Information Needed to Do the Job. *Mental Process*—Analyzing Data or Information; Making Decisions and Solving Problems; Evaluating Information Against Standards. *Work Output*—Repairing and Maintaining Electrical Equipment; Handling and Moving Objects; Controlling Machines and Processes; Implementing Ideas and Programs. *Interacting with Others*—Communicating with Other Workers; Performing Administrative Activities; Providing Consultation and Advice to Others. **Physical Work Conditions:** Using Hands on Objects, Tools, or Controls; Indoors; Hazardous Conditions; Standing. **Other Job Characteristics:** Consequence of Error; Importance of Being Exact or Accurate; Importance of Being Sure All Is Done.

Experience: Job Zone 5. Extensive skill, knowledge, and experience are needed. Very advanced communication and organizational skills are required. **Job Preparation:** SVP 8.0 and above—4 years to more than 10 years. **Knowledge:** Computers and Electronics; Mechanical; Engineering and Technology; Mathematics; English Language; Physics. **Instructional Programs:** 150402 Computer Maintenance Technology/Technician; 470101 Electrical and Electronics Equipment Installer and Repairer, General; 470102 Business Machine Repairer; 470104 Computer Installer and Repairer; 470105 Industrial Electronics Installer and Repairer; 470609 Aviation Systems and Avionics Main. Technologist/Technician.

Related DOT Jobs: 820.261-010 Electrician Apprentice, Powerhouse; 820.261-014 Electrician, Powerhouse; 820.261-018 Electrician, Substation; 821.261-018 Relay Technician.

49-2096.00 Electronic Equipment Installers and Repairers, Motor Vehicles (Electrical Installers and Repairers, Transportation Equipment)

Education: No data available.

Employed: 21,310

Openings: No data available.

Projected Growth: No data available.

Earnings: $33,870

Install, diagnose, or repair communications, sound, security, or navigation equipment in motor vehicles.

Cuts openings and drills holes for fixtures, outlet boxes, and fuse holders, using electric drill and router. Repairs or rebuilds starters, generators, distributors, or door controls, using electrician's tools. Splices wires with knife or cutting pliers, and solders connections to fixtures, outlets, and equipment. Visually inspects and tests electrical system or equipment, using testing devices such as oscilloscope, voltmeter, and ammeter, to determine malfunctions. Measures, cuts, and installs framework and conduit to support and connect wiring, control panels, and junction boxes, using hand tools. Installs electrical equipment such as air-conditioning systems, heating systems, ignition systems, generator brushes, and commutators, using hand tools. Confers with customer to determine nature of malfunction. Estimates cost of repairs based on parts and labor charges. Adjusts, repairs, or replaces defective wiring and relays in ignition, lighting, air-conditioning, and safety-control systems, using electrician's tools. Installs fixtures, outlets, terminal boards, switches, and wall boxes, using hand tools.

GOE Number, Interest Area, and Work Group: 05.02.01; Mechanics, Installers, and Repairers; Electrical and Electronic Systems: Installation and Repair. **Personality Type:** Realistic. Realistic occupations frequently involve work activities that include practical, hands-on problems and solutions. These occupations often deal with plants, animals, and real-world materials like wood, tools, and machinery. Many of the occupations require working outside and do not involve a lot of paperwork or working closely with others. **Work Values:** Moral Values; Security; Supervision, Human Relations; Activity; Company Policies and Practices. **Skills:** Repairing; Installation; Equipment Selection; Testing; Reading Comprehension; Problem Identification. **Abilities:** *Cognitive*—Problem Sensitivity; Information Ordering; Deductive Reasoning; Visualization; Number Facility. *Psychomotor*—Manual Dexterity; Arm-Hand Steadiness; Finger Dexterity. *Physical*—Extent Flexibility; Trunk Strength; Static Strength. *Sensory*—Near Vision; Visual Color Discrimination; Hearing Sensitivity. **General Work Activities:** *Information Input*—Inspecting Equipment, Structures, Materials; Monitoring Processes, Materials, and Surroundings; Getting Information Needed to Do the Job. *Mental Process*—Judging Qualities of Things, Services, Other People's Work; Updating and Using Job-Relevant Knowledge; Making Decisions and Solving Problems. *Work Output*—Repairing and Maintaining Electrical Equipment; Handling and Moving Objects; Implementing Ideas and Programs. *Interacting with Others*—Communicating with Persons Outside Organization; Performing for or Working with the Public; Communicating with Other Workers. **Physical Work Conditions:** Using Hands on Objects, Tools, or Controls; Indoors; Kneeling, Crouching, or Crawling; Standing; Hazardous Equipment. **Other Job Characteristics:** Importance of Being Sure All Is Done; Consequence of Error; Importance of Being Exact or Accurate.

Experience: Job Zone 3. Previous work-related skill, knowledge, or experience is required. **Job Preparation:** SVP 6.0 to less than 7.0—More than 1 year and less than 4 years. **Knowledge:** Mechanical; Computers and Electronics; Engineering and Technology; Building and Construction; Public Safety and Security. **Instructional Programs:** 460302 Electrician; 470604 Auto/Automotive Mechanic/Technician; 470607 Aircraft Mechanic/Technician, Airframe.

Related DOT Jobs: 825.281-022 Electrician, Automotive; 828.381-010 Equipment Installer.

49-2097.00 Electronic Home Entertainment Equipment Installers and Repairers (Electronic Home Entertainment Equipment Repairers)

Education: Postsecondary vocational training

Employed: 35,713

Openings: 3,901

Projected Growth: −11.9%

Earnings: $23,540

Repair, adjust, or install audio or television receivers, stereo systems, camcorders, video systems, or other electronic home-entertainment equipment.

Confers with customers to determine nature of problem or to explain repairs. Makes service calls and repairs units in customers' homes or returns unit to shop for major repair. Installs electronic equipment or instruments such as televisions, radios, audio-visual equipment, and organs, using hand tools. Tunes or adjusts equipment and instruments, according to specifications, to obtain optimum visual or auditory reception. Computes cost estimates for labor and materials. Positions or mounts speakers and wires speakers to console. Disassembles equipment and repairs or replaces loose, worn, or defective components and wiring, using hand tools and soldering iron. Analyzes and tests products and parts to locate defects or source of trouble. Tests circuits, using schematic diagrams, service manuals, and testing instruments such as voltmeters, oscilloscopes, and audiogenerators.

GOE Number, Interest Area, and Work Group: 05.02.02; Mechanics, Installers, and Repairers; Electrical and Electronic Systems: Equipment Repair. **Personality Type:** Realistic. Realistic occupations frequently involve work activities that include practical, hands-on problems and solutions. These occupations often deal with plants, animals, and real-world materials like wood, tools, and machinery. Many of the occupations require working outside and do not involve a lot of paperwork or working closely with others. **Work Values:** Moral Values; Security; Independence; Variety; Compensation. **Skills:** Problem Identification; Installation; Science; Troubleshooting; Critical Thinking. **Abilities:** *Cognitive*—Oral Comprehension; Information Ordering; Written Comprehension; Deductive Reasoning; Oral Expression; Speed of Closure. *Psychomotor*—Finger Dexterity; Arm-Hand Steadiness; Control Precision. *Physical*—Static Strength; Extent Flexibility; Trunk Strength. *Sensory*—Near Vision; Visual Color Discrimination; Sound Localization; Speech Clarity; Hearing Sensitivity. **General Work Activities:** *Information Input*—Inspecting Equipment, Structures, Materials; Getting Information Needed to Do the Job; Monitoring Processes, Materials, and Surroundings. *Mental Process*—Analyzing Data or Information; Judging Qualities of Things, Services, Other People's Work; Evaluating Information Against Standards. *Work Output*—Repairing and Maintaining Electrical Equipment; Handling and Moving Objects; Performing General Physical Activities. *Interacting with Others*—Communicating with Persons Outside Organization; Performing for or Working with the Public; Establishing and Maintaining Relationships. **Physical Work Conditions:** Indoors; Using Hands on Objects, Tools, or Controls; Sitting; Bending or Twisting the Body. **Other Job Characteristics:** Frustrating Circumstances; Importance of Being Sure All Is Done; Consequence of Error; Importance of Being Exact or Accurate.

Experience: Job Zone 3. Previous work-related skill, knowledge, or experience is required. **Job Preparation:** SVP 6.0 to less than 7.0—More than 1 year and less than 4 years. **Knowledge:** Computers and Electronics; Mechanical; Design; Customer and Personal Service; Public Safety and Security; Telecommunications. **Instructional Programs:** 470101 Electrical and Electronics Equipment Installer and Repairer, General; 470103 Communication Systems Installer and Repairer.

Related DOT Jobs: 720.281-010 Radio Repairer; 720.281-014 Tape-Recorder Repairer; 720.281-018 Television-and-Radio Repairer; 729.281-010 Audio-Video Repairer; 730.281-018 Electric-Organ Inspector and Repairer; 823.361-010 Television Installer; 828.261-010 Electronic-Organ Technician.

49-2098.00 Security and Fire Alarm Systems
Installers (All Other Electrical and Electronic Equipment Mechanics, Installers, and Repairers)

Education: No data available.

Employed: 64,500

Openings: No data available.

Projected Growth: No data available.

Earnings: $34,000

Install, program, maintain, and repair security and fire-alarm wiring and equipment. Ensure that work is in accordance with relevant codes.

GOE Number, Interest Area, and Work Group: 06.02.02; Construction, Mining, and Drilling; Construction: Construction and Maintenance. **Instructional Programs:** 150499 Electromechanical Instrumentation and Maintenance Technol./Technicians, Other; 470101 Electrical and Electronics Equipment Installer and Repairer, General; 470401 Instrument Calibration and Repairer. **Note:** The Department of Labor has not collected some data for this job, so it has fewer details than the other descriptions.

49-3000 Vehicle and Mobile Equipment Mechanics, Installers, and Repairers

49-3011.00 Aircraft Mechanics and Service Technicians (Aircraft Mechanics and Service Technicians)

Education: Postsecondary vocational training

Employed: 132,880

Openings: 11,323

Projected Growth: 10.4%

Earnings: No data available.

Diagnose, adjust, repair, or overhaul aircraft engines and assemblies, such as hydraulic and pneumatic systems.

GOE Number, Interest Area, and Work Group: 05.03.01; Mechanics, Installers, and Repairers; Mechanical Work: Vehicles and Facilities. **Instructional Programs:** 470607 Aircraft Mechanic/Technician, Airframe; 470607 Aircraft Mechanic/Technician, Airframe; 470608 Aircraft Mechanic/Technician, Powerplant; 470608 Aircraft Mechanic/Technician, Powerplant. **Note:** The Department of Labor has not collected some data for this job, so it has fewer details than the other descriptions.

49-3011.01 Airframe-and-Power-Plant Mechanics
(Aircraft Mechanics and Service Technicians)

Education: Postsecondary vocational training

Employed: 132,880

Openings: 11,323

Projected Growth: 10.4%

Earnings: No data available.

Inspect, test, repair, maintain, and service aircraft.

Services and maintains aircraft systems by performing tasks such as flushing crankcase, cleaning screens, greasing moving parts, and checking brakes. Repairs, replaces, and rebuilds aircraft structures, functional components, and parts such as wings and fuselage, rigging, and hydraulic units. Removes engine from aircraft or installs engine, using hoist or forklift truck. Modifies aircraft structures, space vehicles, systems, or components, following drawings, engineering orders, and technical publications. Reads and interprets aircraft maintenance manuals and specifications to determine feasibility and method of repairing or replacing malfunctioning or damaged components. Tests engine and system operations, using testing equipment, and listens to engine sounds to detect and diagnose malfunctions. Disassembles and inspects parts for wear, warping, or other defects. Adjusts, aligns, and calibrates aircraft systems, using hand tools, gauges, and test equipment. Examines and inspects engines or other components for cracks, breaks, or leaks. Assembles and installs electrical, plumbing, mechanical, hydraulic, and structural components and accessories, using hand tools and power tools.

GOE Number, Interest Area, and Work Group: 05.03.01; Mechanics, Installers, and Repairers; Mechanical Work: Vehicles and Facilities. **Personality Type:** Realistic. Realistic occupations frequently involve work activities that include practical, hands-on problems and solutions. These occupations often deal with plants, animals, and real-world materials like wood, tools, and machinery. Many of the occupations require working outside and do not involve a lot of paperwork or working closely with others. **Work Values:** Moral Values; Security; Compensation; Company Policies and Practices; Achievement; Supervision, Human Relations. **Skills:** Equipment Maintenance; Installation; Repairing; Testing; Troubleshooting; Equipment Selection. **Abilities:** *Cognitive*—Deductive Reasoning; Information Ordering; Problem Sensitivity; Visualization; Written Comprehension. *Psychomotor*—Manual Dexterity; Control Precision; Finger Dexterity; Arm-Hand Steadiness. *Physical*—Extent Flexibility; Static Strength; Explosive Strength. *Sensory*—Near Vision; Visual Color Discrimination; Hearing Sensitivity. **General Work Activities:** *Information Input*—Inspecting Equipment, Structures, Materials; Getting Information Needed to Do the Job; Monitoring Processes, Materials, and Surroundings. *Mental Process*—Updating and Using Job-Relevant Knowledge; Evaluating Information Against Standards; Making Decisions and Solving Problems; Analyzing Data or Information; Judging Qualities of Things, Services, Other People's Work. *Work Output*—Repairing and Maintaining Mechanical Equipment; Handling and Moving Objects; Controlling Machines and Processes; Repairing and Maintaining Electrical Equipment. *Interacting with Others*—Communicating with Other Workers; Coordinating Work and Activities of Others; Performing Administrative Activities. **Physical Work Conditions:** Using Hands on Objects, Tools, or Controls; Hazardous Equipment; Indoors; Common Protective or Safety Attire; Standing. **Other Job Characteristics:** Consequence of Error; Importance of Being Exact or Accurate; Importance of Being Sure All Is Done.

Experience: Job Zone 4. A minimum of two to four years of work-related skill, knowledge, or experience is needed. **Job Preparation:** SVP 7.0 to less than 8.0—2 years to less than 10 years.

Knowledge: Mechanical; Engineering and Technology; Building and Construction; Design; Mathematics; Physics. **Instructional Program:** 470607 Aircraft Mechanic/Technician, Airframe.

Related DOT Jobs: 621.261-022 Experimental Aircraft Mechanic; 621.281-014 Airframe-and-Power-Plant Mechanic; 621.281-018 Airframe-and-Power-Plant-Mechanic Apprentice.

49-3011.02 Aircraft Engine Specialists (Aircraft Mechanics and Service Technicians)

Education: Postsecondary vocational training
Employed: 132,880
Openings: 11,323
Projected Growth: 10.4%
Earnings: No data available.

Repair and maintain the operating condition of aircraft engines. Includes helicopter engine mechanics.

Tests engine operation, using test equipment such as ignition analyzer, compression checker, distributor timer, and ammeter, to identify malfunction. Listens to operating engine to detect and diagnose malfunctions such as sticking or burned valves. Removes engine from aircraft, using hoist or forklift truck. Reads and interprets manufacturers' maintenance manuals, service bulletins, and other specifications, to determine feasibility and methods of repair. Services, repairs, and rebuilds aircraft structures such as wings, fuselage, rigging, and surface and hydraulic controls, using hand or power tools and equipment. Replaces or repairs worn, defective, or damaged components, using hand tools, gauges, and testing equipment. Services and maintains aircraft and related apparatus by performing activities such as flushing crankcase, cleaning screens, and lubricating moving parts. Reassembles engine and installs engine in aircraft. Disassembles and inspects engine parts such as turbine blades and cylinders, for wear, warping, cracks, and leaks. Adjusts, repairs, or replaces electrical wiring system and aircraft accessories.

GOE Number, Interest Area, and Work Group: 05.03.01; Mechanics, Installers, and Repairers; Mechanical Work: Vehicles and Facilities. **Personality Type:** Realistic. Realistic occupations frequently involve work activities that include practical, hands-on problems and solutions. These occupations often deal with plants, animals, and real-world materials like wood, tools, and machinery. Many of the occupations require working outside and do not involve a lot of paperwork or working closely with others. **Work Values:** Moral Values; Security; Company Policies and Practices; Compensation; Ability Utilization. **Skills:** Equipment Maintenance; Repairing; Troubleshooting; Installation; Problem Identification. **Abilities:** *Cognitive*—Problem Sensitivity; Deductive Reasoning; Written Comprehension; Inductive Reasoning; Speed of Closure. *Psychomotor*—Manual Dexterity; Control Precision; Multilimb Coordination; Finger Dexterity. *Physical*—Extent Flexibility; Static Strength; Explosive Strength. *Sensory*—Hearing Sensitivity; Auditory Attention; Near Vision; Sound Localization. **General Work Activities:** *Information Input*—Getting Information Needed to Do the Job; Inspecting Equipment, Structures, Materials; Identifying Objects, Actions, and Events. *Mental Process*—Updating and Using Job-Relevant Knowledge; Evaluating

Information Against Standards; Analyzing Data or Information. *Work Output*—Repairing and Maintaining Mechanical Equipment; Handling and Moving Objects; Performing General Physical Activities; Repairing and Maintaining Electrical Equipment. *Interacting with Others*—Communicating with Other Workers; Teaching Others; Coaching and Developing Others; Providing Consultation and Advice to Others. **Physical Work Conditions:** Using Hands on Objects, Tools, or Controls; Hazardous Equipment; Standing. **Other Job Characteristics:** Consequence of Error; Importance of Being Sure All Is Done; Importance of Being Exact or Accurate.

Experience: Job Zone 4. A minimum of two to four years of work-related skill, knowledge, or experience is needed. **Job Preparation:** SVP 7.0 to less than 8.0—2 years to less than 10 years. **Knowledge:** Mechanical; Engineering and Technology; Physics; Mathematics; Public Safety and Security; Building and Construction; English Language. **Instructional Programs:** 470607 Aircraft Mechanic/Technician, Airframe; 470607 Aircraft Mechanic/Technician, Airframe; 470608 Aircraft Mechanic/Technician, Powerplant; 470608 Aircraft Mechanic/Technician, Powerplant.

Related DOT Jobs: 621.281-014 Airframe-and-Power-Plant Mechanic; 621.281-030 Rocket-Engine-Component Mechanic; 825.281-038 Experimental-Rocket-Sled Mechanic.

49-3011.03 Aircraft Body and Bonded Structure Repairers (Aircraft Mechanics and Service Technicians)

Education: Postsecondary vocational training
Employed: 132,880
Openings: 11,323
Projected Growth: 10.4%
Earnings: No data available.

Repair body or structure of aircraft according to specifications.

Spreads plastic film over area to be repaired, to prevent damage to surrounding area. Removes or cuts out defective part or drills holes to gain access to internal defect or damage, using drill and punch. Reads work orders, blueprints, and specifications; examines sample or damaged part or structure, to determine repair or fabrication procedures and sequence of operations. Cleans, strips, primes, and sands structural surfaces and materials prior to bonding. Communicates with other workers to fit and align heavy parts or expedite processing of repair parts. Locates and marks dimension and reference lines on defective or replacement part, using templates, scribes, compass, and steel rule. Reinstalls repaired or replacement parts for subsequent riveting or welding, using clamps and wrenches. Trims and shapes replacement section to specified size; fits and secures section in place, using adhesives, hand tools, and power tools. Repairs or fabricates defective section or part, using metal-fabricating machines, saws, brakes, shears, and grinders. Cures bonded structure, using portable or stationary curing equipment.

GOE Number, Interest Area, and Work Group: 05.03.01; Mechanics, Installers, and Repairers; Mechanical Work: Vehicles and Facilities. **Personality Type:** Realistic. Realistic occupations frequently involve work activities that include practical, hands-on problems and solutions. These occupations often deal with plants, animals, and real-world materials like wood, tools, and machinery. Many of the occupations require working outside and do not involve a lot of paperwork or working closely with others. **Work Values:** Moral Values; Security; Compensation; Company Policies and Practices; Supervision, Human Relations; Achievement. **Skills:** Mathematics; Equipment Selection; Installation; Equipment Maintenance; Repairing. **Abilities:** *Cognitive*—Information Ordering; Problem Sensitivity; Visualization; Oral Expression; Memorization; Inductive Reasoning. *Psychomotor*—Manual Dexterity; Wrist-Finger Speed; Finger Dexterity; Control Precision. *Physical*—Extent Flexibility; Trunk Strength; Static Strength. *Sensory*—Near Vision; Far Vision; Visual Color Discrimination; Depth Perception. **General Work Activities:** *Information Input*—Getting Information Needed to Do the Job; Inspecting Equipment, Structures, Materials; Monitoring Processes, Materials, and Surroundings. *Mental Process*—Updating and Using Job-Relevant Knowledge; Making Decisions and Solving Problems; Judging Qualities of Things, Services, Other People's Work. *Work Output*—Handling and Moving Objects; Implementing Ideas and Programs; Controlling Machines and Processes. *Interacting with Others*—Communicating with Other Workers; Coordinating Work and Activities of Others; Establishing and Maintaining Relationships. **Physical Work Conditions:** Using Hands on Objects, Tools, or Controls; Hazardous Equipment; Indoors; Standing. **Other Job Characteristics:** Consequence of Error; Degree of Automation; Importance of Being Exact or Accurate; Importance of Being Sure All Is Done.

Experience: Job Zone 3. Previous work-related skill, knowledge, or experience is required. **Job Preparation:** SVP 6.0 to less than 7.0—More than 1 year and less than 4 years. **Knowledge:** Mechanical; Building and Construction; Design; Engineering and Technology; Mathematics. **Instructional Program:** 470607 Aircraft Mechanic/Technician, Airframe.

Related DOT Jobs: 807.261-010 Aircraft Body Repairer; 807.381-014 Bonded Structures Repairer.

49-3021.00 Automotive Body and Related Repairers
(Automotive Body Repairers)

Education: Long-term O-T-J training

Employed: 226,956

Openings: 33,051

Projected Growth: 15.8%

Earnings: $27,400

Repair and refinish automotive vehicle bodies. Straighten vehicle frames.

Examines vehicle to determine extent and type of damage. Cuts opening in vehicle body for installation of customized windows, using templates and power shears or chisel. Fits and secures windows, vinyl roof, and metal trim to vehicle body, using caulking gun, adhesive brush, and mallet. Removes damaged fenders and panels, using wrenches and cutting torch. Installs replacement parts, using wrenches or welding equipment. Mixes polyester resin and hardener to be used in restoring damaged area. Adjusts or aligns headlights, wheels, and brake system. Cleans work area, using air hose, to remove damaged material and to remove dis-

carded fiberglass strips used in repair procedures. Removes upholstery, accessories, electrical window-and-seat-operating equipment, and trim, to gain access to vehicle body and fenders. Cuts and tapes plastic separating film to outside repair area to avoid damaging surrounding surfaces during repair procedure. Peels separating film from repair area and washes repaired surface with water. Soaks fiberglass matting in resin mixture and applies layers of matting over repair area to specified thickness. Measures and marks vinyl material and cuts material to size for roof installation, using rule, straightedge, and hand shears. Paints and sands repaired surface, using paint spraygun and motorized sander. Fills depressions with body filler and files, grinds, and sands repaired surfaces, using power tools and hand tools. Straightens bent automobile or other vehicle frames, using pneumatic frame-straightening machine. Positions dolly block against surface of dented area and beats opposite surface to remove dents, using hammer. Reads specifications or confers with customer to determine custom modifications to alter appearance of vehicle. Cuts away damaged fiberglass from automobile body, using air grinder.

GOE Number, Interest Area, and Work Group: 05.03.01; Mechanics, Installers, and Repairers; Mechanical Work: Vehicles and Facilities. **Personality Type:** Realistic. Realistic occupations frequently involve work activities that include practical, hands-on problems and solutions. These occupations often deal with plants, animals, and real-world materials like wood, tools, and machinery. Many of the occupations require working outside and do not involve a lot of paperwork or working closely with others. **Work Values:** Moral Values; Security; Independence; Ability Utilization; Compensation; Achievement; Company Policies and Practices; Activity. **Skills:** Repairing; Product Inspection; Installation; Technology Design; Problem Identification. **Abilities:** *Cognitive*—Visualization; Oral Comprehension; Information Ordering; Problem Sensitivity; Written Comprehension; Number Facility. *Psychomotor*—Manual Dexterity; Control Precision; Finger Dexterity; Wrist-Finger Speed; Arm-Hand Steadiness. *Physical*—Extent Flexibility; Static Strength; Trunk Strength. *Sensory*—Near Vision; Visual Color Discrimination; Auditory Attention. **General Work Activities:** *Information Input*—Inspecting Equipment, Structures, Materials; Getting Information Needed to Do the Job; Estimating Needed Characteristics; Identifying Objects, Actions, and Events. *Mental Process*—Updating and Using Job-Relevant Knowledge; Evaluating Information Against Standards; Judging Qualities of Things, Services, Other People's Work; Making Decisions and Solving Problems. *Work Output*—Performing General Physical Activities; Handling and Moving Objects; Controlling Machines and Processes. *Interacting with Others*—Communicating with Persons Outside Organization; Providing Consultation and Advice to Others; Performing for or Working with the Public. **Physical Work Conditions:** Using Hands on Objects, Tools, or Controls; Distracting Sounds and Noise Levels; Standing; Indoors. **Other Job Characteristics:** Consequence of Error; Importance of Being Exact or Accurate; Frustrating Circumstances.

Experience: Job Zone 3. Previous work-related skill, knowledge, or experience is required. **Job Preparation:** SVP 6.0 to less than 7.0—More than 1 year and less than 4 years. **Knowledge:** Mechanical; Engineering and Technology; Building and Construction; Design; Mathematics; Customer and Personal Service; Physics. **Instructional Program:** 470603 Auto/Automotive Body Repairer.

Related DOT Jobs: 807.361-010 Automobile-Body Customizer; 807.381-010 Automobile-Body Repairer; 807.381-030 Auto-Body Repairer, Fiberglass.

49-3022.00 Automotive Glass Installers and Repairers (Automotive Body Repairers)

Education: Long-term O-T-J training
Employed: 226,956
Openings: 33,051
Projected Growth: 15.8%
Earnings: $27,400

Replace or repair broken windshields and window glass in motor vehicles.

Removes broken or damaged windshield or window glass from motor vehicles, using hand tools to remove screws from frame holding glass. Cuts flat safety glass according to specified pattern, using glass cutter. Holds cut or uneven edge of glass against automated abrasive belt to shape or smooth edges. Obtains windshield for specific automobile make and model from stock and examines for defects prior to installation. Replaces or adjusts motorized or manual window-raising mechanisms. Applies moisture-proofing compound along glass edges and installs glass into windshield or window frame in door or side panel of vehicle. Installs precut replacement glass to replace curved or custom-shaped windows. Installs rubber-channeling strip around edge of glass or frame to weather-proof or to prevent rattling.

GOE Number, Interest Area, and Work Group: 05.03.01; Mechanics, Installers, and Repairers; Mechanical Work: Vehicles and Facilities. **Personality Type:** Realistic. Realistic occupations frequently involve work activities that include practical, hands-on problems and solutions. These occupations often deal with plants, animals, and real-world materials like wood, tools, and machinery. Many of the occupations require working outside and do not involve a lot of paperwork or working closely with others. **Work Values:** Moral Values; Independence; Security; Company Policies and Practices; Responsibility; Compensation; Supervision, Human Relations. **Skills:** Installation; Product Inspection; Repairing; Problem Identification; Monitoring; Solution Appraisal; Equipment Selection. **Abilities:** *Cognitive*—Information Ordering; Visualization; Problem Sensitivity; Number Facility; Oral Comprehension; Written Comprehension. *Psychomotor*—Arm-Hand Steadiness; Manual Dexterity; Finger Dexterity; Multilimb Coordination. *Physical*—Static Strength; Extent Flexibility; Trunk Strength. *Sensory*—Night Vision; Glare Sensitivity. **General Work Activities:** *Information Input*—Inspecting Equipment, Structures, Materials; Getting Information Needed to Do the Job; Identifying Objects, Actions, and Events. *Mental Process*—Evaluating Information Against Standards; Judging Qualities of Things, Services, Other People's Work; Updating and Using Job-Relevant Knowledge; Making Decisions and Solving Problems. *Work Output*—Performing General Physical Activities; Handling and Moving Objects; Repairing and Maintaining Mechanical Equipment. *Interacting with Others*—Communicating with Other Workers; Performing for or Working with the Public; Communicating with Persons Outside Organization. **Physical Work Conditions:** Us-

ing Hands on Objects, Tools, or Controls; Standing; Common Protective or Safety Attire. **Other Job Characteristics:** Importance of Being Sure All Is Done; Importance of Being Exact or Accurate; Frustrating Circumstances.

Experience: Job Zone 2. Some previous work-related skill, knowledge, or experience may be helpful, but usually is not needed. **Job Preparation:** SVP 4.00 to 5.99—6 months to less than 2 years. **Knowledge:** Mechanical; Engineering and Technology; Design; Physics; Chemistry; English Language. **Instructional Program:** 470603 Auto/Automotive Body Repairer.

Related DOT Job: 865.684-010 Glass Installer.

49-3023.00 Automotive Service Technicians and Mechanics (Automotive Mechanics)

Education: Postsecondary vocational training
Employed: 789,566
Openings: 119,161
Projected Growth: 16.7%
Earnings: $27,360

Diagnose, adjust, repair, or overhaul automotive vehicles.

GOE Number, Interest Area, and Work Group: 05.03.01; Mechanics, Installers, and Repairers; Mechanical Work: Vehicles and Facilities. **Instructional Programs:** 150803 Automotive Engineering Technology/Technician; 470604 Auto/Automotive Mechanic/Technician. **Note:** The Department of Labor has not collected some data for this job, so it has fewer details than the other descriptions.

49-3023.01 Automotive Master Mechanics (Automotive Mechanics and Service Technicians)

Education: Postsecondary vocational training
Employed: 789,566
Openings: 119,161
Projected Growth: 16.7%
Earnings: $27,360

Repair automobiles, trucks, buses, and other vehicles. Repair virtually any part on the vehicle, or specialize in the transmission system.

Repairs damaged automobile bodies. Repairs radiator leaks. Repairs or replaces shock absorbers. Repairs, relines, replaces, and adjusts brakes. Examines vehicles and discusses extent of damage or malfunction with customer. Rebuilds parts such as crankshafts and cylinder blocks. Replaces and adjusts headlights. Installs and repairs accessories such as radios, heaters, mirrors, and windshield wipers. Repairs manual and automatic transmissions. Overhauls or replaces carburetors, blowers, generators, distributors, starts, and pumps. Repairs or replaces parts such as pistons, rods, gears, valves, and bearings. Repairs and overhauls defective automotive units such as engines, transmissions, or differentials. Rewires ignition system, lights, and instrument panel. Aligns front end.

GOE Number, Interest Area, and Work Group: 05.03.01; Mechanics, Installers, and Repairers; Mechanical Work: Vehicles and Facilities. **Personality Type:** Realistic. Realistic occupations frequently involve work activities that include practical, hands-on problems and solutions. These occupations often deal with plants, animals, and real-world materials like wood, tools, and machinery. Many of the occupations require working outside and do not involve a lot of paperwork or working closely with others. **Work Values:** Moral Values; Security; Ability Utilization; Compensation; Independence. **Skills:** Repairing; Problem Identification; Troubleshooting; Equipment Maintenance; Product Inspection. **Abilities:** *Cognitive*—Information Ordering; Problem Sensitivity; Visualization; Inductive Reasoning; Deductive Reasoning. *Psychomotor*—Wrist-Finger Speed; Control Precision; Manual Dexterity. *Physical*—Extent Flexibility; Static Strength; Trunk Strength. *Sensory*—Hearing Sensitivity; Visual Color Discrimination; Near Vision. **General Work Activities:** *Information Input*—Inspecting Equipment, Structures, Materials; Identifying Objects, Actions, and Events; Getting Information Needed to Do the Job; Monitoring Processes, Materials, and Surroundings. *Mental Process*—Updating and Using Job-Relevant Knowledge; Evaluating Information Against Standards; Making Decisions and Solving Problems; Judging Qualities of Things, Services, Other People's Work. *Work Output*—Repairing and Maintaining Mechanical Equipment; Repairing and Maintaining Electrical Equipment; Handling and Moving Objects; Controlling Machines and Processes. *Interacting with Others*—Communicating with Persons Outside Organization; Communicating with Other Workers; Providing Consultation and Advice to Others; Interpreting Meaning of Information to Others. **Physical Work Conditions:** Using Hands on Objects, Tools, or Controls; Standing; Indoors. **Other Job Characteristics:** Consequence of Error; Importance of Being Sure All Is Done; Importance of Being Exact or Accurate.

Experience: Job Zone 3. Previous work-related skill, knowledge, or experience is required. **Job Preparation:** SVP 6.0 to less than 7.0—More than 1 year and less than 4 years. **Knowledge:** Mechanical; Computers and Electronics; Engineering and Technology; Customer and Personal Service; Physics. **Instructional Programs:** 150803 Automotive Engineering Technology/Technician; 470604 Auto/Automotive Mechanic/Technician.

Related DOT Jobs: 620.261-010 Automobile Mechanic; 620.261-012 Automobile-Mechanic Apprentice; 620.281-062 Transmission Mechanic; 620.364-010 Squeak, Rattle, and Leak Repairer; 620.381-022 Repairer, Heavy.

49-3023.02 Automotive Specialty Technicians
(Automotive Mechanics and Service Technicians)

Education: Postsecondary vocational training

Employed: 789,566

Openings: 119,161

Projected Growth: 16.7%

Earnings: $27,360

Repair only one system or component on a vehicle, such as brakes, suspension, or radiator.

Removes and replaces defective mufflers and tailpipes from automobiles. Repairs and replaces automobile leaf springs. Repairs and rebuilds clutch systems. Repairs and aligns defective wheels of automobiles. Installs and repairs automotive air-conditioning units. Repairs, replaces, and adjusts defective carburetor parts and gasoline filters. Repairs and replaces defective balljoint suspension, brakeshoes, and wheelbearings. Inspects, tests, repairs, and replaces automotive cooling systems and fuel tanks. Tunes automobile engines and tests electronic computer components. Examines vehicle, compiles estimate of repair costs, and secures customer approval to perform repairs. Repairs, installs, and adjusts hydraulic and electromagnetic automatic lift mechanisms used to raise and lower automobile windows, seats, and tops. Converts vehicle fuel systems from gasoline to butane gas operations and repairs and services operating butane fuel units. Aligns and repairs wheels, axles, frames, torsion bars, and steering mechanisms of automobiles. Rebuilds, repairs, and tests automotive injection units. Inspects and tests new vehicles for damage, records findings, and makes repairs. Repairs, overhauls, and adjusts automobile brake systems.

GOE Number, Interest Area, and Work Group: 05.03.01; Mechanics, Installers, and Repairers; Mechanical Work: Vehicles and Facilities. **Personality Type:** Realistic. Realistic occupations frequently involve work activities that include practical, hands-on problems and solutions. These occupations often deal with plants, animals, and real-world materials like wood, tools, and machinery. Many of the occupations require working outside and do not involve a lot of paperwork or working closely with others. **Work Values:** Moral Values; Responsibility; Independence; Security; Ability Utilization; Activity; Achievement. **Skills:** Problem Identification; Repairing; Installation; Troubleshooting; Product Inspection. **Abilities:** *Cognitive*—Information Ordering; Visualization; Problem Sensitivity; Deductive Reasoning; Oral Expression. *Psychomotor*—Manual Dexterity; Reaction Time; Wrist-Finger Speed; Multilimb Coordination; Control Precision. *Physical*—Extent Flexibility; Static Strength; Trunk Strength. *Sensory*—Hearing Sensitivity; Near Vision; Auditory Attention; Visual Color Discrimination. **General Work Activities:** *Information Input*—Inspecting Equipment, Structures, Materials; Identifying Objects, Actions, and Events; Getting Information Needed to Do the Job. *Mental Process*—Updating and Using Job-Relevant Knowledge; Judging Qualities of Things, Services, Other People's Work; Evaluating Information Against Standards. *Work Output*—Repairing and Maintaining Mechanical Equipment; Handling and Moving Objects; Operating Vehicles or Equipment; Performing General Physical Activities. *Interacting with Others*—Communicating with Persons Outside Organization; Interpreting Meaning of Information to Others; Establishing and Maintaining Relationships. **Physical Work Conditions:** Using Hands on Objects, Tools, or Controls; Standing; Indoors; Common Protective or Safety Attire. **Other Job Characteristics:** Consequence of Error; Importance of Being Sure All Is Done; Importance of Being Exact or Accurate.

Experience: Job Zone 2. Some previous work-related skill, knowledge, or experience may be helpful, but usually is not needed. **Job Preparation:** SVP 4.00 to 5.99—6 months to less than 2 years. **Knowledge:** Mechanical; Computers and Electronics; Engineering and Technology; Customer and Personal Service; Physics. **Instructional Programs:** 150803 Automotive Engineering Technology/Technician; 470604 Auto/Automotive Mechanic/Technician.

Related DOT Jobs: 619.380-018 Spring Repairer, Hand; 620.261-030 Automobile-Service-Station Mechanic; 620.261-034 Automotive-Cooling-System Diagnostic Technician; 620.281-010 Air-Conditioning Mechanic; 620.281-026 Brake Repairer; 620.281-034 Carburetor Mechanic; 620.281-038 Front-End Mechanic; 620.281-066 Tune-Up Mechanic; 620.281-070 Vehicle-Fuel-Systems Converter; 620.381-010 Automobile-Radiator Mechanic; 620.682-010 Brake-Drum-Lathe Operator; 620.684-018 Brake Adjuster; 620.684-022 Clutch Rebuilder; 625.281-022 Fuel-Injection Servicer; 706.381-046 Wheelwright; 806.361-026 New-Car Get-Ready Mechanic; 807.664-010 Muffler Installer; 807.684-022 Floor Service Worker, Spring; 825.381-014 Automatic-Window-Seat-and-Top-Lift Repairer.

49-3031.00 Bus and Truck Mechanics and Diesel Engine Specialists (Bus and Truck Mechanics and Diesel Engine Specialists)

Education: Long-term O-T-J training
Employed: 254,820
Openings: 21,502
Projected Growth: 9.8%
Earnings: $29,340

Inspect, repair, and maintain diesel engines used to power machines.

Changes oil, checks batteries, repairs tires and tubes, and lubricates equipment and machinery. Inspects, repairs, and maintains automotive and mechanical equipment and machinery, such as pumps and compressors. Inspects and verifies dimensions and clearances of parts to ensure conformance to factory specifications. Disassembles and overhauls internal combustion engines, pumps, generators, transmissions, clutches, and rear ends. Reads job orders and observes and listens to operating equipment to ensure conformance to specifications or to determine malfunctions. Operates valve-grinding machine to grind and reset valves. Adjusts brakes, aligns wheels, tightens bolts and screws, and reassembles equipment. Attaches test instruments to equipment and reads dials and gauges to diagnose malfunctions. Reconditions and replaces parts, pistons, bearings, gears, and valves. Inspects defective equipment and diagnoses malfunctions, using test instruments such as motor analyzers, chassis charts, and pressure gauges. Examines and adjusts protective guards, loose bolts, and specified safety devices.

GOE Number, Interest Area, and Work Group: 05.03.01; Mechanics, Installers, and Repairers; Mechanical Work: Vehicles and Facilities. **Personality Type:** Realistic. Realistic occupations frequently involve work activities that include practical, hands-on problems and solutions. These occupations often deal with plants, animals, and real-world materials like wood, tools, and machinery. Many of the occupations require working outside and do not involve a lot of paperwork or working closely with others. **Work Values:** Moral Values; Security; Independence; Achievement; Compensation; Responsibility; Activity. **Skills:** Repairing; Troubleshooting; Equipment Maintenance; Installation; Testing; Product Inspection. **Abilities:** *Cognitive*—Problem Sensitivity; Deductive Reasoning; Inductive Reasoning; Written Comprehen-

sion; Information Ordering. *Psychomotor*—Control Precision; Finger Dexterity; Arm-Hand Steadiness. *Physical*—Static Strength; Extent Flexibility; Trunk Strength. *Sensory*—Hearing Sensitivity; Sound Localization. **General Work Activities:** *Information Input*—Inspecting Equipment, Structures, Materials; Identifying Objects, Actions, and Events; Getting Information Needed to Do the Job. *Mental Process*—Making Decisions and Solving Problems; Updating and Using Job-Relevant Knowledge; Evaluating Information Against Standards. *Work Output*—Repairing and Maintaining Mechanical Equipment; Handling and Moving Objects; Performing General Physical Activities. *Interacting with Others*—Communicating with Other Workers; Performing Administrative Activities; Communicating with Persons Outside Organization. **Physical Work Conditions:** Using Hands on Objects, Tools, or Controls; Standing; Indoors. **Other Job Characteristics:** Importance of Being Sure All Is Done; Consequence of Error; Importance of Being Exact or Accurate.

Experience: Job Zone 3. Previous work-related skill, knowledge, or experience is required. **Job Preparation:** SVP 6.0 to less than 7.0—More than 1 year and less than 4 years. **Knowledge:** Mechanical; Engineering and Technology; Mathematics; Computers and Electronics; Public Safety and Security; Design; Customer and Personal Service; Transportation. **Instructional Programs:** 470302 Heavy Equipment Maintenance and Repairer; 470605 Diesel Engine Mechanic and Repairer.

Related DOT Jobs: 620.281-046 Maintenance Mechanic; 620.281-050 Mechanic, Industrial Truck; 620.281-058 Tractor Mechanic; 625.281-010 Diesel Mechanic; 625.281-014 Diesel-Mechanic Apprentice; 629.381-014 Oil-Field Equipment Mechanic.

49-3041.00 Farm Equipment Mechanics (Farm Equipment Mechanics)

Education: Long-term O-T-J training
Employed: 49,408
Openings: 7,611
Projected Growth: –5.2%
Earnings: $22,750

Diagnose, adjust, repair, or overhaul farm machinery and vehicles such as tractors, harvesters, dairy equipment, and irrigation systems.

Reads inspection reports and examines equipment to determine type and extent of defect. Installs and repairs agricultural plumbing systems. Dismantles defective machines, using hand tools. Tests and replaces electrical components and wiring, using test meter, soldering equipment, and wire strippers. Reassembles, adjusts, and lubricates machines and equipment, using hand tools. Installs and maintains self-propelled irrigation system, using truck-mounted crane, wrenches, tube cutter, and pipe threader. Records type and cause of defect on agricultural equipment. Examines and listens to machines, motors, gas and diesel engines, and equipment to detect malfunctioning. Repairs or replaces defective parts, using hand tools, milling and woodworking machines, lathes, welding equipment, grinders, or saws. Drives truck to haul tools and equipment to work site. Fabricates new metal parts, using drill press, engine lathe, and other machine tools.

GOE Number, Interest Area, and Work Group: 05.03.01; Mechanics, Installers, and Repairers; Mechanical Work: Vehicles and Facilities. **Personality Type:** Realistic. Realistic occupations frequently involve work activities that include practical, hands-on problems and solutions. These occupations often deal with plants, animals, and real-world materials like wood, tools, and machinery. Many of the occupations require working outside and do not involve a lot of paperwork or working closely with others. **Work Values:** Moral Values; Security; Independence; Achievement; Ability Utilization; Activity; Responsibility. **Skills:** Installation; Repairing; Troubleshooting; Equipment Maintenance; Testing. **Abilities:** *Cognitive*—Information Ordering; Problem Sensitivity; Deductive Reasoning; Inductive Reasoning; Visualization. *Psychomotor*—Control Precision; Multilimb Coordination; Arm-Hand Steadiness. *Physical*—Extent Flexibility; Static Strength; Trunk Strength. *Sensory*—Hearing Sensitivity; Visual Color Discrimination; Near Vision. **General Work Activities:** *Information Input*—Inspecting Equipment, Structures, Materials; Identifying Objects, Actions, and Events; Monitoring Processes, Materials, and Surroundings. *Mental Process*—Judging Qualities of Things, Services, Other People's Work; Evaluating Information Against Standards; Updating and Using Job-Relevant Knowledge. *Work Output*—Repairing and Maintaining Mechanical Equipment; Handling and Moving Objects; Controlling Machines and Processes. *Interacting with Others*—Communicating with Other Workers; Providing Consultation and Advice to Others; Performing for or Working with the Public. **Physical Work Conditions:** Using Hands on Objects, Tools, or Controls; Hazardous Equipment; Outdoors; Standing. **Other Job Characteristics:** Consequence of Error; Importance of Being Sure All Is Done; Importance of Being Exact or Accurate.

Experience: Job Zone 3. Previous work-related skill, knowledge, or experience is required. **Job Preparation:** SVP 6.0 to less than 7.0—More than 1 year and less than 4 years. **Knowledge:** Mechanical; Engineering and Technology; Transportation; Computers and Electronics; Physics; English Language. **Instructional Programs:** 010201 Agricultural Mechanization, General; 010204 Agricultural Power Machinery Operator; 010299 Agricultural Mechanization, Other.

Related DOT Jobs: 624.281-010 Farm-Equipment Mechanic I; 624.281-014 Farm-Equipment-Mechanic Apprentice; 624.361-014 Sprinkler-Irrigation-Equipment Mechanic; 624.381-010 Assembly Repairer; 624.381-014 Farm-Equipment Mechanic II; 629.281-018 Dairy-Equipment Repairer; 809.381-018 Milking-System Installer.

49-3042.00 Mobile Heavy Equipment Mechanics, Except Engines (Mobile Heavy Equipment Mechanics)

Education: Long-term O-T-J training
Employed: 105,921
Openings: 18,520
Projected Growth: 9.3%
Earnings: $31,520

Diagnose, adjust, repair, or overhaul mobile mechanical, hydraulic, and pneumatic equipment such as cranes, bulldozers, graders, and conveyors used in construction, logging, and surface mining.

Adjusts, maintains, and repairs or replaces engines and subassemblies, including transmissions and crawler heads, using hand tools, jacks, and cranes. Examines parts for damage or excessive wear, using micrometers and gauges. Dismantles and reassembles heavy equipment, using hoists and hand tools. Immerses parts in tanks of solvent or sprays parts with grease solvent to clean parts. Directs workers engaged in cleaning parts and assisting with assembly or disassembly of equipment. Operates and inspects machines or heavy equipment to diagnose defects. Welds or cuts metal, and welds broken parts and structural members, using electric or gas welder. Repairs and replaces damaged or worn parts. Overhauls and tests machines or equipment to ensure operating efficiency.

GOE Number, Interest Area, and Work Group: 05.03.01; Mechanics, Installers, and Repairers; Mechanical Work: Vehicles and Facilities. **Personality Type:** Realistic. Realistic occupations frequently involve work activities that include practical, hands-on problems and solutions. These occupations often deal with plants, animals, and real-world materials like wood, tools, and machinery. Many of the occupations require working outside and do not involve a lot of paperwork or working closely with others. **Work Values:** Moral Values; Compensation; Security; Ability Utilization; Company Policies and Practices. **Skills:** Repairing; Problem Identification; Equipment Maintenance; Product Inspection; Troubleshooting. **Abilities:** *Cognitive*—Problem Sensitivity; Memorization; Deductive Reasoning; Information Ordering; Oral Comprehension. *Psychomotor*—Control Precision; Multilimb Coordination; Arm-Hand Steadiness; Manual Dexterity. *Physical*—Extent Flexibility; Trunk Strength; Static Strength; Explosive Strength. *Sensory*—Hearing Sensitivity; Sound Localization. **General Work Activities:** *Information Input*—Inspecting Equipment, Structures, Materials; Identifying Objects, Actions, and Events; Getting Information Needed to Do the Job. *Mental Process*—Judging Qualities of Things, Services, Other People's Work; Evaluating Information Against Standards; Updating and Using Job-Relevant Knowledge. *Work Output*—Repairing and Maintaining Mechanical Equipment; Performing General Physical Activities; Handling and Moving Objects; Controlling Machines and Processes. *Interacting with Others*—Communicating with Other Workers; Coordinating Work and Activities of Others; Establishing and Maintaining Relationships. **Physical Work Conditions:** Using Hands on Objects, Tools, or Controls; Hazardous Equipment; Outdoors; Kneeling, Crouching, or Crawling; Standing. **Other Job Characteristics:** Consequence of Error; Importance of Being Exact or Accurate; Importance of Being Sure All Is Done.

Experience: Job Zone 4. A minimum of two to four years of work-related skill, knowledge, or experience is needed. **Job Preparation:** SVP 7.0 to less than 8.0—2 years to less than 10 years. **Knowledge:** Mechanical; Engineering and Technology; English Language; Production and Processing; Chemistry; Physics. **Instructional Program:** 470302 Heavy Equipment Maintenance and Repairer.

Related DOT Jobs: 620.261-022 Construction-Equipment Mechanic; 620.281-042 Logging-Equipment Mechanic; 620.381-014 Mechanic, Endless Track Vehicle.

49-3043.00 Rail Car Repairers (Rail Car Repairers)

Education: No data available.
Employed: 13,270
Openings: No data available.
Projected Growth: No data available.
Earnings: $36,330

Diagnose, adjust, repair, or overhaul railroad rolling stock, mine cars, or mass-transit rail cars.

Cleans units and components, using compressed air blower. Repairs window sash frames, attaches weather stripping, and channels to frame, and replaces window glass, using hand tools. Inspects components such as bearings, seals, gaskets, wheels, truck and brake assemblies, air cylinder reservoirs, valves, and coupler assemblies. Installs and repairs interior flooring, fixtures, walls, plumbing, steps, and platforms. Examines car roof for wear and damage, and repairs defective sections, using roofing material, cement, nails, and waterproof paint. Tests units before and after repairs for operability. Aligns car sides, for installation of car ends and crossties, using width gauge, turnbuckle, and wrench. Adjusts repaired or replaced units as needed, following diagrams. Measures sections and drills holes to prepare replacement sections for reassembly. Measures diameter of axle wheel seats, using micrometer; marks dimension on axle for boring of wheels to specified dimensions. Tests electric systems of cars, by using ammeter and by operating light and signal switches. Records condition of cars, repairs made, and other repair work to be performed. Replaces defective wiring and insulation, and tightens electrical connections, using hand tools. Disassembles units such as water pump, control valve, governor, distributor, windshield wiper motor, compressor and roller bearings. Repairs, reassembles, and replaces defective parts, metal sections, or components, using handtools, torque wrench, power tools, and welding equipment. Removes locomotive, car mechanical unit, or other component, using pneumatic hoist and jack, pinch bar, hand tools, and cutting torch.

GOE Number, Interest Area, and Work Group: 05.03.01; Mechanics, Installers, and Repairers; Mechanical Work: Vehicles and Facilities. **Personality Type:** Realistic. Realistic occupations frequently involve work activities that include practical, hands-on problems and solutions. These occupations often deal with plants, animals, and real-world materials like wood, tools, and machinery. Many of the occupations require working outside and do not involve a lot of paperwork or working closely with others. **Work Values:** Moral Values; Independence; Security; Ability Utilization; Variety; Supervision, Human Relations; Company Policies and Practices. **Skills:** Repairing; Equipment Maintenance; Troubleshooting; Installation; Product Inspection. **Abilities:** *Cognitive*—Information Ordering; Problem Sensitivity; Visualization; Deductive Reasoning; Inductive Reasoning. *Psychomotor*—Multilimb Coordination; Control Precision; Manual Dexterity; Finger Dexterity. *Physical*—Extent Flexibility; Static Strength; Explosive Strength. *Sensory*—Near Vision; Depth Perception; Visual Color Discrimination. **General Work Activities:** *Information Input*—Inspecting Equipment, Structures, Materials; Getting Information Needed to Do the Job; Identifying Objects, Actions, and

Events. *Mental Process*—Evaluating Information Against Standards; Updating and Using Job-Relevant Knowledge; Judging Qualities of Things, Services, Other People's Work. *Work Output*—Repairing and Maintaining Mechanical Equipment; Handling and Moving Objects; Performing General Physical Activities. *Interacting with Others*—Communicating with Other Workers; Performing Administrative Activities; Assisting and Caring for Others. **Physical Work Conditions:** Using Hands on Objects, Tools, or Controls; Outdoors; Hazardous Equipment; Hazardous Situations. **Other Job Characteristics:** Consequence of Error; Importance of Being Sure All Is Done; Importance of Being Exact or Accurate.

Experience: Job Zone 3. Previous work-related skill, knowledge, or experience is required. **Job Preparation:** SVP 6.0 to less than 7.0—More than 1 year and less than 4 years. **Knowledge:** Mechanical; Engineering and Technology; Building and Construction; Mathematics; Physics. **Instructional Program:** 470302 Heavy Equipment Maintenance and Repairer.

Related DOT Jobs: 620.381-018 Mechanical-Unit Repairer; 622.381-014 Car Repairer; 622.381-018 Car Repairer, Pullman; 622.381-022 Car-Repairer Apprentice; 622.684-010 Air-Compressor Mechanic; 807.381-026 Streetcar Repairer.

49-3051.00 Motorboat Mechanics (Small Engine Mechanics)

Education: Long-term O-T-J training
Employed: 38,063
Openings: 5,908
Projected Growth: 5%
Earnings: $21,580

Repair and adjust electrical and mechanical equipment of gasoline or diesel-powered inboard or inboard-outboard boat engines.

Mounts motor to boat and operates boat at various speeds on waterway to conduct operational tests. Repairs mechanical equipment of engines, such as power-tilt, bilge pumps, or power take-offs. Replaces parts such as gears, magneto points, piston rings, and spark plugs, and reassembles engine. Analyzes test results, and disassembles and inspects motor for defective parts, using mechanic's hand tools and gauges. Adjusts carburetor mixture, electrical point settings, and timing, while motor is running in water-filled test tank. Idles motor and observes thermometer to determine effectiveness of cooling system. Writes test report to indicate acceptance or reason for rejection of motor. Adjusts generator and replaces faulty wiring, using hand tools and soldering iron. Starts motor and listens to and inspects it for signs of malfunctioning, such as smoke, excessive vibration, misfiring, and missing or broken parts. Examines propeller and propeller shafts; aligns, repairs, or replaces defective parts. Tests motor for conformance to specifications and operations, while motor is running in tank, using tachometers, monometers, voltmeters, ammeter, and stroboscope. Operates machine tools such as lathes, mills, drills, and grinders, to repair or rework parts such as cams, rods, crankshaft, and propeller. Sets starter lock, and aligns and repairs steering or throttle controls, using gauges, screwdrivers, and wrenches.

GOE Number, Interest Area, and Work Group: 05.03.01; Mechanics, Installers, and Repairers; Mechanical Work: Vehicles and Facilities. **Personality Type:** Realistic. Realistic occupations frequently involve work activities that include practical, hands-on problems and solutions. These occupations often deal with plants, animals, and real-world materials like wood, tools, and machinery. Many of the occupations require working outside and do not involve a lot of paperwork or working closely with others. **Work Values:** Moral Values; Security; Company Policies and Practices; Compensation; Ability Utilization. **Skills:** Repairing; Testing; Product Inspection; Troubleshooting; Problem Identification. **Abilities:** *Cognitive*—Problem Sensitivity; Deductive Reasoning; Inductive Reasoning; Information Ordering; Visualization; Written Comprehension. *Psychomotor*—Control Precision; Arm-Hand Steadiness; Manual Dexterity. *Physical*—Static Strength; Extent Flexibility; Trunk Strength. *Sensory*—Hearing Sensitivity; Sound Localization; Depth Perception. **General Work Activities:** *Information Input*—Identifying Objects, Actions, and Events; Getting Information Needed to Do the Job; Monitoring Processes, Materials, and Surroundings. *Mental Process*—Updating and Using Job-Relevant Knowledge; Making Decisions and Solving Problems; Evaluating Information Against Standards. *Work Output*—Repairing and Maintaining Mechanical Equipment; Handling and Moving Objects; Performing General Physical Activities; Controlling Machines and Processes. *Interacting with Others*—Performing Administrative Activities; Communicating with Other Workers; Communicating with Persons Outside Organization; Interpreting Meaning of Information to Others. **Physical Work Conditions:** Using Hands on Objects, Tools, or Controls; Standing; Indoors. **Other Job Characteristics:** Importance of Being Sure All Is Done; Consequence of Error; Importance of Being Exact or Accurate.

Experience: Job Zone 3. Previous work-related skill, knowledge, or experience is required. **Job Preparation:** SVP 6.0 to less than 7.0—More than 1 year and less than 4 years. **Knowledge:** Mechanical; Engineering and Technology; English Language; Physics; Clerical; Mathematics. **Instructional Programs:** 010201 Agricultural Mechanization, General; 470606 Small Engine Mechanic and Repairer.

Related DOT Jobs: 623.261-010 Experimental Mechanic, Outboard Motors; 623.261-014 Outboard-Motor Tester; 623.281-038 Motorboat Mechanic; 623.281-042 Outboard-Motor Mechanic.

49-3052.00 Motorcycle Mechanics (Motorcycle Mechanics)

Education: Long-term O-T-J training
Employed: 13,933
Openings: 2,134
Projected Growth: 3.9%
Earnings: $23,440

Diagnose, adjust, repair, or overhaul motorcycles, scooters, mopeds, dirt bikes, or similar motorized vehicles.

Connects test panel to engine and measures generator output, ignition timing, and other engine performance indicators. Repairs and adjusts motorcycle subassemblies such as forks, transmissions, brakes, and drive chain, according to specifications. Repairs or replaces other parts such as headlight, horn, handlebar controls, gasoline and oil tanks, starter, and muffler. Hammers out dents and bends in frame, welds tears and breaks, and reassembles frame and reinstalls engine. Disassembles subassembly unit and examines condition, movement, or alignment of parts, visually or using gauges. Removes cylinder heads, grinds valves, and scrapes off carbon; replaces defective valves, pistons, cylinders and rings, using hand tools and power tools. Listens to engine, examines vehicle's frame, and confers with customer to determine nature and extent of malfunction or damage. Reassembles and tests subassembly unit. Dismantles engine; repairs or replaces defective parts such as magneto, carburetor, and generator. Replaces defective parts, using hand tools, arbor press, flexible power press, or power tools.

GOE Number, Interest Area, and Work Group: 05.03.01; Mechanics, Installers, and Repairers; Mechanical Work: Vehicles and Facilities. **Personality Type:** Realistic. Realistic occupations frequently involve work activities that include practical, hands-on problems and solutions. These occupations often deal with plants, animals, and real-world materials like wood, tools, and machinery. Many of the occupations require working outside and do not involve a lot of paperwork or working closely with others. **Work Values:** Moral Values; Independence; Security; Compensation; Responsibility; Activity; Achievement. **Skills:** Repairing; Troubleshooting; Problem Identification; Equipment Maintenance; Operation and Control; Testing; Active Listening. **Abilities:** *Cognitive*—Visualization; Problem Sensitivity; Information Ordering; Oral Comprehension; Deductive Reasoning. *Psychomotor*—Control Precision; Manual Dexterity; Finger Dexterity. *Physical*—Static Strength; Gross Body Coordination; Dynamic Strength. *Sensory*—Hearing Sensitivity; Depth Perception; Sound Localization. **General Work Activities:** *Information Input*—Identifying Objects, Actions, and Events; Getting Information Needed to Do the Job; Inspecting Equipment, Structures, Materials. *Mental Process*—Updating and Using Job-Relevant Knowledge; Judging Qualities of Things, Services, Other People's Work; Analyzing Data or Information. *Work Output*—Repairing and Maintaining Mechanical Equipment; Handling and Moving Objects; Performing General Physical Activities. *Interacting with Others*—Communicating with Other Workers; Providing Consultation and Advice to Others; Interpreting Meaning of Information to Others; Communicating with Persons Outside Organization. **Physical Work Conditions:** Using Hands on Objects, Tools, or Controls; Indoors; Kneeling, Crouching, or Crawling. **Other Job Characteristics:** Importance of Being Sure All Is Done; Consequence of Error; Importance of Being Exact or Accurate.

Experience: Job Zone 2. Some previous work-related skill, knowledge, or experience may be helpful, but usually is not needed. **Job Preparation:** SVP 4.00 to 5.99—6 months to less than 2 years. **Knowledge:** Mechanical; Engineering and Technology; Customer and Personal Service; English Language; Mathematics; Design. **Instructional Program:** 470611 Motorcycle Mechanic and Repairer.

Related DOT Jobs: 620.281-054 Motorcycle Repairer; 620.684-026 Motorcycle Subassembly Repairer; 807.381-018 Frame Repairer; 807.484-010 Frame Straightener.

49-3053.00 Outdoor Power Equipment and Other Small Engine Mechanics (Small Engine Mechanics)

Education: Long-term O-T-J training
Employed: 38,063
Openings: 5,908
Projected Growth: 5%
Earnings: $21,580

Diagnose, adjust, repair, or overhaul small engines used to power lawn mowers, chain saws, and related equipment.

Repairs and maintains portable saws powered by internal combustion engines, following manufacturer's repair manuals and using hand tools. Adjusts points, valves, carburetor, distributor and spark plug gaps, using feeler gauges. Repairs fractional-horsepower gasoline engines used to power lawn mowers, garden tractors, and similar machines. Tests and repairs turbo or superchargers. Reassembles engines and listens to engines in action to detect operational difficulties. Dismantles engines, using hand tools; examines parts for defects; cleans parts. Tests and repairs magnetos used in gasoline and diesel engines, using meters, gauges, and hand tools. Repairs and maintains gas internal-combustion engines that power electric generators, compressor, and similar equipment. Tests and inspects engine to determine malfunctions and to locate missing and broken parts, using diagnostic instruments. Grinds, reams, rebores, and retaps parts to obtain specified clearances, using grinders, lathes, taps, reamers, boring machines, and micrometer. Positions and bolts engine to engine stand. Repairs or replaces defective parts such as water pump, carburetor, thermostat, gears, solenoid, pistons, valves, and crankshaft, using hand tools. Records repairs made, time spent, and parts used.

GOE Number, Interest Area, and Work Group: 05.03.01; Mechanics, Installers, and Repairers; Mechanical Work: Vehicles and Facilities. **Personality Type:** Realistic. Realistic occupations frequently involve work activities that include practical, hands-on problems and solutions. These occupations often deal with plants, animals, and real-world materials like wood, tools, and machinery. Many of the occupations require working outside and do not involve a lot of paperwork or working closely with others. **Work Values:** Moral Values; Company Policies and Practices; Security; Activity; Independence; Ability Utilization; Achievement; Compensation. **Skills:** Repairing; Troubleshooting; Equipment Maintenance; Problem Identification; Product Inspection. **Abilities:** *Cognitive*—Problem Sensitivity; Visualization; Information Ordering; Written Comprehension; Deductive Reasoning; Fluency of Ideas. *Psychomotor*—Finger Dexterity; Control Precision; Arm-Hand Steadiness; Multilimb Coordination; Manual Dexterity; Wrist-Finger Speed. *Physical*—Extent Flexibility; Static Strength; Trunk Strength. *Sensory*—Hearing Sensitivity; Sound Localization. **General Work Activities:** *Information Input*—Identifying Objects, Actions, and Events; Inspecting Equipment, Structures, Materials; Monitoring Processes, Materials, and Surroundings. *Mental Process*—Evaluating Information Against Standards; Updating and Using Job-Relevant Knowledge; Analyzing Data or Information. *Work Output*—Repairing and Maintaining Mechanical Equipment; Handling and Moving Objects; Performing General Physical Activities. *Interacting with Others*—Communicating with Other Workers; Communicating with Persons Outside Organization; Providing Consultation and Advice to Others; Interpreting Meaning of Information to Others. **Physical Work Conditions:** Using Hands on Objects, Tools, or Controls; Indoors; Standing; Kneeling, Crouching, or Crawling. **Other Job Characteristics:** Importance of Being Sure All Is Done; Consequence of Error; Importance of Being Exact or Accurate.

Experience: Job Zone 3. Previous work-related skill, knowledge, or experience is required. **Job Preparation:** SVP 6.0 to less than 7.0—More than 1 year and less than 4 years. **Knowledge:** Mechanical; Engineering and Technology; Customer and Personal Service; Clerical; English Language. **Instructional Programs:** 010201 Agricultural Mechanization, General; 470606 Small Engine Mechanic and Repairer.

Related DOT Jobs: 625.281-018 Engine Repairer, Service; 625.281-026 Gas-Engine Repairer; 625.281-030 Power-Saw Mechanic; 625.281-034 Small-Engine Mechanic; 625.381-010 Engine Repairer, Production; 721.281-022 Magneto Repairer.

49-3091.00 Bicycle Repairers (Bicycle Repairers)

Education: Moderate-term O-T-J training
Employed: 10,817
Openings: 1,854
Projected Growth: 22.6%
Earnings: $15,700

Repair and service bicycles.

Repairs holes in tire tubes, using scraper and patch. Shapes replacement parts, using bench grinder. Installs and adjusts speed and gear mechanisms. Assembles new bicycles. Welds broken or cracked frame together, using oxyacetylene torch and welding rods. Installs, repairs, and replaces equipment or accessories such as handle bars, stands, lights, and seats. Disassembles axle to repair, adjust, and replace defective parts, using hand tools. Aligns wheels. Paints bicycle frame, using spray gun or brush.

GOE Number, Interest Area, and Work Group: 05.03.02; Mechanics, Installers, and Repairers; Mechanical Work: Machinery Repair. **Personality Type:** Realistic. Realistic occupations frequently involve work activities that include practical, hands-on problems and solutions. These occupations often deal with plants, animals, and real-world materials like wood, tools, and machinery. Many of the occupations require working outside and do not involve a lot of paperwork or working closely with others. **Work Values:** Moral Values; Independence; Responsibility; Working Conditions; Security; Autonomy. **Skills:** Repairing; Problem Identification; Installation; Technology Design; Solution Appraisal; Reading Comprehension; Active Listening. **Abilities:** *Cognitive*—Visualization; Information Ordering; Oral Comprehension; Oral Expression; Deductive Reasoning. *Psychomotor*—Finger Dexterity; Manual Dexterity; Arm-Hand Steadiness. *Physical*—Extent Flexibility; Static Strength; Explosive Strength; Dynamic Strength. *Sensory*—Speech Clarity; Visual Color Discrimination; Depth Perception. **General Work Activities:** *Information Input*—Getting Information Needed to Do the Job; Inspecting Equipment, Structures, Materials; Identifying Objects, Actions, and Events. *Mental*

Process—Updating and Using Job-Relevant Knowledge; Analyzing Data or Information; Making Decisions and Solving Problems; Evaluating Information Against Standards. *Work Output*—Repairing and Maintaining Mechanical Equipment; Handling and Moving Objects; Performing General Physical Activities. *Interacting with Others*—Performing for or Working with the Public; Influencing Others or Selling; Communicating with Persons Outside Organization; Establishing and Maintaining Relationships. **Physical Work Conditions:** Using Hands on Objects, Tools, or Controls; Indoors; Standing; Kneeling, Crouching, or Crawling. **Other Job Characteristics:** Importance of Being Sure All Is Done; Consequence of Error; Importance of Being Exact or Accurate.

Experience: Job Zone 2. Some previous work-related skill, knowledge, or experience may be helpful, but usually is not needed. **Job Preparation:** SVP 4.00 to 5.99—6 months to less than 2 years. **Knowledge:** Mechanical; Sales and Marketing; Engineering and Technology; Physics; Mathematics; Building and Construction; English Language; Customer and Personal Service. **Instructional Program:** 470610 Bicycle Mechanic and Repairer.

Related DOT Job: 639.681-010 Bicycle Repairer.

49-3092.00 Recreational Vehicle Service Technicians
(Installers and Repairers, Manufactured Buildings, Mobile Homes, and Travel Trailers)

Education: No data available.

Employed: 37,330

Openings: No data available.

Projected Growth: No data available.

Earnings: $21,420

Diagnose, inspect, adjust, repair, or overhaul recreational vehicles, including travel trailers. Specialize in maintaining gas, electrical, hydraulic, plumbing, or chassis/towing systems as well as repairing generators, appliances, and interior components.

Refinishes wood surfaces on cabinets, doors, moldings, and floors, using power sander, putty, spray equipment, brush, paints, or varnishes. Repairs plumbing and propane gas lines, using caulking compounds and plastic or copper pipe. Removes damaged exterior panels, repairs and replaces structural frame members, and seals leaks, using hand tools. Confers with customer or reads work order to determine nature and extent of damage to unit. Opens and closes doors, windows, and drawers to test their operation; trims edges to fit, using jack-plane or drawknife. Resets hardware, using chisel, mallet, and screwdriver. Locates and repairs frayed wiring, broken connections, or incorrect wiring, using ohmmeter, soldering iron, tape, and hand tools. Connects electrical system to outside power source and activates switches to test operation of appliances and light fixtures. Connects water hose to inlet pipe of plumbing system; tests operation of toilets and sinks. Repairs leaks with caulking compound or replaces pipes, using pipe wrench. Inspects, examines, and tests operation of parts or systems to be repaired and verifies completeness of work performed. Seals open side of modular units to prepare them for shipment, using polyethylene sheets, nails, and hammer. Lists parts needed, estimates costs, and plans work procedure, using parts list, technical manuals, and diagrams.

GOE Number, Interest Area, and Work Group: 05.03.01; Mechanics, Installers, and Repairers; Mechanical Work: Vehicles and Facilities. **Personality Type:** Realistic. Realistic occupations frequently involve work activities that include practical, hands-on problems and solutions. These occupations often deal with plants, animals, and real-world materials like wood, tools, and machinery. Many of the occupations require working outside and do not involve a lot of paperwork or working closely with others. **Work Values:** Moral Values; Supervision, Technical; Activity; Variety; Company Policies and Practices; Supervision, Human Relations; Security. **Skills:** Installation; Repairing; Troubleshooting; Problem Identification; Identification of Key Causes. **Abilities:** *Cognitive*—Oral Comprehension; Written Comprehension; Information Ordering; Oral Expression; Problem Sensitivity; Deductive Reasoning. *Psychomotor*—Control Precision; Manual Dexterity; Arm-Hand Steadiness; Wrist-Finger Speed. *Physical*—Extent Flexibility; Static Strength; Trunk Strength. *Sensory*—Depth Perception. **General Work Activities:** *Information Input*—Inspecting Equipment, Structures, Materials; Getting Information Needed to Do the Job; Estimating Needed Characteristics. *Mental Process*—Evaluating Information Against Standards; Making Decisions and Solving Problems; Judging Qualities of Things, Services, Other People's Work. *Work Output*—Repairing and Maintaining Mechanical Equipment; Performing General Physical Activities; Handling and Moving Objects. *Interacting with Others*—Communicating with Persons Outside Organization; Communicating with Other Workers; Establishing and Maintaining Relationships; Providing Consultation and Advice to Others. **Physical Work Conditions:** Using Hands on Objects, Tools, or Controls; Standing; Indoors. **Other Job Characteristics:** Consequence of Error; Importance of Being Sure All Is Done; Importance of Being Exact or Accurate.

Experience: Job Zone 2. Some previous work-related skill, knowledge, or experience may be helpful, but usually is not needed. **Job Preparation:** SVP 4.00 to 5.99—6 months to less than 2 years. **Knowledge:** Building and Construction; Mechanical; Engineering and Technology; Design; Customer and Personal Service. **Instructional Program:** 460401 Building/Property Maintenance and Manager.

Related DOT Jobs: 806.381-070 Custom Van Converter; 869.261-022 Repairer, Recreational Vehicle.

49-3093.00 Tire Repairers and Changers
(Tire Repairers and Changers)

Education: Short-term O-T-J training

Employed: 83,140

Openings: 26,095

Projected Growth: 10.4%

Earnings: $16,810

Repair and replace tires.

Buffs defective area of inner tube, using scraper. Raises vehicle, using hydraulic jack. Hammers required counterweights onto rim of wheel. Rotates tires to different positions on vehicle, using hand tools. Removes inner tube from tire and inspects tire casing for defects such as holes and tears. Reassembles tire onto wheel.

Cleans sides of white-wall tires. Locates puncture in tubeless tire, by visually inspecting or by immersing inflated tire in water bath and observing air bubbles. Places wheel on balancing machine to determine counterweights required to balance wheel. Glues boot (tire patch) over rupture in tire casing, using rubber cement. Inflates inner tube and immerses it in water to locate leak. Unbolts wheel, using lug wrench. Patches tube with adhesive rubber patch, or seals rubber patch to tube, using hot vulcanizing plate. Separates tubed tire from wheel, using rubber mallet and metal bar or mechanical tire changer. Seals puncture in tubeless tire by inserting adhesive material and expanding rubber plug into puncture, using hand tools. Remounts wheel onto vehicle. Removes wheel from vehicle by hand or by use of power hoist.

GOE Number, Interest Area, and Work Group: 05.03.01; Mechanics, Installers, and Repairers; Mechanical Work: Vehicles and Facilities. **Personality Type:** Realistic. Realistic occupations frequently involve work activities that include practical, hands-on problems and solutions. These occupations often deal with plants, animals, and real-world materials like wood, tools, and machinery. Many of the occupations require working outside and do not involve a lot of paperwork or working closely with others. **Work Values:** Moral Values; Security; Independence; Activity; Supervision, Technical; Company Policies and Practices; Responsibility; Supervision, Human Relations. **Skills:** Repairing; Operation and Control; Problem Identification; Equipment Maintenance; Product Inspection; Equipment Selection; Installation. **Abilities:** *Cognitive*—Information Ordering; Problem Sensitivity; Oral Comprehension; Spatial Orientation; Deductive Reasoning; Fluency of Ideas. *Psychomotor*—Control Precision; Wrist-Finger Speed; Finger Dexterity. *Physical*—Static Strength; Extent Flexibility; Trunk Strength. **General Work Activities:** *Information Input*—Identifying Objects, Actions, and Events; Inspecting Equipment, Structures, Materials; Getting Information Needed to Do the Job. *Mental Process*—Making Decisions and Solving Problems; Judging Qualities of Things, Services, Other People's Work; Organizing, Planning, and Prioritizing. *Work Output*—Handling and Moving Objects; Performing General Physical Activities; Controlling Machines and Processes. *Interacting with Others*—Performing for or Working with the Public; Communicating with Persons Outside Organization; Assisting and Caring for Others. **Physical Work Conditions:** Using Hands on Objects, Tools, or Controls; Standing; Special Uniform. **Other Job Characteristics:** Importance of Being Sure All Is Done; Consequence of Error; Importance of Being Exact or Accurate.

Experience: Job Zone 1. No previous work-related skill, knowledge, or experience is needed. **Job Preparation:** SVP Below 4.0—Less than 6 months. **Knowledge:** Mechanical; Customer and Personal Service; Engineering and Technology; Geography; Public Safety and Security. **Instructional Program:** 470699 Vehicle and Mobile Equipment Mechanics and Repairers, Other.

Related DOT Jobs: 750.681-010 Tire Repairer; 915.684-010 Tire Repairer.

49-9000 Other Installation, Maintenance, and Repair Occupations

49-9011.00 Mechanical Door Repairers (Industrial Machinery Mechanics)

Education: Long-term O-T-J training
Employed: 535,469
Openings: 36,778
Projected Growth: 4.4%
Earnings: No data available.

Install, service, or repair opening and closing mechanisms of automatic doors and hydraulic door closers. Includes garage-door mechanics.

Cleans door-closer parts, using caustic soda, rotary brush, and grinding wheel. Studies blueprints and schematic diagrams to determine method of installing and repairing automated door openers. Removes or disassembles defective automatic mechanical door closers, using hand tools. Repairs, replaces, or fabricates worn or broken parts, using welder, lathe, drill press, and shaping and milling machines. Lubricates door closer oil chamber and packs spindle with leather washer. Bores and cuts holes in flooring, using hand tools and power tools. Installs door frames, door closers and electronic-eye mechanisms, using power tools, hand tools, and electronic test equipment. Sets in and secures floor treadle for door-activating mechanism; connects powerpack and electrical panelboard to treadle. Covers treadle with carpeting or other floor covering materials; tests system by stepping on treadle.

GOE Number, Interest Area, and Work Group: 05.03.02; Mechanics, Installers, and Repairers; Mechanical Work: Machinery Repair. **Personality Type:** Realistic. Realistic occupations frequently involve work activities that include practical, hands-on problems and solutions. These occupations often deal with plants, animals, and real-world materials like wood, tools, and machinery. Many of the occupations require working outside and do not involve a lot of paperwork or working closely with others. **Work Values:** Moral Values; Independence; Company Policies and Practices; Supervision, Technical; Activity; Security; Supervision, Human Relations. **Skills:** Installation; Repairing; Equipment Maintenance; Equipment Selection; Troubleshooting; Solution Appraisal; Problem Identification; Product Inspection. **Abilities:** *Cognitive*—Information Ordering; Written Comprehension; Deductive Reasoning; Problem Sensitivity; Visualization. *Psychomotor*—Arm-Hand Steadiness; Manual Dexterity; Control Precision; Finger Dexterity; Wrist-Finger Speed. *Physical*—Extent Flexibility; Static Strength; Trunk Strength. *Sensory*—Visual Color Discrimination; Hearing Sensitivity; Far Vision. **General Work Activities:** *Information Input*—Getting Information Needed to Do the Job; Inspecting Equipment, Structures, Materials; Identifying Objects, Actions, and Events. *Mental Process*—Evaluating Information Against Standards; Analyzing Data or Information; Making Decisions and Solving Problems. *Work Output*—Performing General Physical Activities; Handling and Moving Objects; Repairing and Maintaining Mechanical Equipment. *Interacting with Others*—Communicating with Persons Outside Organization; Performing Administrative Activities; Communicating with Other Workers. **Physical Work Conditions:** Using Hands on Objects, Tools, or Controls; Standing; Hazardous Equipment; Indoors. **Other Job Characteristics:** Consequence of Error; Importance of Being Sure All Is Done; Importance of Being Exact or Accurate; Frustrating Circumstances.

Experience: Job Zone 3. Previous work-related skill, knowledge, or experience is required. **Job Preparation:** SVP 6.0 to less than 7.0—More than 1 year and less than 4 years. **Knowledge:** Mechanical; Engineering and Technology; Building and Construction; Design; Computers and Electronics; Physics; Mathematics. **Instructional Program:** 470303 Industrial Machinery Maintenance and Repairer.

Related DOT Jobs: 630.381-014 Door-Closer Mechanic; 829.281-010 Automatic-Door Mechanic.

49-9012.00 Control and Valve Installers and Repairers, Except Mechanical Door (Precision Instrument Repairers)

Education: Long-term O-T-J training
Employed: 33,310
Openings: 4,910
Projected Growth: –4%
Earnings: $39,580

Install, repair, and maintain mechanical regulating and controlling devices such as electric meters, gas regulators, thermostats, safety and flow valves, and other mechanical governors.

GOE Number, Interest Area, and Work Group: 05.03.02; Mechanics, Installers, and Repairers; Mechanical Work: Machinery Repair. **Instructional Programs:** 150404 Instrumentation Technology/Technician; 150499 Electromechanical Instrumentation and Maintenance Technol./Technicians, Other; 470401 Instrument Calibration and Repairer. **Note:** The Department of Labor has not collected some data for this job, so it has fewer details than the other descriptions.

49-9012.01 Electric Meter Installers and Repairers (Electric Meter Installers and Repairers)

Education: No data available.
Employed: 12,450
Openings: No data available.
Projected Growth: No data available.
Earnings: $40,850

Install electric meters on customer's premises or on pole. Test meters and perform necessary repairs. Turn current on/off by connecting/disconnecting service drop.

Cleans meter parts, using chemical solutions, brushes, sandpaper, and soap and water. Inspects and tests electric meters, relays, and power, to detect cause of malfunction and inaccuracy, using hand tools and testing equipment. Splices and connects cable from meter or current transformer to pull box or switchboard, using hand tools, to provide power. Disconnects and removes electric power meters when defective or when customer accounts are in default, using hand tools. Makes adjustments to meter components such as setscrews or timing mechanism, to conform to specifications. Repairs electric meters and components such as transformers and relays; changes faulty or incorrect wiring, using hand tools. Mounts and installs meter and other electric equipment such as time clocks, transformers, and circuit breakers, using electrician's hand tools. Records meter reading and installation data on meter cards, work orders, or field service orders.

GOE Number, Interest Area, and Work Group: 05.02.02; Mechanics, Installers, and Repairers; Electrical and Electronic Systems: Equipment Repair. **Personality Type:** Realistic. Realistic occupations frequently involve work activities that include practical, hands-on problems and solutions. These occupations often deal with plants, animals, and real-world materials like wood, tools, and machinery. Many of the occupations require working outside and do not involve a lot of paperwork or working closely with others. **Work Values:** Moral Values; Independence; Security; Company Policies and Practices; Activity; Supervision, Human Relations. **Skills:** Troubleshooting; Installation; Repairing; Product Inspection; Problem Identification. **Abilities:** *Cognitive*—Information Ordering; Problem Sensitivity; Visualization; Written Comprehension; Deductive Reasoning. *Psychomotor*—Finger Dexterity; Arm-Hand Steadiness; Manual Dexterity. *Physical*—Extent Flexibility; Gross Body Coordination; Gross Body Equilibrium; Trunk Strength. *Sensory*—Visual Color Discrimination; Near Vision; Far Vision. **General Work Activities:** *Information Input*—Getting Information Needed to Do the Job; Inspecting Equipment, Structures, Materials; Identifying Objects, Actions, and Events; Monitoring Processes, Materials, and Surroundings. *Mental Process*—Making Decisions and Solving Problems; Organizing, Planning, and Prioritizing; Judging Qualities of Things, Services, Other People's Work. *Work Output*—Repairing and Maintaining Electrical Equipment; Handling and Moving Objects; Performing General Physical Activities. *Interacting with Others*—Communicating with Other Workers; Communicating with Persons Outside Organization; Performing Administrative Activities. **Physical Work Conditions:** Hazardous Conditions; Outdoors; Using Hands on Objects, Tools, or Controls. **Other Job Characteristics:** Importance of Being Sure All Is Done; Consequence of Error; Importance of Being Exact or Accurate.

Experience: Job Zone 3. Previous work-related skill, knowledge, or experience is required. **Job Preparation:** SVP 6.0 to less than 7.0—More than 1 year and less than 4 years. **Knowledge:** Mechanical; Computers and Electronics; Engineering and Technology; Public Safety and Security; Mathematics. **Instructional Program:** 470401 Instrument Calibration and Repairer.

Related DOT Jobs: 729.281-014 Electric-Meter Repairer; 729.281-018 Electric-Meter-Repairer Apprentice; 729.281-034 Inside-Meter Tester; 821.361-014 Electric-Meter Installer I; 821.684-010 Electric-Meter Installer II.

49-9012.02 Valve and Regulator Repairers (Mechanical Control and Valve Installers and Repairers)

Education: No data available.

Employed: 20,640

Openings: No data available.

Projected Growth: No data available.

Earnings: $35,640

Test, repair, and adjust mechanical regulators and valves.

Correlates testing data, performs technical calculations, and writes test reports to record data. Cleans corrosives and other deposits from serviceable parts, using solvents, wire brushes, or sandblaster. Lubricates wearing surfaces of mechanical parts, using oils or other lubricants. Records repair work, inventories parts, and orders new parts. Advises customers on proper installation of valves or regulators and related equipment. Measures salvageable parts removed from mechanical control devices for conformance to standards or specifications, using gauges, micrometers, and calipers. Examines valves or mechanical control-device parts for defects, dents, or loose attachments. Replaces, repairs, or adjusts defective valve or regulator parts; tightens attachments, using hand tools, power tools, and welder. Tests valves and regulators for leaks and for temperature and pressure settings, using precision testing equipment. Disassembles mechanical control devices or valves such as regulators, thermostats, or hydrants, using power tools, hand tools, and cutting torch. Dips valves and regulators in molten lead to prevent leakage; paints valves, fittings, and other devices, using spray gun.

GOE Number, Interest Area, and Work Group: 05.03.02; Mechanics, Installers, and Repairers; Mechanical Work: Machinery Repair. **Personality Type:** Realistic. Realistic occupations frequently involve work activities that include practical, hands-on problems and solutions. These occupations often deal with plants, animals, and real-world materials like wood, tools, and machinery. Many of the occupations require working outside and do not involve a lot of paperwork or working closely with others. **Work Values:** Moral Values; Independence; Security; Supervision, Human Relations; Supervision, Technical. **Skills:** Repairing; Writing; Mathematics; Product Inspection; Equipment Maintenance. **Abilities:** *Cognitive*—Information Ordering; Visualization; Problem Sensitivity; Written Comprehension; Deductive Reasoning. *Psychomotor*—Manual Dexterity; Wrist-Finger Speed; Finger Dexterity. *Physical*—Extent Flexibility; Static Strength; Trunk Strength; Explosive Strength. *Sensory*—Near Vision; Hearing Sensitivity; Speech Recognition; Depth Perception. **General Work Activities:** *Information Input*—Getting Information Needed to Do the Job; Inspecting Equipment, Structures, Materials; Identifying Objects, Actions, and Events. *Mental Process*—Analyzing Data or Information; Evaluating Information Against Standards; Making Decisions and Solving Problems; Processing Information. *Work Output*—Repairing and Maintaining Mechanical Equipment; Handling and Moving Objects; Performing General Physical Activities. *Interacting with Others*—Communicating with Persons Outside Organization; Performing Administrative Activities; Providing Consultation and Advice to Others. **Physical Work Conditions:** Using Hands on Objects, Tools, or Controls; Hazardous Equipment; Standing; Indoors. **Other Job Characteristics:** Importance of Being Sure All Is Done; Consequence of Error; Importance of Being Exact or Accurate.

Experience: Job Zone 3. Previous work-related skill, knowledge, or experience is required. **Job Preparation:** SVP 6.0 to less than 7.0—More than 1 year and less than 4 years. **Knowledge:** Mechanical; Engineering and Technology; Mathematics; Physics; Clerical. **Instructional Programs:** 470303 Industrial Machinery Maintenance and Repairer; 470401 Instrument Calibration and Repairer.

Related DOT Jobs: 622.381-010 Air-Valve Repairer; 630.381-030 Valve Repairer; 637.261-022 Industrial-Gas Servicer; 709.684-070 Salvager; 710.381-026 Gas-Regulator Repairer; 710.381-050 Thermostat Repairer; 862.684-030 Water Regulator and Valve Repairer; 953.281-010 Field-Mechanical-Meter Tester.

49-9012.03 Meter Mechanics (Industrial Machinery Mechanics)

Education: Long-term O-T-J training

Employed: 535,469

Openings: 36,778

Projected Growth: 4.4%

Earnings: No data available.

Test, adjust, and repair gas, water, and oil meters.

Cleans plant growth, scale, and rust from meter housing, using wire brush, buffer, sandblaster, or cleaning compounds. Connects gas, oil, water, or air meter to test apparatus, to detect leaks. Lubricates moving meter parts, using oil gun. Records test results, materials used, and meters needing repair on log or card; segregates meters requiring repair. Reassembles meter and meter parts, using soldering gun, power tools, and hand tools. Analyzes test results to determine cause of persistent meter registration errors. Inspects, repairs, and maintains gas meters at wells or processing plants. Adjusts meter and repeats test until meter registration is within specified limits. Caps meter housing and activates controls on paint booth to spray-paint meter case. Dismantles meter and replaces defective parts such as case, shafts, gears, disks, and recording mechanisms, using soldering iron and hand tools.

GOE Number, Interest Area, and Work Group: 05.03.02; Mechanics, Installers, and Repairers; Mechanical Work: Machinery Repair. **Personality Type:** Realistic. Realistic occupations frequently involve work activities that include practical, hands-on problems and solutions. These occupations often deal with plants, animals, and real-world materials like wood, tools, and machinery. Many of the occupations require working outside and do not involve a lot of paperwork or working closely with others. **Work Values:** Moral Values; Independence; Security; Company Policies and Practices; Supervision, Technical; Supervision, Human Relations; Activity. **Skills:** Product Inspection; Repairing; Equipment Maintenance; Installation; Testing. **Abilities:** *Cognitive*—Information Ordering; Problem Sensitivity; Inductive Reasoning; Deductive Reasoning; Written Expression; Visualization. *Psychomotor*—Finger Dexterity; Arm-Hand Steadiness; Control Precision. *Physical*—Extent Flexibility; Static Strength. *Sensory*—Near Vision; Visual Color Discrimination; Glare Sensitivity. **General Work Activities:** *In-*

formation Input—Getting Information Needed to Do the Job; Inspecting Equipment, Structures, Materials; Identifying Objects, Actions, and Events. *Mental Process*—Evaluating Information Against Standards; Making Decisions and Solving Problems; Analyzing Data or Information. *Work Output*—Repairing and Maintaining Mechanical Equipment; Handling and Moving Objects; Performing General Physical Activities. *Interacting with Others*—Performing Administrative Activities; Monitoring and Controlling Resources; Interpreting Meaning of Information to Others; Communicating with Other Workers. **Physical Work Conditions:** Outdoors; Using Hands on Objects, Tools, or Controls; Standing. **Other Job Characteristics:** Consequence of Error; Importance of Being Exact or Accurate; Importance of Being Sure All Is Done.

Experience: Job Zone 2. Some previous work-related skill, knowledge, or experience may be helpful, but usually is not needed. **Job Preparation:** SVP 4.00 to 5.99—6 months to less than 2 years. **Knowledge:** Mechanical; Engineering and Technology; Mathematics; Clerical; English Language; Production and Processing; Design; Physics. **Instructional Program:** 470401 Instrument Calibration and Repairer.

Related DOT Jobs: 710.281-022 Gas-Meter Prover; 710.281-034 Meter Repairer; 710.381-022 Gas-Meter Mechanic I; 710.684-026 Gas-Meter Mechanic II.

49-9021.00 Heating, Air Conditioning, and Refrigeration Mechanics and Installers (Heating, Air Conditioning, and Refrigeration Mechanics and Installers)

Education: Long-term O-T-J training
Employed: 285,922
Openings: 29,552
Projected Growth: 16.9%
Earnings: $29,160

Install or repair heating, central air conditioning, or refrigeration systems, including oil burners, hot-air furnaces, and heating stoves.

GOE Number, Interest Area, and Work Group: 05.03.01; Mechanics, Installers, and Repairers; Mechanical Work: Vehicles and Facilities. **Instructional Programs:** 150501 Heating, Air Conditioning and Refrigeration Technology/Technician; 470201 Heating, Air Conditioning and Refrigeration Mechanic and Repairer. **Note:** The Department of Labor has not collected some data for this job, so it has fewer details than the other descriptions.

49-9021.01 Heating and Air Conditioning Mechanics (Heating, Air Conditioning, and Refrigeration Mechanics and Installers)

Education: Long-term O-T-J training
Employed: 285,922
Openings: 29,552
Projected Growth: 16.9%
Earnings: $29,160

Install, service, and repair heating and air conditioning systems in residences and commercial establishments.

Assembles, positions, and mounts heating or cooling equipment, following blueprints. Inspects inoperative equipment to locate source of trouble. Discusses heating-cooling system malfunctions with users to isolate problems or to verify that malfunctions have been corrected. Inspects and tests system to verify system compliance with plans and specifications and to detect malfunctions. Adjusts system controls to setting recommended by manufacturer, to balance system, using hand tools. Installs auxiliary components to heating-cooling equipment, such as expansion and discharge valves, air ducts, pipes, blowers, dampers, flues, and stokers, following blueprints. Tests pipe or tubing joints and connections for leaks, using pressure gauge or soap-and-water solution. Disassembles system and cleans and oils parts. Studies blueprints to determine configuration of heating or cooling equipment components. Repairs or replaces defective equipment, components, or wiring. Installs, connects, and adjusts thermostats, humidistats, and timers, using hand tools. Lays out and connects electrical wiring between controls and equipment according to wiring diagram, using electrician's hand tools. Reassembles equipment and starts unit to test operation. Measures, cuts, threads, and bends pipe or tubing, using pipefitter's tools. Cuts and drills holes in floors, walls, and roof to install equipment, using power saws and drills. Fabricates, assembles, and installs duct work and chassis parts, using portable metal-working tools and welding equipment. Joins pipes or tubing to equipment and to fuel, water, or refrigerant source, to form complete circuit. Tests electrical circuits and components for continuity, using electrical test equipment. Wraps pipes in insulation and secures it in place with cement or wire bands.

GOE Number, Interest Area, and Work Group: 05.03.01; Mechanics, Installers, and Repairers; Mechanical Work: Vehicles and Facilities. **Personality Type:** Realistic. Realistic occupations frequently involve work activities that include practical, hands-on problems and solutions. These occupations often deal with plants, animals, and real-world materials like wood, tools, and machinery. Many of the occupations require working outside and do not involve a lot of paperwork or working closely with others. **Work Values:** Moral Values; Independence; Security; Activity; Responsibility; Company Policies and Practices. **Skills:** Installation; Troubleshooting; Repairing; Problem Identification; Equipment Maintenance. **Abilities:** *Cognitive*—Deductive Reasoning; Written Comprehension; Problem Sensitivity; Information Ordering; Inductive Reasoning; Visualization. *Psychomotor*—Manual Dexterity; Arm-Hand Steadiness; Finger Dexterity. *Physical*—Extent Flexibility; Static Strength; Trunk Strength. *Sensory*—Depth Perception. **General Work Activities:** *Information Input*—Monitoring Processes, Materials, and Surroundings; Inspecting Equipment, Structures, Materials; Getting Information Needed to Do the Job. *Mental Process*—Making Decisions and Solving Problems; Updating and Using Job-Relevant Knowledge; Evaluating Information Against Standards; Processing Information; Analyzing Data or Information; Organizing, Planning, and Prioritizing. *Work Output*—Performing General Physical Activities; Handling and Moving Objects; Repairing and Maintaining Mechanical Equipment. *Interacting with Others*—Communicating with Persons Outside Organization; Communicating with Other Workers; Interpreting Meaning of Information to Others. **Physical Work Conditions:** Using Hands on Objects, Tools, or Controls; Indoors; Standing. **Other Job Characteristics:** Importance of Being Exact or Accurate; Consequence of Error; Importance of Being Sure All Is Done.

Experience: Job Zone 4. A minimum of two to four years of work-related skill, knowledge, or experience is needed. **Job Preparation:** SVP 7.0 to less than 8.0—2 years to less than 10 years. **Knowledge:** Mechanical; Design; Building and Construction; Engineering and Technology; English Language; Customer and Personal Service. **Instructional Programs:** 150501 Heating, Air Conditioning and Refrigeration Technology/Technician; 470201 Heating, Air Conditioning and Refrigeration Mechanic and Repairer.

Related DOT Jobs: 637.261-014 Heating-and-Air-Conditioning Installer-Servicer; 637.261-030 Solar-Energy-System Installer; 637.261-034 Air and Hydronic Balancing Technician; 637.381-010 Evaporative-Cooler Installer; 862.281-018 Oil-Burner-Servicer-and-Installer; 862.361-010 Furnace Installer; 869.281-010 Furnace Installer-and-Repairer, Hot Air.

49-9021.02 Refrigeration Mechanics (Heating, Air Conditioning, and Refrigeration Mechanics and Installers)

Education: Long-term O-T-J training

Employed: 285,922

Openings: 29,552

Projected Growth: 16.9%

Earnings: $29,160

Install and repair industrial and commercial refrigerating systems.

Tests lines, components, and connections for leaks. Lays out reference points for installation of structural and functional components, using measuring instruments. Dismantles malfunctioning systems and tests components, using electrical, mechanical, and pneumatic testing equipment. Observes system operation, using gauges and instruments, and adjusts or replaces mechanisms and parts, according to specifications. Reads blueprints to determine location, size, capacity, and type of components needed to build refrigeration system. Lifts and aligns components into position, using hoist or block and tackle. Assembles structural and functional components such as controls, switches, gauges, wiring harnesses, valves, pumps, compressors, condensers, cores, and pipes. Adjusts valves according to specifications; charges system with specified type of refrigerant. Keeps records of repairs and replacements made and causes of malfunctions. Fabricates and assembles components and structural portions of refrigeration system, using hand tools, powered tools, and welding equipment. Brazes or solders parts to repair defective joints and leaks. Installs expansion and control valves, using acetylene torch and wrenches. Cuts, bends, threads, and connects pipe to functional components and water, power, or refrigeration system. Replaces or adjusts defective or worn parts to repair system; reassembles system. Mounts compressor, condenser, and other components in specified location on frame, using hand tools and acetylene welding equipment. Drills holes and installs mounting brackets and hangers into floor and walls of building.

GOE Number, Interest Area, and Work Group: 05.03.01; Mechanics, Installers, and Repairers; Mechanical Work: Vehicles and Facilities. **Personality Type:** Realistic. Realistic occupations frequently involve work activities that include practical, hands-on problems and solutions. These occupations often deal with plants, animals, and real-world materials like wood, tools, and machinery. Many of the occupations require working outside and do not involve a lot of paperwork or working closely with others. **Work Values:** Moral Values; Independence; Security; Activity; Company Policies and Practices. **Skills:** Installation; Repairing; Product Inspection; Troubleshooting; Problem Identification; Testing. **Abilities:** *Cognitive*—Information Ordering; Deductive Reasoning; Problem Sensitivity; Visualization; Written Comprehension. *Psychomotor*—Control Precision; Manual Dexterity; Multilimb Coordination. *Physical*—Extent Flexibility; Static Strength; Explosive Strength. **General Work Activities:** *Information Input*—Getting Information Needed to Do the Job; Monitoring Processes, Materials, and Surroundings; Identifying Objects, Actions, and Events. *Mental Process*—Judging Qualities of Things, Services, Other People's Work; Evaluating Information Against Standards; Updating and Using Job-Relevant Knowledge; Analyzing Data or Information. *Work Output*—Repairing and Maintaining Mechanical Equipment; Handling and Moving Objects; Performing General Physical Activities. *Interacting with Others*—Communicating with Other Workers; Performing Administrative Activities; Interpreting Meaning of Information to Others; Communicating with Persons Outside Organization; Establishing and Maintaining Relationships. **Physical Work Conditions:** Indoors; Using Hands on Objects, Tools, or Controls; Standing. **Other Job Characteristics:** Importance of Being Exact or Accurate; Consequence of Error; Importance of Being Sure All Is Done.

Experience: Job Zone 4. A minimum of two to four years of work-related skill, knowledge, or experience is needed. **Job Preparation:** SVP 7.0 to less than 8.0—2 years to less than 10 years. **Knowledge:** Mechanical; Engineering and Technology; Design; Building and Construction; Clerical. **Instructional Programs:** 150501 Heating, Air Conditioning and Refrigeration Technology/Technician; 470201 Heating, Air Conditioning and Refrigeration Mechanic and Repairer.

Related DOT Jobs: 637.261-026 Refrigeration Mechanic; 637.381-014 Refrigeration Unit Repairer; 827.361-014 Refrigeration Mechanic.

49-9031.00 Home Appliance Repairers (Electric Home Appliance and Power Tool Repairers)

Education: No data available.

Employed: 30,220

Openings: No data available.

Projected Growth: No data available.

Earnings: $24,160

Repair, adjust, or install all types of electric or gas household appliances, such as refrigerators, washers, dryers, and ovens.

GOE Number, Interest Area, and Work Group: 05.02.01; Mechanics, Installers, and Repairers; Electrical and Electronic Systems: Installation and Repair. **Instructional Programs:** 470101 Electrical and Electronics Equipment Installer and Repairer, General; 470106 Major Appliance Installer and Repairer; 470199 Electrical and Electronics Equipment Installer and Repairer, Other; 470499 Miscellaneous Mechanics and Repairers, Other. **Note:** The Department of Labor has not collected some data for this job, so it has fewer details than the other descriptions.

49-9031.01 Home Appliance Installers (Electric Home Appliance and Power Tool Repairers)

Education: No data available.

Employed: 30,220

Openings: No data available.

Projected Growth: No data available.

Earnings: $24,160

Install household appliances, such as refrigerators, washing machines, and stoves in mobile homes or customers' homes.

Lights and adjusts pilot lights on gas stoves and examines valves and burners for gas leakage and specified flame. Levels refrigerators, adjusts doors, and connects water lines to water pipes for ice makers and water dispensers, using hand tools. Advises customers regarding use and care of appliance and provides them with emergency service number. Levels washing machines and connects hoses to water pipes, using plumbing and other hand tools. Observes and tests operation of appliances such as refrigerators, washers, and dryers, and makes initial installation adjustments accordingly. Disassembles and reinstalls existing kitchen cabinets; assembles and installs prefabricated kitchen cabinets in conjunction with appliance installation.

GOE Number, Interest Area, and Work Group: 05.02.01; Mechanics, Installers, and Repairers; Electrical and Electronic Systems: Installation and Repair. **Personality Type:** Realistic. Realistic occupations frequently involve work activities that include practical, hands-on problems and solutions. These occupations often deal with plants, animals, and real-world materials like wood, tools, and machinery. Many of the occupations require working outside and do not involve a lot of paperwork or working closely with others. **Work Values:** Moral Values; Security; Activity; Company Policies and Practices; Supervision, Human Relations; Independence; Working Conditions. **Skills:** Troubleshooting; Installation; Problem Identification; Equipment Selection; Operation and Control; Active Listening; Testing; Operation Monitoring; Repairing. **Abilities:** *Cognitive*—Problem Sensitivity; Visualization; Information Ordering; Oral Expression; Deductive Reasoning. *Psychomotor*—Wrist-Finger Speed; Finger Dexterity; Speed of Limb Movement. *Physical*—Static Strength; Extent Flexibility; Dynamic Strength. *Sensory*—Hearing Sensitivity; Sound Localization. **General Work Activities:** *Information Input*—Inspecting Equipment, Structures, Materials; Getting Information Needed to Do the Job; Identifying Objects, Actions, and Events. *Mental Process*—Organizing, Planning, and Prioritizing; Making Decisions and Solving Problems; Updating and Using Job-Relevant Knowledge. *Work Output*—Handling and Moving Objects; Implementing Ideas and Programs; Performing General Physical Activities. *Interacting with Others*—Communicating with Persons Outside Organization; Performing for or Working with the Public; Interpreting Meaning of Information to Others. **Physical Work Conditions:** Using Hands on Objects, Tools, or Controls; Indoors; Standing. **Other Job Characteristics:** Importance of Being Sure All Is Done; Consequence of Error; Importance of Being Exact or Accurate.

Experience: Job Zone 3. Previous work-related skill, knowledge, or experience is required. **Job Preparation:** SVP 6.0 to less than 7.0—More than 1 year and less than 4 years. **Knowledge:** Mechanical; Building and Construction; Engineering and Technology; Public Safety and Security; English Language; Education and Training. **Instructional Programs:** 470101 Electrical and Electronics Equipment Installer and Repairer, General; 470106 Major Appliance Installer and Repairer; 470199 Electrical and Electronics Equipment Installer and Repairer, Other; 470499 Miscellaneous Mechanics and Repairers, Other.

Related DOT Jobs: 827.661-010 Household-Appliance Installer.

49-9031.02 Gas Appliance Repairers (Gas Appliance Repairers)

Education: No data available.

Employed: 11,440

Openings: No data available.

Projected Growth: No data available.

Earnings: $33,140

Repair and install gas appliances and equipment such as ovens, dryers, and hot water heaters.

Measures, cuts, and threads pipe; connects pipe to feeder lines and equipment or to appliance, using rule and hand tools. Assembles new or reconditioned appliances. Tests and examines pipelines and equipment to locate leaks and faulty connections and to determine pressure and flow of gas. Dismantles meters and regulators, and replaces defective pipes, thermocouples, thermostats, valves, and indicator spindles, using hand tools.

GOE Number, Interest Area, and Work Group: 05.03.02; Mechanics, Installers, and Repairers; Mechanical Work: Machinery Repair. **Personality Type:** Realistic. Realistic occupations frequently involve work activities that include practical, hands-on problems and solutions. These occupations often deal with plants, animals, and real-world materials like wood, tools, and machinery. Many of the occupations require working outside and do not involve a lot of paperwork or working closely with others. **Work Values:** Moral Values; Independence; Security; Company Policies and Practices; Supervision, Human Relations; Responsibility. **Skills:** Repairing; Installation; Troubleshooting; Problem Identification; Identification of Key Causes; Operation Monitoring. **Abilities:** *Cognitive*—Visualization; Problem Sensitivity; Speed of Closure; Number Facility; Information Ordering; Deductive Reasoning. *Psychomotor*—Manual Dexterity; Wrist-Finger Speed; Finger Dexterity. *Physical*—Extent Flexibility; Static Strength; Trunk Strength. *Sensory*—Sound Localization; Depth Perception; Hearing Sensitivity. **General Work Activities:** *Information Input*—Inspecting Equipment, Structures, Materials; Getting Information Needed to Do the Job; Monitoring Processes, Materials, and Surroundings. *Mental Process*—Evaluating Information Against Standards; Updating and Using Job-Relevant Knowledge; Analyzing Data or Information; Making Decisions and Solving Problems. *Work Output*—Repairing and Maintaining Mechanical Equipment; Handling and Moving Objects; Performing General Physical Activities. *Interacting with Others*—Performing for or Working with the Public; Interpreting Meaning of Information to Others; Communicating with Persons Outside Organization. **Physical Work Conditions:** Using Hands on Objects, Tools, or Controls; Indoors;

Kneeling, Crouching, or Crawling. **Other Job Characteristics:** Consequence of Error; Importance of Being Sure All Is Done; Importance of Being Exact or Accurate.

Experience: Job Zone 4. A minimum of two to four years of work-related skill, knowledge, or experience is needed. **Job Preparation:** SVP 7.0 to less than 8.0—2 years to less than 10 years. **Knowledge:** Mechanical; Building and Construction; Mathematics; Physics; Engineering and Technology; Public Safety and Security. **Instructional Program:** 470106 Major Appliance Installer and Repairer.

Related DOT Job: 637.261-018 Gas-Appliance Servicer.

49-9041.00 Industrial Machinery Mechanics
(Industrial Machinery Mechanics)

Education: Long-term O-T-J training

Employed: 535,469

Openings: 36,778

Projected Growth: 4.4%

Earnings: No data available.

Repair, install, adjust, or maintain industrial production and processing machinery or refinery and pipeline distribution systems.

Orders or requisitions parts and materials. Cleans and lubricates parts, equipment, and machinery. Test-runs repaired machinery and equipment to verify adequacy of repairs. Welds, to repair broken metal parts, to fabricate new parts, and to assemble new equipment. Repairs and replaces electrical wiring and components of machinery. Enters codes and instructions to program computer-controlled machinery. Fabricates replacement parts. Examines parts for defects such as breakage or excessive wear. Repairs, replaces, adjusts, and aligns components of machinery and equipment. Disassembles machinery and equipment to remove parts and make repairs. Confers with operators and observes, tests, and evaluates operation of machinery and equipment to diagnose cause of malfunction. Records repairs and maintenance performed.

GOE Number, Interest Area, and Work Group: 05.03.02; Mechanics, Installers, and Repairers; Mechanical Work: Machinery Repair. **Personality Type:** Realistic. Realistic occupations frequently involve work activities that include practical, hands-on problems and solutions. These occupations often deal with plants, animals, and real-world materials like wood, tools, and machinery. Many of the occupations require working outside and do not involve a lot of paperwork or working closely with others. **Work Values:** Moral Values; Independence; Activity; Security; Company Policies and Practices. **Skills:** Equipment Maintenance; Repairing; Troubleshooting; Problem Identification; Testing; Product Inspection. **Abilities:** *Cognitive*—Visualization; Information Ordering; Problem Sensitivity; Oral Comprehension; Inductive Reasoning; Deductive Reasoning. *Psychomotor*—Control Precision; Finger Dexterity; Wrist-Finger Speed; Manual Dexterity; Reaction Time. *Physical*—Extent Flexibility; Static Strength; Trunk Strength. *Sensory*—Hearing Sensitivity; Visual Color Discrimination; Auditory Attention. **General Work Activities:** *Information Input*—Inspecting Equipment, Structures, Materials; Getting Information

Needed to Do the Job; Identifying Objects, Actions, and Events. *Mental Process*—Updating and Using Job-Relevant Knowledge; Making Decisions and Solving Problems; Judging Qualities of Things, Services, Other People's Work. *Work Output*—Repairing and Maintaining Mechanical Equipment; Handling and Moving Objects; Performing General Physical Activities; Controlling Machines and Processes. *Interacting with Others*—Communicating with Other Workers; Monitoring and Controlling Resources; Establishing and Maintaining Relationships; Interpreting Meaning of Information to Others. **Physical Work Conditions:** Using Hands on Objects, Tools, or Controls; Indoors; Common Protective or Safety Attire; Hazardous Equipment. **Other Job Characteristics:** Consequence of Error; Importance of Being Exact or Accurate; Importance of Being Sure All Is Done.

Experience: Job Zone 3. Previous work-related skill, knowledge, or experience is required. **Job Preparation:** SVP 6.0 to less than 7.0—More than 1 year and less than 4 years. **Knowledge:** Mechanical; Engineering and Technology; Physics; Computers and Electronics; Public Safety and Security; English Language. **Instructional Programs:** 470303 Industrial Machinery Maintenance and Repairer; 480507 Tool and Die Maker/Technologist.

Related DOT Jobs: 601.281-030 Tool and Fixture Repairer; 620.281-018 Automotive-Maintenance-Equipment Servicer; 626.261-010 Forge-Shop-Machine Repairer; 626.261-014 Repairer, Welding Systems and Equipment; 626.361-010 Repairer, Welding, Brazing, and Burning Machines; 626.381-014 Gas-Welding-Equipment Mechanic; 626.381-018 Hydraulic-Press Servicer; 626.384-010 Repairer, Welding Equipment; 627.261-010 Composing-Room Machinist; 627.261-014 Machinist Apprentice, Composing Room; 627.261-018 Machinist Apprentice, Linotype; 627.261-022 Machinist, Linotype; 629.261-010 Laundry-Machine Mechanic; 629.261-014 Miller, Head, Wet Process; 629.261-018 Powder-Line Repairer; 629.261-022 Electronic-Production-Line-Maintenance Mechanic; 629.280-010 Maintenance Mechanic; 629.281-010 Bakery-Machine Mechanic; 629.281-014 Cellophane-Casting-Machine Repairer; 629.281-030 Maintenance Mechanic (partial list; see the introduction for sources of the complete list).

49-9042.00 Maintenance and Repair Workers, General (General Utility Maintenance Repairers)

Education: Long-term O-T-J training

Employed: 1,232,476

Openings: 180,704

Projected Growth: 7.7%

Earnings: $23,290

Perform work involving the skills of two or more maintenance or craft occupations to keep machines, mechanical equipment, or the structure of an establishment in repair. Perform various duties involving pipe fitting; boiler making; insulating; welding; machining; carpentry; repairing electrical or mechanical equipment; installing, aligning, and balancing new equipment; and repairing buildings, floors, or stairs.

Lays brick to repair and maintain physical structure of establishment. Records repairs made and costs. Cleans and lubricates shafts, bearings, gears, and other parts of machinery. Paints and repairs woodwork and plaster. Sets up and operates machine tools to repair or fabricate machine parts, jigs and fixtures, and tools. Operates cutting torch or welding equipment to cut or join metal parts. Fabricates and repairs counters, benches, partitions, and other wooden structures such as sheds and outbuildings. Dismantles and reassembles defective machines and equipment. Assembles, installs, and/or repairs pipe systems and hydraulic and pneumatic equipment. Installs machinery and equipment. Installs and/or repairs wiring and electrical and electronic components. Inspects and tests machinery and equipment to diagnose machine malfunctions. Installs new or repaired parts. Assembles, installs, and/or repairs plumbing. Estimates costs of repairs.

GOE Number, Interest Area, and Work Group: 05.03.01; Mechanics, Installers, and Repairers; Mechanical Work: Vehicles and Facilities. **Personality Type:** Realistic. Realistic occupations frequently involve work activities that include practical, hands-on problems and solutions. These occupations often deal with plants, animals, and real-world materials like wood, tools, and machinery. Many of the occupations require working outside and do not involve a lot of paperwork or working closely with others. **Work Values:** Moral Values; Company Policies and Practices; Supervision, Human Relations; Independence; Activity. **Skills:** Repairing; Installation; Equipment Maintenance; Problem Identification; Troubleshooting. **Abilities:** *Cognitive*—Visualization; Information Ordering; Problem Sensitivity; Number Facility; Category Flexibility; Deductive Reasoning. *Psychomotor*—Control Precision; Reaction Time; Finger Dexterity. *Physical*—Extent Flexibility; Static Strength; Trunk Strength. *Sensory*—Hearing Sensitivity; Visual Color Discrimination; Near Vision. **General Work Activities:** *Information Input*—Inspecting Equipment, Structures, Materials; Getting Information Needed to Do the Job; Monitoring Processes, Materials, and Surroundings. *Mental Process*—Updating and Using Job-Relevant Knowledge; Judging Qualities of Things, Services, Other People's Work; Making Decisions and Solving Problems; Organizing, Planning, and Prioritizing; Evaluating Information Against Standards. *Work Output*—Repairing and Maintaining Mechanical Equipment; Handling and Moving Objects; Performing General Physical Activities. *Interacting with Others*—Performing Administrative Activities; Communicating with Other Workers; Monitoring and Controlling Resources. **Physical Work Conditions:** Using Hands on Objects, Tools, or Controls; Common Protective or Safety Attire; Indoors. **Other Job Characteristics:** Consequence of Error; Importance of Being Sure All Is Done; Importance of Being Exact or Accurate.

Experience: Job Zone 3. Previous work-related skill, knowledge, or experience is required. **Job Preparation:** SVP 6.0 to less than 7.0—More than 1 year and less than 4 years. **Knowledge:** Building and Construction; Mechanical; Engineering and Technology; Public Safety and Security; Physics; Computers and Electronics; Mathematics; Design. **Instructional Programs:** 010201 Agricultural Mechanization, General; 460401 Building/Property Maintenance and Manager; 479999 Mechanics and Repairers, Other.

Related DOT Jobs: 638.281-010 Fire-Fighting-Equipment Specialist; 899.261-014 Maintenance Repairer, Industrial; 899.381-010 Maintenance Repairer, Building; 899.484-010 Mobile-Home-Lot Utility Worker; 912.364-010 Airport Attendant.

49-9043.00 Maintenance Workers, Machinery
(Industrial Machinery Mechanics)

Education: Long-term O-T-J training
Employed: 535,469
Openings: 36,778
Projected Growth: 4.4%
Earnings: No data available.

Lubricate machinery, change parts, or perform other routine machinery maintenance.

Replaces, empties, or replenishes empty machine and equipment containers such as gas tanks or boxes. Reads work orders and specifications to determine machines and equipment requiring repair or maintenance. Cleans machine and machine parts, using cleaning solvent, cloth, air gun, hose, vacuum, or other equipment. Collects and discards worn machine parts and other garbage to maintain machinery and work areas. Transports machine parts, tools, equipment, and other material between work areas and storage, using crane, hoist, or dolly. Cuts, shapes, smoothes, attaches, or assembles pieces of metal, wood, rubber, or other materials, to repair and maintain machines and equipment. Communicates with or assists other workers to repair or move machines, machine parts or equipment. Starts machine and observes mechanical operation to determine efficiency and to detect defects, malfunctions, or other machine damage. Inventories and requisitions machine parts, equipment, and other supplies to replenish and maintain stock. Sets up and operates machine; adjusts controls that regulate operational functions to ensure conformance to specifications. Marks, separates, ties, aligns, threads, attaches, or inserts material or product, to prepare machine for operation or to identify machine process. Records and maintains production, repair, and machine maintenance information. Inspects or tests damaged machine parts; marks defective area; advises supervisor of need for repair. Dismantles machine, removes machine parts, and reassembles machine, using hand tools, chain falls, jack, crane, or hoist. Replaces or repairs metal, wood, leather, glass, or other lining in machine or equipment compartments or containers. Lubricates, oils, or applies adhesive or other material to machines, machine parts, or other equipment, according to specified procedures. Installs, replaces, or changes machine parts and attachments, according to production specifications.

GOE Number, Interest Area, and Work Group: 05.03.02; Mechanics, Installers, and Repairers; Mechanical Work: Machinery Repair. **Personality Type:** Realistic. Realistic occupations frequently involve work activities that include practical, hands-on problems and solutions. These occupations often deal with plants, animals, and real-world materials like wood, tools, and machinery. Many of the occupations require working outside and do not involve a lot of paperwork or working closely with others. **Work Values:** Moral Values; Variety; Activity; Company Policies and Practices; Security; Supervision, Human Relations. **Skills:** Equipment Maintenance; Troubleshooting; Operation Monitoring; Operation and Control; Repairing. **Abilities:** *Cognitive*—Written Comprehension; Deductive Reasoning; Information Ordering; Problem Sensitivity; Visualization; Written Expression. *Psycho-*

motor—Arm-Hand Steadiness; Manual Dexterity; Reaction Time; Control Precision. *Physical*—Extent Flexibility; Static Strength; Dynamic Strength. *Sensory*—Auditory Attention; Hearing Sensitivity; Sound Localization. **General Work Activities:** *Information Input*—Inspecting Equipment, Structures, Materials; Getting Information Needed to Do the Job; Monitoring Processes, Materials, and Surroundings. *Mental Process*—Evaluating Information Against Standards; Updating and Using Job-Relevant Knowledge; Making Decisions and Solving Problems. *Work Output*—Repairing and Maintaining Mechanical Equipment; Controlling Machines and Processes; Performing General Physical Activities; Handling and Moving Objects. *Interacting with Others*—Communicating with Other Workers; Monitoring and Controlling Resources; Performing Administrative Activities; Assisting and Caring for Others. **Physical Work Conditions:** Indoors; Using Hands on Objects, Tools, or Controls; Hazardous Equipment; Common Protective or Safety Attire; Standing. **Other Job Characteristics:** Consequence of Error; Importance of Being Sure All Is Done; Importance of Being Exact or Accurate.

Experience: Job Zone 1. No previous work-related skill, knowledge, or experience is needed. **Job Preparation:** SVP Below 4.0—Less than 6 months. **Knowledge:** Mechanical; Chemistry; Engineering and Technology; Production and Processing; Building and Construction; Mathematics; Physics. **Instructional Program:** 470303 Industrial Machinery Maintenance and Repairer.

Related DOT Jobs: 514.684-018 Nozzle-and-Sleeve Worker; 519.664-014 Pot Liner; 519.667-010 Carbon Setter; 519.684-014 Leaf Coverer; 529.667-014 Mash-Filter-Cloth Changer; 564.684-010 Knife Setter, Grinder Machine; 590.384-014 Production Technician, Semiconductor Processing Equipment; 622.684-018 Switch Repairer; 628.684-010 Binder and Box Builder; 628.684-014 Frame Bander; 628.684-022 Overhead Cleaner Maintainer; 628.684-042 Spindle Repairer; 628.684-046 Texturing-Machine Fixer; 628.687-010 Flyer Repairer; 629.684-010 Curing-Press Maintainer; 630.584-010 Equipment Cleaner-and-Tester; 638.684-010 Knife Changer; 638.684-014 Knife Setter; 652.385-010 Printing-Roller Handler; 680.684-010 Card Grinder Helper (partial list; see the introduction for sources of the complete list).

49-9044.00 Millwrights (Millwrights)

Education: Long-term O-T-J training

Employed: 82,331

Openings: 5,016

Projected Growth: –1.9%

Earnings: $36,940

Install, dismantle, or move machinery and heavy equipment according to layout plans, blueprints, or other drawings.

Installs robot and modifies its program, using teach pendant. Shrink-fits bushings, sleeves, rings, liners, gears, and wheels to specified items, using portable gas heating equipment. Levels bedplate and establishes centerline, using straightedge, levels, and transit. Inserts shims, adjusts tension on nuts and bolts, or positions parts, using hand tools and measuring instruments, to set specified clearances between moving and stationary parts. Aligns machines and equipment, using hoists, jacks, hand tools, squares,

rules, micrometers, and plumb bobs. Bolts parts such as side and deck plates, jaw plates, and journals, to basic assembly unit. Attaches moving parts and subassemblies to basic assembly unit, using hand tools and power tools. Constructs foundation for machines, using hand tools and building materials such as wood, cement, and steel. Dismantles machinery and equipment for shipment to installation site, usually performing installation and maintenance work as part of team. Dismantles machines, using hammers, wrenches, crowbars, and other hand tools. Signals crane operator to lower basic assembly units to bedplate, and aligns unit to centerline. Assembles machines, and bolts, welds, rivets, or otherwise fastens them to foundation or other structures, using hand tools and power tools. Moves machinery and equipment, using hoists, dollies, rollers, and trucks. Connects power unit to machines or steam piping to equipment, and tests unit to evaluate its mechanical operation. Lays out mounting holes, using measuring instruments, and drills holes with power drill. Positions steel beams to support bedplates of machines and equipment, using blueprints and schematic drawings, to determine work procedures. Replaces defective parts of machine or adjusts clearances and alignment of moving parts. Repairs and lubricates machines and equipment. Operates engine lathe to grind, file, and turn machine parts to dimensional specifications.

GOE Number, Interest Area, and Work Group: 05.03.01; Mechanics, Installers, and Repairers; Mechanical Work: Vehicles and Facilities. **Personality Type:** Realistic. Realistic occupations frequently involve work activities that include practical, hands-on problems and solutions. These occupations often deal with plants, animals, and real-world materials like wood, tools, and machinery. Many of the occupations require working outside and do not involve a lot of paperwork or working closely with others. **Work Values:** Moral Values; Supervision, Human Relations; Activity; Company Policies and Practices; Security; Compensation. **Skills:** Installation; Repairing; Equipment Maintenance; Troubleshooting; Product Inspection. **Abilities:** *Cognitive*—Information Ordering; Visualization; Spatial Orientation; Oral Comprehension; Written Comprehension. *Psychomotor*—Control Precision; Manual Dexterity; Multilimb Coordination. *Physical*—Static Strength; Extent Flexibility; Trunk Strength. *Sensory*—Depth Perception; Near Vision; Peripheral Vision. **General Work Activities:** *Information Input*—Getting Information Needed to Do the Job; Inspecting Equipment, Structures, Materials; Monitoring Processes, Materials, and Surroundings. *Mental Process*—Updating and Using Job-Relevant Knowledge; Evaluating Information Against Standards; Judging Qualities of Things, Services, Other People's Work. *Work Output*—Handling and Moving Objects; Repairing and Maintaining Mechanical Equipment; Controlling Machines and Processes; Performing General Physical Activities. *Interacting with Others*—Communicating with Other Workers; Establishing and Maintaining Relationships; Monitoring and Controlling Resources; Coordinating Work and Activities of Others; Developing and Building Teams. **Physical Work Conditions:** Using Hands on Objects, Tools, or Controls; Hazardous Equipment; Common Protective or Safety Attire; Indoors. **Other Job Characteristics:** Importance of Being Sure All Is Done; Importance of Being Exact or Accurate; Consequence of Error.

Experience: Job Zone 4. A minimum of two to four years of work-related skill, knowledge, or experience is needed. **Job Preparation:** SVP 7.0 to less than 8.0—2 years to less than 10 years.

Knowledge: Mechanical; Design; Building and Construction; Engineering and Technology; Physics; Public Safety and Security. **Instructional Program:** 470303 Industrial Machinery Maintenance and Repairer.

Related DOT Jobs: 638.261-014 Machinery Erector; 638.281-018 Millwright; 638.281-022 Millwright Apprentice.

49-9045.00 Refractory Materials Repairers, Except Brickmasons (Refractory Materials Repairers, Except Brickmasons)

Education: No data available.

Employed: 2,040

Openings: No data available.

Projected Growth: No data available.

Earnings: $29,600

Build or repair furnaces, kilns, cupolas, boilers, converters, ladles, soaking pits, and ovens, using refractory materials.

Transfers clay structures to curing ovens, melting tanks, and drawing kilns, using electric forklift truck. Bolts sections of wooden mold together, using wrench, and lines mold with paper to prevent adherence of clay to mold. Drills holes in furnace wall, bolts overlapping layers of plastic to walls, and hammers surface to compress layers into solid sheets. Tightens locknuts holding assembly together, spreads mortar on jacket to seal sleeve joints, and dries mortar in oven. Spreads mortar on stopper head and rod, using trowel, and slides brick sleeves over rod to form refractory jacket. Fastens stopper head to rod with metal pin, to assemble refractory stopper used to plug pouring nozzles of steel ladles. Dries and bakes new lining by placing inverted lining over burner, building fire in ladle, or by using blowtorch. Disassembles mold, and cuts, chips, and smoothes clay structures such as floaters, drawbars, and L-blocks, using square rule and hand tools. Removes worn or damaged plastic block refractory lining of furnace, using hand tools. Measures furnace wall, and cuts required number of sheets from plastic block, using saw. Climbs scaffolding with hose, and sprays surfaces of cupola with refractory mixture, using spray equipment. Chips slag from lining of ladle, or entire lining when beyond repair, using hammer and chisel. Installs preformed metal scaffolding in interior of cupola, using hand tools. Mixes specified amounts of sand, clay, mortar powder, and water to form refractory clay or mortar, using shovel or mixing machine. Dumps and tamps clay in mold, using tamping tool. Relines or repairs ladle and pouring spout with refractory clay, using trowel. Installs clay structures in melting tanks and drawing kilns to control flow and temperature of molten glass, using hoists and hand tools.

GOE Number, Interest Area, and Work Group: 06.02.03; Construction, Mining, and Drilling; Construction: General. **Personality Type:** Realistic. Realistic occupations frequently involve work activities that include practical, hands-on problems and solutions. These occupations often deal with plants, animals, and real-world materials like wood, tools, and machinery. Many of the occupations require working outside and do not involve a lot of paperwork or working closely with others. **Work Values:** Moral Values; Independence; Company Policies and Practices; Activity;

Security. **Skills:** Repairing; Operation and Control; Equipment Selection; Mathematics; Problem Identification; Product Inspection; Installation. **Abilities:** *Cognitive*—Information Ordering; Visualization; Number Facility; Problem Sensitivity; Deductive Reasoning. *Psychomotor*—Multilimb Coordination; Control Precision; Manual Dexterity; Wrist-Finger Speed. *Physical*—Extent Flexibility; Static Strength; Dynamic Strength. *Sensory*—Depth Perception; Far Vision; Auditory Attention. **General Work Activities:** *Information Input*—Inspecting Equipment, Structures, Materials; Getting Information Needed to Do the Job; Monitoring Processes, Materials, and Surroundings. *Mental Process*—Making Decisions and Solving Problems; Judging Qualities of Things, Services, Other People's Work; Evaluating Information Against Standards. *Work Output*—Handling and Moving Objects; Performing General Physical Activities; Controlling Machines and Processes. *Interacting with Others*—Establishing and Maintaining Relationships; Performing for or Working with the Public; Communicating with Other Workers; Coordinating Work and Activities of Others. **Physical Work Conditions:** Using Hands on Objects, Tools, or Controls; Common Protective or Safety Attire; Hazardous Equipment; Indoors; Standing. **Other Job Characteristics:** Consequence of Error; Importance of Being Sure All Is Done; Frustrating Circumstances; Importance of Being Exact or Accurate.

Experience: Job Zone 1. No previous work-related skill, knowledge, or experience is needed. **Job Preparation:** SVP Below 4.0—Less than 6 months. **Knowledge:** Building and Construction; Mechanical; Engineering and Technology; Physics; Production and Processing; Chemistry. **Instructional Program:** 470303 Industrial Machinery Maintenance and Repairer.

Related DOT Jobs: 519.684-010 Ladle Liner; 519.684-022 Stopper Maker; 579.664-010 Clay-Structure Builder and Servicer; 849.484-010 Boiler Reliner, Plastic Block; 899.684-010 Bondactor-Machine Operator.

49-9051.00 Electrical Power-Line Installers and Repairers (Electrical Powerline Installers and Repairers)

Education: Long-term O-T-J training

Employed: 98,758

Openings: 5,616

Projected Growth: 1.1%

Earnings: $42,600

Install or repair cables or wires used in electrical power or distribution systems. Erect poles and light- or heavy-duty transmission towers.

Cleans, tins, and splices corresponding conductors by twisting ends together or by joining ends with metal clamps and soldering connection. Replaces and straightens poles and attaches crossarms, insulators, and auxiliary equipment to wood poles preparatory to erection. Splices, solders, and insulates conductors and wiring, to join sections of power line and to connect transformers and electrical accessories. Splices cables together or to overhead transmission line, customer-service line, or streetlight line. Opens switches or clamps grounding device, to deenergize disturbed or fallen lines, to facilitate repairs, or to remove electrical hazards. Tests electric power lines and auxiliary equipment, using direct reading and testing instruments to identify cause of disturbances. Cuts and peels lead sheath and insulation from defective or newly installed cables and conducts prior to splicing. Installs watt-hour meters and connects service drops between power line and consumer. Covers conductors with insulating or fireproofing materials. Works on energized lines to avoid interruption of service. Drives conveyance equipped with tools and materials to job site. Strings wire conductors and cable between erected poles; adjusts slack, using winch. Climbs poles and removes and installs hardware, wires, and other equipment. Repairs electrical power cables and auxiliary equipment for electrical power lines. Installs and repairs conduits, cables, wires, and auxiliary equipment, following blueprints. Tests conductors to identify corresponding conductors and to prevent incorrect connections, according to electrical diagrams and specifications.

GOE Number, Interest Area, and Work Group: 05.02.01; Mechanics, Installers, and Repairers; Electrical and Electronic Systems: Installation and Repair. **Personality Type:** Realistic. Realistic occupations frequently involve work activities that include practical, hands-on problems and solutions. These occupations often deal with plants, animals, and real-world materials like wood, tools, and machinery. Many of the occupations require working outside and do not involve a lot of paperwork or working closely with others. **Work Values:** Moral Values; Security; Supervision, Technical; Supervision, Human Relations; Company Policies and Practices. **Skills:** Installation; Troubleshooting; Repairing; Equipment Maintenance; Product Inspection. **Abilities:** *Cognitive*—Information Ordering; Visualization; Perceptual Speed; Problem Sensitivity; Time Sharing; Spatial Orientation. *Psychomotor*—Arm-Hand Steadiness; Manual Dexterity; Multilimb Coordination; Finger Dexterity; Control Precision. *Physical*—Dynamic Strength; Extent Flexibility; Static Strength. *Sensory*—Near Vision; Visual Color Discrimination; Far Vision. **General Work Activities:** *Information Input*—Inspecting Equipment, Structures, Materials; Monitoring Processes, Materials, and Surroundings; Getting Information Needed to Do the Job; Identifying Objects, Actions, and Events. *Mental Process*—Judging Qualities of Things, Services, Other People's Work; Updating and Using Job-Relevant Knowledge; Analyzing Data or Information; Evaluating Information Against Standards. *Work Output*—Performing General Physical Activities; Repairing and Maintaining Electrical Equipment; Handling and Moving Objects. *Interacting with Others*—Communicating with Other Workers; Performing for or Working with the Public; Coordinating Work and Activities of Others. **Physical Work Conditions:** Outdoors; Using Hands on Objects, Tools, or Controls; Common Protective or Safety Attire. **Other Job Characteristics:** Consequence of Error; Importance of Being Sure All Is Done; Importance of Being Exact or Accurate.

Experience: Job Zone 4. A minimum of two to four years of work-related skill, knowledge, or experience is needed. **Job Preparation:** SVP 7.0 to less than 8.0—2 years to less than 10 years. **Knowledge:** Mechanical; Building and Construction; Transportation; Public Safety and Security; Design; Engineering and Technology. **Instructional Programs:** 460301 Electrical and Power Transmission Installer, General; 460303 Lineworker; 460399 Electrical and Power Transmission Installer, Other.

Related DOT Jobs: 821.261-014 Line Maintainer; 821.261-022 Service Restorer, Emergency; 821.261-026 Trouble Shooter II; 821.361-010 Cable Installer-Repairer; 821.361-018 Line Erector; 821.361-022 Line Installer, Street Railway; 821.361-026 Line Repairer; 821.361-030 Line-Erector Apprentice; 821.361-038 Tower Erector; 821.684-022 Trolley-Wire Installer; 825.381-038 Third-Rail Installer; 829.361-010 Cable Splicer; 829.361-014 Cable-Splicer Apprentice.

49-9052.00 Telecommunications Line Installers and Repairers (Telephone and Cable TV Line Installers and Repairers)

Education:	Long-term O-T-J training
Employed:	180,224
Openings:	18,246
Projected Growth:	30.3%
Earnings:	$32,750

String and repair telephone and television cable, including fiber optics and other equipment, for transmitting messages or television programming.

Pulls lines through ducts by hand or with use of winch. Computes impedance of wire from pole to house to determine additional resistance needed for reducing signal to desired level. Ascends poles or enters tunnels and sewers to string lines and install terminal boxes, auxiliary equipment, and appliances, according to diagrams. Repairs cable system, defective lines, and auxiliary equipment. Installs and removes plant equipment such as callboxes and clocks. Digs holes, using power auger or shovel; hoists poles upright into holes, using truck-mounted winch. Cleans and maintains tools and test equipment. Explains cable service to subscriber. Collects installation fees. Connects television set to cable system, evaluates incoming signal, and adjusts system to ensure optimum reception. Measures signal strength at utility pole, using electronic test equipment. Installs terminal boxes and strings lead-in wires, using electrician's tools. Fills and tamps holes, using cement, earth, and tamping device.

GOE Number, Interest Area, and Work Group: 05.02.01; Mechanics, Installers, and Repairers; Electrical and Electronic Systems: Installation and Repair. **Personality Type:** Realistic. Realistic occupations frequently involve work activities that include practical, hands-on problems and solutions. These occupations often deal with plants, animals, and real-world materials like wood, tools, and machinery. Many of the occupations require working outside and do not involve a lot of paperwork or working closely with others. **Work Values:** Moral Values; Security; Supervision, Technical; Independence; Supervision, Human Relations. **Skills:** Installation; Problem Identification; Repairing; Troubleshooting; Active Listening; Equipment Maintenance; Mathematics. **Abilities:** *Cognitive*—Oral Comprehension; Oral Expression; Information Ordering; Deductive Reasoning; Problem Sensitivity. *Psychomotor*—Manual Dexterity; Control Precision; Arm-Hand Steadiness. *Physical*—Static Strength; Trunk Strength; Extent Flexibility; Gross Body Coordination. *Sensory*—Visual Color Discrimination; Depth Perception. **General Work Activities:** *Information Input*—Getting Information Needed to Do the Job; Identifying Objects, Actions, and Events; Inspecting Equipment, Structures, Materials; Monitoring Processes, Materials, and Surroundings.

Mental Process—Evaluating Information Against Standards; Updating and Using Job-Relevant Knowledge; Making Decisions and Solving Problems; Processing Information. *Work Output*—Repairing and Maintaining Electrical Equipment; Performing General Physical Activities; Handling and Moving Objects. *Interacting with Others*—Communicating with Other Workers; Communicating with Persons Outside Organization; Establishing and Maintaining Relationships; Interpreting Meaning of Information to Others. **Physical Work Conditions:** Outdoors; Using Hands on Objects, Tools, or Controls; Standing; Kneeling, Crouching, or Crawling. **Other Job Characteristics:** Importance of Being Sure All Is Done; Consequence of Error; Importance of Being Exact or Accurate.

Experience: Job Zone 3. Previous work-related skill, knowledge, or experience is required. **Job Preparation:** SVP 6.0 to less than 7.0—More than 1 year and less than 4 years. **Knowledge:** Telecommunications; Computers and Electronics; Mechanical; Engineering and Technology; Mathematics. **Instructional Programs:** 460301 Electrical and Power Transmission Installer, General; 460303 Lineworker; 470103 Communication Systems Installer and Repairer.

Related DOT Jobs: 821.281-010 Cable Television Installer; 822.381-014 Line Installer-Repairer.

49-9061.00 Camera and Photographic Equipment Repairers (Camera and Photographic Equipment Repairers)

Education: Moderate-term O-T-J training
Employed: 9,029
Openings: 1,488
Projected Growth: 8.2%
Earnings: $28,320

Repair and adjust cameras and photographic equipment, including commercial video and motion-picture camera equipment.

Fabricates or modifies defective electronic, electrical, and mechanical components, using bench lathe, milling machine, shaper, grinder, and precision hand tools according to specifications. Reads and interprets engineering drawings, diagrams, instructions, and specifications to determine needed repairs, fabrication method, and operation sequence. Assembles aircraft cameras, still and motion picture cameras, photographic equipment, and frames, using diagrams, blueprints, bench machines, hand tools, and power tools. Installs film in aircraft camera and electrical assemblies and wiring in camera housing, following blueprints, using hand tools and soldering equipment. Lays out reference points and dimensions on parts and metal stock to be machined, using precision measuring instruments. Cleans and lubricates cameras and polishes camera lenses, using cleaning materials and work aids. Records test data and documents fabrication techniques on reports. Measures parts to verify specified dimensions/settings, such as camera shutter speed and light meter reading accuracy, using measuring instruments. Recommends design changes or upgrades of microfilming, film-developing, and photographic equipment. Tests equipment performance, focus of lens system, alignment of diaphragm, lens mounts, and film transport, using precision gauges. Calibrates and verifies accuracy of light meters, shutter diaphragm operation, and lens carriers, using timing instruments. Disassembles equipment to gain access to defect, using hand tools. Examines cameras, equipment, processed film, and laboratory reports to diagnose malfunction, using work aids and specifications. Adjusts cameras, photographic mechanisms, and equipment such as range and view finders, shutters, light meters, and lens systems, using hand tools. Requisitions parts and materials.

GOE Number, Interest Area, and Work Group: 05.03.03; Mechanics, Installers, and Repairers; Mechanical Work: Medical and Technical Equipment Fabrication and Repair. **Personality Type:** Realistic. Realistic occupations frequently involve work activities that include practical, hands-on problems and solutions. These occupations often deal with plants, animals, and real-world materials like wood, tools, and machinery. Many of the occupations require working outside and do not involve a lot of paperwork or working closely with others. **Work Values:** Moral Values; Working Conditions; Security; Autonomy; Independence; Ability Utilization. **Skills:** Reading Comprehension; Problem Identification; Repairing; Speaking; Troubleshooting. **Abilities:** *Cognitive*—Deductive Reasoning; Information Ordering; Problem Sensitivity; Visualization; Written Comprehension; Oral Expression. *Psychomotor*—Finger Dexterity; Control Precision; Arm-Hand Steadiness. *Physical*—Extent Flexibility; Dynamic Flexibility; Static Strength. *Sensory*—Near Vision; Speech Clarity; Visual Color Discrimination. **General Work Activities:** *Information Input*—Getting Information Needed to Do the Job; Inspecting Equipment, Structures, Materials; Identifying Objects, Actions, and Events. *Mental Process*—Analyzing Data or Information; Making Decisions and Solving Problems; Updating and Using Job-Relevant Knowledge; Evaluating Information Against Standards. *Work Output*—Repairing and Maintaining Mechanical Equipment; Handling and Moving Objects; Repairing and Maintaining Electrical Equipment. *Interacting with Others*—Communicating with Persons Outside Organization; Establishing and Maintaining Relationships; Providing Consultation and Advice to Others; Performing for or Working with the Public. **Physical Work Conditions:** Using Hands on Objects, Tools, or Controls; Indoors; Sitting. **Other Job Characteristics:** Degree of Automation; Importance of Being Exact or Accurate; Importance of Being Sure All Is Done.

Experience: Job Zone 4. A minimum of two to four years of work-related skill, knowledge, or experience is needed. **Job Preparation:** SVP 7.0 to less than 8.0—2 years to less than 10 years. **Knowledge:** Mechanical; Engineering and Technology; Computers and Electronics; Mathematics; Design. **Instructional Programs:** 470103 Communication Systems Installer and Repairer; 470499 Miscellaneous Mechanics and Repairers, Other.

Related DOT Jobs: 714.281-010 Aircraft-Photographic-Equipment Mechanic; 714.281-014 Camera Repairer; 714.281-018 Machinist, Motion-Picture Equipment; 714.281-022 Photographic Equipment Technician; 714.281-026 Photographic-Equipment-Maintenance Technician; 714.281-030 Service Technician, Computerized-Photofinishing Equipment; 826.261-010 Field-Service Engineer.

49-9062.00 Medical Equipment Repairers (Medical Equipment Repairers)

Education: Long-term O-T-J training

Employed: 10,715

Openings: 1,675

Projected Growth: 13.5%

Earnings: $34,190

Test, adjust, or repair biomedical or electromedical equipment.

Demonstrates and explains correct operation of equipment to medical personnel. Maintains various equipment and apparatus such as patient monitors, electrocardiographs, X-ray units, defibrillators, electrosurgical units, anesthesia apparatus, pacemakers, and sterilizers. Repairs and replaces defective parts such as motors, clutches, tubes, transformers, resistors, condensers, and switches, using hand tools. Disassembles malfunctioning equipment and removes defective components. Solders loose connections, using soldering iron. Installs medical, dental, and related technical equipment in medical and research facilities. Inspects and tests malfunctioning medical and related equipment, using test and analysis instruments and following manufacturers' specifications. Cleans and lubricates equipment, using solvents, rags, and lubricants. Consults with medical or research staff to ensure that equipment functions properly and safely. Safety-tests medical equipment and facility's structural environment to ensure patient and staff safety from electrical or mechanical hazards. Calibrates and adjusts components and equipment, using hand tools, power tools, and measuring devices, and following manufacturers' manuals and troubleshooting techniques. Logs records of maintenance and repair work and approved updates of equipment as required by manufacturer.

GOE Number, Interest Area, and Work Group: 05.03.03; Mechanics, Installers, and Repairers; Mechanical Work: Medical and Technical Equipment Fabrication and Repair. **Personality Type:** Realistic. Realistic occupations frequently involve work activities that include practical, hands-on problems and solutions. These occupations often deal with plants, animals, and real-world materials like wood, tools, and machinery. Many of the occupations require working outside and do not involve a lot of paperwork or working closely with others. **Work Values:** Moral Values; Security; Activity; Compensation; Company Policies and Practices. **Skills:** Installation; Repairing; Equipment Maintenance; Troubleshooting; Instructing. **Abilities:** *Cognitive*—Deductive Reasoning; Problem Sensitivity; Oral Expression; Inductive Reasoning; Visualization; Written Comprehension. *Psychomotor*—Finger Dexterity; Control Precision; Arm-Hand Steadiness. *Physical*—Extent Flexibility; Static Strength; Explosive Strength. *Sensory*—Speech Clarity; Near Vision; Visual Color Discrimination. **General Work Activities:** *Information Input*—Inspecting Equipment, Structures, Materials; Getting Information Needed to Do the Job; Monitoring Processes, Materials, and Surroundings. *Mental Process*—Updating and Using Job-Relevant Knowledge; Evaluating Information Against Standards; Analyzing Data or Information. *Work Output*—Repairing and Maintaining Electrical Equipment; Repairing and Maintaining Mechanical Equipment; Handling and Moving Objects. *Interacting with Others*—Teaching Others; Communicating with Persons Outside Organization; Interpreting Meaning of Information to Others; Communicating with Other Workers. **Physical Work Conditions:** Indoors; Using Hands on Objects, Tools, or Controls; Hazardous Situations; Hazardous Equipment. **Other Job Characteristics:** Consequence of Error; Importance of Being Sure All Is Done; Importance of Being Exact or Accurate.

Experience: Job Zone 3. Previous work-related skill, knowledge, or experience is required. **Job Preparation:** SVP 6.0 to less than 7.0—More than 1 year and less than 4 years. **Knowledge:** Mechanical; Engineering and Technology; Computers and Electronics; Mathematics; Design. **Instructional Program:** 150401 Biomedical Engineering-Related Technology/Technician.

Related DOT Jobs: 019.261-010 Biomedical Equipment Technician; 639.281-022 Medical-Equipment Repairer; 719.261-014 Radiological-Equipment Specialist; 729.281-030 Electromedical-Equipment Repairer; 829.261-014 Dental-Equipment Installer and Servicer.

49-9063.00 Musical Instrument Repairers and Tuners (Musical Instrument Repairers and Tuners)

Education: Long-term O-T-J training

Employed: 12,591

Openings: 2,037

Projected Growth: 6.5%

Earnings: $23,010

Repair percussion, stringed, reed, or wind instruments. Specialize in one area, such as piano tuning.

GOE Number, Interest Area, and Work Group: 05.03.04; Mechanics, Installers, and Repairers; Mechanical Work: Musical Instrument Fabrication and Repair. **Instructional Program:** 470404 Musical Instrument Repairer. **Note:** The Department of Labor has not collected some data for this job, so it has fewer details than the other descriptions.

49-9063.01 Keyboard Instrument Repairers and Tuners (Musical Instrument Repairers and Tuners)

Education: Long-term O-T-J training

Employed: 12,591

Openings: 2,037

Projected Growth: 6.5%

Earnings: $23,010

Repair, adjust, refinish, and tune musical keyboard instruments.

Mixes and measures glue. Adjusts lips, reeds, or toe hole of organ pipes, using hand tools, to regulate airflow and loudness of sound. Adjusts alignment, string spacing, and striking point of hammers of piano, using wrench, burner, shims, and bushings. Inspects and tests parts of pianos, pipe organs, accordions, and concertinas to determine defects, using hand tools, gauges, and electronic testing equipment. Makes wood replacement parts, using woodworking machines and hand tools. Adjusts felt hammers on piano to increase tonal mellowness or brilliance, using sanding paddle, lacquer, or needles. Cleans instruments, using vacuum cleaner. Compares pitch of instruments with specified pitch of tuning tool to tune instrument. Removes irregularities from tuning pins, strings, and hammers of piano, using wood block or filing tool. Disassembles and reassembles instruments and parts to tune and repair, using hand tools and power tools. Repairs or replaces defective, broken, or worn parts, using hand tools, power tools, glue, and nails. Assembles and installs new pipe organs and pianos in buildings.

GOE Number, Interest Area, and Work Group: 05.03.04; Mechanics, Installers, and Repairers; Mechanical Work: Musical Instrument Fabrication and Repair. **Personality Type:** Realistic. Realistic occupations frequently involve work activities that include practical, hands-on problems and solutions. These occupations often deal with plants, animals, and real-world materials like wood, tools, and machinery. Many of the occupations require working outside and do not involve a lot of paperwork or working closely with others. **Work Values:** Moral Values; Independence; Working Conditions; Autonomy; Company Policies and Practices; Responsibility; Security. **Skills:** Repairing; Problem Identification; Installation; Product Inspection; Equipment Selection. **Abilities:** *Cognitive*—Problem Sensitivity; Information Ordering; Deductive Reasoning; Visualization; Category Flexibility. *Psychomotor*—Wrist-Finger Speed; Control Precision; Finger Dexterity. *Physical*—Extent Flexibility; Dynamic Flexibility; Static Strength. *Sensory*—Hearing Sensitivity; Sound Localization; Auditory Attention. **General Work Activities:** *Information Input*—Inspecting Equipment, Structures, Materials; Getting Information Needed to Do the Job; Identifying Objects, Actions, and Events. *Mental Process*—Judging Qualities of Things, Services, Other People's Work; Analyzing Data or Information; Making Decisions and Solving Problems. *Work Output*—Repairing and Maintaining Mechanical Equipment; Handling and Moving Objects; Implementing Ideas and Programs. *Interacting with Others*—Communicating with Persons Outside Organization; Monitoring and Controlling Resources; Communicating with Other Workers; Performing Administrative Activities. **Physical Work Conditions:** Indoors; Using Hands on Objects, Tools, or Controls; Making Repetitive Motions. **Other Job Characteristics:** Importance of Being Exact or Accurate; Importance of Being Sure All Is Done; Consequence of Error.

Experience: Job Zone 3. Previous work-related skill, knowledge, or experience is required. **Job Preparation:** SVP 6.0 to less than 7.0—More than 1 year and less than 4 years. **Knowledge:** Mechanical; Engineering and Technology; Computers and Electronics; Fine Arts; Building and Construction. **Instructional Program:** 470404 Musical Instrument Repairer.

Related DOT Jobs: 730.281-014 Accordion Repairer; 730.281-038 Piano Technician; 730.361-010 Piano Tuner; 730.361-014 Pipe-Organ Tuner and Repairer; 730.381-010 Accordion Tuner; 730.381-038 Organ-Pipe Voicer; 730.681-010 Piano Regulator-Inspector; 730.684-026 Chip Tuner; 730.684-094 Tone Regulator.

49-9063.02 Stringed Instrument Repairers and Tuners (Musical Instrument Repairers and Tuners)

Education: Long-term O-T-J training
Employed: 12,591
Openings: 2,037
Projected Growth: 6.5%
Earnings: $23,010

Repair, adjust, refinish, and tune musical stringed instruments.

Assembles instruments according to specifications, using hand tools. Reassembles instrument or bow with new or repaired part, using glue, hairs, yarn, resin, and clamps. Inspects musical instruments, such as cellos, violins, guitars, and mandolins, to determine defects. Carves wood replacement parts, such as wedges or plugs, according to the shape and dimensions of the instrument or bow. Plays instrument to determine pitch. Tests tubes and pickups in electronic amplifier units, and solders parts and connections. Removes cracked, worn, or broken parts of instrument, using heated knife and hand tools. Disassembles instrument or bow, using hand tools. Adjusts string tension to tune instrument, using hand tools and electronic tuning device. Refinishes instruments to protect and decorate them, using hand tools, buffing tools, and varnish. Repairs broken parts, using glue, clamp, and handpress. Strings instrument and adjusts truss and bridge of instrument to obtain specified string tension and height.

GOE Number, Interest Area, and Work Group: 05.03.04; Mechanics, Installers, and Repairers; Mechanical Work: Musical Instrument Fabrication and Repair. **Personality Type:** Realistic. Realistic occupations frequently involve work activities that include practical, hands-on problems and solutions. These occupations often deal with plants, animals, and real-world materials like wood, tools, and machinery. Many of the occupations require working outside and do not involve a lot of paperwork or working closely with others. **Work Values:** Moral Values; Independence; Working Conditions; Ability Utilization; Autonomy. **Skills:** Repairing; Product Inspection; Problem Identification; Equipment Maintenance; Equipment Selection; Monitoring. **Abilities:** *Cognitive*—Information Ordering; Visualization; Deductive Reasoning; Problem Sensitivity; Perceptual Speed. *Psychomotor*—Arm-Hand Steadiness; Control Precision; Finger Dexterity; Manual Dexterity; Wrist-Finger Speed. *Physical*—Extent Flexibility; Static Strength; Trunk Strength. *Sensory*—Hearing Sensitivity; Auditory Attention; Sound Localization. **General Work Activities:** *Information Input*—Inspecting Equipment, Structures, Materials; Identifying Objects, Actions, and Events; Getting Information Needed to Do the Job. *Mental Process*—Judging Qualities of Things, Services, Other People's Work; Evaluating Information Against Standards; Analyzing Data or Information; Thinking Creatively. *Work Output*—Handling and Moving Objects; Repairing and Maintaining Mechanical Equipment; Repairing and Maintaining Electrical Equipment; Implementing Ideas and Programs; Controlling Machines and Processes. *Interacting with Others*—Communicating with Other Workers; Communicating with Persons Outside Organization; Monitoring and Controlling Resources. **Physical Work Conditions:** Indoors; Using Hands on Objects, Tools, or Controls; Sitting. **Other Job Characteristics:** Importance of Being Sure All Is Done; Importance of Being Exact or Accurate; Consequence of Error.

Experience: Job Zone 3. Previous work-related skill, knowledge, or experience is required. **Job Preparation:** SVP 6.0 to less than 7.0—More than 1 year and less than 4 years. **Knowledge:** Fine Arts; Mechanical; Building and Construction; Engineering and Technology; Physics. **Instructional Program:** 470404 Musical Instrument Repairer.

Related DOT Jobs: 730.281-026 Fretted-Instrument Repairer; 730.281-050 Violin Repairer; 730.381-026 Harp Regulator; 730.684-022 Bow Rehairer.

49-9063.03 Reed or Wind Instrument Repairers and Tuners (Musical Instrument Repairers and Tuners)

Education: Long-term O-T-J training
Employed: 12,591
Openings: 2,037
Projected Growth: 6.5%
Earnings: $23,010

Repair, adjust, refinish, and tune musical reed and wind instruments.

Removes dents and burrs from metal instruments, using mallet and burnishing tool. Repairs cracks in wood or metal instruments, using wire, lathe, filler, clamps, or soldering iron. Replaces worn pads and springs, using hand tools. Inspects mechanical parts of instrument to determine defects. Compares pitch of reed with pitch of tuning bar. Polishes instrument, using rag and polishing compound, buffing wheel, or burnishing tool. Operates bellows to sound metal reed and ascertain its pitch. Lubricates and reassembles instrument, using hand tools and soldering iron or torch. Files reed until pitch corresponds with standard pitch of tuning bar. Disassembles instrument parts such as keys, pistons, and other parts, to tune or repair, using gas torch and hand tools. Shapes old parts and replacement parts to improve tone or intonation, using hand tools, lathe, or soldering iron. Washes metal instruments in lacquer-stripping and cyanide solution to remove lacquer and tarnish.

GOE Number, Interest Area, and Work Group: 05.03.04; Mechanics, Installers, and Repairers; Mechanical Work: Musical Instrument Fabrication and Repair. **Personality Type:** Realistic. Realistic occupations frequently involve work activities that include practical, hands-on problems and solutions. These occupations often deal with plants, animals, and real-world materials like wood, tools, and machinery. Many of the occupations require working outside and do not involve a lot of paperwork or working closely with others. **Work Values:** Moral Values; Independence; Working Conditions; Autonomy; Security; Responsibility; Ability Utilization. **Skills:** Repairing; Problem Identification; Equipment Selection; Troubleshooting; Testing; Monitoring; Product Inspection. **Abilities:** *Cognitive*—Information Ordering; Problem Sensitivity; Visualization; Inductive Reasoning; Deductive Reasoning; Perceptual Speed. *Psychomotor*—Finger Dexterity; Arm-Hand Steadiness; Wrist-Finger Speed; Manual Dexterity. *Physical*—Extent Flexibility; Static Strength; Dynamic Strength; Trunk Strength. *Sensory*—Hearing Sensitivity; Auditory Attention; Near Vision. **General Work Activities:** *Information Input*—Inspecting Equipment, Structures, Materials; Identifying Objects, Actions, and Events; Getting Information Needed to Do the Job. *Mental Process*—Judging Qualities of Things, Services, Other People's Work; Analyzing Data or Information; Evaluating Information Against Standards. *Work Output*—Handling and Moving Objects; Repairing and Maintaining Mechanical Equipment; Controlling Machines and Processes. *Interacting with Others*—Monitoring and Controlling Resources; Establishing and Maintaining Relationships; Performing Administrative Activities; Communicating with Persons Outside Organization; Providing Consultation and Advice to Others; Performing for or Working with the Public. **Physi-**cal Work Conditions: Indoors; Using Hands on Objects, Tools, or Controls; Sitting. **Other Job Characteristics:** Importance of Being Sure All Is Done; Importance of Being Exact or Accurate; Consequence of Error.

Experience: Job Zone 4. A minimum of two to four years of work-related skill, knowledge, or experience is needed. **Job Preparation:** SVP 7.0 to less than 8.0—2 years to less than 10 years. **Knowledge:** Mechanical; Engineering and Technology; Fine Arts; Physics; Chemistry; Production and Processing. **Instructional Program:** 470404 Musical Instrument Repairer.

Related DOT Jobs: 730.281-054 Wind-Instrument Repairer; 730.381-034 Metal-Reed Tuner.

49-9063.04 Percussion Instrument Repairers and Tuners (Musical Instrument Repairers and Tuners)

Education: Long-term O-T-J training
Employed: 12,591
Openings: 2,037
Projected Growth: 6.5%
Earnings: $23,010

Repair and tune musical percussion instruments.

Removes drumhead, using drum key and cutting tools. Repairs breaks in percussion instruments such as drums and cymbals, using drill press, power saw, glues, clamps, or other hand tools. Places rim hoop back onto drum shell to allow drumhead to dry and become taut. Cuts new drumhead from animal skin, using scissors. Soaks drumhead in water to make it pliable. Removes material from bar, using bandsaw, sanding machine, machine grinder, or hand files and scrapers, to obtain the specified tone. Solders or welds frames of mallet instruments and metal drum parts. Cleans, sands, and paints parts of percussion instruments to maintain their condition, in accordance to blueprints and shop drawings. Compares tone of bar with tuned block, stroboscope, or electronic tuner. Removes dents in tympani, using steel block and hammer. Stretches skin over rim hoop, using hand tucking tool. Assembles bar onto instruments. Strikes wood, fiberglass, or metal bars of instruments such as xylophones or vibraharps, to ascertain tone.

GOE Number, Interest Area, and Work Group: 05.03.04; Mechanics, Installers, and Repairers; Mechanical Work: Musical Instrument Fabrication and Repair. **Personality Type:** Realistic. Realistic occupations frequently involve work activities that include practical, hands-on problems and solutions. These occupations often deal with plants, animals, and real-world materials like wood, tools, and machinery. Many of the occupations require working outside and do not involve a lot of paperwork or working closely with others. **Work Values:** Moral Values; Independence; Working Conditions; Autonomy; Responsibility; Security; Ability Utilization. **Skills:** Testing; Repairing; Equipment Selection; Equipment Maintenance; Monitoring; Active Listening; Product Inspection. **Abilities:** *Cognitive*—Information Ordering; Visualization; Problem Sensitivity; Written Comprehension; Inductive Reasoning. *Psychomotor*—Manual Dexterity; Finger Dexterity; Control Precision; Wrist-Finger Speed. *Physical*—Trunk Strength; Extent Flexibility; Static Strength. *Sensory*—Hearing

Sensitivity; Near Vision; Auditory Attention. **General Work Activities:** *Information Input*—Inspecting Equipment, Structures, Materials; Getting Information Needed to Do the Job; Monitoring Processes, Materials, and Surroundings. *Mental Process*—Judging Qualities of Things, Services, Other People's Work; Evaluating Information Against Standards; Analyzing Data or Information. *Work Output*—Handling and Moving Objects; Implementing Ideas and Programs; Controlling Machines and Processes. *Interacting with Others*—Monitoring and Controlling Resources; Providing Consultation and Advice to Others; Performing for or Working with the Public; Interpreting Meaning of Information to Others. **Physical Work Conditions:** Using Hands on Objects, Tools, or Controls; Indoors; Sitting. **Other Job Characteristics:** Importance of Being Exact or Accurate; Importance of Being Sure All Is Done; Consequence of Error.

Experience: Job Zone 3. Previous work-related skill, knowledge, or experience is required. **Job Preparation:** SVP 6.0 to less than 7.0—More than 1 year and less than 4 years. **Knowledge:** Mechanical; Fine Arts; Engineering and Technology; Design; Building and Construction; Physics. **Instructional Program:** 470404 Musical Instrument Repairer.

Related DOT Jobs: 730.381-042 Percussion-Instrument Repairer; 730.381-058 Tuner, Percussion.

49-9064.00 Watch Repairers (Watch Repairers)

Education: Long-term O-T-J training

Employed: 8,449

Openings: 1,244

Projected Growth: –4.2%

Earnings: $24,580

Repair, clean, and adjust mechanisms of timing instruments such as watches and clocks.

Repairs watch cases, surface defects of clocks, and watch bands. Tests accuracy of balance wheel assembly and adjusts timing regulator, using truing calipers, watch-rate recorder, and tweezers. Cleans, rinses, and dries parts, using watch-cleaning machine. Assembles mechanism; oils moving parts; demagnetizes mechanism, using demagnetizing machine. Removes mechanism from case and disassembles parts such as hands, springs, or wheels, using hand tools. Estimates cost of watch for repair. Examines watch mechanism, case, and parts for defects or foreign matter, using loupe (magnifier). Tests and replaces batteries and other electronic components. Repairs or replaces broken, damaged, or worn parts, using watchmaker's lathe, drill press, and hand tools. Records quantity and type of clocks repaired.

GOE Number, Interest Area, and Work Group: 05.03.03; Mechanics, Installers, and Repairers; Mechanical Work: Medical and Technical Equipment Fabrication and Repair. **Personality Type:** Realistic. Realistic occupations frequently involve work activities that include practical, hands-on problems and solutions. These occupations often deal with plants, animals, and real-world materials like wood, tools, and machinery. Many of the occupations require working outside and do not involve a lot of paperwork or working closely with others. **Work Values:** Moral Values; Independence; Working Conditions; Ability Utilization; Security.

Skills: Repairing; Product Inspection; Troubleshooting; Equipment Maintenance; Problem Identification. **Abilities:** *Cognitive*—Number Facility; Mathematical Reasoning; Deductive Reasoning; Problem Sensitivity; Information Ordering. *Psychomotor*—Finger Dexterity; Arm-Hand Steadiness; Manual Dexterity. *Physical*—none met the criteria. *Sensory*—Near Vision; Glare Sensitivity. **General Work Activities:** *Information Input*—Inspecting Equipment, Structures, Materials; Monitoring Processes, Materials, and Surroundings; Getting Information Needed to Do the Job. *Mental Process*—Analyzing Data or Information; Evaluating Information Against Standards; Making Decisions and Solving Problems. *Work Output*—Repairing and Maintaining Mechanical Equipment; Handling and Moving Objects; Controlling Machines and Processes. *Interacting with Others*—Communicating with Persons Outside Organization; Performing for or Working with the Public; Performing Administrative Activities. **Physical Work Conditions:** Using Hands on Objects, Tools, or Controls; Indoors; Sitting. **Other Job Characteristics:** Importance of Being Exact or Accurate; Importance of Being Sure All Is Done; Consequence of Error.

Experience: Job Zone 3. Previous work-related skill, knowledge, or experience is required. **Job Preparation:** SVP 6.0 to less than 7.0—More than 1 year and less than 4 years. **Knowledge:** Mechanical; Mathematics; Customer and Personal Service; Engineering and Technology; Clerical; Production and Processing. **Instructional Program:** 470408 Watch, Clock and Jewelry Repairer.

Related DOT Jobs: 715.281-010 Watch Repairer; 715.281-014 Watch Repairer Apprentice; 715.584-014 Repairer, Auto Clocks.

49-9091.00 Coin, Vending, and Amusement Machine Servicers and Repairers (Coin, Vending, and Amusement Machine Servicers and Repairers)

Education: Long-term O-T-J training

Employed: 27,015

Openings: 4,315

Projected Growth: 15.6%

Earnings: $23,260

Install, service, adjust, or repair coin, vending, or amusement machines, including video games, juke boxes, pinball machines, or slot machines.

Keeps records of machine maintenance and repair. Cleans and oils parts with soap and water, gasoline, kerosene, or carbon tetrachloride. Disassembles and assembles machines, following specifications and using hand tools and power tools. Examines and inspects vending machines and meters to determine cause of malfunction. Tests dispensing, coin-handling, electrical, refrigeration, carbonation, or ice-making systems of machine. Replenishes vending machines with ingredients or products. Shellacs or paints dial markings or mechanisms' exterior, using brush or spray gun. Adjusts and repairs vending machines and meters; replaces defective mechanical and electrical parts, using hand tools, soldering iron, and diagrams. Collects coins from machine and makes settlements with concessionaires.

GOE Number, Interest Area, and Work Group: 05.03.02; Mechanics, Installers, and Repairers; Mechanical Work: Machinery Repair. **Personality Type:** Realistic. Realistic occupations frequently involve work activities that include practical, hands-on problems and solutions. These occupations often deal with plants, animals, and real-world materials like wood, tools, and machinery. Many of the occupations require working outside and do not involve a lot of paperwork or working closely with others. **Work Values:** Moral Values; Independence; Security; Company Policies and Practices; Responsibility. **Skills:** Repairing; Problem Identification; Equipment Maintenance; Troubleshooting; Installation. **Abilities:** *Cognitive*—Number Facility; Problem Sensitivity; Information Ordering; Written Comprehension; Deductive Reasoning; Written Expression. *Psychomotor*—Wrist-Finger Speed; Finger Dexterity; Control Precision. *Physical*—Static Strength; Trunk Strength; Extent Flexibility. *Sensory*—Visual Color Discrimination; Auditory Attention; Peripheral Vision. **General Work Activities:** *Information Input*—Inspecting Equipment, Structures, Materials; Getting Information Needed to Do the Job; Monitoring Processes, Materials, and Surroundings; Identifying Objects, Actions, and Events. *Mental Process*—Making Decisions and Solving Problems; Processing Information; Evaluating Information Against Standards; Analyzing Data or Information. *Work Output*—Repairing and Maintaining Mechanical Equipment; Handling and Moving Objects; Performing General Physical Activities. *Interacting with Others*—Monitoring and Controlling Resources; Performing Administrative Activities; Communicating with Persons Outside Organization; Establishing and Maintaining Relationships. **Physical Work Conditions:** Indoors; Using Hands on Objects, Tools, or Controls; Standing. **Other Job Characteristics:** Importance of Being Exact or Accurate; Consequence of Error; Importance of Being Sure All Is Done.

Experience: Job Zone 2. Some previous work-related skill, knowledge, or experience may be helpful, but usually is not needed. **Job Preparation:** SVP 4.00 to 5.99—6 months to less than 2 years. **Knowledge:** Mechanical; Engineering and Technology; Computers and Electronics; Mathematics; English Language; Customer and Personal Service; Clerical. **Instructional Program:** 470199 Electrical and Electronics Equipment Installer and Repairer, Other.

Related DOT Jobs: 349.680-010 Ticket-Dispenser Changer; 639.281-014 Coin-Machine-Service Repairer; 710.384-026 Parking-Meter Servicer; 710.681-018 Register Repairer; 729.381-014 Pin-Game-Machine Inspector; 729.384-014 Fare-Register Repairer.

49-9092.00 Commercial Divers (All Other Mechanics, Installers, and Repairers)

Education: No data available.
Employed: 299,450
Openings: No data available.
Projected Growth: No data available.
Earnings: $28,260

Work below surface of water, using scuba gear to inspect, repair, remove, or install equipment and structures. Use a variety of power and hand tools such as drills, sledgehammers, torches, and welding equipment. Conduct tests or experiments, rig explosives, or photograph structures or marine life.

Drills holes in rock; rigs explosives for underwater demolitions. Recovers objects by placing rigging around sunken objects and hooking rigging to crane lines. Searches for lost or sunken objects such as bodies, torpedoes, equipment, and ships. Communicates with surface while underwater by signal line or telephone. Sets or guides placement of pilings and sandbags to provide support for structures such as docks, bridges, cofferdams, and platforms. Inspects docks, hulls, and propellers of ships; inspects underwater pipelines, cables, and sewers. Photographs underwater structures or marine life. Levels rails, using wedges and maul or sledgehammer. Repairs ships and other structures below the water line, using caulk, bolts, and hand tools. Cuts and welds steel using underwater welding equipment. Descends into water with aid of diver helper, using scuba gear or diving suit. Removes obstructions from strainers and marine railway or launching ways, using pneumatic and power hand tools.

GOE Number, Interest Area, and Work Group: 06.02.03; Construction, Mining, and Drilling; Construction: General. **Personality Type:** Realistic. Realistic occupations frequently involve work activities that include practical, hands-on problems and solutions. These occupations often deal with plants, animals, and real-world materials like wood, tools, and machinery. Many of the occupations require working outside and do not involve a lot of paperwork or working closely with others. **Work Values:** Moral Values; Ability Utilization; Variety; Responsibility; Achievement. **Skills:** Problem Identification; Repairing; Active Listening; Product Inspection; Coordination; Speaking; Information Gathering. **Abilities:** *Cognitive*—Spatial Orientation; Flexibility of Closure; Information Ordering; Problem Sensitivity; Perceptual Speed. *Psychomotor*—Manual Dexterity; Speed of Limb Movement; Arm-Hand Steadiness; Multilimb Coordination; Wrist-Finger Speed; Finger Dexterity. *Physical*—Gross Body Coordination; Stamina; Dynamic Strength. *Sensory*—Far Vision; Night Vision; Depth Perception. **General Work Activities:** *Information Input*—Inspecting Equipment, Structures, Materials; Identifying Objects, Actions, and Events; Monitoring Processes, Materials, and Surroundings; Getting Information Needed to Do the Job. *Mental Process*—Making Decisions and Solving Problems; Judging Qualities of Things, Services, Other People's Work; Organizing, Planning, and Prioritizing; Updating and Using Job-Relevant Knowledge; Analyzing Data or Information. *Work Output*—Performing General Physical Activities; Handling and Moving Objects; Repairing and Maintaining Mechanical Equipment. *Interacting with Others*—Communicating with Other Workers; Establishing and Maintaining Relationships; Performing Administrative Activities; Monitoring and Controlling Resources; Assisting and Caring for Others; Interpreting Meaning of Information to Others. **Physical Work Conditions:** Common Protective or Safety Attire; Outdoors; Specialized Protective or Safety Attire; Using Hands on Objects, Tools, or Controls. **Other Job Characteristics:** Consequence of Error; Importance of Being Sure All Is Done; Importance of Being Exact or Accurate.

Experience: Job Zone 2. Some previous work-related skill, knowledge, or experience may be helpful, but usually is not needed. **Job Preparation:** SVP 4.00 to 5.99—6 months to less than 2 years. **Knowledge:** Mechanical; Building and Construction; Engineering and Technology; Physics; Telecommunications. **Instructional Programs:** 460401 Building/Property Maintenance and Manager; 470499 Miscellaneous Mechanics and Repairers, Other.

Related DOT Jobs: 379.384-010 Scuba Diver; 899.261-010 Diver.

49-9093.00 Fabric Menders, Except Garment
(Menders, Garments, Linens, and Related)

Education: No data available.

Employed: 8,510

Openings: No data available.

Projected Growth: No data available.

Earnings: $15,990

Repair tears, holes, and other defects in fabrics such as draperies, linens, parachutes, and tents.

Sews fringe, tassels, and ruffles onto drapes and curtains; sews buttons and trimming onto garments. Pulls knots to wrong side of garment, using hook. Repairs holes by weaving thread over them, using needle. Reknits runs and replaces broken threads, using latch needle. Patches holes, sews tears and ripped seams, or darns defects in items, using needle and thread or sewing machine. Trims edges of cut or torn fabric, using scissors or knife, and stitches them together. Measures and hems curtains, garments, and canvas coverings to size, using tape measure. Sews labels and emblems on articles for identification. Stamps grommets into canvas, using mallet and punch or eyelet machine. Cleans stains from fabric or garment, using spray gun and cleaning fluid. Spreads out articles or material and examines for holes, tears, worn areas, and other marked or unmarked defects. Operates sewing machine to restitch defective seams, sew up holes, or replace garment pockets or blanket binding ribbons. Replaces defective shrouds and splices connections between shrouds and harness, using hand tools.

GOE Number, Interest Area, and Work Group: 11.06.01; Recreation, Travel, and Other Personal Services; Apparel, Shoes, Leather, and Fabric Care. **Personality Type:** Realistic. Realistic occupations frequently involve work activities that include practical, hands-on problems and solutions. These occupations often deal with plants, animals, and real-world materials like wood, tools, and machinery. Many of the occupations require working outside and do not involve a lot of paperwork or working closely with others. **Work Values:** Moral Values; Independence; Activity; Supervision, Technical; Security; Supervision, Human Relations. **Skills:** Product Inspection; Operation and Control; Monitoring; Problem Identification. **Abilities:** *Cognitive*—Visualization; Information Ordering; Problem Sensitivity; Flexibility of Closure; Selective Attention; Deductive Reasoning. *Psychomotor*—Finger Dexterity; Arm-Hand Steadiness; Wrist-Finger Speed. *Physical*—none met the criteria. *Sensory*—Near Vision; Visual Color Discrimination. **General Work Activities:** *Information Input*—Inspecting Equipment, Structures, Materials; Identifying Objects, Actions, and Events; Getting Information Needed to Do the Job. *Mental Process*—Evaluating Information Against Standards; Judging Qualities of Things, Services, Other People's Work; Processing Information; Analyzing Data or Information. *Work Output*—Handling and Moving Objects; Controlling Machines and Processes; Performing General Physical Activities. *Interacting with Others*—Communicating with Other Workers; Communicating with Persons Outside Organization; Performing for or Working with the Public. **Physical Work Conditions:** Indoors; Sitting; Using Hands on Objects, Tools, or Controls. **Other Job Characteristics:** Importance of Repeating Same Tasks; Importance of Being Exact or Accurate; Degree of Automation.

Experience: Job Zone 1. No previous work-related skill, knowledge, or experience is needed. **Job Preparation:** SVP Below 4.0—Less than 6 months. **Knowledge:** Mathematics; Production and Processing; Fine Arts; Chemistry; Communications and Media; Building and Construction; Telecommunications; Physics. **Instructional Programs:** 200301 Clothing, Apparel and Textile Workers and Managers, General; 200303 Commercial Garment and Apparel Worker.

Related DOT Jobs: 782.684-010 Canvas Repairer; 782.684-046 Mender, Knit Goods; 784.684-046 Mender; 787.682-030 Mender; 789.684-038 Parachute Mender.

49-9094.00 Locksmiths and Safe Repairers
(Locksmiths and Safe Repairers)

Education: Moderate-term O-T-J training

Employed: 27,146

Openings: 4,557

Projected Growth: 10%

Earnings: $24,890

Repair and open locks; make keys; change locks and safe combinations; install and repair safes.

Keeps record of company locks and keys. Cuts new or duplicate keys, using keycutting machine. Repairs and adjusts safes, vault doors, and vault components, using hand tools, lathes, drill presses, and welding and acetylene-cutting apparatus. Installs safes, vault doors, and deposit boxes according to blueprints, using equipment such as powered drills, taps, dies, truck crane, and dolly. Opens safe locks by drilling. Moves picklock in cylinder to open door locks without keys. Disassembles mechanical or electrical locking devices; repairs or replaces worn tumblers, springs, and other parts, using hand tools. Inserts new or repaired tumblers into lock to change combination. Removes interior and exterior finishes on safes and vaults; sprays on new finishes.

GOE Number, Interest Area, and Work Group: 05.03.01; Mechanics, Installers, and Repairers; Mechanical Work: Vehicles and Facilities. **Personality Type:** Realistic. Realistic occupations frequently involve work activities that include practical, hands-on problems and solutions. These occupations often deal with plants, animals, and real-world materials like wood, tools, and machinery. Many of the occupations require working outside and do not involve a lot of paperwork or working closely with others. **Work Values:** Independence; Moral Values; Security; Responsibility; Compensation; Company Policies and Practices; Working Conditions. **Skills:** Installation; Repairing; Equipment Selection; Problem Identification; Critical Thinking. **Abilities:** *Cognitive*—Written Comprehension; Information Ordering; Visualization; Deductive Reasoning; Memorization. *Psychomotor*—Arm-Hand Steadiness; Finger Dexterity; Manual Dexterity; Control Precision. *Physical*—Gross Body Coordination. **General Work Activities:** *Information Input*—Inspecting Equipment, Structures, Materialss; Getting Information Needed to Do the Job; Identifying Objects, Actions, and Events. *Mental Process*—Making Decisions and Solving Problems; Judging Qualities of Things, Services, Other People's Work;

Updating and Using Job-Relevant Knowledge. *Work Output*—Repairing and Maintaining Mechanical Equipment; Handling and Moving Objects; Performing General Physical Activities. *Interacting with Others*—Communicating with Persons Outside Organization; Performing Administrative Activities; Monitoring and Controlling Resources; Communicating with Other Workers; Providing Consultation and Advice to Others. **Physical Work Conditions:** Using Hands on Objects, Tools, or Controls; Indoors; Standing. **Other Job Characteristics:** Importance of Being Exact or Accurate; Importance of Being Sure All Is Done; Consequence of Error.

Experience: Job Zone 3. Previous work-related skill, knowledge, or experience is required. **Job Preparation:** SVP 6.0 to less than 7.0—More than 1 year and less than 4 years. **Knowledge:** Engineering and Technology; Mechanical; Clerical; Public Safety and Security; Computers and Electronics; Customer and Personal Service; Physics. **Instructional Program:** 470403 Locksmith and Safe Repairer.

Related DOT Jobs: 709.281-010 Locksmith; 709.281-014 Locksmith Apprentice; 869.381-022 Safe-and-Vault Service Mechanic.

49-9095.00 Manufactured Building and Mobile Home Installers (Installers and Repairers, Manufactured Buildings, Mobile Homes, and Travel Trailers)

Education: No data available.

Employed: 37,330

Openings: No data available.

Projected Growth: No data available.

Earnings: $21,420

Move or install mobile homes or prefabricated buildings.

Repairs leaks with caulking compound; replaces pipes, using pipe wrench. Inspects, examines, and tests operation of parts or systems, to determine repairs needed and to verify completeness of work performed. Lists parts needed, estimates costs, and plans work procedure, using parts list, technical manuals, and diagrams. Opens and closes doors, windows, and drawers, to test their operation; trims edges to fit, using jack-plane or drawknife. Refinishes wood surfaces on cabinets, doors, moldings, and floors, using power sander, putty, spray equipment, brush, paints, or varnishes. Resets hardware, using chisel, mallet, and screwdriver. Connects water hose to inlet pipe of plumbing system and tests operation of toilets and sinks. Confers with customer or reads work order to determine nature and extent of damage to unit. Connects electrical system to outside power source and activates switches to test operation of appliances and light fixtures. Removes damaged exterior panels; repairs and replaces structural frame members; and seals leaks, using hand tools. Repairs plumbing and propane gas lines, using caulking compounds and plastic or copper pipe. Locates and repairs frayed wiring, broken connections, or incorrect wiring, using ohmmeter, soldering iron, tape, and hand tools. Seals open side of modular units to prepare them for shipment, using polyethylene sheets, nails, and hammer.

GOE Number, Interest Area, and Work Group: 06.02.03; Construction, Mining, and Drilling; Construction: General. **Personality Type:** Realistic. Realistic occupations frequently involve work activities that include practical, hands-on problems and solutions. These occupations often deal with plants, animals, and real-world materials like wood, tools, and machinery. Many of the occupations require working outside and do not involve a lot of paperwork or working closely with others. **Work Values:** Moral Values; Supervision, Human Relations; Company Policies and Practices; Activity; Variety; Security; Supervision, Technical. **Skills:** Installation; Repairing; Troubleshooting; Problem Identification; Identification of Key Causes. **Abilities:** *Cognitive*—Oral Comprehension; Information Ordering; Written Comprehension; Oral Expression; Problem Sensitivity; Deductive Reasoning. *Psychomotor*—Control Precision; Manual Dexterity; Arm-Hand Steadiness; Wrist-Finger Speed. *Physical*—Extent Flexibility; Static Strength; Trunk Strength. *Sensory*—Depth Perception. **General Work Activities:** *Information Input*—Inspecting Equipment, Structures, Materials; Getting Information Needed to Do the Job; Estimating Needed Characteristics. *Mental Process*—Evaluating Information Against Standards; Making Decisions and Solving Problems; Judging Qualities of Things, Services, Other People's Work. *Work Output*—Performing General Physical Activities; Repairing and Maintaining Mechanical Equipment; Handling and Moving Objects. *Interacting with Others*—Communicating with Persons Outside Organization; Communicating with Other Workers; Establishing and Maintaining Relationships; Providing Consultation and Advice to Others. **Physical Work Conditions:** Using Hands on Objects, Tools, or Controls; Standing; Indoors. **Other Job Characteristics:** Consequence of Error; Importance of Being Sure All Is Done; Importance of Being Exact or Accurate.

Experience: Job Zone 2. Some previous work-related skill, knowledge, or experience may be helpful, but usually is not needed. **Job Preparation:** SVP 4.00 to 5.99—6 months to less than 2 years. **Knowledge:** Building and Construction; Mechanical; Engineering and Technology; Design; Customer and Personal Service. **Instructional Program:** 460401 Building/Property Maintenance and Manager.

Related DOT Jobs: 869.384-010 Repairer, Manufactured Buildings; 869.684-074 Utility Worker.

49-9096.00 Riggers (Riggers)

Education: Long-term O-T-J training

Employed: 11,287

Openings: 1,520

Projected Growth: 0.5%

Earnings: $31,770

Set up or repair rigging for construction projects, manufacturing plants, logging yards, ships and shipyards, or the entertainment industry.

Controls movement of heavy equipment through narrow openings or confined spaces. Attaches load to rigging, to provide support or prepare for moving, using hand and power tools. Attaches pulleys and blocks to fixed overhead structures such as beams, ceilings, and gin pole booms with bolts and clamps. Assembles and installs supporting structures, rigging, hoists, and pulling gear, using hand and power tools. Fabricates and repairs rigging such as slings, tackle, and ladders, using hand and power tools.

Dismantles, maintains, and stores rigging equipment. Selects gear such as cables, pulleys, and winches, according to load weight and size, facilities, and work schedule. Aligns, levels, and anchors machinery. Cleans and dresses machine surfaces and component parts. Signals or gives verbal directions to workers engaged in hoisting and moving loads, to ensure safety of workers and materials. Tests rigging, to ensure safety and reliability. Manipulates rigging lines, hoists, and pulling gear, to move or support materials such as heavy equipment, ships, or theatrical sets.

GOE Number, Interest Area, and Work Group: 06.02.03; Construction, Mining, and Drilling; Construction: General. **Personality Type:** Realistic. Realistic occupations frequently involve work activities that include practical, hands-on problems and solutions. These occupations often deal with plants, animals, and real-world materials like wood, tools, and machinery. Many of the occupations require working outside and do not involve a lot of paperwork or working closely with others. **Work Values:** Moral Values; Company Policies and Practices; Coworkers; Supervision, Technical; Responsibility; Supervision, Human Relations. **Skills:** Coordination; Equipment Selection; Operation and Control; Technology Design; Repairing. **Abilities:** *Cognitive*—Information Ordering; Problem Sensitivity; Visualization; Oral Expression; Written Comprehension. *Psychomotor*—Reaction Time; Manual Dexterity; Multilimb Coordination. *Physical*—Extent Flexibility; Static Strength; Dynamic Strength; Gross Body Equilibrium. *Sensory*—Far Vision; Depth Perception; Near Vision. **General Work Activities:** *Information Input*—Inspecting Equipment, Structures, Materials; Getting Information Needed to Do the Job; Monitoring Processes, Materials, and Surroundings. *Mental Process*—Making Decisions and Solving Problems; Judging Qualities of Things, Services, Other People's Work; Organizing, Planning, and Prioritizing. *Work Output*—Handling and Moving Objects; Controlling Machines and Processes; Performing General Physical Activities. *Interacting with Others*—Communicating with Other Workers; Coordinating Work and Activities of Others; Providing Consultation and Advice to Others. **Physical Work Conditions:** Using Hands on Objects, Tools, or Controls; Outdoors; Standing. **Other Job Characteristics:** Consequence of Error; Importance of Being Exact or Accurate; Importance of Being Sure All Is Done.

Experience: Job Zone 3. Previous work-related skill, knowledge, or experience is required. **Job Preparation:** SVP 6.0 to less than 7.0—More than 1 year and less than 4 years. **Knowledge:** Mechanical; Public Safety and Security; Physics; Building and Construction; Engineering and Technology. **Instructional Programs:** 490202 Construction Equipment Operator; 490306 Marine Maintenance and Ship Repairer.

Related DOT Jobs: 623.381-010 Gear Repairer; 806.261-014 Rigger; 806.261-018 Rigger Apprentice; 921.260-010 Rigger; 921.664-014 Rigger; 962.664-010 High Rigger; 962.684-010 Acrobatic Rigger; 962.684-014 Grip.

49-9097.00 Signal and Track Switch Repairers (Signal or Track Switch Maintainers)

Education: No data available.
Employed: 4,810
Openings: No data available.
Projected Growth: No data available.
Earnings: $38,440

Install, inspect, test, maintain, or repair electric gate crossings, signals, signal equipment, track switches, section lines, or intercommunications systems within a railroad system.

Lubricates moving parts on gate crossing mechanisms and swinging signals. Tightens loose bolts, using wrench, and tests circuits and connections by opening and closing gate. Replaces defective wiring, broken lenses, or burned-out light bulbs. Inspects electrical units of railroad grade crossing gates to detect loose bolts, defective electrical connections and parts. Inspects and tests gate crossings, signals, and signal equipment such as interlocks and hotbox detectors. Cleans lenses of lamps with cloths and solvent. Compiles reports indicating mileage or track inspected, repairs made, and equipment requiring replacement. Tests air lines and air cylinders on pneumatically operated gates. Inspects batteries to ensure that they are filled with battery water or to determine need for replacement. Installs and inspects switch-controlling mechanism on trolley wire and switch in bed of track bed, using hand tools and test equipment. Maintains high-tension lines, deenergizing lines for power company as repairs are requested. Tests signal circuit connections, using standard electrical testing equipment.

GOE Number, Interest Area, and Work Group: 05.02.01; Mechanics, Installers, and Repairers; Electrical and Electronic Systems: Installation and Repair. **Personality Type:** Realistic. Realistic occupations frequently involve work activities that include practical, hands-on problems and solutions. These occupations often deal with plants, animals, and real-world materials like wood, tools, and machinery. Many of the occupations require working outside and do not involve a lot of paperwork or working closely with others. **Work Values:** Moral Values; Supervision, Technical; Security; Supervision, Human Relations; Company Policies and Practices. **Skills:** Installation; Troubleshooting; Equipment Maintenance; Testing; Repairing. **Abilities:** *Cognitive*—Perceptual Speed; Visualization; Information Ordering; Problem Sensitivity; Selective Attention. *Psychomotor*—Finger Dexterity; Control Precision; Manual Dexterity; Wrist-Finger Speed. *Physical*—Extent Flexibility; Static Strength; Gross Body Equilibrium; Explosive Strength. *Sensory*—Visual Color Discrimination; Peripheral Vision; Depth Perception. **General Work Activities:** *Information Input*—Inspecting Equipment, Structures, Materials; Getting Information Needed to Do the Job; Monitoring Processes, Materials, and Surroundings. *Mental Process*—Updating and Using Job-Relevant Knowledge; Making Decisions and Solving Problems; Analyzing Data or Information. *Work Output*—Repairing and Maintaining Mechanical Equipment; Repairing and Maintaining Electrical Equipment; Implementing Ideas and Programs; Performing General Physical Activities. *Interacting with Others*—Communicating with Other Workers; Performing Administrative Activities; Monitoring and Controlling Resources. **Physical Work Conditions:** Outdoors; Using Hands on Objects, Tools, or Controls; Standing. **Other Job Characteristics:** Consequence of Error; Importance of Being Sure All Is Done; Importance of Being Exact or Accurate.

Experience: Job Zone 4. A minimum of two to four years of work-related skill, knowledge, or experience is needed. **Job Preparation:** SVP 7.0 to less than 8.0—2 years to less than 10 years. **Knowledge:** Mechanical; Transportation; Engineering and Technology; Telecommunications; Public Safety and Security. **Instructional Programs:** 460302 Electrician; 460303 Lineworker.

Related DOT Jobs: 822.281-026 Signal Maintainer; 825.261-010 Electric-Track-Switch Maintainer.

49-9098.00 Helpers—Installation, Maintenance, and Repair Workers (Helpers, Mechanics and Repairers)

Education: No data available.

Employed: 228,570

Openings: No data available.

Projected Growth: No data available.

Earnings: $18,230

Help installation, maintenance, and repair workers. Help with maintenance and with parts replacement. Help with repair of vehicles, industrial machinery, and electrical and electronic equipment. Furnish tools, materials, and supplies to other workers. Clean work area, machines, and tools. Hold materials or tools for other workers.

Builds or erects and maintains physical structures, using hand tools or power tools. Cleans or lubricates vehicles, machinery, equipment, instruments, tools, work areas, and other objects, using hand tools, power tools, and cleaning equipment. Furnishes tools, parts, equipment, and supplies to other workers. Assembles and disassembles machinery, equipment, components, and other parts, using hand tools and power tools. Adjusts and connects or disconnects wiring, piping, tubing, and other parts, using hand tools or power tools. Examines and tests machinery, equipment, components, and parts to detect defects and to ensure proper functioning. Positions vehicles, machinery, equipment, physical structures, and other objects, for assembly or installation, using hand tools, power tools, and moving equipment. Applies protective materials to equipment, components, and parts, to prevent defects and corrosion. Installs or replaces machinery, equipment, and new or replacement parts and instruments, using hand tools or power tools. Transfers equipment, tools, parts, and other objects to and from work stations and other areas, using hand tools, power tools, and moving equipment. Helps mechanics and repairers maintain and repair vehicles, industrial machinery, and electrical and electronic equipment. Tends and observes equipment and machinery to verify efficient and safe operation.

GOE Number, Interest Area, and Work Group: 05.03.01; Mechanics, Installers, and Repairers; Mechanical Work: Vehicles and Facilities. Personality Type: Realistic. Realistic occupations frequently involve work activities that include practical, hands-on problems and solutions. These occupations often deal with plants, animals, and real-world materials like wood, tools, and machinery. Many of the occupations require working outside and do not involve a lot of paperwork or working closely with others. Work Values: Moral Values; Activity; Advancement; Coworkers; Supervision, Technical. Skills: Equipment Maintenance; Installation; Repairing; Product Inspection; Operation and Control. Abilities: *Cognitive*—Information Ordering; Oral Comprehension; Visualization; Problem Sensitivity; Selective Attention. *Psychomotor*—Wrist-Finger Speed; Manual Dexterity; Arm-Hand Steadiness. *Physical*—Extent Flexibility; Static Strength; Trunk Strength. *Sensory*—Auditory Attention; Hearing Sensitivity; Visual Color Discrimination. General Work Activities: *Information Input*—Getting Information Needed to Do the Job; Identifying Objects, Actions, and Events; Monitoring Processes, Materials, and Surroundings. *Mental Process*—Evaluating Information Against Standards; Updating and Using Job-Relevant Knowledge; Making Decisions and Solving Problems; Judging Qualities of Things, Services, Other People's Work. *Work Output*—Handling and Moving Objects; Performing General Physical Activities; Repairing and Maintaining Mechanical Equipment. *Interacting with Others*—Assisting and Caring for Others; Communicating with Other Workers; Establishing and Maintaining Relationships. Physical Work Conditions: Using Hands on Objects, Tools, or Controls; Indoors; Standing. Other Job Characteristics: Consequence of Error; Importance of Being Sure All Is Done; Degree of Automation; Importance of Being Exact or Accurate; Importance of Repeating Same Tasks.

Experience: Job Zone 1. No previous work-related skill, knowledge, or experience is needed. Job Preparation: SVP Below 4.0—Less than 6 months. Knowledge: Mechanical; Engineering and Technology; Computers and Electronics; Building and Construction; Mathematics; English Language; Production and Processing. Instructional Program: 470303 Industrial Machinery Maintenance and Repairer.

Related DOT Jobs: 620.664-010 Construction-Equipment-Mechanic Helper; 620.664-014 Maintenance Mechanic Helper; 620.684-014 Automobile-Mechanic Helper; 620.684-030 Tractor-Mechanic Helper; 621.684-010 Airframe-and-Power-Plant-Mechanic Helper; 622.684-014 Car-Repairer Helper; 623.684-010 Motorboat-Mechanic Helper; 623.687-010 Machinist Helper, Outside; 625.684-010 Diesel-Mechanic Helper; 628.664-010 Overhauler Helper; 630.664-010 Repairer Helper; 630.664-018 Service-Mechanic Helper, Compressed-Gas Equipment; 630.684-022 Pump-Servicer Helper; 630.684-034 Spray-Gun-Repairer Helper; 631.364-010 Hydroelectric-Machinery-Mechanic Helper; 631.684-010 Powerhouse-Mechanic Helper; 632.684-010 Ordnance-Artificer Helper; 637.384-010 Industrial-Gas-Servicer Helper; 637.664-010 Heating-and-Air-Conditioning Installer-Servicer Helper; 637.684-010 Gas-Appliance-Servicer Helper (partial list; see the introduction for sources of the complete list).

51-0000
Production Occupations

51-1000 Supervisors, Production Workers

51-1011.00 First-Line Supervisors/Managers of Production and Operating Workers (Blue-Collar Worker Supervisors)

Education: Work experience in a related occupation
Employed: 2,197,772
Openings: 216,115
Projected Growth: 8.9%
Earnings: No data available.

Supervise and coordinate the activities of production and operating workers, such as inspectors, precision workers, machine setters and operators, assemblers, fabricators, and plant and system operators.

Directs and coordinates the activities of employees engaged in production or processing of goods. Demonstrates equipment operations or work procedures to new employees; assigns employees to experienced workers for training. Reviews operations and accounting records or reports to determine the feasibility of production estimates and evaluate current production. Maintains operations data such as time, production, and cost records; prepares management reports. Recommends or implements measures to motivate employees and improve production methods, equipment performance, product quality, or efficiency. Requisitions materials, supplies, equipment parts, or repair services. Interprets specifications, blueprints, job orders, and company policies and procedures for workers. Inspects materials, products, or equipment to detect defects or malfunctions. Monitors or patrols work area and enforces safety or sanitation regulations. Monitors gauges, dials, and other indicators to ensure operators conform to production or processing standards. Sets up and adjusts machines and equipment. Confers with other supervisors to coordinate operations and activities within departments or between departments. Reads and analyzes charts, work orders, or production schedules to determine production requirements. Confers with management or subordinates to resolve worker problems, complaints, or grievances. Plans and establishes work schedules, assignments, and production sequences, to meet production goals. Calculates labor and equipment requirements and production specifications, using standard formulas. Determines standards, production, and rates based on company policy, equipment and labor availability, and workload.

GOE Number, Interest Area, and Work Group: 08.01.01; Industrial Production; Managerial Work in Industrial Production. **Personality Type:** Enterprising. Enterprising occupations frequently involve starting up and carrying out projects. These occupations can involve leading people and making many decisions. They sometimes require risk taking and often deal with business. **Work Values:** Authority; Responsibility; Coworkers; Autonomy; Achievement; Activity; Variety. **Skills:** Management of Personnel Resources; Coordination; Problem Identification; Writ-

ing; Reading Comprehension; Mathematics; Management of Material Resources; Product Inspection. **Abilities:** *Cognitive*—Oral Expression; Written Comprehension; Oral Comprehension; Mathematical Reasoning; Problem Sensitivity; Deductive Reasoning. *Psychomotor*—Response Orientation; Control Precision; Rate Control. *Physical*—Explosive Strength; Dynamic Flexibility; Gross Body Equilibrium. *Sensory*—Auditory Attention; Speech Clarity; Near Vision. **General Work Activities:** *Information Input*—Monitoring Processes, Materials, and Surroundings; Getting Information Needed to Do the Job; Estimating Needed Characteristics. *Mental Process*—Scheduling Work and Activities; Organizing, Planning, and Prioritizing; Analyzing Data or Information; Making Decisions and Solving Problems. *Work Output*—Documenting and Recording Information; Controlling Machines and Processes; Performing General Physical Activities. *Interacting with Others*—Communicating with Other Workers; Guiding, Directing and Motivating Subordinates; Coordinating Work and Activities of Others. **Physical Work Conditions:** Indoors; Sitting; Walking or Running; Standing. **Other Job Characteristics:** Consequence of Error; Frustrating Circumstances; Importance of Being Sure All Is Done.

Experience: Job Zone 3. Previous work-related skill, knowledge, or experience is required. **Job Preparation:** SVP 6.0 to less than 7.0—More than 1 year and less than 4 years. **Knowledge:** Production and Processing; Administration and Management; Personnel and Human Resources; Education and Training; Mathematics. **Instructional Program:** 143001 Engineering/Industrial Management.

Related DOT Jobs: 184.167-046 Incinerator-Plant-General Supervisor; 184.167-142 Superintendent, Cold Storage; 299.137-018 Sample-Room Supervisor; 361.137-010 Supervisor, Laundry; 369.137-010 Supervisor, Dry Cleaning; 369.137-014 Supervisor, Rug Cleaning; 369.167-010 Manager, Laundromat; 500.131-010 Supervisor; 500.132-010 Supervisor, Sheet Manufacturing; 500.134-010 Supervisor, Matrix; 501.130-010 Supervisor, Hot-Dip-Tinning; 501.137-010 Supervisor, Hot-Dip Plating; 502.130-010 Supervisor, Casting-and-Pasting; 503.137-010 Supervisor, Sandblaster; 504.131-010 Heat-Treat Supervisor; 505.130-010 Supervisor, Metalizing; 505.130-014 Supervisor, Vacuum Metalizing; 509.130-010 Supervisor, Powdered Metal; 509.130-014 Supervisor, Power-Reactor; 509.132-010 Supervisor, Soaking Pits (partial list; see the introduction for sources of the complete list).

51-2000 Assemblers and Fabricators

51-2011.00 Aircraft Structure, Surfaces, Rigging, and Systems Assemblers (Aircraft Structure, Surfaces, Rigging, and Systems Assemblers, Precision)

Education: Work experience in a related occupation
Employed: 16,631
Openings: 2,363
Projected Growth: 19.3%
Earnings: $38,400

Assemble, fit, fasten, and install parts of airplanes, space vehicles, or missiles, such as tails, wings, fuselage, bulkheads, stabilizers, landing gear, rigging and control equipment, or heating and ventilating systems.

GOE Number, Interest Area, and Work Group: 08.02.02; Industrial Production; Production Technology: Precision Hand Work. **Instructional Programs:** 150801 Aeronautical and Aerospace Engineering Technology/Technician; 470607 Aircraft Mechanic/Technician, Airframe; 470608 Aircraft Mechanic/Technician, Powerplant; 470609 Aviation Systems and Avionics Maintenance Technologist/Technician. **Note:** The Department of Labor has not collected some data for this job, so it has fewer details than the other descriptions.

51-2011.01 Aircraft Structure Assemblers, Precision
(Aircraft Assemblers)

Education: Work experience in a related occupation

Employed: 16,631

Openings: 2,363

Projected Growth: 19.3%

Earnings: $38,400

Assemble tail, wing, fuselage, or other structural section of aircraft, space vehicles, and missiles, from parts, subassemblies, and components. Install functional units, parts, or equipment, such as landing gear, control surfaces, doors, and floorboards.

Inspects and tests installed units, parts, and equipment for fit, performance, and compliance with standards, using measuring instruments and test equipment. Drills holes in structure and subassemblies; attaches brackets, hinges, or clips to secure installation or to fasten subassemblies. Bolts, screws, or rivets accessories to fasten, support, or hang components and subassemblies. Cuts, trims, and files parts; verifies fitting tolerances to prepare for installation. Aligns structural assemblies. Installs units, parts, equipment, and components in structural assembly, according to blueprints and specifications, using hand tools and power tools. Locates and marks reference points and holes for installation of parts and components, using jigs, templates, and measuring instruments. Positions and aligns subassemblies in jigs or fixtures, using measuring instruments, following blueprint lines and index points.

GOE Number, Interest Area, and Work Group: 08.02.02; Industrial Production; Production Technology: Precision Hand Work. **Personality Type:** Realistic. Realistic occupations frequently involve work activities that include practical, hands-on problems and solutions. These occupations often deal with plants, animals, and real-world materials like wood, tools, and machinery. Many of the occupations require working outside and do not involve a lot of paperwork or working closely with others. **Work Values:** Moral Values; Independence; Company Policies and Practices; Supervision, Human Relations; Activity. **Skills:** Installation; Equipment Selection; Product Inspection; Mathematics; Testing. **Abilities:** *Cognitive*—Visualization; Information Ordering; Problem Sensitivity; Written Comprehension; Spatial Orientation; Perceptual Speed. *Psychomotor*—Arm-Hand Steadiness; Manual Dexterity; Finger Dexterity. *Physical*—Extent Flexibility; Static Strength; Trunk Strength. *Sensory*—Near Vision; Far Vision; Visual Color

Discrimination. **General Work Activities:** *Information Input*—Inspecting Equipment, Structures, Materials; Getting Information Needed to Do the Job; Identifying Objects, Actions, and Events. *Mental Process*—Evaluating Information Against Standards; Updating and Using Job-Relevant Knowledge; Judging Qualities of Things, Services, Other People's Work; Organizing, Planning, and Prioritizing. *Work Output*—Handling and Moving Objects; Implementing Ideas and Programs; Controlling Machines and Processes. *Interacting with Others*—Communicating with Other Workers; Coordinating Work and Activities of Others; Performing Administrative Activities. **Physical Work Conditions:** Using Hands on Objects, Tools, or Controls; Standing; Outdoors. **Other Job Characteristics:** Consequence of Error; Importance of Being Sure All Is Done; Importance of Being Exact or Accurate.

Experience: Job Zone 3. Previous work-related skill, knowledge, or experience is required. **Job Preparation:** SVP 6.0 to less than 7.0—More than 1 year and less than 4 years. **Knowledge:** Mechanical; Engineering and Technology; Production and Processing; Building and Construction; Design. **Instructional Programs:** 150801 Aeronautical and Aerospace Engineering Technology/Technician; 470607 Aircraft Mechanic/Technician, Airframe; 470608 Aircraft Mechanic/Technician, Powerplant; 470609 Aviation Systems and Avionics Maintenance Technologist/Technician.

Related DOT Jobs: 806.361-014 Assembler-Installer, General; 806.381-026 Assembler, Aircraft, Structures and Surfaces.

51-2011.02 Aircraft Systems Assemblers, Precision
(Aircraft Assemblers)

Education: Work experience in a related occupation

Employed: 16,631

Openings: 2,363

Projected Growth: 19.3%

Earnings: $38,400

Lay out, assemble, install, and test aircraft systems such as armament, environmental control, plumbing, and hydraulic.

Measures, drills, files, cuts, bends, and smoothes materials to ensure fit and clearance of parts. Assembles and installs parts, fittings, and assemblies on aircraft, using layout tools, hand tools, power tools, and fasteners. Lays out location of parts and assemblies, according to specifications. Cleans, oils, assembles, and attaches system components to aircraft, using hand tools, power tools, and measuring instruments. Reads and interprets blueprints, illustrations, and specifications to determine layout and sequence of operations, or identity and relationship of parts. Reworks, replaces, realigns, and adjusts parts and assemblies according to specifications. Installs mechanical linkages and actuators, and verifies tension of cables, using tensiometer. Tests systems and assemblies for functional performance; adjusts, repairs, or replaces malfunctioning units or parts. Aligns, fits, and assembles system components such as armament, structural, and mechanical components, using jigs, fixtures, measuring instruments, hand tools, and power tools. Examines parts for defects and for conformance to specifications, using precision measuring instruments.

GOE Number, Interest Area, and Work Group: 08.02.02; Industrial Production; Production Technology: Precision Hand Work.

Personality Type: Realistic. Realistic occupations frequently involve work activities that include practical, hands-on problems and solutions. These occupations often deal with plants, animals, and real-world materials like wood, tools, and machinery. Many of the occupations require working outside and do not involve a lot of paperwork or working closely with others. **Work Values:** Moral Values; Independence; Company Policies and Practices; Activity; Compensation; Supervision, Human Relations. **Skills:** Troubleshooting; Installation; Product Inspection; Equipment Maintenance; Testing; Repairing. **Abilities:** *Cognitive*—Visualization; Written Comprehension; Information Ordering; Problem Sensitivity; Deductive Reasoning. *Psychomotor*—Manual Dexterity; Arm-Hand Steadiness; Control Precision. *Physical*—Static Strength; Extent Flexibility; Trunk Strength; Dynamic Strength; Explosive Strength. *Sensory*—Near Vision; Depth Perception; Visual Color Discrimination. **General Work Activities:** *Information Input*—Inspecting Equipment, Structures, Materials; Getting Information Needed to Do the Job; Identifying Objects, Actions, and Events; Monitoring Processes, Materials, and Surroundings. *Mental Process*—Evaluating Information Against Standards; Updating and Using Job-Relevant Knowledge; Judging Qualities of Things, Services, Other People's Work. *Work Output*—Handling and Moving Objects; Implementing Ideas and Programs; Performing General Physical Activities; Controlling Machines and Processes; Repairing and Maintaining Mechanical Equipment. *Interacting with Others*—Coordinating Work and Activities of Others; Communicating with Other Workers; Performing Administrative Activities. **Physical Work Conditions:** Using Hands on Objects, Tools, or Controls; Indoors; Hazardous Equipment; Standing. **Other Job Characteristics:** Consequence of Error; Importance of Being Sure All Is Done; Importance of Being Exact or Accurate.

Experience: Job Zone 3. Previous work-related skill, knowledge, or experience is required. **Job Preparation:** SVP 6.0 to less than 7.0—More than 1 year and less than 4 years. **Knowledge:** Mechanical; Engineering and Technology; Production and Processing; Design; Building and Construction. **Instructional Programs:** 150801 Aeronautical and Aerospace Engineering Technology/Technician; 470607 Aircraft Mechanic/Technician, Airframe; 470608 Aircraft Mechanic/Technician, Powerplant; 470609 Aviation Systems and Avionics Maintenance Technologist/Technician.

Related DOT Jobs: 806.361-030 Aircraft Mechanic, Armament; 806.381-014 Aircraft Mechanic, Environmental Control System; 806.381-018 Aircraft Mechanic, Rigging and Controls; 806.381-066 Aircraft Mechanic, Plumbing and Hydraulics; 806.381-082 Precision Assembler.

51-2011.03 Aircraft Rigging Assemblers (Aircraft Assemblers)

Education: Work experience in a related occupation

Employed: 16,631

Openings: 2,363

Projected Growth: 19.3%

Earnings: $38,400

Fabricate and assemble aircraft tubing or cable components or assemblies.

Swages fittings onto cable, using swaging machine. Verifies dimensions of cable assembly and position of fittings, using measuring instruments; repairs and reworks defective assemblies. Assembles and attaches fittings onto cable and tubing components, using hand tools. Welds tubing and fittings; solders cable ends, using tack-welder, induction brazing chamber, or other equipment. Measures, cuts, and inspects cable and tubing, using master template, measuring instruments, and cable cutter or saw. Forms loops or splices in cables, using clamps and fittings; reweaves cable strands. Fabricates cable templates. Cleans, lubricates, and coats tubing and cable assemblies. Marks identifying information on tubing or cable assemblies, using electro-chemical etching device, label, rubber stamp, or other methods. Tests tubing and cable assemblies for defects, using pressure-testing equipment and proofloading machines. Selects and installs accessories in swaging machine, using hand tools. Marks location of cutouts, holes, and trim lines of parts and marks relationship of parts, using measuring instruments. Sets up and operates machines and systems to crimp, cut, bend, form, swage, flare, bead, burr, and straighten tubing, according to specifications. Reads and interprets blueprints, work orders, data charts, and specifications, to determine operations and to determine type, quantity, dimensions, configuration, and finish of tubing, cable, and fittings.

GOE Number, Interest Area, and Work Group: 08.02.02; Industrial Production; Production Technology: Precision Hand Work. **Personality Type:** Realistic. Realistic occupations frequently involve work activities that include practical, hands-on problems and solutions. These occupations often deal with plants, animals, and real-world materials like wood, tools, and machinery. Many of the occupations require working outside and do not involve a lot of paperwork or working closely with others. **Work Values:** Moral Values; Independence; Activity; Company Policies and Practices; Supervision, Human Relations. **Skills:** Equipment Selection; Installation; Operation and Control; Mathematics; Product Inspection; Reading Comprehension. **Abilities:** *Cognitive*—Written Comprehension; Visualization; Information Ordering; Problem Sensitivity; Deductive Reasoning. *Psychomotor*—Manual Dexterity; Arm-Hand Steadiness; Control Precision. *Physical*—Static Strength; Explosive Strength; Extent Flexibility. *Sensory*—Visual Color Discrimination; Depth Perception; Far Vision. **General Work Activities:** *Information Input*—Inspecting Equipment, Structures, Materials; Getting Information Needed to Do the Job; Identifying Objects, Actions, and Events. *Mental Process*—Updating and Using Job-Relevant Knowledge; Judging Qualities of Things, Services, Other People's Work; Evaluating Information Against Standards. *Work Output*—Handling and Moving Objects; Implementing Ideas and Programs; Controlling Machines and Processes. *Interacting with Others*—Communicating with Other Workers; Coordinating Work and Activities of Others; Assisting and Caring for Others; Performing Administrative Activities. **Physical Work Conditions:** Using Hands on Objects, Tools, or Controls; Standing; Making Repetitive Motions; Sitting; Outdoors; Hazardous Equipment. **Other Job Characteristics:** Importance of Being Exact or Accurate; Importance of Being Sure All Is Done; Consequence of Error; Degree of Automation.

Experience: Job Zone 3. Previous work-related skill, knowledge, or experience is required. **Job Preparation:** SVP 6.0 to less than 7.0—More than 1 year and less than 4 years. **Knowledge:**

Mechanical; Engineering and Technology; Production and Processing; Building and Construction; Design. **Instructional Programs:** 150801 Aeronautical and Aerospace Engineering Technology/Technician; 470607 Aircraft Mechanic/Technician, Airframe; 470608 Aircraft Mechanic/Technician, Powerplant; 470609 Aviation Systems and Avionics Maintenance Technologist/ Technician.

Related DOT Jobs: 806.381-034 Assembler, Tubing; 806.381-042 Cable Assembler and Swager.

51-2021.00 Coil Winders, Tapers, and Finishers
(Coil Winders, Tapers, and Finishers)

Education: Short-term O-T-J training

Employed: 21,679

Openings: 4,923

Projected Growth: 2.5%

Earnings: $18,660

Wind wire coils used in electrical components such as resistors and transformers and in electrical equipment and instruments such as field cores, bobbins, armature cores, electrical motors, generators, and control equipment.

Observes gauges and stops machine to remove completed components, using hand tools. Reviews work orders and specifications to ascertain material needed and type of part to be processed. Applies solutions or paints to wired electrical components, using hand tools. Attaches, alters, and trims materials such as wire, insulation, and coils, using hand tools. Records production and operational data on specified forms. Repairs and maintains electrical components and machinery parts, using hand tools. Operates or tends wire-coiling machine. Examines and tests wired electrical components, using measuring devices. Selects and loads materials such as workpieces, objects, and machine parts onto equipment used in coiling process.

GOE Number, Interest Area, and Work Group: 08.03.06; Industrial Production; Production Work: Hands-on Work, Assorted Materials. **Personality Type:** Realistic. Realistic occupations frequently involve work activities that include practical, hands-on problems and solutions. These occupations often deal with plants, animals, and real-world materials like wood, tools, and machinery. Many of the occupations require working outside and do not involve a lot of paperwork or working closely with others. **Work Values:** Moral Values; Activity; Company Policies and Practices; Independence; Security; Supervision, Human Relations; Supervision, Technical. **Skills:** Product Inspection; Equipment Maintenance; Equipment Selection; Operation and Control; Operation Monitoring. **Abilities:** *Cognitive*—Problem Sensitivity; Information Ordering; Written Expression; Visualization; Perceptual Speed; Memorization. *Psychomotor*—Control Precision; Manual Dexterity; Arm-Hand Steadiness. *Physical*—Extent Flexibility; Static Strength; Trunk Strength. *Sensory*—Depth Perception; Visual Color Discrimination; Peripheral Vision. **General Work Activities:** *Information Input*—Monitoring Processes, Materials, and Surroundings; Getting Information Needed to Do the Job; Inspecting Equipment, Structures, Materials. *Mental Process*—Evaluating Information Against Standards; Updating and Using Job-Relevant

Knowledge; Judging Qualities of Things, Services, Other People's Work; Analyzing Data or Information; Organizing, Planning, and Prioritizing. *Work Output*—Handling and Moving Objects; Controlling Machines and Processes; Implementing Ideas and Programs. *Interacting with Others*—Communicating with Other Workers; Performing Administrative Activities; Coordinating Work and Activities of Others; Interpreting Meaning of Information to Others. **Physical Work Conditions:** Indoors; Using Hands on Objects, Tools, or Controls; Standing. **Other Job Characteristics:** Degree of Automation; Consequence of Error; Importance of Being Exact or Accurate; Importance of Being Sure All Is Done.

Experience: Job Zone 2. Some previous work-related skill, knowledge, or experience may be helpful, but usually is not needed. **Job Preparation:** SVP 4.00 to 5.99—6 months to less than 2 years. **Knowledge:** Mechanical; Production and Processing; Engineering and Technology; English Language; Physics; Mathematics; Computers and Electronics; Clerical. **Instructional Program:** 470105 Industrial Electronics Installer and Repairer.

Related DOT Jobs: 721.684-018 Coil Connector; 724.362-010 Wire Coiler; 724.381-014 Coil Winder, Repair; 724.684-010 Armature Bander; 724.684-014 Armature Connector II; 724.684-026 Coil Winder; 724.685-010 Element Winding Machine Tender; 726.682-014 Wire-Wrapping-Machine Operator.

51-2022.00 Electrical and Electronic Equipment Assemblers (Electrical and Electronic Equipment Assemblers, Precision)

Education: Work experience in a related occupation

Employed: 200,922

Openings: 38,774

Projected Growth: 6%

Earnings: $21,740

Assemble or modify electrical or electronic equipment such as computers, test equipment, telemetering systems, electric motors, and batteries.

Drills and taps holes in specified locations, to mount control units and to provide openings for elements, wiring, and instruments. Reads and interprets schematic drawings, diagrams, blueprints, specifications, work orders, and reports, to determine materials requirements and assembly instructions. Tests wiring installations, assemblies, and circuits for resistance factors and operational defects; records results. Positions, aligns, and adjusts workpieces and electrical parts to facilitate wiring and assembly. Fabricates and forms parts, coils, and structures according to specifications, using drill, calipers, cutters, and saws. Measures and adjusts voltages to specified value, to determine operational accuracy of instruments. Inspects units to detect malfunctions; adjusts, repairs, or replaces component parts to ensure conformance to specifications. Selects or distributes materials, supplies, and subassemblies to work area. Completes, reviews, and maintains production, time, and component-waste reports. Cleans parts, using cleaning solution, airhose, and cloth. Packs finished assemblies for shipment; transports to storage areas, using hoists or handtrucks. Instructs customers in installation, repair, and maintenance of products; explains assembly procedures or techniques to workers. Paints structures as specified, using paint sprayer. Assembles systems and support structures; installs components, units, and printed circuit boards, following specifications and using hand tools and power tools. Marks and tags components to track and identify stock inventory. Assists or confers with supervisor or engineer to plan and review work activities and to resolve production problems.

GOE Number, Interest Area, and Work Group: 08.02.02; Industrial Production; Production Technology: Precision Hand Work. **Personality Type:** Realistic. Realistic occupations frequently involve work activities that include practical, hands-on problems and solutions. These occupations often deal with plants, animals, and real-world materials like wood, tools, and machinery. Many of the occupations require working outside and do not involve a lot of paperwork or working closely with others. **Work Values:** Moral Values; Company Policies and Practices; Activity; Supervision, Human Relations; Compensation; Working Conditions; Ability Utilization; Achievement. **Skills:** Product Inspection; Installation; Science; Instructing; Equipment Selection. **Abilities:** *Cognitive*—Information Ordering; Problem Sensitivity; Visualization; Perceptual Speed; Deductive Reasoning. *Psychomotor*—Finger Dexterity; Control Precision; Manual Dexterity. *Physical*—Extent Flexibility; Static Strength; Trunk Strength. *Sensory*—Visual Color Discrimination; Near Vision; Auditory Attention. **General Work Activities:** *Information Input*—Getting Information Needed to Do the Job; Inspecting Equipment, Structures, Materials; Identifying Objects, Actions, and Events; Monitoring Processes, Materials, and Surroundings. *Mental Process*—Evaluating Information Against Standards; Making Decisions and Solving Problems; Updating and Using Job-Relevant Knowledge; Processing Information. *Work Output*—Repairing and Maintaining Electrical Equipment; Handling and Moving Objects; Implementing Ideas and Programs; Controlling Machines and Processes. *Interacting with Others*—Communicating with Other Workers; Communicating with Persons Outside Organization; Providing Consultation and Advice to Others. **Physical Work Conditions:** Indoors; Using Hands on Objects, Tools, or Controls; Sitting; Standing. **Other Job Characteristics:** Importance of Being Sure All Is Done; Consequence of Error; Importance of Being Exact or Accurate.

Experience: Job Zone 3. Previous work-related skill, knowledge, or experience is required. **Job Preparation:** SVP 6.0 to less than 7.0—More than 1 year and less than 4 years. **Knowledge:** Computers and Electronics; Production and Processing; Engineering and Technology; Mechanical; Design. **Instructional Programs:** 470102 Business Machine Repairer; 470103 Communication Systems Installer and Repairer; 470105 Industrial Electronics Installer and Repairer.

Related DOT Jobs: 693.381-026 Electrical and Radio Mock-Up Mechanic; 710.281-010 Assembler and Tester, Electronics; 721.381-014 Electric-Motor-Control Assembler; 722.381-010 Assembler; 726.361-014 Group Leader, Printed Circuit Board Assembly; 729.281-042 Wirer; 729.381-022 Wirer, Cable; 730.381-022 Electric-Organ Assembler and Checker; 759.261-010 Prototype-Deicer Assembler; 820.381-014 Transformer Assembler I; 826.361-010 Assembler and Wirer, Industrial Equipment; 826.381-010 Fabricator, Industrial Furnace.

51-2023.00 Electromechanical Equipment Assemblers (Electromechanical Equipment Assemblers, Precision)

Education: Work experience in a related occupation
Employed: 49,541
Openings: 9,529
Projected Growth: 5.7%
Earnings: $23,250

Assemble or modify electromechanical equipment or devices such as servomechanisms, gyros, dynamometers, magnetic drums, tape drives, brakes, control linkage, actuators, and appliances.

Measures parts to determine tolerances, using precision measuring instruments such as micrometers, calipers, and verniers. Inspects, tests, and adjusts completed unit to ensure that unit meets specifications, tolerances, and customer order requirements. Connects electrical wiring according to circuit diagram, using soldering iron. Reads blueprints and specifications to determine component parts and assembly sequence of electromechanical unit. Files, laps, and buffs parts to fit, using hand tools and power tools. Assembles parts or unit; attaches unit to assembly, subassembly, or frame, using hand tools and power tools. Drills, taps, reams, countersinks, and spotfaces bolt holes in parts, using drill press and portable power drill. Disassembles unit to replace parts or to crate for shipping. Cleans and lubricates parts and subassemblies. Attaches name plates and marks identifying information on parts. Positions and aligns parts, using fixtures, jigs, and templates.

GOE Number, Interest Area, and Work Group: 08.02.02; Industrial Production; Production Technology: Precision Hand Work. **Personality Type:** Realistic. Realistic occupations frequently involve work activities that include practical, hands-on problems and solutions. These occupations often deal with plants, animals, and real-world materials like wood, tools, and machinery. Many of the occupations require working outside and do not involve a lot of paperwork or working closely with others. **Work Values:** Moral Values; Independence; Company Policies and Practices; Activity; Supervision, Human Relations. **Skills:** Installation; Product Inspection; Mathematics; Testing; Operation Monitoring; Operation and Control; Equipment Selection; Reading Comprehension. **Abilities:** *Cognitive*—Visualization; Number Facility; Written Comprehension; Problem Sensitivity; Deductive Reasoning. *Psychomotor*—Manual Dexterity; Arm-Hand Steadiness; Finger Dexterity; Control Precision. *Physical*—Extent Flexibility; Static Strength; Trunk Strength. *Sensory*—Near Vision; Visual Color Discrimination; Depth Perception. **General Work Activities:** *Information Input*—Getting Information Needed to Do the Job; Inspecting Equipment, Structures, Materials; Monitoring Processes, Materials, and Surroundings. *Mental Process*—Evaluating Information Against Standards; Updating and Using Job-Relevant Knowledge; Judging Qualities of Things, Services, Other People's Work; Organizing, Planning, and Prioritizing. *Work Output*—Handling and Moving Objects; Controlling Machines and Processes; Repairing and Maintaining Electrical Equipment. *Interacting with*

Others—Communicating with Other Workers; Performing Administrative Activities; Coordinating Work and Activities of Others. **Physical Work Conditions:** Using Hands on Objects, Tools, or Controls; Indoors; Hazardous Equipment. **Other Job Characteristics:** Importance of Being Exact or Accurate; Importance of Being Sure All Is Done; Consequence of Error; Degree of Automation.

Experience: Job Zone 3. Previous work-related skill, knowledge, or experience is required. **Job Preparation:** SVP 6.0 to less than 7.0—More than 1 year and less than 4 years. **Knowledge:** Mechanical; Computers and Electronics; Production and Processing; Engineering and Technology; Design. **Instructional Programs:** 150403 Electromechanical Technology/Technician; 150405 Robotics Technology/Technician; 150499 Electromechanical Instrumentation and Maintenance Technology/Technicians, Other.

Related DOT Jobs: 706.381-018 Final Assembler; 706.381-050 Precision Assembler, Bench; 714.381-010 Assembler, Photographic Equipment; 721.381-018 Governor Assembler, Hydraulic.

51-2031.00 Engine and Other Machine Assemblers
(Machine Builders and Other Precision Machine Assemblers)

Education: Work experience in a related occupation
Employed: 74,418
Openings: 8,532
Projected Growth: 1.7%
Earnings: $29,250

Construct, assemble, or rebuild machines such as engines, turbines, and similar equipment used in such industries as construction, extraction, textiles, and paper manufacturing.

Fastens and installs piping, fixtures, or wiring and electrical components to specifications. Reworks, repairs, and replaces damaged parts or assemblies. Sets and verifies clearance of parts. Verifies conformance of parts to stock list and blueprints, using measuring instruments such as calipers, gauges, and micrometers. Removes rough spots and smoothes surfaces to fit, trim, or clean parts or components, using hand tools and power tools. Inspects and tests parts and accessories for leakage, defect, or functionality, using test equipment. Positions and aligns components for assembly, manually or with hoist. Operates machine to verify functioning, machine capabilities, and conformance to customer's specifications. Sets up and operates metalworking machines such as milling and grinding machines, to shape or fabricate parts. Maintains and lubricates parts and components. Fastens components or parts together, using hand tools, rivet gun, and welding equipment. Lays out and drills, reams, taps, and cuts parts for assembly. Analyzes assembly blueprint and specifications manual; plans assembly or building operations.

GOE Number, Interest Area, and Work Group: 08.02.02; Industrial Production; Production Technology: Precision Hand Work. **Personality Type:** Realistic. Realistic occupations frequently involve work activities that include practical, hands-on problems and solutions. These occupations often deal with plants, animals, and real-world materials like wood, tools, and machinery. Many of the occupations require working outside and do not involve a lot of paperwork or working closely with others. **Work Values:** Moral Values; Independence; Company Policies and Practices; Supervision, Human Relations; Activity. **Skills:** Product Inspection; Operation and Control; Testing; Equipment Maintenance; Equipment Selection; Operation Monitoring. **Abilities:** *Cognitive*—Information Ordering; Visualization; Written Comprehension; Problem Sensitivity; Deductive Reasoning. *Psychomotor*—Control Precision; Finger Dexterity; Multilimb Coordination; Arm-Hand Steadiness; Wrist-Finger Speed. *Physical*—Extent Flexibility; Static Strength; Trunk Strength. *Sensory*—Near Vision; Visual Color Discrimination; Hearing Sensitivity. **General Work Activities:** *Information Input*—Inspecting Equipment, Structures, Materials; Monitoring Processes, Materials, and Surroundings; Getting Information Needed to Do the Job. *Mental Process*—Evaluating Information Against Standards; Analyzing Data or Information; Judging Qualities of Things, Services, Other People's Work. *Work Output*—Handling and Moving Objects; Controlling Machines and Processes; Performing General Physical Activities. *Interacting with Others*—Coordinating Work and Activities of Others; Coaching and Developing Others; Guiding, Directing and Motivating Subordinates; Teaching Others; Communicating with Other Workers; Interpreting Meaning of Information to Others. **Physical Work Conditions:** Hazardous Equipment; Using Hands on Objects, Tools, or Controls; Indoors. **Other Job Characteristics:** Consequence of Error; Importance of Being Sure All Is Done; Importance of Being Exact or Accurate.

Experience: Job Zone 3. Previous work-related skill, knowledge, or experience is required. **Job Preparation:** SVP 6.0 to less than 7.0—More than 1 year and less than 4 years. **Knowledge:** Mechanical; Design; Building and Construction; Engineering and Technology; Physics; Production and Processing; English Language; Computers and Electronics. **Instructional Program:** 470303 Industrial Machinery Maintenance and Repairer.

Related DOT Jobs: 600.261-010 Assembler, Steam-and-Gas Turbine; 600.281-022 Machine Builder; 600.380-026 Turbine-Blade Assembler; 624.381-018 Farm-Machinery Set-Up Mechanic; 638.361-010 Machine Assembler; 706.361-010 Assembler; 706.381-034 Sewing-Machine Assembler; 706.381-038 Subassembler; 706.381-042 Turbine Subassembler; 706.481-010 Internal-Combustion-Engine Subassembler; 801.261-010 Assembler, Mining Machinery; 801.261-018 Rotary-Engine Assembler; 801.361-010 Blower and Compressor Assembler; 806.381-022 Assembler, Aircraft Power Plant; 806.481-014 Assembler, Internal Combustion Engine; 820.361-014 Electric-Motor-and-Generator Assembler.

51-2041.00 Structural Metal Fabricators and Fitters
(Metal Fabricators, Structural Metal Products)

Education: Moderate-term O-T-J training
Employed: 45,790
Openings: 8,551
Projected Growth: 7.5%
Earnings: $24,070

Fabricate, lay out, position, align, and fit parts of structural metal products.

GOE Number, Interest Area, and Work Group: 08.03.03; Industrial Production; Production Work: Equipment Operation, Welding, Brazing, and Soldering. **Instructional Programs:** 480501 Machinist/Machine Technologist; 480503 Machine Shop Assistant; 480506 Sheet Metal Worker. **Note:** The Department of Labor has not collected some data for this job, so it has fewer details than the other descriptions.

51-2041.01 Metal Fabricators, Structural Metal Products (Metal Fabricators, Structural Metal Products)

Education: Moderate-term O-T-J training

Employed: 45,790

Openings: 8,551

Projected Growth: 7.5%

Earnings: $24,070

Fabricate and assemble structural metal products such as frameworks or shells for machinery, ovens, tanks, and stacks. Fabricate and assemble metal parts for buildings and bridges, according to job order or blueprints.

Verifies conformance of workpiece to specifications, using square, ruler, and measuring tape. Hammers, chips, and grinds workpiece to cut, bend, and straighten metal. Positions, aligns, fits, and welds together parts, using jigs, welding torch, and hand tools. Preheats workpieces to render them malleable, using hand torch or furnace. Designs and constructs templates and fixtures, using hand tools. Sets up and operates fabricating machines such as brakes, rolls, shears, flame cutters, and drill presses. Locates and marks bending and cutting lines onto workpiece, allowing for stock thickness and machine and welding shrinkage. Develops layout and plans sequence of operations for fabricating and assembling structural metal products, applying trigonometry and knowledge of metal. Sets up and operates machine tools associated with fabricating shops, such as radial drill, end mill, and edge planer.

GOE Number, Interest Area, and Work Group: 08.03.03; Industrial Production; Production Work: Equipment Operation, Welding, Brazing, and Soldering. **Personality Type:** Realistic. Realistic occupations frequently involve work activities that include practical, hands-on problems and solutions. These occupations often deal with plants, animals, and real-world materials like wood, tools, and machinery. Many of the occupations require working outside and do not involve a lot of paperwork or working closely with others. **Work Values:** Moral Values; Supervision, Human Relations; Activity; Company Policies and Practices; Independence. **Skills:** Mathematics; Product Inspection; Operation and Control; Equipment Selection; Operations Analysis. **Abilities:** *Cognitive*—Visualization; Number Facility; Problem Sensitivity; Deductive Reasoning; Written Comprehension. *Psychomotor*—Control Precision; Arm-Hand Steadiness; Manual Dexterity. *Physical*—Extent Flexibility; Static Strength; Trunk Strength. *Sensory*—Depth Perception. **General Work Activities:** *Information Input*—Getting Information Needed to Do the Job; Identifying Objects, Actions, and Events; Estimating Needed Characteristics. *Mental Process*—Making Decisions and Solving Problems; Evaluating Information Against Standards; Analyzing Data or Information; Judging Qualities of Things, Services, Other People's Work;

Processing Information. *Work Output*—Performing General Physical Activities; Handling and Moving Objects; Controlling Machines and Processes. *Interacting with Others*—Communicating with Other Workers; Establishing and Maintaining Relationships; Coordinating Work and Activities of Others; Performing Administrative Activities; Monitoring and Controlling Resources. **Physical Work Conditions:** Using Hands on Objects, Tools, or Controls; Indoors; Standing. **Other Job Characteristics:** Consequence of Error; Importance of Being Exact or Accurate; Importance of Being Sure All Is Done.

Experience: Job Zone 4. A minimum of two to four years of work-related skill, knowledge, or experience is needed. **Job Preparation:** SVP 7.0 to less than 8.0—2 years to less than 10 years. **Knowledge:** Mechanical; Building and Construction; Design; Production and Processing; Engineering and Technology. **Instructional Programs:** 480501 Machinist/Machine Technologist; 480503 Machine Shop Assistant; 480506 Sheet Metal Worker.

Related DOT Jobs: 619.361-014 Metal Fabricator; 619.361-018 Metal-Fabricator Apprentice.

51-2041.02 Fitters, Structural Metal—Precision (Fitters, Structural Metal, Precision)

Education: Work experience in a related occupation

Employed: 16,713

Openings: 1,750

Projected Growth: –13%

Earnings: $26,180

Lay out, position, align, and fit together fabricated parts of structural metal products, preparatory to welding or riveting.

Examines blueprints and plans sequence of operation, applying knowledge of geometry and understanding of the effects of heat, weld shrinkage, machining, and metal thickness. Aligns parts, using jack, turnbuckles, wedges, drift pins, pry bars, and hammer. Tack-welds fitted parts together. Moves parts into position, by hand or by hoist or crane. Positions or tightens braces, jacks, clamps, ropes, or bolt straps; bolts parts in positions for welding or riveting. Marks reference points onto floor or face block and transposes them to workpiece, using measuring devices, squares, chalk, and soapstone. Removes high spots and cuts bevels, using hand files, portable grinders, and cutting torch. Gives directions to welder to build up low spots or short pieces with weld. Straightens warped or bent parts, using sledge, hand torch, straightening press, or bulldozer. Heat-treats parts with acetylene torch. Sets up face block, jigs, and fixtures. Locates reference points, using transit; erects ladders and scaffolding to fit together large assemblies.

GOE Number, Interest Area, and Work Group: 08.03.03; Industrial Production; Production Work: Equipment Operation, Welding, Brazing, and Soldering. **Personality Type:** Realistic. Realistic occupations frequently involve work activities that include practical, hands-on problems and solutions. These occupations often deal with plants, animals, and real-world materials like wood, tools, and machinery. Many of the occupations require working outside and do not involve a lot of paperwork or working closely with others. **Work Values:** Moral Values; Company Policies and Practices; Independence; Supervision, Human Relations; Activity. **Skills:** Mathematics; Equipment Selection; Product Inspection; Reading Comprehension; Critical Thinking. **Abilities:** *Cognitive*—Mathematical Reasoning; Deductive Reasoning; Visualization; Number Facility; Oral Expression. *Psychomotor*—Control Precision; Multilimb Coordination; Manual Dexterity. *Physical*—Static Strength; Extent Flexibility; Trunk Strength. *Sensory*—Depth Perception; Near Vision; Glare Sensitivity; Speech Clarity. **General Work Activities:** *Information Input*—Getting Information Needed to Do the Job; Identifying Objects, Actions, and Events; Inspecting Equipment, Structures, Materials. *Mental Process*—Analyzing Data or Information; Evaluating Information Against Standards; Organizing, Planning, and Prioritizing; Making Decisions and Solving Problems. *Work Output*—Handling and Moving Objects; Performing General Physical Activities; Drafting and Specifying Technical Devices. *Interacting with Others*—Communicating with Other Workers; Coordinating Work and Activities of Others; Guiding, Directing and Motivating Subordinates. **Physical Work Conditions:** Using Hands on Objects, Tools, or Controls; Common Protective or Safety Attire; Hazardous Equipment; Hazardous Situations. **Other Job Characteristics:** Consequence of Error; Importance of Being Exact or Accurate; Importance of Being Sure All Is Done.

Experience: Job Zone 4. A minimum of two to four years of work-related skill, knowledge, or experience is needed. **Job Preparation:** SVP 7.0 to less than 8.0—2 years to less than 10 years. **Knowledge:** Building and Construction; Mechanical; Mathematics; Engineering and Technology; Physics. **Instructional Program:** 480506 Sheet Metal Worker.

Related DOT Jobs: 801.261-014 Fitter I; 801.381-014 Fitter; 809.261-010 Assembler, Ground Support Equipment.

51-2091.00 Fiberglass Laminators and Fabricators
(Assemblers and Fabricators, Except Machine, Electrical, Electronic, and Precision)

Education: No data available.

Employed: 1,308,670

Openings: No data available.

Projected Growth: No data available.

Earnings: $19,760

Laminate layers of fiberglass on molds to form boat decks and hulls or to form bodies for golf carts, automobiles, or other products.

GOE Number, Interest Area, and Work Group: 08.03.06; Industrial Production; Production Work: Hands-on Work, Assorted Materials. **Instructional Programs:** 200502 Window Treatment Maker and Installer; 480304 Shoe, Boot and Leather Repairer; 480506 Sheet Metal Worker; 480702 Furniture Designer and Maker. **Note:** The Department of Labor has not collected some data for this job, so it has fewer details than the other descriptions.

51-2092.00 Team Assemblers (Assemblers and Fabricators, Except Machine, Electrical, Electronic, and Precision)

Education: No data available.

Employed: 1,308,670

Openings: No data available.

Projected Growth: No data available.

Earnings: $19,760

Work as part of a team having responsibility for assembling an entire product or a component of a product. Perform all tasks conducted by the team in the assembly process. Rotate through all or most of the tasks rather than being assigned to a specific task on a permanent basis. Participate in making management decisions affecting the work. Includes team leaders who work as part of the team.

GOE Number, Interest Area, and Work Group: 08.03.06; Industrial Production; Production Work: Hands-on Work, Assorted Materials. **Instructional Programs:** 200502 Window Treatment Maker and Installer; 480304 Shoe, Boot and Leather Repairer; 480506 Sheet Metal Worker; 480702 Furniture Designer and Maker. **Note:** The Department of Labor has not collected some data for this job, so it has fewer details than the other descriptions.

51-2093.00 Timing Device Assemblers, Adjusters, and Calibrators (Watch, Clock, and Chronometer Assemblers, Adjusters, Calibrators, Precision)

Education: No data available.

Employed: 2,180

Openings: No data available.

Projected Growth: No data available.

Earnings: $17,550

Perform precision assembling or adjusting of timing devices, such as watches, clocks, or chronometers, within narrow tolerances.

Replaces specified parts to repair malfunctioning timepieces, using watchmaker's tools, loupe, and holding fixture. Examines components of timepieces such as watches, clocks, or chronometers, to detect defects, using loupe or microscope. Assembles and installs components of timepieces, using watchmaker's tools and loupe, to complete mechanism. Disassembles timepieces such as watches, clocks, and chronometers, to diagnose and repair malfunctions. Reviews blueprints, sketches, or work orders to gather information about task to be completed. Adjusts size or positioning of timepiece parts, to achieve specified fit or function, using calipers, fixture, and loupe. Tests operation and fit of timepiece parts and subassemblies, using electronic testing equipment, tweezers, watchmaker's tools, and loupe. Observes operation of timepiece parts and subassemblies to determine accuracy of movement and to diagnose cause of defects. Bends parts such as hairsprings, pallets, barrel covers, and bridges, to correct deficiencies in truing or endshake, using tweezers. Cleans and lubricates timepiece parts and assemblies, using solvent, buff stick, and oil. Screws parts or assemblies into position.

GOE Number, Interest Area, and Work Group: 08.02.02; Industrial Production; Production Technology: Precision Hand Work. Personality Type: Realistic. Realistic occupations frequently involve work activities that include practical, hands-on problems and solutions. These occupations often deal with plants, animals, and real-world materials like wood, tools, and machinery. Many of the occupations require working outside and do not involve a lot of paperwork or working closely with others. Work Values: Moral Values; Independence; Working Conditions; Ability Utilization; Company Policies and Practices; Achievement. Skills: Repairing; Reading Comprehension; Equipment Selection; Testing; Installation; Active Learning; Monitoring; Problem Identification. Abilities: *Cognitive*—Visualization; Written Comprehension; Problem Sensitivity; Information Ordering; Deductive Reasoning. *Psychomotor*—Finger Dexterity; Manual Dexterity; Arm-Hand Steadiness. *Physical*—Trunk Strength. *Sensory*—Near Vision. General Work Activities: *Information Input*—Getting Information Needed to Do the Job; Inspecting Equipment, Structures, Materials; Identifying Objects, Actions, and Events. *Mental Process*—Evaluating Information Against Standards; Analyzing Data or Information; Making Decisions and Solving Problems. *Work Output*—Repairing and Maintaining Mechanical Equipment; Handling and Moving Objects; Controlling Machines and Processes; Repairing and Maintaining Electrical Equipment; Implementing Ideas and Programs. *Interacting with Others*—Monitoring and Controlling Resources; Communicating with Persons Outside Organization; Communicating with Other Workers. Physical Work Conditions: Indoors; Using Hands on Objects, Tools, or Controls; Sitting. Other Job Characteristics: Importance of Being Exact or Accurate; Importance of Being Sure All Is Done; Consequence of Error.

Experience: Job Zone 2. Some previous work-related skill, knowledge, or experience may be helpful, but usually is not needed. Job Preparation: SVP 4.00 to 5.99—6 months to less than 2 years. Knowledge: Mechanical; Design; Engineering and Technology; Computers and Electronics; Mathematics. Instructional Program: 470408 Watch, Clock and Jewelry Repairer.

Related DOT Jobs: 715.381-010 Assembler; 715.381-014 Assembler, Watch Train; 715.381-018 Banking Pin Adjuster; 715.381-022 Barrel Assembler; 715.381-026 Barrel-Bridge Assembler; 715.381-030 Barrel-Endshake Adjuster; 715.381-038 Chronometer Assembler and Adjuster; 715.381-042 Chronometer-Balance-and-Hairspring Assembler; 715.381-054 Hairspring Assembler; 715.381-062 Hairspring Vibrator; 715.381-082 Pallet-Stone Inserter; 715.381-086 Pallet-Stone Positioner; 715.381-094 Watch Assembler; 715.681-010 Timing Adjuster.

51-3000 Food Processing Workers

51-3011.00 Bakers (Bakers, Bread and Pastry)

Education:	Moderate-term O-T-J training
Employed:	171,191
Openings:	56,526
Projected Growth:	16.6%
Earnings:	$16,990

Mix and bake ingredients according to recipes to produce breads, rolls, cookies, cakes, pies, pastries, or other baked goods.

GOE Number, Interest Area, and Work Group: 11.05.01; Recreation, Travel, and Other Personal Services; Food and Beverage Services: Preparing. Instructional Program: 120501 Baker/Pastry Chef. Note: The Department of Labor has not collected some data for this job, so it has fewer details than the other descriptions.

51-3011.01 Bakers, Bread and Pastry (Bread and Pastry Bakers)

Education:	Moderate-term O-T-J training
Employed:	171,191
Openings:	56,526
Projected Growth:	16.6%
Earnings:	$16,990

Mix and bake ingredients according to recipes to produce small quantities of breads, pastries, and other baked goods, for consumption on premises or for sale as specialty baked goods.

Mixes ingredients to make icings; decorates cakes and pastries; blends colors for icings, shaped ornaments, and statuaries. Rolls and shapes dough, using rolling pin. Cuts dough in uniform portions with knife, divider, cookie cutter. Mixes ingredients to form dough or batter, by hand or with electric mixer. Molds dough in desired shapes; places dough in greased or floured pans; trims overlapping edges with knife. Checks production schedule to determine variety and quantity of goods to bake. Cuts, peels, and prepares fruit for pie fillings. Spreads or sprinkles toppings on loaves or specialties; places dough in oven, using long-handled paddle (peel). Mixes and cooks pie fillings; pours fillings into pie shells; tops filling with meringue or cream. Weighs and measures ingredients, using measuring cups and spoons. Covers filling with top crust.

GOE Number, Interest Area, and Work Group: 11.05.01; Recreation, Travel, and Other Personal Services; Food and Beverage Services: Preparing. Personality Type: Realistic. Realistic occupations frequently involve work activities that include practical, hands-on problems and solutions. These occupations often deal with plants, animals, and real-world materials like wood, tools, and machinery. Many of the occupations require working outside and do not involve a lot of paperwork or working closely with others. Work Values: Moral Values; Supervision, Human Relations; Independence; Activity; Supervision, Technical; Autonomy; Company Policies and Practices. Skills: Product Inspection; Mathematics; Operation and Control. Abilities: *Cognitive*—Information Ordering; Written Comprehension; Number Facility; Visualization; Problem Sensitivity. *Psychomotor*—Finger Dexterity. *Physical*—none met the criteria. General Work Activities: *Information Input*—Monitoring Processes, Materials, and Surroundings; Getting Information Needed to Do the Job; Estimating Needed Characteristics. *Mental Process*—Judging Qualities of Things, Services, Other People's Work; Organizing, Planning, and Prioritizing; Thinking Creatively. *Work Output*—Handling and Moving Objects; Implementing Ideas and Programs; Controlling Machines and Processes.

Interacting with Others—Communicating with Persons Outside Organization; Monitoring and Controlling Resources; Performing for or Working with the Public. **Physical Work Conditions:** Indoors; Standing; Special Uniform. **Other Job Characteristics:** Importance of Being Sure All Is Done; Degree of Automation; Importance of Being Exact or Accurate.

Experience: Job Zone 3. Previous work-related skill, knowledge, or experience is required. **Job Preparation:** SVP 6.0 to less than 7.0—More than 1 year and less than 4 years. **Knowledge:** Food Production; Customer and Personal Service; Production and Processing; Mathematics; Sales and Marketing. **Instructional Program:** 120501 Baker/Pastry Chef.

Related DOT Jobs: 313.361-010 Baker, Second; 313.361-038 Pie Maker; 313.381-010 Baker; 313.381-018 Cook Apprentice, Pastry; 313.381-026 Cook, Pastry.

51-3011.02 Bakers, Manufacturing (Bakers, Manufacturing)

Education:	Moderate-term O-T-J training
Employed:	54,956
Openings:	11,421
Projected Growth:	8.5%
Earnings:	$22,030

Mix and bake ingredients according to recipes to produce breads, pastries, and other baked goods in large quantities, for sale through establishments such as grocery stores. Use high-volume production equipment.

Dumps ingredients into mixing-machine bowl or steam kettle to mix or cook ingredients according to specific instructions. Measures flour and other ingredients to prepare batters, dough, fillings, and icings, using scale and graduated containers. Decorates cakes. Places dough in pans, molds, or on sheets, and bakes dough in oven or on grill. Rolls, cuts, and shapes dough to form sweet rolls, pie crusts, tarts, cookies, and related products prior to baking. Develops new recipes for cakes and icings. Observes color of products being baked and adjusts oven temperature. Applies glace, icing, or other topping to baked goods, using spatula or brush.

GOE Number, Interest Area, and Work Group: 08.03.02; Industrial Production; Production Work: Equipment Operation, Assorted Materials Processing. **Personality Type:** Realistic. Realistic occupations frequently involve work activities that include practical, hands-on problems and solutions. These occupations often deal with plants, animals, and real-world materials like wood, tools, and machinery. Many of the occupations require working outside and do not involve a lot of paperwork or working closely with others. **Work Values:** Moral Values; Company Policies and Practices; Supervision, Technical; Independence; Supervision, Human Relations. **Skills:** Mathematics; Reading Comprehension; Idea Generation; Idea Evaluation; Operation Monitoring; Operation and Control. **Abilities:** *Cognitive*—Information Ordering; Written Comprehension; Number Facility; Memorization; Originality. *Psychomotor*—Manual Dexterity; Multilimb Coordination; Rate Control. *Physical*—Gross Body Coordination. *Sensory*—Visual Color Discrimination. **General Work Activities:** *Information Input*—Monitoring Processes, Materials, and Surroundings; Getting

Information Needed to Do the Job; Identifying Objects, Actions, and Events. *Mental Process*—Judging Qualities of Things, Services, Other People's Work; Analyzing Data or Information; Thinking Creatively. *Work Output*—Handling and Moving Objects; Controlling Machines and Processes; Performing General Physical Activities. *Interacting with Others*—Communicating with Other Workers; Establishing and Maintaining Relationships; Monitoring and Controlling Resources. **Physical Work Conditions:** Indoors; Hazardous Situations; Standing. **Other Job Characteristics:** Degree of Automation; Importance of Being Exact or Accurate; Consequence of Error; Importance of Repeating Same Tasks.

Experience: Job Zone 3. Previous work-related skill, knowledge, or experience is required. **Job Preparation:** SVP 6.0 to less than 7.0—More than 1 year and less than 4 years. **Knowledge:** Production and Processing; Food Production; Mathematics; Customer and Personal Service; English Language. **Instructional Program:** 120501 Baker/Pastry Chef.

Related DOT Jobs: 520.384-010 Bench Hand; 526.381-010 Baker; 526.381-014 Baker Apprentice.

51-3021.00 Butchers and Meat Cutters (Butchers and Meat Cutters)

Education:	No data available.
Employed:	142,730
Openings:	No data available.
Projected Growth:	No data available.
Earnings:	$22,770

Cut, trim, or prepare consumer-sized portions of meat for use or sale in retail establishments.

Cuts, trims, bones, ties, and grinds meats such as beef, pork, poultry, and fish, to prepare meat in cooking form. Records quantity of meat received and issued to cooks. Estimates requirements and requisitions or orders meat supply. Shapes, laces, and ties roasts, using boning knife, skewer, and twine. Wraps and weighs meat for customers and collects money for sales. Receives, inspects, and stores meat upon delivery. Places meat on trays in display counter.

GOE Number, Interest Area, and Work Group: 11.05.01; Recreation, Travel, and Other Personal Services; Food and Beverage Services: Preparing. **Personality Type:** Realistic. Realistic occupations frequently involve work activities that include practical, hands-on problems and solutions. These occupations often deal with plants, animals, and real-world materials like wood, tools, and machinery. Many of the occupations require working outside and do not involve a lot of paperwork or working closely with others. **Work Values:** Moral Values; Independence; Security; Activity; Responsibility. **Skills:** Product Inspection; Problem Identification; Management of Personnel Resources; Reading Comprehension; Mathematics. **Abilities:** *Cognitive*—Oral Comprehension; Number Facility; Oral Expression; Information Ordering; Problem Sensitivity. *Psychomotor*—Manual Dexterity; Finger Dexterity. *Physical*—Dynamic Strength. **General Work Activities:** *Information Input*—Identifying Objects, Actions, and Events; Estimating Needed Characteristics; Getting Information Needed to

Do the Job. *Mental Process*—Judging Qualities of Things, Services, Other People's Work; Evaluating Information Against Standards; Making Decisions and Solving Problems. *Work Output*—Handling and Moving Objects; Implementing Ideas and Programs; Documenting and Recording Information; Performing General Physical Activities. *Interacting with Others*—Performing for or Working with the Public; Communicating with Persons Outside Organization; Establishing and Maintaining Relationships; Monitoring and Controlling Resources. **Physical Work Conditions:** Indoors; Standing; Using Hands on Objects, Tools, or Controls; Special Uniform. **Other Job Characteristics:** Importance of Being Sure All Is Done; Importance of Being Exact or Accurate; Consequence of Error.

Experience: Job Zone 3. Previous work-related skill, knowledge, or experience is required. **Job Preparation:** SVP 6.0 to less than 7.0—More than 1 year and less than 4 years. **Knowledge:** Customer and Personal Service; Clerical; English Language; Biology; Mathematics; Law, Government and Jurisprudence. **Instructional Program:** 120506 Meatcutter.

Related DOT Jobs: 316.681-010 Butcher, Meat; 316.684-018 Meat Cutter; 316.684-022 Meat-Cutter Apprentice.

51-3022.00 Meat, Poultry, and Fish Cutters and Trimmers (Meat, Poultry, and Fish Cutters and Trimmers)

Education: Short-term O-T-J training
Employed: 142,983
Openings: 33,193
Projected Growth: 24.2%
Earnings: $16,270

Use hand tools to perform routine cutting and trimming of meat, poultry, and fish.

Weighs meats and tags containers for weight and contents. Inspects meat products for defects or blemishes. Cuts and trims meat to prepare for packing. Separates meats and byproducts into specified containers. Obtains and distributes specified meat or carcass. Slaughters live animals. Trims, slices, and sections carcasses for future processing. Cleans carcasses and removes waste products or defective portions. Removes parts such as skin, feathers, scales, or bones from carcass. Seals containers of meat.

GOE Number, Interest Area, and Work Group: 08.03.02; Industrial Production; Production Work: Equipment Operation, Assorted Materials Processing. **Personality Type:** Realistic. Realistic occupations frequently involve work activities that include practical, hands-on problems and solutions. These occupations often deal with plants, animals, and real-world materials like wood, tools, and machinery. Many of the occupations require working outside and do not involve a lot of paperwork or working closely with others. **Work Values:** Moral Values; Activity; Independence; Supervision, Technical; Company Policies and Practices. **Skills:** Product Inspection; Equipment Selection. **Abilities:** *Cognitive*—Information Ordering; Category Flexibility; Spatial Orientation; Selective Attention; Visualization; Perceptual Speed. *Psychomotor*—Manual Dexterity; Wrist-Finger Speed; Arm-Hand Steadiness. *Physical*—Static Strength; Extent Flexibility; Trunk Strength. *Sensory*—Visual Color Discrimination; Peripheral Vision; Depth Perception. **General Work Activities:** *Information Input*—Monitoring Processes, Materials, and Surroundings; Inspecting Equipment, Structures, Materials; Identifying Objects, Actions, and Events. *Mental Process*—Judging Qualities of Things, Services, Other People's Work; Evaluating Information Against Standards; Processing Information. *Work Output*—Handling and Moving Objects; Performing General Physical Activities; Documenting and Recording Information. *Interacting with Others*—Monitoring and Controlling Resources; Communicating with Other Workers; Performing Administrative Activities. **Physical Work Conditions:** Indoors; Using Hands on Objects, Tools, or Controls; Standing. **Other Job Characteristics:** Importance of Being Sure All Is Done; Consequence of Error; Importance of Being Exact or Accurate.

Experience: Job Zone 1. No previous work-related skill, knowledge, or experience is needed. **Job Preparation:** SVP Below 4.0—Less than 6 months. **Knowledge:** Food Production; Biology; Mechanical; Production and Processing; Public Safety and Security. **Instructional Program:** 120506 Meatcutter.

Related DOT Jobs: 521.687-058 Fish Chopper, Gang Knife; 521.687-106 Sausage-Meat Trimmer; 521.687-126 Skin Lifter, Bacon; 522.687-046 Fish Roe Processor; 525.684-010 Boner, Meat; 525.684-014 Butcher, Fish; 525.684-018 Carcass Splitter; 525.684-022 Crab Butcher; 525.684-026 Final-Dressing Cutter; 525.684-030 Fish Cleaner; 525.684-034 Head Trimmer; 525.684-038 Offal Separator; 525.684-042 Poultry Killer; 525.684-046 Skinner; 525.684-050 Sticker, Animal; 525.684-054 Trimmer, Meat; 525.684-058 Turkey-Roll Maker; 525.687-010 Animal Eviscerator; 525.687-014 Casing Splitter; 525.687-030 Gambreler (partial list; see the introduction for sources of the complete list).

51-3023.00 Slaughterers and Meat Packers (Slaughterers and Butchers)

Education: No data available.
Employed: 65,600
Openings: No data available.
Projected Growth: No data available.
Earnings: $18,790

Work in slaughtering, meat packing, or wholesale establishments performing precision functions involving the preparation of meat. Participate in specialized slaughtering tasks. Cut standard or premium cuts of meat for marketing. Make sausage. Wrap meats.

Shackles hind legs of animals to raise them for slaughtering or skinning. Stuns animals prior to slaughtering. Wraps dressed carcasses and/or meat cuts. Removes bone and cuts meat into standard cuts to prepare meat for marketing. Skins sections of animals or whole animals. Severs jugular vein to drain blood and facilitate slaughtering. Trims, cleans, and/or cures animal hides. Saws, splits, or scribes slaughtered animals to reduce carcasses. Trims headmeat and otherwise severs or removes parts of animals heads or skulls. Washes and/or shaves carcasses. Grinds meat into sausage. Slaughters animals in accordance with religious law and determines that carcasses meet specified religious standards when slaughtering is performed for religious purposes. Slits open, eviscerates, and trims carcasses of slaughtered animals. Cuts, trims, skins, sorts, and washes viscera of slaughtered animals to separate edible portions from offal.

GOE Number, Interest Area, and Work Group: 08.03.02; Industrial Production; Production Work: Equipment Operation, Assorted Materials Processing. **Personality Type:** Realistic. Realistic occupations frequently involve work activities that include practical, hands-on problems and solutions. These occupations often deal with plants, animals, and real-world materials like wood, tools, and machinery. Many of the occupations require working outside and do not involve a lot of paperwork or working closely with others. **Work Values:** Security; Independence; Activity; Moral Values; Company Policies and Practices. **Skills:** Product Inspection; Equipment Selection. **Abilities:** *Cognitive*—Information Ordering; Visualization; Perceptual Speed; Memorization; Selective Attention; Category Flexibility. *Psychomotor*—Manual Dexterity; Arm-Hand Steadiness; Wrist-Finger Speed. *Physical*—Static Strength; Extent Flexibility; Trunk Strength. *Sensory*—Visual Color Discrimination; Far Vision; Peripheral Vision. **General Work Activities:** *Information Input*—Monitoring Processes, Materials, and Surroundings; Identifying Objects, Actions, and Events; Inspecting Equipment, Structures, Materials. *Mental Process*—Evaluating Information Against Standards; Judging Qualities of Things, Services, Other People's Work; Updating and Using Job-Relevant Knowledge. *Work Output*—Performing General Physical Activities; Handling and Moving Objects; Controlling Machines and Processes. *Interacting with Others*—Communicating with Other Workers; Assisting and Caring for Others; Coordinating Work and Activities of Others; Monitoring and Controlling Resources; Establishing and Maintaining Relationships. **Physical Work Conditions:** Common Protective or Safety Attire; Using Hands on Objects, Tools, or Controls; Standing. **Other Job Characteristics:** Consequence of Error; Importance of Repeating Same Tasks; Importance of Being Sure All Is Done.

Experience: Job Zone 2. Some previous work-related skill, knowledge, or experience may be helpful, but usually is not needed. **Job Preparation:** SVP 4.00 to 5.99—6 months to less than 2 years. **Knowledge:** Biology; Public Safety and Security; Food Production; Mechanical; Production and Processing. **Instructional Program:** 120506 Meatcutter.

Related DOT Jobs: 525.361-010 Slaughterer, Religious Ritual; 525.381-010 Butcher Apprentice; 525.381-014 Butcher, All-Round; 525.664-010 Meat Dresser.

51-3091.00 Food and Tobacco Roasting, Baking, and Drying Machine Operators and Tenders (Roasting, Baking, and Drying Machine Operators and Tenders, Food and Tobacco)

Education: No data available.

Employed: 13,640

Openings: No data available.

Projected Growth: No data available.

Earnings: $22,110

Operate or tend food or tobacco roasting, baking, or drying equipment, including hearth ovens, kiln driers, roasters, char kilns, and vacuum drying equipment.

Reads work order to determine quantity and type of product to be baked, dried, or roasted. Observes temperature, humidity, and pressure gauges; observes product; adjusts controls and turns valves, to maintain prescribed operating conditions. Opens valve, discharge gates, or hopper chutes, to load or remove product from oven or equipment. Smoothes out product in bin, tray, or conveyor, using rake or shovel. Observes, feels, or tastes products after processing, to ensure that products conform to standards. Weighs product, using scale hopper or scale conveyor. Fills or removes product from trays, carts, hoppers, or equipment, using scoop, peel, or shovel, or by hand. Tests product for moisture content, using moisture meter. Records production data such as weight and amount of product processed, type of product, and time and temperature of processing. Observes and listens for machine malfunctions, and notifies supervisor when corrective actions fail. Clears or dislodges blockages in bins, screens, or other equipment, using pole, brush, or mallet. Pushes racks or carts to transfer product for storage or for further processing. Installs equipment such as spray unit, cutting blades, or screens, using hand tools. Cleans equipment with steam, hot water, and hose. Sets temperature and time controls, lights ovens or gas burners, and starts equipment such as conveyors, blowers, driers, or pumps. Takes sample of product during or after process for laboratory analysis.

GOE Number, Interest Area, and Work Group: 08.03.02; Industrial Production; Production Work: Equipment Operation, Assorted Materials Processing. **Personality Type:** Realistic. Realistic occupations frequently involve work activities that include practical, hands-on problems and solutions. These occupations often deal with plants, animals, and real-world materials like wood, tools, and machinery. Many of the occupations require working outside and do not involve a lot of paperwork or working closely with others. **Work Values:** Moral Values; Company Policies and Practices; Independence; Activity; Supervision, Human Relations. **Skills:** Operation and Control; Product Inspection; Operation Monitoring; Monitoring; Reading Comprehension; Systems Perception. **Abilities:** *Cognitive*—Information Ordering; Written Comprehension; Number Facility; Problem Sensitivity; Time Sharing; Written Expression. *Psychomotor*—Manual Dexterity; Control Precision; Wrist-Finger Speed; Reaction Time; Finger Dexterity. *Physical*—Static Strength; Trunk Strength; Extent Flexibility. *Sensory*—Near Vision; Visual Color Discrimination; Hearing Sensitivity. **General Work Activities:** *Information Input*—Identifying Objects, Actions, and Events; Monitoring Processes, Materials, and Surroundings; Getting Information Needed to Do the Job. *Mental Process*—Judging Qualities of Things, Services, Other People's Work; Evaluating Information Against Standards; Making Decisions and Solving Problems. *Work Output*—Controlling Machines and Processes; Handling and Moving Objects; Documenting and Recording Information. *Interacting with Others*—Communicating with Other Workers; Performing Administrative Activities; Coordinating Work and Activities of Others; Performing for or Working with the Public; Monitoring and Controlling Resources; Interpreting Meaning of Information to Others. **Physical Work Conditions:** Indoors; Using Hands on Objects, Tools, or Controls; Standing. **Other Job Characteristics:** Degree of Automation; Consequence of Error; Importance of Being Sure All Is Done.

Experience: Job Zone 1. No previous work-related skill, knowledge, or experience is needed. **Job Preparation:** SVP Below 4.0—

Less than 6 months. **Knowledge:** Food Production; Mechanical; Mathematics; Production and Processing; Physics. **Instructional Program:** 010401 Agricultural and Food Products Processing Operations and Management.

Related DOT Jobs: 522.662-014 Redrying-Machine Operator; 522.685-038 Curing-Bin Operator; 522.685-066 Fish Smoker; 523.362-010 Cocoa-Bean Roaster I; 523.362-014 Drier Operator; 523.382-010 Gunner; 523.585-022 Drier, Long Goods; 523.585-030 Pulp-Drier Firer; 523.585-034 Roaster, Grain; 523.662-010 Bone-Char Kiln Operator; 523.665-010 Sugar Drier; 523.682-014 Coffee Roaster; 523.682-022 Drier Operator; 523.682-026 Drum Drier; 523.682-030 Kiln Operator, Malt House; 523.682-038 Tobacco Curer; 523.685-026 Coffee Roaster, Continuous Process; 523.685-054 Dehydrator Tender; 523.685-058 Drier Attendant; 523.685-062 Drier Operator (partial list; see the introduction for sources of the complete list).

51-3092.00 Food Batchmakers (Food Batchmakers)

Education: No data available.

Employed: 31,920

Openings: No data available.

Projected Growth: No data available.

Earnings: $23,060

Set up and operate equipment that mixes or blends ingredients used in the manufacturing of food products. Includes candy makers and cheese makers.

Examines, feels, and tastes product to evaluate color, texture, flavor, and bouquet. Fills processing or cooking container such as water-cooled kettle, steam-jacketed rotating cooker, pressure cooker, or vat, with ingredients, following recipe. Determines mixing sequence, based on knowledge of temperature effects and solubility and miscibility properties of specific ingredients. Measures and weighs ingredients, using English or metric measures and balance scales. Operates refining machine to reduce size of cooked batch. Stirs and cooks ingredients at specified temperatures. Mixes or blends ingredients, according to recipe, using paddle or agitator. Calculates ingredient amounts, to formulate or modify recipes to produce food product of specific flavor, texture, clarity, bouquet, and color. Cools food product batch on slabs or in water-cooled kettle. Grades food product according to government regulations or according to type, color, bouquet, and moisture content. Records amounts of ingredients used, test results, and time cycles. Gives directions to other workers who are assisting in batchmaking process. Separates, spreads, kneads, spins, casts, cuts, or rolls food product by hand or using machine. Tests food product sample for moisture content, acidity level, or butter-fat content. Homogenizes or pasteurizes material to prevent separation of substances or to obtain prescribed butterfat content.

GOE Number, Interest Area, and Work Group: 08.03.06; Industrial Production; Production Work: Hands-on Work, Assorted Materials. **Personality Type:** Realistic. Realistic occupations frequently involve work activities that include practical, hands-on problems and solutions. These occupations often deal with plants, animals, and real-world materials like wood, tools, and machinery. Many of the occupations require working outside and do not involve a lot of paperwork or working closely with others. **Work Values:** Moral Values; Supervision, Technical; Company Policies and Practices; Supervision, Human Relations; Activity; Security. **Skills:** Product Inspection; Coordination; Operation and Control; Mathematics; Instructing. **Abilities:** *Cognitive*–Information Ordering; Written Comprehension; Number Facility; Memorization; Inductive Reasoning; Visualization. *Psychomotor*–Manual Dexterity; Wrist-Finger Speed; Control Precision. *Physical*–Extent Flexibility. *Sensory*–Near Vision; Visual Color Discrimination; Hearing Sensitivity. **General Work Activities:** *Information Input*–Identifying Objects, Actions, and Events; Monitoring Processes, Materials, and Surroundings; Getting Information Needed to Do the Job. *Mental Process*–Judging Qualities of Things, Services, Other People's Work; Evaluating Information Against Standards; Making Decisions and Solving Problems. *Work Output*–Controlling Machines and Processes; Handling and Moving Objects; Documenting and Recording Information. *Interacting with Others*–Monitoring and Controlling Resources; Communicating with Other Workers; Performing Administrative Activities. **Physical Work Conditions:** Indoors; Using Hands on Objects, Tools, or Controls; Standing. **Other Job Characteristics:** Importance of Being Sure All Is Done; Importance of Being Exact or Accurate; Consequence of Error.

Experience: Job Zone 3. Previous work-related skill, knowledge, or experience is required. **Job Preparation:** SVP 6.0 to less than 7.0–More than 1 year and less than 4 years. **Knowledge:** Mathematics; Food Production; Production and Processing; Law, Government and Jurisprudence; English Language. **Instructional Programs:** 010401 Agricultural and Food Products Processing Operations and Management; 200401 Institutional Food Workers and Administrators, General.

Related DOT Jobs: 520.361-010 Honey Grader-and-Blender; 529.361-010 Almond-Paste Mixer; 529.361-014 Candy Maker; 529.361-018 Cheesemaker; 529.381-010 Compounder, Flavorings.

51-3093.00 Food Cooking Machine Operators and Tenders (Cooking Machine Operators and Tenders, Food and Tobacco)

Education: No data available.

Employed: 19,690

Openings: No data available.

Projected Growth: No data available.

Earnings: $21,350

Operate or tend cooking equipment such as steam-cooking vats, deep-fry cookers, pressure cookers, kettles, and boilers, to prepare food products.

Admits required amounts of water, steam, cooking oils, or compressed air into equipment. Turns valves or starts pumps to drain product from equipment and to transfer to storage, cooling, or further processing areas. Reads recipes or formulae to determine ingredients or quantities of ingredients needed. Operates auxiliary machines and equipment such as grinders, canners, and molding presses, to prepare or further process products. Places products on conveyor or cart and monitors flow. Activates agitators and paddles to mix or stir ingredients; stops machine when ingredients are thoroughly mixed. Listens for malfunction alarms, shuts down equipment, and notifies supervisor. Operates and controls equipment such as kettles, cookers, vats, and tanks, to cook ingredients or to prepare products for further processing. Starts conveyers, machines, or pumps; sets temperature, pressure, and time controls. Measures or weighs prescribed ingredients, using scales or measuring containers. Pours, adds, or loads prescribed quantities of ingredients or products into cooking equipment, manually or with a hoist. Examines sample of product; tests color, content, consistency, viscosity, acidity, or specific gravity; removes impurities from product. Notifies or signals other workers to operate equipment. Notifies or signals other workers when processing is complete. Removes cooked material or products from equipment. Cleans and washes equipment, using water hoses and using cleaning or sterilizing solutions or rinses. Records production and test data such as processing steps, temperature and steam readings, cooking time, batches processed, and test results. Observes gauges, dials, and product texture or color; adjusts controls to maintain appropriate temperature, pressure, and flow of ingredients.

GOE Number, Interest Area, and Work Group: 08.03.02; Industrial Production; Production Work: Equipment Operation, Assorted Materials Processing. **Personality Type:** Realistic. Realistic occupations frequently involve work activities that include practical, hands-on problems and solutions. These occupations often deal with plants, animals, and real-world materials like wood, tools, and machinery. Many of the occupations require working outside and do not involve a lot of paperwork or working closely with others. **Work Values:** Moral Values; Company Policies and Practices; Supervision, Human Relations; Activity; Independence; Security. **Skills:** Operation and Control; Operation Monitoring; Product Inspection; Mathematics; Reading Comprehension. **Abilities:** *Cognitive*—Written Comprehension; Information Ordering; Problem Sensitivity; Number Facility; Selective Attention; Written Expression. *Psychomotor*—Reaction Time; Control Precision; Arm-Hand Steadiness; Wrist-Finger Speed; Response Orientation. *Physical*—Static Strength. *Sensory*—Auditory Attention; Visual Color Discrimination; Sound Localization. **General Work Activities:** *Information Input*—Monitoring Processes, Materials, and Surroundings; Inspecting Equipment, Structures, Materials; Identifying Objects, Actions, and Events. *Mental Process*—Judging Qualities of Things, Services, Other People's Work; Processing Information; Evaluating Information Against Standards. *Work Output*—Controlling Machines and Processes; Handling and Moving Objects; Performing General Physical Activities. *Interacting with Others*—Communicating with Other Workers; Monitoring and Controlling Resources; Coordinating Work and Activities of Others; Performing Administrative Activities. **Physical Work Conditions:** Indoors; Standing; Using Hands on Objects, Tools, or Controls. **Other Job Characteristics:** Degree of Automation; Importance of Being Sure All Is Done; Consequence of Error.

Experience: Job Zone 1. No previous work-related skill, knowledge, or experience is needed. **Job Preparation:** SVP Below 4.0—Less than 6 months. **Knowledge:** Production and Processing; Food Production; Mathematics; English Language; Mechanical; Public Safety and Security; Clerical. **Instructional Program:** 010401 Agricultural and Food Products Processing Operations and Management.

Related DOT Jobs: 520.685-082 Cooker, Casing; 521.687-090 Nut Steamer; 522.362-010 Yeast Distiller; 522.382-010 Cottage-Cheese Maker; 522.382-022 Mash-Tub-Cooker Operator; 522.382-034 Sugar Boiler; 522.482-010 Masher; 522.682-010 Kettle Operator; 522.682-014 Ordering-Machine Operator; 522.685-018 Brine Maker I; 522.685-034 Corn Cooker; 522.685-094 Steam-Conditioner Operator; 522.685-102 Vacuum-Conditioner Operator; 523.382-022 Processor, Instant Potato; 523.682-010 Chocolate Temperer; 523.682-018 Dextrine Mixer; 523.685-014 Blanching-Machine Operator; 523.685-022 Chocolate Temperer; 523.685-030 Cook-Box Filler; 523.685-034 Cooker, Meal (partial list; see the introduction for sources of the complete list).

51-4000 Metal Workers and Plastic Workers

51-4011.00 Computer-Controlled Machine Tool Operators, Metal and Plastic (Numerical Control Machine Tool Operators and Tenders, Metal and Plastic)

Education: Moderate-term O-T-J training
Employed: 87,978
Openings: 18,908
Projected Growth: 22.6%
Earnings: $27,110

Operate computer-controlled machines or robots to perform one or more machine functions on metal or plastic work pieces.

GOE Number, Interest Area, and Work Group: 08.03.01; Industrial Production; Production Work: Machine Work, Assorted Materials. **Instructional Program:** 480503 Machine Shop Assistant. **Note:** The Department of Labor has not collected some data for this job, so it has fewer details than the other descriptions.

51-4011.01 Numerical Control Machine Tool Operators and Tenders, Metal and Plastic (Numerical Control Machine Tool Operators and Tenders)

Education: Moderate-term O-T-J training
Employed: 87,978
Openings: 18,908
Projected Growth: 22.6%
Earnings: $27,110

Set up and operate numerical control (magnetic- or punched-tape–controlled) machine tools that automatically mill, drill, broach, and ream metal and plastic parts. Adjust machine feed and speed; change cutting tools; adjust machine controls when automatic programming is faulty or when machine malfunctions.

Confers with supervisor or programmer to resolve machine malfunctions and production errors; obtains approval to continue production. Starts automatic operation of numerical control machine to machine parts or test setup, workpiece dimensions, or programming. Maintains machines and removes and replaces broken or worn machine tools, using hand tools. Lifts workpiece to machine, by hand, with hoist or crane, or with tweezers. Stops machine to remove finished workpiece or change tooling, setup, or workpiece placement, according to required machining sequence. Lays out and marks areas of part to be shot-peened, and fills hopper with shot. Loads control media such as tape, card, or disk, in machine controller or enters commands to retrieve programmed instructions. Measures dimensions of finished workpiece to ensure conformance to specifications, using precision measuring instruments, templates, and fixtures. Positions and secures workpiece on machine bed, indexing table, fixture, or dispensing or holding device. Selects, measures, assembles, and sets machine tools such as drill bits and milling or cutting tools, using precision gauges and instruments. Examines electronic components for defects and completeness of laser-beam trimming, using microscope. Enters commands or manually adjusts machine controls to correct malfunctions or tolerances. Monitors machine operation and control panel displays to detect malfunctions and compare readings to specifications. Calculates and sets machine controls to position tools, synchronize tape and tool, or regulate cutting depth, speed, feed, or coolant flow. Determines specifications or procedures for tooling set-up, machine operation, workpiece dimensions, or numerical control sequences, using blueprints, instructions, and machine knowledge. Mounts, installs, aligns, and secures tools, attachments, fixtures, and workpiece on machine, using hand tools and precision measuring instruments.

GOE Number, Interest Area, and Work Group: 08.03.01; Industrial Production; Production Work: Machine Work, Assorted Materials. **Personality Type:** Realistic. Realistic occupations frequently involve work activities that include practical, hands-on problems and solutions. These occupations often deal with plants, animals, and real-world materials like wood, tools, and machinery. Many of the occupations require working outside and do not involve a lot of paperwork or working closely with others. **Work Values:** Moral Values; Activity; Company Policies and Practices; Independence; Supervision, Human Relations. **Skills:** Product Inspection; Operation and Control; Operation Monitoring; Mathematics; Equipment Maintenance; Equipment Selection. **Abilities:** *Cognitive*—Problem Sensitivity; Number Facility; Information Ordering; Written Comprehension; Deductive Reasoning; Visualization. *Psychomotor*—Reaction Time; Wrist-Finger Speed; Control Precision. *Physical*—Dynamic Strength; Static Strength; Explosive Strength. *Sensory*—Speech Clarity; Speech Recognition; Sound Localization. **General Work Activities:** *Information Input*—Monitoring Processes, Materials, and Surroundings; Inspecting Equipment, Structures, Materials; Getting Information Needed to Do the Job. *Mental Process*—Evaluating Information Against Standards; Making Decisions and Solving Problems; Processing Information. *Work Output*—Handling and Moving Objects; Controlling Machines and Processes; Repairing and Maintaining Mechanical Equipment. *Interacting with Others*—Communicating with Other Workers; Establishing and Maintaining Relationships; Coordinating Work and Activities of Others. **Physical Work Conditions:** Indoors; Standing; Using Hands on Objects, Tools, or Controls. **Other Job Characteristics:** Degree of Automation; Importance of Being Exact or Accurate; Consequence of Error.

Experience: Job Zone 2. Some previous work-related skill, knowledge, or experience may be helpful, but usually is not needed. **Job Preparation:** SVP 4.00 to 5.99—6 months to less than 2 years. **Knowledge:** Mechanical; Production and Processing; Engineering and Technology; Mathematics; Computers and Electronics. **Instructional Program:** 480503 Machine Shop Assistant.

Related DOT Jobs: 604.362-010 Lathe Operator, Numerical Control; 605.360-010 Router Set-Up Operator, Numerical Control; 605.380-010 Milling-Machine Set-Up Operator, Numerical Control; 605.382-046 Numerical-Control Router Operator; 606.362-010 Drill-Press Operator, Numerical Control; 606.382-014 Jig-Boring Machine Operator, Numerical Control; 606.382-018 Numerical-Control Drill Operator, Printed Circuit Boards; 606.382-026 Robotic Machine Operator; 609.360-010 Numerical Control Machine Set-Up Operator; 609.362-010 Numerical Control Machine Operator; 617.280-010 Shot-Peening Operator; 699.362-010 Automated Cutting Machine Operator; 726.682-010 Laser-Beam-Trim Operator.

51-4012.00 Numerical Tool and Process Control Programmers (Numerical Control Machine Tool Programmers)

Education: Work experience in a related occupation

Employed: 8,471

Openings: 706

Projected Growth: 6.1%

Earnings: $40,490

Develop programs to control machining or processing of parts by automatic machine tools, equipment, or systems.

Compares encoded tape or computer printout with original program sheet to verify accuracy of instructions. Draws machine tool paths on pattern film, using colored markers and following guidelines for tool speed and efficiency. Enters computer commands to store or retrieve parts patterns, graphic displays, or programs to transfer data to other media. Revises numerical control machine tape programs to eliminate instruction errors and omissions. Writes instruction sheets, cutter lists, and machine instructions programs to guide setup and encode numerical control tape. Moves reference table to align pattern film over circuit board holes with reference marks on enlarger scope. Analyzes drawings, specifications, printed circuit-board pattern film, and design data to calculate dimensions, tool selection, machine speeds, and feed rates. Aligns and secures pattern film on reference table of optical programmer and observes enlarger-scope view of printed circuit board. Depresses pedal or button of programmer to enter coordinates of each hole location into program memory. Loads and unloads disks or tapes and observes operation of machine on trial run to test taped or programmed instructions. Reviews shop orders to determine job specifications and requirements. Sorts shop orders into groups to maximize materials utilization and minimize machine setup. Prepares geometric layout from graphic displays, using computer-assisted drafting software or drafting instruments and graph paper. Determines reference points, machine cutting paths, or hole locations and computes angular and linear dimensions, radii, and curvatures.

GOE Number, Interest Area, and Work Group: 02.08.04; Science, Math, and Engineering; Engineering Technology: General. **Personality Type:** Realistic. Realistic occupations frequently involve work activities that include practical, hands-on problems and solutions. These occupations often deal with plants, animals, and real-world materials like wood, tools, and machinery. Many of the occupations require working outside and do not involve a lot of paperwork or working closely with others. **Work Values:** Moral Values; Independence; Compensation; Autonomy; Company Policies and Practices. **Skills:** Mathematics; Information Organization; Operations Analysis; Programming; Product Inspection; Reading Comprehension; Troubleshooting. **Abilities:** *Cognitive—*Mathematical Reasoning; Information Ordering; Number Facility; Written Comprehension; Deductive Reasoning; Written Expression. *Psychomotor—*Control Precision; Wrist-Finger Speed; Finger Dexterity. *Physical—*Gross Body Equilibrium. *Sensory—*Near Vision; Visual Color Discrimination; Auditory Attention. **General Work Activities:** *Information Input—*Getting Information Needed to Do the Job; Identifying Objects, Actions, and Events; Monitoring Processes, Materials, and Surroundings. *Mental Process—*Making Decisions and Solving Problems; Analyzing Data or Information; Evaluating Information Against Standards. *Work Output—*Drafting and Specifying Technical Devices; Handling and Moving Objects; Interacting with Computers. *Interacting with Others—*Interpreting Meaning of Information to Others; Providing Consultation and Advice to Others; Communicating with Other Workers; Performing Administrative Activities. **Physical Work Conditions:** Indoors; Sitting; Using Hands on Objects, Tools, or Controls. **Other Job Characteristics:** Degree of Automation; Importance of Being Exact or Accurate; Consequence of Error.

Experience: Job Zone 3. Previous work-related skill, knowledge, or experience is required. **Job Preparation:** SVP 6.0 to less than 7.0—More than 1 year and less than 4 years. **Knowledge:** Computers and Electronics; Mathematics; Design; Production and Processing; Engineering and Technology. **Instructional Programs:** 110201 Computer Programming; 110301 Data Processing Technology/Technician.

Related DOT Jobs: 007.167-018 Tool Programmer, Numerical Control; 007.362-010 Nesting Operator, Numerical Control; 609.262-010 Tool Programmer, Numerical Control.

51-4021.00 Extruding and Drawing Machine Setters, Operators, and Tenders, Metal and Plastic (Extruding and Drawing Machine Setters and Set-Up Operators, Metal and Plastic)

Education: No data available.

Employed: 45,010

Openings: No data available.

Projected Growth: No data available.

Earnings: $24,100

Set up, operate, or tend machines to extrude or draw thermoplastic or metal materials into tubes, rods, hoses, wire, bars, or structural shapes.

Tests physical properties of product with testing devices such as acid-bath tester, burst tester, and impact tester. Replaces worn dies when products vary from specifications. Weighs and mixes pelletized, granular, or powdered thermoplastic materials and coloring pigments. Selects nozzles, spacers, and wire guides, according to diameter and length of rod. Adjusts controls to draw or press metal into specified shape and diameter. Studies specifications, determines set-up procedures, and selects machine dies and parts. Examines extruded product for defects such as wrinkles, bubbles, and splits. Measures extruded articles for conformance to specifications; adjusts controls to obtain product of specified dimensions. Installs dies, machine screws, and sizing rings on machine extruding thermoplastic or metal materials. Operates shearing mechanism to cut rods to specified length. Loads machine hopper with mixed materials, using auger; stuffs rolls of plastic dough into machine cylinders. Starts machine and sets controls to regulate vacuum, air pressure, sizing rings, and temperature, and synchronizes speed of extrusion. Reels extruded product into rolls of specified length and weight.

GOE Number, Interest Area, and Work Group: 08.02.01; Industrial Production; Production Technology: Machine Set-up and Operation. **Personality Type:** Realistic. Realistic occupations frequently involve work activities that include practical, hands-on problems and solutions. These occupations often deal with plants, animals, and real-world materials like wood, tools, and machinery. Many of the occupations require working outside and do not involve a lot of paperwork or working closely with others. **Work Values:** Moral Values; Activity; Independence; Company Policies and Practices; Supervision, Human Relations. **Skills:** Product Inspection; Operation and Control; Testing; Operation Monitoring; Equipment Selection; Equipment Maintenance. **Abilities:** *Cognitive—*Information Ordering; Problem Sensitivity; Written Comprehension; Visualization; Number Facility. *Psychomotor—*Control Precision; Multilimb Coordination; Rate Control. *Physical—*Static Strength; Dynamic Strength; Stamina. **General Work Activities:** *Information Input—*Getting Information Needed to Do the Job; Monitoring Processes, Materials, and Surroundings; Inspecting Equipment, Structures, Materials. *Mental Process—*Judging Qualities of Things, Services, Other People's Work; Evaluating Information Against Standards; Making Decisions and Solving Problems. *Work Output—*Handling and Moving Objects; Controlling Machines and Processes; Performing General Physical Activities. *Interacting with Others—*Communicating with Other Workers; Monitoring and Controlling Resources; Performing Administrative Activities. **Physical Work Conditions:** Indoors; Using Hands on Objects, Tools, or Controls; Standing; Common Protective or Safety Attire. **Other Job Characteristics:** Degree of Automation; Consequence of Error; Pace Determined by Speed of Equipment.

Experience: Job Zone 2. Some previous work-related skill, knowledge, or experience may be helpful, but usually is not needed. **Job Preparation:** SVP 4.00 to 5.99—6 months to less than 2 years. **Knowledge:** Production and Processing; Mechanical; Engineering and Technology; Mathematics; Physics. **Instructional Program:** 480501 Machinist/Machine Technologist.

Related DOT Jobs: 557.382-010 Extruder Operator; 614.380-010 Extrusion-Press Adjuster; 614.382-010 Wire Drawer; 614.482-010 Draw-Bench Operator; 614.482-014 Extruder Operator; 614.482-018 Extrusion-Press Operator I.

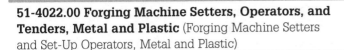

51-4022.00 Forging Machine Setters, Operators, and Tenders, Metal and Plastic (Forging Machine Setters and Set-Up Operators, Metal and Plastic)

Education: No data available.

Employed: 15,540

Openings: No data available.

Projected Growth: No data available.

Earnings: $35,910

Set up, operate, or tend forging machines to taper, shape, or form metal or plastic parts.

Adjusts temperature controls of furnace in which rods are heated. Turns handles or knobs, to set pressure and depth of ram stroke and to synchronize machine operations. Selects, aligns, and bolts positioning fixtures and stops and specified dies to ram and anvil, forging rolls; presses and hammers. Trims and compresses finished forgings to specified tolerances. Sharpens cutting tools and drill bits, using bench grinder. Confers with other workers regarding setup and operational specifications of machines. Marks layout; verifies dimensions; measures, weighs, and inspects machined parts to ensure conformance to product specifications. Positions and moves metal wire or workpiece through series of dies to compress and shape stock to form die impressions. Reads blueprints to determine specified tolerances and sequence of operations to set up machines. Starts machine, produces sample workpiece, and observes operations to detect machine malfunction and to ensure that setup conforms to specifications. Installs and adjusts or removes and replaces dies, synchronizing cams, forging hammer, and stop guides, according to specifications.

GOE Number, Interest Area, and Work Group: 08.02.01; Industrial Production; Production Technology: Machine Set-up and Operation. **Personality Type:** Realistic. Realistic occupations frequently involve work activities that include practical, hands-on problems and solutions. These occupations often deal with plants, animals, and real-world materials like wood, tools, and machinery. Many of the occupations require working outside and do not involve a lot of paperwork or working closely with others. **Work Values:** Moral Values; Activity; Company Policies and Practices; Supervision, Human Relations; Independence. **Skills:** Operation and Control; Operation Monitoring; Product Inspection; Installation; Equipment Selection. **Abilities:** *Cognitive*—Information Ordering; Visualization; Problem Sensitivity; Oral Comprehension; Number Facility. *Psychomotor*—Control Precision; Manual Dexterity; Arm-Hand Steadiness. *Physical*—Static Strength; Extent Flexibility; Trunk Strength. **General Work Activities:** *Information Input*—Getting Information Needed to Do the Job; Inspecting Equipment, Structures, Materials; Monitoring Processes, Materials, and Surroundings. *Mental Process*—Evaluating Information Against Standards; Making Decisions and Solving Problems; Judging Qualities of Things, Services, Other People's Work; Processing Information; Analyzing Data or Information. *Work Output*—Controlling Machines and Processes; Handling and Moving Objects; Repairing and Maintaining Mechanical Equipment; Implementing Ideas and Programs; Performing General Physical Activities. *Interacting with Others*—Communicating with Other Workers; Coordinating Work and Activities of Others; Providing Consultation and Advice to Others; Establishing and Maintaining Relationships. **Physical Work Conditions:** Using Hands on Objects, Tools, or Controls; Indoors; Standing. **Other Job Characteristics:** Degree of Automation; Consequence of Error; Importance of Being Exact or Accurate; Importance of Being Sure All Is Done.

Experience: Job Zone 2. Some previous work-related skill, knowledge, or experience may be helpful, but usually is not needed. **Job Preparation:** SVP 4.00 to 5.99—6 months to less than 2 years. **Knowledge:** Mechanical; Design; Physics; Engineering and Technology; Production and Processing; Mathematics; English Language. **Instructional Program:** 480501 Machinist/Machine Technologist.

Related DOT Jobs: 610.362-010 Drophammer Operator; 611.482-010 Forging-Press Operator I; 611.662-010 Upsetter; 611.682-010 Steel-Shot-Header Operator; 612.260-010 Fastener Technologist; 612.360-010 Die Setter; 612.361-010 Heavy Forger; 612.462-010 Multi-Operation-Machine Operator; 612.462-014 Nut Former; 612.662-010 Spike-Machine Operator; 612.682-010 Buckshot-Swage Operator; 612.682-014 Forging-Roll Operator.

51-4023.00 Rolling Machine Setters, Operators, and Tenders, Metal and Plastic (Rolling Machine Setters and Set-Up Operators, Metal and Plastic)

Education: No data available.

Employed: 18,770

Openings: No data available.

Projected Growth: No data available.

Earnings: $27,000

Set up, operate, or tend machines to roll steel or plastic, forming bends, beads, knurls, rolls, or plate. Set up, operate, or tend machines to flatten, temper, or reduce gauge of material.

Monitors machine cycles and mill operation to detect jamming and to ensure that fabricated products conform to specifications. Activates shear and grinder to trim workpiece, cut steel strips, and monitor forming of gears to specified length and diameter. Manipulates controls and observes dial indicators to monitor, adjust, and regulate speed of machine mechanisms. Sets distance points between rolls, guides, meters, and stops, according to specifications. Resets, adjusts, and corrects machine setup, to reduce thickness, reshape products, and eliminate product defects. Positions, aligns, and secures arbor, spindle, coils, mandrel, dies, and slitting knives onto machine. Reads rolling order and mill schedules to determine set-up specifications, work sequence, product dimensions, and installation procedures. Calculates draft space and roll speed for each mill stand, to plan rolling sequence and specified dimensions and temper. Threads or feeds sheets or rods through rolling mechanism; starts and controls mechanism that automatically feeds steel into rollers. Examines, inspects, measures, and feels raw materials and finished product to verify conformance to specifications, visually or with the use of measurement instruments. Disassembles sizing mills removed from rolling line; sorts and stores parts. Selects rolls, dies, roll stands, and chucks from data charts, to form specified contours and to fabricate products.

Installs equipment such as guides, guards, gears, cooling equipment, and rolls, using hand tools. Starts operation of rolling and milling machines to flatten, temper, form, and reduce sheet-metal sections and produce steel strips. Fills oil cups, adjusts valves, and observes gauges to control flow of metal coolant and lubricants onto workpiece. Signals and assists other workers to remove and position equipment, fill hoppers, and feed materials into machine. Records mill production on schedule sheet.

GOE Number, Interest Area, and Work Group: 08.02.01; Industrial Production; Production Technology: Machine Set-up and Operation. **Personality Type:** Realistic. Realistic occupations frequently involve work activities that include practical, hands-on problems and solutions. These occupations often deal with plants, animals, and real-world materials like wood, tools, and machinery. Many of the occupations require working outside and do not involve a lot of paperwork or working closely with others. **Work Values:** Moral Values; Activity; Company Policies and Practices; Supervision, Human Relations; Independence. **Skills:** Operation and Control; Product Inspection; Operation Monitoring; Mathematics; Equipment Maintenance. **Abilities:** *Cognitive*—Information Ordering; Problem Sensitivity; Written Comprehension; Number Facility; Perceptual Speed; Oral Expression. *Psychomotor*—Manual Dexterity; Control Precision; Rate Control; Arm-Hand Steadiness. *Physical*—Extent Flexibility; Static Strength; Trunk Strength. *Sensory*—Near Vision; Visual Color Discrimination; Depth Perception. **General Work Activities:** *Information Input*—Getting Information Needed to Do the Job; Monitoring Processes, Materials, and Surroundings; Inspecting Equipment, Structures, Materials. *Mental Process*—Evaluating Information Against Standards; Analyzing Data or Information; Making Decisions and Solving Problems; Judging Qualities of Things, Services, Other People's Work. *Work Output*—Controlling Machines and Processes; Performing General Physical Activities; Handling and Moving Objects. *Interacting with Others*—Guiding, Directing and Motivating Subordinates; Communicating with Other Workers; Coordinating Work and Activities of Others; Teaching Others; Interpreting Meaning of Information to Others. **Physical Work Conditions:** Indoors; Using Hands on Objects, Tools, or Controls; Hazardous Equipment; Standing. **Other Job Characteristics:** Degree of Automation; Pace Determined by Speed of Equipment; Consequence of Error.

Experience: Job Zone 2. Some previous work-related skill, knowledge, or experience may be helpful, but usually is not needed. **Job Preparation:** SVP 4.00 to 5.99—6 months to less than 2 years. **Knowledge:** Mechanical; Production and Processing; Mathematics; Engineering and Technology; Education and Training; Clerical. **Instructional Programs:** 480501 Machinist/Machine Technologist; 480506 Sheet Metal Worker; 480599 Precision Metal Workers, Other.

Related DOT Jobs: 613.360-010 Roll-Forming-Machine Set-Up Mechanic; 613.360-014 Roll-Tube Setter; 613.360-018 Tin Roller, Hot Mill; 613.361-010 Guide Setter; 613.382-014 Finisher; 613.462-018 Rolling-Mill Operator; 613.482-014 Piercing-Machine Operator; 613.662-018 Cold-Mill Operator; 613.682-014 Reeling-Machine Operator; 613.682-022 Strip Roller; 613.682-030 Mill Operator, Rolls; 617.480-010 Job Setter, Spline-Rolling Machine; 617.482-014 Forming-Roll Operator I; 617.482-018 Roll-Forming-Machine Operator I; 617.682-022 Setter, Cold-Rolling Machine; 619.462-010 Roll-Threader Operator.

51-4031.00 Cutting, Punching, and Press Machine Setters, Operators, and Tenders, Metal and Plastic
(Machine Tool Cutting Operators and Tenders, Metal and Plastic)

Education: Moderate-term O-T-J training
Employed: 109,331
Openings: 5,844
Projected Growth: –19.9%
Earnings: $24,510

Set up, operate, or tend machines to saw, cut, shear, slit, punch, crimp, notch, bend, or straighten metal or plastic material.

GOE Number, Interest Area, and Work Group: 08.02.01; Industrial Production; Production Technology: Machine Set-up and Operation. **Instructional Programs:** 470408 Watch, Clock and Jewelry Repairer; 480503 Machine Shop Assistant. **Note:** The Department of Labor has not collected some data for this job, so it has fewer details than the other descriptions.

51-4031.01 Sawing Machine Tool Setters and Set-Up Operators, Metal and Plastic (Sawing Machine Tool Setters and Set-Up Operators, Metal and Plastic)

Education: No data available.
Employed: 21,320
Openings: No data available.
Projected Growth: No data available.
Earnings: $23,630

Set up, or set up and operate, metal or plastic sawing machines to cut straight, curved, irregular, or internal patterns in metal or plastic stock or to trim edges of metal or plastic objects. Use machines such as band saws, circular saws, friction saws, hacksawing machines, and jigsaws.

Reads work order for specifications, such as materials to be used, location of cutting lines, and dimensions and tolerances. Removes housings, feed tubes, tool holders, and other accessories to replace worn or broken parts such as springs and bushings. Selects blade according to specifications and installs on machine, using hand tools. Turns valves to start flow of coolant against cutting area and to start airflow which blows cuttings away from kerf. Positions guides, stops, holding blocks, or other fixtures, to secure and direct workpiece, using hand tools and measuring devices. Sharpens dulled blades, using bench grinder, abrasive wheel, or lathe. Starts machine and feeds workpiece against blade, guiding along layout lines, to cut workpiece to specified dimensions. Marks identifying data on workpieces. Measures completed workpiece to verify conformance to specifications, using micrometers, gauges, calipers, templates, or rulers. Places workpiece on cutting table, manually or using hoist; clamps workpiece into position. Replaces defective blades or wheels, using hand tools. Scribes reference lines on workpiece as guide for sawing operations, according to blueprints, templates, sample parts, or specifications. Turns controls to set cutting speed, feed rate, and table angle for specified operation. Examines completed workpieces for defects such as chipped edges and marred surfaces; sorts defective pieces according to defect. Sets blade tension, height, and angle to perform prescribed cut, using wrench.

GOE Number, Interest Area, and Work Group: 08.02.01; Industrial Production; Production Technology: Machine Set-up and Operation. **Personality Type:** Realistic. Realistic occupations frequently involve work activities that include practical, hands-on problems and solutions. These occupations often deal with plants, animals, and real-world materials like wood, tools, and machinery. Many of the occupations require working outside and do not involve a lot of paperwork or working closely with others. **Work Values:** Moral Values; Independence; Supervision, Human Relations; Activity; Company Policies and Practices. **Skills:** Equipment Selection; Product Inspection; Operation and Control; Operation Monitoring; Equipment Maintenance; Mathematics. **Abilities:** *Cognitive*—Visualization; Written Comprehension; Problem Sensitivity; Information Ordering; Perceptual Speed; Spatial Orientation. *Psychomotor*—Arm-Hand Steadiness; Manual Dexterity; Control Precision. *Physical*—Static Strength; Extent Flexibility; Explosive Strength. *Sensory*—Near Vision; Depth Perception; Hearing Sensitivity. **General Work Activities:** *Information Input*—Monitoring Processes, Materials, and Surroundings; Getting Information Needed to Do the Job; Inspecting Equipment, Structures, Materials. *Mental Process*—Judging Qualities of Things, Services, Other People's Work; Evaluating Information Against Standards; Updating and Using Job-Relevant Knowledge; Organizing, Planning, and Prioritizing. *Work Output*—Controlling Machines and Processes; Handling and Moving Objects; Implementing Ideas and Programs. *Interacting with Others*—Communicating with Other Workers; Coordinating Work and Activities of Others; Establishing and Maintaining Relationships; Performing Administrative Activities. **Physical Work Conditions:** Indoors; Hazardous Equipment; Using Hands on Objects, Tools, or Controls. **Other Job Characteristics:** Degree of Automation; Consequence of Error; Importance of Being Exact or Accurate; Importance of Being Sure All Is Done.

Experience: Job Zone 2. Some previous work-related skill, knowledge, or experience may be helpful, but usually is not needed. **Job Preparation:** SVP 4.00 to 5.99—6 months to less than 2 years. **Knowledge:** Mechanical; Production and Processing; Engineering and Technology; Design; Mathematics; Building and Construction. **Instructional Program:** 480501 Machinist/Machine Technologist.

Related DOT Jobs: 607.382-010 Contour-Band-Saw Operator, Vertical; 607.382-014 Saw Operator; 607.682-010 Cut-Off-Saw Operator, Metal; 609.280-010 Trim-Machine Adjuster; 690.482-010 Sawyer; 700.682-018 Profile-Saw Operator.

51-4031.02 Punching Machine Setters and Set-Up Operators, Metal and Plastic (Punching Machine Setters and Set-Up Operators, Metal and Plastic)

Education: Moderate-term O-T-J training
Employed: 47,025
Openings: 5,625
Projected Growth: –7.5%
Earnings: $23,270

Set up, or set up and operate, machines to punch, crimp, or cut blanks, or to notch metal or plastic workpieces between preset dies, according to specifications.

Sets stops, or guides or installs jigs or fixtures, for positioning successive workpieces. Positions, aligns, and secures workpiece against fixtures or stops on machine bed or on die. Adjusts ram stroke of press to specified length, using hand tools. Sets controls or installs gears to synchronize action of feed bar or rollers. Reads job order to determine location of holes or cutting lines. Cleans and lubricates machines. Measures workpiece with rule or tape, or traces from template; marks location with scribe, soapstone, or centerpunch. Installs, aligns, and locks specified punches, dies, and cutting blades in ram or bed of machine, using gauges and hand tools. Activates machine and observes operation to detect misalignment or machine malfunctions. Inspects workpieces for conformance to specifications, visually or with the use of gauges or templates, scale, and compass; adjusts machine to correct errors.

GOE Number, Interest Area, and Work Group: 08.02.01; Industrial Production; Production Technology: Machine Set-up and Operation. **Personality Type:** Realistic. Realistic occupations frequently involve work activities that include practical, hands-on problems and solutions. These occupations often deal with plants, animals, and real-world materials like wood, tools, and machinery. Many of the occupations require working outside and do not involve a lot of paperwork or working closely with others. **Work Values:** Moral Values; Activity; Independence; Company Policies and Practices; Supervision, Human Relations. **Skills:** Operation and Control; Equipment Maintenance; Product Inspection; Installation; Equipment Selection; Problem Identification. **Abilities:** *Cognitive*—Information Ordering; Visualization; Problem Sensitivity; Perceptual Speed; Written Comprehension. *Psychomotor*—Control Precision; Manual Dexterity; Finger Dexterity. *Physical*—Extent Flexibility; Static Strength; Trunk Strength. *Sensory*—Near Vision. **General Work Activities:** *Information Input*—Getting Information Needed to Do the Job; Monitoring Processes, Materials, and Surroundings; Inspecting Equipment, Structures, Materials. *Mental Process*—Evaluating Information Against Standards; Organizing, Planning, and Prioritizing; Judging Qualities of Things, Services, Other People's Work. *Work Output*—Controlling Machines and Processes; Handling and Moving Objects; Performing General Physical Activities. *Interacting with Others*—Teaching Others; Monitoring and Controlling Resources; Staffing Organizational Units; Performing Administrative Activities; Providing Consultation and Advice to Others; Guiding, Directing and Motivating Subordinates. **Physical Work Conditions:** Indoors; Using Hands on Objects, Tools, or Controls; Standing. **Other Job Characteristics:** Importance of Being Exact or Accurate; Importance of Being Sure All Is Done; Degree of Automation.

Experience: Job Zone 2. Some previous work-related skill, knowledge, or experience may be helpful, but usually is not needed. **Job Preparation:** SVP 4.00 to 5.99—6 months to less than 2 years. **Knowledge:** Mechanical; Engineering and Technology; Production and Processing; Physics; Mathematics. **Instructional Programs:** 480501 Machinist/Machine Technologist; 480506 Sheet Metal Worker.

Related DOT Jobs: 615.382-010 Punch-Press Operator I; 615.482-014 Duplicator-Punch Operator; 615.482-018 Ironworker-Machine Operator; 615.482-026 Punch-Press Operator, Automatic; 619.380-014 Punch-Press Setter; 699.380-010 Die Set-Up Operator, Printed Circuit Boards.

51-4031.03 Press and Press Brake Machine Setters and Set-Up Operators, Metal and Plastic (Press and Press-Brake Machine Setters and Set-Up Operators, Metal and Plastic)

Education: No data available.

Employed: 71,700

Openings: No data available.

Projected Growth: No data available.

Earnings: $24,150

Set up, or set up and operate, power-press machines or power-brake machines to bend, form, stretch, notch, punch, or straighten metal or plastic plate and structural shapes, as specified by work order, blueprints, drawing, templates, or layout.

Lubricates workpiece with oil. Selects and positions flat, block, radius, or special-purpose die sets into ram and bed of machine, using hoist, crane, measuring instruments, and hand tools. Operates power press, power brake, apron brake, swaging machine, foot-powered press, hydraulic press, or arbor press according to specifications. Preheats workpiece, using heating furnace or hand torch. Inspects workpiece for defects. Grinds out burrs and sharp edges, using portable grinder, speed lathe, and polishing jack. Installs, aligns, and secures gears, holding fixtures, and dies to machine bed, using gauges, templates, feelers, shims, and hand tools. Lifts, positions, and secures workpiece between dies of machine, using crane and sledge. Plans sequence of operations, applying knowledge of physical properties of metal. Measures workpiece and verifies dimensions and weight, using micrometer, template, straightedge, and scale. Sets stops on machine bed, changes dies, and adjusts components such as ram or power press, when making multiple or successive passes. Hand forms, cuts, or finishes workpiece, using tools such as table saw, hand sledge and anvil, flaring tool, and gauge.

GOE Number, Interest Area, and Work Group: 08.02.01; Industrial Production; Production Technology: Machine Set-up and Operation. **Personality Type:** Realistic. Realistic occupations frequently involve work activities that include practical, hands-on problems and solutions. These occupations often deal with plants, animals, and real-world materials like wood, tools, and machinery. Many of the occupations require working outside and do not involve a lot of paperwork or working closely with others. **Work Values:** Moral Values; Independence; Activity; Supervision, Human Relations; Company Policies and Practices. **Skills:** Science; Operation and Control; Product Inspection; Operation Monitoring; Installation. **Abilities:** *Cognitive*–Information Ordering; Visualization; Written Comprehension; Number Facility; Selective Attention; Problem Sensitivity. *Psychomotor*–Manual Dexterity; Multilimb Coordination; Control Precision. *Physical*–Extent Flexibility; Static Strength; Dynamic Strength; Trunk Strength. *Sensory*–Depth Perception; Auditory Attention; Visual Color Discrimination. **General Work Activities:** *Information Input*–In-specting Equipment, Structures, Materials; Getting Information Needed to Do the Job; Identifying Objects, Actions, and Events. *Mental Process*–Evaluating Information Against Standards; Judging Qualities of Things, Services, Other People's Work; Updating and Using Job-Relevant Knowledge. *Work Output*–Controlling Machines and Processes; Handling and Moving Objects; Performing General Physical Activities. *Interacting with Others*–Communicating with Other Workers; Providing Consultation and Advice to Others; Teaching Others; Coordinating Work and Activities of Others; Performing for or Working with the Public; Resolving Conflict and Negotiating with Others. **Physical Work Conditions:** Indoors; Hazardous Equipment; Using Hands on Objects, Tools, or Controls. **Other Job Characteristics:** Degree of Automation; Consequence of Error; Frustrating Circumstances; Importance of Being Exact or Accurate; Importance of Being Sure All Is Done; Pace Determined by Speed of Equipment.

Experience: Job Zone 2. Some previous work-related skill, knowledge, or experience may be helpful, but usually is not needed. **Job Preparation:** SVP 4.00 to 5.99—6 months to less than 2 years. **Knowledge:** Mechanical; Physics; Production and Processing; Building and Construction; Design. **Instructional Programs:** 480501 Machinist/Machine Technologist; 480506 Sheet Metal Worker.

Related DOT Jobs: 616.682-010 Arbor-Press Operator I; 616.682-026 Kick-Press Operator I; 617.260-010 Press Operator, Heavy Duty; 617.360-010 Brake Operator I; 617.360-014 Swaging-Machine Adjuster; 617.380-010 Kick Press Setter; 617.382-010 Tube Bender, Brass-Wind Instruments; 617.480-014 Press Setter; 617.482-010 Bending-Machine Operator I; 807.684-010 Automobile-Bumper Straightener.

51-4031.04 Shear and Slitter Machine Setters and Set-Up Operators, Metal and Plastic (Shear and Slitter Machine Setters and Set-Up Operators, Metal and Plastic)

Education: No data available.

Employed: 21,920

Openings: No data available.

Projected Growth: No data available.

Earnings: $24,290

Set up, or set up and operate, power-shear or slitting machines to cut metal or plastic material such as plates, sheets, slabs, billets, or bars to specified dimensions and angles.

Threads end of metal coil from reel through slitter; secures ends on recoiler. Selects, cleans, and installs spacers, rubber sleeves, and cutter on arbors. Reads production schedule to determine setup or adjustment of equipment. Operates shear or slitter that cuts or shears metal such as plates, sheets, slabs, billets, or bars, to size. Tests and adjusts cutting speed and action, according to specified length of product, using gauges and hand tools. Measures dimensions of workpiece, using tape, gauge, template, or rule and square, for conformance to specifications. Lifts workpiece manually or by hoist, and positions and secures against guides and stops. Lubricates and cleans machine. Observes machine operation and examines cut strips for flatness, holes, burrs, and surface defects. Hones cutters with oilstone to remove nicks. Installs and aligns knives, disk cutters, or fixtures to shear, bevel, or trim fabricated items. Starts machine, adjusts blade and controls, using wrenches, rule, gauge, or template; monitors operation. Lays out cutting lines on metal stock, to obtain maximum number of pieces from stock.

GOE Number, Interest Area, and Work Group: 08.02.01; Industrial Production; Production Technology: Machine Set-up and Operation. **Personality Type:** Realistic. Realistic occupations frequently involve work activities that include practical, hands-on problems and solutions. These occupations often deal with plants, animals, and real-world materials like wood, tools, and machinery. Many of the occupations require working outside and do not involve a lot of paperwork or working closely with others. **Work Values:** Moral Values; Activity; Independence; Supervision, Human Relations; Company Policies and Practices. **Skills:** Operation Monitoring; Operation and Control; Product Inspection; Testing; Installation. **Abilities:** *Cognitive*—Information Ordering; Written Comprehension; Visualization; Problem Sensitivity; Selective Attention; Perceptual Speed. *Psychomotor*—Control Precision; Finger Dexterity; Reaction Time; Arm-Hand Steadiness. *Physical*—Extent Flexibility; Static Strength; Trunk Strength. *Sensory*—Visual Color Discrimination; Far Vision; Depth Perception. **General Work Activities:** *Information Input*—Getting Information Needed to Do the Job; Estimating Needed Characteristics; Inspecting Equipment, Structures, Materials. *Mental Process*—Evaluating Information Against Standards; Making Decisions and Solving Problems; Updating and Using Job-Relevant Knowledge. *Work Output*—Handling and Moving Objects; Controlling Machines and Processes; Performing General Physical Activities. *Interacting with Others*—Communicating with Other Workers; Coordinating Work and Activities of Others; Resolving Conflict and Negotiating with Others; Establishing and Maintaining Relationships; Interpreting Meaning of Information to Others. **Physical Work Conditions:** Indoors; Hazardous Equipment; Using Hands on Objects, Tools, or Controls. **Other Job Characteristics:** Degree of Automation; Frustrating Circumstances; Consequence of Error.

Experience: Job Zone 2. Some previous work-related skill, knowledge, or experience may be helpful, but usually is not needed. **Job Preparation:** SVP 4.00 to 5.99—6 months to less than 2 years. **Knowledge:** Mechanical; Production and Processing; Engineering and Technology; English Language; Mathematics; Design. **Instructional Programs:** 480501 Machinist/Machine Technologist; 480506 Sheet Metal Worker.

Related DOT Jobs: 615.280-010 Slitter Service and Setter; 615.380-010 Shear Setter; 615.482-010 Angle Shear Operator; 615.662-010 Slitting-Machine Operator II; 615.682-010 Flying-Shear Operator; 615.682-018 Shear Operator I.

51-4032.00 Drilling and Boring Machine Tool Setters, Operators, and Tenders, Metal and Plastic (Drilling and Boring Machine Tool Setters and Set-up Operators, Metal and Plastic)

Education: Moderate-term O-T-J training
Employed: 41,930
Openings: 6,582
Projected Growth: –18.3%
Earnings: $25,630

Set up, operate, or tend drilling machines to drill, bore, ream, mill, or countersink metal or plastic work pieces.

Selects cutting tool according to instructions and knowledge of metal properties. Lays out reference lines and machining locations on work, applying knowledge of shop math and layout techniques, and using layout tools. Positions and secures workpiece on table with bolts, jigs, clamps, shims, or other holding devices, using machining hand tools. Verifies conformance of machined work to specifications, using measuring instruments such as calipers, micrometers, and fixed and telescoping gauges. Operates tracing attachment to duplicate contours from templates or models. Installs tool in spindle. Studies machining instructions to determine dimensional and finish specifications, sequence of operation, setup, and tooling requirements. Operates single- or multiple-spindle drill press to bore holes to perform machining operations on metal, nonmetallic, or plastic workpieces. Lifts workpiece either manually or with hoist onto machine table, or directs crane operator to lift and position workpiece.

GOE Number, Interest Area, and Work Group: 08.02.01; Industrial Production; Production Technology: Machine Set-up and Operation. **Personality Type:** Realistic. Realistic occupations frequently involve work activities that include practical, hands-on problems and solutions. These occupations often deal with plants, animals, and real-world materials like wood, tools, and machinery. Many of the occupations require working outside and do not involve a lot of paperwork or working closely with others. **Work Values:** Moral Values; Independence; Activity; Company Policies and Practices; Supervision, Human Relations. **Skills:** Product Inspection; Mathematics; Operation and Control; Operation Monitoring; Reading Comprehension. **Abilities:** *Cognitive*—Written Comprehension; Visualization; Information Ordering; Number Facility; Mathematical Reasoning; Problem Sensitivity. *Psychomotor*—Arm-Hand Steadiness; Control Precision; Manual Dexterity. *Physical*—Static Strength; Extent Flexibility; Dynamic Strength; Trunk Strength. *Sensory*—Hearing Sensitivity; Depth Perception; Sound Localization. **General Work Activities:** *Information Input*—Getting Information Needed to Do the Job; Inspecting Equipment, Structures, Materials; Identifying Objects, Actions, and Events. *Mental Process*—Evaluating Information Against Standards; Making Decisions and Solving Problems; Judging Qualities of Things, Services, Other People's Work; Processing Information. *Work Output*—Handling and Moving Objects; Controlling Machines and Processes; Performing General Physical Activities. *Interacting with Others*—Communicating with Other Workers; Establishing and Maintaining Relationships; Coordinating Work and Activities of Others; Communicating with Persons Outside Organization. **Physical Work Conditions:** Indoors; Using Hands on Objects, Tools, or Controls; Hazardous Equipment; Standing. **Other Job Characteristics:** Degree of Automation; Consequence of Error; Pace Determined by Speed of Equipment; Importance of Being Exact or Accurate.

Experience: Job Zone 2. Some previous work-related skill, knowledge, or experience may be helpful, but usually is not needed. **Job Preparation:** SVP 4.00 to 5.99—6 months to less than 2 years. **Knowledge:** Mechanical; Engineering and Technology; Building and Construction; Mathematics; Design. **Instructional Program:** 480501 Machinist/Machine Technologist.

Related DOT Jobs: 606.280-010 Boring-Machine Set-Up Operator, Jig; 606.280-014 Boring-Mill Set-Up Operator, Horizontal;

606.380-010 Drill-Press Set-Up Operator, Multiple Spindle; 606.380-014 Drill-Press Set-Up Operator, Radial; 606.380-018 Drill-Press Set-Up Operator, Radial, Tool; 606.382-022 Boring-Machine Operator; 606.682-018 Drill-Press Set-Up Operator, Single Spindle; 606.682-022 Tapper Operator; 676.382-010 Drill-Press Operator, Printed Circuit Boards; 731.381-010 Dice Maker.

51-4033.00 Grinding, Lapping, Polishing, and Buffing Machine Tool Setters, Operators, and Tenders, Metal and Plastic (Grinding, Lapping, and Buffing Machine Tool Setters and Set-Up Operators, Metal and Plastic)

Education: Moderate-term O-T-J training

Employed: 74,996

Openings: 4,007

Projected Growth: –9.6%

Earnings: $24,740

Set up, operate, or tend grinding and related tools that remove excess material or burrs from surfaces, sharpen edges or corners, or buff, hone, or polish metal or plastic work pieces.

GOE Number, Interest Area, and Work Group: 08.02.01; Industrial Production; Production Technology: Machine Set-up and Operation. **Instructional Program:** 480501 Machinist/Machine Technologist. **Note:** The Department of Labor has not collected some data for this job, so it has fewer details than the other descriptions.

51-4033.01 Grinding, Honing, Lapping, and Deburring Machine Set-Up Operators (Grinding, Lapping, and Buffing Machine Tool Setters and Set-up Operators, Metal and Plastic)

Education: Moderate-term O-T-J training

Employed: 74,996

Openings: 4,007

Projected Growth: –9.6%

Earnings: $24,740

Set up and operate grinding, honing, lapping, or deburring machines to remove excess materials or burrs from internal and external surfaces.

Lifts and positions workpiece manually or with hoist; secures in hopper, on machine table, faceplate, or chuck, using clamps. Selects machine tooling to be used in machine operation, utilizing knowledge of machine and production requirements. Studies blueprints, work order, or machining instructions, to determine product dimensions and tooling and to plan operational sequence. Measures workpieces and lays out work, using precision measuring devices. Brushes or sprays lubricating compound on workpiece or turns valve handle and directs flow of coolant against tool and workpiece. Repairs or replaces machine parts, using hand tools or notifies engineering personnel when corrective action is required. Threads and hand feeds materials through machine cutters or abraders. Grinds, sharpens, or hones tools, dies, and products to prescribed dimensions, using power tools, hand tools,

and precision measuring instruments. Mounts and positions tools in machine chuck, spindle, or other tool holding device to specifications, using hand tools. Observes and adjusts machine operation. Computes machine indexing and settings for specified dimension and base reference points. Activates machine start-up switches to grind, lap, hone, debar, shear, or cut workpiece, according to specifications. Moves machine controls to index workpiece and adjust machine for preselected operational settings. Maintains stock of machine parts and machining tools. Inspects or measures workpiece, using measuring instruments such as gauges or micrometers for conformance to specifications.

GOE Number, Interest Area, and Work Group: 08.02.01; Industrial Production; Production Technology: Machine Set-up and Operation. **Personality Type:** Realistic. Realistic occupations frequently involve work activities that include practical, hands-on problems and solutions. These occupations often deal with plants, animals, and real-world materials like wood, tools, and machinery. Many of the occupations require working outside and do not involve a lot of paperwork or working closely with others. **Work Values:** Moral Values; Independence; Activity; Company Policies and Practices; Supervision, Human Relations. **Skills:** Product Inspection; Operation and Control; Mathematics; Equipment Selection; Equipment Maintenance. **Abilities:** *Cognitive*—Visualization; Information Ordering; Written Comprehension; Number Facility; Mathematical Reasoning. *Psychomotor*—Control Precision; Manual Dexterity; Finger Dexterity. *Physical*—Static Strength; Trunk Strength; Extent Flexibility. *Sensory*—Near Vision; Hearing Sensitivity; Depth Perception. **General Work Activities:** *Information Input*—Getting Information Needed to Do the Job; Monitoring Processes, Materials, and Surroundings; Inspecting Equipment, Structures, Materials. *Mental Process*—Evaluating Information Against Standards; Analyzing Data or Information; Making Decisions and Solving Problems; Organizing, Planning, and Prioritizing. *Work Output*—Controlling Machines and Processes; Handling and Moving Objects; Repairing and Maintaining Mechanical Equipment. *Interacting with Others*—Monitoring and Controlling Resources; Communicating with Other Workers; Interpreting Meaning of Information to Others; Assisting and Caring for Others; Coordinating Work and Activities of Others; Establishing and Maintaining Relationships. **Physical Work Conditions:** Indoors; Using Hands on Objects, Tools, or Controls; Hazardous Equipment; Standing. **Other Job Characteristics:** Degree of Automation; Consequence of Error; Importance of Being Exact or Accurate; Importance of Being Sure All Is Done.

Experience: Job Zone 3. Previous work-related skill, knowledge, or experience is required. **Job Preparation:** SVP 6.0 to less than 7.0—More than 1 year and less than 4 years. **Knowledge:** Mechanical; Production and Processing; Engineering and Technology; Mathematics; Clerical. **Instructional Program:** 480501 Machinist/Machine Technologist.

Related DOT Jobs: 601.482-010 Profile-Grinder Technician; 602.360-010 Grinder Set-Up Operator, Gear, Tool; 602.382-034 Grinder, Gear; 602.482-010 Gear-Lapping-Machine Operator; 603.260-010 Grinder Set-Up Operator, Thread Tool; 603.280-026 Grinder Set-Up Operator, Jig; 603.280-034 Job Setter, Honing; 603.380-010 Grinder Machine Setter; 603.382-014 Grinder Set-Up Operator, Centerless; 603.382-018 Honing-Machine Set-Up Operator; 603.382-022 Honing-Machine Set-Up Operator, Tool;

603.382-026 Lapping-Machine Set-Up Operator; 603.382-034 Grinder Set-Up Operator; 603.382-038 Knife Grinder; 603.482-010 Deburrer, Strip; 609.682-026 Nicking-Machine Operator; 628.382-014 Shear-Grinder Operator; 629.682-010 Roll Grinder; 690.280-010 Deburring-and-Tooling-Machine Operator.

51-4033.02 Buffing and Polishing Set-Up Operators
(Grinding, Lapping, and Buffing Machine Tool Setters and Set-up Operators, Metal and Plastic)

Education: Moderate-term O-T-J training

Employed: 74,996

Openings: 4,007

Projected Growth: –9.6%

Earnings: $24,740

Set up and operate buffing or polishing machine.

Removes workpiece and examines finish or luster to ensure surface meets specifications. Selects and attaches workpiece holding fixture to drive mechanism; positions or clamps workpiece to fixture. Holds stick of buffing compound; turns valve and depresses pedal, to administer coolant to workpiece surface. Reads work order to determine parts to be buffed or polished. Starts and observes machine operation for conformance to specifications. Repairs or replaces machine parts to maintain machine in operational condition. Sets and adjusts machine controls according to product specifications, utilizing knowledge of machine operation. Selects buffing or polishing tools and positions and mounts tools to machine tool, chuck, or jig, using hand tools.

GOE Number, Interest Area, and Work Group: 08.02.01; Industrial Production; Production Technology: Machine Set-up and Operation. **Personality Type:** Realistic. Realistic occupations frequently involve work activities that include practical, hands-on problems and solutions. These occupations often deal with plants, animals, and real-world materials like wood, tools, and machinery. Many of the occupations require working outside and do not involve a lot of paperwork or working closely with others. **Work Values:** Moral Values; Independence; Activity; Company Policies and Practices; Supervision, Human Relations. **Skills:** Operation and Control; Repairing; Equipment Maintenance; Product Inspection; Equipment Selection; Reading Comprehension; Operation Monitoring. **Abilities:** *Cognitive*—Written Comprehension; Information Ordering; Problem Sensitivity; Visualization; Deductive Reasoning. *Psychomotor*—Control Precision; Manual Dexterity; Arm-Hand Steadiness. *Physical*—Extent Flexibility; Static Strength; Dynamic Flexibility; Trunk Strength. *Sensory*—Depth Perception; Visual Color Discrimination; Peripheral Vision. **General Work Activities:** *Information Input*—Inspecting Equipment, Structures, Materials; Getting Information Needed to Do the Job; Monitoring Processes, Materials, and Surroundings. *Mental Process*—Evaluating Information Against Standards; Judging Qualities of Things, Services, Other People's Work; Making Decisions and Solving Problems; Analyzing Data or Information. *Work Output*—Controlling Machines and Processes; Handling and Moving Objects; Performing General Physical Activities. *Interacting with Others*—Communicating with Other Workers; Coordinating Work and Activities of Others; Monitoring and Controlling Resources; Assisting and Caring for Others; Establishing and Maintaining Relationships;

Performing Administrative Activities. **Physical Work Conditions:** Using Hands on Objects, Tools, or Controls; Indoors; Standing. **Other Job Characteristics:** Degree of Automation; Consequence of Error; Importance of Being Sure All Is Done.

Experience: Job Zone 2. Some previous work-related skill, knowledge, or experience may be helpful, but usually is not needed. **Job Preparation:** SVP 4.00 to 5.99—6 months to less than 2 years. **Knowledge:** Mechanical; Production and Processing; Engineering and Technology; English Language; Mathematics. **Instructional Program:** 480501 Machinist/Machine Technologist.

Related DOT Jobs: 603.360-010 Buffing-Line Set-Up Worker; 603.382-010 Buffing-Machine Operator; 603.682-010 Buffing-Machine Operator, Silverware; 603.682-022 Mirror-Finishing-Machine Operator; 603.682-026 Polishing-Machine Operator.

51-4034.00 Lathe and Turning Machine Tool Setters, Operators, and Tenders Metal and Plastic (Lathe and Turning Machine Tool Setters and Set-up Operators, Metal and Plastic)

Education: Moderate-term O-T-J training

Employed: 72,226

Openings: 11,957

Projected Growth: –8.4%

Earnings: $28,250

Set up, operate, or tend lathe and turning machines to turn, bore, thread, form, or face metal or plastic materials such as wire, rod, or bar stock.

Computes unspecified dimensions and machine settings, using knowledge of metal properties and shop mathematics. Moves toolholder manually or by turning handwheel; engages automatic feeding mechanism, to feed tools to and along workpiece. Cranks machine through cycle, stopping to adjust tool positions and machine controls, to ensure specified timing, clearance, and tolerances. Moves controls, to set cutting speeds, cutting depths, and feed rates, and to position tool in relation to workplace. Starts machine and turns valve handle to direct flow of coolant on work area; coats disk with spinning compound. Replaces worn tools and sharpens dull cutting tools and dies. Lifts metal stock or workpiece manually or using hoist; positions and secures it in machine, using fasteners and hand tools. Studies blueprint, layout, or chart, to visualize work and determine materials needed, sequence of operations, dimensions, and tooling instructions. Mounts attachments, such as relieving or tracing attachments, to perform operations such as duplicating contours of template or trimming workpiece. Observes operation and stops machine to inspect finished workpiece and to verify conformance with specifications of first-run, using measuring instruments. Selects cutting tools and tooling instructions, according to knowledge of metal properties, shop mathematics, or written specifications. Installs holding fixtures, cams, gears, and stops, to control stock and tool movement, using hand tools, power tools, and measuring instruments. Positions, secures, and aligns cutting tools in toolholders on machine, using hand tools; verifies their position with measuring instruments.

GOE Number, Interest Area, and Work Group: 08.02.01; Industrial Production; Production Technology: Machine Set-up and

Operation. **Personality Type:** Realistic. Realistic occupations frequently involve work activities that include practical, hands-on problems and solutions. These occupations often deal with plants, animals, and real-world materials like wood, tools, and machinery. Many of the occupations require working outside and do not involve a lot of paperwork or working closely with others. **Work Values:** Moral Values; Company Policies and Practices; Independence; Supervision, Human Relations; Activity. **Skills:** Mathematics; Equipment Selection; Equipment Maintenance; Product Inspection; Operation and Control. **Abilities:** *Cognitive*—Visualization; Written Comprehension; Information Ordering; Mathematical Reasoning; Number Facility. *Psychomotor*—Control Precision; Multilimb Coordination; Arm-Hand Steadiness; Manual Dexterity. *Physical*—Static Strength; Trunk Strength; Dynamic Strength; Stamina. *Sensory*—Hearing Sensitivity. **General Work Activities:** *Information Input*—Monitoring Processes, Materials, and Surroundings; Getting Information Needed to Do the Job; Identifying Objects, Actions, and Events. *Mental Process*—Evaluating Information Against Standards; Making Decisions and Solving Problems; Judging Qualities of Things, Services, Other People's Work. *Work Output*—Controlling Machines and Processes; Handling and Moving Objects; Performing General Physical Activities. *Interacting with Others*—Coaching and Developing Others; Assisting and Caring for Others; Establishing and Maintaining Relationships; Communicating with Other Workers; Monitoring and Controlling Resources. **Physical Work Conditions:** Indoors; Using Hands on Objects, Tools, or Controls; Hazardous Equipment. **Other Job Characteristics:** Degree of Automation; Importance of Being Exact or Accurate; Importance of Being Sure All Is Done.

Experience: Job Zone 3. Previous work-related skill, knowledge, or experience is required. **Job Preparation:** SVP 6.0 to less than 7.0—More than 1 year and less than 4 years. **Knowledge:** Production and Processing; Mathematics; Mechanical; Engineering and Technology; Design. **Instructional Program:** 480501 Machinist/ Machine Technologist.

Related DOT Jobs: 604.260-010 Screw-Machine Set-Up Operator, Swiss-Type; 604.280-010 Engine-Lathe Set-Up Operator, Tool; 604.280-014 Screw-Machine Set-Up Operator, Multiple Spindle; 604.280-018 Screw-Machine Set-Up Operator, Single Spindle; 604.280-022 Turret-Lathe Set-Up Operator, Tool; 604.360-010 Setter, Automatic-Spinning Lathe; 604.380-010 Chucking-Machine Set-Up Operator; 604.380-014 Chucking-Machine Set-Up Operator, Multiple Spindle, Vertical; 604.380-018 Engine-Lathe Set-Up Operator; 604.380-022 Screw-Machine Set-Up Operator; 604.380-026 Turret-Lathe Set-Up Operator; 604.682-014 Threading-Machine Operator; 609.380-014 Threading-Machine Setter; 619.362-018 Spinner, Hand; 619.362-022 Spinner, Hydraulic.

51-4035.00 Milling and Planing Machine Setters, Operators, and Tenders, Metal and Plastic (Milling and Planing Machine Setters and Set-Up Operators, Metal and Plastic)

Education: No data available.

Employed: 24,400

Openings: No data available.

Projected Growth: No data available.

Earnings: $28,920

Set up, operate, or tend milling or planing machines to mill, plane, shape, groove, or profile metal or plastic work pieces.

Computes dimensions, tolerances, and angles of workpiece or machine, according to specifications and knowledge of metal properties and shop mathematics. Makes templates or cutting tools. Sharpens dull tools, using bench grinder. Replaces worn tools, using hand tools. Mounts attachments and other tools such as pantograph, engraver, or router, to perform other operations such as drilling or boring. Positions and secures workpiece on machine, using holding devices, measuring instruments, hand tools, and hoists. Verifies conformance of finished workpiece to specifications, using measuring instruments such as microscopes, gauges, calipers, and micrometers. Records production output. Studies blueprint, layout, sketch, or other specifications to determine materials needed, sequence of operations, dimensions, and tooling instructions. Removes workpiece and template or model from machine. Selects and installs cutting tool, stylus, and other accessories according to specifications, using hand tools or power tools. Moves controls to set cutting specifications, to position cutting tool and workpiece in relation to each other, and to start machine. Moves cutter or material manually or by turning handwheel; engages automatic feeding mechanism to mill workpiece to specifications. Observes machine operation and adjusts controls to ensure conformance with specified tolerances. Selects cutting speed, feed rate, and depth of cut, applying knowledge of metal properties and shop mathematics. Verifies alignment of workpiece on machine, using measuring instruments such as rules, gauges, or calipers. Turns valve to begin and regulate the flow of coolant on work area.

GOE Number, Interest Area, and Work Group: 08.02.01; Industrial Production; Production Technology: Machine Set-up and Operation. **Personality Type:** Realistic. Realistic occupations frequently involve work activities that include practical, hands-on problems and solutions. These occupations often deal with plants, animals, and real-world materials like wood, tools, and machinery. Many of the occupations require working outside and do not involve a lot of paperwork or working closely with others. **Work Values:** Moral Values; Independence; Company Policies and Practices; Activity; Supervision, Human Relations. **Skills:** Mathematics; Operation and Control; Equipment Maintenance; Equipment Selection; Operation Monitoring. **Abilities:** *Cognitive*—Number Facility; Written Comprehension; Information Ordering; Visualization; Problem Sensitivity. *Psychomotor*—Control Precision; Wrist-Finger Speed; Manual Dexterity. *Physical*—Static Strength; Stamina; Gross Body Coordination; Dynamic Strength. *Sensory*—Auditory Attention. **General Work Activities:** *Information Input*—Monitoring Processes, Materials, and Surroundings; Getting Information Needed to Do the Job; Inspecting Equipment, Structures, Materials. *Mental Process*—Evaluating Information Against Standards; Processing Information; Analyzing Data or Information. *Work Output*—Controlling Machines and Processes; Handling and Moving Objects; Performing General Physical Activities. *Interacting with Others*—Communicating with Other Workers; Performing Administrative Activities; Establishing and Maintaining Relationships; Monitoring and Controlling Resources. **Physical Work Conditions:** Indoors; Using Hands on Objects, Tools, or Controls; Standing. **Other Job Characteristics:** Degree of Automation; Importance of Being Sure All Is Done; Consequence of Error.

Experience: Job Zone 3. Previous work-related skill, knowledge, or experience is required. **Job Preparation:** SVP 6.0 to less than 7.0—More than 1 year and less than 4 years. **Knowledge:** Production and Processing; Mechanical; Mathematics; Physics; Engineering and Technology. **Instructional Program:** 480501 Machinist/Machine Technologist.

Related DOT Jobs: 605.280-010 Milling-Machine Set-Up Operator I; 605.280-014 Profiling-Machine Set-Up Operator I; 605.280-018 Profiling-Machine Set-Up Operator, Tool; 605.282-010 Milling-Machine Set-Up Operator II; 605.282-014 Planer Set-Up Operator, Tool; 605.282-018 Planer-Type-Milling-Machine Set-Up Operator; 605.382-010 Broaching-Machine Set-Up Operator; 605.382-014 Engraver, Tire Mold; 605.382-018 Keyseating-Machine Set-Up Operator; 605.382-022 Pantograph-Machine Set-Up Operator; 605.382-026 Profiling-Machine Set-Up Operator II; 605.382-030 Rotary-Head-Milling-Machine Set-Up Operator; 605.382-034 Router Operator; 605.382-038 Shaper Set-Up Operator, Tool; 605.382-042 Thread-Milling-Machine Set-Up Operator; 605.482-010 Steel-Wool-Machine Operator; 605.682-010 Barrel-Rib Matting-Machine Operator; 605.682-022 Scalper Operator; 605.682-026 Tooth Cutter, Escape Wheel.

51-4041.00 Machinists (Machinists)

Education: Long-term O-T-J training
Employed: 426,028
Openings: 42,311
Projected Growth: 6.2%
Earnings: $28,860

Set up and operate a variety of machine tools to produce precision parts and instruments. Fabricate and modify parts to make or repair machine tools or to maintain industrial machines, applying knowledge of mechanics, shop mathematics, metal properties, layout, and machining procedures. Includes precision instrument makers who fabricate, modify, or repair mechanical instruments.

Evaluates experimental procedures and recommends changes or modifications for efficiency and adaptability to setup and production. Confers with engineering, supervisory, and manufacturing personnel to exchange technical information. Operates metalworking machine tools such as lathe, milling machine, shaper, or grinder, to machine parts to specifications. Fabricates, assembles, and modifies tooling such as jigs, fixtures, templates, and molds or dies, to produce parts and assemblies. Lays out and verifies dimensions of parts, using precision measuring and marking instruments and knowledge of trigonometry. Installs repaired part into equipment and operates equipment to verify operational efficiency. Dismantles machine or equipment, using hand tools and power tools, to examine parts for defect or to remove defective parts. Installs experimental parts and assemblies, such as hydraulic systems, electrical wiring, lubricants, and batteries into machines and mechanisms. Establishes work procedures for fabricating new structural products, using variety of metalworking machines. Selects, aligns, and secures holding fixtures, cutting tools, attachments, accessories, and materials onto machines. Calculates and sets controls to regulate machining; enters commands to retrieve, input, or edit computerized machine control media. Designs fixtures, tooling, and experimental parts to meet special engineering needs. Assembles parts into completed units, using jigs, fixtures, hand tools, and power tools. Measures, examines, and tests completed units to detect defects and ensure conformance to specifications. Operates brazing, heat-treating, and welding equipment to cut, solder, and braze metal. Cleans, lubricates, and maintains machines, tools, and equipment to remove grease, rust, stains, and foreign matter. Cuts and shapes sheet metal and heats and bends metal to specified shape.

GOE Number, Interest Area, and Work Group: 08.04.01; Industrial Production; Metal and Plastics Machining Technology. **Personality Type:** Realistic. Realistic occupations frequently involve work activities that include practical, hands-on problems and solutions. These occupations often deal with plants, animals, and real-world materials like wood, tools, and machinery. Many of the occupations require working outside and do not involve a lot of paperwork or working closely with others. **Work Values:** Moral Values; Company Policies and Practices; Security; Supervision, Human Relations; Autonomy; Activity; Ability Utilization; Compensation. **Skills:** Mathematics; Installation; Equipment Selection; Testing; Operations Analysis; Product Inspection; Critical Thinking. **Abilities:** *Cognitive*—Visualization; Written Comprehension; Information Ordering; Number Facility; Problem Sensitivity; Deductive Reasoning. *Psychomotor*—Control Precision; Arm-Hand Steadiness; Finger Dexterity; Manual Dexterity. *Physical*—Extent Flexibility; Static Strength; Trunk Strength. *Sensory*—Near Vision; Visual Color Discrimination; Hearing Sensitivity. **General Work Activities:** *Information Input*—Getting Information Needed to Do the Job; Inspecting Equipment, Structures, Materials; Monitoring Processes, Materials, and Surroundings. *Mental Process*—Analyzing Data or Information; Updating and Using Job-Relevant Knowledge; Evaluating Information Against Standards. *Work Output*—Handling and Moving Objects; Controlling Machines and Processes; Repairing and Maintaining Mechanical Equipment; Implementing Ideas and Programs. *Interacting with Others*—Communicating with Other Workers; Providing Consultation and Advice to Others; Establishing and Maintaining Relationships. **Physical Work Conditions:** Indoors; Using Hands on Objects, Tools, or Controls; Common Protective or Safety Attire. **Other Job Characteristics:** Degree of Automation; Consequence of Error; Importance of Being Exact or Accurate.

Experience: Job Zone 4. A minimum of two to four years of work-related skill, knowledge, or experience is needed. **Job Preparation:** SVP 7.0 to less than 8.0—2 years to less than 10 years. **Knowledge:** Mechanical; Design; Engineering and Technology; Mathematics; Production and Processing. **Instructional Programs:** 480501 Machinist/Machine Technologist; 480503 Machine Shop Assistant.

Related DOT Jobs: 019.161-014 Test Technician; 600.260-022 Machinist, Experimental; 600.280-022 Machinist; 600.280-026 Machinist Apprentice; 600.280-030 Machinist Apprentice, Automotive; 600.280-034 Machinist, Automotive; 600.280-042 Maintenance Machinist; 600.281-010 Fluid-Power Mechanic; 600.380-010 Fixture Maker; 693.261-014 Development Mechanic; 693.261-022 Rocket-Motor Mechanic; 806.281-014 Experimental Mechanic, Electrical.

51-4051.00 Metal-Refining Furnace Operators and Tenders (Furnace Operators and Tenders)

Education: Moderate-term O-T-J training

Employed: 23,073

Openings: 2,246

Projected Growth: –5%

Earnings: $25,870

Operate or tend furnaces such as gas, oil, coal, electric-arc, electric induction, open-hearth, or oxygen furnaces, to melt and refine metal before casting or to produce specified types of steel.

Records data and maintains production logs. Sprinkles chemicals over molten metal to bring impurities to surface; removes impurities, using strainers. Kindles fire and shovels fuels and other materials into furnaces or onto conveyors by hand, with hoists, or by directing crane operator. Observes air and temperature gauges or metal color; turns fuel valves or adjusts controls to maintain required temperature. Observes inside of furnace operations by television screen; operates controls to move or discharge metal workpiece. Drains, transfers, or removes molten metal from furnace or into molds, by hoist, pumps, or ladles. Analyzes metal test sample, according to specific instructions, for specific and for specific-element content. Examines and prepares material to load into furnace, including cleaning, crushing, or applying chemicals, using crushing-machine, shovel, rake, or sprayer. Scrapes accumulations of metal oxides from floors, molds, and crucibles; sifts and stores for reclamation. Manipulates controls, to ignite burners, to adjust fuel mixtures, to open and close furnace doors, or to load and discharge materials into or from furnace. Inspects furnace and equipment for defects and wear; directs work crew in cleaning and repairing furnace walls and flooring. Observes color and fluidity of molten metal; obtains test sample of metal from furnace or kettle for analysis. Regulates supply of fuel and air, or controls flow of electric current and water coolant, to heat furnaces. Draws smelted metal samples from furnace for analysis and calculates type and amount of material required to correct smelting process. Weighs materials to be charged into furnace. Weighs materials to maintain prescribed weight, using scales.

GOE Number, Interest Area, and Work Group: 08.03.02; Industrial Production; Production Work: Equipment Operation, Assorted Materials Processing. **Personality Type:** Realistic. Realistic occupations frequently involve work activities that include practical, hands-on problems and solutions. These occupations often deal with plants, animals, and real-world materials like wood, tools, and machinery. Many of the occupations require working outside and do not involve a lot of paperwork or working closely with others. **Work Values:** Moral Values; Independence; Activity; Company Policies and Practices; Supervision, Human Relations. **Skills:** Operation Monitoring; Operation and Control; Problem Identification; Equipment Selection; Equipment Maintenance; Testing. **Abilities:** *Cognitive*—Problem Sensitivity; Information Ordering; Perceptual Speed; Oral Expression; Selective Attention. *Psychomotor*—Manual Dexterity; Control Precision; Multilimb Coordination. *Physical*—Static Strength; Extent Flexibility; Trunk Strength. *Sensory*—Near Vision; Visual Color Discrimination; Far

Vision. **General Work Activities:** *Information Input*—Monitoring Processes, Materials, and Surroundings; Inspecting Equipment, Structures, Materials; Identifying Objects, Actions, and Events; Getting Information Needed to Do the Job. *Mental Process*—Processing Information; Making Decisions and Solving Problems; Judging Qualities of Things, Services, Other People's Work; Evaluating Information Against Standards; Analyzing Data or Information. *Work Output*—Controlling Machines and Processes; Handling and Moving Objects; Performing General Physical Activities. *Interacting with Others*—Communicating with Other Workers; Performing Administrative Activities; Coordinating Work and Activities of Others. **Physical Work Conditions:** Indoors; Using Hands on Objects, Tools, or Controls; Hazardous Equipment. **Other Job Characteristics:** Degree of Automation; Consequence of Error; Importance of Being Sure All Is Done.

Experience: Job Zone 2. Some previous work-related skill, knowledge, or experience may be helpful, but usually is not needed. **Job Preparation:** SVP 4.00 to 5.99—6 months to less than 2 years. **Knowledge:** Production and Processing; Mechanical; Physics; Mathematics; Chemistry. **Instructional Program:** 480599 Precision Metal Workers, Other.

Related DOT Jobs: 504.665-014 Charger Operator; 512.362-010 First Helper; 512.362-014 Furnace Operator; 512.362-018 Furnace Operator; 512.382-010 Oxygen-Furnace Operator; 512.382-014 Stove Tender; 512.382-018 Tin Recovery Worker; 512.662-010 Cupola Tender; 512.684-014 Furnace Charger; 512.685-010 Furnace Tender; 512.685-022 Reclamation Kettle Tender, Metal; 553.685-114 Cadmium Burner.

51-4052.00 Pourers and Casters, Metal (Metal Pourers and Casters, Basic Shapes)

Education: No data available.

Employed: 9,100

Openings: No data available.

Projected Growth: No data available.

Earnings: $24,350

Operate hand-controlled mechanisms to pour and regulate the flow of molten metal into molds to produce castings or ingots.

Repairs and maintains metal forms and equipment, using hand tools, sledges, and bars. Adds metal to molds to compensate for shrinkage. Reads temperature gauges; observes color changes; adjusts furnace flame, torch, or electrical heating unit, to melt metal. Positions equipment or signals workers to position equipment such as ladles, grinding wheels, or crucibles. Skims slag or removes excess metal from ingots or equipment, using hand tools, strainers, rakes, or burners; recycles scrap. Loads specified amount of metal and flux into furnace or clay crucible. Stencils identifying information on ingots and pigs, using special hand tools. Transports metal ingots to storage areas, using forklift. Removes metal ingots or cores from molds, using hand tools, cranes, and chain hoists. Collects samples, or signals workers to sample metal, for analysis. Assembles and imbeds cores in casting frames, using hand tools and equipment. Turns valves to circulate water through core; sprays water on filled molds to cool and solidify metal. Pours molten metal into molds and forms, using ladle. Examines molds to ensure they are clean, smooth, and properly coated.

GOE Number, Interest Area, and Work Group: 08.03.02; Industrial Production; Production Work: Equipment Operation, Assorted Materials Processing. **Personality Type:** Realistic. Realistic occupations frequently involve work activities that include practical, hands-on problems and solutions. These occupations often deal with plants, animals, and real-world materials like wood, tools, and machinery. Many of the occupations require working outside and do not involve a lot of paperwork or working closely with others. **Work Values:** Moral Values; Independence; Company Policies and Practices; Supervision, Human Relations; Supervision, Technical; Activity. **Skills:** Operation Monitoring; Operation and Control; Product Inspection; Repairing; Equipment Maintenance. **Abilities:** *Cognitive*—Information Ordering; Problem Sensitivity; Perceptual Speed; Visualization; Time Sharing; Spatial Orientation. *Psychomotor*—Arm-Hand Steadiness; Manual Dexterity; Control Precision. *Physical*—Static Strength; Trunk Strength; Extent Flexibility; Explosive Strength. *Sensory*—Visual Color Discrimination; Depth Perception; Hearing Sensitivity. **General Work Activities:** *Information Input*—Monitoring Processes, Materials, and Surroundings; Inspecting Equipment, Structures, Materials; Getting Information Needed to Do the Job. *Mental Process*—Judging Qualities of Things, Services, Other People's Work; Evaluating Information Against Standards; Making Decisions and Solving Problems. *Work Output*—Handling and Moving Objects; Controlling Machines and Processes; Performing General Physical Activities. *Interacting with Others*—Communicating with Other Workers; Establishing and Maintaining Relationships; Coordinating Work and Activities of Others. **Physical Work Conditions:** Indoors; Using Hands on Objects, Tools, or Controls; Common Protective or Safety Attire. **Other Job Characteristics:** Consequence of Error; Importance of Being Sure All Is Done; Importance of Being Exact or Accurate.

Experience: Job Zone 1. No previous work-related skill, knowledge, or experience is needed. **Job Preparation:** SVP Below 4.0—Less than 6 months. **Knowledge:** Production and Processing; Mechanical; Physics; Engineering and Technology; Building and Construction. **Instructional Program:** 480599 Precision Metal Workers, Other.

Related DOT Jobs: 502.664-014 Steel Pourer; 502.687-014 Busher; 514.584-010 Ingot Header; 514.684-010 Caster; 514.684-014 Ladle Pourer; 514.684-022 Pourer, Metal; 518.664-010 Mold Maker; 700.687-042 Melter.

51-4061.00 Model Makers, Metal and Plastic (Pattern and Model Makers, Metal)

Education: No data available.

Employed: 4,160

Openings: No data available.

Projected Growth: No data available.

Earnings: $31,590

Set up and operate machines such as lathes, milling and engraving machines, and jig borers to make working models of metal or plastic objects.

Reworks or alters component model or parts as required, to ensure performance of equipment or to ensure that parts meet standards. Devises and constructs own tools, dies, molds, jigs, and fixtures; modifies existing tools and equipment. Determines fixtures, machines, tooling, and sequence of operations, to fabricate parts, dies, and tooling, according to drawings and sketches. Cuts, shapes, and forms metal parts, using lathe, power saw, snips, power brakes and shear, files, and mallets. Lays out and marks reference points and dimension on materials, using measuring instruments and drawing or scribing tools. Drills, countersinks, and reams holes in parts and assemblies for bolts, screws, and other fasteners, using power tools. Fabricates metal or plastic parts, using hand tools. Inspects and tests model or other product to verify conformance to specifications, using precision measuring instruments or circuit tester. Consults and confers with engineering personnel to discuss developmental problems and to recommend modifications to correct or improve performance of product. Sets up and operates machines such as lathes, drill presses, punch presses, or bandsaw, to fabricate prototypes or models. Records specifications, production operations, and final dimensions of model for use in establishing operating standards and machinery procedures. Grinds, files, and sands parts to finished dimensions. Assembles mechanical, electrical, and electronic components into models or prototypes, using hand tools, power tools, and fabricating machines. Wires and solders electrical and electronic connections and components. Aligns, fits, and joins parts, by using bolts or screws or by welding or gluing. Studies blueprints, drawings, or sketches; computes dimensions for laying out materials and planning model production. Makes bridges, plates, wheels, cutting teeth on wheels and pinions, and threaded screws.

GOE Number, Interest Area, and Work Group: 08.04.01; Industrial Production; Metal and Plastics Machining Technology. **Personality Type:** Realistic. Realistic occupations frequently involve work activities that include practical, hands-on problems and solutions. These occupations often deal with plants, animals, and real-world materials like wood, tools, and machinery. Many of the occupations require working outside and do not involve a lot of paperwork or working closely with others. **Work Values:** Moral Values; Ability Utilization; Company Policies and Practices; Achievement; Supervision, Human Relations. **Skills:** Equipment Selection; Testing; Technology Design; Product Inspection; Problem Identification. **Abilities:** *Cognitive*—Information Ordering; Visualization; Written Comprehension; Oral Expression; Mathematical Reasoning. *Psychomotor*—Control Precision; Manual Dexterity; Arm-Hand Steadiness. *Physical*—Trunk Strength; Extent Flexibility; Static Strength. *Sensory*—Near Vision; Visual Color Discrimination; Auditory Attention; Speech Clarity; Far Vision. **General Work Activities:** *Information Input*—Getting Information Needed to Do the Job; Inspecting Equipment, Structures, Materials; Identifying Objects, Actions, and Events. *Mental Process*—Processing Information; Making Decisions and Solving Problems; Evaluating Information Against Standards. *Work Output*—Controlling Machines and Processes; Handling and Moving Objects; Drafting and Specifying Technical Devices. *Interacting with Others*—Communicating with Other Workers; Providing Consultation and Advice to Others; Performing Administrative Activities. **Physical Work Conditions:** Indoors; Using Hands on Objects, Tools, or Controls; Hazardous Equipment; Standing. **Other Job Characteristics:** Importance of Being Exact or Accurate; Importance of Being Sure All Is Done; Degree of Automation.

Experience: Job Zone 4. A minimum of two to four years of work-related skill, knowledge, or experience is needed. **Job Preparation:** SVP 7.0 to less than 8.0—2 years to less than 10 years. **Knowledge:** Design; Engineering and Technology; Mechanical; Building and Construction; Computers and Electronics. **Instructional Programs:** 480501 Machinist/Machine Technologist; 480506 Sheet Metal Worker.

Related DOT Jobs: 600.260-014 Experimental Mechanic; 600.260-018 Model Maker, Firearms; 600.280-054 Sample Maker, Appliances; 693.260-018 Engineering Model Maker; 693.361-014 Mock-Up Builder; 693.380-010 Model Maker; 709.381-014 Model Builder; 710.361-010 Model Maker, Scale; 723.361-010 Model Maker, Fluorescent Lighting.

51-4062.00 Patternmakers, Metal and Plastic (Pattern and Model Makers, Metal)

Education: No data available.

Employed: 4,160

Openings: No data available.

Projected Growth: No data available.

Earnings: $31,590

Lay out, machine, fit, and assemble castings and parts to metal or plastic foundry patterns, core boxes, or match plates.

Designs and develops template or pattern according to work orders, sample parts, or mockups. Cuts, trims, shapes, and forms patterns or templates, using hand tools and power tools. Lays out and draws or scribes pattern onto material, using compass, protractor, ruler, scribe, or other instruments. Studies blueprint of part to be cast or pattern to be made; computes dimensions; plans sequence of operations. Assembles pattern sections, using hand tools, bolts, screws, rivets, or glue. Makes templates or files for own use in inspection and finishing of particular shape. Covers or sprays pattern used in producing plastic with plastic-impregnated fabric or coat of sealing lacquer or wax. Repairs and reworks templates and patterns. Marks identification numbers or symbols onto pattern or template. Sets up and operates machine tools such as milling machines, lathes, drill presses, and grinders, to machine castings or pattern. Cleans and fine-finishes pattern or template, using emery cloth, files, scrapers, and power grinders. Operates welding equipment to weld pattern together. Constructs platforms, fixtures, and jigs for holding and placing patterns. Verifies conformance of pattern or template dimensions to specifications, using measuring instruments such as calipers, scales, and micrometers.

GOE Number, Interest Area, and Work Group: 08.04.01; Industrial Production; Metal and Plastics Machining Technology. **Personality Type:** Realistic. Realistic occupations frequently involve work activities that include practical, hands-on problems and solutions. These occupations often deal with plants, animals, and real-world materials like wood, tools, and machinery. Many of the occupations require working outside and do not involve a lot of paperwork or working closely with others. **Work Values:** Moral Values; Company Policies and Practices; Independence; Ability Utilization; Supervision, Human Relations; Security. **Skills:** Product Inspection; Operation and Control; Operation Monitoring; Mathematics; Technology Design; Operations Analysis. **Abilities:** *Cognitive*—Information Ordering; Visualization; Written Compre-

hension; Number Facility; Mathematical Reasoning. *Psychomotor*—Arm-Hand Steadiness; Wrist-Finger Speed; Control Precision. *Physical*—Static Strength; Trunk Strength; Extent Flexibility. *Sensory*—Near Vision; Auditory Attention; Visual Color Discrimination. **General Work Activities:** *Information Input*—Getting Information Needed to Do the Job; Inspecting Equipment, Structures, Materials; Estimating Needed Characteristics. *Mental Process*—Evaluating Information Against Standards; Judging Qualities of Things, Services, Other People's Work; Organizing, Planning, and Prioritizing. *Work Output*—Handling and Moving Objects; Controlling Machines and Processes; Drafting and Specifying Technical Devices. *Interacting with Others*—Communicating with Persons Outside Organization; Monitoring and Controlling Resources; Providing Consultation and Advice to Others; Guiding, Directing and Motivating Subordinates; Coordinating Work and Activities of Others; Performing for or Working with the Public. **Physical Work Conditions:** Indoors; Using Hands on Objects, Tools, or Controls; Hazardous Equipment; Common Protective or Safety Attire; Standing. **Other Job Characteristics:** Consequence of Error; Importance of Being Exact or Accurate; Importance of Being Sure All Is Done.

Experience: Job Zone 4. A minimum of two to four years of work-related skill, knowledge, or experience is needed. **Job Preparation:** SVP 7.0 to less than 8.0—2 years to less than 10 years. **Knowledge:** Design; Mechanical; Production and Processing; Mathematics; Engineering and Technology. **Instructional Programs:** 480501 Machinist/Machine Technologist; 480506 Sheet Metal Worker.

Related DOT Jobs: 600.280-046 Patternmaker Apprentice, Metal; 600.280-050 Patternmaker, Metal; 601.280-038 Template Maker, Extrusion Die; 601.381-038 Template Maker; 693.281-014 Patternmaker; 693.281-018 Patternmaker, Metal, Bench; 693.281-022 Patternmaker, Sample; 703.381-010 Patternmaker; 709.381-034 Patternmaker; 751.381-010 Patternmaker; 754.381-014 Patternmaker, Plastics.

51-4071.00 Foundry Mold and Coremakers (Foundry Mold Assembly and Shake-Out Workers)

Education: Moderate-term O-T-J training

Employed: 9,295

Openings: 955

Projected Growth: 2.5%

Earnings: $21,910

Make or form wax or sand cores or molds used in the production of metal castings in foundries.

Cleans and smoothes molds, cores, and core boxes; repairs surface imperfections. Positions cores into lower section of mold and reassembles mold for pouring. Sifts sand; packs sand into mold sections, core box, and pattern contours, using hand or pneumatic ramming tools. Sprinkles or sprays parting agent onto pattern and mold sections, to facilitate removal of pattern from mold. Operates ovens to bake cores. Operates furnaces to melt, skim, and flux metal. Rotates sweep board around spindle to make symmetrical molds for convex impressions. Moves and positions workpieces such as mold sections, patterns, and bottom boards, using cranes, or signals others to move workpieces. Lifts upper mold section from lower; removes molded patterns. Positions patterns inside mold sections and clamps sections together. Cuts spouts, runner holes, and sprue holes into mold. Forms and assembles slab cores around pattern; positions wire in mold sections to reinforce mold, using hand tools and glue. Pours molten metal into mold, manually or using crane ladle.

GOE Number, Interest Area, and Work Group: 08.02.02; Industrial Production; Production Technology: Precision Hand Work. **Personality Type:** Realistic. Realistic occupations frequently involve work activities that include practical, hands-on problems and solutions. These occupations often deal with plants, animals, and real-world materials like wood, tools, and machinery. Many of the occupations require working outside and do not involve a lot of paperwork or working closely with others. **Work Values:** Moral Values; Supervision, Human Relations; Company Policies and Practices; Independence; Supervision, Technical. **Skills:** Operation and Control; Product Inspection; Problem Identification; Operations Analysis; Monitoring; Science; Operation Monitoring. **Abilities:** *Cognitive*—Information Ordering; Selective Attention; Visualization; Problem Sensitivity; Oral Comprehension. *Psychomotor*—Arm-Hand Steadiness; Control Precision; Manual Dexterity; Multilimb Coordination. *Physical*—Static Strength; Extent Flexibility; Trunk Strength. *Sensory*—Visual Color Discrimination; Auditory Attention; Glare Sensitivity; Depth Perception. **General Work Activities:** *Information Input*—Monitoring Processes, Materials, and Surroundings; Getting Information Needed to Do the Job; Estimating Needed Characteristics; Inspecting Equipment, Structures, Materials. *Mental Process*—Judging Qualities of Things, Services, Other People's Work; Updating and Using Job-Relevant Knowledge; Evaluating Information Against Standards. *Work Output*—Handling and Moving Objects; Performing General Physical Activities; Controlling Machines and Processes. *Interacting with Others*—Communicating with Other Workers; Coordinating Work and Activities of Others; Establishing and Maintaining Relationships. **Physical Work Conditions:** Indoors; Common Protective or Safety Attire; Using Hands on Objects, Tools, or Controls. **Other Job Characteristics:** Consequence of Error; Degree of Automation; Importance of Being Exact or Accurate.

Experience: Job Zone 2. Some previous work-related skill, knowledge, or experience may be helpful, but usually is not needed. **Job Preparation:** SVP 4.00 to 5.99—6 months to less than 2 years. **Knowledge:** Production and Processing; Building and Construction; Mechanical; Engineering and Technology; Design. **Instructional Program:** 480599 Precision Metal Workers, Other.

Related DOT Jobs: 518.361-010 Molder; 518.361-014 Molder Apprentice; 518.361-018 Molder, Sweep; 518.381-014 Coremaker; 518.381-018 Coremaker Apprentice.

51-4072.00 Molding, Coremaking, and Casting Machine Setters, Operators, and Tenders, Metal and Plastic (Metal Molding, Coremaking, and Casting Machine Setters and Set-Up Operators)

Education: No data available.
Employed: 19,420
Openings: No data available.
Projected Growth: No data available.
Earnings: $25,240

Set up, operate, or tend metal or plastic molding, casting, or coremaking machines to mold or cast metal or thermoplastic parts or products.

GOE Number, Interest Area, and Work Group: 08.02.01; Industrial Production; Production Technology: Machine Set-up and Operation. **Instructional Program:** 480599 Precision Metal Workers, Other. **Note:** The Department of Labor has not collected some data for this job, so it has fewer details than the other descriptions.

51-4072.01 Plastic Molding and Casting Machine Setters and Set-Up Operators (Plastic Molding Machine Setters, Set-Up Operators, Operators, and Tenders)

Education: Moderate-term O-T-J training
Employed: 171,082
Openings: 20,701
Projected Growth: 14.7%
Earnings: No data available.

Set up, or set up and operate, plastic molding machines such as compression or injection molding machines to mold, form, or cast thermoplastic materials to specified shape.

Mixes catalysts, thermoplastic materials, and coloring pigments according to formula, using paddle and mixing machine. Positions, aligns, and secures assembled mold, mold components, and machine accessories onto machine press bed; attaches connecting lines. Removes finished or cured product from dies or mold, using hand tools and airhose. Weighs premixed compounds; dumps compound into die well; fills hoppers of machines that automatically supply compound to die. Trims excess material from part, using knife; grinds scrap plastic into powder for reuse. Repairs and maintains machines and auxiliary equipment, using hand tools and power tools. Observes and adjusts machine setup and operations, to eliminate production of defective parts and products. Reads specifications to determine setup and prescribed temperature and time settings, to mold, form, or cast plastic materials. Installs dies onto machine or press; coats dies with parting agent, according to work order specifications. Presses button or pulls lever to activate machine, to inject dies and compress compounds, to form and cure specified products. Sets machine controls to regulate molding temperature, volume, pressure, and time, according to knowledge of plastics and molding procedures. Measures and visually inspects products for surface and dimension defects, using precision measuring instruments, to ensure conformance to specifications.

GOE Number, Interest Area, and Work Group: 08.02.01; Industrial Production; Production Technology: Machine Set-up and Operation. **Personality Type:** Realistic. Realistic occupations frequently involve work activities that include practical, hands-on problems and solutions. These occupations often deal with plants, animals, and real-world materials like wood, tools, and machinery. Many of the occupations require working outside and do not involve a lot of paperwork or working closely with others. **Work Values:** Moral Values; Independence; Company Policies and Practices; Activity; Supervision, Human Relations. **Skills:** Product Inspection; Operation and Control; Operation Monitoring; Equipment Maintenance; Repairing. **Abilities:** *Cognitive*—Problem Sensitivity; Written Comprehension; Deductive Reasoning; Number Facility; Information Ordering. *Psychomotor*—Control Precision; Manual Dexterity; Wrist-Finger Speed. *Physical*—Static Strength; Explosive Strength; Extent Flexibility. *Sensory*—Near Vision; Visual Color Discrimination; Depth Perception. **General Work Activities:** *Information Input*—Getting Information Needed to Do the Job; Monitoring Processes, Materials, and Surroundings; Inspecting Equipment, Structures, Materials. *Mental Process*—Evaluating Information Against Standards; Processing Information; Analyzing Data or Information; Judging Qualities of Things, Services, Other People's Work; Making Decisions and Solving Problems. *Work Output*—Handling and Moving Objects; Controlling Machines and Processes; Performing General Physical Activities. *Interacting with Others*—Communicating with Other Workers; Monitoring and Controlling Resources; Establishing and Maintaining Relationships. **Physical Work Conditions:** Using Hands on Objects, Tools, or Controls; Indoors; Hazardous Equipment. **Other Job Characteristics:** Degree of Automation; Consequence of Error; Pace Determined by Speed of Equipment.

Experience: Job Zone 2. Some previous work-related skill, knowledge, or experience may be helpful, but usually is not needed. **Job Preparation:** SVP 4.00 to 5.99—6 months to less than 2 years. **Knowledge:** Mechanical; Production and Processing; Chemistry; Mathematics; Computers and Electronics. **Instructional Program:** 150607 Plastics Technology/Technician.

Related DOT Jobs: 556.380-010 Mold Setter; 556.382-014 Injection-Molding-Machine Operator; 556.682-014 Compression-Molding-Machine Operator.

51-4072.02 Plastic Molding and Casting Machine Operators and Tenders (Plastic Molding Machine Setters, Set-Up Operators, Operators, and Tenders)

Education: Moderate-term O-T-J training
Employed: 171,082
Openings: 20,701
Projected Growth: 14.7%
Earnings: No data available.

Operate or tend plastic molding machines such as compression or injection molding machines to mold, form, or cast thermoplastic materials to specified shape.

Stacks molded parts in boxes or on conveyor for subsequent processing; leaves parts in mold to cool. Positions mold frame to correct alignment of tubs containing mixture on top of mold, to facilitate loading of molds. Fills tubs, molds, or cavities of machine with plastic material, in solid or liquid form, prior to activating machine. Trims flashing from product. Signals coworker to synchronize feed of materials into molding process. Reports defect in molds to supervisor. Removes product from mold or conveyor; cleans and reloads mold. Mixes and pours liquid plastic into rotating drum of machine that spreads, hardens, and shapes mixture. Observes meters and gauges to verify specified temperatures, pressures, and press-cycle times. Throws flash and rejected parts into grinder machine to be recycled. Turns valves and dials of machines to regulate pressure and temperature, to set press-cycle time, and to close press. Examines molded product for surface defects such as dents, bubbles, thin areas, and cracks.

Starts machine that automatically liquefies plastic material in heating chamber, injects liquefied material into mold, and ejects molded product. Weighs prescribed amounts of material for molded part and finished product to ensure specifications are maintained. Observes continuous operation of automatic machine and width and alignment of plastic sheeting, to ensure side flanges. Pulls level and toggle latches, to fill mold and regulate tension on sheeting and to release mold covers. Dumps plastic powder, preformed plastic pellets, or preformed rubber slugs into hopper of molding machine. Feels stiffness and consistency of molded sheeting to detect machinery malfunction. Breaks seals that hold plastic product in molds, using hand tool; removes product from mold. Heats plastic material prior to forming product; cools product after processing to prevent distortion.

GOE Number, Interest Area, and Work Group: 08.02.01; Industrial Production; Production Technology: Machine Set-up and Operation. **Personality Type:** Realistic. Realistic occupations frequently involve work activities that include practical, hands-on problems and solutions. These occupations often deal with plants, animals, and real-world materials like wood, tools, and machinery. Many of the occupations require working outside and do not involve a lot of paperwork or working closely with others. **Work Values:** Moral Values; Company Policies and Practices; Activity; Independence; Supervision, Human Relations. **Skills:** Operation and Control; Operation Monitoring; Product Inspection; Mathematics; Problem Identification; Testing. **Abilities:** *Cognitive*—Problem Sensitivity; Perceptual Speed; Information Ordering; Category Flexibility; Oral Expression; Time Sharing. *Psychomotor*—Control Precision; Manual Dexterity; Reaction Time. *Physical*—Static Strength; Trunk Strength; Extent Flexibility. *Sensory*—Near Vision; Visual Color Discrimination; Hearing Sensitivity. **General Work Activities:** *Information Input*—Monitoring Processes, Materials, and Surroundings; Inspecting Equipment, Structures, Materials; Getting Information Needed to Do the Job. *Mental Process*—Judging Qualities of Things, Services, Other People's Work; Evaluating Information Against Standards; Making Decisions and Solving Problems. *Work Output*—Handling and Moving Objects; Controlling Machines and Processes; Performing General Physical Activities. *Interacting with Others*—Communicating with Other Workers; Coordinating Work and Activities of Others; Establishing and Maintaining Relationships; Assisting and Caring for Others. **Physical Work Conditions:** Indoors; Using Hands on Objects, Tools, or Controls; Standing. **Other Job Characteristics:** Degree of Automation; Pace Determined by Speed of Equipment; Importance of Being Sure All Is Done; Frustrating Circumstances.

Experience: Job Zone 1. No previous work-related skill, knowledge, or experience is needed. **Job Preparation:** SVP Below 4.0—Less than 6 months. **Knowledge:** Production and Processing; Mechanical; Mathematics; English Language; Physics; Engineering and Technology. **Instructional Program:** 150607 Plastics Technology/Technician.

Related DOT Jobs: 556.385-010 Centrifugal-Casting-Machine Tender; 556.665-010 Cake-Press Operator; 556.665-014 Corrugator Operator; 556.665-018 Molder, Pipe Covering; 556.685-022 Compression-Molding-Machine Tender; 556.685-038 Injection-Molding-Machine Tender; 556.685-082 Vacuum Plastic-Forming-Machine Operator; 556.685-086 Blow-Molding-Machine Tender; 556.685-090 Centrifugal-Casting-Machine Tender; 690.685-090 Contact-Lens Molder.

51-4072.03 Metal Molding, Coremaking, and Casting Machine Setters and Set-Up Operators (Metal Molding, Coremaking, and Casting Machine Setters and Set-Up Operators)

Education: No data available.

Employed: 19,420

Openings: No data available.

Projected Growth: No data available.

Earnings: $25,240

Set up, or set up and operate, metal casting, molding, and coremaking machines to mold or cast metal parts and products such as tubes, rods, automobile trim, carburetor housings, and motor parts. Use die casting and continuous-casting machines. Use roll-over, squeeze, and shell-molding machines.

Cleans and lubricates casting machine and dies, using airhose and brushes. Inspects castings and core slots for defects, using fixed gauges. Pours molten metal into cold-chamber machine or cylinders, using hand ladle. Connects water hose to cooling system of die, using hand tools. Loads metal ingots or aluminum bars into melting furnace; transfers molten metal to reservoir of die casting machine. Lines cylinder pot with asbestos strips and disk to prevent chilling. Preheats die sections with torch or electric heater. Removes castings from dies and dips castings in water to cool, using pliers or tongs. Obtains and moves specified pattern to work station, manually or using hoist; secures pattern to machine, using wrenches. Repairs or replaces worn or defective machine parts and dies. Moves controls to start, set, or adjust casting, molding, or pressing machines. Stacks and mounts rotor-core laminations over keyed mandrel of casting machine; removes and stamps rotor with identifying data. Loads die sections into machine, using equipment such as chain fall or hoist; secures in position, using hand tools.

GOE Number, Interest Area, and Work Group: 08.02.01; Industrial Production; Production Technology: Machine Set-up and Operation. **Personality Type:** Realistic. Realistic occupations frequently involve work activities that include practical, hands-on problems and solutions. These occupations often deal with plants, animals, and real-world materials like wood, tools, and machinery. Many of the occupations require working outside and do not involve a lot of paperwork or working closely with others. **Work Values:** Moral Values; Independence; Company Policies and Practices; Supervision, Human Relations; Activity. **Skills:** Equipment Selection; Operation Monitoring; Operation and Control; Product Inspection; Equipment Maintenance. **Abilities:** *Cognitive*—Information Ordering; Problem Sensitivity; Perceptual Speed; Memorization; Selective Attention; Visualization. *Psychomotor*—Control Precision; Manual Dexterity; Arm-Hand Steadiness. *Physical*—Extent Flexibility; Static Strength; Explosive Strength. *Sensory*—Depth Perception; Visual Color Discrimination; Far Vision. **General Work Activities:** *Information Input*—Monitoring Processes, Materials, and Surroundings; Inspecting Equipment, Structures, Materials; Getting Information Needed to Do the Job. *Mental Process*—Updating and Using Job-Relevant Knowledge; Judging Qualities of Things, Services, Other People's Work; Making Decisions and Solving Problems; Organizing, Planning, and Pri-

oritizing. *Work Output*—Controlling Machines and Processes; Handling and Moving Objects; Performing General Physical Activities. *Interacting with Others*—Communicating with Other Workers; Coordinating Work and Activities of Others; Performing Administrative Activities; Assisting and Caring for Others. **Physical Work Conditions:** Indoors; Using Hands on Objects, Tools, or Controls; Hazardous Equipment. **Other Job Characteristics:** Degree of Automation; Consequence of Error; Importance of Being Sure All Is Done.

Experience: Job Zone 2. Some previous work-related skill, knowledge, or experience may be helpful, but usually is not needed. **Job Preparation:** SVP 4.00 to 5.99—6 months to less than 2 years. **Knowledge:** Production and Processing; Mechanical; Engineering and Technology; Physics; Public Safety and Security. **Instructional Program:** 480599 Precision Metal Workers, Other.

Related DOT Jobs: 502.482-018 Rotor Casting-Machine Operator; 502.682-014 Casting-Machine Operator; 514.360-010 Die-Casting-Machine Setter; 514.382-010 Die-Casting-Machine Operator I; 518.380-010 Setter, Molding-and-Coremaking Machines.

51-4072.04 Metal Molding, Coremaking, and Casting Machine Operators and Tenders (Metal Molding, Coremaking, and Casting Machine Operators and Tenders)

Education: No data available.

Employed: 36,390

Openings: No data available.

Projected Growth: No data available.

Earnings: $24,640

Operate or tend metal molding, casting, or coremaking machines to mold or cast metal products such as pipes, brake drums, and rods and to mold or cast metal parts such as automobile trim, carburetor housings, and motor parts. Machines include centrifugal casting machines, vacuum casting machines, turnover draw-type coremaking machines, conveyor-screw coremaking machines, and die casting machines.

Assembles shell halves, patterns, and foundry flasks; reinforces core boxes, using glue, clamps, wire, bolts, rams, or machines. Positions, aligns, and secures molds or core boxes in holding devices or under pouring spouts and tubes, using hand tools. Fills core boxes and mold patterns with sand or powders, using ramming tools or pneumatic hammers; removes excess. Cuts spouts and pouring holes in molds, and sizes hardened cores, using saws. Cleans, glues, and racks cores, ingots, or finished products for storage. Inspects metal casts and molds, for cracks, bubbles, or other defects; measures castings to ensure that specifications are met. Skims or pours dross, slag, or impurities from molten metal, using ladle, rake, hoe, spatula, or spoon. Sprays, smokes, or coats molds with compounds to lubricate or insulate mold, using acetylene torches or sprayers. Weighs metals and powders; computes amounts of materials necessary to produce mixture of specified content. Requisitions molds and supplies; inventories and records finished products. Starts and operates furnace, oven, diecasting, coremaking, metal molding, or rotating machines, to pour metal or to create molds and casts. Signals or directs other workers to load conveyor, spray molds, or remove ingots.

Observes and records data from pyrometers, lights, and gauges, to monitor molding process and to adjust furnace temperature. Pours or loads metal or sand into melting pot, furnace, mold, core box, or hopper, using shovel, ladle, or machine. Removes casting from mold, mold from press, or core from core box, with the use of tongs, pliers, or hydraulic ram, or by inversion. Positions ladles or pourers; adjusts controls, to regulate the flow of metal, sand, or coolant into mold. Smoothes and cleans inner surface of mold, using brush, scraper, airhose, or grinding wheel; fills imperfections with refractory material. Repairs or replaces damaged molds, pipes, belts, chains, or other equipment, using hand tools, hand-powered press, or jib crane.

GOE Number, Interest Area, and Work Group: 08.02.01; Industrial Production; Production Technology: Machine Set-up and Operation. **Personality Type:** Realistic. Realistic occupations frequently involve work activities that include practical, hands-on problems and solutions. These occupations often deal with plants, animals, and real-world materials like wood, tools, and machinery. Many of the occupations require working outside and do not involve a lot of paperwork or working closely with others. **Work Values:** Moral Values; Company Policies and Practices; Activity; Supervision, Human Relations; Independence. **Skills:** Product Inspection; Operation and Control; Operation Monitoring; Equipment Maintenance; Testing. **Abilities:** *Cognitive*—Information Ordering; Number Facility; Mathematical Reasoning; Perceptual Speed; Problem Sensitivity. *Psychomotor*—Arm-Hand Steadiness; Reaction Time; Multilimb Coordination. *Physical*—Static Strength; Extent Flexibility; Trunk Strength. *Sensory*—Auditory Attention; Visual Color Discrimination; Far Vision. **General Work Activities:** *Information Input*—Monitoring Processes, Materials, and Surroundings; Inspecting Equipment, Structures, Materials; Getting Information Needed to Do the Job. *Mental Process*—Evaluating Information Against Standards; Judging Qualities of Things, Services, Other People's Work; Processing Information. *Work Output*—Handling and Moving Objects; Controlling Machines and Processes; Performing General Physical Activities. *Interacting with Others*—Communicating with Other Workers; Coordinating Work and Activities of Others; Performing Administrative Activities. **Physical Work Conditions:** Indoors; Using Hands on Objects, Tools, or Controls; Standing. **Other Job Characteristics:** Degree of Automation; Consequence of Error; Importance of Being Sure All Is Done.

Experience: Job Zone 1. No previous work-related skill, knowledge, or experience is needed. **Job Preparation:** SVP Below 4.0—Less than 6 months. **Knowledge:** Mechanical; Production and Processing; Building and Construction; Mathematics; Engineering and Technology. **Instructional Program:** 480599 Precision Metal Workers, Other.

Related DOT Jobs: 502.362-010 Shot Dropper; 502.382-010 Bullet-Slug-Casting-Machine Operator; 502.482-010 Caster; 502.482-014 Casting-Machine Operator, Automatic; 502.682-010 Bullet-Casting Operator; 502.685-010 Molder, Lead Ingot; 502.685-014 Remelter; 514.362-010 Pig-Machine Operator; 514.562-010 Centrifugal-Casting-Machine Operator III; 514.582-010 Vacuum Caster; 514.662-010 Casting Operator; 514.682-010 Casting-Wheel Operator; 514.685-010 Centrifugal-Casting-Machine Operator I; 514.685-014 Centrifugal-Casting-Machine Operator II; 514.685-018 Die-Casting-Machine Operator II; 518.682-010 Machine Molder; 518.685-014 Coremaker, Machine I; 518.685-018 Coremaker, Machine II; 518.685-022 Coremaker, Machine III; 518.685-026 Shell Molder (partial list; see the introduction for sources of the complete list).

51-4072.05 Casting Machine Set-Up Operators (All Other Printing Related Machine Setters and Set-Up Operators)

Education: No data available.

Employed: 10,130

Openings: No data available.

Projected Growth: No data available.

Earnings: $24,330

Set up and operate machines to cast and assemble printing type.

Stops machine when galley is full or when strip is completed. Places reel of controller paper on holder, threads around reels, and attaches to winding roll. Removes and stores assembly stick, controller reel, and matrix case. Forwards galley to appropriate personnel for proofing. Inserts and locks galley or matrix case into place on machine. Sets up matrices in assembly stick, by hand, according to specifications. Starts machine; monitors operation for proper functioning. Positions composing stick to length of line specified in casting instructions.

GOE Number, Interest Area, and Work Group: 08.02.01; Industrial Production; Production Technology: Machine Set-up and Operation. **Personality Type:** Realistic. Realistic occupations frequently involve work activities that include practical, hands-on problems and solutions. These occupations often deal with plants, animals, and real-world materials like wood, tools, and machinery. Many of the occupations require working outside and do not involve a lot of paperwork or working closely with others. **Work Values:** Moral Values; Independence; Activity; Company Policies and Practices; Supervision, Human Relations. **Skills:** Operation and Control; Operation Monitoring; Equipment Maintenance; Equipment Selection; Installation. **Abilities:** *Cognitive*—Information Ordering; Problem Sensitivity; Deductive Reasoning; Written Comprehension; Visualization. *Psychomotor*—Manual Dexterity; Control Precision; Arm-Hand Steadiness. *Physical*—Extent Flexibility; Static Strength; Trunk Strength. *Sensory*—Depth Perception; Peripheral Vision. **General Work Activities:** *Information Input*—Monitoring Processes, Materials, and Surroundings; Getting Information Needed to Do the Job; Identifying Objects, Actions, and Events. *Mental Process*—Evaluating Information Against Standards; Analyzing Data or Information; Making Decisions and Solving Problems; Judging Qualities of Things, Services, Other People's Work; Updating and Using Job-Relevant Knowledge; Organizing, Planning, and Prioritizing. *Work Output*—Controlling Machines and Processes; Handling and Moving Objects; Implementing Ideas and Programs; Performing General Physical Activities. *Interacting with Others*—Communicating with Other Workers; Coordinating Work and Activities of Others; Establishing and Maintaining Relationships. **Physical Work Conditions:** Indoors; Using Hands on Objects, Tools, or Controls; Standing. **Other Job Characteristics:** Degree of Automation; Importance of Being Sure All Is Done; Importance of Being Exact or Accurate.

Experience: Job Zone 3. Previous work-related skill, knowledge, or experience is required. **Job Preparation:** SVP 6.0 to less than 7.0—More than 1 year and less than 4 years. **Knowledge:** Production and Processing; Mechanical; Engineering and Technology; Mathematics; English Language; Physics. **Instructional Program:** 480201 Graphic and Printing Equipment Operator, General.

Related DOT Jobs: 654.382-010 Casting-Machine Operator; 654.582-010 Type-Casting Machine Operator.

51-4081.00 Multiple Machine Tool Setters, Operators, and Tenders, Metal and Plastic (Combination Machine Tool Setters and Set-Up Operators, Metal and Plastic)

Education: No data available.
Employed: 53,000
Openings: No data available.
Projected Growth: No data available.
Earnings: $26,330

Set up, operate, or tend more than one type of cutting or forming machine tool or robot.

GOE Number, Interest Area, and Work Group: 08.02.01; Industrial Production; Production Technology: Machine Set-up and Operation. **Instructional Program:** 480501 Machinist/Machine Technologist. **Note:** The Department of Labor has not collected some data for this job, so it has fewer details than the other descriptions.

51-4081.01 Combination Machine Tool Setters and Set-Up Operators, Metal and Plastic (Combination Machine Tool Setters, Set-Up Operators, Operators, and Tenders)

Education: Moderate-term O-T-J training
Employed: 107,020
Openings: 21,256
Projected Growth: 13.8%
Earnings: No data available.

Set up, or set up and operate, more than one type of cutting or forming machine tool, such as gear hobbers, lathes, press brakes, shearing, and boring machines.

Computes data such as gear dimensions and machine settings, applying knowledge of shop mathematics. Instructs operators or other workers in machine setup and operation. Records operational data such as pressure readings, length of stroke, feeds, and speeds. Makes minor electrical and mechanical repairs and adjustments to machines; notifies supervisor when major service is required. Lifts, positions, and secures workpieces in holding devices, using hoists and hand tools. Inspects first-run workpieces and verifies conformance to specifications to check accuracy of machine setup. Reads blueprint or job order, to determine product specifications and tooling instructions, and to plan operational sequences. Starts machine and turns handwheels or valves to engage feeding, cooling, and lubricating mechanisms. Selects, installs, and adjusts alignment of drills, cutters, dies, guides, and holding devices, using template, measuring instruments, and hand tools. Monitors machine operation and moves controls to align and adjust position of workpieces and action of cutting tools. Sets up and operates lathes, cutters, borers, millers, grinders, presses, drills, and auxiliary machines to make metallic and plastic workpieces. Moves controls, or mounts gears, cams, or templates in machine, to set feed rate and cutting speed, depth, and angle. Measures and marks reference points and cutting lines on workpiece, using traced templates, compasses, and rules.

GOE Number, Interest Area, and Work Group: 08.02.01; Industrial Production; Production Technology: Machine Set-up and Operation. **Personality Type:** Realistic. Realistic occupations frequently involve work activities that include practical, hands-on problems and solutions. These occupations often deal with plants, animals, and real-world materials like wood, tools, and machinery. Many of the occupations require working outside and do not involve a lot of paperwork or working closely with others. **Work Values:** Moral Values; Company Policies and Practices; Activity; Supervision, Human Relations; Independence. **Skills:** Product Inspection; Operation and Control; Testing; Mathematics; Operation Monitoring. **Abilities:** *Cognitive*—Written Comprehension; Information Ordering; Number Facility; Mathematical Reasoning; Oral Expression. *Psychomotor*—Control Precision; Reaction Time; Manual Dexterity. *Physical*—Static Strength; Extent Flexibility; Trunk Strength. *Sensory*—Near Vision; Visual Color Discrimination; Auditory Attention; Far Vision. **General Work Activities:** *Information Input*—Monitoring Processes, Materials, and Surroundings; Inspecting Equipment, Structures, Materials; Getting Information Needed to Do the Job. *Mental Process*—Evaluating Information Against Standards; Processing Information; Judging Qualities of Things, Services, Other People's Work; Making Decisions and Solving Problems. *Work Output*—Controlling Machines and Processes; Handling and Moving Objects; Repairing and Maintaining Mechanical Equipment. *Interacting with Others*—Teaching Others; Communicating with Other Workers; Coaching and Developing Others; Coordinating Work and Activities of Others. **Physical Work Conditions:** Indoors; Using Hands on Objects, Tools, or Controls; Hazardous Equipment. **Other Job Characteristics:** Degree of Automation; Consequence of Error; Importance of Being Exact or Accurate.

Experience: Job Zone 3. Previous work-related skill, knowledge, or experience is required. **Job Preparation:** SVP 6.0 to less than 7.0—More than 1 year and less than 4 years. **Knowledge:** Mechanical; Design; Mathematics; Engineering and Technology; Production and Processing. **Instructional Program:** 480501 Machinist/Machine Technologist.

Related DOT Jobs: 600.360-010 Machine Try-Out Setter; 600.360-014 Machine Setter; 600.380-018 Machine Set-Up Operator; 600.380-022 Machine Setter; 601.280-054 Tool-Machine Set-Up Operator; 602.280-010 Gear-Cutting-Machine Set-Up Operator, Tool; 602.380-010 Gear-Cutting-Machine Set-Up Operator; 602.382-010 Gear Hobber Set-Up Operator; 602.382-014 Gear-Generator Set-Up Operator, Spiral Bevel; 602.382-018 Gear-Generator Set-Up Operator, Straight Bevel; 602.382-022 Gear-Milling-Machine Set-Up Operator; 602.382-026 Gear-Shaper Set-Up Operator; 602.382-030 Gear-Shaver Set-Up Operator; 616.360-022 Machine Setter; 616.380-018 Machine Operator I; 692.682-034 Electrode Turner-and-Finisher.

51-4081.02 Combination Machine Tool Operators and Tenders, Metal and Plastic (Combination Machine Tool Setters, Set-Up Operators, Operators, and Tenders)

Education: Moderate-term O-T-J training

Employed: 107,020

Openings: 21,256

Projected Growth: 13.8%

Earnings: No data available.

Operate or tend more than one type of cutting or forming machine tool that has been previously set up, such as band saws, press brakes, slitting machines, drills, lathes, and boring machines.

Extracts or lifts jammed pieces from machine, using fingers, wire hooks, or lift bar. Performs minor machine maintenance such as oiling or cleaning machines, dies, or workpieces, or adding coolant to machine reservoir. Removes burrs, sharp edges, rust, or scale from workpiece, using file, hand grinder, wire brush, or power tools. Installs machine components such as chucks, boring bars, or cutting tools, according to specifications, using hand tools. Sets machine stops or guides to specified length as indicated by scale, rule, or template. Inspects workpiece for defects; measures workpiece, using rule, template, or other measuring instruments to determine accuracy of machine operation. Aligns layout marks with die or blade. Reads job specifications to determine machine adjustments and material requirements. Positions, adjusts, and secures workpiece against stops, on arbor, or in chuck, fixture, or automatic feeding mechanism, by hand or with the use of hoist. Observes machine operation to detect workpiece defects or machine malfunction. Activates and tends or operates machines to cut, shape, thread, bore, drill, tap, bend, or mill metal or non-metallic material. Adjusts machine components; changes worn accessories such as cutting tools and brushes, using hand tools.

GOE Number, Interest Area, and Work Group: 08.03.01; Industrial Production; Production Work: Machine Work, Assorted Materials. **Personality Type:** Realistic. Realistic occupations frequently involve work activities that include practical, hands-on problems and solutions. These occupations often deal with plants, animals, and real-world materials like wood, tools, and machinery. Many of the occupations require working outside and do not involve a lot of paperwork or working closely with others. **Work Values:** Moral Values; Company Policies and Practices; Activity; Independence; Supervision, Human Relations. **Skills:** Product Inspection; Operation and Control; Operation Monitoring; Equipment Maintenance; Equipment Selection; Installation; Reading Comprehension; Mathematics. **Abilities:** *Cognitive*—Information Ordering; Problem Sensitivity; Written Comprehension; Perceptual Speed; Spatial Orientation; Memorization. *Psychomotor*—Manual Dexterity; Control Precision; Arm-Hand Steadiness; Multilimb Coordination. *Physical*—Static Strength; Extent Flexibility; Explosive Strength; Trunk Strength. *Sensory*—Depth Perception; Peripheral Vision. **General Work Activities:** *Information Input*—Monitoring Processes, Materials, and Surroundings; Getting Information Needed to Do the Job; Inspecting Equipment, Structures, Materials. *Mental Process*—Judging Qualities of Things,

Services, Other People's Work; Evaluating Information Against Standards; Updating and Using Job-Relevant Knowledge. *Work Output*—Controlling Machines and Processes; Handling and Moving Objects; Implementing Ideas and Programs. *Interacting with Others*—Coordinating Work and Activities of Others; Communicating with Other Workers; Performing Administrative Activities. **Physical Work Conditions:** Indoors; Using Hands on Objects, Tools, or Controls; Standing; Hazardous Equipment. **Other Job Characteristics:** Degree of Automation; Pace Determined by Speed of Equipment; Importance of Being Exact or Accurate; Importance of Being Sure All Is Done; Frustrating Circumstances; Consequence of Error.

Experience: Job Zone 2. Some previous work-related skill, knowledge, or experience may be helpful, but usually is not needed. **Job Preparation:** SVP 4.00 to 5.99—6 months to less than 2 years. **Knowledge:** Production and Processing; Mechanical; Mathematics; Engineering and Technology; Building and Construction; Design. **Instructional Program:** 480501 Machinist/Machine Technologist.

Related DOT Jobs: 602.685-010 Gear-Cutting-Machine Operator, Production; 609.682-010 Automatic-Wheel-Line Operator; 609.682-022 Machine Operator, Centrifugal-Control Switches; 609.685-018 Production Machine Tender; 609.685-022 Transfer-Machine Operator; 609.685-026 Trim-Machine Operator; 619.685-062 Machine Operator II.

51-4111.00 Tool and Die Makers (Tool and Die Makers)

Education: Long-term O-T-J training

Employed: 137,802

Openings: 15,309

Projected Growth: -1.5%

Earnings: $37,250

Analyze specifications; lay out metal stock; set up and operate machine tools; fit and assemble parts to make and repair dies, cutting tools, jigs, fixtures, gauges, and machinists' hand tools.

Connects wiring and hydraulic lines to install electrical and hydraulic components. Fits and assembles parts, using bolts, glue, and other fasteners, and using hand tools such as hammers and wrenches. Smoothes and polishes flat and contoured surfaces of parts or tools, using scrapers, abrasive stones, files, emery cloth, or power grinder. Computes dimensions of assembly and plans sequence of operations. Repairs or modifies tools and dies, using machine tools and hand tools. Sets up and operates drill press to drill and tap holes in parts for assembly. Operates power press to test completed dies; applies pigment to die to indicate high spots which require reworking. Inspects die for smoothness, contour conformity, and defects, by touch or visually, using loupe or microscope. Measures, marks, and scribes metal or plastic stock to lay out machining, using instruments such as protractors, micrometers, scribes, and rulers. Fabricates sawblades, using power roller to straighten blade stock, punch press to cut teeth, and power grinder to sharpen teeth. Studies blueprints or specifications and visualizes shape of die, part, or tool. Lifts, positions, and secures machined parts on surface plate or worktable, using hoist, vises, v-blocks, or angle plates. Verifies dimensions, alignments, and clearances of finished parts, using measuring instruments such as calipers, gauge blocks, micrometers, and dial indicators. Sets pyrometer controls of heat-treating furnace; feeds or places parts, tools, or assemblies into furnace to harden. Designs tools, jigs, fixtures, and templates for use as work aids. Casts plastic tools or parts, or casts tungsten-carbide cutting tips, using premade molds. Cuts, shapes, and trims blank or block to specified length or shape, using powersaws, powershears, rule, and hand tools. Sets up and operates machine tools such as lathes, milling machines, shapers, and grinders, to machine parts.

GOE Number, Interest Area, and Work Group: 08.04.01; Industrial Production; Metal and Plastics Machining Technology. **Personality Type:** Realistic. Realistic occupations frequently involve work activities that include practical, hands-on problems and solutions. These occupations often deal with plants, animals, and real-world materials like wood, tools, and machinery. Many of the occupations require working outside and do not involve a lot of paperwork or working closely with others. **Work Values:** Moral Values; Company Policies and Practices; Activity; Supervision, Human Relations; Independence; Security. **Skills:** Operation and Control; Equipment Selection; Product Inspection; Mathematics; Repairing; Installation. **Abilities:** *Cognitive*–Information Ordering; Visualization; Number Facility; Written Comprehension; Mathematical Reasoning. *Psychomotor*–Manual Dexterity; Wrist-Finger Speed; Control Precision. *Physical*–Static Strength; Trunk Strength; Dynamic Strength. *Sensory*–Near Vision; Visual Color Discrimination; Depth Perception. **General Work Activities:** *Information Input*–Getting Information Needed to Do the Job; Inspecting Equipment, Structures, Materials; Monitoring Processes, Materials, and Surroundings. *Mental Process*–Evaluating Information Against Standards; Updating and Using Job-Relevant Knowledge; Judging Qualities of Things, Services, Other People's Work; Organizing, Planning, and Prioritizing. *Work Output*–Handling and Moving Objects; Controlling Machines and Processes; Performing General Physical Activities. *Interacting with Others*–Communicating with Other Workers; Coordinating Work and Activities of Others; Establishing and Maintaining Relationships; Interpreting Meaning of Information to Others; Performing Administrative Activities. **Physical Work Conditions:** Indoors; Using Hands on Objects, Tools, or Controls; Hazardous Equipment; Standing. **Other Job Characteristics:** Importance of Being Sure All Is Done; Importance of Being Exact or Accurate; Consequence of Error.

Experience: Job Zone 4. A minimum of two to four years of work-related skill, knowledge, or experience is needed. **Job Preparation:** SVP 7.0 to less than 8.0—2 years to less than 10 years. **Knowledge:** Mechanical; Production and Processing; Building and Construction; Engineering and Technology; Mathematics. **Instructional Program:** 480507 Tool and Die Maker/Technologist.

Related DOT Jobs: 601.260-010 Tool-and-Die Maker; 601.260-014 Tool-and-Die-Maker Apprentice; 601.280-010 Die Maker, Stamping; 601.280-014 Die Maker, Trim; 601.280-018 Die Maker, Wire Drawing; 601.280-022 Die Sinker; 601.280-030 Mold Maker, Die-Casting and Plastic Molding; 601.280-034 Tap-and-Die-Maker Technician; 601.280-042 Tool Maker; 601.280-058 Tool-Maker Apprentice; 601.281-010 Die Maker, Bench, Stamping; 601.281-014 Die-Try-Out Worker, Stamping; 601.281-026 Tool Maker,

Bench; 601.380-010 Carbide Operator; 601.381-010 Die Finisher; 601.381-014 Die Maker; 601.381-022 Die-Maker Apprentice; 601.381-026 Plastic Tool Maker; 601.381-030 Plastic-Fixture Builder; 601.381-034 Saw Maker (partial list; see the introduction for sources of the complete list).

51-4121.00 Welders, Cutters, Solderers, and Brazers
(Welders and Cutters)

Education:	Long-term O-T-J training
Employed:	367,708
Openings:	37,856
Projected Growth:	8.3%
Earnings:	$25,810

Use hand welding, flame cutting, hand soldering, or brazing equipment to weld or join metal components or to fill holes, indentations, or seams of fabricated metal products.

GOE Number, Interest Area, and Work Group: 08.03.03; Industrial Production; Production Work: Equipment Operation, Welding, Brazing, and Soldering. **Instructional Program:** 480508 Welder/Welding Technologist. **Note:** The Department of Labor has not collected some data for this job, so it has fewer details than the other descriptions.

51-4121.01 Welders, Production (Welders and Cutters)

Education:	Long-term O-T-J training
Employed:	367,708
Openings:	37,856
Projected Growth:	8.3%
Earnings:	$25,810

Assemble and weld metal parts on production line, using welding equipment. Perform tasks that require only a limited knowledge of welding techniques.

Guides and directs flame or electrodes on or across workpiece to straighten, bend, melt, or build up metal. Examines workpiece for defects and measures workpiece with straightedge or template to ensure conformance with specifications. Fuses parts together, seals tension points, and adds metal to build up parts. Connects hoses from torch to tanks of oxygen and fuel gas, and turns valves to release mixture. Selects, positions, and secures torch, cutting tips, or welding rod, according to type, thickness, area, and desired temperature of metal. Dismantles metal assemblies or cuts scrap metal, using thermal-cutting equipment such as flame-cutting torch or plasma-arc equipment. Climbs ladders or works on scaffolds to disassemble structures. Positions and secures workpiece, using hoist, crane, wire and banding machine, or hand tools. Fills cavities or corrects malformation in lead parts; hammers out bulges and bends in metal workpieces. Preheats workpieces, preparatory to welding or bending, using torch. Welds or tack-welds metal parts together, using spot-welding gun or using hand, electric, or gas welding equipment. Ignites torch and regulates flow of gas and air to obtain desired temperature, size, and color of flame. Signals crane operator to move large workpieces.

GOE Number, Interest Area, and Work Group: 08.03.03; Industrial Production; Production Work: Equipment Operation, Welding, Brazing, and Soldering. **Personality Type:** Realistic. Realistic occupations frequently involve work activities that include practical, hands-on problems and solutions. These occupations often deal with plants, animals, and real-world materials like wood, tools, and machinery. Many of the occupations require working outside and do not involve a lot of paperwork or working closely with others. **Work Values:** Moral Values; Activity; Company Policies and Practices; Independence; Security; Supervision, Human Relations. **Skills:** Operation and Control; Operation Monitoring; Product Inspection; Equipment Selection; Mathematics; Equipment Maintenance. **Abilities:** *Cognitive*—Visualization; Information Ordering; Selective Attention; Problem Sensitivity; Spatial Orientation; Perceptual Speed. *Psychomotor*—Manual Dexterity; Arm-Hand Steadiness; Control Precision. *Physical*—Dynamic Strength; Extent Flexibility; Explosive Strength; Trunk Strength. *Sensory*—Near Vision; Depth Perception; Visual Color Discrimination. **General Work Activities:** *Information Input*—Monitoring Processes, Materials, and Surroundings; Inspecting Equipment, Structures, Materials; Getting Information Needed to Do the Job. *Mental Process*—Updating and Using Job-Relevant Knowledge; Evaluating Information Against Standards; Judging Qualities of Things, Services, Other People's Work. *Work Output*—Handling and Moving Objects; Controlling Machines and Processes; Performing General Physical Activities. *Interacting with Others*—Communicating with Other Workers; Coordinating Work and Activities of Others; Performing Administrative Activities; Assisting and Caring for Others; Establishing and Maintaining Relationships; Interpreting Meaning of Information to Others. **Physical Work Conditions:** Indoors; Using Hands on Objects, Tools, or Controls; Standing. **Other Job Characteristics:** Degree of Automation; Importance of Being Sure All Is Done; Consequence of Error.

Experience: Job Zone 1. No previous work-related skill, knowledge, or experience is needed. **Job Preparation:** SVP Below 4.0—Less than 6 months. **Knowledge:** Mechanical; Production and Processing; Building and Construction; Public Safety and Security; Physics; Mathematics. **Instructional Program:** 480508 Welder/Welding Technologist.

Related DOT Jobs: 613.667-010 Liner Assembler; 709.684-086 Torch-Straightener-and Heater; 727.684-022 Lead Burner; 810.664-010 Welder, Gun; 810.684-010 Welder, Tack; 816.684-010 Thermal Cutter, Hand II; 819.684-010 Welder, Production Line.

51-4121.02 Welders and Cutters (Welders and Cutters)

Education: Long-term O-T-J training

Employed: 367,708

Openings: 37,856

Projected Growth: 8.3%

Earnings: $25,810

Use hand welding and flame-cutting equipment to weld together metal components and parts or to cut, trim, or scarf metal objects to dimensions, as specified by layouts, work orders, or blueprints.

Positions workpieces; clamps workpieces together or assembles them in jigs or fixtures. Selects and inserts electrode or gas nozzle into holder; connects hoses and cables to obtain gas or specified amperage, voltage, or polarity. Connects and turns regulator valves to activate and adjust gas flow and pressure to obtain desired flame. Repairs broken or cracked parts, fills holes, and increases size of metal parts, using welding equipment. Welds in flat, horizontal, vertical, or overhead position. Cleans or degreases parts, using wire brush, portable grinder, or chemical bath. Welds metal parts or components together, using brazing, gas, or arc welding equipment. Inspects finished workpiece for conformance to specifications. Preheats workpiece, using hand torch or heating furnace. Ignites torch or starts power supply and strikes arc. Selects and installs torch, torch tip, filler rod, and flux, according to welding chart specifications or type and thickness of metal. Reviews layouts, blueprints, diagrams, or work orders in preparation for welding or cutting metal components. Guides electrodes or torch along weld line at specified speed and angle to weld, melt, cut, or trim metal. Chips or grinds off excess weld, slag, or spatter, using hand scraper or power chipper, portable grinder, or arc-cutting equipment.

GOE Number, Interest Area, and Work Group: 08.03.03; Industrial Production; Production Work: Equipment Operation, Welding, Brazing, and Soldering. **Personality Type:** Realistic. Realistic occupations frequently involve work activities that include practical, hands-on problems and solutions. These occupations often deal with plants, animals, and real-world materials like wood, tools, and machinery. Many of the occupations require working outside and do not involve a lot of paperwork or working closely with others. **Work Values:** Moral Values; Activity; Company Policies and Practices; Supervision, Human Relations; Independence. **Skills:** Operation and Control; Product Inspection; Operation Monitoring; Mathematics; Equipment Selection; Equipment Maintenance. **Abilities:** *Cognitive*—Visualization; Information Ordering; Problem Sensitivity; Memorization; Deductive Reasoning; Perceptual Speed. *Psychomotor*—Arm-Hand Steadiness; Manual Dexterity; Control Precision. *Physical*—Extent Flexibility; Trunk Strength; Static Strength. *Sensory*—Near Vision; Glare Sensitivity; Depth Perception. **General Work Activities:** *Information Input*—Monitoring Processes, Materials, and Surroundings; Getting Information Needed to Do the Job; Inspecting Equipment, Structures, Materials. *Mental Process*—Evaluating Information Against Standards; Making Decisions and Solving Problems; Judging Qualities of Things, Services, Other People's Work. *Work Output*—Handling and Moving Objects; Controlling Machines and Processes; Implementing Ideas and Programs; Performing General Physical Activities. *Interacting with Others*—Communicating with Other Workers; Coordinating Work and Activities of Others; Performing Administrative Activities; Performing for or Working with the Public; Establishing and Maintaining Relationships. **Physical Work Conditions:** Using Hands on Objects, Tools, or Controls; Indoors; Hazardous Equipment; Common Protective or Safety Attire. **Other Job Characteristics:** Consequence of Error; Importance of Being Exact or Accurate; Importance of Being Sure All Is Done.

Experience: Job Zone 2. Some previous work-related skill, knowledge, or experience may be helpful, but usually is not needed. **Job Preparation:** SVP 4.00 to 5.99—6 months to less than 2 years. **Knowledge:** Mechanical; Building and Construction; Production and Processing; Design; Mathematics; Physics; Engineering and Technology. **Instructional Program:** 480508 Welder/Welding Technologist.

Related DOT Jobs: 810.384-010 Welder Apprentice, Arc; 810.384-014 Welder, Arc; 811.684-010 Welder Apprentice, Gas; 811.684-014 Welder, Gas; 816.364-010 Arc Cutter; 816.464-010 Thermal Cutter, Hand I; 819.384-010 Welder, Combination; 819.384-014 Welder Apprentice, Combination.

51-4121.03 Welder-Fitters (Welders and Cutters)

Education: Long-term O-T-J training

Employed: 367,708

Openings: 37,856

Projected Growth: 8.3%

Earnings: $25,810

Lay out, fit, and fabricate metal components to assemble structural forms such as machinery frames, bridge parts, and pressure vessels, using knowledge of welding techniques, metallurgy, and engineering requirements. Includes experimental welders who analyze engineering drawings and specifications to plan welding operations where procedural information is unavailable.

Melts lead bar, wire, or scrap to add lead to joint or to extrude melted scrap into reusable form. Determines required equipment and welding method, applying knowledge of metallurgy, geometry, and welding techniques. Analyzes engineering drawings and specifications to plan layout, assembly, and welding operations. Cuts workpiece, using powered saws, hand shears, or chipping knife. Ignites torch and adjusts valves, amperage, or voltage, to obtain desired flame or arc. Develops templates and other work aids to hold and align parts. Welds components in flat, vertical, or overhead positions. Installs or repairs equipment such as lead pipes, valves, floors, and tank linings. Inspects grooves, angles, or gap allowances, using micrometer, caliper, and precision measuring instruments. Heats, forms, and dresses metal parts, using hand tools, torch, or arc-welding equipment. Tack-welds or welds components and assemblies, using electric, gas, arc, or other welding equipment. Lays out, positions, and secures parts and assemblies according to specifications, using straightedge, combination square, calipers, and ruler. Observes tests on welded surfaces, such as hydrostatic, X-ray, and dimension tolerance tests, to evaluate weld quality and conformance to specifications. Removes rough spots from workpiece, using portable grinder, hand file, or scraper.

GOE Number, Interest Area, and Work Group: 08.03.03; Industrial Production; Production Work: Equipment Operation, Welding, Brazing, and Soldering. **Personality Type:** Realistic. Realistic occupations frequently involve work activities that include practical, hands-on problems and solutions. These occupations often deal with plants, animals, and real-world materials like wood, tools, and machinery. Many of the occupations require working outside and do not involve a lot of paperwork or working closely with others. **Work Values:** Moral Values; Company Policies and Practices; Activity; Supervision, Human Relations; Independence. **Skills:** Equipment Selection; Mathematics; Product Inspection; Repairing; Equipment Maintenance. **Abilities:** *Cognitive*—Written Comprehension; Information Ordering; Number Facility; Mathematical Reasoning; Visualization. *Psychomotor*—Arm-Hand Steadiness; Manual Dexterity; Wrist-Finger Speed; Control Precision. *Physical*—Extent Flexibility; Trunk Strength; Gross Body Equilib-

rium; Dynamic Strength. *Sensory*—Near Vision; Far Vision; Depth Perception. **General Work Activities:** *Information Input*—Getting Information Needed to Do the Job; Inspecting Equipment, Structures, Materials; Identifying Objects, Actions, and Events. *Mental Process*—Judging Qualities of Things, Services, Other People's Work; Evaluating Information Against Standards; Making Decisions and Solving Problems. *Work Output*—Handling and Moving Objects; Controlling Machines and Processes; Implementing Ideas and Programs. *Interacting with Others*—Communicating with Other Workers; Coordinating Work and Activities of Others; Performing Administrative Activities. **Physical Work Conditions:** Using Hands on Objects, Tools, or Controls; Indoors; Common Protective or Safety Attire; Hazardous Equipment. **Other Job Characteristics:** Importance of Being Sure All Is Done; Consequence of Error; Importance of Being Exact or Accurate.

Experience: Job Zone 4. A minimum of two to four years of work-related skill, knowledge, or experience is needed. **Job Preparation:** SVP 7.0 to less than 8.0—2 years to less than 10 years. **Knowledge:** Mechanical; Design; Building and Construction; Engineering and Technology; Production and Processing. **Instructional Program:** 480508 Welder/Welding Technologist.

Related DOT Jobs: 819.281-010 Lead Burner; 819.281-014 Lead-Burner Apprentice; 819.281-022 Welder, Experimental; 819.361-010 Welder-Fitter; 819.361-014 Welder-Fitter Apprentice; 819.381-010 Welder-Assembler.

51-4121.04 Solderers (Solderers and Brazers)

Education: Short-term O-T-J training

Employed: 35,281

Openings: 7,519

Projected Growth: 14.4%

Earnings: $17,600

Solder together components to assemble fabricated metal products, using soldering iron.

Removes workpieces from molten solder and holds parts together until color indicates that solder has set. Dips workpieces into molten solder, or places solder strip between seams and heats seam with iron to band items together. Applies flux to workpiece surfaces in preparation for soldering. Melts and separates soldered joints to repair misaligned or damaged assemblies, using soldering equipment. Cleans workpieces, using chemical solution, file, wire brush, or grinder. Melts and applies solder to fill holes, indentations, and seams of fabricated metal products, using soldering equipment. Grinds, cuts, buffs, or bends edges of workpieces to be joined, to ensure snug fit, using power grinder and hand tools. Aligns and clamps workpieces together, using rule, square, or hand tools, or positions items in fixtures, jigs, or vise. Heats soldering iron or workpiece to specified temperature for soldering, using gas flame or electric current. Melts and applies solder along adjoining edges of workpieces to solder joints, using soldering iron, gas torch, or electric-ultrasonic equipment. Cleans tip of soldering iron, using chemical solution or cleaning compound.

GOE Number, Interest Area, and Work Group: 08.03.03; Industrial Production; Production Work: Equipment Operation, Welding, Brazing, and Soldering. **Personality Type:** Realistic. Realistic occupations frequently involve work activities that include practical, hands-on problems and solutions. These occupations often deal with plants, animals, and real-world materials like wood, tools, and machinery. Many of the occupations require working outside and do not involve a lot of paperwork or working closely with others. **Work Values:** Moral Values; Activity; Company Policies and Practices; Independence; Supervision, Human Relations. **Skills:** Equipment Selection; Operation and Control; Product Inspection; Equipment Maintenance; Operation Monitoring; Monitoring. **Abilities:** *Cognitive*—Information Ordering; Visualization; Category Flexibility; Deductive Reasoning; Perceptual Speed; Number Facility. *Psychomotor*—Manual Dexterity; Finger Dexterity; Arm-Hand Steadiness. *Physical*—Extent Flexibility; Static Strength; Dynamic Strength. *Sensory*—Near Vision; Visual Color Discrimination; Sound Localization. **General Work Activities:** *Information Input*—Monitoring Processes, Materials, and Surroundings; Getting Information Needed to Do the Job; Identifying Objects, Actions, and Events; Inspecting Equipment, Structures, Materials. *Mental Process*—Judging Qualities of Things, Services, Other People's Work; Evaluating Information Against Standards; Analyzing Data or Information. *Work Output*—Handling and Moving Objects; Controlling Machines and Processes; Performing General Physical Activities. *Interacting with Others*—Monitoring and Controlling Resources; Communicating with Other Workers; Performing Administrative Activities; Coordinating Work and Activities of Others. **Physical Work Conditions:** Using Hands on Objects, Tools, or Controls; Indoors; Common Protective or Safety Attire. **Other Job Characteristics:** Consequence of Error; Importance of Being Sure All Is Done; Importance of Being Exact or Accurate.

Experience: Job Zone 1. No previous work-related skill, knowledge, or experience is needed. **Job Preparation:** SVP Below 4.0—Less than 6 months. **Knowledge:** Mechanical; Building and Construction; Production and Processing; Engineering and Technology; Chemistry. **Instructional Program:** 480508 Welder/Welding Technologist.

Related DOT Jobs: 736.684-038 Solderer, Barrel Ribs; 739.684-054 Deicer Finisher; 813.684-014 Solderer-Assembler; 813.684-018 Solderer-Dipper; 813.684-022 Solderer, Production Line; 813.684-026 Solderer, Torch I; 813.684-030 Solderer, Ultrasonic, Hand.

51-4121.05 Brazers (Solderers and Brazers)

Education: Short-term O-T-J training

Employed: 35,281

Openings: 7,519

Projected Growth: 14.4%

Earnings: $17,600

Braze together components to assemble fabricated metal parts, using torch or welding machine and flux.

Removes workpiece from fixture, using tongs; cools workpiece, using air or water. Adjusts electric current and timing cycle of resistance welding machine, to heat metal to bonding temperature. Selects torch tip, flux, and brazing alloy from data charts or work order. Connects hoses from torch to regulator valves and cylinders of oxygen and specified fuel gas, acetylene or natural. Brushes flux onto joint of workpiece or dips braze rod into flux, to prevent oxidation of metal. Cleans joints of workpieces, using wire brush or dipping them into cleaning solution. Cuts carbon

electrodes to specified size and shape, using cutoff saw. Aligns and secures workpieces in fixtures, jigs, or vise, using rule, square, or template. Examines seam and rebrazes defective joints or broken parts. Melts and separates brazed joints to remove and straighten damaged or misaligned components, using hand torch or furnace. Guides torch and rod along joint of workpieces, to heat to brazing temperature, melt braze alloy, and bond workpieces together. Turns valves to start flow of gases; lights flame; adjusts valves to obtain desired color and size of flame.

GOE Number, Interest Area, and Work Group: 08.03.03; Industrial Production; Production Work: Equipment Operation, Welding, Brazing, and Soldering. **Personality Type:** Realistic. Realistic occupations frequently involve work activities that include practical, hands-on problems and solutions. These occupations often deal with plants, animals, and real-world materials like wood, tools, and machinery. Many of the occupations require working outside and do not involve a lot of paperwork or working closely with others. **Work Values:** Moral Values; Activity; Company Policies and Practices; Independence; Security; Supervision, Human Relations. **Skills:** Operation and Control; Equipment Selection; Operation Monitoring; Product Inspection; Installation. **Abilities:** *Cognitive*—Visualization; Information Ordering; Written Comprehension; Problem Sensitivity; Perceptual Speed; Selective Attention. *Psychomotor*—Arm-Hand Steadiness; Control Precision; Manual Dexterity. *Physical*—Extent Flexibility; Trunk Strength; Static Strength. *Sensory*—Near Vision; Visual Color Discrimination; Glare Sensitivity. **General Work Activities:** *Information Input*—Inspecting Equipment, Structures, Materials; Monitoring Processes, Materials, and Surroundings; Getting Information Needed to Do the Job. *Mental Process*—Evaluating Information Against Standards; Making Decisions and Solving Problems; Analyzing Data or Information. *Work Output*—Controlling Machines and Processes; Handling and Moving Objects; Performing General Physical Activities. *Interacting with Others*—Communicating with Other Workers; Monitoring and Controlling Resources; Interpreting Meaning of Information to Others; Coordinating Work and Activities of Others. **Physical Work Conditions:** Using Hands on Objects, Tools, or Controls; Common Protective or Safety Attire; Indoors. **Other Job Characteristics:** Consequence of Error; Importance of Being Exact or Accurate; Importance of Being Sure All Is Done.

Experience: Job Zone 2. Some previous work-related skill, knowledge, or experience may be helpful, but usually is not needed. **Job Preparation:** SVP 4.00 to 5.99—6 months to less than 2 years. **Knowledge:** Engineering and Technology; Mechanical; Production and Processing; Building and Construction; Chemistry. **Instructional Program:** 480508 Welder/Welding Technologist.

Related DOT Jobs: 813.682-010 Brazer, Resistance; 813.684-010 Brazer, Assembler.

51-4122.00 Welding, Soldering, and Brazing Machine Setters, Operators, and Tenders (Welding Machine Setters and Set-Up Operators)

Education: No data available.

Employed: 32,060

Openings: No data available.

Projected Growth: No data available.

Earnings: $26,470

Set up, operate, or tend welding, soldering, or brazing machines or robots that weld, braze, solder, or heat-treat metal products, components, or assemblies.

GOE Number, Interest Area, and Work Group: 08.02.01; Industrial Production; Production Technology: Machine Set-up and Operation. **Instructional Program:** 480508 Welder/Welding Technologist. **Note:** The Department of Labor has not collected some data for this job, so it has fewer details than the other descriptions.

51-4122.01 Welding Machine Setters and Set-Up Operators (Welding Machine Setters and Set-Up Operators)

Education: No data available.

Employed: 32,060

Openings: No data available.

Projected Growth: No data available.

Earnings: $26,470

Set up, or set up and operate, welding machines that join or bond together components to fabricate metal products or assemblies according to specifications and blueprints.

Observes and listens to welding machine and its gauges to ensure welding process meets specifications. Devises and builds fixtures used to bond components, during the welding process. Cleans and maintains workpieces and welding machine parts, using hand tools and equipment. Tends auxiliary equipment used in welding process. Examines metal product or assemblies to ensure that specifications are met. Adds components, chemicals, and solutions to welding machine, using hand tools. Tests products; records test results and operational data on specified forms. Lays out, fits, or tacks workpieces together, using hand tools. Operates welding machine to produce trial workpieces, for examination and testing. Feeds workpiece into welding machine to join or bond components. Turns and presses controls such as cranks, knobs, and buttons, to adjust and activate welding process. Sets up and operates welding machines that join or bond components to fabricate metal products or assemblies. Stops and opens holding device on welding machine, using hand tools. Positions and adjusts fixtures, attachments, or workpieces on machine, using hand tools.

GOE Number, Interest Area, and Work Group: 08.02.01; Industrial Production; Production Technology: Machine Set-up and Operation. **Personality Type:** Realistic. Realistic occupations frequently involve work activities that include practical, hands-on problems and solutions. These occupations often deal with plants, animals, and real-world materials like wood, tools, and machinery. Many of the occupations require working outside and do not involve a lot of paperwork or working closely with others. **Work Values:** Moral Values; Company Policies and Practices; Independence; Activity; Supervision, Human Relations. **Skills:** Equipment Selection; Product Inspection; Operation Monitoring; Testing; Operation and Control; Mathematics. **Abilities:** *Cognitive*—Information Ordering; Problem Sensitivity; Visualization; Perceptual Speed; Written Comprehension; Deductive Reasoning. *Psychomotor*—Manual Dexterity; Arm-Hand Steadiness; Control Precision. *Physical*—Static Strength; Extent Flexibility; Trunk Strength. *Sensory*—Hearing Sensitivity; Auditory Attention; Depth Perception; Sound Localization. **General Work Activities:** *Information Input*—Monitoring Processes, Materials, and Surroundings; Getting Information Needed to Do the Job; Inspecting Equipment, Structures, Materials. *Mental Process*—Judging Qualities of Things, Services, Other People's Work; Evaluating Information Against Standards; Analyzing Data or Information; Organizing, Planning, and Prioritizing; Updating and Using Job-Relevant Knowledge; Making Decisions and Solving Problems. *Work Output*—Controlling Machines and Processes; Handling and Moving Objects; Implementing Ideas and Programs. *Interacting with Others*—Coordinating Work and Activities of Others; Performing Administrative Activities; Communicating with Other Workers. **Physical Work Conditions:** Indoors; Using Hands on Objects, Tools, or Controls; Standing. **Other Job Characteristics:** Degree of Automation; Pace Determined by Speed of Equipment; Consequence of Error.

Experience: Job Zone 3. Previous work-related skill, knowledge, or experience is required. **Job Preparation:** SVP 6.0 to less than 7.0—More than 1 year and less than 4 years. **Knowledge:** Mechanical; Production and Processing; Chemistry; Design; Engineering and Technology. **Instructional Program:** 480508 Welder/Welding Technologist.

Related DOT Jobs: 727.662-010 Lead Burner, Machine; 810.382-010 Welding-Machine Operator, Arc; 811.482-010 Welding-Machine Operator, Gas; 812.360-010 Welder Setter, Resistance Machine; 812.682-010 Welding-Machine Operator, Resistance; 815.380-010 Welder Setter, Electron-Beam Machine; 815.382-010 Welding-Machine Operator, Electron Beam.

51-4122.02 Welding Machine Operators and Tenders (Welding Machine Operators and Tenders)

Education: No data available.

Employed: 78,320

Openings: No data available.

Projected Growth: No data available.

Earnings: $24,400

Operate or tend welding machines that join or bond together components to fabricate metal products and assemblies according to specifications and blueprints.

Adds chemicals or solutions to welding machine to join or bind components. Cleans and maintains workpieces and welding machine parts, using hand tools and equipment. Tends auxiliary equipment used in the welding process. Inspects metal workpiece to ensure that specifications are met, using measuring devices. Stops and opens holding device on welding machine, using hand tools. Positions and adjusts fixtures, attachments, or workpiece on machine, using hand tools and measuring devices. Enters operating instructions into computer to adjust and start welding machine. Observes and listens to welding machine and its controls to ensure that the welding process meets specifications. Operates or tends welding machines that join or bond components to fabricate metal products and assemblies. Turns and presses knobs and buttons to adjust and start welding machine. Reads production schedule and specifications to ascertain product to be fabricated. Transfers components, metal products, and assemblies, using moving equipment.

GOE Number, Interest Area, and Work Group: 08.03.03; Industrial Production; Production Work: Equipment Operation, Welding, Brazing, and Soldering. **Personality Type:** Realistic. Realistic occupations frequently involve work activities that include practical, hands-on problems and solutions. These occupations often deal with plants, animals, and real-world materials like wood, tools, and machinery. Many of the occupations require working outside and do not involve a lot of paperwork or working closely with others. **Work Values:** Moral Values; Independence; Company Policies and Practices; Activity; Supervision, Human Relations. **Skills:** Operation and Control; Operation Monitoring; Product Inspection; Equipment Maintenance; Equipment Selection. **Abilities:** *Cognitive*—Information Ordering; Problem Sensitivity; Perceptual Speed; Written Comprehension; Number Facility; Spatial Orientation. *Psychomotor*—Control Precision; Manual Dexterity; Arm-Hand Steadiness. *Physical*—Static Strength; Trunk Strength; Extent Flexibility. *Sensory*—Hearing Sensitivity; Far Vision; Visual Color Discrimination; Auditory Attention. **General Work Activities:** *Information Input*—Monitoring Processes, Materials, and Surroundings; Inspecting Equipment, Structures, Materials; Getting Information Needed to Do the Job. *Mental Process*—Evaluating Information Against Standards; Judging Qualities of Things, Services, Other People's Work; Organizing, Planning, and Prioritizing. *Work Output*—Handling and Moving Objects; Controlling Machines and Processes; Implementing Ideas and Programs. *Interacting with Others*—Coordinating Work and Activities of Others; Communicating with Other Workers; Performing Administrative Activities. **Physical Work Conditions:** Indoors; Using Hands on Objects, Tools, or Controls; Hazardous Equipment. **Other Job Characteristics:** Degree of Automation; Pace Determined by Speed of Equipment; Consequence of Error.

Experience: Job Zone 2. Some previous work-related skill, knowledge, or experience may be helpful, but usually is not needed. **Job Preparation:** SVP 4.00 to 5.99—6 months to less than 2 years. **Knowledge:** Production and Processing; Mechanical; Engineering and Technology; Computers and Electronics; Mathematics; English Language; Chemistry. **Instructional Program:** 480508 Welder/Welding Technologist.

Related DOT Jobs: 614.684-010 Billet Assembler; 814.382-010 Welding-Machine Operator, Friction; 814.682-010 Welding-Machine Operator, Ultrasonic; 814.684-010 Welder, Explosion; 815.382-014 Welding-Machine Operator, Electroslag; 815.682-010 Laser-Beam-Machine Operator; 815.682-014 Welding-Machine Operator, Thermit; 819.685-010 Welding-Machine Tender.

51-4122.03 Soldering and Brazing Machine Setters and Set-Up Operators (Soldering and Brazing Machine Setters and Set-Up Operators)

Education: No data available.

Employed: 6,920

Openings: No data available.

Projected Growth: No data available.

Earnings: $21,530

Set up, or set up and operate, soldering or brazing machines to braze, solder, heat-treat, or spot-weld fabricated metal products or components as specified by work orders, blueprints, and layout specifications.

Positions, aligns, and bolts holding fixtures, guides, and stops onto or into brazing machine, to position and hold workpieces. Cleans, lubricates, and adjusts equipment to maintain efficient operation, using airhose, cleaning fluid, and hand tools. Examines workpiece for defective seams, solidification, and adherence to specifications; anneals finished workpiece to relieve internal stress. Disconnects electrical current; removes and immerses workpiece into water or acid bath, to cool and clean component. Operates and trains workers to operate heat-treating equipment to bond fabricated metal components according to blueprints, work orders, or specifications. Manipulates levers to synchronize brazing action or to move workpiece through brazing process. Assembles, aligns, and clamps workpieces into holding fixture to bond, heat-treat, or solder fabricated metal components. Fills hoppers and positions spout, to direct flow of flux; manually brushes flux onto seams of workpieces. Sets dials and timing controls to regulate electrical current, gas flow pressure, heating/cooling cycles, and shut-off. Connects, forms, and installs parts to braze, heat-treat, and spot-weld workpiece, metal parts, and components. Selects torch tips, alloy, flux, coil, tubing and wire, according to metal type and thickness, data charts, and records. Starts machine to complete trial run, readjusts machine, and records setup data.

GOE Number, Interest Area, and Work Group: 08.02.01; Industrial Production; Production Technology: Machine Set-up and Operation. **Personality Type:** Realistic. Realistic occupations frequently involve work activities that include practical, hands-on problems and solutions. These occupations often deal with plants, animals, and real-world materials like wood, tools, and machinery. Many of the occupations require working outside and do not involve a lot of paperwork or working closely with others. **Work Values:** Moral Values; Company Policies and Practices; Activity; Independence; Supervision, Human Relations. **Skills:** Product Inspection; Operation and Control; Operation Monitoring; Equipment Selection; Installation; Instructing. **Abilities:** *Cognitive*—Information Ordering; Problem Sensitivity; Written Comprehension; Deductive Reasoning; Oral Expression. *Psychomotor*—Manual Dexterity; Wrist-Finger Speed; Control Precision; Reaction Time. *Physical*—Static Strength; Explosive Strength; Dynamic Flexibility. *Sensory*—Sound Localization; Glare Sensitivity. **General Work Activities:** *Information Input*—Inspecting Equipment, Structures, Materials; Monitoring Processes, Materials, and Surroundings; Getting Information Needed to Do the Job. *Mental Process*—Evaluating Information Against Standards; Judging Qualities of Things, Services, Other People's Work; Making Decisions and Solving Problems. *Work Output*—Handling and Moving Objects; Controlling Machines and Processes; Performing General Physical Activities. *Interacting with Others*—Teaching Others; Communicating with Other Workers; Coaching and Developing Others. **Physical Work Conditions:** Indoors; Common Protective or Safety Attire; Using Hands on Objects, Tools, or Controls. **Other Job Characteristics:** Consequence of Error; Importance of Being Exact or Accurate; Importance of Being Sure All Is Done.

Experience: Job Zone 2. Some previous work-related skill, knowledge, or experience may be helpful, but usually is not needed. **Job Preparation:** SVP 4.00 to 5.99—6 months to less than 2 years. **Knowledge:** Mechanical; Engineering and Technology; Building and Construction; Design; Physics; Education and Training. **Instructional Program:** 480508 Welder/Welding Technologist.

Related DOT Jobs: 813.360-010 Brazing-Machine Setter; 813.360-014 Setter, Induction-Heating Equipment; 813.382-010 Brazer, Induction; 813.382-014 Brazing-Machine Operator.

51-4122.04 Soldering and Brazing Machine Operators and Tenders (Soldering and Brazing Machine Operators and Tenders)

Education: No data available.
Employed: 7,720
Openings: No data available.
Projected Growth: No data available.
Earnings: $20,490

Operate or tend soldering and brazing machines that braze, solder, or spot-weld fabricated metal products or components, as specified by work orders, blueprints, and layout specifications.

Removes workpieces and parts from machinery, using hand tools. Adds chemicals and materials to workpieces or machines, using hand tools. Reads and records operational information on specified production reports. Examines and tests soldered or brazed products or components, using testing devices. Loads and adjusts workpieces, clamps, and parts onto machine, using hand tools. Operates or tends soldering and brazing machines that braze, solder, or spot-weld fabricated products or components. Observes meters, gauges, and machine, to ensure that the solder or brazing process meets specifications. Moves controls to activate and adjust soldering and brazing machines. Cleans and maintains workpieces and machines, using equipment and hand tools.

GOE Number, Interest Area, and Work Group: 08.03.03; Industrial Production; Production Work: Equipment Operation, Welding, Brazing, and Soldering. **Personality Type:** Realistic. Realistic occupations frequently involve work activities that include practical, hands-on problems and solutions. These occupations often deal with plants, animals, and real-world materials like wood, tools, and machinery. Many of the occupations require working outside and do not involve a lot of paperwork or working closely with others. **Work Values:** Moral Values; Independence; Company Policies and Practices; Activity; Supervision, Human Relations. **Skills:** Operation Monitoring; Operation and Control; Product Inspection; Equipment Selection; Equipment Maintenance. **Abilities:** *Cognitive*—Information Ordering; Perceptual Speed; Written Comprehension; Problem Sensitivity; Visualization; Inductive Reasoning. *Psychomotor*—Control Precision; Wrist-Finger Speed; Arm-Hand Steadiness; Manual Dexterity. *Physical*—Extent Flexibility; Static Strength; Trunk Strength. *Sensory*—Near Vision; Sound Localization; Glare Sensitivity. **General Work Activities:** *Information Input*—Monitoring Processes, Materials, and Surroundings; Getting Information Needed to Do the Job; Inspecting Equipment, Structures, Materials. *Mental Process*—Evaluating Information Against Standards; Judging Qualities of Things, Services, Other People's Work; Making Decisions and Solving Problems. *Work Output*—Controlling Machines and Processes; Handling and Moving Objects; Performing General Physical Activities; Documenting and Recording Information. *Interacting with Others*—Performing Administrative Activities; Monitoring and Controlling Resources; Communicating with Other Workers. **Physical Work Conditions:** Indoors; Using Hands on Objects, Tools, or Controls; Common Protective or Safety Attire. **Other Job Characteristics:** Consequence of Error; Degree of Automation; Importance of Being Sure All Is Done.

Experience: Job Zone 1. No previous work-related skill, knowledge, or experience is needed. **Job Preparation:** SVP Below 4.0—Less than 6 months. **Knowledge:** Mechanical; Production and Processing; Design; Clerical; Chemistry. **Instructional Program:** 480508 Welder/Welding Technologist.

Related DOT Jobs: 706.685-010 Type-Soldering-Machine Tender; 715.685-058 Solderer; 726.362-014 Wave-Soldering Machine Operator; 726.684-094 Solder Deposit Operator; 726.685-038 Reflow Operator; 813.482-010 Brazer, Furnace; 813.685-010 Brazer, Controlled Atmospheric Furnace.

51-4191.00 Heat Treating Equipment Setters, Operators, and Tenders, Metal and Plastic (Heat Treating, Annealing, and Tempering Machine Operators and Tenders, Metal and Plastic)

Education: Moderate-term O-T-J training
Employed: 23,344
Openings: 2,265
Projected Growth: –4.1%
Earnings: $25,160

Set up, operate, or tend heating equipment such as heat-treating furnaces, flame-hardening machines, induction machines, soaking pits, or vacuum equipment to temper, harden, anneal, or heat-treat metal or plastic objects.

GOE Number, Interest Area, and Work Group: 08.02.01; Industrial Production; Production Technology: Machine Set-up and Operation. **Instructional Programs:** 480503 Machine Shop Assistant; 480599 Precision Metal Workers, Other. **Note:** The Department of Labor has not collected some data for this job, so it has fewer details than the other descriptions.

51-4191.01 Heating Equipment Setters and Set-Up Operators, Metal and Plastic (Heat Treating, Annealing, and Tempering Machine Operators and Tenders, Metal and Plastic)

Education: Moderate-term O-T-J training
Employed: 23,344
Openings: 2,265
Projected Growth: –4.1%
Earnings: $25,160

Set up, or set up and operate, heating equipment such as heat-treating furnaces, flame-hardening machines, and induction machines, that anneal or heat-treat metal objects.

Estimates flame temperature and heating cycle based on degree of hardness required and metal to be treated. Lights gas burners and adjusts flow of gas and coolant water. Starts conveyors and dial feeder plates; turns setscrews in nozzles to direct flames which anneal specific area of object. Reads work order to determine processing specifications. Sets frequency of current and automatic timer. Instructs new workers in machine operation. Crushes random samples between fingers to determine hardness. Replaces worn dial-feed, burner, and conveyor parts, using hand tools. Mounts fixtures and industrial coil on machine and mounts workpieces in fixture, using hand tools. Visually examines or tests objects, using hardness-testing equipment, to determine flame temperature and degree of hardness.

GOE Number, Interest Area, and Work Group: 08.02.01; Industrial Production; Production Technology: Machine Set-up and Operation. **Personality Type:** Realistic. Realistic occupations frequently involve work activities that include practical, hands-on problems and solutions. These occupations often deal with plants, animals, and real-world materials like wood, tools, and machinery. Many of the occupations require working outside and do not involve a lot of paperwork or working closely with others. **Work Values:** Moral Values; Activity; Company Policies and Practices; Supervision, Human Relations; Independence. **Skills:** Product Inspection; Operation and Control; Operation Monitoring; Equipment Maintenance; Mathematics. **Abilities:** *Cognitive*—Information Ordering; Oral Expression; Problem Sensitivity; Perceptual Speed; Visualization; Written Comprehension. *Psychomotor*—Manual Dexterity; Control Precision; Arm-Hand Steadiness. *Physical*—Extent Flexibility; Static Strength; Explosive Strength; Trunk Strength. *Sensory*—Near Vision; Speech Clarity; Depth Perception; Visual Color Discrimination; Far Vision. **General Work Activities:** *Information Input*—Inspecting Equipment, Structures, Materials; Monitoring Processes, Materials, and Surroundings; Getting Information Needed to Do the Job; Identifying Objects, Actions, and Events. *Mental Process*—Judging Qualities of Things, Services, Other People's Work; Making Decisions and Solving Problems; Organizing, Planning, and Prioritizing; Updating and Using Job-Relevant Knowledge. *Work Output*—Controlling Machines and Processes; Handling and Moving Objects; Implementing Ideas and Programs. *Interacting with Others*—Communicating with Other Workers; Teaching Others; Coaching and Developing Others. **Physical Work Conditions:** Indoors; Using Hands on Objects, Tools, or Controls; Standing; Hazardous Equipment. **Other Job Characteristics:** Degree of Automation; Consequence of Error; Importance of Being Exact or Accurate; Importance of Being Sure All Is Done.

Experience: Job Zone 3. Previous work-related skill, knowledge, or experience is required. **Job Preparation:** SVP 6.0 to less than 7.0—More than 1 year and less than 4 years. **Knowledge:** Mechanical; Production and Processing; Physics; Education and Training; English Language; Engineering and Technology. **Instructional Programs:** 480503 Machine Shop Assistant; 480599 Precision Metal Workers, Other.

Related DOT Jobs: 504.360-010 Flame-Annealing-Machine Setter; 504.380-010 Flame-Hardening-Machine Setter; 504.380-014 Induction-Machine Setter.

51-4191.02 Heat Treating, Annealing, and Tempering Machine Operators and Tenders, Metal and Plastic (Heat Treating, Annealing, and Tempering Machine Operators and Tenders, Metal and Plastic)

Education: Moderate-term O-T-J training
Employed: 23,344
Openings: 2,265
Projected Growth: –4.1%
Earnings: $25,160

Operate or tend machines such as furnaces, baths, flame-hardening machines, and electronic-induction machines, to harden, anneal, and heat-treat metal products or metal parts.

Signals forklift operator to deposit or extract containers of parts into and from furnaces and quenching-rinse tanks. Sets up and operates die-quenching machine to prevent parts from warping. Positions part in fixture, presses buttons to light burners, and tends flame hardening machine, according to procedures, to case-harden metal part. Activates and tends electric furnace that anneals base sections of hardened parts for subsequent machining. Reduces heat and allows parts to cool in furnace. Loads parts into containers, closes furnace door, and inserts parts into furnace when specified temperature is reached. Reads production schedule to determine processing sequence and furnace temperature requirements for objects to be heat treated. Removes parts from furnace after specified time; air dries or cools parts in water or oil brine or in other baths. Tests parts for hardness, using hardness-testing equipment; stamps heat-treatment identification mark on part, using hammer and punch. Cleans oxides and scale from parts or fittings, using steam spray or immersing parts in chemical and water baths. Covers parts with charcoal before inserting in furnace, to prevent discoloration caused by rapid heating. Sets automatic controls, observes gauges, and operates gas or electric furnace used to harden, temper, or anneal metal parts. Adjusts speed and operates continuous furnace through which parts are passed by means of reels and conveyors. Examines parts to ensure that the metal shade and color conform to specifications, utilizing knowledge of metal heat-treating.

GOE Number, Interest Area, and Work Group: 08.02.01; Industrial Production; Production Technology: Machine Set-up and Operation. **Personality Type:** Realistic. Realistic occupations frequently involve work activities that include practical, hands-on problems and solutions. These occupations often deal with plants, animals, and real-world materials like wood, tools, and machinery. Many of the occupations require working outside and do not involve a lot of paperwork or working closely with others. **Work Values:** Moral Values; Independence; Company Policies and Practices; Supervision, Human Relations; Activity. **Skills:** Testing; Operation Monitoring; Product Inspection; Operation and Control; Equipment Selection. **Abilities:** *Cognitive*—Information Ordering; Problem Sensitivity; Written Comprehension; Perceptual Speed; Memorization. *Psychomotor*—Control Precision; Manual Dexterity. *Physical*—Static Strength; Extent Flexibility; Trunk Strength. *Sensory*—Near Vision; Visual Color Discrimination; Far Vision; Depth Perception. **General Work Activities:** *Information Input*—Monitoring Processes, Materials, and Surroundings; Getting Information Needed to Do the Job; Identifying Objects, Actions, and Events; Inspecting Equipment, Structures, Materials. _Mental Process_—Judging Qualities of Things, Services, Other People's Work; Making Decisions and Solving Problems; Evaluating Information Against Standards. _Work Output_—Controlling Machines and Processes; Handling and Moving Objects; Performing General Physical Activities. _Interacting with Others_—Communicating with Other Workers; Coordinating Work and Activities of Others; Establishing and Maintaining Relationships; Assisting and Caring for Others; Performing Administrative Activities. **Physical Work Conditions:** Indoors; Using Hands on Objects, Tools, or Controls; Hazardous Equipment. **Other Job Characteristics:** Degree of Automation; Consequence of Error; Importance of Being Sure All Is Done.

Experience: Job Zone 2. Some previous work-related skill, knowledge, or experience may be helpful, but usually is not needed. **Job Preparation:** SVP 4.00 to 5.99—6 months to less than 2 years. **Knowledge:** Production and Processing; Mechanical; Physics; Chemistry; Mathematics. **Instructional Programs:** 480503 Machine Shop Assistant; 480599 Precision Metal Workers, Other.

Related DOT Jobs: 504.382-010 Hardener; 504.382-014 Heat Treater I; 504.382-018 Heat-Treater Apprentice; 504.682-010 Annealer; 504.682-014 Case Hardener; 504.682-018 Heat Treater II; 504.682-022 Heat-Treating Bluer; 504.682-026 Temperer; 504.685-010 Base-Draw Operator; 504.685-014 Flame-Hardening-Machine Operator; 504.685-022 Induction-Machine Operator; 504.685-026 Production Hardener; 504.687-010 Annealer.

51-4191.03 Heaters, Metal and Plastic (Heaters, Metal and Plastic)

Education: No data available.

Employed: 3,090

Openings: No data available.

Projected Growth: No data available.

Earnings: $24,510

Operate or tend heating equipment such as soaking pits, reheating furnaces, and heating and vacuum equipment, to heat metal sheets, blooms, billets, bars, plates, and rods to a specified temperature for rolling or processing or to heat and cure preformed plastic parts.

Positions part in plastic bag and seals bag with iron. Removes stock from furnace, using cold rod, tongs, or chain hoist; places stock on conveyor for transport to work area. Places part on cart, connects vacuum line to tube, and smoothes bag around part to ensure vacuum. Adjusts controls to maintain temperature and heating time, using thermal instruments and charts, dials and gauges of furnace, and color of stock. Sets oven controls or turns air-pressure valve or autoclave. Inserts vacuum tube into bag; seals bag around tube with tape. Starts conveyors and opens furnace doors, to load stock; signals crane operator to uncover soaking pits and lower ingots into them. Positions stock in furnace, using tongs, chain hoist, or pry bar. Adjusts controls to synchronize speed of feed and take-off conveyors of furnace. Pushes cart to curing oven or places part in autoclave. Impregnates fabric with plastic resins; cuts fabric into strips. Signals coworker to charge steel into furnace. Ignites furnace with torch; turns valve to regu-

late flow of fuel and air to burners. Assists workers in repairing, replacing, cleaning, lubricating, or adjusting furnace equipment, using hand tools. Records time and production data. Removes material from furnace, using crane; or signals crane operator to transfer to next station. Positions plastic sheet and mold in plastic bag, heats material under lamps, and forces confrontation of sheet to mold by vacuum pressure. Removes part and cuts away plastic bag.

GOE Number, Interest Area, and Work Group: 08.03.02; Industrial Production; Production Work: Equipment Operation, Assorted Materials Processing. **Personality Type:** Realistic. Realistic occupations frequently involve work activities that include practical, hands-on problems and solutions. These occupations often deal with plants, animals, and real-world materials like wood, tools, and machinery. Many of the occupations require working outside and do not involve a lot of paperwork or working closely with others. **Work Values:** Moral Values; Supervision, Human Relations; Company Policies and Practices; Activity; Supervision, Technical. **Skills:** Equipment Maintenance; Operation and Control; Repairing; Operation Monitoring; Writing. **Abilities:** _Cognitive_—Information Ordering; Deductive Reasoning; Memorization; Problem Sensitivity; Written Expression; Selective Attention. _Psychomotor_—Control Precision; Arm-Hand Steadiness; Multilimb Coordination. _Physical_—Extent Flexibility; Static Strength; Gross Body Coordination. **General Work Activities:** _Information Input_—Monitoring Processes, Materials, and Surroundings; Identifying Objects, Actions, and Events; Inspecting Equipment, Structures, Materials. _Mental Process_—Evaluating Information Against Standards; Updating and Using Job-Relevant Knowledge; Making Decisions and Solving Problems; Judging Qualities of Things, Services, Other People's Work. _Work Output_—Controlling Machines and Processes; Handling and Moving Objects; Performing General Physical Activities. _Interacting with Others_—Communicating with Other Workers; Assisting and Caring for Others; Performing Administrative Activities. **Physical Work Conditions:** Indoors; Using Hands on Objects, Tools, or Controls; Standing. **Other Job Characteristics:** Consequence of Error; Degree of Automation; Importance of Being Sure All Is Done; Importance of Being Exact or Accurate.

Experience: Job Zone 2. Some previous work-related skill, knowledge, or experience may be helpful, but usually is not needed. **Job Preparation:** SVP 4.00 to 5.99—6 months to less than 2 years. **Knowledge:** Production and Processing; Mechanical; Physics; Engineering and Technology; Mathematics. **Instructional Program:** 480599 Precision Metal Workers, Other.

Related DOT Jobs: 553.685-014 Bagger; 613.362-010 Heater I; 613.462-014 Furnace Operator; 619.682-022 Heater; 619.686-026 Spike-Machine Heater.

51-4192.00 Lay-Out Workers, Metal and Plastic (Precision Lay-Out Workers, Metal)

Education: No data available.

Employed: 13,850

Openings: No data available.

Projected Growth: No data available.

Earnings: $29,800

Lay out reference points and dimensions on metal or plastic stock or workpieces such as sheets, plates, tubes, structural shapes, castings, or machine parts for further processing. Includes shipfitters.

Determines reference points and computes layout dimensions and works, to tolerances as close as 0.001 inch. Adds dimensional details to blueprints or drawings by other workers; designs templates of wood, paper, or metal. Fits and aligns fabricated parts for welding or assembly operations. Inspects machined parts to verify conformance to specifications. Applies pigment to layout surfaces, using paint brush. Plans and develops layout from blueprints and templates, applying knowledge of trigonometry, design, effects of heat, and properties of metal. Examines workpiece and verifies such requirements as dimensions and squareness, using rule, square, and straight-edge. Marks curves, lines, holes, dimensions, and welding symbols onto workpiece, using scribes, soapstone, punches, and hand drill. Locates center line and verifies template position, using measuring instruments including gauge blocks, height gauges, and dial indicators. Details location and sequence of cutting, drilling, bending, rolling, punching, and welding operations, using compass, protractor, dividers, and rule. Lifts and positions workpiece in relation to surface plate, manually or with hoist, using parallel blocks and angle plates. **GOE Number, Interest Area, and Work Group:** 08.04.01; Industrial Production; Metal and Plastics Machining Technology. **Personality Type:** Realistic. Realistic occupations frequently involve work activities that include practical, hands-on problems and solutions. These occupations often deal with plants, animals, and real-world materials like wood, tools, and machinery. Many of the occupations require working outside and do not involve a lot of paperwork or working closely with others. **Work Values:** Moral Values; Independence; Company Policies and Practices; Supervision, Human Relations; Ability Utilization. **Skills:** Mathematics; Product Inspection; Reading Comprehension; Equipment Selection; Technology Design; Active Learning. **Abilities:** *Cognitive*—Number Facility; Visualization; Mathematical Reasoning; Information Ordering; Deductive Reasoning; Written Comprehension. *Psychomotor*—Arm-Hand Steadiness; Manual Dexterity; Finger Dexterity; Multilimb Coordination. *Physical*—Static Strength; Extent Flexibility; Trunk Strength. *Sensory*—Near Vision; Depth Perception. **General Work Activities:** *Information Input*—Getting Information Needed to Do the Job; Inspecting Equipment, Structures, Materials; Estimating Needed Characteristics. *Mental Process*—Evaluating Information Against Standards; Analyzing Data or Information; Making Decisions and Solving Problems. *Work Output*—Drafting and Specifying Technical Devices; Handling and Moving Objects; Implementing Ideas and Programs. *Interacting with Others*—Communicating with Other Workers; Establishing and Maintaining Relationships; Coordinating Work and Activities of Others. **Physical Work Conditions:** Using Hands on Objects, Tools, or Controls; Indoors; Standing. **Other Job Characteristics:** Importance of Being Exact or Accurate; Consequence of Error; Importance of Being Sure All Is Done.

Experience: Job Zone 3. Previous work-related skill, knowledge, or experience is required. **Job Preparation:** SVP 6.0 to less than 7.0—More than 1 year and less than 4 years. **Knowledge:** Production and Processing; Design; Mathematics; Engineering and Technology; Physics. **Instructional Programs:** 480501 Machinist/

Machine Technologist; 480503 Machine Shop Assistant; 480506 Sheet Metal Worker.

Related DOT Jobs: 600.281-018 Lay-Out Worker; 809.281-010 Lay-Out Worker I; 809.381-014 Lay-Out Worker II.

51-4193.00 Plating and Coating Machine Setters, Operators, and Tenders, Metal and Plastic
(Electrolytic Plating and Coating Machine Setters and Set-Up Operators, Metal and Plastic)

Education: No data available.

Employed: 13,770

Openings: No data available.

Projected Growth: No data available.

Earnings: $21,560

Set up, operate, or tend plating or coating machines to coat metal or plastic products with chromium, zinc, copper, cadmium, nickel, or other metal to protect or decorate surfaces. Set up, operate, or tend electrolytic processes.

GOE Number, Interest Area, and Work Group: 08.03.04; Industrial Production; Production Work: Plating and Coating. **Instructional Program:** 480599 Precision Metal Workers, Other. **Note:** The Department of Labor has not collected some data for this job, so it has fewer details than the other descriptions.

51-4193.01 Electrolytic Plating and Coating Machine Setters and Set-Up Operators, Metal and Plastic
(Electrolytic Plating Machine Setters, Set-Up Operators, Operators, and Tenders)

Education: Moderate-term O-T-J training

Employed: 45,050

Openings: 5,108

Projected Growth: 9.6%

Earnings: No data available.

Set up, or set up and operate, electrolytic plating or coating machines such as continuous multistrand electrogalvanizing machines, to coat metal or plastic products electrolytically with chromium, copper, cadmium, or other metal, to provide protective or decorative surfaces or to build up worn surfaces.

Removes plated object from solution at periodic intervals; observes object to ensure conformance to specifications. Measures, marks, and masks areas excluded from plating. Grinds, polishes, or rinses object in water; dries object to maintain clean, even surface. Examines object at end of process to determine thickness of metal deposit; measures thickness, using instruments such as micrometers. Immerses object in cleaning and rinsing baths to complete plating process. Plates small objects such as nuts or bolts, using motor-driven barrel. Suspends stick or piece of plating metal from anode (positive terminal) and immerses metal in plating solution. Suspends object, such as part or mold, from cathode rod (negative terminal) and immerses object in plating solution. Determines size and composition of object to be plated and amount of electrical current and time required, following work order. Adjusts voltage and amperage, based on observations. Moves controls to permit electrodeposition of metal on object or to regulate movement of wire strand to obtain specified thickness. Mixes chemical solutions, fills tanks and charges furnaces.

GOE Number, Interest Area, and Work Group: 08.03.04; Industrial Production; Production Work: Plating and Coating. **Personality Type:** Realistic. Realistic occupations frequently involve work activities that include practical, hands-on problems and solutions. These occupations often deal with plants, animals, and real-world materials like wood, tools, and machinery. Many of the occupations require working outside and do not involve a lot of paperwork or working closely with others. **Work Values:** Moral Values; Independence; Activity; Supervision, Human Relations; Company Policies and Practices. **Skills:** Operation and Control; Product Inspection; Operation Monitoring; Mathematics; Reading Comprehension. **Abilities:** *Cognitive*—Information Ordering; Deductive Reasoning; Oral Comprehension; Written Comprehension; Memorization; Problem Sensitivity. *Psychomotor*—Control Precision; Manual Dexterity; Wrist-Finger Speed; Multilimb Coordination. *Physical*—Extent Flexibility; Static Strength; Trunk Strength. **General Work Activities:** *Information Input*—Inspecting Equipment, Structures, Materials; Monitoring Processes, Materials, and Surroundings; Getting Information Needed to Do the Job. *Mental Process*—Evaluating Information Against Standards; Making Decisions and Solving Problems; Analyzing Data or Information. *Work Output*—Controlling Machines and Processes; Handling and Moving Objects; Performing General Physical Activities. *Interacting with Others*—Communicating with Other Workers; Coordinating Work and Activities of Others; Establishing and Maintaining Relationships; Monitoring and Controlling Resources. **Physical Work Conditions:** Indoors; Using Hands on Objects, Tools, or Controls; Common Protective or Safety Attire; Standing. **Other Job Characteristics:** Consequence of Error; Importance of Being Exact or Accurate; Importance of Being Sure All Is Done.

Experience: Job Zone 3. Previous work-related skill, knowledge, or experience is required. **Job Preparation:** SVP 6.0 to less than 7.0—More than 1 year and less than 4 years. **Knowledge:** Mechanical; Chemistry; Production and Processing; Physics; Engineering and Technology. **Instructional Program:** 480599 Precision Metal Workers, Other.

Related DOT Jobs: 500.362-010 Electrogalvanizing-Machine Operator; 500.380-010 Plater; 500.380-014 Plater Apprentice.

51-4193.02 Electrolytic Plating and Coating Machine Operators and Tenders, Metal and Plastic (Electrolytic Plating Machine Setters, Set-Up Operators, Operators, and Tenders)

Education: Moderate-term O-T-J training

Employed: 45,050

Openings: 5,108

Projected Growth: 9.6%

Earnings: No data available.

Operate or tend electrolytic plating or coating machines, such as zinc-plating machines and anodizing machines, to coat metal or plastic products electrolytically with chromium, zinc, copper, cadmium, or other metal to provide protective or decorative surfaces or to build up worn surfaces.

Mixes and tests plating solution to specified formula and turns valves to fill tank with solution. Measures or estimates amounts of electric current needed and time required to coat objects. Lubricates moving parts of plating conveyor; cleans plating and cleaning-solution tanks. Rinses coated object in cleansing liquids and dries, by using cloth or centrifugal driers or by tumbling in sawdust-filled barrels. Immerses objects to be coated or plated into cleaning solutions, or sprays with conductive solution, to prepare object for plating. Monitors and measures thickness of electroplating on component part, to verify conformance to specifications, using micrometer. Removes object from plating solution after specified time or when desired thickness of metal is deposited on them. Positions objects to be plated in frame or suspends them from positive or negative terminals of power supply. Adjusts dials to regulate flow of current and voltage supplied to terminals, to control plating process. Mixes forming acid solution, treats battery plates, and removes and rinses formed plates.

GOE Number, Interest Area, and Work Group: 08.03.04; Industrial Production; Production Work: Plating and Coating. **Personality Type:** Realistic. Realistic occupations frequently involve work activities that include practical, hands-on problems and solutions. These occupations often deal with plants, animals, and real-world materials like wood, tools, and machinery. Many of the occupations require working outside and do not involve a lot of paperwork or working closely with others. **Work Values:** Moral Values; Independence; Activity; Supervision, Human Relations; Company Policies and Practices. **Skills:** Product Inspection; Operation and Control; Mathematics; Testing; Operation Monitoring; Equipment Maintenance. **Abilities:** *Cognitive*—Information Ordering; Problem Sensitivity; Number Facility; Mathematical Reasoning; Deductive Reasoning. *Psychomotor*—Control Precision; Wrist-Finger Speed; Reaction Time. *Physical*—Dynamic Strength; Explosive Strength; Dynamic Flexibility. *Sensory*—Visual Color Discrimination. **General Work Activities:** *Information Input*—Monitoring Processes, Materials, and Surroundings; Estimating Needed Characteristics; Inspecting Equipment, Structures, Materials. *Mental Process*—Evaluating Information Against Standards; Analyzing Data or Information; Making Decisions and Solving Problems; Judging Qualities of Things, Services, Other People's Work. *Work Output*—Handling and Moving Objects; Controlling Machines and Processes; Implementing Ideas and Programs; Performing General Physical Activities. *Interacting with Others*—Communicating with Other Workers; Assisting and Caring for Others; Monitoring and Controlling Resources; Performing Administrative Activities; Teaching Others; Developing and Building Teams. **Physical Work Conditions:** Indoors; Using Hands on Objects, Tools, or Controls; Common Protective or Safety Attire; Standing; Hazardous Conditions. **Other Job Characteristics:** Degree of Automation; Importance of Being Sure All Is Done; Pace Determined by Speed of Equipment.

Experience: Job Zone 2. Some previous work-related skill, knowledge, or experience may be helpful, but usually is not needed. **Job Preparation:** SVP 4.00 to 5.99—6 months to less than 2 years.

Knowledge: Chemistry; Mathematics; Mechanical; Production and Processing; Physics. **Instructional Program:** 480599 Precision Metal Workers, Other.

Related DOT Jobs: 500.362-014 Plater, Barrel; 500.384-010 Matrix Plater; 500.384-014 Matrix-Bath Attendant; 500.485-010 Zinc-Plating-Machine Operator; 500.682-010 Anodizer; 500.684-010 Electroformer; 500.684-018 Plate Former; 500.684-026 Plater, Printed Circuit Board Panels; 500.684-030 Plater, Semiconductor Wafers and Components; 500.684-034 Plater; 500.685-014 Plating Equipment Tender.

51-4193.03 Nonelectrolytic Plating and Coating Machine Setters and Set-Up Operators, Metal and Plastic (Nonelectrolytic Plating and Coating Machine Setters and Set-Up Operators, Metal and Plastic)

Education: No data available.

Employed: 3,330

Openings: No data available.

Projected Growth: No data available.

Earnings: $21,300

Set up, or set up and operate, nonelectrolytic plating or coating machines, such as hot-dip lines and metal-spraying machines, to coat metal or plastic products or parts with metal.

Positions workpieces, starts operation of machines and conveyors, and feeds workpieces into machines to be coated. Adjusts controls to set temperatures of coating substance, and adjusts speeds of machines and equipment. Operates sandblasting equipment to roughen and clean surface of workpieces. Inspects coated products for defects and specified color and coverage. Preheats workpieces in oven. Operates hoist to place workpieces onto machine feed carriage or spindle. Adjusts controls to synchronize equipment speed with speed of coating or spraying machine. Mixes alodize solution in tank of machine, according to formula; verifies solution concentration, using gauge. Reads production schedule to determine setup of equipment and machines. Installs gears and holding devices on conveyor equipment. Attaches nozzle, positions gun, connects hoses, and threads wire, to set up metal-spraying machine. Measures and sets stops, rolls, brushes, and guides on automatic feeder and conveying equipment or coating machines, using micrometer, rule, and hand tools. Ignites gun and adjusts controls to regulate wire feed, air pressure, and flow of oxygen and fuel to operate metal-spraying machine.

GOE Number, Interest Area, and Work Group: 08.03.04; Industrial Production; Production Work: Plating and Coating. **Personality Type:** Realistic. Realistic occupations frequently involve work activities that include practical, hands-on problems and solutions. These occupations often deal with plants, animals, and real-world materials like wood, tools, and machinery. Many of the occupations require working outside and do not involve a lot of paperwork or working closely with others. **Work Values:** Moral Values; Independence; Supervision, Human Relations; Company Policies and Practices; Activity. **Skills:** Operation and Control; Product Inspection; Operation Monitoring; Installation; Equipment Selection. **Abilities:** *Cognitive*—Written Comprehension; Information Ordering; Visualization; Problem Sensitivity; Selec-

tive Attention; Number Facility. *Psychomotor*—Control Precision; Manual Dexterity; Reaction Time; Multilimb Coordination. *Physical*—Static Strength; Extent Flexibility; Explosive Strength; Dynamic Strength. *Sensory*—Visual Color Discrimination; Depth Perception; Glare Sensitivity. **General Work Activities:** *Information Input*—Monitoring Processes, Materials, and Surroundings; Inspecting Equipment, Structures, Materials; Getting Information Needed to Do the Job. *Mental Process*—Evaluating Information Against Standards; Judging Qualities of Things, Services, Other People's Work; Analyzing Data or Information; Making Decisions and Solving Problems. *Work Output*—Handling and Moving Objects; Controlling Machines and Processes; Performing General Physical Activities. *Interacting with Others*—Communicating with Other Workers; Establishing and Maintaining Relationships; Coordinating Work and Activities of Others; Monitoring and Controlling Resources; Influencing Others or Selling; Performing Administrative Activities. **Physical Work Conditions:** Using Hands on Objects, Tools, or Controls; Indoors; Standing; Common Protective or Safety Attire. **Other Job Characteristics:** Degree of Automation; Consequence of Error; Importance of Being Exact or Accurate.

Experience: Job Zone 3. Previous work-related skill, knowledge, or experience is required. **Job Preparation:** SVP 6.0 to less than 7.0—More than 1 year and less than 4 years. **Knowledge:** Mechanical; Production and Processing; Chemistry; Engineering and Technology; Mathematics; English Language. **Instructional Program:** 480599 Precision Metal Workers, Other.

Related DOT Jobs: 501.362-010 Coating-Machine Operator; 505.382-010 Metal-Spraying-Machine Operator, Automatic I; 509.462-010 Alodize-Machine Operator.

51-4193.04 Nonelectrolytic Plating and Coating Machine Operators and Tenders, Metal and Plastic (Nonelectrolytic Plating and Coating Machine Operators and Tenders, Metal and Plastic)

Education: No data available.

Employed: 4,860

Openings: No data available.

Projected Growth: No data available.

Earnings: $21,500

Operate or tend nonelectrolytic plating or coating machines, such as metal-spraying machines and vacuum metalizing machines, to coat metal or plastic products or parts with metal.

Maintains production records. Cuts metal or other materials, using shears or band saw. Replaces worn parts and adjusts equipment components, using hand tools. Cleans workpieces, using wire brush. Solders equipment and visually examines for completeness. Cleans and maintains equipment, using water hose and scraper. Positions containers to receive parts, and loads or unloads materials in containers, using dolly or handtruck. Measures or weighs materials, using ruler, calculator, and scale. Sprays coating in specified pattern according to instructions; inspects area for defects such as air bubbles or uneven coverage. Removes excess material or impurities from objects, using airhose or grinding machine. Observes gauges and adjusts controls of machine, to regulate functions such as speed and temperature, according to specifications. Presses or turns controls to activate and set equipment operation according to specifications. Positions and feeds materials on plate into machine, manually or automatically, for processing. Fills machine receptacle with coating material or solution. Immerses workpieces in coating solution for specified time. Mixes coating material or solution according to formula, or uses premixed solutions. Places materials on racks and transfers to oven to dry for a specified period of time.

GOE Number, Interest Area, and Work Group: 08.03.04; Industrial Production; Production Work: Plating and Coating. **Personality Type:** Realistic. Realistic occupations frequently involve work activities that include practical, hands-on problems and solutions. These occupations often deal with plants, animals, and real-world materials like wood, tools, and machinery. Many of the occupations require working outside and do not involve a lot of paperwork or working closely with others. **Work Values:** Moral Values; Independence; Supervision, Human Relations; Company Policies and Practices; Activity. **Skills:** Operation Monitoring; Operation and Control; Equipment Maintenance; Product Inspection; Mathematics; Repairing. **Abilities:** *Cognitive*—Information Ordering; Written Comprehension; Selective Attention; Visualization; Number Facility. *Psychomotor*—Control Precision; Arm-Hand Steadiness; Multilimb Coordination; Speed of Limb Movement. *Physical*—Extent Flexibility; Trunk Strength; Static Strength. **General Work Activities:** *Information Input*—Monitoring Processes, Materials, and Surroundings; Inspecting Equipment, Structures, Materials; Getting Information Needed to Do the Job. *Mental Process*—Evaluating Information Against Standards; Updating and Using Job-Relevant Knowledge; Processing Information. *Work Output*—Handling and Moving Objects; Controlling Machines and Processes; Performing General Physical Activities. *Interacting with Others*—Performing Administrative Activities; Communicating with Other Workers; Establishing and Maintaining Relationships. **Physical Work Conditions:** Indoors; Using Hands on Objects, Tools, or Controls; Standing. **Other Job Characteristics:** Consequence of Error; Degree of Automation; Importance of Being Exact or Accurate; Importance of Being Sure All Is Done.

Experience: Job Zone 1. No previous work-related skill, knowledge, or experience is needed. **Job Preparation:** SVP Below 4.0—Less than 6 months. **Knowledge:** Production and Processing; Mechanical; Chemistry; Physics; Mathematics; Engineering and Technology. **Instructional Program:** 480599 Precision Metal Workers, Other.

Related DOT Jobs: 501.485-010 Wire-Coating Operator, Metal; 501.685-010 Plater, Hot Dip; 501.685-014 Tinning-Equipment Tender; 501.685-018 Black Oxide Coating Equipment Tender; 501.685-022 Electroless Plater, Printed Circuit Board Panels; 503.685-010 Coater; 505.382-014 Welding-Rod Coater; 505.482-010 Pasting-Machine Operator; 505.682-010 Sprayer Operator; 505.685-010 Browning Processor; 505.685-014 Metal-Spraying-Machine Operator, Automatic II; 505.685-018 Vacuum-Metalizer Operator; 509.382-010 Coater Operator; 509.685-022 Ceramic Coater, Machine; 509.685-026 Gettering-Filament-Machine Operator; 509.685-030 Impregnator; 509.685-034 Lacquer-Dipping-Machine Operator; 509.685-038 Lubricating-Machine Tender; 554.382-014 Plastics-Spreading-Machine Operator; 554.585-014 Coater Operator (partial list; see the introduction for sources of the complete list).

51-4194.00 Tool Grinders, Filers, and Sharpeners (Tool Grinders, Filers, Sharpeners, and Other Precision Grinders)

Education: No data available.

Employed: 36,820

Openings: No data available.

Projected Growth: No data available.

Earnings: $26,660

Perform precision smoothing, sharpening, polishing, or grinding of metal objects.

Removes finished workpiece from machine and places in boxes or racks, depending on size of workpiece. Forms specified section of workpiece and repairs cracks in workpiece, using welding or brazing equipment. Tends machine that grinds, files, or polishes workpiece. Observes and listens to machine operation, to determine whether adjustments are necessary and to ensure that workpieces meet specifications. Examines and feels surface of workpiece to verify that grinding meets specifications. Turns valves to direct flow of coolant against cutting wheel and workpiece. Places workpiece in electroplating solution or applies pigment to surfaces of workpiece to highlight ridges and grooves. Duplicates workpiece contours, using tracer attachment. Removes and replaces machine parts, using hand tools. Dresses grinding wheel, according to specifications. Straightens workpiece and removes dents in workpiece, using straightening press and hammers. Sets up, operates, and adjusts grinding or polishing machines, to grind metal workpieces such as dies, parts, and tools. Fits parts together in preassembly to ensure that dimensions are accurate. Selects and mounts grinding wheels on machines, according to specifications, using hand tools and applying knowledge of abrasive and grinding procedures. Computes number, width, and angle of cutting tool, micrometer, scales, and gauges; adjusts tool to produce specified cuts. Studies blueprint or layout of metal workpiece, to visualize grinding procedure and to plan sequences of operations. Measures and examines workpiece to verify that dimensions meet specifications. Cleans and lubricates machine parts. Inspects dies to detect defects, assess wear, and verify specifications, using micrometers, steel gauge pins, and loupe. Files or finishes surface of workpiece, using prescribed hand tool.

GOE Number, Interest Area, and Work Group: 08.04.01; Industrial Production; Metal and Plastics Machining Technology. **Personality Type:** Realistic. Realistic occupations frequently involve work activities that include practical, hands-on problems and solutions. These occupations often deal with plants, animals, and real-world materials like wood, tools, and machinery. Many of the occupations require working outside and do not involve a lot of paperwork or working closely with others. **Work Values:** Moral Values; Company Policies and Practices; Supervision, Human Relations; Activity; Independence; Security. **Skills:** Product Inspection; Operation Monitoring; Testing; Operation and Control; Equipment Selection. **Abilities:** *Cognitive*—Information Ordering; Written Comprehension; Visualization; Number Facility; Mathematical Reasoning; Problem Sensitivity. *Psychomotor*—Manual Dexterity; Wrist-Finger Speed; Control Precision. *Physical*—Static Strength; Extent Flexibility; Trunk Strength. *Sensory*—Hearing Sensitivity; Near Vision; Auditory Attention. **General Work**

Activities: *Information Input*—Getting Information Needed to Do the Job; Inspecting Equipment, Structures, Materials; Monitoring Processes, Materials, and Surroundings. *Mental Process*—Evaluating Information Against Standards; Judging Qualities of Things, Services, Other People's Work; Analyzing Data or Information; Organizing, Planning, and Prioritizing; Making Decisions and Solving Problems. *Work Output*—Controlling Machines and Processes; Handling and Moving Objects; Performing General Physical Activities. *Interacting with Others*—Communicating with Other Workers; Establishing and Maintaining Relationships; Performing for or Working with the Public; Resolving Conflict and Negotiating with Others; Assisting and Caring for Others; Communicating with Persons Outside Organization. **Physical Work Conditions:** Indoors; Hazardous Equipment; Using Hands on Objects, Tools, or Controls. **Other Job Characteristics:** Degree of Automation; Consequence of Error; Frustrating Circumstances; Importance of Being Exact or Accurate; Pace Determined by Speed of Equipment.

Experience: Job Zone 3. Previous work-related skill, knowledge, or experience is required. **Job Preparation:** SVP 6.0 to less than 7.0—More than 1 year and less than 4 years. **Knowledge:** Design; Mechanical; Production and Processing; Building and Construction; Mathematics; Engineering and Technology. **Instructional Programs:** 480503 Machine Shop Assistant; 480507 Tool and Die Maker/Technologist.

Related DOT Jobs: 500.381-010 Cylinder Grinder; 601.381-018 Die Polisher; 603.280-010 Grinder Operator, External, Tool; 603.280-014 Grinder Operator, Surface, Tool; 603.280-018 Grinder Operator, Tool; 603.280-022 Grinder Set-Up Operator, Internal; 603.280-030 Grinder Set-Up Operator, Universal; 603.280-038 Tool-Grinder Operator; 680.380-010 Card Grinder; 701.381-014 Saw Filer; 701.381-018 Tool Grinder I; 701.684-030 Tool Filer; 705.381-010 Die Barber; 705.481-010 Filer, Finish; 705.481-014 Lapper, Hand, Tool.

51-5000 Printing Workers

51-5011.00 Bindery Workers (Bindery Machine Operators and Tenders)

Education: No data available.

Employed: 65,490

Openings: No data available.

Projected Growth: No data available.

Earnings: $19,290

Set up or operate binding machines that produce books and other printed materials.

GOE Number, Interest Area, and Work Group: 08.02.01; Industrial Production; Production Technology: Machine Set-up and Operation. **Instructional Program:** 480299 Graphic and Printing Equipment Operators, Other. **Note:** The Department of Labor has not collected some data for this job, so it has fewer details than the other descriptions.

51-5011.01 Bindery Machine Setters and Set-Up Operators (Bindery Machine Operators and Set-Up Operators)

Education: Moderate-term O-T-J training

Employed: 89,554

Openings: 16,466

Projected Growth: 11.5%

Earnings: No data available.

Set up, or set up and operate, machines that perform some or all of the following functions in order to produce books, magazines, pamphlets, catalogs, and other printed materials: gathering, folding, cutting, stitching, rounding and backing, supering, casing-in, lining, pressing, and trimming.

Removes books or products from machine and stacks them. Threads wire into machine to load stitcher head for stapling. Mounts and secures rolls or reels of wire, cloth, paper, or other material onto machine spindles; fills paper feed. Positions and clamps stitching heads on crossarms to space stitches to specified lengths. Reads work order to determine work instructions. Examines product samples for defects. Cleans and lubricates machinery parts and makes minor repairs. Starts machines and makes trial runs to verify accuracy of machine setup. Trains workers to set up, operate, and use automatic bindery machines. Sets machine controls, to adjust length and thickness of folds, stitches, or cuts and to adjust speed and pressure. Fills glue pot; adjusts flow of glue and speed of conveyors. Installs bindery-machine devices such as knives, guides, and clamps, to accommodate sheets, signatures, or books of specified sizes. Observes and monitors machine operations to detect malfunctions; makes required adjustments. Manually stocks supplies such as signatures, books, or paper. Records time spent on specific tasks and number of items produced, for daily production sheet.

GOE Number, Interest Area, and Work Group: 08.02.01; Industrial Production; Production Technology: Machine Set-up and Operation. **Personality Type:** Realistic. Realistic occupations frequently involve work activities that include practical, hands-on problems and solutions. These occupations often deal with plants, animals, and real-world materials like wood, tools, and machinery. Many of the occupations require working outside and do not involve a lot of paperwork or working closely with others. **Work Values:** Moral Values; Activity; Company Policies and Practices; Independence; Supervision, Human Relations. **Skills:** Operation and Control; Operation Monitoring; Product Inspection; Instructing; Monitoring; Reading Comprehension. **Abilities:** *Cognitive*—Information Ordering; Written Comprehension; Perceptual Speed; Visualization; Problem Sensitivity. *Psychomotor*—Control Precision; Arm-Hand Steadiness; Manual Dexterity. *Physical*—Static Strength; Extent Flexibility; Dynamic Flexibility. *Sensory*—Hearing Sensitivity; Depth Perception. **General Work Activities:** *Information Input*—Getting Information Needed to Do the Job; Inspecting Equipment, Structures, Materials; Monitoring Processes, Materials, and Surroundings. *Mental Process*—Evaluating Information Against Standards; Judging Qualities of Things, Services, Other People's Work; Processing Information. *Work Output*—Controlling Machines and Processes; Handling and Moving

Objects; Performing General Physical Activities. *Interacting with Others*—Teaching Others; Communicating with Other Workers; Coaching and Developing Others; Performing Administrative Activities. **Physical Work Conditions:** Indoors; Using Hands on Objects, Tools, or Controls; Standing. **Other Job Characteristics:** Degree of Automation; Importance of Being Sure All Is Done; Importance of Being Exact or Accurate; Consequence of Error.

Experience: Job Zone 2. Some previous work-related skill, knowledge, or experience may be helpful, but usually is not needed. **Job Preparation:** SVP 4.00 to 5.99—6 months to less than 2 years. **Knowledge:** Production and Processing; Mechanical; Education and Training; Clerical; English Language. **Instructional Program:** 480299 Graphic and Printing Equipment Operators, Other.

Related DOT Jobs: 653.360-010 Casing-in-Line Setter; 653.360-018 Bindery-Machine Setter; 653.382-010 Folding-Machine Operator; 653.382-014 Collating-Machine Operator; 653.662-010 Stitching-Machine Operator; 653.682-010 Book-Sewing-Machine Operator II; 653.682-018 Head-Bander-and-Liner Operator; 653.682-022 Tinning-Machine Set-Up Operator.

51-5011.02 Bindery Machine Operators and Tenders
(Bindery Machine Operators and Set-Up Operators)

Education: Moderate-term O-T-J training
Employed: 89,554
Openings: 16,466
Projected Growth: 11.5%
Earnings: No data available.

Operate or tend binding machines that round, back, case, line stitch, press, fold, trim, or perform other binding operations on books and related articles.

Selects, loads, and adjusts workpieces and machine parts, using hand tools. Punches holes in paper sheets and fastens sheets, signatures, or other material, using hand or machine punch or stapler. Rolls, bends, smoothes, and folds sheets, using hands; stacks sheets to be returned to binding machines. Examines printed material and related products to detect defects and to ensure conformance to specifications. Creases or compresses signatures before affixing covers, and places paper jackets on finished books. Applies materials on books or related articles, using machine. Removes printed material or finished products from machines or conveyor belts; stacks material on pallets or skids. Removes broken wire pieces from machine and loads machine with spool of wire. Moves controls to adjust and activate bindery machine to meet specifications. Wraps product in plastic, using machine; packs products in boxes. Inserts illustrated pages, extra sheets, and collated sets into catalogs, periodicals, directories, and other printed products; applies labels to envelopes, using hands or machine. Operates or tends machines that perform binding operations such as pressing, folding, and trimming, on books and related articles. Feeds books and related articles, such as periodicals and pamphlets, into binding machines, following specifications. Stitches or fastens endpapers or bindings, stitches signatures, and applies glue along binding edge of first and last signatures of books. Threads spirals in perforated holes of items to be bound, using spindle or rollers. Opens machine and removes and replaces damaged covers and book, using hand tools.

Cleans work area and maintains equipment and work stations, using hand tools. Maintains records of daily production, using specified forms.

GOE Number, Interest Area, and Work Group: 08.03.05; Industrial Production; Production Work: Printing and Reproduction. **Personality Type:** Realistic. Realistic occupations frequently involve work activities that include practical, hands-on problems and solutions. These occupations often deal with plants, animals, and real-world materials like wood, tools, and machinery. Many of the occupations require working outside and do not involve a lot of paperwork or working closely with others. **Work Values:** Moral Values; Independence; Activity; Company Policies and Practices; Supervision, Human Relations. **Skills:** Product Inspection; Operation and Control; Operation Monitoring; Equipment Maintenance; Equipment Selection; Mathematics. **Abilities:** *Cognitive*—Information Ordering; Problem Sensitivity; Written Comprehension; Memorization; Perceptual Speed; Written Expression. *Psychomotor*—Control Precision; Manual Dexterity; Arm-Hand Steadiness. *Physical*—Static Strength; Extent Flexibility; Trunk Strength. *Sensory*—Far Vision; Depth Perception; Peripheral Vision. **General Work Activities:** *Information Input*—Monitoring Processes, Materials, and Surroundings; Inspecting Equipment, Structures, Materials; Getting Information Needed to Do the Job. *Mental Process*—Judging Qualities of Things, Services, Other People's Work; Evaluating Information Against Standards; Organizing, Planning, and Prioritizing; Making Decisions and Solving Problems; Updating and Using Job-Relevant Knowledge. *Work Output*—Controlling Machines and Processes; Handling and Moving Objects; Implementing Ideas and Programs. *Interacting with Others*—Communicating with Other Workers; Performing Administrative Activities; Coordinating Work and Activities of Others. **Physical Work Conditions:** Indoors; Using Hands on Objects, Tools, or Controls; Standing. **Other Job Characteristics:** Degree of Automation; Pace Determined by Speed of Equipment; Importance of Being Sure All Is Done; Consequence of Error.

Experience: Job Zone 1. No previous work-related skill, knowledge, or experience is needed. **Job Preparation:** SVP Below 4.0—Less than 6 months. **Knowledge:** Production and Processing; Mechanical; Clerical; Communications and Media; Mathematics; Engineering and Technology. **Instructional Program:** 480299 Graphic and Printing Equipment Operators, Other.

Related DOT Jobs: 653.682-014 Covering-Machine Operator; 653.685-010 Bindery Worker; 653.685-014 Book-Sewing-Machine Operator I; 653.685-022 Magazine Repairer; 653.685-026 Rounding-and-Backing-Machine Operator; 653.685-030 Spiral Binder; 692.685-146 Saddle-and-Side Wire Stitcher.

51-5012.00 Bookbinders (Bookbinders)

Education: Moderate-term O-T-J training
Employed: 6,627
Openings: 1,011
Projected Growth: –15.2%
Earnings: $20,690

Perform highly skilled hand-finishing operations, such as grooving and lettering, to bind books.

Packs, weighs, and stacks books on pallet for shipment. Cuts binder board to specified dimension, using board shears, hand cutter, or cutting machine. Glues outside endpapers to cover. Applies color to edges of signatures, using brush, pad, or atomizer. Imprints and embosses lettering, designs, or numbers on cover, using gold, silver, or colored foil and stamping machine. Compresses sewed or glued signatures to reduce book to required thickness, using handpress or smashing machine. Cuts cover material to specified dimensions and fits and glues material to binder board manually or by machine. Places bound book in press that exerts pressure on cover until glue dries. Trims edges of book to size, using cutting or book-trimming machine or hand cutter. Inserts book body in device that forms back edge of book into convex shape and produces grooves to facilitate attachment of cover. Attaches endpapers to top and bottom of book body, using sewing machine; glues endpapers and signatures together along spine, using brush or glue machine. Applies glue to back of book, using brush or glue machine; attaches cloth backing and headband. Folds printed sheets to form signatures (pages) and assembles signatures in numerical order to form book body.

GOE Number, Interest Area, and Work Group: 08.02.02; Industrial Production; Production Technology: Precision Hand Work. **Personality Type:** Realistic. Realistic occupations frequently involve work activities that include practical, hands-on problems and solutions. These occupations often deal with plants, animals, and real-world materials like wood, tools, and machinery. Many of the occupations require working outside and do not involve a lot of paperwork or working closely with others. **Work Values:** Moral Values; Supervision, Technical; Company Policies and Practices; Independence; Working Conditions; Supervision, Human Relations; Security. **Skills:** Operation and Control; Product Inspection; Monitoring; Information Organization; Reading Comprehension; Equipment Selection. **Abilities:** *Cognitive*—Information Ordering; Visualization; Deductive Reasoning; Selective Attention; Perceptual Speed; Number Facility. *Psychomotor*—Manual Dexterity; Wrist-Finger Speed; Arm-Hand Steadiness. *Physical*—Static Strength; Trunk Strength; Extent Flexibility. *Sensory*—Near Vision; Visual Color Discrimination; Depth Perception. **General Work Activities:** *Information Input*—Getting Information Needed to Do the Job; Monitoring Processes, Materials, and Surroundings; Identifying Objects, Actions, and Events. *Mental Process*—Evaluating Information Against Standards; Analyzing Data or Information; Judging Qualities of Things, Services, Other People's Work; Organizing, Planning, and Prioritizing. *Work Output*—Handling and Moving Objects; Performing General Physical Activities; Controlling Machines and Processes. *Interacting with Others*—Communicating with Other Workers; Monitoring and Controlling Resources; Teaching Others; Establishing and Maintaining Relationships; Assisting and Caring for Others; Influencing Others or Selling. **Physical Work Conditions:** Indoors; Using Hands on Objects, Tools, or Controls; Sitting; Contaminants; Hazardous Situations. **Other Job Characteristics:** Degree of Automation; Importance of Being Sure All Is Done; Importance of Being Exact or Accurate.

Experience: Job Zone 4. A minimum of two to four years of work-related skill, knowledge, or experience is needed. **Job Preparation:** SVP 7.0 to less than 8.0—2 years to less than 10 years. **Knowledge:** Production and Processing; Mechanical; English

Language; Mathematics; Engineering and Technology. **Instructional Program:** 480299 Graphic and Printing Equipment Operators, Other.

Related DOT Jobs: 977.381-010 Bookbinder; 977.381-014 Bookbinder Apprentice.

51-5021.00 Job Printers (Job Printers)

Education: Long-term O-T-J training
Employed: 17,049
Openings: 2,756
Projected Growth: 4.3%
Earnings: $24,100

Set type according to copy; operate press to print job order; read proof for errors and clarity of impression; correct imperfections. Commonly work in small establishments where work combines several job skills.

Removes assembled type from galley and places type on composing stone. Selects type from type case and inserts type in printer's stick to reproduce material in copy. Reads proof for errors and clarity of impression. Runs proof sheet through press and examines sheet for clarity of impression. Inserts spacers between words and inserts leads between lines. Slides type from stick into galley. Places chase over type, inserts quoins, and locks chase to hold type. Fills ink fountain and moves lever to adjust flow of ink. Sets feed guides according to size and thickness of paper. Cleans ink rollers at end of run. Corrects errors by resetting type and improves impression by tapping face of type with hammer. Lays form on proof press, inks type, fastens paper to press roller, and pulls roller over form to make proof copy. Pushes button to start press, examines printed sheets, and adjusts press when printing is defective. Positions form (type in locked chase) on bed of press and tightens clamps, using wrench.

GOE Number, Interest Area, and Work Group: 08.03.05; Industrial Production; Production Work: Printing and Reproduction. **Personality Type:** Realistic. Realistic occupations frequently involve work activities that include practical, hands-on problems and solutions. These occupations often deal with plants, animals, and real-world materials like wood, tools, and machinery. Many of the occupations require working outside and do not involve a lot of paperwork or working closely with others. **Work Values:** Moral Values; Independence; Activity; Security; Working Conditions. **Skills:** Reading Comprehension; Operation and Control; Information Organization; Equipment Selection; Problem Identification; Testing. **Abilities:** *Cognitive*—Written Comprehension; Perceptual Speed; Problem Sensitivity; Information Ordering; Visualization. *Psychomotor*—Finger Dexterity; Manual Dexterity; Wrist-Finger Speed. *Physical*—Extent Flexibility; Explosive Strength; Dynamic Flexibility. *Sensory*—Near Vision; Visual Color Discrimination; Glare Sensitivity. **General Work Activities:** *Information Input*—Monitoring Processes, Materials, and Surroundings; Inspecting Equipment, Structures, Materials; Identifying Objects, Actions, and Events. *Mental Process*—Evaluating Information Against Standards; Judging Qualities of Things, Services, Other People's Work; Making Decisions and Solving Problems. *Work Output*—Controlling Machines and Processes; Handling and

Moving Objects; Performing General Physical Activities. *Interacting with Others*—Monitoring and Controlling Resources; Communicating with Other Workers; Establishing and Maintaining Relationships. **Physical Work Conditions:** Indoors; Hazardous Equipment; Using Hands on Objects, Tools, or Controls. **Other Job Characteristics:** Degree of Automation; Importance of Being Exact or Accurate; Frustrating Circumstances; Consequence of Error.

Experience: Job Zone 5. Extensive skill, knowledge, and experience are needed. Very advanced communication and organizational skills are required. **Job Preparation:** SVP 8.0 and above—4 years to more than 10 years. **Knowledge:** Production and Processing; English Language; Communications and Media; Mathematics; Mechanical. **Instructional Program:** 480201 Graphic and Printing Equipment Operator, General.

Related DOT Jobs: 973.381-018 Job Printer; 973.381-022 Job-Printer Apprentice.

51-5022.00 Prepress Technicians and Workers (Hand Compositors and Typesetters)

Education: Long-term O-T-J training
Employed: 13,649
Openings: 2,013
Projected Growth: −18.9%
Earnings: $22,560

Set up and prepare material for printing presses.

GOE Number, Interest Area, and Work Group: 08.03.05; Industrial Production; Production Work: Printing and Reproduction. **Instructional Program:** 480205 Mechanical Typesetter and Composer. **Note:** The Department of Labor has not collected some data for this job, so it has fewer details than the other descriptions.

51-5022.01 Hand Compositors and Typesetters (Compositors and Typesetters, Precision)

Education: Long-term O-T-J training
Employed: 13,649
Openings: 2,013
Projected Growth: −18.9%
Earnings: $22,560

Set up and arrange type by hand. Assemble and lock setup of type, cuts, and headings. Pull proofs.

Removes incorrect portion and manually inserts corrections. Inserts lead, slugs, or lines of quads between lines to adjust length of setup. Selects type from type case and sets it in compositional sequence, reading from copy. Transfers type from stick to galley when setup is complete. Compares symbols on proof with galley symbol, and reads portion of text to locate positions for insertion of corrected slugs. Arranges, groups, and locks galley setups of type, cuts, and headings in chases, according to dummy makeup sheet. Cleans type after use and distributes it to specified boxes

in type case. Arranges galleys of linotype slugs (takes) in sequence on correction table. Measures copy with line gauge to determine length of line. Prepares proof copy of setup, using proof press. Inserts spacers between words or units to balance and justify lines. Compares corrected type slugs against proof to detect errors.

GOE Number, Interest Area, and Work Group: 08.03.05; Industrial Production; Production Work: Printing and Reproduction. **Personality Type:** Realistic. Realistic occupations frequently involve work activities that include practical, hands-on problems and solutions. These occupations often deal with plants, animals, and real-world materials like wood, tools, and machinery. Many of the occupations require working outside and do not involve a lot of paperwork or working closely with others. **Work Values:** Moral Values; Independence; Supervision, Human Relations; Working Conditions; Supervision, Technical; Activity. **Skills:** Product Inspection; Reading Comprehension; Equipment Selection; Solution Appraisal; Problem Identification; Monitoring; Information Organization. **Abilities:** *Cognitive*—Information Ordering; Perceptual Speed; Written Comprehension; Visualization; Category Flexibility; Problem Sensitivity. *Psychomotor*—Finger Dexterity; Wrist-Finger Speed; Arm-Hand Steadiness. *Physical*—none met the criteria. *Sensory*—Near Vision; Depth Perception; Glare Sensitivity; Peripheral Vision. **General Work Activities:** *Information Input*—Getting Information Needed to Do the Job; Inspecting Equipment, Structures, Materials; Identifying Objects, Actions, and Events; Monitoring Processes, Materials, and Surroundings. *Mental Process*—Evaluating Information Against Standards; Making Decisions and Solving Problems; Analyzing Data or Information; Processing Information. *Work Output*—Handling and Moving Objects; Implementing Ideas and Programs; Controlling Machines and Processes. *Interacting with Others*—Communicating with Other Workers; Establishing and Maintaining Relationships; Monitoring and Controlling Resources. **Physical Work Conditions:** Indoors; Using Hands on Objects, Tools, or Controls; Sitting. **Other Job Characteristics:** Importance of Being Exact or Accurate; Importance of Being Sure All Is Done; Degree of Automation.

Experience: Job Zone 4. A minimum of two to four years of work-related skill, knowledge, or experience is needed. **Job Preparation:** SVP 7.0 to less than 8.0—2 years to less than 10 years. **Knowledge:** Production and Processing; Mathematics; English Language; Communications and Media; Mechanical. **Instructional Program:** 480205 Mechanical Typesetter and Composer.

Related DOT Jobs: 973.381-010 Compositor; 973.381-014 Compositor Apprentice; 973.381-026 Make-Up Arranger; 973.381-030 Proofsheet Corrector; 973.681-010 Galley Stripper.

51-5022.02 Paste-Up Workers (Paste-Up Workers)

Education: Long-term O-T-J training
Employed: 9,037
Openings: 1,096
Projected Growth: −51.2%
Earnings: $19,820

Arrange and mount typeset material and illustrations into pasteup for printing reproduction based on artist's or editor's layout.

Covers photographs and artwork with tissue or tracing paper for protection. Tapes transparent plastic overlay to board; positions and applies copy to plastic. Operates phototypesetter to prepare typeset copy for pasteup. Indicates crop marks and enlargement or reduction measurements on photographs with grease pencil, to facilitate processing. Draws functional and decorative borders around layout, using marking and measuring instruments. Writes specifications on tracing paper to provide information for other workers. Removes excess adhesive from board, using scissors, artist's knife, and drafting instruments. Makes negatives or prints of artwork, using photographic equipment, to prepare artwork for pasteup. Applies masking film to artwork layout space on overlay to create clear space on negative for subsequent addition of artwork. Operates electronic plotter to draw artwork positions on pasteup. Compares measurements, using ruler and proportion wheel, to determine proportions needed to make reduced or enlarged photographic prints for pasteup. Cuts typeset copy and artwork to size, applies adhesive, and aligns artwork and typeset copy on board, following position marks. Measures and marks board according to layout to indicate position of artwork, typeset copy, page edges, folds, and colors. Measures artwork and layout space of artwork on pasteup.

GOE Number, Interest Area, and Work Group: 01.07.01; Arts, Entertainment, and Media; Graphic Arts. **Personality Type:** Realistic. Realistic occupations frequently involve work activities that include practical, hands-on problems and solutions. These occupations often deal with plants, animals, and real-world materials like wood, tools, and machinery. Many of the occupations require working outside and do not involve a lot of paperwork or working closely with others. **Work Values:** Moral Values; Independence; Activity; Working Conditions; Security. **Skills:** Reading Comprehension; Product Inspection; Information Organization; Operation and Control; Equipment Selection; Information Gathering; Mathematics; Writing. **Abilities:** *Cognitive*—Information Ordering; Visualization; Written Expression; Perceptual Speed; Deductive Reasoning. *Psychomotor*—Arm-Hand Steadiness; Manual Dexterity; Wrist-Finger Speed. *Physical*—none met the criteria. *Sensory*—Near Vision; Visual Color Discrimination; Depth Perception. **General Work Activities:** *Information Input*—Getting Information Needed to Do the Job; Monitoring Processes, Materials, and Surroundings; Estimating Needed Characteristics. *Mental Process*—Evaluating Information Against Standards; Analyzing Data or Information; Thinking Creatively. *Work Output*—Handling and Moving Objects; Controlling Machines and Processes; Implementing Ideas and Programs. *Interacting with Others*—Communicating with Other Workers; Interpreting Meaning of Information to Others; Establishing and Maintaining Relationships. **Physical Work Conditions:** Indoors; Using Hands on Objects, Tools, or Controls; Sitting. **Other Job Characteristics:** Importance of Being Exact or Accurate; Importance of Being Sure All Is Done; Frustrating Circumstances; Degree of Automation.

Experience: Job Zone 4. A minimum of two to four years of work-related skill, knowledge, or experience is needed. **Job Preparation:** SVP 7.0 to less than 8.0—2 years to less than 10 years. **Knowledge:** Design; English Language; Communications and Media; Mathematics; Production and Processing; Computers and Electronics; Fine Arts. **Instructional Program:** 500402 Graphic Design, Commercial Art and Illustration.

Related DOT Jobs: 970.381-018 Lay-Out Former; 972.381-030 Paste-Up Artist; 972.381-038 Paste-Up Artist Apprentice.

51-5022.03 Photoengravers (Photoengravers)

Education:	Long-term O-T-J training
Employed:	2,747
Openings:	332
Projected Growth:	–51.5%
Earnings:	$28,430

Photograph copy, develop negatives, and prepare photosensitized metal plates for use in letterpress and gravure printing.

Modifies or repairs plates or film, using etching and artist's brush, acid, and hand tools. Transfers images, designs, or patterns onto rollers, plates, or film, using photographic or pantographic equipment and techniques, and hand tools. Brushes protective solution and powder on plate and starts machine, to distribute acid or photosensitizing solution over plate or rollers. Washes rollers and plates to prepare for etching or to remove resistant solution and photographic emulsion, using water, cleaning solution, and brush. Positions, loads, or mounts copy, plates, film, or rollers; secures into place. Mixes caustic or acid solutions. Matches colors with original to produce balanced color values or intensity design. Studies and compares film negatives or positives with originals or design, to determine photographic requirements and verify reproduction. Etches designs on metal rollers and plates, using etching machines, hand tools, and acidic chemicals, to produce printing plates and rollers. Develops and prints negatives, positives, film, or plates, by controlled exposure to light, using exposure equipment, chemical baths, and vacuum. Computes camera machine settings for film exposure or reproduction, using equipment meter, computer, worksheets, and standard formulas and tables. Examines developed film, proof, or engravings, using magnifier, chalk, or charcoal to evaluate quality and detect errors.

GOE Number, Interest Area, and Work Group: 01.07.01; Arts, Entertainment, and Media; Graphic Arts. **Personality Type:** Realistic. Realistic occupations frequently involve work activities that include practical, hands-on problems and solutions. These occupations often deal with plants, animals, and real-world materials like wood, tools, and machinery. Many of the occupations require working outside and do not involve a lot of paperwork or working closely with others. **Work Values:** Moral Values; Independence; Achievement; Autonomy; Working Conditions; Ability Utilization; Supervision, Human Relations. **Skills:** Product Inspection; Operation and Control; Equipment Maintenance; Problem Identification; Monitoring; Information Gathering. **Abilities:** *Cognitive*—Information Ordering; Flexibility of Closure; Visualization; Number Facility; Mathematical Reasoning; Deductive Reasoning. *Psychomotor*—Finger Dexterity; Arm-Hand Steadiness; Manual Dexterity. *Physical*—Dynamic Flexibility. *Sensory*—Visual Color Discrimination; Near Vision; Night Vision. **General Work Activities:** *Information Input*—Monitoring Processes, Materials, and Surroundings; Getting Information Needed to Do the Job; Estimating Needed Characteristics. *Mental Process*—Evaluating Information Against Standards; Judging Qualities of Things, Services,

Other People's Work; Processing Information; Updating and Using Job-Relevant Knowledge. *Work Output*—Controlling Machines and Processes; Handling and Moving Objects; Repairing and Maintaining Mechanical Equipment; Performing General Physical Activities. *Interacting with Others*—Communicating with Other Workers; Communicating with Persons Outside Organization; Establishing and Maintaining Relationships. **Physical Work Conditions:** Indoors; Using Hands on Objects, Tools, or Controls; Contaminants; Sitting. **Other Job Characteristics:** Importance of Being Exact or Accurate; Importance of Being Sure All Is Done; Degree of Automation.

Experience: Job Zone 4. A minimum of two to four years of work-related skill, knowledge, or experience is needed. **Job Preparation:** SVP 7.0 to less than 8.0—2 years to less than 10 years. **Knowledge:** Chemistry; Fine Arts; Mathematics; Computers and Electronics; Design. **Instructional Program:** 480201 Graphic and Printing Equipment Operator, General.

Related DOT Jobs: 970.361-014 Repeat Chief; 970.381-030 Retoucher, Photoengraving; 971.261-010 Etcher, Hand; 971.381-010 Etcher Apprentice, Photoengraving; 971.381-014 Etcher, Photoengraving; 971.381-022 Photoengraver; 971.381-026 Photoengraver Apprentice; 971.381-030 Photoengraving Finisher; 971.381-034 Photoengraving Printer; 971.381-038 Photoengraving Proofer; 971.381-040 Photoengraving-Proofer Apprentice; 971.382-014 Photographer, Photoengraving; 971.382-018 Repeat-Photocomposing-Machine Operator; 972.382-018 Photo Mask Maker, Electron-Beam.

51-5022.04 Camera Operators (Camera Operators)

Education: Long-term O-T-J training
Employed: 9,248
Openings: 1,270
Projected Growth: –31.4%
Earnings: $24,350

Operate process camera and related darkroom equipment to photograph and develop negatives of material to be printed.

Adjusts camera settings, lights, and lens. Immerses film in series of chemical baths to develop images and hangs film on rack to dry. Measures density of continuous tone images to be photographed, to set exposure time for halftone images. Measures original layouts and determines proportions needed to make reduced or enlarged photographic prints for pasteup. Mounts material to be photographed on copyboard of camera. Exposes high contrast film for predetermined exposure time. Selects and installs screens and filters in camera to produce desired effects. Feeds film into automatic film processor that develops, fixes, washes, and dries film. Performs exposure tests to determine line, halftone, and color reproduction exposure lengths for various photographic factors.

GOE Number, Interest Area, and Work Group: 01.07.01; Arts, Entertainment, and Media; Graphic Arts. **Personality Type:** Realistic. Realistic occupations frequently involve work activities that include practical, hands-on problems and solutions. These occupations often deal with plants, animals, and real-world materials like wood, tools, and machinery. Many of the occupations re-

quire working outside and do not involve a lot of paperwork or working closely with others. **Work Values:** Moral Values; Independence; Autonomy; Ability Utilization; Social Status; Creativity; Working Conditions. **Skills:** Equipment Selection; Technology Design; Operation and Control; Product Inspection; Operations Analysis; Testing; Mathematics. **Abilities:** *Cognitive*—Visualization; Information Ordering; Number Facility; Problem Sensitivity; Deductive Reasoning; Inductive Reasoning. *Psychomotor*—Arm-Hand Steadiness; Control Precision; Multilimb Coordination. *Physical*—Extent Flexibility; Gross Body Coordination; Gross Body Equilibrium. *Sensory*—Near Vision; Visual Color Discrimination; Night Vision. **General Work Activities:** *Information Input*—Getting Information Needed to Do the Job; Identifying Objects, Actions, and Events; Monitoring Processes, Materials, and Surroundings. *Mental Process*—Thinking Creatively; Analyzing Data or Information; Making Decisions and Solving Problems; Evaluating Information Against Standards. *Work Output*—Controlling Machines and Processes; Handling and Moving Objects; Implementing Ideas and Programs. *Interacting with Others*—Communicating with Other Workers; Performing Administrative Activities; Providing Consultation and Advice to Others; Monitoring and Controlling Resources; Establishing and Maintaining Relationships; Communicating with Persons Outside Organization. **Physical Work Conditions:** Indoors; Using Hands on Objects, Tools, or Controls; Standing. **Other Job Characteristics:** Importance of Being Sure All Is Done; Importance of Being Exact or Accurate; Consequence of Error.

Experience: Job Zone 4. A minimum of two to four years of work-related skill, knowledge, or experience is needed. **Job Preparation:** SVP 7.0 to less than 8.0—2 years to less than 10 years. **Knowledge:** Fine Arts; Chemistry; Mathematics; Production and Processing; Communications and Media. **Instructional Programs:** 480201 Graphic and Printing Equipment Operator, General; 500406 Commercial Photography.

Related DOT Jobs: 972.382-010 Photographer Apprentice, Lithographic; 972.382-014 Photographer, Lithographic.

51-5022.05 Scanner Operators (Scanner Operators)

Education: No data available.
Employed: 6,880
Openings: No data available.
Projected Growth: No data available.
Earnings: $33,560

Operate electronic or computerized scanning equipment to produce and screen film separations of photographs or art for use in producing lithographic printing plates. Evaluate and correct for deficiencies in the film.

Positions color transparency, negative, or reflection copy on scanning drum and mounts drum and head on scanner. Activates scanner to produce positive or negative films for each primary color and black in original copy. Analyzes original to evaluate color density, gradation highlights, middle tones, and shadows, using densitometer and knowledge of light and color. Unloads exposed film from scanner and places film in automatic processor to develop image on film. Performs tests to determine exposure adjustments on scanner and adjusts scanner controls until specified results are obtained. Inspects developed film for specified results and quality; forwards acceptable negatives or positives to other workers or customer. Types on scanner keyboard or touches mouse to symbols on scanner video display unit to input software, or moves controls to set scanner to specific color density, size, screen ruling, and exposure adjustments. Loads film into holder, places holder in exposing chamber, and starts mechanism that loads and secures film on scanner drum.

GOE Number, Interest Area, and Work Group: 08.03.05; Industrial Production; Production Work: Printing and Reproduction. **Personality Type:** Realistic. Realistic occupations frequently involve work activities that include practical, hands-on problems and solutions. These occupations often deal with plants, animals, and real-world materials like wood, tools, and machinery. Many of the occupations require working outside and do not involve a lot of paperwork or working closely with others. **Work Values:** Moral Values; Independence; Working Conditions; Autonomy; Security. **Skills:** Product Inspection; Testing; Operation and Control; Monitoring; Critical Thinking. **Abilities:** *Cognitive*—Perceptual Speed; Deductive Reasoning; Problem Sensitivity; Visualization; Information Ordering. *Psychomotor*—Control Precision; Finger Dexterity; Response Orientation. *Physical*—none met the criteria. *Sensory*—Visual Color Discrimination; Near Vision; Night Vision. **General Work Activities:** *Information Input*—Getting Information Needed to Do the Job; Monitoring Processes, Materials, and Surroundings; Identifying Objects, Actions, and Events; Inspecting Equipment, Structures, Materials. *Mental Process*—Judging Qualities of Things, Services, Other People's Work; Analyzing Data or Information; Evaluating Information Against Standards. *Work Output*—Interacting with Computers; Controlling Machines and Processes; Handling and Moving Objects. *Interacting with Others*—Communicating with Other Workers; Communicating with Persons Outside Organization; Establishing and Maintaining Relationships. **Physical Work Conditions:** Using Hands on Objects, Tools, or Controls; Sitting; Indoors. **Other Job Characteristics:** Degree of Automation; Importance of Being Exact or Accurate; Importance of Being Sure All Is Done.

Experience: Job Zone 4. A minimum of two to four years of work-related skill, knowledge, or experience is needed. **Job Preparation:** SVP 7.0 to less than 8.0—2 years to less than 10 years. **Knowledge:** Computers and Electronics; Production and Processing; Fine Arts; Communications and Media; Mechanical; Mathematics. **Instructional Program:** 480201 Graphic and Printing Equipment Operator, General.

Related DOT Job: 972.282-010 Scanner Operator.

51-5022.06 Strippers (Film Strippers, Printing)

Education: Long-term O-T-J training
Employed: 22,724
Openings: 3,090
Projected Growth: –33%
Earnings: $32,300

Cut and arrange film into flats (layout sheets resembling a film negative of text in its final form) that are used to make plates. Prepare separate flat for each color.

Sends completed flat to proofing area or platemaking area for preparation of final proof or lithographic plate. Selects and inserts screen tints in film flat, using knowledge of dot percentages required to obtain specific colors. Aligns negatives and masks over unexposed film in vacuum frame to make negatives or positives for final film of each color. Strips negative from base. Applies rubber solution and collodion to toughen negative; cuts to size; and immerses in acid bath to prepare negative for stripping. Examines negatives and photographs to detect defective areas, using lighted viewing table. Determines or approves plans and page sequences to lay out job for specific printing press. Touches up imperfections, using opaque and brush on negatives, and using needle and crayon pencil on photographs. Examines proof returned by customer and makes corrections according to customer specifications. Makes proof from film flat to determine accuracy of flat. Determines proportions needed to reduce or enlarge photographs and graphics to fit in designated area, using calculator or proportion scale. Examines pasteup, artwork, film, prints, and instructions, to determine size and dimensions, number of job colors, and camera work needed. Assembles and aligns negatives or positives to assure register and fit with units of color. Positions film negatives or positives on light table according to art layout, blueprint, and color register to form film flat. Cuts masks and arranges negatives to prepare for contact printing, plate exposure, or proof making. Cuts image window area to allow exposure to plate or film, using razor or artist's knife. Draws ruled lines and borders around negatives or positives.

GOE Number, Interest Area, and Work Group: 08.03.05; Industrial Production; Production Work: Printing and Reproduction. **Personality Type:** Realistic. Realistic occupations frequently involve work activities that include practical, hands-on problems and solutions. These occupations often deal with plants, animals, and real-world materials like wood, tools, and machinery. Many of the occupations require working outside and do not involve a lot of paperwork or working closely with others. **Work Values:** Moral Values; Independence; Responsibility; Autonomy; Working Conditions. **Skills:** Product Inspection; Equipment Selection; Critical Thinking; Problem Identification; Operation and Control; Monitoring. **Abilities:** *Cognitive*—Visualization; Information Ordering; Problem Sensitivity; Fluency of Ideas; Deductive Reasoning; Written Comprehension. *Psychomotor*—Arm-Hand Steadiness; Finger Dexterity. *Physical*—none met the criteria. *Sensory*—Visual Color Discrimination; Near Vision; Night Vision. **General Work Activities:** *Information Input*—Getting Information Needed to Do the Job; Estimating Needed Characteristics; Identifying Objects, Actions, and Events; Monitoring Processes, Materials, and Surroundings. *Mental Process*—Judging Qualities of Things, Services, Other People's Work; Making Decisions and Solving Problems; Thinking Creatively. *Work Output*—Handling and Moving Objects; Implementing Ideas and Programs; Controlling Machines and Processes. *Interacting with Others*—Communicating with Other Workers; Communicating with Persons Outside Organization; Performing Administrative Activities. **Physical Work Conditions:** Indoors; Sitting; Using Hands on Objects, Tools, or Controls. **Other Job Characteristics:** Importance of Being Sure All Is Done; Importance of Being Exact or Accurate; Degree of Automation.

Experience: Job Zone 4. A minimum of two to four years of work-related skill, knowledge, or experience is needed. **Job Prepara-**

tion: SVP 7.0 to less than 8.0—2 years to less than 10 years. **Knowledge:** Fine Arts; Design; Production and Processing; Chemistry; Communications and Media. **Instructional Program:** 480201 Graphic and Printing Equipment Operator, General.

Related DOT Jobs: 971.381-050 Stripper; 971.381-054 Stripper Apprentice; 972.281-022 Stripper, Lithographic I; 972.381-022 Stripper, Lithographic II.

51-5022.07 Platemakers (Platemakers)

Education: Long-term O-T-J training

Employed: 14,537

Openings: 2,307

Projected Growth: –5.2%

Earnings: $28,600

Produce printing plates by exposing sensitized metal sheets to special light through a photographic negative. Operate machines that process plates automatically.

Places plate in vacuum frame to align positives or negatives with each other; places masking paper over uncovered areas. Lowers vacuum frame onto plate-film assembly to establish contact between positive-negative film and plate, and sets timer to expose plate. Examines plate, using light-box and microscope to detect flaws, verify conformity with master plate, and measure dot size and center. Performs tests to determine time required for exposure by exposing plates; compares exposure to scale which measures tone ranges. Repairs defective plates with missing dots, using photographic touch-up tool and ink. Punches holes in light-sensitive plate and inserts pins in holes to prepare plate for contact with positive or negative film. Examines unexposed photographic plate to detect flaws or foreign particles prior to printing pattern of aperture masks on sensitized steel. Removes plate-film assembly from vacuum frame and places exposed plate in automatic processor to develop image and dry plate. Mounts negative and plate in camera that exposes plate to artificial light through photographic negative, thus transferring image. Transfers images by hand and covers surface of plates with photosensitive chemical, using brush, and allows plate to dry. Transfers image from master plate to unexposed plate and immerses plate in developing solution to develop image on plate. Mixes and applies chemical-based developing solution to plates; replenishes solution in processor to maintain it in working order. Installs and aligns plates in printing case.

GOE Number, Interest Area, and Work Group: 08.03.05; Industrial Production; Production Work: Printing and Reproduction. **Personality Type:** Realistic. Realistic occupations frequently involve work activities that include practical, hands-on problems and solutions. These occupations often deal with plants, animals, and real-world materials like wood, tools, and machinery. Many of the occupations require working outside and do not involve a lot of paperwork or working closely with others. **Work Values:** Moral Values; Independence; Responsibility; Autonomy; Working Conditions. **Skills:** Product Inspection; Testing; Operation and Control; Operation Monitoring; Problem Identification; Equipment Selection. **Abilities:** *Cognitive*—Information Ordering; Visualization; Problem Sensitivity; Memorization; Deductive Rea-

soning; Written Comprehension. *Psychomotor*—Arm-Hand Steadiness; Multilimb Coordination. *Physical*—Extent Flexibility. *Sensory*—Glare Sensitivity. **General Work Activities:** *Information Input*—Inspecting Equipment, Structures, Materials; Getting Information Needed to Do the Job; Monitoring Processes, Materials, and Surroundings; Identifying Objects, Actions, and Events. *Mental Process*—Judging Qualities of Things, Services, Other People's Work; Evaluating Information Against Standards; Analyzing Data or Information; Making Decisions and Solving Problems. *Work Output*—Handling and Moving Objects; Controlling Machines and Processes; Implementing Ideas and Programs. *Interacting with Others*—Communicating with Other Workers; Coordinating Work and Activities of Others; Establishing and Maintaining Relationships. **Physical Work Conditions:** Using Hands on Objects, Tools, or Controls; Indoors; Sitting; Standing. **Other Job Characteristics:** Importance of Being Exact or Accurate; Importance of Being Sure All Is Done; Consequence of Error; Degree of Automation.

Experience: Job Zone 3. Previous work-related skill, knowledge, or experience is required. **Job Preparation:** SVP 6.0 to less than 7.0—More than 1 year and less than 4 years. **Knowledge:** Chemistry; Production and Processing; Fine Arts; Engineering and Technology; Mechanical. **Instructional Programs:** 480201 Graphic and Printing Equipment Operator, General; 480206 Lithographer and Platemaker.

Related DOT Jobs: 714.381-018 Photographic-Plate Maker; 972.381-010 Lithographic Platemaker; 972.381-014 Lithographic-Plate-Maker Apprentice; 972.381-026 Transferrer.

51-5022.08 Dot Etchers (All Other Lithography and Photoengraving Workers)

Education: No data available.

Employed: 4,820

Openings: No data available.

Projected Growth: No data available.

Earnings: $34,080

Increase or reduce size of photographic dots by chemical or photomechanical methods to make color corrections on half-tone negatives or positives to be used in preparation of lithographic printing plates.

Compares proof print of color separation negative or positive with customer's original copy and standard color chart to determine accuracy of reproduction. Blocks out or modifies color shades of film, using template, brushes, and opaque. Prepares dyes and other chemical solutions according to standard; applies solution to inaccurately colored areas of film to correct color by chemical method. Prepares photographic masks to protect areas of film not needing correction, using contact frame and automatic film processor or by manually cutting masking material, to correct color by photomechanical method. Identifies and marks color discrepancies on print and film. Applies opaque to defective areas of film to block out blemishes and pinholes. Determines extent of correction and exposure length needed, based on experience or predetermined exposure and color charts. Places masks over separation negatives or positives and exposes film for specified time, using contact frame and automatic film processor to reduce size of photographic dots, to increase or reduce color. Examines film on light table to determine specified color and color balance, using magnifying glass or densitometer.

GOE Number, Interest Area, and Work Group: 01.07.01; Arts, Entertainment, and Media; Graphic Arts. **Personality Type:** Realistic. Realistic occupations frequently involve work activities that include practical, hands-on problems and solutions. These occupations often deal with plants, animals, and real-world materials like wood, tools, and machinery. Many of the occupations require working outside and do not involve a lot of paperwork or working closely with others. **Work Values:** Moral Values; Independence; Autonomy; Working Conditions; Responsibility; Security. **Skills:** Equipment Selection; Product Inspection; Solution Appraisal; Information Organization; Information Gathering; Operations Analysis. **Abilities:** *Cognitive*—Visualization; Information Ordering; Problem Sensitivity; Flexibility of Closure; Deductive Reasoning. *Psychomotor*—Arm-Hand Steadiness. *Physical*—none met the criteria. *Sensory*—Visual Color Discrimination; Near Vision; Night Vision. **General Work Activities:** *Information Input*—Monitoring Processes, Materials, and Surroundings; Getting Information Needed to Do the Job; Inspecting Equipment, Structures, Materials; Identifying Objects, Actions, and Events. *Mental Process*—Making Decisions and Solving Problems; Thinking Creatively; Updating and Using Job-Relevant Knowledge. *Work Output*—Controlling Machines and Processes; Handling and Moving Objects; Implementing Ideas and Programs. *Interacting with Others*—Communicating with Other Workers; Performing Administrative Activities; Monitoring and Controlling Resources; Coaching and Developing Others; Providing Consultation and Advice to Others; Assisting and Caring for Others. **Physical Work Conditions:** Indoors; Using Hands on Objects, Tools, or Controls; Sitting. **Other Job Characteristics:** Importance of Being Exact or Accurate; Importance of Being Sure All Is Done; Degree of Automation.

Experience: Job Zone 5. Extensive skill, knowledge, and experience are needed. Very advanced communication and organizational skills are required. **Job Preparation:** SVP 8.0 and above—4 years to more than 10 years. **Knowledge:** Chemistry; Fine Arts; Production and Processing; Engineering and Technology; Computers and Electronics; Design. **Instructional Programs:** 480201 Graphic and Printing Equipment Operator, General; 480206 Lithographer and Platemaker.

Related DOT Jobs: 972.281-010 Dot Etcher; 972.281-018 Dot Etcher Apprentice.

51-5022.09 Electronic Masking System Operators
(All Other Lithography and Photoengraving Workers)

Education: No data available.

Employed: 4,820

Openings: No data available.

Projected Growth: No data available.

Earnings: $34,080

Operate computerized masking system to produce stripping masks used in production of offset lithographic printing plates.

Studies layout sheet to determine shapes of windows drawn on layout sheet. Removes scored masking material from drafting table. Touches symbol of option selected on menu and activates option with mouse. Selects options on menu of electronic masking system, such as shape, dimensions of designs to be drawn, register marks, and retrieval of stored designs. Touches reference points of designs on layout sheet, using mouse, and presses button of mouse to enter coordinates of design in system memory. Loads drafting unit with masking material to prepare for plotting and scoring of programmed figures; loads film into plotting drum to make photographic mask exposure. Views monitors for feedback and error prompts, for visual representations of work in progress, and for numerical information such as width of line and last point plotted. Places material on light table and peels scored figures from masking material, using needle and tape. Activates plotting drum to make photographic mask exposures. Presses button to transfer data from system memory to disk. Presses button to activate vacuum to hold masking in place and to activate drafting unit that scores masking material with programmed figures. Positions artist's layout on digitizing tables of electronic masking system, to prepare for data entry in system memory. Removes film from plotting drum and puts film in automatic film processor to create masks.

GOE Number, Interest Area, and Work Group: 01.07.01; Arts, Entertainment, and Media; Graphic Arts. **Personality Type:** Realistic. Realistic occupations frequently involve work activities that include practical, hands-on problems and solutions. These occupations often deal with plants, animals, and real-world materials like wood, tools, and machinery. Many of the occupations require working outside and do not involve a lot of paperwork or working closely with others. **Work Values:** Moral Values; Independence; Working Conditions; Security; Activity; Compensation; Supervision, Human Relations; Supervision, Technical. **Skills:** Operation and Control; Equipment Selection. **Abilities:** *Cognitive*—Information Ordering; Visualization; Written Comprehension; Fluency of Ideas; Speed of Closure; Flexibility of Closure. *Psychomotor*—Arm-Hand Steadiness. *Physical*—none met the criteria. *Sensory*—Visual Color Discrimination. **General Work Activities:** *Information Input*—Monitoring Processes, Materials, and Surroundings; Getting Information Needed to Do the Job; Identifying Objects, Actions, and Events. *Mental Process*—Processing Information; Updating and Using Job-Relevant Knowledge; Thinking Creatively. *Work Output*—Interacting with Computers; Controlling Machines and Processes; Handling and Moving Objects. *Interacting with Others*—Communicating with Other Workers; Monitoring and Controlling Resources; Establishing and Maintaining Relationships; Assisting and Caring for Others; Coaching and Developing Others. **Physical Work Conditions:** Indoors; Using Hands on Objects, Tools, or Controls; Sitting. **Other Job Characteristics:** Degree of Automation; Importance of Being Exact or Accurate; Importance of Being Sure All Is Done.

Experience: Job Zone 4. A minimum of two to four years of work-related skill, knowledge, or experience is needed. **Job Preparation:** SVP 7.0 to less than 8.0—2 years to less than 10 years. **Knowledge:** Computers and Electronics; Design; Mathematics; Production and Processing; Fine Arts. **Instructional Programs:** 480201 Graphic and Printing Equipment Operator, General; 480206 Lithographer and Platemaker.

Related DOT Jobs: 972.282-018 Electronic Masking System Operator; 972.382-022 Photo Mask Technician, Electron-Beam.

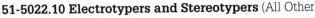

51-5022.10 Electrotypers and Stereotypers (All Other Precision Printing Workers)

Education: No data available.

Employed: 5,140

Openings: No data available.

Projected Growth: No data available.

Earnings: $24,510

Fabricate and finish electrotype and stereotype printing plates.

Trims mat, using trimming machine, by aligning notches of mat with pins on trimming machine. Removes excess metal from edges, back, and nonprinting surface areas of plate, using power shear, milling machines, or routing machine. Pours metal into casting box or plated mold by hand to produce electrotype or stereotype printing plates. Operates automatic casting machine to produce electrotype or stereotype printing plates. Examines plate to detect imperfect formation of lines, type, and halftone dots, using magnifier. Mounts finished plates on wood or metal blocks for flatbed presses, using hammer, nails, or bonding press. Cuts and pastes pieces of paper felt or cardboard in nonprinting areas of wood-fiber mat to prevent collapse during casting. Operates proof press to obtain proof of plate reproduction and registration. Sprays plastic mold with silver solution and immerses mold in plating tank. Aligns and notches mats of color series with key color mat, using matching machine with monocolor magnifier attachment. Corrects defects on plate, using engraver's hand tools, punches, and hammers. Drills matching holes in series of mounted color stereotype plates to be duplicated. Inserts pins in base to register stereotype plates to key plate for mat molding. Curves plates for cylinder presses, using plate-curving machine. Forms mold of composed type, using plastic sheet-molding or wood-fiber mat, and hydraulic press.

GOE Number, Interest Area, and Work Group: 08.03.05; Industrial Production; Production Work: Printing and Reproduction. Personality Type: Realistic. Realistic occupations frequently involve work activities that include practical, hands-on problems and solutions. These occupations often deal with plants, animals, and real-world materials like wood, tools, and machinery. Many of the occupations require working outside and do not involve a lot of paperwork or working closely with others. Work Values: Moral Values; Independence; Supervision, Human Relations; Company Policies and Practices; Supervision, Technical; Activity. Skills: Operation and Control; Product Inspection; Equipment Selection; Problem Identification; Solution Appraisal; Troubleshooting; Operation Monitoring. Abilities: *Cognitive*—Information Ordering; Problem Sensitivity; Visualization; Deductive Reasoning; Category Flexibility. *Psychomotor*—Arm-Hand Steadiness; Manual Dexterity; Finger Dexterity. *Physical*—Extent Flexibility; Static Strength; Explosive Strength. *Sensory*—Near Vision; Visual Color Discrimination. General Work Activities: *Information Input*—Getting Information Needed to Do the Job; Identifying Objects, Actions, and Events; Monitoring Processes, Materials, and Surroundings; Inspecting Equipment, Structures, Materials. *Mental Process*—Evaluating Information Against Standards; Judging Qualities of Things, Services, Other People's Work; Analyzing Data or Information. *Work Output*—Handling and Moving Objects; Controlling Machines and Processes; Performing General Physical Activities. *Interacting with Others*—Performing Administrative Activities; Coordinating Work and Activities of Others; Monitoring and Controlling Resources; Establishing and Maintaining Relationships. Physical Work Conditions: Using Hands on Objects, Tools, or Controls; Indoors; Hazardous Equipment. Other Job Characteristics: Importance of Being Exact or Accurate; Consequence of Error; Importance of Being Sure All Is Done.

Experience: Job Zone 5. Extensive skill, knowledge, and experience are needed. Very advanced communication and organizational skills are required. Job Preparation: SVP 8.0 and above—4 years to more than 10 years. Knowledge: Mechanical; Engineering and Technology; Production and Processing; Mathematics; Building and Construction; Chemistry; Physics. Instructional Programs: 480201 Graphic and Printing Equipment Operator, General; 480299 Graphic and Printing Equipment Operators, Other.

Related DOT Jobs: 974.381-010 Electrotyper; 974.381-014 Electrotyper Apprentice; 974.382-010 Stereotyper Apprentice; 974.382-014 Stereotyper.

51-5022.11 Plate Finishers (All Other Printing Related Machine Setters and Set-Up Operators)

Education: No data available.

Employed: 10,130

Openings: No data available.

Projected Growth: No data available.

Earnings: $24,330

Set up and operate equipment to trim and mount electrotype or stereotype plates.

Operates press to print proof of plate, observing printing quality. Operates cutting tools to shave and smooth plates to specified thickness. Mounts finished plates on wood or metal blocks, using hammer and nails or thermoplastic adhesive and heat press. Rubs surface with finishing material to reveal unevenness. Taps plate with hammer and block to flatten until even. Operates plate curving machine to cut plates to fit printing press. Selects cutting position and sets controls of saws, milling machines, and routers following specifications. Examines plates with magnifier or microscope to detect flaws, using engraver's tools.

GOE Number, Interest Area, and Work Group: 08.03.05; Industrial Production; Production Work: Printing and Reproduction. Personality Type: Realistic. Realistic occupations frequently involve work activities that include practical, hands-on problems and solutions. These occupations often deal with plants, animals, and real-world materials like wood, tools, and machinery. Many of the occupations require working outside and do not involve a lot of paperwork or working closely with others. Work Values: Moral Values; Independence; Activity; Company Policies and Practices; Supervision, Human Relations. Skills: Product Inspection; Operation and Control; Equipment Selection; Equipment Maintenance. Abilities: *Cognitive*—Information Ordering; Deductive Reasoning; Problem Sensitivity; Perceptual Speed; Flexibility of Closure; Speed of Closure. *Psychomotor*—Manual Dexterity; Control Precision; Arm-Hand Steadiness. *Physical*—Static Strength; Trunk Strength; Extent Flexibility. *Sensory*—Near Vision; Depth Perception; Visual Color Discrimination. **General Work Activities:** *Information Input*—Getting Information Needed to Do the Job; Inspecting Equipment, Structures, Materials; Identifying Objects, Actions, and Events. *Mental Process*—Evaluating Information Against Standards; Judging Qualities of Things, Services, Other People's Work; Analyzing Data or Information. *Work Output*—Controlling Machines and Processes; Handling and Moving Objects; Performing General Physical Activities. *Interacting with Others*—Communicating with Other Workers; Coordinating Work and Activities of Others; Interpreting Meaning of Information to Others; Assisting and Caring for Others; Performing Administrative Activities; Establishing and Maintaining Relationships. **Physical Work Conditions:** Using Hands on Objects, Tools, or Controls; Indoors; Standing. **Other Job Characteristics:** Degree of Automation; Importance of Being Exact or Accurate; Importance of Being Sure All Is Done; Consequence of Error.

Experience: Job Zone 5. Extensive skill, knowledge, and experience are needed. Very advanced communication and organizational skills are required. **Job Preparation:** SVP 8.0 and above—4 years to more than 10 years. **Knowledge:** Mechanical; Production and Processing; Engineering and Technology; Physics; Building and Construction; Mathematics. **Instructional Program:** 480201 Graphic and Printing Equipment Operator, General.

Related DOT Job: 659.360-010 Plate Finisher.

51-5022.12 Typesetting and Composing Machine Operators and Tenders (Typesetting and Composing Machine Operators and Tenders)

Education: Moderate-term O-T-J training

Employed: 13,366

Openings: 1,527

Projected Growth: –59.8%

Earnings: $23,050

Operate or tend typesetting and composing equipment, such as phototypesetters, linotype or monotype keyboard machines, photocomposers, linocasters, and photoletterers.

Adjusts feed guides, gauges, and rollers, using hand tools. Mounts materials to be printed onto feed mechanisms and threads materials through guides on machine. Installs printing plates, cylinders, or rollers on machine, using hand tools and gauges. Selects printing plates, dies, or type according to work order. Cleans and lubricates equipment. Measures and records amount of product produced. Mixes colors of paint according to formulas. Inspects product to detect defects. Fills reservoirs with paint or ink. Repairs or replaces worn or broken parts, using hand tools. Monitors machines and gauges to ensure and maintain standards. Adjusts and changes gears, using hand tools.

GOE Number, Interest Area, and Work Group: 09.09.01; Business Detail; Clerical Machine Operation. **Personality Type:** Realistic. Realistic occupations frequently involve work activities that include practical, hands-on problems and solutions. These occupations often deal with plants, animals, and real-world materials

like wood, tools, and machinery. Many of the occupations require working outside and do not involve a lot of paperwork or working closely with others. **Work Values:** Moral Values; Independence; Activity; Company Policies and Practices; Supervision; Human Relations. **Skills:** Operation and Control; Product Inspection; Operation Monitoring; Equipment Selection; Reading Comprehension; Problem Identification. **Abilities:** *Cognitive*—Information Ordering; Written Comprehension; Number Facility; Visualization; Written Expression. *Psychomotor*—Arm-Hand Steadiness; Manual Dexterity; Wrist-Finger Speed; Control Precision. *Physical*—Extent Flexibility; Trunk Strength; Static Strength. *Sensory*—Visual Color Discrimination; Near Vision; Hearing Sensitivity. **General Work Activities:** *Information Input*—Monitoring Processes, Materials, and Surroundings; Inspecting Equipment, Structures, Materials; Getting Information Needed to Do the Job. *Mental Process*—Evaluating Information Against Standards; Judging Qualities of Things, Services, Other People's Work; Updating and Using Job-Relevant Knowledge. *Work Output*—Controlling Machines and Processes; Handling and Moving Objects; Repairing and Maintaining Mechanical Equipment. *Interacting with Others*—Communicating with Other Workers; Establishing and Maintaining Relationships; Performing Administrative Activities. **Physical Work Conditions:** Indoors; Using Hands on Objects, Tools, or Controls; Hazardous Equipment; Sitting. **Other Job Characteristics:** Degree of Automation; Importance of Being Exact or Accurate; Consequence of Error.

Experience: Job Zone 2. Some previous work-related skill, knowledge, or experience may be helpful, but usually is not needed. **Job Preparation:** SVP 4.00 to 5.99—6 months to less than 2 years. **Knowledge:** Computers and Electronics; Mechanical; English Language; Production and Processing; Clerical. **Instructional Programs:** 480205 Mechanical Typesetter and Composer; 480211 Computer Typography and Composition Equipment Operator.

Related DOT Jobs: 650.582-010 Linotype Operator; 650.582-014 Monotype-Keyboard Operator; 650.582-018 Photocomposing-Machine Operator; 650.582-022 Phototypesetter Operator; 650.682-010 Equipment Monitor, Phototypesetting; 650.685-010 Typesetting-Machine Tender; 652.585-010 Photolettering-Machine Operator; 652.685-106 Type-Proof Reproducer.

51-5022.13 Photoengraving and Lithographing Machine Operators and Tenders (Photoengraving and Lithographing Machine Operators and Tenders)

Education: Moderate-term O-T-J training

Employed: 6,769

Openings: 1,020

Projected Growth: –15%

Earnings: $23,960

Operate or tend photoengraving and lithographing equipment, such as plate graining, pantograph, roll varnishing, and routing machines.

Rolls out and hammers used printing plates to remove gripper marks and bent corners. Mounts finished plates on wood, synthetic, or metal blocks, by hand or using automatic plate-mounting equipment. Immerses and turns printing roller in bath solutions to dissolve coating, develop image, and dye, using electric hoist. Cuts excess metal and bevels edges of printing plates using routing machine. Applies acid-resistant ink to varnished copper roller and examines for ink smears or cavities filled with ink. Maintains machinery in working order, such as automatic film processor and exposure machine. Examines printing plates with magnifier for uniformity, size, and structures of grain; washes off excess sediment. Cuts printing plates from sheets of aluminum and zinc, using power shears. Examines finished blueprint for specified color, intensity, and sharpness of line. Grains printing plates by wet or dry sandblasting or by use of glass marbles. Paints over pinholes, scratches, and reference points on roller, using brush and acid-resistant paint. Operates machinery such as film processor, graining machine, and varnishing equipment. Copies printed materials such as documents and drawings, using blueprint machine.

GOE Number, Interest Area, and Work Group: 08.03.05; Industrial Production; Production Work: Printing and Reproduction. **Personality Type:** Realistic. Realistic occupations frequently involve work activities that include practical, hands-on problems and solutions. These occupations often deal with plants, animals, and real-world materials like wood, tools, and machinery. Many of the occupations require working outside and do not involve a lot of paperwork or working closely with others. **Work Values:** Moral Values; Independence; Activity; Company Policies and Practices; Supervision, Human Relations. **Skills:** Product Inspection; Operation and Control; Equipment Maintenance; Equipment Selection; Problem Identification. **Abilities:** *Cognitive*—Information Ordering; Visualization; Problem Sensitivity; Written Comprehension; Deductive Reasoning; Inductive Reasoning. *Psychomotor*—Control Precision; Arm-Hand Steadiness; Finger Dexterity; Speed of Limb Movement. *Physical*—none met the criteria. *Sensory*—Near Vision; Visual Color Discrimination. **General Work Activities:** *Information Input*—Monitoring Processes, Materials, and Surroundings; Getting Information Needed to Do the Job; Inspecting Equipment, Structures, Materials. *Mental Process*—Judging Qualities of Things, Services, Other People's Work; Evaluating Information Against Standards; Thinking Creatively. *Work Output*—Handling and Moving Objects; Controlling Machines and Processes; Repairing and Maintaining Mechanical Equipment. *Interacting with Others*—Monitoring and Controlling Resources; Communicating with Other Workers; Establishing and Maintaining Relationships. **Physical Work Conditions:** Indoors; Using Hands on Objects, Tools, or Controls; Sitting; Standing. **Other Job Characteristics:** Degree of Automation; Importance of Being Exact or Accurate; Consequence of Error; Importance of Being Sure All Is Done.

Experience: Job Zone 2. Some previous work-related skill, knowledge, or experience may be helpful, but usually is not needed. **Job Preparation:** SVP 4.00 to 5.99—6 months to less than 2 years. **Knowledge:** Production and Processing; Chemistry; Mechanical; Engineering and Technology; Fine Arts. **Instructional Program:** 480206 Lithographer and Platemaker.

Related DOT Jobs: 971.685-010 Roller-Print Tender; 972.384-014 Platemaker, Semiconductor Packages; 972.682-010 Plate Grainer; 972.682-014 Plate-Grainer Apprentice; 979.382-022 Pantographer; 979.682-014 Blueprinting-Machine Operator; 979.682-022 Roller Varnisher; 979.682-026 Router.

51-5023.00 Printing Machine Operators (Printing Press Machine Operators and Tenders)

Education: No data available.

Employed: 125,910

Openings: No data available.

Projected Growth: No data available.

Earnings: $26,020

Set up or operate various types of printing machines, such as offset, letterset, intaglio, or gravure presses or screen printers, to produce print on paper or other materials.

GOE Number, Interest Area, and Work Group: 08.03.05; Industrial Production; Production Work: Printing and Reproduction. **Instructional Program:** 480208 Printing Press Operator. **Note:** The Department of Labor has not collected some data for this job, so it has fewer details than the other descriptions.

51-5023.01 Precision Printing Workers (All Other Precision Printing Workers)

Education: No data available.

Employed: 5,140

Openings: No data available.

Projected Growth: No data available.

Earnings: $24,510

Perform variety of precision printing activities, such as duplication of microfilm and reproduction of graphic arts materials.

Reviews layout and customer order to determine size and style of type. Maintains printing machinery and equipment. Positions and aligns negatives to assemble flats for reproduction. Compares test exposures to quality control color guides or exposure guides to determine data for exposure settings. Measures density levels of colors or color guides on proofs, using densitometer, and compares readings to set standards. Operates offset-duplicating machine or small printing press to reproduce single or multicolor copies of lines, drawings, graphs, or similar materials. Mixes powdered ink pigments, using matching book and using measuring and mixing tools. Examines and inspects printed material for clarity of print and specified color. Enters, positions, and alters size of text, using computer, to make up and arrange pages to produce printed materials. Scans artwork, using optical scanner, which changes image into computer-readable form. Hand rubs paper against printing plate to transfer specified design onto paper for use in etching glassware. Puts flats into vacuum frame to produce aluminum plate, microfiche print, or single or multicolor proof. Prepares microfiche duplicates of microfilm, using contact printer and developing machine. Immerses exposed materials into chemical solutions to hand develop single or multicolor proofs or printing plates. Sets up and operates various types of cameras to produce negatives, photostats, or plastic or paper printing plates. Operates automatic processor to develop photographs, plates, or base material used in single or multicolor proofs. Prints paper or film copies of completed material from computer. Sets up and operates bindery equipment to cut, assemble, staple, or bind materials.

GOE Number, Interest Area, and Work Group: 08.03.05; Industrial Production; Production Work: Printing and Reproduction. **Personality Type:** Realistic. Realistic occupations frequently involve work activities that include practical, hands-on problems and solutions. These occupations often deal with plants, animals, and real-world materials like wood, tools, and machinery. Many of the occupations require working outside and do not involve a lot of paperwork or working closely with others. **Work Values:** Moral Values; Independence; Company Policies and Practices; Supervision, Technical; Ability Utilization; Security; Achievement; Working Conditions. **Skills:** Product Inspection; Equipment Selection; Operation and Control; Reading Comprehension; Equipment Maintenance; Information Gathering. **Abilities:** *Cognitive*—Information Ordering; Visualization; Problem Sensitivity; Deductive Reasoning; Written Comprehension. *Psychomotor*—Control Precision; Finger Dexterity; Arm-Hand Steadiness; Manual Dexterity. *Physical*—Extent Flexibility; Dynamic Flexibility. *Sensory*—Visual Color Discrimination; Near Vision; Depth Perception. **General Work Activities:** *Information Input*—Getting Information Needed to Do the Job; Monitoring Processes, Materials, and Surroundings; Inspecting Equipment, Structures, Materials. *Mental Process*—Evaluating Information Against Standards; Judging Qualities of Things, Services, Other People's Work; Processing Information; Analyzing Data or Information. *Work Output*—Handling and Moving Objects; Controlling Machines and Processes; Interacting with Computers. *Interacting with Others*—Communicating with Persons Outside Organization; Establishing and Maintaining Relationships; Performing Administrative Activities; Influencing Others or Selling; Communicating with Other Workers. **Physical Work Conditions:** Using Hands on Objects, Tools, or Controls; Indoors; Standing. **Other Job Characteristics:** Degree of Automation; Importance of Being Exact or Accurate; Importance of Being Sure All Is Done; Consequence of Error.

Experience: Job Zone 2. Some previous work-related skill, knowledge, or experience may be helpful, but usually is not needed. **Job Preparation:** SVP 4.00 to 5.99—6 months to less than 2 years. **Knowledge:** English Language; Computers and Electronics; Production and Processing; Chemistry; Communications and Media; Mathematics. **Instructional Programs:** 480201 Graphic and Printing Equipment Operator, General; 480299 Graphic and Printing Equipment Operators, Other.

Related DOT Jobs: 971.381-046 Screen Maker, Textile; 972.381-034 Proofer, Prepress; 976.381-014 Microfiche Duplicator; 979.381-014 Line-Up Examiner; 979.382-018 Printer; 979.382-026 Computer Typesetter-Keyliner; 979.384-010 Screen Maker, Photographic Process; 979.681-014 Printer.

51-5023.02 Offset Lithographic Press Setters and Set-Up Operators (Offset Lithographic Press Operators)

Education: Moderate-term O-T-J training

Employed: 62,734

Openings: 8,297

Projected Growth: –14.7%

Earnings: $31,000

Set up, or set up and operate, offset printing press, either sheet or web fed, to print single and multicolor copy from lithographic plates. Examine job order to determine press operating time, quantity to be printed, and stock specifications.

Starts press and examines printed copy for ink density, position on paper, and registration. Installs and locks plate into position, using hand tools, to achieve pressure required for printing. Makes adjustments to press, throughout production run, to maintain specific registration and color density. Measures plate thickness and inserts packing sheets on plate cylinder to build up plate to printing height. Loads paper into feeder or installs rolls of paper, adjusts feeder and delivery mechanisms, and unloads printed material from delivery mechanism. Fills ink and dampening solution fountains; adjusts controls to regulate flow of ink and dampening solution to plate cylinder. Applies packing sheets to blanket cylinder to build up blanket thickness to diameter of plate cylinder. Washes plate to remove protective gum coating. Examines job order to determine quantity to be printed, stock specifications, colors, and special printing instructions. Removes and cleans plate and cylinders. Measures paper thickness and adjusts space between blanket and impression cylinders according to thickness of paper stock.

GOE Number, Interest Area, and Work Group: 08.03.05; Industrial Production; Production Work: Printing and Reproduction. **Personality Type:** Realistic. Realistic occupations frequently involve work activities that include practical, hands-on problems and solutions. These occupations often deal with plants, animals, and real-world materials like wood, tools, and machinery. Many of the occupations require working outside and do not involve a lot of paperwork or working closely with others. **Work Values:** Moral Values; Independence; Activity; Company Policies and Practices; Supervision, Human Relations. **Skills:** Operation and Control; Operation Monitoring; Equipment Selection; Product Inspection; Equipment Maintenance. **Abilities:** *Cognitive*—Written Comprehension; Information Ordering; Number Facility; Oral Expression; Visualization; Oral Comprehension. *Psychomotor*—Control Precision; Finger Dexterity. *Physical*—none met the criteria. *Sensory*—Visual Color Discrimination. **General Work Activities:** *Information Input*—Getting Information Needed to Do the Job; Monitoring Processes, Materials, and Surroundings; Estimating Needed Characteristics. *Mental Process*—Judging Qualities of Things, Services, Other People's Work; Evaluating Information Against Standards; Organizing, Planning, and Prioritizing. *Work Output*—Controlling Machines and Processes; Handling and Moving Objects; Performing General Physical Activities. *Interacting with Others*—Coordinating Work and Activities of Others; Communicating with Other Workers; Establishing and Maintaining Relationships; Guiding, Directing and Motivating Subordinates. **Physical Work Conditions:** Indoors; Standing; Using Hands on Objects, Tools, or Controls. **Other Job Characteristics:** Degree of Automation; Importance of Being Exact or Accurate; Importance of Being Sure All Is Done.

Experience: Job Zone 5. Extensive skill, knowledge, and experience are needed. Very advanced communication and organizational skills are required. **Job Preparation:** SVP 8.0 and above—4 years to more than 10 years. **Knowledge:** Production and Processing; Mechanical; English Language; Communications and Media; Engineering and Technology; Mathematics. **Instructional Program:** 480206 Lithographer and Platemaker.

Related DOT Jobs: 651.382-042 Offset-Press Operator I; 651.382-046 Offset-Press-Operator Apprentice.

51-5023.03 Letterpress Setters and Set-Up Operators
(Letterpress Operators)

Education: Moderate-term O-T-J training

Employed: 10,139

Openings: 1,315

Projected Growth: –18.2%

Earnings: $28,620

Set up, or set up and operate, direct relief letterpresses, either sheet or roll (web) fed, to produce single or multicolor printed materials such as newspapers, books, and periodicals.

Reads work orders and job specifications to select ink and paper stock. Positions and installs printing plates, cylinder packing, die, and type forms in press, according to specifications, using hand tools. Mixes colors or inks and fills reservoirs. Dismantles and reassembles printing unit or parts, using hand tools, to repair, clean, maintain, or adjust press. Monitors feeding and printing operations to maintain specified operating levels and detect malfunctions. Pushes buttons or moves controls to start printing press and control operation. Operates specially-equipped presses and auxiliary equipment such as cutting, folding, numbering, and pasting devices. Inspects printed materials for irregularities such as off-level areas, variations in ink volume, register slippage, and poor color register. Records and maintains production logsheet. Directs and monitors activities of apprentices and of feeding or stacking workers. Moves controls to set or adjust ink flow, tension rollers, paper guides, and feed controls. Loads, positions, and adjusts unprinted materials on holding fixtures or in feeding mechanism of press.

GOE Number, Interest Area, and Work Group: 08.03.05; Industrial Production; Production Work: Printing and Reproduction. **Personality Type:** Realistic. Realistic occupations frequently involve work activities that include practical, hands-on problems and solutions. These occupations often deal with plants, animals, and real-world materials like wood, tools, and machinery. Many of the occupations require working outside and do not involve a lot of paperwork or working closely with others. **Work Values:** Moral Values; Activity; Independence; Company Policies and Practices; Supervision, Human Relations. **Skills:** Product Inspection; Operation and Control; Operation Monitoring; Equipment Selection; Equipment Maintenance; Installation. **Abilities:** *Cognitive*—Information Ordering; Perceptual Speed; Visualization; Problem Sensitivity; Deductive Reasoning. *Psychomotor*—Control Precision; Manual Dexterity; Wrist-Finger Speed. *Physical*—Static Strength; Trunk Strength. *Sensory*—Visual Color Discrimination; Near Vision. **General Work Activities:** *Information Input*—Inspecting Equipment, Structures, Materials; Monitoring Processes, Materials, and Surroundings; Getting Information Needed to Do the Job. *Mental Process*—Evaluating Information Against Standards; Organizing, Planning, and Prioritizing; Analyzing Data or Infor-

mation. *Work Output*—Controlling Machines and Processes; Handling and Moving Objects; Documenting and Recording Information; Implementing Ideas and Programs; Repairing and Maintaining Mechanical Equipment. *Interacting with Others*—Communicating with Other Workers; Guiding, Directing and Motivating Subordinates; Coordinating Work and Activities of Others. **Physical Work Conditions:** Indoors; Using Hands on Objects, Tools, or Controls; Standing. **Other Job Characteristics:** Degree of Automation; Importance of Being Sure All Is Done; Consequence of Error.

Experience: Job Zone 3. Previous work-related skill, knowledge, or experience is required. **Job Preparation:** SVP 6.0 to less than 7.0—More than 1 year and less than 4 years. **Knowledge:** Production and Processing; English Language; Mechanical; Communications and Media; Engineering and Technology; Clerical. **Instructional Program:** 480208 Printing Press Operator.

Related DOT Jobs: 651.362-010 Cylinder-Press Operator; 651.362-014 Cylinder-Press-Operator Apprentice; 651.362-018 Platen-Press Operator; 651.362-022 Platen-Press-Operator Apprentice; 651.362-030 Web-Press Operator; 651.362-034 Web-Press-Operator Apprentice; 651.382-034 Tab-Card-Press Operator.

51-5023.04 Design Printing Machine Setters and Set-Up Operators (Specialty Materials Printing Machine Setters and Set-Up Operators)

Education: No data available.

Employed: 11,980

Openings: No data available.

Projected Growth: No data available.

Earnings: $25,220

Set up, or set up and operate, machines to print designs on materials.

Cleans and lubricates equipment. Adjusts feed guides, gauges, and rollers, using hand tools. Adjusts and changes gears, using hand tools. Mixes colors of paint according to formulas. Repairs or replaces worn or broken parts, using hand tools. Inspects product to detect defects. Monitors machines and gauges to ensure and maintain standards. Installs printing plates, cylinders, or rollers on machine, using hand tools and gauges. Fills reservoirs with paint or ink. Measures and records amount of product produced.

GOE Number, Interest Area, and Work Group: 08.03.05; Industrial Production; Production Work: Printing and Reproduction. **Personality Type:** Realistic. Realistic occupations frequently involve work activities that include practical, hands-on problems and solutions. These occupations often deal with plants, animals, and real-world materials like wood, tools, and machinery. Many of the occupations require working outside and do not involve a lot of paperwork or working closely with others. **Work Values:** Moral Values; Independence; Company Policies and Practices; Activity; Supervision, Human Relations. **Skills:** Product Inspection; Operation Monitoring; Operation and Control; Repairing; Equipment Maintenance. **Abilities:** *Cognitive*—Number Facility; Visualization; Problem Sensitivity; Information Ordering; Mathematical Reasoning; Perceptual Speed. *Psychomotor*—Control Precision; Multilimb Coordination; Arm-Hand Steadiness; Manual

Dexterity; Finger Dexterity. *Physical*—Dynamic Strength; Trunk Strength; Extent Flexibility. *Sensory*—Visual Color Discrimination; Near Vision; Depth Perception. **General Work Activities:** *Information Input*—Inspecting Equipment, Structures, Materials; Monitoring Processes, Materials, and Surroundings; Getting Information Needed to Do the Job. *Mental Process*—Evaluating Information Against Standards; Processing Information; Judging Qualities of Things, Services, Other People's Work. *Work Output*—Handling and Moving Objects; Controlling Machines and Processes; Repairing and Maintaining Mechanical Equipment. *Interacting with Others*—Performing Administrative Activities; Communicating with Other Workers; Monitoring and Controlling Resources. **Physical Work Conditions:** Indoors; Using Hands on Objects, Tools, or Controls; Hazardous Equipment. **Other Job Characteristics:** Degree of Automation; Importance of Being Exact or Accurate; Importance of Being Sure All Is Done; Pace Determined by Speed of Equipment.

Experience: Job Zone 3. Previous work-related skill, knowledge, or experience is required. **Job Preparation:** SVP 6.0 to less than 7.0—More than 1 year and less than 4 years. **Knowledge:** Mechanical; Production and Processing; Engineering and Technology; Mathematics; Fine Arts. **Instructional Program:** 480201 Graphic and Printing Equipment Operator, General.

Related DOT Jobs: 651.382-014 Lithograph-Press Operator, Tinware; 651.382-026 Printer, Plastic; 652.382-010 Cloth Printer; 652.662-014 Wallpaper Printer I.

51-5023.05 Marking and Identification Printing Machine Setters and Set-Up Operators (Specialty Materials Printing Machine Setters and Set-Up Operators)

Education:	No data available.
Employed:	11,980
Openings:	No data available.
Projected Growth:	No data available.
Earnings:	$25,220

Set up, or set up and operate, machines to print trademarks, labels, or multicolored identification symbols on materials.

Sets rate of flow of coloring agent, and speed and spacing of materials, to achieve desired product. Mounts materials to be printed onto feed mechanisms and threads materials through guides on machine. Fills reservoirs with ink or specified coloring agents. Selects printing plates, dies, or type according to work order. Examines product to detect defects. Cleans machine and equipment, using solvent and rags. Monitors printing process to detect machine malfunctions. Adjusts machine as needed, using hand tools. Mounts printing plates, dies, or type onto machine. **GOE Number, Interest Area, and Work Group:** 08.03.05; Industrial Production; Production Work: Printing and Reproduction. **Personality Type:** Realistic. Realistic occupations frequently involve work activities that include practical, hands-on problems and solutions. These occupations often deal with plants, animals, and real-world materials like wood, tools, and machinery. Many of the occupations require working outside and do not involve a lot of paperwork or working closely with others. **Work Values:** Moral Values; Independence; Company Policies and Practices; Activity; Supervision, Human Relations. **Skills:** Operation and

Control; Product Inspection; Operation Monitoring; Equipment Selection; Equipment Maintenance; Reading Comprehension. **Abilities:** *Cognitive*—Visualization; Written Comprehension; Information Ordering; Problem Sensitivity; Perceptual Speed. *Psychomotor*—Arm-Hand Steadiness; Control Precision; Finger Dexterity; Manual Dexterity. *Physical*—Extent Flexibility; Dynamic Strength; Dynamic Flexibility. *Sensory*—Visual Color Discrimination. **General Work Activities:** *Information Input*—Getting Information Needed to Do the Job; Monitoring Processes, Materials, and Surroundings; Inspecting Equipment, Structures, Materials. *Mental Process*—Judging Qualities of Things, Services, Other People's Work; Evaluating Information Against Standards; Processing Information; Analyzing Data or Information. *Work Output*—Controlling Machines and Processes; Handling and Moving Objects; Performing General Physical Activities. *Interacting with Others*—Communicating with Other Workers; Performing Administrative Activities; Influencing Others or Selling; Assisting and Caring for Others; Establishing and Maintaining Relationships; Communicating with Persons Outside Organization. **Physical Work Conditions:** Using Hands on Objects, Tools, or Controls; Indoors; Standing. **Other Job Characteristics:** Degree of Automation; Importance of Being Exact or Accurate; Pace Determined by Speed of Equipment.

Experience: Job Zone 1. No previous work-related skill, knowledge, or experience is needed. **Job Preparation:** SVP Below 4.0—Less than 6 months. **Knowledge:** English Language; Mechanical; Production and Processing; Communications and Media; Engineering and Technology; Chemistry. **Instructional Program:** 480201 Graphic and Printing Equipment Operator, General.

Related DOT Jobs: 651.682-022 Tip Printer; 652.662-010 Printing-Machine Operator, Tape Rules; 652.682-010 Box Printer; 652.682-026 Striping-Machine Operator.

51-5023.06 Screen Printing Machine Setters and Set-Up Operators (Screen Printing Machine Setters and Set-Up Operators)

Education:	Moderate-term O-T-J training
Employed:	28,341
Openings:	4,189
Projected Growth:	3%
Earnings:	$18,880

Set up, or set up and operate, screen printing machines to print designs onto articles and materials such as glass or plasticware, cloth, and paper.

Sets and adjusts feed rollers, spindle reel, printing screens, and bolts to specifications. Patrols printing area to monitor production activities and to detect problems such as mechanical breakdowns or malfunctions. Measures, centers, aligns, and positions screen, using gauge and hand tools. Determines, from orders, type and color of designs to print. Reviews print order to determine settings and adjustments required to set up manually controlled or automatic screen printing machine or decorating equipment. Starts dyeing oven and sets thermostat to temperature specified for printing run. Mixes paints according to formula, using bench mixer. Counts and records quantities printed, in production log. Trains workers in use of printing equipment and in quality standards. Adjusts position of design or screen to ensure specified color print registration. Compares ink or paint prepared for printing run with master color swatch to confirm accuracy of match. Examines product for paint smears, position of design, or other defects and adjusts equipment. Inspects printing equipment and replaces damaged or defective parts such as switches, pulleys, fixtures, screws, and bolts.

GOE Number, Interest Area, and Work Group: 08.02.01; Industrial Production; Production Technology: Machine Set-up and Operation. **Personality Type:** Realistic. Realistic occupations frequently involve work activities that include practical, hands-on problems and solutions. These occupations often deal with plants, animals, and real-world materials like wood, tools, and machinery. Many of the occupations require working outside and do not involve a lot of paperwork or working closely with others. **Work Values:** Moral Values; Company Policies and Practices; Activity; Independence; Supervision, Human Relations. **Skills:** Product Inspection; Operation and Control; Instructing; Equipment Maintenance; Repairing; Operation Monitoring; Troubleshooting. **Abilities:** *Cognitive*—Visualization; Perceptual Speed; Problem Sensitivity; Written Comprehension; Oral Expression; Information Ordering. *Psychomotor*—Finger Dexterity; Control Precision; Multilimb Coordination; Wrist-Finger Speed; Arm-Hand Steadiness. *Physical*—Extent Flexibility. *Sensory*—Visual Color Discrimination; Near Vision; Speech Clarity. **General Work Activities:** *Information Input*—Getting Information Needed to Do the Job; Inspecting Equipment, Structures, Materials; Monitoring Processes, Materials, and Surroundings. *Mental Process*—Evaluating Information Against Standards; Judging Qualities of Things, Services, Other People's Work; Updating and Using Job-Relevant Knowledge. *Work Output*—Controlling Machines and Processes; Handling and Moving Objects; Repairing and Maintaining Mechanical Equipment. *Interacting with Others*—Teaching Others; Communicating with Other Workers; Establishing and Maintaining Relationships. **Physical Work Conditions:** Indoors; Using Hands on Objects, Tools, or Controls; Hazardous Equipment; Standing. **Other Job Characteristics:** Degree of Automation; Importance of Being Exact or Accurate; Consequence of Error.

Experience: Job Zone 3. Previous work-related skill, knowledge, or experience is required. **Job Preparation:** SVP 6.0 to less than 7.0—More than 1 year and less than 4 years. **Knowledge:** Production and Processing; Mechanical; Mathematics; Education and Training; Design. **Instructional Program:** 480299 Graphic and Printing Equipment Operators, Other.

Related DOT Jobs: 652.260-010 Section Leader, Screen Printing; 652.380-010 Decorating-Equipment Setter; 979.360-010 Screen-Printing-Equipment Setter.

51-5023.07 Embossing Machine Set-Up Operators
(All Other Printing Related Machine Setters and Set-Up Operators)

Education: No data available.

Employed: 10,130

Openings: No data available.

Projected Growth: No data available.

Earnings: $24,330

Set up and operate embossing machines.

Scrapes high spots on counter die to prevent from puncturing paper. Starts machine to lower ram and impress cardboard. Positions, installs, and locks embossed plate in chase and locks chase in bed of press. Removes and stacks embossed covers. Sets sheets singly in gauge pins and starts press. Mixes embossing composition to putty-like consistency, spreads glue on paten, and applies thin pad of composition over glue. Makes impression of embossing to desired depth in composition on platen, trims off excess, and allows composition to harden. Stamps embossing design on workpiece, using heated work tools. Sets guides to hold cover in position and adjusts table height to obtain correct depth of impression. Cuts surface of cardboard leaving design or letters, using hand tools.

GOE Number, Interest Area, and Work Group: 08.03.05; Industrial Production; Production Work: Printing and Reproduction. **Personality Type:** Realistic. Realistic occupations frequently involve work activities that include practical, hands-on problems and solutions. These occupations often deal with plants, animals, and real-world materials like wood, tools, and machinery. Many of the occupations require working outside and do not involve a lot of paperwork or working closely with others. **Work Values:** Moral Values; Independence; Activity; Company Policies and Practices; Supervision, Human Relations. **Skills:** Operation and Control; Equipment Maintenance; Operation Monitoring; Installation. **Abilities:** *Cognitive*—Information Ordering; Visualization; Perceptual Speed; Problem Sensitivity; Deductive Reasoning. *Psychomotor*—Manual Dexterity; Control Precision; Multilimb Coordination. *Physical*—Trunk Strength. **General Work Activities:** *Information Input*—Monitoring Processes, Materials, and Surroundings; Getting Information Needed to Do the Job; Identifying Objects, Actions, and Events. *Mental Process*—Evaluating Information Against Standards; Analyzing Data or Information; Making Decisions and Solving Problems. *Work Output*—Handling and Moving Objects; Controlling Machines and Processes; Performing General Physical Activities. *Interacting with Others*—Communicating with Other Workers; Coordinating Work and Activities of Others; Establishing and Maintaining Relationships; Assisting and Caring for Others; Monitoring and Controlling Resources; Performing Administrative Activities. **Physical Work Conditions:** Indoors; Using Hands on Objects, Tools, or Controls; Standing. **Other Job Characteristics:** Degree of Automation; Importance of Being Sure All Is Done; Consequence of Error.

Experience: Job Zone 3. Previous work-related skill, knowledge, or experience is required. **Job Preparation:** SVP 6.0 to less than 7.0—More than 1 year and less than 4 years. **Knowledge:** Production and Processing; Mechanical; Mathematics; Engineering and Technology; Physics; English Language; Chemistry. **Instructional Program:** 480201 Graphic and Printing Equipment Operator, General.

Related DOT Jobs: 659.382-010 Embosser; 659.682-014 Embossing-Press Operator; 659.682-018 Embossing-Press-Operator Apprentice.

51-5023.08 Engraver Set-Up Operators (All Other Printing Related Machine Setters and Set-Up Operators)

Education: No data available.

Employed: 10,130

Openings: No data available.

Projected Growth: No data available.

Earnings: $24,330

Set up and operate machines to transfer printing designs.

Determines ground setting according to weight of fabric, type of design, and colors in design. Adjusts and tightens levers in position, using hand tools. Turns screws to align machine components. Examines marks on roller to verify alignment and to detect defects. Records ground setting, length of roller, width of engraving, and circumference of roller on production sheet. Measures depth of engraving and weighs diamond points, using gauges and scales. Inserts mandrel through roller and lifts into position on machine. Positions machine mechanisms and depresses levers to apply marks on roller. Aligns plate with markings on machine table and tacks to table.

GOE Number, Interest Area, and Work Group: 08.03.05; Industrial Production; Production Work: Printing and Reproduction. **Personality Type:** Realistic. Realistic occupations frequently involve work activities that include practical, hands-on problems and solutions. These occupations often deal with plants, animals, and real-world materials like wood, tools, and machinery. Many of the occupations require working outside and do not involve a lot of paperwork or working closely with others. **Work Values:** Moral Values; Independence; Company Policies and Practices; Activity; Supervision, Human Relations. **Skills:** Operation and Control; Equipment Selection; Operation Monitoring; Product Inspection; Mathematics. **Abilities:** *Cognitive*—Information Ordering; Deductive Reasoning; Perceptual Speed; Written Expression; Mathematical Reasoning; Flexibility of Closure. *Psychomotor*—Control Precision; Arm-Hand Steadiness; Manual Dexterity. *Physical*—Extent Flexibility; Gross Body Coordination; Dynamic Flexibility. *Sensory*—Near Vision; Visual Color Discrimination; Auditory Attention. **General Work Activities:** *Information Input*—Getting Information Needed to Do the Job; Identifying Objects, Actions, and Events; Inspecting Equipment, Structures, Materials. *Mental Process*—Analyzing Data or Information; Evaluating Information Against Standards; Making Decisions and Solving Problems; Processing Information; Judging Qualities of Things, Services, Other People's Work. *Work Output*—Controlling Machines and Processes; Handling and Moving Objects; Documenting and Recording Information; Performing General Physical Activities. *Interacting with Others*—Performing Administrative Activities; Communicating with Other Workers; Assisting and Caring for Others; Establishing and Maintaining Relationships; Coordinating Work and Activities of Others. **Physical Work Conditions:** Indoors; Using Hands on Objects, Tools, or Controls; Hazardous Equipment; Standing. **Other Job Characteristics:** Degree of Automation; Importance of Being Exact or Accurate; Importance of Being Sure All Is Done.

Experience: Job Zone 4. A minimum of two to four years of work-related skill, knowledge, or experience is needed. **Job Preparation:** SVP 7.0 to less than 8.0—2 years to less than 10 years. **Knowledge:** Production and Processing; Mechanical; Mathemat-

ics; Engineering and Technology; Clerical. **Instructional Program:** 480201 Graphic and Printing Equipment Operator, General.

Related DOT Jobs: 979.380-010 Pantograph Setter; 979.382-014 Engraver, Machine.

51-5023.09 Printing Press Machine Operators and Tenders (Printing Press Machine Operators and Tenders)

Education: No data available.

Employed: 125,910

Openings: No data available.

Projected Growth: No data available.

Earnings: $26,020

Operate or tend various types of printing machines, such as offset lithographic presses, letter or letterset presses, flexographic or gravure presses, to produce print on paper or other materials such as plastic, cloth, or rubber.

Blends and tests paint, inks, stains and solvents according to type of material being printed and workorder specifications. Dismantles and reassembles printing unit or parts, using hand and power tools, to repair, maintain, or adjust machine. Selects and installs printing plates, rollers, screens, stencils, type, die, and cylinders in machine, according to specifications, using hand tools. Turns, pushes, or moves controls to set and adjust speed, temperature, inkflow, and position and pressure tolerances of press. Monitors feeding, printing, and racking processes of press to maintain specified operating levels and detect malfunctions. Loads, positions, and adjusts unprinted materials on holding fixture or in loading and feeding mechanisms of press. Monitors and controls operation of auxiliary equipment such as cutters, folders, drying ovens, and sanders, to assemble and finish product. Removes printed materials from press, using handtruck, electric lift, or hoist; transports them to drying, storage, or finishing areas. Cleans and lubricates printing machine and components such as rollers, screens, typesetting, and reservoirs, using oil, solvents, brushes, rags, and hoses. Discards or corrects misprinted materials, using ink eradicators or solvents. Accepts orders, calculates and quotes prices, and receives payments from customers. Packs and labels cartons, boxes, or bins of finished products. Keeps daily time and materials usage reports; records identifying information printed on manufactured products and parts. Directs and monitors activities of workers feeding, inspecting, and tending printing machines and materials. Inspects and examines printed products for print clarity, color accuracy, conformance to specifications, and external defects. Reviews work order to determine ink, stock, and equipment needed for production. Pushes buttons, turns handles, or moves controls and levers to start printing machine, or manually controls equipment operation.

GOE Number, Interest Area, and Work Group: 08.03.05; Industrial Production; Production Work: Printing and Reproduction. **Personality Type:** Realistic. Realistic occupations frequently involve work activities that include practical, hands-on problems and solutions. These occupations often deal with plants, animals, and real-world materials like wood, tools, and machinery. Many of the occupations require working outside and do not involve a lot of paperwork or working closely with others. **Work Values:** Moral Values; Activity; Company Policies and Practices; Supervision, Human Relations; Compensation; Achievement. **Skills:** Operation Monitoring; Product Inspection; Operation and Control; Management of Personnel Resources; Testing; Equipment Maintenance. **Abilities:** *Cognitive*—Oral Comprehension; Visualization; Written Expression; Number Facility; Written Comprehension; Mathematical Reasoning. *Psychomotor*—Manual Dexterity; Control Precision; Finger Dexterity. *Physical*—Static Strength; Dynamic Strength; Dynamic Flexibility; Explosive Strength. *Sensory*—Visual Color Discrimination; Near Vision. **General Work Activities:** *Information Input*—Inspecting Equipment, Structures, Materials; Monitoring Processes, Materials, and Surroundings; Estimating Needed Characteristics; Getting Information Needed to Do the Job. *Mental Process*—Judging Qualities of Things, Services, Other People's Work; Analyzing Data or Information; Making Decisions and Solving Problems; Processing Information. *Work Output*—Controlling Machines and Processes; Handling and Moving Objects; Repairing and Maintaining Mechanical Equipment. *Interacting with Others*—Monitoring and Controlling Resources; Coordinating Work and Activities of Others; Communicating with Other Workers; Guiding, Directing and Motivating Subordinates; Establishing and Maintaining Relationships; Assisting and Caring for Others. **Physical Work Conditions:** Indoors; Using Hands on Objects, Tools, or Controls; Common Protective or Safety Attire; Standing. **Other Job Characteristics:** Degree of Automation; Importance of Being Sure All Is Done; Importance of Being Exact or Accurate.

Experience: Job Zone 1. No previous work-related skill, knowledge, or experience is needed. **Job Preparation:** SVP Below 4.0—Less than 6 months. **Knowledge:** Production and Processing; Mechanical; English Language; Chemistry; Engineering and Technology; Mathematics. **Instructional Program:** 480208 Printing Press Operator.

Related DOT Jobs: 651.582-010 Proof-Press Operator; 651.582-014 Lithographic-Proofer Apprentice; 651.585-010 Assistant-Press Operator; 651.682-014 Offset-Duplicating-Machine Operator; 651.682-018 Striper; 651.685-010 Bag Printer; 651.685-014 Design Printer, Balloon; 651.685-018 Offset-Press Operator II; 651.685-022 Platen-Press Feeder; 651.685-026 Assistant Press Operator, Offset; 652.462-010 Rubber-Printing-Machine Operator; 652.582-010 Marker; 652.582-014 Rotary-Screen-Printing-Machine Operator; 652.662-018 Print-Line Operator; 652.682-014 Embossograph Operator; 652.682-018 Screen-Printing-Machine Operator; 652.682-030 Stamping-Press Operator; 652.685-010 Back Tender, Cloth Printing; 652.685-014 Binding Printer; 652.685-018 Carton Marker, Machine (partial list; see the introduction for sources of the complete list).

51-6000 Textile, Apparel, and Furnishings Workers

51-6011.00 Laundry and Dry-Cleaning Workers
(Laundry and Dry-Cleaning Machine Operators and Tenders, Except Pressing)

Education: Moderate-term O-T-J training
Employed: 167,423
Openings: 38,082
Projected Growth: 9.8%
Earnings: $14,670

Operate or tend washing or dry-cleaning machines to wash or dry-clean industrial or household articles such as cloth garments, suede, leather, furs, blankets, draperies, fine linens, rugs, and carpets.

GOE Number, Interest Area, and Work Group: 11.06.01; Recreation, Travel, and Other Personal Services; Apparel, Shoes, Leather, and Fabric Care. **Instructional Programs:** 200301 Clothing, Apparel and Textile Workers and Managers, General; 200309 Drycleaner and Launderer (Commercial). **Note:** The Department of Labor has not collected some data for this job, so it has fewer details than the other descriptions.

51-6011.01 Spotters, Dry Cleaning (Laundry and Dry-Cleaning Machine Operators)

Education: Moderate-term O-T-J training
Employed: 167,423
Openings: 38,082
Projected Growth: 9.8%
Earnings: $14,670

Identify stains in wool, synthetic, and silk garments and household fabrics; apply chemical solutions to remove stain. Determine spotting procedures on basis of type of fabric and nature of stain.

Operates drycleaning machine. Sprinkles chemical solvents over stain and pats area with brush or sponge until stain is removed. Applies bleaching powder to spot; sprays with steam to remove stains from certain fabrics which do not respond to other cleaning solvents. Spreads article on worktable and positions stain over vacuum head or on marble slab. Mixes bleaching agent with hot water in vats; soaks material until it is bleached. Sprays steam, water, or air over spot to flush out chemicals, dry material, raise nap, or brighten color. Inspects spots to ascertain composition and select solvent. Applies chemicals to neutralize effect of solvents. Cleans fabric using vacuum or airhose.

GOE Number, Interest Area, and Work Group: 11.06.01; Recreation, Travel, and Other Personal Services; Apparel, Shoes, Leather, and Fabric Care. **Personality Type:** Realistic. Realistic occupations frequently involve work activities that include practical, hands-on problems and solutions. These occupations often deal with plants, animals, and real-world materials like wood, tools, and machinery. Many of the occupations require working outside and do not involve a lot of paperwork or working closely with others. **Work Values:** Moral Values; Independence; Security; Activity; Supervision, Technical. **Skills:** Product Inspection; Problem Identification; Equipment Selection; Operation Monitoring; Operation and Control; Solution Appraisal. **Abilities:** *Cognitive*—Deductive Reasoning; Information Ordering; Problem Sensitivity; Time Sharing; Category Flexibility; Fluency of Ideas. *Psychomotor*—Wrist-Finger Speed. *Physical*—Dynamic Flexibility. *Sensory*—Visual Color Discrimination; Hearing Sensitivity; Glare Sensitivity; Depth Perception. **General Work Activities:** *Information Input*—Getting Information Needed to Do the Job; Identifying Objects, Actions, and Events; Monitoring Processes, Materials, and Surroundings. *Mental Process*—Analyzing Data or Information; Making Decisions and Solving Problems; Judging

Qualities of Things, Services, Other People's Work. *Work Output*—Handling and Moving Objects; Controlling Machines and Processes; Performing General Physical Activities. *Interacting with Others*—Monitoring and Controlling Resources; Assisting and Caring for Others; Performing for or Working with the Public; Communicating with Other Workers. **Physical Work Conditions:** Indoors; Using Hands on Objects, Tools, or Controls; Hazardous Conditions; Standing. **Other Job Characteristics:** Degree of Automation; Importance of Being Exact or Accurate; Importance of Being Sure All Is Done.

Experience: Job Zone 1. No previous work-related skill, knowledge, or experience is needed. **Job Preparation:** SVP Below 4.0—Less than 6 months. **Knowledge:** Chemistry; Customer and Personal Service; Mathematics; Public Safety and Security; Mechanical. **Instructional Programs:** 200301 Clothing, Apparel and Textile Workers and Managers, General; 200309 Drycleaner and Launderer (Commercial).

Related DOT Jobs: 361.684-018 Spotter I; 362.381-010 Spotter II; 582.684-014 Spot Cleaner; 780.687-058 Upholstery Cleaner.

51-6011.02 Precision Dyers (Precision Dyers)

Education: No data available.

Employed: 4,140

Openings: No data available.

Projected Growth: No data available.

Earnings: $19,620

Change or restore the color of articles such as garments, drapes, and slipcovers, by means of dyes, using knowledge of the textiles' composition and of the chemical properties of bleaches and dyes.

Dissolves dye or bleaching chemicals in water. Tests dye on swatch of fabric to ensure color match. Examines article to identify fabric and original dye by observing or touching, or by testing sample with fire or chemical reagent. Measures and mixes amounts of bleaches, dyes, oils, and acids, following formulas. Sprays or brushes article with prepared solution to remove stains. Operates or directs operation of extractor and drier. Applies dye to article, using spray gun, electrically rotated brush, or handbrush. Rinses article in water and acetic acid solution to remove excess dye and to fix colors. Immerses article in dye solution and stirs with stick, or dyes article in rotary-drum or paddle dyeing machine. Matches sample color, applying knowledge of bleaching agent and dye properties, and type, construction, condition, and color of article. Immerses article in bleaching bath to strip colors.

GOE Number, Interest Area, and Work Group: 11.06.01; Recreation, Travel, and Other Personal Services; Apparel, Shoes, Leather, and Fabric Care. **Personality Type:** Realistic. Realistic occupations frequently involve work activities that include practical, hands-on problems and solutions. These occupations often deal with plants, animals, and real-world materials like wood, tools, and machinery. Many of the occupations require working outside and do not involve a lot of paperwork or working closely with others. **Work Values:** Moral Values; Independence; Security; Supervision, Technical; Supervision, Human Relations; Activity. **Skills:** Product Inspection; Science; Solution Appraisal;

Equipment Selection; Reading Comprehension; Idea Evaluation. **Abilities:** *Cognitive*—Information Ordering; Deductive Reasoning; Memorization; Category Flexibility; Inductive Reasoning. *Psychomotor*—Control Precision. *Physical*—Extent Flexibility; Trunk Strength; Gross Body Coordination. *Sensory*—Visual Color Discrimination. **General Work Activities:** *Information Input*—Getting Information Needed to Do the Job; Identifying Objects, Actions, and Events; Monitoring Processes, Materials, and Surroundings; Inspecting Equipment, Structures, Materials. *Mental Process*—Analyzing Data or Information; Judging Qualities of Things, Services, Other People's Work; Making Decisions and Solving Problems. *Work Output*—Handling and Moving Objects; Controlling Machines and Processes; Implementing Ideas and Programs. *Interacting with Others*—Monitoring and Controlling Resources; Communicating with Other Workers; Coordinating Work and Activities of Others; Establishing and Maintaining Relationships. **Physical Work Conditions:** Indoors; Standing; Using Hands on Objects, Tools, or Controls. **Other Job Characteristics:** Importance of Being Exact or Accurate; Importance of Being Sure All Is Done; Consequence of Error.

Experience: Job Zone 3. Previous work-related skill, knowledge, or experience is required. **Job Preparation:** SVP 6.0 to less than 7.0—More than 1 year and less than 4 years. **Knowledge:** Chemistry; Production and Processing; Mechanical; Mathematics; English Language; Physics. **Instructional Program:** 200309 Drycleaner and Launderer (Commercial).

Related DOT Jobs: 364.361-010 Dyer; 364.361-014 Rug Dyer I; 364.684-010 Rug Dyer II.

51-6011.03 Laundry and Drycleaning Machine Operators and Tenders, Except Pressing (Laundry and Dry-Cleaning Machine Operators)

Education: Moderate-term O-T-J training

Employed: 167,423

Openings: 38,082

Projected Growth: 9.8%

Earnings: $14,670

Operate or tend washing or dry-cleaning machines to wash or dry-clean commercial, industrial, or household articles such as cloth garments, suede, leather, furs, blankets, draperies, fine linens, rugs, and carpets.

Starts washer, dry cleaner, drier, or extractor, and turns valves or levers to regulate and monitor cleaning or drying operations. Examines and sorts articles to be cleaned into lots, according to color, fabric, dirt content, and cleaning technique required. Mixes and adds detergents, dyes, bleach, starch, and other solutions and chemicals to clean, color, dry, or stiffen articles. Loads or directs other workers to load articles into washer or dry cleaning machine. Starts pumps to operate distilling system that drains and reclaims dry cleaning solvents. Cleans machine filters and lubricates equipment. Washes, dry cleans, or glazes delicate articles or fur-garment linings by hand, using mild detergent or dry-cleaning solutions. Presoaks, sterilizes, scrubs, spot-cleans, and dries contaminated or stained articles, using neutralizer solutions and portable machines. Sorts and counts articles removed from dryer;

folds, wraps, or hangs items for airing out, for pickup, or for delivery. Receives and marks articles for laundry or dry cleaning with identifying code number or name, using hand or machine marker. Irons or presses articles, fabrics, and furs, using hand iron or pressing machine. Hangs curtains, drapes, blankets, pants, and other garments on stretch frames to dry, and transports items between specified locations. Mends and sews articles, using hand stitching, adhesive patch, or power sewing machine. Adjusts switches to tend and regulate equipment that fumigates and removes foreign matter from furs. Tends variety of automatic machines that comb and polish furs. Removes or directs other workers to remove items from washer or dry-cleaning machine and into extractor or tumbler.

GOE Number, Interest Area, and Work Group: 11.06.01; Recreation, Travel, and Other Personal Services; Apparel, Shoes, Leather, and Fabric Care. **Personality Type:** Realistic. Realistic occupations frequently involve work activities that include practical, hands-on problems and solutions. These occupations often deal with plants, animals, and real-world materials like wood, tools, and machinery. Many of the occupations require working outside and do not involve a lot of paperwork or working closely with others. **Work Values:** Moral Values; Company Policies and Practices; Activity; Supervision, Human Relations; Security; Independence; Supervision, Technical. **Skills:** Operation and Control; Operation Monitoring; Product Inspection; Equipment Maintenance; Mathematics. **Abilities:** *Cognitive*—Information Ordering; Category Flexibility; Problem Sensitivity; Time Sharing; Oral Expression. *Psychomotor*—Manual Dexterity; Arm-Hand Steadiness; Control Precision. *Physical*—Trunk Strength; Extent Flexibility; Gross Body Coordination; Static Strength; Dynamic Strength. *Sensory*—Visual Color Discrimination; Depth Perception; Peripheral Vision. **General Work Activities:** *Information Input*—Monitoring Processes, Materials, and Surroundings; Identifying Objects, Actions, and Events; Getting Information Needed to Do the Job. *Mental Process*—Judging Qualities of Things, Services, Other People's Work; Making Decisions and Solving Problems; Organizing, Planning, and Prioritizing. *Work Output*—Controlling Machines and Processes; Handling and Moving Objects; Performing General Physical Activities. *Interacting with Others*—Communicating with Other Workers; Guiding, Directing and Motivating Subordinates; Coordinating Work and Activities of Others. **Physical Work Conditions:** Indoors; Using Hands on Objects, Tools, or Controls; Hazardous Equipment; Standing. **Other Job Characteristics:** Degree of Automation; Consequence of Error; Pace Determined by Speed of Equipment; Frustrating Circumstances; Importance of Being Sure All Is Done.

Experience: Job Zone 1. No previous work-related skill, knowledge, or experience is needed. **Job Preparation:** SVP Below 4.0—Less than 6 months. **Knowledge:** Customer and Personal Service; Mechanical; Chemistry; Mathematics; Production and Processing; Clerical. **Instructional Programs:** 200301 Clothing, Apparel and Textile Workers and Managers, General; 200309 Drycleaner and Launderer (Commercial).

Related DOT Jobs: 361.665-010 Washer, Machine; 361.682-010 Rug Cleaner, Machine; 361.684-010 Launderer, Hand; 361.684-014 Laundry Worker I; 361.685-014 Continuous-Towel Roller; 361.685-018 Laundry Worker II; 362.382-010 Dry-Cleaner Apprentice; 362.382-014 Dry Cleaner; 362.684-014 Fur Cleaner; 362.684-026 Leather Cleaner; 362.685-010 Feather Renovator; 369.684-014 Laundry Operator; 369.685-010 Fur Blower; 369.685-014 Fur Cleaner, Machine; 369.685-022 Fur-Glazing-and-Polishing-Machine Operator; 589.685-038 Dry Cleaner.

51-6021.00 Pressers, Textile, Garment, and Related Materials (Pressers, Hand)

Education:	Short-term O-T-J training
Employed:	13,467
Openings:	2,003
Projected Growth:	–11.4%
Earnings:	$14,750

Press or shape articles by hand or machine.

GOE Number, Interest Area, and Work Group: 11.06.01; Recreation, Travel, and Other Personal Services; Apparel, Shoes, Leather, and Fabric Care. **Instructional Programs:** 200301 Clothing, Apparel and Textile Workers and Managers, General; 200309 Drycleaner and Launderer (Commercial). **Note:** The Department of Labor has not collected some data for this job, so it has fewer details than the other descriptions.

51-6021.01 Pressers, Delicate Fabrics (Pressers, Delicate Fabrics)

Education:	No data available.
Employed:	24,580
Openings:	No data available.
Projected Growth:	No data available.
Earnings:	$15,460

Press dry-cleaned and wet-cleaned silk and synthetic-fiber garments by hand or machine, applying knowledge of fabrics and heat to produce high-quality finish. Finish pleated or fancy garments, by hand.

Inserts heated metal form into tie and touches up rough places with hand iron. Finishes velvet garments by steaming them on buck of hot-head press or steamtable and by brushing pile (nap) with handbrush. Finishes fancy garments with hand iron to produce high-quality finishes which cannot be obtained on machine presses. Finishes pleated garments, determining size of pleat from evidence of old pleat or from work order, using machine press or hand iron. Operates machine presses to finish parts that can be pressed flat and completes other parts by pressing with hand iron. Finishes parts that are difficult to reach, such as flounces, by fitting parts over puff irons. Presses ties on small pressing machine.

GOE Number, Interest Area, and Work Group: 11.06.01; Recreation, Travel, and Other Personal Services; Apparel, Shoes, Leather, and Fabric Care. **Personality Type:** Realistic. Realistic occupations frequently involve work activities that include practical, hands-on problems and solutions. These occupations often deal with plants, animals, and real-world materials like wood, tools, and machinery. Many of the occupations require working outside and do not involve a lot of paperwork or working closely with others. **Work Values:** Moral Values; Independence; Security; Activity; Supervision, Technical. **Skills:** Product Inspection. **Abilities:** *Cognitive*—Category Flexibility; Information Ordering; Written Comprehension; Visualization; Selective Attention; Perceptual Speed. *Psychomotor*—Manual Dexterity; Arm-Hand Steadiness; Reaction Time. *Physical*—Dynamic Flexibility; Explosive Strength; Dynamic Strength. *Sensory*—Visual Color Discrimination; Depth Perception; Glare Sensitivity. **General Work Activities:** *Information Input*—Getting Information Needed to Do the Job; Monitoring Processes, Materials, and Surroundings; Inspecting Equipment, Structures, Materials. *Mental Process*—Analyzing Data or Information; Judging Qualities of Things, Services, Other People's Work; Evaluating Information Against Standards. *Work Output*—Handling and Moving Objects; Controlling Machines and Processes; Performing General Physical Activities. *Interacting with Others*—Monitoring and Controlling Resources; Communicating with Other Workers; Establishing and Maintaining Relationships; Assisting and Caring for Others. **Physical Work Conditions:** Indoors; Using Hands on Objects, Tools, or Controls; Standing. **Other Job Characteristics:** Degree of Automation; Importance of Being Exact or Accurate; Importance of Being Sure All Is Done.

Experience: Job Zone 2. Some previous work-related skill, knowledge, or experience may be helpful, but usually is not needed. **Job Preparation:** SVP 4.00 to 5.99—6 months to less than 2 years. **Knowledge:** Customer and Personal Service; Mechanical; Production and Processing; Fine Arts; English Language. **Instructional Programs:** 200301 Clothing, Apparel and Textile Workers and Managers, General; 200309 Drycleaner and Launderer (Commercial).

Related DOT Job: 363.681-010 Silk Finisher.

51-6021.02 Pressing Machine Operators and Tenders—Textile, Garment, and Related Materials
(Pressing Machine Operators and Tenders, Textile, Garment, and Related Materials)

Education: Moderate-term O-T-J training

Employed: 68,791

Openings: 10,249

Projected Growth: –4%

Earnings: $15,140

Operate or tend pressing machines such as hot-head pressing, steam pressing, automatic pressing, ironing, plunger pressing, and hydraulic pressing machines, to press and shape articles such as leather, fur, and cloth garments, drapes, slipcovers, handkerchiefs, and millinery.

Hangs, folds, packages, and tags finished articles for delivery to customer. Lowers iron, ram, or pressing head of machine into position over material to be pressed. Positions materials such as cloth garments, felt, or straw on table, die, or feeding mechanism of pressing machine. Examines and measures finished articles to verify conformance to standards, using measuring devices, including tape measure and micrometer. Sews end of new material to leader or to end of material in pressing machine, using sewing machine. Applies cleaning solvents, and brushes materials made of suede, leather, and felt, to remove spots and to raise and smooth nap. Activates and adjusts machine controls to regulate tempera-

ture and pressure of rollers, ironing shoe, or plates, according to specifications. Cleans and maintains pressing machines, using cleaning solutions and lubricants. Presses materials such as garments, drapes, and slipcovers, using hand iron. Moistens materials to soften; smoothes and straightens materials with hands, to prepare for machine pressing. Removes finished pieces from pressing machine, hangs or stacks for cooling, or forwards for additional processing. Selects, installs, and adjusts machine components, including pressing forms, rollers, and guides, according to pressing instructions, using hoist and hand tools. Activates pressing machine to remove wrinkles from garments and flatwork items or to shape, form, or patch articles. Shrinks, stretches, or blocks articles by hand, to conform to original measurements, using forms, blocks, and steam.

GOE Number, Interest Area, and Work Group: 08.03.02; Industrial Production; Production Work: Equipment Operation, Assorted Materials Processing. **Personality Type:** Realistic. Realistic occupations frequently involve work activities that include practical, hands-on problems and solutions. These occupations often deal with plants, animals, and real-world materials like wood, tools, and machinery. Many of the occupations require working outside and do not involve a lot of paperwork or working closely with others. **Work Values:** Moral Values; Independence; Company Policies and Practices; Activity; Supervision, Human Relations. **Skills:** Product Inspection; Operation and Control; Operation Monitoring; Problem Identification; Equipment Selection. **Abilities:** *Cognitive*—Information Ordering; Selective Attention; Visualization; Deductive Reasoning; Flexibility of Closure; Number Facility. *Psychomotor*—Arm-Hand Steadiness; Control Precision; Manual Dexterity. *Physical*—Extent Flexibility; Static Strength; Trunk Strength. *Sensory*—Visual Color Discrimination; Sound Localization. **General Work Activities:** *Information Input*—Getting Information Needed to Do the Job; Monitoring Processes, Materials, and Surroundings; Inspecting Equipment, Structures, Materials. *Mental Process*—Evaluating Information Against Standards; Judging Qualities of Things, Services, Other People's Work; Processing Information. *Work Output*—Handling and Moving Objects; Controlling Machines and Processes; Performing General Physical Activities. *Interacting with Others*—Communicating with Other Workers; Coordinating Work and Activities of Others; Monitoring and Controlling Resources; Coaching and Developing Others; Resolving Conflict and Negotiating with Others; Establishing and Maintaining Relationships. **Physical Work Conditions:** Indoors; Using Hands on Objects, Tools, or Controls; Hazardous Situations. **Other Job Characteristics:** Degree of Automation; Frustrating Circumstances; Importance of Repeating Same Tasks.

Experience: Job Zone 1. No previous work-related skill, knowledge, or experience is needed. **Job Preparation:** SVP Below 4.0—Less than 6 months. **Knowledge:** Chemistry; Customer and Personal Service; Mechanical; Production and Processing; Physics. **Instructional Programs:** 200301 Clothing, Apparel and Textile Workers and Managers, General; 200309 Drycleaner and Launderer (Commercial).

Related DOT Jobs: 361.685-022 Patching-Machine Operator; 363.682-010 Leather Finisher; 363.682-014 Presser, All-Around; 363.682-018 Presser, Machine; 363.684-010 Blocker; 363.684-014 Hat Blocker; 363.685-010 Press Operator; 363.685-014 Presser,

Automatic; 363.685-018 Presser, Form; 363.685-022 Presser, Handkerchief; 363.685-026 Shirt Presser; 369.685-018 Fur Ironer; 580.685-042 Molder; 583.585-010 Calender-Machine Operator; 583.685-018 Brim Presser I; 583.685-022 Brim-and-Crown Presser; 583.685-050 Hat-Lining Blocker; 583.685-054 Hydraulic-Press Operator; 583.685-058 Hydraulic-Press Operator; 583.685-070 Mangler (partial list; see the introduction for sources of the complete list).

51-6021.03 Pressers, Hand (Pressers, Hand)

Education: Short-term O-T-J training

Employed: 13,467

Openings: 2,003

Projected Growth: –11.4%

Earnings: $14,750

Press articles to remove wrinkles, flatten seams, and give shape, using hand iron. Press drapes, knit goods, millinery parts, parachutes, garments, slip covers, and textiles such as lace, rayon, and silk. Block (shape) knitted garments after cleaning. Press leather goods.

Sprays water over fabric to soften fibers when not using steam iron. Measures fabric to specifications, cuts uneven edges with shears, folds material, and presses with iron to form heading. Smoothes and shapes fabric prior to pressing. Pins, folds, and hangs article after pressing. Places article in position on ironing board or worktable. Fits odd-shaped pieces which cannot be pressed flat over puff iron. Pushes and pulls iron over surface of article, according to type of fabric. Adjusts temperature of iron, according to fabric type; uses covering cloths to prevent scorching or sheen on delicate fabrics.

GOE Number, Interest Area, and Work Group: 11.06.01; Recreation, Travel, and Other Personal Services; Apparel, Shoes, Leather, and Fabric Care. Personality Type: Realistic. Realistic occupations frequently involve work activities that include practical, hands-on problem¶s and solutions. These occupations often deal with plants, animals, and real-world materials like wood, tools, and machinery. Many of the occupations require working outside and do not involve a lot of paperwork or working closely with others. Work Values: Moral Values; Independence; Activity; Security; Company Policies and Practices; Supervision, Human Relations. Skills: Product Inspection. Abilities: *Cognitive*—Selective Attention; Visualization; Information Ordering; Deductive Reasoning; Written Comprehension; Perceptual Speed. *Psychomotor*—Manual Dexterity; Multilimb Coordination; Wrist-Finger Speed. *Physical*—Trunk Strength; Dynamic Strength. *Sensory*—Depth Perception; Visual Color Discrimination; Glare Sensitivity. General Work Activities: *Information Input*—Getting Information Needed to Do the Job; Inspecting Equipment, Structures, Materials; Monitoring Processes, Materials, and Surroundings. *Mental Process*—Analyzing Data or Information; Judging Qualities of Things, Services, Other People's Work; Evaluating Information Against Standards; Making Decisions and Solving Problems. *Work Output*—Handling and Moving Objects; Performing General Physical Activities; Controlling Machines and Processes. *Interacting with Others*—Monitoring and Controlling Resources; Communicating with Other Workers; Establishing and

Maintaining Relationships. Physical Work Conditions: Indoors; Using Hands on Objects, Tools, or Controls; Hazardous Situations; Standing. Other Job Characteristics: Importance of Being Sure All Is Done; Degree of Automation; Consequence of Error.

Experience: Job Zone 1. No previous work-related skill, knowledge, or experience is needed. Job Preparation: SVP Below 4.0—Less than 6 months. Knowledge: Mathematics; Customer and Personal Service; Mechanical; Production and Processing; Engineering and Technology. Instructional Programs: 200301 Clothing, Apparel and Textile Workers and Managers, General; 200309 Drycleaner and Launderer (Commercial).

Related DOT Jobs: 363.684-018 Presser, Hand; 781.684-030 Drapery-Head Former.

51-6031.00 Sewing Machine Operators (Sewing Machine Operators, Garment)

Education: Moderate-term O-T-J training

Employed: 368,701

Openings: 42,318

Projected Growth: –30.3%

Earnings: $14,740

Operate or tend sewing machines to join, reinforce, decorate, or perform related sewing operations in the manufacture of garment or nongarment products.

GOE Number, Interest Area, and Work Group: 08.03.01; Industrial Production; Production Work: Machine Work, Assorted Materials. Instructional Programs: 200301 Clothing, Apparel and Textile Workers and Managers, General; 200303 Commercial Garment and Apparel Worker. Note: The Department of Labor has not collected some data for this job, so it has fewer details than the other descriptions.

51-6031.01 Sewing Machine Operators, Garment (Sewing Machine Operators, Garment)

Education: Moderate-term O-T-J training

Employed: 368,701

Openings: 42,318

Projected Growth: –30.3%

Earnings: $14,740

Operate or tend sewing machines to perform garment-sewing operations such as joining, reinforcing, or decorating garments or garment parts.

Replaces sewing machine parts and performs basic maintenance such as oiling machine. Draws thread through guides, tensions, and needles; adjusts machine functions, according to fabric type. Turns knobs, screws, and dials to adjust settings of machine, according to garment style and observation of operation. Sews replacement parts or missing stitches, according to repair tickets. Observes sewing machine operation to detect defects in stitching or machine malfunction; notifies supervisor. Attaches buttons or fasteners to fabric, using feeding hopper or clamp holder. Folds or stretches edges or length of items, while sewing, to facilitate forming specified sections. Attaches tape, trim, or elastic to specified garments or garment parts, according to item specifications. Positions item under needle, using marks on machine, clamp, template, edges of cloth, or markings on cloth as guides. Removes holding devices and finished item from machine. Starts and operates or tends machines that automatically join, reinforce, or decorate material or fabricated articles. Bastes edges of material to align and temporarily secure garment parts for final assembly. Replaces and rethreads needles. Positions material or article in clamps, template, or hoop frame prior to automatic operation of machine. Guides garment or garment parts under machine needle and presser foot to sew parts together. Records number of garment parts or number of complete garments sewn. Inspects garments and examines repair tags and markings on garment to locate defects or damage. Cuts material and threads, using scissors. Draws markings, or pins applique on fabric, to obtain variation in design; marks stitching errors with pins or tape. Selects supplies such as fasteners and thread, according to specifications or characteristics of fabric.

GOE Number, Interest Area, and Work Group: 08.03.01; Industrial Production; Production Work: Machine Work, Assorted Materials. **Personality Type:** Realistic. Realistic occupations frequently involve work activities that include practical, hands-on problems and solutions. These occupations often deal with plants, animals, and real-world materials like wood, tools, and machinery. Many of the occupations require working outside and do not involve a lot of paperwork or working closely with others. **Work Values:** Moral Values; Activity; Company Policies and Practices; Supervision, Human Relations; Independence. **Skills:** Equipment Selection; Operation and Control; Product Inspection; Repairing; Problem Identification; Operation Monitoring; Equipment Maintenance; Monitoring. **Abilities:** *Cognitive*—Information Ordering; Visualization; Problem Sensitivity; Perceptual Speed; Deductive Reasoning; Spatial Orientation. *Psychomotor*—Arm-Hand Steadiness; Manual Dexterity; Control Precision. *Physical*—Extent Flexibility; Dynamic Flexibility; Gross Body Coordination; Dynamic Strength. *Sensory*—Near Vision; Visual Color Discrimination; Hearing Sensitivity. **General Work Activities:** *Information Input*—Inspecting Equipment, Structures, Materials; Monitoring Processes, Materials, and Surroundings; Getting Information Needed to Do the Job. *Mental Process*—Judging Qualities of Things, Services, Other People's Work; Evaluating Information Against Standards; Thinking Creatively. *Work Output*—Handling and Moving Objects; Controlling Machines and Processes; Repairing and Maintaining Mechanical Equipment. *Interacting with Others*—Communicating with Other Workers; Monitoring and Controlling Resources; Performing Administrative Activities. **Physical Work Conditions:** Indoors; Using Hands on Objects, Tools, or Controls; Sitting. **Other Job Characteristics:** Degree of Automation; Importance of Repeating Same Tasks; Importance of Being Sure All Is Done.

Experience: Job Zone 1. No previous work-related skill, knowledge, or experience is needed. **Job Preparation:** SVP Below 4.0— Less than 6 months. **Knowledge:** Production and Processing; Mechanical; English Language; Mathematics; Clerical; Engineering and Technology. **Instructional Programs:** 200301 Clothing, Apparel and Textile Workers and Managers, General; 200303 Commercial Garment and Apparel Worker.

Related DOT Jobs: 684.682-014 Sewer and Inspector; 689.685-150 Watcher, Automat; 689.685-154 Watcher, Pantograph; 784.682-010 Glove Sewer; 784.682-014 Hat-and-Cap Sewer; 784.685-014 Brim Stitcher I; 786.682-010 Appliquer, Zigzag; 786.682-014 Armhole Baster, Jumpbasting; 786.682-018 Armhole Feller, Handstitching Machine; 786.682-022 Armhole-Sew-and-Trim Operator, Lockstitch; 786.682-026 Back Maker, Lockstitch; 786.682-030 Basting-Machine Operator; 786.682-034 Binder, Chainstitch; 786.682-038 Binder, Coverstitch; 786.682-042 Binder, Lockstitch; 786.682-046 Blindstitch-Machine Operator; 786.682-050 Canvas Baster, Jumpbasting; 786.682-054 Chainstitch Sewing Machine Operator; 786.682-058 Coat Joiner, Lockstitch; 786.682-062 Collar Baster, Jumpbasting (partial list; see the introduction for sources of the complete list).

51-6031.02 Sewing Machine Operators, Non-Garment
(Sewing Machine Operators, Non-Garment)

Education: Moderate-term O-T-J training

Employed: 136,689

Openings: 19,074

Projected Growth: 2.5%

Earnings: $16,990

Operate or tend sewing machines to join together, reinforce, decorate, or perform related sewing operations on nongarment products such as upholstery, draperies, linens, carpets, and mattresses.

Sews materials by hand, using needle and thread. Positions and marks patterns on materials to prepare for sewing. Activates sewing machine to join, gather, hem, reinforce, or decorate materials or fabricated articles such as linens, toys, or luggage. Monitors machine operation to detect problems such as defective stitching, breaks in thread, or machine malfunction. Mounts attachments such as needles, cutting blades, or pattern plates; adjusts machine guides according to specifications. Folds or fits together materials such as cloth, foam rubber, or leather, to prepare for machine sewing. Cuts materials, according to specifications. Cuts excess material or thread from finished product, using blade, scissors, or electric knife. Replaces needles, sands rough areas of needles with sandpaper, and cleans and oils sewing machines to maintain equipment. Tapes or twists together thread or cord to repair breaks. Records amount of materials processed, in production logs. Selects supplies such as binding, cord, or thread, according to specifications or color of material. Places spools of thread, cord, or other materials on spindles; inserts bobbin; threads ends through machine guides and components. Examines and measures finished articles to verify conformance to standards, using ruler. Positions materials through feed rollers and guides, or positions and maneuvers under sewing machine presser foot and needle during operation. Activates and adjusts machine controls to regulate stitching speed and length, dimensions of gathers and tucks, and material or thread tension. Removes finished materials from sewing machine.

GOE Number, Interest Area, and Work Group: 08.03.01; Industrial Production; Production Work: Machine Work, Assorted Materials. **Personality Type:** Realistic. Realistic occupations frequently involve work activities that include practical, hands-on problems and solutions. These occupations often deal with plants, animals, and real-world materials like wood, tools, and machinery. Many of the occupations require working outside and do not involve a lot of paperwork or working closely with others. **Work Values:** Moral Values; Activity; Independence; Company Policies and Practices; Supervision, Human Relations. **Skills:** Product Inspection; Operation and Control; Operation Monitoring; Equipment Maintenance. **Abilities:** *Cognitive*—Visualization; Problem Sensitivity; Information Ordering; Memorization; Perceptual Speed; Deductive Reasoning. *Psychomotor*—Manual Dexterity; Arm-Hand Steadiness; Finger Dexterity; Control Precision. *Physical*—Trunk Strength; Extent Flexibility; Static Strength; Dynamic Strength. *Sensory*—Near Vision; Visual Color Discrimination; Depth Perception. **General Work Activities:** *Information Input*—Monitoring Processes, Materials, and Surroundings; Getting Information Needed to Do the Job; Inspecting Equipment, Structures, Materials. *Mental Process*—Evaluating Information Against Standards; Making Decisions and Solving Problems; Judging Qualities of Things, Services, Other People's Work; Organizing, Planning, and Prioritizing. *Work Output*—Handling and Moving Objects; Controlling Machines and Processes; Implementing Ideas and Programs. *Interacting with Others*—Performing Administrative Activities; Monitoring and Controlling Resources; Communicating with Other Workers; Coordinating Work and Activities of Others. **Physical Work Conditions:** Indoors; Using Hands on Objects, Tools, or Controls; Sitting. **Other Job Characteristics:** Degree of Automation; Importance of Being Sure All Is Done; Importance of Being Exact or Accurate.

Experience: Job Zone 1. No previous work-related skill, knowledge, or experience is needed. **Job Preparation:** SVP Below 4.0—Less than 6 months. **Knowledge:** Mechanical; Production and Processing; Engineering and Technology; Mathematics; Design; Clerical. **Instructional Programs:** 200501 Home Furnishings and Equipment Installers and Consultants, General; 200502 Window Treatment Maker and Installer.

Related DOT Jobs: 689.662-014 Stripe Matcher; 689.682-018 Splicing-Machine Operator; 689.682-022 Stitcher; 689.685-026 Bouffant-Curtain-Machine Tender; 689.685-106 Quilting-Machine Operator; 689.685-118 Sewing-Machine Operator, Special Equipment; 689.685-126 Stitch-Bonding-Machine Tender; 692.685-254 Window-Shade-Ring Sewer; 731.685-010 Rooter Operator; 780.682-010 Sewing-Machine Operator; 780.682-014 Slip-Cover Sewer; 780.682-018 Upholstery Sewer; 782.687-046 Sack Repairer; 783.682-010 Fur-Machine Operator; 783.682-014 Sewing Machine Operator; 787.682-010 Binder; 787.682-014 Carpet Sewer; 787.682-018 Drapery Operator; 787.682-026 Hemmer; 787.682-034 Overedge Sewer (partial list; see the introduction for sources of the complete list).

51-6041.00 Shoe and Leather Workers and Repairers
(Shoe and Leather Workers and Repairers, Precision)

Education: Long-term O-T-J training
Employed: 22,803
Openings: 1,677
Projected Growth: –17.6%
Earnings: $16,610

Construct, decorate, or repair leather and leather-like products such as luggage, shoes, and saddles.

Drills or punches holes and inserts metal rings, handles, and hardware. Reads prescription or specifications; measures item, using calipers, tape measures, or rule. Sews rips or patches holes, by hand or machine, to repair articles such as purses, shoes, and luggage. Attaches accessories or ornamentation to decorate or protect product. Selects material and cuts parts along pattern or outline, with knife, shears, or scissors. Repairs and reconditions products such as trunks, luggage, shoes, and saddles. Assembles product according to specifications, utilizing sewing machine, needle and thread, or leather lacing, glue, clamps, or rivets. Trims and buffs, bevels, or flares workpiece to specified size and shape. Aligns, and stitches or glues, materials such as fabric, fleece, leather, or wood, to join parts. Inspects article for defects and removes damaged or worn parts, using hand tools. Inserts and positions padding, foam cushioning, or lining; glues or stitches into place. Fabricates articles such as purses, wallets, belts, luggage frames, and shoes. Dyes, soaks, paints, stamps, or engraves leather or other materials to obtain desired effect or shape. Draws pattern, using measurements, plaster cast, or customer specifications; positions or outlines pattern on workpiece.

GOE Number, Interest Area, and Work Group: 11.06.01; Recreation, Travel, and Other Personal Services; Apparel, Shoes, Leather, and Fabric Care. **Personality Type:** Realistic. Realistic occupations frequently involve work activities that include practical, hands-on problems and solutions. These occupations often deal with plants, animals, and real-world materials like wood, tools, and machinery. Many of the occupations require working outside and do not involve a lot of paperwork or working closely with others. **Work Values:** Moral Values; Independence; Ability Utilization; Autonomy; Working Conditions; Achievement. **Skills:** Product Inspection; Problem Identification; Information Gathering; Operations Analysis; Critical Thinking; Mathematics; Operation and Control; Reading Comprehension. **Abilities:** *Cognitive*—Written Comprehension; Information Ordering; Visualization; Number Facility; Mathematical Reasoning; Category Flexibility. *Psychomotor*—Arm-Hand Steadiness; Wrist-Finger Speed; Finger Dexterity. *Physical*—Extent Flexibility; Static Strength; Stamina. *Sensory*—Near Vision; Visual Color Discrimination. **General Work Activities:** *Information Input*—Inspecting Equipment, Structures, Materials; Getting Information Needed to Do the Job; Monitoring Processes, Materials, and Surroundings. *Mental Process*—Evaluating Information Against Standards; Judging Qualities of Things, Services, Other People's Work; Processing Information; Making Decisions and Solving Problems. *Work Output*—Handling and Moving Objects; Controlling Machines and Processes; Drafting and Specifying Technical Devices. *Interacting with Others*—Communicating with Persons Outside Organization; Performing for or Working with the Public; Communicating with Other Workers; Monitoring and Controlling Resources; Establishing and Maintaining Relationships. **Physical Work Conditions:** Indoors; Using Hands on Objects, Tools, or Controls; Sitting. **Other Job Characteristics:** Importance of Being Sure All Is Done; Consequence of Error; Importance of Being Exact or Accurate; Importance of Repeating Same Tasks.

Experience: Job Zone 2. Some previous work-related skill, knowledge, or experience may be helpful, but usually is not needed.

Job Preparation: SVP 4.00 to 5.99—6 months to less than 2 years. **Knowledge:** Design; Production and Processing; Fine Arts; Mechanical; Chemistry. **Instructional Programs:** 480304 Shoe, Boot and Leather Repairer; 480399 Leatherworkers and Upholsterers, Other.

Related DOT Jobs: 365.361-010 Luggage Repairer; 365.361-014 Shoe Repairer; 739.684-114 Last-Repairer Helper; 753.381-010 Bootmaker, Hand; 753.684-026 Repairer; 780.381-030 Pad Hand; 781.381-018 Leather Stamper; 783.361-010 Custom-Leather-Products Maker; 783.381-018 Harness Maker; 783.381-022 Luggage Maker; 783.381-026 Saddle Maker; 788.261-010 Orthopedic-Boot-and-Shoe Designer and Maker; 788.381-010 Cobbler; 788.381-014 Shoemaker, Custom; 788.684-046 Finger Cobbler; 788.684-098 Sample Shoe Inspector and Reworker.

51-6042.00 Shoe Machine Operators and Tenders
(Shoe Machine Operators and Tenders)

Education: Moderate-term O-T-J training

Employed: 6,506

Openings: 722

Projected Growth: −35.8%

Earnings: $16,230

Operate or tend a variety of machines to join, decorate, reinforce, or finish shoes and shoe parts.

Selects and places spools of thread or prewound bobbins into shuttles or onto spindles or loupers of stitching machines. Selects and inserts specified cassettes into consoles of stitching machine to stitch decorative designs onto shoe parts. Guides shoe into feeding mechanism that attaches, stitches, joins, or reinforces shoe parts, according to instructions. Cuts excess thread or material from shoe part, using scissors or knife. Removes and examines shoe parts and design to verify conformance to specifications. Aligns parts to be stitched, following seams, edges, or markings; positions parts under needle. Lowers pressure foot or roller to secure parts and starts machine stitching, using hand, foot, or knee controls. Draws thread through machine guide slots and needles. Turns setscrew on needle bar and positions required number of needles in designated stitching machines. Reads shoe part tags to identify appropriate instruction cassette and style and color of thread.

GOE Number, Interest Area, and Work Group: 08.03.01; Industrial Production; Production Work: Machine Work, Assorted Materials. **Personality Type:** Realistic. Realistic occupations frequently involve work activities that include practical, hands-on problems and solutions. These occupations often deal with plants, animals, and real-world materials like wood, tools, and machinery. Many of the occupations require working outside and do not involve a lot of paperwork or working closely with others. **Work Values:** Moral Values; Independence; Activity; Company Policies and Practices; Supervision, Human Relations. **Skills:** Product Inspection; Operation and Control; Reading Comprehension; Operation Monitoring; Equipment Selection. **Abilities:** *Cognitive—* Problem Sensitivity; Visualization; Written Comprehension; Information Ordering; Number Facility; Deductive Reasoning. *Psychomotor—*Finger Dexterity; Arm-Hand Steadiness; Manual

Dexterity. *Physical—*Dynamic Strength; Explosive Strength. *Sensory—*Visual Color Discrimination; Glare Sensitivity. **General Work Activities:** *Information Input—*Getting Information Needed to Do the Job; Inspecting Equipment, Structures, Materials; Monitoring Processes, Materials, and Surroundings. *Mental Process—* Evaluating Information Against Standards; Judging Qualities of Things, Services, Other People's Work; Analyzing Data or Information. *Work Output—*Handling and Moving Objects; Controlling Machines and Processes; Performing General Physical Activities. *Interacting with Others—*Communicating with Other Workers; Performing Administrative Activities; Establishing and Maintaining Relationships. **Physical Work Conditions:** Indoors; Sitting; Using Hands on Objects, Tools, or Controls. **Other Job Characteristics:** Degree of Automation; Importance of Being Sure All Is Done; Importance of Repeating Same Tasks.

Experience: Job Zone 1. No previous work-related skill, knowledge, or experience is needed. **Job Preparation:** SVP Below 4.0— Less than 6 months. **Knowledge:** Production and Processing; Mechanical; Engineering and Technology; English Language; Mathematics; Computers and Electronics. **Instructional Program:** 480304 Shoe, Boot and Leather Repairer.

Related DOT Jobs: 690.682-078 Stitcher, Special Machine; 690.682-082 Stitcher, Standard Machine; 690.685-494 Stitcher, Tape-Controlled Machine; 788.684-114 Thread Laster.

51-6051.00 Sewers, Hand (Sewers, Hand)

Education: Short-term O-T-J training

Employed: 9,790

Openings: 813

Projected Growth: −14.8%

Earnings: $15,520

Sew, join, reinforce, or finish, usually with needle and thread, a variety of manufactured items. Includes weavers and stitchers.

Waxes thread by drawing it through ball of wax. Selects thread, twine, cord, or yarn; threads needles. Joins and reinforces parts of articles such as garments, books, mattresses, toys, and wigs. Measures and aligns parts, fasteners, or trimmings, following seams, edges, or markings on parts. Attaches trimmings and labels to article with cement, using brush or cement gun. Draws and cuts pattern according to specifications. Softens leather or shoe material with water. Ties, knits, weaves, or knots ribbon, yarn, or decorative materials. Smoothes seams with heated iron, flat bone, or rubbing stick. Trims excess threads or edges of parts, using scissors or knife. Sews, using various types of stitches such as felling, tacking, basting, embroidery, and fagoting. Folds, twists, stretches, or drapes material and secures article in preparation for sewing.

GOE Number, Interest Area, and Work Group: 08.03.06; Industrial Production; Production Work: Hands-on Work, Assorted Materials. **Personality Type:** Realistic. Realistic occupations frequently involve work activities that include practical, hands-on problems and solutions. These occupations often deal with plants, animals, and real-world materials like wood, tools, and machinery. Many of the occupations require working outside and do not involve a lot of paperwork or working closely with others. **Work**

Values: Moral Values; Independence; Activity; Supervision, Human Relations; Security; Company Policies and Practices. **Skills:** Product Inspection. **Abilities:** *Cognitive*—Visualization; Information Ordering; Written Comprehension; Perceptual Speed; Selective Attention. *Psychomotor*—Arm-Hand Steadiness; Wrist-Finger Speed; Finger Dexterity. *Physical*—none met the criteria. *Sensory*—Visual Color Discrimination; Near Vision. **General Work Activities:** *Information Input*—Getting Information Needed to Do the Job; Identifying Objects, Actions, and Events; Monitoring Processes, Materials, and Surroundings; Inspecting Equipment, Structures, Materials; Estimating Needed Characteristics. *Mental Process*—Making Decisions and Solving Problems; Evaluating Information Against Standards; Analyzing Data or Information. *Work Output*—Handling and Moving Objects; Performing General Physical Activities; Controlling Machines and Processes; Implementing Ideas and Programs. *Interacting with Others*—Coordinating Work and Activities of Others; Communicating with Other Workers; Monitoring and Controlling Resources; Performing Administrative Activities. **Physical Work Conditions:** Using Hands on Objects, Tools, or Controls; Indoors; Sitting; Making Repetitive Motions. **Other Job Characteristics:** Importance of Being Sure All Is Done; Importance of Being Exact or Accurate; Importance of Repeating Same Tasks.

Experience: Job Zone 1. No previous work-related skill, knowledge, or experience is needed. **Job Preparation:** SVP Below 4.0—Less than 6 months. **Knowledge:** Production and Processing; Design; Fine Arts; Mathematics; English Language; Mechanical; Engineering and Technology. **Instructional Program:** 200301 Clothing, Apparel and Textile Workers and Managers, General.

Related DOT Jobs: 529.687-030 Casing Sewer; 732.684-034 Baseball Sewer, Hand; 732.684-050 Feather Stitcher; 732.684-090 Pelota Maker; 739.384-014 Foundation Maker; 739.684-162 Umbrella Tipper, Hand; 780.684-070 Mattress Finisher; 782.684-030 Hosiery Mender; 782.684-050 Passementerie Worker; 782.684-058 Sewer, Hand; 782.687-018 Cloth-Bale Header; 782.687-058 Thread Marker; 784.684-022 Decorator; 784.684-042 Hat Maker; 787.381-010 Lamp-Shade Sewer; 788.684-054 Hand Sewer, Shoes; 788.684-110 Sole Sewer, Hand; 789.381-010 Beadworker; 789.484-014 Finisher, Hand; 920.687-022 Bale Sewer (partial list; see the introduction for sources of the complete list).

51-6052.00 Tailors, Dressmakers, and Custom Sewers
(Custom Tailors and Sewers)

Education: Work experience in a related occupation
Employed: 73,641
Openings: 6,328
Projected Growth: –8.4%
Earnings: $18,630

Design, make, alter, repair, or fit garments.

GOE Number, Interest Area, and Work Group: 11.06.01; Recreation, Travel, and Other Personal Services; Apparel, Shoes, Leather, and Fabric Care. **Instructional Programs:** 200301 Clothing, Apparel and Textile Workers and Managers, General; 200305 Custom Tailor. **Note:** The Department of Labor has not collected some data for this job, so it has fewer details than the other descriptions.

51-6052.01 Shop and Alteration Tailors (Custom Tailors and Sewers)

Education: Work experience in a related occupation
Employed: 73,641
Openings: 6,328
Projected Growth: –8.4%
Earnings: $18,630

Make tailored garments from existing patterns. Alter, repair, or fit made-to-measure or ready-to-wear garments.

Removes stitches from garment, using ripper or razor blade. Inserts or eliminates padding in shoulders while maintaining drape and proportions of garment. Pins altering folds; marks on cloth at seams, darts, or necklines to indicate alterations to be made. Measures and marks alteration lines. Shortens or lengthens garment parts such as sleeves or legs. Examines tag on garment to ascertain necessary alterations. Fits garment on customer to determine required alterations. Repairs or replaces defective garment parts such as pockets, pocket flaps, and linings. Records required alterations and instructions. Presses garment, using hand iron or pressing machine. Raises or lowers garment parts such as collars or lapels. Resews garment, using needle and thread, or sewing machine. Expands or narrows garment parts such as waist or chest. Studies garment on customer and measures pieces such as sleeves, pants, and hems, using tape measure.

GOE Number, Interest Area, and Work Group: 11.06.01; Recreation, Travel, and Other Personal Services; Apparel, Shoes, Leather, and Fabric Care. **Personality Type:** Realistic. Realistic occupations frequently involve work activities that include practical, hands-on problems and solutions. These occupations often deal with plants, animals, and real-world materials like wood, tools, and machinery. Many of the occupations require working outside and do not involve a lot of paperwork or working closely with others. **Work Values:** Moral Values; Independence; Working Conditions; Autonomy; Ability Utilization; Activity; Security. **Skills:** Product Inspection; Mathematics; Problem Identification; Operation and Control; Operations Analysis. **Abilities:** *Cognitive*—Visualization; Number Facility; Oral Comprehension; Information Ordering; Written Comprehension. *Psychomotor*—Arm-Hand Steadiness; Finger Dexterity; Control Precision. *Physical*—none met the criteria. **General Work Activities:** *Information Input*—Getting Information Needed to Do the Job; Estimating Needed Characteristics; Identifying Objects, Actions, and Events. *Mental Process*—Judging Qualities of Things, Services, Other People's Work; Making Decisions and Solving Problems; Thinking Creatively. *Work Output*—Handling and Moving Objects; Implementing Ideas and Programs; Controlling Machines and Processes. *Interacting with Others*—Performing for or Working with the Public; Communicating with Persons Outside Organization; Communicating with Other Workers; Establishing and Maintaining Relationships; Assisting and Caring for Others. **Physical Work Conditions:** Indoors; Sitting; Using Hands on Objects, Tools, or Controls. **Other Job Characteristics:** Importance of Being Exact or Accurate; Importance of Being Sure All Is Done; Consequence of Error.

Experience: Job Zone 3. Previous work-related skill, knowledge, or experience is required. **Job Preparation:** SVP 6.0 to less than 7.0—More than 1 year and less than 4 years. **Knowledge:** Customer and Personal Service; Production and Processing; Mechanical; Mathematics; Design. **Instructional Programs:** 200301 Clothing, Apparel and Textile Workers and Managers, General; 200305 Custom Tailor.

Related DOT Jobs: 782.361-010 Corset Fitter; 785.261-010 Alteration Tailor; 785.261-018 Tailor Apprentice, Alteration; 785.361-014 Garment Fitter; 785.361-018 Sample Stitcher; 785.361-022 Shop Tailor; 785.361-026 Shop Tailor Apprentice; 969.381-010 Wardrobe-Specialty Worker.

51-6052.02 Custom Tailors (Custom Tailors and Sewers)

Education: Work experience in a related occupation

Employed: 73,641

Openings: 6,328

Projected Growth: –8.4%

Earnings: $18,630

Design or make tailored garments, applying knowledge of garment design, construction, styling, and fabrics.

Presses garment, using hand iron or pressing machine. Fits basted garment on customer and marks areas requiring alterations. Measures customer for size, using tape measure; records measurements. Confers with customer to determine type of material and garment style desired. Sews buttons and buttonholes to finish garment. Draws individual pattern or alters existing pattern to fit customer's measurements. Alters garment and joins parts, using needle and thread or sewing machine, to form finished garment. Assembles garment parts and joins parts with basting stitches, using needle and thread or sewing machine. Develops design for garment, adapts existing design for garment, or copies existing design for garment. Positions pattern of garment parts on fabric, and cuts fabric along outlines, using scissors.

GOE Number, Interest Area, and Work Group: 11.06.01; Recreation, Travel, and Other Personal Services; Apparel, Shoes, Leather, and Fabric Care. **Personality Type:** Realistic. Realistic occupations frequently involve work activities that include practical, hands-on problems and solutions. These occupations often deal with plants, animals, and real-world materials like wood, tools, and machinery. Many of the occupations require working outside and do not involve a lot of paperwork or working closely with others. **Work Values:** Moral Values; Autonomy; Working Conditions; Ability Utilization; Responsibility; Independence. **Skills:** Product Inspection; Mathematics; Equipment Selection; Active Listening; Operation and Control. **Abilities:** *Cognitive*—Originality; Visualization; Information Ordering; Oral Comprehension; Fluency of Ideas; Number Facility. *Psychomotor*—Arm-Hand Steadiness; Finger Dexterity. *Physical*—none met the criteria. **General Work Activities:** *Information Input*—Getting Information Needed to Do the Job; Estimating Needed Characteristics; Identifying Objects, Actions, and Events; Inspecting Equipment, Structures, Materials. *Mental Process*—Thinking Creatively; Organizing, Planning, and Prioritizing; Judging Qualities of Things, Services, Other People's Work. *Work Output*—Handling and Moving Objects; Controlling Machines and Processes; Implementing Ideas and Programs. *Interacting with Others*—Communicating with Persons Outside Organization; Performing for or Working with the Public; Establishing and Maintaining Relationships. **Physical Work Conditions:** Indoors; Using Hands on Objects, Tools, or Controls; Sitting. **Other Job Characteristics:** Importance of Being Exact or Accurate; Importance of Being Sure All Is Done; Consequence of Error.

Experience: Job Zone 4. A minimum of two to four years of work-related skill, knowledge, or experience is needed. **Job Preparation:** SVP 7.0 to less than 8.0—2 years to less than 10 years. **Knowledge:** Customer and Personal Service; Design; Production and Processing; Mathematics; Sales and Marketing. **Instructional Programs:** 200301 Clothing, Apparel and Textile Workers and Managers, General; 200305 Custom Tailor.

Related DOT Jobs: 785.261-014 Custom Tailor; 785.261-022 Tailor Apprentice, Custom; 785.361-010 Dressmaker.

51-6061.00 Textile Bleaching and Dyeing Machine Operators and Tenders (Textile Bleaching and Dyeing Machine Operators and Tenders)

Education: Moderate-term O-T-J training

Employed: 24,487

Openings: 4,021

Projected Growth: –9%

Earnings: $19,350

Operate or tend machines to bleach, shrink, wash, dye, or finish textiles or synthetic or glass fibers.

Observes display screen, control panel and equipment, and cloth entering or exiting process, to determine equipment adjustments. Examines and feels products to determine variation from processing standards. Adjusts equipment controls to maintain standards. Mixes or adds dyes, water, detergents, or chemicals to tanks, to dilute or strengthen solutions as indicated by tests. Creels machine with bobbins or twine. Keys in processing instructions to program electronic equipment. Soaks specified textile products for designated time. Tests solutions used to process textile goods, to detect variations from standards, using standard procedures. Weighs ingredients to be mixed together to process textiles. Removes items such as dyed articles, cloth, cones, and bobbins from tanks and machines, for drying and further processing. Sews ends of cloth together by hand or using machine to form endless length of cloth to facilitate processing. Starts machines and equipment to process and finish textile goods prior to further processing, following instructions. Mounts roll of cloth on machine, using hoist; places textile goods in machines or pieces of equipment. Threads ends of cloth or twine through specified sections of equipment prior to processing. Cleans machines and equipment. Ravels seams connecting cloth ends after processing is completed. Confers with coworkers to ascertain information regarding customer orders, process steps to be completed during shift, or reason for delays. Notifies supervisor of equipment malfunctions. Notifies coworkers to initiate steps in processing of textile goods. Records information such as fabric yardage processed, temperature readings, fabric tensions, machine speeds, and delays caused by range malfunctions.

GOE Number, Interest Area, and Work Group: 08.03.02; Industrial Production; Production Work: Equipment Operation, Assorted Materials Processing. **Personality Type:** Realistic. Realistic occupations frequently involve work activities that include practical, hands-on problems and solutions. These occupations often deal with plants, animals, and real-world materials like wood, tools, and machinery. Many of the occupations require working outside and do not involve a lot of paperwork or working closely with others. **Work Values:** Moral Values; Company Policies and Practices; Supervision, Human Relations; Activity; Supervision, Technical. **Skills:** Operation and Control; Product Inspection; Mathematics; Equipment Selection; Operation Monitoring. **Abilities:** *Cognitive*—Problem Sensitivity; Information Ordering; Written Comprehension; Time Sharing; Perceptual Speed; Memorization. *Psychomotor*—Control Precision; Arm-Hand Steadiness; Wrist-Finger Speed; Manual Dexterity. *Physical*—Static Strength; Extent Flexibility; Trunk Strength. *Sensory*—Visual Color Discrimination; Near Vision; Depth Perception; Far Vision. **General Work Activities:** *Information Input*—Monitoring Processes, Materials, and Surroundings; Getting Information Needed to Do the Job; Inspecting Equipment, Structures, Materials. *Mental Process*—Evaluating Information Against Standards; Judging Qualities of Things, Services, Other People's Work; Processing Information. *Work Output*—Controlling Machines and Processes; Handling and Moving Objects; Implementing Ideas and Programs. *Interacting with Others*—Communicating with Other Workers; Performing Administrative Activities; Coordinating Work and Activities of Others. **Physical Work Conditions:** Indoors; Using Hands on Objects, Tools, or Controls; Hazardous Equipment. **Other Job Characteristics:** Degree of Automation; Consequence of Error; Pace Determined by Speed of Equipment.

Experience: Job Zone 1. No previous work-related skill, knowledge, or experience is needed. **Job Preparation:** SVP Below 4.0— Less than 6 months. **Knowledge:** Production and Processing; Chemistry; Mechanical; Mathematics; English Language. **Instructional Program:** 470303 Industrial Machinery Maintenance and Repairer.

Related DOT Jobs: 582.362-010 Panelboard Operator; 582.362-014 Dye Automation Operator; 582.582-010 Dye-Range Operator, Cloth; 582.665-014 Dye-Reel Operator; 582.665-018 Jigger; 582.685-014 Beam-Dyer Operator; 582.685-018 Bleach-Range Operator; 582.685-022 Boil-Off-Machine Operator, Cloth; 582.685-030 Cloth-Washer Operator; 582.685-034 Coloring-Machine Operator; 582.685-054 Dye-Tank Tender; 582.685-058 Dyed-Yarn Operator; 582.685-070 Felt-Washing-Machine Tender; 582.685-090 Jet-Dyeing-Machine Tender; 582.685-094 Knit-Goods Washer; 582.685-098 Open-Developer Operator; 582.685-102 Package-Dyeing-Machine Operator; 582.685-106 Padding-Machine Operator; 582.685-110 Patch Washer; 582.685-114 Rope-Silica-Machine Operator (partial list; see the introduction for sources of the complete list).

51-6062.00 Textile Cutting Machine Setters, Operators, and Tenders (Textile Cutting Machine Setters and Set-up Operators)

Education: Moderate-term O-T-J training
Employed: 28,220
Openings: 3,603
Projected Growth: –9.6%
Earnings: $21,620

Set up, operate, or tend machines that cut textiles.

Adjusts heating mechanisms, tension, and speed of machine operation, to produce product meeting desired specifications. Repairs or replaces worn or defective parts or components, using hand tools. Starts machine, monitors operation, makes adjustments as needed, and stops machine when specified amount of product has been produced. Operates machine for test run to verify adjustments and to obtain sample of product. Inspects product to ensure that product meets specifications and to determine need for machine adjustment. Installs, levels, and aligns components such as gears, chains, guides, dies, cutters, and needles, to set up machinery for operation. Cleans, oils, and lubricates machines, using airhose, cleaning solutions, rags, oil can and grease gun. Inspects machinery to determine adjustments or repairs needed. Threads yarn, thread, and fabric through guides, needles, and rollers of machines. Studies guides, samples, charts, and specification sheets; confers with supervisor or engineering staff to determine setup requirements.

GOE Number, Interest Area, and Work Group: 08.02.01; Industrial Production; Production Technology: Machine Set-up and Operation. **Personality Type:** Realistic. Realistic occupations frequently involve work activities that include practical, hands-on problems and solutions. These occupations often deal with plants, animals, and real-world materials like wood, tools, and machinery. Many of the occupations require working outside and do not involve a lot of paperwork or working closely with others. **Work Values:** Moral Values; Activity; Company Policies and Practices; Supervision, Human Relations; Independence. **Skills:** Operation and Control; Operation Monitoring; Testing; Product Inspection; Equipment Maintenance. **Abilities:** *Cognitive*—Information Ordering; Written Comprehension; Problem Sensitivity; Visualization; Oral Comprehension. *Psychomotor*—Control Precision; Arm-Hand Steadiness; Finger Dexterity. *Physical*—Extent Flexibility; Trunk Strength; Static Strength. *Sensory*—Near Vision; Auditory Attention; Hearing Sensitivity. **General Work Activities:** *Information Input*—Inspecting Equipment, Structures, Materials; Monitoring Processes, Materials, and Surroundings; Getting Information Needed to Do the Job. *Mental Process*—Evaluating Information Against Standards; Judging Qualities of Things, Services, Other People's Work; Updating and Using Job-Relevant Knowledge; Making Decisions and Solving Problems. *Work Output*—Repairing and Maintaining Mechanical Equipment; Controlling Machines and Processes; Handling and Moving Objects. *Interacting with Others*—Communicating with Other Workers; Establishing and Maintaining Relationships; Providing Consultation and Advice to Others; Communicating with Persons Outside Organization; Interpreting Meaning of Information to Others; Monitoring and Controlling Resources. **Physical Work Conditions:** Indoors; Using Hands on Objects, Tools, or Controls; Standing. **Other Job Characteristics:** Degree of Automation; Consequence of Error; Importance of Being Sure All Is Done; Importance of Being Exact or Accurate.

Experience: Job Zone 3. Previous work-related skill, knowledge, or experience is required. **Job Preparation:** SVP 6.0 to less than 7.0—More than 1 year and less than 4 years. **Knowledge:** Mechanical; Design; Engineering and Technology; Mathematics; English Language. **Instructional Program:** 470303 Industrial Machinery Maintenance and Repairer.

Related DOT Job: 585.380-010 Cutting-Machine Fixer.

51-6063.00 Textile Knitting and Weaving Machine Setters, Operators, and Tenders (Textile Cutting Machine Setters and Set-up Operators)

Education: Moderate-term O-T-J training
Employed: 28,220
Openings: 3,603
Projected Growth: –9.6%
Earnings: $21,620

Set up, operate, or tend machines that knit, loop, weave, or draw in textiles.

Inspects product to ensure that it meets specifications and to determine need for machine adjustment. Starts machine, monitors operation, makes adjustments as needed, and stops machine when specified amount of product has been produced. Threads yarn, thread, and fabric through guides, needles, and rollers of machines. Operates machine for test run, to verify adjustments and to obtain sample of product. Adjusts heating mechanisms, tension, and speed of machine operation, to produce a product meeting desired specifications. Cleans, oils, and lubricates machines, using airhose, cleaning solutions, rags, oil can, and grease gun. Studies guides, samples, charts, and specification sheets; confers with supervisor or engineering staff to determine setup requirements. Installs, levels, and aligns components such as gears, chains, guides, dies, cutters, and needles to set up machinery for operation. Repairs or replaces worn or defective parts or components, using hand tools. Inspects machinery to determine adjustments or repairs needed.

GOE Number, Interest Area, and Work Group: 08.02.01; Industrial Production; Production Technology: Machine Set-up and Operation. **Personality Type:** Realistic. Realistic occupations frequently involve work activities that include practical, hands-on problems and solutions. These occupations often deal with plants, animals, and real-world materials like wood, tools, and machinery. Many of the occupations require working outside and do not involve a lot of paperwork or working closely with others. **Work Values:** Moral Values; Supervision, Human Relations; Company Policies and Practices; Activity; Independence. **Skills:** Operation and Control; Operation Monitoring; Equipment Maintenance; Product Inspection; Testing. **Abilities:** *Cognitive*—Information Ordering; Written Comprehension; Problem Sensitivity; Visualization; Oral Comprehension. *Psychomotor*—Control Precision;

Arm-Hand Steadiness; Finger Dexterity. *Physical*—Extent Flexibility; Static Strength; Trunk Strength. *Sensory*—Near Vision; Auditory Attention; Hearing Sensitivity. **General Work Activities:** *Information Input*—Inspecting Equipment, Structures, Materials; Monitoring Processes, Materials, and Surroundings; Getting Information Needed to Do the Job. *Mental Process*—Evaluating Information Against Standards; Judging Qualities of Things, Services, Other People's Work; Making Decisions and Solving Problems; Updating and Using Job-Relevant Knowledge. *Work Output*—Repairing and Maintaining Mechanical Equipment; Controlling Machines and Processes; Handling and Moving Objects. *Interacting with Others*—Communicating with Other Workers; Establishing and Maintaining Relationships; Providing Consultation and Advice to Others; Monitoring and Controlling Resources; Interpreting Meaning of Information to Others; Communicating with Persons Outside Organization. **Physical Work Conditions:** Indoors; Using Hands on Objects, Tools, or Controls; Standing. **Other Job Characteristics:** Degree of Automation; Consequence of Error; Importance of Being Sure All Is Done; Importance of Being Exact or Accurate.

Experience: Job Zone 3. Previous work-related skill, knowledge, or experience is required. **Job Preparation:** SVP 6.0 to less than 7.0—More than 1 year and less than 4 years. **Knowledge:** Mechanical; Design; Engineering and Technology; Mathematics; English Language. **Instructional Program:** 470303 Industrial Machinery Maintenance and Repairer.

Related DOT Jobs: 683.260-014 Carpet-Loom Fixer; 683.260-018 Loom Fixer; 683.360-010 Loom Changer; 683.381-010 Chain Builder, Loom Control; 683.680-010 Harness Placer; 683.680-014 Heddles Tier, Jacquard Loom; 683.682-018 Drawing-in-Machine Tender; 685.360-010 Knitter Mechanic; 685.380-010 Link-and-Link-Knitting-Machine Operator; 685.381-010 Jacquard-Plate Maker; 685.680-010 Threader; 689.260-014 Quilter Fixer; 689.260-026 Knitting-Machine Fixer; 689.360-010 Needle-Loom Setter; 689.362-010 Needle-Felt-Making-Machine Operator; 689.380-010 Emblem Drawer-in; 689.382-010 Automatic-Pad-Making-Machine Operator; 689.662-010 Needle-Loom Operator.

51-6064.00 Textile Winding, Twisting, and Drawing Out Machine Setters, Operators, and Tenders (Textile Machine Operators and Tenders, Winding, Twisting, Knitting, Weaving, and Cutting)

Education: No data available.
Employed: 174,090
Openings: No data available.
Projected Growth: No data available.
Earnings: $19,440

Set up, operate, or tend machines that wind or twist textiles or that draw out and combine sliver such as wool, hemp, or synthetic fibers.

Repairs or replaces worn or defective parts or components, using hand tools. Starts machine, monitors operation, makes adjustments as needed, and stops machine when specified amount of product has been produced. Adjusts heating mechanisms, tension, and speed of machine operation, to produce a product that meets desired specifications. Threads yarn, thread, and fabric through guides, needles, and rollers of machines. Studies guides, samples, charts, and specification sheets; confers with supervisor or engineering staff to determine set-up requirements. Inspects machinery to determine adjustments or repairs needed. Inspects product to ensure that it meets specifications and to determine need for machine adjustment. Operates machine for test run to verify adjustments and to obtain sample of product. Installs, levels, and aligns components such as gears, chains, guides, dies, cutters, and needles, to set up machinery for operation. Cleans, oils, and lubricates machines, using airhose, cleaning solutions, rags, oil can and grease gun.

GOE Number, Interest Area, and Work Group: 08.02.01; Industrial Production; Production Technology: Machine Set-up and Operation. **Personality Type:** Realistic. Realistic occupations frequently involve work activities that include practical, hands-on problems and solutions. These occupations often deal with plants, animals, and real-world materials like wood, tools, and machinery. Many of the occupations require working outside and do not involve a lot of paperwork or working closely with others. **Work Values:** Moral Values; Supervision, Human Relations; Company Policies and Practices; Activity; Independence. **Skills:** Operation and Control; Operation Monitoring; Product Inspection; Testing; Equipment Maintenance. **Abilities:** *Cognitive*—Information Ordering; Written Comprehension; Problem Sensitivity; Visualization; Oral Comprehension. *Psychomotor*—Control Precision; Arm-Hand Steadiness; Finger Dexterity. *Physical*—Extent Flexibility; Trunk Strength; Static Strength. *Sensory*—Near Vision; Auditory Attention; Hearing Sensitivity. **General Work Activities:** *Information Input*—Monitoring Processes, Materials, and Surroundings; Inspecting Equipment, Structures, Materials; Getting Information Needed to Do the Job. *Mental Process*—Evaluating Information Against Standards; Judging Qualities of Things, Services, Other People's Work; Making Decisions and Solving Problems; Updating and Using Job-Relevant Knowledge. *Work Output*—Repairing and Maintaining Mechanical Equipment; Controlling Machines and Processes; Handling and Moving Objects. *Interacting with Others*—Communicating with Other Workers; Establishing and Maintaining Relationships; Providing Consultation and Advice to Others; Monitoring and Controlling Resources; Interpreting Meaning of Information to Others; Communicating with Persons Outside Organization. **Physical Work Conditions:** Indoors; Using Hands on Objects, Tools, or Controls; Standing. **Other Job Characteristics:** Degree of Automation; Consequence of Error; Importance of Being Sure All Is Done; Importance of Being Exact or Accurate.

Experience: Job Zone 3. Previous work-related skill, knowledge, or experience is required. **Job Preparation:** SVP 6.0 to less than 7.0—More than 1 year and less than 4 years. **Knowledge:** Mechanical; Design; Engineering and Technology; Mathematics; English Language. **Instructional Program:** 470303 Industrial Machinery Maintenance and Repairer.

Related DOT Jobs: 589.360-010 Bonding-Machine Setter; 681.380-010 Rope-Machine Setter; 683.260-010 Braid-Pattern Setter; 689.260-010 Machine Fixer; 689.260-018 Section Leader and Machine Setter; 689.260-022 Section Leader and Machine Setter, Polishing; 689.280-010 Box Tender.

51-6091.00 Extruding and Forming Machine Setters, Operators, and Tenders, Synthetic and Glass Fibers
(Extruding and Forming Machine Setters, Operators and Tenders)

Education: Moderate-term O-T-J training
Employed: 125,555
Openings: 23,246
Projected Growth: 5%
Earnings: No data available.

Set up, operate, or tend machines that extrude and form continuous filaments from synthetic materials such as liquid polymer, rayon, and fiberglass.

GOE Number, Interest Area, and Work Group: 08.03.01; Industrial Production; Production Work: Machine Work, Assorted Materials. **Instructional Program:** 470303 Industrial Machinery Maintenance and Repairer. **Note:** The Department of Labor has not collected some data for this job, so it has fewer details than the other descriptions.

51-6091.01 Extruding and Forming Machine Operators and Tenders, Synthetic or Glass Fibers
(Extruding and Forming Machine Operators and Tenders, Synthetic or Glass Fibers)

Education: Moderate-term O-T-J training
Employed: 32,815
Openings: 6,124
Projected Growth: 7.9%
Earnings: $27,940

Operate or tend machines that extrude and form continuous filaments from synthetic materials such as liquid polymer, rayon, and fiberglass, preparatory to further processing.

Cleans and maintains extruding and forming machines, using hand tools. Moves controls to activate and adjust extruding and forming machines. Presses buttons to stop machine when process is completed or malfunction is detected. Observes machine operation, control board, and gauges to detect malfunctions. Operates or tends machines that extrude and form filaments from synthetic materials. Loads and adjusts materials into extruding and forming machines, using hand tools. Records operational data on tag, and attaches to machine. Notifies workers of defects. Notifies workers to adjust extruding and forming machines. Removes excess or completed filament from machine, using hand tools.

GOE Number, Interest Area, and Work Group: 08.03.01; Industrial Production; Production Work: Machine Work, Assorted Materials. **Personality Type:** Realistic. Realistic occupations frequently involve work activities that include practical, hands-on problems and solutions. These occupations often deal with plants, animals, and real-world materials like wood, tools, and machinery. Many of the occupations require working outside and do not involve a lot of paperwork or working closely with others. **Work Values:** Moral Values; Company Policies and Practices; Independence; Supervision, Human Relations; Activity. **Skills:** Operation Monitoring; Equipment Maintenance; Operation and Control; Product Inspection; Equipment Selection. **Abilities:** *Cognitive*—Perceptual Speed; Information Ordering; Problem Sensitivity; Visualization; Selective Attention. *Psychomotor*—Control Precision; Wrist-Finger Speed; Manual Dexterity. *Physical*—Extent Flexibility; Static Strength; Trunk Strength. *Sensory*—Near Vision; Hearing Sensitivity; Auditory Attention. **General Work Activities:** *Information Input*—Monitoring Processes, Materials, and Surroundings; Inspecting Equipment, Structures, Materials; Identifying Objects, Actions, and Events. *Mental Process*—Judging Qualities of Things, Services, Other People's Work; Evaluating Information Against Standards; Processing Information. *Work Output*—Controlling Machines and Processes; Handling and Moving Objects; Documenting and Recording Information. *Interacting with Others*—Communicating with Other Workers; Performing Administrative Activities; Establishing and Maintaining Relationships; Coordinating Work and Activities of Others. **Physical Work Conditions:** Indoors; Using Hands on Objects, Tools, or Controls; Standing. **Other Job Characteristics:** Degree of Automation; Importance of Being Sure All Is Done; Consequence of Error; Importance of Being Exact or Accurate.

Experience: Job Zone 1. No previous work-related skill, knowledge, or experience is needed. **Job Preparation:** SVP Below 4.0—Less than 6 months. **Knowledge:** Mechanical; Production and Processing; Engineering and Technology; Clerical; Building and Construction. **Instructional Program:** 470303 Industrial Machinery Maintenance and Repairer.

Related DOT Jobs: 557.565-014 Synthetic-Filament Extruder; 557.665-010 Synthetic-Staple Extruder; 557.685-018 Processor; 557.685-022 Second-Floor Operator; 557.685-026 Spinner; 575.685-030 Fiber-Machine Tender; 575.685-082 Test-Skein Winder.

51-6092.00 Fabric and Apparel Patternmakers
(Patternmakers and Layout Workers, Fabric and Apparel)

Education: Long-term O-T-J training

Employed: 15,968

Openings: 1,263

Projected Growth: –3.8%

Earnings: $21,580

Draw and construct sets of precision master fabric patterns or layouts. Mark and cut fabrics and apparel.

Computes dimensions of pattern according to size, considering stretching of material; measures and marks pattern. Draws patterns for range of garment sizes, grading master pattern for each size, using charts or grading device. Draws details on outlined parts to indicate guides in joining parts. Draws lines between reference points, producing outline of graded pattern. Examines sketches, or sample articles and design specifications, to ascertain number, shape, and size of pattern parts. Calculates dimensions and specifications from sales order; enters data on worksheet. Positions master pattern in clamp of grading device, places pa-

perboard under pattern, sets device to specified size, and marks reference points. Traces outline of paper onto cardboard pattern, and cuts pattern into parts to make template. Draws outline of pattern parts, using drafting instruments such as calipers, squares, and straight and curved rules. Positions master pattern on paperboard and drafts reference points based on data from charts. Positions and cuts out pattern, using scissors and knife. Makes drawings of garments and patterns; writes instructions for use in reproducing commercial patterns. Traces outline of specified pattern onto material and cuts fabric, using scissors. Marks finished pattern with garment size, section, and style information. Positions and pins pattern sections onto model form; discusses style lines, details, and revisions with designer. Lays out large patterns on floor and cuts material, according to markings.

GOE Number, Interest Area, and Work Group: 08.03.06; Industrial Production; Production Work: Hands-on Work, Assorted Materials. **Personality Type:** Realistic. Realistic occupations frequently involve work activities that include practical, hands-on problems and solutions. These occupations often deal with plants, animals, and real-world materials like wood, tools, and machinery. Many of the occupations require working outside and do not involve a lot of paperwork or working closely with others. **Work Values:** Moral Values; Independence; Working Conditions; Achievement; Ability Utilization; Supervision, Human Relations; Activity; Security. **Skills:** Mathematics; Writing; Information Organization; Product Inspection; Solution Appraisal; Synthesis/Reorganization; Problem Identification; Monitoring. **Abilities:** *Cognitive*—Visualization; Information Ordering; Number Facility; Mathematical Reasoning; Written Comprehension. *Psychomotor*—Arm-Hand Steadiness; Wrist-Finger Speed; Manual Dexterity. *Physical*—Stamina. *Sensory*—Near Vision; Visual Color Discrimination. **General Work Activities:** *Information Input*—Getting Information Needed to Do the Job; Estimating Needed Characteristics; Identifying Objects, Actions, and Events. *Mental Process*—Evaluating Information Against Standards; Processing Information; Analyzing Data or Information. *Work Output*—Handling and Moving Objects; Drafting and Specifying Technical Devices; Controlling Machines and Processes; Implementing Ideas and Programs. *Interacting with Others*—Communicating with Other Workers; Providing Consultation and Advice to Others; Performing Administrative Activities. **Physical Work Conditions:** Indoors; Using Hands on Objects, Tools, or Controls; Sitting. **Other Job Characteristics:** Importance of Being Exact or Accurate; Consequence of Error; Importance of Being Sure All Is Done.

Experience: Job Zone 2. Some previous work-related skill, knowledge, or experience may be helpful, but usually is not needed. **Job Preparation:** SVP 4.00 to 5.99—6 months to less than 2 years. **Knowledge:** Design; Mathematics; English Language; Telecommunications; Production and Processing. **Instructional Programs:** 200301 Clothing, Apparel and Textile Workers and Managers, General; 200303 Commercial Garment and Apparel Worker.

Related DOT Jobs: 781.361-010 Assistant Designer; 781.361-014 Patternmaker; 781.381-022 Pattern Grader-Cutter; 781.381-030 Sail-Lay-Out Worker; 781.381-034 Grader Marker; 781.484-010 Pleat Patternmaker; 788.281-010 Designer and Patternmaker; 789.381-014 Pattern Chart-Writer; 962.381-010 Draper.

51-6093.00 Upholsterers (Upholsterers)

Education: Long-term O-T-J training

Employed: 66,375

Openings: 5,432

Projected Growth: 0.9%

Earnings: $22,050

Make, repair, or replace upholstery for household furniture or transportation vehicles.

Drills or punches holes in material. Fits, installs, and secures material on workpiece, using hand tools, power tools, glue, cement, or staples. Attaches binding or applies solutions to edges of cut material to prevent raveling. Removes covering, webbing, padding, and defective springs from workpiece, using hand tools. Examines upholstery to locate defects. Repairs frame of workpiece. Stacks, aligns, and smoothes material on cutting table. Operates sewing machine to seam cushions and join various sections of covering material. Maintains records of time required to perform each job. Refinishes wood surfaces on upholstered or reupholstered furniture. Attaches fasteners, grommets, buckles, ornamental trim, and other accessories, to cover or frame, using hand tools. Reads order and applies knowledge and experience with materials to determine type and amount of material required to cover workpiece. Draws cutting lines on material following pattern, templates, sketches, or blueprints, using chalk, pencil, paint, or other method. Sews rips or tears in material, or creates tufting, using needle and thread. Adjusts or replaces webbing, padding, and springs, and secures them in place. Measures and cuts new covering material, using pattern and measuring and cutting instruments. Designs upholstery-cover patterns.

GOE Number, Interest Area, and Work Group: 11.06.01; Recreation, Travel, and Other Personal Services; Apparel, Shoes, Leather, and Fabric Care. **Personality Type:** Realistic. Realistic occupations frequently involve work activities that include practical, hands-on problems and solutions. These occupations often deal with plants, animals, and real-world materials like wood, tools, and machinery. Many of the occupations require working outside and do not involve a lot of paperwork or working closely with others. **Work Values:** Moral Values; Autonomy; Independence; Working Conditions; Achievement; Responsibility; Security. **Skills:** Equipment Selection; Repairing; Monitoring; Problem Identification; Operation and Control. **Abilities:** *Cognitive*—Visualization; Information Ordering; Written Comprehension; Inductive Reasoning; Problem Sensitivity. *Psychomotor*—Manual Dexterity; Finger Dexterity; Wrist-Finger Speed. *Physical*—Static Strength; Extent Flexibility; Trunk Strength. *Sensory*—Near Vision; Visual Color Discrimination. **General Work Activities:** *Information Input*—Getting Information Needed to Do the Job; Estimating Needed Characteristics; Inspecting Equipment, Structures, Materials. *Mental Process*—Thinking Creatively; Making Decisions and Solving Problems; Judging Qualities of Things, Services, Other People's Work. *Work Output*—Handling and Moving Objects; Drafting and Specifying Technical Devices; Performing General Physical Activities. *Interacting with Others*—Performing Administrative Activities; Monitoring and Controlling Resources; Communicating with Other Workers. **Physical Work Conditions:** Indoors; Using Hands on Objects, Tools, or Controls; Standing. **Other Job Characteristics:** Importance of Being Exact or Accurate; Importance of Being Sure All Is Done; Consequence of Error.

Experience: Job Zone 3. Previous work-related skill, knowledge, or experience is required. **Job Preparation:** SVP 6.0 to less than 7.0—More than 1 year and less than 4 years. **Knowledge:** Building and Construction; Production and Processing; Mechanical; Design; Mathematics. **Instructional Programs:** 200501 Home Furnishings and Equipment Installers and Consultants, General; 480303 Upholsterer.

Related DOT Jobs: 780.381-010 Automobile Upholsterer; 780.381-014 Automobile-Upholsterer Apprentice; 780.381-018 Furniture Upholsterer; 780.381-022 Furniture-Upholsterer Apprentice; 780.381-026 Upholsterer, Limousine and Hearse; 780.381-034 Slipcover Cutter; 780.381-038 Upholsterer, Inside; 780.384-014 Upholsterer; 780.684-122 Upholstery Repairer.

51-7000 Woodworkers

51-7011.00 Cabinetmakers and Bench Carpenters
(Cabinetmakers and Bench Carpenters)

Education: Long-term O-T-J training

Employed: 122,957

Openings: 19,927

Projected Growth: 5.2%

Earnings: $22,390

Cut, shape, and assemble wooden articles. Set up and operate a variety of woodworking machines such as power saws, jointers, and mortisers, to surface, cut, or shape lumber or to fabricate parts for wood products.

Studies blueprints, drawings, and written specifications of articles to be constructed or repaired; plans sequence of performing such operations. Bores holes for insertion of screws or dowel, by hand or using boring machine. Glues, fits, and clamps parts and subassemblies together to form complete unit. Trims component parts of joints to ensure snug fit, using hand tools such as planes, chisels, or wood files. Installs hardware such as hinges, catches, and drawer pulls, using hand tools. Drives nails or other fasteners to joints of articles to prepare articles for finishing. Dips, brushes, or sprays assembled articles with protective or decorative materials such as stain, varnish, or lacquer. Sands and scrapes surfaces and joints of articles to prepare articles for finishing. Sets up and operates machines, including power saws, jointers, mortisers, tenoners, molders, and shapers, to cut and shape woodstock. Marks dimensions of parts on paper or lumber stock, following blueprints; matches lumber for color, grain, and texture.

GOE Number, Interest Area, and Work Group: 08.05.01; Industrial Production; Woodworking Technology. **Personality Type:** Realistic. Realistic occupations frequently involve work activities that include practical, hands-on problems and solutions. These occupations often deal with plants, animals, and real-world materials like wood, tools, and machinery. Many of the occupations require working outside and do not involve a lot of paperwork or working closely with others. **Work Values:** Moral Values; Independence; Activity; Ability Utilization; Achievement. **Skills:** Equipment Selection; Operation and Control; Product Inspection; Installation; Mathematics. **Abilities:** *Cognitive*—Written Comprehension; Visualization; Information Ordering; Deductive Reasoning; Number Facility. *Psychomotor*—Arm-Hand Steadiness; Control Precision; Manual Dexterity. *Physical*—Extent Flexibility; Static Strength; Trunk Strength; Explosive Strength. *Sensory*—Depth Perception. **General Work Activities:** *Information Input*—Getting Information Needed to Do the Job; Monitoring Processes, Materials, and Surroundings; Estimating Needed Characteristics; Identifying Objects, Actions, and Events. *Mental Process*—Evaluating Information Against Standards; Organizing, Planning, and Prioritizing; Making Decisions and Solving Problems; Judging Qualities of Things, Services, Other People's Work; Processing Information. *Work Output*—Controlling Machines and Processes; Handling and Moving Objects; Performing General Physical Activities. *Interacting with Others*—Communicating with Other Workers; Teaching Others; Providing Consultation and Advice to Others; Performing Administrative Activities; Monitoring and Controlling Resources. **Physical Work Conditions:** Using Hands on Objects, Tools, or Controls; Indoors; Standing. **Other Job Characteristics:** Importance of Being Exact or Accurate; Importance of Being Sure All Is Done; Consequence of Error.

Experience: Job Zone 3. Previous work-related skill, knowledge, or experience is required. **Job Preparation:** SVP 6.0 to less than 7.0—More than 1 year and less than 4 years. **Knowledge:** Building and Construction; Design; Engineering and Technology; Production and Processing; Mechanical. **Instructional Program:** 480703 Cabinet Maker and Millworker.

Related DOT Jobs: 660.280-010 Cabinetmaker; 660.280-014 Cabinetmaker Apprentice.

51-7021.00 Furniture Finishers (Furniture Finishers)

Education: Long-term O-T-J training
Employed: 38,486
Openings: 5,123
Projected Growth: –1%
Earnings: $19,880

Shape, finish, and refinish damaged, worn, or used furniture or new high-grade furniture, to specified color or finish.

Selects appropriate finishing ingredients such as paint, stain, lacquer, shellac, or varnish, for wood surface. Washes or bleaches surface to return to natural color or to prepare for application of finish. Fills cracks, blemishes, or depressions, and repairs broken parts, using plastic or wood putty, glue, nails, or screws. Smoothes and shapes surfaces with sandpaper, pumice stone, steel wool, or chisel. Treats warped or stained surfaces to restore original contour and color. Removes old finish and damaged or deteriorated parts, using hand tools, abrasives, or solvents. Examines furniture to determine extent of damage or deterioration and determines method of repair or restoration. Mixes finish ingredients to obtain desired color or shade of existing finish. Stencils, gilds, embosses, or paints designs or borders on restored pieces, to reproduce original appearance. Polishes, sprays, or waxes finished pieces to match surrounding finish. Replaces and refurbishes upholstery of item, using tacks, adhesives, softeners, solvents, stains,

or polish. Spreads graining ink over metal portions of furniture to simulate wood-grain finish. Brushes, sprays, or hand rubs finishing ingredients onto and into grain of wood. Disassembles item, masks areas adjacent to those being refinished, and removes accessories, using hand tools, to prepare for finishing. Finishes surfaces of new furniture pieces to replicate antiques by distressing surfaces with abrasives before staining.

GOE Number, Interest Area, and Work Group: 08.05.01; Industrial Production; Woodworking Technology. **Personality Type:** Realistic. Realistic occupations frequently involve work activities that include practical, hands-on problems and solutions. These occupations often deal with plants, animals, and real-world materials like wood, tools, and machinery. Many of the occupations require working outside and do not involve a lot of paperwork or working closely with others. **Work Values:** Moral Values; Independence; Autonomy; Achievement; Compensation; Recognition. **Skills:** Equipment Selection; Problem Identification; Solution Appraisal; Monitoring; Product Inspection; Identification of Key Causes; Judgment and Decision Making; Idea Generation. **Abilities:** *Cognitive*—Information Ordering; Deductive Reasoning; Visualization; Problem Sensitivity; Originality; Category Flexibility. *Psychomotor*—Manual Dexterity; Finger Dexterity; Wrist-Finger Speed; Arm-Hand Steadiness. *Physical*—Extent Flexibility; Dynamic Flexibility; Static Strength. *Sensory*—Visual Color Discrimination; Glare Sensitivity; Depth Perception; Hearing Sensitivity. **General Work Activities:** *Information Input*—Getting Information Needed to Do the Job; Identifying Objects, Actions, and Events; Inspecting Equipment, Structures, Materials. *Mental Process*—Judging Qualities of Things, Services, Other People's Work; Thinking Creatively; Analyzing Data or Information; Making Decisions and Solving Problems. *Work Output*—Handling and Moving Objects; Performing General Physical Activities; Controlling Machines and Processes. *Interacting with Others*—Monitoring and Controlling Resources; Communicating with Persons Outside Organization; Communicating with Other Workers. **Physical Work Conditions:** Indoors; Using Hands on Objects, Tools, or Controls; Standing; Kneeling, Crouching, or Crawling; Contaminants. **Other Job Characteristics:** Importance of Being Sure All Is Done; Importance of Being Exact or Accurate; Consequence of Error.

Experience: Job Zone 2. Some previous work-related skill, knowledge, or experience may be helpful, but usually is not needed. **Job Preparation:** SVP 4.00 to 5.99—6 months to less than 2 years. **Knowledge:** Building and Construction; Chemistry; Production and Processing; Fine Arts; Engineering and Technology; Mechanical. **Instructional Program:** 480702 Furniture Designer and Maker.

Related DOT Jobs: 763.380-010 Furniture Restorer; 763.381-010 Furniture Finisher; 763.381-014 Furniture-Finisher Apprentice; 763.681-010 Frame Repairer; 763.684-022 Caner II; 763.684-034 Finish Patcher.

51-7031.00 Model Makers, Wood (Pattern and Model Makers, Wood)

Education: No data available.
Employed: 9,420
Openings: No data available.
Projected Growth: No data available.
Earnings: $30,490

Construct full-size and scale wooden precision models of products. Includes wood jig builders and loft workers.

Marks identifying information such as colors or codes on patterns, parts, and templates, to indicate assembly method. Fits, fastens, and assembles wood parts together to form pattern, model, or section, using glue, nails, dowels, bolts, and screws. Sets up, operates, and adjusts variety of woodworking machines to cut and shape sections, parts, and patterns, according to specifications. Trims, smoothes, and shapes surfaces, and planes, shaves, files, scrapes, and sands models, to attain specified shapes, using hand tools. Shellacs, lacquers, or waxes finished pattern or model. Reads blueprints, drawings, or written specifications to determine size and shape of pattern and required machine setup. Plans, lays out, and draws outline of unit, sectional patterns, or full-scale mock-up of products. Issues patterns to designated machine operators and maintains pattern record for reference. Constructs wooden models, templates, full-scale mock-up, and molds, for parts of products.

GOE Number, Interest Area, and Work Group: 08.05.01; Industrial Production; Woodworking Technology. **Personality Type:** Realistic. Realistic occupations frequently involve work activities that include practical, hands-on problems and solutions. These occupations often deal with plants, animals, and real-world materials like wood, tools, and machinery. Many of the occupations require working outside and do not involve a lot of paperwork or working closely with others. **Work Values:** Moral Values; Independence; Ability Utilization; Company Policies and Practices; Achievement; Security; Working Conditions. **Skills:** Product Inspection; Mathematics; Equipment Selection; Operation and Control; Reading Comprehension. **Abilities:** *Cognitive*—Written Comprehension; Visualization; Information Ordering; Number Facility; Deductive Reasoning. *Psychomotor*—Control Precision; Multilimb Coordination; Arm-Hand Steadiness. *Physical*—Extent Flexibility; Trunk Strength; Static Strength. *Sensory*—Depth Perception. **General Work Activities:** *Information Input*—Getting Information Needed to Do the Job; Estimating Needed Characteristics; Identifying Objects, Actions, and Events. *Mental Process*—Making Decisions and Solving Problems; Evaluating Information Against Standards; Judging Qualities of Things, Services, Other People's Work; Processing Information. *Work Output*—Drafting and Specifying Technical Devices; Handling and Moving Objects; Controlling Machines and Processes. *Interacting with Others*—Communicating with Other Workers; Establishing and Maintaining Relationships; Coordinating Work and Activities of Others. **Physical Work Conditions:** Indoors; Using Hands on Objects, Tools, or Controls; Standing. **Other Job Characteristics:** Importance of Being Exact or Accurate; Importance of Being Sure All Is Done; Consequence of Error.

Experience: Job Zone 4. A minimum of two to four years of work-related skill, knowledge, or experience is needed. **Job Preparation:** SVP 7.0 to less than 8.0—2 years to less than 10 years. **Knowledge:** Design; Building and Construction; Mechanical; Mathematics; Engineering and Technology. **Instructional Programs:** 480702 Furniture Designer and Maker; 480703 Cabinet Maker and Millworker.

Related DOT Job: 661.380-010 Model Maker, Wood.

51-7032.00 Patternmakers, Wood (Pattern and Model Makers, Wood)

Education: No data available.

Employed: 9,420

Openings: No data available.

Projected Growth: No data available.

Earnings: $30,490

Plan, lay out, and construct wooden unit or sectional patterns used in forming sand molds for castings.

Sets up, operates, and adjusts variety of woodworking machines, to cut and shape sections, parts, and patterns, according to specifications. Fits, fastens, and assembles wood parts together to form pattern, model, or section, using glue, nails, dowels, bolts, and screws. Trims, smoothes, and shapes surfaces, and planes, shaves, files, scrapes, and sands models to attain specified shapes, using hand tools. Shellacs, lacquers, or waxes finished pattern or model. Reads blueprints, drawing, or written specifications to determine size and shape of pattern and required machine setup. Marks identifying information such as colors or codes, on patterns, parts, and templates, to indicate assembly method. Plans, lays out, and draws outline of unit, sectional patterns, or full-scale mock-up of products. Issues patterns to designated machine operators and maintains pattern record for reference. Constructs wooden models, templates, full-scale mock-up, and molds, for parts of products.

GOE Number, Interest Area, and Work Group: 08.05.01; Industrial Production; Woodworking Technology. **Personality Type:** Realistic. Realistic occupations frequently involve work activities that include practical, hands-on problems and solutions. These occupations often deal with plants, animals, and real-world materials like wood, tools, and machinery. Many of the occupations require working outside and do not involve a lot of paperwork or working closely with others. **Work Values:** Moral Values; Independence; Company Policies and Practices; Ability Utilization; Working Conditions; Security; Achievement. **Skills:** Product Inspection; Mathematics; Equipment Selection; Operation and Control; Reading Comprehension. **Abilities:** *Cognitive*—Written Comprehension; Visualization; Information Ordering; Deductive Reasoning; Number Facility. *Psychomotor*—Control Precision; Multilimb Coordination; Arm-Hand Steadiness. *Physical*—Extent Flexibility; Trunk Strength; Static Strength. *Sensory*—Depth Perception. **General Work Activities:** *Information Input*—Getting Information Needed to Do the Job; Estimating Needed Characteristics; Identifying Objects, Actions, and Events. *Mental Process*—Making Decisions and Solving Problems; Evaluating Information Against Standards; Processing Information; Judging Qualities of Things, Services, Other People's Work. *Work Output*—Drafting and Specifying Technical Devices; Handling and Moving Objects; Controlling Machines and Processes. *Interacting with Others*—Communicating with Other Workers; Establishing and Maintaining Relationships; Coordinating Work and Activities of Others. **Physical Work Conditions:** Indoors; Using Hands on Objects, Tools, or Controls; Standing. **Other Job Characteristics:** Importance of Being Exact or Accurate; Importance of Being Sure All Is Done; Consequence of Error.

Experience: Job Zone 4. A minimum of two to four years of work-related skill, knowledge, or experience is needed. **Job Preparation:** SVP 7.0 to less than 8.0—2 years to less than 10 years. **Knowledge:** Design; Building and Construction; Mechanical; Mathematics; Engineering and Technology. **Instructional Programs:** 480702 Furniture Designer and Maker; 480703 Cabinet Maker and Millworker.

Related DOT Jobs: 661.281-018 Patternmaker Apprentice, Wood; 661.281-022 Patternmaker, Wood.

51-7041.00 Sawing Machine Setters, Operators, and Tenders, Wood (Head Sawyers and Sawing Machine Operators and Tenders, Setters and Set-Up Operators)

Education: Moderate-term O-T-J training

Employed: 64,451

Openings: 23,506

Projected Growth: –5.7%

Earnings: No data available.

Set up, operate, or tend wood sawing machines. Includes head sawyers.

GOE Number, Interest Area, and Work Group: 08.03.01; Industrial Production; Production Work: Machine Work, Assorted Materials. **Instructional Programs:** 480701 Woodworkers, General; 480703 Cabinet Maker and Millworker. **Note:** The Department of Labor has not collected some data for this job, so it has fewer details than the other descriptions.

51-7041.01 Sawing Machine Setters and Set-Up Operators (Sawing Machine Setters and Set-Up Operators)

Education: No data available.

Employed: 7,210

Openings: No data available.

Projected Growth: No data available.

Earnings: $20,240

Set up, or set up and operate, wood-sawing machines. Examine blueprints, drawings, work orders, and patterns to determine size and shape of items to be sawed, sawing machines to set up, and sequence of sawing operations.

Places stock in jig and pushes table containing stock into saw, or lays stock on conveyor that carries it into machine. Selects knives to achieve specified diameter of cut, or installs bit and dado saw according to work ticket. Pulls table back against stops and depresses pedal to advance cutterhead that shapes end of stock. Adjusts angle of table by turning handwheel; bolts or clamps holding jigs to table. Aligns and bolts knives in cutterhead and screws it on spindle, using wrenches.

GOE Number, Interest Area, and Work Group: 08.03.01; Industrial Production; Production Work: Machine Work, Assorted Materials. **Personality Type:** Realistic. Realistic occupations frequently involve work activities that include practical, hands-on problems and solutions. These occupations often deal with plants, animals, and real-world materials like wood, tools, and machinery. Many of the occupations require working outside and do not involve a lot of paperwork or working closely with others. **Work Values:** Moral Values; Independence; Company Policies and Practices; Activity; Supervision, Human Relations. **Skills:** Equipment Selection; Operation and Control; Reading Comprehension; Judgment and Decision Making; Product Inspection. **Abilities:** *Cognitive*—Information Ordering; Visualization; Written Comprehension; Number Facility; Selective Attention. *Psychomotor*—Manual Dexterity; Control Precision; Arm-Hand Steadiness. *Physical*—Static Strength; Extent Flexibility; Explosive Strength. *Sensory*—Hearing Sensitivity; Depth Perception; Peripheral Vision. **General Work Activities:** *Information Input*—Getting Information Needed to Do the Job; Identifying Objects, Actions, and Events; Monitoring Processes, Materials, and Surroundings. *Mental Process*—Analyzing Data or Information; Making Decisions and Solving Problems; Evaluating Information Against Standards. *Work Output*—Handling and Moving Objects; Controlling Machines and Processes; Performing General Physical Activities. *Interacting with Others*—Coaching and Developing Others; Assisting and Caring for Others; Interpreting Meaning of Information to Others; Communicating with Other Workers; Establishing and Maintaining Relationships. **Physical Work Conditions:** Indoors; Hazardous Equipment; Using Hands on Objects, Tools, or Controls. **Other Job Characteristics:** Degree of Automation; Consequence of Error; Importance of Being Sure All Is Done.

Experience: Job Zone 2. Some previous work-related skill, knowledge, or experience may be helpful, but usually is not needed. **Job Preparation:** SVP 4.00 to 5.99—6 months to less than 2 years. **Knowledge:** Building and Construction; Mechanical; Mathematics; Production and Processing; Design. **Instructional Program:** 480703 Cabinet Maker and Millworker.

Related DOT Jobs: 669.682-026 Chucking-and-Sawing-Machine Operator; 669.682-030 Corner-Brace-Block-Machine Operator.

51-7041.02 Sawing Machine Operators and Tenders (Sawing Machine Operators and Tenders)

Education: No data available.

Employed: 49,520

Openings: No data available.

Projected Growth: No data available.

Earnings: $18,940

Operate or tend wood-sawing machines such as circular saws, band saws, multiple blade sawing machines, scroll saws, ripsaws, equalizer saws, power saws, and crozer machines. Saw logs to specifications; cut lumber to specified dimensions.

Positions and clamps stock on table, conveyor, or carriage, using hoists, guides, stops, dogs, wedges, and wrench. Sharpens blades or replaces defective or worn blades and bands, using hand tools. Inspects stock for imperfections and estimates grade or quality of stock or workpiece. Counts, sorts, and stacks finished workpieces; disposes of waste material. Unclamps and removes finished workpiece from table. Clears machine jams, using hand tools. Measures workpiece to mark for cuts and to verify accuracy of cuts, using ruler, square, or caliper rule. Moves machine table to specified angle and height by turning handwheels, cranks, or knobs. Unloads and rolls logs from truck to sawmill deck or to carriage; moves logs in pond, using pike pole. Guides workpiece against saw, guides saw over workpiece, or operates automatic feeding device to guide cuts. Mounts and bolts sawing blade or attachments to machine shaft and turns handwheels to set blade tension. Lubricates and cleans machines, using wrench, grease gun, and solvents. Operates and tends saws and machines to cut stock and to adjust machine speed and tension, moving levers and handwheels. Operates panelboard of saw and conveyor system to cut stock to specified dimensions and to move stock through process. Trims defects from stock or workpiece to straighten rough edges of lumber, using circular power saw. Turns knobs, handwheels, setscrews, and panel controls, or uses hand tools to position and adjust cutting stops and guides. Adjusts saw blades by turning handwheels, pressing pedals, levers, and panel buttons, or using wrenches and rulers. Observes approaching lumber on conveyor to determine cut that will produce highest grade. Determines sawing blade, type and grade of stock needed, and cutting procedures, according to work order or supervisor's instructions.

GOE Number, Interest Area, and Work Group: 08.03.01; Industrial Production; Production Work: Machine Work, Assorted Materials. **Personality Type:** Realistic. Realistic occupations frequently involve work activities that include practical, hands-on problems and solutions. These occupations often deal with plants, animals, and real-world materials like wood, tools, and machinery. Many of the occupations require working outside and do not involve a lot of paperwork or working closely with others. **Work Values:** Moral Values; Independence; Activity; Company Policies and Practices; Supervision, Human Relations. **Skills:** Product Inspection; Operation and Control; Equipment Selection; Equipment Maintenance; Operation Monitoring; Repairing. **Abilities:** *Cognitive*—Information Ordering; Visualization; Perceptual Speed; Problem Sensitivity; Oral Comprehension; Category Flexibility. *Psychomotor*—Control Precision; Manual Dexterity; Arm-Hand Steadiness. *Physical*—Static Strength; Trunk Strength; Extent Flexibility. *Sensory*—Near Vision; Far Vision; Depth Perception. **General Work Activities:** *Information Input*—Getting Information Needed to Do the Job; Monitoring Processes, Materials, and Surroundings; Inspecting Equipment, Structures, Materials; Identifying Objects, Actions, and Events. *Mental Process*—Judging Qualities of Things, Services, Other People's Work; Evaluating Information Against Standards; Organizing, Planning, and Prioritizing. *Work Output*—Handling and Moving Objects; Controlling Machines and Processes; Performing General Physical Activities. *Interacting with Others*—Communicating with Other Workers; Performing Administrative Activities; Coordinating Work and Activities of Others. **Physical Work Conditions:** Hazardous Equipment; Using Hands on Objects, Tools, or Controls; Standing. **Other Job Characteristics:** Degree of Automation; Consequence of Error; Pace Determined by Speed of Equipment.

Experience: Job Zone 2. Some previous work-related skill, knowledge, or experience may be helpful, but usually is not needed. **Job Preparation:** SVP 4.00 to 5.99—6 months to less than 2 years. **Knowledge:** Mechanical; Building and Construction; Production and Processing; Engineering and Technology; Mathematics. **Instructional Program:** 480703 Cabinet Maker and Millworker.

Related DOT Jobs: 665.685-046 Shaping Machine Tender; 667.382-010 Stock Grader; 667.482-014 Pocket Cutter; 667.482-018 Stock Cutter; 667.485-010 Shingle Sawyer; 667.662-014 Machine-Tank Operator; 667.682-010 Band-Scroll-Saw Operator; 667.682-014 Bottom-Saw Operator; 667.682-018 Corner-Trimmer Operator; 667.682-022 Cut-Off-Saw Operator I; 667.682-026 Edger, Automatic; 667.682-030 Gang Sawyer; 667.682-042 Jigsaw Operator; 667.682-046 Packager, Head; 667.682-050 Pony Edger; 667.682-054 Radial-Arm-Saw Operator; 667.682-058 Resaw Operator; 667.682-062 Rip-and-Groove-Machine Operator; 667.682-066 Ripsaw Operator; 667.682-070 Shake Sawyer (partial list; see the introduction for sources of the complete list).

51-7042.00 Woodworking Machine Setters, Operators, and Tenders, Except Sawing (Woodworking Machine Operators and Tenders, Setters and Set-Up Operators)

Education: Moderate-term O-T-J training

Employed: 78,792

Openings: 21,462

Projected Growth: −12.5%

Earnings: No data available.

Set up, operate, or tend woodworking machines such as drill presses, lathes, shapers, routers, sanders, planers, and wood-nailing machines.

GOE Number, Interest Area, and Work Group: 08.02.01; Industrial Production; Production Technology: Machine Set-up and Operation. **Instructional Programs:** 480701 Woodworkers, General; 480703 Cabinet Maker and Millworker. **Note:** The Department of Labor has not collected some data for this job, so it has fewer details than the other descriptions.

51-7042.01 Woodworking Machine Setters and Set-Up Operators, Except Sawing (Woodworking Machine Setters and Set-Up Operators, Except Sawing)

Education: No data available.

Employed: 21,280

Openings: No data available.

Projected Growth: No data available.

Earnings: $20,310

Set up, or set up and operate, woodworking machines such as lathes, drill presses, sanders, shapers, and planing machines, to perform woodworking operations.

Examines workpiece visually, by touch, or using tape rule, calipers, or gauges to ensure product meets desired standards. Selects knives, sanding apparatus, cams, cutting heads, bits, chisels and blades. Unclamps and removes workpiece from machine, and stacks workpiece on pallet or in box. Removes and replaces worn machine parts, knives, bits, belts, and sandpaper. Mounts or clamps stock onto machine. Cleans product, machine, or work area, using rags and air hose. Adjusts machine table or cutting devices to produce specified cut or operation. Examines blueprints, drawings, and work orders, to determine characteristics of finished item, materials to be used, and machine setup requirements. Monitors operation of automatic machines and makes adjustments as needed to correct problems and ensure conformance to specifications. Starts machine; feeds stock into machine through feed mechanisms or conveyors. Attaches and adjusts guides, stops, clamps, chucks, and feed mechanisms, using hand tools. Installs knives, sanding apparatus, cams, cutting heads, bits, chisels, and blades, using hand tools. Pushes or holds workpiece against, under, or through cutting, boring, or shaping mechanism. Sharpens knives, bits, and other cutting and shaping tools.

GOE Number, Interest Area, and Work Group: 08.02.01; Industrial Production; Production Technology: Machine Set-up and Operation. **Personality Type:** Realistic. Realistic occupations frequently involve work activities that include practical, hands-on problems and solutions. These occupations often deal with plants, animals, and real-world materials like wood, tools, and machinery. Many of the occupations require working outside and do not involve a lot of paperwork or working closely with others. **Work Values:** Moral Values; Independence; Activity; Company Policies and Practices; Supervision, Human Relations. **Skills:** Operation and Control; Operation Monitoring; Equipment Selection; Installation; Product Inspection. **Abilities:** *Cognitive*—Visualization; Written Comprehension; Problem Sensitivity; Selective Attention; Information Ordering. *Psychomotor*—Manual Dexterity; Control Precision; Arm-Hand Steadiness; Finger Dexterity; Wrist-Finger Speed. *Physical*—Dynamic Strength; Static Strength; Explosive Strength; Dynamic Flexibility. *Sensory*—Depth Perception; Peripheral Vision; Glare Sensitivity. **General Work Activities:** *Information Input*—Getting Information Needed to Do the Job; Monitoring Processes, Materials, and Surroundings; Inspecting Equipment, Structures, Materials. *Mental Process*—Evaluating Information Against Standards; Analyzing Data or Information; Processing Information. *Work Output*—Controlling Machines and Processes; Handling and Moving Objects; Performing General Physical Activities. *Interacting with Others*—Monitoring and Controlling Resources; Communicating with Other Workers; Establishing and Maintaining Relationships. **Physical Work Conditions:** Hazardous Equipment; Using Hands on Objects, Tools, or Controls; Indoors; Common Protective or Safety Attire. **Other Job Characteristics:** Degree of Automation; Importance of Being Sure All Is Done; Consequence of Error.

Experience: Job Zone 2. Some previous work-related skill, knowledge, or experience may be helpful, but usually is not needed. **Job Preparation:** SVP 4.00 to 5.99—6 months to less than 2 years. **Knowledge:** Mechanical; Design; Engineering and Technology; Production and Processing; English Language; Mathematics. **Instructional Programs:** 480701 Woodworkers, General; 480703 Cabinet Maker and Millworker.

Related DOT Jobs: 662.682-010 Molding Sander; 662.682-014 Multiple-Drum Sander; 663.380-010 Knife Setter; 664.382-010 Swing-Type-Lathe Operator; 664.382-018 Trimming Machine Set-Up Operator; 664.662-010 Veneer-Lathe Operator; 665.382-010 Chucking-Machine Operator; 665.382-018 Wood-Carving-Machine Operator; 665.482-014 Mortising-Machine Operator; 665.682-010 Dowel-Machine Operator; 665.682-018 Molder Operator; 665.682-022 Planer Operator; 665.682-026 Profile-Shaper Operator, Automatic; 665.682-030 Router Operator; 665.682-034 Shaper Operator; 665.682-038 Veneer Jointer; 665.682-042 Jointer Operator; 666.382-010 Boring-Machine Operator; 669.280-010

Machine Setter; 669.360-010 Checkering-Machine Adjuster (partial list; see the introduction for sources of the complete list).

51-7042.02 Woodworking Machine Operators and Tenders, Except Sawing (Woodworking Machine Operators and Tenders, Except Sawing)

Education: No data available.

Employed: 51,450

Openings: No data available.

Projected Growth: No data available.

Earnings: $18,780

Operate or tend woodworking machines such as drill presses, lathes, shapers, routers, sanders, planers, and wood-nailing machines to perform woodworking operations.

Selects knives, blades, cutterheads, boring bits, or sanding belts, according to workpiece, machine function, and specifications. Stacks on pallet, by hand or conveyor; controls hoist to remove part or product from work-station. Marks or otherwise identifies completed and inspected workpiece. Cleans machines, work station, or conveyor, using airhose, wax, solvents, brushes, and rags. Examines rollers, sanding belts, knives, cutting or boring devices, and conveyor mechanisms; sharpens or replaces worn parts, using hand tools. Examines raw woodstock to detect defects and to ensure conformity to size and other specification standards. Examines finished workpiece for smoothness, shape, angle, depth-of-cut, and conformity to specifications, visually and using hands, rule, or other gauges. Places water-soaked woodstock into form under hydraulic lift to shape for use in making such items as musical instruments. Places or secures woodstock against guide or into holding device prior to feeding into machine. Installs and adjusts blades, cutterheads, boring bits, or sanding belts in machines, according to workpiece, machine function, and specifications, using hand tools. Readjusts and realigns guides of sanding, cutting, or boring machines to correct defects in finished product, using hand tools. Starts machine and moves lever to engage hydraulic lift to press woodstock into desired form, allows for drying time, and removes. Starts machine, adjusts controls, and moves lever or depresses pedal to bore, shape, smooth, shave, chip, slice or cut woodstock. Examines blueprints, drawings, or samples to determine size, type, and setting of machine tools, stops, jigs, and guides to use.

GOE Number, Interest Area, and Work Group: 08.03.01; Industrial Production; Production Work: Machine Work, Assorted Materials. **Personality Type:** Realistic. Realistic occupations frequently involve work activities that include practical, hands-on problems and solutions. These occupations often deal with plants, animals, and real-world materials like wood, tools, and machinery. Many of the occupations require working outside and do not involve a lot of paperwork or working closely with others. **Work Values:** Moral Values; Independence; Activity; Company Policies and Practices; Supervision, Human Relations. **Skills:** Operation and Control; Product Inspection; Operation Monitoring; Equipment Maintenance; Testing. **Abilities:** *Cognitive*—Written Comprehension; Information Ordering; Visualization; Selective Attention; Number Facility. *Psychomotor*—Arm-Hand Steadiness; Control Precision; Manual Dexterity. *Physical*—Static

Strength; Extent Flexibility; Trunk Strength. *Sensory*—Near Vision; Auditory Attention; Far Vision. **General Work Activities:** *Information Input*—Inspecting Equipment, Structures, Materials; Getting Information Needed to Do the Job; Estimating Needed Characteristics. *Mental Process*—Judging Qualities of Things, Services, Other People's Work; Evaluating Information Against Standards; Analyzing Data or Information. *Work Output*—Controlling Machines and Processes; Handling and Moving Objects; Performing General Physical Activities. *Interacting with Others*—Communicating with Other Workers; Resolving Conflict and Negotiating with Others; Coaching and Developing Others; Monitoring and Controlling Resources; Performing for or Working with the Public; Establishing and Maintaining Relationships. **Physical Work Conditions:** Indoors; Using Hands on Objects, Tools, or Controls; Common Protective or Safety Attire; Hazardous Equipment. **Other Job Characteristics:** Degree of Automation; Consequence of Error; Pace Determined by Speed of Equipment.

Experience: Job Zone 1. No previous work-related skill, knowledge, or experience is needed. **Job Preparation:** SVP Below 4.0— Less than 6 months. **Knowledge:** Mechanical; Building and Construction; Design; Production and Processing; Engineering and Technology. **Instructional Program:** 480703 Cabinet Maker and Millworker.

Related DOT Jobs: 564.682-010 Chipping-Machine Operator; 569.662-010 Incising-Machine Operator; 569.685-014 Bender, Machine; 662.682-018 Stroke-Belt-Sander Operator; 662.685-010 Cork Grinder; 662.685-014 Cylinder-Sander Operator; 662.685-018 Last Scourer; 662.685-022 Sanding-Machine Buffer; 662.685-026 Sanding-Machine Tender; 662.685-030 Sizing-Machine Tender; 662.685-034 Speed-Belt-Sander Tender; 662.685-038 Turning-Sander Tender; 662.685-042 Wood-Heel Back-Liner; 663.585-010 Clipper, Automatic; 663.682-010 Barker Operator; 663.682-018 Veneer-Slicing-Machine Operator; 663.685-014 Excelsior-Machine Tender; 663.685-018 Molding Cutter; 663.685-022 Puncher; 663.685-026 Rounding-Machine Tender (partial list; see the introduction for sources of the complete list).

51-8000 Plant and System Operators

51-8011.00 Nuclear Power Reactor Operators
(Power Generating and Reactor Plant Operators)

Education:	Long-term O-T-J training
Employed:	31,435
Openings:	2,216
Projected Growth:	3.1%
Earnings:	No data available.

Control nuclear reactors.

Monitors computer-operated equipment. Adjusts controls to regulate flow of power between generating stations and substations. Notes malfunctions of equipment, instruments, or controls. Monitors gauges to determine effects of generator loading on other power equipment. Dispatches orders and instructions to personnel through radio-telephone or intercommunication system, to coordinate operation of auxiliary equipment. Corrects abnormal conditions, following standard practices. Regulates equipment according to data provided by recording and indicating instruments or by computers. Monitors and operates boilers, turbines, wells, and auxiliary power-plant equipment.

GOE Number, Interest Area, and Work Group: 08.06.01; Industrial Production; Systems Operation: Utilities and Power Plant. **Personality Type:** Realistic. Realistic occupations frequently involve work activities that include practical, hands-on problems and solutions. These occupations often deal with plants, animals, and real-world materials like wood, tools, and machinery. Many of the occupations require working outside and do not involve a lot of paperwork or working closely with others. **Work Values:** Moral Values; Supervision, Human Relations; Supervision, Technical; Company Policies and Practices; Security. **Skills:** Operation Monitoring; Operation and Control; Problem Identification; Coordination; Reading Comprehension; Speaking. **Abilities:** *Cognitive*—Oral Expression; Written Comprehension; Oral Comprehension; Information Ordering; Problem Sensitivity. *Psychomotor*—Control Precision; Multilimb Coordination; Reaction Time; Arm-Hand Steadiness. *Physical*—none met the criteria. *Sensory*—Speech Clarity; Hearing Sensitivity; Peripheral Vision. **General Work Activities:** *Information Input*—Monitoring Processes, Materials, and Surroundings; Getting Information Needed to Do the Job; Identifying Objects, Actions, and Events. *Mental Process*—Making Decisions and Solving Problems; Evaluating Information Against Standards; Updating and Using Job-Relevant Knowledge; Organizing, Planning, and Prioritizing; Processing Information. *Work Output*—Controlling Machines and Processes; Handling and Moving Objects; Performing General Physical Activities. *Interacting with Others*—Communicating with Other Workers; Coordinating Work and Activities of Others; Establishing and Maintaining Relationships; Interpreting Meaning of Information to Others. **Physical Work Conditions:** Indoors; Using Hands on Objects, Tools, or Controls; Hazardous Conditions; Standing. **Other Job Characteristics:** Consequence of Error; Degree of Automation; Importance of Being Exact or Accurate.

Experience: Job Zone 4. A minimum of two to four years of work-related skill, knowledge, or experience is needed. **Job Preparation:** SVP 7.0 to less than 8.0—2 years to less than 10 years. **Knowledge:** Telecommunications; Engineering and Technology; Computers and Electronics; Physics; Public Safety and Security. **Instructional Program:** 410205 Nuclear/Nuclear Power Technology/Technician.

Related DOT Job: 952.362-022 Power-Reactor Operator.

51-8012.00 Power Distributors and Dispatchers
(Power Distributors and Dispatchers)

Education:	Long-term O-T-J training
Employed:	13,702
Openings:	855
Projected Growth:	-12.2%
Earnings:	$45,690

Coordinate, regulate, or distribute electricity or steam.

Tends auxiliary equipment used in the power distribution process. Controls and operates equipment to regulate or distribute electricity or steam, according to data provided by recording or indicating instruments or computers. Turns and moves controls to adjust and activate power-distribution equipment and machines. Adjusts controls to regulate the flow of power between generating stations, substations, and distribution lines. Calculates and determines load estimates or equipment requirements, to control electrical-distribution equipment or stations. Directs activities of personnel engaged in the controlling and operating of electrical-distribution equipment and machinery. Repairs, maintains, and cleans equipment and machines, using hand tools. Notifies workers or utilities of electrical- and steam-distribution process changes. Compiles and records operational data such as chart and meter readings, power demands, and usage and operating time. Monitors switchboard and control board to ensure equipment operation and electrical and steam distribution. Inspects equipment to ensure that specifications are met and to detect defects.

GOE Number, Interest Area, and Work Group: 08.06.01; Industrial Production; Systems Operation: Utilities and Power Plant. **Personality Type:** Realistic. Realistic occupations frequently involve work activities that include practical, hands-on problems and solutions. These occupations often deal with plants, animals, and real-world materials like wood, tools, and machinery. Many of the occupations require working outside and do not involve a lot of paperwork or working closely with others. **Work Values:** Moral Values; Security; Authority; Company Policies and Practices; Activity; Supervision, Human Relations. **Skills:** Operation Monitoring; Operation and Control; Equipment Maintenance; Repairing; Management of Personnel Resources. **Abilities:** *Cognitive*—Written Comprehension; Information Ordering; Problem Sensitivity; Time Sharing; Selective Attention. *Psychomotor*—Reaction Time; Manual Dexterity; Finger Dexterity; Control Precision; Wrist-Finger Speed. *Physical*—Extent Flexibility; Static Strength; Explosive Strength; Trunk Strength. *Sensory*—Near Vision; Far Vision. **General Work Activities:** *Information Input*—Monitoring Processes, Materials, and Surroundings; Inspecting Equipment, Structures, Materials; Getting Information Needed to Do the Job; Identifying Objects, Actions, and Events; Estimating Needed Characteristics. *Mental Process*—Processing Information; Making Decisions and Solving Problems; Evaluating Information Against Standards; Analyzing Data or Information. *Work Output*—Controlling Machines and Processes; Handling and Moving Objects; Documenting and Recording Information. *Interacting with Others*—Coordinating Work and Activities of Others; Communicating with Other Workers; Guiding, Directing and Motivating Subordinates. **Physical Work Conditions:** Using Hands on Objects, Tools, or Controls; Indoors; Sitting. **Other Job Characteristics:** Consequence of Error; Importance of Being Sure All Is Done; Importance of Being Exact or Accurate.

Experience: Job Zone 4. A minimum of two to four years of work-related skill, knowledge, or experience is needed. **Job Preparation:** SVP 7.0 to less than 8.0—2 years to less than 10 years. **Knowledge:** Mechanical; Mathematics; Engineering and Technology; Telecommunications; Physics. **Instructional Program:** 470501 Stationary Energy Sources Installer and Operator.

Related DOT Jobs: 820.662-010 Motor-Room Controller; 952.167-014 Load Dispatcher; 952.362-014 Feeder-Switchboard Operator; 952.362-026 Substation Operator; 952.362-030 Substation Opera-

tor Apprentice; 952.362-034 Switchboard Operator; 952.362-038 Switchboard Operator; 952.367-014 Switchboard Operator Assistant.

51-8013.00 Power Plant Operators (All Other Plant and System Operators)

Education: Long-term O-T-J training	
Employed: 147,739	
Openings: 11,990	
Projected Growth: 11.1%	
Earnings: No data available.	

Control, operate, or maintain machinery to generate electric power. Includes auxiliary equipment operators.

GOE Number, Interest Area, and Work Group: 08.06.01; Industrial Production; Systems Operation: Utilities and Power Plant. **Instructional Program:** 470501 Stationary Energy Sources Installer and Operator. **Note:** The Department of Labor has not collected some data for this job, so it has fewer details than the other descriptions.

51-8013.01 Power Generating Plant Operators, Except Auxiliary Equipment Operators (Power Generating and Reactor Plant Operators)

Education: Long-term O-T-J training	
Employed: 31,435	
Openings: 2,216	
Projected Growth: 3.1%	
Earnings: No data available.	

Control or operate machinery, such as steam-driven turbo-generators, to generate electric power, often through the use of panelboards, control boards, or semiautomatic equipment.

Adjusts controls on equipment to generate specified electrical power. Operates or controls machinery that generates electric power, using control boards or semiautomatic equipment. Monitors control and switchboard gauges to determine electrical power distribution meets specifications. Compiles and records operational data on specified forms. Examines and tests electrical power distribution machinery and equipment, using testing devices. Maintains and repairs electrical power distribution machinery and equipment, using hand tools.

GOE Number, Interest Area, and Work Group: 08.06.01; Industrial Production; Systems Operation: Utilities and Power Plant. **Personality Type:** Realistic. Realistic occupations frequently involve work activities that include practical, hands-on problems and solutions. These occupations often deal with plants, animals, and real-world materials like wood, tools, and machinery. Many of the occupations require working outside and do not involve a lot of paperwork or working closely with others. **Work Values:** Moral Values; Supervision, Technical; Supervision, Human Relations; Security; Independence. **Skills:** Operation Monitoring; Operation and Control; Troubleshooting; Testing; Equipment Maintenance. **Abilities:** *Cognitive*—Selective Attention; Perceptual

Speed; Deductive Reasoning; Problem Sensitivity; Time Sharing; Information Ordering. *Psychomotor*—Reaction Time; Control Precision; Wrist-Finger Speed; Response Orientation. *Physical*—Static Strength; Trunk Strength; Gross Body Coordination. *Sensory*—Near Vision; Hearing Sensitivity; Auditory Attention; Sound Localization. **General Work Activities:** *Information Input*—Monitoring Processes, Materials, and Surroundings; Getting Information Needed to Do the Job; Identifying Objects, Actions, and Events. *Mental Process*—Making Decisions and Solving Problems; Processing Information; Evaluating Information Against Standards. *Work Output*—Controlling Machines and Processes; Repairing and Maintaining Electrical Equipment; Handling and Moving Objects. *Interacting with Others*—Performing Administrative Activities; Monitoring and Controlling Resources; Communicating with Other Workers. **Physical Work Conditions:** Using Hands on Objects, Tools, or Controls; Indoors; Common Protective or Safety Attire. **Other Job Characteristics:** Consequence of Error; Importance of Being Sure All Is Done; Degree of Automation; Importance of Being Exact or Accurate.

Experience: Job Zone 4. A minimum of two to four years of work-related skill, knowledge, or experience is needed. **Job Preparation:** SVP 7.0 to less than 8.0—2 years to less than 10 years. **Knowledge:** Engineering and Technology; Mechanical; Mathematics; Computers and Electronics; Physics. **Instructional Program:** 470501 Stationary Energy Sources Installer and Operator.

Related DOT Jobs: 952.362-018 Hydroelectric-Station Operator; 952.362-042 Turbine Operator; 952.382-010 Diesel-Plant Operator; 952.382-014 Power Operator; 952.382-018 Power-Plant Operator.

51-8013.02 Auxiliary Equipment Operators, Power
(Power Generating and Reactor Plant Operators)

Education: Long-term O-T-J training
Employed: 31,435
Openings: 2,216
Projected Growth: 3.1%
Earnings: No data available.

Control and maintain auxiliary equipment, such as pumps, fans, compressors, condensers, feedwater heaters, filters, and chlorinators, that supplies water, fuel, lubricants, air, and auxiliary power for turbines, generators, boilers, and other power-generating plant facilities.

Tends portable or stationary high-pressure boilers that supply heat or power for engines, turbines, and steam-powered equipment. Replenishes electrolyte in batteries and oil in voltage transformers and resets tripped electric relays. Reads gauges to verify that units are operating at specified capacity, and listens for sounds warning of mechanical malfunction. Assists in making electrical repairs. Cleans and lubricates equipment and collects oil, water, and electrolyte samples for laboratory analysis, to prevent equipment failure or deterioration. Tightens leaking gland and pipe joints; reports need for major equipment repairs. Opens and closes valves and switches in sequence upon signal from other worker to start or shut down auxiliary units.

GOE Number, Interest Area, and Work Group: 08.06.01; Industrial Production; Systems Operation: Utilities and Power Plant. **Personality Type:** Realistic. Realistic occupations frequently involve work activities that include practical, hands-on problems and solutions. These occupations often deal with plants, animals, and real-world materials like wood, tools, and machinery. Many of the occupations require working outside and do not involve a lot of paperwork or working closely with others. **Work Values:** Moral Values; Supervision, Human Relations; Security; Company Policies and Practices; Supervision, Technical. **Skills:** Operation Monitoring; Operation and Control; Equipment Maintenance; Troubleshooting; Problem Identification. **Abilities:** *Cognitive*—Problem Sensitivity; Inductive Reasoning; Selective Attention; Deductive Reasoning; Information Ordering; Oral Comprehension. *Psychomotor*—Control Precision; Multilimb Coordination; Reaction Time. *Physical*—Extent Flexibility; Trunk Strength; Gross Body Coordination. *Sensory*—Sound Localization; Hearing Sensitivity. **General Work Activities:** *Information Input*—Monitoring Processes, Materials, and Surroundings; Getting Information Needed to Do the Job; Identifying Objects, Actions, and Events. *Mental Process*—Evaluating Information Against Standards; Making Decisions and Solving Problems; Processing Information. *Work Output*—Controlling Machines and Processes; Handling and Moving Objects; Performing General Physical Activities; Repairing and Maintaining Electrical Equipment. *Interacting with Others*—Communicating with Other Workers; Performing Administrative Activities; Interpreting Meaning of Information to Others; Communicating with Persons Outside Organization. **Physical Work Conditions:** Indoors; Using Hands on Objects, Tools, or Controls; Standing. **Other Job Characteristics:** Degree of Automation; Consequence of Error; Importance of Being Exact or Accurate.

Experience: Job Zone 2. Some previous work-related skill, knowledge, or experience may be helpful, but usually is not needed. **Job Preparation:** SVP 4.00 to 5.99—6 months to less than 2 years. **Knowledge:** Mechanical; Engineering and Technology; Physics; Chemistry; Mathematics. **Instructional Program:** 470501 Stationary Energy Sources Installer and Operator.

Related DOT Jobs: 951.685-010 Firer, High Pressure; 952.362-010 Auxiliary-Equipment Operator.

51-8021.00 Stationary Engineers and Boiler Operators (Stationary Engineers)

Education: Long-term O-T-J training
Employed: 31,258
Openings: 1,891
Projected Growth: -5.7%
Earnings: $38,270

Operate or maintain stationary engines, boilers, or other mechanical equipment to provide utilities for buildings or industrial processes. Operate equipment such as steam engines, generators, motors, turbines, and steam boilers.

GOE Number, Interest Area, and Work Group: 08.06.01; Industrial Production; Systems Operation: Utilities and Power Plant. **Instructional Programs:** 460401 Building/Property Maintenance and Manager; 470501 Stationary Energy Sources Installer and

Operator. **Note:** The Department of Labor has not collected some data for this job, so it has fewer details than the other descriptions.

51-8021.01 Boiler Operators and Tenders, Low Pressure (Boiler Operators and Tenders, Low Pressure)

Education: Moderate-term O-T-J training

Employed: 16,005

Openings: 942

Projected Growth: –11%

Earnings: $30,320

Operate or tend low-pressure stationary steam boilers and auxiliary steam equipment, such as pumps, compressors, and air-conditioning equipment, to supply steam heat for office buildings, apartment houses, or industrial establishments and to maintain steam at specified pressure aboard marine vessels.

Cleans and maintains heating and steam boilers and equipment, using hand tools. Moves controls and observes gauges to regulate heat and steam. Ignites fuel in burner using torch or flame. Installs burners and auxiliary equipment, using hand tools. Obtains samples from designated location on boiler and carries samples to testing laboratory. Tests sample quality to ensure sample meets specifications, using testing devices. Records test results on specified form and gives to worker or supervisor. Shovels coal or coke into firebox to feed fuel, using hand tools. Tends boilers and equipment to supply and maintain steam or heat for buildings, marine vessels, or operation of pneumatic tools.

GOE Number, Interest Area, and Work Group: 08.06.01; Industrial Production; Systems Operation: Utilities and Power Plant. **Personality Type:** Realistic. Realistic occupations frequently involve work activities that include practical, hands-on problems and solutions. These occupations often deal with plants, animals, and real-world materials like wood, tools, and machinery. Many of the occupations require working outside and do not involve a lot of paperwork or working closely with others. **Work Values:** Moral Values; Company Policies and Practices; Independence; Security; Supervision, Human Relations; Supervision, Technical. **Skills:** Operation and Control; Equipment Selection; Operation Monitoring; Product Inspection; Equipment Maintenance. **Abilities:** *Cognitive*—Problem Sensitivity; Information Ordering; Perceptual Speed; Memorization; Selective Attention; Spatial Orientation. *Psychomotor*—Control Precision; Manual Dexterity; Arm-Hand Steadiness. *Physical*—Trunk Strength; Extent Flexibility; Static Strength; Explosive Strength. *Sensory*—Near Vision; Far Vision; Depth Perception. **General Work Activities:** *Information Input*—Monitoring Processes, Materials, and Surroundings; Inspecting Equipment, Structures, Materials; Getting Information Needed to Do the Job; Identifying Objects, Actions, and Events. *Mental Process*—Evaluating Information Against Standards; Updating and Using Job-Relevant Knowledge; Judging Qualities of Things, Services, Other People's Work; Organizing, Planning, and Prioritizing; Processing Information. *Work Output*—Controlling Machines and Processes; Handling and Moving Objects; Performing General Physical Activities. *Interacting with Others*—Communicating with Other Workers; Performing Administrative Activities; Coordinating Work and Activities of Others. **Physical Work Conditions:** Using Hands on Objects, Tools, or Controls; Standing; Very Hot; Indoors. **Other Job Characteristics:** Consequence of Error; Degree of Automation; Importance of Being Exact or Accurate; Importance of Being Sure All Is Done.

Experience: Job Zone 2. Some previous work-related skill, knowledge, or experience may be helpful, but usually is not needed. **Job Preparation:** SVP 4.00 to 5.99—6 months to less than 2 years. **Knowledge:** Mechanical; Engineering and Technology; Clerical; Production and Processing; Physics; Mathematics. **Instructional Programs:** 460401 Building/Property Maintenance and Manager; 470501 Stationary Energy Sources Installer and Operator.

Related DOT Jobs: 553.685-066 Firer, Retort; 950.585-014 Boiler-Operator Helper; 950.685-014 Boiler-Room Helper; 951.685-014 Firer, Low Pressure; 951.685-018 Firer, Marine.

51-8021.02 Stationary Engineers (Stationary Engineers)

Education: Long-term O-T-J training

Employed: 31,258

Openings: 1,891

Projected Growth: –5.7%

Earnings: $38,270

Operate and maintain stationary engines and mechanical equipment to provide utilities for buildings or industrial processes. Operate equipment such as steam engines, generators, motors, turbines, and steam boilers.

Tests electrical system to determine voltage, using voltage meter. Lights burners and opens valves on equipment such as condensers, pumps, and compressors, to prepare system for operation. Inspects equipment to determine need for repair, lubrication, or adjustment. Reads dials of temperature, pressure, and ampere gauges and meters to detect malfunctions and ensure specified operation of equipment. Records temperature, pressure, water levels, fuel consumption, and other data at specified intervals in logbook. Adds chemicals or tends equipment to maintain temperature of fluids or atmosphere or to prevent scale buildup. Lubricates, maintains, and repairs equipment, using hand tools and power tools. Adjusts controls and valves on equipment to provide power and to regulate and set operations of system and industrial processes. Cleans equipment, using airhose, brushes, and rags; drains water from pipes and air reservoir.

GOE Number, Interest Area, and Work Group: 08.06.01; Industrial Production; Systems Operation: Utilities and Power Plant. **Personality Type:** Realistic. Realistic occupations frequently involve work activities that include practical, hands-on problems and solutions. These occupations often deal with plants, animals, and real-world materials like wood, tools, and machinery. Many of the occupations require working outside and do not involve a lot of paperwork or working closely with others. **Work Values:** Moral Values; Supervision, Human Relations; Autonomy; Supervision, Technical; Security; Independence. **Skills:** Equipment Maintenance; Operation Monitoring; Operation and Control; Repairing; Testing. **Abilities:** *Cognitive*—Problem Sensitivity; Written Comprehension; Information Ordering; Written Expression; Deductive Reasoning. *Psychomotor*—Control Precision; Finger Dexterity; Manual Dexterity. *Physical*—Static Strength. *Sensory*—

Sound Localization. **General Work Activities:** *Information Input*—Inspecting Equipment, Structures, Materials; Monitoring Processes, Materials, and Surroundings; Getting Information Needed to Do the Job. *Mental Process*—Processing Information; Evaluating Information Against Standards; Analyzing Data or Information. *Work Output*—Controlling Machines and Processes; Repairing and Maintaining Mechanical Equipment; Handling and Moving Objects. *Interacting with Others*—Interpreting Meaning of Information to Others; Communicating with Other Workers; Establishing and Maintaining Relationships. **Physical Work Conditions:** Indoors; Using Hands on Objects, Tools, or Controls; Distracting Sounds and Noise Levels; Standing. **Other Job Characteristics:** Consequence of Error; Degree of Automation; Importance of Being Exact or Accurate; Importance of Being Sure All Is Done.

Experience: Job Zone 3. Previous work-related skill, knowledge, or experience is required. **Job Preparation:** SVP 6.0 to less than 7.0—More than 1 year and less than 4 years. **Knowledge:** Mechanical; Engineering and Technology; Physics; Computers and Electronics; Chemistry. **Instructional Programs:** 460401 Building/Property Maintenance and Manager; 470501 Stationary Energy Sources Installer and Operator.

Related DOT Jobs: 950.362-014 Refrigerating Engineer; 950.382-010 Boiler Operator; 950.382-018 Gas-Engine Operator; 950.382-026 Stationary Engineer; 950.382-030 Stationary-Engineer Apprentice; 950.485-010 Humidifier Attendant; 950.685-010 Air-Compressor Operator.

51-8031.00 Water and Liquid Waste Treatment Plant and System Operators (Water and Liquid Waste Treatment Plant and System Operators)

Education: Long-term O-T-J training

Employed: 98,267

Openings: 12,735

Projected Growth: 14.2%

Earnings: $29,660

Operate or control an entire process or system of machines, often through the use of control boards, to transfer or treat water or liquid waste.

Directs and coordinates plant workers engaged in routine operations and maintenance activities. Collects and tests water and sewage samples, using test equipment and color-analysis standards. Inspects equipment and monitors operating conditions, meters, and gauges to determine load requirements and to detect malfunctions. Maintains, repairs, and lubricates equipment, using hand tools and power tools. Records operational data, personnel attendance, and meter and gauge readings on specified forms. Operates and adjusts controls on equipment to purify and clarify water, process or dispose of sewage, and generate power. Adds chemicals such as ammonia, chlorine, and lime, to disinfect and deodorize water and other liquids. Cleans and maintains tanks and filter beds, using hand tools and power tools.

GOE Number, Interest Area, and Work Group: 08.06.01; Industrial Production; Systems Operation: Utilities and Power Plant. **Personality Type:** Realistic. Realistic occupations frequently involve work activities that include practical, hands-on problems and solutions. These occupations often deal with plants, animals, and real-world materials like wood, tools, and machinery. Many of the occupations require working outside and do not involve a lot of paperwork or working closely with others. **Work Values:** Moral Values; Security; Company Policies and Practices; Supervision, Human Relations; Coworkers; Activity. **Skills:** Operation and Control; Science; Operation Monitoring; Problem Identification; Information Gathering; Systems Perception; Reading Comprehension. **Abilities:** *Cognitive*—Information Ordering; Problem Sensitivity; Time Sharing; Deductive Reasoning; Written Expression; Selective Attention. *Psychomotor*—Control Precision; Manual Dexterity; Arm-Hand Steadiness; Reaction Time. *Physical*—Extent Flexibility; Trunk Strength; Gross Body Coordination; Static Strength; Explosive Strength. *Sensory*—Near Vision; Speech Clarity; Far Vision. **General Work Activities:** *Information Input*—Monitoring Processes, Materials, and Surroundings; Inspecting Equipment, Structures, Materials; Identifying Objects, Actions, and Events. *Mental Process*—Judging Qualities of Things, Services, Other People's Work; Updating and Using Job-Relevant Knowledge; Evaluating Information Against Standards. *Work Output*—Controlling Machines and Processes; Handling and Moving Objects; Documenting and Recording Information. *Interacting with Others*—Coordinating Work and Activities of Others; Communicating with Other Workers; Establishing and Maintaining Relationships. **Physical Work Conditions:** Using Hands on Objects, Tools, or Controls; Indoors; Contaminants. **Other Job Characteristics:** Degree of Automation; Consequence of Error; Importance of Being Sure All Is Done.

Experience: Job Zone 2. Some previous work-related skill, knowledge, or experience may be helpful, but usually is not needed. **Job Preparation:** SVP 4.00 to 5.99—6 months to less than 2 years. **Knowledge:** Chemistry; Mechanical; Production and Processing; Mathematics; Clerical. **Instructional Program:** 150506 Water Quality and Wastewater Treatment Technology/Technician.

Related DOT Jobs: 954.382-010 Pump-Station Operator, Waterworks; 954.382-014 Water-Treatment-Plant Operator; 955.362-010 Wastewater-Treatment-Plant Operator; 955.382-010 Clarifying-Plant Operator; 955.382-014 Waste-Treatment Operator.

51-8091.00 Chemical Plant and System Operators (Chemical Plant and System Operators)

Education: Long-term O-T-J training

Employed: 42,959

Openings: 3,484

Projected Growth: 11%

Earnings: $39,030

Control or operate an entire chemical process or system of machines.

Confers with technical and supervisory personnel to report or resolve conditions affecting safety, efficiency, and product quality. Starts pumps to wash and rinse reactor vessels, to exhaust gases and vapors, and to mix product with water. Monitors recording instruments, flowmeters, panel lights, and other indicators, and listens for warning signals to verify conformity of process conditions. Defrosts frozen valves, using steam hose. Patrols work area to observe level of carbon in thickener tank and wash solutions in overflow troughs to prevent spills. Gauges tank levels, using calibrated rod. Inspects equipment for potential and actual hazards, wear, leaks, and other conditions requiring maintenance shutdown. Draws samples of products and conducts quality control tests to monitor processing and ensure standards are met. Manually regulates or shuts down equipment during emergency situations, as directed by supervisory personnel. Records operating data, such as process conditions, test results, and instruments readings, calculating material requirements or yield according to formulas. Interprets chemical reactions visible through sight glasses or on television monitor and reviews laboratory test reports for process adjustments. Moves control settings to make control adjustments on equipment units affecting speed of chemical reactions and quality and yield. Turns valves to regulate flow of product or byproducts through agitator tanks, storage drums, or neutralizer tanks, according to process. Notifies maintenance, stationary-engineering, and other auxiliary personnel to correct equipment malfunction and adjust power, steam, water, or air supply.

GOE Number, Interest Area, and Work Group: 08.06.02; Industrial Production; Systems Operation: Oil, Gas, and Water Distribution. **Personality Type:** Realistic. Realistic occupations frequently involve work activities that include practical, hands-on problems and solutions. These occupations often deal with plants, animals, and real-world materials like wood, tools, and machinery. Many of the occupations require working outside and do not involve a lot of paperwork or working closely with others. **Work Values:** Moral Values; Security; Company Policies and Practices; Compensation; Supervision, Human Relations. **Skills:** Operation Monitoring; Operation and Control; Science; Problem Identification; Systems Perception; Mathematics; Reading Comprehension. **Abilities:** *Cognitive*—Information Ordering; Written Comprehension; Oral Comprehension; Problem Sensitivity; Oral Expression. *Psychomotor*—Control Precision; Reaction Time; Finger Dexterity. *Physical*—none met the criteria. *Sensory*—Near Vision; Auditory Attention. **General Work Activities:** *Information Input*—Monitoring Processes, Materials, and Surroundings; Inspecting Equipment, Structures, Materials; Getting Information Needed to Do the Job. *Mental Process*—Evaluating Information Against Standards; Analyzing Data or Information; Updating and Using Job-Relevant Knowledge; Making Decisions and Solving Problems. *Work Output*—Controlling Machines and Processes; Handling and Moving Objects; Implementing Ideas and Programs. *Interacting with Others*—Communicating with Other Workers; Interpreting Meaning of Information to Others; Performing Administrative Activities. **Physical Work Conditions:** Indoors; Standing; Using Hands on Objects, Tools, or Controls; Sitting. **Other Job Characteristics:** Consequence of Error; Importance of Being Sure All Is Done; Importance of Being Exact or Accurate.

Experience: Job Zone 2. Some previous work-related skill, knowledge, or experience may be helpful, but usually is not needed. **Job Preparation:** SVP 4.00 to 5.99—6 months to less than 2 years. **Knowledge:** Production and Processing; Chemistry; Mechanical; Mathematics; Engineering and Technology; Public Safety and Security. **Instructional Program:** 410301 Chemical Technology/Technician.

Related DOT Jobs: 558.260-010 Chief Operator; 559.165-010 Checker; 559.382-010 Ammonia-Still Operator; 559.382-038 Naphtha-Washing-System Operator; 559.662-014 Wash Operator.

51-8092.00 Gas Plant Operators (Gas and Petroleum Plant and System Occupations)

Education: Long-term O-T-J training
Employed: 37,526
Openings: 2,335
Projected Growth: –12.6%
Earnings: No data available.

Distribute or process gas for utility companies and others by controlling compressors to maintain specified pressures on main pipelines.

GOE Number, Interest Area, and Work Group: 08.06.02; Industrial Production; Systems Operation: Oil, Gas, and Water Distribution. **Instructional Program:** 470501 Stationary Energy Sources Installer and Operator. **Note:** The Department of Labor has not collected some data for this job, so it has fewer details than the other descriptions.

51-8092.01 Gas Processing Plant Operators (Gas and Petroleum Plant and System Occupations)

Education: Long-term O-T-J training
Employed: 37,526
Openings: 2,335
Projected Growth: –12.6%
Earnings: No data available.

Control equipment, such as compressors, evaporators, heat exchangers, and refrigeration equipment, to process gas for utility companies and for industrial use.

Records gauge readings and test results. Adjusts temperature, pressure, vacuum, level, flow rate, or transfer of gas, according to test results and knowledge of process and equipment. Controls operation of compressors, scrubbers, evaporators, and refrigeration equipment to liquefy, compress, or regasify natural gas. Tests oxygen for purity and moisture content at various stages of process, using burette and moisture meter. Cleans and repairs equipment, using hand tools. Calculates gas ratios, using testing apparatus, to detect deviations from specifications. Reads logsheet to ascertain demand and disposition of product or to detect equipment malfunctions. Observes pressure, temperature, level, and flow gauges to ensure standard operation. Controls fractioning columns, compressors, purifying towers, heat exchangers, and related equipment, to extract nitrogen and oxygen from air. Signals or directs workers tending auxiliary equipment.

GOE Number, Interest Area, and Work Group: 08.06.02; Industrial Production; Systems Operation: Oil, Gas, and Water Distribution. **Personality Type:** Realistic. Realistic occupations frequently involve work activities that include practical, hands-on problems and solutions. These occupations often deal with plants, animals, and real-world materials like wood, tools, and machinery. Many of the occupations require working outside and do not involve a lot of paperwork or working closely with others. **Work Values:** Security; Moral Values; Supervision, Human Relations; Company Policies and Practices; Activity. **Skills:** Operation Monitoring; Operation and Control; Mathematics; Repairing; Equipment Maintenance. **Abilities:** *Cognitive*–Problem Sensitivity; Deductive Reasoning; Written Comprehension; Oral Comprehension; Memorization; Number Facility. *Psychomotor*–Control Precision. *Physical*–Gross Body Coordination. **General Work Activities:** *Information Input*–Getting Information Needed to Do the Job; Monitoring Processes, Materials, and Surroundings; Identifying Objects, Actions, and Events. *Mental Process*–Evaluating Information Against Standards; Analyzing Data or Information; Making Decisions and Solving Problems; Processing Information. *Work Output*–Controlling Machines and Processes; Documenting and Recording Information; Repairing and Maintaining Mechanical Equipment; Handling and Moving Objects; Performing General Physical Activities. *Interacting with Others*–Communicating with Other Workers; Coordinating Work and Activities of Others; Performing Administrative Activities. **Physical Work Conditions:** Indoors; Using Hands on Objects, Tools, or Controls; Standing; Common Protective or Safety Attire. **Other Job Characteristics:** Consequence of Error; Importance of Being Exact or Accurate; Degree of Automation.

Experience: Job Zone 2. Some previous work-related skill, knowledge, or experience may be helpful, but usually is not needed. **Job Preparation:** SVP 4.00 to 5.99–6 months to less than 2 years. **Knowledge:** Mechanical; Chemistry; Production and Processing; Engineering and Technology; Mathematics. **Instructional Program:** 410301 Chemical Technology/Technician.

Related DOT Jobs: 552.362-014 Oxygen-Plant Operator; 559.362-018 Liquefaction-Plant Operator; 953.362-014 Liquefaction-and-Regasification-Plant Operator.

51-8092.02 Gas Distribution Plant Operators
(Gas and Petroleum Plant and System Occupations)

Education: Long-term O-T-J training

Employed: 37,526

Openings: 2,335

Projected Growth: –12.6%

Earnings: No data available.

Control equipment to regulate flow and pressure of gas for utility companies and industrial use. Control distribution of gas for a municipal or industrial plant or a single process in an industrial plant.

Adjusts governors to maintain specified gas pressure and volume. Controls equipment to regulate flow and pressure of gas to feedlines of boilers, furnaces, and related steam-generating or heating equipment. Determines causes of abnormal pressure variances and makes corrective recommendations, such as installation of pipe to relieve overloading. Changes charts in recording meters. Observes, records, and reports flow and pressure-gauge readings on gas mains and fuel feedlines. Determines required governor adjustments, according to customer-demand estimates.

GOE Number, Interest Area, and Work Group: 08.06.02; Industrial Production; Systems Operation: Oil, Gas, and Water Distribution. **Personality Type:** Realistic. Realistic occupations frequently involve work activities that include practical, hands-on problems and solutions. These occupations often deal with plants, animals, and real-world materials like wood, tools, and machinery. Many of the occupations require working outside and do not involve a lot of paperwork or working closely with others. **Work Values:** Moral Values; Security; Supervision, Human Relations; Company Policies and Practices; Independence; Activity; Supervision, Technical. **Skills:** Operation and Control; Operation Monitoring; Equipment Maintenance; Problem Identification; Troubleshooting; Operations Analysis. **Abilities:** *Cognitive*–Information Ordering; Number Facility; Inductive Reasoning; Written Comprehension; Problem Sensitivity. *Psychomotor*–Control Precision. *Physical*–Extent Flexibility. **General Work Activities:** *Information Input*–Monitoring Processes, Materials, and Surroundings; Identifying Objects, Actions, and Events; Getting Information Needed to Do the Job. *Mental Process*–Making Decisions and Solving Problems; Evaluating Information Against Standards; Analyzing Data or Information; Judging Qualities of Things, Services, Other People's Work. *Work Output*–Controlling Machines and Processes; Handling and Moving Objects; Documenting and Recording Information. *Interacting with Others*– Performing Administrative Activities; Interpreting Meaning of Information to Others; Communicating with Other Workers. **Physical Work Conditions:** Indoors; Contaminants; Using Hands on Objects, Tools, or Controls; Hazardous Conditions. **Other Job Characteristics:** Degree of Automation; Consequence of Error; Importance of Being Sure All Is Done; Importance of Being Exact or Accurate.

Experience: Job Zone 3. Previous work-related skill, knowledge, or experience is required. **Job Preparation:** SVP 6.0 to less than 7.0–More than 1 year and less than 4 years. **Knowledge:** Mechanical; Engineering and Technology; Clerical; Production and Processing; Physics. **Instructional Program:** 470501 Stationary Energy Sources Installer and Operator.

Related DOT Jobs: 953.362-010 Fuel Attendant; 953.362-018 Pressure Controller.

51-8093.00 Petroleum Pump System Operators, Refinery Operators, and Gaugers (Petroleum Refinery and Control Panel Operators)

Education: No data available.

Employed: 18,150

Openings: No data available.

Projected Growth: No data available.

Earnings: $45,470

Control the operation of petroleum refining or processing units. Specialize in controlling manifold and pumping systems, gauging or testing oil in storage tanks, or regulating the flow of oil into pipelines.

GOE Number, Interest Area, and Work Group: 08.06.02; Industrial Production; Systems Operation: Oil, Gas, and Water Distribution. **Instructional Program:** 470501 Stationary Energy Sources

Installer and Operator. **Note:** The Department of Labor has not collected some data for this job, so it has fewer details than the other descriptions.

51-8093.01 Petroleum Pump System Operators
(Gas and Petroleum Plant and System Occupations)

Education: Long-term O-T-J training
Employed: 37,526
Openings: 2,335
Projected Growth: –12.6%
Earnings: No data available.

Control or operate manifold and pumping systems to circulate liquids through a petroleum refinery.

Plans movement of products through lines to processing, storage, and shipping units, utilizing knowledge of interconnections and capacities system. Signals other workers by telephone or radio to operate pumps, open and close valves, and check temperatures. Records operating data, such as products and quantities pumped, stocks used, gauging results, and operating time. Reads operating schedules or instructions from dispatcher. Starts battery of pumps, observes pressure meters and flowmeters, and turns valves to regulate pumping speeds according to schedules. Turns handwheels to open line valves and direct flow of product. Synchronizes activities with other pumphouses to ensure continuous flow of products and minimum of contamination between products.

GOE Number, Interest Area, and Work Group: 08.06.02; Industrial Production; Systems Operation: Oil, Gas, and Water Distribution. **Personality Type:** Realistic. Realistic occupations frequently involve work activities that include practical, hands-on problems and solutions. These occupations often deal with plants, animals, and real-world materials like wood, tools, and machinery. Many of the occupations require working outside and do not involve a lot of paperwork or working closely with others. **Work Values:** Moral Values; Security; Company Policies and Practices; Supervision, Human Relations; Supervision, Technical. **Skills:** Operation and Control; Operation Monitoring; Coordination; Repairing; Troubleshooting; Implementation Planning; Systems Perception. **Abilities:** *Cognitive*—Oral Expression; Information Ordering; Written Comprehension; Written Expression; Problem Sensitivity; Deductive Reasoning. *Psychomotor*—Control Precision; Rate Control. *Physical*—Extent Flexibility; Static Strength; Trunk Strength. **General Work Activities:** *Information Input*—Monitoring Processes, Materials, and Surroundings; Getting Information Needed to Do the Job; Inspecting Equipment, Structures, Materials. *Mental Process*—Making Decisions and Solving Problems; Processing Information; Evaluating Information Against Standards. *Work Output*—Controlling Machines and Processes; Handling and Moving Objects; Repairing and Maintaining Mechanical Equipment. *Interacting with Others*—Communicating with Other Workers; Performing Administrative Activities; Establishing and Maintaining Relationships. **Physical Work Conditions:** Indoors; Using Hands on Objects, Tools, or Controls; Standing. **Other Job Characteristics:** Degree of Automation; Consequence of Error; Importance of Being Sure All Is Done.

Experience: Job Zone 3. Previous work-related skill, knowledge, or experience is required. **Job Preparation:** SVP 6.0 to less than 7.0—More than 1 year and less than 4 years. **Knowledge:** Mechanical; Clerical; Chemistry; Telecommunications; Engineering and Technology. **Instructional Program:** 470501 Stationary Energy Sources Installer and Operator.

Related DOT Job: 549.360-010 Pumper.

51-8093.02 Petroleum Refinery and Control Panel Operators (Gas and Petroleum Plant and System Occupations)

Education: Long-term O-T-J training
Employed: 37,526
Openings: 2,335
Projected Growth: –12.6%
Earnings: No data available.

Analyze specifications and control continuous operation of petroleum refining and processing units. Operate control panel to regulate temperature, pressure, rate of flow, and tank level in petroleum refining unit, according to process schedules.

Compiles and records operating data, instrument readings, documents, and results of laboratory analyses. Monitors and adjusts unit controls to ensure safe and efficient operating conditions. Operates auxiliary equipment and controls multiple processing units during distilling or treating operations. Samples and tests liquids and gases for chemical characteristics and color of products, or sends products to laboratory for analysis. Cleans interior of processing units by circulating chemicals and solvents within unit. Repairs, lubricates, and maintains equipment; reports malfunctioning equipment to supervisor to schedule needed repairs. Inspects equipment and listens for automated warning signals, to determine location and nature of malfunction, such as leaks and breakage. Observes instruments, gauges, and meters to verify conformance to specified quality and quantity of product. Reads and analyzes specifications, schedules, logs, and test results to determine changes to equipment controls required to produce specified product. Operates control panel to coordinate and regulate process variables and to direct product flow rate, according to prescribed schedules.

GOE Number, Interest Area, and Work Group: 08.06.02; Industrial Production; Systems Operation: Oil, Gas, and Water Distribution. **Personality Type:** Realistic. Realistic occupations frequently involve work activities that include practical, hands-on problems and solutions. These occupations often deal with plants, animals, and real-world materials like wood, tools, and machinery. Many of the occupations require working outside and do not involve a lot of paperwork or working closely with others. **Work Values:** Moral Values; Security; Company Policies and Practices; Activity; Supervision, Human Relations; Supervision, Technical. **Skills:** Operation Monitoring; Operation and Control; Mathematics; Equipment Maintenance; Product Inspection. **Abilities:** *Cognitive*—Problem Sensitivity; Written Comprehension; Number Facility; Information Ordering; Mathematical Reasoning; Category Flexibility. *Psychomotor*—Reaction Time; Control Precision; Finger Dexterity; Rate Control; Arm-Hand Steadiness.

Physical—Extent Flexibility; Explosive Strength; Dynamic Flexibility; Dynamic Strength. *Sensory*—Sound Localization; Auditory Attention; Hearing Sensitivity. **General Work Activities:** *Information Input*—Inspecting Equipment, Structures, Materials; Monitoring Processes, Materials, and Surroundings; Getting Information Needed to Do the Job. *Mental Process*—Analyzing Data or Information; Processing Information; Evaluating Information Against Standards. *Work Output*—Controlling Machines and Processes; Repairing and Maintaining Mechanical Equipment; Handling and Moving Objects; Documenting and Recording Information. *Interacting with Others*—Interpreting Meaning of Information to Others; Communicating with Other Workers; Performing Administrative Activities. **Physical Work Conditions:** Indoors; Using Hands on Objects, Tools, or Controls; Standing. **Other Job Characteristics:** Degree of Automation; Consequence of Error; Importance of Being Sure All Is Done.

Experience: Job Zone 4. A minimum of two to four years of work-related skill, knowledge, or experience is needed. **Job Preparation:** SVP 7.0 to less than 8.0—2 years to less than 10 years. **Knowledge:** Mechanical; Mathematics; Chemistry; Public Safety and Security; Physics; Engineering and Technology. **Instructional Program:** 470501 Stationary Energy Sources Installer and Operator.

Related DOT Jobs: 546.382-010 Control-Panel Operator; 549.260-010 Refinery Operator.

51-8093.03 Gaugers (Gas and Petroleum Plant and System Occupations)

Education: Long-term O-T-J training
Employed: 37,526
Openings: 2,335
Projected Growth: –12.6%
Earnings: No data available.

Gauge and test oil in storage tanks. Regulate flow of oil into pipelines at wells, tank farms, refineries, and marine and rail terminals, following prescribed standards and regulations.

Tightens connections with wrenches; greases and oils valves, using grease gun and oil can. Starts pumps and opens valves to regulate flow of oil into and out of tanks, according to delivery schedules. Gauges tank containing petroleum and natural gas byproducts, such as condensate or natural gasoline. Records readings and test results. Lowers thermometer into tanks to obtain temperature reading. Records meter and pressure readings at gas well. Reports leaks or defective valves to maintenance. Tests oil to determine amount of bottom sediment, water, and foreign materials, using centrifugal tester. Calculates test results, using standard formulas. Turns bleeder valves or lowers sample container into tank to obtain oil sample. Operates pumps, teletype, and mobile radio. Reads automatic gauges at specified intervals to determine flow rate of oil into or from tanks and amount of oil in tanks. Regulates flow of products into pipelines, using automated pumping equipment. Gauges quality of oil in storage tanks before and after delivery, using calibrated steel tape and conversion. Clamps seal around valves to secure tanks. Inspects pipelines, valves, and flanges to detect malfunctions such as loose connections and leaks.

GOE Number, Interest Area, and Work Group: 08.06.02; Industrial Production; Systems Operation: Oil, Gas, and Water Distribution. **Personality Type:** Realistic. Realistic occupations frequently involve work activities that include practical, hands-on problems and solutions. These occupations often deal with plants, animals, and real-world materials like wood, tools, and machinery. Many of the occupations require working outside and do not involve a lot of paperwork or working closely with others. **Work Values:** Moral Values; Independence; Supervision, Human Relations; Supervision, Technical; Company Policies and Practices. **Skills:** Mathematics; Operation Monitoring; Operation and Control; Reading Comprehension; Problem Identification; Equipment Maintenance; Product Inspection. **Abilities:** *Cognitive*—Problem Sensitivity; Perceptual Speed; Deductive Reasoning; Information Ordering; Mathematical Reasoning; Written Expression. *Psychomotor*—Control Precision; Manual Dexterity; Response Orientation; Wrist-Finger Speed. *Physical*—Extent Flexibility; Static Strength; Explosive Strength. *Sensory*—Auditory Attention; Far Vision; Sound Localization; Hearing Sensitivity; Depth Perception. **General Work Activities:** *Information Input*—Getting Information Needed to Do the Job; Monitoring Processes, Materials, and Surroundings; Inspecting Equipment, Structures, Materials. *Mental Process*—Evaluating Information Against Standards; Processing Information; Analyzing Data or Information; Judging Qualities of Things, Services, Other People's Work; Making Decisions and Solving Problems. *Work Output*—Controlling Machines and Processes; Documenting and Recording Information; Performing General Physical Activities; Handling and Moving Objects. *Interacting with Others*—Communicating with Other Workers; Monitoring and Controlling Resources; Establishing and Maintaining Relationships. **Physical Work Conditions:** Hazardous Conditions; Using Hands on Objects, Tools, or Controls; Contaminants. **Other Job Characteristics:** Consequence of Error; Importance of Being Exact or Accurate; Degree of Automation; Importance of Being Sure All Is Done.

Experience: Job Zone 3. Previous work-related skill, knowledge, or experience is required. **Job Preparation:** SVP 6.0 to less than 7.0—More than 1 year and less than 4 years. **Knowledge:** Mechanical; Mathematics; Production and Processing; Engineering and Technology; Public Safety and Security. **Instructional Program:** 470501 Stationary Energy Sources Installer and Operator.

Related DOT Job: 914.384-010 Gauger.

51-9000 Other Production Occupations

51-9011.00 Chemical Equipment Operators and Tenders (Chemical Equipment Controllers, Operators and Tenders)

Education: Moderate-term O-T-J training
Employed: 100,025
Openings: 19,720
Projected Growth: 11.4%
Earnings: No data available.

Operate or tend equipment such as devulcanizers, steam-jacketed kettles, and reactor vessels, to control chemical changes or reactions in the processing of industrial or consumer products.

GOE Number, Interest Area, and Work Group: 08.03.02; Industrial Production; Production Work: Equipment Operation, Assorted Materials Processing. **Instructional Program:** 470303 Industrial Machinery Maintenance and Repairer. **Note:** The Department of Labor has not collected some data for this job, so it has fewer details than the other descriptions.

51-9011.01 Chemical Equipment Controllers and Operators (Chemical Equipment Controllers, Operators and Tenders)

Education: Moderate-term O-T-J training

Employed: 100,025

Openings: 19,720

Projected Growth: 11.4%

Earnings: No data available.

Control or operate equipment to control chemical changes or reactions in the processing of industrial or consumer products. Use reaction kettles, catalytic converters, continuous or batch-treating equipment, saturator tanks, electrolytic cells, reactor vessels, recovery units, and fermentation chambers.

Opens valves or operates pumps to admit or drain specified amounts of materials, impurities, or treating agents to or from equipment. Weighs or measures specified amounts of materials. Reads plant specifications to ascertain product, ingredient, and prescribed modifications of plant procedures. Dumps or scoops prescribed solid, granular, or powdered materials into equipment. Adds treating or neutralizing agent to product and pumps product through filter or centrifuge to remove impurities or precipitate product. Mixes chemicals according to proportion tables or prescribed formulas. Starts pumps, agitators, reactors, blowers, or automatic feed of materials. Draws samples of product and sends to laboratory for analysis. Moves controls to adjust feed and flow of liquids and gases through equipment in specified sequence. Sets and adjusts indicating, controlling, or timing devices, such as gauging instruments, thermostat, gas analyzers, or recording calorimeter. Flushes or cleans equipment, using steamhose or mechanical reamer. Records operational data such as temperature, pressure, ingredients used, processing time, or test results, in operating log. Makes minor repairs and lubricates and maintains equipment, using hand tools. Directs activities of workers assisting in control or verification of process or in the unloading of materials. Monitors gauges, recording instruments, flowmeters, or product to regulate or maintain specified conditions. Operates or tends auxiliary equipment such as heaters, scrubbers, filters, or driers, to prepare or further process materials. Adjusts controls to regulate temperature, pressure, and time of prescribed reaction, according to knowledge of equipment and process. Tests sample for specific gravity, chemical characteristics, pH level, concentration, or viscosity. Patrols and inspects equipment or unit to detect leaks and malfunctions.

GOE Number, Interest Area, and Work Group: 08.03.02; Industrial Production; Production Work: Equipment Operation, Assorted Materials Processing. **Personality Type:** Realistic. Realistic occupations frequently involve work activities that include practical, hands-on problems and solutions. These occupations often deal with plants, animals, and real-world materials like wood, tools, and machinery. Many of the occupations require working outside and do not involve a lot of paperwork or working closely with others. **Work Values:** Moral Values; Company Policies and Practices; Activity; Supervision, Technical; Supervision, Human Relations. **Skills:** Operation Monitoring; Operation and Control; Reading Comprehension; Product Inspection; Science. **Abilities:** *Cognitive*—Information Ordering; Written Comprehension; Oral Expression; Problem Sensitivity; Selective Attention. *Psychomotor*—Reaction Time; Control Precision; Response Orientation. *Physical*—Extent Flexibility; Static Strength; Dynamic Strength; Stamina; Gross Body Equilibrium. *Sensory*—Near Vision; Speech Clarity; Visual Color Discrimination. **General Work Activities:** *Information Input*—Monitoring Processes, Materials, and Surroundings; Inspecting Equipment, Structures, Materials; Getting Information Needed to Do the Job. *Mental Process*—Updating and Using Job-Relevant Knowledge; Making Decisions and Solving Problems; Evaluating Information Against Standards. *Work Output*—Controlling Machines and Processes; Handling and Moving Objects; Performing General Physical Activities. *Interacting with Others*—Coordinating Work and Activities of Others; Performing Administrative Activities; Communicating with Other Workers. **Physical Work Conditions:** Indoors; Using Hands on Objects, Tools, or Controls; Hazardous Conditions. **Other Job Characteristics:** Degree of Automation; Consequence of Error; Importance of Being Exact or Accurate; Frustrating Circumstances; Importance of Being Sure All Is Done.

Experience: Job Zone 2. Some previous work-related skill, knowledge, or experience may be helpful, but usually is not needed. **Job Preparation:** SVP 4.00 to 5.99—6 months to less than 2 years. **Knowledge:** Chemistry; Mechanical; Mathematics; Engineering and Technology; English Language; Public Safety and Security. **Instructional Program:** 470303 Industrial Machinery Maintenance and Repairer.

Related DOT Jobs: No data available.

51-9011.02 Chemical Equipment Tenders (Chemical Equipment Controllers, Operators and Tenders)

Education: Moderate-term O-T-J training

Employed: 100,025

Openings: 19,720

Projected Growth: 11.4%

Earnings: No data available.

Tend equipment in which a chemical change or reaction takes place in the processing of industrial or consumer products. Use devulcanizers, batch stills, fermenting tanks, steam-jacketed kettles, and reactor vessels.

Notifies maintenance engineer of equipment malfunction. Adjusts valves or controls to maintain system within specified operating conditions. Records data in log from instruments and gauges, concerning temperature, pressure, materials used, treating time, and shift production. Tests samples to determine specific gravity, composition, or acidity, using chemical test equipment such as hydrometer or pH meter. Replaces filtering media or makes minor repairs to equipment, using hand tools. Patrols work area to detect leaks and equipment malfunctions and to monitor operating conditions. Inventories supplies received and consumed. Observes gauges, meters, and panel lights to monitor operating conditions such as temperature or pressure. Drains equipment and pumps water or other solution through, to flush and clean tanks or equipment. Draws sample of products for analysis, to aid in process adjustments and to maintain production standards. Weighs, measures, or mixes prescribed quantities of materials. Loads specified amounts of chemicals into processing equipment. Starts pumps and agitators, turns valves, or moves controls of processing equipment, to admit, transfer, filter, or mix chemicals. Observes safety precautions to prevent fires and explosions. Assists other workers in preparing and maintaining equipment.

GOE Number, Interest Area, and Work Group: 08.03.02; Industrial Production; Production Work: Equipment Operation, Assorted Materials Processing. **Personality Type:** Realistic. Realistic occupations frequently involve work activities that include practical, hands-on problems and solutions. These occupations often deal with plants, animals, and real-world materials like wood, tools, and machinery. Many of the occupations require working outside and do not involve a lot of paperwork or working closely with others. **Work Values:** Moral Values; Company Policies and Practices; Activity; Supervision, Human Relations; Supervision, Technical; Independence. **Skills:** Operation Monitoring; Operation and Control; Product Inspection; Science; Testing. **Abilities:** *Cognitive*—Problem Sensitivity; Information Ordering; Oral Expression; Written Expression; Selective Attention; Deductive Reasoning. *Psychomotor*—Control Precision; Reaction Time; Wrist-Finger Speed; Speed of Limb Movement; Manual Dexterity. *Physical*—Dynamic Flexibility; Explosive Strength; Dynamic Strength. *Sensory*—Speech Clarity; Visual Color Discrimination; Speech Recognition. **General Work Activities:** *Information Input*—Monitoring Processes, Materials, and Surroundings; Inspecting Equipment, Structures, Materials; Getting Information Needed to Do the Job; Identifying Objects, Actions, and Events. *Mental Process*—Evaluating Information Against Standards; Processing Information; Analyzing Data or Information. *Work Output*—Controlling Machines and Processes; Handling and Moving Objects; Performing General Physical Activities; Documenting and Recording Information. *Interacting with Others*—Communicating with Other Workers; Assisting and Caring for Others; Monitoring and Controlling Resources. **Physical Work Conditions:** Indoors; Hazardous Conditions; Using Hands on Objects, Tools, or Controls; Common Protective or Safety Attire. **Other Job Characteristics:** Degree of Automation; Consequence of Error; Importance of Being Exact or Accurate; Importance of Being Sure All Is Done.

Experience: Job Zone 2. Some previous work-related skill, knowledge, or experience may be helpful, but usually is not needed. **Job Preparation:** SVP 4.00 to 5.99—6 months to less than 2 years. **Knowledge:** Chemistry; Mechanical; Mathematics; Production and Processing; Public Safety and Security. **Instructional Program:** 470303 Industrial Machinery Maintenance and Repairer.

Related DOT Jobs: 521.685-190 Ion Exchange Operator; 546.385-010 Gas Treater; 551.465-010 Purification-Operator Helper; 551.585-018 Pan Helper; 551.685-094 Lye Treater; 553.685-026 Cadmium-Liquor Maker; 558.385-010 Cd-Reactor Operator; 558.385-014 Tower Helper; 558.485-010 Caustic Operator; 558.565-010 Acid-Plant Helper; 558.585-010 Catalytic-Converter-Operator Helper; 558.585-018 Contact-Acid-Plant Operator; 558.585-022 Cuprous-Chloride Helper; 558.585-026 Devulcanizer Tender; 558.585-034 Neutralizer; 558.585-042 Twitchell Operator; 558.685-010 Acid-Polymerization Operator; 558.685-014 Ball-Mill Operator; 558.685-030 Ion-Exchange Operator; 558.685-034 Ion-Exchange Operator (partial list; see the introduction for sources of the complete list).

51-9012.00 Separating, Filtering, Clarifying, Precipitating, and Still Machine Setters, Operators, and Tenders (Separating, Filtering, Clarifying, Precipitating, and Still Machine Operators and Tenders)

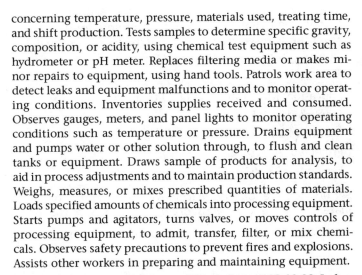

Education: Moderate-term O-T-J training
Employed: 28,492
Openings: 4,827
Projected Growth: –7.2%
Earnings: $29,600

Set up, operate, or tend continuous flow or vat-type equipment; filter presses; shaker screens; centrifuges; condenser tubes; precipitating, fermenting, or evaporating tanks; scrubbing towers; or batch stills. Set up, operate, or tend machines that extract, sort, or separate liquids, gases, or solids from other materials to recover a refined product.

Measures or weighs materials to be refined, mixed, transferred, stored, or otherwise processed. Inspects machines and equipment for hazards, operating efficiency, mechanical malfunctions, wear, and leaks. Lubricates, connects, installs, replaces, or makes minor adjustments or repairs to hoses, pumps, filters, or screens, to maintain processing equipment, using hand tools. Cleans tanks, screens, inflow pipes, and other processing equipment, using hoses, brushes, scrappers, or chemical solutions. Collects samples of material or product for laboratory analysis. Tests samples to determine viscosity, acidity, specific gravity, or degree of concentration, using test equipment such as viscometer, pH meter, and hydrometer. Removes full bags or containers from discharge outlets and replaces them with empty ones. Communicates or signals processing instructions to other workers. Examines samples visually or by hand to verify quality, such as clarity, cleanliness, consistency, dryness, and texture. Removes clogs, defects, and impurities from machines, tanks, conveyors, screen, or other processing equipment. Monitors material flow and control instruments such as gauges, indicators, and meters, to ensure optimal processing conditions and results. Sets or adjusts machine controls to regulate conditions such as material flow, temperature, and pressure, according to specified operating procedures. Dumps, pours, or loads specified amounts of refined or unrefined materials into equipment or containers for further processing or storage. Starts agitators, shakers, conveyors, pumps, or centrifuge machines; turns valves or moves controls, to admit, drain, filter, mix, or transfer materials. Maintains log of instrument readings, test results, and shift production.

GOE Number, Interest Area, and Work Group: 08.03.02; Industrial Production; Production Work: Equipment Operation, Assorted Materials Processing. **Personality Type:** Realistic. Realistic occupations frequently involve work activities that include practical, hands-on problems and solutions. These occupations often deal with plants, animals, and real-world materials like wood, tools, and machinery. Many of the occupations require working outside and do not involve a lot of paperwork or working closely with others. **Work Values:** Moral Values; Supervision, Human Relations; Company Policies and Practices; Activity; Independence; Supervision, Technical. **Skills:** Product Inspection; Operation Monitoring; Operation and Control; Equipment Maintenance; Repairing. **Abilities:** *Cognitive*—Information Ordering; Written Comprehension; Oral Comprehension; Problem Sensitivity; Perceptual Speed; Oral Expression. *Psychomotor*—Control Precision; Wrist-Finger Speed; Response Orientation. *Physical*—Trunk Strength; Static Strength; Stamina. *Sensory*—Near Vision; Visual Color Discrimination; Sound Localization. **General Work Activities:** *Information Input*—Monitoring Processes, Materials, and Surroundings; Inspecting Equipment, Structures, Materials; Getting Information Needed to Do the Job; Identifying Objects, Actions, and Events. *Mental Process*—Evaluating Information Against Standards; Judging Qualities of Things, Services, Other People's Work; Processing Information. *Work Output*—Controlling Machines and Processes; Handling and Moving Objects; Repairing and Maintaining Mechanical Equipment. *Interacting with Others*—Communicating with Other Workers; Performing Administrative Activities; Coordinating Work and Activities of Others; Establishing and Maintaining Relationships; Interpreting Meaning of Information to Others. **Physical Work Conditions:** Using Hands on Objects, Tools, or Controls; Indoors; Standing. **Other Job Characteristics:** Degree of Automation; Importance of Being Sure All Is Done; Consequence of Error.

Experience: Job Zone 1. No previous work-related skill, knowledge, or experience is needed. **Job Preparation:** SVP Below 4.0—Less than 6 months. **Knowledge:** Mechanical; Production and Processing; Mathematics; Chemistry; Clerical; Engineering and Technology. **Instructional Program:** 010401 Agricultural and Food Products Processing Operations and Management.

Related DOT Jobs: 509.685-050 Scrap Handler; 511.385-010 Zinc-Chloride Operator; 511.462-010 Concentrator Operator; 511.465-010 Top-Precipitator Operator; 511.482-014 Cryolite-Recovery Operator; 511.485-010 Molybdenum-Steamer Operator; 511.485-014 Thickener Operator; 511.562-010 Classifier Operator; 511.565-010 Dewaterer Operator; 511.565-018 Iron-Launder Operator; 511.582-010 Leacher; 511.585-010 Hydrate-Control Tender; 511.662-010 Clarifier Operator; 511.664-010 Bottom-Precipitator Operator; 511.685-010 Amalgamator; 511.685-014 Classifier Tender; 511.685-018 Condenser-Tube Tender; 511.685-026 Flotation Tender; 511.685-030 Kettle Tender II; 511.685-034 Kettle Tender, Platinum and Palladium (partial list; see the introduction for sources of the complete list).

51-9021.00 Crushing, Grinding, and Polishing Machine Setters, Operators, and Tenders (Crushing, Grinding, Mixing, and Blending Machine Operators and Tenders)

Education: Moderate-term O-T-J training
Employed: 149,526
Openings: 27,048
Projected Growth: 2.8%
Earnings: $23,350

Set up, operate, or tend machines to crush, grind, or polish materials such as coal, glass, grain, stone, food, or rubber.

Weighs or measures materials, ingredients, and products to ensure conformance to requirements. Collects samples of materials or products for laboratory testing. Examines or feels materials, ingredients, or products, to ensure conformance to established standards. Cleans and maintains machinery, equipment, materials, and products, using hand tools. Tests samples of materials or products to ensure compliance with specifications, using test equipment. Transfers materials, supplies, and products between work areas, using moving equipment and hand tools. Records operational and production data on specified forms. Tends accessory equipment such as pumps and conveyors, to move materials or ingredients through production process. Observes production monitoring equipment to ensure safe and efficient operation. Loads materials into machinery and equipment, using hand tools. Dislodges and clears jammed materials or other items from machinery and equipment, using hand tools. Adds or mixes chemicals and ingredients for processing, using hand tools or other devices. Operates or tends machines and equipment that crush, grind, polish, or blend materials. Moves controls to start, stop, or adjust machinery and equipment that crush, grind, polish, or blend materials. Reads work orders to ascertain production specifications and information.

GOE Number, Interest Area, and Work Group: 08.03.01; Industrial Production; Production Work: Machine Work, Assorted Materials. **Personality Type:** Realistic. Realistic occupations frequently involve work activities that include practical, hands-on problems and solutions. These occupations often deal with plants, animals, and real-world materials like wood, tools, and machinery. Many of the occupations require working outside and do not involve a lot of paperwork or working closely with others. **Work Values:** Moral Values; Independence; Company Policies and Practices; Supervision, Human Relations; Activity. **Skills:** Operation Monitoring; Operation and Control; Product Inspection; Testing; Equipment Maintenance. **Abilities:** *Cognitive*—Problem Sensitivity; Written Expression; Written Comprehension; Information Ordering; Number Facility; Selective Attention. *Psychomotor*—Control Precision; Reaction Time; Manual Dexterity. *Physical*—Static Strength; Explosive Strength; Dynamic Strength. *Sensory*—Sound Localization. **General Work Activities:** *Information Input*—Inspecting Equipment, Structures, Materials; Monitoring Processes, Materials, and Surroundings; Identifying Objects, Actions, and Events; Getting Information Needed to Do the Job. *Mental Process*—Evaluating Information Against Standards; Judging Qualities of Things, Services, Other People's Work; Processing Information. *Work Output*—Controlling Machines and Processes; Handling and Moving Objects; Repairing and Maintaining Mechanical Equipment; Performing General Physical Activities. *Interacting with Others*—Communicating with Other Workers; Performing Administrative Activities; Establishing and Maintaining Relationships; Assisting and Caring for Others; Guiding, Directing and Motivating Subordinates; Coaching and Developing Others. **Physical Work Conditions:** Indoors; Common Protective or Safety Attire; Using Hands on Objects, Tools, or Controls. **Other Job Characteristics:** Degree of Automation; Pace Determined by Speed of Equipment; Consequence of Error.

Experience: Job Zone 1. No previous work-related skill, knowledge, or experience is needed. **Job Preparation:** SVP Below 4.0—Less than 6 months. **Knowledge:** Production and Processing; Mechanical; Mathematics; English Language; Chemistry. **Instructional Program:** 010401 Agricultural and Food Products Processing Operations and Management.

Related DOT Jobs: 515.585-010 Scale-Reclamation Tender; 515.685-010 Batch Maker; 515.685-014 Crusher Tender; 515.685-018 Stamping-Mill Tender; 515.687-010 Hammer-Mill Operator; 519.485-010 Grinder-Mill Operator; 519.685-030 Rod-Mill Tender; 521.362-014 Miller, Distillery; 521.585-014 Miller; 521.585-018 Powder-Mill Operator; 521.662-010 Miller, Wet Process; 521.682-022 Flake Miller, Wheat and Oats; 521.682-026 Grinder Operator; 521.682-034 Refining-Machine Operator; 521.685-074 Cocoa-Room Operator; 521.685-078 Coffee Grinder; 521.685-082 Corn Grinder; 521.685-086 Corn-Grinder Operator, Automatic; 521.685-090 Crusher Operator; 521.685-094 Crushing-Machine Operator (partial list; see the introduction for sources of the complete list).

51-9022.00 Grinding and Polishing Workers, Hand
(Grinding and Polishers, Hand)

Education: Short-term O-T-J training

Employed: 80,628

Openings: 13,334

Projected Growth: 4.3%

Earnings: $20,450

Grind, sand, or polish a variety of metal, wood, stone, clay, plastic, or glass objects, using hand tools or hand-held power tools.

Sharpens abrasive grinding tools, using machines and hand tools. Grinds, sands, cleans, or polishes objects or parts, using hand tools or equipment. Observes and inspects equipment, objects, or parts, to ensure that specifications are met. Selects, loads, and adjusts workpiece or abrasive parts onto equipment or worktable, using hand tools. Trims, scrapes, or deburrs objects or parts, using hand tools or equipment. Moves controls to adjust, start, or stop equipment during grinding and polishing process. Repairs and maintains equipment, objects, or parts, using hand tools. Transfers equipment, objects, or parts, to specified work areas, using moving devices. Records product and processing data on specified forms. Measures and marks equipment, objects, or parts,

to ensure that grinding and polishing standards are met. Applies solutions and chemicals to equipment, objects, or parts, using hand tools. Removes workpiece from equipment or work table, using hand tools.

GOE Number, Interest Area, and Work Group: 08.03.06; Industrial Production; Production Work: Hands-on Work, Assorted Materials. **Personality Type:** Realistic. Realistic occupations frequently involve work activities that include practical, hands-on problems and solutions. These occupations often deal with plants, animals, and real-world materials like wood, tools, and machinery. Many of the occupations require working outside and do not involve a lot of paperwork or working closely with others. **Work Values:** Moral Values; Independence; Supervision, Technical; Activity; Company Policies and Practices. **Skills:** Product Inspection; Operation and Control; Equipment Selection; Operation Monitoring; Equipment Maintenance. **Abilities:** *Cognitive*—Information Ordering; Problem Sensitivity; Number Facility; Written Expression; Deductive Reasoning; Visualization. *Psychomotor*—Control Precision; Wrist-Finger Speed; Manual Dexterity. *Physical*—Trunk Strength; Extent Flexibility; Static Strength. *Sensory*—Depth Perception. **General Work Activities:** *Information Input*—Monitoring Processes, Materials, and Surroundings; Inspecting Equipment, Structures, Materials; Getting Information Needed to Do the Job. *Mental Process*—Evaluating Information Against Standards; Judging Qualities of Things, Services, Other People's Work; Updating and Using Job-Relevant Knowledge; Processing Information; Organizing, Planning, and Prioritizing. *Work Output*—Handling and Moving Objects; Controlling Machines and Processes; Repairing and Maintaining Mechanical Equipment; Performing General Physical Activities. *Interacting with Others*—Performing Administrative Activities; Communicating with Other Workers; Monitoring and Controlling Resources; Establishing and Maintaining Relationships. **Physical Work Conditions:** Using Hands on Objects, Tools, or Controls; Common Protective or Safety Attire; Indoors. **Other Job Characteristics:** Importance of Repeating Same Tasks; Consequence of Error; Importance of Being Sure All Is Done; Importance of Being Exact or Accurate.

Experience: Job Zone 1. No previous work-related skill, knowledge, or experience is needed. **Job Preparation:** SVP Below 4.0—Less than 6 months. **Knowledge:** Mechanical; Engineering and Technology; Production and Processing; Chemistry; Design. **Instructional Program:** 480599 Precision Metal Workers, Other.

Related DOT Jobs: 519.684-018 Mold Dresser; 700.684-034 Filer; 700.687-058 Polisher; 703.687-022 Steel-Barrel Reamer; 705.384-010 Scraper, Hand; 705.484-010 Filer, Hand, Tool; 705.484-014 Final Finisher, Forging Dies; 705.684-022 Grease Buffer; 705.684-026 Grinder I; 705.684-030 Grinder-Chipper I; 705.684-034 Metal Finisher; 705.684-038 Mold Finisher; 705.684-046 Needle Polisher; 705.684-050 Nib Finisher; 705.684-054 Pipe Buffer; 705.684-062 Polisher and Buffer II; 705.687-014 Laborer, Grinding and Polishing; 705.687-018 Metal Sander and Finisher; 706.684-098 Valve Grinder; 709.381-026 Mold Stamper and Repairer (partial list; see the introduction for sources of the complete list).

51-9023.00 Mixing and Blending Machine Setters, Operators, and Tenders (Crushing, Grinding, Mixing, and Blending Machine Operators and Tenders)

Education: Moderate-term O-T-J training
Employed: 149,526
Openings: 27,048
Projected Growth: 2.8%
Earnings: $23,350

Set up, operate, or tend machines to mix or blend materials such as chemicals, tobacco, liquids, color pigments, or explosive ingredients.

Loads materials into machinery and equipment, using hand tools. Records operational and production data on specified forms. Observes production monitoring equipment to ensure safety and efficient operation. Tends accessory equipment such as pumps and conveyors, to move materials or ingredients through production process. Moves controls to start, stop, or adjust machinery and equipment that crush, grind, polish, or blend materials. Weighs or measures materials, ingredients, and products to ensure conformance to requirements. Dislodges and clears jammed materials or other items from machinery and equipment, using hand tools. Adds or mixes chemicals and ingredients for processing, using hand tools or other devices. Examines or feels materials, ingredients, or products to ensure conformance to established standards. Collects samples of materials or products for laboratory testing. Cleans and maintains machinery, equipment, materials, and products, using hand tools. Transfers materials, supplies, and products between work areas, using moving equipment and hand tools. Operates or tends machines and equipment that crush, grind, polish, or blend materials. Reads work orders to ascertain production specifications and information. Tests samples of materials or products to ensure compliance with specifications, using test equipment.

GOE Number, Interest Area, and Work Group: 08.03.02; Industrial Production; Production Work: Equipment Operation, Assorted Materials Processing. **Personality Type:** Realistic. Realistic occupations frequently involve work activities that include practical, hands-on problems and solutions. These occupations often deal with plants, animals, and real-world materials like wood, tools, and machinery. Many of the occupations require working outside and do not involve a lot of paperwork or working closely with others. **Work Values:** Moral Values; Company Policies and Practices; Independence; Activity; Supervision, Human Relations. **Skills:** Operation Monitoring; Operation and Control; Product Inspection; Testing; Equipment Maintenance. **Abilities:** *Cognitive*—Problem Sensitivity; Written Expression; Information Ordering; Written Comprehension; Selective Attention; Number Facility. *Psychomotor*—Control Precision; Reaction Time; Manual Dexterity. *Physical*—Static Strength; Explosive Strength; Dynamic Strength. *Sensory*—Sound Localization. **General Work Activities:** *Information Input*—Inspecting Equipment, Structures, Materials; Monitoring Processes, Materials, and Surroundings; Identifying Objects, Actions, and Events; Getting Information Needed to Do the Job. *Mental Process*—Evaluating Information Against Standards; Judging Qualities of Things, Services, Other People's Work; Pro-

cessing Information. *Work Output*—Controlling Machines and Processes; Handling and Moving Objects; Performing General Physical Activities; Repairing and Maintaining Mechanical Equipment. *Interacting with Others*—Communicating with Other Workers; Coaching and Developing Others; Assisting and Caring for Others; Establishing and Maintaining Relationships; Performing Administrative Activities; Guiding, Directing and Motivating Subordinates. **Physical Work Conditions:** Indoors; Common Protective or Safety Attire; Using Hands on Objects, Tools, or Controls. **Other Job Characteristics:** Degree of Automation; Pace Determined by Speed of Equipment; Consequence of Error.

Experience: Job Zone 1. No previous work-related skill, knowledge, or experience is needed. **Job Preparation:** SVP Below 4.0—Less than 6 months. **Knowledge:** Production and Processing; Mechanical; Mathematics; English Language; Chemistry. **Instructional Program:** 010401 Agricultural and Food Products Processing Operations and Management.

Related DOT Jobs: 509.485-010 Compound Mixer; 510.465-010 Carbide-Powder Processor; 510.465-014 Slurry-Control Tender; 510.685-010 Dust Mixer; 510.685-014 Mix-House Tender; 510.685-018 Mixer; 510.685-022 Pug-Mill Operator; 510.685-026 Sinter-Machine Operator; 510.685-030 Slime-Plant Operator I; 511.685-046 Reagent Tender; 514.685-022 Lime Mixer Tender; 519.685-026 Mud-Mill Tender; 520.362-010 Bulk-Plant Operator; 520.362-014 Dry-Starch Operator; 520.382-010 Cistern-Room Operator; 520.382-014 Liquid-Sugar Melter; 520.385-010 Mixer, Whipped Topping; 520.462-010 Dough-Mixer Operator; 520.485-010 Flour Mixer; 520.485-014 Grain Mixer (partial list; see the introduction for sources of the complete list).

51-9031.00 Cutters and Trimmers, Hand (Cutters and Trimmers, Hand)

Education: Short-term O-T-J training
Employed: 42,145
Openings: 7,488
Projected Growth: –8.3%
Earnings: $17,130

Use hand tools or hand-held power tools to cut and trim a variety of manufactured items such as carpet, fabric, stone, glass, or rubber.

Separates materials or products according to size, weight, type, condition, color, or shade. Routes items to provide cutouts for parts, using portable router, grinder, and hand tools. Positions template or measures material to locate specified point of cut or to obtain maximum yield, using rule, scale, or pattern. Observes, marks, or discards items with defects such as spots, stains, scars, snags, chips, scratches, or unacceptable shape or finish. Transports items to work or storage area by pushing or pulling carts. Counts, weighs, and bundles items. Stacks cut items and loads them on racks, conveyors, or trucks. Marks cutting lines around pattern or template, or follows layout points, using square, rule, straightedge and chalk, pencil, or scribe. Cleans, treats, buffs, or polishes finished items, using grinder, brush, chisel, and cleaning solutions and polishing materials. Folds or shapes materials, preparatory to or after cutting. Marks identification numbers, trademark, grade, marketing data, size, or model number on products. Replaces or sharpens dulled cutting tools such as saws. Lowers table-mounted cutter such as knife blade, cutting wheel, or saw, to cut items to specified size. Adjusts guides and stops to control depth and width of cuts. Cuts materials such as textiles, food, and metal, using hand tools, portable power tools, or bench-mounted tools. Unrolls, lays out, attaches, or mounts material or item on cutting table or machine. Reads work order to determine dimensions, cutting locations, and quantity to cut.

GOE Number, Interest Area, and Work Group: 08.03.06; Industrial Production; Production Work: Hands-on Work, Assorted Materials. **Personality Type:** Realistic. Realistic occupations frequently involve work activities that include practical, hands-on problems and solutions. These occupations often deal with plants, animals, and real-world materials like wood, tools, and machinery. Many of the occupations require working outside and do not involve a lot of paperwork or working closely with others. **Work Values:** Moral Values; Independence; Activity; Company Policies and Practices; Security; Supervision, Technical. **Skills:** Reading Comprehension; Operation and Control; Mathematics; Equipment Selection; Product Inspection; Equipment Maintenance. **Abilities:** *Cognitive*—Visualization; Information Ordering; Number Facility; Written Comprehension; Category Flexibility; Perceptual Speed. *Psychomotor*—Manual Dexterity; Wrist-Finger Speed; Control Precision; Arm-Hand Steadiness. *Physical*—Trunk Strength; Static Strength; Extent Flexibility. *Sensory*—Visual Color Discrimination; Depth Perception. **General Work Activities:** *Information Input*—Getting Information Needed to Do the Job; Monitoring Processes, Materials, and Surroundings; Identifying Objects, Actions, and Events. *Mental Process*—Evaluating Information Against Standards; Judging Qualities of Things, Services, Other People's Work; Processing Information. *Work Output*—Handling and Moving Objects; Controlling Machines and Processes; Performing General Physical Activities. *Interacting with Others*—Performing Administrative Activities; Monitoring and Controlling Resources; Communicating with Other Workers. **Physical Work Conditions:** Indoors; Using Hands on Objects, Tools, or Controls; Hazardous Equipment; Standing. **Other Job Characteristics:** Consequence of Error; Importance of Being Exact or Accurate; Importance of Being Sure All Is Done.

Experience: Job Zone 1. No previous work-related skill, knowledge, or experience is needed. **Job Preparation:** SVP Below 4.0—Less than 6 months. **Knowledge:** Mechanical; Production and Processing; Mathematics; Engineering and Technology; Building and Construction. **Instructional Program:** 200502 Window Treatment Maker and Installer.

Related DOT Jobs: 521.687-014 Binder Cutter, Hand; 521.687-026 Bunch Trimmer, Mold; 521.687-066 Fruit Cutter; 524.687-010 Cherry Cutter; 525.687-046 Hide Trimmer; 539.686-010 Cutter, Wet Machine; 569.684-010 Log Peeler; 569.687-026 Wood Hacker; 575.684-022 Crosscutter, Rolled Glass; 579.684-030 Cutter; 585.684-010 Trimmer, Hand; 590.687-022 Rug Cutter; 673.666-014 Stripper; 689.687-090 Lapper; 700.684-018 Bright Cutter; 700.684-038 Gold Cutter; 700.684-050 Mesh Cutter; 701.687-030 Power-Chisel Operator; 703.684-018 Template Cutter; 709.684-074 Shearer and Trimmer, Wire Screen and Fabric (partial list; see the introduction for sources of the complete list).

51-9032.00 Cutting and Slicing Machine Setters, Operators, and Tenders (Cutting and Slicing Machine Setters, Operators, and Tenders)

Education: Moderate-term O-T-J training
Employed: 95,988
Openings: 18,362
Projected Growth: 6.4%
Earnings: No data available.

Set up, operate, or tend machines that cut or slice materials such as glass, stone, cork, rubber, tobacco, food, paper, or insulating material.

GOE Number, Interest Area, and Work Group: 08.03.01; Industrial Production; Production Work: Machine Work, Assorted Materials. **Instructional Program:** 470303 Industrial Machinery Maintenance and Repairer. **Note:** The Department of Labor has not collected some data for this job, so it has fewer details than the other descriptions.

51-9032.01 Fiber Product Cutting Machine Setters and Set-Up Operators (Cutting and Slicing Machine Setters and Set-Up Operators)

Education: No data available.
Employed: 28,090
Openings: No data available.
Projected Growth: No data available.
Earnings: $22,360

Set up and operate machine to cut or slice fiber material such as paper, wallboard, and insulation material.

Examines, measures, and weighs materials or products to verify conformance to specifications, using measuring devices such as ruler, micrometer, or scale. Reviews work order, blueprints, specifications, or job sample to determine components, settings, and adjustments for cutting and slicing machines. Removes completed materials or products from cutting or slicing machine; stacks or stores for additional processing. Maintains production records such as quantity, type, and dimensions of materials produced. Positions materials such as rubber, paper, or leather on feeding mechanism of cutting or slicing machine. Monitors operation of cutting or slicing machine to detect malfunctions; removes defective or substandard materials; readjusts machine components to conform to standards. Activates machine to cut, slice, slit, perforate, or score fiber products such as paperboard sheets, rubber shoe soles, or plaster wallboard. Adjusts machine controls, to position and align and to regulate speed and pressure of components. Replaces worn or broken parts; cleans and lubricates cutting or slicing machine to maintain equipment in working order. Selects and installs machine components such as cutting blades, rollers, and templates, according to specifications, using hand tools.

GOE Number, Interest Area, and Work Group: 08.03.01; Industrial Production; Production Work: Machine Work, Assorted Materials. **Personality Type:** Realistic. Realistic occupations frequently involve work activities that include practical, hands-on problems and solutions. These occupations often deal with plants, animals, and real-world materials like wood, tools, and machinery. Many of the occupations require working outside and do not involve a lot of paperwork or working closely with others. **Work Values:** Moral Values; Activity; Independence; Company Policies and Practices; Supervision, Human Relations. **Skills:** Operation and Control; Operation Monitoring; Product Inspection; Reading Comprehension; Equipment Maintenance; Equipment Selection. **Abilities:** *Cognitive*—Information Ordering; Visualization; Written Comprehension; Selective Attention; Perceptual Speed; Memorization. *Psychomotor*—Control Precision; Manual Dexterity; Reaction Time. *Physical*—Static Strength; Explosive Strength; Extent Flexibility. *Sensory*—Depth Perception; Far Vision; Visual Color Discrimination. **General Work Activities:** *Information Input*—Monitoring Processes, Materials, and Surroundings; Getting Information Needed to Do the Job; Inspecting Equipment, Structures, Materials. *Mental Process*—Judging Qualities of Things, Services, Other People's Work; Evaluating Information Against Standards; Organizing, Planning, and Prioritizing. *Work Output*—Controlling Machines and Processes; Handling and Moving Objects; Implementing Ideas and Programs. *Interacting with Others*—Communicating with Other Workers; Performing Administrative Activities; Coordinating Work and Activities of Others. **Physical Work Conditions:** Indoors; Using Hands on Objects, Tools, or Controls; Hazardous Equipment. **Other Job Characteristics:** Degree of Automation; Consequence of Error; Pace Determined by Speed of Equipment; Importance of Being Exact or Accurate.

Experience: Job Zone 2. Some previous work-related skill, knowledge, or experience may be helpful, but usually is not needed. **Job Preparation:** SVP 4.00 to 5.99—6 months to less than 2 years. **Knowledge:** Mechanical; Production and Processing; Design; Clerical; Engineering and Technology; Mathematics. **Instructional Program:** 470303 Industrial Machinery Maintenance and Repairer.

Related DOT Jobs: 579.382-018 Knife Operator; 640.360-010 Panel-Machine Setter; 640.682-018 Cutting-Machine Operator; 649.682-026 Platen-Press Operator; 649.682-038 Slitter-Scorer-Cut-Off Operator; 649.682-042 Tablet-Making-Machine Operator; 677.382-010 Batting-Machine Operator, Insulation; 677.682-026 Tenoner Operator; 690.462-010 Outsole Cutter, Automatic; 690.682-010 Arch-Cushion-Skiving-Machine Operator; 690.682-038 Foxing-Cutting-Machine Operator, Automatic; 690.682-042 Heel Breaster, Leather; 690.682-046 Heel-Seat Fitter, Machine; 690.682-050 Hot-Die-Press Operator; 692.360-014 Brush-Machine Setter; 699.382-010 Fluid Jet Cutter Operator.

51-9032.02 Stone Sawyers (Cutting and Slicing Machine Setters and Set-Up Operators)

Education: No data available.

Employed: 28,090

Openings: No data available.

Projected Growth: No data available.

Earnings: $22,360

Set up and operate gang saws, reciprocating saws, circular saws, or wire saws to cut blocks of stone into specified dimensions.

Observes operation to detect uneven sawing and exhausted abrasive supply; tightens pulleys or adds abrasive to maintain cutting speed. Adjusts blade pressure against stone, using ammeter; lowers blade in stone as cut depth increases. Changes or replaces saw blades, cables, and grinding wheels, using wrench. Aligns cable or blades with marks on stone; presses button or turns lever to lower sawing cable or blades to stone. Washes stone, using water hose, and verifies width or thickness of cut stone, using rule. Operates crane or signals crane operator to position or remove stone from car or saw bed. Builds bed of timbers on car, and aligns and levels stone on bed, using crowbar, sledgehammer, wedges, blocks, rule, and spirit level. Turns crank or presses button to move car under sawing cable or saw frame. Starts pump to circulate water and abrasive onto blade or cable during cutting. Starts saw and moves blade across surface of material such as stone, concrete slabs, and asbestos-cement sheets and pipes, to saw. Marks dimensions or traces on stone according to diagram, using chisel and hammer, straightedge, rule, and chalked string.

GOE Number, Interest Area, and Work Group: 08.03.01; Industrial Production; Production Work: Machine Work, Assorted Materials. **Personality Type:** Realistic. Realistic occupations frequently involve work activities that include practical, hands-on problems and solutions. These occupations often deal with plants, animals, and real-world materials like wood, tools, and machinery. Many of the occupations require working outside and do not involve a lot of paperwork or working closely with others. **Work Values:** Moral Values; Company Policies and Practices; Activity; Independence; Supervision, Human Relations. **Skills:** Equipment Selection; Product Inspection; Operation Monitoring; Operation and Control; Equipment Maintenance; Critical Thinking. **Abilities:** *Cognitive*—Problem Sensitivity; Information Ordering; Selective Attention; Deductive Reasoning; Flexibility of Closure; Spatial Orientation. *Psychomotor*—Control Precision; Reaction Time; Manual Dexterity; Multilimb Coordination. *Physical*—Trunk Strength; Static Strength; Stamina; Explosive Strength; Dynamic Strength. *Sensory*—Depth Perception; Peripheral Vision; Visual Color Discrimination. **General Work Activities:** *Information Input*—Monitoring Processes, Materials, and Surroundings; Getting Information Needed to Do the Job; Inspecting Equipment, Structures, Materials; Identifying Objects, Actions, and Events. *Mental Process*—Judging Qualities of Things, Services, Other People's Work; Evaluating Information Against Standards; Updating and Using Job-Relevant Knowledge. *Work Output*—Handling and Moving Objects; Controlling Machines and Processes; Performing General Physical Activities. *Interacting with Others*—Communicating with Other Workers; Coordinating Work and Activities of Others; Performing Administrative Activities. **Physical Work Conditions:** Using Hands on Objects, Tools, or Controls; Standing; Hazardous Equipment. **Other Job Characteristics:** Degree of Automation; Consequence of Error; Importance of Being Exact or Accurate; Importance of Being Sure All Is Done; Frustrating Circumstances.

Experience: Job Zone 2. Some previous work-related skill, knowledge, or experience may be helpful, but usually is not needed. **Job Preparation:** SVP 4.00 to 5.99—6 months to less than 2 years. **Knowledge:** Mechanical; Production and Processing; Building and Construction; Design; Engineering and Technology; Physics. **Instructional Program:** 470303 Industrial Machinery Maintenance and Repairer.

Related DOT Jobs: 670.362-010 Gang Sawyer, Stone; 677.462-010 Circular Sawyer, Stone; 677.462-014 Wire Sawyer.

51-9032.03 Glass Cutting Machine Setters and Set-Up Operators (Cutting and Slicing Machine Setters and Set-Up Operators)

Education: No data available.
Employed: 28,090
Openings: No data available.
Projected Growth: No data available.
Earnings: $22,360

Set up and operate machines to cut glass.

Starts vacuum-cupped crane, to lift and transfer glass. Starts machine to verify setup. Adjusts timing mechanism, to synchronize breaker bar to snap glass at score. Adjusts position, height, and stroke of cutting bridges, manually or by turning controls, to score glass to specific dimensions. Measures glass with tape to verify dimensions and observes glass to detect defects. Removes and replaces worn cutter heads, using hand tools. Operates single cut machine to cut glass. Reviews work order and maintains record of production, using counter. Directs workers on cutting team.

GOE Number, Interest Area, and Work Group: 08.03.01; Industrial Production; Production Work: Machine Work, Assorted Materials. **Personality Type:** Realistic. Realistic occupations frequently involve work activities that include practical, hands-on problems and solutions. These occupations often deal with plants, animals, and real-world materials like wood, tools, and machinery. Many of the occupations require working outside and do not involve a lot of paperwork or working closely with others. **Work Values:** Moral Values; Activity; Company Policies and Practices; Supervision, Technical; Authority; Coworkers; Supervision, Human Relations. **Skills:** Operation and Control; Product Inspection; Operation Monitoring; Mathematics; Equipment Maintenance; Equipment Selection. **Abilities:** *Cognitive*—Information Ordering; Problem Sensitivity; Selective Attention; Visualization; Oral Comprehension; Memorization. *Psychomotor*—Arm-Hand Steadiness; Manual Dexterity; Control Precision. *Physical*—Extent Flexibility; Trunk Strength; Static Strength. *Sensory*—Near Vision; Depth Perception; Speech Recognition; Far Vision; Visual Color Discrimination. **General Work Activities:** *Information Input*—Monitoring Processes, Materials, and Surroundings; Inspecting Equipment, Structures, Materials; Getting Information Needed to Do the Job. *Mental Process*—Evaluating Information Against Standards; Analyzing Data or Information; Judging Qualities of Things, Services, Other People's Work. *Work Output*—Controlling Machines and Processes; Handling and Moving Objects; Implementing Ideas and Programs. *Interacting with Others*—Communicating with Other Workers; Coordinating Work and Activities of Others; Guiding, Directing and Motivating Subordinates. **Physical Work Conditions:** Indoors; Using Hands on Objects, Tools, or Controls; Hazardous Equipment. **Other Job Characteristics:** Degree of Automation; Importance of Being Exact or Accurate; Importance of Being Sure All Is Done; Consequence of Error.

Experience: Job Zone 1. No previous work-related skill, knowledge, or experience is needed. **Job Preparation:** SVP Below 4.0—

Less than 6 months. **Knowledge:** Mechanical; Production and Processing; Engineering and Technology; Mathematics; Education and Training; English Language; Physics; Communications and Media. **Instructional Program:** 470303 Industrial Machinery Maintenance and Repairer.

Related DOT Job: 677.562-010 Glass-Cutting-Machine Operator, Automatic.

51-9032.04 Cutting and Slicing Machine Operators and Tenders (Cutting and Slicing Machine Operators and Tenders)

Education: No data available.
Employed: 67,700
Openings: No data available.
Projected Growth: No data available.
Earnings: $21,420

Operate or tend machines to cut or slice any of a wide variety of products or materials, such as tobacco, food, paper, roofing slate, glass, stone, rubber, cork, and insulation.

Installs or replaces cutting knives, blades, or wheels in cutting machine, using hand tools. Adjusts feeding guides, blades, settings, or speed, to regulate specified depth, length, or width of material, using hand tools or hands. Stops cutting machine when necessary, by pulling lever, pressing button, or depressing pedal; removes debris. Marks cutting lines or identifying information on stock, using marking pencil, ruler, or scribe. Examines and measures stock to ensure conformance to specifications, using ruler, gauge, micrometer, or scale; removes defects. Sharpens cutting blades, knives, or saws, using file, bench grinder, or honing stone. Cuts stock manually, to prepare for machine cutting, using tools such as knife, cleaver, handsaw, or hammer and chisel. Records data concerning amount and type of stock cut from duties performed, including weight, length, and width. Moves stock or scrap to and from machine, transporting either manually or by using cart, handtruck, or lift truck. Stacks and sorts cut material according to type and size, for packaging, further processing, or shipping. Feeds stock into cutting machine, conveyor, or under cutting blades, by threading, guiding, pushing, or turning handwheel. Positions stock along cutting lines or against stops on bed of scoring or cutting machine. Reads work order or receives oral instructions regarding specifications for stock to be cut. Starts cutting machine by pressing button, pulling lever, or depressing pedal to cut stock, following markings or specifications. Cleans and lubricates cutting machine, conveyors, blades, saws, or knives, using steam hose, scrapers, brush, or oil cans. Observes cutting machine in operation, to ensure even flow of stock and to detect jamming, improper feeding, or foreign materials.

GOE Number, Interest Area, and Work Group: 08.03.01; Industrial Production; Production Work: Machine Work, Assorted Materials. **Personality Type:** Realistic. Realistic occupations frequently involve work activities that include practical, hands-on problems and solutions. These occupations often deal with plants, animals, and real-world materials like wood, tools, and machinery. Many of the occupations require working outside and do not involve a lot of paperwork or working closely with others.

Work Values: Moral Values; Activity; Company Policies and Practices; Independence; Supervision, Human Relations. **Skills:** Product Inspection; Operation Monitoring; Operation and Control; Reading Comprehension; Active Listening; Mathematics. **Abilities:** *Cognitive*—Written Comprehension; Perceptual Speed; Problem Sensitivity; Written Expression; Oral Comprehension. *Psychomotor*—Reaction Time; Manual Dexterity; Arm-Hand Steadiness; Control Precision. *Physical*—Extent Flexibility; Static Strength; Explosive Strength. **General Work Activities:** *Information Input*—Monitoring Processes, Materials, and Surroundings; Inspecting Equipment, Structures, Materials; Getting Information Needed to Do the Job. *Mental Process*—Evaluating Information Against Standards; Judging Qualities of Things, Services, Other People's Work; Processing Information. *Work Output*—Controlling Machines and Processes; Handling and Moving Objects; Performing General Physical Activities. *Interacting with Others*—Performing Administrative Activities; Communicating with Other Workers; Coordinating Work and Activities of Others. **Physical Work Conditions:** Indoors; Using Hands on Objects, Tools, or Controls; Hazardous Equipment. **Other Job Characteristics:** Degree of Automation; Pace Determined by Speed of Equipment; Consequence of Error.

Experience: Job Zone 1. No previous work-related skill, knowledge, or experience is needed. **Job Preparation:** SVP Below 4.0—Less than 6 months. **Knowledge:** Production and Processing; Mechanical; Design; Mathematics; Engineering and Technology; Food Production. **Instructional Program:** 470303 Industrial Machinery Maintenance and Repairer.

Related DOT Jobs: 520.682-022 Gum-Scoring-Machine Operator; 521.685-018 Almond-Cutting-Machine Tender; 521.685-098 Cutter, Frozen Meat; 521.685-102 Cutting-Machine Operator; 521.685-158 Granulating-Machine Operator; 521.685-170 Hasher Operator; 521.685-298 Slice-Plug-Cutter Operator; 521.685-302 Slicing-Machine Operator; 521.685-306 Slicing-Machine Operator; 521.685-310 Smoking-Tobacco-Cutter Operator; 521.685-338 Strip-Cutting-Machine Operator; 521.685-342 Stripper-Cutter, Machine; 521.685-354 Sugar-Chipper-Machine Operator; 521.685-386 Scaling Machine Operator; 525.685-010 Band-Saw Operator; 529.585-010 Cheese Cutter; 529.685-018 Binder Layer; 529.685-082 Cutter; 529.685-090 Defective-Cigarette Slitter; 529.685-110 Filler Shredder, Machine (partial list; see the introduction for sources of the complete list).

51-9041.00 Extruding, Forming, Pressing, and Compacting Machine Setters, Operators, and Tenders (Extruding and Forming Machine Setters, Operators and Tenders)

Education: Moderate-term O-T-J training

Employed: 125,555

Openings: 23,246

Projected Growth: 5%

Earnings: No data available.

Set up, operate, or tend machines such as glass-forming machines, plodder machines, and tuber machines, to shape and form products such as glassware, food, rubber, soap, brick, tile, clay, wax, tobacco, or cosmetics.

GOE Number, Interest Area, and Work Group: 08.02.01; Industrial Production; Production Technology: Machine Set-up and Operation. **Instructional Program:** 470303 Industrial Machinery Maintenance and Repairer. **Note:** The Department of Labor has not collected some data for this job, so it has fewer details than the other descriptions.

51-9041.01 Extruding, Forming, Pressing, and Compacting Machine Setters and Set-Up Operators
(Extruding, Forming, Pressing, and Compacting Machine Setters and Set-Up Operators)

Education: No data available.

Employed: 31,440

Openings: No data available.

Projected Growth: No data available.

Earnings: $24,330

Set up, or set up and operate, machines such as glass-forming machines, plodder machines, and tuber machines, to manufacture any of a wide variety of products such as soap bars, formed rubber, glassware, food, brick, and tile, by means of extruding, compressing, or compacting.

Observes operation of machine and product to detect and diagnose cause of faulty operation; monitors gauges and recorders. Threads extruded strip through water tank and holddown bars; attaches strands to wire and draws through tube. Pours, scoops, or dumps specified ingredients, metal assemblies, or mixtures into sections of machine prior to starting machine. Feeds product into machine by hand or conveyor. Ignites burner to preheat product; applies heat, using torch. Removes products from discharge belts and molds, mold components, and feeder tubes from machines. Cleans dies, arbors, compression chambers, and molds, using swabs, sponge, or airhose. Swabs molds with solution to prevent sticking. Collects, examines, measures, weighs, and tests product to verify machine setup and conformance of product to specifications. Selects and measures arbors and dies to verify size specified on work ticket. Synchronizes speed of sections of machine when producing products involving several steps or processes. Installs dies or molds in machines to produce products from variety of materials, according to work order and specifications. Adjusts timer drum to set size of product material and rollers, cutoff knives, and stops, to regulate thickness and length. Installs, aligns, and adjusts neck rings, press plungers, and feeder tubes to molds, to deliver material and form product. Routes sample to lab for analysis, according to procedure. Records product information such as scrap quantity, machine number, and ingredients, to complete work ticket; places tickets with product. Couples air and gas lines to machine to maintain plasticity of material and to regulate solidification of final product. Presses control button to activate machinery and equipment. Operates machines and notifies supervisor or setup personnel of needed adjustments to machines. Turns controls to control machine functions such as air-pressure regulation, vacuum creation, and coolant flow.

GOE Number, Interest Area, and Work Group: 08.02.01; Industrial Production; Production Technology: Machine Set-up and

Operation. **Personality Type:** Realistic. Realistic occupations frequently involve work activities that include practical, hands-on problems and solutions. These occupations often deal with plants, animals, and real-world materials like wood, tools, and machinery. Many of the occupations require working outside and do not involve a lot of paperwork or working closely with others. **Work Values:** Moral Values; Independence; Company Policies and Practices; Supervision, Human Relations; Activity. **Skills:** Operation Monitoring; Operation and Control; Product Inspection; Equipment Maintenance; Installation. **Abilities:** *Cognitive*—Information Ordering; Problem Sensitivity; Written Comprehension; Visualization; Oral Expression; Number Facility. *Psychomotor*—Rate Control; Control Precision; Arm-Hand Steadiness; Reaction Time. *Physical*—Static Strength; Dynamic Strength; Stamina. *Sensory*—Hearing Sensitivity. **General Work Activities:** *Information Input*—Monitoring Processes, Materials, and Surroundings; Inspecting Equipment, Structures, Materials; Getting Information Needed to Do the Job. *Mental Process*—Evaluating Information Against Standards; Judging Qualities of Things, Services, Other People's Work; Making Decisions and Solving Problems. *Work Output*—Controlling Machines and Processes; Handling and Moving Objects; Documenting and Recording Information; Performing General Physical Activities. *Interacting with Others*—Communicating with Other Workers; Performing Administrative Activities; Coaching and Developing Others; Assisting and Caring for Others; Establishing and Maintaining Relationships; Interpreting Meaning of Information to Others. **Physical Work Conditions:** Indoors; Using Hands on Objects, Tools, or Controls; Hazardous Equipment. **Other Job Characteristics:** Degree of Automation; Consequence of Error; Pace Determined by Speed of Equipment.

Experience: Job Zone 2. Some previous work-related skill, knowledge, or experience may be helpful, but usually is not needed. **Job Preparation:** SVP 4.00 to 5.99—6 months to less than 2 years. **Knowledge:** Production and Processing; Mechanical; Engineering and Technology; Mathematics; Physics. **Instructional Program:** 470303 Industrial Machinery Maintenance and Repairer.

Related DOT Jobs: 520.682-014 Center-Machine Operator; 556.682-018 Plodder Operator; 556.682-022 Compressor; 557.382-014 Wink-Cutter Operator; 557.682-010 Graining-Press Operator; 575.380-010 Forming-Machine Upkeep Mechanic; 575.382-010 Brick-and-Tile-Making-Machine Operator; 575.382-014 Forming-Machine Operator; 575.382-022 Glass-Rolling-Machine Operator; 575.682-010 Fiberglass-Dowel-Drawing-Machine Operator; 575.682-022 Ram-Press Operator; 649.582-014 Sizing-Machine Operator; 690.662-014 Tuber-Machine Operator; 692.362-010 Set-Up Mechanic, Crown Assembly Machine.

51-9041.02 Extruding, Forming, Pressing, and Compacting Machine Operators and Tenders

(Extruding, Forming, Pressing, and Compacting Machine Operators and Tenders)

Education: No data available.
Employed: 86,090
Openings: No data available.
Projected Growth: No data available.
Earnings: $22,750

Operate or tend machines to shape and form any of a wide variety of manufactured products such as glass bulbs, molded food and candy, rubber goods, clay products, wax products, tobacco plugs, cosmetics, or paper products, by means of extruding, compressing, or compacting.

Monitors machine operations and observes indicator lights and gauges such as thermometers, voltage meters, and timers, to detect malfunctions. Clears jams, removes defective or substandard materials or products, and readjusts machine components to conform to specifications. Fills molds or positions ingredients or materials such as glass rods, candy, or rolls of paper, on machine-feeding mechanism. Adjusts machine components to regulate speed, pressure, and temperature of machine and to regulate amount, dimensions, and flow of materials or ingredients. Removes materials or products from mold, or from extruding, forming, pressing, or compacting machine; stacks or stores for additional processing. Reviews work orders, specifications, or instructions to determine materials, ingredients, procedures, components, settings, and adjustments for extruding, forming, pressing, or compacting machine. Selects and installs machine components such as dies, molds, and cutters, according to specifications, using hand tools and measuring devices. Examines, measures, and weighs materials or products to verify conformance to standards, using measuring devices such as templates, micrometers, or scales. Moves materials, supplies, components, and finished products between storage and work areas, using work aids such as racks, hoists, and handtrucks. Replaces worn or broken parts such as nozzles, punches, and filters; cleans and lubricates machine components to maintain in working order. Activates machine to shape or form products such as candy bars, light bulbs, silver spoons, balloons, or insulation panels. Records and maintains production data such as meter readings and quantity, type, and dimensions of materials produced. Measures, mixes, cuts, shapes, softens, and joins materials and ingredients such as powder, cornmeal, or rubber to prepare for machine processing.

GOE Number, Interest Area, and Work Group: 08.03.01; Industrial Production; Production Work: Machine Work, Assorted Materials. **Personality Type:** Realistic. Realistic occupations frequently involve work activities that include practical, hands-on problems and solutions. These occupations often deal with plants, animals, and real-world materials like wood, tools, and machinery. Many of the occupations require working outside and do not involve a lot of paperwork or working closely with others. **Work Values:** Moral Values; Independence; Activity; Company Policies and Practices; Supervision, Human Relations. **Skills:** Operation and Control; Operation Monitoring; Product Inspection; Equipment Maintenance; Repairing; Reading Comprehension. **Abilities:** *Cognitive*—Problem Sensitivity; Perceptual Speed; Written Comprehension; Information Ordering; Visualization. *Psychomotor*—Control Precision; Manual Dexterity; Multilimb Coordination; Reaction Time. *Physical*—Trunk Strength; Dynamic Strength; Extent Flexibility. *Sensory*—Depth Perception; Visual Color Discrimination; Hearing Sensitivity; Peripheral Vision. **General Work Activities:** *Information Input*—Monitoring Processes, Materials, and Surroundings; Identifying Objects, Actions, and Events; Getting Information Needed to Do the Job. *Mental Process*—Evaluating Information Against Standards; Judging Qualities of Things, Services, Other People's Work; Making Decisions and Solving Problems; Processing Information. *Work Output*— Handling and Moving Objects; Controlling Machines and Processes; Performing General Physical Activities. *Interacting with Others*—Performing Administrative Activities; Communicating with Other Workers; Monitoring and Controlling Resources. **Physical Work Conditions:** Using Hands on Objects, Tools, or Controls; Indoors; Standing. **Other Job Characteristics:** Degree of Automation; Pace Determined by Speed of Equipment; Importance of Being Sure All Is Done.

Experience: Job Zone 1. No previous work-related skill, knowledge, or experience is needed. **Job Preparation:** SVP Below 4.0— Less than 6 months. **Knowledge:** Production and Processing; Mechanical; Mathematics; Engineering and Technology; Clerical. **Instructional Program:** 470303 Industrial Machinery Maintenance and Repairer.

Related DOT Jobs: 520.682-030 Spinner; 520.682-034 Cracker-and-Cookie-Machine Operator; 520.685-038 Cake Former; 520.685-058 Casting-Machine Operator; 520.685-062 Casting-Machine Operator; 520.685-078 Confectionery-Drops-Machine Operator; 520.685-086 Dividing-Machine Operator; 520.685-102 Flaking-Roll Operator; 520.685-178 Pellet-Mill Operator; 520.685-182 Press Operator, Meat; 520.685-186 Press Tender; 520.685-190 Pretzel-Twisting-Machine Operator; 520.685-198 Rolling-Machine Operator; 520.685-214 Sweet-Goods-Machine Operator; 521.685-330 Stem-Roller-or-Crusher Operator; 521.685-350 Sugar Presser; 529.682-026 Lozenge Maker; 529.685-014 Automatic Lump Making Machine Tender; 529.685-042 Butt Maker; 529.685-054 Chocolate Molder, Machine (partial list; see the introduction for sources of the complete list).

51-9051.00 Furnace, Kiln, Oven, Drier, and Kettle Operators and Tenders (Furnace, Kiln, Oven, Drier, and Kettle Operators and Tenders)

Education: Moderate-term O-T-J training

Employed: 24,909

Openings: 2,417

Projected Growth: –5.6%

Earnings: $25,110

Operate or tend heating equipment other than basic metal, plastic, or food-processing equipment. Anneal glass; dry lumber; cure rubber; remove moisture from materials; boil soap.

Transports materials and products to and from work area, manually or using cart, handtruck, or hoist. Monitors equipment operation, gauges, and panel lights to detect deviation from standards. Presses and adjusts controls to activate, set, and regulate equipment operation according to specifications. Stops equipment and clears blockages or jams, using fingers, wire, or hand tools. Examines or tests sample of processed substance; collects sample for laboratory testing, to ensure conformance to specifications. Replaces worn or defective equipment parts, using hand tools. Cleans, lubricates, and adjusts equipment, using items such as scrapers, solvents, airhose, oil, and hand tools. Loads equipment receptacle or conveyor with material to be processed, manually or using hoist. Confers with supervisor or other equipment operators to report equipment malfunction or to resolve problems resulting from process changes. Reads and interprets work orders and instructions to determine work assignment, process specifications, and production schedule. Removes product from equipment, manually or using hoist, and prepares for storage, shipment, or additional processing. Weighs or measures specified amount of material or substance to be processed, using devices such as scales and calipers. Records gauge readings, test results, and shift production in log book.

GOE Number, Interest Area, and Work Group: 08.03.02; Industrial Production; Production Work: Equipment Operation, Assorted Materials Processing. **Personality Type:** Realistic. Realistic occupations frequently involve work activities that include practical, hands-on problems and solutions. These occupations often deal with plants, animals, and real-world materials like wood, tools, and machinery. Many of the occupations require working outside and do not involve a lot of paperwork or working closely with others. **Work Values:** Moral Values; Company Policies and Practices; Supervision, Human Relations; Security; Independence; Activity. **Skills:** Operation Monitoring; Reading Comprehension; Equipment Maintenance; Product Inspection; Operation and Control. **Abilities:** *Cognitive*—Written Comprehension; Information Ordering; Problem Sensitivity; Oral Comprehension; Deductive Reasoning; Visualization. *Psychomotor*—Control Precision; Rate Control. *Physical*—Static Strength; Trunk Strength; Dynamic Strength; Stamina. **General Work Activities:** *Information Input*— Monitoring Processes, Materials, and Surroundings; Getting Information Needed to Do the Job; Identifying Objects, Actions, and Events; Inspecting Equipment, Structures, Materials. *Mental Process*—Evaluating Information Against Standards; Judging Qualities of Things, Services, Other People's Work; Making Decisions and Solving Problems; Processing Information. *Work Output*— Controlling Machines and Processes; Handling and Moving Objects; Performing General Physical Activities. *Interacting with Others*—Communicating with Other Workers; Performing Administrative Activities; Assisting and Caring for Others; Coaching and Developing Others; Establishing and Maintaining Relationships. **Physical Work Conditions:** Indoors; Standing; Using Hands on Objects, Tools, or Controls. **Other Job Characteristics:** Consequence of Error; Degree of Automation; Importance of Being Sure All Is Done.

Experience: Job Zone 1. No previous work-related skill, knowledge, or experience is needed. **Job Preparation:** SVP Below 4.0— Less than 6 months. **Knowledge:** Production and Processing; Mechanical; Engineering and Technology; Mathematics; Chemistry. **Instructional Program:** 470303 Industrial Machinery Maintenance and Repairer.

Related DOT Jobs: 361.685-010 Conditioner-Tumbler Operator; 369.685-026 Rug-Dry-Room Attendant; 369.685-034 Tumbler Operator; 503.685-022 Flame Degreaser; 504.485-010 Rivet Heater; 504.685-030 Reel-Blade-Bender Furnace Tender; 509.565-010 Kiln Operator; 509.685-018 Burning-Plant Operator; 511.482-010 Control Operator; 511.565-014 Drier Tender; 512.685-018 Pot Tender; 513.362-010 Calciner Operator; 513.462-010 Furnace Operator; 513.565-010 Kiln Operator; 513.682-010 Rotary-Kiln Operator; 518.685-010 Core-Oven Tender; 519.665-014 Standpipe Tender; 519.685-010 Briquetting-Machine Operator; 519.685-018 Kettle Operator; 519.685-022 Kettle Tender I (partial list; see the introduction for sources of the complete list).

51-9061.00 Inspectors, Testers, Sorters, Samplers, and Weighers (Production Inspectors, Testers, Graders, Sorters, Samplers, and Weighers)

Education: No data available.

Employed: 453,750

Openings: No data available.

Projected Growth: No data available.

Earnings: $22,090

Inspect, test, sort, sample, or weigh nonagricultural raw materials or processed, machined, fabricated, or assembled parts or products, to note defects, wear, and deviations from specifications. Use precision measuring instruments and complex test equipment.

GOE Number, Interest Area, and Work Group: 08.02.03; Industrial Production; Production Technology: Inspection. **Instructional Programs:** 150699 Industrial Production Technol./ Technicians, Other; 150702 Quality Control Technology/Technician; 200301 Clothing, Apparel and Textile Workers and Managers, General; 200303 Commercial Garment and Apparel Worker; 480501 Machinist/Machine Technologist; 480503 Machine Shop Assistant; 480506 Sheet Metal Worker; 480599 Precision Metal Workers, Other. **Note:** The Department of Labor has not collected some data for this job, so it has fewer details than the other descriptions.

51-9061.01 Materials Inspectors (Precision Inspectors, Testers, and Graders)

Education: Work experience in a related occupation

Employed: 688,730

Openings: 95,650

Projected Growth: –3.2%

Earnings: No data available.

Examine and inspect materials and finished parts and products, to detect defects and wear and to ensure conformance with work orders, diagrams, blueprints, and template specifications. Specialize in a single phase of inspection.

Supervises testing or drilling activities, and adjusts equipment to obtain sample fluids or to direct drilling. Confers with vendors and others regarding inspection results; recommends corrective procedures; compiles reports of results, recommendations, and needed repairs. Tests and measures finished products, components, or assemblies for functioning, operation, accuracy, or assembly, to verify adherence to functional specifications. Collects samples for testing, and computes findings. Marks items for acceptance or rejection, records test results and inspection data, and compares findings with specifications to ensure conformance to standards. Observes and monitors production operations and equipment to ensure proper assembly of parts; assists in testing and monitoring activities. Inspects materials, products, and work in progress for conformance to specifications; adjusts process or assembly equipment to meet standards. Fabricates, installs, positions, or connects components, parts, finished products, or instruments, for testing or operational purposes. Reads dials and meters to verify functioning of equipment according to specifications. Analyzes and interprets blueprints, sample data, and other materials to determine, change, or measure specifications or inspection and testing procedures. Operates or tends machinery and equipment, and uses hand tools.

GOE Number, Interest Area, and Work Group: 08.02.03; Industrial Production; Production Technology: Inspection. **Personality Type:** Realistic. Realistic occupations frequently involve work activities that include practical, hands-on problems and solutions. These occupations often deal with plants, animals, and real-world materials like wood, tools, and machinery. Many of the occupations require working outside and do not involve a lot of paperwork or working closely with others. **Work Values:** Responsibility; Moral Values; Activity; Independence; Autonomy; Company Policies and Practices; Security; Supervision, Human Relations. **Skills:** Product Inspection; Testing; Mathematics; Operation and Control; Operation Monitoring. **Abilities:** *Cognitive*—Perceptual Speed; Information Ordering; Problem Sensitivity; Selective Attention; Visualization. *Psychomotor*—Manual Dexterity; Control Precision; Reaction Time. *Physical*—Static Strength; Extent Flexibility; Explosive Strength; Trunk Strength. *Sensory*—Near Vision; Visual Color Discrimination; Auditory Attention. **General Work Activities:** *Information Input*—Inspecting Equipment, Structures, Materials; Getting Information Needed to Do the Job; Identifying Objects, Actions, and Events. *Mental Process*—Evaluating Information Against Standards; Updating and Using Job-Relevant Knowledge; Analyzing Data or Information. *Work Output*—Implementing Ideas and Programs; Controlling Machines and Processes; Handling and Moving Objects. *Interacting with Others*—Communicating with Other Workers; Performing Administrative Activities; Providing Consultation and Advice to Others. **Physical Work Conditions:** Indoors; Standing; Using Hands on Objects, Tools, or Controls. **Other Job Characteristics:** Consequence of Error; Importance of Being Sure All Is Done; Degree of Automation.

Experience: Job Zone 3. Previous work-related skill, knowledge, or experience is required. **Job Preparation:** SVP 6.0 to less than 7.0—More than 1 year and less than 4 years. **Knowledge:** Production and Processing; Mechanical; Design; Mathematics; English Language; Engineering and Technology. **Instructional Program:** 410204 Industrial Radiologic Technology/Technician.

Related DOT Jobs: 199.361-010 Radiographer; 504.281-010 Heat-Treat Inspector; 526.381-022 Cake Tester; 529.281-010 Taster; 549.261-010 Mechanical Inspector; 559.381-010 Inspector; 559.381-014 Rubber Tester; 572.360-010 Furnace-Combustion Analyst; 600.281-014 Lay-Out Inspector; 601.261-010 Inspector, Set-Up and Lay-Out; 601.281-022 Inspector, Tool; 609.361-010 Inspector, Floor; 612.261-010 Inspector; 616.361-010 Spring Inspector I; 619.261-010 Inspector, Metal Fabricating; 619.364-010 Inspector I; 619.381-010 Inspector; 619.381-014 Eddy-Current Inspector; 622.381-038 Salvage Inspector; 632.381-014 Inspector, Firearms (partial list; see the introduction for sources of the complete list).

51-9061.02 Mechanical Inspectors (Precision Inspectors, Testers, and Graders)

Education: Work experience in a related occupation

Employed: 688,730

Openings: 95,650

Projected Growth: –3.2%

Earnings: No data available.

Inspect and test mechanical assemblies and systems such as motors, vehicles, and transportation equipment, to detect defects and wear and to ensure compliance with specifications.

Estimates and records operational data. Inspects materials, products, and work in progress for conformance to specifications; adjusts process or assembly equipment to meet standards. Marks items for acceptance or rejection, records test results and inspection data, and compares findings with specifications to ensure conformance to standards. Discards or rejects products, materials, and equipment not meeting specifications. Reads and interprets materials such as work orders, inspection manuals, and blueprints, to determine inspection and test procedures. Installs and positions new or replacement parts, components, and instruments. Starts and operates finished products for testing or inspection. Completes necessary procedures to satisfy licensing requirements, and indicates concurrence with acceptance or rejection decisions. Confers with vendors and others regarding inspection results; recommends corrective procedures; compiles reports of results, recommendations, and needed repairs. Cleans and maintains test equipment and instruments to ensure proper functioning. Reads dials and meters to ensure that equipment is operating according to specifications. Collects samples for testing, and computes findings. Tests and measures finished products, components, or assemblies for functioning, operation, accuracy, or assembly, to verify adherence to functional specifications. Analyzes and interprets sample data.

GOE Number, Interest Area, and Work Group: 08.02.03; Industrial Production; Production Technology: Inspection. **Personality Type:** Realistic. Realistic occupations frequently involve work activities that include practical, hands-on problems and solutions. These occupations often deal with plants, animals, and real-world materials like wood, tools, and machinery. Many of the occupations require working outside and do not involve a lot of paperwork or working closely with others. **Work Values:** Responsibility; Moral Values; Independence; Activity; Security; Company Policies and Practices; Autonomy. **Skills:** Testing; Product Inspection; Reading Comprehension; Science; Problem Identification; Writing; Operation and Control; Operation Monitoring. **Abilities:** *Cognitive*—Written Comprehension; Problem Sensitivity; Perceptual Speed; Number Facility; Flexibility of Closure; Deductive Reasoning. *Psychomotor*—Control Precision; Manual Dexterity; Reaction Time. *Physical*—Extent Flexibility; Static Strength; Trunk Strength. *Sensory*—Near Vision; Hearing Sensitivity; Visual Color Discrimination; Auditory Attention. **General Work Activities:** *Information Input*—Inspecting Equipment, Structures, Materials; Identifying Objects, Actions, and Events; Monitoring Processes, Materials, and Surroundings. *Mental Process*—Evaluating Information Against Standards; Analyzing Data or Information; Updating and Using Job-Relevant Knowledge; Judging Qualities of Things, Services, Other People's Work. *Work Output*—Repairing and Maintaining Mechanical Equipment; Handling and Moving Objects; Documenting and Recording Information; Controlling Machines and Processes. *Interacting with Others*—Communicating with Other Workers; Communicating with Persons Outside Organization; Establishing and Maintaining Relationships; Performing Administrative Activities; Providing Consultation and Advice to Others. **Physical Work Conditions:** Indoors; Standing; Using Hands on Objects, Tools, or Controls. **Other Job Characteristics:** Consequence of Error; Importance of Being Exact or Accurate; Importance of Being Sure All Is Done.

Experience: Job Zone 4. A minimum of two to four years of work-related skill, knowledge, or experience is needed. **Job Preparation:** SVP 7.0 to less than 8.0—2 years to less than 10 years. **Knowledge:** Mechanical; Engineering and Technology; Mathematics; English Language; Design. **Instructional Program:** 480503 Machine Shop Assistant.

Related DOT Jobs: 602.362-010 Gear Inspector; 620.261-014 Automobile Tester; 620.261-018 Automobile-Repair-Service Estimator; 620.281-014 Automotive Technician, Exhaust Emissions; 620.281-030 Bus Inspector; 621.261-010 Airplane Inspector; 621.261-014 Engine Tester; 622.281-010 Locomotive Inspector; 622.381-034 Railroad Wheels and Axle Inspector; 624.361-010 Inspector and Tester; 625.261-010 Diesel-Engine Tester; 710.384-014 Inspector; 736.381-018 Process Inspector; 801.381-018 Major-Assembly Inspector; 806.261-010 Internal-Combustion-Engine Inspector; 806.261-022 Tester, Rocket Motor; 806.261-030 Inspector, Assemblies and Installations; 806.261-038 Inspector, Missile; 806.281-010 Dynamometer Tester, Engine; 806.281-018 Final Inspector, Motorcycles (partial list; see the introduction for sources of the complete list).

51-9061.03 Precision Devices Inspectors and Testers (Precision Inspectors, Testers, and Graders)

Education: Work experience in a related occupation

Employed: 688,730

Openings: 95,650

Projected Growth: –3.2%

Earnings: No data available.

Verify accuracy of and adjust precision devices such as meters and gauges, testing instruments, and clock and watch mechanisms, to ensure that operation of device is in accordance with design specifications.

Computes and/or calculates data and other information. Tests and measures finished products, components, or assemblies for functioning, operation, accuracy, or assembly, to verify adherence to functional specifications. Marks items for acceptance or rejection, records test results and inspection data, and compares findings with specifications to ensure conformance to standards. Operates or tends machinery and equipment, and uses hand tools. Estimates operational data to meet acceptable standards. Disassembles defective parts and components. Confers with vendors and others regarding inspection results and recommends corrective procedures. Completes necessary procedures to satisfy licensing requirements. Analyzes and interprets blueprints, sample data, and other materials, to determine, change, or measure specifications or inspection and testing procedures. Discards or rejects products, materials, and equipment not meeting specifications. Fabricates, installs, positions, or connects components, parts, finished products, or instruments for testing or operational purposes. Cleans and maintains test equipment and instruments and certifies that precision instruments meet standards. Inspects materials, products, and work in progress for conformance to specifications; adjusts process or assembly equipment to meet standards. Reads dials and meters to verify functioning of equipment according to specifications.

GOE Number, Interest Area, and Work Group: 08.02.03; Industrial Production; Production Technology: Inspection. **Personality Type:** Realistic. Realistic occupations frequently involve work activities that include practical, hands-on problems and solutions. These occupations often deal with plants, animals, and real-world materials like wood, tools, and machinery. Many of the occupations require working outside and do not involve a lot of paperwork or working closely with others. **Work Values:** Moral Values; Independence; Responsibility; Activity; Autonomy; Company Policies and Practices; Security. **Skills:** Product Inspection; Testing; Operation Monitoring; Problem Identification; Troubleshooting; Mathematics; Science. **Abilities:** *Cognitive*—Problem Sensitivity; Perceptual Speed; Information Ordering; Number Facility; Written Comprehension; Visualization. *Psychomotor*—Control Precision; Finger Dexterity; Arm-Hand Steadiness. *Physical*—Extent Flexibility; Trunk Strength; Static Strength. *Sensory*—Near Vision; Visual Color Discrimination; Speech Clarity. **General Work Activities:** *Information Input*—Identifying Objects, Actions, and Events; Monitoring Processes, Materials, and Surroundings; Inspecting Equipment, Structures, Materials. *Mental Process*—Evaluating Information Against Standards; Analyzing Data or Information; Updating and Using Job-Relevant Knowledge. *Work Output*—Implementing Ideas and Programs; Drafting and Specifying Technical Devices; Handling and Moving Objects. *Interacting with Others*—Communicating with Other Workers; Performing Administrative Activities; Communicating with Persons Outside Organization. **Physical Work Conditions:** Indoors; Using Hands on Objects, Tools, or Controls; Sitting. **Other Job Characteristics:** Importance of Being Exact or Accurate; Importance of Being Sure All Is Done; Consequence of Error; Degree of Automation.

Experience: Job Zone 3. Previous work-related skill, knowledge, or experience is required. **Job Preparation:** SVP 6.0 to less than 7.0—More than 1 year and less than 4 years. **Knowledge:** Design; Mechanical; Mathematics; Production and Processing; English Language; Engineering and Technology. **Instructional Program:** 480503 Machine Shop Assistant.

Related DOT Jobs: 601.281-018 Inspector, Gauge and Instrument; 710.381-014 Balancer, Scale; 710.381-030 Hydrometer Calibrator; 710.381-034 Calibrator; 710.381-042 Calibrator, Barometers; 710.384-022 Meter Inspector; 711.281-010 Inspector, Optical Instrument; 714.381-014 Inspector, Photographic Equipment; 715.261-010 Mechanical Technician, Laboratory; 715.381-050 Final Inspector; 715.381-058 Hairspring Truer; 715.381-066 Inspector, Hairspring I; 715.381-070 Inspector, Watch Assembly; 715.381-074 Inspector, Watch Train; 715.381-078 Location-and-

Measurement Technician; 715.384-022 Inspector, Watch Parts; 716.381-010 Inspector, Precision; 722.381-014 Instrument Inspector; 729.281-046 X-Ray-Equipment Tester; 729.361-010 Inspector, Electromechanical (partial list; see the introduction for sources of the complete list).

51-9061.04 Electrical and Electronic Inspectors and Testers (Precision Inspectors, Testers, and Graders)

Education: Work experience in a related occupation
Employed: 688,730
Openings: 95,650
Projected Growth: –3.2%
Earnings: No data available.

Inspect and test electrical and electronic systems such as radar navigational equipment, computer memory units, and television and radio transmitters, using precision measuring instruments.

Operates or tends machinery and equipment, and uses hand tools. Writes and installs computer programs to control test equipment. Computes and/or calculates sample data and test results. Confers with vendors and others regarding inspection results; recommends corrective procedures; and compiles reports of results, recommendations, and needed repairs. Disassembles defective parts and components. Reviews maintenance records to ensure that plant equipment functions properly. Installs, positions, or connects new or replacement parts, components, and instruments. Marks items for acceptance or rejection, records test results and inspection data, and compares findings with specifications to ensure conformance to standards. Positions or directs other workers to position products, components, or parts, for testing. Reads dials and meters to verify functioning of equipment according to specifications. Inspects materials, products, and work in progress for conformance to specifications; adjusts process or assembly equipment to meet standards. Analyzes and interprets blueprints, sample data, and other materials, to determine, change, or measure specifications or inspection and testing procedures. Examines, adjusts, or repairs finished products, components, or parts. Cleans and maintains test equipment and instruments to ensure proper functioning. Tests and measures finished products, components, or assemblies for functioning, operation, accuracy, or assembly, to verify adherence to functional specifications.

GOE Number, Interest Area, and Work Group: 08.02.03; Industrial Production; Production Technology: Inspection. **Personality Type:** Realistic. Realistic occupations frequently involve work activities that include practical, hands-on problems and solutions. These occupations often deal with plants, animals, and real-world materials like wood, tools, and machinery. Many of the occupations require working outside and do not involve a lot of paperwork or working closely with others. **Work Values:** Responsibility; Moral Values; Activity; Company Policies and Practices; Security. **Skills:** Product Inspection; Mathematics; Testing; Problem Identification; Troubleshooting. **Abilities:** *Cognitive*—Deductive Reasoning; Perceptual Speed; Visualization; Problem Sensitivity; Oral Expression. *Psychomotor*—Control Precision; Finger Dexterity; Reaction Time; Manual Dexterity. *Physical*—Extent Flexibility;

Trunk Strength; Static Strength. *Sensory*—Near Vision; Visual Color Discrimination; Speech Clarity; Hearing Sensitivity; Auditory Attention. **General Work Activities:** *Information Input*—Monitoring Processes, Materials, and Surroundings; Inspecting Equipment, Structures, Materials; Getting Information Needed to Do the Job. *Mental Process*—Processing Information; Updating and Using Job-Relevant Knowledge; Analyzing Data or Information; Evaluating Information Against Standards. *Work Output*—Repairing and Maintaining Electrical Equipment; Implementing Ideas and Programs; Documenting and Recording Information; Handling and Moving Objects; Controlling Machines and Processes. *Interacting with Others*—Communicating with Other Workers; Providing Consultation and Advice to Others; Interpreting Meaning of Information to Others. **Physical Work Conditions:** Indoors; Using Hands on Objects, Tools, or Controls; Standing. **Other Job Characteristics:** Consequence of Error; Degree of Automation; Importance of Being Sure All Is Done; Importance of Being Exact or Accurate.

Experience: Job Zone 3. Previous work-related skill, knowledge, or experience is required. **Job Preparation:** SVP 6.0 to less than 7.0—More than 1 year and less than 4 years. **Knowledge:** Computers and Electronics; Mechanical; Telecommunications; Design; Engineering and Technology. **Instructional Program:** 470401 Instrument Calibration and Repairer.

Related DOT Jobs: 710.381-046 Tester, Electronic Scale; 721.261-014 Final Tester; 721.281-030 Tester, Motors and Controls; 721.361-010 Inspector, Motors and Generators; 724.281-010 Transformer Tester; 724.364-010 Winding Inspector and Tester; 724.384-010 Armature Tester I; 726.261-018 Electronics Tester; 726.361-018 Group Leader, Printed Circuit Board Quality Control; 726.362-010 Group Leader, Semiconductor Testing; 726.364-010 Lead Hand, Inspecting and Testing; 726.381-010 Electronics Inspector; 726.384-014 Inspector, Circuitry Negative; 726.384-018 Inspector, Semiconductor Wafer Processing; 726.384-022 Photo Mask Inspector; 726.682-018 Coordinate Measuring Equipment Operator; 727.381-018 Dry-Cell Tester; 727.381-022 Storage Battery Inspector and Tester; 729.281-038 Relay Tester; 729.381-010 Electrical-Equipment Tester (partial list; see the introduction for sources of the complete list).

51-9061.05 Production Inspectors, Testers, Graders, Sorters, Samplers, Weighers (Production Inspectors, Testers, Graders, Sorters, Samplers, and Weighers)

Education: No data available.

Employed: 453,750

Openings: No data available.

Projected Growth: No data available.

Earnings: $22,090

Inspect, test, grade, sort, sample, or weigh nonagricultural raw materials or processed, machined, fabricated, or assembled parts or products, before, during, or after processing.

Sets controls, starts machine, and observes machine which automatically sorts or inspects products. Transports inspected or tested products to other work stations, using handtruck or lift truck. Grades, classifies, and sorts products according to size, weight, color, or other specifications. Records inspection or test data such as weight, temperature, grade, or moisture content, and number inspected or graded. Discards or routes defective products or contaminants for rework or reuse. Reads work order to determine inspection criteria and to verify identification numbers and product type. Counts number of product tested or inspected; stacks or arranges for further processing, shipping, or packing. Cleans, trims, makes adjustments, or repairs product or processing equipment, to correct defects found during inspection. Compares color, shape, texture, or grade of product or material with color chart, template, or sample, to verify conformance to standards. Tests samples, materials, or products, using test equipment such as thermometer, voltmeter, moisture meter, or tensiometer, for conformance to specifications. Weighs materials, products, containers, or samples, to verify packaging weight, to determine percentage of each ingredient, or to determine sorting. Wraps and packages product for shipment or delivery. Measures dimensions of product, using measuring instruments such as rulers, calipers, gauges, or micrometers, to verify conformance to specifications. Computes percentages or averages, using formulas and calculator; prepares reports of inspection or test findings. Marks, affixes, or stamps product or container to identify defects or to denote grade or size information. Collects or selects samples for testing or for use as model. Notifies supervisor or specified personnel of deviations from specifications, machine malfunctions, or need for equipment maintenance. Uses or operates product to test functional performance.

GOE Number, Interest Area, and Work Group: 08.02.03; Industrial Production; Production Technology: Inspection. **Personality Type:** Realistic. Realistic occupations frequently involve work activities that include practical, hands-on problems and solutions. These occupations often deal with plants, animals, and real-world materials like wood, tools, and machinery. Many of the occupations require working outside and do not involve a lot of paperwork or working closely with others. **Work Values:** Moral Values; Activity; Company Policies and Practices; Responsibility; Security. **Skills:** Product Inspection; Testing; Operation and Control; Operation Monitoring; Information Gathering. **Abilities:** *Cognitive*—Category Flexibility; Problem Sensitivity; Perceptual Speed; Written Comprehension; Flexibility of Closure; Information Ordering. *Psychomotor*—Control Precision; Manual Dexterity; Finger Dexterity. *Physical*—Extent Flexibility; Static Strength; Trunk Strength. *Sensory*—Near Vision; Visual Color Discrimination; Auditory Attention. **General Work Activities:** *Information Input*—Inspecting Equipment, Structures, Materials; Monitoring Processes, Materials, and Surroundings; Getting Information Needed to Do the Job; Identifying Objects, Actions, and Events. *Mental Process*—Evaluating Information Against Standards; Judging Qualities of Things, Services, Other People's Work; Analyzing Data or Information. *Work Output*—Documenting and Recording Information; Handling and Moving Objects; Controlling Machines and Processes. *Interacting with Others*—Communicating with Other Workers; Interpreting Meaning of Information to Others; Performing Administrative Activities; Monitoring and Controlling Resources. **Physical Work Conditions:** Indoors; Using Hands on Objects, Tools, or Controls; Standing; Sitting. **Other Job Characteristics:** Consequence of Error; Importance of Being Exact or Accurate; Importance of Being Sure All Is Done.

Experience: Job Zone 1. No previous work-related skill, knowledge, or experience is needed. **Job Preparation:** SVP Below 4.0—Less than 6 months. **Knowledge:** Production and Processing; Mathematics; English Language; Mechanical; Engineering and Technology; Clerical. **Instructional Programs:** 150699 Industrial Production Technol./Technicians, Other; 150702 Quality Control Technology/Technician; 200301 Clothing, Apparel and Textile Workers and Managers, General; 200303 Commercial Garment and Apparel Worker; 480501 Machinist/Machine Technologist; 480503 Machine Shop Assistant; 480506 Sheet Metal Worker; 480599 Precision Metal Workers, Other.

Related DOT Jobs: 194.387-010 Quality-Control Inspector; 194.387-014 Record Tester; 199.171-010 Proof Technician; 222.367-046 Petroleum Inspector; 222.384-010 Inspector, Receiving; 222.687-042 Inspector, Handbag Frames; 343.687-010 Plastic-Card Grader, Cardroom; 361.587-010 Flatwork Tier; 361.687-010 Assembler, Wet Wash; 361.687-014 Classifier; 361.687-022 Linen Grader; 369.687-010 Assembler; 369.687-014 Checker; 369.687-022 Inspector; 369.687-026 Marker; 369.687-030 Rug Inspector; 500.287-010 Inspector, Plating; 502.382-014 Fluoroscope Operator; 504.387-010 Hardness Inspector; 509.584-010 Test Preparer (partial list; see the introduction for sources of the complete list).

51-9071.00 Jewelers and Precious Stone and Metal Workers (Jewelers and Precious Stone and Metal Workers)

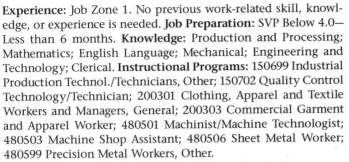

Education: Postsecondary vocational training

Employed: 29,653

Openings: 3,221

Projected Growth: –6%

Earnings: No data available.

Design, fabricate, adjust, repair, or appraise jewelry, gold, silver, other precious metals, or gems. Includes diamond polishers and gem cutters. Includes persons who perform precision casting and modeling of molds, casting metal in molds, or setting precious and semiprecious stones for jewelry and related products.

GOE Number, Interest Area, and Work Group: 08.02.02; Industrial Production; Production Technology: Precision Hand Work. **Instructional Programs:** 470408 Watch, Clock and Jewelry Repairer; 500713 Metal and Jewelry Arts. **Note:** The Department of Labor has not collected some data for this job, so it has fewer details than the other descriptions.

51-9071.01 Jewelers (Jewelers and Silversmiths)

Education: No data available.

Employed: 24,080

Openings: No data available.

Projected Growth: No data available.

Earnings: $24,130

Fabricate and repair jewelry articles.

Examines gemstone surfaces and internal structure to evaluate genuineness, quality, and value, using polariscope, refractometer, and other optical instruments. Forms model of article from wax or metal, using carving tools. Immerses gemstones in chemical solutions, to determine specific gravity and key properties for identification and appraisal. Estimates wholesale and retail value of gemstones, following price guides and market fluctuations. Pours molten metal into mold or operates centrifugal casting machine, to cast article. Forms sand or rubber mold from model for casting article. Places model in casting ring; pours plaster into ring to form mold. Smoothes soldered joints and rough spots, using hand file and emery paper; polishes with polishing wheel or buffing wire. Ties or twists gold or silver wires together; bends to form rings. Repairs, reshapes, and restyles jewelry by replacing broken parts, using hand tools and machines. Solders pieces of jewelry together and enlarges or reduces size of rings, using soldering torch or iron. Arranges jewelry pieces into specified design; softens metal by heating with gas torch; shapes, using hammer and die. Cuts and shapes metal into jewelry pieces, using cutting and carving tools. Grades stones for color, perfection, and quality of cut. Immerses jewelry in cleaning solution or acid to remove stains, or in solution of gold or other metal to color jewelry.

GOE Number, Interest Area, and Work Group: 08.02.02; Industrial Production; Production Technology: Precision Hand Work. **Personality Type:** Realistic. Realistic occupations frequently involve work activities that include practical, hands-on problems and solutions. These occupations often deal with plants, animals, and real-world materials like wood, tools, and machinery. Many of the occupations require working outside and do not involve a lot of paperwork or working closely with others. **Work Values:** Working Conditions; Ability Utilization; Autonomy; Independence; Responsibility. **Skills:** Product Inspection; Repairing; Mathematics; Equipment Selection; Judgment and Decision Making; Problem Identification; Reading Comprehension. **Abilities:** *Cognitive*—Visualization; Category Flexibility; Originality; Information Ordering; Memorization. *Psychomotor*—Finger Dexterity; Arm-Hand Steadiness; Manual Dexterity. *Physical*—Trunk Strength; Explosive Strength; Dynamic Strength. *Sensory*—Near Vision; Visual Color Discrimination; Depth Perception. **General Work Activities:** *Information Input*—Identifying Objects, Actions, and Events; Estimating Needed Characteristics; Getting Information Needed to Do the Job. *Mental Process*—Judging Qualities of Things, Services, Other People's Work; Thinking Creatively; Updating and Using Job-Relevant Knowledge. *Work Output*—Handling and Moving Objects; Controlling Machines and Processes; Implementing Ideas and Programs. *Interacting with Others*—Interpreting Meaning of Information to Others; Monitoring and Controlling Resources; Performing Administrative Activities. **Physical Work Conditions:** Indoors; Using Hands on Objects, Tools, or Controls; Sitting. **Other Job Characteristics:** Consequence of Error; Importance of Being Exact or Accurate; Importance of Being Sure All Is Done.

Experience: Job Zone 4. A minimum of two to four years of work-related skill, knowledge, or experience is needed. **Job Preparation:** SVP 7.0 to less than 8.0—2 years to less than 10 years. **Knowledge:** Fine Arts; Production and Processing; Mechanical; Design; Chemistry. **Instructional Programs:** 470408 Watch, Clock and Jewelry Repairer; 500713 Metal and Jewelry Arts.

Related DOT Jobs: 199.281-010 Gemologist; 700.281-010 Jeweler; 700.281-014 Jeweler Apprentice; 700.381-030 Locket Maker; 700.381-042 Ring Maker; 700.381-046 Sample Maker I.

51-9071.02 Silversmiths (Jewelers and Silversmiths)

Education: No data available.

Employed: 24,080

Openings: No data available.

Projected Growth: No data available.

Earnings: $24,130

Anneal, solder, hammer, shape, and glue silver articles.

Strikes article with small tools, or punches with hammer, to indent or restore embossing. Examines article to determine nature of defects such as dents, uneven bottom, scratches, or holes and to repair. Pierces and cuts open design in ornamentation, using hand drill and scroll saw. Wires parts such as legs, spouts, and handles to body, to prepare article for soldering. Peens edges of scratches or holes to repair defect, using peening hammer. Positions article over snarling tool and raises design area, using foot-powered hammer. Glues plastic separators to handles of coffee and teapots. Verifies levelness of bottom edges of article, by using straightedge or by rocking article back and forth on flat surface. Shapes and straightens damaged or twisted articles by hand or by using pliers. Forms concavity in bottom of article to improve stability, using tracing punches and hammer. Hammers out deformations, selecting and using hammer and dollies with head corresponding in curvature with surface of article. Solders parts together; fills holes and cracks with silver solder, using gas torch. Anneals silverware such as coffeepots, tea sets, and trays, in gas oven for prescribed time to soften metal for reworking. Outlines design from photographs or drawings onto surface of article, using hand tools.

GOE Number, Interest Area, and Work Group: 08.02.02; Industrial Production; Production Technology: Precision Hand Work. **Personality Type:** Realistic. Realistic occupations frequently involve work activities that include practical, hands-on problems and solutions. These occupations often deal with plants, animals, and real-world materials like wood, tools, and machinery. Many of the occupations require working outside and do not involve a lot of paperwork or working closely with others. **Work Values:** Independence; Autonomy; Moral Values; Working Conditions; Variety; Achievement; Ability Utilization. **Skills:** Equipment Selection; Product Inspection; Equipment Maintenance; Problem Identification; Critical Thinking; Judgment and Decision Making; Solution Appraisal. **Abilities:** *Cognitive*—Visualization; Information Ordering; Perceptual Speed; Problem Sensitivity; Memorization; Flexibility of Closure. *Psychomotor*—Arm-Hand Steadiness; Manual Dexterity; Finger Dexterity. *Physical*—Explosive Strength; Extent Flexibility; Static Strength. *Sensory*—Near Vision; Depth Perception; Visual Color Discrimination. **General Work Activities:** *Information Input*—Inspecting Equipment, Structures, Materials; Monitoring Processes, Materials, and Surroundings; Estimating Needed Characteristics. *Mental Process*—Judging Qualities of Things, Services, Other People's Work; Thinking Creatively; Evaluating Information Against Standards. *Work Output*—Handling and Moving Objects; Implementing Ideas and Pro-grams; Controlling Machines and Processes. *Interacting with Others*—Performing Administrative Activities; Communicating with Other Workers; Communicating with Persons Outside Organization; Establishing and Maintaining Relationships; Providing Consultation and Advice to Others; Resolving Conflict and Negotiating with Others. **Physical Work Conditions:** Indoors; Using Hands on Objects, Tools, or Controls; Standing. **Other Job Characteristics:** Importance of Being Sure All Is Done; Frustrating Circumstances; Degree of Automation.

Experience: Job Zone 3. Previous work-related skill, knowledge, or experience is required. **Job Preparation:** SVP 6.0 to less than 7.0—More than 1 year and less than 4 years. **Knowledge:** Mechanical; Production and Processing; Building and Construction; Fine Arts; Design. **Instructional Programs:** 470408 Watch, Clock and Jewelry Repairer; 500713 Metal and Jewelry Arts.

Related DOT Jobs: 700.281-022 Silversmith II; 700.381-022 Hammersmith; 704.381-010 Chaser.

51-9071.03 Model and Mold Makers, Jewelry
(Precision Hand Workers, Jewelry and Related Products)

Education: No data available.

Employed: 11,530

Openings: No data available.

Projected Growth: No data available.

Earnings: $19,060

Make models or molds to create jewelry items.

Examines and measures metal parts for conformance to design specifications on scale drawing. Modifies, sharpens, repairs or fabricates jigs, fixtures, and hand tools such as scrapers, cutter, gougers, and shapers. Computes cost of labor and material to determine production cost of products and articles. Polishes metal surfaces and products, using abrasive wheel. Removes mold from cast article; cleans mold; applies shellac and dry powder to preserve mold for reuse. Presses model into clay; builds up clay around exposed parts of model to retain plaster. Writes or modifies design specifications such as content, weight, and material to be used to cast article. Constructs preliminary model of wax, metal, clay, or plaster; forms sample casting in mold; measures casting to verify dimensions. Cuts design in mold or other material to be used as model to fabricate metal and jewelry products. Builds sand mold in flask, following pattern; heats flask, using furnace or torch to dry and harden mold. Lays out design on metal stock and cuts along markings to fabricate pieces used to cast metal molds. Carves, chisels, scrapes, and files plaster, wax, or other plastic materials to make mold or model, according to design specifications. Mixes or melts clay, metal, plaster, wax, or other material; pours material into mold to cast model or mold. Fits, secures, and solders halves of molds together; drills holes in mold to attach handles and allow gases to escape during casting.

GOE Number, Interest Area, and Work Group: 08.02.02; Industrial Production; Production Technology: Precision Hand Work. **Personality Type:** Realistic. Realistic occupations frequently involve work activities that include practical, hands-on problems and solutions. These occupations often deal with plants, animals, and real-world materials like wood, tools, and machinery. Many of the occupations require working outside and do not involve a lot of paperwork or working closely with others. **Work Values:** Independence; Moral Values; Working Conditions; Ability Utilization; Variety; Security; Achievement. **Skills:** Product Inspection; Writing; Mathematics; Equipment Selection; Operation and Control. **Abilities:** *Cognitive*—Information Ordering; Number Facility; Visualization; Written Expression; Written Comprehension. *Psychomotor*—Arm-Hand Steadiness; Finger Dexterity; Manual Dexterity. *Physical*—Explosive Strength; Gross Body Coordination; Stamina; Dynamic Flexibility. *Sensory*—Near Vision; Visual Color Discrimination; Depth Perception. **General Work Activities:** *Information Input*—Getting Information Needed to Do the Job; Inspecting Equipment, Structures, Materials; Monitoring Processes, Materials, and Surroundings. *Mental Process*—Judging Qualities of Things, Services, Other People's Work; Evaluating Information Against Standards; Thinking Creatively. *Work Output*—Handling and Moving Objects; Drafting and Specifying Technical Devices; Controlling Machines and Processes. *Interacting with Others*—Performing Administrative Activities; Communicating with Other Workers; Monitoring and Controlling Resources. **Physical Work Conditions:** Indoors; Using Hands on Objects, Tools, or Controls; Sitting. **Other Job Characteristics:** Importance of Being Exact or Accurate; Importance of Being Sure All Is Done; Consequence of Error.

Experience: Job Zone 3. Previous work-related skill, knowledge, or experience is required. **Job Preparation:** SVP 6.0 to less than 7.0—More than 1 year and less than 4 years. **Knowledge:** Production and Processing; Design; Mathematics; Mechanical; Fine Arts; Building and Construction. **Instructional Program:** 470408 Watch, Clock and Jewelry Repairer.

Related DOT Jobs: 518.381-010 Bench-Molder Apprentice; 518.381-022 Molder, Bench; 700.281-018 Model Maker I; 700.381-034 Mold Maker I; 700.381-038 Mold-Maker Apprentice; 709.381-018 Model Maker II; 709.381-022 Model-Maker Apprentice; 735.381-018 Sample Maker II; 777.381-022 Mold Maker II.

51-9071.04 Bench Workers, Jewelry (Precision Hand Workers, Jewelry and Related Products)

Education: No data available.

Employed: 11,530

Openings: No data available.

Projected Growth: No data available.

Earnings: $19,060

Cut, file, form, and solder parts for jewelry.

Repairs existing jewelry mountings to reposition jewels or adjust mounting. Sands inside mold pieces, using emery cloth and chalkdust. Assembles and secures mold sections used to cast metal articles and pieces. Brushes, buffs, cleans, and polishes metal items and jewelry pieces, using jeweler's tools, polishing wheel, and chemical bath. Operates machines such as centrifugal-casting, routing, and lathe, to fabricate casting molds, metal parts, or wax models of products. Weighs completed pieces to determine deviation from specifications; records weight and processing time on production records. Researches and analyzes reference materials and consults with interested parties, to develop new products or to modify existing products. Weighs, mixes, and melts metal alloys or material; pours molten material into mold to cast models of jewelry. Designs and fabricates molds, models, and machine accessories; modifies hand tools used to cast metal and jewelry pieces. Forms, joins, or assembles metal pieces, articles, or wire, using soldering iron, gas torch, and hand tools. Examines assembled or finished product, using magnifying glass or precision measuring instruments, to ensure conformance to specifications. Cuts, trims, shapes, and smoothes jewelry stones, pearls, and metal pieces, using abrasives, grinding stone, and power and hand tools. Marks and drills holes in jewelry mounting, to center stones according to design specifications. Positions and aligns stones and metal pieces; sets, mounts, and secures item in place, using setting and hand tools. Manually rotates mold, to distribute molten material and prevent formation of air pockets in mold. Marks, engraves, or embosses designs on metal pieces such as castings, wire, or jewelry, following samples, sketches, or other specifications. Plates articles such as jewelry pieces and clock and watch dials with silver, gold, nickel, or other metals.

GOE Number, Interest Area, and Work Group: 08.02.02; Industrial Production; Production Technology: Precision Hand Work. **Personality Type:** Realistic. Realistic occupations frequently involve work activities that include practical, hands-on problems and solutions. These occupations often deal with plants, animals, and real-world materials like wood, tools, and machinery. Many of the occupations require working outside and do not involve a lot of paperwork or working closely with others. **Work Values:** Independence; Moral Values; Working Conditions; Ability Utilization; Activity. **Skills:** Product Inspection; Active Listening; Operation and Control; Reading Comprehension; Equipment Selection; Operations Analysis; Idea Evaluation; Information Gathering; Monitoring; Critical Thinking. **Abilities:** *Cognitive*—Visualization; Information Ordering; Written Comprehension; Originality; Perceptual Speed; Problem Sensitivity. *Psychomotor*—Finger Dexterity; Arm-Hand Steadiness; Manual Dexterity. *Physical*—none met the criteria. *Sensory*—Near Vision; Visual Color Discrimination. **General Work Activities:** *Information Input*—Getting Information Needed to Do the Job; Inspecting Equipment, Structures, Materials; Identifying Objects, Actions, and Events. *Mental Process*—Judging Qualities of Things, Services, Other People's Work; Evaluating Information Against Standards; Thinking Creatively. *Work Output*—Handling and Moving Objects; Performing General Physical Activities; Controlling Machines and Processes. *Interacting with Others*—Communicating with Persons Outside Organization; Monitoring and Controlling Resources; Communicating with Other Workers. **Physical Work Conditions:** Indoors; Using Hands on Objects, Tools, or Controls; Sitting. **Other Job Characteristics:** Importance of Being Exact or Accurate; Importance of Being Sure All Is Done; Consequence of Error.

Experience: Job Zone 3. Previous work-related skill, knowledge, or experience is required. **Job Preparation:** SVP 6.0 to less than 7.0—More than 1 year and less than 4 years. **Knowledge:** Production and Processing; Fine Arts; Design; Mechanical; Engineering and Technology. **Instructional Program:** 470408 Watch, Clock and Jewelry Repairer.

Related DOT Jobs: 502.381-010 Caster; 502.682-018 Centrifugal-Casting-Machine Operator; 700.381-010 Chain Maker, Hand;

700.381-014 Fancy-Wire Drawer; 700.381-018 Goldbeater; 700.381-026 Lay-Out Worker; 700.381-050 Solderer; 700.381-054 Stone Setter; 700.381-058 Stone-Setter Apprentice; 704.381-018 Engine Turner; 715.381-046 Dial Maker; 735.381-010 Bench Hand; 735.381-014 Pearl Restorer; 735.681-010 Bracelet and Brooch Maker; 770.381-010 Bead Maker.

51-9071.05 Pewter Casters and Finishers (Precision Hand Workers, Jewelry and Related Products)

Education: No data available.

Employed: 11,530

Openings: No data available.

Projected Growth: No data available.

Earnings: $19,060

Cast and finish pewter alloy to form parts for goblets, candlesticks, and other pewterware.

Engraves decorative lines on item, using engraving tool. Sands inside of mold parts, applies glaze to inside surface of mold, and assembles mold. Researches reference materials, analyzes production data, and consults with interested parties to develop ideas for new products. Carries castings or finished item to storage area or next workstation. Designs, drafts, and fabricates models of new casting molds and chipping and turning tools used to finish surface of products. Weighs completed item to determine deviation from specified weight; records weight. Determines placement of auxiliary parts such as handle and spout; marks locations of parts. Strikes mold to separate dried casting from mold. Routes out location of part and solder path where part is joined to item, using routing machine. Weighs and mixes alloy ingredients. Heats ingots or alloy mixture; skims off impurities. Rotates mold to distribute alloy in mold and to prevent formation of air pockets. Secures molded item in chuck of lathe, activates lathe, and finishes inner and outer surfaces of item. Fills casting mold to form parts. Positions and aligns auxiliary part in jig and joins parts, using solder and blowtorch.

GOE Number, Interest Area, and Work Group: 08.02.02; Industrial Production; Production Technology: Precision Hand Work. **Personality Type:** Realistic. Realistic occupations frequently involve work activities that include practical, hands-on problems and solutions. These occupations often deal with plants, animals, and real-world materials like wood, tools, and machinery. Many of the occupations require working outside and do not involve a lot of paperwork or working closely with others. **Work Values:** Independence; Moral Values; Ability Utilization; Working Conditions; Autonomy; Achievement; Creativity. **Skills:** Reading Comprehension; Operation and Control; Product Inspection; Information Gathering; Idea Generation; Mathematics; Technology Design; Idea Evaluation; Active Listening. **Abilities:** *Cognitive*—Information Ordering; Originality; Visualization; Oral Expression; Oral Comprehension; Fluency of Ideas. *Psychomotor*—Arm-Hand Steadiness; Control Precision; Manual Dexterity; Finger Dexterity; Wrist-Finger Speed. *Physical*—Extent Flexibility; Static Strength; Dynamic Strength. *Sensory*—Near Vision; Auditory Attention; Visual Color Discrimination. **General Work Activities:** *Information Input*—Getting Information Needed to Do the Job; Monitoring Processes, Materials, and Surroundings; Identifying Objects, Actions, and Events. *Mental Process*—Thinking Creatively; Organizing, Planning, and Prioritizing; Updating and Using Job-Relevant Knowledge; Analyzing Data or Information; Judging Qualities of Things, Services, Other People's Work; Evaluating Information Against Standards. *Work Output*—Handling and Moving Objects; Implementing Ideas and Programs; Drafting and Specifying Technical Devices; Controlling Machines and Processes; Performing General Physical Activities. *Interacting with Others*—Communicating with Persons Outside Organization; Communicating with Other Workers; Performing Administrative Activities. **Physical Work Conditions:** Indoors; Using Hands on Objects, Tools, or Controls; Very Hot; Hazardous Situations. **Other Job Characteristics:** Degree of Automation; Importance of Repeating Same Tasks; Importance of Being Sure All Is Done; Consequence of Error.

Experience: Job Zone 4. A minimum of two to four years of work-related skill, knowledge, or experience is needed. **Job Preparation:** SVP 7.0 to less than 8.0—2 years to less than 10 years. **Knowledge:** Production and Processing; Fine Arts; Design; Mechanical; Building and Construction. **Instructional Program:** 470408 Watch, Clock and Jewelry Repairer.

Related DOT Jobs: 502.384-010 Pewter Caster; 700.261-010 Pewterer; 700.281-026 Pewter Finisher.

51-9071.06 Gem and Diamond Workers (Gem and Diamond Workers)

Education: No data available.

Employed: 1,100

Openings: No data available.

Projected Growth: No data available.

Earnings: $18,800

Split, saw, cut, shape, polish, or drill gems and diamonds used in jewelry or industrial tools.

Lubricates, dismantles, and cleans lapping, boring, cutting, polishing, and shaping equipment and machinery. Examines diamond or gem to determine shape, cut, and width of stone. Selects shaping wheel; mixes and applies abrasive, bort, or polishing compound. Secures gem or diamond in holder, chuck, dop, lapidary stick, or block, for cutting, polishing, grinding, drilling, or shaping. Examines gem during processing, to ensure accuracy of angle and position of cut or bore, using magnifying glass, loupe, or shadowgraph. Replaces, trues, and sharpens blades, drills, and plates. Measures size of stone's bore holes and cuts, to ensure adherence to specifications, using precision measuring instruments. Laps girdle on rough diamonds, using diamond girdling lathe. Splits gem along premarked lines to remove imperfections, using blade and jeweler's hammer. Bores, laps, and polishes holes in industrial diamonds used for dies, using drill, lathe, lapping machine, and hand tools. Positions gem or diamond against edge of revolving saw, lathe saw, or lapidary slitter, to cut, block, or slit stone. Grinds, drills, and finishes jewel bearings for use in precision instruments such as compasses and chronometers. Holds stone, gem, die, or stylus attached to holder or lapidary stick against rotating plates or wheels, to shape, grind, and polish. Locates and marks drilling position on surface of diamond dies, using diamond chip and power hand drill.

GOE Number, Interest Area, and Work Group: 08.02.02; Industrial Production; Production Technology: Precision Hand Work. **Personality Type:** Realistic. Realistic occupations frequently involve work activities that include practical, hands-on problems and solutions. These occupations often deal with plants, animals, and real-world materials like wood, tools, and machinery. Many of the occupations require working outside and do not involve a lot of paperwork or working closely with others. **Work Values:** Independence; Moral Values; Ability Utilization; Compensation; Working Conditions. **Skills:** Product Inspection; Equipment Selection; Operation and Control; Equipment Maintenance; Problem Identification. **Abilities:** *Cognitive*—Information Ordering; Selective Attention; Category Flexibility; Visualization; Number Facility; Mathematical Reasoning. *Psychomotor*—Arm-Hand Steadiness; Control Precision; Finger Dexterity. *Physical*—Explosive Strength; Dynamic Strength. *Sensory*—Near Vision; Visual Color Discrimination; Depth Perception. **General Work Activities:** *Information Input*—Getting Information Needed to Do the Job; Monitoring Processes, Materials, and Surroundings; Identifying Objects, Actions, and Events. *Mental Process*—Evaluating Information Against Standards; Judging Qualities of Things, Services, Other People's Work; Making Decisions and Solving Problems. *Work Output*—Handling and Moving Objects; Controlling Machines and Processes; Performing General Physical Activities. *Interacting with Others*—Communicating with Other Workers; Performing Administrative Activities; Monitoring and Controlling Resources; Coordinating Work and Activities of Others. **Physical Work Conditions:** Indoors; Using Hands on Objects, Tools, or Controls; Sitting. **Other Job Characteristics:** Importance of Being Exact or Accurate; Consequence of Error; Importance of Being Sure All Is Done.

Experience: Job Zone 2. Some previous work-related skill, knowledge, or experience may be helpful, but usually is not needed. **Job Preparation:** SVP 4.00 to 5.99—6 months to less than 2 years. **Knowledge:** Mechanical; Engineering and Technology; Mathematics; Production and Processing; Physics. **Instructional Programs:** 470408 Watch, Clock and Jewelry Repairer; 500713 Metal and Jewelry Arts.

Related DOT Jobs: 770.261-010 Brilliandeer-Lopper; 770.261-014 Girdler; 770.281-014 Gem Cutter; 770.381-014 Diamond Cleaver; 770.381-018 Diamond Driller; 770.381-022 Diamond-Die Polisher; 770.381-026 Jewel Blocker and Sawyer; 770.381-030 Jewel-Bearing Maker; 770.381-034 Oliving-Machine Operator; 770.381-038 Sapphire-Stylus Grinder; 770.381-042 Spotter; 770.382-010 Lathe Operator; 770.382-014 Phonograph-Needle-Tip Maker.

51-9081.00 Dental Laboratory Technicians (Dental Laboratory Technicians, Precision)

Education: Long-term O-T-J training
Employed: 43,840
Openings: 3,391
Projected Growth: 1%
Earnings: $25,660

Construct and repair full or partial dentures or dental appliances.

Melts metals; mixes plaster, porcelain, or acrylic paste; pours material into molds or over framework to form dental apparatus or prosthesis. Removes excess mixture and investment; polishes surface of prosthesis or framework, using polishing machine. Fills chipped or low spots in surface with acrylic resin. Assembles, carves, grinds, and polishes metal and plastic appliances, using pliers, spatula, grinders, and polishes. Tests appliance for conformance to specifications and accuracy of occlusion, using articulator and micrometer. Applies investments or mixtures such as porcelain paste or wax, over prosthesis framework or setup, using brushes and spatula. Casts plastic, plaster, and metal framework; removes mold from frame. Rebuilds or replaces linings, wire sections, and missing teeth to repair dentures. Reads prescription or specifications and examines models and impressions, to determine design of dental products to be constructed. Fabricates dental appliances or apparatus such as dentures, retainers, or metal bands. Shapes and solders wire and metal frames or bands for dental products, using soldering iron and hand tools.

GOE Number, Interest Area, and Work Group: 08.02.02; Industrial Production; Production Technology: Precision Hand Work. **Personality Type:** Realistic. Realistic occupations frequently involve work activities that include practical, hands-on problems and solutions. These occupations often deal with plants, animals, and real-world materials like wood, tools, and machinery. Many of the occupations require working outside and do not involve a lot of paperwork or working closely with others. **Work Values:** Moral Values; Independence; Working Conditions; Security; Achievement; Ability Utilization; Supervision, Human Relations; Supervision, Technical. **Skills:** Reading Comprehension; Product Inspection; Testing; Science; Problem Identification; Technology Design; Operations Analysis; Mathematics; Writing; Active Listening. **Abilities:** *Cognitive*—Written Comprehension; Visualization; Information Ordering; Number Facility; Deductive Reasoning; Oral Comprehension. *Psychomotor*—Finger Dexterity; Arm-Hand Steadiness; Control Precision. *Physical*—none met the criteria. *Sensory*—Near Vision; Visual Color Discrimination. **General Work Activities:** *Information Input*—Getting Information Needed to Do the Job; Identifying Objects, Actions, and Events; Estimating Needed Characteristics. *Mental Process*—Evaluating Information Against Standards; Analyzing Data or Information; Judging Qualities of Things, Services, Other People's Work. *Work Output*—Handling and Moving Objects; Implementing Ideas and Programs; Controlling Machines and Processes. *Interacting with Others*—Communicating with Other Workers; Establishing and Maintaining Relationships; Communicating with Persons Outside Organization. **Physical Work Conditions:** Indoors; Using Hands on Objects, Tools, or Controls; Sitting. **Other Job Characteristics:** Importance of Being Sure All Is Done; Importance of Being Exact or Accurate; Consequence of Error.

Experience: Job Zone 3. Previous work-related skill, knowledge, or experience is required. **Job Preparation:** SVP 6.0 to less than 7.0—More than 1 year and less than 4 years. **Knowledge:** Medicine and Dentistry; Design; Mechanical; Building and Construction; Mathematics; Physics. **Instructional Program:** 510603 Dental Laboratory Technician.

Related DOT Jobs: 712.381-014 Contour Wire Specialist, Denture; 712.381-018 Dental-Laboratory Technician; 712.381-022 Dental-Laboratory-Technician Apprentice; 712.381-026 Orthodontic Band

Maker; 712.381-030 Orthodontic Technician; 712.381-042 Dental Ceramist; 712.381-046 Denture Waxer; 712.381-050 Finisher, Denture; 712.664-010 Dental Ceramist Assistant.

51-9082.00 Medical Appliance Technicians (Medical Appliance Makers)

Education: No data available.

Employed: 7,130

Openings: No data available.

Projected Growth: No data available.

Earnings: $23,260

Construct, fit, maintain, or repair medical supportive devices such as braces, artificial limbs, joints, arch supports, and other surgical and medical appliances.

Constructs or receives plaster cast of patient's torso or limbs to use as pattern for cutting and fabricating supportive devices. Repairs and maintains medical supportive devices such as artificial limbs, braces, and surgical supports, according to specifications. Fits appliance onto patient and adjusts appliance as necessary. Fabricates wax or plastic impression of amputated area and prepares mold from impression, to form artificial cosmetic ear, nose, or hand. Instructs patient in use of prosthetic or orthotic device. Covers or pads metal or plastic structures and devices, using coverings such as rubber, leather, felt, plastic, or fiberglass. Tests medical supportive device for body fit, alignment, movement, and biomechanical stability, using meters and alignment fixtures. Mixes pigments according to formula to match skin coloring of patient; applies mixture to prosthetic or orthotic device. Polishes artificial limbs, braces, and supports, using grinding and buffing wheels. Drills and taps holes for rivets; glues, welds, bolts, and rivets parts together to form prosthetic or orthotic device. Lays out and marks dimensions of parts, using templates and precision measuring instruments. Carves, cuts, grinds, and welds wood, plastic, or metal material, to fabricate medical supportive devices, using hand and power tools. Reads specifications to determine type of product or device to be fabricated, selects required materials and tools. Bends, forms, and shapes fabric or material to conform to measurements for prescribed contours to fabricate structural components.

GOE Number, Interest Area, and Work Group: 05.03.03; Mechanics, Installers, and Repairers; Mechanical Work: Medical and Technical Equipment Fabrication and Repair. **Personality Type:** Realistic. Realistic occupations frequently involve work activities that include practical, hands-on problems and solutions. These occupations often deal with plants, animals, and real-world materials like wood, tools, and machinery. Many of the occupations require working outside and do not involve a lot of paperwork or working closely with others. **Work Values:** Moral Values; Independence; Achievement; Working Conditions; Supervision, Human Relations; Company Policies and Practices; Compensation; Ability Utilization. **Skills:** Technology Design; Product Inspection; Operations Analysis; Equipment Selection; Reading Comprehension. **Abilities:** *Cognitive*—Oral Expression; Visualization; Information Ordering; Problem Sensitivity; Written Comprehension. *Psychomotor*—Manual Dexterity; Finger Dexterity; Control Precision; Arm-Hand Steadiness. *Physical*—Explosive Strength.

Sensory—Near Vision; Visual Color Discrimination; Speech Clarity. **General Work Activities:** *Information Input*—Getting Information Needed to Do the Job; Inspecting Equipment, Structures, Materials; Identifying Objects, Actions, and Events. *Mental Process*—Updating and Using Job-Relevant Knowledge; Evaluating Information Against Standards; Making Decisions and Solving Problems; Analyzing Data or Information. *Work Output*—Handling and Moving Objects; Repairing and Maintaining Mechanical Equipment; Controlling Machines and Processes. *Interacting with Others*—Assisting and Caring for Others; Teaching Others; Communicating with Persons Outside Organization; Establishing and Maintaining Relationships. **Physical Work Conditions:** Indoors; Using Hands on Objects, Tools, or Controls; Sitting; Hazardous Equipment; Making Repetitive Motions. **Other Job Characteristics:** Importance of Being Exact or Accurate; Importance of Being Sure All Is Done; Consequence of Error.

Experience: Job Zone 2. Some previous work-related skill, knowledge, or experience may be helpful, but usually is not needed. **Job Preparation:** SVP 4.00 to 5.99—6 months to less than 2 years. **Knowledge:** Mechanical; Design; Engineering and Technology; Mathematics; Medicine and Dentistry; Physics. **Instructional Program:** 512307 Orthotics/Prosthetics.

Related DOT Jobs: 712.381-010 Arch-Support Technician; 712.381-034 Orthotics Technician; 712.381-038 Prosthetics Technician.

51-9083.00 Ophthalmic Laboratory Technicians (Ophthalmic Laboratory Technicians)

Education: Long-term O-T-J training

Employed: 22,714

Openings: 1,572

Projected Growth: 4.7%

Earnings: $19,530

Cut, grind, and polish eyeglasses, contact lenses, or other precision optical elements. Assemble and mount lenses into frames; process other optical elements.

GOE Number, Interest Area, and Work Group: 05.03.03; Mechanics, Installers, and Repairers; Mechanical Work: Medical and Technical Equipment Fabrication and Repair. **Instructional Programs:** 511006 Optometric/Ophthalmic Laboratory Technician; 511802 Optical Technician/Assistant; 511803 Ophthalmic Medical Technologist. **Note:** The Department of Labor has not collected some data for this job, so it has fewer details than the other descriptions.

51-9083.01 Precision Lens Grinders and Polishers (Ophthalmic Laboratory Technicians)

Education: Long-term O-T-J training

Employed: 22,714

Openings: 1,572

Projected Growth: 4.7%

Earnings: $19,530

Set up and operate variety of machines and equipment to grind and polish lens and other optical elements.

Immerses eyeglass frames in solutions to harden, soften, or dye frames. Inspects and measures mounted or unmounted lenses to verify alignment and conformance to specifications, using precision measuring instruments. Inspects, weighs, and measures lens blanks or lens, to verify compliance to specifications, using precision instruments. Inspects lens blank to detect flaws, verify smoothness of surface, and ensure thickness of coating on lens. Cuts or blocks lenses, optical glass, and blanks, using cutting machinery or precision hand tools. Controls equipment to coat lenses to alter reflective quality of lens. Adjusts lenses and frames to correct alignment; repairs broken parts, using precision hand tools and soldering iron. Assembles eyeglass frame; attaches shields, nose pads, and temple pieces, using pliers, screwdriver, and drill. Removes lenses from molds and separates lenses in containers for further processing or storage. Mounts, secures, and aligns lenses in frames or optical assemblies, using precision hand tools. Cleans and polishes finished lenses and eyeglasses, using cloth, solvent, and equipment. Lays out lenses and traces lens outline on glass, using template; assembles molds to cast contact lenses. Sets up machines to polish, bevel, edge, and grind lenses, flats, blanks, and other precision optical elements. Mounts and secures lens blanks or optical lens in holding tool or chuck of cutting, polishing, grinding, or coating machine. Holds lens against rotating wheel to grind or polish lens manually or using machine. Positions and adjusts cutting tool to specified curvature, dimensions, and depth of cut. Selects lens blank, molds, tools, or polishing or grinding wheel, according to production specifications. Examines prescription, work order, or broken or used eyeglasses, to determine specifications for lenses, contact lens, and other optical elements. Marks lenses and writes specifications to guide fabricators.

GOE Number, Interest Area, and Work Group: 08.02.02; Industrial Production; Production Technology: Precision Hand Work. **Personality Type:** Realistic. Realistic occupations frequently involve work activities that include practical, hands-on problems and solutions. These occupations often deal with plants, animals, and real-world materials like wood, tools, and machinery. Many of the occupations require working outside and do not involve a lot of paperwork or working closely with others. **Work Values:** Moral Values; Independence; Working Conditions; Compensation; Ability Utilization; Achievement; Security. **Skills:** Product Inspection; Equipment Selection; Operation and Control; Operation Monitoring; Mathematics. **Abilities:** *Cognitive*—Written Comprehension; Information Ordering; Problem Sensitivity; Deductive Reasoning; Number Facility. *Psychomotor*—Arm-Hand Steadiness; Finger Dexterity; Manual Dexterity. *Physical*—Extent Flexibility; Trunk Strength. *Sensory*—Near Vision; Visual Color Discrimination; Depth Perception. **General Work Activities:** *Information Input*—Inspecting Equipment, Structures, Materials; Getting Information Needed to Do the Job; Monitoring Processes, Materials, and Surroundings. *Mental Process*—Evaluating Information Against Standards; Analyzing Data or Information; Judging Qualities of Things, Services, Other People's Work. *Work Output*—Handling and Moving Objects; Controlling Machines and Processes; Implementing Ideas and Programs. *Interacting with Others*—Coordinating Work and Activities of Others; Communicating with Other Workers; Performing Administrative Activities. **Physical Work Conditions:** Indoors; Using Hands on Objects, Tools, or Controls; Sitting. **Other Job Characteristics:** Importance of Be-

ing Exact or Accurate; Importance of Being Sure All Is Done; Degree of Automation.

Experience: Job Zone 3. Previous work-related skill, knowledge, or experience is required. **Job Preparation:** SVP 6.0 to less than 7.0—More than 1 year and less than 4 years. **Knowledge:** Mechanical; Physics; Production and Processing; Mathematics; Engineering and Technology. **Instructional Programs:** 511006 Optometric/Ophthalmic Laboratory Technician; 511802 Optical Technician/Assistant; 511803 Ophthalmic Medical Technologist.

Related DOT Jobs: 713.381-010 Lens-Mold Setter; 713.681-010 Lens Mounter II; 716.280-010 Optician Apprentice; 716.280-014 Optician; 716.381-014 Lay-Out Technician; 716.382-010 Lathe Operator, Contact Lens; 716.382-014 Optical-Element Coater; 716.382-018 Precision-Lens Grinder; 716.382-022 Precision-Lens-Grinder Apprentice; 716.462-010 Precision-Lens Centerer and Edger; 716.681-010 Blocker and Cutter, Contact Lens; 716.681-014 Glass Cutter, Hand; 716.681-018 Lens Polisher, Hand; 716.682-010 Eyeglass-Lens Cutter; 716.682-014 Precision-Lens Generator; 716.682-018 Precision-Lens Polisher.

51-9083.02 Optical Instrument Assemblers
(Ophthalmic Laboratory Technicians)

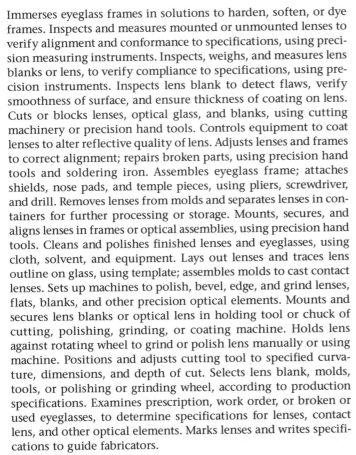

Education: Long-term O-T-J training
Employed: 22,714
Openings: 1,572
Projected Growth: 4.7%
Earnings: $19,530

Assemble optical instruments such as telescopes, level-transits, and gunsights.

Records production, inspection, and test data in logs. Tests and sights instruments to verify compliance to specifications, using precision testing instruments. Paints parts, using brush and spray gun. Computes distance of sighting instruments, using trigonometric formulas. Coats optical elements according to specifications, using coating equipment. Grinds and polishes optics, using hand tools and polishing cloths. Measures and tests optics, using precision measuring and testing instruments. Sets up and operates machines to fabricate fixtures, optics, and tools. Measures and marks dimensions and reference points; lays out stock for machining. Studies work orders, blueprints, and sketches, to formulate plans and sequences for fabricating optical elements, instruments, and systems. Mixes holding compounds; mounts workpiece or optical element on holding fixture and machine. Assembles structural, mechanical, and optical parts of instrument, using hand tools and cement. Cleans elements and parts, using tissue, cleaning solution, and air compressor.

GOE Number, Interest Area, and Work Group: 05.03.03; Mechanics, Installers, and Repairers; Mechanical Work: Medical and Technical Equipment Fabrication and Repair. **Personality Type:** Realistic. Realistic occupations frequently involve work activities that include practical, hands-on problems and solutions. These occupations often deal with plants, animals, and real-world materials like wood, tools, and machinery. Many of the occupations require working outside and do not involve a lot of paperwork or working closely with others. **Work Values:** Moral Values; Independence; Working Conditions; Supervision, Human Relations; Company Policies and Practices; Supervision, Technical; Security. **Skills:** Mathematics; Equipment Selection; Reading Comprehension; Critical Thinking; Operation and Control. **Abilities:** *Cognitive*—Problem Sensitivity; Written Comprehension; Information Ordering; Deductive Reasoning; Mathematical Reasoning; Number Facility. *Psychomotor*—Arm-Hand Steadiness; Manual Dexterity; Finger Dexterity. *Physical*—Trunk Strength; Extent Flexibility; Explosive Strength. *Sensory*—Near Vision; Visual Color Discrimination; Far Vision; Depth Perception. **General Work Activities:** *Information Input*—Getting Information Needed to Do the Job; Inspecting Equipment, Structures, Materials; Monitoring Processes, Materials, and Surroundings. *Mental Process*—Evaluating Information Against Standards; Processing Information; Judging Qualities of Things, Services, Other People's Work. *Work Output*—Controlling Machines and Processes; Handling and Moving Objects; Implementing Ideas and Programs. *Interacting with Others*—Performing Administrative Activities; Interpreting Meaning of Information to Others; Coordinating Work and Activities of Others; Communicating with Other Workers. **Physical Work Conditions:** Indoors; Using Hands on Objects, Tools, or Controls; Sitting; Standing. **Other Job Characteristics:** Degree of Automation; Importance of Being Exact or Accurate; Importance of Being Sure All Is Done.

Experience: Job Zone 4. A minimum of two to four years of work-related skill, knowledge, or experience is needed. **Job Preparation:** SVP 7.0 to less than 8.0—2 years to less than 10 years. **Knowledge:** Physics; Mathematics; Mechanical; Production and Processing; Clerical; Design. **Instructional Programs:** 511803 Ophthalmic Medical Technologist; 511006 Optometric/Ophthalmic Laboratory Technician; 511802 Optical Technician/Assistant.

Related DOT Jobs: 711.381-010 Optical-Instrument Assembler; 716.280-018 Optician.

51-9111.00 Packaging and Filling Machine Operators and Tenders (Packaging and Filling Machine Operators)

Education: Moderate-term O-T-J training

Employed: 376,592

Openings: 88,131

Projected Growth: 12.9%

Earnings: $20,060

Operate or tend machines to prepare industrial or consumer products for storage or shipment. Includes cannery workers who pack food products.

Attaches identification labels to finished packaged items. Cleans, oils, and makes minor repairs to machinery and equipment. Stocks product for packaging or filling machine operation. Stocks packaging material for machine processing. Secures finished packaged items by hand tying, sewing, or attaching fastener. Inspects and removes defective product and packaging material. Counts and records finished and rejected packaged items. Stacks finished packaged items or packs items in cartons or containers. Removes finished packaged items from machine and separates rejected items. Adjusts machine tension and pressure and machine components,

according to size or processing angle of product. Operates mechanism to cut filler product or packaging material. Regulates machine flow, speed, or temperature. Stops or resets machine when malfunction occurs; clears machine jams. Starts machine, by engaging controls. Tends or operates machine that packages product. Tests and evaluates product and verifies product weight or measurement to ensure quality standards. Observes machine operations to ensure quality and conformity of filled or packaged products to standards.

GOE Number, Interest Area, and Work Group: 08.03.01; Industrial Production; Production Work: Machine Work, Assorted Materials. **Personality Type:** Realistic. Realistic occupations frequently involve work activities that include practical, hands-on problems and solutions. These occupations often deal with plants, animals, and real-world materials like wood, tools, and machinery. Many of the occupations require working outside and do not involve a lot of paperwork or working closely with others. **Work Values:** Moral Values; Independence; Activity; Supervision, Human Relations; Company Policies and Practices. **Skills:** Operation and Control; Operation Monitoring; Equipment Maintenance; Product Inspection; Repairing. **Abilities:** *Cognitive*—Perceptual Speed; Information Ordering; Category Flexibility; Selective Attention; Problem Sensitivity. *Psychomotor*—Reaction Time; Control Precision; Manual Dexterity. *Physical*—Static Strength; Extent Flexibility; Trunk Strength. *Sensory*—Near Vision; Hearing Sensitivity; Visual Color Discrimination. **General Work Activities:** *Information Input*—Monitoring Processes, Materials, and Surroundings; Inspecting Equipment, Structures, Materials; Getting Information Needed to Do the Job. *Mental Process*—Judging Qualities of Things, Services, Other People's Work; Processing Information; Evaluating Information Against Standards. *Work Output*—Controlling Machines and Processes; Handling and Moving Objects; Repairing and Maintaining Mechanical Equipment. *Interacting with Others*—Monitoring and Controlling Resources; Communicating with Other Workers; Performing Administrative Activities. **Physical Work Conditions:** Indoors; Using Hands on Objects, Tools, or Controls; Standing. **Other Job Characteristics:** Degree of Automation; Importance of Being Sure All Is Done; Pace Determined by Speed of Equipment.

Experience: Job Zone 1. No previous work-related skill, knowledge, or experience is needed. **Job Preparation:** SVP Below 4.0—Less than 6 months. **Knowledge:** Production and Processing; Mechanical; Mathematics; Physics; Public Safety and Security; Engineering and Technology. **Instructional Program:** 470303 Industrial Machinery Maintenance and Repairer.

Related DOT Jobs: 509.685-046 Scrap Baller; 518.683-010 Sand-Slinger Operator; 520.685-174 Molder, Meat; 520.685-210 Stuffer; 520.685-218 Tray-Casting-Machine Operator; 524.685-030 Filling Machine Tender; 525.685-014 Casing-Running-Machine Tender; 529.665-010 Fruit-Grader Operator; 529.665-022 Yeast-Cutting-and-Wrapping-Machine Operator; 529.685-010 Auto Roller; 529.685-038 Bunch Maker, Machine; 529.685-138 Ham-Rolling-Machine Operator; 529.685-162 Linking-Machine Operator; 529.685-186 Plug-Overwrap-Machine Tender; 529.685-190 Preservative Filler, Machine; 529.685-266 Wrapper Layer; 529.685-270 Wrapper-Layer-and-Examiner, Soft Work; 529.685-282 Can-Filling-and-Closing-Machine Tender; 529.685-286 Cigar-Wrapper Tender, Automatic; 554.684-014 Foam Dispenser (partial list; see the introduction for sources of the complete list).

51-9121.00 Coating, Painting, and Spraying Machine Setters, Operators, and Tenders (Coating, Painting, and Spraying Machine Operators, Tenders, Setters, and Set-Up Operators)

Education: Moderate-term O-T-J training

Employed: 129,051

Openings: 26,434

Projected Growth: 8.7%

Earnings: No data available.

Set up, operate, or tend machines to coat or paint any of a wide variety of products including food, glassware, cloth, ceramics, metal, plastic, paper, or wood, using lacquer, silver, copper, rubber, varnish, glaze, enamel, oil, or rust-proofing materials.

GOE Number, Interest Area, and Work Group: 08.02.01; Industrial Production; Production Technology: Machine Set-up and Operation. **Instructional Program:** 470303 Industrial Machinery Maintenance and Repairer. **Note:** The Department of Labor has not collected some data for this job, so it has fewer details than the other descriptions.

51-9121.01 Coating, Painting, and Spraying Machine Setters and Set-Up Operators (Coating, Painting, and Spraying Machine Setters and Set-Up Operators)

Education: No data available.

Employed: 38,630

Openings: No data available.

Projected Growth: No data available.

Earnings: $22,750

Set up, or set up and operate, machines to coat or paint any of a wide variety of products such as food, glassware, cloth, ceramics, metal, plastic, paper, and wood, using lacquer, silver and copper solution, rubber, paint, varnish, glaze, enamel, oil, or rust-proofing materials.

Selects and loads materials, parts, and workpieces on machine, using hand tools. Observes and adjusts loaded workpiece or machine, according to specifications. Starts pumps to mix solutions and to activate coating or painting machines. Operates auxiliary machines or equipment used on the coating or painting process. Examines and tests solutions, paints, products, and workpieces to ensure that specifications are met. Cleans and maintains coating and painting machines, using hand tools. Measures thickness and quality of coating, using micrometer. Removes materials, parts, or workpieces from painting or coating machines, using hand tools. Weighs or measures chemicals, coatings, or paints; adds to machine. Turns valves and adjusts controls to regulate speed of conveyor, temperature, air pressure and circulation, and flow or spray of coating or paint. Sets up and operates machines to paint or coat products with such materials as silver and copper solution, rubber, paint, glaze, oil, or rust-proofing materials. Records operational data on specified forms.

GOE Number, Interest Area, and Work Group: 08.02.01; Industrial Production; Production Technology: Machine Set-up and Operation. **Personality Type:** Realistic. Realistic occupations frequently involve work activities that include practical, hands-on problems and solutions. These occupations often deal with plants, animals, and real-world materials like wood, tools, and machinery. Many of the occupations require working outside and do not involve a lot of paperwork or working closely with others. **Work Values:** Moral Values; Activity; Independence; Company Policies and Practices; Supervision, Human Relations. **Skills:** Product Inspection; Equipment Selection; Operation Monitoring; Operation and Control; Equipment Maintenance; Problem Identification. **Abilities:** *Cognitive*—Information Ordering; Problem Sensitivity; Visualization; Perceptual Speed; Memorization; Written Expression. *Psychomotor*—Manual Dexterity; Control Precision; Arm-Hand Steadiness. *Physical*—Trunk Strength; Extent Flexibility; Explosive Strength. *Sensory*—Visual Color Discrimination; Depth Perception; Peripheral Vision. **General Work Activities:** *Information Input*—Monitoring Processes, Materials, and Surroundings; Getting Information Needed to Do the Job; Inspecting Equipment, Structures, Materials. *Mental Process*—Judging Qualities of Things, Services, Other People's Work; Evaluating Information Against Standards; Organizing, Planning, and Prioritizing. *Work Output*—Controlling Machines and Processes; Handling and Moving Objects; Implementing Ideas and Programs. *Interacting with Others*—Performing Administrative Activities; Communicating with Other Workers; Coordinating Work and Activities of Others. **Physical Work Conditions:** Indoors; Using Hands on Objects, Tools, or Controls; Standing. **Other Job Characteristics:** Degree of Automation; Pace Determined by Speed of Equipment; Importance of Being Sure All Is Done; Consequence of Error; Frustrating Circumstances; Importance of Being Exact or Accurate.

Experience: Job Zone 2. Some previous work-related skill, knowledge, or experience may be helpful, but usually is not needed. **Job Preparation:** SVP 4.00 to 5.99—6 months to less than 2 years. **Knowledge:** Mechanical; Production and Processing; Chemistry; Mathematics; Clerical. **Instructional Program:** 480599 Precision Metal Workers, Other.

Related DOT Jobs: 534.380-010 Carbon-Paper-Coating-Machine Setter; 574.462-010 Abrasive-Coating-Machine Operator; 574.582-010 Silvering Applicator; 574.682-014 Spray-Machine Operator; 599.382-010 Paint-Sprayer Operator, Automatic; 632.380-018 Primer-Waterproofing-Machine Adjuster; 632.380-026 Varnishing-Unit Tool Setter; 679.682-010 Banding-Machine Operator; 692.682-014 Bead-Forming-Machine Operator.

51-9121.02 Coating, Painting, and Spraying Machine Operators and Tenders (Coating, Painting, and Spraying Machine Operators and Tenders)

Education: No data available.

Employed: 81,320

Openings: No data available.

Projected Growth: No data available.

Earnings: $21,360

Operate or tend machines to coat any of a wide variety of items. Coat food products with sugar, chocolate, or butter. Coat paper and paper products with chemical solutions, wax, or glazes.

Cleans machine, equipment, and work area, using water, solvents, and other cleaning aids. Turns dial, handwheel, valve, or switch, to control and adjust temperature, speed, and flow of product or machine. Attaches specified hose or nozzle to machine, using wrench and pliers. Measures and mixes specified quantities of substances to create coatings, paints, or sprays. Fills hopper, reservoir, trough, or pan with material used to coat, paint, or spray, using conveyor or pail. Starts and stops operation of machine, using lever or button. Observes machine operation and gauges to detect defects or deviations from standards. Transfers completed item or product from machine to drying or storage area, using handcart, handtruck, or crane. Records production data. Places item or product on feedrack, spindle, or reel strand to coat, paint, or spray, using hands, hoist, or trucklift. Examines, measures, weighs, or tests sample product to ensure conformance to specifications. Threads or feeds item or product through or around machine rollers and dryers. Aligns or fastens machine parts such as rollers, guides, brushes, and blades to secure roll, using hand tools.

GOE Number, Interest Area, and Work Group: 08.03.01; Industrial Production; Production Work: Machine Work, Assorted Materials. **Personality Type:** Realistic. Realistic occupations frequently involve work activities that include practical, hands-on problems and solutions. These occupations often deal with plants, animals, and real-world materials like wood, tools, and machinery. Many of the occupations require working outside and do not involve a lot of paperwork or working closely with others. **Work Values:** Moral Values; Independence; Company Policies and Practices; Activity; Supervision, Human Relations. **Skills:** Operation Monitoring; Operation and Control; Product Inspection; Mathematics; Equipment Selection. **Abilities:** *Cognitive*—Problem Sensitivity; Written Expression; Written Comprehension; Information Ordering; Selective Attention; Deductive Reasoning. *Psychomotor*—Control Precision; Arm-Hand Steadiness; Wrist-Finger Speed; Reaction Time; Manual Dexterity. *Physical*—Dynamic Strength; Static Strength; Gross Body Coordination; Stamina; Dynamic Flexibility. *Sensory*—Visual Color Discrimination; Sound Localization; Peripheral Vision. **General Work Activities:** *Information Input*—Monitoring Processes, Materials, and Surroundings; Inspecting Equipment, Structures, Materials; Getting Information Needed to Do the Job. *Mental Process*—Evaluating Information Against Standards; Processing Information; Judging Qualities of Things, Services, Other People's Work. *Work Output*—Controlling Machines and Processes; Handling and Moving Objects; Performing General Physical Activities. *Interacting with Others*—Communicating with Other Workers; Performing Administrative Activities; Monitoring and Controlling Resources; Establishing and Maintaining Relationships. **Physical Work Conditions:** Indoors; Using Hands on Objects, Tools, or Controls; Standing. **Other Job Characteristics:** Degree of Automation; Pace Determined by Speed of Equipment; Importance of Being Sure All Is Done.

Experience: Job Zone 1. No previous work-related skill, knowledge, or experience is needed. **Job Preparation:** SVP Below 4.0—Less than 6 months. **Knowledge:** Production and Processing; Engineering and Technology; Mechanical; Chemistry; Mathematics. **Instructional Program:** 470303 Industrial Machinery Maintenance and Repairer.

Related DOT Jobs: 524.382-010 Coating-Machine Operator; 524.382-014 Enrobing-Machine Operator; 524.665-010 Sanding-Machine Operator; 524.682-010 Depositing-Machine Operator; 524.685-014 Cheese Sprayer; 524.685-018 Coating Operator; 524.685-022 Cracker Sprayer; 524.685-026 Enrobing-Machine Operator; 524.685-034 Icer, Machine; 534.482-010 Waxing-Machine Operator; 534.582-010 Paper-Coating-Machine Operator; 534.682-010 Air-Drier-Machine Operator; 534.682-014 Carbon-Coater-Machine Operator; 534.682-018 Coating-Machine Operator; 534.682-022 Coating-Machine Operator, Hardboard; 534.682-038 Supercalender Operator; 534.685-022 Paper Coater; 534.685-026 Paraffin-Machine Operator; 534.685-030 Varnishing-Machine Operator; 539.482-010 Calender Operator, Insulation Board (partial list; see the introduction for sources of the complete list).

51-9122.00 Painters, Transportation Equipment
(Painters, Transportation Equipment)

Education: Moderate-term O-T-J training

Employed: 41,864

Openings: 8,601

Projected Growth: 9%

Earnings: $29,110

Operate or tend painting machines to paint surfaces of transportation equipment such as automobiles, buses, trucks, trains, boats, and airplanes.

Disassembles sprayer and power equipment such as sandblaster; cleans equipment and hand tools, using solvents, wire brushes, and cloths. Removes accessories from vehicles, such as chrome or mirrors, and masks other surfaces with tape or paper. Mixes, stirs, and thins paint or other coatings, using spatula or power mixing equipment. Lays out logos, symbols, or designs on painted surfaces, according to blueprint specifications, using measuring instruments, stencils, and patterns. Operates lifting and moving devices to move equipment or materials to access areas to be painted. Sets up portable ventilators, exhaust units, ladders, and scaffolding. Regulates controls on portable ventilators and exhaust units to cure and dry paint or other coatings. Selects paint according to company requirements and matches colors of paint following specified color charts. Paints designs, lettering, or other identifying information on vehicles, using paint brush or paint sprayer. Pours paint into spray gun; sprays specified amount of primer, decorative, or finish coatings onto prepared surfaces. Paints areas inaccessible to spray gun or retouches painted surface, using brush. Strips grease, dirt, paint, and rust from vehicle surface, using abrasives, solvents, brushes, blowtorch, or sandblaster.

GOE Number, Interest Area, and Work Group: 05.03.01; Mechanics, Installers, and Repairers; Mechanical Work: Vehicles and Facilities. **Personality Type:** Realistic. Realistic occupations frequently involve work activities that include practical, hands-on problems and solutions. These occupations often deal with plants, animals, and real-world materials like wood, tools, and machinery. Many of the occupations require working outside and do not involve a lot of paperwork or working closely with others. **Work Values:** Moral Values; Independence; Company Policies and Practices; Supervision, Human Relations; Activity. **Skills:** Operation and Control; Reading Comprehension; Equipment Selection. **Abilities:** *Cognitive*—Visualization; Information Ordering; Problem Sensitivity; Selective Attention; Category Flexibility; Written Comprehension. *Psychomotor*—Arm-Hand Steadiness; Control Precision; Manual Dexterity. *Physical*—Static Strength; Extent Flexibility; Dynamic Flexibility. *Sensory*—Visual Color Discrimination; Far Vision; Depth Perception. **General Work Activities:** *Information Input*—Getting Information Needed to Do the Job; Identifying Objects, Actions, and Events; Estimating Needed Characteristics. *Mental Process*—Evaluating Information Against Standards; Judging Qualities of Things, Services, Other People's Work; Processing Information; Analyzing Data or Information; Thinking Creatively; Organizing, Planning, and Prioritizing. *Work Output*—Performing General Physical Activities; Controlling Machines and Processes; Handling and Moving Objects. *Interacting with Others*—Communicating with Other Workers; Influencing Others or Selling; Performing for or Working with the Public; Establishing and Maintaining Relationships. **Physical Work Conditions:** Making Repetitive Motions; Standing; Using Hands on Objects, Tools, or Controls; Bending or Twisting the Body; Contaminants; Common Protective or Safety Attire. **Other Job Characteristics:** Consequence of Error; Importance of Being Exact or Accurate; Importance of Being Sure All Is Done.

Experience: Job Zone 2. Some previous work-related skill, knowledge, or experience may be helpful, but usually is not needed. **Job Preparation:** SVP 4.00 to 5.99—6 months to less than 2 years. **Knowledge:** Mechanical; Mathematics; Design; Fine Arts; Chemistry. **Instructional Program:** 470603 Auto/Automotive Body Repairer.

Related DOT Jobs: 845.381-010 Painter Apprentice, Transportation Equipment; 845.381-014 Painter, Transportation Equipment; 845.381-018 Paint Sprayer, Sandblaster; 845.681-010 Railroad-Car Letterer.

51-9123.00 Painting, Coating, and Decorating Workers (Painting, Coating, and Decorating Workers)

Education: Short-term O-T-J training

Employed: 39,129

Openings: 8,593

Projected Growth: 17.7%

Earnings: $19,060

Paint, coat, or decorate articles such as furniture, glass, plateware, pottery, jewelry, cakes, toys, books, or leather.

Positions and glues decorative pieces in cutout section, following pattern. Immerses workpiece into coating material for specified time. Conceals blemishes in workpiece, such as nicks and dents, using filler such as putty. Cleans surface of workpiece in preparation for coating, using cleaning fluid, solvent, brushes, scraper, steam, sandpaper, or cloth. Cuts out sections in surface of material to be inlaid with decorative pieces, using pattern and knife or scissors. Places coated workpiece in oven or dryer for specified time, to dry or harden finish. Melts or heats coating material to specified temperature. Cleans and maintains tools and equipment, using solvent, brushes, and rags. Drains or wipes workpieces to remove excess coating material or to facilitate setting of finish coat on workpiece. Examines finished surface of workpiece to verify conformance to specifications; retouches defective areas of surface. Rinses coated workpiece to remove excess coating material or to facilitate setting of finish coat on workpiece. Applies coating such as paint, ink, or lacquer, to protect or decorate workpiece surface, using spray gun, pen, or brush. Reads job order and inspects workpiece to determine work procedure and materials required. Selects and mixes ingredients to prepare coating substance according to specifications, using paddle or mechanical mixer.

GOE Number, Interest Area, and Work Group: 08.03.06; Industrial Production; Production Work: Hands-on Work, Assorted Materials. **Personality Type:** Realistic. Realistic occupations frequently involve work activities that include practical, hands-on problems and solutions. These occupations often deal with plants, animals, and real-world materials like wood, tools, and machinery. Many of the occupations require working outside and do not involve a lot of paperwork or working closely with others. **Work Values:** Moral Values; Independence; Activity; Company Policies and Practices; Ability Utilization; Supervision, Human Relations. **Skills:** Product Inspection; Equipment Selection. **Abilities:** *Cognitive*—Information Ordering; Visualization; Written Comprehension; Flexibility of Closure; Perceptual Speed; Number Facility. *Psychomotor*—Manual Dexterity; Arm-Hand Steadiness; Wrist-Finger Speed. *Physical*—Trunk Strength; Stamina. *Sensory*—Near Vision; Visual Color Discrimination. **General Work Activities:** *Information Input*—Getting Information Needed to Do the Job; Monitoring Processes, Materials, and Surroundings; Identifying Objects, Actions, and Events. *Mental Process*—Evaluating Information Against Standards; Judging Qualities of Things, Services, Other People's Work; Making Decisions and Solving Problems. *Work Output*—Handling and Moving Objects; Performing General Physical Activities; Controlling Machines and Processes. *Interacting with Others*—Communicating with Other Workers; Interpreting Meaning of Information to Others; Performing Administrative Activities; Coordinating Work and Activities of Others. **Physical Work Conditions:** Indoors; Using Hands on Objects, Tools, or Controls; Standing. **Other Job Characteristics:** Importance of Being Sure All Is Done; Consequence of Error; Importance of Being Exact or Accurate.

Experience: Job Zone 1. No previous work-related skill, knowledge, or experience is needed. **Job Preparation:** SVP Below 4.0— Less than 6 months. **Knowledge:** Production and Processing; Building and Construction; Fine Arts; Mathematics; Engineering and Technology. **Instructional Program:** 200301 Clothing, Apparel and Textile Workers and Managers, General.

Related DOT Jobs: 364.381-010 Painter, Rug Touch-Up; 500.684-022 Silver Spray Worker; 505.684-010 Electroless Plater; 505.684-014 Metal Sprayer, Production; 509.684-010 Enameler; 554.384-010 Dyer; 554.684-010 Caustic Operator; 562.687-010 Dyer; 562.687-014 Resin Coater; 574.484-010 Optical-Glass Silverer; 574.684-010 Ground Layer; 574.684-014 Silverer; 584.684-010 Latexer; 584.687-010 Leather Coater; 584.687-014 Sprayer, Hand; 589.687-034 Stainer;

589.687-038 Stiffener; 599.682-010 Painter, Electrostatic; 599.687-010 Balloon Dipper; 700.684-054 Oxidizer (partial list; see the introduction for sources of the complete list).

51-9131.00 Photographic Process Workers (Precision Photographic Process Workers)

Education: Moderate-term O-T-J training

Employed: 17,751

Openings: 4,377

Projected Growth: 7%

Earnings: $21,620

Perform precision work involved in photographic processing, such as editing photographic negatives and prints, using photo-mechanical, chemical, or computerized methods.

GOE Number, Interest Area, and Work Group: 08.03.05; Industrial Production; Production Work: Printing and Reproduction. **Instructional Programs:** 100103 Photographic Technology/Technician; 480299 Graphic and Printing Equipment Operators, Other. **Note:** The Department of Labor has not collected some data for this job, so it has fewer details than the other descriptions.

51-9131.01 Photographic Retouchers and Restorers
(Photographic Process Workers, Precision)

Education: Moderate-term O-T-J training

Employed: 17,751

Openings: 4,377

Projected Growth: 7%

Earnings: $21,620

Retouch or restore photographic negatives and prints to accentuate desirable features of subject, using pencils, watercolors, or airbrushes.

Examines drawing, negative, or photographic print to determine coloring, shading, accenting, and changes required to retouch or restore. Paints negative with retouching medium, to ensure that retouching pencil will mark surface of negative. Wipes excess color from portrait to produce specified shade, using cotton swab. Trims edges of print to enhance appearance, using scissors or paper cutter. Applies paint to retouch or enhance negative or photograph, using airbrush, pen, artist's brush, cotton swab, or gloved finger. Mixes ink or paint solutions, according to color specifications, color chart, and consistency desired. Inks borders or lettering on illustration, using pen, brush, or drafting instruments. Rubs eraser or cloth over photograph to reduce gloss, remove debris, or prepare specified areas of illustration for highlighting. Shades negative or photograph with pencil, to smooth facial contours, to conceal blemishes, stray hairs, or wrinkles, and to soften highlights. Cuts out masking template, using shears, and positions templates on picture to mask selected areas.

GOE Number, Interest Area, and Work Group: 08.03.05; Industrial Production; Production Work: Printing and Reproduction. **Personality Type:** Artistic. Artistic occupations frequently involve working with forms, designs, and patterns. These occupations often require self-expression, and the work can be done without following a clear set of rules. **Work Values:** Moral Values; Independence; Working Conditions; Achievement; Autonomy. **Skills:** Product Inspection; Identification of Key Causes; Equipment Selection; Visioning. **Abilities:** *Cognitive*—Visualization; Problem Sensitivity; Information Ordering; Deductive Reasoning; Flexibility of Closure. *Psychomotor*—Arm-Hand Steadiness; Finger Dexterity; Wrist-Finger Speed; Manual Dexterity. *Physical*—none met the criteria. *Sensory*—Visual Color Discrimination; Near Vision; Depth Perception; Glare Sensitivity. **General Work Activities:** *Information Input*—Getting Information Needed to Do the Job; Identifying Objects, Actions, and Events; Inspecting Equipment, Structures, Materials. *Mental Process*—Thinking Creatively; Evaluating Information Against Standards; Judging Qualities of Things, Services, Other People's Work. *Work Output*—Handling and Moving Objects; Controlling Machines and Processes; Performing General Physical Activities. *Interacting with Others*—Communicating with Other Workers; Performing Administrative Activities; Establishing and Maintaining Relationships. **Physical Work Conditions:** Using Hands on Objects, Tools, or Controls; Indoors; Sitting. **Other Job Characteristics:** Importance of Being Exact or Accurate; Importance of Being Sure All Is Done; Consequence of Error.

Experience: Job Zone 3. Previous work-related skill, knowledge, or experience is required. **Job Preparation:** SVP 6.0 to less than 7.0—More than 1 year and less than 4 years. **Knowledge:** Fine Arts; Chemistry; Production and Processing; Design; Mathematics. **Instructional Programs:** 100103 Photographic Technology/Technician; 480299 Graphic and Printing Equipment Operators, Other.

Related DOT Jobs: 970.281-010 Airbrush Artist; 970.281-018 Photograph Retoucher; 970.381-010 Colorist, Photography; 970.381-034 Spotter, Photographic.

51-9131.02 Photographic Reproduction Technicians
(Photographic Process Workers, Precision)

Education: Moderate-term O-T-J training

Employed: 17,751

Openings: 4,377

Projected Growth: 7%

Earnings: $21,620

Duplicate materials to produce prints on sensitized paper, cloth, or film, using photographic equipment.

Rolls exposed section of sensitized paper into developer tank inside machine. Retouches defects in print, using chemicals, inks, brushes, and pens. Places filter over lens to make color separation when copying color work. Reprints original to enlarge, or reprints original in sections to be pieced together. Mounts original photograph, negative, or other printed material in holder or vacuum frame beneath light. Mounts camera on tripod or stand, and loads prescribed type and size film in camera. Reads work order to determine required processes, techniques. materials, and equipment. Rinses developed print in water and places in heated drying cabinet. Estimates exposure time, according to size of lens aperture, grade of sensitized paper, and intensity of light. Examines developed print for defects such as broken lines, spots, and blurs. Starts exposure to duplicate original, photograph, or negative. Mixes developing and processing solutions for use in developing, processing, and rinsing prints. Places sensitized paper in frame of projection printer, photostat, or other reproduction machine. Selects lens assembly according to size and type of negative or photograph to be printed. Measures material to be copied; computes percentage of enlargement or reproduction necessary, using rule, chart, or percentage scale. Examines negative for contrast, to determine grade of sensitized paper required for print. Sets automatic timer, lens opening, and carriage of printer to specified focus and exposure time. Develops exposed paper or material.

GOE Number, Interest Area, and Work Group: 08.03.05; Industrial Production; Production Work: Printing and Reproduction. **Personality Type:** Realistic. Realistic occupations frequently involve work activities that include practical, hands-on problems and solutions. These occupations often deal with plants, animals, and real-world materials like wood, tools, and machinery. Many of the occupations require working outside and do not involve a lot of paperwork or working closely with others. **Work Values:** Independence; Moral Values; Working Conditions; Autonomy; Achievement; Supervision, Human Relations; Supervision, Technical. **Skills:** Mathematics; Equipment Selection; Reading Comprehension; Product Inspection; Operation and Control. **Abilities:** *Cognitive*—Information Ordering; Written Comprehension; Mathematical Reasoning; Number Facility; Deductive Reasoning. *Psychomotor*—Arm-Hand Steadiness; Wrist-Finger Speed; Control Precision. *Physical*—Stamina. *Sensory*—Near Vision; Visual Color Discrimination; Night Vision. **General Work Activities:** *Information Input*—Getting Information Needed to Do the Job; Estimating Needed Characteristics; Monitoring Processes, Materials, and Surroundings. *Mental Process*—Evaluating Information Against Standards; Processing Information; Analyzing Data or Information. *Work Output*—Handling and Moving Objects; Controlling Machines and Processes; Implementing Ideas and Programs. *Interacting with Others*—Communicating with Other Workers; Interpreting Meaning of Information to Others; Assisting and Caring for Others; Performing Administrative Activities; Coordinating Work and Activities of Others; Establishing and Maintaining Relationships. **Physical Work Conditions:** Indoors; Using Hands on Objects, Tools, or Controls; Hazardous Conditions. **Other Job Characteristics:** Importance of Being Exact or Accurate; Importance of Being Sure All Is Done; Consequence of Error.

Experience: Job Zone 3. Previous work-related skill, knowledge, or experience is required. **Job Preparation:** SVP 6.0 to less than 7.0—More than 1 year and less than 4 years. **Knowledge:** Production and Processing; Chemistry; Mathematics; Fine Arts; Engineering and Technology. **Instructional Programs:** 100103 Photographic Technology/Technician; 480299 Graphic and Printing Equipment Operators, Other.

Related DOT Jobs: 976.361-010 Reproduction Technician; 976.381-018 Projection Printer; 976.381-022 Template Reproduction Technician; 976.382-022 Photostat Operator.

51-9131.03 Photographic Hand Developers
(Photographic Process Workers, Precision)

Education: Moderate-term O-T-J training
Employed: 17,751
Openings: 4,377
Projected Growth: 7%
Earnings: $21,620

Develop exposed photographic film or sensitized paper in series of chemical and water baths to produce negative or positive prints.

Immerses negative paper, film, or print in hyposolution to fix image. Dries prints or negatives, using sponge, squeegee, or mechanical air dryer. Produces color photographs, negatives, and slides, using color reproduction processes. Mixes developing and fixing solutions, following formula. Immerses negative paper, film, or print in water to remove chemicals. Immerses exposed film or photographic paper in developer solution, to bring out latent image. Immerses negative paper, film, or print in stop bath to arrest developer action.

GOE Number, Interest Area, and Work Group: 08.03.05; Industrial Production; Production Work: Printing and Reproduction. **Personality Type:** Realistic. Realistic occupations frequently involve work activities that include practical, hands-on problems and solutions. These occupations often deal with plants, animals, and real-world materials like wood, tools, and machinery. Many of the occupations require working outside and do not involve a lot of paperwork or working closely with others. **Work Values:** Moral Values; Independence; Supervision, Technical; Working Conditions; Security. **Skills:** Reading Comprehension; Mathematics. **Abilities:** *Cognitive*—Information Ordering; Problem Sensitivity; Perceptual Speed; Deductive Reasoning; Written Comprehension. *Psychomotor*—Wrist-Finger Speed; Control Precision; Manual Dexterity. *Physical*—Extent Flexibility; Trunk Strength. *Sensory*—Night Vision; Near Vision; Visual Color Discrimination. **General Work Activities:** *Information Input*—Monitoring Processes, Materials, and Surroundings; Getting Information Needed to Do the Job; Identifying Objects, Actions, and Events. *Mental Process*—Analyzing Data or Information; Evaluating Information Against Standards; Judging Qualities of Things, Services, Other People's Work. *Work Output*—Handling and Moving Objects; Controlling Machines and Processes; Performing General Physical Activities. *Interacting with Others*—Communicating with Other Workers; Coordinating Work and Activities of Others; Assisting and Caring for Others; Monitoring and Controlling Resources; Interpreting Meaning of Information to Others; Performing Administrative Activities. **Physical Work Conditions:** Indoors; Using Hands on Objects, Tools, or Controls; Standing. **Other Job Characteristics:** Importance of Being Sure All Is Done; Importance of Being Exact or Accurate; Consequence of Error.

Experience: Job Zone 2. Some previous work-related skill, knowledge, or experience may be helpful, but usually is not needed. **Job Preparation:** SVP 4.00 to 5.99—6 months to less than 2 years. **Knowledge:** Chemistry; Fine Arts; Production and Processing;

Mathematics; Computers and Electronics. **Instructional Programs:** 100103 Photographic Technology/Technician; 480299 Graphic and Printing Equipment Operators, Other.

Related DOT Job: 976.681-010 Developer.

51-9131.04 Film Laboratory Technicians (Photographic Process Workers, Precision)

Education: Moderate-term O-T-J training

Employed: 17,751

Openings: 4,377

Projected Growth: 7%

Earnings: $21,620

Evaluate motion picture film to determine characteristics such as sensitivity to light, density, and exposure time required for printing.

Threads film strip through densitometer and exposes film to light to determine density of film. Threads film strip through sensitometer and exposes film to light. Records test data; routes film to film developer and film printer for further processing. Exposes film strip to progressively timed lights to compare effects of various exposure times. Computes amount of light intensity needed to compensate for density of film, using standardized formulas. Reads gauges on sensitometer to determine film's sensitivity to light. Examines developed film strip to determine optimal exposure time and light intensity required for printing.

GOE Number, Interest Area, and Work Group: 08.03.05; Industrial Production; Production Work: Printing and Reproduction. **Personality Type:** Realistic. Realistic occupations frequently involve work activities that include practical, hands-on problems and solutions. These occupations often deal with plants, animals, and real-world materials like wood, tools, and machinery. Many of the occupations require working outside and do not involve a lot of paperwork or working closely with others. **Work Values:** Moral Values; Independence; Working Conditions; Supervision, Technical; Autonomy. **Skills:** Product Inspection; Mathematics; Solution Appraisal; Science; Information Gathering; Information Organization; Reading Comprehension; Judgment and Decision Making; Operation and Control. **Abilities:** *Cognitive*—Number Facility; Information Ordering; Inductive Reasoning; Written Expression; Mathematical Reasoning. *Psychomotor*—Arm-Hand Steadiness; Control Precision; Wrist-Finger Speed; Finger Dexterity. *Physical*—none met the criteria. *Sensory*—Near Vision; Visual Color Discrimination; Far Vision. **General Work Activities:** *Information Input*—Getting Information Needed to Do the Job; Monitoring Processes, Materials, and Surroundings; Identifying Objects, Actions, and Events. *Mental Process*—Judging Qualities of Things, Services, Other People's Work; Evaluating Information Against Standards; Processing Information. *Work Output*—Documenting and Recording Information; Handling and Moving Objects; Controlling Machines and Processes. *Interacting with Others*—Interpreting Meaning of Information to Others; Performing Administrative Activities; Communicating with Other Workers. **Physical Work Conditions:** Indoors; Using Hands on Objects, Tools, or Controls; Sitting. **Other Job Characteristics:** Importance of Being Sure All Is Done; Importance of Being Exact or Accurate; Consequence of Error.

Experience: Job Zone 4. A minimum of two to four years of work-related skill, knowledge, or experience is needed. **Job Preparation:** SVP 7.0 to less than 8.0—2 years to less than 10 years. **Knowledge:** Mathematics; Production and Processing; Physics; Clerical; Fine Arts; Mechanical. **Instructional Programs:** 100103 Photographic Technology/Technician; 480299 Graphic and Printing Equipment Operators, Other.

Related DOT Job: 976.381-010 Film Laboratory Technician I.

51-9132.00 Photographic Processing Machine Operators (Photographic Processing Machine Operators and Tenders)

Education: Short-term O-T-J training

Employed: 45,741

Openings: 9,985

Projected Growth: −11.4%

Earnings: $17,800

Operate photographic processing machines such as photographic printing machines, film-developing machines, and mounting presses.

Measures and mixes chemicals according to formula to prepare solutions for processing. Fills tanks of processing machines with solutions such as developer, dyes, stop-baths, fixers, bleaches, and washes. Monitors equipment operation to detect malfunctions. Sets and adjusts machine controls, according to specifications, type of operation, and material requirements. Discards or cleans and repairs defective film or circuit patterns on photographic plates, using cleaning solutions and hand tools. Cleans and maintains photoprocessing equipment, using cleaning and rinsing solutions and ultrasonic equipment. Maintains records such as number and types of processing completed, rate of materials usage, and customer charges. Reads work orders and examines negatives and film to determine machine settings and processing requirements. Places film in labeled containers; numbers film for identification, using numbering machine or by hand. Removes completed work from equipment and examines circuit boards, plates, film, and prints for conformance to quality standards. Loads circuit boards, racks or rolls of film, negatives, or printing paper into processing or printing machines. Starts and operates machines to prepare circuit boards and expose, develop, etch, fix, wash, dry, and print film or plates.

GOE Number, Interest Area, and Work Group: 08.03.05; Industrial Production; Production Work: Printing and Reproduction. **Personality Type:** Realistic. Realistic occupations frequently involve work activities that include practical, hands-on problems and solutions. These occupations often deal with plants, animals, and real-world materials like wood, tools, and machinery. Many of the occupations require working outside and do not involve a lot of paperwork or working closely with others. **Work Values:** Moral Values; Independence; Working Conditions; Company Policies and Practices; Supervision, Human Relations. **Skills:** Product Inspection; Operation and Control; Operation Monitoring; Mathematics; Equipment Selection; Reading Comprehension. **Abilities:** *Cognitive*—Information Ordering; Problem Sensitivity; Perceptual Speed; Written Comprehension; Written Expression.

Psychomotor—Manual Dexterity; Control Precision; Arm-Hand Steadiness. *Physical*—Extent Flexibility; Trunk Strength; Dynamic Flexibility; Gross Body Coordination; Dynamic Strength. *Sensory*—Night Vision; Near Vision; Visual Color Discrimination. **General Work Activities:** *Information Input*—Monitoring Processes, Materials, and Surroundings; Inspecting Equipment, Structures, Materials; Getting Information Needed to Do the Job. *Mental Process*—Judging Qualities of Things, Services, Other People's Work; Evaluating Information Against Standards; Updating and Using Job-Relevant Knowledge. *Work Output*—Handling and Moving Objects; Controlling Machines and Processes; Implementing Ideas and Programs. *Interacting with Others*—Performing Administrative Activities; Communicating with Other Workers; Coordinating Work and Activities of Others. **Physical Work Conditions:** Using Hands on Objects, Tools, or Controls; Standing; Contaminants; Indoors. **Other Job Characteristics:** Degree of Automation; Importance of Being Exact or Accurate; Consequence of Error.

Experience: Job Zone 2. Some previous work-related skill, knowledge, or experience may be helpful, but usually is not needed.
Job Preparation: SVP 4.00 to 5.99—6 months to less than 2 years.
Knowledge: Production and Processing; Mechanical; Chemistry; Computers and Electronics; Clerical. **Instructional Program:** 100103 Photographic Technology/Technician.

Related DOT Jobs: 976.380-010 Computer-Controlled-Color-Photograph-Printer Operator; 976.382-014 Color-Printer Operator; 976.382-018 Film Developer; 976.382-030 Photographic Aligner, Semiconductor Wafers; 976.382-034 Step-and-Repeat Reduction Camera Operator; 976.382-038 Photo Mask Pattern Generator; 976.384-010 Photo Technician; 976.384-014 Photo Mask Processor; 976.385-010 Microfilm Processor; 976.665-010 Take-Down Sorter; 976.682-010 Film Printer; 976.682-014 Printer Operator, Black-and-White; 976.682-018 Rectification Printer; 976.684-014 Film Laboratory Technician; 976.684-030 Contact Printer, Printed Circuit Boards; 976.684-038 Contact Worker, Lithography; 976.685-014 Developer, Automatic; 976.685-018 Film Laboratory Technician II; 976.685-022 Mounter, Automatic; 976.685-026 Print Developer, Automatic (partial list; see the introduction for sources of the complete list).

51-9141.00 Semiconductor Processors (Electronic Semiconductor Processors)

Education: Moderate-term O-T-J training
Employed: 63,367
Openings: 10,615
Projected Growth: 45.2%
Earnings: $24,810

Perform various functions in the manufacture of electronic semiconductors. Load semiconductor material into furnace; saw formed ingots into segments; load individual segment into crystal-growing chamber; monitor controls; locate crystal axis in ingot, using X-ray equipment; and saw ingots into wafers. Clean, polish, and load wafers into series of special-purpose furnaces, chemical baths, and equipment used to form circuitry and change conductive properties.

Cleans and dries materials and equipment using solvent, etching equipment, sandblasting equipment, and drying equipment, to remove contaminants or photoresist. Places semiconductor wafers in processing containers or equipment holders, using vacuum wand or tweezers. Maintains processing, production, and inspection information and reports. Stamps or etches identifying information on finished component. Counts, sorts, and weighs processed items. Inspects materials, components, or products for surface defects; measures circuitry, using electronic test equipment, precision measuring instruments, and standard procedures. Loads and unloads equipment chambers; transports finished product to storage or to area for further processing. Studies work order, instructions, formulas, and processing charts to determine specifications and sequence of operations. Etches, laps, polishes, or grinds wafers or ingots, using etching, lapping, polishing, or grinding equipment. Measures and weighs amounts of crystal-growing materials; mixes and grinds materials; loads materials into container, following procedures. Monitors operation; adjusts controls of processing machines and equipment, to produce compositions with specific electronic properties. Manipulates valves, switches, and buttons; keys commands into control panels to start semiconductor processing cycles. Attaches ampoule to diffusion pump to remove air from ampoule; seals ampoule, using blowtorch. Aligns photo mask pattern on photoresist layer, exposes pattern to ultraviolet light, and develops pattern, using specialized equipment. Forms seed crystal for crystal growing or locates crystal axis of ingot, using X-ray equipment, drill, and sanding machine. Operates saw to cut remelt into sections of specified size or to cut ingots into wafers.

GOE Number, Interest Area, and Work Group: 08.03.02; Industrial Production; Production Work: Equipment Operation, Assorted Materials Processing. **Personality Type:** Realistic. Realistic occupations frequently involve work activities that include practical, hands-on problems and solutions. These occupations often deal with plants, animals, and real-world materials like wood, tools, and machinery. Many of the occupations require working outside and do not involve a lot of paperwork or working closely with others. **Work Values:** Moral Values; Independence; Company Policies and Practices; Activity; Supervision, Human Relations. **Skills:** Operation Monitoring; Operation and Control; Equipment Selection; Science; Product Inspection. **Abilities:** *Cognitive*—Information Ordering; Written Comprehension; Inductive Reasoning; Number Facility; Problem Sensitivity; Deductive Reasoning. *Psychomotor*—Control Precision; Wrist-Finger Speed; Finger Dexterity; Manual Dexterity. *Physical*—Trunk Strength. *Sensory*—Near Vision; Far Vision; Glare Sensitivity. **General Work Activities:** *Information Input*—Monitoring Processes, Materials, and Surroundings; Inspecting Equipment, Structures, Materials; Getting Information Needed to Do the Job. *Mental Process*—Processing Information; Making Decisions and Solving Problems; Evaluating Information Against Standards. *Work Output*—Controlling Machines and Processes; Handling and Moving Objects; Documenting and Recording Information; Implementing Ideas and Programs. *Interacting with Others*—Performing Administrative Activities; Communicating with Other Workers; Monitoring and Controlling Resources. **Physical Work Conditions:** Indoors; Using Hands on Objects, Tools, or Controls; Standing. **Other Job Characteristics:** Importance of Being Exact or Accurate; Importance of Being Sure All Is Done; Consequence of Error.

Experience: Job Zone 1. No previous work-related skill, knowledge, or experience is needed. **Job Preparation:** SVP Below 4.0—Less than 6 months. **Knowledge:** Production and Processing; Mathematics; Mechanical; Computers and Electronics; Engineering and Technology. **Instructional Program:** 470105 Industrial Electronics Installer and Repairer.

Related DOT Jobs: 590.362-018 Group Leader, Semiconductor Processing; 590.382-022 Ion Implant Machine Operator; 590.384-010 Charge Preparation Technician; 590.684-014 Electronic-Component Processor; 590.684-022 Semiconductor Processor; 590.684-042 Integrated Circuit Fabricator; 590.685-070 Diffusion Furnace Operator, Semiconductor Wafers; 590.685-086 Metallization Equipment Tender, Semiconductors.

51-9191.00 Cementing and Gluing Machine Operators and Tenders (Cementing and Gluing Machine Operators and Tenders)

Education: Moderate-term O-T-J training

Employed: 32,144

Openings: 5,210

Projected Growth: –15.6%

Earnings: $20,720

Operate or tend cementing and gluing machines to join items for further processing or to form a completed product. Join veneer sheets into plywood; glue paper; join rubber and rubberized fabric parts; join plastic, simulated leather, or other materials.

Starts machine; turns valves or moves controls, to feed, admit, or transfer materials and adhesive. Monitors machine operation to detect malfunctions, to remove jammed materials, and to readjust machine components to conform to specifications. Adjusts machine components according to specifications such as width, length, and thickness of materials to be joined. Positions materials being joined, to ensure accurate application of adhesive. Mounts or loads material such as paper, plastic, wood, or rubber in feeding mechanism of cementing or gluing machine. Measures and mixes ingredients according to specifications, to prepare glue. Examines and measures completed materials or products to verify conformance to specifications, using measuring devices such as tape measure, gauge, or calipers. Cleans and maintains gluing and cementing machines, using cleaning solutions, lubricants, brushes, and scrapers. Maintains production records such as number, dimensions, and thickness of materials processed. Transports materials, supplies, and finished products between storage and work areas, using forklift. Adjusts machine to apply specified amount of glue, cement, or adhesive. Monitors and fills machine with glue, cement, or adhesive as needed. Reads work orders and communicates with coworkers to determine machine and equipment settings and adjustments, and supply and product specifications. Observes gauges, meters, and control panels, to regulate temperature, pressure, or speed of feeder or conveyor. Removes completed materials or products and restocks materials to be joined.

GOE Number, Interest Area, and Work Group: 08.03.01; Industrial Production; Production Work: Machine Work, Assorted Materials. **Personality Type:** Realistic. Realistic occupations frequently involve work activities that include practical, hands-on problems and solutions. These occupations often deal with plants, animals, and real-world materials like wood, tools, and machinery. Many of the occupations require working outside and do not involve a lot of paperwork or working closely with others. **Work Values:** Moral Values; Supervision, Human Relations; Company Policies and Practices; Activity; Independence. **Skills:** Product Inspection; Operation Monitoring; Operation and Control; Equipment Maintenance; Equipment Selection. **Abilities:** *Cognitive*—Problem Sensitivity; Written Comprehension; Visualization; Deductive Reasoning; Information Ordering. *Psychomotor*—Arm-Hand Steadiness; Control Precision; Manual Dexterity. *Physical*—Static Strength; Trunk Strength; Extent Flexibility. *Sensory*—Visual Color Discrimination; Depth Perception. **General Work Activities:** *Information Input*—Monitoring Processes, Materials, and Surroundings; Inspecting Equipment, Structures, Materials; Getting Information Needed to Do the Job. *Mental Process*—Evaluating Information Against Standards; Processing Information; Analyzing Data or Information. *Work Output*—Handling and Moving Objects; Controlling Machines and Processes; Repairing and Maintaining Mechanical Equipment. *Interacting with Others*—Communicating with Other Workers; Establishing and Maintaining Relationships; Interpreting Meaning of Information to Others; Performing Administrative Activities. **Physical Work Conditions:** Indoors; Using Hands on Objects, Tools, or Controls; Hazardous Equipment. **Other Job Characteristics:** Degree of Automation; Pace Determined by Speed of Equipment; Importance of Being Sure All Is Done.

Experience: Job Zone 1. No previous work-related skill, knowledge, or experience is needed. **Job Preparation:** SVP Below 4.0—Less than 6 months. **Knowledge:** Production and Processing; Mechanical; Mathematics; Physics; Chemistry; Building and Construction; Engineering and Technology. **Instructional Program:** 470303 Industrial Machinery Maintenance and Repairer.

Related DOT Jobs: 554.682-014 Masking-Machine Operator; 554.685-030 Laminator; 569.565-010 Crew Leader, Gluing; 569.685-018 Core Feeder, Plywood Layup Line; 569.685-022 Core-Composer-Machine Tender; 569.685-026 Core-Laying-Machine Operator; 569.685-034 Edge-Glue-Machine Tender; 569.685-042 Glue Spreader, Veneer; 569.685-054 Hot-Plate-Plywood-Press Operator; 569.685-062 Splicer Operator; 579.685-022 Glass-Wool-Blanket-Machine Feeder; 584.665-014 Glue-Spreading-Machine Operator; 584.685-026 Hat-Stock-Laminating-Machine Operator; 620.685-010 Bonder, Automobile Brakes; 640.685-014 Book-Jacket-Cover-Machine Operator; 641.662-010 Box-Sealing-Machine Operator; 641.682-010 Blanket-Winder Operator; 641.682-014 Gluing-Machine Operator, Automatic; 641.685-014 Board-Liner Operator; 641.685-018 Box-Lining-Machine Feeder (partial list; see the introduction for sources of the complete list).

51-9192.00 Cleaning, Washing, and Metal Pickling Equipment Operators and Tenders (Cleaning, Washing, and Pickling Equipment Operators and Tenders)

Education: No data available.

Employed: 24,970

Openings: No data available.

Projected Growth: No data available.

Earnings: $20,910

Operate or tend machines to wash or clean products such as barrels or kegs, glass items, tin plate, food, pulp, coal, plastic, or rubber, to remove impurities.

Measures, weighs, or mixes specified quantity of cleaning solutions, using measuring tank, calibrated rod or suction tube. Adds specified amounts of chemicals into equipment at required time to maintain level and concentration of solution. Sets controls to regulate temperature and length of cycle; starts conveyors, pumps, agitators, and machines. Drains, cleans, and refills machine or tank at designated intervals, with cleaning solution or water. Records gauge readings, materials used, processing time, or test results in production log. Adjusts, cleans, and lubricates mechanical parts of machine, using hand tools and grease gun. Draws sample for laboratory analysis or tests solutions for conformance to specifications such as acidity or specific gravity. Loads and unloads objects to and from machine, conveyor, or rack. Observes machine operation, gauges, or thermometer; adjusts controls to maintain operation, according to specifications. Examines and inspects machine for malfunctions; examines and inspects product for conformance to processing specifications.

GOE Number, Interest Area, and Work Group: 08.03.02; Industrial Production; Production Work: Equipment Operation, Assorted Materials Processing. **Personality Type:** Realistic. Realistic occupations frequently involve work activities that include practical, hands-on problems and solutions. These occupations often deal with plants, animals, and real-world materials like wood, tools, and machinery. Many of the occupations require working outside and do not involve a lot of paperwork or working closely with others. **Work Values:** Moral Values; Independence; Company Policies and Practices; Activity; Supervision, Human Relations. **Skills:** Operation Monitoring; Operation and Control; Product Inspection; Problem Identification; Equipment Maintenance. **Abilities:** _Cognitive_—Information Ordering; Number Facility; Problem Sensitivity; Written Comprehension; Selective Attention; Mathematical Reasoning. _Psychomotor_—Control Precision; Multilimb Coordination; Arm-Hand Steadiness. _Physical_—Dynamic Flexibility. **General Work Activities:** _Information Input_—Inspecting Equipment, Structures, Materials; Monitoring Processes, Materials, and Surroundings; Identifying Objects, Actions, and Events. _Mental Process_—Evaluating Information Against Standards; Processing Information; Updating and Using Job-Relevant Knowledge; Analyzing Data or Information. _Work Output_—Controlling Machines and Processes; Handling and Moving Objects; Performing General Physical Activities. _Interacting with Others_—Performing Administrative Activities; Monitoring and Controlling Resources; Establishing and Maintaining Relationships; Communicating with Other Workers. **Physical Work Conditions:** Indoors; Standing; Using Hands on Objects, Tools, or Controls. **Other Job Characteristics:** Degree of Automation; Consequence of Error; Pace Determined by Speed of Equipment.

Experience: Job Zone 1. No previous work-related skill, knowledge, or experience is needed. **Job Preparation:** SVP Below 4.0—Less than 6 months. **Knowledge:** Production and Processing; Mechanical; Chemistry; Mathematics; Engineering and Technology; Physics. **Instructional Program:** 470303 Industrial Machinery Maintenance and Repairer.

Related DOT Jobs: 503.685-026 Furnace-and-Wash-Equipment Operator; 503.685-030 Metal-Cleaner, Immersion; 503.685-034 Metal-Washing-Machine Operator; 509.685-014 Branner-Machine Tender; 511.685-022 Dust-Collector Attendant; 511.685-066 Trommel Tender; 521.685-110 Dried Fruit Washer; 529.665-014 Washroom Operator; 529.685-074 Container Washer, Machine; 529.685-226 Steamer; 529.685-254 Wash-House Worker; 529.685-258 Washer, Agricultural Produce; 529.685-262 Wheat Cleaner; 529.685-278 Yeast Washer; 533.362-010 Bleacher, Pulp; 533.665-010 Blow-Pit Operator; 533.685-010 Bleach-Boiler Filler; 533.685-014 Brown-Stock Washer; 533.685-034 Washer Engineer; 549.685-010 Air-Table Operator (partial list; see the introduction for sources of the complete list).

51-9193.00 Cooling and Freezing Equipment Operators and Tenders (Cooling and Freezing Equipment Operators and Tenders)

Education: No data available.

Employed: 6,140

Openings: No data available.

Projected Growth: No data available.

Earnings: $19,400

Operate or tend equipment such as cooling and freezing units, refrigerators, batch freezers, and freezing tunnels, to cool or freeze products, food, blood plasma, and chemicals.

Stirs material with spoon or paddle to mix ingredients or to allow even cooling and prevent coagulation. Monitors pressure gauges, flowmeters, thermometers, or product; adjusts controls to maintain specified conditions. Starts equipment to blend contents or mix with air to prevent sticking to vat. Adjusts machine or freezer speed and air intake to obtain desired consistency and amount of product. Assembles or attaches pipes, fittings, or valves, using hand tools. Loads and positions wrapping paper, sticks, bags, or cartons into dispensing machines; removes jammed sticks, using pliers or picks. Inserts forming fixture; starts machine that cuts frozen product into measured portions or specified shapes. Positions molds on conveyor; measures and adjusts level of fill, using depth gauge. Flushes lines with solutions or steam to clean and sterilize equipment. Cleans, maintains, and repairs machines. Records temperatures, amount of materials processed, or test results on report form. Places or positions containers into equipment; removes container after cooling or freezing process. Measures or weighs specified amounts of ingredients or material; adds into tanks, vats, or equipment. Starts pumps, agitators, and conveyors; turns valves to admit or transfer product, refrigerant, or mix. Scrapes, dislodges, or breaks excess frost or ice from equipment. Draws sample of product and tests for specific gravity, acidity, or sugar content, using hydrometer, pH meter, or refractometer.

GOE Number, Interest Area, and Work Group: 08.03.02; Industrial Production; Production Work: Equipment Operation, Assorted Materials Processing. **Personality Type:** Realistic. Realistic occupations frequently involve work activities that include practical, hands-on problems and solutions. These occupations often deal with plants, animals, and real-world materials like wood, tools, and machinery. Many of the occupations require working outside and do not involve a lot of paperwork or working closely with others. **Work Values:** Moral Values; Independence; Company

Policies and Practices; Supervision, Human Relations; Security. **Skills:** Operation Monitoring; Operation and Control; Repairing; Product Inspection; Equipment Maintenance. **Abilities:** *Cognitive*—Information Ordering; Problem Sensitivity; Perceptual Speed; Number Facility; Deductive Reasoning. *Psychomotor*—Manual Dexterity; Finger Dexterity; Control Precision. *Physical*—Extent Flexibility; Static Strength; Trunk Strength; Stamina. *Sensory*—Near Vision; Visual Color Discrimination; Hearing Sensitivity. **General Work Activities:** *Information Input*—Monitoring Processes, Materials, and Surroundings; Inspecting Equipment, Structures, Materials; Identifying Objects, Actions, and Events. *Mental Process*—Evaluating Information Against Standards; Making Decisions and Solving Problems; Judging Qualities of Things, Services, Other People's Work; Scheduling Work and Activities. *Work Output*—Controlling Machines and Processes; Performing General Physical Activities; Handling and Moving Objects. *Interacting with Others*—Communicating with Other Workers; Performing Administrative Activities; Coordinating Work and Activities of Others; Establishing and Maintaining Relationships. **Physical Work Conditions:** Indoors; Using Hands on Objects, Tools, or Controls; Standing. **Other Job Characteristics:** Degree of Automation; Consequence of Error; Importance of Being Exact or Accurate; Frustrating Circumstances.

Experience: Job Zone 1. No previous work-related skill, knowledge, or experience is needed. **Job Preparation:** SVP Below 4.0— Less than 6 months. **Knowledge:** Mechanical; Engineering and Technology; Mathematics; Chemistry; Production and Processing. **Instructional Program:** 470303 Industrial Machinery Maintenance and Repairer.

Related DOT Jobs: 522.685-014 Brewery Cellar Worker; 523.585-014 Chiller Tender; 523.585-018 Crystallizer Operator; 523.685-010 Batch Freezer; 523.685-018 Chilling-Hood Operator; 523.685-038 Cooler Tender; 523.685-042 Cooling-Machine Operator; 523.685-046 Cooling-Pan Tender; 523.685-050 Crystallizer Operator; 523.685-082 Freezer Tunnel Operator; 523.685-102 Ice Maker; 529.482-010 Freezer Operator; 529.482-014 Novelty Maker I; 529.482-018 Novelty Maker II; 529.485-010 Barrel Filler; 529.685-250 Votator-Machine Operator; 551.685-042 Chiller Operator; 556.685-054 Paradichlorobenzene Tender; 559.685-090 Freezing-Machine Operator; 559.685-170 Spreading-Machine Operator.

51-9194.00 Etchers and Engravers (Precision Etchers and Engravers, Hand or Machine)

Education: No data available.

Employed: 3,290

Openings: No data available.

Projected Growth: No data available.

Earnings: $22,180

Engrave or etch metal, wood, rubber, or other materials for identification or for decorative purposes. Includes etcher-circuit processors, pantograph engravers, and silk screen etchers.

GOE Number, Interest Area, and Work Group: 01.07.01; Arts, Entertainment, and Media; Graphic Arts. **Instructional Programs:** 470408 Watch, Clock and Jewelry Repairer; 480201 Graphic and

Printing Equipment Operator, General. **Note:** The Department of Labor has not collected some data for this job, so it has fewer details than the other descriptions.

51-9194.01 Precision Etchers and Engravers, Hand or Machine (Precision Etchers and Engravers, Hand or Machine)

Education: No data available.

Employed: 3,290

Openings: No data available.

Projected Growth: No data available.

Earnings: $22,180

Engrave or etch flat or curved metal, wood, rubber, or other materials by hand or by machine, for printing, identification, or decorative purposes. Includes etchers and engravers of both hard and soft metals or materials. Includes jewelry and seal engravers.

Transfers design from sleet or film to die or roller by decimal staining. Polishes and oils surface of plate or die; brushes with acid proof paint. Sharpens and forms cutting edge of gravers or cutter grinder. Scrapes plate or die to remove imperfections and to smooth surface. Casts male die from engraved female die for use in seals. Sketches original design or pattern for use in printing or engraving. Prints proof or examines design to verify accuracy; reworks engraving as required. Reviews sketches, diagrams, blueprints, or photographs, to determine design to be cut or engraved. Trims precut designs or cuts around design, to remove undesirable part, using graver. Operates machine to engrave design into steel rollers or plates. Determines machine settings and moves bars or levers, to reproduce designs on rollers or plates. Sketches, traces, or scribes layout lines and design on workpiece, plates, dies, or rollers, using compass, scriber, graver, or pencil. Engraves or cuts lettering, design, or characters in workpiece surface, using hand tools and engraving tool. Measures and computes dimensions of lettering, designs, or patterns to be engraved. Positions and clamps workpiece, plate, or roller in holding fixture.

GOE Number, Interest Area, and Work Group: 01.07.01; Arts, Entertainment, and Media; Graphic Arts. **Personality Type:** Realistic. Realistic occupations frequently involve work activities that include practical, hands-on problems and solutions. These occupations often deal with plants, animals, and real-world materials like wood, tools, and machinery. Many of the occupations require working outside and do not involve a lot of paperwork or working closely with others. **Work Values:** Moral Values; Independence; Activity; Working Conditions; Achievement; Ability Utilization. **Skills:** Equipment Selection; Product Inspection; Operation and Control; Monitoring. **Abilities:** *Cognitive*—Visualization; Written Comprehension; Mathematical Reasoning; Information Ordering; Number Facility. *Psychomotor*—Arm-Hand Steadiness; Control Precision; Finger Dexterity; Manual Dexterity. *Physical*—Gross Body Coordination. *Sensory*—Depth Perception. **General Work Activities:** *Information Input*—Getting Information Needed to Do the Job; Monitoring Processes, Materials, and Surroundings; Estimating Needed Characteristics. *Men-*

tal Process–Thinking Creatively; Judging Qualities of Things, Services, Other People's Work; Evaluating Information Against Standards. *Work Output*–Handling and Moving Objects; Controlling Machines and Processes; Implementing Ideas and Programs. *Interacting with Others*–Communicating with Other Workers; Monitoring and Controlling Resources; Communicating with Persons Outside Organization; Establishing and Maintaining Relationships. **Physical Work Conditions:** Indoors; Using Hands on Objects, Tools, or Controls; Standing. **Other Job Characteristics:** Importance of Being Exact or Accurate; Importance of Being Sure All Is Done; Consequence of Error.

Experience: Job Zone 3. Previous work-related skill, knowledge, or experience is required. **Job Preparation:** SVP 6.0 to less than 7.0–More than 1 year and less than 4 years. **Knowledge:** Design; Mechanical; Fine Arts; Production and Processing; Engineering and Technology. **Instructional Programs:** 470408 Watch, Clock and Jewelry Repairer; 480201 Graphic and Printing Equipment Operator, General.

Related DOT Jobs: 704.381-022 Engraver Apprentice, Decorative; 704.381-026 Engraver, Hand, Hard Metals; 704.381-030 Engraver, Hand, Soft Metals; 704.381-034 Engraver, Seals; 972.381-018 Sketch Maker II; 972.681-010 Music Engraver; 979.281-010 Die Maker; 979.281-014 Engraver, Block; 979.281-018 Engraver, Picture; 979.381-010 Engraver I; 979.381-030 Siderographer.

51-9194.02 Engravers/Carvers (Artists and Commercial Artists)

Education: Work experience, plus degree
Employed: 308,496
Openings: 58,769
Projected Growth: 25.7%
Earnings: $31,690

Engrave or carve designs or lettering onto objects, using hand-held power tools.

Carves design on workpiece, using electric hand tool. Polishes engravings, using felt and cork wheels. Suggests original designs to customer or management. Attaches engraved workpiece to mount, using cement. Dresses and shapes cutting wheels by holding dressing stone against rotating wheel. Prepares workpiece to be engraved or carved, such as glassware, rubber, or plastic product. Cuts outline of impression with graver and removes excess material with knife. Holds workpiece against outer edge of wheel and twists and turns workpiece to grind glass according to marked design. Traces, sketches, or presses design or facsimile signature on workpiece, by hand or by using artist equipment. Selects and mounts wheel and miter on lathe; equips lathe with water to cool wheel and prevent dust.

GOE Number, Interest Area, and Work Group: 01.07.01; Arts, Entertainment, and Media; Graphic Arts. **Personality Type:** Realistic. Realistic occupations frequently involve work activities that include practical, hands-on problems and solutions. These occupations often deal with plants, animals, and real-world materials like wood, tools, and machinery. Many of the occupations require working outside and do not involve a lot of paperwork or working closely with others. **Work Values:** Moral Values; Independence; Ability Utilization; Working Conditions; Achievement. **Skills:** Equipment Selection; Product Inspection; Operation and Control; Judgment and Decision Making; Equipment Maintenance. **Abilities:** *Cognitive*–Visualization; Originality; Information Ordering; Problem Sensitivity; Fluency of Ideas. *Psychomotor*–Arm-Hand Steadiness; Finger Dexterity; Manual Dexterity. *Physical*–Trunk Strength; Extent Flexibility; Dynamic Flexibility; Dynamic Strength. *Sensory*–Near Vision; Depth Perception; Visual Color Discrimination. **General Work Activities:** *Information Input*–Monitoring Processes, Materials, and Surroundings; Getting Information Needed to Do the Job; Inspecting Equipment, Structures, Materials. *Mental Process*–Thinking Creatively; Judging Qualities of Things, Services, Other People's Work; Evaluating Information Against Standards. *Work Output*–Handling and Moving Objects; Controlling Machines and Processes; Implementing Ideas and Programs. *Interacting with Others*–Communicating with Persons Outside Organization; Communicating with Other Workers; Establishing and Maintaining Relationships; Providing Consultation and Advice to Others. **Physical Work Conditions:** Indoors; Using Hands on Objects, Tools, or Controls; Hazardous Equipment. **Other Job Characteristics:** Importance of Being Exact or Accurate; Importance of Being Sure All Is Done; Degree of Automation.

Experience: Job Zone 3. Previous work-related skill, knowledge, or experience is required. **Job Preparation:** SVP 6.0 to less than 7.0–More than 1 year and less than 4 years. **Knowledge:** Fine Arts; Design; Production and Processing; Mechanical; Customer and Personal Service. **Instructional Programs:** 500201 Crafts, Folk Art and Artisanry; 500402 Graphic Design, Commercial Art and Illustration; 500502 Technical Theater/Theater Design and Stagecraft; 500701 Art, General; 500702 Fine/Studio Arts; 500705 Drawing; 500706 Intermedia; 500708 Painting; 500709 Sculpture; 500710 Printmaking; 500711 Ceramics Arts and Ceramics; 500712 Fiber, Textile and Weaving Arts; 500713 Metal and Jewelry Arts; 500799 Fine Arts and Art Studies, Other; 512703 Medical Illustrating.

Related DOT Jobs: 733.381-010 Engraver, Rubber; 754.381-010 Internal Carver; 775.381-010 Engraver.

51-9194.03 Etchers (Artists and Commercial Artists)

Education: Work experience, plus degree
Employed: 308,496
Openings: 58,769
Projected Growth: 25.7%
Earnings: $31,690

Etch or cut artistic designs in glass articles, using acid solutions, sandblasting equipment, and design patterns.

Immerses ware in hot water to remove wax or peels off tape. Coats glass in molten wax or masks glassware with tape. Positions pattern against waxed or taped ware and sprays ink through pattern to transfer design to wax or tape. Immerses waxed ware in hydrofluoric acid to etch design on glass surface. Removes wax or tape, using stylus or knife, to expose glassware surface to be etched. Sandblasts exposed area of glass, using spray gun, to cut design in surface.

GOE Number, Interest Area, and Work Group: 01.07.01; Arts, Entertainment, and Media; Graphic Arts. **Personality Type:** Realistic. Realistic occupations frequently involve work activities that include practical, hands-on problems and solutions. These occupations often deal with plants, animals, and real-world materials like wood, tools, and machinery. Many of the occupations require working outside and do not involve a lot of paperwork or working closely with others. **Work Values:** Independence; Moral Values; Creativity; Achievement; Ability Utilization; Autonomy; Working Conditions. **Skills:** Product Inspection; Equipment Selection; Operation Monitoring; Operation and Control; Equipment Maintenance. **Abilities:** *Cognitive*—Information Ordering; Visualization; Problem Sensitivity; Memorization; Selective Attention; Deductive Reasoning. *Psychomotor*—Arm-Hand Steadiness; Manual Dexterity; Wrist-Finger Speed. *Physical*—Trunk Strength; Static Strength; Stamina; Explosive Strength. *Sensory*—Depth Perception; Peripheral Vision; Glare Sensitivity. **General Work Activities:** *Information Input*—Monitoring Processes, Materials, and Surroundings; Getting Information Needed to Do the Job; Inspecting Equipment, Structures, Materials. *Mental Process*—Thinking Creatively; Judging Qualities of Things, Services, Other People's Work; Evaluating Information Against Standards; Organizing, Planning, and Prioritizing. *Work Output*—Handling and Moving Objects; Controlling Machines and Processes; Implementing Ideas and Programs. *Interacting with Others*—Communicating with Other Workers; Performing Administrative Activities; Communicating with Persons Outside Organization; Performing for or Working with the Public; Coordinating Work and Activities of Others. **Physical Work Conditions:** Indoors; Using Hands on Objects, Tools, or Controls; Sitting; Hazardous Equipment; Making Repetitive Motions; Common Protective or Safety Attire. **Other Job Characteristics:** Importance of Being Exact or Accurate; Consequence of Error; Importance of Being Sure All Is Done.

Experience: Job Zone 3. Previous work-related skill, knowledge, or experience is required. **Job Preparation:** SVP 6.0 to less than 7.0—More than 1 year and less than 4 years. **Knowledge:** Fine Arts; Chemistry; Production and Processing; Mechanical; Design. **Instructional Programs:** 500201 Crafts, Folk Art and Artisanry; 500402 Graphic Design, Commercial Art and Illustration; 500502 Technical Theater/Theater Design and Stagecraft; 500701 Art, General; 500702 Fine/Studio Arts; 500705 Drawing; 500706 Intermedia; 500708 Painting; 500709 Sculpture; 500710 Printmaking; 500711 Ceramics Arts and Ceramics; 500712 Fiber, Textile and Weaving Arts; 500713 Metal and Jewelry Arts; 500799 Fine Arts and Art Studies, Other; 512703 Medical Illustrating.

Related DOT Job: 775.381-014 Glass Decorator.

51-9194.04 Pantograph Engravers (Engraving and Printing Workers, Hand)

Education: No data available.

Employed: 7,810

Openings: No data available.

Projected Growth: No data available.

Earnings: $16,450

Affix identifying information onto a variety of materials and products, using engraving machines or equipment.

Verifies conformance to specifications, using micrometers and calipers. Sets stylus at beginning of pattern. Adjusts depth and size of cut by adjusting height of worktable or adjusting gauge on machine arms. Selects and inserts letter or design template beneath stylus attached to machine cutting tool or router, according to work order. Brushes acid over designated engraving to darken or highlight inscription. Examines engraving for quality of cut, burrs, rough spots, and irregular or incomplete engraving. Sharpens cutting tools on cutter grinder. Sets reduction scale to obtain required reproduction ratio on workpiece. Inserts cutting tool or bit into machine and secures with wrench. Positions and secures work piece such as nameplate, stamp, seal, badge, trophy, or bowling ball, in holding fixture, using measuring instruments. Starts machine; guides stylus over template, causing cutting tool to simultaneously duplicate design or letters on workpiece. Observes action of cutting tool through microscope; adjusts movement of stylus to ensure accurate reproduction.

GOE Number, Interest Area, and Work Group: 01.07.01; Arts, Entertainment, and Media; Graphic Arts. **Personality Type:** Realistic. Realistic occupations frequently involve work activities that include practical, hands-on problems and solutions. These occupations often deal with plants, animals, and real-world materials like wood, tools, and machinery. Many of the occupations require working outside and do not involve a lot of paperwork or working closely with others. **Work Values:** Moral Values; Independence; Supervision, Technical; Activity; Company Policies and Practices; Security. **Skills:** Product Inspection; Operation and Control; Equipment Selection; Equipment Maintenance; Reading Comprehension; Operation Monitoring. **Abilities:** *Cognitive*—Visualization; Information Ordering; Perceptual Speed; Selective Attention; Time Sharing; Memorization. *Psychomotor*—Arm-Hand Steadiness; Control Precision; Manual Dexterity. *Physical*—Trunk Strength; Dynamic Strength; Gross Body Coordination; Dynamic Flexibility. *Sensory*—Near Vision; Depth Perception; Visual Color Discrimination. **General Work Activities:** *Information Input*—Monitoring Processes, Materials, and Surroundings; Inspecting Equipment, Structures, Materials; Getting Information Needed to Do the Job. *Mental Process*—Judging Qualities of Things, Services, Other People's Work; Organizing, Planning, and Prioritizing; Evaluating Information Against Standards. *Work Output*—Handling and Moving Objects; Controlling Machines and Processes; Implementing Ideas and Programs. *Interacting with Others*—Coordinating Work and Activities of Others; Communicating with Other Workers; Performing Administrative Activities; Establishing and Maintaining Relationships. **Physical Work Conditions:** Indoors; Using Hands on Objects, Tools, or Controls; Hazardous Equipment. **Other Job Characteristics:** Degree of Automation; Importance of Being Exact or Accurate; Consequence of Error; Importance of Being Sure All Is Done.

Experience: Job Zone 1. No previous work-related skill, knowledge, or experience is needed. **Job Preparation:** SVP Below 4.0—Less than 6 months. **Knowledge:** Mechanical; Production and Processing; Design; Mathematics; Engineering and Technology. **Instructional Program:** 480299 Graphic and Printing Equipment Operators, Other.

Related DOT Jobs: 704.382-010 Engraver, Pantograph I; 704.582-010 Engraver, Machine II; 704.682-010 Engraver, Machine I; 704.682-014 Engraver, Pantograph II; 732.584-010 Bowling-Ball Engraver.

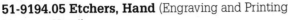

51-9194.05 Etchers, Hand (Engraving and Printing Workers, Hand)

Education: No data available.

Employed: 7,810

Openings: No data available.

Projected Growth: No data available.

Earnings: $16,450

Etch patterns, designs, lettering, or figures onto a variety of materials and products.

Inspects etched work for uniformity, using calibrated microscope and gauge. Compares workpiece design such as lettering, trademark, numerals, or lines to sample, to verify development of pattern. Neutralizes workpiece to remove acid, wax, or enamel, using water or solvents. Prepares etching solution according to formula. Positions and secures workpiece to be etched on setup board. Measures and marks workpiece such as plastic, fiberglass, epoxy board, metal, or glass, using measuring and calibrating equipment. Exposes workpiece to acid to develop etch pattern such as designs, lettering, or figures. Transfers image to workpiece, using contact printer, pantograph stylus, silkscreen printing device, or stamp pad. Fills etched characters with opaque paste to improve readability. Prepares workpiece for etching by cutting, sanding, cleaning, or treating with wax, acid resist, lime, etching powder, or light-sensitive enamel. Reduces artwork, using reduction camera.

GOE Number, Interest Area, and Work Group: 01.07.01; Arts, Entertainment, and Media; Graphic Arts. **Personality Type:** Realistic. Realistic occupations frequently involve work activities that include practical, hands-on problems and solutions. These occupations often deal with plants, animals, and real-world materials like wood, tools, and machinery. Many of the occupations require working outside and do not involve a lot of paperwork or working closely with others. **Work Values:** Moral Values; Independence; Company Policies and Practices; Supervision, Technical; Activity; Achievement; Security. **Skills:** Equipment Selection; Product Inspection; Identification of Key Causes; Mathematics; Judgment and Decision Making; Visioning; Equipment Maintenance; Monitoring. **Abilities:** *Cognitive*—Visualization; Information Ordering; Perceptual Speed; Memorization; Written Comprehension; Problem Sensitivity. *Psychomotor*—Arm-Hand Steadiness; Manual Dexterity; Control Precision. *Physical*—Static Strength; Dynamic Strength; Dynamic Flexibility; Explosive Strength. *Sensory*—Near Vision; Visual Color Discrimination; Depth Perception. **General Work Activities:** *Information Input*—Monitoring Processes, Materials, and Surroundings; Inspecting Equipment, Structures, Materials; Getting Information Needed to Do the Job. *Mental Process*—Judging Qualities of Things, Services, Other People's Work; Evaluating Information Against Standards; Thinking Creatively; Updating and Using Job-Relevant Knowledge; Organizing, Planning, and Prioritizing. *Work Output*—Handling and Moving Objects; Implementing Ideas and Programs; Controlling Machines and Processes. *Interacting with Others*—Communicating with Other Workers; Coordinating Work and Activities of Others; Performing Administrative Activities. **Physical Work Conditions:** Indoors; Using Hands on Objects, Tools, or Controls; Hazardous Conditions. **Other Job Characteristics:** Importance of Being Exact or Accurate; Importance of Being Sure All Is Done; Consequence of Error.

Experience: Job Zone 1. No previous work-related skill, knowledge, or experience is needed. **Job Preparation:** SVP Below 4.0—Less than 6 months. **Knowledge:** Design; Fine Arts; Production and Processing; Chemistry; Mechanical. **Instructional Program:** 480299 Graphic and Printing Equipment Operators, Other.

Related DOT Jobs: 590.684-018 Etched-Circuit Processor; 704.684-010 Etcher; 704.684-014 Silk-Screen Etcher; 704.687-014 Etcher, Hand; 716.681-022 Optical-Glass Etcher; 775.584-010 Glass Calibrator.

51-9194.06 Engravers, Hand (Engraving and Printing Workers, Hand)

Education: No data available.

Employed: 7,810

Openings: No data available.

Projected Growth: No data available.

Earnings: $16,450

Engrave designs and identifying information onto rollers or plates used in printing.

Punches holes in plate to fasten plate to press, using hand tools. Traces pattern of design and letters in reverse on linoleum or two- or three-ply rubber, using ruler, pencil, drawing instruments, or cutting tools. Prepares additional rubber plates for jobs requiring colors, by omitting different portions of design or lettering on each plate. Glues rubber or linoleum pattern to wood block. Cuts around drawn pattern leaving raised design or letters, using cutting tools. Refers to sketch to ensure that lines of only one printing color are engraved into each roller. Cuts strip of engraving gum (two- or three-ply rubber, cemented to cloth backing) using knife. Presses sketch on copper printing roller to produce impression of design. Cuts grooves of specified depth and uniformity into printing roller following lines of design impression. Inspects designs for defective engraving and reengraves to meet specifications.

GOE Number, Interest Area, and Work Group: 01.07.01; Arts, Entertainment, and Media; Graphic Arts. **Personality Type:** Realistic. Realistic occupations frequently involve work activities that include practical, hands-on problems and solutions. These occupations often deal with plants, animals, and real-world materials like wood, tools, and machinery. Many of the occupations require working outside and do not involve a lot of paperwork or working closely with others. **Work Values:** Moral Values; Independence; Activity; Supervision, Technical; Company Policies and Practices; Security. **Skills:** Product Inspection; Mathematics; Problem Identification; Judgment and Decision Making; Equipment Selection. **Abilities:** *Cognitive*—Visualization; Information Ordering; Problem Sensitivity; Memorization; Perceptual Speed. *Psychomotor*—Arm-Hand Steadiness; Manual Dexterity; Finger Dexterity. *Physical*—Extent Flexibility; Trunk Strength; Explosive Strength. *Sensory*—Near Vision; Visual Color Discrimination; Depth Perception. **General Work Activities:** *Information Input*—Inspecting Equipment, Structures, Materials; Getting Information Needed to Do the Job; Monitoring Processes, Materials, and Surroundings. *Mental Process*—Judging Qualities of Things, Services, Other People's Work; Thinking Creatively; Evaluating Information Against Standards. *Work Output*—Handling and Moving Objects; Implementing Ideas and Programs; Drafting and Specifying Technical Devices. *Interacting with Others*—Coordinating Work and Activities of Others; Performing Administrative Activities; Communicating with Other Workers. **Physical Work Conditions:** Indoors; Using Hands on Objects, Tools, or Controls; Sitting. **Other Job Characteristics:** Importance of Being Exact or Accurate; Consequence of Error; Importance of Being Sure All Is Done.

Experience: Job Zone 3. Previous work-related skill, knowledge, or experience is required. **Job Preparation:** SVP 6.0 to less than 7.0—More than 1 year and less than 4 years. **Knowledge:** Design; Fine Arts; Production and Processing; Communications and Media; Mechanical. **Instructional Program:** 480299 Graphic and Printing Equipment Operators, Other.

Related DOT Jobs: 979.581-010 Engraver, Rubber; 979.681-018 Roller Engraver, Hand; 979.684-014 Engraver II.

51-9195.00 Molders, Shapers, and Casters, Except Metal and Plastic (Precision Molders, Shapers, Casters, and Carvers, Except Jewelry and Foundry)

Education: No data available.

Employed: 13,420

Openings: No data available.

Projected Growth: No data available.

Earnings: $21,260

Mold, shape, form, cast, or carve food, figurine, tile, pipe, and candle products consisting of clay, glass, plaster, concrete, stone, or combinations of materials.

GOE Number, Interest Area, and Work Group: 08.02.02; Industrial Production; Production Technology: Precision Hand Work. **Instructional Program:** 480599 Precision Metal Workers, Other. **Note:** The Department of Labor has not collected some data for this job, so it has fewer details than the other descriptions.

51-9195.01 Precision Mold and Pattern Casters, except Nonferrous Metals (Precision Foundry Mold and Coremakers)

Education: No data available.

Employed: 11,950

Openings: No data available.

Projected Growth: No data available.

Earnings: $24,620

Cast molds and patterns from a variety of materials except nonferrous metals, according to blueprints and specifications.

Combines or melts ingredients to attain specified viscosity and shape. Patches broken edges and fractures, using clay or plaster;

molders hand tools. Trims or removes excess material, using scraper, knife, or bandsaw. Mixes ingredients according to standard formula. Verifies dimensions, using measuring instruments such as calipers, vernier gauge, and protractor. Removes casting from mold after specified time, using tools and equipment such as hand tools, power tools, and crane. Locates and scribes parting line on patterns, using measuring instruments such as calipers, square, and depth gauge. Constructs or assembles wooden mold, using clamps and bolts, hand tools, and power tools. Applies lubricant or parting agent to mold or pattern. Reviews specifications, blueprint, or sketch, to plan and lay out work. Applies reinforcing strips and additional layers of materials to form pattern of model. Pours, packs, spreads, or presses plaster, concrete, liquid plastic, or other materials into or around model or mold. Positions and secures reinforcing structure or materials, flask, mold, model, or pattern.

GOE Number, Interest Area, and Work Group: 08.02.02; Industrial Production; Production Technology: Precision Hand Work. **Personality Type:** Realistic. Realistic occupations frequently involve work activities that include practical, hands-on problems and solutions. These occupations often deal with plants, animals, and real-world materials like wood, tools, and machinery. Many of the occupations require working outside and do not involve a lot of paperwork or working closely with others. **Work Values:** Moral Values; Supervision, Human Relations; Independence; Activity; Supervision, Technical; Company Policies and Practices. **Skills:** Mathematics; Equipment Selection; Reading Comprehension; Problem Identification; Product Inspection. **Abilities:** *Cognitive*—Visualization; Information Ordering; Written Comprehension; Number Facility; Deductive Reasoning; Mathematical Reasoning. *Psychomotor*—Wrist-Finger Speed; Arm-Hand Steadiness; Manual Dexterity. *Physical*—Explosive Strength; Stamina. **General Work Activities:** *Information Input*—Getting Information Needed to Do the Job; Monitoring Processes, Materials, and Surroundings; Inspecting Equipment, Structures, Materials. *Mental Process*—Evaluating Information Against Standards; Making Decisions and Solving Problems; Organizing, Planning, and Prioritizing. *Work Output*—Performing General Physical Activities; Handling and Moving Objects; Controlling Machines and Processes. *Interacting with Others*—Communicating with Other Workers; Establishing and Maintaining Relationships; Monitoring and Controlling Resources; Performing Administrative Activities. **Physical Work Conditions:** Indoors; Standing; Using Hands on Objects, Tools, or Controls; Distracting Sounds and Noise Levels. **Other Job Characteristics:** Consequence of Error; Importance of Being Exact or Accurate; Importance of Being Sure All Is Done.

Experience: Job Zone 3. Previous work-related skill, knowledge, or experience is required. **Job Preparation:** SVP 6.0 to less than 7.0—More than 1 year and less than 4 years. **Knowledge:** Design; Production and Processing; Mechanical; Building and Construction; Mathematics. **Instructional Program:** 480599 Precision Metal Workers, Other.

Related DOT Jobs: 575.461-010 Concrete-Stone Fabricator; 739.381-046 Mannequin-Mold Maker; 769.381-010 Compo Caster; 777.081-010 Modeler; 777.381-034 Plaster Molder I; 777.381-038 Plaster-Pattern Caster.

51-9195.02 Precision Pattern and Die Casters, Nonferrous Metals (Foundry Mold Assembly and Shake-Out Workers)

Education: Moderate-term O-T-J training

Employed: 9,295

Openings: 955

Projected Growth: 2.5%

Earnings: $21,910

Cast metal patterns and dies, according to specifications, from a variety of nonferrous metals such as aluminum or bronze.

Operates hoist to position dies or patterns on foundry floor. Machines metal patterns to exact dimensions. Constructs wood patterns used to form sand molds for metal casts. Operates foundry furnaces and ovens. Lowers metal jig into molten metal in prescribed manner, to attach anchor bolts to punch. Preheats dies or patterns, using blowtorch or other equipment; applies parting compound. Tilts melting pot or uses ladle to pour molten alloy, bronze, or other nonferrous metal into sand mold. Shapes mold to specified contours with sand, using trowel and related tools. Clamps metal and plywood strips around die or pattern to form mold.

GOE Number, Interest Area, and Work Group: 08.02.02; Industrial Production; Production Technology: Precision Hand Work. **Personality Type:** Realistic. Realistic occupations frequently involve work activities that include practical, hands-on problems and solutions. These occupations often deal with plants, animals, and real-world materials like wood, tools, and machinery. Many of the occupations require working outside and do not involve a lot of paperwork or working closely with others. **Work Values:** Moral Values; Independence; Supervision, Human Relations; Activity; Company Policies and Practices. **Skills:** Operation and Control; Equipment Selection; Product Inspection. **Abilities:** *Cognitive*—Information Ordering; Problem Sensitivity; Deductive Reasoning; Selective Attention; Spatial Orientation; Number Facility. *Psychomotor*—Manual Dexterity; Wrist-Finger Speed; Reaction Time. *Physical*—Static Strength; Explosive Strength; Dynamic Strength. *Sensory*—Depth Perception; Glare Sensitivity; Sound Localization. **General Work Activities:** *Information Input*—Monitoring Processes, Materials, and Surroundings; Getting Information Needed to Do the Job; Inspecting Equipment, Structures, Materials. *Mental Process*—Evaluating Information Against Standards; Updating and Using Job-Relevant Knowledge; Judging Qualities of Things, Services, Other People's Work. *Work Output*—Handling and Moving Objects; Controlling Machines and Processes; Performing General Physical Activities. *Interacting with Others*—Communicating with Other Workers; Establishing and Maintaining Relationships; Providing Consultation and Advice to Others; Coaching and Developing Others; Assisting and Caring for Others. **Physical Work Conditions:** Indoors; Using Hands on Objects, Tools, or Controls; Common Protective or Safety Attire; Very Hot. **Other Job Characteristics:** Consequence of Error; Degree of Automation; Pace Determined by Speed of Equipment; Importance of Being Sure All Is Done; Frustrating Circumstances; Importance of Being Exact or Accurate.

Experience: Job Zone 4. A minimum of two to four years of work-related skill, knowledge, or experience is needed. **Job Preparation:** SVP 7.0 to less than 8.0—2 years to less than 10 years. **Knowledge:** Building and Construction; Engineering and Technology; Production and Processing; Design; Mechanical; Mathematics. **Instructional Program:** 480599 Precision Metal Workers, Other.

Related DOT Jobs: 502.381-014 Molder, Punch; 693.381-022 Molder, Pattern.

51-9195.03 Stone Cutters and Carvers (Bricklayers, Blockmasons, and Stonemasons)

Education: Long-term O-T-J training

Employed: 156,986

Openings: 29,721

Projected Growth: 12.3%

Earnings: No data available.

Cut or carve stone according to diagrams and patterns.

Selects chisels, pneumatic or surfacing tools, or sandblasting nozzles; determines sequence of their use according to intricacy of design or figure. Moves fingers over surface of carving to ensure smoothness of finish. Verifies depth and dimensions of cut or carving, using measuring instruments to ensure adherence to specifications. Guides nozzle over stone following stencil outline; chips along marks to create design or work surface down to desired finish. Removes or adds stencil during blasting to create differences in depth of cuts, intricate designs, or rough, pitted finish. Lays out designs or dimensions on stone surface, by freehand or by transferring from tracing paper, using scribe or chalk and measuring instruments. Studies artistic objects or graphic materials such as models, sketches, or blueprints; plans carving or cutting technique. Drills holes; cuts molding and grooves in stone. Loads sandblasting equipment with abrasive, attaches nozzle to hose, and turns valves to admit compressed air and activate jet.

GOE Number, Interest Area, and Work Group: 06.02.01; Construction, Mining, and Drilling; Construction: Masonry, Stone, and Brick Work. **Personality Type:** Realistic. Realistic occupations frequently involve work activities that include practical, hands-on problems and solutions. These occupations often deal with plants, animals, and real-world materials like wood, tools, and machinery. Many of the occupations require working outside and do not involve a lot of paperwork or working closely with others. **Work Values:** Moral Values; Independence; Achievement; Ability Utilization; Autonomy. **Skills:** Product Inspection; Equipment Selection; Operation and Control; Mathematics. **Abilities:** *Cognitive*—Visualization; Information Ordering; Written Comprehension; Problem Sensitivity; Deductive Reasoning; Inductive Reasoning. *Psychomotor*—Arm-Hand Steadiness; Wrist-Finger Speed. *Physical*—Extent Flexibility; Trunk Strength; Static Strength. *Sensory*—Near Vision; Depth Perception. **General Work Activities:** *Information Input*—Getting Information Needed to Do the Job; Monitoring Processes, Materials, and Surroundings; Identifying Objects, Actions, and Events. *Mental Process*—Thinking Creatively; Evaluating Information Against Standards; Judging Qualities of Things, Services, Other People's Work. *Work Out-*

put—Handling and Moving Objects; Controlling Machines and Processes; Performing General Physical Activities. *Interacting with Others*—Communicating with Other Workers; Coaching and Developing Others; Coordinating Work and Activities of Others; Establishing and Maintaining Relationships; Assisting and Caring for Others. **Physical Work Conditions:** Indoors; Using Hands on Objects, Tools, or Controls; Common Protective or Safety Attire; Standing. **Other Job Characteristics:** Importance of Being Sure All Is Done; Consequence of Error; Importance of Being Exact or Accurate.

Experience: Job Zone 3. Previous work-related skill, knowledge, or experience is required. **Job Preparation:** SVP 6.0 to less than 7.0—More than 1 year and less than 4 years. **Knowledge:** Fine Arts; Design; Physics; Mechanical; Building and Construction. **Instructional Program:** 500201 Crafts, Folk Art and Artisanry.

Related DOT Jobs: 673.382-010 Sandblaster, Stone; 673.382-014 Sandblaster, Stone Apprentice; 771.281-014 Stone Carver; 771.381-010 Stonecutter Apprentice, Hand; 771.381-014 Stonecutter, Hand.

51-9195.04 Glass Blowers, Molders, Benders, and Finishers (Artists and Commercial Artists)

Education: Work experience, plus degree

Employed: 308,496

Openings: 58,769

Projected Growth: 25.7%

Earnings: $31,690

Shape molten glass according to patterns.

Cuts length of tubing to specified size, using file or cutting wheel. Strikes neck of finished article to separate article from blowpipe. Determines type and quantity of glass required to fabricate product. Develops sketch of glass product into blueprint specifications, applying knowledge of glass technology and glass blowing. Examines gob of molten glass for imperfections, utilizing knowledge of molten glass characteristics. Inspects and measures product to verify conformance to specifications, using instruments such as micrometers, calipers, magnifiers, and rulers. Preheats or melts glass pieces; anneals or cools glass products and components, using ovens and refractory powder. Dips end of blowpipe into molten glass to collect gob on pipe head; cuts gob from molten glass, using sheers. Places glass into die or mold of press; controls press to form products such as glassware components or optical blanks. Blows tubing into specified shape, using compressed air or own breath. Shapes, bends, or joins sections of glass, using paddles, pressing and flattening hand tools, or cork. Heats glass to pliable stage, using gas flame or oven. Adjusts press stroke length and pressure; regulates oven temperatures according to glass type processed.

GOE Number, Interest Area, and Work Group: 01.06.01; Arts, Entertainment, and Media; Craft Arts. **Personality Type:** Realistic. Realistic occupations frequently involve work activities that include practical, hands-on problems and solutions. These occupations often deal with plants, animals, and real-world materials like wood, tools, and machinery. Many of the occupations require working outside and do not involve a lot of paperwork or working closely with others. **Work Values:** Moral Values; Inde-

pendence; Achievement; Ability Utilization; Compensation; Supervision, Technical; Autonomy; Recognition. **Skills:** Product Inspection; Equipment Selection; Operation and Control; Mathematics. **Abilities:** *Cognitive*—Visualization; Information Ordering; Problem Sensitivity; Mathematical Reasoning; Deductive Reasoning. *Psychomotor*—Arm-Hand Steadiness; Manual Dexterity; Control Precision; Wrist-Finger Speed. *Physical*—Extent Flexibility; Stamina; Dynamic Flexibility. **General Work Activities:** *Information Input*—Getting Information Needed to Do the Job; Monitoring Processes, Materials, and Surroundings; Estimating Needed Characteristics. *Mental Process*—Evaluating Information Against Standards; Thinking Creatively; Judging Qualities of Things, Services, Other People's Work. *Work Output*—Handling and Moving Objects; Controlling Machines and Processes; Performing General Physical Activities. *Interacting with Others*—Communicating with Other Workers; Coaching and Developing Others; Establishing and Maintaining Relationships; Assisting and Caring for Others. **Physical Work Conditions:** Indoors; Using Hands on Objects, Tools, or Controls; Standing. **Other Job Characteristics:** Importance of Being Exact or Accurate; Importance of Repeating Same Tasks; Importance of Being Sure All Is Done; Consequence of Error.

Experience: Job Zone 4. A minimum of two to four years of work-related skill, knowledge, or experience is needed. **Job Preparation:** SVP 7.0 to less than 8.0—2 years to less than 10 years. **Knowledge:** Production and Processing; Design; Engineering and Technology; Mechanical; Physics. **Instructional Programs:** 500201 Crafts, Folk Art and Artisanry; 500402 Graphic Design, Commercial Art and Illustration; 500502 Technical Theater/Theater Design and Stagecraft; 500701 Art, General; 500702 Fine/Studio Arts; 500705 Drawing; 500706 Intermedia; 500708 Painting; 500709 Sculpture; 500710 Printmaking; 500711 Ceramics Arts and Ceramics; 500712 Fiber, Textile and Weaving Arts; 500713 Metal and Jewelry Arts; 500799 Fine Arts and Art Studies, Other; 512703 Medical Illustrating.

Related DOT Jobs: 006.261-010 Scientific Glass Blower; 575.381-010 Molder; 772.281-010 Glass Blower, Laboratory Apparatus; 772.381-010 Glass Bender; 772.381-018 Ware Finisher; 772.381-022 Glass Blower.

51-9195.05 Potters (Artists and Commercial Artists)

Education: Work experience, plus degree

Employed: 308,496

Openings: 58,769

Projected Growth: 25.7%

Earnings: $31,690

Mold clay into ware as clay revolves on potter's wheel.

Positions ball of clay in center of potters wheel. Moves piece from wheel to dry. Verifies size and form, using calipers and templates. Starts motor, or pumps treadle with foot, to revolve wheel. Adjusts speed of wheel according to feel of changing firmness of clay. Smoothes surfaces of finished piece, using rubber scrapers and wet sponge. Raises and shapes clay into ware such as vases, saggers, and pitchers, on revolving wheel, using hands, fingers, and thumbs. Pulls wire through base of article and wheel to separate finished piece.

GOE Number, Interest Area, and Work Group: 01.06.01; Arts, Entertainment, and Media; Craft Arts. **Personality Type:** Realistic. Realistic occupations frequently involve work activities that include practical, hands-on problems and solutions. These occupations often deal with plants, animals, and real-world materials like wood, tools, and machinery. Many of the occupations require working outside and do not involve a lot of paperwork or working closely with others. **Work Values:** Moral Values; Independence; Autonomy; Achievement; Creativity. **Skills:** Operation and Control; Product Inspection. **Abilities:** *Cognitive*—Visualization; Originality; Fluency of Ideas; Flexibility of Closure; Selective Attention; Information Ordering. *Psychomotor*—Arm-Hand Steadiness; Manual Dexterity; Finger Dexterity. *Physical*—Extent Flexibility; Dynamic Flexibility. **General Work Activities:** *Information Input*—Monitoring Processes, Materials, and Surroundings; Getting Information Needed to Do the Job; Estimating Needed Characteristics. *Mental Process*—Thinking Creatively; Evaluating Information Against Standards; Updating and Using Job-Relevant Knowledge; Judging Qualities of Things, Services, Other People's Work. *Work Output*—Handling and Moving Objects; Controlling Machines and Processes; Implementing Ideas and Programs. *Interacting with Others*—Monitoring and Controlling Resources; Coaching and Developing Others; Communicating with Other Workers. **Physical Work Conditions:** Using Hands on Objects, Tools, or Controls; Indoors; Making Repetitive Motions. **Other Job Characteristics:** Importance of Repeating Same Tasks; Importance of Being Exact or Accurate; Pace Determined by Speed of Equipment.

Experience: Job Zone 4. A minimum of two to four years of work-related skill, knowledge, or experience is needed. **Job Preparation:** SVP 7.0 to less than 8.0—2 years to less than 10 years. **Knowledge:** Fine Arts; Production and Processing; Engineering and Technology; Physics; Building and Construction. **Instructional Programs:** 500201 Crafts, Folk Art and Artisanry; 500402 Graphic Design, Commercial Art and Illustration; 500502 Technical Theater/Theater Design and Stagecraft; 500701 Art, General; 500702 Fine/Studio Arts; 500705 Drawing; 500706 Intermedia; 500708 Painting; 500709 Sculpture; 500710 Printmaking; 500711 Ceramics Arts and Ceramics; 500712 Fiber, Textile and Weaving Arts; 500713 Metal and Jewelry Arts; 500799 Fine Arts and Art Studies, Other; 512703 Medical Illustrating.

Related DOT Job: 774.381-010 Thrower.

51-9195.06 Mold Makers, Hand (Molders and Casters, Hand)

Education: No data available.

Employed: 20,450

Openings: No data available.

Projected Growth: No data available.

Earnings: $18,920

Construct or form molds from existing forms for use in casting objects.

Covers model or pattern of object from which mold is to be made with lubricant or parting agent to prevent mold from sticking to model. Examines mold for accuracy. Covers portions of model with layers of modeling or casting material treated to harden when allowed to set or dry. Places form around model and separately immerses each half portion of model in plaster, wax, or other mold-making material. Assembles hardened molds; seals joints. Removes excess modeling or mold material such as plaster, wax, or rubber, using straightedge. Separates model or pattern from mold. Repairs cracks and broken edges of mold, using hand tools. Melts metal pieces, using torch; casts products such as inlays and crowns, using centrifugal casting machine. Bores holes or cuts grates and risers in mold, using power tools. Smoothes surfaces of mold, using scraping tool and sandpaper. Allows mold to harden or dry in oven and repeats process until mold is complete. Constructs molds used for casting metal, clay, or plaster objects, using plaster, fiberglass, rubber, casting machine, patterns, and flasks. Mixes modeling material such as plaster powder and water, or mud, sand, and loam, to specified formula.

GOE Number, Interest Area, and Work Group: 08.03.06; Industrial Production; Production Work: Hands-on Work, Assorted Materials. **Personality Type:** Realistic. Realistic occupations frequently involve work activities that include practical, hands-on problems and solutions. These occupations often deal with plants, animals, and real-world materials like wood, tools, and machinery. Many of the occupations require working outside and do not involve a lot of paperwork or working closely with others. **Work Values:** Moral Values; Independence; Supervision, Human Relations; Company Policies and Practices; Supervision, Technical; Security. **Skills:** Equipment Selection; Product Inspection; Repairing; Monitoring; Operation and Control. **Abilities:** *Cognitive*—Information Ordering; Visualization; Deductive Reasoning; Perceptual Speed; Flexibility of Closure; Spatial Orientation. *Psychomotor*—Arm-Hand Steadiness; Manual Dexterity; Finger Dexterity; Wrist-Finger Speed. *Physical*—Extent Flexibility; Static Strength; Explosive Strength. *Sensory*—Hearing Sensitivity; Depth Perception; Visual Color Discrimination. **General Work Activities:** *Information Input*—Monitoring Processes, Materials, and Surroundings; Inspecting Equipment, Structures, Materials; Getting Information Needed to Do the Job. *Mental Process*—Judging Qualities of Things, Services, Other People's Work; Evaluating Information Against Standards; Making Decisions and Solving Problems; Organizing, Planning, and Prioritizing. *Work Output*—Handling and Moving Objects; Controlling Machines and Processes; Implementing Ideas and Programs; Performing General Physical Activities. *Interacting with Others*—Communicating with Other Workers; Performing Administrative Activities; Establishing and Maintaining Relationships. **Physical Work Conditions:** Indoors; Using Hands on Objects, Tools, or Controls; Common Protective or Safety Attire. **Other Job Characteristics:** Consequence of Error; Importance of Being Exact or Accurate; Importance of Being Sure All Is Done.

Experience: Job Zone 2. Some previous work-related skill, knowledge, or experience may be helpful, but usually is not needed. **Job Preparation:** SVP 4.00 to 5.99—6 months to less than 2 years. **Knowledge:** Building and Construction; Production and Processing; Mechanical; Chemistry; Engineering and Technology. **Instructional Program:** 480506 Sheet Metal Worker.

Related DOT Jobs: 518.484-010 Plaster Molder II; 518.684-014 Coremaker, Pipe; 575.684-038 Mold Maker, Terra Cotta; 712.684-046 Denture-Model Maker; 777.684-014 Mold Maker; 777.684-018 Mold Maker.

51-9195.07 Molding and Casting Workers (Molders and Casters, Hand)

Education: No data available.

Employed: 20,450

Openings: No data available.

Projected Growth: No data available.

Earnings: $18,920

Perform a variety of duties such as mixing materials, assembling mold parts, and filling and stacking molds, to mold and cast a wide range of products.

Opens mold and removes finished products. Molds parts or products using vibrator, handpress, or casting equipment; taps or tilts mold to ensure uniformity. Inspects and tests parts or products to detect defects and to verify accuracy and adherence to standards. Measures and cuts product to specified dimensions, using measuring and cutting instruments. Brushes or sprays surface of mold with parting agent, or inserts paper, to ensure smoothness and to prevent sticking or seepage. Assembles, inserts, and adjusts wires, tubes, cores, fittings, rods, or patterns into mold, using hand tools and depth gauge. Fastens metal inserts such as drainage tubes, bolts, or electrical connections to product, using hand tools and power tools. Cleans, trims, smoothes, and polishes products or parts. Loads or stacks filled molds in oven, drier, or curing box, or on storage racks or carts. Engraves or stamps identifying symbols, letters, or numbers on product. Selects size and type of mold according to instructions. Installs and secures mold or mold parts together. Reads work order or examines part to determine part or section of product to be produced. Removes excess material and levels and smoothes wet mold mixture. Measures ingredients and mixes molding or casting material or sealing compound, to prescribed consistency according to formula. Operates and adjusts controls of heating equipment to melt material or to cure, dry, or bake filled molds according to specifications. Fills mold with mixed material or applies material to mold to specified thickness. Aligns and assembles parts to produce completed product, using gauges and hand tools. Cleans and lubricates mold and mold parts.

GOE Number, Interest Area, and Work Group: 08.03.06; Industrial Production; Production Work: Hands-on Work, Assorted Materials. **Personality Type:** Realistic. Realistic occupations frequently involve work activities that include practical, hands-on problems and solutions. These occupations often deal with plants, animals, and real-world materials like wood, tools, and machinery. Many of the occupations require working outside and do not involve a lot of paperwork or working closely with others. **Work Values:** Moral Values; Independence; Supervision, Human Relations; Company Policies and Practices; Activity. **Skills:** Operation and Control; Product Inspection; Operation Monitoring; Equipment Selection; Testing. **Abilities:** *Cognitive*—Visualization; Information Ordering; Inductive Reasoning; Perceptual Speed; Written Comprehension. *Psychomotor*—Manual Dexterity; Control Precision; Finger Dexterity; Arm-Hand Steadiness. *Physical*—Static Strength; Trunk Strength; Explosive Strength. *Sensory*—Near Vision; Depth Perception. **General Work Activities:** *Information Input*—Inspecting Equipment, Structures, Materials; Getting Information Needed to Do the Job; Monitoring Processes, Materials, and Surroundings. *Mental Process*—Evaluating Information Against Standards; Processing Information; Analyzing Data or Information; Making Decisions and Solving Problems; Judging Qualities of Things, Services, Other People's Work. *Work Output*—Handling and Moving Objects; Controlling Machines and Processes; Performing General Physical Activities. *Interacting with Others*—Performing Administrative Activities; Communicating with Other Workers; Coordinating Work and Activities of Others; Establishing and Maintaining Relationships. **Physical Work Conditions:** Indoors; Using Hands on Objects, Tools, or Controls; Standing. **Other Job Characteristics:** Importance of Being Exact or Accurate; Importance of Being Sure All Is Done; Consequence of Error.

Experience: Job Zone 2. Some previous work-related skill, knowledge, or experience may be helpful, but usually is not needed. **Job Preparation:** SVP 4.00 to 5.99—6 months to less than 2 years. **Knowledge:** Production and Processing; Mechanical; Building and Construction; Mathematics; Engineering and Technology. **Instructional Program:** 480506 Sheet Metal Worker.

Related DOT Jobs: 502.684-010 Lead Caster; 502.684-014 Mill Helper; 502.684-022 Needle Leader; 556.484-010 Scagliola Mechanic; 556.684-014 Encapsulator; 556.684-018 Mold-Filling Operator; 556.684-026 Rubber Molder; 556.684-030 Loader-Demolder; 556.687-022 Molder, Toilet Products; 556.687-030 Mold Filler; 575.684-014 Caster; 575.684-018 Caster; 575.684-030 Handle Maker; 575.684-034 Laundry-Tub Maker; 575.684-042 Molder, Hand; 575.684-046 Terrazzo-Tile Maker; 575.684-050 Cultured-Marble-Products Maker; 579.684-010 Concrete-Vault Maker; 579.684-018 Kiln-Furniture Caster; 579.684-026 Caster (partial list; see the introduction for sources of the complete list).

51-9196.00 Paper Goods Machine Setters, Operators, and Tenders (Paper Goods Machine Setters and Set-Up Operators)

Education: Moderate-term O-T-J training

Employed: 61,894

Openings: 9,308

Projected Growth: –4.1%

Earnings: $25,990

Set up, operate, or tend paper-goods machines that perform a variety of functions such as converting, sawing, corrugating, banding, wrapping, boxing, stitching, forming, or sealing paper or paperboard sheets into products.

Examines completed work to detect defects and to verify conformance to work orders. Installs attachments to machines for gluing, folding, printing, or cutting. Observes operation of various machines to detect machine malfunctions; makes corrections for product to meet specifications. Fills glue and paraffin reservoirs; loads automatic stapling mechanism. Places roll of paper or cardboard on machine feedtrack; threads paper through gluing, coating, and slitting rollers. Starts machine and regulates tension on pressure rolls; synchronizes speed of machine components and temperature of glue or paraffin. Cuts products to specified dimensions, using hand or power cutters. Measures, spaces, and sets saw blades, cutters, and perforators, according to product specifications. Removes finished cores; stacks or places them on conveyor for transfer to other work areas. Adjusts guide assembly and folding mechanism according to specifications, using hand tools. Disassembles machines to repair or replace broken or worn parts using hand or power tools.

GOE Number, Interest Area, and Work Group: 08.02.01; Industrial Production; Production Technology: Machine Set-up and Operation. **Personality Type:** Realistic. Realistic occupations frequently involve work activities that include practical, hands-on problems and solutions. These occupations often deal with plants, animals, and real-world materials like wood, tools, and machinery. Many of the occupations require working outside and do not involve a lot of paperwork or working closely with others. **Work Values:** Moral Values; Supervision, Human Relations; Company Policies and Practices; Independence; Activity. **Skills:** Operation and Control; Operation Monitoring; Equipment Maintenance; Installation; Product Inspection. **Abilities:** *Cognitive*—Problem Sensitivity; Information Ordering; Oral Comprehension; Written Comprehension; Deductive Reasoning; Visualization. *Psychomotor*—Control Precision; Manual Dexterity; Finger Dexterity. *Physical*—Static Strength. **General Work Activities:** *Information Input*—Monitoring Processes, Materials, and Surroundings; Getting Information Needed to Do the Job; Inspecting Equipment, Structures, Materials. *Mental Process*—Evaluating Information Against Standards; Judging Qualities of Things, Services, Other People's Work; Making Decisions and Solving Problems. *Work Output*—Handling and Moving Objects; Controlling Machines and Processes; Performing General Physical Activities. *Interacting with Others*—Communicating with Other Workers; Monitoring and Controlling Resources; Performing Administrative Activities. **Physical Work Conditions:** Indoors; Using Hands on Objects, Tools, or Controls; Standing. **Other Job Characteristics:** Degree of Automation; Consequence of Error; Importance of Being Sure All Is Done.

Experience: Job Zone 2. Some previous work-related skill, knowledge, or experience may be helpful, but usually is not needed. **Job Preparation:** SVP 4.00 to 5.99—6 months to less than 2 years. **Knowledge:** Production and Processing; Mechanical; Engineering and Technology; Computers and Electronics; Mathematics. **Instructional Program:** 470303 Industrial Machinery Maintenance and Repairer.

Related DOT Jobs: 640.682-010 Convolute-Tube Winder; 640.682-022 Spiral-Tube Winder; 641.380-010 Envelope-Folding-Machine Adjuster; 649.380-010 Machine Set-Up Operator, Paper Goods; 649.682-010 Box-Folding-Machine Operator.

51-9197.00 Tire Builders (Tire Building Machine Operators)

Education:	Moderate-term O-T-J training
Employed:	17,648
Openings:	1,749
Projected Growth:	–1.4%
Earnings:	$36,430

Operate machines to build tires from rubber components.

Positions ply stitcher rollers and drum according to width of stock, using hand tools and gauges. Pulls ply from supply rack and aligns ply with edge of drum. Cuts ply at splice point and presses ends together to form continuous band. Rubs cement stick on drum edge to provide adhesive surface for plies. Winds chafers and breaker onto plies. Brushes solvent onto ply to ensure adhesion; repeats process as specified, alternating direction of each ply to strengthen tire. Aligns tread with guide, starts drum to wind tread onto plies, and slices ends. Depresses pedal to collapse drum; lifts tire onto conveyor. Activates bead setters that press prefabricated beads onto plies; activates position-rollers that turn ply edges under and over beads. Depresses pedal to rotate drum; winds specified number of plies around drum to form tire body. Turns ends of plies under and over beads with steel rod. Starts rollers that bond tread and plies as drum revolves.

GOE Number, Interest Area, and Work Group: 08.03.06; Industrial Production; Production Work: Hands-on Work, Assorted Materials. **Personality Type:** Realistic. Realistic occupations frequently involve work activities that include practical, hands-on problems and solutions. These occupations often deal with plants, animals, and real-world materials like wood, tools, and machinery. Many of the occupations require working outside and do not involve a lot of paperwork or working closely with others. **Work Values:** Moral Values; Independence; Activity; Supervision, Human Relations; Company Policies and Practices. **Skills:** Operation and Control; Operation Monitoring. **Abilities:** *Cognitive*—Information Ordering; Deductive Reasoning; Visualization; Selective Attention; Mathematical Reasoning; Problem Sensitivity. *Psychomotor*—Wrist-Finger Speed; Manual Dexterity; Control Precision. *Physical*—Static Strength; Extent Flexibility; Explosive Strength; Trunk Strength. *Sensory*—Hearing Sensitivity; Depth Perception; Peripheral Vision; Sound Localization. **General Work Activities:** *Information Input*—Monitoring Processes, Materials, and Surroundings; Getting Information Needed to Do the Job; Inspecting Equipment, Structures, Materials. *Mental Process*—Analyzing Data or Information; Evaluating Information Against Standards; Processing Information; Judging Qualities of Things, Services, Other People's Work. *Work Output*—Handling and Moving Objects; Controlling Machines and Processes; Performing General Physical Activities. *Interacting with Others*—Communicating with Other Workers; Monitoring and Controlling Resources; Coaching and Developing Others; Establishing and Maintaining Relationships. **Physical Work Conditions:** Indoors; Using Hands on Objects, Tools, or Controls; Hazardous Equipment; Standing. **Other Job Characteristics:** Degree of Automation; Importance of Being Sure All Is Done; Pace Determined by Speed of Equipment.

Experience: Job Zone 1. No previous work-related skill, knowledge, or experience is needed. **Job Preparation:** SVP Below 4.0—Less than 6 months. **Knowledge:** Production and Processing; Mechanical; Mathematics; Engineering and Technology; Public Safety and Security. **Instructional Program:** 470303 Industrial Machinery Maintenance and Repairer.

Related DOT Jobs: 750.384-010 Tire Builder, Automobile; 750.684-014 Bead Builder.

51-9198.00 Helpers—Production Workers (All Other Helpers, Laborers, and Material Movers, Hand)

Education: Short-term O-T-J training
Employed: 1,933,840
Openings: 653,577
Projected Growth: 13.4%
Earnings: No data available.

Help production workers by performing duties of lesser skill. Supply or hold materials or tools; cleaning work area and equipment.

GOE Number, Interest Area, and Work Group: 08.03.02; Industrial Production; Production Work: Equipment Operation, Assorted Materials Processing. **Instructional Programs:** No data available. **Note:** The Department of Labor has not collected some data for this job, so it has fewer details than the other descriptions.

51-9198.01 Production Laborers (All Other Helpers, Laborers, and Material Movers, Hand)

Education: No data available.
Employed: 1,749,540
Openings: No data available.
Projected Growth: No data available.
Earnings: $17,860

Perform variety of routine tasks to assist in production activities.

Loads and unloads items from machines, conveyors, and conveyance. Inserts parts into partial assembly, during various stages of assembly, to complete product. Examines product to verify conformance to company standards. Records information such as number of product tested, meter readings, and date and time product placed in oven. Weighs raw materials for distribution. Ties product in bundles for further processing or shipment, following prescribed procedure. Lifts raw materials, final products, and items packed for shipment, manually or using hoist. Carries or handtrucks supplies to work stations. Feeds item into processing machine. Attaches slings, ropes, cables, or identification tags to objects such as pipes, hoses, and bundles. Threads ends of items such as thread, cloth, and lace through needles and rollers and around takeup tube. Breaks up defective products for reprocessing. Positions spout or chute of storage bin to fill containers during processing. Places product in equipment or on worksurface for further processing, inspecting, or wrapping. Cuts or breaks flashing from materials or products. Separates product according to weight, grade, size, and composition of material used to produce product. Folds parts of product and final product during processing. Washes machines, equipment, vehicles, and products such as prints, rugs, and table linens. Counts finished product to determine completion of production order. Mixes ingredients, according to formula.

GOE Number, Interest Area, and Work Group: 08.03.02; Industrial Production; Production Work: Equipment Operation, Assorted Materials Processing. **Personality Type:** Realistic. Realistic occupations frequently involve work activities that include practical, hands-on problems and solutions. These occupations often deal with plants, animals, and real-world materials like wood, tools, and machinery. Many of the occupations require working outside and do not involve a lot of paperwork or working closely with others. **Work Values:** Moral Values; Activity; Coworkers; Supervision, Human Relations; Company Policies and Practices; Supervision, Technical. **Skills:** Product Inspection; Equipment Selection; Operation and Control. **Abilities:** *Cognitive*—Information Ordering; Category Flexibility; Problem Sensitivity; Spatial Orientation; Perceptual Speed. *Psychomotor*—Manual Dexterity; Arm-Hand Steadiness; Multilimb Coordination. *Physical*—Static Strength; Dynamic Strength; Trunk Strength; Extent Flexibility. *Sensory*—Visual Color Discrimination; Depth Perception; Peripheral Vision. **General Work Activities:** *Information Input*—Identifying Objects, Actions, and Events; Inspecting Equipment, Structures, Materials; Monitoring Processes, Materials, and Surroundings; Getting Information Needed to Do the Job. *Mental Process*—Evaluating Information Against Standards; Updating and Using Job-Relevant Knowledge; Processing Information. *Work Output*—Performing General Physical Activities; Handling and Moving Objects; Documenting and Recording Information. *Interacting with Others*—Assisting and Caring for Others; Performing Administrative Activities; Monitoring and Controlling Resources. **Physical Work Conditions:** No data available.

Experience: Job Zone 1. No previous work-related skill, knowledge, or experience is needed. **Job Preparation:** SVP Below 4.0—Less than 6 months. **Knowledge:** Production and Processing; Clerical; Mathematics; Mechanical; English Language. **Instructional Programs:** No data available.

Related DOT Jobs: 230.667-014 Telephone-Directory Deliverer; 230.687-010 Advertising-Material Distributor; 299.667-010 Billposter; 299.687-010 Porter, Sample Case; 361.687-018 Laundry Laborer; 361.687-026 Shaker, Wearing Apparel; 361.687-030 Washer, Hand; 362.686-010 Dry-Cleaner Helper; 362.686-014 Rug-Cleaner Helper; 362.687-010 Glove Cleaner, Hand; 362.687-014 Lining Scrubber; 362.687-018 Shaver; 363.687-010 Glove Former; 363.687-014 Ironer, Sock; 363.687-018 Puff Ironer; 363.687-022 Stretcher-Drier Operator; 364.687-010 Dyer Helper; 364.687-014 Rug-Dyer Helper; 369.387-010 Laundry Worker III; 369.687-018 Folder (partial list; see the introduction for sources of the complete list).

51-9198.02 Production Helpers (All Other Helpers, Laborers, and Material Movers, Hand)

Education: No data available.
Employed: 1,749,540
Openings: No data available.
Projected Growth: No data available.
Earnings: $17,860

Perform variety of tasks requiring limited knowledge of production processes in support of skilled production workers.

Places or positions equipment or partially assembled product for further processing, manually or using hoist. Measures amount of ingredients, length of extruded article, or work, to ensure conformance to specifications. Observes operation and notifies equipment operator of malfunctions. Starts machines or equipment to begin process. Turns valves to regulate flow of liquids or air, to reverse machine, to start pump, and to regulate equipment. Mixes ingredients, according to procedure. Tends equipment to facilitate process. Replaces damaged or worm equipment parts. Signals coworkers to facilitate moving product, during processing. Removes product, machine attachments, and waste material from machine. Marks or tags identification on parts. Loads and unloads processing equipment or conveyance used to receive raw materials or to ship finished products. Dumps materials into machine hopper prior to mixing. Cleans and lubricates equipment. Reads gauges and charts and records data.

GOE Number, Interest Area, and Work Group: 08.03.02; Industrial Production; Production Work: Equipment Operation, Assorted Materials Processing. **Personality Type:** Realistic. Realistic occupations frequently involve work activities that include practical, hands-on problems and solutions. These occupations often deal with plants, animals, and real-world materials like wood, tools, and machinery. Many of the occupations require working outside and do not involve a lot of paperwork or working closely with others. **Work Values:** Moral Values; Activity; Supervision, Human Relations; Supervision, Technical; Coworkers; Security. **Skills:** Equipment Maintenance; Operation and Control; Operation Monitoring; Repairing; Equipment Selection; Product Inspection. **Abilities:** *Cognitive*—Information Ordering; Problem Sensitivity; Oral Expression; Oral Comprehension; Written Comprehension; Written Expression. *Psychomotor*—Control Precision; Reaction Time; Wrist-Finger Speed. *Physical*—Static Strength; Extent Flexibility; Trunk Strength; Stamina. *Sensory*—Auditory Attention; Hearing Sensitivity; Far Vision. **General Work Activities:** *Information Input*—Monitoring Processes, Materials, and Surroundings; Getting Information Needed to Do the Job; Identifying Objects, Actions, and Events. *Mental Process*—Evaluating Information Against Standards; Processing Information; Organizing, Planning, and Prioritizing; Analyzing Data or Information; Making Decisions and Solving Problems; Updating and Using Job-Relevant Knowledge. *Work Output*—Handling and Moving Objects; Performing General Physical Activities; Repairing and Maintaining Mechanical Equipment; Controlling Machines and Processes. *Interacting with Others*—Communicating with Other Workers; Assisting and Caring for Others; Coordinating Work and Activities of Others. **Physical Work Conditions:** Using Hands on Objects, Tools, or Controls; Indoors; Standing. **Other Job Characteristics:** Consequence of Error; Degree of Automation; Importance of Being Sure All Is Done.

Experience: Job Zone 1. No previous work-related skill, knowledge, or experience is needed. **Job Preparation:** SVP Below 4.0—Less than 6 months. **Knowledge:** Production and Processing; Mechanical; Engineering and Technology; Mathematics; Clerical; English Language. **Instructional Programs:** No data available.

Related DOT Jobs: 365.674-010 Shoe-Repairer Helper; 500.686-010 Laborer, Electroplating; 502.664-018 Steel-Pourer Helper; 503.686-010 Pickler Helper, Continuous Pickling Line; 504.685-018 Heat-Treater Helper; 509.685-010 Alodize-Machine Helper; 511.685-058 Slime-Plant-Operator Helper; 512.684-010 Second Helper; 518.684-010 Core Setter; 519.485-014 Recovery-Operator Helper; 529.685-146 Ice Cream Freezer Assistant; 540.686-010 Compounder Helper; 542.362-014 Refinery Operator Helper; 542.665-010 Oven-Heater Helper; 543.664-010 Carbon-Furnace-Operator Helper; 549.684-010 Pumper Helper; 549.685-030 Treater Helper; 549.685-034 Wash-Oil-Pump Operator Helper; 557.564-010 Extruder-Operator Helper; 558.585-038 Polymerization Helper (partial list; see the introduction for sources of the complete list).

53-0000

Transportation and Material Moving Occupations

53-1000 Supervisors, Transportation and Material Moving Workers

53-1011.00 Aircraft Cargo Handling Supervisors
(First-Line Supervisors and Managers/Supervisors—Helpers, Laborers, and Material Movers, Hand)

Education: No data available.

Employed: 148,990

Openings: No data available.

Projected Growth: No data available.

Earnings: $30,320

Direct ground crew in the loading, unloading, securing, and staging of aircraft cargo or baggage. Determine the quantity and orientation of cargo; compute aircraft center of gravity. Accompany aircraft as member of flight crew; monitor and handle cargo in flight; assist and brief passengers on safety and emergency procedures.

GOE Number, Interest Area, and Work Group: 11.01.01; Recreation, Travel, and Other Personal Services; Managerial Work in Recreation, Travel, and Other Personal Services. **Instructional Programs:** 520205 Operations Management and Supervision; 520203 Logistics and Materials Management. **Note:** The Department of Labor has not collected some data for this job, so it has fewer details than the other descriptions.

53-1021.00 First-Line Supervisors/Managers of Helpers, Laborers, and Material Movers, Hand
(Blue-Collar Worker Supervisors)

Education: Work experience in a related occupation

Employed: 2,197,772

Openings: 216,115

Projected Growth: 8.9%

Earnings: No data available.

Supervise and coordinate the activities of helpers, laborers, or material movers.

Informs designated employee or department of items loaded; reports loading deficiencies. Observes work procedures to ensure quality of work. Assigns duties and work schedules. Examines freight to determine sequence of loading; examines equipment to determine compliance with specifications. Inspects equipment for wear; inspects completed work for conformance to standards. Inventories and orders supplies. Resolves customer complaints. Records information such as daily receipts, employee time and wage data, description of freight, and inspection results. Verifies materials loaded or unloaded against work order; schedules times of shipment and mode of transportation. Trains and instructs workers. Supervises and coordinates activities of workers performing assigned tasks. Determines work sequence and equipment needed, according to work order, shipping records, and experience. Quotes prices to customers.

GOE Number, Interest Area, and Work Group: 08.01.01; Industrial Production; Managerial Work in Industrial Production. **Personality Type:** Enterprising. Enterprising occupations frequently involve starting up and carrying out projects. These occupations can involve leading people and making many decisions. They sometimes require risk taking and often deal with business. **Work Values:** Authority; Responsibility; Coworkers; Activity; Autonomy. **Skills:** Instructing; Social Perceptiveness; Systems Perception; Problem Identification; Critical Thinking. **Abilities:** *Cognitive*—Oral Expression; Oral Comprehension; Problem Sensitivity; Information Ordering; Written Comprehension. *Psychomotor*—none met the criteria. *Physical*—Static Strength. *Sensory*—Speech Clarity. **General Work Activities:** *Information Input*—Inspecting Equipment, Structures, Materials; Getting Information Needed to Do the Job; Monitoring Processes, Materials, and Surroundings. *Mental Process*—Evaluating Information Against Standards; Scheduling Work and Activities; Processing Information; Making Decisions and Solving Problems. *Work Output*—Documenting and Recording Information; Handling and Moving Objects; Performing General Physical Activities. *Interacting with Others*—Guiding, Directing and Motivating Subordinates; Communicating with Other Workers; Teaching Others. **Physical Work Conditions:** Indoors; Sitting; Standing. **Other Job Characteristics:** Consequence of Error; Importance of Being Exact or Accurate; Importance of Being Sure All Is Done.

Experience: Job Zone 3. Previous work-related skill, knowledge, or experience is required. **Job Preparation:** SVP 6.0 to less than 7.0—More than 1 year and less than 4 years. **Knowledge:** Production and Processing; Administration and Management; Personnel and Human Resources; Mathematics; Economics and Accounting. **Instructional Programs:** 520201 Business Administration and Management, General; 520205 Operations Management and Supervision.

Related DOT Jobs: 189.167-042 Superintendent, Labor Utilization; 519.137-014 Supervisor, Scrap Preparation; 559.137-050 Supervisor, Tank Cleaning; 570.132-022 Supervisor; 699.137-010 Supervisor, Cleaning; 860.137-010 Carpenter-Labor Supervisor; 891.137-014 Supervisor, Aircraft Cleaning; 891.137-018 Supervisor, Tank Cleaning; 899.131-022 Utility Supervisor, Boat and Plant; 910.137-014 Car-Cleaning Supervisor; 910.137-018 Circus-Train Supervisor; 910.137-026 Freight-Loading Supervisor; 915.137-010 Car-Wash Supervisor; 922.137-018 Supervisor, Loading and Unloading.

53-1031.00 First-Line Supervisors/Managers of Transportation and Material-Moving Machine and Vehicle Operators (Blue-Collar Worker Supervisors)

Education: Work experience in a related occupation

Employed: 2,197,772

Openings: 216,115

Projected Growth: 8.9%

Earnings: No data available.

Directly supervise and coordinate activities of transportation and material-moving machine and vehicle operators and helpers.

Maintains or verifies time, transportation, financial, inventory, and personnel records. Recommends or implements personnel actions such as hiring, firing, and performance evaluations. Interprets transportation and tariff regulations, shipping orders, safety regulations, and company policies and procedures, for workers. Resolves worker problems or assists workers in solving problems. Reviews orders, production schedules, and shipping/receiving notices, to determine work sequence and material shipping dates, type, volume, and destinations. Receives telephone or radio reports of emergencies; dispatches personnel and vehicle in response to request. Explains and demonstrates work tasks to new workers; assigns workers to experienced workers for further training. Requisitions needed personnel, supplies, equipment, parts, or repair services. Plans and establishes transportation routes, work schedules, and assignments; allocates equipment to meet transportation, operations, or production goals. Recommends and implements measures to improve worker motivation, equipment performance, work methods, and customer services. Directs workers in transportation or related services such as pumping, moving, storing, and loading/unloading of materials or people. Confers with customers, supervisors, contractors, and other personnel to exchange information and resolve problems. Computes and estimates cash, payroll, transportation, personnel, and storage requirements, using calculator. Inspects or tests materials, stock, vehicles, equipment, and facilities, to locate defects, to meet maintenance or production specifications, and to verify safety standards. Prepares, compiles, and submits reports on work activities, operations, production, and work related accidents. Drives vehicles or operates machines or equipment. Examines, measures, and weighs cargo or materials, to determine specific handling requirements. Repairs or schedules repair and preventive maintenance of vehicles and other equipment.

GOE Number, Interest Area, and Work Group: 07.01.01; Transportation; Managerial Work in Transportation. **Personality Type:** Enterprising. Enterprising occupations frequently involve starting up and carrying out projects. These occupations can involve leading people and making many decisions. They sometimes require risk taking and often deal with business. **Work Values:** Authority; Responsibility; Autonomy; Coworkers; Variety; Activity. **Skills:** Reading Comprehension; Management of Financial Resources; Management of Personnel Resources; Coordination; Problem Identification; Identifying Downstream Consequences; Active Listening; Speaking. **Abilities:** *Cognitive*—Oral Expression; Written Comprehension; Written Expression; Oral Comprehension; Information Ordering. *Psychomotor*—Control Precision; Multilimb Coordination; Rate Control. *Physical*—Trunk Strength; Explosive Strength; Gross Body Coordination. *Sensory*—Speech Recognition; Speech Clarity. **General Work Activities:** *Information Input*—Inspecting Equipment, Structures, Materials; Getting Information Needed to Do the Job; Estimating Needed Characteristics. *Mental Process*—Evaluating Information Against Standards; Making Decisions and Solving Problems; Scheduling Work and Activities; Processing Information; Organizing, Planning, and Prioritizing. *Work Output*—Documenting and Recording Information; Operating Vehicles or Equipment; Repairing and Maintaining Mechanical Equipment; Implementing Ideas and Programs; Performing General Physical Activities; Handling and Moving Objects. *Interacting with Others*—Communicating with Other Workers; Coordinating Work and Activities of Others; Guiding,

Directing and Motivating Subordinates. **Physical Work Conditions:** Indoors; Sitting; Standing. **Other Job Characteristics:** Consequence of Error; Importance of Being Exact or Accurate; Importance of Being Sure All Is Done.

Experience: Job Zone 3. Previous work-related skill, knowledge, or experience is required. **Job Preparation:** SVP 6.0 to less than 7.0—More than 1 year and less than 4 years. **Knowledge:** Transportation; Administration and Management; Personnel and Human Resources; Mathematics; Economics and Accounting. **Instructional Program:** 080709 General Distribution Operations.

Related DOT Jobs: 185.167-018 Manager, Distribution Warehouse; 187.167-150 Manager, Storage Garage; 292.137-014 Supervisor, Route Sales-Delivery Drivers; 579.137-030 Dispatcher, Concrete Products; 859.137-010 Supervisor, Grading; 909.137-010 Driver Supervisor; 909.137-014 Garbage-Collection Supervisor; 909.137-018 Truck Supervisor; 910.137-022 Conductor, Yard; 910.137-034 Road Supervisor of Engines; 910.137-046 Yard Manager; 911.131-010 Boatswain; 911.137-018 Header; 911.137-022 Superintendent, Stevedoring; 911.137-026 Supervisor, Ferry Terminal; 913.133-010 Road Supervisor; 913.133-014 Supervisor, Cab; 913.167-014 Dispatcher, Bus and Trolley; 914.131-010 Supervisor, Pumping; 914.132-010 Compressor-Station Engineer, Chief (partial list; see the introduction for sources of the complete list).

53-2000 Air Transportation Workers

53-2011.00 Airline Pilots, Copilots, and Flight Engineers (Aircraft Pilots and Flight Engineers)

Education:	Bachelor's degree
Employed:	93,585
Openings:	4,555
Projected Growth:	5.9%
Earnings:	$91,750

Pilot and navigate the flight of multiengine aircraft in regularly scheduled service for the transport of passengers and cargo. Obtain required Federal Air Transport rating and certification in specific aircraft type used.

Holds commercial pilot's license issued by Federal Aviation Administration. Conducts preflight checks and reads gauges, to verify that fluids and pressure are at prescribed levels. Orders changes in fuel supply, load, route, or schedule, to ensure safety of flight. Coordinates flight activities with ground-crew and air-traffic control; informs crew members of flight and test procedures. Operates radio equipment and contacts control tower for takeoff, clearance, arrival instructions, and other information. Obtains and reviews data such as load weight, fuel supply, weather conditions, and flight schedule. Plots flight pattern and files flight plan with appropriate officials. Logs information such as flight time, altitude flown, and fuel consumption. Gives training and instruction in aircraft operations for students and other pilots. Conducts in-flight tests and evaluations, at specified altitudes, in all types of weather, to determine receptivity and other characteristics of equipment and systems. Starts engines, operates controls, and pilots airplane, to transport passengers, mail, or freight, adhering to flight plan, regulations, and procedures. Plans and formulates flight activities and test schedules; prepares flight evaluation reports.

GOE Number, Interest Area, and Work Group: 07.03.01; Transportation; Air Vehicle Operation. **Personality Type:** Realistic. Realistic occupations frequently involve work activities that include practical, hands-on problems and solutions. These occupations often deal with plants, animals, and real-world materials like wood, tools, and machinery. Many of the occupations require working outside and do not involve a lot of paperwork or working closely with others. **Work Values:** Ability Utilization; Company Policies and Practices; Compensation; Achievement; Recognition. **Skills:** Operation and Control; Operation Monitoring; Instructing; Coordination; Judgment and Decision Making; Systems Perception. **Abilities:** *Cognitive*—Spatial Orientation; Problem Sensitivity; Oral Expression; Oral Comprehension; Written Comprehension. *Psychomotor*—Reaction Time; Response Orientation; Rate Control. *Physical*—Extent Flexibility; Trunk Strength; Gross Body Coordination. *Sensory*—Far Vision; Night Vision; Depth Perception. **General Work Activities:** *Information Input*—Getting Information Needed to Do the Job; Monitoring Processes, Materials, and Surroundings; Inspecting Equipment, Structures, Materials. *Mental Process*—Making Decisions and Solving Problems; Evaluating Information Against Standards; Organizing, Planning, and Prioritizing; Updating and Using Job-Relevant Knowledge; Analyzing Data or Information; Processing Information. *Work Output*—Operating Vehicles or Equipment; Documenting and Recording Information; Handling and Moving Objects. *Interacting with Others*—Communicating with Other Workers; Coordinating Work and Activities of Others; Teaching Others. **Physical Work Conditions:** Special Uniform; Using Hands on Objects, Tools, or Controls; Sitting. **Other Job Characteristics:** Consequence of Error; Degree of Automation; Importance of Being Sure All Is Done.

Experience: Job Zone 4. A minimum of two to four years of work-related skill, knowledge, or experience is needed. **Job Preparation:** SVP 7.0 to less than 8.0—2 years to less than 10 years. **Knowledge:** Transportation; Public Safety and Security; Geography; Physics; Telecommunications; Mathematics. **Instructional Programs:** 490102 Aircraft Pilot and Navigator (Professional); 490107 Aircraft Pilot (Private).

Related DOT Jobs: 196.263-030 Executive Pilot; 196.263-034 Facilities-Flight-Check Pilot.

53-2012.00 Commercial Pilots (Aircraft Pilots and Flight Engineers)

Education: Bachelor's degree

Employed: 93,585

Openings: 4,555

Projected Growth: 5.9%

Earnings: $91,750

Pilot and navigate the flight of small fixed- or rotary-winged aircraft, primarily for the transport of cargo and passengers. Obtain required Commercial Rating.

Plans and formulates flight activities and test schedules; prepares flight evaluation reports. Plots flight pattern; files flight plan with appropriate officials. Obtains and reviews data such as load weight, fuel supply, weather conditions, and flight schedules. Conducts in-flight tests and evaluations, at specified altitudes, in all types of weather, to determine receptivity and other characteristics of equipment and systems. Coordinates flight activities with ground crew and air-traffic control; informs crew members of flight and test procedures. Logs information such as flight time, altitude flown, and fuel consumption. Conducts preflight checks and reads gauges to verify that fluids and pressure are at prescribed levels. Holds commercial pilot's license issued by Federal Aviation Administration. Operates radio equipment; contacts control tower for takeoff, clearance, arrival instructions, and other information. Orders changes in fuel supply, load, route, or schedule to ensure safety of flight. Starts engines, operates controls, and pilots airplane, to transport passengers, mail, or freight, adhering to flight plan and regulations and procedures. Gives training and instruction in aircraft operations for students and other pilots.

GOE Number, Interest Area, and Work Group: 07.03.01; Transportation; Air Vehicle Operation. **Personality Type:** Realistic. Realistic occupations frequently involve work activities that include practical, hands-on problems and solutions. These occupations often deal with plants, animals, and real-world materials like wood, tools, and machinery. Many of the occupations require working outside and do not involve a lot of paperwork or working closely with others. **Work Values:** Compensation; Company Policies and Practices; Ability Utilization; Achievement; Recognition. **Skills:** Operation and Control; Instructing; Operation Monitoring; Coordination; Systems Perception; Judgment and Decision Making. **Abilities:** *Cognitive*—Spatial Orientation; Problem Sensitivity; Oral Expression; Oral Comprehension; Written Comprehension. *Psychomotor*—Reaction Time; Response Orientation; Rate Control. *Physical*—Extent Flexibility; Trunk Strength; Gross Body Coordination. *Sensory*—Far Vision; Night Vision; Depth Perception. **General Work Activities:** *Information Input*—Getting Information Needed to Do the Job; Inspecting Equipment, Structures, Materials; Monitoring Processes, Materials, and Surroundings. *Mental Process*—Making Decisions and Solving Problems; Evaluating Information Against Standards; Updating and Using Job-Relevant Knowledge; Organizing, Planning, and Prioritizing; Judging Qualities of Things, Services, Other People's Work; Processing Information. *Work Output*—Operating Vehicles or Equipment; Documenting and Recording Information; Handling and Moving Objects. *Interacting with Others*—Communicating with Other Workers; Teaching Others; Coordinating Work and Activities of Others. **Physical Work Conditions:** Special Uniform; Sitting; Using Hands on Objects, Tools, or Controls. **Other Job Characteristics:** Consequence of Error; Degree of Automation; Importance of Being Sure All Is Done.

Experience: Job Zone 4. A minimum of two to four years of work-related skill, knowledge, or experience is needed. **Job Preparation:** SVP 7.0 to less than 8.0—2 years to less than 10 years. **Knowledge:** Transportation; Geography; Physics; Public Safety and Security; Telecommunications; Mathematics. **Instructional Programs:** 490102 Aircraft Pilot and Navigator (Professional); 490107 Aircraft Pilot (Private).

Related DOT Job: 196.263-014 Airplane Pilot, Commercial.

53-2021.00 Air Traffic Controllers (Air Traffic Controllers)

Education: Long-term O-T-J training
Employed: 29,739
Openings: 2,321
Projected Growth: 2.3%
Earnings: $64,880

Control air traffic on and within vicinity of airport. Control movement of air traffic between altitude sectors and control centers according to established procedures and policies. Authorize, regulate, and control commercial airline flights, according to government or company regulations, to expedite and ensure flight safety.

Transfers control of departing flights to traffic control center; accepts control of arriving flights from air traffic control center. Controls air traffic at and within vicinity of airport. Relays air traffic information such as altitude, expected time of arrival, and course of aircraft, to control centers. Analyzes factors such as weather reports, fuel requirements, and maps, to determine flights and air routes. Inspects, adjusts, and controls radio equipment and airport lights. Reviews records and reports, for clarity and completeness; maintains records and reports. Directs radio searches for aircraft; alerts control centers emergency facilities of flight difficulties. Determines timing of and procedure for flight vector changes in sector. Recommends flight path changes to planes traveling in storms or fog or in emergency situations. Issues landing and take-off authorizations and instructions; communicates other information to aircraft. Communicates with, relays flight plans to, and coordinates movement of air traffic between control centers. Completes daily activity report and keeps record of messages from aircraft.

GOE Number, Interest Area, and Work Group: 07.02.01; Transportation; Vehicle Expediting and Coordinating. **Personality Type:** Conventional. Conventional occupations frequently involve following set procedures and routines. These occupations can include working with data and details more than with ideas. Usually there is a clear line of authority to follow. **Work Values:** Authority; Security; Responsibility; Achievement; Ability Utilization; Company Policies and Practices. **Skills:** Operation and Control; Active Listening; Coordination; Critical Thinking; Operation Monitoring. **Abilities:** *Cognitive*—Written Comprehension; Oral Comprehension; Oral Expression; Selective Attention; Time Sharing; Problem Sensitivity. *Psychomotor*—Reaction Time; Response Orientation; Rate Control. *Physical*—Gross Body Coordination; Gross Body Equilibrium. *Sensory*—Auditory Attention; Near Vision; Speech Clarity. **General Work Activities:** *Information Input*—Monitoring Processes, Materials, and Surroundings; Getting Information Needed to Do the Job; Identifying Objects, Actions, and Events. *Mental Process*—Analyzing Data or Information; Making Decisions and Solving Problems; Processing Information. *Work Output*—Documenting and Recording Information; Controlling Machines and Processes; Handling and Moving Objects. *Interacting with Others*—Communicating with Other Workers; Assisting and Caring for Others; Providing Consultation and Advice to Others; Communicating with Persons Outside Organization. **Physical Work Conditions:** Indoors; Sitting; Using Hands on Objects, Tools, or Controls. **Other Job Characteristics:** Consequence of Error; Importance of Being Exact or Accurate; Importance of Being Sure All Is Done; Importance of Being Aware of New Events.

Experience: Job Zone 4. A minimum of two to four years of work-related skill, knowledge, or experience is needed. **Job Preparation:** SVP 7.0 to less than 8.0—2 years to less than 10 years. **Knowledge:** Transportation; Telecommunications; English Language; Physics; Computers and Electronics; Mathematics. **Instructional Program:** 490105 Air Traffic Controller.

Related DOT Jobs: 193.162-010 Air-Traffic Coordinator; 193.162-014 Air-Traffic-Control Specialist, Station; 193.162-018 Air-Traffic-Control Specialist, Tower; 193.167-010 Chief Controller; 912.167-010 Dispatcher.

53-2022.00 Airfield Operations Specialists (All Other Transportation and Related Workers)

Education: No data available.
Employed: 131,040
Openings: No data available.
Projected Growth: No data available.
Earnings: $23,730

Ensure the safe takeoff and landing of commercial and military aircraft. Coordinate duties of air-traffic control and maintenance personnel; dispatch; use airfield landing and navigational aids; implement airfield safety procedures; monitor and maintain flight records; apply knowledge of weather information.

GOE Number, Interest Area, and Work Group: 07.02.01; Transportation; Vehicle Expediting and Coordinating. **Instructional Program:** 080709 General Distribution Operations. **Note:** The Department of Labor has not collected some data for this job, so it has fewer details than the other descriptions.

53-3000 Motor Vehicle Operators

53-3011.00 Ambulance Drivers and Attendants, Except Emergency Medical Technicians (Ambulance Drivers and Attendants)

Education: Short-term O-T-J training
Employed: 19,294
Openings: 4,191
Projected Growth: 35%
Earnings: $16,960

Drive ambulance or assist ambulance driver in transporting sick, injured, or convalescent persons. Assist in lifting patients.

Places patients on stretcher and loads stretcher into ambulance, usually with help of ambulance attendant. Reports facts concerning accident or emergency to hospital personnel or law enforcement officials. Administers first aid as needed. Transports sick or injured persons to hospital or transports convalescents to destination, avoiding sudden motions detrimental to patients. Changes equipment to maintain sanitary conditions. Replaces supplies and disposable items on ambulance.

GOE Number, Interest Area, and Work Group: 07.07.01; Transportation; Other Services Requiring Driving. **Personality Type:** Social. Social occupations frequently involve working with, communicating with, and teaching people. These occupations often involve helping or providing service to others. **Work Values:** Social Service; Security; Achievement; Variety; Moral Values. **Skills:** Service Orientation; Active Listening; Speaking; Critical Thinking; Operation and Control; Coordination. **Abilities:** *Cognitive*—Spatial Orientation; Oral Expression; Selective Attention; Time Sharing; Memorization; Perceptual Speed. *Psychomotor*—Reaction Time; Response Orientation; Control Precision. *Physical*—Static Strength; Gross Body Coordination; Gross Body Equilibrium. *Sensory*—Far Vision; Sound Localization; Near Vision. **General Work Activities:** *Information Input*—Getting Information Needed to Do the Job; Monitoring Processes, Materials, and Surroundings; Identifying Objects, Actions, and Events. *Mental Process*—Updating and Using Job-Relevant Knowledge; Making Decisions and Solving Problems; Processing Information; Analyzing Data or Information; Judging Qualities of Things, Services, Other People's Work. *Work Output*—Operating Vehicles or Equipment; Performing General Physical Activities; Handling and Moving Objects. *Interacting with Others*—Assisting and Caring for Others; Communicating with Other Workers; Establishing and Maintaining Relationships; Performing for or Working with the Public. **Physical Work Conditions:** Special Uniform; Diseases or Infections; Using Hands on Objects, Tools, or Controls. **Other Job Characteristics:** Consequence of Error; Frustrating Circumstances; Importance of Being Exact or Accurate.

Experience: Job Zone 1. No previous work-related skill, knowledge, or experience is needed. **Job Preparation:** SVP Below 4.0—Less than 6 months. **Knowledge:** Medicine and Dentistry; Geography; Customer and Personal Service; Transportation; Therapy and Counseling. **Instructional Program:** 510904 Emergency Medical Technology/Technician.

Related DOT Jobs: 355.374-010 Ambulance Attendant; 913.683-010 Ambulance Driver.

53-3021.00 Bus Drivers, Transit and Intercity
(Bus Drivers)

Education: Moderate-term O-T-J training
Employed: 203,323
Openings: 29,885
Projected Growth: 15.8%
Earnings: $24,370

Drive bus or motor coach, including regular route operations, charters, and private carriage. Assist passengers with baggage. Collect fares or tickets.

Reports delays or accidents. Assists passengers with baggage; collects tickets or cash fares. Loads and unloads baggage in baggage compartment. Advises passengers to be seated and orderly while

on vehicle. Inspects vehicle; checks gas, oil, and water before departure. Records cash receipts and ticket fares. Regulates heating, lighting, and ventilating systems for passenger comfort. Parks vehicle at loading area for passengers to board. Drives vehicle over specified route or to specified destination, according to time schedule, to transport passengers, complying with traffic regulations. Makes minor repairs to vehicle and changes tires.

GOE Number, Interest Area, and Work Group: 07.07.01; Transportation; Other Services Requiring Driving. **Personality Type:** Realistic. Realistic occupations frequently involve work activities that include practical, hands-on problems and solutions. These occupations often deal with plants, animals, and real-world materials like wood, tools, and machinery. Many of the occupations require working outside and do not involve a lot of paperwork or working closely with others. **Work Values:** Company Policies and Practices; Supervision, Human Relations; Supervision, Technical; Independence; Security. **Skills:** Operation and Control; Repairing; Operation Monitoring; Service Orientation; Social Perceptiveness; Time Management; Problem Identification. **Abilities:** *Cognitive*—Spatial Orientation; Oral Expression; Number Facility; Problem Sensitivity; Selective Attention; Written Comprehension. *Psychomotor*—Control Precision; Reaction Time; Response Orientation. *Physical*—Static Strength. *Sensory*—Far Vision; Night Vision; Depth Perception. **General Work Activities:** *Information Input*—Inspecting Equipment, Structures, Materials; Monitoring Processes, Materials, and Surroundings; Identifying Objects, Actions, and Events. *Mental Process*—Making Decisions and Solving Problems; Updating and Using Job-Relevant Knowledge; Organizing, Planning, and Prioritizing. *Work Output*—Operating Vehicles or Equipment; Handling and Moving Objects; Repairing and Maintaining Mechanical Equipment. *Interacting with Others*—Performing for or Working with the Public; Communicating with Persons Outside Organization; Assisting and Caring for Others. **Physical Work Conditions:** Sitting; Special Uniform; Using Hands on Objects, Tools, or Controls. **Other Job Characteristics:** Consequence of Error; Importance of Being Sure All Is Done; Importance of Being Exact or Accurate.

Experience: Job Zone 1. No previous work-related skill, knowledge, or experience is needed. **Job Preparation:** SVP Below 4.0—Less than 6 months. **Knowledge:** Transportation; Geography; Mechanical; Public Safety and Security; Customer and Personal Service. **Instructional Program:** 490205 Truck, Bus and Other Commercial Vehicle Operator.

Related DOT Jobs: 913.363-010 Bus Driver, Day-Haul or Farm Charter; 913.463-010 Bus Driver; 913.663-014 Mobile-Lounge Driver.

53-3022.00 Bus Drivers, School (School Bus Drivers)

Education: Short-term O-T-J training
Employed: 434,753
Openings: 65,136
Projected Growth: 17.6%
Earnings: $18,820

Transport students or special clients such as elderly or disabled persons. Ensure adherence to safety rules. Assist passengers in boarding or exiting.

Makes minor repairs to bus. Complies with local traffic regulations. Regulates heating, lighting, and ventilating systems for passenger comfort. Reports delays or accidents. Drives bus to transport pupils over specified routes. Maintains order among pupils during trip. Inspects bus; checks gas, oil, and water levels.

GOE Number, Interest Area, and Work Group: 07.07.01; Transportation; Other Services Requiring Driving. **Personality Type:** Realistic. Realistic occupations frequently involve work activities that include practical, hands-on problems and solutions. These occupations often deal with plants, animals, and real-world materials like wood, tools, and machinery. Many of the occupations require working outside and do not involve a lot of paperwork or working closely with others. **Work Values:** Supervision, Human Relations; Company Policies and Practices; Supervision, Technical; Independence; Moral Values. **Skills:** Operation and Control; Operation Monitoring; Repairing; Equipment Maintenance; Problem Identification; Speaking. **Abilities:** *Cognitive*—Time Sharing; Selective Attention; Spatial Orientation; Oral Expression; Written Comprehension. *Psychomotor*—Response Orientation; Reaction Time; Rate Control. *Physical*—Trunk Strength; Gross Body Coordination; Explosive Strength. *Sensory*—Sound Localization; Far Vision; Peripheral Vision. **General Work Activities:** *Information Input*—Getting Information Needed to Do the Job; Monitoring Processes, Materials, and Surroundings; Inspecting Equipment, Structures, Materials. *Mental Process*—Making Decisions and Solving Problems; Updating and Using Job-Relevant Knowledge; Analyzing Data or Information. *Work Output*—Operating Vehicles or Equipment; Handling and Moving Objects; Repairing and Maintaining Mechanical Equipment. *Interacting with Others*—Assisting and Caring for Others; Performing for or Working with the Public; Resolving Conflict and Negotiating with Others; Establishing and Maintaining Relationships; Communicating with Other Workers. **Physical Work Conditions:** Sitting; Distracting Sounds and Noise Levels; Outdoors. **Other Job Characteristics:** Consequence of Error; Degree of Automation; Importance of Being Aware of New Events.

Experience: Job Zone 2. Some previous work-related skill, knowledge, or experience may be helpful, but usually is not needed. **Job Preparation:** SVP 4.00 to 5.99—6 months to less than 2 years. **Knowledge:** Transportation; Public Safety and Security; Customer and Personal Service; Geography; Law, Government and Jurisprudence. **Instructional Program:** 490205 Truck, Bus and Other Commercial Vehicle Operator.

Related DOT Job: 913.463-010 Bus Driver.

53-3031.00 Driver/Sales Workers (Driver/Sales Workers)

Education: Short-term O-T-J training

Employed: 304,768

Openings: 22,801

Projected Growth: 4.7%

Earnings: $19,330

Drive truck or other vehicle over established routes or within an established territory. Sell goods such as food products, including restaurant take-out items. Pick up and deliver items such as laundry. Take orders and collect payments. Includes newspaper delivery drivers.

Reviews list of dealers, customers, or station drops; loads truck. Collects coins from vending machines, refills machine, and removes aged merchandise. Collects money from customers, makes change, and records transactions on customer receipt. Records sales or deliveries information on daily sales or delivery record. Listens to and resolves customers' complaints regarding product or services. Arranges merchandise and sales promotion displays; issues sales promotion materials to customers. Writes customer order and sales contracts according to company guidelines. Informs regular customers of new products or services and of price changes. Calls on prospective customers to explain company services and to solicit new business. Sells food specialties such as sandwiches and beverages, to office workers and patrons of sports events. Drives truck to deliver such items as food, medical supplies, or newspapers. Maintains truck and food-dispensing equipment; cleans inside of machines that dispense food or beverages.

GOE Number, Interest Area, and Work Group: 07.07.01; Transportation; Other Services Requiring Driving. **Personality Type:** Enterprising. Enterprising occupations frequently involve starting up and carrying out projects. These occupations can involve leading people and making many decisions. They sometimes require risk taking and often deal with business. **Work Values:** Independence; Moral Values; Activity; Supervision, Human Relations; Autonomy; Supervision, Technical. **Skills:** Active Listening; Reading Comprehension; Critical Thinking; Problem Identification; Speaking; Mathematics; Negotiation. **Abilities:** *Cognitive*—Oral Expression; Oral Comprehension; Number Facility; Written Comprehension; Spatial Orientation. *Psychomotor*—Manual Dexterity. *Physical*—Static Strength; Trunk Strength; Stamina. *Sensory*—Speech Recognition; Glare Sensitivity. **General Work Activities:** *Information Input*—Estimating Needed Characteristics; Identifying Objects, Actions, and Events; Getting Information Needed to Do the Job. *Mental Process*—Organizing, Planning, and Prioritizing; Processing Information; Making Decisions and Solving Problems; Updating and Using Job-Relevant Knowledge. *Work Output*—Operating Vehicles or Equipment; Handling and Moving Objects; Documenting and Recording Information. *Interacting with Others*—Performing for or Working with the Public; Influencing Others or Selling; Establishing and Maintaining Relationships; Communicating with Persons Outside Organization. **Physical Work Conditions:** Standing; Outdoors; Using Hands on Objects, Tools, or Controls. **Other Job Characteristics:** Importance of Being Sure All Is Done; Consequence of Error; Importance of Being Exact or Accurate.

Experience: Job Zone 1. No previous work-related skill, knowledge, or experience is needed. **Job Preparation:** SVP Below 4.0—Less than 6 months. **Knowledge:** Sales and Marketing; Transportation; Mathematics; Customer and Personal Service; English Language. **Instructional Program:** 080705 General Retailing Operations.

Related DOT Jobs: 292.353-010 Driver, Sales Route; 292.363-010 Newspaper-Delivery Driver; 292.463-010 Lunch-Truck Driver; 292.483-010 Coin Collector; 292.667-010 Driver Helper, Sales Route; 292.687-010 Coin-Machine Collector.

53-3032.00 Truck Drivers, Heavy and Tractor-Trailer
(Truck Drivers, Heavy or Tractor-Trailer)

Education: No data available.

Employed: 1,480,780

Openings: No data available.

Projected Growth: No data available.

Earnings: $27,980

Drive a tractor-trailer combination or a truck with a capacity of at least 26,000 GVW to transport and deliver goods, livestock, or materials, in liquid, loose, or packaged form. Unload truck. Use automated routing equipment. Obtain required commercial driver's license.

GOE Number, Interest Area, and Work Group: 07.05.01; Transportation; Truck Driving. **Instructional Programs:** 010501 Agricultural Supplies Retailing and Wholesaling; 490205 Truck, Bus and Other Commercial Vehicle Operator. **Note:** The Department of Labor has not collected some data for this job, so it has fewer details than the other descriptions.

53-3032.01 Truck Drivers, Heavy (Truck Drivers)

Education: Short-term O-T-J training

Employed: 2,969,641

Openings: 535,419

Projected Growth: 16.6%

Earnings: No data available.

Drive truck with capacity of more than three tons to transport materials to specified destinations.

Positions blocks and ties rope around items to secure cargo for transport. Obtains customer signature or collects payment for goods delivered and for delivery charges. Assists in loading and unloading truck, manually. Cleans, inspects, and services vehicle. Maintains truck log according to state and federal regulations. Maintains radio or telephone contact with base or supervisor, to receive instructions or to be dispatched to new location. Drives truck with capacity of more than 3 tons, to transport and deliver cargo, materials, or damaged vehicles. Keeps record of materials and products transported. Operates equipment on vehicle, to load, unload, or disperse cargo or materials.

GOE Number, Interest Area, and Work Group: 07.05.01; Transportation; Truck Driving. **Personality Type:** Realistic. Realistic occupations frequently involve work activities that include practical, hands-on problems and solutions. These occupations often deal with plants, animals, and real-world materials like wood, tools, and machinery. Many of the occupations require working outside and do not involve a lot of paperwork or working closely with others. **Work Values:** Independence; Compensation; Company Policies and Practices; Autonomy; Activity; Supervision, Human Relations; Security. **Skills:** Equipment Maintenance; Operation and Control; Operation Monitoring; Reading Comprehension; Repairing; Writing. **Abilities:** *Cognitive*—Spatial Orientation; Oral Comprehension; Written Comprehension; Problem Sensitivity; Time Sharing; Information Ordering. *Psychomotor*—Reaction Time; Response Orientation; Control Precision. *Physical*—Static Strength; Extent Flexibility; Explosive Strength; Trunk Strength. *Sensory*—Far Vision; Depth Perception; Near Vision; Night Vision. **General Work Activities:** *Information Input*—Inspecting Equipment, Structures, Materials; Getting Information Needed to Do the Job; Identifying Objects, Actions, and Events. *Mental Process*—Evaluating Information Against Standards; Processing Information; Updating and Using Job-Relevant Knowledge. *Work Output*—Operating Vehicles or Equipment; Performing General Physical Activities; Handling and Moving Objects; Documenting and Recording Information. *Interacting with Others*—Performing Administrative Activities; Communicating with Persons Outside Organization; Monitoring and Controlling Resources. **Physical Work Conditions:** Sitting; Using Hands on Objects, Tools, or Controls; Indoors; Outdoors. **Other Job Characteristics:** Consequence of Error; Degree of Automation; Frustrating Circumstances.

Experience: Job Zone 1. No previous work-related skill, knowledge, or experience is needed. **Job Preparation:** SVP Below 4.0—Less than 6 months. **Knowledge:** Transportation; Geography; Mechanical; Law, Government and Jurisprudence; Clerical; Public Safety and Security. **Instructional Program:** 490205 Truck, Bus and Other Commercial Vehicle Operator.

Related DOT Jobs: 900.683-010 Concrete-Mixing-Truck Driver; 902.683-010 Dump-Truck Driver; 903.683-010 Explosives-Truck Driver; 903.683-014 Powder-Truck Driver; 903.683-018 Tank-Truck Driver; 905.483-010 Milk Driver; 905.663-010 Garbage Collector Driver; 905.663-014 Truck Driver, Heavy; 905.683-010 Water-Truck Driver II; 909.663-010 Hostler; 919.663-018 Driver-Utility Worker; 919.663-026 Tow-Truck Operator; 953.583-010 Drip Pumper.

53-3032.02 Tractor-Trailer Truck Drivers (Truck Drivers)

Education: Short-term O-T-J training

Employed: 2,969,641

Openings: 535,419

Projected Growth: 16.6%

Earnings: No data available.

Drive tractor-trailer truck to transport products, livestock, or materials to specified destinations.

Reads bill of lading to determine assignment. Gives directions to helper in packing and moving goods to trailer. Wraps goods using pads, packing paper, and containers; secures load to trailer wall, using straps. Inventories and inspects goods to be moved. Obtains customer's signature or collects payment for services. Services truck with oil, fuel, and radiator fluid, to maintain tractor-trailer. Works as member of two-person team driving tractor with sleeper bunk behind cab. Fastens chain or binders to secure load on trailer during transit. Inspects truck before and after trips; submits report indicating truck condition. Maintains driver log according to I.C.C. regulations. Drives truck to weigh station before and after loading and along route, to document weight and conform to state regulations. Maneuvers truck into loading or unloading position, following signals from loading crew as needed. Drives tractor-trailer combination, applying knowledge of commercial driving regulations, to transport and deliver products, livestock, or materials, usually over long distance. Loads or unloads truck, or assists in loading and unloading.

GOE Number, Interest Area, and Work Group: 07.05.01; Transportation; Truck Driving. **Personality Type:** Realistic. Realistic occupations frequently involve work activities that include practical, hands-on problems and solutions. These occupations often deal with plants, animals, and real-world materials like wood, tools, and machinery. Many of the occupations require working outside and do not involve a lot of paperwork or working closely with others. **Work Values:** Compensation; Company Policies and Practices; Independence; Activity; Supervision, Human Relations. **Skills:** Operation and Control; Reading Comprehension; Equipment Maintenance; Writing; Troubleshooting. **Abilities:** *Cognitive*–Spatial Orientation; Information Ordering; Oral Expression; Visualization; Time Sharing. *Psychomotor*–Reaction Time; Response Orientation; Rate Control. *Physical*–Static Strength; Extent Flexibility; Explosive Strength. *Sensory*–Far Vision; Depth Perception; Near Vision; Hearing Sensitivity. **General Work Activities:** *Information Input*–Inspecting Equipment, Structures, Materials; Getting Information Needed to Do the Job; Identifying Objects, Actions, and Events. *Mental Process*–Processing Information; Evaluating Information Against Standards; Judging Qualities of Things, Services, Other People's Work; Updating and Using Job-Relevant Knowledge. *Work Output*–Operating Vehicles or Equipment; Documenting and Recording Information; Handling and Moving Objects; Repairing and Maintaining Mechanical Equipment. *Interacting with Others*–Performing Administrative Activities; Communicating with Other Workers; Establishing and Maintaining Relationships. **Physical Work Conditions:** Sitting; Using Hands on Objects, Tools, or Controls; Indoors. **Other Job Characteristics:** Consequence of Error; Degree of Automation; Frustrating Circumstances.

Experience: Job Zone 2. Some previous work-related skill, knowledge, or experience may be helpful, but usually is not needed. **Job Preparation:** SVP 4.00 to 5.99—6 months to less than 2 years. **Knowledge:** Transportation; Geography; Mechanical; Law, Government and Jurisprudence; Public Safety and Security. **Instructional Program:** 490205 Truck, Bus and Other Commercial Vehicle Operator.

Related DOT Jobs: 904.363-010 Tractor-Trailer Moving Van Driver; 904.383-010 Tractor-Trailer-Truck Driver; 904.683-010 Log-Truck Driver.

53-3033.00 Truck Drivers, Light or Delivery Services
(Truck Drivers)

Education: Short-term O-T-J training
Employed: 2,969,641
Openings: 535,419
Projected Growth: 16.6%
Earnings: No data available.

Drive a truck or van with a capacity of under 26,000 GVW, primarily to deliver or pick up merchandise or to deliver packages within a specified area. Use automatic routing or location software. Load and unload truck.

Communicates with base or other vehicles, using telephone or radio. Performs emergency roadside repairs. Presents billing invoice and collects receipt or payment. Inspects and maintains vehicle equipment and supplies. Loads and unloads truck, van, or automobile. Drives truck, van, or automobile with capacity under 3 tons, to transport materials, products, or people. Maintains records such as vehicle log, record of cargo, or billing statements, in accordance with regulations.

GOE Number, Interest Area, and Work Group: 07.05.01; Transportation; Truck Driving. **Personality Type:** Realistic. Realistic occupations frequently involve work activities that include practical, hands-on problems and solutions. These occupations often deal with plants, animals, and real-world materials like wood, tools, and machinery. Many of the occupations require working outside and do not involve a lot of paperwork or working closely with others. **Work Values:** Independence; Compensation; Company Policies and Practices; Activity; Supervision, Human Relations. **Skills:** Equipment Maintenance; Operation and Control; Repairing; Operation Monitoring; Writing; Product Inspection; Reading Comprehension. **Abilities:** *Cognitive*–Spatial Orientation; Information Ordering; Oral Expression; Oral Comprehension; Time Sharing. *Psychomotor*–Reaction Time; Response Orientation; Control Precision. *Physical*–Static Strength; Extent Flexibility; Trunk Strength. *Sensory*–Far Vision; Near Vision; Depth Perception; Hearing Sensitivity. **General Work Activities:** *Information Input*–Inspecting Equipment, Structures, Materials; Getting Information Needed to Do the Job; Monitoring Processes, Materials, and Surroundings. *Mental Process*–Processing Information; Evaluating Information Against Standards; Organizing, Planning, and Prioritizing; Judging Qualities of Things, Services, Other People's Work. *Work Output*–Operating Vehicles or Equipment; Handling and Moving Objects; Repairing and Maintaining Mechanical Equipment. *Interacting with Others*–Communicating with Persons Outside Organization; Performing Administrative Activities; Communicating with Other Workers. **Physical Work Conditions:** Sitting; Outdoors; Indoors; Using Hands on Objects, Tools, or Controls. **Other Job Characteristics:** Consequence of Error; Degree of Automation; Importance of Being Aware of New Events; Frustrating Circumstances.

Experience: Job Zone 1. No previous work-related skill, knowledge, or experience is needed. **Job Preparation:** SVP Below 4.0—Less than 6 months. **Knowledge:** Transportation; Geography; Mechanical; Public Safety and Security; Clerical. **Instructional Program:** 490205 Truck, Bus and Other Commercial Vehicle Operator.

Related DOT Jobs: 906.683-010 Food-Service Driver; 906.683-014 Liquid-Fertilizer Servicer; 906.683-018 Telephone-Directory-Distributor Driver; 906.683-022 Truck Driver, Light; 913.663-018 Driver; 919.663-022 Escort-Vehicle Driver.

53-3041.00 Taxi Drivers and Chauffeurs (Taxi Drivers and Chauffeurs)

Education: Short-term O-T-J training
Employed: 131,576
Openings: 26,739
Projected Growth: 20%
Earnings: $15,540

Drive automobiles, vans, or limousines to transport passengers. Carry cargo.

Maintains vehicle by performing such duties as regulating tire pressure and adding gasoline, oil, and water. Makes minor repairs on vehicle, such as fixing punctures, cleaning spark plugs, or adjusting carburetor. Vacuums, sweeps, and cleans interior, and washes and polishes exterior of automobile. Performs errands for customers, such as carrying mail to and from post office. Delivers automobiles to customers from rental agency, car dealership, or repair shop. Assists passengers in entering and exiting vehicle; assists with luggage; holds umbrellas in wet weather. Collects and documents fees, payments, and deposits determined by rental contracts or taximeter recordings. Communicates with taxicab dispatcher by radio or telephone, to receive requests for passenger service. Drives taxicab, limousine, company car, hearse, or privately owned vehicle to transport passengers. Tests performance of vehicle accessories, such as lights, horn, and windshield wipers.

GOE Number, Interest Area, and Work Group: 07.07.01; Transportation; Other Services Requiring Driving. **Personality Type:** Realistic. Realistic occupations frequently involve work activities that include practical, hands-on problems and solutions. These occupations often deal with plants, animals, and real-world materials like wood, tools, and machinery. Many of the occupations require working outside and do not involve a lot of paperwork or working closely with others. **Work Values:** Independence; Social Service; Moral Values; Compensation; Security; Supervision, Human Relations; Autonomy. **Skills:** Operation and Control; Service Orientation; Repairing; Operation Monitoring; Testing. **Abilities:** *Cognitive*—Oral Comprehension; Number Facility; Written Comprehension; Time Sharing; Spatial Orientation; Memorization. *Psychomotor*—Reaction Time; Response Orientation; Multilimb Coordination. *Physical*—Gross Body Coordination; Dynamic Strength; Gross Body Equilibrium. *Sensory*—Near Vision; Sound Localization; Speech Clarity; Peripheral Vision. **General Work Activities:** *Information Input*—Getting Information Needed to Do the Job; Monitoring Processes, Materials, and Surroundings; Inspecting Equipment, Structures, Materials. *Mental Process*—Processing Information; Analyzing Data or Information; Making Decisions and Solving Problems; Organizing, Planning, and Prioritizing. *Work Output*—Operating Vehicles or Equipment; Repairing and Maintaining Mechanical Equipment; Performing General Physical Activities. *Interacting with Others*—Communicating with Other Workers; Performing for or Working with the Public; Communicating with Persons Outside Organization. **Physical Work Conditions:** Outdoors; Sitting; Special Uniform. **Other Job Characteristics:** Consequence of Error; Importance of Being Aware of New Events; Frustrating Circumstances.

Experience: Job Zone 1. No previous work-related skill, knowledge, or experience is needed. **Job Preparation:** SVP Below 4.0—Less than 6 months. **Knowledge:** Transportation; Customer and Personal Service; Geography; Mechanical; Law, Government and Jurisprudence; English Language. **Instructional Program:** 490205 Truck, Bus and Other Commercial Vehicle Operator.

Related DOT Jobs: 359.673-010 Chauffeur; 359.673-014 Chauffeur, Funeral Car; 913.463-018 Taxi Driver; 913.663-010 Chauffeur; 919.663-010 Deliverer, Car Rental; 919.683-014 Driver.

53-4000 Rail Transportation Workers

53-4011.00 Locomotive Engineers (Locomotive Engineers)

Education: Work experience in a related occupation
Employed: 33,179
Openings: 2,394
Projected Growth: 4.8%
Earnings: $39,800

Drive electric, diesel-electric, steam, or gas-turbine–electric locomotives to transport passengers or freight. Interpret train orders, electronic or manual signals, and railroad rules and regulations.

Drives diesel-electric rail-detector car to transport rail-flaw–detecting machine over railroad. Observes track to detect obstructions. Confers with conductor or traffic control center personnel via radiophone, to issue or receive information concerning stops, delays, or oncoming trains. Calls out train signals to assistant for verification of meaning, to avoid errors in interpretation. Synchronizes watch with that of conductor, to ensure that departure time from station or terminal is in accordance with time schedule. Inspects locomotive after run, to detect damaged or defective equipment. Inspects locomotive before run, to verify specified fuel, sand, water, and other supplies. Interprets train orders, train signals, and railroad rules and regulations, to drive locomotive, following safety regulations and time schedule. Receives starting signal from conductor; moves controls such as throttle and air brakes, to drive locomotive. Prepares reports to explain accidents, unscheduled stops, or delays.

GOE Number, Interest Area, and Work Group: 07.06.01; Transportation; Rail Vehicle Operation. **Personality Type:** Realistic. Realistic occupations frequently involve work activities that include practical, hands-on problems and solutions. These occupations often deal with plants, animals, and real-world materials like wood, tools, and machinery. Many of the occupations require working outside and do not involve a lot of paperwork or working closely with others. **Work Values:** Supervision, Human Relations; Company Policies and Practices; Security; Supervision, Technical; Compensation; Moral Values. **Skills:** Operation and Control; Operation Monitoring; Reading Comprehension; Systems Perception; Problem Identification. **Abilities:** *Cognitive*—Selective Attention; Problem Sensitivity; Oral Comprehension; Oral Expression; Spatial Orientation; Written Expression. *Psychomotor*—Reaction Time; Response Orientation; Control Precision. *Physical*—Explosive Strength; Gross Body Coordination; Dynamic Strength. *Sensory*—Auditory Attention; Far Vision; Night Vision. **General Work Activities:** *Information Input*—Inspecting Equipment, Structures, Materials; Getting Information Needed to Do the Job; Monitoring Processes, Materials, and Surroundings. *Mental Process*—Making Decisions and Solving Problems; Evaluating Information Against Standards; Analyzing Data or Information. *Work Output*—Operating Vehicles or Equipment; Handling and

Moving Objects; Documenting and Recording Information; Performing General Physical Activities. *Interacting with Others*—Communicating with Other Workers; Establishing and Maintaining Relationships; Interpreting Meaning of Information to Others. **Physical Work Conditions:** Using Hands on Objects, Tools, or Controls; Hazardous Equipment; Special Uniform. **Other Job Characteristics:** Consequence of Error; Frustrating Circumstances; Importance of Being Sure All Is Done.

Experience: Job Zone 4. A minimum of two to four years of work-related skill, knowledge, or experience is needed. **Job Preparation:** SVP 7.0 to less than 8.0—2 years to less than 10 years. **Knowledge:** Transportation; Public Safety and Security; Telecommunications; Mathematics; Mechanical. **Instructional Program:** 490299 Vehicle and Equipment Operators, Other.

Related DOT Job: 910.363-014 Locomotive Engineer.

53-4012.00 Locomotive Firers (Locomotive Firers)

Education: No data available.

Employed: 3,700

Openings: No data available.

Projected Growth: No data available.

Earnings: $37,290

Monitor locomotive instruments. Watch for dragging equipment, obstacles on rights-of-way, and train signals during run. Watch for and relay traffic signals from yard workers to yard engineer, in railroad yard.

Operates locomotive during emergency. Observes signal from workers in rear of train and relays information to engineer. Observes train as it goes around curves, to detect dragging equipment and smoking journal boxes. Observes train signals along route and verifies their meaning for engineer. Inventories supplies such as fuel, water, and sand, to ensure safe, efficient operation during run. Starts diesel engine to warm engine before run. Signals other worker to set brakes and to throw track switches when switching cars from train to way stations. Inspects locomotive to detect damaged or worn parts. Observes oil, temperature, and pressure gauges on dashboard, to ascertain if engine is operating safely and efficiently. Observes track from left side of locomotive, to detect obstructions on tracks.

GOE Number, Interest Area, and Work Group: 07.06.01; Transportation; Rail Vehicle Operation. **Personality Type:** Realistic. Realistic occupations frequently involve work activities that include practical, hands-on problems and solutions. These occupations often deal with plants, animals, and real-world materials like wood, tools, and machinery. Many of the occupations require working outside and do not involve a lot of paperwork or working closely with others. **Work Values:** Moral Values; Company Policies and Practices; Supervision, Human Relations; Supervision, Technical; Security. **Skills:** Operation Monitoring; Operation and Control; Problem Identification; Systems Perception; Coordination. **Abilities:** *Cognitive*—Problem Sensitivity; Perceptual Speed; Time Sharing; Oral Expression; Speed of Closure; Selective Attention. *Psychomotor*—Reaction Time; Response Orientation; Manual Dexterity. *Physical*—Extent Flexibility; Explosive Strength; Dynamic Flexibility; Gross Body Coordination. *Sensory*—Far Vision; Night

Vision; Peripheral Vision. **General Work Activities:** *Information Input*—Monitoring Processes, Materials, and Surroundings; Getting Information Needed to Do the Job; Inspecting Equipment, Structures, Materials. *Mental Process*—Evaluating Information Against Standards; Making Decisions and Solving Problems; Processing Information. *Work Output*—Operating Vehicles or Equipment; Performing General Physical Activities; Handling and Moving Objects. *Interacting with Others*—Communicating with Other Workers; Interpreting Meaning of Information to Others; Monitoring and Controlling Resources; Establishing and Maintaining Relationships. **Physical Work Conditions:** Hazardous Equipment; Outdoors; Distracting Sounds and Noise Levels. **Other Job Characteristics:** Consequence of Error; Degree of Automation; Importance of Being Sure All Is Done.

Experience: Job Zone 3. Previous work-related skill, knowledge, or experience is required. **Job Preparation:** SVP 6.0 to less than 7.0—More than 1 year and less than 4 years. **Knowledge:** Transportation; Mechanical; Public Safety and Security; Engineering and Technology; Geography; English Language; Telecommunications. **Instructional Program:** 490299 Vehicle and Equipment Operators, Other.

Related DOT Job: 910.363-010 Firer, Locomotive.

53-4013.00 Rail Yard Engineers, Dinkey Operators, and Hostlers (Rail Yard Engineers, Dinkey Operators, and Hostlers)

Education: No data available.

Employed: 3,110

Openings: No data available.

Projected Growth: No data available.

Earnings: $35,720

Drive switching or other locomotive or dinkey engines within railroad yard, industrial plant, quarry, construction project, or similar location.

Inspects track for defects; assists in installation or repair of rails and ties. Drives locomotives to and from various stations in roundhouse, to have locomotives cleaned, serviced, repaired, or supplied. Receives switching orders from yard conductor; talks with conductor and other workers via radio-telephone, to exchange switching information. Operates flatcar equipped with derrick, or operates railcar, to transport personnel or equipment. Operates and controls dinkey engine to transport and shunt cars at industrial or mine site. Operates switching diesel engine to switch railroad cars, using remote control. Observes oil, air, and steam pressure gauges, and observes water level, to ensure operating efficiency. Reads daily car schedule to determine number of cars needed for next day's run. Inspects engine at start and end of shift; refuels and lubricates engine as needed. Drives switching locomotive within railroad yard or other establishment to switch railroad cars. Records number of cars available or number of cars sent to repair station and type of service needed.

GOE Number, Interest Area, and Work Group: 07.06.01; Transportation; Rail Vehicle Operation. **Personality Type:** Realistic. Realistic occupations frequently involve work activities that include practical, hands-on problems and solutions. These occupations often deal with plants, animals, and real-world materials like wood, tools, and machinery. Many of the occupations require working outside and do not involve a lot of paperwork or working closely with others. **Work Values:** Moral Values; Supervision, Human Relations; Supervision, Technical; Company Policies and Practices; Security. **Skills:** Operation and Control; Operation Monitoring; Equipment Maintenance; Active Listening; Speaking; Problem Identification. **Abilities:** *Cognitive*—Oral Comprehension; Problem Sensitivity; Written Comprehension; Oral Expression; Perceptual Speed. *Psychomotor*—Control Precision; Reaction Time; Rate Control; Response Orientation. *Physical*—Static Strength; Gross Body Coordination. *Sensory*—Speech Clarity; Depth Perception; Far Vision. **General Work Activities:** *Information Input*—Getting Information Needed to Do the Job; Monitoring Processes, Materials, and Surroundings; Inspecting Equipment, Structures, Materials. *Mental Process*—Evaluating Information Against Standards; Organizing, Planning, and Prioritizing; Processing Information. *Work Output*—Operating Vehicles or Equipment; Handling and Moving Objects; Controlling Machines and Processes; Repairing and Maintaining Mechanical Equipment. *Interacting with Others*—Communicating with Other Workers; Interpreting Meaning of Information to Others; Coordinating Work and Activities of Others. **Physical Work Conditions:** Outdoors; Using Hands on Objects, Tools, or Controls; Distracting Sounds and Noise Levels. **Other Job Characteristics:** Degree of Automation; Consequence of Error; Importance of Being Exact or Accurate.

Experience: Job Zone 2. Some previous work-related skill, knowledge, or experience may be helpful, but usually is not needed. **Job Preparation:** SVP 4.00 to 5.99—6 months to less than 2 years. **Knowledge:** Transportation; Mechanical; Engineering and Technology; Public Safety and Security; Mathematics; Telecommunications. **Instructional Program:** 490299 Vehicle and Equipment Operators, Other.

Related DOT Jobs: 910.363-018 Yard Engineer; 910.583-010 Laborer, Car Barn; 910.683-010 Hostler; 919.663-014 Dinkey Operator.

53-4021.00 Railroad Brake, Signal, and Switch Operators (Railroad Brake, Signal, and Switch Operators)

Education: Work experience in a related occupation

Employed: 14,164

Openings: 708

Projected Growth: –47.8%

Earnings: $36,550

Operate railroad track switches. Couple or uncouple rolling stock to make up or break up trains. Signal engineers by hand or by flagging. Inspect couplings, air hoses, journal boxes, and hand brakes.

GOE Number, Interest Area, and Work Group: 07.02.01; Transportation; Vehicle Expediting and Coordinating. **Instructional Program:** 470302 Heavy Equipment Maintenance and Repairer. **Note:** The Department of Labor has not collected some data for this job, so it has fewer details than the other descriptions.

53-4021.01 Train Crew Members (Railroad Brake, Signal, and Switch Operators)

Education: Work experience in a related occupation

Employed: 14,164

Openings: 708

Projected Growth: –47.8%

Earnings: $36,550

Inspect couplings, airhoses, journal boxes, and handbrakes on trains to ensure that they function properly.

Answers questions from passengers concerning train rules, station, and timetable information. Signals locomotive engineer to start or stop train when coupling or uncoupling cars. Observes signals from other crewmembers. Collects tickets, fares, and passes from passengers. Assists passengers in boarding and leaving train. Adjusts controls to regulate air conditioning, heating, and lighting on train, for comfort of passengers. Reports to conductor any equipment requiring major repair. Pulls or pushes track switch to reroute cars. Sets flares, flags, lanterns, or torpedoes in front and at rear of train during emergency stops, to warn oncoming trains. Makes minor repairs to couplings, airhoses, and journal boxes, using hand tools. Climbs ladder to top of car to set brakes or to ride atop to control car's speed when shunted. Inspects couplings, airhoses, journal boxes, and handbrakes to ensure that they are securely fastened and function properly. Places passengers' baggage in rack above seats on train.

GOE Number, Interest Area, and Work Group: 07.08.01; Transportation; Support Work in Transportation. **Personality Type:** Realistic. Realistic occupations frequently involve work activities that include practical, hands-on problems and solutions. These occupations often deal with plants, animals, and real-world materials like wood, tools, and machinery. Many of the occupations require working outside and do not involve a lot of paperwork or working closely with others. **Work Values:** Moral Values; Supervision, Human Relations; Supervision, Technical; Company Policies and Practices; Security. **Skills:** Product Inspection; Problem Identification; Service Orientation; Equipment Maintenance; Operation and Control. **Abilities:** *Cognitive*—Oral Expression; Problem Sensitivity; Oral Comprehension; Information Ordering; Deductive Reasoning. *Psychomotor*—Reaction Time; Manual Dexterity; Control Precision. *Physical*—Static Strength; Dynamic Strength; Trunk Strength; Extent Flexibility; Gross Body Coordination. *Sensory*—Auditory Attention; Far Vision; Speech Clarity. **General Work Activities:** *Information Input*—Inspecting Equipment, Structures, Materials; Getting Information Needed to Do the Job; Identifying Objects, Actions, and Events. *Mental Process*—Analyzing Data or Information; Making Decisions and Solving Problems; Evaluating Information Against Standards. *Work Output*—Performing General Physical Activities; Repairing and Maintaining Mechanical Equipment; Handling and Moving Objects. *Interacting with Others*—Communicating with Other Workers; Interpreting Meaning of Information to Others; Communicating with Persons Outside Organization; Performing for or Working with the Public. **Physical Work Conditions:** Using Hands on Objects, Tools, or Controls; Standing; Walking or Running; Special Uniform. **Other Job Characteristics:** Consequence of Error;

Importance of Being Sure All Is Done; Frustrating Circumstances; Importance of Being Exact or Accurate.

Experience: Job Zone 2. Some previous work-related skill, knowledge, or experience may be helpful, but usually is not needed. **Job Preparation:** SVP 4.00 to 5.99—6 months to less than 2 years. **Knowledge:** Customer and Personal Service; Transportation; Mechanical; English Language; Public Safety and Security. **Instructional Program:** 470302 Heavy Equipment Maintenance and Repairer.

Related DOT Jobs: 910.364-010 Braker, Passenger Train; 910.367-010 Brake Coupler, Road Freight.

53-4021.02 Railroad Yard Workers (Railroad Brake, Signal, and Switch Operators)

Education: Work experience in a related occupation

Employed: 14,164

Openings: 708

Projected Growth: –47.8%

Earnings: $36,550

Perform a variety of activities such as coupling railcars and operating railroad-track switches in railroad yard, to facilitate the movement of railcars within the yard.

Signals engineer to start and stop engine. Watches for and relays traffic signals to start and stop cars during shunting, using arm or lantern. Opens and closes chute gates to load and unload cars. Raises lever to couple and uncouple cars for makeup and breakup of trains. Receives oral or written instructions indicating which cars are to be switched and indicating track assignments. Opens and closes ventilation doors. Attaches cable to cars being hoisted by cable or chain, in mines, quarries, or industrial plants. Connects airhose to car, using wrench. Throws track switches to route cars to different sections of yard. Rides atop cars that have been shunted and turns handwheel to control speed or to stop car at specified position.

GOE Number, Interest Area, and Work Group: 07.08.01; Transportation; Support Work in Transportation. **Personality Type:** Realistic. Realistic occupations frequently involve work activities that include practical, hands-on problems and solutions. These occupations often deal with plants, animals, and real-world materials like wood, tools, and machinery. Many of the occupations require working outside and do not involve a lot of paperwork or working closely with others. **Work Values:** Moral Values; Company Policies and Practices; Supervision, Technical; Supervision, Human Relations; Security. **Skills:** Operation and Control; Active Listening; Reading Comprehension; Coordination. **Abilities:** *Cognitive*—Written Comprehension; Oral Comprehension; Information Ordering; Oral Expression; Perceptual Speed. *Psychomotor*—Response Orientation; Reaction Time; Control Precision. *Physical*—Extent Flexibility; Gross Body Equilibrium; Static Strength; Dynamic Strength. *Sensory*—Far Vision; Auditory Attention; Depth Perception. **General Work Activities:** *Information Input*—Getting Information Needed to Do the Job; Monitoring Processes, Materials, and Surroundings; Identifying Objects, Actions, and Events. *Mental Process*—Analyzing Data or Information; Organizing, Planning, and Prioritizing; Making Decisions and

Solving Problems; Processing Information. *Work Output*—Performing General Physical Activities; Handling and Moving Objects; Controlling Machines and Processes. *Interacting with Others*—Communicating with Other Workers; Coordinating Work and Activities of Others; Interpreting Meaning of Information to Others; Establishing and Maintaining Relationships; Performing Administrative Activities. **Physical Work Conditions:** Outdoors; Using Hands on Objects, Tools, or Controls; Standing. **Other Job Characteristics:** Consequence of Error; Importance of Being Exact or Accurate; Importance of Being Sure All Is Done.

Experience: Job Zone 1. No previous work-related skill, knowledge, or experience is needed. **Job Preparation:** SVP Below 4.0—Less than 6 months. **Knowledge:** Transportation; Mechanical; Engineering and Technology; Physics; English Language. **Instructional Program:** 470302 Heavy Equipment Maintenance and Repairer.

Related DOT Jobs: 910.367-022 Locomotive Operator Helper; 910.664-010 Yard Coupler; 910.667-026 Switch Tender; 932.664-010 Brake Holder.

53-4031.00 Railroad Conductors and Yardmasters (Railroad Conductors and Yardmasters)

Education: Work experience in a related occupation

Employed: 25,421

Openings: 1,614

Projected Growth: –6.7%

Earnings: $38,500

Conductors: Coordinate activities of train crew on passenger or freight train. Coordinate activities of switch-engine crew within yard of railroad, industrial plant, or similar location. Yardmasters: Coordinate activities of workers engaged in railroad traffic operations such as the makeup or breakup of trains, and yard switching. Review train schedules and switching orders.

Observes lights on panelboard to monitor location of trains. Documents and prepares reports of accidents, unscheduled stops, or delays, at completion of train run. Records departure and arrival times, messages, tickets and revenue collected, and passenger accommodations and destinations. Verifies accuracy of timekeeping instruments with engineer to ensure that station departure time complies with timetable schedules. Inspects freight cars for compliance with sealing procedures, records car and corresponding seal number, and confirms route and destination information. Collects tickets, fares, or passes from passengers; answers questions concerning train rules, regulations, and schedules; provides destination information. Charts train movements to estimate arrival times. Operates controls to electrically activate track switches and traffic signals. Confers with traffic control personnel, engineer, and other workers engaged in transporting freight, to receive and convey instructions. Instructs workers to set warning signals in front and rear of train during emergency stops, to warn oncoming trains. Observes yard traffic, to determine tracks available for accommodating inbound and outbound traffic. Reviews schedules, switching orders, way bills, and shipping records, to obtain cargo loading and unloading information. Signals engineer to begin train run, stop train, or change speed, using radiotelephone, lantern, teletypewriter, or hand movement. Coordinates crew activities to transport and provide boarding, porter, maid, and meal services to passengers. Directs and instructs workers engaged in yard activities such as switching track, coupling and uncoupling cars, and routing inbound and outbound traffic. Inspects or supervises workers in inspection and maintenance of mechanical equipment, to ensure efficient and safe train operation. Observes and communicates with passengers and instructs workers to regulate air conditioning, lighting, and heating, to ensure passenger safety and comfort.

GOE Number, Interest Area, and Work Group: 07.01.01; Transportation; Managerial Work in Transportation. **Personality Type:** Realistic. Realistic occupations frequently involve work activities that include practical, hands-on problems and solutions. These occupations often deal with plants, animals, and real-world materials like wood, tools, and machinery. Many of the occupations require working outside and do not involve a lot of paperwork or working closely with others. **Work Values:** Security; Company Policies and Practices; Authority; Supervision, Technical; Autonomy. **Skills:** Coordination; Operation and Control; Management of Personnel Resources; Operation Monitoring; Reading Comprehension; Active Listening; Product Inspection; Systems Perception; Information Gathering; Problem Identification. **Abilities:** *Cognitive*—Oral Expression; Problem Sensitivity; Written Expression; Written Comprehension; Deductive Reasoning; Oral Comprehension. *Psychomotor*—Rate Control; Reaction Time; Multilimb Coordination; Control Precision. *Physical*—Gross Body Equilibrium. *Sensory*—Speech Clarity; Near Vision; Far Vision. **General Work Activities:** *Information Input*—Getting Information Needed to Do the Job; Monitoring Processes, Materials, and Surroundings; Inspecting Equipment, Structures, Materials. *Mental Process*—Scheduling Work and Activities; Organizing, Planning, and Prioritizing; Making Decisions and Solving Problems. *Work Output*—Documenting and Recording Information; Controlling Machines and Processes; Handling and Moving Objects. *Interacting with Others*—Coordinating Work and Activities of Others; Communicating with Other Workers; Performing for or Working with the Public; Communicating with Persons Outside Organization. **Physical Work Conditions:** Standing; Outdoors; Special Uniform; Walking or Running. **Other Job Characteristics:** Consequence of Error; Degree of Automation; Importance of Being Exact or Accurate; Importance of Being Aware of New Events.

Experience: Job Zone 4. A minimum of two to four years of work-related skill, knowledge, or experience is needed. **Job Preparation:** SVP 7.0 to less than 8.0—2 years to less than 10 years. **Knowledge:** Administration and Management; Transportation; Public Safety and Security; English Language; Mathematics. **Instructional Programs:** 520201 Business Administration and Management, General; 520203 Logistics and Materials Management.

Related DOT Jobs: 184.167-262 Train Dispatcher; 184.167-278 Yard Manager; 198.167-010 Conductor, Passenger Car; 198.167-014 Conductor, Pullman; 198.167-018 Conductor, Road Freight; 910.167-010 Car Chaser.

53-4041.00 Subway and Streetcar Operators
(Subway and Streetcar Operators)

Education: Moderate-term O-T-J training
Employed: 3,329
Openings: 250
Projected Growth: 7.1%
Earnings: $43,330

Operate subway or elevated suburban train with no separate locomotive, to transport passengers. Operate electric-powered streetcar, to transport passengers. Handle fares.

Drives rail-guided public transportation such as subways, elevated suburban trains, or electric-powered streetcars, to transport passengers. Records readings of coin receptor at beginning and end of shift, to verify amount of money received during shift. Collects fares from passengers and issues change and transfers. Opens and closes doors of train or streetcar to allow passengers to enter or leave vehicle. Answers questions from passengers concerning fares, schedules, and routings.

GOE Number, Interest Area, and Work Group: 07.06.01; Transportation; Rail Vehicle Operation. **Personality Type:** Realistic. Realistic occupations frequently involve work activities that include practical, hands-on problems and solutions. These occupations often deal with plants, animals, and real-world materials like wood, tools, and machinery. Many of the occupations require working outside and do not involve a lot of paperwork or working closely with others. **Work Values:** Supervision, Human Relations; Moral Values; Supervision, Technical; Independence; Company Policies and Practices; Security. **Skills:** Operation and Control; Operation Monitoring; Active Listening; Reading Comprehension; Speaking. **Abilities:** *Cognitive*—Oral Expression; Oral Comprehension; Number Facility; Memorization; Spatial Orientation. *Psychomotor*—Reaction Time; Control Precision; Multilimb Coordination; Response Orientation. *Physical*—Trunk Strength; Gross Body Coordination. *Sensory*—Far Vision; Depth Perception; Night Vision; Glare Sensitivity. **General Work Activities:** *Information Input*—Getting Information Needed to Do the Job; Monitoring Processes, Materials, and Surroundings; Identifying Objects, Actions, and Events. *Mental Process*—Processing Information; Analyzing Data or Information; Making Decisions and Solving Problems. *Work Output*—Operating Vehicles or Equipment; Handling and Moving Objects; Documenting and Recording Information. *Interacting with Others*—Performing for or Working with the Public; Communicating with Persons Outside Organization; Performing Administrative Activities; Communicating with Other Workers; Interpreting Meaning of Information to Others. **Physical Work Conditions:** Special Uniform; Sitting; Using Hands on Objects, Tools, or Controls; Indoors. **Other Job Characteristics:** Consequence of Error; Degree of Automation; Importance of Repeating Same Tasks.

Experience: Job Zone 2. Some previous work-related skill, knowledge, or experience may be helpful, but usually is not needed. **Job Preparation:** SVP 4.00 to 5.99—6 months to less than 2 years. **Knowledge:** Transportation; Customer and Personal Service; Clerical; Geography; Mathematics; English Language; Public Safety and Security. **Instructional Program:** 490299 Vehicle and Equipment Operators, Other.

Related DOT Jobs: 910.683-014 Motor Operator; 913.463-014 Streetcar Operator.

53-5000 Water Transportation Workers

53-5011.00 Sailors and Marine Oilers (Ordinary Seamen and Marine Oilers)

Education: No data available.

Employed: 12,850

Openings: No data available.

Projected Growth: No data available.

Earnings: $22,160

Stand watch to look for obstructions in path of vessel; measure water depth; turn wheel on bridge; use emergency equipment as directed by captain, mate, or pilot. Break out, rig, overhaul, and store cargo-handling gear, stationary rigging, and running gear. Perform a variety of maintenance tasks to preserve the painted surface of the ship and to maintain line and ship equipment. Obtain required government-issued certification and tankerman certification for work done aboard liquid-carrying vessels.

GOE Number, Interest Area, and Work Group: 07.04.01; Transportation; Water Vehicle Operation. **Instructional Programs:** 490306 Marine Maintenance and Ship Repairer; 490399 Water Transportation Workers, Other. **Note:** The Department of Labor has not collected some data for this job, so it has fewer details than the other descriptions.

53-5011.01 Able Seamen (Able Seamen)

Education: No data available.

Employed: 8,060

Openings: No data available.

Projected Growth: No data available.

Earnings: $26,790

Stand watch at bow or on wing of bridge to look for obstructions in path of vessel. Measure water depth. Turn wheel on bridge or use emergency equipment as directed by mate. Break out, rig, overhaul, and store cargo-handling gear, stationary rigging, and running gear. Chip rust from and paint deck or ship's structure. Obtain required government-issued certification. Obtain required certification for work done aboard liquid-carrying vessels.

Steers ship under direction of ship's commander or navigating officer, or directs helmsman to steer, following designated course. Steers ship and maintains visual communication with other ships. Stands watch from bow of ship or wing of bridge to look for obstruction in path of ship. Overhauls lifeboats and lifeboat gear, and lowers or raises lifeboats with winch or falls. Paints and chips rust on deck or superstructure of ship. Breaks out, rigs, overhauls, and stows cargo-handling gear, stationary rigging, and running gear. Stows or removes cargo from ship's hold. Maintains ship's log while in port, and stands gangway watch to prevent unauthorized persons from boarding ship. Gives directions to crew engaged in cleaning wheelhouse and quarter deck. Relays specified signals to ships in vicinity, using visual signaling devices such as blinker light and semaphore. Measures depth of water in shallow or unfamiliar waters, using leadline; telephones or shouts information to bridge. Stands by wheel when ship is on automatic pilot; verifies accuracy of course by comparing with magnetic compass.

GOE Number, Interest Area, and Work Group: 07.04.01; Transportation; Water Vehicle Operation. **Personality Type:** Realistic. Realistic occupations frequently involve work activities that include practical, hands-on problems and solutions. These occupations often deal with plants, animals, and real-world materials like wood, tools, and machinery. Many of the occupations require working outside and do not involve a lot of paperwork or working closely with others. **Work Values:** Moral Values; Coworkers; Supervision, Technical; Advancement; Supervision, Human Relations. **Skills:** Coordination; Operation and Control; Operation Monitoring; Monitoring; Systems Perception; Equipment Selection; Reading Comprehension; Equipment Maintenance. **Abilities:** *Cognitive*—Oral Expression; Spatial Orientation; Oral Comprehension; Selective Attention; Perceptual Speed. *Psychomotor*—Control Precision; Reaction Time; Response Orientation; Rate Control; Speed of Limb Movement. *Physical*—Static Strength; Extent Flexibility; Trunk Strength. *Sensory*—Far Vision; Glare Sensitivity; Night Vision. **General Work Activities:** *Information Input*—Getting Information Needed to Do the Job; Monitoring Processes, Materials, and Surroundings; Identifying Objects, Actions, and Events; Inspecting Equipment, Structures, Materials. *Mental Process*—Processing Information; Making Decisions and Solving Problems; Evaluating Information Against Standards. *Work Output*—Performing General Physical Activities; Operating Vehicles or Equipment; Handling and Moving Objects. *Interacting with Others*—Communicating with Other Workers; Establishing and Maintaining Relationships; Coordinating Work and Activities of Others; Interpreting Meaning of Information to Others. **Physical Work Conditions:** Standing; Using Hands on Objects, Tools, or Controls; Outdoors; Special Uniform. **Other Job Characteristics:** Consequence of Error; Frustrating Circumstances; Importance of Being Aware of New Events; Importance of Being Sure All Is Done.

Experience: Job Zone 2. Some previous work-related skill, knowledge, or experience may be helpful, but usually is not needed. **Job Preparation:** SVP 4.00 to 5.99—6 months to less than 2 years. **Knowledge:** Transportation; Mechanical; Geography; Telecommunications; Public Safety and Security; Mathematics. **Instructional Program:** 490399 Water Transportation Workers, Other.

Related DOT Jobs: 911.363-014 Quartermaster; 911.364-010 Able Seaman.

53-5011.02 Ordinary Seamen and Marine Oilers
(Ordinary Seamen and Marine Oilers)

Education: No data available.

Employed: 12,850

Openings: No data available.

Projected Growth: No data available.

Earnings: $22,160

Stand deck department watches; perform a variety of tasks to preserve the painted surface of the ship and to maintain lines and ship equipment, such as running and cargo-handling gear. Oil and grease moving parts of engines and auxiliary equipment. Obtain required government-issued certification. Obtain required certification for work done aboard liquid-carrying vessels.

Records data in ship's log, such as weather conditions and distance traveled. Handles lines to moor vessel to wharf, to tie up vessel to another vessel, or to rig towing lines. Sweeps and washes deck, using broom, mops, brushes, and hose. Examines machinery for specified pressure and flow of lubricants. Reads pressure and temperature gauges or displays; records data in engineering log. Turns wheel while observing compass, to maintain ship on course. Assists engineer in overhauling and adjusting machinery. Loads or unloads materials from vessel. Stands watch from bow of ship or wing of bridge, to look for obstructions in path of ship. Splices and repairs cables and ropes, using marlinespike, wirecutters, twine, and hand tools. Lubricates machinery, equipment, and engine parts, such as gears, shafts, and bearings. Paints or varnishes decks, superstructures, lifeboats, or sides of ship. Cleans and polishes wood trim, brass, and other metal parts. Chips and cleans rust spots on deck, superstructure, and sides of ship, using wire brush and hand or air chipping machine. Lowers and mans lifeboat in case of emergency.

GOE Number, Interest Area, and Work Group: 07.04.01; Transportation; Water Vehicle Operation. **Personality Type:** Realistic. Realistic occupations frequently involve work activities that include practical, hands-on problems and solutions. These occupations often deal with plants, animals, and real-world materials like wood, tools, and machinery. Many of the occupations require working outside and do not involve a lot of paperwork or working closely with others. **Work Values:** Moral Values; Advancement; Supervision, Technical; Coworkers; Activity. **Skills:** Equipment Maintenance; Repairing; Operation and Control; Operation Monitoring; Systems Perception. **Abilities:** *Cognitive*—Spatial Orientation; Problem Sensitivity; Written Expression; Visualization; Information Ordering. *Psychomotor*—Control Precision; Manual Dexterity; Multilimb Coordination; Wrist-Finger Speed. *Physical*—Trunk Strength; Extent Flexibility; Static Strength. *Sensory*—Far Vision; Depth Perception; Night Vision. **General Work Activities:** *Information Input*—Getting Information Needed to Do the Job; Monitoring Processes, Materials, and Surroundings; Inspecting Equipment, Structures, Materials. *Mental Process*—Analyzing Data or Information; Judging Qualities of Things, Services, Other People's Work; Evaluating Information Against Standards; Updating and Using Job-Relevant Knowledge. *Work Output*—Performing General Physical Activities; Handling and Moving Objects;

Repairing and Maintaining Mechanical Equipment. *Interacting with Others*—Communicating with Other Workers; Performing Administrative Activities; Establishing and Maintaining Relationships. **Physical Work Conditions:** Outdoors; Special Uniform; Using Hands on Objects, Tools, or Controls; Standing. **Other Job Characteristics:** Consequence of Error; Importance of Being Sure All Is Done; Importance of Being Exact or Accurate; Importance of Being Aware of New Events.

Experience: Job Zone 2. Some previous work-related skill, knowledge, or experience may be helpful, but usually is not needed. **Job Preparation:** SVP 4.00 to 5.99—6 months to less than 2 years. **Knowledge:** Transportation; Mechanical; Public Safety and Security; Building and Construction; Mathematics; Engineering and Technology. **Instructional Programs:** 490306 Marine Maintenance and Ship Repairer; 490399 Water Transportation Workers, Other.

Related DOT Jobs: 911.584-010 Marine Oiler; 911.664-014 Sailor, Pleasure Craft; 911.687-022 Deckhand; 911.687-030 Ordinary Seaman.

53-5021.00 Captains, Mates, and Pilots of Water Vessels (Captains and Pilots, Water Vessels)

Education: Work experience in a related occupation

Employed: 18,552

Openings: 3,581

Projected Growth: 3%

Earnings: No data available.

Command or supervise operations of ships and water vessels such as tugboats and ferryboats that travel into and out of harbors, estuaries, straits, and sounds and that travel on rivers, lakes, bays, and oceans. Obtain required license issued by U.S. Coast Guard.

GOE Number, Interest Area, and Work Group: 07.04.01; Transportation; Water Vehicle Operation. **Instructional Programs:** 490306 Marine Maintenance and Ship Repairer; 490399 Water Transportation Workers, Other. **Note:** The Department of Labor has not collected some data for this job, so it has fewer details than the other descriptions.

53-5021.01 Ship and Boat Captains (Water Vessel Captains and Pilots)

Education: Work experience in a related occupation

Employed: 18,552

Openings: 3,581

Projected Growth: 3%

Earnings: No data available.

Command vessels in oceans, bays, lakes, rivers, and coastal waters.

Inspects vessel to ensure safety of crew and passengers, efficient and safe operation of vessel and equipment, and conformance to regulations. Purchases supplies and equipment, contacts buyers to sell fish, and resolves questions or problems with customs officials. Signals passing vessels, using whistle, flashing lights, flags, and radio. Tows and maneuvers barge or signals tugboat to tow barge to destination. Interviews, hires, and instructs crew; assigns watches and living quarters. Maintains records of daily activities, movements, and ports-of-call; prepares progress and personnel reports. Calculates sighting of land, using electronic sounding devices and following contour lines on chart. Signals crew or deckhands to rig tow lines, open or close gates and ramps, and pull guard chains across entry. Collects fares from customers or signals ferryboat helper to collect fares. Computes position, sets course, and determines speed, using charts, area plotting sheets, compass, sextant, and knowledge of local conditions. Steers and operates vessel, or orders helmsperson to steer vessel, using radio, depth finder, radar, lights, buoys, and lighthouses. Directs and coordinates activities of crew or workers, such as loading and unloading, operating signal devices, fishing, and repairing defective equipment. Commands water vessels such as passenger and freight vessels, fishing vessels, yachts, tugboats, barges, deep submergence vehicles, and ferryboats. Monitors sonar and navigational aids and reads gauges to verify sufficient levels of hydraulic fluid, air pressure, and oxygen.

GOE Number, Interest Area, and Work Group: 07.04.01; Transportation; Water Vehicle Operation. **Personality Type:** Enterprising. Enterprising occupations frequently involve starting up and carrying out projects. These occupations can involve leading people and making many decisions. They sometimes require risk taking and often deal with business. **Work Values:** Authority; Responsibility; Autonomy; Ability Utilization; Achievement; Compensation; Recognition. **Skills:** Management of Personnel Resources; Coordination; Operation and Control; Judgment and Decision Making; Problem Identification; Operation Monitoring. **Abilities:** *Cognitive*—Problem Sensitivity; Spatial Orientation; Number Facility; Oral Expression; Mathematical Reasoning; Information Ordering. *Psychomotor*—Response Orientation; Reaction Time; Control Precision. *Physical*—Gross Body Equilibrium; Gross Body Coordination; Stamina. *Sensory*—Far Vision; Night Vision; Glare Sensitivity; Depth Perception. **General Work Activities:** *Information Input*—Getting Information Needed to Do the Job; Identifying Objects, Actions, and Events; Monitoring Processes, Materials, and Surroundings. *Mental Process*—Making Decisions and Solving Problems; Analyzing Data or Information; Processing Information. *Work Output*—Operating Vehicles or Equipment; Implementing Ideas and Programs; Controlling Machines and Processes; Documenting and Recording Information. *Interacting with Others*—Communicating with Other Workers; Coordinating Work and Activities of Others; Monitoring and Controlling Resources. **Physical Work Conditions:** Outdoors; Using Hands on Objects, Tools, or Controls; Standing. **Other Job Characteristics:** Consequence of Error; Importance of Being Exact or Accurate; Importance of Being Sure All Is Done.

Experience: Job Zone 4. A minimum of two to four years of work-related skill, knowledge, or experience is needed. **Job Preparation:** SVP 7.0 to less than 8.0—2 years to less than 10 years. **Knowledge:** Transportation; Geography; Mathematics; Administration and Management; Law, Government and Jurisprudence; Physics. **Instructional Program:** 490303 Fishing Tech./Commercial Fishing.

Related DOT Jobs: 197.133-010 Captain, Fishing Vessel; 197.133-014 Master, Yacht; 197.133-030 Tugboat Captain; 197.161-010 Dredge Captain; 197.163-010 Ferryboat Captain; 197.163-014 Master, Passenger Barge; 197.163-018 Master, Riverboat; 197.167-010 Master, Ship; 911.137-010 Barge Captain; 911.137-014 Derrick-Boat Captain; 911.263-010 Deep Submergence Vehicle Operator; 911.363-010 Ferryboat Operator.

53-5021.02 Mates—Ship, Boat, and Barge (Mates, Ship, Boat, and Barge)

Education: Work experience in a related occupation
Employed: 8,054
Openings: 1,631
Projected Growth: 7.9%
Earnings: $29,310

Supervise and coordinate activities of crew aboard ships, boats, barges, or dredges.

Inspects equipment such as cargo-handling gear, lifesaving equipment, fishing gear, towing gear, dredging gear, and visual-signaling equipment, for defects. Determines geographical position of ship, using loran and azimuths of celestial bodies. Steers vessel, using navigation devices such as compass and sexton, and using navigational aids such as lighthouses and buoys. Observes water from masthead and advises navigational direction. Assumes command of vessel in event ship master becomes incapacitated. Supervises activities of crew engaged in ship's activity, such as barging, towing, dredging, or fishing. Observes loading and unloading of cargo and equipment to ensure that handling and storage are according to specifications. Supervises crew in repair or replacement of defective vessel gear and equipment. Stands watch on vessel during specified periods while vessel is underway. Supervises crew in cleaning and maintaining decks, superstructure, and bridge.

GOE Number, Interest Area, and Work Group: 07.04.01; Transportation; Water Vehicle Operation. **Personality Type:** Realistic. Realistic occupations frequently involve work activities that include practical, hands-on problems and solutions. These occupations often deal with plants, animals, and real-world materials like wood, tools, and machinery. Many of the occupations require working outside and do not involve a lot of paperwork or working closely with others. **Work Values:** Authority; Company Policies and Practices; Advancement; Coworkers; Autonomy; Moral Values; Activity. **Skills:** Coordination; Operation and Control; Systems Perception; Management of Personnel Resources; Implementation Planning. **Abilities:** *Cognitive*—Oral Comprehension; Oral Expression; Spatial Orientation; Deductive Reasoning; Information Ordering; Problem Sensitivity. *Psychomotor*—Control Precision; Reaction Time; Response Orientation. *Physical*—Gross Body Equilibrium; Gross Body Coordination. *Sensory*—Far Vision; Glare Sensitivity; Night Vision. **General Work Activities:** *Information Input*—Inspecting Equipment, Structures, Materials; Getting Information Needed to Do the Job; Monitoring Processes, Materials, and Surroundings. *Mental Process*—Making Decisions and Solving Problems; Organizing, Planning, and Prioritizing; Judging Qualities of Things, Services, Other People's Work; Evaluating Information Against Standards; Analyzing Data or Information. *Work Output*—Operating Vehicles or Equipment; Performing General Physical Activities; Handling and Moving Objects. *Interacting with Others*—Communicating with Other Workers; Coordinating Work and Activities of Others; Guiding, Directing and Motivating Subordinates. **Physical Work Conditions:** Outdoors; Standing; Using Hands on Objects, Tools, or Controls. **Other Job Characteristics:** Consequence of Error; Importance of Being Exact or Accurate; Importance of Being Aware of New Events.

Experience: Job Zone 3. Previous work-related skill, knowledge, or experience is required. **Job Preparation:** SVP 6.0 to less than 7.0—More than 1 year and less than 4 years. **Knowledge:** Transportation; Mechanical; Administration and Management; Geography; Public Safety and Security. **Instructional Programs:** 490303 Fishing Tech./Commercial Fishing; 490309 Marine Science/Merchant Marine Officer; 490399 Water Transportation Workers, Other.

Related DOT Jobs: 197.133-018 Mate, Fishing Vessel; 197.133-022 Mate, Ship; 197.133-034 Tugboat Mate; 197.137-010 Dredge Mate; 911.133-010 Cadet, Deck.

53-5021.03 Pilots, Ship (Water Vessel Captains and Pilots)

Education: Work experience in a related occupation
Employed: 18,552
Openings: 3,581
Projected Growth: 3%
Earnings: No data available.

Command ships to steer them into and out of harbors, estuaries, straits, and sounds, and to steer them on rivers, lakes, and bays. Obtain required license from U.S. Coast Guard, with limitations indicating class and tonnage of vessels for which license is valid and route and waters that may be piloted.

Signals tugboat captain to berth and unberth ship. Directs course and speed of ship on basis of specialized knowledge of local winds, weather, tides, and current. Orders worker at helm to steer ship. Navigates ship to avoid reefs, outlying shoals, and other hazards, utilizing aids to navigation, such as lighthouses and buoys.

GOE Number, Interest Area, and Work Group: 07.04.01; Transportation; Water Vehicle Operation. **Personality Type:** Realistic. Realistic occupations frequently involve work activities that include practical, hands-on problems and solutions. These occupations often deal with plants, animals, and real-world materials like wood, tools, and machinery. Many of the occupations require working outside and do not involve a lot of paperwork or working closely with others. **Work Values:** Autonomy; Responsibility; Authority; Achievement; Ability Utilization. **Skills:** Operation and Control; Judgment and Decision Making; Systems Perception; Monitoring; Mathematics; Active Listening. **Abilities:** *Cognitive*—Spatial Orientation; Oral Expression; Inductive Reasoning; Time Sharing; Selective Attention. *Psychomotor*—Control Precision; Rate Control; Reaction Time. *Physical*—Trunk Strength; Gross Body Equilibrium; Stamina. *Sensory*—Far Vision; Night Vision; Depth Perception. **General Work Activities:** *Information Input*—Getting Information Needed to Do the Job; Monitoring

Processes, Materials, and Surroundings; Identifying Objects, Actions, and Events. *Mental Process*—Making Decisions and Solving Problems; Analyzing Data or Information; Updating and Using Job-Relevant Knowledge. *Work Output*—Operating Vehicles or Equipment; Performing General Physical Activities; Handling and Moving Objects. *Interacting with Others*—Communicating with Other Workers; Interpreting Meaning of Information to Others; Communicating with Persons Outside Organization. **Physical Work Conditions:** Using Hands on Objects, Tools, or Controls; Standing; Special Uniform. **Other Job Characteristics:** Consequence of Error; Frustrating Circumstances; Degree of Automation.

Experience: Job Zone 5. Extensive skill, knowledge, and experience are needed. Very advanced communication and organizational skills are required. **Job Preparation:** SVP 8.0 and above—4 years to more than 10 years. **Knowledge:** Transportation; Geography; Telecommunications; Mathematics; Engineering and Technology. **Instructional Program:** 490309 Marine Science/Merchant Marine Officer.

Related DOT Job: 197.133-026 Pilot, Ship.

53-5022.00 Motorboat Operators (Motorboat Operators)

Education: No data available.
Employed: 1,220
Openings: No data available.
Projected Growth: No data available.
Earnings: $24,750

Operate small motor-driven boats to carry passengers and freight between ships, or ship to shore. Patrol harbors and beach areas. Assist in navigational activities.

Maintains desired course, using compass or electronic navigational aides. Performs routine maintenance on boat engine and equipment. Cleans and repairs boat hull and superstructure. Gives directions for loading and seating in boat. Operates engine throttle and steering mechanism to guide boat on desired course. Secures boat to dock with mooring lines; casts off lines to depart.

GOE Number, Interest Area, and Work Group: 07.04.01; Transportation; Water Vehicle Operation. **Personality Type:** Realistic. Realistic occupations frequently involve work activities that include practical, hands-on problems and solutions. These occupations often deal with plants, animals, and real-world materials like wood, tools, and machinery. Many of the occupations require working outside and do not involve a lot of paperwork or working closely with others. **Work Values:** Autonomy; Independence; Moral Values; Responsibility; Recognition. **Skills:** Equipment Maintenance; Repairing; Operation and Control; Operation Monitoring; Troubleshooting; Problem Identification. **Abilities:** *Cognitive*—Spatial Orientation; Oral Expression; Information Ordering; Deductive Reasoning; Visualization; Inductive Reasoning. *Psychomotor*—Reaction Time; Control Precision; Response Orientation. *Physical*—Extent Flexibility; Static Strength; Gross Body Equilibrium; Explosive Strength. *Sensory*—Far Vision; Sound Localization; Night Vision. **General Work Activities:** *Information Input*—Monitoring Processes, Materials, and Surroundings; Inspecting Equipment, Structures, Materials; Getting Information Needed to Do the Job. *Mental Process*—Updating and Using Job-Relevant Knowledge; Making Decisions and Solving Problems; Evaluating Information Against Standards; Analyzing Data or Information. *Work Output*—Operating Vehicles or Equipment; Repairing and Maintaining Mechanical Equipment; Performing General Physical Activities; Handling and Moving Objects. *Interacting with Others*—Performing for or Working with the Public; Communicating with Persons Outside Organization; Communicating with Other Workers; Establishing and Maintaining Relationships. **Physical Work Conditions:** Outdoors; Common Protective or Safety Attire; Using Hands on Objects, Tools, or Controls. **Other Job Characteristics:** Consequence of Error; Importance of Being Sure All Is Done; Frustrating Circumstances.

Experience: Job Zone 2. Some previous work-related skill, knowledge, or experience may be helpful, but usually is not needed. **Job Preparation:** SVP 4.00 to 5.99—6 months to less than 2 years. **Knowledge:** Mechanical; Transportation; Public Safety and Security; Geography; Engineering and Technology. **Instructional Program:** 490399 Water Transportation Workers, Other.

Related DOT Jobs: 911.663-010 Motorboat Operator; 919.683-010 Dock Hand.

53-5031.00 Ship Engineers (Ship Engineers)

Education: Work experience in a related occupation

Employed: 6,236

Openings: 1,219

Projected Growth: 4.3%

Earnings: $40,150

Supervise and coordinate activities of crew engaged in operating and maintaining engines, boilers, deck machinery, and electrical, sanitary, and refrigeration equipment aboard ship.

Inspects engines and other equipment. Repairs machinery, using hand tools and power tools. Maintains engineering log and bellbook (orders of changes in speed and direction of ship). Stands engine-room watch, observing that lubricants and water levels are maintained in machinery and that load on generators is within limits. Orders crew to repair or replace defective parts of engines and other equipment. Starts engines to propel ship; regulates engines and power transmission to control speed of ship.

GOE Number, Interest Area, and Work Group: 08.06.01; Industrial Production; Systems Operation: Utilities and Power Plant. **Personality Type:** Realistic. Realistic occupations frequently involve work activities that include practical, hands-on problems and solutions. These occupations often deal with plants, animals, and real-world materials like wood, tools, and machinery. Many of the occupations require working outside and do not involve a lot of paperwork or working closely with others. **Work Values:** Authority; Responsibility; Compensation; Autonomy; Ability Utilization; Company Policies and Practices. **Skills:** Operation and Control; Operation Monitoring; Coordination; Repairing; Equipment Maintenance. **Abilities:** *Cognitive*—Problem Sensitivity; Oral Expression; Written Comprehension; Written Expression; Information Ordering; Oral Comprehension. *Psychomotor*—Control Precision; Multilimb Coordination; Reaction Time. *Physical*—Extent Flexibility; Explosive Strength; Trunk Strength; Gross Body

Coordination. *Sensory*—Auditory Attention; Glare Sensitivity; Hearing Sensitivity. **General Work Activities:** *Information Input*—Inspecting Equipment, Structures, Materials; Getting Information Needed to Do the Job; Monitoring Processes, Materials, and Surroundings. *Mental Process*—Making Decisions and Solving Problems; Evaluating Information Against Standards; Analyzing Data or Information. *Work Output*—Controlling Machines and Processes; Performing General Physical Activities; Handling and Moving Objects; Repairing and Maintaining Mechanical Equipment. *Interacting with Others*—Coordinating Work and Activities of Others; Communicating with Other Workers; Establishing and Maintaining Relationships; Developing and Building Teams. **Physical Work Conditions:** Indoors; Standing; Using Hands on Objects, Tools, or Controls. **Other Job Characteristics:** Consequence of Error; Importance of Being Exact or Accurate; Importance of Being Aware of New Events.

Experience: Job Zone 5. Extensive skill, knowledge, and experience are needed. Very advanced communication and organizational skills are required. **Job Preparation:** SVP 8.0 and above—4 years to more than 10 years. **Knowledge:** Mechanical; Transportation; Engineering and Technology; Public Safety and Security; Administration and Management. **Instructional Programs:** 490306 Marine Maintenance and Ship Repairer; 490309 Marine Science/Merchant Marine Officer.

Related DOT Job: 197.130-010 Engineer.

53-6000 Other Transportation Workers

53-6011.00 Bridge and Lock Tenders (Bridge, Lock, and Lighthouse Tenders)

Education: No data available.

Employed: 3,810

Openings: No data available.

Projected Growth: No data available.

Earnings: $30,300

Operate and tend bridges, canal locks, and lighthouses to permit marine passage on inland waterways, near shores, and at danger points in waterway passages. Supervise such operations. Includes drawbridge operators, lock tenders and operators, and slip bridge operators.

Writes and submits maintenance work requisitions. Turns valves to increase or decrease water level in lock. Records names, type, and destinations of vessels passing through bridge opening or locks. Records number of trains or vehicles crossing bridge. Cleans, oils, greases, and makes minor repairs and adjustments to equipment. Prepares accident reports. Logs data such as water levels and weather conditions. Inspects bridge, and inspects bridge or canal auxiliary equipment. Attaches rope or cable lines to bitt on lock deck or wharf to secure vessel. Observes positions of vessels, to ensure optimum utilization of lock space or bridge opening space. Signals vessels to proceed. Observes approaching vessels to determine size and speed; listens for whistle signal indicating desire to pass. Operates gas, steam, and hydroelectric generating units, to control mechanisms to open locks or bridge. Controls machinery to open and close canal locks and dams, railroad or highway drawbridges, or horizontally or vertically adjustable bridges. Moves levers to activate traffic signals, navigation lights, and alarms. Relays messages to vessels in waterway.

GOE Number, Interest Area, and Work Group: 05.03.01; Mechanics, Installers, and Repairers; Mechanical Work: Vehicles and Facilities. **Personality Type:** Realistic. Realistic occupations frequently involve work activities that include practical, hands-on problems and solutions. These occupations often deal with plants, animals, and real-world materials like wood, tools, and machinery. Many of the occupations require working outside and do not involve a lot of paperwork or working closely with others. **Work Values:** Moral Values; Independence; Security; Supervision, Human Relations; Autonomy. **Skills:** Repairing; Equipment Maintenance; Operation and Control; Installation; Troubleshooting. **Abilities:** *Cognitive*—Written Expression; Spatial Orientation; Selective Attention; Oral Expression; Problem Sensitivity; Oral Comprehension. *Psychomotor*—Reaction Time; Control Precision; Manual Dexterity. *Physical*—Extent Flexibility; Static Strength; Trunk Strength. *Sensory*—Far Vision; Depth Perception; Night Vision. **General Work Activities:** *Information Input*—Monitoring Processes, Materials, and Surroundings; Getting Information Needed to Do the Job; Inspecting Equipment, Structures, Materials. *Mental Process*—Making Decisions and Solving Problems; Processing Information; Analyzing Data or Information. *Work Output*—Controlling Machines and Processes; Repairing and Maintaining Mechanical Equipment; Repairing and Maintaining Electrical Equipment. *Interacting with Others*—Communicating with Persons Outside Organization; Assisting and Caring for Others; Performing for or Working with the Public; Performing Administrative Activities; Communicating with Other Workers. **Physical Work Conditions:** Using Hands on Objects, Tools, or Controls; Hazardous Equipment; Outdoors; Indoors. **Other Job Characteristics:** Consequence of Error; Degree of Automation; Importance of Being Aware of New Events.

Experience: Job Zone 2. Some previous work-related skill, knowledge, or experience may be helpful, but usually is not needed. **Job Preparation:** SVP 4.00 to 5.99—6 months to less than 2 years. **Knowledge:** Mechanical; Transportation; Clerical; Mathematics; English Language; Engineering and Technology. **Instructional Program:** 470302 Heavy Equipment Maintenance and Repairer.

Related DOT Jobs: 371.362-010 Drawbridge Operator; 911.131-014 Lock Tender, Chief Operator; 911.362-010 Lock Operator; 919.682-010 Bridge Operator, Slip.

53-6021.00 Parking Lot Attendants (Parking Lot Attendants)

Education: Short-term O-T-J training
Employed: 86,006
Openings: 17,725
Projected Growth: 31.2%
Earnings: $13,930

Park automobiles or issue tickets for customers in a parking lot or garage. Collect fee.

Takes numbered tag from customer, locates car, and delivers it to customel; directs customer to parked car. Keeps new car lot in order and maximizes use of space. Services cars in storage, to protect tires, battery, and finish against deterioration. Inspects vehicles to detect damage. Services vehicles with gas, oil, and water. Lifts, positions, and removes barricades to open or close parking areas. Parks automobiles in parking lot, storage garage, or new car lot. Collects parking fee from customer, based on charges for time automobile is parked. Patrols area to prevent thefts of parked automobiles or of items in automobiles. Places numbered tag on windshield of automobile to be parked; hands customer similar tag to be used in locating parked automobile. Signals or directs vehicle drivers to parking area, with hands or flashlight.

GOE Number, Interest Area, and Work Group: 07.07.01; Transportation; Other Services Requiring Driving. **Personality Type:** Realistic. Realistic occupations frequently involve work activities that include practical, hands-on problems and solutions. These occupations often deal with plants, animals, and real-world materials like wood, tools, and machinery. Many of the occupations require working outside and do not involve a lot of paperwork or working closely with others. **Work Values:** Moral Values; Independence; Social Service; Security; Supervision, Human Relations. **Skills:** Writing; Product Inspection; Problem Identification; Social Perceptiveness; Service Orientation. **Abilities:** *Cognitive*—Oral Expression; Oral Comprehension; Written Comprehension; Information Ordering; Spatial Orientation; Problem Sensitivity. *Psychomotor*—Control Precision. *Physical*—none met the criteria. **General Work Activities:** *Information Input*—Monitoring Processes, Materials, and Surroundings; Identifying Objects, Actions, and Events; Inspecting Equipment, Structures, Materials. *Mental Process*—Processing Information; Judging Qualities of Things, Services, Other People's Work; Organizing, Planning, and Prioritizing; Making Decisions and Solving Problems. *Work Output*—Operating Vehicles or Equipment; Performing General Physical Activities; Handling and Moving Objects. *Interacting with Others*—Performing for or Working with the Public; Communicating with Persons Outside Organization; Assisting and Caring for Others. **Physical Work Conditions:** Outdoors; Standing; Special Uniform. **Other Job Characteristics:** Consequence of Error; Importance of Being Sure All Is Done; Importance of Being Exact or Accurate.

Experience: Job Zone 1. No previous work-related skill, knowledge, or experience is needed. **Job Preparation:** SVP Below 4.0—Less than 6 months. **Knowledge:** Customer and Personal Service; Mathematics; Public Safety and Security; Mechanical; Clerical. **Instructional Program:** 129999 Personal and Miscellaneous Services, Other.

Related DOT Jobs: 915.473-010 Parking-Lot Attendant; 915.583-010 Lot Attendant; 915.667-014 Parking Lot Signaler.

53-6031.00 Service Station Attendants (Service Station Attendants)

Education: Short-term O-T-J training
Employed: 140,679
Openings: 40,321
Projected Growth: –1.2%
Earnings: $14,310

Service automobiles, buses, trucks, boats, and other automotive or marine vehicles, using fuel, lubricants, and accessories. Collect payment for services and supplies. Lubricate vehicle, change motor oil, install antifreeze, or replace lights or other accessories such as windshield wiper blades or fan belts. Repair or replace tires.

Adjusts brakes, replaces spark plugs, and makes other minor repairs. Sells accessories and services such as batteries, tires, lubrication services, and safety inspections. Cleans parking area, offices, and equipment; removes trash. Maintains customer records; follows up periodically, with telephone, mail, or personal reminders of service due. Assists in arranging merchandise displays and taking inventories. Cleans windshield or washes and waxes vehicle. Changes, tests, and repairs or replaces tires. Fills, or allows customer to fill, fuel tank of vehicle with gasoline or diesel fuel, to specified level. Greases and lubricates vehicles or specified units such as springs, universal joints, and steering knuckles, using grease gun or spray lubricant. Prepares daily report of fuel, oil, and accessories sold in service station. Collects cash from customer and makes change; charges purchases to customer's credit card. Installs accessories such as air or oil filter, battery, windshield wiper blades, fan belt, or lights. Checks air pressure in tires, levels of fuel, motor oil, and other fluids; adds air, oil, water, and required fluids.

GOE Number, Interest Area, and Work Group: 10.03.01; Sales and Marketing; General Sales. **Personality Type:** Realistic. Realistic occupations frequently involve work activities that include practical, hands-on problems and solutions. These occupations often deal with plants, animals, and real-world materials like wood, tools, and machinery. Many of the occupations require working outside and do not involve a lot of paperwork or working closely with others. **Work Values:** Moral Values; Social Service; Supervision, Human Relations; Coworkers; Security. **Skills:** Repairing; Problem Identification; Speaking; Product Inspection; Operation and Control. **Abilities:** *Cognitive*—Number Facility; Oral Comprehension; Problem Sensitivity; Oral Expression; Mathematical Reasoning; Information Ordering. *Psychomotor*—Reaction Time; Wrist-Finger Speed; Multilimb Coordination; Manual Dexterity. *Physical*—Extent Flexibility; Static Strength; Trunk Strength. *Sensory*—Hearing Sensitivity; Auditory Attention; Sound Localization. **General Work Activities:** *Information Input*—Inspecting Equipment, Structures, Materials; Monitoring Processes, Materials, and Surroundings; Getting Information Needed to Do the Job. *Mental Process*—Evaluating Information Against Standards; Processing Information; Judging Qualities of Things, Services, Other People's Work; Analyzing Data or Information. *Work Output*—Handling and Moving Objects; Repairing and Maintaining Mechanical Equipment; Performing General Physical Activities. *Interacting with Others*—Communicating with Persons Outside Organization; Performing for or Working with the Public; Assisting and Caring for Others; Establishing and Maintaining Relationships. **Physical Work Conditions:** Contaminants; Outdoors; Using Hands on Objects, Tools, or Controls; Hazardous Conditions; Standing. **Other Job Characteristics:** Consequence of Error; Importance of Being Sure All Is Done; Frustrating Circumstances; Importance of Being Exact or Accurate.

Experience: Job Zone 1. No previous work-related skill, knowledge, or experience is needed. **Job Preparation:** SVP Below 4.0—

Less than 6 months. **Knowledge:** Customer and Personal Service; Sales and Marketing; Mechanical; Mathematics; Clerical. **Instructional Programs:** 081209 Petroleum Products Retailing Operations; 480506 Sheet Metal Worker.

Related DOT Jobs: 915.467-010 Automobile-Service-Station Attendant; 915.477-010 Automobile-Self-Serve-Service-Station Attendant; 915.587-010 Gas-and-Oil Servicer; 915.687-014 Garage Servicer, Industrial; 915.687-018 Lubrication Servicer; 915.687-030 Taxi Servicer.

53-6041.00 Traffic Technicians (Traffic Technicians)

Education: No data available.

Employed: 6,790

Openings: No data available.

Projected Growth: No data available.

Earnings: $34,290

Conduct field studies to determine traffic volume, speed, effectiveness of signals, adequacy of lighting, and other factors influencing traffic conditions, under direction of traffic engineer.

Recommends changes in traffic control devices and regulations, on basis of findings. Conducts statistical studies of traffic conditions. Times stoplight or other delays, using stopwatch. Determines average speed of vehicles, using electrical timing devices or radar equipment. Analyzes traffic volume and interviews motorists at intersections or areas where congestion exists or disproportionate number of accidents have occurred. Prepares drawings of proposed signal installations or other control devices, using drafting instruments. Computes mathematical factors for adjusting timing of traffic signals, speed restrictions, and related data, using standard formulas. Observes factors affecting traffic conditions, such as lighting, visibility of signs and pavement markings, traffic signals, and width of street. Draws graphs, charts, diagrams, and similar aids to illustrate observations and conclusions.

GOE Number, Interest Area, and Work Group: 07.02.01; Transportation; Vehicle Expediting and Coordinating. **Personality Type:** Realistic. Realistic occupations frequently involve work activities that include practical, hands-on problems and solutions. These occupations often deal with plants, animals, and real-world materials like wood, tools, and machinery. Many of the occupations require working outside and do not involve a lot of paperwork or working closely with others. **Work Values:** Moral Values; Independence; Company Policies and Practices; Supervision, Human Relations; Security. **Skills:** Information Gathering; Mathematics; Problem Identification; Critical Thinking; Writing. **Abilities:** *Cognitive*—Number Facility; Mathematical Reasoning; Inductive Reasoning; Deductive Reasoning; Written Expression; Fluency of Ideas. *Psychomotor*—Reaction Time; Finger Dexterity; Multilimb Coordination. *Physical*—Gross Body Coordination; Dynamic Flexibility; Gross Body Equilibrium. *Sensory*—Far Vision; Speech Clarity; Glare Sensitivity. **General Work Activities:** *Information Input*—Getting Information Needed to Do the Job; Monitoring Processes, Materials, and Surroundings; Identifying Objects, Actions, and Events. *Mental Process*—Analyzing Data or Information; Processing Information; Making Decisions and Solving Problems. *Work Output*—Drafting and Specifying Technical Devices; Documenting and Recording Information; Implementing Ideas and Programs. *Interacting with Others*—Communicating with Other Workers; Providing Consultation and Advice to Others; Interpreting Meaning of Information to Others; Communicating with Persons Outside Organization. **Physical Work Conditions:** Standing; Indoors; Using Hands on Objects, Tools, or Controls. **Other Job Characteristics:** Importance of Being Exact or Accurate; Consequence of Error; Importance of Being Sure All Is Done.

Experience: Job Zone 4. A minimum of two to four years of work-related skill, knowledge, or experience is needed. **Job Preparation:** SVP 7.0 to less than 8.0—2 years to less than 10 years. **Knowledge:** Mathematics; Transportation; Engineering and Technology; Design; Public Safety and Security. **Instructional Program:** 150201 Civil Engineering/Civil Technology/Technician.

Related DOT Job: 199.267-030 Traffic Technician.

53-6051.00 Transportation Inspectors (Transportation Inspectors)

Education: No data available.

Employed: 19,930

Openings: No data available.

Projected Growth: No data available.

Earnings: $39,560

Inspect equipment or goods in connection with the safe transport of cargo or people. Includes rail transport inspectors such as freight inspectors, car inspectors, rail inspectors, and other nonprecision inspectors of other types of transportation vehicles.

GOE Number, Interest Area, and Work Group: 07.08.01; Transportation; Support Work in Transportation. **Instructional Program:** 470302 Heavy Equipment Maintenance and Repairer. **Note:** The Department of Labor has not collected some data for this job, so it has fewer details than the other descriptions.

53-6051.01 Aviation Inspectors (Inspectors and Compliance Officers)

Education: Work experience in a related occupation

Employed: 176,175

Openings: 19,910

Projected Growth: 10.5%

Earnings: $36,820

Inspect aircraft, maintenance procedures, air navigational aids, air traffic controls, and communications equipment to ensure conformance with federal safety regulations.

Conducts flight test program to test equipment, instruments, and systems under various conditions, including adverse weather, using both manual and automatic controls. Investigates air accidents to determine cause. Approves or disapproves issuance of certificate of airworthiness. Prepares reports to document flight activities and inspection findings. Analyzes training program; conducts examinations to ensure competency of persons operating, installing, and repairing equipment. Starts aircraft; observes gauges, meters, and other instruments to detect evidence of malfunction. Examines access plates and doors for security. Examines maintenance record and flight log to determine if service and maintenance checks and overhauls were performed at prescribed intervals. Inspects aircraft and components to identify damage or defects and to determine structural and mechanical airworthiness, using hand tools and test instruments. Recommends purchase, repair, or modification of equipment. Schedules and coordinates inflight testing program with ground crews and air traffic control, to ensure ground tracking, equipment monitoring, and related services.

GOE Number, Interest Area, and Work Group: 04.04.02; Law, Law Enforcement, and Public Safety; Public Safety: Regulations Enforcement. **Personality Type:** Realistic. Realistic occupations frequently involve work activities that include practical, hands-on problems and solutions. These occupations often deal with plants, animals, and real-world materials like wood, tools, and machinery. Many of the occupations require working outside and do not involve a lot of paperwork or working closely with others. **Work Values:** Supervision, Human Relations; Responsibility; Company Policies and Practices; Security; Compensation; Autonomy; Supervision, Technical. **Skills:** Reading Comprehension; Product Inspection; Writing; Information Gathering; Operation Monitoring; Testing; Critical Thinking; Problem Identification. **Abilities:** *Cognitive*—Problem Sensitivity; Written Expression; Information Ordering; Written Comprehension; Oral Expression. *Psychomotor*—Control Precision; Response Orientation; Reaction Time; Manual Dexterity. *Physical*—Extent Flexibility; Trunk Strength; Gross Body Coordination. *Sensory*—Near Vision; Far Vision; Speech Clarity. **General Work Activities:** *Information Input*—Inspecting Equipment, Structures, Materials; Getting Information Needed to Do the Job; Monitoring Processes, Materials, and Surroundings. *Mental Process*—Updating and Using Job-Relevant Knowledge; Evaluating Information Against Standards; Making Decisions and Solving Problems. *Work Output*—Documenting and Recording Information; Handling and Moving Objects; Implementing Ideas and Programs. *Interacting with Others*—Communicating with Other Workers; Coordinating Work and Activities of Others; Interpreting Meaning of Information to Others; Providing Consultation and Advice to Others. **Physical Work Conditions:** Standing; Using Hands on Objects, Tools, or Controls; Distracting Sounds and Noise Levels; Outdoors; Indoors. **Other Job Characteristics:** Consequence of Error; Importance of Being Sure All Is Done; Importance of Being Exact or Accurate.

Experience: Job Zone 4. A minimum of two to four years of work-related skill, knowledge, or experience is needed. **Job Preparation:** SVP 7.0 to less than 8.0—2 years to less than 10 years. **Knowledge:** Engineering and Technology; Public Safety and Security; Mechanical; English Language; Law, Government and Jurisprudence. **Instructional Programs:** 030203 Natural Resources Law Enforcement and Protective Services; 150701 Occupational Safety and Health Technology/Technician; 521601 Taxation.

Related DOT Jobs: 168.264-010 Inspector, Air-Carrier; 196.163-014 Supervising Airplane Pilot.

53-6051.02 Public Transportation Inspectors
(Inspectors and Compliance Officers)

Education: Work experience in a related occupation

Employed: 176,175

Openings: 19,910

Projected Growth: 10.5%

Earnings: $36,820

Monitor operation of public transportation systems to ensure good service and compliance with regulations. Investigate accidents, equipment failures, and complaints.

Inspects company vehicles and other property for evidence of abuse, damage, and mechanical malfunction; directs repair. Recommends promotions and disciplinary actions involving transportation personnel. Assists in dispatching equipment when necessary. Reports disruptions to service. Submits written reports to management with recommendations for improving service. Determines need for changes in service, such as additional vehicles, route changes, and revised schedules, to improve service and efficiency. Investigates schedule delays, accidents, and complaints. Observes and records time required to load and unload passengers or freight volume of traffic on vehicle and at stops. Observes employees performing assigned duties, to note their deportment, treatment of passengers, and adherence to company regulations and schedules. Drives automobile along route to detect conditions hazardous to equipment and passengers; negotiates with local governments to eliminate hazards.

GOE Number, Interest Area, and Work Group: 04.04.02; Law, Law Enforcement, and Public Safety; Public Safety: Regulations Enforcement. **Personality Type:** Enterprising. Enterprising occupations frequently involve starting up and carrying out projects. These occupations can involve leading people and making many decisions. They sometimes require risk taking and often deal with business. **Work Values:** Supervision, Human Relations; Security; Company Policies and Practices; Responsibility; Independence; Moral Values; Autonomy. **Skills:** Writing; Monitoring; Reading Comprehension; Speaking; Product Inspection; Operations Analysis. **Abilities:** *Cognitive*—Oral Expression; Problem Sensitivity; Written Expression; Oral Comprehension; Inductive Reasoning; Deductive Reasoning. *Psychomotor*—Response Orientation; Rate Control. *Physical*—none met the criteria. *Sensory*—Far Vision; Hearing Sensitivity. **General Work Activities:** *Information Input*—Getting Information Needed to Do the Job; Inspecting Equipment, Structures, Materials; Monitoring Processes, Materials, and Surroundings. *Mental Process*—Evaluating Information Against Standards; Processing Information; Analyzing Data or Information. *Work Output*—Documenting and Recording Information; Operating Vehicles or Equipment; Handling and Moving Objects; Repairing and Maintaining Mechanical Equipment. *Interacting with Others*—Communicating with Other Workers; Performing Administrative Activities; Providing Consultation and Advice to Others; Communicating with Persons Outside Organization; Interpreting Meaning of Information to Others; Monitoring and Controlling Resources. **Physical Work Conditions:** Sitting; Outdoors; Indoors. **Other Job Characteristics:** Importance of Being Sure All Is Done; Consequence of Error; Importance of Being Exact or Accurate.

Experience: Job Zone 4. A minimum of two to four years of work-related skill, knowledge, or experience is needed. **Job Preparation:** SVP 7.0 to less than 8.0—2 years to less than 10 years. **Knowledge:** Transportation; Public Safety and Security; Mathematics; English Language; Law, Government and Jurisprudence; Administration and Management. **Instructional Programs:** 030203 Natural Resources Law Enforcement and Protective Services; 150701 Occupational Safety and Health Technology/Technician; 521601 Taxation.

Related DOT Jobs: 168.167-082 Transportation Inspector; 184.163-010 Traffic Inspector.

53-6051.03 Marine Cargo Inspectors (Inspectors and Compliance Officers)

Education: Work experience in a related occupation

Employed: 176,175

Openings: 19,910

Projected Growth: 10.5%

Earnings: $36,820

Inspect cargoes of seagoing vessels to certify compliance with health and safety regulations in cargo handling and stowage.

Writes certificates of admeasurement; lists details such as design, length, depth, and breadth of vessel, and method of propulsion. Advises crew in techniques of stowing dangerous and heavy cargo, according to knowledge of hazardous cargo. Analyzes data, formulates recommendations, and writes reports of findings. Times roll of ship, using stopwatch. Examines blueprints of ship; takes physical measurements to determine capacity and depth of vessel in water, using measuring instruments. Determines type of license and safety equipment required, and computes applicable tolls and wharfage fees. Calculates gross and net tonnage, hold capacities, volume of stored fuel and water, cargo weight, and ship stability factors, using mathematical formulas. Reads vessel documents to ascertain cargo capabilities according to design and cargo regulations. Inspects loaded cargo in holds and cargo-handling devices, to determine compliance with regulations and need for maintenance. Issues certificate of compliance when no violations are detected; recommends remedial procedures to correct deficiencies.

GOE Number, Interest Area, and Work Group: 04.04.02; Law, Law Enforcement, and Public Safety; Public Safety: Regulations Enforcement. **Personality Type:** Conventional. Conventional occupations frequently involve following set procedures and routines. These occupations can include working with data and details more than with ideas. Usually there is a clear line of authority to follow. **Work Values:** Responsibility; Autonomy; Independence; Security; Moral Values. **Skills:** Mathematics; Reading Comprehension; Information Gathering; Writing; Active Listening. **Abilities:** *Cognitive*—Problem Sensitivity; Written Comprehension; Number Facility; Oral Expression; Written Expression; Deductive Reasoning. *Psychomotor*—Multilimb Coordination. *Physical*—Extent Flexibility; Trunk Strength; Gross Body Coordination. *Sensory*—Near Vision; Far Vision; Visual Color Discrimination; Depth Perception. **General Work Activities:** *Information Input*—Inspecting

Equipment, Structures, Materials; Getting Information Needed to Do the Job; Identifying Objects, Actions, and Events. *Mental Process*—Making Decisions and Solving Problems; Processing Information; Evaluating Information Against Standards. *Work Output*—Documenting and Recording Information; Implementing Ideas and Programs; Handling and Moving Objects. *Interacting with Others*—Interpreting Meaning of Information to Others; Communicating with Other Workers; Communicating with Persons Outside Organization. **Physical Work Conditions:** Outdoors; Standing; Using Hands on Objects, Tools, or Controls; Walking or Running. **Other Job Characteristics:** Consequence of Error; Importance of Being Sure All Is Done; Importance of Being Exact or Accurate.

Experience: Job Zone 5. Extensive skill, knowledge, and experience are needed. Very advanced communication and organizational skills are required. **Job Preparation:** SVP 8.0 and above—4 years to more than 10 years. **Knowledge:** Mathematics; Public Safety and Security; English Language; Transportation; Design. **Instructional Programs:** 030203 Natural Resources Law Enforcement and Protective Services; 150701 Occupational Safety and Health Technology/Technician; 521601 Taxation.

Related DOT Jobs: 168.267-094 Marine-Cargo Surveyor; 169.284-010 Admeasurer.

53-6051.04 Railroad Inspectors (Transportation Inspectors)

Education: No data available.

Employed: 19,930

Openings: No data available.

Projected Growth: No data available.

Earnings: $39,560

Inspect railroad equipment, roadbed, and track to ensure safe transport of people or cargo.

Places lanterns or flags in front and rear of train to signal that inspection is being performed. Packs brake bearings with grease. Makes minor repairs. Notifies train dispatcher of railcar to be moved to shop for repair. Seals leaks found during inspection that can be sealed with caulking compound. Directs crews to repair or replace defective equipment or to reballast roadbed. Fills paint container on rail-detector car used to mark section of defective rail with paint. Tags rail cars needing immediate repair. Starts machine and signals worker to operate rail-detector car. Tests and synchronizes rail-flaw detection machine, using circuit tester and hand tools; reloads machine with paper and ink. Inspects signals and track wiring to determine continuity of electrical connections. Operates switches to determine working conditions. Inspects and tests completed work. Examines locomotives and cars to detect damage or structural defects. Examines roadbed, switches, fishplates, rails, and ties to detect damage or wear. Prepares reports on repairs made and on equipment, railcars, or roadbed needing repairs. Replaces defective brake rod pins; tightens safety appliances.

GOE Number, Interest Area, and Work Group: 05.03.01; Mechanics, Installers, and Repairers; Mechanical Work: Vehicles and Facilities. **Personality Type:** Realistic. Realistic occupations frequently involve work activities that include practical, hands-on problems and solutions. These occupations often deal with plants, animals, and real-world materials like wood, tools, and machinery. Many of the occupations require working outside and do not involve a lot of paperwork or working closely with others. **Work Values:** Moral Values; Responsibility; Security; Activity; Supervision, Human Relations; Coworkers; Company Policies and Practices; Autonomy. **Skills:** Problem Identification; Troubleshooting; Writing; Testing; Operation Monitoring; Repairing; Product Inspection. **Abilities:** *Cognitive*—Problem Sensitivity; Oral Expression; Written Expression; Deductive Reasoning; Oral Comprehension; Inductive Reasoning. *Psychomotor*—Control Precision; Arm-Hand Steadiness; Manual Dexterity. *Physical*—Extent Flexibility; Static Strength; Gross Body Coordination; Trunk Strength. *Sensory*—Near Vision; Far Vision; Hearing Sensitivity; Speech Clarity. **General Work Activities:** *Information Input*—Inspecting Equipment, Structures, Materials; Monitoring Processes, Materials, and Surroundings; Getting Information Needed to Do the Job; Identifying Objects, Actions, and Events. *Mental Process*—Judging Qualities of Things, Services, Other People's Work; Evaluating Information Against Standards; Making Decisions and Solving Problems. *Work Output*—Repairing and Maintaining Mechanical Equipment; Performing General Physical Activities; Handling and Moving Objects. *Interacting with Others*—Coordinating Work and Activities of Others; Communicating with Other Workers; Providing Consultation and Advice to Others. **Physical Work Conditions:** Outdoors; Standing; Using Hands on Objects, Tools, or Controls. **Other Job Characteristics:** Consequence of Error; Importance of Being Exact or Accurate; Importance of Being Sure All Is Done.

Experience: Job Zone 2. Some previous work-related skill, knowledge, or experience may be helpful, but usually is not needed. **Job Preparation:** SVP 4.00 to 5.99—6 months to less than 2 years. **Knowledge:** Transportation; Public Safety and Security; Mechanical; Building and Construction; Engineering and Technology. **Instructional Program:** 470302 Heavy Equipment Maintenance and Repairer.

Related DOT Jobs: 168.287-018 Inspector, Railroad; 910.263-010 Rail-Flaw-Detector Operator; 910.367-030 Way Inspector; 910.384-010 Tank-Car Inspector; 910.387-014 Railroad-Car Inspector; 910.667-010 Car Inspector.

53-6051.05 Motor Vehicle Inspectors (Transportation Inspectors)

Education: No data available.

Employed: 19,930

Openings: No data available.

Projected Growth: No data available.

Earnings: $39,560

Inspect automotive vehicles to ensure compliance with governmental regulations and safety standards.

Examines vehicles for damage, and drives vehicle to detect malfunctions. Services vehicles with fuel and water. Notifies authorities of owners having illegal equipment installed on vehicle. Positions trailer and drives car onto truck trailer. Prepares and keeps record of vehicles delivered. Prepares report on each vehicle for follow-up action by owner or police. Tests vehicle components for wear, damage, or improper adjustment, using mechanical or electrical devices. Inspects truck accessories, air lines, and electric circuits; reports needed repairs. Applies inspection sticker to vehicles that pass inspection; applies rejection sticker to vehicles that fail.

GOE Number, Interest Area, and Work Group: 08.02.03; Industrial Production; Production Technology: Inspection. **Personality Type:** Realistic. Realistic occupations frequently involve work activities that include practical, hands-on problems and solutions. These occupations often deal with plants, animals, and real-world materials like wood, tools, and machinery. Many of the occupations require working outside and do not involve a lot of paperwork or working closely with others. **Work Values:** Responsibility; Moral Values; Security; Independence; Company Policies and Practices; Activity; Autonomy. **Skills:** Product Inspection; Problem Identification; Troubleshooting; Identification of Key Causes; Science. **Abilities:** *Cognitive*—Problem Sensitivity; Oral Expression; Written Expression; Information Ordering; Flexibility of Closure. *Psychomotor*—Control Precision; Manual Dexterity; Multilimb Coordination. *Physical*—Extent Flexibility; Static Strength; Trunk Strength; Gross Body Coordination. *Sensory*—Hearing Sensitivity; Visual Color Discrimination; Sound Localization. **General Work Activities:** *Information Input*—Inspecting Equipment, Structures, Materials; Getting Information Needed to Do the Job; Identifying Objects, Actions, and Events. *Mental Process*—Evaluating Information Against Standards; Judging Qualities of Things, Services, Other People's Work; Making Decisions and Solving Problems. *Work Output*—Operating Vehicles or Equipment; Documenting and Recording Information; Repairing and Maintaining Mechanical Equipment; Performing General Physical Activities; Handling and Moving Objects. *Interacting with Others*—Communicating with Persons Outside Organization; Performing Administrative Activities; Communicating with Other Workers; Performing for or Working with the Public. **Physical Work Conditions:** Standing; Using Hands on Objects, Tools, or Controls; Outdoors. **Other Job Characteristics:** Importance of Being Exact or Accurate; Consequence of Error; Importance of Being Sure All Is Done.

Experience: Job Zone 2. Some previous work-related skill, knowledge, or experience may be helpful, but usually is not needed. **Job Preparation:** SVP 4.00 to 5.99—6 months to less than 2 years. **Knowledge:** Public Safety and Security; Mechanical; English Language; Transportation; Computers and Electronics. **Instructional Program:** 470302 Heavy Equipment Maintenance and Repairer.

Related DOT Jobs: 168.267-058 Inspector, Motor Vehicles; 379.364-010 Automobile Tester; 919.363-010 New-Car Inspector; 919.687-018 Safety Inspector, Truck.

53-6051.06 Freight Inspectors (Transportation Inspectors)

Education: No data available.
Employed: 19,930
Openings: No data available.
Projected Growth: No data available.
Earnings: $39,560

Inspect freight for proper storage according to specifications.

Measures height and width of loads that will pass over bridges or through tunnels. Prepares and submits report after trip. Posts warning signs on vehicles containing explosives or inflammatory or radioactive materials. Notifies workers of special treatment required for shipments. Monitors temperature and humidity of freight storage area. Observes loading of freight to ensure that crews comply with procedures. Inspects shipment to ascertain that freight is securely braced and blocked. Records freight condition and handling; notifies crews to reload freight or insert additional bracing or packing.

GOE Number, Interest Area, and Work Group: 07.08.01; Transportation; Support Work in Transportation. **Personality Type:** Conventional. Conventional occupations frequently involve following set procedures and routines. These occupations can include working with data and details more than with ideas. Usually there is a clear line of authority to follow. **Work Values:** Moral Values; Supervision, Technical; Company Policies and Practices; Security; Supervision, Human Relations; Activity. **Skills:** Writing; Reading Comprehension; Product Inspection; Mathematics; Monitoring; Problem Identification; Active Listening. **Abilities:** *Cognitive*—Oral Expression; Problem Sensitivity; Written Expression; Information Ordering; Written Comprehension. *Psychomotor*—none met the criteria. *Physical*—Extent Flexibility; Trunk Strength; Gross Body Coordination; Stamina. *Sensory*—Far Vision; Speech Clarity; Speech Recognition. **General Work Activities:** *Information Input*—Getting Information Needed to Do the Job; Inspecting Equipment, Structures, Materials; Monitoring Processes, Materials, and Surroundings. *Mental Process*—Evaluating Information Against Standards; Judging Qualities of Things, Services, Other People's Work; Making Decisions and Solving Problems. *Work Output*—Documenting and Recording Information; Performing General Physical Activities; Handling and Moving Objects. *Interacting with Others*—Coordinating Work and Activities of Others; Performing Administrative Activities; Communicating with Other Workers. **Physical Work Conditions:** Standing; Outdoors; Using Hands on Objects, Tools, or Controls. **Other Job Characteristics:** Consequence of Error; Importance of Being Exact or Accurate; Importance of Being Sure All Is Done.

Experience: Job Zone 2. Some previous work-related skill, knowledge, or experience may be helpful, but usually is not needed. **Job Preparation:** SVP 4.00 to 5.99—6 months to less than 2 years. **Knowledge:** Transportation; English Language; Public Safety and Security; Production and Processing; Mathematics; Clerical. **Instructional Program:** 470302 Heavy Equipment Maintenance and Repairer.

Related DOT Jobs: 910.387-010 Perishable-Fruit Inspector; 910.667-018 Loading Inspector; 910.667-022 Perishable-Freight Inspector.

53-7000 Material Moving Workers

53-7011.00 Conveyor Operators and Tenders
(Conveyor Operators and Tenders)

Education: No data available.

Employed: 35,320

Openings: No data available.

Projected Growth: No data available.

Earnings: $21,800

Control or tend conveyors or conveyor systems that move materials or products to and from stockpiles, processing stations, departments, or vehicles. Control speed and routing of materials or products.

Repairs or replaces equipment components or parts such as blades, rolls, and pumps. Manipulates controls, levers, and valves, to start pumps, auxiliary equipment, or conveyors, and to adjust equipment positions, speed, timing, and material flow. Observes conveyor operations and monitors lights, dials, and gauges, to maintain specified operating levels and detect equipment malfunctions. Stops equipment or machinery and clears jams, using poles, bars, and hand tools, or removes damaged materials from conveyors. Signals workers in other departments to move materials, products, or machinery, or notifies work stations of shipments enroute and estimated delivery times. Moves, assembles, and connects hoses or nozzles to material hoppers, storage tanks, conveyor sections or chutes, and pumps. Inspects equipment and machinery to prevent loss of materials or products during transit. Reads production and delivery schedules; confers with supervisor to determine processing procedures. Cleans, sterilizes, and maintains equipment, machinery, and work stations, using hand tools, shovels, brooms, chemicals, hoses, and lubricants. Weighs or measures materials and products, using scales or other measuring instruments, to verify specified tonnage and prevent overloads. Collects samples of materials or products for laboratory analysis, to ensure conformance to specifications. Affixes identifying information to materials or products, using hand tools. Records production data such as weight, type, quantity, and storage locations of materials; documents equipment downtime. Distributes materials, supplies, and equipment to work stations, using lifts and trucks. Loads, unloads, or adjusts materials or products on conveyors by hand or using lifts and hoists.

GOE Number, Interest Area, and Work Group: 08.07.01; Industrial Production; Hands-on Work: Loading, Moving, Hoisting, and Conveying. **Personality Type:** Realistic. Realistic occupations frequently involve work activities that include practical, hands-on problems and solutions. These occupations often deal with plants, animals, and real-world materials like wood, tools, and machinery. Many of the occupations require working outside and do not involve a lot of paperwork or working closely with others. **Work Values:** Moral Values; Supervision, Human Relations; Activity;

Company Policies and Practices; Supervision, Technical. **Skills:** Operation and Control; Operation Monitoring; Equipment Maintenance; Troubleshooting; Repairing. **Abilities:** *Cognitive*—Perceptual Speed; Problem Sensitivity; Information Ordering; Number Facility; Selective Attention. *Psychomotor*—Multilimb Coordination; Wrist-Finger Speed; Control Precision. *Physical*—Static Strength; Trunk Strength; Extent Flexibility. *Sensory*—Near Vision; Depth Perception; Peripheral Vision; Sound Localization. **General Work Activities:** *Information Input*—Monitoring Processes, Materials, and Surroundings; Inspecting Equipment, Structures, Materials; Getting Information Needed to Do the Job. *Mental Process*—Evaluating Information Against Standards; Processing Information; Judging Qualities of Things, Services, Other People's Work; Analyzing Data or Information. *Work Output*—Controlling Machines and Processes; Handling and Moving Objects; Repairing and Maintaining Mechanical Equipment; Documenting and Recording Information. *Interacting with Others*—Communicating with Other Workers; Performing Administrative Activities; Coordinating Work and Activities of Others. **Physical Work Conditions:** Using Hands on Objects, Tools, or Controls; Indoors; Standing. **Other Job Characteristics:** Degree of Automation; Consequence of Error; Pace Determined by Speed of Equipment.

Experience: Job Zone 1. No previous work-related skill, knowledge, or experience is needed. **Job Preparation:** SVP Below 4.0—Less than 6 months. **Knowledge:** Production and Processing; Mechanical; Clerical; Transportation; English Language; Physics; Engineering and Technology. **Instructional Programs:** No data available.

Related DOT Jobs: 524.565-010 Trolley Operator; 529.682-030 Silo Operator; 529.685-050 Char-Conveyor Tender; 553.685-078 Milled-Rubber Tender; 575.687-038 Tip-Out Worker; 579.685-050 Silo Tender; 579.685-062 Brick Unloader Tender; 613.685-034 Bed Operator; 669.685-090 Tipple Tender; 921.382-010 Conveyor Operator, Pneumatic System; 921.563-010 Coke Loader; 921.565-010 Cement Loader; 921.662-018 Conveyor-System Operator; 921.662-026 Tipple Operator; 921.682-014 Palletizer Operator I; 921.683-014 Boom-Conveyor Operator; 921.685-014 Bull-Chain Operator; 921.685-022 Chip-Bin Conveyor Tender; 921.685-026 Conveyor Tender; 921.685-030 Cooker Loader (partial list; see the introduction for sources of the complete list).

53-7021.00 Crane and Tower Operators (Crane and Tower Operators)

Education: Moderate-term O-T-J training

Employed: 48,564

Openings: 6,139

Projected Growth: 0.5%

Earnings: $30,510

Operate mechanical boom and cable, or tower and cable, equipment, to lift and move materials, machines, or products in many directions.

Inspects bundle packaging for conformance to customer requirements; removes and batches packaging tickets. Reviews daily truck-delivery schedule to ascertain orders, sequence of deliveries, and special loading instructions. Loads and unloads bundles from trucks and moves containers to storage bins, using moving equipment. Inspects and compares load weights with lifting capacity to ensure against overload. Inspects and adjusts crane mechanisms and accessory equipment, to prevent malfunctions and wear. Cleans, lubricates, and maintains mechanisms such as cables, pulleys, and grappling devices. Inspects cables and grappling devices for wear; installs or replaces cables. Weighs bundles, using floor scale; records weight for company records. Operates cranes, cherry pickers, or other moving equipment, to lift and move loads such as machinery or bulk materials. Directs helpers engaged in placing blocking and outrigging under crane when lifting loads. Directs truck drivers backing vehicles into loading bays. Covers, uncovers, and secures loads for delivery.

GOE Number, Interest Area, and Work Group: 08.07.01; Industrial Production; Hands-on Work: Loading, Moving, Hoisting, and Conveying. **Personality Type:** Realistic. Realistic occupations frequently involve work activities that include practical, hands-on problems and solutions. These occupations often deal with plants, animals, and real-world materials like wood, tools, and machinery. Many of the occupations require working outside and do not involve a lot of paperwork or working closely with others. **Work Values:** Moral Values; Company Policies and Practices; Supervision, Human Relations; Supervision, Technical; Activity. **Skills:** Operation and Control; Equipment Selection; Product Inspection; Coordination; Repairing. **Abilities:** *Cognitive*—Oral Expression; Information Ordering; Problem Sensitivity; Deductive Reasoning; Number Facility; Spatial Orientation. *Psychomotor*—Control Precision; Multilimb Coordination; Reaction Time. *Physical*—Static Strength; Extent Flexibility; Trunk Strength. *Sensory*—Depth Perception; Far Vision; Auditory Attention. **General Work Activities:** *Information Input*—Getting Information Needed to Do the Job; Inspecting Equipment, Structures, Materials; Monitoring Processes, Materials, and Surroundings. *Mental Process*—Evaluating Information Against Standards; Making Decisions and Solving Problems; Updating and Using Job-Relevant Knowledge; Processing Information; Analyzing Data or Information. *Work Output*—Controlling Machines and Processes; Handling and Moving Objects; Performing General Physical Activities. *Interacting with Others*—Communicating with Other Workers; Coordinating Work and Activities of Others; Establishing and Maintaining Relationships; Performing Administrative Activities. **Physical Work Conditions:** Outdoors; Using Hands on Objects, Tools, or Controls; Hazardous Equipment. **Other Job Characteristics:** Consequence of Error; Degree of Automation; Importance of Being Sure All Is Done.

Experience: Job Zone 2. Some previous work-related skill, knowledge, or experience may be helpful, but usually is not needed. **Job Preparation:** SVP 4.00 to 5.99—6 months to less than 2 years. **Knowledge:** Mechanical; Engineering and Technology; Transportation; Clerical; Physics. **Instructional Program:** 490202 Construction Equipment Operator.

Related DOT Jobs: 519.683-010 Dross Skimmer; 921.663-010 Overhead Crane Operator; 921.663-014 Cherry-Picker Operator; 921.663-022 Derrick Operator; 921.663-038 Locomotive-Crane Operator; 921.663-042 Monorail Crane Operator; 921.663-054 Tower-Crane Operator; 921.663-058 Tractor-Crane Operator; 921.663-062 Truck-Crane Operator; 921.663-070 Truck Loader, Overhead Crane; 921.683-018 Cantilever-Crane Operator; 921.683-034 Derrick-Boat Operator; 921.683-066 Sorting-Grapple Operator; 921.683-074 Tower-Loader Operator.

53-7031.00 Dredge Operators (Dredge Operators)

Education: No data available.
Employed: 1,740
Openings: No data available.
Projected Growth: No data available.
Earnings: $27,340

Operate dredge to remove sand, gravel, or other materials from lakes, rivers, or streams and to excavate and maintain navigable channels in waterways.

Directs workers placing shore anchors and cables, laying additional pipes from dredge to shore, and pumping water from pontoons. Starts power winch that draws in or lets out cable to change position of dredge, or pulls in and lets out cable manually. Lowers anchor pole to verify depth of excavation, using winch, or scans depth gauge to determine depth of excavation. Starts and stops engines to operate equipment. Moves levers to position dredge for excavation, to engage hydraulic pump, to raise and lower suction boom, and to control rotation of cutterhead.

GOE Number, Interest Area, and Work Group: 07.04.01; Transportation; Water Vehicle Operation. **Personality Type:** Realistic. Realistic occupations frequently involve work activities that include practical, hands-on problems and solutions. These occupations often deal with plants, animals, and real-world materials like wood, tools, and machinery. Many of the occupations require working outside and do not involve a lot of paperwork or working closely with others. **Work Values:** Moral Values; Supervision, Human Relations; Independence; Authority; Supervision, Technical; Compensation; Company Policies and Practices. **Skills:** Operation and Control; Operation Monitoring; Management of Personnel Resources; Coordination; Speaking. **Abilities:** *Cognitive*—Information Ordering; Oral Expression; Selective Attention; Spatial Orientation; Visualization. *Psychomotor*—Control Precision; Multilimb Coordination; Reaction Time. *Physical*—Static Strength; Extent Flexibility; Trunk Strength. *Sensory*—Depth Perception; Speech Clarity; Glare Sensitivity. **General Work Activities:** *Information Input*—Monitoring Processes, Materials, and Surroundings; Getting Information Needed to Do the Job; Identifying Objects, Actions, and Events. *Mental Process*—Making Decisions and Solving Problems; Analyzing Data or Information; Updating and Using Job-Relevant Knowledge. *Work Output*—Controlling Machines and Processes; Handling and Moving Objects; Performing General Physical Activities. *Interacting with Others*—Coordinating Work and Activities of Others; Communicating with Other Workers; Guiding, Directing and Motivating Subordinates. **Physical Work Conditions:** Outdoors; Using Hands on Objects, Tools, or Controls; Hazardous Equipment. **Other Job Characteristics:** Degree of Automation; Consequence of Error; Frustrating Circumstances.

Experience: Job Zone 2. Some previous work-related skill, knowledge, or experience may be helpful, but usually is not needed. **Job Preparation:** SVP 4.00 to 5.99—6 months to less than 2 years. **Knowledge:** Mechanical; Engineering and Technology; Geography; Transportation; Mathematics; Physics; Public Safety and Security. **Instructional Program:** 490399 Water Transportation Workers, Other.

Related DOT Job: 850.663-010 Dredge Operator.

53-7032.00 Excavating and Loading Machine and Dragline Operators (Excavating and Loading Machine Operators)

Education: Moderate-term O-T-J training
Employed: 105,966
Openings: 6,199
Projected Growth: 15.3%
Earnings: $27,090

Operate or tend machinery equipped with scoops, shovels, or buckets to excavate and load loose materials.

GOE Number, Interest Area, and Work Group: 08.07.01; Industrial Production; Hands-on Work: Loading, Moving, Hoisting, and Conveying. **Instructional Program:** 490202 Construction Equipment Operator. **Note:** The Department of Labor has not collected some data for this job, so it has fewer details than the other descriptions.

53-7032.01 Excavating and Loading Machine Operators (Excavation and Loading Machine Operators)

Education: Moderate-term O-T-J training
Employed: 105,966
Openings: 6,199
Projected Growth: 15.3%
Earnings: $27,090

Operate machinery equipped with scoops, shovels, or buckets to excavate and load loose materials.

Observes hand signals, grade stakes, and other markings when operating machines. Operates power machinery such as powered shovel, stripping shovel, scraper loader (mucking machine), or backhoe (trench-excavating machine), to excavate and load material. Measures and verifies levels of rock or gravel, base, and other excavated material. Lubricates and repairs machinery; replaces parts such as gears, bearings, and bucket teeth. Directs ground workers engaged in activities such as moving stakes or markers. Receives written or oral instructions to move or excavate material.

GOE Number, Interest Area, and Work Group: 06.03.01; Construction, Mining, and Drilling; Mining and Drilling. **Personality Type:** Realistic. Realistic occupations frequently involve work activities that include practical, hands-on problems and solutions. These occupations often deal with plants, animals, and real-world materials like wood, tools, and machinery. Many of the occupations require working outside and do not involve a lot of paperwork or working closely with others. **Work Values:** Moral Values; Compensation; Company Policies and Practices; Supervision, Human Relations; Activity. **Skills:** Operation and Control; Operation Monitoring; Repairing; Equipment Selection; Equipment Maintenance; Coordination. **Abilities:** *Cognitive*—Oral Comprehension; Written Comprehension; Spatial Orientation; Oral Expression; Problem Sensitivity. *Psychomotor*—Control Precision; Multilimb Coordination; Reaction Time. *Physical*—Trunk Strength;

Static Strength; Dynamic Strength; Gross Body Coordination. *Sensory*—Depth Perception; Speech Clarity; Far Vision. **General Work Activities:** *Information Input*—Getting Information Needed to Do the Job; Monitoring Processes, Materials, and Surroundings; Identifying Objects, Actions, and Events. *Mental Process*—Evaluating Information Against Standards; Processing Information; Making Decisions and Solving Problems; Updating and Using Job-Relevant Knowledge; Developing Objectives and Strategies; Judging Qualities of Things, Services, Other People's Work. *Work Output*—Operating Vehicles or Equipment; Controlling Machines and Processes; Handling and Moving Objects. *Interacting with Others*—Communicating with Other Workers; Coordinating Work and Activities of Others; Establishing and Maintaining Relationships. **Physical Work Conditions:** Outdoors; Using Hands on Objects, Tools, or Controls; Whole Body Vibration. **Other Job Characteristics:** Degree of Automation; Consequence of Error; Importance of Being Sure All Is Done; Importance of Being Exact or Accurate.

Experience: Job Zone 2. Some previous work-related skill, knowledge, or experience may be helpful, but usually is not needed. **Job Preparation:** SVP 4.00 to 5.99—6 months to less than 2 years. **Knowledge:** Mechanical; Engineering and Technology; Physics; Mathematics; English Language. **Instructional Program:** 490202 Construction Equipment Operator.

Related DOT Jobs: 850.663-026 Stripping-Shovel Operator; 850.683-026 Mucking-Machine Operator; 850.683-030 Power-Shovel Operator; 850.683-042 Tower-Excavator Operator; 851.663-010 Septic-Tank Installer; 921.683-022 Coal-Equipment Operator; 930.683-022 Harvester Operator.

53-7032.02 Dragline Operators (Dragline Operators)

Education: No data available.
Employed: 2,610
Openings: No data available.
Projected Growth: No data available.
Earnings: $27,960

Operate power-driven crane equipment with dragline bucket to excavate or move sand, gravel, mud, or other materials.

Directs workers engaged in placing blocks and outriggers, to prevent capsizing of machine when lifting heavy loads. Drives machine to work site. Moves controls to position boom, lower and drag bucket through material, and release material at unloading point.

GOE Number, Interest Area, and Work Group: 08.07.01; Industrial Production; Hands-on Work: Loading, Moving, Hoisting, and Conveying. **Personality Type:** Realistic. Realistic occupations frequently involve work activities that include practical, hands-on problems and solutions. These occupations often deal with plants, animals, and real-world materials like wood, tools, and machinery. Many of the occupations require working outside and do not involve a lot of paperwork or working closely with others. **Work Values:** Moral Values; Independence; Company Policies and Practices; Supervision, Human Relations; Supervision, Technical. **Skills:** Operation and Control; Coordination; Speaking; Monitoring; Operation Monitoring. **Abilities:** *Cognitive*—Oral Expression; Spatial Orientation; Information Ordering; Time Sharing; Problem Sensitivity; Oral Comprehension. *Psychomotor*—Control Precision; Multilimb Coordination; Reaction Time. *Physical*—Static Strength; Gross Body Coordination; Explosive Strength; Dynamic Flexibility. *Sensory*—Depth Perception; Far Vision; Peripheral Vision. **General Work Activities:** *Information Input*—Getting Information Needed to Do the Job; Monitoring Processes, Materials, and Surroundings; Identifying Objects, Actions, and Events. *Mental Process*—Making Decisions and Solving Problems; Organizing, Planning, and Prioritizing; Analyzing Data or Information. *Work Output*—Controlling Machines and Processes; Operating Vehicles or Equipment; Performing General Physical Activities. *Interacting with Others*—Communicating with Other Workers; Establishing and Maintaining Relationships; Coordinating Work and Activities of Others. **Physical Work Conditions:** Outdoors; Using Hands on Objects, Tools, or Controls; Hazardous Equipment. **Other Job Characteristics:** Degree of Automation; Consequence of Error; Importance of Being Sure All Is Done.

Experience: Job Zone 2. Some previous work-related skill, knowledge, or experience may be helpful, but usually is not needed. **Job Preparation:** SVP 4.00 to 5.99—6 months to less than 2 years. **Knowledge:** Mechanical; Building and Construction; Engineering and Technology; Transportation; Public Safety and Security; Physics; Geography. **Instructional Program:** 490202 Construction Equipment Operator.

Related DOT Job: 850.683-018 Dragline Operator.

53-7033.00 Loading Machine Operators, Underground Mining (Loading Machine Operators, Underground Mining)

Education: No data available.

Employed: 3,210

Openings: No data available.

Projected Growth: No data available.

Earnings: $29,990

Operate underground loading machine to load coal, ore, or rock into shuttle or mine car or onto conveyors. Operate equipment such as power shovels, hoisting engines equipped with cable-drawn scraper or scoop, or machines equipped with gathering arms and conveyor.

Operates levers to move conveyor boom or shovel, to move mine contents into car or onto conveyor. Drives machine into pile of material blasted from working face. Pries off loose material from roof and moves it into path of machine with crowbar. Starts conveyor boom and gathering-arm motors. Moves trailing electrical cable clear of obstructions, using rubber safety gloves. Advances machine to gather material and convey it into car at rear. Stops gathering arms when car is full.

GOE Number, Interest Area, and Work Group: 06.03.01; Construction, Mining, and Drilling; Mining and Drilling. **Personality Type:** Realistic. Realistic occupations frequently involve work activities that include practical, hands-on problems and solutions. These occupations often deal with plants, animals, and real-world materials like wood, tools, and machinery. Many of the occupa-

tions require working outside and do not involve a lot of paperwork or working closely with others. **Work Values:** Moral Values; Independence; Supervision, Human Relations; Supervision, Technical; Company Policies and Practices. **Skills:** Operation and Control; Repairing; Equipment Maintenance; Operation Monitoring; Equipment Selection. **Abilities:** *Cognitive*—Spatial Orientation; Problem Sensitivity; Visualization; Category Flexibility; Deductive Reasoning; Information Ordering. *Psychomotor*—Control Precision; Multilimb Coordination; Reaction Time. *Physical*—Static Strength; Extent Flexibility; Trunk Strength. *Sensory*—Depth Perception; Night Vision; Auditory Attention. **General Work Activities:** *Information Input*—Monitoring Processes, Materials, and Surroundings; Inspecting Equipment, Structures, Materials; Getting Information Needed to Do the Job. *Mental Process*—Making Decisions and Solving Problems; Judging Qualities of Things, Services, Other People's Work; Organizing, Planning, and Prioritizing. *Work Output*—Operating Vehicles or Equipment; Controlling Machines and Processes; Handling and Moving Objects. *Interacting with Others*—Communicating with Other Workers; Assisting and Caring for Others; Monitoring and Controlling Resources; Establishing and Maintaining Relationships. **Physical Work Conditions:** Common Protective or Safety Attire; Using Hands on Objects, Tools, or Controls; Outdoors. **Other Job Characteristics:** Degree of Automation; Consequence of Error; Pace Determined by Speed of Equipment; Importance of Being Exact or Accurate; Importance of Being Sure All Is Done.

Experience: Job Zone 2. Some previous work-related skill, knowledge, or experience may be helpful, but usually is not needed. **Job Preparation:** SVP 4.00 to 5.99—6 months to less than 2 years. **Knowledge:** Mechanical; Engineering and Technology; Public Safety and Security; Production and Processing; Physics. **Instructional Program:** 490299 Vehicle and Equipment Operators, Other.

Related DOT Jobs: 932.683-014 Loading-Machine Operator; 932.683-018 Mechanical-Shovel Operator.

53-7041.00 Hoist and Winch Operators (Hoist and Winch Operators)

Education: Moderate-term O-T-J training

Employed: 10,627

Openings: 1,619

Projected Growth: 6%

Earnings: $28,030

Operate or tend hoists or winches to lift and pull loads, using power-operated cable equipment.

Repairs, maintains, and adjusts equipment, using hand tools. Observes equipment gauges and indicators and hand signals to verify depth of materials, instruments, or position of load. Selects loads or materials according to weight and size specifications. Climbs ladder to facilitate positioning and setup of vehicle-mounted derrick. Attaches, fastens, and disconnects cables or lines to loads and materials, using hand tools. Moves or repositions hoists, winches, loads, and materials, manually or using equipment and machines such as trucks, cars, and handtrucks. Starts engine of hoist or winch, to move loads or materials, using controls such as levers, pedals, and buttons. Operates equipment such as hoist, winch, or hydraulic boom, to lift and pull loads and materials. Tends auxiliary equipment such as jacks, slings, cables, or stop blocks, to facilitate moving items or materials for further processing.

GOE Number, Interest Area, and Work Group: 08.07.01; Industrial Production; Hands-on Work: Loading, Moving, Hoisting, and Conveying. **Personality Type:** Realistic. Realistic occupations frequently involve work activities that include practical, hands-on problems and solutions. These occupations often deal with plants, animals, and real-world materials like wood, tools, and machinery. Many of the occupations require working outside and do not involve a lot of paperwork or working closely with others. **Work Values:** Moral Values; Independence; Supervision, Human Relations; Company Policies and Practices; Supervision, Technical. **Skills:** Repairing; Operation and Control; Equipment Maintenance; Operation Monitoring; Equipment Selection. **Abilities:** *Cognitive*—Information Ordering; Visualization; Spatial Orientation; Selective Attention; Written Comprehension; Written Expression. *Psychomotor*—Control Precision; Multilimb Coordination; Reaction Time. *Physical*—Static Strength; Extent Flexibility; Trunk Strength. *Sensory*—Depth Perception; Far Vision; Visual Color Discrimination; Peripheral Vision. **General Work Activities:** *Information Input*—Monitoring Processes, Materials, and Surroundings; Estimating Needed Characteristics; Identifying Objects, Actions, and Events. *Mental Process*—Evaluating Information Against Standards; Analyzing Data or Information; Updating and Using Job-Relevant Knowledge; Judging Qualities of Things, Services, Other People's Work; Making Decisions and Solving Problems. *Work Output*—Handling and Moving Objects; Performing General Physical Activities; Controlling Machines and Processes. *Interacting with Others*—Performing Administrative Activities; Communicating with Other Workers; Establishing and Maintaining Relationships. **Physical Work Conditions:** Outdoors; Using Hands on Objects, Tools, or Controls; Hazardous Equipment. **Other Job Characteristics:** Consequence of Error; Degree of Automation; Importance of Being Exact or Accurate; Pace Determined by Speed of Equipment.

Experience: Job Zone 1. No previous work-related skill, knowledge, or experience is needed. **Job Preparation:** SVP Below 4.0— Less than 6 months. **Knowledge:** Mechanical; Physics; Transportation; Public Safety and Security; Engineering and Technology. **Instructional Program:** 490202 Construction Equipment Operator.

Related DOT Jobs: 663.686-022 Lathe Spotter; 869.683-014 Rigger; 911.687-018 Coal Trimmer; 921.662-022 Marine Railway Operator; 921.663-026 Hoist Operator; 921.663-030 Hoisting Engineer; 921.663-046 Pneumatic-Hoist Operator; 921.663-050 Scraper-Loader Operator; 921.663-066 Yarding Engineer; 921.682-022 Transfer Controller; 921.683-010 Boat-Hoist Operator; 921.683-030 Cupola Hoist Operator; 921.683-046 Hydraulic-Boom Operator; 921.683-054 Jammer Operator; 921.683-058 Log Loader; 921.683-082 Winch Driver; 921.683-086 Yard Worker; 921.685-010 Boat Loader II; 921.685-042 Electric-Fork Operator; 930.363-010 Clean-Out Driller (partial list; see the introduction for sources of the complete list).

53-7051.00 Industrial Truck and Tractor Operators
(Industrial Truck and Tractor Operators)

Education: Short-term O-T-J training
Employed: 415,443
Openings: 80,758
Projected Growth: 9.2%
Earnings: $23,360

Operate industrial trucks or tractors equipped to move materials around a warehouse, storage yard, factory, construction site, or similar location.

Signals workers to discharge, dump, or level materials. Positions lifting device under, over, or around loaded pallets, skids, and boxes; secures material or products for transport to designated areas. Moves levers and controls to operate lifting devices such as forklifts, lift beams, swivel hooks, hoists, and elevating platforms, to load, unload, transport, and stack material. Performs routine maintenance on vehicles and auxiliary equipment, such as cleaning, lubricating, recharging batteries, fueling, or replacing liquefied-gas tank. Operates or tends automatic stacking, loading, packaging, or cutting machines. Weighs materials or products; records weight and other production data on tags or labels. Manually loads or unloads materials onto or off pallets, skids, platforms, cars, or lifting devices. Turns valves and opens chutes to dump, spray, or release materials from dump cars or storage bins into hoppers. Moves controls, to drive gasoline- or electric-powered trucks, cars, or tractors, and to transport materials between loading, processing, and storage areas. Hooks tow trucks to trailer hitches; fastens attachments such as graders, plows, rollers, and winch cables to tractor, using hitchpins.

GOE Number, Interest Area, and Work Group: 08.07.01; Industrial Production; Hands-on Work: Loading, Moving, Hoisting, and Conveying. **Personality Type:** Realistic. Realistic occupations frequently involve work activities that include practical, hands-on problems and solutions. These occupations often deal with plants, animals, and real-world materials like wood, tools, and machinery. Many of the occupations require working outside and do not involve a lot of paperwork or working closely with others. **Work Values:** Moral Values; Supervision, Human Relations; Company Policies and Practices; Supervision, Technical; Activity. **Skills:** Operation and Control; Equipment Selection; Operation Monitoring; Repairing; Troubleshooting; Coordination. **Abilities:** *Cognitive*—Spatial Orientation; Information Ordering; Problem Sensitivity; Visualization; Time Sharing; Selective Attention. *Psychomotor*—Control Precision; Multilimb Coordination; Manual Dexterity. *Physical*—Static Strength; Extent Flexibility; Trunk Strength. *Sensory*—Depth Perception; Far Vision; Auditory Attention. **General Work Activities:** *Information Input*—Monitoring Processes, Materials, and Surroundings; Inspecting Equipment, Structures, Materials; Getting Information Needed to Do the Job. *Mental Process*—Making Decisions and Solving Problems; Evaluating Information Against Standards; Organizing, Planning, and Prioritizing; Updating and Using Job-Relevant Knowledge; Processing Information; Analyzing Data or Information. *Work Output*—Operating Vehicles or Equipment; Controlling Machines and

Processes; Repairing and Maintaining Mechanical Equipment; Performing General Physical Activities; Handling and Moving Objects. *Interacting with Others*—Communicating with Other Workers; Monitoring and Controlling Resources; Performing Administrative Activities; Coordinating Work and Activities of Others. **Physical Work Conditions:** Using Hands on Objects, Tools, or Controls; Common Protective or Safety Attire; Outdoors. **Other Job Characteristics:** Consequence of Error; Importance of Being Sure All Is Done; Importance of Being Exact or Accurate.

Experience: Job Zone 1. No previous work-related skill, knowledge, or experience is needed. **Job Preparation:** SVP Below 4.0— Less than 6 months. **Knowledge:** Transportation; Mechanical; Mathematics; Clerical; Physics; Production and Processing. **Instructional Program:** 490299 Vehicle and Equipment Operators, Other.

Related DOT Jobs: 519.663-014 Hot-Car Operator; 519.683-014 Larry Operator; 569.683-010 Kiln-Transfer Operator; 921.583-010 Transfer-Car Operator, Drier; 921.683-042 Front-End Loader Operator; 921.683-050 Industrial-Truck Operator; 921.683-070 Straddle-Truck Operator; 921.683-078 Transfer-Car Operator; 929.583-010 Yard Worker; 929.683-014 Tractor Operator.

53-7061.00 Cleaners of Vehicles and Equipment
(Cleaners of Vehicles and Equipment)

Education: Short-term O-T-J training
Employed: 287,607
Openings: 116,789
Projected Growth: 25%
Earnings: $14,540

Wash or otherwise clean vehicles, machinery, and other equipment. Use such materials as water, cleaning agents, brushes, cloths, and hoses.

Transports materials, equipment, or supplies to and from work area, using carts or hoists. Places objects on drying racks or dyes surfaces, using cloth, squeegees, or air compressors. Turns valves or disconnects hoses to eliminate water, cleaning solutions, or vapors from machinery or tanks. Connects hoses and lines to pumps and other equipment. Disassembles and reassembles machines or equipment; removes and reattaches vehicle parts and trim, using hand tools. Examines and inspects parts, equipment, and vehicles for cleanliness, damage, and compliance with standards or regulations. Applies paints, dyes, polishes, reconditioners, and masking materials to vehicles, to preserve, protect, or restore color and condition. Lubricates machinery, vehicles, and equipment; performs minor repairs and adjustments, using hand tools. Presoaks or rinses machine parts, equipment, or vehicles, by immersing objects in cleaning solutions or water, manually or using hoists. Records production and operational data on specified forms. Mixes cleaning solutions and abrasive compositions and other compounds according to formula. Monitors operation of cleaning machines; stops machine or notifies supervisor when malfunctions occur. Sweeps, shovels, or vacuums loose debris and salvageable scrap into containers; removes from work area.

Scrubs, scrapes, or sprays machine parts, equipment, or vehicles, using scrapers, brushes, cleaners, disinfectants, insecticides, acid, and abrasives. Turns valves or handles on equipment to regulate pressure and flow of water, air, steam, or abrasives from sprayer nozzles. Maintains inventories of supplies. Presses buttons to activate cleaning equipment or machines. Collects and tests samples of cleaning solutions and vapors.

GOE Number, Interest Area, and Work Group: 11.08.01; Recreation, Travel, and Other Personal Services; Other Personal Services. **Personality Type:** Realistic. Realistic occupations frequently involve work activities that include practical, hands-on problems and solutions. These occupations often deal with plants, animals, and real-world materials like wood, tools, and machinery. Many of the occupations require working outside and do not involve a lot of paperwork or working closely with others. **Work Values:** Moral Values; Independence; Activity; Coworkers; Company Policies and Practices; Supervision, Technical; Supervision, Human Relations. **Skills:** Equipment Selection; Operation and Control; Equipment Maintenance; Repairing; Operation Monitoring; Monitoring; Reading Comprehension; Writing. **Abilities:** *Cognitive*— Information Ordering; Problem Sensitivity; Inductive Reasoning; Perceptual Speed; Visualization. *Psychomotor*—Wrist-Finger Speed; Manual Dexterity; Finger Dexterity; Control Precision; Multilimb Coordination; Speed of Limb Movement. *Physical*—Extent Flexibility; Trunk Strength; Static Strength. *Sensory*—Near Vision; Depth Perception. **General Work Activities:** *Information Input*— Monitoring Processes, Materials, and Surroundings; Inspecting Equipment, Structures, Materials; Identifying Objects, Actions, and Events. *Mental Process*—Evaluating Information Against Standards; Processing Information; Judging Qualities of Things, Services, Other People's Work. *Work Output*—Performing General Physical Activities; Controlling Machines and Processes; Handling and Moving Objects. *Interacting with Others*—Monitoring and Controlling Resources; Performing Administrative Activities; Communicating with Other Workers. **Physical Work Conditions:** Using Hands on Objects, Tools, or Controls; Standing; Outdoors. **Other Job Characteristics:** Consequence of Error; Importance of Being Sure All Is Done; Degree of Automation.

Experience: Job Zone 1. No previous work-related skill, knowledge, or experience is needed. **Job Preparation:** SVP Below 4.0— Less than 6 months. **Knowledge:** Mechanical; Chemistry; Clerical; Mathematics; Engineering and Technology; English Language. **Instructional Program:** 200601 Custodial, Housekeeping and Home Services Workers and Managers.

Related DOT Jobs: 503.687-010 Sandblaster; 511.687-010 Blanket Washer; 519.664-010 Assembly Cleaner; 521.687-030 Char Puller; 521.687-054 Filter-Screen Cleaner; 521.687-114 Shaker Washer; 529.685-230 Stem-Dryer Maintainer; 529.687-014 Bin Cleaner; 529.687-018 Box-Truck Washer; 529.687-054 Cooker Cleaner; 529.687-062 Die Cleaner; 529.687-190 Stone Cleaner; 529.687-194 Suction-Plate-Carrier Cleaner; 529.687-206 Trolley Cleaner; 529.687-210 Washer; 529.687-214 Washroom Cleaner; 557.684-010 Jet Handler; 559.684-022 Tank Cleaner; 559.687-018 Casting-Machine-Service Operator; 559.687-022 Cell Cleaner (partial list; see the introduction for sources of the complete list).

53-7062.00 Laborers and Freight, Stock, and Material Movers, Hand (Freight, Stock, and Material Movers, Hand)

Education: Short-term O-T-J training
Employed: 822,119
Openings: 306,549
Projected Growth: 1.5%
Earnings: No data available.

Manually move freight, stock, or other materials. Perform other unskilled general labor. Includes all unskilled manual laborers not elsewhere classified.

GOE Number, Interest Area, and Work Group: 08.07.01; Industrial Production; Hands-on Work: Loading, Moving, Hoisting, and Conveying. **Instructional Programs:** No data available. **Note:** The Department of Labor has not collected some data for this job, so it has fewer details than the other descriptions.

53-7062.01 Stevedores, Except Equipment Operators (Stevedores, Except Equipment Operators)

Education: No data available.
Employed: 26,540
Openings: No data available.
Projected Growth: No data available.
Earnings: $41,400

Manually load and unload ship cargo. Stack cargo in transit shed or in hold of ship, using pallet or cargo board. Attach and move slings to lift cargo. Guide load lift.

Shores cargo in ship's hold to prevent shifting during voyage. Attaches and moves slings used to lift cargo. Stacks cargo in transit shed or in hold of ship, as directed. Carries or moves cargo by handtruck to wharf; stacks cargo on pallets to facilitate transfer to and from ship. Guides load being lifted, to prevent swinging.

GOE Number, Interest Area, and Work Group: 07.08.01; Transportation; Support Work in Transportation. **Personality Type:** Realistic. Realistic occupations frequently involve work activities that include practical, hands-on problems and solutions. These occupations often deal with plants, animals, and real-world materials like wood, tools, and machinery. Many of the occupations require working outside and do not involve a lot of paperwork or working closely with others. **Work Values:** Moral Values; Supervision, Technical; Company Policies and Practices; Supervision, Human Relations; Security; Activity; Coworkers. **Skills:** none met the criteria. **Abilities:** *Cognitive*—Spatial Orientation; Visualization; Information Ordering; Selective Attention; Category Flexibility; Problem Sensitivity. *Psychomotor*—Speed of Limb Movement; Manual Dexterity; Multilimb Coordination. *Physical*—Static Strength; Dynamic Strength; Trunk Strength. *Sensory*—Depth Perception; Peripheral Vision; Night Vision; Glare Sensitivity; Auditory Attention. **General Work Activities:** *Information Input*—Monitoring Processes, Materials, and Surroundings; Estimating Needed Characteristics; Getting Information Needed to Do the Job. *Mental Process*—Organizing, Planning, and Prioritizing; Evaluating Information Against Standards; Analyzing Data

or Information. *Work Output*—Handling and Moving Objects; Performing General Physical Activities; Implementing Ideas and Programs. *Interacting with Others*—Communicating with Other Workers; Establishing and Maintaining Relationships; Assisting and Caring for Others; Coordinating Work and Activities of Others. **Physical Work Conditions:** Standing; Outdoors; Using Hands on Objects, Tools, or Controls. **Other Job Characteristics:** Consequence of Error; Importance of Being Sure All Is Done; Frustrating Circumstances.

Experience: Job Zone 1. No previous work-related skill, knowledge, or experience is needed. **Job Preparation:** SVP Below 4.0—Less than 6 months. **Knowledge:** Production and Processing; Transportation; Physics; Public Safety and Security; Mechanical; Building and Construction. **Instructional Programs:** No data available.

Related DOT Job: 922.687-090 Stevedore II.

53-7062.02 Grips and Set-Up Workers, Motion Picture Sets, Studios, and Stages (All Other Freight, Stock, and Material Movers, Hand)

Education: No data available.
Employed: 838,720
Openings: No data available.
Projected Growth: No data available.
Earnings: $18,260

Arrange equipment; raise and lower scenery.

Reads work orders and follows oral instructions to determine specified material and equipment to be moved and its relocation. Rigs and dismantles stage or set equipment such as frames, scaffolding, platforms, or backdrops, using carpenter's hand tools. Adjusts controls to raise and lower scenery and stage curtain during performance, following cues. Adjusts controls to guide, position, and move equipment such as cranes, booms, and cameras. Erects canvas covers to protect equipment from weather. Orders equipment and maintains equipment storage areas. Sews and repairs items, using materials and hand tools such as canvas and sewing machines. Produces special lighting and sound effects during performances, using various machines and devices. Arranges equipment preparatory to sessions and performances, following work order specifications; handles props during performances. Connects electrical equipment to power source; tests equipment before performance.

GOE Number, Interest Area, and Work Group: 06.04.01; Construction, Mining, and Drilling; Hands-on Work: Construction, Extraction, and Maintenance. **Personality Type:** Realistic. Realistic occupations frequently involve work activities that include practical, hands-on problems and solutions. These occupations often deal with plants, animals, and real-world materials like wood, tools, and machinery. Many of the occupations require working outside and do not involve a lot of paperwork or working closely with others. **Work Values:** Moral Values; Company Policies and Practices; Coworkers; Supervision, Human Relations; Activity; Supervision, Technical; Working Conditions. **Skills:** Reading Comprehension; Active Listening; Monitoring; Coordination; Operation and Control. **Abilities:** *Cognitive*—Visualization; Information Ordering; Spatial Orientation; Problem Sensitivity; Oral Comprehension; Written Comprehension. *Psychomotor*—Manual Dexterity; Arm-Hand Steadiness; Control Precision. *Physical*—Static Strength; Extent Flexibility; Trunk Strength. *Sensory*—Near Vision; Depth Perception; Auditory Attention. **General Work Activities:** *Information Input*—Getting Information Needed to Do the Job; Identifying Objects, Actions, and Events; Inspecting Equipment, Structures, Materials; Monitoring Processes, Materials, and Surroundings. *Mental Process*—Organizing, Planning, and Prioritizing; Making Decisions and Solving Problems; Evaluating Information Against Standards. *Work Output*—Performing General Physical Activities; Handling and Moving Objects; Implementing Ideas and Programs; Controlling Machines and Processes. *Interacting with Others*—Communicating with Other Workers; Establishing and Maintaining Relationships; Monitoring and Controlling Resources. **Physical Work Conditions:** Using Hands on Objects, Tools, or Controls; Standing; Indoors. **Other Job Characteristics:** Consequence of Error; Importance of Being Sure All Is Done; Importance of Being Exact or Accurate.

Experience: Job Zone 2. Some previous work-related skill, knowledge, or experience may be helpful, but usually is not needed. **Job Preparation:** SVP 4.00 to 5.99—6 months to less than 2 years. **Knowledge:** Building and Construction; Engineering and Technology; Mechanical; English Language; Fine Arts; Design. **Instructional Programs:** 500501 Drama/Theater Arts, General; 500502 Technical Theater/Theater Design and Stagecraft.

Related DOT Jobs: 962.384-010 Microphone-Boom Operator; 962.664-014 Recording Studio Set-Up Worker; 962.684-018 Motor-Power Connector; 962.684-022 Prop Attendant; 962.687-018 Flyer; 962.687-022 Grip.

53-7062.03 Freight, Stock, and Material Movers, Hand (Freight, Stock and Material Movers)

Education: Short-term O-T-J training

Employed: 822,119

Openings: 306,549

Projected Growth: 1.5%

Earnings: No data available.

Load, unload, and move materials at plant, yard, or other work site.

Assembles product containers and crates, using hand tools and precut lumber. Sorts and stores items according to specifications. Installs protective devices such as bracing, padding, or strapping, to prevent shifting or damage to items being transported. Cleans work area, using brooms, rags, and cleaning compounds. Attaches identifying tags or marks information on containers. Loads and unloads materials to and from designated storage areas such as racks, shelves, or vehicles such as trucks. Adjusts or replaces equipment parts such as rollers, belts, plugs, and caps, using hand tools. Reads work orders, or receives and listens to oral instructions, to determine work assignment. Shovels materials such as gravel, ice, or spilled concrete, into containers or bins or onto conveyors. Transports receptacles to and from designated areas, by hand or using dollies, handtrucks, and wheelbarrows. Secures lifting attachments to materials and conveys load to destination, using crane or hoist. Stacks or piles materials such as lumber, boards, or pallets. Directs spouts and positions receptacles such as bins, carts, and containers, to receive loads. Bundles and bands material such as fodder and tobacco leaves, using banding machines. Records number of units handled and moved, using daily production sheet or work tickets.

GOE Number, Interest Area, and Work Group: 08.07.01; Industrial Production; Hands-on Work: Loading, Moving, Hoisting, and Conveying. **Personality Type:** Realistic. Realistic occupations frequently involve work activities that include practical, hands-on problems and solutions. These occupations often deal with plants, animals, and real-world materials like wood, tools, and machinery. Many of the occupations require working outside and do not involve a lot of paperwork or working closely with others. **Work Values:** Moral Values; Supervision, Human Relations; Activity; Supervision, Technical; Company Policies and Practices; Security. **Skills:** Active Listening; Equipment Selection; Reading Comprehension; Operation and Control. **Abilities:** *Cognitive*—Oral Comprehension; Written Comprehension; Information Ordering; Category Flexibility; Memorization. *Psychomotor*—Multilimb Coordination; Manual Dexterity. *Physical*—Static Strength; Trunk Strength; Extent Flexibility. *Sensory*—Depth Perception; Peripheral Vision. **General Work Activities:** *Information Input*—Getting Information Needed to Do the Job; Inspecting Equipment, Structures, Materials; Estimating Needed Characteristics. *Mental Process*—Processing Information; Evaluating Information Against Standards; Organizing, Planning, and Prioritizing; Updating and Using Job-Relevant Knowledge; Making Decisions and Solving Problems. *Work Output*—Handling and Moving Objects; Performing General Physical Activities; Documenting and Recording Information. *Interacting with Others*—Performing Administrative Activities; Communicating with Other Workers; Coordinating Work and Activities of Others; Assisting and Caring for Others; Communicating with Persons Outside Organization; Establishing and Maintaining Relationships. **Physical Work Conditions:** Using Hands on Objects, Tools, or Controls; Standing; Indoors. **Other Job Characteristics:** Importance of Repeating Same Tasks; Importance of Being Sure All Is Done; Degree of Automation; Importance of Being Exact or Accurate.

Experience: Job Zone 1. No previous work-related skill, knowledge, or experience is needed. **Job Preparation:** SVP Below 4.0—Less than 6 months. **Knowledge:** Production and Processing; Engineering and Technology; Mechanical; Clerical; Physics. **Instructional Programs:** No data available.

Related DOT Jobs: 412.687-010 Commissary Assistant; 520.687-010 Blender Laborer; 520.687-038 Gum Puller; 523.687-022 Freezing-Room Worker; 525.687-054 Offal Icer, Poultry; 525.687-086 Shackler; 529.687-138 Leaf Tier; 542.667-010 Wharf Tender; 573.687-030 Setter Helper; 575.687-026 Pipe Stripper; 579.665-014 Laborer, Concrete-Mixing Plant; 579.687-018 Floor Attendant; 669.687-018 Lumber Straightener; 677.687-010 Log Roller; 684.687-022 Collector; 727.687-030 Battery Stacker; 860.684-018 Car Blocker; 904.687-010 Tractor-Trailer Moving Van Driver Helper; 905.687-010 Truck-Driver Helper; 910.667-030 Transfer-Table Operator Helper (partial list; see the introduction for sources of the complete list).

53-7063.00 Machine Feeders and Offbearers (Machine Feeders and Offbearers)

Education: Short-term O-T-J training

Employed: 212,822

Openings: 40,239

Projected Growth: –0.9%

Earnings: $18,810

Feed materials into or remove materials from machines or equipment that is automatic or that is tended by other workers.

Moves controls to start, stop, or adjust machinery and equipment. Modifies materials and products during manufacturing process to meet requirements. Inspects materials and products to detect defects and to ensure conformance to specifications. Sorts and selects materials and products; rejects defective pieces, following specified instructions and standards. Adds chemicals, solutions, or ingredients to machines or equipment, to ensure that manufacturing process meets specifications. Off bears materials and products from machines and equipment, using hand tools. Loads materials and products into machines and equipment, using hand tools and moving devices. Removes materials and products from machines and equipment, using hand tools and moving devices. Identifies and marks materials, products, and samples, following instructions. Records production and operational information and data on specified forms. Weighs or measures materials or products to ensure conformance to specifications. Fastens, packages, or stacks materials and products, using hand tools and fastening equipment. Transfers materials and products between storage areas and machinery and equipment. Feeds materials into machines and equipment, to process and manufacture products. Shovels or scoops materials into containers or machines, or into equipment for processing, storage or transport. Cleans and maintains machinery, equipment, and work areas, to ensure proper functioning and safe working conditions.

GOE Number, Interest Area, and Work Group: 08.07.01; Industrial Production; Hands-on Work: Loading, Moving, Hoisting, and Conveying. **Personality Type:** Realistic. Realistic occupations frequently involve work activities that include practical, hands-on problems and solutions. These occupations often deal with plants, animals, and real-world materials like wood, tools, and machinery. Many of the occupations require working outside and do not involve a lot of paperwork or working closely with others. **Work Values:** Moral Values; Activity; Security; Supervision, Human Relations; Coworkers; Supervision, Technical; Company Policies and Practices. **Skills:** Product Inspection; Operation and Control; Equipment Maintenance; Operation Monitoring. **Abilities:** *Cognitive*—Problem Sensitivity; Information Ordering; Category Flexibility; Perceptual Speed; Spatial Orientation. *Psychomotor*—Manual Dexterity; Multilimb Coordination; Control Precision. *Physical*—Static Strength; Extent Flexibility; Trunk Strength. *Sensory*—Depth Perception; Far Vision; Visual Color Discrimination. **General Work Activities:** *Information Input*—Inspecting Equipment, Structures, Materials; Monitoring Processes, Materials, and Surroundings; Getting Information Needed to Do the Job. *Mental Process*—Evaluating Information Against Standards; Judging Qualities of Things, Services, Other People's Work; Processing Information. *Work Output*—Handling and Moving Objects; Performing General Physical Activities; Controlling Machines and Processes. *Interacting with Others*—Performing Administrative Activities; Communicating with Other Workers; Monitoring and Controlling Resources. **Physical Work Conditions:** Using Hands on Objects, Tools, or Controls; Indoors; Standing. **Other Job Characteristics:** Degree of Automation; Pace Determined by Speed of Equipment; Importance of Being Aware of New Events.

Experience: Job Zone 1. No previous work-related skill, knowledge, or experience is needed. **Job Preparation:** SVP Below 4.0—Less than 6 months. **Knowledge:** Production and Processing; Mechanical; Mathematics; Chemistry; Clerical; Engineering and Technology. **Instructional Programs:** No data available.

Related DOT Jobs: 361.686-010 Washing-Machine Loader-and-Puller; 363.686-010 Flatwork Finisher; 369.686-010 Folding-Machine Operator; 429.686-010 Press Feeder, Broomcorn; 504.686-014 Furnace Helper; 504.686-022 Heat Treater; 509.666-010 Compound-Coating-Machine Offbearer; 509.686-014 Pasting-Machine Offbearer; 509.687-026 Laborer, General; 512.686-010 Cupola Charger; 515.686-010 Battery-Wrecker Operator; 519.686-010 Laborer, General; 520.686-010 Ball-Machine Operator; 520.686-014 Dessert-Cup-Machine Feeder; 520.686-030 Molding-Machine-Operator Helper; 520.686-034 Plug Shaper, Machine; 521.686-014 Cake Puller; 521.686-018 Chicle-Grinder Feeder; 521.686-022 Cotton Puller; 521.686-030 Cut-in Worker (partial list; see the introduction for sources of the complete list).

53-7064.00 Packers and Packagers, Hand (Hand Packers and Packagers)

Education: Short-term O-T-J training

Employed: 984,044

Openings: 249,421

Projected Growth: 21.7%

Earnings: $14,540

Pack or package by hand a wide variety of products and materials.

Seals containers or materials, using glues, fasteners, and hand tools. Assembles and lines cartons, crates, and containers, using hand tools. Obtains and sorts products, materials, and orders, using hand tools. Examines and inspects containers, materials, and products, to ensure that the packaging process meets specifications. Records product and packaging information on specified forms and records. Removes and places completed or defective product or materials on moving equipment or in specified area. Tends packing machines and equipment that prepare and package materials and products. Measures, weighs, and counts products and materials, using equipment. Loads materials and products into package-processing equipment. Marks and labels containers or products, using marking instruments. Fastens and wraps products and materials, using hand tools. Places or pours products or materials into containers, using hand tools and equipment. Cleans containers, materials, or work area, using cleaning solutions and hand tools.

GOE Number, Interest Area, and Work Group: 08.07.01; Industrial Production; Hands-on Work: Loading, Moving, Hoisting, and Conveying. **Personality Type:** Realistic. Realistic occupations frequently involve work activities that include practical, hands-on problems and solutions. These occupations often deal with plants, animals, and real-world materials like wood, tools, and machinery. Many of the occupations require working outside and do not involve a lot of paperwork or working closely with others. **Work Values:** Moral Values; Activity; Supervision, Technical; Supervision, Human Relations; Company Policies and Practices. **Skills:** Operation and Control; Product Inspection. **Abilities:** *Cognitive*—Information Ordering; Category Flexibility; Problem Sensitivity; Visualization; Perceptual Speed; Number Facility. *Psychomotor*—Manual Dexterity; Wrist-Finger Speed; Control Precision. *Physical*—Static Strength; Extent Flexibility; Trunk Strength. **General Work Activities:** *Information Input*—Inspecting Equipment, Structures, Materials; Getting Information Needed to Do the Job; Monitoring Processes, Materials, and Surroundings. *Mental Process*—Organizing, Planning, and Prioritizing; Evaluating Information Against Standards; Judging Qualities of Things, Services, Other People's Work. *Work Output*—Handling and Moving Objects; Performing General Physical Activities; Documenting and Recording Information; Controlling Machines and Processes. *Interacting with Others*—Performing Administrative Activities; Monitoring and Controlling Resources; Communicating with Other Workers; Coordinating Work and Activities of Others; Assisting and Caring for Others; Establishing and Maintaining Relationships. **Physical Work Conditions:** Indoors; Using Hands on Objects, Tools, or Controls; Standing. **Other Job Characteristics:** Importance of Being Sure All Is Done; Consequence of Error; Importance of Repeating Same Tasks; Importance of Being Exact or Accurate.

Experience: Job Zone 1. No previous work-related skill, knowledge, or experience is needed. **Job Preparation:** SVP Below 4.0—Less than 6 months. **Knowledge:** Production and Processing; Clerical; Mathematics; Physics; Mechanical; English Language. **Instructional Programs:** No data available.

Related DOT Jobs: 522.687-010 Barrel Filler I; 522.687-018 Bulker; 525.687-082 Poultry-Dressing Worker; 525.687-118 Tier; 529.687-022 Bulk Filler; 529.687-086 Fish-Egg Packer; 529.687-150 Linker; 559.687-014 Ampoule Sealer; 585.687-030 Singer; 700.687-038 Laborer, Gold Leaf; 710.687-034 Tie-Up Worker; 737.587-018 Primer Boxer; 737.687-014 Bag Loader; 737.687-030 Core Loader; 737.687-094 Packer-Fuser; 753.687-038 Packing-Line Worker; 784.687-042 Inspector-Packer; 789.687-106 Mophead Trimmer-and-Wrapper; 794.687-034 Paper-Pattern Folder; 920.587-010 Cloth-Bolt Bander (partial list; see the introduction for sources of the complete list).

53-7071.00 Gas Compressor and Gas Pumping Station Operators (Gas Pumping Station Operators)

Education: No data available.

Employed: 1,340

Openings: No data available.

Projected Growth: No data available.

Earnings: $27,170

Operate steam, gas, electric motor, or internal-combustion engine-driven compressors. Transmit, compress, or recover gases such as butane, nitrogen, hydrogen, and natural gas.

GOE Number, Interest Area, and Work Group: 08.06.02; Industrial Production; Systems Operation: Oil, Gas, and Water Distribution. **Instructional Program:** 470501 Stationary Energy Sources Installer and Operator. **Note:** The Department of Labor has not collected some data for this job, so it has fewer details than the other descriptions.

53-7071.01 Gas Pumping Station Operators
(Gas Pumping Station Operators)

Education: No data available.

Employed: 1,340

Openings: No data available.

Projected Growth: No data available.

Earnings: $27,170

Control the operation of steam, gas, or electric-motor–driven compressor to maintain specified pressures on high- and low-pressure mains, dispensing gas from gasholders.

Cleans, lubricates, and adjusts compressors, using hand tools. Observes pressure gauges to determine consumption-rate variations; turns knobs or switches to regulate pressures. Reads gas meters and records amount of gas received and dispensed from holders. Opens valve to allow gas to flow into and out of compressors.

GOE Number, Interest Area, and Work Group: 08.06.02; Industrial Production; Systems Operation: Oil, Gas, and Water Distribution. **Personality Type:** Realistic. Realistic occupations frequently involve work activities that include practical, hands-on problems and solutions. These occupations often deal with plants, animals, and real-world materials like wood, tools, and machinery. Many of the occupations require working outside and do not involve a lot of paperwork or working closely with others. **Work Values:** Independence; Moral Values; Supervision, Human Relations; Company Policies and Practices; Security. **Skills:** Operation and Control; Operation Monitoring; Equipment Maintenance; Problem Identification. **Abilities:** *Cognitive*—Information Ordering; Written Comprehension; Memorization; Number Facility; Problem Sensitivity. *Psychomotor*—Control Precision; Reaction Time. *Physical*—Static Strength. *Sensory*—Glare Sensitivity. **General Work Activities:** *Information Input*—Monitoring Processes, Materials, and Surroundings; Getting Information Needed to Do the Job; Identifying Objects, Actions, and Events. *Mental Process*—Processing Information; Evaluating Information Against Standards; Making Decisions and Solving Problems. *Work Output*—Documenting and Recording Information; Controlling Machines and Processes; Handling and Moving Objects. *Interacting with Others*—Performing Administrative Activities; Performing for or Working with the Public; Communicating with Other Workers; Monitoring and Controlling Resources. **Physical Work Conditions:** Standing; Indoors; Using Hands on Objects, Tools, or Controls. **Other Job Characteristics:** Degree of Automation; Consequence of Error; Importance of Being Sure All Is Done; Importance of Being Exact or Accurate.

Experience: Job Zone 2. Some previous work-related skill, knowledge, or experience may be helpful, but usually is not needed. **Job Preparation:** SVP 4.00 to 5.99—6 months to less than 2 years. **Knowledge:** Mechanical; Engineering and Technology; Clerical; Computers and Electronics; Mathematics. **Instructional Program:** 470501 Stationary Energy Sources Installer and Operator.

Related DOT Job: 953.382-010 Gas-Pumping-Station Operator.

53-7071.02 Gas Compressor Operators (Gas Compressor Operators)

Education: No data available.

Employed: 3,080

Openings: No data available.

Projected Growth: No data available.

Earnings: $38,620

Operate steam or internal-combustion engines to transmit, compress, or recover gases such as butane, nitrogen, hydrogen, and natural gas, in various production processes.

Operates equipment to control transmission of natural gas through pipelines. Monitors meters, gauges, and recording instrument charts, to ensure specified temperature, pressure, and flow of gas through system. Operates or tends equipment to purify gases. Records instrument readings and operational changes in operating log. Performs minor repairs on equipment, using hand tools. Observes operation of equipment to detect malfunctions. Moves controls and turns valves to start compressor engines, pumps, and auxiliary equipment. Conducts chemical tests to evaluate quality of gas.

GOE Number, Interest Area, and Work Group: 08.06.02; Industrial Production; Systems Operation: Oil, Gas, and Water Distribution. **Personality Type:** Realistic. Realistic occupations frequently involve work activities that include practical, hands-on problems and solutions. These occupations often deal with plants, animals, and real-world materials like wood, tools, and machinery. Many of the occupations require working outside and do not involve a lot of paperwork or working closely with others. **Work Values:** Moral Values; Supervision, Human Relations; Independence; Security; Supervision, Technical; Company Policies and Practices. **Skills:** Operation and Control; Operation Monitoring; Repairing; Troubleshooting; Mathematics; Problem Identification. **Abilities:** *Cognitive*—Problem Sensitivity; Information Ordering; Written Expression; Inductive Reasoning; Deductive Reasoning; Perceptual Speed. *Psychomotor*—Control Precision; Multilimb Coordination. *Physical*—Extent Flexibility. **General Work Activities:** *Information Input*—Monitoring Processes, Materials, and Surroundings; Identifying Objects, Actions, and Events; Inspecting Equipment, Structures, Materials. *Mental Process*—Making Decisions and Solving Problems; Evaluating Information Against Standards; Analyzing Data or Information. *Work Output*—Controlling Machines and Processes; Handling and Moving Objects; Documenting and Recording Information. *Interacting with Others*—Performing Administrative Activities; Communicating with Other Workers; Establishing and Maintaining Relationships; Interpreting Meaning of Information to Others. **Physical Work Conditions:** Indoors; Contaminants; Using Hands on Objects,

Tools, or Controls; Standing. **Other Job Characteristics:** Consequence of Error; Degree of Automation; Importance of Being Sure All Is Done; Importance of Being Exact or Accurate.

Experience: Job Zone 4. A minimum of two to four years of work-related skill, knowledge, or experience is needed. **Job Preparation:** SVP 7.0 to less than 8.0—2 years to less than 10 years. **Knowledge:** Mechanical; Chemistry; Clerical; Physics; Production and Processing. **Instructional Program:** 470501 Stationary Energy Sources Installer and Operator.

Related DOT Job: 950.382-014 Gas-Compressor Operator.

53-7072.00 Pump Operators, Except Wellhead Pumpers (Pump Operators)

Education: No data available.

Employed: 8,610

Openings: No data available.

Projected Growth: No data available.

Earnings: $32,370

Tend, control, or operate power-driven, stationary, or portable pumps and manifold systems to transfer gases, oil, other liquids, slurries, or powdered materials to and from various vessels and processes.

Records information such as type and quantity of material, and operating data. Turns valves and starts pump to commence or regulate flow of substances such as gases, liquids, slurries, or powdered materials. Observes gauges and flowmeter to ascertain that specifications are met, such as tank level, chemical amounts, and pressure. Tends vessels that store substances such as gases, liquids, slurries, or powdered materials. Tends auxiliary equipment such as water treatment and refrigeration units and heat exchanges. Cleans and maintains pumps and vessels, using hand tools and equipment. Inspects and reports vessel and pump abnormalities such as leaks, pressure, and temperature fluctuations. Transfers materials to and from vessels, using moving equipment. Collects and delivers sample solutions for laboratory analysis. Communicates with workers to start flow of materials or substance. Connects hoses and pipes to pumps and vessels, using hand tools. Tests materials and solutions, using testing equipment. Adds chemicals and solutions to tank to ensure that specifications are met.

GOE Number, Interest Area, and Work Group: 08.07.01; Industrial Production; Hands-on Work: Loading, Moving, Hoisting, and Conveying. **Personality Type:** Realistic. Realistic occupations frequently involve work activities that include practical, hands-on problems and solutions. These occupations often deal with plants, animals, and real-world materials like wood, tools, and machinery. Many of the occupations require working outside and do not involve a lot of paperwork or working closely with others. **Work Values:** Moral Values; Supervision, Human Relations; Supervision, Technical; Company Policies and Practices; Activity. **Skills:** Operation and Control; Operation Monitoring; Equipment Maintenance; Equipment Selection; Testing; Mathematics. **Abilities:** *Cognitive*—Information Ordering; Problem Sensitivity; Oral Expression; Time Sharing; Selective Attention. *Psychomotor*—

Control Precision; Manual Dexterity; Arm-Hand Steadiness. *Physical*—Trunk Strength; Extent Flexibility; Static Strength. *Sensory*—Near Vision; Visual Color Discrimination; Far Vision; Depth Perception. **General Work Activities:** *Information Input*—Monitoring Processes, Materials, and Surroundings; Identifying Objects, Actions, and Events; Inspecting Equipment, Structures, Materials. *Mental Process*—Judging Qualities of Things, Services, Other People's Work; Evaluating Information Against Standards; Processing Information; Making Decisions and Solving Problems; Updating and Using Job-Relevant Knowledge. *Work Output*—Controlling Machines and Processes; Handling and Moving Objects; Implementing Ideas and Programs. *Interacting with Others*—Communicating with Other Workers; Coordinating Work and Activities of Others; Performing Administrative Activities; Establishing and Maintaining Relationships. **Physical Work Conditions:** Using Hands on Objects, Tools, or Controls; Indoors; Hazardous Equipment; Standing. **Other Job Characteristics:** Degree of Automation; Importance of Being Sure All Is Done; Pace Determined by Speed of Equipment; Consequence of Error; Importance of Being Exact or Accurate.

Experience: Job Zone 2. Some previous work-related skill, knowledge, or experience may be helpful, but usually is not needed. **Job Preparation:** SVP 4.00 to 5.99—6 months to less than 2 years. **Knowledge:** Mechanical; Physics; Chemistry; Production and Processing; English Language. **Instructional Program:** 470399 Industrial Equipment Maintenance and Repairers, Other.

Related DOT Jobs: 521.565-010 Liquor-Bridge Operator; 522.662-010 Receiver, Fermenting Cellars; 529.585-014 Tank Tender; 529.685-242 Tank Pumper, Panelboard; 529.685-246 Tapper; 549.362-010 Still-Pump Operator; 549.382-018 Wash-Oil-Pump Operator; 549.685-042 Utility Operator III; 559.585-014 Grease-and-Tallow Pumper; 559.665-038 Tank-Farm Attendant; 559.684-034 Utility Worker, Production; 559.685-026 Brine-Well Operator; 914.585-010 Gas-Transfer Operator; 914.665-010 Pigment Pumper; 914.665-014 Pumper, Brewery; 914.682-010 Pumper; 939.682-010 Monitor Car Operator; 950.362-010 Engineer, Exhauster; 952.464-010 Cable Maintainer.

53-7073.00 Wellhead Pumpers (Wellhead Pumpers)

Education: No data available.

Employed: 7,040

Openings: No data available.

Projected Growth: No data available.

Earnings: $33,610

Operate power pumps and auxiliary equipment to produce flow of oil or gas from wells in oil field.

Opens valves to return compressed gas to bottoms of specified wells, to repressurize them and to force oil to surface. Operates engines and pumps from central powerplant, to shut off wells and to switch flow of oil into storage tanks. Reads tank gauges and pump meters, and keeps production records. Starts compressor engines and diverts oil from storage tanks into compressor units and auxiliary equipment to recover natural gas from oil. Starts pumps and opens valves, to pump oil from wells into storage tanks.

GOE Number, Interest Area, and Work Group: 08.06.02; Industrial Production; Systems Operation: Oil, Gas, and Water Distribution. **Personality Type:** Realistic. Realistic occupations frequently involve work activities that include practical, hands-on problems and solutions. These occupations often deal with plants, animals, and real-world materials like wood, tools, and machinery. Many of the occupations require working outside and do not involve a lot of paperwork or working closely with others. **Work Values:** Moral Values; Independence; Supervision, Human Relations; Supervision, Technical; Company Policies and Practices. **Skills:** Operation Monitoring; Operation and Control; Writing; Product Inspection. **Abilities:** *Cognitive*—Information Ordering; Problem Sensitivity; Memorization; Deductive Reasoning; Written Comprehension; Oral Comprehension. *Psychomotor*—Control Precision; Rate Control. *Physical*—Gross Body Coordination. **General Work Activities:** *Information Input*—Monitoring Processes, Materials, and Surroundings; Getting Information Needed to Do the Job; Identifying Objects, Actions, and Events. *Mental Process*—Making Decisions and Solving Problems; Evaluating Information Against Standards; Processing Information; Analyzing Data or Information. *Work Output*—Controlling Machines and Processes; Handling and Moving Objects; Documenting and Recording Information. *Interacting with Others*—Performing Administrative Activities; Communicating with Other Workers; Coordinating Work and Activities of Others. **Physical Work Conditions:** Common Protective or Safety Attire; Standing; Contaminants. **Other Job Characteristics:** Consequence of Error; Degree of Automation; Importance of Being Sure All Is Done.

Experience: Job Zone 4. A minimum of two to four years of work-related skill, knowledge, or experience is needed. **Job Preparation:** SVP 7.0 to less than 8.0—2 years to less than 10 years. **Knowledge:** Clerical; Production and Processing; Engineering and Technology; Mechanical; Physics. **Instructional Program:** 470399 Industrial Equipment Maintenance and Repairers, Other.

Related DOT Job: 914.382-022 Pumper, Head.

53-7081.00 Refuse and Recyclable Material Collectors (Refuse and Recyclable Material Collectors)

Education: Short-term O-T-J training

Employed: 98,801

Openings: 38,604

Projected Growth: 3.9%

Earnings: $21,860

Collect and dump refuse or recyclable materials from containers into truck. Drive truck.

Drives truck. Starts hoisting device that raises refuse bin attached to rear of truck; dumps contents into opening in enclosed truck body.

GOE Number, Interest Area, and Work Group: 08.07.01; Industrial Production; Hands-on Work: Loading, Moving, Hoisting, and Conveying. **Personality Type:** Realistic. Realistic occupations frequently involve work activities that include practical, hands-on problems and solutions. These occupations often deal with plants, animals, and real-world materials like wood, tools, and machinery. Many of the occupations require working outside and do not involve a lot of paperwork or working closely with others. **Work Values:** Moral Values; Company Policies and Practices; Security; Supervision, Human Relations; Activity. **Skills:** Operation and Control. **Abilities:** *Cognitive*—Spatial Orientation; Category Flexibility; Problem Sensitivity; Written Comprehension; Memorization; Flexibility of Closure. *Psychomotor*—Multilimb Coordination; Rate Control. *Physical*—Static Strength; Trunk Strength; Dynamic Strength; Stamina; Gross Body Coordination. *Sensory*—Glare Sensitivity. **General Work Activities:** *Information Input*—Monitoring Processes, Materials, and Surroundings; Identifying Objects, Actions, and Events; Getting Information Needed to Do the Job. *Mental Process*—Organizing, Planning, and Prioritizing; Making Decisions and Solving Problems; Evaluating Information Against Standards. *Work Output*—Performing General Physical Activities; Handling and Moving Objects; Operating Vehicles or Equipment. *Interacting with Others*—Communicating with Other Workers; Coordinating Work and Activities of Others; Establishing and Maintaining Relationships; Performing for or Working with the Public. **Physical Work Conditions:** Outdoors; Standing; Using Hands on Objects, Tools, or Controls. **Other Job Characteristics:** Degree of Automation; Importance of Repeating Same Tasks; Consequence of Error; Importance of Being Sure All Is Done.

Experience: Job Zone 1. No previous work-related skill, knowledge, or experience is needed. **Job Preparation:** SVP Below 4.0—Less than 6 months. **Knowledge:** Transportation; Geography; Mechanical; Public Safety and Security; Customer and Personal Service. **Instructional Program:** 490299 Vehicle and Equipment Operators, Other.

Related DOT Job: 955.687-022 Garbage Collector.

53-7111.00 Shuttle Car Operators (Shuttle Car Operators)

Education: No data available.
Employed: 2,880
Openings: No data available.
Projected Growth: No data available.
Earnings: $35,090

Operate diesel or electric-powered shuttle car in underground mine to transport materials from working face to mine cars or conveyor.

Positions shuttle car under discharge conveyor of loading machine; observes that materials are loaded according to specifications. Controls conveyor which runs entire length of shuttle car, to apportion load as loading progresses. Drives loaded shuttle car to ramp and moves controls to discharge load into mine car or onto conveyor. Maneuvers shuttle car to keep its nose under discharge conveyor. Moves mine cars into position to be loaded from shuttle car.

GOE Number, Interest Area, and Work Group: 06.03.01; Construction, Mining, and Drilling; Mining and Drilling. **Personality Type:** Realistic. Realistic occupations frequently involve work activities that include practical, hands-on problems and solutions. These occupations often deal with plants, animals, and real-world materials like wood, tools, and machinery. Many of the occupa-

tions require working outside and do not involve a lot of paperwork or working closely with others. **Work Values:** Moral Values; Independence; Supervision, Human Relations; Supervision, Technical; Company Policies and Practices. **Skills:** Operation and Control; Operation Monitoring. **Abilities:** *Cognitive*—Visualization; Spatial Orientation; Problem Sensitivity; Time Sharing; Perceptual Speed. *Psychomotor*—Control Precision; Multilimb Coordination; Manual Dexterity; Rate Control. *Physical*—Gross Body Coordination. *Sensory*—Depth Perception; Night Vision; Far Vision; Peripheral Vision. **General Work Activities:** *Information Input*—Monitoring Processes, Materials, and Surroundings; Getting Information Needed to Do the Job; Estimating Needed Characteristics. *Mental Process*—Evaluating Information Against Standards; Analyzing Data or Information; Making Decisions and Solving Problems. *Work Output*—Operating Vehicles or Equipment; Handling and Moving Objects; Controlling Machines and Processes. *Interacting with Others*—Communicating with Other Workers; Establishing and Maintaining Relationships; Coaching and Developing Others; Monitoring and Controlling Resources; Assisting and Caring for Others. **Physical Work Conditions:** Outdoors; Using Hands on Objects, Tools, or Controls; Distracting Sounds and Noise Levels; Common Protective or Safety Attire. **Other Job Characteristics:** Degree of Automation; Consequence of Error; Importance of Being Sure All Is Done.

Experience: Job Zone 2. Some previous work-related skill, knowledge, or experience may be helpful, but usually is not needed. **Job Preparation:** SVP 4.00 to 5.99—6 months to less than 2 years. **Knowledge:** Transportation; Mechanical; Engineering and Technology; Public Safety and Security; Production and Processing. **Instructional Program:** 490299 Vehicle and Equipment Operators, Other.

Related DOT Job: 932.683-022 Shuttle-Car Operator.

53-7121.00 Tank Car, Truck, and Ship Loaders (Tank Car and Truck Loaders)

Education: No data available.
Employed: 3,980
Openings: No data available.
Projected Growth: No data available.
Earnings: $31,170

Load and unload chemicals and bulk solids such as coal, sand, and grain into or from tank cars, trucks, or ships, using material-moving equipment. Perform a variety of other tasks relating to shipment of products. Gauge or sample shipping tanks; test them for leaks.

Operates blenders and heaters, to mix, blend, and heat products. Starts pumps and adjusts valves, to regulate flow of product to vessel, utilizing knowledge of loading procedures. Monitors product movement to and from storage tanks; coordinates with other workers to ensure constant product flow. Unloads cars by connecting hose to outlet plugs and pumping compressed air into car, forcing liquid into storage tank. Verifies tank car, barge, or truck load number, to ensure car placement accuracy based on written or verbal instructions. Weighs and inspects vessels, to prevent contamination and to ensure cleanliness and compliance to loading procedures. Tests vessels for leaks, damage, and defects; repairs or replaces defective parts. Reads meter to verify content, temperature, and volume of liquid load. Copies and tacks load specifications onto tank; seals outlet valves on tank car, barge, or truck. Records operating data such as products and quantities pumped, gauge readings, and operating time, manually or using computer. Retrieves liquid sample and performs tests on contents; delivers sample to laboratory for testing.

GOE Number, Interest Area, and Work Group: 08.07.01; Industrial Production; Hands-on Work: Loading, Moving, Hoisting, and Conveying. **Personality Type:** Realistic. Realistic occupations frequently involve work activities that include practical, hands-on problems and solutions. These occupations often deal with plants, animals, and real-world materials like wood, tools, and machinery. Many of the occupations require working outside and do not involve a lot of paperwork or working closely with others. **Work Values:** Moral Values; Independence; Company Policies and Practices; Supervision, Human Relations; Supervision, Technical. **Skills:** Operation Monitoring; Operation and Control; Product Inspection; Testing; Repairing; Reading Comprehension; Equipment Selection. **Abilities:** *Cognitive*—Written Comprehension; Problem Sensitivity; Written Expression; Number Facility; Deductive Reasoning. *Psychomotor*—Reaction Time; Control Precision; Rate Control; Manual Dexterity. *Physical*—Static Strength; Explosive Strength; Dynamic Strength; Gross Body Coordination. *Sensory*—Sound Localization; Peripheral Vision. **General Work Activities:** *Information Input*—Getting Information Needed to Do the Job; Monitoring Processes, Materials, and Surroundings; Inspecting Equipment, Structures, Materials. *Mental Process*—Judging Qualities of Things, Services, Other People's Work; Evaluating Information Against Standards; Processing Information. *Work Output*—Controlling Machines and Processes; Handling and Moving Objects; Documenting and Recording Information. *Interacting with Others*—Communicating with Other Workers; Coordinating Work and Activities of Others; Monitoring and Controlling Resources. **Physical Work Conditions:** Hazardous Conditions; Standing; Contaminants; Outdoors. **Other Job Characteristics:** Consequence of Error; Importance of Being Exact or Accurate; Importance of Being Sure All Is Done.

Experience: Job Zone 3. Previous work-related skill, knowledge, or experience is required. **Job Preparation:** SVP 6.0 to less than 7.0—More than 1 year and less than 4 years. **Knowledge:** Production and Processing; Chemistry; Mechanical; Engineering and Technology; Physics; Mathematics; Public Safety and Security; English Language. **Instructional Programs:** No data available.

Related DOT Jobs: 914.382-014 Pumper-Gauger; 914.382-018 Pumper-Gauger Apprentice; 914.667-010 Loader I.

55-0000
Military Specific Occupations

55-1000 Military Officer Special and Tactical Operations Leaders/Managers

55-1011.00 Air Crew Officers

Perform and direct in-flight duties to ensure the successful completion of combat, reconnaissance, transport, and search-and-rescue missions. Operate aircraft communications and radar equipment; establish satellite linkages and jam enemy communications capabilities; operate aircraft weapons and defensive systems; conduct preflight, in-flight, and postflight inspections of onboard equipment; direct cargo and personnel drops.

GOE Number, Interest Area, and Work Group: 04.05.01; Law, Law Enforcement, and Public Safety; Military: Officers and Supervisors. **Instructional Programs:** 280101 Air Force R.O.T.C./ Air Science; 280301 Army R.O.T.C./Military Science; 280401 Navy/ Marine Corps R.O.T.C./Naval Science. **Note:** The Department of Labor has not collected some data for this job, so it has fewer details than the other descriptions.

55-1012.00 Aircraft Launch and Recovery Officers

Plan and direct the operation and maintenance of catapults, arresting gear, and associated mechanical, hydraulic, and control systems involved primarily in aircraft carrier takeoff and landing operations. Supervise readiness and safety of arresting gear, launching equipment, barricades, and visual landing aid systems. Plan and coordinate the design, development, and testing of launch and recovery systems. Prepare specifications for catapult and arresting gear installations. Evaluate design proposals, determining handling equipment needed for new aircraft. Prepare technical data and instructions for operation of landing aids. Train personnel in carrier takeoff and landing procedures.

GOE Number, Interest Area, and Work Group: 04.05.01; Law, Law Enforcement, and Public Safety; Military: Officers and Supervisors. **Instructional Programs:** 280101 Air Force R.O.T.C./ Air Science; 280301 Army R.O.T.C./Military Science; 280401 Navy/ Marine Corps R.O.T.C./Naval Science. **Note:** The Department of Labor has not collected some data for this job, so it has fewer details than the other descriptions.

55-1013.00 Armored Assault Vehicle Officers

Direct the operation of tanks, light armor, and amphibious assault vehicle units during combat situations on land or in aquatic environments. Direct crew members in the operation of targeting and firing systems. Coordinate the operation of advanced onboard communications and navigation equipment. Direct the transport of personnel and equipment during combat. Formulate and implement battle plans, including the tactical employment of armored vehicle units; coordinate with infantry, artillery, and air support units.

GOE Number, Interest Area, and Work Group: 04.05.01; Law, Law Enforcement, and Public Safety; Military: Officers and Supervisors. **Instructional Programs:** 280101 Air Force R.O.T.C./ Air Science; 280301 Army R.O.T.C./Military Science; 280401 Navy/ Marine Corps R.O.T.C./Naval Science. **Note:** The Department of Labor has not collected some data for this job, so it has fewer details than the other descriptions.

55-1014.00 Artillery and Missile Officers

Manage personnel and weapons operations to destroy enemy positions, aircraft, and vessels. Plan, target, and coordinate the tactical deployment of field artillery and air-defense artillery missile-systems units. Direct the establishment and operation of fire-control communications systems. Target and launch intercontinental ballistic missiles. Direct the storage and handling of nuclear munitions and components. Oversee security of weapons storage and launch facilities. Manage maintenance of weapons systems.

GOE Number, Interest Area, and Work Group: 04.05.01; Law, Law Enforcement, and Public Safety; Military: Officers and Supervisors. **Instructional Programs:** 280101 Air Force R.O.T.C./ Air Science; 280301 Army R.O.T.C./Military Science; 280401 Navy/ Marine Corps R.O.T.C./Naval Science. **Note:** The Department of Labor has not collected some data for this job, so it has fewer details than the other descriptions.

55-1015.00 Command and Control Center Officers

Manage the operation of communications, detection, and weapons systems essential for controlling air, ground, and naval operations. Manage critical communication links between air, naval, and ground forces. Formulate and implement emergency plans for natural and wartime disasters. Coordinate emergency response teams and agencies. Evaluate command-center information and the need for high-level military and government reporting. Manage the operation of surveillance and detection systems. Provide technical information and advice on capabilities and operational readiness. Direct operation of computerized weapons, including targeting, firing, and launching.

GOE Number, Interest Area, and Work Group: 04.05.01; Law, Law Enforcement, and Public Safety; Military: Officers and Supervisors. **Instructional Programs:** 280101 Air Force R.O.T.C./ Air Science; 280301 Army R.O.T.C./Military Science; 280401 Navy/ Marine Corps R.O.T.C./Naval Science. **Note:** The Department of Labor has not collected some data for this job, so it has fewer details than the other descriptions.

55-1016.00 Infantry Officers

Direct, train, and lead infantry units in ground combat operations. Direct deployment of infantry weapons, vehicles, and equipment. Direct location, construction, and camouflage of infantry positions and equipment. Manage field communications operations; coordinate with armor, artillery, and air support units. Perform strategic and tactical planning, including developing battle plans and leading basic reconnaissance operations.

GOE Number, Interest Area, and Work Group: 04.05.01; Law, Law Enforcement, and Public Safety; Military: Officers and Supervisors. **Instructional Programs**: 280101 Air Force R.O.T.C./ Air Science; 280301 Army R.O.T.C./Military Science; 280401 Navy/ Marine Corps R.O.T.C./Naval Science. **Note**: The Department of Labor has not collected some data for this job, so it has fewer details than the other descriptions.

55-1017.00 Special Forces Officers

Lead elite teams that implement unconventional operations by air, land, or sea during combat or peacetime. Lead offensive raids, demolitions, reconnaissance, search and rescue, and counterterrorism. Perform duties involving specialized training in swimming, diving, parachuting, survival, emergency medicine, and foreign languages. Direct advanced reconnaissance operations; evaluate intelligence information. Recruit, train, and equip friendly forces. Lead raids and invasions on enemy territories. Train personnel to implement individual missions and contingency plans. Perform strategic and tactical planning for politically sensitive missions. Operate sophisticated communications equipment.

GOE Number, Interest Area, and Work Group: 04.05.01; Law, Law Enforcement, and Public Safety; Military: Officers and Supervisors. **Instructional Programs**: 280101 Air Force R.O.T.C./ Air Science; 280301 Army R.O.T.C./Military Science; 280401 Navy/ Marine Corps R.O.T.C./Naval Science. **Note**: The Department of Labor has not collected some data for this job, so it has fewer details than the other descriptions.

55-2000 First-Line Enlisted Military Supervisor/Managers

55-2011.00 First-Line Supervisors/Managers of Air Crew Members

Supervise and coordinate the activities of air crew members. Perform the same activities as the workers they supervise.

GOE Number, Interest Area, and Work Group: 04.05.01; Law, Law Enforcement, and Public Safety; Military: Officers and Supervisors. **Instructional Program**: 290101 Military Technologies. **Note**: The Department of Labor has not collected some data for this job, so it has fewer details than the other descriptions.

55-2012.00 First-Line Supervisors/Managers of Weapons Specialists/Crew Members

Supervise and coordinate the activities of weapons specialists/ crew members. Perform the same activities as the workers they supervise.

GOE Number, Interest Area, and Work Group: 04.05.01; Law, Law Enforcement, and Public Safety; Military: Officers and Supervisors. **Instructional Program**: 290101 Military Technologies. **Note**: The Department of Labor has not collected some data for this job, so it has fewer details than the other descriptions.

55-2013.00 First-Line Supervisors/Managers of All Other Tactical Operations Specialists

Supervise and coordinate the activities of all other tactical operations specialists not classified separately above. Perform the same activities as the workers they supervise.

GOE Number, Interest Area, and Work Group: 04.05.01; Law, Law Enforcement, and Public Safety; Military: Officers and Supervisors. **Instructional Program**: 290101 Military Technologies. **Note**: The Department of Labor has not collected some data for this job, so it has fewer details than the other descriptions.

55-3000 Military Enlisted Tactical Operations and Air/ Weapons Specialists and Crew Members

55-3011.00 Air Crew Members

Perform in-flight duties to ensure the successful completion of combat, reconnaissance, transport, and search-and-rescue missions. Operate aircraft communications and detection equipment, establishing satellite linkages and jamming enemy communications capabilities. Conduct preflight, in-flight, and postflight inspections of onboard equipment. Operate and maintain aircraft weapons and defensive systems. Operate and maintain aircraft in-flight refueling systems. Execute aircraft safety and emergency procedures. Compute and verify data reflecting weight and balance of passengers, cargo, fuel, and emergency and special equipment. Conduct cargo and personnel drops.

GOE Number, Interest Area, and Work Group: 04.05.02; Law, Law Enforcement, and Public Safety; Military: Specialists. **Instructional Program**: 290101 Military Technologies. **Note**: The Department of Labor has not collected some data for this job, so it has fewer details than the other descriptions.

55-3012.00 Aircraft Launch and Recovery Specialists

Operate and maintain catapults, arresting gear, and associated mechanical, hydraulic, and control systems involved primarily in aircraft carrier takeoff and landing operations. Install and maintain visual landing aids. Test and maintain launch and recovery equipment, using electric and mechanical test equipment and hand tools. Activate airfield arresting systems, such as crash barriers and cables, during emergency landing situations. Direct aircraft launch and recovery operations, using hand or light signals. Maintain logs of airplane launches, recoveries, and equipment maintenance.

GOE Number, Interest Area, and Work Group: 04.05.02; Law, Law Enforcement, and Public Safety; Military: Specialists. **Instructional Program**: 290101 Military Technologies. **Note**: The Department of Labor has not collected some data for this job, so it has fewer details than the other descriptions.

55-3013.00 Armored Assault Vehicle Crew Members

Operate tanks, light armor, and amphibious assault vehicles during combat situations on land or in aquatic environments. Drive armored vehicles that require specialized training. Operate and maintain targeting and firing systems. Operate and maintain advanced onboard communications and navigation equipment. Transport personnel and equipment in a combat environment. Operate and maintain auxiliary weapons, including machine guns and grenade launchers.

GOE Number, Interest Area, and Work Group: 04.05.02; Law, Law Enforcement, and Public Safety; Military: Specialists. Instructional Program: 290101 Military Technologies. Note: The Department of Labor has not collected some data for this job, so it has fewer details than the other descriptions.

55-3014.00 Artillery and Missile Crew Members

Target, fire, and maintain weapons used to destroy enemy positions, aircraft, and vessels. Use guns, cannons, and howitzers predominantly in ground combat operations; use missiles and rockets predominantly in air defense operations; use torpedoes and missiles predominantly in operations launched from a ship or submarine. Test, inspect, and store ammunition, missiles, and torpedoes. Conduct preventive and routine maintenance on weapons and related equipment. Establish and maintain radio and wire communications. Operate computerized weapons, including targeting, firing, and launching.

GOE Number, Interest Area, and Work Group: 04.05.02; Law, Law Enforcement, and Public Safety; Military: Specialists. Instructional Program: 290101 Military Technologies. Note: The Department of Labor has not collected some data for this job, so it has fewer details than the other descriptions.

55-3015.00 Command and Control Center Specialists

Operate and monitor communications, detection, and weapons systems essential for controlling air, ground, and naval operations. Maintain and relay critical communications between air, naval, and ground forces. Implement emergency plans for natural and wartime disasters. Relay command center information to high-level military and government decision makers. Monitor surveillance and detection systems such as those involved in air defense. Interpret and evaluate tactical situations. Make recommendations to superiors. Operate computerized weapons, including targeting, firing, and launching.

GOE Number, Interest Area, and Work Group: 04.05.02; Law, Law Enforcement, and Public Safety; Military: Specialists. Instructional Program: 290101 Military Technologies. Note: The Department of Labor has not collected some data for this job, so it has fewer details than the other descriptions.

55-3016.00 Infantry

Operate weapons and equipment in ground combat operations. Operate and maintain weapons such as rifles, machine guns, mortars, and hand grenades. Locate, construct, and camouflage infantry positions and equipment. Evaluate terrain; record topographical information. Operate and maintain field communications equipment. Assess need for and directing supporting fire. Place explosives and perform minesweeping activities on land. Participate in basic reconnaissance operations.

GOE Number, Interest Area, and Work Group: 04.05.02; Law, Law Enforcement, and Public Safety; Military: Specialists. Instructional Program: 290101 Military Technologies. Note: The Department of Labor has not collected some data for this job, so it has fewer details than the other descriptions.

55-3017.00 Radar and Sonar Technicians

Operate equipment, using radio or sound-wave technology to identify, track, and analyze objects or natural phenomena of military interest. Perform minor maintenance. Includes airborne, shipboard, and terrestrial positions.

GOE Number, Interest Area, and Work Group: 04.05.02; Law, Law Enforcement, and Public Safety; Military: Specialists. Instructional Program: 290101 Military Technologies. Note: The Department of Labor has not collected some data for this job, so it has fewer details than the other descriptions.

55-3018.00 Special Forces

Implement unconventional operations by air, land, or sea during combat or peacetime, as members of elite teams. Participate in offensive raids, demolitions, reconnaissance, search and rescue, and counterterrorism. Participate in operations requiring specialized training in swimming, diving, parachuting, survival, emergency medicine, and foreign languages. Conduct advanced reconnaissance operations. Collect intelligence information. Recruit, train, and equip friendly forces. Conduct raids and invasions on enemy territories. Lay and detonate explosives for demolition targets. Locate, identify, defuse, and dispose of ordnance. Operate and maintain sophisticated communications equipment.

GOE Number, Interest Area, and Work Group: 04.05.02; Law, Law Enforcement, and Public Safety; Military: Specialists. Instructional Program: 290101 Military Technologies. Note: The Department of Labor has not collected some data for this job, so it has fewer details than the other descriptions.

Appendix

Exploring Careers Based on Interests

This Is *Not* Another Boring Appendix

Most appendixes are boring, so few people pay much attention to them. But we think this one is different. Yes, it does *look* boring, but what you can do with it is quite interesting. You see, you can use this appendix as a career-assessment instrument to help you identify options to consider in more detail.

It starts with a very simple question: "What are you interested in?" and then leads you to career possibilities that match those interests. As you will soon see, this appendix is very easy to use. And you can use it to accomplish the same thing an expensive test session might do.

The interest areas listed in this appendix are from the *Guide for Occupational Exploration,* Third Edition (JIST Works, 2001).

Quick Tips on Using This Appendix to Identify Career Options

We included this appendix so that you can use it to quickly identify career options to explore more fully. Here are some quick tips on how you can use it:

- **Begin with the 14 GOE interest areas.** Look over the 14 interest areas presented in just a bit. Read the brief descriptions for each and select your 2 or 3 top choices.

- **Review the work groups and job titles in your top interest areas.** Later in this appendix is a list of more specific GOE work groups for each interest area. Within these groups are related job titles. Carefully review these lists for your top interest areas.

- **Select specific work groups and titles.** Because others are likely to use this book, use a separate sheet of paper to write specific GOE work groups and related job titles that interest you most. Or photocopy these pages and checkmark those that interest you. (Permission to photocopy pages from this book is granted only to individual users. For groups and other uses, you must obtain permission in writing from the publisher.)

- **Look over the other interest areas.** Do the same thing for the interest areas you did not select as your top ones. Doing this sometimes uncovers an option you would otherwise overlook.

- **Select your top work groups or job titles for more exploration.** Select the 5 to 10 top work groups or job titles that you want to learn more about. You can select more, of course, but you should limit it to ones that are *most* interesting to you.

- **Research your selections.** You can use a variety of sources to obtain additional information on the career options you select. Besides this book, two other major resources are the *Occupational Outlook Handbook* and the *Guide for Occupational Exploration.* Both are described in the introduction to this book. You can also access the complete database of detailed information on the O*NET jobs on the Internet at http://online.onetcenter.org.

- **Develop a plan of action.** Thinking and researching are important, but don't stop there. When you identify a career, training, or education option that motivates you, decide to do something to move toward that goal. A variety of good career and life-planning resources are available, so decide to take action—soon.

This Appendix Is Based on a Career Exploration System Developed by the U.S. Department of Labor

Lots of research suggests that following your interests is one of the most reliable ways to identify a career or learning objective.

This appendix is based on a system developed by the U.S. Department of Labor called the *Guide for Occupational Exploration.* The GOE is based on substantial research into creating a useful and easy-to-use system to help people explore career alternatives. Although this appendix is not a career assessment test, it provides information that can help you clarify your career goals.

The GOE was first released in the late 1970s; however, this appendix uses new GOE interest areas and work groups first released in the 2001 revision of the *Guide for Occupational Exploration.*

A variety of occupational reference books, career assessment tests, and career information software use the GOE system for organizing occupations. You may use some of these GOE-based materials already. Even if you don't, the information in here can help you clarify your career objectives.

Brief Descriptions of the 14 GOE Interest Groups

The 14 interest areas are presented here, along with brief descriptions for each. Look over the interest areas and select the 2 or 3 that interest you most.

01 Arts, Entertainment, and Media. *An interest in creatively expressing feelings or ideas, in communicating news or information, or in performing.* You can satisfy this interest in several creative, verbal, or performing activities. For example, if you enjoy literature, perhaps writing or editing would appeal to you. Do you prefer to work in the performing arts? If so, you could direct or perform in drama, music, or dance. If you especially enjoy the visual arts, you could become a critic in painting, sculpture, or ceramics. You may want to use your hands to create or decorate products. You may prefer to model clothes or develop sets for entertainment. Or you may want to participate in sports professionally, as an athlete or coach.

02 Science, Math, and Engineering. *An interest in discovering, collecting, and analyzing information about the natural world; in applying scientific research findings to problems in medicine, the life sciences, and the natural* sciences; in imagining and manipulating quantitative data; and in applying technology to manufacturing, transportation, mining, and other economic activities. You can satisfy this interest by working with the knowledge and processes of the sciences. You may enjoy researching and developing new knowledge in mathematics; or perhaps solving problems in the physical or life sciences would appeal to you. You may want to study engineering and help create new machines, processes, and structures. If you want to work with scientific equipment and procedures, you could seek a job in a research or testing laboratory.

03 Plants and Animals. *An interest in working with plants and animals, usually outdoors.* You can satisfy this interest by working in farming, forestry, fishing, and related fields. You may like doing physical work outdoors, such as on a farm. You may enjoy animals; perhaps training or taking care of animals would appeal to you. If you have management ability, you could own, operate, or manage a farm or related business.

04 Law, Law Enforcement, and Public Safety. *An interest in upholding people's rights, or in protecting people and property by using authority, inspecting, or monitoring.* You can satisfy this interest by working in law, law enforcement, fire-fighting, and related fields. For example, if you enjoy mental challenge and intrigue, you could investigate crimes or fires for a living. If you enjoy working with verbal skills, you may want to defend citizens in court or research deeds, wills, and other legal documents. You may prefer to fight fires and respond to other emergencies. Or, if you want more routine work, perhaps a job in guarding or patrolling would appeal to you; if you have management ability, you could seek a leadership position in law enforcement and the protective services. Work in the military gives you the chance to use technical or leadership skills while serving your country.

05 Mechanics, Installers, and Repairers. *An interest in applying mechanical and electrical/electronic principles to practical situations by use of machines or hand tools.* You can satisfy this interest working with a variety of tools, technologies, materials, and settings. If you enjoy making machines run efficiently or fixing them when they break down, you could seek a job installing or repairing such devices as copiers, aircraft engines, automobiles, or watches. You may instead prefer to deal directly with certain materials and find work cutting and shaping metal or wood. Or if electricity and electronics interest you, you could install cables, troubleshoot telephone networks, or repair videocassette recorders. If you prefer routine or physical work in settings other than factories, perhaps work repairing tires or batteries would appeal to you.

06 Construction, Mining, and Drilling. *An interest in assembling components of buildings and other structures, or in using mechanical devices to drill or excavate.* If construction interests you, you can find fulfillment in the many building projects that are being undertaken at all times. If you like to organize and plan, you can find careers in management. On the other hand, you can play a more direct role in putting up and finishing buildings by doing jobs such as plumbing, carpentry, masonry, painting, or roofing. You may like working at a mine or oilfield, operating the powerful drilling or digging equipment. There are also several jobs that let you put your hands to the task.

07 Transportation. *An interest in operations that move people or materials.* You can satisfy this interest by managing a transportation service, by helping vehicles keep on their assigned schedules and routes, or by driving or piloting a vehicle. If you enjoy taking responsibility, perhaps managing a rail line would appeal to you. If you work well with details and can take pressure on the job, you might consider being an air traffic controller. Or would you rather get out on the highway, on the water, or up in the air? If so, you could drive a truck from state to state, sail down the Mississippi on a barge, or fly a crop duster over a cornfield. If you prefer to stay closer to home, you could drive a delivery van, taxi, or school bus. You can use your physical strength to load freight and arrange it so that it gets to its destination in one piece.

08 Industrial Production. *An interest in repetitive, concrete, organized activities most often done in a factory setting.* You can satisfy this interest by working in one of many industries that mass-produce goods, or for a utility that distributes electric power, gas, and so on. You may enjoy manual work, using your hands or hand tools. Perhaps you prefer to operate machines. You may like to inspect, sort, count, or weigh products. Using your training and experience to set up machines or supervise other workers may appeal to you.

09 Business Detail. *An interest in organized, clearly defined activities requiring accuracy and attention to details, primarily in an office setting.* You can satisfy this interest in a variety of jobs in which you attend to the details of a business operation. You may enjoy using your math skills; if so, perhaps a job in billing, computing, or financial record-keeping would satisfy you. If you prefer to deal with people, you may want a job in which you meet the public, talk on the telephone, or supervise other workers. You may like to do word processing on a computer, turn out copies on a duplicating machine, or work out sums on a calculator. Perhaps a job in filing or recording would satisfy you. Or you may want to use your training and experience to manage an office.

10 Sales and Marketing. *An interest in bringing others to a particular point of view by personal persuasion, using sales and promotional techniques.* You can satisfy this interest in a variety of sales and marketing jobs. If you like using technical knowledge of science or agriculture, you may enjoy selling technical products or services. Or perhaps you are more interested in selling business-related services such as insurance coverage, advertising space, or investment opportunities. Real estate offers several kinds of sales jobs. Perhaps you'd rather work with something you can pick up and show to people. You may work in stores, sales offices, or customers' homes.

11 Recreation, Travel, and Other Personal Services. *An interest in catering to the personal wishes and needs of others, so that they may enjoy cleanliness, good food and drink, comfortable lodging away from home, and enjoyable recreation.* You can satisfy this interest by providing services for the convenience, feeding, and pampering of others in hotels, restaurants, airplanes, and so on. If you enjoy improving the appearance of others, perhaps working in the hair and beauty care field would satisfy you. You may want to provide personal services such as taking care of small children, tailoring garments, or ushering. Or you may use your knowledge of the field to manage workers who are providing these services.

12 Education and Social Service. *An interest in teaching people or improving their social or spiritual well-being.* You can satisfy this interest by teaching students, who may be preschoolers, retirees, or any age between. Or if you are interested in helping people sort out their complicated lives, you may find fulfillment as a counselor, social worker, or religious worker. Working in a museum or library may give you opportunities to expand people's understanding of the world. If you also have an interest in business, you may find satisfaction in managerial work in this field.

13 General Management and Support. *An interest in making an organization run smoothly.* You can satisfy this interest by working in a position of leadership, or by specializing in a function that contributes to the overall effort. The organization may be a profit-making business, a nonprofit, or a government agency. If you especially enjoy working with people, you may find fulfillment from working in human resources. An interest in numbers may cause you to consider accounting, finance, budgeting, or purchasing. Or perhaps you would enjoy managing the organization's physical resources (for example, land, buildings, equipment, and utilities).

14 Medical and Health Services. *An interest in helping people be healthy.* You can satisfy this interest by working on a health-care team as a doctor, therapist, or nurse. You might specialize in one of the many different parts of the body or types of care, or you might be a generalist who deals with the whole patient. If you like technology, you might find satisfaction working with X rays, one of the electronic means of diagnosis, or clinical laboratory testing. You might work with healthy people, helping them stay in condition through exercise and eating right. If you like to organize, analyze, and plan, a managerial role might be right for you.

Limitations of Database Information

In this book's introduction, we mention that there are limitations to what we can do with the databases we used to create this book. And the information in this appendix demonstrates some of these limitations.

For example, some GOE work groups list no related OOH jobs, or are missing O*NET or OOH job titles you would expect to see. One example of this is in the Arts, Entertainment, and Media interest area. One of the work groups there is called Graphic Arts, and you would expect to find the OOH job title Visual Artists there. Unfortunately, that job title is not listed there, although Visual Artists is listed in another work group within Arts, Entertainment, and Media.

This is not a mistake. It has to do with the limitations of the database. In this case, the problem results from each job title in the database being assigned to one and only one GOE work group. The Visual Artists job title might fit into several GOE work groups, but it appears in only one.

But there are other problems. For example, you do not find the OOH job title of Jewelers, Precious Stone and Metal Workers, in the GOE interest area of Arts, Entertainment, and Media at all. This is because the database assigns that job to the GOE interest area of Industrial Production. People who make jewelry do in fact work in factory settings, but artists also make jewelry. So the difference here has to do with work setting and other factors, where the same job could fit into several GOE interest groups. But you won't see it in the Arts area, because the database has it assigned to another group.

Yet another limitation comes from the Department of Labor linking only 782 of the 1,094 jobs in the O*NET database to the jobs listed in the OOH. Which means that some jobs in the O*NET do not have OOH jobs listed with them.

These are limitations that come from the database provided by the Department of Labor. Even so, we think the wide variety of job titles listed within each GOE interest area and work group will give you a good idea of the types of jobs they cover. Just understand that these lists are not perfect, just pretty darned good.

GOE Work Groups with Related Job Titles

The 14 GOE interest areas are divided into 132 more specific groups of related jobs, called *work groups*. All job titles in the various government databases can be organized into these groupings.

The GOE uses a system of number codes for the various work groups. These numbers, which are called *GOE codes,* can be used to cross-reference to other occupational information systems that use the GOE's structure.

The listing that follows provides the following:

1. **Each of the 14 GOE interest areas.** The two-digit number before each interest area is the one assigned to it in the GOE system.

2. **GOE work groups.** Each interest area is divided into work groups. These work groups are presented in bold letters under each interest area. The six-digit number before each work group is the GOE number assigned to that group. You can use this number to cross-reference other GOE-based information systems.

3. **O*NET job titles.** Under each work group is one or more related job titles from the O*NET database. We include the O*NET code number for each job title to allow you to cross-reference other systems using the O*NET information, including this book. The O*NET database of occupations is explained in more detail in this book's introduction.

4. *Occupational Outlook Handbook* **job titles.** Following the O*NET job titles are one or more additional titles that are also related to each work group. These are jobs listed in the OOH.

The job titles from the O*NET and OOH give you a good idea of the types of jobs that are related to each GOE work group. Keep in mind, though, that there are many more specialized jobs that are not listed.

GOE Interest Area 01: Arts, Entertainment, and Media

GOE Work Groups and Related Job Titles

01.01.01 Managerial Work in Arts, Entertainment, and Media

O*NET Jobs: 13-1011.00 Agents and Business Managers of Artists, Performers, and Athletes; 27-1011.00 Art Directors; 27-2012.00 Producers and Directors; 27-2012.01 Producers; 27-2012.03 Program Directors; 27-2012.05 Technical Directors/Managers. **OOH Jobs:** Actors, Directors, and Producers; Visual Artists.

01.02.01 Writing and Editing

O*NET Jobs: 27-3041.00 Editors; 27-3042.00 Technical Writers; 27-3043.00 Writers and Authors; 27-3043.01 Poets and Lyricists; 27-3043.02 Creative Writers; 27-3043.04 Copy Writers. **OOH Jobs:** Writers and Editors, Including Technical Writers.

01.03.01 News, Broadcasting, and Public Relations

O*NET Jobs: 27-3021.00 Broadcast News Analysts; 27-3022.00 Reporters and Correspondents; 27-3031.00 Public Relations Specialists; 27-3043.03 Caption Writers; 27-3091.00 Interpreters and Translators. **OOH Jobs:** News Analysts, Reporters, and Correspondents; Public Relations Specialists.

01.04.01 Visual Arts: Studio Art

O*NET Jobs: 27-1013.00 Fine Artists, Including Painters, Sculptors, and Illustrators; 27-1013.01 Painters and Illustrators; 27-1013.02 Sketch Artists; 27-1013.03 Cartoonists; 27-1013.04 Sculptors. **OOH Jobs:** Visual Artists.

01.04.02 Visual Arts: Design

O*NET Jobs: 27-1014.00 Multi-Media Artists and Animators; 27-1021.00 Commercial and Industrial Designers; 27-1022.00 Fashion Designers; 27-1023.00 Floral Designers; 27-1024.00 Graphic Designers; 27-1025.00 Interior Designers; 27-1026.00 Merchandise Displayers and Window Trimmers; 27-1027.00 Set and Exhibit Designers; 27-1027.01 Set Designers; 27-1027.02 Exhibit Designers. **OOH Jobs:** Designers; Visual Artists.

01.05.01 Performing Arts: Drama: Directing, Performing, Narrating, and Announcing

O*NET Jobs: 27-2011.00 Actors; 27-2012.02 Directors—Stage, Motion Pictures, Television, and Radio; 27-3011.00 Radio and Television Announcers; 27-3012.00 Public Address System and Other Announcers. **OOH Jobs:** Actors, Directors, and Producers; Announcers.

01.05.02 Performing Arts: Music: Directing, Composing and Arranging, and Performing

O*NET Jobs: 27-2012.04 Talent Directors; 27-2041.00 Music Directors and Composers; 27-2041.01 Music Directors; 27-2041.02 Music Arrangers and Orchestrators; 27-2041.03 Composers; 27-2042.00 Musicians and Singers; 27-2042.01 Singers; 27-2042.02 Musicians, Instrumental. **OOH Jobs:** Actors, Directors, and Producers; Musicians, Singers, and Related Workers.

01.05.03 Performing Arts: Dance: Performing and Choreography

O*NET Jobs: 27-2031.00 Dancers; 27-2032.00 Choreographers. **OOH Jobs:** Dancers and Choreographers.

01.06.01 Craft Arts

O*NET Jobs: 27-1012.00 Craft Artists; 51-9195.04 Glass Blowers, Molders, Benders, and Finishers; 51-9195.05 Potters. **OOH Jobs:** None listed.

01.07.01 Graphic Arts

O*NET Jobs: 43-9031.00 Desktop Publishers; 51-5022.02 Paste-Up Workers; 51-5022.03 Photoengravers; 51-5022.04 Camera Operators; 51-5022.08 Dot Etchers; 51-5022.09 Electronic Masking System Operators; 51-9194.00 Etchers and Engravers; 51-9194.01 Precision Etchers and Engravers, Hand or Machine; 51-9194.02 Engravers/Carvers; 51-9194.03 Etchers; 51-9194.04 Pantograph Engravers; 51-9194.05 Etchers, Hand; 51-9194.06 Engravers, Hand. **OOH Jobs:** Prepress Workers.

01.08.01 Media Technology

O*NET Jobs: 27-4011.00 Audio and Video Equipment Technicians; 27-4012.00 Broadcast Technicians; 27-4013.00 Radio Operators; 27-4014.00 Sound Engineering Technicians; 27-4021.00 Photographers; 27-4021.01 Professional Photographers; 27-4031.00 Camera Operators, Television, Video, and Motion Picture; 27-4032.00 Film and Video Editors. **OOH Jobs:** Broadcast and Sound Technicians; Photographers and Camera Operators.

01.09.01 Modeling and Personal Appearance

O*NET Jobs: 39-3092.00 Costume Attendants; 39-5091.00 Makeup Artists, Theatrical and Performance; 41-9012.00 Models. **OOH Jobs:** Barbers, Cosmetologists, and Related Workers; Demonstrators, Product Promoters, and Models.

01.10.01 Sports: Coaching, Instructing, Officiating, and Performing

O*NET Jobs: 27-2021.00 Athletes and Sports Competitors; 27-2022.00 Coaches and Scouts; 27-2023.00 Umpires, Referees, and Other Sports Officials; 39-9031.00 Fitness Trainers and Aerobics Instructors. **OOH Jobs:** Instructors and Coaches, Sports and Physical Training.

GOE Interest Area 02: Science, Math, and Engineering

GOE Work Groups and Related Job Titles

02.01.01 Managerial Work in Science, Math, and Engineering

O*NET Jobs: 11-3021.00 Computer and Information Systems Managers; 11-9041.00 Engineering Managers; 11-9121.00 Natural Sciences Managers. **OOH Jobs:** Engineering, Natural Science, and Computer and Information Systems Managers.

02.02.01 Physical Sciences

O*NET Jobs: 19-2011.00 Astronomers; 19-2012.00 Physicists; 19-2021.00 Atmospheric and Space Scientists; 19-2031.00 Chemists; 19-2032.00 Materials Scientists; 19-2042.00 Geoscientists, Except Hydrologists and Geographers; 19-2042.01 Geologists; 19-2043.00 Hydrologists; 19-3092.00 Geographers. **OOH Jobs:** Atmospheric Scientists; Chemists; Geologists, Geophysicists, and Oceanographers; Physicists and Astronomers; Social Scientists, Other.

02.03.01 Life Sciences: Animal Specialization

O*NET Jobs: 19-1011.00 Animal Scientists; 19-1023.00 Zoologists and Wildlife Biologists; 19-1041.00 Epidemiologists; 19-1042.00 Medical Scientists, Except Epidemiologists. **OOH Jobs:** Agricultural and Food Scientists; Biological and Medical Scientists.

02.03.02 Life Sciences: Plant Specialization

O*NET Jobs: 19-1013.01 Plant Scientists; 19-1013.02 Soil Scientists; 19-1031.01 Soil Conservationists; 19-1031.02 Range Managers; 19-1032.00 Foresters. **OOH Jobs:** Agricultural and Food Scientists; Conservation Scientists and Foresters.

02.03.03 Life Sciences: Plant and Animal Specialization

O*NET Jobs: 19-1020.01 Biologists; 19-1021.00 Biochemists and Biophysicists; 19-1021.01 Biochemists; 19-1021.02 Biophysicists; 19-1022.00 Microbiologists; 19-1031.00 Conservation Scientists; 19-2041.00 Environmental Scientists and Specialists, Including Health. **OOH Jobs:** Biological and Medical Scientists.

02.03.04 Life Sciences: Food Research

O*NET Jobs: 19-1012.00 Food Scientists and Technologists; 19-4011.00 Agricultural and Food Science Technicians; 19-4011.01 Agricultural Technicians; 19-4011.02 Food Science Technicians. **OOH Jobs:** Agricultural and Food Scientists; Science Technicians.

02.04.01 Social Sciences: Psychology, Sociology, and Anthropology

O*NET Jobs: 19-3032.00 Industrial-Organizational Psychologists; 19-3041.00 Sociologists; 19-3091.00 Anthropologists and Archeologists; 19-3091.01 Anthropologists; 19-3091.02 Archeologists. **OOH Jobs:** Psychologists; Social Scientists, Other.

02.04.02 Social Sciences: Economics, Public Policy, and History

O*NET Jobs: 19-3011.00 Economists; 19-3022.00 Survey Researchers; 19-3051.00 Urban and Regional Planners; 19-3093.00 Historians; 19-3094.00 Political Scientists; 19-4061.00 Social Science Research Assistants; 19-4061.01 City Planning Aides. **OOH Jobs:** Economists and Marketing Research Analysts; Social Scientists, Other; Urban and Regional Planners.

02.05.01 Laboratory Technology: Physical Sciences

O*NET Jobs: 19-4031.00 Chemical Technicians; 19-4041.00 Geological and Petroleum Technicians; 19-4041.01 Geological Data Technicians; 19-4041.02 Geological Sample Test Technicians; 19-4051.00 Nuclear Technicians; 19-4051.01 Nuclear Equipment Operation Technicians. **OOH Jobs:** Science Technicians.

02.05.02 Laboratory Technology: Life Sciences

O*NET Jobs: 19-4021.00 Biological Technicians; 19-4091.00 Environmental Science and Protection Technicians, Including Health; 27-4021.02 Photographers, Scientific. **OOH Jobs:** Photographers and Camera Operators; Science Technicians.

02.06.01 Mathematics and Computers: Data Processing

O*NET Jobs: 15-1011.00 Computer and Information Scientists, Research; 15-1021.00 Computer Programmers; 15-1041.00 Computer Support Specialists; 15-1051.00 Computer Systems Analysts; 15-1061.00 Database Administrators; 15-1071.00 Network and Computer Systems Administrators; 15-1071.01 Computer Security Specialists; 15-1081.00 Network Systems and Data Communications Analysts. **OOH Jobs:** Computer Programmers; Computer Systems Analysts, Engineers, and Scientists.

02.06.02 Mathematics and Computers: Data Analysis

O*NET Jobs: 15-2011.00 Actuaries; 15-2021.00 Mathe-maticians; 15-2031.00 Operations Research Analysts; 15-2041.00 Statisticians; 15-3011.00 Mathematical Technicians; 43-9111.00 Statistical Assistants. **OOH Jobs:** Actuaries; Mathematicians; Operations Research Analysts; Science Technicians; Statisticians.

02.07.01 Engineering: Research and Systems Design

O*NET Jobs: 15-1031.00 Computer Software Engineers, Applications; 15-1032.00 Computer Software Engineers, Systems Software; 17-2021.00 Agricultural Engineers; 17-2041.00 Chemical Engineers; 17-2061.00 Computer Hardware Engineers; 17-2121.01 Marine Engineers; 17-2161.00 Nuclear Engineers. **OOH Jobs:** Chemical Engineers; Computer Systems Analysts, Engineers, and Scientists; Nuclear Engineers.

02.07.02 Engineering: Industrial and Safety

O*NET Jobs: 17-2111.01 Industrial Safety and Health Engineers; 17-2111.02 Fire-Prevention and Protection Engineers; 17-2111.03 Product Safety Engineers; 17-2112.00 Industrial Engineers; 17-2131.00 Materials

Engineers; 17-2151.00 Mining and Geological Engineers, Including Mining Safety Engineers. **OOH Jobs:** Industrial Engineers, Except Safety Engineers; Materials Engineers; Mining Engineers, Including Mine Safety Engineers.

02.07.03 Engineering: Design

O*NET Jobs: 17-1011.00 Architects, Except Landscape and Naval; 17-1012.00 Landscape Architects; 17-2121.00 Marine Engineers and Naval Architects; 17-2121.02 Marine Architects. **OOH Jobs:** Architects, Except Landscape and Marine; Landscape Architects.

02.07.04 Engineering: General Engineering

O*NET Jobs: 17-2011.00 Aerospace Engineers; 17-2031.00 Biomedical Engineers; 17-2051.00 Civil Engineers; 17-2071.00 Electrical Engineers; 17-2072.00 Electronics Engineers, Except Computer; 17-2081.00 Environmental Engineers; 17-2111.00 Health and Safety Engineers, Except Mining Safety Engineers and Inspectors; 17-2141.00 Mechanical Engineers; 17-2171.00 Petroleum Engineers; 41-9031.00 Sales Engineers. **OOH Jobs:** Aerospace Engineers; Civil Engineers; Electrical and Electronics Engineers; Manufacturers' and Wholesale Sales Representatives; Mechanical Engineers; Petroleum Engineers.

02.08.01 Engineering Technology: Surveying

O*NET Jobs: 17-1022.00 Surveyors; 17-3031.00 Surveying and Mapping Technicians; 17-3031.01 Surveying Technicians; 17-3031.02 Mapping Technicians. **OOH Jobs:** Surveyors, Cartographers, Photogrammetrists, and Surveying Technicians.

02.08.02 Engineering Technology: Industrial and Safety

O*NET Jobs: 13-1041.05 Pressure Vessel Inspectors; 17-3026.00 Industrial Engineering Technicians; 47-4011.00 Construction and Building Inspectors. **OOH Jobs:** Construction and Building Inspectors; Engineering Technicians; Inspectors and Compliance Officers, Except Construction.

02.08.03 Engineering Technology: Design

O*NET Jobs: 17-1021.00 Cartographers and Photogrammetrists; 17-3011.00 Architectural and Civil Drafters; 17-3011.01 Architectural Drafters; 17-3011.02 Civil Drafters; 17-3012.00 Electrical and Electronics Drafters; 17-3012.01 Electronic Drafters; 17-3012.02 Electrical Drafters; 17-3013.00 Mechanical Drafters. **OOH Jobs:** Drafters; Surveyors, Cartographers, Photogrammetrists, and Surveying Technicians.

02.08.04 Engineering Technology: General

O*NET Jobs: 17-3021.00 Aerospace Engineering and Operations Technicians; 17-3022.00 Civil Engineering Technicians; 17-3023.00 Electrical and Electronic Engineering Technicians; 17-3023.01 Electronics Engineering Technicians; 17-3023.02 Calibration and Instrumentation Technicians; 17-3023.03 Electrical Engineering Technicians; 17-3024.00 Electro-Mechanical Technicians; 17-3025.00 Environmental Engineering Technicians; 17-3027.00 Mechanical Engineering Technicians; 51-4012.00 Numerical Tool and Process Control Programmers. **OOH Jobs:** Engineering Technicians; Machinists and Numerical Control Machine Tool Programmers.

GOE Interest Area 03: Plants and Animals

GOE Work Groups and Related Job Titles

03.01.01 Managerial Work: Farming and Fishing

O*NET Jobs: 11-9011.02 Agricultural Crop Farm Managers; 11-9011.03 Fish Hatchery Managers; 11-9012.00 Farmers and Ranchers; 19-4093.00

Forest and Conservation Technicians; 45-1011.00 First-Line Supervisors/ Managers of Farming, Fishing, and Forestry Workers; 45-1011.01 First-Line Supervisors and Manager/Supervisors—Agricultural Crop Workers; 45-1011.02 First-Line Supervisors and Manager/Supervisors—Animal Husbandry Workers; 45-1011.03 First-Line Supervisors and Manager/Supervisors—Animal Care Workers, Except Livestock; 45-1011.06 First-Line Supervisors and Manager/Supervisors—Fishery Workers; 45-2031.00 Farm Labor Contractors. **OOH Jobs:** Farmers and Farm Managers.

03.01.02 Managerial Work: Nursery, Groundskeeping, and Logging

O*NET Jobs: 11-9011.01 Nursery and Greenhouse Managers; 37-1012.00 First-Line Supervisors/Managers of Landscaping, Lawn Service, and Groundskeeping Workers; 37-1012.01 Lawn Service Managers; 37-1012.02 First-Line Supervisors and Manager/Supervisors—Landscaping Workers; 45-1011.04 First-Line Supervisors and Manager/Supervisors—Horticultural Workers; 45-1011.05 First-Line Supervisors and Manager/Supervisors—Logging Workers. **OOH Jobs:** Landscaping, Groundskeeping, Nursery, Greenhouse, and Lawn Service Occupations.

03.02.01 Animal Care and Training

O*NET Jobs: 29-1131.00 Veterinarians; 29-2056.00 Veterinary Technologists and Technicians; 31-9096.00 Veterinary Assistants and Laboratory Animal Caretakers; 39-2011.00 Animal Trainers; 39-2021.00 Nonfarm Animal Caretakers; 45-2021.00 Animal Breeders. **OOH Jobs:** Veterinarians; Veterinary Assistants and Nonfarm Animal Caretakers.

03.03.01 Hands-on Work: Farming

O*NET Jobs: 45-2091.00 Agricultural Equipment Operators; 45-2092.00 Farmworkers and Laborers, Crop, Nursery, and Greenhouse; 45-2092.02 General Farmworkers; 45-2093.00 Farmworkers, Farm and Ranch Animals **OOH Jobs:** None listed.

03.03.02 Hands-on Work: Forestry and Logging

O*NET Jobs: 19-4093.00 Forest and Conservation Technicians; 45-4011.00 Forest and Conservation Workers; 45-4021.00 Fallers; 45-4022.00 Logging Equipment Operators; 45-4022.01 Logging Tractor Operators. **OOH Jobs:** Forestry, Conservation, and Logging Occupations.

03.03.03 Hands-on Work: Hunting and Fishing

O*NET Jobs: 45-3011.00 Fishers and Related Fishing Workers; 45-3021.00 Hunters and Trappers. **OOH Jobs:** Fishers and Fishing Vessel Operators.

03.03.04 Hands-on Work: Nursery, Groundskeeping, and Pest Control

O*NET Jobs: 37-2021.00 Pest Control Workers; 37-3011.00 Landscaping and Groundskeeping Workers; 37-3012.00 Pesticide Handlers, Sprayers, and Applicators, Vegetation; 37-3013.00 Tree Trimmers and Pruners; 45-2092.01 Nursery Workers. **OOH Jobs:** Landscaping, Groundskeeping, Nursery, Greenhouse, and Lawn Service Occupations; Pest Controllers.

GOE Interest Area 04: Law, Law Enforcement, and Public Safety

GOE Work Groups and Related Job Titles

04.01.01 Managerial Work in Law, Law Enforcement, and Public Safety

O*NET Jobs: 13-1061.00 Emergency Management Specialists; 33-1011.00 First-Line Supervisors/Managers of Correctional Officers; 33-1012.00 First-Line Supervisors/Managers of Police and Detectives; 33-1021.00 First-Line Supervisors/Managers of Fire Fighting and Prevention

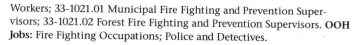

Workers; 33-1021.01 Municipal Fire Fighting and Prevention Supervisors; 33-1021.02 Forest Fire Fighting and Prevention Supervisors. **OOH Jobs:** Fire Fighting Occupations; Police and Detectives.

04.02.01 Law: Legal Practice and Justice Administration

O*NET Jobs: 23-1011.00 Lawyers; 23-1021.00 Administrative Law Judges, Adjudicators, and Hearing Officers; 23-1022.00 Arbitrators, Mediators, and Conciliators; 23-1023.00 Judges, Magistrate Judges, and Magistrates. **OOH Jobs:** Lawyers and Judicial Workers.

04.02.02 Law: Legal Support

O*NET Jobs: 23-2011.00 Paralegals and Legal Assistants; 23-2092.00 Law Clerks; 23-2093.00 Title Examiners, Abstractors, and Searchers; 23-2093.01 Title Searchers; 23-2093.02 Title Examiners and Abstractors. **OOH Jobs:** Paralegals.

04.03.01 Law Enforcement: Investigation and Protection

O*NET Jobs: 33-2021.02 Fire Investigators; 33-3011.00 Bailiffs; 33-3012.00 Correctional Officers and Jailers; 33-3021.00 Detectives and Criminal Investigators; 33-3021.01 Police Detectives; 33-3021.03 Criminal Investigators and Special Agents; 33-3021.04 Child Support, Missing Persons, and Unemployment Insurance Fraud Investigators; 33-3021.05 Immigration and Customs Inspectors; 33-3031.00 Fish and Game Wardens; 33-3041.00 Parking Enforcement Workers; 33-3051.00 Police and Sheriff's Patrol Officers; 33-3051.01 Police Patrol Officers; 33-3051.02 Highway Patrol Pilots; 33-3051.03 Sheriffs and Deputy Sheriffs; 33-3052.00 Transit and Railroad Police. **OOH Jobs:** Correctional Officers; Fire Fighting Occupations; Police and Detectives.

04.03.02 Law Enforcement: Technology

O*NET Jobs: 19-4092.00 Forensic Science Technicians; 33-3021.02 Police Identification and Records Officers. **OOH Jobs:** Police and Detectives; Science Technicians.

04.03.03 Law Enforcement: Security

O*NET Jobs: 33-9011.00 Animal Control Workers; 33-9021.00 Private Detectives and Investigators; 33-9031.00 Gaming Surveillance Officers and Gaming Investigators; 33-9032.00 Security Guards; 33-9091.00 Crossing Guards; 33-9092.00 Lifeguards, Ski Patrol, and Other Recreational Protective Service Workers. **OOH Jobs:** Guards; Private Detectives and Investigators.

04.04.01 Public Safety: Emergency Responding

O*NET Jobs: 29-2041.00 Emergency Medical Technicians and Paramedics; 33-2011.00 Fire Fighters; 33-2011.01 Municipal Fire Fighters; 33-2011.02 Forest Fire Fighters. **OOH Jobs:** Emergency Medical Technicians; Fire Fighting Occupations.

04.04.02 Public Safety: Regulations Enforcement

O*NET Jobs: 13-1041.00 Compliance Officers, Except Agriculture, Construction, Health and Safety, and Transportation; 13-1041.01 Environmental Compliance Inspectors; 13-1041.02 Licensing Examiners and Inspectors; 13-1041.03 Equal Opportunity Representatives and Officers; 13-1041.04 Government Property Inspectors and Investigators; 13-2061.00 Financial Examiners; 19-4051.02 Nuclear Monitoring Technicians; 29-9011.00 Occupational Health and Safety Specialists; 29-9012.00 Occupational Health and Safety Technicians; 33-2021.00 Fire Inspectors and Investigators; 33-2021.01 Fire Inspectors; 33-2022.00 Forest Fire Inspectors and Prevention Specialists; 45-2011.00 Agricultural Inspectors; 53-6051.01 Aviation Inspectors; 53-6051.02 Public Transportation Inspectors; 53-6051.03 Marine Cargo Inspectors. **OOH Jobs:** Fire Fighting Occupations; Inspectors and Compliance Officers, Except Construction; Science Technicians.

04.05.01 Military: Officers and Supervisors

O*NET Jobs: 55-1011.00 Air Crew Officers; 55-1012.00 Aircraft Launch and Recovery Officers; 55-1013.00 Armored Assault Vehicle Officers; 55-1014.00 Artillery and Missile Officers; 55-1015.00 Command and Control Center Officers; 55-1016.00 Infantry Officers; 55-1017.00 Special Forces Officers; 55-2011.00 First-Line Supervisors/Managers of Air Crew Members; 55-2012.00 First-Line Supervisors/Managers of Weapons Specialists/Crew Members; 55-2013.00 First-Line Supervisors/Managers of All Other Tactical Operations Specialists. **OOH Jobs:** Job Opportunities in the Armed Forces.

04.05.02 Military: Specialists

O*NET Jobs: 55-3011.00 Air Crew Members; 55-3012.00 Aircraft Launch and Recovery Specialists; 55-3013.00 Armored Assault Vehicle Crew Members; 55-3014.00 Artillery and Missile Crew Members; 55-3015.00 Command and Control Center Specialists; 55-3016.00 Infantry; 55-3017.00 Radar and Sonar Technicians; 55-3018.00 Special Forces. **OOH Jobs:** Job Opportunities in the Armed Forces.

GOE Interest Area 05: Mechanics, Installers, and Repairers

GOE Work Groups and Related Job Titles

05.01.01 Managerial Work in Mechanics, Installers, and Repairers

O*NET Jobs: 49-1011.00 First-Line Supervisors/Managers of Mechanics, Installers, and Repairers. **OOH Jobs:** Blue-Collar Worker Supervisors.

05.02.01 Electrical and Electronic Systems: Installation and Repair

O*NET Jobs: 47-4021.00 Elevator Installers and Repairers; 49-2022.00 Telecommunications Equipment Installers and Repairers, Except Line Installers; 49-2022.01 Central Office and PBX Installers and Repairers; 49-2022.02 Frame Wirers, Central Office; 49-2022.03 Communication Equipment Mechanics, Installers, and Repairers; 49-2022.04 Telecommunications Facility Examiners; 49-2022.05 Station Installers and Repairers, Telephone; 49-2091.00 Avionics Technicians; 49-2093.00 Electrical and Electronics Installers and Repairers, Transportation Equipment; 49-2094.00 Electrical and Electronics Repairers, Commercial and Industrial Equipment; 49-2096.00 Electronic Equipment Installers and Repairers, Motor Vehicles; 49-9031.00 Home Appliance Repairers; 49-9031.01 Home Appliance Installers; 49-9051.00 Electrical Power-Line Installers and Repairers; 49-9052.00 Telecommunications Line Installers and Repairers; 49-9097.00 Signal and Track Switch Repairers. **OOH Jobs:** Aircraft Mechanics and Service Technicians; Electronics Repairers, Commercial and Industrial Equipment; Elevator Installers and Repairers; Home Appliance and Power Tool Repairers; Line Installers and Repairers; Telecommunications Equipment Mechanics, Installers, and Repairers.

05.02.02 Electrical and Electronic Systems: Equipment Repair

O*NET Jobs: 49-2011.00 Computer, Automated Teller, and Office Machine Repairers; 49-2011.02 Data Processing Equipment Repairers; 49-2011.03 Office Machine and Cash Register Servicers; 49-2021.00 Radio Mechanics; 49-2092.00 Electric Motor, Power Tool, and Related Repairers; 49-2092.01 Electric Home Appliance and Power Tool Repairers; 49-2092.02 Electric Motor and Switch Assemblers and Repairers; 49-2092.03 Battery Repairers; 49-2092.04 Transformer Repairers; 49-2092.05 Electrical Parts Reconditioners; 49-2095.00 Electrical and Electronics Repairers, Powerhouse, Substation, and Relay; 49-2097.00 Electronic Home Entertainment Equipment Installers and Repairers; 49-9012.01 Electric Meter Installers and Repairers. **OOH Jobs:** Computer, Automated Teller, and

Office Machine Repairers; Electronic Home Entertainment Equipment Repairers; Home Appliance and Power Tool Repairers; Telecommunications Equipment Mechanics, Installers, and Repairers.

05.03.01 Mechanical Work: Vehicles and Facilities

O*NET Jobs: 47-3013.00 Helpers—Electricians; 49-3011.00 Aircraft Mechanics and Service Technicians; 49-3011.01 Airframe-and-Power-Plant Mechanics; 49-3011.02 Aircraft Engine Specialists; 49-3011.03 Aircraft Body and Bonded Structure Repairers; 49-3021.00 Automotive Body and Related Repairers; 49-3022.00 Automotive Glass Installers and Repairers; 49-3023.00 Automotive Service Technicians and Mechanics; 49-3023.01 Automotive Master Mechanics; 49-3023.02 Automotive Specialty Technicians; 49-3031.00 Bus and Truck Mechanics and Diesel Engine Specialists; 49-3041.00 Farm Equipment Mechanics; 49-3042.00 Mobile Heavy Equipment Mechanics, Except Engines; 49-3043.00 Rail Car Repairers; 49-3051.00 Motorboat Mechanics; 49-3052.00 Motorcycle Mechanics; 49-3053.00 Outdoor Power Equipment and Other Small Engine Mechanics; 49-3092.00 Recreational Vehicle Service Technicians; 49-3093.00 Tire Repairers and Changers; 49-9021.00 Heating, Air Conditioning, and Refrigeration Mechanics and Installers; 49-9021.01 Heating and Air Conditioning Mechanics; 49-9021.02 Refrigeration Mechanics; 49-9042.00 Maintenance and Repair Workers, General; 49-9044.00 Millwrights; 49-9094.00 Locksmiths and Safe Repairers; 49-9098.00 Helpers—Installation, Maintenance, and Repair Workers; 51-9122.00 Painters, Transportation Equipment; 53-6011.00 Bridge and Lock Tenders; 53-6051.04 Railroad Inspectors. OOH Jobs: Aircraft Mechanics and Service Technicians; Automotive Body Repairers; Automotive Mechanics and Service Technicians; Diesel Mechanics and Service Technicians; Farm Equipment Mechanics; Handlers, Equipment Cleaners, Helpers, and Laborers; Heating, Air Conditioning, and Refrigeration Mechanics and Installers; Inspectors, Testers, and Graders; Maintenance Mechanics, General Utility; Millwrights; Mobile Heavy Equipment Mechanics; Motorcycle, Boat, and Small-Engine Mechanics; Painting and Coating Machine Operators.

05.03.02 Mechanical Work: Machinery Repair

O*NET Jobs: 49-2092.06 Hand and Portable Power Tool Repairers; 49-3091.00 Bicycle Repairers; 49-9011.00 Mechanical Door Repairers; 49-9012.00 Control and Valve Installers and Repairers, Except Mechanical Door; 49-9012.02 Valve and Regulator Repairers; 49-9012.03 Meter Mechanics; 49-9031.02 Gas Appliance Repairers; 49-9041.00 Industrial Machinery Mechanics; 49-9043.00 Maintenance Workers, Machinery; 49-9091.00 Coin, Vending, and Amusement Machine Servicers and Repairers. OOH Jobs: Coin and Vending, and Amusement Machine Servicers and Repairers; Home Appliance and Power Tool Repairers; Industrial Machinery Repairers.

05.03.03 Mechanical Work: Medical and Technical Equipment Fabrication and Repair

O*NET Jobs: 49-9061.00 Camera and Photographic Equipment Repairers; 49-9062.00 Medical Equipment Repairers; 49-9064.00 Watch Repairers; 51-9082.00 Medical Appliance Technicians; 51-9083.00 Ophthalmic Laboratory Technicians; 51-9083.02 Optical Instrument Assemblers. OOH Jobs: None listed.

05.03.04 Mechanical Work: Musical Instrument Fabrication and Repair

O*NET Jobs: 49-9063.00 Musical Instrument Repairers and Tuners; 49-9063.01 Keyboard Instrument Repairers and Tuners; 49-9063.02 Stringed Instrument Repairers and Tuners; 49-9063.03 Reed or Wind Instrument Repairers and Tuners; 49-9063.04 Percussion Instrument Repairers and Tuners. OOH Jobs: Musical Instrument Repairers and Tuners.

GOE Interest Area 06: Construction, Mining, and Drilling

GOE Work Groups and Related Job Titles

06.01.01 Managerial Work in Construction, Mining, and Drilling

O*NET Jobs: 11-9021.00 Construction Managers; 47-1011.00 First-Line Supervisors/Managers of Construction Trades and Extraction Workers; 47-1011.01 First-Line Supervisors and Manager/Supervisors—Construction Trades Workers; 47-1011.02 First-Line Supervisors and Manager/Supervisors—Extractive Workers. OOH Jobs: Blue-Collar Worker Supervisors; Construction Managers.

06.02.01 Construction: Masonry, Stone, and Brick Work

O*NET Jobs: 47-2021.00 Brickmasons and Blockmasons; 47-2022.00 Stonemasons; 47-2042.00 Floor Layers, Except Carpet, Wood, and Hard Tiles; 47-2044.00 Tile and Marble Setters; 47-2051.00 Cement Masons and Concrete Finishers; 47-2053.00 Terrazzo Workers and Finishers; 51-9195.03 Stone Cutters and Carvers. OOH Jobs: Bricklayers and Stonemasons; Carpet, Floor, and Tile Installers and Finishers; Cement Masons, Concrete Finishers, and Terrazzo Workers.

06.02.02 Construction: Construction and Maintenance

O*NET Jobs: 47-2011.00 Boilermakers; 47-2031.00 Carpenters; 47-2031.01 Construction Carpenters; 47-2031.02 Rough Carpenters; 47-2031.04 Ship Carpenters and Joiners; 47-2031.05 Boat Builders and Shipwrights; 47-2041.00 Carpet Installers; 47-2043.00 Floor Sanders and Finishers; 47-2081.00 Drywall and Ceiling Tile Installers; 47-2081.01 Ceiling Tile Installers; 47-2081.02 Drywall Installers; 47-2111.00 Electricians; 47-2121.00 Glaziers; 47-2131.00 Insulation Workers, Floor, Ceiling, and Wall; 47-2132.00 Insulation Workers, Mechanical; 47-2141.00 Painters, Construction and Maintenance; 47-2142.00 Paperhangers; 47-2152.00 Plumbers, Pipefitters, and Steamfitters; 47-2152.01 Pipe Fitters; 47-2152.02 Plumbers; 47-2161.00 Plasterers and Stucco Masons; 47-2181.00 Roofers; 47-2211.00 Sheet Metal Workers; 49-2098.00 Security and Fire Alarm Systems Installers. OOH Jobs: Boilermakers; Carpenters; Carpet, Floor, and Tile Installers and Finishers; Drywall Installers and Finishers; Electricians; Glaziers; Insulation Workers; Painters and Paperhangers; Plasterers and Stucco Masons; Plumbers, Pipefitters, and Steamfitters; Roofers; Sheet Metal Workers.

06.02.03 Construction: General

O*NET Jobs: 47-2031.06 Brattice Builders; 47-2071.00 Paving, Surfacing, and Tamping Equipment Operators; 47-2072.00 Pile-Driver Operators; 47-2073.00 Operating Engineers and Other Construction Equipment Operators; 47-2073.01 Grader, Bulldozer, and Scraper Operators; 47-2073.02 Operating Engineers; 47-2082.00 Tapers; 47-2151.00 Pipelayers; 47-2152.03 Pipelaying Fitters; 47-2171.00 Reinforcing Iron and Rebar Workers; 47-2221.00 Structural Iron and Steel Workers; 47-4031.00 Fence Erectors; 47-4041.00 Hazardous Materials Removal Workers; 47-4061.00 Rail-Track Laying and Maintenance Equipment Operators; 47-4091.00 Segmental Pavers; 47-5031.00 Explosives Workers, Ordnance Handling Experts, and Blasters; 49-9045.00 Refractory Materials Repairers, Except Brickmasons; 49-9092.00 Commercial Divers; 49-9095.00 Manufactured Building and Mobile Home Installers; 49-9096.00 Riggers. OOH Jobs: Carpenters; Construction Equipment Operators; Drywall Installers and Finishers; Structural and Reinforcing Metal Workers.

06.03.01 Mining and Drilling

O*NET Jobs: 47-5011.00 Derrick Operators, Oil and Gas; 47-5012.00 Rotary Drill Operators, Oil and Gas; 47-5013.00 Service Unit Operators,

Oil, Gas, and Mining; 47-5021.00 Earth Drillers, Except Oil and Gas; 47-5021.01 Construction Drillers; 47-5021.02 Well and Core Drill Operators; 47-5041.00 Continuous Mining Machine Operators; 47-5042.00 Mine Cutting and Channeling Machine Operators; 47-5051.00 Rock Splitters, Quarry; 47-5061.00 Roof Bolters, Mining; 47-5071.00 Roustabouts, Oil and Gas; 53-7032.01 Excavating and Loading Machine Operators; 53-7033.00 Loading Machine Operators, Underground Mining; 53-7111.00 Shuttle Car Operators. **OOH Jobs:** Material Moving Equipment Operators.

06.04.01 Hands-on Work: Construction, Extraction, and Maintenance

O*NET Jobs: 47-2031.03 Carpenter Assemblers and Repairers; 47-2061.00 Construction Laborers; 47-3011.00 Helpers—Brickmasons, Blockmasons, Stonemasons, and Tile and Marble Setters; 47-3012.00 Helpers—Carpenters; 47-3014.00 Helpers—Painters, Paperhangers, Plasterers, and Stucco Masons; 47-3015.00 Helpers—Pipelayers, Plumbers, Pipefitters, and Steamfitters; 47-3016.00 Helpers—Roofers; 47-4051.00 Highway Maintenance Workers; 47-4071.00 Septic Tank Servicers and Sewer Pipe Cleaners; 47-5081.00 Helpers—Extraction Workers; 53-7062.02 Grips and Set-Up Workers, Motion Picture Sets, Studios, and Stages. **OOH Jobs:** Carpenters; Handlers, Equipment Cleaners, Helpers, and Laborers.

GOE Interest Area 07: Transportation

GOE Work Groups and Related Job Titles

07.01.01 Managerial Work in Transportation

O*NET Jobs: 11-3071.01 Transportation Managers; 53-1031.00 First-Line Supervisors/Managers of Transportation and Material-Moving Machine and Vehicle Operators; 53-4031.00 Railroad Conductors and Yardmasters. **OOH Jobs:** Blue-Collar Worker Supervisors; Rail Transportation Occupations.

07.02.01 Vehicle Expediting and Coordinating

O*NET Jobs: 53-2021.00 Air Traffic Controllers; 53-2022.00 Airfield Operations Specialists; 53-4021.00 Railroad Brake, Signal, and Switch Operators; 53-6041.00 Traffic Technicians. **OOH Jobs:** Air Traffic Controllers.

07.03.01 Air Vehicle Operation

O*NET Jobs: 53-2011.00 Airline Pilots, Copilots, and Flight Engineers; 53-2012.00 Commercial Pilots **OOH Jobs:** None listed.

07.04.01 Water Vehicle Operation

O*NET Jobs: 53-5011.00 Sailors and Marine Oilers; 53-5011.01 Able Seamen; 53-5011.02 Ordinary Seamen and Marine Oilers; 53-5021.00 Captains, Mates, and Pilots of Water Vessels; 53-5021.01 Ship and Boat Captains; 53-5021.02 Mates—Ship, Boat, and Barge; 53-5021.03 Pilots, Ship; 53-5022.00 Motorboat Operators; 53-7031.00 Dredge Operators. **OOH Jobs:** None listed.

07.05.01 Truck Driving

O*NET Jobs: 53-3032.00 Truck Drivers, Heavy and Tractor-Trailer; 53-3032.01 Truck Drivers, Heavy; 53-3032.02 Tractor-Trailer Truck Drivers; 53-3033.00 Truck Drivers, Light or Delivery Services. **OOH Jobs:** Truckdrivers.

07.06.01 Rail Vehicle Operation

O*NET Jobs: 53-4011.00 Locomotive Engineers; 53-4012.00 Locomotive Firers; 53-4013.00 Rail Yard Engineers, Dinkey Operators, and Hostlers; 53-4041.00 Subway and Streetcar Operators. **OOH Jobs:** Rail Transportation Occupations.

07.07.01 Other Services Requiring Driving

O*NET Jobs: 53-3011.00 Ambulance Drivers and Attendants, Except Emergency Medical Technicians; 53-3021.00 Bus Drivers, Transit and Intercity; 53-3022.00 Bus Drivers, School; 53-3031.00 Driver/Sales Workers; 53-3041.00 Taxi Drivers and Chauffeurs; 53-6021.00 Parking Lot Attendants. **OOH Jobs:** Busdrivers; Handlers, Equipment Cleaners, Helpers, and Laborers; Taxi Drivers and Chauffeurs; Truckdrivers.

07.08.01 Support Work in Transportation

O*NET Jobs: 53-4021.01 Train Crew Members; 53-4021.02 Railroad Yard Workers; 53-6051.00 Transportation Inspectors; 53-6051.06 Freight Inspectors; 53-7062.01 Stevedores, Except Equipment Operators. **OOH Jobs:** Handlers, Equipment Cleaners, Helpers, and Laborers; Inspectors, Testers, and Graders; Rail Transportation Occupations.

GOE Interest Area 08: Industrial Production

GOE Work Groups and Related Job Titles

08.01.01 Managerial Work in Industrial Production

O*NET Jobs: 11-3051.00 Industrial Production Managers; 51-1011.00 First-Line Supervisors/Managers of Production and Operating Workers; 53-1021.00 First-Line Supervisors/Managers of Helpers, Laborers, and Material Movers, Hand. **OOH Jobs:** Blue-Collar Worker Supervisors; Industrial Production Managers.

08.02.01 Production Technology: Machine Set-up and Operation

O*NET Jobs: 51-4021.00 Extruding and Drawing Machine Setters, Operators, and Tenders, Metal and Plastic; 51-4022.00 Forging Machine Setters, Operators, and Tenders, Metal and Plastic; 51-4023.00 Rolling Machine Setters, Operators, and Tenders, Metal and Plastic; 51-4031.00 Cutting, Punching, and Press Machine Setters, Operators, and Tenders, Metal and Plastic; 51-4031.01 Sawing Machine Tool Setters and Set-Up Operators, Metal and Plastic; 51-4031.02 Punching Machine Setters and Set-Up Operators, Metal and Plastic; 51-4031.03 Press and Press Brake Machine Setters and Set-Up Operators, Metal and Plastic; 51-4031.04 Shear and Slitter Machine Setters and Set-Up Operators, Metal and Plastic; 51-4032.00 Drilling and Boring Machine Tool Setters, Operators, and Tenders, Metal and Plastic; 51-4033.00 Grinding, Lapping, Polishing, and Buffing Machine Tool Setters, Operators, and Tenders, Metal and Plastic; 51-4033.01 Grinding, Honing, Lapping, and Deburring Machine Set-Up Operators; 51-4033.02 Buffing and Polishing Set-Up Operators; 51-4034.00 Lathe and Turning Machine Tool Setters, Operators, and Tenders, Metal and Plastic; 51-4035.00 Milling and Planing Machine Setters, Operators, and Tenders, Metal and Plastic; 51-4072.00 Molding, Coremaking, and Casting Machine Setters, Operators, and Tenders, Metal and Plastic; 51-4072.01 Plastic Molding and Casting Machine Setters and Set-Up Operators; 51-4072.02 Plastic Molding and Casting Machine Operators and Tenders; 51-4072.03 Metal Molding, Coremaking, and Casting Machine Setters and Set-Up Operators; 51-4072.04 Metal Molding, Coremaking, and Casting Machine Operators and Tenders; 51-4072.05 Casting Machine Set-Up Operators; 51-4081.00 Multiple Machine Tool Setters, Operators, and Tenders, Metal and Plastic; 51-4081.01 Combination Machine Tool Setters and Set-Up Operators, Metal and Plastic; 51-4122.00 Welding, Soldering, and Brazing Machine Setters, Operators, and Tenders; 51-4122.01 Welding Machine Setters and Set-Up Operators; 51-4122.03 Soldering and Brazing Machine Setters and Set-Up Operators; 51-4191.00 Heat Treating Equipment Setters, Operators, and Tenders, Metal and Plastic; 51-4191.01 Heating Equipment Setters and Set-Up Operators, Metal and Plastic; 51-4191.02 Heat Treating, Annealing, and

Tempering Machine Operators and Tenders, Metal and Plastic; 51-5011.00 Bindery Workers; 51-5011.01 Bindery Machine Setters and Set-Up Operators; 51-5023.06 Screen Printing Machine Setters and Set-Up Operators; 51-6062.00 Textile Cutting Machine Setters, Operators, and Tenders; 51-6063.00 Textile Knitting and Weaving Machine Setters, Operators, and Tenders; 51-6064.00 Textile Winding, Twisting, and Drawing Out Machine Setters, Operators, and Tenders; 51-7042.00 Woodworking Machine Setters, Operators, and Tenders, Except Sawing; 51-7042.01 Woodworking Machine Setters and Set-Up Operators, Except Sawing; 51-9041.00 Extruding, Forming, Pressing, and Compacting Machine Setters, Operators, and Tenders; 51-9041.01 Extruding, Forming, Pressing, and Compacting Machine Setters and Set-Up Operators; 51-9121.00 Coating, Painting, and Spraying Machine Setters, Operators, and Tenders; 51-9121.01 Coating, Painting, and Spraying Machine Setters and Set-Up Operators; 51-9196.00 Paper Goods Machine Setters, Operators, and Tenders. **OOH Jobs:** Bindery Workers; Metalworking and Plastics-Working Machine Operators; Painting and Coating Machine Operators; Printing Press Operators; Textile Machinery Operators; Welders, Cutters, and Welding Machine Operators; Woodworking Occupations.

08.02.02 Production Technology: Precision Hand Work

O*NET Jobs: 51-2011.00 Aircraft Structure, Surfaces, Rigging, and Systems Assemblers; 51-2011.01 Aircraft Structure Assemblers, Precision; 51-2011.02 Aircraft Systems Assemblers, Precision; 51-2011.03 Aircraft Rigging Assemblers; 51-2022.00 Electrical and Electronic Equipment Assemblers; 51-2023.00 Electromechanical Equipment Assemblers; 51-2031.00 Engine and Other Machine Assemblers; 51-2093.00 Timing Device Assemblers, Adjusters, and Calibrators; 51-4071.00 Foundry Mold and Coremakers; 51-5012.00 Bookbinders; 51-9071.00 Jewelers and Precious Stone and Metal Workers; 51-9071.01 Jewelers; 51-9071.02 Silversmiths; 51-9071.03 Model and Mold Makers, Jewelry; 51-9071.04 Bench Workers, Jewelry; 51-9071.05 Pewter Casters and Finishers; 51-9071.06 Gem and Diamond Workers; 51-9081.00 Dental Laboratory Technicians; 51-9083.01 Precision Lens Grinders and Polishers; 51-9195.00 Molders, Shapers, and Casters, Except Metal and Plastic; 51-9195.01 Precision Mold and Pattern Casters, except Nonferrous Metals; 51-9195.02 Precision Pattern and Die Casters, Nonferrous Metals. **OOH Jobs:** Bindery Workers; Dental Laboratory Technicians; Jewelers and Precious Stones and Metal Workers; Precision Assemblers.

08.02.03 Production Technology: Inspection

O*NET Jobs: 45-4023.00 Log Graders and Scalers; 51-9061.00 Inspectors, Testers, Sorters, Samplers, and Weighers; 51-9061.01 Materials Inspectors; 51-9061.02 Mechanical Inspectors; 51-9061.03 Precision Devices Inspectors and Testers; 51-9061.04 Electrical and Electronic Inspectors and Testers; 51-9061.05 Production Inspectors, Testers, Graders, Sorters, Samplers, Weighers; 53-6051.05 Motor Vehicle Inspectors. **OOH Jobs:** Forestry, Conservation, and Logging Occupations; Inspectors, Testers, and Graders.

08.03.01 Production Work: Machine Work, Assorted Materials

O*NET Jobs: 51-4011.00 Computer-Controlled Machine Tool Operators, Metal and Plastic; 51-4011.01 Numerical Control Machine Tool Operators and Tenders, Metal and Plastic; 51-4081.02 Combination Machine Tool Operators and Tenders, Metal and Plastic; 51-6031.00 Sewing Machine Operators; 51-6031.01 Sewing Machine Operators, Garment; 51-6031.02 Sewing Machine Operators, Non-Garment; 51-6042.00 Shoe Machine Operators and Tenders; 51-6091.00 Extruding and Forming Machine Setters, Operators, and Tenders, Synthetic and Glass Fibers; 51-6091.01 Extruding and Forming Machine Operators and Tenders, Synthetic or Glass Fibers; 51-7041.00 Sawing Machine Setters, Operators, and Tenders, Wood; 51-7041.01 Sawing Machine Setters and Set-Up

Operators; 51-7041.02 Sawing Machine Operators and Tenders; 51-7042.02 Woodworking Machine Operators and Tenders, Except Sawing; 51-9021.00 Crushing, Grinding, and Polishing Machine Setters, Operators, and Tenders; 51-9032.00 Cutting and Slicing Machine Setters, Operators, and Tenders; 51-9032.01 Fiber Product Cutting Machine Setters and Set-Up Operators; 51-9032.02 Stone Sawyers; 51-9032.03 Glass Cutting Machine Setters and Set-Up Operators; 51-9032.04 Cutting and Slicing Machine Operators and Tenders; 51-9041.02 Extruding, Forming, Pressing, and Compacting Machine Operators and Tenders; 51-9111.00 Packaging and Filling Machine Operators and Tenders; 51-9121.02 Coating, Painting, and Spraying Machine Operators and Tenders; 51-9191.00 Cementing and Gluing Machine Operators and Tenders. **OOH Jobs:** Apparel Workers; Metalworking and Plastics-Working Machine Operators; Painting and Coating Machine Operators; Textile Machinery Operators; Woodworking Occupations.

08.03.02 Production Work: Equipment Operation, Assorted Materials Processing

O*NET Jobs: 51-3011.02 Bakers, Manufacturing; 51-3022.00 Meat, Poultry, and Fish Cutters and Trimmers; 51-3023.00 Slaughterers and Meat Packers; 51-3091.00 Food and Tobacco Roasting, Baking, and Drying Machine Operators and Tenders; 51-3093.00 Food Cooking Machine Operators and Tenders; 51-4051.00 Metal-Refining Furnace Operators and Tenders; 51-4052.00 Pourers and Casters, Metal; 51-4191.03 Heaters, Metal and Plastic; 51-6021.02 Pressing Machine Operators and Tenders—Textile, Garment, and Related Materials; 51-6061.00 Textile Bleaching and Dyeing Machine Operators and Tenders; 51-9011.00 Chemical Equipment Operators and Tenders; 51-9011.01 Chemical Equipment Controllers and Operators; 51-9011.02 Chemical Equipment Tenders; 51-9012.00 Separating, Filtering, Clarifying, Precipitating, and Still Machine Setters, Operators, and Tenders; 51-9023.00 Mixing and Blending Machine Setters, Operators, and Tenders; 51-9051.00 Furnace, Kiln, Oven, Drier, and Kettle Operators and Tenders; 51-9141.00 Semiconductor Processors; 51-9192.00 Cleaning, Washing, and Metal Pickling Equipment Operators and Tenders; 51-9193.00 Cooling and Freezing Equipment Operators and Tenders; 51-9198.00 Helpers—Production Workers; 51-9198.01 Production Laborers; 51-9198.02 Production Helpers. **OOH Jobs:** Materials Processing; Apparel Workers; Butchers and Meat, Poultry, and Fish Cutters; Electronic Semiconductor Processors; Handlers, Equipment Cleaners, Helpers, and Laborers; Metalworking and Plastics-Working Machine Operators; Textile Machinery Operators.

08.03.03 Production Work: Equipment Operation, Welding, Brazing, and Soldering

O*NET Jobs: 51-2041.00 Structural Metal Fabricators and Fitters; 51-2041.01 Metal Fabricators, Structural Metal Products; 51-2041.02 Fitters, Structural Metal—Precision; 51-4121.00 Welders, Cutters, Solderers, and Brazers; 51-4121.01 Welders, Production; 51-4121.02 Welders and Cutters; 51-4121.03 Welder-Fitters; 51-4121.04 Solderers; 51-4121.05 Brazers; 51-4122.02 Welding Machine Operators and Tenders; 51-4122.04 Soldering and Brazing Machine Operators and Tenders. **OOH Jobs:** Metalworking and Plastics-Working Machine Operators; Precision Assemblers; Welders, Cutters, and Welding Machine Operators.

08.03.04 Production Work: Plating and Coating

O*NET Jobs: 51-4193.00 Plating and Coating Machine Setters, Operators, and Tenders, Metal and Plastic; 51-4193.01 Electrolytic Plating and Coating Machine Setters and Set-Up Operators, Metal and Plastic; 51-4193.02 Electrolytic Plating and Coating Machine Operators and Tenders, Metal and Plastic; 51-4193.03 Nonelectrolytic Plating and Coating Machine Setters and Set-Up Operators, Metal and Plastic; 51-4193.04 Nonelectrolytic Plating and Coating Machine Operators and Tenders, Metal and Plastic. **OOH Jobs:** Metalworking and Plastics-Working Machine Operators.

08.03.05 Production Work: Printing and Reproduction

O*NET Jobs: 51-5011.02 Bindery Machine Operators and Tenders; 51-5021.00 Job Printers; 51-5022.00 Prepress Technicians and Workers; 51-5022.01 Hand Compositors and Typesetters; 51-5022.05 Scanner Operators; 51-5022.06 Strippers; 51-5022.07 Platemakers; 51-5022.10 Electrotypers and Stereotypers; 51-5022.11 Plate Finishers; 51-5022.13 Photoengraving and Lithographing Machine Operators and Tenders; 51-5023.00 Printing Machine Operators; 51-5023.01 Precision Printing Workers; 51-5023.02 Offset Lithographic Press Setters and Set-Up Operators; 51-5023.03 Letterpress Setters and Set-Up Operators; 51-5023.04 Design Printing Machine Setters and Set-Up Operators; 51-5023.05 Marking and Identification Printing Machine Setters and Set-Up Operators; 51-5023.07 Embossing Machine Set-Up Operators; 51-5023.08 Engraver Set-Up Operators; 51-5023.09 Printing Press Machine Operators and Tenders; 51-9131.00 Photographic Process Workers; 51-9131.01 Photographic Retouchers and Restorers; 51-9131.02 Photographic Reproduction Technicians; 51-9131.03 Photographic Hand Developers; 51-9131.04 Film Laboratory Technicians; 51-9132.00 Photographic Processing Machine Operators. OOH Jobs: Bindery Workers; Photographic Process Workers; Prepress Workers; Printing Press Operators.

08.03.06 Production Work: Hands-on Work, Assorted Materials

O*NET Jobs: 45-2041.00 Graders and Sorters, Agricultural Products; 51-2021.00 Coil Winders, Tapers, and Finishers; 51-2091.00 Fiberglass Laminators and Fabricators; 51-2092.00 Team Assemblers; 51-3092.00 Food Batchmakers; 51-6051.00 Sewers, Hand; 51-6092.00 Fabric and Apparel Patternmakers; 51-9022.00 Grinding and Polishing Workers, Hand; 51-9031.00 Cutters and Trimmers, Hand; 51-9123.00 Painting, Coating, and Decorating Workers; 51-9195.06 Mold Makers, Hand; 51-9195.07 Molding and Casting Workers; 51-9197.00 Tire Builders. OOH Jobs: Apparel Workers.

08.04.01 Metal and Plastics Machining Technology

O*NET Jobs: 51-4041.00 Machinists; 51-4061.00 Model Makers, Metal and Plastic; 51-4062.00 Patternmakers, Metal and Plastic; 51-4111.00 Tool and Die Makers; 51-4192.00 Lay-Out Workers, Metal and Plastic; 51-4194.00 Tool Grinders, Filers, and Sharpeners. OOH Jobs: Machinists and Numerical Control Machine Tool Programmers; Tool and Die Makers.

08.05.01 Woodworking Technology

O*NET Jobs: 51-7011.00 Cabinetmakers and Bench Carpenters; 51-7021.00 Furniture Finishers; 51-7031.00 Model Makers, Wood; 51-7032.00 Patternmakers, Wood. OOH Jobs: Woodworking Occupations.

08.06.01 Systems Operation: Utilities and Power Plant

O*NET Jobs: 51-8011.00 Nuclear Power Reactor Operators; 51-8012.00 Power Distributors and Dispatchers; 51-8013.00 Power Plant Operators; 51-8013.01 Power Generating Plant Operators, Except Auxiliary Equipment Operators; 51-8013.02 Auxiliary Equipment Operators, Power; 51-8021.00 Stationary Engineers and Boiler Operators; 51-8021.01 Boiler Operators and Tenders, Low Pressure; 51-8021.02 Stationary Engineers; 51-8031.00 Water and Liquid Waste Treatment Plant and System Operators; 53-5031.00 Ship Engineers. OOH Jobs: Electric Power Generating Plant Operators and Power Distributors and Dispatchers; Stationary Engineers; Water and Wastewater Treatment Plant Operators; Water Transportation Occupations.

08.06.02 Systems Operation: Oil, Gas, and Water Distribution

O*NET Jobs: 51-8091.00 Chemical Plant and System Operators; 51-8092.00 Gas Plant Operators; 51-8092.01 Gas Processing Plant Opera-tors; 51-8092.02 Gas Distribution Plant Operators; 51-8093.00 Petroleum Pump System Operators, Refinery Operators, and Gaugers; 51-8093.01 Petroleum Pump System Operators and Control Panel Operators; 51-8093.03 Gaugers; 53-7071.00 Gas Compressor and Gas Pumping Station Operators; 53-7071.01 Gas Pumping Station Operators; 53-7071.02 Gas Compressor Operators; 53-7073.00 Wellhead Pumpers. OOH Jobs: Material Moving Equipment Operators.

08.07.01 Hands-on Work: Loading, Moving, Hoisting, and Conveying

O*NET Jobs: 47-4041.01 Irradiated-Fuel Handlers; 53-7011.00 Conveyor Operators and Tenders; 53-7021.00 Crane and Tower Operators; 53-7032.00 Excavating and Loading Machine and Dragline Operators; 53-7032.02 Dragline Operators; 53-7041.00 Hoist and Winch Operators; 53-7051.00 Industrial Truck and Tractor Operators; 53-7062.00 Laborers and Freight, Stock, and Material Movers, Hand; 53-7062.03 Freight, Stock, and Material Movers, Hand; 53-7063.00 Machine Feeders and Offbearers; 53-7064.00 Packers and Packagers, Hand; 53-7072.00 Pump Operators, Except Wellhead Pumpers; 53-7081.00 Refuse and Recyclable Material Collectors; 53-7121.00 Tank Car, Truck, and Ship Loaders. OOH Jobs: Handlers, Equipment Cleaners, Helpers, and Laborers; Hazardous Materials Removal Workers; Material Moving Equipment Operators.

GOE Interest Area 09: Business Detail

GOE Work Groups and Related Job Titles

09.01.01 Managerial Work in Business Detail

O*NET Jobs: 11-3011.00 Administrative Services Managers; 43-1011.00 First-Line Supervisors/Managers of Office and Administrative Support Workers; 43-1011.01 First-Line Supervisors, Customer Service; 43-1011.02 First-Line Supervisors, Administrative Support. OOH Jobs: Administrative Services and Facility Managers; Office and Administrative Support Supervisors and Managers.

09.02.01 Administrative Detail: Administration

O*NET Jobs: 43-4031.00 Court, Municipal, and License Clerks; 43-4031.01 Court Clerks; 43-4031.02 Municipal Clerks; 43-4031.03 License Clerks. OOH Jobs: None listed.

09.02.02 Administrative Detail: Secretarial Work

O*NET Jobs: 43-6011.00 Executive Secretaries and Administrative Assistants; 43-6012.00 Legal Secretaries; 43-6013.00 Medical Secretaries; 43-6014.00 Secretaries, Except Legal, Medical, and Executive. OOH Jobs: Secretaries.

09.02.03 Administrative Detail: Interviewing

O*NET Jobs: 43-4061.00 Eligibility Interviewers, Government Programs; 43-4061.01 Claims Takers, Unemployment Benefits; 43-4061.02 Welfare Eligibility Workers and Interviewers; 43-4111.00 Interviewers, Except Eligibility and Loan; 43-4131.00 Loan Interviewers and Clerks. OOH Jobs: Adjusters, Investigators, and Collectors; Interviewing and New Account Clerks; Loan Clerks and Credit Authorizers, Checkers, and Clerks.

09.03.01 Bookkeeping, Auditing, and Accounting

O*NET Jobs: 13-2082.00 Tax Preparers; 43-3021.00 Billing and Posting Clerks and Machine Operators; 43-3021.01 Statement Clerks; 43-3021.02 Billing, Cost, and Rate Clerks; 43-3031.00 Bookkeeping, Accounting, and Auditing Clerks; 43-3051.00 Payroll and Timekeeping Clerks; 43-4011.00 Brokerage Clerks. OOH Jobs: Billing Clerks and Billing Machine Operators; Bookkeeping, Accounting, and Auditing Clerks; Brokerage Clerks and Statement Clerks; Payroll and Timekeeping Clerks.

09.04.01 Material Control

O*NET Jobs: 43-5041.00 Meter Readers, Utilities; 43-5061.00 Production, Planning, and Expediting Clerks;. OOH Jobs: None listed.

09.05.01 Customer Service

O*NET Jobs: 41-2011.00 Cashiers; 41-2012.00 Gaming Change Persons and Booth Cashiers; 41-2021.00 Counter and Rental Clerks; 43-3011.00 Bill and Account Collectors; 43-3041.00 Gaming Cage Workers; 43-3071.00 Tellers; 43-4051.00 Customer Service Representatives; 43-4051.01 Adjustment Clerks; 43-4051.02 Customer Service Representatives, Utilities; 43-4141.00 New Accounts Clerks; 43-4151.00 Order Clerks; 43-4171.00 Receptionists and Information Clerks; 43-4181.01 Travel Clerks. OOH Jobs: Adjusters, Investigators, and Collectors; Bank Tellers; Cashiers; Counter and Rental Clerks; Interviewing and New Account Clerks; Order Clerks; Receptionists; Reservation and Transportation Ticket Agents and Travel Clerks.

09.06.01 Communications

O*NET Jobs: 43-2011.00 Switchboard Operators, Including Answering Service; 43-2021.00 Telephone Operators; 43-2021.01 Directory Assistance Operators; 43-2021.02 Central Office Operators; 43-5031.00 Police, Fire, and Ambulance Dispatchers; 43-5032.00 Dispatchers, Except Police, Fire, and Ambulance. OOH Jobs: Communications Equipment Operators.

09.07.01 Records Processing: Verification and Proofing

O*NET Jobs: 43-4041.00 Credit Authorizers, Checkers, and Clerks; 43-4041.01 Credit Authorizers; 43-4041.02 Credit Checkers; 43-9041.00 Insurance Claims and Policy Processing Clerks; 43-9041.01 Insurance Claims Clerks; 43-9041.02 Insurance Policy Processing Clerks; 43-9081.00 Proofreaders and Copy Markers. OOH Jobs: Adjusters, Investigators, and Collectors; Loan Clerks and Credit Authorizers, Checkers, and Clerks.

09.07.02 Records Processing: Preparation and Maintenance

O*NET Jobs: 23-2091.00 Court Reporters; 29-2071.00 Medical Records and Health Information Technicians; 31-9094.00 Medical Transcriptionists; 43-3061.00 Procurement Clerks; 43-4021.00 Correspondence Clerks; 43-4071.00 File Clerks; 43-4161.00 Human Resources Assistants, Except Payroll and Timekeeping; 43-9061.00 Office Clerks, General OOH Jobs: File Clerks; Health Information Technicians; Human Resources Clerks, Except Payroll and Timekeeping; Office Clerks, General.

09.08.01 Records and Materials Processing

O*NET Jobs: 43-5011.00 Cargo and Freight Agents; 43-5021.00 Couriers and Messengers; 43-5052.00 Postal Service Mail Carriers; 43-5053.00 Postal Service Mail Sorters, Processors, and Processing Machine Operators; 43-5071.00 Shipping, Receiving, and Traffic Clerks; 43-5081.00 Stock Clerks and Order Fillers; 43-5081.02 Marking Clerks; 43-5081.03 Stock Clerks—Stockroom, Warehouse, or Storage Yard; 43-5081.04 Order Fillers, Wholesale and Retail Sales; 43-5111.00 Weighers, Measurers, Checkers, and Samplers, Recordkeeping; 43-9051.02 Mail Clerks, Except Mail Machine Operators and Postal Service. OOH Jobs: Mail Clerks and Messengers; Postal Clerks and Mail Carriers; Shipping, Receiving, and Traffic Clerks.

09.09.01 Clerical Machine Operation

O*NET Jobs: 43-3021.03 Billing, Posting, and Calculating Machine Operators; 43-5051.00 Postal Service Clerks; 43-9011.00 Computer Operators; 43-9021.00 Data Entry Keyers; 43-9022.00 Word Processors and Typists; 43-9051.00 Mail Clerks and Mail Machine Operators, Except Postal Service; 43-9051.01 Mail Machine Operators, Preparation and Handling; 43-9071.00 Office Machine Operators, Except Computer; 43-9071.01 Duplicating Machine Operators; 49-2011.01 Automatic Teller Machine Servicers; 51-5022.12 Typesetting and Composing Machine Operators and Tenders. OOH Jobs: Billing Clerks and Billing Machine Operators; Computer Operators; Postal Clerks and Mail Carriers; Prepress Workers; Word Processors, Typists, and Data Entry Keyers.

GOE Interest Area 10: Sales and Marketing

GOE Work Groups and Related Job Titles

10.01.01 Managerial Work in Sales and Marketing

O*NET Jobs: 11-2011.00 Advertising and Promotions Managers; 11-2021.00 Marketing Managers; 11-2022.00 Sales Managers; 41-1011.00 First-Line Supervisors/Managers of Retail Sales Workers; 41-1012.00 First-Line Supervisors/Managers of Non-Retail Sales Workers. OOH Jobs: Advertising, Marketing, and Public Relations Managers; Retail Sales Worker Supervisors and Managers.

10.02.01 Sales Technology: Technical Sales

O*NET Jobs: 41-4011.00 Sales Representatives, Wholesale and Manufacturing, Technical and Scientific Products; 41-4011.01 Sales Representatives, Agricultural; 41-4011.02 Sales Representatives, Chemical and Pharmaceutical; 41-4011.03 Sales Representatives, Electrical/Electronic; 41-4011.04 Sales Representatives, Mechanical Equipment and Supplies; 41-4011.05 Sales Representatives, Medical; 41-4011.06 Sales Representatives, Instruments. OOH Jobs: Manufacturers' and Wholesale Sales Representatives.

10.02.02 Sales Technology: Intangible Sales

O*NET Jobs: 41-3011.00 Advertising Sales Agents; 41-3021.00 Insurance Sales Agents; 41-3031.00 Securities, Commodities, and Financial Services Sales Agents; 41-3031.01 Sales Agents, Securities and Commodities; 41-3031.02 Sales Agents, Financial Services. OOH Jobs: Insurance Sales Agents; Securities, Commodities, and Financial Services Sales Representatives; Services Sales Representatives.

10.03.01 General Sales

O*NET Jobs: 41-2022.00 Parts Salespersons; 41-2031.00 Retail Salespersons; 41-3041.00 Travel Agents; 41-4012.00 Sales Representatives, Wholesale and Manufacturing, Except Technical and Scientific Products; 41-9021.00 Real Estate Brokers; 41-9022.00 Real Estate Sales Agents; 43-5081.01 Stock Clerks, Sales Floor; 53-6031.00 Service Station Attendants. OOH Jobs: Manufacturers' and Wholesale Sales Representatives; Real Estate Agents and Brokers; Retail Salespersons; Travel Agents.

10.04.01 Personal Soliciting

O*NET Jobs: 41-9011.00 Demonstrators and Product Promoters; 41-9041.00 Telemarketers; 41-9091.00 Door-To-Door Sales Workers, News and Street Vendors, and Related Workers. OOH Jobs: Demonstrators, Product Promoters, and Models; Services Sales Representatives.

GOE Interest Area 11: Recreation, Travel, and Other Personal Services

GOE Work Groups and Related Job Titles

11.01.01 Managerial Work in Recreation, Travel, and Other Personal Services

O*NET Jobs: 11-9051.00 Food Service Managers; 11-9071.00 Gaming Managers; 11-9081.00 Lodging Managers; 13-1121.00 Meeting and Convention Planners; 35-1012.00 First-Line Supervisors/Managers of Food

Preparation and Serving Workers; 37-1011.00 First-Line Supervisors/Managers of Housekeeping and Janitorial Workers; 37-1011.01 Housekeeping Supervisors; 37-1011.02 Janitorial Supervisors; 39-1011.00 Gaming Supervisors; 39-1021.00 First-Line Supervisors/Managers of Personal Service Workers; 53-1011.00 Aircraft Cargo Handling Supervisors. **OOH Jobs:** Hotel Managers and Assistants; Janitors and Cleaners and Institutional Cleaning Supervisors; Restaurant and Food Service Managers.

11.02.01 Recreational Services

O*NET Jobs: 39-1012.00 Slot Key Persons; 39-3011.00 Gaming Dealers; 39-3012.00 Gaming and Sports Book Writers and Runners; 39-3021.00 Motion Picture Projectionists; 39-3031.00 Ushers, Lobby Attendants, and Ticket Takers; 39-3091.00 Amusement and Recreation Attendants; 39-6021.00 Tour Guides and Escorts; 39-6022.00 Travel Guides; 39-9032.00 Recreation Workers. **OOH Jobs:** Recreation Workers.

11.03.01 Transportation and Lodging Services

O*NET Jobs: 39-6011.00 Baggage Porters and Bellhops; 39-6012.00 Concierges; 39-6031.00 Flight Attendants; 39-6032.00 Transportation Attendants, Except Flight Attendants and Baggage Porters; 43-4081.00 Hotel, Motel, and Resort Desk Clerks; 43-4181.00 Reservation and Transportation Ticket Agents and Travel Clerks; 43-4181.02 Reservation and Transportation Ticket Agents. **OOH Jobs:** Flight Attendants; Hotel, Motel, and Resort Desk Clerks; Reservation and Transportation Ticket Agents and Travel Clerks.

11.04.01 Barber and Beauty Services

O*NET Jobs: 39-5011.00 Barbers; 39-5012.00 Hairdressers, Hairstylists, and Cosmetologists; 39-5092.00 Manicurists and Pedicurists; 39-5093.00 Shampooers; 39-5094.00 Skin Care Specialists. **OOH Jobs:** Barbers, Cosmetologists, and Related Workers.

11.05.01 Food and Beverage Services: Preparing

O*NET Jobs: 35-1011.00 Chefs and Head Cooks; 35-2011.00 Cooks, Fast Food; 35-2012.00 Cooks, Institution and Cafeteria; 35-2014.00 Cooks, Restaurant; 35-2015.00 Cooks, Short Order; 35-2021.00 Food Preparation Workers; 35-9021.00 Dishwashers; 51-3011.00 Bakers; 51-3011.01 Bakers, Bread and Pastry; 51-3021.00 Butchers and Meat Cutters. **OOH Jobs:** Butchers and Meat, Poultry, and Fish Cutters; Chefs, Cooks, and Other Kitchen Workers.

11.05.02 Food and Beverage Services: Serving

O*NET Jobs: 35-3011.00 Bartenders; 35-3021.00 Combined Food Preparation and Serving Workers, Including Fast Food; 35-3022.00 Counter Attendants, Cafeteria, Food Concession, and Coffee Shop; 35-3031.00 Waiters and Waitresses; 35-3041.00 Food Servers, Nonrestaurant; 35-9011.00 Dining Room and Cafeteria Attendants and Bartender Helpers; 35-9031.00 Hosts and Hostesses, Restaurant, Lounge, and Coffee Shop. **OOH Jobs:** Food and Beverage Service Occupations.

11.06.01 Apparel, Shoes, Leather, and Fabric Care

O*NET Jobs: 49-9093.00 Fabric Menders, Except Garment; 51-6011.00 Laundry and Dry-Cleaning Workers; 51-6011.01 Spotters, Dry Cleaning; 51-6011.02 Precision Dyers; 51-6011.03 Laundry and Drycleaning Machine Operators and Tenders, Except Pressing; 51-6021.00 Pressers, Textile, Garment, and Related Materials; 51-6021.01 Pressers, Delicate Fabrics; 51-6021.03 Pressers, Hand; 51-6041.00 Shoe and Leather Workers and Repairers; 51-6052.00 Tailors, Dressmakers, and Custom Sewers; 51-6052.01 Shop and Alteration Tailors; 51-6052.02 Custom Tailors; 51-6093.00 Upholsterers. **OOH Jobs:** Apparel Workers; Shoe and Leather Workers and Repairers; Upholsterers.

11.07.01 Cleaning and Building Services

O*NET Jobs: 37-2011.00 Janitors and Cleaners, Except Maids and Housekeeping Cleaners; 37-2012.00 Maids and Housekeeping Cleaners; 39-3093.00 Locker Room, Coatroom, and Dressing Room Attendants. **OOH Jobs:** Janitors and Cleaners and Institutional Cleaning Supervisors.

11.08.01 Other Personal Services

O*NET Jobs: 35-2013.00 Cooks, Private Household; 39-4011.00 Embalmers; 39-4021.00 Funeral Attendants; 39-9021.00 Personal and Home Care Aides; 53-7061.00 Cleaners of Vehicles and Equipment. **OOH Jobs:** Funeral Directors and Morticians; Handlers, Equipment Cleaners, Helpers, and Laborers.

GOE Interest Area 12: Education and Social Service

GOE Work Groups and Related Job Titles

12.01.01 Managerial Work in Education and Social Service

O*NET Jobs: 11-9031.00 Education Administrators, Preschool and Child Care Center/Program; 11-9032.00 Education Administrators, Elementary and Secondary School; 11-9033.00 Education Administrators, Post-secondary; 11-9151.00 Social and Community Service Managers; 19-1031.03 Park Naturalists; 25-9031.00 Instructional Coordinators. **OOH Jobs:** Conservation Scientists and Foresters; Education Administrators.

12.02.01 Social Services: Religious

O*NET Jobs: 21-2011.00 Clergy; 21-2021.00 Directors, Religious Activities and Education. **OOH Jobs:** Clergy; Protestant Ministers; Rabbis; Roman Catholic Priests.

12.02.02 Social Services: Counseling and Social Work

O*NET Jobs: 19-3031.00 Clinical, Counseling, and School Psychologists; 19-3031.02 Clinical Psychologists; 19-3031.03 Counseling Psychologists; 21-1011.00 Substance Abuse and Behavioral Disorder Counselors; 21-1013.00 Marriage and Family Therapists; 21-1014.00 Mental Health Counselors; 21-1015.00 Rehabilitation Counselors; 21-1021.00 Child, Family, and School Social Workers; 21-1022.00 Medical and Public Health Social Workers; 21-1023.00 Mental Health and Substance Abuse Social Workers; 21-1092.00 Probation Officers and Correctional Treatment Specialists; 21-1093.00 Social and Human Service Assistants; 39-9041.00 Residential Advisors. **OOH Jobs:** Human Service Workers and Assistants; Psychologists; Social Workers.

12.03.01 Educational Services: Counseling and Evaluation

O*NET Jobs: 13-2052.00 Personal Financial Advisors; 19-3031.01 Educational Psychologists; 21-1012.00 Educational, Vocational, and School Counselors **OOH Jobs:** Counselors; Psychologists.

12.03.02 Educational Services: Postsecondary and Adult Teaching and Instructing

O*NET Jobs: 25-1011.00 Business Teachers, Postsecondary; 25-1021.00 Computer Science Teachers, Postsecondary; 25-1022.00 Mathematical Science Teachers, Postsecondary; 25-1031.00 Architecture Teachers, Postsecondary; 25-1032.00 Engineering Teachers, Postsecondary; 25-1041.00 Agricultural Sciences Teachers, Postsecondary; 25-1042.00 Biological Science Teachers, Postsecondary; 25-1043.00 Forestry and Conservation Science Teachers, Postsecondary; 25-1051.00 Atmospheric, Earth, Marine, and Space Sciences Teachers, Postsecondary; 25-1052.00 Chemistry Teachers, Postsecondary; 25-1053.00 Environmental Science Teachers, Postsecondary; 25-1054.00 Physics Teachers, Postsecondary;

25-1061.00 Anthropology and Archeology Teachers, Postsecondary; 25-1062.00 Area, Ethnic, and Cultural Studies Teachers, Postsecondary; 25-1063.00 Economics Teachers, Postsecondary; 25-1064.00 Geography Teachers, Postsecondary; 25-1065.00 Political Science Teachers, Postsecondary; 25-1066.00 Psychology Teachers, Postsecondary; 25-1067.00 Sociology Teachers, Postsecondary; 25-1071.00 Health Specialties Teachers, Postsecondary; 25-1072.00 Nursing Instructors and Teachers, Postsecondary; 25-1081.00 Education Teachers, Postsecondary; 25-1082.00 Library Science Teachers, Postsecondary; 25-1111.00 Criminal Justice and Law Enforcement Teachers, Postsecondary; 25-1112.00 Law Teachers, Postsecondary; 25-1113.00 Social Work Teachers, Postsecondary; 25-1121.00 Art, Drama, and Music Teachers, Postsecondary; 25-1122.00 Communications Teachers, Postsecondary; 25-1123.00 English Language and Literature Teachers, Postsecondary; 25-1124.00 Foreign Language and Literature Teachers, Postsecondary; 25-1125.00 History Teachers, Postsecondary; 25-1126.00 Philosophy and Religion Teachers, Postsecondary; 25-1191.00 Graduate Teaching Assistants; 25-1192.00 Home Economics Teachers, Postsecondary; 25-1193.00 Recreation and Fitness Studies Teachers, Postsecondary; 25-1194.00 Vocational Education Teachers, Postsecondary; 25-3011.00 Adult Literacy, Remedial Education, and GED Teachers and Instructors; 25-3021.00 Self-Enrichment Education Teachers; 25-9021.00 Farm and Home Management Advisors. OOH Jobs: Adult and Vocational Education Teachers; College and University Faculty.

12.03.03 Educational Services: Preschool, Elementary, and Secondary Teaching and Instructing

O*NET Jobs: 25-2011.00 Preschool Teachers, Except Special Education; 25-2012.00 Kindergarten Teachers, Except Special Education; 25-2021.00 Elementary School Teachers, Except Special Education; 25-2022.00 Middle School Teachers, Except Special and Vocational Education; 25-2023.00 Vocational Education Teachers, Middle School; 25-2031.00 Secondary School Teachers, Except Special and Vocational Education; 25-2032.00 Vocational Education Teachers, Secondary School; 25-2041.00 Special Education Teachers, Preschool, Kindergarten, and Elementary School; 25-2042.00 Special Education Teachers, Middle School; 25-2043.00 Special Education Teachers, Secondary School; 25-9041.00 Teacher Assistants; 39-9011.00 Child Care Workers. OOH Jobs: Preschool Teachers and Child-Care Workers; School Teachers—Kindergarten, Elementary, and Secondary; Special Education Teachers; Teacher Assistants.

12.03.04 Educational Services: Library and Museum

O*NET Jobs: 25-4011.00 Archivists; 25-4012.00 Curators; 25-4013.00 Museum Technicians and Conservators; 25-4021.00 Librarians; 25-4031.00 Library Technicians; 25-9011.00 Audio-Visual Collections Specialists; 43-4121.00 Library Assistants, Clerical. OOH Jobs: Archivists, Curators, Museum Technicians, and Conservators; Librarians; Library Assistants and Bookmobile Drivers; Library Technicians.

GOE Interest Area 13: General Management and Support

GOE Work Groups and Related Job Titles

13.01.01 General Management Work and Management of Support Functions

O*NET Jobs: 11-1011.00 Chief Executives; 11-1011.01 Government Service Executives; 11-1011.02 Private Sector Executives; 11-1021.00 General and Operations Managers; 11-1031.00 Legislators; 11-2031.00 Public Relations Managers; 11-3031.00 Financial Managers; 11-3031.01 Treasurers,

Controllers, and Chief Financial Officers; 11-3031.02 Financial Managers, Branch or Department; 11-3040.00 Human Resources Managers; 11-3041.00 Compensation and Benefits Managers; 11-3042.00 Training and Development Managers; 11-3061.00 Purchasing Managers; 11-3071.00 Transportation, Storage, and Distribution Managers; 11-3071.02 Storage and Distribution Managers; 11-9011.00 Farm, Ranch, and Other Agricultural Managers; 11-9061.00 Funeral Directors; 11-9131.00 Postmasters and Mail Superintendents; 11-9141.00 Property, Real Estate, and Community Association Managers. OOH Jobs: Financial Managers; Funeral Directors and Morticians; General Managers and Top Executives; Government Chief Executives and Legislators; Human Resources, Training, and Labor Relations Specialists and Managers; Property, Real Estate, and Community Association Managers; Purchasing Managers, Buyers, and Purchasing Agents.

13.02.01 Management Support: Human Resources

O*NET Jobs: 13-1071.00 Employment, Recruitment, and Placement Specialists; 13-1071.01 Employment Interviewers, Private or Public Employment Service; 13-1071.02 Personnel Recruiters; 13-1072.00 Compensation, Benefits, and Job Analysis Specialists; 13-1073.00 Training and Development Specialists. OOH Jobs: Employment Interviewers, Private or Public Employment Service; Human Resources, Training, and Labor Relations Specialists and Managers.

13.02.02 Management Support: Purchasing

O*NET Jobs: 13-1021.00 Purchasing Agents and Buyers, Farm Products; 13-1022.00 Wholesale and Retail Buyers, Except Farm Products; 13-1023.00 Purchasing Agents, Except Wholesale, Retail, and Farm Products. OOH Jobs: Purchasing Managers, Buyers, and Purchasing Agents.

13.02.03 Management Support: Accounting and Auditing

O*NET Jobs: 13-2011.00 Accountants and Auditors; 13-2011.01 Accountants; 13-2011.02 Auditors; 13-2081.00 Tax Examiners, Collectors, and Revenue Agents. OOH Jobs: Accountants and Auditors.

13.02.04 Management Support: Investigation and Analysis

O*NET Jobs: 13-1031.00 Claims Adjusters, Examiners, and Investigators; 13-1031.01 Claims Examiners, Property and Casualty Insurance; 13-1031.02 Insurance Adjusters, Examiners, and Investigators; 13-1032.00 Insurance Appraisers, Auto Damage; 13-1051.00 Cost Estimators; 13-1081.00 Logisticians; 13-1111.00 Management Analysts; 13-2021.00 Appraisers and Assessors of Real Estate; 13-2021.01 Assessors; 13-2021.02 Appraisers, Real Estate; 13-2031.00 Budget Analysts; 13-2041.00 Credit Analysts; 13-2051.00 Financial Analysts; 13-2053.00 Insurance Underwriters; 13-2071.00 Loan Counselors; 13-2072.00 Loan Officers; 19-3021.00 Market Research Analysts. OOH Jobs: Adjusters, Investigators, and Collectors; Budget Analysts; Cost Estimators; Economists and Marketing Research Analysts; Insurance Underwriters; Loan Officers and Counselors; Management Analysts.

GOE Interest Area 14: Medical and Health Services

GOE Work Groups and Related Job Titles

14.01.01 Managerial Work in Medical and Health Services

O*NET Jobs: 11-9111.00 Medical and Health Services Managers; 13-1041.06 Coroners. OOH Jobs: Health Service Managers; Inspectors and Compliance Officers, Except Construction.

14.02.01 Medicine and Surgery

O*NET Jobs: 29-1051.00 Pharmacists; 29-1061.00 Anesthesiologists; 29-1062.00 Family and General Practitioners; 29-1063.00 Internists,

General; 29-1064.00 Obstetricians and Gynecologists; 29-1065.00 Pediatricians, General; 29-1066.00 Psychiatrists; 29-1067.00 Surgeons; 29-1071.00 Physician Assistants; 29-1111.00 Registered Nurses; 29-2052.00 Pharmacy Technicians; 29-2055.00 Surgical Technologists; 31-9092.00 Medical Assistants; 31-9095.00 Pharmacy Aides. **OOH Jobs:** Medical Assistants; Pharmacists; Pharmacy Technicians and Assistants; Physicians; Physician's Assistants; Registered Nurses; Surgical Technologists.

14.03.01 Dentistry

O*NET Jobs: 29-1021.00 Dentists, General; 29-1022.00 Oral and Maxillofacial Surgeons; 29-1023.00 Orthodontists; 29-1024.00 Prosthodontists; 29-2021.00 Dental Hygienists; 31-9091.00 Dental Assistants. **OOH Jobs:** Dental Assistants; Dental Hygienists; Dentists.

14.04.01 Health Specialties

O*NET Jobs: 29-1011.00 Chiropractors; 29-1041.00 Optometrists; 29-1081.00 Podiatrists; 29-2081.00 Opticians, Dispensing. **OOH Jobs:** Chiropractors; Opticians, Dispensing; Optometrists; Podiatrists.

14.05.01 Medical Technology

O*NET Jobs: 29-2011.00 Medical and Clinical Laboratory Technologists; 29-2012.00 Medical and Clinical Laboratory Technicians; 29-2031.00 Cardiovascular Technologists and Technicians; 29-2032.00 Diagnostic Medical Sonographers; 29-2033.00 Nuclear Medicine Technologists; 29-2034.00 Radiologic Technologists and Technicians; 29-2034.01 Radiologic Technologists; 29-2034.02 Radiologic Technicians; 29-2091.00 Orthotists and Prosthetists; 31-9093.00 Medical Equipment Preparers. **OOH Jobs:** Cardiovascular Technologists and Technicians; Clinical

Laboratory Technologists and Technicians; Nuclear Medicine Technologists; Radiologic Technologists.

14.06.01 Medical Therapy

O*NET Jobs: 29-1121.00 Audiologists; 29-1122.00 Occupational Therapists; 29-1123.00 Physical Therapists; 29-1124.00 Radiation Therapists; 29-1125.00 Recreational Therapists; 29-1126.00 Respiratory Therapists; 29-1127.00 Speech-Language Pathologists; 29-2054.00 Respiratory Therapy Technicians; 31-2011.00 Occupational Therapist Assistants; 31-2012.00 Occupational Therapist Aides; 31-2021.00 Physical Therapist Assistants; 31-2022.00 Physical Therapist Aides; 31-9011.00 Massage Therapists. **OOH Jobs:** Occupational Therapists; Occupational Therapy Assistants and Aides; Physical Therapists; Physical Therapists Assistants and Aides; Recreational Therapists; Respiratory Therapists; Speech-Language Pathologists and Audiologists.

14.07.01 Patient Care and Assistance

O*NET Jobs: 29-2053.00 Psychiatric Technicians; 29-2061.00 Licensed Practical and Licensed Vocational Nurses; 31-1011.00 Home Health Aides; 31-1012.00 Nursing Aides, Orderlies, and Attendants; 31-1013.00 Psychiatric Aides. **OOH Jobs:** Home Health and Personal Care Aides; Licensed Practical Nurses; Nursing and Psychiatric Aides.

14.08.01 Health Protection and Promotion

O*NET Jobs: 21-1091.00 Health Educators; 29-1031.00 Dietitians and Nutritionists; 29-2051.00 Dietetic Technicians; 29-9091.00 Athletic Trainers. **OOH Jobs:** Dietitians and Nutritionists.

INDEX
of O*NET Job Titles

© JIST Works

E

F

G

H

I

© JIST Works

Contents

Contents

If You Want More Details About the O*NET Occupations

You may want more detailed information about occupations than we can provide in this book. For example, you may want to know the rate control measures for an occupation. If so, we suggest that you access the O*NET database. It is available on the Internet at http://online.onetcenter.org.

The O*NET database on the Internet can be difficult to use and understand, since it includes an enormous amount of detailed information on each job. Software from other sources, including JIST Publishing, will include the O*NET information in electronic form. In some cases, this software will make it much easier to find and use the details in the O*NET you really want. Please contact JIST if you are interested in software that includes the O*NET data; the company's information appears on page ii.

A Sample O*NET Description —and What It Includes

It would take more than 10 pages to print all the data on one job in the O*NET database. And much of that data would be in coded form that is not easy to understand without study. That's simply too much information for most people and would result in a book of more than 10,000 pages. So our challenge was to create a description of each O*NET occupation that would be useful to most people and that would be practical in book form.

We stayed up late many nights considering how to do this. The result is the carefully thought-out job descriptions you find in this book. Because a picture is worth a thousand words, we provide a sample O*NET job description next. To help you understand all that it includes, we point out its many elements and then explain each one.

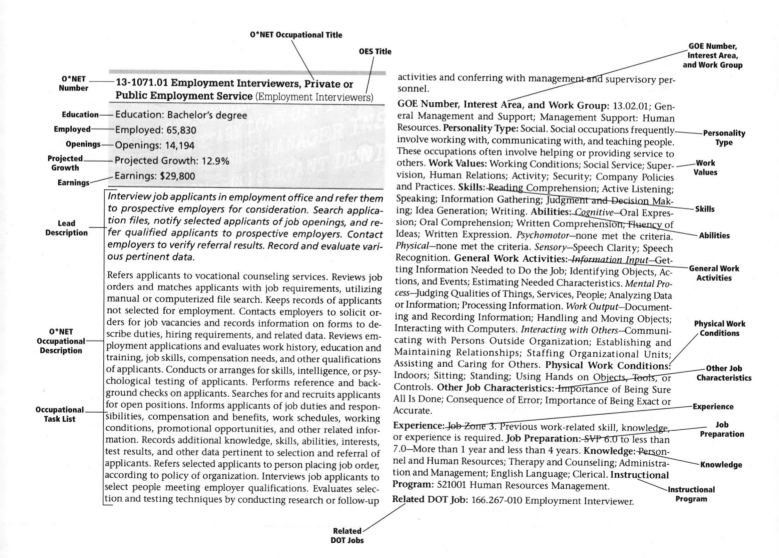

O*NET Occupational Title

OES Title

O*NET Number — **13-1071.01 Employment Interviewers, Private or Public Employment Service** (Employment Interviewers)

Education — Education: Bachelor's degree

Employed — Employed: 65,830

Openings — Openings: 14,194

Projected Growth — Projected Growth: 12.9%

Earnings — Earnings: $29,800

Lead Description — *Interview job applicants in employment office and refer them to prospective employers for consideration. Search application files, notify selected applicants of job openings, and refer qualified applicants to prospective employers. Contact employers to verify referral results. Record and evaluate various pertinent data.*

O*NET Occupational Description — Refers applicants to vocational counseling services. Reviews job orders and matches applicants with job requirements, utilizing manual or computerized file search. Keeps records of applicants not selected for employment. Contacts employers to solicit orders for job vacancies and records information on forms to describe duties, hiring requirements, and related data. Reviews employment applications and evaluates work history, education and training, job skills, compensation needs, and other qualifications of applicants. Conducts or arranges for skills, intelligence, or psychological testing of applicants. Performs reference and background checks on applicants. Searches for and recruits applicants for open positions. Informs applicants of job duties and responsibilities, compensation and benefits, work schedules, working conditions, promotional opportunities, and other related information. Records additional knowledge, skills, abilities, interests, test results, and other data pertinent to selection and referral of applicants. Refers selected applicants to person placing job order, according to policy of organization. Interviews job applicants to select people meeting employer qualifications. Evaluates selection and testing techniques by conducting research or follow-up activities and conferring with management and supervisory personnel.

GOE Number, Interest Area, and Work Group: 13.02.01; General Management and Support; Management Support: Human Resources. **Personality Type:** Social. Social occupations frequently involve working with, communicating with, and teaching people. These occupations often involve helping or providing service to others. **Work Values:** Working Conditions; Social Service; Supervision, Human Relations; Activity; Security; Company Policies and Practices. **Skills:** Reading Comprehension; Active Listening; Speaking; Information Gathering; Judgment and Decision Making; Idea Generation; Writing. **Abilities:** *Cognitive*—Oral Expression; Oral Comprehension; Written Comprehension; Fluency of Ideas; Written Expression. *Psychomotor*—none met the criteria. *Physical*—none met the criteria. *Sensory*—Speech Clarity; Speech Recognition. **General Work Activities:** *Information Input*—Getting Information Needed to Do the Job; Identifying Objects, Actions, and Events; Estimating Needed Characteristics. *Mental Process*—Judging Qualities of Things, Services, People; Analyzing Data or Information; Processing Information. *Work Output*—Documenting and Recording Information; Handling and Moving Objects; Interacting with Computers. *Interacting with Others*—Communicating with Persons Outside Organization; Establishing and Maintaining Relationships; Staffing Organizational Units; Assisting and Caring for Others. **Physical Work Conditions:** Indoors; Sitting; Standing; Using Hands on Objects, Tools, or Controls. **Other Job Characteristics:** Importance of Being Sure All Is Done; Consequence of Error; Importance of Being Exact or Accurate.

Experience: Job Zone 3. Previous work-related skill, knowledge, or experience is required. **Job Preparation:** SVP 6.0 to less than 7.0—More than 1 year and less than 4 years. **Knowledge:** Personnel and Human Resources; Therapy and Counseling; Administration and Management; English Language; Clerical. **Instructional Program:** 521001 Human Resources Management.

Related DOT Job: 166.267-010 Employment Interviewer.

(Labels pointing to sample description:) GOE Number, Interest Area, and Work Group; Personality Type; Work Values; Skills; Abilities; General Work Activities; Physical Work Conditions; Other Job Characteristics; Experience; Job Preparation; Knowledge; Instructional Program; Related DOT Jobs; Occupational Task List; Lead Description; O*NET Occupational Description; Education; Employed; Openings; Projected Growth; Earnings

Details on Each Information Element in the Job Descriptions

While short, each description is packed with useful information that will be quite helpful for most readers. Most content is easy enough to understand, although some details will interest only those who require it. Other elements require some explanation. Following are details on each information element included in the job descriptions. Some of this information may be more detail than you need, so skim the content to find what you want to know.

We tried to keep our explanation nontechnical. Unfortunately, some of the O*NET is technical, and some readers have inquiring minds that want to know such details. For this reason, we felt compelled to add more information than some of you might want. Too much, too little—it's a balancing act we hope gives most of you what you need.

O*NET Number

Each O*NET occupation is assigned a unique number. These are not random numbers, because they are based on the Standard Occupational Classification (SOC) system established by the federal government. The SOC is a new structure for organizing jobs based on the work performed, and it is being adopted by all federal agencies that collect and distribute data. Since the O*NET numbering system puts job titles into groupings of related jobs, it's pretty logical to use. You can see how this system works by looking at the list of O*NET occupations in the table of contents. Occupations in this book are presented in numerical order, using their assigned O*NET number. Although some numbers appear to be missing, these absent numbers allow for future expansion of the numbering system.

Quick tip on how to use this information: The O*NET number allows you to quickly cross-reference other O*NET information sources, including the government's Web site that provides more details on the O*NET jobs.

O*NET Occupational Title

This title, which appears in bold, is assigned to the job by the Department of Labor. We include the newest O*NET titles, which are based on those used in the SOC system.

OES Title

In parenthesis is the job title used in the Occupational Employment Survey (OES) system that most closely relates to the O*NET job title. The government currently employs several systems to track information on occupations. The OES is used by U.S. Bureau of Labor Statistics (BLS) to collect wage and employment data. The O*NET system is used for most information in this book, but we used the OES system as the information source for the education requirements, employment data, projected growth, and earnings for each occupation. Therefore, you see the same education level, employment data and projections, and earnings data for jobs that share OES titles, even though their O*NET titles differ.

Quick tip on how to use this information: This alternate title may help you learn other names for this job. But the title is here more to let technical users know where we obtained key data, such as earnings.

Education

This line lists the education or training typically required for entry into a job. Please note, however, that some (or many) who work in the job may have higher or lower levels of education than indicated. Certification or licensing may be required for some jobs, but accurate information on such requirements is not available yet from the O*NET database. You need to determine such requirements from other sources, such as the *Occupational Outlook Handbook*.

The Department of Labor uses 11 levels of education or training to classify the education, training, and experience needs of a job. One of these levels is assigned to each job in this book.

The 11 Education and Training Levels

Short-term O-T-J (on-the-job) training. It is possible to work in these occupations and achieve an average level of performance within a few days or weeks through on-the-job training.

Moderate-term O-T-J (on-the-job) training. Occupations that require this type of training can be performed adequately after a 1- to 12-month period of combined on-the-job and informal training. Typically, untrained workers observe experienced workers perform tasks and are gradually moved into progressively more difficult assignments.

Long-term O-T-J (on-the-job) training. This training requires more than 12 months of on-the-job training or combined work experience and formal classroom instruction. This includes occupations that use formal apprenticeships for training workers that may take up to 4 years. It also includes intensive occupation-specific, employer-sponsored training like police academies. Furthermore, it includes occupations that require natural talent that must be developed over many years.

(continued)

Status. Occupations that satisfy these work values offer advancement, potential for leadership, and are often considered prestigious.

Advancement. Workers on this job have opportunities for advancement.

Authority. Workers on this job give directions and instructions to others.

Recognition. Workers on this job receive recognition for the work they do.

Social Status. Workers on this job are looked up to by others in their company and their community.

Quick tips on how to use this information: While often overlooked by job seekers, work values are a very important part of what makes a job enjoyable or miserable. So think about which work values are particularly important to include in your career, and then write down those that are most important to you. Later, as you review the job descriptions, look for ones that meet your criteria.

Skills

This section lists skills needed to perform in each job. Depending on the occupation, some of these skills are quite complex, while others are relatively basic. All of us possess thousands of skills, although we take most of them for granted. For example, have you ever considered the complexity of physical skills needed to drive a car? This task is so complex that the most sophisticated machines cannot do it nearly as well as most 16-year olds. While all of the many skills we possess are not listed in the O*NET database, it does include many skills that are important across a range of jobs. To avoid overwhelming you with details, only those skills with higher numerical ratings in the database are listed for each job.

The O*NET database provides measures for 46 skills for each job. Each skill is rated on 2 scales. One rates the skill on its importance to the job, and the other on the level of performance required for the job. To create useful skills information for the job descriptions, we used the level-of-performance measure, since that is, we believe, the more useful measure.

For each job, we included skills with a score higher than the average for all jobs. Next, we selected the 5 skills with the highest numerical ratings and listed them in the descriptions. In some cases, when 2 or more skills were tied in their measure for fifth place, we included up to 10 skills in the description.

Some jobs have fewer than 5 and sometimes no skills with numeric measures higher than the average measure for all jobs for each skill. For example, no skill is rated higher than average for Maids. Skills with the highest ratings include equipment selection, information organization, problem identification, identification of key causes, and social perceptiveness. However, the respective ratings for these 5 skills are 24, 24, 24, 21, and 21. Using a scale of 0 to 100, all are considerably below the average. You can understand why listing these skills would not be an accurate representation of skills needed to perform this job. So, in these situations, we include the phrase, "none met the criteria."

Following are the 46 skills used in the job descriptions, along with brief explanations for each one. These skills are classified as either Basic Skills or Cross-Functional Skills.

The 46 Skills

Basic Skills. These capacities facilitate the acquisition of new knowledge and skills.

Active Learning. Working with new material or information to grasp its implications.

Active Listening. Listening to what other people are saying and asking questions as appropriate.

Critical Thinking. Using logic and analysis to identify the strengths and weaknesses of different approaches.

Learning Strategies. Using multiple approaches when learning or teaching new things.

Mathematics. Using mathematics to solve problems.

Monitoring. Assessing how well one is doing when learning or doing something.

Reading Comprehension. Understanding written sentences and paragraphs in work-related documents.

Science. Using scientific methods to solve problems.

Speaking. Talking to others to effectively convey information.

Writing. Communicating effectively with others in writing as indicated by the needs of the audience.

Cross-Functional Skills. These skills facilitate performance in a variety of job settings.

Coordination. Adjusting actions in relation to others' actions.

Equipment Maintenance. Performing routine maintenance and determining when and what kind of maintenance is needed.

Equipment Selection. Determining the kind of tools and equipment needed to do a job.

Idea Evaluation. Evaluating the likely success of an idea in relation to the demands of the situation.

Idea Generation. Generating a number of different approaches to problems.

13-2061.00 Financial Examiners (Inspectors and Compliance Officers)

Education: Work experience in a related occupation
Employed: 176,175
Openings: 19,910
Projected Growth: 10.5%
Earnings: $36,820

Enforce or ensure compliance with laws and regulations governing financial and securities institutions and governing financial and real estate transactions. Examine, verify correctness of, or establish authenticity of records.

Recommends action to ensure compliance with laws and regulations or to protect solvency of institution. Investigates activities of institutions to enforce laws and regulations and to ensure legality of transactions and operations or financial solvency. Determines if application action is in public interest and in accordance with regulations, and recommends acceptance or rejection of application. Establishes guidelines for and directs implementation of procedures and policies to comply with new and revised regulations. Reviews applications for merger, acquisition, establishment of new institution, acceptance in Federal Reserve System, or registration of securities sales. Reviews, analyzes, and interprets new, proposed, or revised laws, regulations, policies, and procedures. Directs workers engaged in designing, writing, and publishing guidelines, manuals, bulletins, and reports. Conducts or arranges for educational classes and training programs. Confers with officials of real estate, securities, or financial institution industries to exchange views and discuss issues or pending cases. Schedules audits and examines records and reports to determine regulatory compliance.

GOE Number, Interest Area, and Work Group: 04.04.02; Law, Law Enforcement, and Public Safety; Public Safety: Regulations Enforcement. **Personality Type:** Enterprising. Enterprising occupations frequently involve starting up and carrying out projects. These occupations can involve leading people and making many decisions. They sometimes require risk taking and often deal with business. **Work Values:** Working Conditions; Activity; Security; Compensation; Advancement; Autonomy; Social Status; Responsibility. **Skills:** Reading Comprehension; Problem Identification; Writing; Judgment and Decision Making; Information Gathering. **Abilities:** *Cognitive*—Written Comprehension; Oral Expression; Problem Sensitivity; Number Facility; Deductive Reasoning; Oral Comprehension. *Psychomotor*—none met the criteria. *Physical*—Trunk Strength. *Sensory*—Near Vision; Speech Clarity; Speech Recognition. **General Work Activities:** *Information Input*—Getting Information Needed to Do the Job; Identifying Objects, Actions, and Events; Monitoring Processes, Materials, and Surroundings. *Mental Process*—Evaluating Information Against Standards; Judging Qualities of Things, Services, People; Making Decisions and Solving Problems. *Work Output*—Implementing Ideas and Programs; Documenting and Recording Information; Interacting with Computers. *Interacting with Others*—Communicating with Persons Outside Organization; Communicating with Other Workers; Providing Consultation and Advice to Others;

Interpreting Meaning of Information to Others. **Physical Work Conditions:** Indoors; Sitting; Using Hands on Objects, Tools, or Controls. **Other Job Characteristics:** Consequence of Error; Importance of Being Sure All Is Done; Importance of Being Exact or Accurate.

Experience: Job Zone 4. A minimum of two to four years of work-related skill, knowledge, or experience is needed. **Job Preparation:** SVP 7.0 to less than 8.0—2 years to less than 10 years. **Knowledge:** Economics and Accounting; Mathematics; English Language; Education and Training; Law, Government and Jurisprudence. **Instructional Programs:** 030203 Natural Resources Law Enforcement and Protective Services; 150701 Occupational Safety and Health Technology/Technician; 521601 Taxation.

Related DOT Jobs: 160.167-046 Chief Bank Examiner; 186.117-090 Compliance Officer; 188.167-038 Director, Securities and Real Estate.

13-2071.00 Loan Counselors (Loan Counselors and Officers)

Education: Bachelor's degree
Employed: 227,410
Openings: 39,836
Projected Growth: 21.2%
Earnings: $35,340

Provide guidance to prospective loan applicants who have problems qualifying for traditional loans, including determining the best type of loan and explaining loan requirements or restrictions.

Confers with underwriters to aid in resolving mortgage application problems. Interviews applicant and requests specified information for loan application. Computes payment schedule. Ensures loan agreements are complete and accurate according to policy. Approves loan within specified limits. Refers loan to loan committee for approval. Arranges for maintenance and liquidation of delinquent property. Negotiates payment arrangements with customers for delinquent loan balance. Supervises loan personnel. Submits application to credit analyst for verification and recommendation. Petitions court to transfer title and deeds of collateral to bank. Analyzes applicant's financial status, credit, and property evaluation to determine feasibility of granting loan. Contacts applicant or creditors to resolve questions regarding application information. Analyzes potential loan markets to develop prospects for loans.

GOE Number, Interest Area, and Work Group: 13.02.04; General Management and Support; Management Support: Investigation and Analysis. **Personality Type:** Enterprising. Enterprising occupations frequently involve starting up and carrying out projects. These occupations can involve leading people and making many decisions. They sometimes require risk taking and often deal with business. **Work Values:** Working Conditions; Advancement; Coworkers; Responsibility; Company Policies and Practices. **Skills:** Reading Comprehension; Information Gathering; Speaking; Active Listening; Problem Identification; Mathematics; Writing; Judgment and Decision Making; Critical Thinking.

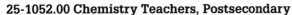

Acts as adviser to student organizations. Compiles bibliographies of specialized materials for outside reading assignments. Stimulates class discussions. Compiles, administers, and grades examinations, or assigns this work to others. Advises students on academic and vocational curricula. Conducts research in particular field of knowledge and publishes findings in professional journals. Directs research of other teachers or graduate students working for advanced academic degrees. Prepares and delivers lectures to students. Serves on faculty committee providing professional consulting services to government and industry.

GOE Number, Interest Area, and Work Group: 12.03.02; Education and Social Service; Educational Services: Postsecondary and Adult Teaching and Instructing. **Personality Type:** Artistic. Artistic occupations frequently involve working with forms, designs, and patterns. These occupations often require self-expression, and the work can be done without following a clear set of rules. **Work Values:** Achievement; Ability Utilization; Authority; Autonomy; Working Conditions; Responsibility; Social Service. **Skills:** Reading Comprehension; Speaking; Instructing; Learning Strategies; Writing. **Abilities:** *Cognitive*—Oral Expression; Oral Comprehension; Written Comprehension; Written Expression; Fluency of Ideas. *Psychomotor*—none met the criteria. *Physical*—none met the criteria. *Sensory*—Speech Clarity; Speech Recognition; Sound Localization. **General Work Activities:** *Information Input*—Getting Information Needed to Do the Job; Identifying Objects, Actions, and Events; Estimating Needed Characteristics. *Mental Process*—Judging Qualities of Things, Services, Other People's Work; Processing Information; Organizing, Planning, and Prioritizing. *Work Output*—Implementing Ideas and Programs; Documenting and Recording Information; Interacting with Computers. *Interacting with Others*—Teaching Others; Communicating with Other Workers; Establishing and Maintaining Relationships; Interpreting Meaning of Information to Others. **Physical Work Conditions:** Indoors; Sitting; Standing. **Other Job Characteristics:** Importance of Being Sure All Is Done; Importance of Being Exact or Accurate; Consequence of Error.

Experience: Job Zone 5. Extensive skill, knowledge, and experience are needed. Very advanced communication and organizational skills are required. **Job Preparation:** SVP 8.0 and above—4 years to more than 10 years. **Knowledge:** Education and Training; English Language; Foreign Language; Communications and Media; Computers and Electronics; Clerical. **Instructional Programs:** 160103 Foreign Language Interpretation and Translation; 160301 Chinese Language and Literature; 160302 Japanese Language and Literature; 160399 East and Southeast Asian Languages and Literatures, Other; 160402 Russian Language and Literature; 160499 East European Languages and Literatures, Other; 160501 German Language and Literature; 160502 Scandinavian Languages and Literatures; 160599 Germanic Languages and Literatures, Other; 160601 Greek Language and Literature (Modern); 160703 South Asian Languages and Literatures; 160901 French Language and Literature; 160902 Italian Language and Literature; 160904 Portuguese Language and Literature; 160905 Spanish Language and Literature.

Related DOT Job: 090.227-010 Faculty Member, College or University.

25-1125.00 History Teachers, Postsecondary (College and University Faculty)

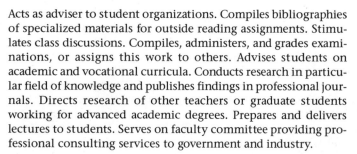

Education: Doctoral degree
Employed: 865,356
Openings: 139,101
Projected Growth: 22.6%
Earnings: No data available.

Teach courses in human history and historiography.

Conducts research in particular field of knowledge and publishes findings in professional journals. Compiles bibliographies of specialized materials for outside reading assignments. Serves on faculty committee providing professional consulting services to government and industry. Directs research of other teachers or graduate students working for advanced academic degrees. Stimulates class discussions. Advises students on academic and vocational curricula. Compiles, administers, and grades examinations, or assigns this work to others. Prepares and delivers lectures to students. Acts as adviser to student organizations.

GOE Number, Interest Area, and Work Group: 12.03.02; Education and Social Service; Educational Services: Postsecondary and Adult Teaching and Instructing. **Personality Type:** Social. Social occupations frequently involve working with, communicating with, and teaching people. These occupations often involve helping or providing service to others. **Work Values:** Achievement; Authority; Ability Utilization; Autonomy; Responsibility. **Skills:** Reading Comprehension; Instructing; Speaking; Active Learning; Learning Strategies; Writing; Active Listening. **Abilities:** *Cognitive*—Oral Expression; Written Comprehension; Written Expression; Oral Comprehension; Deductive Reasoning. *Psychomotor*—none met the criteria. *Physical*—none met the criteria. *Sensory*—Speech Clarity; Speech Recognition; Far Vision. **General Work Activities:** *Information Input*—Getting Information Needed to Do the Job; Estimating Needed Characteristics; Identifying Objects, Actions, and Events. *Mental Process*—Judging Qualities of Things, Services, Other People's Work; Organizing, Planning, and Prioritizing; Developing Objectives and Strategies; Updating and Using Job-Relevant Knowledge; Processing Information. *Work Output*—Implementing Ideas and Programs; Documenting and Recording Information; Interacting with Computers. *Interacting with Others*—Teaching Others; Communicating with Other Workers; Coaching and Developing Others. **Physical Work Conditions:** Indoors; Sitting; Standing. **Other Job Characteristics:** Importance of Being Sure All Is Done; Consequence of Error; Importance of Being Exact or Accurate.

Experience: Job Zone 5. Extensive skill, knowledge, and experience are needed. Very advanced communication and organizational skills are required. **Job Preparation:** SVP 8.0 and above—4 years to more than 10 years. **Knowledge:** Education and Training; Sociology and Anthropology; History and Archeology; English Language; Psychology. **Instructional Programs:** 450801 History, General; 450802 American (United States) History; 450803 European History; 450804 History and Philosophy of Science and Tech.; 450805 Public/Applied History and Archival Administration.

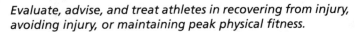

ues: Social Service; Security; Moral Values; Achievement; Supervision, Human Relations. **Skills:** Social Perceptiveness; Reading Comprehension; Service Orientation; Speaking; Active Listening. **Abilities:** *Cognitive*—Problem Sensitivity; Oral Expression; Oral Comprehension; Written Comprehension; Memorization; Deductive Reasoning. *Psychomotor*—Multilimb Coordination; Rate Control. *Physical*—Static Strength; Extent Flexibility; Trunk Strength; Gross Body Coordination. *Sensory*—Speech Recognition; Speech Clarity; Hearing Sensitivity. **General Work Activities:** *Information Input*—Getting Information Needed to Do the Job; Identifying Objects, Actions, and Events; Monitoring Processes, Materials, and Surroundings. *Mental Process*—Analyzing Data or Information; Making Decisions and Solving Problems; Thinking Creatively; Processing Information; Judging Qualities of Things, Services, Other People's Work; Updating and Using Job-Relevant Knowledge. *Work Output*—Performing General Physical Activities; Documenting and Recording Information; Implementing Ideas and Programs. *Interacting with Others*—Assisting and Caring for Others; Communicating with Other Workers; Teaching Others. **Physical Work Conditions:** Indoors; Standing; Using Hands on Objects, Tools, or Controls; Sitting. **Other Job Characteristics:** Consequence of Error; Importance of Being Sure All Is Done; Importance of Being Aware of New Events.

Experience: Job Zone 2. Some previous work-related skill, knowledge, or experience may be helpful, but usually is not needed. **Job Preparation:** SVP 4.00 to 5.99—6 months to less than 2 years. **Knowledge:** Therapy and Counseling; Education and Training; Medicine and Dentistry; Psychology; English Language; Customer and Personal Service. **Instructional Program:** 510803 Occupational Therapy Assistant.

Related DOT Job: 076.364-010 Occupational Therapy Assistant.

31-2012.00 Occupational Therapist Aides
(Occupational Therapy Assistants and Aides)

Education: Associate degree
Employed: 18,619
Openings: 3,106
Projected Growth: 39.8%
Earnings: $28,690

Perform only delegated, selected, or routine tasks in specific situations. Prepare patient and treatment room. Work under close supervision of an occupational therapist or occupational therapy assistant.

Designs and adapts equipment and working-living environment. Assists occupational therapist to plan, implement, and administer educational, vocational, and recreational activities to restore, reinforce, and enhance task performances. Helps professional staff demonstrate therapy techniques, such as manual and creative arts, and games. Assists educational specialist or clinical psychologist in administering situational or diagnostic tests to measure client's abilities or progress. Prepares work material, assembles and maintains equipment, and orders supplies. Maintains observed information in client records and prepares written reports. Transports patient to and from occupational therapy work area. Reports information and observations to supervisor verbally. Instructs or assists in instructing patient and family in home programs and

basic living skills as well as care and use of adaptive equipment. Assists in evaluation of physically, developmentally, mentally retarded, or emotionally disabled client's daily living skills and capacities. Fabricates splints and other assistant devices.

GOE Number, Interest Area, and Work Group: 14.06.01; Medical and Health Services; Medical Therapy. **Personality Type:** Social. Social occupations frequently involve working with, communicating with, and teaching people. These occupations often involve helping or providing service to others. **Work Values:** Social Service; Security; Moral Values; Achievement; Supervision, Human Relations. **Skills:** Social Perceptiveness; Reading Comprehension; Active Listening; Service Orientation; Speaking. **Abilities:** *Cognitive*—Problem Sensitivity; Oral Comprehension; Oral Expression; Written Comprehension; Deductive Reasoning; Memorization. *Psychomotor*—Multilimb Coordination; Rate Control. *Physical*—Static Strength; Extent Flexibility; Trunk Strength; Gross Body Coordination. *Sensory*—Speech Recognition; Speech Clarity; Hearing Sensitivity. **General Work Activities:** *Information Input*—Getting Information Needed to Do the Job; Identifying Objects, Actions, and Events; Monitoring Processes, Materials, and Surroundings. *Mental Process*—Analyzing Data or Information; Making Decisions and Solving Problems; Judging Qualities of Things, Services, Other People's Work; Thinking Creatively; Updating and Using Job-Relevant Knowledge; Processing Information. *Work Output*—Performing General Physical Activities; Documenting and Recording Information; Implementing Ideas and Programs. *Interacting with Others*—Assisting and Caring for Others; Communicating with Other Workers; Teaching Others. **Physical Work Conditions:** Indoors; Standing; Sitting; Using Hands on Objects, Tools, or Controls. **Other Job Characteristics:** Importance of Being Sure All Is Done; Consequence of Error; Importance of Being Aware of New Events.

Experience: Job Zone 2. Some previous work-related skill, knowledge, or experience may be helpful, but usually is not needed. **Job Preparation:** SVP 4.00 to 5.99—6 months to less than 2 years. **Knowledge:** Therapy and Counseling; Education and Training; Medicine and Dentistry; Customer and Personal Service; English Language; Psychology. **Instructional Program:** 510803 Occupational Therapy Assistant.

Related DOT Job: 355.377-010 Occupational Therapy Aide.

31-2021.00 Physical Therapist Assistants (Physical Therapy Assistants and Aides)

Education: Associate degree
Employed: 82,147
Openings: 14,195
Projected Growth: 43.7%
Earnings: $21,870

Assist physical therapists in providing physical therapy treatments and procedures. In accordance with state laws, assist in the development of treatment plans, carry out routine functions, document the progress of treatment, and modify specific treatments in accordance with patient status and within the scope of treatment plans established by a physical therapist. Obtain required formal training.

fowl, or shellfish; cuts and bones meat prior to cooking. Estimates food consumption and requisitions; purchases supplies or procures food from storage. Portions, arranges, and garnishes food; serves food to waiter or patron. Bakes, roasts, broils, and steams meats, fish, vegetables, and other foods. Regulates temperature of ovens, broilers, grills, and roasters. Seasons and cooks food according to recipes or personal judgment and experience. Weighs, measures, and mixes ingredients according to recipe or personal judgment, using various kitchen utensils and equipment. Bakes bread, rolls, cakes, and pastry. Washes, peels, cuts, and seeds fruits and vegetables to prepare fruits and vegetables for use.

GOE Number, Interest Area, and Work Group: 11.05.01; Recreation, Travel, and Other Personal Services; Food and Beverage Services: Preparing. **Personality Type:** Realistic. Realistic occupations frequently involve work activities that include practical, hands-on problems and solutions. These occupations often deal with plants, animals, and real-world materials like wood, tools, and machinery. Many of the occupations require working outside and do not involve a lot of paperwork or working closely with others. **Work Values:** Moral Values; Co-workers; Responsibility; Achievement; Creativity. **Skills:** Active Learning; Coordination; Speaking; Learning Strategies; Monitoring. **Abilities:** *Cognitive*—Information Ordering; Memorization; Written Comprehension; Oral Expression; Number Facility; Visualization. *Psychomotor*—Wrist-Finger Speed; Manual Dexterity; Arm-Hand Steadiness. *Physical*—Static Strength; Extent Flexibility; Trunk Strength. *Sensory*—Near Vision; Visual Color Discrimination; Peripheral Vision; Night Vision. **General Work Activities:** *Information Input*—Identifying Objects, Actions, and Events; Estimating Needed Characteristics; Monitoring Processes, Materials, and Surroundings. *Mental Process*—Thinking Creatively; Judging Qualities of Things, Services, Other People's Work; Organizing, Planning, and Prioritizing. *Work Output*—Handling and Moving Objects; Performing General Physical Activities; Controlling Machines and Processes. *Interacting with Others*—Monitoring and Controlling Resources; Coordinating Work and Activities of Others; Guiding, Directing and Motivating Subordinates. **Physical Work Conditions:** Indoors; Standing; Special Uniform. **Other Job Characteristics:** Importance of Being Sure All Is Done; Consequence of Error; Importance of Being Exact or Accurate.

Experience: Job Zone 3. Previous work-related skill, knowledge, or experience is required. **Job Preparation:** SVP 6.0 to less than 7.0—More than 1 year and less than 4 years. **Knowledge:** Customer and Personal Service; Mathematics; Public Safety and Security; Food Production; Education and Training; Production and Processing; Personnel and Human Resources. **Instructional Program:** 120503 Culinary Arts/Chef Training.

Related DOT Jobs: 313.281-010 Chef De Froid; 313.361-014 Cook; 313.361-018 Cook Apprentice; 313.361-030 Cook, Specialty, Foreign Food; 313.361-034 Garde Manger; 313.381-022 Cook, Barbecue; 313.381-034 Ice-Cream Chef; 315.361-022 Cook, Station; 315.381-014 Cook, Larder; 315.381-018 Cook, Railroad.

35-2015.00 Cooks, Short Order (Short Order and Fast Food Cooks)

Education: Short-term O-T-J training
Employed: 676,576
Openings: 226,320
Projected Growth: 18.4%
Earnings: No data available.

Prepare and cook to order a variety of foods that require only a short preparation time. Take orders from customers and serve patrons at counters or tables.

Completes order from steamtable and serves customer at table or counter. Accepts payment and makes change, or writes charge slip. Cleans food preparation equipment, work area, and counter or tables. Takes order from customer and cooks foods requiring short preparation time, according to customer requirements. Carves meats, makes sandwiches, and brews coffee.

GOE Number, Interest Area, and Work Group: 11.05.01; Recreation, Travel, and Other Personal Services; Food and Beverage Services: Preparing. **Personality Type:** Realistic. Realistic occupations frequently involve work activities that include practical, hands-on problems and solutions. These occupations often deal with plants, animals, and real-world materials like wood, tools, and machinery. Many of the occupations require working outside and do not involve a lot of paperwork or working closely with others. **Work Values:** Moral Values; Activity; Co-workers; Security; Company Policies and Practices; Supervision, Human Relations. **Skills:** Service Orientation; Operation and Control. **Abilities:** *Cognitive*—Oral Comprehension; Number Facility; Time Sharing; Information Ordering; Mathematical Reasoning; Problem Sensitivity. *Psychomotor*—Wrist-Finger Speed. *Physical*—none met the criteria. **General Work Activities:** *Information Input*—Getting Information Needed to Do the Job; Monitoring Processes, Materials, and Surroundings; Estimating Needed Characteristics. *Mental Process*—Organizing, Planning, and Prioritizing; Judging Qualities of Things, Services, Other People's Work; Processing Information. *Work Output*—Handling and Moving Objects; Controlling Machines and Processes; Implementing Ideas and Programs. *Interacting with Others*—Performing for or Working with the Public; Communicating with Persons Outside Organization; Establishing and Maintaining Relationships. **Physical Work Conditions:** Indoors; Standing; Using Hands on Objects, Tools, or Controls. **Other Job Characteristics:** Importance of Being Exact or Accurate; Importance of Being Sure All Is Done; Consequence of Error.

Experience: Job Zone 1. No previous work-related skill, knowledge, or experience is needed. **Job Preparation:** SVP Below 4.0—Less than 6 months. **Knowledge:** Customer and Personal Service; Mathematics; English Language; Food Production; Law, Government and Jurisprudence. **Instructional Program:** 120505 Kitchen Personnel/Cook and Assistant Training.

Related DOT Job: 313.374-014 Cook, Short Order.

35-2021.00 Food Preparation Workers (Food Preparation Workers)

Education: Short-term O-T-J training
Employed: 1,256,251
Openings: 529,498
Projected Growth: 10.4%
Earnings: $13,700

Perform a variety of food preparation duties other than cooking, such as preparing cold foods and shellfish, slicing meat, and brewing coffee or tea.

Cleans, cuts, slices, or disjoints meats and poultry to prepare for cooking. Requisitions, stores, and distributes food supplies, equipment, and utensils. Distributes food to waiters and waitresses to serve to customers. Butchers and cleans fowl, fish, poultry, and shellfish to prepare for cooking or serving. Cleans and maintains work areas, equipment, and utensils. Stores food in designated containers and storage areas to prevent spoilage. Prepares variety of foods according to customers' orders or instructions of superior, following approved procedures. Prepares and serves variety of beverages such as coffee, tea, and soft drinks. Cleans and portions, and cuts or peels various foods to prepare for cooking or serving. Portions and arranges food on serving dishes, trays, carts, or conveyor belts. Carries food supplies, equipment, and utensils to and from storage and work areas.

GOE Number, Interest Area, and Work Group: 11.05.01; Recreation, Travel, and Other Personal Services; Food and Beverage Services: Preparing. **Personality Type:** Realistic. Realistic occupations frequently involve work activities that include practical, hands-on problems and solutions. These occupations often deal with plants, animals, and real-world materials like wood, tools, and machinery. Many of the occupations require working outside and do not involve a lot of paperwork or working closely with others. **Work Values:** Moral Values; Activity; Co-workers; Supervision, Human Relations; Security; Supervision, Technical; Company Policies and Practices. **Skills:** Service Orientation; Active Listening; Writing. **Abilities:** *Cognitive*—Information Ordering; Oral Comprehension; Memorization; Visualization; Oral Expression. *Psychomotor*—Wrist-Finger Speed; Manual Dexterity; Arm-Hand Steadiness. *Physical*—Trunk Strength; Extent Flexibility; Static Strength. *Sensory*—Visual Color Discrimination; Speech Recognition; Hearing Sensitivity. **General Work Activities:** *Information Input*—Monitoring Processes, Materials, and Surroundings; Estimating Needed Characteristics; Getting Information Needed to Do the Job. *Mental Process*—Evaluating Information Against Standards; Judging Qualities of Things, Services, Other People's Work; Organizing, Planning, and Prioritizing. *Work Output*—Handling and Moving Objects; Performing General Physical Activities; Controlling Machines and Processes. *Interacting with Others*—Communicating with Other Workers; Establishing and Maintaining Relationships; Monitoring and Controlling Resources. **Physical Work Conditions:** Indoors; Using Hands on Objects, Tools, or Controls; Standing. **Other Job Characteristics:** Importance of Being Sure All Is Done; Consequence of Error; Importance of Being Exact or Accurate.

Experience: Job Zone 1. No previous work-related skill, knowledge, or experience is needed. **Job Preparation:** SVP Below 4.0—Less than 6 months. **Knowledge:** Customer and Personal Service; Food Production; Public Safety and Security; Mechanical; Chemistry. **Instructional Programs:** 120505 Kitchen Personnel/Cook and Assistant Training; 200401 Institutional Food Workers and Administrators, General; 200405 Food Caterer.

Related DOT Jobs: 311.674-014 Raw Shellfish Preparer; 313.684-010 Baker Helper; 313.687-010 Cook Helper, Pastry; 316.661-010 Carver; 316.684-010 Butcher, Chicken and Fish; 316.684-014 Deli Cutter-Slicer; 317.384-010 Salad Maker; 317.664-010 Sandwich Maker; 317.684-010 Coffee Maker; 317.684-014 Pantry Goods Maker; 317.687-010 Cook Helper; 319.484-010 Food Assembler, Kitchen; 319.677-010 Caterer Helper.

35-3000 Food and Beverage Serving Workers

35-3011.00 Bartenders (Bartenders)

Education: Short-term O-T-J training
Employed: 403,828
Openings: 85,583
Projected Growth: 1.9%
Earnings: $12,990

Mix and serve drinks to patrons, directly or through waitstaff.

Serves wine and draft or bottled beer. Cleans glasses, utensils, and bar equipment. Prepares appetizers such as pickles, cheese, and cold meats. Arranges bottles and glasses to make attractive display. Slices and pits fruit for garnishing drinks. Collects money for drinks served. Mixes ingredients such as liquor, soda, water, sugar, and bitters, to prepare cocktails and other drinks. Orders or requisitions liquors and supplies.

GOE Number, Interest Area, and Work Group: 11.05.02; Recreation, Travel, and Other Personal Services; Food and Beverage Services: Serving. **Personality Type:** Enterprising. Enterprising occupations frequently involve starting up and carrying out projects. These occupations can involve leading people and making many decisions. They sometimes require risk taking and often deal with business. **Work Values:** Moral Values; Social Service; Working Conditions; Supervision, Technical; Co-workers. **Skills:** Service Orientation; Mathematics; Social Perceptiveness; Active Listening; Speaking; Writing. **Abilities:** *Cognitive*—Memorization; Information Ordering; Number Facility; Oral Comprehension; Oral Expression. *Psychomotor*—Wrist-Finger Speed; Manual Dexterity; Arm-Hand Steadiness. *Physical*—Extent Flexibility; Trunk Strength; Static Strength. *Sensory*—Speech Recognition; Auditory Attention; Night Vision. **General Work Activities:** *Information Input*—Getting Information Needed to Do the Job; Monitoring Processes, Materials, and Surroundings; Identifying Objects, Actions, and Events. *Mental Process*—Updating and Using Job-Relevant Knowledge; Thinking Creatively; Evaluating Information Against Standards. *Work Output*—Handling and Moving Objects; Controlling Machines and Processes; Performing General Physical Activities. *Interacting with Others*—Establishing and Maintaining Relationships; Performing for or Working with the Public; Communicating with Persons Outside Organization; Monitoring and Controlling Resources. **Physical Work Conditions:** Stand-

Office and Administrative Support Occupations 43-0000 335

Farming, Fishing, and Forestry Occupations 45-0000 378

Arts, Design, Entertainment, Sports, and Media Occupations 27-0000 193

Life, Physical, and Social Science Occupations 19-0000 112

Community and Social Services Occupations 21-0000 146

Legal Occupations 23-0000 155

Education, Training, and Library Occupations 25-0000 162

Table of Contents

Quick Summary of Major Sections

Introduction. A brief overview of the O*NET system and this book. Includes a sample O*NET job description and reviews its many elements, such as job duties, education required, earnings, skills, abilities, personality type, working conditions, and more. Offers tips to help students, job seekers, career changers, employers, career counselors and others use this reference. *The introduction starts on page 1.*

O*NET Occupational Descriptions. The book's main section, providing information-packed descriptions for over 1,000 jobs in the O*NET database. Descriptions are arranged by their O*NET number and within logical groupings of related jobs. The major job groups and their corresponding code numbers are listed below. *The job descriptions start on page 23.*

Appendix: Exploring Careers Based on Interests. Very useful for uncovering career and learning options based on interests. *The appendix starts on page 665.*

Index of O*NET Job Titles. All job titles in the O*NET database (and, therefore, in this book) appear here in alphabetic order. *The index starts on page 681.*

List of O*NET Occupations in Related Job Groupings

We include this list to help you quickly locate the job descriptions that interest you. It uses the current O*NET structure that groups similar jobs together. All jobs in the current O*NET database are shown in this list within the groupings. The O*NET uses a numbering system to organize its groupings and subgroupings, and these numbers appear in the list. Finally, the O*NET assigns a unique number code to each job title, and these codes are shown also. The job descriptions are arranged in the book in the same sequence you see here. The list provides the page number where you can find each job description.

Important Notice on the Limitations of Use of This Book

Occupational information in this book reflects jobs as they have been found to occur, but they may not coincide in every respect with jobs as performed in particular establishments or at certain localities. Readers demanding specific job information should supplement it with local data.

Note that the U.S. Department of Labor and JIST Publishing have no responsibility for establishing wage levels or settling jurisdictional matters for occupations. In preparing vocational definitions, no data were collected concerning these and related matters. Therefore, the occupational information in this book cannot be regarded as determining standards for any aspect of the employer-employee relationship. Data contained in this publication should not be considered a judicial or legislative standard for wages, hours, or other contractual or bargaining elements.

Credits

Although several people have their names on the cover, this book represents many years of work by hundreds of dedicated individuals. The O*NET database that serves as this book's basis was created by researchers and developers under the direction of the U.S. Department of Labor. They, in turn, were assisted by thousands of employers who provided details on the nature of work in thousands of job samplings used in the database's development.

While the O*NET database was first released several years ago, it is based on the substantial work done on an earlier database used to develop the *Dictionary of Occupational Titles* (DOT). That DOT database was first used in the 1939 DOT edition and has been continuously updated since. The DOT formed the basis for much of the occupational information used by employers, job seekers, career counselors, educational and training institutions, researchers, policy makers, and others.

Because of their large numbers, most who worked on the occupational material used in this book are not credited. Even so, we appreciate their efforts and present this book in their honor and in the honor of the good people at the U.S. Department of Labor who made the O*NET database and earlier sources of career information possible. Thanks.

This Book Is Easier to Use Than It Looks

Please don't be intimidated by the formal look of this book. We have worked hard to make it an easy-to-use and valuable resource for a variety of nontechnical purposes.

We believe this reference will be of great help to job seekers, students, businesses, educators, career counselors, and many others. It provides, in a practical format, a major new standard for organizing and describing occupations. It describes over 1,000 jobs and includes data on earnings, education and training required, growth, skills required, and much more.

This Book Uses the Latest Information Sources

The information database used to create this book was developed by the U.S. Department of Labor (DOL) and replaces an older information system. This new source of occupational information, called the O*NET (for the Occupational Information Network), represents a major change from the past. Many governmental, business, educational, and other organizations rely on the standardized occupational classification system developed by the DOL. The O*NET system is the standard now used in collecting data on wages, job growth, and related facts.

The O*NET is clearly an important new information source. But the amount of information in the electronic database—and the way it is presented—has limited use for many people. As a result, the DOL releases the O*NET database to developers, so they can adapt the data into print and software formats that reach a wide audience.

This book was the first to provide the O*NET material in printed form, and we hope it serves as a beneficial tool. This edition is the first to use the O*NET's new Standard Occupational Classification (SOC) structure (explained in the introduction) and other features available in the most recent O*NET database update. The changes in the latest version of the O*NET make the original O*NET system, used in the first edition of this book, obsolete.

This book is the result of cooperation between a private organization and governmental agencies. In this case, we think your taxes are being spent wisely.

O*NET Dictionary of Occupational Titles, Second Edition

© 2002 by JIST Publishing, Inc.

Published by JIST Works, an imprint of JIST Publishing, Inc.
8902 Otis Avenue
Indianapolis, IN 46216-1033

Phone: 1-800-648-JIST   Fax: 1-800-JIST-FAX
E-mail: editorial@jist.com   Web site: www.jist.com

About Career Materials Published by JIST

For the best information on occupations, many people—including experienced career professionals—rely on JIST. JIST has published information about careers and job search since the 1970s. JIST offers occupational references plus hundreds of other books, videos, assessment devices, and software.

Quantity discounts are available for this reference and other JIST books. Please call the JIST sales staff at 1-800-648-JIST weekdays for details.

Visit www.jist.com to find out about JIST products, get free book chapters, and link to other career-related sites. You can also learn more about JIST authors and JIST training available to professionals.

A free catalog is available to professionals at schools, institutions, and other programs. It presents hundreds of helpful publications on career, job search, self-help, and business topics from JIST and other publishers. Please call 1-800-648-JIST or visit www.jist.com to request the JIST catalog.

Editors: Susan Pines, Veda Dickerson, Lori Cates
Interior Designer: Aleata Howard
Interior Layout: Carolyn J. Newland
Cover Designer: Honeymoon Image & Design, Inc.
Proofreader: Paula Lowell

Printed in the United States of America
06 05 04 03 02 01   9 8 7 6 5 4 3 2 1

Library of Congress Cataloging-in-Publication Data

O*NET dictionary of occupational titles.—2nd ed.
    p.cm.
    "Based on information obtained from the U.S. Department of Labor, the U.S. Census Bureau, and other reliable sources."
    "Developed under the direction of J. Michael Farr and LaVerne L. Ludden, Ed.D., with database work by Laurence Shatkin, Ph.D."
    ISBN 1-56370-845-0—ISBN 1-56370-846-9
        1. Occupations—United States—Dictionaries. 2. Occupations—United States—Classification. I. Farr, J. Michael. II. Ludden, LaVerne, 1949- III. Shatkin, Laurence. IV. United States. Dept. of Labor. V. JIST Works, Inc.

HB2595 .016 2001
331.7'003—dc21   2001038356

ISBN 1-56370-845-0 Softcover
ISBN 1-56370-846-9 Hardcover

SECOND EDITION

O*NET

Dictionary of Occupational Titles

Based on information obtained from the U.S. Department of Labor, the U.S. Census Bureau, and other reliable sources

Developed under the direction of J. Michael Farr and LaVerne L. Ludden, Ed.D., with database work by Laurence Shatkin, Ph.D.

DISCARD

jist
Works

GLOSSARY

This glossary provides definitions for many of the specialized literacy terms in this book. These terms are highlighted in boldface type on first occurrence.

alphabetic principle: The understanding that letters of the alphabet are used to represent the sounds heard in words. Prior to developing the alphabetic principle, children use nonphonemic letter strings.

directionality: Understanding about the left-to-right, top-to-bottom convention of placing English writing on a page.

discovery center: A tabletop area in a classroom stocked with nature (e.g., shells, rocks, and nests) and other items (e.g., magnifying lenses) for children to handle and observe.

dramatic play: An advanced form of play in which children take on roles and act out make-believe stories and situations.

mock letters: Designs made with lines found in standard alphabet letters but composed to create a unique symbol that is not a standard letter (e.g., an *E* with five horizontal lines, not three).

mock words: Arrangements of letters that closely follow the *look* of actual words, even though they do not represent real words in the English language.

nonphonemic letter strings: A series of letters used by children to represent words without consideration of the sounds represented by those letters. Children use nonphonemic letter strings to approximate conventional writing based on its appearance.

oral language: Communication based on speech.

phonemic awareness: The awareness of the sounds in speech, including words, syllables, and phonemes.

phonological awareness: The awareness of the constituent sounds of words in learning to read and spell.

writing center: A classroom area stocked with materials that invite children to engage in writing.

Where Young Children Start in Learning to Write

• • • • • • • • • • • • •

As another day begins, children arrive at their preschool. Four-year-old Gretchen stands in the doorway, head bowed, eyes aimed at the floor. Her mother nudges her gently and says, "Go ahead. Tell your teacher."

Gretchen: I got stitches. [walks through the doorway and turns her head to expose the right side of her chin]

Teacher: [looks at stitches and also notices a bruise above her right eye] What happened, Gretchen?

Gretchen: I falled.

Teacher: You fell? Did you fall someplace at your house, or did you fall at the park across the street?

Gretchen: In my room. And I can't jump on my bed anymore.

Teacher: Oh, you fell while jumping on your bed?

Gretchen: I falled on the rocking chair.

Teacher: Oh, you fell off your bed while jumping on it, and you hit the rocking chair?

Gretchen I can't jump on the rocking chair anymore.

Teacher: [in an incredulous tone] Did you try to jump from your bed to a rocking chair? [Gretchen nods] Oh, my. So, you tried to jump into a rocking chair, and then what happened?

Gretchen: I, I, like this [uses hand motions to trace her fall's trajectory], and then the...the...the rocking chair... the rocking chair, like this [uses hands again to indicate object falling over], and the thing on the...that thing on the...on the bottom...the chair, the rocking chair hit my eye [hand up to eye] and my chin bumped the floor and bleeded [hand on chin], and then my mommy came and I had to sit in my car seat for the hospital.

Teacher: So, you jumped up off your bed into the rocking chair, and then the rocking chair fell over, with you in it. When the rocking chair fell over, you fell onto the floor, and the bottom part that makes the chair rock hit you in the eye, and then your chin hit the floor. Is that what happened?

Gretchen: Yes, yes, and then I had to...had to...had to go to the hospital and they did stitches. My mommy took me.

Teacher: Your mommy came to your room and then she took you to the hospital?

Gretchen: Yes, and my brother.

Teacher: Oh, your brother went, too. Well, I'm sorry that you hurt yourself and had to have stitches. I bet you were scared.

Gretchen: Yes, I was.

Teacher: That would be a wonderful story for our class book. Maybe you'd like to draw some pictures about falling and going to the hospital to get stitches, and I could write down what you say. Then, we could add this story to our class book. What do you think?

Gretchen does not answer. By this time, several children have gathered around to listen to the news, and Gretchen's best friend is clutching her hand. As the children head to a table to play, they continue talking about Gretchen's adventure of the night before.

• • • • • • • • • • • • • • •

Gretchen's experience was a topic of conversation several times throughout the day. Other children told of similar experiences, and a hospital theme emerged in the **dramatic play** center. As the children took the roles of parents, they called the doctor, took sick children to the hospital, and warned about dangerous activities such as jumping on beds and running out into the street. As the children played, they created stories, pulling from their own experience to create fictionalized roles for themselves and the dolls serving as their "children."

Composing Without Writing/ Writing Without Composing

Gretchen never composed a written account of her fall and stitches for the class book. Four-year-olds have a strong desire to tell all about something or to capture the events in play, but less interest in creating a record of experiences once the story has been told or reenacted. They do not yet realize that written records help people save, recall, and share past experiences. However, Gretchen's teacher understood that talking about events and creating related scenarios in play help children like Gretchen to convey their intentions—their meanings. Although Gretchen did not actually record her experience in writing, these early social interactions with interested adults and peers help children learn to think and compose—an essential element in writing.

> Preschoolers create large quantities of writing that involve no composing. When children write without composing, they simply explore the physical forms of writing.

Interestingly, preschoolers also create large quantities of writing that involve no composing. When children write without composing, they simply explore the physical forms of writing. Figure 1a shows writing of this kind created by a 4-year-old.

Figure 1
Writing Devoid of Specific Content: Experimentation With Form

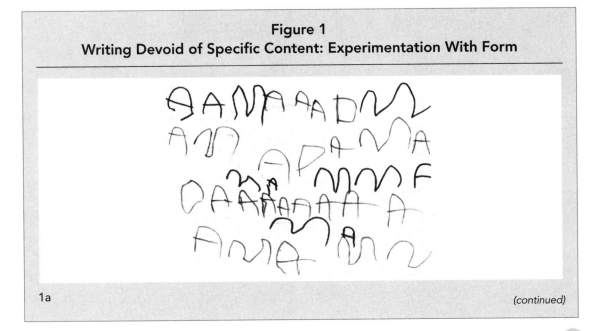

1a

(continued)

Figure 1 *(continued)*

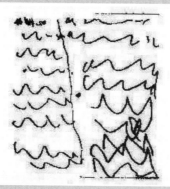

1b

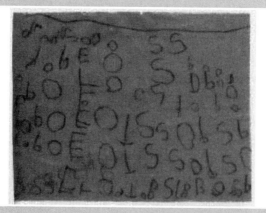

1c

1d

When the teacher asked the child to tell her about his writing, the child said, "It's nothing." Apparently, the child was simply practicing some of the letters in his name (*ADAM*), or stringing letters together to create something that looked like writing, not attempting to communicate a specific message. In another example, Figure 1b is a single page of a 14-page "storybook" written by another 4-year-old. Although the child said it was a storybook, it had no specific story. This child, too, was simply creating an artifact that resembled a storybook. He even drew a line down the center of each sheet of paper to indicate where the bound pages of an actual book come together!

Figure 1c is a child's experiment in making a lot of letters and letter-like forms, none of which represented any thoughts. Figure 1d shows a child's "words," which were not any words in particular. These **mock words** were the products of the 4-year-old's experimentation with putting letters together to make collections that look like words.

Creating print markings is a skill that develops in conjunction with a child's budding picture-making skills. Development in both domains proceeds by leaps and bounds between 3 and 5 years of age. Three-year-olds, especially, often combine both writing and picture marks in the same performance. As Howard Gardner noted in *Artful Scribbles: The Significance of Children's Drawings* (1980), these combination pieces typically do not convey a message. Instead, children use these to inventory many of the graphic forms they have in their repertoires. Figures 2a and 2b are examples of this kind of performance. Each was produced by a different young 3-year-old.

Bridging the Oral and Graphic Worlds

When preschoolers first use marks to convey meaning, whether in the pictures they draw or in the scribble writing they create, they must tell us what their marks "say"—what they mean. Preschoolers cannot at first capture all of their thoughts and feelings in graphic form—their pictures and writing at first fall short of the conventional, and cannot easily be interpreted by others. Only with the help of their verbal explanations can others find out about preschoolers' intended meanings. Beginning during the preschool years and continuing through kindergarten and the primary grades, children gradually become more skilled in both drawing and writing. Little by little, the marks children put on a page begin to stand more on their own to represent the messages they wish to

> Preschoolers cannot at first capture all of their thoughts and feelings in graphic form—their pictures and writing at first fall short of the conventional, and cannot easily be interpreted by others.

Figure 2
Children's Inventories of Drawing and Writing Marks

2a

2b

convey. In this way, the graphic world becomes a bridge to the oral world, because drawings and writing capture more of the meaning a child tries to communicate.

Conclusions: A Child's Journeys in Writing Development

This book, intended for teachers of 3-, 4-, and young 5-year-olds, describes the preschool child's journey in learning to write and the preschool teacher's important contributions to this journey. Actually, several journeys are described. As we have already suggested, the child's writing development rests on the gradual coming together of various strands of knowledge and skills. One journey involves the child's first steps in moving from **oral language** and pictures to writing. Other journeys involve the child's movement from scribble marks to recognizable alphabet letters, and from letter string words to actual words. There is also the journey from the use of short, simple messages to messages that are reasonably detailed and coherent. As these journeys are described, the reader also gains information about the settings in which writing takes place, and about the importance of support from both materials and people. Children must be assisted in many ways in making their journeys, if the story is to end as we would hope, with competent children, full of ideas, eager to record them, and confident in their ability to write.

All names used in this book are pseudonyms. Descriptions of students and teachers are composite sketches that represent real classroom situations that we have encountered in our studies.

CHAPTER 2

Helping Children to Convey Meaning in Words

This chapter focuses on children's first steps in representing their meanings and on the ways that teachers can support them. The development considered in this chapter sometimes begins early in the preschool years—around 3 years of age or a bit younger. Sometimes, it begins much later than this. The starting point depends on when the child is introduced to the idea that writing is intentional—that it represents meaning—and the support a child receives in attempting to use writing. When adults model and interpret writing, children can begin to understand that a special graphic system—writing—is used to convey meaning, as in the following example.

> When adults model and interpret writing, children can begin to understand that a special graphic system—writing—is used to convey meaning.

. . . .

This is a list of things we need at the store. This word says "milk." This word says "eggs." This one says "bread," and this one says "lettuce." Will you open the cupboard door and check the cereal boxes? I think some are nearly empty. We might need to add cereal to our list.

. . . .

Children also learn about the function and power of the written word when adults talk with them about important events in their lives (recall Gretchen from the opening vignette in Chapter 1), or about their drawings of objects and events, and offer to write down what children say.

This chapter focuses specifically on situations in which young children created pictures to capture meaning and then elaborated on the meaning through conversations with a teacher. In the instances considered, the teacher added writing by taking dictation after talking with the child.

Is a Picture Really Worth a Thousand Words?

Everyone is familiar with this old adage, which suggests that words alone, no matter how well selected, fail to convey information with the clarity that might come from viewing a picture. Indeed, this is true in many situations. Pictures, though, are open to a variety of interpretations. Words, in contrast, can convey meaning more precisely.

Consider the drawings in Figure 3. Even if we knew that the drawing in Figure 3a depicted a trolley on its tracks and the drawing in Figure 3b depicted a road taken to the trolley stop, we would not know the significance of either picture for the child simply from viewing the drawings. Only after the child explains that he rode the trolley train to the science museum and took the road by car to get to the trolley stop do we know the specific meaning of each drawing. Similarly, the significance of the butterfly in Figure 3c, drawn by a child and then cut out and glued onto his page of a class book about the children's experiences in raising caterpillars, was not apparent from the drawing. His teacher learned about the specific meaning of the butterfly drawing when the child told about his personal experience as the butterflies were set free.

Figure 3
Illustrations of How Words Capture a Child's Specific Message in Pictures

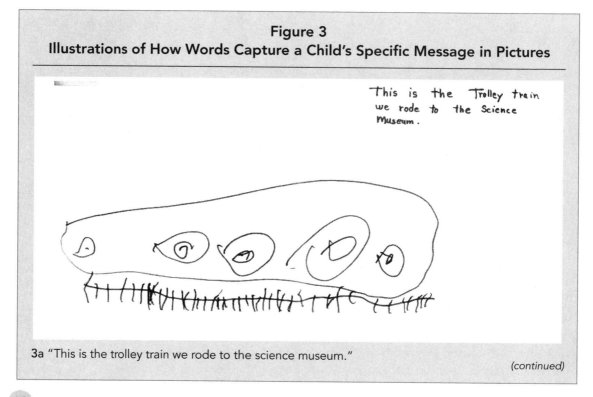

This is the Trolley train we rode to the Science Museum.

3a "This is the trolley train we rode to the science museum."

(continued)

Figure 3 *(continued)*

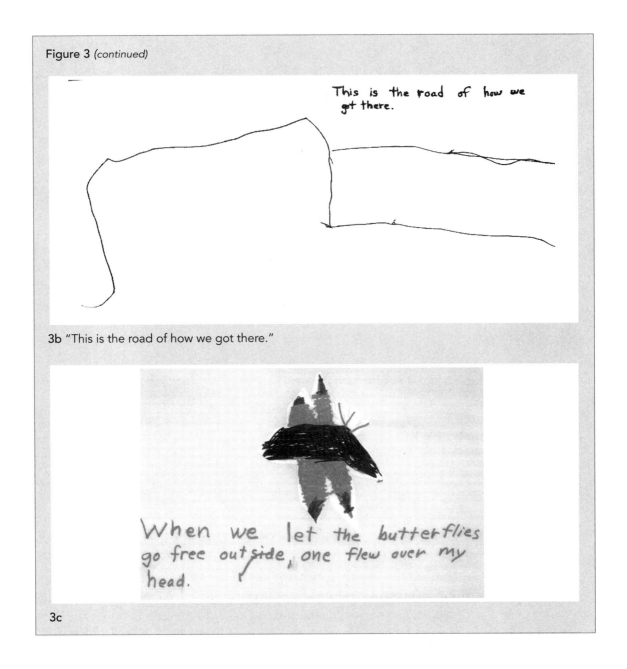

This is the road of how we got there.

3b "This is the road of how we got there."

When we let the butterflies go free outside, one flew over my head.

3c

When teachers or parents talk with children about their drawings and then offer to write down what they say, children have opportunities to learn that the written word can convey meaning. The earlier these experiences are provided, the earlier children get the idea that words are powerful. For example, Figure 4 is a scribble picture created by a very young 3-year-old, with scribble writing added in the lower right. When asked to explain the

Figure 4
Scribble Drawing With Scribble Writing Message

marks, the child said, "Those are words. They say, 'Dear Mommy, I love you. Dear Daddy, I love you too. And my name.'"

It is interesting that such a young child, with no skill yet in drawing realistic pictures or creating conventional writing, felt compelled to add the scribble writing beside his picture. Perhaps children do this because they have learned that adults notice such marks and ask, "What does this say?" which gives children a good opening to convey their specific and full meaning through oral language. Anne Dyson (1986, 1991, 1992) has written extensively about how early forms of both drawing and writing serve as "props" or "supplements" to other kinds of symbolic activity, such as talk, play, and gestures, upon which children must first rely to convey their meanings. This child's addition of scribble writing beside his picture seems to have been such a prop. The full and elaborated meaning was then conveyed verbally to his parents.

Getting the Story

Through talking about their drawings, children learn far more about writing than the mere fact that what they say can be written down. For example, they develop skill in constructing more elaborated meanings and gain greater understanding of what others must be told if they are to understand all that a child wants them to know. Recall that Gretchen (the child in the opening vignette from Chapter 1) was at first a minimalist when she told her teacher what happened. "I got stitches," was all that she said. Gradually, in response to her teacher's genuine interest and concern, Gretchen provided most of the details about her ordeal.

Taking the time to talk with children about their pictures helps children reflect about the meanings they want to convey. It is not necessary for a teacher to record the first words that come out of a child's mouth, as these words rarely tell all. Writing these down, as if it is all that is on a child's mind, shortchanges a child. For example, the child's dictated message about the trolley train in Figures 3a and 3b tells what is depicted by the drawings (trolley train and a road) and the specific significance of each for this child on a specific occasion. But surely the child had even more memories of the trolley train ride than these first brief comments indicate. For example, the portion of the trolley leading to the science museum is elevated, which provides interesting views. What did the child see during the ride to the science museum? How did the child like riding in a trolley on elevated tracks? A few more prompts for conversation often encourage a child to relate more.

A wise teacher, of course, is careful not to take the discussion of a drawing in directions that a child does not wish to go. Sometimes repeating a child's first comments in a tone that indicates genuine interest and commenting on some specific detail the child captured in the drawing will be enough to invite the child to tell more, as in the following example.

• • • • • • • • • • • • • •

Teacher: Oh, so this is the trolley that you rode to the science museum. These look like the windows in the trolley car. And I see the tracks, right here. The trolley rides on tracks.

Child: Yeah. When you look out, you see people and cars and trucks down there. This trolley is way, way up high, not on the ground. Did you know that?

Through talking about their drawings, children learn far more about writing than the mere fact that what they say can be written down.

Teacher:	Yes, I've seen that trolley when driving in my car. I've never been on that trolley. I've only been on the trolleys that run on the ground or go underground.
Child:	You don't like the science museum?
Teacher:	Oh, I love the science museum, but I always drive there in my car.
Child:	You should take the trolley. You'd like it.
Teacher:	I might do that.

• • • • • • • • • • • • • • •

Providing the opportunity for a child to talk about the experience and to elaborate on all that the picture might actually mean is more important than writing down a first short statement. If the conversation is fairly extensive and includes discussions that veer away from the child's core experience and message (e.g., whether the teacher has taken the trolley to the science museum, or likes the museum), the teacher can ask, after the conversation, "What would you like for me to write down about your trip to the science museum?"

Using a separate piece of paper is sometimes more appropriate than writing directly on the child's picture, especially if the child's meaning is fairly extensive. Of course, if the picture and dictation are part of a class book, such as was the case with the butterfly picture in Figure 3c, the teacher writes on the page, because book pages have both words and pictures.

Peer Support

Several children often choose to go to the **writing center** at the same time to draw and write. While there, the children often share many of their experiences from both inside and outside of school. These shared experiences help children discuss their thoughts with peers, while they work at representing them through drawing and writing. Sometimes, children also talk out loud as they create drawings that support fictional stories. Occasionally, two children decide to work together to spin a tale.

In one preschool classroom, two young 5-year-olds composed a long story in which they combined firefighting, a favorite play theme of one author, with knowledge about various injuries and the role of doctors in treating them. The pair composed the story together, aloud, taking turns drawing pictures on the pages of a blank book they found in the classroom writing center. They worked on the book for two days during the daily activity time, using only drawings to represent the story.

They were concerned when the story was finally finished because they knew that most books have words as well as pictures. "We can't write it all!" one of the authors proclaimed to the other. "It's too long!" A teacher overhead the discussion and offered to write down the story, if the children would retell it to her. Using the illustrations to prompt their recall, the children retold the story, page by page. The teacher later typed the text for each page on strips and worked with the children the following day to help them match the strips of text to the pages (see Figure 5).

In the story, a young boy suffers a series of injuries, each of which requires a visit to a doctor's office. In the first problem, a child eats lollipops that were on fire and had to visit the doctor. Soon after the boy had recovered from his burned tongue, he tripped on a stone, hit his mouth, and knocked out all his teeth. He put his teeth under his pillow that night, and the tooth fairy left $20. Unfortunately, the boy had two more accidents the next day. His mom forgot to take her purse to the doctor this time, and the child had to pay the doctor with his own money. The story continues with more unfortunate events, each of which was solved. Then, suddenly, it was Christmas and the boy was happy again because he received lots of presents, which is where the story ended.

Figure 5
Pages From Students' Drawn Story, "Fire, Fire!"

Four lollipops were on fire.

5a

(continued)

Figure 5 *(continued)*

A little boy ate one lollipop and his tongue caught on fire.

5b

Then, he had to go see the doctor at the doctor's office.

5c

The doctor poked a hose in the little boy's mouth to put out the fire. The little boy spit the water out after the fire got out.

hose

5d

The task of transcribing such a long story was overwhelming to these two young children. They knew from past experience, however, that they could create a story together and anchor their composition with pictures. They probably also knew they could enlist a teacher's help in recording the story, had she not offered before they could ask. It was customary for teachers in this classroom to offer to take dictation, after children drew pictures and talked about them with a teacher. Their prior experience in using oral language to talk about their drawings with their teachers no doubt helped the children build their language and narrative skill capacity. Knowing that teachers were willing to take dictation gave them the latitude they needed on this occasion to spin quite a tale.

Teacher Support: Even When They Write, Keep Talking

Figure 6 shows another page of the class book about raising caterpillars and butterflies. This child added some writing alongside his picture. Preschoolers, of course, do not yet have enough skill in writing to capture their meaning. The picture carries the load, but as we've already seen, it rarely conveys everything. Talk still carries the day. This child explained that the caterpillar was inside its chrysalis, waiting to come out as a butterfly. There also was some discussion about how long caterpillars stay

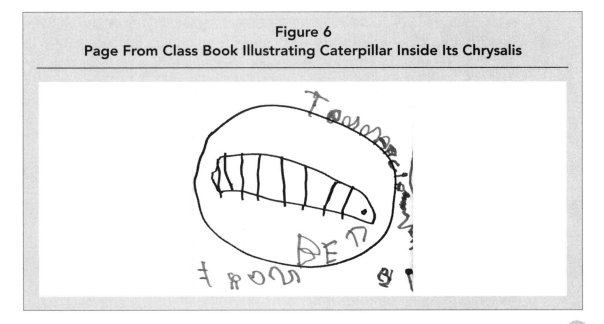

Figure 6
Page From Class Book Illustrating Caterpillar Inside Its Chrysalis

inside a chrysalis and what happens while it is inside. In this case, the teacher did not offer to write down what the child said during their discussion, as she had done many times in the past because, on most occasions, he drew or added a bit of his own writing, and she thought transcribing his stories might discourage his attempts to add more writing of his own. She also knew that the caterpillar and butterfly book would be placed in the classroom library and that children often asked one another about their pictures, as they looked at class books together.

A teacher must judge when to take a child's dictation, and when to talk without adding conventional writing as a supplement to the child's own writing. Had the children been drawing pictures for display on a bulletin board in a school hallway, the teacher might have added the child's dictation to inform parents and other teachers and children in the school about the specific meanings represented by this child's picture and rudimentary writing; however, a page in a class book destined for the classroom library is a different situation. In this case, the child could explain the meaning of the picture and writing, verbally, to other children in the class, as they looked at the book. If the dictation were there, they might simply ask a teacher to read it and not engage the child in discussing it.

Conclusions: Oral Language, Writing, and Drawing Connections

When working with preschool children, it is important to understand that rudimentary drawing and writing cannot begin to capture all that children mean. These graphic representations serve as placeholders—props, in Dyson's words—for more than meets the eye. It takes a very long time before children's drawing and writing can stand on their own to convey a child's full intentions. In the meantime, oral language is our link to knowing what children intend. We can offer to write down what children say if they wish, or we can judge only to discuss their pictures and writing without recording the messages in our mature hand. Of course, we should create an atmosphere in which children know that we would be happy to take down their dictation when they ask.

CHAPTER 3

From Scribble to Script

This chapter chronicles the development of marks used for writing, from children's first intentional use of lines intended as writing to the point at which they exert a measure of control over these forms. The development we consider here typically spans from 2 or 2½ years of age to a little over 5 years of age—from the late toddler stage through the end of the preschool years (Baghban, 1984; Clay, 1987; Schickedanz, 1990).

The First Discovery: "I Can Make Marks"

The young child's world is full of designs on paper and many other surfaces. Writing materials and the physical forms of writing and drawing fascinate young children. Children's discovery that writing and drawing tools leave tracks and that their form is under their control sparks curiosity. The child moves the tool in one way and looks. The child moves it in a different way and looks. The child moves the tool in a flurry, back and forth, round and round, jab, jab, jab, and looks. To anyone watching, it appears that the child is thinking, "Different actions produce different results. How interesting!"

For several months, toddlers experiment and take great delight in their actions no matter the results. Then, a question seems to occur to the exploring child: "How do I re-create a certain effect, the design I want? What is the action that results in a *specific* effect?" This question sometimes emerges as marks produced in free exploration begin to remind the child of something. Consider the drawing in Figure 7, which was created by a 2-year-old as he explored with a marker on white notepaper. The child was silent, absorbed in the doing, until he finished drawing. He looked a long time at this drawing, touched it several times, and then said, "A man." Then, he pointed to the two spots in the top portion and said, "Eyes," and next to the large inside circle in the middle and said, "Mouth."

It is doubtful that the child intended to create any specific design when he first put pen to paper. But suddenly, there it was—a happy

Figure 7
A Child's Free Exploration Drawing: "A Man"

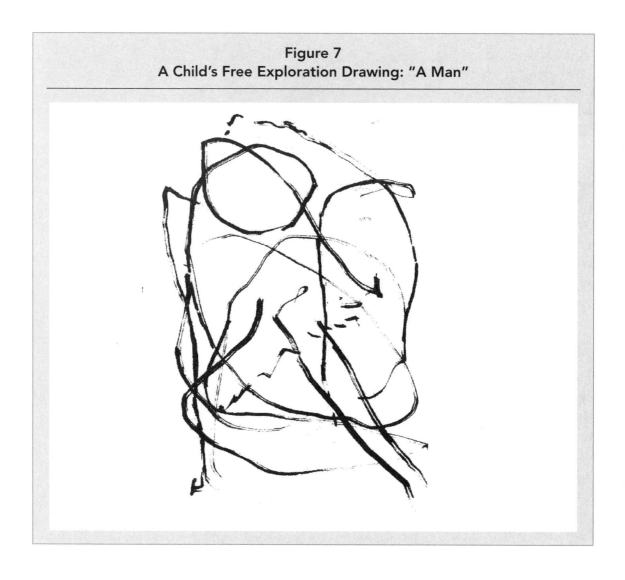

accident—the result of a series of random, exploratory movements. With new interest in the marks, the child began to wonder, "I want to do that again, but how? What did I do to produce this?"

Marking becomes more deliberate after this question comes to the child's mind. Of course, not every occasion of marking is guided by such thoughts. Before 2½ or 3 years of age, the thought is probably rarely there as the child creates marks. The sheer joy of doing dominates the child's marking, and it remains a motivation for writing throughout the early childhood years. The difference, though, after some point in the third year of life, are the moments, and soon an ever-increasing number of them, when action is deliberate. The child wants to make a line look a certain way, or wants to create a particular form to represent a specific image. Or the child wants to make it clear that marks made on a specific occasion are not a picture of something, but "say" something. Marking and meaning become joined on these occasions of deliberate action. The child tries to control marks to serve his or her representational purposes. Sometimes, the representation is a picture; sometimes the marks are intended as writing.

This Is Writing, Not a Picture

If someone were to show you the four samples in Figure 8, odds are you would know at a glance that Figure 8a is writing. Figure 8b, on the other hand, might require some study: Did the form result from a child's random exploration with a marker, or was it intended to be a picture of something, such as a face with bangs covering the forehead? Or might it be a bowl of spaghetti with a noodle hanging over its edge? As it turns out, Figure 8b is a phone message, written by a 3-year-old in the midst of dramatic play. The

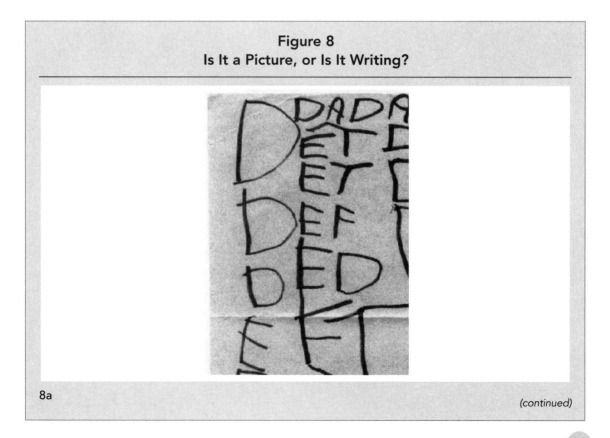

Figure 8
Is It a Picture, or Is It Writing?

8a

(continued)

Figure 8 *(continued)*

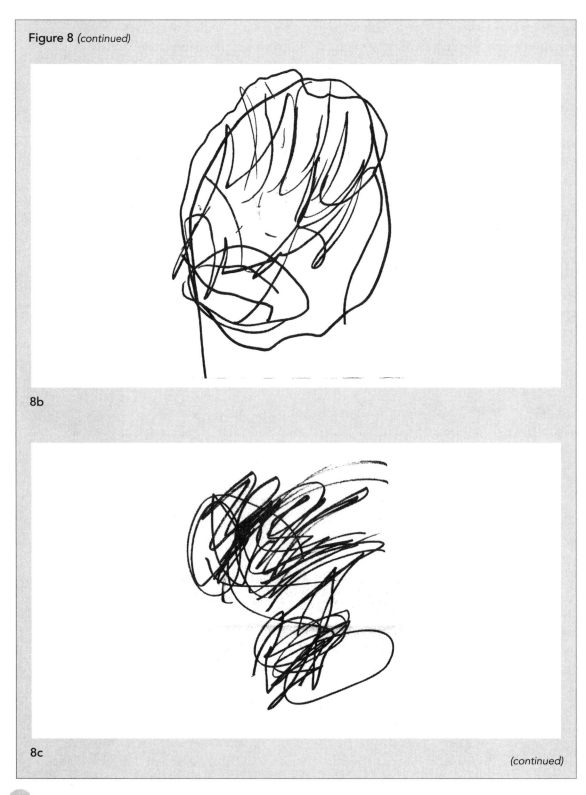

8b

8c

(continued)

Figure 8 *(continued)*

8d

marks in Figures 8c and 8d also are writing, both signatures. Figure 8c was used to label a block building, while Figure 8d was written on the back of the child's paper collage. All of these scribble samples were created by children who were between 2½ and 3½ years of age.

These representations are typical of children who are at the very beginning of their journey into learning how to mark meanings. In Figures 8c and 8d, we see no difference between the marks the child uses to draw pictures and those that are intended to "say" something. We know the child's intention only by listening to what the child says or by watching the context in which the child applies the marking tool to paper or uses the item after its creation.

Almost on the heels of the dawning of representational intentions, however, we see evidence that the child now understands that marks used for writing look different from those used for drawing pictures. Figure 9 illustrates this insight. First, the child drew a scribble picture covering most of the paper's surface, using lines that went here and there and round and

Figure 9
Writing Marks Are Lined Up, Picture Marks Are Not

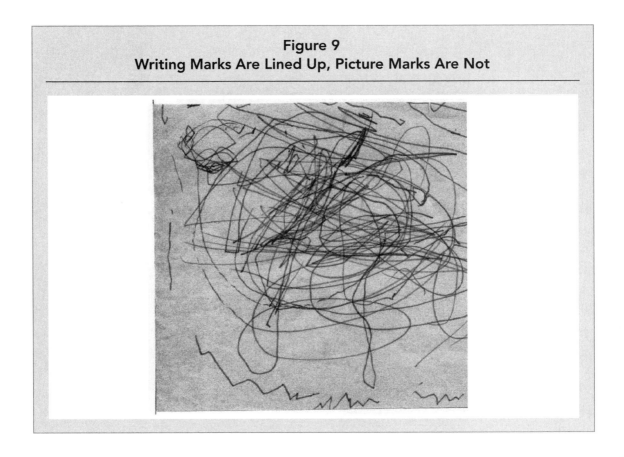

round. Then, the child placed marks at the bottom of the page and said they were her name (see the zigzag, scribble writing there). These marks were separated a bit from the picture and arranged in a linear pattern. We also see some writing marks along the far left of the paper. These resemble the letters *J*, *l*, and *i*, all of which were used in the child's name. Though arranged vertically, not horizontally, on the page, as is the convention for English writing, the letters are in a line and stand apart from the scribbled picture.

We see that the child exerted a different kind of control over the marks intended as writing than she applied to the lines in her drawing. Writing marks were not allowed to go all over the place. The internal variations in lines of the child's writing are fairly uniform, as if she had noticed that the same details repeat frequently in a way that details do not typically repeat in a picture. Lines in a picture can meander and intertwine, as if each is allowed to have a mind of its own. As a consequence, pictures contain greater variation in form than writing does. Clearly, the child who created this sample was aware of two general worlds of marks—a world of pictures and a world of print. This distinction is a major discovery for the young child.

Details, Details: Increasing Focus on the Features of Print Symbols

In the world of writing, individual designs—alphabet letters—make up the lines of print that children notice. At first, the line itself, the fact of a linear arrangement, is all that seems to register with young children, or it is the only feature they try to capture in their writing. This, after all, is what makes a collection of marks *look* like writing and not a picture. As was noted earlier, however, even in their first scribbles children indicate that they perceive some degree of detail within lines of print. For a while, though, they represent this perception only with zigs and zags varying in density. In Figure 9 the zigs and zags are sometimes rather dense, and sometimes more spread out. Most "details" look very much alike, although the peaks and valleys of the zigs and zags vary a bit, as does the distance in between them.

The scribble lines making up the "letter to Daddy" shown in Figure 10a also have very little variation, just like the writing in Figure 9. In contrast, the lines in Figure 10b, which were created by a 4-year-old who was playing at producing writing, have very dense zigs and zags that vary considerably. Yet the child is still using *only* zigs and zags.

When we compare Figure 10b with both Figures 10c and 10d, we notice something new in the last two. The marks in their lines of print contain not only a few zigs and zags but also some loops. The first line even starts with a separate small form, a closed curve—a circle. There are a few other marks that stand alone—the small closed curve with a tail at the beginning of line five, and the small vertical line at the beginning of line six. In line four, we also can see that the child started with a zigzag that looks very much like *W*. It was followed with a closed curve (similar to *O*), not with another zigzag. This closed curve is followed by a zigzag line that is open at the bottom rather than at the top, which looks like *M*. This detail is followed by another closed loop, one that differs somewhat from the loops used earlier. The variation in the forms included here shows the child's awareness that lines of print are comprised of different symbols.

Figure 10d was created by the same 4-year-old who created Figure 10c. She turned over her paper to write "a letter." But here, she used almost no

Figure 10
Scribble Writing and Looped Mock Letters

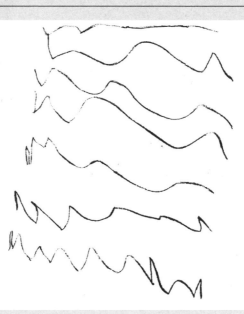

10a

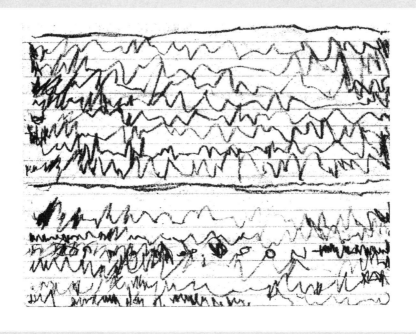

10b

(continued)

Figure 10 *(continued)*

10c

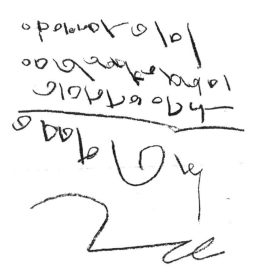

10d

scribble writing. Many of these marks are **mock letters**. The letters *a*, *c*, and *e* appeared in her name, which adults in her family wrote in lowercase (as none of these letters was the first letter in her name). The noncurved lines in her name were *t* and *y*. We can see the influence of all these letters in the child's writing, although she also took some liberties. When writing her letters, she created some new forms that are not found in the English alphabet.

The children who created the samples shown in Figure 11 also created new forms. Figure 11a is a 4-year-old's grocery list. We see among some lines of scribble a few distinct little forms, some of which are mock letters. In Figure 11b there are many mock letters and a few actual letters (*A*, *R*, *V*, and *O*). In Figure 11c, we see many actual letters and a few mock letters, especially those that resemble *E*s but with extra horizontal lines. We also see what appear to be upside-down *T*s, plus a few long vertical lines with a closed circle placed in the middle of their lower ends, not to one side or the other as in actual letters, such as *b* and *d*.

Mock letters contain the segments that are the building blocks of actual letters. To understand what children are probably thinking when they create mock letters, let's consider Legos, Tinker Toys, and wooden blocks—three popular construction toys. These toys are packaged with an insert that shows a few specific items that can be made with the materials provided. Of course, the possibilities are vast and the child invents many original designs, not just those shown in packaging material. But no matter what a child builds, the basic materials of a particulate construction toy make all the varied structures look like they belong together. They are of the same kind, because the basic pieces used to make any item come from the same basic set of materials as are used to make other items.

A limited set of lines—building blocks—is also available to make all letters of the alphabet. Some lines are used in some letters; other lines are used in others. Often the same kinds of lines are used in many letters, but their number (compare *E* and *F*) or placement vary (compare *d* and *b*). Creating letters is the same as creating structures with blocks—the possibilities for creating different forms are almost endless. The child does not know at first that there are only 26 letters—that all the possibilities for creating forms with this set of lines are not exploited. For all the child knows, there could be 50 or 100 letters in the English alphabet, just as there are endless possibilities for different block constructions from the same set of basic blocks.

Figure 11
From Mock Letters to Real Letters

11a

11b

11c

It is no wonder that children first combine lines in many ways. They might very well think, "Surely this is a letter, although I haven't actually seen one like this before." Until a child has several years of experience, including exposure to a variety of alphabet puzzles, alphabet books, and words in the environment, we are likely to see mock letters in the child's writing.

When a child builds with construction toys, teachers praise creativity and encourage unique constructions. With writing, the rules change—socialization narrows the possibilities. Eventually, the almost infinite number of possible marks is winnowed out to a standard set. During the preschool years, as children devise new letter forms, teachers must accept and celebrate their good thinking. After all, the child is working within the set of lines used to produce letters. In time, and rather quickly actually, children narrow the designs of their creations so that even mock letters look very much like actual letters.

> During the preschool years, as children devise new letter forms, teachers must accept and celebrate their good thinking.

Children Realize There Is a Limited Set of Letters

One day, after finishing an alphabet puzzle, a child who was almost 5 years old asked his teacher, "Are these all the alphabet letters in the whole wide world?" She asked what made him think that this might be all of them. "Because," he said, "I see the same ones everywhere!" The teacher explained that the puzzle the child had just completed did indeed contain all the English alphabet letters in the whole wide world, but that there are other languages in the world with different alphabet symbols.

This child's question reveals an insight: Everywhere we look, we see the same letters. In time, the young child concludes that there is a limited set of alphabet letters, not an endless variety of forms. "People don't approach the set of lines used to create alphabet letters the way I approach my blocks," a child concludes, "and I won't either."

Creating Scribbles, Mock Letters, and Actual Letters

Once children have attained the insight that there are a limited rather than an endless number of letters, mock letters seldom appear in their writing, except during play. When children make props for play scenarios, they generally recognize that the props are "just pretend" and that written marks needn't be "real" letters. Writing for this purpose, even among 5-year-olds, may be a combination of scribbles, mock letters, and actual letters. More often, though, we see actual letters, or good approximations to them, combined with scribble writing, which is easier and faster to produce than are mock or actual letters. We see just this combination of marks on a ticket a child prepared for a classroom production of *The Three Little Pigs* (see Figure 12). Notice that the forms at the top of the ticket are the numerals 1 through 10.

In nonplay situations, the older 4-year-old and younger 5-year-old typically use forms that are actual letters, although their skill in creating them is limited in many ways. Consider the samples provided in Figure 13. Figure 13a comes from a sign-up sheet provided in a block area. When the block area was full (occupants were limited to four at a time), children who wanted turns wrote their names on a sheet of paper attached to a clipboard. The name at the top of this list is *SARAH*. She started in the middle of the paper with the letter *S*, wrote the letters *A* and *R*, and then ran out of room. She returned to the middle of the paper and wrote *A* to the left of *S,* then added *H* to the left of that. Budding knowledge of **directionality** collides with the challenges encountered in specific situations.

Sarah's print placement strategies are very typical among preschoolers. She started in a place that did not give her enough space to write all of a word on one line. Then she fit in the rest of the letters as best she could. Sometimes, children rotate the paper and write the remaining letters on

---

Figure 12
Ticket for Classroom Production of *The Three Little Pigs*

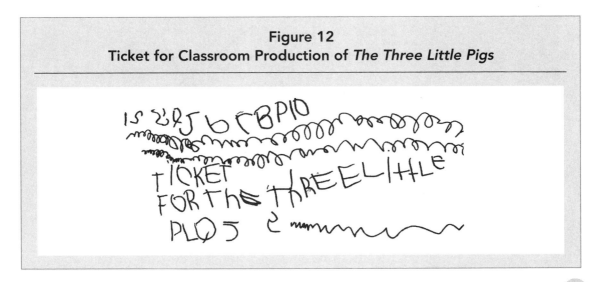

Figure 13
Where to Start, and Where to Go?

13a

13b

what first had been the right side of the paper, but ends up, at least for a time, as the top.

Notice that Sarah knew the letters of her name, wrote them in the correct temporal order, and started out writing from left to right. Had Sarah started at the left-hand margin (rather than in the middle of the page), she might have returned to the left to finish writing. But there was space, right there on the original line, so why not fill it?

Had Sarah's teacher not observed her, she might have drawn the conclusion that Sarah started with *H* and went from there, jumbling the order of the letters in her name. Not so. Sarah did not yet know that she should always sweep to the left and write the remaining letters from left to right under her top row. Such a strategy might actually seem very inefficient to a young child in Sarah's situation: "Why waste all that space I left on the first line?" "Why separate my name by putting letters on two different lines?"

Thinking of this kind caused a different child to resist her teacher's suggestion that she put the *A* that follows *R* in the word *library* under the *L* she had written in the first line (see Figure 13b). She wanted the *R* and *A* to be "together," she explained, "because they come together in the word." Children have their reasons for doing things. Gradually, they begin to see things as adults see them, because they realize that abiding by conventions allows others to interpret their writing. In the meantime, we can enjoy their efforts and accept some of their thoughtful accommodations to the challenges they encounter.

A Close Look at the Letters Preschoolers Create

Preschoolers form letters in interesting ways. Notice that in Figure 13a Sarah reversed the *S* in her name. *S* is a difficult letter for young children to orient correctly, because making the first move in the wrong direction reverses the letter. Notice that the only other curved line in Sarah's name is in the upper portion of *R* and that the movement for this curved line starts in the opposite direction needed to write *S*.

Reversed letters are very common in the writing of preschool and kindergarten children. In most cases, there is no confusion about which letter they have written, and it must seem to preschoolers that orientation should not matter. Teachers can support children's acquisition of knowledge about letter orientation by commenting that "*M* and *W* are just alike, except one faces up and the other faces down." For older preschoolers, teachers might contrast the direction of movement when making *S* and *2* in quick demonstrations provided at the writing table, as appropriate to the children's current endeavors. When writing an experience chart with a group of children, a teacher also might comment, when starting the letter *S*, "I start here and then go this way, and then back around like this. If I go the other way, my *S* will be backward. We would still know that it is *S*, but I want my *S* to go the way it is supposed to go."

We also see a lot of imprecision in the marks that preschoolers use to compose alphabet letters. Notice the *B* in *library* in Figure 13b. The child did splendidly with the top closed curve but had some difficulty with the bottom portion. (It is possible she thought *P* at first, and then repaired it to form a *B*, but we cannot be certain.) The *R*s in *library* are also interesting. The diagonal line that makes up the lower right half of *R* caused the child some trouble. Diagonal lines are difficult, as we will see again in some later samples. Sarah's *H* and one *A* are also interesting. In the *H*, the horizontal bar is placed about as low as it can go on the right line. The *A* between the *H* and the *S* also is pushing the limits a bit. *A*'s are closed at the top, not open. When open, they begin to pass into *H* territory. But Sarah uses straight lines for *H* and diagonal lines for *A*, which diminishes any possibility of confusion between these two letters in her writing. Besides, there's just a small gap in the top of the *A*, nothing serious.

We see some of the same difficulties and a few others in the samples in Figure 14. All of these samples are color names devised by children for a class book on colors. Figure 14a says, "Zebra black." Notice the difficulty with diagonal lines in both *Z* and *k*. Notice how well formed the other letters are, and that they are in lowercase as well, except for the second *A* (the one in the middle of *black*). We can see the child's struggle with the lowercase *a* at the end of *Zebra*. Perhaps the child did not want to attempt another one in the next word (*black*).

Trying to make new letter forms, and then returning to the more familiar, especially with writing they consider important and know is public, is characteristic of preschoolers. Preschoolers have a variety of strategies at their disposal, and select their use to fit specific purposes (Siegler, 1996). Teachers model both uppercase and lowercase letters in their own writing, and children gain further exposure to both kinds of letters through environmental print and books. Slowly, they give each a try. We shouldn't worry in the preschool

> Trying to make new letter forms, and then returning to the more familiar, especially with writing they consider important and know is public, is characteristic of preschoolers.

Figure 14
Typical Errors in Preschoolers' Letter Formation

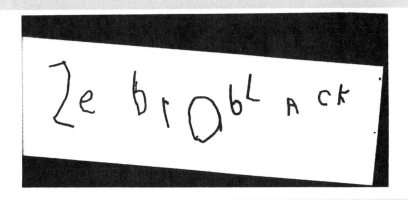

14a

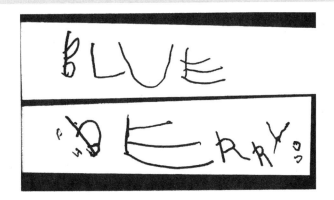

14b

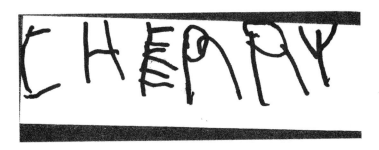

14c

years about where children use lowercase and uppercase letters. Knowing that there are two kinds of letters, big ones and little ones, and having a familiarity with how each looks, is plenty for children to know in these early years.

Figure 14b ("BLUE BERRY") was also created by a child for the class color book. Look at the *E*s. The first horizontal line does not start right at the top of the vertical left post, and the horizontal lines are larger than usual. The curved lines at the top of both the *B*s and *R*s also don't start at the top. What was the child thinking? We don't know, nor does it matter. We know what letters the child intended.

Figure 14c ("CHERRY") was created by a third child. Notice the fancy *E*. Mock letter *E*s of this kind are almost universal in children's writing. Children add lines in an apparent attempt to amplify the letter *E*. Perhaps they think there is more "*E*-ness" this way. They have a good point, and there is no confusion between this *E* and any other letter in the alphabet. All children stop doing this, in time. It's something to enjoy while it lasts, not something to worry about.

Notice the struggle in Figure 14c with the diagonal line for the right side of the *R*. Diagonal lines present a challenge for preschoolers, as we have already seen. The *C* in this sample is also interesting, given that it was formed out of three lines, not the conventional one. First, the child made a vertical line at the left, and then added the two short horizontal lines, one at the top and one at the bottom. This color name, like all the others, was written on strips of paper. How does a child make sure she doesn't go over the left edge of the strip, especially when forming a curved line, which requires a good bit of control? A child might think, "Don't even attempt it. Make the *C* in a different way that I can control better." Children are always thinking about ways to solve the problems they encounter as they write.

Why Preschoolers Write the Way They Write

Some of the imprecision we see in young children's letter formation is cognitive. In other words, preschool children judge whether the marks they make will be interpreted as intended or will be confused with another letter. Had Sarah thought there was any question about the *A* with the open top that she had formed in writing her name on the sign-up sheet (see Figure 13a), she might have used another mark to close its top. Children quite often go back and tidy up their work if they think it matters for how a letter will be interpreted.

"Where do I start?" "Where do I aim?" Making diagonal lines is a projective space problem. The child must imagine the line needed, before starting. Adults often think that children can easily transfer mental images of alphabet letters onto paper. Although children do work from visual images, re-creating these on paper—in two-dimensional space—is not easy. Even a physical model to copy does not really help. The lines in the copy are already formed. The child might wonder, "How did someone *do* that?" "How do I move my marker to re-create that shape?" If a young child wants help, an adult can draw the letter on another piece of paper, while describing each move he or she makes. Then, the adult can draw it again, line segment by line segment, while the child does the same segments on his or her paper, after the teacher draws each one. Then, for a diagonal line, such as in *R* or *K*, the teacher can place strategic dots. For *R*, place one dot on the vertical line where the child starts, and the other at the stopping point. For the first vertical line in the letter *K*, place one dot where the child can start the line and another at the midpoint of the vertical line.

Formal handwriting lessons do not belong in the preschool, although explicit instruction can be given in response to a child's requests. Preschoolers often make such requests, in time, as they strive to get their representations of specific letters to look the way these letters look everywhere else they see them. "I can't do *R*," they say. Or someone announces, "My *S* is going the wrong way again. Help me!"

Some of the young child's difficulty in forming letters is not cognitive but a consequence of immature fine-motor skills. When the marking tool is held in a rigid fist grip and the movement comes from the muscle of the upper arm, it's difficult, if not impossible, to create and combine lines with precision or to make letters that are small rather than large. It's still difficult to be precise when the writing tool is held rigidly in the fingers and the movement comes by moving the entire hand at the wrist. Thus, preschoolers write big letters that look wobbly and whose lines overrun where they are supposed to stop. Notice the *H*, *A*'s, and *R* in Sarah's name (see Figure 13a). Lines that meet do not stop at the meeting point. They go beyond. Look at the *A* in *library* and you will see the same thing (see Figure 13b).

We see no overruns in Figure 14a. This child had exceptional fine-motor skill for a preschooler, which explains not only the absence of major line overruns, but also the use of many lowercase letters, which are more difficult to form than uppercase. Making lowercase letters requires considerable finger dexterity, which this child had.

We see a few line overruns in Figure 14b, although it's not a problem. This is not careless or sloppy writing. Indeed, this is wonderful writing, given the typical preschool child's level of motor control. It's rather amazing how hard preschoolers try to keep their writing within reasonable bounds, despite their motor limitations. They try to avoid overlapping and overrunning lines, even though precision of movement is difficult for them. No matter the various imperfections in the letters preschoolers form, we can recognize the letters with ease. There's no point in fussing at children about writing letters perfectly. Their time is better spent in other endeavors.

Conclusions: Celebrating a Child's Scribbles and Everything That Follows

The preschool years are remarkable years for learning and development. As we have seen in this chapter, a young child's writing evolves from scribble to script in a matter of only two or three years. To be sure, the child still has much to learn. But any child who travels the distance described here is off to a wonderful start.

The preschool teacher and the child's family have a front row seat for observing these remarkable achievements. They also set the stage for the opportunities a child has to write, and they provide the support children need along the way. The most important thing for adults to do during these years is celebrate a child's writing attempts and respond to what children attempt to *communicate*.

CHAPTER 4

From Letter Strings to Real Words

We discussed in Chapter 3 how the marks children use for writing gradually change first from scribble to mock letters and then to reasonable approximations of conventional forms. Just as preschool children develop their skill in creating marks and forming letters, they also develop skill using letters first to approximate and then to create actual words.

Beginning at approximately age 3, once children are making mock letters and rudimentary approximations of some actual letters, they begin to put their letter-like designs together to make "words." They make considerable progress in developing a beginning understanding of word making throughout the rest of their preschool years. In kindergarten and beyond, as they continue to acquire more knowledge about how print actually works to represent sounds in spoken words, their word creations are closer to conventional word making—spelling. Children very slowly begin to grasp the pivotal importance of the selection of specific letters and their sequencing in written communication as they develop **phonological awareness**), learn letter names, and observe their teacher's demonstrations of breaking spoken words into their individual sounds and linking these to the letter or letters that represent them. Children also learn more about word making as they talk about their writing with teachers, and as they observe and interact with the print that surrounds them.

We know, however, that simply immersing children in a print-rich environment is not enough. Children "read" the entire physical context that surrounds environmental print, to determine what it "says" or means, without looking much at the print itself (Masonheimer, Drum, & Ehri, 1984; Reutzel, Fawson, Young, Morrison, & Wilcox, 2003). This is why it is important to engage preschoolers in other activities in which the code-based nature of print is made more obvious.

At first, preschoolers have no understanding that print is mapped onto oral language. Their experimentation with word creation is more visual, with environmental print serving as an important source of knowledge about how words look, though not of why each word looks exactly as it looks—why those letters, in that order. Even after children acquire the basic insight that print and speech are related, the precise way in which they are related eludes them. Only gradually do preschoolers begin to realize that letters represent the individual sounds in spoken words. Skill in isolating sounds in words and knowing which letters represent them are beyond the capability of most preschoolers, especially younger ones. With older 4-year-olds, however, we often do see the beginnings of an understanding of the basic processes involved in conventional word making.

This chapter examines the development of children's understanding about how letters are used to make words and offers teachers suggestions for supporting children's learning. It is based on the systematic work by Baghban (1984), Clay (1975, 1987), and Invernizzi (2003), and on the countless contributions of others who have studied young children's writing.

Use of Environmental Print

There is no question that children are surrounded by environmental print, both in and outside of school. Imagine all the products with printed labels that children see in their homes on a daily basis—their toothpaste, cereal, milk cartons, and snack containers. In addition, most are exposed to other printed materials that adults use, such as the mail delivered each day, advertising circulars left on doorsteps, and perhaps newspapers, magazines, and books. On their way to school or to the grocery store, children see street signs and the print on the fronts of commercial establishments. The latter include fast food outlets and grocery stores with words that they may already "read" when they see them in context. When taken out of context, preschoolers typically cannot read words that they have seen many times, and "read" in their typical context (Reutzel et al., 2003).

Preschool classrooms offer even more environmental print, most of it actively created and used by the children and the teachers (see Figure 15). In some classrooms, there are posters or sign-in sheets listing the names of all the children. A morning message is used in some preschool classrooms, which might have a greeting from the teacher and a simple statement about one of the day's activities. As the teacher reads the morning message with the children in a morning circle, words are underlined. Thus, the print becomes a tool for children's learning. Classrooms also may be filled with displays of print that the teachers and children have constructed together. For example, the teacher might have written down on a chart each child's

Figure 15
Preschool Classroom Environmental Print

favorite animal from a recent trip to the zoo, or the teacher might have written a statement on a chart every few days to record the significant progress made by seeds the children had planted. In addition to posters, charts, and a morning message, which are created and used in a whole-group setting, many preschool classrooms contain a variety of manipulative materials, including alphabet puzzles, puzzles with pictures' names labeled, letter tiles, and picture cards with labels, among the choices provided to children for center time. And of course, print-rich classrooms are filled with books and poem charts. Many predictable text books are oversized with print that is large enough for children to see easily as the teacher points to the print as it is read aloud, and most poem charts also have large print.

As children inspect print that is around them, they notice, for example, that words usually consist of more than one letter, and create mock words that usually contain three to seven letters—the typical range of letters in the words they see in their environment. They also recognize that words contain a variety of letters, and therefore rarely create mock words by repeating just one letter three or four times. They also realize that the same letters appear in many different words and that the very same letters can be used to make different words, if the letters are reordered. Their mock words reflect these insights. Children also sometimes use letters from familiar words, especially their own names and those of their classmates, as a base from which to form new mock words, and they also "borrow" whole words from environmental print to create their own messages, often without regard for what the words actually say (Fields, 1998; Invernizzi, 2003). Sometimes, children simply want to create print artifacts, and because in these cases there is no specific message being conveyed anyway, any "words" will work.

The writing in Figure 16 illustrates the variety of ways children incorporate environmental print into their own creations. After visiting an aquarium as part of their investigation of ocean life, these 4-year-olds were invited to draw their favorite ocean animals in fish bowls. The teacher modeled the activity, labeling her own drawings with the words *shark*, *octopus*, and *eel*. Some children produced drawings but did not label them. The only print on their papers was their own name, which served to identify the creator of each paper. Some children used classmates' names in their drawings and writing, confidently asserting that those were the names of the fish—animals are sometimes given human-like names, so why not their fish? Notice that one child did not draw any fish, but filled her bowl with print—some copied from a list of classmates' names, and one word, *pizza*, copied twice from a chart created as a shared writing activity during which children listed their favorite pizza toppings. It seems that this child just wanted to create words, and copied some from the environment. Two children created their own "words" in addition to copying names and other words. Note that not a single child demonstrated understanding of the **alphabetic principle**—that to form words, we must select letters that represent the specific sounds in a spoken word. The absence of this insight is quite typical among preschool children.

The individual variations in the children's performances also illustrate how preschoolers often stray from a teacher's assignment to engage in drawing and writing. Their teacher accepted each child's creation, knowing that motivation to write and draw comes from having considerable control over what and when to do one or the other, or both. It is probably worthwhile for preschool teachers occasionally to model and suggest specific

Figure 16
Children's Use of Environmental Print

things that children might do. Preschoolers then need freedom to take things in the direction they wish.

Children's Names as a Special Source of Knowledge About Word Making

We saw in Figure 16 that children's names are often prominent in their writing and drawing. In fact, children probably first become aware of both letters and words through engagement with their names, and we know that the first letters a child is likely to know are those from their names (Treiman & Broderick, 1998; Treiman, Cohen, Mulqueeny, Kessler, & Schechtman, 2007). As we see in

> Children probably first become aware of both letters and words through engagement with their names, and we know that the first letters a child is likely to know are those from their names.

Figure 17, pictures and letter shapes are often equally prominent in a child's earliest attempts to use letters to convey specific meanings. This sample was produced by 3-year-old Brianna in a post office dramatic play center. Together, the pictures and letters constituted a letter to her aunt. When her teacher asked what the letter said, Brianna read, "Dear Auntie Shante, I am coming to see you. Me and Mommy and Henry. We coming. Love, Brianna."

For Brianna, meaning was represented as much by the picture as by the print, and she relied on oral language to explain both pictures and letters. The important thing to know about the letters was that almost all were from her name. She indicated that the *NA* at the bottom of the page said "love Brianna." Apparently, Brianna knew that letters were needed to write

Figure 17
Brianna's Letter

"Dear Auntie Shante, I am coming to see you. Me and Mommy and Henry. We coming. Love, Brianna."

the rest of her message to her aunt. She borrowed letters from her name, no doubt because there were those she knew best how to write. The understanding that the same letters used to write our name can be used in other words is a rare insight among young 3-year-olds. They typically consider letters in their name as "theirs" and often claim, as theirs, every word they see that begins with their name's first letter. Brianna's willingness to reuse letters from her name to create other "words" (mock ones, to be sure) demonstrates a budding understanding that letters in her name also can be used in other words.

As described in Chapter 3, and as we have seen here in Brianna's letter, the first letters to appear in children's writing are often those found in words that are most familiar to them—especially their names. At age 3, Billy, a classmate of Brianna, had shown a lot of interest in his name. He could spell it aloud, letter by letter, and he tried to write it, too, although he wasn't always able to write each letter as he recited it. Billy wrote a letter to his older brother, Odell, who had gone on a trip with their father. Figure 18 shows that Billy used variations of his name, over and over again, to complete his letter. He read it to his teacher as follows: "Odell, I been missing you. Come home tomorrow. Love, Billy. Come home now."

While still relying on his name as the basic source of letters to write to his brother, Billy nonetheless demonstrated a more sophisticated understanding of writing than did Brianna. For example, he reused letters in his

Figure 18
Billy's Letter

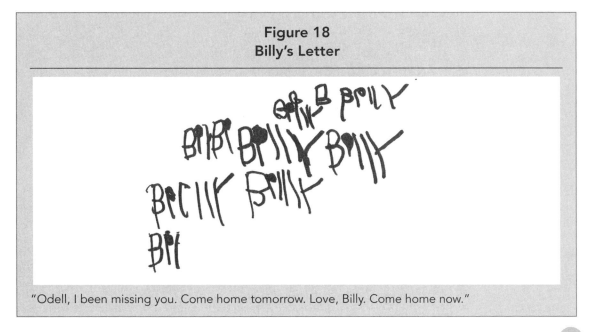

"Odell, I been missing you. Come home tomorrow. Love, Billy. Come home now."

name and altered their sequence in his name to create other "words." Apparently, he had observed that the same letters can be used to spell many different words and that some words differ by only one letter (e.g., *cake* and *Coke*, *Mike* and *Ike*). In many cases Billy added just one new mark to *Billy* (e.g., *Billly*, *BiClly*, and *Belly*). In *Belly*, the addition of a letter *e* substituted for the letter that occupies that spot in his name (*i*). In one "word," Billy used a second strategy—recombining letters in a new sequence (*BilBi*). He also used a third strategy—deleting letters to create a shorter "word" (*Bil*).

As children begin to move beyond relying on the letters in their names to create new "words," their awareness of general visual characteristics of words, obtained from observation of environmental print, frequently leads them to produce mock words. These strings of letters certainly look like real words, even though their letters do not represent the sound sequences of actual words in our language.

In this phase of stringing letters together to create words, without any knowledge of the need to select and order letters to represent the order of sounds heard in spoken words, children have not yet discovered how print works in English and other alphabetic languages. We say that children lack an understanding of the alphabetic principle, which means that they do not understand that letters represent sounds. Their intention is to make their writing look like it is composed of words, and they believe at first that the mock words they create are actual words. They often show their mock words to adults and ask, "What words are these?" Adults typically try to read them—sound them out—with the result that the adult says mostly nonsense words. Children typically laugh at this result, and adults can tell them, "These look like words, but they are not real words." Children typically continue this kind of exploration for months until they finally realize that this approach doesn't work very well for making actual words. They then begin to ask for spellings, they copy words from the environment, or they ask adults, "How do you spell *bird's nest*?"

The writing sample in Figure 19 was produced by 5-year-old Marisol in her preschool classroom's writing center. According to Marisol, her writing says, "I like my dog. I take good care of him." Her writing, like Billy's, uses **nonphonemic letter strings**—letters arranged in a string, but not selected and sequenced to match the sound structure of an actual word. Unlike Billy, however, Marisol uses many letters, not just those drawn mostly from her name. In fact, there are 11 distinct letters among the 25 symbols she created in this sample. Her writing looks a lot more like "real" writing than Billy's because she has written many more different "words,"

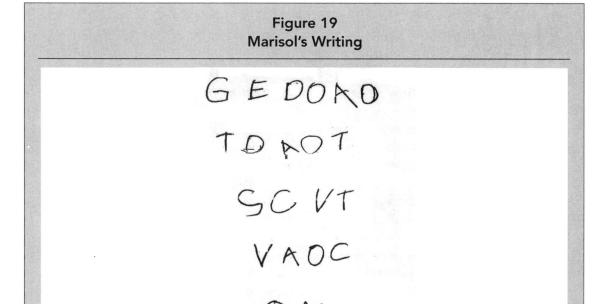

Figure 19
Marisol's Writing

G E DOAD

T D AOT

SC VT

VAOC

O N

NO

B V

"I like my dog. I take good care of him."

given her larger repertoire of letters to use. We get the impression that Marisol has carefully inspected a wider range of real words than has Billy.

Like Billy and Marisol, Jeffrey wrote letter strings (see Figure 20) to represent the message, "My mom and dad like to play. They like to play with my sisters and my dog, too." Note that Jeffrey attempted to make his writing appear more conventional by adding periods at the end of each line of print. Sometimes, children even draw lines under their mock words, apparently thinking that these marks are somehow essential for "real" writing, given that some of the writing they've seen (e.g., older siblings' homework, a teacher's writing on lined chart paper) has been done on lines. Children pay close attention to the print they see and they try to incorporate visual elements that make their efforts resemble the real thing.

Figure 20
Jeffrey's Composition

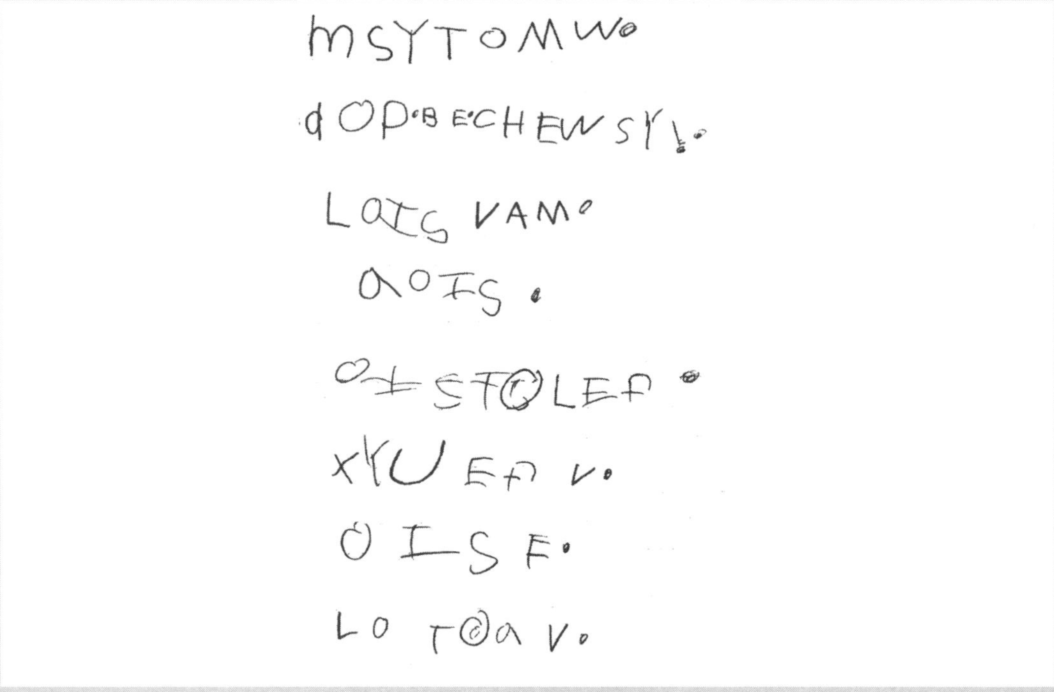

MSYTOMWo
dOP·BECHEWSY!·
LOIG VAMo
AoFS .
o±ST@LEP ⊕
XYU EP V·
O I S F·
Lo T@a V·

"My mom and dad like to play. They like to play with my sisters and my dog, too."

Beginnings of Phonemic Spelling

A major developmental leap in writing occurs when children discover that spoken words are made up of sounds, and that these have some connection to letters in printed words. A beginning awareness of the sounds in words, called phonological awareness, is first demonstrated when children begin to divide words into syllables, and syllables into onsets (all of the sounds prior to the first vowel, such as /b/ in *boy* and /str/- in *string*) and rimes (the vowel and all that follows, such as /oy/ in /b/-/oy/, and -/ing/ in /str/-/ing/). These levels of phonological processing precede **phonemic awareness**, which is awareness of individual sounds in words, not awareness of larger chunks, such as syllables or onset-rime units. Phonemic awareness develops gradually as children are engaged in experiences that bring these smaller units of sound in words to their attention.

> A major developmental leap in writing occurs when children discover that spoken words are made up of sounds, and that these have some connection to printed words.

During the preschool years, beginning levels of phonological awareness develop as children engage in language play such as play with rhyming words and words that begin with the same sound (i.e., alliteration). Children's phonemic-level awareness can be enhanced in a number of ways that focus children's attention on this level of speech (Invernizzi, 2003). One way teachers can do this is by including engagement in singing songs that call children's attention to the individual sounds in oral language (Invernizzi, 2003), such as by singing songs that manipulate sounds in words. Consider "Apples and Bananas," a song by Raffi: "I like to eat, eat, eat, apples and bananas...I like to eat, eat, eat, eeples and beeneenees...I like to ote, ote, ote, opels and bononoes...." As children sing this song and others (e.g., "Willoughby Wallaby Woo"), they experience the changing of some individual sounds in words while others remain constant. Such experiences provide a level of support—scaffolding—that enables children to successfully manipulate sounds, as they sing along, even though they are not likely at first to be skilled in isolating and manipulating phonemes on their own. Repeated engagement in this type of playful activity, as well as others, leads over time to growth in phonological awareness.

Preschool teachers can also enhance children's phonemic-level awareness by reciting poems with a lot of alliteration and then talking about the words that begin with the same sound, after a poem has been recited. Teachers can also engage children in playing games like "I Spy," in which children are encouraged to find objects in the classroom that begin with particular sounds. For example, a teacher might say, "I spy something that starts with /m/, like Marisol's name.../m/ *Marisol*. I want you to think about objects in our classroom and decide whether any of them have names that start with /m/." To participate, children must say the names of objects they see or know about and then isolate the first sound of an object's name. They must then match it to /m/, the target sound the teacher has provided. As you can see, this activity requires children to isolate the individual sound—the phoneme—at the beginning of a word.

It is also the case, however, that isolating an initial sound in a word when a single consonant phoneme constitutes all of a syllable's onset (e.g., *b-oy*, *d-og*) is much easier for children to detect than is isolating the first phoneme of an onset that is a consonant cluster (e.g., /s/ in *str*, which is the onset of *string*), or to separate the individual sounds in a syllable's rime unit (e.g., /k/ separated from *ack*, the rime unit in *black*) (Treiman, 1985).

Still, the practice of isolating the first sound in words with a single consonant phoneme is still worthwhile for children, and it is most beneficial to their writing when paired with writing the letter that represents the sound isolated. In this way, children learn letter names, as a teacher says, "That's right. The first sound we hear in the word *bird* is /b/. We use the letter *B* to write /b/, so I will write that letter, right here." They also learn the alphabetic principle (i.e., letters function to represent sounds in spoken words) and some specific sound–letter matches.

Connecting letters to specific sounds is not a simple task for preschoolers. To do this, they must distinguish among letter shapes and know each letter's name, and must know that letters are used to write sounds we hear in words (i.e., understand the alphabetic principle). Many young children can recognize and name all the letters of the alphabet but have no idea how to use them to make words. As a consequence, they continue to create mock words by stringing letters together, because they have no idea how letters are actually used to make words.

Teachers can help children understand the alphabetic principle if they demonstrate writing by sounding out words and then represent each sound with a letter or letters. This thinking out loud as the teacher writes can be done as a natural part of preschool classroom routines. A teacher might say, for example, when involving children in making labels for art-center supplies, "This sign is for the markers. Let's see, /m/, /m/, /m/, /m/...*markers*. The word *markers* starts with the letter *m*, so I'll write the *m* first, right here." The teacher might then say, "I hear /r/ next, but I know there's an *a* before it that we don't hear, so I will write that first and then write *r* for /r/. Then, I hear /k/, mark /k/, and we use *i* to write /k/, so I'll write *k* next...." By transcribing a spoken word into its written form, the teacher explicitly models the most fundamental of literacy concepts—the fact that print conveys meaning—and also precisely how print works to represent meaning in languages with alphabetic writing systems. Such an authentic use of print serves many important literacy purposes and also serves the social purpose of helping to keep the art center neat.

Teachers can help children develop alphabetic knowledge through a combination of direct small-group instruction and whole-group activities, such as dictated or shared writing in which sounding out spoken words to spell them is demonstrated. Figure 21 shows another example of an experience that involved the teacher demonstrating writing. This time, a dictation activity followed a read-aloud of the picture book *Raccoon on His Own* (Arnosky, 2001). The teacher elicited from the children lists of animals that

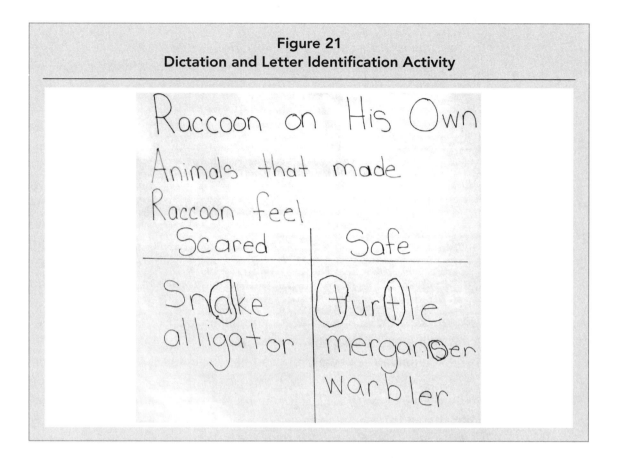

Figure 21
Dictation and Letter Identification Activity

made raccoon feel either safe or scared. After the teacher and children discussed a suggestion, the teacher wrote it down, by sounding it out and selecting a letter for each sound. After doing this, the teacher called a few individual children to step up to the chart to circle a beginning letter in one of the words. As children did this, they were asked to name the letter. Then, the teacher led the children in reading the word, focusing on sounding out the first letter, and then reading the rest while underlining all of the remaining letters. The letter at the beginning of some words was not circled. Doing so would have required children to sit too long in a whole group, and would not have left any letters for children to circle on their own during center time, if they were interested. This proved to be a very popular activity!

Learning center activities can also engage children in sorting small items or pictures onto mats or into bowls labeled with the appropriate letters according to their beginning sounds. Learning center activities should be introduced and modeled in a large-group setting. This instruction and practice provide children with the background they need to successfully use the materials in an independent learning center.

Preschool teachers will also want to label children's drawings or paintings after talking with children about them, as was discussed in Chapter 2. Here, again, the teacher can think aloud the spelling of some of the most prominent words as they are written. A teacher has yet another opportunity when a child "anchors" a message in scribble writing and then approaches the teacher to talk about it. If the child is agreeable, and if it serves the child's purposes, the teacher can help in writing some actual words to go with the scribble the child has created. Perhaps the child would like the teacher to write "Dear Mommy" or some other part of the message. Using the highly informative think-aloud strategy the teacher can help the child. All of these activities—songs, teacher-demonstrated writing, individual writing assistance, and practice games, introduced to the whole group and then put out in learning centers—help children develop phonological awareness, letter name knowledge, the alphabetic principle, and some specific sound–letter connections.

When children begin to understand the way that sounds are connected to letters from having seen teachers demonstrate these connections, they often begin to create phonemic-based spellings on their own. Sometimes, this occurs while they are still writing letters that are not very conventional. Four-year-old Helen demonstrated her budding phonemic awareness and sound–letter connections in the message shown in Figure 22, which she created for her best friend, Cameron. She explained to her teacher that the print on the left says, "I love Cameron." When asked about the symbols on the right side of the page, she pointed out the hearts and indicated that those show how much she loves her friend. Then she said, the rest of the writing says, "I want you to play at my house."

Helen's representation of just two of the three sounds in a word is typical of children who first begin to use phonemic spelling. The /l/ and /v/ are dominant sounds in the word *love*, and are also the first and last sounds, which are easiest for children to focus on. The middle phoneme in *love*, a vowel, is harder for children to detect.

CM for *Cameron* is also an interesting example of abbreviated word making. The second phoneme in *Cameron* is a soft vowel, which is relatively hard to hear. Helen did not represent any of the sounds in the second and third syllables of Cameron's name. Since the first syllable of the Cameron's name is the one accented, it is likely that Helen was not as aware of the sounds in the unaccented syllables that followed. Often, children

Figure 22
Helen's Message to Cameron

"I love Cameron. I want you to play at my house."

only represent the most obvious sounds they hear in words, and also include just enough to satisfy their intent of writing the word. Even if Helen had heard some of the sounds in the last two syllables of Cameron's name, she might have decided it wasn't necessary to represent them.

Children do not immediately abandon earlier forms of word making when they first create some phonemic-based spellings. We can see Helen's use of scribbled symbols in the second part of her message. Figure 23 likewise illustrates that even older preschool children mix writing forms. Five-year-old Jackson read this journal entry as, "My mom fixes me spinach and turkey and gravy. It is good." This appears at first glance to be a mix of letter string words and scribble writing. Closer examination, however, reveals that Jackson engaged in significant phonemic spelling. The *mi* on the first line may represent *my*, while the *fes* is for *fixes*. The word *me* is represented with a single letter *m*, and *spinach* is spelled *snh*, representing the three

Figure 23
Jackson's Journal Entry

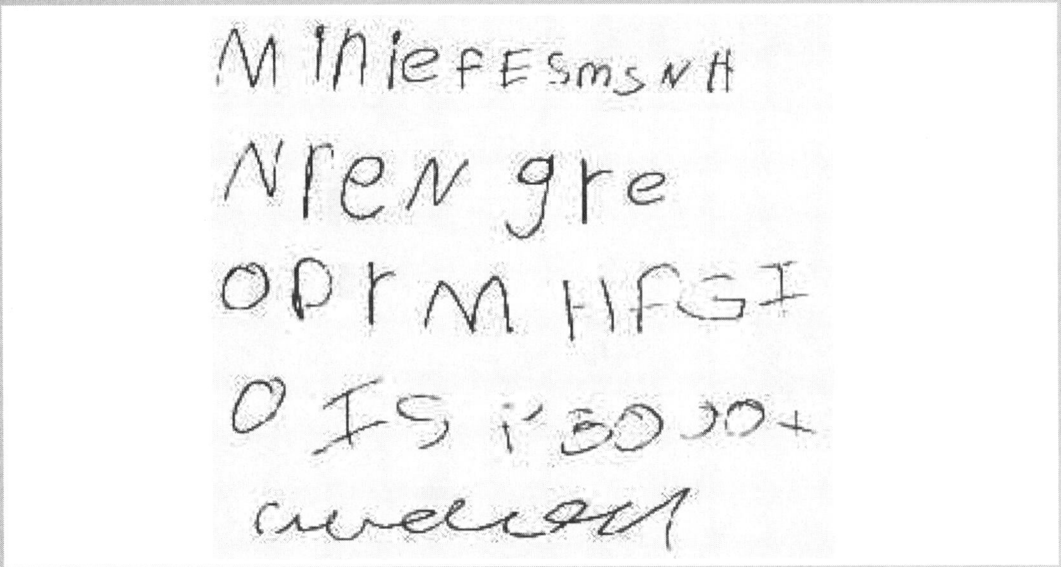

"My mom fixes me spinach and turkey and gravy. It is good."

major consonant sounds in the word. The name of the letter *H* contains /aich/, which explains his selection of that letter as the last in spinach. Use of the letter-name strategy is also evident in children's use of single letters to represent entire words, as when they write *C* for *see*, *R* for *are*, and *U* for *you*. In these cases, the letter names have in them the sequence of two sounds heard in these words.

The letter strings and scribble that follow the first two lines in Jackson's message suggest that he wanted to create lots of writing but couldn't sustain the level of effort needed to continue sounding out words and selecting letters. It is very common for preschoolers to tire as they write messages; it is hard work for them.

Movement Along a Developmental Continuum

Once children fully understand that writing involves organizing letters into clusters based on the sound sequence in words, they follow a very common progression from representing only the most prominent sounds in words to representing most of the sounds they hear. Most preschool children are only able to represent most or all of the sounds in words if they have significant support. Moreover, regardless of the extent to which all children in a class participate in the same activities, they will develop the ability to produce phonemic spelling at different rates. Figure 24 illustrates the variation in the spelling skills of a group of 4-year-old preschoolers in the same classroom at the end of the year before they were to enter kindergarten. After the teacher demonstrated spelling four words, sounding out and representing each sound with a single letter, children could then select a picture to paste onto the poster and write a label for it. The teacher assisted children by slowly enunciating each child's word. Some children were able to represent all of the phonemes in their words, while others represented only beginning and ending consonants. Some children showed more control than others over letter formation, although fine motor control did not seem to be related to the child's ability to match letters to sounds.

Preschool children rarely move beyond the beginning stages of phoneme-based spelling. Many will reach that phase of spelling in kindergarten; others not until first grade. If preschool teachers are aware of the full progression of word-creation development, they can support the continued growth of all children in their classrooms, wherever they fall on the developmental continuum. If teachers know what kind of word-creation strategy a child is likely to use next, they can plan activities and interact with individual children in ways that nudge them toward the next level for them.

Conclusions: Learning That Looks Aren't Everything in Making Words

The samples in this chapter illustrate how much preschoolers learn about using written language, and how much is left for most of them to learn as they continue on in kindergarten (and beyond). They first attempt to write words by using the letters in their names and copying letters and words from the environment. Until children figure out that letters are mapped to speech, their "words" are mock letter strings that look like words but are not. As children realize that sounds in words are represented by letters, they begin to attempt phoneme-based spellings, but first represent very few of the sounds in a word, often only the first. Gradually, they begin to isolate more sounds in words and include more and more letters in the

Figure 24
Invented Spelling

Invented Spelling
Our 1st time to spell

be (bee)

frog (frog)

bar (bear)

hat (hat)

Bt (bat) Alston

KAT (cat) Eqa

B F D (bird) Shardrell

bot (boat) Deborah

t re (tree) Angel

F R K (fork) Anastasia

C K (cake) Tiffany

Got (goat) Faith

MPs (mouse) Steven

MMON (moon) Noah

Q s (dog) Ashton

BED (bed) Teyonna

raD (rabbit) Johnathan

R (star) Katelyn

BIL (ball) Da'Kerian

AAS (house) Christian

words they try to write. Eventually, and usually not until they are in kindergarten or first grade, children represent most of the sounds that actually make up a word they try to spell.

Teachers can help children by offering opportunities for them to play with language, to explore letters and sounds, and to experiment with writing. Teachers also can write with children, using a process in which words are sounded out and letters are used to write them after they are named. Specific ways to structure the classroom to facilitate writing development will be elaborated on in Chapter 5.

Supporting Preschool Children's Writing

C hildren's progress in moving from scribbles to script and from let-ter strings to phonemic spelling addresses only part of a child's de-velopment as a writer. As we have indicated in previous chapters, while children grapple with symbol formation and word making, they also develop an increasingly sophisticated understanding of how meaning can be conveyed. They figure out that writing has many purposes and takes many forms. Preschool teachers can help children develop this aspect of writing, just as they can help with other aspects.

Supporting Oral Composition

One of the most important things to understand about preschool children's message creation is that it rests on oral language. As was discussed in Chapter 2, children first learn to compose through talk—when they tell stories about events in their lives at home, retell stories from favorite books or television shows, act out story lines in their dramatic play, explain their drawings or paintings, or talk about something of interest in the classroom. As part of encouraging children to talk, teachers often ask for more infor-mation. As Roberto tells about the hedgehog he encountered in the petting zoo, he is likely to be asked, "Did you pet it? What did it feel like? Did it stick you? How big was it? Did the lady feed it? What did it eat?" As Roberto responds, he learns to extend his explanations to include more informa-tion. He is also learning to consider what his audience—classmates and teacher—wants to know. Roberto and his classmates are socialized into thinking through what they say during shared interactions. Teachers can also help children more directly to extend their oral language, as we saw in Chapter 1 when Gretchen's teacher elicited the full story of her stitches. The skills that children develop through these kinds of oral language inter-actions are exactly those they need if they are to grow as writers.

As children are drawn into oral language in preschool classrooms, they begin to internalize the many functions that it serves. For example, they learn to use language to name and label things, and to describe things and events. They also learn to use language to make their needs known, to request help, and to persuade others to join them in play. Once engaged in play, they use language to create scenarios and to direct play actions. All of these functions of language are also accomplished later through writing.

The more varied the young children's uses of oral language, the more varied are their later uses of written language. A child who has learned to speak up to ask classmates to leave his block structure standing will eventually recognize that he can make a sign that says, "Don't knock this down!" A child who wants to tell everyone all about her pet tarantula will discover that she can draw a picture and compose a message about the tarantula to share. What children learn to do with oral language, they also do in writing.

Providing Opportunities for Oral and Written Composition

Teachers can do many things to help young children move from oral composition to graphic expressions of meaning, including writing. In dramatic play centers, for example, children explore storytelling as they act out scenarios from their everyday lives or reenact stories they have heard from books. Equally important, they create fantasy scenarios in which story lines are developed and plots are carried forward by actions (Edwards, 1990; Kavanaugh & Engle, 1998; McCaslin, 1996). Teachers can extend the language in children's play by participating occasionally in it. One teacher, having observed that two children playing veterinarian in a dramatic play center were losing interest in their roles, brought over a stuffed dog and said, "My dog got hit by a car! Can you help?" The children promptly began examining the dog, giving each other directions for taking X-rays, bandaging a hurt paw, and prescribing medicine for the injured animal. One child even offered advice to the pet owner about preventing her dog from getting out of the yard. By intervening briefly and responsively in the children's play, the teacher extended their play scenario and the actions and language they used.

This play scenario can easily be extended to incorporate written language. A veterinarian's office (or a shoe store, restaurant, or bakery), if equipped with relevant literacy props, will prompt writing. A veterinarian's office, for example, could include prescription pads, receipts, an appointment book, and a notepad for writing instructions for follow-up care. Children will use all forms of writing that we have described in earlier chapters, which range from scribbles to letter strings and early phonemic spelling. Just as in extending oral language in dramatic play, teachers can join the play in strategic ways to nudge children toward using writing props. For example, the teacher who took her dog to the vet could have asked the children for a receipt and to schedule a follow-up appointment. Such requests would help children experiment with specific functions of writing and also encourage them to include writing as an integral part of their pretend play (Christie, 1991; Kieff & Casbergue, 1999; Roskos & Neuman, 1993).

Figure 25 is an example of the kind of writing that can result when preschool dramatic play centers are equipped with appropriate writing materials. Hannah's classroom's housekeeping center was equipped with a notepad and a small bulletin board on the "kitchen" counter. Hannah and her friends were getting ready to go out for the evening, which included leaving their children with a babysitter. Hannah began the note to the baby sitter by writing the name of her child, Ben (actually the name of her older brother—a very familiar word indeed). She then explained that she could be reached at the phone number on the first line. Note that she did not write her real phone number but rather something visually similar to a phone number. This behavior is similar to the mock word behavior, based

Figure 25
Hannah's Note to a Babysitter

on visual knowledge about words, which we described in Chapter 4. The phone number contained six digits, although the final digit was a letter not a number. The remaining lines of apparent scribble were instructions for feeding the baby and putting him to bed. Hannah confided that she wrote the instructions in script like her mommy's handwriting. Clearly the dramatic play center and one of the writing props included functioned to bring an opportunity for composing into Hannah's play.

Children can also be prompted to incorporate writing into their block play. Block play includes considerable dramatic play, as children build pretend skyscrapers, houses, and hospitals, and use miniature cars, trucks, police cruisers, ambulances and play figures to enact scenes from city life. It is common for preschoolers to supplement model traffic signs that are provided with their own handwritten signs and to create labels for buildings and streets. Simply placing markers and appropriately sized paper, tongue depressors, and masking tape in the block center is sometimes enough to encourage writing for these purposes, although teachers sometimes need to suggest such activities in order to nudge children to do the same. Children also sometimes create bus tickets, and "do not enter" or "open" and "closed" signs to support their block play.

Teachers also sometimes directly prompt writing in the block center. In the midst of the construction boom that followed a hurricane in one community, a teacher noticed that children were very aware of the large numbers of construction workers gathered each morning in the parking lot of a nearby building supply store. She considered setting up a home construction store as a dramatic play area in which children could work through their ideas about the influx of strangers into their community. She realized, however, that the block center was already serving that purpose as the children acted out stopping at the store (the block shelves) to select lumber before heading to their "job sites."

She capitalized on the children's interests by sharing nonfiction picture books about construction and engaging children in a shared writing activity in which they created lists of building supplies and construction equipment. Finally, she joined the children in the block center as they played, using writing materials already there, to model writing out an order for building supplies. She also drew a simple plan for rebuilding a garage—a frequently seen construction project in the area around the school. The children quickly joined in, filling her order with blocks and tools and then helping her build her garage. Almost immediately after she left her order form and plan on the top of the block shelf, children began to use her models to create orders of their own before selecting blocks. Figure 26 shows 4-year-old Tyler in the process of doing just that. Over the next few weeks, children's own lists of supplies and plans for buildings filled the block area.

Even though Tyler's block center writing was mostly conventional in form—real words—it is important to remember that many children will use scribble writing or letter string words to fulfill the same purposes. Frequently, the writing children do in dramatic play is not intended to represent a specific message. Rather, writing is simply part of acting out a pretend scenario that emulates adult activities, not much different from cooking and serving pretend meals. Pretending to create an order form is much more important to the play than what the form actually says.

Figure 26
Tyler's Block Center Writing

Just as teachers have a role in encouraging writing during play, it is also important for preschool teachers to foster children's ability to share information through informational (expository) writing. While some children may engage fairly easily in sharing information, most need encouragement. Preschoolers are generally accustomed to talking about their immediate activities and surroundings. This type of talk is most often narrative in form. Informational composition, however, requires children to use a less familiar style of language. This type of writing is best supported when children are provided with lots of content to talk and write about.

To engage children with interesting content, teachers can provide a well-equipped **discovery center**. Such a center contains objects for children to observe and handle (for example, a pet canary in a cage, a bird nest, and some feathers), as well as informational picture books related to the objects. These books should be shared with the children during read-aloud sessions and also displayed in a way that invites children to explore them in the discovery center. It doesn't matter that the children can't read the books independently. Considerable information can be obtained and discussed as children examine the pictures and compare them to the artifacts in the discovery center. Figure 27 shows how simple and inviting such a display can be.

The information children derive from the artifacts and books in the classroom can be shared through both oral and written language. Inviting children to dictate pages to create "all about" books related to specific topics extends both oral language and children's recognition that what they say can be written down. In one preschool classroom, the 4-year-olds spent three weeks studying "creepy crawlies." The discovery center contained an aquarium housing a tarantula on loan from one of the families; a Japanese cricket cage with a live cricket, also from a child's home; and a variety of insects mounted in magnifying boxes purchased from a teaching supply store. Children went on "bug hunts" in the play yard to find out where different creatures lived and to observe them in their natural habitats. They shared many books with their teachers about insects, spiders, worms, and centipedes. Periodically throughout this time of exploration, children were invited to draw pictures and dictate information about their favorite creatures for inclusion in a class book. As the following examples illustrate, children's contributions at the beginning of their investigation included simple phrases or personalized narrations, possibly reflecting children's relative lack of knowledge about the topic, and lack of interest.

Figure 27
Discovery Center Display

• • • • • • • • • • • • • •

Eric: Lizard. I like a lizard.

Max: I like spiders. And I like spider webs too. I like spiders when they're on the spider webs.

Gabriella: Doodlebugs always roll up when you touch them. They always tickle when they're on your hand.

• • • • • • • • • • • • • •

Many children included more information for dictations that were taken later in their investigation of creepy crawlies, which suggested that the more knowledge children gained, the more information they had to share, and the more interested they became in the topic. As the investigation continued, the teacher also engaged in more extended conversations with children about what they were learning and used those conversations to draw out more information as children dictated what they wanted to say about the pictures they drew. The increase in information can be seen in the following example.

• • • • • • • • • • • • • • • •

Teacher: Kate, what do you want me to write to go with your picture?

Kate: [pointing to her picture of three snakes] Snakes.

Teacher: Is there anything else you want me to write?

Kate: I like snakes.

Teacher: I know you really like looking at our books about snakes. What snakes do you like best?

Kate: I like purple ones and rattlesnakes and milk snakes and coral snakes.

• • • • • • • • • • • • • • • •

Thus, in response to brief discussion about her picture, Kate was able to express very specific knowledge that would not have been evident from either her picture or her first responses to her teacher's query about what should be written on her page of the class book. Similar conversations about their pictures resulted in even more detailed dictations from Leo, Caitlin, and Tyrone as seen in the information they dictated.

• • • • • • • • • • • • • • • •

Leo: Ladybugs. They spit a yellow liquid so birds can't eat them. They eat bad bugs. They eat leaves. They're red and orange. They have a back with spots and red.

Caitlin: Butterflies. They fly and they eat other bugs. And they eat plants. They lay their eggs on plants.

Tyrone: Ladybugs. I learned about not to mush them. To hold them careful. They live in the grass. They eat those green bugs.

• • • • • • • • • • • • • • • •

Written Composition and the Writing Center

While it is clear from the preschoolers' dictations that some children have a lot to say about topics in which they have an interest, it is also clear, upon examination of these children's written attempts, that their writing lags behind their oral language. This is typical. Just as babies can understand many more words than they are able to say, so too can preschoolers construct oral compositions that are more sophisticated than they can convey in writing.

The writing sample in Figure 28 is Christopher's attempt to write his page for the class book about insects. He read it to his teacher as, "Spiders. Poison. Spiders live on rocks." Christopher indicated that the objects on the left in his composition were rocks and spider webs, while other lines were the words. While he had not yet developed a conventional understanding of writing, he was beginning to develop a good sense of how to convey information about a specific topic.

The gap between what children can write and their oral composition ability is equally evident in their narratives. Figure 29 represents 4-year-old Emily's story about a flower. The only conventional writing in this sample is her name. She asked her teacher to write down the story that went with her picture, signaling an understanding of the difference between drawing and writing. Emily's dictations revealed that she was developing into a competent storyteller.

Figure 28
Christopher's Page for an Insect Book

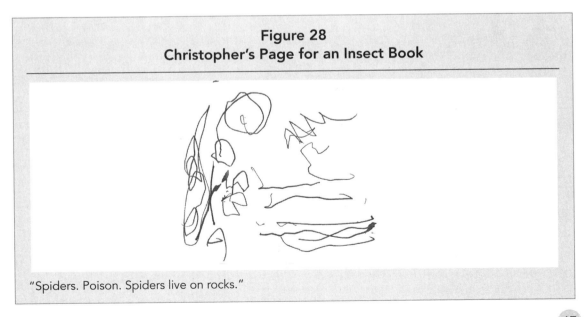

"Spiders. Poison. Spiders live on rocks."

Figure 29
Emily's Flower Story

- - - - - - - - - - - - - - -

Once upon a time, there was a flower. It was snowing and it froze to death. It didn't have any water forever and ever. And then one day it did get some water because the person saw it wasn't going to get any water. "Mom, our flower did get some." And along came an ant that said, "I'm going to eat you, flower." But the ant was joking. And I hope you feel better flower because it's still freezing but it did get water. The flower felt better because it found a lake and thought it would be fun.

- - - - - - - - - - - - - - -

While the plot of her story is somewhat disjointed, it is clear that Emily understood that stories have conflict—in this case a flower freezing to death without water and being threatened by an ant—and that stories end when the conflict is resolved. While she didn't yet have the ability to write her story using print, she was nonetheless successful in composing it.

Both Christopher and Emily's compositions were created in their classroom writing centers. Just as children benefit from opportunities to write in dramatic play centers, block areas, and at discovery tables—all with teacher's support and encouragement—they also benefit from time and materials that enable them to write independently, for their own purposes, using whatever form of writing they wish. While Emily's "writing" was composed entirely of pictures, with the exception of her name, Christopher included writing, in the form of scribble placed beside his picture of rocks and spider webs. In both cases, the writing center offered the children the freedom to experiment with composition or forms of writing.

A well-equipped writing center contains a variety of writing implements, including thin and thick markers, regular and colored pencils, and pens. It also has paper of different sizes, colors, and textures, to encourage children's exploration. White paper cut in half and stapled together to make blank books invites extended writing that moves well beyond simple labeled drawings or lists, to stories, descriptions and explanations.

This was certainly the case for one a 4-year-old girl, who taped three blank books together to create a book with 36 pages. Figure 30 includes examples of the kinds of writing she used to fill her pages. She had decided to write a book about fairies and labeled her cover page as such (Figure 30a). Her story begins on the second page where she writes, "One day the fairies went out and they saw a toad" (Figure 30b). Careful examination of that page reveals that the child was aware of the alphabetic principle and used it to invent spellings for the words *one* ("we"), *and* ("ad"), *saw* ("sald"), and *toad* ("tad"). She spelled three words conventionally: *the, out,* and *they.* The remaining letters may be less obvious attempts to spell the remaining words. It is also possible that the child wrote more words than she remembered when she later read her composition aloud to her teacher, thus accounting for the apparent mismatch between her reading and the words on the page.

As shown in Figure 30c, the child continued her story on page 3 with a brief attempt at invented spelling for *there was* ("the wys") followed by a string of letters and then very detailed lines of scribble writing. This page

Figure 30
Child's Fairy Book

30a Book cover: "The Fairies"

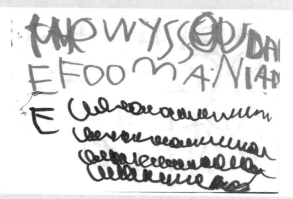

30b p. 2: "One day, the fairies went out and they saw a toad."

30c p. 3: One page of mixed letters and scribble—"There was…"

(continued)

Figure 30 *(continued)*

30d 8 pages of this—6 lines of detailed scribble per page.

30e 13 pages like this—4 lines of less detailed scribble per page.

30f 10 pages like this—only 3 lines of scribble per page, and not detailed.

(continued)

Figure 30 *(continued)*

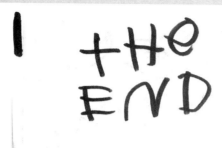

30g Back cover: "The End"—child knew these words as sight words from having seen them in many stories.

is followed by 8 pages of scribble with 6 lines per page (Figure 30d), then 13 pages containing 4 lines each of less detailed scribble (Figure 30e), and finally 10 pages with only 3 lines each of sprawling, apparently hastily drawn scribble (Figure 30f). The back cover of her book returns to conventional writing with "The End" (Figure 30g). It is evident that this child tried to complete the task she had set for herself—writing a 36-page book about fairies—she found that she could not sustain the level of attention to detail with which she began.

The use of multiple strategies and forms of writing within a single sample is not uncommon among preschoolers. Even as children discover more advanced ways to write, they simply add those forms at first to the kinds of writing they already know best how to use. They move back and forth freely among forms, depending on their intentions and the functions they want their writing to serve. The availability of several strategies in children's repertoires is a well-documented phenomenon in all aspects of development. Changes in development occur as the dominance of the various strategies change and as new ones are added to a child's repertoire (Siegler, 1996). What matters most during the preschool years is providing opportunities that allow children to follow their intentions. Teachers can offer the materials and support children as they attempt to write in new ways. Without a well stocked writing center and ample time during the day to choose their own activities, it is unlikely that children will be able to engage in explorations of writing that are as extensive the child who wrote the book about fairies.

Conclusions: Connecting Oral Composing and Writing

The samples of children's oral and written compositions in this chapter offer compelling evidence that young children can and will write for a variety of purposes and will use a variety of different forms. Their ability is supported by teachers who provide many opportunities for both oral language and writing in their classrooms. Children will express themselves through dramatic play, if teachers join the play in ways that encourage children to extend the scenarios they enact and provide materials that encourage writing as an integral part of their pretense.

Teachers can further enhance children's oral and written language abilities by engaging them with interesting content. The more children that have to talk about, the more they will eventually have to write about—whether they dictate it to their teachers or write it independently, in some form. Classrooms filled with interesting objects, books, and activities invite children to talk—to their parents, their teachers, and to one another. With the support of caring teachers, all of this language can be channeled into opportunities for children to engage with written language.

CHAPTER 6

Assessing Writing Development in the Early Years

Educators at every level are faced with increasing calls for account-ability, which often translate into requirements to assess children's learning. In the United States, federal mandates have focused a spot-light on literacy learning, which has heightened discussion about the im-portance of ensuring that all children arrive at kindergarten ready to benefit from the more focused literacy instruction that characterizes the start of formal schooling.

Preschool teachers, too, must assess children's progress. While rarely required to administer formal, standardized assessments, they are expected to be aware of each child's progress and to design teacher-directed instruc-tion as well as play opportunities that accommodate children's varying lev-els of skill. At the preschool level, this can be done by carefully observing and documenting children's demonstrations of progress. In terms of writ-ing development, teachers document changes by taking note of the varied ways that children attempt to write and by preserving samples of children's drawing and writing, over a period of time.

Capturing Multiple Dimensions of Writing

The previous chapters have demonstrated that children's writing develop-ment is multidimensional. That is, children must learn how to make marks, moving from scribbles to recognizable alphabet letters. They must also learn to create words, starting with strings of symbols (i.e., mock letters), without any consideration of representing sounds, and moving gradually to the use of letters that are selected to represent sounds in spoken words. At the same time, they are also learning how to create messages that range from simple labels to stories and other kinds of compositions that share information. Full assessment of children's writing development requires a teacher to examine all of these dimensions simultaneously because—as il-lustrated in previous chapters—children might, for example, be fairly advanced in message creation, while using only rudimentary drawings with little use of print, sometimes at the scribble level.

Comprehensive writing assessment also requires careful attention to the contexts within which children write. A child might use early phonemic spelling when writing a story at the writing center but use lines of letter strings or scribble to create a pretend grocery list in dramatic play. If samples from dramatic play are the only ones considered, teachers might underestimate children's level of skill. Conversely, examining children's written products without observing how they were produced can lead to a teacher to conclude that children know more than they actually do.

Consider the picture in Figure 31. The child on the left wanted to write an invitation for a pretend party. Her teacher explained that an invitation should include the time and place of the event, as well as the hostesses' names. In other words, the child did not create this message by herself. Instead, she was told what this cultural artifact should say. Given the circumstances, the teacher would not be able to judge, on the basis of this writing sample alone, the child's true message-creation skill. But the teacher watched as the child wrote: "6:30 Com To the PRPt FROm Lara Beth Grayson" by herself. Her marks, all conventional numbers and letters, and words—both invented and conventionally spelled—were produced independently and revealed very sophisticated skill on these dimensions of writing.

Notice that the child on the right in Figure 31 is also creating an invitation. She used her classmate's model, however, carefully copying the lines of print. It is not possible, therefore, to draw conclusions about the second child's independent level of skill given her reliance on the support offered by both the teacher and the first child. Had the teacher examined the two pieces of writing, without having observed their creation, she might have drawn some erroneous conclusions about the skills of each child.

As this example illustrates, simply gathering and preserving writing samples as the only means of documenting children's writing development is insufficient. All samples, or at least a majority, should be accompanied by anecdotal notes—brief descriptions of how and where the writing was produced, including who was present, what help they provided, the questions a child asked, whether the child copied writing from some source, and so on. Only then can a teacher analyze the samples accurately to determine the child's understandings and skills. An anecdotal note to accompany the first child's invitation might read as follows.

Figure 31
Writing an Invitation During Dramatic Play

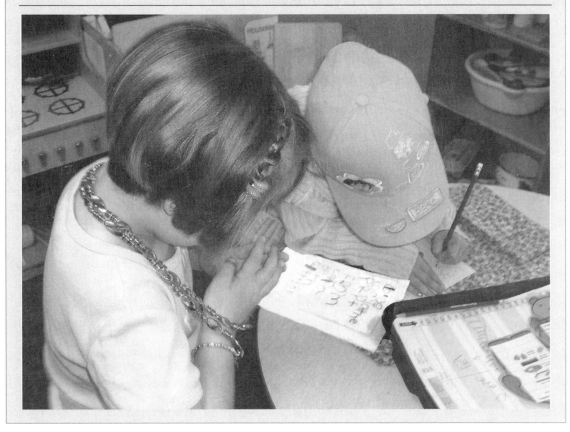

Grayson initiated invitation writing during dramatic play. Teacher helped decide what to write. Wrote independently after discussion. First time she included vowels in invented spelling (*com*). Later helped Laura copy invitation.

To be useful, a good anecdotal note should provide enough context for the teacher to later remember the situation in which the writing occurred. A collection of such samples and anecdotal notes, gathered over time, serves multiple purposes. The samples capture and make visible children's writing development, provide tangible documentation to support a teacher's conclusions about children's skill levels, and provide evidence to share with parents, the child's future teachers, and administrators who might not otherwise understand the rich variety of ways in which children's writing develops.

The Continuum of Development for Early Writing

While it is fairly easy to describe the context within which specific writing samples are created, analyzing the samples is trickier, precisely because so many different skills develop simultaneously, and because specific contexts affect what and how children write. The continuum of writing development that follows provides an overview of each dimension (marks, word creation, and messages) and includes samples of writing to illustrate movement from simple to more advanced skills levels within each dimension. Preschool teachers can compare samples of writing and drawing collected from children in their own classrooms to the examples in the continuum to determine each child's developmental progress. Teachers can use this knowledge of children's writing development to tailor the instructional activities and manipulative materials they provide and to structure their interactions with children according to individual strengths and needs.

Marks

This part of the continuum concerns the physical characteristics of the marks children use when their intention is to write. Typically, when young children first intend to represent meanings, they draw rather than write. The continuum provided here, however, includes only levels of writing marks, not levels of picture making. You may wish to consult other resources to learn about levels of development for drawing and painting, such as Gardner (1980) or Kellogg and O'Dell (1967). Writing mark levels include (1) scribble, (2) mock letters, (3) actual letters (rudimentary approximations), (4) actual letters (closer approximations), and (5) actual letters (conventional). The most common levels seen in the preschool years are levels 1 through 3—which we discuss in the sections that follow—although some older preschoolers reach levels 4 and 5.

Children first use scribble marks for writing. Development within scribble writing moves from (1) marks organized very much like scribble drawings (i.e., no linear arrangement), to (2) continuous linear scribble without much internal detail, to (3) continuous linear scribble with internal detail, to (4) discrete scribble marks arranged in a line (see Figure 32). Determining whether a picture-like scribble is writing rather than drawing requires knowledge of the context and the child's intentions (e.g., child turns a collage paper over, scribbles on the back, and says, "I did my name").

When children notice the ways that lines are combined to make alphabet letters, they begin to create mock letters—forms that look very much like the "real thing" (see Figure 33). Many preschoolers do not yet

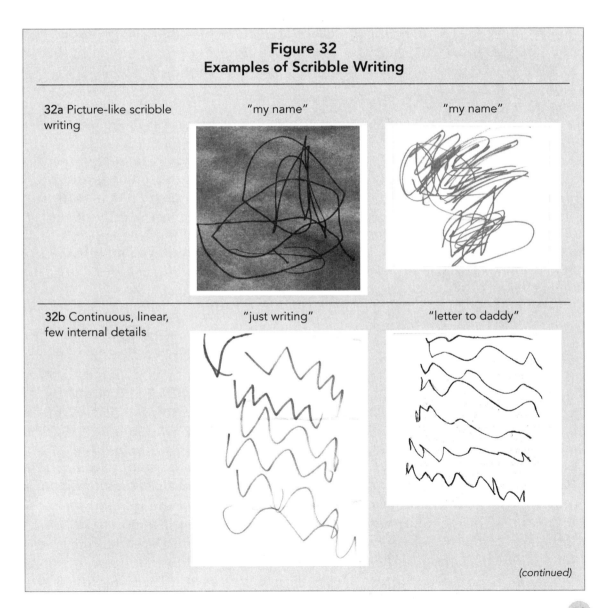

Figure 32
Examples of Scribble Writing

32a Picture-like scribble writing   "my name"   "my name"

32b Continuous, linear, few internal details   "just writing"   "letter to daddy"

(continued)

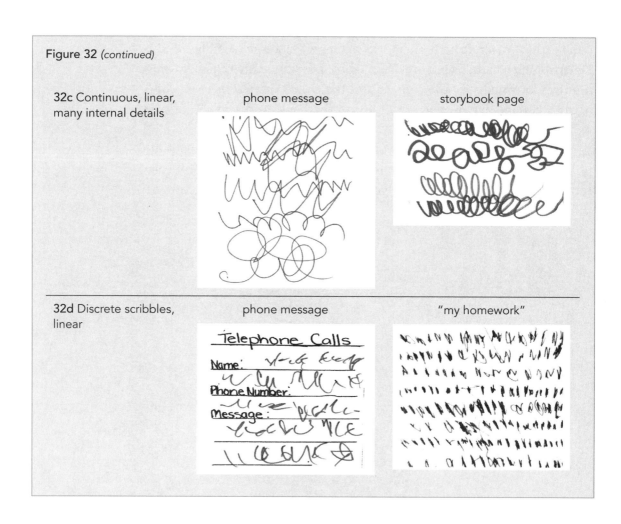

Figure 32 *(continued)*

32c Continuous, linear, many internal details

phone message

storybook page

32d Discrete scribbles, linear

phone message

"my homework"

Telephone Calls
Name:
Phone Number:
Message:

know that there are only 26 alphabet letters in the English alphabet, with a big and small form for each one. They might think there are countless letters that they have not yet seen and they create forms that are good possibilities! Often, preschoolers' mock letters are mixed in with actual letter forms, because they seem to assume that the mock letters they create *could* be real letters, just ones they have not yet encountered in their environment.

Children's first actual letters are rudimentary—just a beginning. Their lines "wobble," overrun stopping points, are sometimes substitutions for a line in the conventional letter, are placed to create atypical proportions, and are often reversed (see Figure 34a). Over the preschool and kindergarten years, children's letters gradually develop into forms that resemble the conventional forms more closely (see Figure 34b) and then match the conventional forms (see Figure 34c). Children's skill in forming specific letters

Figure 33
Examples of Mock Letters

33a

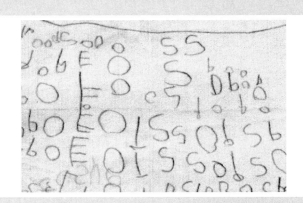

33b

33c

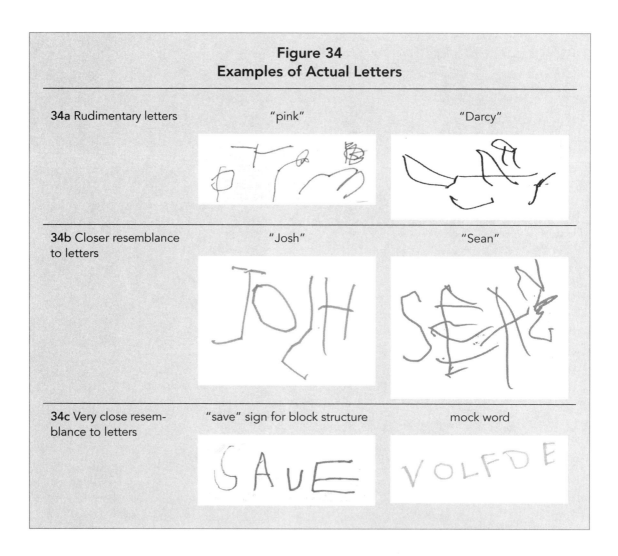

Figure 34
Examples of Actual Letters

34a Rudimentary letters | "pink" | "Darcy"

34b Closer resemblance to letters | "Josh" | "Sean"

34c Very close resemblance to letters | "save" sign for block structure | mock word

is not "all or none" but varies across different letters. Some are harder to form than others, and a child's experience with different letters also affects skill in writing them. Preschoolers often can form best the first letter in their names, perhaps because they have focused on this letter the most when viewing their names, or because they have written only this letter for a period of time to stand for their entire name.

Even though a few preschool children write letters that are fully conventional, this is the exception not the rule. Forming letters conventionally requires fine motor skill beyond what is typical for most preschoolers, along with very detailed knowledge of letter features and how to combine lines to create these.

Word-Creation Strategies

This part of the continuum concerns the process children use to combine letters to make words. At first, children only have knowledge of how words look from having seen words in their environment, and they string letters together to make what looks like a word. The words created in this way are called mock words because they are nonphonemic—do not take into account the sound a letter actually represents (see Figure 35a). Children who create mock words have no idea why specific letters make up various words.

When children first realize that speech and print are related, their level of phonological awareness is typically only at the syllabic level. Children sometimes write words that reflect this awareness, but use any

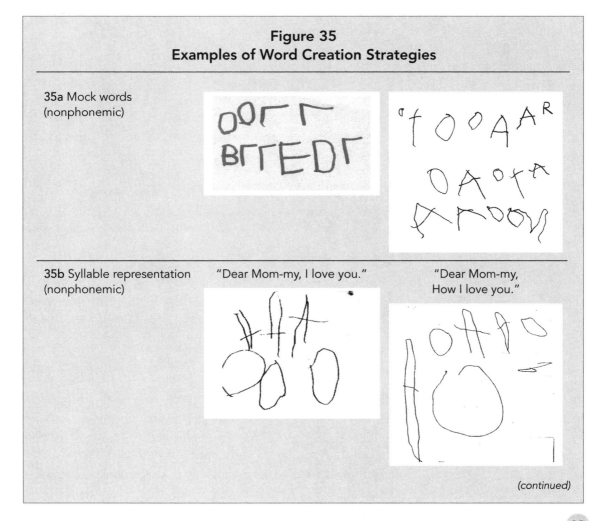

Figure 35
Examples of Word Creation Strategies

35a Mock words
(nonphonemic)

35b Syllable representation
(nonphonemic)

"Dear Mom-my, I love you."

"Dear Mom-my, How I love you."

(continued)

Figure 35 *(continued)*

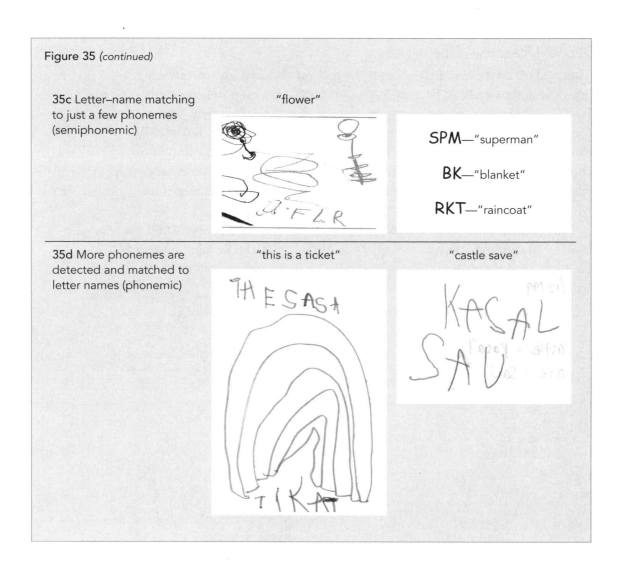

35c Letter–name matching to just a few phonemes (semiphonemic)	"flower"	SPM—"superman" BK—"blanket" RKT—"raincoat"
35d More phonemes are detected and matched to letter names (phonemic)	"this is a ticket"	"castle save"

letter in their repertoire to represent the syllable "beats" they hear in a word (see Figure 35b). These words are also nonphonemic because letters are still used without regard to their assigned sound values.

In time, children do begin to create spellings that are based on an awareness of sound in words at the phoneme level and on the knowledge that letters are used selectively to represent specific sounds in spoken words. Children often use their letter–name knowledge to select letters to represent a sound or two they hear in a word (see Figure 35c). Soft vowels and other sounds in the middle of words are omitted. Children usually represent some sounds from the beginning and end of a word. Gradually, children develop more skill in detecting more of the individual sounds they hear in words, and they also know more letter names to use in matching to these sounds (see Figure 35d). This level of development is sometimes seen in some preschoolers, but not in most.

Levels of Messages

This part of the continuum concerns the content of a child's writing—the meaning a child wants to capture—and the kind of representation used to convey the meaning. One way to judge a message's content level is to consider its length and complexity (see Figure 36). A long story is a higher level message than is a single label for an item drawn; a sentence dictated to describe a drawing is a higher level message than is a label. The appropriateness of a message, of course, depends in part on context. For example, a sign for a play grocery store might have a single label for each food pictured, because this is suitable for a sign. If a child is writing a story, however, or describing how caterpillars grew into butterflies, a more detailed

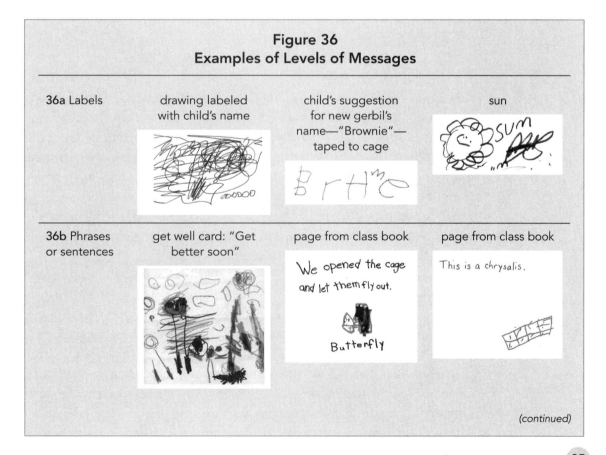

Figure 36
Examples of Levels of Messages

36a Labels

drawing labeled with child's name

child's suggestion for new gerbil's name—"Brownie"— taped to cage

sun

36b Phrases or sentences

get well card: "Get better soon"

page from class book

We opened the cage and let them fly out.

Butterfly

page from class book

This is a chrysalis.

(continued)

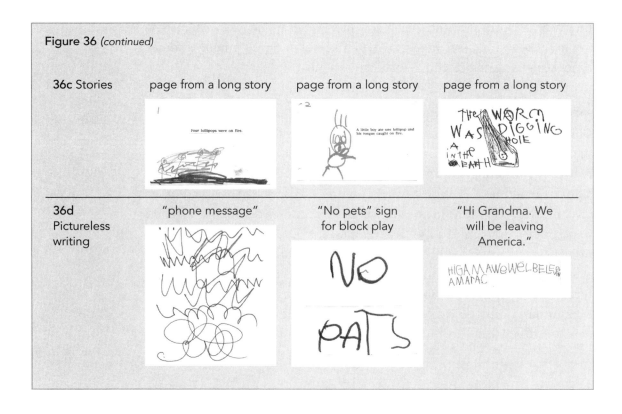

Figure 36 *(continued)*

36c Stories

page from a long story | page from a long story | page from a long story

36d
Pictureless
writing

"phone message" | "No pets" sign for block play | "Hi Grandma. We will be leaving America."

message is both possible and suitable. To judge the length and complexity of a child's messages, one considers the context and uses the highest level where it is appropriate to create a long message. To determine program support for message creation, one looks at whether most samples from a class are simple labels or include messages that go beyond these to descriptions of events and to whole stories. It does not matter in judging a message's content level whether the child uses writing-like marks or actual letters, or whether the teacher wrote down the message a child dictated. The focus is the level of the message the child composes.

A second way to look at the level of written messages is to consider the kind of representational vehicle a child uses. Often, preschoolers use pictures alone to represent their meaning and then support the message with oral explanations. Sometimes, preschoolers combine pictures and writing marks to represent their meaning while continuing to rely on oral language to convey the full meaning, given that neither graphic system alone or even the two combined can do this. Sometimes, preschoolers use only writing marks to convey their meanings, and these can be understood without oral support. More often, however, preschoolers' writing marks need the child's oral interpretation because the marks are unconventional. Sometimes, when a child's writing could convey a meaning by itself, it is customary for the artifact created to have illustrations. For all of these reasons, levels of message must be judged with care by considering a variety of samples, collected from a wide variety of social circumstances.

Conclusions: Understanding What Children Are Learning

Preschool teachers must be able to assess children's writing development, simultaneously, across multiple dimensions. Accurate assessment requires capturing and analyzing examples of children's writing, over time, and from multiple contexts. Teachers must note details of the situations in which writing is produced, including the child's intentions and any support the child received, from written sources in the environment, from peers, or from adults.

For this type of assessment information to be useful, teachers must analyze writing examples for indications of progress in development. Teachers can use the continuum of writing development provided in this chapter to help them recognize significant developmental differences among various pieces of writing. Use of this continuum helps a teacher assess all dimensions of writing skill, which is necessary if a complete and rich picture of a child's writing development is to be obtained.

CHAPTER 7

Home–School Connections

A s we discussed in Chapter 6, teachers can assess children's develop-ing understanding of writing through careful observation of chil-dren's writing behavior and examination of the artifacts they produce. Teachers must always keep in mind that the writing children do in the classroom tells only part of the story. A child's drawing and writing at home add rich information to the overall picture of the child's writing inter-ests and progress. Some children even produce more writing at home than at school, perhaps because, for some children, the home setting provides different and more inspiring purposes for writing. Enlisting parents and other primary caregivers as partners in assessing and supporting preschool-ers' writing development helps everyone gain a clearer picture of how a child understands the functions, forms, and meanings of written language.

Fully engaging all of the adults in children's lives in supporting and assessing a preschoolers' literacy development acknowledges that all fami-lies have strengths and can help their children achieve (Rockwell, Andre, & Hawley, 1996). As teachers communicate with parents and other caregivers about children's literacy development, they also gain insight into how fam-ily situations help shape each child's learning. Moreover, as they learn what prompts children to write at home, they gain insights for adapting class-room activities for use with diverse populations.

Strategies for Connecting Home and School

As we demonstrated in Chapter 6, the most appropriate literacy assess-ments for young children are informal and observational (Morrow & Smith, 1990). It is relatively easy for teachers to enlist parents' help in gath-ering information that will increase their understanding of children's writ-ing development. In both home and school settings, children's writing behavior can be observed, with samples then shared and discussed. Teachers can encourage parents to watch for any signs of drawing and writing by children at home and to share samples and information about what they observed with teachers at school. Hannah's mother brought the sample shown in Figure 37 to school. She had watched and listened while Hannah gathered stuffed animals and dolls, "conducted a meeting," and took notes on a stenographer's pad, borrowed from her mom's desk.

Hannah's meeting "minutes" are a series of linear scribbles. During a brief interaction with Hannah's mother when she dropped Hannah off at school, Hannah's teacher was able to point out that Hannah knew that writing was created in lines, from left to right, and that writing could be used to write down things to be remembered, such as an important discussion at a meeting.

Not long after this, Hannah's mom sent in the sample shown in Figure 38 with a note that said, "Hannah had another meeting." When Hannah's mother picked her up that afternoon, she also pointed out to Hannah's teacher that Hannah had attempted to write her name at the top of the page. The teacher then noted that unlike in the first sample, Hannah had written a series of separate figures this time. Her writing behavior suggested that she had made an important discovery—that print is composed of distinct letters.

Hannah's teacher also drew the mother's attention to what appeared to be Hannah's name, printed again at the bottom of the page, and also to the writing on the left side of the page, which appeared to move in a different

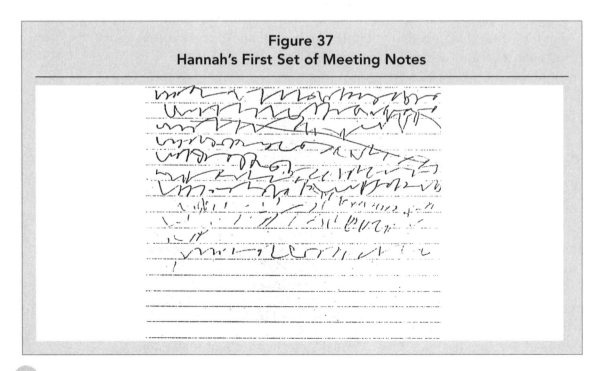

Figure 37
Hannah's First Set of Meeting Notes

Figure 38
Hannah's Second Set of Meeting Notes

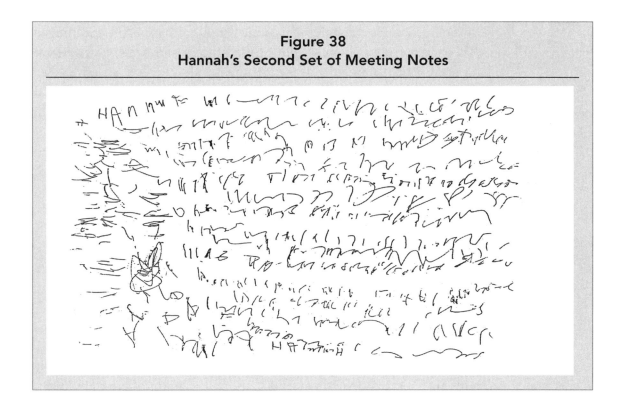

direction than the rest of the lines. The teacher explained that children Hannah's age often use space creatively, turning the paper to fill up empty margins when they run out of space at the bottom of a page. Hannah's mother confirmed that she had often seen Hannah turning a paper around and around as she wrote, and both women agreed that Hannah must have had a long meeting!

The pleasurable, collaborative sharing of stories about Hannah's writing exemplifies the type of interaction with parents and the classroom—a bulletin board just inside the door—on which she posted copies of notes to be sent home, pages for parents to sign up to help in the classroom or to chaperone outings, and space for parents to post pictures and artifacts from home to share with children, teachers, and other parents. When writing samples were brought in, the teacher summarized the parent's story of the writing and placed a copy of the sample and the summary in a folder for the child. The original sample was then posted on the parents' corner display.

This process allowed the teacher to capture a picture of the children's home literacy, to which she could return later for comparison, and it demonstrated the importance of all forms of writing to everyone who perused the board. Samples brought in by some parents also probably encouraged other parents to watch for similar efforts at home and to help them notice more the ways that preschoolers experiment with writing. The desire to see their own children represented on the board might even have prompted some parents to provide their children with writing materials and to join in writing with them.

Establishing comfortable routines for sharing stories of literacy development also can help parents and other caregivers feel comfortable enough with the teacher to discuss their concerns about their child's writing. Parents sometimes are concerned about backward letters or other errors, such as in directionality. These concerns sometimes cause parents to worry that their children might have a learning disability. Teachers can assure parents that letter reversals and inconsistent directionality are perfectly normal during the preschool years, and, in fact, persist for many letters well into first and second grades.

The coloring book pages shown in Figure 39 might cause concern had Daniel's mother not been aware of the normal course of writing development. Three-year-old Daniel colored the page on the left (Figure 39a) by himself at home and then wrote his name on the bottom from right to left, reversing most of the letters. At his request, his aunt colored the page on the right. When both had finished coloring, Daniel proclaimed that his aunt's coloring was better and promptly signed his name to that picture, too, this time writing it from left to right (Figure 39b). When his teacher saw this sample and heard the story about its production, she was able to point out that Daniel was probably using solid logic to determine how to write his name in the coloring book. His rule was to start from the center binding, not from the left, and work out from there. His teacher also marveled at Daniel's ability to flip the letters around spatially to write them. Few adults have that skill!

Daniel's mom laughed as she described Daniel taking credit for his aunt's coloring, and the teacher noted that Daniel seemed to understand the power that writing his name can serve. The teacher's note about this brief sharing included the fact that Daniel was coloring with his aunt, a sign that the extended family was involved in his literacy development. She was sure to post this sample in the parents' corner, knowing that it would provide some reassurance to other parents about the common use of backward writing by preschoolers.

As noted, the parents' corner also allowed parents or other primary caregivers to post pictures of the children engaged in activities at home or

Figure 39
Daniel's Coloring Book Pages

39a

39b

Note. Book pages from Rudin, H. (Ed.). *Big value coloring book.* Copyright 1975 by Waldman Publishing Corp.

on family outings. Photographs of special events, such as a new brother's bris or a Japanese child's celebration of Children's Day with his siblings, prompted both parents and children to share personal stories. Children were encouraged to tell about the people in the pictures and what was happening, a kind of oral storytelling that we discussed in Chapter 5. The teacher also encouraged parents to bring in pictures of the ordinary days in children's lives to affirm the value of everyday family interaction.

Recognizing that not all families had the financial resources to take and print photographs, the teacher obtained an easy-to-operate digital camera through a donation and sent it home each week with a different family. She asked parents to try to "catch" their children reading and writing. Other parents could print pictures on their own. For those using the borrowed camera, the teacher set aside time when it was returned to download and discuss pictures, and to print some for posting in the Parent's Corner.

Figure 40, a photo brought in by Emily's mother, shows Emily and her classmate Stephanie, absorbed with their writing, working amid a variety of paints, paper, and markers on the kitchen table. Figure 41 is a writing sample that Emily's mother brought in to accompany the picture. She described how Emily and Stephanie both contributed to it, alternately drawing and writing, using a variety of scribbles, mock letters, a signature, and other actual letters. This sample provided yet another chance for the teacher to demonstrate that all of these forms of writing were valued. Its placement on the board prompted other parents to bring in similar samples that they recognized as significant after seeing the bulletin board display.

When teachers and parents begin to collaborate about literacy development early on in children's lives, many parents carry forward expectation for involvement as their children move into kindergarten. These expectations encourage parents to advocate for their children and to remain involved in their learning. Hannah's parents demonstrated this when Hannah turned 4 and moved to a new preschool class. Assuming that the new teacher would also want to share observations about Hannah's writing, the child's mother brought in the sample in Figure 42 without waiting for the teacher to ask. The teacher happily discussed the sample with her and learned that Hannah and her dad had written it together, at Hannah's request. At this point, Hannah was aware that writing is done with letters; she spent lots of time, both at home and at school, practicing writing letters. She also knew that words have correct spellings and often asked adults to spell words she wanted to write. Hannah's mother reported that her husband provided all the conventional spellings evident in this piece, while Hannah wrote some words herself, with no effort to map sounds to letters.

Examining this writing sample with Hannah's parents allowed her teacher to see that Hannah's literacy efforts were well supported at home. Adding a copy of this sample and a summary of her conversation with Hannah's mother to Hannah's writing folder provided valuable assessment information. As the folder was filled with additional samples from both home and school, over the course of the school year, a clear picture of Hannah's progress emerged.

Challenges to Collaboration

Teachers who involve parents in observing, documenting, and sharing their preschoolers' experimentation with writing must be prepared for a

Figure 40
Children Writing at Home

Figure 41
Emily and Stephanie's Collaborative Writing

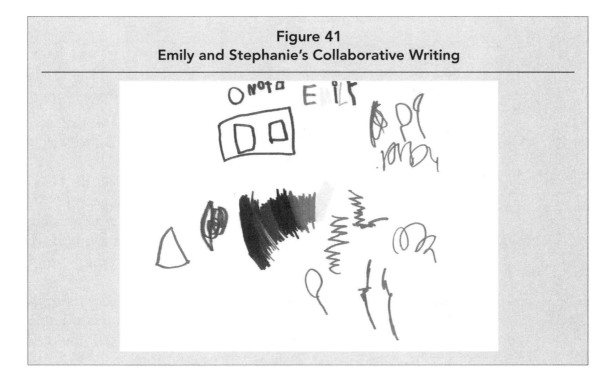

Figure 42
Hannah's Third Writing Sample

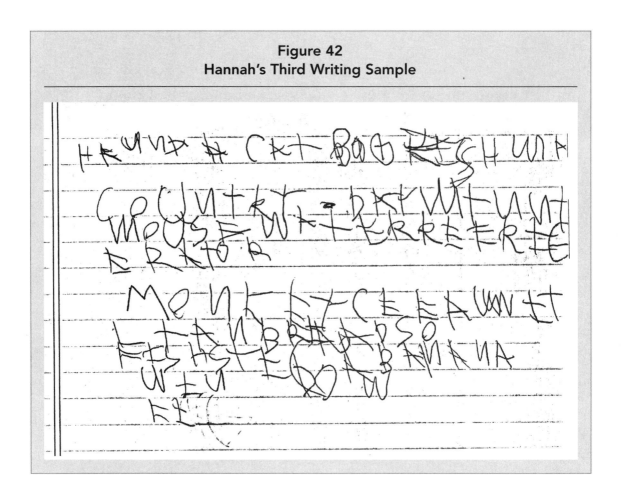

number of challenges. They must recognize how differences in culture, family composition, literacy levels, language, and beliefs about how children become literate affect how parents and caregivers interact with teachers (Lilly & Green, 2004). Teachers need to examine carefully their own assumptions about parents' and caregivers' roles in their children's education and make sure that they keep an open mind they as they hear family stories and find strengths in what is shared (Kieff & Wellhousen, 2000). This is especially true if the behaviors described don't fit the teacher's own experiences and beliefs about home literacy.

Daniel's teacher, for example, frowns on coloring books, preferring open-ended art activities. When Daniel's mother brought in the coloring book pages in Figure 39, his teacher could have used the opportunity to suggest that encouraging the child to color on blank paper might be better. But doing so would have ignored the fact that the child engaged in a valid and valuable literacy interaction with his aunt as part of the coloring book activity. The teacher's choice not to include coloring books in her own classroom, though wise, does not negate the fact that in many homes, these books offer opportunities for wonderful interaction between parents and children.

There are differences of opinion about computer use. Most early childhood educators agree that children benefit little from spending hours of independent, unstructured time in front of a computer screen, especially when the activity replaces more active play with interaction, oral language, and drawing, writing and building. Parents, however, often encourage their preschoolers to spend time with programs designed to foster early literacy. Rather than disapprove of computer use completely, teachers can help parents put computer use into perspective and perhaps consider more carefully what types of computer activity are age appropriate. In terms of writing, most preschoolers will benefit from simply playing with a keyboard in an open-ended word-processing program. If an adult sets the program to use a large font, children can experiment with typing letters and can watch them appear on the screen. Parents can join in this play to name letters as they appear, thus helping children learn to recognize and name letters.

Finally, teachers might discover that parents' views about getting their children ready for kindergarten involve some unrealistic expectations about literacy development. For example, some parents worry that their children aren't developing at a proper rate, and they sometimes ask teachers to engage children in activities that are not appropriate. The previous chapters in this book provide a guide to the typical progression of writing in young children. Teachers can share this information with parents to help them understand and support their children's literacy development.

For more information regarding developmentally appropriate practices, teachers can turn to sources, such as *Learning to Read and Write: Developmentally Appropriate Practices for Young Children* (International Reading Association & National Association for the Education of Young Children, 1998). This position statement includes expectations for children's literacy achievement at different ages, beginning in preschool, and suggests a variety of activities that support this achievement. Also, a national panel on preventing reading difficulties led to the development of a guide for promoting children's early literacy that includes developmental expectations and supportive activities for parents and teachers (Burns, Griffin, & Snow, 1999).

Conclusions: The Promise of Home–School Partnerships

Collaboration with parents requires work, but the results are worth the effort. All parents can offer insight into how their children engage in writing outside the classroom. Bringing parents into frequent conversations about their children, and sharing the joys and concerns embedded in their stories, can unite teachers and families in their resolve to do what is best for individual children. These exchanges also provide opportunities for teachers and parents to develop an appreciation for each other's perspectives on children's learning. This exchange sometimes led families to bring more of the literacy interactions that occur at school into their homes. Equally important, exchanges with families also helps teachers to provide opportunities and interactions in the preschool that match those with which children are comfortable at home.

REFERENCES

Baghban, M. (1984). *Our daughter learns to read and write: A case study from birth to three*. Newark, DE: International Reading Association.

Burns, M.S., Griffin, P., & Snow C.E. (Eds.). (1999). *Starting out right: A guide to promoting children's reading success*. Washington, DC: National Academy Press.

Christie, J.F. (Ed.). (1991). *Play and early literacy development*. Albany: State University of New York Press.

Clay, M.M. (1975). *What did I write? Beginning writing behaviour*. Portsmouth, NH: Heinemann.

Clay, M.M. (1987). *Writing begins at home: Preparing children for writing before they go to school*. Portsmouth, NH: Heinemann.

Dyson, A.H. (1986). Transitions and tensions: Interrelationship between the drawing, talking, and dictating of young children. *Research in the Teaching of English, 20*(4), 379–409.

Dyson, A.H. (1991). The word and the world: Reconceptualizing written language development or, do rainbows mean a lot to little girls? *Research in the Teaching of English, 25*(1), 97–123.

Dyson, A.H. (1992). *From prop to mediator: The changing role of written language in children's symbolic repertoires* (Occasional Paper No. 32). Berkeley: National Center for the Study of Writing, University of California at Berkeley. Retrieved July 21, 2008, from www.nwp.org/cs/public/download/nwp_file/54/OP32.pdf?x-r=pcfile_d

Edwards, L.C. (1990). *Affective development and the creative arts: A process approach to early childhood education*. Columbus, OH: Merrill.

Fields, M.V. (1998). *Your child learns to read and write*. Olney, MD: Association for Childhood Education International.

Gardner, H. (1980). *Artful scribbles: The significance of children's drawings*. New York: Basic Books.

International Reading Association & National Association for the Education of Young Children. (1998). *Learning to read and write: Developmentally appropriate practices for young children*. Newark, DE; Washington, DC: Authors.

Invernizzi, M. (2003). Concepts, sounds, and the ABCs: A diet for the very young reader. In D.M. Barone & L.M. Morrow (Eds.), *Literacy and young children: Research-based practices* (pp. 140–156). New York: Guilford.

Kavanaugh, R., & Engle, S. (1998). The development of pretense and narrative in early childhood. In O.N. Saracho & B. Spodek (Eds.), *Multiple perspectives on play in early childhood education* (pp. 80–99). Albany: State University of New York Press.

Kellogg, R., & O'Dell, S. (1967). *The psychology of children's art*. San Diego, CA: Random House.

Kieff, J.E., & Wellhousen, K. (2000). Planning family involvement in early childhood programs. *Young Children, 55*(3), 18–25.

Kieff, J.E., & Casbergue, R.M. (1999). *Playful learning and teaching: Integrating play into preschool and primary programs.* Boston: Allyn & Bacon.

Lilly, E., & Green, C. (2004). *Developing partnerships with families through children's literature.* Upper Saddle River, NJ: Merrill/Prentice Hall.

Masonheimer, P.E., Drum, P.A., & Ehri, L.C. (1984). Does environmental print identification lead children into word reading? *Journal of Reading Behavior, 16*(4), 257–271.

McCaslin, N. (1996). *Creative drama in the classroom and beyond* (6th ed.). White Plains, NY: Longman.

Morrow, L.M., & Smith, J.K. (1990). *Assessment for instruction in early literacy.* Englewood Cliffs, NJ: Prentice Hall.

Reutzel, D.R., Fawson, P.C., Young, J.R., Morrison, T.G., & Wilcox, B. (2003). Reading environmental print: What is the role of concepts about print in discriminating young readers' responses? *Reading Psychology, 24*(2), 123–162. doi:10.1080/02702710308232

Rockwell, R.E., Andre, L.C., & Hawley, M.K. (1996). *Parents and teachers as partners: Issues and challenges.* Fort Worth, TX: Harcourt.

Roskos, K., & Neuman, S.B. (1993). Descriptive observations of adults' facilitation of literacy in young children's play. *Early Childhood Research Quarterly, 8*(1), 77–97. doi:10.1016/S0885-2006(05)80099-7

Schickedanz, J.A. (1990). *Adam's righting revolutions: One child's literacy development from infancy through grade one.* Portsmouth, NH: Heinemann.

Siegler, R.S. (1996). *Emerging minds: The process of change in children's thinking.* New York: Oxford University Press.

Treiman, R. (1985). Onsets and rimes as units of spoken syllables: Evidence from children. *Journal of Experimental Child Psychology, 39*(1), 161–181. doi:10.1016/0022-0965(85)90034-7

Treiman, R., & Broderick, V. (1998). What's in a name: Children's knowledge about the letters in their own names. *Journal of Experimental Child Psychology, 70*(2), 97–116. doi:10.1006/jecp.1998.2448

Treiman, R., Cohen, J., Mulqueeny, K., Kessler, B., & Schechtman, S. (2007). Young children's knowledge about printed names. *Child Development, 78*(5), 1458–1471. doi:10.1111/j.1467-8624.2007.01077.x

LITERATURE CITED

Arnosky, J. (2001). *Raccoon on his own.* New York: Puffin.

INDEX

Note: Page numbers followed by *f* indicate figures.

A

B

C